Submarine Periscope

THERMAL IMAGING
NIGHT VISION
LASER RANGEFINDING &
OTHER OPTRONIC SYSTEMS

Glasgow and London

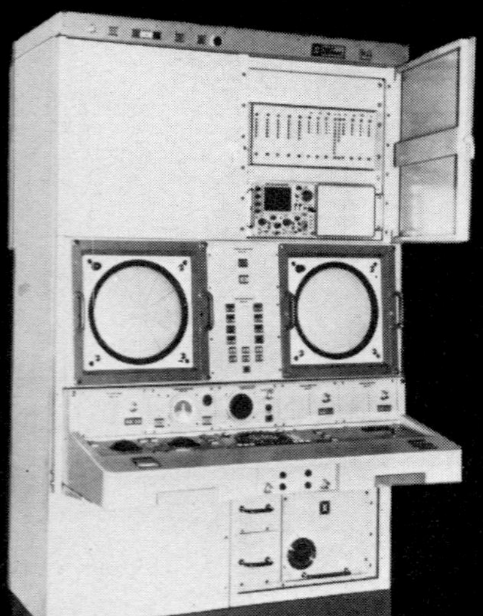

E 17. ENGINES, DIESEL

Blohm & Voss AG
Chantiers de l'Atlantique
C.R.M. Fabbrica Motori Marini
D.T.C.N.
Grandi Motori Trieste
Hatch & Kirk, Inc.
Howaldtswerke-Deutsche Werft
Korody-Colyer Corporation
M.T.U. (Motoren-und-Turbinen-Union)
Netherlands United Shipbuilding Bureaux Ltd.
Rhine-Schelde Verolme
S.A.C.M.

E 18. ENGINES, GAS TURBINE

D.T.C.N.
Netherlands United Shipbuilding Bureaux Ltd.
Rhine-Schelde Verolme

E 19. ENGINES, STEAM TURBINE

Blohm & Voss AG
D.T.C.N.
Netherlands United Shipbuilding Bureaux Ltd.
Yarrow (Shipbuilders) Ltd.

E 20. EPICYCLIC GEARS

E 21. ESCORT VESSELS

Blohm & Voss AG
Brooke Marine Ltd.
Dubigeon Normandie
Fr. Lürssen Werft
Netherlands United Shipbuilding Bureaux Ltd.
Vosper Thornycroft Group, The
Yarrow (Shipbuilders) Ltd.

F 1. FAST PATROL BOATS

Alinavi
Batservice Verft A/S
Bell Aerospace Canada
British Hovercraft Corp.
Brooke Marine Ltd.
David Cheverton
Fairey Marine Ltd.
Fr. Lürssen Werft
Karlskronavarvet AB
Netherlands United Shipbuilding Bureaux Ltd.
L. Rodriquez Shipyard
Sofrexan
Vosper Thornycroft Group, The
Yarrow (Shipbuilders) Ltd.

F 2. FAST WARSHIP DESIGN SERVICE

Brooke Marine Ltd.
C.S.E.E.
Netherlands United Shipbuilding Bureaux Ltd.
Karlskronavarvet AB
Vosper Thornycroft Group, The
Yarrow (Shipbuilders) Ltd.

F 3. FEED WATER HEATERS

Blohm & Voss AG

F 4. FERRIES

Bell Aerospace Canada
British Hovercraft Corp.
Brooke Marine Ltd.
David Cheverton
D.T.C.N.
Dubigeon Normandie
Netherlands United Shipbuilding Bureaux Ltd.
Rhine-Schelde Verolme
Yarrow (Shipbuilders) Ltd.

F 5. FIBRE OPTICS

Barr & Stroud
Ferranti Ltd.

F 6. FIBREGLASS VESSELS AND OTHER PRODUCTS

Batservice Verft A/S
D.T.C.N.
Fairey Marine Limited
Karlskronavarvet AB
Vosper Thornycroft Group, The
Yarrow (Shipbuilders) Ltd.

F 7. FIRE AND SALVAGE VESSELS

Bell Aerospace Canada
Brooke Marine Ltd.
David Cheverton
Vosper Thornycroft Group, The
Yarrow (Shipbuilders) Ltd.

F 8. FIRE CONTROL AND GUNNERY EQUIPMENT

AB Bofors
C.I.T. Alcatel
D.T.C.N.
Ferranti Ltd.
Hollandse Signaalapparaten B.V.
Laurence Scott & Electromotors Ltd.
Singer Librascope
Thomson C.S.F.

F 9. FIRE PUMPS

F 10. FITTINGS, SHIPS

F 11. FLEXIBLE CONDUIT COVERINGS

F 12. FLOODLIGHTS

F 13. FORK LIFT TRUCKS

F 14. FRESH WATER DISTILLING PLANT

Netherlands United Shipbuilding Bureaux Ltd.

F 15. FRIGATES

Blohm & Voss AG
Brooke Marine Ltd.
Dubigeon Normandie
Netherlands United Shipbuilding Bureaux Ltd.
Rhine-Schelde Verolme
Sofrexan
Vosper Thornycroft Group, The
Yarrow (Shipbuilders) Ltd.

F 16. FUEL OIL INJECTORS

Hatch & Kirk, Inc.
Korody-Colyer Corporation

G 1. GAS TURBINE BOATS

Alinavi
Bell Aerospace Canada
Blohm & Voss AG
Brooke Marine Ltd.
D.T.C.N.
Karlskronavarvet AB
Netherlands United Shipbuilding Bureaux Ltd.
Vosper Thornycroft Group, The
Yarrow (Shipbuilders) Ltd.

G 2. GAS TURBINES

D.T.C.N.
Rhine-Schelde Verolme
Yarrow (Shipbuilders) Ltd.

G 3. GEAR CASINGS

Korody-Colyer Corporation
Yarrow (Shipbuilders) Ltd.

G 4. GEARS AND GEARING

C.R.M. Fabbrica Motori Marini
Korody-Colyer Corporation
Netherlands United Shipbuilding Bureaux Ltd.
Yarrow (Shipbuilders) Ltd.

G 5. GEARS-HYPOID

Barr & Stroud
Korody-Colyer Corporation

G 6. GEARS-SPIRAL BEVEL

Barr & Stroud
Korody-Colyer Corporation

G 7. GEARS, REVERSE-REDUCTION

C.R.M. Fabbrica Motori Marini
Korody-Colyer Corporation
M.T.U. (Motoren-und-Turbinen-Union)
Netherlands United Shipbuilding Bureaux Ltd.
Zahnradfabrik Friedrichshafen AG

G 8. GEARS-SPUR

Korody-Colyer Corporation

G 9. GEARS, VEE DRIVE

C.R.M. Fabbrica Motori Marini
Korody-Colyer Corporation
Vosper Thornycroft Group, The
Zahnradfabrik Friedrichshafen

G 10. GENERATORS, ELECTRIC

Ferranti Ltd.
Laurence Scott & Electromotors Ltd.
Unelec

G 11. GOVERNORS

D.T.C.N.
Hatch & Kirk, Inc.
Korody-Colyer Corporation

G 12. GOVERNORS, ENGINE SPEED

Hatch & Kirk, Inc.
Korody-Colyer Corporation

G 13. GUIDED MISSILE SERVICING EQUIPMENT

Aerospatiale
British Aircraft Corporation
Cossor Electronics
Korody-Colyer Corporation
Thomson C.S.F.

G 14. GUIDED MISSILE SHIPS

Alinavi
Blohm & Voss AG
Brooke Marine Ltd.
D.T.C.N.
Fr. Lürssen Werft
General Dynamics Corporation
Karlskronavarvet AB
Netherlands United Shipbuilding Bureaux Ltd.
Sofrexan
Vosper Thornycroft Group, The
Yarrow (Shipbuilders) Ltd.

P 4. PERISCOPE FAIRINGS
D.T.C.N.
Edo Corporation
MacTaggart Scott Co. Ltd.

P 5. PERISCOPES
Barr & Stroud
D.T.C.N.

P 6. PIPES, COPPER AND BRASS

P 7. PIPES, SEA WATER

P 8. PIPE BENDING MACHINES

P 9. PISTONS, PISTON RINGS AND GUDGEON PINS
Hatch & Kirk, Inc.
Korody-Colyer Corporation

P 10. PLOTTING TABLES
Hollandse Signaalapparaten B.V.
Laurence Scott & Electromotors Ltd.
Selenia

P 11. PLUGS AND SOCKETS
Plessey Company Ltd., The
Thomson C.S.F.

P 12. PONTOONS, SELF PROPELLED
Brooke Marine Ltd.
David Cheverton
Netherlands United Shipbuilding Bureaux Ltd.
Yarrow (Shipbuilders) Ltd.

P 13. PRESSURE VESSELS
Netherlands United Shipbuilding Bureaux Ltd.
Yarrow (Shipbuilders) Ltd.

P 14. PROPELLENTS
AB Bofors

P 15. PROPELLERS, SHIPS'
AB Bofors
Split Shipyard

P 16. PROPELLERS, SHIPS' RESEARCH
Vosper Thornycroft Group, The

P 17. PROPULSION MACHINERY
Blohm & Voss AG
Korody-Colyer Corporation
M.T.U. (Motoren-und-Turbinen-Union)
Netherlands United Shipbuilding Bureaux Ltd.
Ruston Paxman Diesels Ltd.
Yarrow (Shipbuilders) Ltd.

P 18. PUBLISHERS
David and Charles
Ian Allan Ltd.
McGraw-Hill Book Company
Macdonald and Jane's

P 19. PUMPS
Korody-Colyer Corporation
MacTaggart Scott Co. Ltd.
Unelec

P 20. PUMPS, COMPONENT PARTS
Korody-Colyer Corporation

R 1. RADAR AERIALS
Aeromaritime Systems Limited
British Aircraft Corp.
Cossor Electronics
Decca Radar Ltd.
Hollandse Signaalapparaten B.V.
Plessey Company Ltd.
R.F. Communications
Selenia
Thomson C.S.F.

R 2. RADAR FOR FIRE CONTROL
Cossor Electronics
Ferranti Ltd.
Hollandse Signaalapparaten B.V.
Marconi Radar Systems Ltd.
Plessey Company Ltd.
Selenia
Thomson C.S.F.

R 3. RADAR FOR HARBOUR SUPERVISION
Decca Radar Ltd.
Ferranti Ltd.
Hollandse Signaalapparaten B.V.
Selenia
Thomson C.S.F.

R 4. RADAR FOR NAVIGATION WARNING INTERCEPTION
Aeromaritime Systems Limited
Ferranti Ltd.
Hollandse Signaalapparaten B.V.
Selenia
Thomson C.S.F.

R 5. RADIO, AIR
Aeromaritime Systems Limited
Plessey Company Ltd.
R.F. Communications
Thomson C.S.F.

R 6. RADIO EQUIPMENT
Aeromaritime Systems Limited
D.T.C.N.
Marconi Communications Systems Ltd.
Plessey Company Ltd.
R.F. Communications
Thomson C.S.F.

R 7. RADIO TRANSMITTERS AND RECEIVERS
Aeromaritime Systems Limited
Marconi Communications Systems Ltd.
Plessey Company Ltd.
R.F. Communications
Thomson C.S.F.

R 8. RADOMES
British Aircraft Corp.

R 9. RAMJETS
Aerospatiale

R 10. RANGEFINDERS
Barr & Stroud

R 11. RE-ENTRY DEVICE
C.I.T. Alcatel

R 12. RELOCALISATION DEVICE
C.I.T. Alcatel

R 13. REMOTE CONTROLS
Aeromaritime Systems Limited
C.S.E.E.
Dubigeon Normandie
Howaldtswerke-Deutsche Werft
Plessey Company Ltd.
Thomson C.S.F.
Vosper Thornycroft Group, The

R 14. REMOTE POWER CONTROL SYSTEMS
Aeromaritime Systems Limited

R 15. REPLACEMENT PARTS FOR DIESEL ENGINES
Blohm & Voss AG
Chantiers de l'Atlantique
Hatch & Kirk, Inc.
Korody-Colyer Corporation
MacTaggart Scott Co. Ltd.
M.T.U. (Motoren-und-Turbinen-Union)
Netherlands United Shipbuilding Bureaux Ltd.

R 16. RESEARCH SHIPS
Brooke Marine Ltd.
Karlskronavarvet AB
Thomson C.S.F.
Yarrow (Shipbuilders) Ltd.

R 17. REVERSE REDUCTION GEARS OIL OPERATED
Hatch & Kirk, Inc.
Korody-Colyer Corporation
M.T.U. (Motoren-und-Turbinen-Union)

R 18. REVERSING ENGINES, STEAM AND AIR OPERATED

R 19. REVERSING GEARS
C.R.M. Fabbrica Motori Marini
Korody-Colyer Corporation
M.T.U. (Motoren-und-Turbinen-Union)
Netherlands United Shipbuilding Bureaux Ltd.

R 20. ROLL DAMPING FINS
Blohm & Voss AG
Howaldtswerke-Deutsche Werft
Thomson C.S.F.
Vosper Thornycroft Group, The

R 21. RUDDERS
Howaldtswerke-Deutsche Werft
Karlskronavarvet AB
Yarrow (Shipbuilders) Ltd.

S 1. SALVAGE AND BOOM VESSELS
Brooke Marine Ltd.
David Cheverton
Karlskronavarvet AB
Yarrow (Shipbuilders) Ltd.

S 2. SCIENTIFIC INSTRUMENTS
Barr & Stroud
Ferranti Ltd.
Thomson C.S.F.

S 3. SEALS (MECHANICAL)

S 4. SHIP BUILDERS AND SHIP REPAIRERS
Alinavi
Blohm & Voss AG
Brooke Marine Ltd.
Cantiere Navali Del Tirreno e Riuniti
Dubigeon Normandie
Fr. Lürssen Werft
Howaldtswerke-Deutsche Werft
Karlskronavarvet AB
L. Rodriquez Shipyard
Netherlands United Shipbuilding Bureaux Ltd.
Split Shipyard
Thomson C.S.F.
Vosper Thornycroft Group, The
Yarrow (Shipbuilders) Ltd.

S 5. SHIP AND SUBMARINE DESIGN
Brooke Marine Ltd.
Howaldtswerke-Deutsche Werft
Ingenieurkontor Lübeck
Karlskronavarvet AB
Netherlands United Shipbuilding Bureaux Ltd.
Thomson C.S.F.
Vosper Thornycroft Group, The
Yarrow (Shipbuilders) Ltd.

S 6. SHIP MACHINERY
Blohm & Voss AG
M.T.U. (Motoren-und-Turbinen-Union)
Netherlands United Shipbuilding Bureaux Ltd.
Yarrow (Shipbuilders) Ltd.

S 7. SHIPS MAGNETIC COMPASS TEST TABLES

S 8. SHIP STABILISERS
Blohm & Voss AG
Howaldtswerke-Deutsche Werft
Vosper Thornycroft Group, The

S 9. SHIP SYSTEMS ENGINEERING
Aeromaritime Systems Limited
Alinavi
Ferranti Ltd.
Singer Librascope
Yarrow (Shipbuilders) Ltd.

S 10. SHIPS' BRASS FOUNDRY FOR SONAR AND RADAR
C.S.E.E.
Van Der Heem Electronics N.V.

S 11. SIMULATORS
C.I.T. Alcatel
C.S.E.E.
Ferranti Ltd.
Laurence Scott & Electromotors Ltd.
Van Der Heem Electronics N.V.

S 12. SLIP RING ASSEMBLIES

S 13. SMOKE INDICATORS
Barr & Stroud

S 14. SOCKETS AND PLUGS, ELECTRIC WATERTIGHT
Plessey Company Ltd.
Thomson C.S.F.

S 15. SOCKETS AND PLUGS, MULTI-PIN PATTERNS
Thomson C.S.F.

S 16. SOCKET TERMINATIONS
Thomson C.S.F.

S 17. SONAR EQUIPMENT
British Aircraft Corporation
C.I.T. Alcatel
D.T.C.N.
Edo Corporation
Ferrograph Co. Ltd.
Rhine-Schelde Verolme
Selenia
Thomson C.S.F.
Van Der Heem Electronics Ltd.

S 18. SONAR EQUIPMENT (PASSIVE ACTIVE-INTERCEPT)
Van Der Heem Electronics N.V.

S 19. SONAR EQUIPMENT, HULL FITTINGS AND HYDRAULICS
C.I.T. Alcatel
D.T.C.N.
Laurence Scott & Electromotors Ltd.
Thomson C.S.F.

S 20. SPARE PARTS FOR DIESEL ENGINES
Blohm & Voss AG
C.R.M. Fabbrica Motori Marini
D.T.C.N.
Grandi Motori Trieste
Hatch & Kirk, Inc.
Korody-Colyer Corporation
M.T.U. (Motoren-und-Turbinen-Union)
Netherlands United Shipbuilding Bureaux Ltd.
Ruston Paxman Diesels Ltd.

S 21. SPEED BOATS
Alinavi
Batservice Verft S/A
Bell Aerospace Canada
Brooke Marine Ltd.
Fairey Marine Ltd.
Fr. Lürssen Werft
L. Rodriquez Shipyard
Vosper Thornycroft Group, The

S 22. STABILISING EQUIPMENT
Blohm & Voss AG
Ferranti Ltd.
Howaldtswerke-Deutsche Werft
Vosper Thornycroft Group, The

S 23. STABILISING EQUIPMENT FOR FIRE CONTROL
Ferranti Ltd.
Hollandse Signaalapparaten B.V.

S 24. STEAM-RAISING PLANT, CONVENTIONAL
Blohm & Voss AG
Netherlands United Shipbuilding Bureaux Ltd.
Rhine-Schelde Verolme
Yarrow (Shipbuilders) Ltd.

S 25. STEAM-RAISING PLANT, NUCLEAR

S 26. STEAM TURBINES
Blohm & Voss AG
Netherlands United Shipbuilding Bureaux Ltd.
Yarrow (Shipbuilders) Ltd.

S 27. STEEL, ALLOY AND SPECIAL
AB Bofors

S 28. STEEL FORGINGS, PLATES AND SECTIONS, STAMPINGS
AB Bofors

S 29. STEEL, MANGANESE, WEAR RESISTING
AB Bofors

S 30. STEERING GEAR
Riva Calzoni

S 31. STRESS RELIEVING
Yarrow (Shipbuilders) Ltd.

S 32. SUBMARINE DISTRESS BUOY
Barr & Stroud
C.I.T. Alcatel
Singer Librascope

S 33. SUBMARINE FIRE CONTROL
C.I.T. Alcatel
D.T.C.N.
Laurence Scott & Electromotors Ltd.
Rhine-Schelde Verolme
Thomson C.S.F.

S 34. SUBMARINE PERISCOPES
Barr & Stroud
D.T.C.N.
Dubigeon Normandie
Rhine-Schelde Verolme
Thomson C.S.F.

S 35. SUBMARINES
D.T.C.N.
Howaldtswerke-Deutsche Werft
Ingenieurkontor Lübeck
Karlskronavarvet AB
Netherlands United Shipbuilding Bureaux Ltd.
Split Shipyard
Vickers Limited

S 36. SUBMARINES (CONVENTIONAL)
D.T.C.N.
Ingenieurkontor Lübeck
Karlskronavarvet AB
Netherlands United Shipbuilding Bureaux Ltd.
Thomson C.S.F.
Vickers Limited

S 37. SUPERHEATERS
Blohm & Voss AG
Yarrow (Shipbuilders) Ltd.

S 38. SUPPORT SERVICES
Vosper Thornycroft Group, The

S 39. SURVEY EQUIPMENT
C.S.E.E.
D.T.C.N.
Thomson C.S.F.
Van Der Heem Electronics N.V.

S 40. SWITCHBOARDS
Blohm & Voss AG
C.S.E.E.
Laurence Scott & Electromotors Ltd.
Plessey Company Ltd., The
Whipp & Bourne Ltd.

S 41. SWITCHBOARDS AND SWITCHGEAR
Laurence Scott & Electromotors Ltd.
Vosper Thornycroft Group, The

T 1. TACTICAL TRAINING SIMULATORS
C.S.E.E.
Hollandse Signaalapparaten B.V.
Laurence Scott & Electromotors Ltd.
Marconi Radar Systems Ltd.
Thomson C.S.F.
Van Der Heem Electronics N.V.

T 2. TANKERS
Batservice Verft A/S
Blohm & Voss AG
Howaldtswerke-Deutsche Werft
Netherlands United Shipbuilding Bureaux Ltd.
Rhine-Schelde Verolme
Split Shipyard
Yarrow (Shipbuilders) Ltd.

T 3. TANKERS (SMALL)
Brooke Marine Ltd.
Dubigeon Normandie
Fr. Lürssen Werft
Rhine-Schelde Verolme
Split Shipyard
Yarrow (Shipbuilders) Ltd.

M 5. MARINE FUELS AND LUBRICANTS
B.P. Trading Limited

M 6. MARINE ENGINE MONITORING AND DATA RECORDING SYSTEM
Decca Radar Ltd.

M 7. MARINE RADAR
Decca Radar Ltd.
D.T.C.N.
Hollandse Signaalapparaten B.V.
Selenia
Thomson C.S.F.

M 8. MATERIALS HANDLING EQUIPMENT
MacTaggart, Scott & Co. Ltd.

M 9. MERCHANT SHIPS
Blohm & Voss AG
Brooke Marine Ltd.
Dubigeon Normandie
Fr. Lürssen Werft
Howaldtswerke-Deutsche Werft
Split Shipyard
Yarrow (Shipbuilders) Ltd.

M 10. MICROPHONE EQUIPMENT
D.T.C.N.
R.F. Communications

M 11. MINE LAYERS
Bell Aerospace Canada
Blohm & Voss AG
Brooke Marine Ltd.
Dubigeon Normandie
Karlskronavarvet AB
Netherlands United Shipbuilding Bureaux Ltd.
Vosper Thornycroft Group, The
Yarrow (Shipbuilders) Ltd.

M 12. MINESWEEPERS
Batservice Verft A/S
Bell Aerospace Canada
Blohm & Voss AG
Brooke Marine Ltd.
Edo Corporation
Karlskronavarvet AB
Netherlands United Shipbuilding Bureaux Ltd.
Sofrexan
Thomson C.S.F.
Vosper Thornycroft Group, The
Yarrow (Shipbuilders) Ltd.

M 13. MISSILE CONTROL SYSTEMS
Aerospatiale
British Aircraft Corporation
C.I.T. Alcatel
D.T.C.N.
Ferranti Ltd.
Hollandse Signaalapparaten B.V.
Selenia
Thomson C.S.F.

M 14. MISSILE INSTALLATIONS
Aerospatiale
British Aircraft Corporation
C.S.E.E.
D.T.C.N.
Selenia
Thomson C.S.F.

M 15. MISSILE LAUNCHING SYSTEMS
Aerospatiale
British Aircraft Corporation
D.T.C.N.
Selenia

M 16. MISSILE SHIPS
Alinavi
Bell Aerospace Canada
Blohm & Voss AG
Brooke Marine Ltd.
D.T.C.N.
Fr. Lürssen Werft
Karlskronavarvet AB
Netherlands United Shipbuilding Bureaux Ltd.
Vosper Thornycroft Group, The
Yarrow (Shipbuilders) Ltd.

M 17. MODEL MAKERS AND DESIGNERS
Ingenieurkontor Lübeck
Split Shipyard
Thomson C.S.F.
Vosper Thornycroft Group, The
Yarrow (Shipbuilders) Ltd.

M 18. MODEL TEST TOWING TANK SERVICE

M 19. MOTOR CONTROL GEAR
C.S.E.E.
Korody-Colyer Corporation
Laurence Scott & Electromotors Ltd.
Thomson C.S.F.

M 20. MOTOR STARTERS
Hatch & Kirk, Inc.
Korody-Colyer Corporation
Laurence Scott & Electromotors Ltd.
Thomson C.S.F.

M 21. MOTOR TORPEDO BOATS
Batservice Verft A/S
Bell Aerospace Canada
Brooke Marine Ltd.
Dubigeon Normandie
Fr. Lürssen Werft
Karlskronavarvet AB
Thomson C.S.F.
Vosper Thornycroft Group, The
Yarrow (Shipbuilders) Ltd.

M 22. MOTORS, ELECTRIC
Ferranti Ltd.
Laurence Scott & Electromotors Ltd.
Unelec

M 23. MOVING WEIGHT STABILISERS

M 24. MULTI PLAN PLUGS

N 1. NAVAL GUNS
AB Bofors
D.T.C.N.

N 2. NAVAL RADAR
Aeromaritime Systems Limited
Cossor Electronics
Decca Radar Ltd.
D.T.C.N.
Hollandse Signaalapparaten B.V.
R.F. Communications
Selenia
Thomson C.S.F.

N 3. NAVIGATION AIDS
Aeromaritime Systems Limited
Decca Radar Ltd.
Ferranti Ltd.
Laurence Scott & Electromotors Ltd.
R.F. Communications
Singer Librascope
Thomson C.S.F.
Ven Der Heem Electronics N.V.

N 4. NIGHT VISION SYSTEMS
Aeromaritime Systems Limited
Barr & Stroud
Singer Librascope
Thomson C.S.F.

N 5. NON-MAGNETIC MINESWEEPERS
Bell Aerospace Canada
Brooke Marine Ltd.
Dubigeon Normandie
Karlskronavarvet AB
Netherlands United Shipbuilding Bureaux Ltd.
Vosper Thornycroft Group, The
Yarrow (Shipbuilders) Ltd.

O 1. OCEANOGRAPHIC SURVEY SHIPS
Brooke Marine Ltd.
C.I.T. Alcatel
D.T.C.N.
Karlskronavarvet AB
Netherlands United Shipbuilding Bureaux Ltd.
Van Der Heem Electronics N.V.
Yarrow (Shipbuilders) Ltd.

O 2. OIL DRILLING RIGS
Howaldtswerke-Deutsche Werft
Netherlands United Shipbuilding Bureaux Ltd.

O 3. 'OILFREE' COMPRESSORS

O 4. OIL FUEL HEATERS
Blohm & Voss AG

O 5. OIL FUEL SYSTEMS AND BURNERS

O 6. OIL RIG SUPPLY VESSELS AND WORK BOATS
Batservice Verft A/S
Brooke Marine Ltd.
David Cheverton
Vosper Thornycroft Group, The

O 7. OPTICAL EQUIPMENT
Barr & Stroud

O 8. OPTICAL FILTERS

O 9. ORDNANCE
AB Bofors

P 1. PARTS FOR DIESELS ENGINES
Blohm & Voss AG
D.T.C.N.
Grandi Motori Trieste
Hatch & Kirk, Inc.
Korody-Colyer Corporation
M.T.U. (Motoren-und-Turbinen-Union)
Netherlands United Shipbuilding Bureaux Ltd.
Ruston Paxman Diesels Ltd.

P 2. PASSENGER SHIPS
Alinavi
Batservice Verft A/S
Blohm & Voss AG
Brooke Marine Ltd.
D.T.C.N.
Dubigeon Normandie
Howaldtswerke-Deutsche Werft
Netherlands United Shipbuilding Bureaux Ltd.
L. Rodriquez Shipyard
Split Shipyard
Yarrow (Shipbuilders) Ltd.

P 3. PATROL BOATS, LAUNCHES, TENDERS AND PINNACES
Alinavi
British Aircraft Corp.
Bell Aerospace Canada
Brooke Marine Ltd.
David Cheverton
D.T.C.N.
Dubigeon Normandie
Fairey Marine Ltd.
Fr. Lürssen Werft
Karlskronavarvet AB
Netherlands United Shipbuilding Bureaux Ltd.
Sofrexan
Vosper Thornycroft Group, The
Yarrow (Shipbuilders) Ltd.

GENERAL DYNAMICS
Submarines . . . Shipboard Missile Systems . . . Surface Ships
Ocean Data and Navigation Systems . . . Electronics

Fairey Marine
FAST PATROL BOATS

30 foot (9 m) SPEAR in police service

53 foot (16 m) LANCE Coastal Patrol Boat

Fairey Marine design and build a range (20 ft to 85 ft) of high speed patrol boats for offshore deterrent patrols and interception duties.

In service with three Navies, Coastguards, Police and other civil authorities worldwide.

Fairey Marine Fast Patrol Boats are backed by a comprehensive support organisation. Services provided include; co-ordination of spares and maintenance facilities and planning and implementation of training programmes.

For full details please contact: Manager, Military Sales

Fairey Marine Limited

Hamble, Southampton SO3 5NB, England. Tel: Hamble 2661
Telex: 47546. Telegrams: Airily, Hamble.

DUBIGEON-NORMANDIE

NANTES ★ ROUEN ★ LE HAVRE ★ DIEPPE

Shipbuilding of naval surface ships and submarines.

Modernization and conversion of navals ships.

G 15. GUIDED MISSILES
AB Bofors
Aerospatiale
British Aircraft Corporation
D.T.C.N.
Thomson C.S.F.

G 16. GUN BOATS
Alinavi
Batservice Verft A/S
Bell Aerospace Canada
Brooke Marine Ltd.
D.T.C.N.
Fairey Marine Ltd.
Fr. Lürssen Werft
Karlskronavarvet AB
Netherlands United Shipbuilding Bureaux Ltd.
L. Rodriquez Shipyard
Sofrexan
Vosper Thornycroft Group, The
Yarrow (Shipbuilders) Ltd.

G 17. GUNS AND MOUNTINGS
AB Bofors
Sofrexan

G 18. GUN MOUNTS
AB Bofors

G 19. GUN-SIGHTING APPARATUS AND HEIGHT FINDERS
Barr & Stroud
Hollandse Signaalapparaten B.V.
Thomson C.S.F.

G 20. GYROSCOPIC COMPASSES
D.T.C.N.
Ferranti Ltd.
Thomson C.S.F.

H 1. HEAT EXCHANGERS
Blohm & Voss AG
Hatch & Kirk, Inc.
Howaldtswerke-Deutsche Werft
Korody-Colyer Corporation
Split Shipyard

H 2. HEATED WINDOWS
Barr & Stroud

H 3. HELM INDICATORS
Laurence Scott & Electromotors Ltd.

H 4. HOVERCRAFT
Bell Aerospace Canada
British Hovercraft Corp.
D.T.C.N.
Vosper Thornycroft Group, The

H 5. HYDRAULIC EQUIPMENT
MacTaggart, Scott & Co. Ltd.
Riva Calzoni
Vosper Thornycroft Group, The

H 6. HYDRAULIC MACHINERY
MacTaggart, Scott & Co. Ltd.
Riva Calzoni

H 7. HYDRAULIC PLANT
MacTaggart, Scott & Co. Ltd.
Riva Calzoni

H 8. HYDROFOILS
Aerospatiale
Alinavi
Blohm & Voss AG
D.T.C.N.
Edo Corporation
L. Rodriquez Shipyard

H 9. HYDROGRAPHIC SURVEY EQUIPMENT
D.T.C.N.
Edo Corporation
Karlskronavarvet AB
Plessey Company Ltd., The

I 1. INDICATORS, ELECTRIC
Korody-Colyer Corporation
Laurence Scott & Electromotors Ltd.

I 2. I.F.F. RADAR
Cossor Electronics

I 3. IFF Mk10 SYSTEMS
Aeromaritime Systems Limited
Cossor Electronics Limited
Plessey Company Ltd.

I 4. INFRA-RED MATERIALS
Barr & Stroud
Thomson C.S.F.

I 5. INFRA-RED SYSTEMS
Barr & Stroud

I 6. INJECTORS
Hatch & Kirk, Inc.
Korody-Colyer Corporation

I 7. INSTRUMENT COMPONENTS (MECHANICAL)
Korody-Colyer Corporation
Laurence Scott & Electromotors Ltd.
Thomson C.S.F.

I 8. INSTRUMENTS, ELECTRONIC
AB Bofors
Barr & Stroud
Cossor Electronics
D.T.C.N.
Ferranti Ltd.
Van Der Heem Electronics N.V.

I 9. INSTRUMENTS, NAUTICAL
D.T.C.N.
Laurence Scott & Electromotors Ltd.
Van Der Heem Electronics N.V.

I 10. INSTRUMENT PANELS
D.T.C.N.
Karlskronavarvet AB
Korody-Colyer Corporation
Laurence Scott & Electromotors Ltd.
Singer Librascope
Thomson C.S.F.
Vosper Thornycroft Group, The
Whipp & Bourne Ltd.

I 11. INSTRUMENT, PRECISION
Barr & Stroud
D.T.C.N.
Ferranti Ltd.
Korody-Colyer Corporation
Laurence Scott & Electromotors Ltd.

I 12. INSTRUMENTS, TEST EQUIPMENT
Cossor Electronics Limited
D.T.C.N.
Ferranti Ltd.
Korody-Colyer Corporation
Laurence Scott & Electromotors Ltd.
Selenia
Thomson C.S.F.
Van Der Heem Electronics N.V.

I 13. INTERIOR DESIGN AND FURNISHING FOR SHIPS
Blohm & Voss AG
Brooke Marine Ltd.
Vosper Thornycroft Group, The

I 14. INVERTERS AND BATTERY CHARGERS
Ferranti Ltd.
Vosper Thornycroft Group, The

L 1. LAMPHOLDERS

L 2. LANDING CRAFT
Bell Aerospace Canada
British Hovercraft Corp.
Brooke Marine Ltd.
David Cheverton
D.T.C.N.
Netherlands United Shipbuilding Bureaux Ltd.
Sofrexan
Yarrow (Shipbuilders) Ltd.

L 3. LASER RANGEFINDERS
AB Bofors
Barr & Stroud
Ferranti Ltd.

L 4. LASER SYSTEMS
Barr & Stroud
D.T.C.N.
Ferranti Ltd.
Selenia
Singer Librascope
Thomson C.S.F.

L 5. LIFTS-HYDRAULIC
MacTaggart, Scott & Co. Ltd.

L 6. LIGHTS AND LIGHTING

L 7. LIQUID PETROLEUM GAS CARRIERS
Brooke Marine Ltd.
Fr. Lürssen Werft
General Dynamics Corporation
Rhine-Schelde Verolme

L 8. LOUDSPEAKER EQUIPMENT
Aeromaritime Systems Limited
Thomson C.S.F.

M 1. MACHINED PARTS, FERROUS
Blohm & Voss AG
Laurence Scott & Electromotors Ltd.
Yarrow (Shipbuilders) Ltd.

M 2. MACHINED PARTS, NON-FERROUS
Blohm & Voss AG
Laurence Scott & Electromotors Ltd.
Yarrow (Shipbuilders) Ltd.

M 3. MAINTENANCE AND REPAIR SHIPS
Brooke Marine Ltd.
Dubigeon Normandie
Fr. Lürssen Werft
Karlskronavarvet AB
Rhine-Schelde Verolme
Vosper Thornycroft Group, The
Yarrow (Shipbuilders) Ltd.

M 4. MARINE ARCHITECTS
D.T.C.N.
General Dynamics Corporation
Ingenieurkontor Lübeck
Netherlands United Shipbuilding Bureaux Ltd.
Vosper Thornycroft Group, The
Yarrow (Shipbuilders) Ltd.

JANE'S FIGHTING SHIPS

Edited by **Captain John E. Moore**
RN, FRGS

Order of Contents

Alphabetical List of Advertisers
Classified List of Advertisers*
Frontispiece
Contents List
Foreword
Acknowledgements
The Use of Jane's Fighting Ships
Identification Silhouettes
Ship Reference Section
Table of Naval Strengths
Naval Aircraft and Missiles
Index of Named Ships
Index of Classes

World Sales Distribution

Jane's Yearbooks,
St. Giles House, 49/50 Poland Street,
London W1A 2LG, England

All the World
except

North, Central and South America:
McGraw-Hill Book Company,
1221 Avenue of the Americas,
New York, NY 10020, USA

and

Canada:
McGraw-Hill Company of Canada Ltd, 330 Progress Avenue, Scarborough, Ontario, Canada

Editorial communication to:

The Editor, Jane's Fighting Ships
Jane's Yearbooks, St. Giles House, 49/50 Poland Street
London W1A 2LG, England
Telephone 01-437 9844

Advertisement communication to:

Jane's Advertising Department
Haymarket Publishing Group,
Gillow House, 5 Winsley Street,
London W1A 2HG, England
Telephone 01-636 3600

***Classified List of Advertisers**

The various products available from the advertisers in this edition are listed alphabetically in about 350 different headings.

Alphabetical list of advertisers

1973/74 edition

12m.
Fast Patrol Craft,
one of twelve built
for various overseas
governments.

33m.
Fast Patrol Craft,
one of four built
for the Libyan Arab
Republic Navy.

One of four
33m.
Fast Patrol Craft
for the
Pakistan Navy.

HMAFV Seal,
one of three
37.5m Long Range
Recovery and
Support Craft
now in service
with the Ministry
of Defence (Air).

Al Said
Flagship Oman Navy.

Now building three 37.5m Fast Patrol Craft for two overseas navies and six 33m Fast Patrol Craft for two overseas navies

Alphabetical list of advertisers

1973/74 edition—*continued*

ITALIAN NAVY - Guided-missile Destroyer AUDACE

ELETTRONICA SAN GIORGIO S.p.A. Genova Sestri · Italy

Press Dep. Elettronica San Giorgio · Esa 16-72 · DEL PINO

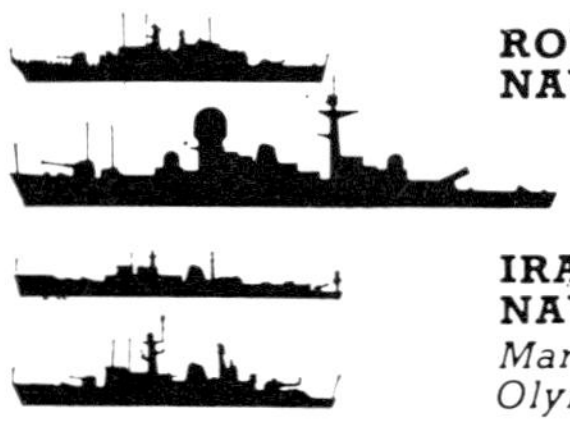

JANE'S YEARBOOKS

These fully comprehensive reference works, each one highly recommended in its own particular field, reflect every year the development and progress of the industry or service they describe. It is difficult to find elsewhere such a high standard of consistent accuracy—up to fifty per cent of the information covered by Jane's is revised and updated with each new edition. Year after year, since 1897, Jane's have produced a stock of unexpected or little-known information, frequently making publication day headlines. Readers have been amazed at the ever increasing bulk of indispensable information offered to them. Reviewers have commented that the impossible has again been achieved, and Jane's have once more improved their standards.

Jane's now number seven, and an eighth is on the way for 1974, JANE'S OCEAN TECHNOLOGY, edited by Robert Trillo. This volume will describe and illustrate with the traditional wealth of detail, activity both on and beneath the surface of the world's oceans. We hope that it too will become the "bible of its field".

JANE'S ALL THE WORLD'S AIRCRAFT

Edited by John W. R. Taylor — 64th Year of issue

The annual record of aviation development and progress.

'We thought that last year's Jane's could not be improved upon. It has been.'

Air Force Magazine

JANE'S WEAPON SYSTEMS

Edited by R. T. Pretty and D. H. R. Archer — 5th Edition

The international reference book on modern weapon development.

'the latest volume . . . has been expanded and thoroughly revised, with more illustrations than ever.'

Navy News

JANE'S SURFACE SKIMMERS

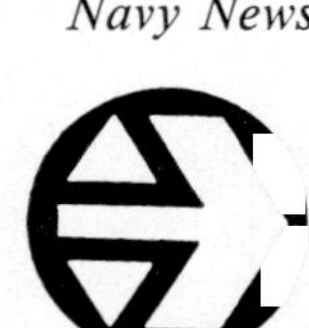

Hovercraft and Hydrofoils — 7th Edition

Edited and compiled by Roy McLeavy

'*Jane's Surface Skimmers* covers the complete range of the world's hovercraft and hydrofoil concepts from kits for homebuilt single-seaters to multi-thousand tonners.' *The Diplomatist*

JANE'S FREIGHT CONTAINERS

Ports - Operators - Manufacturers — 6th Edition

Edited by Patrick Finlay

'. . . a comprehensive survey of developments past, present and future in the international sphere . . . The section devoted to "Trends for the Future" also makes fascinating reading . . .'

Dock and Harbour Authority

JANE'S WORLD RAILWAYS

A world-wide survey of railway operation and equipment — 22nd Year of issue

Edited by Henry Sampson

'. . . this world-wide survey of railway operation and equipment remains an essential guide for suppliers and an invaluable reference work for anyone involved in railway management.'

International Railway Journal

JANE'S MAJOR COMPANIES OF EUROPE

Edited by Jonathan Love and Lionel F. Gray — 9th Edition

'. . . more than ever essential reading for those in the City . . . . The book will prove a key requirement for the year ahead . . . Jane's is an essentially European work.' *City Press*

CLASSIFIED LIST OF ADVERTISERS

A 1. ACTION INFORMATION SYSTEMS
D.T.C.N.
Ferranti Ltd.
Hollandse Signaalapparaten B.V.
Plessey Company Ltd.
Singer Librascope

A 2. ACTION INFORMATION TRAINERS
Ferranti Ltd.
Hollandse Signaalapparaten B.V.
Plessey Company Ltd.
Rhine-Schelde Verolme

A 3. AIR COMPRESSORS
C.I.T. Alcatel
Split Shipyard

A 4. AIRCRAFT ARRESTING GEAR
MacTaggart, Scott & Co. Ltd.

A 5. AIRCRAFT CARRIERS
Netherlands United Shipbuilding Bureaux Ltd.

A 6. AIRCRAFT INSTRUMENTS
Edo Corporation
Ferranti Ltd.

A 7. AIR CUSHION VEHICLES
Bell Aerospace Canada
British Hovercraft Corp.
D.T.C.N.
Vosper Thornycroft Group, The

A 8. AIRFRAME MANUFACTURERS
Hawker Siddeley

A 9. ALIGNMENT EQUIPMENT
British Aircraft Corp.

A 10. ALTERNATORS
Laurence Scott & Electromotors Ltd.
Unelec

A 11. AMMUNITION
AB Bofors
Aeromaritime Systems Limited

A 12. AMMUNITION HOISTS
Aeromaritime Systems Limited
Blohm & Voss AG
MacTaggart, Scott & Co. Ltd.

A 13. ANTI-SUBMARINE LAUNCHES
D.T.C.N.
Netherlands United Shipbuilding Bureaux Ltd.
Vosper Thornycroft Group, The
Yarrow (Shipbuilders) Ltd.

A 14. ANTI SUBMARINE ROCKET LAUNCHERS
AB Bofors
D.T.C.N.

A 15. ANTI-SUBMARINE ROCKETS
AB Bofors
D.T.C.N.

A 16. ARMOUR PLATES
AB Bofors

A 17. ASSAULT CRAFT
Bell Aerospace Canada
Blohm & Voss AG
Brooke Marine Ltd.
David Cheverton
D.T.C.N.
Vosper Thornycroft Group, The
Yarrow (Shipbuilders) Ltd.

A 18. ASSAULT SHIPS
Blohm & Voss AG
Brooke Marine Ltd.
D.T.C.N.
Vosper Thornycroft Group, The
Yarrow (Shipbuilders) Ltd.

A 19. AUTOMATIC CONTROL SYSTEMS
C.I.T. Alcatel
D.T.C.N.
Ferranti Ltd.
Laurence Scott & Electromotors Ltd.
Rhine-Schelde Verolme
Singer Librascope

A 20. AUTOMATIC STEERING
C.S.E.E.

A 21. AUXILIARY MACHINERY
Blohm & Voss AG
D.T.C.N.
Korody-Colyer Corporation
Laurence Scott & Electromotors Ltd.
M.T.U. (Motoren-und-Turbinen-Union)
Rhine-Schelde Verolme
Ruston Paxman Diesels Ltd.
Unelec

B 1. BINOCULARS
Barr & Stroud
Rhine-Schelde Verolme

B 2. BOILERS
Blohm & Voss AG
Howaldtswerke-Deutsche Werft
Netherlands United Shipbuilding Bureaux Ltd.
Yarrow (Shipbuilders) Ltd.

B 3. BOOKS (NAVAL)
Ian Allan Ltd.

B 4. BULK CARRIERS
Blohm & Voss AG
Brooke Marine Ltd
Dubigeon Normandie
Fr. Lürssen Werft
General Dynamics Corporation
Howaldtswerke-Deutsche Werft
Rhine-Schelde Verolme
Split Shipyard

C 1. CABLE LOOMS (WITH OR WITHOUT)
Laurence Scott & Electromotors Ltd.

C 2. CAISSONS
Brooke Marine Ltd.

C 3. CAPSTANS AND WINDLASSES
MacTaggart, Scott & Co. Ltd.
Riva Calzoni

C 4. CAR FERRIES
Bell Aerospace Canada
Blohm & Voss AG
British Hovercraft Corp. Ltd.
Brooke Marine Ltd.
D.T.C.N.
Dubigeon Normandie
Fr. Lürssen Werft
Rhine-Schelde Verolme
Yarrow (Shipbuilders) Ltd.

C 5. CARGO HANDLING EQUIPMENT
Blohm & Voss AG
MacTaggart, Scott & Co. Ltd.

C 6. CARGO SHIPS
Batservice Verft A/S
Blohm & Voss AG
Brooke Marine Ltd.
D.T.C.N.
Dubigeon Normandie
Fr. Lürssen Werft
General Dynamics Corporation
Howaldtswerke-Deutshe Werft
Netherlands United Shipbuilding Bureaux Co.
Rhine-Schelde Verolme
Yarrow (Shipbuilding) Ltd.

C 7. CARGO SPACE MONITORS
D.T.C.N.

C 8. CASTINGS, ALUMINIUM-BRONZE

C 9. CASTINGS, HIGH DUTY IRON

C 10. CASTINGS, NON-FERROUS

C 11. CASTINGS, SHELL, MOULDED
Ferranti Ltd.

C 12. CASTINGS, S.G. IRON
Ferranti Ltd.

C 13. CASTINGS, S.G. NI-RESIST IRON
Ferranti Ltd.

C 14. CASTINGS, STEEL
AB Bofors
Rhine-Schelde Verolme

C 15. CATHODIC PROTECTION EQUIPMENT
Marconi Radar Systems Ltd.

C 16. CENTRALISED AND AUTOMATIC CONTROL
C.I.T. Alcatel
Ferranti Ltd.
M.T.U. (Motoren-und-Turbinen-Union)
Thomson C.S.F.

C 17. COASTAL AND INSHORE MINESWEEPERS
Batservice Verft A/S
Bell Aerospace Canada
Brooke Marine Ltd.
Karlskronavarvet AB
Netherlands United Shipbuilding Bureaux Ltd.
Rhine-Schelde Verolme
Yarrow (Shipbuilders) Ltd.

C 18. COMPRESSED AIR STARTERS FOR GAS TURBINES AND DIESEL ENGINES
Korody-Colyer Corporation

C 19. COMPRESSORS
C.I.T. Alcatel
Ferranti Ltd.
Rhine-Schelde Verolme
Split Shipyard

C 20. COMPUTER SERVICES
C.S.E.E.
Ferranti Ltd.
Thomson C.S.F.
Yarrow (Shipbuilders) Ltd.

C 21. COMPUTERS
Ferranti Ltd.
Hollandse Signaalapparaten N.V.
Selenia
Singer Librascope
Thomson C.S.F.
Yarrow (Shipbuilders) Ltd.

C 22. CONDENSER TUBES

C 23. CONDENSERS
Blohm & Voss AG
Yarrow (Shipbuilders) Ltd.

C 24. CONTAINER SHIPS
Blohm & Voss AG
Brooke Marine Ltd.
Dubigeon Normandie
Fr. Lürssen Werft
General Dynamics Corporation
Howaldtswerke-Deutsche Werft
Netherlands United Shipbuilding Bureaux Ltd.
Split Shipyard
Yarrow (Shipbuilders) Ltd.

C 25. CONTROL DESKS (ELECTRIC)
C.S.E.E.
Laurence Scott & Electromotors Ltd.
Vosper Thornycroft Group, The
Whipp & Bourne Ltd.

C 26. CONTROL GEAR
Korody-Colyer Corporation
Laurence Scott & Electromotors Ltd.
Vosper Thornycroft Group, The

C 27. CORVETTES
Blohm & Voss AG
Dubigeon Normandie
Fr. Lürssen Werft
Netherlands United Shipbuilding Bureaux Ltd.
Sofrexan
Vosper Thornycroft Group, The
Yarrow (Shipbuilders) Ltd.

C 28. CRANES, SHIPS'
Dubigeon Normandie

C 29. CRUISERS
Dubigeon Normandie
Netherlands United Shipbuilding Bureaux Ltd.

C 30. COUPLINGS
Yarrow (Shipbuilders) Ltd.

D 1. DECK MACHINERY
MacTaggart, Scott & Co. Ltd.

D 2. DESTROYERS
Blohm & Voss AG
Brooke Marine Ltd.
D.T.C.N.
Dubigeon Normandie
Netherlands United Shipbuilding Bureaux Ltd.
Vosper Thornycroft Group, The
Yarrow (Shipbuilders) Ltd.

D 3. DIESEL ENGINES, AUXILIARY
Blohm & Voss AG
Chantiers de l'Atlantique
D.T.C.N.
Grandi Motori Trieste
Hatch & Kirk, Inc.
Howaldtswerke-Deutsche Werft
Korody-Colyer Corporation
M.T.U. (Motoren-und-Turbinen-Union)
Netherlands United Shipbuilding Bureaux Ltd.
Ruston Paxman Diesels Ltd.
S.A.C.M.

D 4. DIESEL ENGINES, MAIN PROPULSION
Blohm & Voss AG
Chantiers de l'Atlantique
C.R.M. Fabbrica Motori Marini
D.T.C.N.
Grandi Motori Trieste
Hatch & Kirk Inc.
Korody-Colyer Corporation
M.T.U. (Motoren-und-Turbinen-Union)
Ruston Paxman Diesels Ltd.
S.A.C.M.
Split Shipyard

D 5. DIESEL ENGINE SPARE PARTS
Blohm & Voss AG
Chantiers de l'Atlantique
C.R.M. Fabbrica Motori Marini
D.T.C.N.
Grandi Motori Trieste
Hatch & Kirk, Inc.
Korody-Colyer Corporation
M.T.U. (Motoren-und-Turbinen-Union)
Netherlands United Shipbuilding Bureaux Ltd.
Ruston Paxman Diesels Ltd.
Split Shipyard

D 6. DIESEL FUEL INJECTION EQUIPMENT
D.T.C.N.
Hatch & Kirk, Inc.
Korody-Colyer Corporation

D 7. DIVING EQUIPMENT
Thomson C.S.F.

D 8. DOCK GATES
Brooke Marine Ltd.
Dubigeon Normandie
Netherlands United Shipbuilding Bureaux Ltd.

D 9. DREDGERS
Brooke Marine Ltd.

D 10. DRY CARGO VESSELS
Batservice Verft A/S
Blohm & Voss AG
Brooke Marine Ltd.
Fr. Lürssen Werft
General Dynamics Corporation
Howaldtswerke-Deutsche Werft
Netherlands United Shipbuilding Bureaux Ltd.
Split Shipyard
Yarrow (Shipbuilders) Ltd.

D 11. DRY DOCK PROPRIETORS
Blohm & Voss AG
Howaldtswerke-Deutsche Werft
Netherlands United Shipbuilding Bureaux Ltd.

D 12. DYNAMIC POSITIONING
C.I.T. Alcatel

D 13. ECHO SOUNDERS
Van Der Heem Electronics N.V.

E 1. ECONOMISERS
Netherlands United Shipbuilding Bureaux Ltd.
Yarrow (Shipbuilders) Ltd.

E 2. ELECTRIC CABLES

E 3. ELECTRICAL AUXILIARIES
Laurence Scott & Electromotors Ltd.

E 4. ELECTRONIC COUNTERMEASURE
Aeromaritime Systems Limited

E 5. ELECTRICAL EQUIPMENT
C.S.E.E.
Ferranti Ltd.
Laurence Scott & Electromotors Ltd.
Unelec

E 6. ELECTRICAL FITTINGS

E 7. ELECTRICAL INSTALLATIONS AND REPAIRS
Cossor Electronics Limited
C.S.E.E.
Karlskronavarvet AB
Plessey Company Ltd.
Vosper Thornycroft Group, The
Yarrow (Shipbuilders) Ltd.

E 8. ELECTRICAL SWITCHGEAR
Laurence Scott & Electromotors Ltd.
Whipp & Bourne Ltd.

E 9. ELECTRO-HYDRAULIC AUXILIARIES
MacTaggart, Scott & Co. Ltd.

E 10. ELECTRONIC EQUIPMENT
Cossor Electronics Limited
C.S.E.E.
Decca Radar Ltd.
D.T.C.N.
Edo Corporation
Ferranti Ltd.
Hollandse Signaalapparaten B.V.
Plessey Company Ltd.
Selenia
Singer Librascope
Thomson C.S.F.
Van Der Heem Electronics N.V.

E 11. ELECTRONIC EQUIPMENT REFITS
Ferranti Ltd.
Plessey Company Ltd.

E 12. ENGINE MONITORS AND DATA LOGGERS
Decca Radar Ltd.
M.T.U. (Motoren-und-Turbinen-Union)

E 13. ENGINE PARTS, DIESEL
C.R.M. Fabbrica Motori Marini
Grandi Motori Trieste
Hatch & Kirk, Inc.
Korody-Colyer Corporation
M.T.U. (Motoren-und-Turbinen-Union)
Netherlands United Shipbuilding Bureaux Ltd.

E 14. ENGINE SPEED CONTROLS
C.S.E.E.
Hatch & Kirk, Inc.

E 15. ENGINE START AND SHUT-DOWN CONTROLS
C.S.E.E.
Hatch & Kirk, Inc.

E 16. ENGINES, AIRCRAFT
M.T.U. (Motoren-und-Turbinen-Union)

Der Antrieb kommt von mtu

power to the power of experience

T 4. TANKS, OIL AND WATER STORAGE
Howaldtswerke-Deutsche Werft
Split Shipyard
Rhine-Schelde Verolme

T 5. TECHNICAL PUBLICATIONS
Aeromaritime Systems Limited
Ferranti Ltd.
B.P.C. Publishing Ltd.
McGraw-Hill Book Company

T 6. TELECOMMUNICATION EQUIPMENT
Aeromaritime Systems Limited
C.I.T. Alcatel
Ferranti Ltd.
Selenia
R.F. Communications
Thomson C.S.F.
Van Der Heem Electronics N.V.

T 7. TELEGRAPH SYSTEMS
Aeromaritime Systems Limited

T 8. TELEMOTORS

T 9. TELEPHONES, BATTERY-LESS

T 10. TELEPHONES, LOUD-SPEAKING
Plessey Company Ltd., The

T 11. TENDERS
Blohm & Voss AG
Brooke Marine Ltd.
David Cheverton
Fr. Lürssen Werft
Vosper Thornycroft Group, The
Yarrow (Shipbuilders) Ltd.

T 12. TEST EQUIPMENT FOR FIRE CONTROL SYSTEMS
C.S.E.E.
Ferranti Ltd.
Hollandse Signaalapparaten B.V.
Laurence Scott & Electromotors Ltd.
Singer Librascope

T 13. TEXTILE FIBRES

T 14. TORPEDO CONTROL SYSTEMS
C.I.T. Alcatel
D.T.C.N.
Ferranti Ltd.
Hollandse Signaalapparaten B.V.
Laurence Scott & Electromotors Ltd.
Thomson C.S.F.

T 15. TORPEDO CRAFT BUILDERS
Alinavi
Batservice Verft A/S
Brooke Marine Ltd.
C.I.T. Alcatel
D.T.C.N.
Fr. Lürssen Werft
Karlskronavarvet AB
Netherlands United Shipbuilding Bureaux Ltd.
Yarrow (Shipbuilders) Ltd.

T 16. TORPEDO DEPTH AND ROLL RECORDERS
C.I.T. Alcatel
D.T.C.N.

T 17. TORPEDO ORDER AND DEFLECTION CONTROL
C.I.T. Alcatel
D.T.C.N.

T 18. TORPEDO SIDE-LAUNCHERS
D.T.C.N.

T 19. TORPEDOES AND TORPEDO TUBES
D.T.C.N.
Karlskronavarvet AB
Netherlands United Shipbuilding Bureaux Ltd.

T 20. TRAINING EQUIPMENT
C.I.T. Alcatel
C.S.E.E.
Ferranti Ltd.
Hollandse Signaalapparaten B.V.
Van Der Heem Electronics N.V.

T 21. TRAWLERS
Brooke Marine Ltd.
C.S.E.E.
Dubigeon Normandie
Yarrow (Shipbuilders) Ltd.

T 22. TUGS
Brooke Marine Ltd.
Dubigeon Normandie
Yarrow (Shipbuilders) Ltd.

T 23. TURBINE GEARS
Netherlands United Shipbuilding Bureax Ltd.

T 24. TURBINES
Blohm & Voss AG
Netherlands United Shipbuilding Bureaux Ltd.
Yarrow (Shipbuilders) Ltd.

T 25. TURBINES, EXHAUST

T 26. TURBINES, GAS MARINE
D.T.C.N.
Netherlands United Shipbuilding Bureaux Ltd.
Yarrow (Shipbuilders) Ltd.

T 27. TURBINES, STEAM MARINE
Blohm & Voss AG
Yarrow (Shipbuilders) Ltd.

U 1. UNDERWATER LIGHTS

U 2. UNDERWATER TELEVISION EQUIPMENT
Edo Corporation
Thomson C.S.F.

V 1. VALVES AND COCKS
Cockburns Ltd.
Split Shipyard

V 2. VALVES AND COCKS, HYDRAULIC
Cockburns Ltd.
MacTaggart, Scott & Co. Ltd.
Split Shipyard

V 3. VALVES, AUTOMATIC PLATE OR DISC
Cockburns Ltd.

V 4. VALVES, BUTTERFLY FLUID AND VENTILATION
Cockburns Ltd.

V 5. V/STOL AIRCRAFT
Hawker Siddeley

V 6. VOLTAGE REGULATORS, AUTOMATIC
Korody-Colyer Corporation

W 1. WARSHIP REPAIRERS
AB Bofors
Alinavi
Brooke Marine Ltd.
Dubigeon Normandie
Fr. Lürssen Werft
Howaldtswerke-Deutsche Werft
Karlskronavarvet AB
Netherlands United Shipbuilding Bureaux Ltd.
Plessey Company Ltd., The
Vickers Limited
Vosper Thornycroft Group, The
Yarrow (Shipbuilders) Ltd.

W 2. WARSHIPS
Alinavi
Blohm & Voss AG
Brooke Marine Ltd.
Dubigeon Normandie
Fr. Lürssen Werft
General Dynamics Corporation
Howaldtswerke-Deutsche Werft
Netherlands United Shipbuilding Bureaux Ltd.
Sofrexan
Vickers Limited
Vosper Thornycroft Group, The
Yarrow (Shipbuilders) Ltd.

W 3. WATER TUBE BOILERS
Blohm & Voss AG
Howaldtswerke-Deutsche Werft
Netherlands United Shipbuilding Bureaux Ltd.
Yarrow (Shipbuilders) Ltd.

W 4. WEAPON SYSTEMS
AB Bofors
Aerospatiale
C.S.E.E.
Ferranti Ltd.
General Dynamics Corporation
Hollandse Signaalapparaten B.V.
Selenia
Thomson C.S.F.
Vosper Thornycroft Group, The

W 5. WEAPON SYSTEMS (SONAR COMPONENTS)
Dubigeon Normandie
Edo Corporation
General Dynamics Corporation
Hollandse Signaalapparaten B.V.
Laurence Scott & Electromotors Ltd.
Thomson C.S.F.
Van Der Heem Electronics N.V.
Vosper Thornycroft Group, The

W 6. WELDING, ARC, ARGON ARC OR GAS
Karlskronavarvet A.B.
Yarrow (Shipbuilders) Ltd.

W 7. WINCHES
MacTaggart, Scott & Co. Ltd.

X 1. X-RAY WORK
Karlskroavarvet A.B.
Split Shipyard
Yarrow (Shipbuilders) Ltd.

Y 1. YACHTS (POWERED)
Brooke Marine Ltd.
Dubigeon Normandie
Fairey Marine Ltd.
Fr. Lürssen Werft
Vosper Thornycroft Group, The
Yarrow (Shipbuilders) Ltd.

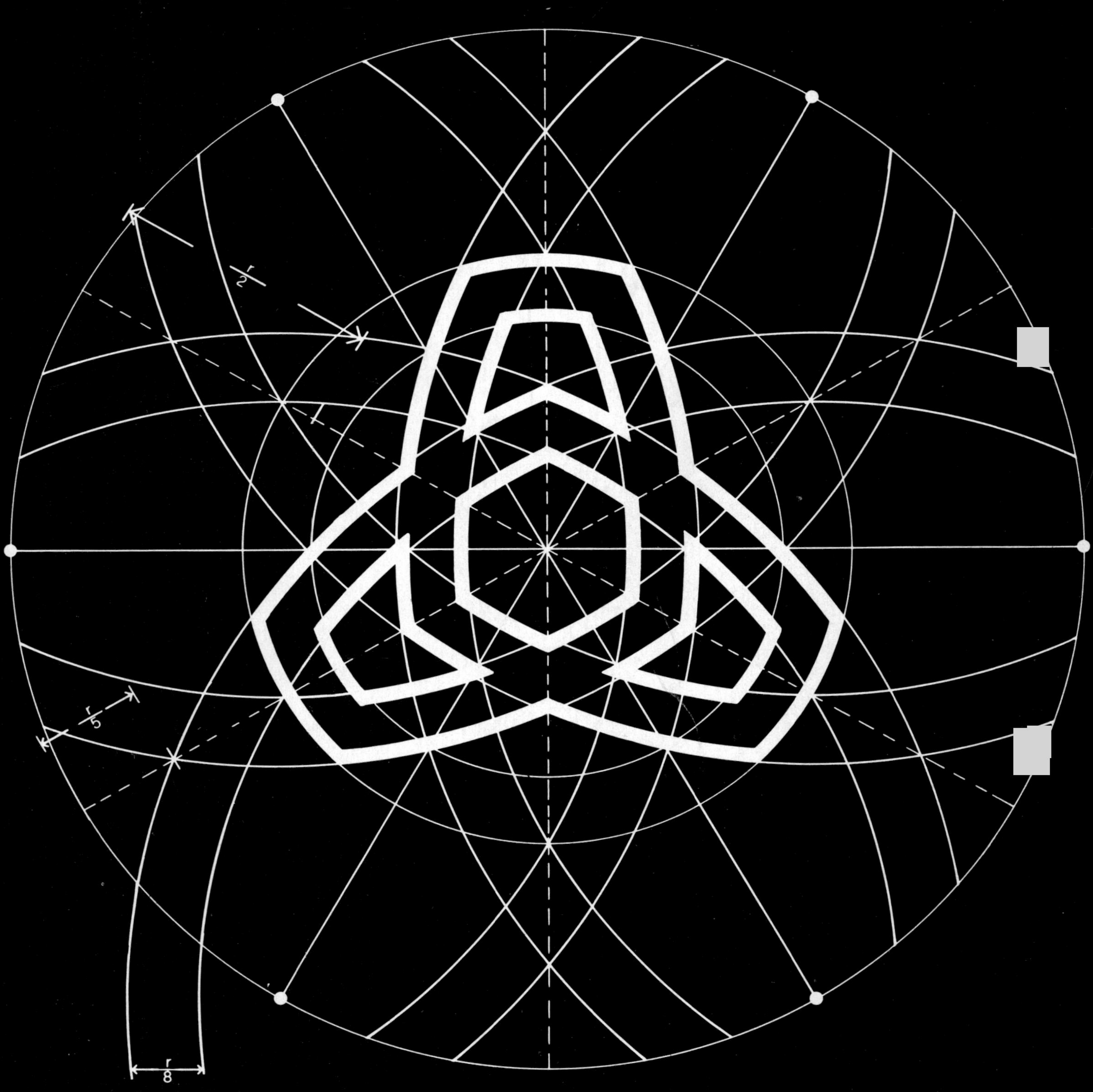

Grandi Motori Trieste
FIAT-ANSALDO-C.R.D.A.-S.p.A.

THE SUBMARINES

BUILT BY

SHIPYARD & DIESEL ENGINE FACTORY •SPLIT•

SPLIT - YUGOSLAVIA

We predict that you'll need this sound ray path analyser for Sonar operations.

The SPI-03 is efficient, reliable and, above all, versatile. Use it to predict the optimum mode for fixed transducer operation and VDS transducer depth for surface ships: to predict optimum listening and escape depths for submarines: to predict optimum transducer depths for helicopters and effective operating areas for sonobuoys. As a trainer, use it to teach sonar operators in acoustic ray path relationship.

CONVERGENCE ZONE

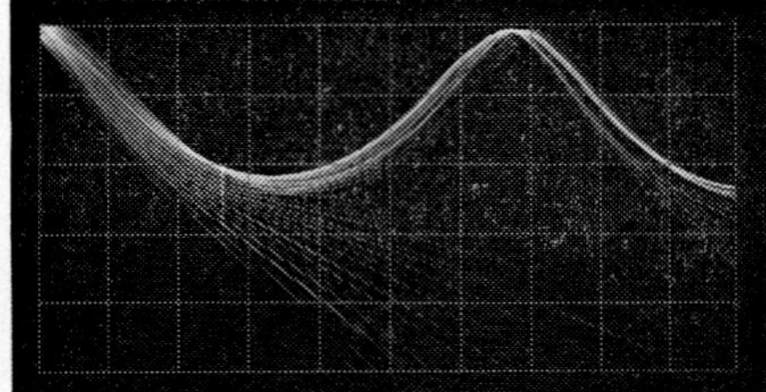

Bottom reflections off

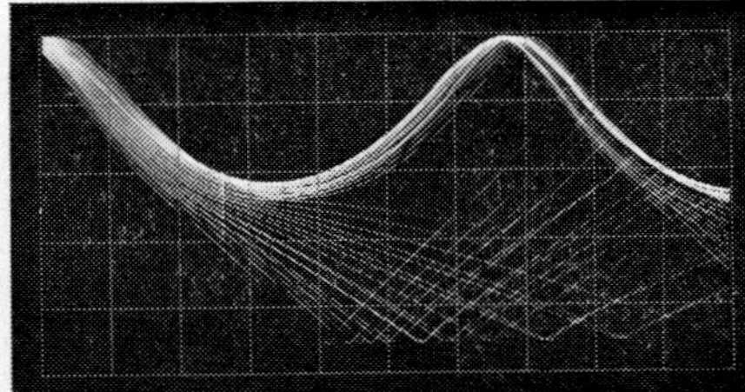

Bottom reflections on

PREDICTION FOR VDS ADJUSTMENT

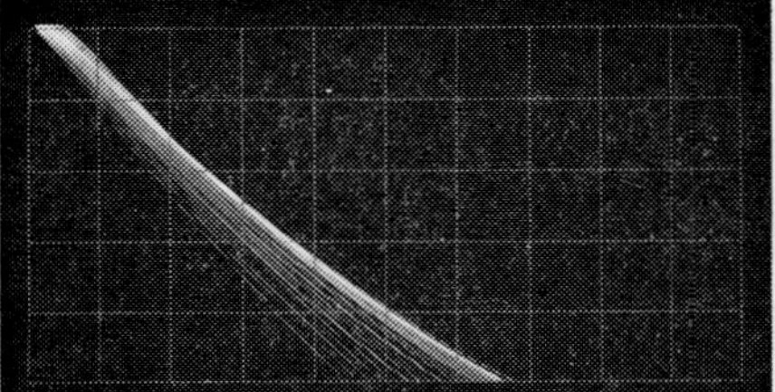

Hull mounted sonar

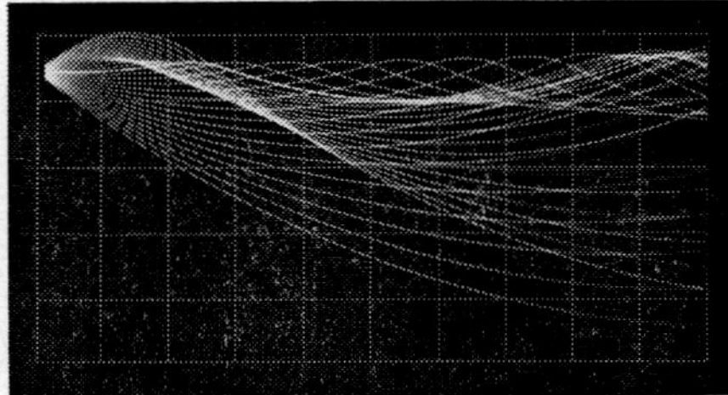

Variable depth sonar, same conditions

SOUND CHANNELS

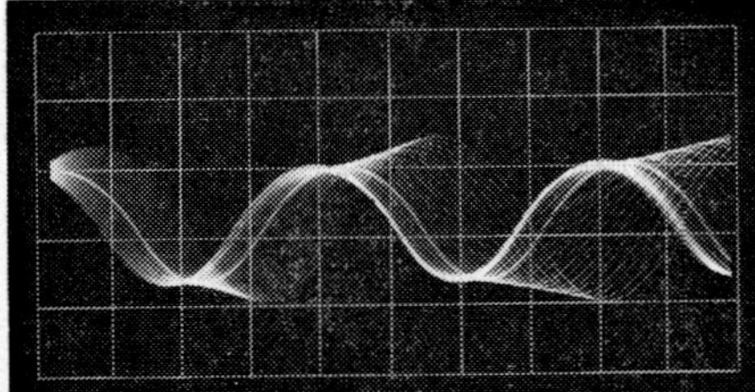

Deep sound channel

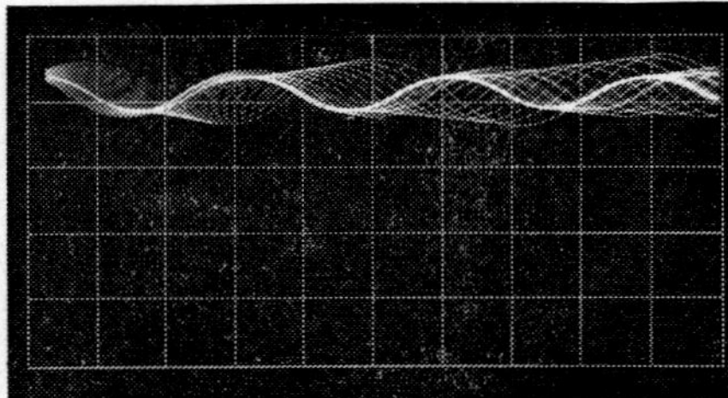

Shallow sound channel

It features:

7 in x 3½ in sound ray path CRT display
5 adjustable water layers and constant gradient in the sixth or bottom layer
maximum calculation time 74 ms.
adjustable beam widths from 5° - 40°
5-position test switch
easy alignment and maintenance
compact construction
all solid state.

For full details, please ask for our SPI-03 leaflet.

Program:

- Sound ray path analysers
- Sonar
- Shipborne simulators
- Shorebased training systems
- Echo sounders
- Sub bottom profilers

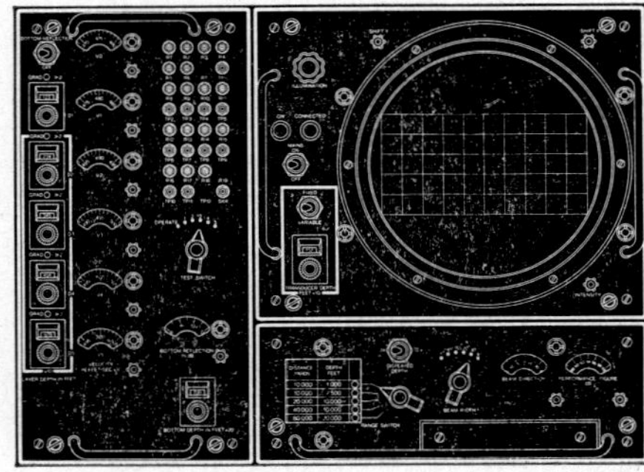

VAN DER HEEM ELECTRONICS B.V.
P.O. BOX 1060, THE HAGUE,
THE NETHERLANDS

A MEMBER OF THE
PHILIPS GROUP OF COMPANIES

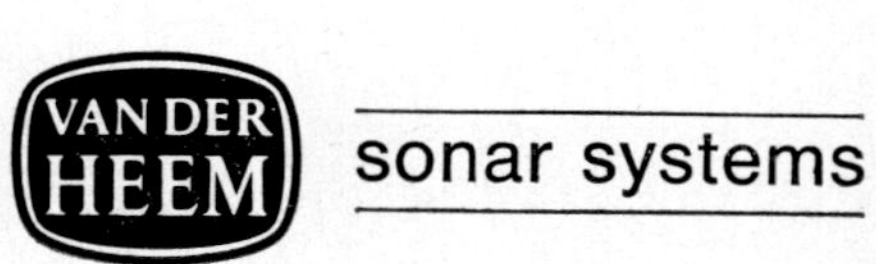

H2

Original design Worldwide success.

With 18 licensees, 11 production centers, more than 50 maintenance bases in the world, the S.E.M.T.-Pielstick diesel engines offer you the following advantages :

- A wide range of power of high speed and medium speed engines - from 900 to 17.100 HP.

- Two types of modern reliable and compact engines :
- S.E.M.T.- Pielstick, PA type : from 900 to 6.300 HP
- S.E.M.T.- Pielstick, PC type : from 3000 to 17.100 HP.

10.8 million HP of S.E.M.T.-Pielstick engines are in service or on order, including 50% of the total power installed in the medium speed range.

Due to their great flexibility the S.E.M.T-Pielstick engines are used for :

- merchant marine propulsion - power plants - generating sets - railway traction - drilling & pumping sets - offshore platforms - fishing vessels - tugs

Chantiers de l'Atlantique département moteurs
2, Quai de Seine - 93-Saint-Denis Tél. 820 61 91 Télex 62 333 F Motlan

A magic carpet for modern Persia

How to move troops, vehicles and stores over deep water, shoals, beaches and marshland – fast?

The Imperial Iranian Navy's answer is the amphibious hovercraft and they now have ten in service. This Wellington (BH.7) Class can carry 170 fully-equipped troops, or a combination of troops, guns and vehicles, at over 60 knots.

For strike and off-shore interception with surface-to-surface weapon systems, for assault and logistic support, for reconnaissance and casualty evacuation, the hovercraft gives real flexibility to defence forces.

WORLD HOVERCRAFT LEADERS

british hovercraft corporation

EAST COWES · ISLE OF WIGHT · ENGLAND

A member of the Westland Group of Companies

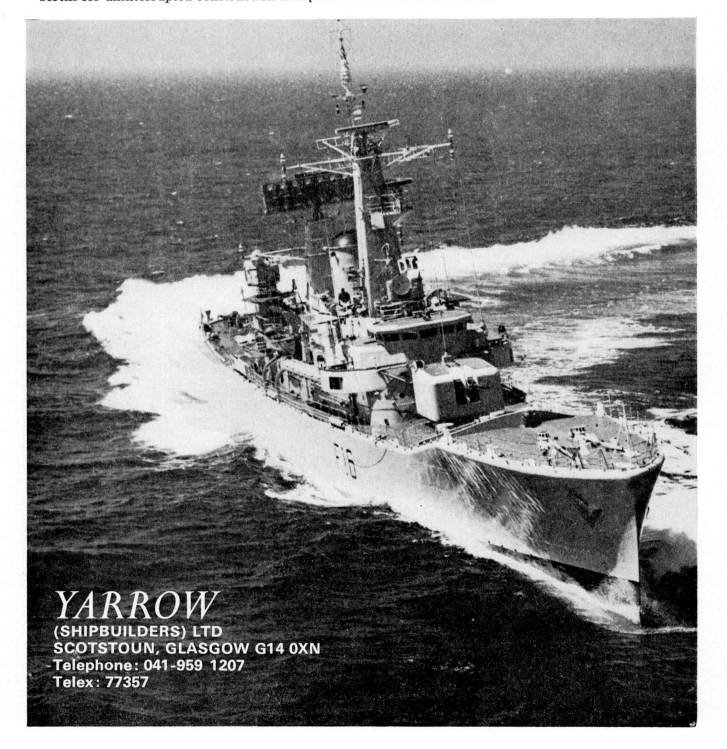

M22 weapon control system on board Royal Swedish Navy 'Spica' class MTB.

M20

Signaal's integrated weapon control systems:

ultimate compactness

Each weapon control system of the M 20 family is designed for use on board ships ranging from motorgunboats up to destroyers. An M 20 is an autonomous weapon cell. Depending on its configuration, it controls guns, torpedoes and/or guided weapons simultaneously. Air and surface targets can be handled at the same time. The spherical radome, which covers the fully stabilized warning and tracking antenna system is now characteristic in a large number of navies.

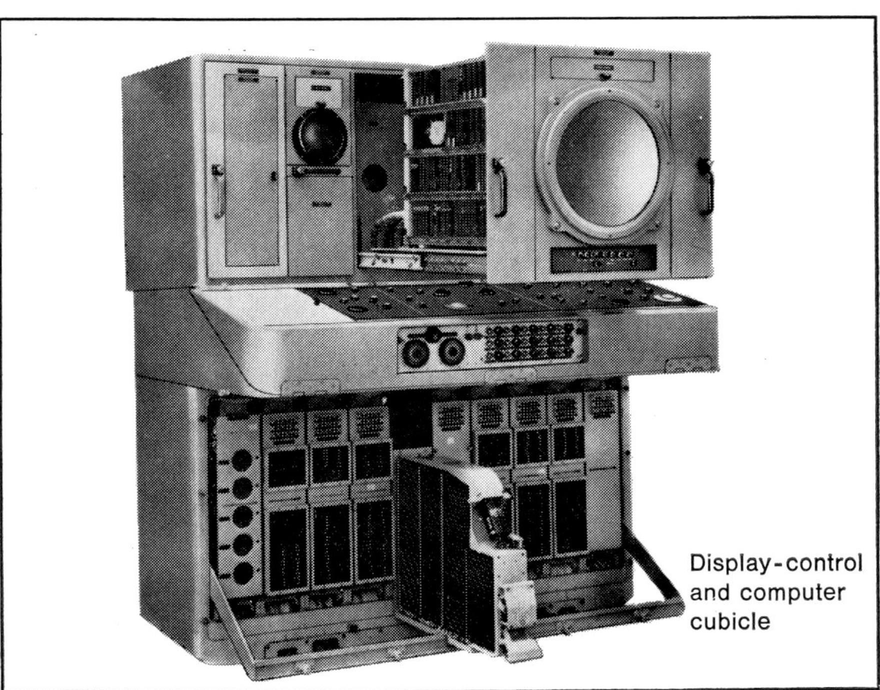

Display-control and computer cubicle

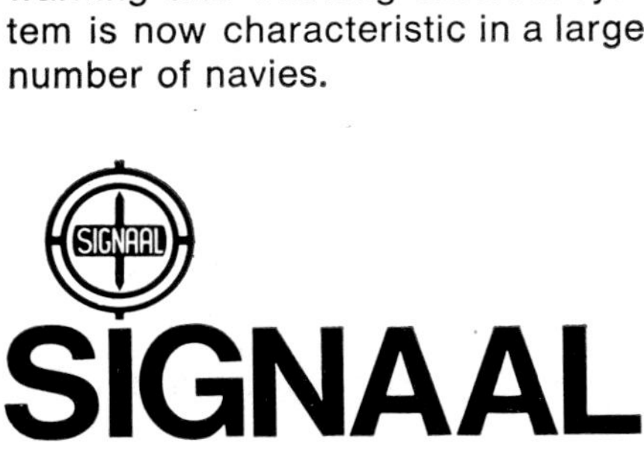

SIGNAAL

radar, weapon control, data handling and air traffic control systems

B.V. HOLLANDSE SIGNAALAPPARATEN HENGELO

For over three decades, Librascope has helped to pioneer technological advancements in all aspects of Naval weapon systems. Our first product was an aircraft weight and balance computer for use in aircraft operation. From this beginning in mechanical linkage computers, Librascope worked with the Navy to develop electro-mechanical analog computers for Naval antiaircraft and antisubmarine weapon control systems. The alliance between Librascope and the Navy has paid off in progress. Today, virtually every ASW weapon control system installed aboard surface ships and submarines of the U. S. Navy was designed and manufactured by Librascope.

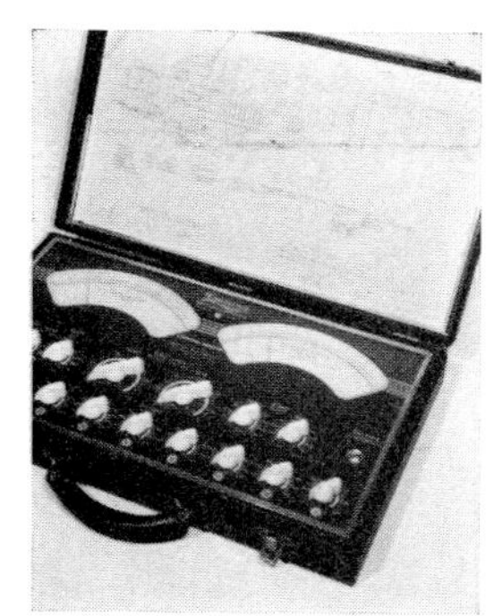

To keep pace with the rapidly

Good ideas...

OFFICIAL U.S. NAVY PHOTO

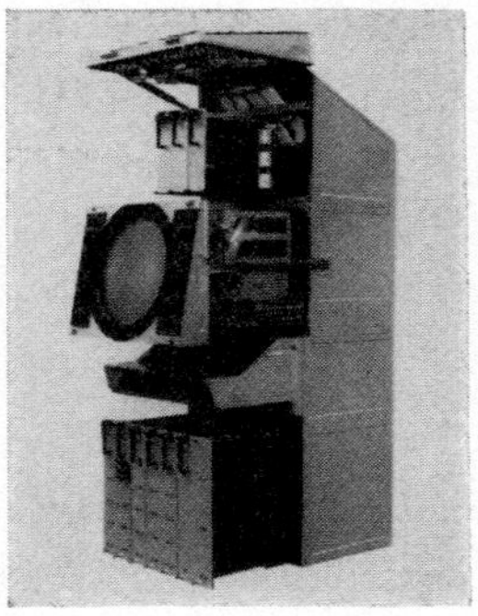

The Harrier is free.

Every battle commander who uses conventional strike aircraft is stuck with the fact that they're dependent on runways. They're helpless without them. Vulnerable on them. Now Harrier has forced a fundamental change on all modern tactical thinking.

Its unique V/STOL capability gives a battle commander a new tactical weapon. Harrier is not tied to vulnerable static sites, with their easily spotted, easily eliminated concrete runways.

By using Harrier's freedom and independence to the full, he can operate effectively from unsophisticated, dispersed sites over a wide area. Harrier can submerge into a wood or under camouflage nets and disappear. It's

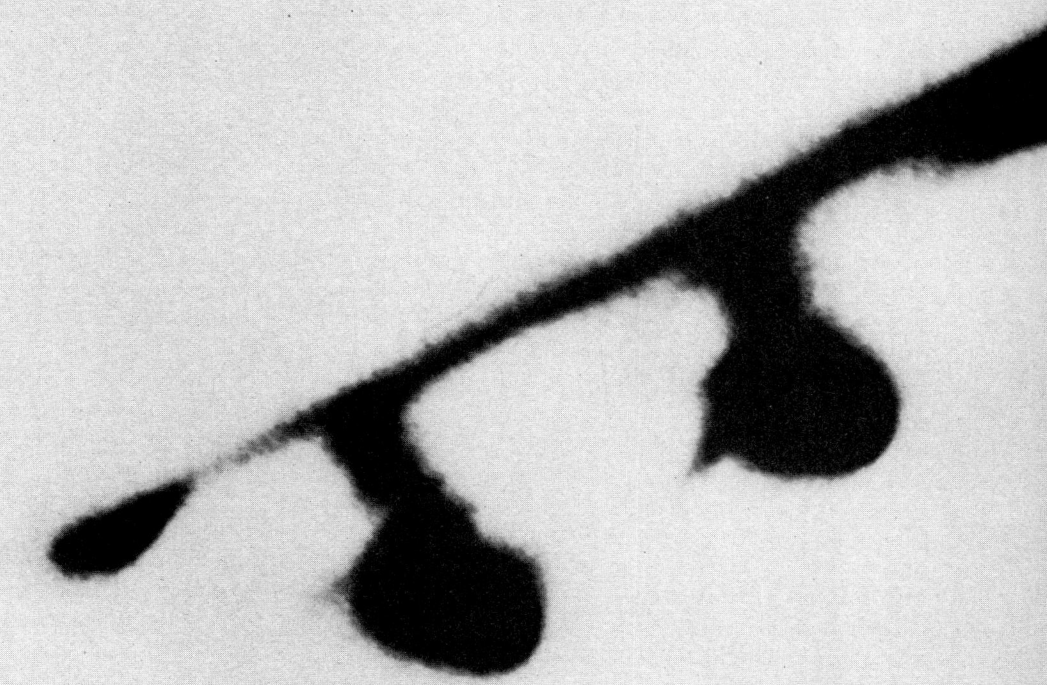

Triton radar antenna
surveillance radar of Vega system

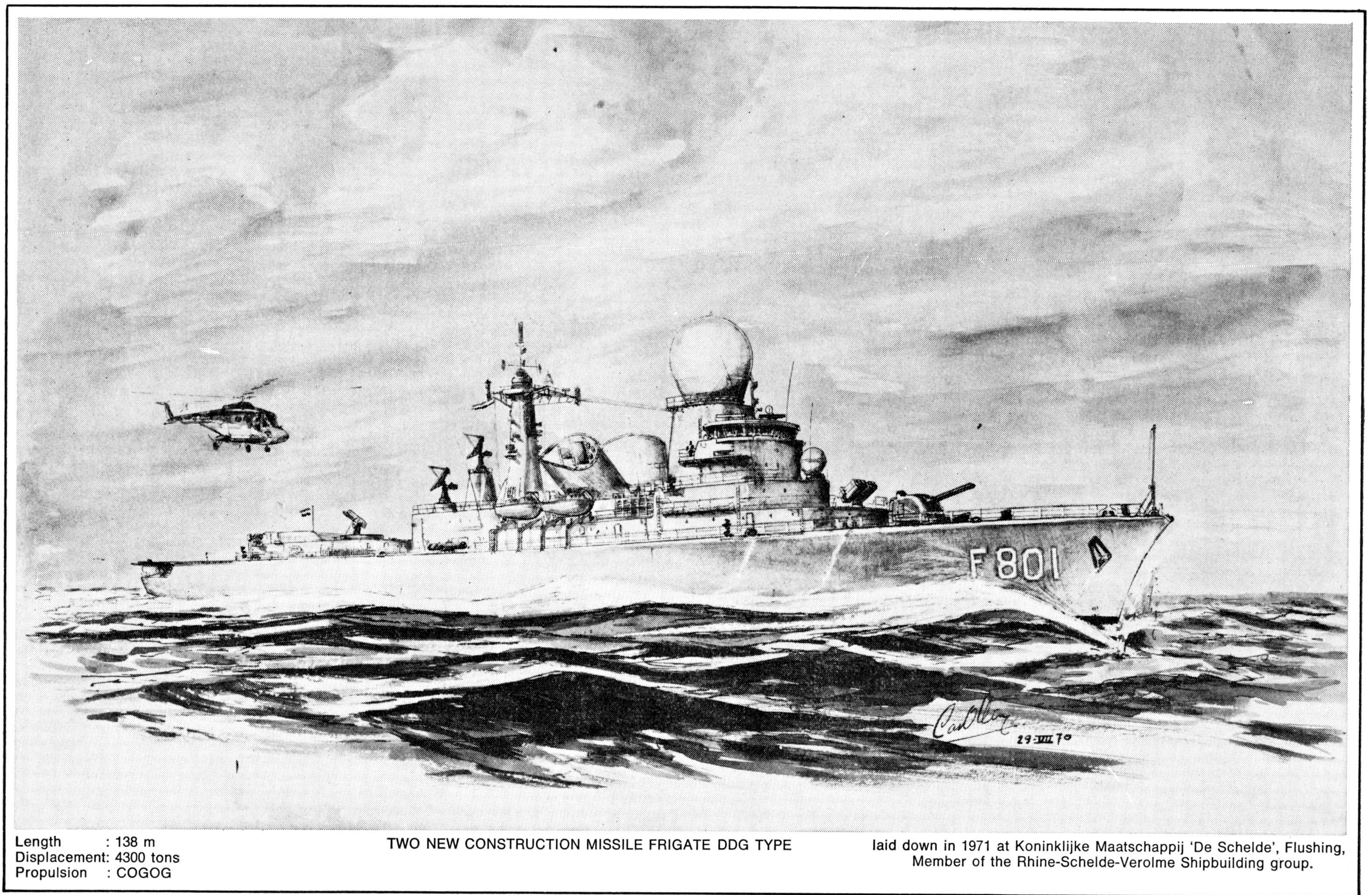

Length : 138 m
Displacement: 4300 tons
Propulsion : COGOG

TWO NEW CONSTRUCTION MISSILE FRIGATE DDG TYPE

laid down in 1971 at Koninklijke Maatschappij 'De Schelde', Flushing, Member of the Rhine-Schelde-Verolme Shipbuilding group.

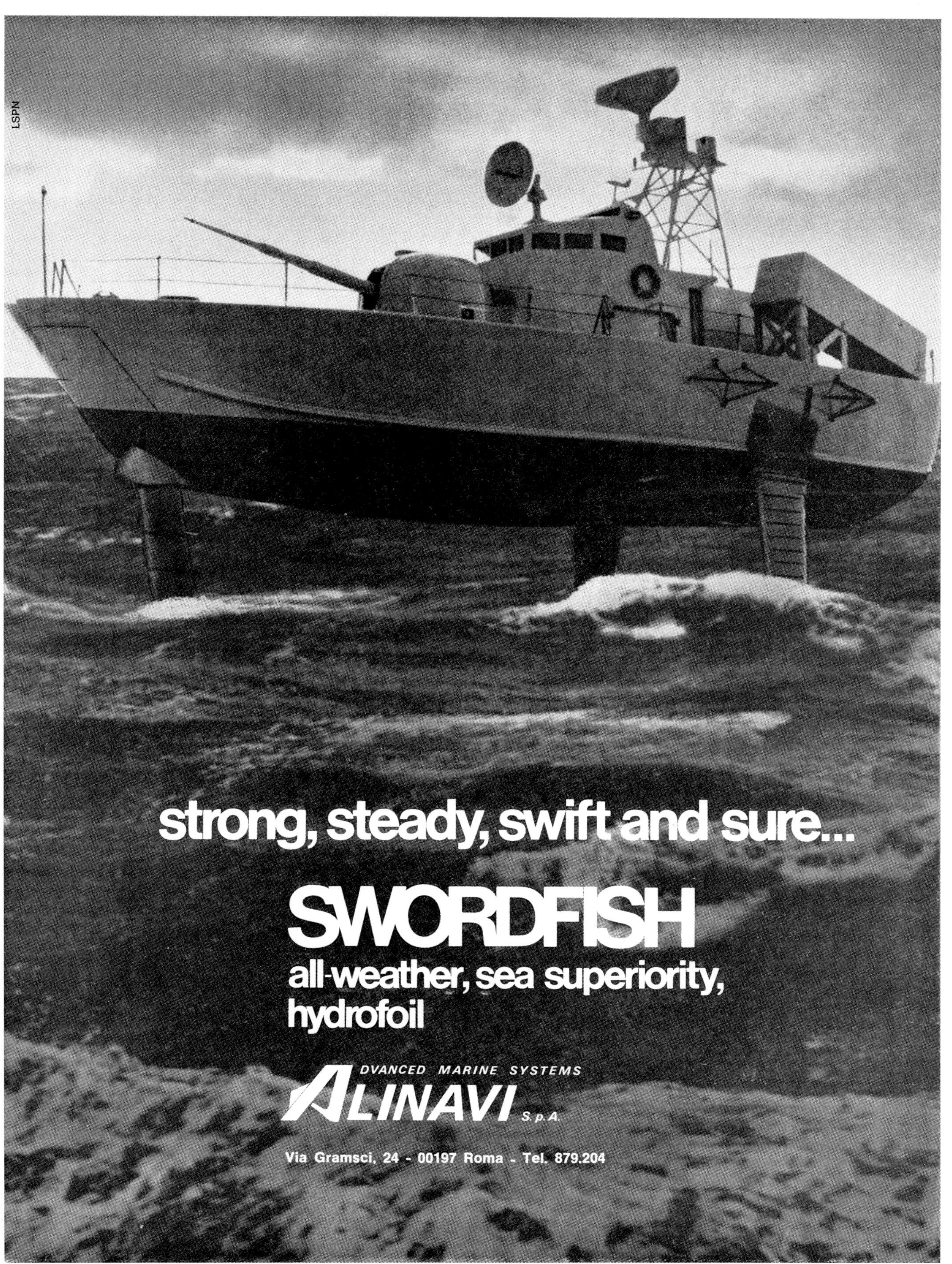
LSPN
strong, steady, swift and sure...
SWORDFISH
all-weather, sea superiority, hydrofoil
DVANCED MARINE SYSTEMS
ALINAVI S.p.A.
Via Gramsci, 24 - 00197 Roma - Tel. 879.204

BP Marine International have been supplying a comprehensive bunkering service for a great many years. With a past like ours just imagine what the future holds.
BP
BP marine international
Fuels and Lubricants Services
3
B
TRANS
Boyd
BP marine international
BP

Vittorio Veneto *International Defence Review/Italian Ministry of Defence*

JANE'S FIGHTING SHIPS

FOUNDED IN 1897 BY FRED T. JANE

EDITED BY
CAPTAIN JOHN E. MOORE RN, FRGS

1973-74

I.S.B.N. 0 354 00119 1

JANE'S YEARBOOKS

LONDON

SAMPSON LOW, MARSTON & Co., LTD.

Cossor Naval IFF Systems

CRS 357 R.C.U.

SSR 1520 Transponder

11 ft Aerial

SSR 1503 C.U.

IFF 800 Interrogator

Cossor manufacture a range of IFF Systems to meet all Naval requirements ranging from the IFF 800 System, for Escort ships offering comprehensive facilities coupled with high reliability and ease of maintainance, to the newly introduced IFF 825 M – a miniature solid state rugged diesel equipment designed for Fast Patrol Boats.

Cossor Electronics Limited,
Sales Division — Aviation & Surface Electronics.
The Pinnacles, Harlow, Essex, England.
Telephone: Harlow 26862 Telex: 81228 Cables: Cossor, Harlow.

JANE'S FIGHTING SHIPS 1973-74

EDITED BY

CAPTAIN JOHN E. MOORE

Except for the United States of America, Philippines, South Korea, South Vietnam, and Taiwan China which were edited and compiled by:

NORMAN POLMAR

CONTENTS

Refits and Modernisation

Integrated systems packages (turnkey projects).

Worldwide technical support services and training.

When your Navy is involved in ship refits, or purchasing ships needing modernisation, you will need services and facilities during planning and implementation of your weapon and electronics systems.

All these services and facilities are available from Plessey whose teams of specialists will take full responsibility for design, engineering and implementation of weapons and electronics systems. Additionally we will provide ship survey facilities, commissioning engineers and overhaul technicians—all under the direct control of an experienced Plessey project manager.

First step is to invite Plessey Services, together with a ship repairer, to inspect the ship, assess its role, staffing, terms of payment, delivery, guarantees, etc.

Plessey Services will undertake training courses for officers and ratings at Plessey and other equipment manufacturers' establishments, and plan harbour and sea trials.

Plessey Services provide ship maintenance engineers working either on board or ashore. They instruct your engineers on land or at sea. We also help you create an efficient shore-based training and maintenance organisation.

This organisation has arrangements for providing spares for all weapons and electronic installations.

1. *The Almirante Williams undergoing a major refit for the Chilean Navy.*
2. *A section of the operations room of the Type 42 guided-missile destroyer, fully equipped with Plessey Naval Displays.*

The Plessey Company Limited
Addlestone, Weybridge, Surrey, England
Tel: Weybridge 47282. Telex: 262329

687 PRS

FOREWORD

This book is about fighting ships, of which some 15,000 of all classes are listed, from vast aircraft carriers to the myriad support ships which are vital to a fleet's existence. Unless one's interest is solely that of the model maker the existence of these ships must prompt, first, the question "Why?" and, if that is satisfactorily answered, the further query "Do they meet the need?"

Certainly we shall find varying reasons in different countries but one basic cause is the fear of conflict. It is as essential for the well-informed layman as it is for the naval planner to be quite clear about the impact of this fear in the countries concerned. There is little point in crying "Deterrence" if the ships constructed for this purpose lack adequate fighting capabilities.

One does not need to be a political commentator or a professional man of government to realise the few basic facts which govern the "Fear" situation in this brutal and complicated world. To do so we must accept the division of the world as it is today and not as the liberal idealists would have us believe. We must accept the fact that many governments and leaders are human, fallible, greedy and power-loving. It is in these failings that we will find the roots of our fear. It is no exaggeration to say that the world is at war today. We are all at war against brutality, murder and violence whether it be in minor forms or in the international sphere where it has support from ambitious and, in many cases, inexperienced leaders. This all tends to destroy stability and to make the likelihood of major hostilities even greater. It gives more chance of a polarisation of interests and less chance for the peaceful improvement of the less fortunate countries. It results in greater sums being spent on armaments and is one of the main reasons for the existence of the world's fleets.

When Lenin laid the pattern for the advance of world communism, the world he saw was one very different from that of today. The great increase in the number of new small independent states has multiplied the points of possible friction; and too many of these new states, rejecting colonialism, have substituted violent dictatorships steeped in nationalism. This fragmentation has given opportunities for external interference unknown for many years and has opened a path for a new form of imperialism, disguised as political idealism. In this imbroglio nations have built fleets for different reasons—all, in one way or another, based on the fear of violence.

In this book it is possible to differentiate five major types of fleet:

(a) the status symbol navy;
(b) the coast defence fleet;
(c) the minor naval power;
(d) the major naval power;
(e) the super-power.

Taking these in turn it is instructive to examine how the various countries have approached their problems and, in their solution, to discover whether they have obtained "value for money".

The first type of navy need concern us little. It is probably best exemplified by ex-President Nkrumah's order of the *Black Star* for Ghana. This ship was never delivered and is now HMS *Mermaid* but was intended as a floating display with Nkrumah as the centre-piece.

Passing to more serious applications of naval power we come to the coast defence fleets of which there are a number now in existence. They range in size from a few gunboats to those comparable to that of the Philippines with a frigate leading a force of some twenty-five major patrol vessels, the same number of inshore patrol craft and a force of landing ships. These are clearly not intended for prolonged operations beyond coastal waters and would be adequate for support of military activity in the seven thousand odd islands which make up the Philippines group. There is a sensible balance in the types of ships included and a similarity in the training required, and this represents a navy which should be providing a fair return for capital and running expenses.

The minor naval powers represent the largest number of countries in this book and the varying methods of approach are most interesting. Starting from the west we find included in this category the navies of the main countries of South and Central America, amongst them Argentina, Brazil, Chile, Colombia, Ecuador, Mexico, Uruguay and Venezuela. With aircraft carriers owned by Argentina and Brazil one cannot help wondering whether the considerable capital and running costs are justified and whether the tasks set them could not be carried out as efficiently by shore-based LRMP aircraft. This would free escorts and provide capital for more smaller ships to cover greater areas with embarked helicopters. Such vessels are shortly to enter service in Brazil, the six "Niteroi" class DLGs representing the latest and, possibly, the most powerful ships in South American waters. In addition to surface ships several new submarines are joining these navies as well as missile boats and FPBs. These have obvious roles but the best financial return for these navies, which all have considerable coastlines and riverine areas for their operations, would seem to be in an increased number of smaller, faster vessels designed for their roles rather than for prolonged action in a major war.

Moving eastwards, and leaving the NATO navies for later consideration, the Swedish navy presents many points of interest. New patrol submarines, missile and torpedo-boats and shore-based helicopters present a formidable barrier to any operations against their coasts. Now that the cruisers have gone, the backing for these forces is provided by destroyers and frigates, with a new class of minelayers to operate off the coast. This at present appears a well balanced navy designed for a specific task, but uncertain of its future as the politicians, hopeful of peace, cut its financial support.

Egypt must be considered in this category with the main bulk of its navy provided by the USSR. Its twelve submarines and the Light Forces with "Osas", "Komars", "Shershens" and P6s could be a formidable outfit if well manned and led. They represent a fair return for money if considered as support for operations against Israel, which is rapidly building up a navy whose emphasis is similarly on submarines and Light Forces. Both are well suited for interdiction, raiding and reconnaissance.

In the Indian Ocean the navies of India and Pakistan have already shown their capabilities in the war of December 1971. Both have submarines, cruisers and destroyers/frigates; the Indians have Osa missile boats and Pakistan is reported to be considering missiles for Chinese-built "Shanghai" class. In the war of 1971 the aircraft carrier Vikrant was very active but a successful submarine attack would have deprived the Indians not only of their only operating centre but also of the twenty to thirty aircraft embarked. The main query in both navies, however, is the value of the cruisers. Large ships with ships' companies of seven to eight hundred represent a tying up of resources which, in an area of great distances, could be used for more smaller ships covering greater areas.

Two other navies operate in the southern corners of the Indian Ocean, those of Australia and South Africa. The latter relies on LRMP aircraft and Buccaneers of the Air Force to support a growing fleet of destroyers/frigates and submarines, whilst the former still retains an ageing carrier and one which can operate helicopters. Both are planning

new classes of destroyers/frigates, those of Australia being larger than might have been expected. But in this part of the world distances are immense and the endurance of both men and ships must be considered. With two helicopters, missiles and gas turbines the Australian DDL is a most interesting advance.

Finally, in the Pacific, there are two navies of great interest and importance. Both belong to countries which must be considered, for different reasons, as very major powers: China and Japan. Whilst the latter's navy is known as the Maritime Self-defence Force, that of the former, by its actions, has also held a claim to a similar title. However, the roles of the two are very different. China with its vast area and huge population is far more self-sufficient than Japan, which relies overwhelmingly on imports for her raw materials. For China the term "self-defence" has meant the protection of her coast-line, some 2,500 miles, varying in winter from sub-zero to tropical temperatures. To this end she has built a fleet based on submarines and Light Forces. With the arrival of the new missile-destroyers it is questionable whether this navy is any longer in the "self-defence" category. New submarines, possibly nuclear, have been seen and, with her ability to rival the Western nations in missile and nuclear matters, there seems no reason why she should not embark on a Polaris-type building programme. There is, therefore, every likelihood that the next few years will see the Chinese navy spreading its influence abroad.

Her neighbour, Japan, has a different connotation for the term "self-defence". This must include both the protection of at least the four main islands with their huge coastlines as well as the sea-lanes carrying her exports and imports. China has internal lines of communication—Japan has none. In a difficult Japanese political situation the creation of a navy adequate for these tasks is probably impossible. But the introduction of the "Haruna" class with helicopters may foreshadow improvements, though protection with SAMs and increases in LRMP aircraft, submarines and fleet support are clearly necessary.

So to the major naval powers, and among these are the major maritime powers of NATO with the exception of the USA. In the Mediterranean both Turkey and Greece are steadily modernising their fleets, the former including locally built ships such as the frigates of the "Berk" class, whilst the latter is now taking the very sensible step of purchasing "La Combattante" missile boats, invaluable amongst the Aegean islands.

Further west Italy is once again proving not only that she has imaginative planners and designers but that she can build good ships. Foremost amongst these is the *Vittorio Veneto,* a ship possessing not only reasonable speed and long range but also a combined SAM-A/S launcher and the capability to carry nine A/S helicopters, possibly Sea Kings, in the future. All this is included in a hull of 8,850 tons full load displacement with a complement of 530. Her smaller consorts of the "Andrea Doria" class carry four helicopters in a 6,500-ton hull whilst, another 2,000 tons smaller, the "Audace" class has two helicopters. In a submarine environment these three classes have the ability to deploy a large force of helicopters, still one of the submarine's two most effective adversaries. By keeping down size and cost the Italians have produced ships which can deploy over large areas for ASW operations and have shown the value of smaller and, therefore, more numerous ships.

Spain, with coastlines both in the Mediterranean and in the Atlantic, is building the new "Andalucia" frigates at Ferrol and "Daphne" class submarines at Cartagena. Meanwhile nearly 3,000 men are embarked in the aircraft carrier and cruiser which are amongst the oldest ships in the fleet and it is questionable whether they are really earning their keep. More Orion LRMP aircraft would seem a good plan for Spain.

Four more "Daphnes" and a force of modern frigates and corvettes make up the bulk of Portugal's navy, which, with present colonial commitments, has a considerable number of landing craft.

To the north, and with the same dual-ocean problem as Spain, is the considerable French navy. Here we find for the first time a force of ballistic missile submarines: with five built or building instead of the original four, France will ensure that one is always on patrol. The shape of the remainder of the fleet shows the world-wide calls on this navy. Two aircraft carriers are backed by a growing force of fast modern frigates/destroyers and submarines. In the surface fleet the provision of French-produced missiles, SSM, SAM and A/S, is a notable feature whilst considerable numbers of minesweepers/hunters and amphibious forces help to make this a strong, well-balanced fleet. There is, however, some cause for concern in the lack, except in a few ships, of embarked helicopters. Perhaps their appearance in the *Duguay-Trouin* and the *Georges Leygues* suggests that this is being remedied. Nevertheless France is once again possessed of a formidable fleet.

Belgium is at last breaking free from her long-standing addiction to minesweepers, and the new E-71 frigates, though lacking in speed and helicopters, will make an interesting addition to her fleet.

In the Netherlands, even more radical ideas are in train. Building to a plan of ASW and MCM groups, the Netherlands, which shed their carrier in 1968 and have only one cruiser remaining, are building new destroyers, frigates and MCM vessels, whilst they increase their strength of LRMP aircraft and helicopters. Abjuring the cost of nuclear submarines and large ships the Dutch will, in the next ten years, have a modern fleet designed for stated roles and well supported both afloat and in the air.

West Germany, so far with eyes more on the Baltic than elsewhere, has a large submarine and Light Forces building programme. Small, fast patrol submarines have been Germany's main contribution to Western naval construction and currently she is involved in the largest building programme of this type in the world, with the possible exception of China. Her "Jaguar" class FPBs are fine craft but are being overtaken by the Type 143 and 148 missile boats, 30 in all. With a backing of destroyers, MCM vessels, amphibious craft and support ships this is a well-founded and efficient navy. Whether West Germany will turn more to the ocean areas with ships of similar type to the "Lutjens" class instead of concentrating on the very vulnerable Baltic flank remains to be seen. At least her Naval Air Arm can operate in both directions, though Atlantics will be vulnerable in the Baltic.

The small Danish fleet is primarily concerned with local defence. Small submarines, frigates, corvettes, a number of missile boats under construction and both torpedo-boats and mine warfare craft make up the bulk of this force.

The other northern member of NATO, Norway, has a fleet of similar make-up, stronger in submarines and missile-boats armed with the native Penguin missile. This is hardly surprising in view of the problems of being NATO's northern flank. These are both sound, small navies which are valuable additions to the NATO whole but unlikely to effect very much on their own in anything more than a state of harassment.

The Canadian navy has been the subject of much adverse comment from "liberal" politicians who conceive its task as "Home Defence". Others, more realistic, have acknowledged that, as in World War II, its task in war would include oceanic operations. No longer having to operate her single aircraft carrier Canada has purchased new submarines and has designed and is building the "Iroquois" (D280) class of destroyers. These are much larger than

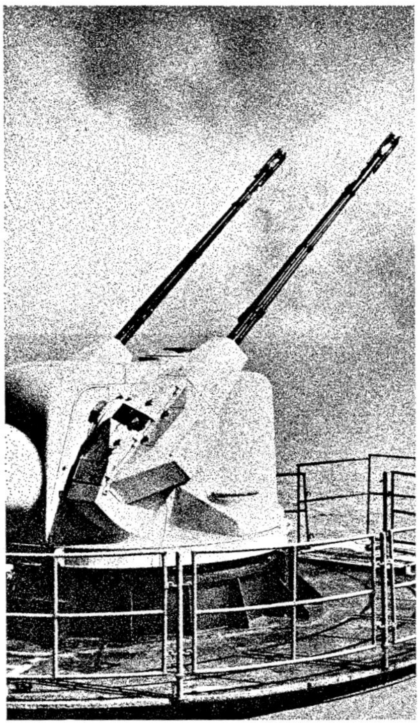

their predecessors, have a fair range, carry two Sea King helicopters, will mount Sea Sparrow missiles and are deficient only in speed. They are the leaders of a small but competent fleet, which as the pioneer of helicopter operations in rough weather needs more of these aircraft embarked. Alongside this need is the lack of missiles in Canadian ships, a necessity if they are to engage in oceanic operations.

Apart from the USA the last maritime nation in NATO is the United Kingdom. Like France she has a string of widely-scattered commitments throughout the world, but unlike any of the other maritime European members of the Organisation, she relies on voluntary service. Financial restraints have imposed severe limitations on her armed forces and these appear to be the controlling elements in the shape and size of her fleet. The role of this fleet has been the subject of much political debate, and though it became popular to speak of it as a "European Navy", the British commitments world-wide must be remembered, as well as the fact that the geographic boundaries of NATO are no indication of the breadth of that alliance's needs and interests.

Like all other navies that of Great Britain should be able to support governmental decisions and requirements in peacetime, it should be capable of acting in emergencies abroad or internal security crises, if called for, and at the same time be a deterrent to hostilities by possessing a fleet capable of exercising maritime control and the successful protection of shipping should this deterrence fail. All this in the wide areas which the Royal Navy is called on to cover requires ships and aircraft in quantity as well as of quality. In a fleet where political decisions have already whittled down numbers this balance is a delicate one.

Costs have kept the Polaris force to four submarines when five are necessary to guarantee one on station at all times. This is as simple a sum as that which shows that £65 million per Through-Deck Cruiser means a limited deployment of a helicopter force at sea in the future. The Royal Navy has already cut the Type 82 building programme from four to one because of vastly increased costs and the new MCM vessels are already spoken of as reaching the £5 million mark.

In a navy needing ships in quantity it is questionable whether the enormously expensive ships in the present programme will, in the search for quality, give full value for money. The Italians have put nine helicopters at sea in the *Vittorio Veneto,* well under half the size of the TDC and saving not only in capital costs but in running costs, as she needs only two-thirds of the latter's complement. In a world where half the overall expenditure on a ship (capital plus running costs throughout her life) are spent on her manning, and in a navy needing many ships, such a vessel would seem to be a justifiable economy.

Other large sums are expended on the amphibious forces. With two commando carriers and two assault ships as the main body of the amphibious element the project of conveying and landing the Royal Marines abroad is very vulnerable to material defects or enemy action. With more, cheaper, faster ships built to commercial standards such activities would have greater chances of success. Were there greater numbers of helicopter cruisers of the *Vittorio Veneto* type these, too, would be a valuable addition in emergencies.

Over-complication is a sure way of achieving inflated costs. Other contributory factors are delays in design, ordering, building and maintenance. These result not only in price increases but also in inefficiency. The delays in converting HMS *Tiger* so that she could carry only four helicopters brought her final price to the absurd figure of £13.5 million. No accurate estimate has been given of the amount lost over the development of the useless mark 23 torpedo and its predecessors but the result was that Britain's latest submarines were operating until 1973 with torpedoes designed in the mid-1930s as their most accurate armament. The costs of the development of four surface-to-air weapons are not available en bloc but appear to have precluded the production of either long range A/S weapons or SSMs. As a result of these delays a few frigates are only now receiving the thirteen-year-old Australian Ikara to back up the single helicopter which is the most that even the more modern destroyers and frigates carry, and some of the "County" class are now embarking the commercially-designed French Exocet SSM.

In a situation where, as Nicholas Whitestone says in his new book *The Submarine,* "The dominant reality of naval warfare today and for the foreseeable future is the fighting superiority of the submarine," the British nuclear Fleet boats are amongst the best afloat and are the natural opposition to similar enemy submarines. Although HMS *Dreadnought* finally joined the fleet in 1963 only six others have so far followed her. The other deadly enemy of the submarine is the helicopter and, although the Lynx is replacing the Wasp and the Sea King the Wessex, embarked numbers are still low. This is partly due to the fact that all but a few British ships accommodate only one helicopter whilst certain other navies have designed their ships for two in a 4,000-ton hull. Combined with the fact that if the three TDCs are eventually completed their availability will only allow three very occasionally, two more frequently, and one regularly at sea this means a serious deficiency in this very threatening A/S weapon system.

Finally, the Royal Navy is lacking in air cover. The Royal Air Force provides magnificent support with its Nimrod LRMP aircraft but fighter cover is another matter. The 1966 claim that the RAF would provide all that was needed was doubted at the time and these doubts have been proved painfully true in later exercises. It is a simple arithmetical fact that one cannot protect ships beyond the range of land-based fighters, and at the limits of that range reaction time is generally too great. Whilst in the civil-air world the Government has seen fit to spend £600 millions on Concorde before a firm market has been established, apparently little progress has been made with the development of a seaborne VTOL. An important role for such an aircraft is foreseen by the Government. It is to be hoped that there will be less procrastination than usual in ordering, should the 1973 project definition study be successful.

There are thus many gaps remaining in today's Royal Navy, partly as the result of financial stringency and partly because of cumulative delays and inefficiencies. Now that more ship-design work is being undertaken by contractors perhaps the design of components and weapons will be similarly delegated, as is so often the case in other navies. The resultant savings could be directed to building more ships.

Lastly in this survey are the two super-powers, with the two greatest navies in the world, those of the USA and the USSR. Both have to watch costs, each has approached its problems differently.

A lot said about the Royal Navy applies equally to the USN, but in the USA great efforts are being made towards the development of new types of ship and new weapons. These were discussed by Norman Polmar in last year's edition. Here it will probably suffice to return to the original query: are the navies getting value for money? More important, are the countries to which those navies belong getting value for money? Is the policy of the USA being enhanced by the spending of some £420 million ($1 billion) on CVN 70? All this article is entitled to ask is whether this vast sum could not be better spent on smaller, less complicated and cheaper ships which would still be as fast or faster and still carry a well worthwhile number of aircraft.

Perhaps some of this money might go towards the development of the hovercraft and underwater fleet, fields in which the USN is today a leader. The former is one line of development which could revolutionise naval warfare, if

the large hovercraft proves practicable as the nuclear submarine has already done. A large helicopter-carrying hovercraft moving at 60-100 knots would be a formidable enemy to the submarine, could act in the amphibious role and would be readily and swiftly deployed in peacetime for a multitude of roles.

This year, however there is little to be added about the USN beyond last year's comments.

Not so with the USSR. Here the indefatigable Admiral Gorshkov has produced a new cruiser of the "Kara" class, two new classes of submarine, "Delta" and "Papa", and western observers wait to see how near prediction the new aircraft carrier *Kiev* will be when she appears.

To consider *Kiev* first. Last year it seemed unlikely that, if she existed, she would be designed to carry fixed-wing aircraft. This now seems to be a fair assessment. So she will probably carry helicopters and VTOL. What therefore will be her role? This depends to some extent on the capabilities of Soviet VTOL aircraft, which have hitherto been closely guarded. However, a ship of her size will have a world-wide capability and will be able to provide anti-submarine and air-strike power at any point where the Soviets deem intervention to be necessary. In other, and USN, words she will be capable of "projection of power ashore". In wartime her role is fairly clear but she will certainly add a new dimension to Soviet maritime capability.

The new "Kara" class cruiser *Nikolayev* has preceded *Kiev* from the same yard. She is a 10,000-ton cruiser with every available type of missile, gun, radar and electronic warfare device, with the exception of long-range SSMs. Very fast, she too clearly has a world-wide capability and it seems likely that a considerable number of this class of cruiser and the "Krivak" destroyers will be built.

In the Soviet submarine world the "Papa" class is now reported, possibly an enlargement of the "Charlie" class or an improvement with different missiles. The slow building rate of the "Charlies" might suggest the latter. There is, however, no doubt about the "Delta". A platform was needed for the new SS-N-8 which had been test fired from the single "Hotel III". A reconstruction of the "Yankee" class, carrying twelve 4,000-n.-mile missiles instead of sixteen SS-N-6s, has filled this requirement, giving the Soviets far greater flexibility in the Atlantic and Pacific deployments of their seaborne nuclear deterrent.

Other significant additions to the Fleet are the second "Chilikin" class support ship and her smaller cousin. Having achieved a global naval capability for all major classes of ships and submarines the Soviets are giving proper consideration to their future stores and fuel support. In the past this has relied largely on tankers, both naval and mercantile. The new ships have a general purpose role and more must be expected.

In considering staff problems it has long been the habit to "take the worst possible case". As this today is the obliteration of the civilised, if not the whole, world this aspect of naval warfare is a highly specialised one in which undetectability, weapon efficiency and invulnerable communications are prime factors. Should the deterrent effect of well over a hundred ballistic-missile-carrying submarines fail there is no point in considering the functions of the remainder of the fleets. A large proportion of mankind will have been killed or be dying painful deaths.

It is therefore at a lower level of hostilities that we must consider this matter. We must consider what threat there is to our "peace", such as it is. A "threat" is frequently defined as "capability" plus "intention". We have already discussed the instability of world politics, and, whilst this book gives the naval "capability" of every maritime nation, no book ever written can successfully predict any nation's "intention". This can change overnight with changing circumstances and, whilst certain countries pursue long-term aims, these can be radically altered as the result of elections, assassinations, miscalculations or a hundred other causes. The reader should, therefore, consider the fighting ships listed here in the light of the capability they give their owner-countries to threaten to pursue or to pursue courses of action which may well alter in the wake of changing situations.

John E. Moore

AN EDITORIAL NOTE

from

RAYMOND V. B. BLACKMAN, MBE, CEng, MIMarE, FRINA

Editor, JANE'S FIGHTING SHIPS, 1949-50 to 1972-73 editions

When my successor was appointed Editor of JANE'S FIGHTING SHIPS towards the end of last year I wrote to him: "My heartiest congratulations (and my deepest sympathy)". For JANE'S FIGHTING SHIPS is both a dear octopus and a hard task-master. It absorbs its editor and consumes him. It beckons him at first dawn and reluctantly releases him when he has long burned the midnight oil. More appositely named than Fred T. Jane himself could have foreseen, "Jane" demanded more than any woman.

A quarter of a century in the chair is a long time. Indeed my stint has been longer than any previous editorship of FIGHTING SHIPS, including that of the founder. However, things have changed since I became editor. The then smaller publishing house gave me a great deal of autonomy. For nearly twenty years I personally wrote to all the naval authorities in the world, prepared all copy, obtained all photographs, corrected all galleys, made up all pages and read all proofs. There was a direct traffic between my study at Portsmouth and the printers.

During the last five years or so, however, Jane's has been big business as part of a much bigger organisation. Converted from letterpress and blocks to litho, all Jane's traffic was centralised in London with executive, editorial and production staff. The size of the volume has almost doubled and its world-wide distribution multiplied. An editor of the United States and associated countries was appointed and successive assistant compilers and editorial assistants were brought in to reduce the editorial year from the full twelve months required by a sole editor to the first six months of the year and to bring the publication date forward from the end of the year to the end of July when the first of all the Jane's Yearbooks now appears. There is now a spider-web postal network to and from the publishers, editors and contributors of FIGHTING SHIPS, and all material is channelled through the London offices for registry, progress chasing and despatch to all people concerned.

If I might strike a personal note, this apportionment of JANE'S FIGHTING SHIPS, which I had successively regarded over the years as my baby, my teenager and my woman come-of-age, was like having one's limbs parted one by one and seeing them incorporated in another body.

It was not only with these thoughts in mind, but taking a precautionary measure in view of my two tours of the Far East during which I travelled in many military and civil aircraft and ships, that I agreed with the publishers that a deputy was required and accordingly in 1971 an Assistant Editor was appointed who was envisaged as (and has now become) my successor.

Fred Jane was a prolific journalist and a competent artist. Oscar Parkes was a doctor and artist. Francis McMurtrie was a journalist and a ship lover with an encyclopaedic memory. They all had a bond of dedication to the annual which Jane created, a dedication which I like to think rubbed off the two latter, whom I knew and assisted since 1930, on to me, who had graduated through service in the Royal Navy and at the Admiralty as a marine engineer and naval architect and as a naval and technical writer on both sides of the Atlantic.

Captain John Moore is the first full-career naval officer to be appointed as editor of JANE'S FIGHTING SHIPS, and he brings to it his experience as a submariner and a naval intelligence officer. Since I handed over to him last November he has done things his way and I am sure everybody concerned joins me in wishing him well.

I would like to give a valedictory salute to all those who have helped me during the last twenty-five years.

Raymond V. B. Blackman

ACKNOWLEDGEMENTS

In the first year of editorship of FIGHTING SHIPS the task has been made far easier because of the great help given by correspondents world-wide who have taken much time and great pains to provide accurate information and numerous photographs. If some are disappointed that their offerings have not been included this is only because they have arrived too late for publication. As Mr. Blackman explained last year publishers' dead-lines are strict, and once copy has been sent to the printers between January and late April alterations are both time-consuming and expensive. Where possible everything is included but sometimes correspondence is just too late.

Great help has, as always, been given by the Ministries in various countries and their Defence and Naval Attachés in London. The full tally of these reads like a diplomatic list, and in the interests of space-reduction I trust they will excuse lack of individual mention.

There are many who have forwarded help and information, and amongst these most valued correspondents the following have rendered most signal assistance: Mr. C. W. E. Richardson; Lieutenant Erminio Bagnasco; Captain F. de Blocq van Kuffeler; Mr. John S. Rowe; Mr. S. L. Morison; Lieutenant Toshio Tamura; Mr. G. K. Jacobs; Lieutenant-Cdr. A. Hague, VRD; Dr. A. Fraccaroli; Dr. G. Arra; Commodore H. B. M. Ronneberg; Mr. R. F. Winfield; Mr. E. Tsang; Rear-Admiral M. J. Adam, C.V.O., C.B.E. These are only a few, but will the others please accept our joint thanks and continue their invaluable assistance?

Mr. R. V. B. Blackman and Mr. Norman Polmar have done their best to keep me on the rails, whilst my wife has provided so much help and encouragement that we have produced the copy reasonably on time. This would have been of little avail without the great efforts of the production staff at Jane's Yearbooks, led by Mr. Mervyn Worthington, and the superhuman deciphering ability of the compositors at Netherwood and Dalton Ltd., the printers, who have been associated with Jane's publications for seventy-six years.

The United States section has been compiled and edited for the sixth consecutive year by Mr. Norman Polmar. In addition, he again has undertaken the listings for South Korea, the Philippines, Taiwan China, and South Vietnam.

Mr. Polmar is grateful to many individuals for providing assistance in the preparation of this year's edition, especially Captains John W. King Jnr, Gerald H. Barkalow, and Robert K. Ripley, and Lieutenant Commander William T. Dannheim of the Ship Acquisition and Improvement Division, Office of the Chief of Naval Operations; Mr. Nathan Gilbert of the Office of the Deputy CNO (Air Warfare); Commander Don Walsh of the Office of the Secretary of the Navy; Mr. Samuel L. Morison of the Naval History Division; Mr. Robert Carlisle, Chief Yeoman Ronald G. Woll, and Miss Anna Urban of the Office of Navy Information; Mr. Norman Hanson of Headquarters, Naval Material Command; Mr. Richard C. Bassett of the Naval Ship Systems Command; Mr. H. A. Taylor of the Bureau of Naval Personnel; Captain Berry Meaux, Chief Warrant Officer Joseph Greco, and Miss Elizabeth Segedi of the Public Information Division, US Coast Guard; Mr Raymond Wilcove of the National Ocean Survey; and Messrs. A. D. Baker III and Robert Widder.

Finally it would be both ungracious and dishonest not to mention the role, particularly as a last-minute check, of the other naval annuals: *Flottes de Combat* edited by M. Henri Le Masson; Weyer's *Flottentaschenbuch* edited by Herr Gerhard Albrecht; *Almanacco Navale* edited by Dr. Giorgio Giorgerini and Signor Augusto Nani; and *Marinkalender* edited by Captain Allan Kull.

Contributions for the next edition, which is already in preparation, should be sent as soon as possible to:

The Editor,
Jane's Fighting Ships,
c/o Jane's Yearbooks,
Sampson Low, Marston & Co.,
St. Giles House,
49-50, Poland Street,
London W1A 2LG, England.

THE USE OF JANE'S FIGHTING SHIPS

As there have been certain changes of format in this edition it seems sensible to offer some form of guide to the reader.

Firstly, to assist recognition from ship, shore or air, sixteen pages of silhouettes have been included in the front. The criteria for selection of these ships are importance and likelihood of sighting.

Secondly, after a ship is recognised the new Index of Classes at the back will give the reader the page number for more detailed study. This index contains many more classes than the silhouette section; inevitable, when considering over 15,000 ships.

Thirdly, the various countries' sections have been re-arranged for two purposes. One is to provide, within the constraints of size, a photograph or drawing with the details of each major class. The other is to give a standard arrangement of types of ship to make comparisons easier. This has not always been possible and has resulted in what may seem an unusual order of priority, particularly for submarines. These are not kept rigidly to their position, particularly in the case of the USSR.

Fourthly, an attempt has been made to group those ships with similar tasks under one heading, e.g. Light Force and Mine Warfare Forces.

Fifthly, an arbitrary use of the various classifications, e.g. frigate, corvette etc., has been adopted. This is necessary as no two countries agree on nomenclature and if national usage were adopted, confusion could well result. The bureaucratic habit of changing a ship's designation at frequent intervals has been ignored except where the function of that ship has changed through modernisation or conversion.

Sixthly, the section on Naval Aircraft and missiles has been rearranged and these are now listed under countries rather than functions.

Lastly, please note that the scale of the drawings in the main text, unless otherwise stated, varies according to the requirements of space.

These alterations have been designed to assist the readers whose comments and suggestions for improvement are welcome at all times.

John E. Moore

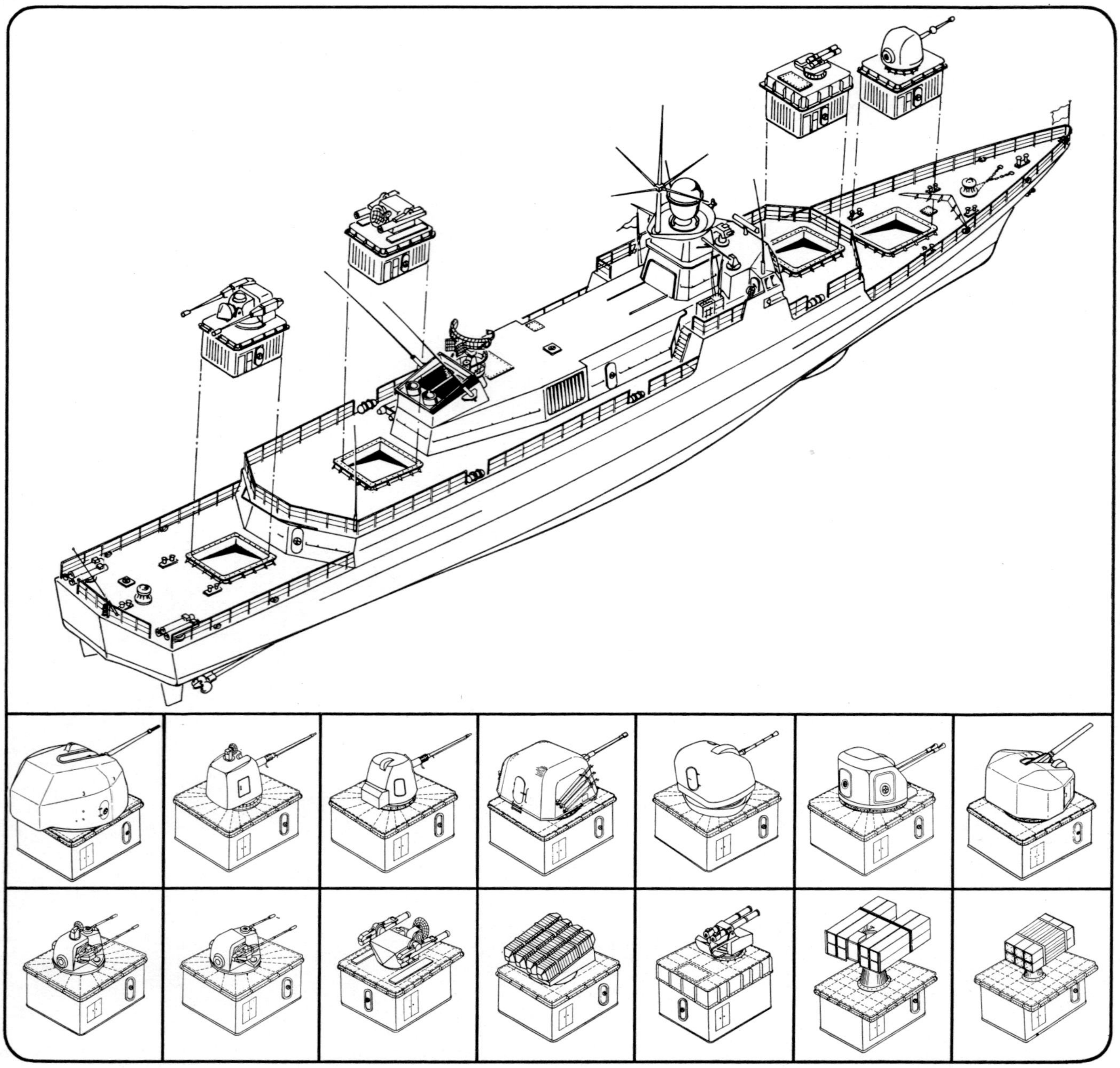

CG3

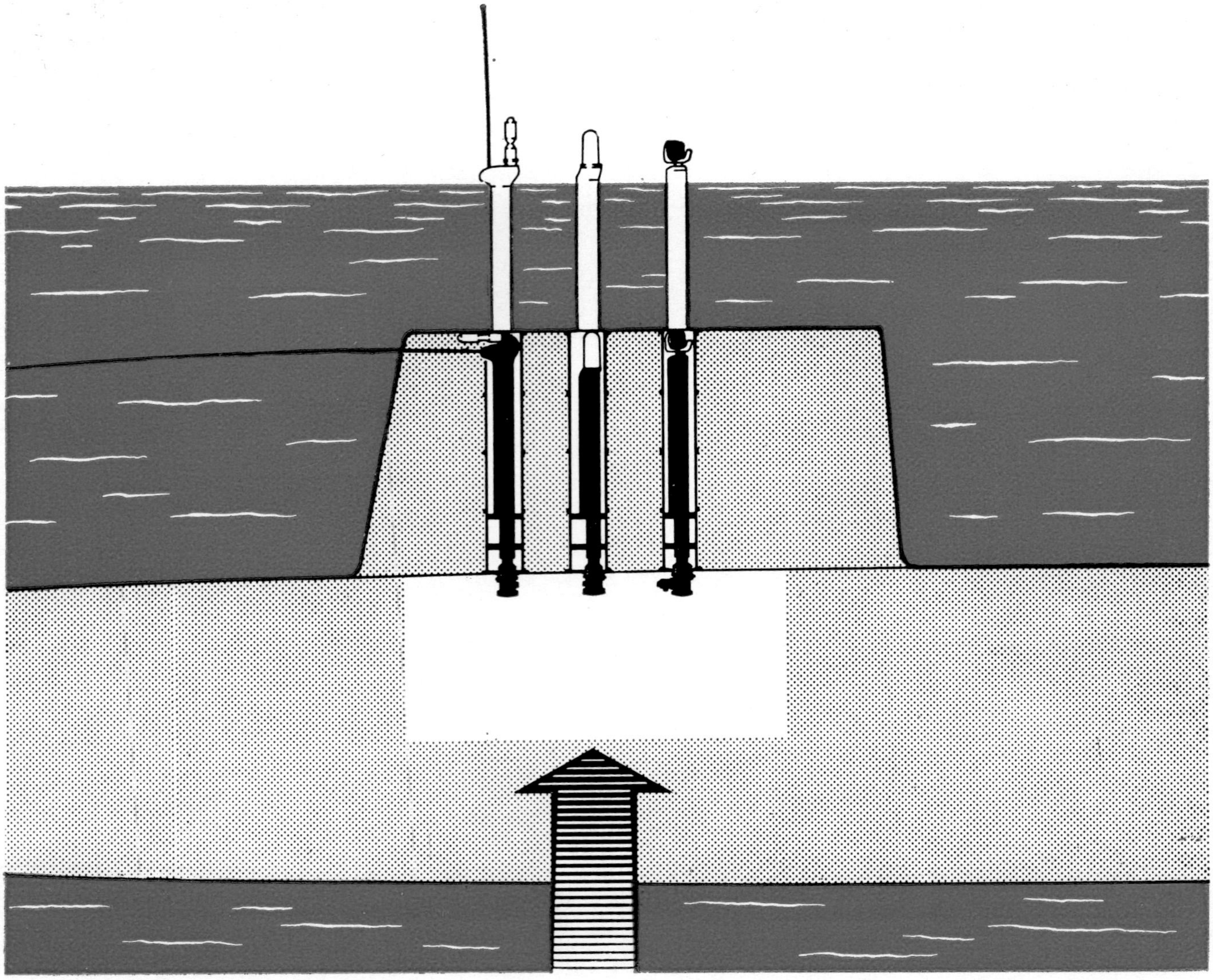

If he'd been around today
he'd have used our know how.

IDENTIFICATION SILHOUETTES

The scale of these silhouettes varies and they should be used only for identification.

Battleship

IOWA *Class*

Aircraft Carriers

COLOSSUS *Class*

MAJESTIC *Class*

CLEMENCEAU *Class*

BULWARK *Class*

ARK ROYAL *Class*

HERMES *Class*

Aircraft Carriers

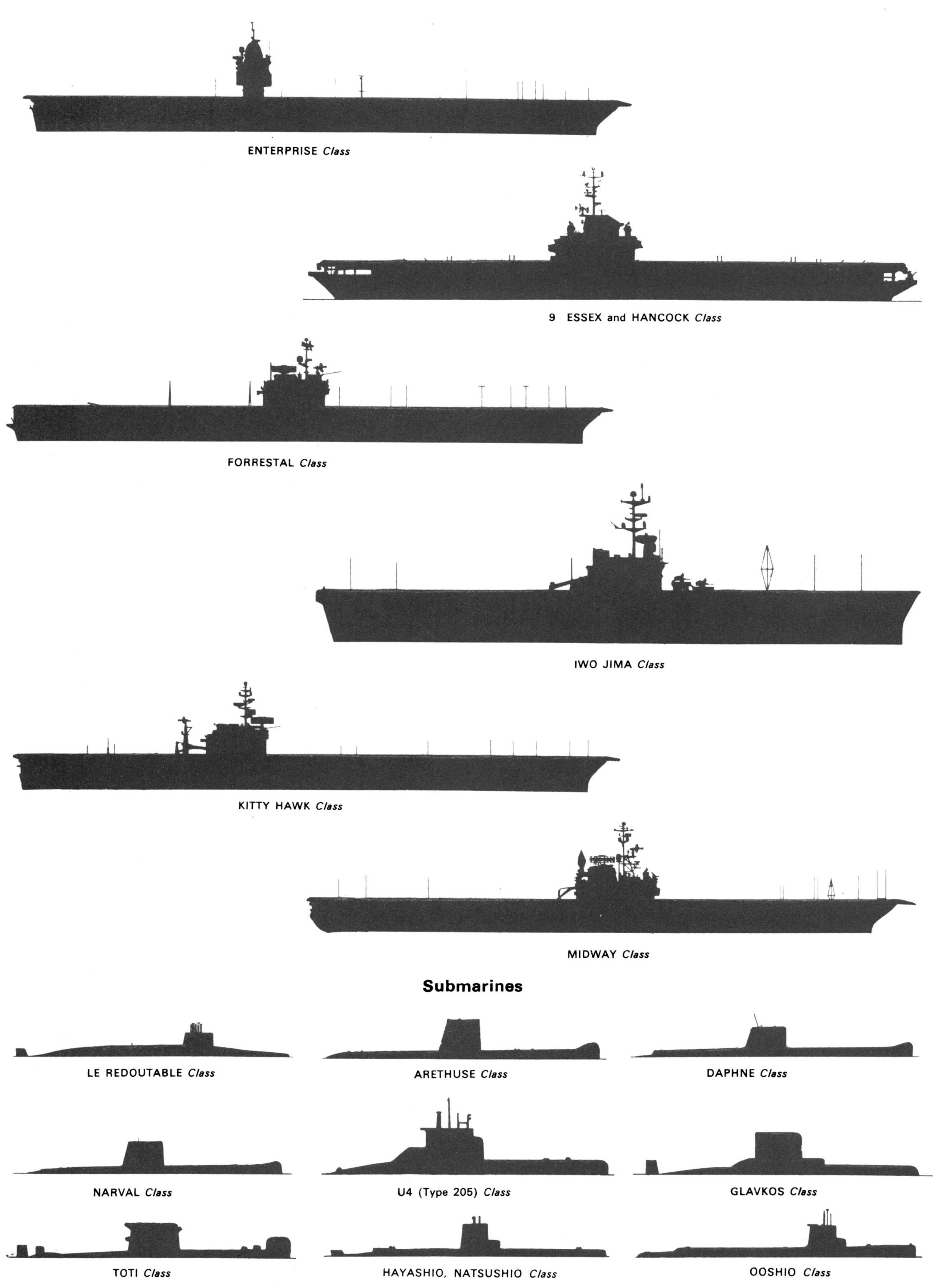

ENTERPRISE *Class*

9 ESSEX and HANCOCK *Class*

FORRESTAL *Class*

IWO JIMA *Class*

KITTY HAWK *Class*

MIDWAY *Class*

Submarines

LE REDOUTABLE *Class*

ARETHUSE *Class*

DAPHNE *Class*

NARVAL *Class*

U4 (Type 205) *Class*

GLAVKOS *Class*

TOTI *Class*

HAYASHIO, NATSUSHIO *Class*

OOSHIO *Class*

Submarines

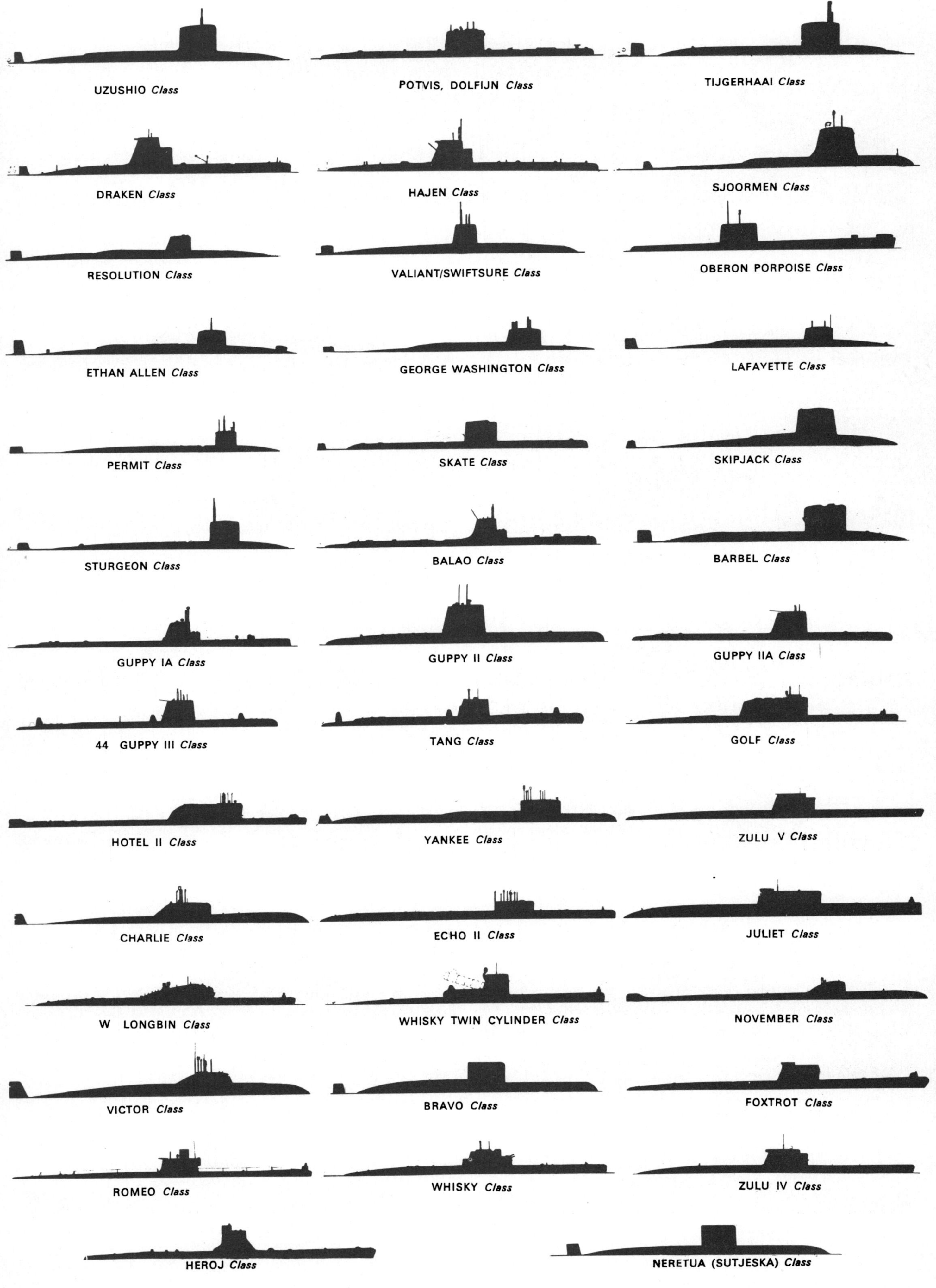
UZUSHIO Class
POTVIS, DOLFIJN Class
TIJGERHAAI Class
DRAKEN Class
HAJEN Class
SJOORMEN Class
RESOLUTION Class
VALIANT/SWIFTSURE Class
OBERON PORPOISE Class
ETHAN ALLEN Class
GEORGE WASHINGTON Class
LAFAYETTE Class
PERMIT Class
SKATE Class
SKIPJACK Class
STURGEON Class
BALAO Class
BARBEL Class
GUPPY IA Class
GUPPY II Class
GUPPY IIA Class
44 GUPPY III Class
TANG Class
GOLF Class
HOTEL II Class
YANKEE Class
ZULU V Class
CHARLIE Class
ECHO II Class
JULIET Class
W LONGBIN Class
WHISKY TWIN CYLINDER Class
NOVEMBER Class
VICTOR Class
BRAVO Class
FOXTROT Class
ROMEO Class
WHISKY Class
ZULU IV Class
HEROJ Class
NERETUA (SUTJESKA) Class

Cruisers

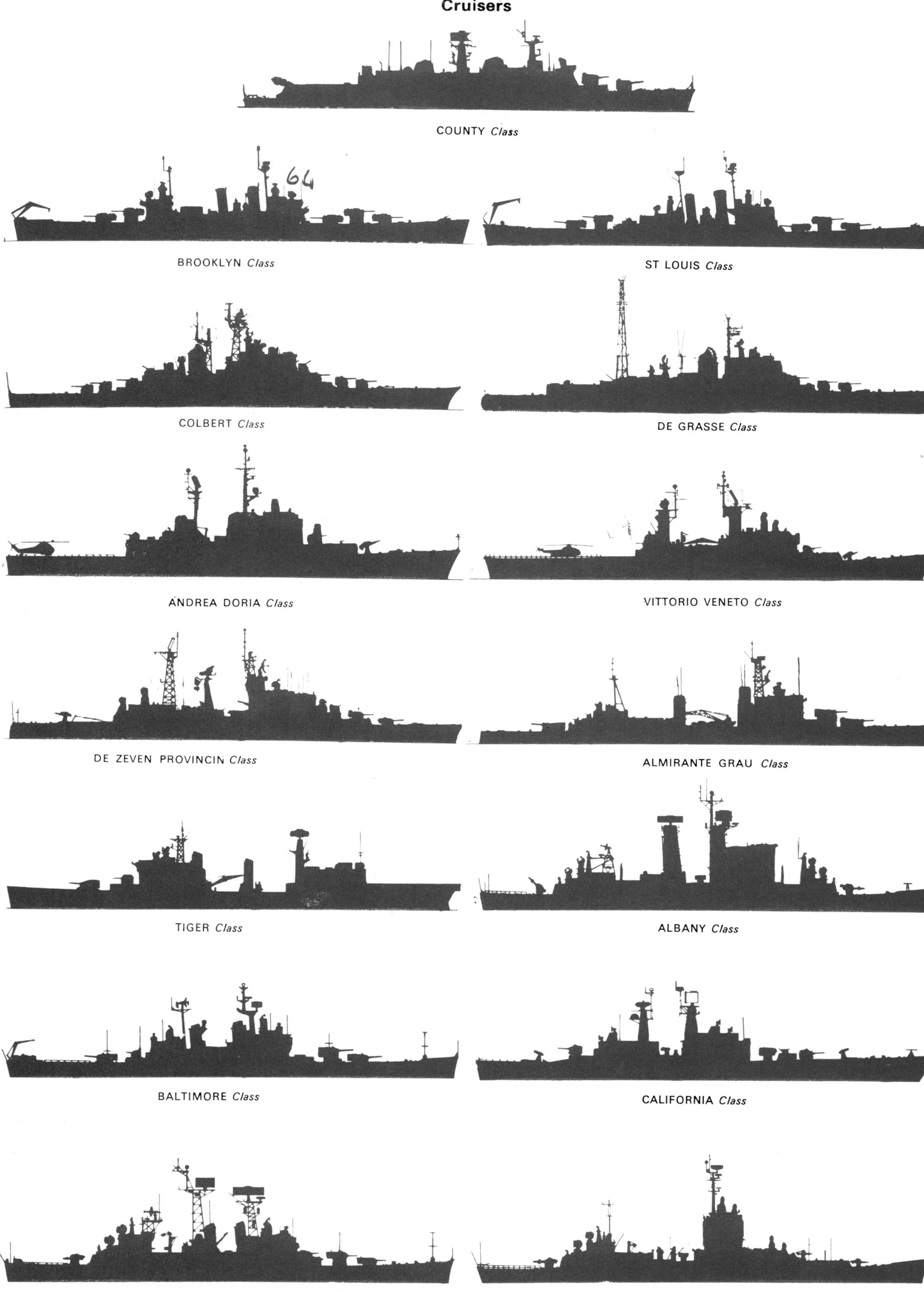
COUNTY *Class*
BROOKLYN *Class*
ST LOUIS *Class*
COLBERT *Class*
DE GRASSE *Class*
ANDREA DORIA *Class*
VITTORIO VENETO *Class*
DE ZEVEN PROVINCIN *Class*
ALMIRANTE GRAU *Class*
TIGER *Class*
ALBANY *Class*
BALTIMORE *Class*
CALIFORNIA *Class*
GALVESTON *Class*
LONG BEACH *Class*

Cruisers

SALEM *Class*

KRESTA I *Class*

KRESTA II *Class*

KYNDA *Class*

MOSKVA *Class*

SVERDLOV *Class*

Assault Ships

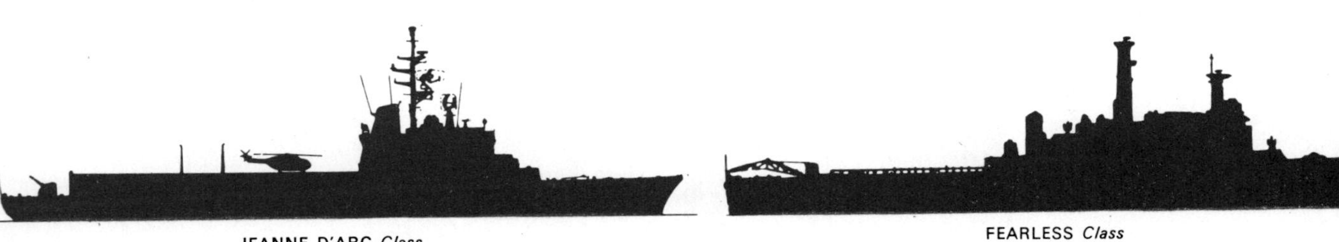

JEANNE D'ARC *Class*

FEARLESS *Class*

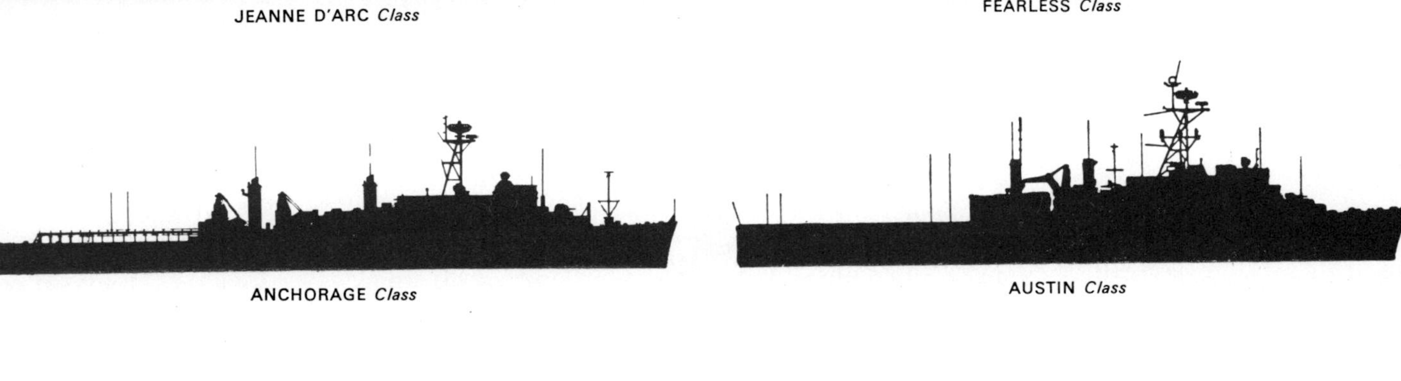

ANCHORAGE *Class*

AUSTIN *Class*

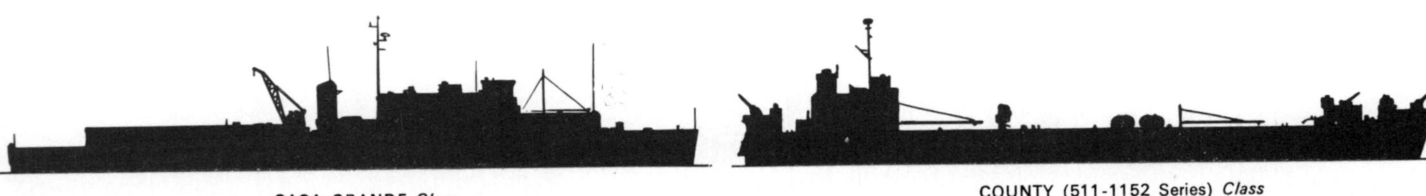

CASA GRANDE *Class*

COUNTY (511-1152 Series) *Class*

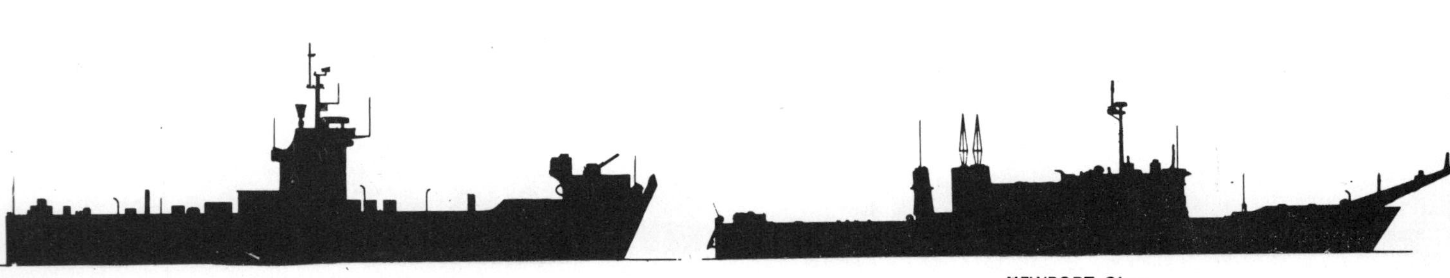

LSM *Class*

NEWPORT *Class*

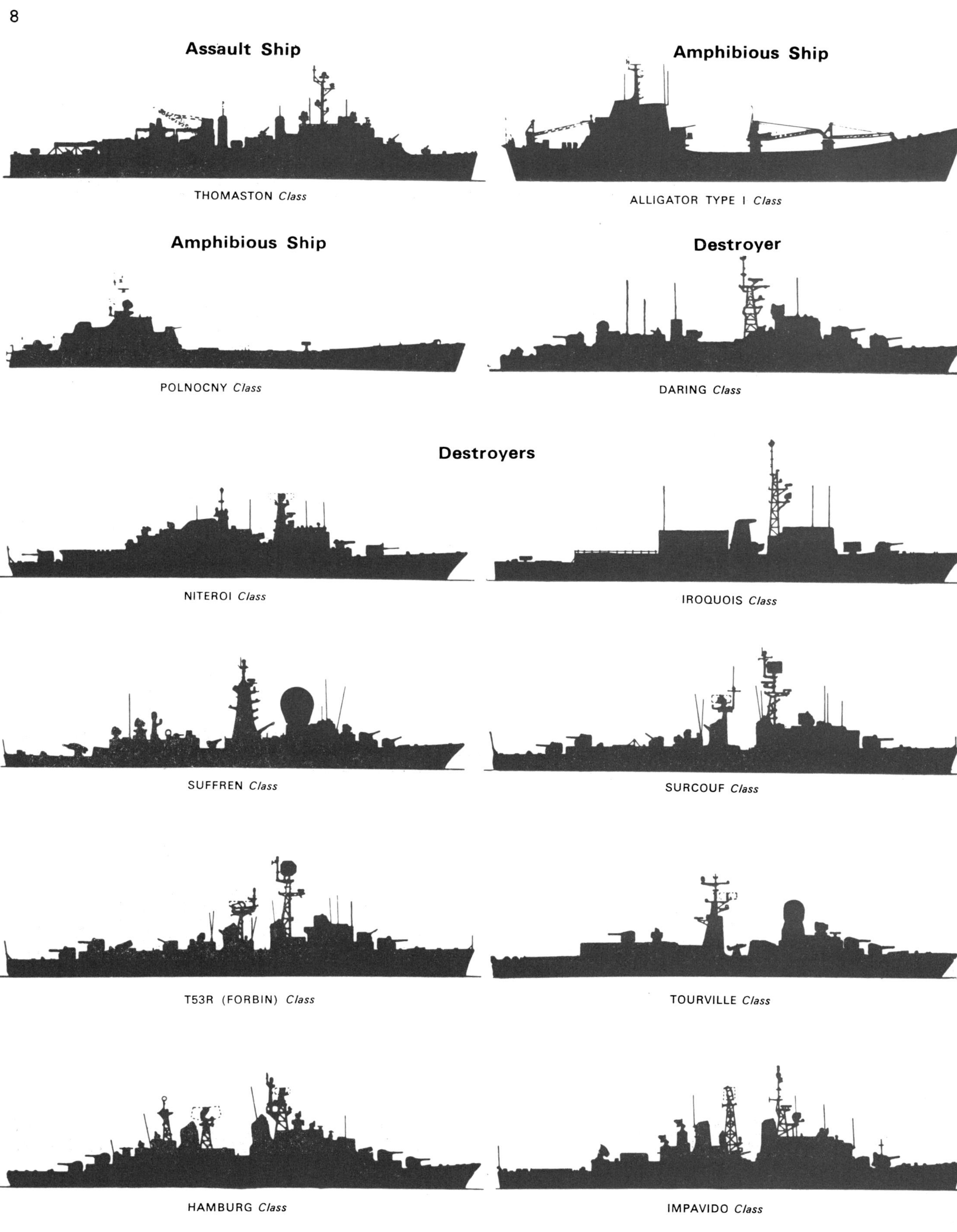

Assault Ship

THOMASTON *Class*

Amphibious Ship

ALLIGATOR TYPE I *Class*

Amphibious Ship

POLNOCNY *Class*

Destroyer

DARING *Class*

Destroyers

NITEROI *Class*

IROQUOIS *Class*

SUFFREN *Class*

SURCOUF *Class*

T53R (FORBIN) *Class*

TOURVILLE *Class*

HAMBURG *Class*

IMPAVIDO *Class*

IMPETUOSO *Class*

YAMAGUMO *Class*

Destroyers

AKIZUKI *Class*

AYANAMI *Class*

HARUKAZE *Class*

FRIESLAND *Class*

HOLLAND *Class*

AUDAZ *Class*

112 MODIFIED OQUENDO *Class*

HALLAND *Class*

ÖLAND *Class*

ÖSTERGÖTLAND *Class*

SHEFFIELD (Type 42) *Class*

ALLEN M. SUMNER *Class*

BELKNAP *Class*

Destroyers

CHARLES F. ADAMS *Class*

COONTZ *Class*

FLETCHER *Class*

FORREST SHERMAN *Class*

GEARING (FRAM I) *Class*

GEARING (FRAM II) *Class*

LEAHY *Class*

KANIN *Class*

KASHIN *Class*

KILDIN *Class*

KOTLIN *Class*

KOTLIN SAM I and II

KRIVAK *Class*

KRUPNY *Class*

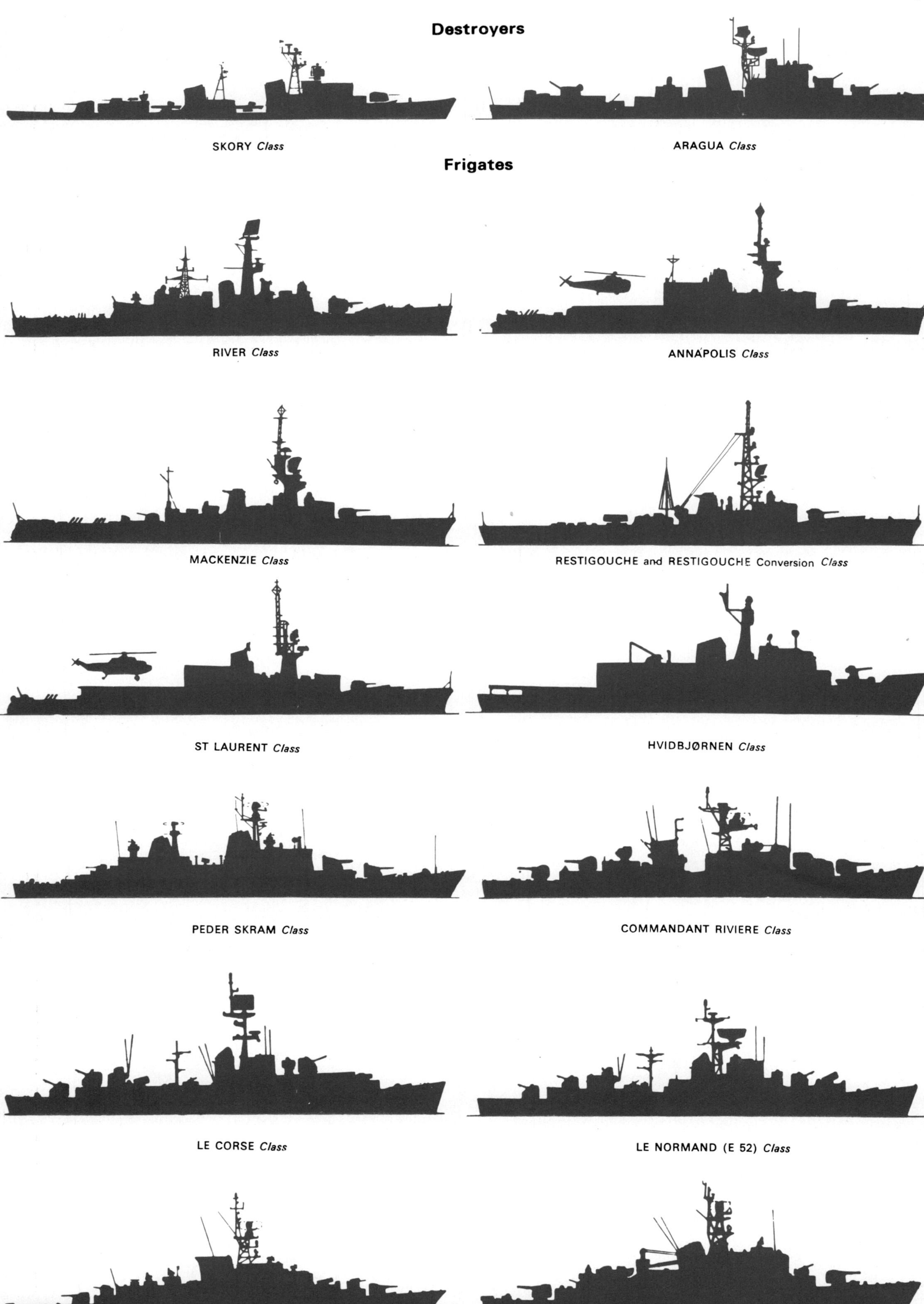
Destroyers
SKORY Class
ARAGUA Class
Frigates
RIVER Class
ANNAPOLIS Class
MACKENZIE Class
RESTIGOUCHE and RESTIGOUCHE Conversion Class
ST LAURENT Class
HVIDBJØRNEN Class
PEDER SKRAM Class
COMMANDANT RIVIERE Class
LE CORSE Class
LE NORMAND (E 52) Class
KÖLN Class
RHTEIN Class

Frigates

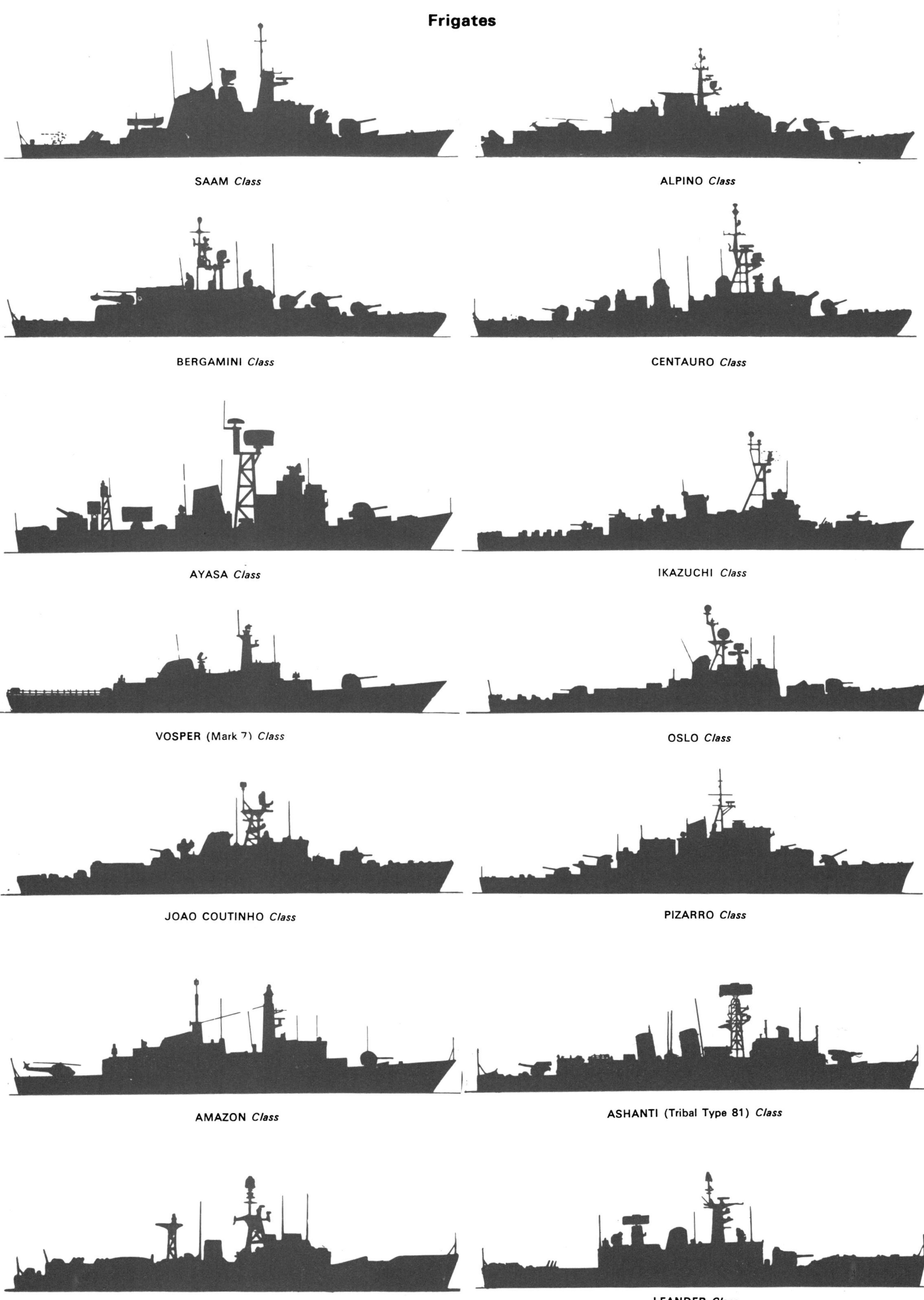

SAAM *Class*

ALPINO *Class*

BERGAMINI *Class*

CENTAURO *Class*

AYASA *Class*

IKAZUCHI *Class*

VOSPER (Mark 7) *Class*

OSLO *Class*

JOAO COUTINHO *Class*

PIZARRO *Class*

AMAZON *Class*

ASHANTI (Tribal Type 81) *Class*

BLACKWOOD (Type 14) *Class*

LEANDER *Class*

Frigates

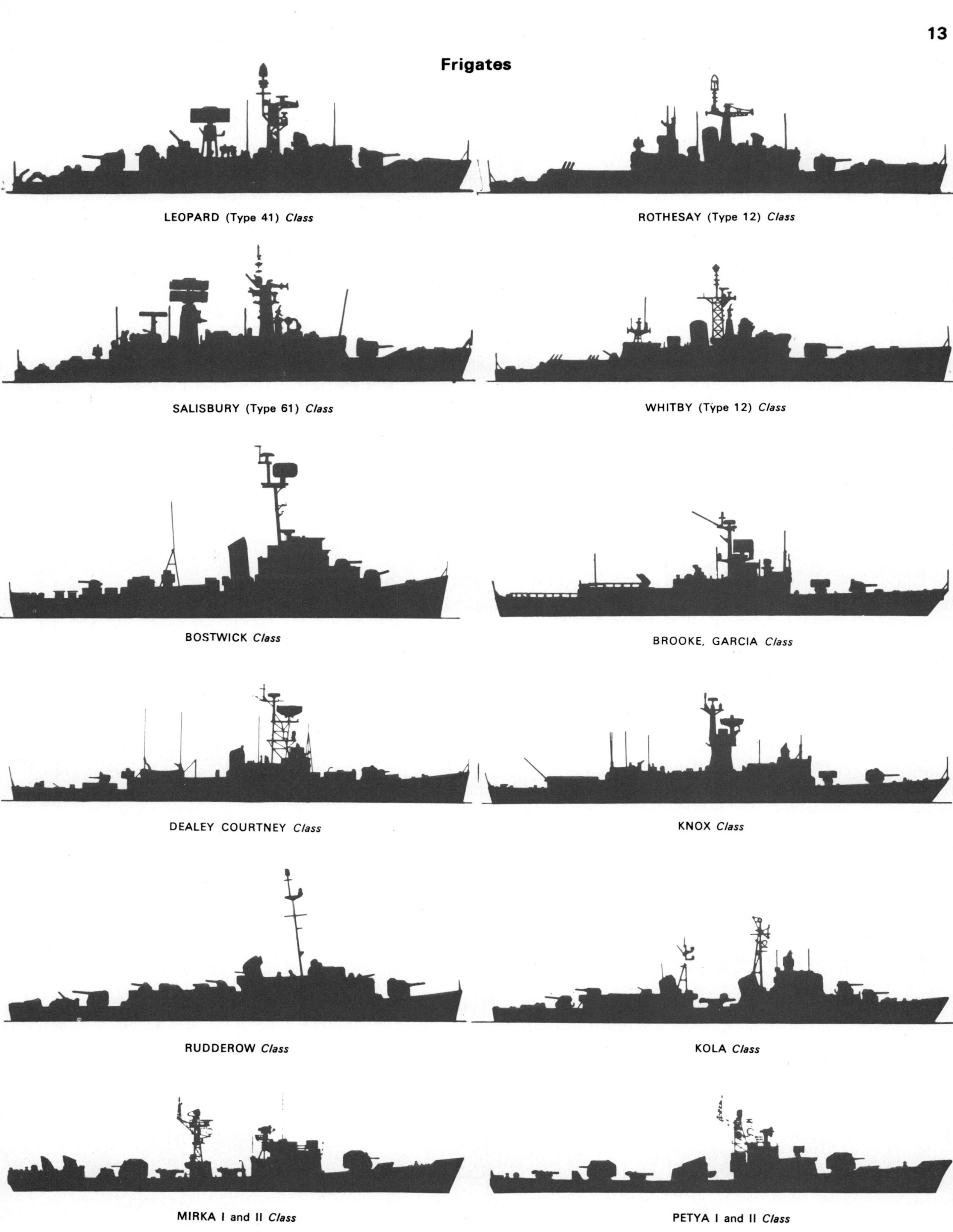

LEOPARD (Type 41) *Class*

ROTHESAY (Type 12) *Class*

SALISBURY (Type 61) *Class*

WHITBY (Type 12) *Class*

BOSTWICK *Class*

BROOKE, GARCIA *Class*

DEALEY COURTNEY *Class*

KNOX *Class*

RUDDEROW *Class*

KOLA *Class*

MIRKA I and II *Class*

PETYA I and II *Class*

RIGA *Class*

ALMIRANTE CLEMENTÉ *Class*

Corvettes

TRITON *Class*

ALBATROS *Class*

APE *Class*

DE CRISTOFARO *Class*

MIZUTORI *Class*

Ex-US PCE Type (185 ft) *Class*

MK 3 Vosper Thornycroft Type (DORINA) *Class*

ATREVIDA *Class*

KRONSTADT *Class*

POTI *Class*

SO I *Class*

STENKA *Class*

Type 143 *Class*

SAAR *Class*

PERKASA *Class*

SNÖGG *Class*

STORM *Class*

KOMAR *Class*

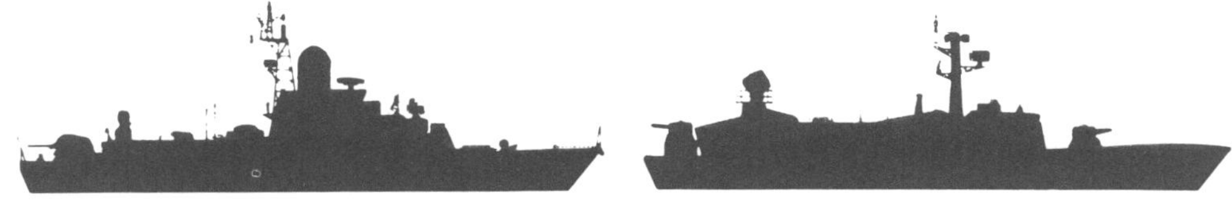

NANUCHKA *Class*

OSA *Class*

Torpedo Boats

JAGUAR (Types 140 and 141) *Class*

Type 142 (Modernised ZOBEL) *Class*

FALKEN *Class*

FLYVEFISKEN *Class*

SØLØVEN *Class*

TJELD *Class*

SPICA *Class*

T 32 *Class*

T 42 *Class*

BRAVE *Class*

P 4 *Class*

P 6, P 8, P 10 *Class*

PSHELA *Class*

SHERSHEN *Class*

SHANGHAI I and II *Class*

Vosper Thornycroft Type A (INDEPENDENCE) *Class*

Vosper Thornycroft Type B (SOVEREIGNTY) *Class*

Patrol Craft

US PC Type (173 ft) *Class*

ASHVILLE CLASS *Class*

Minelayers

SOOYA *Class*

FALSTER *Class*

Fleet Minesweepers

KROGULEC *Class*

ALMANZORA *Class*

AGILE *Class*

AUK *Class*

T 43 *Class*

T 58 *Class*

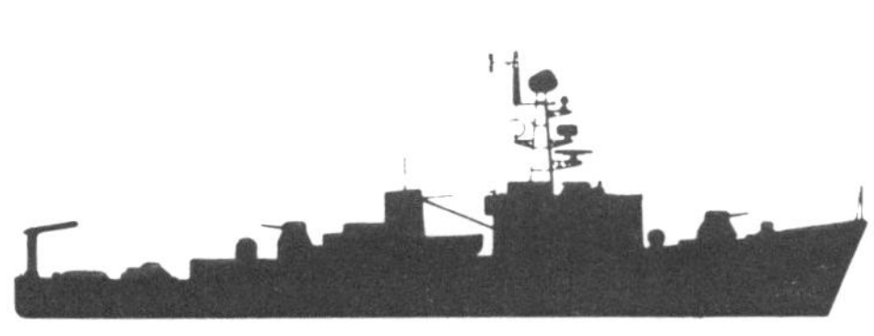

YURKA *Class*

KRAKE *Class*

HABICHT II *Class*

Coastal Minesweepers

LINDAU *Class*

SCHÜTZE *Class*

KASADA *Class*

KONDOR *Class*

DOKKUM WILDERVANK *Class*

Minehunter

CIRCE *Class*

Coastal Minesweepers

TON *Class*

WILTON *Class*

BLUEBIRD *Class*

SASHA *Class*

VANYA *Class*

LAMA *Class*

Submarine Support Ships

UGRA *Class*

DON *Class*

Survey Ship

SAMARA *Class*

Survey Ships

MOMA *Class*

HECLA *Class*

NIKOLAI, ZUBOV *Class*

Research Ships

LEBEDEV *Class*

VOSTOK Class

AKADEMIK *Class*

Space Event Ship

KOMAROV *Class*

Coastal Survey Ship

BEAGLE *Class*

Experimental Hydrofoil

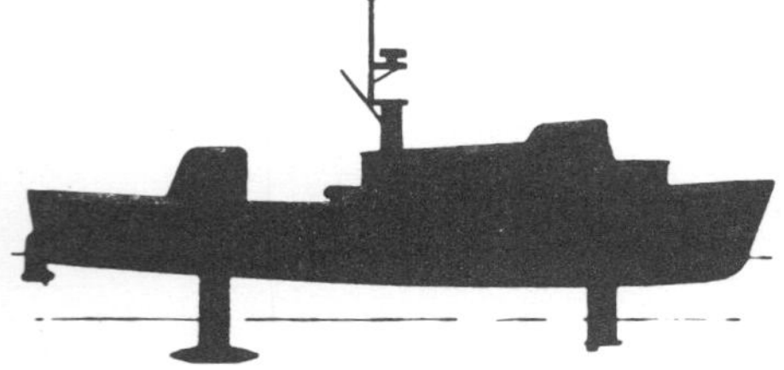
HIGH POINT *Class*

Hovercraft

WINCHESTER (SR. N6) *Class*

ABU DHABI

SEA WING, ABU DHABI DEFENCE FORCE

Administration

Sea Wing Commander:
Commander G. A. St. G. Poole

The Sea Wing of the Abu Dhabi Defence Force was formed in March 1968. The Wing's function is to patrol territorial waters and oil installations in Abu Dhabi marine areas. The Wing is locally recruited with the exception of some ex-Royal Naval Officers, and Officers on secondment from the Pakistan Navy.

LIGHT FORCES

3 "KAWKAB" TYPE (PATROL CRAFT)

BANIYAS (July 1969) **KAWKAB** (Jan 1969) **THOABAN** (Jan 1969)

Displacement, tons	32
Dimensions, feet	57 × 16·5 × 4·5
Guns	2—20 mm
Main engines	2 Caterpillar diesels. 750 bhp = 19 knots
Range, miles	**300**
Complement	**2 officers, 9 men**

Built by Keith Nelson & Co. Ltd, Bembridge, Isle of Wight. Launch dates above. Of glass fibre hull construction.

THOABAN *1970, Abu Dhabi Defence Force*

6 "DHAFEER" TYPE (PATROL CRAFT)

DHAFEER (Feb 1968)
DURGHAM (Sep 1968)
GHADUNFAR (May 1968)
HAZZA (May 1968)
MURAYJIB (Feb 1970)
TIMSAH (Sep 1968)

Displacement, tons	10
Dimensions, feet	41 × 12 × 3·5
Guns	1 × 7·62 MG, 2 light MG
Main engines	2 Cummins diesels; 370 bhp = 19 knots
Range, miles	150
Complement	6 (1 officer, 5 men)

All built by Keith Nelson & Co Ltd, Bembridge, Isle of Wight. Of glass fibre hull construction. Launch dates above.

DURGHAM *1970, Abu Dhabi Defence Force*

ALGERIA

Strength of the Fleet

6 Corvettes	2 Fleet Minesweepers
9 Missile Boats	1 Training Ship
12 Torpedo Boats	5 Harbour Craft

Personnel

1972: Total 3 300 (230 officers and cadets and 3 070 men)
1973: Total 3 200 (230 officers and cadets and 2 970 men)

Mercantile Marine

Lloyd's Register of Shipping: 17 vessels of 56 523 tons gross

CORVETTES

6 Ex-SOVIET "SOI" CLASS

Displacement, tons	215 light; 250 normal
Dimensions, feet	137·8 × 19·4 × 9·2
Guns	4—25 mm (2 twin mounts)
A/S weapons	4—5 barrelled rocket launchers
Main engines	3 diesels; 6 000 bhp = 29 knots
Complement	30

Delivered by USSR on 7 and 8 Oct 1967, first two, and the other four since 1968.

Soviet "SOI" Class

LIGHT FORCES

3 Ex-SOVIET "OSA" CLASS (MISSILE BOATS)

Displacement, tons	165 standard; 200 full load
Dimensions, feet	127·9 oa × 24·9 × 5·9
Missiles	4 SSN 2A (Styx)
Guns	4—30 mm
Main engines	3 diesels; 13 000 hp = 34 knots

One boat was delivered by USSR on 7 Oct 1967. Two others have been reported since.

"Osa" I Class

6 Ex-SOVIET "KOMAR" CLASS (MISSILE BOATS)

Displacement, tons	70 standard; 80 full load
Dimensions, feet	83·6 × 19·7 × 5·0
Missiles	2 SSN 2A (Styx)
Guns	2—25 mm
Main engines	4 diesels, 4 shafts, 4 800 hp = 40 knots

Acquired in 1967 from USSR. The number of serviceable boats is reported to be six or seven.

12 Ex-SOVIET "P6" CLASS (TORPEDO BOATS)

Displacement, tons	66 standard; 75 full load
Dimensions, feet	83·6 × 19·7 × 6·0
Tubes	2—21 inch
Guns	4—25 mm
Main engines	4 Diesels, 4 shafts, 4 800 hp = 45 knots

Six were acquired from the USSR in 1964. Two more boats reported to be in reserve were received from Egypt in 1963.

MINESWEEPERS

2 Ex-SOVIET "T 43" CLASS (FLEET TYPE)

Displacement, tons	500 standard; 610 full load
Dimensions, feet	190·2 × 27·9 × 6·9
Guns	4—37 mm; 4—25 mm
Main engines	2 Diesels; 2 shafts; 2 000 hp = 17 knots
Range, miles	1 600 at 10 knots
Complement	40

Soviet "T 43" *Class*

Minesweepers—*continued*

T 43 *Class* (& Radar Picket)

TRAINING SHIP (*Ex-Coastal Minesweeper*)

SIDI FRADJ (ex-*Darfour*)

Displacement, tons	215 standard; 270 full load
Dimensions, feet	136 oa × 24·5 × 6
Guns	1—3 in; 2—20 mm AA
Main engines	Diesels; 1 000 bhp = 13 knots

Two ex-US BYMS type coastal minesweepers were presented to Algeria by Egypt to form the nucleus of the new Algerian Navy. Both *Darfour* (ex-BYMS 2041) and *Tor* (ex-BYMS 2175) arrived in Algiers on 4 Nov 1962, being officially handed over on 6 Nov and renamed *Sidi Fradj* and *Djebel Aures*, respectively, but the latter was wrecked off Algiers in Apr 1963 and *Sidi Fradj* has been used as a training ship since 1965. Now considered obsolescent.

ALBANIA

Strength of the Fleet

4 Corvettes
4 Submarines
42 Torpedo Boats
2 Fleet Minesweepers
6 Inshore Minesweepers
10 MSB
4 Oilers
20 Small Auxiliaries

Personnel

1973: Total 3 000 including 300 coastal frontier guards

Mercantile Marine

Lloyd's Register of Shipping: 17 vessels of 56 523 tons gross

CORVETTES

4 Ex-USSR "KRONSTADT" CLASS

Displacement, tons	310 standard; 380 full load
Dimensions, feet	170·6 × 21·3 × 9·0 (*52·0 × 6·5 × 2·7 metres*)
Guns	1—3·4 in (*85 mm*); 2—37 mm AA (single); 6—12·7 AA MG (3 vertical twin)
A/S weapons	2 depth charge projectors; 2 DC rails
Main engines	3 Diesels; 3 shafts; 3 300 bhp = 24 knots
Range, miles	1 500 at 12 knots
Complement	65

Equipped for minelaying: 2 rails; about 40 mines. Four were transferred from the USSR in 1958. Albania sent two for A/S updating in 1960 and two others in 1961.

"KRONSTADT" Class Ex-USSR

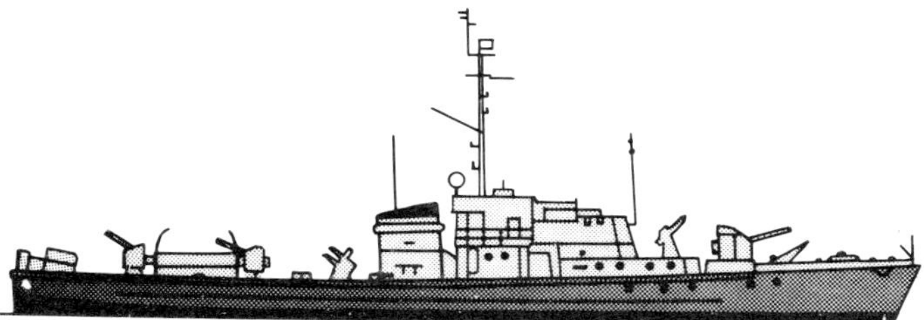

"KRONSTADT" Class

SUBMARINES

4 Ex-USSR "W" CLASS

Displacement, tons	1 050 surface; 1 350 submerged
Dimensions, feet	247·0 × 19·0 × 15·2 (*75·3 × 5·8 × 4·6 metres*)
Tubes	6—21 in (4 bow, 2 stern)
Main engines	Diesels; 4 000 bhp; 2 shafts = 17 knots surface
Range, miles	13 000 at 8 knots surfaced)
	Electric motors; 2 500 hp = 15 knots dived
Complement	60

Submarines—*continued*

Three of the four "W" class submarines are operational and one is now used as a stationary training hulk. All are based at Vlore. Two were transferred from the USSR in 1960, and two others were reportedly seized from the USSR in mid-1961 upon the withdrawal of Soviet ships from their Albanian base.

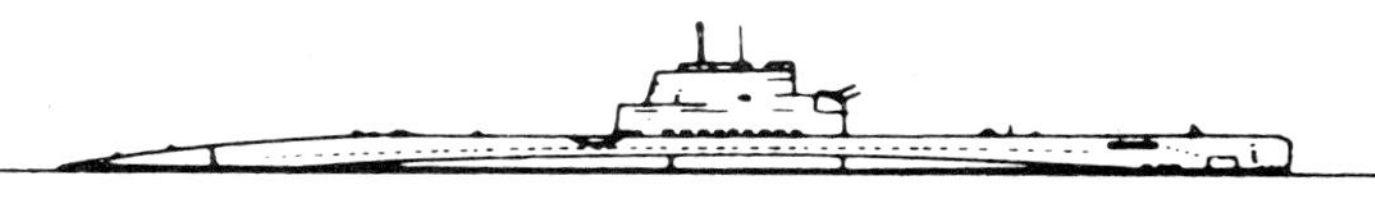

"W" *Class*

LIGHT FORCES

12 USSR "P-4" CLASS (TORPEDO BOATS)

Displacement, tons	25
Dimensions, feet	62·3 × 11·5 × 5·6 (*19·0 × 3·5 × 1·7 metres*)
Guns	2 or 4—12·7 mm AA MG (see notes)
Tubes	2—18 in (*450 mm*)
Main engines	2 Diesels; 2 Shafts; 2200bhp = 50 knots

Six were transferred from the USSR in 1956 (with radar and 2—12·7 mm MG) and six from China, three in April 1965 and three in Sep 1965, without radar and 4—12·7 mm MG (2 twin).

"P-4" Class **Ex-USSR**

30 Ex-CHINESE HU CHWAN CLASS (TORPEDO BOATS)

Displacement, tons	45
Dimensions, feet	70 × 16·5 × 3·1 (*21·3 × 5·0 × ·9 metres*)
Guns	4—12·7 mm
Torpedo tubes	2—21 inch
Main engines	2 M50 Diesels; 2 shafts 2 200 hp = 55 knots

Built in Shanghai and transferred in 1968-70.

MINESWEEPERS

2 Ex-USSR "T 43" CLASS (FLEET TYPE)

Displacement, tons	500 standard; 610 full load
Dimensions, feet	190·2 × 27·9 × 6·9 (*58·0 × 8·5 × 2·1 metres*)
Guns	4—37 mm AA (2 twin); 4—25 mm AA
Main engines	2 Diesels; 2 shafts; 2 000 bhp = 17 knots
Range, miles	1 600 at 10 knots
Complement	40

"T 43" class fleet minsweepers acquired from the USSR. Transferred in Aug 1960.

Minesweepers—*continued*

"T 43" Class Ex-USSR

6 Ex-USSR "T 301" CLASS (INSHORE TYPE)

Displacement, tons	150 standard; 180 full load
Dimensions, feet	124·6 × 19·7 × 4·9 (*38·0 × 6·8 × 1·5 metres*)
Guns	2—37 mm AA; 2—25 mm AA
Main engines	2 diesels; 2 shafts; 1 440 bhp = 17 knots
Range, miles	2 200 at 10 knots
Complement	25

Transferred from USSR—two in 1957, two in 1959 and two in 1960.

"T 301" Class Ex-USSR

10 Ex-SOVIET PO 2 CLASS (MSB)

Displacement, tons	40 to 45 standard; 45 to 50 full load
Dimensions, feet	82·0 × 16·7 × 5·6
Guns	2—25 mm or 2—13 mm
Main engines,	Diesels = 30 knots

There are reports of some 10 PO2 class in service and possibly 3 ex-Italian MS 501. The PO2 class, though primarily Minesweeping boats are also general utility craft.

DEGAUSSING SHIP

1 Ex-USSR "SEKSTAN" CLASS

Dimensions, feet	134·0 × 40·0 × 14·0 max
Main engines	Diesels; 400 bhp = 11 kts
Complement	35

Built in Finland in 1956. Transferred from the USSR in 1960. The two landing craft of the utility transport type were deleted from the list in 1971.

OILERS

2 Ex-USSR "KHOBI" CLASS

Displacement, tons	800
Measurement, tons	1 600 deadweight; 1 500 oil
Dimensions, feet	220·0 × 33·0 × 15·0
Main engines	2 diesels; 1 600 bhp = 12 knots

Launched in 1956. Transferred from the USSR in Sep 1958 and Feb 1959. In addition to the above there are reported to be a number of small auxiliaries.

1 Ex-USSR "TOPLIVO 1" CLASS

Displacement, tons 280

Transferred from the USSR in March 1960. Similar to "Khobi" class in appearance.

1 Ex-USSR "TOPLIVO 3" CLASS

Displacement, tons 275

Transferred from the USSR in 1960. Both the above oilers have funnel aft as in the "Khobi" class.

TENDERS

There are reported to be a dozen or so harbour and port tenders including, YPs, a water carrier and torpedo recovery vessel of the Soviet "Poluchat 1" class. The "Atrek" class submarine tender transferred from USSR in 1961 as a depot ship was converted into a merchant ship.

TUGS

Several small tugs are employed in local duties or harbour service.

ARGENTINA

Administration

Commander in Chief of the Navy:
Almirante Carlos Guido Natal Coda

Chief of Naval Staff:
Vicealmirante Eugenio Fuenterrosa

Chief of Naval Operations:
Vicealmirante Ruben Raul Giavedoni

Diplomatic Representation

Naval Attaché in London and The Netherlands:
Contraalmirante Fernando Vazquez Maiztegui

Naval Attaché in Washington:
Contraalmirante Carlos Alvarez

Naval Attaché in Paris:
Capitan de Navio H. Meyer Arana

Deletions and Transfers

Corvette

1967 *Republica* deleted—scrapped 1968

Coastal Minesweepers

Bouchard Class
1963 *Drummond* and *Spiro* laid up
1964 *Bouchard* and *Parker* transferred to Paraguay
1967 *Granville* and *Robinson* deleted
1969 *Py* and *Seaver* transferred to Paraguay

Strength of the Fleet

1 Aircraft Carrier
3 Cruisers
10 Destroyers
3 Frigates
2 Corvettes
2 Submarines
6 Landing Ships
2 LCTS
27 Minor Landing Craft
11 Patrol Vessels
3 Patrol Craft
2 FPBs
4 Coastal Minesweepers
2 Minehunters
3 Survey Ships
5 Transports
3 Oilers
1 Icebreaker
1 Training Ship
1 Salvage Ship
13 Tugs

Minelayer Support Ships

1971 *Corrientes* sold

Survey Ship

1970 *Commodoro Augusto Lasserre* Q 9 (ex-*Santissima Trinidad* P 34 ex-*HMS Caicos* ex-*HMS Hannam*) deleted

Landing Ships (Medium)

1971 (Jan) BDM1 Q 69 (ex-*USS LSM* 267) deleted

Ships

The names of Argentine warships and naval auxiliaries are preceded by "A.R.A." (Armada Republica Argentina)

New Constuction Programme

2 Modified Type 42 Guided Missile Destroyers
2 Patrol Submarines (German design)
2 Fast Patrol Vessels

Personnel

1973: 31 126 (2 616 officers, 16 510 petty officers and ratings and 12 000 conscripts)

Mercantile Marine

Lloyd's Register of Shipping:
335 vessels of 1 311 874 tons gross

Oilers

1961 *Punta Ciguena* (ex-*Sulphur Bluff*) deleted
1971 *Punta Rasa* (ex-*Salt Creek*) and *Punta Lara* (ex USS LC IL 688) deleted

Tugs

1958 (Oct) *Guarani* (Salvage Tug) lost in Straits of Magellan
1960 (May) *Ronquel* (Salvage Tug) deleted
1963 *Charrua* (Salvage Tug) ex-US Army LT 224 deleted
1967 (11 July) *Ona* deleted
1971 *Querandi* deleted

AIRCRAFT CARRIER

1 Ex-BRITISH "COLOSSUS" CLASS

Name	Builders	Laid down	Launched	Completed
25 DE MAYO (ex-*HNMS Karel Doorman*, ex-*HMS Venerable*)	Cammell Laird & Co Ltd Birkenhead	3 Dec 1942	30 Dec 1943	17 Jan 1945

Displacement, tons	**15 892 standard; 19 896 full load**
Length, feet (*metres*)	**630 (*192·0*) pp 693·2 (*211·3*) oa**
Beam, feet (*metres*)	**80 (*24·4*)**
Draught, feet (*metres*)	**25 (*7·6*)**
Width, feet (*metres*)	**121·3 (*37·0*) overall**
Hangar:	
Length, feet (*metres*)	455 (*138·7*)
Width, feet (*metres*)	52 (*15·8*)
Height, feet (*metres*)	17·5 (*5·3*)
Aircraft	Capacity 21; normal complement: 14 (8 fixed-wing and 6 helicopters)
Guns, AA	10—40 mm
Main engines	Parsons geared turbines; 40 000 shp; 2 shafts
Boilers	4 three-drum; working pressure 400 psi (*28·1 kg/cm²*); Superheat 700°F (*371°C*)
Speed, knots	24·25 designed
Oil fuel, tons	3 200
Range, miles	12 000 at 14 knots, 6 200 at 23 knots
Complement	1 500

GENERAL
Purchased from Great Britain on 1 Apr 1948 and commissioned in the Royal Netherlands Navy on 28 May 1948. Badly damaged by boiler room fire on 29 Apr 1968. Sold to Argentina on 15 Oct 1968 and refitted at Rotterdam by N. V. Dok en Werf Mij Wilton Fijenoord. Commissioned in the Argentine Navy on 12 Mar 1969. Completed refit on 22 Aug 1969 and sailed for Argentina on 1 Sep 1969. With modified island superstructure and bridge, lattice tripod radar mast, and tall raked funnel, she differs considerably from her former appearance and from her original sister ships in the British, French and Brazilian Navies.

RECONSTRUCTION. Underwent extensive refit modernisation in 1955-1958 including angled flight deck and steam catapult, mirror sight landing system, and new anti-aircraft battery of ten 40 mm guns, at the Wilton-Fijenoord Shipyard, at a cost of 25 million guilders. Conversion completed in July 1958.

ENGINEERING. The turbine sets and boilers are arranged *en echelon*, the two propelling-machinery spaces having two boilers and one set of turbines in each space, on the unit system. She was reboilered in 1965-1966 with boilers removed from HMS *Leviathan*. During refit for Argentina in 1968-1969 she received new turbines, also from HMS *Leviathan*.

RADAR
Search: Two Philips LWO series early warning radars with associated height finders for air interception.
Tactical: S Band tactical and navigation radar.

DISPOSALS
It was officially stated in Jan 1971 that the aircraft carrier *Independencia* (ex-HMS *Warrior*), No. V 1, a near-sister-ship of *25 de Mayo*, was no longer operational and had been withdrawn from service.

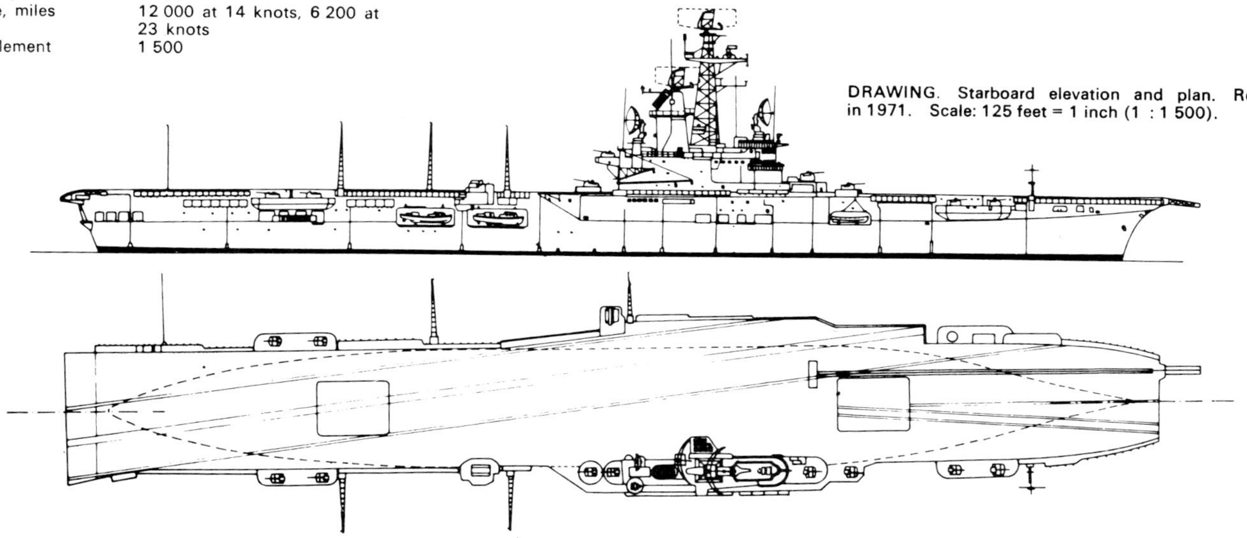

DRAWING. Starboard elevation and plan. Redrawn in 1971. Scale: 125 feet = 1 inch (1 : 1 500).

25 DE MAYO (Harrier VTOL aircraft demonstration on flight deck) — *1970, Argentine Navy*

25 DE MAYO — *1970, Wright & Logan*

CRUISERS

Name	*No.*	*Builders*	*Laid down*	*Launched*	*Completed*
GENERAL BELGRANO (*ex-17 de Octubre, ex-Phoenix*, CL 46)	C 4	New York S.B. Corp Camden	15 Apr 1935	12 Mar 1938	18 Mar 1939
NUEVE DE JULIO (*ex-Boise*, CL 47)	C 5	Newport News S.B. & D.D. Co	1 Apr 1935	3 Dec 1936	1 Feb 1939

2 Ex-US "BROOKLYN" CLASS

Displacement, tons	*Gen. Belgrano:* 10 800 standard; 12 650 normal; 13 645 full load *Nueve de Julio:* 10 500 standard 12 300 normal; 13 645 full load
Length, feet (*metres*)	608·3 (*185·4*) oa
Beam, feet (*metres*)	69 (*21·0*)
Draught, feet (*metres*)	24 (*7·3*) max
Aircraft	2 helicopters
Missiles, AA	2 quadruple "Sea Cat" launchers (*General Belgrano* only).
Guns, surface	15—6 in (*153 mm*) 47 cal; 8—5 in (*127 mm*) 25 cal.
Guns, AA	28—40 mm; 16—20 mm;
Guns, saluting	4—47 mm
Armour	Belt 4 in—1½ in (*100—38 mm*) Decks 3 in + 2 in (*76 + 51 mm*) Turrets 5 in—3 in (*127—76 mm*) Conning Tower 8 in (*203 mm*)
Boilers	8 Babcock & Wilcox Express type
Main engines	Parsons geared turbines; 100 000 shp; 4 shafts
Speed, knots	32·5
Range, miles	7 600 at 15 knots
Oil fuel (tons)	2 200
Complement	1 200

DRAWING: Starboard elevation and plan. Re-drawn in 1971. Scale 125 feet = 1 inch. (1 : 1 500). "Sea-cats" abreast bridge in *General Belgrano* only.

GENERAL

Former "light" cruisers of the United States Navy "Brooklyn" class. Superstructure was reduced, bulges added, beam increased, and mainmast derricks and catapults removed. Purchased from the United States in 1951 at a cost of $7 800 000 representing 10 per cent of their original cost ($37 000 000) plus the expense of reconditioning them. Both were transferred to the Argentine Navy on 12 Apr 1951. *General Belgrano* was commissioned under the name *17 de Octubre* at Philadelphia on 17 Oct 1951. *9 de Julio* was commissioned into the Argentine Navy at Philadelphia on 11 Mar 1952. *9 de Julio* refers to 9 July 1816, when the Argentine provinces signed the Declaration of Independence. *17 de Octubre* was renamed *General Belgrano* in 1956 following the overthrow of President Peron the year before.

RADAR

Search: L Band early warning radar, Type SPS 12. Tactical: Probably SPS 10.

HANGAR. The hangar in the hull right aft accommodates two helicopters together with engine spares and duplicate parts, though 4 aircraft was the original complement.

9 DE JULIO, *1969, Argentine Navy*

Name	*No.*	*Builders*	*Laid down*	*Launched*	*Completed*
LA ARGENTINA	C 3	Vickers-Armstrongs Ltd, Barrow-in Furness	Jan 1936	16 Mar 1937	31 Jan 1939

Displacement, tons	6 000 standard; 7 610 normal 8 630 full load
Length, feet (*metres*)	510 (*155·5*) pp; 541·2 (*164·9*) oa
Beam, feet (*metres*)	56·5 (*17·2*)
Draught, feet (*metres*)	16·5 (*5·0*) max
Guns, surface	9—6 in (*153 mm*)
Guns, AA	14—40 mm
Torpedo tubes	6—21 in (*533 mm*), tripled
Armour	Side and C.T. 3 in (*76 mm*); deck and gunhouses 2 in (*51 mm*)
Boilers	4 Yarrow; 300 psi (*21 kg/cm²*)
Main engines	Parsons geared turbines 54 000 shp; 4 shafts.
Speed, knots	30
Range, miles	7 500 at 12 knots
Oil fuel (tons)	1 500
Complement	800

GENERAL

Designed as Training Cruiser. Cost 6 000 000 gold pesos (about £1 750 000). Best recent speed 25 knots. Now in reserve with skeleton crew.

GUNNERY. Original 4 inch guns were removed in 1950 and 40 mm guns added.

DRAWING. Starboard elevation and plan. Re-drawn in 1971. Scale 125 feet = 1 inch (1 : 1 500).

LA ARGENTINA *1969 Argentine Navy*

DESTROYERS

2 NEW CONSTRUCTION TYPE 42

HERCULES

Displacement, tons	3 500 full load
Length, feet (*metres*)	392·0 (*119·5*) wl; 410·0 (*125·0*) oa
Beam, feet (*metres*)	47·0 (*14·3*)
Draught, feet (*metres*)	22·0 (*6·7*)
Missile launchers	2 "Sea Dart" (1 twin)
Aircraft	1 anti-submarine helicopter
Guns	1—4·5 in automatic; 2—20 mm Oerlikon
Main engines	Rolls Royce Olympus gas turbines for full power; Rolls Royce Tyne gas turbines for cruising; 2 shafts; 50 000 shp
Speed, knots	30 designed
Range, miles	4 000 at 18 knots
Complement	300

HERCULES (TYPE 42)

GENERAL

Guided missile armed destroyers of the British "Sheffield" class. The Argentine Navy signed the contract with Vickers Ltd, Barrow-in-Furness, announced on 18 May 1970, for the construction of two "Type 42" destroyers or frigates, one to be built in Great Britain and the other in Argentina with British oversight of construction.

5 Ex-US "FLETCHER" CLASS

Name	No.	Builders	Laid down	Launched	Commissioned
BROWN (ex-USS *Heermann*, DD 532)	D 20	Bethlehem Steel Co, San Francisco	8 May 1942	5 Dec 1942	6 July 1943
ESPORA (ex-USS *Dortch*, DD 670)	D 21	Federal S.B. & D.D. Co, Port Newark	2 Mar 1943	20 June 1943	7 Aug 1943
ROSALES (ex-USS *Stembel*, DD 644)	D 22	Bath Iron Works Corporation, Bath, Maine	21 Dec 1942	8 May 1943	16 July 1943
DOMECQ GARCIA (ex-USS *Braine*, DD 630)	D 23	Bath Iron Works Corp.	12 Oct 1942	7 Mar 1943	11 May 1943
ALMIRANTE STORNI (ex-USS *Cowell*, DD 547)	D 24	Bethlehem Co, San Pedro	7 Sep 1942	18 Mar 1943	23 Aug 1943

ex-Fletcher

Displacement, tons	2 100 standard; 3 050 full load
Length, feet (*metres*)	376·5 (*114·8*) oa
Beam, feet (*metres*)	39·5 (*12·0*)
Draught, feet (*metres*)	12·2 (*3·7*) mean; 18 (*5·5*) max
Guns, surface	4—5 in (*127 mm*) 38 cal.
Guns, AA	6—3 in (*76 mm*) 50 cal.
Torpedo tubes	5—21 in (*533 mm*) quintupled
A/S depth charges	2 fixed Hedgehogs; 1 DC rack
A/S torpedo racks	2 side-launching
Boilers	4 Babcock & Wilcox
Main engines	2 sets GE or AC geared turbines 60 000 shp; 2 shafts
Speed, knots	35
Range, miles	6 000 at 15 knots
Oil fuel (tons)	650
Complement	300

ROSALES 1971

GENERAL

First three transferred to the Argentine Navy on 1 Aug 1961. *Espora* is of the later "Fletcher" class. Last pair transferred 17 Aug 1971. *Brown* is division leader.

RADAR. Search: L Band SPS 6. Tactical: C Band SPS 10. Fire Control: X Band, antenna on Director.

2 Ex-US ALLEN M. SUMNER CLASS

Name	Builders	Launched	Commissioned
BOUCHARD (ex-USS *Borie* DD 704)	Federal SB & DD Co.	4 July 1944	21 Sep 1944
— (ex-USS *Hank* DD 702)	Federal SB & DD Co.	21 May 1944	28 Aug 1944

Displacement, tons	2 200 standard; 3 320 full load
Length, feet (*metres*)	376·5 (*114·8*) oa
Beam, feet (*metres*)	40·9 (*12·5*)
Draught, feet (*metres*)	19 (*5·8*)
Guns	6—5 in (*127 mm*) 38 cal; DP (twin) 4—3 in (*Hank* only)
A/S Weapons	2 Triple torpedo tubes (Mk 32); 2 ahead-firing Hedgehogs Facilities for small helicopter
Main engines	2 geared turbines; 60 000 shp; 2 shafts
Boilers	4
Speed, knots	34
Complement	274

Transferred to Argentina 1 July 1972. *Bouchard* is modernised—*Hank* is not.

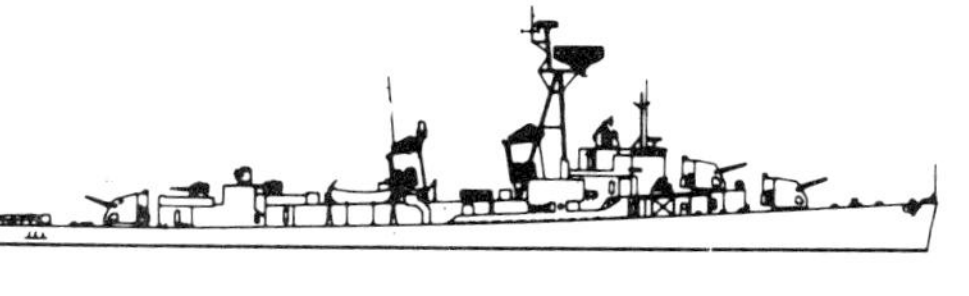

BOUCHARD (ex-USS *Borie* DD 704)

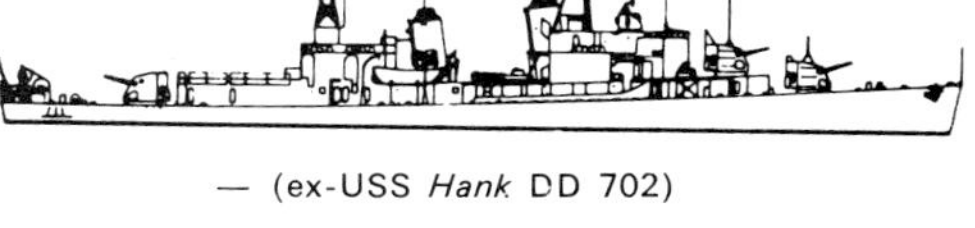

— (ex-USS *Hank* DD 702)

3 "BUENOS AIRES" CLASS

Name	No.	Builders	Laid down	Launched	Completed
ENTRE RIOS	D 7	Vickers-Armstrongs Ltd, Barrow-in-Furness	1936	21 Sep 1937	Mar 1938
SAN JUAN	D 9	John Brown & Co Ltd, Clydebank	1936	24 June 1937	Mar 1938
SANTA CRUZ	D 12	Cammell Laird & Co Ltd, Birkenhead	1936	3 Nov 1937	Oct 1938

Displacement, tons	1 375 standard; 1 820 to 1 850 normal; 1 980 to 2 010 full load
Length, feet (*metres*)	312 (*95·1*) pp; 320 (*97·5*) wl; 323 (*98·5*) oa
Beam, feet (*metres*)	34·8 (*10·6*)
Draught, feet (*metres*)	10·7 (*3·3*) mean
Guns, surface	3 or 4—4·7 in (*120 mm*)
Guns, AA	6—40 mm; 5 MG
A/S weapons	1 Hedgehog; 4—DCT
Torpedo tubes	4—21 in (*533 mm*) quadrupled
Boilers	3 three-drum type
Main engines	Parsons geared turbines 34 000 shp; 2 shafts
Speed, knots	35
Range, miles	4 100 at 14 knots
Oil fuel (tons)	450
Complement	200

TORPEDOES. One quadruple torpedo mount removed in 1956.

DISPOSALS AND TRANSFERS

Corrientes of this class was lost by collision with the cruiser *Almirante Brown* on 3 Oct 1941. *Buenos Aires*, *Misiones* and *San Luis* were withdrawn from service in 1971.

ENTRE RIOS 1971.

FRIGATES

2 "AZOPARDO" CLASS

Name	No.	Builders	Laid down	Launched	Completed
AZOPARDO	P 35	Astillero Nav. Rio Santiago	Nov 1950	11 Dec 1953	7 July 1957
PIEDRABUENA	P 36	Astillero Nav. Rio Santiago	Nov 1950	17 Dec 1954	16 Dec 1958

AZOPARDO, PIEDRABUENA

AZOPARDO — *1966, Argentine Navy*

Displacement, tons	1 160 standard; 1 400 full load
Length, feet (*metres*)	278·5 (*84·9*)
Beam, feet (*metres*)	31·5 (*9·6*)
Draught, feet (*metres*)	10·2 (*3·1*)
Guns, surface	1—4·1 in (*105 mm*)
Guns, AA	6—40 mm
A/S weapons	1 Hedgehog; 4 DC mortars
Boilers	2 water tube 3-drum type
Main engines	2 Parsons geared turbines; 5 000 shp; 2 shafts
Speed, knots	20 max
Oil fuel, tons	340
Range, miles	5 400 at 12 knots
Complement	160

GENERAL
Both built at Astillero Nav. Rio Santiago. Improved "King" type. *Azopardo* named after the Argentine naval hero.

Ex-US PF TYPE

JUAN B AZOPARDO (ex-*Hercules*, ex-USS *Asheville* PF 1 ,ex-*HMCS Nadur*, ex-*HMS Adur*) GC 11

JUAN B. AZOPARDO

JUAN B. AZOPARDO — *1969, Argentine Navy*

Displacement, tons	1 445 standard; 1 920 normal; 2 415 full load
Length, feet (*metres*)	283 (*86·3*) wl; 301 (*91·8*) oa
Beam, feet (*metres*)	37·5 (*10·1*)
Draught, feet (*metres*)	13·7 (*4·2*)
Guns, AA	2—40 mm
Boilers	2 three-drum type
Main engines	Triple expansion 5 500 ihp; 2 shafts
Speed, knots	20 (max now 14)
Oil fuel, tons	700
Range, miles	7 800 at 12 knots
Complement	175

GENERAL
Former US patrol escort of the "Tacoma" class, built by Canadian Vickers, Montreal; laid down on 10 Mar 1942, launched on 22 Aug 1942 and completed on 1 Dec 1942. Operated by National Maritime Prefectura and bears prefix P.N.M. to name.

DISPOSALS AND TRANSFERS
Heronia (ex-USS *Reading*, PF 66) was withdrawn from active service and scrapped in 1966. *Sarandi* (ex-USS *Uniontown*, ex-*Chattanooga*, PF 65) was removed from service in 1968.

CORVETTES

2 "KING" CLASS

Name	No.	Builders	Laid down	Launched	Completed
KING	P 21	Astillero Nav. Rio Santiago	Dec 1938	Dec 1943	28 July 1946
MURATURE	P 20	Astillero Nav. Rio Santiago	June 1938	July 1945	18 Nov 1946

Displacement, tons	913 standard; 1 000 normal; 1 032 full load
Length, feet (*metres*)	252·7 (*77·0*)
Beam, feet (*metres*)	29 (*8·8*)
Draught, feet (*metres*)	7·5 (*2·3*)
Guns, surface	3—4·1 (*105 mm*)
Guns, AA	4—40 mm Bofors; 2—MG
A/S	4—DCT
Main engines	2—Werkspoor 4-stroke diesels; 2 500 bhp; 2 shafts
Speed, knots	18
Oil fuel (tons)	90
Range, miles	6 000 at 12 knots
Complement	130

KING — *1970, Argentine Navy*

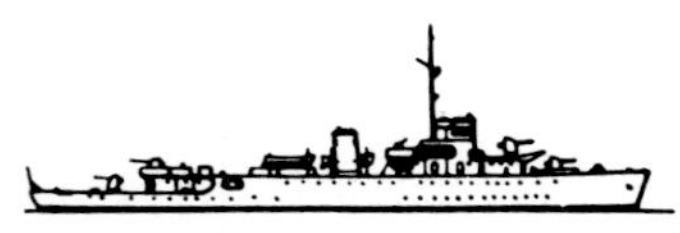

KING, MURATURE

GENERAL
Both built at Astillero Nav. Rio Santiago. Named after Captain John King, an Irish follower of Admiral Brown, who distinguished himself in the war with Brazil, 1826-28; and Captain Murature, who performed conspicuous service against the Paraguayans at the Battle of Cuevas on Aug 6 1865. For river service.

SUBMARINES

2 NEW CONSTRUCTION

Displacement, tons	1 000 surface; 1 290 dived
Length, feet (*metres*)	183·4 (*55·9*)
Beam, feet (*metres*)	20·5 (*6·25*)
Torpedo tubes	8—21 in; bow tubes
Main engines	Diesel electric; 1 shaft; 5 000 hp
Speed, knots	22 dived

Building by Howaldswerke Deutsche Werft AG, Kiel. Double hull with MTU diesels—4 generators.

1 000 ton submarine of Howaldswerke class

2 Ex-US "BALAO" CLASS

SANTA FE (ex-USS *Catfish* SS 339) S 21
SANTIAGO DEL ESTERO (ex-USS *Chivo* SS 341) S 22

Displacement, tons	1 870 surface; 2 430 submerged
Length, feet (*metres*)	307·5 (*93·6*) oa
Beam, feet (*metres*)	27·2 (*8·3*)
Draught, feet (*metres*)	18·0 (*5·5*)
Torpedo tubes	10—21 in (*533 mm*); 6 fwd, 4 aft
Main engines	3 diesels; 4 800 shp; 2 electric motors; 5 400 shp
Speed, knots	18 on surface; 15 submerged
Range miles	12 000 at 10 knots
Oil fuel, tons	300
Complement	82

GENERAL
Both of the "Balao" class built by Electric Boat Co being launched on 19 Nov 1944 and 14 Jan 1945 and commissioned on 19 Mar 1945 and 28 April 1945, respectively. *Catfish* was modified under the Guppy II programme (1948-50) and *Chivo* under the Guppy 1A programme (1951). Both transferred to Argentina at Mare Island on 7 Jan 1971.

SANTA FE — *1970, A. & J. Pavia*

DISPOSALS
Previous submarines of these names S 11 and S 12 (ex-USS *Lamprey* SS 372 and *Macabi* SS 375) have been paid off and are to be scrapped for spares.

AMPHIBIOUS FORCES

CANDIDO DE LASALA Q 43 (ex-USS *Gunston Hall, LSD* 5)

Displacement, tons	5 480 standard; 9 375 full load
Dimensions, feet	457·8 oa × 72·2 × 18·0
Guns	12—40 mm AA
Main engines	2 Skinner Unaflow; 2 shafts; 7 400 shp = 15·4 knots
Boilers	2 Two drum
Range, miles	8 000 at 15 knots
Complement	Accommodation for 326 (17 officers and 309 men)

GENERAL
Built by Moor Dry Dock Co, Oakland, Calif. Laid down on 28 Dec 1942, launched on 1 May 1943 and completed on 10 Nov 1943. Transferred from the US Navy on 1 May 1970. Arcticized in 1948/9.

CANDIDO DE LASALA — *1972, Argentine Navy*

1 NEW CONSTRUCTION LANDING SHIP

CABO SAN ANTONIO

Displacement, tons	4 300 light; 8 000 full load
Dimensions, feet	445 oa × 62 × 16·5
Guns	6—3 in (3 twin)
Main engines	Diesels; 2 shafts; 13 700 bhp = 11 knots
Complement	124

Built at the Naval Shipyard in Rio Santiago. Reported to be designed to carry a helicopter and two landing craft.

4 Ex-US LST TYPE

CABO SAN BARTOLOME BDT 11 (ex-US *LST*)
CABO SAN GONZALO BDT 4 (ex-US *LST* 872)
CABO SAN ISIDRO BDT 6 (ex-US *LST* 919)
CABO SAN PIO BDT 10 (ex-US *LST* 1044)

Displacement, tons	2 366 beaching; 4 080 full load
Dimensions, feet	316 wl; 328 oa × 50 × 14
Guns	4—40 mm (2 twin) *Cabo San Bartolome* only
Main engines	2 diesels; 2 shafts; 1 800 bhp = 11 knots
Oil fuel (tons)	700
Range, miles	9 500 at 9 knots
Complement	80

GENERAL
Built by Puget Sound Bridge and Dredging Co., Seatle, USA. Launched in 1944. All ships have two rudders

DISPOSALS AND TRANSFER
BDT 5, BDT 8, BDT 9, and BDT 12, were withdrawn from service in 1958-60, and BDT 2, BDT 7, BDT 11 and BDT 13 in 1964. BDT 14 withdrawn in 1971. *Cabo San Fransisco de Paula*, BDT 3 has been used as a store ship since 1966.

MEDIUM LANDING SHIPS

Of the former United States landing ships, (medium) BDM 2 (ex-USN *LSM* 86) was converted into a minelayer support vessel in 1968.

2 Ex-US LCT TYPE

BDI 1 Q 56 (ex-USS *LC/L* 583) **BDI 4** Q 57 (ex-USS *LC/L* 606)

Displacement, tons	230 light; 387 full load
Dimensions, feet	153 wl; 159 oa × 23·2 × 5
Guns	2—20 mm AA (only in BDI 4)
Main engines	8 sets diesels; 3 200 bhp = 14 knots. Two reversible propellers
Oil fuel, tons	110
Range, miles	6 000 at 12 knots
Complement	30

DISPOSALS AND TRANSFERS
BDI 3, BDI 6, BDI 8, BDI 9, BDI 11 and BDI 13 were withdrawn from service in 1958. BDI 1 and BDI 4 were given new Q numbers as shown above instead of Q 64 and 67. BDI 10 (Q 63) was converted into an oiler in 1960 and renamed *Punta Lara*. BDI 5, BDI 7, BDI 12 and BDI 14 were officially deleted from the list in 1961, BDI 2 in 1963, and BDI 15 (Q68) in 1971.

BDI — *1970 Argentine Navy*

31 MINOR LANDING CRAFT

LCM 1 **LCM 2** **LCM d** **LCM 4**

It was officially stated in Jan 1971 that four LCMs had been incorporated in the Fleet.

8 EDVP's

Units incorporated into the Argentine Navy at the end of 1970 included eight vehicle and personnel landing craft.

EDVP 1, 3, 4, 5, 6, 7, 8, 9, 10, 11, 12, 13, 20, 21, 22, 24, 27, 28, 29

Displacement, tons	12
Dimensions, feet	39·5 × 10·5 × 5·5
Main engines	Diesel, 9 knots

Ex USN LCVPs. EDVP Numbers 16, 23, 25 and 26 were withdrawn from service in 1966.

LIGHT FORCES

2 NEW CONSTRUCTION (FAST PATROL VESSELS)

Displacement, tons	240
Guns	1—3 in (*76 mm*) AA, 2—40 mm AA
Main engines	Diesels; 4 shafts; speed 40 knots
Complement	35

It was officially stated by the Argentine Navy in Jan 1971 that the two fast patrol vessels were ordered in 1970 and are under construction by Lurssen of Hamburg, and at Astill Nav. Rio Santiago.

2 Ex-US TUG TYPE (PATROL VESSELS)

THOMPSON (ex-US *Sombrero Key*) A 4 **GOYENA** (ex-US *Dry Tortugas*) A 3

Displacement, tons	1 863 full load
Dimensions, feet	191·3 × 37 × 18
Guns	2—40 mm (1 twin) Bofors; 2—20 mm, 70 cal (single)
Main engines	2 Enterprise diesels; 2 250 bhp = 12 knots
Oil fuel (tons)	532
Complement	60

Built by Pendleton Shipyard Co., New Orleans. Launched in 1943 and leased to the Argentine Navy in 1965.

2 Ex-US ATF TYPE (PATROL VESSELS)

COMMANDANTE GENERAL IRIGOYEN (ex-USS *Cahuilla*, ATF 152) A 1
COMMANDANTE GENERAL ZAPIOLA (ex-USS *Arpaho*, ATF 68) A 2

Displacement, tons	1 235 standard; 1 675 full load
Dimensions, feet	195 wl; 205 oa × 38·2 × 15·3
Guns	1—3 in; 4—40 mm AA;
Main engines	4 sets diesels with electric drive; 3 000 bhp = 16 knots
Complement	85

Former US fleet ocean tugs of the "Cherokee" class. Fitted with powerful pumps and other salvage equipment. Both built by Charleston S.B. & D.D. Co., Charleston, S.C. Launched on 2 Nov 1944 and 22 June 1942, respectively, and completed on 10 Mar 1945 and 20 Jan 1943. Transferred to Argentina at San Diego, California, in 1961. Classified as tugs untill 1966 when they were re-rated as patrol vessels.

COMMANDANTE GENERAL IRIGOYEN *1969, Argentine Navy*

6 Ex-US ATA TYPE (PATROL VESSELS)

ALFEREZ SOBRAL (ex-US *ATA* 210) A 9
CHIRIGUANO (ex-US *ATA* 227) A 7
COMODORO SOMELLERA (ex-US *ATA* 187) A 10
DIAGUITA (ex-US *ATA* 124) A 5
SANAVIRON (ex-US *ATA* 228) A 8
YAMANA (ex-US *ATA* 126) A 6

Displacement, tons	689 standard; 800 full load
Dimensions, feet	134·5 wl; 143 oa × 34 × 12
Guns	2—20 mm AA
Main engines	Diesel-electric; 1 500 bhp = 12·5 knots
Oil fuel (tons)	154
Radius, miles	16 500
Complement	49

YAMANA *1969, Argentine Navy*

Former US auxiliary ocean tugs. Built by Levingstone Shipbuilding Co., Orange Texas, USA, in 1945. *Diaguita* and *Yamana* are fitted as rescue ships. A 5, A 6, A 7 and A 8 bear names of South American Indian tribes. Classified as ocean salvage tugs until 1966 when they were re-rated as patrol vessels. A 9 and A 10 were added to the list in 1972.

SPIRO GC 12 (ex-Bouchard class)

Displacement, tons	560 normal; 650 full load
Dimensions, feet	197 oa × 24 × 11½
Guns	4 × 40 mm
Main engines	2 MAN Diesels; 2 000 bhp = 13 knots
Complement	77

GENERAL
Former minesweeper of the "Bouchard" class, now operated by the Prefectura Nacional Maritima. Built by the Rio Santiago Navy Yard. Launched on 7 June 1937. Sister ships *Bouchard*, *Parker*, *Py* and *Seaver* were transferred to the Paraguayan Navy. They were the first warships built in Argentine yards.

SPIRO *1969, Argentine Navy*

3 "LYNCH" TYPE (COASTAL PATROL VESSELS)

EREZCANO GC 23 **LYNCH** GC 21 **TOLL** GC 22

Displacement, tons	100 normal; 117 full load
Dimensions, feet	90 × 19 × 6
Guns	1 — 20 mm
Main engines	2 Maybach Diesels; 2 700 bhp = 22 knots
Complement	16

GENERAL
Patrol craft operated by the Prefectura Nacional Maritima. Pennant numbers GC 23, GC 21, and GC 22, respectively, were assigned when they were under construction at Rio Santiago shipyards in 1964. GC 31 of similar characteristics, see photograph below.

LYNCH *1969, Argentine Navy*

GC 31 *1971*

2 Ex US HIGGINS CLASS (FPBs)

P 82 **P 84**

Displacement, tons	45
Dimensions, feet	78·7 × 9·8 × 4·6
Guns	2—40 mm 4MG
Torpedo launchers	4—21 inch
Main engines	3 Packard; 4 050 hp = 45 knots
Range, miles	1 000 at 20 knots
Complement	12

DISPOSALS
P 81, 83, 85, 87 and 89 deleted in 1963 and P 86 and 88 in 1968.

MINESWEEPERS

6 Ex-BRITISH "TON" CLASS (CMS)

CHACO (ex-HMS *Rennington*) M 5
CHUBUT (ex-HMS *Santon*) M 3
FORMOSA (ex-HMS *Ilmington*) M 6
NEUQUEN (ex-HMS *Hickleton*) M 1
RIO NEGRO (ex-HMS *Tarlton*) M 2
TIERRA DEL FUEGO (ex-HMS *Bevington*) M 4

Displacement, tons	360 standard; 425 full load
Dimensions, feet	140 pp; 153 oa × 28·8 × 8·2
Guns	1—40 mm AA
Main engines	2 Diesels; 2 shafts; 3 000 bhp = 15 knots
Oil fuel (tons)	45
Range, miles	2 300 at 13 knots; 3 000 at 8 knots
Complement	Minsweepers 27; Minehunters 36

Former British coastal minesweepers of the "Ton" class. Of composite wooden and non-magnetic metal construction. Purchased in 1967. In 1968 *Chaco* and *Formosa* were converted into minehunters in HM Dockyard, Portsmouth, and the other four were refitted and modernised as minesweepers by the Vosper Thornycroft Group with Vosper activated fin stabiliser equipment.

CHACO (hunter) *1970, Wright & Logan*

TIERRA DEL FUEGO (sweeper) *1969, Wright & Logan*

SURVEY SHIPS

1 Ex-CANADIAN FLOWER CLASS

CAPITAN CANEPA (ex-HMCS *Barrie*) Q 8

Displacement, tons	995 standard; 1 265 full load
Dimensions, feet	208 × 33·5 × 16·5
Main engines	Triple expansion; 2 750 ihp = 15 knots
Boilers	2
Oil fuel (tons)	271
Range, miles	7 200 at 10 knots
Complement	54

GENERAL
Former Canadian corvette of the "Flower" class. Launched in Canada on 12 Nov. 1940. Completed on 12 May 1941.

CAPITAN CANEPA *1969, Argentine Navy*

1 TRANSPORT TYPE

USHUAIA No. Q 10

Displacement, tons	1 275 standard; 1 500 full load
Dimensions, feet	211 × 31·5 × 11·5
Guns	removed
Main engines	2 sets diesels; 2 shafts; 1 200 bhp = 12.7 knots
Oil fuel (tons)	60
Range, miles	3 500 at 12 knots
Complement	65

GENERAL
Built at Rio Santiago. Launched in 1939. Named after the capital of the territory of Tierra del Fuego. Formerly rated as a transport until 1959, when she was reclassified as a survey ship. She also lays and services buoys and light buoys.

Survey Ships—*continued*

USHUAIA *1969, Argentine Navy*

1 AUXILIARY SAILING SHIP

EL AUSTRAL (ex-US *Atlantis*) Q 7

Displacement, tons	571
Dimensions, feet	110 pp 141 oa × 27 × 20
Main engines	Diesel; 400 bhp
Oil fuel (tons)	22
Complement	19

GENERAL
Built by Burmeister & Wain, Copenhagen. Launched and completed in 1931. Incorporated into the Argentine Navy on 30 April ,1966. Acquired from USA. Officially rated as *Buque Oceanagrafico*.

TRANSPORTS

BAHIA AGUIRRE (Q2) **BAHIA BUEN SUCESO** (Q6) **BAHIA THETIS** (Q8)

Displacement, tons	3 100 standard; 5 000 full load
Dimensions, feet	334·7 × 47 × 13·8
Guns	2—4·1 in; 2—40 mm Bofors AA; 2—20 mm AA; 4—47 mm saluting (Q6 only)
Main engines	2 sets Nordberg diesels; 2 shafts; 3 750 bhp =16 knots
Oil fuel (tons)	500 (Q8); 442 (Q6), 355 (Q2)
Complement	100

GENERAL
Built in Canada by Halifax shipyards. *Bahia Buen Suceso* was completed at Halifax, Nova Scotia, in June 1950. The first two are troop transports, *Bahia Thetis* used as a training ship and armed (see above).

BAHIA THETIS *1967, Werner Schiefer*

SAN JULIAN (ex-*FS* 281) B 7

Displacement, tons	930
Dimensions, feet	176 × 32·5 × 11
Main engines	2 sets diesels; 2 shafts; 1 000 bhp = 10 knots
Oil fuel (tons)	75
Complement	40

GENERAL
Ex-US Army small cargo carrier. Built by Wheeler Shipbuilding Corpn. Launched in 1944. It was officially stated in May 1960 that this vessel, formerly rated as a transport was to be converted into a salvage vessel, but in Dec 1961 it was officially stated that she would continue to be a transport ship.

LA PATAIA B 10

Displacement, tons	3 825 standard; 6 000 full load
Dimensions, feet	335·2 × 50·2 × 23
Main engines	2 sets diesels; 2 shafts; 3 400 bhp = 16 knots
Oil fuel (tons)	500
Complement	100

GENERAL
Built in Italy by C. R. del Adriatico (CRDA). Laid down on 25 Apr 1948, launched on 25 June 1949, completed in June 1950 and delivered on 2 Oct 1951. Troop transport. Sister ships *Le Maier* and *Les Eclaireurs* were scrapped in 1964.

LA PATAIA *1970, Argentine Navy*

SALVAGE SHIP

GUARDIAMARINA ZICARI (ex-*Tehuelche*, ex-HMS *Kingfisher*, ex-*King Salvor*) (Q81)

Displacement, tons	1 600
Dimensions, feet	200·2 pp; 216 oa × 37·8 × 13
Main engines	Triple expansion, 2 shafts; 1 500 ihp = 12 knots
Oil fuel, (tons)	310
Complement	82

GENERAL
Former British submarine rescue ship. Built as an Admiralty ocean salvage vessel by Wm. Simons & Co. Ltd. Renfrew, Scotland, and laid down on 17 May 1941, launched on 18 May 1942 and completed on 17 July 1942. Converted into a Submarine Rescue Bell and Target ship in 1953-54. Paid off as Bell Rescue Ship in 1958 and subsequently employed as Submarine Support Ship and Tender. Purchased from Great Britain in Dec 1960, and sailed from Chatham to Argentina in Apr 1961, and renamed *Tehuelche*, Again renamed *Guardiamarina Zicari* in Apr 1963.

GUARDIAMARINA ZICARI *Argentine Navy*

OILERS

PUNTA MEDANOS B 18

Displacement, tons	14 352 standard; 16 331 full load
Measurement, tons	8 250 deadweight,
Dimensions, feet	470 pp; 502 oa × 62 × 28·5
Main engines	Double reduction geared turbines. 2 shafts; 9 500 shp = 18 knots (over 19 knots attained on trials)
Boilers	2 Babcock & Wilcox two-drum integral furnace water-tube
Oil fuel (tons)	1 500
Range, miles	13 700 at 15 knots
Complement	99

GENERAL
Built by Swan, Hunter & Wigham Richardson Ltd, Wallsend on-Tyne. Launched on 20 Feb 1950. Completed on 10 Oct 1950. A unit of the Argentine Navy available as a training vessel for personnel. She embodied experience gained in previous fleet oilers, and was then the finest equipped and fastest of her type afloat. Fitted for fuelling warships at sea. Boilers built under licence by the Wallsend Slipway & Engineering Company. Steam conditions of 400 lb. per sq. in pressure and 750 deg F

PUNTA MEDANOS *1969, Argentine Navy*

PUNTA DELGADA (ex-*Sugarland*, ex-*Nanticoke, AOG* 66) B 16

Displacement, tons	5 930 standard; 6 090 full load
Dimensions, feet	325 × 48·2 × 20
Main engines	Westinghouse diesel; 1 shaft; 1 400 bhp = 11·5 knots
Oil fuel (tons)	150
Range, miles	9 000 at 11 knots
Complement	72

GENERAL
Named after geographical location. USMS type T1-M-BT1. Built by St. John's River SB Corp, Jacksonville, Fla. Launched on 7 Apr 1945.

DISPOSALS
Of two sister ships of this class *Punta Ninfas* (ex-*Black Bayou*, ex-*Michigamme*, AOG 65) was scrapped in 1964, and *Punta Loyola* (ex-*Capitain*, ex-*Klikitat*, AOG 64) was withdrawn from active service in 1966.

PUNTA ALTA B 12

Displacement, tons	1 600 standard; 1 900 full load
Measurement, tons	800 deadweight
Dimensions, feet	210 × 33·8 × 12·5
Main engines	Diesel; 1 shaft; 1 850 bhp = 8 knots
Oil fuel (tons)	146

GENERAL
Built at Puerto Belgrano. Launched in 1937. Named after a headland.

ICEBREAKER

GENERAL SAN MARTIN Q 4

Displacement, tons	4 854 standard; 5 301 full load
Measurement, tons	1 600 deadweight
Dimensions, feet	279 × 61 × 21
Guns	1—4 in; 2—40 mm AA Bofors
Aircraft	1 reconnaissance aircraft and 1 helicopter
Main engines	4 diesel-electric; 2 shafts; 7 100 hp = 16 knots
Range, miles	35 000 at 10 knots
Oil fuel (tons)	1 100
Complement	160

GENERAL
Built by Seebeck Yard of Weser AG. Launched on 24 June 1954. Completed in Oct 1954. Used by the Antarctic Institute. Fitted for research. Specially insulated against cold.

TRAINING SHIP

LIBERTAD Q 2

Displacement, tons	3 025 standard; 3 765 full load
Dimensions, feet	262 wl; 301 oa × 47 × 21·8
Guns	1—3 in; 4—40 mm AA; 4—47 mm saluting
Main engines	2 Sulzer diesels; 2 400 bhp ≐ 13·5 knots
Complement	370 (crew) plus 150 cadets

GENERAL
Built in the state owned shipyards at Rio Santiago. Launched on 30 June 1956. The former training ship *Madryn* was removed from the list on 29 June 1967.

LIBERTAD *1971*

TUGS

GUAYCURU R 33 **QUILMES** R 32

Displacement, tons	368 full load
Dimensions, feet	107·2 × 24·4 × 12·5
Main engines	Skinner Unaflow engines; 645 ihp = 9 knots
Boilers	Cylindrical
Oil fuel (tons)	52
Range, miles	2 200 at 7 knots
Complement	14

GENERAL
"Quilmes" class tugs built at Rio Santiago, Argentina, in the State Naval Shipyards. Laid down on 23 Aug and 15 Mar 1956, respectively launched on 27 Dec 1959 and 8 July 1957 and completed on 29 July and 30 Mar 1960.

PEHUENCHE R 29 **TONOCOTE** R 30

Displacement, tons	330
Dimensions, feet	105 × 24·7 × 12·5
Main engines	Triple expansion; 600 ihp = 11 knots
Boiler	2
Oil fuel (tons)	36
Range, miles	1 200 at 9 knots
Complement	13

GENERAL
Both built in Rio Santiago Naval Yard. Commissioned for service in 1954.

MATACO R 3 **TOBA** R 4

Displacement, tons	600
Measurement, tons	339 gross
Dimensions, feet	130·5 pp; 137 wl; 139 oa × 28·5 × 11.5
Main engines	Triple expansion; 2 shafts; 1 200 ihp = 12 knots
Boilers	2
Oil fuel (tons)	95
Range, miles	3 900 at 10 knots
Complement	34

GENERAL
Both built by Hawthorn Leslie, Ltd, Hebburn-on-Tyne. Launched on 24 Jan 1928 and 23 Dec 1927, respectively. Both completed in Mar 1928.

HUARPE R 12

Displacenemt, tons	370
Dimensions, feet	107 × 27·2 × 12
Main engines	Triple expansion; 800 ihp
Boilers	1 cylindrical (Howaldt Werke)
Oil fuel (tons)	58
Complement	13

GENERAL
Built by Howaldt Werke in 1927. Entered service in the Argentine Navy in 1942.

DISPOSAL
Sister ship *Puelche*, R 13, was withdrawn from service, it was officially stated in Jan 1971.

CALCHAQUI	R 6	(ex-US 445)	**MOCOVI**	R 5	(ex-US 441)
CAPAYAN	R 16	(ex-US 443)	**MORCOYAN**	R 19	(ex-US 448)
CHULUPI	R 10	(ex-US 426)	**QUIQUIYAN**	R 18	(ex-US 444)

Displacement, tons	70
Dimensions, feet	67 × 14 × 13
Main engines	Diesel; 310 bhp = 10 knots
Oil fuel (tons)	8·7
Complement	5

Built in USA and officially allocated the above pennant numbers in 1969.

AUSTRALIA

Minister for Defence (and Navy):
Mr. L. H. Barnard

Chairman of the Chiefs of Staff:
Admiral Sir Victor Smith, KBE, CB, DSC

Naval Board

Chief of Naval Staff:
Vice-Admiral Sir Richard I. Peek, KBE, CB, DSC

Chief of Naval Personnel:
Rear-Admiral Hugh David Stevenson, CBE

Chief of Naval Technical Services:
Rear-Admiral Brynmore W. Mussared, CBE

Chief of Supply and Works:
Rear-Admiral Gordon John Branstone Crabbe, CBE, DSC

Deputy Chief of the Naval Staff:
Rear-Admiral William John Dovers, CBE, DSC

Secretary, Department of the Navy:
Mr. Samuel Landau, CBE, MA

Senior Appointments

Flag Officer Commanding Australian Fleet:
Rear-Admiral Anthony M. Synnot, CBE

Flag Officer Commanding Eastern Area:
Rear-Admiral W. D. H. Graham, CBE

Diplomatic Representation

Australian Naval Representative: in London
Captain David W. Leach, CBE, MVO

Naval Attaché in Washington:
Commodore Alan G. McFarlane

Naval Attache in Tokyo:
Captain F. E. Irvine

Strength of the Fleet

2 Aircraft Carriers (1 as Transport Ship)
7 Destroyers (3 armed with guided missiles)
6 Frigates
4 Patrol Submarines
6 Coastal Minesweepers and Minehunters
20 Patrol Craft
6 Oceanographic and Survey Ships
2 Fleet Support Ships
6 Small Craft

New Construction Programme

3 Destroyers (DDL)
2 Patrol Submarines (*Orion, Otama*)
1 Combat Support Ship (20 270 tons) (*Protector*)
1 Oceanographic Ship (*Cook*)
1 Hydrographic Vessel (*Flinders*)

Navy Estimates

$A
1968-69: 223 721 500 *
1969-70: 239 252 100 *
1970-71: 243 010 000 *
1971-72: 282 741 000 *
1972-73: 316 655 000 *

*Includes United States Credits

Personnel

1 January 1969: 16 638 officers and sailors
1 January 1970: 17 030 officers and sailors
1 January 1971: 17 090 officers and sailors
1 January 1972: 17 000 officers and sailors
1 January 1973: 17 128 officers and sailors

Mercantile Marine

Lloyd's Register of Shipping:
370 vessels of 1 184 010 tons gross

Naval Procurement

Under the 1972-73 Defence authorization the following have been, or are to be ordered:
3 Destroyers (DDL type) to be built at Williamstown at a cost of $A355 million.
3 Destroyers (DLGs *Hobart, Perth* and *Brisbane*) to be modernized at a cost of $A33 million
4 Frigates (*Parramatta, Stuart, Yarra* and *Derwent*) to have extended refits at a cost of $A50 million
10 Sea King helicopters in lieu of 20 Wessex at a cost of $A43 million (delivery in 1974)
6 Lynx helicopters at a cost of $A4 million

Disposals

Destroyers (Battle class)
1957 *Bataan*
1962 *Warramunga*
1968 *Arunta* (sank on tow to breakers)
1970 *Tobruk*

Frigates (Type 15)
4/1958 *Quality* 1/1963 *Quadrant*
1970 *Quiberon, Quickmatch*
1972 *Queenborough*

SDBs
1953 SDML 1322. 1960 SDB 1327
1972 SDBs 1321, 1324, 1325

BDVs
1965 *Karangi, Kookaburra*
1966 *Kangaroo*
1968 *Koala*

Tugs
1969 *Emu, Sprightly*

Fleet Air Arm

Squadrons	*Duty*	*Aircraft*
HT 273	Helo aircrew Training and Pilot continuation training. Fleet support and SAR.	Iroquois and Scout helos
VC 724	Fixed wing fighter pilot training and fleet requirement flying and trials.	Macchi jet trainers. TA4G Skyhawk Trainers. A4G Skyhawks
HT 725	A/S helo training and fleet requirement duties.	Wessex 31B helos
VF 805	Front line strike fighters.	A4G Skyhawks
VS 816	Front line fixed wing A/S.	S2E Trackers
HS 817	Front line helo A/S.	Wessex 31B helos
VC 851	Training squadron for aircrew. Twin engine conversion, communication and Fleet requirement duties.	S2E Trackers and Dakotas (to be replaced by Hawker-Siddeley 748 trainers)

HULL NUMBERS

Aircraft Carriers

Melbourne	21

Submarines

Oxley	57
Otway	59
Ovens	70
Onslow	60

Guided Missile Destroyers

Perth	38
Hobart	39
Brisbane	41

Destroyers

Vampire	11
Vendetta	08
Duchess	154

Destroyer Escorts

Yarra	45
Parramatta	46
Stuart	48
Derwent	49
Swan	50
Torrens	53

Training Ships

Sydney	214
Anzac	59

Minehunters

Snipe	1102
Curlew	1121

Coastal Minesweepers

Hawk	1139
Teal (O)	1152
Gull (O)	1185
Ibis (O)	1183

Survey Ships

Moresby	573
Paluma	337
Diamantina	266
Kimbla	314

Support Ships

Stalwart	215
Supply	195

Reserve Training Ships

Bass	247
Banks	244

Patrol Boats

Advance	83
Assail	89
Attack	90
Barbette	97
Barricade	98
Bayonet	101
Aitape (P)	84
Ladava (P)	92
Lae (P)	93
Madang (P)	94
Samarai (P)	85
Aware	91
Ardent	87
Bombard	99
Buccaneer	100
Archer (R)	86
Adroit (R)	82
Arrow (R)	88
Acute (R)	81
Bandolier (O)	95

Notes
O=Operational Reserve
P=Papua-New Guinea Division
R=Reserve Training

AIRCRAFT CARRIER

Name	*No.*	*Builders*	*Laid down*	*Launched*	*Commissioned*
MELBOURNE (ex-*Majestic*)	21	Vickers-Armstrong, Barrow-in-Furness	15 Apr 1943	28 Feb 1945	28 Oct 1955

1 MODIFIED "MAJESTIC" CLASS

Displacement, tons	16 000 standard; 19 966 full load
Length, feet (*metres*)	650·0 (*198·1*)wl; 701·5 (*213·8*)oa
Beam, feet (*metres*)	80·2 (*24·5*) hull
Draught, feet (*metres*)	25·5 (*7·8*)
Width, feet (*metres*)	80·0 (*24·4*) flight deck 126·0 (*38·4*) oa including 6 deg angled deck and mirrors
Hangar, feet (*metres*)	444×52×17·5 (*135·3×15·8×5·3*)
Aircraft	8 Sky Hawk jet fighters; 6 Tracker aircraft; 10 Westland Wessex A/S helicopters (see *Aircraft* notes)
Guns, AA	12—40 mm (4 twin, 4 single) Bofors
Boilers	4 Admiralty 3-drum type
Main engines	Parsons single reduction geared turbines; 2 shafts; 42 000 shp
Speed, knots	24; sea speed 23 max
Range, miles	12 000 at 14 knots; 6 200 at 23 knots
Complement	1 335 (includes 347 Carrier Air Group personnel); 1 070 (75 officers and 995 sailors) as Flagship

MELBOURNE — *1970, Royal Australian Navy*

GENERAL
At the end of the Second World War, when she was still incomplete, work on this ship was virtually brought to a standstill pending a decision as to future naval requirements. When full-scale work was resumed during 1949-55, and after her design had several times been re-cast, she underwent reconstruction and modernisation in Great Britain, including the fitting of the angled deck, steam catapult and mirror deck landing sights, and was transferred to the RAN on completion. She was commissioned and renamed at Barrow-in-Furness on 28 Oct 1955, sailed from Portsmouth on 5 Mar 1956, and arrived at Fremantle, Australia, on 23 April 1956. She became flagship of the Royal Australian Navy at Sydney on 14 May 1956. She cost £A8 309 000.

MODERNISATION. *Melbourne* completed her extended refit during 1969 at a cost of over $A8 750 000 (25 per cent over estimate) to enable her to operate with S2E Tracker and A4G Skyhawk aircraft, and to improve habitability.

REFITS. In 1971 the catapult was rebuilt and a bridle-catcher fitted, and the flight deck was strengthened. Under refit from November 1972 to May 1973.

AIRCRAFT. The aircraft complement formerly comprised 8 Sea Venom jet fighters, 17 Gannet turbo-prop anti-submarine aircraft, and 2 Sycamore helicopters, later 4 Sea Venom, 6 Gannet and 10 Wessex A/S helicopters. Fourteen S2E Tracker anti-submarine aircraft and ten A4G Skyhawk fighter/bombers were purchased in 1966 in the USA (in service 1967) at a cost of $A46 000 000. Another 10 A4G Skyhawk (including 2 TA4G Trainers) were delivered during 1971. *Melbourne* now carries Skyhawks, Trackers and Wessex.

ENGINEERING. Boilers work at a pressure of 430 lb per sq in and a temperature of 700 degrees Fahrenheit of superheat.

RADAR. Search: Philips LWO series early warning and associated height finders for aircraft direction. Tactical: Type 293 Target Indication and surface warning. E.W.: Electronic intelligence and warfare equipment also fitted. Carrier controlled approach Radar. (Dome on island.)

DRAWING. Starboard elevation and plan as converted with the angled deck. Scale: 128 feet = 1 inch.

MELBOURNE — *1970, Royal Australian Navy*

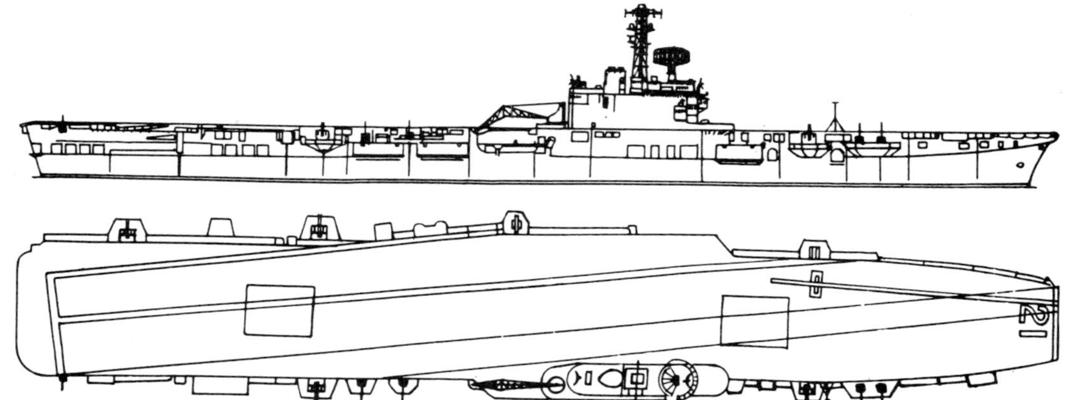

DESTROYERS

3 "PERTH" CLASS (DLGs)

Name	No.	Builders	Laid down	Launched	Commissioned
BRISBANE	41	Defoe Shipbuilding Co, Bay City, Mich.	15 Feb 1965	5 May 1966	16 Dec 1967
HOBART	39	Defoe Shipbuilding Co, Bay City, Mich.	26 Oct 1962	9 Jan 1964	18 Dec 1965
PERTH	38	Defoe Shipbuilding Co, Bay City, Mich.	21 Sep 1962	26 Sep 1963	17 July 1965

Displacement, tons	3 370 standard; 4 618 full load
Length, feet (*metres*)	431·0 (*131·4*)wl; 437·0 (*132·2*)oa
Beam, feet (*metres*)	47·1 (*14·3*)
Draught, feet (*metres*)	20·1 (*6·1*)
Missile launchers	1 single for "Tartar"
A/S weapons	2 single launchers for long range "Ikara" system
Guns	2—5 in (*127 mm*) 54 cal, dp, single-mount, rapid fire
Torpedo tubes	6 (2 triple) for A/S torpedoes
Boilers	4 Foster Wheeler "D" type; 1 200 psi; 950°F
Main engines	2 GE double reduction turbines; 2 shafts; 70 000 shp
Speed, knots	35
Range, miles	6 000 at 14 knots 1 600 at 30 knots
Complement	333 (21 officers, 312 sailors)

GENERAL
On 6 Jan 1962, in Washington, US defence representatives and Australian military officials (on behalf of the Royal Australian Navy) and executives of the Defoe Shipbuilding Company, of Bay City, Michigan, signed a $A25 726 700 contract for the construction of two guided-missile destroyers (shipbuilding cost only). On 22 Jan 1963 it was officially announced by the Navy Minister in Canberra, Australia, that a third guided-missile destroyer was to be built in USA for Australia. The first of their kind for the Australian Navy, they constitute the 1st Destroyer Squadron, RAN. All three ships have been in action off Vietnam where they served with the US 7th fleet

DESIGN. Generally similar to the US "Charles F. Adams" class, but they differ by the addition of a broad deckhouse between the funnels enclosing the Ikara anti-submarine torpedo-carrying missile system, and the mounting of a single-arm launcher, instead of a twin, for the Tartar surface-to-air guided missiles. As compared with previous destroyers, the ships have greater length overall, more beam and heavier displacement. They have a new hull design with aluminium superstructures. The most recent habitability improvements have been incorporated into their construction, including air conditioning of all living spaces.

COST. Original estimate $A12 800 000 to $A14 000 000 each (with missiles and electronics $A40 000 000 each). The total cost of *Perth* was reported to be $A50 000 000.

MODERNISATION. All three ships will return to the USA for modernisation, including the fitting of Mk. 10 mountings for the 5 inch guns and a Naval Data System. *Hobart* returned in 1972 and the other two will follow in turn.

RADAR. Search: SPS 40 and 3 D SPS 52 for aircraft Tactical: SPS 10 surface search and tactical radar. Fire Control: C Band for Tartar system, X band for guns.

BRISBANE, HOBART, PERTH

PERTH — *1971, Royal Australian Navy*

BRISBANE — *1970, Royal Australian Navy*

3 "DARING" CLASS (DD)

Name	No.	Builders	Begun	Launched	Completed
VAMPIRE	11	Cockatoo Island Dockyard, Sydney	1 July 1952	27 Oct 1956	23 June 1959
VENDETTA	08	HMA Naval Dockyard, Williamstown	4 July 1949	3 May 1954	26 Nov 1958
DUCHESS	154	John I. Thornycroft & Co. Southampton	2 July 1948	9 Apr 1951	23 Oct 1952

Displacement, tons	2 800 standard; 3 600 full load
Length, feet (*metres*)	366 (*111·3*)pp; 388·5 (*118·4*)oa
Beam, feet (*metres*)	43 (*13·1*)
Draught, feet (*metres*)	12·8 (*3·9*)
Guns, surface	6—4·5 in (*115 mm*) in 3 twin turrets, two forward and one aft
Guns, AA	6—40 mm (2—40 mm in *Duchess*)
A/S weapons	1 3-barrelled DC mortar (see *Design* notes)
Boilers	2 Foster Wheeler; 650 psi; 850°F
Main engines	English Electric geared turbines; 2 shafts; 54 000 shp
Speed, knots	30·5
Range, miles	3 700 at 20 knots; 3 000 at 20 knots (*Duchess*)
Oil fuel, tons	584
Complement	320 (14 officers, 306 sailors)

GENERAL
The above particulars refer to *Vampire* and *Vendetta*. *Duchess* has "Squid" instead of "Limbo" depth charge mortars. The three ships constitute the 2nd Destroyer Squadron, R.A.N. *Vampire* and *Vendetta* are the largest destroyers ever built in Australia. They were ordered in 1946. Their sister ship, *Voyager*, the prototype of the

Destroyers—*continued*

class, collided with the aircraft carrier *Melbourne* and sank off the southern coast of New South Wales on the night of 10 Feb 1964. She was replaced by the British destroyer *Duchess*, lent to Australia by the United Kingdom for four years on 8 May 1964, later extended to 1971 and purchased by RAN in 1972.
Four large destroyers of this type were originally projected, to have been named after the Royal Australian Navy's famous "Scrap Iron Flotilla" of destroyers which won renown in the Mediterranean on the Tobruk ferry run and in other areas during the Second World War, but *Waterhen* was cancelled in 1954.

DESIGN. *Vampire* and *Vendetta* were of similar design, including all welded construction, to that of the "Daring" class, built in Great Britain, but were modified to suit Australian conditions and have "Limbo" instead of "Squid" anti-submarine mortars. The superstructure is of light alloy, instead of steel, to reduce weight.

MODERNISATION. *Vampire* completed in Dec 1971. *Vendetta* started half-life refit in Sept 1971. To complete in 1973. The $A20 million programme for both ships includes new Mk 22 fire-control systems, new LW02 air-warning and navigation radars, new action-information centre, modernised communications, fitting modernised turrets, improved habitability, the fitting of an enclosed bridge and new funnels.

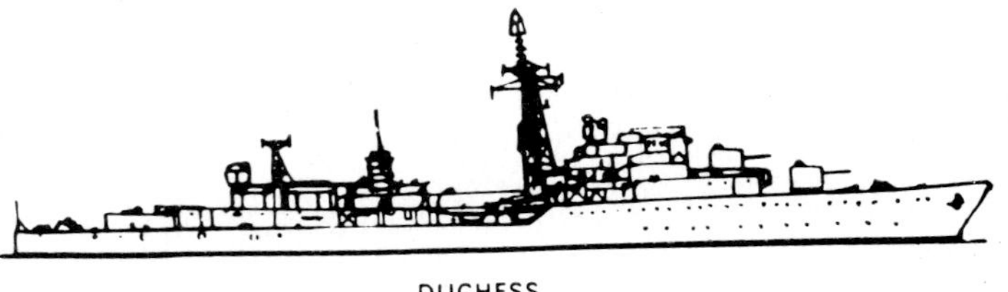

DUCHESS

VAMPIRE, VENDETTA

REFIT. *Duchess* has been converted for training duties and has had X turret removed.

RADAR
Search: Type 293 S Band air and surface warning radar.
Fire Control: X Band for both forward and after systems.

GUNNERY. "B" and "X" 4·5-inch twin turrets were removed from *Vampire* during her 1968 refit, pending major refit in 1970-71 (see *Anzac Gunnery* notes).

TUBES. The five 21-inch torpedo tubes in a quintuple mounting in *Duchess* were removed in 1970.

VAMPIRE — *1970, Royal Australian Navy*

DUCHESS — ***1970, Royal Australian Navy***

Destroyers—*continued*

3 DDL CLASS

Displacement, tons	4 200 standard
Length, feet (*metres*)	425 wl (*129·6*)
Beam, feet (*metres*)	48 (*14·6*)
Aircraft	2 helicopters
Missiles	Probably single Standard SAM's and up to six SSMs of undecided type
Guns	1—5 in (possibly OTO 127/54) 2—35 mm
Torpedo tubes	2 triple ASW mountings
Main engines	2 Olympus gas turbines with 2 Tyne gas turbines for cruising. COCOG arrangement; total 50 000 shp
Speed, knots	30
Range, miles	6 000 at 18 knots
Complement	205

The RAN's replacement programme for their destroyers and frigates presents a number of problems unique to the Antipodes. An enormous coastline, great distances to other theatres, combined with a restricted budget offered the designers many difficulties. The result is probably as good as could be asked for and, even under new governmental restrictions, approval has been given for the design of three new ships of this type. A powerful SSM and SAM armament combined with high performance radars, Australian designed sonar and two helicopters make this a potent class of ships which have a good range and are deficient only in speed. In this they are by no means alone. The usual confusion exists in their title of DDL—"Light Destroyer" for a ship of 4 200 tons is a complete misnomer. They have therefore been classed as "Destroyers".

DDL, new general purpose destroyer, preliminary design

1 "BATTLE" CLASS (DD)

Displacement, tons	2 400 standard; 3 400 full load
Length, feet (*metres*)	355 (*108·2*) pp; 379 (*115·5*) oa
Beam, feet (*metres*)	41·0 (*12·5*)
Draught, feet (*metres*)	17·5 (*5·3*) max
Guns, surface	2—4·5 in (1 twin turret)
Guns, AA	5—40 mm
A/S weapons	1 "Squid" 3-barrelled DC mortar
Boilers	2 Admiralty 3-drum 400 psi; 650°F
Main engines	Parsons geared turbines; 2 shafts; 50 000 shp
Speed, knots	31
Oil fuel, tons	680
Range, miles	3 000 at 20 knots
Complement	332 (20 officers, 312 sailors)

Name	*No.*	*Builders*	*Laid down*	*Launched*	*Completed*
ANZAC	59	Williamstown Naval Dockyard	23 Sep 1946	20 Aug 1948	14 Mar 1951

ANZAC

DISPOSALS

Sister ship *Tobruk* was placed on the disposal list in 1970. Of the three destroyers of the "Tribal" class, *Bataan* was listed for disposal in 1957 (and scrapped), *Warramunga* in 1962, and *Arunta* in 1968, (*Arunta* sank on 13 Feb, 1969, off E. Australia whilst in tow to breakers in Taiwan).

GENERAL

Ordered in 1946. Originally similar to the "Battle" class destroyers in the Royal Navy, but several alterations were incorporated, including sleeping accommodation for officers and men fore and aft, improved mess layout and other amenities, modern radar fire control, close range Staag armament (new type of twin 40 mm Bofors gun mounting) and contemporary anti-submarine weapons.

GUNNERY. *Anazc* had the first "Daring" type 4·5 inch guns and mountings of completely Australian manufacture (weight of twin mount is approx 50 tons). They are fully automatic, with a rate of fire of 25 rounds per minute, and an accurate range of over ten miles, firing a shell weighing 53 lb. (The 4·5 inch guns for *Tobruk* were imported from Great Britain.)

Original main armament was two twin 4·5 inch turrets. *Anzac* became a Fleet Training ship in Mar 1961. In 1966 "B" turret in *Anzac* was suppressed and replaced by a chartroom for training purposes.

RADAR. Search: Type 293 S Band combined air and surface warning radar.

ANZAC ("B" turret replaced by chartroom)

1972, Royal Australian Navy

FRIGATES

6 "RIVER" CLASS

Name	No.	Builders	Laid down	Launched	Commissioned
YARRA	45	Williamstown Naval Dockyard, Melbourne	9 Apr 1957	30 Sep 1958	27 July 1961
PARRAMATTA	46	Cockatoo Island Dockyard, Sydney	3 Jan 1957	31 Jan 1959	4 July 1961
STUART	48	Cockatoo Island Dockyard, Sydney	20 Mar 1959	8 Apr 1961	28 June 1963
DERWENT	49	Williamstown Naval Dockyard, Melbourne	16 June 1958	17 Apr 1961	30 Apr 1964
SWAN	50	Williamstown Naval Dockyard, Melbourne	18 Aug 1965	16 Dec 1967	20 Jan 1970
TORRENS	53	Cockatoo Island Dockyard, Sydney	18 Aug 1965	28 Sep 1968	19 Jan 1971

Displacement, tons	2 100 standard; 2 700 full load
Length, feet (*metres*)	360·0 (*109·7*) pp; 370·0 (*112·8*) oa
Beam, feet (*metres*)	41·0 (*12·5*)
Draught, feet (*metres*)	17·3 (*5·3*)
Missile launchers	1 quadruple for "Seacat"
A/S weapons	1 launcher for "Ikara" long range system 1 "Limbo" 3-barrelled DC mortar
Guns, dual purpose	2—4·5 in (*115 mm*)
Boilers	2 Babcock & Wilcox; 550 psi; 850°F
Main engines	2 double reduction geared turbines; 2 shafts; 30 000 shp
Speed, knots	30
Range, miles	4 500 at 12 knots
Complement	247 (13 officers, 234 sailors) in *Swan* and *Torrens*; 250 (13 officers, 237 sailors) in other four ships

YARRA *1972, Royal Australian Navy*

GENERAL
The design is basically similar to that of British "Type 12" anti-submarine frigates, but modified by the Royal Australian Navy to incorporate improvements in equipment and habitability. The enclosed tower foremast differs from that in "Rothesay" class frigates in the Royal Navy. All six ships were standardised to uniform armament and layout. *Stuart* was the first ship fitted with the "Ikara" anti-submarine guided missile, trial ship for the system. *Derwent* was the first RAN ship to be fitted with "Seacat". The variable depth sonar has been removed from *Derwent* and *Stuart*. Note difference in silhouette between *Swan* and *Torrens* and the earlier ships of the class, the former pair having a straight-run upper deck.

RADAR. Search: All ships fitted with Philips LWO series of L Band early warning radars. Type 293 combined air and surface warning, except *Swan* which has Philips/HSA X Band radar. Fire Control: MRS 3 or HSA systems, X Band radar.

SWAN, TORRENS

DERWENT

STUART

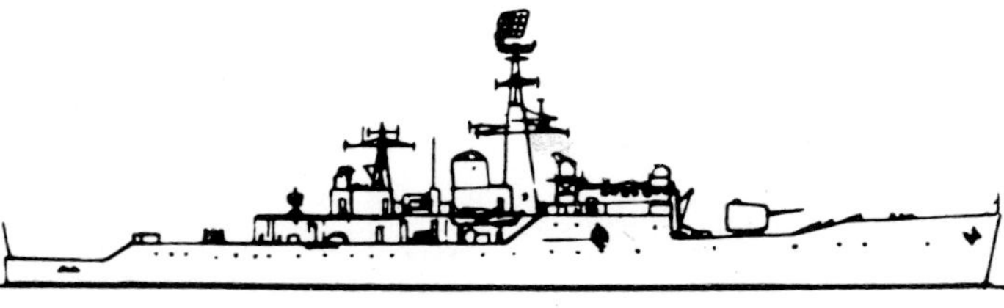

PARRAMATTA, YARRA.

SWAN *1972, Royal Australian Navy*

SUBMARINES

4 + 2 "OXLEY" CLASS (BRITISH "OBERON" TYPE)

Name	No.	Builders	Laid down	Launched	Commissioned
ONSLOW	60	Scotts' Shipbuilding & Eng Co Ltd, Greenock	4 Dec 1967	3 Dec 1968	22 Dec 1969
OTWAY	59	Scotts' Shipbuilding & Eng Co Ltd, Greenock	29 June 1965	29 Nov 1966	23 Apr 1968
OVENS	70	Scotts' Shipbuilding & Eng Co Ltd, Greenock	17 June 1966	4 Dec 1967	18 Apr 1969
OXLEY	57	Scotts' Shipbuilding & Eng Co Ltd, Greenock	2 July 1964	24 Sep 1965	18 Apr 1967
ORION		Scotts' Shipbuilding & Eng Co Ltd, Greenock	6 Oct 1972	Due 1974	Due 1975
OTAMA		Scotts' Shipbuilding & Eng Co Ltd, Greenock	1973	Due 1975	Due 1976

Displacement, tons	1 610 standard; 2 196 surface; 2 417 submerged (revised official figures)
Length, feet (*metres*)	241 (*73·5*) pp; 295·5 (*90·1*) oa
Beam, feet (*metres*)	26·5 (*8·1*)
Draught, feet (*metres*)	18 (*5·5*)
Torpedo tubes	8—21 in (*533 mm*) (6 bow, 2 stern)
Main engines	2 Admiralty Standard Range diesels, 3 600 bhp; 2 shafts; 2 electric motors, 6 000 shp; Electric drive
Speed, knots	16 surface; 18 dived (official figure)
Oil fuel, tons	300
Range, miles	12 000 at 10 knots
Complement	62 (7 officers, 55 sailors)

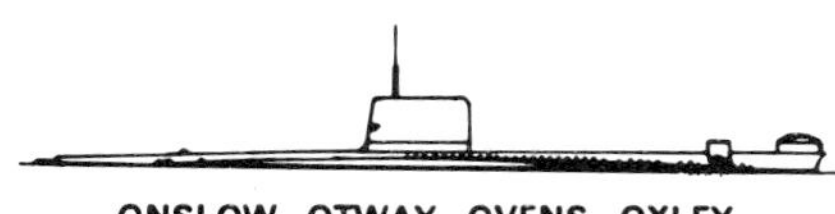

ONSLOW, OTWAY, OVENS, OXLEY

GENERAL
It was officially announced by the Minister for the Navy in Canberra, Australia, on 22 Jan 1963 that four submarines of the "Oberon" class were to be built in British shipyards under Admiralty supervision at an overall cost of £A5 000 000 each, with deliveries spread over 3 years. These constitute the 1st Submarine Squadron, R.A.N. based at HMAS Platypus, Neutral Bay, Sydney.

NAMES. *Oxley* and *Otway* are named after two earlier RAN submarines, completed in 1927. *Otama* will be named after the Queensland aboriginal word for Dolphin.

R.N. SQUADRON. The last unit of the Fourth Submarine Squadron of the Royal Navy, *Trump*, was withdrawn from Balmoral, Sydney in Jan 1969.
But in 1970 RN submarines were again based on Sydney, "on detachment" from the Far East Fleet, and one British submarine will be maintained on station from 1971, it was officially stated in the 1971-72 Navy Estimates. *Odin* arrived in Australian waters in late 1972 for a three year attachment.

OXLEY *1971, Royal Australian Navy*

OTWAY *1971, John Mortimer*

MINE WARFARE SHIPS

CURLEW (ex-HMS *Chediston*, ex-*Montrose*) 1121
GULL (ex-HMS *Swanston*) 1185
HAWK (ex-HMS *Somerleyton*, ex-*Gamston*) 1139
IBIS (ex-HMS *Singleton*) 1183
SNIPE (ex-HMS *Alcaston*) 1102
TEAL (ex-HMS *Jackton*) 1152

Displacement, tons	375 standard; 445 full load (revised official figures)
Dimensions, feet	140 pp; 152 oa × 28·8 × 8·2
Guns	2—40 mm AA, *Curlew* and *Snipe* 1—40 mm
Main engines	Napier Deltic diesels; 2 shafts; 3 000 bhp = 16 knots
Range, miles	2 300 at 13 knots; 3 000 at 8 knots
Complement	34 (4 officers; 30 sailors); Minehunters 38 (3 officers, 35 sailors)

"Ton" class coastal minesweepers. Purchased from the United Kingdom in 1961, and modified in British Dockyards to suit Australian conditions. Turned over to the Royal Australian Navy, commissioned and re-named on 21 Aug, 19 July, 18 July, 7 Sept, 11 Sept, and 30 Aug 1962 respectively. Mirrlees diesels were replaced by Napier Deltic, and ships air conditioned and fitted with stabilisers. Sailed from Portsmouth to Australia on 1 Oct 1962. Constitute the 1st Mine Countermeasures Squadron. *Curlew* and *Snipe* have been converted into minehunters.

FUTURE. It is understood that replacements for these ships are now being considered

HAWK *1970, Royal Australian Navy*

PATROL BOATS

Australia									
ACUTE	81	**ARCHER**	86	**ASSAIL**	89	**BANDOLIER**	95	**BAYONET**	101
ADROIT	82	**ARDENT**	87	**ATTACK**	90	**BARBETTE**	97	**BOMBARD**	99
ADVANCE	83	**ARROW**	88	**AWARE**	91	**BARRICADE**	98	**BUCCANEER**	100
New Guinea									
AITAPE	84	**LADAVA**	92	**LAE**	93	**MADANG**	94	**SAMARAI**	85

Displacement, tons	146 full load
Dimensions, feet	107·5 oa × 20 × 7·3 (max)
Guns	1—40 mm; 2 medium MG (no guns in *Aware, Bandolier* and *Madang*)
Main engines	Paxman 16 YJCM Diesels 3 500 hp; 2 shafts = 21-24 knots
Complement	19 (3 officers, 16 sailors). New Guinea boats: 2 officers 14 sailors

Five patrol boats for the formation of the New Guinea coastal security force and fifteen for general duties have been built. Steel construction. Builders: Evans Deakin & Co, Pty Ltd, Brisbane, and Walkers Ltd, Maryborough. Ordered in Nov 1965. First vessel was originally scheduled for delivery in Aug 1966, but was not launched until Mar 1967. Cost $A800 000 each.

LAE — *1972, Royal Australian Navy*

OCEANOGRAPHIC AND SURVEY SHIPS

1 NEW CONSTRUCTION

COOK 291

Displacement, tons	1 750 standard; 2 300 full load
Length, feet (*metres*)	315·0 (*90·6*)
Beam, feet (*metres*)	44·0 (*13·4*)
Draught, feet (*metres*)	15·1 (*4·6*)
Aircraft	1 helicopter
Main engines	Diesels; 2 shafts; 4 000 bhp
Speed, knots	20 approx
Oil fuel, tons	400
Range, miles	10 000 at 10 knots
Complement	140 including 13 scientists

GENERAL
Intended to replace HMAS *Diamantina*, the design is basically similar to that of HMAS *Moresby*. Her cost is estimated to be nearly $A12 000 000 (nearly $A18 000 000 with spares. shore support and initial maintenance). The helicopter and hangar will provide facilities for use in the hydrographic role, but the ship will have a dual oceanographic and hydrographic research capacity with accommodation and laboratory research facilities for up to 13 scientists in addition to the ship's company.

COOK — *1972, Official, revised artists impression*

Name	*No.*	*Builders*	*Laid down*	*Launched*	*Commissioned*
MORESBY	573	State Dockyard, Newcastle NSW	June 1961	7 Sep 1963	6 Mar 1964

Displacement, tons	1 714 standard; 2 351 full load
Length, feet (*metres*)	284·5 (*86·7*) pp; 314·0 (*95·7*) oa
Beam, feet (*metres*)	42·0 (*12·8*)
Draught, feet (*metres*)	15·0 (*4·6*)
Guns	2—40 mm Bofors AA (single)
Aircraft	1 Westland Scout Helicopter
Main engines	Diesel-electric; 3 diesels; 3 990 bhp; 2 electric motors; 2 shafts; 5 000 shp = 19 knots
Complement	146 (13 officers, 133 sailors)

GENERAL
The Royal Australian Navy's first specifically designed survey ship. Built at a cost of £A2 000 000 ($A4 000 000).

MORESBY

MORESBY — *Royal Australian Navy*

Name	*No.*	*Builders*	*Laid down*	*Launched*	*Completed*
DIAMANTINA	266 (ex-F 377)	Walkers Ltd, Maryborough, Queensland	12 Apr 1943	6 Apr 1944	27 Apr 1945

Displacement, tons	1 340 standard; 2 127 full load
Length, feet (*metres*)	283 (*86·3*) pp; 301·3 (*91·8*) oa
Beam, feet (*metres*)	36·7 (*11·2*)
Draught, feet (*metres*)	12·5 (*3·8*)
Guns	1—40 mm
Boilers	2 Admiralty 3-drum
Main engines	Triple expansion 5 500 ihp; 2 shafts
Speed, knots	19·5
Range, miles	7 700 at 12 knots
Complement	125 (6 officers, 119 sailors)

GENERAL
Frigate converted in 1959-60 for survey and completed conversion for oceanographic research in June 1969. The conversion included the provision of special laboratories. Sister ship *Lachlan* was sold to the Royal New Zealand Navy.

ARMAMENT. The two 4-inch guns and two "Squid" A/S mortars in "B" position were removed. The forward 4-inch gun was in "A" position with the 40 mm gun superimposed.

DIAMANTINA

KIMBLA A 314

Displacement, tons	762 standard; 1 021 full load
Dimensions, feet	150 pp; 179 oa × 32 × 12 mean
Main engines	Triple expansion; Oil fuel; 1 shaft; 350 ihp = 9·5 knots
Complement	40 (4 officers and 36 sailors)

Built as a boom defence vessel by Walkers Ltd., Maryborough. Laid down on 4 Nov 1953. Launched 23 Mar 1955. Completed on 26 Mar 1956. Converted to a Trials Vessel in 1959. Is now employed on trials. Guns removed (1—40 mm AA; 2—20 mm AA.)

FLINDERS

Displacement, tons	800
Dimensions, feet	150·0 × 33·0
Complement	36 officers and men

Similar in design to *Atyimba* built for the Philippines, she will replace *Paluma*. Laid down at Williamstown in Dec 1970. Her functional design will allow a 50% increase in output over *Paluma* which is a converted stores tender. Notable for bow anchor in the eyes of the ship.

PALUMA

Displacement, tons	336
Dimensions, feet	120 × 24 × 6·8 mean
Main engines	Ruston & Hornsby diesels; 2 shafts = 9·5 knots
Complement	3 officers and 25 sailors

Built at the Newcastle State Dockyard during the Second World War as a motor stores lighter. Commissioned on 18 March 1957. Conversion into a survey vessel was completed on 10 May 1959.

FAST TRANSPORT (*ex-Aircraft Carrier*)

1 "MAJESTIC" CLASS

Name	No.	Deck Letter	Builders	Laid down	Launched	Commissioned
SYDNEY (ex-*Terrible*)	P 214 (ex-A 214, ex-R 17)	S (ex-K)	H.M. Dockyard, Devonport	19 Apr 1943	30 Sep 1944	16 Dec 1948

Displacement, tons	12 569 standard; 17 233 full load (revised official figure)
Length, feet (*metres*)	630·0 (*192·0*)pp; 696·8 (*212·4*)oa
Beam, feet (*metres*)	80·0 (*24·4*)
Draught, feet (*metres*)	18·25 (*5·6*) mean; 25·0 (*7·6*) max
Flight deck,	
Length feet (*metres*)	690·7 (*210·5*)
Width, feet (*metres*)	112·5 (*34·3*)
Guns, AA	4—40 mm, single mountings
Boilers	4 Admiralty 3-drum; 400 psi; 700°F
Main engines	Parsons single reduction geared turbines; 2 shafts; 42 000 shp
Speed, knots	24·5
Range, miles	12 000 at 14 knots
Complement	607 (40 officers, 567 sailors) as transport. 550 (36 officers and 514 sailors) as training ship

SYDNEY — *1972, Royal Australian Navy*

GENERAL
This ship was handed over to the Royal Australian Navy on 16 Dec 1948, accepted for service on 5 Feb 1949, sailed from Devonport on 12 April and arrived in Australia in May 1949.

As an operational aircraft carrier she displaced 15 740 tons standard, carried the 21st CAG of Sea Fury fighters and Firefly anti-submarine and reconnaissance squadrons with a stowage capacity of 37 machines. She mounted 30 Bofors 40 mm AA guns, and her complement was 1 100 officers and sailors (peace), 1 300 (war). Served off Korea 1951-52 and 1953-54.

RADAR
Search: Type 293 combined air and surface warning.

TRAINING AND CONVERSION. In May 1955 *Sydney* landed her aircraft and entered her training role. It was officially announced on 4 Apr 1957 that she would have a flying training role, but the ship was converted to a fast military transport in 1962, and was recommissioned after conversion on 7 Mar 1962. She also still serves as a training ship, and can operate Wessex anti-submarine helicopters. Has carried out many return trooping trips to Vietnam earning the title of "Vung Tau ferry".

SUPPORT SHIPS

1 PROJECTED AOE

PROTECTOR

Displacement, tons	20 270 full load
Dimensions, feet	536·0 pp; 593·0 oa × 72·0
Aircraft	2 helicopters
Main engines	4 medium speed diesels driving 2 controllable pitch propellers through reduction gearing
Complement	335

GENERAL
Approval in principle given for the building of this ship in Australia but only after re-examination of the design. Planned to replenish ships of all sizes and to carry all kinds of fuel oils, ammunition, consumable stores, machinery spares, missiles and victualling stores. To be fitted for probe refuelling.

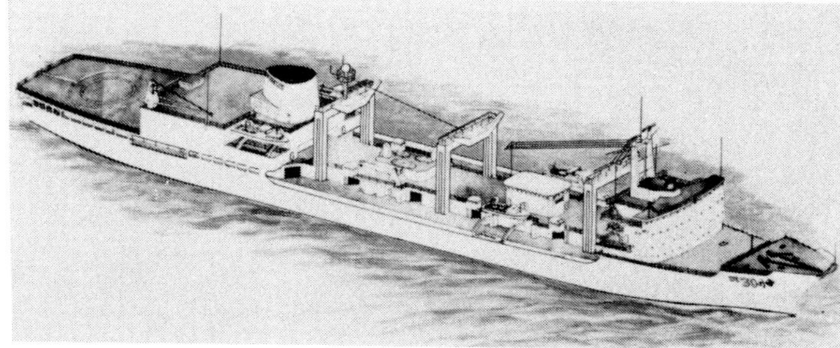

PROTECTOR — *1972, Royal Australian Navy*

STALWART 215

Displacement, tons	10 000 standard; 15 500 full load
Length, feet (*metres*)	515·5 (*157·1*) oa
Beam, feet (*metres*)	67·5 (*20·6*)
Draught, feet (*metres*)	29·5 (*9·0*)
Missiles	Provision for Seacat
Guns, AA	4—40 mm (2 twin)
Main engines	2 Scott-Sulzer 6-cyl turbo-diesels 2 shafts; 14 400 bhp
Speed, knots	20
Complement	396 (23 officers and 373 sailors)

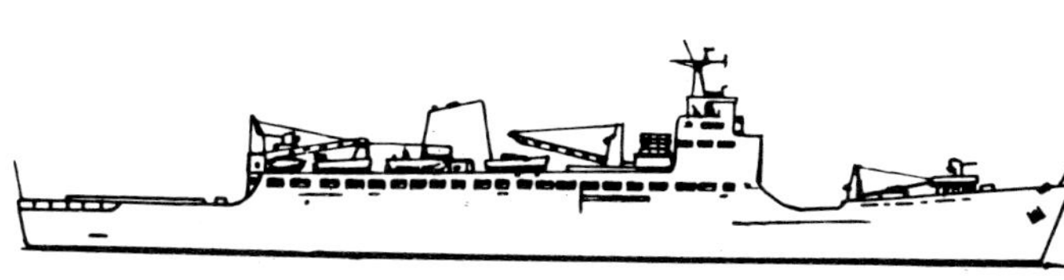

STALWART

GENERAL
Largest naval vessel designed and built in Australia. Built at Cockatoo Island Dockyard by Vickers (Australia) Pty Ltd, Sydney. Ordered on 11 Sep 1963. Laid down in June 1964 and launched on 7 Oct 1966. Commissioned 9 Feb 1968. Designed to maintain destroyers and frigates, and advanced weapons systems, including guided missiles. She has a helicopter flight deck and is defensively armed. High standard of habitability. Formerly rated as Escort Maintenance Ship. Redesignated Destroyer Tender in 1968. Cost officially estimated at just under $A15 000 000.

STALWART — *1972, Royal Australian Navy*

SUPPLY (ex-*Tide Austral*) 195

Displacement, tons	15 000 standard; 25 941 full load
Measurement, tons	17 600 deadweight; 11 200 gross
Dimensions, feet	550 pp; 583 oa × 71 × 32 max
Guns	6—40 mm AA (2 twin, 2 single)
Main engines	Double reduction geared turbines; 15 000 shp = 17·25 knots
Complement	13 officers, 187 sailors

Built for Australia by Harland & Wolff, Ltd, Belfast. Launched 1 Sep 1954, completed March 1955. British "Tide" Class. Lent to Great Britain until 1 Sep 1962, when *Tide Austral* was re-named HMAS *Supply* and commissioned in the Royal Australian Navy at Portsmouth 15 Aug 1962. Sailed for Australia 1 Oct 1962.

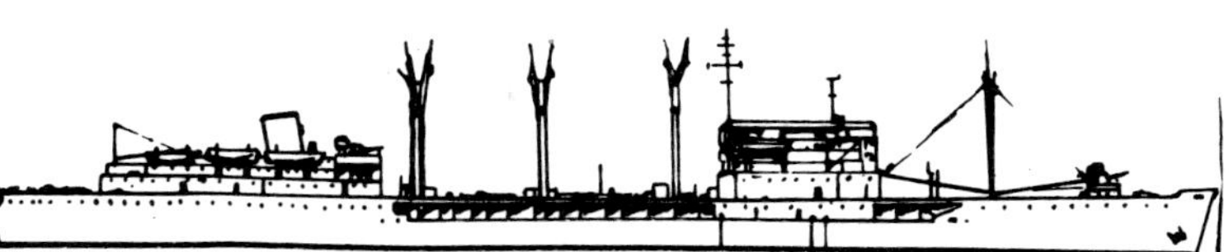

SUPPLY

Support Ships—*continued*

SUPPLY *1972, Royal Australian Navy*

DIVING TENDERS

OTTER (ex-*Wintringham*) Y 299 **SEAL** (ex-*Popham*) Y 298 **TORTOISE** (ex-*Neasham*) Y 280

SEAL *1971, Royal Australian Navy*

Tenders—*continued*

Displacement, tons	120 standard; 159 full load
Dimensions, feet	100 pp × 22 × 5·8
Main engines	2 Paxman diesels; 1 100 bhp = 14 knots
Range, miles	2 000 at 9 knots; 1 500 at 12 knots

Transferred from Royal Navy, these ex-inshore Minesweepers were converted to Diving Tenders and attached to the Diving School at Sydney.

GENERAL PURPOSE VESSELS

BANKS **BASS**

Displacement, tons	207 standard; 255 and 260 full load respectively
Dimensions, feet	90 pp; 101 oa × 22 × 8
Main engines	Diesel; speed = 10 knots
Complement	14 (2 officers, 12 sailors)

"Explorer" class. Of all steel construction. *Banks* was fitted for fishery surveillance and *Bass* for surveying, but both were used for other duties. Reserve training.

TUG

BRONZEWING

Displacement, tons	250
Dimensions, feet	98·8 oa × 21·2 × 8·2
Main engines	Diesel; 1 shaft; 480 bhp = 10 knots

Launched by Mort's Dock, Sydney 25 June 1946.

BUILDING PROGRAMME. 4 new harbour tugs and 8 LCHs are now building.

BAHAMAS

PATROL CRAFT

4 "60 ft" GRP TYPE

ACKLINS **ANDROS** **ELEUTHERA** **SAN SALVADOR**

Displacement, tons	30 standard approx
Dimensions, feet	62·0 oa × 15·8 × 4·6
Guns	2—20 mm (not yet fitted)
Main engines	2 Caterpillar diesels = 19·5 knots
Complement	11

Standard "60 ft" Keith Nelson patrol craft in glass reinforced plastic, built in 1971.

ANDROS *1972, Vosper Thornycroft*

BANGLADESH

Administration

Minister for Air Shipping and Waterways,
General Osmani

Chief of staff
Commander Nurul Huq

Administrative Officer
Captain Kashedul Islam Chowdhury

Strength:	3 Armed River Steamers 1 Poluchat class
Personnel:	700—1000
Bases:	Chittagong, Kulna, Dacca

The Bangladesh Navy was the last of the three services to be formed, Commander Nurul Huq (a 37 year old engineering specialist trained at Manadon Royal Naval Engineering College) being appointed Chief of Staff at the end of March 1972. The first armed river steamer was commissioned by General Osmani on 12 June 1972 as P101. Two more, P102 and 103, were commissioned in late July being followed by P104, an ex-Soviet Poluchat class. Four Soviet Vanya class coastal minesweepers will be operating in Bangladesh waters until late 1973. It is possible that these will be transferred to the navy on completion of their current tasks, but meanwhile the Bangladesh authorities are enquiring abroad for new construction tenders, presumably to carry our their stated intention of building up a force of gunboats and destroyers/frigates. The activities of the Soviet Navy in this area suggest that, if adequate credit is not available in Western countries, the Bangladesh navy may be based on Russian ships.

3 ARMED RIVER STEAMERS

Displacement, tons	100 tons (approx)
Dimensions, feet	100 × 18 × 6 (approx)
Guns	1—25 mm

1 Ex-SOVIET POLUCHAT PATROL BOAT

Displacement, tons	100 standard
Dimensions, feet	98·4 × 19·0 × 5·9
Guns	2—25 mm

GENERAL
As no other announcement has been made it is assumed that this ship has been transferred by India.

BELGIUM

Administration

Chief of Naval Staff:
Commodore L. J. J. Lurquin

Diplomatic Representation

Naval Military and Air Attaché in London:
Colonel (BEM) Jules Kaisin

Naval, Military and Air Attaché in Washington:
Lt. General Avi. van Rolleghem

Naval, Military and Naval Attaché in Paris:
Colonel (BEM) Hugo Rel

New Construction Plan For 1975-1978

4 Frigates projected, service by 1978 (see specification below)
1 Training Corvette projected, service by 1975

Strength of the Fleet

7 Ocean Minesweepers
2 Command and Logistic Support Ships
9 Coastal Minesweepers (Non-Magnetic)
12 Inshore Minesweepers
6 River Patrol Boats
2 Research Ships
13 Auxiliaries and Service Craft

Personnel

1973: 330 officers and 4 700 men
1972: 330 officers and 4 681 men
1971: 316 officers and 3 969 men
1970: 330 officers and 4 500 men
1969: 330 officers and 4 400 men

Mercantile Marine

Lloyd's Register of Shipping:
224 vessels of 1 191 555 tons gross

Disposals (d) and Transfers

Escorts
1966 *AF Dufour, De Brouwer*
1969 *De Moor, C Lecointe*

Support Ships
1967 *Kamina*
1969 *Adriende Gerlache*

Coastal Minesweepers
1966 *Roeslaere, Arlon, Bastogne* to Norway
29/6/1969 *Malmedy, Blankenberge, Laroche* to USA for transfer to Greece
29/7/1969 *St. Truiden, Herve* to USA for transfer to Greece
30/10/1969 *Diest, Eeklo, Lier, Maaseik, Charleroi, St. Niklaas, Diksmuide, Dd Panne* to USA for transfer to Taiwan

Inshore Minesweepers
1970 *Temse, Hasselt, Kortrijk, Townai* to USA

Research Ship
1964 *Eupen*

FRIGATES

4 "E-71" CLASS

F 910 **F 911** **F 912** **F 913**

Displacement, tons	2 200 full load
Length, feet (*metres*)	351·1 (*106·4*)
Beam, feet (*metres*)	40·6 (*12·3*)
Draught, feet (*metres*)	12·07 (*3·66*)
Guns	1—100 mm AA Provision for Close-in-defence-system
Missiles	1 NATO Sea Sparrow SAM; Provision for SS missile system
Torpedo Launchers	2 L-5 Torpedo Launchers
Rocket Launcher	1 6 × 375 mm LR Bofors
Main engines	1 Rolls Royce Olympus TM3 gas turbine; 28 000 bhp; 2 Cockerill diesels 6 000 bhp
Speed, knots	28 (15 on 1 diesel, 20 on 2 diesels)
Range, miles	4 000 at 18 knots; 5 000 at 14 knots
Complement	15 officers, 145 men

Programme of building by Cockerill Yards Hoboken (Antwerp) and Boelwerf N.V. (Temse). 910 and 911 to be laid down in 1974 for completion the first in 1976 and the second in 1977. 912 and 913 to be laid down in 1975. All to be fitted with hull mounted sonar and two dynamic fin stabilisers. All expected to be in service by 1978.

TYPE E 71 FRIGATE *1973, Belgian Navy*

OCEAN MINESWEEPERS

7 U.S. MSO (Ex-AM) TYPE 498

Name	*Pennant No.*	*Builders*	*Laid down*	*Launched*	*Completed*	*Transferred*
A.F. DUFOUR (ex-*Lagen*, M 950 ex-*MSO* 498)	M 903	Bellingham Shipyard Inc. Wash	1954	13 Aug 1954	27 Sep 1955	15 Apr 1966
ARTEVELDE (ex-*MSO* 503, ex-*AM* 503)	M 907	Tacoma Boatbuilding Co. Tacoma, Wash	1953	19 June 1954	15 Dec 1955	15 Dec 1955
BREYDEL (ex-*MSO* 504, ex-*AM* 504)	M 906	Tacoma Boatbuilding Co. Tacoma, Wash	1954	25 Mar 1955	15 Feb 1956	15 Feb 1956
DE BROUWER (ex-*Namsen*, M 951, ex-*MSO* 499)	M 904	Bellingham Shipyard Inc. Wash	1954	15 Oct 1954	1 Nov 1955	15 Apr 1966
F. BOVESSE (ex-*MSO* 516, ex-*AM* 516)	M 909	Tampa Shipbuilding Co Inc, Tampa, Fla.	1954	2 Aug 1956	25 Jan 1957	25 Jan 1957
G. TRUFFAUT (ex-*MSO* 515, ex-*AM* 515)	M 908	Tampa Shipbuilding Co Inc, Tampa, Fla.	1955	11 Nov 1955	12 Oct 1956	12 Oct 1956
VAN HAVERBEKE (ex-*MSO* 522)	M 902	Petersen Builders Inc, Sturgeon Bay, Wisc.	1959	29 Oct 1959	7 Nov 1960	9 Dec 1960

Displacement, tons	720 standard; 780 full load
Length, feet (*metres*)	165·0 (*50·3*) wl; 172·5 (*52·6*) oa
Beam, feet (*metres*)	35·0 (*10·7*)
Draught, feet (*metres*)	11·0 (*3·4*)
Guns	1—40 mm AA
Main engines	2 GM diesels; 2 shafts; 1 600 bhp
Speed, knots	14 approx
Range, miles	2 400 at 12 knots; 3 000 at 20 knots
Oil fuel, tons	50
Complement	72 (5 officers, 67 men)

Wooden hulls and non-magnetic structure. Capable of sweeping mines of all types. Diesels of non-magnetic stainless steel alloy. Controllable pitch propellers.

Artevelde and *Breydel* were transferred at Seattle, Wash. *Van Haverbeke* berthed at Ostend on 2 May 1961, *F. Bovesse* in Sep 1957, *G. Truffaut* in Aug 1957, *Breydel* in Sep 1956, and *Artevelde* in June 1956.

VAN HAVERBEKE *1971, Giorgio Arra*

Ocean Minesweepers—*continued*

A. F. Dufour (ex-*Lagen*) and *De Brouwer* (ex-*Namsen*), handed over by USA to Norway on 27 Sep and 1 Nov 1955, respectively, were transferred to Belgium in 1966.

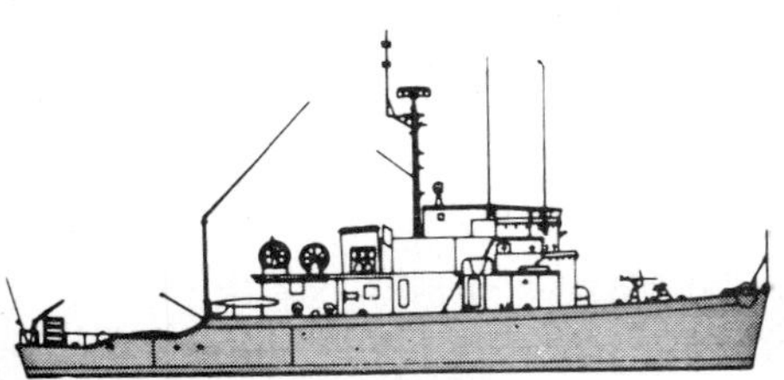

AGILE *Class*

F. BOVESSE *1970, John G. Callis*

COASTAL MINESWEEPERS

9 U.S. MSC (ex-AMS) TYPE 60

M 929 HEIST
M 931 KNOKKE
M 933 KOKSIJDE
M 932 NIEUWPOORT
M 930 ROCHEFORT
M 927 SPA
M 928 STAVELOT
M 934 VERVIERS (ex-*MSC* 259)
M 935 VEURNE (ex-*MSC* 260)

Displacement, tons	330 light; 390 full load
Dimensions, feet	139 pp; 144 oa × 27·9 × 7·5 (8 max)
Guns	1—40 mm AA
Main engines	2 GM Diesels; 2 shafts; 880 bhp = 13·5 knots max
Oil fuel, tons	28
Range, miles	2 700 at economical speed (10·5 knots)
Complement	39

Coastal minesweepers with wooden hulls and constructed throughout of materials with the lowest possible magnetic attraction to attain the greatest possible safety factor when sweeping for magnetic mines. M 910-925, 934 and 935 were built in USA, under MDAP, and M 926-933 of same type were built in Belgium under MAP with machinery and equipment from USA. M 934 (ex-MSC 259) turned over 19 June 1956, M 935 (ex-MSC 260) was transferred on 7 Sep 1956. M 926 to 933 were all laid down in 1953-54 and launched and completed in 1954-55.

RECLASSIFICATION. *Mechelen*, M 926, former coastal minesweeper of this class, was re-rated as a research ship and re-numbered A 962 in 1968 (see next page).

KNOKKE *1970, Belgian Navy*

INSHORE MINESWEEPERS

12 "HERSTAL" CLASS MSI

M 485 ANDENNE (ex-*MSI* 97) May 1958
M 484 DINANT (ex-*MSI* 96) 5 Apr 1958
M 478 HERSTAL (ex-*MSI* 90) 6 Aug 1956
M 479 HUY (ex-*MSI* 91) 17 Nov 1956
M 473 LOKEREN 18 May 1957
M 476 MERKSEM 5 Apr. 1958
M 477 OUDENAERDE May 1958
M 483 OUGREE (ex *MSI* 95) 16 Nov 1957
M 480 SERAING (ex-*MSI* 92) 16 Mar 1957
M 475 TONGEREN 16 Nov 1957
M 474 TURNHOUT 7 Sep 1957
M 482 VISE (ex-*MSI* 94) 7 Sep 1957

Displacement, tons	160 light (190 full load)
Dimensions, feet	106·7 pp; 113·2 oa × 22·3 × 6 (7 max)
Guns	1—13 mm AA
Main engines	2 diesels; 2 shafts; 1 260 bhp = 15 knots max
Oil fuel (tons)	18
Range, miles	2 300 at 10 knots
Complement	17

MSI type. Modified AMI "100-foot" class. All built in Belgium. The first four MSI were launched in 1956. *Herstal* and *Temse* were both launched at the Mercantile Marine Yard, Kruibche, on 6 Aug 1956, followed by another pair in 1956, and four more pairs in 1957 (see launch dates above). *Herstal* was completed in June 1957.

The first group of eight (M 478 to 485) was a United States "off shore order", the remaining eight (M 470 to 477) being financed under the Belgian Navy Estimates.

VISE *1971, Belgian Navy*

SUPPORT SHIPS

ZINNIA A 961

Displacement, tons	1 705 light; 2 435 full load
Length, feet (*metres*)	299·2 (*91·2*) pp; 309 (*94·2*) wl; 326·4 (*99·5*) oa
Beam, feet (*metres*)	49·9 (*14·0*)
Draught, feet (*metres*)	11·8 (*3·6*)
Guns	3—40 mm AA (single)
Aircraft	1 helicopter
Main engines	2 Cockerill V 12 RT 240 CO diesels; 5 000 bhp; 1 shaft
Speed, knots	20 max; 18 sea
Oil fuel, tons	500
Range, miles	4 400 at 14 knots
Complement	125

Laid down at Hoboken by J. Cockerill on 8 Nov 1966. Launched on 6 May 1967. Completed on 12 Sep 1967 Controllable pitch propeller. Design includes a platform and a retractable hangar for one light liaison-helicopter. Rated as Command and Logistic Support Ship.

ZINNIA *1970, Lt. Cdr. (R) J F. van Puyvelde*

Support Ships—*continued*

GODETIA A 960

Displacement, tons	1 700 light; 2 300 full load
Dimensions, feet	289 wl; 301 oa × 46 × 11·5
Guns	4—40 mm (2 twin) AA
Aircraft	Provision for light helicopter
Main engines	4 ACEC—MAN diesels; 2 shafts; 5 400 bhp = 19 knots max
Oil fuel, tons	500
Range, miles	4 500 at 15 knots
Complement	100 plus 35 spare billets

Built at Temse by J. Boel and Sons. Laid down on 15 Feb 1965, launched on 7 Dec 1965 and completed on 2 June 1966. Controllable pitch propellers. Provided with a platform which can take a light liaison-helicopter, and has Royal Apartments.

GODETIA *1972, Belgian Navy*

GODETIA *1970, Belgian Navy*

RIVER PATROL BOATS

LEIE **LIBERATION** **MEUSE** **SAMBRE** **SCHELDE** **SEMOIS**

Displacement, tons	25 light; 27·5 full load
Dimensions, feet	75·5 pp; 82 oa × 12·5 × 3 feet (*Liberation* 85·5 × 13·1 × 3·2)
Guns	2—13 mm MG
Main engines	2 diesels; 2 shafts; 440 bhp = 19 knots
Complement	7

LEIE *1970, John G. Callis*

River Patrol Boats—*continued*

Built at the Theodor Shipyards of Regensburg, Germany, in 1953, except *Liberation* in 1954. *Dender, Ourthe* and *Rupel* were officially deleted from the list in 1965. *Yser* was deleted from the list on 27 Aug 1969 and sold on 9 Sep 1969.

RESEARCH SHIPS

MECHELEN A 962 (ex-M 926)

Displacement, tons	330 light; 390 full load
Dimensions, feet	139 pp; 144 oa × 27·9 × 7·5 (8 max)
Main engines	2 GM diesels; 2 shafts; 880 bhp = 13·5 knots max
Oil fuel (tons)	28
Radius, miles	2 700 at economical speed (10·5 knots)
Complement	39

Former coastal minesweeper built in 1954. Re-rated as a research ship in 1968.

MECHELEN *1970, Belgian Navy*

ZENOBE GRAMME A 958

Displacement, tons	149
Dimensions, feet	92/76 × 22·5 × 7 feet
Main engines	1 MWM diesel; 1 shaft; 200 bhp = 10 knots
Complement	14

Auxiliary sail schooner. Built by J. Boel in Temse, Belgium, in 1961. Designed for scientific research.

TUGS

SUB-LIEUTENANT VALCKE A 950

Displacement, tons	110
Dimensions, feet	78·8 pp; 95 oa × 21 × 5·5
Main engines	1 diesel; 1 shaft; 600 bhp = 12 knots
Complement	14

Built in Haarlem, Netherlands in 1951.

There are also two port tugs, *Bij* and *Krekel*, displacement 71 tons, length 57·8 feet. 2 Voith-Schneider propellers, 400 hp; three harbour tugs, *Hommel* and *Wesp*, displacement 22 tons, length 43 feet, with 300 bhp diesels and Voith-Schneider propellers, built in Germany in 1953; and *Mier*, displacement 17·5 tons, length 41 feet, with 90 bhp diesels and Voith-Schneider propellers, built in Belgium in 1962.

AUXILIARY CRAFT

HARBOUR CRAFT. There are three barges, namely *FN 4*, *FN 5* and *FN 6*, displacement 300 tons, length, 105 feet, built in the Netherlands; the ammunition ship *Ekster*, displacement 140 tons, length 118 feet, built in Belgium in 1953; two diving cutters, ZM 3 and ZM 4, displacement 8 tons, length 33 feet, built in Belgium in 1953; and the harbour transport cutter *Spin*, displacement 32 tons, length 47·8 feet, with 250 bhp diesels = 8 knots and Voith-Schneider propeller, built in the Netherlands in 1958.

BRAZIL

Administration

Minister of the Navy:
Admiral Adalberto de Barros Nunes

Chief of Naval Staff:
Admiral Antonio Borges da Silveira Lobo

Chief of Naval Material:
Admiral Francisco de Alcantara

Chief of Naval Personnel:
Admiral Ramos de Azevedo Leite

Diplomatic Representation

Naval Attaché in London:
Captain Hugo Regis Veiga

Naval Attaché in Washington:
Rear Admiral Eddy Sampaio Espellet

Naval Attaché in Paris:
Captain Murillo Rubens Habema de Maia

Strength of the Fleet

1 Aircraft Carrier
2 Cruisers
13 Destroyers
5 Frigates
10 Corvettes
3 Patrol Submarines
1 Amphibious Ship
6 Coastal Minesweepers
1 River Monitor
7 Gunboats
6 Survey Ships
6 Survey Launches
1 Repair Ship
2 Oilers
4 Transports
3 Tugs
3 Floating Docks

New Construction

6 Destroyers (DLG) (+4)
3 Patrol Submarines
6 Coastal Minesweepers
5 River Patrol Ships

Proposed New Construction

10 Frigates
8 Coastal Minesweepers
25 FPBs
1 LPD
1 Survey Ship
1 Cargo Ship
1 Fleet Tug

Naval Bases

There are naval bases at Rio de Janeiro, Belem, Natal, Ricife and Salvadore, and a River base at Ladario.

Naval Aviation

A Fleet Air Arm was formed on 26 January 1965, exclusively of helicopters. Current strength:—
15 Whirlwind, 5 Wasps, 2 Bell 47, 13 Hughes 269A, 9 Hughes 200, 6 Hughes 500, 3 SH-3D helicopters. Fixed-wing aircraft afloat are operated by the Brazilian Air Force.

Personnel

1971: 40 600 (3 800 officers and 36 800 men) including marines

1972: 42 125 (3 264 officers and 38 861 men) including marines and auxiliary corps.

Mercantile Marine

Lloyd's Register of Shipping
420 vessels of 1 730 877 tons gross

Disposals

Submarines

1967 *Humaita* (ex-USS *Muskallung*) returned to USN—expended as target in 1968.
1968 *Riachuelo* (ex-USS *Paddle*) broken up
1972 *Rio Grande do Sul* (ex-USS *Sandlance*)

River Monitor

1972 *Paraguacu* (ex-*Victoria*, ex-*Esperito Santo*)

Gunboats

1968 Rio class of six small gunboats deleted

Tankers

1963 *Anita Garibaldi*, *Gastão Moutinho*, *Mataripe*, and *Taubate* plus the water-carriers *Itaupra* and *Paulo Alfonso*
1970 *Raza* (ex-*Klaskamine*) and *Rijo* (ex-*Gualula*)

Training Ships

1968 *Albatros*

AIRCRAFT CARRIER

1 Ex-BRITISH TYPE
("COLOSSUS" CLASS)

	Pennant No.	*Builders*	*Laid down*	*Launched*	*Completed*	*Reconstructed*
MINAS GERAIS (ex-HMS *Vengeance*)	A 11	Swan, Hunter & Wigham Richardson, Ltd, Wallsend on-Tyne	16 Nov 1942	23 Feb 1944	15 Jan 1945	Verolme Dock, Rotterdam, 1957-60

Displacement, tons	15 890 standard; 17 500 normal; 19 890 full load (see *Displacement* note)
Length, feet (*metres*)	630 (*192·0*) pp; 695 (*211·8*) oa
Beam, feet (*metres*)	80 (*24·4*)
Draught, feet (*metres*)	21·5 (*6·6*) mean; 24·5 (*7·5*) max
Flight deck,	
Length, feet (*metres*)	690 (*210·3*)
Width, feet (*metres*)	121 (*37·0*) oa as reconstructed
Height, feet (*metres*)	39 (*11·9*) above water line
Catapults	1 steam
Aircraft	20 aircraft including 7 S2A, 4 Sea Kings
Guns, AA	10—40 mm (2 quadruple, 1 twin)
Guns, saluting	2—47 mm
Boilers	4 Admiralty 3-drum type; Working pressure 400 psi (*28 kg/cm²*); max superheat 700°F (371°C)
Main engines	Parsons geared turbines; 2 shafts; 40 000 shp
Speed, knots	24; 25·3 on trials after reconstruction
Range, miles	12 000 at 14 knots; 6 200 at 23 knots
Oil fuel, tons	3 200
Complement	1 000 (1 300 with air group)

MINAS GERAIS *1971, Brazilian Navy*

GENERAL AND CONVERSION

Served in the British Navy from 1945 onwards. Insulated for tropical service and partially air-conditioned. Fitted out in late 1948 to early 1949 for experimental cruise to the Arctic. Lent to the Royal Australian Navy early in 1953, but returned to the Royal Navy in Aug 1955. Purchased by the Brazilian Government on 14 Dec 1956 (date announced by British Admiralty). Reconstructed at Verolme Dock, Rotterdam (Verolme United Shipyard's Rozenburg yard) from summer 1957 to Dec 1960. The conversion and overhaul included the installation of the angled deck, steam catapult, mirror sight deck landing system, armament fire control and radar equipment. The ship was purchased for $9 000 000 and the reconstruction cost $27 000 000. Commissioned in the Brazilian Navy at Rotterdam on 6 Dec 1960. Left Rotterdam for Rio de Janeiro on her maiden voyage as *Minas Gerais* on 13 Jan 1961. Used primarily for anti-submarine aircraft and helicopters.

ENGINEERING. Engines and boilers arranged *en echelon*, the two propelling machinery spaces having one set of turbines and two boilers installed side by side in each space, on the unit system. Maximum speed at 120 rpm. Steam capacity was increased when the boilers were retubed during reconstruction in 1957-60.

ELECTRICAL. During reconstruction an alternating current system was installed with a total of 2 500 kW supplied by four turbo-generators and one diesel generator.

RADAR. Search: SPS 8 and SPS 12 systems. Tactical: SPS 10.

DAMAGE CONTROL. No great measure of vertical sub-division on the sandwich system as it was reckoned that it is better for ships to settle evenly in the event of damage and flooding than to foster capsizing.

OPERATIONAL. Single track catapult for launching, and arrester wires for recovering, 20 000 lb aircraft at 60 knots. Catapult accelerator gear port side forward. Flight deck originally designed for 14 000 lb aircraft reinforced to take heavier machines.

HANGAR. Dimensions: length, 445 feet; width, 52 feet; clear depth, 17·5 feet. Aircraft lifts: 45 feet by 34 feet. During reconstruction in 1957-60 new lifts replaced the original units.

DISPLACEMENT. Before reconstruction: 13 190 tons standard; 18 010 tons full load.

Aircraft Carrier —*continued*

DRAWING. Starboard elevation and plan. Re-drawn in 1971. Scale: 125 feet = 1 inch (1 : 1 500).

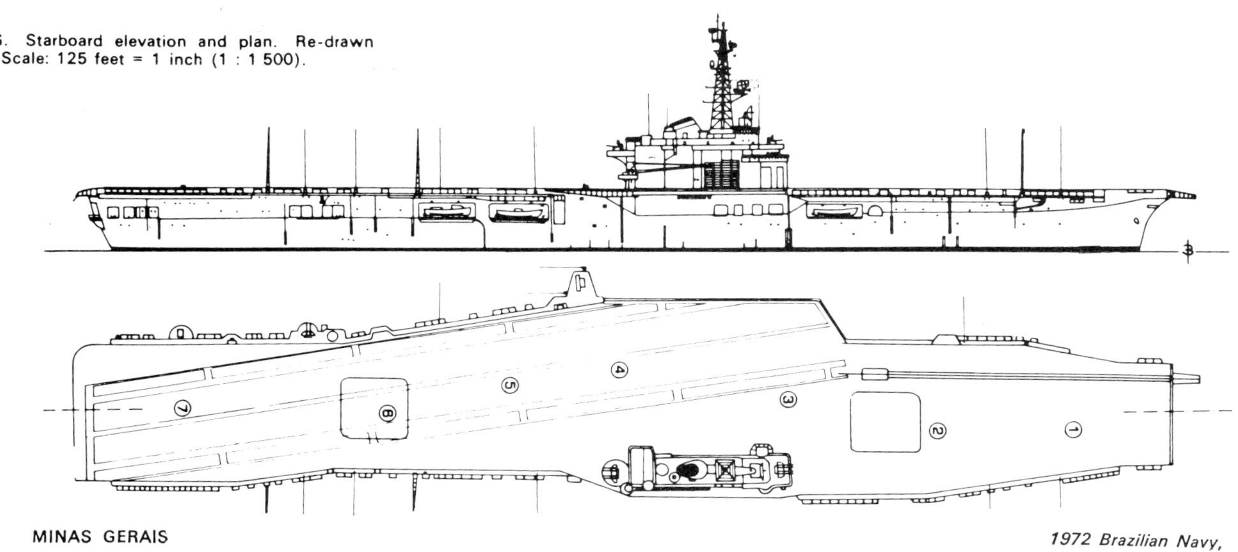

MINAS GERAIS

1972 Brazilian Navy,

CRUISERS

TAMANDARE (ex-USS *St. Louis, CL* 49)	*Pennant No.*	*Builders*	*Laid down*	*Launched*	*Completed*
	C 12	Newport News S.B. & DD.. Co.	10 Dec 1936	15 Apr 1938	10 Dec 1939

Displacement, tons	10 000 standard; 13 500 full load	Guns, dual purpose	8—5 in (*127 mm*) 38 cal (4 twin)	Main engines	Parson's geared turbines; 100 000 shp; 4 shafts
Length, feet (*metres*)	608·5 (*185·5*) oa	Guns, AA	28—40 mm, 8—20 mm	Speed, knots	32·5
Beam, feet (*metres*)	69 (*21·0*)	Armour, inches (*mm*)	Belt 5 in—1½ in (*127 mm—38 mm*); Decks 3 in—2 in (*76 mm—51 mm*); Turrets 5 in—3 in (*127 mm—76 mm*); C.T. 8 in (*203 mm*)	Range, miles	14 500 at 15 knots
Draught, feet (*metres*)	24 (*7·3*) max			Oil fuel, tons	2 100
Aircraft	1 Helicopter (see *Hangar notes*)			Complement	975
Guns, surface	15—6 in (*153 mm*) (47 cal (5 triple)	Boilers	8 Babcock & Wilcox Express		

TAMANDARE

1972, Brazilian Navy

GENERAL
"St. Louis class". Transferred from USA on 29 Jan 1951. Differs from *Barroso* in having 5-inch guns paired in roomy gunhouses on high bases, different boat stowage, small tripod mast immediately abaft 2nd funnel, and after gunnery control redistributed.

RADAR. SPS 12 search and SPS 10 tactical radar.

HANGAR. The hangar in the hull right aft could originally accommodate 6 aircraft if necessary together with engine spares and duplicate parts, though 4 aircraft was the normal capacity.

DRAWING. Starboard elevation and plan: Re-drawn in 1971. Scale: 125 feet = 1 inch. (1 : 1 500).

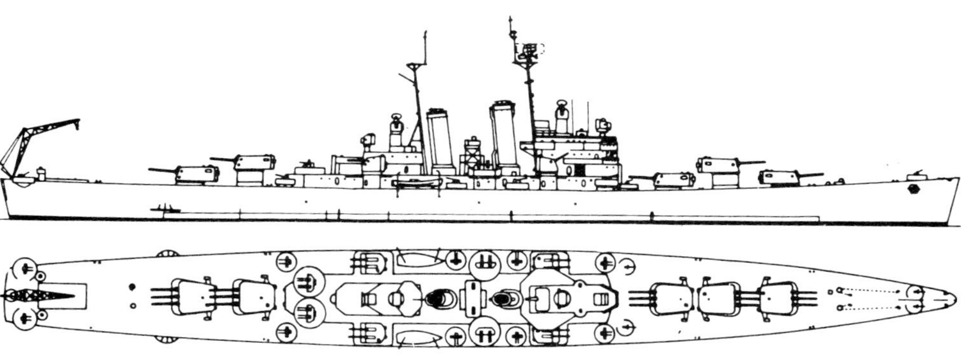

Cruisers—*continued*

BARROSO (ex-USS *Philadelphia*, CL 41)	*Pennant No.*	*Builders*	*Laid down*	*Launched*	*Completed*
	C 11	Philadelphia Navy Yard	28 May 1935	17 Nov 1936	28 July 1938

Displacement, tons	9 700 standard; 13 400 full load
Length, feet (*metres*)	600 (*182·9*) wl; 608·5 (*185·5*) oa
Beam, feet (*metres*)	69 (*21·0*) with bulges
Draught, feet (*metres*)	19·8 (*6·0*) mean; 24 (*7·3*) max
Aircraft	1 Helicopter
Guns, surface	15—6 in (*153 mm*) 47cal (5 triple) 8—5 in (*127 mm*) 38 cal single
Guns, AA	28—40 mm, 20—20 mm
Armour, inches (*mm*)	Belt 4 in—1½ in (*102—38*); decks 3 in and 2 in (*76* and *51*) Turrets 5 in—3 in (*127—76*); C.T. 8 in (*203*)
Boilers	8 Babcock & Wilcox Express
Main engines	Parson's geared turbines; 100 000 shp; 4 shafts
Speed, knots	32·5
Range, miles	14 500 at 15 knots
Oil fuel (tons)	2 100
Complement	888

GENERAL
"Brooklyn" class. Purchased from the United States in 1951. Originally two catapults were mounted on the quarter deck for launching the aircraft (see *Hangar Notes* under *Tamandaré*). Commissioned in the Brazilian Navy on 21 Aug 1951. Originally a sister ship of *General Belgrano* (ex-17 *de Octubre*, ex-USS *Phoenix*) and *Nueve de Julio*, (ex-USS *Boise*) in the Argentine Navy, and *O'Higgins* (ex-USS *Brooklyn*) and *Prat* (ex-USS *Nashville*) in the Chilean Navy.

RADAR. Search: SPS 4. Tactical: SPS 10. Air Search: SPS 6C.

DRAWING. Starboard elevation and plan. Re-drawn in 1971. Scale: 125 feet = 1 inch. (1 : 1 500).

BARROSO — *1971, Brazilian Navy*

DESTROYERS (CT)

6 "NITEROI" CLASS
VOSPER THORNYCROFT MARK 10

CONSTITUIÇÃO INDEPENDENCIA NITEROI
DEFENSORA LIBERAL UNIAO

Displacement, tons	3 300 standard; 3 900 full load
Length, feet (*metres*)	400 (*121·9*) wl; 424 (*129·2*) oa
Beam, feet (*metres*)	44·2 (*13·5*)
Draught, feet (*metres*)	18·2 (*5·5*)
Aircraft	One WG 13 A/S helicopter
Missile launchers	2 twin Exocet surface-to-surface in General Purpose version; 2 triple Seacat; Ikara in Anti-Submarine version
Guns	2—4·5 inch Mark 8 in General Purpose version; 2—40 mm L/70; 1—4·5 inch Mark 8 in Anti-Submarine version
A/S weapons	One Bofors 375 mm twin tube A/S rocket launcher; Two triple Mark 32 torpedo tubes; 1 DC rail
Main engines	CODOG system; 2 Rolls Royce Olympus Gas turbines = 56 000 bhp = 30 knots 4 MTU diesels, 15 760 hp = 22 knots
Range, miles	5 300 at 17 knots (2 diesels); 4 200 at 19 knots (4 diesels); 1 300 at 29 knots (Gas)
Complement	200 officers and ratings

GENERAL
A very interesting design of singularly handsome, symmetrical, raked and low-lying clean-cut appearance. The moulded depth is 28½ feet (*8·8 metres*). Exceptionally economical in personnel complement, amounting to a fifty per cent reduction of manpower in relation to previous warships of this size and complexity.

CONTRACT. A contract, announced on 29 Sep 1970, valued at about £100 000 000, was signed between the Brazilian Government and Vosper Thornycroft Ltd, Portsmouth, England for the design and building of these six Vosper Thornycroft Mark 10 frigates comparable with the British type 42 guided missile destroyers being built for the Royal Navy.

CONSTRUCTION. Four of the ships will be built at Vosper Thornycroft's Woolston, Southampton shipyard and two by the Naval Dockyard in Brazil with materials, equipment and lead-yard services supplied by Vosper Thornycroft. Of the four ships to be built in Great Britain two will be general purpose fleet escorts equivalent to destroyer leaders and the other two will be highly specialised anti-submarine DLG type vessels.
The two ships being built in Brazil are both anti-submarine destroyers (*Liberal* and *Uniao*) both being laid down on 11 June 1972. Building practice will be generally similar to that for the Royal Navy but modified to suit Brazilian naval requirements.
DELIVERY. Design work was scheduled for construction of the first British-built ship to be started at Woolston early in 1972. The estimated building time for each ship is about four years, ships being laid down at yearly intervals so that these six vessels will be completed between 1976 and 1979.

CLASS. It is envisaged that the originally formulated new construction scheme for six units of this "Niteroi" class will be extended eventually to ten ships. In that case Vosper Thornycroft will build the first six of the Mark 10 Type and the remaining four will be assembled in the Naval Dockyard in Brazil, as the Brazilian Government is anxious to establish the construciton of such ships in Brazil.

ELECTRONICS. CAAIS. Equipment by Ferranti (2 FM1600B computers) ECM by Decca.

RADAR. 1 Plessey AWS-2 Air Warning with Mk 10 IFF. 1 Signaal ZWO-6 Surface Warning and navigation. 2 Selenia RTN-10X Weapon control and tracking. 1 Ikara Tracker radar (A/S ships).

SONAR. 1 Edo 610E medium range. 1 Edo 700E VDS (A/S ships).

NAMES. The name *Niteroi* was previously borne by the Brazilian Submarine chaser *Joao Pessoa Niteroi* built at Rio in 1943. The names of the six ships as originally allocated in 1971 were: *Campista, Constituição, Defensora, Imperatriz, Isabel* and *Niteroi*.

NITEROI *Class*

NITEROI — *1971, Vosper Thornycroft Group and Brazilian Navy*

Destroyers—*continued*

4 "AMAZONAS" CLASS

Name		*Laid down*	*Launched*	*Completed*
ACRE	D 10	28 Dec 40	30 May 45	10 Dec 51
AMAZONAS	D 12	20 July 40	29 Nov 43	10 Nov 49
ARAGUAIA	D 14	20 July 40	24 Nov 43	3 Sep 49
ARAGUARI	D 15	28 Dec 40	14 July 46	23 June 51

Displacement, tons: 1 450 standard; 2 180 full load
Length, feet (*metres*): 323·0 (*98·5*) oa
Beam, feet (*metres*): 35·0 (*10·7*)
Draught, feet (*metres*): 10·5 (*3·2*)
Guns, surface: 3—5 in (*127 mm*) 38 cal
Guns, AA: 4—40 mm (2 twin); 2—20 mm
A/S weapons: 4 DCT
Torpedo tubes: 6—21 in (*533 mm*), two triple
Boilers: 3 three-drum type
Main engines: Parsons geared turbines; 2 shafts; 34 000 shp
Speed, knots: 35·5 designed; 34 sea
Range, miles: 6 000 at 15 knots
Oil fuel, tons: 450
Complement: 190

AMAZONAS *Class*

ARAGUARI

1972, Brazilian Navy

All built by Ilha das Cobras, Rio de Janeiro, to British design. Named after rivers. Refitted with tripod mast.
RADAR. Search: SPS 4. Tactical: SPS 10.

DISPOSALS
Of this class, *Ajuricaba*, D 11 and *Apa*, D 13, were removed from the list in 1964.

1 "MARCILIO DIAS" CLASS

MARIZ E BARROS D 26

Displacement, tons: 1 500 standard; 2 200 full load
Length, feet (*metres*): 360 (*109·7*) oa
Beam, feet (*metres*): 35 (*10·7*)
Draught, feet (*metres*): 12 (*3·7*)
Guns, dual purpose: 2—5 in (*127 mm*) 38 cal
Guns, AA: 4—40 mm
Missile launchers: 1 quadruple "Seacat" in X position
A/S weapons: 2 hedgehogs; 4 DCT
Torpedo tubes: 4—21 in (*533 mm*) quadruple
Boilers: 4 Babcock & Wilcox Express
Main engines: GE geared turbines; 2 shafts; 42 800 shp
Speed, knots: 36·5 designed, now 32 max
Range, miles: 6 000 at 15 knots
Oil fuel, tons: 500
Complement: 190

MARIZ E BARROS

MARIZ E BARROS

1971, Brazilian Navy

GENERAL
Built at Ilha das Cobras, Rio de Janeiro, with design, guns and material from USA. Laid down in 1937, launched on 28 Dec 1940, commissioned on 29 Nov 1943, and completed in 1944.

DISPOSALS
Sister ships *Greenhalgh*, D 24 and *Marcilio Dias*, D 25, were deleted from the list in 1966.

7 Ex-US "FLETCHER" TYPE

"PARA" CLASS

Name	*Pennant No.*	*Builders*	*Laid down*	*Launched*	*Completed*
PARA (ex-USS *Guest*, DD 472)	D 27	Boston Navy Yard	27 Sep 1941	20 Feb 1942	15 Dec 1942
PARAIBA (ex-USS *Bennett*, DD 473)	D 28	Boston Navy Yard	10 Dec 1941	16 Apr 1942	9 Feb 1943
PARANA (ex-USS *Cushing*, DD 797)	D 29	Bethlehem Steel Co (Staten Island)	3 May 1943	30 Sep 1943	17 Jan 1944
PERNAMBUCO (ex-USS *Hailey*, DD 556)	D 30	Seattle-Tacoma S.B. Corpn, (Seattle)	1 Apr 1942	9 Mar 1943	30 Sep 1943
PIAUI (ex-USS *Lewis Hancock*, DD 675)	D 31	Federal S.B. & D.D. Co.	24 Sep 1942	1 Aug 1943	24 Sep 1943
SANTA CATARINA (ex-USS *Irwin*, DD 794)	D 32	Bethlehem Steel Co. (San Pedro)	14 Feb 1943	31 Oct 1943	14 Feb 1944
NARANHAO (ex-USS *Shields*, DD 596)	D 33	Puget Sound Navy Yard	10 Aug 1943	25 Sep 1944	8 Feb 1945

Displacement, tons: 2 050 standard; 3 050 full load
Length, feet (*metres*): 376·5 (*114·8*) oa
Beam, feet (*metres*): 39·3 (*12·0*)
Draught, feet (*metres*): 18 (*5·5*) max
Guns, dual purpose: 5—5 in (*127 mm*) 38 cal; except *Pernambuco:* 4—5 in
Guns, AA: 10—40 mm (2 quadruple and 1 twin) except *Pernambuco* 6—3 in (*76 mm*) 50 cal (3 twin) and *Para:* 6—40 mm (3 twin
Torpedo tubes: 5—21 in (*533 mm*)
A/S weapons: 2 Hedgehogs; 1 DC rack; 2 side launching torpedo racks
Boilers: 4 Babcock & Wilcox
Main engines: 2 GE geared turbines; 2 shafts; 60 000 shp
Speed, knots: 35
Range, miles: 5 000 at 15 knots; 1 260 at 30 knots
Oil fuel, tons: 650
Complement: 260

PERNAMBUCO (four 5-inch guns)

1969, Brazilian Navy

Destroyers—*continued*

GENERAL
Parana, Piaui and *Santa Catarina* are of the later "Fletcher" class and *Para, Paraiba, Pernambuco* are of the "Fletcher" class. *Para, Paraiba, Parana* and *Pernambuco* were acquired from USA on loan for five years, subsequently extended. *Para* was transferred to Brazil on 5 June 1959 *Pariba* on 15 Dec 1959 at Bremerton, Washington, *Parana* and *Pernambuco* on 20 July 1961, at Norfolk Naval Shipyard, Portsmouth, Virginia *Piaui* was transferred on 1 Aug 1967, *Santa Caterina* on 10 May 1968 and *Naranhao* on 1 July 1972.
Sister ships *Yarnall* (DD-541) and *Irwin* (DD-794) were selected as replacements for *Sigsbee* (DD 502) and *Melvin* (DD 680), originally scheduled for transfer; but in the event *Yarnall* was transferred to Taiwan.

RADAR. Search: SPS 6. Tactical: SPS 10. Fire Control: X Band.

PIAUI (five 5-inch guns) *1972, Brazilian Navy*

PERNAMBUCO

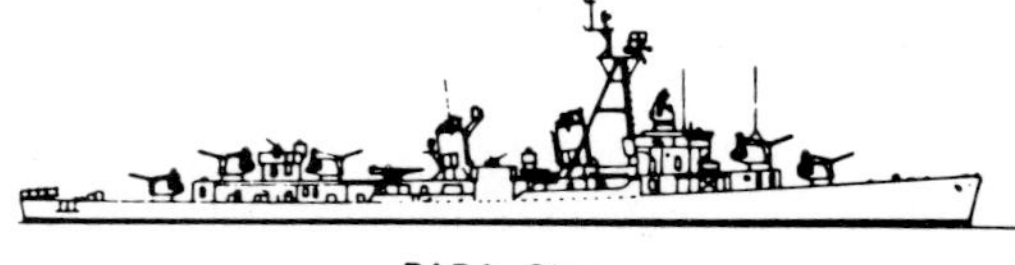

PARA *Class*

1 Ex-US "ALLEN M. SUMNER" CLASS

Name	*Pennant No.*	*Builder*	*Launched*	*Commissioned*
MATO GROSSO (ex-USS *Compton*, DD 705)	D 34	Federal S.B. & D.D. Co.	17 Sep 1944	4 Nov 1944

Displacement, tons	2 200 standard; 3 320 full load
Length, feet (*metres*)	376·5 (*114·8*) oa
Beam, feet (*metres*)	40·9 (*12·4*)
Draught, feet (*metres*)	19 (*5·8*)
Guns	6—5 in (*127 mm*) 38 cal DP (twins)
A/S weapons	2 fixed Hedgehogs; depth charges; 2 triple torpedo launchers (Mk 32)
Main engines	2 geared turbines; 60 000 shp; 2 shafts
Speed, knots	34
Range, miles	4 600 at 15 knots; 1 260 at 30 knots
Complement	274

GENERAL
Transferred to Brazil on 27 Sep 1972.

GUNNERY. 3 inch guns removed before transfer.

USS COMPTON (now MATO GROSSO with 3 inch guns removed) *1969, USN*

FRIGATES

5 Ex-US DE TYPE "BERTIOGA" CLASS

Name	*Pennant No.*	*Laid down*	*Launched*	*Completed*
BAEPENDI (ex-USS *Cannon*, DE 99)	U 27 (ex-D 17)	14 Nov 1942	25 May 1943	26 Sep 1943
BAURU (ex-USS *Reybold*, DE 177)	U 28 (ex-D 18)	17 May 1943	22 Aug 1943	11 Oct 1943
BENEVENTE (ex-USS *Christopher*, DE 100)	U 30 (ex-D 20)	7 Dec 1942	June 1943	23 Oct 1943
BOCAINA (ex-USS *Marts*, DE 174)	U 32 (ex-D 22)	26 Apr 1943	8 Aug 1943	3 Sep 1943
BRACUI (ex-USS *McAnn*, DE 179)	U 31 (ex-D 23)	3 May 1943	5 Sep 1943	24 Sep 1943

Displacement, tons	1 240 standard; 1 900 full load
Length, feet (*metres*)	306 (*93·3*) oa
Beam, feet (*metres*)	36·7 (*11·2*)
Draught, feet (*metres*)	12 (*3·7*)
Guns, dual purpose	3—3 in (*76 mm*)
Guns, AA	2—40 mm, 4—20 mm
Torpedo tubes	3—21 in (*533 mm*)
A/S weapons	2 DC racks
Main engines	4 GM diesels; 2 electric motors; diesel-electric drive; 2 shafts; 6 000 bhp
Speed, knots	21
Range, miles	11 500 at 11 knots
Oil fuel, tons	300
Complement	200

BAEPENDI *1970, Brazilian Navy*

BERTIOGA *Class*

GENERAL
Former US "Bostwick" class destroyer escorts, transferred in 1944. Built by Dravo, Wilmington, Del. (*Baependi*) and Federal, Port Newark (other four). Formerly designated CTE (Destroyer Escorts) but reclassified as *Avisos Oceanicos* in 1965.

DISPOSALS
Of this class, *Babitonga*, D 16 (ex-USS *Alger*, DE 101) and *Bertioga*, D 21 (ex-USS *Pennewill*, DE 175) were officially removed from the list in 1964, and *Beberibe* D 19 (ex-USS *Herzog*, DE 178) in 1968.

CORVETTES

10 "IMPERIAL MARINHEIRO" CLASS

ANGOSTURA V 20
BAHIANA V 21
CABOCLO V 19
FORTE DE COIMBRA V 18
IGUATEMI V 16
IMPERIAL MARINHEIRO V 15
IPIRANGA V 17
MEARIM V 22
PURUS V 23
SOLIMOES V 24

Displacement, tons	911 standard
Dimensions, feet	184 × 30·5 × 11·7
Guns	1—3 in, 50 cal; 4—20 mm AA
Main engines	2 Sulzer diesels; 2 160 bhp = 16 knots
Oil fuel (tons)	135
Complement	60

IMPERIAL MARINHEIRO *Class*

All built in the Netherlands, launched in 1954-55, and incorporated into the Brazilian Navy in 1955. Actually fleet tugs. Some can be used as fire boats.

SOLIMOES *1972, Brazilian Navy*

SUBMARINES

3 NEW CONSTRUCTION BRITISH "OBERON" CLASS

HUMAITA
1 unnamed
TONELERO

Displacement, tons	1 610 standard estimated; 2 060 full buoyancy surface; 2 200 normal surface; 2 420 submerged, official figure
Length, feet (*metres*)	295·5 (*90·1*) overall
Beam, feet (*metres*)	26·5 (*8·1*)
Draught, feet (*metres*)	18·0 (*5·5*)
Tubes	8—21 in (*533 mm*), 6 bow and 2 stern for homing torpedoes
Main engines	2 Admiralty Standard Range 1 16-cyl diesels; 3 680 bhp; 2 electric motors; 6 000 shp; 2 shafts; electric drive
Speed, knots	15 on surface max; 17·5 submerged designed
Complement	70 (6 officers and 64 men)

GENERAL
It was officially stated that two submarines of the British "Oberon" class were ordered from Vickers, Barrow in 1969. They are expected to be in service in 1972 and 1974. *Humaita* was launched on 5 Oct 1971 and *Tonelero* laid down on 18 Nov 1971, being launched on 22 Nov 1972. Diesels by Vickers Shipbuilding Group. Electric motors by AEI-English Electric. Sonar, modern navigational aids and provision for modern fire control system developed by Vickers. A third boat was ordered in 1972.

HUMAITA *1972, Brazilian Navy*

HISTORICAL. The name *Humaita* commemorates a naval action in the river war against Paraguay on 21 Feb 1868. It was previously borne by a submarine of much the same dimensions launched in 1927, and by S 14 (ex-USS *Muskallung*, SS 262).

1 Ex-US "BALAO" CLASS

BAHIA (ex-USS *Plaice*, SS 390) S 12

Displacement, tons	**1 526 standard; 1 816 surface; 2 400 submerged**
Length, feet (*metres*)	**311·5 (*94·9*)**
Beam, feet (*metres*)	**27 (*8·2*)**
Draught, feet (*metres*)	**17 (*5·2*)**
Torpedo tubes	**10—21 in (*533 mm*); 6 bow, 4 stern**
Main engines	**6 500 bhp FM 2-stroke diesels; 5 500 hp electric motors**
Speed, knots	20 on surface; 10 submerged
Radius, miles	12 000 at 10 knots
Oil fuel, tons	300
Complement	85

Built by Portsmouth Navy Shipyard. Launched on 15 Nov 1943 and completed on 12 Feb 1944. Lent to Brazil for five years after overhaul at Pearl Harbour Navy Shipyard in Sep 1963 and loan subsequently extended at regular intervals.

3 Ex-US "GUPPY II" TYPE

GUANABARA (ex-USS *Dogfish* SS 350) S 10
RIO DE JANEIRO (ex-USS *Odax* SS 484) S 13
RIO GRANDE DO SUL (ex-USS *Grampus* SS 523) S 11

Displacement, tons	1 870 standard; 2 420 dived
Length, feet (*metres*)	307·5 (*93·8*) oa
Beam, feet (*metres*)	27·2 (*8·3*)
Draught, feet (*metres*)	18 (*5·5*)
Torpedo Tubes	10—21 in (6 bow, 4 stern)
Main engines	3 diesels, 4 800 shp; 2 motors; 5 400 shp; 2 shafts
Speed, knots	18 surfaced; 15 dived
Range, miles	12 000 at 10 knots (surfaced)
Complement	82

GENERAL
Dogfish built by Electric Boat Co. Commissioned 29 April 1946 and *Odax* built by Portsmouth Navy Yard, commissioned 11 July 1945. *Grampus* built in Boston Navy Yard and commissioned 26 Oct 1949. Transferred 13 May 1972 (*Rio Grande do Sul*), 10 July 1972 (*Rio de Janeiro*), 28 July 1972 (*Guanabara*).

RIO GRANDE DE SUL *1972, Brazilian Navy*

AMPHIBIOUS SHIP

1 TANK LANDING SHIP (LST) (511-1152 Series)

GARCIA D'AVILA G 28 (ex-USS *Outagamie County* LST 1073)

Displacement, tons	1 653 standard; 2 366 beaching; 4 080 full load
Dimensions, feet	316 wl; 328 oa × 50 × 14
Guns	8—40 mm AA (2 twin, 4 single)
Main engines	GM diesels; 2 shafts; 1 700 bhp = 11·6 knots
Complement	119
Troops	147

Transferred on loan to Brazli by USN 21 May 1971.

GARCIA D'AVILA *1973, Brazilian Navy*

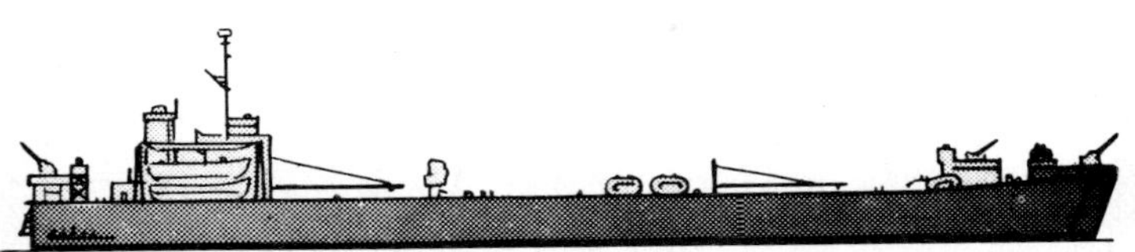

COUNTY (511-1152 Series) *Class*

LIGHT FORCES

1 THORNYCROFT TYPE (RIVER MONITOR)

PARNAIBA U 17 (ex-P 2)

Displacement, tons	620 standard; 720 full load
Dimensions, feet	180·5 oa × 33·3 × 5·1 max
Guns	1—3 in, 50 cal; 2—47 mm; 2—40 mm AA; 6—20 mm AA
Armour	3 in side and partial deck protection
Main engines	2 Thornycroft triple expansion; 2 shafts; 1 300 ihp = 12 knots
Boilers	2 three drum type, working pressure 250 psi
Oil fuel, tons	70
Range, miles	1 350 at 10 knots
Complement	90

Built at Rio de Janeiro. Laid down on 11 June 1936. Launched on 2 Sep 1937 and completed in Nov 1937. In Mato Grosso Flotilla. Rearmed with the above guns in 1960.

PARNAIBA *1971, Brazilian Navy*

2 PEDRO TEIXEIRA CLASS (RIVER PATROL SHIPS)

PEDRO TEIXEIRA (completes June 1973)
RAPOSO TAVARES (completes Feb 1974)

Displacement, tons	700 standard
Dimensions, feet	203·4 × 30·7 × 6·3
Guns	1—40 mm AA 2—81 mm mortars 6—·50 cal MG
Main engines	4 diesels; 2 shafts = 16 knots

Both building in Arsenal de Marinha do Rio de Janeiro. Helicopter platforms to be fitted.

Light Forces—*continued*

3 RORAIMA CLASS (RIVER PATROL SHIPS)

AMAPA **RORAIMA** **RONDONIA**

Displacement, tons	340 standard
Dimensions, feet	147·6 × 27·7 × 4·2
Guns	1—40 mm AA 2—81 mm mortars 6—·50 cal MGs
Main engines	Diesels; 2 shafts = 14 knots

Building by Shipyard Maclaren, Brazil for completion in late 1973.

6 "PIRATINI" CLASS (GUNBOATS)

PAMPEIRO P 12 **PENEDO** P 14 **PIRATINI** P 10
PARATI P 13 **PIRAJA** P 11 **POTI** P 15

Displacement, tons	105 standard;
Dimensions, feet	95 × 19 × 6
Guns	3—·50 cal MG; 1—81 mm mortar
Main engines	4 diesels; 1 100 bhp = 17 knots
Range, miles	1 700 at 12 knots
Complement	15 officers and men

Six coastal gunboats of the "Piratini" class were built in the Arsenal de Marinha do Rio de Janeiro. *Piratini* entered service in Nov 1970 and the remainder between Mar and Oct 1971.

POTI *1972, Brazilian Navy*

1 "P" CLASS (GUNBOAT)

PIRAQUE J 32 (ex-P 4)

Displacement, tons	130 standard
Dimensions, feet	128·0 × 19·5 × 6·0
Guns	1—3 in, 23 cal; 2—20 mm AA; 2 DCT
Main engines	3 diesels; 3 shafts; 1 890 bhp = 20 knots
Complement	30

GENERAL
Launched in 1948. Built at Rio de Janeiro. The hull is of wooden construction.

DISPOSALS
Of this class *Pirambu* P 2, and *Pirapia*, P 5 were officially removed from the list in 1964, *Pirauna*, P 6 in 1960 and *Piraju*, P 1 and *Piranha*, P 3 in 1971.

PIRAQUE *1968, Brazilian Navy*

COASTAL MINESWEEPERS

4 NEW CONSTRUCTION "SCHÜTZE" CLASS

ANHATOMIRIM M 16 **ARATU** M 15
ARACATUBA M 18 **ATALAIA** M 17

Displacement, tons	230 standard; 280 full load
Dimensions, feet	154·9 × 23·6 × 6·9
Guns	1—40 mm AA
Main engines	4 Maybach diesels; 2 shafts; 4 500 bhp = 24 knots
Range, miles	710 at 20 knots
Complement	31

Builders: Abeking & Rasmussen, Lemwerder. Ordered in Apr 1969. Six more are projected. Aratu and Anhatomirim entered service on 5 May 1971 and 30 November 1971 respectively, the other pair in late 1972.

ARATU 1972, *Brazilian Navy*

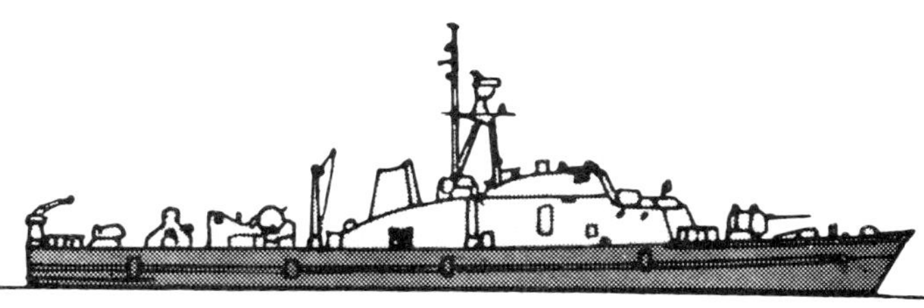
229 SCHÜTZE *Class*

2 Ex-US MSC TYPE "JAVARI" CLASS

JURUENA (ex-USS *Grackle*) M 14 **JURUA** (ex-USS *Jackdaw*) M 13

Displacement, tons	270 standard; 350 full load
Dimensions, feet	136 × 24·5 × 8 max
Guns	4—20 mm in two twin mountings
A/S weapons	2 DCT
Main engines	2 GM diesels; 2 shafts; 1 000 bhp = 15 knots
Oil fuel (tons)	16
Range, miles	2 300 at 8·5 knots
Complement	50

GENERAL
Coastal minesweepers of wooden construction. Both launched in 1942-43. Originally known in USA as Auxiliary Motor minesweepers (AMS). Reclassified as Minesweepers, Coastal (old), MSC (o), in Feb 1955. *Javari*, ex-*Cardinal*, MSCo 4 and, *Jutai*, ex-*Egret*, MSCo 13, were transferred to Brazil by USA at Charleston Naval Shipyard on 15 Aug 1960 as the nucleus of a Brazilian mine force, and renamed after Brazilian rivers. *Jackdaw* MSCo 21, was transferred in Jan 1963, and *Grackle* MSCo 13, in Apr 1963. Used for patrol and escort duties.
DISPOSALS
Javari, M 11, and *Jutai*, M 12, were declared for disposal in 1969.

JURUENA 1972, *Brazilian Navy*

SURVEY SHIPS

2 FRIGATE TYPE

Name	*Pennant No.*	*Laid down*	*Launched*	*Completed*
CANOPUS	H 22	13 Dec 1956	20 Nov 1957	15 Mar 1958
SIRIUS	H 21	13 Dec 1956	30 July 1957	1 Jan 1958

Displacement, tons	1 463 standard; 1 800 full load
Dimensions, feet	236·2 pp; 246 wl; 255·7 oa × 39·3 × 12.2
Guns	1—3 in AA; 4—20 mm MG
Main engines	2 Sulzer diesels; 2 shafts; 2 700 bhp = 15·75 knots
Range, miles	12 000 at cruising speed of 11 knots
Complement	102

GENERAL
Built by Ishikawajima Heavy Industries Co. Ltd., Tokyo, Japan. Helicopter platform aft. Special surveying apparatus, echo sounders, Raydist equipment, sounding machines installed, and helicopter, landing craft (LCVP), jeep, and survey launches carried. All living and working spaces are air-conditioned. Controllable pitch propellers.

SIRIUS 1970, *Brazilian Navy*

3 COASTAL TYPE

Name	*Pennant No.*	*Laid down*	*Launched*	*Commissioned*
ARGUS	H 31	12 Dec 1955	6 Dec 1957	29 Jan 1959
ORION	H 32	12 Dec 1955	5 Feb 1958	11 June 1959
TAURUS	H 33	12 Dec 1955	7 Jan 1958	23 Apr 1959

Displacement, tons	250 standard; 300 full load
Dimensions, feet	138 pp; 147·7 oa × 20 × 6·6
Guns	2—20 mm AA
Main engines	2 diesels coupled to two shafts; 1 200 bhp = 15 knots
Oil fuel, tons	35
Range, miles	1 200 at 15 knots

All built by Arsenal da Marinha, Rio de Janeiro.

TAURUS 1972, *Brazilian Navy*

ALMIRANTE SALDANHA U 10 (ex-NE 1)

Displacement, tons	3 325 standard; 3 825 full load
Dimensions, feet	262 pp; 307·2 oa × 52 × 18·2 mean
Main engines	Diesel; 1 400 bhp = 11 knots
Range, miles	12 000 at 10 knots
Complement	356

Former training ship with a total sail area of 25 990 sq ft and armed with four 4-in guns one 3-in AA gun and four 3-pounders. Built by Vickers Armstrongs Ltd, Barrow. Launched on 19 Dec 1933. Cost £314 500. Instructional minelaying gear was included in equipment. The single 21-in torpedo tube was removed. Re-classified as an Oceanographic Ship (NOc) Aug 1959, and completly remodelled by 1964. A photograph as sailing ship appears in the 1952-53 to 1959-60 editions.

ALMIRANTE SALDANHA 1972, *Brazilian Navy*

SURVEY LAUNCHES

CAMOCIS	H 16	**ITACURUSSA**	H 15	**PARAIBANO**	H 11
CARAVELAS	H 17	**JACEGUAI**	H 14	**RIO BRANCO**	H 12

Displacement, tons 32 standard; 50 full load
Dimensions, feet 52·5 × 15·1 × 4·3
Main engines 1 diesel; 165 bhp = 11 knots
Range, miles 600 at 11 knots

Small wooden hulled coastal survey launches. Built by Borman, Rio in 1968-71.

PARAIBANO *1972, Brazilian Navy*

REPAIR SHIP

BELMONTE G 24 (ex-USS *Helios*, ARB 12, ex-*LST* 1127)

Displacement, tons 1 625 light; 2 030 standard; 4 100 full load
Dimensions, feet 316 wl; 328 oa × 50 × 11
Guns 8—40 mm AA
Main engines GM diesels; 2 shafts; 1 800 bhp = 11·6 knots
Oil fuel, tons 1 000
Range, miles 6 000 at 9 knots

GENERAL
Former United States battle damage repair ship. Built by Maryland DD Co, Baltimore Md. Laid down on 23 Nov 1944. Launched on 14 Feb 1945. Completed on 26 Feb 1945. Loaned to Brazil by USA in Jan 1962 under MAP.

BELMONTE *1969, Brazilian Navy*

OILERS

MARAJO G 27

Measurement, tons 10 500 deadweight
Dimensions, feet 440·7 × 63·3 × 24
Main engines Diesel; one shaft = 13·6 knots
Capacity, *cu metres* 14 200
Complement 80
Range, miles 9 200 at 13 knots

Laid down on 13 Dec 1966 and launched on 31 Jan 1968. Built by Ishikawajima Do Brasil-Estaleisos SA. Completed on 22 Oct 1968.

MARAJO *1969, Brazilian Navy*

POTENGI G 17

Displacement, tons 600
Dimensions, feet 175·5 pp; 178·8 oa × 24·5 × 6
Main engines Diesels, 2 shafts; 550 bhp = 10 knots
Oil, tons 450
Complement 19

Built at the Papendrecht yard in the Netherlands. Launched on 16 Mar 1938. Employed in the Mato Grosso Flotilla on river service.

TRANSPORTS

4 "PEREIRA" CLASS

Name	*Pennant No.*	*Laid down*	*Launched*	*Completed*
ARY PARREIRAS	G 21	13 Dec 1955	24 Aug 1956	29 Dec 1956
BARROSO PEREIRA	G 16	13 Dec 1953	10 Aug 1954	1 Dec 1954
CUSTÓDIO DE MELLO	U 26	13 Dec 1953	10 June 1954	30 Dec 1954
SOARES DUTRA	G 22	13 Dec 1955	13 Dec 1956	23 Mar 1957

Displacement, tons 4 800 standard; 7 300 full load
Measurement, tons 4 200 deadweight; 4 879 gross (Panama)
Dimensions, feet 362 pp; 391·8 oa × 52·5 × 20·5 max
Guns 4—3 in (U 26); 2—3 in (others); 2/4—20 mm
Main engines Ishikawajima double reduction geared turbines; 2 shafts; 4 800 shp = 17·67 knots (sea speed 15 knots)
Boilers 2 Ishikawajima two drum water tube type, oil fuel
Complement 127 (Troop capacity 497)

GENERAL
All built in Japan by Ishikawajima Heavy Industries Co, Ltd, Tokyo. Transports and cargo vessels. Flush deckers with forecastle and long poop. Elevator type helicopter landing platform aft. Troop carrying capacity for 497, with commensurate medical, hospital and dental facilities. Working and living quarters are mechanically ventilated with partial air conditioning. Refrigerated cargo space 15 500 cubic feet. Can carry 4 000 tons of cargo. *Barroso Pereira* and *Custódio de Mello* were incorporated into the Brazilian Navy on 22 Mar 1955 and 8 Feb 1955 respectively. Formerly armed with eight 40 mm AA guns. *Custódio de Mello* has been classified as a training ship since July 1961.

SOARES DUTRA *1972, Brazilian Navy*

TUGS

TRIDENTE R 22 (ex-*ATA 235*)
TRITÃO R 21 (ex-*ATA 234*)
TRIUNFO R 23 (ex-*ATA 236*)

Displacement, tons 534 standard; 835 full load
Dimensions, feet 133·7 wl; 143 oa × 33 × 13·2
Guns 2—20 mm AA
Main engines GM diesel-electric; 1 500 hp = 13 knots

GENERAL
All built by Gulfport Boiler & Welding Works, Inc, Port Arthur, Texas, and launched in 1954. Ex-US *ATRs*. Nos. *Tridente* R 22, *Tritao* R 21, *Triunfo* R 23 (ex-R1, R 2, R 3).

TRIDENTE *1972, Brazilian Navy*

FLOATING DOCKS

2 FLOATING DOCKS

CIDADE DE NATAL (ex-AFDL 39)

Displacement, tons 7 600
Length, feet (*metres*) 390·3 (119)
Beam, feet (*metres*) 86·9 (26·5)
Capacity, tons 2 800

Concrete floating dock loaned to Brazil by USN ,10 Nov. 1966.

GOIAS (ex-AFDL 4)

Displacement, tons 3 000
Length, feet (*metres*) 200 (52·6)
Beam, feet (*metres*) 44 (13·4)
Capacity, tons 1 000

Steel floating dock acquired by Brazil from USN, 10 Nov. 1966.

CEARA (ex-*ARD* 14)

Displacement, tons 5 200
Dimensions, feet 402·0 × 81·0

Formerly the United States auxiliary repair dry dock *ARD* 14. Transferred from the US Navy to the Brazilian Navy and allocated the name *Ceara* in 1968.

BRUNEI

Askar Melayu Diraja Brunei (Royal Brunei Malay Regiment) Flotilla:
Commanding Officer: Lieutenant Commander P. G. King, R.N.

FAST PATROL BOAT

PAHLAWAN

Displacement, tons	95 standard; 114 full load
Dimensions, feet	90·0 pp; 96·0 wl; 99·0 oa × 25·2 × 7·0
Missiles	8—SS 12 on 2 launchers
Guns	1—40 mm; 1—20 mm Hispano Suiza
Main engines	3 Bristol Siddeley Proteus gas turbines; 3 shafts; 12 750 bhp = 57 knots max; 2 diesels for cruising and manoeuvring.
Range, miles	450 at full speed; 2 300 at 10 knots
Complement	20

Ordered from Vosper Ltd, Portsmouth, England, on 10 Dec 1965. Launched on 5 Dec 1966. Completed 19 Oct 1967. Constructed of resin bonded timber with aluminium alloy superstructure. Missile launchers fitted in May 1972.

PAHLAWAN *1968, Vosper Limited*

COASTAL PATROL BOATS

MASNA **SALEHA** **NORAIN**

Displacement, tons	25
Dimensions, feet	62·0 × 16·0 × 4·5
Guns	2—20 mm Hispano Suiza; 2 MG
Main engines	2 GM diesels; 1 240 bhp = 26 knots *max*
Range, miles	600 at 23 knots
Complement	8

These boats were built specially for the Flotilla by Vosper Thornycroft (Private) Ltd. Singapore. Fitted with Decca 202 radar. *Norain*, last of the three, completed August 1972.

NORAIN *1972, Vosper Thornycroft*

ARMED LAUNCHES

BENDAHARA **KEMAINDERA** **MAHARAJALELA**

Displacement, tons	10
Dimensions, feet	47·0 × 12·0 × 3·0
Guns	2 MG
Main engines	2 GM diesels; 334 bhp = 20 knots
Range, miles	200
Complement	6

Rated as armed motor launches. Fitted with Decca 202 radar.

HOVERCRAFT

SRN 6 with a speed of 60 knots and a range of 150 miles armed with one machine gun
There are also 25 armed river boats, it was officially stated in Jan 1972.

BULGARIA

Administration

Commander-in-Chief, Navy:
Vice-Admiral Dobrev

Diplomatic Representation

Naval, Military and Air Attaché in London:
Colonel Dimiter Simov

Strength of the Fleet

2 Frigates
8 Corvettes
2 Submarines
3 Missile Boats
12 Torpedo Boats
2 Fleet Minesweepers
4 Coastal Minesweepers
4 Inshore Minesweepers
24 Minesweeping Boats
20 Landing Craft

Personnel

1973 7 000 officers and ratings

Mercantile Marine

Lloyd's Register of Shipping:
148 vessels of 703 878 tons gross

FRIGATES

2 "RIGA" TYPE

DRUZKI **SMELI**

Displacement, tons	1 200 standard; 1 600 full load
Length, feet (*metres*)	298·8 (*91·0*) oa
Beam, feet (*metres*)	33·5 (*10·2*)
Draught, feet (*metres*)	11·2 (*3·4*)
Guns	3—3·9 in (*100 mm*); 4—37 mm
A/S Weapons	2 16 barrelled rocket launchers
Tubes	3—21 in (*533 mm*)
Main engines	Geared turbines; 2 shafts; 25 000 shp
Speed, knots	28
Range, miles	2 500 at 15 knots
Complement	150

Transferred from USSR in 1957-8. S Band search radar.

"Riga" Type

CORVETTES

6 "SOI" TYPE

Displacement, tons	215 light; 250 full load
Dimensions, feet	137·8 × 19·4 × 9·2
Guns	4—25 mm (2 twin)
A/S weapons	4 five-barrelled ahead throwing rocket launchers
Main engines	3 diesels; 6 000 bhp = 29 knots
Range, miles	1 100 at 13 knots
Complement	30

Steel hulled patrol vessel transferred from USSR in 1963.

2 "KRONSTADT" TYPE

Displacement, tons	310 standard; 380 full load
Dimensions, feet	170·6 × 21·3 × 9·0
Guns	1—3·4 in; 2—37 mm AA; 3—20 mm AA
A/S weapons	Depth charge throwers
Main engines	3 Diesels; 3 shafts; 3 300 hp = 24 knots
Guns	1—3·4 in; 2—37 mm AA; 3—20 mm AA
A/S weapons	Depth charge throwers
Main engines	3 Diesels; 3 shafts; 3 300 hp = 24 knots
Oil fuel, tons	20
Range, miles	1 500 at 12 knots
Complement	65

Transferred from USSR in 1957.

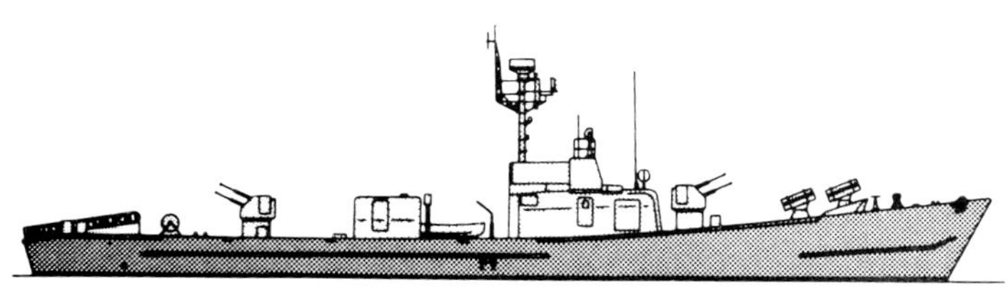

"SIO" type.

SUBMARINES

2 "W" CLASS

POBEDA **SLAVA**

Displacement, tons	1 050 surface; 1 350 submerged
Length, feet (*metres*)	247·0 (*75·3*) oa
Beam, feet (*metres*)	19·0 (*5·8*)
Draught, feet (*metres*)	15·1 (*4·6*)
Torpedo tubes	6—21 in (*533 mm*), 4 bow, 2 stern
Main engines	4 000 hp diesels (surface) 2 500 hp motors (submerged)
Speed, knots	17 on surface, 15 submerged
Range, miles	13 000 at 8 knots (surface)
Complement	60

Transferred from the USSR in 1958. The Soviet "MV" type coastal submarine was deleted from the list in 1967.

"W" Type

LIGHT FORCES

3 "OSA" CLASS (MISSILE BOATS)

Displacement, tons	165 standard; 200 full load
Dimensions, feet	127·9 × 24·9 × 5·9
Missiles launcher	4 in two pairs abreast for "SS-N-2"
Guns	4—30 mm (2 twin, 1 forward, 1 aft)
Main engines	3 diesels; 13 200 bhp = 28 knots
Complement	25

Reported to have been transferred from the USSR in 1971.

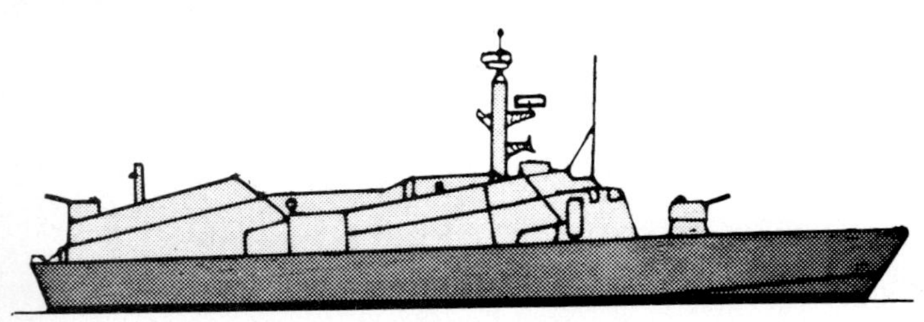

"Osa" type.

8 "P 4" TYPE (TORPEDO BOATS)

Displacement, tons	25 full load
Dimensions, feet	62·3 × 11·5 × 5·6
Guns	2—25 mm AA
Torpedo tubes	2—18 in
Main engines	2 diesels; 2 shafts; 2 200 bhp = 50 knots

Transferred from the USSR in 1956. The boats of the Soviet "PA 2" type, of which there were originally reported to have been 12, were deleted from the list in 1967.

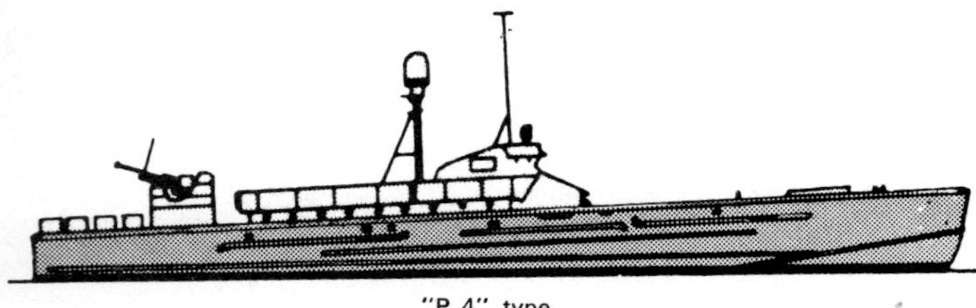

"P 4" type.

4 "SHERSHEN" TYPE (TORPEDO BOATS)

Displacement, tons	150 standard; 160 full load
Dimensions, feet	114·8 × 23·0 × 5·0
Guns	4—30 mm AA (2 twin)
Tubes	4—21 in (single)
Main engines	3 Diesels; 3 shafts; 13 000 bhp = 41 knots
Complement	16

Transferred in 1971.

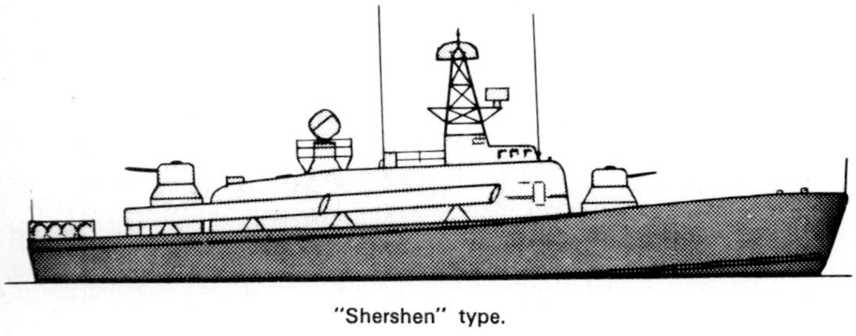

"Shershen" type.

MINESWEEPERS

2 "T 43" (FLEET) TYPE

Displacement, tons	500 standard; 610 full load
Dimensions, feet	190·2 × 27·9 × 6·9
Guns	4—37 mm AA; 4—25 mm
Main engines	2 diesels; 2 shafts; 2 000 bhp = 17 knots
Range, miles	1 600 at 10 knots
Complement	40

Three were transferred from the USSR in 1953, of which one was cannibalised.

4 "VANYA" (CMS) TYPE

Displacement, tons	250 standard; 275 full load
Dimensions, feet	129·9 × 24·3 × 6·9
Guns	2—30 mm AA (twin)
Main engines	2 Diesels; 2 200 bhp = 18 knots
Complement	30

Transferred from USSR in 1971-72.

4 "T 301" (IMS) TYPE

Displacement, tons	150 standard; 180 full load
Dimensions, feet	124·6 × 19·7 × 4·9
Guns	2—37 mm AA; 2—25 mm AA
Main engines	2 diesels; 2 shafts; 1 440 hp = 17 knots
Range, miles	2 200 at 10 knots

Transferred from the USSR in 1955. These have probably reached the end of their seagoing lives.

24 "PO 2" TYPE (MSB)

Former Soviet craft. 12 were reported to have been acquired in 1950 and 12 in 1956 for general purpose duties.

LANDING CRAFT

10 "VYDRA" TYPE

Displacement, tons	300 standard; 500 full load
Dimensions, feet	164·0 × 26·2 × 7·2
Main engines	2 diesels; 2 shafts; 400 bhp = 10 knots

Transferred from the USSR in 1970.

10 MFP TYPE

Dimensions, feet	164·0 oa × 20·0 × 6·6
Guns	1—37 mm AA or none

Built in Bulgaria in 1954. Based on a German Second World War MFP design.

AUXILIARIES

A number of auxiliaries, harbour oilers and tugs have been reported.

BURMA

Administration

Vice-Chief of Staff, Defence Services (Navy):
Commodore Thaung Tin

Diplomatic Representation

Naval, Military and Air Attaché in London:
Lieutenant-Colonel Kyee Myint

Naval, Military and Air Attaché in Washington:
Colonel Tin Htut

Strength of the Fleet

2 Frigates
2 Patrol Vessels
5 Torpedo Boats
72 Gunboats
2 Survey Vessels
11 Auxiliary Ships and Service Craft

Personnel

1973: 6 200 (300 officers and 5 900 ratings) including reserves

Mercantile Marine

Lloyd's Register of Shipping:
40 vessels of 54 877 tons gross

FRIGATES

1 Ex-BRITISH "RIVER" CLASS

Name	*Builders*	*Laid down*	*Launched*	*Completed*
MAYU (ex-HMS *Fal*)	Smiths Dock Co Ltd, South Bank-on-Tees, Middlesborough, England	20 May 1942	9 Nov 1942	2 July 1943

Displacement, tons	1 460 standard; 2 170 full load
Length, feet (*metres*)	283 (*86·3*) pp; 301·3 (*91·8*) oa
Beam, feet (*metres*)	36·7 (*11·3*)
Draught, feet (*metres*)	12 (*3·7*)
Guns, dual purpose	1—4 in (*102 mm*)
Guns, AA	4—40 mm
Boilers	2—three drum type
Main engines	Triple expansion 5 500 ihp; 2 shafts
Speed, knots	19
Range, miles	4 200 at 12 knots
Oil fuel (tons)	440
Complement	140

"River" class frigate. Acquired from Great Britain and renamed in March 1948.

MAYU *Burmese Navy*

1 Ex-BRITISH "ALGERINE" CLASS

Name	*Builders*	*Laid down*	*Launched*	*Completed*
YAN MYO AUNG (ex-HMS *Mariner*, ex-*Kincardine*)	Port Arthur Shipyards, Canada	26 Aug 1943	9 May 1944	23 May 1945

Displacement, tons	1 040 standard; 1 335 full load
Length, feet (*metres*)	225 (*68·6*) pp; 235 (*71·6*) oa
Beam, feet (*metres*)	35·5 (*19·8*)
Draught, feet (*metres*)	11·5 (*3·5*)
Guns, surface	1—4 in (*102 mm*)
Guns, AA	4—40 mm
Boilers	2 three-drum type
Main engines	Triple expansion 2 000 shp; 2 shafts
Speed, knots	16·5
Range, miles	4 000 at 12 knots
Complement	140

Former ocean minesweeper in the British Navy, used as escort vessel. Handed over to Burma in London and renamed *Yan Myo Aung*, on 18 Apr 1958. Fitted for minelaying and can carry 16 mines, eight on each side.

YAN MYO AUNG *1964, Burmese Navy*

CORVETTES

1 Ex-US PCE TYPE

YAN TAING AUNG, PCE 41 (ex-USS *Farmington*, PCE 894)

Displacement, tons	640 standard; 903 full load
Dimensions, feet	180 wl; 184 oa × 33 × 9·5
Guns	1—3 in, 50 cal dp; 2—40 mm AA (1 twin); 8—20 mm AA (4 twin)
A/S weapons	1 hedgehog; 2 DCT; 2 DC tracks
Main engines	GM diesels; 2 shafts; 1 800 bhp = 15 knots

Former US Patrol ship (escort). Built by Willamette Iron & Steel Corp, Portland, Oregon. Laid down on 7 Dec 1942, launched on 15 May 1943 and completed 10 Aug 1943. Transferred on 18 June 1965.

1 Ex-US MSF TYPE

YAN GYI AUNG, PCE 42 (ex-USS *Craddock*, MSF 356)

Displacement, tons	650 standard; 945 full load
Dimensions, feet	180 wl; 184·5 oa × 33 × 9·8 max
Guns	1—3 in 50 cal single forward; 4—40 mm AA (2 twin); 4—20 mm AA (2 twin)
Main engines	Diesels; 2 shafts; 1 710 shp = 14·8 knots
Range, miles	4 300 at 10 knots

Former US steel hulled fleet minesweeper of the "Admirable" class. Built by Willamette Iron & Steel Corp, Portland, Oregon. Laid down on 10 Nov 1943 and launched on 22 July 1944. Transferred at San Diego on 31 Mar 1967.

LIGHT FORCES

5 SAUNDERS ROE CONVERTIBLE TORPEDO BOATS

T 201 (ex-*PTS 101*) **T 203** (ex-*PTS 103*) **T 205** (ex-*PTS 105*)
T 202 (ex-*PTS 102*) **T 204** (ex-*PTS 104*)

Displacement, tons	50 standard; 64 full load
Dimensions, feet	67 pp; 71·5 oa × 19·5 × 6 max
Guns	As MGB: 1—4·5 in; 1—40 mm AA; As MTB: 2—20 mm AA
Tubes	As MTB: 4—21 in
Main engines	2 Napier Deltic diesels; 5 000 shp = 42 knots
Complement	13

T 202 *1966, Burmese Navy,*

Light Forces—*continued*

Interchangeable motor torpedo boats/motor gunboats built by Saunders Roe (Anglesey) Ltd, England. Convertible craft of aluminium construction, with riveted skin and aluminium alloy framework. As well as main engines, auxiliary power is also provided by diesels. The Saunders-Roe slow-speed electric drive was fitted to facilitate manoeuvring in the confined inland waters where the craft may be required to operate. Armament and layout of the vessels were similar to the British fast patrol boats of the "Dark" Class. The cost including engines, equipment, and spares of the five boats was over £1 800 000. T 201 was launched 24 Mar 1956. All were completed in 1956-57.

4 Ex-BRITISH LCG (M) TYPE

INDAW **INLAY** **INMA** **INYA**

Displacement, tons	381
Dimensions, feet	154·5 oa × 22·5 × 7·8
Guns	2—25 pdr; 2—2 pdr
Main engines	Paxman Ricardo diesels; 2 shafts; 1 000 bhp = 13 knots
Complement	39

Former British *LCG* (M). Landing craft, gun (medium). Employed as gunboats.

INMA *Burmese Navy*

2 BURMESE-BUILT GUNBOATS

NAGAKYAY **NAWARAT**

Displacement, tons	400 standard; 450 full load
Dimensions, feet	163 × 26·8 × 5·8
Guns	2—25 pdr QF; 2—40 mm AA
Main engines	2 Paxman-Ricardo turbo-charged diesels; 2 shafts; 1 160 bhp = 12 knots
Complement	43

Built at the Government Dockyard, Dawbon, Rangoon, Burma, *Nagakyay* was completed on 3 Dec 1960 and *Nawarat* on 26 Apr 1960.

NAGAKYAY *1962, Burmese Navy*

10 YUGOSLAVIAN-BUILT "Y" TYPE GUNBOATS

Y 301 Y 302 Y 303 Y 304 Y 305 Y 306 Y 307 Y 308 Y 309 Y 310

Displacement, tons	120
Dimensions, feet	100 pp; 104·8 oa × 24 × 3
Guns	2—40 mm AA; 1—2 pdr
Main engines	2 Mercedes-Benz diesels; 2 shafts; 1 000 bhp = 13 knots
Complement	29

All ten of these boats were completed in 1958 at the "Uljanik" Shipyard, Pula, in Yugoslavia. For detailed building dates see 1966-67 and earlier editions.

Y 310 *1964, Burmese Navy*

2 IMPROVED YUGOSLAV TYPE GUNBOATS

Y 311 **Y 312**

Dimensions approximately as Y-type above. Built in Burma 1969.

8 GUNBOATS (ex-TRANSPORTS)

SABAN **SEINDA** **SETYAHAT** **SHWETHIDA**
SAGU **SETKAYA** **SHWEPAZUN** **SINMIN**

Displacement, tons	98
Dimensions, feet	94·5 × 22 × 4·5
Guns	1—40 mm; 3—20 mm
Main engines	Crossley ERL—6 diesel; 160 bhp = 12 knots
Complement	32

SHWEPAZUN *1971, Burmese Navy*

6 US-BUILT PGM TYPE GUNBOATS

PGM 401 PGM 402 PGM 403 PGM 404 PGM 405 PGM 406

Displacement, tons	100
Dimensions, feet	95 × 19 × 5
Guns	1—40 mm AA; 2—0·5 US Browning MG
Main engines	4 GM diesels; 2 shafts; 1 000 bhp = 16 knots
Complement	17

Built by the Marinette Marine Corporation, USA. Ex-US PGM 43-46, 51 and 52 respectively. Machinery comprises 2-stroke, 6-cylinder, tandem geared twin diesel propulsion unit—1 LH and 1 RH; 500 bhp per unit.

PGM 401 *1962, Burmese Navy*

7 Ex-UNITED STATES CGC TYPE GUNBOATS

MGB 101 MGB 102 MGB 104 MGB 105 MGB 106 MGB 108 MGB 110

Displacement, tons	49 standard; 66 full load
Dimensions, feet	78 pp; 83 oa × 16 × 5·5
Guns	1—40 mm AA; 1—20 mm AA
Main engines	4 GM diesels; 2 shafts; 800 bhp = 11 knots
Complement	16

Ex-USCG 83-ft type cutters with new hulls built in Burma. Completed in 1960. For detailed building dates see 1966-67 and earlier editions. Machinery comprises 2-stroke, 6 cylinder, tandem geared, twin diesel propulsion units—1 LH and 1 RH drive; 400 bhp per unit. Three of this class are reported to have been sunk.

MGB 102 *1962, Burmese Navy*

10 BURMESE-BUILT RIVER PATROL CRAFT

Small craft, 50 feet long, built in Burma in 1951-52.

25 YUGOSLAV-BUILT RIVER PATROL CRAFT

Small craft, 52 feet long, acquired from Yugoslavia in the mid 1960's.

SURVEY VESSELS

THU TAY THI

Ocean Survey ship, 204 feet overall and 1 100 tons displacement, acquired from Yugoslavia in the mid-1960's. Complement 99.

YAY BO (UBHL 807)

Coastal survey vessel, possibly Dutch built with complement of 25 and a displacement of 108 tons.

SUPPORT SHIP

YAN LON AUNG

Light forces support ship of 520 tons, acquired from Japan in 1967.

TRANSPORTS

PYIDAWAYE

Measurement, tons	2 217·31 gross
Dimensions, feet	270 × 47 × 15
Main engines	Fleming & Ferguson triple expansion 2 000 ihp
Boilers	2 Scotch (return type)
Range, miles	2 000
Complement	88

Former passenger ship. In service since 1962. Wears the Burmese naval ensign.

PYIDAWAYE *1964, Burmese Navy*

1 Ex-US LCU TYPE

LCU 1626 (ex-USS *LCU 1626*)

Displacement, tons	200 light; 342 full load
Dimensions, feet	135·2 oa × 29 × 5·5
Main engines	Diesels; 2 shafts; 1 000 bhp = 11 knots

Ex-US utility landing craft. Transferred under MAP in 1967. Used as transport.

Transports—*continued*

8 Ex-US LCM TYPE

LCM 701 LCM 702 LCM 703 LCM 704 LCM 705 LCM 706 LCM 707 LCM 708

Displacement, tons	28
Dimensions, feet	56 × 14 × 4
Main engines	2 Gray Marine diesels; 225 bhp

US-built LCM type landing craft. Used as local transports for stores and personnel.

CAMEROON

Complete independence was proclaimed on 1 Jan 1960

Mercantile Marine

Lloyd's Register of Shipping: 13 vessels of 2 334 tons gross

PATROL BOATS

VIGILANT (ex-*VC 6*, P 756) **AUDACIEUX** (ex-*VC 8*, P 758)

Displacement, tons	75 standard; 82 full load
Dimensions, feet	104·2 × 15·5 × 5·5
Guns	2—20 mm AA
Main engines	Mercedes-Benz diesels; 2 shafts; 2 700 bhp = 28 knots
Range, miles	1 500 at 15 knots
Complement	15

Former French seaward defence motor launches of the VC type. Built by Constructions Mécaniques de Normandie, Cherbourg. Completed in 1957-58 *Vigilant* was officially handed over from France to the Republic of Cameroon on 7 Mar 1964.

BRIGADIER M'BONGA TOUNDA

Displacement, tons	20 full load
Dimensions, feet	60 × 13·5 × 4
Guns	1—12·7 mm MG
Main engines	Caterpillar Diesel; 2 shafts; 540 bhp = 21 knots
Complement	8

Built by Ch Navals de L'Esterel in 1967. Customs duties.

VALEUREUX

Displacement, tons	45 full load
Dimensions, feet	78·1 × 16·3 × 5·1
Guns	2—20 mm AA
Main engines	2 Diesels; 2 shafts; 960 hp = 25 knots
Complement	9

Built by Ch Navals de L'Esterel in 1970.

CANADA

Administration

Minister of National Defence:
The Hon. James Richardson MP

On 1 Aug 1964 the Naval Board was dissolved, and Naval Headquarters was integrated with Canadian Forces Headquarters. On 1 Feb 1968, the Canadian Forces Reorganization Act unified the three branches of the Canadian Forces and the title Royal Canadian Navy was dropped. Maritime Command, one of five commands comprising the Canadian Armed Forces, is made up of the bulk of what was the Royal Canadian Navy plus Maritime patrol aircraft squadrons and bases.

Senior Naval Appointments

Chief of Maritime Operations:
Rear Admiral J. A. Charles, CD

Commander Maritime Forces Pacific:
Rear Admiral R. H. Leir, C.D.

Commander Canadian Flotilla Atlantic:
Commodore A. L. Collier, DSC, CD

Diplomatic Representation

Senior Naval Liaison Officer, London:
Captain (N) J. W. Mason, CD

Canadian Forces Attaché and Senior Naval Liaison Officer, Washington:
Commodore R. J. Pickford, CD

Canadian Forces Attaché (Naval) Moscow:
Lt. Col .W. Draper CD

Establishment

The Royal Canadian Navy was officially established on 4 May 1910, when Royal Assent was given to the Naval Service Act.

Senior Officers Pennant

The senior ship of a squadron wears a command broad pennant. This is a swallow-tailed pennant, white, with blue borders top and bottom, and bearing the squadron number in blue.

Strength of the Fleet

4 Destroyers (DDH)
18 Frigates
4 Patrol Submarines
5 Replenishment Ships (2 small)
2 Maintenance Ships
6 Research Vessels
13 Miscellaneous
27 Tugs

Personnel

1971: 16 906 (2 379 officers, 14 527 men and women)
1972: 15 223 (2 590 officers, 12 633 men and women)

Navy Estimates

1968-69: $283 201 000 (Maritime Command)
1969-70: $359 701 000 (Maritime Command)
1970-71: $360 000 000 (Maritime Command)
1971-72: $348 000 000 (Maritime Command)
1972-73: $363 000 000 (Maritime Command)

Mercantile Marine

Lloyd's Register of Shipping:
1 235 vessels of 2 380 635 tons gross

Disposals and Transfers

Aircraft Carrier

1 April, 1970 *Bonaventure* paid off. Sold for scrap to M. W. Kennedy Ltd., Vancouver, BC and towed to Taiwan from Halifax 27 Oct.

Destroyers

1963 *Crusader* and *Sioux*
1966 *Iroquois, Cayuga, Huron, Micmac, Nootka, Haida* to Toronto as floating museum.
1969 *Crescent Algonquin* and *Athabaskan*

Hydrofoil

1972 *Bras d'or* discarded due to lack of funds for this project

DESTROYERS (DDH)

4 "IROQUOIS" CLASS

Displacement, tons	4 200 full load
Length, feet (*metres*)	398 (*121·3*) pp 426 (*129·8*) oa
Beam, feet (*metres*)	50 (*15·2*)
Draught, feet (*metres*)	14·5 (*4·4*)
Aircraft	2 "Sea King" CHSS-2 A/S helicopters
Missiles	(see note)
Guns, dual purpose	1—5 in (*127 mm*) LA, single Oto-Melara
A/S	1 Mk 10 "Limbo"
Torpedo tubes	2 triple for A/S homing torpedoes
Main engines	Gas turbines; 2 Pratt & Whitney FT4A2 50 000 shp + 2 Pratt & Whitney FT12AH3 7 400 shp for cruising; 2 shafts
Speed, knots	29 +
Range, miles	4 500 at 20 knots
Complement	280 (20 officers, 260 men)

Name	*No.*	*Builders*	*Laid down*	*Launched*	*Completion*
ALGONQUIN	283	Davie SB Co, Lauzon	1 Sep 1969	27 Nov 1970	30 Sept 1973
ATHABASKAN	282	Davie SB Co, Lauzon	1 June 1969	mid Apr 1971	30 Nov 1972
HURON	281	Marine Industries Ltd, Sorel	15 Jan 1969	3 Apr 1971	30 June 1973
IROQUOIS	280	Marine Industries Ltd, Sorel	15 Jan 1969	28 Nov 1970	29 July 1972

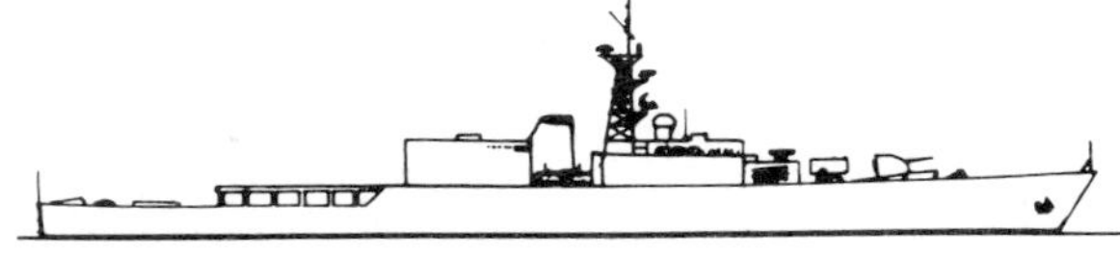

IROQUOIS *Class* (twin funnels)

GENERAL
It will be observed that these ships have the same hull design, dimensions and basic characteristics as the large general purpose frigates cancelled at the end of 1963 (see particulars and illustration in the 1963-64 edition). Designed as anti-submarine ships, they are fitted with variable depth and conventional sonar, landing deck equipped with double hauldown and beartrap, flume type anti-rolling tanks to stabilise the ships at low speed, pre-wetting system to counter radio-active fallout, enclosed citadel, and bridge control of machinery.

ENGINEERING. The gas turbines feed through a Swiss double reduction gearbox to two five bladed CP propellers.

ELECTRONICS. Mk 22 Weapon System Control by Hollandse Signaal.

RADAR. SPQ 2D Surface warning and Navigation SPS 501 (SPS 12) long range warning M 22 fire control.

MISSILES. Launch system (GMLS) by Raytheon for Mk III Sea Sparrow missiles. Two launchers in forward end of the superstructure.

SONAR. SQS 505 Hull mounted in 14 ft dome VDS. 18 ft towed body aft. SQS 501 Bottomed target classification.

TORPEDOES. The Mk 32 tubes are to be used with Mk 46 torpedoes.

IROQUOIS *1972 Canadian Forces*

FRIGATES

2 "ANNAPOLIS" CLASS

Displacement, tons	2 400 standard; 3 000 full load
Length, feet (*metres*)	371·0 (*113·1*) oa
Beam, feet (*metres*)	42·0 (*12·8*)
Draught, feet (*metres*)	14·4 (*4·4*)
Aircraft	1 CHSS-2 "Sea King" helicopter
Guns, AA	2—3 in (*76 mm*) 50 cal (1 twin)
A/S weapons	1 Mk 10 "Limbo" in after well
Boilers	2 water tube
Main engines	Geared turbines; 2 shafts; 30 000 shp
Speed, knots	28 (official figure) 30 trials
Complement	246 (12 officers, 234 ratings)

Name	*No.*	*Builders*	*Work Commenced*	*Launched*	*Completed*
ANNAPOLIS	265	Halifax Shipyards Ltd, Halifax	July 1960	27 Apr 1963	19 Dec 1964
NIPIGON	266	Marine Industries Ltd, Sorel Q	Apr 1960	10 Dec 1961	30 May 1964

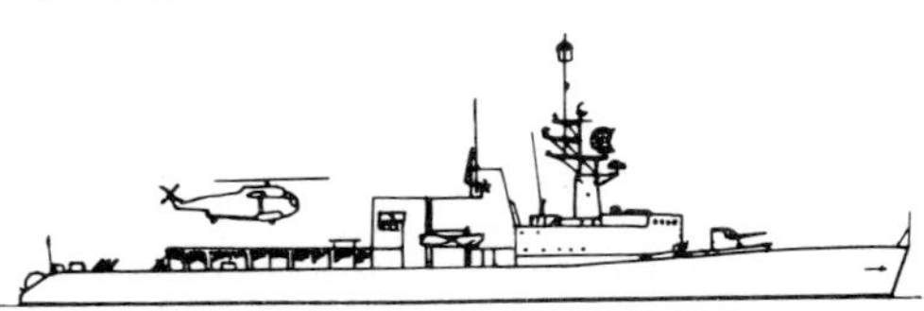

ANNAPOLIS, NIPIGON

These two ships represented the logical development of the original "St Laurent" class, through the "Restigouche" and "Mackenzie" designs. Due to the erection of a helicopter hangar and flight deck, and variable depth sonar only one "Limbo" mounting could be installed. Also the 50 cal 3 inch mounting had to be moved forward to replace the 70 cal mounting in the original design.

RADAR. Search: SPS 12. Tactical: SPS 10. Fire Control: X Band.

CONSTRUCTION. As these are largely prefabricated no firm laying down date is officially given. Work on hull units commenced under cover long before components were laid on the slip.

NIPIGON *1971, Canadian Forces*

Frigates—*continued*

4 "MACKENZIE" CLASS

Displacement, tons	2 380 standard; 2 890 full load
Length, feet (*metres*)	366·0 (*111·5*) oa
Beam, feet (*metres*)	42·0 (*12·8*)
Draught, feet (*metres*)	13·5 (*4·1*)
Guns, AA	4—3 in (*76 mm*) 2 twin
A/S weapons	2 Mk 10 "Limbo" in well aft
Boilers	2 water tube
Main engines	Geared turbines; 2 shafts; 30 000 shp
Speed, knots	28
Complement	245 (12 officers, 233 ratings)

Name	No.	Builders	Laid down	Launched	Completed
MACKENZIE	261	Canadian Vickers Ltd, Montreal	15 Dec 1958	25 May 1961	6 Oct 1962
QU'APPELLE	264	Davie Shipbuilding & Repairing	14 Jan 1960	2 May 1962	14 Sep 1963
***SASKATCHEWAN**	262	Victoria Machinery (and Yarrow)	16 July 1959	1 Feb 1961	16 Feb 1963
YUKON	263	Burrard DD & Shipbuilding	25 Oct 1959	27 July 1961	25 May 1963

MACKENZIE, YUKON

MACKENZIE — *1970, Canadian Maritime Command.*

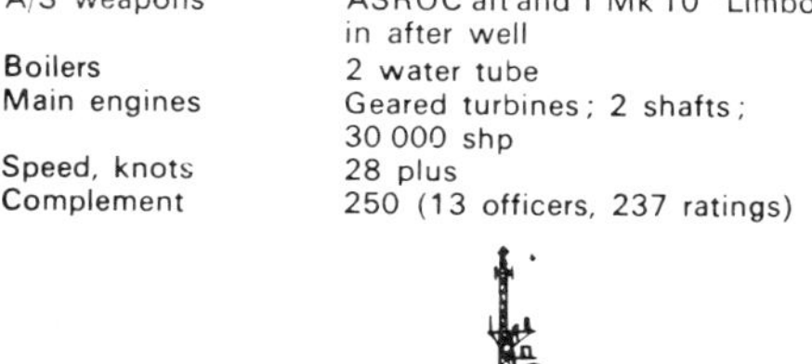

QU'APPELLE

RADAR. Search: SPS 12. Tactical: SPS 10. Fire Control: X Band.

**Saskatchewan* was launched by Victoria Machinery Depot Co Ltd, but completed by Yarrow's Ltd.

4 "IMPROVED RESTIGOUCHE"

Displacement, tons	2 390 standard; 2 900 full load
Length, feet (*metres*)	371·0 (*113·1*)
Beam, feet (*metres*)	42·0 (*12·8*)
Draught, feet (*metres*)	14·1 (*4·3*)
Guns, AA	2—3 in (*76 mm*) 70 cal forward
A/S weapons	ASROC aft and 1 Mk 10 "Limbo" in after well
Boilers	2 water tube
Main engines	Geared turbines; 2 shafts; 30 000 shp
Speed, knots	28 plus
Complement	250 (13 officers, 237 ratings)

Name	No.	Builder	Laid down	Launched	Completed
GATINEAU	236	Davie Shipbuilding & Repairing	30 Apr 1953	3 June 1957	17 Feb 1959
KOOTENAY	258	Burrard DD & Shipbuilding	21 Aug 1952	15 June 1954	7 Mar 1959
RESTIGOUCHE	257	Canadian Vickers, Montreal	15 July 1953	22 Nov 1954	7 June 1958
TERRA NOVA	259	Victoria Machinery Depot Co	14 Nov 1952	21 June 1955	6 June 1959

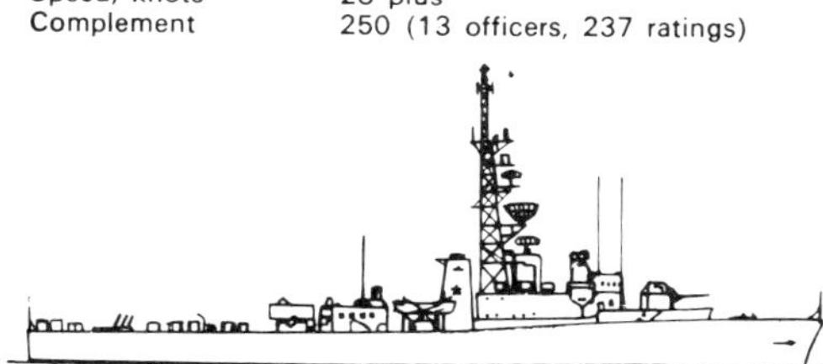

GATINEAU — *1972, Canadian Forces*

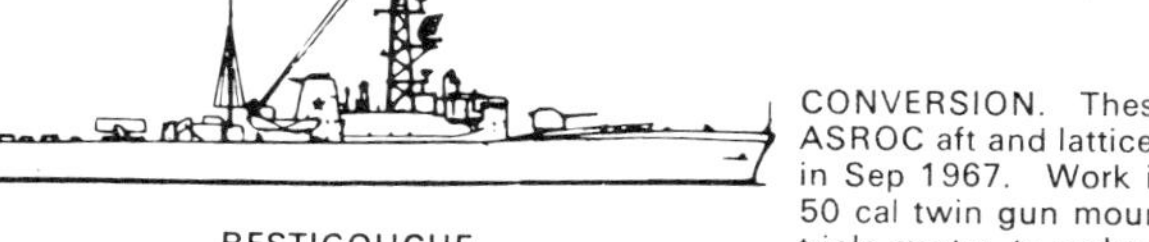

RESTIGOUCHE

CONVERSION. These four ships were refitted with ASROC aft and lattice foremast, *Terra Nova* commencing in Sep 1967. Work included removing the after 3 inch 50 cal twin gun mounting and one "Limbo" A/S Mk 10 triple mortar, to make way for ASROC and variable depth sonar. Dates of refits *Terra Nova* was completed on 18 Oct 1968; *Gatineau* commenced on 15 Sep 1969, *Kootenay* in May 1970 and *Restigouche* in August 1970.

RADAR. Search: SPS 12. Tactical: SPS 10. Fire Control: X Band.

3 "RESTIGOUCHE" CLASS

Displacement, tons	2 370 standard; 2 880 full load
Length, feet (*metres*)	366·0 (*111·5*) oa
Beam, feet (*metres*)	42·0 (*12·8*)
Draught, feet (*metres*)	13·5 (*4·1*)
Guns, AA	4—3 in (*76 mm*) 2 twin
A/S weapons	2 Mk 10 "Limbo" in well aft
Boilers	2 water tube
Main engines	Geared turbines; 2 shafts; 30 000 shp
Speed, knots	28
Complement	248 (12 officers, 236 ratings)

Name	No.	Builder	Laid down	Launched	Completed
CHAUDIERE	235	Halifax Shipyards Ltd	30 July 1953	13 Nov 1957	14 Nov 1959
COLUMBIA	260	Burrard DD & Shipbuilding	11 June 1953	1 Nov 1956	7 Nov 1959
ST. CROIX	256	Marine Industries Ltd, Sorel, Q	15 Oct 1954	17 Nov 1957	4 Oct 1958

CHAUDIERE — *1970, Canadian Maritime Command*

CHAUDIERE, COLUMBIA, ST. CROIX

RADAR. Search: SPS 12. Tactical: SPS 10. Fire Control: X Band.

Frigates—*continued*

7 "ST. LAURENT" CLASS

Displacement, tons	2 260 standard; 2 800 full load
Length, feet (*metres*)	366·0 (*111·5*) oa
Beam, feet (*metres*)	42·0 (*12·8*)
Draught, feet (*metres*)	13·2 (*4·0*)
Aircraft	1 A/S helicopter
Guns, AA	2—3 in (*76 mm*) 50 cal (1 twin)
A/S weapons	1 Mk 10 "Limbo" in after well
Boilers	2 water tube
Main engines	English Electric geared turbines; 2 shafts; 30 000 shp
Speed, knots	28·5 (official figure)
Complement	250 (13 officers, 237 ratings)

Name	*No.*	*Builders*	*Laid down*	*Launched*	*Completed*
ST. LAURENT	DDE 205	Canadian Vickers, Ltd, Montreal	22 Nov 1950	20 Nov 1951	29 Oct 1955
SAGUENAY	DDE 206	Halifax Shipyards, Ltd, Halifax	4 Apr 1951	30 July 1953	15 Dec 1956
SKEENA	DDE 207	Burrard Dry Dock & Shipbuilding	1 June 1951	19 Aug 1952	30 Mar 1957
OTTAWA	DDE 229	Canadian Vickers, Ltd, Montreal	8 June 1951	29 Apr 1953	10 Nov 1956
MARGAREE	DDE 230	Halifax Shipyards Ltd, Halifax	12 Sep 1951	29 Mar 1956	5 Oct 1957
***FRASER**	DDE 233	Yarrows, Ltd, Esquimalt, B.C.	11 Dec 1951	19 Feb 1953	28 June 1957
ASSINIBOINE	DDE 234	Marine Industries Ltd, Sorel, Q	19 May 1952	12 Feb 1954	16 Aug 1956

GENERAL
The first major warships to be designed in Canada. In design, much assistance was received from the Royal Navy (propelling machinery of British design) and the US Navy. In function they supersede the frigates of the Second World War and like the latter they were designed so that in the event of emergency they could be produced rapidly and in quantity.

* *Fraser* was launched by Burrard Dry Dock & Shipbuilding but completed by Yarrows Ltd.

RADAR. Search: SPS 12. Tactical: SPS 10.

RECONSTRUCTION. All have helicopter platforms and VDS. *St. Laurent* was equipped with VDS in 1961 and platform added later. Twin funnels were stepped to permit forward extension of the helicopter hangar. Gunhouses are of fibreglass. In providing helicopter platforms and hangars it was possible to retain only one three barrelled "Limbo" mortar and only one twin 3-inch gun mounting. Dates of recommissioning after conversion: *Assiniboine* 28 June 1963, *St. Laurent* 4 Oct 1963, *Ottawa* 21 Oct 1964, *Saguenay* 14 May 1965, *Skeena* 15 Aug 1965, *Margaree* 15 Oct 1965, *Fraser* 31 Aug 1966.

Fraser has lattice radar mast by the funnels.

GUNNERY. Original armament was 4—3 inch, 50 cal AA (2 twin), 2—40 mm AA (single), and 2 "Limbo" mortars.

FRASER

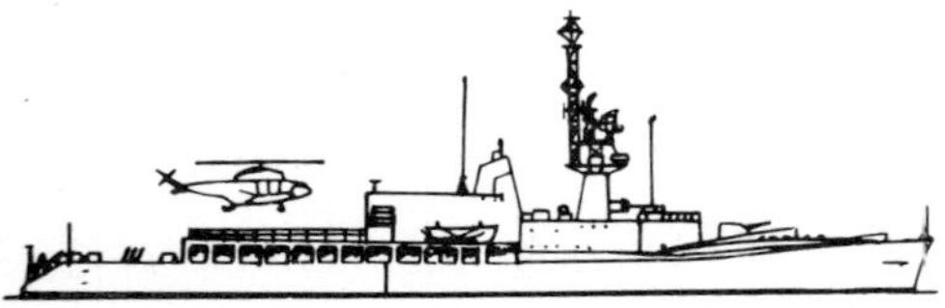

FRASER *1972, Canadian Forces*

SKEENA *1971, Wright & Logan*

OVERHEAD PLAN VIEW SKEENA

SUBMARINES

3 BRITISH-BUILT "OBERON" TYPE

Name	No.	Builders	Laid down	Launched	Commissioned
OJIBWA (ex-*Onyx*)	72	HM Dockyard, Chatham	27 Sep 1962	29 Feb 1964	23 Sep 1965
OKANAGAN	74	HM Dockyard, Chatham	25 Mar 1965	17 Sep 1966	22 June 1968
ONONDAGA	73	HM Dockyard, Chatham	18 June 1964	25 Sep 1965	22 June 1967

Displacement, tons	2 060 full buoyancy surface; 2 200 normal surface; 2 420 submerged
Length, feet (*metres*)	241 (*73·5*) pp; 294·2 (*90·0*) oa
Beam, feet (*metres*)	26·5 (*8·1*)
Draught, feet (*metres*)	18 (*5·5*)
Torpedo tubes	8—21 in (*533 mm*), 6 bow and 2 stern
Main engines	2 Admiralty Standard Range diesels; 3 680 bhp; 2 shafts; 2 electric motors; 6 000 hp
Speed, knots	12 on surface; 17 submerged
Complement	65 (7 officers, 58 ratings)

GENERAL

The procurement of three submarines for the Royal Canadian Navy was announced by the Minister of National Defence on 11 Apr 1962, all of the "Oberon" class built in Great Britain. The first of these patrol submarines was obtained by the Canadian Government from the Royal Navy construction programme. She was laid down as *Onyx* but launched as *Ojibwa*. The other two were specifically Canadian procurements. There were some design changes to meet specific new requirements including installation of RCN communications equipment and enlargement of de-icing and air-conditioning systems to meet the wide extremes of climate encountered in Canadian operating areas.

NAMES. The name *Ojibwa* is that of a tribe of North American Indians now widely dispersed in Canada and the USA and one of the largest remnants of aboriginal population. *Okanangan* and *Onondaga* are also well known Canadian Indian tribes.

ELECTRONICS. The equipment includes sonar with forecastle mounted array and X band surveillance radar installations.

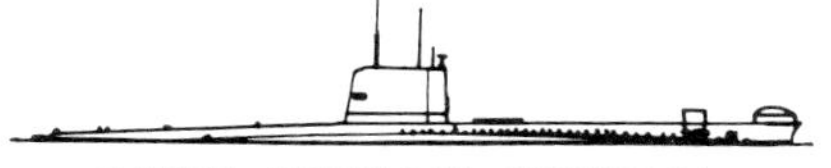

OJIBWA, OKANAGAN, ONONDAGA

OKANAGAN — *1969, Canadian Maritime Command*

ONONDAGA — *1970 Canadian Maritime Command*

1 Ex-US "TENCH" TYPE

RAINBOW SS 75 (ex-*USS Argonaut* SS 475)

Displacement, tons	1 800 surface; 2 500 submerged
Length, feet (*metres*)	311·2 (*95·0*)
Beam, feet (*metres*)	27·2 (*8·2*)
Draught, feet (*metres*)	17·1 (*5·2*)
Torpedo tubes	10—21 in (*533 mm*) 6 fwd 4 aft
Main engines	6 500 hp diesels (surface); 4 610 hp motors (submerged)
Speed, knots	20 on surface; 10 submerged
Range, miles	12 000 at 10 knots surface
Complement	82 (8 officers, 74 men)

RAINBOW — ***1970, Canadian Maritime Command***

Built by Navy Yard, Portsmouth, New Hampshire. Laid down on 28 June 1944, launched on 1 Oct 1944 and completed on 15 Jan 1945. Purchased in Dec 1968 as a replacement for *Grilse*. Commissioned on 2 Dec 1968. Based at Esquimalt for anti-submarine training.

The training submarine *Grilse* (ex-USS *Burrfish*) was returned to the USN in Dec 1968 after having been on loan to Canada since May 1961.

RAINBOW

REPLENISHMENT SHIPS

Name	No.	Builders	Laid down	Launched	Completed
PRESERVER	AOR 510	Saint John Dry Dock Co Ltd, N.B.	17 Oct 1967	29 May 1969	30 July 1970
PROTECTEUR	AOR 509	Saint John Dry Dock Co Ltd, N.B.	17 Oct 1967	18 July 1968	30 Aug 1969

Displacement, tons 9 000 light; 24 000 full load
Measurement, tons 22 100 gross; 13 250 deadweight
Length, feet (*metres*) 546 (*168·4*) oa
Beam, feet (*metres*) 76 (*23·2*)
Draught, feet (*metres*) 30 (*9·1*)
Guns, AA 1—3 in (*76 mm*)
A/S launcher 1 Sea Sparrow fitted
Aircraft 3 CHSS-2 helicopters
Boilers 2 forced draught water tube
Main engines Geared turbine; 21 000 shp; 1 shaft
Range, miles 4 100 at 20, 7 500 at 11·5 knots
Complememt 227 (15 officers, 212 ratings)

Provided for under the Five Year Programme. Contract price $47 500 000 for both ships. In design they are an improvement on that of the prototype *Provider*. They could carry spare anti-submarine helicopters, military vehicles and bulk equipment for sealift purposes. 12 000 tons fuel, 1 250 tons ammunition.

PRESERVER *1971, Canadian Forces*

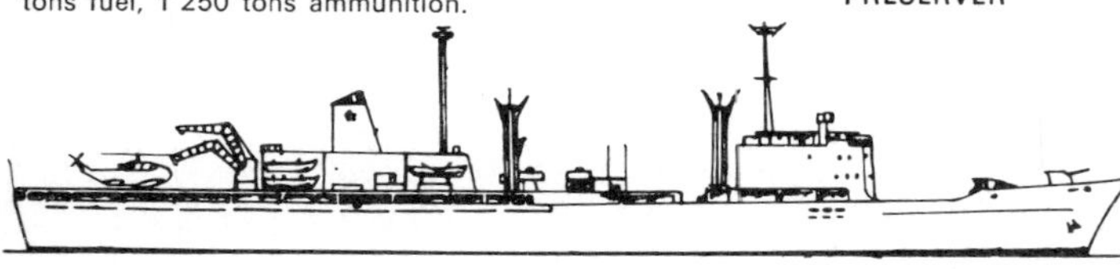

PRESERVER, PROTECTEUR

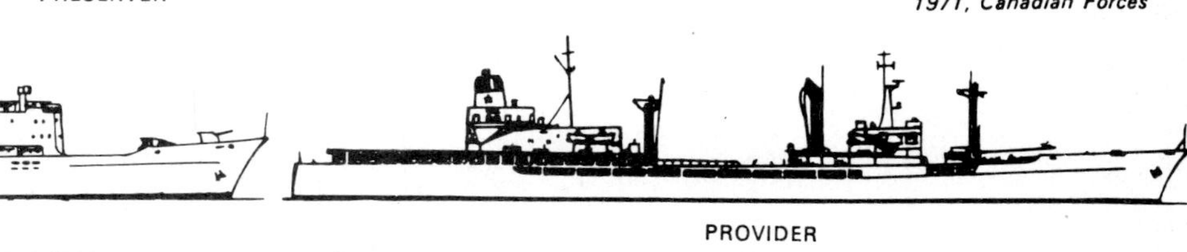

PROVIDER

PROVIDER AOR 508

Displacement, tons 7 300 light; 22 700 full load
Measurement, tons 20 000 gross; 14 700 deadweight
Length, feet (*metres*) 523 (*159·4*) pp; 555 (*169·2*) oa
Beam, feet (*metres*) 76 (*23·2*)
Draught, feet (*metres*) 32 (*9·8*) max
Aircraft 3 HSS 2 helicopters
Boilers 2 water tube
Main engines Double reduction geared turbine; 21 000 shp; 1 shaft
Speed, knots 20
Range, miles 5 000 at 20 knots
Oil fuel, (tons) 1 200
Complement 142 (11 officers, 131 ratings)

Authorised (announced) on 15 Apr 1958. Built by Davie Shipbuilding Ltd, Lauzon, Quebec. Preliminary construction work began in Sep 1960. Laid down on 1 May 1961. Launched on 5 July 1962. Commissioned for service on 28 Sep 1963. Cost $15 700 000.

DESIGN. The helicopter flight deck is aft with the hangar on this deck and immediately below the funnel. At least three Sikorsky helicopters can be accommodated in the hangar. The flight deck can receive the largest and heaviest helicopters. A total of 20 electro-hydraulic winches are fitted on deck for ship-to-ship movements of cargo and supplies, as well as shore-to-ship requirements when alongside.

PROVIDER *1971, Canadian Forces*

2 "DUN" CLASS OILERS

DUNDALK AOC 501 **DUNDURN** AOC 502

Displacement, tons 950
Dimensions, feet 178·8 × 32·2 × 13
Main engines Diesel; 700 bhp = 10 knots

Small vessels designated tankers, and classed as fleet auxiliaries.

DUNDURN *1969, courtesy Mr. G. R. Hooper (Master)*

MAINTENANCE SHIPS

2 "CAPE" CLASS

Name	No.	Builders	Laid down	Launched	Completed
CAPE BRETON	100	Burrard Dry Dock Co, Vancouver, BC	5 July 1944	7 Oct 1944	25 Apr 1945
CAPE SCOTT	101	Burrard Dry Dock Co, Vancouver, BC	8 June 1944	27 Sep 1944	20 Mar 1945

Displacement, tons 8 580 standard; 11 270 full load
Dimensions, feet 441·5 × 57 × 20 mean at standard displacement
Main engines Triple expansion; 1 shaft; 2 500 ihp = 11 knots
Boilers 2 Foster Wheeler
Complement *Cape Breton* 220; *Cape Scott* 270 officers and men

CAPE SCOTT *1971, Canadian Forces*

CAPE BRETON CAPE SCOTT

Cape Breton (ex-*HMS Flamborough Head*) transferred in 1953—in reserve since 1964. *Cape Scott* (ex- *HMS Beachy Head*) transferred in 1952.

RESEARCH VESSELS

BLUETHROAT AGOR 114

Displacement, tons	785 standard; 870 full load
Dimensions, feet	150·7 pp; 157 oa × 33 × 10
Main engines	Diesel; 2 shafts; 1 200 bhp = 13 knots

Authorised under 1951 Programme. Built by Geo. T. Davie & Sons Ltd, Lauzon PQ. Laid down on 31 Oct 1952. Launched on 15 Sep 1955. Completed on 28 Nov 1955. Built as Mine and Loop Layer, but under NATO standardised nomenclature listed as Harbour Mineplanter. In 1957 she was rated Controlled Minelayer, NPC 114. Redesignated as Cable Layer (ALC) in 1959, and as Research Vessel (AGOR) in 1964.

SACKVILLE AGOR 113

Displacement, tons	1 085 standard; 1 350 full load
Dimensions, feet	190 pp; 205 oa × 33 × 14·5
Main engines	Triple expansion; 2 750 ihp = 16 knots
Boilers	2 SE

Built by St. John Dry Dock Co, NB. Launched on 15 May 1941. Completed on 30 Dec 1941. Ex-"Flower" class corvette converted to loop layer. Employed by Naval Research Laboratories for oceanographic work.

FORT FRANCES AGOR 170

Displacement, tons	1 040 standard; 1 335 full load
Dimensions, feet	225 ca × 35 × 11 max
Main engines	Triple expansion; 2 shafts; 2 000 ihp = 16·5 knots
Boilers	2, of 3-drum type

Built by Port Arthur Shipbuilding Co, Ontario. Launched on 30 Oct 1943. Former "Algerine" class Ocean Minesweeper (AM). Redesignated Coastal Escort (FSE) in 1953. Refitted as survey ship and redesignated AGH in 1959. Again redesignated AGOR in 1964. A photograph appears in the 1964-65 to 1966-67 editions. Sister ship *Oshawa*, AGOR 174 was disposed of when *Endeavour* commissioned. *Kapuskasing*, FSE 171, was lent to Dept of Mines and Technical Surveys. *New Liskeard* was discarded on 1 Dec 1969.

QUEST AGOR 172

Displacement, tons	2 130
Dimensions, feet	235 oa × 42 × 15·5
Aircraft	Light helicopter
Main engines	Diesel electric; 2 shafts; 2 950 shp = 16 knots max; Bow thruster propeller
Range, miles	10 000 at 12 knots
Complement	55

Built by Burrard Dry Dock Co, Vancouver for the Naval Research Establishment of the Defence Research Board for acoustic hydrographic and general oceanographic work, in particular as related to anti-submarine warfare. Capable of operating in heavy ice in the company of an icebreaker. A large 5-ton crane is fitted forward so that the jib-head can be lowered to surface level and thus reduce the swing on scientific instruments. Design is slightly enlarged version of *Endeavour* (see below) with similar main engines, speed and range. Construction began in 1967. Launched on 9 July 1968. Completed on 21 Aug 1969. Based at Halifax.

QUEST *1972, Canadian Forces*

ENDEAVOUR AGOR 171

Displacement, tons	1 560
Dimensions, feet	215 wl; 236 oa × 38·5 × 13
Aircraft	1 light helicopter
Main engines	Diesel electric; 2 shafts; 2 960 shp = 16 knots
Range, miles	10 000 at 12 knots
Complement	10 officers, 13 scientists, 25 ratings (plus helicopter pilot and engineer)

A naval research ship specifically designed to meet the scientific requirements for undertaking programmes in anti-submarine research. Flight deck 48 by 31 feet. Stiffened for operating in ice-covered areas. Designed by the Director General Ships and the Pacific Naval Laboratory. Built by Yarrows Ltd, Esquimalt, BC. Contract let in Nov 1963. Accepted for service on 9 Mar 1965. She is able to turn in 2·5 times her own length. Her crowsnest is fitted with engine and steering controls for navigation in ice. A bulbous bow reduces pitch and she has anti-roll tanks. Two 9-ton Austin-Weston telescopic cranes are fitted. There are two oceanographical winches each holding 5 000 fathoms of wire, two bathythermograph winches and a deep-sea anchoring and coring winch. She has acoustic insulation in her machinery spaces.

ENDEAVOUR *1970, Canadian Maritime Command*

Research Vessels—*continued*

LAYMORE AGOR 516 (ex-AKS 516)

Measurement, tons	560 gross, 262 net
Dimensions, feet	176·5 × 32 × 8
Main engines	GM diesels; 1 000 bhp = 10·8 knots

Former coastal supply vessel, rated as fleet auxiliary and designated AKS. Converted to research vessel 2 Aug 1965 to Mar 1966 and reclassified AGOR. Her original sister ship *Eastore* was sold on 30 July 1964.

MISCELLANEOUS

GRANBY FSE 180 (ex-*Victoriaville*, DE 320) (DIVING SUPPORT SHIP)

Displacement, tons	1 570 standard; 2 360 full load (as frigate)
Dimensions, feet	310·5 oa × 36·5 × 16·0
Guns, surface	2—4 in (1 twin)
Guns, AA	6—40 mm (4 single, 1 twin) as frigate
A/S weapons	2 "Squid" triple barrelled depth charge mortars
Boilers	2 Admiralty 3-drum type
Main engines	Triple expansion; 2 shafts; 5 500 ihp = 19 knots max
Range, miles	9 600 at 12 knots
Oil fuel, tons	720 bunkerage capacity
Complement	140 (as frigate)

Depot ship for Fleet Diving Unit, Atlantic. Sole survivor of the 21 of this class, all built in Canada, which originally of similar design to the British "River" class frigates, including three transferred to Norway, were modernised and reconstructed to flush deckers (completed anti-submarine conversion in 1953-58). All redesignated FFE (instead of PF) in 1953. Again redesignated, DE, in 1964 and FSE in 1968.

Lauzon was declared surplus in 1963, *Buckingham*, *Fort Erie* and *Lanark* in 1965, *Cap de la Madeleine*, *Inch Arran*, *La Hulloise* and *Outremont* in 1966, *Antigonish*, *Jonquiere*, *New Glasgow*, *New Waterford*, *Ste. Theresa*, *Stettler*, *Sussexvale* and *Swansea* in 1967, and *Beacon Hill* in 1968.

TRANSFERS. *Penetang* (ex-*Rouyn*), *Prestonian* (ex-*Beauharnois*), and *Toronto* (ex-*Gifford*) were lent to Norway in 1956, being renamed *Draug*, *Troll* and *Garm* respectively, and transferred outright on 27 June 1958.

The diving depot ship *Granby*, YMT 180, originally a "Bangor" (Diesel) class fleet minesweeper (AM), redesignated coastal escort (FSE) in 1953 and clearance diving depot ship (YMT) in 1959 after having been employed as a submarine rescue vessel, was declared surplus in 1967 and replaced by the ocean escort *Victoriaville*, converted to a diving depot ship and renamed *Granby* (see previous page).

YMT 11 **YMT 12** (DIVING TENDERS)

Displacement, tons	110
Dimensions, feet	88 × 20 × 4·8 mean
Main engines	GM diesels; 228 bhp = 10·75 knots

YMT 11 was completed in Jan 1962 and YMT 12 on 7 Aug 1963, both by Ferguson Industries Ltd, Picton, Nova Scotia. They can dive four men at a time to a depth of 250 feet and are fitted with a recompression chamber. A photograph of YMT 11 appears in the 1962-63 edition.

There are small diving tenders YMT 6, YMT 8, YMT 9 and YMT 10, 70 tons, 75 × 18·5 × 8·5 feet, 2 diesels 165 bhp. YMT 1 (46 ft) was transferred to the Naval Research Establishment as a yard craft. YMT 3 and YMT 5 were declared surplus and sold in 1963. YMT 2 and YMT 7 are 46-ft, wooden hulled single screw vessels. Two new diving tenders, YSD 1 and YSD 2, entered service in 1965.

Also torpedo recovery vessels *Nimpkish*, YMR 120, and *Songhee*, YMR 1. The yacht *Oriole*, QW 3, used for officer cadet training, has been in commission since 1953.

6 "BAY" CLASS Ex-CMS (TRAINING SHIPS)

Name	*No.*	*Builders*	*Laid down*	*Launched*	*Completed*
CHALEUR	164	Marine Industries	20 Feb 56	17 Nov 56	12 Sep 57
CHIGNECTO	160	Geo. T. Davie	25 Oct 55	26 Feb 57	1 Aug 57
COWICHAN	162	Yarrows	10 July 56	26 Feb 57	19 Dec 57
FUNDY	159	Davie Shipbuilding	7 Mar 55	14 June 56	27 Nov 56
MIRAMICHI	163	Victoria Machinery	2 Feb 56	22 Feb 57	28 Oct 57
THUNDER	161	Port Arthur	1 Sep 55	27 Oct 56	3 Oct 57

Displacement, tons	390 standard; 412 full load
Dimensions, feet	140·0 pp; 152·0 oa × 28·0 × 7·0 aft
Guns	1—40 mm AA
Main engines	2 GM V-12 diesels; 2 shafts; 2 400 bhp = 16 knots
Oil fuel, tons	52
Range, miles	4 500 at 11 knots
Complement	38 (3 officers, 35 ratings)

Extensively built of aluminium, including frames and decks. There were originally 14 vessels of this class. Named after Canadian straits and bays. Designation changed from AMC to MCB in 1954. *Chaleur*, *Chignecto*, *Cowichan* and *Miramichi* are employed as training ships. *Thunder* and *Fundy* commissioned for midshipman training in summer 1970.

TRANSFERS. *Chaleur* (144), *Chignecto* (156), *Cowichan* (147), *Fundy* (145), *Miramichi* (150), and *Thunder* (153) of this class were transferred to the French Navy in 1954; but six more of the same class with the same names were built for the Royal Canadian Navy to replace those transferred. *Comax* (146), *Gaspe* (143), *Trinity* (157), and *Ungava* (148) of this class were transferred to the Turkish Navy in 1958.

Fortune, *James Bay*, *Quinte* and *Resolute* were declared surplus in 1965. *Fortune* (renamed *Offshore*) and *James Bay* were sold commercially for oil exploration.

Miscellaneous—*continued*

4 "PORTE" CLASS (GATE VESSELS)

Name	*No.*	*Builders*	*Laid down*	*Launched*	*Completed*
PORTE DE LA REINE	184	Victory Machinery	4 Mar 51	28 Dec 51	19 Sep 52
PORTE QUEBEC	185	Burrard Dry Dock	15 Feb 51	28 Aug 51	7 Oct 52
PORTE ST. JEAN	180	Geo. T. Davie	16 May 50	21 Nov 50	4 June52
PORTE ST. LOUIS	183	Geo. T. Davie	21 Mar 51	22 July 52	28 Aug 52

Displacement, tons 429 full load
Dimensions, feet 125·5 × 26·3 × 13
Guns 1—40 mm AA
Main engines Diesel; A/C Electric; 1 shaft; 600 bhp = 11 knots
Complement 3 officers; 20 ratings

Of trawler design. Multi-purpose vessels used for operating gates in A/S booms, fleet auxiliaries, anti-submarine netlayers for entrances to defended harbours. Can be fitted for minesweeping. Designation changed from YNG to YMG in 1954. All four used during summer for training Reserves. *Port Dauphine* was taken over by the Coast Guard.

PORTE DE LA REINE *1971, Canadian Forces*

TUGS

3 "SAINT" CLASS

Name	*No.*	*Laid down*	*Launched*	*Completed*
SAINT ANTHONY	ATA 531	15 July 1954	2 Nov 1955	22 Feb 1957
SAINT CHARLES	ATA 533	28 Apr 1954	10 July 1956	7 June 1957
SAINT JOHN	ATA 535	1 Dec 1953	14 May 1956	23 Nov 1956

Displacement, tons 840 full load
Dimensions, feet 151·5 × 33 × 17
Guns 2—40 mm Bofors AA
Main engines Diesel; 1 shaft; 1 920 bhp = 14 knots

Ocean tugs. Authorised under the 1951 Programme. All built by the St. John Dry Dock Co.

SAINT JOHN *1970, Canadian Maritime Command*

3 "TON" CLASS

CLIFTON (ATA 529) **HEATHERTON** (ATA 527) **RIVERTON** (ATA 528)

Displacement, tons 462
Dimensions, feet 104 pp; 111·2 oa × 28 × 11
Main engines Dominion Sulzer diesel; 1 000 bhp = 11 knots
Complement 17

Large harbour tugs. *Clifton* was launched on 31 July 1944. A photograph of *Heatherton* appears in the 1952-53 to 1959-60 editions.

5 "GLEN" CLASS

GLENBROOK **GLENDYNE** **GLENEVIS** **GLENLIVIT II** **GLENSIDE**

Dimensions, feet 80 × 20·7 × 7·2 (aft full load)
Main engines Diesel; 300 bhp = 9 knots

Big harbour tugs. *Glenlivit II* is loaned to Halfax Department of Public Works. Hull numbers are YTB 501, 503, 502, 504 and 500, respectively. Sister tugs *Glendevon*, Y 505 and *Glendon*, Y 506 were taken out of service on 31 Mar 1964 and sold to commercial interests.

3 "WOOD" CLASS

EASTWOOD **GREENWOOD** **OAKWOOD**

Dimensions, feet 60 oa × 16 × 5 (aft full load)
Main engines 250 hp = 10 knots

Medium harbour tugs. Used as A/S Target Towing Vessels. Launched 1944. Hull numbers are YMT 550, 551 and 554 respectively. *Wildwood* was stricken from the Navy List in 1959. *Lakewood* was declared surplus in 1966.
Other medium harbour tugs are:

FT1, FT2. Employed as fire tugs, Hull numbers YMT 556 and 557 respectively. Sister fire tug FT3, YMT 558, was taken out of service on 31 Mar 1964 and transferred to Dept of Public Works, St. John's Newfoundland.

Tugs—*continued*

13 "VILLE" CLASS

ADAMSVILLE **BEAMSVILLE** **LAWRENCEVILLE** **LISTERVILLE** **LOGANVILLE** **MANNVILLE** **MARYSVILLE** **MERRICKVILLE** **OTTERVILLE** **PARKSVILLE** **PLAINSVILLE** **QUEENSVILLE** **YOUVILLE**

Dimensions, feet 40 × 10·5 × 4·8
Main engines Diesel; 1 shaft; 150 bhp

Small harbour tugs. Majority employed on towing duties at Esquimalt and Halifax: Hull numbers are YTS 582, 583, 584, 578, 589, 577, 585, 581, 590, 579, 587, 586 and 588 respectively. Sister tugs *Colville*, Y 576, and *Eckville*, Y 580, were taken out of service on 31 Mar 1964 for disposal. The small harbour tugs *Shoveller* and *Valliant* Nos YTS 591 and 575, were disposed of in 1966.

The supply vessel *Seatari* (ex-*Malahat*), AKS 514, was officially deleted from the list in 1969.

R.C.M.P. MARINE DIVISION

1 "FORT" CLASS

FORT STEELE MP 34

Displacement, tons 85
Dimensions, feet 110 wl; 118 oa × 21 × 7
Main engines Two Paxman Ventura 12 YJCM diesels; 2 shafts; Kamewa controllable pitch propellers; 2 800 bhp = over 18 knots.
Complement 16

Completed by Canadian Shipbuilding & Engineering Ltd in Nov 1958. Patrol craft on the east coast. Built of steel with aluminium superstructure. Twin rudders.

The large "Commissioner" class patrol vessel of the corvette type, *Wood*, MP 17, was transferred from the Royal Canadian Mounted Police Division to the Ministry of Transport in 1971 and renamed *Daring*, see Coast Guard on later page.

1 "BIRD" CLASS

VICTORIA MP 31

Displacement, tons 66 full load
Dimensions, feet 92 × 17 × 5·3
Main engines 2 diesels; 1 200 bhp = 14 knots
Complement 20

Victoria was built for the RCMP by Yarrows Limited, Victoria. Completed in Dec 1955. She was a steel copy of the wooden "Bird" class inshore patrol vessels built for the Navy.

VICTORIA *1971*

2 75 ft "DETACHMENT" CLASS

STAND OFF **NICHOLSON**

Displacement, tons 55
Dimensions, feet 75 oa × 17 × 6·5
Main engines 2 diesel; 1 400 bhp = 16 knots
Complement 5

Both of wood construction. Both built by Smith & Rhuland, Lunenburg NS and completed in 1967 and 1968 respectively. Intended for service on the Atlantic coast.

13 65 ft "DETACHMENT" CLASS

ACADIAN **ADVERSUS** **ALERT** **BURIN** **CAPTOR** **DETECTOR** **GANGES** **INTERCEPTOR** **MASSET** **NANAIMO** **TAHSIS** **TOFINO** **WESTVIEW**

Displacement, tons 48
Dimensions, feet 65 × 15 × 4
Main engines 1 Cummins diesel; 1 shaft; 410 bhp = 12 knots

Coastal patrol police boats built for service on the east and west coasts.

2 "TURBOJET" TYPE

LITTLE BOW II **SIDNEY**

Displacement, tons 27
Dimensions, feet 55 × 14 × 4
Main engines 2 General Motors turbojet engines; 600 bhp = 16 knots

These turbojet craft were built as an experiment and no additions are contemplated.

6 "DETACHMENT" CLASS (GREAT LAKES)

CARNDUFF II **CHILCOOT II** **CUTKNIFE II** **MOOSOMIN II** **SHAUNAVON II** **TAGISH II**

Dimensions, feet 50 × 15 × 3
Main engines 2 diesel engines; 600 bhp = over 17 knots

A class of small, fast patrol craft built for service on the Great Lakes.
There are also *Advance, Athabasca, Beaver, Fort Erie, Fort Francis II, Kenora III, Sorel* and *Valleyfield*, 26 to 36 feet in length with petrol motors, speeds up to 27 knots. Six are on the Great Lakes and four on the West Coast. In addition to these there are also the following, *Battleford, Slide Out, Dauphine, Lac La Ronge, Moose Jaw, Bruce* and *Reliance*.

CANADIAN COAST GUARD

Administration

Minister of Transport:
Hon Don Jamieson PC, MP

Deputy Minister of Transport:
Mr. O. G. Stoner, BA

Administrator, Marine Transportation Administration:
Dr. P. Camu

Director Marine Operations (Canadian Coast Guard):
Rear Admiral Anthony H. G. Storrs, DSC & Bar, CD, RCN (Ret'd)

Establishment

In January 1962 all ships owned and operated by the Federal Department of Transport with the exception of pilotage and canal craft, were amalgamated into the Canadian Coast Guard, a civilian service.

Ships

The Canadian Coast Guard comprises 150 vessels of all types (including 61 barges), of which about 60 are of watch-keeping size. They operate in Canadian waters from the Great Lakes to the northernmost reaches of the Arctic Archipelago.

There are heavy icebreakers, icebreaking ships for tending buoys and lighthouses, marine survey craft, weather-oceanographic ships, and many specialized vessels for tasks such as search and rescue, cable lifting and repair, marine research and shallow-draft operations in areas such as the Mackenzie River system and some parts of the Arctic.

The Ship Building and Heavy Equipment Branch of the Department of Defence Productions arranges for the design, construction and repair of Coast Guard ships and also provides this service for a number of other Canadian Government departments.

Principal bases for the ships are the department's 11 District offices, located at— St. John's, Newfoundland; Dartmouth, N.S.; Saint John, N.B.; Charlottetown, P.E.I.; Quebec and Sorel, Que.; Prescott and Parry Sound, Ont.; Victoria and Prince Rupert, B.C.; and at Hay River, on Great Slave Lake.

Flag

The Canadian Coast Guard has its own distinctive jack, a red maple leaf on a white ground at the hoist and two gold dolphins on a blue ground at the fly.

Canadian Coast Guard vessels have a red maple leaf on the funnel. It is now standard practice to have the funnel white with a red band at the top and the red maple leaf against the white.

Missions

The Canadian Coast Guard carries out the following missions:

1. Icebreaking and Escort. Icebreaking is carried out in the Gulf of St. Lawrence and River St. Lawrence and the Great Lakes in winter to assist shipping and fc. flood control, and in Arctic waters in summer.
2. Icebreaker-Aids to Navigation Tenders. Installation, supply and maintenance of fixed and floating aids-to-navigation in Canadian waters.
3. Organize and provide icebreaker support and some cargo vessels for the annual Northern sealift which supplies bases and settlements in the Canadian Arctic and Hudson Bay.
4. Provide and operate special patrol cutters and lifeboats for marine search and rescue.
5. Provide and operate survey and sounding vessels for the St. Lawrence River Ship Channel.
6. Provide and operate weatherships for Ocean Station "Papa" in the Pacific.
7. Provide and operate vessel for the repairing of undersea cables.
8. Provide and operate vessel for environmental research.
9. Provide and operate vessel for Marine Traffic Control on the St. Lawrence river.
10. Operate a small fleet of aircraft primarily for aids to navigation ice reconnaissance, and pollution control work.

Fleet Strength

Heavy Icebreakers	5
Medium Icebreakers	1
Medium Icebreaking aid to navigation vessels	7
Light Icebreaking aid to navigation vessels	7
Ice strengthened aid to navigation vessels	4
Aid-to-navigation tenders	12
Northern supply vessels	12
Sealift stevedore depot vessel	1
Search and Rescue—Offshore patrol cutters	6
Great Lakes patrol cutters	3
Shore-based hovercraft	1
Shore-based lifeboats	6
Shore-based launches	6
St. Lawrence light icebreaking survey and sounding vessel	1
St. Lawrence ship channel survey and sounding vessels	6
Weather ships for ocean station Papa in the Pacific	2
Cable repair ship	1
Environmental research vessel	1
St. Lawrence River marine traffic control vessel	1
Training vessels	2
Total	85

Aircraft

Fixed wing	1
Helicopters	28

WEATHER SHIPS

Name	*Laid down*	*Launched*	*Completed*
QUADRA	Feb 1965	4 July 1966	Mar 1967
VANCOUVER	Mar 1964	29 June 1965	4 July 1966

Displacement, tons	5 600 full load
Dimensions, feet	361·2 pp; 404·2 oa × 50 × 17·5
Aircraft	1 helicopter
Main engines	Turbo-electric; 2 shafts; 7 500 shp = 18 knots
Boilers	2 automatic Babcock & Wilcox D type
Range, miles	8 400 at 14 knots
Complement	96

New type, turbo-electric twin screw weather and oceanographic vessels for Pacific Ocean service. Both built by Burrard Drydock Limited, North Vancouver, B.C. They replace the Coast Guard weather ships, former frigates, which have been in service for many years, on loan from the Royal Canadian Navy, for Ocean Station "Papa" 900 miles west of the British Columbia coast. They have bow water jet reaction system to assist steering at slow speeds. Flume stabilization systems are fitted. They are turbo-electric powered, with oil-fired boilers to provide the quiet operation needed for vessels housing much scientific equipment. Their complement includes 15 technical officers such as meteorologists, oceanographers and electronics technicians.

The three former "River" class frigates, *St. Catherines, Stonetown* and *St Stephen,* acquired by the Department of Transport from the Royal Canadian Navy and converted into weather ships in 1950, were taken out of service in 1968 and sold in 1969.

VANCOUVER — *1970, Canadian Coast Guard, Official*

JOHN CABOT

Displacement, tons	6 375 full load
Dimensions, feet	313·3 × 60 × 21·5
Aircraft	1 helicopter
Main engines	Diesel-electric; 2 shafts; 9 000 shp = 15 knots
Range, miles	10 000 at 12 knots
Complement	85 officers and men

Combination cable repair ship and icebreaker. Built by Canadian Vickers Limited, Montreal. Laid down in May 1963, launched on 15 Apr 1964 and completed in July 1965. Designed to repair and lay cable over the bow only. For use in East Coast and Arctic waters. Bow water jet reaction manoeuvring system, heeling tanks and Flume stabilisation system. Three circular storage holds handle a total of 400 miles of submarine cable. Personnel include technicians and helicopter pilots.

JOHN CABOT — *1970, Canadian Coast Guard*

NORTHERN SUPPLY VESSELS

2 FORMER TANK LANDING CRAFT (LCT 8s)

EIDER **SKUA**

Measurement, tons	1 083 to 1 104 gross
Dimensions, feet	225 pp; 231·2 oa × 38 × 3
Main engines	Diesel; 1 000 shp = 9 knots

Converted LCT (8)s, acquired from Great Britain in 1957-61. Built by Harland & Wolff, Belfast (*Puffin* and *Raven*) and Sir Wm. Arrol & Co Ltd, Glasgow (*Eider*). All completed in 1946.
Of sister ships, *Nanook*, officially rated as a Northern Service Depot Ship, was disposed of in 1969, *Auk* and *Gannet* were declared for disposal in 1970, *Raven* put on the disposal list in 1971 and *Puffin* in 1972.

SKUA *Canadian Coast Guard*

2 FORMER TANK LANDING CRAFT (LCT 4s)

MARMOT **MINK**

Displacement, tons	586 full load
Dimensions, feet	187·2 × 33·8 × 4
Main engines	Diesel; 920 shp = 8 knots

Converted LCT (4)s acquired from Great Britain in 1958. Completed in 1944. Formerly officially rated as Steel Landing Craft for Northern Service, now re-rated as Aids to Navigation Tenders, in reserve.

MINK *1963, Canadian Coast Guard*

ICEBREAKERS

NORMAN MCLEOD ROGERS

Displacement, tons	6 320 full load
Dimensions, feet	295 oa × 62·5 × 20
Aircraft	1 helicopter
Landing craft	2
Main engines	4 diesels and 2 gas turbines powering 2 electric motors; 2 shafts; 12 000 shp = 15 knots
Complement	55

A new type of icebreaker for use in the Gulf of St Lawrence and East Coast waters. Built at the yard of Canadian Vickers Limited, Montreal. This is the world's first application of gas turbine electric propulsion for booster power in an icebreaker. Completed in Oct 1969. Officially rated as a Heavy Icebreaker.

NORMAN MCLEOD ROGERS *1970, Canadian Coast Guard*

LOUIS S. ST. LAURENT

Displacement, tons	13 000 full load
Dimensions, feet	366·5 oa × 80 × 31
Aircraft	2 helicopters
Main engines	Turbo-electric; 3 shafts; 24 000 shp = 17·75 knots *trials*
Range, miles	16 000 miles at 13 knots cruising speed
Complement	Total accommodation for 216

Icebreakers—*continued*

This new icebreaker for service in the Arctic and the Gulf of St. Lawrence was built at Canadian Vickers Limited, Montreal. She is larger than any of the former Coast Guard icebreakers. This triple screw ship with a steam turbo-electric propulsion system is the world's most powerful non-nuclear powered icebreaker. She has a helicopter hangar below the flight deck, with an elevator to raise the two helicopters to the deck when required. She was launched on 3 Dec 1966 and completed in Oct 1969. She is officially rated as a heavy icebreaker.

LOUIS S. ST. LAURENT *1971, Canadian Coast Guard*

JOHN A. MACDONALD

Displacement, tons	9 160 full load
Measurement, tons	6 186 gross
Dimensions, feet	315 × 70 × 28
Main engines	Diesel-electric; 15 000 shp = 15·5 knots designed

Completed by Davie Shipbuilding Limited, Lauzon Port Quebec, in Sep 1960. Officially rated as a heavy icebreaker.

DISPOSAL
The old icebreaker *Saurel* was removed from the Canadian Coast Guard list and disposed of in 1967.

JOHN A. MACDONALD *1971, Canadian Coast Guard*

MONTCALM **WOLFE**

Displacement, tons	3 005 full load
Measurement, tons	2 022 gross
Dimensions, feet	220 × 48 × 16
Main engines	Steam reciprocating; 4 000 ihp = 13 knots designed

Wolfe was built by Canadian Vickers Limited, Montreal, and completed in Nov 1959, *Montcalm* was built by Davie Shipbuilding Ltd, Lauzon, P.Q., and completed in June 1957. Officially rated as Medium Icebreaking Aids to Navigation Vessels.

MONTCALM ***1972, Canadian Coast Guard***

Icebreakers—*continued*

CAMSELL

Displacement, tons	3 072 full load
Measurement, tons	2 020 gross
Dimensions, feet	223·5 × 48 × 16
Main engines	Diesel-electric; 4 250 shp = 13 knots designed

Completed by Burrard Dry Dock Company Limited, Vancouver, BC in Oct 1959. Officially rated as Medium Icebreaking Aids to Navigation Vessel.

CAMSELL *1972, Canadian Coast Guard*

SIR HUMPHREY GILBERT

Displacement, tons	3 000 full load
Measurement, tons	1 930 gross
Dimensions, feet	220 × 48 × 16·3
Main engines	Diesel-electric; 4 250 shp = 13 knots designed

Completed by Davie Shipbuilding Limited, Lauzon, Port Quebec, in June 1959. Officially rated as Medium Icebreaking Aids to Navigation Vessel.

SIR HUMPHREY GILBERT *1970, Canadian Coast Guard*

.ABRADOR

Displacement, tons	6 490 full load
Measurement, tons	3 823 gross
Dimensions, feet	269·0 pp; 290·0 oa × 63·5 × 29·0
Aircraft	Provision for 2 helicopters
Main engines	Diesel-electric; 10 000 shp = 16 knots designed

Built by Marine Industries Limited, Sorel, Quebec. Ordered in Feb 1949, laid down on 18 Nov 1949, launched on 14 Dec 1951 and completed for the Royal Canadian Navy on 8 July 1954, but transferred to the Department of Transport in Feb 1958. Officially rated as a Heavy Icebreaker. She was the first naval vessel to traverse the North West passage and circumnavigate North America, when she was Canada's largest and most modern icebreaker. High-tensile steel sides 1·6 inches thick and heeling tanks. Aircraft hanger and flight deck aft for operating helicopters. Carries two landing craft strengthened to resist ice. Latest navigational devices, and equipped with instruments for hydrography, oceanography, meteorology, cosmic ray research, ice reconnaissance and other scientific purposes. Fitted with Denny Brown stabilisers. Propelling machinery can be controlled from bridge. She was transferred, on loan to the Department of Transport and subsequently acquired from the Royal Canadian Navy outright. Mounting for two 40 mm guns forward, but guns were removed.

LABRADOR *1970, Canadian Coast Guard*

d'IBERVILLE

Displacement, tons	9 930 full load
Measurement, tons	5 678 gross
Dimensions, feet	310 × 66·5 × 30·2
Main engines	Steam reciprocating; 10 800 ihp = 15 knots designed

Completed by Davie Shipbuilding Limited Lauzon, Port Quebec, in May 1953. Officially rated as a Heavy Icebreaker.

d'IBERVILLE *1972, Canadian Coast Guard*

ERNEST LAPOINTE

Displacement, tons	1 675 full load
Measurement, tons	1 179 gross
Dimensions, feet	184 × 36 × 15·5
Main engines	Steam reciprocating; 2 000 iph = 13 knots designed

Completed by Davie Shipbuilding Limited, Lauzon, Port Quebec in Feb 1941. Officially rated as St. Lawrence Ship Channel Icebreaking Survey and Sounding Vessel.

ERNEST LAPOINTE *1971, Canadian Coast Guard*

N. B. McLEAN

Displacement, tons	5 034 full load
Measurement, tons	3 254 gross
Dimensions, feet	277 × 60·5 × 19·6
Main engines	Steam reciprocating; 6 500 ihp = 13 knots max

Completed by Halifax Shipyards Limited, Halifax, NS, in 1930. Officially rated as Medium Icebreaker.

GRIFFON

Displacement, tons	3 096
Dimensions, feet	234 × 49 × 15·5
Main engines	Diesel; 4 000 bhp; 13·5 knots designed

Completed in Dec 1970. Officially rated as a Medium Icebreaking Aid to Navigation Vessel.

J. E. BERNIER

Displacement, tons	3 096
Dimensions, feet	231 × 49 × 16
Aircraft	1 helicopter
Main engines	Diesel Electric; 4 250 bhp = 13·5 knots (trial speed)

Built by Davie Shipbuilding Co. Ltd, Lauzon, Quebec; completed in Aug 1967. Officially rated as Medium Icebreaking Aid to Navigation Vessel.

J. E. BERNIER *1971, Canadian Coast Guard*

Icebreakers—*continued*

SIMCOE

Displacement, tons 1 300 full load
Dimensions, feet 179·5 × 38 × 12
Main engines Diesel-electric; 2 000 shp = 12 knots

Completed by Canadian Vickers in 1962. Officially rated as Ice Strengthened Aid to Navigation Vessel.

SIMON FRASER **TUPPER**

Displacement, tons 1 876 full load
Measurements, tons 1 357 gross
Dimensions, feet 204·5 × 42 × 14
Main engines Diesel-electric; 2 900 shp = 13·5 knots designed

Simon Fraser was completed by Burrard Dry Dock Company Limited, N. Vancouver in Feb 1960 and *Tupper* by Marine Industries Limited, Sorel, Quebec in Dec 1959. Both officially rated as Light Icebreaking Aid to Navigation Vessels.

THOMAS CARLETON

Displacement, tons 1 532 full load
Dimensions, feet 180 × 42 × 13
Main engines Diesel; 2 000 bhp = 12 knots designed

Built by Saint John Dry Dock Limited Saint John, NB. Completed in 1960. Officially rated as a light Icebreaking Aid to Navigation Vessel.

THOMAS CARLETON *1970, Canadian Coast Guard*

ALEXANDER HENRY

Displacement, tons 2 497 full load
Measurements, tons 1 647 gross
Dimensions, feet 210 × 43·5 × 16
Main engines Diesel; 3 550 bhp = 13 knots designed

Built by Port Arthur Shipbuilding Limited, Port Arthur. Completed in July 1959. Officially rated as a Medium Icebreaking Aid to Navigation Vessel.

SIR WILLIAM ALEXANDER

Displacement, tons 3 555 full load
Measurements, tons 2 153 gross
Dimensions, feet 227·5 × 45 × 17·5
Main engines Diesel electric; 4 250 shp = 15 knots designed

Built by Halifax Shipyards, Limited, Halifax. Completed in June 1959. Equipped with Flume Stabilisation System. Officially rated as a Medium Icebreaking Aid to Navigation Vessel.

SIR WILLIAM ALEXANDER *1970, Canadian Coast Guard*

WALTER E. FOSTER

Displacement, tons 2 715 full load
Measurement, tons 1 672 gross
Dimensions, feet 229·2 × 42·5 × 16
Main engines Steam reciprocating; 2 000 ihp = 12·5 knots designed

WALTER E. FOSTER *1970, Canadian Coast Guard,*

Built by Canadian Vickers, Limited, Montreal. Completed in Dec 1954. Officially rated as a Light Icebreaking Aid to Navigation Vessel.

EDWARD CORNWALLIS

Displacement, tons 3 700 full load
Measurement, tons 1 965 gross
Dimensions, feet 259 × 43·5 × 18
Main engines Steam reciprocating; 2 800 ihp = 13·5 knots designed

Built by Canadian Vickers Limited, Montreal. Completed in Dec 1949. Photograph in the 1963-64 to 1965-66 editions. In reserve. Officially rated as a Light Icebreaking Aid to Navigation Vessel.

DISPOSAL
The Arctic Service Vessel *C. D. Howe* was officially deleted from the Coast Guard List in 1969.

EDWARD CORNWALLIS *1971, Canadian Coast Guard*

DEPOT SHIP

NARWHAL

Measurement, tons 2 064 gross
Dimensions, feet 251·5 × 42·0 × 12·0
Main engines Diesel; 2 000 bhp
Complement 32

Built by Canadian Vickers, Montreal. Completed in July 1963. Officially rated as Sealift Stevedore Depot Vessel. Cruising range: 9 200 miles.

NARWHAL *1970, Canadian Coast Guard*

SEARCH AND RESCUE CUTTERS

ALERT

Displacement, tons 2 025
Dimensions, feet 234·3 × 39·9 × 15·1
Aircraft 1 helicopter
Main engines Diesel Electric; 7 716 hp = 18·75 knots
Range, miles 6 000

Ordered from Davie Shipbuilding Ltd Lauzon Feb 1967. For offshore duties.

ALERT *1971, Canadian Coast Guard*

DARING (ex-*Wood*, ex-MP 17)

Displacement, tons 600 standard
Dimensions, feet 178 oa × 29 × 9·2
Main engines 2 Fairbanks- Morse diesels; 2 shafts; 2 660 bhp = 16 knots
Complement 60 as RCMP vessel

Corvette type. Built by Geo. T. Davie and Sons Ltd Lauzon, Levis, Quebec. Completed in July 1958. Used for patrol on the east coast of Canada, this ship is built of steel, strengthened against ice, with aluminium superstructure. Transferred from the Royal Canadian Mounted Police Marine Division to the Ministry of Transport in 1971, and renamed *Daring*.

DARING (ex-*Wood*) *1966, Director of Marine Services*

Search, Rescue Cutter—*continued*

RACER **RALLY** **RAPID** **READY** **RELAY** **RIDER**

Measurement, tons 153 gross
Dimensions, feet 95·2 × 20 × 6·5
Main engines Diesel; 2 400 bhp = 20 knots designed

Built by Yarrows Ltd, Esquimalt, BC; Davie Shipbuilding Ltd, Lauzon, PQ; Ferguson Industries, Picton, NS; Burrard Dry Dock, Vancouver; and Kingston Shipyard, respectively. All completed in 1963. *Rider*, completed for the Dept of Fisheries, was taken over by the Coast Guard in Mar 1969. *Rapid* was placed in reserve in 1970

RAPID *Maurice Crosby, 1971*

SPINDRIFT **SPRAY** **SPUME**

Measurement, tons 57 gross
Dimensions, feet 70 × 16·8 × 4·7
Main engines 2 diesels; 1 500 bhp = 19 knots designed

Built by Cliff Richardson Boats Ltd. Meaford, Ont; J. J. Taylor & Sons, Ltd, Toronto; and Grew Ltd, Penetanguishene, Ont, respectively. Completed in 1963-64 for service on Great Lakes Patrol.

SPINDRIFT *1966, Canadian Coast Guard, Official*

SUPPLY VESSELS

BARTLETT **PROVO WALLIS**

Displacement, tons 1 620
Dimensions, feet 189·3 × 42·5 × 12·5
Engines Diesel; 1 760 bhp = 12 knots

In service since 1970. Classed as Ice Strengthened Aid to Navigation Vessels.

BARTLETT *1971, Canadian Coast Guard*

MONTMORENCY

Displacement, tons 1 006 full load
Measurement, tons 750 gross
Dimensions, feet 163 × 34 × 11
Main engines Diesel; 1 200 bhp

Built by Davie Shipbuilding Limited, Lauzon, Port Quebec. Completed in Aug 1957. Officially rated as an Ice Strengthened Aid to Navigation Vessel.

MONTMAGNY

Displacement, tons 565 full load
Dimensions, feet 148·0 × 29·0 × 8·0
Main engines Diesels; 1 000 bhp

Built by Russel Bros. Owen Sound, Ont. Completed in May 1963.

MONTMAGNY *1970, Canadian Coast Guard*

Supply Vessels—*continued*

VERENDRYE

Displacement, tons 400 full load
Dimensions, feet 125·0 × 26·0 × 7·0
Main engines Diesels; 760 bhp

Built by Geo. T. Davie & Sons.Ltd, Lauzon. Completed in Oct 1959.

ALEXANDER MACKENZIE **SIR JAMES DOUGLAS**

Displacement, tons 720 full load
Dimensions, feet 150·0 × 30·0 × 10·3
Main engines Diesels; 1 000 bhp

564 tons gross. Built by Burrard Dry Dock Vancouver and completed 1950 and Nov 1956 respectively. These two, and *Montmagny* and *Verendrye*, are officially rated as Aid to Navigation Tenders.

SIR JAMES DOUGLAS *1970, Canadian Coast Guard*

SURVEY AND SOUNDING VESSELS

VILLE MARIE

Displacement, tons 493 full load
Dimensions, feet 134·0 × 28·0 × 9·5
Main engines Diesel electric; 1 000 hp

BEAUFORT

Displacement, tons 767 full load
Dimensions, feet 167·5 × 24·0 × 9·0
Main engines Diesels; 1 280 bhp

NICOLET

Displacement, tons 935 full load
Dimensions, feet 166·5 × 35·0 × 9·6
Main engines Diesels; 1 350 bhp

DETECTOR

Displacement, tons 584 full load
Dimensions feet 140·0 × 35·0 × 10·0
Main engines Steam reciprocating

Beaufort and *Ville Marie* were completed in 1960. There are also two smaller vessels *Glenada* and *Jean Bourdon* for the St. Lawrence Ship Channel.

ENVIRONMENTAL RESEARCH VESSEL

PORTE DAUPHINE

Displacement, tons 447
Dimensions, feet 119·3 × 25 × 11·3
Main engines Diesel; 1 shaft; 600 bhp = 12·5 knots

Former gate vessel of the "Porte" class in the Royal Canadian Navy, taken over in 1958.

PORTE DAUPHINE *1970, Canadian Coast Guard*

DUMIT **ECKALOO** **MISKANAW** **TEMBAH**

Four vessels to assist navigation in Mackenzie River operations. Small tug/buoy tender type.

MALLARD **MOORHEN**

Shore based craft: For search and rescue and patrol duties: Six lifeboats (CG 101-106), six launches (*Mallard, Moorhen*, CG 110-113) and one Hovercraft (CG 021).

DISPOSALS

Supply vessels: *Estevan* was for disposal in 1970. *Brant* deleted from list in 1967 and *Chesterfield* in 1968, *Grenville* sank in St. Lawrence River in Dec 1968 due to ice action.

CEYLON *(Sri Lanka)*

Administration

The Royal Ceylon Navy was formed on 9 Dec 1950 when the Navy Act was proclaimed.

Captain of the Navy:
Commodore D. V. Hunter

Diplomatic Representation

Services Attaché in London:
Withdrawn from 1 November 1970

Naval Base

The Naval Base is established at Trincomalee, which was a British base from 1795 until 1957.

Strength of the Fleet

1 Frigate	27 Patrol boats
5 Fast Gunboats	1 Tug
1 Hydrofoil Craft	

Personnel

1973: 2 000 (160 officers and 1 840 sailors)

Mercantile Marine

1973: Lloyds' Register of Shipping:
28 vessels of 13 107 tons gross

Defence Expenditure and Policy

Since the Indo-Pakistan war visits by US, British and Russian ships have taken place. It is reported that Defence spending has been doubled and that "20 small police and gunboats" have been acquired.

FRIGATES

1 Ex-CANADIAN "RIVER" CLASS

Name	*No.*	*Builders*	*Launched*
GAJABAHU (ex-*Misnak*, ex-HMCS *Hallowell*)	F 232	Canadian Vickers Ltd, Montreal	8 Aug 1944

Displacement, tons: 1 445 standard; 2 360 full load
Lenght, feet (*metres*): 283 (*86·3*) pp; 295·5 (*90·1*) wl; 310·5 (*91·9*) oa
Beam, feet (*metres*): 36·5 (*11·1*)
Draught, feet (*metres*): 13·8 (*4·2*)
Guns, surface: 1—4 in (*102 mm*)
Guns, AA: 3—40 mm
Boilers: 2 three-drum type
Main engines: Triple expansion; 5 500 ihp; 2 shafts
Speed, knots: 20
Range, miles: 4 200 at 12 knots
Oil fuel, tons: 585
Complement: 160

GENERAL
Acquired by Israel in 1950 and sold by Israel to Ceylon in 1959. Guns above replaced 3—4·7 inch, 8—20 mm in 1965. Reportedly now non-operational. Sister ship *Mahasena* (ex-*Mivtakh*, ex-Canadian *Violetta*, ex-HMCS *Orkney*) was sold early in June 1964 to a Hong Kong shipbreaker.

GAJABAHU — *1971, Royal Ceylon Navy*

5 Ex-CHINESE SHANGHAI IV CLASS

Displacement, tons: 120 full load
Dimensions, feet: 130 × 18 × 5·6
Guns: 4—37 mm (2 twin)
4—25 mm (2 twin abaft the bridge) 1—small mortar forward
Main engines: 4 Diesels; 5 000 bhp = 30 knots
Complement: 25

B *Class*

GENERAL
The first pair was transferred by China in Feb 1972, the remainder over the next few months. In monsoonal conditions off the Ceylonese coast these boats will be lively and uncomfortable.

PATROL BOATS

21 THORNYCROFT TYPE

Displacement, tons: 15
Dimensions, feet: 45·5 × 12 × 3
Main engines: 2 boats: Thornycroft K6SMI engines; 500 bhp = 25 knots
7 boats: General Motors 6 71-Series; 560 bhp = 25 knots

GENERAL
Fast twin screw motor launches built by Thornycroft (Malasyia) Limited in Singapore The hulls are of hard chine type with double skin teak planking. Equipped with radar, radio, searchlight etc. Two ordered in 1965 and completed in 1966. Seven ordered in 1966 and completed in 1967. 12 more assembled in Ceylon and completed by Sep 1968.

PC 102 — *1970, Royal Ceylon Navy*

HANSAYA LIHINIYA

HANSAYA — *1971, Royal Ceylon Navy*

Displacement, tons: 36
Dimensions, feet: 63·5 pp; 66 oa × 14 × 4
Main engines: 3 General Motors diesels; 450 bhp = 16 knots

"Hansaya" class long patrol boats built at Venice by the Korody Marine Corporation.

DIYAKAWA KORAWAKKA SERUWA TARAWA

Displacement, tons: 13
Dimensions, feet: 46 pp; 48 oa × 12 × 3
Main engines: 2 Foden FD.6 diesels; 240 bhp = 15 knots

Diyakawa and *Korawakka* were rated as harbour launches in June 1970. *Seruwa* and *Tarawa* were rated as hydrographic vessels.

SERUWA — *1971, Royal Ceylon Navy*

1 SHORT HYDROFOIL TYPE

Dimensions, feet: 22·2 × 9·9 hull; 10·2 oa. Depth over side moulded; 3; Draught at anchor, 3·7, Draught at speed, 1·7 official figures.
Main engines: 2 Volvo Penta Aquamatic 100 hp engines. Total 200 hp = 40 knots

A short type of hydrofoil craft added to the Royal Ceylon Navy List in 1964.

Patrol Boats—*continued*

HYDROFOIL CRAFT *1964, Royal Ceylon Navy*

TUG

ALIYA (ex-*Adept*, ex-*Empire Barbara*)

Displacement, tons	503 full load
Dimensions, feet	105 × 26·5 × 12·8
Main engines	Triple expansion; 850 ihp = 10 knots

Built by Cochrane & Sons Ltd., Selby, Yorks, England. Transferred from Great Britain Decommisioned in 1964 to be sold, but this intention was rescinded. She was re-commisioned in 1966, and underwent major refit in 1967.

ESCORT MINESWEEPERS. *Parakrama* (ex-HMS *Pickle*) was sold in June 1964 to a Hong Kong scrapyard and *Vijaya* (ex-HMS *Flyingfish*, ex-*Tillsonburg*) was returned to Britain.

SEAWARD DEFENCE BOAT. *Kotiya* (ex-HMS *Doxford*) sank in Trincomalee Harbour during the cyclone of 22 Dec 1964, and was disposed of after salvaging.

BOOM DEFENCE VESSEL. *Baron* was purchased from Great Britain by the Colombo Port Commission.

CHILE

Administration

Minister of National Defence:
Sr José Tohá

Commander-in-Chief of the Navy
Admiral Raul Montero Cornejo

Chief of the Naval Staff:
Rear-Admiral Hugo Cabezas

New Construction

Two submarines of the British "Oberon" class.
Two frigates of the British "Leander" class.

Disposals

Destroyers (Thornycroft Serrano class)
1958 *Aldea, Videla*
1963 *Hyatt, Orella, Riquelsne, Serrano*

Diplomatic Representation

Chief of the Chilean Naval mission in Great Britain and Naval Attaché in London, Paris, The Hague and Stockholm:
Rear Admiral Oscar Buzeta

Chief of the Chilean Naval Mission in USA and Naval Attaché in Washington:
Rear-Admiral Luis Eberhard

Personnel

1972: 20 000 (1 200 officers, 18 300 ratings,500 marines
1973: 22 000 (1 300 officers, 18 500 ratings, 2 200 marines)

Frigates (Canadian River Class)
1963 *Buquedano, Iquique*
1968 *Covadonga*

Corvettes (Canadian Flower Class)
1967 *Papudo*
1969 *Casma, Chipana*

Strength of the Fleet

3 Cruisers
4 Destroyers
4 Frigates & 2 Building
2 Patrol Submarines & 2 Building
1 Tank Landing Ship
4 Landing Craft
4 Torpedo Boats
6 Patrol Vessels
1 Survey Ship
11 Support Ships and Service Craft

Mercantile Marine

Lloyd's Register of Shipping
134 vessels of 382 013 tons gross

Transports
1968 *Presidente Pinto* to harbour duties, *Angamos* deleted

Tugs
1968 *Contramaeste Breto* lost
Huemul

CRUISERS

	No.	Builders	Laid down	Launched	Completed
LATORRE (ex-*Göta Lejon*)	CL 04	Eriksberg Mekaniska Verkstad, Göteborg	27 Sep 1943	17 Nov 1945	15 Dec 1947

1 "TRE KRONOR" CLASS

Displacement, tons	8 200 standard; 9 200 full load
Length, feet (*metres*)	590·5 (*180·0*) wl; 597 (*182·0*) oa
Beam, feet (*metres*)	54 (*16·5*)
Draught, feet (*metres*)	21·5 (*6·6*) max
Guns, surface	7—6 in (*150 mm*) 53 cal.
Guns, AA	4—57 mm; 11—40 mm
Tubes	6—21 inch
Armour	3 in—5 in (*75—125 mm*)
Boilers	4 Swedish 4-drum type
Main engines	2 sets De Laval geared turbines; 100 000 shp; 2 shafts
Speed, knots	33 designed
Complement	610

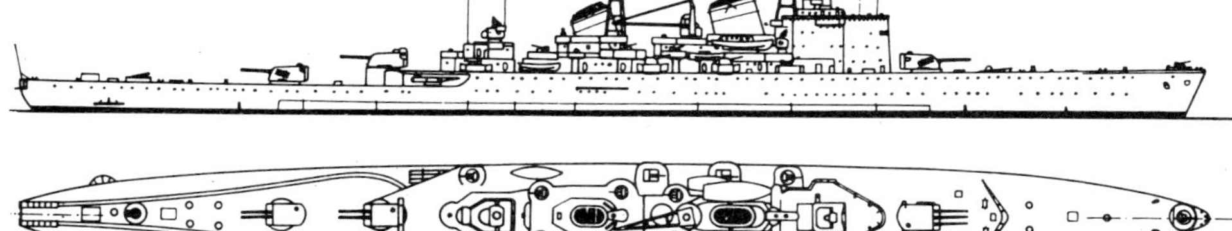

GENERAL
Radar control arrangements were installed for 6-inch guns. Fitted for minelaying with a capacity of 120 mines. Reconstructed in 1951-52, modernised in 1958, with new radar, 57 mm guns etc. Sister ship *Tre Kronor* was paid off in Sweden on 1 Jan 1964.

RADAR. Search: LWO 3, Type 227. Tactical: Type 293. Fire Control: X band.

GUNNERY. The 6 inch guns are high angle automatic anti-aircraft weapons with an elevation of 70 degrees. The 9—25 mm AA formerly mounted were suppressed in 1951 and 7—40 mm AA added.

TRANSFER. The purchase by Chile of the Swedish cruiser *Göta Lejon* was announced on 15 July 1971.

DRAWING. Starboard elevation and plan. Redrawn in 1970. Scale 125 feet = 1 inch (1 : 1 500).

APPEARANCE. Light tripod masts have been stepped as shown in photo. Enclosed tower bridge structure.

LATOIRE *1973, Chilean Navy*

Cruisers—*continued*

Name	*No.*	*Builders*	*Laid down*	*Launched*	*Completed*
O'HIGGINS (ex-USS *Brooklyn*, CL 40)	CL 02	New York Navy Yard	12 Mar 1935	30 Nov 1936	18 July 1938
PRAT (ex-USS *Nashville*, CL 43)	CL 03	New York S.B. Corp.	24 Jan 1935	2 Oct 1937	25 Nov 1938

2 "PRAT" CLASS
Ex-US "BROOKLYN" CLASS

Displacement, tons
O'Higgins 9 700 standard; 13 000 full load
Prat 10 000 standard; 13 500 full load
Length, feet (*metres*) 608·3 (*185·4*) oa
Beam, feet (*metres*) 69 (*21·0*)
Draught, feet (*metres*) 24 (*7·3*) max
Aircraft 1 Bell helicopter (see *Hangar*)
Guns, surface 15—6 in (*153 mm*) 47 cal (5 triple); 8—5 in (*127 mm*) 25 cal (single)
Guns, AA 28—40 mm; 24—20 mm
Armour, inches (*mm*) Belt 4 in—1½ in (*102—38*); Decks 3 in+2 in (*76+51*); Turrets 5 in—3 in (*127—76*); C.T. 8 in (*203*)
Boilers 8 Babcock & Wilcox Express type
Main engines Westinghouse geared turbines 100 000 shp; 4 shafts
Speed, knots 32·5
Range, miles 14 500 at 15 knots
Oil fuel (tons) 2 100
Complement 888 to 975 (peace)

Former "light" cruisers of the US "Brooklyn" Class. Purchased from the United States in 1951 at a price representing 10 per cent of their original cost ($37 000 000) plus the expense of reconditioning them.

HANGER. The hanger in the hull right aft could accommodate 6 aircraft if necessary together with engine spares and duplicate parts, though 4 aircraft was the normal capacity. Above the hanger two catapults were mounted as far outboard as possible, and a revolving crane was placed at the stern extremity overhanging the aircraft hatch.

RADAR
Search: SPS 12. Tactical: SPS 10.

DRAWING. Starboard elevation and plan. Drawn in 1971. Scale: 125 feet = 1 inch (1 : 1 500).

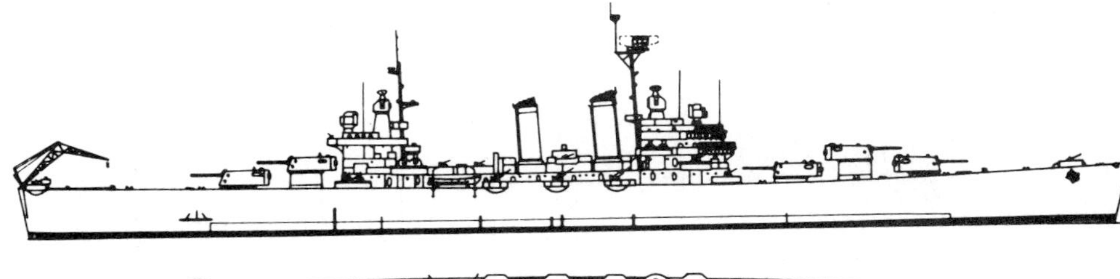

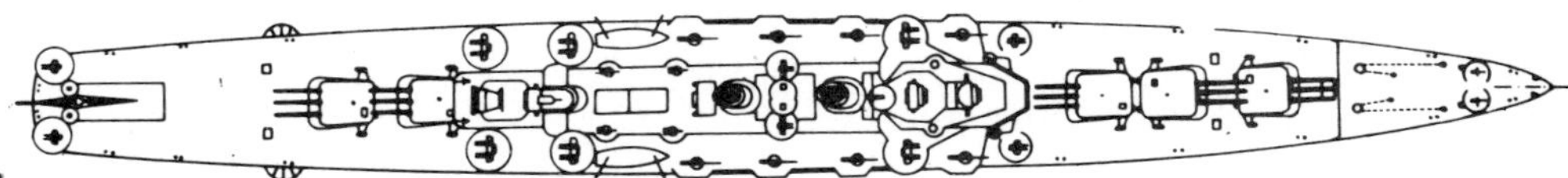

PRAT *1971, Chilean Navy,*

DESTROYERS

Name	*No.*	*Builders*	*Laid down*	*Launched*	*Completed*
RIVEROS	DD 18	Vickers-Armstrongs Ltd, Barrow	12 Apr 1957	12 Dec 1958	31 Dec 1960
WILLIAMS	DD 19	Vickers-Armstrongs Ltd, Barrow	20 June 1956	5 May 1958	26 Mar 1960

2 "ALMIRANTE" CLASS

Displacement, tons 2 730 standard; 3 300 full load
Length, feet (*metres*) 402 (*122·5*) oa
Beam, feet (*metres*) 43 (*13·1*)
Draught, feet (*metres*) 13·3 (*4·0*)
Missiles, AA 4 Exocet Launchers; Quadruple launcher for "Seacat"
Guns, AA 4—4 in (*102 mm*); 6—40 mm
A/S 2 Squid 3-barrelled DC mortars
Torpedo tubes 5—21 in (*533 mm*) quintupled
Boilers 2 Babcock & Wilcox
Main engines Parsons Pametrada geared turbine 54 000 shp; 2 shafts
Speed, knots 34·5
Range, miles 6 000 at 16 knots
Complement 266

GENERAL
Ordered in May 1955. Layout and general arrangements are conventional. Bunks fitted for entire crew. Both modernised by Swan Hunter, *Williams* in 1971 and *Riveros* in 1972.

ELECTRICAL. The electrical system is on alternating current. Galleys are all electric. There is widespread use of fluorescent lighting. Degaussing cables are fitted.

RADAR. Plessey AWSI and Target Indication radar with A10 autonomous displays being fitted at refits.

MISSILES. British "Seacat" radar controlled short range surface-to-air weapon installations were fitted at the Chilean Navy Yard at Talcahuano in 1964. Exocet fitted during 1971-72 modernisations.

GUNNERY. The four inch guns are disposed in four single mountings, two superimposed forward and two aft. They are automatic with a range of 12 500 yards (11 400 metres) and an elevation of 75 degrees.

WILLIAMS *1972, Wright & Logan*

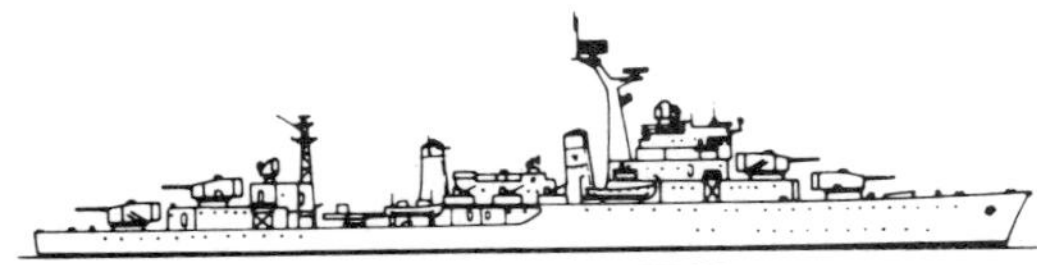

WILLIAMS, RIVEROS

OPERATIONAL. The operations room and similar spaces are air-conditioned. Twin rudders for exceptional manoeuvrability. Ventilation and heating systems designed to suit the Chilean coastline, extending from the tropics to Cape Horn. Latest type of warship radar fitted, specially developed to work in conjunction with new fire control systems developed by Vickers-Armstrongs.

RIVEROS *1971, Chilean Navy,*

Destroyers—*continued*

2 Ex-US "FLETCHER" CLASS

BLANCO ENCALADA (ex-USS *Wadleigh* DD 689)
COCHRANE (ex-USS *Rooks*, DD 804)

No.	*Builder*	*Launched*	*Completed*
DD 14	Bath Iron Works Corpn. Bath	7 Aug 1943	19 Oct 1943
DD 15	Todd Pacific Shipyards	6 June 1944	2 Sep 1944

Displacement, tons	2 100 standard; 2 750 full load
Length, feet (*metres*)	376·5 (110·5) oa
Beam, feet (*metres*)	39·5 (12·0)
Draught, feet (*metres*)	18 (5·5) max
Guns, dual purpose	4—5 in (127 *mm*) 38 cal.
Guns, AA	6—3 in (*76 mm*) 50 cal.
Torpedo tubes	5—21 in (quintupled)
A/S	2 Hedgehogs; 2 side launching torpedo racks; 1 DC rack; 6 "K" DCT
Boilers	4 Babcock & Wilcox
Main engines	2 GE geared turbines 60 000 shp ; 2 shafts
Range, miles	5 000 at 15 knots; 1 260 at 30 knots
Oil fuel (tons)	650
Speed, knots	35
Complement	250 (14 officers, 236 men). Accommodation for 324 (24 officers, 300 men)

COCHRANE *1972, Chilean Navy,*

BLANCO ENCALADA, COCHRANE

GENERAL

Former United States destroyers of the "Fletcher" class. Transferred to Chile under the Military Aid Program in 1963. Three more destroyers were scheduled for transfer from the United States Navy to the Chilean Navy under a new transfer law signed by the President of the United States in 1966. The ships were to have been refitted and modernised and adapted to Chilean requirements before transfer to the new flag, but the four Frigates of the "Serrano" class were transferred instead.

RADAR. Search: SPS 6. Tactical: SPS 10. Fire Control: X Band.

FRIGATES

2 NEW CONSTRUCTION BRITISH "LEANDER" CLASS

CONDELL PF 06 **LYNCH** PF 07

Displacement, tons	2 500 standard; 2 962 full load
Length, feet (*metres*)	360·0(*109·7*)wl; 372·0(*113·4*) oa
Beam, feet (*metres*)	43·0 (*13·1*)
Draught, feet (*metres*)	18·0 (*5·5*) max (props)
Aircraft	1 light helicopter
Missile launchers	4 Exocet launchers; 1 quacruple "Seacat"
Guns, duel purpose	2—4·5 in (1 twin)
Boilers	2
Main engines	2 geared turbines; 30 000 shp
Speed, knots	30
Range, miles	4 500 at 12 knots
Complement	263

GENERAL

Ordered from Yarrow & Co Ltd, Scotstoun in the modernisation programme of the Chilean Navy. Until the Swedish cruiser was acquired *Condell*, laid down on 5 June 1971, was to have been named *Latorre*.

CONDELL, LYNCH

4 APD TRANSPORT TYPE

SERRANO APD 26 (ex-USS *Odum* APD 71, ex-DE 670)
ORELLA APD 27 (ex-USS *Jack C. Robinson* APD 72, ex-DE 671)
RIQUELME APD 28 (ex-USS *Joseph E. Campbell* APD 49, ex-DE 70)
URIBE APD 29 (ex-USS *Daniel Griffin* APD 38, ex-DE 54)

ORELLA *1970, Chilean Navy,*

Displacement, tons	1 400 standard; 2 130 full load
Length, feet (*metres*)	300·0 (*91·4*) wl; 306·0 (*93·3*) oa
Beam, feet (*metres*)	37·0 (*11·3*)
Draught, feet (*metres*)	12·6 (*3·8*)
Guns	1—5 in 38 cal dp; 6—40 mm AA
Main engines	GE turbo-electric; 2 shafts; 12 000 shp = 23·6 knots; 2 turbines 6 000 hp each; 2 generators 4 500 kW each
Boilers	2 Foster Wheeler "D" type
Range, miles	5 000 at 15 knots; 2 000 at 23 knots
Complement	209

GENERAL

These former destroyer escort transports were purchased from the USA, transferred at Orange, Texas 25 Nov 1966 (first three) and Norfolk Va 1 Dec 1966 (*Uribe*). They have been modernised, except *Requelme*.

SUBMARINES

2 NEW CONSTRUCTION BRITISH "OBERON" CLASS

HYATT SS 23 **O'BRIEN** SS 22

Displacement, tons	1 610 standard; 2 030 surface; 2 410 submerged
Length, feet (*metres*)	241·0 (*73·5*) pp; 295·2 (*90·0*) oa
Beam, feet (*metres*)	26·5 (*8·1*)
Draught, feet (*metres*)	18·1 (*5·5*)
Torpedo tubes	8—21 in (*533 mm*)
Main engines	2 diesels 3 680 bhp; 2 electric motors 6 000 shp; 2 shafts, electric drive
Speed, knots	12 surface, 17 submerged

Ordered from Scott's Shipbuilding & Engineering Co, Ltd, Greenock, late 1969 as part of a new fleet replacement and modernisation programme. *Hyatt* was originally to have been named *Condell.*

2 Ex-US "BALAO" CLASS

SIMPSON SS 21 (ex-USS *Spot*, SS 413)
THOMPSON SS 20 (ex-USS *Springer*, SS 414)

Displacement, tons	1 526 standard; 1 816 surface; 2 425 submerged
Length, feet (*metres*)	311·6 (*95·0*)
Beam, feet (*metres*)	27·0 (*8·2*)
Draught, feet (*metres*)	17·0 (*5·2*)
Torpedo tubes	10—21 in (*533 mm*), 6 bow; 4 stern
Main engines	6 500 hp GM 2-stroke diesels; 4 610 hp electric motors
Speed, knots	20 on surface, 10 submerged
Complement	80

THOMSON *1971, Chilean Navy, Official*

SIMPSON *1972, Chilean Navy*

Both built at Mare Island Navy Yard. *Thomson* launched on 3 Aug 1944, completed on 18 Oct 1944, was transferred at San Francisco, on 23 Jan 1961, and overhauled in USA in 1966. *Simpson*, launched on 20 May 1944 and completed on 3 Aug 1944, was transferred end of 1961. Both Guppy conversions.

REPAIR SHIP

AGUILA LST 91, ex-ARV 135 (ex-USS *Aventinus*, ARVE 3, ex-LST 1092)

Displacement, tons	1 625 light; 4 100 full load
Dimensions, feet	316 wl; 328 oa × 50 × 11·2
Guns	8—40 mm AA
Main engines	GM diesels; 2 shafts; 1 800 bhp = 11·6 knots

Former United States aircraft repair ship (Engine). Built by American Bridge Co. Ambridge, Pa. Laid down on 8 Jan 1945, launched on 24 Mar 1945, and completed on 19 May 1945. Transferred to the Chilian Navy by USA in 1963 under the Military Aid Program. Also used as a destroyer tender and submarine repair ship.

AGUILA *1971, Chilean Navy*

LANDING CRAFT

ASPIRANTE MOREL LSM 92 (ex-USS *Aloto, LSM 444*)

Displacement, tons	743 standard; 1 095 full load
Dimensions, feet	196·5 wl; 203·5 oa × 34·5 × 7·3
Main engines	Diesel; 2 shafts; 2 800 bhp = 12 knots
Oil fuel (tons)	60
Range, miles	2 500 at 9 knots
Complement	60

Former United States medium landing ship launched in 1945. *Aspirante Morel* (ex-*Aloto*) was leased to Chile on 2 Sep 1960 at Pearl Harbour to replace the older LSM of the same name.
Sister ships original *Aspirante Morel* (ex-USS *LSN 417*) withdrawn from service in 1958 *Guardiamarine Contreras* (ex-USS *LSM 113*) in 1959. *Aspirante Izaza* (ex-USS *LSM 295*) and *Aspirante Goicolea* (ex-USS *LSM 400*) in use as harbour craft.

ASPURANTE NOREL *1972, Chilean Navy*

ELICURA LSM 90 **OROMPELLO** LSM 94

Displacement, tons	290 light; 750 full load
Dimensions, feet	138 wl; 145 oa × 34 × 12·8
Main engines	Diesels; 2 shafts; 900 bhp = 10·5 knots
Oil fuel (tons)	77
Range, miles	2 900 at 9 knots
Complement	20

Orompello wqs built for the Chilean Government by Dade Drydock Corporation, Miami, Florida, and transferred on 15 Sep 1964. *Elicura* was built at Talcahuano, launched on 21 April 1967, and handed over on 10 Dec 1968.

OROMPELLO *1971, Chilean Navy*

GRUMETE DIAZ LCU 96 (ex-LCU 1396)

Displacement, tons	143 to 160 light; 309 to 329 full load
Dimensions, feet	105 wl; 119 oa × 32·7 × 5 max
Main engines	Diesel; 3 shafts; 675 bhp = 10 knots
Oil fuel (tons)	11
Range, miles	700 at 7 knots
Complement	12

Landing Craft—*continued*

Former United States tank landing craft of the LCT (6) type. Launched in 1944. Transferred in 1960. *Grumete Bolados* LCU 95 was withdrawn from service in 1971 and *Grumete Tellez* in 1972. *Diaz* now in service as a harbour craft.

Of the six landing craft of the "Cabo Bustos" class, *Cabo Bustos* was converted into a harbour ammunition barge and renamed *Polvorera*, and *Eduardo Llanos* and *Soldado Canaves* were officially withdrawn from service in 1965, and sister ships *Grumete Bolados, Grumete Diaz* and *Grumete Tellez* were withdrawn from service in 1959.

LIGHT FORCES

FRESIA 81 **GUACOLDA** 80 **QUIDORA** 82 **TEGUALDA** 83

Displacement, tons	134
Dimensions, feet	118·1 × 18·4 × 7·2
Guns	2—40 mm AA
Tubes	4—21 in
Main engines	Diesels; 2 shafts; 4 800 bhp = 32 knots
Range, miles	1 500 at 15 knots
Complement	20

Built in Spain at Cadiz to German Lürssen design. *Fresia* and *Guacolda* were delivered on 9 Dec 1965 and 30 July 1965, respectively, *Quidora* and *Tegualda* in 1966. A photograph od *Guacolda* appears in the 1968-69 edition, and of *Quidora* in the 1969-70 and 1970-71 editions.

FRESIA *1971, Chilean Navy*

PAPUDO

Displacement, tons	450
Dimensions, feet	173·0 × 23·0 × 12·0
Guns	1—40 mm; 4—20 mm
A/S weapons	1 Hedgehog; 4 "K" DCT; 1 DC rack
Complement	69 (4 officers, 65 men)

Built in Asmar, Talcahuano, Chile. Launched on 7 Jan 1970. Rated as PC. Handed over on 27 Nov 1971.

PAPUDO *1972, Chilean Navy*

	Pennant No.	Launched
LAUTARO (ex-USS *ATA 122*)	PP 62	27 Nov 1942
LIENTUR (ex-USS *ATA 177*)	PP 60	5 June 1944

Displacement, tons	534 standard; 835 full load
Dimensions, feet	134·5 wl; 143 oa × 33 × 13·2 max
Guns	1—3 in AA; 2—20 mm AA
Main engines	GM diesel-electric; 1 500 shp = 12·5 knots
Oil fuel, tons	187
Complement	33

LAUTARO *1969, Chilean Navy*

Light Forces—*continued*

Former United States Navy auxiliary ocean tugs of the ATA type ("Maricopa" class), originally ocean rescue tugs (ATRs), transferred to the Chilian Navy and reclassified as patrol vessels. Launch dates above. Built by Levingstone Shipbuilding Co, Orange, Texas, USA.
LOSS. Sister ship *Leucoton* (ex-USS *ATA 200*) PP 61 ran aground on a sand bank on 15 Aug 1965 and was lost as a result of a heavy coastal storm during salvage operations.

ALDEA ATF 63 (ex-US *ATF* 98, *Arikara*)

Displacement, tons	1 235 standard; 1 675 full load
Dimensions, feet	195·0 wl; 205·0 oa × 38·5 × 15·5 max
Guns	1—3 in 50 cal AA
Main engines	Diesel Electric; 1 shaft; 3 000 bhp = 15 knots
Complement	85

Former USN fleet ocean tug, launched on 22 June 1943. Transferred on 7 Jan 1971.

ALDEA — *1972, Chilean Navy*

FUENTEALBA WPC 75 — **ODGER** WPC 76

Displacement, tons	215 max
Dimensions, feet	80 × 21 × 9
Guns	1—20 mm AA
Main engines	One Cummins diesel 340 hp = 9 knots
Range, miles	2 600 at 9 knots
Complement	19

Both these vessels were built in Chile by Astilleros Y Maeslronzas De La Armada (ASMAR); *Fuentealba* was completed in 22 July 1966 and *Odger* 21 April 1967.

FUENTEALBA — *1972, Chilean Navy, Offiical*

SURVEY SHIP

YELCHO (ex-USS *Tekesta*, ATF 93) Pennant No. AGS 64

Displacement, tons	1 235 standard; 1 675 full load
Dimensions, feet	195 wl; 205 oa × 38·5 × 15·3 max
Guns	2—40 mm AA
Main engines	4 diesels with electric drive shaft; 3 000 bhp = 16·5 knots
Complement	85

Survey Ships—*continued*

Former United States fleet ocean tug of the ATF type ("Apache" class) fitted with powerful pumps and other salvage equipment. *Yelcho* was built by Commercial Iron Works, Portland, Oregon, laid down on 7 Sep 1942, launched on 20 Mar 1943, completed on 16 Aug 1943, and loaned to Chile by the USA on 15 May 1960, having since been employed as Antarctic research ship and surveying vessel.

LOSS. Sister ship *Janequo* (ex-USS *Potawatomi, ATF 109*) AGS 65 sank with all hands on 15 Aug 1965 during the salvage operations on *Leucoton*, see above.

YETCHO — *1972, Chilean Navy*

TRANSPORTS

AQUILES AP-47 (ex-Danish *Tjaldur*)

Displacement, tons	2 660 registered; 1 462 net; 1 395 dw
Dimensions, feet	288 × 44 × 17
Main engines	1 Slow Burmeister and Wain Diesel; 3 600 bhp = 16 knots
Range, miles	5 500 at 16 knots
Complement	60 crew plus 447 troops

Ex-Danish MV *Tjaldur* built in 1953 by Aalborg Verft, Denmark, bought by Chile in 1967.

AQUILES — *1968, Chilean Navy*

PILOTO PARDO AP 45

Displacement, tons	1 250 light; 2 000 standard; 3 000 full load
Dimensions, feet	269 × 39 × 15
Aircraft	1 helicopter
Guns	1—101·6/50; 2—20 mm
Main engines	2 diesel-electric; 2 000 hp = 14 knots
Complement	44 (plus 24 passengers)
Range, miles	6 000 at 10 knots

Built by Haarlemsche Scheepsbouw Mij, Haarlem, Netherlands. Antarctic patrol ship, transport and research vessel with reinforced hull to navigate in ice. Officially listed as transport. Delivered in 1959.

PILOTO PARDO — *1969, Chilean Navy, Official*

OILERS

ARAUCANO — *1972, U.S. Navy*

ARAUCANO AO 53

Displacement, tons	17 300
Measurement, tons	18 030 deadweight
Dimensions, feet	497·6 × 74·9 × 28·8
Guns	4—40 mm
Main engines	B and W diesels; 10 800 bhp = 15·5 knots (17 on trials)
Range, miles	12 000 at 15·5 knots

Naval tanker built by Burmeister & Wain, Copenhagen, Denmark. Launched on 21 June 1967.

ALMIRANTE JORGE MONTT AO 52

Displacement, tons	9 000 standard; 17 500 full load
Measurement, tons	11 800 gross; 17 750 deadweight
Dimensions, feet	548 × 67·5 × 30
Main engines	Rateau Bretagne geared turbine; 1 shaft; 6 300 shp = 14 knots
Boilers	2 Babcock & Wilcox
Range, miles	16 500 at 14 knots

Naval supply tanker. Built by Ateliers et Chantiers de la Seine Maritime, Le Trait, France Laid down in 1954. Launched on 14 Jan 1956. Completed in Mar 1956.

ALMIRANTE JORGE MONTT — *1969, Chilean Navy*

BEAGLE AO 54 (ex-AOG 8 USS *Genesse*)

Displacement, tons	4 240 standard
Dimensions, feet	310 × 48·7 × 16
Guns	2—3 inch 50 cal; 4—20 mm
Range, miles	6 670 at 10 knots

BEAGLE — *1972, Chilean Navy*

TRAINING SHIP

ESMERALDA (ex-*Don Juan de Austria*) BE 43

Displacement, tons	3 040 standard; 3 673 full load
Dimensions, feet	308·8 oa; 260 pp × 43 × 23 max
Guns	2—57 mm
Sail area	Total 26 910 sq feet
Main engines	1 Fiat Auxiliary diesel; 1 shaft; 1 400 bhp = 11 knots
Range, miles	8 000 at 8 knots
Complement	271 plus 80 cadets

Training Ships—*continued*

Four-masted schooner completed in 1952. Built in Spain by the Echevarrieta Yard, Cadiz, and originally intended for the Spanish Navy. Transferred to Chile on 12 May 1953. Near sister ship of *Juan Sebastian de Elcano* in the Spanish Navy. Similar to the Brazilian training ship *Almirante Saldanha* before her major reconstruction. Replaced transport *Presidente Pinto* as training ship.

ESMERALDA — *1971, A. & J. Pavia*

FLOATING DOCK

MUTILLA ARD 132 (ex-US *ARD 32*)

Displacement, tons	5 200
Capacity, tons	3 000
Dimensions, feet	492 × 84 × 5·7 to 33·2 feet

Leased to Chile 15 May 1960.

TUGS

COLOCOLO ATA 73

Displacement, tons	790
Dimensions, feet	126·5 × 27·0 × 12·0 mean
Main engines	Triple expansion; 1 050 shp = 11 knots
Oil fuel, tons	155

Built by Bow, McLachlan & Co, Paisley. Formerly classed as coastguard vessel. Rebuilt in 1962-63. Of four sister ships *Janequeo* was withdrawn from service in 1958, *Sobenes* in 1965, *Galvarino* in 1968 and *Cabrales* in 1971.

ANCUD (YT 104)
CAUPOLICAN (YT 127)
CORTEZ (YT 128)
MONREAL (YT 105)
REYES (YT 120)

Fortuna (YT 123) and *Galvez* (YT 102) were withdrawn from service in 1965, *Moctezuma* (YT 108) in 1968 and *Ugarte* (YT 107) in 1971. *Yagan* (YT 126) was lost in 1964 while assisting a merchant ship during a storm.

3 Ex-US FLEET TUGS

ex-**TEKESTA** ATF 93
ex-**POTOWATOMII** ATF 109
ex-**ARIKARA** ATF 92

Displacement, tons	1 235 standard; 1 675 full load
Dimensions, feet	205 oa × 38·5 × 15·5
Guns	1—3 in
Main engines	Diesel electric; 1 shaft; 3 000 bhp = 15 knots
Complement	85

Transferred in 1960 (ATF 93), 1963 (ATF 109) and 1972 (ATF 92).

CHINA

Administration

Commander-in-Chief of the Navy:
Vice-Admiral Hsiao Ching Kuang

Pennant Numbers

Block numbering system:—
Submarines: 100 series; Major Surface Ships: 200 series; Amphibious Ships: 300 series.

Strength of the Fleet

44 Submarines
8 Destroyers
9 Frigates
11 Escorts (Sloops and Corvettes)
17 Fast Missile Boats
20 Submarine Chasers (Patrol Vessels)
315 Fast Gunboats
200 Fast Torpedo Boats
22 Coast and River Defence Vessels
27 Medium and Coastal Minesweepers
54 Amphibious Types (Landing Ships and Craft)
33 Auxiliaries and Support Ships
375 Miscellaneous and Service Craft

Personnel

1973: 160 000 officers and men, including 20 000 naval air force and 28 000 marines

Mercantile Marine

Lloyd's Register of Shipping:
265 vessels of 1 022 256 tons gross

The Chinese Navy

Despite setbacks under the Manchus, the Chinese have possessed a navy in some force since 200BC. In addition they have had the will and capability to use their fleet, as their expeditions to the Persian Gulf and Africa in the 15th Century bear witness. So today's navy has a tradition older than any other exept the Greek and Italian and a modern, rapidly expanding force capable of operations abroad. In the following pages the Chinese Navy is shown in two parts—the new fleet of Hsiao Ching Kuang and the antique remnants of the Nationalist navy. While studying these it must be remembered that not only is there a steady building programme of all classes in the modernised Chinese Yards but also the Chinese have an advanced nuclear and missile capability. This combination will make the Chinese navy, already twice as strong in manpower as the Royal Navy, an important element in the future balance of power East of Suez.

Chinese Naval Air Force

With 20 000 officers and men and over 450 aircraft, this is a considerable land-based naval air force. Equipped with MIG 17 and 19 (and possibly MIG 21) fighter aircraft and SA2-SAM, with 100 IL 28 Torpedo bombers, Madge flying boats, Hound M14 helicopters and transport and communication aircraft this is primarily a defensive force. Chinese ingenuity should find little difficulty in getting a proportion of these aircraft afloat, particularly in view of the increasing tempo of their shipbuilding programme.

"THE NEW NAVY"

DESTROYERS

4 NEW CONSTRUCTION

Displacement, tons	3 500
Dimensions, feet	450 × 45 × 15
Missiles	2 surface to surface launchers
Guns	4—130 mm (2 twins) 8—37 mm 8—25 mm
A/S weapons	2—A/S rocket launches
Speed	30+

GENERAL
All the above figures are approximate, designed to show the possible capability of this new class, which is being built in Shanghai (and other yards). It has been reported several times during the year and is probably now in series production. What the missiles are is doubtful, although the Chinese experience with Styx makes this a logical and likely choice.

New Construction DDG — *1972 Chinese*

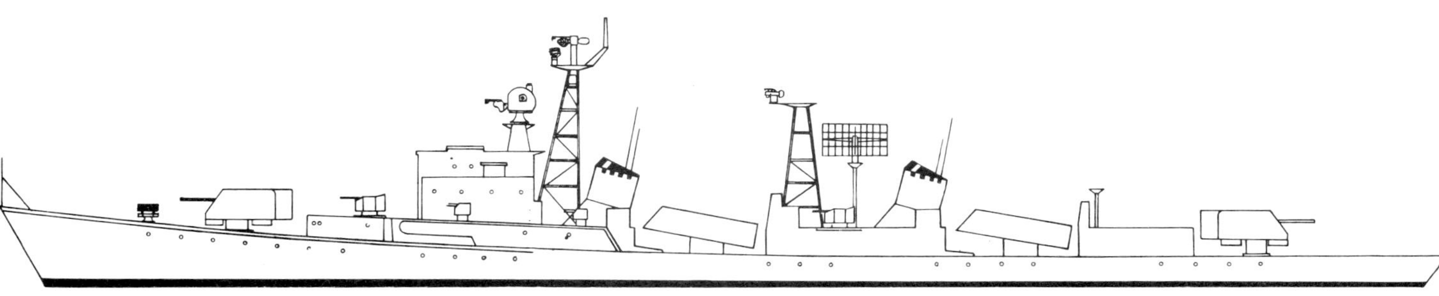

New Construction

4 Ex-SOVIET "GORDY" CLASS

ANSHAN **CHI LIN**
CHANG CHUN **FU CHUN**

Displacement, tons	1 657 standard; 2 150 full load
Length, feet (*metres*)	357·7 (*109·0*) pp; 377 (*114·9*) oa
Beam, feet (*metres*)	33·5 (*10·2*)
Draught, feet (*metres*)	13 (*4·0*)
Guns, surface	4—5·1 in (*130 mm*)
Guns, AA	8—37 mm
A/S	8 DCT
Torpedo tubes	6—21 in (*533 mm*) tripled
Boilers	3-drum type
Main engines	Tosi geared turbines 50 000 shp; 2 shafts
Speed, knots	36
Oil fuel (tons)	500
Complement	250

CHANG CHUN — *Hajime Fukaya*

GENERAL
Of Odero-Terni-Orlando design. All launched in 1936-41. Fitted for minelaying. Transferred 1954.

FRIGATES

5 "KIANGNAN" CLASS

No. 209

Displacement, tons	1 350 standard; 1 800 full load
Length, feet (*metres*)	298 (*90·8*)
Beam, feet (*metres*)	33·5 (*10·2*)
Draught, feet (*metres*)	12 (*3·7*)
Guns, dual purpose	6—3·9 in (*100 mm*) (3 twin)
Speed, knots	30

GENERAL
Built at Canton since 1968 with two twin mountings forward and one aft.

The Communist Chinese Navy has embarked on a building programme of which this class started in 1968 is the beginning. These good-sized ships with a deep-water capability are a sensible complement to the growing submarine fleet and the enormous number of short range missile boats and FPBs with which the Chicom navy is now equipped. With these in mind it would be no surprise to see this and future classes fitted with surface to surface missiles. (see Destroyers)

4 "RIGA" CLASS

CH'ENG TU **KUEI YANG**
KUEI LIN **K'UN MING**

Displacement, tons	1 200 standard; 1 600 full load
Length, feet (*metres*)	295 (*89·9*) oa
Beam, feet (*metres*)	31·5 (*9·6*)
Draught, feet (*metres*)	10 (*3·0*)
Guns, dual purpose	3—3·9 in (*100 mm*) single mounts
Guns, AA	4—37 mm
A/S	4 DC projectors
Torpedo tubes	3—21 in (*533 mm*); 3 torpedoes
Mines	50 capacity, fitted with rails
Boilers	2
Main engines	Geared turbines 24 000 shp; 2 shafts
Speed, knots	28
Oil fuel (tons)	300

GENERAL
First of the class, launched on 28 Apr 1956 at Hutang Shipyard, Shanghai, had light tripod mast, but was later converted with heavier mast and larger bridge as in the other three. Second vessel was launched on 26 Sep 1956. Third vessel was built at Shanghai and the fourth in 1957. Somewhat similar to the Soviet "Riga" class destroyer escorts. Two were redesigned with modified superstructure.

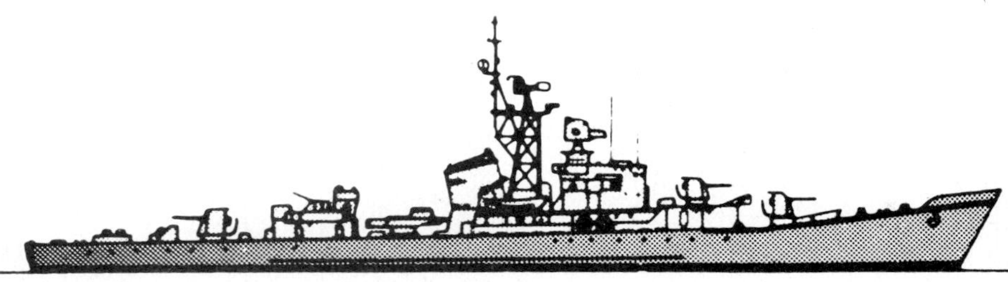

RIGA CLASS

"Riga" Class *1971*

CORVETTES

20 "KRONSTADT" TYPE SUBMARINE CHASERS

579 611 612 615 618 622

Displacement, tons	310 standard; 380 full load
Dimensions, feet	170·6 × 21·5 × 9
Guns	1—3·9 in; 2—37 mm AA; 3—20 mm AA
A/S Weapons	2 Rocket launchers
Main engines	Diesels; 2 shafts; speed 24 knots

Six built in 1950-53 were received from USSR in 1956-57. Remainder were built at Shanghai and Canton, with 12 completed in 1956. The last was assembled by 1957. Flush decked, squat funnel, slightly raked, block bridge structure.

The six old former Soviet patrol vessels of the "Artillerist" class, and the three former British patrol trawlers of the "Isles" class were deleted from the list in 1967, and the two former Soviet submarine chasers of the "S.O.1." class in 1969.

KRONSTADT 579 *1969*

KRONSTADT *Class*

SUBMARINES

NEW CONSTRUCTION

Reported sightings of an Albacore-hulled type of submarine, which apparently was started in 1969, plus the Chinese nuclear capability suggest that this may be the first of a class of nuclear-propelled submarines. If so, and in view of their current missile programme, the production of a class of ballistic-missile nuclear submarines may be seen within the 1970's

1 "G" CLASS BALLISTIC MISSILE TYPE

Displacement, tons	2 350 surface; 2 800 submerged
Length, feet (*metres*)	320·0 (*97·5*)
Beam, feet (*metres*)	28·2 (*8·6*)
Draught, feet (*metres*)	22·0 (*6·7*)
Missile launchers	3 vertical tubes
Torpedo tubes	6—21 in (*533 mm*) bow
Main engines	3 diesels, total 6 000 hp Electric motors
Speed, knots	17·6 surface, 17 submerged
Radius, miles	22 700 surface cruising
Complement	86 (12 officers, 74 men)

Ballistic missile submarine similar to the Soviet "G" class. Built at Dairen in 1964. The missile tubes are fitted in the conning tower. It is not known whether this boat has been fitted with missiles, although it is possible and well within Chinese technical capability.

"G" Class *1972*

18 SOVIET "R" CLASS

Displacement, tons	1 100 surface; 1 600 submerged
Length, feet (*metres*)	246·0 (*75·0*)
Beam, feet (*metres*)	27·9 (*8·5*)
Draught, feet (*metres*)	14·1 (*4·3*)
Torpedo tubes	6—21 in (bow) 18 torpedoes
Main engines	Diesels; electric motors
Speed, knots	18·5 surface; 15 submerged

The Chinese are now building their own Soviet design "R" class submarines possibly at a rate of 4 a year.

"R" Class *1972*

21 SOVIET "W" CLASS

Displacement, tons	1 300 surface; 1 600 submerged
Length, feet (*metres*)	272·3 (*83·0*) oa
Beam, feet (*metres*)	24·3 (*7·3*)
Draught, feet (*metres*)	15·7 (*4·8*)
Torpedo tubes	6—21 in (*533 mm*); 4 bow 2 aft (20 torpedoes or 40 mines)
Main engines	Diesel-electric; 2 shafts; 4 000 bhp diesels; 2 500 hp electric motors
Speed, knots	17 surface; 15 submerged
Radius, miles	13 000
Complement	60

Medium size streamlined, long range submarines similar to the "W" class built in the USSR. Equipped with snort. Fitted for minelaying. Assembled from Soviet components in Chinese yards between 1956 and 1964.

"W" Class *1972*

1 Ex-SOVIET "S-1" CLASS

Displacement, tons	840 surface; 1 050 submerged
Length, feet (*metres*)	256 (*78·0*)
Beam, feet (*metres*)	21 (*6·4*)
Draught, feet (*metres*)	13 (*4·0*)
Torpedo tubes	6—21 in (*533 mm*)
Main engines	4 200 hp diesels; 2 200 hp electric motors
Speed, knots	19 surface; 8·5 submerged
Radius, miles	9 800 at 9 knots
Oil fuel, tons	105
Complement	50

Launched in 1939. Transferred from the USSR in 1955.

3 Ex-SOVIET "M-V" CLASS

Displacement, tons	350 surface; 420 submerged
Length, feet (*metres*)	167·3 (*51·0*)
Beam, feet (*metres*)	16·0 (*4·9*)
Draught, feet (*metres*)	12·1 (*3·7*)
Guns, AA	1—45 mm 1 MG;
Torpedo tubes	2—21 in (*533 mm*)
Main engines	1 000 hp diesels; 800 hp electric motors
Speed, knots	13 surface; 10 submerged
Radius, miles	4 000 at 8·5 knots
Oil fuel, tons	21
Complement	24

Designed for coastal operations, latterly used for training and instruction but nearing the end of their usefulness owing to age. Four were transferred from the USSR in 1954-55, but *M 200* was deleted from the list in 1963.

The two smaller submarines built for coastal operations, one of the ex-Soviet "M IV" class, and one of the ex-Soviet "M 1" class, latterly used only for training and instruction, were deleted from the list in 1963.

LIGHT FORCES

17 SOVIET "OSA" TYPE (MISSILE BOATS)

Displacement, tons	165 standard; 200 full load
Dimensions, feet	128·7 × 25·1 × 5·9
Missiles, surface	4 "Styx" type launchers in two pairs abreast aft
Guns	4—30 mm (2 twin, 1 forward and 1 aft)
Main engines	3 diesels; 13 000 bhp = 32 knots

It was reported in Jan 1965 that one "Osa" class guided missile patrol boat had been incorporated in the Navy. Four more were acquired in 1966-67, and two in 1968. A building programme of 10 boats a year is assumed.

"Osa" Class 1972

20 SOVIET "KOMAR" TYPE (MISSILE BOATS)

Displacement, tons	70 standard; 80 full load
Dimensions, feet	83·7 oa × 19·8 × 5
Missiles, surface	2 "Styx" type launchers
Guns	2—25 mm AA (1 twin forward)
Main engines	Diesels; 2 shafts; 4 800 bhp = 40 knots

One "Komar" class guided missile boat is reported to have joined the fleet In 1965. Two more were delivered in 1967 and seven in 1968 to 1971. A building programme of 10 a year is assumed.

"Komar" Class 1972

5 "HAINAN" CLASS

Dimensions, feet	135 × 20 × 10
Guns	4—37 mm (2 pairs superimposed, 1 forward, 1 aft) 4—25 mm (2 pairs superimposed, amidships)

Chinese built improved Soviet "S.O.I." type. Low freeboard. The 25 mm guns are abaft the bridge.

200 "SHANGHAI" II, III and IV TYPES (GUNBOATS)

Displacement, tons	120 full load
Dimensions, feet	130 × 18 × 5·6
Guns	4—37 mm, 2 twin, 1 forward, 1 aft (1—57 mm forward in Type II only 4—25 mm, 2 twin aft of bridge 1 mortar forward
Torpedo tubes	2 (not fitted in later boats)
Main engines	4 diesels; 5 000 bhp = 30 knots
Complement	25

Two centreline trainable torpedo tubes were mounted abaft the superstructure. Construction continuing at Shanghai and other yards. Three units were transferred to North Korea and four to North Vietnam.

SHANGHAI II *Class*

SHANGHAI IV Class 1970

25 "SHANGHAI" I TYPE (GUNBOATS)

Displacement, tons	100 full load
Dimensions, feet	120 × 18 × 5·5
Guns	4—37 mm in twin mountings fore and aft
Main engines	4 diesels; 4 800 bhp = 28 knots
Complement	21

The prototype of these convertible motor gun/torpedo boats appeared in 1959.

60 "SWATOW" TYPE (GUNBOATS)

Displacement, tons	67 full load
Dimensions, feet	83·5 × 20 × 6
Guns	4—37 mm, in twin mountings; 2—12·7 mm
A/S weapons	8 depth charges
Main engines	4 diesels; 4 800 bhp = 40 knots
Complement	17

"P 6" type motor torpedo boat hulls with torpedo tubes removed. In 1958 "P-6" hulls were converted to "Swatow" class motor gunboats at Dairen, Canton, and Shanghai.

30 "WHAMPOA" (MODIFED) TYPE (GUNBOATS)

It is understood that 30 boats of the "Whampoa" type, similar to the "Swatow" class, are in the fleet.

70 "HU CHWAN" CLASS (TORPEDO BOATS)

Displacement, tons	45
Dimensions, feet	70 × 16·5 × 3·1
Torpedo tubes	2—21 inch
Guns	4—12·7 mm (2 twins)
Main engines	Possibly 2 M50 12 Cylinder Diesels; 2 shafts; 2 200 hp = 55 knots (calm conditions)

Hydrofoil torpedo boats, designed and built by China, in the HUTANG yard, Shanghai having been under construction since 1966. One unit reported transferred to North Vietnam. At least 25 motor torpedo boats of the hydrofoil type were reported to be in the South China Fleet in 1968. Of all-metal construction with a bridge well forward and a low super-structure extending aft. The guns are mounted one on the main deck and one on the superstructure. Forward pair of foils can apparantly be withdrawn into recesses in the hull. Painted olive green. 30 transfered to Albania.

70 "P4" TYPE (TORPEDO BOATS)

Displacement, tons	25
Dimensions, feet	63 × 11 × 5·6
Guns	2 or 4—25 mm AA
Torpedo tubes	2—18 in
Main engines	Diesels; 2 200 bhp = 50 knots

This class have aluminium hulls. The German-built *Kual 102* was deleted from the list in 1963.

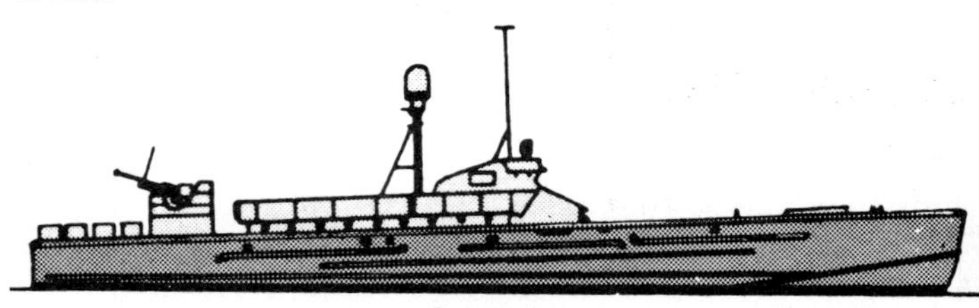

P 4 *Class*

80 "P6" TYPE (TORPEDO BOATS)

153 154 155 159

Displacement, tons	66
Dimensions, feet	82 × 20 × 6
Guns	4—25 mm AA
Torpedo tubes	2—21 in
Main engines	Diesels, 5 000 bhp = 45 knots
Complement	25

This class have wooden hulls. Some were constucted in Chinese republican yards. All have been built since 1966. Above pennant numbers observed *en flotille*.

P 6. *Class*

FLEET MINESWEEPERS

20 SOVIET "T 43" CLASS

Displacement, tons	500 standard; 610 full load
Dimensions, feet	190·2 × 28·2 × 6·9
Guns	4—37 mm AA (2 twin)
Main engines	2 diesels; 2 shafts; 2 200 bhp = 17 knots

Two were acquired from USSR im 1954-55. Eighteen more were built in Chinese shipyards, two in 1956, and the remainder since. The construction of "T 43" class fleet minesweepers was terminated at Wuchang, but continued at Canton.

"T 43" class *1972*

"THE OLD NAVY"

ESCORTS

Note The existence of the 11 ships is uncertain. In a navy with an expanding building programme it is likely that all have been scrapped thus releasing some 1 500 officers and men for the modern fleet. Full details and photographs are in the 1971-72 edition.

Class	*No.*	*Names*	*Displacement tons standard*	*Speed (knots)*	*Guns*	*Date (launched)*
Ex-Japanese "Ukuru"	1	**HUI AN** (ex-*Shisaka*)	940	19·5	2—4·7 in	1943
Ex-Japanese "Etorofu"	1	**CHANG PAI** (ex-*Oki*)	870	19·5	2—3·9 in	1942
Ex-Japanese "Uji"	1	**NAN CHANG** (ex-*Uji*)	950	20	2—3·9 in	1940
Ex-Japanese "C"	1	**SHEN YANG**	745	16·5	2—3·9 in	1945
Ex-Japanese "D"	4	**CHANG SHA** **CHI NAN** **HSI AN** **WU CHANG**	740	17·5	3—3 in or 3/6—37 mm	1944 1945
Ex-Canadian "Castle"	1	**KUANG CHOU** (ex-*Bowmanville*)	1 100	16·5	2—5·1 in	1944
Ex-British "Flower"	2	**KAI FENG** (ex-*Clover*) **LIN I** (ex-*Heliotrope*)	1 020	16	2—3·9 in	1941

COAST DEFENCE VESSELS

Class	*No.*	*Names*	*Displacement (tons standard)*	*Speed (knots)*	*Guns*	*Date*
Ex-US PGM	3	**KAN TANG** + 2 (ex-PGMs 12 & 14)	280	20	1—3 in 2—40 mm	1945 (US)
Chinese	1	**CH'ANG CHIANG**	464	12	4—40 mm 4—25 mm	1929
ex-Japanese	1	**CHAING YUAN**	550	12	1—20 mm	1905
Chinese	2	**TING HSIN** **TUNG TEH**	500	11	1—3 in 4—47 mm	—

RIVER DEFENCE VESSELS

Class	*No.*	*Names*	*Displacement*	*Speed*	*Guns*	*Date*
Ex-Japanese	2	ex-**YUNG AN** ex-**YUNG PING**	170	12	1—47 mm 5—25 mm	1929
Ex-Japanese	1	ex-**CHANG TEH**	305	14	2—3 in	1923
Ex-Japanese	2	**FU CHIANG** Ex-**CHIANG HSI**	320	16·5	1—3·1 in 8—25 mm	1939
Ex-British *Sandpiper*	1	Ex-**YING HAO**	185	11	1—3·7 in how.	1933
Ex-British *Falcon*	1	Ex-**NAN CHIAN**	372	15	1—3·7 in how. 2—6 pdr.	1931
Ex-British *Gannet*	1	Ex-**YING SHAN**	310	16	2—3 in	1927
Ex-US *Totuila*	2	Ex-**MEI YUAN** Ex-**TAI YUAN**	370	12	2—3 in	1927
Ex-Japanese	1	Ex-**KIANG KUN**	180	14	2—3 in	1921
Ex-French	1	Ex-**FAHU**	201	14	1—3 in	1921
Ex-Japanese	1	Ex-**HO HSUEH**	215	9	2—3 in	1911

Note. The existence of the majority of this list of Old Ming above must be in doubt. The 1 000 or so men required to man them would be better employed in the very large numbers of small craft in this fleet. Full details and some photographs of the above ships appeared in the 1971-72 edition.

FLEET MINESWEEPERS

1 Ex-BRITISH "BATHURST" CLASS

Ex-SS **CHEUNG HING** (ex-HMAS *Bendigo*)

Displacement, tons	815 standard; 1 025 full load
Dimensions, feet	162 pp; 186 oa × 31 × 8·5
Guns	2—5·1 in; 2—37 mm AA
Main engines	Triple expansion; 2 shafts; 1 800 ihp = 15 knots
Boilers	2 Admiralty 3-drum small tube type
Oil fuel (tons)	170
Range, miles	4 300 at 10 knots

Built as a fleet minesweeper but employed as an escort vessel. Launched in Mar 1941 at Sydney, Australia. Disposed of as surplus after the Second World War. Converted from a merchant vessel.

COASTAL MINESWEEPERS

4 Ex-US YMS TYPE

Ex-**YMS 346** Ex-**YMS 367** Ex-**YMS 393** Ex-**YMS 2017**

Displacement, tons 270 standard; 350 full load
Dimensions, feet 136 × 24·5 × 6
Guns 1—3 in; 2—20 mm; 2 DCT
Main engines 2 GM Diesels; 1 000 bhp = 13 knots

Built of wood in USA in 1942-43, and transferred to the Chinese Navy in 1948. Some are fitted as gunboats. Ex-YMS 339 was deleted from the list in 1963.

2 Ex-JAPANESE AMS TYPE

Ex-**No. 4** **No. 201** (ex-No. 14)

Displacement, tons 222
Dimensions, feet 97·1 oa × 19·3 × 7·3 max
Guns 1—3·1 in; 4—25 mm (No, 201. 1—40 mm; 1—25 mm; 2—13 mm; 3—7·7 mm)
Main engines 1 Diesel; 300 bhp = 9·5 knots
Range, miles 1 700 at 9·5 knots

Ex-Japanese auxiliary minesweepers. Trawler type No 201, completed in 1943, was delivered to China at Tsingtau on 3 Oct 1947, and taken over by the Chinese Republic.

BOOM DEFENCE VESSELS

1 Ex-BRITISH "BAR" TYPE

Ex-Japanese No. 101 (ex-HMS *Barlight*)

Displacement, tons 750 standard; 1 000 full load
Dimensions, feet 150 pp; 173·8 oa × 32·2 × 9·5
Guns 1—3 in dp; 6 MG
Main engines Triple expansion; 850 ihp = 11·75 knots
Boilers 2 single-ended

Boom defence vessel of British "Bar" Class. Built by Lobnitz & Co Ltd, Renfrew. Launched on 10 Sep 1938. Captured by Japanese in 1941. Acquired by China in 1945.

5 Ex-US "TREE" CLASS

Displacement, tons 560 standard; 805 full load
Dimensions, feet 146 wl; 163 oa × 30·5 × 11·8
Guns 1—3 in AA
Main engines Diesel-electric; 800 bhp = 13 knots

Former United States netlayers of the "Tree" class taken over by the Peoples Republic.

SURVEY CRAFT

Ex-**CHUNG NING** (ex-Japanese *Takebu Maru*)

Displacement, tons 200 standard
Dimensions, feet 115 × 16 × 6
Main engines Speed; 10 knots

Former Japanese. Employed for hydrographic and general purpose duties.

Ex-**FUTING**

Displacement, tons 160 standard
Dimensions, feet 90 × 20 × 8
Main engines Speed; 11 knots

REPAIR SHIP

TAKU SHAN (ex-*Hsing An*, ex-USS *Achilles, ARL* 41, ex-*LST* 455)

Displacement, tons 1 625 light; 4 100 full load
Dimensions, feet 316 wl; 328 oa × 50 × 11
Guns 1—3 in; 8—40 mm AA
Main engines Diesel-electric; 2 shafts; 1 800 bhp = 11 knots

Launched on 17 Oct 1942. Burned and grounded in 1949, salvaged and refitted.

LANDING SHIPS

16 Ex-US LST TYPE

CHANG PAI SHAN
CHING KANG SHAN
CHUNG (ex-USS *LST* 355)
Ex-**CHUNG 101** (ex-USS *LST* 804)
Ex-**CHUNG 102** (ex-USS *LST*)
Ex-**CHUNG 107** (ex-USS *LST* 1027)
Ex-**CHUNG 110**
Ex-**CHUNG 111** (ex-USS *LST* 805)
Ex-**CHUNG 116** (ex-USS *LST* 406)
Ex-**CHUNG 122** (ex-*Ch'ing Ling*)
Ex-**CHUNG 125**
I MENG SHAN (ex-*Chung* 106 ex-USS *LST* 589)
No. 16
No. 258
TA PIEH SHAN
TAI HSING SHAN
SZU CH'ING SHAN

Landing Ships—*continued*

Displacement, tons 1 653 standard; 4 080 full load
Dimensions, feet 316 wl; 328 oa × 50 × 14
Main engines Diesel; 2 shafts; 1 700 bhp = 11 knots

There were reported to be 20 ex-US LSTs in naval service, but several are out of commission. Eleven other ex-US LSTs were in the merchant service.

13 Ex-US LSM TYPE

Ex-**CHUAN SHIH SHUI**
Ex-**HUA 201** (ex-USS *LSM* 112)
Ex-**HUA 202** (ex-USS *LSM* 248)
Ex-**HUA 204** (ex-USS *LSM* 430)
Ex-**HUA 205** (ex-USS *LSM* 336)
Ex-**HUA 207** (ex-USS *LSM* 282)
Ex-**HUA 208** (ex-USS *LSM* 42)
Ex-**HUA 209** (ex-USS *LSM* 153)
Ex-**HUA 211**
Ex-**HUA 212**
Ex-**HUAI HO** (ex-Chinese *Wan Fu*)
Ex-**HUANG HO** (ex-Chinese *Mei Sheng* ex-USS *LSM* 433)
Ex-**YUN HO** (ex-Chinese *Wang Chung*)

Displacement, tons 743 beaching; 1 095 full load
Dimensions, feet 196·5 wl; 203·5 oa × 34·5 × 8·8
Main engines Diesel; 2 shafts; 2 800 12 knots

Built in USA in 1944-45. Some were converted for minelaying Armament varies.

LANDING CRAFT

15 Ex-US LSIL TYPE

Ex-**CHU TIEN** (ex-Chinese *Lien Kuang* ex-USS *LCI* 517)
Ex-**KU CHOU**
Ex-USS **LCI 488**
Ex-**LIEN PI** (ex-USS *LCI* 514)
MIN 301
MIN 303
MIN 306
MIN 311
MIN 312
MIN 313
MIN 319
MIN 321
MIN 325
MIN 331
Ex-**YUNG KAN** (ex-Chinese *Lien Yung*, ex-USS *LCI* 632)

Displacement, tons 230 light; 387 full load
Dimensions, feet 159 × 23·7 × 5·7
Main engines Diesel; 2 shafts; 1 320 bhp = 14 knots

Built in USA in 1943-45. Reported to be fitted with rocket launchers. Some are fitted as minesweepers. Armament varies.

10 Ex-US LCU (ex-LCT) TYPE

Ex-**HO CHIEN** (ex-USS *LCT* 515) Ex-**HO YUNG** (ex-USS *LCT* 1171)

Displacement, tons 160 light; 320 full load
Dimensions, feet 105 wl; 119 oa × 33 × 5
Main engines Diesel; 3 shafts; 475 bhp = 10 knots
Oil fuel (tons) 80

Former United States Navy Tank Landing Craft later reclassified as Utility Landing Craft. There are reported to be ten utility landing craft comprising two of the ex-British LCT (3) class and eight of the ex-US LCT (5) and LCT (6) class.

SUPPLY SHIPS

8 Ex-US ARMY FS TYPE

Ex-US Army FS 146 (ex-*Clover*)
Ex-US Army FS 155 (ex-*Violet*)
Ex-**TA CHEN** (ex-US)
Ex-US Army FS——
Ex-US Army FS——

Displacement, tons 1 000 standard
Dimensions, feet 175 oa × 32 × 10
Main engines GM diesels; 1 000 bhp = 12 knots

Built in USA in 1944-54. Two are reported to be employed as motor torpedo boat tenders. The transport *Chiao Jen* was stricken from the list in 1967.

OILERS

There are reported to be two ex-US "Mattawee" Class petrol tankers and three ex-US 174 ft yard oilers of the "YO" type.

TUGS

There are reported to be at least two tugs of the USSR type, two of the US Navy ATA type, two of the US Army type, and five of the US Army harbour tug type.

SERVICE CRAFT

There are also reported to be 125 armed motor junks, 100 armed motor launches and 150 service craft and miscellaneous boats.

COLOMBIA

Administration

Fleet Commander:
Vice Admiral Jaime Parra Ramirez

Chief of Naval Operations:
Rear Admiral Eduardo Wills Olaya

Chief of Naval Staff:
Rear Admiral Alfonso Diaz Osorio

Diplomatic Representative

Naval Attaché in Washington:
Captain Hernando Salas Ramirez

Strength of the Fleet

4 Destroyers
5 Frigates
2 Submarines (70 tons)
22 Patrol Boats
4 Gunboats
2 Survey Vessels
6 Transports (Small)
4 Oilers
13 Tugs
2 Floating Docks

New Construction

2 Patrol Submarines

Disposals

Frigates (ex-Tacoma class)
Dec 1962 *Capitan Tono*
Jan 1965 *Almirante Padilla*
1968 *Almirante Brion*

Designation

Ships names are prefaced by the letters "ARC" (Armada Republica de Colombia)

Personnel

1973: 700 officers and 6 500 men

Mercantile Marine

Lloyd's Register of Shipping
54 vessels of 231 994 tons gross

DESTROYERS

2 MODIFIED "HALLAND" TYPE

Name	*No.*	*Builders*	*Laid down*	*Launched*	*Completed*
SIETE DE AGOSTO	06	Götaverken, Göteberg	Nov 1955	19 June 1956	31 Oct 1958
VEINTE DE JULIO	05	Kockums Mek Verkstads A/B, Malmo	Oct 1955	26 June 1956	15 June 1958

Displacement, tons: 2 650 standard; 3 300 full load
Length, feet (*metres*): 380·5 (*116·0*)pp; 397·2 (*121·1*)oa
Beam, feet (*metres*): 40·7 (*12·4*)
Draught, feet (*metres*): 15·4 (*4·7*)
Guns: 6—4·7 in (*120 mm*) (3 twin turrets); 4—40 mm (single)
Torpedo tubes: 4—21 in (*533 mm*)
A/S weapons: 1 quadruple DC rocket launcher
Main engines: De Laval double reduction geared turbines; 2 shafts; 55 000 shp
Speed, knots: 30 nominal, 16 economical
Boilers: 2 Penhöet, Motala Verkstad; 568 psi; 840°F
Range, miles: 445 at full power
Oil fuel, tons: 524
Complement: 260 (20 officers, 240 men)

GENERAL
Modified Swedish "Halland" type ordered in 1954. The hull and machinery are similar to the Swedish class but they have different armament (six 4·7 inch instead of four, no 57 mm guns, four 40 mm guns instead of six, and four torpedo tubes instead of eight) and different accommodation arrangements. They have an anti-submarine rocket projector, more radar and communication equipment, and air conditioned living spaces, having been designed for the tropics.

ENGINEERING. Although the designed speed was 35 knots, it is officially stated that the maximum sustained speed does not exceed 25 knots.

RADAR. Search: HSA LWO 3—SGR 114. Tactical: HSA DA 02—SGR 105. Fire Control: X Band, probably HSA M 20 series.

7 DE AGOSTO *1971, Colombian Navy*

20 DE JULIO *1970, Colombian Navy*

1 Ex-FLETCHER" " CLASS

Name	*No.*	*Builders*	*Laid down*	*Launched*	*Completed*
ANTIOQUIA (ex-USS *Hale*, DD 642)	DD 01	Bath Iron Works Corporation, Bath, Maine	23 Nov 1942	4 Apr 1943	15 June 1943

Displacement, tons: 2 100 standard; 2 952 full load
Length, feet (*metres*): 369·0 (*112·5*)pp; 376·0 (*114·8*)oa
Beam, feet (*metres*): 39·5 (*12·0*)
Draught, feet (*metres*): 18·0 (*5·5*) max
Guns: 4—5 in (*127 mm*) 38 cal; 6—3 in (*76 mm*) 50 cal (3 twin)
Torpedo tubes: 5—21 in (*533 mm*) quintupled
A/S weapons: 2 fixed Hedgehogs; 1 DC rack; 2 side-launching torpedo racks
Main engines: 2 sets GE geared turbines; 2 shafts; 60 000 shp
Speed, knots: 35 designed, 37 max, 14 econ
Boilers: 4 Babcock & Wilcox; 615 psi; 850°F
Range, miles: 6 000 at 14 knots
Oil fuel, tons: 650
Complement: 300

Former US destroyer of the "Fletcher class". Transferred from the US Navy at Boston, Massachussetts, on 23 Jan 1961.

RADAR. Search: SPS 6. Tactical: SPS 10. Fire Control: X Band.

ANTIOQUIA *1970, Colombian Navy*

Destroyers—*continued*

1 Ex-US ALLEN M. SUMNER CLASS

Name	*Builder*	*Launched*	*Commissioned*
CALDAS (ex-USS *Willard Keith* DD 775)	Bethlehem (San Pedro)	29 Aug 1944	27 Dec 1944

Displacement, tons 2 200 standard; 3 320 full load
Length, feet (*metres*) 376 (*114·8*) oa
Beam, feet (*metres*) 40·9 (*12·4*)
Draught, feet (*metres*) 19 (*5·8*)
Guns 6—5 in (twins); 4—3 in (twins)
A/S Weapons 2 Fixed Hedgehogs
2 triple torpedo tubes (Mk 32)
Main engines 2 geared turbines; 2 shafts; 60 000 shp
Boilers 4
Speed, knots 34
Range, miles 2 400 at 25 knots; 4 800 at 15 knots
Complement 274

Transferred 1 July 1972

A. M. SUMNER Class

FRIGATES

4 Ex-US APDs

ALMIRANTE BRION (ex-*USS Burke APD* 65, ex-*DE* 215) DT 07
ALMIRANTE PADILLA (ex-*USS Tollberg APD* 103, ex-*DE* 593) DT 12
ALMIRANTE TONO (ex-*USS Bassett APD* 73, ex-*DE* 672) DT 04
CORDOBA (ex-*USS Ruchamkin LPP* 89, ex-*APD* 89, ex-*DE* 228) DT 15

Displacement, tons 1 400 standard; 2 130 full load
Dimensions, feet 300 wl; 306 oa × 37 × 12·7 max
Guns 1—5 in, 38 cal dp; 6—40 mm AA
Main engines GE turbo-electric; 2 shafts; 12 000 shp = 23·6 knots
Boilers 2 "D" Express
Oil fuel (tons) 350
Range, miles 5 500 at 15 knots; 2 000 at 23 knots
Complement 204 accommodation plus 162 troop capacity

GENERAL
Former US high speed transports (converted destroyer escorts). *Almirante Padilla* was built by Bethlehem SB Co, Hingham, Mass, laid down on 30 Dec 1943, launched on 12 Feb 1944, completed on 31 Jan 1945 and transferred on 14 Aug 1965. *Almirante Tono* was built by Consolidated Steel Co, Orange, Tex, laid down on 28 Nov 1943, launched on 15 Jan 1944, completed on 23 Feb 1945 and transferred at Boston, Mass, on 6 Sep 1968. *Almirante Brion* was built by Philadelphia Navy Yard, laid down on 1 Jan 1943, launched on 3 Apr 1943, completed on 20 Aug 1943 and transferred on 8 Dec 1968. *Cordoba* was built by Philadelphia Navy Yard, laid down on 14 Feb 1944, launched on 15 June 1944 and transferred on 24 Nov 1969. DT 07 now serving as riverine hospital ship.

ALMIRANTE BRION *1971, Colombian Navy*

1 Ex-US "DEALEY" CLASS

BOYACA DE 16 (ex-USS *Hartley* DE 1029)

Displacement, tons 1 450 standard; 1 914 full load
Dimensions, feet 314·5 oa × 36·8 × 13·6
Guns 2—3 in; 50 cal
A/S Weapons 2 triple torpedo tubes
Main engines 1 De Laval geared turbine; 20 000 shp; 1 shaft
Boilers 2 Foster Wheeler
Speed, knots 25
Complement 165

Transferred 8 July 1972.

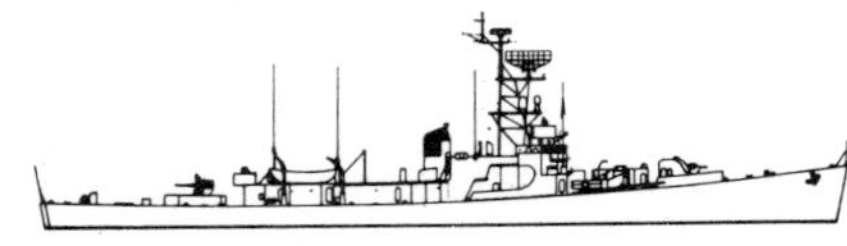

DEALEY (DE 1006)

SUBMARINES

2 HOWALDTSWERKE TYPE PATROL SUBMARINES

Displacement, tons 1 000 surface; 1 290 dived
Length, feet (*metres*) 183·4 (*55·9*)
Beam, feet (*metres*) 20·5 (*6·52*)
Torpedo tubes 8—21 in bow
Main engines Diesel electric; 1 shaft; 5 000 hp
Speed, knots 22 dived

Building by Howaldtswerke, Kiel.

2 MIDGET SUBMARINES

These boats, purchased from Italy and of about 70 tons were delivered in July-August 1972 for assembly in Cartagena.

LIGHT FORCES

CARLOS E. RESTREPO AN 206 **PEDRO GUAL** AN 204
ESTEBAN JARAMILLO AN 205

Displacement, tons 123·5
Dimensions, feet 107·8 pp × 18 × 6
Guns 1—20 mm AA
Main engines 2 Maybach diesels; 2 450 bhp = 26 knots

Built by Werft Gebr. Schurenstedt KG Bardenfleth in 1964.

PEDRO GUAL *1965, Colombian Navy*

OLAYA HERRERA AN 203

Displacement, tons 40
Dimensions, feet 68·8 pp × 12·8 × 3·5
Guns 1—·50 mm Browning AA
Main engines 2 Merbens diesels; 570 bhp

Built by Astilleros Magdalena Barranquilla, in 1960.

GENERAL RAFAEL REYES AN 01 **GENERAL VASQUES COBO** AN 02

Displacement, tons 146
Dimensions, feet 118 pp; 124·7 oa × 23 × 5
Guns 1—40 mm
Main engines 2 Maybach diesels; 2 400 bhp = 18 knots

Built by Lürssen Werft, Vegesack. Launched on 10 Nov and 27 Sep 1955, respectively. Delivered in May 1956.

ESPARTANA GC 100

Displacement, tons 50
Dimensions, feet 90 wl; 96 oa × 13·5 × 4
Guns 1—20 mm AA
Main engines 2 diesels; 300 bhp = 13·5 knots

Launched on 22 June 1950 at Cartagena Naval Dockyard.

CAPITAN R. D. BINNEY GC 101

Displacement, tons 23
Dimensions, feet 67 × 10·7 × 3·5
Main engines Diesels; 115 bhp = 13 knots

Built at Cartagena in 1947. Buoy and lighthouse inspection boat. Named after first head of Colombian Naval Academy, Lt-Commander Ralph Douglas Binney, RN.

CAPITAN R. D. BINNEY *1971, Colombian Navy*

Light Forces—*continued*

ALBERTO RESTREPO LR 125 (1 Oct 1952)
CARLOS GALINDO LR 128 (1954)
HUMBERTO CORTES LR 126 (26 Nov 1952)
JUAN LUCIO LR 122 (2 May 1953)

Displacement, tons	35
Dimensions, feet	76·8 pp; 81·8 oa × 12 × 2·8
Guns	1—20 mm AA; 4 MG
Main engines	2 GM diesels; 260 bhp = 13 knots
Complement	13

Built at Cartagena. Launch dates above.

ALFONSO VARGAS LR 123 (3 July 1952)
FRITZ HAGALE LR 124 (19 July 1952)

Displacement, tons	33
Dimensions, feet	72 pp; 76 oa × 12 × 2·8
Guns	1—20 mm AA; 4 GM
Main engines	2 GM diesels 280 bhp = 13 knots
Complement	10

Built at Cartagena naval base. Designed for operations on rivers. Named after naval officers. Launch dates above.

DILIGENTE LR 132
INDEPENDIENTE LR 134
PALACE LR 130
TORMENTOSA LR 136
TRIUNFANTE LR 133
VALEROSA LR 137
VENGADORA LR 131
VOLADORA LR 135

Launched af the Naval Base, Cartagena, in 1952-54. The boats vary in detail.

3 "ARAUCA" CLASS GUNBOATS

ARAUCA CF 37 **LETICIA** CF 36 **RIOHACHA** CF 35

Displacement, tons	184 full load
Dimensions, feet	163·5 oa × 23·5 × 2·8
Guns	2—3 in, dp, 50 cal; 4—20 mm
Main engines	2 Caterpillar diesels; 916 bhp = 13 knots
Range, miles	1 000 at 12 knots
Complement	43

Built by Union Industrial de Barranquilla (Unial) Colombia. Launched in 1955. Completed in 1956. *Leticia* has been equipped as a hospital ship.

LETICIA *1971, Colombian Navy*

RIOHACHA *1966, Colombian Navy*

1 BARRANQUILLA CLASS GUNBOAT

CARTAGENA CF 33

Displacement, tons	142
Dimensions, feet	130 pp; 137·8 oa × 23·5 × 2·8 max
Guns	2—3 in; 1—20 mm AA; 4 MG
Main engines	2 Gardner semi-diesels; 2 shafts working in tunnels; 600 hp = 15·5 knots
Oil fuel (tons)	24
Complement	39

Built by Yarrow & Co. Ltd., Scotstoun, Glasgow, and launched on 22 Mar 1930. Sister ship *Santa Marta*, CF 32, was withdrawn from service in Dec 1962. and Barranquilla in 1970.

CARTAGENA *1971, Colombian Navy*

SURVEY VESSELS

SAN ANDREAS (ex-USS *Rockville*, PCER 851)

Displacement, tons	674 standard; 858 full load
Dimensions, feet	180·0 wl; 184·5 oa × 33·6 × 7·0
Main engines	2 diesels; 2 shafts; 1 800 bhp = 15 knots
Complement	60

Former US patrol recue escort vessel built by Pullman Standard Car Mfg Co. Chicago, laid down on 18 Oct 1943, launched on 22 Feb 1944, completed on 15 May 1944. acquired on 5 June 1969 for conversion to a surveying vessel.

GORGONA FB 161

Displacement, tons	560
Dimensions, feet	135 × 29·5 × 9·3
Main engines	2 Nohab diesels; 910 bhp = 13 knots

Built by Astilliero Lidingoverken. Launched in May 1954. Formerly classified as a tender.

GORGONA *1971, Colombian Navy*

QUINDIO (ex-USY443)

Displacement, tons	600
Dimensions, feet	131 × 29·8 × 8
Main engines	1 diesel; 700 hp = 10 knots
Complement	17

Launched in 1943.

BOCAS DE CENIZA

Displacement, tons	675
Complement	20

Launched in 1943.

TRANSPORTS

CIUDAD DE QUIBDO TM 43

Displacement, tons	633
Dimensions, feet	165 × 23·5 × 9
Main engines	1 Mai diesel; 1 shaft; 390 bhp = 11 knots
Oil fuel (tons)	32
Complement	12

Built by Gebr. Sander Delfzijl, in the Netherlands.

CIUDAD DE QUIBDO *1971, Colombian Navy*

BELL SALTER (ex-*Souris*, ex-*Leccarmaro II*). TM 41.

Displacement, tons	60
Dimensions, feet	82 × 14 × 5·5
Main engines	2 GM diesels; 1 500 rpm; speed 8 knots

HERNANDO GUTIERREZ TF 52
MARIO SERPA TF 51
SOCORRO (ex-*Alberto Gomez*)

HERNANDO GUTIERREZ *1971, Colombian Navy*

Transports—*continued*

Displacement, tons	70
Dimensions, feet	82 × 18 × 2·8
Main engines	2 GM diesels; 260 bhp = 9 knots
Oil fuel (tons)	4
Complement	10 (berths for 56 troops)

River transports. Launched at Cartagena in 1954, 1953 and 1955 respectively. Named after Army Officers. *Socorro* was converted in July 1967 into a floating surgery. *Hernando Gutierrez* and *Mario Serpa* were also converted into dispensary ships in 1970.

RAFAEL MARTINEZ

Displacement, tons	38
Dimensions	57·5 oa × 15 × 8
Main engines	2 six-cylinder diesels = 120 bhp

OILERS

TUMACO BT 57

Displacement, tons	9 214 light; 22 316 full load
Dimensions, feet	602·3 × 76 × 32·1
Main engines	Rush-Sulzer diesels; 1 shaft; 10 500 bhp = 15·5 knots
Complement	65 (10 officers, 55 men)

Sister ship *Barrancabermeja* was withdrawn from fleet service and officially deleted from the list in 1972.

BARRANCABERMEJA (TUMACO similar) *1970, Colombian Navy*

COVENAS (ex-MT *Randfonn*) BT 65

Measurement, tons	22 096 gross; 5 096 net; 14 000 deadweight
Dimensions, feet	515·3 oa × 64 × 30·5 max
Main engines	Diesel; 1 shaft; 6 000 bhp = 14·5 knots
Complement	49 (7 officers, 42 men)

Built by Gotaverken in 1950. Acquired in 1966. Capacity 136 250 barrels. The oiler *Antonio de Arevalo* was withdrawn from service in 1967.

COVENAS *1971, Colombian Navy*

MAMONAL (ex-US *Tonti,* AOG 76) BT 62
SANCHO JIMENO (ex-*Transmere,* ex-USS *Kiamichi,* AOG 73) BT 63

Displacement, tons	5 984 full load
Measurement, tons	3 150 gross; 3 925 deadweight; 2 063 net
Dimensions, feet	309 wl, 325 oa × 48·2 × 21·7
Main engines	Diesel; 1 shaft; 1 400 bhp = 10 knots
Complement	33

Built by Todd Shipyard, Houston, and St. John's River S.B. Corp., Jacksonville, respectively. *Sancho Jimeno* was purchased in 1952. *Mamonal* was transferred in Jan 1965.

SANCHO JIMENO *1970, Colombian Navy*

TRAINING SHIP

GLORIA

Displacement, tons	1 300
Dimensions, feet	212 × 34·8 × 21·7
Main engines	Auxiliary diesel; 500 bhp = 10·5 knots

Sail training ship. Built at Bilbao in 1968. Barque rigged. Hull is entirely welded. Sail area: 1 675 sq yards (*1,400 sq. metres*).

GLORIA *1971, Colombian Navy*

TUGS

PEDRO DE HEREDIA (ex-USS *Choctaw,* ATF 70) RM 72

Displacement, tons	1 235 standard; 1 764 full load
Dimensions, feet	195 wl; 205 oa × 38·5 × 15·5 max
Main engines	4 diesels, electrical drive; 3 000 bhp = 16·5 knots

Former United States ocean tug of the "Apache" class. Launched on 18 Oct 1942.

BAHIA HONDA RM 74 (ex-USS *Umpqua* ATA 209)
BAHIA UTRIA RM 75 (ex-USS *Kalmia* ATA 184)

Displacement, tons	534 standard; 858 full load
Dimensions, feet	134·5 wl; 143·0 oa × 31·0 × 8·0
Guns	1—3 in dp
Main engines	2 GM diesel-electric; 1 shaft; 1 500 bhp = 13 knots
Complement	45

Transferred from the United States Navy in 1971.

PEDRO DE HEREDIA *1971, Colombian Navy*

TENIENTE SORZANO

Displacement, tons	54
Dimensions, feet	60 pp; 65·7 oa × 17·5 × 9
Main engines	6-cylinder diesel; 240 bhp

ANDAGOYA RM 71

Displacement, tons	100
Main engines	Caterpillar diesel; 80 bhp = 8 knots

Launched in 1928. Re-engined in 1955.

ABADIA MENDEZ

Displacement, tons	39
Dimensions, feet	52·5 × 11 × 4
Main engines	Caterpillar diesel; 80 bhp = 8 knots

Built in Germany in 1924. Harbour tug. There are also the harbour tug, *La Colombiana* and the river tug *Joves Fiallo,* RR 90.

CANDIDO LEGUIZAMO
CAPITAN ALVARO RUIZ
CAPITAN CASTRO
CAPITAN RIGOBERTO GIRALDO
CAPITAN VLADIMAR VALEK
TENIENTE LUIS BERNAL

Displacement, tons	50
Dimensions, feet	63 × 14 × 2·5
Main engines	2 GM diesels; 260 bhp = 9 knots

TENIENTE MIGUEL SILVA RM 89

Dimensions, feet	73·3 × 17·5 × 3
Main engines	2 diesels; 260 bhp = 9 knots

River tug. Built by Union Industrial (Unial) of Barranquilla.

FLOATING DOCKS AND WORKSHOP

RODRIGUEZ ZAMORA (ex-USN ARD 28)

Displacement, tons	6 700 full load
Capacity, tons	3 000
Dimensions, feet	488 × 81
Complement	109

Auxiliary Floating Dock.

MANUEL LARA

Small Floating Dock.

CAPITAN ELOY MANTILLA (ex-USN YR 66)

Displacement, tons	516 standard
Dimensions, feet	150 × 34
Complement	24

Floating Workshop.

In addition there is the repair craft *Victor Cubillos.*

CONGO

The Republic of Congo (formerly Middle Congo, of French Equatorial Africa), which became independant on 15 Aug 1960, formed a naval service, but the patrol vessel *Reine N'Galifowou* (ex-French P 754) which was transferred 16 Nov, 1962 was returned to France on 18 Feb ,1965 and then re-transferred to Senegal as *Siné Saloum.* Since 1970 at least twelve river patrol boats have been delivered.

COSTA RICA

The Coast Guard includes two 90 ft wooden patrol boats and an armed tug.

CUBA

Strength of the Fleet

3 Frigates
20 Corvettes
20 Missile Boats
24 Torpedo Boats
34 Miscellaneous

Naval Establishments

Naval Academy:
At Mariel, for officers and cadets

Naval school:
At Morro Castle, for petty officers and men

Naval Bases:
Mariel and Cienfuegos

Personnel

1973; 6 000 (380 officers, 220 subordinate officers, and 5 400 men)

Mercantile Marine

Lloyd's Register of Shipping:
267 vessels of 398 030 tons gross

Disposals

CRUISER (so called)
1972 *Cuba*

CORVETTE
1972 *Patria*

Note: The US embargo on exports to Cuba has been running for some ten years. As a result all ex-USN ships in the Cuban Navy are expected to be in poor condition through lack of spares.

"THE NEW NAVY"

CORVETTES

12 Ex-USSR "SOI" TYPE

Displacement, tons	215 standard; 250 full load
Dimensions, feet	138·6 × 20 × 9·2
Guns	4—25 mm (2 twin)
A/S weapons	4 five-barrelled rocket launchers
Range, miles	1 100 at 13 knots
Complement	30
Main engines	3 diesels; 6 000 bhp = 29 knots

Six were transferred from the USSR by Sep 1964, and six more in 1967.

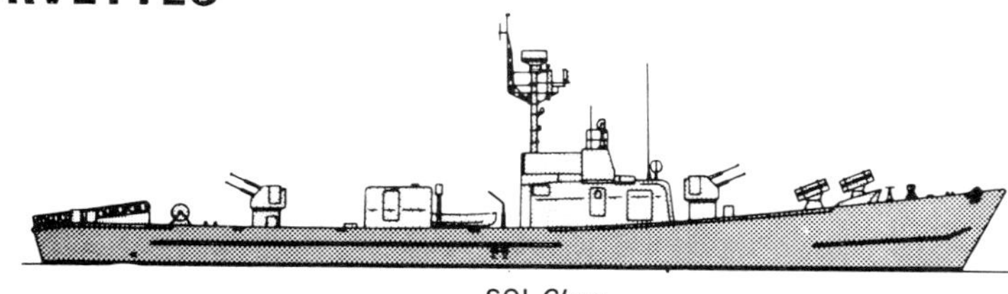

SOI *Class*

6 Ex-USSR "KRONSTADT" TYPE

Displacement, tons	310 standard; 380 full load
Dimensions, feet	170·6 × 21·3 × 9
Guns	1—3·9 in; 2—37 mm AA; 3—20 mm AA; DC
A/S weapons	1 DC Thrower
Mines	6 on two racks at the stern
Main engines	3 diesels; 3 shafts; 3 300 hp = 24 knots
Range, miles	1 500 at 12 knots
Complement	65

Former Soviet submarine chasers reported transferred from the USSR in 1962. First twelve transferred from USSR in 1962. Last pair arrived in 1967.

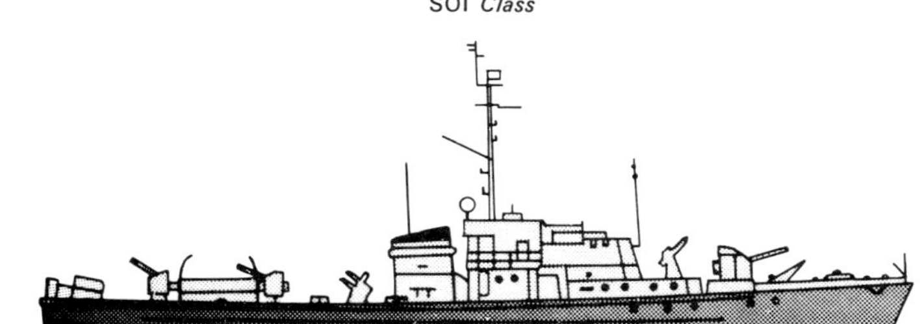

KRONSTADT *Class*

LIGHT FORCES

2 Ex-USSR "OSA" TYPE MISSILE BOATS

Displacement, tons	165 standard; 200 full load
Dimensions, feet	128·7 × 25·1 × 5·9
Missiles	4 SSN-2 launchers in two pairs
Guns	4—30 mm (2 twin, 1 forward, 1 aft)
Main engines	3 diesels; 13 000 bhp = 32 knots
Complement	25

Two boats of this class were transferred to Cuba from the USSR in January 1972. With the obvious rundown of the ex-USN ships in the Cuban Navy and the determination of the Cuban Government to maintain an independent Naval presence in the Caribbean these could be the forerunners of further reinforcements. With the "Komar" class units below there are now twenty hulls mounting 44 of the proven and effective "Styx" missiles in a highly sensitive area.

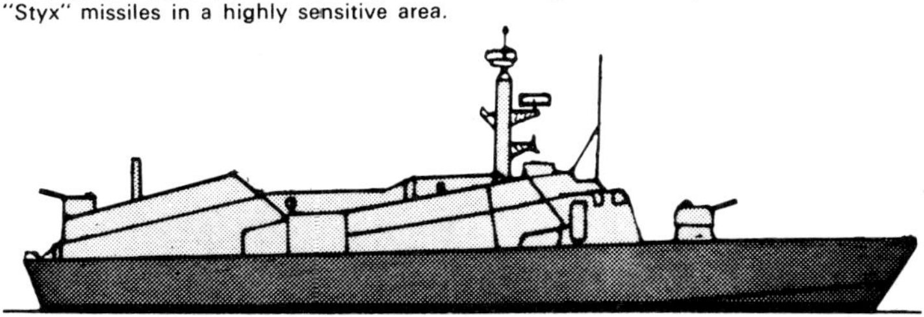

OSA *Class*

18 Ex-USSR "KOMAR" TYPE MISSILE BOATS

Displacement, tons	70 standard; 180 full load
Dimensions, feet	83·6 × 19·6 × 4·9
Missiles	2 SSN-2
Guns	2—25 mm AA
Main engines	4 diesels; 4 shafts; 4 800 bhp = 40 knots

"KOMAR" Type

Light Forces—*continued*

12 Ex-USSR "P 6" TYPE TORPEDO BOATS

Displacement, tons	66 standard; 75 full load
Dimensions, feet	84·2 × 20 × 6
Guns	4—25 mm AA (two twin)
Tubes	2—21 in (two single)
Main engines	4 diesels; 4 shafts; 4 800 hp = 45 knots
Complement	25

P 6 *Class*

12 Ex-USSR "P 4" TYPE TORPEDO BOATS

Displacement, tons	25
Dimensions, feet	62·7 × 11·6 × 5·6
Guns	2—25 mm AA
Tubes	2—18 in
Main engines	2 diesels; 2 200 bhp = 50 knots

Former Soviet motor torpedo boats, transferred from the USSR in 1962-64.

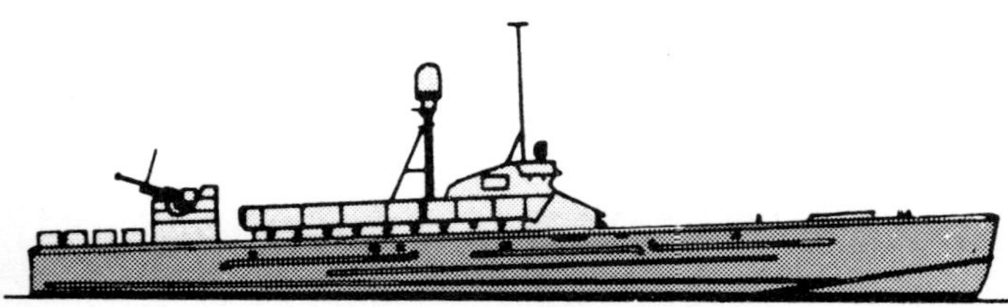

P 4 *Class*

"THE OLD NAVY"

FRIGATES

ANTONIO MACEO (ex-USS *Peoria*, PF 67) F 302
JOSE MARTI (ex-USS *Eugene*, PF 40) F 301
MAXIMO GOMEZ (ex-USS *Grand Island*, PF 14) F 303

3 Ex-US PF TYPE

Displacement, tons	1 430 standard; 2 415 full load
Dimensions, feet	304 oa × 37·5 × 13·7
Guns, dual purpose	3—3 in (*76 mm*)
Guns, AA	*Antonio Maceo*: 4—40 mm; 4—12·7 mm *José Marti*: 4—40mm ; 6—20 mm; *Maximo Gomez*: 4—40 mm; 9—20 mm
A/S weapons	Hedgehog; DCT; racks
Boilers	2 three-drum type
Main engines	Triple expansion; 2 shafts; 5 500 ihp
Speed, knots	18
Range, miles	9 500 at 12 knots
Complement	135 (*José Marti*)

All three were completed in 1944 and acquired from the US Navy in 1947. Refitted in 1956 at Key West.

CORVETTES

2 Ex-US PCE TYPE ESCORT PATROL VESSELS

CARIBE (ex-USS *PCE 872*) PE 201 **SIBONY** (ex-USS *PCE 893*) PE 302

Displacement, tons	640 standard; 903 full load
Dimensions, feet	180 wl; 184·5 oa × 33 × 9·5
Guns	1—3 in dp; 3—40 mm AA; 4—20 mm AA
A/S weapons	Hedgehog; DCT and racks
Main engines	12 cylinder diesels; 2 shafts; 1 800 bhp = 14 knots
Complement	99

Built in USA. Completed 1943-44. Refitted at Key West 1956.

CARIBE *Cuban Navy*

LIGHT FORCES

HABANA *GC* 107 (ex-*SC* 1291) **ORIENTE** *GC* 104 (ex-*SC* 1 000)
LAS VILLAS *GC* 106 (ex-*SC* 1290) **PINAR DEL RIO** *GC* 108 (ex-*SC* 1301)

Displacement, tons	95
Dimensions, feet	107·5 wl; 111 oa × 17 × 6.5
Guns	2—20 mm AA
Main engines	GM diesels; 2 shafts; 1 000 bhp = 15 knots

Built in the United States by Dingle Boat Works (*Oriente*), W.A. Robinson, Inc, Ipswich, Mass. (*Havana* and *Las Villas*), and Perkins & Vaughn Inc, Wickford, RI (*Pinar del Rio*). *Camaguey* GC 105, was removed from the effective list in 1960.

HABANA *Cuban Navy*

LEONCIO PRADO *GC* 101

Displacement, tons	80
Dimensions, feet	110 × 17·7 × 6·2
Guns	1—20 mm AA
Main engines	2 sets 8-cycle, 2 stroke diesels; 1 000 bhp = 15 knots
Oil	2 232 gallons for a cruising radius of 16 000 miles

Built at Havana. Launched in 1946. Of wooden hulled construction.

LEONCIO PRADO *1966, Cuban Navy*

GC 11 (ex-USCGC 83351) **GC 13** (ex-USCGC 83385) **GC 14** (ex-USCGC 83395)

Displacement, tons	45
Dimensions, feet	83 × 16 × 4·5
Guns	1—20 mm AA
Main engines	2 Sterling Viking petrol motors; 1 200 hp = 18 knots
Complement	12

Former *CS* of same numbers. Built in USA. Ex-Coast Guard Cutters. Launched in 1942-43. Of wooden hulled construction. Received from US Navy in March 1943. Rated as *Guardacostas*, 83 ft. GC 12 and GC 22 were disposed of.

GC 13 *Cuban Navy*

GC 32 (ex-USCGC 56191) **GC 33** (ex-USCGC 56190) **GC 34** (ex-USCGC 56192)

Displacement, tons	45
Dimensions, feet	83 × 16 × 4·5
Guns	1—20 mm AA
Main engines	2 Superior diesels; 460 bhp = 12 knots
Complement	12

Built in USA. Ex-Coast Guard cutters. Launched in 1942-43. Of wooden hulled construction. GC 31 was disposed of.

DONOTIVO (ex-*Capitan Fernandez Quevedo*) GC 102

Displacement, tons	130
Dimensions, feet	101 × 18 × 7
Main engines	2 sets diesels; 360 bhp = 12 knots

Built at Havana. Launched in 1932.

MATANZAS *GC* 103

Displacement, tons	80
Dimensions, feet	100 × 18 × 6
Guns	1—1 pdr
Main engines	2 Fairbanks Morse diesels; 180 bhp = 12 knots

Wooden hulled. Built at Havana. Launched in 1912.

Light Forces—*continued*

R 41 (ex-*PT* 715) **R 42** (ex-*PT* 716)

Displacement, tons	35
Dimensions, feet	71 × 19·2 × 5
Guns	2 MG
Main engines	2 Packard gas engines; 3 shafts; 3 600 bhp = 35 knots

Former US motor torpedo boats of the PT type. Built in the USA by Annapolis Yacht Yard Inc, Annapolis, Md. Launched on 9 July 1945 (R 41) and 17 July 1945 (R 42). Sunk during a hurricane on 5 Oct 1948, but were salvaged and put into service as sea-air rescue craft. Rated as *Buques-Auxiliaries, ex-Torpederos*. Sister R 43 sank on 6 May 1961 after hitting a submerged object off Western Cuba.

R 41 *Cuban Navy*

SV 7 **SV 8** **SV 9** **SV 10** **SV 12** **SV 14**

Dimensions, feet	Length 40
Guns	1—50 cal MG
Main engines	2 GM diesels; speed 25 knots

Later boats of the SV type assigned to naval stations for coastal vigilance, to deal with contraband, and for auxiliary services, rescue and navigation. Equipped with radar.

SV 1 **SV 2** **SV 3** **SV 4** **SV 5** **SV 6**

Displacement, tons	6·15
Dimensions, feet	32 × 10 × 2·8
Main engines	2 Chrysler Crown, 230 bhp = 18 knots

Auxiliary patrol boats for port vigilance, launched in 1953.

ENRIQUE COLLAZO (ex-*Joaquin Godoy*)

Displacement, tons	815
Dimensions, feet	211 × 34 × 9
Main engines	Triple expansion; 2 shafts; 672 ihp = 8 knots

Built at Paisley, Scotland. Launched in 1906. Acquired in 1950 from Cuban mercantile marine. Lighthouse tender.

BERTHA SF 10

Displacement, tons	98
Dimensions, feet	104 × 19 × 11
Main engines	2 Gray Marine diesels; 450 bhp = 10 knots

Launched in 1944. Lighthouse tender.

10 DE OCTUBRE (ex-*ATR* 4)

Displacement, tons	852 standard; 1 315 full load
Dimensions, feet	155 wl; 165·5 oa × 33·3 × 16
Main engines	Triple expansion; 1 600 ihp = 12 knots
Boilers	2 Babcock & Wilcox D-type; oil burning

Former US ocean rescue tug. Built in the USA. Launched in 1943. Largely of wooden construction. Guns removed. Pennant No. RS 210. Rated as *Buque de Rescate y Salvamento*. Sister ship *20 de Mayo* was removed from the effective list.

GRANMA A 11

Yacht which landed in Cuba on 2 Dec 1956 with Dr Fidel Castro and the men who began the liberation war. Historical vessel incorporated into the Navy as an auxiliary. The former Presidential Yacht *10 de Marzo* (ex-*Wakitty*) was removed from the list.

A1 **A2** **A3**

Displacement, tons	60
Dimensions, feet	74 × 15 × 5
Guns	1 MG
Main engines	2 diesel engines

Formerly yachts. A photograph of A3 appears in the 1954-55 to 1957-58 editions.

CYPRUS

PATROL BOATS

Mercantile Marine

Lloyd's Register of Shipping: 394 vessels of 2 014 675 tons gross

6 "P 4" CLASS

Displacement, tons	25
Dimensions, feet	62·7 × 11·6 × 5·6
Guns	2—25 mm
Tubes	2—18 in
Main engines	2 diesels; 2 200 bhp = 50 knots

Four of these were transferred by USSR in Oct 1964 and two in Feb 1965. Also reported that two extra engines have been supplied since that time.

2 Ex-GERMAN "R" TYPE

Displacement, tons	125
Dimensions, feet	124 × 19 × 4·5
Guns	1—40 mm; 1—20 mm
Main engines	2 MAN diesels; 1 800 bhp = 20 knots

Originally three of this class were taken up from mercantile use and re-armed. One was destroyed by Turkish air attack on 8 Aug 1964 at Xeros. It was reported that there were 10 small craft of about 50 tons, armed with one or two 20 mm guns.

No. 15 *1972, Dr. Giorgio Arra*

DENMARK

Administration

Commander-in-Chief:
Vice-Admiral S. Thostrup, RDN

Diplomatic Representation

Defence Attaché, London:
Colonel H.H. Prince Georg of Denmark, CVO

Assistant Defence Attaché, London:
Captain Jorgen E. Haack-Moeller, RDN

Defence Attaché, Washington:
Colonel P. B. Nissen, RDAF

Disposals and Transfers

FRIGATES
1963 Rolfkrake, Valdemar Sejr, Niels Ebbesen
1965 Huitfeld
1966 Willemoes, Esbern Snare

CORVETTE
1963 Thetis

Strength of the Fleet

- 6 Frigates
- 4 Corvettes
- 6 Patrol Submarines
- 8 Missile Boats (under construction)
- 16 Torpedo Boats
- 35 Patrol Craft
- 7 Minelayers
- 8 Coastal Minesweepers
- 4 Inshore Minesweepers
- 2 Depot Ships
- 2 Oilers
- 5 Icebreakers
- 1 Royal Yacht

Navy Estimates

1968-69: 390 900 000 Kr.
1969-70: 418 800 000 Kr.
1970-71: 441 800 000 Kr.
1971-72: 478 500 000 Kr.
1972-73: 520 400 000 Kr.

Personnel

January 1973; 6 600 officers and men
(Reserve of 3 000 Maritime Home Guard)

Mercantile Marine

Lloyd's Register of Shipping
1 331 vessels of 4 019 927 tons gross

FRIGATES

2 "PEDER SKRAM" CLASS

Displacement, tons	2 030 standard; 2 720 full load
Length, feet (*metres*)	354·3 (108) pp; 396·5 (*112·6*) oa
Beam, feet (*metres*)	39·5 (*12*)
Draught, feet (*metres*)	11·8 (*3·6*)
Guns, surface	4—5 in (*127 mm*) 38 cal
Guns, AA	4—40 mm
A/S weapons	DC
Main engines	CODAG; 2 shafts:— 2 GM 16-567 D diesels; 4 800 hp; 2 Pratt & Whitney PWA GG 4A-3 gas turbines; 44 000 hp total output
Speed, knots	28 designed; over 30 max; 18 economical sea
Complement	112

Name	*No.*	*Builders*	*Laid down*	*Launched*	*Completed*
HERLUF TROLLE	F 353	Helsingörs J. & M.	18 Dec 1964	8 Sep 1965	16 Apr 1967
PEDER SKRAM	F 352	Helsingörs J. & M.	25 Sep 1964	20 May 1965	30 June 1966

GENERAL
Fast frigates of Danish design built at Helsingör. They were to have been armed, additionally to guns, with three 21 inch torpedo tubes and the "Terne" anti-submarine weapon. There is space on the quarter deck for possible future surface-to-air guided missile launcher installation.

HERLUF TROLLE *1972, Royal Danish Navy.*

PENNANT NOS. The pennant numbers allocated originally were D 320 and D 321, when they were designated DE (Destroyer Escorts).

RADAR. Search: Two S Band air and surface search. Tactical: X Band. Fire Control: Three X Band and HSA or Contraves.

Frigates—*continued*

4 "HVIDBJØRNEN" CLASS

Name	No.	Builders	Laid down	Launched	Completed
FYLLA	F 351	Aalborg Værft	27 June 1962	18 Dec 1962	10 July 1963
HVIDBJØRNEN	F 348	Aarhus Flydedok	4 June 1961	23 Nov 1961	15 Dec 1962
INGOLF	F 350	Svendborg Værft	5 Dec 1961	27 July 1961	27 July 1963
VÆDDEREN	F 349	Aalborg Værft	30 Oct 1961	6 Apr 1962	19 Mar 1963

Displacement, tons	1 345 standard; 1 650 full load
Length, feet (*metres*)	219·8 (*67·0*) pp; 238·2 (*72·6*) oa
Beam, feet (*metres*)	38·0 (*11·6*)
Draught, feet (*metres*)	16 (*4·9*)
Aircraft	1 Alouette III helicopter
Guns, dual purpose	1—3 in (*76 mm*)
Main engines	4 GM 16—567C diesels; 6 400 bhp; 1 shaft
Speed, knots	18
Range, miles	6 000 at 13 knots
Complement	75

GENERAL
Ordered in 1960-61. Of frigate type for fishery protection and surveying duties in the North Ses, Faroe Islands and Greenland waters. They are equipped with a helicopter platform aft.

RADAR. Search: S Band combined air and surface Navigation: X Band.

FYLLA — *1972, Royal Danish Navy*

CORVETTES

4 "TRITON" CLASS

Name	No.	Builders	Launched	Transferred
BELLONA	F 344	Naval Meccanicia, Castellammare	9 Jan 1955	31 Jan 1957
DIANA	F 345	Cantiere del Tirreno, Riva, Trigoso	19 Dec 1954	30 July 1955
FLORA	F 346	Cantiere del Tirreno, Riva, Trigoso	25 June 1955	28 Aug 1956
TRITON	F 347	Cantiere Navali di Taranto	12 Sep 1954	10 Aug 1955

Displacement, tons	760 standard; 873 full load
Length, feet (*metres*)	242·8 (*74·0*) pp; 250·3 (*76·3*) oa
Beam, feet (*metres*)	31·5 (*9·6*)
Draught, feet (*metres*)	9 (*2·7*)
Guns, surface	2—3 in (*76 mm*)
Guns, AA	1—40 mm
A/S	2 Hedgehogs; 4 DCT
Main engines	2 Ansaldo Fiat 409T diesels 4 400 bhp; 2 shafts
Speed, knots	18 designed, 20 max 16 sea
Range, miles	3 000 at 18 knots
Complement	110

GENERAL
All four vessels were built in Italy for the Danish Navy under the United States "offshore" account in the Mutual Defence Assistance Programme. Sisters of the Italian "Albatros" class.

RADAR. Search: Plessey AWS 1. Navigation: S Band.

CLASSIFICATION. Officially classified as corvettes in 1954, but have "F" pennant numbers like frigates.

FLORA — *1972, Royal Danish Navy*

SUBMARINES

2 "NARHVALEN" CLASS

Name	No.	Laid down	Launched	Completed
NARHVALEN	S 320	16 Feb 1965	10 Sep 1968	27 Feb 1970
NORDKAPEREN	S 321	20 Jan 1966	18 Dec 1969	22 Dec 1970

Displacement, tons	**370 surface; 450 submerged**
Length, feet (*metres*)	**144·4 (*44·0*)**
Beam, feet (*metres*)	**15 (*4·6*)**
Draught, feet (*metres*)	**12·5 (*3·8*)**
Torpedo tubes	**8—21 in (*533 mm*) bow, internal**
Main engines	**Diesels; 1 200 bhp surface; electric motors; 1 200 hp submerged**
Speed, knots	**10 surface; 17 submerged**
Complement	**21**

These coastal submarines are similar to the German "U-4" class and were built under licence at the Royal Dockyard, Copenhagen. They are fitted with snort. Originally numbered S 330 and S 331.

NARHVALEN — *1970, Royal Danish Navy*

4 "DELFINEN" CLASS

Name	No.	Laid down	Launched	Completed
DELFINEN	S 326	1 July 1954	4 May 1956	16 Sep 1958
SPÆKHUGGEREN	S 327	1 Dec 1954	20 Feb 1957	27 June 1959
SPRINGEREN	S 329	3 Jan 1961	26 Apr 1963	22 Oct 1964
TUMLEREN	S 328	22 May 1956	22 May 1958	15 Jan 1960

Displacement, tons	**550 standard; 595 surface; 643 submerged**
Length, feet (*metres*)	**117·2 (*54·0*)**
Beam, feet (*metres*)	**15·4 (*4·7*)**
Draught, feet (*metres*)	**13·1 (*4·0*)**
Torpedo tubes	**4—21 in (*533 mm*)**
Main engines	**2 Burmeister & Wain diesels 1 200 bhp surface; electric motors; 1 200 hp submerged**
Speed, knots	**15 surface and submerged**
Range, miles	**4 000 at 8 knots**
Complement	**33**

Built in the Royal Dockyard, Copenhagen. Engined with diesels of a new type. Equipped with snort.

SPRINGEREN — *1972, Royal Danish Navy*

LIGHT FORCES

8 200 ton TYPE MISSILE BOATS

Displacement, tons	*circa* 240
Guided weapons	To be installed
Guns	1—76 mm Oto Melara or 1—57 mm L 70 Bofors
Torpedo tubes	4—21 in
Main engines	CODAG arrangement of 3 Rolls Royce Proteus gas turbines plus diesels for cruising.
Speed, knots	40 max approx

First four ordered from Royal Dockyard Copenhagen, 1971 to complete in 1975-76. Further four now building. Lürssen Werft design. Controllable pitch propellers.

6 "SØLØVEN" CLASS TORPEDO BOATS

Name	Pennant No.	Laid down	Launched	Completed
SØLØVEN	P 510	27 Aug 1962	19 Apr 1963	June 1964*
SØRIDDEREN	P 511	4 Oct 1962	22 Aug 1963	June 1964*
SØBJORNEN	P 512	9 July 1963	19 Aug 1964	Sep 1965
SØHESTEN	P 513	5 Sep 1963	31 Mar 1965	June 1966
SØHUNDEN	P 514	18 Aug 1964	12 Jan 1966	Dec 1966
SØULVEN	P 515	30 Mar 1965	27 Apr 1966	Mar 1967

Displacement, tons	95 standard; 114 full load
Dimensions, feet	90 pp; 96 wl; 99 oa × 25·5 × 7
Guns	2—40 mm Bofors AA
Tubes	4—21 in (side)
Main engines	3 Bristol Siddeley Proteus gas turbines; 3 shafts; 12 750 bhp = 54 knots GM diesels on wing shafts for cruising = 10 knots
Range, miles	400 at 46 knots
Complement	29

The design is a combination of the "Brave" class hull form and "Ferocity" type construction. *Søløven* ("Sea Lion") and *Søridderen* ("Sea Knight") were built by Vosper Limited, Portsmouth, England (*delivered to the Royal Danish Navy on 12 and 10 Feb 1965, respectively); and the remaining four under licence by the Royal Dockyard, Copenhagan.

SØULVEN *1970, Royal Danish Navy*

4 "FALKEN" CLASS TORPEDO BOATS

Name	Pennant No.	Laid down	Launched	Completed
FALKEN	P 506	1 Nov 1960	19 Dec 1961	4 Oct 1962
GLENTEN	P 507	3 Jan 1961	15 Mar 1962	15 Dec 1962
GRIBBEN	P 508	15 May 1961	18 July 1962	26 Apr 1963
HØGEN	P 509	1 Sep 1961	4 Oct 1962	6 June 1963

Displacement, tons	119
Dimensions, feet	118 × 17·8 × 6
Guns	1—40 mm AA; 1—20 mm AA
Tubes	4—21 in (side)
Main engines	3 diesels; 3 shafts; 9 000 bhp = 40 knots
Complement	23

Ordered under US offshore procurement in the Military Aid Programme. All built at the Royal Dockyard, Copenhagen. Named after birds.

GRIBBEN *1970, Royal Danlsh Navy*

6 "FLYVEFISKEN" CLASS TORPEDO BOATS

FLYVEFISKEN P 500 **HAJEN** P 501 **HAVKATTEN** P 502 **LAXEN** P 503 **MAKRELEN** P 504 **SVÆRDFISKEN** P 505

Displacement, tons	110
Dimensions, feet	120 × 18 × 6
Guns	1—40 mm AA; 1—20 mm AA
Tubes	2—21 in
Main engines	3 diesels; 3 shafts; 7 500 bhp = 40 knots
Complement	22

Three built in Royal Dockyard, Copenhagen, three in Frederikssund Vaerft. All units are named after fishes. Ordered in 1952, laid down in 1953 and launched in 1954-55.

SVÆRDFISKEN *1970, Royal Danish Navy*

9 "DAPHNE" CLASS PATROL BOATS

Name	Pennant No.	Laid down	Launched	Completed
DAPHNE	P 530	1 Apr 1960	10 Nov 1960	19 Dec 1961
DRYADEN	P 531	1 July 1960	1 Mar 1961	4 Apr 1962
HAVFRUEN	P 533	15 Mar 1961	4 Oct 1961	20 Dec 1962
HAVMANDEN	P 532	15 Nov 1960	16 May 1961	30 Aug 1962
NAJADEN	P 534	20 Sep 1961	20 June 1962	26 Apr 1963
NEPTUN	P 536	1 Sep 1962	29 May 1963	18 Dec 1963
NYMFEN	P 535	1 Apr 1962	1 Nov 1962	4 Oct 1963
RAN	P 537	1 Dec 1962	10 July 1963	15 May 1964
ROTA	P 538	19 July 1963	25 Nov 1963	20 Jan 1965

Displacement, tons	170
Dimensions, feet	121·3 × 20 × 6·5
Guns	1—40 mm AA
A/S weapons	2—51 mm rocket launchers, depth charges
Main engines	Diesels; 2 shafts; 2 600 bhp = 20 knots (plus 1 cruising engine; 100 bhp)
Complement	23

All built at the Royal Dockyard, Copenhagen.

NEPTUN *1970. Royal Danish Navy*

6 "BARSØ" CLASS PATROL CRAFT

BARSØ Y 300 **DREJØ** Y 301 **ROMSØ** Y 302 **SAMSØ** Y 303 **THURØ** Y 304 **VEJRØ** Y 305

Displacement, tons	155
Dimensions, feet	83·7 × 19·7 × 9·8
Speed	11 knots

Rated as patrol cutters. All launched and completed in 1969.

BARSØ *1970, Royal Danish Navy*

2 "MAGAEN" CLASS PATROL CRAFT

MAAGEN (Y 384) **MALLEMUKKEN** (Y 385)

Displacement, tons	190
Dimensions, feet	88·5 × 21·7 × 9·5
Guns	1—40 mm AA
Main engines	385 hp; 1 shaft; speed 11 knots

Of steel construction. Built at Helsingor, laid down 15 Jan 1960, launched 1960.

1 "SKARVEN" CLASS PATROL CRAFT

TEJSTEN (Y 383)

Displacement, tons	130
Dimensions, feet	82 × 20·7 × 9·4
Guns	1—37 mm
Main engines	Alfa Diesel; 180 bhp = 9 knots

Of wooden construction. Built by Holbaek Skibsbyggeri. Launched 1951. Sister boat *Skarven*, Y 382, was disabled by grounding in the Faroes on 7 May 1966 and officially deleted from the list. All three above for service in Greenland waters.

1 "ALHOLM" CLASS PATROL CRAFT

ERTHOLM Y 371 (ex-*MSK* 3)

Displacement, tons	70
Dimensions, feet	69 × 17 × 9
Guns	1—20 mm AA
Main engines	Diesel; 120 bhp = 10 knots

Built by Frederikssund Vaerft. Launched in 1945. A photograph of this class (*Alholm*) appears in the 1968-69 edition. Of sister boats *Birkholm* Y 370 (ex-MSK 2) was officially deleted from the list in 1969, and *Alholm* Y 369 (ex-MSK 1) in 1972.

1 "FYRHOLM" CLASS PATROL CRAFT

LINDHOLM Y 374 (ex-*MSK* 6)

Displacement, tons	68
Dimensions, feet	65·7 × 16·8 × 7·5
Main engines	Diesel; 120 bhp = 9 knots

Built by Sydhavns Vaerft. Launched in 1945. Of sister boats *Græsholm* Y 373 (ex-MSK 5) was officially deleted from the list in 1968 and *Fyrholm* T 372 (ex-MSK 4) in 1969.

Light Forces—*continued*

7 "FÆNØ" CLASS PATROL CRAFT

ASKØ MHV 81 (ex-Y 386, ex-M 560, ex-MS 2)
BAAGØ MHV 84 (ex-Y 387, ex-M 561, ex-MS 3)
ENØ MHV 82 (ex-Y 388, ex-M 562, ex-MS 5)
FÆNØ MHV 69 (ex-M 563, ex-MS 6)
HJORTØ MHV 85 (ex-Y 389, ex-M 564, ex-MS 7)
LYØ MHV 86 (ex-Y 390, ex-M 565, ex-MS 8)
MANØ MHV 83 (ex-Y 391, ex-M 566, ex-MS 9)

Displacement, tons 74
Dimensions, feet 78·8 × 21 × 5
Guns 1—20 mm
Main engines Diesel; 1 shaft; 350 bhp = 11 knots

Of wooden construction. All launched in 1941. Former inshore minesweepers. Used by the Maritime Home Guard.

FÆNO 1969, *Royal Danish Navy*

MHV 60 **MHV 71** **MHV 72**

Displacement, tons 76
Guns 1—20 mm AA
Main engines 200 bhp = 10 knots

Built in 1958. Patrol boats and training craft for the Naval Home Guard. Of the fishing cutter type. Formerly designated DMH, but allocated MHV numbers in 1969. In addition there are some 20 small vessels of the trawler and other types.

5 "Y" TYPE

Y 338 **Y 339** **Y 343** **Y 354** **Y 359**

Miscellaneous patrol cutters (ex-fishing vessels) all built in 1944-45. Y 342 and Y 347 were removed from the list in 1971.

MINE WARFARE FORCES

4 "FALSTER" CLASS MINELAYERS

Name	*No.*	*Builders*	*Laid down*	*Launched*	*Completed*
FALSTER	N 80	Nakskov Skibsvaerft	12 Apr 1962	19 Sep 1962	7 Nov 1963
FYEN	N 81	Frederikshavn Værft	12 Apr 1962	3 Oct 1962	18 Sep 1963
MØEN	N 82	Frederikshavn Værft	4 Oct 1962	6 Mar 1963	29 Apr 1964
SJÆLLAND	N 83	Nakskov Skibsvaerft	17 Jan 1963	14 June 1963	7 July 1964

Displacement, tons 1 900 full load
Length, feet (*metres*) 238 (*72·5*) pp; 252·6 (*77·0*) oa
Beam, feet (*metres*) 41 (*12·5*)
Draught, feet (*metres*) 10 (*3·0*)
Guns, duel purpose 4—3 in (*76 mm*), 2 twin mountings
Mines 400
Main engines 2 GM—567D 3 diesels; 4 800 shp 2 shafts
Speed, knots 17
Complement 120

GENERAL
Minelayers of a novel Scandinavian-NATO design. Ordered in 1960-61. All are named after Danish islands. The steel hull is flush-decked with a raking stem, a full stern and a prominent knuckle forward. The super structure has a block outline surmounted by a squat streamlined funnel, two light lattice masts, high angle director control towers fore and aft and whip aerials. The hull has been specially strengthened for ice navigation.

RADAR. Search: C Band low coverage. Navigation: S and X Band.

SJÆLLAND 1972 *Royal Danish Navy*

1 "LANGELAND" CLASS COASTAL MINELAYER

LANGELAND N 42

Displacement, tons 310 standard; 332 full load
Dimensions, feet 133·5 oa; 128·2 pp × 23·7 × 7·2
Guns 2—40 mm; 2—20 mm Madsen
Main engines Diesel; 2 shafts; 385 bhp = 11·6 knots
Complement 37

Built at the Royal Dockyard, Copenhagen. Laid down in 1950. Launched on 17 May 1950. Completed in 1951

LANGELAND 1971, *Royal Danish Navy*

2 "LOUGEN" CLASS COASTAL MINELAYERS

LAALAND N 40 **LOUGEN** N 41

Displacement, tons 240 standard; 260 full load
Dimensions, feet 105·5 × 21·2 × 6·5
Guns 2—20 mm AA
Main engines B & W diesel; 2 shafts; 350 bhp = 10 knots
Complement 31

Built at the Royal Dockyard, Copenhagen. Both laid down in 1940, launched in 1941 and completed in 1946. The old coastal minelayer *Lindormen*, N 39, was officially stricken from the list in 1970.

LOUGEN 1971, *Royal Danish Navy*

8 "SUND" CLASS COASTAL MINESWEEPERS

AARØSUND (ex-*AMS* 127) M 571
ALSSUND (ex-*AMS* 128) M 572
EGERNSUND (ex-*AMS* 129) M 573
GRØNSUND (ex-*MSC* 256) M 574
GULDBORGSUND (ex-*MSC* 257) M 575
OMØSUND (ex-*MSC* 221) M 576
ULVSUND (ex-*MSC* 263) M 577
VILSUND (ex-*MSC* 264) M 578

Displacement, tons 350 standard; 376 full load
Dimensions, feet 138 pp; 144 oa × 27 × 8·5
Guns 2—20 mm
Main engines Diesels; 2 shafts; 1 200 bhp = 13 knots
Range, miles 2 500 at 10 knots
Complement 35

MSC (ex-AMS) 60 class NATO coastal minesweepers all built in USA. Completed in 1954-56. *Aarøsund* was transferred on 24 Jan 1955, *Alssund* on 5 Apr 1955, *Egernsund* on 3 Aug 1955, *Grønsund* on 21 Sep 1956, *Guldborgsund* on 11 Nov 1956. *Omøsund* on 20 June 1956, *Ulvsund* on 20 Sep 1956 and *Vilsund* on 15 Nov 1956.

GULDBORGSUND has been fitted with a charthouse between bridge and funnel and is employed on surveying duties.

Mine Warfare Forces—*continued*

ALSSUND *1970, Royal Danish Navy*

4 "VIG" CLASS INSHORE MINESWEEPERS

Displacement, tons	180
Dimensions, feet	113·5 × 22·5 × 6·2
Guns	2—20 mm AA
Main engines	2 diesels; 2 shafts; 11 000 bhp = 13 knots
Range, miles	2 000 at 9 knots
Complement	18

All built at the Royal Dockyard, Copenhagen.

MOSVIG *1970, Royal Danish Navy*

DEPOT SHIPS

HJÆLPEREN (ex-US *LSM* 500) A 563

Displacement, tons	1 030 standard; 1 170 full load
Dimensions, feet	203·5 oa × 34·5 × 8·3
Guns	2—40 mm
Main engines	Diesels; 2 shafts; 2 800 bhp = 12 knots
Complement	60

Former United States medium landing ship. Built by Brown Shipbuilding Co, Houston. Texas. Laid down on 17 Mar 1945. Launched on 7 Apr 1945. Completed on 17 May 1945. Transferred to the Royal Danish Navy on 15 May 1953. Depot and repair ship for motor torpedo boats.

HJÆLPEREN *1971, Royal Danish Navy*

HENRIK GERNER (ex-M/S *Hammershus*) A 542

Displacement, tons	2 200 standard
Dimensions, feet	252·7 × 40 × 18·3
Guns	6—40 mm AA
Main engines	Burmeister & Wain diesel; speed = 15 knots
Complement	230

Former Danish passenger ship. Built in 1936. Transferred to the Royal Danish Navy on 8 Jan 1964, refitted at the Royal Dockyard, Copenhagen, and commissioned as a depot ship for submarines.

HENRIK GERNER *1971, Royal Danish Navy*

Depot Ships—*continued*

The tenders *Hollaenderdybet* (ex-*Den Lille Havfrue*), A 554, and *Kongedybet* (ex-*Kirsten Pill*), A 555, were officially stricken from the list in 1970.

The depot ship *Aegir*, ex-German *Tanga*, was officially deleted from the list in Jan 1967.

OILERS

RIMFAXE (ex-US *YO* 226) A 568 **SKINFAXE** (ex-US *YO* 229) A 569

Displacement, tons	422 light; 1 390 full load
Dimensions, feet	174 oa × 32 × 13·2
Main engines	1 GM diesel; 560 bhp = 10 knots
Complement	23

Yard oilers transferred to the Royal Danish Navy from the USA on 2 Aug 1962. A photograph of *Skinfaxe* appears in the 1968-69 to 1970-71 editions.

RIMFAXE *1971, Royal Danish Navy*

ICEBREAKERS

(Icebreakers are controlled by the Ministry of Trade and Shipping.)

DANBJØRN **ISBJØRN**

Displacement, tons	3 685
Dimensions, feet	252 × 56 × 20
Main engines	Diesels; Electric drive; 11 880 bhp = 14 knots
Complement	34

Built in 1965. The old two-funnelled icebreaker *Isbjørn* was discarded in 1969.

DANBJØRN *1970, Royal Danish Navy*

ELBJØRN

Displacement, tons	893 standard; 1 400 full load
Dimensions, feet	156·5 × 40·3 × 14·5
Main engines	Diesels; electric drive; 3 600 bhp = 12 knots

Built in 1953.

STOREBJØRN

Displacement, tons	2 540
Dimensions, feet	197 × 49·2 × 19

Built in 1931.

LILLEBJØRN

Displacement, tons	1 000
Dimensions, feet	144·3 × 36·5 × 18

Built in 1926. The small icebreaker *Mjolner* was removed from the list in 1960.

ROYAL YACHT

DANNEBROG A 540

Displacement, tons	1 130
Dimensions, feet	246 oa × 34 × 11·2
Guns	2—37 mm
Main engines	2 sets Burmeister & Wain 8 cylinder; 2 cycle diesels. 1 800 bhp = 14 knots
Complement	57

Built at the Royal Dockyard, Copenhagen. Launched on 10 Oct 1931.

DANNEBROG *1971, Royal Danish Navy*

DOMINICAN REPUBLIC

Administration

Under Secretary for the Navy:
Commodore Francisco A. Amiama Castillo

Chief of Naval Staff:
Commodore Manuel A. Logroño Contin

Vice-Chief of Naval Staff:
Captain Francisco A. Marte Victoria

Disposals

DESTROYERS
1968 Sanchez (ex-*Fame*)
1972 Duarte (ex-*Hotspur*)

CORVETTES
Ex-US PCs
1962 Patria
1968 27 de Febrero Constitucion

Strength of the Fleet

3 Frigates
5 Corvettes
3 Landing Craft
9 Patrol Craft
2 Survey Craft
2 Oilers
10 Tugs
2 Minesweepers

New Construction

Five corvettes are projected to replace the "Flower" Type.

Personnel

1973: 3 810 officers and men

Mercantile Marine

Lloyd's Register of Shipping
17 vessels of 8 881 tons gross

FRIGATES

2 Ex-US "TACOMA" CLASS

Name	*Pennant No.*	*Builders*	*Laid down*	*Launched*	*Completed*
CAP. GENERAL PEDRO SANTANA (ex-*Presidente Troncoso*, ex-USS *Knoxville*, PF 64)	453 (ex-F 104)	Kaiser S.Y. Richmond, Cal.	14 Nov 1943	20 Jan 1944	27 May 1944
GREGORIO LUPERON (ex-*Presidente Peynado*, ex-USS *Pueblo*, PF 13)	452 (ex-F 103)	Leatham D. Smith S.B. Co, Wis.	15 Apr 1943	10 July 1943	29 Apr 1944

Displacement, tons: 1 430 standard; 2 415 full load
Length, feet (*metres*): 298·0 (*90·8*) wl; 304·0 (*92·7*) oa
Beam, feet (*metres*): 37·5 (*11·4*)
Draught, feet (*metres*): 12·0 (*3·7*); 13·7 (*4·2*)
Guns: 3—3 in (*76 mm*) single; 4—40 mm (2 twin); 6—20 mm; 4—0·5 in (*12·7 mm*) MG (2 twin)
Main engines: Triple expansion; 2 shafts; 5 500 ihp
Speed, knots: 19 (designed)
Boilers: 2 of three-drum type
Oil fuel, tons: 760
Range, miles: 9 500 at 12 knots
Complement: 140

Formerly United States patrol frigates, PF of the "Tacoma" class similar to the contempory British frigates of the "River" class. Transferred from the US Navy to the Dominican Republic Navy in 1949. Renamed in 1962.

GREGORIO LUPERON — *1972, Dominican Navy*

1 Ex-CANADIAN "RIVER" TYPE

MELLA (ex-*Presidente Trujillo*, ex-HMS *Carlplace*) 451

Displacement, tons: 1 400 standard; 2 125 full load
Length, feet (*metres*): 301·5 (*91·9*)
Beam, feet (*metres*): 36·7 (*11·2*)
Draught, feet (*metres*): 12·0 (*3·7*) mean
Guns: 1—4 in; 2—47 mm; 1—40 mm; 4—20 mm (2 twin)
Main engines: Triple expansion; 2 shafts; 5 500 ihp
Speed, knots: 20
Boilers: 2 of three-drum type
Oil fuel, tons: 645
Range, miles: 4 200 at 12 knots
Complement: 195 (15 officers, 130 ratings, 50 midshipmen)

MELLA — *1972, Dominican Navy*

Built by Davies SB & Repairing Co, Lauzon, Canada. Launched on 6 July 1944. Completed on 13 Dec 1944. Transferred to the Dominican Navy in 1946. Original Dominican frigate. Modified for use as Presidental Yacht with extra accommodation and deck-houses built up aft. Pennant number as a frigate was F 101, but as the Presidential Yacht it was no longer worn. Now carries pennant number 451 as training ship. Renamed *Mella* in 1962. Used for training midshipmen.

CORVETTES

2 Ex-CANADIAN "FLOWER" TYPE

Name	*Pennant No.*	*Builders*	*Launched*	*Completed*
CRISTOBAL COLON (ex-HMCS *Lachute*)	401 (ex-C 101)	Morton Ltd, Quebec City, P.Q.	9 June 1944	24 Oct 1944
JUAN ALEJANDRO ACOSTA (ex-HMCS *Louisbourg*)	402 (ex-C 102)	Morton Ltd, Quebec City, P.Q.	13 July 1943	13 Dec 1943

Displacement, tons: 1 060 standard; 1 350 full load
Length, feet (*metres*): 193·0 (*58·8*) pp; 208·0 (*63·4*) oa
Beam, feet (*metres*): 33·0 (*10·0*)
Draught, feet (*metres*): 13·3 (*4·0*) mean
Guns, surface: 1—4 in (*102 mm*)
Guns, AA: *C. Colon:* 2—40 mm (twin) 6—20 mm; 4—0·5 in MG (2 twin) *J. A. Acosta*: 1—40 mm; 6—20 mm; 2—0·5 in MG
Main engines: Triple expansion; 2 750 ihp
Speed, knots: 16
Boilers: 2 of three-drum type
Oil fuel, tons: 282
Range, miles: 2 900 at 15 knots
Complement: 53

Built in Canadian shipyards under the emergency construction programme during the Second World War. Transferred to the Dominican Navy in 1947. Pennant numbers were changed in 1968, 300 being added to all numbers and letter C suppressed.

DISPOSALS
Of three sister ships *Gerardo Jansen* (ex-HMCS *Peterborough*), 404 (ex-C 104), *Juan Bautista Cambiaso* (ex-HMCS *Belleville*), 403 (ex-C 103) and *Juan Bautista Maggiolo* (ex-HMCS *Riviere du loup*, 405 (ex-C 105) were officially deleted from the list in 1972. The sixth ship of the class, *Asbestos*, was wrecked *en route* from Canada.

JUAN ALEJANDRO ACOSTA — *1972, Dominican Navy*

AMPHIBIOUS CRAFT

1 Ex-US LSM

SIRIO (ex-USS *LSM* 483) 301 (ex-BA 104)

Displacement, tons	734 standard; 1 100 full load
Dimensions, feet	196 wl; 203·5 oa × 34 × 10 mean
Main engines	2 General Motors diesels; 2 shafts; 1 800 bhp = 14 knots
Oil fuel, tons	164
Complement	30

Ex-United States *LSM* (Medium Landing Ship). Built by Brown Shipbuilding Co. Houston, Texas. Laid down on 17 Feb 1945, launched on 10 Mar 1945 and completed on 13 April 1945. Transferred to the Dominican Navy in 1960. Pennant number changed from BA 104 to 301 in 1968. Refitted in Dominica in 1970.

SIRIO *1972, Dominican Navy*

2 LCUs

ENRIQUILLO (ex-*17 de Julio*) 303 (ex-LA 3) **SAMANA** 302 (ex-LA 2)

Displacement, tons	150 standard; 310 full load
Dimensions, feet	105 wl; 119·5 oa × 36 × 3 mean
Guns	1 AA, 50 cal
Main engines	3 General Motors diesels; 441 bhp = 8 knots
Oil fuel, tons	80
Complement	17

Both built by Astilleros Navales Dominicanos in 1957-58. The new *Samana*, LA 2, replaced the *Samana* LA 2 lost in bad weather. *Enriquilla* (ex-17 *de Julio*) was launched on 24 Oct 1957. Renamed in 1962. Pennant numbers changed from LA 3 and LA 2 to 303 and 302, respectively, in 1968.

SAMANA *1972, Dominican Navy*

LIGHT FORCES

3 Ex-USCG WPC TYPE

	Pennant No.	Launched
INDEPENDENCIA (ex-USCGC *Icarus*)	204 (ex-P 105)	1931
LIBERTAD (ex-*Rafael Atoa*, ex-USCGC *Thetis*)	205 (ex-P 106)	1931
RESTAURACION (ex-USCGC *Galathea*)	203 (ex-P 104)	1932

Displacement, tons	337 standard
Dimensions, feet	165·0 × 25·2 × 9·5
Guns	1—3 in; 1—40 mm AA; 1—20 mm AA
Main engines	2 Diesels; 1 280 bhp = 15 knots
Range, miles	1 300 at 15 knots
Complement	49 (5 officers, 44 men)

Ex-US Coastguard Cutters. *Independencia* was completed by Bath Iron Works in 1932, and *Restauracion* by John H. Machis & Co, Camden, NJ, in 1933. Pennant numbers were changed from P 105, P 106, P 104 to 200 series in 1968.

RESTAURACION *1972, Dominican Navy*

Light Forces—*continued*

1 US PGM TYPE

BETELGEUSE (ex-US *PGM* 77) GC 102

Displacement, tons	145·5
Dimensions, feet	101·5 × 21·0 × 5·0
Guns	1—40 mm; 4—20 mm AA (2 twin); 2—0·5 in 50 cal MG
Main engines	8 diesels; 2 shafts; 2 200 bhp = 21 knots
Range, miles	1 500 at 10 knots
Complement	20

Built in the USA and transferred to the Dominican Republic under the Military Aid Programme. Completed in 1966 by Peterson Builders. Transferred on 14 Jan 1966.

BETELGEUSE *1972, Dominican Navy*

RIGEL GC 101 (ex-US AVR)

Displacement, tons	27 standard; 32·2 full load
Dimensions, feet	63·0 × 15·5 × 5·0
Guns	2—50 cal MG
Main engines	General Motors V8—71 diesels = 18·5 knots
Complement	9

Originally built in 1953. Reconditioned by NAUSTA, Keywest, USA.

DISPOSALS

The former GC 102, *Las Carreras*, ex-*Sanchez*, ex-*Patria*, ex-*SC 1153*, and her sister boat GC 101, *30 de Marzo*, ex-*Mella*, ex-*Rosa*, ex-*SC 1351*, were discarded in 1966-67. *Las Calderas* (ex-*Luberon*, GC 9) and *Bahia Ocoa* (ex-*22 de Junio*, GC 10) were discarded in 1968. Sister boat *Bahia Manzanillo* GC 11 (ex-*16 de Agosto*, ex-USCG cutter 56199) was discarded in 1962. The coastguard vessel *Trinidad*, GC 8, was also discarded in 1962, and *Boya*, GC 2, in 1960. The training ship *Duarte* (ex-*Nueva Tioditie*), GA 1 was discarded in 1962.

RIGEL *1969, Dominican Navy*

3 "BELLATRIX" CLASS

BELLATRIX GC 106 **CAPELLA** GC 108 **PROCYON** GC 103

Displacement, tons	60
Dimensions, feet	85 × 18 × 5
Guns	3—·5 mg
Main engines	2 GM Diesels; 500 bhp = 18·7 knots

Built by Sewart Seacraft Inc. at Berwick, Louisiana. Transferred to the Dominican Navy by USA, *Bellatrix* on 18 Aug 1967, *Procyon* on 1 May 1957 and *Capella* on 15 Oct 1968.

BELLATRIX *1970, Dominican Navy*

Light Forces—*continued*

2 "ATLANTIDA" TYPE

PUERTO HEMOSA LA 7 **ATLANTIDA** LA 8

The motor launch *Altogracia*, LA-1 (ex-*Laura*), was discarded in 1960 and *Najaya*, LA 4, in 1962.

CAPITAN LASINA GC 105 (ex-LR 101)

Displacement, tons	100 standard
Dimensions, feet	92·0 wl; 104·8 oa × 19·2 × 5·8
Guns	2—20 mm AA
Main engines	2 GM diesels; 2 shafts; 1 000 hp = 17 knots
Complement	20

Of wooden construction. Launched in 1944. Named as above in 1957. LR 102 was lost in 1956. Sister boat *Capitan Maduro*, LR 103 was discarded in 1968.

CAPITAN LASINA *1972, Dominican Navy*

DISPOSALS. The auxiliary ships (*Buques Auxiliaries*) *18 de Decembre*, BA-101 (ex-US *WPC* 587), converted patrol vessel, and *Leonor*, BA-102 (ex-*Romanita*), were discarded in 1960. The Presidential yacht *Patria* (ex-*Angelita*) was sold in 1968.

1 BROOKE MARINE LAUNCH

Displacement, tons	15
Dimensions, feet	40 × 12 × 2
Guns	3 MG
Main engines	2 Diesels; 370 bhp = 22 knots

Ordered 30 March 1971 and delivered Sept 1972.

FLEET MINESWEEPERS

2 Ex-US MSF TYPE

SEPARACION (ex-USS *Skirmish*, MSF 303) BM 454 **TORTUGERO** (ex-USS *Signet*, MSF 302) BM 455

Displacement. tons	650 standard; 900 full load
Dimensions, feet	180·0 wl; 184·5 oa × 33·0 × 14·5
Guns	1—3 in; 2—40 mm AA; 6—20 mm AA
Main engines	2 diesels; 2 shafts; 1 710 bhp = 14 knots
Range, miles	5 600 at 9 knots
Complement	90 (8 officers, 82 men)

Former US fleet minesweepers of the "Admirable" class. Purchased on 13 Jan 1965.

SEPARACION *1972, Dominican Navy*

SURVEY CRAFT

1 SURVEY VESSEL

CAPOTILLO (ex-*Camillia*) (ex-FB 101) 1

Displacement, tons	337
Dimensions, feet	117 × 24 × 7·8
Main engines	2 Diesels; 880 bhp = 10 knots
Complement	29

Built in the United States in 1911. Acquired from the United States Coast Guard in 1949. Underwent a major refit in Dominica in 1970.

CAPOTILLO *1972, Dominican Navy*

Survey Craft—*continued*

1 SURVEY LAUNCH

CAONABO LA 5

Displacement, tons	12
Dimensions, feet	53 × 9 × 4
Main engines	2 motors; 500 hp = 14 knots
Complement	6

Acquired for the Hydrographic Service of the Navy in 1960.

1971

OILERS

2 Ex-US YO TYPE COASTAL TANKERS

CAPITAN W ARVELO BT 4 (ex-USS *YO 215*) **CAPITAN BEOTEGUI** BT 5 (ex-US *YO 213*)

Displacement, tons	370 light; 1 400 full load
Dimensions, feet	174·0 × 32·0 × 13·0
Guns	1—20 mm
Main engines	1 Fairbanks-Morse diesel; 525 bhp = 8 knots max
Capacity	6 570 barrels
Complement	27

Former United States self-propelled fuel oil barges. Both built by Ira S. Bushey & Sons, Inc, Brooklyn, New York. Loaned by the USA in Mar 1964.

CAPITAN W. ARVELO *1969, Dominican Navy*

DISPOSALS. The oiler *San Carlos*, BT 102, was officially deleted from the list in Feb 1965 and *Ulises Heureaux* (ex-*24 de Octubre*, ex-YO 2) BT 101, in 1968.

TUGS

1 Ex-US MARICOPA CLASS

CAONABO RM 18 (ex-USS *Sagamore* ATA 208)

Displacement, tons	534 standard; 835 full load
Dimensions, feet	143 oa × 33·9 × 13
Guns	1—3 in 50 cal
Main engines	2 GM diesel-electric; 1 shaft; 1 500 bhp = 13 knots

Transferred 1 Feb 1972.

2 "HERCULES" TYPE

HERCULES RP 12 (ex-R 2) **GUACANAGARIX** RP 13 (ex-R 5)

Dimensions, feet	70·0 × 15·6 × 9·0
Main engines	1 Caterpillar motor; 500 hp; 1 225 rpm
Complement	8 to 11

Small tugs of coastal type built by Astilleros Navalis Dominicos in 1960.

HERCULES *1971*

Tugs—*continued*

1 US TYPE

ISABELA RP 20 (ex-R 1)

Displacement, tons	40
Dimensions, feet	65 × 14 × 9
Main engines	2 diesel motors; 300 bhp = 8 knots
Complement	8

Built in the United States. Named *Isabela* in 1957. A photograph appears in the 1951-52 to 1957-58 editions. The tug *Hercules* (ex-*Heracles*), Pennant No. R 2, transferred from the Dominican mercantile marine in 1952, was lost in 1956.

6 "BERGANTIN" TYPE

BOHECHIO RP 16 **CONSUELO** RP 18 **HAINA** RP 17
CALDERAS RP 19 **MAGUANA** RP 14 (ex-R 10) **SANTANA** RP 15 (ex-R 7)

Small tugs for harbour and coastal use. Not all of uniform type and dimensions.

DISPOSALS. The tugs *Bergantin*, R-6, *Catalina*, R-3, *Leonidas*, R-8 and *Luperon* R-4 were discarded in 1960-62.

ECUADOR

Administration

Minister of Defence:
Senor Luis Robles Plaza

Commander-in-Chief of the Navy:
Rear Admiral Reinaldo Vallejo Vivas

Diplomatic Representation

Naval Attaché in London:
Vacant

Naval Attaché in Washington:
Commander M. Valviviezo

Strength of the Fleet

4 Frigates
2 Corvettes
3 Torpedo Boats (PTB)
2 Motor Gunboats (PGM Type)
6 Patrol Boats (Motor Launches)
2 Medium Landing Ships (LSM Type)
1 Supply Ship (Cargo)
1 Survey Ship (ex-Netlayer)
1 Water Carrier (YW Type)
3 Tugs (1 Ocean, 2 Harbour)

Ships

The names of Ecuadorian naval vessels are prefaced by "BAE".

Establishments

The Naval Academy is in Salinas

Naval Bases

Guayaquil, Salinas, and San Lorenzo y Galapagos

Personnel

1973: Total 3 800 (300 officers and 3 500 men)

Mercantile Marine

Lloyd's Register of Shipping:
21 vessels of 56 807 tons gross

FRIGATES

1 Ex-US "TACOMA" CLASS

Name	Pennant No.	Builders	Laid down	Launched	Completed
GUAYAS (ex-USS *Covington* PF 56)	E 21 (ex-E 01)	Globe S.B, Co. Superior, Wis.	1 Mar 1943	15 July 1943	7 Aug 1944

Displacement, tons	1 430 standard; 2 415 full load
Length, feet (*metres*)	304·0 (*92·7*) oa
Beam, feet (*metres*)	37·5 (*11·4*)
Draught, feet (*metres*)	13·7 (*4·2*)
Guns, surface	2—3 in (*76 mm*) single
Guns, AA	2—40 mm; 4—20 mm
A/S weapons	3 DCT
Boilers	2 small tube
Main engines	Triple expansion; 2 shafts; 5 500 ihp
Speed, knots	19 max; 16 sea
Radius, miles	9 500 at 12 knots
Oil fuel, tons	290 normal; 645 max
Complement	150

Purchased from the USA in 1947.

GUAYAS *1967, Ecuadorian Navy*

2 Ex-BRITISH "HUNT" CLASS (TYPE 1)

Name	Pennant No.	Builders	Laid down	Launched	Completed
PRESIDENTE ALFARO (ex-HMS *Quantock*)	D 2 (ex-D 01)	Scotts' S.B. & Eng Co Ltd, Greenock	26 July 1939	22 Apr 1940	6 Feb 1941
PRESIDENTE VELASCO IBARRA (ex-HMS *Meynell*)	D 3 (ex-D 02)	Swan Hunter & Wigham Richardson, Wallsend	10 Aug 1939	7 June 1940	30 Dec 1940

Displacement, tons	1 000 standard; 1 490 full load
Length, feet (*metres*)	272·3 (*83·0*) pp, 280 (*85·4*) oa
Beam, feet (*metres*)	29 (*8·8*)
Draught, feet (*metres*)	14 (*4·3*)
Guns, surface	4—4 in (*102 mm*)
Guns, AA	2—20 mm
A/S weapons	DC throwers; DC racks
Boilers	2 Admiralty 3-drum
Main engines	Parsons geared turbines (by Wallsend Slipway in *Presidente Velasco Ibarra*) 19 000 shp; 2 shafts
Speed, knots	23 sea
Radius, miles	2 000 at 12 knots; 800 at 25 knots
Oil fuel (tons)	280
Complement	146

PRESIDENTE ALFARO *1970, Ecuadorian Navy*

Former British frigates (ex-escort destroyers) of the "Hunt" class, Type 1, purchased by Ecuador from Great Britain on 18 Oct 1954, and refitted by J. Samuel White & Co. Ltd. Cowes, Isle of Wight. *Quantock* was taken over by the Ecuadorian Navy in Portsmouth Dockyard on 16 Aug 1955, when she was renamed *Presidente Alfaro*. Sister ship *Meynell* was transferred to the Ecuadorian Navy and renamed *Presidente Velasco Ibarra* in Aug 1955.

1 Ex-US APD TYPE

25 DE JULIO D 1 (ex-E 12) (ex-*Enright*, APD 66, ex-DE 216)

Displacement, tons	1 400 standard; 2 130 full load
Dimensions, feet	306·0 oa × 37·0 × 12·6
Guns	1—5 in 38 cal; 4—40 mm
Boilers	2 "D" Express
Main engines	GE geared tubines with electric drive; 2 shafts; 12 000 shp = 23 knots
Range, miles	2 000 at 23 knots
Complement	204

Former US high speed transport (modified destroyer escort). Built by the Navy Yard, Philadelphia, Pa. Laid down on 22 Feb 1943, launched on 29 May 1943 and completed on 21 Sep 1943. Transferred to Ecuador on 14 July 1967 under MAP. Could carry 162 troops.

25 DE JULIO *1968, Ecuadorian Navy*

CORVETTES

2 Ex-US PCE TYPE

Name	ESMERALDAS (ex-USS *Eunice*, PCE 846)	MANABI (ex-USS *Pascagoula*, PCE 874)
Pennant No.	P 21 (ex-E 22, ex-E 03)	P 22 (ex-E 23, ex-E 02)
Builders	Pullman Standard Car Manufacturing Co, Chicago, Ill	Albina Eng & Mach Works, Portland, Oreg
Laid down	10 Aug 1943	1 Mar 1943
Launched	20 Dec 1943	11 May 1943
Completed	4 Mar 1944	31 Dec 1943
Transferred	29 Nov 1960	5 Dec 1960

Displacement, tons	640 standard; 903 full load
Dimensions, feet	180 wl; 184·5 oa × 33 × 9·5
Guns	1—3 in dual purpose; 6—40 mm AA
A/S weapons	4 DCT; 2 DC Racks
Main engines	GM diesels; 2 shafts; 1 800 bhp = 15·4 knots
Range, miles	4 300 at 10 knots
Complement	100 officers and men

Former United States patrol vessels (180 ft Escorts) transferred from the US Navy to the Ecuadorian Navy on 29 Nov and 5 Dec 1960, respectively.

MANABI *1972, Ecuadorian Navy*

AMPHIBIOUS SHIPS

JAMBELI (ex-USS *LSM* 539) T 31 **TARQUI** (ex-USS *LSM* 555) T 32

Displacement, tons	743 beaching; 1 095 full load
Dimensions, feet	196·5 wl; 203·0 oa × 34·0 × 10
Guns	2—40 mm AA
Range, miles	2 500 at 12 knots
Main engines	Diesels; 2 shafts; 2 800 bhp = 12·5 knots

Former US Landing Ships. Medium. *Jambeli* was laid down by Brown S.B. Co, Houston, on 10 May 1945. *Tarqui* was laid down by the Navy Yard, Charleston, SC on 3 Mar 1945 and launched on 22 Mar 1945. Purchased from USA in 1958 and transferred to the Ecuadorian Navy at Green Cove Springs, Florida in Nov 1958. Crew 60.

JAMBELI *1967, Ecuadorian Navy*

SURVEY SHIP

ORION (ex-USS *Mulberry*, AN 27) O 111 (ex-101)

Displacement, tons	560 standard; 805 full load
Dimensions, feet	146 wl; 163 oa × 30·5 × 11·8 max
Guns	1—3 in AA
Main engines	Diesel-electric; 800 bhp = 13 knots
Complement	35

Former United States netlayer. Built by Commercial Iron Works, Portland, Oregon. Launched on 26 Mar 1941. Loaned by US under MAP. Transferred to Ecuador in Nov 1965.

ORION *1970, Ecuadorian Navy*

LIGHT FORCES

2 Ex-US PGM TYPE

GUAYAQUIL (ex-US *PGM* 76) LC 62 (ex-LC 72)
QUITO (ex-US *PGM* 75) LC 61 (ex-LC 71)

Displacement, tons	101
Dimensions, feet	95 oa × 19 × 5
Guns	1—40 mm AA; 2—20 mm
Main engines	4 diesels; 2 shafts; 2 200 bhp = 21 knots
Range, miles	1 500 at cruising speed
Complement	15

US built. Transferred to the Ecuadorian Navy under MAP on 30 Nov 1965.

GUAYAQUIL *1967, Ecuadorian Navy*

3 PTB TYPE

MANTA LT 91 **TENA** LT 93 **TULCAN** LT 92

Displacement, tons	119 standard; 134 full load
Dimensions, feet	119·4 × 19·1 × 6·6
Guns	1—40 mm AA; 1—20 mm AA
Torpedo tubes	2—21 inch
Machinery	Diesels; 3 shafts; 9 000 bhp = 35 knots
Range, miles	700 at 30 knots; 1 500 at 15 knots
Complement	19

Built by Lurssen Werft, Bremen 1970-71. Further boats of this class are projected.

MANTA *1972, Ecuadorian Navy*

6 ML TYPE

LSP 1 **LSP 2** **LSP 3** **LSP 4** **LSP 5** **LSP 6**

Displacement, tons	45 standard; 64 full load
Dimensions, feet	76·8 × 13·5 × 4·2 mean (6·3 max)
Guns	Light MG AA
Main engines	Bohn & Kähier diesel; 2 shafts; 1 200 bhp = 22 knots
Range, miles	550 at 16 knots
Complement	9

Built by Hermann Havighorst, Bremen-Blumenthal. Ordered in 1954. First two were delivered in Aug 1954 and the remainder in 1955. Pennant Nos. LP 81 to LP 86.

LSP 6 *1963, Ecuadorian Navy*

TUGS

CAYAMBE (ex-*Lois Rios*, ex-USS *Cusabo*, *ATF* 155) R 101 (ex-R 51, ex-R 01)

Displacement, tons	1 235 standard; 1 675 full load
Dimensions, feet	195 wl; 205 oa × 38·5 × 15·5 max
Guns	1—3 in; 4—40 mm AA; 2—20 mm AA
Main engines	4 diesels with electric drive; 3 000 bhp = 16·5 knots
Complement	85

Tugs—*continued*

Former US "Apache" class fleet ocean tug. Launched on 26 Feb 1945. Fitted with powerful pumps and other salvage equipment. Transferred to Ecuador by lease on 2 Nov 1960 and renamed *Los Rios*. Again renamed *Cayambe* in 1966.

CAYAMBE *1970, Ecuadorian Navy*

COTOPAXI (ex-*R. T. Ellis*) R 103 (ex-R 53)

Displacement, tons	150
Dimensions, feet	82 × 21 × 8
Main engines	Diesel; 1 shaft; 650 bhp = 9 knots

Former US tug. Built by Equitable Building Co, Incorp. Purchased from the United States in 1947.

SANGAY (ex-*Loja*) R 102 (ex-R 52)

Displacement, tons	295 light; 390 full load
Dimensions, feet	107 × 26 × 14
Main engines	Fairbanks Morse diesel; speed = 12 knots

Built in 1952. Acquired by the Ecuadorian Navy in 1964. Renamed in 1966.

MISCELLANEOUS

CALICUCHIMA (ex-US *FS* 525) T 34 (ex-T 42) (SUPPLY SHIP).

Displacement, tons	650 light; 950 full load
Dimensions, feet	176 × 32 × 14 max
Main engines	Diesels; 2 shafts; 500 bhp = 11 knots

Former United States small cargo ship of the Army FS type. Leased to Ecuador on 8 Apr 1963 and purchased in April 1969. Provides service to the Galapagos Islands.

Miscellaneous—*continued*

CALICUCHIMA *1970, Ecuadorian Navy*

ATAHUALPA (ex-US *YW* 131) T 33 (ex-T 41, ex-A 01) (WATER BOAT)

Displacement, tons	415 light; 1 235 full load
Dimensions, feet	174·0 × 32·0 × 15·0
Main engines	GM diesels; 750 bhp = 11·5 knots

Built by Leatham D. Smith SB Co, Sturgeon Bay in 1945. Transferred from USA in Mar 1963. Acquired by the Ecuadorian Navy on 2 May 1963.

AMAZONAS (ex-US *ARD* 17) (AUXILIARY DOCK)

Measurement, tons	3 500 lifting capacity
Dimensions, feet	491·7 oa × 81·0 oa × 32·9 max

Former United States auxiliary floating dock. Built in 1943-44. Transferred on loan on 7 Jan 1961. Suitable for docking destroyers and landing ships. Dry dock companion craft YFND 20 was leased on 2 Nov 1961.

EGYPT

Administration

Commander Naval Forces:
Commodore Fuad Zekry

Diplomatic Representation

Defence Attaché in London:
Major-General A. Mounir

Strength of the Fleet

5 Destroyers	18 Missile Boats
3 Frigates	36 Torpedo Boats
12 Corvettes	10 Minesweepers
12 Submarines	2 Inshore Minesweepers
14 Amphibious Craft	6 Miscellaneous

Personnel

1973; 14 500 officers and men, including the Coast Guard

Mercantile Marine

Lloyd's Register of Shipping
127 vessels of 242 745 tons gross

DESTROYERS

4 Ex-USSR "SKORY" TYPE

AL NASSER
AL ZAFR
DAMIET
SUEZ

Displacement, tons	2 600 standard; 3 500 full load
Length, feet (*metres*)	395·2 (120·5)
Beam, feet (*metres*)	38·7 (*11·8*)
Draught, feet (*metres*)	15·1 (*4·6*)
Guns, surface	4—5·1 in (*130 mm*)
Guns, AA	2—3·4 in (*76 mm*); 8—37 mm
A/S weapons	4 DCT
Torpedo tubes	10—21 in (*533 mm*) quintupled
Mines	80 can be carried
Boilers	3
Main engines	Geared turbines; 2 abafts; 60 000 shp
Speed, knots	35
Range, miles	4 000 at 15 knots
Complement	260

SKORY Type *1966*

Former Skory class destroyers of the Soviet Navy. Launched in 1951. *Al Nasser* and *Al Zafr* were delivered to the Egyptian Navy on 11 June 1956 at Alexandria. The implication of each name in Arabic is "victory". It was reported in Dec 1959 that six destroyers were being transferred from the USSR to Egypt. Two were delivered at Alexandria in Jan 1962.

RADAR. Search: Probably S Band. Tactical: Probably C Band. Fire Control: X Band.

Destroyers—*continued*

1 Ex-BRITISH "Z" TYPE

EL FATEH (ex-HMS *Zenith*)

Displacement, tons	1 730 standard; 2 575 full load
Length, feet (*metres*)	350 (*106·8*) wl; 362·8 (*110·6*) oa
Beam, feet (*metres*)	35·7 (*10·9*)
Draught, feet (*metres*)	17·1 (*5·2*) max
Guns, dual purpose	4—4·5 in (*115 mm*)
Guns, AA	6—40 mm
A/S weapons	4 DCT
Boilers	2 Admiralty 3-drum
Main engines	Parsons geared turbines; 2 shafts; 40 000 shp
Speed, knots	36·75 designed; 31·25 sea
Radius, miles	2 800 at 20 knots
Oil fuel, tons	580
Complement	250

Former "Z" class destroyer in the British Navy. Built by Wm. Denny & Bros Ltd, Dumbarton. Laid down on 19 May 1942, launched on 5 June 1944 and completed on 22 Dec 1944. Purchased from Great Britain in 1955. Before being taken over by Egypt. *El Fateh* was refitted by John I. Thornycroft & Co Ltd, Woolston, Southampton in July 1956.

RADAR. Search: Type 960 Metric wavelength. Tactical: Type 293. S Band. Fire Control: X Band.

EL FATEH

MODERNISATION. Refitted and modernised by J. Samuel White & Co Ltd, at Cowes, Isle of Wight from May 1963 until July 1964.

LOSS
Sister ship *El Qaher* (ex-HMS *Myngs*) was sunk by Israeli aircraft on 16 May 1970 at Berenice (Ras Banas).

FRIGATES

1 Ex-BRITISH "BLACK SWAN" TYPE

Displacement, tons	1 490 standard; 1 925 full load
Length, feet (*metres*)	283 (*86·3*) pp; 299·5 (*91·3*) oa
Beam, feet (*metres*)	38·5 (*11·7*)
Draught, feet (*metres*)	14·0 (*4·3*) max
Guns, surface	6—4 in (*102 mm*)
Guns, AA	4—40 mm; 2—20 mm
A/S weapons	4 DCT
Boilers	2 three-drum type
Main engines	Geared turbines; 2 shafts; 4 300 shp
Speed, knots	19·75 designed; 18 sea
Range, miles	4 500 at 12 knots
Oil fuel, tons	370
Complement	180

Former "Black Swan" class sloop (later re-rated as frigate) in the British Navy. Transferred from Great Britain in Nov 1949. As flotilla leader she had a broad band painted on her funnel and a thinner flotilla band.

Name	*No.*	*Builders*	*Laid down*	*Launched*	*Completed*
TARIK (ex-*Malek Farouq*, ex-HMS *Whimbrel*)	42	Yarrow & Co Ltd, Glasgow	31 Oct 1941	25 Aug 1942	13 Jan 1943

TARIK

1 Ex-BRITISH "RIVER" TYPE

Displacement, tons	1 490 standard; 2 216 full load
Length, feet (*metres*)	283 (*86·3*) pp; 301·5 (*91·9*) oa
Beam, feet (*metres*)	36·7 (*11·2*)
Draught, feet (*metres*)	14·1 (*4·3*)
Guns, surface	1—4 in (*102 mm*)
Guns, AA	2—40 mm; 6—20 mm
A/S weapons	4 DCT
Boilers	2 Admiralty 3-drum type
Main engines	Triple expansion; 2 shafts; 5 500 ihp
Speed, knots	18
Range, miles	7 700 at 12 knots
Oil fuel, tons	640
Complement	180

Former "River" class frigate of the British Navy. Purchased from Great Britain in Nov 1948. Refitted by Willoughby (Plymouth) Ltd. Sailed for Egypt in Apr 1950. Formerly mounted two 4-inch guns.

CLASS. Of her two sister ships *Abikir* (ex-HMS *Usk*) was sunk as a blockship in the Suez Canal in Nov 1956. (raised and dumped in Apr 1957); and *Domiat* (ex-HMS *Nith*) was sunk by the British cruiser *Newfoundland* off Suez on 1 Nov 1956.

Name	*No.*	*Builders*	*Laid down*	*Launched*	*Completed*
RASHID (ex-HMS *Spey*)	43	Smith's Dock Co Ltd,	18 July 1941	10 Dec 1941	19 May 1942

RASHID *1968*

1 Ex-BRITISH "HUNT" TYPE

Displacement, tons	1 000 standard; 1 490 full load
Length, feet (*metres*)	273 (*83·2*) wl; 280 (*85·3*) oa
Beam, feet (*metres*)	29 (*8·8*)
Draught, feet (*metres*)	15·1 (*4·3*) max
Guns, surface	4—4 in (*103 mm*)
Guns, AA	2—40 mm; 2—20 mm
A/S weapons	2 DCT
Boilers	2 three-drum type
Main engines	Parsons geared turbines; 2 shafts; 19 000 shp
Speed, knots	25 max
Range, miles	2 000 at 12 knots
Oil fuel, tons	280
Complement	146

Former British "Hunt" Class, Type 1 escort destroyer (later re-rated as frigate). Served in the British Navy from 1940. Transferred from the British Navy to the Egyptian Navy in July 1950: Sailed for Egypt in April 1951, after a nine months' refit by J. Samuel White & Co Ltd, Cowes. She was first renamed *Ibrahim el Awal* but was renamed *Mohamed Ali el Kebir* about 1951.

	No.	*Builders*	*Laid down*	*Launched*	*Completed*
PORT SAID (ex-*Mohamed Ali*, ex-*Ibrahim el Awal*, ex-HMS *Cottesmore*)	11	Yarrow & Co. Ltd, Scotstoun, Glasgow	12 Dec 1939	5 Sep 1940	29 Dec 1940

PORT SAID (ex-*Mohamed Ali*)

CLASS. Sister ship *Ibrahim el Awal* served in the British Navy as HMS *Mendip* until 1948, when she was transferred to the Chinese Navy and renamed *Lin Fu*; she was returned to the British Navy at Hong Kong a year later and reverted to her original name, but was transferred to the Egyptian Navy in Nov 1949, when she was first renamed *Mohamed Ali el Kebir* but was afterwards again renamed *Ibrahim el Awal*, exchanging names with her sister ship about 1951-52. *Ibrahim el Awal* surrendered to Israeli forces off Haifa on 31 Oct 1956; she was rehabilitated and incorporated into the Israeli Navy and renamed *Haifa* (see later page).

CORVETTES

12 Ex-USSR "SOI" TYPE

Displacement, tons 215 light; 250 full load
Dimensions, feet 138·6 × 20 × 9·2
Guns 4—25 mm (2 twin mountings)
A/S weapons 4 five-barrelled ahead throwing rocket launchers
Main engines 3 diesel; 6 000 bhp = 29 knots
Range, miles 1 100 at 13 knots
Complement 30

Former Soviet submarine chasers. Eight reported to have been transferred by the USSR to Egypt in 1962 to 1967 and four others later.

SUBMARINES

6 Ex-USSR "R" TYPE

Displacement, tons 1 100 surface; 1 600 submerged
Length, feet (*metres*) 246·0 (*75·0*)
Beam, feet (*metres*) 24·0 (*7·3*)
Draught, feet (*metres*) 14·5 (*4·4*)
Torpedo tubes 6—21 in (*533 mm*) bow
Main engines Diesels, 4 000 bhp
Electric motors, 2 500 hp
Speed, knots 19 surface; 16 submerged
Complement 65

Two "R" class units replaced two "W" class boats which returned to the USSR in May 1966. Another "R" class boat was transferred to Egypt in Feb 1966, and five "R" class submarines had been delivered by the end of 1966. Six "R" boats were transferred by 1969.

R Type *1968, Skyfotos*

6 Ex-USSR "W" TYPE

Displacement, tons 1 030 surface; 1 180 submerged
Length, feet (*metres*) 247 (75·3) oa
Beam, feet (*metres*) 19 (5·8)
Draught, feet (*metres*) 15 (4·6)
Guns, AA 4—25 mm
Torpedo tubes 6—21 in (*533 mm*); 4 forward 2 aft
Main engines 4 000 bhp diesels; 2 500 hp electric motors
Speed, knots 17 on surface; 15 submerged
Range, miles 13 000 at 8 knots surfaced
Complement 60

The first "W" class units were transferred from the Soviet Navy to the Egyptian Navy in June 1957. Three more arrived at Alexandria on 24 Jan 1958. Another was transferred to Egypt at Alexandria in Jan 1962.

Two W class submarines sailed from Alexandria to Leningrad in late 1971 under escort, apparently for refit. The "MV" Type submarine transferred by USSR in June 1957 has now been scrapped.

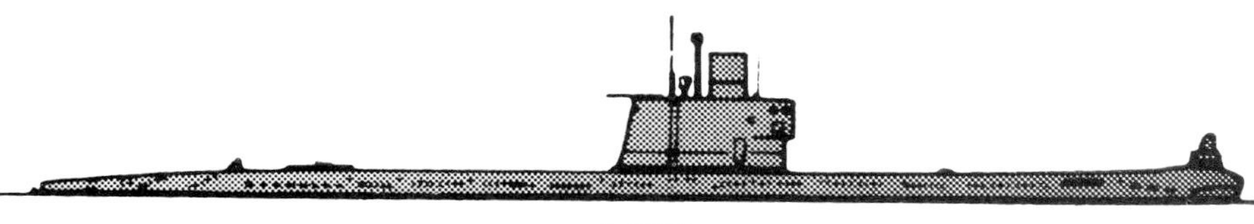

R *Class*

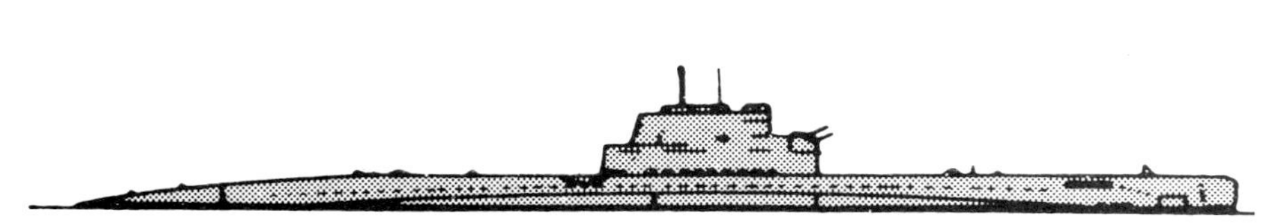

W *Class*

AMPHIBIOUS CRAFT

10 Ex-USSR "VYDRA" TYPE

Displacement, tons 300 standard; 500 full load
Dimensions, feet 157·4 × 24·6 × 7·2
Main engines 2 diesels; 2 shafts; 400 bhp = 15 knots

Can carry and land up to 250 tons of military equipment and stores

4 Ex-USSR "SMB 1" TYPE

Displacement, tons 200 standard; 420 full load
Dimensions, feet 157·5 × 21·3 × 5·6
Main engines 2 diesels; 2 shafts; 400 hp speed = 11 knots

Several utility landing craft of the MP-SMB 1, delivered to the Egyptian Navy in 1965. Predecessors of the "Vydra" type. Can carry 150 tons of military equipment.
(The tank landing ship *Aka* (ex-LST 178) was sunk as a block-ship near Lake Timsah in the Suez canal on 1 Nov 1956). The LCM type was deleted in 1971.

LIGHT FORCES

12 Ex-USSR "OSA" TYPE MISSILE BOATS

Displacement, tons 165 standard; 200 full load
Dimensions, feet 128·7 × 25·1 × 5·9
Missiles 4 launchers in two pairs abreast for SSN 2 A (Styx)
Guns 4—30 mm (2 twin, 1 forward, 1 aft)
Main engines 3 diesels; 13 000 bhp = 32 knots
Complement 25

Reported to have been delivered to Egypt by the Soviet Navy in 1966.

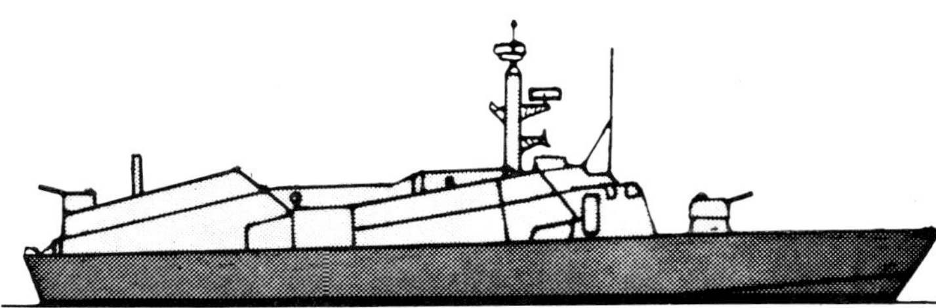

OSA *Class*

6 Ex-USSR "KOMAR" TYPE MISSILE BOATS

Displacement, tons 70 standard; 80 × full load
Dimensions, feet 83·6 × 19·6 × 4·9
Missiles 2 launchers for SSN-2A (Styx)
Guns 2—25 mm
Main engines 4 diesels; 4 shafts; 4 800 hp = 40 knots

Former Soviet missile boats transferred from the USSR in 1962 to 1967. One of this type was sunk by Israeli jets on 16 May 1970. Two patrol boats named *Nisr* 1 and 2 110 tons, are reported to have been launched at Port Said on 16 May 1963 *et seq* by the Castro Naval Shipyard.

KOMAR Type *1966, Col. Bjorn Borg*

6 Ex-USSR "SHERSHEN" TYPE TORPEDO BOATS

Displacement, tons 150 standard; 160 full load
Dimensions, feet 115·5 × 23 × 5
Guns 4—30 mm AA (2 twin)
Torpedo tubes 4—21 in (single)
A/S weapons 12 DC
Main engines 3 diesels; 3 shafts; 13 000 hp = 38 knots

Light forces—*continued*

One delivered from USSR in Feb 1967, two more (326,328) in Oct 1967, and three since.

SHERSHEN *Class*

P 6 *Class*

24 Ex-USSR "P 6" TYPE TORPEDO BOATS

Displacement, tons	66 standard; 75 full load
Dimensions, feet	84·2 × 20 × 6
Guns	4—25 mm AA MG
Tubes	2—21 in
Main engines	4 diesels; 4 shafts; 4 800 hp = 45 knots
Complement	25

The first twelve boats arrived at Alexandria on 19 Apr 1956. Two boats were destroyed by British naval aircraft on 4 Nov 1956, two were sunk by the Israeli destroyer *Elath* off Sinai on 12 July 1967, two by Israeli MTBs off Sinai coast on 11 July 1967, two by Israeli air attacks in 1969, and two in the Red Sea on 22 Jan 1970.

The above particulars refer to the early arrivals. Six former Soviet motor torpedo boats of the "P6" class are reported to have been transferred by the USSR in 1960.

6 Ex-YUGOSLAVIAN TYPE TORPEDO BOATS

Displacement, tons	56 full load
Dimensions, feet	78 × 20·7 × 5·2
Guns	1—40 mm AA
Tubes	4
Main engines	3 Packard motors; 3 shafts; 4 500 bhp = 35 knots

Purchased from Yugoslavia in 1956. Similar to the boats of the US Higgins type.

The two motor torpedo boats of the British Fairmile "D" type, *El Naser* and *El Zafer*, are reported to have been disposed of, and the three motor launches of the British Fairmile "B" type, *Hamza* (ex-ML 134), *Sab el Bahr* and *Saker el Baher* are hulks. The transport *El Quseir* (ex-*El Amira Fawzia*) and the yachts *Ntisar* (ex-*Fakhr le Bihar*) and *El Horria* (ex-Royal yacht *Mahroussa*), latterly used as training ships, were deleted from the list in 1967, although the latter was still in service in 1970.

MINEWARFARE FORCES

6 Ex-USSR "T 43" TYPE MINESWEEPERS

ASSIUT **BAHAIRA** **CHARKIEH** **DAQHALIA** **GARBIA** **SINAI**

Displacement, tons	500 standard; 610 full load
Dimensions, feet	190·2 × 28·2 × 6·9
Guns	4—37 mm AA; 4—25 mm
Main engines	2 diesels; 2 shafts; 2 000 hp = 17 knots
Range, miles	1 600 at 10 knots
Complement	40

Four were transferred from the Soviet Navy and delivered to Egypt in 1956, and two others later. *Miniya* was sunk by Israeli air attack in the Gulf of Suez on 6 Feb 1970. Sister ships *Hittine* and *Yarmouk* were allocated to Syria.

T 43 *Class*

4 Ex-USSR "YURKA" TYPE

ASWAN **GIZA** **SOHAG** **QENA**

Displacement, tons	500 standard; 550 full load
Dimensions, feet	172 × 31 × 8·9
Guns	4—30 mm AA (2 twin)
Main engines	2 diesels; 4 000 bhp = 18 knots

Steel-hulled minesweepers transferred from USSR 1970-71.

2 Ex-USSR "T 301" TYPE INSHORE MINESWEEPERS

Displacement, tons	130 standard; 180 full load
Dimensions, feet	124·6 × 19·7 × 4·9
Guns	2—37 mm AA; 2—25 mm AA
Main engines	2 Diesels; 2 shafts; 1 440 hp = 17 knots
Range, miles	2 200 at 10 knots
Complement	30

Reported to have been transferred by the USSR to Egypt in 1962; possibly a third ship transferred also.

BYMS TYPE

Of the wooden coastal minesweepers, *Gaza* (ex-*BYMS* 2013) was lost on 26 July 1950, as a result of a fuel-tank explosion off Mersa Matrouh, sister ships *Darfour* (ex-*BYMS* 2041) and *Tor* (ex-*BYMS* 2175) were transferred to the Algerian Navy on 6 Nov 1962, and the remaining six, *Arish* (ex-*BYMS* 2028), *Kaisaria* (ex-*BYMS* 2075), *Kordofan* (ex-*BYMS* 2212), *Malek Fuad* (ex-*BYMS* 2035), *Naharia* (ex-*BYMS* 2069) and *Rafah* (ex-*BYMS* 2149) are no more than mouldering hulks.

MISCELLANEOUS

4 Ex-USSR "OKHTENSKY" TYPE TUGS

A number of Soviet fleet tugs was reported transferred to the Egyptian Navy in 1966

1 Ex-BRITISH "BANGOR" TYPE

NASR (ex-HMS *Bude*)

Displacement, tons	672 standard; 900 full load
Dimensions, feet	180·0 oa × 28·5 × 9·5
Guns	1—4 in; 1—3 in; 2—40 mm AA
A/S weapons	2 DCT
Main engines	Triple expansion; 2 shafts; 2 400 ihp = 16 knots (designed) sea speed 14 knots
Boilers	2 Admiralty 3-drum type
Oil fuel, tons	170
Range, miles	4 300 at 10 knots
Complement	60

Former "Bangor" class fleet minesweeper acquired from Great Britain. Built by Lobnitz & Co, Ltd, Renfrew. Laid down on 2 April 1940, launched on 4 Sep 1940 and completed on 12 Dec 1941, now virtually a hulk. Sister ship *Sollum* sank in heavy weather off Alexandria on 7 Mar 1953. *Matrouth* (ex-HMS *Stornoway*) believed sunk 1968-69.

1 Ex-BRITISH "FLOWER" TYPE

Displacement, tons	**1 060 standard; 1 340 full load**
Length, feet (*metres*)	**190 (*57·9*) pp; 205 (*62·5*) oa**
Beam, feet (*metres*)	**33 (*10·0*)**
Draught, feet (*metres*)	**14·5 (*4·4*) max**
Guns, surface	**1—4 in (*102 mm*)**
Guns, AA	**2—20 mm**
Boilers	**2 SE**
Main engines	**Triple expansion; 2 750 shp**
Speed, knots	**16**
Range, miles	7 000 at 10 knots
Oil fuel (tons)	230
Complement	85

Name	*Builders*	*Laid down*	*Launched*	*Completed*
EL SUDAN (ex-*Mallow*, ex-*Partizanka* ex-*Nada*, ex-HMS *Mallow*)	**Harland & Wolff, Ltd, Belfast**	**14 Nov 1939**	**22 May 1940**	**2 July 1940**

Former "Flower" class corvette (later re-rated as frigate) of the British Navy. Taken over by Yugoslavia in 1943 (loaned). Returned to the British Navy early in 1949 and transferred to Egypt on 28 Oct 1949. Now used for training.

CLASS. Sister ship *Misr* (ex-SS *Malrouk*) was rammed and sunk by collision south of Suez 16th-17th May 1953.

None of the above four old WW2-built vessels is any longer of considerable military value.

EL SUDAN

A. & J. Pavia

ETHIOPIA

Administration

The Imperial Ethiopian Navy, founded in 1955, is one of the three Services under the Ministry of National Defence. The Commander-in-Chief is His Imperial Majesty. The Deputy Commander-in-Chief has his Naval Headquarters in Addis Ababa.

Deputy Commander-in-Chief of the Imperial Ethiopian Navy:
Rear Admiral H.I.H. Prince Alexander Desta
Chief of Staff:
Colonel Taye Telahun

Naval Officer in Charge, Haile Selassie I Naval Base, Massawa:
Captain P. W. Stewart, RN(Retd)

Naval Establishments

"Haile Selassie I" Massawa: Naval Base and College, established in 1956.
Embaticalla: Marine Commando Training School.
Assab: Naval Base, expanding to include a ship repair facility.

Personnel

1973: 1 380 officers and men.

Mercantile Marine

Lloyds Register of Shipping: 23 vessels of 45 903 tons gross

COASTAL MINESWEEPER

1 Ex-NETHERLANDS "WILDERVANK" CLASS

MS 41 (ex-*Elst*, M 829)

Displacement, tons	373 standard; 417 full load
Dimensions, feet	149·8 oa × 28·0 × 7·5
Guns	2—40 mm AA
Main engines	2 diesels; 2 shafts; 2 500 bhp = 14 knots
Oil fuel, tons	25 tons
Radius, miles	2 500 at 10 knots
Complement	38

Western Union type non-magnetic coastal minesweeper of the "Wildervank" class built in the Netherlands in 1954-56. Purchased by Ethiopia and transferred from the Royal Netherlands Navy in 1971.

MS 41 1972

TRAINING SHIP

ETHIOPIA (ex-USS *Orca*, AVP 49) A 01

Displacement, tons	1 766 standard; 2 800 full load
Dimensions, feet	300 wl; 310·8 oa × 41 × 13·5 max
Guns	1—5 in 38 cal; 5—40 mm AA
Main engines	2—sets diesels; 2 shafts; 6 080 bhp = 18·2 knots
Complement	215

Former United States seaplane tender. Built by Lake Washington Shipyard, Houghton Wash. Laid down 13 July 1942, launched on 4 Oct 1942 and completed on 23 Jan 1944. Transferred from the US Navy in Jan 1962.

ETHIOPIA *1972, Imperial Ethiopian Navy*

PATROL BOATS

5 PGM TYPE

PC11 (ex-USN *WVP* 95304)
PC 12 (ex-USN *WVP* 95310)
PC 13 (ex-USN *PGM* 53)
PC 14 (ex-USN *PGM* 54)
PC 15 (ex-USN *PGM* 58)

Displacement, tons	101
Dimensions, feet	95 oa × 19 × 5
Guns	1—40 mm AA; 1—50 cal MG
Main engines	4 diesels; 2 shafts; 2 200 bhp = 21 knots
Range, miles	1 500 at cruising speed
Complement	15

Ex-*PGM* 53 and ex-*PGM* 54 were built by Petersen Builders for transfer on 25 Aug 1961 and ex-*PGM* 58 built by Marinette was transferred on 19 July 1962, under MAP. All are steel-hulled and twin-screwed.

The former Yugoslavian motor torpedo boats *Barracuda* and *Shark*, received in Jan 1960, were removed from the Ethiopian Navy list in 1969.

PC 12 *1970, Imperial Ethiopian Navy*

HARBOUR DEFENCE CRAFT

4 "CAROLINE" CLASS

CAROLINE GB 22
JACQUELINE GB 24
JOHN GB 21
PATRICK GB 23

Length, feet	40
Guns	2—·50 calibre machine guns
Speed, knots	20 approx
Complement	7

Patrol craft or very light gunboats. Built by Steward Seacraft Inc, Berwick, La. *Caroline* and *John* were delivered in 1966, *Jacqueline* and *Patrick* in 1967. Their complement is 3 officers and 4 ratings or 2 officers and 5 ratings.

JOHN *1970, Imperial Ethiopian Navy*

LANDING CRAFT

There are 4 of the US LCM type.

LC 34 *1972, Imperial Ethiopian Navy*

EL SALVADOR

Personnel

130 officers and men

Mercantile Marine

Lloyds Register of Shipping: 10 vessels of 1 506 tons gross

PATROL BOATS

GC 1 (ex-*Fle-Ja-Lis*)
GC 2 (ex-*Nohaba*)

Displacement, tons	46
Dimensions, feet	72 oa × 16 × 5·5
Guns	1—20 mm
Main engines	2 diesels; 2 shafts; speed = 12 knots
Complement	16

Former British HDML type. Purchased from commercial sources in 1959.

FINLAND

Administration

Commander-in-Chief, Finnish Navy:
Rear-Admiral J. K. Pirhonen

Diplomatic Representation

Naval Attaché in London:
Vacant

Naval Attaché in Washington:
Colonel T. O. Lehti

Naval Attaché in Moscow:
Colonel Henrik Anttila

Naval Attaché in Paris:
Lieutenant-Colonel Niilo Palmén

Strength of the Fleet

3 Frigates (including 1 for training)
2 Corvettes (Fast Gunboats)
2 Coastal Minelayers
1 Missile Craft
4 Coast Guard Patrol Vessels
15 Fast Patrol Boats
14 Patrol Boats
5 Patrol Boats, ex-Inshore Minesweepers
1 Cable Ship
14 Support Ships and Service Craft
9 Icebreakers

New Construction Programme

4 80-ton GRP Inshore Minesweepers
1 Tender

Treaty Limitations

The Finnish Navy is limited by the treaty of Paris 1947 to 10 000 tons of ships and 4 500 personnel. Submarines and motor torpedo boats are prohibited.

Coast Guard

All Coast Guard Vessels come under the Ministry of the Interior.

Hydrographic Department

This office and the Survey Ships come under the Ministry of Trade and Industry.

Icebreakers

All these ships work for the Board of Navigation except OTSO which belongs to Helsinki.

Personnel

1972: 2 000 (150 officers and1 850 ratings)
1973: 2 500 (200 officers and 2 300 ratings)

Mercantile Marine

Lloyd's Register of Shipping:
390 vessels of 1 470 825 tons gross

Disposals

LIGHT FORCES
1963 Hurja 1-5 Taisto 2, 4 and 5
1966 Taisto 3, 6-8

MINEWARFARE FORCES
1958 Tammenpää, Vaterpää. (CMS)
1959 Purunpää (CMS), Ajonpää (MSB)
1960 Katanpää (CMS)
1961 Kuha 10 and 11 (MSB) Ahven 1 and 5 (MSB)
1963 Kallaupää, Kuha 2, 5, 7, 8, 12-18 Ahuen 2, 3, 4, 6

COASTGUARD VESSELS
1958 VMV 18
1960 Merikotka
1970 VMV 11, 13, 19 and 20
1971 Aura

LCUs
1963 Lonna

ICEBREAKERS
1961 Sampo
1969 Apu (renamed Tarmo to act as museum ship in Helsinki).

Note (a) Names of icebreakers are perpetuated thereby causing confusion
(b) Kuha 3 and 6 are unaccounted for but are probably scrapped.
(c) For other disposals see 1966-67 edition.

FRIGATES

2 "UUSIMAA" CLASS

HÄMEENMAA **UUSIMAA**

Displacement, tons	1 200 standard; 1 600 full load
Length, feet (*metres*)	298·8 (*91*)
Beam, feet (*metres*)	33·7 (*10·2*)
Draught, feet (*metres*)	11 (*3·4*)
Guns	3—3·9 in (*100 mm*) dp single; 4—37 mm
A/S weapons	1 Hedgehog; 4 DC projectors
Torpedo tubes	3—21 in (*533 mm*)
Mines	50 (capacity)
Main engines	Geared turbines; 2 shafts; 25 000 shp
Speed, knots	28
Boilers	2
Complement	150

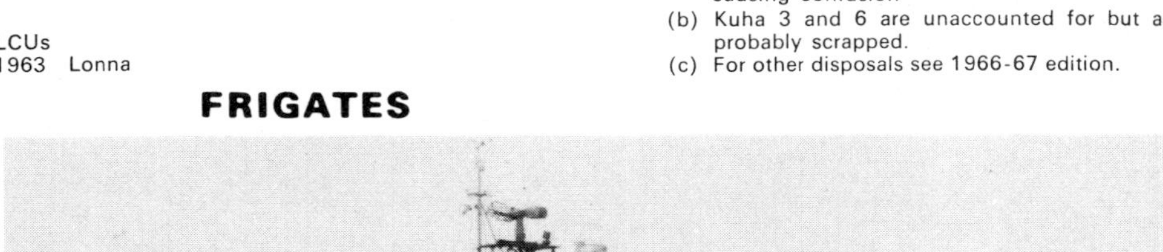

UUSIMAA *1972, Finnish Navy*

Former Soviet frigates of the "Riga" class. Purchased from the USSR and transferred to the Finnish Navy on 28 Apr 1964 and 12 May 1964, respectively.
RADAR. Search: S Band. Fire Control: X Band.

MATTI KURKI (ex-HMS *Porlock Bay*, ex-*Loch Seaforth*, ex-*Loch Muick*)

Displacement, tons	1 580 standard; 2 420 full load
Length, feet (*metres*)	286·0 (*87·2*) pp; 307·5 (*93·7*) oa
Beam, feet (*metres*)	38·5 (*11·7*)
Draught, feet (*metres*)	15·2 (*4·6*)
Guns	4—4 in (*102 mm*); 2 twin; 6—40 mm AA (2 twin, 2 single)
Main engines	Triple expansion; 2 shafts; 5 500 ihp
Speed, knots	18
Boilers	2 Admiralty 3-drum
Range, miles	9 500 at 12 knots
Oil fuel, tons	724
Complement	160

Former British frigate of the "Bay" class. Built by Charles Hill & Sons, Bristol. Laid down on 22 Nov 1944, launched on 14 June 1945 and completed on 8 Mar 1946. Transferred in Mar 1962. Employed as a training ship (*Koululaiva*).

RADAR. Search and Tactical. Type 293.

MATTI KURKI *1972, Wright & Logan*

CORVETTES

KARJALA **TURUNMAA**

Displacement, tons	660 standard: 770 full load
Dimensions, feet	243·1 × 25·6 × 7·9
Guns	1—4·7 in automatic dp forward; 2—40 mm AA (single); 2—30 mm AA (1 twin) aft
A/S weapons	Depth charge projectors
Main engines	CODOG (combined diesel or gas turbine). 3 Mercedes-Benz diesels; 3 990 bhp; 1 Rolls Royce Olympus gas turbine; 22 000 hp = 35 knots
Complement	70

Ordered on 23 Feb 1956 from Wärtsilä-yhtymä Oy Shipyard, Helsinki. Flush-decked. Rocket flare guide rails on sides of 4·7 in turret. Fitted with Vosper Thorny-Croft fin stabilisers equipment. *Karjala* was launched on 16 Aug 1967 and completed on 21 Oct 1968. *Turunmaa* was launched on 11 July 1967 and completed on 29 Aug 1968.

RADAR. Search and Tactical: X Band. (HSA).

TURUNMAA *1971, Finnish Navy*

LIGHT FORCES

ISKU

Displacement, tons	115
Dimensions, feet	86·5 × 28·6 × 6·6
Missile launchers	4 "Styx" surface-to-surface in two pairs abreast
Guns, anti-aircraft	2—30 mm (1 twin)
Main engines	4 diesels; 4 800 bhp = 25 knots

Guided missile craft of novel design completed for the Finnish Navy in 1970. Built at the "Reposaaren kenepoja". The construction combines a missile boat armament on a landing craft hull. The missile launchers are of similar type to those mounted in the Soviet "Osa" class.

ISKU *1972, Finnish Navy*

13 "NUOLI" CLASS

NUOLI 1 **NUOLI 2** **NUOLI 3** **NUOLI 4** **NUOLI 5** **NUOLI 6** **NUOLI 7** **NUOLI 8** **NUOLI 9** **NUOLI 10** **NUOLI 11** **NUOLI 12** **NUOLI 13**

Displacement, tons	45 standard; 64 full load
Dimensions, feet	72·2 × 21·7 × 5·0
Guns	1—40 mm AA; 1—20 mm AA
Main engines	3 diesels; 2 700 bhp = 40 knots
Complement	15

Designed and built by Laivateollisuus Oy, Turku. First four were launched in 1961, five more in 1962, and two more in 1963. Fitted with X Band radar.

NUOLI 10 *1969, Finnish Navy*

NUOLI 7 *1972, Finnish Navy*

2 "VASAMA" CLASS

VASAMA 1 **VASAMA 2**

Displacement, tons	50 standard; 70 full load
Dimensions, feet	67·0 pp; 71·5 oa × 19·5 × 6·0
Guns	2—40 mm AA
Main engines	2 Napier Deltic diesels; 5 000 bhp = 42 knots
Complement	20

British "Dark" type built by Saunders Roe (Anglesey) Ltd, Beaumaris, in 1955-57.

VASAMA 2 *1970, Finnish Navy*

VALPAS

Displacement, tons	540
Dimensions, feet	159·1 × 27·9 × 12·5.
Main engines	Diesel; 1 800 bhp = 15 knots

Officially stated to be slightly larger than the Coast Guard vessel *Silmä*, see below. Completed in 1971.

SILMÄ

Displacement, tons	500
Dimensions, feet	160·8 × 27·2 × 11·8
Main engines	1 800 bhp = 15 knots

Coast Guard vessel built by Laivateollisuus Oy, Turku, in 1962-63. Prototype for an improved patrol vessel, see *Valpas* above.

SILMA *1964, Finnish Navy*

UISKO

Displacement, tons	400
Dimensions, feet	141 × 24 × 12·8
Main engines	1 800 bhp = 15 knots

Coast Guard vessel built by Valmet Oy, Helsinki. Launched in 1958. Completed in 1959.

UISKO *Finnish Navy*

TURSAS

Displacement, tons	400
Dimensions, feet	131·2 × 23·5 × 14
Guns	1—3 in; 1—40 mm AA; 2—20 mm AA
Main engines	Diesel; 620 bhp = 12 knots

Built by Crichton-Vulkan. Launched in 1933. Belongs to the Coast Guard.

TURSAS *1968, Finnish Navy*

Light Forces—*continued*

VIIMA

Displacement, tons	135
Dimensions, feet	118·1 × 21·7 × 7·5
Gun	1—20 mm AA
Main engines	3 diesels; 4 050 bhp = 24 knots

Coast Guard patrol boat built by Laivateollisuus Oy Ab, Turku, Finland in 1964. Formerly rated as *Vartiomoottoriveneet*.

VIIMA *1971, Finnish Navy*

8 "KOSKELO" CLASS

KAAKKURI **KIILSA** **KOSKELO** **KUOVI** **TELKKA** **KUIKKA** **KURKI** **TAVI**

Displacement, tons	75 standard; 97 full load
Dimensions, feet	95·1 × 16·4 × 4·9
Guns	2—20 mm AA
Main engines	2 Mercedes-Benz diesels; 2 shafts; 1 000 bhp = 16 knots
Complement	8

Built of steel and strengthened against ice, *Koskelo* and *Kuikka* were completed in 1956. Remaining six were completed in 1958-60.

KUIKKA *1968, Finnish Navy*

5 "R" CLASS

RAISIO (No. 4) **RÖYTTA** (No. 5) **RUISSALO** (No. 3)

Displacement, tons	110 standard; 130 full load
Dimensions, feet	108·3 × 18·0 × 5·9
Guns	1—40 mm Bofors AA; 1—20 mm Madsen AA
Main engines	2 Mercedes-Benz diesels; 2 500 bhp = 17 knots

Built by Laivateollisuus, Turku, in 1959.

RÖYTTA *1969, Finnish Navy*

RIHTNIEMI (No. 1) **RYMÄTTYLÄ** (No. 2)

Displacement, tons	90 standard; 110 full load
Dimensions, feet	101·7 × 18·7 × 5·9
Guns	1—40 mm Bofors AA; 1—20 mm Madsen AA
Main engines	2 Mercedes-Benz diesels; 1 400 bhp = 15 knots

Built by Rauma-Repela Oy Shipyard. Ordered in July 1955, launched in 1956 and delivered on 20 May 1957. Controllable pitch propellers.

Light Forces—*continued*

RIHTNIEMI *1968, Finnish Navy*

MINE WARFARE SHIPS

KEIHÄSSALMI

Displacement, tons	360
Dimensions, feet	168 × 23 × 6
Guns	2—40 mm AA; 2—20 mm AA
Mines	Up to 100 capacity
Main engines	2 Wärtsilä diesels; 2 shafts; 2 000 bhp = 15 knots
Complement	60

Of improved "Ruotsinsalmi" type, built at Valmet Oy Shipyard, Helsinki under contract dated June 1955. Launched on 16 Mar 1957. Diesel type officially revised in 1971. X Band Search and Tactical radar.

KEIHASSALMI *1972, Finnish Navy*

RUOTSINSALMI

Displacement, tons	310
Dimensions, feet	150 × 23 × 5
Guns	2—40 mm AA; 2—20 mm AA
Mines	Up to 100 capacity
Main engines	2 MAN diesels; 2 shafts; 1 200 bhp = 15 knots
Complement	60

Built by Crichton-Vulcan Shipyard, Turku. Laid down in 1937. Launched in May 1940. Completed in Feb 1941. Diesel type officially revised in 1971.

RUOTSINSALMI *1969, Finnish Navy*

MISCELLANEOUS

KORSHOLM (HQ SHIP)

Displacement, tons	650
Dimensions, feet	160·8 × 27·9 × 10·8
Speed, knots	10·5

Adapted merchant ship of the small passenger and cargo type. Built in 1931.

KORSHOLM *1970, Finnish Navy,*

Miscellaneous—*continued*

6 "KALA" CLASS

KALA 1 **KALA 2** **KALA 3** **KALA 4** **KALA 5** **KALA 6**

Displacement, tons	60
Dimensions, feet	81·8 × 26·2 × 6
Main engines	2 diesels; 360 bhp = 9 knots

Launched in 1956. Completed in 1959. Of LCU (utility landing craft) type. Officially classed as transport craft.

KALA 6 *1963, Finnish Navy.*

SEILI (ex-F 177) LCU

Displacement, tons	180 standard
Dimensions, feet	143·0 × 20·0 × 4·0
Guns	1—1·4 in (*105 mm*)
Main engines	Speed = 10 knots

Former German MFP type landing craft converted and armoured. Launched in 1942. *Lonna* was scrapped in 1963.

SEILI *1970, Finnish Navy.*

3 "PANSIO" CLASS (TUG TYPE)

PANSIO (1947) **PORKKALA** (1940) **PUKKIO** (1939)

Displacement, tons	162 standard
Dimensions, feet	92·0 × 21·5 × 9·0
Guns	1—40 mm AA; 1—20 mm AA
Main engines	Diesels; 300 bhp = 9 knots

Built by Valmet Oy, Turku. Launch dates above. Vessels of the tug type used as transports, minesweeping tenders, minelayers and patrol vessels. Can carry 20 mines.

TRAINING SHIP

The training ship *Suomen Joutsen* (ex-*Oldenburg*, ex-*Laennec*) was converted into a stationary seaman's school ship, and sold to the Finnish Mercantile School in 1960.

3 "PIRTTISAARI" CLASS TUGS

PIRTTISAARI (ex-*DR* 7) **PYHTÄÄ** (ex-*DR* 2) **PURHA** (ex-*DR* 10)

Displacement, tons	106
Dimensions, feet	69 × 20 × 8·5
Guns	1—20 mm
Main engines	1 diesel; 400 bhp = 9 knots

Former US Army Tugs. Launched in 1943-44. General purpose vessels used as minesweepers, minelayers, patrol vessels, tenders, tugs or personnel transports. *DR 2* and *DR 7*, were adapted as the Coast Artillery transports *Pyhtää* and *Pirttisaari* in 1958 and 1959, respectively.

PIRTTISAARI *1970, Finnish Navy.*

PUTSAARI

Displacement, tons	430
Dimensions, feet	147·6 × 38·5 × 9·8
Main engines	Diesel; 450 bhp = 10 knots

Built by Rauma-Repola Oy Shipyard, Rauma. Launched in Dec 1965.

ICEBREAKERS

1 PROJECTED GIANT TYPE

Displacement, tons	50 000
Length, feet	639·76 (*195·0 metres*)
Main engines	140 000 hp

The Wärtsilä yard is reported to be planning to build a giant icebreaker if a buyer can be found. Machinery estimated to cost £ 3·6 million. This icebreaker has been offered to the USA for 60 000 000 US dollars, but not negotiated. Possibly STAL-LAVAL will deliver the machinery.

2 NEW CONSTRUCTION

URHO

Displacement, tons	7 800
Dimensions, feet	337·8 × 77·1 × 24·6
Aircraft	1 helicopter
Main engines	Diesel-electric; 5 diesels 20 000 bhp = 17 knots

The first icebreaker of new construction considerably larger than the "Tarmo" class icebreaker was ordered on 11 Dec 1970. She is scheduled to be completed towards the end of 1974. The second was ordered on 14 April 1971 for completion in Jan 1976. Fitted with two screws aft, taking 60% of available power and one forward, taking the remainder. Both from the Wärtsilä yard.

3 "TARMO" CLASS

TARMO **VARMA** **APU**

Displacement, tons	4 890
Dimensions, feet	281·0 × 71·0 × 21·0
Aircraft	1 helicopter
Main engines	Wärtsilä-Sulzer diesels; electric drive; 4 shafts (2 screws forward 2 screws aft); 12 000 bhp = 17 knots

Built by Wärtsilä-yhtymä Oy Shipyard, Helsinki. *Tarmo* was completed in 1963, *Varma* in 1968 (launched 29 Mar) and *Apu* on 25 Nov 1970.

TARMO *1968, Finnish Navy*

3 (4) "KARHU" CLASS

KARHU **MURTAJA** **SAMPO**

Displacement, tons	3 540
Dimensions, feet	243·2 × 57 × 20
Main engines	Diesel-electric; 4 shafts; 7 500 bhp = 16 knots

Built by Wärtsilä-yhtymä Oy Shipyard, Helsinki. *Karhu* was launched on 22 Oct 1957, and completed at the end of 1958. *Murtaja* was launched on 23 Sep 1958. *Sampo* was completed in 1960. There is also the combined Finnish/West German owned, Finnish manned, icebreaker *HANSA*, of the "Sampo" class, completed on 25 Nov 1966, which operates off Germany in winter and off Finland otherwise.

VOIMA

Displacement, tons	4 415
Dimensions, feet	254·8 wl; 274 oa × 63·7 × 20·3
Main engines	Diesels with electric drive; 4 shafts; 14 000 bhp = 16·5 knots
Oil fuel (tons)	740

Built by Wärtsilä-yhtyma Oy Shipyard, Helsinki. Launched and completed in 1953. Built for deep-sea work. Two propellers forward and aft.

SISU

Displacement, tons	2 075
Dimensions, feet	194·8 wl; 210·2 oa × 46·5 × 16·8
Guns	2—3·9 in AA
Main engines	2 sets Atlas Polar Diesels with electric drive; 2 shafts and a bow propeller; 4 000 hp = 16 knots
Complement	100

Built by Wärtsilä-yhtymä Oy Shipyard, Helsinki. Launched on 24 Sep 1938.

OTSO

Displacement, tons	900
Dimensions, feet	134·5 pp; 144·3 oa × 37·5 × 16·5
Main engines	Triple expansion, with bow propeller; 1 860 ihp = 13 knots
Oil fuel, tons	60

Launched in 1936. Belongs to the town of Helsinki.

FRANCE

Administration

Chief of the Naval Staff:
Amiral M. F. M. de Joybert

Conseil Superieur de la Marine:
Amiral Iehlé

Vice-Amiraux d'Escadre Daille, Clotteau and Brasseur-Kermadec

Vice Amiraux Midoux, Guillou, and Joire-Noulens

C in C Atlantic Theatre (CECLANT) and Préfet Maritime de la DeuxièmeRégion (PREMAR DEUX):
Vice-Amiral Daille

Prefet Maritime de la Première Région (PREMAR UN):
Contre-Amiral Frédéric Moreau

C in C Mediterranean Theatre (CECMED) and Préfet Maritime de la Troisième Région (PREMAR TROIS):
Vice-Amiral d'Escadre Brasseur-Kermadec

Diplomatic Representation

Naval Attaché in London:
Contre-Amiral Paul Delahousse

Naval Attaché in Washington:
Contre-Amiral Gelinet

Naval Attaché in Moscow:
Capitaine de Vaisseau Leroux

Naval Attaché in Ottawa:
Lieutenant-Colonel Berg

Submarine Service

Now known as Force Océanique Stratégique (FOST) with HQ at Houilles near Paris. SSBN (*SNLE*) force based at Ile Longue Brest with a training base at Roche-Douvres and VLF W/T station at Rosay. Patrol submarines are based at Lorient and Toulon. Plans for nuclear fleet submarines are included in the 15 year plan.

Strength of the Fleet

3 Aircraft Carriers (I LPH)
3 Cruisers (1 CLH)
19 Destroyers
28 Frigates
2 SSBNs
20 Patrol Submarines
2 Landing Ships (Assault)
5 LSTs
14 LCTs
33 Minor Landing Craft
1 Missile Boat
14 Patrol Craft
6 Patrol Boats
14 Ocean Minesweepers
5 Minehunters
61 Coastal Minesweepers
10 Inshore Minesweepers
13 Survey Vessels
4 Maintenance and Repair Ships
5 Logistic Support Ships
4 Experimental Ships
14 Transports and Fleet Supply Ships
9 Oilers
16 Boom Defence Vessels
60 Tugs
20 Miscellaneous

15-Year Re-equipment Plan

This programme provides for the following fleet by 1985:

2 Aircraft carriers
2 Helicopter carriers
30 Frigates or corvettes
35 Avisos
5 SSBN
20 Patrol Submarines (or Fleet)
30 Patrol craft
MHC and MSC as necessary
5 Replenishment Oilers
Logistic Support and Maintenance Ships
2 Assault Ships
Landing Ships and craft
Transports
50 LRMP aircraft
Carrier borne aircraft
Helicopters

1971-75 New Construction Plan

1 Helicopter Carrier
3 Guided Missile Destroyers ("Corvettes") "C 70" Type
3 Guided Missile Destroyers ("Corvettes") "C 67" Type
14 Escorts (officially rated as *Avisos*) "A 69" Type
3 Nuclear Powered Ballistic Missile Submarines
4 Patrol Submarines
2 Patrol Boats (for overseas service)
1 Fleet Replenisnment Ship
2 Small Landing Ships (Transports)

Personnel

1969: 70 200 (5 400 officers, 64 800 ratings)
1970: 69 300 (4 880 officers, 64 420 ratings)
1971: 68 586 (4 732 officers, 63 854 ratings)
1972: 68 308 (4 604 officers, 63 704 ratings)
1973: 67 600 (4 400 officers, 63 200 ratings)
(personnel to be increased by 5 000 under the 15-year re-equipment plan)

Mercantile Marine

Lloyd's Register of Shipping:
1 390 vessels of 7 419 596 tons gross

Disposals and Transfers

Destroyers

6/1971 *Surcouf*. Foreward section sank after collision—after section used for spares

Frigates

1961 *La Croix de Lorraine, L'Ailette, La Confiance, L'Aventure*
1964 *La Surprise* to Morocco
1971 *Gustave Zédé* (Command Ship)

Submarines

British S-class
10/1952 *Sibylle* (ex-*Sportsman*) lost off Toulon
10/1958 *Sirène* (ex-*Spiteful*) returned to UK
11/1959 *Sultane* (ex-*Statesman*) returned to UK
8/1961 *Saphir* (ex-*Satyr*) returned to UK

German Classes
1957 *Blaison* (ex-U 123) Type IX B
1958 *Bouan* (ex-U 510) Type IXC
1961 *Laubie* (ex-U 766) Type VIIC
1963 *Mille* (ex-U 471) Type VIIC
1968 *Roland Morillot* (ex-U 2518) type XXI
La Créole Class
7/1961 *L'Africaine*
3/1963 *La Créole*
1965 *L'Andromède, L'Astrée*
1966 *L'Artemis*

PENNANT NUMBERS

R Aircraft and Helicopter Carriers
95 Arromanches
97 Jeanne d'Arc
98 Clemenceau
99 Foch

S Submarines
610 Le Foudroyant
611 Le Redoutable
612 Le Terrible
613 L'Indomptable
614 Le Tonnant
631 Narval
632 Marsouin
633 Dauphin
634 Requin
635 Aréthuse
636 Argonaute
637 Espadon
638 Morse
639 Amazone
640 Ariane
641 Daphné
642 Diane
643 Doris
645 Flore
646 Galatée
648 Junon
649 Venus
650 Psyche
651 Sirène
655 Gymnote

C Cruisers and Command Ships
610 de Grasse
611 Colbert

D Missile Leaders and Destroyers
602 Suffren
603 Duquesne
604 Tourville
605 Duguay-Trouin
622 Kersaint
623 Cassard
624 Bouvet
625 Dupetit Thouars
626 Chevalier Paul
627 Maillé Brézé

D Missile Leaders and Destroyers —*continued*
628 Vauquelin
629 D'Estrées
630 Du Chayla
631 Casabianca
632 Guépratte
633 Duperré
634 La Bourdonnais
635 Forbin
636 Tartu
637 Jauréguiberry
638 La Galissonnière

F Frigates, Escorts and Corvettes
703 Aconit
725 Victor Schoelcher
726 Commandant Bory
727 Amiral Charner
728 Doudart de La Grée
729 Balny
733 Commandant Rivière
740 Commandante Bourdais
748 Protet
749 Ensigne de Vaisseau Henry
761 Le Corse
762 Le Brestois
763 Le Boulonnais
764 Le Bordelais
765 Le Normand
766 Le Picard
767 Le Gascon
768 Le Lorrain
769 Le Bourguignon
770 Le Champenois
771 Le Savoyard
772 Le Breton
773 Le Basque
774 L'Agenais
775 Le Béarnais
776 L'Alsacien
777 Le Provençal
778 Le Vendéen

M Coastal and Inshore Minesweepers
609 Narvik
610 Ouistreham
612 Alençon
613 Berneval

M Minesweepers—*continued*
615 Cantho
616 Dompaire
617 Garigliano
618 Mytho
619 Vinh-long
620 Berlaimont
621 Origny
622 Autun
623 Baccarat
624 Colmar
632 Pervenche
633 Pivoine
635 Réséda
638 Acacia
639 Acanthe
640 Marjolaine
667 Ajonc
668 Azalée
669 Bégonia
670 Bleuet
671 Camélia
672 Chrysanthème
673 Coquelicot
674 Cyclamen
675 Eglantine
676 Gardénia
677 Giroflée
678 Glaieul
679 Glycine
680 Jacinthe
681 Laurier
682 Lilas
683 Liseron
684 Lobelia
685 Magnolia
687 Mimosa
688 Muguet
691 ex-SC 525
701 Sirius
702 Rigel
703 Antarès
704 Algol
705 Aldebaran
706 Régulus
707 Véga
708 Castor
710 Pégase
712 Cybèle

M Minesweepers—*continued*
713 Calliope
714 Clio
715 Circe
716 Ceres
726 La Dunkerquoise
727 La Malouine
728 La Bayonnaise
729 La Paimpolaise
730 La Dieppoise
731 La Lorientaise
734 Croix du Sud
735 Etoile Polaire
736 Altair
737 Capricorne
740 Cassiopée
741 Eridan
743 Sagittaire
746 Arcturus
747 Bételgeuse
748 Persée
749 Phénix
750 Bellatrix
751 Dénébola
754 Canopus
755 Capella
756 Céphée
757 Verseau
758 Aries
759 Lyre
765 Mercure
771 Tulipe
772 Armoise
773 Violette
774 Oeillet
775 Paquerette
776 Jasmin
781 Aubépine
782 Capucine
783 Hortensia
784 Géranium
785 Hibiscus
786 Dahlia
787 Jonquille
788 Myosotis
789 Pétunia

P Patrol Vessels, Coastal Escorts
630 L'Intrépide

P Patrol Vessels—*continued*

635 L'Ardent
637 L'Etourdi
638 L'Effronté
639 Le Frondeur
640 Le Fringant
641 Le Fougueux
642 L'Opiniatre
643 L'Agile
644 L'Adroit
645 L'Alerte
646 L'Attentif
647 L'Enjoué
648 Le Hardi
730 La Combattante
752 VC2
760 VC10
780 Oiseau des Isles
9785 PB
9786 PB

L Landing Ships

9003 Argens
9004 Bidassoa
9007 Trieux
9008 Dives
9009 Blavet
9021 Ouragan
9022 Orage
9061 LCT
9070 LCT
9071 LCT
9072 LCT
9073 LCT
9074 LCT
9081 Workshop
9082 Workshop
9083 Workshop
9084 Workshop
9091 LCT
9092 LCT

L Landing Ships—*continued*

9093 LCT
9094 LCT
9095 LCT
9096 LCT
9097 Issole
9099 LCT

A Auxiliaries and Support Ships

603 Henry Poincaré
607 Arago
608 Moselle
610 Ile d'Oléron
612 Médoc
614 Falleron
615 Loire
617 Garonne
618 Rance
619 Aber Wrach
620 Acheron
621 Rhin
622 Rhone
625 Papenoo
626 La Charente
627 La Seine
628 La Saone
629 Lac Chambon
630 Lac Tchad
632 Punaruu
634 Verdon
635 Rummel

A Auxiliaries—*continued*

637 Maurienne
638 Sahel
643 Aunis
644 Berry
646 Triton
648 Archimède
649 Etoile
650 La Belle Poule
652 Mutin
653 La Grande Hermine
660 Hippopotame
661 Infatigable
665 Goliath
666 Eléphant
667 Hercule
668 Rhinocéros
669 Tenace
670 Implacable
673 Lutteur
674 Acharné
675 Isère
678 La Coquille
682 Alidade
683 Octant
684 Coolie
685 Robuste
686 Actif
687 Laborieux
688 Valeureux
692 Travailleur
698 Petrel
699 Pelican
706 Courageux
718 Pachyderme
719 Bélier
724 Belouga
727 Araignée
728 Scorpion
730 Libellule
731 Persistante

A Auxiliaries—*continued*

733 Saintonge
748 Cataracte
749 La Prudente
750 Liamone
751 Oasis
753 La Découverte
755 Commandant Robert Giraud
756 L'Espérance
757 D'Entrecasteaux
758 La Recherche
759 Marcel Le Bihan
760 Cigale
761 Criquet
762 Fourmi
763 Grillon
764 Scarabée
765 Locuste
766 L'Estafette
777 Luciole
780 Astrolabe
781 Boussole
785 Zelée
789 Archéonaute
791 Corail

Y

604 Ariel
613 Faune
661 Korrigan
664 Lutin
696 Alphée
710 Sylphe
712 Tréberon
735 Merlin
736 Mélusine
741 Elfe
743 Palangrin

AIRCRAFT CARRIERS

2 "CLEMENCEAU" CLASS

Name	*No.*	*Builders*	*Laid down*	*Launched*	*Completed*
CLEMENCEAU (PA 54)	R 98	Brest	Nov 1955	21 Dec 1957	22 Nov 1961
FOCH (PA 55)	R 99	Chantier de L'Atlantique	Feb 1957	28 July 1960	15 July 1963

Displacement, tons	27 307 normal; 32 780 full load
Length, feet (*metres*)	780·8 (*238·0*)pp; 869·4 (*265·0*)oa
Beam, feet (*metres*)	104·1 (*31·7*) hull (with bulges)
Width, feet (*metres*)	168·0 (*51·2*) oa
Draught, feet (*metres*)	24·6 (*7·5*) 28·2 (*8·6*) screws
Aircraft	Capacity 40, including jet aircraft. Each carries 3 Flights—1 of *Etendard IV*, 1 of *Crusader*, 1 of Breguet *Alizé*
Catapults	2 Mitchell-Brown steam, Mk BS 5
Armour	Flight deck, island superstructure and bridges, hull (over machinery spaces and magazines)
Guns	8—3·9 in (*100 mm*) AA automatic in single turrets
Main engines	2 sets Parsons geared turbines; 2 shafts; 126 000 shp
Speed, knots	32 max (33·4 trials); 24 sustained sea
Boilers	6; steam pressure 640 psi (*45 kg/cm²*), superheat 842°F (450°C)
Range, miles	7 500 at 18 knots; 4 800 at 24 knots; 3 500 at full power
Oil fuel, tons	3 720
Complement	2 239 (179 officers, 2 060 men)

CLEMENCEAU — *1971, Dr. Giorgio Arra*

GENERAL
First aircraft carriers designed as such and built from the keel to be completed in France. Authorised in 1953 and 1955, respectively. *Clemenceau* ordered from Brest Dockyard on 28 May 1954 and begun in Nov 1955. *Foch* begun at Chantiers de l'Atlantique a St. Nazaire, Penhoet-Loire, in a special dry dock (contract provided for the construction of the hull and propelling machinery) and completed by Brest Dockyard.

FLIGHT DECK. Angled deck incorporated, two lifts, measuring 52·5 × 36 feet, one on the starboard deck edge, two steam catapults for aircraft up to 11 tons, and two deck landing aids. The flight deck measures 543 × 96·8 feet and is angled at 8 degrees.

HANGAR. Dimensions of the hangar are 590·6 × 78·7 × 23·0 feet.

RADAR. One DRBV21 lower L-Band long range air surveillance; one DRBV 10 three dimensional air search and height finders S-band for aircraft direction; one NRBA 50 aircraft approach control radar in dome, four DRBC 31/2 fire control radars mounted on gun directors; Tacan beacon.

ELECTRONICS. Comprehensive DF and ECM equipment. Both to be fitted with SENIT 4 Tactical data automation system.

DRAWING. Starboard elevation and plan. Scale: 125 feet = 1 inch (1 : 1 500).

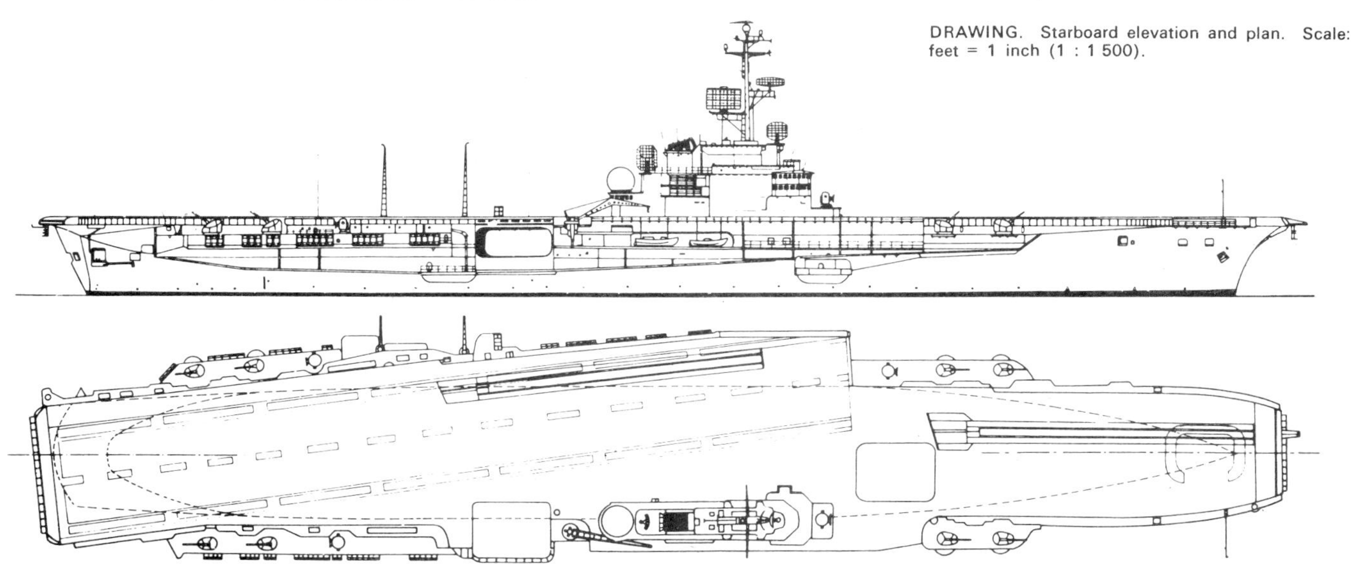

Aircraft Carrier —*continued*

GUNNERY. Originally to have been armed with 24—2·25 inch guns in twin mountings, but the armament was revised to 12—3·9 inch (*100 mm*) in 1956 and to 8—3·9 inch (*100 mm*) in 1958. The 100 mm guns were of a new design. Rate of fire 60 rounds per minute.

BULGES. *Foch* was completed with bulges. These having proved successful, *Clemenceau* was modified similarly on first refit, increasing her beam by 6 feet.

FOCH — *1971, French Navy,*

1 Ex-BRITISH "COLOSSUS" CLASS (LPH)

Name	*Pennant No.*	*Builders*	*Laid down*	*Launched*	*Completed*
ARROMANCHES (ex-HMS *Colossus*)	R 95	Vickers-Armstrong Ltd, Newcastle-on-Tyne	1 June 1942	30 Sep 1943	16 Dec 1944

Displacement, tons	14 000 standard; 18 500 full load
Length, feet (*metres*)	648·8 (*197·8*) pp; 694·5 (*211·7*) oa
Beam, feet (*metres*)	80·2 (*24·5*)
Width, feet (*metres*)	118 (*36·0*) oa
Draught, feet (*metres*)	23 (*7·0*)
Aircraft	40
Boilers	4 three-drum type; 400 psi (*28 kg/cm²*); 680°F (360°C)
Main engines	Parsons geared turbines 40 000 shp; 2 shafts
Speed, knots	25
Range, miles	12 000 at 14 knots; 6 200 at 23 knots
Oil fuel (tons)	3 200
Complement	1 019 (42 officers and 777 men, plus 200 for air service)

This ship was lent to the French Navy for five years from August 1946 with the option of purchase in 1951. This was taken up and she was permanently transferred from Great Britain in that year. Extensively refitted 1950/51; and again refitted in 1957-58.

RECONSTRUCTION. Modernised and partially rebuilt in 1957-58 with the angled deck at 4 degrees, and mirror sight deck landing aid sponsons, the overall width being increased from 112·5 feet to just over 118 feet (*36 metres*). In consequence of these modifications the ship was able to receive Breguet Alizé ASM aircraft of the 1050 type. Extensively refitted in 1968 and rearmed in Sep 1969, being redesignated a helicopter carrier for several years more service in a quadruple role; to operate intervention and anti-submarine helicopters, as a fast operational transport and a sea training carrier.

DRAWING. Starboard elevation and plan. Redrawn in 1970. Scale: 125 feet = 1 inch (1 : 1 500).

ARROMANCHES — *1971, French Navy*

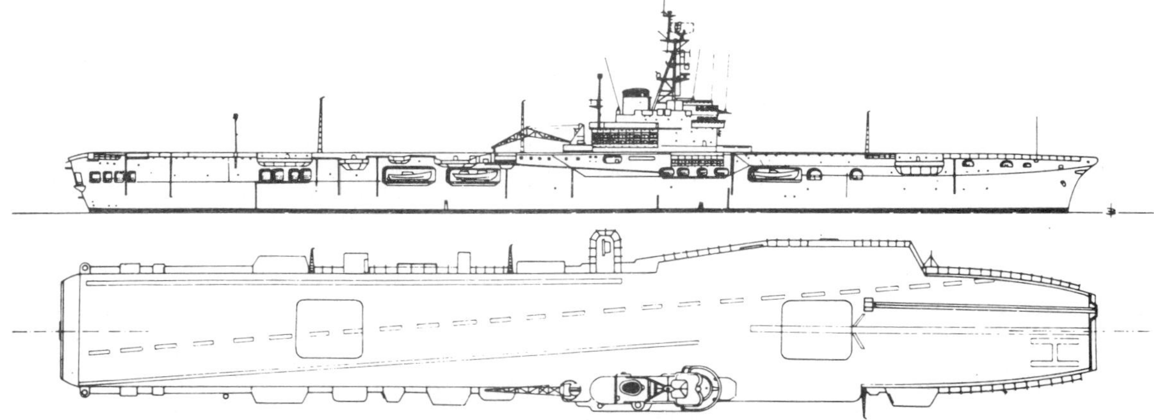

Aircraft Carrier —*continued*

ARROMANCHES *1971, Dr. Giorgio Arra*

ENGINEERING. Engines and boilers are arranged *en echelon*, one set of turbines and two boilers being installed side by side in each of the two main propelling machinery spaces, on the unit system, so that the starboard propeller shaft is longer than the port.

RADAR. Search: DRBV 22 Air/surface surveillance.

GUNNERY. She formerly mounted 43—40 mm AA guns (as refitted) but these were removed when she became a training and helicopter carrier.

CRUISERS

Name	*No.*	*Builders*	*Ordered*	*Laid down*	*Launched*	*Completed*
JEANNE D'ARC (ex-*La Résolue*)	R 97	Brest Dockyard	8 Mar 1957	7 July 1960	30 Sep 1961	1 July 1963 (trials) 30 June 1964 (service)

Displacement, tons	10 000 standard; 12 365 full load
Length, feet (*metres*)	564·2 (*172*) pp; 597·1 (*182·0*) oa
Beam, feet (*metres*)	78·7 (*24·0*) hull
Draught, feet (*metres*)	24·0 (*7·3*) max
Flight deck	203·4 × 68·9 (*62·0* × *21·0*)
Aircraft	Heavy A/S helicopters (4 in peacetime as training ship; 8 in wartime)
Guns	4—3·9 in (*100* mm) AA single
Main engines	Rateau-Bretagne geared turbines; 2 shafts; 40 000 shp
Speed, knots	26·5 designed
Boilers	4; working pressure 640 psi (*45 kg/cm²*); 842°F (*450°C*)
Range miles	6 000 at 15 knots
Oil fuel, tons	1 360
Complement	906 (44 officers, 670 ratings and 192 cadets)

GENERAL

Authorised under the 1957 estimates. Used for training officer cadets in peacetime in place of the old training cruiser *Jeanne d'Arc* (which was decommissioned on 28 July 1964 and sold for scrap in Dec 1965 at Brest). In wartime, after rapid modification, she would be used as a commando ship, helicopter carrier or troop transport with commando equipment and a battalion of 700 men. The lift has a capacity of 12 tons. The ship is almost entirely air-conditioned.

MODIFICATIONS. Between first steaming trials and completion for operational service the ship was modified with a taller funnel to clear the superstructure and obviate the smoke and exhaust gases swirling on to the bridges.

ELECTRONICS. The ship is almost as well equipped with electronic apparatus as the aircraft carrier *Clemenceau*. She also has long range sonar gear.

RADAR. Search: DRBI 10 3D and DRBV 23. Tactical: S Band with cheese type antenna. Fire Control: X band.

GUNNERY. She was originally designed to mount six 100 mm (3·9 inch) guns (now four).

NAMES. The name *La Résolue* was only a temporary one until the decommissioning of the training cruiser *Jeanne d'Arc* which was relieved by *La Résolue* in 1964 when the latter ship took the name *Jeanne d'Arc*, on 16 July.

JEANNE D'ARC

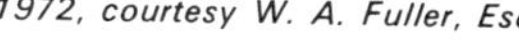

1972, courtesy W. A. Fuller, Esq

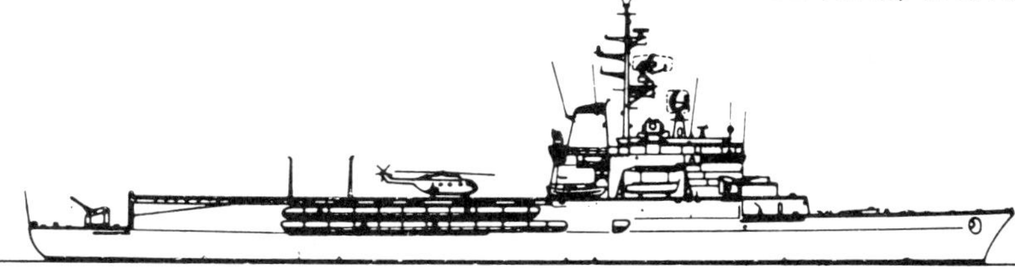

JEANNE D'ARC

JEANNE D'ARC *French Navy*

Cruisers—*continued*

Name	Pennant No.	Builders	Laid down	Launched	Completed	Commissioned	Reconstruction
COLBERT	C 611	Brest Dockyard	Dec 1953	24 Mar 1956 (floated out of dry dock)	1958 (trials end of 1957)	5 May 1959	Apr 1970-Oct 1972

Displacement, tons	8 500 standard; 11 300 full load
Length, feet (*metres*)	593·2 (*180·8*) oa
Beam, feet (*metres*)	64·6 (*19·7*)
Draught, feet (*metres*)	25·2 (7·7) screws
Missile launchers	4 Exocet launchers; 1 twin "Masurca" surface-to-air aft
Guns	2—3·9 in (*100 mm*) single automatic; 12—57 mm in 6 twin mountings, 3 on each side
Armour	Has some protection. See notes
Main engines	2 sets CEM-Parsons geared turbines; 2 shafts; 86 000 shp
Speed, knots	32·4 max (33·7 trials); 15 economical sea
Boilers	4 Indret multitubular; 640 psi (*45 kg/cm²*); 842°F (450°C)
Range, miles	4 000 at 25 knots
Oil fuel, tons	1 492
Complement	800 (70 officers, 730 men) as Flagship after reconstruction

Provision was made in the original design for her to be fitted with guided missiles. New scheme of protection, and platform for helicopter. She was equipped as command ship and for radar control of air strikes.

REARMAMENT. *Colbert* has been undergoing a major refit since Apr 1970. She will have SENIT tactical information system, new radar including decimetric improved DRB 23 as in *Foch*, and air-conditioned accommodation. The ship started trials in October 1972. Reductions in armament during reconstruction saved 80 mill. francs from original refit cost of 350 mill. francs.

ELECTRONICS. Senit I data automation system. ECM.

RADAR. One navigation set; one DRBV 21 lower L band surveillance set; one warning set;; one DRBV 23 L band search set; one DRBI 10 three dimensional air-search and height finder. Two DRBC 32 fire control for 57 mm guns; one DRBC 32 for 100 mm guns; two DRBC 51 for Masurca control.

MISSILES. Exact details of Exocet fitting not available. *Colbert* carries 48 Masurca missiles probably a mix of M2 mod 2 "line-of-sight" beam riders and Mk 2 mod 3 semi-active radar homing versions.

GUNNERY. Prior to Apr 1970 the armament comprised sixteen 5 inch (*127 mm*) dual purpose guns in eight twin mountings, and twenty 57 mm Bofors anti-aircraft guns in ten twin mountings.

SONAR. Hull mounted set.

COLBERT (1970-73 rearmament model) *1971, French Navy,*

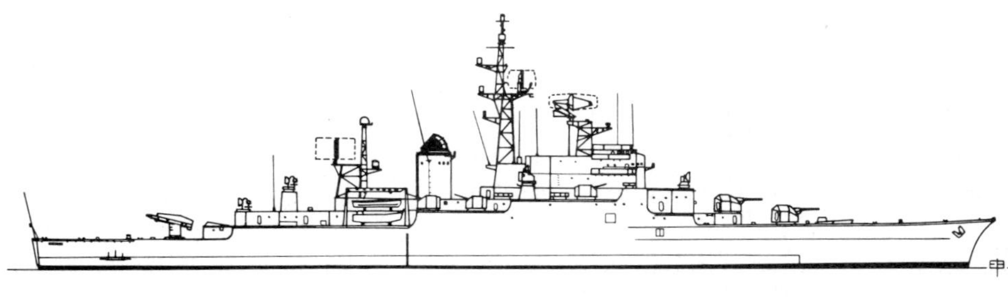

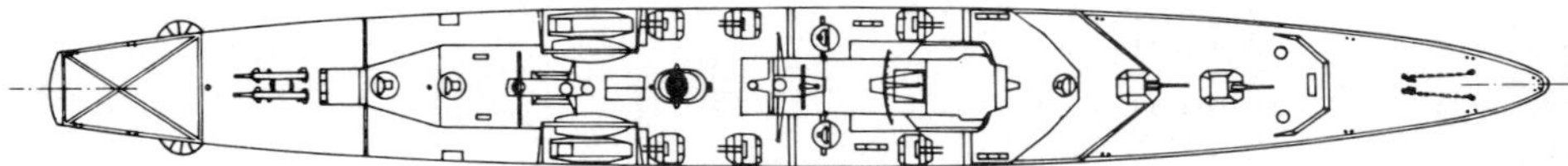

Name	Pennant No.	Builders	Laid down	Launched	Completed	Commissioned
DE GRASSE	C 610	Lorient Dockyard and Brest Dockyard (see notes)	Nov 1938	11 Sep 1946	Aug 1955 (trials)	3 Sep 1956 (operational)

Displacement, tons	9 000 standard; 12 350 full load
Length, feet (*metres*)	617·8 (*188·3*)pp; 563·7 (*199·3*)oa
Beam, feet (*metres*)	69·9 (*21·3*)
Draught, feet (*metres*)	20·7 (*6·3*) aft
Guns	12—5 in (*127 mm*) dp; (6 twin mountings)
Main engines	2 sets Rateau-Chantiers de Bretagne geared turbines 105 000 shp (120 000 max); 2 shafts
Speed, knots	33 max (33·8 trials); 18 cruising
Boilers	4 A & C de B Indret multitubular; 500 psi (*35 kg/cm²*). 725°F (*385°C*)
Range, miles	6 000 at 18 knots; 2 000 at full power
Oil fuel, tons	1 900 normal
Complement	560 plus accommodation for 120 engineers and technicians

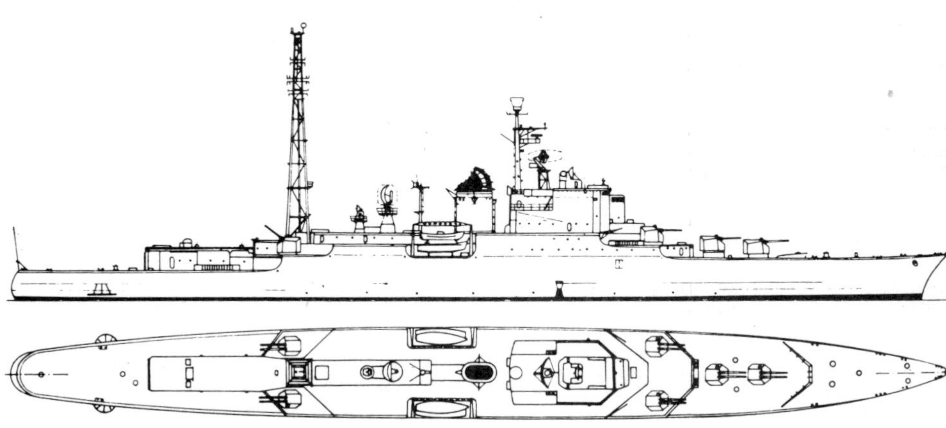

GENERAL
Ordered under the 1937 Estimates. Her construction was suspended during the German occupation of Lorient. but was resumed in 1946 until her launch when building was stopped. Construction was again resumed on 9 Jan 1951. Completed in Brest Dockyard as an anti-aircraft cruiser to a modified design. She is equipped as a fleet command ship and for radar control of air strikes.

MODIFICATIONS. Refitted at Brest as Flagship of the Pacific Experimental Nuclear Centre in 1966. Signal department enlarged and 57 mm armament removed. Equipped against fall out.

RADAR. One DRBV 23 L Band Search set; one DRBI 10 three dimensional air search and height finder; one DRBC 32 fire control radar; Tacan beacon.

GUNNERY. All the 57 mm Bofors AA guns (six twin mountings) and two twin 5 inch guns were removed during the conversion as flagship of the Pacific Experimental centre.

DRAWING. Starboard elevation and plan. Redrawn in 1970. Scale: 125 feet = 1 inch (1 : 1 500).

DE GRASSE *1967, French Navy*

DESTROYERS

2 "SUFFREN" CLASS

(FLE 60 TYPE DDG)

Name	No.	Builders	Laid down	Launched	Trials	Operational
DUQUESNE	D 603	Brest Dockyard	Nov 1964	12 Feb 1966	July 1968	Apr 1970
SUFFREN	D 602	Lorient Dockyard	Dec 1962	15 May 1965	Dec 1965	July 1967

Displacement, tons	5 090 standard; 6 090 full load
Length, feet (*metres*)	517·1 (*157·6*) oa
Beam, feet (*metres*)	50·9 (*15·5*)
Draught, feet (*metres*)	20·0 (*6·1*)
Missile launchers	Twin "Masurca" surface-air
Guns	2—3·9 in (*100 mm*) automatic, single AA; 2—30 mm (automatic, single) AA
A/S weapons	"Malafon" rocket/homing torpedo single launcher 13 missiles carried
Torpedo tubes	4 (2 each side) for A/S homing torpedoes
Main engines	Double reduction geared turbines; 2 shafts; 72 500 shp
Speed, knots	34
Boilers	4 automatic; working pressure 640 psi (*45 kg/cm²*); superheat 842°F (450°C)
Range, miles	5 000 at 18 knots
Complement	426 (38 officers, 388 men)

DUQUESNE — *1971, Wright & Logan*

DUQUESNE, SUFFREN

GENERAL
Ordered under the 1960 Programme. The structure provides best possible resistance to atomic blast. Equipped with gyro controlled stabilisers. Air conditioning of accommodation and operational areas.

ELECTRONICS. *Senit I* action data automatic system.

RADAR. One DRBN 32 search and navigation set; one DRBI 23 L band stacked-beam three dimensional air surveillance and target designator in radome; one DRBV 50 surface surveillance radar; two DRBR 51 Masurca fire control; one DRBC 32 fire control for forward guns.

MISSILES. Carry 48 *Masurca* missiles, probably a mix of Mk 2 Mod 2 beam riders and Mk 2 Mod 3 semi-active homers.

SONAR. One DUBV 23 hull-mounted set and a DUBV 43 VDS.

SUFFREN — *1970, French Navy*

3 NEW CONSTRUCTION (C70 TYPE)

GEORGES LEYGUES +2

Displacement, tons	3 950
Length, feet (*metres*)	438·0 (*133·5*)
Aircraft	2 WG 13 helicopters with Mk L6 torpedoes & ASM
Missile launchers	4 "MM 38" ("Exocet"); Masurca in A/A version
Guns	2—3·9 in (*100 mm*)
A/S Weapons	Malafon in A/S version
Torpedoes	10 tubes for Mk L5
Main engines	CODOG (combined diesels of gas turbines); 2 shafts
Speed, knots	30 (19·5 on diesels)
Complement	circa 220

A new C 70 type of so-called "corvette" is projected. Three are included in the new construction programme, the lead ship laid down late 1972.
A total of 24 is planned for completion by 1985, half being an A/S version like *G. Leygues* and half A/A.

TOURVILLE model — *1971, French Navy*

3 "TOURVILLE" CLASS

(F67 TYPE F DDG)

DUGUAY-TROUIN F 605 **TOURVILLE** F 604
DE GRASSE F 606

Displacement, tons	4 580 standard; 5 745 full load
Length, feet (*metres*)	510·3 (*152·8*) oa
Beam, feet (*metres*)	50·2 (*15·3*)
Draught, feet (*metres*)	18·7 (*5·7*)
Aircraft	2 WG 13 ON ASW helicopters
Missile launchers	6 "MM 38" ("Exocet")
Torpedoes	Auto guided A/S
A/S Weapons	"Malafon" rocket/homing torpedo
Guns	3—3·9 in (*100 mm*) AA
Main engines	Geared turbines; 2 shafts; 54 400 shp
Speed, knots	31
Boilers	4 automatic
Range, miles	5 000 at 18 knots
Complement	303 (25 officers, 278 men)

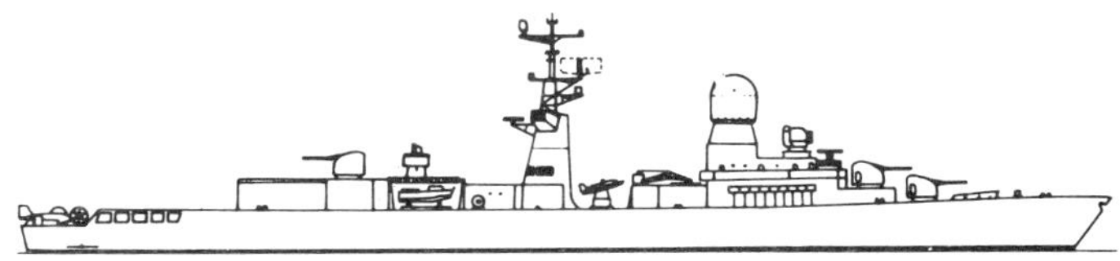

TOURVILLE

Developed from the "Aconit" design. *Tourville* was laid down at Lorient on 16 Mar 1970 and launched May 13 1972 for completion in 1974. *Duguay-Trouin* was laid down in Jan 1971 for launching in 1973 and completion in 1974. *De Grasse* begun in 1972. For completion in 1975. Originally rated as "corvettes" but reclassified as frigates on 8 July 1971 and given "D" pennant numbers like destroyers.

Destroyers—*continued*

1 ANTI-SUBMARINE (T 56) TYPE

Name	*Pennant No.*	*Builders*	*Laid down*	*Launched*	*Completed*
LA GALISSONNIÈRE	D 638	Lorient Naval Dockyard	Nov 1958	12 Mar 1960	July 1962

LA GALISSONIÈRE

Displacement, tons	2 750 standard; 3 740 full load;
Length, feet (*metres*)	435·7 (*132·8*) oa
Beam, feet (*metres*)	41·7 (*12·7*)
Draught, feet (*metres*)	15·4 (*4·7*) aft; 18·0 (*5·5*) screws
Aircraft	1 A/S helicopter
A/S weapons	"Malafon" rocket/homing torpedoes, 1 launcher
Guns	2—3·9 in (*100 mm*) AA automatic, single
Torpedo tubes	6—21·7 in (*550 mm*) ASM, 2 triple
Main engines	2 sets geared turbines; 2 shafts; 63 000 shp (72 000 on trials, light)
Boilers	4 A & C de B Indret; 500 psi (*35 kg/cm²*); 617°F (*380°C*)
Speed, knots	34 (*38·2* on trials, light)
Range, miles	5 000 at 18 knots
Oil fuel, tons	725
Complement	333 (20 officers, 313 men)

GENERAL
Designed as a flotilla leader. Same characteristics as regards hull and machinery as T 47 and T 53 R types, but different armament. She has a hangar and a platform for landing a helicopter. When first commissioned she was used as an experimental ship for new sonars and anti-submarine weapons.

ARMAMENT. She is fitted with French makes of guided missiles and was the first French combatant ship to be so armed. This is the reason for the two 3·9 in (*100 mm*) guns instead of the 3 or 4 previously planned. As redesigned she was France's first operational guided missile ship.

ELECTRONICS. Tacan beacon and full DF and ECM fit.

RADAR. One navigation set; one DRBV 50 search/navigation set; one DRBV 22 L-band search set; one DRBC 32 X band fire-control.

SONAR. One hull-mounted DUBV 23; one VDS DUBV 43.

LA GALISSONNIÈRE — *1972, A. & J. Pavia*

16 SURCOUF CLASS

Name	*No.*	*Builders*	*Laid down*	*Launched*	*Completed*	
CASSARD	D 623	A. C. Bretagne	Nov 1951	12 May 1953	14 Apr 1956	Group A
CHEVALIER PAUL	D 626	F. C. Gironde	Feb 1952	28 July 1953	22 Dec 1956	
KERSAINT	D 622	Lorient Naval Dockyard	Nov 1951	3 Oct 1953	20 Mar 1956	Group B Type 47
BOUVET	D 624	Lorient Naval Dockyard	June 1952	3 Oct 1953	13 May 1956	
DUPETIT THOUARS	D 625	Brest Naval Dockyard	Mar 1952	4 Feb 1954	15 Sep 1956	
DU CHAYLA	D 630	Brest Naval Dockyard	July 1953	27 Nov 1954	4 June 1957	
MAILLÉ BRÉZÉ	D 627	Lorient Naval Dockyard	Oct 1953	26 Sep 1954	4 May 1957	Group C Type 47
VAUQUELIN	D 628	Lorient Naval Dockyard	Mar 1953	26 Sep 1954	3 Nov 1956	
D'ESTRÉES	D 629	Brest Naval Dockyard	May 1953	27 Nov 1954	19 Mar 1957	
CASABIANCA	D 631	A. C. Bretagne	Oct 1953	13 Nov 1954	4 May 1957	
GUÉPRATTE	D 632	F. C. Gironde	Aug 1953	9 Nov 1954	6 June 1957	
LA BOURDONNAIS	D 634	Brest Naval Dockyard	Aug 1954	15 Oct 1955	Mar 1958	Group D Type 53R
FORBIN	D 635	Brest Naval Dockyard	Aug 1954	15 Oct 1955	1 Feb 1958	
TARTU	D 636	Ateliers et Chantiers de Bretagne	Nov 1954	2 Dec 1955	5 Feb 1958	
JAURÉGUIBERRY	D 637	Forges et Chantiers de la Gironde	Sep 1954	5 Nov 1955	July 1958	
DUPERRÉ	D (ex-A, ex-D) 633	Lorient Naval Dockyard	Nov 1954	2 July 1955	8 Oct 1957	Group E

	Group A (Leaders)	*Group B (DDG)*	*Group C (A/S)*	*Group D (A/D)*	*Group E (ex-Trials)*
Displacement, tons	2 750 (standard); 3 740 full load	As Group A	2 750 standard; 3 900 full load	As Group A	As Group A
Length, feet (*metres*)	421·3 (*128·4*)		434·6 (*132·5*)		
Beam, feet (*metres*)	41·7 (*12·7*)		41·7 (*12·7*)		
Draught, feet (*metres*)	17·7 (*5·4*)		14·4 (*4·4*)		
Missiles, AA	Nil	Single Mk 13 Tartar (40 missiles)	Malafon	Nil	
Guns, dual purpose	6—5 in (*127 mm*)	Nil	2—3·9 in (*100 mm*)	6—5 in (*127 mm*)	As Group C (after conversion)
Guns, AA	4—57 mm	6—57 mm	2—20 mm	6—57 mm	
Torpedo Tubes	6—21·7 in A/S	As Group A			
A/S weapons	A/S rocket projector 375 mm		As Group A		
Boilers	4 Indret	As Group A	As Group A	As Group A	
Main engines	2 Parsons geared turbines; 63 000 shp; 2 shafts				
Speed, knots	34		32		
Range, miles	5 000 at 18 knots		As Group A	As Group A	As Group A
Oil fuel (tons)	800				
Complement	293 (336 with staff)	310	320	293	320

SURCOUF *Class* (Group B)

SURCOUF *Class* (Group D)

SURCOUF *Class* (Group A)

Destroyers—*continued*

GENERAL
Since 1963 this class has undergone various conversions as above. *Duperre* still converting from trials ship, completing 1974.

RADAR
Group B. One SPS-52 three dimensional air surveillance and target designation radar. Two SPG-51 Tartar control sets . One DRBV 20 search set; one DRBC 32 X-band fire control. Senit 2.
Group C. One DRBV 32 navigation set; one DRBV 50 surface warning; one DRBV 22 air surveillance; two DRBC 32 X-band fire control for 100 mm guns and Malafon.
Group D. One DRBI three dimensional air search and height finder set; one DRBV 22 air search set. Tacan. Senit 2.

SONAR
Group C. Hull-mounted DUBV 23 and VDS DUBV 43.

D'ESTRÉES *Class* (A/S Type)

KERSAINT DDG Type — *1972, Dr. Giorgio Arra*

D'ESTRÉES (A/S type) — *1972, Dr. Giorgio Arra*

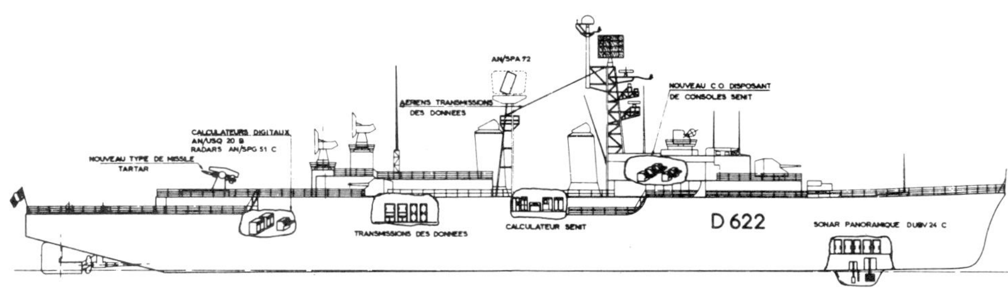

SURCOUF class (converted DDG) — *1973, Cols Bleus*

FRIGATES

1 "ACONIT" CLASS

ACONIT F 703

Displacement, tons	3 000 standard; 3 560 full load
Length, feet (*metres*)	416·7 (*127·0*) oa
Beam, feet (*metres*)	44·0 (*13·4*)
Draught, feet (*metres*)	18 (*5·5*)
Missiles, A/S	"Malafon" rocket/homing torpedo
Guns	2—3·9 in (*100 mm*) AA
A/S weapons	1 quadruple 12 in (*305 mm*) mortar
Torpedoes	2 launchers for A/S
Main engines	Geared turbines; 1 shaft; 28 650 shp
Boilers	2 automatic
Speed, knots	27
Range, miles	5 000 at 18 knots
Complement	258 (20 officers, 238 men)

ACONIT

ACONIT as completed — *1972, French Navy*

Officially rated as "Corvette" but from size and armament must be described as frigate. Laid down at Lorient in Jan 1966 and launched on 7 Mar 1970, commissioned 15 May 1971 for service in 1972. SENIT 3 equipment fitted.

RADAR. One DRBV 13 S-band surveillance set; one DRBC 32 X-band fire control set; one DRBN 32 search/navigation set;

SONAR. One hull-mounted DUBV 23; one VDS type DUBV 43.

Frigates—*continued*

9 "COMMANDANT" RIVIERE CLASS

Name	No.	Launched	Completed
COMMANDANT RIVIÈRE	F 733	Oct 58	Dec 62
VICTOR SCHOELCHER	F 725	Oct 58	Oct 62
COMMANDANT BORY	F 726	Oct 58	Mar 64
AMIRAL CHARNER	F 727	Mar 60	Dec 62
DOUDART DE LA GRÉE	F 728	Apr 61	Mar 63
BALNY	F 729	Mar 62	Feb 71
COMMANDANT BOURDAIS	F 740	Apr 61	Mar 63
PROTET	F 748	Dec 62	May 64
ENSEIGNE DE VAISSEAU HENRY	F 749	Dec 63	Jan 65

Displacement, tons: 1 750 standard; 2 250 full load (*Balny* 1 650 standard; 1 950 full load)
Length, feet (*metres*): 321·5 (*98·0*) pp; 338 (*103*) oa
Beam, feet (*metres*): 37·8 (*11·5*)
Draught, feet (*metres*): 12·5 (*3·8*) mean; 14·1 (*4·3*) max
Aircraft: 1 light helicopter can land aft
Guns, AA: 3—3·9 in (*100 mm*) automatic, singles (*Balny* 2 only); 2—30 mm
A/S: 1—12 in (*305 mm*) quadruple mortar
Torpedo tubes: 6—21 in (*533 mm*) ASM
Main engines: 4 SEMT-Pielstick diesels; 16 000 bhp; 2 shafts; except *Commandant Bory:* Sigma free piston generators and gas turbines *Balny:* CODAG; 1 shaft
Speed, knots: 25 max (26·6 trials)
Range, miles: 4 500 at 15 knots (*Balny* 8 000 at 12 knots)
Complement: 214 (15 officers, 199 men)

COMMANDANT RIVIÈRE *Class*

VICTOR SCHOELCHER — *1972, Dr. Giorgio Arra*

GENERAL
All built by Lorient Dockyard. Fitted for operations under widely differing conditions. Capable of accepting a light helicopter aft. Can carry a force of up to 80 soldiers in an emergency, as well as two 30 ft LCAs. *Balny's* trials continued for several years. *Commandant Bourdais* commissioned as fishery protection ship for Newfoundland and Greenland in Mar 1963. *Victor Schoelcher* acts as training ship. *Com. Belo* class of Portugal is similar.

RADAR. Search: DRBV 22. Tactical: S Band. Fire Control: X Band DRBC 32.

BALNY (with CODAG propulsion system and only two 3·9 inch guns) — *1971, Wright & Logan*

14 "LE NORMAND" CLASS (E 52 TYPE)

Name	*No.*	*Builders*	*Laid down*	*Launched*	*Completed*
LE NORMAND	F 765	F. Ch. de la Medit	July 1953	13 Feb 1954	3 Nov 1956
LE LORRAIN	F 768	F. Ch. de la Medit	Feb 1954	19 June 1954	1 Jan 1957
LE PICARD	F 766	A. C. Loire	Nov 1953	31 May 1954	20 Sep 1956
LE GASCON	F 767	A. C. Loire	Feb 1954	23 Oct 1954	29 Mar 1957
LE CHAMPENOIS	F 770	A. C. Loire	May 1954	12 Mar 1955	1 June 1957
LE SAVOYARD	F 771	F. Ch. de la Medit	Nov 1953	7 May 1955	14 June 1956
LE BOURGUIGNON	F 769	Penhoët	Jan 1954	28 Jan 1956	11 July 1957
LE BRETON	F 772	Lorient Navy Yard	June 1954	2 Apr 1955	20 Aug 1957
LE BASQUE	F 773	Lorient Navy Yard	Dec 1954	25 Feb 1956	18 Oct 1957
L'AGENAIS	F 774	Lorient Navy Yard	Aug 1955	23 June 1956	14 May 1958
LE BÉARNAIS	F 775	Lorient Navy Yard	Dec 1955	23 June 1956	18 Oct 1958
L'ALCACIEN	F 776	Lorient Navy Yard	July 1956	26 Jan 1957	27 Aug 1960
LE PROVENCAL	F 777	Lorient Navy Yard	Feb 1957	5 Oct 1957	6 Nov 1959
LE VENDÉEN	F 778	F. Ch. de la Medit	Mar 1957	27 July 1957	1 Oct 1960

Displacement, tons: 1 295 standard; 1 795 full load
Length, feet (*metres*): 311·7 (*95·0*) pp; 325·8 (*99·3*) oa
Beam, feet (*metres*): 33·8 (*10·3*)
Draught, feet (*metres*): 11·2 (*3·4*) aft; 13·5 (*4·1*) screws
Guns, AA: 6—2·25 in (*57 mm*), in twin mountings (4 only in F 776, 777, 778); 2—20 mm
A/S: Heavy sextuple Bofors ASM (*lance-roquettes*) mortar of Hedgehog type forward (*except* F 776, 777, 778 with 1—12 in (*305 mm*) quadruple mortar) 2 DC mortars; 1 DC rack
Torpedo tubes: 12 ASM (4 triple mountings aft) for homing torpedoes
Boilers: 2 Indret; pressure 500 psi (*35·2 kg/cm²*); superheat 725°F (385°C)
Main engines: Parsons or Rateau geared turbines 20 000 shp
Speed, knots: 28 (on trials they exceeded 29 kts)
Radius, miles: 4 500 at 12 knots
Oil fuel (tons): 310
Complement: 175 peace; 200 war

LE VENDÉEN — *1972, Dr. Giorgio Arra*

GENERAL
The E 52 type have similar characteristics to the E 50 type as regards hull and machinery but are easily distinguished in that they have the ASM tubes aft and the heavy hedgehog or ASM howitzer forward while the E 50 type have the ASM torpedo tubes forward. *L'Agenais, L'Alsacien, Le Béarnais, Le Provencal* and *Le Vendéen* have a different arrangement of bridges. *L'Alsacien, Le Provencal* and *Le Vendéen* are of the E 52B type and have the Strombos-Velensi type modified funnel cap.

RADAR. Search: DRBV 22. Fire Control: One DRBV 31/32 X-band.

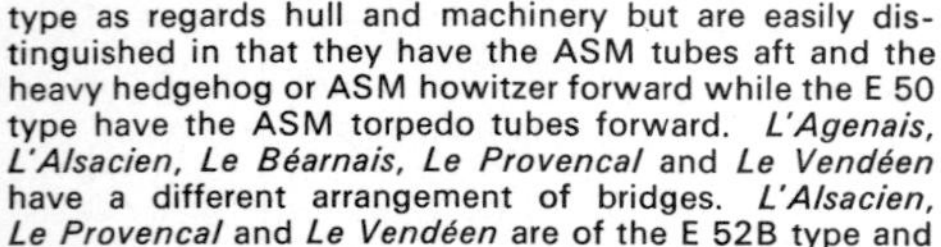

L'ALSACIEN, LE PROVENCAL, LE VENDÉEN

LE NORMAND *Class*

Frigates—*continued*

LE BÉARNAIS

1972, Dr. Giorgio Arra

4 "LE CORSE" CLASS (E 50 TYPE)

Name	No.	Builders	Laid down	Launched	Completed
LE BORDELAIS	F 764	F. Ch. de la Medit	May 1952	11 July 1953	7 Apr 1955
LE BOULONNAIS	F 763	A. C. Loire	Mar 1952	12 May 1953	5 Aug 1955
LE BRESTOIS	F 762	Lorient Navy Yard	Nov 1951	16 Aug 1952	19 Jan 1956
LE CORSE	F 761	Lorient Navy Yard	Oct 1951	5 Aug 1952	15 Apr 1955

Displacement, tons	1 290 standard; 1 528 for trials; 1 680 full load
Length, feet (*metres*)	311·7 (*95·0*) pp 325·5 (*99·2*) oa
Beam, feet (*metres*)	33·8 (*10·3*)
Draught, feet (*metres*)	13·5 (*4·1*) screws
Guns, AA	6—2·25 in (*57 mm*), 3 twin 2—20 mm
A/S weapons	2 mortars; 1 DC rack; 1 sextuple "lance roquettes"
Torpedo tubes	12 ASM tubes (four triple mounts forward) for homing torpedoes
Boilers	2 Indret; pressure 500 psi (*35·2 kg/cm²*); superheat 725°F (385°C)
Main engines	Rateau A & C de B geared turbines 20 000 shp
Speed, knots	28·5 max, 28·9 trials (*Bordelais* 29·5 on trials); economical sea speed 14
Range, miles	4 000 at 15 knots
Oil fuel, tons	292
Complement	174

GENERAL
Le Bordelais has Strombos-Velensi type modified funnel cap. *Le Brestois* has similar mast arrangement to that in *Le Provencal*. *Le Boulonnais* and *Le Corse* in reserve since 1 Dec 1964, *Le Bordelais* since Aug 1966.

RADAR. Search: DRBV 22.

GUNNERY. *Le Brestois* had a single 3·9 in (*100 mm*) automatic AA gun mounted in place of the after twin 57 mm mounting for experimental purposes and after her refit, completed in 1963, she retained this mounting.

LE CORSE *Class*, E 50 Type

LE BRESTOIS (showing 100 mm gun)

1971, Dr. Giorgio Arra

LE CORSE (as reactivated)

1972, Dr. Giorgio Arra

14 NEW CONSTRUCTION TYPE A69 (TYPE A70 SIMILAR)

D'ESTIENNE-D'ORVES, AMYOT-D'INVILLE, DROGOU, DETROYAT +10

Displacement, tons	950 standard; 1 260 full load
Length, feet (*metres*)	262·5 (*80·0*) oa; 249·3 (*76·0*) pp
Beam, feet (*metres*)	33·8 (*10·3*)
Draught, feet (*metres*)	9·8 (*3·0*)
Guns	1—3·9 in (*100 mm*) AA; 2—20 mm AA
A/S weapons	1 sextuple mortar (375 mm); 4 fixed torpedo tubes
Main engines	2 SEMT Pielstick PC2V diesels; 2 shafts; controllable pitch propellers; 11 000 bhp
Speed, knots	24 (22 with 80% power)
Range, miles	4 500 at 15 knots
Complement	62 (4 officers, 58 men)

GENERAL
Small escorts of a new type rated as *"Avisos"*, but also officially described as "Dispatch Vessels", a new category of ships to be ranked after the fast frigates of the "E 50" type. The first pair were ordered at the Lorient yard in 1971 to complete in 1974. To be followed by three each year in 1972, 1973, 1974 and 1975. To be named after Naval officers who distinguished themselves in WW II. In addition the A70 class will mount two Exocet launchers.

RADAR. One Decca type 202 navigation set; one DRBV 51 stabilised surveillance and target designator set. One DRBC 32E fire control set.

SONAR. One hull mounted sonar either Plessey MS 26 or Alcatel Premo.

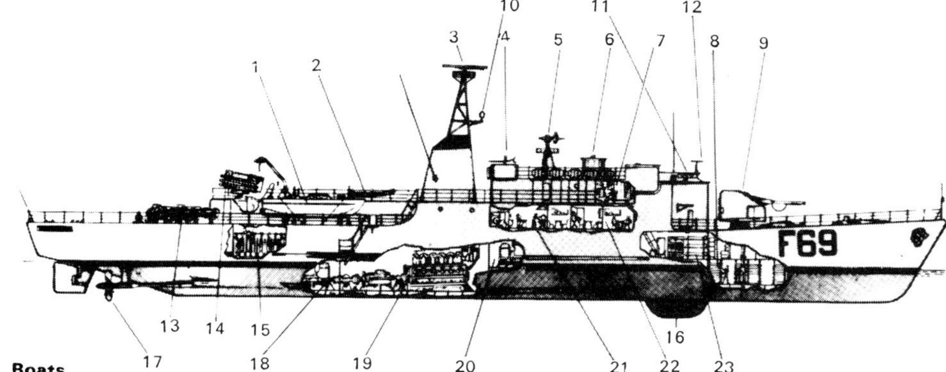

Boats
1 Utility boat (LCPS)
2 Inflatable rubber dinghy

Anti-Aircraft & Surface Defence
3 Surveillance radar
4 2—20 mm guns
5 Fire control radar
6 Target indication position
7 Operations room
8 100 mm ammunition magazine
9 100 mm turret

Navigation
10 D/f loop
11 Navigation bridge
12 Navigation radar

Anti-submarine Defence
13 Torpedo tubes (4)
14 A/S rcoket launcher, 6 barrelled
15 A/S rocket magazine
16 Sonar dome

Propulsion
17 Variable pitch screws
18 After auxiliary compartment
19 Main engine room
20 Forward auxiliary compartment

Accommodation
21 Galley
22 Crew's mess deck
23 Crew space

A 69 TYPE *AVISO* (A70 similar hull)

1972, French Navy

SUBMARINES

Name	No.	Builders	Laid down	Launched	Completion	Operational
LE REDOUTABLE	Q 252 (S 611)	Cherbourg Naval Dockyard	30 Mar 1964	29 Mar 1967	Trials 1969	1 Dec 1971
LE TERRIBLE	Q 253 (S 612)	Cherbourg Naval Dockyard	24 June 1967	12 Dec 1969	Trials 1971	
LE FOUDROYANT	Q 257 (S 610)	Cherbourg Naval Dockyard	1969	4 Dec 1971		Scheduled 1974
L'INDOMPTABLE	Q 258 (S 613)	Cherbourg Naval Dockyard	Scheduled 1971	Scheduled 1973	Scheduled 1975	Scheduled 1976
LE TONNANT	Q 259 (S 614)	Cherbourg Naval Dockyard	Scheduled 1974	Scheduled 1976	Scheduled 1977	Scheduled 1978

5 NUCLEAR POWERED BALLISTIC MISSILE TYPE

Displacement, tons	7 500 surface; 9 000 submerged
Length, feet (*metres*)	420 (*128·0*)
Beam, feet (*metres*)	34·8 (*10·6*)
Draught, feet (*metres*)	32·8 (*10·0*)
Missile launchers	16 tubes amidships for "Polaris" type ICBM's; range 1 900 miles
Torpedo tubes	4—21·7 inch (18 torpedoes)
Nuclear reactors	1 pressurised water-cooled
Main engines	2 turbo-alternators; 1 electric motor; 15 000 hp; 1 shaft
Auxiliary propulsion	1 diesel
Speed, knots	20 on surface; 25 submerged (conservative estimate)
Complement	Two alternating crews each of 135 (15 officers, 120 men)

GENERAL
Le Redoutable was the first French nuclear powered, ballistic missile armed submarine and the prototype of the *"Force de dissuasion"* of five such vessels which the Navy plans to have in the late 1970s. The vessels have a submerged cruise duration of about three months. The diesel has oil bunkerage for a range of 5 000 miles. The decision to build a fourth unit of this class was officially announced on 7 Dec 1967. It was officially stated in Feb 1972 that a fifth deterrent submarine of this type is included in the Third Construction Programme; ordered from Brest in autumn 1972.

MISSILES. First boats armed with MSBS M-1 of 18 tons launch weight with a range of 1 400 miles. The last three boats will have M-2 missiles (19·9 tons and 1 875 miles range). Both M-1 and M-2 have a 500 KT head. Further improvements planned include the M-20 missile (M2 with thermonuclear head) and M-4 with a range in the 3 000 mile bracket and fitted with MRV or MIRV. Both these developments are unlikely until the late 1970s.

RADAR. *Le Redoutable* is equipped with Calypso X Band radar for navigation and attack. Has passive ECM and DF systems.

LE REDOUTABLE *1972, French Navy*

LE TERRIBLE *1972, French Navy*

1 EXPERIMENTAL MISSILE TYPE

Name	No.	Builders	Laid down	Launched	Completed
GYMNOTE	S 655	Cherbourg Naval Dockyard	17 Mar 1963	17 Mar 1964	17 Oct 1966

Displacement, tons	3 000 surface; 3 250 submerged
Length, feet (*metres*)	275·6 (*84·0*)
Beam, feet (*metres*)	34·7 (*10·6*)
Draught, feet (*metres*)	25 (*7·6*)
Missile launchers	4 tubes for MSBS
Main engines	4 sets 620 kW diesel electric, 2 electric motors; 2 shafts; 2 600 hp
Speed, knots	11 surface; 10 submerged
Complement	78 (8 officers, 70 men)

An experimental submarine for testing ballistic missiles for the first French nuclear powered deterrent submarines, and for use as an underwater laboratory to prove equipment and arms for nuclear powered submarines.

HULL. *Gymnote* was the hull laid down in 1958 as the nuclear powered submarine Q 244 which was cancelled in 1959. The hull was still available when a trials vessel for the French "Polaris" type missiles was required and was completed as *Gymnote*.

GYMNOTE *1970, French Navy*

4 NEW CONSTRUCTION

AGOSTA **LA PRAYA**
BÉVÉZIERS **OUESSANT**

Displacement, tons	1 200 standard; 1 450 surface; 1 725 submerged
Length, feet (*metres*)	213·3 (*65·0*)
Beam, feet (*metres*)	22·3 (*6·8*)
Draught, feet (*metres*)	16·7 (*5·7*)
Tubes	4—21·7 in (*550 mm*) 20 reload torpedoes
Main engines	Diesel-electric; 2 SEMT Peilstick diesels 3 600 hp; 1 main motor 4 600 hp; 1 cruising motor; 1 shaft.

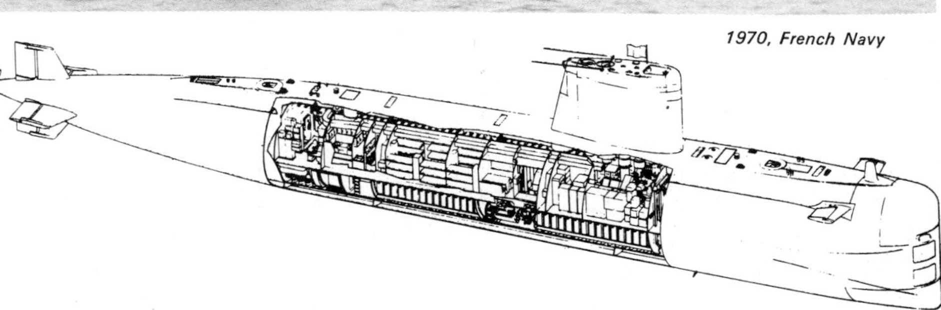

BEVEZIERS *1973, Cols Bleus*

Submarines—*continued*

Speed, knots	12 surfaced; 20 submerged
Range, miles	9 000 at 9 knots (snorting); 350 at 3·5 knots (dived)
Endurance	45 days
Complement	50 (6 officers, 44 men)

GENERAL
New type of conventional ocean-going submarines of high performance the building of which was officially announced in 1970 under the third five-year new construction plan 1971-75. All to be built at Cherbourg, keels being laid one each year. *Agosta* laid down Feb 7 1972.

RADAR. Possibly X Band Calypso Th D 1030 or 1031 for search/navigation.

SONAR. DUUA 1 active sonar with transducers forward and aft; DSUV passive sonar with 36 hydrophones; passive ranging; intercept set.

PSYCHE *1971, Wright & Logan*

9 "DAPHNE" CLASS

Name	*No.*	*Launched*	*Completed*
DAPHNÉ	S 641	20 June 1959	1 June 1964
DIANE	S 642	4 Oct 1960	20 June 1964
DORIS	S 643	14 May 1960	26 Aug 1964
FLORE	S 645	21 Dec 1960	21 May 1964
GALATÉE	S 646	22 Sep 1961	25 July 1964
JUNON	S 648	11 May 1964	25 Feb 1966
VENUS	S 649	24 Sep 1964	1 Jan 1966
PSYCHÉ	S 650	28 June 1967	July 1969
SIRÈNE	S 651	28 June 1967	Mar 1970

Displacement, tons	**869 surface; 1 043 submerged**
Length, feet (*metres*)	**189·6 (*57·8*)**
Beam, feet (*metres*)	**22·3 (*6·8*)**
Draught, feet (*metres*)	**15·1 (*4·6*)**
Torpedo tubes	**12—21·7 in (*550 mm*) 8 bow 4 stern**
Main engines	**SEMT-Pielstick diesel-electric 1 300 bhp surface; 1 600 hp motors submerged; 2 shafts**
Range, miles	2 700 at 12·5 knots (surfaced); 4 500 at 5 knots (snorting); 3 000 at 7 knots (snorting)
Speed, knots	**13·5 surface; 16 submerged**
Complement	45 (6 officers, 39 men)

VENUS (showing new sonar dome) *1972, Dr. Georgio Arra*

BUILDERS. *Daphné* and *Diane* were built by Dubigeon, Nantes, *Doris*, *Flore*, *Galatée*, *Junon* and *Venus* by Cherbourg and *Psyché* and *Sirène* by Brest.

RADAR. X Band Calypso II for search/navigation.

SONAR. DUUA 1 active sonar with transducers forward and aft; passive ranging; intercept set.

MODERNISATION. In hand from 1971 to improve sonar and armament.

FOREIGN ORDERS. South Africa (3), Pakistan (3), Portugal (4), Spain (building in Spain) (4).

LOSSES. Of the "Daphne" class *Minerve*, S 647 was lost in the Western Mediterranean on 27 Jan 1968 and *Eurydice*, S 644, was lost in that area on 4 Mar 1970. *Sirène* sank at Keroman, Lorient on 11 Oct 1972 after flooding through a torpedo tube. Raised on 22 Oct for refit.

4 "ARÉTHUSE" CLASS

Name	*No.*	*Programme*	*Builders*	*Laid down*	*Launched*	*Completed*
AMAZONE	S 639	1954	Cherbourg	Dec 1955	3 Apr 1958	1 July 1959
ARÉTHUSE	S 635	1953	Cherbourg	Mar 1955	9 Nov 1957	23 Oct 1958
ARGONAUTE	S 636	1953	Cherbourg	Mar 1955	29 June 1957	11 Feb 1959
ARIANE	S 640	1954	Cherbourg	Dec 1955	12 Sep 1958	16 Mar 1960

Displacement, tons	400 standard; 543 surface; 669 submerged
Length, feet (*metres*)	162·7 (*49·6*)
Beam, feet (*metres*)	19 (*5·8*)
Draught, feet (*metres*)	13·1 (*4·0*)
Torpedo tubes	4—21·7 in (*550 mm*) bow, 4 reloads
Main engines	12-cyl. SEMT-Pielstick diesel-electric; 1 060 bhp surface; 1 300 hp motors dived; 1 shaft
Speed, knots	12·5 surface; 16 submerged
Complement	40 (6 officers, 34 men)

An excellent class of small submarines with a minimum number of ballast tanks and a diving depth of about 600 feet.

ARIANE *1972, Dr. Giorgio Arra*

6 "NARVAL" CLASS

Name	*No.*	*Programme*	*Builders*	*Laid down*	*Launched*	*Completed*
NARVAL	S 631	1949	Cherbourg	June 1951	11 Dec 1954	1 Dec 1957
MARSOUIN	S 632	1949	Cherbourg	Sept 1951	21 May 1955	1 Oct 1957
DAUPHIN	S 633	1950	Cherbourg	May 1952	17 Sep 1955	1 Aug 1958
REQUIN	S 634	1950	Cherbourg	June 1952	3 Dec 1955	1 Aug 1958
ESPADON	S 637	1954	Normand	Dec 1955	15 Sep 1958	2 Apr 1960
MORSE	S 638	1954	Seine Maritime	Feb 1956	10 Dec 1958	2 May 1960

Displacement, tons	1 320 standard; 1 635 surface; 1 910 submerged
Length, feet (*metres*)	257·2 (*77·6*)
Beam, feet (*metres*)	25·6 (*7·8*)
Draught, feet (*metres*)	18·5 (*5·4*)
Torpedo tubes	6—21·7 in (*550 mm*) bow; 14 reload torpedoes; capable of minelaying
Main engines	Three 12-cyl SEMT-Pielstick diesels; two 2 400 hp electric motors; 2 shafts
Speed, knots	15 surface; 18 submerged
Range, miles	15 000 at 8 knots (snorting)
Endurance	45 days
Complement	63 (7 officers, 56 men)

Designed as oceangoing standard submarines. Improved versions based on the German XXI type. *Dauphine*, *Marsouin*, *Narval* and *Requin* were built in seven prefabricated parts each of 10 metres in length.

RECONSTRUCTION. During a five-year reconstruction programme, announced in 1965 and completed by the end of 1970, these submarines, *Requin* in Spring 1967 and *Espadon* and *Morse* in succession at Lorient followed by the other three, were given a new diesel electric power plant as well as new weapon and detection equipment. Sonar similar to that in the *Daphne* class. Alcatel DLT-8-4E torpedo control system. See altered appearance of *Morse* and *Narval*.

ENGINEERING. New main propelling machinery installed on reconstruction during 1965 to 1970 includes diesel-electric drive on the surface with SEMT-Pielstick diesels. The original main engines comprised Schneider 4 000 bhp 7 cyl. 2 str. diesels for surface propulsion and 5 000 hp electric motors submerged.

MORSE (showing modified conning fin) *1972, Dr. Giorgio Arra*

DORIS *1972, Dr. Giorgio Arra*

AMPHIBIOUS VESSELS

OURAGAN L 9021 **ORAGE** L 9022

Displacement, tons	5 800 light; 8 500 full load; 15 000 when fully immersed
Length, feet (*metres*)	488·9 (*149·0*)
Beam, feet (*metres*)	70·5 (*21·5*)
Draught, feet (*metres*)	16·1 (*4·9*); 28·5 (*8·7*) max
Guns	2—4·7 in (*120 mm*) mortars; 6—30 mm
Main engines	2 diesels; 2 shafts; 8 640 bhp
Speed, knots	17
Range, miles	4 000 at 15 knots
Complement	239 (16 officers, 223 men)

Built at Brest Dockyard. *Ouragan* was laid down in June 1962, launched on 9 Nov 1963, completed for trials in 1964. and commissioned in Jan 1965. *Orage* was laid down in June 1966, launched on 22 Apr 1967 and completed in Mar 1968. Bridge is on the starboard side. Fitted with a platform for four heavy helicopters. Able to carry EDICs loaded with eleven light tanks each, or 18 loaded LCMs, also 1 500 tons of material and equipment handled by two 35 ton cranes. Allocated to the Pacific Nuclear Experimental Centre.

OURAGAN *1970, courtesy Admiral M. Adam*

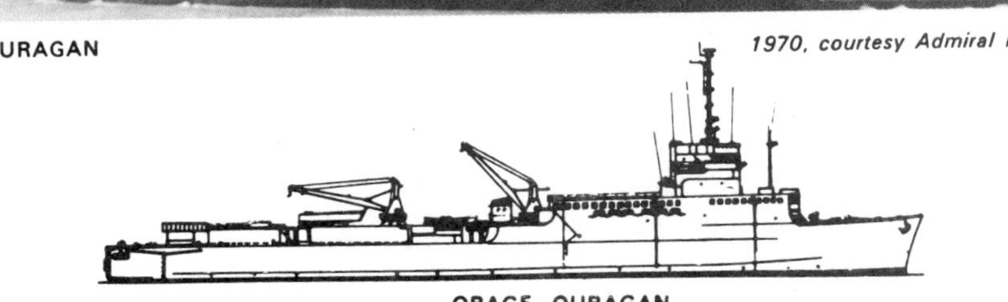

ORAGE, OURAGAN

ORAGE *1969, French Navy,*

5 LANDING SHIPS

ARGENS L 9003 **BIDASSOA** L 9004 **BLAVET** L 9009 **DIVES** L 9008 **TRIEUX** L9007

Displacement, tons	1 400 standard; 1 765 normal; 4 225 full load
Dimensions, feet	328 oa × 50 × 14
Guns	2—40 mm AA; 4—20 mm AA (*Argens, Trieux*) 1—4·7 in mortar; 3—40 mm AA (*Bidassoa, Blavet, Dives*)
Main engines	SEMT-Pielstick diesels; 2 shafts; 2 000 bhp = 11 knots
Range, miles	18 500 at 10 knots
Complement	85 (6 officers and 79 men.) Plus 170 troops (normal)

Built by Chantiers Seine Maritime (*Bidassoa, Dives*) and Chantiers de Bretagne, Nantes (others). Launched on 7 Apr 1959, 30 Dec 1960, 15 Jan 1960, 29 June 1960 and 6 Dec 1958, respectively. All commissioned in 1960-61. Can carry: 4 LCVP's, 1 800 tons of freight, 335 (up to 870 if required) troops (329 in bunks, 552 in hammocks). *Blavet* and *Trieux* are fitted as light helicopter carriers with a hanger before the bridge.

ARGENS *1971, Dr. Giorgio Arra*

The former US tank landing ships *Chéliff* (ex-US *LST* 874) and *Odet* (ex-US *LST* 815) were officially deleted from the list in 1970 and 1969, respectively.

LANDING SHIP DOCK. The dock landing ship *Foudre* (ex-Greek *Okeanos*, ex-British *Oceanway*, ex-US *LSD* 12), A 646, was officially deleted from the list in 1969.

NOTE. 2 650 ton Landing Craft are planned.

11 EDIC (LCT)

L 9091 (7 Jan 1968)
L 9092 (21 Feb 1958)
L 9093 (17 Apr 1958)
L 9094 (24 July 1958)
L 9095 (11 Apr 1958)
L 9096 (11 Oct 1958)
L 9070 (30 Oct 1967)
L 9071 (30 Jan 1968)
L 9072 (1968)
L 9073 (1968)
L 9074 (1970)

Displacement, tons	292 standard; 642 full load
Dimensions, feet	193·5 × 39·2 × 4·5
Guns	2—20 mm AA
Main engines	MGO diesels; 2 shafts; 1 000 bhp = 8 knots
Complement	16 (1 officer, and 15 men)

9091, 9094, 9070 were built by C. N. Franco Belges, 9095, 9096 by Toulon Dockyard, 9071 by La Perrière. Launch dates above.

L 9092 *1970, French Navy,*

ISSOLE L 9097

Displacement, tons	600 full load
Dimensions, feet	160·8 × 23 × 7·2
Main engines	2 diesels; 1 000 bhp = 12 knots

Built at Toulon in 1957-58. Coaster with bow doors and ramp.

ISSOLE *1969, courtesy Godfrey H. Walker, Esq.*

LCT 9099

Former British tank landing craft. Fitted as a workshop in 1964. *LCT* 9062, *LCT* 9063 (ex-*Alkyon*), *LCT* 9064 (ex-*Salvor*), *LCT* 9098 deleted from list in 1969.

LCT 9061 (ex-HMS *Buttress*, LCT(8) 4099)

Former British tank landing craft purchased in July 1965, see LCT(8)s, UK section.

4 EDA (*Engins de Débarquement Ateliers*)

Same hull and engine characteristics as the EDIC type, but equipped as repair ships. Built in 1964 and 1965.

L 9081 and **L 9082** are *bâtiments-annexe atelier* (B A A), **L 9083** is *bâtiment-annexe-électronique* (B A E), **L 9084** is *bâtiment-annexe-magasin électrique* (B A M E).

LIGHT FORCES

14 "LE FOUGUEUX" CLASS (PATROL CRAFT)

L'ADROIT (6 Sep 1958)
L'AGILE (26 June 1954)
L'ALERTE (5 Oct 1957)
L'ATTENTIF (10 July 1958)
L'ARDENT (17 July 1958)
L'EFFRONTÉ (27 Jan 1959)
L'ENJOUÉ (5 Oct 1957)
L'ÉTOURDI (5 Feb 1958)
LE FOUGUEUX (31 May 1954)
LE FRINGANT (6 Feb 1958)
LE FRONDEUR (26 Feb 1959)
LE HARDI (17 Sep 1958)
L'INTRÉPIDE (12 Dec 1958)
L'OPINIATRE (4 May 1954)

Displacement, tons	325 standard, 400 full load
Dimensions, feet	170 pp × 23 × 6·5
Guns	2—40 mm Bofors AA, 2—20 mm AA
A/S weapons	1 hedgehog, 4 DC mortars (and 2 DC racks). Sonar in *L'Agile, Le Fougueux, L'Opiniatre*, others have a new 120 mm ASM mortar forward, 2 DCT, 1 DC rack
Tubes	*L'Intrepide* has a tube mounted on the stern
Main engines	4 SEMT-Pielstick light and fast diesel engines coupled 2 by 2 3 240 bhp = 18·7 knots (22 knots on trial)
Radius, miles	3 000 at 12 knots, 2 000 at 15 knots
Complement	62 (4 officers, 58 men)

L'Agile, Le Fougueux and *L'Opiniatre* were built in France under a USA offshore order. Five more were built under the 1955 and six under the 1956 estimates. These have a different armament, slightly different appearance and modified bridge. *L'Agile* is employed on fishery protection duties in the North Sea, English Channel, Bristol Channel, off Shetland and Orkney Islands and Norway.

L'INTREPIDE (tube on stern) *1972, Dr. Giorgio Arra*

LA COMBATTANTE (MISSILE BOAT)

Displacement, tons	180 standard; 202 full load
Dimensions, feet	147·8 × 24·2 × 6·5
Guns	1—30 mm AA
Launchers	1 quadruple for SS 11; has carried "Exocet; 1 for 14 flares
Main engines	2 SEMT-Pielstick diesels; 2 shafts; controllable pitch propellers; 3 200 bhp = 23 knots
Range, miles	2 000 at 12 knots
Complement	25

Patrouilleur garde-côte or light patrol vessel. Authorised under the 1960 Programme. Built by Constructions Mécaniques de Normandie. Laid down in Apr 1962, launched on 20 June 1963, and completed on 1 Mar 1964. Of wooden and plastic laminated non-magnetic construction. Fitted for trials of the MM 38 missile system (Exocet).

LA COMBATTANTE *1972, Dr. Giorgio Arra*

1 Ex-US SC TYPE (PATROL CRAFT)

M 691 (ex-*CH* 101, ex-*SC* 524)

Displacement, tons	110 standard; 138 full load
Dimensions, feet	107·5 wl; 110·6 oa × 18·8 × 6·5
Main engines	2 GM diesels; 2 shafts; 1 000 bhp = 15 knots

Of wooden construction. Launched in 1943. Acquired from the USN in 1944. Formerly rated as Submarine Chasers, but re-rated as patrol vessels in 1951. *P* 690, 691, 695, 696, 697, 711, 713, 714, 715 were converted into inshore minesweepers in 1954, but were discarded as such in 1958-59. P 706 was officially deleted from the list in 1969. For full list of disposals see 1967-68 and earlier editions.

TRANSFERS
P 699 was transferred to the Ivory Coast Republic and re-named *Patience* (now defunct) and P 700 was transferred to the Senegalian Republic and re-named *Senegal*.

1 FAIRMILE ML TYPE

OISEAU DES ILES P 78C

Displacement, tons	130
Dimensions, feet	111·5 × 18·4 × 4·3
Speed, knots	11·5

This former Fairmile motor launch was seized by the Customs Authority and allocated to the Navy for training frogmen.

2 VC TYPE (PATROL CRAFT)

VC 2 P 752 **VC 10** P 760

Displacement, tons	75 standard; 82 full load
Dimensions, feet	104·2 × 15·5 × 5·5
Guns	2—20 mm AA
Main engines	2 Mercedes-Benz diesels; 2 shafts; 2 700 bhp = 28 knots
Radius, miles	1 500 at 15 knots
Complement	15

Light Forces—*continued*

Seaward defence motor launches of new type. All completed in 1958 and 1959. Built by the Constructions Mécaniques de Normandie, Cherbourg (VC 3 and 10) and Lürrsens in Germany (VC 2).

TRANSFERS
VC 1 (P 751). To Mauritania 1969. VC 3 (753). To Mediterranean Trials Centre. VC 4 (P 754). To Congo and subsequently to Senegal (*Sine Saloum*) in 1966. VC 5 (P 755). To Senegal (*Casamance*) Jan 1963. VC 5 (P 756). To Cameroon (*Vigilante*) Jan 1964. VC 7 (P 757). To Mediterranean Trials Centre. VC 8. (P 758) To Madagascar in 1963, returned and subsequently to Cameroon (*Audacieux*) 1968. VC 9 (P 759). To Ivory Coast (*Perseverance*) 1963. VC 11 (P 761). To Tunisia (*Istiklal*) 1960., VC 12 (P762). To Morocco (*El Sabiq*) 1960.

VC 10 *1971, Dr. Giorgio Arra*

P 9785 **P 9786**

Displacement, tons	45
Dimensions, feet	79·3 × 14·8 × 4·2
Guns	8—0·5 MG (four twin mountings)
Main engines	2 Daimler-Benz diesels; 2 shafts; 1 000 bhp = 18 knots

Built by Burmeister-Brême (P 9785) and Bodenwerft-Kressbronn. Completed in 1954. Sister boats P 9783, P 9784 P 9787 and P 9788 were officially deleted from the list in 1969.

NOTE. 2 Patrol Boats authorised for construction for overseas service. Delivery 1974. The auxiliary patrol launch *Rambervillers* was deleted from the list in 1963. She was a war prize with the *Ormont* which was retired from service in Feb 1958. The former Rhine Flotilla support ships *Hoche*, L 981, *Kleber*, L 982, and *Marceau*, L 980, were officially deleted from the list in 1965. The former Rhine Flotilla patrol boats P 9781 and P 9782 (35 tons, duralumin hull), P 9796 (ex-41), P 9787 (ex-42) and P 9798 (ex-43), all 23 tons, P 9740, P 9741, P 9742 and P 9743 (12 tons, peralumin hull), P 9794 (10 tons, hydrofoil), and P 9790 and P9791 (2 tons, fixed foils) were also officially deleted from the list in 1965, and P 9792 and P 9793 (6 tons, fixed foils) in 1966. The patrol boats *Enclume* A 790, old German LCM, and *Amiral Exelmans* (ex-*Germania*), A 73, ex-river passenger boat used for training pilots, were officially deleted from the list in 1969.

MINE WARFARE FORCES

5 "CIRCE" CLASS (MINEHUNTERS)

CYBÈLE	M 712	**CALLIOPE**	M 713	**CLIO**	M 714
CIRCE	M 715	**CERES**	M 716		

Displacement, tons	460 standard; 495 normal; 510 full load
Dimensions, feet	152·6 × 29·2 × 8·0
Guns	1—20 mm
Main engines	Diesels; single axial screw; 1 800 bhp = 15 knots
Range, miles	3 000 at 12 knots
Complement	48 (4 officers, 44 men)

A new design. Ordered in 1968. Built by Constructions Mécaniques de Normandie, Cherbourg. Active rudder on each side for working at slow speeds. Fitted with Mk DUBM 20 minehunting sonar. *Circe* was launched on 15 Dec 1970, *Clio* on 10 June 1971, *Calliope* on 21 Oct 1971, *Cybèle* on Jan 1972 and *Ceres* in April 1972.

CIRCE as completed *May 1971, courtesy M. Henri Le Massion*

14 US MSO (ex-AM) TYPE "BERNEVAL" CLASS (OCEAN MINESWEEPERS)

NARVIK (ex-*AM* 512)	M 609	**MYTHO** (ex-*AM* 475)	M 618
OUISTREHAM (ex-*AM* 513)	M 610	**VINH LONG** (ex-*AM* 477)	M 619
ALENCON (ex-*AM* 453)	M 612	**BERLAIMONT** (ex-*AM* 500)	M 620
BERNEVAL (ex-*AM* 450)	M 613	**ORIGNY** (ex-*AM* 501)	M 621
CANTHO (ex-*AM* 476)	M 615	**AUTUN** (ex-*AM* 502)	M 622
DOMPAIRE (ex-*AM* 454)	M 616	**BACCARAT** (ex-*AM* 505)	M 623
GARIGLIANO (ex-*AM* 452)	M 617	**COLMAR** (ex-*AM* 514)	M 624

Displacement, tons	700 standard; 780 full load
Dimensions, feet	165 wl; 171 oa × 35 × 10·3
Guns	1—40 mm AA
Main engines	2 GM diesels; 2 shafts; 1 600 bhp = 13·5 knots
Range, miles	3 000 at 10 knots
Complement	56 (4 officers, 52 men)

The USA transferred to France eight new AMs in 1953, and four in 1954. Three more transferred in 1956. *Origny* is classified and fitted as an oceanographic research vessel but is Navy owned and manned. *Bir Hacheim* M614 (ex-*AM* 451) was returned to the US Navy at Brest on 4 Sept 1970 and transferred to Uruguayan Navy, being renamed *Maldonado*.

APPEARANCE. *Autun, Baccarat, Berlaimont, Colmar, Narvik, Origny* and *Ouistreham* have a taller funnel.

Mine Warfare Forces—*continued*

AUTUN (tall funnel type) *1971, A. & J. Pavia*

27 BRITISH TYPE "SIRIUS" CLASS (CMS)

SIRIUS (6 Oct 52)	M 701	**SAGITTAIRE** (12 Jan 55)	M 743
RIGEL (13 May 53)	M 702	**ARCTURUS** (12 Mar 54)	M 746
ANTARÈS (21 Jan 54)	M 703	**BÉTELGEUSE** (12 July 54)	M 747
ALGOL (15 Apr 53)	M 704	**PERSÉE** (23 May 55)	M 748
ALDÉRBARAN (27 June 53)	M 705	**PHÉNIX** (23 May 55)	M 749
RÉGULUS (18 Nov 52)	M 706	**DÉNÉBOLA** (12 July 56)	M 751
VEGA (14 Jan 53)	M 707	**BELLATRIX** (21 July 55)	M 750
CASTOR (19 Nov 53)	M 708	**CANOPUS** (31 Dec 53)	M 754
PÉGASE (21 June 55)	M 710	**CAPELLA** (6 Sep 55)	M 755
CROIX DU SUD (13 June 56)	M 734	**CÉPHÉE** (3 Jan 56)	M 756
ÉTOILE POLAIRE (5 Mar 57)	M 735	**VERSEAU** (26 Apr 56)	M 757
ALTAIR (27 Mar 56)	M 736	**ARIES** (13 Mar 56)	M 758
CASSIOPÉE (16 Nov 53)	M 740	**LYRE** (3 May 56)	M 759
ÉRIDAN (18 May 54)	M 741		

Displacement, tons	365 standard; 424 full load
Dimensions, feet	140 pp; 152 oa × 28 × 8·2
Guns	1—40 mm Bofors AA; 120 mm Oerlikon AA (several have 2—20 mm AA)
Main engines	SIGMA free piston generators and Alsthom or Rateau-Bretagne gas turbines or SEMT-Pielstick 16-cyl fast diesels; 2 shafts; 2 000 bhp = 15 knots (11·5 knots when sweeping)
Oil fuel (tons)	48
Range, mlies	3 000 at 15 knots
Complement	38

Of wooden and aluminium alloy construction. Launch dates above. Of same general characteristics as the British "Ton" class, but of different hull construction. Propelled by Alsthom or Rateau gas turbines with SIGMA free piston generators ,except *Altair, Arcturus, Aries, Bételgeuse, Canopus, Capella, Céphée, Croix du Sud, Étoile Polaire, Lyre, Phénix* and *Verseau*, which have SEMT-Pielstick light diesels. 16 vessels were built under the "off-shore" programme. *Altair, Arcturus* and *Croix du Sud* have been station-ships in the West Indies since 1960. D 25, D 26 and D 27 were allocated to Yugoslavia. *Fomalhaut, Orion, Pollux* and *Procyon* were returned to the USN in 1970, *Achernar* and *Centaure* in 1971. *Capricorne* sold to Senegal March 1970. 1 more of this class deleted 1972.

ANTARES *1971, courtesy Admiral M. Adam*

27 US MSC (Ex-AMS) TYPE. "ACACIA" CLASS (CMS)

PERVENCHE (ex-*AMS* 141)	M 632	**CYCLAMEN** (ex-*AMS* 119)	M 674
PIVOINE (ex-*AMS* 125)	M 633	**EGLANTINE** (ex-*AMS* 117)	M 675
RÉSÉDA (ex-*AMS* 126)	M 635	**GARDÉNIA** (ex-*AMS* 114)	M 676
ACACIA (ex-*AMS* 69)	M 638	**GIROFLÉE** (ex-*AMS* 85)	M 677
ACANTHE (ex-*AMS* 70)	M 639	**GLAIEUL** (ex-*AMS* 120)	M 678
MARJOLAINE (ex-*Aconit*, ex-*AMS* 66)	M 640	**GLYCINE** (ex-*AMS* 118)	M 679
AJONC (ex-*AMS* 71)	M 667	**JACINTHE** (ex-*AMS* 115)	M 680
AZALÉE (ex-*AMS* 67)	M 668	**LAURIER** (ex-*AMS* 86)	M 681
BÉGONIA (ex-*AMS* 83)	M 669	**LILAS** (ex-*AMS* 93)	M 682
BLEUÉT (ex-*AMS* 116)	M 670	**LISERON** (ex-*AMS* 98)	M 683
CAMÉLIA (ex-*AMS* 68)	M 671	**LOBÉLIA** (ex-*AMS* 96)	M 684
CHRYSANTHÈME (ex-*AMS* 113)	M 672	**MAGNOLIA** (ex-*AMS* 87)	M 685
COQUELICOT (ex-*AMS* 84)	M 673	**MIMOSA** (ex-*AMS* 99)	M 687
		MUGUET (ex-*AMS* 97)	M 688

Displacement, tons	320 standard; 370 full load
Dimensions, feet	136·2 pp; 141 oa × 26 × 8·3
Guns	2—20 mm AA
Main engines	2 GM diesels; 2 shafts; 1 200 bhp = 13 knots (8 sweeping)
Oil fuel, tons	40
Range, miles	2 500 at 10 knots
Complement	38 (3 officers, 35 men)

The USA agreed in Sep 1952 to allocate to France in 1953, 36 new AMS (later re-designated MSC) under the Mutual Defence Assistance Programme, but only 30 were finally transferred to France in 1953-55. Three were returned to the USA after delivery to Saigon for Indo-China, and two of these were allocated to Japan (AMS 95 and 144). Three were not delivered, two having been allocated to Spain (139 and 143) and one to Taiwan (140). Constructed throughout of wood or other materials with the lowest possible magnetic signature. All built in USA in 1951-54. All named after flowers. *Aconit* was renamed *Marjolaine* in 1967 (name *Aconit* assigned to new frigate). *Jacinthe* was converted into a minelayer in 1968. *Marguerite* (ex-*AMS* 94) was returned to the USN at Toulon in Nov 1969 and transferred to the Uruguayan Navy, renamed *Rio Negro. Pavot* (ex-*MSC* 124) and *Renocule* (ex-*MSC* 142) were returned to the USN on 24 March 1970 and transferred to the Turkish Navy.

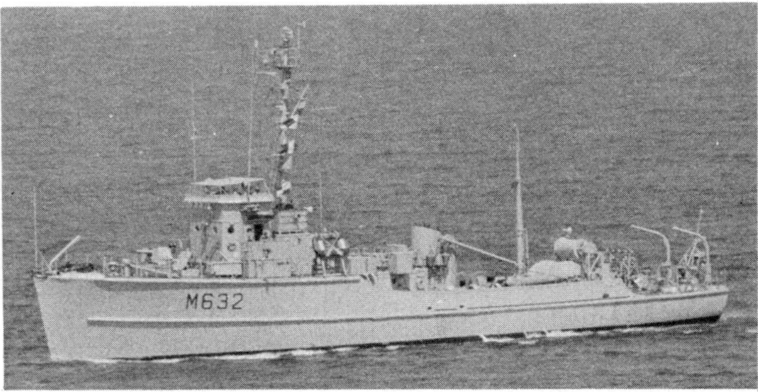

PERVENCHE *1971, Dr. Giorgio Arra*

1 SPECIAL TYPE (CMS)

MERCURE M 765

Displacement, tons	333 light; 362 normal; 400 full load
Dimensions, feet	137·8 pp; 145·5 oa × 27 × 8·5
Guns	2—20 mm AA
Main engines	2 Mercedes-Benz diesels; 2 shafts; Kamewa variable pitch propellers; 4 000 bhp = 15 knots
Oil fuel, tons	48
Range, miles	3 000 at 15 knots
Complement	48

Ordered in France from Mécaniques de Normandie (who have built six sister ships for the Federal German Navy) under the "off-shore" programme. Laid down in Jan 1955. Launched on 21 Dec 1957. Completed in Dec. 1958. Somewhat different from the "Sirius" class and with the same method of construction as the United States-built "Acacia" class. Stated to be a very successful model.

MERCURE *1968, French Navy.*

6 Ex-CANADIAN "BAY" TYPE "LA DUNKERQUOISE" CLASS (CMS)

LA DUNKERQUOISE (ex-*Fundy*)	M 726
LA MALOUINE (ex-*Cowlcham*)	M 727
LA BAYONNAISE (ex-*Chignecto*)	M 728
LA PAIMPOLAISE (ex-*Thunder*)	M 729
LA DIEPPOISE (ex-*Chaleur*)	M 730
LA LORIENTAISE (ex-*Miarmachi*)	M 731

Displacement, tons	370 full load; 470 standard;
Dimensions, feet	140 pp; 152 oa × 28 × 8·7
Guns	1—40 mm AA
Main engines	General Motors diesls; 2 shafts; 2 500 bhp = 15 knots max
Oil fuel (tons)	52
Range, miles	4 500 at 11 knots
Complement	43 (4 officers, 39 men)

La Bayonnaise (launched 12 May 1952), *La Malouine* (launched 12 Nov 1951) and *La Palmpolaise* (launched 17 July 1953) were transferred to the French flag at Halifax on 1 Apr 1954 *Dunkerquoise* (launched 17 July 1953) on 30 Apr 1954, and *La Dieppoise* (launched 21 June 1952) and *La Orientaise* (launched in 1953) on 10 Oct 1954. All similar to the "Bay" class in the Royal Canadian Navy.

As these ships are used on "colonial" service. They have been air conditioned.

LA DIEPPOISE ***1971, French Navy.***

Mine Warfare Forces—*continued*

10 Ex-BRITISH "HAM" CLASS (IMS)

ARMOISE (ex-*Wexham*)	M 772		**JASMIN** (ex-*Stedham*)	M 776
AUBÉPINE (ex-*Rendlesham*)	M 781		**JONQUILLE** (ex-*Sulham*)	M 787
CAPUCINE (ex-*Petersham*)	M 782		**MYOSOTIS** (ex-*Ripplingham*)	M 788
DAHLIA (ex-*Whippingham*)	M 786		**OEILLET** (ex-*Isham*)	M 774
GÉRANIUM (ex-*Tibenham*)	M 784		**PAQUERETTE** (ex-*Kingham*)	M 775
HIBISCUS (ex-*Sparham*)	M 785		**PÉTUNIA** (ex-*Pineham*)	M 789
HORTENSIA (ex-*Mileham*)	M 783		**TULIPE** (ex-*Frettenham*)	M 771
			VIOLETTE (ex-*Mersham*)	M 773

Displacement, tons	120 standard; 140 full load
Dimensions, feet	100 pp; 106·5 oa × 21·2 × 5·5
Guns	1—40 mm Bofors AA or 1—20 mm Oerlikon AA forward
Main engines	2 Paxman diesels; 550 bhp = 14 knots (9 knots when sweeping)
Oil fuel (tons)	15
Complement	12 (2 officers, 10 men)

Former British inshore minesweepers of the "Ham" class transferred to France under the US "off-shore" procurement programme. The first, *Tulipe* M 771, was delivered in Dec 1954, and the last *Pétunia* M 789, was handed over at Hythe on 10 Nov. 1955. In 1972 five of the above were deleted (names not known).

ARMOISE *1972, Dr. Giorgio Arra*

SURVEY SHIPS

1 NEW CONSTRUCTION

D'ENTRECASTEAUX A 757

Displacement, tons	2 200
Dimensions, feet	295·2 × 42·7 × 12·8
Main engines	2 diesel-electric; 1 000 kW; 2 controllable pitch propellers; Speed—15 knots
Auxiliary engines	2 Schottel orientable and retractable
Complement	93 (8 officers, 85 men)

This ship was specially designed for oceanographic surveys. Completed 10 Oct 1970. Accommodation for 38 scientists.

D'ENTRECASTEAUX *1971, Courtesy Admiral M. Adam*

2 TROPICAL TYPE

ASTROLABE A 780 (ex-P 680) **BOUSSOLE** A 781 (ex-P 681)

Displacement, tons	350 standard; 440 full load
Dimensions, feet	137·8 × 27 × 8·2
Guns	1—40 mm AA; 2 MG
Main engines	2 Baudouin DV.8 diesels. 1 shaft; controllable pitch propeller; 800 bhp = 13 knots max
Radius, miles	4 000
Complement	36 (3 officers, 33 men)

Authorised under the 1961 Programme. Specially designed for the Hydrographic Service for surveys in tropical waters. Built by Chantiers de la Seine Maritime, Le Trait. Laid down in 1962, launched on 27 May and 11 Apr 1963 respectively, and commissioned in 1964.

ASTROLABE *1970, French Navy,*

Survey Ships—*continued*

1 RESEARCH TYPE

LA RECHERCHE (ex-*Guyane*) A 758 (ex-P 660)

Displacement, tons	780 standard; 1 047 full load
Measurement, tons	965 gross
Dimensions, feet	203·5 pp; 221·5 oa × 34·2 × 13
Main engines	1 Werkspoor diesel; 1 535 bhp = 13·5 knots
Complement	42 (5 officers, 37 men)

Former passenger motor vessel built by Chantiers Zeigler at Dunkirk. Launched on 17 Sep 1951. Purchased in 1960 and converted by Cherbourg Dockyard into a surveying ship. Commissioned into the French Navy in Mar 1961 and her name changed from *Guyane* to *La Recherche*. To improve stability she was fitted with bulges.

LA RECHERCHE *1970, French Navy,*

2 CONVERTED TRAWLER TYPE

L'ESPÉRANCE (ex-*Jacques Coeur*) A 756
L'ESTAFETTE (ex-*Jacques Cartier*) A 766

Displacement, tons	800 standard; 1 400 full load
Dimensions, feet	196·1 × 32·2 × 14·8
Main engines	MAN diesels; 1 850 bhp = 15 knots
Complement	29 (5 officers, 24 men)

Former trawlers built in 1962 and purchased in 1968-69 and adapted as survey ships.

1 EXPERIMENTAL TYPE

LA COQUILLE (ex-*Atlantic Dolphin*) A 678

Displacement, tons	394 standard; 555 full load
Dimensions, feet	121·3 × 26·2 × 14·1
Main engines	Paxman diesel-electric; 1 shaft; speed 12 knots
Complement	23 (2 officers, 21 men)

Former British trawler. Built by J. S. Doig, Grimsby, in 1963. Purchased in May 1965 and converted by Cherbourg Dockyard as a survey and scientific research ship for the Pacific Nuclear Experimental Centre.

OCTANT *1970,*

2 TENDER TYPE

ALIDADE (ex-*Evelyne Marie*) P 682 **OCTANT** (ex-*Michel Marie*) P 683

Displacement, tons	110 standard; 120 full load
Dimensions, feet	Length 78
Main engines	2 diesels; 1 shaft; controllable pitch; 250 bhp = 9 knots
Complement	11

Two small fishing trawlers purchased by the Navy and converted into survey craft of a new type by the Constructions Mécaniques de Normandie at Cherbourg as tenders to *La Recherche*. Wooden hull and steel upperworks. *Alidade* floated up after conversion on 15 Nov 1962 and *Octant* on 20 Dec 1962. Commissioned in 1963.

ALIDADE *1969,*

Survey Ships—*continued*

1 SURVEY LAUNCH

CORAIL A 791

Launched in 1957. 50 tons with complement of 7.

NOTE. (a) *Origny* (M 621) of 800 tons and launched in 1954 refitted for oceanographic research. (b) *Archéonaute* (A 789) of 120 tons employed in archaeological research.

1 Ex-BRITISH "NET" CLASS

LA DÉCOUVERTE (ex-*Amalthée*, ex-*Plantagenet*, ex-*Barwood*) A 753

Displacement, tons	605 standard; 790 full load
Dimensions, feet	159·7 × 30·7 × 13
Main engines	Triple expansion; 850 ihp = 10 knots
Boilers	Cylindrical

Formerly the British boom defence vessel HMS *Plantagenet* (ex-*Barwood*) built by Lobnitz & Co Ltd, Renfrew and launched on 23 Feb 1939. She became the commercial oil research ship *Amalthée* under the French flag in 1960. She was purchased for the French Navy in 1969 and converted as a survey ship.

LA DÉCOUVERTE *1970, courtesy Admiral M. Adam*

MAINTENANCE SHIPS

3 CONVERTED LINERS

MÉDOC (ex-*Sidi Ferruch*) A 612

Displacement, tons	4 430 standard; 5 300 full load
Measurement, tons	3 988 gross
Dimensions, feet	372·2 × 49·2 × 23
Main engines	2 Rateau turbines; 2 shafts; 4 750 shp = 15 knots
Boilers	2
Complement	123 (8 officers, 115 men)

Passenger vessel designed and built for Algeria by F.C. Medit. Built by Bretagne/Loire. Launched on 14 May 1949. Purchased in Sep 1963 and fitted out as barrack and accommodation ship for the maintenance of the Nuclear Establishment of Polynesia, the experimental base in the Pacific, manned by naval personnel. *Maine* (ex-*El Mansour*) A 611 and near sister ship *Morvan* (ex-*Sidi Mabrouk*) A 613 were officially deleted from the list in 1971.

MEDOC *1969, French Navy.*

MAURIENNE (ex-M/S *Brazza*) A 637 **MOSELLE** (ex-*Foucauld*) A 608

Displacement, tons	8 700 standard; 9 100 full load
Measurement, tons	9 065 gross; 5 946 deadweight
Dimensions, feet	480 oa × 62 × 22·3
Main engines	2 Doxford diesels; 2 shafts; 8 800 bhp = 17·5 knots

Former motor passenger ships of the *Chargeurs Réunis* (West Africa Coast Service). Built by Swan, Hunter & Wigham Richardson Ltd, Wallsend-on Tyne. Launched on 14 Oct and 17 July 1947. Completed in 1948. *Maurienne* was purchased in Nov 1964, converted at Brest in 1965 and admitted to active service on 8 Mar 1966; helicopter landing platform aft. *Moselle* was converted in 1967 (no platform).

MOSELLE *1972, Dr. Giorgio Arra*

Maintenance Ships—*continued*

1 NEW CONSTRUCTION (REPAIR SHIP)

ACHERON A 620

Displacement, tons	6 485 standard; 10 250 full load
Dimensions, feet	482·2 × 70·5 × 21·3
Main engines	2 SEMT-Pielstick diesels; 1 shaft; 11 500 bhp = 18 knots

Provided for under the 1961 Programme. Built at Brest Dockyard. Laid down in 1969. Launched on 30 May 1970. Intended to be an ammunition ship but reclassified as a repair ship, it was officially stated in Feb 1972.

LOGISTIC SUPPORT SHIPS

5 "RHIN" TYPE

GARONNE Repair Workshop (*Bâtiment de soutien logistique, version Atelier*)
LOIRE Minesweeper Support (*Bâtiment de soutien logistique, version Dragueurs*)
RANCE Damage Control (*Bâtiment de soutien logistique, version Sécurité*)
RHIN Electronic Service (*Bâtiment de soutien logistique, version Électronique*)
RHÔNE Submarine Depot (*Bâtiment de soutien logistique, version Sousmarins*)

Displacement, tons	2 075 standard; 2 445 full load; see notes
Dimensions, feet	302·0 pp; 331·5 oa × 43·0 × 12·1 (*Garonne, Loire*, see notes)
Guns	3—40 mm AA
Aircraft	2 Alouette helicopters
Landing craft	2 (LCP)
Main engines	2 SEMT-Pielstick diesels; 1 shaft; 3 300 bhp = 16·5 knots
Range, miles	6 000 at 12 knots
Complement	71 (5 officers, 66 men) plus *circa* 100 technicians, except *Garonne* 221 (10 officers, 211 men); *Loire* 175

These ships have the same basic characteristics, hull and machinery, differing only in their respective specialisation, except *Garrone* which has one more deck, larger workshops and a heavier displacement of 2 320 tons standard, as a repair ship for the Pacific Nuclear Experimental Station (CEP), and *Rance*, radiological security ship (radioactive decontamination) with extended bridge and different silhouette and hanger for three helicopters. All were built by Lorient.

Name	*No.*	*Programme*	*Laid down*	*Launched*	*Completed*
Garonne	A 617	1963	Nov 1963	8 Aug 1964	1 Sep 1965
Loire	A 615	1962	July 1965	1 Oct 1966	10 Oct 1967
Rance	A 618	1963	Aug 1964	15 May 1965	5 Feb 1966
Rhin	A 621	1959	May 1961	17 Mar 1962	1 Mar 1964
Rhone	A 622	1960	Feb 1962	8 Dec 1962	1 Dec 1964

RHIN (LOIRE and RHÔNE similar) *1972, Dr. Giorgio Arra*

RHÔNE

RHIN

RANCE *1969, French Navy.*

GARONNE *French Navy.*

EXPERIMENTAL SHIPS

HENRI POINCARÉ (ex-*Maina Marasso*) A 603

Displacement, tons	23 430 full load
Measurement, tons	12 835 gross
Dimensions, feet	565·0 pp; 590·6 oa × 72·8 × 28·9
Main engines	1 Parsons geared turbine; 1 shaft; 10 000 shp = 15 knots
Boilers	2 Foster Wheeler high pressure water tube

Built by Cantieri Riuniti de Adriaticos, Monfalcone. Launched in Oct 1960. Former Italian tanker. Purchased in Sep 1964. Converted in Brest dockyard from 1 Oct 1964 to Mar 1968 into a radar picket ship and guidance vessel for the experimental guided missile station in the Landes (SW France). Named after the mathematician and scientist.

HENRI POINCARÉ *1969, French Navy.*

ILE d'OLÉRON (ex-*München*, ex-*Mur*)

Displacement, tons	5 500 standard; 6 500 full load
Length, feet (*metres*)	350·0 (*106·7*pp; 377·5 (*115·2*)oa
Beam, feet (*metres*)	50·0 (*15·2*)
Draught, feet (*metres*)	21·3 (*6·5*)
Main engines	MAN 6-cylinder diesels; 1 shaft; 3 500 bhp
Speed, knots	14·5
Oil fuel, tons	340
Range, miles	7 200 at 12 knots
Complement	195 (15 officers, 180 men)

Launched in Germany in 1939. Taken as a war prize. Formerly rated as a transport. Converted to experimental guided missile ship in 1957-58 by Chantiers de Provence et l'Arsenal de Toulon. Commissioned as test bed early in 1959. Equipped with stabilisers.

ILE d'OLÉRON *1970, French Navy*

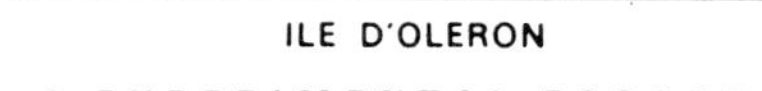

ILE D'OLERON

EXPERIMENTAL. When converted was designed for experiments with two launchers for ship to air missiles, the medium range "Masurca" and the long range "Masalca", and one launcher for ship to shore missiles, the "Malaface". Latterly fitted with one launcher for target planes. Now fitted for trials on MM 38 ("Exocet").

RADAR. The photograph shows the ship fitted with an L band early warning radar and an S band stacked beam air and surface 3 D radar. The missile system tracking radar operates in C band.

1 EXPERIMENTAL ESCORT

ARAGO (ex-*Somali*, ex-USS DE 111) A 607

Displacement, tons	1 265 standard, 1 600 full load
Length, feet (*metres*)	300·0 (*91·4*) pp; 306·0 (*93·3*) wl
Beam, feet (*metres*)	36·8 (*11·2*)
Draught feet (*metres*)	10·7 (*3·3*)
Main engines	4 GE diesels, 2 electric motors; diesel-electric drive; 2 shafts; 6 000 bhp
Speed, knots	19 (economical 11)
Range, miles	11 500 at 11 knots
Complement	150 (10 officers, 140 men)

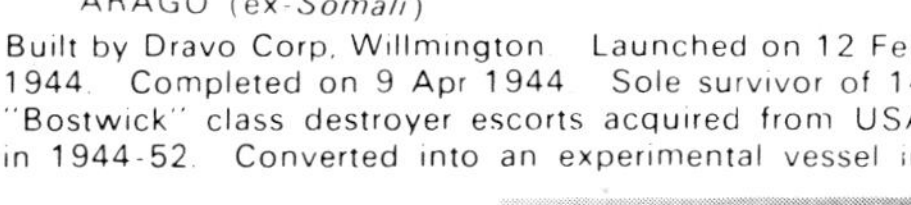

ARAGO (ex-*Somali*) *1972, Dr. Giorgio Arra*

ARAGO

Built by Dravo Corp, Willmington. Launched on 12 Feb 1944. Completed on 9 Apr 1944. Sole survivor of 14 "Bostwick" class destroyer escorts acquired from USA in 1944-52. Converted into an experimental vessel in 1956 and armament removed pennant number changed from F 703 to A 607. Name changed from *Somali* to *Arago* on 1 Apr 1968. Fitted with S band combined air and surface search radar.

TRITON A 646

Displacement, tons	1 300 standard; 1 500 full load
Dimensions, feet	223·1 × 39·4 × 11·8
Main engines	Diesels 2 Voith Schneider = 13 knots
Radius, miles	4 000 at 13 knots
Complement	50 (4 officers, 29 men + 17 scientists)

Under sea recovery and trials ship to replace *Elie Monnier*. To be equipped with a helicopter. Launched at Lorient on 7 Mar 1970 and completed by 1971. Support ship for the 2-man submarine *Griffon*.

TRITON *1972, French Navy*

BOOM DEFENCE VESSELS

LA FIDÈLE A 751 **LA PERSÉVÉRANTE** A 750 **LA PRUDENTE** A 749

Displacement, tons	446 standard; 626 full load
Dimensions, feet	142·8 × 32·8 × 9·2
Main engines	2 Badouin diesels; 1 shaft; 620 bhp = 10 knots
Radius, miles	4 000 at 10 knots
Complement	30 (1 officer, 29 men)

Net layers and tenders built by Atel. Ch. La Manche, Dieppe, (*La Fidèle* and *La Prudente*) and Atel. Ch. La Rochelle (*La Persévétante*). Launched on 13 May 1968 (*La Fidèle*), 14 May 1968 (*La Persévérante*) and 26 Aug 1968 (*La Prudente*). Diesel-electric drive, 440 kW.

LA PRUDENTE *1970, French Navy.*

Boom Defence Vessels—*continued*

5 "GRILLON" CLASS

CIGALE (ex-*AN* 98) A 760
CRIQUET (ex-*AN* 96) A 761
FOURMI (ex-*AN* 97) A 762
GRILLON (ex-*AN* 95) A 763
SCARABÉE (ex-*AN* 94) A 764

Displacement, tons	770 standard; 850 full load
Dimensions, feet	151·9 oa × 33·5 × 10·5
Guns	1—40 mm Bofors AA; 4—20 mm AA
Main engines	2, 4-stroke diesels, electric drive, 1 shaft; 1 600 bhp = 12 knots
Complement	45

US type off-shore orders. Sister ship *G* 6 was allocated to Spain. *Criquet* was launched on 3 June 1954, *Cigale* on 23 Sep 1954, *Fourmi* on 6 July 1954, *Grillon* on 18 Feb 1954 and *Scarabée* on 21 Nov 1953. Rated as *Garbarres* (*Mouilleur de Filets*). A photograph of *Criquet* appears in the 1957-58 to 1964-65 editions, and of *Scarabée* in the 1968-69 to 1970-71 editions.

CIGALE *1971, French Navy,*

5 Ex-US-AN TYPE NETLAYERS

ARAIGNÉE (ex-*Hackberry*, ex-*Maple*, *AN* 727)	A 727
LIBELLULE (ex-*Rosewood*, AN 31)	A 730
LOCUSTE (ex-*Locust*, *AN* 765)	A 765
LUCIOLE (ex-*Sandalwood*, *AN* 32)	A 777
SCORPION (ex-*Yew*, *AN* 37)	A 728

Displacement, tons	560 standard; 850 full load
Dimensions, feet	146·0 wl; 163·0 oa × 30·5 × 11·7
Guns	1—3 in AA; some MG
Main engines	2 GM diesels; 2 shafts; 4 500 bhp = 16 knots
Range, miles	2 000 at 13 knots

Launched on 6 Mar 1941, 1 Apr 1941, 1 Feb 1941, 6 Mar 1941 and 25 Sep 1941 respectively. *Locuste* was purchased in 1966, *Luciole* in 1967, *Libellule* in 1969. The others were transferred in 1944. Sister ship *Tarentule* (ex-*Pepperwood*, ex-*Walnut*, AN 729) A 729 was officially deleted from the list in 1972.

ARAIGNEE *1970, French Navy*

MARCEL LE BIHAN (ex-German *Greif*) A 759

Displacement, tons	800 standard; 1 000 full load
Dimensions, feet	236·2 × 34·8 × 10·5 max
Guns	4—20 mm AA
Main engines	2 GM diesels 2 shafts, 4 400 bhp = 16 knots
Radius miles	2 000 at 13 knots

Former German aircraft tender. Built by Lubecker Fleudewerke. Launched in 1936. Completed in 1937. Transferred by USA in Feb 1948. Re-rated Escorteur de Deuxième Classe early 1953, Aviso Escorteur 11 Aug 1953, Aviso 1955 and Gabarre 1 Nov 1959, 4·1 in gun and 2—40 mm removed. Tender for bathysphere *Archimède*.

MARCEL LE BIHAN *1971, Dr. Giorgio Arra*

COMMANDANT ROBERT GIRAUD
(ex-*Immelmann*) A 755 (ex-F 755)

Displacement, tons	1 142 standard; 1 380 full load
Length, feet (*metres*)	239·0 (*72·9*) pp; 256·0 (*78·0*) oa
Beam, feet (*metres*)	36·0 (*11·0*)
Draught, feet (*metres*)	12·0 (*3·7*)
Main Engines	4 MAN diesels; 2 shafts; 8 800 bhp
Range, miles	7 800 at 12 knots
Oil fuel, tons	236

Former *dépanneur d'hydravions*, ex-German aircraft tender. Built by Norderwerft, Hamburg. Launched in 1941. Completed in Dec 1941. Transferred by Great Britain in Aug 1946, with *Paul Goffeny*. Re-rated as *Escorteur de Deuxième Classe* early in 1953, as *Aviso Escorteur* on 11 Aug 1953, as *Aviso* in 1955, as *Gabarre* in 1963, and *Aviso Hydrograph* on 1969. Formerly used as patrol and escort vessel, support gunboat and carrier for commandos. The diesels are coupled two by two with hydraulic transmission on two shafts. Sister ship *Paul Goffeny* was officially deleted from the list in 1969.

COMMANDANT ROBERT GIRAUD *1972. Dr. Giorgio Arra*

PERSISTANTE A 731

Displacement, tons	350
Main engines	500 hp = 8 knots

Girafe and *Persévérante* were scrapped in 1957, *Fidèle* in 1958 *Puissant* in 1960, *Agissante* in 1961, *Victorieuse* in 1964, *Patiente* in 1972.

OILERS

LA CHARENTE (ex-*Beaufort*) A 626

Displacement, tons	7 084 light; 26 000 full load
Measurement, tons	12 373 gross; 18 800 deadweight
Dimensions, feet	587·2 × 72 × 30·3
Main engines	1 General Electric geared turbine
Boilers	2

Former Norwegian tanker built by Kaldnes Mek. Verksted Tönsberg, in 1957. Purchased by the French Navy in May 1965 and adapted for the Pacific Experimental Station.

LA CHARENTE *1969, courtesy Admiral M. Adam*

PAPENOO (ex-Norwegian *Bow Queen*) **PUNARUU** (ex Norwegian *Bow Cecil*)

Measurement, tons	3 000 *deadweight*

Two small oilers purchased in Dec 1971 and officially added to the navy list in Feb 1972, for the Pacific Experimental Station. The names are those of Tahiti rivers.

ISÈRE (ex-*La Mayenne*, ex-*Caltex Strasbourg*) A 675

Displacement, tons	10 172 light
Measurement, tons	18 000 deadweight
Dimensions, feet	559 × 71·2 × 30·3
Main engines	1 single geared Parsons turbine; 8 260 shp = 16 knots
Boilers	2

Built by Seine Maritime. Launched on 22 June 1959. Former French tanker. Purchased late in 1964 for the Pacific Nuclear Experimental Centre.

LAC CHAMBON (ex-*Anticline*) A 629
LAC TCHAD (ex-*Syncline*) A 630

Displacement tons	800 light 2 670 full load
Dimensions, feet	235 × 37 × 15·8
Guns	3—20 mm AA
Main engines	2 Fairbanks-Morse diesels, 1 150 bhp = 11 knots

Oilers—*continued*

Ex-US oil barges. Acquired in Dec 1944 and Mar 1945. *Lac Noir* was scrapped in 1951 and *Lac Pavin* in 1953. A photograph of *Lac Tchad* appears in the 1968-69 to 1970-71 editions.

LAC TONLE SAP — *1971, French Navy*

LA SAÔNE A 628 — **LA SEINE** A 627

Displacement, tons	7 350 light; 23 800 full load
Measurement, tons	16 870 deadweight
Dimensions, feet	525 × 72·5 × 33
Main engines	Parsons geared turbines; 2 shafts; 15 800 shp = 17 knots
Boilers	3 Penhoet

Ordered as fleet tankers. Completed as merchant tankers after the Second World War. Returned to the French Navy from charter company in Sep 1953. *La Seine* was fitted as a fleet replenishment ship in 1961, *La Saône* in 1962. Now rated as *Pétroliers Ravitailleurs d'Escadre*. They carry 11 500 tons of fuel, 330 tons of food and have wine tanks.

LA SAONE — *1972 Dr. Giorgio Arra*

ABER-WRACH (ex-*CA* 1) A 619

Displacement, tons	1 380 standard; 3 400 full load
Dimensions, feet	284 oa × 40 × 15·8
Guns	1—40 mm AA
Main engines	1 diesel; controllable pitch propeller; 2 000 bhp = 12 knots

Built at Cherbourg. Authorised in 1956. Ordered in 1959. Laid down in 1961. The after part with engine room was launched on 24 Apr 1963. The fore part was built on the vacated slip, launched and welded to the after part. Complete hull floated up on 21 Nov 1963. Commissioned in 1964.

ABER WRACH — *1970, French Navy,*

FLEET TUGS

TENACE

Displacement, tons	936 light; 1 454 full load
Dimensions, feet	167·3 oa × 37·8
Main engines	2 diesels; Kort engines 4 600 hp = 15 knots
Range, miles	9 500 at 15 knots

A new oceangoing tug. Built by Joelkers, Hamburg. Launched on 9 Dec 1971, and completed May 1972.

LE FORT — **L'UTILE**

Displacement, tons	311
Dimensions, feet	91·9 × 26·2 × 10·3
Main engines	MGO diesel; 980 shp = 11·5 knots
Range, miles	2 400 at 10 knots

Two fleet tugs officially added to the navy list in June and April 1971.

ACTIF	A 686	**HERCULE**	A 667	**ROBUSTE**	A 685
COURAGEUX	A 706	**LABORIEUX**	A 687	**TRAVAILLEUR**	A 692
		LUTTEUR	A 673	**VALEUREUX**	A 688

Displacement, tons	230
Dimensions, feet	92 × 26 × 13
Main engines	1 MGO diesel; 1 050 bhp = 11 knots
Radius, miles	2 400 nautical
Complement	15

Courageux, Hercule, Robuste and *Valeureux* were completed in 1960 and the other four in 1962-63 at Le Havre, F. Ch. de la Méditerranée for service at Cherbourg (*Lutteur*). Toulon (*Actif, Robuste* and *Travailleur*) and Brest (*Hercule, Laborieux* and *Valeureux*).

HIPPOPOTAME (ex-*Utrecht*) A 660

Displacement, tons	640
Measurement, tons	524 gross
Main engines	Diesel-electric; 1 850 shp

Tugs—*continued*

Built as USN ATA of *Maricopa* class. Former Netherlands high sea tug. Built in 1943. Purchased by the French Navy in Jan 1964 to be used at the Experimental Base in the Pacific. Admitted to active service on 5 Mar 1964.

BÉLIER A 719 — **PACHYDERME** A 718

Displacement, tons	900 standard; 1 185 and 1 115 full load, respectively
Main engines	2 000 ihp = 12 knots
Oil fuel (tons)	180
Radius, miles	3 000

A photograph of *Pachyderme* appears in the 1957-58 edition.

BUFFLE A 700

Displacement, tons	900 standard; 1 180 full load
Dimensions, feet	167·5 × 33 × 10
Main engines	2 sets triple expansion; 2 000 ihp = 12 knots
Complement	32

Launched on 4 May 1939. *Erable* was officially deleted from the list in 1969.

ACHARNÉ A 674

Displacement, tons	500 standard; 682 full load
Dimensions, feet	114·8 × 27·8 × 10
Main engines	Triple expansion; 1 000 ihp = 11 knots

Laid down in 1937 at Brest. *Actif, Appliqué* and *Capét* were scrapped in 1957-58. *Contentin* was withdrawn from service in 1960. *Champion* was condemned in 1961, *Obstiné* in 1965, *Entente* and *Tetu* in 1966, *Utile* in 1969 and *Ytile* in 1972.

INFATIGABLE (ex-*Polangen*) A 661

Displacement, tons	715
Main engines	1 300 ihp = 11 knots

Coolie was officially deleted from the list in 1969 and sister tug *Malabar* in 1969.

IMPLACABLE (ex-*Fohn II*) A 670

Displacement, tons	800
Main engines	1 300 ihp = 11 knots

DISPOSALS
Intraitable (ex-*Nordergrunde*) was condemned in Mar 1961, and *Mammouth* in July 1963. *Imbattable* (ex-*Nesserland*) was officially deleted in 1965.

ÉLÉPHANT (ex-*Bar*) A 666

Displacement, tons	810 standard; 1 180 full load
Main engines	2 000 ihp = 12 knots

The tug *Samson* (ex-German *Suder Hever*) was officially condemned Mar 1961.

RHINOCÉROS A 668

Displacement, tons	640
Main engines	Diesels; 1 850 bhp = 12 knots

A photograph of *Rhinocéros* appears in the 1953-54 to 1957-58 editions.

NOTE. A new tug of 1 150 tons (193·8 feet × 36 × 16·7) with main engines of 4 600 hp and a speed of 15 knots was ordered from A & C du Havre (*La Rochelle*) in late 1972 for delivery in 1974.

DISPOSALS. *Locmine* was condemned in 1964, *Efficace* was officially deleted from the list in 1966, and *Tenace* (ex-*ATA* 226) A 669 in Feb 1972.

HARBOUR TUGS. *Acajou, Balsa Bouleau Charme Chêne Cormier, Équeurdreville, Érable, Frene, Hetre Hevea, Latanier, Melcze, Mérisier Okoume, Olivier Peuplier Pin, Platane Saule, Sycomore*

Châtaignier, Manguier, Marronnier, Noyer Paletuvier, Papayer:
Built at Cherbourg in 1967 for service at Brest (*Châtaignier, Manguier, Papayer*) Toulon (*Marronnier, Noyer*) and Cherbourg (*Paletuvier*) 700 hp.

Ane, Bengali, Eider, Grand Duc, Macreuse Marabort, Martin Pecheur:
All eight 60·2 × 18·8 × 9 feet, diesel 250 hp = 9 knots. Five based at Lorient, three at St. Malo. *Alouette, Sarcelle, Vanneau* and three more ordered in Oct 1967.

TRAINING SHIPS

LA BELLE-POULE A 650 — **L'ÉTOILE** A 649

Displacement, tons	227
Dimensions, feet	128 oa × 23·7 × 11·8
Main engines	Sulzer diesel; 120 bhp = 6 knots

Auxiliary sail vessels. Built by Chantiers de Normandie (Fécamp) in 1932. Accommodation for 3 officers, 30 cadets, 5 petty officers, 12 men. Attached to Navy School.

LA GRANDE HERMINE (ex-*Ménestrel*)

Ex fishing boat built in 1936 Purchased in 1963 in replacement for *Dolphin* (ex-*Simone Marcelle*) as the School of Manoeuvre Training ship.

MUTIN A 652

A small coastal tender attached to *l'École de pilotage* (the School of Pilotage).

TORPEDO RECOVERY CRAFT

PELICAN (ex-*Kerfany*) A 699 — **PETREL** (ex- *Cap Lopez*) A 698

Displacement, tons	362 standard; 425 full load (*Petrel* 277/318)
Dimensions, feet	121·4 × 28·0 × 13·1 (*Petrel* 98·4 × 25·6 × 11·5)
Tubes	One
Main engines	Diesel; 1 shaft; 650 bhp = 10 knots
Complement	19 (5 officers, 14 men)

Purchased in 1965-66 and converted from tuna clippers into torpedo recovery craft.

Torpedo Recovery Craft—*continued*

PÉLICAN *1972, Dr. Giorgio Arra*

TRANSPORTS

BERRY (ex-M/S *Médoc*) A 644

Displacement, tons	2 700
Measurement, tons	1 203 gross; 1 552 deadweight
Dimensions, feet	284·5 oa × 38 × 15
Main engines	2 MWM diesels coupled on one shaft; 2 400 bhp = 15 knots

Built by Roland Werft Bremen. Launched on 10 May 1958. Purchased in Oct 1964 from Cie. Worms for the Pacific experimental station, renamed in 1964 and refitted in 1965. Classed as refrigerated transport. For CEP (Centre Experimental Pacific). Sister ship *Anjou* (ex-*Leoville*) A 645 was officially deleted from the list in Feb 1972.

BERRY *1969, French Navy*

AUNIS (ex-*Regina Pacis*) A 643

Displacement, tons	2 700 full load
Measurement, tons	1 250 gross
Dimensions, feet	284·5 × 31 × 15
Main engines	2 4-str 8-cyl oil geared to 1 shaft; 2 000 bhp = 16·6 knots

Built by Roland Werft, Bremen. Launched on 3 July 1956. Purchased in Nov 1966 from Seatto, Ambrosino & Pugliese for Pacific Experimental Station.

Verdon (ex-*Josta*) A 634 was officially deleted from the list in Feb 1972.

ALPHÉE Y 696 **ELFE** Y 741 **KORRIGAN** Y 661
ARIEL Y 604 **FAUNE** Y 613

Displacement, tons	225 full load
Dimensions, feet	132·8 × 24·5 × 10·8
Main engines	MGO diesels; 2 shafts; 1 640 bhp = 16 knots

Ariel was laid down in Dec 1963, launched on 27 Apr 1964 and delivered in Dec 1964 by Villeneuve (La Garonne). *Korrigan* was launched on 6 Mar 1964, *Alphée* on 10 June 1969, *Elfe* on 14 Apr 1970, *Faune* on 15 Apr 1971. Can carry 400 passengers. Sixth ship ordered 1972.

ALPHÉE *1972, courtesy Admiral M. Adam*

SYLPHE Y 710

Displacement, tons	171 standard; 189 full load
Dimensions, feet	126·5 × 22·7 × 8·2
Main engines	MGO diesel; 1 shaft; 600 bhp = 12 knots

Small transport for personnel, built by Chantiers Franco-Belge in 1959-60.

SAINTONGE (ex-*Santa Maria*) A 733

Measurement, tons	294 gross; 500 deadweight
Dimensions, feet	177 × 28 × 10·5
Main engines	1 diesel; 1 shaft; 520 bhp = 9 knots

Transports—*continued*

Built by Chantiers Duchesne et Bossière, Le Havre, for a Norwegian owner under the name of *Sven Germa*. Launched on 12 July 1956. Purchased in Apr 1965 from the firm of H. Beal & Co, Fort de France for the Pacific Nuclear Experimental Centre. The CEP support transports Guyenne (ex-*Douce France*, ex-*Sunfarer*) A 735 and *Tarn* (ex-*Orgeval*, ex-*Colomb Bechar*, ex-*Maria Laetitia*) A 771 were officially deleted from the list (*Tarn* sunk as target ship off Tahiti on 18 June 1970).

FALLERON (ex-German *Welle*) A 614

Displacement, tons	210 standard; 429 full load
Dimensions, feet	128·0 × 22·0 × 7·8
Main engines	1 Sulzer diesel; 280 bhp = 8 knots

Cap Ferrat was stricken in 1960. *Ter* (ex-German *Heinrich*) was condemned in 1964. *Molène* (ex-German B 262, ex-V 620, ex-*Köln*) was officially deleted from the list in Aug 1963, and *Gapeau* (ex-German B 264, ex-V 625, ex-*Johan Shultz*) in 1969.

MÉLUSINE Y 736 **MERLIN** Y 735

Displacement, tons	170
Dimensions, feet	103·3 × 23·2 × 7·9
Main engines	MGO diesels; 2 shafts; 960 bhp = 11 knots

Small transports for 400 personnel built in 1966 by Chantiers Navals Franco-Belges at Chalon sur Saône. Both laid down in Dec 1966 and accepted on 1 June 1968. *Mélusine* was launched on 23 Dec 1967 and *Merlin* on 8 Nov 1967. Their home port is Toulon.

TRÉBÉRON (ex-B 254) Y 712)

Displacement, tons	120 standard; 140 full load
Dimensions, feet	82·0 × 19·7 × 9·5
Main engines	Diesel; 1 shaft; 120 bhp = 8·5 knots

Former German danlayer used as small personnel transport for local port service.

LUTIN (ex-*Georges Clemenceau*)

Displacement, tons	68
Main engines	400 hp = 10 knots

Purchased in 1965. Ex-vedette. Detection school, Toulon.

SSBN TENDER. A 1 200-ton service lighter of 1 000 hp for nuclear fuel elements of SSBNs was launched on 26 Oct 1967 for delivery in May 1968.

DIVING TENDER

BELOUGA A 724 (ex-*Côte d'Argent*)

Displacement, tons	225 standard; 270 full load
Dimensions, feet	85·3 × 22·6 × 9·8
Main engines	1 Baudouin DV 8 diesel; 400 bhp = 9·5 knots
Complement	11 (1 officer, 10 men)

Tuna clipper built 1958, purchased in 1966 for conversion into a diving tender. The diving tender *Ingénieur Élie Monnier* A 647 (ex-German Trawler *Albatross*) was officially deleted from the list in 1972.

WATER CARRIERS

LIAMONE (ex-*Arrosoir*) A750

Displacement, tons	450 light; 1 369 full load
Dimensions, feet	184 × 28·9 × 13·8
Main engines	Sulzer diesels; 1 000 bhp = 11·5 knots

Rated as regional supply ship. Crew 27. Renamed *Liamone* in Mar 1954. Photograph in 1957-58 edition. Of two sister ships *Giboulée* was officially deleted from the list in 1969 and *Hanap* in 1971.

SAHEL A 638

Displacement, tons	630 light; 1 450 full load
Measurement, tons	650 deadweight
Dimensions, feet	176·2 × 29·5 × 14·5
Guns	2—20 mm AA
Main engines	2 diesels; 700 bhp = 12 knots

Completed in Aug 1951 by Chantiers Naval de Caen. Sister ship *Rummel* A 635 was officially deleted from the list in 1972.

SAHEL *1972, Dr. Giorgio Arra*

OASIS A 751

Displacement, tons	335 standard; 683 full load
Displacement, feet	164·8 × 27 × 9
Guns	2—20 mm AA
Main engines	Triple expansion; 1 shaft; 800 ihp = 10 knots

Built by A. C. Bretagne. In reserve. Sister *Torrent* was scrapped in 1964.

CATARACTE

Small water carrier of 330 tons. *Cascade*, *Durance* and *Fraiche* were scrapped in 1957, *Aube* in 1958, *Ardèche* in 1960, *Casamance* and *Zöghouan* in 1963, *Aiguade* in 1964, *Benzène* in 1967, *Bruine* in 1969, *Averse*, *Déluge*, *Fontaine*, *Formène*, *Mirage* and *Ondée* in 1970.

GERMANY (Federal Republic)

Bundesmarine Administration

Chief of Naval Staff, Federal German Navy:
Vice-Admiral Heinz Kühnle

Commander-in-Chief of the Fleet:
Konter-Admiral Paul Hartwig

Diplomatic Representation

Naval Attaché in London:
Rear Admiral Dr. Schuenemann

Naval Attaché in Washington:
Captain Andreas Wiese

Naval Attaché in Paris:
Captain Carl Hoffmann

Strength of the Fleet

11 Destroyers (including 3 DDG)
6 Frigates
6 Corvettes
12 Patrol submarines
2 Landing Ships
22 Landing Craft
38 Torpedo Boats
24 Coastal Minesweepers
29 Fast Minesweepers
21 Inshore Minesweepers
17 Depot & Maintenance Ships
14 Logistic Support Ships
19 Oilers
12 Tugs (+12 Harbour Tugs)
18 Tenders & Training Ships

New Construction

18 U13 Class Patrol Submarines
Guided missile craft under construction includes:
10 Fast patrol boats of 550 tons displacement
20 Fast patrol boats of 365 tons displacement

Future Development

Interest is being shown by the Naval Staff in various and varied projects.
(a) Development of more powerful ship-to-ship missiles.
(b) Development of SAM's and ASM's.
(c) Installation of coastal missiles.
(d) Construction of 250 ton hydrofoils of US *Tucumcari* type.

Personnel

1969: 37 500 (3 750 officers, 33 750 men)
1970: 39 000 (3 900 officers, 35 100 men)
1971: 35 000 (3 200 officers, 31 800 men)
1972: 35 900 (4 500 officers, 31 400 men)
1973: 36 000 (4 550 officers, 31 450 men)
(Includes Naval Air Arm)

Naval Air Arm

6 000 men total
2 LRMP squadrons (15 Breguet Atlantic)
4 Fighter bomber squadrons (60 F104G)
3 Helicopter squadrons (re-equipping with 22 Sea King Mk 41)
Communication aircraft (20 DO 28 and others)

Mercantile Marine

Lloyd's Register of Shipping:
2 546 vessels of 8 515 669 tons gross

Hydrographic Service

This service is under the direction of the Ministry of Transport, is civilian manned with HQ at Hamburg. Survey ships are listed at the end of the section.

Disposals and Losses

Frigates
1972 *Scharnhorst* and *Gneisenau*

Submarines
1966 *Hai* (ex-U 2365) Type XXIII lost off Dogger Bank. Raised and scrapped
1968 *Hecht* (ex-U 2367) Type XXIII

Depot Ship
1966 WST (ex-USS LSD 11) sold to Greek M.N.

DESTROYERS

3 MODIFIED "ADAMS" CLASS DDG

Name	*No.*	*Builders*	*Laid down*	*Launched*	*Completion*
LÜTJENS	D 185 (USN-DDG 28)	Bath Iron Works Corp	1 Mar 1966	11 Aug 1967	12 Mar 1969
MÖLDERS	D 186 (USN-DDG 29)	Bath Iron Works Corp	12 Apr 1966	13 Apr 1968	12 Sep 1969
ROMMEL	D 187 (USN-DDG 30)	Bath Iron Works Corp	22 Aug 1967	1 Feb 1969	24 Apr 1970

Displacement, tons	3 370 standard; 4 500 full load
Length, feet (*metres*)	431 (*131·4*) wl; 440 (*134·1*) oa
Beam, feet (*metres*)	47 (*14·3*)
Draught, feet (*metres*)	20 (*6·1*)
Missile launchers	1 "Tartar" single
Guns, dual purpose	2—5 in (*127 mm*) single
A/S launchers	"Asroc"; 2 triple torpedo; 1 DCT
Boilers	4 Combustion Engineering; 1 200 psi (*84·4 kg/cm²*)
Main engines	Geared steam turbines 70 000 shp; 2 shafts
Oil fuel, tons	900
Range, miles	4 500 at 20 knots
Speed, knots	35
Complement	340 (21 officers, 319 men)

GENERAL

Destroyers basically of the "Charles F. Adams" type; but modified to suit Federal German requirements and practice and presenting a considerably different silhouette. 1965 contract. Cost $43 754 000.

LÜTJENS 1970

RADAR. SPS 52 three dimensional air search and target designator with aerial on after funnel. SPS 50 air surveillance with aerial on mainmast. Two SPG 51 Tartar fire control aerials abaft after funnel. One SPS 10 surface warning set. One GFCS 68 for gun armament Tacan beacon. Satir 2 ADA system (believed similar to Senit 2).

SONAR. Probably SQS 23.

LÜTJENS *Class*

Destroyers—*continued*

ROMMEL 1972

4 "HAMBURG" CLASS

Displacement, tons	3 400 standard; 4 400 full load
Length, feet (*metres*)	420 (*128*) wl; 439·7 (*134·0*) oa
Beam, feet (*metres*)	44 (*13·4*)
Draught, feet (*metres*)	17 (*5·2*)
Guns, dual purpose	4—3·9 in (*100 mm*) single
Guns, AA	8—40 mm, 4 twin
A/S weapons	2 Bofors 4-barrel DC Mortars; 1 DCT
Torpedo tubes	5—21 in (*533 mm*), 3 bow and 2 stern; 2—12 in for AS torpedoes
Boilers	4 Wahodag; 910 psi (*64 kg/cm²*), 860°F (460°C)
Main engines	2 Wahodag dr geared turbines; 68 000 shp; 2 shafts
Speed, knots	35·8 max; 18 economical sea
Range, miles	6 000 at 13 knots; 920 at 35 knots
Complement	280 (17 officers, 263 men)

Name	*No.*	*Builders*	*Laid down*	*Launched*	*Completed*
BAYERN	D 183	H. C. Stülcken Sohn, Hamburg	1962	14 Aug 1962	6 July **1965**
HAMBURG	D 181	H. C. Stülcken Sohn, Hamburg	1959	26 Mar 1960	23 Mar **1964**
HESSEN	D 184	H. C. Stülcken Sohn, Hamburg	1962	4 May 1963	8 Oct **1968**
SCHLESWIG-HOLSTEIN	D 182	H. C. Stülcken Sohn, Hamburg	1959	20 Aug 1960	12 Oct **1964**

GENERAL
All named after countries of the German Federal Republic. Capable of minelaying.

ELECTRONICS. FCS for Bofors A/S launcher, Torpedoes and DC from Hollandse. ECM fitted.

RADAR. All Radar by Hollandse Signaalapparaten. One air warning LW 02/3. One DAO 2 target designator. One nav/surface warning set. Two M45 100 mm fire control sets. Two M45 40 mm fire control sets.

HAMBURG (with HSA LW 04 instead of LW 02/3 radar aerial) *1971, Stefan Terzibaschitsch*

HAMBURG *Class*

BAYERN *1971, Wright & Logan*

Destroyers—*continued*

4 Ex-US "FLETCHER" CLASS

Name	No.	Builders	Laid down	Launched	Completed	German commissioned
Z 2 (ex-USS *Ringgold, DD* 500)	D 171	Federal SB & DD Co, Port Newark	25 June 1942	11 Nov 1942	24 Dec 1942	14 July 1959
Z 3 (ex-USS *Wadsworth, DD* 516)	D 172	Bath Iron Works Corporation, Maine	18 Aug 1942	10 Jan 1943	16 Mar 1943	6 Oct 1959
Z 4 (ex-USS *Claxton, DD* 571)	D 178	Consolidated Steel Corporation, Orange	25 June 1941	1 Apr 1942	8 Dec 1942	15 Dec 1959
Z 5 (ex-USS *Dyson, DD* 572)	D 179	Consolidated Steel Corporation, Orange	25 June 1941	15 Apr 1942	30 Dec 1942	23 Feb 1960

Displacement, tons	2 100 standard; 2 750 full load
Length, feet (*metres*)	368·4 (*112·3*) wl; 376·5 (*114·8*) oa
Beam, feet (*metres*)	39·5 (*12*)
Draught, feet (*metres*)	18 (*5·5*) max
Guns, dual purpose	4—5 in (*127 mm*) 38 cal.
Guns, AA	6—3 in (*76 mm*) 50 cal., 3 twin mountings
A/S	2 hedgehogs; 1 DC rack
Torpedo tubes	5—21 in (*533 mm*), quintuple bank; 2 ASW tubes
Boilers	4 Babcock & Wilcox; 569 psi (*40 kg/cm²*); 851°F (*455°C*)
Main engines	2 sets GE geared turbines 60 000 shp; 2 shafts
Speed, knots	35 max; 17 economical sea speed
Range, miles	6 000 at 15 knots
Oil fuel (tons)	540
Complement	250

Z1 *Class*

GENERAL
Former US "Fletcher" class destroyers. Their loan from the United States for five years was extended. First ship arrived at Bremerhaven on 14 Apr 1958. *Ringgold* was transferred by the USA at Charleston, S.C. on 14 July 1969. Capable of minelaying.

RADAR. Search: SPS 6. Tactical: SPS 10. Fire Control: GFCS 56 and 68.

DISPOSALS. Z 6, No. D 180 (ex-USS *Charles Ausburn, DD* 570) was decommissioned on 15 Dec 1967 and scrapped in 1969. Z 1, No. D 170 (ex-USS *Anthony, DD* 515) was decommissioned in Feb 1972 for cannibalisation to provide spare parts for her four sister ships.

Z 3 *1972,*

FRIGATES

6 "KOLN" CLASS

Name	No.	Builders	Launched	Completed
AUGSBURG	F 222	H. C. Stülcken Sohn, Hamburg	15 Aug 1959	7 Apr 1962
BRAUNSCHWEIG	F 225	H. C. Stülcken Sohn, Hamburg	3 Feb 1962	16 June 1964
EMDEN	F 221	H. C. Stülcken Sohn, Hamburg	21 Mar 1959	24 Oct 1961
KARLSRUHE	F 223	H. C. Stülcken Sohn, Hamburg	24 Oct 1959	15 Dec 1962
KÖLN	F 220	H. C. Stülcken Sohn, Hamburg	6 Dec 1958	15 Apr 1961
LUBECK	F 224	H. C. Stülcken Sohn, Hamburg	23 July 1960	6 July 1963

Displacement, tons	2 100 standard; 2 550 full load
Length, feet (*metres*)	360·9 (*110*)
Beam, feet (*metres*)	36·1 (*11·0*)
Draught, feet (*metres*)	11·2 (*3·4*)
Guns, dual purpose	2—3·9 in (*100 mm*)
Guns, AA	6—40 mm; 2 twin and 2 single
A/S	2 Bofors 4-barrel DC mortars (rocket launchers)
Torpedo tubes	2 for ASW torpedoes
Main engines	Combined diesel and gas turbine plant: 4 MAN 16-cyl. diesels, total 12 000 bhp; 2 Brown-Boveri gas turbines, 24 000 bhp; total 36 000 shp; 2 shafts
Speed, knots	32 max; 23 economical sea speed;
Range, miles	920 at full power
Oil fuel, tons	333
Complement	210

GENERAL
Streamlined and flushdecked fast anti-submarine frigates or escort destroyers with low freeboard aft. Ordered in Mar 1957. All ships of this class are named after towns of West Germany. Capable of minelaying.

LUBECK *1972*

ELECTRONICS. Hollandse FCS for Bofors A/S launchers M9 torpedo fire control.

RADAR. All by Hollandse. One DA 02 target designator. One nav/surface warning set. Two M45 100 mm fire control sets. Two M45 40 mm fire control sets.

ENGINEERING. Each of the two shafts is driven by two diesels coupled and geared to one BBC gas turbine. Controllable pitch propellers. A speed of 32 knots is reported to have been attained on full power trials.

CATAGORY. These ships were originally designated *Geleitboote*, but are now rated as *Fregatten*.

KÖLN *Class*

Frigates—*continued*

BRAUNSCHWEIG 1971, Skyfotos

CORVETTES

HANS BÜRKNER Y 879

Displacement, tons	982 standard; 1 100 full load
Dimensions, feet	265·2 oa × 30·8 × 10
Guns	2—40 mm AA (twin mounting)
A/S weapons	1 DC mortar (four-barrelled); 2 DC racks
Main Engines	4 MAN diesels; 2 shafts; 13 600 shp = 25 knots
Complement	50

Torpedofangboot. Built by Atlaswerke, Bremen. Launched on 16 July 1961. Completed on 18 May 1963. Named after designer of German pre-First World War battleships.

HANS BÜRKNER 1970

THESEUS (blockbridge type) 1970

5 "THETIS" CLASS

HERMES A 1431 (ex-P 6112)
HAJADE A 1432 (ex-P 6113)
THESEUS A 1434 (ex-P 6115)
THETIS A 1430 (ex-P 6111)
TRITON A 1433 (ex-P 6114)

Displacement, tons	564 standard; 680 full load
Dimensions, feet	229·7 × 27 × 7·5
Guns	2—40 mm AA (twin mounting) (To be replaced by 1—3 in Oto Melara)
A/S weapons	Bofors DC mortar (*Hermes* 2 tubes)
Main engines	2 MAN diesels; 2 shafts; 6 800 bhp = 24 knots
Complement	48

Built by Roland Werft, Bremen-Hemelingen. Some have computer house before bridge. *Thetis* commissioned on 1 July 1961, *Hermes* on 16 Dec 1961, *Najada* on 12 May 1962, *Triton* on 10 Nov 1962, *Theseus* on 15 Aug 1963. Combined nav/surface warning radar. HSA M9 series torpedo control.

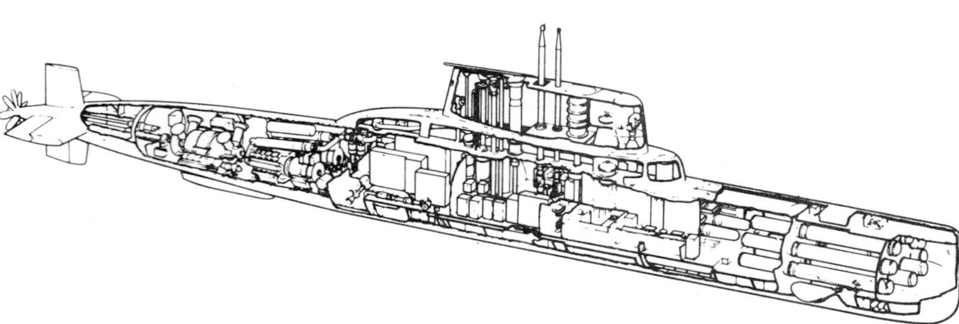

NAJADE (forebridge type) 1970, Skyfotos

SUBMARINES

18 NEW CONSTRUCTION TYPE 206

U 13 S 192	**U 20** S 199	**U 27** S 176
U 14 S 193	**U 21** S 170	**U 28** S 177
U 15 S 194	**U 22** S 171	**U 29** S 178
U 16 S 195	**U 23** S 172	**U 30** S 179
U 17 S 196	**U 24** S 173	
U 18 S 197	**U 25** S 174	
U 19 S 198	**U 26** S 175	

Displacement, tons	500 nominal; 600 submerged
Length, feet (*metres*)	147·6 (*45·0*)
Beam, feet (*metres*)	15·4 (*4·7*)
Torpedo tubes	8 forward facing
Main engines	Diesel-electric; 1 shaft; 1 800 hp
Speed, knots	17 max submerged
Complement	22

Authorised on 7 June 1969 from Howaldtswerke/Deutsche Werft and Reinstahl/Nordseewerke.

U 13 was completed in 1972. Launch dates: U 13 28 Sep 1971, U 14 1 Feb 1972, U 15 15 June 1972, U 16 29 Aug 1972, U 17 10 Oct 1972. All 18 are to be completed by end 1974.

Cutaway impression of the Vickers/AKL 500-ton oceangoing submarine 1972, Vickers Limited

Submarines—*continued*

11 COASTAL TYPE 205

U 1 (21 Oct 1961) S 180
U 2 (25 Jan 1962) S 181
U 4 (22 Aug 1962) S 183
U 5 (22 Nov 1962) S 184
U 6 (22 Apr 1963) S 185
U 7 (29 May 1963) S 186
U 8 (11 Oct 1963) S 187
U 9 (20 Oct 1966) S 188
U 10 (20 July 1967) S 189
U 11 (9 Feb 1968) S 190
U 12 (10 Sep 1968) S 191

Displacement, tons	370 surface; 450 submerged
Length, feet (*metres*)	142·7 (*43·5*) oa
Beam, feet (*metres*)	15·1 (*4·6*)
Draught, feet (*metres*)	13·5 (*4·3*)
Torpedo tubes	8 in bow
Main engines	2 MB diesels; total 1 200 bhp 2 electric motors, total 1 700 bhp; single screw
Speed, knots	10 on surface; 17 submerged
Complement	21

GENERAL

All built by Howaldtswerke, Kiel in floating docks. Original launch dates above. "Teardrop" hull. Fitted with schnorkel. First submarines designed and built by Germany since the end of the Second World War. U 4-12 were built to a heavier and improved design. U 1 and U 2 were modified accordingly and refloated on 17 Feb 1967 and 15 July 1966 respectively. U 1 was reconstructed late 1963 to 4 Mar 1965. (See original appearance in the 1962-63 and 1963-64 editions.) U 4-8 are sheathed with zinc. U-9-12 have hulls of different steel alloys of non-magnetic properties. U 7 and U 11 entered service on 22 May 1968 and 21 June 1968, respectively. U 12 was completed on 14 Jan 1969. U 3 of this class lent to Norway on 10 July 1962 and temporarily named *Kobben* (S 310), was returned to Germany in 1964 and decommissioned on 15 Sep 1967 for disposal.

U 11 *1970*

RADAR. French Thomson-CSF Calypso, nav/att. set. Passive DF.

TORPEDO EQUIPMENT. The boats are trimmed by the stern to load through the bow caps. Also fitted for minelaying. Fire control by Hollandse Sig. Mk 8.

1 CONVERTED TYPE XXI

WILHELM BAUER (ex-U 2540) Y 880

Displacement, tons	1 620 surface; 1 820 submerged
Length, feet (*metres*)	252·7 (*77·0*) pp
Beam, feet (*metres*)	21·7 (*6·6*)
Draught, feet (*metres*)	20·3 (*6·2*)
Torpedo tubes	4—21 in (*533 mm*) in bow
Main engines	Diesel-electric drive 2 diesels total 4 200 bhp 2 electric motors total 5 000 hp
Speed, knots	15·5 surface; 17·5 submerged

WILHELM BAUER *1971*

Launched in 1944 by Blohm & Voss, Hamburg. Sunk on 3 May 1945. Raised in 1957. Rebuilt in 1958-59 at Howaldtswerke, Kiel. Commissioned on 1 Sep 1960. Used for experiments on electronic equipment in the *Erpobungsstelle fur Marinewaffen* (Experimental Stati. for Naval Weapons). Conning tower was modified.

AMPHIBIOUS VESSELS

2 Ex-US LSM TYPE

EIDECHSE (ex-USS *LSM* 491) L 751 **KROKODIL** (ex-USS *LSM* 537) L 750

Displacement, tons	743 light; 1 095 full load
Dimensions, feet	196·5 wl; 203·5 oa × 34·5 × 8·3
Guns	2—40 mm AA (1 twin)
Main engines	GM diesel; 2 shafts; 2 800 bhp = 12·5 knots

Rated as Lundungsboote. Survivors of six medium landing ships (two LSM(R) and four LSM) purchased from USA for about $6 000 000 and transferred to Germany on 5 Sep 1958 at Charleston SC. Refitted in 1959.

DISPOSALS.
Two medium landing ships of this class, *Salamander* (ex-USS *LSM* 553) L 752 and *Viper* (ex-USS *LSM* 558) L 753 were officially deleted from the list in Feb and Mar 1969. The two medium landing ships (rocket) of the US LSMR type, *Natter* L 755 (ex-*Thames River*, LSM(R) 534 and *Otter* L 754 (ex-*Smyrna River*, LSM(R) 532), were decommissioned on 15 Dec 1967 and scrapped.

The two landing ships of the former United States LST type, ex-USS *Millard Count* LST 987, and ex-USS *Montgomery County*, LST 1041, purchased in 1960 for co. version into repair ships similar to the US ARB type, above, were scrapped in 196

KROKODIL (helicopter deck aft) ***Wright & Logan***

22 LCU TYPE

BARBE	L 790	**FELCHEN**	L 793	**LACHS**	L 762	**SALM**	L 799
BRASSE	L 789	**FLUNDER**	L 760	**MAKRELE**	L 796	**SCHLEIE**	L 765
BUTT	L 788	**FORELLE**	L 794	**MURANE**	L 797	**STOR**	L 766
DELPHIN	L 791	**INGER**	L 795	**PLOTZE**	L 763	**TUMMLER**	L 767
DORSCH	L 792	**KARPFEN**	L 761	**RENKE**	L 798	**WELS**	L 768
				ROCHEN	L 764	**ZANDER**	L 769

Displacement, tons	200 light; 403 full load
Dimensions, feet	136·5 × 28·9 × 5·2
Guns	1—20 mm AA
Main engines	GM diesels; 2 shafts; 1 380 bhp = 12 knots
Complement	17

Similar to the United States LCU (Landing Craft, Utility) type. Provided with bow and stern ramp. Built by Howaldt, Hamburg, all launched in 1965-66. A photograph of *Delphin* appears in the 1967-68 to 1969-70 editions.

The utility landing craft LCU 1 (ex-USS LCU 779, ex-LCT(6) 779), transferred from the USA under MAP was scrapped in 1968.

SCHLEIE *1970, Stefan Terzibaschitsch*

LIGHT FORCES

10 NEW CONSTRUCTION TYPE 143 (MISSILE BOATS)

S 11	P 6111	**S 12**	P 6112	**S 13**	P 6113	**S 14**	P 6114
S 15	P 6115	**S 16**	P 6116	**S 17**	P 6117	**S 18**	P 6118
S 19	P 6119	**S 20**	P 6120				

Displacement, tons	360 nominal; 550 full load
Dimensions, feet	200·0 × 24·6 × 8·5
Guided weapons	4 launchers for "Exocet" surface-to-surface missiles
Guns	2—76 mm AA (Italian Oto Melara)
Torpedoes	2—21 in wire guided
Main engines	4 MTU diesels; 4 shafts = 38 knots
Complement	40

GENERAL
Ordered in 1971. To be completed from 1975 to 1977 to replace ten torpedo boats of the "Jaguar" class. Final funds allocated 13 July 1972. First laid down late 1972. Builders; 7 at Lürssen and 3 at Kroger, Rendsberg.

ELECTRONICS.
Believed that data automation system AGIS is being fitted to permit use of Type 143 as control ship for concerted operation of Type 148 boats.

RADAR.
All by Hollandse. Two WM 27 in radome for Exocet, gun and torpedo control.

MODEL TYPE 143 *1970,*

20 NEW CONSTRUCTION TYPE 148 (MISSILE BOATS)

S 41	P 6141	**S 42**	P 6142	**S 43**	P 6143	**S 44**	P 6144
S 45	P 6145	**S 46**	P 6146	**S 47**	P 6147	**S 48**	P 6148
S 49	P 6149	**S 50**	P 6150	**S 51**	P 6151	**S 52**	P 6152
S 53	P 6153	**S 54**	P 6154	**S 55**	P 6155	**S 56**	P 6156
S 57	P 6157	**S 58**	P 6158	**S 59**	P 6159	**S 60**	P 6160

Displacement, tons	234 standard; 265 full load
Dimensions, feet	154·2 × 23·0 × 5·9
Guided weapons	4 launchers for "Exocet" surface-to-surface missiles
Guns	1—76 mm AA (Oto Melara); 1—40 mm AA (Bofors)
Torpedoes	2—21 in (or 8 mines)
Main engines	4 MTU diesels; 4 shafts; 12 000 bhp = 38·5 knots
Oil fuel, tons	39
Range, miles	600 at 30 knots
Complement	30 (4 officers, 26 men)

GENERAL.
Ordered in Oct 1970. To be completed from 1973 onwards to replace torpedo boats of the "Jaguar" class. Builders: Constructions Mecaniques de Normandy, Cherbourg. S 41 was laid down on Oct 1971 and launched 27 Mar 1972, arrived in Germany for fitting out July 14 1972 and commissioned 30 Oct 1972. Trials until March 1973.

RADAR. X-Band nav radar. Triton C-band air and surface search and target designator with IFF aerial POLLUX X-band tracking radar. Thomson-CSF VEGA-POLLUX PCET control system and radar for control of EXOCET, torpedoes and guns. Less sophisticated than type 143.

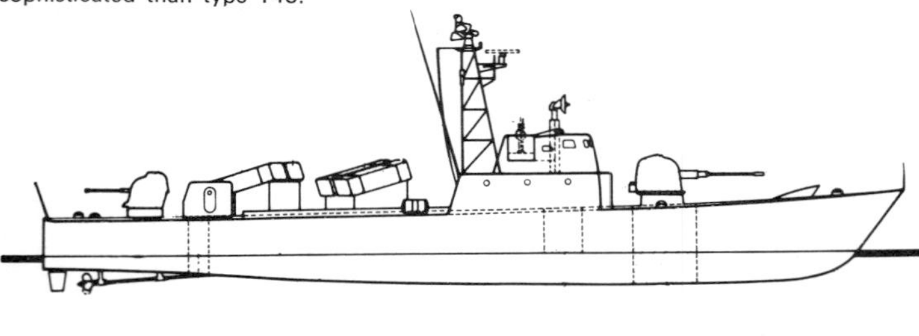

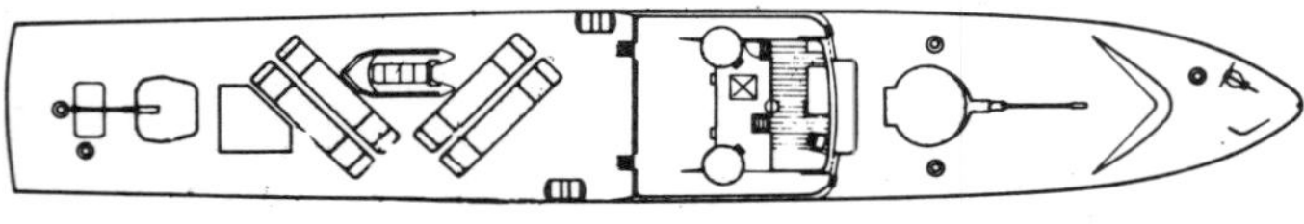

TYPE 148 *1972*

10 NEW CONVERSION TYPE 142 (TORPEDO BOATS)

DACHS	P 6094	**HERMELIN**	P 6095	**OZELOT**	P 6101
FRETTCHEN	P 6100	**HYÄNE**	P 6099	**PUMA**	P 6097
GEPARD	P 6098	**NERZ**	P 6096	**WIESEL**	P 6093
				ZOBEL	P 6092

Displacement, tons	225 full load
Dimensions, feet	137·8 × 23 × 7·5
Guns	2—40 mm AA Bofors L 70 (single)
Tubes	2—21 in wire guided
Main engines	4 Mercedes-Benz 20 cyl diesels; 4 shafts; 12 000 bhp = 40 knots
Complement	38

Originally units of the "Jaguar" class, but now officially known as the modernised "Zobel" class. Two M 20 series Radars in radome for control of guns and torpedoes.

FRETTCHEN (TYPE 142) *1972,*

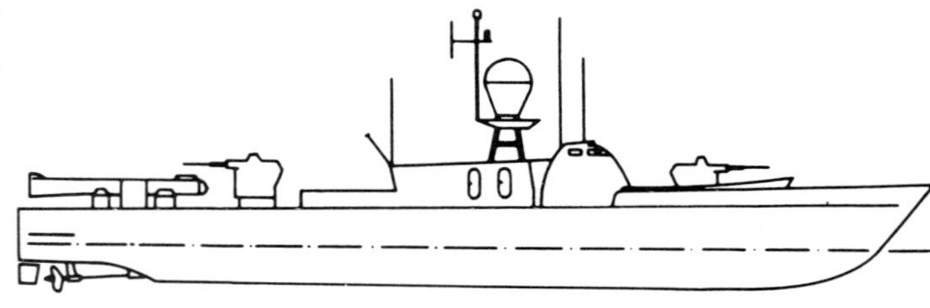

28 "JAGUAR" CLASS (TORPEDO BOATS)

ALBATROS *	P 6069	**HÄHER**	P 6087	**PANTHER**	P 6064
ALK	P 6084	**ILTIS**	P 6058	**PELIKAN**	P 6086
BUSSARD *	P 6074	**JAGUAR**	P 6059	**PINGUIN**	P 6090
DOMMEL	P 6091	**KONDOR ***	P 6070	**REIHER**	P 6089
ELSTER	P 6088	**KORMORAN ***	P 6077	**SEEADLER ***	P 6068
FALKE *	P 6072	**KRANICH**	P 6083	**SPERBER ***	P 6076
FUCHS	P 6066	**LEOPARD**	P 6060	**STORCH**	P 6085
GEIER *	P 6073	**LÖWE**	P 6065	**WOLF**	P 6062
GREIF *	P 6071	**LUCHS**	P 6061		
HABICHT *	P 6075				

Displacement, tons	160 standard; 190 full load
Dimensions, feet	138 × 22 × 5
Guns	2—40 mm AA Bofors L 70 (single)
Tubes	4—21 in (2 torpedo tubes can be removed for 4 mines)
Main engines	Mercedes-Benz 20 cyl or Maybach 16 cyl diesels; 4 shafts; 12 000 bhp = 42 knots
Complement	38

32 boats were built by Fr. Lürssen, Bremen-Vegasack in 1957-62 and eight by Krögerwerft Rendsburg in 1958-64. Of composite construction, with steel frames, mahogany diagonal carvel hulls, alloy bulkheads and superstructure. Units marked * are Type 141 with Maybach diesels. Remaining 20 are Type 140 with Mercedes-Benz diesels. Ten were converted into Type 142, see above. *Marder* and *Weihe* paid off 22 June 1972 for cannibalization.

DOMMEL *1971, Giorgio Arra*

MINE WARFARE FORCES

18 "LINDAU" CLASS (CMS)

CUXHAVEN	M 1078	**KONSTANZ**	M 1081	**TÜBINGEN**	M 1074
DÜREN	M 1079	**LINDAU**	M 1072	**ULM**	M 1083
FLENSBURG	M 1084	**MARBURG**	M 1080	**VÖLKLINGEN**	M 1087
FULDA	M 1068	**MINDEN**	M 1085	**WEILHEIM**	M 1077
GÖTTINGEN	M 1070	**PADERBORN**	M 1076	**WETZLAR**	M 1075
KOBLENZ	M 1071	**SCHLESWIG**	M 1073	**WOLFSBURG**	M 1082

Displacement, tons	370 standard; 425 full load
Dimensions, feet	137·8 pp; 147·7 oa × 27·2 × 8·5
Guns	1—40 mm AA
Main engines	Maybach diesels; 2 shafts; 4 000 bhp = 17 knots
Complement	46

Lindau, first German built vessel for the Federal German Navy since the Second World War, launched on 16 Feb 1957. Basically of NATO WU type but modified for German requirements. Built by Yacht- & Bootswerft, Burmester, Bremen-Berg. Seventeen similar Kustenminensuchboote were built in German yards in 1958-60. The hull is of wooden construction, laminated with plastic glue. The engines are of non-magnetic materials. The first six, *Göttingen, Koblenz, Lindau, Schleswig, Tübingen* and *Wetzlar*, were modified with lower bridges in 1958-59. *Schleswig* was lengthened by 6·8 feet in 1960 in all others in 1960-64. *Flensburg* and *Fulda* were converted into mine-hunters in 1968-69 as part of a total of ten ships to be so converted.

SCHLESWIG *1972*

6 "VEGESACK" CLASS (CMS)

DETMOLD	M 1252	**PASSAU**	M 1255	**VEGESACK**	M 1250
HAMELN	M 1251	**SIEGEN**	M 1254	**WORMS**	M 1253

Displacement, tons	362 standard; 378 full load
Dimensions, feet	137·8 pp; 144·3 oa × 26·2 × 9
Guns	2—20 mm AA
Main engines	2 Mercedes-Benz diesels; 2 shafts; 1,500 bhp = 15 knots Kamewa controllable pitch propellers

Built in Cherbourg. All launched and completed in 1959-60. Near sisters to French *Mercure*.

WORMS *1972*

29 "SCHUTZE" CLASS (FAST IMS)

ATAIR	M 1067	**NEPTUN**	M 1093	**SPICA**	M 1059
CAPELLA	M 1098	**ORION**	M 1053	**STEINBOCK**	M 1091
CASTOR	M 1051	**PEGASUS**	M 1066	**STIER**	Y 849
DENEB	M 1064	**PERSEUS**	M 1090	**URANUS**	M 1099
FISCHE	M 1096	**POLLUX**	M 1054	**WAAGE**	M 1063
GEMMA	M 1097	**PLUTO**	M 1092	**WEGA**	M 1089
HERKULES	M 1095	**REGULUS**	M 1057	**WIDDER**	M 1094
JUPITER	M 1065	**RIGEL**	M 1056	**WAAGE**	M 1063
KREBS	M 1055	**SCHUTZE**	M 1062	**WEGA**	M 1089
MARS	M 1058	**SIRIUS**	M 1055	**WIDDER**	M 1094
MIRA	M 1050	**SKORPION**	M 1060		

Displacement, tons	200 standard; 226 full load
Dimensions, feet	144·5 pp; 154·5 oa × 22·3 × 7·2
Guns	1—40 mm AA (some still have the designed 2—40 mm) *Pegasus* have 2—40 mm
Main engines	Maybach diesels; 2 shafts; Escher-Wyss propellers 3 600 bhp = 24·5 knots
Complement	39

Algol, Capella, Castor, Fische, Gemma, Krebs, Mars, Mira, Orion, Pollux, Regulus, Rigel, Schütze, Sirius, Skorpion, Spica, Steinbock, Stier, Waage, and *Wega* were built by Abeking & Rasmussen, Lemwerder; *Deneb, Jupiter, Pluto, Uranus* and *Widder* by Schurenstedt, Bardenfl; *Atair, Herkules, Neptun, Pegasus* and *Perseus* by Schlichting, Travemünde. The design is a development of the "R" boats of the Second World War. All this class are named after stars. *Stier*, former hull number M 1061, carries no weapons, but has a decompression chamber, being security vessel for submarines. All completed in 1959-64. Formerly classified as inshore minesweepers, but re-rated as fast minesweepers in 1966.

DISPOSALS. *Algol* M 1068 was scrapped in 1972.

STIER (decompression chamber) *1972*

STEINBOCK *1971*

10 "FRAUENLOB" CLASS (IMS)

ACHERON	Y 1661	**FRAUENLOB**	Y 1652	**MEDUSA**	Y 1655
ATLANTIS	Y 1660	**GEFION**	Y 1654	**MINERVA**	Y 1657
DIANA	Y 1658	**LORELEY**	Y 1659	**NAUTILUS**	Y 1653
				UNDINE	Y 1656

Displacement, tons	204 standard; 230 tons full load
Dimensions, feet	124·7 × 27·2 × 7·2
Guns	1—40 mm AA
Main engines	Diesels = 14 knots
Complement	24

Built by Kröger Werft, Rendsberg. Launched in 1965-67. Completed in 1965-68. Originally designed as *Kustenwachboote* or coastguard boats with "W" pennant numbers. Rated as inshore minesweepers in 1968 with the "M" hull numbers. Re-allocated "Y" numbers in 1970.

NAUTILUS *1971*

Mine Warfare —*continued*

HOLNIS Y 836 (ex- M 2651) (IMS)

Displacement, tons	180
Dimensions, feet	116·8 × 24·3 × 6·9
Guns	1—20 mm AA
Main engines	2 Mercedes-Benz diesels; 2 shafts; 2 000 bhp = 14·5 knots
Complement	21

Now serving for test and evaluation purposes, *Holnis* was launched on 22 May 1965 and completed in 1966 by Abeking & Rasmussen, Lemwerde, as the prototype of a new design of *Binnenminensuchboote* projected as a class of 20 such vessels but she is the only unit of this type, the other 19 boats having been cancelled. Hull number changed from M 2651 to Y 836 in 1970.

HOLNIS *1972*

2 "NIOBE" CLASS (IMS)

HANSA Y 806, ex-W 22 (18 Nov 1957) **NIOBE** Y 1643, ex-W 21 (18 Aug 1957)

Displacement, tons	150 standard; 180 full load
Dimensions, feet	115·2 × 21·3 × 5·6
Guns	1—40 mm AA
Main engines	*Hansa:* 1 Mercedes-Benz diesel; 1 shaft; 950 bhp = 14 knots *Niobe:* 2 Mercedes-Benz diesels; 2 shafts; 1 900 bhp = 16 knots
Complement	*Hansa* 19; *Niobe* 22

Built by Kröger Werft, Rendsburg. Launch dates above. Completed in 1958. The post-war prototype vessels of the category, formerly designated *Küstenwachboote* or coastal patrol vessels but re-rated as *Binnenminensuchboote* or inshore minesweepers in 1966. Named after former cruisers. *Hansa* serves as support ship for minedivers. *Niobe* (photograph in the 1967-68 edition) serves for test and evaluation purposes.

HANSA *1970, Stefan Terzibaschitsch*

8 ARIADNE CLASS (IMS)

AMAZONE	(27 Feb 1963)	Y 1650	**HERTHA**	(18 Feb 1961)	Y 1647
ARIADNE	(23 Apr 1960)	Y 1644	**NIXE**	(3 Dec 1962)	Y 1649
FREYA	(25 June 1966)	Y 1645	**NYMPHE**	(20 Nov 1962)	Y 834
GAZELLE	(14 Aug 1963)	Y 1651	**VINETA**	(17 Sep 1960)	Y 1646

Displacement, tons	184 standard; 210 full load
Dimensions, feet	124·3 × 27·2 × 6·6
Guns	1—40 mm AA
Main engines	2 Mercedes-Benz diesels; 2 shafts; 2 000 bhp = 14 knots
Complement	23

Launch dates above. All completed by Krögerwerft, Rendsburg, in 1960-63. All named after former cruisers, 1897-1900. Formerly classified as patrol boats (*Küstenwachboote*) but re-rated as inshore minesweepers in 1966, and given new M hull numbers in Jan 1968, and Y hull numbers in 1970. In reserve.

FREYA *1970*

DEPOT MAINTENANCE SHIPS

13 "RHEIN" CLASS

DONAU	69	**LECH**	56	**RHEIN**	58
ELBE	61	**MAIN**	63	**RUHR**	64
ISAR	54	**MOSEL**	67	**SAAR**	65
LAHN	55	**NECKAR**	66	**WERRA**	68
				WESER	62

Displacement, tons	2 370 standard; 2 540 full load except *Lahn* and *Lech* 2 460 standard; 2 680 full load
Length, feet (*metres*)	304·5 (*92·8*) wl; 323·5 (*98·6*) oa
Beam, feet (*metres*)	38·8 (*11·8*)
Draught, feet (*metres*)	11·2 (*3·4*)
Guns, AA	2—3·9 in (*100 mm*); none in *Lahn, Lech*; 4—40 mm
Main engines	6 Maybach or Daimler diesels; Diesel-electric drive in *Isar, Lahn, Lech, Mosel, Saar* 11 400 bhp; 2 shafts
Speed, knots	21·7 max, 15 economical sea speed
Radius, miles	1 625 at 15 knots
Oil fuel, tons	334
Complement	110 (accommodation for 200)

GENERAL

Elbe, Mosel, Rhein, and *Ruhr* were built by Schliekerwerft, Hamburg, *Isar* by Blohm & Voss, Hamburg, *Weser* by Elsflether Werft, *Neckar* by Lürssen, Bremen-Vegesack, *Saar* by Norderwerft, Hamburg, *Donau* by Schlichting, Travemünde, *Lahn* and *Lech* by Flender, Lübeck, *Main, Werra* by Lindenau, Kiel-Friedrichsort. All completed in 1961-64. Rated as *Belgleitschiffe* (tenders) for minesweepers (*Isar, Mosel, Saar*), submarines (*Lahn, Lech*), training (*Donau, Ruhr, Weser*), and motor torpedo boats (others) but these handsome and symmetrical ships of very interesting design, with their 3·9 in (100 mm) guns could obviously be used in lieu of frigates, although their flag superior is A.

SAAR *1971*

STATUS. Five of these comparatively new ships, namely *Donau, Isar, Lahn, Lech* and *Weser*. were placed in reserve by July 1968 it was officially stated. This was part of the economy programme announced by the Federal German Navy in Sep 1967.

RADAR. All by Hollandse. Search: HSA DA 02. Fire Control: Two HSA M 45 for 100 mm and 40 mm.

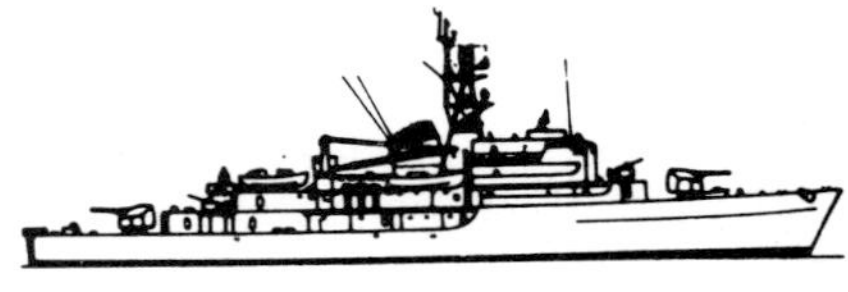

RHEIN *Class*

Depot Maintenance—*continued*

ODIN (ex-USS *Diomedes, ARB* 11, ex-*LST* 1119) A 512
WOTAN (ex-USS *Ulysses, ARB* 9, ex-*LST* 967) A 513

Displacement, tons	1 625 light; 3 600 full load; (revised official figures)
Dimensions, feet	316 wl; 328 oa × 50 × 11
Guns	4—20 mm AA
Main engines	2 GM diesels; 2 shafts; 1 800 bhp = 11·6 knots
Oil fuel (tons)	600
Range, miles	15 000 at 9 knots

WOTAN 1970

Repair Ships. Transferred under MAP in June 1961. *Odin* commissioned in Jan 1966 and *Wotan* on 2 Dec 1965.

DISPOSALS OF MINELAYERS (ex-LANDING SHIPS)
The two former United States landing Ships (similar to the above repair ships) converted into minelayers, *Bochum* (ex-USS *Rice County, LST* 1089) N 120 (ex-A 1404) and *Bottrop* (ex-USS *Saline County,* LST 1101) N 121 (ex-A 1504) were transferred to Turkey in November 1972. The third ship of this type, *Bamberg* (ex-USS *Greer County*), LST 799 N 122 (ex-A 1403) was scrapped in 1968.

WIELAND Y 804 **MEMMERT** Y 805

The two small repair ships, *Wieland* Y 804, 130 tons, rated as a *Schwimmwerkstattschiff* or floating workshop, and *Memmert* Y 805 (ex-USN 106, ex-*India*, ex-BP 34), 165 tons, rated as a *Torpedoklarmachschiff* or torpedo repair ship, salvage vessel with a derrick, were officially stated in 1971 to be still in service and on the Navy List.

LOGISTIC SUPPORT SHIPS

2 MINE CARRIER TYPE

SACHSENWALD A 1437 **STEIGERWALD** A 1438

Displacement, tons	3 850 full load
Dimensions, feet	363·5 × 45·6 × 11·2
Guns	4—40 mm AA (two twin mountings)
Main engines	2 diesels; 2 shafts; 5 600 hp = 17 knots (revised official figure)
Radius, miles	3 500 nautical
Complement	65

Built by Blohm & Voss, Hamburg as mine transports. Laid down on 1 Aug 1966 and 9 May 1966. Launched on 10 Dec 1966 and 10 Mar 1967. Both commissioned on 20 Aug 1969. Rated as *Minentransporter*. Have mine ports in the stern and can be used as minelayers.

CANCELLATIONS. The project for *Torpedotransporter*, designed as a supply ship and transport for torpedoes, etc. was abandoned in 1968. The project for three *Grosse Versorger*, or heavy maintenance, support and provision ships, was abandoned in 1970.

SACHSENWALD 1970

STEIGERWALD 1971, *Stefan Terzibaschitsch*

2 "WESTERWALD" CLASS

ODENWALD A 1436 **WESTERWALD** A 1435

Displacement, tons	3 460
Dimensions, feet	347·8 × 46 × 12·2
Guns	4—40 mm AA
Main engines	Diesels; 5 600 bhp = 17 knots
Complement	60

Ammunition transports built by Lübecker Masch in 1966-67. *Odenwald* was launched on 5 May 1966 and commissioned on 23 Mar 1967 and *Westerwald* was launched on 25 Feb 1966 and commissioned on 1 Feb 1967. Rated as *Munitionstransporter*.

ODENWALD 1971

WESTERWALD 1972

8 "LÜNEBURG" CLASS

COBURG	A 1412	**LÜNEBURG**	A 1411	**OFFENBURG**	A 1417
FREIBURG	A 1413	**MEERSBURG**	A 1418	**SAARBURG**	A 1415
GLÜCKSBURG	A 1414	**NIENBURG**	A 1416		

Displacement, tons	3 254
Dimensions, feet	341·2 × 43·3 × 13·8
Guns	4—40 mm AA
Main engines	2 Maybach diesels; 2 shafts; 5 600 bhp = 17 knots
Complement	103

Lüneberg, Coburg, Glücksburg, Meersburg and *Nienburg* were built by Flensburger Schiffbau and Vulkan, Bremen, others by Blohm & Voss, Hamburg. Commissioned on 9 July, 27 May, 9 July, 9 July, 25 June, 1 Aug, 27 May and 30 July, respectively, 1968.

OFFENBURG 1972, *Wright & Logan*

Logistic Support Ships—*continued*

NIENBURG *1971*

SAARBURG *1970*

1 "ANGELN" CLASS

DITHMARSCHEN (ex-*Hébé*) A 1409

Measurement, tons 2 101 gross
Dimensions, feet, 296·9 × 43·6 × 20·3
Main engines Pielstick diesels; 1 shaft; 3 000 bhp = 14 knots
Complement 57

Built by Ateliers et Chantiers de Bretagne, Nantes. Purchased from shipowners S. N. Caënnaise, Caen. Launched on 7 May 1955 and commissioned on 19 Dec 1959. Rated as *Materialtransporter*. Sister ship *Angeln* (ex-*Borée*) A 1408 was decommissioned in 1971 and officially deleted from the list in Feb 1972. Handed over to Turkey 22 March 1972.

DITHMARSCHEN *1972, Wright & Logan*

SCHWARZWALD (ex-*Amalthee*) A 1400

Measurement, tons 1 667 gross (revised official figure)
Dimensions, feet 263·1 × 39 × 15·1
Guns 4—40 mm AA Bofors
Main engines Sulzer diesel; 3 000 bhp = 15 knots (official figure)

Built by Ch. Dubigeon, Nantes. Launched on 31 Jan 1956. Purchased from the Soc Navale Caënnaise in Feb 1960. Commissioned as an ammunition transport.

SCHWARZWALD *1971*

DISPOSALS

Three supply ships were stricken from the Navy List: *Pfälzerland* (ex-*Lucetta*) Y 831 on 15 Apr 1969; *Siegerland* (ex-*Leuchtenburg 3*) Y 832 on 31 March 1969; and *Sauerland* (ex-*Rolandseck*) Y 830 on 14 May 1969.

OILERS

AMMERSEE A 1425 **WALCHENSEE** A 1424
TEGERNSEE A 1426 **WESTENSEE** A 1427

Displacement, tons 2 000 (revised official figure)
Dimensions, feet 233 × 36·7 × 13·5
Main engines Diesels; 2 shafts; 1 400 bhp = 12·6 knots

Built by Lindenau, Friedrichsort. Launched on 22 Sep 1966, 22 Oct 1966, 10 July 1965 and 25 Feb 1966 and commissioned on 2 Mar 1967, 23 Mar 1967, 29 June 1966 and 6 Oct 1967 respectively.
A photograph of *Tegernsee* appears in the 1968-69 to 1970-71 editions.

WESTENSEE *1971*

EIFEL (ex-*Friedrich Jung*) A 1429

Displacement, tons 2 279 light; 4 700 full load
Measurement, tons 3 444 gross, 4 720 deadweight
Dimensions, feet 334 × 47·2 × 23·3
Main engines 3 360 hp = 14 knots

Built by Norder-Werft, Hamburg. Launched on 29 Mar 1958. Purchased in 1963 for service as an oiler in the Bundesmarine. Commissioned on 27 May 1963.

EIFEL *1970*

HARZ (ex-*Claere Jung*) A 1428

Displacement, tons 1 308 light; 3 696 full load
Measurement, tons 2 594 gross; 3 755 deadweight
Dimensions, feet 303·2 × 43·5 × 21·7
Main engines 2 520 hp = 13 knots

Built in 1953 by Norder-Werft, Hamburg. Purchased in 1963 for service as an oiler in the Bundesmarine. Commissioned on 27 May 1963.

HARZ *1970*

FRANKENLAND (ex-*Münsterland*, ex-*Powell*) A 1439 (ex-Y 827)

Displacement, tons 16 310
Measurement, tons 11 700 gross
Dimensions, feet 521·8 × 70·2 × 37·5
Main engines Diesels; 5 800 bhp = 13·5 knots

Built by Lithgows, Glasgow. Launched in 1950. Commissioned on 29 Apr 1959.

FRANKENLAND *1972*

Oilers—*continued*

BODENSEE (ex-*Unkas*) A 1406 (ex-A 54) **WITTENSEE** (ex-*Sioux*) A 1407

Displacement, tons	1 200
Measurement, tons	1 230 deadweight: 980 gross
Dimensions, feet	208·3 × 32·5 × 15
Main engines	Diesels; 1 050—1 250 bhp = 12 knots

Built by P. Lindenau, Kiel-Friedrichsort. Launched on 19 Nov 1955 and on 23 Sep 1958, respectively. Commissioned on 26 Mar 1959. These ships are nearly identical. A photograph of *Bodensee* appears in the 1968-69 to 1971-72 editions.

WITTENSEE *1972*

BORKUM (ex-USN 105, ex- *Borkum*) Y 824

Displacement, tons	450
Measurement, tons	265 gross
Dimensions, feet	124·7 × 26·5 × 12
Main engines	Diesels; Speed = 6 knots

Built by Flender Lübeck. Launched in 1939. Former German motor tanker.

EUTIN (ex-*Ramsöy*) Y 825

Displacement, tons	410
Main engines	Speed = 6 knots

Built by Menzer, Geesthact. Launched in 1943. Commissioned on 1 July 1956

EMSLAND (ex-*Antonio Zotti*) A 1440 (ex-Y 828)
MÜNSTERLAND (ex-*Angela Germona*) A 1441 (ex-Y 829)

Measurement, tons	6 200 gross (*Emsland*); 6 191 (*Münsterland*)
Dimensions, feet	461 × 54·2 × 25·8
Main engines	Diesel; CRDA; 4 800 bhp (*Emsland*); Fiat 5 500 bhp (*Münsterland*) = 13 knots

Built by CRDA Monfalcone, and Ansaldo, Genoa, respectively. Both launched in 1943. Completed in 1947 and 1946, respectively. Purchased in 1960 from Italian owners. Converted in 1960-61 by Schliekerwerft, Hamburg, and Howaldtswerke, Hamburg, respectively. Commissioned 7 Nov 1961 and 16 Oct 1961. Civilian crew.

EMSLAND *1970*

MÜNSTERLAND *1972*

FW 1 **FW 2** **FW 3** **FW 4** **FW 5** **FW 6**

Displacement, tons	590 (revised official figure)
Dimensions, feet	144·4 × 25·6 × 8·2
Main engines	MWM diesel, 230 bhp = 9 knots

Built by Germania in 1963-64. Actually employed as Frischwasserboote.
The oiler *Jeverland* (ex-*Ammerland*. ex-*Kongsdal*) Y 826 was sold in Dec 1968 and broken up at Santander, Spain early in 1969.

FW 2 *1970*

TRAINING SHIPS

1 DEUTSCHLAND CLASS

Name	*No.*	*Builders*	*Laid down*	*Launched*	*Completed*
DEUTSCHLAND	A 59	Nobiskrug, Rendsburg	1959	5 Nov 1960	25 May 1963

Displacement, tons	4 880 normal; 5 500 full load
Length, feet (*metres*)	452·8 (*138·0*) pp; 475·8 (*145·0*) oa
Beam, feet (*metres*)	52·5 (*16·0*)
Draught, feet (*metres*)	15·7 (*4·8*)
A/S weapons	2 Bofors 4-barrel rocket launchers
Guns, dual purpose	4—3·9 in (*100 mm*) single
Guns, AA	6—40 mm; 2 twin and 2 single
Torpedo tubes	4 for A/S; 2 for surface
Boilers	2 Wahodag; 768 psi (*54km/cm²*); 870°F (*465*°C)
Main engines	6 680 bhp diesels (2 Daimler-Benz and 2 Maybach); 2 shafts 8 000 shp double reduction MAN geared turbines; 1 shaft
Speed, knots	22 max (3 shafts); 17 (2 shafts) 14 economical (1 shaft)
Range, miles	1 700 at 17 knots
Oil fuel, tons	230 furnace; 410 diesel
Complement	554 (33 officers, 271 men, 250 cadets)

GENERAL

First West German naval ship to exceed the post-war limit of 3 000 tons. Designed with armament and machinery of different types for training purposes. The name originally planned for this ship was *Berlin*. Ordered in 1956. Carried out her first machinery sea trials on 15 Jan 1963.

DEUTSCHLAND *1970, Skyfotos*

Training Ships—*continued*

RADAR. All by Hollandse. Search: HSA LW 02/3. Tactical: HSA DA 02. One nav/surface warning radar. Fire Control: HSA 2 M45 100 mm and 40 mm fire control. HSA fire control for Bofors A/S launcher, torpedoes and DC.

DEUTSCHLAND

GORCH FOCK A 60

Displacement, tons	1 760 standard; 1 870 full load
Dimensions, feet	229·7 wl; 257 oa × 39·2 × 15·8
Main engines	Auxiliary MAN diesel; 800 bhp = 11 knots
Sail area, sq ft	21 141 (speed of up to 15 knots under sail)
Radius, miles	1 990
Complement	206 (10 officers, 56 ratings, 140 cadets)

Sail training ship of the improved "Horst Wessel" type. Barque rig. Launched by Blohm & Voss, Hamburg, on 23 Aug 1958 and commissioned on 17 Dec 1958. A photograph appears in the 1968-69 to 1970-71 editions.

NORDWIND Y 834

Displacement, tons	100
Dimensions, feet	78·8 × 22 × 9
Main engines	Diesel; 150 bhp = 8 knots. (Sail area 2 037·5 sq ft)

Ketch, ex-Kreigsfischkutter (KFK). Photograph in the 1954-55 edition. There are over 70 other sailing vessels of various types serving for sail training and recreational purposes. *Achat, Alarich, Amsel, Argonaut, Borasco, Brigant, Dankwart, Diamont Dietrich, Drossel, Dompfaff, Fafnir, Fink, Flibustier, Freibeuter, Gernot, Geiserich, Geuse, Giselher, Gödicke, Gunnar, Gunter, Hadubrand, Hagen, Hartnaut Hildebrand, Horand, Hunding, Jaspis, Kaper, Klipper, Korsar, Kuchkuch, Lerche, Likendeeler, Magellan, Michel, Mime, Meise, Mistral, Monsun, Nachtigall, Ortwin, Ostwind, Pampero, Pirol, Ruediger, Samum, Saphir, Schirocco, Seeteufel, Siegfried, Siegmund, Siegura Smaragd, Star, Stieglitz, Störtebecker, Taifun, Teja, Topas, Tornadon, Totila, Vitalienbrüder, Volker, Walter, Wate, Westwind, Wiking, Wittigo, Zeisig.*

TENDERS

EIDER (ex-*Catherine*, ex-*Dochet*) Y 1663 (ex-A 50)

Displacement, tons	480 standard; 750 full load
Dimensions, feet	164·0 pp; 177·2 oa × 27·5 × 14·0
Guns	1—40 mm AA; 1—20 mm AA
Main engines	Triple expansion; 1 shaft; 750 ihp = 12 knots
Oil fuel, tons	130

Former British "Isles" type minesweeping trawler. Built in Canada by Davie & Sons, Lauzon, in 1942. Employed as a mine clearance training vessel. She has been civilian manned since 1 Jan 1968. Her near sister ship *Trave* (ex-*Caroline*, ex-*Flint*) A 51 was decommissioned for good in Nov 1971.

EIDER 1972

OSTE (ex-USN 101, *Puddefjord*) A 52

Measurement, tons	567 gross
Dimensions, feet	160 × 29·7 × 17
Guns	2—20 mm AA
Main engines	2 Sulzer diesels; 1 shaft; 1 400 bhp = 14 knots

Built in 1943 at Akers Mekaniske Vaerkstad, Oslo. Taken over from the US Navy. Converted into a radar research and testing vessel in 1968.

OSTE (as radar testing ship) *1970, Stefan Terzibaschitsch*

EMS (ex-USN 104, ex-*Harle*) Y 1662 (ex-A 53)

Measurement, tons	660 gross
Dimensions, feet	185·7 oa × 29 × 15·5
Guns	4—20 mm
Main engines	Sulzer diesels; 1 000 bhp = 12 knots

Built in 1941 by Kremer & Sohn, Elmshorn. Officially stated in 1971 to be still in service with the Navy.

EMS 1972

WALTHER VON LEDEBUR Y 841

Displacement, tons	725
Dimensions, feet	219·8 × 34·8 × 8·9
Main engines	Maybach diesels; 2 shafts; 5 000 bhp = 19 knots

Wooden hulled vessel. Built by Burmester, Bremen-Berg. Launched on 30 June 1966. The largest of several civilian manned experimental vessels including *Friedrich Voge* (ex-*Kurefjord*) Y 888, former tug, 179 tons gross; *Karl Kolls* (ex-*Salmo*, ex-*Gerda 1*, ex-*Margarethe*, ex-*Nora*) Y 887, former small freighter, 189 tons gross; *Otto Meycke* Y 882, former trawler; *Wilhelm Pullwer* Y 838; and *Wilhelm Laudahn* Y 839 (ex-UW 9, ex-*Seeschwalbe* P 6057, ex-S 3) serving different agencies.

WALTHER VON LEDEBUR 1971

4 Ex-COASTAL MINESWEEPERS

ADOLF BESTELMEYER (ex-*BYMS* 2213) **HERMAN VON HELMOLTZ**
H. C. OERSTED (ex-*Vinstra*, ex-*NYMS* 247) **RUDOLF DIESEL** (ex-*BYMS* 2279

Displacement, tons	270 standard; 350 full load
Dimensions, feet	136 × 24·5 × 8
Main engines	2 diesels; 2 shafts; 1 000 bhp = 15 knots;

Of US YMS type. Built in 1943. *Adolf Bestelmeyer*, Y 881, and *Rudolph Diesel* Y 889, are used for gunnery purposes. *H. C. Oersted*, Y 877, was acquired from the Royal Norwegian Navy. *Herman von Helmholtz*, Y 878, commissioned on 18 Dec 1962, is used as a degaussing ship. A photograph of *H. C. Oersted* appears in the 1967-68 edition, and of *Adolf Bestelmeyer* in the 1968-69 to 1970-71 editions.

RUDOLF DIESEL 1971

SURVEYING VESSELS include *Planet* (1967), military research ship temporarily commissioned as a survey ship, Y 843, in the Bundesmarine; and *Meteor* (1964). *Süderoog, Gauss, Hooge, Ruden, Atair, Rungholt, Alkor* and *Wega*, administered by the Federal Ministry of Transport.

TRIALS VESSELS include *Viktoria* (ex-*Herzog Friederich*) Y 808; TF 101 (Y 883), TF 102 (Y 884), TF 103 (Y 885), TF 104 (Y886) and TF 105 (Y 835); TF 25 (Y 806) and TF 26 (Y 807); and EF 1 (ex-*Süderoog*) Y 890, but these were all officially deleted from the strength in 1968 as none of them are on the Navy List, all being manned by civilians as experimental vessels for various agencies, as are the four YMS type vessels above which are retained in this edition, since as former minesweepers they are still naval defence potential.

FISHERY PROTECTION VESSELS include *Poseidon, Anton Dohrn, Meerkatze, Frithjof Walther Herwig* and *Uthorn*, administered by the Federal Ministry for Agriculture and Fisheries.

TANK CLEANING VESSELS include *Forde* and *Jade* of 1 100 tons completed in late 1967.

RESCUE LAUNCHES

4 "KW" TYPE

FL 5 Y 857 (ex-W 11)
FL 6 Y 858 (ex-W 12)
FL 7 Y 859 (ex-W 13)
FL 8 Y 860 (ex-W 14)

Displacement, tons	45 standard; 60 full load
Dimensions, feet	83·0 pp; 93·5 oa × 15·5 × 4·0
Main engines	2 Mercedes-Benz diesels; 2 000 bhp = 25 knots
Complement	14

FL 1 (ex-*FL* 51, ex-*MSM* 2) was disposed of in 1962. *FL 4* (ex-*Falke*, ex-*FL* 4), a smaller type of aircraft rescue boat, was also disposed of in 1962. *FL 2* (ex-*FL* 52, ex-*MSM* 3) and *FL 3* (ex-*FL* 50, ex-*MSM* 1), ex-German Air Force sea rescue launches, were disposed of on 2 Aug and 1 Aug 1963 respectively.

Built in 1951-52. All are similar to US Coast Guard 93-ft type. Formerly rated as harbour defence vessels, but re-rated as Flugsicherungsboote (employed as air/sea rescue launches) in 1959. Guns removed. Formerly H 11 (ex-P 1) H 12 (ex-P 2), H 13 (ex-P 3) and H 14 (ex- P4) respectively. A photograph of FL 6 appears in the 1968-69 to 1971-72 editions.

FL 6 1968

FL 9 Y 861 (ex-D 2763) **FL 10** Y 862 (ex-D 2765) **FL 11** Y 963 (ex-D 2766)

Displacement, tons	70
Dimensions, feet	95·2 × 16·5 × 4·2
Main Engines	Maybach diesels; 2 shafts; 3 200 bhp = 30 knots
Radius, miles	600 at 20 knots

Built by Kröger, Rendsburg. Former Flugsicherungsboote of the RAF station List/Sylt Commissioned on 1 Sep 1961.

FL 10 1972

TUGS

BALTRUM **JUIST** **LANGEOOG** **NORDERNEY** **SPIEKEROOG** **WANGEROOGE**

Displacement, tons	854 standard; 1 024 full load
Dimensions, feet	170·6 × 39·4 × 12·8
Guns	1—40 mm AA
Main engines	Diesel-electric; 2 shafts; 2 400 hp = 13·6 knots
Complement	35

Built by Schichau, Bremerhaven. *Wangerooge*, prototype, salvage tug, was launched on 4 July 1966. *Wangerooge* commissioned on 9 Apr 1968, *Langeoog* and *Spiekeroog* on 14 Aug 1968, *Baltrum* on 8 Oct 1968.

FEHMARN A 1458 **HELGOLAND** A 1457

Displacement, tons	1 310 standard; 1 619 full load
Dimensions, feet	223·1 × 41·7 × 14·4
Guns	1—40 mm AA
Main engines	Diesel-electric; 4 MWM diesels; 2 shafts; 3 800 hp = 16·6 knots

Bergungsschlepper or salvage tugs. Built by Unterweser, Bremerhaven. Launched on 25 Nov 1965 and 8 Apr 1965 and commissioned on 1 Feb 1967 and 8 Mar 1966. A photograph of *Fehmarn* appears in the 1968-69 to 1971-72 editions.

AMRUM Y 822 **FÖHR** Y 821 **NEUWERK** Y 823 **SYLT** Y 820

Displacement, tons	262 standard
Dimensions, feet	100·7 oa × 25·2
Main engines	1 Deutz diesel 1 100 bhp = 12 knots

Built by Fr. Schichau, Bremerhaven. Launched in 1961. All completed in 1962-63.

Tugs—*continued*

HELGOLAND 1972

DISPOSALS. *Passat* (ex-USN 103, ex-*Passat*) Y 800 was scrapped in 1968. *Pellworm* (ex-USN 102, ex-*Pellworm*) Y 801 was stricken from the active list in 1968. *Plön* (ex-*Bombay*, ex-*Bodden*) Y 802 was stricken from the list in 1970.

HARBOUR TYPE. There are also nine small harbour tugs all completed in 1958-60;—*Blauort* Y 803, *Knechtsand* Y 814, *Langeness* Y 819, *Lütje Horn* Y 812, *Mellum* Y 813, *Nordstrand* Y 817, *Scharhörn* Y 815 *Trischen* Y 818 and *Vogelsand* Y 816 and three completed in 1970 by Schichau, Bremerhaven of 122 tons and 800 hp;- *Neuende, Eller Bek, Heppens.*

ICEBREAKERS

HANSE

Displacement, tons	3 700
Dimensions, feet	243·2 × 57 × 20
Main engines	Diesel-electric; 4 shafts; 7 500 bhp = 16 knots

Built by Wärtsilä Oy, Helsinki, Finland. Laid down on 12 Jan 1965. Launched on 17 Oct 1966. Completed on 25 Nov 1966. Commissioned on 13 Dec 1966. Although owned by West Germany she sails under the Finnish flag, manned by a Finnish crew. Only when the winter is so severe that icebreakers are needed in the southern Baltic will she be transferred under the German flag and command. She is of improved "Karhu" class. She does not belong to the Bundesmarine.

EISBAR A 1402 **EISVOGEL** A 1401

Displacement, tons	560 standard
Dimensions, feet	125·3 oa × 31·2 × 7·9 (15·1 max)
Guns	Can carry 1—40 mm AA Bofors
Main Engines	2 Maybach diesels; 2 shafts; 2 400 bhp = 13 knots

Built by J. G. Hitzler, Lauenburg. Launched on 9 June and 28 Apr 1960, and commissioned on 1 Nov and 11 Mar 1961, respectively. Icebreakers and tugs.

EISVOGEL 1970

SURVEY SHIPS

METEOR (Research Ship) 3 085 tons, launched 1964, Complement 55
KOMET (Survey and Research) 1 595 tons, launched 1969, Complement 42
GAUSS (Survey and Research) 1 074 tons, launched 1949, Complement 40
SÜDEROOG (Survey Ship) 211 tons, launched 1956, Complement 16
ATAIR (Survey and Wrecks) 148 tons, launched 1962, Complement 13
WEGA (Survey and Wrecks) 148 tons, launched 1962, Complement 12

GERMANY (Democratic Republic)

Administration

Commander-in-Chief, Volksmarine:
Vice Admiral Willi Ehm

Chief of Naval Staff
Rear Admiral Gustav Hesse

Strength of the Fleet

2	Frigates	26	Corvettes
22	Landing craft	12	Missile Boats
63	Torpedo Boats	12	Fleet Minesweepers
41	Coastal Minesweepers	10	Inshore Minesweepers
12	Patrol Craft (GBK)	10	Survey Vessels
4	Oilers	12	Auxiliaries
12	Tugs		

Personnel

1973: 1 700 officers and 15 200 men (including GBK)

Mercantile Marine

Lloyds Register of Shipping
436 vessels of 1 198 365 tons gross

GRENZBRIGADE KUSTE (GBK)

The seaborne branch of the Frontier Guards, this is a force of about 3 000 men. Their various craft are difficult to disentangle from those of the Navy, many being taken from that list. Where possible mention of this is made in the notes.

FRIGATES

2 Ex-SOVIET "RIGA" TYPE

ERNEST THÄLMANN 141 **KARL MARX** 142

Displacement, tons	1 200 standard; 1 600 full load
Dimensions, feet	298·8 × 33·7 × 11
Guns	3—3·9 in single; 4—37 mm AA paired vertically
Tubes	3—21 in
A/S weapons	4 depth charge projectors; 2 rocket launchers
Main engines	Geared turbines; 2 shafts; 25 000 shp = 28 knots
Oil fuel (tons)	300
Range, miles	2 500 at 15 knots
Complement	150

Designed to carry 50 mines. Fitted with Haymarket search radar. Sister ships *Friedrich Engels* 124 and *Karl Liebnecht* 123 have been scrapped, it was stated in 1971. A fifth ship of this type was burnt out at the end of 1959 and became a total wreck.

KARL MARX *1965, Werner Kähling*

CORVETTES

12 USSR "SO-I" TYPE

ADLER, BUSSARD, FALKE, HABICHT, HAI, KORMORAN, KRANICH, MÖWE, REIHER, SCHWALBE, SPERBER, WEIHE

Displacement, tons	215 standard; 250 full load
Dimensions, feet	138 × 20 × 9·2 max
Guns	4—25 mm AA (2 twin mounts)
A/S weapons	4 ahead throwing launchers; 2 DCT
Main engines	3 diesels; 6 000 bhp = 29 knots
Complement	30

Submarine chasers. Fitted with mine rails. Pennant numbers run in a G 40 and G 60 series. These vessels now belong to the coast guard. Some may have been deleted.

G22 *1970, Niels Gartig*

14 "HAI" CLASS

BAD DOBEREN, GREVESMÜHLEN, GADEBUSCH, LÜDZ, LUDWIGSLUST, PARCHIM, PERLEBERG, RIBNITZ-DAMGARTEN, STERNBERG, TETEROW, WISMAR

Displacement, tons	300 standard; 370 full load
Dimensions, feet	174 pp; 187 oa × 19 × 10
Guns	4—25 or 37 mm (2 twin)
A/S weapons	2—4 barrelled rocket launchers
Main engines	2 gas turbines; diesels; 8 000 bhp = 25 knots
Complement	45

Submarine chasers built at Peenewerft, Wolgast. The prototype vessel completed construction in 1963. All were in service by the end of 1969, and the programme is now completed. Pennant numbers are in the 400 series.

HAI No. 411 *1971, S. Breyer*

AMPHIBIOUS CRAFT

4 "KROKODIL" CLASS (LSM)

Displacement, tons	about 800
Length, feet	226·9
Guns	2—57 mm
Speed, knots	15+

A new class of amphibious ships developed by Peenewerft for Warsaw Pact countries Have ramps fore and aft.

6 "ROBBE" CLASS

EBERSWALDE, ELSENHÜTTENSTADT, GRIMMEN, HOYERSWERDA, LÜBBEN, SCHWEDT

Displacement, tons	600 standard; 800 full load
Dimensions, feet	196·8 × 32·8 × 6·6
Guns	2—57 mm AA (1 twin); 4—25 mm AA (2 twin)
Main engines	Diesels = 12 knots

Amphibious vessels of a type midway between the landing ship and landing craft categories. Launched in 1962-64.

"ROBBE CLASS" *1971, S. Breyer*

Amphibious Craft—*continued*

12 "LABO" CLASS

GERHARD PRENZLER **HEINZ WILKOWSKI** **ROLF PETERS**

Displacement, tons	150 standard; 200 full load
Dimensions, feet	131·2 × 27·9 × 5·9
Guns	4—25 mm AA (2 twin)
Main engines	Diesels = 10 knots

Landing craft of a lighter type. Built by Peenewerft, Wolgast. Launched in 1961-63.

"LABO" Class 1969, *S. Breyer*

LIGHT FORCES

12 SOVIET "OSA" CLASS (MISSILE BOATS)

ALBERT GAST **ALBIN KÖBIS** **AUGUST LÜTTGENS** **FRITZ GAST** **KARL MESEBERG** **MAX REICHPIETSCH** **PAUL EISENSCHNEIDER** **PAUL SCHULZ** **PAUL WIECZOREK** **RICHARD SORGE** **RUDOLF EGELHUFER** **WALTER KRÄMER**

Displacement, tons	165 standard; 200 full load
Dimensions, feet	128·7 × 25·1 × 5·9
Missile launchers	4 mountings in 2 pairs abreast aft for "Styx"; SSN-2A
Guns	4—30 mm (2 twin, 1 forward, 1 aft)
Main engines	3 diesels; 13 000 hp = 32 knots

Most valuable and powerful boats for coastal operations. Pennant numbers in the 700 series.

OSA Type 1965, *Reinecke*

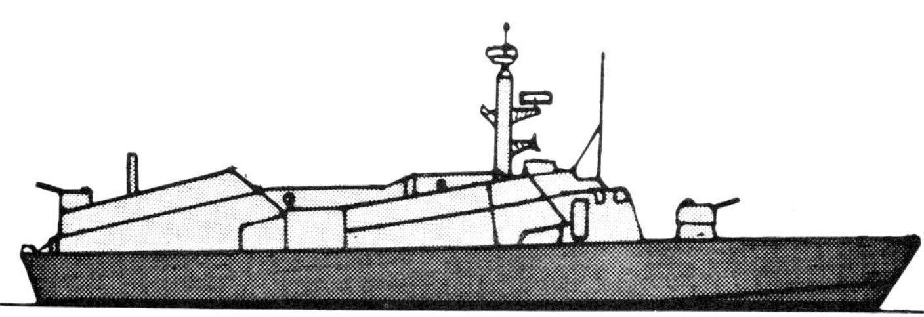

OSA *Class*

15 SOVIET "SHERSHEN" CLASS (TORPEDO BOATS)

ARTHUR BECKER **EDGAR ANDRÉ**

Displacement, tons	150 standard; 160 full load
Dimensions, feet	115·5 × 23·1 × 5
Guns	4—30 mm (2 twin)
Tubes	4—21 in (single)
Main engines	Diesels; 13 000 bhp; 3 shafts = 38 knots
Complement	16

Acquired from the USSR. Four were delivered in 1968-69, the first instalment of a flotilla. They do not differ from the Soviet boats of the class. Pennant numbers 811-5, 831-5, 851-5

Light Forces—*continued*

SHERSHEN Class 1970, *Niels Gartig*

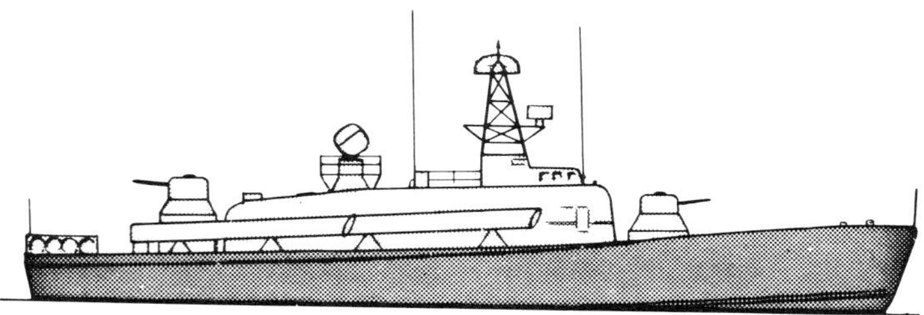

SHERSHEN *Class*

40 "ILTIS" CLASS (TORPEDO BOATS)

Displacement, tons	20
Dimensions, feet	55·8 × 10·5 × 2·5
Tubes	2—21 in (torpedos fired over stern). Some have three tubes
Main engines	Diesels; 3 000 bhp = 50 knots

Leichte Torpedoschnellboote or light torpedo fast boats of the PT type. No anti-aircraft guns. Numbered in a 900 series. Several different types of this class exist, varying in hull material and silhouette. eg. Type 1 are flush-decked and Type 2 have a raised forecastle. With the torpedo tubes removed these boats are used to land frogmen and raiding parties. Displacement and dimensions given are for Type 2. Others vary slightly.

No. 912 1971, *S. Breyer*

8 Ex-SOVIET "P6" CLASS (TORPEDO BOATS)

Displacement, tons	66 standard; 75 full load
Dimensions, feet	84·2 × 20 × 6 max
Guns	4—25 mm (2 twin mountings)
Tubes	2—21 in
Main engines	4 diesels; 4 800 bhp = 45 knots max
Complement	25

Interchangable torpedo/gunboats acquired in 1957-60 from the USSR. Wooden hull. Pennant numbers now run in an 800 series. Most of this originally more numerous class has been scrapped or converted. Four of these boats have had their tubes removed and been transferred to the GBK with pennant Nos G81-84.

P 6 Class No. 864 1970, *Niels Gartig*

MINE WARFARE FORCES

10 "KRAKE" CLASS (FLEET MINESWEEPERS)

BERLIN **ERFURT** **DRESDEN** **GERA** **HALLE** **KARL-MARX-STADT** **LIEPZIG** **MAGDEBURG** **POTSDAM** **ROSTOCK**

Displacement, tons	650 standard
Dimensions, feet	229·7 × 26·5 × 12·2
Guns	1—3·4 in; 10—25 mm AA paired vertically
A/S weapons	4 DCT
Main engines	Diesels; 2 shafts; 3 400 bhp = 18 knots
Complement	90

Built in 1956-58 at Peenewerft, Wolgast. Four completed in 1958, were originally for Poland. Appearance is different compared with the first type, the squat wide funnel being close to the bridge with lattice mast and radar. Fitted for minelaying. On 1 Mar 1961 they were given the names of the capitals of districts etc, of East Germany. Pennant numbers 221 to 224 and 241 to 243 and S11-13.

"Krake" Class No. 222 *1970, Niels Gartig*

2 "HABICHT" II CLASS

211 **212**

Displacement, tons	550 standard
Dimensions, feet	213 oa × 26·5 × 11·8
Guns	1—3·4 in; 8—25 mm AA paired vertically
A/S weapons	4 DCT
Main engines	2 diesels; 2 shafts; 2 800 bhp = 17 knots
Complement	80

The design was a modification of that of the "Habitch 1" class, but lengthened by 20 feet amidships. Built at Wolgast Peenyard. Both completed in 1955-56. All welded. Fitted for minelaying. Four vessels of this class were deleted from the list in 1970. It is doubtful whether any remain on the active list.

"HABICHT 1" CLASS

The six fleet minesweepers of the "Habicht 1' class Ncs. 213, 214, 215 and 216, employed as patrol escort ships and minesweepers, and R 11 and R 21, converted into rescue ships, were deleted from the list in 1972 having been scrapped or discarded.

"Habicht II" Class *1969*

41 "KONDOR" I and II CLASS (CMS)

AHRENSHOOP **ANKLAM** **BERGEN** **BITTERFELD** **BUTZOW** **DEMMIN** **DESSAU** **GENTHIN** **GRAAL-MÜRITZ** **GREIFSWALD** **KLÜTZ** **KUHLUNGSBORN** **KYRITZ** **NEUSTRELITZ** **PASEWALK** **PREROW** **ROBEL** **ROSSLAU** **STRASSBURG** **TANGERHÜTTE** **TEMPLIN** **UCKERMUNDE** **VITTE** **WARNEMUNDE** **WEISSWASSER** **WOLGAST** **ZERBST** **ZINGST**

Displacement, tons	245 standard; 280 full load
Dimensions, feet	154·2 × 23·0 × 6·6
Guns	2—25 mm or 2—30 mm
Main engines	Diesels; 2 shafts; 4 000 bhp = 24 knots

GENERAL

A new class of medium fast minesweepers and patrol vessels built at Peenewerft. Five units were operational in 1970 and 15 by the end of 1971. They replace the small minesweepers of the "Schwalbe" class. Type II has additional length and extra MG's. First appearing in 1971. Production continues.

PENNANT NUMBERS

These have been changed with some frequency. At present the following is as near as can be offered:

Type I. Prototype-V31. Active minesweepers 311-312 (total 25). Attached to GBK-G11-16. G21-26. Possible conversion for torpedo recovery-B73. Training ships-S24-26. Conversion to AGi's Meteor and Komet.

Type II (Total 16) Prototype-V32. Active minesweepers - 321-326 and 331-336 Training ships S21-23.

W 316 *1971*

10 "SCHWALBE II" CLASS (IMS)

Displacement, tons	100 standard
Dimensions, feet	105 oa × 18 × 3·5 max
Main engines	2 diesels; 3800 bhp = 12·5 knots

Small minesweepers of medium speed built in 1955-57 at VEB Yachtwerft, Berlin. The pennant numbers run in 300 series. Being phased out and replaced by "Kondor" class coastal minesweepers; see previous page. Six boats were deleted from the list in 1971 and ten in 1972. A number of units of this class are used as torpedo retrievers and buoy tenders. All this class is being paid off.

The minesweeping boats of the original "Schwalbe" class were deleted from the effective list in 1968.

SCHWALBE CLASS *1968*

2 PARTISAN CLASS

PARTISAN **PIONIER**

Displacement, tons	79
Main engines	Speed = 13 knots

Built in 1957. Coastal boats rated as *schulschiffe* or training vessels. The 20 boats of the "KS 1" class in the GBK were deleted from the list in 1971.

Mine Warfare Forces—*continued*

PIONIER 1969

12 NEW CONSTRUCTION PATROL CRAFT

A new class of some 60 tons is now under construction for the use of the GBK and police. Twelve now in service.

SURVEY VESSELS

HYDROGRAPH

Of 700 tons and 11 knots. Built in 1953.

JOHANN L. KRÜGER **HELMUT JUST**

Displacement, tons	475
Measurement, tons	260 gross
Dimensions, feet	128 × 24 × 11
Main engines	Diesel; 400 bhp = 10·5 knots

Also *Alfred Merz* and *Karl F. Gauss* (1952-55), 200 tons, 9·5 knots (seiner type); *Jordan* (1954), 135 tons, 10 knots (German KFK type); *Arkona, Darsser Ort* and *Stubbenkammer* (1956), 55 tons, 10 knots (cutter type); and *Flaggtief* (ex-*Stralsund*) 30 tons, 8 knots.

OILERS

1 BASKUNCHAK CLASS

USEDOM

Displacement, tons	2 500
Dimensions, feet	277 × 39 × 15
Speed, knots	13

USEDOM 1970, *Niels Gartig*

3 TYPE 600

HIDDENSEE **POEL** **RIEMS**

Displacement, tons	600 DWT
Dimensions, feet	195 oa × 29·5 × 12·5 max
Main engines	2 diesels; 2 800 bhp = 14 knots

Built at Peenewerft, Wolgast, in 1960-61. Crew 26. Speed in service 9 knots.

RIEMS 1971, *S. Breyer*

1 VILM TYPE

VILM

Displacement, tons	585
Dimensions, feet	118 × 24 × 8·9
Main engines	Speed = 9 knots

Built by Mathias-Thesen-W, Wismor in 1955 to 1957.

MISCELLANEOUS

RUGEN
Torpedo Trials Ship

1 KÜMO CLASS

RUDEN

Of 265 tons and capable af 11 knots. General tender.

1 KAMENKA CLASS

BUK

AGS of 500 tons built in 1950.

DORNBUSCH
Cable layer of 700 tons

LUMME

Small diving tender.

8 BUOY TENDERS

BREITLING, ESPERORT, GOLWITZ, RAMZOW

+ 4

Displacement, tons	158
Dimensions, feet	97 × 20·3 × 6·2
Main engines	1 diesel; 580 hp = 11·5 knots

WILHELM PIECK

Displacement, tons	200
Main engines	Diesel; 1 shaft; 106 bhp = 8 knots

Brigantine employed as a pre-naval school ship. Built in 1951. A photograph appears in the 1955-56 edition. Also yachts, *Ernst Thälmann*, 150 tons, *Jonny Scheer*, 120 tons, *Max Riechpietsch* and *Knechtsand*.

The old training ship *Albin Köbis* (ex-escort vessel *Ernst Thälmann*, ex-*Dorsch*, ex-Danish fishery protection ship *Hbidvjornen*) was deleted from the list in 1968.

The fishery protection vessels *Robert Koch*, *Professor Henking* (ex-*Neues Deutschland*) and *Dr Friedrich Wolf* were deleted from the Navy List in 1968.
The tenders H 41 and H 43, the netlayer H 42, and the experimental vessels *Karl Liebknecht*, *Rosa Luxemburg* and *Saturn* were also deleted in 1968.

Several GBK Training boats. Small craft, including *Ernst Schneller*.

NOTE
There are one 700 class seagoing tug and eleven harbour tugs.

GHANA

Administration

Commander of the Navy: Commodore Kelvin Dzang

Personnel

1973: 1 000 (100 officers, 900 ratings)

Mercantile Marine

Lloyd's Register of Shipping: 74 vessels of 166 183 gross tons

CORVETTES

KROMANTSE 1971

2 "KROMANTSE" CLASS

KROMANTSE F 17 **KETA** F 18

Displacement, tons	380 light; 440 standard; 500 full load
Dimensions, feet	162 wl; 177 oa × 28·5 × 13 (props)
Guns	1—4 in; 1—40 mm AA (see notes)
A/S weapons	1 Squid triple-barrelled depth charge mortar
Main engines	2 Bristol Siddeley Maybach diesels; 2 shafts; 390 rpm; 7 100 bhp = 20 knots (5 700 hp = 18 knots sea)
Oil fuel, tons	60
Range, miles	2 000 at 16 knots; 2 900 at 14 knots
Complement	54 (6 + 3 officers, 45 ratings)

Anti-submarine vessels of a novel type designed by Vosper Ltd, Portsmouth, a joint venture with Vickers-Armstrongs, Ltd, one ship being built by each company. Comprehensively fitted with sonar, air and surface warning radar. Vosper roll damping fins, and air conditioning throughout excepting machinery spaces. Generators 360 kW The electrical power supply is 440 volts, 60 cycles ac. The originally proposed twin 40 mm mounting was suppressed to save top weight. A very interesting patrol vessel design, an example of what can be achieved on a comparatively small platform to produce an inexpensive and quickly built anti-submarine vessel. *Kromantse* was launched by Vosper Ltd at the Camber Shipyard, Portsmouth, on 5 Sep 1963, and commissioned on 27 July 1964. *Keta* was launched at Newcastle on 18 Jan 1965, and commissioned on 18 May 1965.

RADAR. Search. Plessey AWS 1.

RESCINDMENT. The order to Yarrow & Co Ltd, Scotstoun, Glasgow for the construction of a frigate to have been called *The Black Star*, (the Ghana national flag emblem) was rescinded in 1966, but the ship was launched without ceremony or name on Clydeside on 29 Dec 1966 and completed in 1968 for sale. Commissioned in the Royal Navy as HMS *Mermaid*.

KROMANTSE *1969, Ghana Navy,*

COASTAL MINESWEEPERS

1 "TON" CLASS

EJURA (ex-*Aldington*) M 16

Displacement, tons	360 standard; 425 full load
Dimensions, feet	140 pp; 153 oa × 28·8 × 8·2
Guns	1—40 mm AA forward; 2—20 mm AA aft
Main engines	Deltic diesels; 2 shafts; 3 000 bhp = 15 knots max
Oil fuel (tons)	45
Range	2 300 at 13 knots
Complement	27

Former Royal Navy non-magnetic type vessel. Lent to Ghana by Britain in 1964.

EJURA *1971, Ghana Navy,*

INSHORE MINESWEEPERS

AFADZATO (ex-*Ottringham*) M 12 **YOGAGA** (ex-*Malham*) M 11

Displacement, tons	120 standard; 159 full load
Dimensions, feet	100 pp; 107·5 oa × 22 × 5·8
Guns	1—15 mm AA
Main engines	2 Paxman diesels; 1 100 = 14 knots
Oil fuel, tons	15
Range, miles	2 000 at 9 knots
Complement	22

Malham, commissioned on 2 Oct 1959, and *Ottringham* commissioned on 30 Oct 1959, sailed for Ghana on 31 Oct 1959, and were officially transferred from the Royal Navy to the Ghana Navy at Takoradi at the end of Nov 1959 and renamed after hills in Ghana. Now fitted with funnel.

YOGAGA *1966, Ghana Navy*

SEAWARD DEFENCE BOATS

2 "FORD" CLASS

ELMINA P 13 **KOMENDA** P 14

Displacement, tons	120 standard; 142 full load
Dimensions, feet	110 wl; 117·5 oa × 20 × 7 (screws)
Guns	1—40 mm, 60 cal Bofors AA
A/S weapons	Depth charge throwers
Main engines	2 Davey Paxman diesels; 2 shafts; 1 000 bhp = 18 knots (max).
Complement	19

KOMENDA *1969, Ghana Navy*

PATROL BOATS

3 USSR BUILT

P 20 **P 21** **P 23**

Displacement, tons	86 standard; 91 full load
Dimensions, feet	98 pp × 15 × 4·8
Guns, AA	2—14·5 mm (twin mounting)
Main engines	2 model M50-3 diesels; 2 shafts; 1 600 rpm. 1 200 bhp = 18 knots
Oil fuel, rons	9·25
Range, miles	460 at 17 knots
Complement	16 (2 officers, 14 ratings)

Built in the USSR. Completed in Aug 1963. Acquired in 1967. Sister boat *P 22* has been scrapped, it was officially stated in 1970.

P 23 *1969, Ghana Navy.*

MAINTENANCE REPAIR CRAFT

ASUANTSI (ex-*MRC* 1122)

Displacement, tons	657
Dimensions, feet	225 pp; 231·3 oa × 39 × 3·3 forward, 5 aft
Main engines	4 Paxman, 1 840 bhp = 9 knots cruising

Acquired from Britain in 1965 and arrived in Ghana waters in July 1965. Used as a base workshop at Tema Naval Base. Is kept operational, and does a fair amount of seatime in general training and exercise tasks.

ASUANTSI — *1966, Ghana Navy.*

GREECE

Administration

Commander-in-Chief, Hellenic Navy:
Vice-Admiral K. Margaritis

Deputy Commander-in-Chief:
Rear-Admiral T. Manolopoulos

Commander of the Fleet:
Rear Admiral P. Atapakis

Personnel

1973: 17 900 (1 900 officers and 16 000 ratings) (Conscript, 24 months or enlistment)

Strength of the Fleet

9 Destroyers
4 Frigates
5 Corvettes
6 Patrol Submarines
14 Landing Ships
8 LCU's
4 Missile Boats
12 Torpedo Boats
5 Patrol Vessels
21 Coastal Minesweepers
2 Coastal Minelayers
5 Survey Vessels
8 Oilers (6 small)
13 Miscellaneous

Disposals

Cruiser
1964 *Elli* (ex-*Eugenio di Savoia*)

Destroyers
1972 *Doxa, Niki* (Gleaves class)

Frigates
1959 *Aegaion, Kriti, Themistocles* (Hunt II)
1960 *Pindos, Miaoulis* (Hunt III)
1963 *Adrion, Astings* (Hunt III)

Submarine
1972 *Poseidon* (Balao class)

Diplomatic Representation

Naval Attaché in London:
Captain J. Papageorgiou

Naval Attaché in Washington:
Captain S. Kapsalis

Naval Attaché in Cairo:
Captain G. Roussias

Naval Attaché in Bonn:
Captain A. Damiralis

Mercantile Marine

Lloyd's Register of Shipping:
2 241 vessels of 15 328 860 tons gross

DESTROYERS

2 Ex-US "GEARING" CLASS

KANARIS (ex-USS *Stickell* DD 888)

THEMISTOCLES D 210 (ex-USS *Frank Knox*, DDR/DD 742)

Displacement, tons	2,425 standard; 3 500 full load
Length, feet (*metres*)	390·5 (*119 0*) oa
Beam, feet (*metres*)	40·9 (*12·4*)
Draught, feet (*metres*)	19·0 (*5·8*)
Guns	6—5 in (*127 mm*) 38 cal. dp
A/S weapons	2 triple torpedo launchers, Mk 32
Torpedo tubes	2 fixed, Mk 25
Main engines	2 Westinghouse geared turbines; 2 shafts; 60 000 shp
Boilers	4 Babcock & Wilcox
Speed, knots	34
Complement	269 (16 officers, 253 men)
Range, miles	4 800 at 15 knots
Complement	269 (16 officers, 253 men)

THEMISTOCLES — *1972, Hellenic Navy.*

Former US destroyers of the "Gearing" class. *Frank Knox* had been modified to serve as radar picket. Built by Bath Iron Works. Launched on 17 Sep 1944. Completed on 11 Dec 1944. Transferred 3 Feb 1971. *Stickell* built by Consolidated Steel Corp. Launched on 16 June 1945. Completed 30 Oct 1945. Transferred 1 July 1972.

1 Ex-US "ALLEN M. SUMNER" CLASS

MIAOULIS D 211 (ex-USS *Ingraham*, DD 694)

Displacement, tons	2 200 standard; 3 320 full load
Length, feet (*metres*)	376·5 (*114·8*) oa
Beam, feet (*metres*)	40·9 (*12·4*)
Draught, feet (*metres*)	19·0 (*5·8*)
Guns	6—5 in (*127 mm*) 38 cal dp
A/S weapons	2 triple torpedo launchers, Mk 32; 2 ahead throwing hedgehogs
Torpedo tubes	2 fixed, Mk 25
Main engines	2 geared turbines; 2 shafts; 60 000 shp
Boilers	4
Speed, knots	34 approx
Range, miles	4 600 at 15 knots
Complement	269 (16 officers, 94 POs, 159 men)

MIAOULIS — *1972, Hellenic Navy.*

Former fleet destroyer of the "Allen M. Sumner" class which had been modernised under the FRAM II programme. Built by Federal SB & DD Co. Launched on 16 Jan 1944. Completed on 10 Mar 1944. Transferred to Greece in July 1971.

Destroyers—*continued*

6 Ex-US "FLETCHER" CLASS

Name	No.	Builder	Laid down	Launched	Completed
ASPIS (ex-USS *Conner, DD* 582)	D 06	Boston Navy Yard	16 Apr 1942	18 July 1942	8 June 1943
LONCHI (ex-USS *Hall, DD* 583)	D 56	Boston Navy Yard	16 Apr 1942	18 July 1942	6 July 1943
NAVARINON (ex-USS *Brown, DD* 546)	D 63	Bethlehem (S. Pedro)	27 June 1942	22 Feb 1943	10 July 1943
SFENDONI (ex-USS *Aulick, DD* 569)	D 85	Consolidated Steel Corp, Texas	14 May 1941	2 Mar 1942	27 Oct 1942
THYELLA (ex-USS *Bradford, DD* 545)	D 28	Bethlehem (S. Pedro)	28 Apr 1942	12 Dec 1942	12 June 1943
VELOS (ex-USS *Charette, DD* 581)	D 16	Boston Navy Yard	20 Feb 1941	3 June 1942	18 May 1943

Displacement, tons	2 100 standard; 3 050 full load
Length, feet (*metres*)	376·5 (*114·7*) oa
Beam, feet (*metres*)	39·5 (*12·0*)
Draught, feet (*metres*)	18 (*5·5*) max
Guns, dual purpose	4—5 in (*127 mm*) 38 cal. in *Aspis, Lonchi, Sfendoni* and *Velos*, 5 in *Navarinon* and *Thyella*
Guns, AA	6—3 in (*76 mm*), 3 twin, in *Aspis, Lonchi, Sfendoni* and *Velos*. 10—40 mm (2 quadruple, 1 twin) in *Navarinon* and *Thyella*
A/S weapons	Hedgehogs; DC's
Torpedo tubes	5—21 in (*533 mm*), quintuple bank, in *Aspis, Lonchi, Sfendoni* and *Velos*, none in *Navarinon* and *Thyella*
Torpedo racks	Side-launching for A/S torpedoes
Boilers	4 Babcock & Wilcox; 615 psi (*43·3 kg/cm²*) 800°F (*427°C*)
Main engines	2 sets GE geared turbines; 2 shafts; 60 000 shp
Speed, knots	35 designed, 30 to 32 max
Range, miles	6 000 at 15 knots; 1 260 to 1 285 at 30 to 32 knots
Oil fuel, tons	506
Complement	250

Transferred from USA, *Aspis, Lonchi* and *Velos* at Long Beach, Cal, on 15 Sep 1959, 9 Feb 1960 and 15 June 1959, respectively, *Sfendoni* at Philadelphia on 21 Aug 1959. *Navarinon* and *Thyella* at Seattle, Wash, on 27 Sep 1962. *Aspis* means Shield.

RADAR. Search: SPS 6, SPS 10. Fire Control: GFC 56 and 63 systems.

SFENDONI — *1971, Major Aldo Fraccaroli*

ex-FLETCHER Class

FRIGATES

4 Ex-US "BOSTWICK" DE TYPE

Name	No.	NATO No.	Builders	Laid down	Launched	Completed
AETOS (ex-USS *Slater*, DE 766)	01	D 212	Tampa SB Co	9 Mar 1943	13 Feb 1944	1 May 1944
IERAX (ex-USS *Elbert*, DE 768)	31	D 213	Tampa SB Co	1 Apr 1943	23 May 1944	12 July 1944
LEON (ex-USS *Eldridge*, DE 173)	54	D 217	Federal SB & DD Co	22 Feb 1943	25 June 1943	27 Aug 1943
PANTHIR (ex-USS *Garfield Thomas*, DE 193)	67	D 227	Federal SB & DD Co	23 Sep 1943	12 Dec 1943	24 Jan 1944

Displacement, tons	1 240 standard; 1 900 full load
Length, feet (*metres*)	306 (*93·3*) oa
Beam, feet (*metres*)	36·7 (*11·2*)
Draught, feet (*metres*)	14 (*4·3*)
Guns, dual purpose	3—3 in (*76 mm*) 50 cal.
Guns, AA	6—40 *mm*, 3 twin 14—20 *mm*, 7 twin
A/S weapons	Hedgehog; 8 DCT; 1 DC rack
Torpedo racks	Side launching for A/S torpedoes
Main engines	4 sets GM diesel-electric 6 000 bhp; 2 shafts
Speed, knots	19·25 max
Range, miles	9 000 at 12 knots
Oil fuel (tons)	316
Complement	220 (war)

Former US destroyer escorts of the "Bostwick" class. *Aetos* and *Ierax* were transferred on 15 Mar 1951 and *Leon* and *Panthir* on 15 Jan 1951. Their 3—21 inch torpedo tubes in a triple mount were removed. Meanings of names are Eagle, Falcon, Lion and Panther, respectively.

LEON — *1972, Hellenic Navy.*

CORVETTES

5 Ex-BRITISH "ALGERINE" TYPE

Name	No.	Builders	Launched
ARMATOLOS (ex-HMS *Aries*)	M 12	Toronto Shipyard	19 Sep 1942
MAHITIS (ex-HMS *Postillion*)	M 58	Redfern Construction Co	14 Nov 1942
NAVMACHOS (ex-HMS *Lightfoot*)	M 64	Redfern Construction Co	31 Aug 1942
POLEMISTIS (ex-HMS *Gozo*)	M 74	Redfern Construction Co	18 Mar 1943
PYRPOLITIS (ex-HMS *Arcturus*)	M 76	Redfern Construction Co	27 Jan 1943

Displacement, tons	1 030 standard; 1 325 full load
Length, feet (*metres*)	225 (*68·6*) oa
Beam, feet (*metres*)	35·5 (*10·8*)
Draught, feet (*metres*)	11·5 (*3·5*) max
Guns, dual purpose	2—3 in (*76 mm*) US Mark 21 (1 in *Pirpolitis*, none in *Mahitis*)
Guns, AA	4—20 mm (US), 2MG
A/S weapons	2 to 4 DCT
Main engines	2 triple expansion; 2 shafts; 2 700 ihp = 16 knots max
Boilers	2 Yarrow, 250 psi (*17·6 kg cm²*)
Oil fuel, tons	235
Range, miles	5 000 at 10 knots; 2 270 at 14·5 knots
Complement	85

Former British ocean minesweepers of the "Algerine" class. Acquired from the Executive Committee of Surplus Allied Material. Latterly employed as Corvettes. The armament of *Mahitis* was removed when she became a training ship. *Armatolos* and *Navmachos* were used as auxiliaries and others as personnel transports.

ex-ALGERINE Class

POLEMISTIS — *1971, Royal Hellenic Navy.*

SUBMARINES

NEW CONSTRUCTION

GLAVKOS S 110 **PROTEUS** S 113
NEREUS S 111 **TRITON** S 112

Displacement, tons	1 000 surface; 1 290 submerged
Length, feet (*metres*)	183·4 (*55·9*)
Beam, feet (*metres*)	20·5 (*6·25*)
Torpedo tubes	8—21 in (*533 mm*) bow
Main engines	4 MTU Diesels; diesel-electric; 1 shaft; 5 000 hp
Speed, knots	22 submerged max
Complement	32

Built by Howaldtswerke Deutsche Werft AG, Kiel. Double hull construction. Retractable bow planes. Endurance, 50 days. Low rev screw. Fitted with Omega. *Glavkos* launched Sept 1970, completed Sept 1971. *Nereus* launched Sept 1971, completed Feb 1972. *Triton* completed Sept 1972.

GLAVKOS *1972, Stefan Terzebaschitsch*

1 Ex-US "BALAO" CLASS

TRIAINA (ex-USS *Scabbardfish*, SS 397) S 86

Displacement, tons	1 816 surface; 2 425 submerged
Length, feet (*metres*)	311·5 (*94·9*) oa
Beam, feet (*metres*)	27·0 (*8·2*)
Draught, feet (*metres*)	17·0 (*5·2*)
Torpedo tubes	10—21 in (*533 mm*), 6 bow, 4 stern
Main engines	6 500 bhp diesels (surface) 4 610 hp motors (submerged)
Speed, knots	20 on surface, 10 submerged
Range, miles	12 000 at 10 knots (surface)
Complement	85

Built at Portsmouth Navy Yard, USA. Launched on 27 Jan 1944 and completed on 29 Apr 1944. Transferred on 26 Feb 1965 at San Francisco (lent by US in 1964).

TRIAINA *1970, Royal Hellenic Navy,*

1 Ex-US "GUPPY" CLASS

PAPANIKOLIS (ex-*Hardhead* SS 365 IIA) S 114

Displacement, tons	1 840 standard; 2 445 dived
Length, feet (*metres*)	306 (*93·2*)
Beam, feet (*metres*)	27 (*8·3*)
Draught, feet (*metres*)	17 (*5·2*)
Torpedo tubes	10—21 inch; 6 bow, 4 stern
Main engines	3 Diesels; 4 800 shp/2 Motors, 5 400 shp; 2 shafts
Speed	17 surface; 15 dived
Range, miles	12 000 at 10 knots (surface)
Complement	84

Hardhead built by Manitowoc SB Co. Commissioned April 1944. Transferred 26 July 1972.

AMPHIBIOUS VESSELS

1 Ex-US LSD

NAFKRATOUSSA (ex-USS *Fort Mandan, LSD* 21) L 153

Displacement, tons	4 790 light; 9 375 full load
Dimensions, feet	457·8 oa × 72·2 × 18 max
Guns	8—40 mm AA
Main engines	Geared turbines; 2 shafts; 7 000 shp = 15·4 knots
Boilers	2

Built at Boston Navy Yard. Laid down on 2 Jan 1945. Launched on 22 May 1945. Completed on 31 Oct 1945. This dock landing ship taken over from USA in 1971 replacing the previous *Nafkratoussa* (ex-*Hyperion*, ex-*LSD* 9) out of service in 1971 as Headquarters ship of Captain, Landing Forces.

NAFKRATOUSSA (ex-*LSD* 9) *1970, A. & J. Pavia*

8 Ex-US LST's

KRITI (ex-USS *Page County, LST* 1076)	L 171
IKARIA (ex-USS *Potter County, LST* 1086)	L 154
LESBOS (ex-USS *Boone County, LST* 389)	L 172
RODOS (ex-USS *Bowman County, LST* 391)	L 157
SYROS (ex-USS *LST* 325)	L 144
CHIOS (ex *LST* 35)	L 195
LIMNOS (ex *LST* 36)	L 158
SAMOS (ex *LST* 33)	L 179

Former United States tank landing ships. Cargo capacity 2 100 tons. *Ikaria, Lesbos* and *Rodos* were transferred to the Royal Hellenic Navy on 9 Aug 1960. *Syros* was transferred on 29 May 1964 at Portsmouth, Virginia, under MAP. *Kriti* was transferred in Mar 1971. Last three under lease-lend in 1943. Of the original LST (3) type landing ships on loan from Great Britain, *Alfios* (ex-*LST* 3020), *Axios* (ex-*LST* 3007) and *Strymon* (ex-LST 3502) were returned to the Royal Navy, refitted at Malta and taken over by the Ministry of Transport. *Acheloos* (which replaced *Acheloos*, ex-LST 2503 in 1964) and *Aliakmon* L 104 (ex-LST 3002) were officially deleted from the list in 1939, and *Pinios* L 171 (ex-*LST* 3506) in 1971.

LIMNOS *1972, Royal Hellenic Navy*

5 Ex-US LSM's

IPOPLIARKHOS CRYSTALIDIS (ex-USS *LSM* 541)	L 165
IPOPLIARKHOS DANIOLOS (ex-USS *LSM* 227)	L 163
IPOPLIARKHOS GRIGOROPOULOS (ex-USS *LSM* 45)	L 161
IPOPLIARKHOS ROUSSEN (ex-USS *LSM* 399)	L 164
IPOPLIARKHOS TOURNAS (ex-USS *LSM* 102)	L 162

Displacement, tons	743 beaching; 1 095 full load
Dimensions, feet	196·5 wl; 203·5 oa × 34·2 × 8·3
Guns	2—40 mm AA; 8—20 mm AA
Main engines	Diesel direct drive; 2 shafts; 3 600 bhp = 13 knots

Former US Medium Landing Ships. *LSM* 541 and *LSM* 557 were handed over to Greece at Salamis on 30 Oct 1958 and *LSM* 45, *LSM* 102, *LSM* 227 and *LSM* 399 at Portsmouth, Virginia on 3 Nov 1958. All were renamed after naval heroes killed during World War 2. *Ipopliarkhos Merlin* L 166 sunk in collision 15 Nov 1972.

IPOPLIARKHOS TOURNAS *1971, Royal Hellenic Navy,*

Amphibious Vessels—*continued*

KITHNOS, LCU 763 (L 149) *1971, Royal Hellenic Navy,*

8 Ex-US LCU's

LCU 763 (*Kithnos*) **LCU 827**(*Sciathos*) **LCU 1229** (*Kea*)
LCU 655 (*Sifnos*) **LCU 852** (*Scopelos*) **LCU 1379** (*Karpathos*)
LCU 971 (*Kimolos*) **LCU 1382** (*Kassos*)

Displacement, tons	143 standard; 309 full load
Dimensions, feet	105 wl; 119 oa × 32·7 × 5 max
Guns	2—20 mm AA
Main Engines	Diesel; 3 shafts; 440 bhp = 8 knots
Complement	13

Former US Utility Landing Craft of the *LCU* (ex-*LST* (6)) type. *Sciathos* and *Scopelos* were acquired in 1959. *Kea, Kithnos* (original No. 149) and *Sifnos* were transferred from USA in 1961. and *Karpathos* (original No. 146) *Kassos* and *Kimolos* in 1962. These LCUs are referred to by their hull numbers and not by name. There are also 13 LCMs and 34 *LCVPs*. all transferred from USA

LIGHT FORCES

4 NEW CONSTRUCTION (MISSILE BOATS)

CALYPSO P 54 **EUNIKI** P 55 **KYMOTHOI** P 53 **NAVSITHOI** P 56

Displacement, tons	234 standard; 255 full load
Dimensions, feet	154·2 × 23·3 × 8·2
Missiles	4 MM 38 Exocet surface-to-surface
Guns	4—35 mm AA (2 twin)
Torpedo tubes	2 anti-submarine
Main engines	4 diesels; 4 shafts; 12 000 bhp = 36·5 knots
Oil fuel, tons	39 bunkerage
Range, miles	850 at 25 knots
Complement	40 (4 officers, and 36 men)

Ordered in 1969 from Constructions Mécaniques de Normandie Cherbourg. Similar to the Israeli "Saar" class.

Calypso launched 26 Apr 1971, completed Apr 1972. *Euniki* launched 8 Sept 1971, completed June 1972. *Kymothoi* launched 26 Jan 1971, completed Dec 1971. *Navsithoi* launched 20 Dec 1971, completed July 1972.

CALYPSO as launched. *Apr 1971, courtesy Admiral M. Adam*

"TJELD" TYPE (TORPEDO BOATS)

ANDROMEDA P 21 **KASTOR** P 23 **PYGASOS** P 25
KYKØNOS P 24 **TOXOTIS** P 26

Displacement, tons	69 standard; 76 full load
Dimensions, feet	75 pp; 80·4 oa × 24·6 × 6·9
Torpedo tubes	4—21 In
Guns	2—40 mm AA
Main engines	2 Napier Deltic T 18-37 K diesels; 3 100 bhp = 43 knots
Complement	22

Andromeda and *Inionos* were taken over in Feb 1967 from Mandal, Norway. *Kastor* and *Kykonos*, and the third pair, *Pigassos* and *Toxotis*, were delivered in succession in 1967. *Inionos* was officially deleted from the list.

ANDROMEDA *1971. Royal Hellenic Navy,*

1 VOSPER "BRAVE" TYPE (TORPEDO BOAT)

ASTRAPI P 20 (ex-*Strahl* P 6194)

Displacement, tons	95 standard; 110 full load
Dimensions, feet	96 (full); 99 oa × 25 × 7 (props)
Torpedo chutes	4—21 in side launching
Guns	2—40 mm AA
Main engines	3 Bristol Siddeley Marine Proteus gas turbines; 3 shafts; 12 750 bhp = 55·5 knots

Built by Vosper, Portsmouth. Launched on 10 Jan 1962. Commissioned in Federal German Navy on 21 Nov 1962. Transferred to Royal Hellenic Navy in Apr 1967. Refitted by Vosper in 1968. Of similar design to British "Brave" class.

ASTRAPI *1972, Hellenic Navy,*

1 VOSPER "FEROCITY" TYPE (TORPEDO BOAT)

AIOLOS P 19 (ex-*Pfeil* P 6193)

Displacement, tons	75 standard; 80 full load
Dimensions, feet	92 wl; 95 oa × 23·9 × 6·5
Torpedo chutes	4—21 in side launching
Guns	2—40 mm AA
Main engines	2 Bristol Siddeley Marine Proteus gas turbines; 2 shafts; 8 500 bhp = 50 knots

Built by Vosper, Portsmouth. Launched on 26 Oct 1961. Commissioned in German Navy on 27 June 1962. Transferred to Royal Hellenic Navy in Apr 1967. Refitted by Vosper in 1968. Based on design of Vosper prototype *Ferocity*.

AIOLOS *1972, Hellenic Navy,*

5 "SILBERMOWE" TYPE (TORPEDO BOATS)

DOLPHIN (ex-*Sturmmöwe*) P 15 **PHOENIX** (ex-*Eismöwe*) P 27
DRAKON (ex-*Silbermöwe*) P 16 **POLIKOS** (ex-*Raubmöwe*) P 17
POLIDEFKIS (ex-*Wildschwan*) P 18

Displacement, tons	119 standard; 155 full load
Dimensions, feet	116·1 × 16·7 × 5·9
Torpedo tubes	2—21 in
Guns	1—40 mm AA; 2—20 mm AA (1 twin)
Main engines	3 diesels; 3 shafts; 9 000 bhp = 38 knots

Old S-Boote taken over from Germany 17 Dec 1968. Built by Lurssen, Vegesack, 1951-56.

3 PGM TYPE

ANTIPLOIARKHOS PEZOPOULOS (ex-*PGM* 21, ex-*PC* 1552) P 70
PLOTARKHIS ARSLANOGLOU (ex-*PGM* 25, ex-*PC* 1556) P 14
PLOTARKHIS CHANTZIKONSTANDIS (ex-*PGM* 29, ex-*PC* 1565) P 96

Displacement, tons	335 standard; 439 full load
Dimensions, feet	170 wl; 174·7 oa × 23 × 10·8 (max)
Guns	1—3 in; 6—20 mm AA
A/S weapons	Hedgehog; side launching torpedo racks; depth charges
Main engines	2 GM diesels; 2 shafts; 3 600 bhp = 19 knots

Light Forces—*continued*

All launched in 1943-44. Acquired from USA in Aug 1947. The two 40 mm AA guns were removed and a hedgehog was installed in 1963. Of these sister ships *Plotarkhis Blessas* (ex-PGM 28, ex-PC 1559) P 61, was sold in 1963 and *Antiploiarkhos Laskos* (ex-*PGM* 16, ex-*PC* 1448) P 53 and *Ploiarkhos Meletopoulos* (ex-*PGM* 22, ex-*PC* 1553) P 57 were out of service in 1971.

ANTIPLOIARKHOS PEZOPOULOS *1970, Royal Hellenic Navy,*

2 LSSL TYPE

PLOTARKHIS MARIDAKIS (ex-USS *LSSL* 65) L 94 (ex-P 94)
PLOTARKHIS VLACHAVAS (ex-USS *LSSL*) 35 L 95 (ex-P 95)

Displacement, tons	257 standard; 395 full load
Dimensions, feet	157·0 × 23·2 × 5·7
Guns	1—3 in; 4—40 mm AA (2 twin); 4—20 mm AA
Main engines	Diesels; 2 shafts; 1 600 bhp = 14·4 knots

Built by Albina Engine & Machinery Works Inc. Portland, Oreg, and Commercial Iron Works, Portland, and launched on 14 Nov and 17 Sep 1944, respectively. *Plotarkhis Vlachavas* was transferred from USA on 12 Aug 1957 and *Plotarkhis Maridakis* in June 1958. Given L instead of P pennant numbers in 1971.

PLOTARKHIS VLACHAVAS *1972, Dr. Giorgio Arra*

MINE WARFARE FORCES

2 COASTAL MINELAYERS

AKTION (ex-*LSM* 301, ex-MMC 6) N 04
AMVRAKIA (ex-*LSM* 303, ex-MMC 7) N 05

Displacement, tons	720 standard; 1 100 full load
Dimensions, feet	196·5 wl · 203·5 oa × 34·5 × 8·3 max
Guns	8—40 mm dp (4 twin); 6—20 mm AA (single)
Mines	Capacity 100 to 130
Main engines	2 diesels; 2 shafts; 3 600 bhp = 12·5 knots
Range, miles	3 000 at 12 knots
Complement	65

Former US Medium Landing Ships. Both built at Charleston Naval Shipyard. *Aktion* was launched on 1 Jan 1945 and *Amvrakia* on 14 Nov 1944. Converted in the USA into all purpose seagoing minelayers for the Royal Hellenic Navy. Underwent extensive rebuilding from the deck up. Twin rudders. The Greek flag was hoisted on 1 Dec 1953.

DORIS *1971, Royal Hellenic Navy*

AMVRAKIA *1970, Royal Hellenic Navy*

10 COASTAL MINESWEEPERS

AIDON (ex-*MSC* 310) M 248
AIGLI (ex-*MSC* 299) M 246
ARGO (ex-*MSC* 317) M 213
AVRA (ex-*MSC* 318) M 214
ALKYON (ex-*MSC* 319) M 211
DAPHNI (ex-*MSC* 307) M 247
DORIS (ex-*MSC* 298) M 245
KICHLI (ex-*MSC* 308) M 241
PLEIAS (ex-*MSC* 314) M 240
KISSA (ex-*MSC* 309) M 242

Displacement, tons	320 standard; 370 full load
Dimensions, feet	138 pp; 144 oa × 28 × 8·5
Guns	2—20 mm AA (twin)
Main engines	2 GM diesels; 2 shafts; 880 bhp = 13 knots
Complement	39

Built in USA for Greece. *Aidon, Aigli, Daphni, Doris, Kichli* and *Kissa*, were completed and transferred in 1964-65, *Argo* and *Avra* in 1968, *Alkyon* and *Pleias* in 1969-70. Built of wood and non-magnetic materials. *Kichu* M 249 was officially deleted in 1972.

5 ex.-US MSC TYPE 60

ANTIOPI (ex-Belgian *Herve, M* 921, ex-USS *MSC* 153) M 205
ATALANTI (ex-Belgian *St. Truiden, M* 919 ex-USS *MSC* 169) M 202
NIOVI (ex-Belgian *Laroche, M* 924, ex-USS *MSC* 171) M 254
PHEDRA (ex-Belgian *Malmedy, M* 922, ex-USS *MSC* 154) M 206
THALIA (ex-Belgian *Blankenberge, M* 923, ex-USS *MSC* 170) M 210

Displacement, tons	330 standard; 402 full load
Dimensions, feet	145·0 oa × 27·9 × 8·0 feet
Guns	2—20 mm Oerlikon (1 twin)
Main engines	2 GM diesels; 2 shafts; 900 bhp = 14 knots
Complement	38 officers and men

Former Belgian vessels taken over on 29 July 1969 (*Herve* and *St. Truiden*) and 26 Sep 1969 (*Laroche, Malmedy* and *Blankenberge*). Of USN *MSC* (ex-*AMS*). Type 60

NIOVI *1971, Michael D. J. Lennon*

Mine Warfare. Forces—*continued*

6 ex-US BYMS TYPE

AFROESSA (ex-*BYMS* 2185) M 209
KALYMNOS (ex-*BYMS* 2033) M 201
KARTERIA (ex-*BYMS* 2065) M 203
KERKYRA (ex-*BYMS* 2172) M 208
PARALOS (ex-*BYMS* 2066) M 204
ZAKYNTHOS (ex-*BYMS* 2209) M 212

Displacement, tons	270 standard; 350 full load
Dimensions, feet	136 × 24·5 × 8
Guns	1—3 in; 2—20 mm AA; 4 MG; 2 DCT
Main Engines	Diesel; 1 000 bhp = 12 knots
Complement	33

Of wooden construction. Known by numbers, *Karteria* was launched on 21 Dec 1942. *Ithaki* (ex-*BYMS* 2240). *Kefallinia* (ex-*BYMS* 2171), *Lefkas* (ex-*BYMS* 2086), *Patmos* (ex-*BYMS* 2229), *Salaminia* (ex- *BYMS* 2067), and *Simi* (ex-*BYMS* 2190) were deleted from the list in 1966 and *Leros* (ex-*BYMS* 2186) and *Paxi* (ex-*BYMS* 2056) in 1969.

NOTE. 4 ex-US MSL's taken over in 1972. These of 36 feet and 10 tons with single diesels giving a speed up to 12 knots.

AFROESSA *1971, Royal Hellenic Navy, Official*

SURVEY VESSELS

ATALANTI

Of 383 tons, launched in 1954 with a complement of 35.

VEGAS (ex-*BYMS* 2078) A 478

Of 350 tons and with a complement of 33.

Former coastal minesweeper of the wooden hulled BYMS type. Of eight sister ships used as coastal patrol vessels, *Aura* (ex-*BYMS* 2054) was deleted from the list in 1962, *Andromeda* (ex-*BYMS* 2261), *Kleio* (ex-*BYMS* 2152) and *Thalia* (ex-*BYMS* 2252) in 1967, *Lambadias* (ex-*BYMS* 2182), *Pigassos* (ex-*BYMS* 2221) and *Prokyon* (ex-*BYMS* 2076) in 1968, and *Ariadne* (ex-*BYMS* 2058) in1971.

ANEMOS A 469 (ex-German *KFK KW7*)

Officially added to the Royal Hellenic Navy List in 1969. The coastal survey vessel *Alykoni* was discarded in 1961. Displaces 112 tons, was launched in 1944 and has a complement of 16.

A. IDHI (BB15)

Of 38 tons, launched in 1945. Complement 9.

1 SURVEYING LAUNCH

Of 25 tons, launched in 1940. Complement 9.

ST LYKOUDIS (ex-*Chania*, ex-HMS *Nasturtium*) A 481

Displacement, tons	1 020 standard; 1,280 full load
Dimensions, feet	190 pp; 205 oa × 33 × 14·5
Main Engines	Triple expansion; 2 750 ihp = 14 knots
Boilers	2 SE
Oil fuel (tons)	230

Former corvette of the British "Flower" type. Launched in 1940. Sold to Greece as a merchant ship in 1948. Now acts as Lighthouse Tender.

ST. LYKOUDIS *1969, Royal Hellenic Navy*

OILERS

ARETHOUSA (ex-USS *Natchaug*, AOG 54) A 377
ARIADNI (ex-USS *Tombigbee*, AOG 11)

Displacement, tons	1 850 light; 4 335 full load
Measurement, tons	2 575 deadweight; cargo capacity 2 040
Dimensions, feet	292 wl; 310·8 oa × 48·5 × 15·7 max
Guns	4—3 in dp; 50 cal
Main engines	GM diesels; 2 shafts; 3 300 bhp = 14 knots
Complement	43 (6 officers, 37 men)

Former US petrol carriers. A 377 built by Cargill Inc, Savage, Minn. Laid down on 15 Aug 1944. Launched on 16 Dec 144. Transferred from the USA to Greece under the Mutual Defense Assistance Program at Pearl Harbour, Hawaii, in July 1959. *Ariadni* transferred mid-1972.

ARETHOUSA *1972, Hellenic Navy*

ZEUS (ex-YOG 98) A 372

Dimensions, feet 165 × 35 × 10

Former US yard petrol carrier. Launched in 1944. Capacity 900 tons.

SIRIOS (ex-*Poseidon*, ex-*Empire Faun*) A 345

Formerly on loan from Great Britain, but purchased outright in 1962. This ship was renamed *Sirios* when the name *Poseidon* was given to the submarine *Lapon* acquired from the USA in 1958. Capacity 850 tons.

VIVIIS A 471

Originally a water carrier but now employed as an oiler. Capacity 687 tons.

PROMETHEUS A 374

Small yard oil tanker. Launched in 1959. Capacity 520 tons.

KRONOS (ex-*Islay*, ex-*Dresden*) A 373

Displacement, tons 311

Capacity 110 tons. *Khalki* and *Xanthi* were officially stricken from the list in 1958.

ORION (ex-US tanker Y 126) A 376

Formerly small United States yard tanker. Capacity 700 tons.

ORION *1969, Royal Hellenic Navy*

11 TUGS

ACCHILEUS (ex-*Confident*)
AIAS
ANTAIOS (ex-*Busy*)
ATLAS (ex-*F* 5)
ATROMITOS A 410
CIGAS
MINOTAVROS (ex-*Theseus*, ex-*ST* 539)
PERSEUS (ex-*ST*772)
ROMALEOS
TITAN
SAMSON (ex-*F* 16)

Heraklis was officially deleted from the list in 1966, *Aegeus* in 1968, *Kentravros* in 1969 and *Aegeus* in 1972.

MISCELLANEOUS

HEPHESTUS (ex-USS *Josiah Willard Gibbs*, T-AGOR 1, ex-USS *San Carlos*, AVP 51) A 413

Displacement, tons	1 750 standard; 2 800 full load
Dimensions, feet	300·0 wl; 310·8 oa × 41·2 × 13·5
Main engines	2 Fairbanks-Morse diesels. 2 shafts; 6 080 bhp = 18 knots
Complement	75 (10 officers and 65 men)

Former US seaplane tender converted for oceanographic research. Built by Lake Washington Shipyard, Houghton, Wash. Laid down on 7 Sep 1942, launched on 20 Dec 1942 and completed on 21 Mar 1944. Transferred to the Hellenic Navy on 7 Dec 1971. Used as a general support ship.

HEPHESTUS *Dr. Giorgio Arra*

SOTIR (ex-*Salventure*) A 384

Displacement, tons	1,440 standard; 1 700 full load
Measurement, tons	1 112 gross
Dimensions, feet	216 oa × 37·8 × 13 max
Main Engines	Triple expansion; 2 shafts; 1 500 ihp = 12 knots
Oil fuel (tons)	310
Complement	60

Former British Royal Fleet Auxiliary ocean salvage vessel of the "Salv" class. On loan from Great Britain. Equipped with a decompression chamber.

SOTIR *1972, Dr Giorgio Arra*

SAKIPIS (ex-*KNM Ellida*, ex-USS *ARB* 13, ex-USS *LST* 50) A 329

Displacement, tons	3 800 standard; 5 000 full load
Dimensions, feet	316 wl; 328 oa × 50 × 11 max
Guns	12—40 mm AA; 12—20 mm AA
Main Engines	GM diesels; 2 shafts; 1 800 bhp = 10 knots
Complement	200

Former US tank landing ship. Built by Dravo Corporation, Pittsburgh. Laid down on 29 Aug 1943, launched on 16 Oct 1943, completed on 27 Nov 1943. Converted to a battle damage repair ship in 1952 by Puget Sound Bridge & Dry Dock Co. Taken over by the Royal Norwegian Navy at Seattle on 14 Nov 1952 to serve as a battle damage repair ship for surface vessels. Returned to the US Navy on 1 July 1960. Transferred to Greece on 16 Sep 1960 at Bergen, Norway.

SAKIPIS *1972, Hellenic Navy,*

HERMES (ex-*Product*, ex-*Port Jackson*) A 324

Displacement, tons	550 standard; 650 full load
Dimensions, feet	133 × 27·8 × 11
Main Engines	Diesel; 4-stroke; 560 bhp = 11 knots

Former British trawler. Launched in 1941. On loan from Great Britain. Acts as Minesweeper Depot Ship.

HERMES *1969, Royal Hellenic Navy*

THETIS (ex-USS *AN* 103) A 307

Displacement, tons	680 standard; 805 full load
Dimensions, feet	146 wl; 169·5 oa × 33·5 × 11·8 max
Guns	1—40 mm AA; 4—20 mm AA
Main engines	MAN diesels; 1 shaft; 1 400 bhp = 12 knots
Complement	48

Netlayer of the US type. Built by Kröger, Rendsburg, as a US offshore order. Launched in 1959. Taken over by the Royal Hellenic Navy on 9 Apr 1960.

THETIS *1971, Royal Hellenic Navy*

SKYROS A 485

Displacement, tons 350

SERRAI (ex-*Anna Raeder*) A 487

Displacement, tons 725

Both act as Lighthouse Tenders.

5 WATER BOATS

ILIKI **KASTORIA** **STYMPHALIA** **TRIHONIS** **VOLVI**

Capacity: *Iliki* and *Stymphalia* 120 tons, *Trihonis* 300 tons, *Volvi* 350 tons, *Kastoria* 520 tons, *Kaliroe* was officially deleted from the list in 1972.

GABON

Mercantile Marine

Lloyd's Register of Shipping: 6 vessels of 1 519 tons gross.

PATROL BOATS

PRESIDENT ALBERT BERNARD BONGO

An 85 ton patrol boat built by Chant. Navals d'Esterel and delivered March 1972.

PRESIDENT LEON M'BA GCO 1

Displacement, tons	85 standard
Dimensions, feet	92 × 20·5 × 5
Guns	1—75 mm; 1—12·7 mm MG
Main engines	Diesel = 12·5 knots
Complement	16

Built in Gabon, launched on 16 Jan 1968.

BOUET-WILLAUMEZ (ex-HDML 1021).

Displacement, tons	40
Dimensions, feet	70·8 × 15·3 × 5·9
Guns	2—20 mm AA
Main engines	2 Diesels; 300 hp = 12·5 knots
Complement	8

Launched in 1943. Transferred in 1961 by France and still, apparently, going strong.

NOTE. Plans exist for a 60 ft Patrol Boat and four LCVP s.

GRENADA

Mercantile Marine

Lloyd's Register of Shipping: 3 vessels of 343 tons gross

PATROL BOAT

Displacement, tons	15
Dimensions, feet	40 × 12 × 2
Guns	3 MG
Main engines	2 Diesels; 370 hp = 22 knots

Delivered by Brooke Marine, Lowestoft early in 1972.

GUATEMALA

On 5 Jan 1959 Guatemala announced the establishment of a navy, with the primary duty of routing poaching fishing boats and smugglers. There are four small patrol craft (ex-US 40 ft Coast Guard cutters). A 63 ft aircraft rescue boat (AVR) was transferred from USA to Guatemala on 8 Oct 1964. The patrol boat *Barrunda* was deleted in 1971.

Personnel

1973: 180 officers, non-commissioned officers and men

Mercantile Marine

1973: Lloyd's Register of Shipping: 2 vessels of 3 629 tons gross

GUINEA

Personnel

1973: 350 officers and men.

Mercantile Marine

Lloyd's Register of Shipping: 9 vessels of 15 538 tons gross

TORPEDO BOATS

4 Ex-USSR "P 6" CLASS

Displacement, tons	66 standard; 75 full load
Dimensions, feet	84·2 × 20·0 × 6·0
Guns	4—25 mm AA
Tubes	2—21 in (or mines or depth charges)
Main engines	Diesels; 4 shafts; 4 800 bhp = 45 knots
Complement	25

PATROL BOATS

2 USSR-BUILT

P 215 **P 425**

Displacement, tons	86 standard; 91 full load
Dimensions, feet	98·0 pp × 15·0 × 4·8
Guns	2 14·5 mm AA (1 twin)
Main engines	2 diesels; 2 shafts; 12 00 bhp = 18 knots
Oil fuel, tons	9·25
Range, miles	460 at 17 knots
Complement	16 (2 officers, 14 ratings)

LANDING CRAFT

2 SMALL UTILITY TYPE

All the above craft were observed in Conakry Harbour in 1970. Recent visits by considerable numbers of Soviet ships may have increased these numbers.

GUYANA

Mercantile Marine

Lloyd's Register of Shipping: 42 vessels of 13 735 tons gross

PATROL LAUNCHES

JAGUAR, MARGAY, OCELOT

Displacement, tons	10
Dimensions, feet	40 × 12 × 3·5
Guns	7·62 mm general purpose machine guns
Main engines	2 D 336A diesels; 370 hp = 21 knots
Complement	6

They have steel hulls with aluminium superstructures. Completed 29 Apr 1971 (*Jaguar*) 21 May 1971 (*Margay*) 22 June 1971 (*Ocelot*).

NOTE. Three 110 ft Patrol Craft ordered from Vosper Thornycraft in 1970.

HAITI

Personnel

1972: Total 290 (40 officers and 250 men)

COAST GUARD VESSELS

DESSALINES (ex-USS *Tonawanda AN* 89) GC 10

Displacement, tons	650 standard, 785 full load
Dimensions, feet	168·5 × 33 × 10·8
Main Engines	Busch-Sulzer diesel-electric; 1 500 shp = 12 knots

Former United States Navy netlayer of the "Cohoes" class. Built by Leatham D. Smith S.B. Co. Launched on 14 Nov 1944. Loaned to Haiti in 1960 for five years.

AMIRAL KILLICK (ex-USCG *Black Rock, WAGL* 367) GC 7

Displacement, tons	160
Dimensions, feet	Length 114

Former buoy tender purchased from the US Coast Guard in 1955, commissioned in Jan 1956.

LA CRETE A PIERROT (ex-USCG 95315) GC 8 **VERTIERES** GC 9

Displacement, tons	100
Dimensions, feet	95 × 19 × 5
Guns	1—40 mm AA
Main Engines	4 diesels; 2 shafts; 2 200 bhp = 21 knots
Radius, miles	1 500
Complement	15

Former US Coast Guard steel cutters. Built at US Coast Guard Yard, Curtiss Bay, Maryland. *La Crête à Pierrot* was acquired on 26 Feb 1956. *Vertières* was transferred to Haiti at Norfolk, Virginia, in Oct 1956 and commissioned in Dec 1956

16 AOUT 1946 (ex-*SC* 453) GC 2

Displacement, tons	110 standard, 138 full load
Dimensions, feet	110·5 × 18·8 × 6·5
Guns	2—40 mm; 2—20 mm
Main Engines	Diesels, 2 shafts; 1 000 bhp = 15 knots

Submarine chaser of the SC type acquired during 1947 from the US Navy. Launched in 1943. Laid up in reserve. *Amiral Killick* GC 4 was discarded in 1954. *Toussaint L'Ouverture* (ex-SC 1064) was sold in 1959.

SAVANNAH GC 1

Displacement, tons	47
Dimensions, feet	83 × 16 × 4·2
Main Engines	Diesels; 2 shafts; 200 bhp = 9 knots
Complement	12

Ex-USCG cutter 56200, built in the USA in 1944 and acquired in 1944.

ARTIBONITE (ex-US *LCT*) GC 5

Displacement, tons	134 standard; 285 full load
Dimensions, feet	120·3 oa × 32 × 4·2
Main Engines	3 diesels; 675 bhp = 8 knots
Complement	12

Former US tank landing craft. Salvaged by Haitian Coast Guard after grounding and converted. Laid up in reserve having been damaged by grounding in Mar 1956. *Vertières* GC 6 (ex-USS *APC* 92) was lost at sea.

SANS SOUCI (ex-*Captain James Taylor*)

Displacement, tons	161
Main Engines	Diesels; 2 shafts; 300 bhp = 10 knots

Employed, when required, as the Presidential Yacht.

HONDURAS

Coast Guard

There are three small coastguard cutters.

Mercantile Marine

Lloyd's Register of Shipping: 58 vessels of 74 030 tons gross

HONDURAS, BRITISH

2 PATROL CRAFT

BELIZE PBM 01 **BELMOPAN** PBM 02

Displacement, tons	15
Dimensions, feet	40 × 12 × 2
Guns	3 MG
Main engines	2 Diesels; 370 hp = 22 knots

Built by Brooke Marine, Lowestoft.

HONG KONG

7-78 FT VOSPER THORNYCROFT PATROL CRAFT

Displacement, tons	80
Dimensions, feet	78·5 oa × 17·2 × 5·5
Guns	1—·50 cal MG
Main engines	Two Cummins diesels; 1 500 hp = 20 knots
Range, miles	700 at 15 knots
Complement	16

Steel hulled craft built by Vosper Thornycroft Private Ltd, Singapore. Delivered May-Nov 1972 to the Royal Hong Kong Police.

HUNGARY

Diplomatic Representation

Military and Air Attaché London: Lieut Colonel Károly Mészaros

Mercantile Marine

Lloyd's Register of Shipping: 18 vessels of 33 061 tons gross

River Guard

Until late in 1968 naval vessels listed included the river patrol vessel *Baya* (ex-*Barsch*), the parent ship *Csobanc*, the training ship *Badascony*, ten patrol launches, ten river minesweepers, and two minesweeping launches (see full particulars of all these vessels in the 1968-69 and earlier editions; but in 1969 it was officially stated by the Hungarian Embassy in London that there were no longer any fighting ships in Hungary since the small fleet had been dispersed, and in 1970 it was stated that there were no plans to enter new naval vessels into service. But it is reported that there still remains a residue of a flotilla of river monitors and watch pickets forming the River Guard (some 500 strong) under the Ministry of the Interior which constitutes a para-military marine service, and army vessels are very active along the Danube.

No. 542-007 *1972, Hungarian River Guard,*

ICELAND

Duties

The Coast Guard Service (Landhelgisgaezlan) deals with fishery protection, salvage, rescue, hydrographic research, surveying and lighthouse duties.

Strength of the Coast Guard

1973: 120 officers and men

Personnel

5 Patrol Vessels; Prefix: v/s; colour: dark grey
2 Whalecatchers
1 Patrol Aircraft and helicopter

Mercantile Marine

Lloyd's Register of Shipping:
301 vessels of 130 561 tons gross

COAST GUARD PATROL VESSELS

ÆGIR

Displacement, tons	1 150
Dimensions, feet	204 × 33 × 13
Guns	1—57 mm
Main engines	2 diesels; 2 shafts; 8 000 bhp = 19 knots
Complement	22

The first new construction patrol vessel for the Icelandic Coast Guard Service for about eight years. Projected in Feb 1965. Built by Aalborg Vaerft, Denmark. Laid down in May 1967. Completed in 1968.

ÆGIR *1969, Icelandic Coast Guard Service*

ODINN

Measurement, tons	1 000
Dimensions, feet	187 pp × 33 × 13
Guns	1—57 mm
Main Engines	2 diesels; 2 shafts; 5 000 bhp = 18 knots
Complement	22

Designed as a coast guard vessel. Built at Aalborg Vaerft A/S, Denmark. Laid down in Jan 1959. Launched in Sep 1959. Completed in Jan 1960. To be refitted with a new tripod mast in 1972.

ODINN *1967, Icelandic Coast Guard Service*

ALBERT

Measurement, tons	200 gross
Dimensions, feet	Length: 111·2
Guns	1—47 mm
Main engines	1 Nohab diesel; 650 bhp = 12·5 knots
Complement	15

Launched in 1956. Completed and commissioned for service in Apr 1957. To be refitted in 1972.

THOR

Displacement, tons	920
Dimensions, feet	183·3 pp; 206 oa × 31·2 × 13
Guns	2—57 mm
Main engines	2 diesels; 3 200 bhp = 17 knots
Complement	22

Built at Aalborg, Denmark. Launched in 1951. Completed and commissioned in late 1951. Rated as coastal inspection and salvage vessel. Fitted with helicopter platform during refit in 1972.

THOR *1969, Icelandic Coast Guard Service*

ARVAKUR

Displacement, tons	716
Dimensions, feet	106 × 33 × 13
Guns	1 small to be mounted
Main engines	1 diesel; 1 000 bhp = 12 knots
Complement	12

Built as a lighthouse tender in the Netherlands in 1962. Acquired by Iceland for duty in the Coast Guard Service in 1969.

ARVAKUR *1969, Icelandic Coast Guard Service*

NOTE. Two 20 knot whale-catchers requisitioned in 1972.

DISPOSALS

Gautur (ex-*Odinn*) was officially deleted from the Coast Guard List on 1 Jan 1963, *Tyr* in 1964, and *Sæbjorg* in Aug 1965. The old *Aegir* (built in 1929) was broken up in 1968, and the small *Maria Julia* was sold in 1969.

LOSS. The fishery protection patrol vessel and lighthouse tender *Hermodur* foundered off the south-west coast of Iceland on 17 Feb 1959.

INDIA

Administration

Chief of the Naval Staff:
Admiral S. N. Kohli

Flag Officer C in C, West Coast:

Flag Officer Commanding Western Fleet:
Rear-Admiral E. C. Kuruvila

Flag Officer C in C, East Coast:
Vice-Admiral N. Krishnan

Flag Officer, Southern Naval Area:
Rear-Admiral V. A. Kamath

Flag Officer Commanding Eastern Fleet:
Rear-Admiral S. H. Sarma

Diplomatic Representation

Naval Adviser in London:
Commodore Russom Ghandi

Naval Attaché in Paris and Bonn:
Commodore B. K. Dang

Naval Attaché in Moscow:
Commodore G. K. Nadkar

Naval Attaché in Washington:
Major General A. Naidu

Strength of the Fleet

1 Aircraft Carrier
2 Cruisers
6 Destroyers (3 DDE's)
24 Frigates (includes 4 building)
4 Patrol Submarines
1 Landing Ship
2 Landing Craft
8 Missile Boats
21 Patrol Craft
4 CMS
4 IMS
4 Survey Vessels
2 Submarine Tenders
4 Oilers
1 Repair Ship
1 Store Ship
1 Tug

Colour of Warships

In 1969 the active vessels of the Indian Fleet assumed a darker shade of grey than previously used.

Personnel

1973: 24 000 officers and ratings

Naval Bases and Establishments

Bombay (C in C Western Fleet, barracks and main Dockyard);
Vishakapatnam (C in C Eastern Command, submarine base, dockyard and barracks);
Cochin (Naval Air Station, barracks and professional schools);
Lonavala and Jamnagar (professional schools);
Calcutta, Goa, and Port Blair small bases only.

Mercantile Marine

Lloyd's Register of Shipping:
412 vessels of 2 649 677 tons gross

AIRCRAFT CARRIER

Name	*No.*	*Builders*	*Engineers*	*Laid down*	*Launched*	*Completed*
VIKRANT (ex-HMS *Hercules*)	R 11	Vickers-Armstrong Ltd, Tyne	Parsons Marine Steam Turbine Co	14 Oct 1943	22 Sep 1945	4 Mar 1961

1 Ex-BRITISH "MAJESTIC" CLASS

Displacement, tons	16 000 standard; 19 500 full load
Length, feet (*metres*)	630 (*192·0*) pp; 700 (*213·4*) oa
Beam, feet (*metres*)	80 (*24·4*) hull
Width, feet (*metres*)	128 (*39·0*)
Draught, feet (*metres*)	24 (*7·3*)
Aircraft	21 capacity
Guns, AA	15—40 mm; 4 twin, 7 single
Boilers	4 Admiralty 3-drum; 400 psi; 700°F
Main engines	Parsons single reduction geared turbines; 40 000 shp; 2 shafts
Speed, knots	24·5 designed
Complement	1 343, designed accommodation

Acquired from Great Britain in Jan 1957 after having been suspended in May 1946 when structurally almost complete and 75% fitted out. Taken in hand by Harland & Wolff Ltd, Belfast, in Apr 1957 for completion in 1961 Commissioned on 4 Mar 1961 and renamed *Vikrant*.

HABITABILITY. Partially air-conditioned and insulated for tropical service, the ship's sides being sprayed with asbestos cement instead of being lagged. Separate messes and dining halls.

AIRCRAFT. Still equipped with Seahawks although re-equipment is planned. Harrier trials in mid-1972 showed promise.

ENGINEERING. Engines and boilers are arranged *en echelon*, one set of turbines and two boilers being installed side by side in each of the two propelling machinery spaces, on the unit system, so that the starboard propeller shaft is longer than the port.

FLIGHT DECK. The aircraft including strike and anti-submarine aircraft, operate from an angled deck with steam catapult, landing sights and two electrically operated lifts.

RADAR. Search: Type 960, Type 277. Tactical: Type 293. Miscellaneous: Type 963 Carrier Controlled Approach.

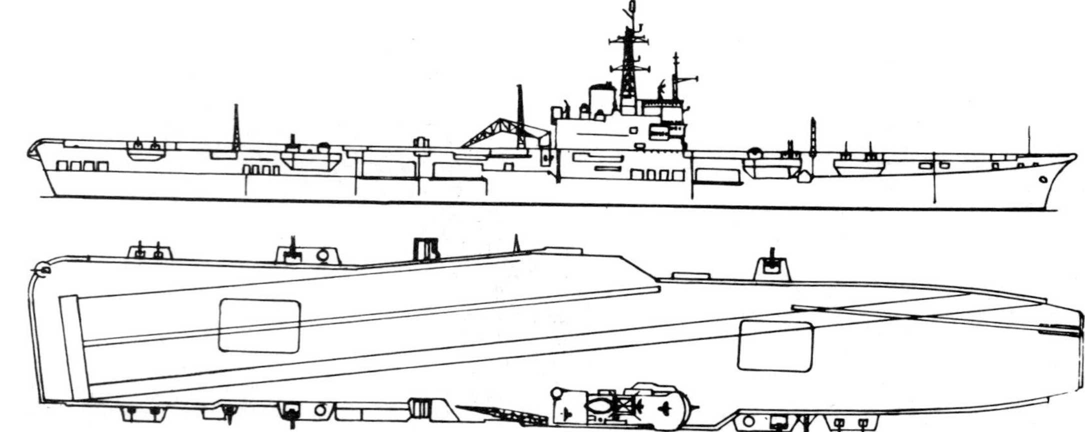

DRAWING. Starboard elevation and plan. Drawn in 1971. Scale: 125 feet = 1 inch (1 : 1 500).

VIKRANT *1971, John G. C. llis*

CRUISERS

Name	No.	Builders	Engineers	Laid down	Launched	Completed
MYSORE (ex- HMS *Nigeria*)	C 60	Vickers-Armstrongs, Ltd, Tyne	Parsons	8 Feb 1938	18 July 1939	23 Sep 1940

Displacement, tons	8 700 standard; 11 040 full load
Length, feet (*metres*)	538·0 (*164·0*)pp; 549·0 (*167·3*)wl 555·5 (*169·3*) oa
Beam, feet (*metres*)	62·0 (*18·9*)
Draught, feet (*metres*)	21·0 (*6·4*) max
Guns	9—6 in (*152 mm*), 3 triple; 8—4 in (*102 mm*) LP, 4 twin; 12—40 mm AA; 5 twin, 2 single
Armour	Side 4½ in—3 in (*114—76 mm*); Deck 2 in (*51 mm*); Conning tower 4 in (102 *mm*); Turrets 2 in (*51 mm*)
Main engines	Parsons geared turbines; 4 shafts; 72 500 shp
Speed, knots	31·5
Boilers	4 Admiralty 3-drum type
Complement	800

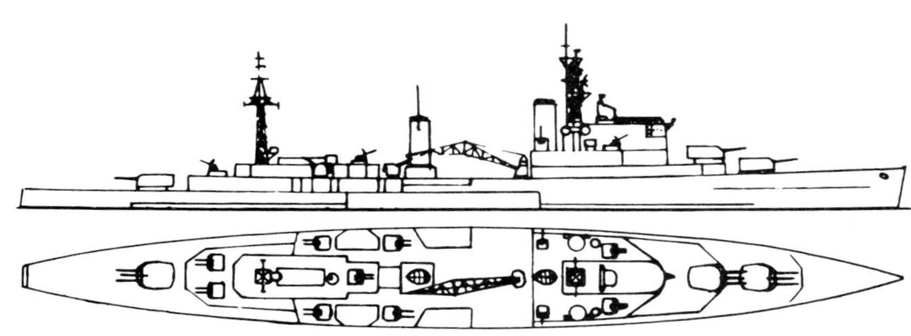

GENERAL

Formerly a "Colony" class cruiser in the Royal Navy. Purchased from Great Britain on 8 Apr 1954 for £300 000. Extensively refitted and reconstructed by Cammell Laird & Co Ltd, Birkenhead, before commissioning. Formally handed over to the Indian Navy at Birkenhead and renamed *Mysore* on 29 Aug 1957. Involved in two serious collisions, the second in late 1972 with *Beas*, resulting in two months of repairs.

RADAR. Search: Type 960, Type 277. Tactical: Type 293. Fire Control: X Band.

RECONSTRUCTION. Ship formerly had tripod masts. During reconstruction the triple 6 inch turret in "X" position and the 6—21 inch torpedo tubes (tripled) were removed, the bridge was modified, two lattice masts were stepped, all electrical equipment was replaced and the engine room and other parts of the ship were refitted.

DRAWING. Starboard elevation and plan. Drawn in 1971. Scale: 125 feet = 1 inch (1 : 1 500).

MYSORE *1971, Roland Rodwell*

Name	No.	Builders	Laid down	Launched	Completed
DELHI (ex HMS *Achilles*)	C 74	Cammell Laird & Co Ltd, Birkenhead	11 June 1931	1 Sep 1932	5 Oct 1933

Displacement, tons	7 114 standard; 9 740 full load
Length, feet (*metres*)	522·0 (*159·1*)pp; 544·5 (*166·0*)oa
Beam, feet (*metres*)	55·2 (*16·8*)
Draught, feet (*metres*)	20·0 (*6·1*) max
Guns	6—6 in (*152 mm*); 8—4 in (*102 mm*) AA; 14—40 mm AA; 4—3 pdr saluting
Armour	4 in-2 in side; 1 in gunhouses; 1 in bridge; 2 in deck
Main engines	Parsons geared turbines; 4 shafts 72 000 shp
Speed, knots	32
Boilers	4 Admiralty 3-drum type
Oil fuel, tons	1 800
Complement	800

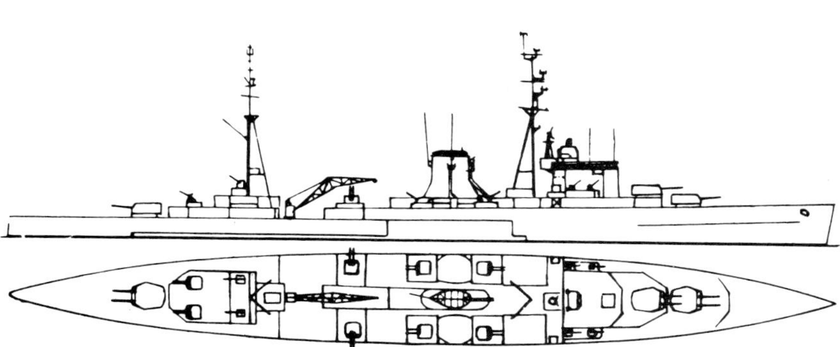

Formerly a "Leander" class light cruiser in the Royal Navy. Purchased from Great Britain and delivered on 5 July 1948. Refitted in 1955. Now used for training.

RADAR. Search: Type 960, Type 277. Tactical: Type 293. Fire Control: Early design.

TORPEDO TUBES. In 1958 the original eight 21 inch torpedo tubes, in two quadruple banks, were removed, and the forecastle deck plating was consequently extended aft to the twin 40 mm AA gun mounting abreast the boat stowage.

HISTORICAL. As HMS *Achilles*, then lent to the Royal New Zealand Navy, this ship, with HMS *Ajax* and HMS *Exeter*, defeated the German battleship *Admiral Graf Spee* in the Battle of the River Plate on 13 Dec 1939.

DRAWING. Starboard elevation and plan. Drawn in 1971. Scale: 125 feet = 1 inch (1 : 1 500).

DELHI

DESTROYERS

3 Ex-BRITISH "R" CLASS

Name	No.	Builders	Begun	Launched	Completed	Transferred
RANA (ex-HMS *Raider*)	D 115	Cammell Laird & Co Ltd, Birkenhead	16 Apr 1941	1 Apr 1942	16 Nov 1942	9 Sep 1949
RAJPUT (ex-HMS *Rotherham*)	D 209	John Brown & Co Ltd, Clydebank	10 Apr 1941	21 Mar 1942	27 Aug 1942	29 July 1949
RANJIT (ex-HMS *Redoubt*)	D 141	John Brown & Co Ltd, Clydebank	19 June 1941	2 May 1942	1 Oct 1942	4 July 1949

Displacement, tons	1 725 standard; 2 424 full load
Length, feet (*metres*)	339·5 (*103·5*) wl; 362·0 (*110·3*) oa
Beam, feet (*metres*)	35·7 (*10·9*)
Draught, feet (*metres*)	17·1 (*5·2*)
Guns	4—4·7 in (*120 mm*); 4—40 mm AA
A/S weapons	4 DCT
Torpedo tubes	8—21 in (2 quadruple) in *Rana*
Main engines	Parsons geared turbines; 2 shafts 40 000 shp
Speed, knots	32
Boilers	2 Admiralty 3-drum type
Oil fuel, tons	490
Range, miles	2 500 at 20 knots
Complement	240

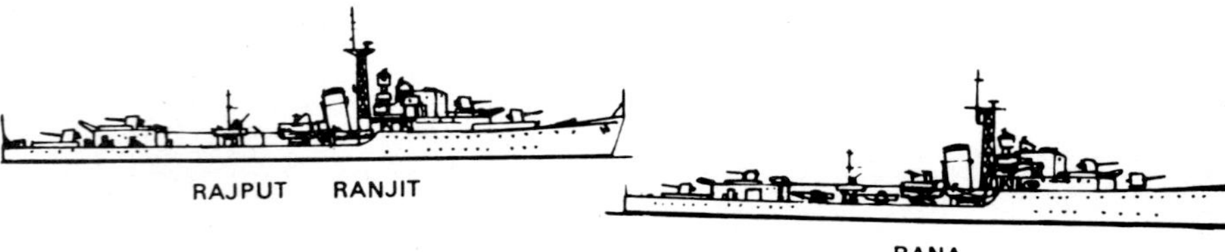

RAJPUT RANJIT

RANA

First British destroyers with officers' accommodation forward instead of aft. Refitted and modernised before transfer. Arrived in Indian waters in Jan 1950. Constitute 11th Destroyer Squadron of which *Rajput* is Leader.

RADAR. Search: Type 293. Fire Control: Early design.

RAJPUT

3 "HUNT" CLASS TYPE II

Name	No.	Builders	Laid down	Launched	Completed
GANGA (ex-HMS *Chiddingfold*)	D 94	Scott's Shipbuilding & Engineering Co Ltd, Greenock	1 Mar 1940	10 Mar 1941	16 Oct 1941
GODAVARI (ex-HMS *Bedale*, ex-*Slazak*, ex-*Bedale*)	D 92	R. & W. Hawthorn, Leslie & Co Ltd, Hebburn	29 May 1940	5 Sep 1941	18 June 1944
GOMATI (ex-HMS *Lamerton*)	D 93	Swan, Hunter & Wigham Richardson Ltd, Wallsend	10 Apr 1939	14 Dec 1940	16 Aug 1944

Displacement, tons	1 050 standard; 1 610 full load
Length, feet (*metres*)	264·2 (*80·5*) pp; 280·0 (*85·3*) oa
Beam, feet (*metres*)	31·5 (*9·6*)
Draught feet (*metres*)	14·0 (*4·3*)
Guns	6—4 in (*102 mm*) dp; 4—20 mm AA
Main engines	Parsons geared turbines; 2 shafts; 19 000 shp
Speed, knots	25
Boilers	2 Admiralty 3-drum
Oil fuel, tons	280
Range, miles	3 700 at 14 knots
Complement	150

GANGA, GODAVARI, GOMATI

GANGA *Added 1971, A. & J. Pavia*

Former "Hunt" class, Type II frigates F 131, F 126 and F 88, respectively, (ex-Escort Destroyers). Transferred from Great Britain in Apr/May 1953. Lent to the Indian Navy for three years, subject to extension by agreement. Officially rated as destroyers with D pennant Nos. Constitute the 22nd Destroyer Squadron of which *Godavari* is leader. Now used for training.

FRIGATES

6 NEW CONSTRUCTION "LEANDER" CLASS

HIMGIRI + 4 **NILGIRI**

Displacement, tons	2 450 standard; 2 800 full load
Length, feet (*metres*)	360 (*109·7*) wl; 372 (*113·4*) oa
Beam, feet (*metres*)	43 (*13·1*)
Draught, feet (*metres*)	18 (*5·5*)
Aircraft	1 Wasp helicopter
Missiles, AA	2 "Seacat" quadruple launchers
Guns, dual purpose	2—4·5 in (*115 mm*) 1 twin 2—40 mm
A/S weapons	1 "Limbo" 3 barrelled DC mortar
Boilers	2
Main engines	2 geared turbines; 30 000 shp
Speed, knots	30 max
Oil fuel, tons	460
Range, miles	4 500 at 12 knots
Complement	263

First major warships built in Indian yards. Of similar design to later (broad beam) "Leander" class general purpose frigates in the Royal Navy. All ordered from Mazagon Docks Ltd, Bombay. *Nilgiri* was laid down in Oct 1966, launched on 23 Oct 1968 and was commissioned on 3 June 1972. *Himgiri* was launched on 6 May 1970. The third ship was laid down on 14 Sep 1970. Three further ships of the class are projected to complete at yearly intervals.

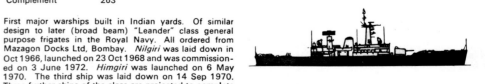

LEANDER *Class*

3 "LEOPARD" CLASS

Name	No.	Builders	Launched	Completed
BEAS	F 137	Vickers-Armstrongs Ltd, Newcastle-on-Tyne	9 Oct 1958	24 May 1960
BETWA	F 139	Vickers-Armstrongs Ltd, Newcastle-on-Tyne	15 Sep 1959	8 Dec 1960
BRAHMAPUTRA (ex-*Panther*)	F 31	John Brown & Co Ltd, Clydebank	15 Mar 1957	28 Mar 1958

Displacement, tons	2 251 standard; 2 515 full load
Length, feet (*metres*)	320·0 (*97·5*) pp; 330·0 (*100·6*) wl; 339·8 (*103·6*) oa
Beam, feet (*metres*)	40·0 (*12·2*)
Draught, feet (*metres*)	16·0 (*4·9*) max
Guns	4—4·5 in (*114 mm*), 2 twin; 4—40 mm AA
A/S weapons	1 Squid 3-barrelled DC mortar
Main engines	Admiralty standard range diesels 2 shafts; 12 380 bhp
Speed, knots	25
Range, miles	7 500 at 16 knots
Complement	210

BEAS, BETWA, BRAHMAPUTRA

Frigates—*continued*

Brahmaputra (Leader), originally ordered as *Panther* for the Royal Navy on 28 June 1951, was the first major warship to be built in Great Britain for the Indian Navy since India became independent. All three ships are generally similar to the British frigates of the "Leopard" class, but modified to suit Indian conditions.

RADAR. Search: Type 960. Tactical: Type 293. Fire Control: X Band forward and aft.

BRAHMAPUTRA — *1971, Indian Navy,*

2 "WHITBY" CLASS. 1st RATE

Name	*No.*	*Builders*	*Launched*	*Completed*
TALWAR	F 140	Cammell Laird & Co Ltd, Birkenhead	18 July 1958	1960
TRISHUL (*Leader*)	F 143	Harland & Wolff Ltd, Belfast	18 June 1959	1960

Displacement, tons	2 144 standard; 2 545 full load (*Talwar*), 2 557 (*Trishul*)
Length, feet (*metres*)	360 (*109·7*) pp 369·8 (*112·7*) oa
Beam, feet (*metres*)	41 (*12·5*)
Draught, feet (*metres*)	17·8 (*5·4*)
Guns, surface	2—4·5 in (*115 mm*)
Guns, AA	4—40 mm (1 twin before "Limbos", 2 singles abaft funnel)
A/S weapons	2 "Limbo" 3-barrelled DC mortars
Boilers	2 Babcock & Wilcox
Main engines	2 sets geared turbines; 30 000 shp; 2 shafts
Speed, knots	30 max
Oil fuel, tons	400
Range, miles	4 500 at 12 knots
Complement	231 (11 officers, 220 men)

TALWAR, TRISHUL

GENERAL
Built in Great Britain and generally similar to the British frigates of the "Whitby" class, but slightly modified tc suit Indian conditions.

RADAR. Tactical: Type 293. Fire Control: X Band.

TORPEDO TUBES. Provision was made in the original design for twelve 21 inch (eight single A/S and two twin) but they were not fitted.

TALWAR — *A. & J. Pavia*

2 "BLACKWOOD" CLASS 2nd RATE

Name	*No*	*Builders*	*Launched*	*Completed*
KIRPAN	F 144	Alex Stephen & Sons Ltd Govan, Glasgow	19 Aug 1958	July 1959
KUTHAR	F 146	J. Samuel White & Co Ltd Cowes, Isle of Wight	14 Oct 1958	1959

Displacement, tons	1 180 standard; 1 456 full load
Length, feet (*metres*)	300 (*91·4*) pp; 310 (*94·5*) oa
Beam, feet (*metres*)	33 (*10·0*)
Draught, feet (*metres*)	15·5 (*4·7*)
Guns, AA	3—40 mm (single)
A/S weapons	2 "Limbo" 3-barrelled DC mortars
Boilers	Babcock & Wilcox
Main engines	1 set geared turbines; 15 000 shp; 1 shaft
Speed, knots	27·8 max; 24·5 sustained sea
Range, miles	4 000 at 12 knots
Oil fuel, tons	300
Complement	150

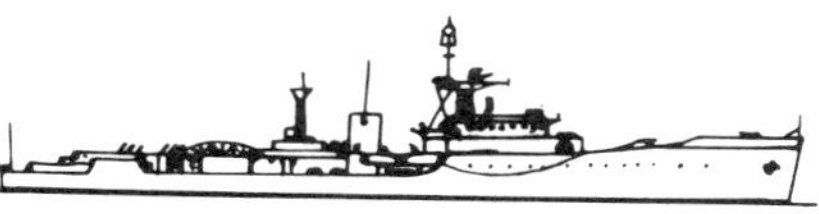

KIRPAN, KUTHAR

Built in Great Britain, and generally similar to the British frigates of the "Blackwood" class, but slightly modified to suit Indian requirements. Kirpan means Sword. *Khukri* was sunk in the Pakistan war on 9 Dec 1971.

RADAR. Fitted with S band air and surface surveillance radar.

TORPEDO TUBES. Provision was made for four 21-inch (2 twin), but they were not fitted.

KUTHAR — *A. & J. Pavia*

2 "KISTNA" CLASS

Name	*No.*	*Builders*	*Laid down*	*Launched*	*Completed*
KAVERI	F 110	Yarrow & Co. Ltd, Scotstoun, Glasgow	28 Oct 1942	15 June 1943	21 Oct 1943
KISTNA	F 46	Yarrow & Co. Ltd, Scotstoun, Glasgow	14 July 1942	22 Apr 1943	23 Aug 1943

Displacement, tons	1 470 standard; 1 925 full load
Length, feet (*metres*)	283·0 (*86·3*) pp; 295·5 (*90·1*) wl 299·5 (*91·3*) oa
Beam, feet (*metres*)	38·5 (*11·7*)
Draught, feet (*metres*)	11·2 (*3·4*)
Guns	4—4 in (*102 mm*); 4—40 mm AA
A/S weapons	2 DCT
Main engines	Parsons geared turbines; 2 shafts; 4 300 shp
Speed, knots	19
Boilers	2 three-drum type
Range, miles	4 500 at 12 knots
Oil fuel, tons	370
Complement	210

Former sloops of the British "Black Swan" class built for India and modified to suit Indian conditions. *Cauvery* was renamed *Kaveri* in 1968.

RADAR. Fitted with S band air and surface surveillance radar and ranging radar for the gunfire control system.

KAVERI, KISTNA

1 "RIVER" CLASS

TIR F 256 (ex-HMS *Bann*)

Displacement, tons	1 463 standard; 1 934 full load
Length, feet (*metres*)	283·0 (*86·3*) pp; 303 (*92·4*) oa
Beam, feet (*metres*)	36·7 (*11·2*)
Draught, feet (*metres*)	14·5 (*4·4*)
Guns	1—4 in (*102 mm*); 1—40 mm AA; 2—20 mm AA
Main engines	Triple expansion; 2 shafts; 5 500 ihp
Speed, knots	18
Boilers	2 Admiralty 3-drum type
Range, miles	4 200 at 12 knots
Oil fuel, tons	385
Complement	120

TIR

Frigates—*continued*

Former "River" class frigate in the Royal Navy. Built by Charles Hill & Sons Ltd, Bristol. Laid down on 18 June 1942, launched on 29 Dec 1942, completed on 7 May 1942 and transferred on 3 Dec 1945. Converted to a Midshipman's Training Frigate by Bombay Dockyard in 1948. Originally the sister ship of *Investigator*, see under Survey Ships.

8 "PETYA" CLASS

KADMATT **KATCHAL** **KILTAN**
KAMORTA **KAVARATTI** **+ 3**

Displacement, tons	950 standard; 1 150 full load
Length, feet (*metres*)	250·0 (*76·2*) wl; 270 (*82·3*) oa
Beam, feet (*metres*)	29·9 (*9·1*)
Draught, feet (*metres*)	10·5 (*3·2*)
Guns	4—3 in (*76 mm*) dp, 2 twin
Torpedo tubes	5—16 in
Main engines	2 gas turbines; 30 000 hp; 2 diesels; 2 shafts; 6 000 hp
Speed, knots	34

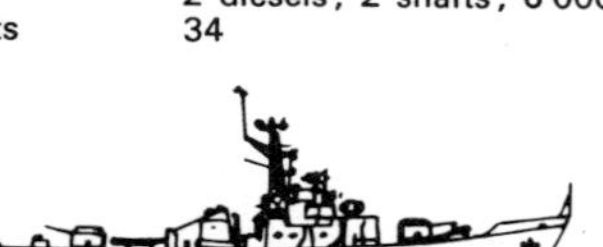

KADMATT

"PETYA" CLASS *Ex-Soviet*

Transferred to the Indian Navy since 1969. Pennant numbers of two units are reported to be P 179 and P 181. Fitted with Head Net "A" radar.

SUBMARINES

4 EX SOVIET "F" CLASS

KALVARI **KARANJ** **KURSURA**
KANDERI

Displacement, tons	2 000 surface; 2 300 dived
Length, feet (*metres*)	296·8 (*90·5*)
Beam, feet (*metres*)	24·1 (*7·3*)
Draught, feet (*metres*)	19·0 (*5·8*)
Tubes	10—21 in (20 torpedoes carried)
Main engines	Diesels; 3 shafts; 6 000 bhp; 3 electric motors; 6 000 hp
Speed, knots	20 surface; 15 dived
Complement	70

KALVARI

KANDERI *1971, Dr. Louis Th. Berge*

Kalvari arrived in India on 16 July 1968 and *Kanderi* in May 1969. *Karanj* in Jan 1970 and *Kursura* in Apr 1970.

AMPHIBIOUS VESSELS

SOVIET "POLOCNY" CLASS

GHARIAL 1 (1966) **GULDAR 2** (1966)

Displacement, tons	900 to 1 000
Dimensions, feet	246 × 39·3 × 9·8
Armament	Rocket projector
Main Engines	Diesels; 4 000 bhp = 15 knots

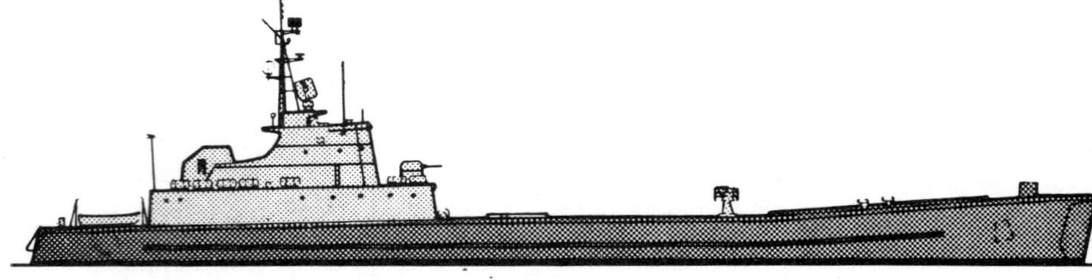

POLNOCNY *Class*

MAGAR (ex-HMS *Avenger*, LST (3) 3011)

Displacement, tons	2 256 light; 4 980 full load
Dimensions, feet	347·5 oa × 55·2 × 11·2
Guns	2—40 mm AA; 6—20 mm AA; (2 twin, 2 single)
Main Engines	Triple expansion; 2 shafts; 5 500 ihp = 13 knots

Former British tank landing ship of the LST (3) type transferred in 1949. There is also LCT 4294 (ex-1294), yard craft of 200 tons, 187·2 × 38·8 × 3·5 feet, speed 9·5 knots.

MAGAR *1964, A. & J. Pavia*

LIGHT FORCES

8 "OSA" TYPE (MISSILE BOATS)

MTB 1 **MTB 2** **MTB 3** **MTB 4** **MTB 5** **MTB 6** **MTB 7** **MTB 8**

Displacement, tons	165 standard; 200 full load
Dimensions, feet	128·7 × 25·1 × 5·9
Guns	4—30 mm (2 twin)
Main engines	3 diesels; 3 shafts; 13 000 bhp = 32 knots
Missile launchers	4 in two pairs for SSN 2A (Styx)

Reported to be of similar type to the Soviet missile boats of the "Osa" class.

OSA *Class*

DHARINI A 306 (ex-*Hermine*)

Displacement, tons	**4 625**
Dimensions, feet	**328 × 46 × 19**
Main Engines	**Triple expansion**
Oil fuel (tons)	**621**

Cargo ship converted to a tender. Officially rated as a repair and store ship. Commissioned in May 1960.

DHARINI *1964, Indian Navy*

Light Forces—*continued*

5 Ex-USSR POLUCHAT CLASS

PANBAN **PANAJI** **PANVEL** **PULICAT** **PURI**

Displacement, tons	100 standard
Dimensions, feet	98·4 × 19 × 5·9
Guns	2—25 mm

4 HDML TYPE

SPC 3110 (ex-*HDML* 1110) **SPC 3117** (ex-*HDML* 1117)
SPC 3112 (ex-*HDML* 1112) **SPC 3118** (ex-*HDML* 1118)

Displacement, tons	48 standard; 54 full load
Dimensions, feet	72 oa × 16 × 4·7
Guns	2—20 mm AA
Main Engines	Diesel; 2 shafts; 320 bhp = 12 knots
Complement	14

Former British Harbour Defence Motor Launches. These boats, formerly known as Seaward Defence Motor Launches, constitute the 321st Sea/Land Patrol Craft Squadron.

The seaward patrol craft *SPC* 6420 (ex-*ML* 6420, ex-*ML* 420) of the Fairmile "B" motor launch type, was stricken from the Navy list in 1963.
Six were ordered from USSR five of which were reportedly delivered in 1967. One on loan to Bangladesh.

SPC 3112 *Indian Navy.*

MINE WARFARE FORCES

4 "TON" CLASS

CANNANORE (ex-*Whitton*) M 1191 **KAKINADA** (ex-*Durweston*) M 1201
CUDDALORE (ex-*Wennington*) M 1190 **KARWAR** (ex-*Overton*) Leader M 1197

Displacement, tons	360 standard; 425 full load
Dimensions, feet	140·0 pp; 153·0 oa × 28·8 × 8·2
Guns	2—20 mm AA
Main engines	Napier Deltic diesels; 2 shafts; 1 250 bhp = 15 knots
Oil fuel, tons	45
Range, miles	3 000 at 8 knots
Complement	40

"Ton" class coastal minesweepers of wooden construction built for the Royal Navy, but transferred from Great Britain to the Indian Navy in 1956. *Cannanore* was built by Fleetlands Shipyard, Ltd Gosport and launched 30 Jan 1956; *Karwar* was built by Camper & Nicholson, Ltd, Gosport, and launched 30 Jan 1956. *Cuddalore*, built by J. S. Doig Ltd, Grimsby, and *Kakinada*, built by Dorset Yacht Co Ltd, Hamworthy were taken over in Aug 1956, and sailed for India in Nov Dec 1956. Named after minor ports in India. Constitute the 18th Mine Counter Measures Squadron, together with the inshore minesweepers. Four more were reportedly to be acquired.
A photograph of *Cannanore* appears in the 1957-58 to 1963-64 editions and of *Kakinada* in the 1967-68 to 1970-71 editions.

KARWAR *1971, Wright & Logan*

4 "HAM" CLASS (IMS)

BASSEIN (ex-*Littleham*) M 2707 **BIMLIPITAN** (ex-*Hildersham*) M 2705
BHATKAL M 89 **BULSAR**

Displacement, tons	120 standard; 170 full load
Dimensions, feet	98·0 pp; 107·0 oa × 22·0 × 6·7
Guns	1—20 mm AA
Main engines	2 Paxman diesels; 550 bhp = 14 knots (9 knots sweeping)
Oil fuel, tons	15
Complement	16

"Ham" class inshore minesweepers of wooden construction built for the Royal Navy but transferred from Great Britain to the Indian Navy in 1955. *Bassein* was built by Brooke Marine Ltd, Oulton Broad, Lowestoft, and launched on 4 May 1954; *Bimlipitan* was built by Vosper Ltd, Portsmouth, and launched on 5 Feb 1954. Two further units were built at Magazon Dockyard Bombay. *Bhaktal* was launched in Apr 1967, and *Bulsar* on 17 May 1969. Two more ships are projected.
Barq (ex-*MMS* 132), *MMS* 130 and *MMS* 154, former British motor minesweepers of the "105 ft" type of wooden construction, transferred from Great Britain, are employed as yard craft. *MMS* 1632 and *MMS* 1654 are yard craft in Bombay.

BASSEIN *1971, A. & J. Pavia*

SURVEY SHIPS

1 INDIAN BUILT

DARSHAK

Displacement, tons	2 790
Length, feet (*metres*)	319 (*97·2*) oa
Beam, feet (*metres*)	49 (*14·9*)
Draught, feet (*metres*)	28·8 (*8·8*)
Main engines	2 diesel-electric units, 3 000 bhp
Speed, knots	16
Complement	150

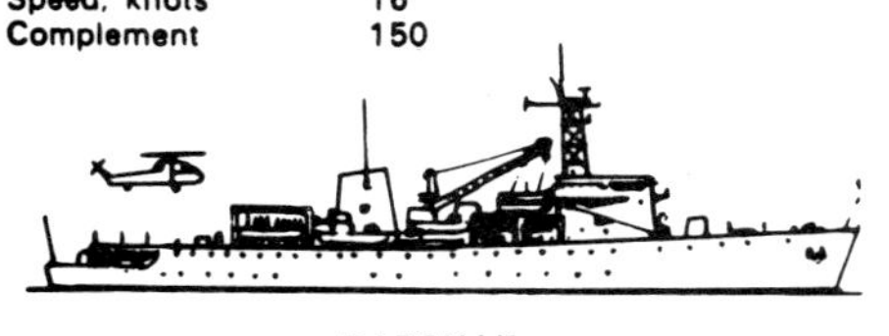

DARSHAK

DARSHAK *1967*

First ship built by Hindustan Shipyard, Vizagapatam for the Navy. Launched on 2 Nov 1959 and commissioned on 28 Dec 1964. Provision was made to operate a helicopter. The ship is all welded.

1 "RIVER" CLASS (Ex-FRIGATE)

INVESTIGATOR F 243 (ex-*Khukri*, ex-HMS *Trent*)

Displacement, tons	1 460 standard; 1 930 full load
Length, feet (*metres*)	283 (*86·3*) pp; 303 (*92·4*) oa
Beam, feet (*metres*)	36·7 (*11·2*)
Draught, feet (*metres*)	14 (*4·3*)
Boilers	2 Admiralty 3-drum
Main engines	Triple expansion 5 500 shp; 2 shafts
Speed, knots	18 max
Range, miles	5 000 at 10 knots
Oil fuel, tons	400
Complement	172

INVESTIGATOR

INVESTIGATOR *1965, Indian Navy*

Former "River" class frigate in the Royal Navy. Built by Charles Hill & Sons Ltd, Bristol. Laid down on 31 Jan 1942, launched on 10 Oct 1942, completed on 15 Feb 1943, and transferred in April 1946. Converted to a survey ship and renamed *Investigator* in 1951. Originally the sister ship of the training frigate *Tir*, see previous page.

Survey Ships—*continued*

2 "SUTLEJ" CLASS
(Ex-FRIGATES, Ex-SLOOPS)

JUMNA F 11 **SUTLEJ** F 95

Displacement, tons	1 300 standard; 1 750 full load
Length, feet (*metres*)	276 (*84·1*) wl; 292·5 (*89·2*) oa
Beam, feet (*metres*)	37·5 (*11·4*)
Draught, feet (*metres*)	11·5 (*3·5*)
Boilers	2 Admiralty 3-drum
Main engines	Parsons geared turbines 3 600 shp; 2 shafts
Speed, knots	18
Range, miles	5 600 at 12 knots
Oil fuel, tons	370
Complement	150

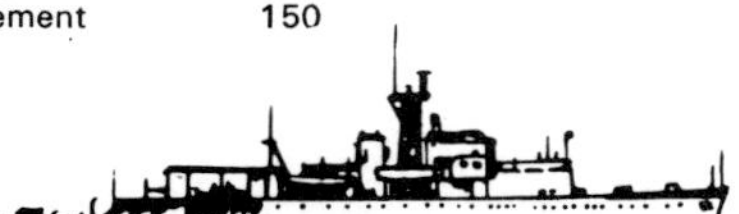
JUMNA

JUMNA 1971, Indian Navy

Former frigates employed as survey ships since 1957 and 1955 respectively. Both ships are generally similar to the former British frigates of the "Egret" class. *Jumna* and *Sutlej* together with *Kaveri* and *Kistna* (see previous page) formerly constituted the 12th Frigate Squadron.

CONSTRUCTION. Both built by Wm. Denny & Bros Ltd, Dumbarton. *Jumna* was laid down on 20 Feb 1940, launched on 16 Nov 1940 and completed on 13 May 1941. *Sutlej* was laid down on 4 Jan 1940, launched on 10 Oct 1940 and completed on 23 Apr 1941.

SUBMARINE TENDERS

AMBA A 14

Displacement, tons	6 000 light; 9 000 full load
Dimensions, feet	370 pp; 420 oa × 65 × 20
Guns, dual purpose	4—2·3 in (*57 mm*) 2 twin
Main engines	Diesels; 2 shafts; 7 000 bhp = 17 knots

Modified "Ugra" type acquired from the USSR in 1968. Provision for helicopter.

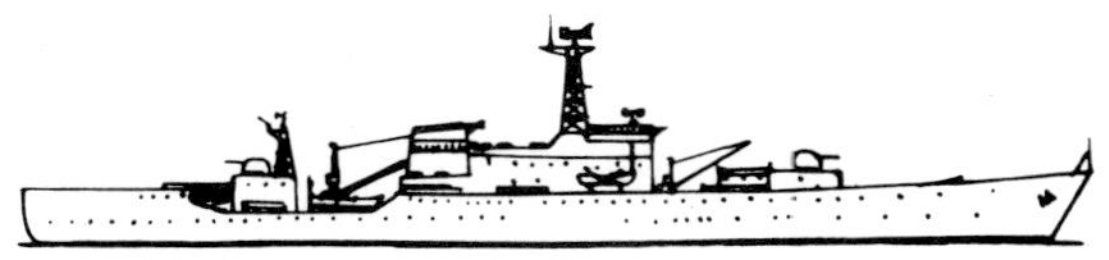
AMBA

NISTAR

Displacement, tons	790 standard; 900 full load
Dimensions, feet	220·0 × 29·5 × 7·9
Main engines	2 diesels; 2 shafts; 5 000 bhp = 18 knots

Converted from a fleet minesweeper of the Soviet "T 58" type to a submarine rescue ship and transferred from USSR late-1971.

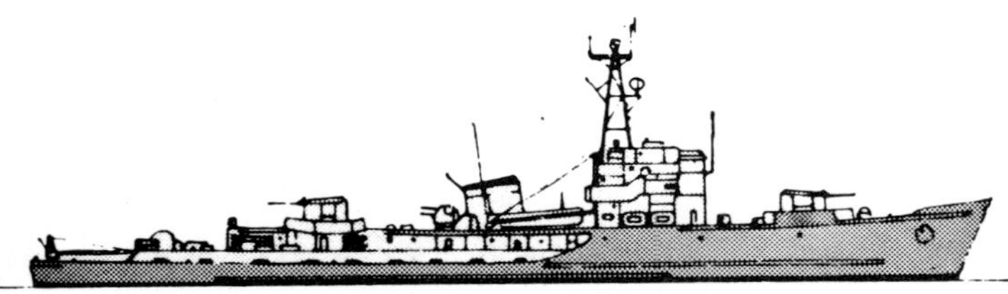

OILERS

SHAKTI A 136

Displacement, tons	3 500
Dimensions, feet	323 × 44 × 20
Main Engines	Diesel; speed: 13 knots max; 9 knots economical

Rated as Fleet Replenishment Group Tanker. Acquired from Italy in Nov 1953.

HOOGHLY

Formerly *"Baqir"* of Gulf Shipping Corp. Ltd. Acquired in 1972.

CHILKA **SAMBHAR**

Displacement, tons	1 530 (oil capacity 1 000)
Dimensions, feet	202 × 30·7 × 13
Main Engines	Triple expansion; 809 ihp = 9 knots

Chilka built by Blythwood Shipbuilding Co, Scotstoun. *Sambhar* by A. & J. Inglis, Ltd, Glasgow, launched 1942. Both acquired in 1948. Engined by David Rowan & Co. Two steam dynamos, two steam pumps, ballast pump. Rated as yard craft.

DEEPAK A 1750

On charter to Indian Navy from Mogul Lines. Fleet replenishment tanker. Fitted with a helicopter landing platform aft, but no hangar.

TUG

HATHI

Displacement, tons	668
Dimensions, feet	147·5 × 23·7 × 15
Main Engines	Triple expansion; speed = 13 knots

Built by the Taikoo Dock & Engineering Company, Hong Kong. Launched in 1932.

SEAWARD DEFENCE BOATS

6 "AJAY" CLASS

ABHAY **AJAY** **AJIT** **AKSHAY** **AMAR** **ASIT**

Displacement, tons	120 standard; 151 full load (*Ajay* 146)
Dimensions, feet	110 pp; 117·2 oa × 20 × 5
Guns	1—40 mm AA
Main Engines	2 diesels; speed = 18 knots

Generally similar to the "Ford" class in the Royal Navy. *Ajay* was built by Garden Reach Workshop, Calcutta and commissioned on 21 Sep 1960. *Abhay* and *Akshay* were both built by Hoogly Docking and Engineering Company Ltd. Calcutta and commissioned on 13 Nov 1961 and 8 Jan 1962, respectively. *Asit* launched 27 Sept 1969. Two more under construction.

AJAY 1964, Indian Navy.

2 "SHARADA" CLASS

SHARADA SPB 3133 **SUKANYA** SPB 3132

Displacement, tons	86
Dimensions, feet	103·2, length
Guns	Small arms
Main Engines	Diesels

Built in Yugoslavia. Commissioned on 5 Dec 1959 and 12 Dec 1959, respectively.

SHARADA 1964, Indian Navy.

4 "SAVITRI" CLASS

SAVITRI SPB 3128 **SHARAYU** SPB 3129 **SUBHADRA** SPB 3130 **SUVARNA** SPB 3131

Displacement, tons	63
Dimensions, feet	85·3 pp; 90·2 oa × 20 × 5
Guns	Small Arms
Main Engines	2 diesels; 2 shafts; 1 900 bhp = 21 knots

Built in Italy. Commissioned on 6 Feb 1958, 28 Oct 1957, 20 Aug 1957 and 28 Aug 1957, respectively. Constitute the 322nd SDB Squadron. *Sharayu* is Leader.

INDONESIA

Administration

Commander-in-Chief of the Navy and Chief of the Naval Staff:
Vice-Admiral R. Sudomo

Deputy Chief of the Naval Staff Operations:
Rear-Admiral L. M. Abdul Kadir

Inspector General of the Navy:
Rear Admiral Subroto Judono

Chief for Naval Material:
Rear Admiral Sudiono

Chief for Naval Personnel:
Rear Admiral Suprapto

Commander of Navy Marine Corps:
Brigadier General Moch. Anwar

Commander-in-Chief Indonesian Fleet:
Vice-Admiral Samsjul Bachri

Strength of the Fleet

- 3 Destroyers
- 10 Frigates
- 18 Corvettes
- 10 Submarines
- 17 Amphibious Vessels (includes 8 LST)
- 12 Missile Boats
- 18 Gunboats
- 21 Torpedo Boats
- 34 Patrol Craft (plus 48 auxiliary patrol craft)
- 6 Fleet Minesweepers
- 20 Coastal Minesweepers
- 4 Survey Vessels
- 4 Depot Ships
- 9 Oilers
- 10 Auxiliaries

Diplomatic Representation

Naval Attaché and Naval Attaché for air in London:
Colonel D. U. Martojo

Naval Attaché and Naval Attaché for Air in Washington:
Colonel Kko. Santoso

Personnel

Navy: 25 000; and 14 000 Marine Commando Corps

Disposals

CRUISER
1972 *Irian*
CORVETTES
1958 *Hang Tuah*, sunk by rebel aircraft
1968 *Banteng, Radjawali*
1969 *Pati Unus*

Mercantile Marine

Lloyd's Register of Shipping:
513 vessels of 618 589 tons gross

DESTROYERS

SANDJAJA *Indonesian Navy*

3 Ex-USSR "SKORY" CLASS

BRAWIDJAJA 306
SANDJAJA
SULTAN BADARUDIN 303

Displacement, tons	2 600 standard; 3 500 full load
Length, feet (*metres*)	395·2 (*120·5*)
Beam, feet (*metres*)	38·9 (*11·8*)
Draught, feet (*metres*)	15·1 (*4·6*)
Guns, surface	4—5·1 in (*130 mm*); 2 twin
Guns, AA	2—3·4 in (*76 mm*); 7—37 mm; certain ships have 8—37 mm (4 twin)
A/S weapons	4 DCT
Torpedo tubes	10—21 in (*533 mm*)
Mines	Could carry up to 80
Boilers	3
Main engines	Geared turbines; 2 shafts; 60 000 shp
Speed, knots	33
Range, miles	3 900 at 13 knots
Complement	260

Former Soviet destroyers of the "Skory" type. Built in 1951-56. Four (201, 202, 203, 204,) were purchased from Poland and transferred to the Indonesian Navy in 1959. One more was transferred in 1962 and a pair in 1964. Deletions occurred in 1969 and 1971.

FRIGATES

1 Ex-US "CLAUD JONES" CLASS

SAMADIKUN (ex-USS *John R. Perry* DE 1034)

Displacement, tons	1 450 standard; 1 750 full load
Length, feet (*metres*)	310 (*95*) oa
Beam, feet (*metres*)	37 (*11·3*)
Draught, feet (*metres*)	18 (*5·5*)
Guns	1—3 in 50 cal
A/S weapons	2 triple Torpedo Tubes (Mk 32)
Main engines	4 diesels; 9 200 hp; 1 shaft
Speed, knots	22
Complement	175

Purchased from USN 20 Feb 1973

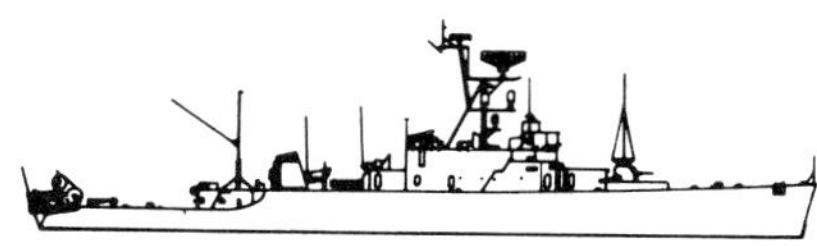

SAMADIKUN

6 Ex-USSR "RIGA" CLASS

JOS SUDARSO 351
KAKIALI 359
LAMBUNG MANGKURAT 357
NGURAH RAI 353
NUKU 360
SLAMET RIJADI 352

Displacement, tons	1 200 standard; 1 600 full load
Length, feet (*metres*)	298·8 (*91*)
Beam, feet (*metres*)	33·7 (*10·2*)
Draught, feet (*metres*)	11 (*3·4*)
Guns, dual purpose	3—3·9 in (*100 mm*) single mounts
Guns, AA	4—37 mm
A/S weapons	4 DC projectors
Torpedo tubes	3—21 in (*533 mm*)
Mines	Fitted with mine rails
Boilers	2
Main engines	Geared steam turbines; 2 shafts; 25 000 shp
Speed, knots	28
Complement	150

RIGA Class *Sergei Romanov*

Two "Riga" class frigates, pennant Nos. 405 and 406, were transferred from the USSR to Indonesia with the cruiser *Irian* in Sep 1962. Two more were transferred in 1963 and four more in 1964. *Monginsidi* was placed in reserve in 1969 and subsequently deleted. *Hang Tuah* was deleted from the list in 1971.

RADAR
SLIM NET search and warning; fire control radar on Wasp Head director; navigation radar.

2 "SURAPATI" CLASS

SURAPATI 251
IMAN BONDJOL 250

	6—20 mm (3 twin)
A/S weapons	2 hedgehogs; 4 DCT
Torpedo tubes	3—21 in (*533 mm*)
Boilers	2 Foster Wheeler
Main engines	2 sets Parsons geared turbines; 2 shafts; 24 000 shp
Speed, knots	32
Range, miles	2 800 at 22 knots
Oil fuel, tons	350
Complement	200

Both completed in May 1958 by Ansaldo, Genoa Near sisters of the *Almirante Clemente* class of Venezuela

Name	*No.*	*Builders*	*Laid down*	*Launched*	*Completed*
IMAN BONDJOL	250	Ansaldo, Leghorn	8 Jan 1956	5 May 1956	19 May 1958
SURAPATI	251	Ansaldo, Leghorn	8 Jan 1956	5 May 1956	28 May 1958

IMAN BONDJOL *courtesy Dr Ing Luigi Accorsi*

Frigates—*continued*

2 "PATTIMURA" CLASS

	Launched	Completed
PATTIMURA 252	1 July 1956	28 Jan 1958
SULTAN HASANUDIN 253	24 Mar 1957	8 Mar 1958

Displacement, tons	950 standard; 1 200 full load
Length, feet (*metres*)	246 (*75·0*) pp; 270·2 (*82·4*) oa
Beam, feet (*metres*)	34 (*10·4*)
Draught, feet (*metres*)	9 (*2·7*)
Guns, AA	2—3 in (*76 mm*) 40 cal. 2—30 mm 70 cal twin
A/S weapons	2 hedgehogs; 4 DCT
Main engines	3 Ansaldo-Fiat diesels; 3 shafts; 6 900 bhp
Speed, knots	22
Range, miles	2 400 at 18 knots
Oil fuel, tons	100
Complement	110

Both laid down on 8 Jan 1956 by Ansaldo, Leghorn. Similar to Italian *Albatross* class.

PATTIMURA *Dr Ing Luigi Accorsi*

CORVETTES

14 Ex-USSR "KRONSTADT" TYPE

BARAKUDA 817
KAKAP 816
KATULA 811
LANDJURU
LAPAI
LUMBA LUMBA
MADIDIHANG
MOMARE
PALU 818
PANDRONG 814
SURA 815
TOHOK 829
TONGKOL
TJUTJUT

Displacement, tons	310 standard; 380 full load
Dimensions, feet	170·6 × 21·5 × 9
Guns	1—3·9 in; 2—37 mm AA; 3—20 mm AA
A/S weapons	Depth charge projectors
Mines	Fitted for laying
Main engines	Diesels; 3 shafts; 3 300 bhp = 24 knots
Oil fuel, tons	20
Range, miles	1 500 at 12 knots
Complement	65

Built in 1951-54. Transferred to the Indonesian Navy on 30 Dec 1958. *Landjuru, Lapai, Lumba Lumba, Madidihang, Momare* and *Tongkol* were withdrawn from active service in 1970.

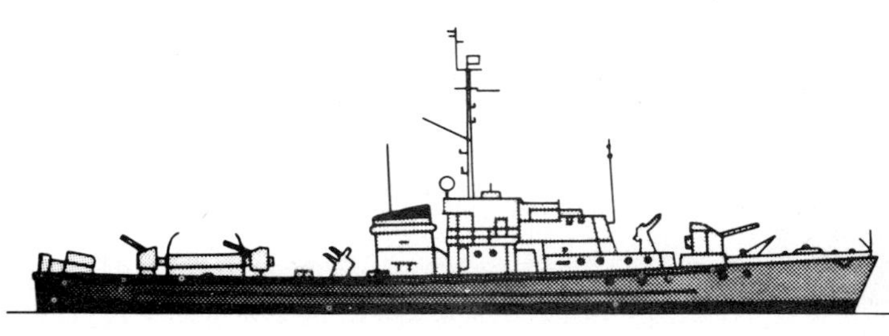

KRONSTADT *Class*

4 Ex-US PC TYPE

HUI (ex-USS *Malvern, PC* 580) 318
TENGGIRI (ex-USS *PC* 1183) 309
TJAKALANG (ex-USS *Pierre, PC* 1141) 313
TORANI (ex-USS *Manville, PC* 581) 317

Displacement, tons	280 standard; 450 full load
Dimensions, feet	170 wl; 173·7 oa × 23 × 10·8 max
Guns	1—3 in; 1—40 mm AA; 2—20 mm AA; 4 DCT
Main engines	2 GM diesels; 2 shafts; 2 880 bhp = 20 knots
Oil fuel, tons	60
Range, miles	5 000 at 10 knots
Complement	54 (4 officers, 50 men)

Built in 1942-43. *Pierre* transferred from the US Navy at Pearl Harbour, Hawaii in Oct 1958 and *Malvern* and *Manville* in Mar 1960. Sister ship *Alu-Alu* (ex-USS *PC* 787) was removed from the effective list in 1961.

TENGGIRI *1966, Indonesian Navy*

SUBMARINES

10 Ex-USSR "W" CLASS

ALUGORO 406
BRAMASTRA 412
HENDRADJALA 405
NAGABANDA 403
NAGARANGSANG 404
PASOPATI 410
TJANDRASA 408
TJUNDMANI 411
TRISULA 402
WIDJAJADANU 409

Displacement, tons	1 030 surface; 1 180 submerged
Length, feet (*metres*)	248·5 (*75·3*) oa
Beam, feet (*metres*)	19·1 (*5·8*)
Draught, feet (*metres*)	15 (*4·6*) max
Guns, AA	2—2·4 in (*57 mm*); 2—25 mm
Torpedo tubes	6—21 in (*533 mm*) 4 forward, 2 aft; 18 torpedos carried
Mines	40 in lieu of torpedos
Main engines	4 000 bhp diesels; 2 500 hp electric motors, diesel-electric drive; 2 shafts
Speed, knots	17 on surface; 15 submerged
Range, miles	13 000 to 16 500
Complement	60

W *Class*

Former Soviet submarines of the medium sized, long range "W" class. *Nanggala* and *Tjakra* were purchased from Poland and transferred to the Indonesian Navy in Aug 1959. *Nanggala* was overhauled at Surabaja in 1960. The four Soviet submarines of the "W" class, which arrived in Indonesia on 28 June 1962, brought the total number of this class transferred to Indonesia to 14 units, but it was reported that only six would be maintained operational, while six would be kept in reserve and two used for spare parts. *Tjundmani* was placed in reserve in 1969. *Nanggala* and *Tjakra* were deleted from the list in 1972.

AMPHIBIOUS VESSELS

7 Ex-US LST "511-1152" TYPE

Name	Former name	No.
TANDJUNG NUSANIVE	(ex-USS *LAWRENCE CITY*)	887
TELUK BAJUR	(ex-USS *LST 616*)	502
TELUK KAU	(ex-USS *LST 652*)	504
TELUK SALEH	(ex-USS *CLARKE COUNTY*)	510
TELUK MANADO	(ex-USS *LST 657*)	505
TELUK BOME	(ex-USS *IREDELL COUNTY*)	511
TELUK LANGSA	(ex-USS *LST 1128*)	501

Displacememt, tons: 1 653 standard; 4 080 full load
Dimensions, feet: 316 wl; 328 oa × 50 × 14
Guns: 7—40 mm AA; 2—20 mm AA
Main Engines: GM diesels; 2 shafts; 1 700 bhp = 11·6 knots
Oil fuel (tons): 600
Radius, miles: 7 200 at 10 knots
Cargo capacity: 2 100 tons
Complement: 119 (accommodation for 266)

TRANSFERS:
505 in Mar 1960, 887 in Dec 1960, 502, 510 and 511 in June 1961, 504 and 501 in July 1970.

1 JAPANESE TYPE

TELUK AMBOINA LST 869

Displacement, tons: 2 200 standard; 4 800 full load
Dimensions, feet: 327 × 50 × 15
Guns: 2—85 mm; 4—40 mm
Main Engines: MAN diesels; 2 shafts; 3 000 bhp = 13·1 knots
Oil fuel (tons): 1 200
Radius, miles: 4 000 at 13·1 knots
Complement: 88 (accommodation for 300)

Built in Japan. Launched on 17 Mar 1961 and transferred in June 1961.

3 Ex-US LCT TYPE

AMAHAI (ex-*Tropenvogel, LCI* 467) 864
MARICH (ex-*Zeemeeuw*) 866
PIRU (ex-*Zeearend, LCI* 420) 868

Displacement, tons: 250 standard; 381 full load
Dimensions, feet: 158 × 23 × 7
Guns: 1—37 mm; 2 Vickers MG
Main engines: GM diesels; 1 800 bhp = 15 knots
Complement: 60

Former US infantry landing craft. Turned over from Netherlands East Indies Government on formation of Indonesian Navy in 1950. Sister ship *Baruna* (ex-*Ijsvogel* LCI 948) and *Namlea* (ex-*Stormvogel* LCI 588) were rerated as pilot ship and light ship in 1961.

3 Ex-YUGOSLAV LCT TYPE

TELUK KATURAI 862 **TELUK WEDA** 861 **TELUK WORI** 863

Displacement, tons: 110 standard; 250 full load
Dimensions, feet: 166 × 21·5 × 5·5
Guns: 1—40 mm; 2—20 mm
Main engines: 2 diesels; 2 shafts; 375 bhp = 7 knots
Oil fuel (tons): 6
Complement: 15

Transferred form Yugoslavia on 1 Nov 1958. Sister ship *Teluk Wadjo* 860 was deleted from the list in 1971. The remainder are in non-operational reserve.

2 Ex- "LCVT" TYPE

DORE **AMURANG**

Displacement, tons: 182 standard; 275 full load
Dimensions, feet: 125·7 × 32·8 × 5·9
Main engines: Diesels; 210 hp = 8 knots
Complement: 17

1 Ex-USSR LCT TYPE

TELUK PARIGI

Displacement, tons: 600 standard; 800 full load
Dimensions, feet: 246·0 × 39·3 × 9·8
Main engines: Diesels; 2 shafts; 2 200 hp = 10 knots

LIGHT FORCES

12 Ex-USSR "KOMAR" CLASS (MISSILE BOATS)

GRIWIDJAJA	**KATJABOLA**	**SAROTAMA**
HARDADALI	**KOLAPLINTAH**	**SARPAMINA**
KALAMISANI	**PULANGGENI**	**SARPAWISESA**
KALANADA	**NAGAPASA**	**TRITUSTA**

Displacement, tons: 70 standard; 80 full load
Dimensions, feet: 83·7 × 19·8 × 5
Guns: 2—25 mm AA (1 twin)
Guided weapons: 2 launchers for SSN2A (Styx)
Main engines: 4 diesels; 4 800 hp = 40 knots

Former Soviet guided missile patrol boats of the "Komar" class. Six were transferred to Indonesia in 1961-63, four more in Sep 1964 and two in 1965.

18 Ex-USSR "BK" CLASS (GUNBOATS)

Displacement, tons: 120
Dimensions, feet: 124·7 × 19 × 4·6
Guns: 1—85 mm; 4—25 mm AA
Main engines: Diesels; speed 20 knots

Reported to have been transferred from the USSR to Indonesia in 1962. Fitted with large gun mounting. Ten Soviet-built gunboats were reported to have been transferred to Indonesia at Djakarta 11 Oct 1961.

3 Ex-USN "PGM" TYPE (GUNBOATS)

SILUNGKANG (ex-*PGM 65*) 1319
WAITATIRE (ex-*PGM 56*) 1320
KALAKUANG (ex-*PGM 57*) 1321

Displacement, tons: 122 full load
Dimensions, feet: 100 × 21 × 8·5
Guns: 2—20 mm AA 2 MG
Main engines: 2 diesels, 2 shafts = 17 knots
Transferred 1965.

7 GERMAN-BUILT "JAGUAR" TYPE (TORPEDO BOATS)

ADJAK **BIRUANG** **MADJAN KUMBANG** **SERIGALA**
ANOA **HARIMAU** **SINGA**

Displacement, tons: 160 standard; 190 full load
Dimensions, feet: 131 pp; 138 oa × 22 × 7·5
Guns: 2—40 mm AA (single)
Torpedo tubes: 4—21 in
Main engines: 4 Daimler-Benz diesels; 4 shafts; 12 000 bhp = 42 knots
Complement: 39

Built by Lürssen, Bremen-Vegesack in 1959-60. The first four boats had wooden hulls, but the second four were built of steel. Pennant Nos. 601, 602, 603, 604, 605, 607, and 608. A photograph of *Singa* appears in the 1961-62 to 67-68 editions. *Matian Tutul* 606 of this class was sunk on 15 Jan 1962 by Dutch warships off New Guinea.

HARIMAU *Indonesia*

14 Ex-USSR "P6" TYPE (TORPEDO BOATS)

ANGIN BADAI	**ANGIN GRENGGONG**	**ANGIN RIBUT**
ANGIN BOHOROK	**ANGIN KUMBANG**	**ANGIN TAUFAN**
ANGIN BRUBU	**ANGIN PASAT**	**ANGIN TONGGI**
ANGIN GENDING	**ANGIN PRAHARA**	**ANGIN WAMANDAIS**
	ANGIN PUJUH	**ANGIN WAMBRAU**

Displacement, tons: 66 standard; 75 full load
Dimensions, feet: 84·2 × 20 × 6
Guns: 4—25 mm AA (2 twin)
Tubes: 2—21 in (single)
Main engines: Diesels; 4 800 bhp = 45 knots
Complement: 25

A total of 14 were reported delivered since 1961, including eight in 1961, and six in 1962. Fitted with *Skinhead* target detection radar.

ANGIN KUMBANG *1968, Indonesian Navy*

Light Forces—*continued*

6 Ex-YUGOSLAVIAN "KRALJEVICA" TYPE

BUBARA **DORANG** **KRAPU** **LAJANG** **LEMADANG** **TODAK**

Displacement, tons	190 standard; 245 full load
Dimensions, feet	134·5 × 20·8 × 7
Guns	1—3 in; 1—40 mm AA; 6—20 mm AA
A/S weapons	DC
Main Engines	2 MAN diesels; 2 shafts; 3 300 bhp = 20 knots
Oil fuel (tons)	15
Radius, miles	1 500 at 12 knots
Complement	54

Former Yugoslavian submarine chasers of the "Kraljevica" class. Purchased and transferred on 27th Dec 1958. Nos 310, 311 (*Dorang*), 312 (*Lajang*) and 314 to 316. *Bubara* was withdrawn from active service in 1970.

DORANG *1968, Indonesian Navy*

3 "MAWAR" CLASS

KALAHITAM **KELABANG** **KOMPAS**

Displacement, tons	147
Guns	40 mm AA
Main engines	2 diesels; speed 21 knots

Indonesia was reported to be building five submarine chasers of the "Mawar" class in her own yards. Similar to the prototype *Kelabang*. At least two, *Kompas* and *Kalahitam*, have been completed.

KALAHITAM *1968, Indonesian Navy*

25 Ex-HDML PATROL BOAT TYPES

PP 01	**PP 06**	**PP 011**	**PP 016**	**PP 021**
PP 02	**PP 07**	**PP 012**	**PP 017**	**PP 022**
PP 03	**PP 08**	**PP 013**	**PP 018**	**PP 023**
PP 04	**PP 09**	**PP 014**	**PP 019**	**PP 024**
PP 05	**PP 10**	**PP 015**	**PP 020**	**PP 025**

Displacement, tons	46 standard; 54 full load
Dimensions, feet	72 × 16 × 5·5
Guns	1—37 mm; 2—20 mm Oerlikon MG
Main Engines	2 diesels; 2 shafts; 300 bhp = 11 knots
Complement	10

All ex-Netherlands patrol boats. Built in 1943-46. Formerly Britiah HDML type *RP* 109, *RP* 111, *RP* 112, *RP* 114, and *RP* 118 (ex-*HDML* 1451, *HDML* 1472, *HDML* 1473, *HDML* 1454 and *HDML* 1449).

9 Ex-US MOTOR LAUNCHES

Displacement, tons	44 standard, 56 full load
Dimensions, feet	62 oa × 18·3 × 4
Guns	1—20 mm AA; 1 MG
Main Engines	1 diesel; 165 bhp = 10 knots
Complement,	10

Built in 1945-46. Former American Higgins type motor launches, later Netherlands *RP* 120, *RP* 121, *RP* 122, *RP* 125, *RP* 127, *RP* 128, *RP* 130, *RP* 134, and *RP* 136, ..ansferred to Indonesia in 1950.

1 Ex-DUTCH MOTOR LAUNCH

Displacement, tons	54
Guns	1—40 mm AA; 2—20 mm AA
A/S weapons	3 DCT
Main Engines	Speed = 11 knots
Complement	10

Former Netherlands motor launch *RP* 138, transferred by the Royal Netherlands Navy in 1950. A photograph of this type appears in the 1951-52 to 1960-61 editions.

MINE WARFARE FORCES

6 Ex-USSR "T43" TYPE (FLEET TYPE)

PULAU RANI **PULAU RADJA** **PULAU RATENO** **PULAU RONDO** **PULAU ROON** **PULAU RORBAS**

Displacement, tons	500 standard; 610 full load
Dimensions, feet	190·2 × 28·2 × 6·9
Guns	4—37 mm AA; 4—25 mm AA
Main engines	2 diesels; 2 shafts; 2 000 bhp = 17 knots
Complement	40

Former Soviet fleet minesweepers of the "T 43" type transferred to Indonesia by the USSR, four in 1962 and two in 1964. *Pulau Rondo* is in reserve.

T 43 *Class*

10 "R" CLASS (CMS)

PULAU RAAS **PULAU RANGSANG** **PULAU RAU** **PULAU REMPANG** **PULAU RENGAT** **PULAU RINDJA** **PULAU ROMA** **PULAU ROTI** **PULAU RUPAT** **PULAU RUSA**

Displacement, tons	139·4 standard
Dimensions, feet	129 × 18·7 × 5
Guns	1—40 mm AA; 2—20 mm AA
Main engines	2 MAN diesels; 12 cyl; 2 800 bhp = 24·6 knots
Complement	26

Built by Abeking & Rasmussen Jacht-und Bootswerft, Lemwerder IO in 1945-57. These boats have a framework of light metal covered with wood. *Pulau Raas, Pulau Rempang* and *Pulau Roti* in reserve in 1969.

PULAU ROTI *Indonesian Navy*

4 Ex-DUTCH (CMS)

DJAMPEA **DJOMBANG** **ENGGANO** (ex-*Hino Maru*) **FLORES**

Displacement, tons	175
Dimensions, feet	106·7 pp; 113·7 (*Flores*) 114·1 oa × 18·8 × 6·2
Main Engines	1 Enterprise diesel; 360 bhp = 12·5 knots

First three were commissioned in 1941. *Flores* was completed by the Japanese during the occupation of Java. First two were built at Droogdok, Maatschappij, Soerabaya and the other two at Droogdok Mij, Tandjong Priok. Used as auxiliary minesweepers by the Royal Netherlands Navy. *Enggano* was re-named by Japanese. These ships were recovered after the war. *Enggano* in reserve in 1969.

6 Ex-US "BLUEBIRD" CLASS (CMS)

PULAU ALOR (ex-*Meadowlark*)	717
PULAU ANJER (ex-*Limpkin*)	719
PULAU ANTANG (ex-*Frigate Bird*)	721
PULAU ARU (ex-*Falcon*)	722
PULAU ARUAN (ex-*Jacana*)	718
PULAU IMPALASA (ex-*Humming Bird*)	720

Displacement, tons	320 light; 370 full load
Dimensions, feet	138·0 pp; 144·0 oa × 28·0 × 8·2
Guns	2—20 mm AA (1 twin)
Main engines	Packard diesels; 2 shafts; 1 200 bhp = 12·5 knots
Complement	39

The following were transferred from the USN in 1971: *Falcon* (MSC 190), *Frigate Bird* (MSC 191), *Humming Bird* (MSC 192), *Jacana* (MSC 193), *Limpkin* (MSC 195), *Meadowlark* (MSC 196). All have wooden hulls with low magnetic signature.

BLUEBIRD *Class*

SURVEY SHIPS

BURUDJULASAD

Displacement, tons	2 150 full load
Dimensions, feet	269·5 × 37·4 × 11·5
Machinery	4 MAN diesels; 2 shafts; 6 850 bhp = 19·1 knots
Complement	113

Burudjulasad was launched in 1966; her equipment includes laboratories for oceanic and meteorological research, a cartographic room, and a helicopter.

BURUDJULASAD *1968, Indonesian Navy*

BURDIAMHAL

Displacement, tons	1 500 full load
Dimensions, feet	211·7 oa; 192 pp × 33·2 × 10
Main engines	2 Werkspoor diesels; 1 160 bhp = 10 knots
Complement	90

Built by Schweepserf De Waal, Zalthomme. Launched on 6 Sep 1952. Completed on 6 July 1953.

JALANIDHI

Displacement, tons	985
Complement	58

Launched in 1962.

ARIES (ex-*Samudera*)

Measurement, tons	200 gross
Dimensions, feet	125·2 × 21·5 × 9·8
Main engines	Werkspoor diesel engines; 450 bhp

Built by Ferus Smit, Foxol. Launched on 28 May 1952. Completed on 28 Aug 1952. Same type as "Bango" class motor patrol vessels. Equipped as a laboratory ship, used for deep sea exploration in Indonesian waters. Another survey ship, *Dewa Kembar*, was laid up in reserve, and *Hidral* was deleted in Feb 1972.

DEPOT/MAINTENANCE SHIPS

MULTATULI 476

Displacement, tons	3 220
Dimensions, feet	338 pp; 365·3 oa × 52·5 × 23
Guns	1—85 mm, 4—40 mm (single mountings)
Main engines	B & W diesel, 5 500 bhp = 18·5 knot max
Oil fuel (tons)	1 400
Radius, miles	6 000 at 16 knots cruising speed
Complement	134

Built in Japan by Ishikawajima-Harima Heavy Industries Co. Ltd, as a submarine tender. Launched on 15 May 1961. Delivered to Indonesia Aug 1961. Pennant No. 476. Flush decker. Capacity for replenishment at sea (fuel oil, fresh water, provisions, ammunition, naval stores and personnel). Medical and hospital facilities. Equipment for supplying compressed air, electric power and distilled water to submarines. Air conditioning and mechanical ventilation arrangements for all living and working quarters

1 Ex-USSR "DON" CLASS

RATULANGI

Displacement, tons	6 700 standard; 9 000 full load
Dimensions, feet	458·9 × 57·7 × 22·3
Guns	4—3·9 in; 8—57 mm AA
Main engines	Diesels; 14 000 bhp = 21 knots approx
Complement	300

A submarine support ship, escort vessel and maintenance tender of the "Don" class transferred from the USSR to Indonesia in 1962, arriving in Indonesia in July with Soviet pennant No. 441. Fitted with SLIM NET search and warning radar and with fire control radar.

RATULANGI *1968, Indonesian Navy*

Depot/Maintenance Ships—*continued*

1 Ex-USSR "ATREK" CLASS

THAMRIN

Displacement, tons	3 500 standard; 6 700 full load
Measurement, tons	3 258 gross
Dimensions, feet	336 × 49 × 20
Main engines	Steam expansion and exhaust turbine; 2 450 ihp = 13 knots
Boilers	2
Range, miles	3 500 at 13 knots

Former Soviet advanced submarine parent ship of the smaller tender type. Built in 1955-57 and converted to naval use from a mercantile freighter. Arrived in Indonesia on 28 June 1962.

DJAJA WIDJAJA (ex-US *Askari* 9109, ex-*ARL* 30, ex-*LST* 1131) 9017.

Displacement, tons	1 625 light; 4 100 full load
Dimensions, feet	316·0 wl; 328·0 oa × 50·0 × 11·0
Guns	8—40 mm AA (2 quadruple)
Main engines	General Motors diesels; 2 shafts; 1 800 bhp = 11·6 knots
Complement	280

Of wartime construction, this ship was in reserve from 1956-66. She was recommissioned and reached Vietnam in 1967 to support River Assault Flotilla One. She was used by the USN and Vietnamese Navy working up the Mekong in support of the Cambodian operations in May 1970. Transferred on lease to Indonesia at *Guam* in Sep 1971.

DUMAI (ex-USS *Tidewater*) 562

Displacement, tons	8 165 standard; 16 635 full load
Dimensions, feet	465 wl; 492 oa × 69·5 × 27·2
Guns	1—5 in; 38 cal dp
Main engines	Geared turbines; 1 shaft; 8 500 shp = 18·4 knots
Boilers	2 Babcock & Wilcox
Complement	778

Transferred January 1971, as destroyer depot ship.

OILERS

2 Ex-USSR TYPE

BUNJU **SAMBU**

Displacement, tons	2 170 standard; 6 170 full load
Dimensions, feet	350·5 × 49·2 × 20·2
Guns	2—20 mm
Main Engines	Polar diesel; 1 shaft; 2 650 bhp = 10 knots
Oil fuel (tons)	390
Cargo capacity	4 739 tons
Complement	71

Former Soviet tankers transferred to the Indonesian Navy on 29 June 1959. Pennant Nos. 904 and 903. Both laid up in 1969.

TJEPU (ex-*Scandus*, ex-*Nordhem*)

Displacement, tons	1 372
Measurement, tons	1 042 gross
Dimensions, feet	226·5 × 34 × 14·2
Main Engines	Polar diesel; 1 shaft; 850 bhp = 11 knots

Built in Sweden in 1949. Acquired in 1951. Pennant No. 901. Laid up in 1969.

PLADU

Displacement, tons	1 412 standard; 4 062 full load
Dimensions, feet	294·7 × 42·2 × 15·5
Guns	2—20 mm
Main Engines	Compound engines; 1 700 ihp = 10 knots
Oil fuel (tons)	449
Cargo capacity, tons	3 132
Complement	70

Purchased from Singapore in 1958. Pennant No. 902. Withdrawn from active service in 1970.

5 Ex-USSR TYPE

BALIKAPAN **PANGKALAN BRANDAN**

Displacement, tons	3 500 standard; 7 115 full load
Dimensions, feet	400·3 × 52·5 × 21·0
Main engines	Diesels; 2 shafts; 4 500 bhp = 17 knots max

TARAKAN **BULA**

Displacement, tons	1 340 full load
Dimensions, feet	352·0 × 37·7 × 14·8
Main engines	Diesels; 1 shaft; 1 500 bhp = 13 knots

PAKAN BARU

Displacement, tons	1 500 full load
Dimensions, feet	63 × 11·5 × 4·5
Main engines	Diesels; 2 shafts; 800 bhp = 11 knots

TUGS

RAKATA (ex-USS *Menominee, ATF* 73)

Displacement, tons 1,235 standard; 1,675 full load
Dimensions, feet 195 wl; 205 oa × 38·5 × 15·5 max
Guns 1—3 in; 4—40 mm AA; 2—20 mm AA
Main engines 4 diesels with electric drive; 3 000 bhp = 16·5 knots
Complement 85

Former American fleet ocean tug of the "Apache" class. Launched on 14 Feb 1942. Transferred from the United States Navy to the Indonesian Navy at San Diego in Mar 1961. Pennant No. 928.

LAMPO BATANG

Displacement, tons 250
Dimensions, feet 92·3 oa; 86·7 pp × 23·2 × 11·3
Main engines 2 diesels; 1 200 bhp = 11 knots
Oil fuel (tons) 18
Radius, miles 1 000 at 11 knots
Complement 43

Ocean tug. Built in Japan. Launched in April 1961. Delivered in Nov 1961. Pennant No. 934.

GANDENG

Measurement, tons 610 gross
Main Engines Speed = 7·5 knots

Launched in 1940. Reported to have been given a new Indonesian name.

BROMO **TAMBORA**

Displacement, tons 150
Dimensions, feet 71·7 wl; 79 oa × 21·7 × 9·7
Main Engines MAN diesel; 2 shafts; 600 bhp = 10·5 knots
Oil fuel (tons) 9
Radius, miles 690 at 10·5 knots
Complement 15

Harbour tugs. Built in Japan. Launched in June 1961. Delivered in Aug 1961. Pennant Nos 936 and 935.

SALVAGE VESSEL

TRITON (ex-*Mutsunoura Maru*)

Displacement, tons 384
Measurement, tons 383 gross
Dimensions, feet 182·5 × 30 × 15
Main Engines Triple expansion reciprocating; 700 ihp = 7 knots
Complement 43

Former Japanese vessel renamed. Launched in 1941. Pennant No. 926. Laid up in reserve in 1969.

CABLE SHIP

BIDUK

Displacement, tons 1 250 standard
Dimensions, feet 213·2 oa × 39·5 × 11·5
Main Engines 1 Triple expansion engine; 1 600 ihp = 12 knots
Complement 66

Cable Layer, Lighthouse Tender, and multi-purpose naval auxiliary. Built by J. & K. Smit, Kinderijk. Launched on 30 Oct 1951. Completed on 30 July 1952.

TRANSPORTS

2 "BANGGAI" TYPE

BANGGAI (ex-*Biscaya*) **NUSA TELU** (ex-*Casa Blanca*)

Measurement, tons 750
Dimensions, feet 168 × 27·9 × 7·8

Dual purpose troop and cargo ships. Renamed in 1961. Pennant Nos 925, 924.

MOROTAI TYPE. The transports *Halmahera*, No 921, and *Merotai*, No. 922, reverted to the Merchant Navy as *Djati Roto* and *Djati Bono* in 1968. Acquired from merchant service on 23 Nov 1957.

AUXILIARY PATROL CRAFT

5 DKN TYPE

DKN 901 **DKN 902** **DKN 903** **DKN 904** **DKN 905**

Displacement, tons 140
Dimensions, feet 128 × 19 × 5·2
Guns 4—20 mm AA
Main Engines Maybach diesels; 2 shafts; 3 000 bhp = 24·5 knots

Patrol craft and police boats. Projected as a class of ten units. 901, 902 and 904 were built by Lürssen, Vergesack, 903 and 905 by Abeking & Rasmussen Lemwerder.

6 "PAT" CLASS

PAT 01 **PAT 02** **PAT 03** **PAT 04** **PAT 05** **PAT 06**

Dimensions, feet 91·9 pp; 100 oa × 17 × 6
Main Engines 2 Caterpillar diesels; 340 bhp

The auxiliary patrol craft *Kelabang* was deleted from the list in Feb 1972.

Auxiliary Patrol Craft—*continued*

6 "BALAM" CLASS

BALAM **BARAU** **BEKAKA** **BELATIK** **BENDALU** **BOGA**

Measurement, tons 200 gross
Dimensions, feet 125·2 oa × 21·3 × 6·5
Main Engines Werkspoor diesel engine; 400-430 bhp = 11 knots

All launched in 1953. *Balam* and others were commissioned for service in 1953.

7 "BANGO" CLASS

BANGO **BABUT** **BEO** **BETTET** **BIDO** **BLEKOK** **BLIBIS**

Measurement, tons 194 gross
Dimensions, feet 120·5 pp; 125·2 oa × 21·3 × 6·6
Main Engines Werkspoor diesel engine; 430 bhp = 11 knots

All launched in 1952. A photograph of *Bettet* appears in the 1953-54 to 1960-61 editions.

7 "DURIAN" CLASS

DAIK **DAGONG** **DAMARA** **DATA** **DUATA** **DUKU** **DURIAN**

Displacement, tons 90
Dimensions, feet 78·2 × 16 × 6·8
Main Engines Caterpillar diesel; 190 bhp

All launched in 1952.

12 "ALKAI" CLASS

ALKAI **ALULU** **AMPIS** **ANKANG** **ANTANG** **ARYAT**
ALLAP **AMPOK** **ANDIS** **ANKLOENG** **AROKWES** **ATTAT**

Displacement, tons 143; 247 full load
Dimensions, feet 124·3 × 18·5 × 5·5
Guns 1—37 mm AA; 4 MG
Main engines Enterprise diesel; 400-450 = 12 knots
Complement 20

Built in the Netherlands. *Ampok* and *Alkai* were shipped to Indonesia on 17 Mar 1950. *Ampis* in reserve in 1969.

3 Ex-US SC TYPE

BHAYAMKARA 1 **BHAYAMKARA II** **BHAYAMKARA III**

Displacement, tons 116 (trials); 148 full load
Dimensions, feet 107·5 wl; 110·8 oa × 17 × 6·5
Main Engines Diesel; 800 bhp = 15·5 knots

Former US submarine chasers of the 110 SC type. Operated by Indonesian Marine Police. A photograph appears in the 1954-55 to 1960-61 editions.

2 MERABU TYPE

MERABU (ex-*Merbaboe*) **RINDJANI**

Displacement, tons 80
Dimensions, feet 74·5 × 14·5 × 5
Main Engines Diesel; 135 bhp = 10 knots
Complement 20

Merabu is laid up in reserve it was officially stated in 1969 (removed from the effective list).

TRAINING SHIP

DEWARUTJI

Displacement, tons 810 standard; 1 500 full load
Dimensions, feet 191·2 oa; 136·2 pp × 31·2 × 13·9
Main Engines MAN diesel engines; 600 bhp = 10·5 knots
Complement 110 (32 + 78 midshipmen)

Built in Germany by H. C. Stülcken & Sohn, Hamburg. Launched on 24 Jan 1953. Completed on 9 July 1953. Barquentine of iron construction. Sail area, 1 305 sq yds (*1 091 sq metres*). Speed with sails 12·8 knots. The training ship *Nanusa* a former freighter, has been returned to mercantile service.

DEWARUTJI *Indonesia*

IRAN

Administration

Commander-in Chief Imperial Iranian Navy:
Rear Admiral Attaie

Diplomatic Representation

Naval Attaché in London:
Captain Ali Ashgar Bahram

Naval Attaché in Washington:
Captain Movaghari

Strength of the Fleet

3 Destroyers
4 Frigates
4 Corvettes
2 Landing Craft
10 Patrol Boats
4 Coastal Minesweepers
2 Inshore Minesweepers
14 Hovercraft (2 Building)
2 Repair Ships
2 Yachts
1 Oiler
6 Harbour Launches
2 Auxiliaries
2 Store Ships (Building)

New Construction

Interest is being shown by Iranian authorities in the building of both frigates and submarines. No details or orders have yet been released.

Personnel

1973: 13 000 officers and men

Mercantile Marine

Lloyd's Register of Shipping
88 vessels of 180 659 tons

DESTROYERS

1 Ex-BRITISH "BATTLE" CLASS

Name	*No.*	*Builders*	*Laid down*	*Launched*	*Completed*
ARTEMIZ (ex-HMS *Sluys*, D 60)	D 5	Cammell Laird & Co Ltd, Birkenhead	24 Nov 1943	28 Feb. 1945	30 Sep 1946

Displacement, tons	2 325 standard; 3 360 full load
Length, feet (*metres*)	355·0 (*108·2*) pp; 379·0 (*115·5*) oa
Beam, feet (*metres*)	40·5 (*12·3*)
Draught, feet (*metres*)	17·5 (*5·2*) max
Guns	4—4·5 in (*115 mm*) 2 twin forward
Guns	8—40 mm Bofors AA
Missile launchers	1 quadruple "Seacat" AA aft
A/S weapons	1 "Squid" 3-barrelled DC mortar
Main engines	Parsons geared turbines; 2 shafts; 50 000 shp
Speed, knots	35·5 max; 31 sustained sea
Boilers	2 Admiralty 3-drum type
Oil fuel, tons	680
Range, miles	3 000 at 20 knots
Complement	270

ARTEMIZ *1971*

Transferred to Iran at Southampton on 26 Jan 1967, and handed over to the Imperial Iranian Navy after a 3-year modernisation refit by the Vosper Thornycroft Group.

RADAR. Search: Plessey AWS 1. Air surveillance with on-mounted IFF; Contraves Sea-Hunter fire control; Decca RDL 1 radar intercept; Racal DF equipment.

ARTEMIZ

2 Ex-US ALLEN M. SUMNER CLASS

Name	*No.*	*Builders*	*Launched*	*Commissioned*
BABR (ex-USS *Zellars*, DD 777)	D 7	Todd Pacific Shipyards	19 July 1944	25 Oct 1944
PALANG (ex-USS *Stormes*, DD 780)	D 9	Todd Pacific Shipyards	4 Nov 1944	27 Jan 1945

Displacement, tons	2 200 standard; 3 320 full load
Length, feet (*metres*)	376·5 (*114·8*) oa
Beam, feet (*metres*)	40·9 (*12·4*)
Draft, feet (*metres*)	19 (*5·8*)
Guns	6—5 inch (*127 mm*) 38 calibre dual-purpose (twin)
ASW weapons	2 fixed Hedgehogs; depth charges 2 triple torpedo launchers (Mk 32) 2 fixed torpedo launchers (Mk 25) 2 Drone A/S helicopters
Main engines	2 geared turbines; 60 000 shp; 2 shafts
Boilers	4
Speed, knots	34
Complement	274 (14 officers, 260 ratings) (designed wartime 345)

Two "FRAM II" conversion destroyers of the "Allen M. Sumner" class nominally transferred to Iran from the USN in 1971 for delivery in 1972. Renamed on transfer with names previously used for the ex-British "Loch" class (*Babr*) and the ex-British "Algerine" class (*Palang*) paid off on 30 Oct 1969 and Dec 1966 respectively and officially deleted from the effective list in 1972. USS *Gainard* (DD 706) was taken over in Mar 1971 but, being beyond repair, was used for spares and training; being replaced by USS *Stormes* (DD 780).

RADAR. SPS 10 search; SPS 37 air-surveillance with on-mounted IFF; Gun fire control system Mk 56 with radar on director.

SONAR. SQS 23 or SQS 29 Sonar; VDS.

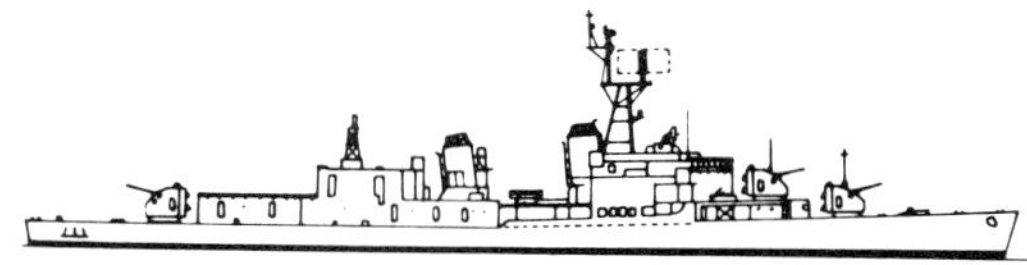

BABR and PALANG

BABR (as ZELLARS) *United States Navy*

FRIGATES

4 "SAAM" CLASS

Name	No.	Builders	Laid down	Launched	Completed
FARAMAZ	DE 13	Vosper Thornycroft, Woolston	25 July 1968	30 July 1969	28 Feb 1972
ROSTAM	DE 15	Vickers, Newcastle & Barrow	10 Dec 1967	4 Mar 1969	June 1972
SAAM	DE 12	Vosper Thornycroft, Woolston	22 May 1967	25 July 1968	20 May 1971
ZAAL	DE 14	Vickers, Barrow	3 Mar 1968	4 Mar 1969	1 Mar 1971

Displacement, tons	1 110 standard; 1 290 full load
Length, feet (*metres*)	310·0 (*94·4*) oa
Beam, feet (*metres*)	34·0 (*10·4*)
Draught, feet (*metres*)	11·2 (*3·4*)
Missile launchers	1 quintuple "Seakiller" SS; 1 triple "Seacat" AA
Guns	1—4·5 in (*115 mm*) Mk 8. (Mk 5 in *Saam, Zaal*); 2—35 mm Oerlikon (1 twin) AA
A/S weapons	1 "Limbo" 3-barrelled DC mortar
Main engines	2 Rolls-Royce "Olympus" gas turbines; 2 Paxman diesels; 2 shafts; 46 000 + 3 800 shp
Speed, knots	40 designed
Complement	125 (accommodation for 146)

SAAM — *1972, Vosper Thornycroft*

SAAM *Class*

GENERAL
It was announced on 25 Aug 1966 that Vosper Ltd, Portsmouth, received an order for four "destroyers" for the Iranian Navy. Of small frigate type, high speed from gas turbines, with diesels for long range cruising. Air conditioned throughout.Fitted withVosper stabilisers. *Rostam* was towed to Barrow for completion.

RADAR. Plessey AWS 1 air surveillance with on-mounted IFF. Two Contraves Seahunter systems for control of 35 mm, Seakillers and Seacats. Decca RDL 1 passive DF equipment.

CORVETTES

4 US PF TYPE

Name	No.	Builders	Laid down	Launched	Completed
BAYANDOR	F 25 (ex-USS *PF* 103)	Levingstone Shipbuilding Co, Orange, Texas	20 Aug 1962	7 July 1963	18 May 1964
KAHNAMUIE	F 28 (ex-USS *PF* 106)	Levingstone Shipbuilding Co, Orange, Texas	12 June 1967	4 Apr 1968	13 Feb 1969
MILANIAN	F 27 (ex-USS *PF* 105)	Levingstone Shipbuilding Co, Orange, Texas	1 May 1967	4 Jan 1968	13 Feb 1969
NAGHDI	F 26 (ex-USS *PF* 104)	Levingstone Shipbuilding Co, Orange, Texas	12 Sep 1962	10 Oct 1963	22 July 1964

Displacement, tons	900 standard; 1 135 full load
Length, feet (*metres*)	275·0 (*83·8*) oa
Beam, feet (*metres*)	33·0 (*10·0*)
Draught, feet (*metres*)	10·2 (*3·1*)
Guns	2—3 in (*76 mm*); 2—40 mm AA
A/S weapons	1 Hedgehog, 4 DCT
Main engines	F-M diesels; 2 shafts; 6 000 bhp
Speed, knots	20 max
Complement	140

MILANIAN — *1972, Imperial Iranian Navy*

BAYANDOR *Class*

Built as two pairs, five years apart. Transferred from the USA to Iran under the Mutual Assistance Programme in 1964 (*Bayandor* and *Naghdi*) and 1969 (*Kahnamuie* and *Milanian*). SPS 12 Search radar and navigation radar.

COASTAL MINESWEEPERS

4 MSC TYPE

KARKAS (ex-USS *MSC* 292) 34
SHAHBAZ (ex-USS *MSC* 275) 32
SHAHROKH (ex-USS *MSC* 276) 31
SIMORGH (ex-USS *MSC* 291) 33

Displacement, tons	320 light; 378 full load
Dimensions, feet	138 pp; 145·8 oa × 28 × 8·3
Guns	1—20 mm
Main engines	2 GM diesels; 2 shafts; 890 bhp = 12·8 knots
Oil fuel (tons)	27
Radius, miles	2 400 at 11 knots
Complement	40 (4 officers, 2 midshipmen, 34 men)

Built by Bellingham Shipyards Co (*Shahbaz* and *Shakrokh*), Petersen Builders Inc. (*Karkas*) and Tacoma Boatbuilding Co, (*Simorgh*). Of wooden construction. Launched in 1958-61 and transported from US to Iran under MAP in 1959-62. "Shahbaz" means Eagle and "Shahrokh" means Bird of Prey.

SHAHROKH — *1971, John G. Callis*

INSHORE MINESWEEPERS

2 US MSI TYPE

HARISCHI (ex-*Kahnamuie*) 301 (ex-*MSI* 14)
RIAZI 302 (ex-*MSI* 13)

Displacement, tons	180 standard; 235 full load
Dimensions, feet	111 × 23 × 6
Guns	MG
Main engines	diesels; 650 bhp = 13 knots
Oil fuel, tons	20
Radius, miles	1 000 at 9 knots
Complement	23 (5 officers, 18 men)

Built in USA by Tacoma Boatbuilding Co and delivered to Iran under MAP. Laid down on 22 June 1962 and 1 Feb 1963, and transferred at Seattle, Washington, on 3 Sep 1964 and 15 Oct 1964, respectively. In Aug 1967 *Kahnamuie* was renamed *Harischi* as the name was required for one of the new US PFs, see above.

RIAZI — *1971.*

LIGHT FORCES

3 IMPROVED PGM TYPE

BATTRAAM (ex-US PGM 112) PGM 66
NAHID (ex-US PGM 122) PGM 67
PARVIN (ex-US PGM 103) PGM 65

Displacement, tons	105 standard; 146 full load
Dimensions, feet	100 × 22 × 10
Guns	1—40 mm; 2—20 mm, 2—50 cal MG
Main engines	8 MG diesels; 2 000 bhp = 15 knots

Motor gunboats of an enlarged design, compared with the "Kayvan" class below. Built in USA by Tacoma Boatbuilding Co of Tacoma and Petersen Builders Inc of Sturgeon Bay, Wisconsin, and transferred to Iran under MAP in 1970

PARVIN *1971*

4 PGM TYPE

KAYVAN (MDA1) **MAHAN** 64 **MEHRAN** **TIRAN**

Displacement, tons	85 standard; 107 full load
Dimensions, feet	90 pp; 95 oa × 20·2 × 6·8 max
Guns	1—40 mm AA
A/S weapons	8-barrelled 7·2 in projector, 8—300 lb depth charges
Main engines	4 Cummins diesels; 2 shafts; 2 200 bhp = 20 knots
Radius, miles	500 cruising range
Complement	15

Kayvan, built in USA in 1955, was delivered to Iran on 14 Jan 1956. *Tiran* was built by the US Coast Guard at Curtis Bay, Maryland, and transferred to Iran in 1957. *Mahan* and *Mehran* were delivered to Iran in 1959.

MAHAN *1969, Imperial Iranian Navy*

3 PATROL BOATS

GOHAR **SHAHPAR** **No. 3**

Displacement, tons	70
Dimensions, feet	75·2 × 16·5 × 6
Main engines	2 diesels; 1 100 hp; 2 shafts = 27 knots

Built by Abeking and Rasmussen. *Gohar* launched 22 Jan 1970, *Shahpar* on 19 Mar 1970.

REPAIR SHIPS

1 Ex-US ARL (Ex-LST) TYPE

SOHRAB (ex-USS *Gordius, ARL* 36, ex-*LST* 1145)

Displacement, tons	1 625 light; 4 100 full load
Dimensions, feet	316 wl; 328 oa × 50 × 11·2
Guns	8—40 mm AA
Main engines	GM diesels; 2 shafts; 1 800 bhp = 11·6 knots

Former US repair ship for landing craft. Built by Chicago Bridge & Iron Co, Seneca Ill. Laid down on 5 Feb 1945. Launched on 7 May 1945. Completed on 18 May 1945. Transferred by the USA under the Military Aid Programme in Sep 1961.

SOHRAB *1971*

Repair Ships—*continued*

1 Ex-US AR TYPE

CHAHBAHAR (ex-USS *Amphion*) AR 13

Displacement, tons	7 826 standard; 14 490 full load
Dimensions, feet	456·0 wl; 492·0 oa × 70·0 × 27·5
Guns	2—3 in 50 cal AA
Main engines	Westinghouse turbines; 1 shaft; 8 500 shp = 16·5 knots
Boilers	2 Foster-Wheeler
Complement	Accommodation for 921.

Built by Tampa Shipbuilding Co. Launched on 15 May 1945. Commissioned on 30 Jan 1946. Transferred to IIN on 1 Oct 1971. Based at Bandar Abbas.

CHAHBAHAR *1972, Imperial Iranian Navy*

HOVERCRAFT

4+2 "WELLINGTON (BH.7) CLASS

101 **102** 103 104

Displacement, tons	50 max weight, 33 empty
Dimensions, feet	76 × 45 × 42 (height inflated)
Guns	2 Browning MG
Main engines	1 Proteus 15 M/541 gas turbine = 60 knots max
Oil fuel tons	10 max

First pair are BH 7 Mk 4 (delivered Nov 70 and Mar 71) and the next four are Mk 5 craft (two for delivery in the second half of 1973, one in late 1974 and one in early 1975).

101 *1971*

8 WINCHESTER (SR.N6) CLASS

01 02 03 04 05 06 07 08

Displacement, tons	10 normal gross weight (basic weight 14 200 lbs; disposable load 8 200 lbs)
Dimensions, feet	48·4 × 25·3 × 15·9 (height)
Main engines	1 Gnome Model 1050 gas turbine = 58 knots max.
	1 Peters diesel as auxiliary power unit.

The Imperial Iranian Navy has the world's largest fully operational hovercraft squadron, which is used for coastal defence and logistic duties.

03 *1971*

LANDING CRAFT

QUESM (ex-USS *LCU* 1431) LCU 47

Displacement, tons	160 light; 320 full load
Dimensions, feet	119 × 32 × 5·7
Guns	2—20 mm AA
Main engines	Diesels; 675 bhp = 10 knots
Complement	14

LCU 1431 was transferred to Iran by US in 1964 under the Military Aid Programme.

QUESM *1971*

LARAK (ex-US *LSIL* 710) LSIL 42

Transferred Dec 1958.

IMPERIAL YACHTS

KISH

Displacement, tons	178
Dimensions, feet	122 × 25 × 7
Main engines	2 sets by Motor und Turbinen Union Friedrichshafen GMBH MAN-Maybach-Mercedes-Benz; 2 920 hp

A smaller and more modern Imperial Yacht built by Yacht und Bootswerft, Burmester, Germany. Commissioned in 1970. In the Persian Gulf.

KISH *1971*

SHASAVAR

Displacement, tons	530
Dimensions, feet	176 × 25·3 × 10·5
Main engines	2 sets diesels; 1 300 bhp

Built by N. V. Boele's Scheepwerven, Boines, Netherlands. Engined by Gebr Stork of Hengelo. Launched in 1936. In the Caspian Sea.

SHAHSAVAR *1971, Imperial Iranian Navy*

COASTAL LAUNCHES

6 HARBOUR TYPE

MAHNAVI-HAMRAZ **MAHNAVI-TAHERI** **MAHNAVI-VAHEDI** **MARDJAN** **MORVARID** **SADAF**

Displacement, tons	10 standard
Dimensions, feet	40·0 × 11·0 × 3·7
Guns	Light MG
Main engines	2 General Motors diesels

Small launches for port duties. The three coastal launches of the Caspian type, *Babolsar, Gorgan* and *Sefidroude* were stated in 1972 to be out of service.

2 STORE SHIPS

2 ships of 300 feet, twin-screw diesel, ordered from Yarrow in 1972 for delivery in mid 1974 as store ships and transports.

OILERS

HORMUZ (ex-*YO* 247) 43

Displacement, tons	1 250 standard; 1 700 full load
Dimensions, feet	171·2 wl; 178·3 oa × 32·2 × 14
Main engines	1 Ansaldo Q 370, 4 cycle diesel
Oil fuel, tons	25

Hormuz was built by Cantiere Castellamare di Stabia. Own oil fuel: 25 tons. Cargo oil capacity: 5 000 to 6 000 barrels.

HORMUZ *1970, Imperial Iranian Navy*

WATER CARRIER

LENGEH 46 (ex-USS *YW* 88)

Displacement, tons	1 250 standard
Dimensions, feet	178 × 32 × 14
Main engines	Diesels; speed = 10 knots

Transferred to Iran by US in 1964. Similar to oiler *Hormuz* above.

TUGS

BAHMANSHIR 45

Harbour tug (ex-US Army ST 1002), 150 tons, transferred in 1962. The tug *Yadakbar* (ex-*Neyrou*) was officially deleted from the list in 1971.

IRAQ

Personnel

1973. 2 000 officers and men

SOVIET-IRAQI TREATY

Under this treaty, signed in April 1972, the Soviet fleet will have access to the Iraqi base of UMM QASR. In return Soviet assistance will be given to strengthen Iraq's defences. From the naval aspect, taking into account the small number of personnel, this is most likely to be confined to light forces. With *SO*'s and *P6*'s already in the strength the most likely "assistance" would logically be the provision of *KOMARS* or *OSAs*. Either would notably affect the balance of power in the Persian Gulf.

CORVETTES

3 Ex-USSR "SO-I" TYPE

Displacement, tons	215 light; 250 full load
Dimensions, feet	138·6 × 20 × 9·2
Guns	4—25 mm AA
A/S weapons	4 five-barrelled ahead-throwing rocket launchers.
Main engines	3 diesels; 6 000 bhp = 29 knots
Complement	30

Former Soviet submarine chasers delivered by the USSR to Iraq in 1962.

LIGHT FORCES

12 Ex-USSR "P 6" TYPE

Displacement, tons	66 standard; 75 full load
Dimensions, feet	84·2 × 20 × 6
Guns	4—25 mm
Tubes	2—21 in
Main engines	Diesels; 4 800 bhp = 45 knots
Complement	25

Presented by the USSR. Two were received in 1959, four in Nov 1960, and six in Jan 1961. Some remain non-operational.

No. 1 No. 2 No. 3 No. 4

Displacement, tons	**67**
Dimensions, feet	**100 × 17 × 3 mean**
Guns	**1—3·7 in howitzer; 2—3 in mortars; 4 MG**
Main engines	**2 Thornycroft diesels; 2 shafts; 280 bhp = 12 knots**

Protected by bullet-proof plating. All built by John I. Thornycroft & Co Ltd, Woolston, Southampton. All launched, completed and delivered in 1937.

No. 1 *John I. Thornycroft & Co. Ltd*

Mercantile Marine

Lloyd's Register of Shipping: 41 vessels of 121 399 tons gross

6 Ex-USSR SMALL TYPE

Six small patrol boats are also reported to have been delivered by the USSR.

8 PORTS ADMINISTRATION TYPE

Length, feet	**36**
Main engines	**1 diesel; 125 bhp**

Patrol boats built by John I. Thornycroft & Co for the Iraqi Ports Administration.

4 PILOT DESPATCH TYPE

Length, feet	**21**
Main engines	**1 diesel; 40 bhp**

Pilot despatch launches built by John I. Thornycroft & Co for the Iraqui Ports Administration.

TUG

ALARM (ex-*St Ewe*)

Displacement, tons	570 standard; 820 full load
Dimensions, feet	135 × 30 × 14·5
Main engines	Triple expansion; 1 shaft; 1 200 ihp = 12 knots
Boilers	2 oil-fired

Former British "Rescue" type tug of the "Saint" class. Built by Murdock & Murray. Launched in 1919.

LIGHTHOUSE TENDER

FAISAL 1 (ex-*Sans Peur*, ex-*Restless*)

Displacement, tons	1 025
Dimensions, feet	186 × 29·5 × 14·5
Main engines	Triple expansion; 2 shafts; 850 ihp = 13 knots
Boilers	1 oil-fired

Former Royal Yacht. Designed by G. L. Watson Ltd. Built by John Brown & Co Ltd, Clydebank. Launched in 1923. A photograph appears in the 1937 to 1959-60 editions.

PRESIDENTIAL YACHT

AL THAWRA (ex-*Melike Aliye*)

Displacement, tons	746
Main engines	Diesels; 2 shafts; 1 800 shp = 14 knots

Royal Yacht before assassination of King Faisal II in 1958, after which she was renamed *Al Thawra* (*The Revolution*) instead of *Malika Aliye* (*Queen Aliyah*)

AL THAWRA *Added 1966, Aldo Fraccaroli*

IRELAND (REPUBLIC OF)

Administration

Minister for Defence: Mr. J. Cronin, TD

Commanding Officer and Director Naval Service: Captain T. McKenna

The Irish Naval Service is administered from Naval Headquarters, Department of Defence, Dublin, by the Commanding Officer and Director of the Service. The naval base and dockyard are on Haulbowline Island in Cork Harbour.

Personnel

1973, 480 officers and men

DISPOSALS

Cliona (ex-HMS *Bellwort*) and *Macha* (ex-HMS *Borage*), both built by George Brown, & Co (Marine) Ltd, Greenock, were sold for breaking up in 1970-71. *Maev* (ex-HMS *Oxlip*) deleted 1972. Tender *Wyndham* sold in 1968 and *General McHardy* in 1971.

Mercantile Marine

Lloyd's Register of Shipping: 97 vessels of 182 319 tons gross

FISHERY PROTECTION VESSEL

1 NEW CONSTRUCTION

DEIRDRE FP 20

Displacement, tons	972
Dimensions, feet	184·5 pp × 34·0 × 14·5
Guns	1—40 mm Bofors
Main engines	2 British Polar diesels coupled to 1 shaft; 4 200 bhp = approx 18 knots
Oil fuel	170 bunker capacity
Complement	42

Designed as an all weather ship. Built by Verolme, Cork. Controllable pitch propeller stabilisers and sonar. The first vessel ever built for the Naval Service in the Republic of Ireland. Launched on 29 Dec 1971. Completed May 1972.

COASTAL MINESWEEPERS

FOLA *1972, Irish Naval Service*

3 Ex-BRITISH "TON" CLASS

BANBA CM 11 (ex-HMS *Alverton*, M 1104)
FÓLA CM 12 (ex-HMS *Blaxton* M 1132)
GRAINNE CM 10 (ex-HMS *Oulston*, M 1129)

Displacement, tons	360 standard; 425 full load
Dimensions, feet	140·0 pp; 153·0 oa × 28·8 × 8·2
Guns	1—40 mm AA; 2—20 mm AA
Main engines	2 diesels; 2 shafts; 3 000 bhp = 15 knots max
Oil fuel, tons	45
Range, miles	2 300 at 13 knots
Complement	30 average

Former British "Ton" class coastal minesweepers. Built in 1954-59. Double mahogany hulls and otherwise constructed of aluminium alloy and other materials with the lowest possible magnetic attraction to attain the greatest possible safety factor when sweeping. Purchased from Great Britain in 1971. See fuller particulars of the numerous "Ton" class in the United Kingdom section on later page. Acquired for fishery protection duties as replacements for the old corvettes. Arrived in Irish Republican waters in Spring 1971.

JOHN ADAMS

Measurement, tons	94 gross
Dimensions, feet	85 × 18·5 × 7
Main engines	diesel; 125 bhp = 8 knots

Built by Richard Dunston, Ltd, Thorne, Doncaster, Yorks. Launched in 1934.

ISRAEL

Administration

Commander in Chief of the Israeli Navy:
Rear Admiral Benjamin Telem

Diplomatic Representation

Naval, Military and Air Attaché in London and Paris:
Major General S. Eyal

Naval, Military and Air Attaché in Washington:
Major General E. Zaira

Strength of the Fleet

2 Patrol Submarines (+3 building)
13 Missile Boats (+5 building)
9 Torpedo Boats
30 Patrol Vessels
9 Landing Craft
2 Transports
7 Attack Boats

Personnel

4 000 (250 officers and 3 750 men)

Mercantile Marine

Lloyd's Register of Shipping:
99 vessels of 698 068 tons gross

SUBMARINES

3 VICKERS 500-ton CLASS

A contract was signed in April 1972 for the construction of these submarines by Vickers Ltd, Barrow-in-Furness.

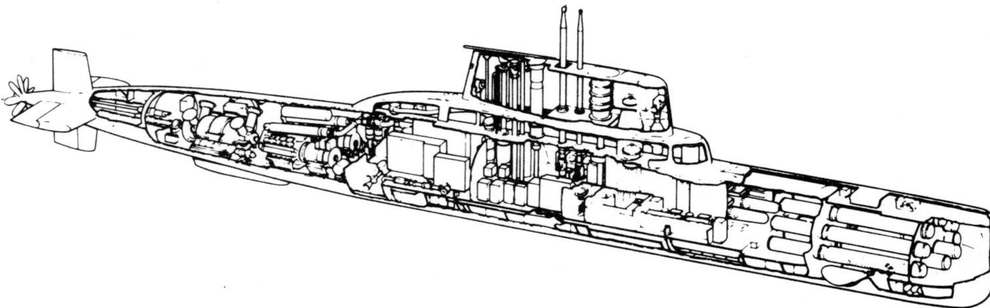

Cutaway impression of the Vickers/AKL 500-ton oceangoing submarine *1972, Vickers Limited*

2 Ex-BRITISH "T" CLASS

Displacement, tons	*Dolphin:* 1 310 standard; 1 535 surface; 1 740 submerged *Leviathan:* 1 280 standard; 1 505 surface; 1 700 submerged
Length, feet (*metres*)	*Dolphin:* 293·5 (*89·5*) oa *Leviathan:* 285·5 (*87·0*) oa
Beam, feet (*metres*)	26·5 (*8·1*)
Draught, feet (*metres*)	14·8 (*4·5*)
Torpedo tubes	6—21 m (*533 mm*) 4 bow, 2 stern
Main engines	Diesels; 2 500 bhp (surface); Electric Motors: 2 900 hp (submerged)
Speed, knots	15·25 on surface; 15 to 18 submerged
Complement	*Dolphin:* 65 *Leviathan:* 69

Name	*No.*	*Builders*	*Laid down*	*Launched*	*Completed*
LEVIATHAN (ex-HMS *Turpin*)	75	HM Dockyard, Chatham	24 May 1943	5 Aug 1944	18 Dec 1944
DOLPHIN (ex-HMS *Truncheon*)	77	HM Dockyard, Devonport	5 Nov 1942	22 Feb 1944	25 May 1945

Both aged T class who were lengthened and modernised during conversion (*Leviathan* plus 12 feet *Dolphin* plus 20 feet). Handed over after extensive refit. *Leviathan* on 19 May 1967, *Dolphin* on 9 Jan 1968.

LOSS. Original sister ship *Dakar* (ex-HMS *Totem*), handed over to Israel on 10 Nov 1967, was lost in the Eastern Mediterranean on 25 Jan 1968.

LEVIATHAN *1972, Israeli Navy*

LIGHT FORCES

6 "SAAR IV" CLASS (MISSILE BOATS)

RESHEF +5

Displacement, tons	415 standard
Dimensions, feet	190·6 × 25 × 8
Missile launchers	7 Gabriel
Guns	2—76 mm Oto Melara. 2 MGs
A/S weapons	4 DC
Engines	4 Maybach diesels; 5 340 hp
Speed,	32 knots
Range, miles	approx 1 500 at 30 knots
Complement	45

Built in Israel these steel-hulled boats carry Israeli-made missiles and electronics. The first was launched on 19 Feb 1973 for service in April 1973.

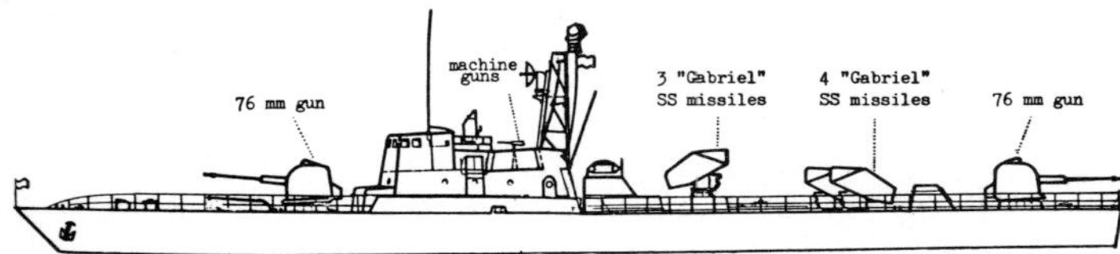

RESHEF *1973, Israeli Navy*

RESHEF *1973, Israeli Navy*

Light Forces—*continued*

12 "SAAR" CLASS (MISSILE BOATS)

ACCO **HAIFA** **HETZ** **MIZNAG**
EILAT **HANIT** **MIFGAV** **SAAR**
GAASH **HEREV** **MIVTACH** **SOUFA**

Displacement, tons	220 standard; 250 full load
Dimensions, feet	147·6 oa × 23·0 × 5·9 (8·2) max
Missile launchers	Gabriel surface to surface (see notes)
Guns, AA	40 mm or 76 mm (see notes)
Tubes	2 side launchers for 21 in torpedoes (surface or A/S)
Main engines	4 Maybach diesels; 13 500 bhp 4 shafts = 40+ knots
Oil fuel, tons	30
Range, miles	2 500 at 15 knots; 1 600 at 20 knots; 1 000 at 30 knots
Complement	35 to 40

Built by Ch de Normandie, Cherbourg, from designs by Lürssen Werft of Bremen. Political problems caused their building in France instead of Germany—a political embargo kept the last five in France until their journey to Israel began on Christmas Eve 1969. Two batches were built, the first six (*Acco, Eilat, Haifa, Misgav, Miznak, Mivtach*) being fitted originally with three 40 mm AA guns and ordered in 1965. The second six (*Gaash, Hanit, Herev Hetz, Saar, Soufa*) were ordered in 1966 and fitted with 76 mm O.T.O. Melara AA guns. Five of these ships were delivered to Israel and two (*Acco* and *Saar*) made the journey on completion of local trials after the 1969 French arms embargo. The last five arrived off Haifa in January 1970 after a much-publicised passage which proved the remarkable endurance of this class.
The first batch was fitted for sonar but this was omitted from the 76 mm gun fitted group.. Since their arrival in Israel provision of Gabriel surface to surface missiles has progressed. The first group can mount an armament varying from one 40 mm gun and eight Gabriel missiles (two single fixed mounts forward and two triple trainable mounts amidships) to three 40 mm guns and two 21 inch torpedo launchers. The second group can mount the two triple Gabriel launchers amidships as well as the 76 mm Oto Melara gun forward.
The Gabriel missile system is controlled by radar and optical sights and launches a low-altitude missile with a 150 lb. HE head to a range of 12·5 miles.

HANIT *1971, Israeli Navy*

3 "OPHIR" CLASS (TORPEDO BOATS)

OPHIR T 150 **SHVA** T 151 **TARSHISH** T 152

Displacement, tons	40
Dimensions, feet	70 × 17 × 5
Guns,	1—40 mm AA; 2—20 mm AA
Torpedoes	2—17·7 in
Main engines	High octane petrol engines; 4 000 bhp = 40 knots.

Motor torpedo Boats/Gunboats built for the Israeli Navy by Cantieri Baglieto, Varraze, Italy, in 1956-57. In reserve.

SHVA *1964, Israeli Navy*

6 "AYAH" CLASS (TORPEDO BOATS)

AYA T 207 **DAYA** T 202 **TAHMASS** T 204
BAZ T 201 **PERESS** T 203 **YASOOR** T 205

Displacement, tons	62 standard
Dimensions, feet	85·3 oa × 20·7 × 5
Guns	1—40 mm; 4—20 mm AA (see notes)
Torpedoes	2—17·7 in
Main engines	2 Napier Deltic diesels; 2 shafts; 4 600 bhp = 42 knots
Complement	15

Built by Chantiers de Meulan, France. Launched in 1950-56. It now appears that at least two boats mount 20 mm guns forward as well as aft. All are probably in reserve prior to disposal.

AYA *1972, Israeli Navy*

4 "KEDMA" CLASS

KEDMA 46 **NEGBA** 52 **YAMA** 48 **ZAFONA** 60

Displacement, tons	32
Dimensions, feet	67·0 × 15·0 × 4·8
Guns	2—20 mm
Main engines	2 diesels; 2 shafts; 1 540 bhp = 25 knots
Complement	10

Built in Japan during 1968. Handy boats of the small seaward defence type. Used for coastguard and police work in peace time.

KEDMA *1970, Israeli Navy*

2 "YAR" CLASS

YARDEN 42 **YARKON** 44

Displacement, tons	96 standard; 109 full load
Dimensions, feet	100 × 20 × 6
Guns,	2—20 mm AA
Main engines	Diesels; 2 shafts; speed 22 knots
Complement	16

Both built by Yacht & Bootswerft, Burmester Bremen-Burg, Germany. *Yarkon* was launched on 25 July 1956 and *Yarden* in 1957. Present status uncertain.

YARDEN *Israeli Navy*

10 SWIFT TYPE (ex-USN PCF)

Displacement, tons	22·5 full load
Dimensions, feet	50·0 oa × 13·0 × 3·5
Guns	1—81 mm mortar; 3—50 cal MG
Main engines	2 geared diesels; 960 shp; 2 shafts = 28 knots (max)
Complement	6

N 854 *1972, Dr. Giorgio Arra*

Light Forces—*continued*

12 "PBR" TYPE

Displacement, tons	7·5
Length, feet	30·2 oa
Guns	1—0·5 MG
Main engines	Diesels; speed = 24 knots
Complement	5

New vessels in service with the Israeli Navy and added to the official list in 1971.

PBR *Israeli Navy*

FIREFISH MODEL III

Displacement, tons	6
Dimensions, feet	28 × 7·5
Main engines	2 Mercruiser V-8; 430 hp
Speed, knots	52 max
Range, miles	250 cruising; 150 max speed

Under construction by Sandaire, San Diego. Glass fibre craft, can carry five men. Capable of being radio-controlled for attack missions or minesweeping under ship or aircraft control.

FIREFISH Model III *1972, Courtesy Sandaire*

2 "HDML" TYPE

DROR 21 **TIRTSA** 25

Displacement, tons	46 standard; 54 full load
Dimensions, feet	72 oa × 16 × 5·5
Guns	2—20 mm AA
A/S	8 DC
Main engines	2 diesels; 2 shafts; 320 bhp = 12 knots
Complement	12

Former British harbour defence motor launches. Built in Great Britain in 1943. Used for coastguard and police work in peacetime.

LANDING CRAFT

3 "ASH" CLASS

ASHDOD 61 **ASHKELON** 63 **ACHZIV** 65

Displacement, tons	400 standard; 730 full load
Dimensions, feet	180·5 pp; 205·5 oa × 32·8 × 5·8
Guns	2—20 mm AA
Main engines	3 MWM diesels; 3 shafts; 1 900 bhp = 10·5 knots
Oil fuel, tons	37
Complement	20

These three landing craft were completed during 1966-67 by Israel Shipyards, Haifa.

Landing Craft—*continued*

ASHDOD *Israeli Navy*

3 "LC" TYPE

ETZION GUEBER 51 **SHIKOMONA** 53 **LC 55**

Displacement, tons	182 standard; 230 full load
Dimensions, feet	120·0 × 23·2 × 4·7
Guns, AA	2—20 mm
Main engines	2 diesels; 2 shafts; 1 280 bhp = 10 knots
Complement	12

In lieu of the landing craft of the LCI and LCT types, which were taken out of commission for disposal (with the exception of one LCT, which was given to the Israeli National Museum in Haifa) three new landing craft were built in the Israeli Dockyard.

SHIKOMONA *Israeli Navy*

3 "LCM" TYPE

LCM

Displacement, tons	22 tons standard; 60 full load
Dimensions, feet	50 × 14 × 3·2
Main engines	2 diesels; 450 bhp = 11 knots

Former United States vessels of the LCM (Landing Craft Mechanised) type. There are a number of other landing craft.

BEIT SHAFEI

Dimensions, feet	225·0 × 38·9 × 5·0
Capacity	16 tanks
Speed	12·5 knots

TRANSPORTS

1 "BAT SHEVA" TYPE

BAT SHEVA

Displacement, tons	900
Dimensions, feet	311·7 × 36·7 × 26·9
Guns	4—20 mm AA
Main engines	diesels; speed = 10 knots
Complement	26

Bat Golim was sunk by Frogman attack in Eilat in 1971.

BAT SHEVA *1971, Israeli Navy*

1 "BAT YAM" TYPE

BAT YAM

A small armed merchant ship used as a transport.

ITALY

Administration

Chief of Naval Staff:
Ammiraglio di Squadra Giuseppe Roselli Lorenzini

Commander, Allied Naval Forces, Southern Europe (Naples):
Ammiraglio di Squadra Giuseppe Pighini

Commander-in-Chief of Fleet (and Comedcent)
Ammiraglio di Squadra Gino De Giorgi

Director General Navy Personnel:
Ammiraglio di Squadra Mario Gambetta

Deputy Chief of Naval Staff:
Ammiraglio di Squadra Aldo Baldini

Diplomatic Representation

Naval Attaché in London:
Rear Admiral Corrado Vittori

Naval Attaché in Washington:
Captain Mario Porta

Naval Attaché in Moscow:
Captain Ubaldo Garagnani

Naval Attaché in Paris:
Captain Giuseppe Colombo

Naval Attaché in Bonn:
Captain Giancarlo Lombardi

Strength of the Fleet

3 Cruisers
10 Destroyers (DLGs)
11 Frigates
11 Corvettes
9 Submarines
1 Landing Ship
18 Light Forces
4 Fleet Minesweepers
37 Coastal Minesweepers
20 Inshore Minesweepers
2 Netlayers
1 Oiler
4 Training Ships
113 Auxiliaries
25 Tugs

Disposals

Cruisers

1961. *Luigi di Savoia*
1972. *Giuseppe Garibaldi*

Destroyers

1971. *San Marco, Artigliere*

Submarines

1965. *Giada*
1967. *Vortice*
1972. *Pietro Calvi, Leonardo da Vinci, Enrico Tazzoli.*

Coastal Minesweepers

1966-67. 17 ships of Azalea and Anemone classes.

Personnel

1973. 44 300 (including Naval Air Arm and an expanding Force of Marines).

Naval Air Arm

3 LRMP Squadrons. Originally with S-2 Trackers. Re-equipping with 18 Breguet Atlantics (first delivered 27 June 1972).

Helicopters. SH-3D, SH-34, AB-204B, Bell 47, HU-16A.

Mercantile Marine

Lloyd's Register of Shipping:
1 684 vessels of 8 187 323 tons gross

CRUISERS

1 HELICOPTER CARRIER TYPE

Name	*No.*	*Builders*	*Laid down*	*Launched*	*Completed*
VITTORIO VENETO	C 550	Navalmeccanica Castellammare di Stabia	10 June 1965	5 Feb 1967	30 Apr 1969

Displacement, tons	7 500 standard; 8 350 full load
Length, feet (*metres*)	557·7 (*170·0*) oa
Beam, feet (*metres*)	63·6 (*19·4*)
Draught, feet (*metres*)	17·2 (*5·2*)
Aircraft	9 A/B 240B ASW helicopters
Missiles, AA	1 "Terrier"/"Asroc" twin launcher forward
Guns, AA	8—3 in (*76 mm*) 62 cal.
Torpedo tubes	2 triple for A/S torpedoes
Boilers	4 Foster-Wheeler; 711 psi (*50 kg/cm²*); 842°F (*450°C*)
Main engines	2 Tosi double reduction geared turbines; 73 000 shp; 2 shafts
Speed, knots	32 designed
Range, miles	6 000 at 20 knots
Oil fuel, tons	1 200
Complement	530 (60 officers, 470 men)

GENERAL
Multi-purpose guided missile armed cruiser and helicopter carrier. Developed from the "Doria" class, but with much larger helicopter squadron and improved facilities for anti-submarine operations. Projected under the 1959-60 New Construction Programme, but her design was recast several times: see official artist's impression in the 1963-64 to 1966-67 editions. She was commissioned for service on 12 July 1969.

RADAR. SBS 48 3-dimensional air search and target designator on fore funnel SPS 29 long range search set on after funnel. One SMA/SPQ-2 combined search and navigation set-X band. 2 SPG-55A fire control groups forward for Terrier. 4 Orion fire-control sets for guns.

VITTORIO VENETO — *1971, Dr Aldo Fraccaroli*

VITTORIO VENETO — *1970 Italian Navy*

Cruisers—*continued*

DRAWING. Scale 125 feet = 1 inch (1 : 1 500)

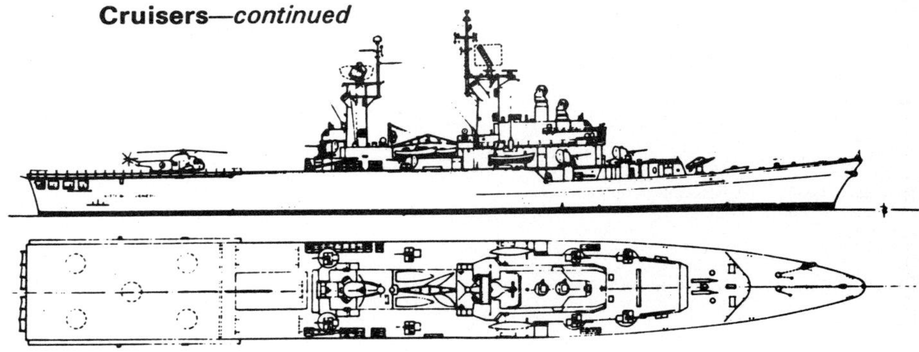

RESCINDMENT. The projected improved guided missile cruiser/helicopter carrier/assault ship *Trieste* (ex-*Italia*) was officially deleted from the New Construction Programme in 1968.

2 "ANDREA DORIA" CLASS

Name	No.	Builders	Laid down	Launched	Completed
ANDREA DORIA	553	Cantieri del Tirreno, Riva Trigoso	11 May 1958	27 Feb 1963	23 Feb 1964
CAIO DUILIO	554	Navalmeccanica Castellammare di Stabia	16 May 1958	22 Dec 1962	30 Nov 1964

Displacement, tons	5 000 standard; 6 500 full load (official figures)
Length, feet (*metres*)	489·8 (*149·3*) oa
Beam, feet (*metres*)	56·4 (*17·2*)
Draught, feet (*metres*)	16·4 (*5·0*)
Aircraft	4 A/B 204B ASW helicopters
Missiles, AA	1 "Terrier" twin launcher forward
Guns, AA	8—3 in (*76 mm*) 62 cal.
Torpedo tubes	2 triple for 12 in (*305 mm*) A/S torpedoes
Boilers	4 Foster-Wheeler; 711 psi (*50 kg/cm²*); 842°F (*450°C*)
Main engines	2 double reduction geared turbines 60 000 shp; 2 shafts
Speed, knots	31 designed, 30 sustained
Radius, miles	6 000 at 20 knots
Oil fuel, tons	1 100
Complement	478 (53 officers, 425 men)

CAIO DUILIO *1972, Dr Aldo Fraccaroli*

Escort cruisers of novel design and generous beam with a good helicopter capacity in relation to their size. *Enrico Dandolo* was the name originally allocated to *Andrea Doria*.

GUNNERY. The anti-aircraft battery includes eight 3-inch fully automatic guns of a new pattern, disposed in single turrets, four on each side amidships abreast the funnels and the bridge.

HELICOPTER PLATFORM. Helicopters operate from a large platform aft measuring 98·5 feet by 52·5 feet (30 by *16 metres*). The Harrier, designed and built by Hawker Siddeley, demonstrated its capabilities of operating from shipborne platforms when it completed a two-day demonstration with a vertical landing on the comparatively small helicopter flight deck of the *Andrea Doria*.

ROLL DAMPING. Both ships have Gyrofin-Salmoiraghi stabilisers.

RADAR. SPS 39 three dimensional air surveillance and target designator on main mast. SPS-12 search set forward. Nav radar. Two SPG-55 control groups for Terrier. Four Orion fire control radars for guns. LSAG NA-9 gun fire control system. ECM and DF. Tacan beacon.

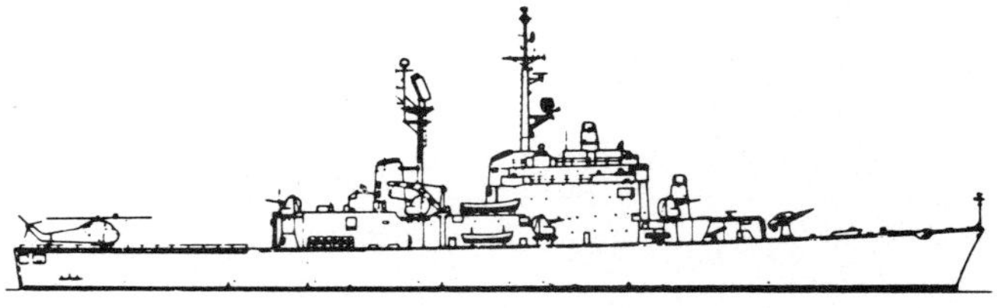

ANDREA DORIA, CAIO DUILIO

ANDREA DORIA *1972, Dr. Aldo Fraccaroli*

DESTROYERS *(DDG)*

2 "AUDACE" CLASS

Name	No.	Builders	Laid Down	Launched
ARDITO	D 550	Navalmeccanica Castellamare	19 July 1968	27 Nov 1971
AUDACE	D 551	Cantieri del Tirreno, Riva Trigoso	27 April 1968	2 Oct 1971

Displacement, tons	3 600 standard; 4 400 full load
Length, feet (*metres*)	446·4 (*136·6*)
Beam, feet (*metres*)	47·1 (*14·5*)
Draught, feet (*metres*)	15 (*4·6*)
Aircraft	2 A/S helicopters
Missile launchers	1 RIM-66A Standard
Guns, dual purpose	2—5 in (*127 mm*) 54 cal single
Guns, AA	4—3 in (*76 mm*) 62 cal
Torpedo tubes	6 A/S (two tripled) 4 fixed tubes
Boilers	4 Foster Wheeler type
Main engines	2 geared turbines; 73 000 shp; 2 shafts
Speed, knots	33

GENERAL
It was announced in Apr 1966 that two new guided missile destroyers would be built. They are basically similar to, but an improvement in design on that of the "Impavido" class.

AIRCRAFT. Originally planned to carry two AB 204 AS helicopters carrying two A/S torpedoes. These may be replaced by two Sea King SH3Ds.

ELECTRONICS. Fitted with SCLAR control and launch units for 105 mm rockets which can be fitted with chaff dispensers, flares or HE heads having a range of 7 miles.

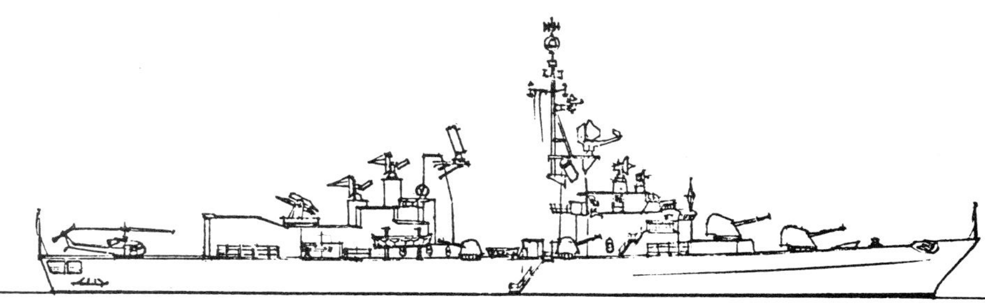

AUDACE *Class*

RADAR. SPS-52 three dimensional air surveillance on after funnel; two SPG 51 tracking and missile guidance; three Orion RTN 10X for Argo NA 10 fire control system. SPS 12 nav radar Elsag NA 10 fire control system.

TORPEDO TUBES. The two triple Mk 32 launchers for Mk 44 torpedoes are on either beam amidships. The four fixed torpedo tubes (Canguro System) for A/S or anti ship torpedoes are built into the transom, a pair being fitted high on either quarter.

AUDACE — *1972, Aviazione e Marina Genova*

2 "IMPAVIDO" CLASS

Name	No.	Builders	Laid down	Launched	Completed
IMPAVIDO	D 570	Cantieri del Tirreno, Riva Trigoso	10 June 1957	25 May 1962	16 Nov 1963
INTREPIDO	D 571	Ansaldo, Leghorn	16 May 1959	21 Oct 1962	30 Oct 1964

Displacement, tons	3 201 standard; 3 851 full load
Length, feet (*metres*)	429·5 (*131·3*)
Beam, feet (*metres*)	44·7 (*13·6*)
Draught, feet (*metres*)	14·8 (*4·5*)
Aircraft	1 AB 204 AS helicopter
Missiles, AA	1 "Tartar" launcher, aft
Guns, AA	2—5 in (*127 mm*) 38 cal. forward; 4—3 in (*76 mm*) 62 cal.
Torpedo tubes	2 triple for A/S torpedoes
Boilers	4 Foster Wheeler; 711 psi (*50 kg/cm²*); 842°F (*450°C*)
Main engines	2 double reduction geared turbine; 70 000 shp; 2 shafts
Speed, knots	34 designed, see *Engineering*
Range, miles	3 300 at 20 knots; 2 900 at 25 knots
Oil fuel, tons	650
Complements	344 (15 officers, 319 men)

GENERAL
Rated as *Caccia Lanciamissili*. Built under the 1956-57 and 1958-59 programmes, respectively. Both ships have stabilisers.

ENGINEERING. On first full power trials *Impavido*, at light displacement, reached 34·5 knots (33 knots at normal load). Sustained sea speed: 30 knots.

IMPAVIDO — *1972, Dr Giorgio Arra*

RADAR. Search: SPS 12 and SPS 39 3 D. Fire Control: SPG 51 for "Tartar", X Band for guns.

IMPAVIDO, INTREPIDO

INTREPIDO — *1968, Dr. Giorgio Arra*

Destroyers—*continued*

Name	*No.*	*Builders*	*Laid down*	*Launched*	*Completed*
SAN GIORGIO (ex-*Pompeo Magno*)	D 562	Cantieri N. Riuniti Ancona	23 Sep 1939	28 Aug 1941	24 June 1943

Displacement, tons 3 950 standard; 4 350 full load
Length, feet (*metres*) 455·2 (*138·8*)wl; 466·5 (*142·3*)oa
Beam, feet (*metres*) 47·2 (*14·4*)
Draught, feet (*metres*) 21·0 (*4·5*)
Guns 4—5 in (*127 mm*) 38 cal; 3—3 in (*76 mm*) 62 cal
A/S weapons 1 three-barrelled mortar; 2 triple torpedo tubes
Main engines 2 Tosi Metrovick gas turbines; 15 000 hp; and 4 Fiat diesels; 16 600 bhp; 2 shafts
Speed, knots 20 (diesels), 28 (diesel and gas)
Range, miles 4 800 at 20 knots
Oil fuel, tons 500 (diesel oil)
Complement 314 plus 130 cadets

Built as *Esploratore Oceanice* (Ocean Scout). Converted into fleet destroyer in 1951 by Cantieri del Tirreno, Genova, being completed 1 July 1955. Underwent complete re-construction at the Naval Dockyard, La Spezia, in 1963-65. The modernisation included her adaptation as a Training Ship for 130 cadets of the Accademia Navale. Changes were made in the armament and new machinery was fitted, gas turbines and diesels replacing steam turbines and boilers.

RADAR. Search: SPS 6. Fire control: 4 X Band Nav set.

CLASS. Original sister ship *San Marco*, D 563 (ex-*Guilio Germanico*) was officially deleted from the list in Jan 1971.

SAN GIORGIO *1972, Dr Giorgio Arra*

SAN GIORGIO

2 "IMPETUOSO" CLASS

Name	*No.*	*Builders*	*Ordered*	*Laid down*	*Launched*	*Completed*
IMPETUOSO	D 558	Cantieri del Tirreno, Riva Trigoso	Nov 1950	7 May 1952	16 Sep 1956	25 Jan 1958
INDOMITO	D 559	Ansaldo, Leghorn (formerly OTO)	Nov 1950	24 Apr 1952	7 Aug 1955	23 Feb 1958

Displacement, tons 2 755 standard; 3 800 full load
Length, feet (*metres*) 405 (*123·4*) pp; 418·7 (*127·6*) oa
Beam, feet (*metres*) 43·5 (*13·3*)
Draught, feet (*metres*) 17·5 (*4·5*)
Guns, AA 4—5 in (*127 mm*) 38 cal. 16—40 mm, 56 cal.
A/S weapons 1 three-barrelled mortar; 4 DCT; 1 DC rack
Tubes 6 (2 triple) for A/S torpedoes
Main engines 2 double reduction geared turbines; 2 shafts; 65 000 shp
Boilers 4 Foster-Wheeler; 711 psi (*50 kg/cm²*) working pressure; 842°F (*450°C*) superheat temperature
Speed, knots 34, see *Engineering* notes
Range, miles 3 400 at 20 knots
Oil fuel, tons 650
Complement 393 (25 officers, 368 men)

Italy's first destroyers built since Second World War. Armament if and when converted: 1 single "Tartar" launcher 2—5 in, 4—3 in guns

ENGINEERING. On their initial sea trials these ships attained a speed of 35 knots at full load.

RADAR. Search: SPS 6. Fire Control: US Mk 57 on fore director, US Mk 37 aft. Surface warning/nav set.

INDOMITO *1971, Dr. Aldo Fraccaroli*

IMPETUOSO, INDOMITO

2 Ex-US "FLETCHER" CLASS

Name	*No.*	*Builders*	*Laid down*	*Launched*	*Completed*
FANTE (ex-USS *Walker*, DD 517)	**D 561**	**Bath Iron Works Corpn**	**31 Aug 1942**	**31 Jan 1943**	**2 Apr 1943**
GENIERE (ex-USS *Pritchett*, DD 561)	**D 555**	**Seattle-Tacoma SB Corpn**	**20 July 1942**	**31 July 1943**	**15 Jan 1944**

Displacement, tons 2 080 standard; 2 940 full load
Length, feet (*metres*) 376·5 (*114·3*) oa
Beam, feet (*metres*) 39·5 (*12·0*)
Draught, feet (*metres*) 18 (*5·5*)
Guns, surface 2—5 inch, 38 cal (4 in *Geniere*)
Guns, AA 4—3 inch, 50 cal (6 in *Geniere*) in twin mountings
A/S weapons 1 DC rack, 2 side-launching torpedo racks, 2 fixed Hedgehogs
Main engines GE geared turbines; 2 shafts; 60 000 shp
Boilers 4 Babcock & Wilcox
Speed, knots 35 designed (32 sea)
Oil, fuel tons 650
Range, miles 6 000 at 15 knots
Complement 250

GENERAL
Walker was transferred from the United States Navy and commissioned as *Fante* on 2 July 1969. *Prichett* was transferred at San Diego on 10 Jan 1970 and renamed *Geniere*. She left San Francisco Navy Yard for Italy in the late summer 1970.

RADAR. Search: SPS 6 and SPS 10. Fire Control: US Mk 57 forward.

TORPEDO TUBES. The five 21-inch torpedo tubes (originally ten, in two quintuple banks) were removed.

DEACTIVATION. A third destroyer of this class, *Lanciere*, D 560 (ex-USS *Taylor*, DD 468) was transferred from the United States Navy on 2 July 1969 (with *Fante*, ex-*Walker*, see above) and commissioned into the Italian Navy, but in Jan 1971 she was officially deleted from the list. It has been stated that this 30-year old veteran will probably be cannibalised to provide spare parts to keep her two almost equally old sister ships in effective condition.

GENIERE *1971, Italian Navy.*

Destroyers—*continued*

Name	*No.*	*Builders*	*Laid down*	*Launched*	*Completed*
AVIERE (ex-USS *Nicholson, DD* 442)	D 554	Boston Navy Yard	1 Nov 1939	31 May 1940	3 June 1941

Displacement, tons	1 700 standard; 2 580 full load
Length, feet (*metres*)	341 (*103·9*) wl; 348·3 (*1Q6·1*) oa
Beam, feet (*metres*)	36·0 (*11·0*)
Draught, feet (*metres*)	18 (*5·5*) max
Guns, surface	4—5 in (see *Gunnery*)
Guns, AA	12—40 mm; 6—20 mm
A/S weapons	4 DC throwers; 2 DC racks
Main engines	GE geared turbines; 2 shafts; 50 000 shp
Boilers	4 Babcock & Wilcox
Speed, knots	30 (26 sustained)
Oil fuel, tons	600
Range, miles	6 000 at 12 knots
Complement	240

Former US "Gleaves" class destroyer. Transferred from USA and commissioned on 25 May 1951. Officially turned over to Italy on 11 June 1951. The 5—21 in torpedo tubes were removed.

GUNNERY. In 1970 she was fitted with OTO Melara 127/54 (5-inch) gun mounting in "B" position and new OTO Melara 76/62 (3-inch) gun mounting in "X" position, these new mountings having been adopted by the Italian navy.

AVIERE — 1972, *Italian Navy*

RADAR. Search: SPS 6. Fire Control: US Mk 57.

STATUS. Classification officially changed from Fleet Destroyer to Experimental Ship in 1971.

FRIGATES

2 "ALPINO" CLASS

Name	*No.*	*Builders*	*Laid down*	*Launched*	*Completed*
ALPINO (ex-*Circe*)	F 580	Cantiere Navali del Tirreno, Riva Trigoso	27 Feb 1963	10 June 1967	14 Jan 1968
CARABINIERE (ex-*Climene*)	F 581	Cantiere Navali del Tirreno, Riva Trigoso	9 Jan 1965	30 Sep 1967	28 Apr 1968

Displacement, tons	2 700 full load
Length, feet (*metres*)	349·0 (*106·4*) pp; 352·0 (*107·3*) wl; 371·7 (*113·3*) oa
Beam, feet (*metres*)	43·6 (*13·3*)
Draught, feet (*metres*)	12·7 (*3·9*)
Aircraft	2 A/B 204B ASW helicopters
Guns	6—3 in (*76 mm*) dp 62 cal single
A/S weapons	1 single depth charge mortar
Tubes	6 (2 triple) 12 in (*305 mm*) for A/S torpedoes
Main engines	4 Tosi diesels = 16 800 hp; 2 Tosi Metrovick gas turbines = 15 000 hp; 2 shafts; 31 800 hp
Speed, knots	22 (diesel), 29 (diesel and gas)
Range, miles	4 200 at 18 knots
Oil fuel, tons	275
Complement	254 (21 officers, 233 men)

CARABINIERE — 1972, *Italian Navy*

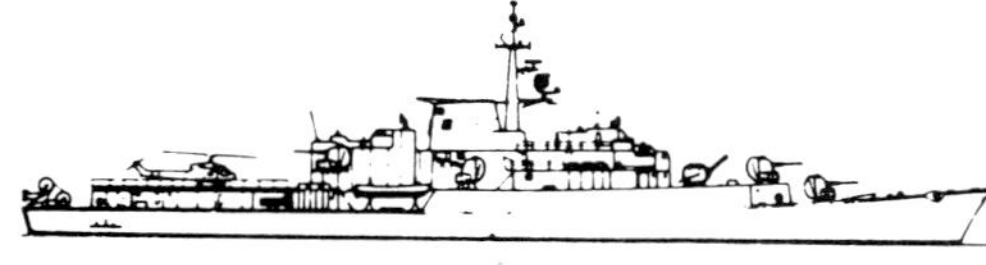

ALPINO CARABINIERE

Circe and *Climene* were provided for under the 1959-60 programme. The original "Circe" class project was modified in 1962, in respect of both machinery and armament. The originally allocated names *Circe* and *Climene* were changed to *Alpino* and *Carabiniere*, respectively in June 1965. The new design is an improved version of that of the "Centauro" class combined with that of the "Bergamini" class. They have similar basic characteristics but a heavier displacement and increased engine power. Two other ships of the same type, to have been named *Perseo* and *Polluce* were provided for under the 1960-61 programme, but they were suspended owing to fiscal considerations.

RADAR. Search: SPS 12. SMA/SPQ-2 combined air/surface search/nav radar-X band. MM/SPR-A radar intercept. 3 Orion fire-control radars in ELSAG Argo "O" fire control system.

SONAR. Possibly SQS-4, SQS-30, SQS-36 with ELSAG fire control system DLB-1.

4 "BERGAMINI" CLASS

Name	*No.*	*Builders*	*Laid down*	*Launched*	*Completed*
CARLO BERGAMINI	F 593	San Marco, CRDA Trieste	19 May 1957	16 June 1960	23 June 1962
CARLO MARGOTTINI	F 595	Navalmeccanica, Castellammare	26 May 1957	12 June 1960	5 May 1962
LUIGI RIZZO	F 596	Navalmeccanica, Castellammare	26 May 1957	6 Mar 1957	15 Dec 1961
VIRGINIO FASAN	F 594	Navalmeccanica, Castellammare	6 Mar 1960	9 Oct 1960	10 Oct 1962

Displacement, tons	1 650 full load
Length, feet (*mteres*)	311·7 (*95·0*) oa
Beam, feet (*metres*)	37·4 (*11·4*)
Draught, feet (*metres*)	10·5 (*3·2*)
Aircraft	1 A/B-47-J3 helicopter
Guns	2—3 in (*76 mm*) dp 62 cal single
A/S weapons	1 single depth charge mortar
Tubes	6 (2 triple) 12 in (*305 mm*) for A/S torpedoes
Main engines	4 diesels (Fiat in *Fasan* and *Margottini*, Tosi in others); 2 shafts; 15 000 bhp
Speed, knots	26 max; 24·5 sustained
Range, miles	4 000 at 18 knots
Complement	160

VIRGINIO FASAN (after conversion) — 1972, *Dr. Giorgio Arra*

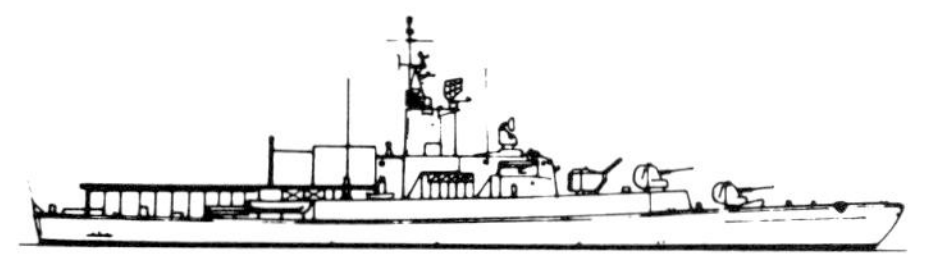

BERGAMINI *Class*

RADAR. Search: SPS 12. Fire Control: X Band. Single ARGO NA2 fire control system and radar. MM/SPR-A radar intercept. Nav-Surface warning.

MODIFICATION. The anit-submarine capability was augmented in *Carlo Margottini* in 1968, *Virginio Fasan* in 1969, *Carlo Bergamini* in 1970 and *Luigi Rizzo* in 1971 by the allocation of an AB-204 A/S helicopter for the operation of which the enlargement of the flight deck was necessary together with the removal of the 3-inch gun aft.

ANTI-SUBMARINE. The single-barrelled automatic depth charge mortars have a range of 1 000 yards. Rate of fire is 15 DC per minute. The 12-inch torpedoes have a life of six minutes at 30 knots. ELSAG DLB-1 fire control system.

ROLL DAMPING. Two Denny-Brown stabilisers reduce inclination in heavy seas from 20 to 5 degrees.

Frigates—*continued*

4 "CENTAURO" CLASS

Name	No.	Builders	Laid down	Launched	Completed
CANOPO	F 551 (ex-D 570)	Cantieri Navali di Taranto	15 May 1952	20 Feb 1955	1 Apr 1958
CENTAURO	F 554 (ex-D 571)	Ansaldo, Leghorn	31 May 1952	4 Apr 1954	5 May 1957
CIGNO	F 555 (ex-D 572)	Cantieri Navali di Taranto	10 Feb 1954	20 Mar 1955	7 Mar 1957
CASTORE	F 553 (ex-D 573)	Cantieri Navali di Taranto	14 Mar 1955	8 July 1956	14 July 1957

Displacement, tons	1 807 standard; 2 250 full load
Length, feet (*metres*)	308·4 (*94*) pp; 338·4 (*103·1*) oa
Beam, feet (*metres*)	39·5 (*12*)
Draught, feet (*metres*)	12·6 (*3·8*)
Guns, AA	3—3 in (*76 mm*) 62 cal single
A/S weapons	1 three-barrelled depth charge mortar
Tubes	6 (2 triple) 12 in (*305 mm*) for A/S torpedoes
Main engines	2 double reduction geared turbines 2 shafts; 22 000 shp
Speed, knots	25
Boilers	2 Foster Wheeler; 626 psi (*44 kg/cm²*) working pressure; 842°F (*450°C*) superheat temperature
Oil fuel, tons	400
Range, miles	3 660 at 20 knots
Complement	255 (16 officers, 239 men)

The above data refers to *Castore*, *Canopo* and *Centauro* see *Conversion*. *Cigno* (US hull No. DE 1020) and *Castore* (DE 1031) were built to Italian plans and specifications under the US off-shore programme. All four ships have automatic anti-submarine and medium anti-aircraft armament, and are fitted with US sonar gear.

RADAR. Search: SPS 6. Fire Control: X Band. SMA/SPQ-2 combined surface and air search-navigation—X band. MM/SPR-A intercept.

SONAR. SQS-11.

CONVERSION. *Castore* underwent medium anti-aircraft conversion in 1966-67, *Canopo* in 1968-69, and *Centauro* in 1970-71. See former particulars (still applicable to *Cigno*) in the 1966-67 and earlier editions. The changes include the mounting of three 3-inch 62 cal single guns, replacing the two 2 barrelled 76 mm 62 cal and the four 40 mm 70 cal AA guns.

CASTORE — *1972, Dr. Giorgio Arra*

CENTAURO *Class* as converted

CIGNO (CENTAURO *Class* original)

ALDEBARAN

Name	No.	Builders	Laid down	Launched	Completed
ALDEBARAN (ex-USS *Thornhill, DE* 195)	F 590	Federal SB & DD Co, P. Newark	7 Oct 1943	30 Dec 1943	1 Feb 1944

Displacement, tons	**1 900 full load**
Length, feet (*metres*)	**306 (*93·3*) oa**
Beam, feet (*metres*)	**36·7 (*11·2*)**
Draught, feet (*metres*)	**14 (*4·3*)**
Guns, surface	**3—3 in (*76 mm*) 50 cal.**
Guns, AA	**6—40 mm; 18—20 mm**
A/S weapons	**1 Hedgehog; 8 DCT; 2 DC racks**
Main engines	**GM diesel-electric; 2 shafts; 6 000 hp**
Speed, knots	**21 designed; 16·5 actual sea**
Radius, miles	**11 500 at 11 knots**
Oil fuel, tons	**300**
Complement	**160**

ALDEBARAN — *Italian Navy*

Ex-US destroyer escort of the "Bostwick" class. Transferred on 10 Jan 1951. In 1956 a pentapod foremast was stepped in place of the former polemast.

RADAR. Search: SPS 6. Fire Control: X Band.

DISPOSALS. Sister ships *Altair*, F 591 (ex-USS *Gandy, DE* 764) and *Andromeda*, F 592 (ex-USS *Wesson, DE* 184) were officially deleted from the list in Jan 1972.

CORVETTES

4 "DE CRISTOFARO" CLASS

Name	No.	Builders	Laid down	Launched	Completed
LICIO VISINTINI	F 546	CRDA Monfalcone	30 Sep 1963	30 May 1965	25 Aug 1966
PIETRO DE CRISTOFARO	F 540	Cantiere Navali de Tirreho, Riva Tregoso	30 Apr 1963	29 May 1965	19 Dec 1965
SALVATORE TODARO	F 550	Cantiere Ansaldo, Leghorn	21 Oct 1962	24 Oct 1964	25 Apr 1966
UMBERTO GROSSO	F 541	Cantiere Ansaldo, Leghorn	21 Oct 1962	12 Dec. 1964	25 Apr. 1966

Displacement, tons	850 standard; 1 020 full load
Length, feet (*metres*)	246 (*75·0*) pp; 263·2 (*80·2*) oa
Beam, feet (*metres*)	33·7 (*10·3*)
Draught, feet (*metres*)	9 (*2·7*)
Guns, dual purpose	2—3 in (*76 mm*), 62 cal, single
A/S weapons	1 single-barrelled DC mortar
Tubes	2 triple for A/S torpedoes
Main engines	2 diesels = 8 400 bhp; 2 sha/ts
Speed, knots	23·5 max; 21·5 sustained sea
Range, miles	4 000 at 18 knots
Oil fuel, tons	100
Complement	131 (8 officers, 123 men)

The design is an improved version of the "Albatros" class.

RADAR. Air and surface surveillance radar with antenna mounted at top of foremast. Gunfire control system has director mounted aft, above compass platform, with X band tracker radar.

SONAR. SQS-36. ELSAG DLB-1 fire control system.

LICIO VISINTINI — *1972, Italian Navy*

RESCINDMENT. The projected improved type of "corvette" *circa* 1 200 tons, gas turbines, 20 000 hp, 30-31 knots, was deleted from the New Construction Programme in 1968.

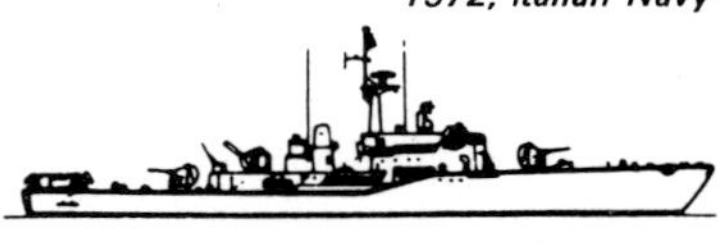

DE CRISTOFARO *Class*

Corvettes—*continued*

4 "ALBATROS" CLASS

Name	No.	Builders	Launched	Completed
AIRONE (ex-*PCE* 1621)	F 545	Navalmeccanica, Castellammare di Stabia	21 Nov 1954	29 Dec 1955
ALBATROS (ex-*PCE* 1619)	F 543	Navalmeccanica, Castellammare di Stabia	18 July 1954	1 June 1955
ALCIONE (ex-*PCE* 1620)	F 544	Navalmeccanica, Castellammare di Stabia	19 Sep 1954	23 Oct 1955
AQUILA (ex-*Lynx*, ex-*PCE* 1626)	F 542	Breda Marghera Yard, Mestre, Venice	31 July 1954	2 Oct 1956

Displacement, tons	800 standard; 950 full load
Length, feet (*metres*)	250·3 (*76·3*) oa
Beam feet (*metres*)	31·5 (*9·6*)
Draught, feet (*metres*)	9·2 (*2·8*)
Guns, AA	4—40 mm 70 cal. Bofors (see *Gunnery*)
A/S weapons	2 Hedgehogs Mk II; 2 DCT; 1 DC rack; 2 triple tubes
Tubes	2 triple A/S to be fitted
Main engines	2 Fiat diesels; 2 shafts 5 200 bhp
Speed, knots	19
Range, miles	3 000 at 18 knots
Oil fuel, tons	100
Complement	109

AQUILA 1972, Dr. Aldo Fraccaroli

Eight ships of this class were built in Italy under US offshore MDAP orders. 3 for Italy, 4 for Denmark and 1 for the Netherlands, *Aquila*, laid down on 25 July 1953, which was ceded to the Italian Navy on 18 Oct 1961 at Den Helder.

RADAR. SMA/SPQ-2 X band combined air and surface navigation set. ELSAG NA-2 fire control.

GUNNERY. The two 3-inch guns originally mounted, one forward and one aft, were temporarily replaced by two 40 mm guns in 1963. The ultimate armament will include two 3-inch guns of the OTO Melara model.

ALBATROS *Class*

3 "APE" CLASS

BOMBARDA F 549 **SFINGE** F 579
CHIMERA F 569

Displacement, tons	670 standard; 771 full load
Length, feet (*metres*)	192.8 (*58·8*) wl; 212·6 (*64·8*) oa
Beam, feet (*metres*)	28·5 (*8·7*)
Draught, feet (*metres*)	8·9 (*2·7*)
Guns, AA	4—40 mm 56 cal in *Chimera* and *Sfinge*; 2—40 mm 56 cal and 2—20 mm 70 cal in *Bombarda*
A/S weapons	1 Hedgehog Mk 10
Main engines	2 Fiat diesels; 2 shafts; 3 500 bhp
Speed, knots	15
Range, miles	2 450 at 15 knots
Oil fuel, tons	64
Complement	100 to 108

Completed in 1951 (*Bombarda*) and 1943. Originally fitted for minesweeping. Modified with navigating bridge. *Ape* is now support ship (*nave appoggio*) for frogmen and commandos (see photograph under Support Ships in later page).

RADAR. Search: SPS 6 in *Sfinge* (see photograph in the 1968-69 to 1971-72 editions).

CHIMERA 1972, Dr Giorgio Arra

CLASS. *Fenice*, F 577, *Folga*, F 576, and *Pomona*, F 573, were officially deleted from the list in 1965, *Driade*, F 568, on 1 Aug 1966, *Danaide*, F 563, in 1968, *Minerva*, F 562, in 1969, *Flora*, F 572, *Gru*, F 566, and *Pellicano*, F 574, in 1970, *Baionetta*, F 578, *Cormorano*, F 575, *Crisalide*, F 547, *Farfella*, F 548, *Gabbiano*, F 571, *Ibis*, F 561, *Scimitarra*, F 564, *Sibilla*, F 565, and *Urania*, F 570, in 1972.

SUBMARINES

4 "TOTI" CLASS

Name	No.	Builders	Laid down	Launched	Completed
ATTILIO BAGNOLINI	S 505	CRDA Monfalcone	15 Apr 1965	26 Aug 1967	16 June 1968
ENRICO DANDOLO	S 513	CRDA Monfalcone	10 Mar 1967	16 Dec 1967	25 Sep 1968
LAZZARO MOCENIGO	S 514	CRDA Monfalcone	12 June 1967	20 Apr 1968	11 Jan 1969
ENRICO TOTI	S 506	CRDA Monfalcone	15 Apr 1965	12 Mar 1967	22 Jan 1968

Displacement, tons	460 standard; 524 surface 582 submerged
Length, feet (*metres*)	153·2 (*46·7*)
Beam, feet (*metres*)	15·4 (*4.7*)
Draught, feet (*metres*)	13·1 (*4·0*)
Torpedo tubes	4—21 in
Main engines	2 Fiat MB 820 N/I diesels, 1 electric motor, Diesel-electric drive; 2 200 hp; 1 shaft
Speed, knots,	9 on surface; 14 submerged
Range, miles	3 000 at 5 knots
Complement	24

Italy's first indigenously-built submarines since the Second World War. The design was recast several times, being finalised as coastal submarines of the hunter-killer type.

ELECTRONICS. WT, HF, UHF and VLF equipment. Computer based fire control.

RADAR. Search/nav set. IFF, ECM.

SONAR. Passive set in stem. Active set in bow dome. Passive range finding. Ray path analyzer.

TOTI with new hydroplanes 1972, Dr Giorgio Arra

NEW CONSTRUCTION. The two projected patrol submarines of the Sauro class, officially deleted from the New Construction Programme in 1968, were restored to the building schedule in 1972. Names under consideration: *Cesare Battisti*, *Guglielmo Marconi*, *Nazario Sauro*. To be fitted with Selenia passive and active sonars, search/nav radar, ECM.

3 Ex-US "BALAO" CLASS

Name	No.	Builders	Launched	Completed	Transferred
ALFREDO CAPPELLINI (ex-USS *Capitaine*, *SS* 336)	S 507	Electric Boat Div, General Dynamics Corpn	1 Oct 1944	26 Jan 1945	5 Mar 1966
EVANGELISTA TORRICELLI (ex-USS *Lizardfish*, *SS* 373)	S 512	Manitowoc SB Co, Manitowoc, Wisconsin	16 July 1944	30 Dec 1944	9 Jan 1960
FRANCESCO MOROSINI (ex-USS *Besugo*, *SS* 321)	S 508	Electric Boat Div, General Dynamics Corpn	27 Feb 1944	19 June 1944	31 Mar 1966

Displacement, tons	1 600 standard; 1 816 surface; 2 425 submerged
Length, feet (*metres*)	311·5 (*95·0*)
Beam, feet (*metres*)	27 (*8·2*))
Draught, feet (*metres*)	17 (*5·2*)
Torpedo tubes	10—21 in (*533 mm*) 6 bow and 4 stern
Main engines	4 GM 16/278 diesels, 6 000 hp; 4 electric motors; 2 750 hp
Speed, knots	18 on surface; 10 submerged
Range, miles	14 000 at 10 knots
Oil fuel, (tons)	300
Complement	85

Lizardfish was originally to have been renamed *Luigi Torelli*.

ALFREDO CAPPELLINI 1972, Dr. Giorgio Arra

Submarines—*continued*

2 Ex-US GUPPY III TYPE

Name	*Builders*	*Laid down*	*Launched*	*Completed*	*Transferred*
GIANFRANCO PRIAROGGIA GAZZANA (ex-USS *Volador* SS 490)	Portsmouth Navy Yard	15 June 1945	17 Jan 1946	10 Jan 1948	18 Aug 1972
PIERO LONGOBARDO (ex-USS *Pickerel* SS 524)	Boston Navy Yard	8 Feb 1944	15 Dec 1944	4 Apr 1949	18 Aug 1972

Displacement, tons	1 975 standard; 2 450 dived
Length, feet (*metres*)	326·5 (*99·4*) oa
Beam, feet (*metres*)	27 (*8·2*)
Draught, feet (*metres*)	17 (*5·2*)
Torpedo tubes	10—21 in; 6 bow, 4 stern
Main engines	4 diesels; 6 400 bhp—2 electric motors; 5 400 shp; 2 shafts
Speed, knots	20 surface; 15 dived
Range, miles	12 000 at 10 knots (surfaced)
Oil fuel, tons	300
Complement	85

Transferred to Italy instead of USS *Jallao* and *Quillback* as originally planned.

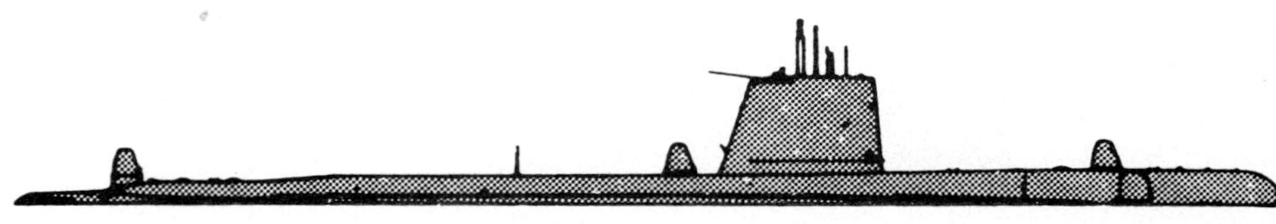

GUPPY III *Class*

LANDING SHIP

QUARTO

Displacement, tons	764 standard; 980 full load
Dimensions, feet	226·4 × 31·3 × 6
Guns	4—40 mm AA (2 twin)
Main engines	3 diesels; 2 300 bhp = 13 knots
Range, miles	1 300 at 13 knots

Quarto was laid down on 19 Mar 1966 at Taranto Naval Shipyard and launched on 18 Mar 1967. The design is intermediate between that of LSM and LCT.

QUARTO *1971, Dr. Aldo Fraccaroli*

LIGHT FORCES

MISSILE BOATS. The five vessels of the large MGB type projected under the 1969 new construction programme were officially deleted from the naval schedule in Jan 1972.

VEDETTA (ex-*Belay Deress*, ex-USS **PC 1616**) **F 597**

Displacement, tons	325 standard; 450 full load
Dimensions, feet	170 pp; 174 oa × 23 × 10
Guns	2—40 mm; 56 cal Bofors AA; 2—20 mm AA
Main engines	4 diesels; 2 shafts; 3 240 bhp = 19 knots
A/S weapons	1 Hedgehog ; 4 DCT; 2 DC racks
Range, miles	3 000 at 12 knots
Complement	60

She was sold to Italy, being transferred on 3 Feb 1959, and officially classified as a *nave pattuglia* (patrol vessel). Air-conditioning equipment is installed. Refitted in La Spezia Navy Yard in 1959. Employed as a Fishery Protection Vessel.

VEDETTA *1969, Italian Navy*

MS 441 (ex-841) **MS 443** (ex-843) **MS 453** (ex-853)

Displacement, tons	64 full load
Dimensions, feet	78 × 20 × 6
Guns	1—40 mm, 56 cal; 2 or 3—20 mm, 70 cal
Torpedoes	2—17·7 in (no tubes)
Main engines	3 petrol motors; 3 shafts; 4 500 bhp = 34 knots
Range, miles	1 000 at 20 knots

Former US PT boats of Higgins type. Refitted in Italy in 1949-53. New radar installed. MS 441 converted into a fast transport for commandos and frogmen.
MS 442 (ex-842), MS 451 (ex-851) and MS 452 (ex-852) transferred to Customs in 1966, and MS 444 (ex-844) was removed from the effective list in 1966.

Light Forces—*continued*

MS 453 *1969, Italian Navy*

MS 472 (ex-612) **MS 473** (ex-813) **MS 474** (ex-614) **MS 481** (ex-615)

Displacement, tons	72 full load
Dimensions, feet	92 × 15 × 5
Guns	1 or 2—40 mm, 56 cal
Torpedoes	2—17·7 in
Main engines	Petrol motors; 3 shafts; 3 450 bhp = 27 knots
Range, miles	600 at 16 knots

Built in 1942-43 at CRDA Monfalcone yard; converted as MV (motovedette) with no tubes under the Peace Treaty. Reconverted in 1951-53. MS 472 and MS 473 were refitted as convertible boats in 1960 and MS 474 and MS 481 in 1961.

MS 481 *1971, Dr. Giorgio Arra*

MS 482 (ex-616), MS 483 (ex-617) and MS 484 (ex-618) were removed from the effective list in 1963, and MS 471 (ex-611) and MS 475 (ex-619) in 1965.

The British MTBs *Dark Avenger*, *Dark Biter*, *Dark Hunter* and *Dark Invader* were taken over in 1967 for the Guardia di Finanza.

2 "FRECCIA" CLASS (FPBs)

FRECCIA (ex-*MC* 590) P 493 **SAETTA** (ex-*MC* 591) P 494

Displacement, tons	188 standard; 205 full load
Dimensions, feet	150 × 23·8 × 5·5
Guns	*As Gunboat*: 3—40 mm, 70 cal or 2—40 mm, 70 cal
	As Fast Minelayer: 1—40 mm AA with 8 mines
	As Torpedo Boat: 1—40 mm, 70 cal
Tubes	*As Torpedo Boat*: 2—21 in
Main engines	2 diesels; 7 600 bhp; 1 Bristol Siddeley Proteus gas turbine. 4 250 shp; Total hp 11 850 = 40 knots

Freccia was laid down by Cantiere del Tirreno, Riva Trigosa on 30 Apr 1963, launched on 9 Jan 1965 and commissioned on 6 July 1965. *Saetta* was laid down by CRDA, Monfalcone on 11 June 1963, launched on 11 Apr 1965, and completed in 1966. Special convertible version designed to carry mines or depth charges. Can be converted in 24 hours to gunboat, torpedo boat, fast minelayer, or missile boat. Fitted with S band navigation and tactical radar employing a slotted waveguide antenna. The gunfire control system has a director with X band tracker radar. *Saetta* has been

SAETTA experimentally armed with 5 short range missiles *1970*

Light Forces—*continued*

armed with Sea Killer Mk I system with 5 round trainable launcher. Contraves fire control including target-tracking radar with TV camera mounted on top. It is planned to fit *Freccia* with Otomat, Selina radar, and Ecograph sonar. See photograph. *Dardo* (ex-*MC* 592, ex-493) P 495 and *Strale* (ex-*MC* 593, ex-494) P 496 were officially deleted from the programme in Jan 1972.

FRECCIA *1972, Dr. Giorgio Arra*

2 "LAMPO" CLASS (FPBs)

BALENO (ex-*MC* 492) P 492 **LAMPO** (ex-*MC* 491) P. 491

Displacement, tons	170 standard; 196 full load
Dimensions, feet	131·5 × 21 × 5
Guns	*As Gunboat:* 3—40 mm, 70 cal or 2—40 mm, 70 cal *As Torpedo Boat:* 1—40 mm, 70 cal
Tubes	*As Torpedo Boat:* 2—21 in
Main engines	2 Fiat diesels, 1 Metrovick gas turbine; 3 shafts; total 11 700 hp = 39 knots.

Convertible gunboats, improved versions of the *Folgore* prototype. Both built by Arsenale MM Taranto. *Lampo* was laid down on 4 Jan 1958, launched on 22 Nov 1960 and commissioned in July 1963. A photograph of her as torpedo boat appears in the 1968-69 edition. *Baleno* was laid-down on the same slip on 22 Nov 1960, launched on 10 May 1964 and commissioned on 16 July 1965. She has been converted to an improved design.

LAMPO with modified funnel *1972, Dr. Giorgio Arra*

BALENO *1972, Dr. Giorgio Arra*

FOLGORE (ex-*MC* 490) P490 (MGB)

Displacement, tons	160 standard; 190 full load
Dimensions, feet	129·5 × 19·7 × 5
Guns	2—40 mm AA
Tubes	2—21 in
Main engines	4 diesels; 4 shafts; 10 000 bhp = 38 knots (accelerating from 20 knots to full speed very rapidly)

Authorised in Nov 1950, launched on 21 Jan 1954 from CRDA Monfalcone Yard, and commissioned on 21 July 1955. Two rudders.

FOLGORE *1972, Dr. Giorgio Arra*

Light Forces—*continued*

5 "ALANO" CLASS

(Ex-US LANDING SHIPS, SUPPORT/LARGE)

BRACCO (ex-*LSSL* 38) **MASTINO** (ex-*LSSL* 62) **SEGUGIO** (ex-*LSSL* 64)
MOLOSSO (ex-*LSSL* 63) **SPINONE** (ex-*LSSL* 118)

Displacement, tons	246 standard; 430 full load
Dimensions, feet	153 wl; 158·5 oa × 23·7 × 5·7
Guns	5—40 mm; 56 cal; 4—20 mm, 70 cal; 4—12·7 mm
Main engines	8 Gray Marine diesels; 2 shafts; 1 800 bhp = 12 knots
Oil fuel, tons	87
Range, miles	4 660 at 10 knots

Transferred from the USN on 25 July 1951, under the Mutual Defense Assistance Program. NATO pennant numbers L9852 to L 9856, respectively. A photograph of *Segugio* appears in the 1967-68 to 1968-69 editions, of *Mastino* in the 1963-64 to 1967-68 editions, and of *Spinone* in the 1968-69 and 1969-70 editions. *Alano* (ex-*LSSL* 34) L 9851, was officially deleted from the list in Jan 1972.

MOLOSSO *1970, Italian Navy*

4 "SALMONE" CLASS (Ex-US MSO TYPE) (FMS)

SALMONE (ex-*MSO* 507) M 5430 **SQUALO** (ex-*MSO* 518) M 5433
SGOMBRO (ex-*MSO* 517) M 5432 **STORIONE** (ex-*MSO* 506) M 5431

Displacement, tons	665 standard; 750 full load
Dimensions, feet	165 wl; 173 oa × 35 × 13·1
Guns	1—40 mm; 56 cal AA
Main engines	2 diesels; 2 shafts; 1 600 bhp = 14 knots
Oil fuel, tons	46
Range, miles	3 000 at 10 knots

Former US "Agile" class. Wooden hulls and non-magnetic diesels of stainless steel alloy. Controllable pitch propellers. *Storione*, launched on 13 Nov 1954, was built by Martinolich SB Company, San Diego, and transferred on 23 Feb, 1956. *Salmone*, launched on 19 Feb 1955 was built by Martinolich SB Co, and transferred at San Diego, on 17 June 1956. *Sgombro* and *Spualo* were delivered in June 1957.

SGOMBRO *1972, Dr Aldo Fraccaroli*

MINE WARFARE FORCES

18 "ABETE" CLASS (CMS)

ABETE	M 5501	**FAGGIO**	M 5507	**OLMO**	M 5512
ACACIA	M 5502	**FRASSINO**	M 5508	**ONTANO**	M 5513
BETULLA	M 5503	**GELSO**	M 5509	**PINO**	M 5514
CASTAGNO	M 5504	**LARICE**	M 5510	**PIOPPO**	M 5515
CEDRO	M 5505	**MANDORLO**	M 5519	**PLATANO**	M 5516
CILIEGIO	M 5506	**NOCE**	M 5511	**QUERCIA**	M 5517

ONTANO *1972, Dr. Giorgio Arra*

Mine Warfare Forces—*continued*

Displacement, tons	378 standard; 405 full load (*Mandorlo* 360)
Dimensions, feet	138 pp; 144 oa × 26·5 × 8·5
Guns	2—20 mm, 70 cal AA
Main engines	2 diesels; 2 shafts; 1 200 bhp = 13·5 knots
Oil fuel (tons)	25
Range, miles	2 500 at 10 knots

Wooden hulled *Dragomine Costieri* constructed throughout of materials with the lowest possible magnetic attraction to attain the greatest safety factor when sweeping for magnetic mines. All transferred by the US in 1953-54. Original hull numbers AMS 72-76, 79-82, 88-90, 133-137. *Mandorlo* (ex-*Salice*, ex-USS *MSC* 280), transferred at Seattle on 16 Dec 1960, is of slightly different type and is used as MHC (minehunter).

19 "AGAVE" CLASS (CMS)

AGAVE	M 5531	**GLICINE**	M 5537	**BAMBÙ**	*M 5521
ALLORO	M 5532	**LOTO**	M 5538	**EBANO**	*M 5522
EDERA	M 5533	**MIRTO**	M 5539	**MANGO**	*M 5523
GAGGIA	M 5534	**TIMO**	M 5540	**MOGANO**	*M 5524
GELSOMINO	M 5535	**TRIFOGLIO**	M 5541	**PALMA**	*M 5525
GIAGGIOLO	M 5536	**VISCHIO**	M 5542	**ROVERE**	*M 5526
				SANDALO	*M 5527

Displacement, tons	375 standard; 405 full load
Dimensions, feet	144 oa × 26·5 × 8·5
Guns	2—20 mm; 70 cal AA
Main engines	2 diesels; 2 shafts; 1 200 bhp = 13·5 knots
Oil fuel (tons)	25
Range, miles	2 500 at 10 knots

Non-magnetic minesweepers of composite wooden and alloy construction similar to those transferred from the US but built in Italian yards. *Last 7 were built by CRDA, Monfalcone, and launched in 1956.

TRIFOGLIO — *1972 Dr. Giorgio Arra*

20 "ARAGOSTA" CLASS (IMS)

ARAGOSTA	M 5450	**GAMBERO**	M 5457	**POLIPO**	M 5463
ARSELLA	M 5451	**GRANCHIO**	M 5458	**PORPORA**	M 5464
ASTICE	M 5452	**MITILO**	M 5459	**RICCIO**	M 5465
ATTINIA	M 5453	**OSTRICA**	M 5460	**SCAMPO**	M 5466
CALAMARO	M 5454	**PAGURO**	M 5461	**SEPPIA**	M 5467
CONCHIGLIA	M 5455	**PINNA**	M 5462	**TELLINA**	M 5468
DROMIA	M 5456			**TOTANO**	M 5469

Displacement, tons	119 standard; 188 full load
Dimensions, feet	106 × 21 × 6
Main engines	2 diesels; 1 000 bhp = 14 knots
Oil fuel (tons)	15
Range, miles	2 000 at 9 knots
Complement	14

Similar to the British "Ham" class. All constructed in Italian yards to the order of NATO in 1955-57. All names of small sea creatures. Designed armament of one 20 mm gun not mounted. *Polipo* was originally named *Polpo*.

POLIPO — *1971, Italian Navy*

HYDROFOIL

1 P-420 SWORDFISH

Displacement, tons	62·5
Dimensions, feet	75 × 36·5 × 14·4 (length and beam foils extended, draught hullborne)
Missile launchers	2 fixed for "Otomat" ship-to-ship missiles
Guns	1 Oto Melara 76 mm automatic anti-aircraft
Main engines	Rolls Royce "Proteus" gas turbine driving waterjet pump; 4 500 bhp; diesel and retractable propeller unit for hullborne propulsion
Range, miles	400 at 45 knots; 1 200 at 8 knots
Speed, knots	50 max, 42 cruising (sea state 4)
Complement	10

To be delivered to the Italian Navy in 1973 by Alinavi, Naples. Missiles made by Oto Melara Matra. Fitted with Elsag NA-10 Mod 1 fire control system with Orion RTN-10X radar.

Hydrofoil—*continued*

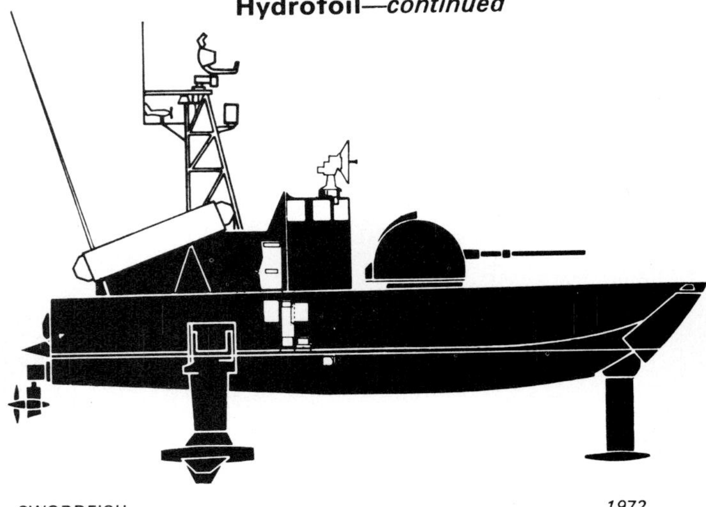

SWORDFISH — *1972*

SURVEY VESSEL

1 NEW CONSTRUCTION

Displacement, tons — **1 582 full load**

To be built under the 1972 new construction programme. It is officially stated that her name is still under consideration.

NOTE. In addition *Pioppo* and *Mirto* minesweepers are used for surveying.

OILERS

1 Ex-US "T2" TYPE

STEROPE (ex-*Enrico Insom*) A 5368

Displacement, tons	5 350 light; 21 800 full load
Dimensions, feet	523·5 oa × 68 × 30·8
Main engines	Turbo-electric; 6 000 shp = 15 knots
Boilers	2 Babcock & Wilcox

Former United States built oiler of the T 2 type acquired by the Italian Navy in 1959 and refitted at La Spezia Navy Yard in April 1959.
The oiler *Dalmazia* A 5367 was officially deleted from the list in Jan 1972.

STEROPE — *1970, Aldo Fraccaroli*

NETLAYERS

2 "ALICUDI" CLASS

ALICUDI A 5304 (ex-USS AN 99) **FILICUDI** A 5305 (ex-USS AN 100)

Displacement, tons	680 standard; 834 full load
Dimensions, feet	151·8 pp; 165·3 oa × 33·5 × 10·5
Guns	1—40 mm, 70 cal AA; 4—20 mm, 70 cal AA
Main engines	Diesel-electric; 1 200 hp = 12 knots

Built to the order of NATO. Laid down on 22 Apr 1954 and 19 July 1954, respectively, by Ansaldo, Leghorn, launched on 11 July 1954 and 26 Sep 1954.

ALICUDI — *Italian Navy*

SUPPORT SHIPS

1 AVP TYPE

PIETRO CAVEZZALE (ex-USS *Oyster Bay, AVP* 28, ex-*AGP* 6) A 5301

Displacement, tons	1 766 standard; 2 800 full load
Dimensions, feet	300 wl; 311·8 oa × 41 × 13·5 max
Guns	1—76 mm; 2—40 mm, 56 cal AA
Main engines	2 sets diesels; 2 shafts; 6 080 bhp = 16 knots
Oil fuel (tons)	400
Range, miles	10 000 at 11 knots
Complement	200

Former United States seaplane tender (previously motor torpedo boat tender) of the "Barnegat" class, built at Lake Washington Shipyard and launched on 7 Sep 1942. Transferred to the Italian Navy on 23 Oct 1957 and renamed.

PIETRO CAVEZZALE *1972, Italian Navy*

TRANSPORTS

1 AV TYPE

ANDREA BAFILE (ex-USS *St. George*, AV 16) A 5314

Displacement, tons	8 510 standard; 14 000 full load
Dimensions, feet	492 oa × 69·5 × 26 max
Guns	2—5 in 38 cal
Main engines	Allis-Chalmers geared turbines; 1 shaft; 8 500 shp = 17 knots
Boilers	2 Foster-Wheeler
Range, miles	13 400 at 13 knots

Former USN seaplane carrier, launched on 14 Feb 1944. Purchased and commissioned in the Italian Navy on 17 May 1969 and modified. Troop transport and command ship. Serves as a depot ship for "Special Forces" (frogmen etc).

ANDREA BAFILE *1972, Italian Navy*

1 AKA TYPE

ETNA (ex-USS *Whitley, AKA* 91) A 5328

Displacement, tons	7 430 light; 14 200 full load
Measurement, tons	5 145 gross; 7 700 deadweight
Dimensions, feet	435·0 wl; 459·2 oa × 63·0 × 26·3 max
Guns	4—40 mm
Main engines	GE geared turbines; 1 shaft; 6 000 shp = 15 knots
Boilers	2 Combustion Engineering
Range, miles	18 900 at 12 knots

Transports—*continued*

Former US Navy attack cargo ship of the "Andromeda" class. Built by Moore DD Co, Oakland, California. Launched on 22 June 1944. Completed on 21 Sep 1944. C2—S—B 1 type. Transferred to Italy in Feb 1962. Rated as *Nave trasporto mezzi da sbarco.*

ETNA *1970, Italian Navy*

1 AVB TYPE

ANTEO (ex-USS *Alameda County*, AVB 1, ex-*LST* 32) A 5306

Displacement, tons	1 625 light; 2 366 beaching; 4 080 full load
Dimensions, feet	316 wl; 328 oa × 50 × 14 max
Guns	7—40 mm AA; 2—20 mm AA
Main engines	GM diesels; 2 shafts; 1 700 bhp = 11·6 knots max
Range, miles	15 900 at 9 knots

Former US tank landing ship. Built by Dravo Corp, Neville Island, Pa. Laid down on 17 Feb 1943. Launched on 23 May 1943. Completed on 12 July 1943. Reclassified from LST 32 to AVB 1 (Advance Aviation Base ship) on 28 Sep 1957. Transferred to the Italian Navy in Nov 1962 as a transport.

ANTEO *1972, Dr. Giorgio Arra*

ANTEO *1970, Italian Navy*

TRAINING SHIPS

AMERIGO VESPUCCI A 5312

Displacement, tons	3 543 standard; 4 146 full load
Dimensions, feet	229·5 pp; 270 oa hull; 330 oa bowsprit × 51 × 22
Guns	4—3 in, 50 cal; 1—20 mm
Main engines	Two Fiat diesels with electric drive to 2 Marelli motors. 1 shaft; 2 000 hp = 10 knots
Sail area	22 604 square feet
Endurance	5 450 miles at 6·5 knots
Complement, tons	400 + 150 midshipmen

Built at Castellammare. Launched on 22 March 1930 and completed in 1931. Hull, masts and yards are of steel. Loud speakers and echo-sounding gear are included in her equipment. Extensively refitted at La Spezia Naval Dockyard in 1964.

Training Ships—*continued*

AMERIGO VESPUCCI *1968, Italian Navy*

PALINURO (ex-*Commandant Louis Richard*) A 5311.

Displacement, tons	1 042 standard; 1 450 full load
Measurement, tons	858 gross
Dimensions, feet	204 pp; 226·3 oa × 32 × 18·7
Main engines	1 diesel; 1 shaft; 450 bhp = 7·5 knots
Endurance, miles	5 390 at 7·5 knots
Sail area, square feet	1 152

Barquentine, ex-French, launched in 1920. Purchased in 1950. Rebuilt and commissioned in Italian Navy on 16 July 1955.

PALINURO *1968, Italian Navy*

CORSARO II

Measurement, tons	41
Dimensions, feet	68·6 × 15·4 × 9·5
Auxiliary engines	1 Mercedes-Benz diesel, 96 bhp
Sail area	2117 square feet

Special yacht for sail training and oceanic navigation. RORC class. Built by Costaguta Yard, Voltri, in 1959-60.

STELLA POLARE

Measurement, tons	47
Dimensions, feet	69 × 15·4 × 9·8
Sail area, square feet	2 200
Complement	14

Yawl. Built by Santgerm. Chiavari in 1964-65 as a sail training vessel for the Italian Navy.

MOTOR TRANSPORTS

10 Ex-GERMAN MFP TYPE

MTC 1001	**MTC 1004**	**MTC 1006**	**MTC 1008**	**MTC 1010**
MTC 1003	**MTC 1005**	**MTC 1007**	**MTC 1009**	**MTC 1102**

Displacement, tons	240 standard
Dimensions, feet	164 × 21·3 × 5·7
Guns	2 or 3—20 or 37 mm
Main engines	2 or 3 diesels; 500 bhp = 10 knots

Moto-Trasporti Costieri, MTC 1001 to 1010 are Italian MZ (*Motozattere*). MTC 1102 and 1103 are ex-German built in Italy. MTC 1002 was removed from the effective list in 1964, MTC 1101 and MTC 1104 in 1970, and MTC 1103 in 1971.

MTC 1010 *1971, Dr. Giorgio Arra*

Motor Transports—*continued*

23 Ex-US LCM TYPE

MTM 9901	**MTM 9905**	**MTM 9911**	**MTM 9916**	**MTM 9921**
MTM 9902	**MTM 9906**	**MTM 9912**	**MTM 9917**	**MTM 9922**
MTM 9903	**MTM 9908**	**MTM 9913**	**MTM 9918**	**MTM 9923**
MTM 9904	**MTM 9909**	**MTM 9914**	**MTM 9919**	**MTM 9924**
		MTM 9915	**MTM 9920**	**MTM 9925**

Displacement, tons	20 standard
Dimensions, feet	49·5 × 14·8 × 4·2
Guns	2—20 mm AA
Main engines	diesels; speed 10 knots

Rated as *Moto-Trasporti Medi.* Former US landing craft of the LCM type. MTM 9907 was removed from the effective list in 1967, and MTM 9910 in 1971.

39 Ex-US LCVP TYPE

MTP 9701	**MTP 9709**	**MTP 9717**	**MTP 9726**	**MTP 9734**
MTP 9702	**MYP 9710**	**MTP 9718**	**MTP 9727**	**MTP 9735**
MTP 9703	**MTP 9711**	**MTP 9719**	**MTP 9728**	**MTP 9736**
MTP 9704	**MTP 9712**	**MTP 9720**	**MTP 9729**	**MTP 9737**
MTP 9705	**MTP 9713**	**MTP 9721**	**MTE 9730**	**MTP 9738**
MTP 9706	**MTP 9714**	**MTP 9722**	**MTP 9731**	**MTP 9739**
MTP 9707	**MTP 9715**	**MTP 9723**	**MTP 9732**	**MTP 9740**
MTP 9708		**MTP 9724**	**MTP 9733**	**MTP 9741**

Displacement, tons	8 to 10 standard
Dimensions, feet	36·5 × 10·8 × 3
Guns	2 MG
Main engines	Diesels; Speed: 10 knots

Rated as *Moto-Trasporti Piccoli.* MTP 9701 to 9724 are former US landing craft of the LCVP type. MTP 9726 of 10 tons displacement and similar characteristics is of Italian construction. MTP 9725 was officially removed from the effective list in 1963, and MTP 9716 in 1971.

LIGHTHOUSE TENDERS

BUFFOLUTO A 5327

Displacement, tons	930 standard
Dimensions, feet	172·5 pp; 184·2 oa × 29·5 × 11
Main engines	2 triple expansion; 1 400 ihp = 10 knots
Boilers	2 Thornycroft

Built by S. Giorgio, La Spezia. Launched in 1922. Sister ship *Panigaglia* blew up in July 1947.

RAMPINO A 5309

Displacement, tons	350 standard; 645 full load
Dimensions, feet	158·8 × 24·2 × 13
Main engines	Triple expansion = 7 knots

Buoy tender. Of netlayer type. Built at Osaka. Classed as *Nave Ausiliarie.*

3 Ex-BRITISH LCT(3) TYPE

MTF 1301 **MTF 1302** **MTF 1303**

Displacement, tons	296 light; 700 full load
Dimensions, feet	192 × 31 × 7
Guns	1—40 mm, 56 cal AA; 2—20 mm, 70 cal AA
Main engines	diesel; 1 shaft; speed = 8 knots

Converted landing craft of the British LCT (3) type. Lighthouse motor transports (Moto-Trasporti Fari). NATO Pennant Nos.: A 5361, A 5362 and A 5363.

MFT 1301 *1968, Italian Navy*

SALVAGE SHIP

PROTEO (ex-*Perseo*, ex-*Proteo*) A 5310

Displacement, tons	1 865 standard; 2 147 full load
Dimensions, feet	220·5 pp; 248 oa × 38 × 21 max
Main engines	2 diesels; 4 800 bhp = 16 knots (see Notes)
Radius, miles	7 500 at 13 knots

Laid down at Cantieri Navali Riuniti, Ancona, in 1943. Suspended in 1944. Seized by Germans and transferred to Trieste. Construction recommenced at Cantieri Navali Riuniti, Ancona, in 1949. Diesels at 250 rpm drive a single propeller through hydraulic couplings and reduction gearing. Formerly mounted one 3·9 inch AA gun and two 20 mm, 70 cal AA guns.

PROTEO *1969, Italian Navy*

REPAIR CRAFT

MOC 1201 **MOC 1202** **MOC 1203** **MOC 1204** **MOC 1205** **MOC 1207** **MOC 1208**

Displacement, tons 350 standard; 640 full load
Dimensions, feet 192 × 31 × 7
Guns 2—40 mm; 2—20 mm (2 ships have 2—40 mm and 1 ship has 3—20 mm)
Main engines diesel = 8 knots

Former British LCT (3) type landing craft converted to repair craft. MOC 1207 and 1208 are ammunition transports. NATO Nos.: A 5331 to 5338, respectively.

WATER CARRIERS

2 NEW CONSTRUCTION

PIAVE **TEVERE**

Displacement, tons 4 973 full load
Dimensions, feet 301·2 × 43·8 × 19·3
Main engines 2 Fiat 13 306/55 diesels; 2 shafts; 2 560 bhp = 13·7 knots
Range, miles 1 500 at 12·5 knots
Water capacity, tons 3 528

Piave was built by Orlando, Livorno, and *Tevere* by Pellegrino, Napoli. *Piave* was laid down on 14 Apr 1971 and launched on 18 Dec 1971.

3 "INMA" TYPE

BASENTO A 5256 **BRADANO** A 5357 **BRENTA** A 5358

Displacement, tons 1 914
Dimensions, feet 216·9 × 33 × 12·8 ·0
Main engines 2 Fiat A 236 diesels; 2 shafts; 1 730 hp = 12·5 knots
Water capacity, tons 1 200
Radius 1650 miles at 12·5 knots

Built by Inma di La Spezia. Laid down in 1969-70 and launched and completed in 1970-71.

ADIGE (ex-*YW* 92) **FLEGETONTE** (ex-*YW* 95) **ISONZO** (ex-*YW* 77) **TICINO** (ex-*YW* 79) **TANARO** (ex-*YW* 99)

Displacement, tons 436 standard; 1 470 full load
Guns 3—20 mm, 70 cal AA
Main engines 2 diesels; 315 hp = 8 knots
Water capacity, tons 850

Ex-US Army YW type. NATO Pennant Nos.: A 5369, A 5371, A 5372, A 5376 and A 5377 respectively.

PO A 5365 **VOLTURNO** A 5366

Displacement, tons 1 556 light; 3 541 standard; 6 000 full load
Dimensions, feet 270·7 × 38·8 × 16·8
Guns 1—4 in, 35 cal; 2—40 mm; 2—20 mm (*Po*)
1—4·7 in, 45 cal; 2—40 mm; 2—20 mm AA (*Volturno*)
Main engines Triple expansion; 1 700 ihp = 11·5 knots
Boilers 2 oil-fired watertube
Oil fuel (tons) 226
Cargo capacity, tons 2 200

Po was launched by Cant Nav Riuniti, Ancona, on 21 Dec 1936. *Volturno* was built by Cantieri del Tirreno, Riva, Trigoso, in 1936-37, and rebuilding was completed in 1951. *Volturno* has radar mast. A photograph of *Volturno* appears in the 1967-68 and earlier editions.

PO *1970, Italian Navy*

SESIA A 5375

Displacement, tons 1 050
Dimensions, feet 213·2 × 33 × 11·2
Guns 3—20 mm, 70 cal AA
Main engines Fiat diesels; 2 shafts; 600 bhp = 8 knots

Built by Adriatico. Launched in 1933. Fitted for minelaying.

SESIA *1972, Italian Navy*

Water Carriers—*continued*

METAURO A 5373

Displacement, tons 592
Dimensions, feet 133·2 × 26·5 × 10·5
Guns 1—20 mm, 70 cal AA
Main engines Tosi diesels; 400 bhp = 8 knots

Built by C. N. Quarnaro-Fiume. Launched in 1933.

ARNO A 5370

Displacement, tons 634
Dimensions, feet 138·8 × 26 × 10
Guns 1—20 mm, 70 cal AA
Main engines 1 Fiat diesel; 350 bhp = 8 knots

Built by Odero-Terni-Orlando, La Spezia. Launched in 1929.

MINCIO A 5374

Displacement, tons 645
Dimensions, feet 138·5 × 26·2 × 10
Guns 1—20 mm, 70 cal AA
Main engines Tosi diesels; 350 bhp = 8 knots

Built in Venice. Launched in 1929.

TIMAVO

Displacement, tons 265
Main engines 1 Tosi diesel; 200 bhp = 8 knots

Built by COMI, Venezia, 1926. Sister ship *Vipacco* was removed from the effective list in 1961.

FRIGIDO (ex-*Fukuiu Maru*)

Displacement, tons 398
Dimensions, feet 116·5 × 21·5 × 10
Guns 2 MG
Main engines Triple expansion; 221 ihp = 7 knots
Boilers 1 cylindrical

Built by Osaka. Launched in 1912. Purchased in 1916.

OFANTO

Displacement, tons 250
Dimensions, feet 105·5 × 19·7 × 7·5
Main engines 1 Triple expansion; 165 ihp = 6 knots
Boilers 1

Built by SEB, Riva Trigoso, 1913-14.

LENO **SIMETO** **SPRUGOLA** **STURA**

Small water carriers of 270, 167, 212 and 126 displacement, respectively. *Tronto* was officially deleted from the list in 1970.

TUGS

PORTO D'ISCHIA **RIVA TRIGOSO**

Displacement, tons 296 full load
Dimensions, feet 83·7 × 23·3 × 10·8
Main engines Diesel; 1 shaft; 850 bhp = 12·1 knots

Both launched in Sep 1969. Controllable pitch propeller.

CIRCEO **TAVOLARA**

Both completed in 1955. Minor tugs for local and general purposes.

AUSONIA **PANARIA**

Displacement, tons 240

Both launched in 1948. Coastal tugs for general utility duties.

CICLOPE A 5319 **TITANO** A 5320

Displacement, tons 1 200
Dimensions, feet 157·5 × 32·5 × 13
Main engines Triple expansion; 1 shaft; 1 000 ihp = 8 knots

Both were launched in 1948. Sister ship *Nereo* was discarded in 1957.

MISENO **MONTE CRISTO**

Displacement, tons 285

Former United States Navy harbour tugs. The tug *Atlante* A 5317 was officially deleted from the list in 1970.

GAGLIARDO A 5322 **ROBUSTO** A 5323

Displacement, tons 389 standard; 506 full load
Main engines 1 000 ihp = 8 knots

Both launched in 1939.

Tugs—*continued*

PORTO EMPEDOCLE

Displacement, tons	330 standard
Main engines	500 ihp = 11 knots

Launched in 1934. Employed as a harbour tug. Armament of 1—3 in gun removed.

PORTO FOSSONE **PORTO PISANO** **PORTO RECANATI** **PORTO TORRES** **PORTO VECCHIO** **SALVORE** **TINO**

Displacement, tons	226 to 270
Dimensions, feet	88·8 × 22 × 10
Main engines	600 ihp = 9 knots

All launched in 1936-37, except *Tino*, 1931. Principally employed as harbour tugs. Armament of 1—3 inch gun removed. *Porto Rosso* was deleted from the list in 1965.

ATLETA (ex-*LT* 152) **COLOSSO** (ex-*LT* 214) **FORTE** (ex-*LT* 159) **TENACE** (ex-*LT* 154)

Displacement, tons	525 standard; 835 full load
Dimensions, feet	142·8 × 32·8 × 11
Main engines	2 diesel-electric; 690 hp = 11 knots

Ex-US Army. Pennant Nos.: A 5318, A 5320, A 5321, A 5324, respectively.

VENTIMIGLIA

Displacement, tons	230 standard
Dimensions, feet	108·2 × 23 × 7·2
Main engines	550 hp = 10 knots

Near sister ship *Lipari* was officially deleted from the list in Jan 1972. There are also 55 harbour tugs, ferry tugs, lagoon tugs, numbered tugs and minor tugs.

IVORY COAST

Mercantile Marine

1973 Lloyd's Register of Shipping: 36 vessels of 82 316 tons gross

PATROL BOATS

1 FRANCO-BELGE TYPE

VIGILANT

Displacement, tons	240 normal
Dimensions, feet	149·3 pp; 155·8 oa × 23·6 × 8·2
Guns	2—40 mm AA
Missiles	8 SS12
Main engines	2 diesels; 2 shafts; 2 400 bhp = 18·5 knots
Range, miles	2 000 at 15 knots
Complement	25 (3 officers and 22 men)

Built by Franco-Belge. Laid down in Feb 1967. Launched on 23 May 1967. Completed in 1968. Sister ship to *Malaika* of Madagascan Navy.

1 Ex-FRENCH VC TYPE

PERSEVERANCE (ex-*VC* 9, *P* 759)

Displacement, tons	75 standard; 82 full load
Dimensions, feet	104·5 × 15·5 × 5·5
Guns	2—20 mm AA
Main engines	2 Mercedes-Benz diesels; 2 shafts; 2 700 bhp = 28 knots
Oil fuel, tons	10
Range, miles	1 100 at 16·5 knots; 800 at 21 knots
Complement	15

Former French seaward defence motor launch. Built by Constructions Mecaniques de Normandie. Cherbourg. Completed in 1958. Transferred from France to Ivory Coast 26 April 1963.

PERSEVERANCE *1964, Ivory Coast Armed Forces*

8 PATROL BOATS

These are 30 ft craft for coastal and river patrols.

LANDING CRAFT

1 TRAWLER TYPE

LOKDJO

There are six landing craft of the LCVP type, 7 tons, 2 machine guns and Mercedes diesels 200 hp, 9 knots. 2 were built in Abidjan in 1970.

JAMAICA

Defence Force Coast Guard

Jamaica, which became independent within the Commonwealth, on 6 Aug 1962, formed the Coast Guard as the Maritime Arm of the Defence Force. This is based at HMJS Cagway, Port Royal.
The Jamaican Government signed an agreement with the USA for the transfer of a small number of coastguard vessels for the new navy.
Great Britain lent several RN petty officers for technical assistance. The British Mission included a technical team to survey sites for the establishment of local naval bases.

Administration

Officer Commanding Jamaican Defence Force Coast Guard:
Captain J. E. Farnol D.S.C., R.N.(Retd)

Personnel

1973: 12 officers, 62 Petty officers and ratings (*Coast Guard Reserve*: 8 officers, 27 men)

Mercantile Marine

1973: Lloyd's Register of Shipping: 7 vessels of 13 819 tons gross

PATROL BOATS

DISCOVERY BAY P 4 **HOLLAND BAY P 5** **MANATEE BAY P 6**

Displacement, tons	60
Dimensions, feet	85 × 18·8 × 5·9
Guns	3—·50 cal Browning
Main engines	3 GM 12 V71 TI diesels; 3 shafts; 2 000 shp = 26·5 knots
Oil fuel, tons	13
Range, miles	1 000 at 20 knots
Complement	10

Built by Teledyne Sewart Seacraft Inc, Berwick, La, USA. All aluminium construction. *Discovery Bay*, the prototype was launched in Aug 1966 and commissioned on 3 Nov 1966. *Holland Bay*, commissioned 4 Apr 1967, and *Manatee Bay*, commissioned 9 Aug 1967, were supplied under the US Military Assistance Programme. All three boats were extensively refitted and modified in 1972-73 by the builders with GM 12V 71 Turbo-injected engines to give greater range, speed and operational flexibility.

DISCOVERY BAY *1973, Jamaica C G*

3 NEW CONSTRUCTION

Displacement, tons	104
Dimensions, feet	105 × 19 × 7
Guns	2—20 mm; 3—·50 cal MG; 1—81 mm mortar
Main engines	2 Maybach MB 16V 538 TB90; 6 000 shp = 32 knots
Complement	15

Designed by Teledyne Sewart Inc, Berwick, La USA. First boat to be delivered in 1974. Boats will have accommodation for 24 soldiers and may be used as mobile hospitals in an emergency.

AVR TYPE
The former 3 ex-US AVR type patrol boats have been disposed of.

JORDAN

Coastal Guard

It was officially stated in 1969 that Jordan had no naval force known as such, but the Jordan Coastal Guard, sometimes called the Jordan Sea Force, took orders direct from the Director of Operations at General Headquarters.
The force of two Bertram fibre glass patrol boats, two Polson aluminium motor boats and four wooden motor boats is based at Aqaba. There is no flotilla in the Dead Sea.

JAPAN

Administration

Chief of the Maritime Staff, Defence Agency:
Admiral Kazutomi Uchida

Commander-in-Chief, Self-Defence Fleet:
Vice Admiral T. Motomura

Chief Administration Division Maritime Staff Office:
Rear Admiral Kiyonori Kunishima

Diplomatic Representation

Defence (Naval) Attaché in London:
Captain Keizo Ohashi

Defence (Naval) Attaché in Washington:
Captain Yasuhiro Tamagawa

Defence Attaché in Moscow:
Coloneol Keitaro Watanabe

Defence Attaché in Paris:
Coloneol Akira Kashiwagi

Five Year Defence Plan

The tourth 5-year defence programme (1973-77) announced 9 October 1972 provides for the building of the following.

- 2 Haruna class DDH of 5 200 tons
- 1 SAM DDG of 3 900 tons
- 1 SSM DDG of 3 600 tons
- 3 DDs of 2 500 tons
- 3 Frigates of 1 450 tons
- 3 Frigates of 1 500 tons,
- 3 Isoshio class submarines of 1 800 tons.
- 2 Submarines of 2 200 tons
- 19 Minesweepers
- 3 Missile Boats of 200 tons
- 3 Torpedo Boats of 100 tons
- 2 LSTs of 1 500 tons
- 3 LSTs of 2 000 tons
- 1 Supply Ship of 5 000 tons
- 1 Submarine Tender of 2 700 tons
- 1 Oceanographic Research Ship of 2 000 tons
- 18 Patrol Boats
- Plus miscellaneous craft

At the end of this programme (1977) the fleet should consist of 170 modern ships totalling 214 000 tons.

NUCLEAR POWER STUDY. The Director of the Japanese Defence Agency stated on 5 May 1955 that Japan was studying the possibility of building a nuclear powered submarine. In the meantime, conventional submarines would be ordered.

Strength of the Fleet

- 32 Destroyers (3 Building)
- 19 Frigates (4 Building)
- 20 Corvettes
- 16 Submarines (2 Building)
- 7 Landing Ships
- 48 Landing Craft
- 7 Torpedo Boats
- 3 Minelayers
- 1 MCM Support Ship
- 39 Coastal Minesweepers
- 10 Minesweeping Boats
- 2 Training Ships
- 2 Submarine Rescue Vessels
- 7 Auxiliaries
- 1 Oiler

Personnel

1973: 44 000 (7 000 officers, 32 000 men, 5 000 civil)

Names

The practice of painting the ship's names on the broadsides of the hulls was discontinued in 1970.

Maritime Safety Agency (Coast Guard)

- **10 Large Patrol Vessels**
- 40 Medium Patrol Vessels
- **38 Small Patrol Vessels**
- **2 Fire Fighting Craft**
- **29 Patrol Craft**
- 7 Surveying Vessels
- **5 Tenders**
- **1 Underwater Research Vessel**
- **114 Coastal Patrol Craft**
- **49 Harbour Patrol Craft**

Mercantile Marine

Lloyd's Register of Shipping
9 433 vessels of 34 929 214 tons gross

Deletions and Transfers

Frigates

1970 *Kiri, Keyaki, Nire, Sugi, Shii* to US.
1972 *Kaya, Bura, Kashi, Moni, Tochi, Ume, Maki, Kusu, Matsu, Nata, Sakura* (All ex-US PFs). *Wakaba*.

Submarines

1971 *Kuroshio* to US.

Light Forces

1972 PT 2, 3, 4 and 9. *Kosoku* 1, 22-28, 30.

LST

1972 *Hayatomo*.

Tug

1965 *Toba*.

DESTROYERS

1 NEW CONSTRUCTION DDG

DD 168

Displacement, tons	3 850
Dimensions, feet	443 × 47 × 15
Aircraft	1 helicopter
Missiles	Standard RIM 60A SAM and HARPOON SSM
Guns	2—5 in (twin)
A/S weapons	ASROC and 2 triple A/S torpedo tubes
Main engines	2 turbines; 60 000 hp
Speed	32 knots

Laid down Feb 1973. To be fitted with VDS.

2 "HARUNA" CLASS

Displacement, tons	**4 700 (official figure)**
Length, feet (*metres*)	**502·0 (*153·0*)**
Beam, feet (*metres*)	**57·4 (*17·5*)**
Draught, feet (*metres*)	**16·7 (*5·1*)**
Aircraft	**3 anti-submarine helicopters**
A/S weapons	**Asroc multiple launcher**
Guns	**2—5 in (*127 mm*) single, rapid fire**
Torpedo tubes	**6—21 in (*533 mm*) 2 triple**
Main engines	**70 000 shp**
Speed, knots	**32**
Complement	**364**

Name	*No.*	*Builders*	*Laid down*	*Launched*	*Completed*
HARUNA	141	Mitsubishi (Nagasaki)	19 Mar 1970	1 Feb 1972	Feb 1973
——	142	Ishikawajima (Tokyo)	8 Mar 1972	(Sep 1973)	(Nov 1974)

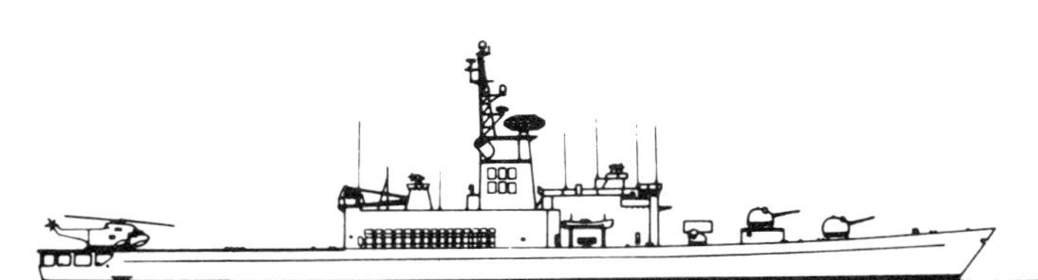

HARUNA (DDH Helocarrier)

Ordered under the third five-year defence programme (from 1968 to 1972).

4 "TAKATSUKI" CLASS

Name	*No.*	*Builders*	*Laid down*	*Launched*	*Completed*
KIKUZUKI	DD 165	Mitsubishi Jyuko Co, Nagasaki	15 Mar 1966	25 Mar 1967	27 Mar 1968
MOCHIZUKI	DD 166	Ishikawajima Jyuko Co, Tokyo	25 Nov 1966	15 Mar 1968	25 Mar 1969
NAGATSUKI	DD 167	Mitsubishi Jyuko Co, Nagasaki	2 Mar 1968	19 Mar 1969	12 Feb 1970
TAKATSUKI	DD 164	Ishikawajima Jyuko Com Tokyo	8 Oct 1964	7 Jan 1966	15 Mar 1967

Displacement, tons	3 050 (official figure)
Length, feet (*metres*)	446·2 (*136·0*) oa
Beam, feet (*metres*)	44·0 (*13·4*)
Draught, feet (*metres*)	14·5 (*4·4*)
Aircraft	1 helicopter
A/S weapons	Octuple Asroc; 1 four barrelled rocket launcher
Guns, dual purpose	2—5 in (*127 mm*) 54 cal. single
Torpedo launchers	2 triple for A/S homing torpedoes
Boilers	2 Mitsubishi CE
Main engines	2 Mitsubishi WH geared turbines 60 000 shp; 2 shafts
Speed, knots	32
Complement	270

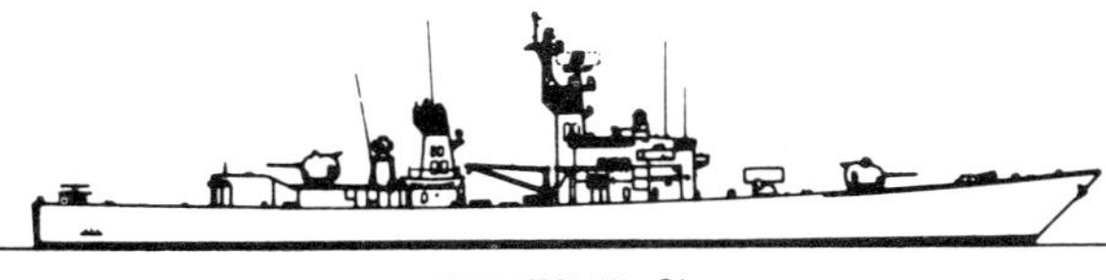

TAKATSUKI *Class*

Anti-submarine type. *Takatsuki* (High Moon) was provided unoer the 1963 programme. Equipped with drone anti-submarine helicopter and hangar.

RADAR. Search: Metric wavelength. Tactical: Probably C Band. Fire Control: GFCS 56 with X Band.

KIKUZUKI *1971, S. Woodrifle*

Destroyers—*continued*

3 "YAMAGUMO" CLASS

Name	*No.*	*Builders*
YAMAGUMO	DD 113	Mitsui Zosen Co, Tamano
MAKIGUMO	DD 114	Uraga Dock Co, Yokosuka
ASAGUMO	DD 115	Maizuru Jyuko Co, Maizuru

Laid down	*Launched*	*Completed*
23 Mar 1964	27 Feb 1965	29 Jan 1966
10 June 1964	26 July 1965	19 Mar 1966
24 June 1965	25 Nov 1966	29 Aug 1967

Displacement, tons	2 150
Length, feet (*metres*)	377 (*115*)
Beam, feet (*metres*)	38·7 (*11·8*)
Draught, feet (*metres*)	13·*1* (*4*)
Guns	4—3 in; 50 cal (2 twin)
A/S weapons	1 Asroc; 1 four barrelled rocket launcher
Torpedo tubes	2 triple mountings for A/S torpedoes
Main engines	6 Diesels; 26 500 bhp; 2 shafts
Speed, knots	27
Complement	210

RADAR. Search; Metric.Tactical; C Band-Fire Control; GFCS 56 with X Band.

SONAR. *Yamagumo* and *Makigumo* fitted with VDS.

YAMAGUMO *Class*

YAMAGUMO *1972, Toshio Tamura*

5 "MINEGUMO" CLASS

MINEGUMO	DD 116
NATSUGUMO	DD 117
MURAKUMO	DD 118
AOKUMO	DD 119
YUUGUMO	DD 120

Mitsui Zosen Co, Tamano
Uraga Dock Co, Yokosuka
Maizuru Jyuko Co
Sumitamo Co, Uraga

Laid down	*Launched*	*Completed*
14 Mar 1967	16 Dec 1967	31 Aug 1968
26 June 1967	25 July 1968	25 Apr 1969
19 Oct 1968	15 Nov 1969	21 Aug 1970
12 Nov 1970	30 Mar 1972	25 Nov 1972
1 Nov 1972	(Sept 1973)	(June 1974)

All details as for *Yamagumo* class except:

A/S weapons	1 Dash helicopter in place of ASROC

Note difference in silhouettes between this and the *Yamagumo* class.

MINEGUMO *Class*

NATSUGUMO *1972, Japanese Maritime Self-Defence Force*

1 "AMATSUKAZE" CLASS (DDG)

AMATSUKAZE DD 163

Displacement, tons	**3 050 standard; 4 000 full load**
Length, feet (*metres*)	**429·8 (*131·0*)**
Beam, feet (*metres*)	**44 (*13·4*)**
Draught, feet (*metres*)	**13·8 (*4·2*)**
Aircraft	Can operate helicopter
Missile launchers	**1 single "Tartar" (US)**
Guns	**4—3 in (*76 mm*) 50 cal, 2 twin**
A/S weapons	**ASROC; 2 Hedgehogs**
Torpedo mountings	**1 each side for A/S short torpedoes**
Main engines	**2 Ishikawajima GE geared turbines 2 shafts; 60 000 shp**
Speed, knots	**33**
Boilers	**2 Ishikawajima Foster Wheeler**
Oil fuel, tons	**900**
Complement	**290**

Ordered under the 1960 programme. Built by Mitsubishi, Nagasaki. Laid down on 29 Nov 1962, launched on 5 Oct 1963 and completed on 15 Feb 1965.

RADAR. Search: SPS 37 and SPS 39 3 D. Fire Control: SPS 51 for "Tartar", X Band for guns.

AMATSUKAZE

AMATSUKAZE *1969, Japanese Maritime Self-Defence Force*

2 "AKIZUKI" CLASS

Displacement, tons	2 350 standard; 2 890 full load
Length, feet (metres)	387·2 (*118·0*) oa
Beam, feet (*metres*)	39·4 (*12·0*)
Draught, feet (*metres*)	13·1 (*4·0*)
Guns, dual purpose	3—5 in (*127 mm*) 54 cal. single
Guns, AA	4—3 in (*76 mm*) 50 cal., 2 twin
Torpedo tubes	4—21 in (*533 mm*) quadrupled
A/S	1—US model Mk 108 rocket launcher; 2 hedgehogs; 2 Y-mortars; 2 DCT

Name	*No.*	*Builders*	*Laid down*	*Launched*	*Completed*
AKIZUKI	DD 161	Mitsubishi Zosen Co, Nagasaki	31 July 1958	26 June 1959	13 Feb 1960
TERUZUKI	DD 162	Shin Mitsubishi Jyuko Co, Kobe	15 Aug 1958	24 June 1959	29 Feb 1960

AKIZUKI, TERUZUKI

Destroyers—*continued*

Boilers	2 Mitsubishi CE type
Main engines	2 geared turbines:— *Akizuki:* Mitsubishi Escher-Weiss *Teruzuki:* Westinghouse 45 000 shp, 2 shafts
Speed, knots	32
Complement	330

Destroyers of unusual design with long forecastle hull. Received from USA as part of the 1957 Military Aid Programme, but built in Japanese shipyards under an off-shore procurement agreement. US Navy hull numbers DD 960 and DD 961.

RADAR
Search: SPS 6. Tactical: SPS 10. Fire Control: X Band

TERUZUKI *1971, courtesy Mr. Michael D. J. Lennon*

3 "MURASAME" CLASS

Displacement, tons	1 800 standard; 2 500 full load
Length, feet (*metres*)	354·3 (*108·0*) oa
Beam, feet (*metres*)	36 (*11·0*) oa
Draught, feet (*metres*)	12·2 (*3·7*)
Guns, dual purpose	3—5 in (*127 mm*) 54 cal
Guns, AA	4—3 in (*76 mm*) 50 cal, 2 twin
A/S	8 short torpedoes; 1 Hedgehog 1 DC rack; 1 Y-gun
Boilers	2 (see *Engineering* notes)
Main engines	2 sets geared turbines 30 000 shp; 2 shafts
Speed, knots	30
Complement	250

Name	*No.*	*Builders*	*Laid down*	*Launched*	*Completed*
HARUSAME	DD 109	Uraga Dock Co, Yokosuka	17 June 1958	18 June 1959	15 Dec 1959
MURASAME	DD 107	Mitsubishi Zosen Co, Nagasaki	17 Dec 1957	31 July 1958	28 Feb 1959
YUDACHI	DD 108	Ishakawajima Jyuko Co, Tokyo	16 Dec 1957	29 July 1958	25 Mar 1959

MURASAME *Class*

Murasame and *Yudachi* were built under the 1956 Programme, *Harusame* 1957 Programme.

ENGINEERING. *Murusame* has *Mitsubishi* Jyuko turbines and Mitsubishi CE boilers; and the other two have Ishikawajima Harima Jyuko turbines and Ishikawajima FW-D boilers.

RADAR. Search: SPS 6. Tactical: SPS 10. Fire Control: X Band.

MURASAME *1972, Japanese Maritime Self-Defence Force*

7 "AYANAMI" CLASS

Displacement, tons	1 700 standard; 2 500 full load
Length, feet (*metres*)	357·6 (*109·0*) oa
Beam, feet (*metres*)	35·1 (*10·7*)
Draught, feet (*metres*)	12 (*3·7*)
Guns	6—3 in (*76 mm*) 50 cal (3 twin)
A/S weapons	2 US Model Mk 15 Hedgehogs; 2 Y-guns; 2 DC racks
Torpedo tubes	4—21 in (*533 mm*) quadruple
Torpedo launchers	4 fixed, for A/S homing torpedoes
Main engines	2 Mitsubishi Escher-Weiss geared turbines; 2 shafts; 35 000 shp
Speed, knots	32
Boilers	2 (see *Engineering*)
Complement	230

Name	*No.*	*Builders*	*Laid down*	*Launched*	*Completed*
AYANAMI	DD 103	Mitsubishi Zosen Co, Nagasaki	20 Nov 1956	1 June 1957	12 Feb 1958
ISONAMI	DD 104	Shin Mitsubishi Jyuko Co, Kobe	14 Dec 1956	30 Sep 1957	14 Mar 1958
MAKINAMI	DD 112	Iino Jyuko Co, Maizuru	20 Mar 1959	25 Apr 1960	30 Oct 1960
ONAMI	DD 111	Ishikawajima Jyuko Co, Tokyo	20 Mar 1959	13 Feb 1960	29 Aug 1960
SHIKINAMI	DD 106	Mitsui Zosen Co, Tamano	24 Dec 1956	25 Sep 1957	15 Mar 1958
TAKANAMI	DD 110	Mitsui Zosen Co, Tamano	8 Nov 1958	8 Aug 1959	30 Jan 1960
URANAMI	DD 105	Kawasaki Jyuko Co, Tokyo	1 Feb 1957	29 Aug 1957	27 Feb 1958

AYANAMI *Class*

ANTI-SUBMARINE. Trainable Hedgehogs forward of the bridge. Originally all ships fitted with A/S torpedo launchers on quarter-deck but in *Shikinami* (1972) *Isonami* (1971) *Uranami* (1970) and *Ayanami* (1969) these were removed and two triple A/S torpedo tubes were fitted.

RADAR. Search: SPS 12. Tactical: SPS 10. Fire Control: X Band.

ENGINEERING. Types of boilers installed are as follows. Mitsubishi CE in *Ayanami*, *Isonami* and *Uranami*; Hitachi Babcock & Wilcox in *Ōnami*, *Shikinami* and *Takanami*; Kawasaki Jyuko BD in *Makinami*.

MAKINAMI *1972, Japanese Maritime Self-Defence Force*

2 "HARUKAZE" CLASS

Name	*No.*	*Builders*	*Laid down*	*Launched*	Completed
HARUKAZE	DD 101	Mitsubishi Zosen Co, Nagasaki	15 Dec 1954	20 Sep 1955	26 Apr 1956
YUKIKAZE	DD 102	Mitsubishi Jyuko Co, Kobe	17 Nov 1954	20 Aug 1955	31 July 1956

Displacement, tons	1 700 standard; 2 340 full load
Length, feet (*metres*)	347·8 (*106·0*) wl; 358·5 (*109·3*) oa
Beam, feet (*metres*)	34·5 (*10·5*)
Draught, feet (*metres*)	12·0 (*3·7*)
Guns	3—5 in (*127 mm*) 38 cal dp 8—40 mm (2 quadruple) AA
A/S weapons	Tubes for short homing torpedoes; 2 Hedgehogs; 1 DC rack; 4 K-guns
Main engines	2 sets geared turbines; *Harukaze:* 2 Mitsubishi Escher Weiss; *Yukikaze:* 2 Westinghouse; 2 shafts; 30 000 shp
Speed, knots	30
Boilers	*Harukaze:* 2 Hitachi-Babcock; *Yukikaze:* 2 Combustion Engineering
Range, miles	6 000 at 18 knots
Oil fuel, tons	557
Complement	240

HARUKAZE *1972, Japanese Maritime Self-Defence Force*

Destroyer Escorts—*continued*

Authorised under the 1953 programme. First destroyer hulled vessels built in Japan after the Second World War. Electric welding was extensively used in hull construction; development of weldable high tension steel in main hull and light alloy in superstructure were also novel.

RADAR. Search: L Band. Tactical: SPS 10. Fire Control: X Band.

ANTI-SUBMARINE. Armament was modified in Mar 1969 when homing torpedo tubes were mounted and depth charge equipment correspondingly reduced. Nearly all the armament was supplied from the USA under the MSA clause.

HARUKAZE, YUKIKAZE

US LATER "FLETCHER" TYPE

2 "ARIAKE" CLASS

Name	No.	Builders	Launched	Completed
ARIAKE (ex-USS *Heywood L. Edwards, DD 663*)	DD 183	Boston Navy Yard	6 Oct 1943	26 Jan 1944
YUGURE (ex-USS *Richard P. Leary, DD 664*)	DD 184	Boston Navy Yard	6 Oct 1943	23 Feb 1944

Displacement, tons	2 050 standard; 3 040 full load
Length, feet (*metres*)	376·5 (*114·8*)
Beam, feet (*metres*)	39·3 (*12·0*)
Draught, feet (*metres*)	18 (*5·5*) max
Guns, dual purpose	*Ariake:* 3—5 in (*127 mm*) 38 cal. *Yugure:* 4—5 in (*127 mm*) 38 cal.
Guns, AA	3—40 mm
A/S weapons	*Ariake:* Mk 108 rocket launcher dropping gear for short homing torpedoes on each side; *Yugure:* 2 Hedgehogs; 1 DC; 2 short torpedo launchers
Main engines	2 GE geared turbines; 2 shafts; 60 000 shp
Speed, knots	35
Boilers	4 Foster Wheeler
Range, miles	1 260 at 30 knots 5 000 at 15 knots
Complement	300

..ansferred on loan from the US Navy on 10 Mar 1959 and towed to Japan for refit, during which No. 3 5 inch gun was removed. Both ships completed a more extensive refit in Mar 1962 with improved bridges, larger combat information centre, newer radar aerials and tripod masts. No. 2 5 inch gun in *Ariake* was replaced by Weapon A. In 1971 *Ariake* was transferred to trials duty with Yamagumo class bow and bow sonar. No 1 5 inch gun removed.

RADAR. Search: SPS 12. Tactical: SPS 10. Fire Control: Probably GFCS 68.

ARIAKE

YUGURE 1972, *Japanese Maritime Self-Defence Force*

The destroyers *Asakaze* (ex-USS *Ellyson*) and *Hatakaze* (ex-USS *Macomb*) taken over on 19 Oct 1954 were returned to the United States Navy in 1969. They were transferred later to Taiwan, *Hatakaze* as *Hsien Yang* and *Asakaze* to be used for spares.

FRIGATES

6+4 "CHIKUGO" CLASS

AYASE DE 216	**IWASE** DE 219
CHIKUGO DE 215	**MIKUMA** DE 217
CHITOSE DE 220	**TOKACHI** DE 218

Displacement, tons	1 470 standard; 1 750 full load
Length, feet (*metres*)	305·5 (*93·0*) oa
Beam, feet (*metres*)	35·5 (*10·8*)
Draught, feet (*metres*)	11·5 (*3·5*)
Guns, dual purpose	2—3 in (*76 mm*) 50 cal, (1 twin)
Guns, AA	2—40 mm (1 twin)
A/S weapons	Octuple ASROC
Torpedo launchers	2 triple 12·7 in (*324 mm*)
Main engines	4 Mitsui B & W diesels; 2 shafts; 16 000 shp
Speed, knots	25
Complement	165

Chikugo laid down by Mitsui oosen on 9 Dec 1968, launched 13 Jan 1970, completed 31 July 1970. *Ayase* laid down 5 Dec 1969, launched 16 Sep 1970, and completed 20 May 1971. *Mikuma* laid down 17 Mar 1970, launched 16 Feb 1971 and completed 26 Aug 1971. *Tokachi* laid down by Mitsui oosen on 11 Dec 1970, launched 25 Nov 1971 and completed 17 May 1972. *Iwase* laid down by Mitsui oosen on 6 Aug 1971, launched 29 June 1972, completed 12 Dec 1972. *Chitose* laid down by Hitachi Maizuru 7 Oct 1971, launched Jan 1973 for completion in Sep 1973. DE 221 laid down by Mitsui oosen 20 Sep 1972, launched April 1973 for completion Dec 1973. DE 222, 223, 224 to be laid down in 1973 for completion in 1975.

MIKUMA 1972, *Toshio Tamura*

RADAR. Search: L Band. Tactical: SPS 10. Fire Control: X Band.

SONAR. Fitted with VDS.

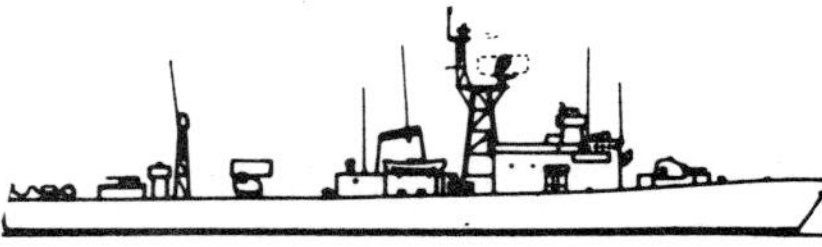

CHIKUGO *Class*

4 "ISUZU" CLASS

Name	No.	Builders	Laid down	Launched	Completed
ISUZU	DE 211	Mitsui Zosen Co, Tamano	16 Apr 1960	17 Jan 1961	29 July 1961
KITAKAMI	DE 213	Ishikawajima-Harima Co, Tokyo	7 June 1962	21 June 1963	27 Feb 1964
MOGAMI	DE 212	Mitsubishi Zosen Co, Nagasaki	4 Aug 1960	7 Mar 1961	28 Oct 1961
ŌI	DE 214	Maizuru (former Iino) Co, Maizuru	10 June 1962	15 June 1963	22 Jan 1964

Displacement, tons	1 490 standard; 1 700 full load
Length, feet (*metres*)	308·5 (*94·0*) oa
Beam, feet (*metres*)	34·2 (*10·4*)
Draught, feet (*metres*)	11·5 (*3·5*)
Guns, dual purpose	4—3 in (*76 mm*) 50 cal. 2 twin
A/S weapons	1 4-barrelled rocket launcher; 1 DCT; 1 DC rack *Isuzu* Mk 108 rocket launcher (Weapon A)
Torpedo tubes	4—21 in (*533 mm*) quadrupled
Torpedo launchers	2 triple for A/S homing torpedoes
Main engines	4 diesels, Mitsui in *Oi, Isuzu*, Mitsubishi in *Kitakami, Mogami;* 16 000 hp; 2 shafts
Speed, knots	25
Complement	180

ISUZU, MOGAMI

ISUZU 1970, courtesy, *Toshio Tamura*

Frigates—*continued*

RADAR. Search: SPS 6. Tactical: SPS 10.

CLASS VARIATION. The second pair of this type, *Kitakami* and *Ōi*, have a number of improvements in armament and equipment and are of slightly different dimensions.

KITAKAMI, OI

KITAKAMI — 1972, *Japanese Maritime Self-Defence Force*

2 "IKAZUCHI" CLASS

Name	*No.*	*Builders*	*Laid down*	*Launched*	*Completed*
IKAZUCHI	DE 202	Kawasaki Jyuko Co, Kobe	18 Dec 1954	6 Sep 1955	29 May 1956
INAZUMA	DE 203	Mitsui Zosen Co, Tamano	25 Dec 1954	4 Aug 1955	5 Mar 1956

Displacement, tons	1 070 standard; 1 300 full load
Length, feet (*metres*)	287 (*87·5*) wl; 288·7 (*88·0* oa)
Beam, feet (*metres*)	28·5 (*8·7*)
Draught, feet (*metres*)	10·2 (*3·1*)
Guns	2—3 in (*76 mm*) 50 cal. dp; 2—40 mm AA
A/S weapons	1 Hedgehog; 8 K-guns; 2 DC racks
Main engines	12 000 hp diesels; Mitsubishi in *Ikazuchi*; Mitsui B & W in *Inazuma*; 2 shafts
Range, miles	5 500 at 15 knots
Speed, knots	25
Complement	160

IKAZUCHI, INAZUMA

INAZUMA — 1967, *Japanese Maritime Self-Defence Force*

GUNNERY. The original 2—3 inch guns and 4—40 mm guns were removed in Mar 1959 and replaced by 2—3 inch quick firing guns and 2—40 mm guns.

RADAR. Search: SPS 6. Tactical: SPS 10. Fire Control: X Band.

1 "AKEBONO" CLASS

Name	*No.*	*Builders*	*Laid down*	*Launched*	*Completed*
AKEBONO	DE 201	Ishikawajima Jyuko Co, Tokyo	10 Dec 1954	15 Oct 1955	20 Mar 1956

Displacement, tons	1 060 standard; 1 350 full load
Length, feet (*metres*)	295 (*90·0*) oa
Beam, feet (*metres*)	28·5 (*8·7*)
Draught, feet (*metres*)	11 (*3·4*)
Guns, AA	2—3 in (*76 mm*) 50 cal.; 1—40 mm
A/S weapons	4 K-guns; 1 Hedgehog; 1 DC rack
Main engines	Ishikawajima geared turbines; 2 shafts; 18 000 shp
Speed, knots	28
Boilers	2 Ishikawajima-Foster Wheeler
Complement	190

AKEBONO

AKEBONO — 1972, *Japanese Maritime Self-Defence Force*

GUNNERY. The original 2—3 inch guns and 4—40 mm guns were removed in March 1959 when 2—3 inch quick firing guns were mounted.

RADAR. Search: SPS 6. Tactical: SPS 10. Fire Control: X Band.

2 "ASAHI" CLASS

Name	*No.*	*Builders*	*Laid down*	*Launched*	*Completed*
ASAHI (ex-USS *Amick, DE* 168)	DE 262	Federal Port, Newark	30 Nov 1942	27 May 1943	26 July 1943
HATSUHI (ex-USS *Atherton, DE* 169)	DE 263	Federal Port, Newark	14 Jan 1943	27 May 1943	29 Aug 1943

Displacement, tons	1 250 standard; 1 900 full load
Length, feet (*metres*)	306 (*93·3*) oa
Beam, feet (*metres*)	36·1 (*11·0*)
Draught, feet (*metres*)	12 (*3·7*)
Guns	3—3 in (*76 mm*) 50 cal. dp;
A/S weapons	8 K-guns; 1 DCT
Main engines	GM diesels; electric drive; 2 shafts; 6 000 hp
Range, miles	11 500 at 11 knots 5 500 at 18 knots
Speed, knots	20
Complement	220

ASAHI, HATSUHI

Former US "Bostwick" class destroyer escorts. Taken over from the US Navy on 14 June 1955.

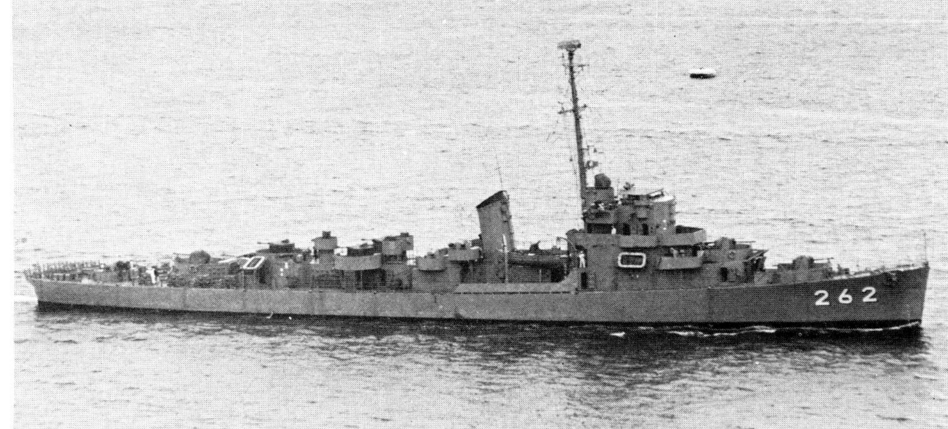

ASAHI — 1972, *Toshio Tamura*

CORVETTES

8 "MIZUTORI" CLASS (PC)

Name	No.	Builders	Laid down	Launched	Completed
HATSUKARI	315	Sasebo Shipyard	25 Jan 1960	24 June 1960	15 Nov 1960
HIYODORI	320	Sasebo Shipyard	26 Feb 1965	25 Sep 1965	28 Feb 1966
KASASAGI	314	Fujinagata, Osaka	18 Dec 1959	31 May 1960	31 Oct 1960
MIZUTORI	311	Kawasaki, Kobe	13 Mar 1959	22 Sep 1959	26 Feb 1965
ŌTORI	313	Kure Shipyard	16 Dec 1959	27 May 1960	30 Mar 1963
SHIRATORI	319	Sasebo Shipyard	29 Feb 1964	8 Oct 1964	30 Mar 1963
UMIDORI	316	Sasebo Shipyard	15 Feb 1962	15 Oct 1962	15 Mar 1960
YAMADORI	312	Fujinagata, Osaka	14 Mar 1959	22 Oct 1959	15 Mar 1960

Displacement, tons	**420 to 450 standard**
Dimensions, feet	**197·0 × 23·3 × 7·5**
Guns	**2—40 mm (1 twin) AA**
A/S weapons	**1 hedgehog; 1 DC rack; 6 homing torpedo launchers Triple**
Main engines	**2 MAN diesels; 2 shafts; 3 800 bhp = 20 knots**
Complement	**80**
Range, miles	2 000 at 12 knots

***Mizutori* and *Yamadori* built under 1958 programme, *Ōtori, Kasasagi* and *Hatsukari* 1959, *Umidori* (Sea Bird) and *Wahataka* (Young Hawk) 1961, *Kumataka* 1962, *Shirātori* (White Bird) 1963, *Hiyodori* 1964.**

4 "UMITAKA" CLASS (PC)

Name	No.	Builders	Laid down	Launched	Completed
ŌTAKA	310	Kure Shipyard	18 Mar 1959	3 Sep 1959	14 Jan 1960
UMITAKA	309	Kawasaki, Kobe	13 Mar 1959	25 July 1959	30 Nov 1959
KUMATAKA	318	Fujinagata, Osaka	20 Mar 1963	21 Oct 1963	25 Mar 1964
WAKATAKA	317	Kure Shipyard	5 Mar 1962	13 Nov 1962	30 Mar 1963

KUMATAKA *1972, Japanese Maritime Self-Defence Force*

ŌTAKA *1967, Hajime Fukaya*

Displacement, tons	440 to 480 standard
Dimensions, feet	197·0 × 23·3 × 8·0
Guns	2—40 mm (1 twin) AA
A/S weapons	1 Hedgehog, 1 DC rack; 2 triple A/S torpedo launchers
Main engines	2 B & W diesels; 2 shafts; 4 000 bhp = 20 knots
Complement	80

1 "HAYABUSA" CLASS (PC)

HAYABUSA 308

Displacement, tons	360 standard
Dimensions, feet	190·2 × 25·7 × 7
Guns	2—40 mm AA (1 twin)
A/S weapons	1 hedgehog; 2 Y Guns; 2 DC racks
Main engines	2 diesels; 4 000 bhp; 2 shafts = 20 knots
Complement	75

Built under the 1954 fiscal year programme by Mitsubishi Shipbuilding & Engineering Co Ltd, Nagasaki. Laid down on 23 May 1956. Launched on 20 Nov 1956. Completed on 10 June 1957. A gas turbine was installed in Mar 1962 and removed in 1972.

HAYABUSA *1972, Japanese Maritime Self-Defence Force*

7 "KARI" and "KAMOME" CLASS (PC)

Name	No.	Builders	Laid down	Launched	Completed
KAMOME	305	Uraga	27 Jan 1956	3 Sep 1956	14 Jan 1957
KARI	301	Fujinagata, Osaka	18 Jan 1956	26 Sep 1956	8 Feb 1957
KIJI	302	Iino, Maizuru	14 Dec 1955	11 Sep 1956	29 Jan 1957
MISAGO	307	Uraga	27 Jan 1956	1 Nov 1956	11 Feb 1957
TAKA	303	Fujinagata, Osaka	18 Jan 1956	17 Nov 1956	11 Mar 1957
TSUBAME	306	Kure Shipyard	15 Mar 1956	10 Oct 1956	31 Jan 1957
WASHI	304	Iino, Maizuru	14 Dec 1955	12 Nov 1956	20 Mar 1957

Displacement, tons	330 standard; (*Kari, Kiji, Taka, Washi,* 310)
Dimensions, feet	173·3 oa × 21·8 × 6·8
Guns	2—40 mm (1 twin)
A/S weapons	1 Hedgehog; 2-Y guns; 2 DC racks
Main engines	2 diesels (*Kari, Kiji, Taka,* and *Washi* Kawasaki-MAN; others Mitsui-Burmeister & Wain). 2 shafts; 4 000 bhp = 20 knots
Oil fuel (tons)	21·5
Range, miles	2 000 at 12 knots
Complement	70

MISAGO *1970, Japanese Maritime Self Defence Force*

Authorised under the 1954 programme. At the time they were an entirely new type of fast patrol vessels, reminiscent of the United States PC type but modified and improved in many ways. *Kari* class (301-304). *Kamome* class (305-307).

SUBMARINES

4 + 2 UZUSHIO CLASS

Name	No.	Builders
UZUSHIO	SS 566	Kawasaki
MAKISHIO	SS 567	Mitsubishi
ISOSHIO	SS 568	Kawasaki
NARUSHIO	SS 569	Mitsubishi
570		Kawasaki
571		

Laid down	Launched	Completed
25 Sep 1968	11 Mar 1970	21 Jan 1971
21 June 1969	27 Jan 1971	2 Feb 1972
9 July 1970	18 Mar 1972	25 Nov 1972
8 May 1971	Nov 1972	Feb 1973
5 July 1972	Nov 1973	Feb 1975
1973	1974	1976

Displacement, tons	**1 850 standard**
Length, feet (*metres*)	**236·2 (*72·0*)**
Beam, feet (*metres*)	**32·5 (*9·9*)**
Draught, feet (*metres*)	**24·6 (*7·5*)**
Torpedo tubes	**6—21 in (*533 mm*); bow**
Main engines	**2 diesels; 3 400 bhp; 1 shaft; 1 electric motor; 7 200 hp**
Speed, knots	**12 on surface, 20 submerged**
Complement	**80**

Of double-hull construction and "tear-drop" form.

UZUSHIO *1972, Japanese Maritime Self-Defence Force*

Submarines—*continued*

5 "OOSHIO" CLASS

Name	No.	Builders	Laid down	Launched	Completed
ARASHIO	SS 565	Mitsubishi Jyuko, Kobe	5 July 1967	24 Oct 1968	25 July 1969
ASASHIO	SS 562	Kawasaki Jyuko Co, Kobe	10 Oct 1964	27 Nov 1965	13 Oct 1966
HARUSHIO	SS 563	Mitsubishi Jyuko Co, Kobe	12 Oct 1965	25 Feb 1967	1 Dec 1967
MICHISHIO	SS 564	Kawasaki Jyuko, Kobe	26 July 1966	5 Dec 1967	29 Aug 1968
OOSHIO	SS 561	Mitsubishi Jyuko Co, Kobe	29 June 1963	30 Apr 1964	31 Mar 1965

Displacement, tons	1 650 standard; *Ooshio* 1 600
Length, feet (*metres*)	288·7 (*88·0*)
Beam, feet (*metres*)	26·9 (*8·2*)
Draught, feet (*metres*)	16·2 (*4·9*), *Ooshio* 15·4 (*4·7*)
Torpedo tubes	8—21 in (*533 mm*); 6 bow 2 stern
Main engines	2 diesels; 2 900 bhp; 2 shafts; 2 electric motors; 6 300 hp
Speed, knots	14 on surface; 18 submerged
Complement	80

Double-hulled boats. This class is the first ever built in Japanese yards with a deep-diving capability. A bigger design to obtain improved seaworthiness, a larger torpedo capacity and more comprehensive sonar and electronic devices. *Ooshio* was built under the 1961 programme, *Asashio* 1963. Cost $5 600 000.

MICHISHIO *1972, Japanese Maritime Self-Defence Force*

4 "HAYASHIO" and "NATSUSHIO" CLASS

Name	No.	Builders	Laid down	Launched	Completed
FUYUSHIO	SS 524	Kawasaki Jyuko Co, Kobe	6 Dec 1961	14 Dec 1962	17 Sep 1963
HAYASHIO	SS 521	Shin Mitsubishi Jyuko Co, Kobe	6 June 1960	31 July 1961	30 June 1962
NATSUSHIO	SS 523	Shin Mitsubishi Jyuko Co, Kobe	5 Dec 1961	18 Sep 1962	29 June 1963
WAKASHIO	SS 522	Kawasaki Jyuko Co, Kobe	7 June 1960	28 Aug 1961	17 Aug 1962

Displacement, tons	750 standard (SS 521, 522); 780 standard (SS 523, 524)
Length, feet (*metres*)	193·6 (*59·0*) oa (SS 521, 522); 200·1 (*61·0*) oa (SS 523, 524)
Beam, feet (*metres*)	21·3 (*6·5*)
Draught, feet (*metres*)	13·5 (*4·1*)
Torpedo tubes	3—21 in (*533 mm*); bow
Main engines	2 diesels, total 1 350 hp; 2 shafts; 2 electric motors, total 1 700 hp
Speed, knots	11 on surface; 14 submerged
Complement	40

Medium submarines of improved type, with more efficient sonar devices, giving them slightly increased displacement. Very handy and successful boats, with a large safety factor, complete air conditioning and good habitability.

Hayashio class SS 521-522.
Natsushio class SS 523-524.

NATSUSHIO *1971, Japanese Maritime Self-Defence Force*

1 "OYASHIO" CLASS

OYASHIO SS 511

Displacement, tons	1 130 surface; 1 420 submerged
Length, feet (*metres*)	258·5 (*78·8*)
Beam, feet (*metres*)	23 (*7·0*)
Draught, feet (*metres*)	15·2 (*4·6*)
Torpedo tubes	4—21 in (*533 mm*); 10 torpedoes
Main engines	2 diesels, total 2 700 hp; 2 electric motors, total 5 960 hp
Speed, knots	13 on surface; 19 submerged
Range, miles	5 000 at 10 knots
Complement	65

OYASHIO *1972, Japanese Maritime Self-Defence Force*

Ordered under the 1956 Programme. Built by Kawasaki Jyuko Co Kobe. Laid down on 25 Dec 1957, launched on 25 May 1959 and completed on 30 June 1960. The first submarine built in a Japanese shipyard after the Second World War, *Oyashio* is the name of a tide stream in the Pacific off Honshu. First estimated to cost £2 718 000, but this figure was exceeded. Of double-hull construction.

AMPHIBIOUS SHIPS

2000 TON CLASS (LST)

Displacement, tons	2 000
Guns	2—3 in (singles)
Main engines	6 000 hp = 17 knots or 4 400 hp = 13·5 knots

Fitted with bow doors.

2 "ATSUMI" CLASS (LST)

ATSUMI 4101 +1

Displacement, tons	1 480
Dimensions, feet	291·9 × 42·6 × 8·5
Guns	4—40 mm AA (twins)
Main engines	2 diesels; 4 400 hp = 14 knots
Complement	100

Completed 27 Nov 1972 at Sasebo Jyuko Co, Sasebo. A second will be built at Sasebo under 1972 programme.

ATSUMI *1972, Toshio Tamura*

3 "OOSUMI" CLASS

OOSUMI 4001 **SHIMOKITA** 4002 **SHIRETOKO** 4003

Displacement, tons	1 650 standard; 4 080 full load
Dimensions, feet	316·0 wl; 328·0 oa × 50·0 × 14·0
Guns	4—40 mm single; 2—40 mm twin; 12—20 mm AA single
Main engines	GM diesels; 2 shafts; 1 700 bhp = 11 knots
Range, miles	9 500 at 9 knots
Complement	100

Former US *Dagget County, LST* 689, *Hillsdale County, LST* 835, and *Nansemond County, LST* 1064, built by Jeffersonville B. & M. Co, Ind; American Bridge Co, Ambridge; Pa; and Bethlehem Steel Co, Hingham, Mass. respectively, in 1954-55. Commissioned in the Japanese MSDF on 1 Apr 1961.

SHIMOKITA *1972, Japanese Maritime Self-Defence Force*

Amphibious Ships—*continued*

LSM 3001 (ex-French *LSM* 9013, ex-USS *LSM* 125)

Displacement, tons	743 beaching; 1 095 full load
Dimensions, feet	196·5 wl; 203·5 oa × 34·5 × 5·2 beaching; (8·5 max)
Guns	2—40 mm AA; 6—20 mm AA
Main engines	diesels; 2 shafts; 2 800 bhp = 12 knots
Complement	50

Transferred from USA to France in 1954 for use in Indo-China. Returned by France in 1957 to USA, and then transferred to Japan in 1958.

LCU 2001 LCU 2002 LCU 2003 LCU 2004 LCU 2005 LCU 2006

Ex-US LCU 1602 to 1607 of 187 tons transferred on 2 June 1955.

LCM 1001—1042

29 LCMs of 22 tons and 20 LCVPs of 8 tons were transferred from USA on 2 June 1955 and 13 LCMs, Nos 1030—1042 in 1961.

LSM 3001 *1971, Japanese Maritime Self-Defence Force*

LIGHT FORCES

PT 11 PT 12 PT 13 PT 14

Displacement, tons	100
Dimensions, feet	116·4 × 30·2 × 3·9
Guns	2—40 mm AA
Tubes	4—21 inch
Main engines	2 Mitsubishi diesels; 2 IHI gas turbines; 3 shafts; 11 200 hp (PT 11 10 500 hp) = 40 knots
Complement	28

Built by Mitsubishi, Snimonoseki. PT 11 laid down 11 Mar 1970, completed 27 Mar 1971. PT 12 laid down 22 April 1971, completed 28 Mar 1972. PT 13 laid down 28 Mar 1972, completed 16 Dec 1972. PT 14 1973-74.

PT 10

Displacement, tons	90 standard; 120 full load
Dimensions, feet	105 × 27·8 × 3·7
Guns	2—40 mm AA (1 forward, 1 aft)
Tubes	4—21 in (single, amidships)
Main engines	3 Napier Deltic diesels; 9 400 bhp = 40 knots
Complement	26

1960 programme. Built by Mitsubishi, Shimonoseki. Laid down on 30 Jan 1961 Launched on 28 July 1961. Completed on 25 May 1962. Light metal hull.

PT 10 *1971, Japanese Maritime Self-Defence Force*

PT 7 PT 8

Displacement, tons	100
Dimensions, feet	112 × 24·7 × 4
Guns	2—40 mm AA
Tubes	4—21 in
Main engines	3 Mitsubishi diesels; 3 shafts; 6 000 bhp = 33 knots
Complement	30

Authorised in the 1954 fiscal year. Built by Mitsubishi Zosen Co, Shimonoseki Works. Both laid down on 23 Aug 1956, launched on 2 Feb and 20 July 1957, respectively, and completed on 19 Dec 1957 and 10 Jan 1958. Light metal hulls.

PT 7 *1970, Japanese Maritime Self-Defence Force*

HAYATE (HYDROFOIL)

Displacement, tons	78
Dimensions, feet	78·8 × 18 × 8·5
Main engines	2 Gas Turbines; 1 Diesel; 6 500 bhp = 50 knots
Complement	19

Completed March 1970.

PB 19, 20, 21, 22, 23, 24, 25, 26, 27.

Displacement, tons	18
Dimensions, feet	55·8 × 14·1 × 2·7
Gun	1—20 mm
Main engines	2 diesels; 760 hp = 20 knots
Complement	6

19-22 completed 31 Mar 1971, 23-24 31 Mar 1972, 25-27 Mar 1973. All built by Ishikawajima Yokohama. GRP hulls.

KOSOKU 4 ASH 04 **KOSOKU 5** ASH 05

Displacement, tons	30
Dimensions, feet	75·5 × 18 ×2·5
Main engines	2 Packard engines; 1 600 bhp = 30 knots

Of aluminium construction. Laid down on 10 Oct 1958 and 11 Dec 1958 at Mitsubishi, Shimonoseki Works under the 1957 and 1958 Programme, launched on 11 Dec 1958 and 2 Mar 1959, and completed on 11 May ,1959 and 12 June 1959, respectively.

KOSOKU 2 KOSOKU 3

Displacement, tons	30
Dimensions, feet	65·7 × 17 × 2·7
Main engines	2 Packard petrol engines; 3 000 bhp = 42 knots

ASH category. Of wooden construction. All are Maritime Self-Defence Force Auxiliaries.

MINE WARFARE FORCES

1 "SOOYA" CLASS MINELAYER

SOOYA 951

Displacement, tons	**2 150 standard**
Length, feet (*metres*)	**324·8 (*99·0*)**
Beam, feet (*metres*)	**49·2 (*15·0*)**
Draught, feet (*metres*)	**13·8 (*4·2*)**
Guns	**2—3 in (*76 mm*) 50 cal. (1 twin); 2—20 mm**
Torpedo tubes	**6 anti-submarine type (2 triple)**
Main engines	**4 diesels; 6 400 bhp**
Speed, knots	**18**
Complement	**185**

Laid down by Hitachi Zosen, Maizuru on 9 July 1970, launched 31 Mar 1971 and completed 30 Sept 1971. With twin rails can carry 200 buoyant mines. Has helicopter platform aft and acts at times as command ship for MCM forces.

SOOYA *1972, Maizuru Jukogyo*

Minewarfare Forces—*continued*

MINESWEEPER SUPPORT SHIP

HAYASE 462

Displacement, tons	2 150 standard
Dimensions, feet	324·8 × 49·2 × 13·8
Guns	2—3 in (*76 mm*); 2—20 mm
Main engines	4 diesels; 6 400 bhp; 2 screws = 18 knots
Torpedo tubes	6 anti-submarine
Complement	185

Laid down by Ishikawajima Haruna 16 Sep 1970, launched 21 June 1971, completed 6 Nov 1971. Has helicopter platform aft.

HAYASE *1972, Japanese Maritime Self Defence Force*

MINELAYER AND CABLE LAYER

TSUGARU 481

Displacement, tons	950 standard
Dimensions, feet	216·3 × 34·1 × 11
Guns	1—3 in, 50 cal dp; 2—20 mm AA;
A/S weapons	4 K-guns (DC mortars)
Mines	4 mine launchers, capacity of 40 mines
Main engines	Diesel; 2 shafts; 3 200 bhp = 16 knots
Complement	100

Dual purpose cable layer and coastal minelayer. Built under the 1953 programme by Yokohama Shipyard & Engine Works, Mitsubishi Nippon-Heavy Industries Ltd. Laid down on 18 Dec 1954. Launched on 19 July 1955. Completed on 15 Dec 1955.

TSUGARU *1966, Japanese Maritime Self-Defence Force*

UTILITY MINELAYER

ERIMO 491

Displacement, tons	630 standard
Dimensions, feet	210 × 26 × 8
Guns	2—40 mm AA; 2—20 mm AA
A/S weapons	1 Hedgehog; 2 K-guns; 2 DC racks
Main engines	Diesel; 2 shafts; 2 500 bhp = 18 knots
Complement	80

Multi-purpose minelayer, ocean minesweeper (non-magnetic) and submarine chaser. Authorised under 1953 fiscal programme. Built by Uraga Dock Co. Laid down on 10 Dec 1954. Launched on 12 July 1955. Completed on 28 Dec 1955.

ERIMO ***1970, Japanese Maritime Self-Defence Force***

25 "KASADO" CLASS (CMS)

Name	*No.*	*Laid down*	*Launched*	*Completed*
AMAMI	MSC 625	1 Mar 1966	31 Oct 1966	6 Mar 1967
CHIBURI	MSC 620	27 Mar 1963	29 Nov 1963	25 Mar 1964
HABUSHI	MSC 608	25 Aug 1958	19 June 1959	22 Sep 1959
HARIO	MSC 618	19 Mar 1962	10 Dec 1962	23 Mar 1963
HIRADO	MSC 614	14 Mar 1960	3 Oct 1960	17 Dec 1960
HOTAKA	MSC 616	22 Mar 1961	23 Oct 1961	24 Feb 1962
IBUKI	MSC 628	27 Feb 1967	2 Dec 1967	27 Feb 1968
KANAWA	MSC 606	25 Aug 1958	22 Apr 1959	24 July 1959
KARATO	MSC 617	15 Mar 1962	11 Dec 1962	23 Mar 1963
KASADO	MSC 604	9 July 1956	19 Mar 1958	26 June 1958
KATSURA	MSC 629	10 Feb 1967	18 Sep 1967	15 Feb 1968
KOSHIKI	MSC 615	20 Mar 1961	9 Nov 1961	29 Jan 1962
KUDAKO	MSC 622	17 Mar 1964	8 Dec 1964	24 Mar 1965
MIKURA	MSC 612	30 Mar 1959	14 Mar 1960	27 May 1960
MINASE	MSC 627	1 Feb 1966	10 Jan 1967	25 Mar 1967
MUTSURE	MSC 619	28 Mar 1963	16 Dec 1963	24 Mar 1964
OOTSU	MSC 621	25 Mar 1964	6 Nov 1964	24 Feb 1965
REBUN	MSC 624	17 Feb 1964	18 Dec 1964	25 Mar 1965
RISHIRI	MSC 623	9 Mar 1964	22 Nov 1965	5 Mar 1966
SAKITO	MSC 607	16 Aug 1958	22 Apr 1959	25 Aug 1959
SHIKINE	MSC 613	12 Jan 1960	22 July 1960	15 Nov 1960
SHISAKA	MSC 605	20 July 1956	20 Mar 1958	16 Aug 1958
TATARA	MSC 610	25 Aug 1958	14 Jan 1960	26 Mar 1960
TSUKUMI	MSC 611	24 Mar 1959	12 Jan 1960	27 Apr 1960
URUME	MSC 626	1 Feb 1966	12 Nov 1966	30 Jan 1967

Displacement, tons	340 standard
Dimensions, feet	150·9 × 27·6 × 7·5; 170·6 × 28·9 × 7·9 later ships
Guns	1—20 mm AA
Main engines	2 diesels; 2 shafts; 1 200 bhp, 1 440 later ships= 14 knots

Hull is of wooden construction. Otherwise built of non-magnetic materials. *Habushi, Kanawa, Kasado* and *638* were built by Hitachi, Kanawaga Works, *Shishaka, Sakito* and *639* by Nippon Steel Tube Co, Tsurumi.

12 "TAKAMI" CLASS

TAKAMI	MSC 630	25 Sep 1968	15 July 1969	15 Dec 1969
IOU	MSC 631	21 Sep 1968	12 Aug 1969	22 Jan 1970
MIYAKE	MSC 632	14 Aug 1969	3 June 1970	19 Nov 1970
UTONE	MSC 633	6 Aug 1969	6 Apr 1970	3 Sep 1970
AWAJI	MSC 634	20 Apr 1970	11 Dec 1970	29 Mar 1971
TOOSHI	MSC 635	14 May 1970	12 Oct 1970	18 Mar 1971
TEURI	MSC 636	12 Apr 1971	19 Oct 1971	14 Mar 1972
MUROTSO	MSC 637	16 Apr 1971	16 Dec 1971	31 Mar 1972
638		26 May 1972	Apr 1973	July 1973
639		22 Apr 1972	Apr 1973	July 1973
640		(1973)	(1974)	(1974)
641		(1973)	(1974)	(1974)

Of similar dimensions to "Kasado" class but of slightly different construction and with a displacement of 380 tons.

TAKAMI *1972, Japanese Maritime Self-Defence Force*

1 "KOOZU" CLASS

KOOZU MST 473

Similar to "Kasado" class but has had minesweeping gear removed and was fitted as MCM Command Ship in July 1972.

4 "YASHIMA" CLASS (CMS)

HASHIMA (ex-USS *AMS* 95) YAS 47
TOSHIMA (ex-USS *MSC* 258)
TSUSHIMA (ex-USS MSC, ex-*AMS* 255)
YASHIMA (ex-USS *AMS* 144) YAS 46

Displacement, tons	335 standard; 375 full load
Dimensions, feet	138 pp; 144 oa × 26·5 × 8·3
Guns	1—20 mm AA
Main engines	2 GM diesels; 880 bhp = 13 knots
Range, miles	2 500 at 10 knots

Former US auxiliary minesweepers *Hashima* and *Yashima* now used as accommodation ships.

Minewarfare Ships—*continued*

10 "ICHIGO" CLASS (MSBs)

701 702 703 704 705 706 707 708 709 710

Displacement, tons	40 (50 for 7-10)
Dimensions, feet	62·3 oa × 16 × 4 (7-10 73·8 × 17·7 × 3·6)
Main engines	2 diesels; 2 shafts; 320 bhp = 10 knots (7-10 480 hp = 11 knots)
Complement	10

Nos. 701-3 were launched in Jan and Feb 1957 and completed in Mar and Apr 1957. 704 was launched in Apr 1957 and completed in June 1957. 705-6 were laid down in Aug 1958 and completed in Feb-Mar 1959. 701, 702 and 707 were built by Hitachi, Kanagawa; and the others by Nippon Steel Tube Co, Tsurumi. No. 707 laid down 26 May 1972 and completed Mar 1973. No. 708 laid down 3 Aug 1972 and completed Mar 1973. Nos. 709 and 710 to be built 1973-74.

MB 5 *1963*

TRAINING SHIPS

AZUMA 4201

Displacement, tons	1 950 standard; 2 500 full load
Length, feet (*metres*)	325 (*99·0*)
Beam, feet (*metres*)	42·7 (*13·0*)
Draught, feet (*metres*)	12·5 (*3·8*)
Aircraft	1 helicopter
Guns	1—3 in (*76 mm*) 50 cal.
A/S weapons	2 short torpedo launchers
Main engines	2 diesels; 2 shafts; 4 000 bhp
Speed, knots	18
Complement	185

Built by Maizuru Jyuko Co, Maizuru as a training support ship. Laid down on 30 July 1968, launched on 14 Apr 1969 and completed 26 Nov 1969. Has helicopter hangar amidships. Acts as drone carrier.

AZUMA

KATORI 3501

Displacement, tons	3 372 standard; 4 000 full load
Length, feet (*metres*)	418·5 (*127·0*)
Beam, feet (*metres*)	49·3 (*14·6*)
Draught, feet (*metres*)	14·6 (*4·3*)
Aircraft	1 helicopter
Guns, dual purpose	4—3 in (*76 mm*) 50 cal
A/S weapons	1 four barrelled rocket launcher
Torpedo launchers	6 (2 triple mounts) for homing torpedoes
Main engines	geared turbines; 2 shafts; 20 000 shp
Range, miles	7 000 at 18 knots
Speed, knots	25
Complement	460 including trainees

Built by Ishikawajima Harima, Tokyo. Laid down 8 Dec 1967, launched on 19 Nov 1968 and completed on 10 Sep 1969. Provided with a landing deck aft for a helicopter and amidships hangar.

RADAR Search: SPS 12. Tactical: SPS 10.

KATORI

KATORI *1970, Courtesy, Toshio Tamura*

SUBMARINE RESCUE VESSELS

FUSIMI ASR 402

Displacement, tons	1 430 standard
Dimensions, feet	249·5 × 41 × 12
Main engines	2 diesels; 1 shaft; 3 000 bhp = 16 knots
Complement	100

Built by Sumnitomo SB & Machinery Co, laid down on 5 Nov 1968, launched 10 Sep 1969, completed 10 Feb 1970. Has a rescue chamber and two decompression chambers.

FUSIMI *1972, Japanese Maritime Self-Defence Force*

CHIHAYA ASR 401

Displacement, tons	1 340 standard
Dimensions, feet	239·5 × 39·3 × 12·7
Main engines	Diesels; 2 700 bhp = 15 knots
Complement	90

Authorised under the 1959 programme. The first vessel of her kind to be built in Japan. Laid down on 15 Mar 1960. Launched by Mitsubishi Nippon Heavy Industries Co, Yokohama on 4 Oct 1960. Completed on 15 Mar 1961. Has rescue chamber, 2 decompression chambers, four-point mooring equipment and a 12 ton derrick.

CHIHAYA *1972, Japanese Maritime Self-Defence Force*

SALVAGE VESSEL

SHOBO 41

Displacement, tons 45
Dimensions, feet 75 × 18 × 3·3
Main engines 4 diesels; Speed = 19 knots

A fire defence boat. Built by Azumo Zosen, Yokosuka. Completed 28 Feb 1964.

OILERS

HAMANA

Displacement, tons 2 900 light; 7 550 full load
Dimensions, feet 420 × 51·5 × 20·5
Guns 2—40 mm AA
Main engines Diesel; 5 000 bhp = 16 knots

Built by Uraga Dock Co under the 1960 programme. Laid down on 17 Apr 1961 launched on 24 Oct 1961, and completed on 10 Mar 1962. Named after the lake.

MISCELLANEOUS

2 "NASAMI" CLASS

MIHO (ex-USS *FS* 524) YAS 59 **NASAMI** (ex-USS *FS* 408) YAS 51

Displacement, tons 706
Dimensions, feet 177 × 30 × 10
Main engines Diesels; 2 shafts; 1 000 bhp = 11 knots

Transferred from the United States in 1955. *Nasami* is rated as a minesweeper tender (MST), *Miho*, formerly rated as ASS, was refitted as an inshore minesweeper depot ship in August 1959.

YAS 48 **YAS 54** **YAS 55**

Displacement, tons 75
Dimensions, feet 82 × 20 × 6
Main engines diesel engines; 13 knots

PBs converted to Harbour auxiliaries.

2 "ATADA" CLASS

Name	*No.*	*Laid down*	*Launched*	*Completed*
ATADA	YAS 56	20 June 1955	12 Mar 1956	30 Apr 1956
ITSUKI	YAS 57	22 June 1955	12 Mar 1956	20 June 1956

Displacement, tons 240 standard; 260 full load
Dimensions, feet 118 pp; 123·3 oa × 21 × 6·8
Guns 1—20 mm AA
Main engines Diesel; 2 shafts; 1 200 bhp = 13 knots

Of wood and light metal construction. Authorised under the 1953 fiscal yaar programme. Built by the Hitachi Zosen Co. Now used as auxiliaries.

ATADA *1970, Japanese Maritime Self-Defence Force*

Miscellaneous—*continued*

1 "YASHIRO" CLASS

YASHIRO YAS 58

Displacement, tons 230 standard; 255 full load
Dimensions, feet 118 pp × 22·7 × 6·2
Guns 1—20 mm AA
Main engines diesel; 2 shafts; 1 200 bhp = 13 knots

Built under the 1963 Programme by the Nippon Steel Tube Co, Tsurumi. Laid down on 22 June 1955, launched on 26 Mar 1956 and completed on 10 July 1956. Now used as auxiliary.

DISPOSALS

Of the nine coastal minesweepers of the "Ujishima" class, ex-US AMS of the "Albatross" class, *Moroshima*, *Ogishima*, *Ninoshima*, *Yugoshima*, *Nuwajima*, *Yurishima* were officially deleted from the list in 1957; *Etajima* and *Yjishima* in 1966 and returned to USN in 1967. *Yakishima* returned to USN on 31 Mar 1970.

YASHIRO *1970, Japanese Maritime Self-Defence Force*

ICEBREAKER (AGB)

FUJI 5001

Displacement, tons 5 250 standard; 7 760 normal; 8 566 full load
Dimensions, feet 328 × 72·2 × 29
Aircraft 3 helicopters
Main engines 4 diesel-electric; 2 shafts; 12 000 shp = 16 knots
Radius, miles 5 000 at 15 knots
Complement 200 plus 35 scientists and observers

Antarctic Support Ship. Built by Tsurumi Shipyard, Yokohama, Nippon Kokan Kabushiki Kaisha. Laid down on 28 Aug 1964, launched on 18 Mar 1965, delivered on 15 July 1965. Hangar and flight deck aft. Named after the mountain.

FUJI *1968, Japanese Maritime Self-Defence Force*

TUGS

SUMA YAS 45

Displacement, tons 115
Dimensions, feet 70·5 × 19 × 5
Main engines 1 diesel; 600 bhp = 12 knots

ATR category. Steel construction. Former name YTL 749. The small harbour tugs 72, 167, 203, 244, 749 and 750 were transferred by the USA. 748 was scrapped. in 1971.

MARITIME SAFETY AGENCY

Established in May 1948. *Commandant:* Yoshinari Tezuka Personnel 1973: 11 100

LARGE PATROL VESSELS

2 "IZU" CLASS

IZU PL 31 **MIURA** PL 32

Displacement, tons	2 080 normal
Dimensions, feet	295·3 wl × 38 × 12·8
Main engines	diesel; 2 shafts; 10 400 bhp = 21·6 knots
Range, miles	14 500 at 12·7 knots; 5 000 at 21 knots
Complement	72

Izu was laid down in Aug 1966, launched in Jan 1967 and completed in July 1967. *Miura*, built by Maizuru Jukogyo Ltd, was laid down in May 1968, launched in Oct 1968 and completed in Mar 1969. Employed in long range rescue and patrol and weather observation duties. Equipped with weather observation radar, various types of marine instruments. Ice proof hull for winter work.

MIURA *1970, Japanese Maritime Safety Agency*

ERIMO PL 13 **SATSUMA** PL 14

Displacement, tons	1 009 normal
Dimensions, feet	239·5 wl × 30·2 × 9·9
Guns	1—3 in, 50 cal; 1—20 mm AA
Main engines	diesels; 2 shafts; 4 800 bhp = 19·78 knots
Range, miles	6 000 at 18 knots

Both built by Hitachi Zosen Co Ltd. *Erimo* was laid down on 29 Mar 1965, launched on 14 Aug 1965 and completed on 30 Nov 1965. Her structure is strengthened against ice. Employed as a patrol vessel off northern Japan. *Satsuma*, completed on 30 July 1966, is assigned to guard and rescue south of Japan.

SATSUMA *1970, Japanese Maritime Safety Agency*

KOJIMA PL 21

Displacement, tons	1 100
Dimensions, feet	228·3 × 33·8 × 10·5
Guns	1—3 In; 1—40 mm AA; 1—20 mm AA
Main engines	diesels; 2 600 hp = 17 knots
Range, miles	6 000 at 13 knots
Complement	17 officers, 42 men, 47 cadets

Maritime Safety Agency training ship. Completed on 21 May 1964 at Kure Zosen.

KOJIMA *1965, Japanese Maritime Safety Agency*

Large Patrol Vessels—*continued*

2 "NOJIMA" CLASS

NOJIMA PL 11 **OJIKA** PL 12

Displacement, tons	950 standard; 980 normal; 1 100 full load
Dimensions, feet	208·8 pp; 226·5 oa × 30·2 × 10·5
Main engines	2 sets diesels; 3 000 bhp = 17·5 knots
Complement	51

Nojima was built by Uraga Dock Co Ltd. Laid down on 27 Oct 1961, launched on 12 Feb 1962, and completed on 30 Apr 1962. *Ojika* was completed on 10 June 1963. Both employed as patrol vessels and weather ships.

OJIKA *1972, Japanese Maritime Safety Agency*

2 "MUROTO" CLASS

DAIO PL 02 **MUROTO** PL 01

Displacement, tons	750 standard; 840 normal
Dimensions, feet	182 pp; 200 oa × 30·5 × 10·2
Guns	1—3 in, 50 cal; 2—20 mm AA
Main engines	2—4 cycle single acting diesels; 1 500 bhp = 15·37 knots

Muroto, built by Uraga Dock Company Ltd, Tokyo, was laid down on 16 Aug 1949, launched on 5 Dec 1949, and delivered on 20 Mar 1950. Vertical tubular donkey boiler, three generators, wireless, radar, direction finder, echo-sounder, streamlined bridge wings.

MUROTO *1970, Japanese Maritime Safety Agency*

SOYA PL 107

Displacement, tons	4 364 normal; 4 818 full load
Dimensions, feet	259·2 wl × 51·9 (*including bulge*) × 18·9
Aircraft	4 helicopters (see *notes*)
Main engines	2 sets diesels; 4 800 bhp = 12·5 knots on trials
Range, miles	10 000 at 12 knots
Complement	96

Originally a Lighthouse Supply Ship and Navigational Aid Vessel (LL) but converted by Nippon Kokan Kabashiki Kaisha, Asano into a South Pole Research Ship. Her first conversion, begun on 12 Mar 1956 was completed on 10 Oct, 1956. The second conversion, begun on 1 July 1957, was completed on 30 Sep 1957. The third conversion was completed on 5 Oct 1958. She carried two Sikorsky S—58 helicopters and two Bell 47G-2 helicopters on a flight platform laid on the quarter deck for exploration and surveying in the Antarctic. She was designed for breaking ice more than 4 feet thick. Upon completion of her Antarctic research mission in 1963 she was assigned to guard and rescue service as a patrol vessel.

SOYA *1970, Japanese Maritime Safety Agency*

MEDIUM PATROL VESSELS

4 "KUNASHIRI" CLASS

KUNASHIRI PM 65 **MINABE** PM 66 PM 67 PM 68

Displacement, tons	498 normal
Dimensions, feet	190·4 oa × 24·2 × 7·9
Gun	1—20 mm AA
Main engines	2 sets diesels; 2 600 bhp = 17·6 knots
Range, miles	3 000 at 16·9 knots
Complement	40

Kunashiri was built by Maizuru Jukogyo Ltd. Laid down in Oct 1968, launched in Dec 1968 and completed in Mar 1969. *Minabe*, laid down in Oct 1969, and completed in Mar 1970.

KUNASHIRI *1970, Japanese Maritime Safety Agency*

5 "CHIFURI" CLASS

CHIFURI PM 18 **KOZU** PM 20 **SHIKINE** PM 21
DAITO PM 22 **KUROKAMI** PM 19

Displacement, tons	465 standard; 483 normal
Dimensions, feet	169 pp; 177 wl × 25·2 × 8·5 (normal)
Guns	1—3 in 50 cal; 1—20 mm AA
Main engines	2 sets diesels; 1 300 bhp = 15·8 knots
Range, miles	3 000 at 12 knots

DAITO *1970, Japanese Maritime Safety Agency*

14 "REBUN" CLASS

AMAKUSA	PM 09	**HIRADO**	PM 17	**NOTO**	PM 13
GENKAI	PM 07	**IKI**	PM 05	**OKI**	PM 06
HACHIJO	PM 08	**KOSHIKI**	PM 16	**OKUSHIRI**	PM 10
HEKURA	PM 14	**KUSAKAKI**	PM 11	**REBUN**	PM 04
		MIKURA	PM 15	**RISHIRI**	PM 12

Displacement, tons	450 standard; 488 trials; 495 normal
Dimensions, feet	155·2 pp; 164 wl; 170 oa × 26·5 × 8·5
Guns	1—3 in 50 cal; 1—20 mm AA
Main engines	2 sets diesels; 1 300 bhp = 15 knots
Range, miles	3 000 at 12 knots

A development of the original "Awaji" class medium patrol vessel design. All completed in 1951.

HIRADO *1972, Japanese Maritime Safety Agency*

Medium Patrol Vessels—*continued*

3 "AWAJI" CLASS

AWAJI PM 01 **MIYAKE** PM 02 **SADO** PM 03

Displacement, tons	510 standard; 550 normal
Dimensions, feet	172 oa × 26·7 × 9·2
Guns	1—3 in 50 cal; 1—20 mm AA
Main engines	2 sets diesels; 1 300 bhp = 15 knots
Range, miles	6 000 at 12 knots

Of a design resembling United States Coast Guard Cutters. All completed in 1950.

MIYAKE *1971, Maritime Safety Agency*

5 "MATSUURA" CLASS

AMAMI PM 62 **MATSUURA** PM 60 **SENDAI** PM 61
KARATSU PM 64 **NATORI** PM 63

Displacement, tons	420 standard; 425 normal
Dimensions, feet	163·3 pp; 181·5 oa × 23 × 7·5
Gun	1—20 mm AA
Main engines	2 sets diesels; 1 400 bhp = 16·5 knots (*Matsuura, Sendai*); 1 800 bhp = 16·8 knots (*Amami, Natori*); 2 600 bhp (*Karatsu*)
Range, miles	3 500 at 12 knots
Complement	37

Matsuura and *Sendai* were built by Osaka Shipbuilding Co Ltd. *Matsuura* was laid down on 16 Oct 1960, launched on 24 Dec 1960 and completed on 18 Mar 1961. *Sendai* was laid down on 23 Aug 1961, launched on 18 Jan 1962 and completed on 21 Apr 1962. *Amami* completed on 29 Mar 1965, *Natori*, completed in 1966, and *Karatsu*, delivered to MSA on 31 Mar 1967, were built by Hitachi Zosen Co Ltd.

MATSUURA *1970, Japanese Maritime Safety Agency*

TESHIO PM 53

Displacement, tons	421·5 normal
Dimensions, feet	149·4 pp; 159 wl × 23 × 8·2
Gun	1—40 mm AA
Main engines	2 sets diesels; 1 400 bhp = 15·71 knots
Range, miles	3 800 at 12 knots
Complement	37

Built by Uraga Dock Co Ltd. Laid down on 15 Sep 1954, launched on 12 Jan 1955, completed on 19 Mar 1955.

6 "Y·AHAGI" CLASS

CHITOSE	PM 56	**SORACHI**	PM 57	**YAHAGI**	PM 54
HORONAI	PM 59	**SUMIDA**	PM 55	**YUBARI**	PM 58

Displacemment, tons	333·15 standard; 375·7 normal
Dimensions, feet	147·3 pp; 157·2 wl × 24 × 7·4 (normal)
Gun	1—40 mm AA
Main engines	2 sets diesels; 1 400 bhp = 15·5 knots
Range, miles	3 500 at 12 knots
Complement	37

All built by Niigata Engineering Co Ltd, *Yahagi* was laid down on 9 Dec 1955, launched on 19 May 1956 and completed on 31 July 1956. *Sumida* was completed on 30 June 1957. *Chitose* was laid down on 20 Sep 1957, launched on 24 Feb 1958 and completed on 30 Apr 1958. *Sorachi* was completed in Mar 1959, *Yubari* on 15 Mar 1960 *Horonai* on 4 Feb 1961.

SORACHI *1972, Japanese Maritime Safety Agency*

Medium Patrol Vessels—*continued*

2 "TOKACHI" CLASS

TATSUTA PM 52 **TOKACHI** PM 51

Displacement, tons	336 standard; 381 normal (*Tokachi*) 324 standard; 369 normal (*Tatsuta*)
Dimensions, feet	157·5 pp; 164 wl; 170 oa × 21·9 × 11·2
Gun	1—40 mm AA
Main engines	2 sets of 4 cycle single acting diesels 1 500 bhp = 16 knots (max); 12 knots (service) (*Tokachi*) 1 400 bhp = 15 knots (max); 12 knots (service) (*Tatsuta*)
Range, miles	3 800 at 12 knots
Complement	37

***Tokachi* was built by Harima Dockyard, Kure. Laid down on 14 Nov 1953, launched on 8 May 1954 and completed on 31 July 1954. *Tatsuta* was completed on 10 Sep 1954.**

TOKACHI *1972, Japanese Maritime Safety Agency*

SMALL PATROL VESSELS

3 "NAGARA" CLASS

KITAKAMI PS 20 **NAGARA** PS 18 **TONE** PS 19

Displacement, tons	260
Dimensions, feet	131·2 × 23 × 7·2
Gun	1—40 mm AA
Main engines	2 diesels; 2 shafts; 800 bhp = 13·5 knots
Range, miles	2 000 at 12 knots
Complement	35

Improved versions of the "Kuma" class. All launched and completed in 1952.

NAGARA *1970 Japanese Maritime Safety Agency*

17 "KUMA" CLASS

ABUKUMA	PS 08	**KIKUCHI**	PS 10	**NOSHIRO**	PS 13
CHIKUGO	PS 16	**KISO**	PS 14	**OYODO**	PS 07
FUJI	PS 02	**KUMA**	PS 01	**SAGAMI**	PS 06
ISHIKARI	PS 05	**KUMANO**	PS 17	**SHINANO**	PS 15
ISUZU	PS 04	**KUZURYU**	PS 09	**TENRYU**	PS 03
		MOGAMI	PS 11	**YOSHINO**	PS 12

Displacement, tons	258 standard; 275 normal
Dimensions, feet	122 pp; 126·3 wl; 132·2 oa × 23 × 7·5
Gun	1—40 mm AA
Main engines	2 sets diesels; 800 bhp = 13·6 knots
Range, miles	2 000 at 12 knots
Complement	35

***Kuma* was built by Nippon Kokan Kabushiki Kaisha, Tsurumi Dockyard, laid down on 29 Sep 1950, launched on 12 Jan 1951 and completed on 24 Mar 1951.**

MOGAMI *1970, Japanese Maritime Safety Agency*

Small Patrol Vessels—*continued*

13 "HIDAKA" CLASS

ASHITAKA	PS 43	**IBUKI**	PS 45	**ROKKO**	PS 35
AKIYOSHI	PS 37	**KAMUI**	PS 41	**TAKANAWA**	PS 36
HIDAKA	PS 32	**KUNIMI**	PS 38	**TAKATSUKI**	PS 39
HIYAMA	PS 33	**KURAMA**	PS 44	**TOUMI**	PS 46
				TSURUGI	PS 34

Displacement, tons	166·2 to 164·4 standard; 169·4 normal
Dimensions, feet	100 pp; 111 oa × 20·8 × 5·5
Main engines	1 set diesels; 1 shaft; 690 to 700 bhp = 13·5 knots
Range, miles	1 200 at 12 knots

Hidaka was built by Azuma Shipbuilding Co. Laid down on 4 Oct 1961, launched on 2 Mar 1962 and completed on 23 Apr 1962. Both *Hiyama* and *Tsurugi* were completed in Mar 1963 by Hitachi Shipbuilding Co. *Kunimi* was built under the 1964 fiscal year programme by Hayashikane Shipbuilding & Engineering Co, Shimoneseki, laid down on 15 Nov 1964, launched on 19 Dec 1964 and completed on 15 Feb 1965. Three more local patrol ships were completed in 1965, two in 1966, two in 1967 and two in 1968.

ASHITAKA *1972, Japanese Maritime Safety Agency*

5 SPECIAL RESCUE TYPE

AKAGI PS 40

Displacement, tons	42
Dimensions, feet	78·8 oa × 17·8 ×3·2
Main engines	2 Mercedes Benz diesels; 2 200 bhp = 28 knots
Range, miles	350 at 21 knots

Completed by Hitachi Zosen Kanagawa in 1965.

TSUKUBA PS 31

Displacement, tons	65
Dimensions, feet	80·5 × 21·5 × 3·7
Main engines	2 Niigata diesels; 1 800 bhp = 18·4 knots trials
Range, miles	230 at 15 knots

Built by Hitachi Zosen, Kanagawa and completed on 30 May 1962.

ASAMA PS 47 **BIZAN** PS 42 **SHIRAMINE** PS 48

Displacement, tons	40 normal; *Shiramine* 48 normal
Dimensions, feet	80·5 × 18·3 × 2·8
Guns	1 MG aft
Main engines	2 Mitsubishi diesels; 1 140 bhp = 21·6 knots; *Shiramine*, 2 Benz diesels; 2 200 bhp = 25 knots
Range, miles	400 at 18 knots; *Shiramine* 250 at 25 knots

Bizan and *Asama* were built by Shimonoseki Shipyard & Engine Works, Mitsubishi Heavy Industries Ltd. Completed in Mar 1966 and in Feb 1969 respectively. *Shiramine* was built by the same shipyard and completed in Dec 1969. Of light metal construction.

SHIRAMINE *1972, Japanese Maritime Safety Agency*

The small patrol vessel *Kabashima*, PS 100, was scrapped in 1970. Of this group *Fujitaka*, PS 151, and *Hayabusa*, PS 153, were deleted from the list in 1965, and *Komadori*, PS 152, in 1966.

The six small patrol vessels of the "Kawachidori" type, *Asachidori*, *Hamachidori*, *Haruchidori*, *Miochidori*, *Sawachidori* and *Tomochidori* were officially deleted from the list in 1969. Previous disposals were *Namichidori* and *Sayochidori* in 1965, *Okichidori* and *Shimachidori* in 1966, *Kawachidori*, *Musachidori* and *Iwachidori* in 1967 and *Wakachidori* and *Isochidori* in 1968.

FIRE FIGHTING CRAFT

3 "HIRYU" CLASS

HIRYU FL 01 | **NANRYU** FL 03 | **SHYORYU** FL 02

Displacement, tons	251 normal
Dimensions, feet	90·2 oa × 34·1 × 7·2
Main engines	2 sets diesels; 2 200 bhp = 13·5 knots
Range, miles	395 at 13·4 knots
Complements	14

Hiryu, a catamaran type fire boat, was built by Nippon Kokan Kabushiki Kaisha, Asano Dockyard. Laid down in Oct 1968, launched in Feb 1969 and completed in Mar 1969. Designed and built for fire fighting services to large tankers. Seven water nozzles (6 000 l/min × 2, 3 000 l/min × 4 and 1 800 l/min × 1) are installed and fire extinguishing foamy liquid of 14·5 cubic metres is carried and to be discharged from these nozzles. A sister ship, *Shoryu* was completed in Mar 1970, and a third vessel *Nanryu*, in Mar 1971, both at the same Asano dockyard.

HIRYU *1970, Japanese Maritime Safety Agency*

PATROL CRAFT

7 "SHINONOME" CLASS, 3 "HANAYUKI" CLASS

ASAGUMO	PC 34	**ISOYUKI**	PC 39	**NATSUGUMO**	PC 35
HANAYUKI	PC 37	**MAKIGUMO**	PC 32	**SHINONOME**	PC 30
HATAGUMO	PC 31	**MINEYUKI**	PC 38	**TATSUGUMO**	PC 36
				YAEGUMO	PC 33

Displacement, tons	43 to 46 normal (*Hanayuki* 37 to 40)
Dimensions, feet	69 × 17·2 × 3·2 (*Hatagumo, Makigumo, Shinonome, Yaegumo, Asagumo, Natsugumo, Tatsugumo*) 68·9 oa × 16·7 × 3·1 (*Hanayuki, Mineyuki, Isoyuki*)
Main engines	2 diesels; 1 400 bhp = 20 knots 2 diesels; 1 000 bhp = 18·8 knots (*Shinonome*) 2 diesels; 1 500 bhp = 21 knots (*Hanayuki* class)
Complement	9 to 10

Isoyuki on 29 Feb 1960, *Hanayuki* and *Mineyuki* in Mar 1959, *Asagumo* on 15 Mar 1955, *Natsugumo* on 31 Mar 1955, *Tatsugumo* on 31 May 1955 and the others before Oct 1954. Of light alloy framework and wooden hulls.

HANAYUKI *1970, Japanese Maritime Safety Agency*

14 "MATSUYUKI" CLASS, 5 "SHIKINAMI" CLASS

ASAGIRI	PC 47	**KOMAYUKI**	PC 45	**SHIMAYUKI**	PC 41
HAMAGIRI	PC 48	**MATSUNAMI**	PC 53	**TAKANAMI**	PC 58
HAMANAMI	PC 52	**MATSUYUKI**	PC 40	**TAMAYUKI**	PC 42
HAMAYUKI	PC 43	**SAGIRI**	PC 49	**TOMONAMI**	PC 55
HAYAGIRI	PC 51	**SETOGIRI**	PC 50	**UMIGIRI**	PC 46
ISENAMI	PC 57	**SHIKINAMI**	PC 54	**WAKANAMI**	PC 56
				YAMAYUKI	PC 44

Displacement, tons	40 for 41-47 and 49-51, 51 for 48, 57 for 52, 55 for 53, 44 for 54-58
Dimensions, feet	65·6 wl × 16·7 × 3·2 (73·8 × 19·0 × 43·0 for PC 53)
Guns	One 13 mm AA
Main engines	Two Mercedes Benz diesels; 2 200 bhp = 25·8 knots; PC 48 1 140 bhp = 14·6 knots; PC 52 = 21·8 knots; PC 53 = 20·8 knots
Range, miles	About 500 miles at near maximum speed
Complement	10

Since 1964 two or three craft of this type have been built per year by Hitachi Kanagawa Factory. PC's 40-47 and 49-51 were built of light alloy frames with wooden hulls. PC's 48 and 52 were built of steel whilst PC's 53-58 (the last five termed *Shikinami* class) were built completely of light alloy. The resultant variations in speed are shown above.

SURVEYING VESSELS

AKASHI (HL 07)

Displacement, tons	1 420
Dimensions, feet	242·7 × 42·6 × 14·1
Main engines	2 diesels; 2 shafts; 3 200 bhp = 16 knots
Complement	65

Built by Nippon Steel Tube Co, Tsurumi. Laid down 21 Sep 1968, completed 25 Dec 1969.

SHOYO HL 01

Displacement, tons	2 000
Dimensions, feet	262·4 × 40·3 × 13·8
Main engines	2 Fuji V-12; 4 800 hp; 1 shaft = 17·4 knots
Complement	73

Built by Hitachi Zosen, Maizuru. Completed March 1972. Fully equipped for all types of hydrographic and oceanographic work.

TENYO HM 05

Displacement, tons	181
Dimensions, feet	95 × 19·2 × 9·2
Main engines	Diesels; 230 bhp = 10 knots
Range, miles	3 160 at 10 knots

HEIYO HM 04

Displacement, tons	69
Dimensions, feet	73·5 × 14·5 × 8
Main engines	Diesel; 150 bhp = 9 knots
Range, miles	670 at 9 knots

Completed by Shimuzu Dockyard of Nippon Kokan Kabushiki Kaisha in Mar 1955. There are 21 other smaller vessels of HS type ranging from 5 to 8 tons displacement.

MEIYO HL 03

Displacement, tons	486 normal
Measurements, tons	360 gross
Dimensions, feet	133 wl; 146 oa × 26·5 × 9·5
Main engines	1 set diesel; 700 bhp = 12 knots
Range, miles	5 000 at 11 knots
Complement	40

Built by Nagoya Shipbuilding & Engineering Co, Nagoya. Laid down on 14 Sep 1962, launched 22 Dec 1962 and completed 15 Mar 1963. Controllable pitch propeller. The old *Meiyo* (HL 01) was discarded on 1 Mar 1963 and replaced by the new *Meiyo*, HL 03.

MEIYO *1971, Maritime Safety Agency*

TAKUYO HL 02

Displacement, tons	880 standard; 930 normal
Dimensions, feet	185 pp; 192·8 wl × 31·2 × 10·7 normal
Main engines	2 sets diesels; 1 300 bhp = 14 knots max
Range, miles	8 000 at 12 knots

Built for the Maritime Safety Agency, by Niigata Engineering Co Ltd. Laid down on 19 May 1956, launched on 19 Dec 1956, and completed in March 1957.

TAKUYO *1971, Japanese Maritime Safety Agency*

KAIYO HM 06

Displacement, tons	378 normal
Dimensions, feet	132·5 wl; 146 oa ××26·5 × 7·8
Main engines	1 set diesels; 450 bhp = 12 knots
Range, miles	6 100 at 11 knots

Built by Nagoya Shipbuilding & Engineering Co, Nagoya. Completed on 14 Mar 1964. Rated as Medium Surveying Vessel. Controllable pitch propeller.

KAIYO *1972, Japanese Maritime Safety Agency*

TENDERS

WAKAKUSA *1971, Maritime Safety Agency*

WAKAKUSA LL 01

Displacement, tons	1 815
Dimensions, feet	204 × 32·2 × 19·1
Main engines	1 850 hp

Built by Hitachi Innoshima Dockyard in Mar 1946. Purchased from Osaka Shosen Kaisha, in Jan 1956. Rated as Navigation Aid Vessel (Lighthouse Supply Ship).

GINGA LL 12 **HOKUTO** LL 11 **KAIO** LL 13

Displacements, tons	500
Dimensions, feet	128·7 × 31·2 × 13·9
Main engines	2 diesels; 420 bhp = 11·26 knots
Range, miles	2 800 at 10 knots

The above three are not sister ships. The above particulars refer to *Ginga* which was built by Osaka Shipbuilding Co Ltd. Laid down on 11 Nov 1953, launched on 6 May 1954 and completed on 30 June 1954. Equipped with 15 ton derrick for laying buoys. Rated as Navigation Aid Vessels (Buoy Tenders). A photograph of *Ginga* appears in the 1955-56 to 1964-65 editions.

There are also 7 LMs (LM 101 to LM 109) and 15 navigation and buoy tenders for miscellaneous service.

GINGA *1971, Maritime Safety Agency*

MYOJO LM 11

Displacements, tons	318 normal
Dimensions, feet	78·8 pp; 87·1 oa × 39·4 × 8·8
Main engines	2 sets diesels; 600 bhp = 11·1 knots
Range, miles	3 679 at 10 knots

Built by Nippon Kokan Kabushiki Kaisha, Asano Dockyard. Laid down in Nov 1966, launched in Feb 1967 and delivered in Mar 1967. The first catamaran type buoy tender, propelled by controllable pitch propeller, this ship is employed in maintenance and position adjustment service to floating aids to navigation.

There are also 8 LM's for the same maintenance service, 87 LS's and 18 HS's. Eight LS class tenders were scrapped and eight replacements built, and one was purchased.

MYOJO *1970, Japanese Maritime Safety Agency*

UNDER WATER RESEARCH VESSEL

SHINKAI HU 06

Displacement, tons	91
Dimensions, feet	54·2 oa × 21·6 × 13
Main engines	1 set electric motor; 11 kW
Range, hours	4·6 at 2·3 knots
Complement	4

Laid down in Sep 1967, launched in Mar 1968 and completed in March 1969 by Kawasaki Heavy Industries Ltd. An underwater vehicle designed for making researches of biological and underground resources of the continental shelves. With a main propeller and two auxilary ones installed on each side of the hull, this ship can dive 2 000 feet and stay on the sea bed for sampling, observing and photographing.

SHINKAI *1970, Japanese Maritime Safety Agency*

COASTAL PATROL CRAFT

114 MOTOR LAUNCH TYPE

SOYOKAZE	CL 03	**HATAKAZE**	CL 17	**KOTOKAZE**	CL 31
SAWAKAZE	CL 04	**MATSUKAZE**	CL 18	**KITAKAZE**	CL 32
OKIKAZE	CL 05	**IWAKAZE**	CL 19	**ISOKAZE**	CL 33
YAMAKAZE	CL 06	**NATSUKAZE**	CL 20	**KISOKAZE**	CL 34
MINEKAZE	CL 07	**YUKEKAZE**	CL 21	**MICHIKAZE**	CL 35
UMIKAZE	CL 08	**SHIMAKAZE**	CL 22	**TSURUKAZE**	CL 36
NOKAZE	CL 09	**YUKAZE**	CL 23	**AMATSUKAZE**	CL 37
NUMAKAZE	CL 10	**YODOKAZE**	CL 24	**KUKIKAZE**	CL 38
KAWAKAZE	CL 11	**ASAKAZE**	CL 25	**SAGIKAZE**	CL 39
TANIKAZE	CL 12	**YAKAZE**	CL 26	**SHIOKAZE**	CL 40
HATSUKAZE	CL 13	**KIYAKAZE**	CL 27	**NIIKAZE**	CL 41
ARAKAZE	CL 14	**IYOKAZE**	CL 28	**TOMOKAZE**	CL 42
HARUKAZE	CL 15	**FUSAKAZE**	CL 29	**WAKAKAZE**	CL 43
SACHIKAZE	CL 16	**TACHIKAZE**	CL 30	and **CL 44-97 105-157**	

CL 03 to **CL 97** (95 boats) and **CL 105** to **CL 157** (19 boats)

For coastal patrol and rescue duties. *Arakaze* CL 14, of light alloy construction, was laid down in Nov 1953, launched in Feb 1954 and completed in Mar 1954. The others are of steel or wooden construction. Nineteen sister boats were built in 1971.

KUKIKAZE *1971, Maritime Safety Agency*

HARBOUR PATROL CRAFT

CS 06 to **CS 58** (35 boats) and **CS 100** to **CS 126** (14 boats)
For harbour patrol and seaward defence duties. Of various types and displacements. CS 01, 02, 03, 04, 05, 08, 10, 13, 17, 21, 28, 31, 34, 35, 36, 45 and 47 were scrapped. A photograph of this type, *Isagiku* CS 63, appears in the 1960-61 to 1964-65 editions.

SALVAGE CRAFT

FS 01 to **FS 07** (7 boats) for fire-fighting service, rescue and salvage duties.

UTILITY LAUNCHES

There are 14 local and miscellaneous boats of various sizes and employment.

KENYA

Establishment

The Kenya Navy, which is based in Mombasa, was inaugurated on 12 Dec 1964, the first anniversary of Kenya's independence.

Administration

Commander, Kenya Navy: Commander William Alan Edward Hall, RN

Personnel

1973: 300 officers and men

Mercantile Marine

Lloyd's Register of Shipping: 23 vessels of 21 857 tons gross

PATROL CRAFT

3 BRITISH VOSPER TYPE

CHUI P 3112 **NDOVU** P 3117 **SIMBA** P 3110

Displacement, tons	96 standard; 109 full load
Dimensions, feet	95 wl; 103 oa × 19·8 × 5·8
Guns	2—40 mm Bofors AA
Main engines	2 Paxman Ventura diesels; 2 800 bhp = 24 knots
Range, miles	1 000 at economical speed; 1 500 at 16 knots
Complement	23 (3 officers and 20 ratings)

The first ships specially built for the Kenya Navy. Designed and built by Vosper Ltd. Portsmouth. Ordered on 28 Oct 1964. *Simba* was launched on 9 Sep 1965 and completed on 23 May 1966. *Chui* was handed over on 7 July 1966 and *Ndovu* was handed over on 27 July 1966. All three left Portsmouth on 22 Aug 1966 and arrived at their base in Mombasa on 4 Oct 1966. Air conditioned. Fitted with modern radar communications equipment and roll damping fins. *Chui* means Leopard, *Ndovu* means Elephant, *Simba* means Lion.

SEAWARD DEFENCE BOAT
It was officially stated in Jan 1972 that the seaward defence boat of the British "Ford" class, *Nyati* (ex-HMS *Aberford*) P 3102, was sold in late 1971.

NDOVU *1970, Kenya Navy*

KHMER REPUBLIC

The Marine Royale Khmer was established on 1 March 1954 and became Marine Nationale Khmer on 9 October 1970.

Chief of Staff of Marine Nationale Khmere (MNK): Commodore Vong Sarendy

Personnel

1973: Navy 3 400 officers and men. Marine Corps: 2 000 officers and men

Mercantile Marine

1973: Lloyds' Register of Shipping: 2 vessels of 1 880 tons gross

PATROL VESSELS

2 Ex-US PC TYPE

E 311 (ex-*Flamberge, P 631*, ex-*PC 1086*) **E 312** (ex-*L'Inconstant, P 636*, ex-*PC 1171*)

Displacement, tons	325 standard; 400 full load
Dimensions, feet	170 wl; 173·7 oa × 23 × 6·5
Guns	1—3 in dp; 1—40 mm AA, 4—20 mm AA
Main engines	2 GM diesels, 2 shafts; 3 600 bhp = 18 knots
Oil fuel (tons)	62
Range, miles	2 300 at 18 knots; 6 000 at 10 knots
Complement	63

Former US submarine chasers of the PC type. Transferred from the US Navy to the French Navy in 1951 and served in Indo-China and again transferred to the Marine Nationale Khmer in 1955-56. Built of steel.

E 312

SUPPORT GUNBOATS

2 EX-US LSIL TYPE

P 111 (ex-*LSIL 9039*, ex-*LSIL 875*)

Displacement, tons	230 standard; 387 full load
Dimensions, feet	169 × 23·7 × 5·7
Guns	1—3 in; 1—40 mm AA; 2—20 mm AA
Main engines	2 GM diesels; 2 shafts; 1 000 bhp = 15 knots
Oil fuel (tons)	100
Range, miles	8 000 at 12 knots
Complement	58

Former US infantry landing ship of the LSIL type. Transferred from the US Navy to the French Navy, on 2 Mar 1951 and stationed in Indo-China; and again transferred to the Marine Nationale Khmer in 1957.

P 112 (ex-*Medecin Capitaine Le Gall*)

Displacement, tons	230 standard; 350 full load
Dimensions, feet	160 × 23 × 6
Guns	1—3 in; 5—20 mm AA
Main engines	2 GM diesels; 2 shafts; 1 800 bhp = 15 knots
Oil fuel	120 tons
Range, miles	8 000 at 12 knots
Complement	40

TORPEDO BOATS

2 Ex-YUGOSLAV 108 TYPE

VR 1 **VR 2**

Displacement, tons	55 standard; 60 full load
Dimensions, feet	69 pp; 78 oa × 21·3 × 7·8
Guns	1—40 mm AA; 4—12·7 mm MG
Tubes	2—21 in
Main engines	3 Packard petrol motors; 5 000 bhp = 36 knots
Complement	14

Torpedo boats presented by Yugoslavia in 1965 and numbered by the Cambodian Navy. Similar to US "Higgins" class.

PATROL BOATS

2 Ex-US AVR TYPE

VR 3 **VR 4**

Displacement, tons	30
Dimensions, feet	63 × 13 × 4·6
Guns	4—12·7 mm MG
Main engines	GM Diesel 500 bhp = 15 knots
Complement	12

3 Ex-CHINESE CPB TYPE

VP 1 **VP 2** **VP 3**

Displacement, tons	7·7 standard; 9·7 full load
Dimensions, feet	42 × 9 × 3·9
Guns	2—12·7 mm MG
Main engines	Diesel, 300 bhp = 20 knots
Complement	10

Coastal patrol boats transferred from the People's Republic of China in Jan 1968. A photograph of these in company appears in the 1969-70 edition.

1 Ex-HDML TYPE

VP 212 (*ex-VP 748*, ex-*HDML 1223*)

Displacement, tons	46 standard; 54 full load
Dimensions, feet	72 oa × 16 × 5·5
Guns	2—20 mm AA; 4—7·5 mm MG
Main engines	2 diesels; 2 shafts; 300 bhp = 10 knots
Complement	8

Former British harbour defence motor launch of the HDML type. Transferred from the British Navy to the French Navy in 1950 and again transferred from the French Navy to the Marine Nationale Khmere in 1956. VP 749 and VP 642 were discarded in 1968.

LANDING CRAFT

1 EDIC TYPE

T 916 (ex-*EDIC 606*)

Displacement, tons	292 standard; 650 full load
Dimensions, feet	193·5 × 39·2 × 4·5
Guns	1—81 mm mortar; 2—12·7 mm MG
Main engines	2 MGO diesels; 2 shafts; 1 000 bhp = 10 knots
Complement	16 (1 officer, 15 men)

Completed and transferred from the French Government in Aug 1969.

2 Ex-US LCU TYPE

T 914 (ex-USS *LCU 783*) **T 915** (ex-USS *LCU 1421*)

Displacement, tons	180 standard, 360 full load
Dimensions, feet	115 wl; 119 oa × 34 × 6
Guns	2—20 mm AA
Main engines	3 diesels; 3 shafts; 675 bhp = 8 knots
Complement	12

Former US utility landing craft of the LCU type. LCU 783 and LCU 1421 were transferred on 31 May 1962. T 919 (ex-USS *LCU* 1577) was sunk by a mine on 5 May 1970. Former LCT(6)s 9085 (ex-622) and 9091 (ex-720) were deleted from the list in 1969, with ex-LCU 9073 (ex-USS *LCU* 1420). All now believed deleted.

Landing Craft—*continued*

T 913 — *1969, Marine Nat. Khmere*

TUG

PINGOUIE R 911 (ex-USS *YTL* 556)

KUWAIT

Personnel

1973: 200 (Coastguard)

Mercantile Marine

Lloyd's Register of Shipping: 164 vessels of 656 403 tons gross

PATROL BOATS

10 "78 ft" TYPE

AL-SALEMI **AL-SHURTI** **AL-MUBARAKI** **AMAN** **INTISAR** **MARZOOK** **MASHHOOR** **MAYMOON** **MURSHED** **WATHAH**

Displacement, tons	40
Dimensions, feet	78 oa × 15·5 × 4·5 mean
Main engines	2 Rolls Royce 8-cylinder 90° V form marine diesels; 1 340 shp at 1 800 rpm, 1 116 shp at 1 700 rpm = 20 knots
Guns	1 MG
Range, miles	700 at 15 knots
Complement	12 (5 officers, 7 men)

INTISAR — *1972, Vosper Thornycroft*

Patrol Boats—*continued*

Two were built by Thornycroft before the merger and six by Vosper afterwards (first two of which were ordered from the Group on 12 Sep 1966). Designed and built by John I. Thornycroft & Co Ltd, Woolston, Southampton. *Al-Salemi* and *Al-Mubaraki* were ordered in Aug 1965 and shipped to Kuwait on 8 Sep 1966. Specially designed for operational duties in the Arabian Gulf. Hulls are of welded steel construction, with superstructures of aluminium alloy. Twin hydraulically operated rudders, giving good manoeuvrability. Decca type D 202 radar. Two Lister Blackstone air-cooled diesel generators, 220 volts.

The later boats are slightly different in appearance with modified superstructure and funnel suppressed; see photograph of *Intisar*.

PATROL LAUNCHES

Built by the Singapore Yard of Thornycroft (Malaysia) Limited, now the Tanjong Rhu, Singapore, Yard of Vosper Thornycroft Private Ltd. Known as 50-foot patrol craft. Completed in 1962.

8 "35 ft" TYPE

Built by Vosper Thornycroft Private Ltd, Singapore. Of double-skinned teak construction with twin turbo-charged Perkins diesels they are capable of 24 knots. Ordered July 1972.

"35 ft" type — *1972, Vosper Thornycroft*

LANDING CRAFT

Two 88-ft landing craft have been built for the Ministry of the Interior, Kuwait by Vosper Thornycroft Private Ltd, Singapore.

KOREA (North)

Administration

Commander of the Navy: Rear Admiral Yu Chang Kwon

Personnel

1973: 12 000 officers and men

Mercantile Marine

Lloyd's Register of Shipping 12 vessels of 50 556 tons gross

SUBMARINES

4 Ex-SOVIET "W" CLASS

Displacement, tons	1 030 surface; 1 180 submerged
Dimensions, feet	248·5 × 19·1 × 15
Tubes	6—21 in (4 bow, 2 stern); 18 torpedoes carried normally (or up to 40 mines)
Main engines	diesels: 4 000 bhp = 17 knots surface; Electric motors: 2 500 hp = 15 knots submerged; 2 shafts
Range, miles	13 000 at 8 knots
Complement	60

CORVETTES

10 SOVIET "SO-1" CLASS

Displacement, tons	215 light; 250 normal
Dimensions, feet	147 oa × 20 × 10
Guns	4—25 mm (2 twin)
A/S weapons	4 five barrelled launchers
Main engines	3 diesels; 3 500 bhp = 26 knots

Soviet designed craft similar to the "SO-1" class steel hulled submarine chasers.

"SO-1" Type — *1971*

4 PATROL TYPE

Displacement, tons	*circa* 130
Dimensions, feet	Length 100

Small craft for seaward defence and local duties, rated as submarine chasers. The two patrol vessels of the ex-Soviet "Artillerist" type and the four patrol launches of the ex-Soviet "MO I" type were deleted from the list in 1971-72.

LIGHT FORCES

4 Ex-SOVIET "OSA" CLASS MISSILE BOATS

Displacement, tons	165 standard, 200 full load
Dimensions, feet	123·0 × 27·9 × 5·9
Missile launchers	4 in two pairs abreast for *Styx* missiles
Guns	4—30 mm (2 twin forward, 1 aft)
Main engines	3 diesels; 13 200 bhp = 38 knots

The combination of the "Osa" flotilla and the "Komar" units (below), both armed with the very potent 15 mile range "Styx" missiles, provides a powerful striking force on the South Korean border and within 250 miles of Japan.

6 Ex-SOVIET "KOMAR" CLASS MISSILE BOATS

Displacement, tons	75 standard; 100 full load
Dimensions, feet	83·7 × 21·0 × 4·9
Missile launchers	2 for "Styx" missiles
Guns	2—25 mm AA (1 twin forward)
Main engines	4 diesels; 4 shafts; 4 800 bhp = 40 knots

See note under "Osa" type above.

12 "SHANGHAI" CLASS GUNBOATS

Displacement, tons	120 full load
Dimensions, feet	128·6 × 18 × 5·5
Guns	4—37 mm (2 twin); 4—25 mm (2 twin)
Main engines	4 diesels; 5 000 bhp = 30 knots
Range, miles	800 at 17 knots
Complement	25

Fast patrol boats or motor gunboats reported acquired from China in 1967.

4 "SWATOW" CLASS GUNBOATS

Displacement, tons	67
Dimensions, feet	83·5 × 20 × 6
Guns	4—37 mm; 2—12·7 mm
A/S weapons	8 DC
Main engines	4 diesels 4 800 bhp = 40 knots
Complement	17

7 MGB TYPE

Reported to have been incorporated into the North Korean Navy since 1 Jan 1967.

4 PTG TYPE

Larger vessels of the patrol gunboat type reported to have been acquired in 1967-68.

20 LIGHT GUNBOATS

Believed to be for inshore patrols.

3 PTF TYPE TORPEDO BOATS

Displacement, tons	160 approx
Dimensions, feet	120 approx length
Guns	4

Commissioned 1967-68.

10 Ex-SOVIET "P 6" CLASS TORPEDO BOATS

Displacement, tons	66 standard; 75 full load
Dimensions, feet	84·2 × 20 × 6
Guns	4—25 mm
Torpedo tubes	2—21 in (or mines or DC)
Main engines	diesels; 4 800 hp; 4 shafts = 45 knots
Complement	25

40 Ex-SOVIET "P 4" CLASS TORPEDO BOATS

Displacement, tons	50
Dimensions, feet	85·5 × 20 × 6
Guns	4—25 mm AA
Main engines	diesels; 2 000 bhp = 42 knots

Former Soviet motor torpedo boats. Built in 1951-57. Aluminium hulls.

"P-4" Type *1971*

KOREA (REPUBLIC OF)

Administration

Chief of Naval Operations:
Rear Admiral Kyu-Sop Kim

Vice Chief of Naval Operations:
Rear Admiral Su-Kap Cha

Commander-in-Chief of Fleet:
Commodore Yun-Kyong Oh

Personnel

1972: 18 900 (2 400 officers and 16 500 enlisted men) in Navy; 29 600 (2 300 officers and 27 300 enlisted men) in Marine Corps

Strength of the Fleet

5 Destroyers
4 Frigates (3 Destroyer Escort Type)
6 Escort Transports
15 Patrol Vessels
21 Patrol Boats
12 Coastal Minesweepers
8 Tank Landing Ships
12 Medium Landing Ships
1 Survey Ship
13 Fleet Support Ships

Diplomatic Representation

Naval Attache in London:
Colonel Tong-Lo Kim (Air Force)

Naval Attache in Paris
Colonel Sang-Kil Sin (Army)

Naval Attache in Washington:
Captain Ki-Kyong Hong (Navy)

Mercantile Marine

Lloyd's Register of Shipping:
446 vessels of 1 057 408 tons gross

DESTROYERS

2 Ex-US "GEARING" CLASS

Name	*No.*	*Launched*	*US Comm*	*Transferred*
CHUNG BUK (ex-USS *Chevalier*, DD 805)	DD 95	29 Oct 1944	9 Jan 1945	5 July 1972
JEONG BUK (ex-USS *Everett F. Larson*, DD 830)	DD 96	28 Jan 1945	6 Apr 1945	30 Oct 1972

Displacement, tons	2 425 standard; approx 3 500 full load
Length, feet (*metres*)	383 (*116·7*) wl; 390·5 (*119·0*) oa
Beam, feet (*metres*)	40·9 (*12·4*)
Draught, feet (*metres*)	19 (*5·8*)
Guns	6—5 inch (*127 mm*) 38 cal DP (twin)
A/S weapons	6—12·75 inch (*324 mm*) torpedo tubes (Mk 32 triple); 2 fixed hedgehogs
Main engines	2 geared turbines (General Electric); 60 000 shp; 2 shafts
Boilers	4 (Babcock & Wilcox)
Speed, knots	34
Complement	approx 275

Former US "Gearing" class destroyers. Both ships built by Bath Iron Works Corp, Bath, Maine.
These ships were converted to radar picket destroyers (DDR) in 1949; subsequently modernised under the US Navy's Fleet Rehabilitation and Modernisation (FRAM II) programme. Fitted with small helicopter hangar and flight deck. Anti-ship torpedo tubes and secondary gun armament have been removed.

JEONG BUK (as USS *Everett F. Larson*) *1972, United States Navy*

ELECTRONICS. These ships have SPS-40 and SPS-10 search radars on their tripod mast. Fitted with SQS-29 series hull-mounted sonar.

Destroyers—*continued*

3 Ex-US "FLETCHER" CLASS

Name	*No.*	*Launched*	*US Comm.*	*Transferred*
CHUNG MU (ex-USS *Erben*, DD 631)	DD 91	21 Mar 1943	28 May 1943	1 May 1963
SEOUL (ex-USS *Halsey Powell*, DD 686)	DD 92	30 June 1943	25 Oct 1943	15 Nov 1968
PUSAN (ex-USS *Hickox*, DD 590)	DD 93	4 July 1943	10 Sep 1943	27 Apr 1968

Displacement, tons: 2 050 standard; 3 050 full load
Length, feet (*metres*): 360 (*110·3*) wl; 376·5 (*114·8*) oa
Beam, feet (*metres*): 39·6 (*12·0*)
Draught, feet (*metres*): 18 (*5·5*)
Guns: 5—5 inch (*127 mm*) 38 cal DP; 10—40 mm AA (2 quad, 1 twin) except *Seoul* (none)
A/S weapons: 6—12·75 inch (*324 mm*) torpedo tubes (Mk 32 triple); 2 hedgehogs depth charges
Main engines: Geared turbines (General Electric); 60 000 shp; 2 shafts
Boilers: 4 (Babcock & Wilcox)
Speed, knots: 35
Complement: approx 320

Former US "Fletcher" class destroyers. *Chung Mu* built by Bath Iron Works, Bath, Maine; *Seoul* built by Bethlehem Steel, Staten Island, New York; *Pusan* built by Federal Shipbuilding, Kearny, New Jersey.
Tripod masts have been fitted to support larger radar antennas; the two 21 inch quintuple torpedo tube mounts originally fitted have been removed as have the 20 mm light anti-aircraft guns.

ELECTRONICS. SPS-10 and SPS-6 search radars are fitted.

SEOUL *1968, United States Navy*

FRIGATES

1 Ex-US "RUDDEROW" CLASS

Name	*No.*	*Launched*	*US Comm.*	*Transferred*
CHUNG NAM (ex-USS *Holt*, DE 706)	DE 73	15 Feb 1944	9 June 1944	19 June 1963

Displacement, tons: 1 450 standard; 1 890 full load
Length, feet (*metres*): 300 (*91·5*) wl; 306 (*83·2*) oa
Beam, feet (*metres*): 37 (*11·3*)
Draught, feet (*metres*): 14 (*4·3*)
Guns: 2—5 inch (*127 mm*) 38 cal DP; 4—40 mm AA (twin)
A/S weapons: 6—12·75 inch (*324 mm*) torpedo tubes (Mk 32 triple) 1 hedgehog; depth charges
Main engines: Turbo-electric drive (General Electric geared turbines); 12 000 shp; 2 shafts
Boilers: 2 (Combustion Engineering)
Speed, knots: 24
Complement: approx 210

Former US destroyer escort of the TEV design. Built by Defoe Shipbuilding, Bay City, Michigan. Triple 21 inch torpedo tube mount originally fitted was removed shortly after completion.

ELECTRONICS. SPS-5 and SPS-6 search radars are fitted.

CHUNG NAM *1971, Korean Navy*

2 Ex-US "BOSTWICK" CLASS

Name	*No.*	*Launched*	*US Comm.*	*Transferred*
KYONG KI (ex-USS *Muir*, DE 770)	DE 71	4 June 1944	30 Aug 1944	Feb 1956
KANG WON (ex-USS *Sutton*, DE 771)	DE 72	6 Aug 1944	22 Dec 1944	Feb 1956

Displacement, tons: 1 265 standard; 1 700 full load
Length, feet (*metres*): 300 (*91·5*) wl; 306 (*93·3*) oa
Beam, feet (*metres*): 36·6 (*11·2*)
Draught, feet (*metres*): 14 (*4·3*)
Guns: 3—3 inch (*76 mm*) 50 cal AA; 6—40 mm AA (twin); 4—20 mm AA (single)
A/S weapons: 6—12·75 inch (*324 mm*) torpedo tubes (Mk 32 triple); 1 hedgehog; depth charges
Main engines: Diesel-electric (4 General Motors diesels); 6 000 bhp; 2 shafts
Speed, knots: 21
Complement: approx 210

Former US destroyer escort of DET design. Built by Tampa Shipbuilding, Tampa, Florida. Triple 21 inch torpedo tube mount originally fitted was removed shortly after completion. Refitted at Pearl Harbour, Hawaii, in 1964, being provided with tripod masts to support improved radar antennas; also fitted with more modern sonar and anti-submarine weapons.

ELECTRONICS. Fitted with SPS-6 and SPS-5 search radars.

KYONG KI *1971, Korean Navy*

Ex-US "TACOMA" CLASS

All Ships of this type have been stricken from the Korean Navy.

Former US "Tacoma" class patrol frigate, similar in desgn to the British "River" class. Built by Kaiser Co, Richmond, California, as Maritime Commission type S2-S2-AQ1.

Apnok (PF 62, ex-USS *Rockford*, PF 48), transferred to South Korea in 1950, was damaged in a collision on 21 May 1952; returned to US Navy and sunk as target in 1953. *Du Man* (PF 61, ex-USS *Muskogee*, PF 49) *Nak Tong* (PF 65, ex-USS *Hoquiam*, PF 5), *Tae Tong* (PF 63 ex-USS *Tacoma*, PF 3), and *Im Chin* (PF 66, ex-USS *Sausalito*, PF 4), transferred to South Korea in 1950-1952, scrapped in 1972-1973.

Ex-USS *Pasco* (PF 6) and *Gloucester* (PF 22) were towed from storage in Japan to Korea for spare parts cannibalisation.

See 1972-1973 and previous editions for characteristics and photographs.

ESCORT TRANSPORTS

6 Ex-US APD TYPE

Name	No.	Launched	US Comm.	Transferred
KYONG NAM (ex-USS *Cavallaro*, APD 128)	APD 81	15 June 1944	13 Mar 1945	Oct 1959
AH SAN (ex-USS *Harry L. Corl*, APD 108)	APD 82	1 Mar 1944	5 June 1945	June 1966
UNG PO (ex-*Julius A. Raven*, APD 110)	APD 83	3 Mar 1944	28 June 1945	June 1966
KYONG PUK (ex-USS *Kephart*, APD 61)	APD 85	6 Sep 1943	7 Jan 1944	Aug 1967
JONNAM (ex-USS *Hayter*, APD 80)	APD 86	11 Nov 1943	16 Mar 1944	Aug 1967
CHR JU (ex-*William M. Hobby*, APD 95)	APD 87	11 Feb 1944	4 Apr 1945	Aug 1967

Displacement, tons	1 400 standard; 2 130 full load
Length, feet (*metres*)	300 (*91·4*) wl; 306 (*93·3*) oa
Beam, feet (*metres*)	37 (*11·3*)
Draught, feet (*metres*)	12·6 (*3·2*)
Guns	1—5 inch (*127 mm*) 38 cal DP 6—40 mm AA (twin)
A/S weapons	depth charges
Main engines	Turbo-electric (General Electric turbines); 12 000 shp; 2 shafts
Boilers	2 (Foster Wheeler "D" Express)
Speed, knots	23·6
Complement	approx 200
Troop capacity	approx 160

All begun as destroyers escorts (DE), but converted during construction or after completion to high-speed transports (APD). APD 81 built by Defoe Shipbuilding Co. Bay City, Michigan; APD 82 and APD 83 by Bethlehem, Shipbuilding Co. Hingham, Massachusetts; APD 85-87 by Charleston Navy Yard, South Carolina.
In Korean service four latter ships originally rated as gunboats (PG); changed in 1972 to APD. All are fitted to carry approximately 160 troops.

PHOTOGRAPHS. Note davits aft of funnel for carrying four LCVP-type landing craft or other small boats. Two different configurations: ex-APD 37 class with high bridge and lattice mast supporting 10-ton capacity boom; ex-APD 87 class with low bridge and tripod mast supporting 10-ton capacity boom.

KYONG NAM

PATROL VESSELS

1 Ex-US "ASHEVILLE" CLASS

PAEK KU (ex-USS *Benicia*, PG 96) PGM 11 20 Dec 1969

Displacement, tons	225 standard; 245 full load
Dimensions, feet	164·5 oa × 23·8 × 9·5
Guns	1—3 inch (*76 mm*) 50 cal AA (forward); 1—40 mm AA (aft); 4—·50 cal MG (twin)
Main engines	CODAG: 2 diesels (Cummins); 1 450 bhp; 2 shafts = 16 knots; 1 gas turbine (General Electric); 13 300 shp; 2 shafts = 40+ knots
Complement	approx 25

Former US "Asheville" class patrol gunboat Built by Tacoma Boatbuilding Co, Tacoma, Washington; launch date above; commissioned in US Navy on 25 Apr 1970; transferred to ROK Navy on 15 Oct 1971 and arrived in Korea in January 1972. This is the first ship of the class to be transferred to a foreign navy by the United States. See United States section for design, engineering, and gunnery notes. No anti-submarine sensors or weapons are fitted.

MISSILES. During 1971, while in US Navy service, this ship was fitted experimentally with one launcher for the Standard surface-to-surface missile. The box-like container/launcher held two missiles. See 1971-1972 edition for additional photo of *Benicia* in missile configuration (page 706); view below shows Standard missile containers aft, and 3 inch gun trained aft.

PAEK KU (as USS BENICIA) *1971, United States Navy*

3 Ex-US "AUK" CLASS MSF TYPE

SHIN SONG (ex-USS *Ptarmigan*, MSF 376)	PCE 1001	15 July 1944
SUNCHON (ex-USS *Speed*, MSF 116)	PCE 1002	18 Apr 1942
KOJE (ex-USS *Dextrous*, MSF 341)	PCE 1003	17 Jan 1943

Displacement, tons	890 standard; 1 250 full load
Dimensions, feet	215 wl; 221·2 oa × 32·2 × 10·8
Guns	2—3 inch (*76 mm*) 50 cal AA (single); 4—40 mm AA (twin); 4—20 mm AA (twin)
A/S weapons	3—12·75 inch (*324 mm*) torpedo tubes (Mk 32 triple); 1 hedgehog; depth charges
Main engines	Diesel-electric (General Motors diesels); 3 532 bhp; 2 shafts = 18 knots
Complement	approx 110

Former US Navy minesweepers (originally designated AM). Built by Savannah Machine & Foundry Co, Savannah, Georgia; American SB Co, Lorain, Ohio; and Gulf SB Corp. Madisonville, Texas, respectively. Launch dates above; PCE 1001 commissioned in US Navy on 15 Jan 1944, PCE 1002 on 15 Oct 1942, and PCE 1003 on 8 Sep 1943; PCE 1001 transferred to ROK Navy in July 1963, PCE 1002 in Nov 1967, and PCE 1003 in Dec 1967.
Upon transfer the minesweeping gear was removed and a second 3 inch gun fitted aft; additional anti-submarine weapons also fitted.

SUNCHON *1969*

8 Ex-US 185-ft PCE TYPE

KO JIN (ex-USS *Report*, MSF 289)	PCEC 50	8 Aug 1944
RO RYANG (ex-USS PCEC 882)	PCEC 51	3 Dec 1943
MYONG RYANG (ex-USS PCEC 896)	PCEC 52	22 May 1943
HAN SAN (ex-USS PCEC 873)	PCEC 53	5 May 1943
OK PO (ex-USS PCEC 898)	PCEC 55	3 Aug 1943
PYOK PA (ex-USS *Dania*, PCE 870)	PCE 57	27 Feb 1943
RYUL PO (ex-USS *Somerset*, PCE 892)	PCE 58	1 May 1943
SA CHON (ex-USS *Batesburg*, PCE 903)	PCE 59	6 Sep 1943

Displacement, tons	640 standard; 950 full load
Dimensions, feet	180 wl; 184·5 oa × 33 × 9·5
Guns	1—3 inch (*76 mm*) 50 cal AA; 6—40 mm AA (twin) except *Ko Jin* only 4—40 mm; 4 or 8—20 mm AA (single or twin)
A/S weapons	1 hedgehog (except *Ko Jin*); depth charges
Main engines	Diesels (General Motors); 2 000 bhp; 2 shafts = 15 knots
Complement	approx 100

OK PO *1969*

Patrol Vessels—*continued*

Former US Navy patrol craft. Launch dates above. Four units had been modified in US service as "control" ships (PCEC) for operation with landing craft, being fitted with additional communications equipment in an enlarged bridge area.
The USS *Report* was transferred to the US Army after World War II for experimental work; refitted with additional electronic equipment and subsequently transferred to South Korea as *Ko Jin* (designated PCEC).
Ro Ryang and *Myong Ryang* transferred to South Korea in Feb 1955; *Han San* and *Ok Po* in Sep 1955; *Pyok Pa, Ryul Po,* and *Sa Chon* in Dec 1961.
Tang Po (PCE 56, ex-USS *Maria,* PCE 842) was sunk by North Korean coastal guns on 19 Jan 1967.

O TAE SAN *1961*

3 Ex-US 173-ft PC TYPE

O TAE SAN (ex-USS *Winnemuca,* PC 1145) PC 707 27 Oct 1943
KUM CHONG SAN (ex-USS *Grosse Point,* PC 1546) PC 708 30 Jan 1944
SOL AK (ex-USS *Chadron,* PC 564) PC 709 12 Apr 1942

Displacement, tons	280 standard; 450 full load
Dimensions, feet	170 wl; 173·66 oa × 23 × 10·8
Guns	1—3 inch (*76 mm*) 50 cal AA; 1—40 mm AA; 4—20 mm AA (single) reduced or removed from some units
A/S weapons	1 mousetrap; depth charges
Main engines	Diesels (General Motors in PC 707 and 708; Fairbanks Morse in PC 709); 2 880 bhp; 2 shafts = 20 knots
Complement	approx 70

Former US Navy patrol craft. Launch dates above. *Kum Chong San* and *Sol Ak* transferred to South Korea in Nov 1960; *O Tae San* in Jan 1964.
Pak Tu San PC 701 (ex-US Merchant Marine Academy *Ensign Whitehead,* ex-USS PC 823), *Kum Kang San* PC 702 (ex-USS PC 810), and *Sam Kak San* PC 703 (ex-USS PC 802) decommissioned in 1960 and scrapped; *Han Ra San* PC 705 (ex-USS PC 485) sunk in typhoon off Guam in Nov 1962, subsequently raised but scrapped in 1964; *Myo Hyang San* PC 706 (ex-USS PC 600) decommissioned in 1968 and scrapped.

Ex-US 136-ft PCS TYPE

The former US wood-hulled PCS type submarine chasers loaned to South Korea in 1952 have been returned to US custody and discarded: *Hwa Song* PCS 201 (ex-USS PCS 1426), *Kum Song* PCS 202 (ex-USS PCS 1445), *Mok Song* PCS 203 (ex-USS PCS 1446), and *Su Song* PCS 205 (ex-USS PCS 1448).

8 Ex-US COAST GUARD 95-ft TYPE

PB 3 (ex-USCGC *Cape Rosier,* WPB 95333)
PB 5 (ex-USCGC *Cape Sable,* WPB 95334)
PB 6 (ex-USCGC *Cape Providence,* WPB 95335)
PB 8 (ex-USCGC *Cape Porpoise,* WPB 95327)
PB 9 (ex-USCGC *Cape Falcon,* WPB 95330)
PB 10 (ex-USCGC *Cape Trinity,* WPB 95331)
PB 11 (ex-USCGC *Cape Darby,* WPB 95323)
PB 12 (ex-USCGC *Cape Kiwanda,* WPB 95329)

Displacement, tons	98 full load
Dimensions, feet	95 oa × 19 × 6
Guns	1—·50 cal MG/1—81 mm mortar; 2—·30 cal MG
Main engines	4 diesels (General Motors); 2 200 bhp; 2 shafts = 20 knots max
Complement	13

Former US Coast Guard steel-hulled patrol craft. Built in 1958-1959. Nine units transferred to South Korea in Sep 1968. PB 7 (ex-USCGC *Cape Florida,* WPB 95325) stricken after grounding in May 1971.
Combination machinegun/mortar mount is forward; single light machineguns are aft. See US Coast Guard listings for additional details.

PB 5

1 COASTAL PATROL AND INTERDICTION CRAFT

Displacement, tons	approx 70 full load
Dimensions, feet	99·1 oa × 18 × 6
Guns	light cannon and machine guns planned; see notes
Main engines	3 gas turbines (Avco Lycoming TF 35); 5 400 hp; 3 shafts = 40+ knots maximum; 2 diesels (300 bhp) with outboard drive for low-speed cruising

The prototype Coastal Patrol and Interdiction Craft (CPIC) sponsored by the US Navy was constructed by Tacoma Boatbuilding, Tacoma, Washington; after completion in mid-1973 the craft was to undergo brief trials for the US Navy and then transfer to South Korea.

The CPIC was designed to intercept infiltration attempts into South Korea and other nations with long and vulnerable coastlines. Plans for additional craft for US and foreign use are under study. See United States section for preliminary drawing. Twin 30 mm rapid-fire gun mount planned for these craft reportedly is encountering development problems.

9 65-ft SEWART TYPE

FB 1 **FB 2** **FB 3** **FB 5** **FB 6** **FB 7** **FB 8** **FB 9** **FB 10**

Displacement, tons	33 full load
Dimensions, feet	65 oa × 16
Guns	2—20 mm (single)
Main engines	3 diesels (General Motors 12V71); 1 590 bhp; 3 shafts = 25 knots
Complement	5

These craft were built in the United States by Sewart. The design is adapted from a commercial 65-foot craft. Referred to as "Toksuuri" No. 1 through 10 by the South Koreans (with the No. 4 being considered unlucky and not assigned). Transferred to South Korea in August 1967.

FB 10 on marine railway

4 US 40-ft SEWART TYPE

SB 1 **SB 2** **SB 3** **SB 5**

Displacement, tons	9·25 full load
Dimensions, feet	40 oa × 12 × 3
Guns	1—·50 cal MG; 2—·30 cal MG
Main engines	2 diesels (General Motors); 500 bhp; 2 shafts = 31 knots
Complement	7

These are aluminium-hulled craft built in the United States by Sewart. Transferred to South Korea in 1964. No. 4 not assigned.

MOTOR TORPEDO BOATS

Ol Pe Mi (ex-USS PT 812) stricken in 1969; *Kal Mae Ki* (ex-USS PT 616) stricken in 1969. Latter craft returned to United States for use as a memorial.

KO CHANG —see following page *Korean Navy*

COASTAL MINESWEEPERS

8 Ex-US MSC TYPE

KUM SAN (ex-US MSC 284) MSC 522
KO HUNG (ex-US MSC 285) MSC 523
KUM KOK (ex-US MSC 286) MSC 525
NAM YANG (ex-US MSC 295) MSC 526
NA DONG (ex-US MSC 296) MSC 527
SAM CHOK (ex-US MSC 316) MSC 528
(ex-US MSC 320) MSC 529
(ex-US MSC 321) MSC 530

Displacement, tons	320 light; 370 full load
Dimensions, feet	144 oa × 28 × 8·2
Guns	2—20 mm AA
Main engines	2 diesels; 1 200 bhp; 2 shafts = 14 knots
Complement	approx 40

"Bluebird" class coastal minesweepers built by the United States specifically for transfer under the Military Aid Programme. Wood hulled with non-magnetic metal fittings.
Kum San transferred to South Korea in June 1959, *Ko Hung* in Sep 1959, *Kum Kok* in Nov 1959, *Nam Yang* in Sep 1963, *Ha Dong* in Nov 1963, and *Sam Chok* in July 1968.

Two additional units under construction at Peterson Builders, Sturgeon Bay, Wisconsin, in 1973.

KUM SAN *1967, Korean Navy*

4 Ex-US YMS TYPE

KWANG CHU (ex-USS YMS 413) MSC 503
KUM HWA (ex-USS *Curlew*, MSCO 8, ex-AMS 8, ex-YMS 218) MSC 519
KIM PO (ex-USS *Kite*, MSCO 22, ex-AMS 22, ex-YMS 375) MSC 520
KO CHANG (ex-USS *Mockingbird*, MSCO 27, ex-AMS 27, ex-YMS 419) MSC 521

Displacement, tons	270 standard; 350 full load
Dimensions, feet	136 oa × 24·5 × 8
Guns	1—40 mm AA; 2—20 mm AA
Main engines	diesels; 1 000 bhp = 15 knots
Complement	approx 50

Former US Navy auxiliary motor minesweepers built 1941-1942. Wood hulled. *Kum Hwa, Kim Po*, and *Ko Chang* transferred to South Korea in Jan 1956.

Yong Kung MSC 518 (ex-US BYMS 8) scrapped in 1955, *Kil Chu* MSC 514 (ex-US BYMS 5) scrapped in 1959, *Kang Wha* MSC 508 (ex-USS YMS 245) lost in 1959, *Kim Chon* MSC 513 (ex-USS YMS 258) scrapped in 1968, *Ka Pyong* MSC 509 (ex-USS YMS 210) sunk in 1950, *Kupo* MSC 512 (ex-USS YMS 323) scrapped in 1956, *Kang Kyong* MSC 510 (ex-USS YMS 330) scrapped in 1963, *Ko Yung* MSC 515 (ex-USS BYMS 55) scrapped in 1959; *Kang Jim* MSC 501 (ex-USS YMS 354) scrapped in 1959, *Kyoung Chu* MSC 502 (ex-USS YMS 358) scrapped in 1962, *Ka Ya San* MSC 511 (ex-USS YMS 423) lost in 1949, *Kang Nung* MSC 507 (ex-YMS 463) scrapped in 1959, *Ko Won* MSC 517 (ex-US YMS type unnumbered) lost in 1948 *Kong City* MSC 516 (ex-US BYMS 6) sunk in 1950.

MINESWEEPING BOATS

MSB 1 (ex-US MSB 2)

Displacement, tons	30 light; 39 full load
Dimensions, feet	57·2 oa × 15·3 × 4
Guns	machineguns
Main engines	2 geared diesels (Packard); 600 bhp; 2 shafts = 12 knots

Former US Navy Minesweeping boat transferred on 1 Dec 1961. Wood hulled.

LANDING SHIPS

8 Ex-US LST TYPE

UN PONG	(ex-USS LST 1010)	LST 807	29 Mar 1944
DUK BONG	(ex-USS LST 227)	LST 808	21 Sep 1943
BI BONG	(ex-USS LST 218)	LST 809	20 July 1943
KAE BONG	(ex-USS *Berkshire County*, LST 288)	LST 810	7 Nov 1943
WEE BONG	(ex-USS *Johnson County*, LST 849)	LST 812	30 Dec 1944
SU YONG	(ex-USS *Kane County*, LST 853)	LST 813	17 Nov 1944
BUK HAN	(ex-USS *Lynn County*, LST 900)	LST 815	9 Dec 1944
HWA SAN	(ex-USS *Pender County*, LST 1080)	LST 816	2 May 1945

Displacement, tons	1 653 standard; 2 366 beaching; 4 080 full load
Dimensions, feet	316 wl; 328 oa × 50 × 14
Guns	10 or 8—40 mm AA
Main engines	diesels; 1 700 bhp; 2 shafts = 11·6 knots
Complement	approx 110

Former US Navy tank landing ships. Cargo capacity 2 100 tons. Launch dates above. *Un Bong* transferred to South Korea in Feb 1955, *Duk Bong* in Mar 1955, *Bi Bong* in May 1955, *Kae Bong* in Mar 1956, *Wee Bong* in Jan 1959, *Su Yong* and *Buk Han* in Dec 1958, and *Hwa San* in Oct 1958.

LSTs previously operated by South Korea and stricken were: ex-USS LST 120, ex-USS LST 213, *Dan Yang* ex-USS LST 343, ex-USS LST 378, ex-USS LST 380, *Ryong Pi* LST 806 ex-USS LST 388, *An Tong* LST 803 ex-USS LST 491 sunk in 1952, ex-USS LST 536, ex-USS LST 594, *Chon Po* LST 805 ex-USS LST 595, ex-USS LST 624 *Ryong Hwa* LST 801 ex-USS LST 659, *Lyung Wha* ex-USS LST 805.

1 Ex-US LSMR TYPE

SI HUNG (ex-USS *St Joseph River*, LSMR 527) LSMR 311

Displacement, tons	944 standard; 1 084 full load
Dimensions, feet	204·5 wl; 206·2 oa × 34·5 × 10
Guns	1—5 inch (*127 mm*) 38 cal DP; 2—40 mm AA; 4—20 mm AA
Rocket launchers	8 twin rapid-fire launchers for 5 inch rockets
Main engines	2 diesels (General Motors); 2 800 bhp; 2 shafts = 12·6 knots
Complement	approx 140

Former US Navy landing ship completed as a rocket-firing ship to support amphibious landing operations. Transferred to South Korea on 15 Sep 1960. Configuration differs from conventional LSM type with "island" bridge structure and 5 inch gun aft; no bow doors.

SI HUNG *1967, Korean Navy.*

11 Ex-US LSM TYPE

TAE CHO (ex-USS LSM 546) LSM 601
TYO TO (ex-USS LSM 268) LSM 602
KA TOK (ex-USS LSM 462) LSM 605
KO MUN (ex-USS LSM 30) LSM 606
PIAN (ex-USS LSM 96) LSM 607
PUNG TO (ex-USS LSM 54) LSML 608
WOL MI (ex-USS LSM 57) LSM 609
KI RIN (ex-USS LSM 19) LSM 610
NUNG RA (ex-USS LSM 84) LSM 611
SIN MI (ex-USS LSM 316) LSM 612
UL RUNG (ex-USS LSM 17) LSM 613

Displacement, tons	743 beaching; 1 095 full load
Dimensions, feet	196·5 wl; 203·5 oa × 34·6 × 8·5
Guns	2—40 mm AA (twin); several 20 mm AA
Main engines	2 diesels (direct drive; Fairbanks Morse except *Tyo To* General Motors); 2 800 bhp; 2 shafts = 12·5 knots
Complement	approx 60

TYO TO *1969*

DUK BONG

Landing Ships—*continued*

Ex-US LST TYPE — *continued*

Former US Navy medium landing ships. Built 1944-1945. LSM 601, 602, and 605 transferred to South Korea in 1955; others in 1956. *Sin Mi* served in Indochina as French L 9014 and *Ul Rung* as French L 9017 during 1954-1955; returned to United States in Oct 1955 and retransferred to South Korea in fall 1956.
Pung To serves as mine force flagship fitted with mine-laying rails and designated LSML. Arrangement of 20 mm guns differs; some ships have two single mounts adjacent to forward 40 mm mount on forecastle; other 20 mm guns along sides of cargo well.
Tok To LSM 603 (ex-USS LSM 419) scrapped in 1963.

1 Ex-US LCU TYPE

LCU 1 (ex-USS LCU 531)

Displacement, tons 309 full load
Dimensions, feet 105 wl; 119·1 oa × 32·66 × 5
Main engines diesels (Gray Marine); 675 bhp; 3 shafts = 10 knots

Former US Navy utility landing craft. Built in 1943 as LCT(6) 531. Transferred to South Korea in Dec 1960. No name assigned.

Po Song Man LSSL 109 (ex-USS LSSL 54), *Yung Hung Man* LSSL 107 (ex-USS LSSL 77), *Yong Il Man* LSSL 110 (ex-USS LSSL 84), and *Kang Hwa Man* LSSL 108 (ex-USS LSSL 91) have been scrapped.

REPAIR SHIPS

1 Ex-US ARL TYPE

TUK SU (ex-USS *Minotaur*, ARL 15, ex-LST 645) ARL 1

Displacement, tons 2 366 standard; 4 100 full load
Dimensions, feet 316 wl; 328 oa × 50 × 11·2
Guns 8—40 mm AA; 12—20 mm AA
Main engines diesels (General Motors); 1 800 bhp; 2 shafts = 11·6 knots
Complement approx 250

Former US Navy landing craft repair ship. Converted during construction from an LST. Launched on 20 Sep 1944 and commissioned in US Navy on 30 Sep 1944. Transferred to South Korea in Oct 1955.

TUK SU

SUPPLY SHIPS

6 Ex-US FREIGHT SUPPLY TYPE

IN CHON	(ex-US Army FS 198)	AKL 902
CHIN NAM PO	(ex-US Army FS 356)	AKL 905
MOK PO	(ex-USCGC *Trillium*, WAK 170, ex-US Army FS 397)	AKL 907
KUN SAN	(ex-USS *Sharps*, AKL 10, ex-AG 139, ex-US Army FS 385)	AKL 908
MA SAN	(ex-USS AKL 35, ex-US Army FS 383)	AKL 909
UL SAN	(ex-USS *Brule*, AKL 28, ex-US Army FS 370)	AKL 910

Displacement, tons approx 700
Dimensions, feet 176·5 oa × 32·8 × 10
Guns 2—20 mm AA (single) in most ships
Main engines diesel; 1 000 bhp; 1 shaft = 10 knots
Complement approx 20

Originally US Army freight and supply ships built in World War II for coastal operation. *In Chon* built by Higgins Industries, *Chin Nam Po* by J. K. Welding, *Ul San* by Sturgeon Bay, others by Ingalls (Dectaur, Alabama).
Many subsequently served in US Navy and Military Sea Transportation Service (now Military Sealift Command). Details and configurations differ.
In Chon and *Chin Nam Po* transferred to South Korea in 1951; *Mok Po*, *Kin San*, and *Ma San* in 1956; *Ul San* on 1 Nov 1971.

Pusan AKL 901 (ex-US Army FS 162), *Wonsan* AKL 903 (ex-US Army FS 254), *Song Chin* AKL 906 (ex-US Army FS 285) scrapped in 1958.

MA SAN 1957

OILERS

1 NORWEGIAN TYPE

CHUN JI (ex-*Birk*) AO 2

Displacement, tons 1 400 standard; 4 160 full load
Dimensions, feet 297·5 oa × 44·5 × 18·2
Guns 1—40 mm AA; several 20 mm AA
Main engines 2 diesels; 1 800 bhp; 1 shaft = 12 knots
Complement approx 70

Former Norwegian tankers built by A/S Berken Mek Verks, Bergen, Norway, in 1951. Transferred to South Korea in Sep 1953. Sister ship *Pujon* AO 3 (ex-*Hassel*) ran aground and was lost on 24 May 1971.

Oilers—*continued*

CHUN JI 1969

1 Ex-US 235-ft YO TYPE

HWA CHON (ex-*Paek Yeon* AO 5, ex-USS *Derrick* YO 59) AO 5

Displacement, tons 890 standard; 2 700 full load
Dimensions, feet 236 oa × 37·9 × 15
Guns several 20 mm AA
Main engines diesel (Fairbanks Morse); 1 150 bhp; 1 shaft = 10·5 knots
Complement approx 45

Former US Navy self-propelled fuel barge. Transferred to South Korea on 14 Oct 1955. Capacity 10 000 barrels petroleum. Reportedly, the ship has been laid up in reserve.

HWA CHON 1969

2 Ex-US 174-ft YO TYPE

KU YONG (ex-USS YO 118) YO 1 (ex-USS YO 179) YO 6

Displacement, tons 1 400 full load
Dimensions, feet 174 oa × 32
Guns several 20 mm AA
Main engines diesel (Union); 500 bhp; 1 shaft = 7 knots
Complement approx 35

Former US Navy self-propelled fuel barges. Transferred to South Korea on 3 Dec 1946 and 13 Sep 1971, respectively. Cargo capacity 6 570 barrels.

OCEAN TUGS

2 Ex-US ATA TYPE

YONG MUN	(ex-USS *Keosanqua*, ATA 198)	ATA 2	17 Jan 1945
DO BONG	(ex-USS *Pinola*, ATA 206)	ATA (S) 3	14 Dec 1944

Displacement, tons 538 standard; 835 full load
Dimensions, feet 133·66 wl; 143 oa × 33·8
Guns 1—3 inch (*76 mm*) 50 cal AA; 4—20 mm AA
Main engines diesel (General Motors); 1 500 bhp; 1 shaft = 13 knots
Complement approx 45

Former US Navy auxiliary ocean tugs. Launch dates above. Both transferred to South Korea in February 1962. *Do Bong* modified for salvage work.

The South Korean Navy also operates nine small harbour tugs (designated YTL). These are one ex-US Navy craft (YTL 550) and five ex-US Army craft.

DO BONG (YONG MUN alongside) 1969

SERVICE CRAFT

The South Korean Navy operates approximately 35 small service craft in addition to the YO-type oilers listed above and the harbour tugs noted above. These craft include open lighters, floating cranes, diving tenders, dredges, ferries, non-self-propelled fuel barges, pontoon barges, and sludge removal barges. Most are former US Navy craft.

HYDROGRAPHIC SERVICE

The following craft are operated by the Korean Hydrographic Service and are not rated as Navy. All are engaged in surveying operations.

1 Ex-US ATA TYPE

TAN YUNG (ex-USS *Tillamook*, ATA 192) 15 Nov 1944

Characteristics similar to the two ex-US ocean tugs listed previously. Launch date above. Transferred to South Korea on 25 July 1971 for use as surveying ship.

2 Ex-BELGIAN MSI TYPE

SURO 5 (ex-Belgian *Temse*) **SURO 6** (ex-Belgian *Tournai*, ex-US MSI 93)

Displacement, tons	160 light; 190 full load
Dimensions, feet	113·2 oa × 22·3 × 6
Main engines	Diesels; 1 260 bhp; 2 shafts = 15 knots

Former Belgian inshore minesweepers. Built in Belgium, the *Tournai* being financed by United States. Launched on 6 Aug 1956 and 18 May 1957, respectively. Transferred to South Korea in March 1970

1 Ex-US YMS TYPE

SURO 3 (ex-USC & GS *Hodgson*)

Displacement, tons	289 full load
Dimensions, feet	136 oa × 24·5 × 9·25
Main engines	2 diesels; 1 000 bhp; 2 shafts = 15 knots

YMS type transferred to South Korea from US Coast & Geodetic Survey in 1968.

COAST GUARD

The Korean Coast Guard operates about 25 small ships and craft including several tugs and small rescue craft.

LEBANON

Diplomatic Representation

Naval, Military and Air Attaché in London: Brigadier General Antoine Raphael

Mercantile Marine

Lloyd's Register of Shipping: 70 vessels of 116 571 tons gross

PATROL BOATS

TARABLOUS

Displacement, tons	105 standard
Dimensions, feet	124·7 × 18 × 5·8
Guns	2—40 mm
Main engines	2 Mercedes-Benz diesels; 2 shafts; 2 700 bhp = 27 knots
Radius, miles	1 500
Complement	19 (3 officers, 16 men)

Tarablous was built by Ch. Navals de l'Estérel. Laid down in June 1958. Launched in June 1959. Completed in 1959.

TARABLOUS *1968 Lebanese Navy*

3 "BYBLOS" CLASS

BYBLOS 11 **SIDON** 12 **BEYROUTH** (ex-*TIR*) 13

Displacement, tons	28 standard
Dimensions, feet	66 × 13·5 × 4
Guns	1—20 mm AA; 2 MG
Main engines	General Motors diesels; 2 shafts; 530 bhp = 18·5 knots

French built ML type craft. Built by Ch. Navals de l'Estérel. Launched in 1954-55

DJOUNIEH

Displacement, tons	82 standard; 130 full load
Dimensions, feet	112 × 18 × 7·5
Guns	1—20 mm; 2—12·7 mm MG
Main engines	2 GM diesels; 2 shafts = 16 knots
Complement	16

Ex-Fairmile "B" motor launch of the Royal Navy built in 1940-41.

DJOUNIEH *1970, Lebanese Navy*

LANDING CRAFT

SOUR (ex-LCU 1474)

Displacement, tons	180 standard; 360 full load
Dimensions, feet	115 × 34 × 6
Guns	2—20 mm AA
Main engines	3 diesels; 3 shafts; 675 bhp = 10 knots

Former United States utility landing craft built in 1957, transferred in Nov 1958.

SOUR *1968, Lebanese Navy*

LAOS

Administration

Commander, Royal Lao Navy and Chief of Naval Staff:
Colonel Prince Sinthanavong Kindavong

RIVER PATROL CRAFT

7 LCM (6) Type	28 tons	4 in commission, 3 in reserve
6 Cabin Type	21 tons	2 in commission, 4 in reserve
2 Chris Craft Type	15 tons	2 in commission
12 11 metre Type	10 tons	5 in commission, 7 in reserve
8 8 metre Type	6 tons	8 in reserve
7 Cargo Transport	50 tons	1 in commission, 6 in reserve

It was officially stated in 1972 that the above craft are formed into four squadrons.

LIBERIA

Personnel

The small naval service or coast guard has about 200 officers and men.

Mercantile Marine

Lloyd's Register of Shipping: 2 234 vessels of 44 443 652 tons gross

MOTOR GUNBOAT

ALERT (Ex USN *PGM* 102)

Displacement, tons	100
Dimensions, feet	95 oa × 19 × 5
Guns	1—40 mm AA
Main engines	4 diesels; 2 shafts; 2 200 bhp = 21 knots
Complement	15

PGM 102 (US number) was built in the United States for transfer under the Military Aid Programme in 1967.

PRESIDENTIAL YACHT

LIBERIAN (ex-*Virginia*)

Measurement, tons	742 (*Thames* measurement); 692·27 gross; 341·6 net
Dimensions, feet	173 wl; 209 oa × 29·7 × 13·1

Motor yacht of 742 tons (yacht measurement) built in 1930 by William Beardmore & Co Ltd, Dalmuir. Purchased by Liberia for use as the Presidential Yacht in 1957. (Her previous owners were the Trustees of the Estate of the late Viscount Camrose.) Extensively refitted by Cammell Laird & Co Ltd, Birkenhead, at the end of 1962.

PATROL BOATS

ML 4001 **ML 4002**

Displacement, tons	11·5
Dimensions, feet	40·5 oa × 11·5 × 3·5
Guns	2 MG
Main engines	2 GM diesels; 2 shafts; 380 bhp = 23 knots max

Coastguard cutters built at the United States Coast Guard Yard, Curtis Bay, Maryland, presented by the USA and transferred during 1957.

ML 4002 *Courtesy Dr Giorgio Arra*

LANDING CRAFT

Landing craft reported to be used for transport and general utility purposes.

LIBYA

Establishment

The Libyan Navy was established in Nov 1962 when a British Naval Mission was formed and first recruits were trained at HMS *St Angelo*, Malta. Cadets were also trained at the Britannia Royal Naval College, Dartmouth, and technical ratings at HMS *Sultan*, Gosport, and HMS *Collingwood*, Fareham, England.

Personnel

1973: Total 2 000 officers and ratings, including Coast Guard

Administration

Senior Officer, Libyan Navy: Lieutenant-Commander A. Shaksuki

Mercantile Marine

Lloyd's Register of Shipping: 13 vessels of 5 932 tons gross

FRIGATE

1 V-T MARK 7

DAT-ASSAWARI

Displacement, tons	1 325 standard; 1 625 full load
Length, feet (*metres*)	310·0 (*94·5*) pp; 330·0 (*100·6*) oa
Beam, feet (*metres*)	36·0 (*11·0*)
Draught, feet (*metres*)	11·2 (*3·4*)
A/S weapons	1 Mortar Mark 10
Missile launchers	6 (2 triple) "Seacat" close range ship-to-air
Guns	1—4·5 in; 2—40 mm (twin); 2—35 mm (twin)
Main engines	CODOG arrangement; 2 shafts; 2 Rolls Royce gas turbines; 23 200 shp = 37·5 knots max 2 Paxman diesels; 3 500 bhp = 17 knots economical cruising speed
Range, miles	5 700 at 17 knots

DAT-ASSAWARI 1972, *Vosper Thornycroft*

Mark 7 Fast Frigate ordered from Vosper Thornycroft on 6 Feb 1968. Generally similar in design to the two Iranian ships built by this firm, but larger and with different armament. She was launched without ceremony in Sep 1969. Trials completed late 1972 prior to work-up at Portland, England.

RADAR. AWS-1 air surveillance set; fire control radar and RDL-1 radar direction finder.

LOGISTIC SUPPORT SHIP

1 DOCK TYPE

ZELTIN

Displacement, tons	2 200 standard; 2 470 full load
Ship:	
Length, feet (*metres*)	300·0 (*91·4*) wl; 324·0 (*98·8*) oa
Beam, feet (*metres*)	48·0 (*14·6*)
Draught, feet (*metres*)	10·2 (*3·1*); 19·0 (*5·8*) aft when flooded
Dock:	
Length, feet (*metres*)	135·0 (*41·1*)
Width, feet (*metres*)	40·0 (*12·2*)
Guns	2—40 mm AA
Main engines	2 Paxman 16 cyl diesels; 3 500 bhp; 2 shafts
Speed, knots	15
Range, miles	3 000 at 14 knots
Complement	As Senior Officer Ship: 101 (15 officers and 86 ratings)

ZELTIN *1969*

The Vosper-Thornycroft Group received the order for this novel dock ship on 31 Jan 1967 (announced) for delivery in late 1968. She was designed and built by John I. Thornycroft & Co Ltd, at the Group's Woolston Shipyard. Launched on 29 Feb 1968. Commissioned (with *Sirte* and *Susa*) on 23 Jan 1969.

The ship provides full logistic support, including mobile docking maintenance and repair facilities for the Libyan fleet and acts as parent ship for the corvette *Tobruk* and the three fast patrol boats *Sebha*, *Sirte* and *Susa*. Craft up to 120 ft can be docked.

Fitted with accommodation for a flag officer or a senior officer and staff. Operational and administrative base of the squadron. Workshops with a total area of approx 4 500 sq ft are situated amidships with ready access to the dock, and there is a 3-ton travelling gantry fitted with outriggers to cover ships berthed alongside up to 200 feet long.

ZELTIN *1969, Vosper Thornycroft*

CORVETTE

TOBRUK

Displacement, tons	440 standard; 500 full load
Dimensions, feet	162 wl; 177 oa × 28·5 × 10 mean (13 props)
Guns	1—4 in; 4—40 mm AA (single)
Main engines	2 Paxman Ventura 16 YJCM diesels; 2 shafts; 3 800 bhp = 18 knots
Range, miles	2 900 at 14 knots
Complement	63 (5 officers and 58 ratings)

Designed and built by Vosper Limited, Portsmouth, in association with Vickers Limited. Launched on 29 July 1965, completed on 30 Mar 1966, commissioned for service at Portsmouth on 20 Apr 1966, sailed for Libya on 30 May 1966 and arrived in Tripoli on 15 June 1966. A gun corvette fitted with surface warning radar, Vosper roll damping fins and air-conditioning. Duties for which she was designed include protection of shipping from air and sea attack, training officers and men of the Libyan Navy, and State visiting. A suite of State apartments is included in the accommodation.

TOBRUK *1971, A. & J. Pavia*

LIGHT FORCES

3 "SUSA" CLASS (MISSILE BOATS)

SEBHA (ex-*Sokna*) **SIRTE** **SUSA**

Displacement, tons	95 standard; 114 full load
Dimensions, feet	90·0 pp; 96·0 wl; 100·0 oa × 25·5 × 7·0
Missiles	8—SS 12
Guns	2—40 mm AA (single)
Main engines	3 Bristol Siddeley "Proteus" gas turbines; 3 shafts; 12 750 bhp = 54 knots
Complement	20

The order for these three fast patrol boats from Vosper Limited, Portsmouth, England, was announced on 12 Oct 1966. They are generally similar to the motor torpedo boats designed and built by Vosper for the Royal Danish Navy. Built at the Vosper-Thornycroft Group's Portchester shipyard. Fitted with air conditioning and modern radar and radio equipment. *Susa* was launched on 31 Aug 1967, *Sirte* on 10 Jan 1968 and *Sokna* (renamed *Sebha*) on 29 Feb 1968. First operational vessels in the world to be armed with Nord-Aviation SS 12(M) guided weapons with sighting turret installation and other equipment developed jointly by Vosper and Nord. These weapons, of which eight can be fired by each boat without reloading, have a destructive power equivalent to a six-inch shell.

SEBHA *1969, Wright & Logan*

SUSA discharging one of her eight Nord-Aviation missiles *1969, Vosper*

4 "GARIAN" TYPE (PATROL BOATS)

GARIAN **KHAWLAN** **MERAWA** **SABRATHA**

Displacement, tons	120 standard; 159 full load
Dimensions, feet	100 pp; 106 oa × 21·2 × 5·5
Guns	1—20 mm AA
Main engines	2 Paxman diesels; 1 100 bhp = 14 knots
Range, miles	1 500 at 12 knots
Complement	15 to 22

Built by Brooke Marine, Lowestoft. Launched on 21 Apr, 29 May, 25 Oct and 30 Sep 1969, respectively, and completed on 30 Aug 1969 (*Garian* and *Khawlan*) and early 1970 (other two).

KHAWLAN *1970, Courtesy Brooke Marine*

INSHORE MINESWEEPERS

2 BRITISH "HAM" TYPE

BRAK (ex-HMS *Harpham*) **ZUARA** (ex-HMS *Greetham*)

Displacement, tons	100
Dimensions, feet	102·0 × 20·0 × 5·0
Guns	1—40 mm; 1—20 mm
Main engines	2 Paxman 12 YJCM diesels; 3 600 bhp = 24 knots
Range, miles	1 800 at 13 knots
Complement	20

Lent by Great Britain in 1963 to form the nucleus of a navy for Libya, and given outright to the Royal Libyan Navy in 1966. Given Libyan names in Sep 1966.

BRAK *A. & J. Pavia*

MAINTENANCE REPAIR CRAFT

ZLEITEN (ex-*MRC* 1013, ex-LCT)

Displacement, tons	657 standard; 900 approx full load
Dimensions, feet	225·0 pp, 231·3 oa × 39·0 × 3·3 forward, 5·0 aft
Main engines	4 Paxman diesels; 2 shafts; 1 840 bhp = 9 knots cruising

Built in 1944-45. Purchased from Great Britain on 5 Sep 1966. Depot ship for minesweepers.

COAST GUARD VESSELS

SECURITY PATROL VESSELS. *Ar-Rakib* and *Farwa* were completed on 4 May 1967 by John I Thornycroft, Woolston, 100 tons, 100 × 21 × 5·5 feet, 3 Rolls Royce DV8TLM diesels, 1 740 bhp = 18 knots, 1—20 mm gun, 1 800 miles range at 14 knots, fuel 20 tons. Designed specifically for operation in North African waters. Welded steel construction. Four similar craft were ordered from the Vosper Thornycroft Group (announced on 3 Jan 1968), *Benina*, *Misurata*, both completed on 29 Aug 1968, *Akrama* and *Homs*, both completed early in 1969.

FARWA *1969, Thornycroft*

CUSTOMS LAUNCHES

There are also three fast patrol launches for customs and fishery protection: see full particulars in the 1963-64 and 1964-65 editions.

MALAWI

It was reported that Great Britain was to supply Malawi with at least three gunboats to patrol the disputed waters of Lake Malawi (which has an extent of 11 460 sq miles and a length of 360 miles with an outlet to the River Zambesi).

MALAYSIA

Administration

Chief of the Naval Staff:
Rear-Admiral Dato K. Thanabalasingam, DPMT JMN, SMJ

Deputy to the Chief of the Naval Staff:
Captain Mohd Zain bin Mohd Salleh, KMN

Commander Naval Forces West Malaysia:
Captain P. K. Nettur, AMN

Commander Naval Forces East Malaysia:
Captain Cheah Leong Voon, AMN

Diplomatic Representation

Services Adviser in London:
Colonel Michael Pekteck Foo

Strength of the Fleet

2 Frigates
6 Coastal Minesweepers
4 Missile Boats
24 Patrol Craft (3 Gunboats ordered)
1 Survey Vessel
1 Diving Tender
1 Support Ship
24 Police Launchers

New Construction

4 Fast Missile Boats

Personnel

1973: 5 090 (460 officers and 4 630 ratings)

Ships

The names of Malaysian warships are prefixed by KD.. (Kapal Diraja) meaning Royal Ship

Mercantile Marine

Lloyd's Register of Shipping:
99 vessels of 149 304 tons gross

FRIGATES

1 YARROW TYPE

RAHMAT (ex-*Hang Jebat*) F 24

Displacement, tons	1 250 standard; 1 600 full load
Length, feet (*metres*)	300·0 (*91·44*)pp; 308 (*93·9*) oa
Beam, feet (*metres*)	34·1 (*10·4*)
Draught, feet (*metres*)	14·8 (*4·5*)
Aircraft	1 helicopter
Missile launchers	1 quadruple "Seacat" surface-to-air
Guns, dual purpose	1—4·5 in (*114 mm*)
Guns, AA	2—40 mm
A/S weapons	1 "Limbo" three-barrelled mortar
Main engines	1 Bristol Siddeley Olympus gas turbine; 19 500 shp; Crossley Pielstick diesel; 3 850 bhp; 2 shafts
Speed, knots	26 boosted by gas turbine; 16 on diesel alone
Range, miles	6 000 at 16 knots 1 000 at 26 knots
Complement	140

General purpose frigate of new design developed by Yarrow. Fully automatic with saving in complement. Delivered mid-1971.

RAHMAT *1972, Wright & Logan*

Ordered from Yarrow & Co Ltd, Scotstoun, on 11 Feb 1966. Launched on 18 Dec 1967. Delivered 13 Sep 1972.

RADAR. Air Surveillance: HSA LW 02. Fire control; M 20 with radar in spherical radome for guns; M 44 for Seacat.

1 Ex-BRITISH "LOCH" CLASS

HANG TUAH (ex-HMS *Loch Insh*) F 433

Displacement, tons	1 575 standard; 2 400 full load
Length, feet (*metres*)	297·2 (*90·6*) wl; 307·0 (*93·6*) oa
Beam, feet (*metres*)	38·5 (*11·7*)
Draught, feet (*metres*)	14·8 (*4·5*)
Guns, AA	6—40 mm
Boilers	2 Admiralty 3-drum
Main engines	2 triple expansion; 5 500 ihp; 2 shafts
Speed, knots	19·5 designed
Range, miles	6 400 at 10 knots
Complement	140

Built by Henry Robb Ltd, Leith. Laid down on 17 Nov 1943, launched on 10 May 1944 and completed on 20 Oct 1944. On transfer refitted with helicopter deck, air-conditioning, modern radar and extra accommodation in Portsmouth Dockyard. Re-commissioned on 12 Oct

HANG TUAH *1972, Royal Malaysian Navy*

1964. Sailed on 12 Nov 1964. Converted into a training ship in Apr 1971, the two 4-inch guns and the two "Squid" mortars having been removed. *Hang Tuah* was the name of a Malay Admiral of the 15th century.

RADAR: Search: Type 227.

COASTAL MINESWEEPERS

6 Ex-BRITISH "TON" CLASS

BRINCHANG (ex-*Thankerton*) M 1172
JERAI (ex-*Dilston*) M 1168
KINABALU (ex-*Essington*) M 1134
LEDANG (ex-*Hexton*) M 1143
MAHAMIRU (ex-*Darlaston*) M 1127
TAHAN (ex-*Lullington*) M 1163

Displacement, tons	360 standard; 425 full load
Dimensions, feet	140 pp; 152 oa × 28·8 × 8·2
Guns	1—40 mm AA forward; 2—20 mm AA aft
Main engines	Diesels; 2 shafts; 2 500 bhp = 15 knots max
Oil fuel, tons	45
Range, miles	2 300 at 13 knots
Complement	39

***Mahamiru* transferred from the Royal Navy on 24 May 1960. *Ledang*, refitted at Chatham Dockyard before transfer, commissioned for Malaysia in Oct 1963. *Jerai* and *Kinabalu*, refitted in Great Britain, arrived in Malaysia summer 1964. *Brinchang* and *Tahan*, refitted in Singapore, transferred to Malaysian Navy in May and Apr 1966, respectively.**

MAHAMIRU *1972, Royal Malaysian Navy*

SURVEY VESSEL

1 Ex-BRITISH "TON" CLASS

PERANTAU (ex-HMS *Myrmidon*, ex-HMS *Edderton*) A 151

Displacement, tons	360 standard; 420 full load
Dimensions, feet	153 oa × 28·8 × 8·5
Main engines	Diesels; 2 shafts; 3 000 bhp = 15 knots
Range, miles	2 300 at 13 knots
Complement	35

A former coastal minesweeper of the "Ton" type, converted by the Royal Navy into a survey ship, renamed *Myrmidon* in Apr 1964, and commissioned for service on 20 July 1964. Paid off in 1968 and purchased by Malaysia in 1969. Service in Malaysian waters since 1970. *Perantau* means "a rover".

PERANTAU *1972, Royal Malaysian Navy*

LIGHT FORCES

4 "PERDANA" CLASS (MISSILE BOATS)

PERDANA **GANAS** **SERANG** **GANYANG**

Displacement, tons	234 standard; 265 full load
Dimensions, feet	154·2 × 23·1 × 12·8
Missile launchers	2 MM38 ("Exocet") surface-to-surface
Guns	1—57 mm Bofors; 1—40 mm 70 cal Bofors
Main engines	4 MTU diesels; 4 shafts; 14 000 bhp = 36·5 knots
Range, miles	800 at 25 knots

First pair built by Constructions Mécaniques de Normandie, *Perdana* launched 31 May 1972 completed December 1972 and *Ganas* launched 26 Oct 1972 for completion May 1973. Second pair built by Société Francaise de Constructions Navales (ex-Franco-Belge), *Serang* launched 22 Dec 1971, completing Jan 1973 and *Ganyang* launched 16 March 1972, completing March 1973. All of basic "La Combattante II" design.

4 "PERKASA" CLASS (MISSILE BOATS)

GEMPITA P 152 **HANDALAN** P 151 **PENDEKAR** P 153 **PERKASA** P 150

Displacement, tons	95 standard; 114 full load
Dimensions, feet	90 pp; 96 wl; 99 oa × 25·5 × 7
Guns	1—40 mm AA; 1—20 mm AA
Missiles	8—SS 12(M) in 2 quadruple launchers
Main engines	3 Rolls Royce Proteus gas turbines; 3 shafts; 12 750 bhp = 54 knots GM diesels on wing shafts for cruising = 10 knots

The design is a combination of the "Brave" class hull form and "Ferocity" type construction. Ordered from Vosper Limited, Portsmouth, England, on 22 Oct 1964. Generally similar to the motor torpedo boats built by Vosper for the Royal Danish Navy. They can also operate in the gunboat role or a minelaying role. *Perkasa* (Valiant) was launched on 26 Oct 1965, *Handalan* (Reliant) on 18 Jan 1966, *Gempita* (Thunderer) on 6 Apr 1966 and *Pendekar* (Champion) on 24 June 1966. The hull is entirely of glued laminated wooden construction, with upperworks of aluminium alloy. Equipment includes Rover gas turbine generating sets, full air conditioning, Decca radar, and comprehensive navigation and communications system. The craft were shipped to Malaysia in mid-1967. They were re-armed with eight SS.12 missiles in place of four 21-inch torpedoes in 1971.

GEMPITA (Firing SS 12 missile) *1972, Royal Malaysian Navy*

3 "LA COMBATTANTE II" TYPE (GUNBOATS)

It was reported in October 1972 that the Malaysian Government intended to order these craft which would be fitted with additional guns in place of missiles.

6 "KEDAH" CLASS (PATROL CRAFT)

SRI KEDAH	P 3138	**SRI PAHANG**	P 3141	**SRI SELANGOR**	P 3139
SRI KELANTAN	P 3142	**SRI PERAK**	P 3140	**SRI TRENGGANU**	P 3143

4 "SABAH" CLASS (PATROL CRAFT)

SRI MELAKA	P 3147	**SRI SABAH**	P 3144
SRI NEGRI SEMBILAN	P 3146	**SRI SARAWAK**	P 3145

14 "KRIS" CLASS (PATROL CRAFT)

		KRIS	P 34	**SERAMPANG**	P 41
BADEK	P 37	**LEMBING**	P 40	**SRI JOHOR**	P 49
BELEDAU	P 44	**PANAH**	P 42	**SRI PERLIS**	P 47
KELEWANG	P 45	**RENCHONG**	P 38	**SUNDANG**	P 36
KERAMBIT	P 43	**RENTAKA**	P 46	**TOMBAK**	P 39

Displacement, tons	96 standard; 109 full load
Dimensions, feet	95 wl; 103 oa × 19·8 × 5·5
Guns	2—40 mm; 70 cal AA
Main engines	2 Bristol Siddeley/Maybach MD 655/18 diesels; 3 500 bhp = 27 knots max
Range, miles	1 400 (*Sabah* class 1 660) at 14 knots
Complement	22 (3 officers, 19 ratings)

All 24 craft were built by Vosper Limited, Portsmouth. The first six boats, constituting the "Kedah" class were ordered in 1961 for delivery in 1963. The four boats of the "Sabah" class were ordered in 1963 for delivery in 1964. The remaining 14 boats of the "Kris" class were ordered in 1965 for delivery between 1966 and 1968. All are of prefabricated steel construction and are fitted with Decca radar, air conditioning and Vosper roll damping equipment. The difference between the three classes are minor, the later ones having improved radar, communications, evaporators and engines

Light Forces—*continued*

of Maybach, as opposed to Bristol Siddeley construction. *Sri Johor*, the last of the 14 boats of the "Kris" class, was launched on 22 June 1967.

BADEK ("Kris" Class) *1972, Royal Malaysian Navy*

SUPPORT SHIP

SRI LANGKAWI (ex-USS *Hunterdon County* LST 838)

Displacement, tons	1 653 standard; 2 366 beaching; 4 080 full load
Dimensions, feet	316·0 wl; 328·0 oa × 50·0 × 14·0
Guns	8—40 mm (2 twin, 4 single)
Main engines	GM diesels; 2 shafts; 1 700 bhp = 11·6 knots
Complement	138 (11 officers, 127 ratings)

An LST of the 511-1152 series built in 1945. Transferred from the US Navy and commissioned in the Royal Malaysian Navy on 1 July 1971.

SRI LANGKAWI *1972, Royal Malaysian Navy*

DIVING TENDER

DUYONG

Displacement, tons	120 standard; 140 full load
Dimensions, feet	99·5 wl; 110·0 oa × 21·0 × 5·8
Guns	1—20 mm
Main engines	2 Cummins diesels; 1 900 rpm; 500 bhp = 10 knots
Complement	23

Built by Kall Teck (Pte) Ltd, Singapore. Launched on 18 Aug 1970. Commissioned on 5 Jan 1971.

DUYONG *1972, Royal Malaysian Navy*

Royal Malaysian Police

18 PX CLASS

Mahkota, Temenggong, Hulubalang, Maharajasetia, Maharajalela, Pahlawan, Bentara, Perwira, Pertanda, Shahbandar, Sangsetia, Laksamana, Pekan, Kelang, Kuala Kangsar, Arau, Sri Gumantong, Sri Labuan, (Numbered PX 1-18).

Displacement, tons	85
Dimensions, feet	87·5 oa × 19 × 4·8
Guns	2—20 mm
Main engines	2 Mercedes Benz diesels; 2 shafts; 2 700 hp = 25 knots
Range, miles	700 at 15 knots
Complement	15

6 IMPROVED PX CLASS

Alor Star, Kota Bahru, Kuala Trengganu, Johore Bahru, Sri Menanti, Kuching (Numbered PX 19-24).

Displacement, tons	92
Dimensions, feet	91 oa
Guns	2—20 mm
Main engines	2 diesels; 2 460 hp = 25 knots
Range, miles	750 at 15 knots
Complement	18

All 24 boats built by Vosper Thornycroft Private, Singapore, PX class between 1963 and 1970, Improved PX class 1972-73. *Sri Gumantong* and *Sri Labuan* operated by Sabah Government, remainder by Royal Malaysian Police.

MEXICO

Administration

Secretary of the Navy:
Admiral C. G. Demn. Luis M. Bravo Carrera

Under-Secretary of the Navy:
Rear-Admiral Ing. M. N. Ricardo Chazaro Lara

Commander-in-Chief of the Navy:
Vice-Admiral C. G. Demn. Humberto Uribe Escandon

Chief of the Naval Staff:
Rear-Admiral C. G. Demn. Miguel A. Gomez Ortega

Director of Services:
Rear-Admiral C. G. Demn. Mario Artigas Fernandez

Diplomatic Representation

Naval Attaché in London:
Rear-Admiral J. Blanco Peyrefitte

Naval Attaché in Washington:
Vice-Admiral Miguel Manzarraga

Personnel

1973: Total 13 000 officers and men (including Naval Air Force and Marines)

Strength of the Fleet

2 Destroyers
10 Frigates, Escorts, Transport and Gunboats
2 Landing Ships
15 Escorts and Fleet Minesweepers
10 Patrol Boats and Launches
2 Survey Ships
2 Oilers
5 Tugs

Naval Air Force

5 Catalina PBY-5A
Grumman J2F-6
6 Bell H-13 helicopters
6 Alouette III helicopters

Mercantile Marine

Lloyd's Register of Shipping:
216 vessels of 416 832 tons gross

DESTROYERS

2 Ex-US "FLETCHER" CLASS

Name	Builders	Laid down	Launched	Completed
CUAUTHEMOC F 1 (ex-*Harrison* DD 574)	Consolidated Steel	25 Jan 41	7 May 43	25 Jan 43
CUITLAHUAC F 2 (ex-*John Rodgers* DD 573)	Consolidated Steel	25 July 41	7 May 43	9 Feb 43

Displacement, tons	2 100 standard; 3 050 full load
Length, feet (*metres*)	376·5 (*114·7*) oa
Beam, feet (*metres*)	39·5 (*12·0*)
Draught, feet (*metres*)	18·0 (*5·5*)
Guns (*original*)	5—5 in (*127 mm*); 14—40 mm
Torpedo tubes	5—21 in (*533 mm*) quintupled
A/S weapons	8 DCT, 2 Hedgehogs
Main engines	2 geared turbines; 2 shafts; 60 000 shp
Boilers	4
Speed, knots	34
Oil fuel, tons	650
Range, miles	5 000 at 15 knots
Complement	250

Former US standard destroyers of the original "Fletcher" class. Transferred to the Mexican Navy in Aug 1970 after being paid off in USN 1 May 1968.

CUAUTHEMOC *1972, Mexican Navy*

FRIGATES

5 Ex-US "RUDDEROW" CLASS

Name	No.	Builders	Laid down	Launched	Completed
CHIHUAHUA (ex-USS *Rednour*, APD 102, ex-DE 592)	B 8	Bethlehem SB Co, Hingham	9 Jan 1944	1 Mar 1944	15 Mar 1945
COAHUILA (ex-USS *Barber*, LPR, ex-APD 57, ex-*DE* 161)	B 7	Norfolk Navy Yard, Norfolk, Va	27 Apr 1943	20 May 1943	10 Oct 1943
PAPALOAPAN (ex-USS *Earhart*, APD 113, ex-*DE* 603)	B 4 (ex-H 4)	Bethlehem SB Co, Hingham	20 Mar 1945	12 May 1945	26 July 1945
TEHUANTEPEC (ex-USS *Joseph M. Auman*, APD 117, ex-DE 674)	B 5 (ex-H 5)	Consolidated Steel Corp, Orange	8 Nov 1943	5 Feb 1944	25 Apr 1945
USUMACINTA (ex-USS *Don O. Woods*, APD 118, ex-DE 721)	B 6 (ex-H 6)	Consolidated Steel Corp, Orange	1 Dec 1943	19 Feb 1944	28 May 1945

Displacement, tons	1 400 standard; 2 130 full load
Length, feet (*metres*)	300·0 (*91·5*) wl; 306·0 (*93·3*) oa
Beam, feet (*metres*)	37·0 (*11·3*)
Draught, feet (*metres*)	12·7 (*3·9*)
Guns	1—5 in (*127 mm*) 38 cal. dp; 6—40 mm AA (3 twin)
Main engines	GE turbo-electric; 2 shafts; 12 000 shp
Speed, knots	23·6 full; 13 economical sea
Boilers	2 Foster Wheeler "D" with superheater; 475 psi (*33·4 kg/cm²*) 750°F (*399°C*)
Range, miles	5 000 at 15 knots
Oil fuel, tons	350
Complement	204 plus 162 troops

The first four were purchased by Mexico in December 1963 and *Chihuahua* and *Coahuila* on 17 Feb 1969. The first four replaced the four ex-US "Tacoma" type frigates bearing the same names, which were deleted in June and Aug 1964. *California* stranded and lost 16 Jan 1972 on Bahia Peninsula.

PAPALOAPAN *1972, Mexican Navy*

1 "DURANGO" TYPE

Name	No.	Builders	Launched	Completed
DURANGO	B—1 (ex-128)	Union Naval de Levante, Valencia	28 June 1935	1936

Displacement, tons	1 600 standard; 2 000 full load
Length, feet (*metres*)	282·0 (*86·0*) pp; 303·0 (*92·4*) oa
Beam, feet (*metres*)	40·0 (*12·2*)
Draught, feet (*metres*)	10·0 (*3·1*)
Guns	2—4 in (*102 mm*); 2—2·24 in (*57 mm*); 2—20 mm
Main engines	2 Enterprise DMR-38 diesels, electric drive; 2 shafts; 5 000 bhp
Speed, knots	18 max, 12 sea (cruising)
Range, miles	3 000 at 12 knots
Oil fuel, tons	140
Complement	149 (24 officer and 125 men)

Originally designed primarily as an armed transport with accommodation for 20 officers and 450 men. The two Yarrow boilers and Parsons geared turbines of 6 500 shp installed when first built were replaced with two 2 500 bhp diesels in 1967 when the ship was re-rigged with remodelled funnel. Carries a lighter armament than the "Guanajuato" class (see next page) which besides troop carrying and transport capacity are equivalent to frigates in many ways. *Durango* replaced *Zaragoza* as training ship in Mar 1964.

DURANGO *1972, Mexican Navy*

Frigates—*continued*

3 "GUANAJUATO" CLASS

Name	*No.*	*Builders*	*Launched*
GUANAJUATO	C-7	Sociedad Espanol de Construction Naval, Ferrol	29 May 1934
POTOSI	C-9	Sociedad Espanol de Construction Naval, Motagorda, Cadiz	24 Aug 1934
QUERETARO	C-8	Sociedad Espanol de Construction Naval, Ferrol	29 June 1934

Displacement, tons	1 300 standard; 1 950; full load
Length, feet (*metres*)	264·0 (*80·5*)
Beam, feet (*metres*)	37·8 (*11·5*)
Draught, feet (*metres*)	11·5 (*3·5*)
Guns	3—4 in (*102 mm*) single; 4—20 mm, single
Main engines	2 Enterprise DMR-38 diesels; 2 shafts; 5 000 bhp
Speed, knots	14
Oil fuel, tons	140
Complement	140 (20 officers and 120 men)

Officially classified as gunboats (*canoneros*), but can be used as transports with berths for 120 troops. The Parsons geared turbines (2 shafts; 5 000 shp=19 knots, and Yarrow boilers installed when originally built in 1934 were replaced with two diesels each of 2 500 bhp: *Querétaro* in 1958, *Potosi* in 1961, and *Guanajuato* in 1964.

GUANAJUATO — *1970, Wright & Logan*

ESCORT MINESWEEPERS

10 Ex-US "AUK" CLASS

EX-US Name and No.

PIONEER	MSF 105	**DEVASTATOR**	MSF 318
SYMBOL	MSF 123	**GLADIATOR**	MSF 319
CHAMPION	MSF 314	**SPEAR**	MSF 322
COMPETENT	MSF 316	**ARDENT**	MSF 346
DEFENSE	MSF 317	**SCOTER**	MSF 318

Displacement, tons	890 standard; 1 250 full load
Dimensions, feet	215 wl; 221·2 oa × 32·2 × 10·8
Guns	1—3 in 50 cal; 2 or 4—40 mm
Main engines	Diesel electric; 2 shafts; 3 500 bhp = 18 knots
Complement	9 officers and 96 ratings

All purchased 19 Sept 1972. In addition one *Admirable* class and nine more *Auk* class to be purchased during 1973 for spare parts.

15 Ex-MSF TYPE

Name	*No.*	*Ex-US Name & No.*		*Name*	*No.*	*Ex-US Name & No*	
DM-01	D-1	*Jubilant*	255	**DM-13**	E-3	*Knave*	256
DM-02	D-2	*Hilarity*	241	**DM-14**	E-4	*Rebel*	284
DM-03	D-3	*Execute*	232	**DM-15**	E-5	*Crag*	214
DM-05	D-5	*Scuffle*	298	**DM-16**	E-6	*Dour*	223
DM-06	D-6	*Eager*	224	**DM-17**	E-7	*Diploma*	221
DM-10	D-0	*Instill*	252	**DM-18**	E-8	*Invade*	254
DM-11	E-1	*Device*	220	**DM-19**	E-9	*Intrigue*	253
DM-12	E-2	*Ransom*	283	**DM-20**	E-0	*Harlequin*	365

Displacement, tons	650 standard; 945 full load
Dimensions, feet	180 wl; 184·5 oa × 33 × 10
Guns	1—3 in, 50 cal dp; 2—40 mm AA; 4—6 20 mm
Main engines	2 diesels; 2 shafts; 1 710 bhp = 15 knots
Range, miles	4 300 at 10 knots
Complement	104

Former US steel-hulled "180-ft" fleet minesweepers of the "Admirable" class. MSF, ex-AM type. All completed in 1943-44. Of the twenty vessels transferred at Orange, Texas, on 2 Oct 1962 ten were designated *dragaminas* for minesweeping duties, with D pennant numbers, and ten *escoltas* for escort and general purpose duties with E pennant numbers. DM 04 (D-4) ex-*Facility* 233, DM 07 (D-7) ex-*Recruit* 285, DM 08 (D-8) ex-*Success* 310, and DM 09 (D-9) ex-*Scout* 296 were removed from the list in 1971 and DM 11 (E-1) ex-*Device* 220 in 1972. To be used for spare parts.

DM 17 — *1970, Mexican Navy*

OCEANOGRAPHIC SHIP

1 Ex-US PCE TYPE

VIRGILIO URIBE (ex-*Tomas Marin*, ex-PCE 875) **C 1** (ex-C 3)

Displacement, tons	600 standard; 903 full load
Dimensions, feet	180 wl; 184·5 oa × 33·1 × 9·5
Guns	1—3 in, 50 cal; 6—40 mm AA (3 twin); 4—20 mm AA (single)
A/S weapons	2 DCT
Main engines	GM diesels; 2 shafts; 1 800 bhp = 15 knots
Range, miles	4 300 at 10 knots
Complement	80

Sole survivor of five former US patrol vessels of the PCE type, all completed in 1943-44

Escort Minesweepers—*continued*

and purchased from US Navy in 1947. Formerly rated as *Corbeta*. Now employed on oceanographic research. Sister ships *Blass Godinez* (ex-*PCE* 871) C 2, *David Porter* (ex-*PCE* 847) C 4, *Pedro Saina de Baranda* (ex-*PCE* 844) C 1, and *Virgilio Uribe* (ex-*PCE* 868) C 5 were scrapped in 1955. For disposals of *PC* type see 1971-72 and earlier editions.

VIRGILIO URIBE — *1972, Mexican Navy*

SURVEY SHIP

SOTAVENTO 1 A

Displacement, tons	300 standard; 400 full load
Dimensions, feet	165·5 × 28 × 10
Main engines	Diesels; 1 800 bhp = 17 knots
Complement	30

Built by Higgins, New Orleans. Launched in 1947. Handsome, streamlined, with truncated funnel, air conditioned and equipped with radar. Formerly the Presidential Yacht, but officially reclassified as *Buque Hidrografico* in 1966.

SOTAVENTO — *1967, Mexican Navy*

PATROL BOATS

2 "AZUETA" CLASS

AZUETA G 9 **VILLAPANDO** G 6

Displacement, tons	80 standard; 85 full load
Dimensions, feet	85·3 × 16·4 × 7·0
Guns	2—13·2 mm AA (1 twin)
Main engines	Superior diesels; 600 bhp = 12 knots

Of all steel construction. Built at Astilleros de Tampico in 1959 and 1960 respectively.

AZUETA — *Mexican Navy*

Patrol Boats—*continued*

5 RIVER TYPE

AM 4 **AM 5** **AM 6** **AM 7** **AM 8**

Displacement, tons 35
Main engines Diesel; speed = 10 knots

River patrol craft of steel construction. Built in Tampico and Veracruz. Entered service from 1960 to 1962.

POLIMAR 1 G 1 **POLIMAR 2** G 2 **POLIMAR 3** G 3

Displacement, tons 37 standard; 57 full load
Dimensions, feet 60·1 × 15·1 × 4·0
Main engines 2 diesels; 456 bhp = 16 knots

Small patrol craft of steel construction. *Polimar 1* was built at Astilleros de Tampico in 1961 and entered service on 1 Oct 1962. *Polimar 2* and *Polimar 3* were built at Icacas Shipyard, Guerrero and entered service in 1966.

POLIMAR III *1972, Mexican Navy*

TRANSPORT

ZACATECAS B 2

Displacement, tons 780 standard
Dimensions, feet 158 × 27·2 × 9
Guns 1—40 mm AA; 2—20 mm AA (single)
Main engines 1 MAN diesel; 560 hp = 10 knots
Complement 50 (13 officers and 37 men)

Built at Ulua Shipyard, Veracruz. Launched in 1959. Cargo ship type. The hull is of welded steel construction.

LANDING SHIPS

2 Ex-US LST (511-1152 Series)

RIO PANUCO (ex-USS *Park County* LST 1077)
MANZILLO ((ex-USS *Clearwater County*)

Displacement, tons 1 653 standard; 2 366 beaching; 4 080 full load
Dimensions, feet 316 wl; 328 oa × 50 × 14
Guns 6—40 mm
Main engines GM diesels; 2 shafts; 1 700 bhp = 11·6 knots
Range, miles 6 000 at 11 knots
Complement 119
Troop capacity 147

Transferred to Mexico on 13 Aug 1971 and 25 May 1972 respectively. Both employed as rescue ships.

OILERS

2 Ex-US YO TYPE

AGUASCALIENTES (ex-YOG 6) A 5 **TLAXCALA** (ex-YO 107) A 6

Displacement, tons 440 light; 1 480 to 1 800 full load
Dimensions, feet 174·5 oa × 33·0 × 11·8 max
Main engines Union diesel direct; 500 bhp = 8 knots
Capacity 6 570 barrels
Complement 26 (5 officers and 21 ratings)

Former US self-propelled fuel oil barges. Built by Geo. H. Mathis Co Ltd, Camden, N.J. and Geo. Lawley & Son, Neponset, Mass. respectively, in 1943. Purchased in 1964. Entered service in Nov 1964.

TUGS

R-1 (ex-*Farallon*) **R-3** (ex-*Point Vicente*) **R-5** (ex-*Burnt Island*)
R-2 (ex-*Montauk*) **R-4** (ex-*Moose Teak*)

Remolcadores acquired by the Mexican Navy in 1968.

MALAGASY

Mercantile Marine

Lloyd's Register of Shipping: 48 vessels of 52 162 tons gross

PATROL VESSELS

MALAIKA

Displacement, tons 235 light
Dimensions, feet 149·3 pp; 155·8 oa × 23·6 × 8·2
Guns 2—40 mm AA
Main engines 2 MGO diesels; 2 shafts; 2 400 bhp = 18·5 knots
Range, miles 4 000 at 18 knots
Complement 25

Patrol Vessels—*continued*

Ordered by the French Navy to be built by Chantiers Navals Franco-Belges for delivery to Madagascar. Laid down in Nov 1966, launched on 22 Mar 1967 and completed in Dec 1967. A second unit is planned.

FANANTENANA (ex-*Richelieu*)

Displacement, tons 1 040 standard; 1 200 full load
Dimensions, feet 183·7 pp; 206·4 oa × 30 × 14·8
Guns 2—40 mm AA
Main engines 2 Deutz diesels; 1 shaft; 1 060 + 500 bhp = 12 knots

Trawler purchased and converted in 1966-67 to Coast Guard and training ship. 691 tons gross. Built in 1959 by A. G. Weser, Bremen, Germany.

JASMINE (ex-*D* 385, ex-*D* 211, ex-*YMS* 31)

Displacement, tons 280 standard; 325 full load
Dimensions, feet 134·5 × 24·5 × 12
Main engines 2 diesels; 2 shafts; 1 000 bhp = 12 knots
Oil fuel, tons 22

Former coastal minesweeper of the YMS type launched on 10 Apr 1942 and acquired by France in 1954. Acquired by Madagascar on 19 Aug 1965 as a light tender. Same type originally as *Tanamasoandro* (ex-*Marjolaine*, ex-*D* 337, ex-*YMS* 69) which was discarded on delivery of *Malaika* (ex-*P* 758, *VC* 8) and returned to the French Navy in 1967.

5 PATROL BOATS

Displacement, tons 46
Guns 1—40 mm
Main engines 2 diesels = 22 knots

Used by the Maritime Police.

TRANSPORT

One 810 ton Transport is building at Diego-Suarez. With a complement of 27 she will be capable of carrying 120 troops and their transport.

MAURITANIA

Mercantile Marine

Lloyd's Register of Shipping: 4 vessels of 1 681 tons gross

PATROL BOATS

DAR EL BARKA **TICHITT**

Displacement, tons 75 standard; 82 full load
Dimensions, feet 105 × 18·9 × 5·5
Guns 1—20 mm AA 1 MG
Main engines 2 Mercedes Maybach diesels; 2 shafts; 2 700 bhp = 28 knots
Range, miles 1 500 at 15 knots
Complement 19

Built by Ch Navales de L'Estérel, in service June and April 1969 respectively.

IM RAQ'NI **SLOUGHI**

Displacement, tons 20
Dimensions, feet 59 × 13·5 × 3·8
Guns 1—12·7 mm
Main engines 2 GM diesels; 512 bhp = 21 knots
Range, miles 860 at 12 knots

Built by Ch. Navales de L'Estérel in 1965 and 1968, respectively

OMAN, SULTANATE OF

Commander of the Navy:
Commander D. R. Williams, MBE, SON

Mercantile Marine

Lloyd's Register of Shipping: 3 vessels of 2 013 tons gross

PATROL VESSEL

AL SAID

Displacement, tons 900
Dimensions, feet 203·4 × 35·1 × 9·8
Guns 1—40 mm
Main engines 2 Paxman Ventura 12 cyl diesels; 2 shafts; 2 470 bhp
Complement 32 + 7 staff + 32 troops

AL SAID *Brooke Marine, 1971*

Patrol Vessels—*continued*

Built by Brooke Marine, Lowestoft. Launched 7 Apr 1970 as a yacht for the Sultan of Muscat and Oman, she was converted for a dual purpose role with a gun on her forecastle as flagship of the new navy and as ship of state. Completed in 1971.

FAST PATROL BOATS

3 BROOKE MARINE TYPE

AL BUSHRA **AL MANSUR** **AL NEJAH**

Displacement, tons	135 standard; 153 full load
Dimensions, feet	123 oa × 22·5 × 5·5
Guns	2—40 mm
Main engines	2 Paxman Ventura diesels; 4 800 bhp = 29 knots
Range, miles	3 300 at 15 knots
Complement	25

Built by Brooke Marine, Lowestoft, England. Ordered 5 Jan 1971, completed from mid 1972.

Fast Patrol Boats—*continued*

AL BUSHRA *1972, Ford Jenkins*

MOROCCO

Personnel

1973: 1 500 officers and ratings (including Marines)

Mercantile Marine

Lloyd's Register of Shipping:
39 vessels of 46 907 tons gross

FRIGATE

Name	*Builders*	*Laid down*	*Launched*	*Completed*
AL MAOUNA (ex-*La Surprise*, ex-HMS *Torridge*) 31 (ex-033)	Blyth Dry Docks & Ship building Co	17 Oct 1942	16 Aug 1943	6 Apr 1944

Displacement, tons	1 450 standard; 2 150 full load
Length, feet (*metres*)	283·0 (*86·3*) pp; 301·3 (*91·8*) oa
Beam, feet (*metres*)	36·5 (*11·1*)
Draught, feet (*metres*)	12·5 (*3·8*)
Aircraft	1 helicopter
Guns, surface	2—4·1 in (*105 mm*)
Guns, AA	3—40 mm; 2—20 mm
A/S weapons	1 "Hedgehog"; 4 DCT; 2 DC racks
Main engines	Triple expansion; 2 shafts; 5 500 ihp
Boilers	2 Admiralty 3-drum
Speed, knots	18
Oil fuel, tons	645
Range, miles	14 400 at 12 knots
Complement	123 (10 officers, 113 men)

Former British "River" class frigate purchased by France in 1944. Sold to Morocco in June 1964 and converted as flagship and Royal yacht by Chantiers Dubigeon at Brest. A helicopter landing deck and extra accommodation were provided aft. SPS 6 search radar. Accepted on 5 March 1965.

AL MAOUNA *1968, Royal Moroccan Navy*

PATROL VESSELS

AL BACHIR 22 (ex-12)

Displacement, tons	125 light; 154 full load
Dimensions, feet	124·7 pp; 133·2 oa × 20·8 × 4·7
Guns	2—40 mm AA and MG
Main engines	2 SEMT-Pielstick diesels; 2 shafts; 3 600 bhp = 25 knots
Oil fuel, tons	21
Range, miles	4 000 at 15 knots
Complement	23

Ordered in 1964 from Constructions Mécaniques de Normandie, Cherbourg, launched 25 Feb 1967, delivered 30 Mar 1967.

LIEUTENANT RIFFI 32

Displacement, tons	325 standard; 374 full load
Dimensions, feet	170 wl; 173·8 oa × 23 × 6·3
Guns	1—3 in dp; 2—40 mm AA
A/S weapons	2 ASM mortars; 1 DC rack
Main engines	SEMT-Pielstick diesels; 2 shafts: 3 600 bhp = 19 knots
Range, miles	6 000 at 12 knots; 4 000 at 15 knots
Complement	59 (4 officers, 55 men)

AL BACHIR *1967, Royal Moroccan Navy*

Of modified "Fougueux" design. Built by Constructions Mécaniques de Normandie, Cherbourg. Laid down in May 1963. Launched on 1 Mar 1964. Completed in May 1964. Controllable pitch propellers.

The corvette (*aviso*) *El Lahiq* (ex-*Chamois*, ex-*Annamite*) was returned to France in 1967 and hulked as a breakwater at the Ile de Levant. She was transferred from the French Navy on 7 Nov 1961. The patrol vessel *Agadir* (ex-French *Gaumier*, ex-USS *PC* 545) was returned to France on 19 Aug 1964 and became Q 390. Sold for scrap at Brest on 15 Nov 1965.

SEAWARD PATROL CRAFT

ES SABIQ (ex-*P* 762, *VC* 12) 11

Displacement, tons	60 standard; 82 full load
Dimensions, feet	104·5 × 15·5 × 5·5
Guns	2—20 mm AA
Main engines	Mercedes-Benz diesels; 2 shafts; 2 700 bhp = 28 knots
Range, miles	3 000 at 15 knots
Complement	17

Former French seaward defence motor launch of the VC type. Built by Chantiers Navals d'Estérel. Launched on 13 Aug 1957. Completed in 1958. Transferred from the French Navy to the Moroccan Navy on 15 Nov 1960 and renamed *Es Sabiq*.

LANDING CRAFT

LIEUTENANT MALGHAGH 21

Displacement, tons	292 standard; 642 full load
Dimensions, feet	193·6 × 39·2 × 4·3
Guns	2—20 mm AA
Main engines	MGO diesels; 2 shafts; 1 000 bhp = 8 knots
Complement	16 (1 officer, 15 men)

Ordered early in 1963 from Chantiers Navals Franco-Belges and completed in 1964. Similar to the French landing craft of the EDIC type built at the same yard.

LIEUTENANT MALGHAGH *1971, Royal Moroccan Navy*

There are also the yacht *Essaoira*, 60 tons, from Italy in 1967, used as a training vessel for watchkeepers; and twelve customs boats, four of 40 tons, 82 feet, diesels 940 bhp = 23 knots, and eight 42·7 feet; all built in 1963. The *Murene*, Coast Guard Cutter, has also been reported.

NETHERLANDS

Administration

Minister of Defence: H. J. de Koster

Chairman Joint Chiefs of Staff:
Lt-Gen. W. van Rijn

Chairman Joint Services Material Board:
Vice-Admiral J. C. H. van den Bergh

Chief of the Naval Staff and Commander-in-Chief:
Vice-Admiral E. Roest

Flag Officer Naval Personnel:
Rear-Admiral F. H. Heckman

Flag Officer Naval Material:
Vice-Admiral Mr. Ir. P. P. van de Vijver

Command

Admiral Netherlands Home Command:
Rear-Admiral B. Veldkamp

Commander Netherlands Task Group:
Rear Admiral P. J. F. van der Meer Mohr

Commandant Royal Netherlands Marine Corps:
Major-General A. C. Lamers

Flag Officer Netherlands Antilles:
Commodore F. B. Hamilton

Diplomatic Representation

Naval Attaché in London:
Captain J. B. Genet

Naval Attaché in Washington and NLR SACLANT:
Rear-Admiral H. van Mastrigt

Naval Attaché in Paris:
Captain M. G. Zuidijk

Naval Attaché in Bonn:
Captain J. P. L. de Rouw

Strength of the Fleet
(including new construction)

1 Cruiser
2 Destroyers DDG (Building)
22 Frigates (4 Building)
11 Corvettes
6 Patrol Submarines
6 MCM Support and Escort Ships
31 Coastal Minesweepers
4 Minehunters
5 MCM Diving Vessels
16 Inshore Minesweepers
4 Survey Ships (1 Building)
2 Fast Combat Support Ships (1 Building)
27 Miscellaneous

Future New Construction Programme

1 Destroyer (DDG type)
8 Frigates (ASW)
2 Patrol Submarines
15 MCM Vessels
1 Fast Combat Support Ship
26 Helicopters
LRMP Aircraft

Planned Strength in 1980 s

3 ASW Groups each of 6 ASW frigates, 1 DDG, 1 Support Ship (helicopters in all ships) to operate in *Eastlant* Area and Western approaches to Channel.
1 ASW Group of 4 ASW frigates to operate in Channel command.
6 Patrol Submarines
25 LRMP Aircraft
2 MCM Groups of 12 ships each operating off Dutch ports.
1 MCM Group of 7 ships for Channel command.

Naval Air Force

Personnel: 2 000 with 44 aircraft

2 LRMP Squadrons with Atlantics and Neptunes
18 Wasps and AB-204B helicopters
23 S-58 helicopters for SAR, being replaced by SH-3Ds

Personnel

1 January 1973: 20 000 officers and ratings (including the Navy Air Service, Royal Netherlands Marine Corps and about 360 officers and women of the W.R.NL.N.S.)

Disposals and Transfers

Aircraft Carrier

Oct 1968. *Karel Doorman* to Argentina as *25 de Mayo*

Frigates

Dec 1967 *De Bitter, De Zeeuw, Dubois, Van Amstel, Van Ewijck, Van Zijll* returned to US and scrapped.

Corvette

Oct 1961 *Lynx* returned to USS for transfer to Italy

Submarines

July 1963 *Zwaardvis* (ex-*Talent*)
1966 *Tijgerhaai* (ex-*Tarn*)
Nov 1970 *Zeeleuw* (ex-*Hawkbill*)
Nov 1971 *Walrus* (ex-*Icefish*)

Storeships

1968 *Zuiderkruis*
1972 *Woendi*

Netlayer

Sept 1970 *Cerberus* returned to US for transfer to Turkey

Mercantile Marine

Lloyd's Register of Shipping:
1 452 vessels of 4 972 244 tons gross

LIST OF PENNANT NUMBERS

Submarines

S 804 Potvis
S 805 Tonijn
S 806 Zwaardvis
S 807 Tijgerhaai
S 808 Dolfijn
S 809 Zeehond

Cruisers

C 802 De Zeven Provincien

Destroyers

D 808 Holland
D 809 Zeeland
D 810 Noord Brabant
D 811 Gelderland
D 812 Friesland
D 813 Groningen
D 814 Limburg
D 815 Overijssel
D 816 Drenthe
D 817 Utrecht
D 818 Rotterdam
D 918 Amsterdam

Frigates

F 802 Van Speyck
F 803 Van Galen
F 804 Tjerk Hiddes
F 805 Van Nes
F 814 Isaac Sweers
F 815 Evertsen

Corvettes

F 817 Wolf
F 818 Fret
F 819 Hermelijn
F 820 Vos
F 821 Panter
F 822 Jaguar

Escorts:

A 854 Onversaagd
A 855 Onbevreesd
A 858 Onvervaard

MCM Command Support Ships

A 856 Onverschrokken
A 857 Onvermoeid
A 859 Onverdroten

Mine Hunters:

M 801 Dokkum
M 818 Drunen
M 842 Veere

Coastal Minesweepers:

M 802 Hoogezand
M 803 Wildervank
M 808 Axel
M 809 Naaldwijk
M 810 Abcoude
M 811 Aalsmeer
M 812 Drachten
M 813 Ommen
M 814 Meppel
M 815 Giethoorn
M 817 Venlo
M 819 Goes
M 823 Naarden
M 826 Grijpskerk
M 827 Hoogeveen
M 828 Staphorst
M 830 Sittard
M 841 Gemert
M 845 Beemster
M 846 Bolsward
M 847 Bedum
M 848 Beilen
M 849 Borculo
M 850 Borne
M 851 Brummen
M 852 Breukelen
M 853 Blaricum
M 854 Brielle
M 855 Breskens
M 856 Bruinisse
M 857 Boxtel
M 858 Brouwershaveh

Inshore Minesweepers:

M 868 Alblas
M 869 Bussemaker
M 870 Lacomblé
M 871 Van Hamel
M 872 Van Straelen
M 873 Van Moppes
M 874 Chömpff
M 875 Van Well-Groeneveld
M 876 Schuiling
M 877 Van Versendaal
M 878 Van Der Wel
M 879 Van 't Hoff
M 880 Mahu
M 881 Staverman
M 882 Houtepen
M 883 Zomer

Diving Vessels:

M 806 Roermond
M 807 Waalwijk
M 820 Woerden
M 822 Leersum
M 844 Rhenen

Patrol Vessels:

P 802 Balder
P 803 Bulgia
P 804 Freijer
P 805 Hadda
P 806 Hefring

Auxiliary Ships:

A 830 Pelikaan
A 835 Poolster
A 847 Argus
A 848 Triton
A 849 Nautilus
A 850 Hydra
A 870 Wamandai
A 871 Wambrau
A 872 Westgat
A 873 Wielingen
A 902 Luymes
A 907 Snellius
A 912 Dreg 4

Nos. 879 to 892 are allocated to stationary accommodation ships.

CRUISER

Name	No.	Builders	Laid down	Launched	Completed
DE ZEVEN PROVINCIEN (ex-*De Ruyter*, ex-*Eendracht*, ex-*Kijkduin*)	C 802	Rotterdam Drydock Co	19 May 1939	22 Aug 1950	17 Dec 1953

Displacement, tons	9 529 standard; 11 850 full load
Length, feet (*metres*)	590·5 (*180·0*) pp; 614·5 (*190·3*) oa
Beam, feet (*metres*)	56·7 (*17·3*)
Draught, feet (*metres*)	22·0 (*6·7*) max
Missile launchers	1 twin "Terrier" aft
Guns	4—6 in (*152 mm*) in twin turrets; 6—57 mm in twin turrets; 4—40 mm AA
Main engines	2 De Schelde-Parsons geared turbines; 85 000 shp; 2 shafts
Speed, knots	32
Boilers	4 Werkspoor-Yarrow
Complement	*De Zeven Provincien:* 940

Machinery by K. M. de Schelde. Construction resumed in 1946. Tripod mast originally abaft after funnel, is now before after funnel.

DE ZEVEN PROVINCIEN *1972, Royal Netherlands Navy*

RADAR. Search: LW 01, SPS 39 3-D, SGR 104 Height Finder. Tactical: DA 02. Fire Control: HSA M 20 series for larger guns. 2 SPG 55 for "Terrier". 2 M 45 for 40 mm guns.

Scale 125 feet = 1 inch. (1 : 1 500)

MISSILE CONVERSION. *De Zeven Provincien* was converted in 1962-64 by Rotterdamsche Droogdok Mij, Rotterdam with "Terrier" installation by NV Dok en Werf Mij Wilton-Fijenoord Schiedam. She was again refitted and modernised in 1971-72. *De Ruyter* will not be converted. She will be replaced in 1975 by two guided missile armed frigates (DDG) the construction of which was started in 1971.

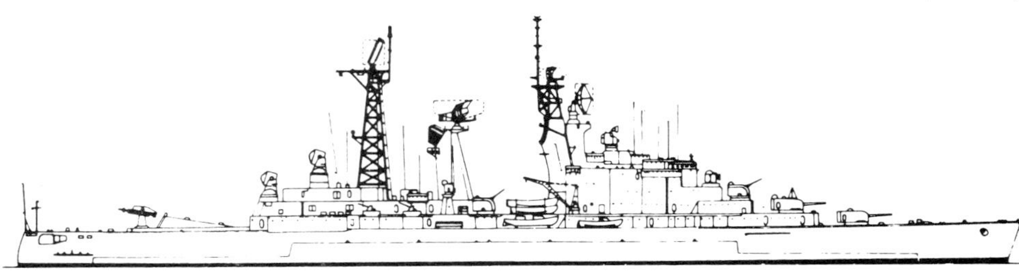

GUNNERY. Main armament has 60 degrees elevation. All guns are fully automatic and radar controlled. The 6 inch guns have a rate of fire of 15 rounds per minute.

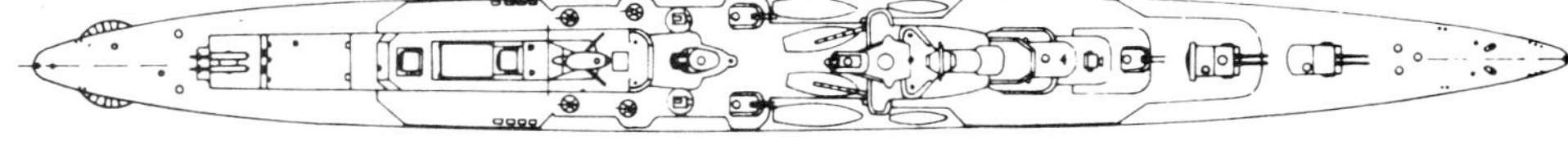

DISPOSAL. *De Ruyter* removed from the active list 13 Oct 1972. Being transferred to Peru.

DESTROYERS

2 "TROMP" CLASS (DDG)

Name	Builders	Laid down
DE RUYTER	Koninklijke Maatschappij De Schelde, Flushing	22 Dec 1971
TROMP	Koninklijke Maatschappij De Schelde, Flushing	4 Sep 1971

Displacement, tons	4 300 standard; 5 400 full load
Length, feet (*metres*)	429·5 (*130·9*) pp; 454·1 (*138·4*) oa
Beam, feet (*metres*)	48·6 (*14·8*)
Draught, feet (*metres*)	15·1 (*4·6*)
Guns	2—4·7 in (twin turret)
Missile launchers	1 "Tartar" aft; Seasparrow Point defence missile system
Aircraft	1 light weight helicopter armed with homing torpedoes
Main engines	2 main gas turbines, 40 000 hp; 2 cruising gas turbines, 8 000 hp
Speed, knots	circa 30 max
Complement	306

TROMP class *1971, Royal Netherlands Navy*

GENERAL
First design allowance was voted for in 1967 estimates. Ordered (announced on 27 July 1970) for laying down in 1971 and completion in 1975. Hangar and helicopter spot landing platform aft.
The cruiser *De Ruyter* (see previous page) will be paid off before the frigate of this name is commissioned.

TROMP *Class*

RADAR. HSA 3D search and target designator in main radome: WM 25 fire control with co-mounted search and tracker in smaller radome for Seasparrow and 4·7 in: 2 SPG-51 for Tartar; Sewaco 1 automated A.I.O.

FRIGATES

6 "VAN SPEYCK" CLASS

Name	No.	Builders	Laid down	Launched	Completed
TJERK HIDDES	F 804	Nederlandse Dok en Scheepsbouw Mij, Amsterdam	1 June 1964	17 Dec 1965	16 Aug 1967
VAN GALEN	F 803	Koninklijke Maatschappij De Schelde, Flushing	25 July 1963	19 June 1965	1 Mar 1967
VAN NES	F 805	Koninklijke Maatschappij De Schelde, Flushing	25 July 1963	26 Mar 1966	9 Aug 1967
VAN SPEYCK	F 802	Nederlandse Dok en Scheepsbouw Mij, Amsterdam	1 Oct 1963	5 Mar 1965	14 Feb 1967
EVERTSEN	F 815	Koninklijke Maatschappij De Schelde, Flushing	6 July 1965	18 June 1966	21 Dec 1967
SAAC SWEERS	F 814	Nederlandse Dok en Scheepsbouw Mij, Amsterdam	5 May 1965	10 Mar 1967	15 May 1968

Displacement, tons	2 200 standard; 2 850 full load
Dimensions, feet	360 wl, 372 oa × 41 × 18
Guns	2—4·5 in (twin turret)
Missile launchers	2 quadruple "Seacat" anti-aircraft
A/S weapons	1 "Limbo" three-barrelled depth charge mortar
Aircraft	1 lightweight helicopter armed with homing torpedoes
Boilers	2 Babcock & Wilcox
Main engines	2 double reduction geared turbines; 2 shafts; 30 000 shp
Speed, knots	28·5 sea, 30 max
Complement	254

GENERAL. Four ships were ordered in Oct 1962 and two later. Built to replace the six frigates of the "Van Amstel" class (DEs) returned to USA and subsequently scrapped. Have ECM and VDS.

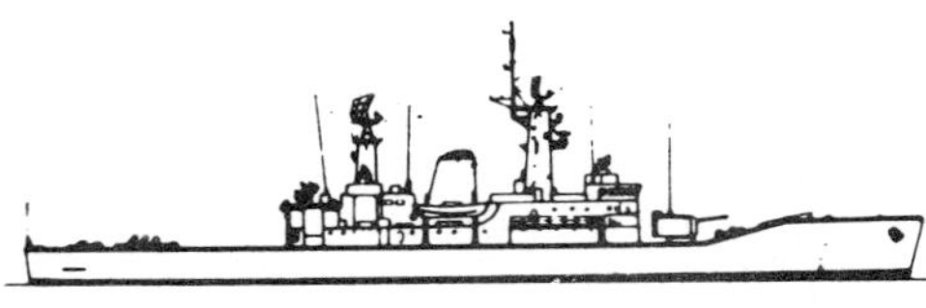

VAN SPEYCK class

DESIGN. Although in general these ships are based on the design of the British Improved Type 12 ("Leander" class), there are a number of modifications to suit the requirements of the Royal Netherlands Navy. As far as possible equipment of Netherlands manufacture was installed. This resulted in a number of changes in the ship's superstructure compared with the British "Leander" class. To avoid delay these ships were in some cases fitted with equipment already available, instead of going through long development stages.

RADAR. LW 02 air surveillance on mainmast; DA 05 target indicator on foremast; surface-warning/nav set on foremast; 1-M45 for 4·5 in guns; 2-M44 for Seacat.

VAN GALEN — 1971, Royal Netherlands Navy

8 "FRIESLAND" CLASS

Name	No.	Builders	Laid down	Launched	Completed
FRIESLAND	D 812	Nederlandse Dok en Scheepsbouw Mij, Amsterdam	17 Dec 1951	21 Feb 1953	22 Mar 1956
GRONINGEN	D 813	Nederlandse Dok en Scheepsbouw Mij, Amsterdam	21 Feb 1952	9 Jan 1954	12 Sep 1956
LIMBURG	D 814	Koninklijke Maatschappij De Schelde, Flushing	28 Nov 1953	5 Sep 1955	31 Oct 1956
OVERIJSSEL	D 815	Dok-en-Werfmaatschappij Wilton-Fijenoord	15 Oct 1953	8 Aug 1955	4 Oct 1957
DRENTHE	D 816	Nederlandse Dok en Scheepsbouw Mij, Amsterdam	9 Jan 1954	26 Mar 1955	1 Aug 1957
UTRECHT	D 817	Koninklijke Maatschappij De Schelde, Flushing	15 Feb 1954	2 June 1956	1 Oct 1957
ROTTERDAM	D 818	Rotterdamse Droogdok Mij, Rotterdam	7 Jan 1954	26 Jan 1956	28 Feb 1957
AMSTERDAM	D 819	Nederlandse Dok en Scheepsbouw Mij, Amsterdam	26 Mar 1955	25 Aug 1956	10 Aug 1958

Displacement, tons	2 497 standard; 3 070 full load
Length, feet (*metres*)	370 (*112·8*) pp; 380·5 (*116·0*) oa
Beam, feet (*metres*)	38·5 (*11·7*)
Draught, feet (*metres*)	17 (*5·2*)
Guns, surface	4—4·7 in (*120 mm*) twin turrets
Guns, AA	4—40 mm (2 removed during recent refits)
A/S weapons	2 four-barrelled depth charge mortars. Bofors rocket launchers
Boilers	4 Babcock
Main engines	2 Werkspoor geared turbines, 60 000 shp; 2 shafts
Speed, knots	36
Complement	284

GENERAL

These ships have side armour as well as deck protection. "Limbo" type anti-submarine rocket throwers. Twin rudders. Propellers 370 rpm. Named after provinces of the Netherlands, and the two principal cities. To be replaced by a new class of frigates after 1975.

RADAR. Search: LW 03. Tactical: DA 05. Fire Control HSA M 45 for 4·7 in. HSA fire control for 40 mm and A/S rockets.

GUNNERY. The 4·7 inch guns are fully automatic with a rate of fire of 50 rounds per minute. All guns are radar controlled. Originally six 40 mm guns were mounted.

OVERIJSSEL — 1972, Royal Netherlands Navy

TORPEDO TUBES. *Utrecht* was equipped with eight 21 inch A/S torpedo tubes (single, four on each side) in 1960 and *Overijssel* in 1961, and the others were to have been, but the project was dropped and tubes already fitted were removed.

FRIESLAND *Class*

FRIESLAND — 1971, Royal Netherlands Navy

Frigates—*continued*

4 "HOLLAND" CLASS

Name	No.	Builders	Laid down	Launched	Completed
HOLLAND	D 808	Rotterdamse Droogdok Mij, Rotterdam	21 Apr 1950	11 Apr 1953	31 Dec 1954
ZEELAND	D 809	Koninklijke Maatschappij De Schelde, Flushing	12 Jan 1951	27 June 1953	1 Mar 1955
NOORD BRABANT	D 810	Koninklijke Maatschappij De Schelde, Flushing	1 Mar 1951	28 Nov 1953	1 June 1955
GELDERLAND	D 811	Dok-en-Werfmaatschappij Wilton-Fijenoord	10 Mar 1951	19 Sep 1953	17 Aug 1955

Displacement, tons	2 215 standard; 2 765 full load
Length, feet (*metres*)	360·5 (*109·9*) pp; 371·1 (*113·1*) oa
Beam, feet (*metres*)	37·5 (*11·4*)
Draught, feet (*metres*)	16·8 (*5·1*)
Guns	4—4·7 in (*120 mm*); 1—40 mm
A/S weapons	2 four-barrelled DC mortars. Bofors rocket launchers
Main engines	Werkspoor Parsons geared turbines; 2 shafts; 45 000 shp
Speed, knots	32
Boilers	4 Babcock
Complement	247

HOLLAND *Class*

GENERAL

Two ships of this class are equipped with engines of the pre-war "Callenburgh" class and two with similar engines built during the war in the Netherlands, intended for German destroyers that were never built. (The four "Callenburgh" class destroyers were being built in 1940. *Isaac Sweers* was towed to England and completed there. *Tjerk Hiddes* was completed by the Germans as ZH 1. The other two, *Callenburgh* and *Van Almonde*, were too severely damaged for further use and were scrapped, the engines being installed in the "Holland" class).

RADAR. Search: LW 03. Tactical: DA 02. Fire Control: HSA M 45 for 4·7 in. HSA fire control for A/S rocket launcher.

GUNNERY. The 4·7 inch guns are fully automatic with a rate of fire of 50 rounds per minute. All guns are radar controlled.

HOLLAND — *1970, Courtesy Godfrey H. Walker, Esq.*

4 NEW CONSTRUCTION ASW TYPE

Displacement, tons	circa 3 000 (revised official figures)
Aircraft	1 helicopter
Missile launchers	Surface-to-air and surface-to-surface
Main engines	Gas turbines
Speed, knots	circa 30 max

The 1970 Estimates included a vote for the construction of four new anti-submarine frigates to replace the four "Holland" class DDEs in 1975-76.

CORVETTES

6 "WOLF" CLASS

Name	No.	Builders	Laid down	Launched	Completed
FRET (ex-*PCE* 1604)	F 818	General Shipbuilding and Engineering Works, Boston	18 Dec 1952	30 July 1953	4 May 1954
HERMELIJN (ex-*PCE* 1605)	F 819	General Shipbuilding and Engineering Works, Boston	2 Mar 1953	6 Mar 1954	5 Aug 1954
JAGUAR (ex-*PCE* 1609)	F 822	Avondale Marine Ways, Inc, New Orleans, Louisiana	10 Dec 1952	20 Mar 1954	11 June 1954
PANTER (ex-*PCE* 1608)	F 821	Avondale Marine Ways, Inc, New Orleans, Louisiana	1 Dec 1952	30 Jan 1954	11 June 1954
VOS (ex-*PCE* 1606)	F 820	General Shipbuilding and Engineering Works, Boston	3 Aug 1952	1 May 1954	2 Dec 1954
WOLF (ex-*PCE* 1607)	F 817	Avondale Marine Ways, Inc, New Orleans, Louisiana	15 Nov 1952	2 Jan 1954	26 Mar 1954

Displacement, tons	808 standard; 975 full load
Length, feet (*metres*)	180 (*54·9*) pp; 184·5 (*56·2*) oa
Beam, feet (*metres*)	33 (*10·0*)
Draught, feet (*metres*)	9·5 (*2·9*) mean; 14·5 (*4·4*) max
Guns, dual purpose	1—3 in (*76 mm*)
Guns, AA	6—40 mm (*Jaguar, Panter:* 4—40 mm); 8—20 mm
A/S	1 Hedgehog; 2 DCT (*Jaguar, Panter:* 4); 2 DC racks
Main engines	2 GM diesels; 1 600 bhp; 2 shafts
Range, miles	4 300 at 10 knots
Speed, knots	15
Complement	96

PCE type escorts built in USA. *Lynx* (ex-*PCE* 1626) of a different type, similar to the Italian "Albatros" and Danish "Triton" classes, was returned to USN on 18 Oct 1961, and handed over to the Italian Navy and renamed *Aquila*. 20 mm guns not fitted in peacetime.

WOLF *Class*

PANTER — *1972, Wright & Logan*

Corvettes—*continued*

5 "BALDER" CLASS

Name	*No.*	*Laid down*	*Launched*	*Completed*
BALDER	P 802	12 Sep 1953	24 Feb 1954	6 Aug 1954
BULGIA	P 803	10 Oct 1953	24 Apr 1954	9 Aug 1954
FREYR	P 804	24 Feb 1954	21 July 1954	1 Dec 1954
HADDA	P 805	24 Apr 1954	2 Oct 1954	3 Feb 1955
HEFRING	P 806	21 July 1954	1 Dec 1954	23 Mar 1955

Displacement, tons 149 standard; 225 full load
Dimensions, feet 114·9 pp; 119·1 oa × 20·2 × 5·9
Guns 1—40 mm; 3—20 mm
A/S weapons 2 DGT, Mousetrap
Main engines Diesels; 2 shafts; 1 050 shp = 15·5 knots
Range, miles 1 000 at 13 knots
Complement 27

Built in the Netherlands by Rijkswerf Willemsoord on US account. US submarine chaser type, SC Nos 1627-1631.

HEFRING *1971, Royal Netherlands Navy*

SUBMARINES

2 "ZWAARDVIS" CLASS

Name	*No.*	*Builders*	*Laid down*	*Launched*	*Completed*
TIJGERHAAI	S 807	Rotterdamse Droogdok Mij, Rotterdam	14 July 1966	25 May 1971	20 Oct 1972
ZWAARDVIS	S 806	Rotterdamse Droogdok Mij, Rotterdam	14 July 1966	2 July 1970	18 Aug 1972

Displacement, tons 2 350 surface; 2 640 submerged
Length, feet (*metres*) 213·3 (*65·0*)
Beam, feet (*metres*)) 27·5 (*8·4*)
Draught, feet (*metres*) 23·3 (*7·1*)
Torpedo tubes 6—21 in (*533 mm*)
Main engines Diesel-electric; 3 diesel generators; 1 shaft
Speed, knots 13 on surface; 20 submerged
Complement 67

In the 1964 Navy Estimates a first instalment was approved for the construction of two conventionally powered submarines. Scheduled to be commissioned one year after launch. HSA M8 Fire Control.

ZWAARDVIS *1972, Royal Netherlands Navy*

2 "POTVIS" CLASS
2 "DOLFIJN" CLASS

Name	*No.*	*Builders*	*Laid down*	*Launched*	*Completed*
POTVIS	S 804	Wilton-Fijenoord, Schiedam	17 Sep 1962	12 Jan 1965	2 Nov 1965
TONIJN	S 805	Wilton-Fijenoord, Schiedam	27 Nov 1962	14 June 1965	24 Feb 1966
DOLFIJN	S 808	Rotterdamse Droogdok Mij, Rotterdam	30 Dec 1954	20 May 1959	16 Dec 1960
ZEEHOND	S 809	Rotterdamse Droogdok Mij, Rotterdam	30 Dec 1954	20 Feb 1960	16 Mar 1961

Displacement, tons 1 140 standard; 1 494 surface
1 826 submerged
Length, feet (*metres*) 260·9 (*79·5*)
Beam, feet (*metres*) 25·8 (*7·8*)
Draught, feet (*metres*) 15·8 (*4·8*)
Torpedo tubes 8—21 in (*533 mm*)
Main engines 2 MAN diesels; total 3 100 bhp
Electric motors, 4 200 hp; 2 shafts
Speed, knots 14·5 on surface; 17 submerged
Complement 64

These submarines are of a triple-hulled design. Maximum depth 980 feet (*300 metres*). *Potvis* and *Tonijn*, originally voted for in 1949 with the other pair, but suspended for some years, had several modifications compared with *Dolfijn* and *Zeehond* and were officially considered to be a separate class; but modernisation of both classes had been completed, and all four boats are now almost identical. HSA M8 Fire Control.

CONSTRUCTION. The hull consists of three cylinders arranged in a triangular shape. The upper cylinder accommodates the crew, navigational equipment and armament. The lower two cylinders house the propulsion machinery comprising diesel engines, batteries and electric motors. See Frontispiece of the 1959-1960 edition for scale models—cutaway longitudinal section showing double decker roominess, and cross section showing triple hull permitting greater diving depth.

DOLFIJN *1972, Edmund Moroney*

ZEEHOND *1971, Royal Netherlands Navy*

MINE WARFARE FORCES

6 "ONVERSAAGD" CLASS (MCM SUPPORT SHIPS and ESCORTS)

Name	*No.*	*Laid down*	*Completed*
ONVERSAAGD (ex-AM 480)	A 854 (ex-M 884)	1952	27 May 1954
ONBEVREESD (ex-AM 481)	A 855 (ex-M 885)	1952	21 Sep 1954
ONVERSCHROKKEN (ex-AM 483)	A 856 (ex-M 886)	1952	22 July 1954
ONVERMOEID (ex-AM 484)	A 857 (ex-M 887)	1952	23 Sep 1954
ONVERVAARD (ex-AM 482)	A 858 (ex-M 888)	1952	31 Mar 1955
ONVERDROTEN (ex-AM 485)	A 859 (ex-M 889)	1952	22 Nov 1954

Displacement, tons	735 standard; 790 full load
Dimensions, feet	165·0 pp; 172·0 oa × 36·0 × 10·6
Guns	1—40 mm AA
A/S weapons	2 DC
Main engines	Diesels; 1 600 bhp = 15·5 knots
Oil fuel, tons	46
Range, miles	2 400 at 12 knots
Complement	70

Built in USA for the Netherlands, *Onversaagd, Onbevreesd* and *Onvervaard* by Astoria Marine Construction Co. and the remaining three by Peterson, Builders, Wisconsin. Of wooden and non-magnetic construction.

RECLASSIFICATION. Originally designed as Ocean Minesweepers, but used as Escorts and re-numbered with "A" pennants in 1966. Reclassified in 1968 as Escorts *Onversaagd, Onbevreesd* and *Onvervaard,* and MCM Group Command and Support Ships *Onverschrokken, Onvermoeid* and *Onverdroten.* The last converted in 1972 to serve as Torpedo Trials vessel in place of *Mercuu.*

ONVERVAARD (Escort type) *1972, Royal Netherlands Navy*

18 "DOKKUM" CLASS (CMS and MINEHUNTERS)

ABCOUDE	M 810	**HOOGEZAND**	M 802	**ROERMOND***	M 806
DOKKUM	M 801 H	**HOOGEVEEN**	M 827	**SITTARD**	M 830
DRACHTEN	M 812	**NAALDWIJK**	M 809	**STAPHORST**	M 828 H
DRUNEN	M 818 H	**NAARDEN**	M 823	**VEERE**	M 842 H
GEMERT	M 841	**OMMEN**	M 813	**VENLO**	M 817
GIETHOORN	M 815	**RHENEN***	M 844	**WOERDEN***	M 820

8 "WILDERVANK" CLASS (CMS)

AALSMEER	M 811	**GOES**	M 819	**MEPPEL**	M 814
AXEL	M 808	**GRIJPSKERK**	M 826	**WAALWIJK***	M 807
		LEERSUM*	M 822	**WILDERVANK**	M 803

Displacement, tons	373 standard; 417 full load
Dimensions, feet	149·8 oa × 28 × 6·5
Guns	2—40 mm
Main engines	2 diesels; Fyenoord MAN or Werkspoor; 2 500 bhp = 16 knots
Range, miles	2 500 at 10 knots
Complement	38

Of 32 Western Union type non-magnetic coastal minesweepers built in the Netherlands (*Kustmynenvegers*), 18 were on US account as the "Dokkum" class, with MAN engines, and 14 on Netherlands account as the "Wildervank" class, with Werkspoor diesels. All launched in 1954-56 and completed in 1955-56. Named after small towns in the Netherlands. *Dokkum* and *Drunen* converted to minehunters *Mijnenjagers* (MHC) in 1968-70, *Veere* in 1970-71 and *Staphorst* in 1972-73. *Leersum, Rhenen, Waalwijk,* and *Woerden* were converted to MCM diving vessels (*Duikvaartuigen*) in 1962-65, and *Roermond* in 1968. *Gieten, Lisse, Lochem, Sneek* and *Steenwijk* of the "Wildervank" class were deleted from the list in 1970, and *Elst* was sold to Ethiopia in 1971. HSA surface/nav radar.

DOKKUM (Hunter) *1971, Royal Netherlands Navy*

Mine Warfare Forces—*continued*

SITTARD (Sweeper) *1972, Royal Netherlands Navy*

14 "BEEMSTER" CLASS (CMS)

BEEMSTER (ex-*AMS* 105)	M 845	**BREUKELEN** (ex-*AMS* 100)	M 852
BOLSWARD (ex-*AMS* 109)	M 846	**BLARICUM** (ex-*AMS* 112)	M 853
BEDUM (ex-*Beerta* ex-*AMS* 106)	M 847	**BRIELLE** (ex-*AMS* 167)	M 854
BEILEN (ex-*AMS* 110)	M 848	**BRESKENS** (ex-*AMS* 148)	M 855
BORCULO (ex-*AMS* 107)	M 849	**BRUINISSE** (ex-*AMS* 168)	M 856
BORNE (ex-*AMS* 108)	M 850	**BOXTEL** (ex-*AMS* 149)	M 857
BRUMMEN (ex-*AMS* 111)	M 851	**BROUWERSHAVEN** ex-*AMS* 150)	M 858

Displacement, tons	330 standard; 384 full load
Dimensions, feet	138 pp; 144·7 oa × 27·9 × 7·5
Guns	2—20 mm AA
Main engines	2 diesels; 880 bhp = 13·6 knots
Range, miles	2 500 at 10 knots
Complement	37

All completed and transferred from USA in 1953-54. Of non-magnetic construction. Named after small towns in the Netherlands.

BROUWERSHAVEN *1971, Courtesy Mr. Michael D. J. Lennon*

16 "VAN STRAELEN" CLASS (IMS)

ALBLAS	M 868	**MAHU**	M 880	**VAN MOPPES**	M 873
BUSSEMAKER	M 869	**SCHUILING**	M 876	**VAN STRAELEN**	M 872
CHÖMPFF	M 874	**STAVERMAN**	M 881	**VAN VERSENDAAL**	M 877
HOUTEPEN	M 882	**VAN DER WEL**	M 878	**VAN WELL GROENVELD**	M 875
LACOMBLÉ	M 870	**VAN HAMEL**	M 871		
		VAN 'T HOFF	M 879	**ZOMER**	M 883

Displacement, tons	151 light; 169 full load
Dimensions, feet	90 pp; 99·3 oa × 18·2 × 5·2
Guns	1—20 mm AA
Main engines	Werkspoor diesels; 2 shafts; 1 100 bhp = 13 knots
Complement	12

Built, 6 by Werf de Noord at Albasserdam; 5 by N.V. de Arnhemse Scheepsbouw Maatschappij at Arnhem; and 5 by Amsterdamsche Scheepswerft G. de Vries Lentsch Jr at Amsterdam. Eight were built under the offshore procurement programme, with MDAP funds, and the remaining eight were paid for by Netherlands. All ordered in mid-1957. Built of non-magnetic materials. *Alblas,* the first, was laid down at Werf de Noord N.V. at Albasserdam on 26 Feb 1958, launched on 29 June 1959, started trials on 15 Jan 1960 and completed on 12 Mar 1960. All the others were laid down in 1958-61, launched in 1958-61 and commissioned in 1960-62.

VAN WELL GROENVELD *1972, Wright & Logan*

SURVEY SHIPS

1 NEW CONSTRUCTION OCEANOGRAPHIC TYPE

The 1971 Estimates announced the construction of an oceanographic/hydrographic ship to replace *Snellius*. The 1972 Estimates stated she will be ordered in late 1972/ early 1973 and will be larger than *Snellius*.

2 "BUYSKES" CLASS

BLOMMENDAL A 905 **BUYSKES** A 904

Displacement tons	1 050
Dimensions, feet	177·2 × 35·4 × 11·4
Main engines	Diesel electric; 2 100 hp (3 × 700) = 13 knots max
Complement	45

The projected two survey ships, the construction of which was announced in the 1971 Defence Estimates, were ordered in Feb 1971 from the yard of Boele Scheepswerven en Machinenfabriek, Bolnes. Their design is based on that of the very successful pilot cutters of the "Capella" class. Have a helicopter deck. Both ships primarily have been designed for survey work, but can also be used for extensive oceanographic and meteorological work. They will operate mainly in the North Sea and other shallow waters off the Continental Shelf. Their cost is estimated to be 10·5 million guilders per ship. Completed in Nov 1972 and March 1973. *Buyskes* launched 11 July 1972.

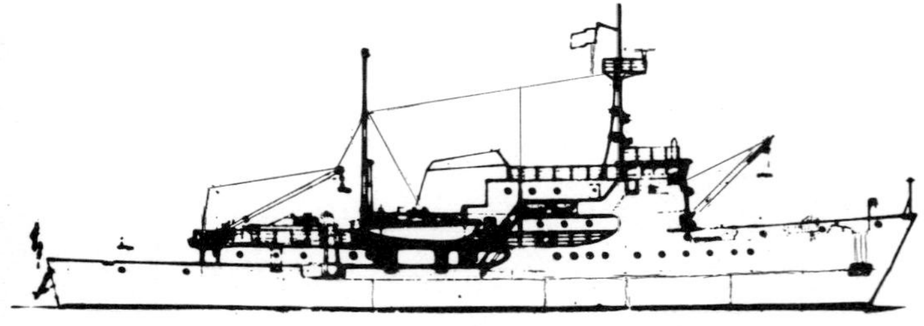

BUYSKES 1971

Name	*No.*	*Builders*	*Laid down*	*Launched*	*Completed*
SNELLIUS	A 907	P. Smit, Jr, Rotterdam	3 Jan 1949	14 Apr 1951	4 Feb 1952

Displacement, tons	1 100 standard; 1 540 full load
Dimensions, feet	234·2 × 35·5 × 12·8
Guns	1—40 mm AA; 2—20 mm AA
Main engines	2 Stork 6 cyl, 4 str diesels; 2 shafts; 2 000 bhp = 15 knots
Complement	80

Sloop type. Fitted for service in the tropics with special upper deck access and habitability.

DREG IV A 920

Displacement, tons	46 standard; 48 full load
Dimensions, feet	65·7 × 15·1 × 4·9
Main engines	120 hp = 9·5 knots
Complement	10

Sister boats *Dreg I*, *Dreg II* and *Dreg III* of this class were scrapped in 1969-70.

FAST COMBAT SUPPORT SHIP

2 "POOLSTER" CLASS

POOLSTER A 835 **ZUIDERKRUIS**

Displacement, tons	16 800 full load
Measurements, tons	10 000 deadweight
Dimensions, feet	515 pp; 556 oa × 66·7 × 27
Guns	2—40 mm AA
Aircraft	Capacity: 5 helicopters (official complement 3 SH-34 J)
Main engines	22 500 shp turbines = 21 knots (18 service) (Werkspoor diesels in Zuiderkruis)
Complement	200

Fast fleet replenishment ship (*Bevoorradingsschip*). *Poolster* built by Rotterdam se Droogdok Mij. Laid down on 18 Sep 1962. Launched on 16 Oct 1963. Trials mid-1964. Commissioned on 10 Sep 1964. Helicopter deck aft. Funnel heightened by 4·5 m. *Zuiderkruis* building by Rhine-Scheldt-Verolme. Ordered Oct 1972.

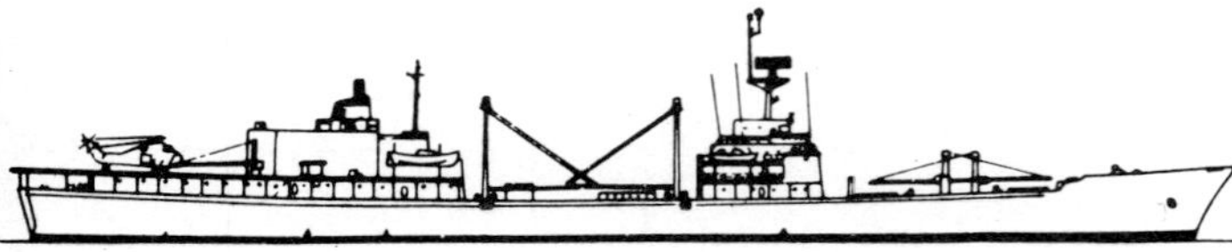

POOLSTER

POOLSTER (note modified funnel) *1972, Wright & Logan*

SUPPLY SHIPS

1 Ex-BRITISH LST TYPE

PELIKAAN (ex-HMS *Thruster*, ex-*LST*) A 830

Displacement, tons	2 840 light; 4 250 standard; 6 538 full load
Dimensions, feet	390 × 49 × 13
Guns	2—40 mm AA; 10—20 mm AA
Main engines	Turbine; 7 000 shp = 17 knots
Oil fuel, tons	2 100 max
Range, miles	8 000 at 14 knots
Complement	127

Built by Harland & Wolff Ltd, Belfast. Laid down on 31 July 1941. Launched on 24 Sep 1942. Completed on 14 Mar 1943. Purchased from Great Britain in 1947. Commissioned in the Royal Netherlands Navy in July 1948. Store ship at Den Helder.

PELIKAAN *1969, Royal Netherlands Navy*

ACCOMMODATION SHIPS

Cornelis Drebbel is the name of the new "Boatel"—775 tons, length 206·7 feet, beam 38·7 feet, draught 3·6 feet, complement 200, cost 3m guilders. Ordered in 1969 from Scheepswerf Voorwaarts at Hoogezand, launched on 19 Nov 1970 and completed in 1971. Serves as accommodation vessel for crews of ships refitting at private yards in the Rotterdam area. *Luymes* (ex survey ship) also used for accommodation.

LANDING CRAFT

L 9521 **L 9526**

Displacement, tons	20
Dimensions, feet	50 × 11·8 × 5·8
Main engines	2 Kromhout diesels; 75 bhp = 8 knots
Complement	3

Now officially rated as LCA Type. The landing craft L 9609 (ex-*Kais*) was sold in 1970.

L 9510 **L 9512** **L 9514** **L 9517** **L 9520**
L 9511 **L 9513** **L 9515** **L 9518** **L 9522**

Displacement, tons	13·6
Dimensions, feet	46·2 × 11·5 × 6
Main engines	Rolls Royce diesel; Schottel propeller; 200 bhp = 12 knots
Complement	3

New landing craft made of plastic (polyester), all commissioned in 1962-63, except L 9520 in 1964.

TRAINING SHIPS

HENDRIK KARSSEN (ex-*Y* 807, ex-*RC* 11, ex-*De Mok* 1) Y 8102

Displacement, tons	172 standard; 185 full load
Dimensions, feet	137·8 oa; 114 pp × 20·7 × 5·5
Guns	2—20 mm AA
Main engines	2 Kromhout diesels; 180 bhp = 11 knots
Complement	18

Built by Rijkswerf Willemsoord. Launched in 1939. Equipped with water monitors for fire fighting. Renamed *Hendrik Karssen* in 1954. Training and ferry vessel for local use at Den Helder.

HOBEIN (ex-*Doornbos*, ex-German *Dornbusch*) Y 8101

Displacement, tons	132
Dimensions, feet	92 oa; 83·3 pp × 19·7 × 5·5
Guns	1—40 mm AA; 1—20 mm AA
Main engines	Diesel; 250 bhp = 8·5 knots
Complement	10

Navigational training ship for midshipmen and other naval personnel, and ferry vessel for local use at Den Helder. Renamed *Hobein* in July 1952.

URANIA (ex-*Tromp*) Y 8050

Displacement, tons	38
Dimensions, feet	72 × 16·3 × 10
Main engines	Diesel; 65 hp
Complement	15

Schooner used for training in seamanship. Commissioned on 23 Apr 1938.

TENDERS

VAN BOCHOVE A 923

Displacement, tons	150
Dimensions, feet	97·2 × 18·2 × 6
Main engines	Kromhout diesel; Schottel propeller; 140 bhp = 8 knots
Complement	8

Torpedo recovery vessel. Built by Zaanlandse Scheepsbouw Mij, Zaandam. Ordered Oct 1961, launched on 20 July 1962 and completed in Aug 1962.

DIVING TENDER (NETLAYER)
The diving tender *Cerebus*, A 895, former netlayer, was returned to the US Navy on 17 Sep 1970. The ship was then immediately handed over to the Turkish Navy and named *AG 6*.

TUGS

WESTGAT A 872 **WIELINGEN** A 873

Displacement, tons	185
Dimensions, feet	90·6 × 22·7 × 7·7
Guns	2—20 mm AA
Main engines	Bolnes diesel; 720 bhp = 12 knots

Built by Rijkswerf, Willemsoord. Launched on 22 Aug 1967 and 6 Jan 1968 and completed on 10 Jan 1968 and 4 Apr 1968, respectively. Equipped with salvage pumps and fire fighting equipment. Stationed at Den Helder. The tug *Hercules* (ex-*Walcheren* XII, ex-*Atlas*) A 828, was sold to private interests in 1968.

WAMANDAI A 870 (ex-Y 8035)

Displacement, tons	159 standard; 185 full load
Dimensions, feet	89·2 × 21·3 × 7·5
Guns	2—20 mm AA
Main engines	Diesel; 500 bhp = 11 knots

Built by Rijkswerf, Willemsoord, Den Helder. Launched on 28 May 1960. Equipped with salvage pumps and fire fighting equipment. In the Netherlands Antilles since 1964.

WAMBRAU A 871

Displacement, tons	154 standard; 184 full load
Dimensions, feet	86·5 oa × 20·7 × 7·5
Guns	2—20 mm AA
Main engines	Werkspoor diesel and Kort nozzle; 500 bhp = 10·8 knots

Built by Rijkswerf Willemsoord. Launched on 27 Aug 1956. Completed on 8 Jan 1957. Equipped with salvage pumps and fire fighting equipment. Stationed at Den Helder.

BERKEL Y 8037 **DINTEL** Y 8038 **DOMMEL** Y 8039 **IJSSEL** Y 8040

Displacement, tons	139 standard; 163 full load
Dimensions, feet	82 oa × 20·5 × 7·3
Main engines	Werkspoor diesel and Kort nozzle; 500 bhp

Harbour tugs built by H. H. Bodewes, Millingen. Specially designed for use at Den Helder. Completed in 1956-57.

NEW ZEALAND

Defence Headquarters Naval Staff

Chief of Naval Staff:
Rear Admiral E. C. Thorne, CBE

Deputy Chief of Naval Staff:
Commodore N. D. Anderson, OBE

The three New Zealand Service Boards were formally abolished in 1971 as part of the Defence Headquarters reorganization. The former three Service Headquarters and Defence Office have been reorganised into functional branches and offices.
On 1 June 1970 the command and control of the three New Zealand Services was vested in the Chief of Defence Staff who exercises this authority through the three Service Chiefs of Staff.

Diplomatic Representation

Head of New Zealand Defence Liaison Staff, London and Senior Naval Liason Officer:
Commodore M. J. McDowell

Deputy Head of New Zealand Defence Staff, Washington and Naval Attaché:
Commander K. M. Saul

Personnel

January 1969: 2 959 officers and ratings
January 1970: 3 074 officers and ratings
January 1971: 2 870 officers and ratings
January 1972: 2 993 officers and ratings
January 1973: 2 966 officers and ratings

Strength of the Fleet

4 Frigates
1 Survey Ship
2 Escort Minesweepers
15 Patrol Craft (four building)
1 Research Vessel
2 Tenders

Mercantile Marine

Lloyd's Register of Shipping:
120 vessels of 181 901 tons gross

Disposals

Cruisers

Dec 1971	*Black Prince*
July 1966	*Royalist*

Frigates

April 1971	*Blackpool* returned to Royal Navy
Dec 1961	*Taupo, Tutira*
Sept 1965	*Hawea, Pukaki*
1966	*Rotoiti, Kaniere*

Corvettes

1962	*Kiwi*
1967	*Tui*

Miscellaneous

1961	*Coastguard Endeavour* (ex-*John Biscoe*)
1964	*Hauraki, Maori, Philomel, Lander* /
June 1971	*Endeavour* (ex-USS *Namakagon*) returned to USN for transfer to Taiwan. (now *Lung Chuan*)

FRIGATES

2 "LEANDER" CLASS

Displacement, tons	2 450 standard; 2 860 full load *Waikato*: 2 470 standard; 2990 full load *Canterbury*
Length, feet (*metres*)	360·0 (*109·7*) pp; 372·0 (*113·4*) oa *Waikato*; 370·0 (*112·8*) pp *Canterbury*
Beam, feet (*metres*)	41·0 (*12·5*) *Waikato*; 43·0 (*13·1*) *Canterbury*
Draught, feet (*metres*)	18 (*5·5*)
Aircraft	1 Wasp helicopter armed with homing torpedo
Missile launchers	1 quadruple "Seacat"
Guns	2—4·5 in (*155 mm*) in twin turret; 2—20 mm AA
A/S weapons	1 Limbo 3-barrelled DC mortar *Waikato*; 2—TF Mk 32 Mod 5 torpedo tubes *Canterbury*
Main engines	2 sets d.r. geared turbines; 2 shafts; 30 000 shp

Name	*No.*	*Builders*	*Laid down*	*Launched*	*Completed*
CANTERBURY	F 421	Yarrow Ltd, Clyde	12 Apr 1969	6 May 1970	22 Oct 1971
WAIKATO	F 55	Harland & Wolff Ltd, Belfast	10 Jan 1964	18 Feb 1965	19 Sep 1966

Speed, knots	30 *Waikato*; 28 *Canterbury*
Boilers	2 Babcock & Wilcox
Complement	248 (14 officers, 234 ratings) *Waikato*; 243 (14 officers 229 ratings) *Canterbury*

Waikato, ordered on 14 June 1963. Commissioned on 16 Sep 1966, trials in the United Kingdom until spring 1967, arrived in New Zealand waters in May 1967. *Canterbury* was ordered in Aug 1968, arrived in New Zealand in Aug 1972.

RADAR. Search: Type 965. Tactical 993. Fire Control MRS 3 System and X Band.

WAIKATO

CANTERBURY 1972, Wright & Logan

Frigates—*continued*

Name	*No.*	*Builders*	*Launched*	*Completed*
OTAGO (ex-*Hastings*)	F 111	John I. Thornycroft & Co, Ltd Woolston, Southampton	11 Dec 1958	22 June 1960
TARANAKI	F 148	J. Samuel White & Co Ltd, Cowes, Isle of Wight	19 Aug 1959	28 Mar 1961

2 "ROTHESAY" CLASS TYPE 12

Scale: 150 feet = 1 inch (1 : 1 800)

Displacement, tons	2 144 standard; 2 557 full load
Length, feet (*metres*)	360·0 (*109·7*) pp; 370·0 (*112·8*) oa
Beam, feet (*metres*)	41·0 (*12·5*)
Draught, feet (*metres*)	17·3 (*5·3*) max (props)
Missile launchers	1 quadruple "Seacat"
Guns	2—4·5 in (*115 mm*) in twin turret; 2—40 mm (*Taranaki* only)
A/S weapons	2 Limbo 3-barrelled DC mortars
Main engines	2 sets d.r. geared turbines; 2 shafts; 30 000 shp
Speed, knots	30
Boilers	2 Babcock & Wilcox
Complement	240 (13 officers, 227 ratings)

OTAGO, TARANAKI

Anti-submarine frigates. *Taranaki* was ordered direct (announced by J. Samuel White & Co on 22 Feb 1957). For *Otago* New Zealand took over the contract (officially stated on 26 Feb 1957) for *Hastings* originally ordered from John I. Thornycroft & Co in Feb 1956 for the Royal Navy Both vessels are generally similar to those in the Royal Navy, but were modified to suit New Zealand conditions. *Otago* has had enclosed foremast since 1967 refit; *Taranaki* was similarly fitted during 1969.

RADAR. Search Type 993 and Type 277. Fire Control X Band

TUBES. The original twelve 21 in (*533 mm*) A/S torpedo tubes (8 single and 2 twin) were suppressed.

TARANAKI

1971, Royal New Zealand Navy

ESCORT MINESWEEPERS

2 "BATHURST" CLASS

Name	*No.*	*Builders*	*Laid down*	*Launched*	*Completed*
INVERELL	M 233	Mort's Dock, Sydney	7 Dec 1941	2 May 1942	2 May 1943
KIAMA	M 353	Evans Deakins, Brisbane	2 Nov 1942	3 July 1943	26 Jan 1944

Displacement, tons	790 standard; 1 025 full load
Length, feet (*metres*)	162·0 (*49·4*) pp; 186·0 (*56·7*) oa
Beam, feet (*metres*)	31·0 (*9·4*)
Draught, feet (*metres*)	9·5 (*2·9*)
Guns	2—40 mm AA
Main engines	Triple expansion; 2 shafts; 1 800 ihp
Speed, knots	15
Boilers	2 Admiralty 3-drum small tube
Complement	71

Originally four vessels of this class were given to New Zealand by Australia in 1952 (see disposal note below).

Kiama was recommissioned on 15 Mar 1966 for training and fishery protection duties, her 4-inch gun being replaced by a 40 mm AA gun, and a deckhouse being built aft.

Inverell was recommissioned on 15 Aug 1965 as a training ship for new entry ratings, replacing the frigate *Rotoiti*. Her sweeping gear was removed and her deckhouse extended further aft. 4-inch gun replaced by 40 mm.

DISPOSALS
Echuca was scrapped at Auckland in April 1968, and *Stawell* in Aug 1968.

KIAMA

1972, Royal New Zealand Navy

SURVEY SHIPS

LACHLAN F 364

Displacement, tons	1 420 standard; 2 220 full load
Length, feet (*metres*)	301·2 (*91·8*)
Beam, feet (*metres*)	36·7 (*11·2*)
Draught, feet (*metres*)	16·0 (*4·9*)
Main engines	Triple expansion; 2 shafts; 5 500 ihp
Speed, knots	20
Boilers	2 Admiralty 3-drum type
Complement	143

Former Australian "River" class frigate. Built by Mort's Dock, Sydney, NSW, launched on 25 Mar 1944, transferred on loan from RAN in 1948 and purchased outright in 1962. Her forecastle deck was subsequently extended aft from the shelter deck to the quarter deck. Guns were removed on conversion for survey duties. A helicopter platform 50 feet by 30 feet, 7 feet above the quarter deck, was laid in 1966. An enclosed bridge was fitted during 1970 refit. Due to end her service in 1975 and consideration for a replacement is now being given.

LACHLAN

1972, Royal New Zealand Navy

PATROL CRAFT

4 LAKE CLASS

PUKAKI P 3568
ROTOITI P 3569
TAUPO P 3570
HAWEA P 3571

Displacement, tons	105 standard; 138 full load
Dimensions, feet	107·7 oa × 20 × 11·8
Guns	Possibly 2—40 mm
Main engines	2 Paxman 12YJCM Diesels; 1 200 hp = 28 knots
Complement	3 officers, 16 ratings

Under construction by Brooke Marine, Lowestoft, England. the first to complete on 14 Feb 1974 and the remainder at two monthly intervals.

11 HDML TYPE

HAKU P 3565 (ex-*Wakefield* ex-Q 1197)
KAHAWAI P3553 (ex-*Tamaki*)
KOURA P 3564 (ex-*Toroa* ex-Q 1350)
KUPARU P 3563 (ex-*Pegasus* ex-Q 1349)
MAKO P3551 (ex-Q 1183)
MANGA P3567 (ex-Q 1185)
PAEA P3552 (ex-Q 1184)
PARORE P3562 (ex-Q 1190 ex *Olphert*)
TAKAPU P3556 (ex-Q 1188)
TAMURE P3555 (ex-*Ngapona* ex-Q 1193)
TARAPUNGA (P 3566 ex-Q 1387)

Displacement, tons	46 standard; 54 full load
Dimensions, feet	72 × 16 × 5·5
Guns	1—20 mm AA; several MG (not fitted at present)
Main engines	Diesel; 2 shafts; 320 bhp = 12 knots
Complement	9

Originally known as Harbour Defence Motor Launches. All built in various yards in the United States and Canada and shipped to New Zealand.

Takapu and *Tarapunga* are commissioned as surveying MLs and operate with *Lachlan*. All others have been converted with lattice masts surmounted by a radar serial, *Mako*, *Paea*, *Kahawai* and *Haku* are employed on Fishery Protection duties, others are attached to RNZNVR Divisions. *Maroro* was disposed of in 1972. From 1974 onwards some of these will be phased-out to provide the manpower for the "Lake" class.

KAHAWI and MAKO — *1970, Royal New Zealand Navy*

RESEARCH VESSEL

TUI A 2 (ex-USS *Charles H. Davis*, T-AGOR 5)

Displacement, tons	1 200 standard; 1 380 full load
Dimensions, feet	208·9 × 37·4 × 15·3
Main engines	Diesel-electric; 1 shaft; 10 000 hp = 12 knots
Complement	8 officers, 16 ratings, 15 scientists

Oceanographic research ship built by Christy Corp, Sturgeon Bay, Wis. Laid down on 15 June 1961, launched on 30 June 1962 and completed on 25 Jan 1963. On loan from US since 28 July 1970 for 5 years. Commissioned in the Royal New Zealand Navy on 11 Sep 1970. Bow propeller 175 hp.

TUI — *1971, Royal New Zealand Navy*

TENDERS

ARATAKI **MANAWANUI**

Dimensions, feet	Length: 75
Main engines	Diesel

Steel tugs. *Arataki* is used as a dockyard tug and *Manawanui* as a diving tender.

NICARAGUA

Mercantile Marine

Lloyd's Register of Shipping: 11 vessels of 21 845 tons gross

COAST GUARD BOATS

RIO CRUTA

Dimensions, feet	Length: 85
Guns	1—20 mm automatic cannon in bow
Main engines	Diesels; speed = 9 knots maximum
Complement	11

A wooden *guardacosta* of the Marine Section of the Guardia Nacional of Nicaragua. Another *guardacosta* without name or number is a diesel launch of approx 26 ft with a 20 mm gun, a designed speed of 25 knots and a crew of 5 or 6. Also reported were six wooden patrol boats, four 90 ft and two about 80 ft, and a former patrol boat, 75 ft, wooden, built in 1925, used for training.

NIGERIA

Administration

Chief of the Naval Staff:
Rear-Admiral Joseph Etim Akinwole Wey, OFR

Naval Officer-in-Charge (Lagos):
Commodore Nelson Bossman Soroh

Chief of Staff:
Commander Mugibi Ayinde Adelanwa

Diplomatic Representation

Naval Attaché (Assistant Defence Adviser) in London:
Lieutenant Commander Emmanuel Oladipo Makinde

Strength of the Fleet

1 Frigate, 2 Corvettes, 6 Seaward Defence Boats, 3 Fast Patrol Boats, 2 Patrol Craft (building), 8 Patrol Launches, 1 Landing Craft, 2 Survey Craft.

Personnel

1968: 100 Officers and 1 200 ratings
1970: 120 Officers and 1 600 ratings
1971: 180 Officers and 2 000 ratings
1972: 190 Officers and 2 000 ratings
1973: 200 Officers and 2 100 ratings

Mercantile Marine

Lloyd's Register of Shipping:
56 vessels of 99 226 tons gross

FRIGATE

1 A/S AND AA TYPE

Displacement, tons	1 724 standard; 2 000 full load
Length, feet (*metres*)	341·2 (*104·0*) pp; 360·2 (*109·8*) oa
Beam, feet (*metres*)	37·0 (*11·3*)
Draught, feet (*metres*)	11·5 (*3·5*)
Guns	2—4 in (*102 mm*) dp (1 twin) 5—40 mm AA single
A/S weapons	1—triple-barrelled DC mortar
Main engines	4 MAN Diesels; 2 shafts; 16 000 bhp
Speed, knots	26
Range, miles	3 500 at 15 knots
Complement	216

Anti-aircraft and anti-submarine frigate built in the Netherlands by Wilton, Fijenoord. Cost £3 500 000. Commissioned in Sep 1965. Helicopter platform laid on aft.

Name	*No.*	*Builders*	*Laid down*	*Launched*	*Completed*
NIGERIA	F 87	Wilton, Fijenoord NV	9 Apr 1964	12 Apr 1965	16 Sep 196[illegible]

NIGERIA — *1970, Nigerian Navy*

CORVETTES

2 Mk 3 VOSPER THORNYCROFT TYPE

DORINA **OTOBO**

Displacement, tons	500 standard; 650 full load
Dimensions, feet	202 oa × 31 × 11·33 (over props)
Guns	2—4 in (1 twin); 2—40 mm Bofors (single) 2—20 mm cannons
Main engines	2 MAN diesels; = 23 knots max
Range, miles	3 500 at 14 knots
Complement	66 (7 officers and 59 ratings)

Ordered on 28 Mar 1968. *Dorina* laid down 26 Jan 1970, launched 16 Sep 1970, completed June 1972. *Otobo* laid down 28 Sep 1970, launched 25 May 1971, completed November 1972. Known as the "Hippopotamus" class as each name means "hippopotamus" in one of the principal Nigerian languages Plessey AWS-1 air search radar; HSA M 20 fire control. Decca TM 626 navigation radar. Plessey M 26 Sonar. HSA M 22 Fire Control.

OTOBO *1972, Wright and Logan*

SEAWARD DEFENCE BOATS

6 "FORD" CLASS

BENIN (ex-HMS *Hinksford*)
BONNY (ex-HMS *Difford*) P 3111
ENUGU P 3137
KADUNA (ex-HMS *Axford*) P 03
SAPELE (ex-HMS *Dubford*) P 3119
IBADAN II (ex-HMS *Bryansford*)

Displacement, tons	120 standard; 160 full load
Dimensions, feet	110 pp; 117·2 oa × 20 × 5
Guns	1—40 mm Bofors AA; 2—20 mm Oerlikon
A/S weapons	DC rails and DC
Main engines	Davey Paxman diesels; Foden engine on centre shaft; 1 100 bhp = 18 knots max; 15 knots sea speed
Complement	26

Enugu was the first warship built for the Nigerian Navy. Ordered from Camper and Nicholson's Gosport, in 1960. Completed on 14 Dec 1961. Sailed from Portsmouth for Nigeria on 10 Apr 1962. Fitted with Vosper roll damping fins. *Benin, Ibadan* and *Kaduna* were purchased from Great Britain on 1 July 1966 and transferred at Devonport on 9 Sep 1966. *Ibadan* was seized by the Eastern Region prior to its declaration of independence as the Republic of Biafra on 30 May 1967 and renamed *Vigilance* but was sunk at Port Harcourt on 10 Sep 1967 by Nigerian Navy, salved but later scrapped at Lagos. *Dubford* and *Gifford* were purchased from Great Britain during 1967-68 and *Bryansford* in 1968-69.

KADUNA *1970, Nigerian Navy*

DISPOSALS AND LOSSES

The seaward defence motor launch *Kaduna* (ex-HMS *SDML* 3515) was deleted from the Navy List in 1965. Presidential Yacht *Valiant* was transferred to Inland Waterways Department in 1966. Of the two minesweeping launches, *Sapele* (ex-*MSML* 2217) was disposed of in Feb 1967 and *Calabar* (ex-*MSML* 2223) was deleted from the list in 1969. The customs vessel *Challenger*, P 10, was deleted in 1970.
The patrol vessel *Ogoja*, former Netherlands *Queen Wilhelmina*,(ex-USS *PC* 468) was wrecked off Brass in October 1969.

FAST PATROL BOATS

3 Ex-SOVIET "P 6" CLASS

Displacement, tons	66 standard; 75 full load
Dimensions, feet	84·2 × 20 × 6
Guns	4—25 mm (2 twin)
A/S weapons	2 DCT; 2 DC racks
Main engines	4 12 cyl diesels; 4 800 bhp = 45 knots
Complement	24

Fast Patrol Boats—*continued*

Soviet built fast patrol boats of the small submarine chaser type purchased from the USSR in 1967. Torpedo tubes removed. POT HEAD search/navigation radar.

EKPEN *1969, Nigerian Navy*

2 BROOKE-MARINE PATROL CRAFT

No details available from Nigerian sources. The following is approximately correct.

Displacement, tons	105 standard
Dimensions, feet	107 × 20 × 12
Guns	Possibly 2—40 or 20 mm
Main engines	2 Diesels = 28 knots
Complement	20

Building by Brooke Marine, Lowestoft, England. Ordered in 1971.

8 VOSPER-THORNYCROFT PATROL LAUNCHES

Displacement, tons	15
Dimensions, feet	34 oa × 10 × 2·8
Guns	1 machine gun
Main engines	2 Diesels; 290 hp = 19 knots
Complement	6

Ordered for Nigerian Police March 1971, completed 1971-72. GRP hulls.

LANDING CRAFT

LOKOJA (ex-*LCT* (4) 1213)

Displacement, tons	350 standard; 586 full load
Dimensions, feet	187·5 × 38·8 × 4·5
Guns	2—20 mm AA
Main engines	2 Paxman diesels; 920 bhp = 10 knots

Purchased from Great Britain in 1959. Allocated the name *Lokoja* in 1961. Underwent a major refit in 1966-67, including complete replating of the bottom.

LOKOJA *1971, Nigerian Navy*

SURVEY VESSELS

PATHFINDER P 06

Measurement, tons	544 gross
Dimensions, feet	154·2 × 27 × 11
Guns	1—40 mm AA
Main engines	2 triple expansion; 200 ihp = 8 knots

Built by J. Samuel White & Co Ltd, Cowes, Isle of Wight. Launched on 23 Oct 1953 and completed in 1954.

PENELOPE P 11

Measurement, tons	79 gross
Dimensions, feet	79·5 × 7·8 × 4·5
Main engines	2 Gardner diesels; speed 10 knots

Built by Aldous Successors, Brightlingsea in 1958. Used for local survey duties.

NORWAY

Administration

Commander-in-Chief (Inspector-General):
Rear Admiral Hans Sigurd Skjong

Commander Naval Logistics Services:
Rear-Admiral Thorleif Petersen, KCVO, MBE

Commander Coastal Fleet:
Commodore Øivind Schau

Diplomatic Representation

Defence Attaché in London:
Lieutenant-Colonel Ivar Kollbotn

Naval Attaché in Washington:

Naval Attaché in Moscow:
Commodore S. N. Østervold, DSC

Strength of the Fleet

15 Coastal Submarines (Diesel Powered)
5 Frigates (Destroyer Escort Type)
4 Coastal Minelayers (ex-Ocean Minesweepers)
2 Patrol Vessels (Submarine Chasers)
10 Coastal Minesweepers (Non-Magnetic)
26 Missile Torpedo Boats (Fast Patrol Boats)
20 Missile Gunboats (Fast Patrol Boats)
14 Fleet Support Ships and Service Craft

Ships

Norwegian warships are referred to officially with the prefix KNM, equivalent to HMS. Since Mar 1959 the suffix "RNoN" has been used instead of "RNorN".

Personnel

1973: 8 500 officers and ratings
1972: 8 000 officers and ratings
1971: 9 000 officers and ratings
1970: 8 500 officers and ratings
1969: 7 200 officers and ratings

Mercantile Marine

Lloyd's Register of Shipping:
2 826 ships of 23 507 108 tons gross

Disposals

Destroyers

1959 *Stord* (ex-*Success*)
1961 *Trondheim* (ex-*Croziers*)
Arendal (ex-*Badsworth*)
Narvik (ex-*Glaisdale*)
1965 *Haugesund* (ex-*Beaufort*)
Tromso (ex-*Zetland*)
1966 *Oslo* (ex-*Crown*)
1967 *Bergen* (ex-*Cromwell*)
Stavanger (ex-*Crystal*)
(All above ex-RN ships)

Frigates

1966 *Draug* (ex-*Penetang*)
1972 *Horten* (ex-*Troll*, ex-*Prestonian*)

Submarines

1961 *Kinn* (ex-U1202 VII C)
1962 *Utsira* (ex-*Variance*)
1963 *Kaura* (ex-U 905 VII C)
1964 *Utstein* (ex-*Venturer*)
Ula (ex-*Varne*)
Utvaer (ex-*Viking*)
Kya (ex-U 926 VII C)
1965 *Uthaug* (ex-*Votary*)
(German U-3 lent to Norway as *Kobben* S 310 from 1962-64 for training for the new "Kobben" class)

OSLO *Class*

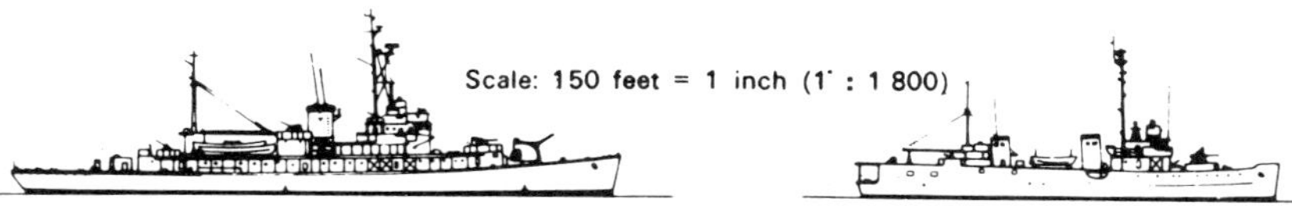

Scale: 150 feet = 1 inch (1' : 1 800)

HAAKON VII

BRAGE, GOR, TYR, ULLER

FRIGATES

5 "OSLO" CLASS

DESTROYER ESCORT TYPE

Name	*No.*	*Builders*	*Laid down*	*Launched*	*Completed*
BERGEN	F 301	Marinens Hovedverft, Horten	1964	23 Aug 1965	15 June 1967
NARVIK	F 304	Marinens Hovedverft, Horten	1964	8 Jan 1965	30 Nov 1966
OSLO	F 300	Marinens Hovedverft, Horten	1963	17 Jan 1964	29 Jan 1966
STAVANGER	F 303	Marinens Hovedverft, Horten	1965	4 Feb 1966	1 Dec 1967
TRONDHEIM	F 302	Marinens Hovedverft, Horten	1963	4 Sep 1964	2 June 1966

Displacement, tons	1 450 standard; 1 745 full load
Length, feet (*metres*)	308 (*93·9*) pp; 317 (*96·6*) oa
Beam, feet (*metres*)	36·7 (*11·2*)
Draught, feet (*metres*)	17·4 (*5·3*)
Guns, dual purpose	4—3 in (*76 mm*) 2 twin mounts
Missile launches	"Penguin" to be installed in 1972
A/S weapons	"Terne" system
Torpedo launchers	2
Boilers	2 Babcock & Wilcox
Main engines	1 set De Laval Ljungstron double reduction geared turbines; 1 shaft; 20 000 shp
Speed, knots	25
Complement	151 (11 officers, 140 ratings)

Built under the five-year naval construction programme approved by the Norwegian "Storting" (Parliament) late in 1960. Although all the ships of this class were constructed in the Norwegian Naval Dockyard, half the cost was borne by Norway and the other half by the United States. The design of these ships is similar to that of the "Dealey" class destroyer escorts in the United States Navy, but slightly modified to suit Norwegian requirements. They have traditional Norwegian destroyer names or torpedo boat names.

RADAR. Search: DRBV 22. Tactical and Fire Control: HSA M 24 system.

ENGINEERING. The main turbines and auxiliary machinery were all built by De Laval Ljungstrom, Sweden at the company's works in Stockholm-Nacka.

BERGEN *1971, Royal Norwegian Navy*

F300

OSLO *1972, Royal Norwegian Navy*

CORVETTES

2 "SLEIPNER" CLASS

ÆGER F 311 **SLEIPNER** F 310

Displacement, tons	600 standard; 780 full load
Dimensions, feet	227·8 oa × 26·2
Guns	1—3 in; 1—40 mm
A/S weapons	"Terne" ASW system
Main engines	4 Maybach diesels; 2 shafts; 9 000 bhp = over 20 knots
Complement	62

Under the five-year programme only two instead of the originally planned five new patrol vessels were built. *Sleipner* was launched on 9 Nov 1963 at the Nylands Verksted shipyard, Oslo, and completed on 29 Apr 1965. *Aeger*, originally to have been named *Balder*, was launched on 24 Sep 1965, and completed on 31 Mar 1967.

SLEIPNER *1972, Royal Norwegian Navy*

SUBMARINES

15 "KOBBEN" CLASS

Name	No.	Launched	Completed
KAURA	S 315	16 Oct 1964	5 Feb 1965
KINN	S 316	30 Nov 1963	8 Apr 1964
KOBBEN	S 318	25 Apr 1964	17 Aug 1964
KUNNA	S 319	16 July 1964	1 Oct 1964
KYA	S 317	20 Feb 1964	15 June 1964
SKLINNA	S 305	21 Jan 1966	27 May 1966
SKOLPEN	S 306	24 Mar 1966	17 Aug 1966
STADT	S 307	10 June 1966	15 Nov 1966
STORD	S 308	2 Sep 1966	9 Feb 1967
SVENNER	S 309	27 Jan 1967	1 July 1967
ULA	S 300	19 Dec 1964	7 May 1965
UTHAUG	S 304	8 Oct 1965	16 Feb 1966
UTSIRA	S 301	11 Mar 1965	1 July 1965
UTSTEIN	S 302	19 May 1965	9 Sep 1965
UTVAER	S 303	30 June 1965	1 Dec 1965

Displacement, tons	350 standard; 472 submerged
Length, feet (*metres*)	149 (*45·4*)
Beam, feet (*metres*)	15 (*4·6*)
Draught, feet (*metres*)	14 (*4·3*)
Tubes	8—21 in (*533 mm*) bow
Main engines	2 MB 820 Maybach-Mercedes-Benz diesels; 1 200 bhp; electric drive; 1 200 hp; 1 shaft
Speed, knots	17
Complement	18 (5 officers, 13 men)

GENERAL
It was announced in July 1959 that the USA and Norway would share equally the cost of these submarines ordered under a modernisation programme, for delivery in 1964-67. All were built by Rheinstahl-Nordseewerke in Emden, West Germany. Of the same type as the German U 4 class but with stronger hulls to dive deeper. *Svenner* has a second periscope for COs training operations.

NAMES. All names except *Kobben* are Norwegian coastal features. *Kobben* was the name of the first submarine in the Royal Norwegian Navy. Commissioned on 28 Nov 1909.

KINN 1970, *Royal Norwegian Navy*

SVENNER 1972, *Royal Norwegian Navy*

LIGHT FORCES

(N.B Armament varies in all classes as Penguin SSM is installed)

6 "SNÖGG" CLASS (MISSILE BOATS)

KJAPP P 985 **RAPP** P 981 **SNAR** P 982
KVIKK P 984 **RASK** P 983 **SNOGG** (ex-Lyr) P 980

Displacement, tons	100 standard; 125 full load
Dimensions, feet	120·0 × 20·5 × 5·0
Missile launchers	4 "Penguin" SSM; range 20 km plus
Guns	1—40 mm
Tubes	4—21 in
Main engines	2 Maybach diesels; 2 shafts; 7 200 bhp = 32 knots
Complement	18

These steel hulled torpedo boats of a new design ordered from Batservice Werft, A/S, Mandal, Norway, started coming into service in 1970. Hulls are similar to those of the "Storm" class gunboats: see next column. Armed with missiles in addition to gun and tubes. The six torpedo boats of the "Rapp" class, of the same names, were deleted from the the list in 1970.

SNAR (with Penguins) 1972, *Royal Norwegian Navy*

RAPP 1971, *Royal Norwegian Navy*

20 "STORM" CLASS (MISSILE BOATS)

ARG	P 968	**DJERV**	P 966	**ODD**	P 975	**STEIL**	P 969
BLINK	P 961	**GLIMT**	P 962	**PIL**	P 976	**STORM**	P 960
BRANN	P 970	**GNIST**	P 979	**ROKK**	P 978	**TRAUST**	P 973
BRASK	P 977	**HVASS**	P 972	**SKJOLD**	P 963	**TROSS**	P 971
BROTT	P 974	**KJEKK**	P 965	**SKUDD**	P 967	**TRYGG**	P 964

Light Forces—*continued*

Displacement, tons	100 standard; 125 full load
Dimensions, feet	120·0 × 20·5 × 5·0
Missile launchers	6 "Penguin" SSM; range 20 km plus
Guns	1—3 in; 1—40 mm
A/S weapons	DC throwers
Main engines	2 Maybach diesels; 2 shafts; 7 200 bhp = 32 knots

The first of 20 (instead of the 23 originally planned) gunboats of a new design built under the five-year programme was *Storm*, launched on 8 Feb 1963, and completed on 31 May 1963, but this prototype was eventually scrapped and replaced by a new series construction boat as the last of the class. The first of the production boats was *Blink*, launched on 28 June 1965 and completed on 18 Dec 1965. Formerly known as Motor Gunboats, but officially reclassified as Gunboats in 1965. The first was armed with "Penguin" surface-to-surface guided missile launchers in 1970, in addition to originally designed armament.

TRAUST with 6 Penguins fitted 1971, *A/S Kongsberg Vapenfabrikk*

PENGUIN SSM missile being launched 1971, *A/S Kongsberg Vapenfabrikk*

Light Forces—*continued*

20 "TJELD" CLASS (TORPEDO BOATS)

DELFIN	P 386	**HAI**	P 381	**LAKS**	P 384	**SKARV**	P 344
ERLE	P 390	**HAUK**	P 349	**LOM**	P 347	**SKREI**	P 380
FALK	P 350	**HVAL**	P 383	**LYR**	P 387	**STEGG**	P 348
GEIR	P 389	**JO**	P 346	**RAVN**	P 357	**TEIST**	P 345
GRIBB	P 388	**KNURR**	P 385	**SEL**	P 382	**TJELD**	P 343

Displacement, tons	70 standard; 82 full load
Dimensions, feet	75·5 pp; 80·3 oa × 24·5 × 6·8 max
Guns	1—40 mm AA; 1—20 mm AA
Tubes	4—21 in
Main engines	2 Napier Deltic Turboblown diesels; 2 shafts; 6 200 bhp = 45 knots
Radius, miles	450 at 40 knots; 600 at 25 knots
Complement	18

Built by Boatservice Ltd, Oslo. The first boat, *Tjeld* commissioned in June 1960, and the last of the first group of twelve in 1962. The first of the second group of eight, *Sel*, was launched on 7 Mar 1963 and the last, *Delfin*, on 7 Jan 1966 (commissioned on 20 May 1966).

SKARV *1969, Wright & Logan*

MINE WARFARE SHIPS

4 "GOR" CLASS (COASTAL MINELAYERS)

BRAGE (ex-USS *Triumph*, MMC 3, ex-*MSF* 323, ex-*AM* 323) transferred 1960
GOR (ex-USS *Strive*, MMC 1 ex-*MSF* 117, ex-*AM* 117) transferred 1959
TYR (ex-USS *Sustain*, MMC 2, ex-*MSF* 119, ex-*AM* 119) transferred 1959
ULLER (ex-USS *Seer*, MMC 5, ex-*MSF* 112, ex-*AM* 112) transferred 1960

Displacement, tons	890 standard; 1 250 full load
Dimensions, feet	215 wl; 221·2 oa × 32·2 × 16 max
Guns	*Brage, Gor, Tyr:* 1—3 in, 50 cal; 4—20 mm AA (2 twin); *Uller:* 1—3 in, 50 cal; 1—40 mm AA
A/S weapons	*Brage, Gor, Tyr:* 2 Hedgehogs; 3 DCT *Uller:* "Terne" ASW system; 1 DCT
Main engines	GM diesels; electric drive; 2 shafts; 2 070 bhp = 16 knots
Complement	83

Former US Coastal Minelayers (MMC) built as Ocean Minesweepers (AM) but reclassified as Fleet Minesweepers (MSF) in Feb 1955. *Gor, Tyr* and *Uller* were built by American Shipbuilding Co. and *Brage* by Associated Shipbuilders. *Gor* and *Tyr* converted 1959 and *Brage* 1960 into coastal minelayers at Charleston Naval Shipyard, but *Uller* was converted in Norway.

Name	*No.*	*Laid down*	*Launched*	*Completed*
Brage	N 49	27 Oct 1942	25 Feb 1943	3 Feb 1944
Gor	N 48	17 Nov 1941	16 May 1942	27 Oct 1942
Tyr	N 47	17 Nov 1941	23 June 1942	9 Nov 1942
Uller	N 50	28 Nov 1941	23 May 1942	21 Oct 1942

BRAGE *1972, Royal Norwegian Navy*

BORGEN N 51 (CONTROLLED MINELAYER)

Displacement, tons	**282 standard**
Dimensions, feet	**94·5 pp; 102·5 oa × 26·2 × 11**
Main engines	**2 GM diesels; 2 Voith-Schneider propellers; 330 bhp = 9 knots**

BORGEN *1972, Royal Norwegian Navy*

Mine Warfare Ships—*continued*

10 "SAUDA" CLASS (CMS)

ALTA (ex-*Arlon* M 915, ex-*MSC* 104)	M 314	31 Jan 1953
GLOMMA (ex-*Bastogne* M 916, ex-*MSC* 151)	M 317	13 June 1953
KVINA	M 332	21 July 1954
OGNA	M 315	18 June 1954
SAUDA (ex-USS *AMS* 102)	M 311	4 Oct 1952
SIRA (ex-USS *MSC* 132)	M 312	26 Oct 1954
TANA (ex-*Roeselaere* M 914, ex-*MSC* 103)	M 313	6 Dec 1952
TISTA	M 331	1 June 1954
UTLA	M 334	2 Mar 1955
VOSSO	M 316	16 June 1954

Displacement, tons	333 standard; 384 full load
Dimensions, feet	144 × 28 × 8·5 max
Guns	2—20 mm AA
Main engines	GM diesels; 880 bhp = 13·5 knots
Oil fuel, tons	25
Complement	38

Sauda, built by Hodgeson Bros, Gowdy & Stevens, East Boothbay, Maine, was completed on 25 Aug 1953 and *Sira* on 28 Nov 1955. Hull of wooden construction. Five coastal minesweepers of the non-magnetic type were built in Norway with US engines. Launch dates above. Completed on 5 Mar 1955 (*Ogna*), 16 Mar 1955 (*Vosso*), 27 Apr 1955 (*Tista*), 12 July 1955 (*Kvina*) and 15 Nov 1955 (*Utla*). *Kvina*, *Ogna* and *Utla* were built by Båtservice Ltd, Mandal, *Tista* by Forende Batbyggeriex, Risör, and *Vosso* by Skaaluren Skibsbyggeri, Rosendal.

***Alta*, *Glomma* and *Tana* were taken over from the Royal Belgian Navy in May, Sep and Mar 1966, respectively, having been exchanged for two Norwegian ocean minesweepers of the US MSO type, *Lagen* (ex-*MSO* 498) and *Namsen* (ex-*MSO* 499).**

VOSSO *1970, Royal Norwegian Navy*

AMPHIBIOUS FORCES

2 "KVALSUND" CLASS

5 "IMPROVED KVALSUND" CLASS

BORGSUND	**RAFTSUND**	**ROTSUND**
KVALSUND	**REINOYSUND**	**SORÖYSUND**
MAURSUND		

Displacement, tons	560
Dimensions, feet	167·3 × 33·5 × 5·9
Guns	2—20 mm
Speed, knots	11

Built by Mjöllem and Karlsen Bergen. First pair delivered in 1970 remainder in following two years.

1 Ex-US LCU

Displacement, tons	180 light; 360 full load
Dimensions, feet	119 oa × 34 × 6
Guns	2—20 mm
Main engines	3 Diesels; 3 shafts; 6 758 bhp = 10 knots
Complement	14

Transferred from US on completion 1952.

DEPOT SHIP

1 Ex-CANADIAN FRIGATE TYPE

VALKYRIEN (ex-*Garm*, ex-*Toronto*) Pennant No. A 535 (ex-F 315)

Displacement, tons	1,570 standard; 2 240 full load
Dimensions, feet	301·3 × 36·5 × 16
Guns	*Horten:* 3—40 mm; *Valkyrien:* 2—4 in, 2—40 mm
Main engines	Triple expansion; 2 shafts; 5 500 ihp = 19 knots
Complement	*Horten:* 86; *Valkyrien:* 104

Former Canadian modernised "River" class frigate. Built by Davie Shipbuilding Co., Lauzon, Port Quebec, Canada. Launched on 18 Sep 1943, and completed 6 May 1944. Loaned to Norway on 10 Mar 1956 and renamed, transferred outright early in 1959, and converted for use as depot ship and again renamed in 1964, *Valkyrien* as parent ship for torpedo boats and gunboats. *Horten* disposed of in 1972.

VALKYRIEN *1972, Royal Norwegian Navy*

DRAUG

Small depot ship for frogmen and divers. Completed in 1972 by Nielsen of Harstad.

TRAINING SHIP

HAAKON VII (ex-US *Gardiners Bay*, *AVP* 39) A 537

Displacement, tons	1 766 standard; 2 800 full load
Length, feet (*metres*)	300 (*91·4*) wl; 310·8 (*94·7*) oa
Beam, feet (*metres*)	41·2 (*12·7*)
Draught, feet (*metres*)	13·5 (*4·1*) max
Guns, surface	1—5 in (*127 mm*)
Guns, AA	8—40 mm; 4—20 mm
Main engines	2 F-M diesels 6 080 bhp; 2 shafts
Speed, knots	18·2
Complement	215, plus 86 officer cadets and petty officer apprentices

Former US seaplane tender (small) of the AVP type, Built by Lake Washington Shipyard, Houghton, Wash. Laid down on 14 Mar 1944, launched on 2 Dec 1944 and completed on 11 Feb 1945. Transferred from the US Navy to the Royal Norwegian Navy on 17 May 1958 and converted and rearmed as a training ship for midshipmen and naval cadets. Accommodation for 367.

HAAKON VII — *1970, Royal Norwegian Navy*

FISHERY PROTECTION SHIPS

NORNEN

Measurement, tons	930 gross
Dimensions, feet	201·8 × 32·8 × 15·8
Guns	1—3 in (*76 mm*)
Main engines	4 diesels; 3 500 bhp = 17 knots
Complement	32

Built by Mjellem & Karlsen, Bergen, Norway. Launched and completed in 1963.

NORNEN — *1970, Royal Norwegian Navy*

FARM **HEIMDAL**

Measurement, tons	600 gross
Dimensions, feet	177 × 26·2 × 16·5
Guns	1—3 in (*76 mm*)
Main engines	2 diesels; 2 700 bhp = 16 knots
Complement	29

Farm was built by Ankerlokken Veft, Fioro and *Heimdal* by Bolsones Verft, Molde, in 1962.

FARM — *1970, Royal Norwegian Navy*

ANDENES **NORDKAPP** **SENJA**

Measurement, tons	500 gross
Dimensions, feet	186 × 31 × 16
Guns	1—3 in (*76 mm*)
Main engines	MAN diesel; 2 300 bhp = 16 knots
Complement	29

All three built in the Netherlands in 1957 as whalers. Acquired by Norway in 1965 and converted into Fishery Protection Ships.

NORDKAPP — *1970, Royal Norwegian Navy*

OCEANOGRAPHIC RESEARCH SHIPS

H. U. SVERDRUP

Displacement, tons	400
Measurement, tons	295 gross
Dimensions, feet	127·7 oa; 111·5 pp × 25 × 13
Main engines	Wichmann diesel; 600 bhp = 11·5 knots
Oil fuel (tons)	65
Range, miles	5 000 at 10 knots cruising speed
Complement	10 crew; 9 scientists

Built by Orens Mekaniske Verksted, Trondheim. Laid down in Sep 1959, launched in Feb 1960, completed on 15 June 1960. Financed by the US Mutual Weapon Development Programme and operated by the Norwegian Defence Research Establishment. Steel hull, welded construction, controllable pitch propeller. She does not belong to the Royal Norwegian Navy, but is a Defence project.

ROYAL YACHT

NORGE (ex-*Philante*) A 533

Measurement, tons	1 686 (*Thames yacht measurement*)
Dimensions, feet	250·2 pp; 263 oa × 28 × 15·2
Main engines	8-cyl diesels; 2 shafts; 3 000 bhp = 17 knots

Built by Camper & Nicholson's Ltd, Gosport, England, to the order of the late Mr T. O. M. Sopwith as escort and store vessel for the yachts *Endeavour I* and *Endeavour II*. Launched on 17 Feb 1937. Served in the British Navy as an anti-submarine escort during the Second World War, after which she was purchased by the Norwegian people for King Haakon at a cost of nearly £250 000 and reconditioned as a Royal Yacht at Southampton. Can accommodate about 50 people in addition to crew.

NORGE — *1971, Royal Norwegian Navy*

NOTE. 2 small personnel transports completed in 1971.

PANAMA

Mercantile Marine

Lloyd's Register of Shipping: 1 337 ships of 7 793 598 tons gross

PATROL BOATS

2 VOSPER TYPE

PANQUIACO GC 10 **LIGIA ELENA**

Displacement, tons	96 standard; 123 full load
Dimensions, feet	95·0 wl; 103·0 oa × 18·9 × 5·8
Guns	2—20 mm
Main engines	2 Paxman Ventura 12 cyl diesels; 2 800 bhp = 24 knots
Complement	23

Constructed with hull of welded mild steel and upperworks of welded or buck-bolted aluminium alloy. Vosper fin stabiliser equipment. *Panquiaco* was launched on 22 July 1970 and *Ligia Elena* on 25 Aug 1970 at Porchester, Portsmouth, England. Both completed March 1971.

2 US SMALL CG UTILITY TYPE

Displacement, tons	35
Dimensions, feet	69 × 14 × 5
Guns	1 MG
Main engines	400 hp = 13 knots
Complement	10

Transferred to Panama by the USA at the US Naval Station, Rodman, Canal Zone, in June 1962. Under the 1955 Treaty the USA occupied the Rio Hato base.

PAKISTAN

Administration

Chief of the Naval Staff:
Vice-Admiral Hasan Hafeez Ahmad TQA

Commodore Commanding P. N. Flotilla:
Commodore R. M. Shaikh

Strength of the Fleet

1 Light Cruiser
4 Destroyers
2 Frigates
3 Patrol Submarines
6 Gunboats
1 Patrol Boat
7 Coastal Minesweepers
1 Survey Ship
7 Auxiliaries

Diplomatic Representation

Naval Attaché in London:
Commodore Leslie Norman Mungavin, SK

Naval Attaché in Washington:
Captain Syed Quamar Raza, SJ

Personnel

1969: 9 200 (850 officers; 8 350 ratings)
1970: 9 870 (870 officers; 9 000 ratings)
1971: 9 900 (900 officers; 9 000 ratings)
1972: 10 500 (950 officers; 9 550 ratings)
1973: 10 000 (950 officers; 9 050 ratings)

Mercantile Marine

Lloyd's Register of Shipping:
131 vessels of 532 637 tons gross

LIGHT CRUISER (*Cadet Training Ship*)

Name	*No.*	*Builders and Engineers*	*Laid down*	*Launched*	*Completed*
BABUR (ex-HMS *Diadem*)	84	R. & W. Hawthorn Leslie & Co Ltd, Hebburn-on-Tyne	15 Nov 1939	26 Aug 1942	6 Jan 1944

Displacement, tons	5 900 standard; 7 560 full load
Length, feet (*metres*)	485 (*147·9*) pp; 512 (*156·1*) oa
Beam, feet (metres)	52·0 (*15·8*)
Draught, feet (*metres*)	18·5 (*5·6*)
Guns, surface	8—5·25 in (*133 mm*) 4 twin
Guns, AA	14—40 mm
Torpedo tubes	6—21 in (*533 mm*) 2 triple
Armour	3 in (*76 mm*) sides; 2 in (*51 mm*) decks and turrets
Boilers	4 Admiralty 3-drum
Main engines	Parsons s.r. geared turbines; 4 shafts; 62 000 shp
Speed, knots	32
Oil fuel, tons	1 100
Complement	588

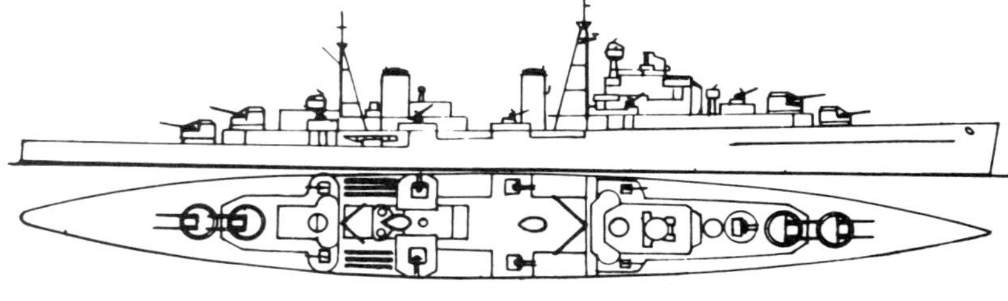

Former British Improved "Dido" class anti-aircraft light cruiser. Purchased on 29 Feb 1956. Refitted at HM Dockyard, Portsmouth and there transferred to Pakistan and renamed *Babur* on 5 July, 1957. Adapted as cadet training ship in 1961.

RADAR. Search: Type 960, Type 293. Fire Control: Early British design.
DRAWING. Starboard elevation and plan. Scale: 125 feet = 1 inch (1 : 1 500).

BABUR — 1966, *Pakistan Navy*

DESTROYERS

Name	*No.*	*Builders*	*Laid down*	*Launched*	*Completed*
BADR (ex-HMS *Gabbard*)	161 (ex-D 47)	Swan, Hunter & Wigham Richardson Ltd, Wallsend-on-Tyne	2 Feb 1944	16 Mar 1945	10 Dec 1946

1 "BATTLE" CLASS

Displacement, tons	2 325 standard; 3 361 full load
Length, feet (*metres*)	355·0(*108·2*) pp; 379·0(*115·5*) oa
Beam, feet (*metres*)	40·2 (*12·3*)
Draught, feet (*metres*)	17·0 (*5·2*)
Guns	4—4·5 in (*115 mm*); 10—40 mm AA
A/S weapons	"Squid" triple DC mortar
Torpedo tubes	8—21 in (*533 mm*) quadrupled
Main engines	Parsons geared turbines; 2 shafts; 50 000 shp
Speed, knots	35·75 designed; 31 sea
Boilers	2 Admiralty 3-drum type
Range, miles	6 000 at 20 knots
Oil fuel, tons	680
Complement	270

BADR — 1972, *Pakistan Navy*

Purchased from Britain on 29 Feb 1956. Modernised with US funds under MDAP. Refitted at Palmers Hebburn, Yarrow, transferred to Pakistan on 24 Jan 1957 and sailed from Portsmouth for Karachi on 17 Feb 1957.

RADAR. Search: Type 277, Type 293. Fire Control: X Band.
PENNANT No. Changed from D 47 to 161 in 1963.

LOSS
Sister ship *Khaibar* (ex-HMS *Cadiz*) No. 163 (ex-D 79) was sunk during the Indo-Pakistan War in Dec 1971.

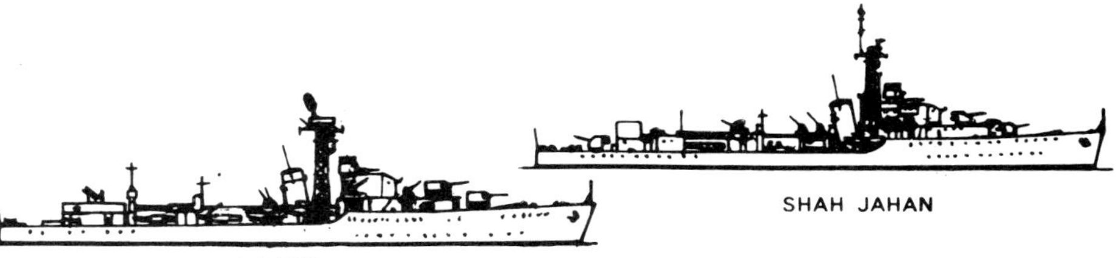

SHAH JAHAN

BADR

Destroyers—*continued*

1 "CH" CLASS

SHAH JAHAN (ex-HMS *Charity*) 164 (ex-D 29)

Displacement, tons	1 710 standard; 2 545 full load
Length, feet (*metres*)	350·0(*106·7*) wl; 362·7(*110·5*) oa
Beam, feet (*metres*)	35·7 (*10·9*)
Draught, feet (*metres*)	17·0 (*5·2*)
Guns	3—4·5 in (*115 mm*); 6—40 mm AA
A/S weapons	2 "Squid" triple DC mortars
Torpedo tubes	4—21 in (*533 mm*) quadrupled
Main engines	Parsons geared turbines; 2 shafts; 40 000 shp
Speed, knots	36·75 designed; 31·25 sea
Boilers	2 Admiralty 3-drum type
Complement	200

Built by John I. Thornycroft, Co Ltd, Woolston, laid down on 9 July 1943, launched on 30 Nov 1944 and completed on 19 Nov 1945. Purchased by USA and handed over to Pakistan on 16 Dec 1958, under MDAP, at yard of J. Samuel White & Co Ltd, Cowes, who refitted her.

SHAH JAHAN *1972, Pakistan Navy*

Sister ship *Taimur* (ex-HMS *Chivalrous*) was returned to the Royal Navy and scrapped in 1960-61.

RADAR. Search: Type 293. Fire Control: X Band.

2 "CR" CLASS

Name	*No.*	*Builders*	*Laid down*	*Launched*	*Completed*
ALAMGIR (ex-HMS *Creole*)	160 (ex-D 82)	J. Samuel White & Co Ltd, Cowes	3 Aug 1944	22 Nov 1945	14 Oct 1946
JAHANGIR (ex-HMS *Crispin*, ex-*Craccher*)	162 (ex-D 168)	J. Samuel White & Co Ltd, Cowes	1 Feb 1944	23 June 1945	10 July 1946

Displacement, tons	1 730 standard; 2 560 full load
Length, feet (*metres*)	350·0(*106·7*) wl; 362·8(*110·5*) oa
Beam, feet (*metres*)	35·7 (*10·9*)
Draught, feet (*metres*)	17·0 (*5·2*)
Guns	3—4·5 in (*115 mm*); 6—40 mm AA
A/S weapons	2 "Squid" triple DC mortars
Torpedo tubes	4—21 in (*533 mm*) quadrupled
Main engines	Parsons geared turbines; 2 shafts 40 000 shp
Speed, knots	36·75 designed; 31·25 sea
Boilers	2 Admiralty 3-drum type
Range, miles	5 600 at 20 knots
Oil fuel, tons	580
Complement	200

ALAMGIR *1965, Pakistan Navy*

ALAMGIR, JAHANGIR

Purchased by Pakistan (announced by the Royal Navy) on 29 Feb 1956. Refitted and modernised in Great Britain by John I. Thornycroft & Co Ltd, Woolston, Southampton, in 1957-58 with US funds under MDAP Turned over to the Pakistan Navy at Southampton in 1958 (*Crispin* on 18 Mar and *Creole* 20 June) and renamed.

RADAR. Search: Type 293. Fire Control: X Band.

JAHANGIR *1972, Pakistan Navy*

GUNNERY. There was formerly a W/T cabin in place of "B" gun and a gun in "X" position, but during the refit before joining the Pakistan Navy the 4·5 inch gun was restored to "B" position, the 4·5 inch gun in "X" position was suppressed and two "Squids" were substituted.

PENNANT Nos. Changed from D 82 and D 168 to 160 and 162, respectively, in 1963.

FRIGATES

2 LIMITED CONVERSION TYPE 16

Name	*No.*	*Builders*	*Laid down*	*Launched*	*Completed*
TIPPU SULTAN (ex-HMS *Onslow*, ex-*Pakenham*)	260 (ex-F 249)	John Brown & Co Ltd, Clydebank	1 July 1940	31 Mar 1941	8 Oct 1941
TUGHRIL (ex-HMS *Onslaught*, ex-*Pathfinder*)	261 (ex-F 204)	Fairfield SB & Eng Co Ltd, Glasgow	14 Jan 1941	9 Oct 1941	19 June 1942

Displacement, tons	1 800 standard; 2 300 full load
Length, feet (*metres*)	328·7(*100·2*) pp; 345·0(*10·72*) oa
Beam, feet (*metres*)	35·0 (*10·7*)
Draught, feet (*metres*)	15·7 (*4·8*)
Guns	2—4 in (*102 mm*); 5—40 mm AA
A/S weapons	2 "Squid" triple DC mortars
Torpedo tubes	4—21 in (*533 mm*)
Main engines	Parsons geared turbines; 2 shafts; 40 000 shp
Speed, knots	34
Boilers	2 Admiralty 3-drum type
Complement	170

TUGHRIL *1972, Pakistan Navy*

Originally three "O" class destroyers were acquired from Great Britain, *Tippu Sultan* being handed over on 30 Sep 1949; *Tariq* on 3 Nov 1949; and *Tughril* on 6 Mar 1951. An agreement was signed in London between Great Britain and USA for refit and conversion in the United Kingdom of *Tippu Sultan* and *Tughril* (announced 29 Apr 1957) with US funds. All three ships were scheduled for conversion into fast anti-submarine frigates. *Tippu Sultan* and *Tughril* were converted at Liverpool by Grayson Rolls & Clover Docks Ltd, Birkenhead, and C. & H. Crighton Ltd, respectively. *Tariq* was not converted. She was handed back to Great Britain at Portsmouth on 10 July 1959 and broken up at Sunderland, arriving there in Oct 1959.

RADAR. Equipped with Type 293 search radar.

PENNANT Nos. changed from D 49 and D 204 to F 249 and F 204 respectively, in 1959, and to 260 and 261 in 1963.

TIPPU SULTAN, TUGHRIL

SUBMARINES

3 "HANGOR" CLASS

(FRENCH "DAPHNE" TYPE)

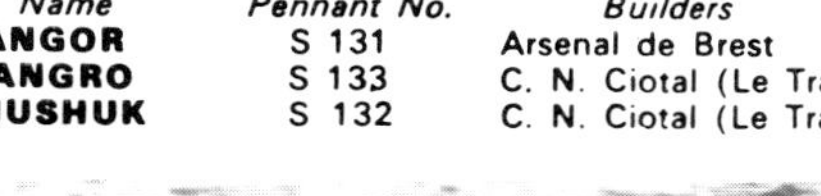

Name	Pennant No.	Builders	Laid Down	Launched	Completed
HANGOR	S 131	Arsenal de Brest	1 Dec 1967	28 June 1969	12 Jan 1970
MANGRO	S 133	C. N. Ciotal (Le Trait)	8 July 1968	7 Feb 1970	8 Aug 1970
SHUSHUK	S 132	C. N. Ciotal (Le Trait)	1 Dec 1967	30 July 1969	12 Jan 1970

Displacement, tons	700 standard; 869 surface; 1 043 submerged
Length, feet (*metres*)	189·6 (*57·8*)
Beam, feet (*metres*)	22·3 (*6·8*)
Draught, feet (*metres*)	15·1 (*4·6*)
Torpedo tubes	12—21 in (*550 mm*) 8 bow, 4 stern (external)
Main engines	Diesel electric (SEMT-Pielstick); 1 300 bhp surface; electric motors 1 600 hp submerged; 2 shafts
Speed, knots	13 surface; 15·5 submerged
Complement	45

These are the first submarines built for the Pakistan Navy. They are basically of the French "Daphne" class design, but slightly modified internally to suit Pakistan requirements and naval conditions. They are broadly similar to the submarines built in France for Portugal and South Africa and the submarines being constructed to the "Daphne" design in Spain.

SHUSHUK — *1972*

MANGRO — *1971, Courtesy Admiral M. J. Adam*

SURVEY SHIP

Name	No.	Builders	Laid down	Launched	Completed
ZULFIQUAR (*ex-Dhanush, ex-Deveron*)	262 (ex-F 265)	Smith's Dock Co Ltd, South Bank-on-Tees	16 Apr 1942	12 Oct 1942	2 Mar 1943

1 "RIVER" CLASS

Displacement, tons	1 370 standard; 2 100 full load
Length, feet (*metres*)	283·0 (*85·3*) pp; 301·5 (*91·9*) oa
Beam, feet (*metres*)	36·7 (*11·2*)
Draught, feet (*metres*)	12·5 (*3·8*)
Guns	1—4 in (*102 mm*); 2—40 mm AA
Main engines	Triple expansion; 5 500 ihp
Speed, knots	20
Boilers	2 Admiralty 3-drum type
Range, miles	6 000 at 12 knots
Oil fuel, tons	400
Complement	150

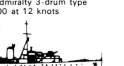

ZULFIQUAR

ZULFIQUAR — *1972, Pakistan Navy*

Former British frigate of the "River" class converted into a survey ship, with additional charthouse aft. She has strengthened davits and carries survey motor boats. The after 4-inch gun was removed.

PENNANT No. was changed from F 265 to 262 in 1963.

DISPOSAL. Sister ship *Shamsher* (ex-*Nadder*) of the "River" class (training ship) was disposed of in 1960.

LIGHT FORCES

6 G2-C (Ex-Chinese "SHANGHAI") GUNBOATS

Displacement, tons	120 full load
Dimensions, feet	130 × 18 × 5·6
Guns	4—37 mm; 4—25 mm
Main engines	4 Diesels; 5 000 bhp = 30 knots
Complement	25

Reportedly transferred early 1972. Discussions on fitting missiles have taken place, presumably referring to Styx-type.

1 "TOWN" CLASS

RAJSHAHI P 140

Displacement, tons	115 standard; 143 full load
Dimensions, feet	100 wl; 107 oa × 20 × 11
Guns	2—40 mm; 70 cal Bofors AA
Main engines	2 Maybach/Mercedes MD 655/18 diesels; 3 400 bhp (tropical) = 24 knots
Complement	19

Four fast patrol craft named after towns in East Pakistan were built by Brooke Marine Limited, Lowestoft, England, to the order of the Pakistan Government. The contract was placed on 5 Oct 1963, *Jessore* and *Comilla* were commissioned on 20 May, 1965 and *Rajshahi* and *Sylhet* on 2 Aug 1965. The hulls were of special design, being longitudinally and traversely strengthened. All-welded steel construction with superstructures of all welded sea resistant aluminium alloy.

LOSSES. Sister boats *Comilla* P 142, *Jessore* P 141, and *Sylhet* P 143 were sunk in the Bay of Bengal during the Indo-Pakistan war Dec 1971.

JESSORE (RAJSHAHI similar) — *1966, A. & J. Pavia*

SDML 3517 (ex-*SDML* 1261) **SDML 3520** (ex-*SDML* 1266)

Displacement, tons	**46 standard; 54 full load**
Dimensions, feet	**72 oa × 15·8 × 15·3**
Guns	**1—3 pdr; 1—20 mm AA**
Main engines	**Diesels; 2 shafts; 320 bhp = 12 knots**
Complement	**14**

Former British Harbour Defence Motor Launches of wooden construction, built under the emergency programme during the Second World War, and re-designated Seaward Defence Motor Launches after the war. SDML 3518 and SDML 3519 were scrapped in 1965.

Light Forces—*continued*

SDML 3520 — ***1965, Pakistan Navy***

COASTAL MINESWEEPERS

7 MSC TYPE

MAHMOOD	**(ex-*MSC* 267) M 160**	**MUHAFIZ**	**(ex-*AMS* 138) M 163**
MOMIN	**(ex-*MSC* 293) M 161**	**MUJAHID**	**(ex-*MSC* 261) M 164**
MOSHAL	**(ex-*MSC* 294) M 167**	**MUKHTAR**	**(ex-*MSC* 274) M 165**
MURABAK	**(ex-*MSC* 262) M 162**	**MUNSIF**	**(ex-*MSC* 273) M 166**

Displacement, tons	335 light; 375 full load
Dimensions, feet	138 pp; 144 oa × 27 × 8·5
Guns	2—20 mm
Main engines	GM diesels; 2 shafts; 880 bhp = 14 knots
Complement	39

Transferred to Pakistan by the US under MAP. *Mukhtar* and *Munsif* on 25 June 1959, *Muhafiz* on 25 Feb 1955, *Mujahid* in Nov 1956, *Mahmood*, M 160, in May 1957, *Murabak* in 1957, *Momin* in Aug 1962 and *Moshal* M 167, on 13 July 1963. *Muhafiz* M 163 sunk during Indo-Pakistan War Dec 1971.

MUNSIF — *1972, Pakistan Navy*

OILERS

DACCA (ex-USNS *Mission Santa Clara*, AO 132) A 41

Displacement, tons	5 730 light; 22 380 full load
Dimensions, feet	503 wl; 523·5 oa × 68 × 30·9 max
Main engines	Turbo-electric; 6 000 shp = 15 knots
Boilers	2 Babcock & Wilcox
Oil capacity	20 000 tons (official figure); 134 000 barrel capacity
Complement	160 (15 officers and 145 men)

Former US fleet tanker of the "T2-SE-A1" Type ("Mission" Class). Transferred on loan to Pakistan under MDAP. Handed over from the US on 17 Jan 1963.

DACCA *1964, Pakistan Navy*

ATTOCK (ex-USS YO 249) A 298

Displacement, tons	600 standard; 1,255 full load
Dimensions, feet	177·2 oa × 32 × 15 max
Main engines	Direct coupled diesel; speed 8·5 knots
Complement	26

A harbour oiler of 6 500 barrels capacity built in Trieste, Italy, in 1960 for the Pakistan Navy, under the Mutual Defence Assistance Programme of USA. A photograph appears in the 1964-63 to 1970-71 editions.

WATER CARRIERS

ZUM ZUM YW 15

Built in Italy under US off-shore procurement of the MDA Programme.

Water Carriers—*continued*

ZUM ZUM *1971, W. H. Davis*

TUGS

MADADGAR (ex-USS *Yuma, ATF* 94) A 42

Displacement, tons	1 235 standard; 1 675 full load
Dimensions, feet	195 wl; 205 oa × 38·5 × 15·3 max
Main engines	4 GM diesels; electric drive; 1 shaft; 3 000 bhp = 16·5 knots
Complement	85

Ocean-going salvage tug. Built by Commercial Iron Works, Portland, Oregon. Laid down on 13 Feb 1943. Launched on 17 July 1943. Completed on 31 Aug 1943. Transferred from the US Navy to the Pakistan Navy on 25 Mar 1959 under MDAP. Fitted with powerful pumps and other salvage equipment.

RUSTOM

Dimensions, feet	105·0 × 30·0 × 11·0
Main engines	Crossley diesel; 1 000 bhp = 9·5 knots (max)
Range, miles	3 000 at economic speed
Complement	21

General purpose tug for the Pakistan Navy originally ordered from Werf-Zeeland at Hansweert, Netherlands, in Aug 1952, but after the liquidation of this yard the order was transferred to Worst & Dutmer at Meppel. Launched on 29 Nov 1955.

BHOLU (ex-US YTL 755) **GAMA** (ex-US YTL 754)

These are small harbour tugs built under an "off-shore" order by Costaguta-Voltz.

PARAGUAY

Strength of the Fleet

2 River Defence Vessels
3 Patrol vessels
2 Patrol launches
3 River Patrol Boats
1 Tug
3 Service Craft

Personnel

1973 1 900 officers and men including coastguard and marines.

Mercantile Marine

Lloyd's Register of Shipping:
26 vessels of 21 884 tons gross

RIVER DEFENCE VESSELS

RATED AS GUNBOATS

2 "HUMAITA" CLASS

HUMAITA (ex-*Capitan Cabral*) C 2 **PARAGUAY** (ex-*Comodor Meya*) C 1

Displacement, tons	636 standard; 865 full load
Dimensions, feet	231 × 35 × 5·3
Guns	4—4·7 in; 3—3 in AA; 2—40 mm AA
Mines	6
Armour	·5 in side amidships, ·3 in deck, ·8 in CT
Main engines	Parsons geared turbines; 2 shafts; 3 800 shp = 17 knots
Boilers	2
Oil fuel, tons	150
Range, miles	3 400 at 16 knots
Complement	86

Rated as gunboats but also fitted for minelaying. The armour is of high tensile steel. Both built by Odero, Genoa, laid down in Apr 1929, launched in 1930, and completed in May 1931.

PARAGUAY

PATROL VESSELS

3 "BOUCHARD" CLASS

FORMER MEDIUM MINESWEEPERS

HERNANDEZ (ex-*Seaver*) **MESA** (ex-*Parker*) **NANAHUA** (ex-*Bouchard*)

Patrol Vessels—*continued*

Displacement, tons	450 standard; 620 normal; 650 full load
Dimensions, feet	164 pp; 197 oa × 24 × 8·5 max
Guns	4—40 mm Bofors AA; 2 MG
Main engines	2 sets MAN 2-cycle diesels; 2 000 bhp = 16 knots
Oil fuel, tons	50
Radius, miles	6 000 at 12 knots
Complement	70

Former Argentinian minesweepers of the "Bouchard" class. Built at Sanchez Shipyard, San Fernando, Rio Santiago Naval Yard, and Hansen & Puccini, San Fernando, respectively. Laid down in 1936, 1935 and 1937. Launched on 2 May 1937, 20 Mar 1936 and 18 Aug 1938. Can carry mines. Transferred from the Argentinian Navy to the Paraguayan Navy in Apr 1964 et seq.

MESA (*Parker*)

PATROL LAUNCHES

2 CG TYPE

P1 (ex-USCGC 20417) **P 2** (ex-USCGC 20418)

Displacement, tons	16
Dimensions, feet	45·5 oa × 13·5 × 3·5
Guns	2—20 mm AA
Main engines	2 petrol motors; 2 shafts; 190 hp = 20 knots
Complement	10

Of wooden construction. Built in the United States in 1944. Acquired from the United States Coast Guard in 1944.

RIVER PATROL BOATS

CORONEL MARTINEZ A 2

Displacement, tons	80
Dimensions, feet	71·5 × 18 × 8·2
Guns	1—3 in; 2—37 mm
Main engines	150 ihp = 6·5 knots

Medium type of river patrol boat, military transport and general utility craft.

CAPITAN CABRAL (ex-*Adolfo Riquelme*) A 1

Displacement, tons	180 standard; 206 full load
Dimensions, feet	98·5 pp; 107·2 oa × 23·5 × 9·8
Guns	1—3 in Vickers; 2—37 mm Vickers; 4 MG
Main engines	Triple expansion; 1 shaft; 300 ihp = 9 knots
Complement	47

CAPITAN CABRAL

River Patrol Boats—*continued*

Former tug. Built by Werf-Conrad, Haarlem. Launched in 1907. Of wooden construction.

TENIENTE HERREROS A 3

Displacement, tons	41
Dimensions, feet	63·2 × 11 × 6·8
Guns	4 MG
Main engines	300 ihp = 5·5 knots

Small type of river patrol boat and service craft. Built in the Netherlands in 1908.

TUGS

YLT 559 A 4 (ex-USS YTL 211)

Dimensions, feet	66·2 × 17 × 5
Main engines	Diesel; 300 bhp

Small harbour tug YLT 559 transferred to Paraguay by the USA under the Military Aid Programme in March 1967. Built by Everett Pacific SB & DD Co, Wash.

The floating dock AFDL 26 of 1 000 tons and of steel construction was leased by the USN to Paraguay in March 1956.

Two ferries YFB 82 and 86 were leased by the USN to Paraguay in June 1970.

PERU

Administration

Minister of Marine and Chief of Naval Operations:
Vice Admiral Luis E. Vargas Caballero

Chief of Naval Staff:
Vice Admiral Fernando Zapater Vantosse

Commander-in-Chief of the Fleet:
Rear Admiral Oscar Cuadros

Strength of the Fleet

2 Cruisers
4 Destroyers
3 Frigates
2 Corvettes
5 Patrol Submarines (2 building)
6 Fast Patrol Craft
2 Coastal Gunboats
2 Coastal Minesweepers
7 River Gunboats
3 Patrol Launches
7 Amphibious Vessels
3 Transports
6 Oilers
7 Support Ships and Service Craft

NOTE. Peru is taking over the cruiser *De Ruyter* from the Netherlands.

Disposals

Frigates

1961 *Galvez* (ex-USS *Woonsocket*)
1966 *Ferré* (ex-HMCS *Poundmaker*) *Palacios* (ex-HMCS *Sr Pierre*)

Submarines

1960 *Arica, Casma, Islay, Pacocha*

Auxiliaries

1960 *Rimac*
1961 *Cabo Blanco, Organus*

Diplomatic Representation

Naval Attaché in London and Paris:
Rear Admiral Cesar Barandiaran

Naval Attaché in Washington:
Vice Admiral Jose Arce Larco

Personnel

1973: 8 000 (730 officers, 7 270 men)

Mercantile Marine

Lloyd's Register of Shipping:
655 vessels of 446 374 tons gross

CRUISERS

Name	*No.*	*Builders*	*Laid down*	*Launched*	*Completed*
ALMIRANTE GRAU (ex-HMS *Newfoundland*)	81	Swan, Hunter & Wigham Richardson, Ltd, Wallsend on-Tyne	9 Nov 1939	19 Dec 1941	31 Dec 1942
CORONEL BOLOGNESI (ex-HMS *Ceylon*)	82	Alexander Stephen & Sons, Ltd, Govan, Glasgow	27 Apr 1939	30 July 1942	13 July 1943

2 "ALMIRANTE GRAU" CLASS

Displacement, tons	*Almirante Grau:* 8 800 standard; 11 090 full load *Col. Bolognesi:* 8 781 standard; 11 110 full load
Length, feet (*metres*)	538 (*164·0*) wl; 549 (*167·4*) wl; 555·5 (*169·3*) oa
Beam, feet (*metres*)	63·6 (*19·4*)
Draught, feet (*metres*)	16·5 (*5·0*) mean; 20·5 (*6·2*) max
Guns, surface	9—6 in (*152 mm*) three triple
Guns, dual purpose	8—4 in (4 twin)
Guns, AA	12—40 mm *Almirante Grau* 18—40 mm *Col. Bolognesi*
Armour	4 in (*102 mm*) sides and CT; 2 in (*51 mm*) turrets and deck
Boilers	4 Admiralty 3-drum; 400 psi (*28 kg/cm²*); 720°F (*382°C*)
Main engines	Parsons s.r. geared turbines 72 500 shp; 4 shafts
Speed, knots	31·5
Range, miles	6 000 at 13 knots; 2 800 at full power
Oil fuel (tons)	1 620
Complement	*Almirante Grau:* 743 *Col. Bolognesi:* 766

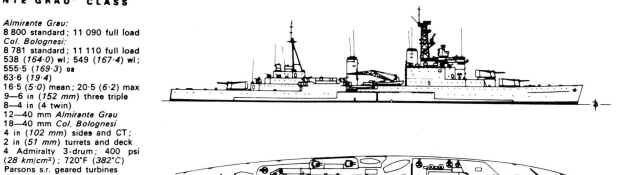

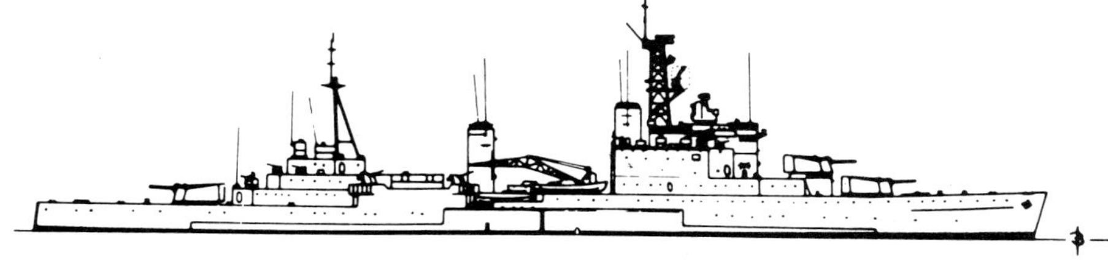

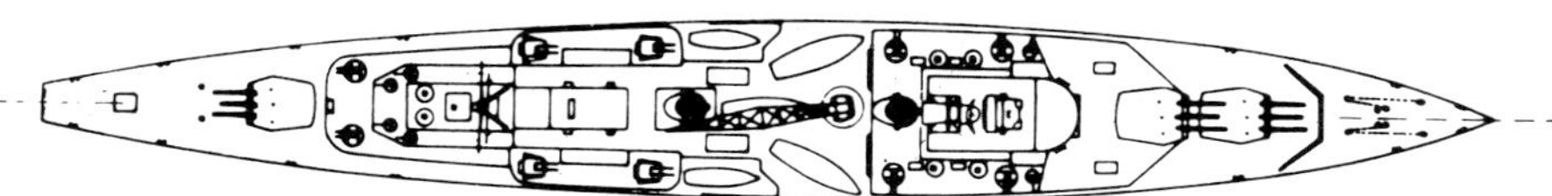

Former British cruisers of the "Ceylon" class, a modification of the original 8 000-ton "Colony" class design, one 6-inch turret having been suppressed, and the number of light AA. guns augmented *Almirante Grau* was engined by Wallsend Slipway & Engineering Co Ltd.

RECONSTRUCTION. *Almirante Grau* was reconstructed in 1951-53 at HM Dockyard, Devonport, with two lattice masts, new bridge and improved AA armament, her torpedo tubes being removed. *Coronel Bolognesi* was refitted with lattice foremast and covered modified bridge in 1955-56, and her torpedo tubes were removed.

Cruisers—*continued*

ALMIRANTE GRAU — *1971, Peruvian Navy*

RADAR. Search: Type 960, Type 277, Type 293 Fire Control: S Band for surface fire, X Band for AA fire.

TRANSFER. *Almirante Grau* (incorporated in the Peruvian Navy on 19 Dec 1959) was formally transferred from the British Navy at Portsmouth on 30 Dec 1959, and *Coronel Bolognesi* was transferred from the British Navy at Portsmouth on 9 Feb 1960.

DESTROYERS

2 "FERRÉ" CLASS
Ex-BRITISH "DARING" CLASS

Name	Builders	Laid down	Launched	Completed
FERRÉ (ex-HMS *Decoy*)	Yarrow, Co Ltd, Scotstoun	22 Sep 1946	29 Mar 1949	28 Apr 1953
PALACIOS (ex-HMS *Diana*)	Yarrow, Co Ltd, Scotstoun	3 Apr 1947	8 May 1952	29 Mar 1954

Displacement, tons: 2 800 standard; 3 600 full load
Length, feet (*metres*): 366 (*111·7*) pp; 375 (*114·3*) wl; 390 (*118·9*) oa
Beam, feet (*metres*): 43 (*13·1*)
Draught, feet (*metres*): 18 (*5·5*) max
Guns, surface: 6—4·5 in (*115 mm*); 2 twin fwd; 1 twin aft; Mk VI
Guns, AA: 2—40 mm
A/S weapons: 1 Squid 3 barrelled DC mortar
Torpedo tubes: 5—21 in (*533 mm*)
Boilers: 2 Foster Wheeler; Pressure 650 psi (*45·7 kg/cm²*); Superheat 850°F (454°C)
Main engines: English Electric dr geared turbines 2 shafts
Speed, knots: 34·75 designed; 31·5 deep
Range, miles: 3 000 at 20 knots
Oil fuel (tons): 580
Complement: 297

Purchased by Peru in 1969 and refitted by Cammel Laird (Ship repairers) Ltd, Birkenhead, for further service. *Palacios* was towed from Plymouth for refit on 9 Dec 1969. Formerly units of the "Daring" class of the Royal Navy, the largest orthodox destroyers ever built in Great Britain. Completed trials late 1972.

FERRÉ (as HMS *Decoy*) — *1970, Skyfotos*

RADAR. Tactical: Type 293. Fire Control: X Band for both forward and after-fire control systems.

FERRÉ, PALACIOS

GUISE, VILLAR

2 "VILLAR" CLASS
Ex-US "FLETCHER" CLASS

Name	No.	Builders	Launched	Completed
GUISE (ex-USS *Isherwood, DD* 520)	72	Bethlehem Steel Co, Staten Island	24 Nov 1942	10 Apr 1943
VILLAR (ex-USS *Benham, DD* 796)	71	Bethlehem Steel Co, Staten Island	29 Aug 1943	20 Dec 1943

Displacement, tons: 2 120 standard; 2 715 normal; 3 050 full load
Length, feet (*metres*): 360·2 (*109·8*) pp; 370 (*112·8*) wl; 376·2 (*114·7*) oa
Beam, feet (*metres*): 39·7 (*12·1*)
Draught, feet (*metres*): 12·2 (*3·7*) mean; 18 (*5·5*) max
Guns, dual purpose: 4—5 in (*127 mm*) 38 cal
Guns, AA: 6—3 in (*76 mm*) 50 cal, 3 twin
A/S weapons: 2 fixed Hedgehogs; 1 DC rack
Torpedo tubes: 5—21 in (*533 mm*) quintupled
Torpedo racks: 2 side-launching for A/S torpedoes
Boilers: 4 Babcock & Wilcox: 600 psi (*42 kg/cm²*); 850°F (*455°C*)
Main engines: 2 GE impulse reaction geared turbines; 60 000 shp; 2 shafts
Speed, knots: 34 max; 15 economical sea
Range, miles: 5 000 at 15 knots; 900 at full power
Oil fuel (tons): 650
Complement: Allowance; 245 (15 officers and 230 men) Max accommodation: 275 (15 officers and 260 men)

Former United States destroyers of the later "Fletcher" class (*Villar*) and "Fletcher" class (*Guise*).

VILLAR — *1971, Peruvian Navy*

RADAR. Search: SPS 6, SPS 10. Fire Control: GFCS 68 system forward, GFCS 56 system aft.

TRANSFER. Transferred from the United States Navy to the Peruvian Navy at Boston, Massachusetts, on 15 Dec 1960, and at San Diego, California, on 8 Oct 1961 respectively.

FRIGATES

3 "CASTILLA" CLASS

Ex-US "CANNON" CLASS

Name	No.	Launched	Completed
AGUIRRE (ex-USS *Waterman, DE* 740)	62	4 July 1943	31 Dec 1943
CASTILLA (ex-USS *Bangust, DE* 739)	61	6 June 1943	30 Oct 1943
RODRIQUEZ (ex-USS *Weaver, DE* 741)	63	20 June 1943	30 Nov 1943

Displacement, tons	1 240 standard; 1 900 full load
Length, feet (*metres*)	300 (*91·4*) pp; 302·2 (*92·1*) wl; 306 (*93·3*) oa
Beam, feet (*metres*)	36·9 (*11·2*)
Draught, feet (*metres*)	12 (*3·6*) mean; 14·1 (*4·3*) max
Guns, dual purpose	3—3 in (*76 mm*) 50 cal
Guns, AA	6—40 mm, 3 twin; 10—20 mm
A/S weapons	1 Mk 10 ahead-throwing mortar; 8 K mortars; 2 DC racks aft
Main engines	4 GM diesel-electric sets 60 000 hp; 2 shafts
Speed, knots	21 designed; 19 max continuous
Range, miles	10 500 at 12 knots; 3 000 at full power
Oil fuel (tons)	322
Complement	Allowance: 172 (12 officers and 160 men); Max accommodation: 212 (12 officers and 200 men)

Former United States destroyer escorts, DE, of the "Cannon" class. All built by the Western Pipe & Steel Co, San Pedro, California, in 1943. Transferred to Peru on 26 Oct 1951, under the Mutual Defence Assistance Programme. Reconditioned and modernised at Green Cove Springs and Jacksonville, Flor. Actually arrived in Peru on 24 May 1952.

TORPEDO TUBES. The original three 21 inch torpedo tubes in a triple mounting were removed.

CASTILLA *1970, Peruvian Navy*

AGUIRRE, CASTILLA, RODRIGUEZ

CORVETTES

2 "GALVEZ" CLASS. Ex-US MSF TYPE

Name	No.	Laid down	Launched	Completed
DIEZ CANSECO (ex-USS *Shoveler, MSF* 382)	69	1 Apr 1944	10 Dec 1944	28 June 1945
GALVEZ (ex-USS *Ruddy, MSF* 380)	68	24 Feb 1944	29 Oct 1944	28 Apr 1945

Displacement, tons	890 standard; 1 250 full load
Dimensions, feet	215 wl; 221·2 oa × 32·2 × 11 max
Guns	1—3 in, 50 cal dp; 2—40 mm AA
A/S weapons	1 Hedgehog
Main engines	Diesel electric; 2 shafts; 3 532 bhp = 18 knots
Range, miles	4 300 at 10 knots
Complement	100

Former US "Auk" class fleet minesweepers, MSF (ex-ocean minesweepers, AM), of the large steel hulled type. Both built by the Gulf Shipbuilding Corp. Activated at San Diego, California, and transferred to the Peruvian Navy under the Mutual Defence Assistance Programme on 1 Nov 1960. Sonar equipment was fitted so that they could be used as patrol vessels. The 3 inch gun director was removed.

DIEZ CANSECO, GALVEZ

GALVEZ *1970, Peruvian Navy*

SUBMARINES

2 HOWALDTSWERKE TYPE

Displacement, tons	1 000 surface; 1 290 dived
Dimensions, feet	183·4 × 20·5 × 19·8
Torpedo Tubes	8—21 in bow tubes
Main machinery	Diesel-electric; 5 000 hp; 1 shaft
Speed, knots	22 dived
Complement	32

Building by Howaldtswerke DW. AG, Kiel. To be fitted with Hollandse SA M8 Torpedo fire control system

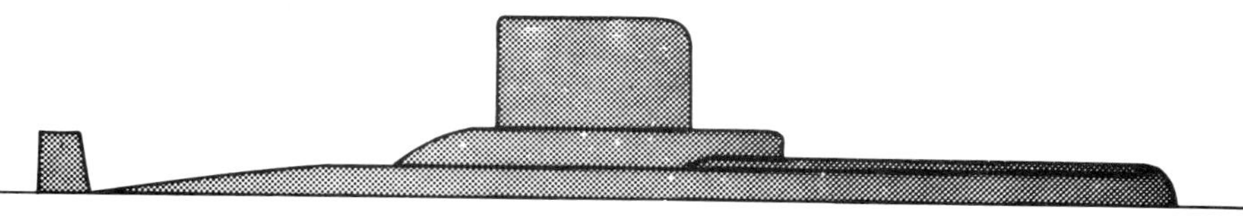

Howaldtswerke Type

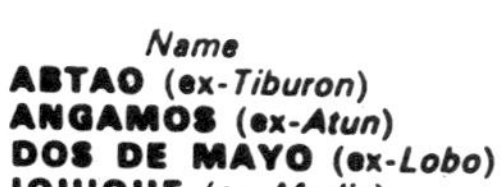

4 "ABTAO" CLASS (US BUILT)

Name	No.	Laid down	Launched	Completed
ABTAO (ex-*Tiburon*)	42	12 May 1952	27 Oct 1953	20 Feb 1954
ANGAMOS (ex-*Atun*)	43	27 Oct 1955	5 Feb 1957	1 July 1957
DOS DE MAYO (ex-*Lobo*)	41	12 May 1952	6 Feb 1954	14 June 1954
IQUIQUE (ex-*Merlin*)	44	27 Oct 1955	5 Feb 1957	1 Oct 1957

Displacement, tons	825 standard; 1 400 submerged
Length, feet (*metres*)	243 (*74·1*) oa
Beam, feet (*metres*)	22 (*6·7*)
Draught, feet (*metres*)	14 (*4·3*)
Guns, surface	1—5 in (*127 mm*) 25 cal (*Abtao* and *Dos de Mayo*)
Torpedo tubes	6—21 in (*533 mm*); 4 bow, 2 stern
Main engines	2 GM 278A diesels; 2 400 bhp; Electric motors; 2 shafts
Speed, knots	16 on surface; 10 submerged
Range, miles	5 000 at 10 knots (surfaced)
Oil fuel (tons)	45
Complement	40

All built by Electric Boat Division. General Dynamics Corporation, Groton, Connecticut. They are of modified US "Mackerel" class.

DOS DE MAYO *1970, Peruvian Navy*

LIGHT FORCES

6 VOSPER TYPE (FPBs)

DE LOS HEROS	23	**LARREA**	25	**SANTILLANA**	22
HERRERA	24	**SANCHEZ CARRION**	26	**VELARDE**	21

Displacement, tons	100 standard; 130 full load
Dimensions, feet	103·7 wl; 109·7 oa × 21 ×5·7
Guns	2—20 mm AA
Main engines	2 Napier Deltic 18 cyl, turbocharged diesels; 6 200 bhp = 30 knots
Range, miles	1 100 at 15 knots
Complement	25 (4 officers and 21 ratings)

Designed and built by Vosper Ltd, Portsmouth, England, for the Peruvian Navy. Of all-welded steel construction with aluminium upperworks. Designed for coastal patrol, air-sea-rescue, and fishery protection. Equipped with Vosper roll damping fins, Decca Type 707 true motion radar, comprehensive radio, up-to-date navigation aids, sonar, depth charges in racks aft, and air-conditioning. The first boat, *Velarde*, was launched on 10 July 1964, the last, *Sanchez Carrion*, on 18 Feb 1965. Can be armed as gunboat, torpedo boat (four side-launched torpedoes) or minelayer. A twin rocket projector can be fitted forward instead of gun.

SANCHEZ CARRION *1971, Peruvian Navy*

3 "RIO" CLASS (PATROL LAUNCHES)

RIO PIURA 04 **RIO TUMBES** 02 **RIO ZARUMILLA** 01

Displacement, tons	37 full load
Dimensions, feet	65·7 × 17 × 3·2
Guns	2—40 mm
Main engines	2 GM diesels; 2 shafts; 1 200 bhp = 18 knots

Built by Viareggio, Italy. Ordered in 1959, laid down on 15 July 1959, and entered service on 5 Sep 1960. *Rio el Salto*, 03, was deleted from the list in 1966.

RIO PIURA *1967, Peruvian Navy*

2 GUNBOATS

RIO SAMA PC 11 (ex-USS *PGM* 78)
RIO CHIRA PC 12 (ex-USS *PGM* 111)

Displacement, tons	130 standard; 147 full load
Dimensions, feet	101 × 21 × 6
Guns	2—40 mm, 4—20 mm, 2—0·5 cal MG
Main engines	2 Diesels; 2 shafts; 1 800 hp = 18·5 knots
Range, miles	1 500 at 10 knots
Complement	15

PC 11 transferred in Sep 1966 from the United States under the Military Aid Programme. PC 12 transferred 30 June 1972.

RIO SAMA *1971, Peruvian Navy*

Light Forces—*continued*

2 "MARANON" CLASS (RIVER GUNBOATS)

MARANÓN	13	John I. Thornycroft & Co	23 Apr 1951	July 1951
UCAYALI	14	Ltd. Southampton, England	7 Mar 1951	June 1951

Displacement, tons	365 full load
Dimensions, feet	154·8 wl × 32 × 4 max
Guns	2—3 in 50 cal dp; 7—20 mm AA (2 twin, 3 single)
Main engines	British Polar M 441 diesels; 800 bhp = 12 knots
Range, miles	6 000 at 10 knots
Complement	40

Ordered early in 1950. Employed on police duties in Upper Amazon. Specially designed for carrying naval officers and men under tropical conditions. Very shallow draught. Superstructure of aluminium alloy. Mechanical ventilation. Based at Iquitos.

2 "LORETO" CLASS (RIVER GUNBOATS)

AMAZONAS 11

Displacement, tons	250 standard
Dimensions, feet	145 × 22 × 4
Guns	2—3 in; 1—47 mm; 2—20 mm AA
Main engines	Diesel; 750 bhp = 15 knots
Range, miles	4 000 at 10 knots
Complement	35

Designed and built by the Electric Boat Co, Groton, Conn. Launched in 1934. A photograph of *Loreto* appears in the 1958-59 edition and of *Amazonas* in the 1959-60 to 1970-71 editions.

NAPO 301 (RIVER GUNBOAT)

Displacement, tons	98
Dimensions, feet	100 pp; 101·5 oa × 18 × 3
Main engines	Triple expansion; 250 ihp = 12 knots
Boilers	Yarrow
Complement	22

Built by Yarrow Co Ltd, Scotstoun, Glasgow. Launched in 1920. Built of steel. Converted from wood to oil fuel burning. In the Upper Amazon Flotilla. Pennant No. 16 was changed to 301 in 1967. Converted to a Dispensary Vessel in 1968.

AMERICA 15 (RIVER GUNBOAT)

Displacement, tons	240
Dimensions, feet	133 × 19·5 × 4·5
Guns	2—3 pdr; 4—12·7 mm AA
Main engines	Triple expansion; 350 ihp = 14 knots
Complement	26

Built by Tranmere Bay Development Co Ltd, Birkenhead. Built of steel. Launched and completed in 1904. Converted from coal to oil fuel burning. In the Upper Amazon Flotilla. The river gunboat *Iquitos* was discarded in 1967 after 92 years service.

COASTAL MINESWEEPERS

2 "BONDY" CLASS

BONDY (ex-*YMS* 25) 137 **SAN MARTIN** (ex-*YMS* 35) 138

Displacement, tons	300 standard; 325 full load
Dimensions, feet	136 × 24·5 × 6
Guns	1—3 in; 2—20 mm AA
Main engines	2 GM diesels; 1 000 bhp = 13 knots (11 knots econ)
Complement	30

Former US wooden motor minesweepers, YMS. *Bondy* was built by Greenport Basin & Construction Co, Long Island, NY, and launched on 28 Jan 1943, *San Martin* by C. Hilterbandt Drydock Co, Kingston, NY, and acquired from USA in 1947. Formerly known as *Alferez de Fragata Bondy* and *Guardiamarina San Martin.*

BONDY *1966, Peruvian Navy*

AMPHIBIOUS VESSELS

CHIMBOTE (ex-M/S *Rawhiti*, ex-USS *LST* 283) 34

Displacement, tons	1 625 standard; 4 050 full load
Dimensions, feet	316 wl; 328 oa × 50 × 14·1
Guns	1—3 in
Main engines	GM diesels; 2 shafts; 1 700 bhp = 10 knots
Oil fuel, tons	600 oil tanks; 1 100 ballast tanks
Range, miles	9 500 at 9 knots
Complement	Accommodation for 16 officers and 130 men

Former US tank landing ship of the 1-510 Series. Built by American Bridge Co Ambridge, Pennsylvania. Laid down on 2 Aug 1943, launched on 10 Oct 1943 and completed on 18 Nov 1943. Sold to Peru by a British firm in 1951.

Amphibious Vessels—*continued*

CHIMBOTE 1970, *Peruvian Navy*

PAITA (ex-USS *Burnett County, LST* 512) 35 (ex-*AT* 4)

Displacement, tons	1 653 standard; 4 080 full load
Dimensions, feet	316 wl; 328 oa × 50 × 14·5 max
Guns	6—40 mm AA; 6—20 mm AA
Main engines	GM diesels; 2 shafts; 1 700 bhp = 10 knots
Range, miles	9 500 at 9 knots
Complement	13 officers, 106 men

Former US tank landing ship of the 511-1152 Series. Built by Chicago Bridge & Iron Co. Seneca, Illinois. Laid down on 29 July 1943. Launched on 10 Dec 1943 and completed on 8 Jan 1944. Purchased by Peru in 1957

PAITA 1972, *Peruvian Navy*

2 "LOMAS" CLASS

ATICO (ex-USS *LSM* 554) **LOMAS** (ex-USS *LSM* 396)

Displacement, tons	513 standard; 913 full load
Dimensions, feet	196·5 wl; 203·5 oa × 34·5 × 7
Guns	2—40 mm AA; 4—20 mm AA
Main engines	Diesels; 800 rpm; 2 shafts; 3 600 bhp = 12 knots
Oil fuel, tons	165 oil tanks
Complement	Accommodation for 116 (10 officers and 106 men)

Former US medium landing ships of the LSM type. Both built by Charleston Navy Yard, Charleston, SC, USA. Purchased in 1959. A photograph of *Lomas* appears in the 1967-68 to 1971-72 editions.

Name	*No.*	*Laid down*	*Launched*	*Completed*
Atico	37	3 Mar 1945	22 Mar 1945	14 Sep 1945
Lomas	36	13 Dec 1944	2 Jan 1945	23 Mar 1945

ATICO 1972, *Peruvian Navy*

3 Ex-US LCUs

PIRURA BT 4 (ex-US LCU 1161) **SALTO** BT 3 (ex-US LCU 855)
ZARUMILLA BT 1 (ex-US LCU 501)

Displacement, tons	160 light; 315 full load
Dimensions, feet	119 oa × 32·7 × 5
Guns	2—20 mm
Main engines	Gray Marine diesels; 3 shafts; 675 bhp = 10 knots
Complement	15

Sold to Peru Aug 1947.

SURVEY VESSELS

BAP UNANUE

Of 858 tons, launched in 1944, with a complement of 29.

BAP CARDENAS

Of 19 tons, launched in 1950, with a compliment of 4.

TRANSPORTS

INDEPENDENCIA (ex-USS *Bellatrix, AKA* 3, ex-*Raven, SKA* 20) 31 (ex-21)

Displacement, tons	6 194 light
Measurement, tons	Maritime Commission deadweight, 8 656
Guns	1—5 in 38 cal; 3—3 in 50 cal. 10—20 mm
Dimensions, feet	435 wl; 459 oa × 63 × 26·5
Main engines	1 Nordberg diesel; 1 shaft; 6 000 bhp = 16·5 knots

Former US attack cargo ship. Built by Tampa Shipbuilding Co, Tampa, Florida, in 1941. Transferred to Peru at Bremerton, Washington on 20 July 1963 under the Military Aid Program. Training ship for the Peruvian Naval Academy. Pennant number was changed from 21 to 31 in 1969.

INDEPENDENCIA 1970, *Peruvian Navy*

ILO **RIMAC**

Displacement, tons	18 400 full load
Measurement, tons	13 000 deadweight
Dimensions, feet	507·7 × 67·3 × 27·2
Main engines	Diesels; Speed = 15·6 knots

The name *Ilo* was assigned to a new vessel launched on 15 July 1970 by the Servicio Industrial de la Marina in Callao. The new transport *Ilo* completed in Dec 1971. Her sister ship *Rimac* was launched at the same yard on 12 Dec 1971.
The old *Ilo* (ex-*Norlindo*) No. 133 (ex-33) was removed from the effective list in 1968.

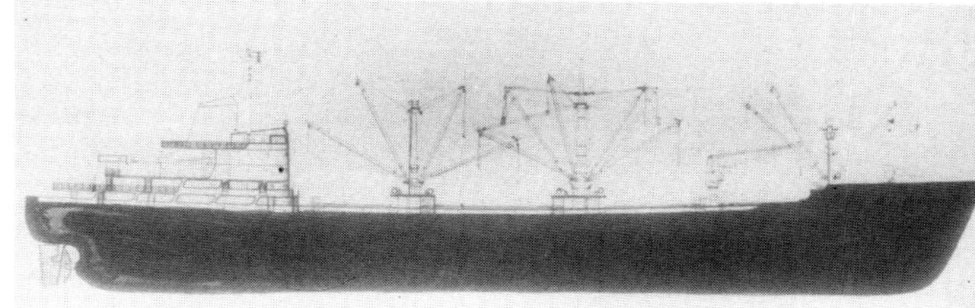

ILO 1971, *Peruvian Navy*

CALLAO (ex-*Monserrate*) 132

Displacement, tons	7 790 full load
Measurement, tons	5 578 gross
Dimensions, feet	459 × 56 × 22
Main engines	2 diesel motors; speed = 14 knots
Complement	100 (13 officers, 87 ratings)

Former Hamburg America liner. Built by Bremen Vulkan Yard, Bremen-Vegesack. Launched in 1938. Salved and seized on 1 Apr 1941 by the Peruvian Government after scuttling by the Germans. Employed as a troop transport and cargo carrier. Pennant No. changed from 32 to 132 in 1964.

CALLAO 1972, *Peruvian Navy*

FLOATING DOCKS

The former US auxiliary floating dry dock *ARD 8* was transferred to Peru in Feb 1961: displacement 5 200 tons; length 492 feet; beam 84 feet; draught 5·7 to 33·2 feet. Pennant No. changed from WY 20 to ADF 112 in 1964.
The former US floating dock *AFDL 33* launched in Oct 1964 was transferred to Peru in July 1959; displacement 1 900 tons; length 288 feet; beam 64 feet, draught 8·2 to 31·5 feet. Pennant No. changed from WY 19 to ADF 111 in 1964.

OILERS

3 "PARINAS" CLASS

Name	No.	Launched	Completed
PARINAS	155	2 May 1967	13 June 1968
PIMENTAL	156	30 Dec 1967	27 June 1969
+1		Building	

Displacement, tons: 3 434 light; 13 600 full load
Measurement, tons: 10 000 deadweight
Dimensions, feet: 410·9 × 63·1 × 26
Main engines: Burmeister and Wain Type 750 diesel; 5 400 bhp = 14·5 knots

Built by the Servicio Industrial de la Marina in the Naval Arsenal at Callao. In service 1969.

PARINAS — *1970, Peruvian Navy*

2 "SECHURA" CLASS

LOBITOS 159 — **ZORRITOS** 158

Displacement, tons: 8 700 full load
Measurement, tons: 4 300 gross; 6 000 deadweight
Dimensions, feet: 360·0 wl; 385·0 oa × 52·0 × 21·2 max
Main engines: Burmeister & Wain diesels; 2 400 bhp = 12 knots (13·25 knots on trials)
Boilers: 2 Scotch with Thornycroft oil burners for cargo tank cleaning

Designed for transferring fuel to warships at sea. *Zorritos*, built by Servicio Industrial de la Marina in the Arsenal Naval del Callao, Peru, was laid down on 8 Oct 1955 and launched on 8 Oct 1958. Pennant No. was changed from 58 to 158 in 1964. *Lobitos* built by Servicio Industrial de la Marina in the Arsenal Naval del Callao, Peru, was launched in May 1965. Sister ship *Sechura*, No. 154 (ex-54) was laid up in 1968 (officially removed from the effective list).

LOBITOS — *1969, US Navy*

TALARA 153

Displacement, tons: 7 000
Measurement tons: 4 800 deadweight, (about 35 000 barrels)
Dimensions, feet: 336·2 × 50·9 × 22·5
Main engines: Burmeister & Wain diesel; Type 562 *VT-F115*; 2 400 bhp = 12 knots

Built to requirements of Lloyd's Register. Laid down in 1953 by Burmeister & Wain's Maskin-Og Skibsbygger, Copenhagen. Completed in 1955. No. changed from 53 to 153 in 1964. A photograph appears in the 1955-56 to 1966-67 editions. Laid up in reserve in 1969 (removed from the effective list).

MOLLENDO (ex-*Amalienborg*) ATP 151

Displacement, tons: 6 084 standard; 25 670 full load
Dimensions, feet: 534·8 × 72·2 × 30
Main engines: 674-VTFS-160 diesels; 7 500 bhp = 14·5 knots

This Japanese built tanker, completed Sep 1962, was acquired by Peru in Apr 1967.

MOLLENDO — ***1970, Peruvian Navy***

WATER CARRIER

MANTILLA (ex-US *YW* 122) 141

Displacement, tons: 1 235 full load
Dimensions, feet: 174 × 32
Guns: 1 MG forward
Capacity, gallons: 200,000

Former US water barge. Built by Henry C. Grebe & Co Inc, Chicago, Ill. Lent to Peru in July 1963.

MANTILLA — *1970, Peruvian Navy*

TUGS

RIOS (ex-USS *Pinto, ATF* 90) 123

Displacement, tons: 1 235 standard; 1 675 full load
Measurement, tons: 195 wl; 205 oa × 38·5 × 15·5 max
Main engines: 4 GM diesel electric; 3 000 bhp = 16·5 knots

Former United States fleet ocean tug of the "Apache" class. Launched on 5 Jan 1943. Transferred to Peru in 1960 and delivered in Jan 1961. Fitted with powerful pumps and other salvage equipment.

RIOS — *1967, Peruvian Navy*

UNANUE (ex-USS *Wateree, ATA* 174) 136

Displacement, tons: 534 standard; 852 full load; official revised figure
Dimensions, feet: 133·7 wl, 143 oa × 33·9 × 13·2
Main engines: GM diesel-electric; 1 500 bhp = 13 knots

Former United States auxiliary ocean tug of the "Maricopa" class. Built by Levingston SB Co, Orange, Texas. Laid down on 5 Oct 1943, launched on 18 Nov 1943 and completed on 20 July, 1944. Purchased from the USA in Nov 1961 under MAP.

UNANUE — ***1970, Peruvian Navy***

PHILIPPINES

Administration

Flag Officer in Command, Philippine Navy:
Commodore Ismael C. Lomibao.

Diplomatic Representation

Naval, Military and Air Attaché in London:
Colonel Pedro L. Los Baños

Naval Attaché in Washington:
Captain Ramon Madrid

Personnel

1972: 1 640 officers and 16 360 men including Coast Guard

Strength of the Fleet

1	Frigate	18	Patrol Boats
11	Patrol Vessels	4	Minesweepers
9	Patrol Gunboats	2	Command Ships
4	Hydrofoil Patrol Boats	11	Landing Ships

DESTROYERS

The Philippine Navy can be expected to begin operating ships of destroyer size during the 1970s in view of the increasing level of competence of the Philippine Navy and the reduction of US naval forces in the Western Pacific.

Ships

Most names are those of geographical locations and are prefixed by RPS (Republic of Philippines Ship).

Coast Guard

Established Oct 1967 as a specialised branch within the Navy.
Commandant: Commodore Dioscero E. Papa

Mercantile Marine

Lloyds' Register of Shipping:
327 vessels of 924 564 tons

FRIGATES

1 Ex-US "BOSTWICK" CLASS

Name	*No.*	*Launched*	*US Comm.*	*Transferred*
DATU KALANTIAW (ex-USS *Booth*, DE 170)	PS 76	21 June 1943	21 July 1943	15 Dec 1967

Displacement, tons	1 220 standard; 1 620 full load
Length, feet (*metres*)	300 (*91·5*) wl; 306 (*93·2*) oa
Beam, feet (*metres*)	36·6 (*11·2*)
Draught, feet (*metres*)	14 (*4·3*)
Guns	3—3 inch (*76 mm*) 50 cal AA 6—40 mm AA (twin) 2—20 mm AA (single)
A/S weapons	6—12·75 inch (*324 mm*) torpedo tubes (Mk 32 triple); depth charges
Main engines	Diesel-electric drive (General Motors diesels); 6 000 bhp; 2 shafts
Speed, knots	21
Complement	Approx 165

Former US destroyer escort of the DET design. Built by Federal Shipbuilding & Dry Dock Co, Newark, New Jersey, and completed by the Norfolk Navy Yard. Triple 21 inch torpedo tube mount originally fitted has been removed. Equipped with SPS-5 and SPS-6 search radars.

DISPOSALS
Rajah Soliman D 66 (ex-USS *Bowers*, APD 40), which had been transferred to the Philippines in 1961, was sunk in a typhoon in the Philippines in June 1962; raised but stricken on 3 Dec 1964.

PATROL VESSELS

2 Ex-US "AUK" CLASS MSF TYPE

RIZAL (ex-USS *Murrelet*, MSF 372)	PS 69	29 Dec 1944
QUEZON (ex-USS *Vigilance*, MSF 324)	PS 70	5 Apr 1943

Displacement, tons	890 standard; 1 250 full load
Dimensions, feet	215 wl; 221·2 oa × 32·2 × 10·8
Guns	2—3 inch (*76 mm*) 50 cal AA (single); 4—40 mm AA (twin); 4—20 mm AA (twin)
A/S weapons	3—12·75 inch (*324 mm*) torpedo tubes (Mk 32 triple); 1 hedgehog; depth charges
Main engines	Diesel-electric (General Motors diesels); 3 532 bhp; 2 shafts = 18 knots
Complement	approx 100

Former US Navy minesweepers (originally designated AM). Built by Savannah Machine & Foundry Co, Savannah, Georgia, and Associated Shipbuilders, Seattle, Washington, respectively. Launch dates above. PS 69 commissioned in US Navy on 21 Aug 1945 and PS 70 on 28 Feb 1944; PS 69 transferred to the Philippines on 18 June 1965 and PS 70 on 19 Aug 1967.
Upon transfer the minesweeping gear was removed and a second 3 inch gun fitted aft; additional anti-submarine weapons also fitted.

RIZAL *1971, Philippine Navy*

5 Ex-US 185-ft PCE TYPE

CEBU (ex-USS PCE 881)	PS 28	10 Nov 1943
NEGROS OCCIDENTAL (ex-USS PCE 884)	PS 29	24 Feb 1944
LEYTE (ex-USS PCE 885)	PS 30	30 Apr 1945
PANGASINAN (ex-USS PCE 891)	PS 31	15 June 1944
ILOILO (ex-USS PCE 897)	PS 32	3 Aug 1943

Displacement, tons	640 standard; 850 full load
Dimensions, feet	180 wl; 184·5 oa × 34 × 9·5
Guns	1—3 inch (*76 mm*) 50 cal AA; 3 or 6—40 mm AA (single or twin); 4—20 mm AA (single)
A/S weapons	2—12·75 inch (*324 mm*) torpedo tubes (Mk 32 single); depth charges; hedgehog in some
Main engines	Diesels (General Motors); 2 000 bhp; 2 shafts = 15 knots
Complement	approx 100

Former US Navy patrol craft. PS 28, 29, and 30 built by Albina Engineering & Machine Works, Portland, Oregon; PS 31 and 32 built by Willamette Iron & Steel Corp, Portland, Oregon. Launch dates above; completed 1944-1945. All five units transferred to the Philippines in July 1948.

Patrol Vessels—*continued*

CEBU *1971, Philippine Navy*

LEYTE *Philippine Navy*

4 Ex-US 173-ft PC TYPE

BATANGAS (ex-USS PC 1134)	PS 24	18 Jan 1943
NUEVA ECIJA (ex-USS PC 1241)	PS 25	24 Dec 1942
CAPIZ (ex-USS PC 1564)	PS 27	19 Apr 1944
NUEVA VISCAYA (ex-USAF *Altus*, ex-USS PC 568)	PS 80	25 Apr 1942

Displacement, tons	280 standard; 450 full load
Dimensions, feet	170 wl; 173·66 oa × 23 × 10·8
Guns	1—3 inch (*76 mm*) 50 cal AA; 1—40 mm AA; several—20 mm AA (single or twin)
A/S weapons	depth charges
Main engines	Diesels (General Motors); 2 880 bhp; 2 shafts = 20 knots
Complement	Approx 70

Former US Navy patrol craft. Launch dates above; completed 1942-1944. *Batangas* and *Capiz* transferred to the Philippines in July 1948; *Nueva Ecija* in Oct 1958; and *Nueva Viscaya* in Mar 1968. The *Nueva Viscaya* was stricken from the US Navy on 15 Mar 1963 and subsequently served with the US Air Force until transferred.

Bohol PS 22 (ex-USS PC 1131) scrapped in 1969, *Camarines Sur* C 21 (ex-USS PC 1121) stricken in 1953, *Negros Oriental* C 26 (ex-USS PC 1563) sunk in typhoon at Guam in Nov 1962 (raised and stricken in 1963).

Tatlac PG 11 (ex-USS PCS 1399, ex-YMS 450) and *Laguna* PG 12 (ex-USS PCS 1403) scrapped in 1969.

110ft SC TYPE

Cagayan R 14 (ex-USS SC 731), *Mountain Province* P 15 (ex-USS SC 736), *Liocus Sup* P 16 (ex-USS SC 739), *Surigao* P 17 (ex-USS SC 747), *Isabella* P 18 (ex-USS SC 750), *Cavite* P 19 (ex-USS SC 981) scrapped; *Alert* PY 54 (ex-USS SC 1267) sunk in 1956; *Malampay Sound* AF 20 (ex-USS SC 1274) stricken.

Patrol Vessels—*continued*

BOHOL—now stricken *1968, Philippine Navy*

4 100-ft PGM TYPE

AGUSAN G 61 **ROMBLON** G 63
CATANDUANES G 62 **PALAWAN** G 64

Displacement, tons	122 full load
Dimensions, feet	100·33 oa × 21·1 × 8·5
Guns	2—20 mm AA; 2—·50 cal MG
Main engines	Diesels (Mercedes Benz); 950 bhp; 2 shafts = 17 knots

Steel-hulled patrol gunboats built under US military assistance programme for the Philippines. Built by Tacoma Boatbuilding Co, Tacoma, Washington, and transferred to the Philippines upon completion, G 61 and 62 in Mar 1960, and G 63 and 64 in June 1960. Assigned US designations PGM 39-42 while under construction.
These craft are lengthened versions of the US Coast Guard 85-foot "Cape" class patrol boat design. *Catanduanes* is operated by the Philippine Coast Guard.

ROMBLON *1968, Philippine Navy*

5 110-ft PGM TYPE

CAMARINES PG 48 **ANTIQUE** PG 51
SULU PG 49 **MISMAMIS OCCIDENTAL** PG 53
LA UNION PG 50

Displacement, tons	100 standard; 144 full load
Dimensions, feet	110 oa × 17 × 6·5
Guns	1—60 mm mortar; 1—40 mm AA; 4—·50 cal MG
Main engines	Diesels; 2 shafts = 18 knots

Wood-hulled patrol gunboats built under US military assistance programme for the Philippines. Built by Georgia Shipbuilding Co, St Mary's Georgia, and transferred to the Philippines upon completion, PG 48 in Jan 1955, PG 49 and 50 in April 1955, and PG 51 and 53 in Aug 1956. Assigned US designations PGM 33-36 and 38 while under construction.
The design of these craft is based on the 110-foot wood submarine chasers of World War II construction.
Masbate PG 52 (built as PGM 37) sunk in 1965.

LA UNION *1968*

HYDROFOIL PATROL BOATS

2 ITALIAN DESIGN

CAMIGUIN H 72 **SIQUIJOR** H 73

Displacement, tons	36
Dimensions, feet	67·75 × 15·3 (24·1 overfoils) × 8·9 (3 8 foilborne)
Guns	1—20 mm AA
Main engines	Diesel (Mercedes Benz); 1 250 bhp; 2 shafts = 38 knots

Built by Cantiere Navale Leopoldo Rodriquez, Messina, Sicily. Laid down on 26 May and 28 Oct 1964. Completed in Apr 1965. For military and police patrol.

Hydrofoil Patrolboats—*continued*

CAMIGUIN Type on foils *1965*

CAMIGUIN *1969, Philippine Navy*

2 JAPANESE DESIGN

BALER H 75 **BONTOC** H 74

Displacement, tons	32 full load
Dimensions, feet	68·9 × 15·7 × 24·6 over foils
Guns	MG fore and aft
Main engines	Ikegai-Mercedes Benz diesel; 3 200 bhp = 37·8 knots (32 cruising). Also auxiliary engine
Complement	15 (3 officers, 12 ratings)

Built by Hitachi Zosen, Kanawaga, Japan. Completed in Dec 1966. For smuggling prevention.

INSHORE PATROL CRAFT

6 65-ft SEWART TYPE

Displacement, tons	33 full load
Dimensions, feet	65 oa × 16
Guns	6 machineguns
Main engines	3 diesels (General Motors 12V71); 1 590 bhp; 3 shafts = 25 knots

These craft were ordered in the United States from Sewart in 1971. The design is adopted from a commercial 65-foot boat. Similar to the FB 1-10 operated by the South Korean Navy.

18 "SWIFT" TYPE

PCF 300 (ex-USN PCF 6633)
PCF 301 (ex-USN PCF 6634)
PCF 302 (ex-USN PCF 35)
PCF 303 (ex-USN PCF 36)
PCF 304 (ex-USN PCF 37)
PCF 305 (ex-USN PCF 38)
PCF 306 (ex-USN PCF 681)
PCF 307 (ex-USN PCF 682)
PCF 308 (ex-USN PCF 683)
PCF 309 (ex-USN PCF 684)
PCF 310 (ex-USN PCF 685)
PCF 311 (ex-USN PCF 686)
PCF 312 (ex-USN PCF 687)
PCF 313 (ex-USN PCF 688)
PCF 314 (ex-USN PCF 6911)
PCF 315 (ex-USN PCF 6912)
PCF 316 (ex-USN PCF 6913)
PCF 317 (built 1970)

Displacement, tons	22·5 full load
Dimensions, feet	51·3 × 13·6
Guns	2—50 cal MG
Main engines	2 geared diesels (General Motors); 860 bhp; 2 shafts = 28 knots

Inshore patrol craft of the "Swift" type built in the United States. PCF 302-305 served in US Navy prior to transfer to the Philippines; others built for US military assistance programmes. PCF 300 and 301 transferred to Philippines in Mar 1966, PCF 302-305 in Aug 1966, PCF 306-313 in Feb 1968, PCF 314-316 in July 1970. PCF 317 is Philippine built (ferro concrete).

Inshore Patrol Craft—*Continued*

PCF 310 — *1969, Philippine Navy*

PATROL MINESWEEPERS

2 Ex-US MSO TYPE

DAVAO DEL NORTE (ex-USS *Energy*, MSO 436)	PM 91	13 Feb 1953
DAVAO DEL SUR (ex-USS *Firm*, MSO 444)	PM 92	15 Apr 1953

Displacement, tons	665 light; 750 full load
Dimensions, feet	165 wl; 172 oa × 36 × 13·6
Guns	2—20 mm AA
Main engines	4 diesels (Packard); 2 280 bhp; 2 shafts (controllable-pitch propellers) = 15·5 knots

Former US Navy ocean minesweepers of the "Agile" class. Built by J. M. Martinac Shipbuilding Corp, Tacoma, Washington; launch dates above. Commissioned in US Navy on 16 July 1954 and 12 Oct 1954, respectively. Wood-hulled with non-magnetic engines and fittings.

Both ships transferred to the Philippine Navy on 5 July 1972; designated PM for patrol-minesweepers.

DAVAO DEL NORTE (as US *Energy*) — *1968, US Navy*

2 Ex-US MSC TYPE

ZAMBALES (ex-USS MSC 218)	PM 55
ZAMBOANGA DEL NORTE (ex-USS MSC 219)	PM 56

Displacement, tons	320 light; 385 full load
Dimensions, feet	144 oa × 28 × 8·2
Guns	2—20 mm AA
Main engines	2 diesels; 880 bhp; 2 shafts = 12 knots

"Bluebird" class coastal minesweepers built by the United States specifically for transfer under the military aid programme. Transferred on 7 Mar 1956 and 23 Apr 1956, respectively. Wood hulled with non-magnetic metal fittings.

ZAMBALES — *1969, Philippine Navy*

COMMAND SHIPS

THE PRESIDENT (ex-*Roxas*, ex-*Lapu-Lapu*) TP 777

Dimensions, feet	275 oa × 42·6 × 21
Guns	2—20 mm AA
Main engines	Diesels; 5 000 bhp; 2 shafts = 18 knots

Built at Ishikawajima, Japan, as war reparation; launched in 1958 and completed in 1959. Used as presidential yacht and command ship.

Originally named *Lapu-Lapu* after the chief who killed Magellan; renamed *Roxas* on 9 Oct 1962 after the late Manuel Roxas, the first President of the Philippines Republic renamed *The President* in 1967.

THE PRESIDENT — *1968, Philippine Navy.*

MOUNT SAMAT (ex-*Pagasa*, ex-*Santa Maria* ex-*Pagasa*, ex-APO 21, ex-USS *Quest*, AM 281) TK 21 16 Mar 1944

Displacement, tons	650 standard; 945 full load
Dimensions, feet	184·5 wl; 180 oa × 33 × 9·8
Main engines	Diesels (Cooper Bessemer); 1 710 bhp; 2 shafts = 14·8 knots

Former US Navy minesweeper (AM). Built by Gulf Shipbuilding Corp. Launch date above; commissioned on 25 Oct 1944. Transferred to the Philippines in July 1948. Used as presidential yacht and command ship. A sister ship serves as a surveying ship in the coast guard as the *Samar*.

MOUNT SAMAT — *1971*

LANDING SHIPS

9 Ex-US LST TYPE

BULACAN (ex-USS LST 843)	LT 38	29 Nov 1944
ALBAY (ex-USS LST 865)	LT 39	22 Nov 1944
MISAMIS ORIENTAL (ex-USS LST 875)	LT 40	29 Nov 1944
BATAAN (ex-USS *Caddo Parish*, LST 515)	LT 85	31 Dec 1943
CAGAYAN (ex-USS *Hickman County*, LST 825)	LT 86	11 Nov 1944
ILCOS NORTE (ex-USS *Madera County*, LST 905)	LT 87	30 Dec 1944
MONDRO OCCIDENTAL (ex-USNS LST 222)	LT 93	17 Aug 1943
SURAGO DEL NORTE (es-USNS LST 546)	LT 94	16 Feb 1944
SURAGO DEL SUR (ex-USNS LST 488)	LT 95	5 Mar 1943

Displacement, tons	1 620 standard; 2 366 beaching; 4 080 full load
Dimensions, feet	316 wl; 328 oa × 50 × 14
Guns	8—40 mm AA (two twin, four single)
Main engines	Diesels (General Motors); 1 700 bhp; 2 shafts = 11·6 knots

Former US Navy tank landing ships. Cargo capacity 2 100 tons. Launch dates above. Three ships transferred in July 1948; three ships on 29 Nov 1969; and three ships on 15 July 1972.

Cutabato T 36 ex-USS LST 75 and *Pampanga* T 37 ex-USS LST 842 have been scrapped.

MISAMIS ORIENTAL — *1968, Philippine Navy*

2 Ex-US LSM TYPE

ISABELA	(ex-USS LSM 463)	LP 41
ORIENTAL MINDORO	(ex-USS LSM 320)	LP 68

Displacement, tons	743 beaching; 1 095 full load
Dimensions, feet	196·5 wl; 203·5 oa × 34·6 × 8·5
Guns	2—40 mm AA (twin); several 20 mm AA
Main engines	Diesels (direct drive; General Motors except Fairbanks Morse in *Isabela*); 2 800 bhp; 2 shafts = 12·5 knots

Former US Navy medium landing ships. Built 1944-1945. Transferred to the Philippines in Mar 1961, and Apr 1962, respectively. *Batanes* LP 65 ex-USS LSM 236 ran aground and stricken in 1972.

Landing Ships—*continued*

BATANES—now stricken *1962, Courtesy Mr W. H. Davis*

REPAIR SHIPS

2 Ex-US ARL TYPE

AKLAN (ex-USS *Romulus*, ARL 22, ex-LST 926) AR 67
NARRA (ex-USS *Krishna*, ARL 38, ex-LST 1149) AR 88

Displacement, tons	2 366 standard; 4 100 full load
Dimensions, feet	316 wl; 328 oa × 50 × 11·2
Guns	8—40 mm AA (quad); several 20 mm AA
Main engines	Diesels (General Motors); 1 800 bhp; 2 shafts = 11·6 knots

Former US Navy landing craft repair ships. Converted during construction from LSTs; launched on 15 Nov 1944 and 25 May 1945, respectively. Transferred to the Philippines in Nov 1961 and on 30 Oct 1971, respectively.

AKLAN *1968, Philippine Navy*

OILERS

2 Ex-US YO and YOG TYPE

LAKE MAUJAN (ex-USS YO 173) YO 43
LAKE BOHI (ex-USS YOG 73) YO 78

Displacement, tons	520 standard; 1 400 full load
Dimensions, feet	174 oa × 32 × 13·2
Guns	2—20 mm AA (single)
Main engines	Diesel; 560 bhp; 1 shaft = 8 knots

Former US Navy self-propelled fuel oil barges. Built in 1943-1944. Cargo capacity 6 570 barrels. *Lake Maujan* carries fuel oil and *Lake Bohi* carries gasoline and diesel fuel. *Lake Lanao* of same design (see photo). Transferred to the Philippines in July 1948 and July 1967, respectively.

WATER CARRIER

LAKE LANAO

Displacement, tons	1 235 full load
Dimensions, feet	174 oa × 32 × 15
Guns	2—20 mm AA
Main engines	Diesel; 560 bhp; 1 shaft = 8 knots

Former US Navy self-propelled water barge. Cargo capacity 200 000 gallons fresh water. Transferred to the Philippines in July 1948.

LAKE LANAO *1969, Philippine Navy*

TUGS

1 Ex-US ATR TYPE

IFUGAO (ex-HMS *Emphatic*, ex-USS ATR 96) AQ 44

Displacement, tons	783 full load
Dimensions, feet	134·6 wl; 143 oa × 33·8 × 13·5
Guns	1—3 inch (*76 mm*) 50 cal AA; 2—20 mm AA
Main engines	Diesel; 1 500 bhp; 1 shaft = 13 knots

Rescue tug transferred to Royal Navy upon launching on 27 Jan 1944; subsequently returned to US Navy and retransferred to the Philippines in July 1948.

6 Ex-US HARBOUR TYPE

MARANAO (ex-YTL 554)	YQ 221	**AETA** (ex-YTL 449)	YQ 224
IGOROT (ex-YTL 572)	YQ 222	**ILONGOT**((ex-YTL 427)	YQ 225
TAGBANUA (ex-YTL 429)	YQ 223	**TASADAY** (ex-YTL 425)	YQ 226

Former US Navy 66-foot harbour tugs.

SERVICE CRAFT

The Philippines Navy operates several former US and Australian floating dry docks and a number of non-self-propelled service craft. The former includes the ex-US Navy. **AFDL 20** and **AFDL 44**.

SUPPLY SHIPS AND TENDERS

1 Ex-US COAST GUARD C1-M-AV1 TYPE

MACTAN (ex-USCGC *Kukui*, WAK 186, ex-USS *Colquitt*, AK 174) TK 90

Displacement, tons	4 900 light; 5 636 full load
Dimensions, feet	320 wl; 338·5 oa × 50 × 18
Guns	Unarmed
Main engines	Diesel (Nordberg); 1 750 bhp; 1 shaft = 11·5 knots

Cargo-ship built by Froemming Brothers, Milwaukee, Wisconsin; launched on 21 Jan 1945 and commissioned in US Navy on 22 Sep 1945 and transferred to the Coast Guard two days later. Subsequently served as Coast Guard supply ship in Pacific until transferred to Philippines on 1 Mar 1972. These ships are used to supply military posts and lighthouses in the Philippine archipelago.

1 Ex-US COAST GUARD TENDER

KALINGA (ex-USCGC *Redbud*, WLB 398, ex-USNS *Redbud*, T-AKL 398) TK 89

Displacement, tons	935 standard
Dimensions, feet	180 oa × 37 × 13
Guns	Unarmed
Main engines	Diesel-electric; 1 200 bhp; 1 shaft = 13 knots

Originally US Coast Guard buoy tender (WAGL 398) built by Marine Iron & Shipbuilding Co, Duluth, Minnesota; launched on 11 Sep 1943. Transferred to US Navy on 25 Mar 1949 as AG 398; redesignated AKL 398 on 31 Mar 1949; transferred to Military Sea Transportation Service on 20 Feb 1952 (T-AKL 398); reacquired by Coast Guard on 20 Nov 1970 and transferred to Philippines on 1 Mar 1972. (Corrected from previous edition.)

3 Ex-US ARMY FS TYPE

BOJEADOE (ex-US Army FS 203) TK 46
LAUIS LEDGE (ex-US Army FS 185) TK 45
LIMASAWA (ex-USCGC *Nettle* WAK 169, ex-US Army FS 169) TK

Displacement, tons	470 standard; 811 full load
Dimensions, feet	180 oa × 23 × 10
Main engines	Diesels; 1 000 shp; 1 shaft = 11 knots

Former US Army freight and supply ships.

LAUIS LEDGE *1969, Philippine Navy*

1 Ex-AUSTRALIAN TYPE

PEARL BANK (ex-US Army LO 4, ex-Australian MSL)

Displacement, tons	160 standard; 300 full load
Dimensions, feet	120 oa × 24·5 × 8
Main engines	Diesels (Fairbanks Morse); 240 bhp; 2 shafts = 7 knots

Originally an Australian motor stores lighter; subsequently transferred to the US Army and then to the Philippines.

COAST AND GEODETIC SERVICE

SAMAR (ex-USS *Project*, AM 278) M 33 20 Nov 1943

Former US Navy minesweeper, similar to the *Mount Samat*. Built by Gulf Shipbuilding Corp. Transferred to the Philippines in July 1948. Subsequently adapted for surveying and now operated by the Coast & Geodetic Service.

COAST GUARD

2 PATROL BOATS

ABRA FB 83 **BUKIDNON** FB 84

Displacement, tons	40 standard
Dimensions, feet	87·5 oa × 19 × 4·75
Guns	2—20 mm AA
Main engines	Diesels (Mercedes-Benz); 2 460 bhp; 2 shafts = approx 25 knots
Complement	15 (3 officers, 12 enlisted men)

One acquired from Singapore in late 1969. *Bukidnon* built at Cavite. Wood hull and aluminium superstructure.

The Coast Guard also has 14 40-foot utility boats, all transferred from the US Coast Guard except for the *CGC 127*, a 40-foot, 11-ton craft built in the Philippines with a ferro-concrete hull.

POLAND

Administration

Commander-in-Chief of the Polish Navy:
Vice-Admiral Ludwik Janczyszyn

Chief of the Naval Staff:
Rear-Admiral Henryk Pietraszkiewicz

Diplomatic Representation

Naval, Military and Air Attaché in London:
Colonel Witold Lokuciewski

Naval, Military and Air Attaché in Washington:
Colonel Henryk Nowaczyk

Naval, Military and Air Attaché in Moscow:
Brigadier General Waclaw Jagas

Naval, Military and Air Attaché in Paris:
Colonel Marian Bugaj

Strength of the Fleet

4 Submarines (Diesel Powered)
4 Destroyers
24 Fleet Minesweepers (Medium)
12 Fast Missile Boats
8 Patrol Vessel (Submarine Chasers)
20 Fast Torpedo Boats
38 Patrol Boats
16 Landing Ships
27 Minesweeping Boats
8 Training Ships
6 Surveying Vessels
7 Oilers
12 Support Ships and Auxiliaries

Ships

Polish warships are referred to officially with the prefix ORP, equivalent to HMS, for *Okrety Polska Rzeczpospolita*

Naval Aviation

There is a Fleet Air Arm of about 50 fixed-wing aircraft (mainly MiG-17 and IL-28) and helicopters.

Personnel

1973: 20 000 (1 800 officers and 18 200 men)

Mercantile Marine

Lloyd's Register of Shipping:
617 vessels of 2 012 659 tons gross

DESTROYERS

1 Ex-SOVIET SAM "KOTLIN" TYPE

WARSZAWA 275

Displacement, tons	2 850 standard; 3 885 full load
Length, feet (*metres*)	415·0 (*126·5*) oa
Beam, feet (*metres*)	42·3 (*12·9*)
Draught, feet (*metres*)	16·1 (*4·9*) max
Missile launchers	1 twin SAN-1 (Goa) aft for surface-to-air missiles
Guns	2—3·9 in (*100 mm*) dp (1 twin); 4—57 mm (1 quadruple)
A/S weapons	6 side thrown DC projectors
Main engines	Geared turbines; 2 shafts; 72 000 shp
Speed, knots	36
Complement	285

Transferred from the USSR to the Polish Navy in 1970

SAM "KOTLIN" CLASS *1972*

2 Ex-SOVIET "SKORY" CLASS

GROM (ex-*Smetlivy*) 273 **WICHER** (ex-*Skory*) 274

Displacement, tons	2 600 standard; 3 500 full load
Length, feet (*metres*)	393·8 (*120·0*) pp; 420 (*128·0*) oa
Beam, feet (*metres*)	41 (*12·5*)
Draught, feet (*metres*)	15 (*4·5*)
Guns, surface	4—5·1 in (*130 mm*), 2 twin mounts
Guns, AA	2—3 in (*76 mm*); 7—37 mm
A/S weapons	4 DCT
Torpedo tubes	10—21 in (*533 mm*) 2 quintuple
Mines	80 capacity
Boilers	4 high pressure
Main engines	Geared turbines; 2 shafts; 70 000 shp
Speed, knots	36
Radius, miles	4 000 at 15 knots
Oil fuel, tons	700
Complement	280

Former Soviet destroyers of the first "Skory" type. *Wicher* was in fact the prototype of the class. Two were delivered by the USSR to Poland on 15 Dec 1957 (*Grom*) and 28 June 1958 (*Wicher*).

PENNANT NUMBERS. Former identification numerals were 53 and 54, respectively.

RADAR. Search: An obsolescent S Band radar. Tactical: Square tie. Fire Control: Obsolescent type.

GROM *1968*

1 BRITISH BUILT

BLYSKAWICA 271

Displacement, tons	2 144 standard; 3 383 full load
Length, feet (*metres*)	357 (*108·8*) pp; 374 (*114·0*) oa
Beam, feet (*metres*)	37 (*11·3*)
Draught, feet (*metres*)	10·2 (*3·1*)
Guns, dual purpose	8—4 in (*102 mm*)
Guns, AA	10—37 mm
A/S weapons	4 DCT; 22 DC and racks
Torpedo tubes	3—21 in (*533 mm*) tripled
Boilers	4 three-drum type
Main engines	Parsons geared turbines; 2 shafts; 54 000 shp
Speed, knots	39
Complement	180

Built by J. Samuel White & Co Ltd, Cowes, Isle of Wight. Laid down on 1 Oct 1935, launched on 1 Oct 1936 and completed on 1 Oct 1937. Name means Lightning. Originally fitted for minelaying, and could carry 7 mines; but no longer has minelaying capabilities. Bows were strengthened for ice navigation. Possibly now non-operational.

ARMAMENT. The original armament was 7—4·7 mm AA, 4 MG, 6—21 inch tubes (tripled), 2 DCT.

BLYSKAWICA *1965, Polish Navy*

RECONSTRUCTION. The ship was completely dismantled in 1958 down to the hull, and superstructure was entirely rebuilt and armament modified in 1959-60.

PRESERVATION. The old destroyer *Burza*, 1 515 tons standard, 2 430 tons full load, was officially withdrawn from active service with the Polish Navy in 1962 and put in a state of preservation to be used as a museum ship.

CORVETTES

8 Ex-SOVIET "KRONSTADT" CLASS

CZUINY 368	**NIEUGIETY** 361	**ZAWZIETY** 363	**ZWINNY** 365
GROZNY 362	**WYTRWALY** 367	**ZRECZNY** 366	**ZWROTNY** 364

Displacement, tons	310 standard; 380 full load
Dimensions, feet	170·6 × 21·5 × 9
Guns	1—3·9 in; 2—37 mm AA; 4—13 mm MG AA
Main engines	3 diesels;; 3 screws; 3 300 bhp = 27 knots
Complement	65

Former Soviet submarine chasers. Four built in 1953 were acquired by Poland in 1957. *Grozny Wytrwaly Zrecany* and *Zwinny* (Strong, Energetic, Clever and Speedy), were delivered on 15 Dec 1957. Six of these may have been reduced to reserve.

ZAWZIETY *1968*

SUBMARINES

4 Ex-USSR "W" TYPE

BIELIK 295	**ORZEL** 292
KONDOR 294	**SOKOL** 293

Displacement, tons	1 030 surface; 1 180 submerged
Length, feet (*metres*)	248·5 (*75·3*)
Beam, feet (*metres*)	19·1 (5·8)
Draught, feet (*metres*)	15 (*4·6*)
Torpedo tubes	6—21 in (*533 mm*), 4 bow, 2 stern 18 torpedoes carried
Mines	40 mines in lieu of torpedoes
Main engines	2 Diesels; 4 000 hp; 2 shafts Electric motors, 2 500 hp
Speed, knots	17 on surface; 15 submerged
Range, miles	13 000 at 8 knots (surfaced)
Complement	60

A class of medium size long range submarines built in the USSR and transferred to the Polish Navy.

SOKOL *1971, Polish Navy*

KONDOR *1972*

LIGHT FORCES

12 SOVIET "OSA" TYPE (MISSILE BOATS)

Displacement, tons	165 standard; 200 full load
Dimensions, feet	128·7 × 25·1 × 5·9
Missiles	4 launchers for SSN-2A
Guns	4—30 mm (2 twin, 1 forward, 1 aft)
Main engines	3 diesels; 13 000 bhp = 32 knots
Complement	25

All pennant numbers are in the 100 series and are carried on side-boards on the bridge.

RADAR. Search: Square Tie and Strut Curve. Fire Control: Drum Tilt.

"Osa" class No. 164 *1969*

19 Ex-SOVIET "P 6" TYPE (TORPEDO BOATS)

401	**404**	**407**	**410**	**413**	**417**
402	**405**	**408**	**411**	**414**	**418**
403	**406**	**409**	**412**	**415**	**419**
				416	

Displacement, tons	66 standard; 75 full load
Dimensions, feet	84·2 × 20 × 6
Guns	4—25 mm AA; 8 DC
Tubes	2—21 in
Main engines	4 diesels; 4 800 bhp = 45 knots
Complement	25

Acquired from the USSR in 1957-58. Torpedo tubes removed in some. SKIN HEAD surface search and navigation radar.

Light Forces—*continued*

No. 408 *1970*

No. 410 *1971, Polish Navy*

4 "WISLA" CLASS (TORPEDO BOATS)

Displacement, tons	70 full load
Dimensions, feet	82·0 × 18·0 × 6·0
A/S weapons	4 DC
Guns	2—30 mm AA Twin
Tubes	4—21 in (*533 mm*)
Main engines	Diesels; speed 30 knots max

Polish built in a continuing programme.

Light Forces—*continued*

4 "OKSYWIE" CLASS (PATROL CRAFT)

301 **302** **303** **304**

Displacement, tons	170 standard
Dimensions, feet	134·5 × 19·0 × 6·9
Guns	4—37 mm (2 twin)
Main engines	Diesels; speed = 20 knots

Improved versions of earlier patrol boats of the type. Depth charge racks fitted.

7 "MODIFIED OBLUZE" CLASS (PATROL CRAFT)

351 **352** **353** **354** **355**

"OBLUZE" Class *1972, S. Breyer*

5 "OBLUZE" CLASS

321 **322** **323** **324** **325**

Displacement, tons	170
Dimensions, feet	134·0 × 19·0 × 7·0
Guns	2—37 mm AA

Built since 1965 at Oksywie Shipyard. 351 to 355 are slightly different. Belong to WOP (coastguard).

OBLUZE (old number) *1969*

9 "GDANSK" CLASS (PATROL CRAFT)

311 **313** **315** **317** **319**
312 **314** **316** **318**

Displacement, tons	120
Dimensions, feet	124·7 × 19·2 × 5·0
Guns	2—37 mm AA
Main engines	Diesels; speed 20 knots

Built in 1960. Depth charges carried. Belong to WOP (coastguard).

20 "K8" CLASS (PATROL CRAFT)

KP 118 **KP 120** **KP 122** **KP 124** **KP 126**
KP 119 **KP 121** **KP 123** **KP 125**

Displacement, tons	60
Guns	2 MG AA (in twin mounting)
Main engines	3 motors; speed 15 knots

Small patrol boats reported to be under the jurisdiction of the WOP.

MINE WARFARE FORCES

12 "KROGULEC" CLASS (FLEET MINESWEEPERS)

ORLIK	613	**KORMORAN**	616		**619**	**622**
KROGULEC	614	**CZAPLA**	617	**TUKAN**	620	**623**
JASTRAB	615	**ALABATROS**	618		**621**	**624**

Displacement, tons	500
Dimensions, feet	190·3 × 24·6 × 8·2
Guns	6—25 mm AA
Main engines	Diesels; speed = 16 knots

Flushdecked minesweepers of a new type built at the Stocznia Yard from 1963 onwards. *Jastrab* and *Orlik* commissioned in 1964.

KROGULEC *1972, S. Breyer*

12 SOVIET "T 43" TYPE (FLEET MINESWEEPERS)

BIZON	605	**DZIK**	604	**MORS**	610	**TUR**	602
BOBR	606	**FOKA**	609	**ROSOMAK**	607	**ZBIK**	612
DELFIN	608	**LOS**	603	**RYS**	611	**ZUBR**	601

Displacement, tons	500 standard; 610 full load
Dimensions, feet	190·2 × 28·2 × 6·9
Guns	4—37 mm AA; 4—25 mm
Main engines	2 diesels; 2 shafts; 2 000 hp = 17 knots
Complement	40

Soviet "T43" type but built in Poland at Stocznia Gdynska. Gdynia in 1957-62.

DELFIN *1969, Polish Navy*

MINESWEEPING BOATS

20 "K 8" CLASS (MSBs)

Displacement, tons	20 approx
Dimensions, feet	54·1 × 19·0 × 5·0

Minesweeping boats built in Poland. Pennant numbers run in 800 and 900 series.

AMPHIBIOUS VESSELS

22 "POLNOCNY" CLASS LSM

800-810 **888-899**

Displacement tons	780 standard; 1 000 full load
Dimensions, feet	225 × 27·7 × 9·8
Armament	2—18 barrelled rocket projectors 1—30 mm
Main engines	2 diesels; 5 000 bhp = 18 knots

Polish built, in Gdansk, but same as the Soviet "Polnocny" type can carry six tanks of varying types.

Amphibious Vessels—*continued*

LANDING CRAFT. It was officially stated by the Polish naval authorities in Feb 1971 that all of the landing craft of the US LCT (5) type have been removed from the effective list.

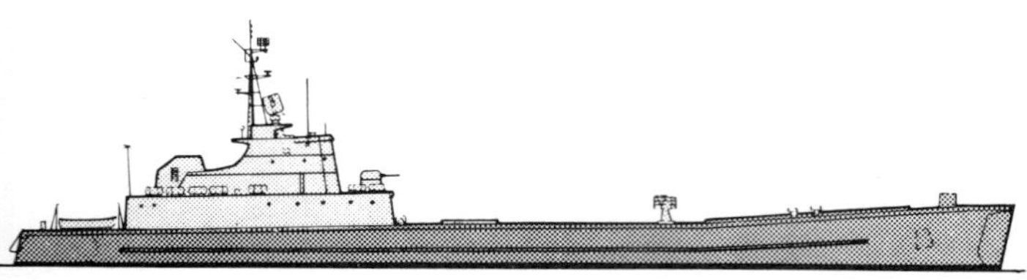

POLNOCNY

TRAINING SHIPS

GRYF (ex-*Zetempowiec*, ex-*Opplem*, ex-*Omsk*, ex-*Empire Contees*, ex-*Irene Oldendorf*)

Measurement, tons	1 959 gross
Dimensions, feet	282·2 × 44·2 × 18·8
Guns	2—3·9 in; 4—37 mm AA
Main engines	Steam; 1 200 hp = 10 knots

Former German "Hansa" class ship. Built by Burmeister & Wain. Launched in 1944. Taken over in 1947. Transferred to the Navy in 1949. The name was changed from *Zetempowiec* to *Gryf* in 1957. Used as a cadet training ship.

GRYF *1969*

ISKRA (ex-*Pigmy*, ex-*Iskra*, ex-*St Blanc*, ex-*Vlissingen*)

Displacement, tons	560
Dimensions, feet	128 × 25 × 10
Main engines	Diesels; 250 bhp = 7·5 knots
Complement	30, plus 40 cadets

A three masted schooner with auxiliary engines. Built by Muller, Foxhol, Holland. Launched in 1917. Cadet training ship.

ISKRA *1969*

Training Ships—*continued*

DAR POMORZA (ex-*Prinz Eitel Friedrich*)

Displacement, tons	1 561
Measurement, tons	1 566 gross
Dimensions, feet	240 × 41 × 21
Main engines	Diesel

An auxiliary motored fully rigged sailing ship of the Polish Mercantile Marine. Built by Blohm & Voss, Hamburg. Launched in 1909. Provides personnel and training for the Merchant Navy, but is not on the Polish Navy List.

DAR POMORZA *Skyfotos*

SURVEYING VESSELS

"MOMA CLASS"

KOPERNIK

Of 1 580 tons, launched in 1971.

BALTYK

Displacement, tons	1 200
Measurements, tons	658 gross; 450 deadweight
Dimensions, feet	194·3 oa; 175·3 pp × 29·5 × 14
Main engines	Steam; 1 000 hp = 11 knots

Trawler of B-10 type. Built in 1954 in Gdansk. Converted and structure altered. The hydrographic vessels *Zodiac* and *Koziorozec* (see details in the 1961-62 edition) are no longer on the Navy List. They belong to the Shipping Board of Gdansk.

BALTYK *1968*

OILERS

Z 3 **Z 8** **Z 9**

Displacement, tons approx 700

Z 5 **Z 6** **Z 7**

Lighters of 300 tons gross with diesels, converted into tankers for coastal service.

DEGAUSSING VESSELS

URAN **URANIA**

Displacement, tons 254
Main engines Speed = 8 knots

Degaussing vessel of the British MMS minesweeper 11 type, classed as auxiliaries.

ICEBREAKER

PERCUN

Displacement, tons 800
Main engines Diesel-electric; 2 shafts; 3 500 bhp = 12 knots

Icebreaker built in 1962 by P. K. Harris & Sons, Appledore, Devon, England. Not a naval vessel but can be employed with and for the Navy.

PERCUN 1972

NOTE. All the following are used for pre-Naval training.

TENDERS

JOWISZ **JUPITER** **MARS** **ORION**

Displacement, tons 130
Dimensions, feet 100 × 16 × 4·2
Main engines Diesel; 3 shafts; 400 bhp = 10 knots
Complement 32

All built in USSR in 1944-45. Soviet "T 301" type. Formerly named *Kormoran, Kania, Krogulec* and *Orlik*. Training tenders.

YACHTS

ZAWISZA CZARNY

Measurement, tons 150 gross
Dimensions, feet 107 × 23
Main engines Diesel; 300 bhp = 9 knots

Three masted schooner with a sail area of 514 sq. yards. Built in 1952. Training yacht.

JANEK KRASNICKI **ZEW MORZA**

Measurement, tons 70 gross
Dimensions, feet 82 × 21
Main engines Diesel; speed 5 knots

Two masted schooners with a sail area of 418 sq. yards. Built at Neptun, Rostock. Formerly named *Edit* and *Jutta*. Training yachts.

MARIUS ZARUSKI (ex-*Kryssaren*)

Measurement, tons 71 gross
Dimensions, feet 83 × 19
Main engines Petrol engine; 150 bhp = 5 knots

Ketch with a sail area of 368 sq. yards. Purchased from Sweden. Training boat.

PORTUGAL

Administration

Minister of Marine:
Vice-Admiral Manuel Pereira Crespo

Chief of Naval Staff:
Admiral Fernando Ornelas e Vasconcelos

Diplomatic Representation

Naval Attaché in London:
Commander C. A. Salgueiro Rego

Naval Attaché in Washington:
Commander Jose Ferraz de Carvalho

Naval Attaché in Paris:
Commander Silvano J. Freitas-Braneo

Strength of the Fleet

8 Frigates
23 Corvettes (4 Building)
4 Submarines
36 Patrol Craft
4 Ocean Minesweepers
12 Coastal Minesweepers
66 Landing Craft
7 Survey Vessels
4 Fishery Protection Vessels
1 Training Ship
4 Support Ships and Auxiliaries

Personnel

1970: 17 700 (1 650 officers and 16 050 men) including marines
1971: 18 300 (1 700 officers and 16 600 men) including marines
1972: 19 000 (1 800 officers and 17 200 men) including marines
1973: 19 000 (1 800 officers and 17 200 men) including marines

Disposals

Destroyers

1959 *Douro*
1960 *Dao*
1965 *Tejo, Lima*
1967 *Vouga*

Frigates

1968 *Corte Real, Diogo Cão*
1969 *Nuno Tristao, D. Fernando, S. Cristovao*
1970 *Francisco de Almeida, Pacheco Pereira*
1971 *Alvares Cabral, Vasco da Gama*

Corvettes

1971 *Cacheu*

Submarines

1967 *Neptuno*
1969 *Nautilo, Narval*

Mercantile Marine

Lloyd's Register of Shipping:
407 vessels of 1 027 070 tons gross

FRIGATES

4 "COMANDANTE JOÃO BELO" CLASS

Name	*No.*	*Builders*	*Laid down*	*Launched*	*Completed*
COMANDANTE HERMENEGILDO CAPELO	F 481	At et Ch de Nantes	13 May 1966	29 Nov 1966	26 Apr 1968
COMANDANTE JOÃO BELO	F 480	At et Ch de Nantes	6 Sep 1965	22 Mar 1966	1 July 1967
COMANDANTE ROBERTO IVENS	F 482	At et Ch de Nantes	13 Dec 1966	8 Aug 1967	23 Nov 1968
COMANDANTE SACADURA CABRAL	F 483	At et Ch de Nantes	18 Aug 1967	15 Mar 1968	25 July 1969

Displacement, tons 1 990 standard; 2 230 full load
Length, feet (*metres*) 321·5 (*98*) pp; 338 (*103·0*) oa
Beam, feet (*metres*) 37·7 (*11·5*)
Draught, feet (*metres*) 12·5 (*3·8*) mean; 14·5 (*4·42*) max
Guns 3—3·9 in (*100 mm*) AA single; 2—40 mm AA
A/S weapons 1—12 in (*305 mm*) quadruple
Torpedo tubes 6—21·7 in (*550 mm*) ASM, 2 triple
Main engines SEMT-Pielstick diesels; 2 shafts; 18 760 bhp
Speed, knots 25 (26·1 max)
Radius, miles 4 500 at 15 knots; 2 300 at 25 knots
Complement 200 (14 officers, 186 men)

COMANDANTE ROBERTO IVENS *1970, Portuguese Navy*

Frigates—*continued*

DESIGN. They are similar to the French "Commandant Riviere" type except for the 30 mm AA guns which were replaced by 40 mm AA guns.

CONSTRUCTION. The prefabricated construction of these frigates was begun on 1 Oct 1964 at the Ateliers et Chantiers de Nantes, France.

RADAR. Search: DRBV 22. Tactical: Probably S Band. Fire Control: DRBC 32 radar director.

COMANDANTE JOAO BELO *Class*

SACADURA CABRAL *1972, Portuguese Navy*

3 "ALMIRANTE PEREIRA DA SILVA" CLASS

Name	*No.*	*Builders*	*Laid down*	*Launched*	*Completed*
ALMIRANTE GAGO COUTINHO	F 473 (ex-US DE 1042)	Estaleiros Navais Lisnave, Lisbon	2 Dec 1963	13 Aug 1965	29 Nov 1967
ALMIRANTE MAGALHÃES CORREA	F 474 (ex-US DE 1046)	Estaleiros Navais de Viana do Castelo	30 Aug 1965	26 Apr 1966	4 Nov 1968
ALMIRANTE PEREIRA DA SILVA	F 472 (ex-US DE 1039)	Estaleiros Navais Lisnave, Lisbon	14 June 1962	2 Dec 1963	20 Dec 1966

Displacement, tons	1 450 standard; 1 914 full load
Length, feet (*metres*)	314·6 (*95·9*)
Beam, feet (*metres*)	36·68 (*11·18*)
Draught, feet (*metres*)	14 (*4·3*) hull; 17·5 (*5·33*) max
Guns	4—3 in (*76 mm*) 50 cal. dp;
A/S weapons	2 Bofors 4-barrelled mortars 2 DC throwers
Torpedo tubes	6 (2 triple) for A/S torpedoes
Main engines	De Laval dr geared turbines; 1 shaft; 20 000 shp
Speed, knots	27 designed
Boilers	2 Foster Wheeler, 300 psi, 850°F
Range, miles	3 220 at 15 knots
Oil fuel, tons	400
Complement	166 (12 officers, 154 men)

ALMIRANTE PEREIRA DA SILVA *1968, Portuguese Navy*

DESIGN. Medium-fast frigates similar to the United States destroyer escorts of the "Dealey" class, but modified to suit Portuguese requirements.

RADAR. Search: SPS 6. Tactical: X Band. Surface warning and navigation Air surveillance: S band. Extensive EW.

CONSTRUCTION. The prefabrication of *Almirante Pereira da Silva* and *Almirante Gago Coutinho* was begun in 1961 at Lisnave (formerly Navalis Shipyard, Lisbon) and of *Almirante Magalhães Correa* in 1962.

SONAR. Probably DUBV-43.

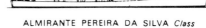

ALMIRANTE PEREIRA DA SILVA *Class*

PERO ESCOBAR F 335

Displacement, tons	1 270 standard; 1 390 full load
Length, feet (*metres*)	306·7 (*93·5*) wl; 321·5 (*98·0*) oa
Beam, feet (*metres*)	35·5 (*10·8*)
Draught, feet (*metres*)	10 (*3·0*); 12·2 (*3·7*) deep
Guns	4—3 in (*76 mm*) 50 cal. dp
A/S weapons	2 "Squid" triple DC mortars
Torpedo tubes	6 (2 triple) for A/S torpedoes
Main engines	2 Ansaldo-Genova sr geared turbines; 2 shafts; 24 000 shp
Speed, knots	32·6 max
Boilers	2 Ansoldo-Foster Wheeler "D" 32 *kg/cm²*, 400°C
Complement	165 (10 officers, 155 men)

PERO ESCOBAR *1969, Portuguese Navy*

Built for the Portuguese Navy by Navalmeccanica, Castellammare di Stabia, Italy. Laid down on 9 Jan 1955. Launched on 25 Sep 1955. Completed on 30 June 1957.

RADAR. Search S Band air surveillance. Fire Control: Elsag X Band.

MODERNISATION in 1970-71 included new guns, sonar and A/S torpedo tubes similar to those in the "Almirante Pereira da Silva" class. Armament before modernisation: 2 single 3 inch guns, 1 twin 40 mm AA, 2 twin 20 mm AA, 3—21 inch torpedo tubes.

PERO ESCOBAR

CORVETTES

6+4 "JOAO COUTINHO" CLASS

Name		Builders	Launched	Completed
ANTONIO ENES	F 471	Empresa Nacional Bazan, Spain	16 Aug 1969	18 June 1971
AUGUSTO DE CASTILHO	F 484	Empresa Nacional Bazan, Spain	4 July 1969	14 Nov 1970
GENERAL PEREIRA D'ECA	F 477	Blohm and Voss A.G., Hamburg, Germany	26 July 1969	10 Oct 1970
HONORIO BARRETO	F 485	Empresa Nacional Bazan, Spain	11 Apr 1970	15 Apr 1971
JACINTO CANDIDO	F 476	Blohm and Voss A.G., Hamburg, Germany	16 June 1969	16 June 1970
JOÃO COUTINHO	F 475	Blohm and Voss A.G., Hamburg, Germany	2 May 1969	7 Mar 1970

Displacement, tons	1 203 standard; 1 380 full load
Length, feet (*metres*)	227·5 (*84·6*)
Beam, feet (*metres*)	33·8 (*10·3*)
Draught, feet (*metres*)	10·0 (*3·07*); 11·8 (*3·6*) deep
Guns	2—3 in (*76 mm*) dp; 2—40 mm AA
A/S weapons	1 Hedgehog; 2 DC throwers; 2 DC tracks
Main engines	2 OEW 12 cyl. Pielstick diesels; 10 560 bhp
Speed, knots	24·4
Range, miles	5 900 at 18 knots
Complement	97 (9 officers, 88 men) plus 34 marine detachment

RADAR. Equipped with SPS 10 search radar. S-Band air surveillance and X-band surface warning and navigation.

NEW CONSTRUCTION. Four similar corvettes are under construction at Empres Nacional Bazan, Spain. They will carry one French 3·9 inch gun in place of the two 3 inch above and will have Plessey AWS-2 air surveillance radar.

JOÃO COUTINHO *1971, Portuguese Navy*

JOÃO COUTINHO *Class*

4 PORTUGUESE BUILT "MAIO" CLASS

Name	No.	Builders	Launched	Completed
BOAVISTA	P 592	Est Nav do Mondego	10 July 1956	17 May 1957
BRAVA	P 590	EN de Viana do Castelo	2 May 1956	27 Dec 1956
FOGO	P 591	EN de Viana do Castelo	2 May 1956	11 Apr 1957
SANTA LUZIA	P 594	Arsenal do Alfeite	17 Jan 1957	24 Oct 1958

Displacement, tons	366 standard; 400 full load
Dimensions, feet	170 pp; 173·8 oa × 23 × 10 mean
Guns	2—40 mm AA; 2—20 mm AA
A/S weapons	1 Hedgehog, 4 DCT; 2 depth charge tracks
Main engines	4 SEMT-Pielstick diesels (4-stroke, 14 cylinder V); 2 shafts; 3 500 bhp = 19 knots
Oil fuel, tons	45
Range, miles	3 900 at 19 knots
Complement	67 (5 officers, 62 men)

Built in Portugal under the US off-shore procurement programme. Of all-welded construction. Sister ship *Santo Antão* was discarded 1 Oct 1971

FOGO *1972, Portuguese Navy*

3 FRENCH BUILT "MAIO" CLASS

Name	No.	Builders	Launched
MAIO (ex-*Funchal*, ex-*P* 4)	P 587	Dubigeon, Nantes	27 Sep 1954
PORTO SANTO (ex-*P* 5)	P 588	Normand (Le Havre)	9 Feb 1955
S NICOLAU (ex-*P* 8)	P 589	Normand (Le Havre)	7 June 1955

Displacement, tons	366 standard; 400 full load
Dimensions, feet	170 pp; 173·7 oa × 23 × 10
Guns	2—40 mm AA; 2—20 mm AA
A/S weapons	1 Hedgehog; 4 DCT; 2 depth charge tracks
Main engines	4 SEMT-Pielstick diesels; 2 shafts; 3 240 bhp = 17·5 knots
Range, miles	4 000 at 10 knots
Complement	67 (5 officers, 62 men)

Of PC design, but built in France as a US offshore procurement order under the Mutual Defense Assistance Programme. Fitted with two mine rails.

S. NICOLAU *Dr. Giorgio Arra*

8 "CACINE" CLASS

CACINE	P 1140	**CUANZA**	P 1144	**ROVUMA**	P 1143
CUNENE	P 1141	**GEBA**	P 1145	**ZAIRE**	P 1146
		MANDOVI	P 1142	**ZAMBEZE**	P 1147

Displacement, tons	292·5 official figure; 310 full load
Dimensions, feet	144·0 oa × 25·2 × 7·1
Guns	2—40 mm AA 1—32 barrelled rocket-launcher 37 mm
Main engines	2 Maybach diesels; 2 000 bhp = 20 knots
Complement	33 (3 officers, 30 men)

Cacine, Cunene Mandovi and *Rovuma* were built in Arsenal do Alfeita in 1969, the other four in Estaleiros Navais do Mondego in 1969-72.

CACINE *1970, Portuguese Navy*

SUBMARINES

4 "ALBACORA" CLASS (FRENCH "DAPHNE" TYPE)

Name	No.	Builders	Laid down	Launched	Completed
ALBACORA	S 163	Dubigeon-Normandie	6 Sep 1965	13 Oct 1966	1 Oct 1967
BARRACUDA	S 164	Dubigeon-Normandie	19 Oct 1965	24 Apr 1967	4 May 1968
CACHALOTE	S 165	Dubigeon-Normandie	27 Oct 1966	16 Feb 1968	25 Jan 1969
DELFIM	S 166	Dubigeon-Normandie	14 May 1967	23 Sep 1968	1 Oct 1969

Displacement, tons	700 standard; 869 surface; 1 043 submerged
Length, feet (*metres*)	189·6 (*57·8*)
Beam, feet (*metres*)	22·3 (*6·8*)
Draught, feet (*metres*)	15·1 (*4·6*)
Torpedo tubes	12—21·7 in (*550 mm*); 8 bow, 4 stern
Main engines	SEMT-Pielstick diesels, 1 300 bhp Electric motors, 450 kW, 1 600 hp; 2 shafts
Speed, knots	13·2 on surface and 16 submerged
Range, miles	2 710 at 12·5 knots on surface; 2 130 at 10 knots snorting
Oil fuel, tons	90
Complement	50 (5 officers; 45 men)

The prefabricated construction of these medium size submarines was begun during 1 Oct 1964 to 6 Sep 1965 at the Dubigeon-Normandie Shipyard, Nantes, France. They are basically similar to the French "Daphne" type, but slightly modified to suit Portuguese requirements.

BARRACUDA — *1970, Captain Aluino Martins da Silva*

DELFIN — *1972, Portuguese Navy*

LIGHT FORCES

10 "ARGOS" CLASS

ARGOS	P 372	**DRAGÃO**	P 374	**LIRA**	P 361
CASSIOPEIA	P 373	**ESCORPIÃO**	P 375	**ORION**	P 362
CENTAURO	P 1130	**HIDRA**	P 376	**PEGASO**	P 379
				SAGITARIO	P 1131

Displacement, tons	180 standard; 210 full load
Dimensions, feet	131·2 pp; 136·8 oa × 20·5 × 7
Guns	2—40 mm AA
Main engines	2 Maybach diesels; 1 200 bhp = 17 knots
Oil fuel, tons	16
Complement	24 (2 officers, 22 men)

Six built by Arsenal do Alfeite, Lisbon, and four by Estaleiros Navais de Viana do Castelo. All completed June 1963 to Sep 1965. Named after constellations. A photograph of *Dragão* appears in the 1964-65 to 1966-67 editions.

ARGOS — *1967, Portuguese Navy*

2 "DOM ALEIXO" CLASS

DOM ALEIXO P 1148 — **DOM JEREMIAS** P 1149

Displacement, tons	60 standard; 67·69 full load (officially revised figures)
Dimensions, feet	82·1 oa × 17·0 × 5·2
Guns	1—20 mm AA
Main engines	2 Cummins diesels; 1 270 bhp = 16 knots
Complement	10 (2 officiers, 8 men)

Dom Aleixo was commissioned on 7 Dec 1967 and *Dom Jeremias* on 22 Dec 1967.

DOM ALEIXO — *1969, Portuguese Navy*

3 "ALVOR" CLASS

ALBUFEIRA P 1157 — **ALJEZUR** P 1158 — **ALVOR** P 1156

Displacement, tons	35·7 full load
Dimensions, feet	68 oa × 18 × 5·1
Guns	1—20 mm AA
Main engines	2 Cummins diesels; 235 bhp = 12·3 knots.
Complement	7 (1 officer)

They were all built at Arsenal do Alfeite and commissioned in 1967-68.

ALVOR — *1968, Portuguese Navy*

11 "BELLATRIX" CLASS

ALDEBARAN	P 1152	**ESPIGA**	P 366	**PROCION**	P 1153
ALTAIR	P 377	**FOMALHAUT**	P 367	**RIGEL**	P 378
ARCTURUS	P 1151	**POLLUX**	P 368	**SIRIUS**	P 1154
BELLATRIX	P 363			**VEGA**	P 1155

Displacement, tons	23 light; 27·6 full load (officially revised figures)
Dimensions, feet	62·8 wl; 68·0 oa × 15·2 × 4·0
Guns	1—20 mm Oerlikon AA
Main engines	2 Cummins diesels; 470 bhp = 15 knots
Complement	7 (1 officer, 6 men)

The first batch was completed in 1961-62 in Germany by Beyerische Schiffbaugesellschaft and the last five (*Arcturus*, *Aldebaran* and *Procion*, commissioned on 17 May 1968, *Sirius* and *Vega*) were built in Arsenal do Alfeite, Lisbon. A photograph of *Bellatrix* appears in the 1962-63 to 1967-68 editions, and of *Espiga* in the 1969-70 edition. Sister launches *Canopus* P 364 and *Deneb* P 365 were discarded on 1 Feb 1971 and 15 Oct 1971, respectively.

ARCTURUS — *1972, Portuguese Navy*

Light Forces—*continued*

6 "JUPITER" CLASS

JUPITER P 1132	**MERCURIO** P 1135	**URANO** P 1137
MARTE P 1134	**SATURNO** P 1136	**VENUS** P 1133

Displacement, tons	32 standard; 43·5 full load
Dimensions, feet	69·0 oa × 16·5 × 4·3
Guns	1—20 mm Oerlikon AA
Main engines	2 Cummins diesels; 1 270 bhp = 20 knots
Complement	8 (1 officer, 7 men)

Built during 1964-65. All commissioned between 10 Mar 1965 and 12 Aug 1965. The patrol launch *Algol* P 1138 was officially deleted from the list in 1972.

JUPITER *Portuguese Navy*

CASTOR P 580

Displacement, tons	**22**
Dimensions, feet	**53·5 wl; 58 oa × 13·1 × 3·3**
Guns	**1—20 mm Oerlikon AA**
Main engines	**2 Cummins diesels; 500 bhp = 15 knots**
Complement	**7**

Built at the Estaleiros Navais do Mondego and commissioned on 3 Feb 1964.

ANTARES P 360 **REGULUS P 369**

Displacement, tons	**18**
Dimensions, feet	**56 oa: 51·5 wl × 15·2 × 4 aft**
Guns	**1—20 mm Oerlikon quick firing AA**
Main engines	**2 Cummins diesels; 2 shafts; 460 bnp = 18·2 knots**
Complement	7

Antares was built in 1959 by James Taylor (Shipbuilders) Ltd, Shoreham, Sussex, England. The hull is of Deborine resinglass fibre moulding. *Regulus* was built in Portugal by Navalis Shipyard, the hull being imported from England. Completed on 27 Jan 1962. Of this class, *Sirius* and *Vega* were lost in action in Dec 1961 during the Indian invasion of Goa.

RIO MINHO P 370

Displacement, tons	14
Dimensions, feet	49·2 × 10·5 × 2·3
Guns	2 light MG
Main engines	2 Alfa Romeo; 130 bhp = 9 knots
Complement	7

Built at Arsenal do Alfeite in 1955-57 for the River Minho on the Spanish border.

DISPOSALS
The gunboat *Dio* was discarded on 20 Apr 1969. The patrol launch *Tete,* P 371, former river gunboat, was to have been discarded in 1971, but continued in service. To be replaced by *Chire* a converted river steamer.

Of the six "Isles" class trawlers purchased from Great Britain in 1947, and named after islands in the Azores, originally classified as patrol vessels but later rated as minesweepers. *Miguel* (ex-*Brurey*) was discarded in 1956, *Terceira* (ex-*Haling*) in 1957, *Salvador Correia* (ex-*Saltarelo*) in 1961, and *Faial* (ex-*Mangrove*) M 391 was decommissioned on 27 Mar 1967, *Baldaque da Silva* (ex-*Ruskholm*) changed her name to *Salvador Correia* was reclassified as a survey ship and was scrapped March 1967. *Santa Maria* (ex-P4, ex-*Whalsay*) M 392 was discarded on 15 Apr 1971.

MINE WARFARE FORCES

4 "S. JORGE" CLASS (OCEAN MINESWEEPER)

CORVO (ex-USS *MSO* 487) M 418 **PICO** (ex-USS *MSO* 479) M 416
GRACIOSA (ex-USS *MSO* 486) M 417 **S. JORGE** (ex-USS *MSO* 478) M 415

Name	*Builders*	*Laid down*	*Launched*	*Completed*
Corvo	Burger Boat Co	18 Aug 1953	28 July 1954	23 Nov 1955
Graciosa	Burger Boat Co	16 May 1953	19 Nov 1953	15 Aug 1955
Pico	Bellingham SY	1 Oct 1953	18 June 1954	1 June 1955
S. Jorge	Bellingham SY	26 Aug 1953	30 Apr 1954	1 June 1955

Displacement, tons	720 standard; 780 full load
Dimensions, feet	165·0 pp; 172·0 oa × 35·0 × 10·4
Guns	1—40 mm AA
Main engines	2 GM diesels; 2 shafts; 1 600 bhp = 13·7 knots max
Oil fuel, tons	46
Range, miles	3 800 at 10 knots (economical speed)
Complement	69 (5 officers, 64 men)

Minewarfare Forces—*continued*

"MSO 421" class built in the USA under the Mutual Defense Assistance Programme. Constructed of wooden and non-magnetic materials. The diesels of non-magnetic stainless steel alloy, are model 8-278A, two stroke cycle, non-reversible 8-cylindar V engines. Controllable pitch propellers.

GRACIOSA *1969, Portuguese Navy*

4 "S. ROQUE" CLASS (BRITISH "TON" TYPE) (CMS)

Name	*No.*	*Launched*	*Completed*
LAGOA	M 403	15 Sep 1955	10 Aug 1956
RIBEIRA GRANDE	M 402	14 Oct 1955	8 Feb 1957
ROSARIO	M 404	29 Nov 1955	8 Feb 1956
S ROQUE	M 401	15 Sep 1955	6 June 1956

Displacement, tons	394·4 standard; 451·9 full load (revised official figures)
Dimensions, feet	140·0 pp; 152·0 oa × 28·8 × 7·0
Guns	2—20 mm AA (twin mount)
Main engines	2 Mirrlees diesels; 2 shafts; 2 500 bhp = 15 knots
Complement	47 (4 officers, 43 men)

Similar to British "Ton" class coastal minesweepers, but built in Portugal. All laid down at CUF Shipyard, Lisbon, on 7 Sep 1954, under the OSP-MAP. *Lagoa* and *S Roque* were financed by USA and the other two by Portugal. 40 mm AA gun removed.

LAGOA *1972, Portuguese Navy*

8 "PONTA DELGADA" CLASS (CMS)

ANGRA DO HEROISMO	(ex-*AMS* 62)	M 407
HORTA	(ex-*AMS* 61)	M 406
LAJES	(ex-*AMS* 146)	M 411
PONTA DELGADA	(ex-*Adjutant, AMS* 60)	M 405
SANTA CRUZ	(ex-*AMS* 92)	M 409
S. PEDRO	(ex-*AMS* 147)	M 412
VELAS	(ex-*AMS* 145)	M 410
VILA DO PORTO	(ex-*AMS* 91)	M 408

Displacement, tons	338 standard; 370 full load (officially revised figures)
Dimensions, feet	138·0 pp; 144·0 oa × 27·0 × 8·0
Guns	2—20 mm AA (twin mount)
Main engines	GM diesels; 900 bhp = 13 knots
Complement	40 (4 officers, 36 men)

Of wooden and non-magnetic construction. *Ponta Delgada* was transferred from USA on 7 Apr 1953. Four more were delivered in 1953-54 and remaining three in 1955.

HORTA *1971, Portuguese Navy*

LANDING CRAFT

2 "BOMBARDA" CLASS LDG

ALABARDA LDG 202 **BOMBARDA** LDG 201 (ex-105)

The LDG *Alabarda* is under construction at the Estaleiros Navais do Mondego, *Bombarda* was commissioned in 1969.

BOMBARDA *1970, Portuguese Navy*

4 "ALFANGE" CLASS LDG

ALFANGE LDG 101
ARIETE LDG 102
CIMITARRA LDG 103
MONTANTE LDG 104

Displacement, tons	500
Dimensions, feet	Length: 187
Main engines	2 diesels; 1 000 bhp
Complement	20

Landing craft similar to the LCT (4) type built at the Estaleiros Navais do Mondego and commissioned during 1965.

ALFANGE *1968, Portuguese Navy*

16 LDM 400 CLASS

LDM 401 LDM 404 LDM 407 LDM 410 LDM 413
LDM 402 LDM 405 LDM 408 LDM 411 LDM 414
LDM 403 LDM 406 LDM 409 LDM 412 LDM 415
LDM 416

10 LDM 300 CLASS

LDM 301 LDM 303 LDM 306 LDM 309 LDM 311
LDM 302 LDM 304 LDM 308 LDM 310 LDM 312

LDM 305 and LDM 313 were discarded on 11 June 1971 and LDM 307 on 22 June 1971.

3 LDM 200 CLASS

LDM 201 LDM 202 LDM 204

LDM 203 and LDM 205 were discarded on 22 June 1971.

17 LDM 100 CLASS

LDM 101 LDM 105 LDM 108 LDM 111 LDM 115
LDM 102 LDM 106 LDM 109 LDM 112 LDM 116
LDM 103 LDM 107 LDM 110 LDM 113 LDM 117
LDM 114 LDM 118

Displacement, tons	50 full load
Dimensions, feet	Length: 50 feet
Main engines	2 diesels; 450 bhp

29 LCM type landing craft were commisisoned in 1964 to 1966 setting up four classes in LDM 100, 200, 300, and 400 series as above. All built at the Estaleiros Navais do Mondego. LDM 104 was discarded on 11 June 1971.

3 LDP 300 (Ex-LD) CLASS

LDP 301 LDP 302 LDP 303

LDP (ex-LD) 304 of this class was officially discarded on 15 Oct 1971.

16 LDP 200 CLASS

LDP 201 LDP 203 LDP 206 LDP 209 LDP 212 LDP 215
LDP 204 LDP 207 LDP 210 LDP 213 LDP 216
LDP 205 LDP 208 LDP 211 LDP 214 LDP 217

Thirteen LDP 200 class were commissioned in 1965-67, four in Jan-Feb 1969. Of this class LDP 202 was discarded on 9 Mar 1970.

3 LDP 100 (Ex-LD) CLASS

LDP 105 LDP 107 LDP 108

Displacement, tons	12 light; 18 full load
Dimensions, feet	Length: 46 oa
Main engines	2 diesels; 180 bhp

The nine LD class landing craft (of the LCA type) were redesignated LDP 103, 105, 107, 108 and 109 and LDP 301, 302, 303 and 304. Built at the Estaleiros Navais do Mondego and commissioned on 16 June 1961 (LDP 103), 22 Feb 1963 (LDP 105), 1964 (LDP 107, 108, 109, 301, 302, 303, 304). LPD 103 and LPD 109 were discarded on 15 Nov 1969.

SURVEY SHIPS

AFONSO DE ALBUQUERQUE A 526
(ex-HMS *Dalrymple*, ex-*Luce Bay*, ex-*Loch Class*)

Displacement, tons	1 590 standard; 2 230 full load
Length, feet (*metres*)	286·0 (*87·2*) pp; 307·0 (*93·6*) oa
Beam, feet (*metres*)	38·5 (*11·7*)
Draught, feet (*metres*)	14·2 (*4·3*)
Main engines	4-cylinder triple expansion; 2 shafts; 5 500 ihp
Speed, knots	19·5
Boilers	2 Admiralty 3-drum type
Range, miles	7 055 at 9·1 knots
Complement	109 (9 officers, 100 men)

AFONSO DE ALBUQUERQUE *1970, Portuguese Navy*

AFONSO DE ALBUQUERQUE

Modified "Bay" class frigate. Built by Wm. Pickersgill & Sons Ltd, Sunderland, but completed at HM Dockyard Devonport. Laid down on 29 Apr 1944. Launched on 12 Apr 1945, completed on 10 Feb 1949. Equipped with radar and sonar. Purchased from Great Britain in Apr 1966. Main machinery by George Clark Ltd. Sunderland. Power at 220 volts DC from two 120 kw turbogenerators and two 150 kw diesel generators.

1 Ex-US "KELLAR" CLASS

ALMEIDA CARVALHO (ex-USNS *Kellar*, T-AGS 25)

Displacement, tons	1 200 standard; 1 400 full load
Dimensions, feet	191·5 wl; 109·0 oa × 39·0 × 15·0
Main engines	Diesel-electric; 1 shaft; 1 200 bp = 15 knots
Complement	30 (5 officers, 25 men)

Laid down on 20 Nov 1962, launched on 30 July 1964 and completed on 31 Jan 1969. On loan from the US Navy since 21 Jan 1972.

1 "PEDRO NUNES" CLASS (Ex-SLOOP)

PEDRO NUNES A 528

Displacement, tons	1 162 standard; 1 217 full load
Dimensions, feet	223·0 pp; 234·3 oa × 32·8 × 10·2
Guns	1—4·7 in, 50 cal; 4—20 mm AA (see Notes)
Main engines	2 sets MAN 8 cyl diesels; 2 400 bhp = 16·5 knots
Oil fuel, tons	110 normal; 126 max
Range, miles	6 400 at 13·4 knots
Complement	100 (7 officers, 93 men)

Survey Ships—*continued*

Built as a second class sloop (*aviso de segundo classe*) at Lisbon Naval Yard. Laid down on 5 Nov 1931, launched on 17 Mar 1934 and completed on 11 Apr 1935. Converted into a survey ship (*navio hidrografico*) in 1956, when the forward 4·7 inch gun was removed. Working off Guinea. Sister ship *Joao de Lisboa* (ex-*Infante D. Henrique*), A 5200, was discarded on 17 Aug 1966.

PEDRO NUNES 1968, *Portuguese Navy*

1 Ex-BRITISH "FLOWER" CLASS FRIGATE

CARVALHO ARAUJO (ex-*Terje Ten* ex-*Commandant Drogou*, ex-*Chrysanthemum*) A 524

Displacement, tons	1 020 standard, 1 340 full load
Dimensions, feet	190 pp; 205 oa × 33 × 16·5
Guns	1—3 inch; 4—20 mm AA
Main engines	Triple expansion; 2 750 ihp = 16 knots
Boilers	2 cylindrical
Oil fuel, tons	288
Complement	100 (7 officers, 93 men)

Former British "Flower" class corvette (later re-rated frigate). Built by Harland & Wolff Ltd, Belfast. Laid down on 17 Feb 1940, launched on 11 Apr 1941, completed on 26 Jan 1942. Served in the French Navy during the Second World War. Sold out of the service after hostilities. Purchased by Portugal from the Hector Whaling Company, at Capetown, in Mar 1969, and equipped as a survey ship to replace the former *Carvalho Araujo* (ex-British "Flower" class minesweeping sloop *Jonquil*) discarded in 1959. Working off Angola and São Tomé. The survey ship *Salvador Correia*, former minesweeper and patrol vessel *Baldaque da Silva*, ex-minesweeping trawler *Ruskholm* of the British "Isles" class, discarded on 27 Mar 1967.

1 Ex-BRITISH "BANGOR" CLASS FLEET MINESWEEPER

ALMIRANTE LACERDA (ex-*Caraquet*) A 525

Displacement, tons	672 standard; 830 full load
Dimensions, feet	171·5 pp; 180·0 oa × 28·5 × 9·5 max
Guns	1—3 in; 2—20 mm AA
Main engines	Triple expansion; 2 shafts; 2 400 ihp = 16 knots
Boilers	2, of 3-drum small-tube type
Oil fuel, tons	160
Complement	100 (7 officers, 93 men)

Former British fleet minesweeper of the "Bangor" class, steam type. Built in Canada, launched on 2 June 1941, and purchased from Great Britain in 1946. Working off Mozambique.

CRUZEIRO DO SUL (ex-*Giroflée*)

Displacement, tons	120 standard
Dimensions, feet	93·2 × 17·8 × 8
Main engines	2 Gleenifer diesels; 320 bhp = 12 knots max
Range, miles	2 000 at 10 knots (economical speed)
Complement	8 (1 officer, 7 men)

Launched 1935.

MIRA (ex-*Formalhaut*, ex-*Arrabida*)

Displacement, tons	30 standard
Dimensions, feet	62·9 × 15·2 × 4
Main engines	3 Perkins diesels; 300 bhp = 15 knots max
Range, miles	650 at 8 knots (economical speed)
Complement	6 men

Launched 1961.

FISHERY PROTECTION VESSELS

4 "AZEVIA" CLASS

AZEVIA P595 **BICUDA** P596 **CORVINA** P 597 **DOURADA** P598

Displacement, tons	230 standard; 275 full load (revised official figures)
Dimensions, feet	134·5 pp; 139·8 oa × 21·3 × 7·0
Guns	2—20 mm AA
Main engines	2 Sulzer 7-cyl 2-stroke diesels except first pair; 2 MAN 10-cyl 4-stroke diesels; 2 shafts; 2 400 bhp = 17 knots
Oil fuel, tons	25
Range, miles	2 250 at 12·8 knots; 1 080 at 17·3 knots
Complement	30 (2 officers, 28 men)

All launched in 1942-42. A photograph of *Bicuda* appears in the 1953-54 to 1959-60 editions. Sister ship *Espadilha* was discarded on 20 Apr 1969.

AZEVIA *1968, Portuguese Navy*

TRAINING SHIP

SAGRES (ex-*Guanabara*, ex-*Albert Leo Schlageter*) A 520

Displacement, tons	1 725 standard; 1 869 full load (official revised figures)
Dimensions, feet	229·7 pp; 249·0 oa × 39·3 × 17·0
Main engines	2 MAN auxiliary diesels; 1 shaft; 750 bhp = 10 knots
Oil fuel, tons	52
Range, miles	3 500 at 6·5 knots
Complement	153 (10 officers, 143 men)

Former German sail training ship. Built by Blohm & Voss, Hamburg. Launched in June 1937 and completed on 1 Feb 1938. Sister of US Coast Guard training ship *Eagle* (ex-German *Horst Wessel*). Taken by USA as a reparation after the Second World War in 1945 and sold to Brazil in 1948. Purchased from Brazil and commissioned in the Portuguese Navy on 2 Feb 1962 at Rio de Janeiro and renamed *Sagres*. Sail area 20 793 sq ft. Height of mast 142 ft.

SAGRES *1971, Portuguese Navy*

DEPOT SHIP

Former Training Ship

SANTO ANDRÉ (ex-*Sagres*, ex-*Flores*, ex-*Max*, ex-*Rickmer Rickmers*) A 5207

Displacement, tons	3 385 standard; 3 866 full load (officially revised figures)
Dimensions, feet	263·5 × 40·3 × 19·0
Guns	4—47 mm saluting
Main engines	2 Krupp diesels; 2 shafts; 700 bhp = 8 knots

Former German sailing vessel. Built at Bremerhaven. Launched in 1896. Captured during the First World War. Re-rigged as a barque and adapted as a naval training ship during 1924-27. Auxiliary motors were fitted in 1931. Reclassified as a depot ship and renamed *Santo André* by decree of 31 Jan 1962. Replaced on 8 Feb 1962 by the training ship *Guanabara*, purchased from Brazil which took the name and number of the former *Sagres*.

FLEET OILER

S. GABRIEL A 5206

Displacement, tons	9 000 standard; 14 626 full load (officially revised figures)
Measurement, tons	9 854 gross; 9 000 deadweight
Dimensions, feet	452·8 pp 479·0 oa × 59·8 × 26·2
Main engines	1 Pametrada-geared turbine; 1 shaft; 9 500 shp = 17 knots
Boilers	2
Range, miles	6 000 at 15 knots
Complement	84 (10 officers, 74 men)

Built at Estaleiros de Viana do Castelo. Commissioned on 27 Mar 1963. The oiler *Cimarron* was officially deleted from the list in Mar 1971.

S. GABRIEL *1969, Portuguese Navy*

LOGISTIC SHIPS

1 Ex-US ARC/LSM TYPE

S. RAFAEL (ex-*Medusa*, ex-USS *Portunus*, *ARC* 1, ex-*LSM* 275, ex-*LCT* (7) 1773) A 5214

Displacement, tons	743 standard; 1 220 full load
Dimensions, feet	196·5 pp; 221·1 oa × 34·5 × 10·5
Guns	2—40 mm; 2—20 mm
Main engines	GM direct drive diesel; 2 shafts; 2 800 bhp = 12 knots
Radius, miles	5 240 at 10 knots
Complement	56 (6 officers, 50 men)

Former US medium landing ship, LSM type. Built by Federal Sbipbuilding and Drydock Co, Newark, New Jersey. Laid down on 1 Aug 1944, launched on 11 Sep 1944, and completed on 6 Oct 1944. Converted to a cable repairing or laying ship by the US Navy in 1952. Transferred to the Portuguese Navy under MAP in 1959. Delivered to Portugal on 16 Nov and commissioned on 18 Nov as a diving tender (***navio-apoio de mergulhadores***). **Converted to a logistic ship in 1969 and guns mounted as above.**

Logistic Ships—*continued*

S. RAFAEL (ex-*Medusa*) *Portuguese Navy*

1 FLEET OILER TYPE

SAM BRAS A 523

Displacement, tons	5 766 standard; 6 374 full load (officially revised figures)
Dimensions, feet	333·1 pp; 356·8 oa × 47·3 × 16·5 (officially revised figures)
Guns	1—3 in (*76 mm*); 2—40 mm; 2—20 mm
Main engines	B & W 2-stroke diesel; 1 shaft; 2 820 bhp = 12 knots
Oil fuel, tons	568
Radius, miles	11 000 at 12 knots
Complement	101 (11 officers, 90 men)

Built at Arsenal do Alfeite. Laid down on 22 Feb 1941. Launched on 17 Mar 1942. Former fleet oiler converted to logistic ship and armed as above in Arsenal do Alfeite.

S. BRAS *1971, Portuguese Navy*

TUG/BUOY TENDER

1 NEW CONSTRUCTION

SCHULTZ XAVIER

Displacement, tons	900
Main engines	2 400 hp = 14·5 knots
Range, miles	3 000 at 12·5 knots

A dual purpose fleet tug and buoy tender is reported to have been ordered late in 1968 from the Alfeite Naval Yard. The old lighthouse tender *Almirante Schultz*, A 521, was discarded on 10 Nov 1969. See full particulars and photograph in the 1969-70 edition.

ROMANIA

Commander-in-Chief of the Navy:
Vice Admiral Grigore Martes

Diplomatic Representation

Naval Attaché in London:
Captain 1st Rank A. A. Dusa

Naval, Military and Air Attaché in Washington
Colonel Nicolae Gheorghe Plesa

Strength of the Fleet

3 Coastal Escorts	22 Inshore Minesweepers
5 Missile Boats	8 Minesweeping Boats
4 Medium Minesweepers	2 Training Ships
8 Torpedo Boats	15 Auxiliary Vessels
3 Patrol Vessels	10 Landing Craft

Personnel

1973: 5 000 officers and ratings

Mercantile Marine

Lloyd's Register of Shipping:
71 vessels of 363 996 tons gross

COASTAL ESCORTS

3 Ex-USSR "POTI" CLASS

V 31 **V 32** **V 33**

Displacement, tons	550 standard; 650 full load
Dimensions, feet	196·9 × 26·2 × 9·2
Guns	2—57 mm AA (1 twin mounting)
Tubes	4—16 in anti-submarine
A/S weapons	2—12 barrelled rocket launchers
Main engines	2 gas turbines; 2 diesels; 4 shafts; total 20 000 hp = 28 knots

PCs, i.e. coastal escort vessels of the patrol vessel or submarine chaser type transferred from the USSR in 1970. Similar to the Soviet "Poti" class in all respects.

MISSILE BOATS

5 Ex-USSR "OSA" CLASS

PENNANTS 194 to 198

Displacement, tons	165 standard; 200 full load
Dimensions, feet	128·7 × 25·1 × 5·9
Missile launchers	4 for SSN 2A
Guns, AA	4—30 mm (2 twin, 1 forward, 1 aft)
Main engines	3 diesels; 13 000 bhp = 32 knots

Built since 1959.

MINESWEEPERS

4 Ex-GERMAN "M 40" TYPE

DESCATUSARIA DESROBIERA DEMOCRATIA DREPTATEA

Displacement, tons	543 standard; 775 full load
Dimensions, feet	188 pp; 203·5 oa × 28 × 7·5 (max)
Guns	6—37 mm AA (twin)
A/S weapons	2 DCT
Main engines	Triple expansion; 2 shafts; 2 400 ihp = 17 knots
Boilers	2 three-drum water tube
Fuel, tons	152 coal
Radius, miles	4 000 at 10 knots
Complement	80

Former German "M 40" type coal-burning minesweepers. Built in 1943. Taken over by USSR at the end of the Second World War. Transferred to Rumania in 1956-1957. Pennant numbers DB-13, DB-14, DB-15 and DB-16.

DB-15 and DB-16 *1968*

DB-14 and DB-15 *1964, P. H. Silverstone*

TORPEDO BOATS

6 Ex-USSR "P 4" CLASS

PENNANTS 87 to 92.

Displacement, tons	25
Dimensions, feet	62·7 × 11·6 × 5·6
Guns	2 MG
Tubes	2—18 in
Main engines	2 diesels; 2 200 bhp = 50 knots

Former Soviet motor torpedo boats transferred to Romania from the USSR.

PATROL VESSELS

3 Ex-USSR "KRONSTADT" CLASS

V-1 V-2 V-3

Displacement, tons	310 standard; 380 full load
Dimensions, feet	170·6 × 21·5 × 9
Guns	1—3·9 in dual purpose forward; 2—37 mm AA single aft; 6—12·7 mm in twin mounts
A/S weapons	2 ahead throwing launchers; 2 side projectors; 2 depth charge tracks
Main engines	3 diesels; 3 shafts; 3 300 bhp = 27 knots

Former Soviet submarine chasers transferred to Romania from the USSR.

INSHORE MINESWEEPERS

22 Ex-USSR "T 301" CLASS

Displacement, tons	130
Dimensions, feet	100 × 16 × 4·5
Guns	2—45 mm AA; 4—12·7 mm MG
Main engines	Diesel; 480 bhp = 10 knots
Complement	30

Former Soviet coastal minesweepers transferred to Romania by the USSR in 1956-60. Probably half of these are non-operational.

TRAINING SHIPS

MIRCEA

Displacement, tons	1 604
Dimensions, feet	239·5 oa; 267·3 (with bowsprit) × 39·3 × 16·5
Sail area	18 830 sq ft
Main engines	Auxiliary MAN, 6-cylinder Diesel; 500 bhp = 9·5 knots
Complement	83 + 140 midshipmen for training

Built by Blohm & Voss, Hamburg. Laid down on 30 Apr 1938. Launched on 22 Sep 1938. Completed on 29 Mar 1939. Refitted at Hamburg in 1966.

MIRCEA *1970, courtesy Mr Michael D. J. Lennon*

RASARITUL (ex-*Taifun*)

Measurement, tons	34 (*Thames* measurement)
Dimensions, feet	54·0 × 12·5 × 3·0
Main engines	2 petrol motors; 2 shafts

Built by J. Samuel White & Co Ltd, Cowes, Isle of Wight, England. Launched in 1938. Of wooden construction. Yacht used as sail training ship. The training ship *Liberatea* (ex-*Luceafarul*, ex-*Nahlin*), former Royal Yacht, and the training ship *Constanta* (former submarine depot ship) were removed from the list in 1968.

MINESWEEPING BOATS

8 "TR-40 CLASS"

VD-241 VD-242 VD-243 VD-244 VD-245 VD-246 VD-247 VD-248

Eight "TR-40" Class minesweeping boats are employed on shallow water and river duties. Two survey craft, ten transports and three oilers are also reported.

SAUDI ARABIA

Diplomatic Representation

Defence Attaché in London:
Brigadier Abdullah Al-Saheal

Mercantile Marine

Lloyd's Register of Shipping: 35 vessels of 50 369 tons gross

LIGHT FORCES

2 JAGUAR CLASS (TORPEDO BOATS)

Displacement, tons	160 standard; 190 full load
Dimensions, feet	138 oa × 23·0 × 7·3
Guns	2—40 mm
Torpedo tubes	4—21 in
Main engines	4 diesels; 12 000 bhp = 42 knots
Complement	33 (3 officers; 30 men)

Built in Germany and delivered in 1969.

RIYADH

Displacement, tons	100 standard
Dimensions, feet	95·0 × 19·0 × 6·0
Guns	1—40 mm AA
Main engines	4 diesels; 2 shafts; 2 200 bhp = 21 knots

Steel-hulled patrol boat of US CG design transferred to Saudi Arabia in 1960

Light Forces—*continued*

20 45 ft PATROL BOATS

Built by Whittingham and Mitchell, Chertsey, England. Armed with one ·5 cal MG and powered with two 362 hp diesels.

10 23 ft HUNTRESS PATROL BOATS

Built by Fairey Marine, Hamble, England. Capable of 20 knots with a cruising range of 150 miles and a complement of four.

20 ft PATROL BOATS

Smaller editions of the 45 ft craft above. By the same builder.

8 SRN-6 HOVERCRAFT

Displacement, tons	10 normal (load 8 200 lbs)
Dimensions, feet	48·4 × 25·3 × 15·9 (height)
Main machinery	1 Gnome model 1050 gas turbine
Speed, knots	58

Acquired from British Hovercraft Corporation Ltd, between Feb and Dec 1970.

2 AIR SEA-RESCUE LAUNCHES

ASR 1 **ASR 2**

With two diesels of 1 230 hp and capable of 25 knots.

SENEGAL

Mercantile Marine

Lloyd's Register of Shipping: 39 vessels of 16 280 tons gross

PATROL VESSELS

SAINT LOUIS

Displacement, tons	235 standard
Dimensions, feet	149·3 pp; 155·8 oa × 23·6 × 8·2
Guns	2—40 mm AA
Missiles	8—SS12 SSM
Main engines	2 MGO diesels; 2 shafts; 2 400 bhp = 18·5 knots
Range, miles	2 000 at 15 knots

Ordered from Ch Navales Franco-Belges. Laid down on 20 Apr 1970, launched on 5 Aug 1970 and commissioned on 1 Mar 1971. Sister to *Malaika* of Malagasy, *Vigilant* of Ivory Coast and *Bizerte* of Tunisian Navy.

2 Ex-FRENCH "VC" TYPE

CASAMANCE (ex-*VC* 5, *P* 755)
SINE-SALOUM (ex-*Reine N'Galifourou*, ex-*VC* 4, *P* 754)

Displacement, tons	75 standard; 82 full load
Dimensions, feet	104·5 × 15·5 × 5·5
Guns	2—20 mm AA
Main engines	2 Mercedes-Benz diesels; 2 shafts; 2 700 bhp = 28 knots max

Former French patrol craft (Vedettes de Surveillance Côtière). Built by the Constructions Mécaniques de Normandie, Cherbourg. Completed in 1958. *Casamance* was transferred from France to Senegal in 1963. *Sine-Saloum* was given to Senegal on 24 Aug 1965 after having been returned to France by the Congo in Feb 1965.

SINE-SALOUM *1967, Senegalese Navy*

1 Ex-US "SC" TYPE

SÉNÉGAL (ex-*P* 700, ex-*CH* 62, ex-US *SC* 1344)

Displacement, tons	110 standard; 138 full load
Dimensions, feet	107·5 wl; 110·9 × 17 × 6·5
Guns	1—40 mm AA; 3—20 mm AA
Main engines	2 GM diesels; 2 shafts; 1 000 bhp = 13 knots max
Complement	25

Former US submarine chaser transferred to France on 19 Nov 1943, and from France to Senegal on 12 July 1961. First ship of Senegalese naval force.

12 VOSPER PATROL BOATS

Built by Vosper Thornycroft, Singapore. 45 ft boats of standard pattern.

SABAH

In addition to two PX-class 87 ft patrol boats on detachment from the Royal Malaysian Police the following have been provided direct to Sabah by Vosper Thornycroft Private Ltd, Singapore.

2 55 ft PATROL BOATS

SRI SEMPORNA **SRI BANGJI**

Displacement, tons	50
Dimensions, feet	55 × 15 × 30
Guns	1—MG
Main engines	Diesels; 1 200 hp = 20 knots
Range, miles	300 at 15 knots
Complement	11

2 91 ft PATROL BOATS

For delivery in 1973.

1 YACHT

PUTRI SABAH

Displacement, tons	117
Dimensions, feet	91 × 19 × 5·5
Main engines	1 Diesel = 12 knots
Complement	22

ST. LUCIA

Mercantile Marine

Lloyd's Register of Shipping: 1 vessel of 507 tons gross

1 BROOKE MARINE PATROL CRAFT

CHATOYER

Displacement, tons	15
Dimensions, feet	40 × 12 × 2
Guns	3 MG
Main engines	2 Diesels; 370 hp = 22 knots

ST. VINCENT

Mercantile Marine

Lloyd's Register of Shipping: 4 vessels of 1 477 tons gross

1 BROOKE MARINE PATROL CRAFT

HELEN

Details as *Chatoyer*, St Lucia.

SIERRA LEONE

Mercantile Marine

Lloyd's Register of Shipping: 8 vessels of 1 795 tons gross

PATROL VESSEL

It has been officially stated that Sierra Leone is acquiring at least one fighting vessel.

SOMALI REPUBLIC

Mercantile Marine

Lloyd's Register of Shipping: 148 vessels of 873 209 tons gross

TORPEDO BOATS

4 Ex-USSR "P4" CLASS

Displacement, tons	25
Dimensions, feet	62·7 × 11·6 × 5·6
Torpedo tubes	2—18 in
Guns	2 MG (twin)
Main engines	2 diesels; 2 shafts; 2 200 bhp = 50 knots

12 or more of the ex-USSR "P 6" type were to be transferred by the USSR or UAR.

PATROL BOATS

6 Ex-USSR "POLUCHAT" I CLASS

Displacement, tons	100 standard, 120 full load
Dimensions, feet	98·4 × 20·0 × 5·9
Guns	2—25 mm AA
Main engines	Diesels = 15 knots

Two of these boats were reported to have been transferred from the USSR in 1968.

SOUTHERN YEMEN

Mercantile Marine

1973: Lloyd's Register of Shipping: 5 vessels of 1 417 tons gross

INSHORE MINESWEEPERS

3 "HAM" CLASS

Displacement, tons	120 standard; 160 full load
Dimensions, feet	106·5 oa × 21·2 × 5·5
Guns	1—20 mm AA
Main engines	2 Paxman diesels; 1 100 bhp = 14 knots
Oil fuel, tons	15
Complement	15 officers and men

The British inshore minesweepers *Bodenham, Blunham* and *Elsenham* were transferred to the South Arabian Navy established by the Federal Government.

PATROL BOATS

15 COASTAL TYPE

Fifteen small diesel engined patrol boats were ordered in the United Kingdom in 1969.

SINGAPORE

Mercantile Marine

Lloyd's Register of Shipping: 281 vessels of 870 513 tons gross

LIGHT FORCES

4 LÜRSSEN VEGESACK DESIGN MISSILE BOATS

SEA WOLF **SEA LION** **SEA SERPENT**

Approximate details:

Displacement, tons	120
Dimensions, feet	120 × 20 × 6
Main engines	Diesels = 35 knots
Complement	20

Designed by Lürssen Werft who built the first pair which arrived Autumn 1972. *Sea Serpent* built by Singapore Shipbuilding and Engineering Co launched 16 November 1972.

6 VOSPER THORNYCROFT DESIGN FPBs

3 "TYPE A"

INDEPENDENCE (15 July 1969) P 69
FREEDOM (18 Nov 1969) P 70
JUSTICE (15 May 1970) P 72

Displacement, tons	100 standard
Dimensions, feet	103·6 wl; 109·6 × 21·0 × 5·6
Guns	1—40 mm AA (forward); 1—20 mm AA aft
Main engines	2 Maybach diesels; 2 × 3 600 bhp = 32 knots (max)
Range, miles	1 100 at 15 knots
Complement	19 to 22

On 21 May 1968 the Vosper Thornycroft Group announced the receipt of an order for six of their 110-foot fast patrol boats for the Republic of Singapore. In design these vessels are of a hybrid type between that of the fast patrol craft built for the Malaysian Navy and those built for the Peruvian Navy. Two sub types, the first of each (*Independence* and *Sovereignty*) built in UK, the remainder in Singapore. Second type have more advanced armament. *Independance* was completed in 1970.

INDEPENDENCE *1971, Vosper Thornycroft*

3 "TYPE B"

SOVEREIGNTY (25 Nov 1969) P 71
DARING (28 Nov 1970) P 73
DAUNTLESS (21 Feb 1971) P 74

Displacement, tons	100 standard; 130 full load
Dimensions, feet	103·6 wl; 109·6 × 21·0 × 5·6
Guns	1—76 mm Bofors; 1—20 mm Oerlikon
Main engines	2 Maybach MD 872 diesels; 2 × 3 600 bhp = 32 knots max; continuous sea speed over 25 knots
Range, miles	1 100 at 15 knots
Complement	19 (3 officers, 16 ratings)

Sovereignty was built by Vosper Thornycroft Ltd, Portsmouth, England and completed in 1971. *Daring* and *Dauntless* built by Vosper Thornycroft Private Ltd (formerly Uniteers Yard) in Singapore. Steel hulls of round bilge form with spray strake and spray deflecting knuckle extending for more than half the length. Aluminium alloy superstructure.

Light Forces—*continued*

SOVEREIGNTY *1971, Vosper Thornycroft*

SEAWARD DEFENCE BOAT

1 "FORD" TYPE

PANGLIMA P 48

Displacement, tons	119 standard; 134 full load
Dimensions, feet	117·0 × 20·0 × 6·0
Guns	1—40 mm; 60 cal AA forward
Main engines	Paxman YHAXM supercharged B 12 diesels = 14 knots
Oil fuel, tons	15
Complement	15 officers and men

Built by United Engineers, Singapore. Laid down in 1954. Launched on 14 Jan 1956. Accepted by the Singapore Government in May 1956. Similar to the British seaward defence boats of the "Ford" class. Transferred to the Royal Malaysian Navy on the formation of Malaysia. Transferred to the Singapore Government (independent Republic of Singapore) in 1967.

PANGLIMA *1964*

PATROL BOATS

PX 10 **PX 11** **PX 12** **PX 13**

Displacement, tons	40 standard
Length, feet	87·0
Guns	2—20 mm

Built by Vosper Thornycroft Group, Portsmouth, England for marine police duties. There is also the former Netherlands boat *Endeavor*, built in 1955.

LANDING SHIP

1 US LST TYPE

ENDURANCE A 81 (ex-USS *Holmes County*, LST 836)

Displacement, tons	1 653 light; 4 080 full load
Dimensions, feet	316·0 wl; 328·0 oa × 50·0 × 14·0
Guns	8—40 mm (4 twin)
Main engines	GM diesels; 2 shafts; 1 700 bhp = 11·6 knots
Complement	120

Tank landing craft transferred from the United States Navy on 1 July 1971.

LANDING CRAFT

2 LCT (8) TYPE

CAIRNHILL (ex-*Ardennes*) **TANGLIN** (ex-*Arromanches*)

Displacement, tons	657 light; 1 017 full load
Dimensions, feet	225·0 pp; 231·2 oa × 39·0 × 5·0
Main engines	4 Paxman diesels; 1 840 bhp = 12·6 knots max (9 knots economical cruising speed)
Complement	37

Originally in the Royal Navy but transferred to the British Army. Acquired by Singapore in 1970. There are also six small landing craft.

TANGLIN *1971, A. & J. Pavia*

SOUTH AFRICA

Administration

Commandant General South African Defence Force:
Admiral H. H. Biermann SSA, OBE

Commander, Maritime Defence and Chief of the Navy:
Vice-Admiral J. Johnson, SM, DSC

Chief of Naval Staff:
Rear-Admiral S. C. Biermann, SM

Diplomatic Representation

Armed Forces Attaché in London:
Rear Admiral M. R. Terry Lloyd, SM

Naval Attaché in London:
Commander C. H. Bennett

Defence and Armed Forces Attaché in Washington:
Brigadier F. A. Beeton, SM

Strength of the Fleet

2 Destroyers
7 Frigates
3 Patrol Submarines
10 Coastal Minesweepers
1 Survey Ship
5 Seaward Defence Craft
5 Support Ships and Auxiliaries
5 Air Sea Rescue Launches

Naval Base

HM Dockyard at Simonstown was transferred to the Republic of South Africa on 2 Apr 1957. The new submarine base building at Simonstown, SAS Drommedaris, incorporating offices, accommodation and operations centre alongside a Synchrolift marin eelevator, capable of docking all South African ships except the *Tafelberg*, was opened in July 1972.
A new Maritime Headquarters was opened in March 1973 at Silvermine on the Cape Peninsula.

New Construction

It is reported that plans are being considered for the construction of six new corvettes.

Personnel

1973: Total 4 665 (427 officers, 3 038 ratings and 1 200 national service ratings)

Air Sea Rescue Base

The SAAF Maritime Group base at Langebaan was transferred to the South African Navy on 1 Nov 1969, becoming SAN Sea Rescue Base (SAS *Flamingo*). The ASR launches were launches given Naval Coastal Forces numbers to replace SAF "R" numbers.

Mercantile Marine

Lloyd's Register of Shipping:
255 vessels of 511 190 tons gross

DESTROYERS

2 FORMER BRITISH "W" CLASS

Name	No.	Builders	Laid down	Launched	Completed
JAN VAN RIEBEECK (ex-HMS *Wessex*, ex-*Zenith*)	D 278	Fairfield SB & Eng Co Ltd, Govan, Glasgow	20 Oct 1942	2 Sep 1943	11 May 1944
SIMON VAN DER STEL (ex-HMS *Whelp*)	D 237	R. & W. Hawthorn Leslie & Co Ltd	1 May 1942	3 June 1943	25 Apr 1944

Displacement, tons	2 205 standard; 2 850 full load
Length, feet (*metres*)	339·5 (103·6)pp; 362·8 (*110·6*)oa
Beam, feet (*metres*)	35·7 (*10·9*)
Draught, feet (*metres*)	17·1 (*5·2*) max (props)
Aircraft	2 Westland "Wasp" helicopters
Guns, surface	4—4 in (*102 mm*) 2 twin
Guns, AA	2—40 mm (single)
Guns, saluting	4—3 pdr.
Torpedo tubes	4—21 in (quadruple)
Torpedo tubes, A/S	6 (2 triple)
A/S weapons	2 DCT; 2 DC racks
Boilers	2 Admiralty 3-drum type; 300 psi; 670°F
Main engines	2 Parsons sr geared turbines; 2 shafts; 40 000 shp
Speed, knots	36·75 designed; 31·25 sea
Range, miles	3 260 at 14 knots; 1 000 at 30 knots
Oil fuel, tons	579 (95%)
Complement	192 (11 officers, 181 men)

Purchased from Great Britain, *Jan van Riebeeck* was transferred to South Africa on 29 Mar 1950, and *Simon van der Stel* early in 1952.

MODERNISATION. *Simon Van der Stel* was modernised in 1962-64 and *Jan van Riebeeck* in 1964-66.

RADAR. Search: Type 293. Fire Control: X Band (NSG NA 9 system)

GUNNERY. The main armament formerly comprised four 4·7 inch guns.

JAN VAN RIEBEECK — *South African Navy*

JAN VAN RIEBEECK & SIMON VAN DER STEL

FRIGATES

3 "PRESIDENT" CLASS

Name	No	Builders	Laid down	Launched	Completed
PRESIDENT KRUGER	F 150	Yarrow & Co. Scotstoun	6 Apr 1959	20 Oct 1960	1 Oct 1962
PRESIDENT PRETORIUS	F 145	Yarrow & Co. Scotstoun	21 Nov 1960	28 Sep 1962	4 Mar 1964
PRESIDENT STEYN	F 147	Alex Stephen & Sons. Govan	20 May 1960	23 Nov 1961	25 Apr 1963

Displacement, tons	2 250 standard; 2 800 full load
Length, feet (*metres*)	360 (*109·7*) wl; 370 (*112·8*) oa
Beam, feet (*metres*)	41·0 (*12·5*)
Draught, feet (*metres*)	17·1 (*5·2*) max (props)
Guns, surface	2—4·5 in (*115 mm*) 1 twin
Guns, AA	2—40 mm Bofors
Guns, saluting	4—3 pdr.
Aircraft	1 "Wasp" helicopter
A/S weapons	1 "Limbo" 3-barrel DC mortar
Boilers	2 Babcock & Wilcox; 550 psi; 850°F
Main engines	2 sets double reduction geared turbines; 2 shafts; 30 000 shp
Speed, knots	over 30 max, 28 sustained sea
Range, miles	4 500 at 12 knots
Oil fuel, tons	430
Complement	203 (13 officers, 190 men)

Originally "Whitby" Type 12 frigates. *President Kruger* arrived in South Africa on 27 Mar 1963.

MODERNISATION. Refitted to carry a "Wasp" A/S helicopter, with hangar and landing deck. To accommodate this, one "Limbo" A/S mortar was removed and the two single 40 mm remounted on the hangar roof. *President Kruger* completed refit and recommissioned on 5 Aug 1969, *President Steyn* completed refit in 1971, when *President Pretorius* was taken in hand. The refits were carried out at S.A. Naval Dockyard, Simonstown and included replacement of the lattice foremast by a truncated pyramid tower.

PRESIDENT STEYN — *1972, South African Navy*

PRETORIUS — *1973*

Frigates—*continued*

ENGINEERING. Geared turbines of advanced design and high power start on a cruising turbine and switch over to the main turbines at a predetermined speed.

ELECTRICAL. System is alternating current, 440 volts, three phase, 60 cycles per second.

RADAR. Thomson CSF Jupiter 23 cm surveillance; Type 293 air/surface warning; nav set. Elsag NA9C fire control (Kruger with original fire control radar) ECM and DF.

GUNNERY. The two 40 mm guns were on the main deck, a deck lower than in the "Whitby" class original design.

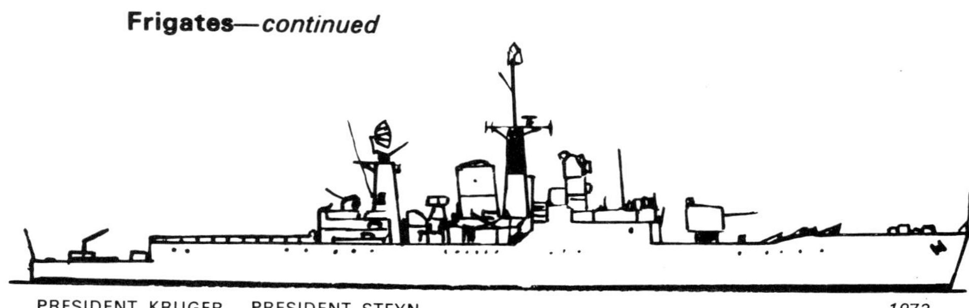

PRESIDENT KRUGER PRESIDENT STEYN 1973

PRESIDENT KRUGER 1971, South African Navy

1 FORMER BRITISH TYPE 15

VRYSTAAT (ex-HMS *Wrangler*) F 157

Displacement, tons	2 240 standard; 2 880 full load
Length, feet (*metres*)	339·5 (*103·5*) pp; 362·8 (*110·6*) oa
Beam, feet (*metres*)	35·7 (*10·9*)
Draught, feet (*metres*)	17·1 (*5·2*) max props
Guns, surface	2—4 in (*102 mm*) 1 twin
Guns, AA	2—40 mm Bofors
Guns, saluting	4—3 pdr
A/S weapons	2 Squid DC mortars
Boilers	2 Admiralty 3-drum; 300 psi; 675°F
Main engines	Parsons single reduction geared turbines; 2 shafts; 40 000 shp
Speed, knots	36·75 designed; 31·25 sea
Range, miles	3 200 at 14 knots 1 300 at full power
Oil fuel, tons	505
Complement	195 (13 officers, 182 men)

Built by Vickers-Armstrongs, Barrow. Laid down on 23 Sep 1942, launched on 30 Dec 1943, completed on 14 June 1944. Fully converted into a Type 15 fast anti-submarine frigate from a fleet destroyer of the "W" class in 1951-52 by Harland & Wolf Ltd, Belfast. Refitted by the Mount Stuart Dry Dock Ltd, Cardiff, and taken over from the Royal Navy on 29 Nov 1956 as a unit of the South African Navy and renamed *Vrystaat*. Sailed for South Africa at the end of Jan 1957.

RADAR. Search: Type 277, Type 293. CM and DF.

VRYSTAAT 1970, South African Navy

VRYSTAAT 1973

2 FORMER BRITISH "LOCH" CLASS

Name	No.	Builders	Laid down	Launched	Completed
GOOD HOPE (ex-HMS *Loch Boisdale*)	F 432	Blyth Dry Docks & SB Co Ltd	8 Nov 1943	5 July 1944	1 Dec 1944
TRANSVAAL (ex-HMS *Loch Ard*)	F 602	Harland & Wolff, Ltd, Belfast	20 Jan 1944	2 Aug 1944	21 May 1945

Displacement, tons	1 610 standard; 2 450 full load
Length, feet (*metres*)	286 (*87·2*) pp; 307 (*93·6*) oa
Beam, feet (*metres*)	38·5 (*11·7*)
Draught, feet (*metres*)	15·1 (*4·6*) max
Guns, surface	2—4 in (*102 mm*) 1 twin
Guns, AA	*Transvaal:* 6—40 mm Bofors *Good Hope:* 2—40 mm Bofors
Guns, saluting	*Good Hope:* 4—3 pdr
A/S weapons	2 "Squid" triple DC mortars
Boilers	2 Admiralty 3-drum; 225 psi
Main engines	2 sets triple expansion; 2 shafts; 5 500 ihp
Speed, knots	19 max
Range, miles	9 500 at 12 knots
Oil fuel, tons	720
Complement	165 (10 officers, 155 men)

These two anti-submarine frigates, and a sister ship, *Natal*, were presented to South Africa by Great Britain in 1944-45.

TRANSVAAL 1971, South African Navy

CONSTRUCTION. *Transvaal* was completed by Lobnitz & Co Ltd, Renfrew.

MODIFICATION. When *Transvaal* was modernised she had her forecastle deck extended aft to provide extra accommodation (see photograph).

CONVERSION. *Good Hope* was converted into a despatch vessel in 1955 as Administrative Flagship of the South African Navy. She has deckhouse super-

Frigates—*continued*

structure for extra cabins, and reception platform above built on aft, and mainmast. Refitted in 1961. Sister ship *Natal* (survey ship). Sunk on 19 Sep 1972.

RADAR. Equipment includes Type 277 search radar installation.

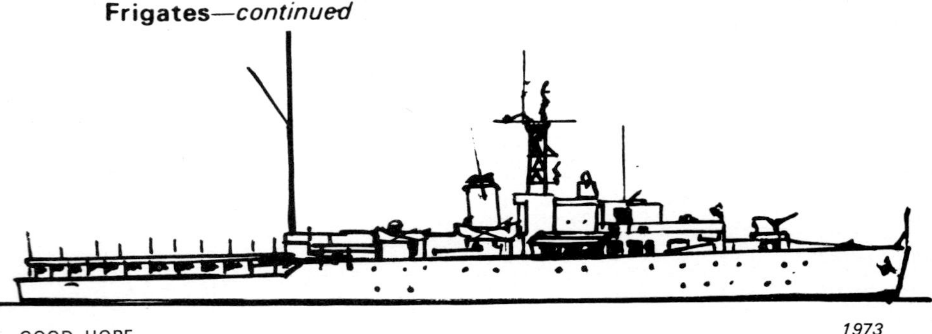

GOOD HOPE 1973

1 FORMER BRITISH "ALGERINE" CLASS

PIETERMARITZBURG (ex-HMS *Pelorus*) M 291

Displacement, tons	**1 040 standard; 1 330 full load**
Length, feet (*metres*)	**212·5 (*64·8*) pp; 225 (*68·6*) oa**
Beam feet (*metres*)	**35·5 (*10·8*)**
Draught, feet (*metres*)	**11·5 (*3·5*)**
Guns, surface	**2—4 in (*102 mm*) 1 twin**
Guns, AA	**2—40 mm Bofors**
A/S weapons	**4 DCT**
Boilers	**2 three-drum type; 250 psi**
Main engines	**2 sets triple expansion; 2 shafts; 2 400 ihp**
Speed, knots	16 max, 14 sustained
Range, miles	5 500 at 10 knots
Oil fuel, tons	270
Complement	115 (8 officers, 107 men)

Built as ocean minesweeper by Lobnitz & Co Ltd. Renfrew. Laid down on 8 Oct 1942, launched on 18 June 1943, completed on 7 Oct 1943. Also used as escort vessel. Purchased from Great Britain in 1947 Re-commissioned as midshipmen's training ship on 30 Aug 1962. The twin 4 inch mount, replacing a single 4 inch, was refitted in 1958. Refitted in 1971. Sister ship *Bloemfontein* (ex-HMS *Rosamund*) was sunk as a target by *Johannesburg* and *President Kruger* on 5 June 1967 off Simonstown.

PIETERMARITZBURG 1969, South African Navy

SUBMARINES

3 "FRENCH" "DAPHNE" CLASS

Name	*No.*	*Builders*	*Laid down*	*Launched*	*Completed*
EMILY HOBHOUSE	S 98	Dubigeon—Normandie (Nantes-Chantenay)	18 Nov 1968	24 Oct 1969	25 Jan 1971
JOHANNA VAN DER MERWE	S 99	Dubigeon—Normandie (Nantes-Chantenay)	24 Apr 1969	21 July 1970	21 July 1971
MARIA VAN RIEBEECK	S 97	Dubigeon—Normandie (Nantes-Chantenay)	14 Mar 1968	18 Mar 1969	22 June 1970

Displacement, tons	850 surface; 1 040 submerged
Length, feet (*metres*)	190·3 (*58*)
Beam, feet (*metres*)	22·3 (*6·8*)
Draught, feet (*metres*)	15·4 (*4·7*)
Torpedo tubes	12—21·7 in (*550 mm*) (8 bow, 4 stern)
Main engines	SEMT-Pielstick diesel electric; 1 300 bhp surface; 1 600 hp submerged; 2 shafts
Speed, knots	16 surface and submerged
Range, miles	4 500 at 5 knots (snorting)
Complement	47 (6 officers, 41 men)

First submarines ordered for the South African Navy. They are of the French "Daphne" design, similar to those built in France for Pakistan and Portugal.

MARIA VAN RIEBEECK 1971, South African Navy

SURVEY SHIP

1 YARROW NEW CONSTRUCTION

PROTEA

Displacement, tons	**1 930 standard; 2 750 full load**
Length, feet (*metres*)	**235 (*71·6*); 260·1 (*79·3*)**
Beam, feet (*metres*)	**49·1 (*15·0*)**
Draught, feet (*metres*)	**15·1 (*4·6*)**
Aircraft	**1 helicopter**
Main engines	**4 Paxman/Ventura diesels geared to 1 shaft and controllable pitch propeller; 4 880 bhp**
Speed, knots	Designed for 16 on trials
Range, miles	12 000 at 11 knots
Oil fuel, tons	560 bunkerage capacity
Complement	Total 123 (12 officers, 104 ratings plus 7 scientists)

PROTEA 1973

An order was placed with Yarrow (Shipbuilders) Ltd, for a "Hecla" class survey ship on 7 Nov 1969. Equipped for hydrographic survey with limited facilities for the collection of oceanographical data and for this purpose fitted with special communications equipment, naval surveying gear, survey launches and facilities for helicopter operations. Hull strengthened for navigation in ice and fitted with a transverse bow thrust unit and passive roll stabilisation system. Capable of undertaking long ocean passages in any part of the world including winter passages in the North Atlantic. Laid down 20 July 1970, launched 14 July 1971, commissioned 23 May 1972.

COASTAL MINESWEEPERS

10 BRITISH "TON" CLASS

DURBAN	M 1499	**MOSSELBAAI** (ex-*Oakington*)	M 1213
EAST LONDON (ex-*Chilton*)	M 1215	**PORT ELIZABETH** (*Dumbleton*)	M 1212
JOHANNESBURG (*Castleton*)	M 1207	**PRETORIA** (ex-*Dunkerton*)	M 1144
KAAPSTAD (ex-*Hazleton*)	M 1142	**WALVISBAAI** (ex-*Packington*)	M 1214
KIMBERLEY (ex-*Stratton*)	M 1210	**WINDHOEK**	M 1498

Displacement, tons	360 standard; 425 full load
Dimensions, feet	140·0 pp; 152·0 oa × 28·8 × 8·2
Guns	1—40 mm Bofors AA; 2—20 mm AA
Main engines	Mirrlees diesels in *Kaapstad* and *Pretoria*, 2 500 bhp; Deltic diesels in remainder; 3 000 bhp = 15 knots
Range, miles	2 300 at 13 knots

Kaapstad and *Pretoria*, open bridge and lattice mast, were purchased in 1955. *Windhoek*, frigate bridge and tripod mast, was launched by Thornycroft, Southampton, on 27 June 1957. *Durban*, covered bridge and tripod mast, was launched at Camper & Nicholson, Gosport, on 12 June 1957. *East London* and *Port Elizabeth*, transferred from the Royal Navy at Hythe on 27 Oct 1958, sailed for South Africa in Nov 1958. *Johannesburg*, *Kimberley* and *Mosselbaai* were delivered in 1959. *Walvisbaai* was launched by Harland & Wolff, Belfast on 10 Dec 1958 and delivered in 1959.

DURBAN 1971

SEAWARD DEFENCE BOATS

5 BRITISH "FORD" CLASS

GELDERLAND (ex-*Brayford*)	P 3105	**NAUTILUS** (ex-*Glassford*)	P 3120
HAERLEM	P 3126	**OOSTERLAND**	P 3127
		RIJGER	P 3125

Displacement, tons	120 standard; 160 full load
Dimensions, feet	110·0 wl; 117·2 oa × 20·0 × 4·5
Guns	1—40 mm AA
A/S weapons	2 DCT in *Haerlem*, *Oosterland* and *Rijger*
Main engines	2 Davey Paxman diesels; Foden engine on centre shaft; 1 100 bhp = 18 knots max; sea speed 15 knots

Gelderland built by A. & J. Inglis Ltd, Glasgow, was purchased from Britain, and handed over to South Africa at Portsmouth on 30 Aug 1954. Second ship, *Nautilus* was purchased in 1955, *Rijger* was launched on 6 Feb 1958, *Haerlem* on 18 June 1958, *Oosterland* on 27 Jan 1959. All three of these later ships, built by Vosper Ltd, Portsmouth, are fitted with Vosper roll damping fins. *Haerlem* had a charthouse added aft (see photograph in the 1966-67 to 1970-71 editions) as an inshore survey boat.

RIJGER 1971

TRAINING VESSELS

HDML 1204

Displacement, tons	45 standard; 54 full load (revised official figures)
Dimensions, feet	72·0 × 15·5 × 5·3
Main engines	2 Gardner 8-cylinder diesels; 300 bhp = 11 knots

Sole survivor of the former British Admiralty type HDMLs (Harbour Defence Motor Launches) later designated Seaward Defence Motor Launches. Built in South Africa 1941-42. Guns removed. Attached to Military Academy, Saldanha, as Midshipmen's training vessel. SDML 1202 was converted to a gunnery target. SDML 1330 and 1331 were scrapped in 1953, SDML 1199 and 1201 in 1955, SDML 1198 in 1956, SDML 1332 in 1958 and SDMLs 1197, 1200, 1202 and 1203 in 1968.

NAVIGATOR

Navigational Training Vessel. 75 tons displacement; 63 × 20 feet; 2 Foden diesels, 200 bhp = 9·5 knots. Based at Naval College, Gordon's Bay. Round bilge fishing boat wooden hull. Built by Fred Nicholls (Pty) Ltd, Durban in 1964.

BOOM DEFENCE VESSELS

SOMERSET (ex-HMS *Barcross*) P 285

Displacement, tons	750 standard; 960 full load
Dimensions, feet	150·0pp; 182·0 oa × 32·2 × 11·5
Main engines	Triple expansion; 850 hp = 11 knots
Boilers	2 single ended
Oil fuel, tons	186

Built by Blyth Dry Dock & SB Co Ltd. Laid down on 15 Apr 1941, launched on 21 Oct 1941, completed on 14 Apr 1942. Engined by Swan, Hunter & Wigham Richardson Ltd, Tyne. Renamed in 1951 after Dick King's horse. Sister ship *Fleur* (ex-HMS *Barbrake*) P 273 was sunk as a target in False Bay on 8th Oct 1965.

FLEET REPLENISHMENT SHIP

TAFELBERG (ex-*Annam*) A 243

Measurement, tons	12 500 gross; 18 430 deadweight
Main engines	B & W diesels; 8 420 bhp = 15·5 knots
Complement	100 as naval vessel (40 as tanker)

Built by Nakskovs Skibsvaert as Danish East Asiatic Co tanker. Launched on 20 June 1958. Purchased by the Navy in 1965. Accommodation rehabilitated by Barens Shipbuilding & Engineering Co, Durban with extra accommodation, air conditioning, re-wiring for additional equipment, new upper RAS (replenishment at sea) deck to contain gantries, re-fuelling pipes. Provision for helicopters. Remainder of conversion by Jowies, Brown & Hamer, Durban. Name means Table Mountain.

TAFELBERG 1970, South African Navy

TAFELBERG 1973

TORPEDO RECOVERY VESSEL

FLEUR P 3148

Displacement, tons	220 standard; 257 full load
Dimensions, feet	115·0 wl; 121·5 oa × 27·5 × 11·1
Main engines	2 Paxman Ventura diesels; 1 400 bhp

Built by Dorman Long (Africa) Ltd at Durban and completed on 28 Nov 1969. Commissioned 3 Dec 1969. Combined Torpedo Recovery Vessel and Diving Tender.

FLEUR 1970. South African Navy

NAVAL TUGS

DE NEYS **DE NOORDE**

Displacement, tons	180 and 170, respectively
Dimensions, feet	94·0 × 26·5 × 15·75 and 104·5 × 25·0 × 15·0
Main engines	2 Lister Blackstone diesels; 2 shafts; 608 bhp = 9 knots
Complement	10

Both built by Globe Engineering Works Ltd, CapeTown. Completed on 23 July 1969 and Dec 1961.

AIR SEA RESCUE LAUNCHES (ex-SAAF)

P 1551 (ex-*R* 31) **P 1552** (ex-*R* 30) **P 1554** **P 1555**

P 1554 and 1555: 26 tons, 64 × 16 × 5 feet, 2 diesels, 1 120 bhp = 28 kts. Built by Groves and Gutteridge, Cowes. P 1551 & 1552: 87 tons, 96 × 19 × 4 feet, 2 diesels, 4 480 bhp = 30 kts. (1962, 1961). There are also 2 ex-seaplane tenders, 41 ft, and 2 ex-marine tenders, 24 ft.

PASELBERG 1973, South African Navy

SPAIN

Administration

Minister of Marine:
Admiral Excmo Sr Don Adolfo Baturone Colombo

Chief of Naval Staff:
Admiral Excmo Sr Don Enrique Barbudo Duarte

Deputy Chief of Naval Staff:
Vice-Admiral Excmo Sr Don José R. González López

Commander-in-Chief of the Fleet:
Vice-Admiral Excmo Sr Don Gabriel Pita de Veiga y Sanz

Diplomatic Representation

Naval Attaché in London:
Captain Sr Don Salvador Moreno Reyna

Naval Attaché in Washington:
Captain Sr Don Angel Liberal Lucini

Strength of the Fleet

1 Helicopter Carrier
1 Heavy Cruiser
18 Destroyers
4 Frigates
5 Corvettes
8 Patrol Submarines
11 Ocean Minesweepers
12 Coastal Minesweepers
14 Patrol and Coastguard Vessels
3 Fast Torpedo Boats
3 Anti-Submarine Launches
6 Landing Ships
8 Landing Craft
47 Support Ships and Service Craft

Personnel

1973: Total 52 100 (4 400 officers, 36 700 ratings, 4 600 civil branch, 6 400 marines)

Replacement Programmes

The first phase comprised 5 frigates of US design and 4 submarines of French design.
The second phase, approved in Jan 1972, provides for 3 guided missile armed destroyers, 2 fleet submarines, 10 corvettes, 13 heavy patrol vessels, 10 light patrol vessels, 6 missile boats, 2 logistic support ships for submarines and minesweepers, 1 survey ship and 1 auxiliary, a total of 48 ships by 1979.
Under the Agreement of 6 Aug 1970 the USA agreed to provide 2 submarines, 5 destroyers, 4 MSO's, 3 LST's, 1 AE and 1 AO. Except for the last two all these ships were transferred in 1971-72.

Mercantile Marine

Lloyd's Register of Shipping:
2 313 vessels of 4 300 055 tons gross

Disposals

Cruisers

1956 *Navarra*
1963 *Mendez Nuñez*
1966 *Am. Cervera, Galicia, Miguel de Cervantes*

Destroyers

1957 *Lepanto, Alcala Gallano, Am. Valdes, Alsedo, Velasco*
1958 *Ciscar*
1959 *Jorge Juan*
1961 *Lazaga*
1964 *Escaña, Gravina, Ulloa, Churruca*
1965 *Sanchez Barcaiztegui*
1968 *Martin A. Pinzon, Pizarro*
1969 *Am. Antequere*
1970 *Am. Miranda*
1971 *Magallanes, Vasco Nuñez de Balbao, Hernan Cortes*
1972 *Sarmiento de Gambos*

Frigates

1957 *Calvo Sotelo*
1959 *Canovas del Castilla*
1971 *Mate*
1972 *Neptune, Eolo, Triton*

Submarines

1966 D 1 (S 11)
1971 D 2 (S 21), D 3 (S 22), G 7 (ex-U573 VII C) Midget submarines SA 41 (F 1), SA 42 (F 2)

Minesweepers

1954 *Guadalete* sunk in gale
1971 *Lerez*
1972 *Bidasoa, Nervion, Segura, Tambre, Ter*

Patrol Vessels

1970 *Arcila, Xanen*
1971 *Javier Quiroga*

HELICOPTER CARRIER

Ex-AIRCRAFT CARRIER (CVL)

Name	*No*	*Builders*	*Laid down*	*Launched*	*Completed*
DÉDALO (ex-USS *Cabot*, AVT 3, ex-CVL 28, ex-*Wilmington*, CL 79)	PH 01	New York Shipbuilding Corporation	16 Aug 1942	4 Apr 1943	24 July 1943

Displacement, tons	11 000 standard; 15 800 full load
Length, feet (*metres*)	600·0 (*182·8*) wl; 623·0 (*189·9*) oa
Beam, feet (*metres*)	71·5 (*21·8*) hull
Width, feet (*metres*)	109·0 (*33·2*) extreme
Draught, feet (*metres*)	26·0 (*7·9*)
Aircraft	20 A/S, combat and transport helicopters
Guns	26—40 mm AA (2 quadruple, 9 twin)
Armour	2 to 5 in sides; 2 to 3 in deck
Main engines	GE geared turbines; 4 shafts; 100 000 shp
Speed, knots	32 sea, 33·5 max
Boilers	4 Babcock & Wilcox
Range, miles	7 200 at 15 knots
Oil fuel, tons	1 800
Complement	800 (50 officers, 750 men)

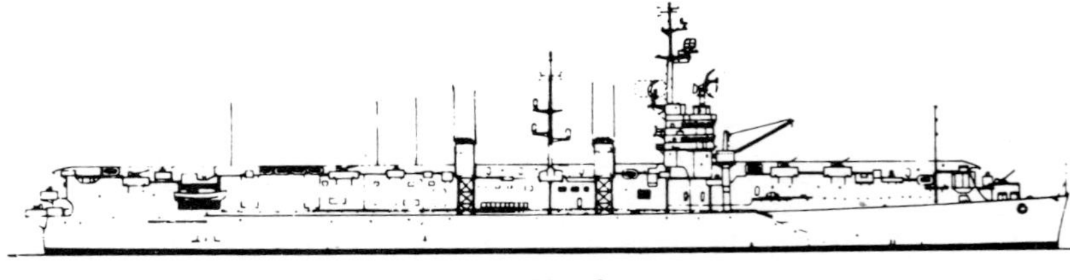
DEDALO

Completed as an aircraft carrier from the hull of a "Cleveland" class cruiser. Originally carried over 40 aircraft. Converted with strengthened flight and hangar decks, large port side catapult, revised magazine arrangements, new electronic gear, corrected stability to counter added top weight, and 20 aircraft. Since conversion has only two of her original four funnels.

Flight deck: 545 × 108 feet (*166·1 × 32·9 metres*). Reactivated and modernised at Philadelphia Naval Shipyard, where she was transferred to Spain on 30 Aug 1967, on loan for five years.

RADAR. SPS 6 and SPS 40 search radar; SPS 10 tactical; SPS 6 heightfinder.

DEDALO *1969 Spanish Navy*

CRUISER

Name	No.	Builders	Laid down	Launched	Completed
CANARIAS	C 21	Sociedad Espanola de Construction Naval, El Ferrol	15 Aug 1928	28 May 1931	1 Oct 1936

Displacement, tons	10 282 standard; 13 280 full load
Length, feet (*metres*)	636·5 (*194·0*)
Beam, feet (*metres*)	64·0 (*19·5*)
Draught, feet (*metres*)	21·3 (*6·5*)
Guns	8—8 in (*203 mm*) 50 cal (4 twin); 8—4·7 in (*120 mm*) 45 cal. single; 2—1·5 in (*38 mm*) 70 cal AA; 5—40 mm AA; 2—20 mm AA
Armour	sides 1·5—2 in (*38—50 mm*); turrets and deck 1 in (25 *mm*); magazines 4 in (*100 mm*)
Main engines	Parsons geared turbines; 2 shafts; 92 000 shp
Speed, knots	31 max; 11 economical sea
Boilers	8 Yarrow type
Range, miles	8 000 at 15 knots
Oil fuel, tons	2 794
Complement	1 000 (40 officers, 960 men)

This ship was designed by the late Sir Philip Watts on the basic pattern of the contemporary British heavy cruisers of the later "County" classes. From initial completion until 1952 she had trunked funnels, but she emerged from refit in 1953 with two separate funnels, this being a reversion to the original design which had never been carried out.

RADAR. S-band air surveillance; Marconi surface warning/navigation set.

CANARIAS *1970, Spanish Navy*

TORPEDO TUBES. The twelve 21 inch torpedo tubes in four triple mountings were removed in 1960.

GUNNERY. Elevation of the 8 inch guns is 70 degrees.

CLASS. Only sister ship *Baleares* was torpedoed and sunk on 6 Mar 1938 during the Spanish Civil War.

DRAWING. Starboard elevation and plan. Scale 125 feet = 1 inch (1 : 1 500).

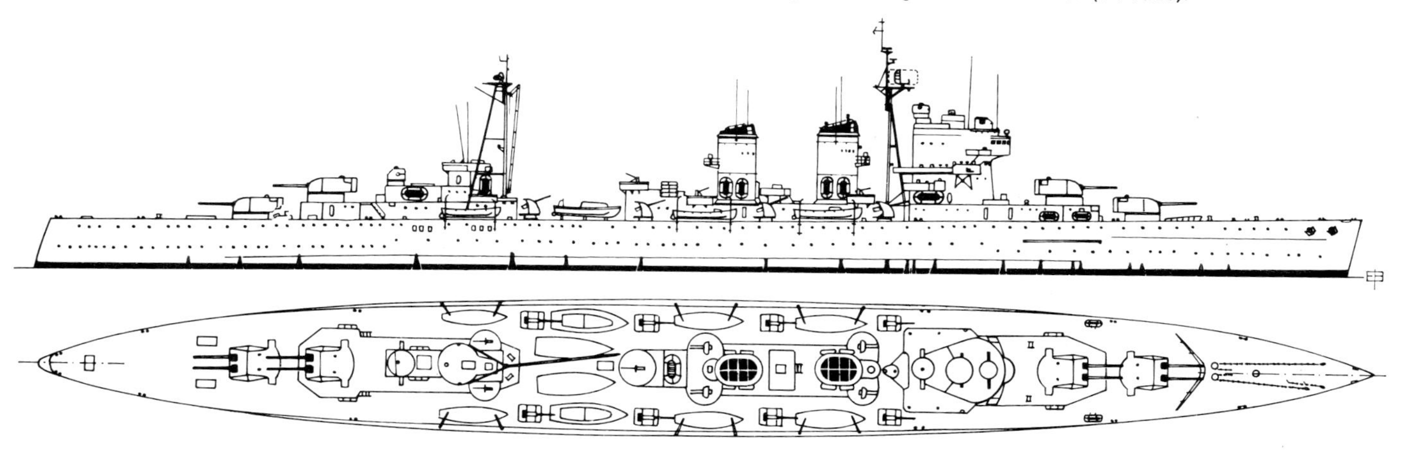

DESTROYERS

5 Ex-US "GEARING" CLASS

Name	No.	Launched	Completed
GRAVINA (ex-USS *Furse*, DD 882)	D 62	9 Mar 1945	10 July 1945
CHURRUCA (ex-USS *Eugene A. Greene* DD 711)	D 61	18 Mar 1945	8 June 1945
(ex-USS *James E. Kyes* ,DD 787)		14 Aug 1945	8 Feb 1946
(ex-USS *Shelton*, DD 790)		8 Mar 1946	21 June 1946
(ex-USS *Hanson*, DD 832)		11 Mar 1945	11 May 1945

Displacement, tons	2 425 standard; 3 480 full load
Length, feet (*metres*)	390·5 (*119·0*) oa
Beam, feet (*metres*)	40·9 (*12·4*)
Draught, feet (*metres*)	19 (*5·8*)
Guns	4—5 in (*127 mm*) 38 cal DP twin
A/S weapons	1 Asroc launcher 2 Triple Mk 32 tubes; Facilities for small helicopter
Main engines	2 geared turbines (GE or Westinghouse) 60 000 shp; 2 shafts
Boilers	4 Babcock and Wilcox
Speed, knots	34
Range, miles	4 800 at 15 knots
Complement	274

Transferred as follows—first pair 31 Aug 1972, Last ships March 1973.

2 MODIFIED "OQUENDO" TYPE

Name	No.	Laid down	Launched	Completed
MARQUÉS DE LA ENSENADA	D 43	4 Sep 1951	15 July 1959	(D 43) 30 Aug 1970
ROGER DE LAURIA	D 42	4 Sep 1951	12 Nov 1958	(D 42) 22 Dec 1969

Displacement, tons	3 000 standard; 3 587 full load
Lenght, feet (*metres*)	391·5 (*119·3*)
Beam, feet (*metres*)	42·7 (*13·0*)
Draught, feet (*metres*)	18·4 (*5·6*)
Aircraft	1 anti-submarine helicopter
Guns	6—5 in (*127 mm*) 38 cal (3 twin)
A/S weapons	2 triple launchers for 324 mm homing torpedoes
Torpedo tubes	2—21 in (*533 mm*) fixed single
Main engines	2 Rateau-Bretagne geared turbines; 2 shafts; 60 000 shp
Speed, knots	31
Boilers	3 three-drum type
Oil fuel, tons	673
Range, miles	4 500 at 15 knots
Complement	296 (20 officers, 276 men)

Ordered at Ferrol in 1948. Originally of the same design as *Oquendo*, see next page. Towed to Cartagena for reconstruction to a new design. *Roger de Lauria* was re-launched after being lengthened and widened on 29 Aug 1967 and *Marqués de la Ensenada* on 2 Mar 1968. *Roger de Lauria* started trials on 30 May 1969 and *Marqués de la Ensenada* on 10 Sep 1970, and both ships in service in 1971.

MARQUÉS DE LA ENSENADA, ROGER DE LAURIA

ROGER DE LAURIA *1970, Spanish Navy*

RADAR. Search: SPS 40. Tactical: SPS 10. Fire Control: GFCS 68 system, X Band.

SONAR. One hull, one variable depth towed.

Destroyers—*continued*

8 "AUDAZ" CLASS

Name	No.	Laid down	Launched	Completed
AUDAZ	D 31	26 Sep 1945	24 Jan 1951	30 June 1953
FUROR	D 34	3 Aug 1945	24 Feb 1955	7 Sep 1960
INTRÉPIDO	D 38	14 July 1945	15 Feb 1961	25 Mar 1965
METEORO (ex-*Atrevido*)	D 33	3 Aug 1945	4 Sep 1951	30 Nov 1955
OSADO	D 32	3 Aug 1945	4 Sep 1951	13 Dec 1961
RAYO	D 35	3 Aug 1945	4 Sep 1951	20 May 1958
RELÁMPAGO	D 39	14 July 1945	26 Sep 1961	7 July 1965
TEMERARIO	D 37	14 July 1945	29 Mar 1960	16 Mar 1964

Displacement, tons: 1 227 standard; 1 550 full load
Length, feet (*metres*): 295·2 (*90·0*) pp; 308·2 (*94·0*) oa
Beam, feet (*metres*): 30·5 (*9·3*)
Draught, feet (*metres*): 17·1 (*5·2*) max
Guns: 2—3 in (*76 mm*) 50 cal dp; 2—40 mm 70 cal AA
A/S weapons: 2 Hedgehogs; 8 mortars; 2 DC racks
Torpedo racks: 2 side launching for A/S torpedoes (6 torpedoes)
Main engines: Rateau-Bretagne geared turbines; 2 shafts; 28 000 shp
Speed, knots: 32 (see *Engineering*)
Boilers: 2 La Seine 3-drum type
Range, miles: 3 800 at 15 knots, 900 at 32 knots
Oil fuel, tons: 290
Complement: 198 (13 officers, 185 men)

Based on the French "Le Fier" design. All built at Ferrol. Allocated D Pennant numbers in 1961.

AUDAZ *Class*

MODERNISATION. Delivery dates after modernisation: *Audaz* 28 June 1961, *Furor* 9 Sep 1960, *Meteoro* 21 Feb 1963, *Osado* 21 Aug 1961, *Rayo* 21 Feb 1963. All fitted with US electronic and ASW equipment.

RADAR. Search and tactical: S-band. Fire Control: Mk 63. Surface search; SPS 10.

INTREPIDO — 1969, *Spanish Navy*

ENGINEERING. The boilers are in two compartments separated by the engine rooms. Steam is superheated to 375 degrees Fahrenheit. Working pressure is 500 lb. per sq in. Engines have developed 30 800 shp on trials and 32,500 shp max = 33 knots.

LOSS. Sister ship *Ariete* grounded on 25 Feb 1966 and was declared a total loss.

1 "OQUENDO" TYPE

Name	No.	Laid down	Launched	Completed
OQUENDO	D 41	15 June 1951	5 Sep 1956	22 Dec 1964

Displacement, tons: 2 582 standard; 3 005 full load
Length, feet (*metres*): 382 (*116·4*)
Beam, feet (*metres*): 36·5 (*11·1*)
Draught, feet (*metres*): 12·5 (*3·8*)
Guns: 4—4·7 (*120 mm*) 50 cal (2 twin); 6—40 mm, 70 cal. single
A/S weapons: 2 Hedgehogs
Torpedo racks: 2 Mk 4 with 3 Mk 32 homing torpedoes each
Main engines: 2 Rateau-Bretagne geared turbines; 2 shafts; 60000 shp
Speed, knots: 32·4 max
Boilers: 3 three-drum type
Oil fuel, tons: 659
Range, miles: 5 000 at 15 knots
Complement: 249

OQUENDO — 1971, *Spanish Navy*

Ordered at Ferrol in 1947. Initially completed on 13 Sep 1960. Completed modernisation on 22 Dec 1964.

CONSTRUCTION. Designed as a conventional destroyer but modified during construction. Seven 21-inch torpedo tubes and two depth charge throwers were suppressed in favour of later anti-submarine weapons. *Roger de Lauria* and *Marqués de la Ensenada*, see previous page, were originally of the "Oquendo" design. Sister ships *Blas de Lezo, Blasco de Garay, Bonifaz, Gelmirez, Langara* and *Recalde* were cancelled in 1953.

RADAR. Search: British 293 type. Tactical: 293 type. Fire Control: Mk 8 and close range blind fire British types.

5 "LEPANTO" CLASS

Name	No.	Builders	Laid down	Launched	Completed
ALCALA GALIANO (ex-USS *Jarvis*, DD 799)	D 24	Todd Pacific Shipyards	—	14 Feb 1944	3 June 1944
ALMIRANTE FERRANDIZ (ex-USS *David W. Taylor*, DD 551)	D 22	Gulf SB Corpn, Chickasaw, Ala	12 June 1941	4 July 1942	18 Sep 1943
ALMIRANTE VALDES (ex-USS *Converse*, DD 509)	D 23	Bath Iron Works Corp, Maine	23 Feb 1942	30 Aug 1942	8 June 1943
JORGE JUAN (ex-USS *McGowan*, DD 678)	D 25	Federal SB & DD Co	—	14 Nov 1943	20 Dec 1943
LEPANTO (ex-USS *Capps*, DD 550)	D 21	Gulf SB Corpn, Chickasaw, Ala	12 June 1941	31 May 1942	23 June 1943

Displacement, tons: 2 080 standard; 2 750 normal; 3 050 full load
Length, feet (*metres*): 376·5 (*114·8*) oa
Beam, feet (*metres*): 39·5 (*12·0*)
Draught, feet (*metres*): 18·0 (*5·5*)
Guns, surface: *D21, D22:* 5—5 in (*127 mm*) 38 cal; *Others:* 4—5 in (*127 mm*) single
Guns, AA: *D21, D22:* 6—40 mm, 60 cal, 3 twin; 6—20 mm, 70 cal, single; *Others:* 6—3 in (*76 mm*) 50 cal, 3 twin
A/S weapons: 2 "Hedgehogs"; 6 DCT in D21, D22, 4 in D23; 2 DC racks in D21, D22, 1 in others
Torpedo tubes: 5—21 in (*533 mm*) quintupled in D23 (2 exterior tubes blinded), 3 (tripled) in others
Torpedo racks: 2 side launching Mk 4 each with 3 Mk 32 A/S torpedoes
Main engines: Geared turbines; Westinghouse in D21, D22, GE in others; 2 shafts; 60 000 shp
Speed, knots: 35 max, 16 economical sea
Boilers: 4 Babcock & Wilcox
Range, miles: 5 000 at 15 knots
Oil fuel, tons: 650
Complement: 290 (17 officers, 273 men)

JORGE JUAN (from 5 inch) — 1972, *Spanish Navy*

ALMIRANTE FERRANDIZ, LEPANTO

ALCALA GALIANO, JORGE JUAN, VALDES

Former US destroyers. *Lepanto*, and *Almirante Ferrandiz*, were reconditioned at San Francisco, Cal, and there turned over to the Spanish Navy on 15 May 1957, sailing for Spain on 1 July 1957. *Valdes* was transferred at Philadelphia on 1 July 1959. *Jorge Juan*, was transferred at Barcelona on 1 Dec 1960 and *Alcala Galiano*, at Philadelphia on 3 Nov 1960, both being of the later "Fletcher" class.

RADAR. Search. SPS 6C. Tactical: SPS 10. Fire Control: Mk 37 with round scanner in D 21, D 22; GFCS 68, Mk 37 and Mk 56, and 2 Mk 63 for 3 in guns.

Destroyers—*continued*

2 "ALAVA" CLASS

Name	No.	Builders	Laid down	Launched	Completed	Modernised
ALAVA	D 52 (ex-23)	Cartagena	21 Dec 1944	19 May 1947	21 Dec 1950	17 Jan 1962
LINIERS	D 51 (ex-21)	Cartagena	1 Jan 1945	1 May 1946	27 Jan 1951	18 Sep 1962

Displacement, tons	1 842 standard; 2 287 full load
Length, feet (*metres*)	336·3 (*102·5*)
Beam, feet (*metres*)	31·5 (*9·6*)
Draught, feet (*metres*)	19·7 (*6·0*)
Guns	3—3 in (*76 mm*) 50 cal, Mk 22; 3—40 mm, 70 cal AA
A/S weapons	2 "Hedgehogs"; 8 DC mortars; 2 DC racks
Torpedo racks	2 side launching, 6 A/S torpedoes
Main engines	Parsons geared turbines; 2 shafts; 31 500 shp
Speed, knots	29 max, 12 economical sea
Boilers	4 Yarrow 3-drum type
Range, miles	4 100 at 15 knots
Oil fuel, tons	370
Complement	224 (17 officers, 207 men

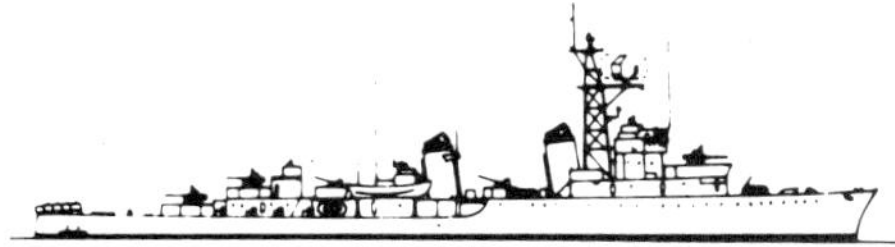

ALAVA, LINIERS

LINIERS — *1972, Admiral M. Adam*

Ordered in 1936, but construction was held up by the Civil War. After being resumed, was again suspended in 1940, but restarted at Empresa Nacional Bazan in 1944.

RADAR. Search and Tactical: S-band. Fire Control: Mk 63.

TORPEDO TUBES. These ships have had no tubes since modernisation in 1962. They formerly carried 6—21 inch (tripled), but now have torpedo racks.

GUNNERY. Before modernisation these ships mounted 4—4·7 inch, 6—37 mm AA and 3—20 mm AA guns.

FRIGATES

5 "BALEARES" CLASS

Name	No	Laid down	Launched	Completed
ANDALUCIA	F 72 (DEG 8)	2 July 1969	30 Mar 1971	to be 1974
ASTURIAS	F 74 (DEG 10)	30 Mar 1971	May 1972	to be 1975
BALEARES	F 71 (DEG 7)	31 Oct 1968	20 Aug 1970	to be 1974
CATALUÑA	F 73 (DEG 9)	20 Aug 1970	3 Nov 1971	to be 1975
ESTREMADURA	F 75 (DEG 11)	3 Nov 1971	Jan 1973	to be 1976

Displacement, tons	3 000 standard; 4 100 full load
Length, feet (*metres*)	415·0 (*126·5*)pp; 438·0 (*133·5*)oa
Beam, feet (*metres*)	46·9 (*14·3*)
Draught, feet (*metres*)	25·9 (*7·9*) max
Missile launchers	1 single for "Standard" missiles
Guns	1—5 in (*127 mm*) 54 cal dp
A/S weapons	1 eight-tube ASROC launcher
Torpedo tubes	4 anti-submarine (2 twin); 2 general purpose (single)
Main engines	1 set geared turbines; 1 shaft; 35 000 shp
Boilers	2 high pressure V2M type; 1 200 psi (84·4 *kg/cm²*)
Speed, knots	28 plus (sea)
Range	Over 4 000 miles at 20 knots
Complement	256 (15 officers, 241 men)

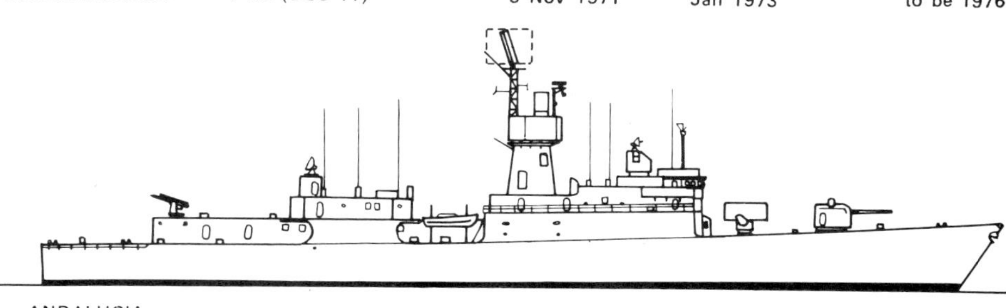

ANDALUCIA — 1973

In June 1966 Spain and USA signed an agreement for the construction of five frigates in Spain with technical and material assistance by USA. Being built by Empresa Nacional Bazán at El Ferrol. Generally similar in appearance to the US escort ships of the "Knox" class but with modified weapons system and other characteristics to meet the requirements of the Spanish Navy. Equipped with weapons and electronic equipment furnished by USA, including anti-submarine warfare torpedoes and rockets.

RADAR. Search: SPS 52 (3D). Tactical: SPS 10. Fire Control: SPG 51 continuous wave.

SONAR. SQS 23 bow mounted; SQA 13 VDS.

2 "PIZARRO" CLASS

Name	No.	Launched	Completed
LEGAZPI	F 42	8 Aug 1944	8 Aug 1951
VICENTE YAÑEZ PINZON	F 41	3 Aug 1944	5 Aug 1949

Displacement, tons	1 924 standard; 2 228 full load
Length, feet (*metres*)	279·0 (*85·0*) pp; 312·5 (*95·3*) oa
Beam, feet (*metres*)	39·5 (*12·0*)
Draught, feet (*metres*)	17·7 (*5·4*)
Guns, surface	2—5 in (*127 mm*) 38 cal.
Guns, AA	4—40 mm, 70 cal.
A/S weapons	2 "Hedgehogs"; 8 mortars; 2 racks
Torpedo racks	2 side launching for A/S
Main engines	2 sets Parsons geared turbines; 2 shafts; 6 000 shp
Speed, knots	18·5
Boilers	2 Yarrow type
Range, miles	3 000 at 15 knots
Oil fuel, tons	390
Complement	291 (14 officers, 277 men)

LEGAZPI, VICENTE YANEZ PINZON

VICENTE YAÑEZ PINZON — *1971, Spanish Navy*

All built at Ferrol. Originally designed to carry 30 mines *Legazpi* and *Vicente Yañez Pinzon* completed modernisation on 14 Jan and 25 Mar 1960 respectively. S-band search and SPS-10 tactical radar. Of five sister ships *Martin Aloñso Pinzon* and *Pizarro* were discarded in 1968, *Magallanes* and *Vasco Nuñez de Balboa* were removed from the active list in 1971, and *Hernan Cortes* on 2 Dec 1971. *Sarmiento de Gamboa* discarded in 1972.

"JUPITER" CLASS

Name	No.	Launched	Completed
JUPITER	F 11	14 Sep 1935	1937
VULCANO	F 12	12 Oct 1935	1937

Displacement, tons	2 103 standard; 2 360 full load
Length, feet (*metres*)	302·8 (*92·3*) pp; 328·1 (*100·0*) oa
Beam, feet (*metres*)	41·5 (*12·6*)
Draught, feet (*metres*)	11·5 (*3·5*)
Guns	4—3 in (*76 mm*) Mk 26, single; 4—40 mm, 70 cal AA
A/S weapons	2 "Hedgehogs"; 8 mortars; 2 DC racks
Mines	*Jupiter* 254, *Vulcano* 238
Main engines	2 sets Parsons geared turbines; 2 shafts; 5 000 shp
Speed, knots	17·4 max, 10 economical sea
Boilers	2 Yarrow type
Range, miles	5 700 at 12 knots
Oil fuel, tons	340
Complement	243 (16 officers, 227 men)

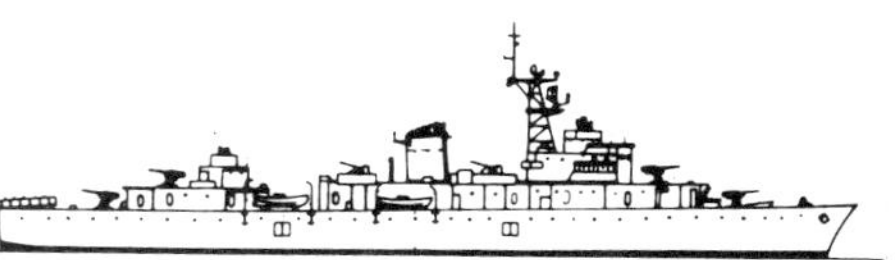

JUPITER, VULCANO

Both built by the Sociedad Española de Construccion Naval, Ferrol. Originally multi-purpose frigates or

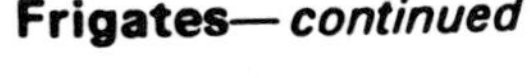

Frigates—*continued*

gunboats and cruising type minelayers. Latterly classified as frigate minelayers, but now officially re-classified as frigates. The modernisation of *Jupiter* with lattice mast and four 3-inch guns was completed on 28 Oct 1960, and of *Vulcano* on 28 Feb 1961. Both allocated F pennant numbers in 1961.

RADAR. Search: S band. Tactical: SPS 10. Fire Control: Mk 51 and Mk 52.

VULCANO *1971, Spanish Navy*

CORVETTES

5 "ATREVIDA" CLASS

Name	No.	Laid down	Launched	Completed
ATREVIDA	F 61	26 June 1950	2 Dec 1952	19 Aug 1954
DIANA	F 63	27 July 1953	29 Apr 1955	13 May 1960
NAUTILUS	F 64	27 July 1953	23 Aug 1956	15 Dec 1959
PRINCESA	F 62	18 Mar 1953	31 Mar 1956	3 Oct 1959
VILLA DE BILBAO	F 65	18 Mar 1953	19 Feb 1958	2 July 1960

Displacement, tons	1 031 standard; 1 135 full load
Length, feet (*metres*)	247·8 (*75·5*) oa
Beam, feet (*metres*)	33·5 (*10·2*)
Draught, feet (*metres*)	9·8 (*3·0*)
Guns	1—3 in (*76 mm*) 50 cal dp; 3—40 mm, 70 cal AA
A/S weapons	2 Hedgehogs; 8 mortars; 2 DC racks
Mines	20 can be carried
Main engines	Sulzer diesels; 2 shafts; 3 000 bhp
Speed, knots	18·5 max
Range, miles	8 000 at 10 knots
Oil fuel, tons	100
Complement	113 (10 officers, 103 men)

ATREVIDA *Class*

ATREVIDA *1971, Michael D. J. Lennon*

Atrevida commissioned on 19 Aug 1954. All have been modernised since 1959, *Princesa* being delivered on 3 Oct 1959, *Nautilus* on 10 Dec 1959, *Diana* on 13 May 1960, *Atrevida* on 14 June 1960 and *Villa de Bilbao* on 2 Sep 1960. No funnel, the diesel exhaust being on the starboard side waterline. Combined air and surface search radar. Allocated F pennant numbers in 1961. SPS 10 radar.

CLASS. The sixth ship of this class *Descubierta*, F 51 the only one not modernised, was officially removed from the effective list in 1971.

SUBMARINES

NEW CONSTRUCTION
4 FRENCH "DAPHNE" TYPE

No.	Builders	Laid down	Launched	Completed
S 61	E.N. Bazan, Cartagena	13 Aug 1968	1972	1973
S 62	E.N. Bazan, Cartagena	1969	1972	1973
S 63	E.N. Bazan, Cartagena	1972	to be 1973	to be 1974
S 64	E.N. Bazan, Cartagena	1972	to be 1973	to be 1974

Displacement, tons	870 surface; 1 040 submerged
Length, feet (*metres*)	189·6 (*57·8*)
Beam, feet (*metres*)	22·3 (*6·8*)
Draught, feet (*metres*)	15·1 (*4·6*)
Tubes	12—21·7 in (*550 mm*) (8 bow, 4 stern)
Main engines	SEMT- Pielstick diesel-electric; 1 300 bhp surface; 1 600 hp submerged; 2 shafts
Speed, knots	13 on surface; 15·5 submerged
Range, miles	3 000 at 7 knots 4 500 at 5 knots
Complement	50 (5 officers, 45 men)

Basically similar to the French "Daphne" class and being built with extensive French assistance n the Cartagena Yard.

"DAPHNE" TYPE *1971*

1 Ex-US "BALAO" CLASS

ALMIRANTE GARCIA DE LOS REYES S31
(ex-USS *Kraken, SS* 370)

Displacement, tons	1 880 surface; 2 ;60 submerged
Length, feet (*metres*)	311·5 (*95·0*)
Beam, feet (*metres*)	27·2 (*8·3*)
Draught, feet (*metres*)	17·2 (*5·2*)
Torpedo tubes	6—21 in (*533 mm*), and 4 for acoustic torpedoes
Main engines	4 diesels, total 6 400 bhp; 2 shafts; 2 electric motors, 4 600 shp
Speed, knots	20 on surface; 10 submerged
Oil fuel, tons	300
Range, miles	12 000 at 10 knots
Complement	80

ALMIRANTE GARCIA DE LOS REYES *1969, Spanish Navy*

Former US Navy submarine of the "Balao" class. Built by Manitowoc SB Co. Launched on 30 Apr 1944 and completed on 8 Sep 1944. Transferred on 24 Oct 1959 after modernisation and overhaul at Pearl Harbour.

Submarines—*continued*

3 Ex-US "BALAO" GUPPY IIA TYPE

Name	No.	Ex-Name & No.	Laid down	Launched	Completed
ISAAC PERAL	S 32	(ex-USS *Ronquil*, SS 396)	9 Sep 1943	27 June 1944	23 Apr 1944
NARCISO MONTURIOL	S 33	(ex-USS *Picuda*, SS 382)	15 Mar 1943	12 July 1943	16 Oct 1943
COSME GARCIA	S 34	(ex-USS *Bang*, SS 385)			

Displacement, tons	1 840 surface; 2 445 submerged
Length, feet (*metres*)	306·0 (*93·3*) oa
Beam, feet (*metres*)	27·0 (*8·2*)
Draught, feet (*metres*)	17·0 (*5·2*)
Torpedo tubes	10—21 in (*533 mm*), 6 bow, 4 stern
Main engines	3 diesels; total 4 800 bhp; 2 shafts; 2 electric motors; 5 400 shp
Speed, knots	18 on surface; 15 submerged
Range, miles	12 000 at 10 knots
Complement	84

Built by Portsmouth Navy Yard. Transferred to Spain on 1 July 1971 (*Ronquil*) 1 Oct 1972 (*Bang* and *Picuda*).

PICUDA (before transfer) *Added 1972, Dr. Giorgio Arra*

2 "TIBURON" CLASS

SA 51 **SA 52**

Displacement, tons	78 surface; 81 submerged
Length, feet (*metres*)	70·5 (*21·5*)
Beam, feet (*metres*)	9 (*2·7*)
Draught, feet (*metres*)	9 (*2·7*)
Torpedo tubes	2—21 in (*533 mm*)
Main engines	Pegaso diesels; 400 hp Electric motors; 400 hp
Speed, knots	10 on surface; 14·5 submerged
Range, miles	2 000 at 6 knots (surfaced) 150 at 7 knots (dived)
Complement	5

Midget submarines launched in 1958. Originally rated as *Submarinos Experimentales*, but in 1963 designated Assault Submarines with "SA" numbers.
ENGINEERING. The diesels were built by ENASA (formerly Hispano-Suiza) Barcelona, 200 hp each, at 2 000 rpm, with reduction gear on the single screw disposed in a nozzle in continuation of the conic after hull.

LIGHT FORCES

LT 30 **LT 31** **LT 32**

3 TORPEDO BOATS

Displacement, tons	100 standard; 116 full load
Dimensions, feet	114 × 16·8 × 5
Gun	1—20 mm AA
Tubes	2—21 in
Main engines	3 diesel; 3 shafts; 7 500 bhp = 41 knots
Oil fuel, tons	20
Range, miles	650 at 30 knots
Complement	26

Built at La Carraca, Cadiz, to the design of Lurssens of Bremen. LT 31 was commissioned on 21 July 1956. L 32 was launched in 1956, (photograph in 1960-61 to 1966-67 editions). LT 27, LT 28 and LT 29 were discarded in 1963.

LT 31 *1970, Spanish Navy*

LA COMBATTANTE II TYPE

Several of these missile boats are to be built by France for Spain under an agreement signed between M. Debré and Sr. Lopez Bravo on 15 Feb 1973. Will probably mount Otomat SSMs.

CANDIDO PEREZ (ex-*SC* 679)

Displacement, tons	108 standard; 138 full load
Dimensions, feet	107·5 wl; 111·0 oa × 19·0 × 7·0
Guns	1—40 mm AA; 3—20 mm AA
A/S weapons	2 DCT; 2 Mouse Trap Mk 20
Main engines	GM diesels; 2 shafts; 1 000 bhp = 15·6 knots
Range, miles	2 300 at 10 knots

Built by Walter E. Abrams Shipyard, Inc. Laid down on 4 Mar 1942. Launched on 29 Aug 1942. Completed on 19 Dec 1942. Transferred to Spain on 24 Oct 1956 by USA. Frogmen tender.

CANDIDO PEREZ *Spanish Navy*

CABO FRADERA

Displacement, tons	25 standard; 28 full load
Dimensions, feet	58·5 × 14 × 5·2
Main engines	2 diesels; 760 bhp = 12 knots
Complement	9

Built at La Carraca, in 1963. (River patrol boat *Cabo Fradera* was disposed of)

LAS 10 (ex-LAS 1) **LAS 20** (ex-LAS 2) **LAS 30** (ex-LAS 3)

Displacement, tons	49 standard; 63 full load
Dimensions, feet	78·0 pp; 83·3 oa × 16·1 × 6·6
Guns	1—20 mm AA; 2—7 mm (single)
A/S launchers	2 Mk 20 for 8 light rockets of "Hedgehog" type
Main engines	800 bhp = 15 knots
Complement	15

Seaward defence vessels. Of wooden hull construction. First units were built by E. N. Bazan, Cadiz in 1963-64. There are also five smaller launches, LPI 1 to LPI 5, of 25 tons, 16 knots, 46·0 × 15·4 feet.

LAS 10 *1971*

CENTINELA W 21 **SERVIOLA** W 22

Displacement, tons	255 standard, 282 full load
Dimensions, feet	117·5 × 22·5 × 9·8
Guns	2—37 mm
Main engines	1 diesel; 430 bhp = 12 knots

Completed at Ferrol, in 1953. Trawlers rated as Fishery Protection Vessels (*Guardapescas*). Given pennant numbers as above in 1972.

SERVIOLA *1969, Spanish Navy*

Light Forces—*continued*

PEGASO **PROCYON**

Displacement, tons	436 standard; 498 full load
Dimensions, feet	137·8 × 27·0 × 9·5
Guns	2—20 mm AA
Main engines	Reciprocating; 1 shaft; 532 bhp = 12 knots
Fuel, tons	200 coal
Range, miles	3 500 at 9 knots
Complement	39

Both were commissioned at Cartegena in Jan 1951. Attached to the Naval School.

PROCYON *1971, Spanish Navy*

AZOR

Displacement, tons	442 standard; 486 full load
Dimensions, feet	153·0 × 25·2 × 12·5
Main engines	2 diesels; 1 200 bhp = 12 knots
Range, miles	4 000

Originally a Fishery Protection Vessel (*Guardapescas*). Used as the Caudillo's yacht. Built by E. N. Bazan at El Ferrol. Launched on 9 June 1949. Commissioned on 20 July 1949. Underwent an extensive refit, her hull being cut to admit an extension in length.

AZOR *1969, Spanish Navy.*

CIES W 31 **SALVORA** W 32

Displacement, tons	180 standard; 275 full load
Dimensions, feet	107·0 × 20·5 × 9·0
Guns	1—20 mm MG
Main engines	1 Sulzer diesel; 400 bhp = 12 knots
Complement	24

Purchased in Dec 1952. Trawlers rated as Fishery Protection Vessels

SALVORA *1969, Spanish Navy*

MINEWARFARE FORCES

4 Ex-US "AGILE" CLASS (MSO)

Name	*No.*	*Ex-Name & No.*		*Launched*	*Completed*
GUADALETE	M 41	*Dynamic*	MSO 432	17 Dec 1952	15 Dec 1953
GUADALMEDINA	M 42	*Pivot*	MSO 463	9 Jan 1954	12 July 1954
GUADALQUIVIR	M 43	*Persistant*	MSO 491	23 Apr 1955	3 Feb 1956
GUADIANA	M 44	*Vigor*	MSO 473	24 June 1953	8 Nov 1954

Minewarfare Forces—*continued*

Displacement, tons	665 standard; 750 full load
Dimensions, feet	165·0 wl; 172·0 oa × 36·0 × 13·6
Guns	1—40 mm AA; 2—20 mm AA
Main engines	4 Packard diesels; 2 shafts; controllable pitch propellers; 2 280 bhp = 15·5 knots
Range, miles	3 000 at 10 knots
Complement	71 (6 officers, 65 men)

The first three were transferred and commissioned on 1 July 1971. The fourth unit was delivered in April 1972. SPS 10 surface search radar.

GUADALQUIVIR (as *Persistant*) *1972*

7 "GUADIARO" CLASS (MSO)

Name	*No.*	*Builders*	*Launched*	*Completed*	*Modernised*
ALMANZORA	M 14	Cartagena	27 July 1953	Nov 1954	20 May 1960
EO	M 17	Cadiz	22 Sep 1953	Mar 1955	22 Mar 1961
EUME	M 13	Cartagena	27 July 1953	Dec 1953	20 July 1960
GUADALHORCE	M 16	Cartagena	18 Feb 1953	Dec 1953	18 Feb 1960
GUADIARO	M 11	Cartagena	26 June 1950	Apr 1953	14 Dec 1959
NAVIA	M 15	Cadiz	28 July 1953	Mar 1955	22 Nov 1960
TINTO	M 12	Cartagena	26 June 1950	May 1953	28 July 1959

Displacement, tons	671 standard; 770 full load
Dimensions, feet	243·8 × 33·5 × 12·3 max
Guns	2—20 mm AA
Main engines	Triple expansion and exhaust turbines; 2 shafts; 2 400 hp = 13 knots after modernisation
Boilers	2 Yarrow
Oil fuel, tons	90
Range, miles	1 000 at 6 knots
Complement	79

ALMANZORA *1971 Aldo Fraccaroli*

12 Ex-US AMS TYPE (CMS)

DUERO (ex-*Spoonbill, MSC* 202)	M 28	**NALÓN** (ex-*AMS* 139)	M 21
EBRO (ex-*MSC* 269)	M 26	**ODIEL** (ex-*MSC* 288)	M 32
GENIL (ex-*MSC* 279)	M 31	**SIL** (ex-*Redwing, MSC* 200)	M 29
JUCAR (ex-*AMS* 220)	M 23	**TAJO** (ex-*MSC* 287)	M 30
LLOBREGAT (ex-*AMS* 143)	M 22	**TURIA** (ex-*AMS* 130)	M 27
MIÑO (ex-*AMS* 266)	M 22	**ULLA** (ex-*AMS* 265)	M 24

Displacement, tons	355 standard; 384 full load
Dimensions, feet	138·0 pp; 144·0 oa × 27·2 × 8·0
Guns	2—20 mm AA (1 twin)
A/S weapons	2 Mouse Trap Mk 20 rocket launchers
Main engines	2 diesels; 2 shafts; 900 bhp = 14 knots
Oil fuel, tons	30
Range, miles	2 700 at 10 knots
Complement	39

EBRO, Class A, small crane *1970, Spanish Navy*

Minewarfare Forces—*continued*

Transferred from the USA, *Nalón* on 16 Feb 1954, *Llobregat* on 5 Nov 1954, *Turia* on 1 June 1955, *Jucar* on 22 June 1956, *Ulla* on 24 July 1956, *Miño* on 25 Oct 1956, *Sil* and *Duero* on 16 June 1959, *Ebro* on 19 Dec 1958, *Genil* on 11 Sep 1959, *Tajo* on 9 July 1959 and *Odiel* on 9 Oct 1959.

Two sub-types: with crane at mainmast: M 21, 22, 23, 24, 25, 27, 28, 29; with small crane abreast the funnel: M 26, 30, 31, 32. Tactical radar of various types. AN/UQS-1 sonar.

ULLA, Class B, with mainmast *1971, Spanish Navy*

AMPHIBIOUS VESSELS

1 Ex-US "CASA GRANDE" CLASS (LSD)

GALICIA TA 31 (ex-USS *San Marcos*, LSD 25)

Displacement, tons	4 790 standard; 9 375 full load
Dimensions, feet	475·4 oa × 76·2 × 18·0 max
Guns	12—40 mm, 60 cal AA (2 quadruple, 2 twin)
Main engines	Geared turbines; 2 shafts; 7 000 shp = 15·4 knots
Boilers	2
Range, miles	8 000 at 15 knots
Complement	265 (15 officers, 250 men)

Transferred to Spain on 1 July 1971. Fitted with helicopter platform. Can carry 3 LCUs or 18 LCMs.

GALICIA (as *San Marcos*) *A. & J. Pavia*

3 Ex-US LST

CONDE DE VENADITO L 13 (ex-USS *Tom Green County*, LST 1159)
MARTIN ALVAREZ L 12 (ex-USS *Wexford County*, LST 1168)
VELASCO L 11 (ex-USS *Terrebonne Parish*, LST 1156)

Displacement, tons	2 590 standard; 5 800 full load
Dimensions, feet	384·0 oa × 55·0 × 17·0
Guns	6—3 in, 50 cal (3 twin, 2 forward, 1 aft)
Main engines	4 GM diesels; 2 shafts; 6 000 bhp = 15 knots
Range, miles	15 000 at 9 knots
Complement	116 (troops 395)

LST 1156 transferred on 1 June 1971, LST 1159 and LST 1168 on 29 Oct 1971.

VELASCO (as *Terrebonne Parish*) *A. & J. Pavia*

LSM 1 (ex-USS *LSM* 329) **LSM 2** (ex-USS *LSM* 331) **LSM 3** (ex-USS *LSM* 343)

Displacement, tons	930 standard; 1 094 full load
Dimensions, feet	196·5 wl × 203·5 oa × 34·5 × 8·3
Guns	1—40 mm AA; 2—40 mm AA
Main engines	2 diesels; 2 shafts; 3 600 bhp = 12·5 knots

Medium landing ships transferred at Bremerton, Washington, on 25 Mar 1960. A photograph of LSM 2 appears in the 1965-66 to 1967-68 editions.

Amphibious Vessels—*continued*

LSM 3 *1969*

BDK 1 **BDK 2** **BDK 3** **BDK 4** **BDK 5**

Displacement, tons	440 to 481 standard; 868 to 894 full load
Dimensions, feet	187·0 × 38·8 × 5·5
Main engines	2 diesels; 2 shafts; 920 to 1 000 bhp = 7 to 10 knots
Range, miles	1 000 at 7 knots

BDK 3 to 5 were built by Bazan, Ferrol. BDK 1 and 2 are British built LCT (4).

BDK 5 *1971, Spanish Navy*

BDK 6 **BDK 7** **BDK 8** +2

Displacement, tons	315 standard; 665 full load
Dimensions, feet	193·5 × 39·0 × 5·0
Guns	1—20 mm AA; 2—12·7 mm AA MG
Main engines	2 diesels; 2 shafts; 1 040 bhp = 9·5 knots
Range, miles	1 500 at 9 knots

Landing craft of the French EDIC type built at La Carraca. Completed in Dec 1966.

K 6 *1970, Spanish Navy*

SURVEY SHIPS

CASTOR H 4 **POLLUX** H 5

Displacement, tons	327 standard; 383 full load
Dimensions, feet	111 pp; 125·9 oa × 24·9 × 8·9
Main engines	1 Sulzer 4TD-36 diesel; 720 hp = 11·7 knots
Range, miles	3 620 at 8 knots
Complement	36

Built by E. N. Bazan La Carraca. Completed on 10 Nov 1966 and 6 Dec 1966.

CASTOR *1970, Spanish Navy*

TOFINO

Displacement, tons	998 standard; 1 255 full load
Dimensions, feet	224·5 × 35 × 11
Gun	1—37 mm
Main engines	Triple expansion; 2 shafts; 810 ihp = 12·5 knots
Boilers	2 Yarrow
Complement	88

Built at Ferrol. Launched on 21 Aug 1933. Sister ship *Malaspina* (ex-*Bausa*) was officially deleted from the effective list in 1971.

Survey Ships—*continued*

TOFINO *1970, Professor Alfredo Aguileru*

JUAN DE LA COSA (ex-*Artabro*)

Displacement, tons	770 standard; 1 100 full load
Dimensions, feet	188 × 35·5 × 8·8
Main engines	B & W diesels; electric drive; 500 bhp = 9 knots
Complement	51

Launched by UNL, Valence in 1935. The small survey craft *H 2* and *H 3* (see photograph in the 1969-70 edition) were withdrawn from the active list in 1969-70.

JUAN DE LA COSA *1969, Spanish Navy*

TRANSPORTS

ALMIRANTE LOBO (ex-*Torrelaguna*)

Displacement, tons	5 662 standard; 8 038 full load
Dimensions, feet	362·5 × 48·2 × 25·7
Guns	1—1·5 in, 85 cal
Main engines	1 triple expansion; 2 000 ihp = 12 knots

Ex-cargo vessel. Built at Astilleros Echevarrieta, Cadiz. Commissioned 4 Oct 1954.

ALMIRANTE LOBO

1 Ex-US "HASKELL" CLASS

ARAGON TA 11) ex-USS *Noble*, APA 218)

Displacement, tons	6 720 light; 12 450 full load
Dimensions, feet	436·5 wl; 455 oa × 63·5 × 24 max
Main engines	Geared turbines; 8 500 shp = 17 knots
Boilers	2 Babcock & Wi cox
Range, miles	14 700 at 16 knots

Former US Attack Transport, transferred at San Francisco on 19 Dec 1964.

ARAGON *1971, Michael D. J. Lennon*

Transports—*continued*

1 Ex-US "ANDROMEDA" CLASS

CASTILLA TA 21 (ex-USS *Achernar*, AKA 53)

Displacement, tons	7 430 light; 11 416 full load
Dimensions, feet	435 wl; 457·8 oa × 63 × 24
Guns	1—5 in, 38 cal; 8—40 mm, 60 cal
Main engines	2 GE geared turbines; 12 000 shp = 16 knots
Boilers	2 Foster-Wheeler

Former US Attack Cargo Ship, transferred at New York on 2 Feb 1965.

CASTILLA *1970, Spanish Navy*

TRAINING SHIP

JUAN SEBASTIAN DE ELCANO

Displacement, tons	3 420 standard, 3 754 full load
Dimensions, feet	269·2 pp; 308·5 oa × 43 × 23 full load
Guns	2—37 mm
Main engines	1 Sulzer diesel; 1 shaft; 1 500 bhp = 9·5 knots
Oil fuel, tons	230
Endurance, miles	10 000 at 9·5 knots
Complement	224 + 80 cadets

Four masted schooner. Named after the first circumnavigator of the world (1519-26) who succeeded to the command of the expedition led by Magallanes after the latter's death. Built by Echevarrieta Yard, Cadiz. Launched on 5 Mar 1927. Completed in 1928.

JUAN SEBASTIAN DE ELCANO *1972 US Navy*

COASTAL LAUNCHES

V 2	Displacement: 22 tons	Guns: 1—7 mm	Speed: 6·7 knots
V 4	Displacement: 65 tons	Guns: 1—7 mm	Speed: 9 knots
V 5	Displacement: 4·5 tons	Guns: 1—7 mm	Speed: 5 knots
V 6	Displacement: 42 tons	Guns: 2—20 mm	Speed: 19·2 knots
V 7	Displacement: 20 tons	Guns: 1—7 mm	Speed: 8·5 knots
V 8	Displacement: 26·5 tons	Guns: 1—7 mm	Speed: 7·8 knots
V 9	Displacement: 15·6 tons	Guns: 1—7 mm	Speed: 9 knots
V 10	Displacement: 11·69 tons	Guns: 1—7 mm	Speed: 9·5 knots
V 11	Displacement: 11·69 tons	Guns: 1—7 mm	Speed: 9·5 knots
V 12	Displacement: 28 tons	Guns: 1—7 mm	Speed: 7·8 knots
V 13	Displacement: 45·1 tons	Guns: 1—7 mm	Speed: 7·8 knots
V 17	Displacement: 110·9 tons	Guns: 1—20 mm	Speed: 10·5 knots
V 18	Displacement: 116 tons	Guns: 1—13 mm	Speed: 6 knots
V 21	Displacement: 16 tons	Guns: 1—13 mm	Speed: 17·6 knots

Coastal Launches—*continued*

LANZON (V 18) *1969, Spanish Navy*

There are also V 1, yacht, ex-*Azor*, and V 6 (ex-V 22, 25 metres, 2 diesels, 800 bhp, see above). Coastal launches employed on surveillance and fishery protection duties, *Lanchos guardapescas*, except V 17 and V 21, rated as *patrulleros*. V 4 is named *Alcatraz*; V 12 *Esturión* and V 18 *Lanzón*. V 19 was officially removed from the list in 1963, V 20 in 1965, and V 3 on 26 Oct 1968.

V 21 *1969, Spanish Navy*

BOOM DEFENCE VESSEL

CALAHEDES I CR (ex-*G 6*)

Displacement, tons	630 standard; 831 full load
Dimensions, feet	165·5 × 34 × 10·5
Guns	1—40 mm AA; 4—20 mm AA single
Main engines	2 diesels; electric drive; 1 shaft; 1 500 bhp = 12 knots
Range, miles	5 200 at 12 knots

Built by Penhoët, France, as a US off-shore order. Launched on 28 Sep 1954. Transferred from the US in 1955 under MDAP.

AUXILIARY PATROL VESSELS

RR 10 **RR 19** **RR 20** **RR 28** **R 29**

Displacement, tons	364 standard; 498 full load
Dimensions, feet	124·0 × 29·0 × 10·0
Guns	1—1·5 in, 85 cal or 1—47 mm; 1—20 mm AA
Main engines	Triple expansion; 1 shaft; 800 ihp = 11·5 knots
Boilers	1 cylindrical, 13 kg/cm
Fuel, tons	200 coal
Range, miles	620 at 10 knots

Former tugs. All launched in 1941-42. All classed as *Patrulleros* except RR 28, classed as *remolcador de rada*, some have navigation radar. Some to be discarded shortly. A photograph appears in the 1957-58 edition.

OILERS

TEIDE BP 11

Displacement, tons	2 747 light; 8 030 full load
Oil capacity, tons	5 350
Dimensions, feet	385·5 × 48·5 × 20·3
Guns	1—4·1 in, not mounted, but provision for AA
Main engines	2 diesels; 3 360 bhp = 12 knots

Ordered from Factoria de Bazan, Cartagena, in December 1952. Laid down on 11 Nov 1954. Launched on 20 June 1955. In service October 1956. Rated as *Petrolero de Escuadra*. Modernised in 1962 with refuelling at sea equipment.

Oilers—*continued*

TEIDE 1968, *Spanish Navy*

PP 1 **PP 2**

Displacement, tons	470
Dimensions, feet	138 pp; 147·5 oa × 25 × 9·5
Main engines	Deutz diesel; 220 bhp = 10 knots
Complement	12

Both built at Santander and launched in 1939. There are also 14 other small service tankers. The oiler *Pluton* (ex-*Campilo*) BP 01, was officially removed from the list on 2 May 1971.

TUGS

RR 50 **RR 51** **RR 52** **RR 53** **RR 54** **RR 55**

Displacement, tons	205 standard; 227 full load
Dimensions, feet	91·2 × 23 × 11
Main engines	Diesels; 1 shaft; 1 400 bhp (53 to 55), 800 bhp (50 to 52)

All built at Cartagena for naval service, first three in 1963, last three in 1967.

BS 1 (ex-RA 6) **RA 4** **RA 5**

Displacement, tons	951 standard; 1 069 full load
Dimensions, feet	183·5 × 32·8 × 15·8
Main engines	2 Sulzer diesels; 3 200 bhp = 15 knots

All built at La Carraca, in 1963. RA 6 was renumbered BS 1 when she became a frogman base.

RA 1 **RA 2**

Displacement, tons	757 standard; 1 039 full load
Dimensions, feet	184 × 33·5 × 12
Guns	2 MG
Main engines	2 Sulzer diesels; 3 200 bhp = 15 knots

Ordered in 1949. Built at Factoria de Bazan, Cartagena. Launched on 2 Sep 1954 and 5 Oct 1954, commissioned on 9 July 1955 and 12 Sep 1955, respectively.

RA 2

RA 3 (ex-*Metinda III*)

Displacement, tons	762 standard; 1 080 full load
Dimensions, feet	137 × 33·1 × 15·5
Main engines	Triple expansion; 12 knots max; 10 knots service

A photograph of RA 3 appears in the 1969-70 to 1971-72 editions.

RR 15

Displacement, tons	434
Dimensions, feet	124 × 27·5 × 10
Main engines	800 ihp = 11·5 knots

Of this class RR 17 was deleted from the Navy List in 1968 and RR 16 in 1969.

RR 16

Built at EN Bazan La Carraca in 1962. Length 88·6 feet. RR 11 stricken 1967.

SWEDEN

Administration

General Inspector:
Rear-Admiral Hans Skjong

Chief of Naval Material Department:
Thorleif Petterson

Commander-in-Chief of Coastal Fleet
Rear-Admiral Christer Kierkegaard

Commodore Robert Helseth

Chief of Naval Staff:
Major-General Bo Varenius

Chief of Staff Coastal Fleet (Acting)
Captain S. Hakanson

Diplomatic Representation

Naval Attaché in London:
Captain N. U. Rydström

Naval Attaché in Washington:
Captain N. L. Lindgren

Strength of the Fleet

8 Destroyers
5 Frigates
22 Patrol Submarines
2 Minelayers
1 Submarine Support Ship
42 Torpedo Boats
23 Patrol Boats
18 Coastal Minesweepers
17 Inshore Minesweepers
9 Mining Tenders
1 Staff Communications Ship
2 Training Ships
6 Surveying Vessels
1 Salvage Vessel
2 Mine Transports
48 Landing Craft
5 Icebreakers
2 Icebreaking Tugs
14 Support Ships and Service Craft

Future Plans

In June 1972 the Swedish Parliament approved the Government's Defence Plan for the next 5 years. The proposals of the Defence Minister, Mr Andersson, reduced the service vote by a tenth below the minimum requirement of General Stig Synnergren, the Supreme Commander. The effects of this reduction on the Navy may be the scrapping of all frigates without replacement by 1978, leaving only helicopters in the A/S role and a reduction of submarines from 22 to 11.

Personnel

1973: Active list of Navy and Coast Artillery: total 15 000 officers and men, including conscripts.

Composition of the Navy

In addition to seagoing personnel the Navy includes the Coastal Artillery, manning 20 mobile and 45 coastal batteries of both major guns and SSMs. The Naval Air Arm operates 10 Boeing Vertol 107 helicopters, 10 A/B OH-58A and a number of Alouette II helicopters.

New Construction Programme

5 Conventional Submarines (New design A14 Type)
2 Minelayers
2 Anti-submarine Corvettes
12 Torpedo Boats (Modified "Spica" type) Building,
16 to 24 Fast Gunboats (New Design)
3 Coastal Minesweepers (Modified M 44 type)
1 Icebreaker (Diesel Electric)

Disposals and Transfers

Cruisers

1964 *Tre Kronor*
1971 *Göta Lejon* to Chile (*Latorre*)

Destroyers

1958 *Klas Horn*
1963 *Ehrensköld, Nordensköld*

Submarines

1960 *Dykaren, Sjöborren, Sjöhunden, Sjölejonet, Svärdfisken*
1964 *Sjörbjörnen, Sjöormen, Tumlaren*

Depot Ships

1972 *Patricia*

Surveying Vessels

1972 *Johen Nordenankar, Petter Gedda*

Mercantile Marine

Lloyd's Register of Shipping:
875 vessels of 5 632 336 tons gross

DESTROYERS

4 "ÖSTERGÖTLAND" CLASS

Name	No.	Builders	Laid down	Launched	Completed
GÄSTRIKLAND	J 22	Götaverken, Göteborg	1 Oct 1955	6 June 1956	14 Jan 1959
HÄLSINGLAND	J 23	Kockums Mek Verkstads A/B	1 Oct 1955	14 Jan 1957	17 June 1959
ÖSTERGÖTLAND	J 20	Götaverken, Göteborg	1 Sep 1955	8 May 1956	3 Mar 1958
SÖDERMANLAND	J 21	Eriksberg Mekaniska Verkstad	1 June 1955	28 May 1956	27 June 1958

Displacement, tons: 2 100 standard; 2 600 full load (officially revised figures)
Length, feet (*metres*): 367·5 (*112·0*) oa
Beam, feet (*metres*): 36·8 (*11·2*)
Draught, feet (*metres*): 12·0 (*3·7*)
Missile launchers: 1 quadruple "Seacat" surface-to-air
Guns: 4—4·7 in (*120 mm*), 2 twin; 4—40 mm AA single
A/S weapons: Triple barrelled DC mortar
Torpedo tubes: 6—21 in (*533 mm*), 2 triple
Mines: 60 can be carried
Main engines: De Laval turbines; 2 shafts; 40 000 shp
Speed, knots: 35
Boilers: 2 Babcock & Wilcox
Range, miles: 2 200 at 20 knots
Oil fuel, tons: 330
Complement: 244 (18 officers, 226 men)

ÖSTERGÖTLAND *Class*

These ships have improved anti-aircraft defence and anti-submarine weapons of the Bofors type. J (for *Jagare*) painted on bows with number in 1966.

MODERNISATION. *Gästrikland* in 1965, *Södermanland* in 1967, *Hälsingland* in 1968, *Östergötland* in 1969.

RADAR. Thomson CSF Saturn S-band long-range search and target designator; HSA M 44 series for Seacat; M 45 series for guns.

HÄLSINGLAND *1972, Royal Swedish Navy*

2 "HALLAND" CLASS

Name	No.	Builders	Laid down	Launched	Completed
HALLAND	J 18	Götaverken, Göteborg	1951	16 July 1952	8 June 1955
SMÅLAND	J 19	Eriksberg Mekaniska Verkstad, Göteborg	1951	23 Oct 1952	12 Jan 1956

Displacement, tons: 2 800 standard; 3 400 full load
Length, feet (*metres*): 380·5 (*116·0*)wl; 397·2 (*121·0*)oa
Beam, feet (*metres*): 41·3 (*12·6*)
Draught, feet (*metres*): 14·8 (*4·5*)
Missiles, surface: 1 rocket launcher RB 08
Guns: 4—4·7 in (*120 mm*) dp (2 twin) 2—57 mm AA; 6—40 mm AA
A/S weapons: 2 four-barrelled DC mortars
Torpedo tubes: 8—21 in (*533 mm*) 2 quadruple
Mines: Can be fitted for minelaying
Main engines: De Laval double reduction geared turbines; 2 shafts; 58 000 shp
Speed, knots: 35
Boilers: 2 Penhöet
Range, miles: 3 000 at 20 knots
Oil fuel, tons: 500
Complement: 290 (18 officers, 272 men)

Both ordered in 1948. The first Swedish destroyers of post-war design and construction. Fully automatic gun

Destroyers—*continued*

turrets forward and aft, ahead throwing anti-submarine weapons of the Bofors type forward, and ship-to-ship guided missiles launcher abaft the after funnel.

RADAR. Thomson CSF Saturn S-band long-range search and target designator on foremast; LW 02/03 air warning radar on main mast M 22 series with co-mounted search and tracking radars in radome. ECM.

HALLAND *Class*

HALLAND *1968, Royal Swedish Navy*

2 "ÖLAND" CLASS

Name	*No.*	*Builders*	*Laid down*	*Launched*	*Completed*	*Modernised*
ÖLAND	J 16	Kockums Mek Verkstads A/B, Malmö	1943	15 Dec 1945	5 Dec 1947	1960, 1969
UPPLAND	J 17	Karlskrona Dockyard	1943	5 Nov 1946	31 Jan 1949	1963

Displacement, tons	2 000 standard; 2 400 full load
Length, feet (*metres*)	351 (*107·0*) pp; 367·5 (*112·0*) oa
Beam, feet (*metres*)	36·8 (*11·2*)
Draught, feet (*metres*)	11·2 (*3·4*)
Guns	4—4·7 in (*120 mm*) dp (2 twin); 6—40 mm AA single
A/S weapons	1 triple-barrelled DC mortar
Torpedo tubes	6—21 in (*533 mm*) 2 triple
Mines	60 capacity, fitted for laying
Main engines	De Laval geared turbines; 2 shafts; 44 000 shp
Speed, knots	35
Boilers	2 Penhöet
Range, miles	2 500 at 20 knots
Oil fuel, tons	300
Complement	210

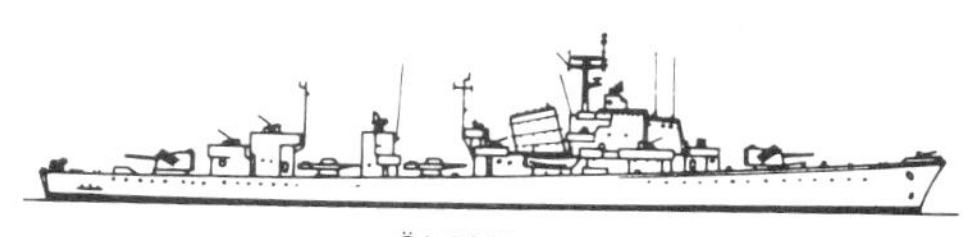

ÖLAND

Superstructure and machinery spaces lightly armoured.

RADAR. Thomson CSF Saturn S-band long-range search and target-designator; Two M 45 series fire control radars for guns; navigation set.

GUNNERY. 4·7 inch guns semi-automatic with 80° elevation. 40 mm AA gun near jackstaff was removed in 1962, and eight 20 mm AA guns in 1964.

RECONSTRUCTION. *Öland* was modernised with new bridge in 1960 and again in 1969; and *Uppland* with new bridge and helicopter platform in 1963.

OLAND *1970, Royal Swedish Navy*

FRIGATES

4 "VISBY" CLASS

Name	*No.*	*Builders*	*Launched*	*Completed*
HÄLSINGBORG	13	Götaverken	23 Mar 43	30 Nov 43
KALMAR	14	Eriksberg	20 July 43	3 Feb 44
SUNDSVALL	F 12	Eriksberg	20 Oct 42	17 Sep 43
VISBY	F 11	Götaverken	16 Oct 42	10 Aug 43

Displacement, tons	1 150 standard; 1 320 full load
Length, feet (*metres*)	310·0 (*94·5*) wl; 321·5 (*98·0*) oa
Beam, feet (*metres*)	30 (*9·1*)
Draught, feet (*metres*)	12·5 (*3·8*)
Aircraft	1 helicopter (F 11 and F 12)
Guns	3—4·7 in (*120 mm*); 3—40 mm AA (2—57 mm only in F 11 and F 12)
A/S weapons	1 four-barrelled DC mortar
Torpedo tubes	5—21 in (*533 mm*) F 11 F 12
Main engines	De Laval geared turbines; 2 shafts; 36 000 shp
Speed, knots	39
Boilers	3 three-drum type
Range, miles	1 600 at 20 knots
Oil fuel, tons	150
Complement	140

SUNDSVALL *1972, Royal Swedish Navy*

Kalmar was laid down on 16 Nov 1942, and *Visby* on 29 Apr 1942. All were originally fitted for minelaying.

RADAR. Thomson CSF Saturn S-band long-range search and target designator; M 24 fire control systems with co-mounted radars for search and tracking for guns.

VISBY *Class*

Frigates—*continued*

KARLSKRONA F 79

Displacement, tons	1 200 standard; 1 400 full load
Length, feet (*metres*)	304·1 (*92·7*) wl; 310·5 (*94·6*) oa
Beam, feet (*metres*)	31·8 (*9·7*)
Draught, feet (*metres*)	12·5 (*3·8*)
Guns	3—4·7 in (*120 mm*) do single; 4—40 mm AA single
A/S weapons	2 triple-barrelled DC mortars
Main engines	De Laval geared turbines; 2 shafts; 32 000 shp
Speed, knots	39
Boilers	3 Penhöet
Range, miles	1 200 at 20 knots
Oil fuel, tons	150
Complement	130

Built by Karlskrona Dockyard. Launched on 16 June 1939 and completed on 12 Sep 1940. Originally carried 20 to 60 mines. Refitted for anti-submarine warfare, and officially reclassified as frigate on 1 Jan 1961. Converted in 1963. Of this class *Göteborg* was discarded in 1958, *Stockholm* on 1 Jan 1964, *Malmö* and *Norrkoping* in 1967, and *Gavle* in 1969.

RADAR. Equipped with Type 293 search installation.

KARLSKRONA *1970, Stefan Terzibaschitsch*

SUBMARINES

Five submarines of a streamlined, long-range type, are included in the new construction programme. Three ordered from Kokums in 1972 for delivery 1977-78.

NEW CONSTRUCTION PATROL TYPE

5 "A 14" CLASS

Displacement, tons	980 surfaced; 1 125 submerged
Length, feet (*metres*)	167·3 (*51·0*)
Beam, feet (*metres*)	20·0 (*6·1*)
Draught, feet (*metres*)	16·7 (*5·1*)
Torpedo tubes	21 in (*533 mm*)
Main engines	Diesels, electric motors; 1 shaft
Speed, knots	*circa* 20 surface and submerged
Complement	25

SJÖHUNDEN *1972, Royal Swedish Navy*

5 "SJÖORMEN" CLASS (A11B)

Name	Builders	Launched	Completed
SJÖORMEN	Kockums	25 Jan 67	31 July 67
SJÖLEJONET	Kockums	29 June 67	16 Dec 68
SJÖHUNDEN	Kockums	21 Mar 68	25 June 69
SJÖHÄSTEN	Karlskrona	6 Aug 68	15 Sep 69
SJÖBJÖRNEN	Karlskrona	9 Jan 68	28 Feb 69

Displacement, tons	11 00 standard (officially revised figures, 1972); 1 400 submerged
Length, feet (*metres*)	167·3 (*51·0*)
Beam, feet (*metres*)	20·0 (*6·1*)
Draught, feet (*metres*)	19·7 (*6·0*)
Torpedo tubes	4—21 in (*533 mm*) 2 A/S tubes
Main engines	Pielstick diesels; 1 large 5-bladed propeller; 1 900 bhp; electric motors
Speed, knots	15 surface; 20 submerged
Endurance	3 weeks
Complement	23

Of whale shaped hull configuration. Twin-decked. Diving depth 500 ft.

APPEARANCE. Distinctive letters painted on the conning tower fin or "sail" are Sor, Sbj, She, Shu, Sle.

6 "DRAKEN" CLASS (A11)

Name	Builders	Launched	Completed
DELFINEN	Karlskrona	7 Mar 61	7 June 62
DRAKEN	Kockums	1 Apr 60	4 Apr 62
GRIPEN	Karlskrona	31 May 60	28 Apr 62
NORDKAPAREN	Kockums	8 Mar 61	4 Apr 62
SPRINGAREN	Kockums	31 Aug 61	7 Nov 62
VARGEN	Kockums	20 May 60	15 Nov 61

Displacement, tons	770 standard; 835 surface; 1 110 submerged
Length, feet (*metres*)	226·4 (*69·0*)
Beam, feet (*metres*)	16·7 (*5·1*)
Draught, feet (*metres*)	17·4 (*5·3*)
Torpedo tubes	4—21 in (*533 mm*) bow
Main engines	Pielstick diesels; 1 700 bhp; electric motors
Speed, knots	17 surface; 20 submerged
Complement	36

NORDKAPAREN *1971, Royal Swedish Navy*

These six submarines have fast-diving capabilities and are equipped with snort.

APPEARANCE. Distinctive letters painted on the conning tower are: Del. *Delfinen*; Dra. *Draken*; Gri. *Gripen*; Nor. *Nordkaparen*; Spr. *Springaren*; Vgn. *Vargen*.

6 "HAJEN" CLASS

Name	Builders	Launched	Completed
BÄVERN	Kockums	3 Feb 1958	29 May 1959
HAJEN	Karlskrona	11 Dec 1954	28 Feb 1957
ILLERN	Kockums	14 Nov 1957	31 Aug 1959
SÄLEN	Kockums	3 Oct 1955	8 Apr 1957
UTTERN	Kockums	14 Nov 1958	15 Mar 1960
VALEN	Kockums	24 Apr 1955	4 Mar 1957

Displacement, tons	720 standard; 785 surface; 1 000 submerged
Length, feet (*metres*)	216·5 (*66·0*)
Beam, feet (*metres*)	16·7 (*5·1*)
Draught, feet (*metres*)	16·4 (*5·0*)
Guns	1—20 mm AA
Torpedo tubes	4—21 in (*533 mm*) bow (8 torpedoes)

HAJEN *1970, Royal Swedish Navy*

Submarines—*continued*

Main engines	SEMT-Pielstick diesels; 1 700 bhp; Electric motors; electric drive on surface
Speed, knots	16 on surface, 17 submerged
Complement	44

All built by Kockums Mekaniska Verkstads Aktiebolag, Malmo, except *Valen* built by the Royal Swedish Naval Dockyard, Karlskrona.

OPERATIONAL. Equipped with Schnorkel, and have fast-diving capabilities.

APPEARANCE. Distinctive letters painted on the conning tower are: Bäv, *Bävern*; Haj, *Hajen*; Iln, *Illern*; Sa, *Sälen*; Utn, *Uttern*; Val, *Valen*.

5 "ABBORREN" CLASS

ABBORREN (ex-U5)
GÄDDAN (ex-U7)
LAXEN (ex-U8)
MAKRILLEN (ex-U9)
SIKEN (ex-U6)

Displacement, tons	400 standard; 430 surface; 460 submerged
Length, feet (*metres*)	164·0 (*50·0*)
Beam, feet (*metres*)	14·1 (*4·3*)
Draught, feet (*metres*)	12·5 (*3·8*)
Torpedo tubes	4—21 in (*533 mm*) 3 bow and 1 stern
Main engines	2 MAN diesels, total 1 500 bhp; Electric motors, 750 hp
Speed, knots	14 on surface; 9 submerged
Complement	23

All were built by Kokums Mek. Verkstads, Malmö (*U* 4 on 5 June 1943, *U* 5 on 8 July 1943, *U* 6 on 18 Aug 1943, *U* 7 on 23 Nov 1943), and by Karlskrona Naval Dockyard (*U* 8 on 25 Apr 1944, *U* 9 on 23 May 1944), (original launch dates). Reconstructed in 1960-64. Launching dates after reconstruction: *Abborren* in 1962, *Makrillen* in 1963, *Forellen* in 1963, *Laxen* in 1964, *Gäddan* in 1963, *Siken* in 1964. All have been streamlined. Officially rated as *Kustubåtar* (coastal submarines). Distinctive letters Abb, For, Gad, Lax, Mak, Sik.

CLASS. Of four sister submarines of this class. *U 1* was scrapped in 1961, *U 2* was for sale in 1962, and *U 3* in 1964. *Forellen* (ex-*U 4*) was deleted officially from the list in 1971.

ILLERN *1972, Royal Swedish Navy*

MAKRILLEN *1969, Royal Swedish Navy*

LAXEN *1972, Royal Swedish Navy*

LIGHT FORCES

2 PROJECTED MTB FLOTILLA LEADERS

K 1 **K 2**

Displacement, tons	circa 700
Dimensions, feet	246·0 × 26·2 × 8·0
Guns	1—57 mm forward; 1—40 mm aft
A/S weapons	1 single barrelled depth charge mortar forward
Main engines	Gas turbines for power; diesels for cruising
Complement	70

A new type of corvette is planned to fill the need for ships to act as flotilla leaders for fast torpedo boats and missile gunboats and for escort duties to relieve old destroyers and frigates. It is reported they may turn out at 800 to 1 000 tons displacement.

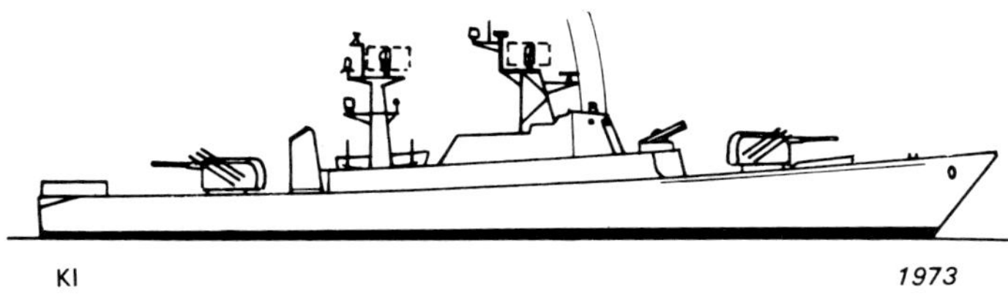

KI *1973*

16 PROJECTED MISSILE BOATS

JÄGAREN P 151 **P 152**

Displacement, tons	145
Dimensions, feet	119·75 × 20·3 × 4·9
Guns	1—57 mm Bofors
Missile launchers	4 "Penguin" surface-to-surface
Main engines	2 MTU MB20V 672 TY90 diesels; 2 shafts; 7 000 bhp = 35 knots
Complement	20

Instead of the motor gunboats projected for several years it is intended to order sixteen fast patrol boats similar to the Norwegian motor torpedo boats of the "Snögg" class armed with "Penguin" missiles. *Jägaren* was built in Norway, completing on 8 June 1972. Currently undergoing extensive trials before the remainder of the class is confirmed. Fitted for alternative minelaying capability aft.

JÄGAREN *1972*

12 "REPEAT SPICA" CLASS (FPBs)

HALMSTAD	T 140	**NYNÄSHAMN**	T 132	**VARBERG**	T 134
LULEÅ	T 139	**PITEÅ**	T 138	**VÄSTERÅS**	T 135
NORRKÖPING	T 131	**STRÖMSTAD**	T 141	**VÄSTERUIK**	T 136
NORRTÄLJE	T 133	**UMEÅ**	T 137	**YSTAD**	T 142

Displacement, tons	235 normal trim
Dimensions, feet	144·4 × 23·9 × 5·3
Guns	1—57 mm Bofors
Torpedo tubes	6—21 in for wire-guided torpedoes
Main engines	3 Rolls Royce Proteus gas turbines; 3 shafts; 12 900 bhp = 40·5 knots

Otherwise similar to the original "Spica" class from which they were developed. Building by Karlskronavarvet AB. Guided missiles are not included in the design to date. *Norrköping* launched 16 Nov 1972. Completed Feb 1973. Commissioned March 1973.

6 "SPICA" CLASS (FPBs)

CAPELLA	T 123	**SIRIUS**	T 122	**VEGA**	T 125
CASTOR	T 124	**SPICA**	T 121	**VIRGO**	T 126

Displacement, tons	200 standard; 230 full load
Dimensions, feet	139·5 hull; 141 oa × 23·3 × 5·2
Guns	1—57 mm Bofors AA
Torpedo tubes	6—21 in single, fixed
Rocket launchers	For flare rockets
Main engines	3 Bristol Siddeley Proteus 1 274 gas turbines; 3 shafts; 12 720 shp = 40 knots
Complement	28 (7 officers, 21 ratings)

Light Forces—*continued*

The lead vessel of a group of six, *Spica*, was completed in 1966 by Götaverken, Göteborg, and the other five in 1966 to 1968. Designed to operate in areas contaminated by nuclear fall-out. *Sirius* and *Capella* were built by Götaverken and *Castor*, *Vega* and *Virgo* by Karlskronavarvet. The 57 mm gun is in a power operated turret controlled by a radar equipped director, with 57 mm rocket flare projector placed before, and a 10·3 mm launcher on each side, of the totally enclosed bridge. The turret is mounted in the centre of a long foredeck to give wide and clear arcs of fire.

RADAR. M 22 fire control system with co-mounted radars in radome for guns and torpedoes.

CAPELLA *1970, Royal Swedish Navy*

VEGA *1971, Royal Swedish Navy*

VIRGO *1971, Royal Swedish Navy*

11 "PLEJAD" CLASS MTB—MGB CONVERTIBLES

ALDEBARAN	T 107	**ARCTURUS**	T 110	**POLARIS**	T 103
ALTAIR	T 108	**ARGO**	T 111	**POLLUX**	T 104
ANTARES	T 109	**ASTREA**	T 112	**REGULUS**	T 105
		PLEJAD	T 102	**RIGEL**	T 106

Displacement, tons	155 standard; 170 full load
Dimensions, feet	157·5 × 18·3 × 5·2
Guns	2—40 mm Bofors AA
Tubes	6—21 in (2 forward, 4 aft)
Main engines	3 Mercedes-Benz diesels; 3 shafts; 9 000 bhp = 37·5 knots
Range, miles	600 at 30 knots
Complement	33

All built at Lurssen, Vegesack, launched between 1954 and 1959 and completed by 1960.

***Perseus*, T 101, built at Karlskrona, completed in 1951, the first of a convertible type of torpedo and gunboat of experimental design, re-engined with Götaverken machinery to give greater power, differing in appearance from the other boats, but funnel later removed, was discarded in 1967.**

ARGO *1971, Royal Swedish Navy*

POLLUX *1970, Royal Swedish Navy*

15 "T 42" TYPE (FPBs)

T 42	**T 45**	**T 48**	**T 51**	**T 54**
T 43	**T 46**	**T 49**	**T 52**	**T 55**
T 44	**T 47**	**T 50**	**T 53**	**T 56**

Displacement, tons	40 to 45 standard
Dimensions, feet	75·5 × 19·4 × 4·6
Guns	1—40 mm Bofors AA; 2 MG
Tubes	2—21 in
Main engines	Petrol engines; speed = 45 knots

Built by Kockums Mekaniska Verkstads Aktiebolag, Malmö. All launched and completed between 1956 and 1959.

T 45 *1970, Royal Swedish Navy*

10 "T 32" TYPE (FPBs)

T 32	**T 34**	**T 36**	**T 38**	**T 40**
T 33	**T 35**	**T 37**	**T 39**	**T 41**

Displacement, tons	40 standard (T 41: 45 standard)
Dimensions, feet	75·5 × 18·4 × 4·5 (T 41: 76·0 × 18·7 × 4·6)
Guns	1—40 mm Bofors AA; 4 MG
Tubes	2—21 in
Main engines	Petrol engines; speed = 40 knots

Launched in 1950-52 and completed in 1951-53. Built by Kockums Mekaniska Verkstads Aktiebolag, Malmö. Of all welded steel construction. T 41, of slightly different design, provided under the 1952 Programme, was launched and completed in 1962.

Of the smaller torpedo boats, *T 21*, *T 22*, *T 23*, *T 24*, *T 25*, *T 26* and *T 27* were scrapped in 1959, and *T 28*, *T 29*, *T 30* and *T 31* in 1960. The older torpedo boats *T 15*, *T 16*, *T 17* and *T 18* were discarded in 1967.

T 34 *1972, Royal Swedish Navy*

V 57

Displacement, tons	115 standard
Dimensions, feet	98 pp; 105 oa × 17·3 × 7·5
Guns	2—20 mm AA
Main engines	Diesel; 500 bhp = 13·5 knots
Complement	12

Built at Stockholm. Launched in 1953. Fitted for minelaying. In Coast Artillery. *V 51*, *V 52*, *V 53*, *V 54*, *V 55* and *V 56*, 125 tons coal burning triple expansion steam engined type manned by Coast Artillery, were officially discarded in 1967.

7 "70" SERIES

71	**72**	**73**	**74**	**75**	**76**	**77**

Displacement, tons	28 standard
Dimensions, feet	69 × 15 × 5
Guns	1—20 mm
Main engines	Diesel; speed = 18 knots

Launched in 1966-67 and completed in 1968.

Light Forces—*continued*

10 "60" SERIES

61 62 63 64 65 66 67 68 69 70

Displacement, tons	30 standard
Dimensions, feet	62·3 × 15 × 4
Guns	1—20 mm
Main engines	Diesel; speed = 19 knots

Guard boats of the coast artillery (*Bevakningsbåtar*) launched in 1960-61.

5 "SVK" TYPE

SVK 1 SVK 2 SVK 3 SVK 4 SVK 5

Displacement, tons	19 standard
Dimensions, feet	55·8 × 12·1 × 3·9
Guns	1—20 mm AA
Main engines	Diesels; 100 to 135 bhp = 10 to 11 knots

Patrol launches of the Sjovarnskarens type. All launched in 1944. Sjovarnskaren = RNVR. *Tumlaren*, a small fishing cutter, also belongs to the SVK.

6 "TV" 101 CLASS

TV 101 TV 102 TV 103 TV 104 TV 105 TV 106

Displacement, tons	80
Main engines	2 Diesels; 1 000 hp

Aluminium hulled vessels.

MINEWARFARE FORCES

1 + 2 NEW CONSTRUCTION (MINELAYERS)

ÄLVSBORG M 02 VISBORG M 03 M 04

Displacement, tons	2 650 (revised official figure)
Length, feet (*metres*)	303·15 (*92·40*)
Beam, feet (*metres*)	48·2 (*14·7*)
Draught, feet (*metres*)	13·2 (*4·0*)
Guns	3—40 mm Bofors AA
Main engines	2 Nohab-Polar 12 cyl diesels; 1 shaft; 4 200 bhp
Speed, knots	15 max
Cost	Estimated about 34 000 000 kr
Complement	95 (accommodation for 205 more)

ÄLVSBORG

The *Älvsborg* was ordered in 1968 from the Naval Dockyard in Karlskrona, launched on 11 Nov 1969, and completed on 10 Apr 1971. The novel ship replaced the submarine depot ship *Patricia* which was sold in 1972.

Visborg, laid down at Karlskrona in 1972 will succeed *Marieholm* as Command Ship for C-in-C Active Fleet. M 04 will succeed *Alvsnabben* as minelayer and training ship.

ALVSBORG 1972, *Royal Swedish Navy*

ÄLVSNABBEN M 01 (MINELAYER)

Displacement, tons	4 250 standard
Length, feet (*metres*)	317·6 (*96·8*) wl; 334·7 (*102·0*) oa
Beam, feet (*metres*)	44·6 (*13·6*)
Draught, feet (*metres*)	16·4 (*5·0*)
Guns	2—6 in (*152 mm*); 2—57 mm Bofors; 2—40 mm AA; 4—37 mm saluting
Main engines	Diesels; 1 shaft; 3 000 bhp
Speed, knots	14
Complement	255 (63 cadets)

ÄLVSNABBEN

ÄLVSNABBEN ***1969 Royal Swedish Navy***

Built on a mercantile hull by Eriksberg Mekaniska Verkstad Göteborg. Laid down on 31 Oct 1942, launched on 19 Jan 1943, completed on 8 May 1943. Employed as a training ship during 1953-58. Relieved the anti-aircraft cruiser *Gotland* as Cadet's Seagoing Training Ship in 1959. Re-armed in 1961. Formerly carried 4—6 inch, 8—40 mm AA, 6—20 mm AA.

RADAR. Thomson CSF Saturn S-band long-range search and target designator; M 45 fire control system for guns.

12 "ARKO" CLASS (CMS)

ARKÖ	M 57	**HASSLÖ**	M 64	**NÄMDÖ**	M 67	**STYRSÖ**	M 61
ASPÖ	M 63	**IGGÖ**	M 60	**SKAFTÖ**	M 62	**VÄLLÖ**	M 66
BLIDÖ	M 68	**KARLSÖ**	M 59	**SPÅRÖ**	M 58	**VINÖ**	M 65

Displacement, tons	285 standard; 300 full load
Dimensions, feet	131 pp; 144·5 oa × 23 × 8 max
Guns	1—40 mm AA
Main engines	Mercedes-Benz diesels; 2 shafts; 2 000 bhp = 14·5 knots

Of wooden construction. There is a small difference in the deck-line between M 57-59 and M60-68. *Arkö* was launched on 21 Jan 1957. *Arkö*, *Karlsö* and *Spårö* were completed in 1958, *Iggö* in 1961 *Aspö*, *Hasslö*, *Vinö*, *Skaftö* and *Styrsö* in 1962 *Vällö* 1963, *Bildö* and *Nämdö* in 1964.

NÄMDÖ 1972, *Royal Swedish Navy*

Minewarfare Forces—*continued*

6 "HANÖ" CLASS (CMS)

HANÖ M 51	**STURKÖ** M 54	**TJURKÖ** M 53
ORNÖ M 55	**TÄRNÖ** M 52	**UTÖ** M 56

Displacement, tons 270 standard
Dimensions, feet 131·2 × 23 × 8
Guns 2—40 mm AA
Main engines Diesels; 2 shafts; 2 400 bhp = 14·5 knots

All of this class were built at Karlskrona and launched in 1953.

TÄRNÖ *1970, Royal Swedish Navy*

PROJECTED MINEHUNTERS

PROJECTED NON-MAGNETIC TYPE *Courtesy Captain Allan Kull*

9 MINING TENDERS

MUL 12 (1952)	**MUL 14** (1953)	**MUL 16** (1956)	**MUL 18** (1956)
MUL 13 (1952)	**MUL 15** (1953)	**MUL 17** (1956)	**MUL 19** (1956)

Displacement, tons 245 fulll load
Dimensions, feet 102·3 × 24·3 × 10·2 max
Guns 1—40 mm AA
Main engines 1 Nohab diesel-electric; 360 bhp = 10·5 knots

Launch dates above. Coastal Artillery personnel.

MUL 11

Displacement, tons 200 full load
Dimensions, feet 98·8 × 23·7 × 11·8 max
Guns 2—20 mm AA
Main engines 2 Atlas diesels; 300 bhp = 10 knots

Launched in 1946. *MUL 10* was officially deleted from the list in 1970.

MUL 11 degaussing *1971, Royal Swedish Navy*

"M 31" CLASS (IMS)

M 31 GASSTEN **M 32 NORSTEN** **M 33 VIKSTEN**

Displacement, tons 120 standard (official figure)
Guns 1—40 mm AA
Main engines Diesels = 9 knots

Minewarfare Forces—*continued*

Ordered 1972. Approximately of the same design as the M 44 class: see below. Built in glass reinforced plastic as forerunners to the new minehunters.

9 "M41" AND "M 44" CLASSES (IMS)

BLACKAN M 44	**GILLÖGA** M 47	**RÖDLÖGA** M 48
DÄMMAN M 45	**HISINGEN** M 43	**SVARTLÖGA** M 49
GALTEN M 46	**ORUST** M 41	**TJÖRN** M 42

Displacement, tons *Orust, Tjörn:* 110 standard; *Hisingen:* 115; others 140
Dimensions, feet *Orust, Tjörn:* 62·3 × 19·7 × 4·5; others 76·2 × 21 × 4·7
Guns *Orust, Tjörn:* 1—20 mm AA; others 1—40 mm AA
Main engines 2 diesels; 600 bhp = 9 knots

Orust and *Tjörn* were launched in 1948. Similar to fishing cutter type. *Blackan, Dämman, Galten* and *Hisingen* were launched in 1957. Three authorised in Apr 1962 were built in 1964.

SVARTLOGA *1970, Royal Swedish Navy*

8 "M 15" CLASS (IMS)

M 15 **M 16** **M 21** **M 22** **M 23** **M 24** **M 25** **M 26**

Displacement, tons 70 standard
Dimensions, feet 85·3 × 16·5 × 4·5
Guns 1—20 mm
Main engines Diesel; 600 bhp = 13 knots

All launched in 1941. M 17, M 18 and M 20 of this large motor launch type were re-rated as tenders and renamed *Lommen, Spoven* and *Skuld* respectively: see later page. M 19 was officially deleted from the list in 1969.

M 26 *1972, Royal Swedish Navy*

LANDING CRAFT

BORE **GRIM** **HEIMDAL**

Displacement, tons 340 full load
Dimensions, feet 118·1 × 27·9 × 8·5
Main engines Diesels; 800 bhp = 12 knots

General utility landing craft of improved design. Launched in 1961 (*Grim*) and 1966.

BORE *1969, Royal Swedish Navy*

SKAGUL A 333 **SLEIPNER** A 335

Displacement, tons 335 standard
Dimensions, feet 114·8 × 27·9 × 9·5
Main engines Diesels; 640 bhp = 10 knots

Sleipner was launched in 1959 and completed in 1960. *Skagul* was launched and completed in 1960.

Landing Craft—*continued*

Nos. 201-204 **205-238** **239-243**

Displacement, tons 31
Dimensions, feet 69 × 13·8 × 4·2
Main engines Speed = 18 knots

A series of 43 landing craft rated as Landstigningfarkoster. Launched in 1957 *et seq.*

L 51 **L 52** **L 53** **L 54** **L 55**

Displacement, tons 32 standard
Dimensions, feet 50·8 × 16 × 3·2
Main engines Diesel; 140 bhp = 8 knots

Landing craft of general utility type. Launched in 1948,

ANE **BALDER** **LOKE** **RING**

Displacement, tons 135 standard
Dimensions, feet 91·9 × 26·2 × 6·0
Main engines Speed = 8·5 knots (*Loke* 9·2 knots; *Ring* 11 knots)

SURVEY SHIPS

ANDERS BURE (ex-*Rali*)

Displacement, tons 54
Dimensions, feet 82·0 × 19·4 × 6·9
Main engines Diesels = 15 knots
Complement 11

Rali was built in 1968. She was purchased in 1971 and renamed.

JOHAN MÅNSSON

Displacement, tons 977 standard; 1 030 full load (official figure)
Dimensions, feet 183·7 × 36·1 × 11·5
Main engines Diesels; 3 300 bhp = 15 knots
Complement 85

Launched on 14 Jan 1966. A new survey ship is planned in the near future.

JOHAN MANSSON *1971, Royal Swedish Navy*

RAN

Displacement, tons 285 standard
Dimensions, feet 98·4 × 23·0 × 8·5
Main engines Diesels; 260 bhp = 9 knots
Complement 37

Ran was launched in 1945 and completed and commissioned for service in 1946.

GUSTAV AF KLINT

Displacement, tons 750 standard
Dimensions, feet 170·6 × 28·5 × 15·4
Main engines Diesels; 640 bhp = 10 knots
Complement 66

Launched in 1941. Reconstructed in 1963. She formerly displaced 650 tons with a length of 154 feet.

GUSTAV AV KLINT *1970, Royal Swedish Navy*

Survey Ships—*continued*

ANDEN (ex-*M* 9)

Displacement, tons 53 standard
Dimensions, feet 78·8 × 16·5 × 4·5
Main engines Diesel; 400 bhp = 13 knots

NILS STRÖMCRONA

Displacement, tons 140 standard
Dimensions, feet 88·6 × 17·0 × 8·2
Guns None in peacetime
Main engines Diesels; 300 bhp = 9 knots

Launched in 1894. The older survey ships will eventually be replaced.

Former inshore minesweeper of the motor launch type, launched in 1940 and subsequently converted into survey craft. M 7 and M 8 were taken over as patrol boats. Sister boats *Grisslan* (ex-*M* 6), *Svårtan* (ex-*M* 5), *Tårnan* (ex-*M* 4) and *Viggen* (ex-*M* 10) were officially deleted from the list in 1971 and *Måsen* (ex-*M* 3) in 1972.

MINE TRANSPORTS

FÄLLAREN A 236 **MINÖREN** A 237

Displacement, tons 165 standard
Dimensions, feet 105 × 20·3 × 7·2
Main engines Speed = 9 knots

Launched in 1941 and 1940 respectively.

EXPERIMENTAL CRAFT

URD (ex-*Capella*) A 271

Displacement, tons 63 standard; 90 full load
Dimensions, feet 73·8 × 18·3 × 9·2
Main engines Diesels; 200 bhp = 8 knots

Experimental vessel added to the official list in 1970. Launched in 1969

OILERS

OLJAREN (ex-*Martha*) A 227

Displacement, tons 1 100 standard
Dimensions, feet 180·5 × 27·6 × 12·1
Guns 2—25 mm AA
Main engines Diesels; 400 bhp = 10 knots

Launched in 1939. Cargo capacity 695 tons. Her pennant number was formerly 267. The oiler *Tankaren* (ex-*Lister*) 269 was officially deleted from the list in 1969 and the oiler *Eldaren* (ex-*Muron*) A 226 (ex-266) was deleted in 1970.

OLJAREN *1971, Royal Swedish Navy*

BRAENNAREN

Displacement, tons 857
Speed, knots 11

Ex-German merchant tanker *Indio* purchased early 1972. Built 1965.

SUPPLY SHIP

FREJA A 221

Displacement, tons 415 standard; 450 full load
Dimensions, feet 160·8 × 27·9 × 12·1
Main engines Diesels; 600 bhp = 11 knots

Built by Kroger, Rendsburg. Launched in 1953. Employed as a provision ship.

STAFF SHIP

MARIEHOLM A 201

Displacement, tons 1 400 standard
Dimensions, feet 210 × 32·5 × 11·5 max
Aircraft 1 helicopter
Guns 2 MG (1—40 mm removed, see notes below)
Main engines Steam reciprocating; 950 ihp = 12 knots

Former passenger ship. Completed in 1934. Converted during the Second World War to serve as a Base Communication Centre for the Commander-in-Chief of the

Staff Ship—*continued*

Active Fleet. Recently used as a Staff Ship for the Commander-in-Chief in winter time, flying his flag. The ship had her mainmast removed and a helicopter platform installed aft in 1959 for employment as flagship of the Active Fleet (the "Coast Fleet"). The 40 mm Bofors on the forecastle has been landed for the time being.

MARIEHOLM *1972, Royal Swedish Navy*

SALVAGE VESSEL

BELOS A 211

Displacement, tons	1 000 standard (officially revised figure, 1972)
Dimensions, feet	204·4 × 37·0 × 12·0
Aircraft	1 helicopter
Main engines	Diesels; 2 shafts; 1 200 bhp = 13 knots

Built to replace the old *Belos*, discarded on 1 Aug 1963. Launched on 15 Nov 1961. Completed on 29 May 1963. Equipped with decompression chamber.

BELOS *1972, Wright & Logan*

TRAINING SHIPS

FALKEN (12 June 1947) **GLADAN** (14 Nov 1946)

Displacement, tons	220 standard
Dimensions, feet	93 wl; 129·5 oa × 23·5 × 13·5
Main engines	Auxiliary diesel; 120 bhp

Sail training ships. Schooners. Launch dates above. Sail area 5 511 square feet.

ICEBREAKERS

1 NEW CONSTRUCTION

Displacement, tons	8 000
Dimensions, feet	341·2 × 78·0 × 24·0
Main engines	4 Diesel-electric; 23 000 hp = 18 knots

This new icebreaker is under construction by the Wärtsilä concern in Finland. Near sister of Finnish "Urho" class.

NJORD

Displacement, tons	5 150 standard; 5 686 full load
Dimensions, feet	260·8 pp; 283·8 oa × 69·6 × 20·3
Main engines	Wärtsilä diesel-electric; 4 shafts, 2 forward, 2 aft; 12 000 hp = 18 knots

Built by Wärtsilä, Finland. Launched on 20 Oct 1968 and completed in Dec 1969 Near sister ship of *Tor*.

NJORD *1971, Royal Swedish Navy*

Icebreakers—*continued*

TOR

Displacement, tons	4 980 standard; 5 290 full load
Dimensions, feet	254·3 pp; 277·2 oa × 69·5 × 20·3
Main engines	Wärtsilä-Sulzer diesel-electric; 4 shafts; 2 forward; 2 aft; 12 000 hp = 18 knots

Launched from Wärtsilä's Crichton-Vulcan yard, Turku, on 25 May 1963. Towed to Sandvikens Skeppsdocka, Helsingfors, for completion. Delivered on 31 Jan 1964. Larger but generally similar to *Oden*, and a near-sister to *Tarmo* built for Finland.

TOR *1972, Royal Swedish Navy*

ODEN

Displacement, tons	4 950 standard; 5 220 full load
Dimensions, feet	255·9 pp; 273·5 oa × 63·7 × 22·7
Main engines	Diesel-electric; 4 shafts (2 for'd); 10 500 bhp = 16 knots
Oil fuel, tons	740
Complement	75

Similar to the Finnish *Voima* and 3 Soviet icebreakers. 4 screws, 2 forward, 2 aft. Built at Sandviken, Helsingfors. Launched on 16 Oct 1956. Completed in 1958.

ODEN *1972, Royal Swedish Navy*

THULE

Displacement, tons	2 200 standard; 2 280 full load
Dimensions, feet	187·0 wl; 204·2 oa × 52·8 × 19·4
Main engines	Diesel-electric; 3 shafts (1 for'd); 4 800 bhp = 14 knots
Complement	43

Launched at the Naval Dockyard, Karlskrona, in Oct 1951. Completed in 1953. A photograph appears in the 1969-70 and earlier editions. The icebreaker *Atle* was officially discarded in 1967.

YMER

Displacement, tons	4 330 standard; 4 645 full load
Dimensions, feet	240 wl; 258 oa × 63·1 × 22·3
Main engines	6 Atlas diesel-electric; 9 000 hp = 16 knots
Complement	44

Launched by Kockums MV A/B, Malmö in 1932. First large icebreaker with diesel-electric propulsion. Designed to carry a seaplane for ice spotting and survey.

YMER *1969, Royal Swedish Navy*

TENDERS

1 NEW CONSTRUCTION

Displacement, tons	144
Dimensions, feet	109·2 × 20
Main engines	2 diesels; 1 100 hp = 13 knots

Ordered 1972 from Lundevarv-Ocverkstads AB, Kramfors for delivery in 1974.

PELIKANEN A 247

Displacement, tons	130 standard (officially revised figure)
Dimensions, feet	108·2 × 19·0 × 6·0
Main engines	Speed = 15 knots

Torpedo recovery and rocket trials vessel. Delivered on 26 Sep 1963.

SIGRUN A 256

Displacement, tons	250 standard
Dimensions, feet	105·0 × 22·3 × 11·8
Main engines	Diesels; 320 bhp = 11 knots

Launched in 1961.

HECTOR A 321 **HERMES** A 253 **HEROS** A 322

Displacement, tons	185 standard
Dimensions, feet	75·5 × 22·6 × 11·1
Main engines	Diesels; 630 bhp = 11 knots

Launched in 1953-57. The pennant number of *Hermes* was changed from 318.

HERA **HERCULES** A 323

Displacement, tons	127 tons
Dimensions, feet	65·3 ×21·3 × 12·5
Main engines	Diesels; 615 bhp = 11·5 knots

HÄGERN (ex-*Torpedbargaren*) A246

Displacement, tons	50 standard
Dimensions, feet	88·6 × 16·4 × 4·9
Main engines	Diesels; 270 bhp = 10 knots

Hägern was launched in 1951. Her pennant number was changed from 274 to 246.

LOMMEN (ex-*M* 17) A 231
SKULD (ex-*M* 20) A 371
SPOVEN (ex-*M* 18) A 232

Displacement, tons	70 standard
Dimensions, feet	85·3 × 16·5 × 4·5
Main engines	Diesel; 600 bhp = 13 knots

Former inshore minesweepers of the large motor launch type. All launched in 1941.

TUGS

ACHILLES A 251 **AJAX** A 252

Displacement, tons	450
Dimensions, feet	108·2 × 28·5 × 12
Main engines	Diesel, 1650 bhp = 12 knots

Achilles was launched in 1962 and *Ajax* in 1963. Both are icebreaking tugs. Former pennant numbers were 276 and 277, respectively.

AJAX 1970, Royal Swedish Navy

WATER CARRIERS

FRYKEN A 217

Displacement, tons	307 standard
Dimensions, feet	105·0 × 18·7 × 8·9
Main engines	Diesels; 370 bhp = 10 knots

A naval construction water carrier. Launched in 1959 and completed in 1960. Former pennant number was 263.

1970, Royal Swedish Navy

UNDEN A 216

Displacement, tons	540 standard (officially revised figure)
Dimensions, feet	121·4 × 23·3 × 9·8 max
Main engines	Steam reciprocating; 225 ihp = 9 knots

Launched in 1946. The pennant number of *Unden* was formerly 268.

GÄLNAN

Displacement, tons	98 standard
Dimensions, feet	95·1 × 19·0 × 9·2
Main engines	Speed = 8 knots

Launched in 1942. Small water tanker for harbour and local services.

SUDAN

Establishment

The navy was established in 1962 to guard the Red Sea coast with a training staff from Yugoslavian Navy.

Diplomatic Representation

Naval Military and Air Attaché in London:
Col. Hassan Yousef El Hassan

Mercantile Marine

Lloyd's Register of Shipping: 14 vessels of 35 502 tons gross

PATROL BOATS

2 YUGOSLAV PBR 512 TYPE

FASHER PBR 1 **KHARTOUM** PBR 2

Displacement, tons	190 standard; 245 full load
Dimensions, feet	134·5 × 20·7 × 7·0
Guns	2—40 mm AA; 2—20 mm AA
Main engines	Diesel; 2 shafts; 3 300 bhp = 20 knots
Range, miles	1 500 at 12 knots

Submarine chasers of the "500" class. Transferred from the Yugoslavian Navy during 1969.

Patrol Boats—*continued*

4 YUGOSLAV MOSOR PB TYPE

GIHAD PB 1 **HORRIYA** PB 2 **ISTIQLAL** PB 3 **SHAAB** PB 4

Displacement, tons	100
Dimensions, feet	115 × 16·5 × 5·2
Guns	1—40 mm AA; 1—20 mm AA; 2—7·6 mm MG
Main engines	Mercedes-Benz diesels; 2 shafts; 1 800 bhp = 20 knots
Range, miles	1 400 at 12 knots
Complement	20 officers and men

Built by Mosor Shipyard, Trogir, Yugoslavia, in 1961-62. Of steel construction. First craft acquired by the newly established Sudanese Navy.

GIHAD *Sudanese Navy*

HORRIYA *Sudanese Navy*

LANDING CRAFT

Two ex-Yugoslavian landing craft of the DTK 221 type were taken over during 1969.

OILER

FASHODA (ex-PN 17)

Displacement, tons	420 standard; 650 full load
Dimensions, feet	141·5 × 22·8 × 13·6
Main engines	300 bhp = 7 knots

Former Yugoslavian oiler rehabilitated and transferred to the Sudanese Navy in 1969.

WATER CARRIER

BARAKA (ex-PV 6)

A small water carrier, transferred from Yugoslavia to the Sudanese Navy in 1969.

SURVEY SHIP

IENAGA

A small vessel, converted into a hydrographic ship, acquired from Yugoslavia in 1969.

SYRIA

Mercantile Marine

Lloyd's Register of Shipping: 7 vessels of 1 659 tons gross

LIGHT FORCES

2 Ex-USSR "OSA" CLASS (MISSILE BOATS)

Displacement, tons	165 standard; 200 full load
Dimensions, feet	128.7 × 25·1 × 5·9
Missile launchers	4, two pairs abreast, for SSN 2-A (Styx)
Guns	4—30 mm twins 1 forward, 1 aft
Main engines	3 diesels; 13 000 bhp = 32 knots
Complement	25

Transferred December 1972.

Light Forces—*continued*

SYRIAN OSA CLASS *Dec. 1972*

6 Ex-USSR "KOMAR" CLASS (MISSILE BOATS)

Displacement, tons	70 standard; 80 full load
Dimensions, feet	83·7 × 19·8 × 5
Missile launchers	2 for SSN 2A (Styx)
Guns	2—25 mm AA
Main engines	4 diesels; 4 shafts; 4 800 bhp = 40 knots

Transferred between 1963 and 1966.

17 Ex-USSR P 4 TYPE (TORPEDO BOATS)

Displacement, tons	25 standard
Dimensions, feet	62·7 × 11·6 × 5·6
Tubes	2—18 in
Guns	2— MG (twin)
Main engines	2 diesels; 2 200 bhp 2 shafts = 50 knots

Five torpedo boats were transferred from the USSR at Latakia on 7 Feb 1957, and at least twelve subsequently. Only approximately ten of these can be considered operational.

3 Ex-FRENCH "CH" TYPE

Name	*Builders*	*Laid down*	*Launched*	*Completed*
ABABEH IBN NEFEH	A. C. de France	1938	Jan 1940	Apr 1940
ABDULLAH IBN ARISSI	A.C. Seine Maut	1938	1939	1940
TAREK IBN ZAYED	A.C. Seine Maut	1938	1939	1940

Displacement, tons	107 standard; 131 full load
Dimensions, feet	116·5 pp; 121·8 oa × 17·5 × 6·5
Guns	1—3 in; 2—20 mm AA
A/S weapons	Depth charges
Main engines	MAN diesels; 2 shafts; 1 130 bhp = 16 knots
Oil fuel, tons	50
Range, miles	1 200 at 8 knots; 680 at 13 knots
Complement	28

Rebuilt in 1955-56 when the funnels were removed.
These former French submarine chasers were transferred in 1962 to form the nucleus of the Syrian Navy. Respectively ex-*Ch* 10, ex-*Ch* 19, and ex-*Ch* 130. Two of these ships are no longer fit for service.

"Ch" Type *M Henri Le Masson*

MINESWEEPERS

2 Ex-USSR "T 43" TYPE

HITTINE **YARMOUK**

Displacement, tons	500 standard; 610 full load
Dimensions, feet	191·5 × 28·1 × 6·9
Guns	4—37 mm AA; 4—25 mm AA
Main engines	2 diesel motors; 2 shafts 2 000 hp = 17 knots
Range, miles	1 600 at 10 knots
Complement	40

Reported in 1962 to have transferred from the Soviet Navy to the Syrian Navy

TAIWAN (REPUBLIC OF CHINA)

Administration

Commander-in-Chief of the Navy:
Admiral Soong Chang-chih

Deputy Commander-in-Chief, Operations:
Vice Admiral Huang Hsi-lin

Deputy Commander-in-Chief, Administration:
Vice Admiral Lee Tun-chien

Commander, Fleet Command:
Vice Admiral Chen Ching-kun

Diplomatic Representation

Naval Attaché in Washington, D.C.:
Rear-Admiral Wang Hsi-ling

Personnel

1972: 38 000 officers and enlisted men in Navy plus 34 000 officers and enlisted men in Marine Corps

Mercantile Marine

Lloyd's Register of Shipping:
399 vessels of 1 494 903 tons gross

Strength of the Fleet

2 Submarines
19 Destroyers
11 Frigates
1 Frigate/Transport
4 Patrol Vessels
1 Coastal Minelayer
13 Coastal Minesweepers
9 Mine Boats & Launches
6 Torpedo Boats
1 Dock Landing Ship
2 Amphibious Flagships
21 Tank Landing Ships
4 Medium Landing Ships
22 Utility Landing Craft
20 Auxiliary Ships
5 Floating Dry Docks

SUBMARINES

2 Ex-US GUPPY II TYPE

Name	*No.*	*Builder*	*Launched*	*US Comm*	*Transferred*
HAI SHIH (ex-USS *Cutlass*, SS 478)	SS 1	Portsmouth Navy Yard	5 Nov 1944	17 Mar 1945	12 Apr 1973
(ex-USS *Tusk*, SS 426)	SS 2	Cramp Shipbuilding Co	8 July 1945	11 Apr 1946	1973

Displacement, tons	1 870 standard; 2 420 submerged
Length, feet (*metres*)	307·5 (*93·6*) oa
Beam, feet (*metres*)	27·2 (*8·3*)
Draught, feet (*metres*)	18 (*5·5*)
Torpedo tubes	10—21 inch (*533 mm*); 6 fwd; 4 aft
Main engines	3 diesels (Fairbanks Morse); 4 800 bhp/ 2 electric motors (Elliott); 5 400 shp; 2 shafts
Speed, knots	18 surface; 15 submerged
Complement	approx 80

Originally fleet-type submarines of the US Navy "Tench" class; extensively modernised under the GUPPY II programme. (See United States section for additional GUPPY II notes).
These submarines each have four 126-cell electric batteries; fitted with snorkel.

HAI SHIH *1972, United States Navy*

The *Cutlass* was the first US submarine to be transferred to an allied navy in the Western Pacific; provided primarily to improve anti-submarine training capabilities of the Republic of China Navy.

DESTROYERS

4 Ex-US "GEARING" CLASS

Name	*No.*	*Builder*	*Launched*	*US Comm*	*Transferred*
DANG YANG (ex-USS *Lloyd Thomas*, DD 764)	DD 11	Bethlehem Steel (San Francisco)	5 Oct 1945	21 Mar 1947	12 Oct 1972
LIAO YANG (ex-USS *Hanson*, DD 832)	DD 21	Bath Iron Works Corp	11 Mar 1945	11 May 1945	18 Apr 1973
LAO YANG (ex-USS *Shelton*, DD 790)	DD 20	Todd Pacific Shipyards	8 Mar 1946	21 June 1946	18 Apr 1973
CHIEN YANG (ex-USS *James E. Kyes*, DD 787)	DD 12	Todd Pacific Shipyards	4 Aug 1945	8 Feb 1946	18 Apr 1973

Displacement, tons	2 425 standard; approx 3 500 full load
Length, feet (*metres*)	390·5 (*119·0*) oa
Beam, feet (*metres*)	40·9 (*12·4*)
Draught, feet (*metres*)	19 (*5·8*)
Guns	4—5 inch (*127 mm*) 38 cal DP (twin)
A/S weapons	1 ASROC 8-tube launcher except in *Dang Yang* which has trainable hedgehog (Mk 15) 6—12·75 inch (*324 mm*) torpedo tubes (Mk 32 triple)
Main engines	2 geared turbines (General Electric); 60 000 shp; 2 shafts
Boilers	4
Speed, knots	34
Complement	approx 275

Former US Navy destroyers of the "Gearing" class. The *Dang Yang* was modified to a special anti-submarine configuration and reclassified as a "hunter-killer" destroyer (DDK) in 1949; changed to "escort" destroyer (DDE) in 1950; changed again to "straight" DD upon modernisation in 1962. These ships have been extensively modernised under the Fleet Rehabilitation and Modernisation programme, all to FRAM I standard except *Dang Yang* which was FRAM II (no ASROC). All have helicopter platform and hangar.
Armament listed above was at time of transfer. The ex-*Shelton* has twin 5 inch gun mounts in "A" and "B" positions with A/S torpedo tubes alongside second funnel; other ships have the "A" and "Y" gun mounts with torpedo tubes in "B" position except *Dang Yang* has torpedo tubes between funnels.
The three FRAM I ships initially were scheduled for transfer to Spain; however; they were declined by Spain and allocated to Taiwan China.

Ex-USS *Warrington* (DD 843) sold to Taiwan China in 1973 for transfer of bow section to *Hua Yang* (damaged in collision) and scrapping.

ELECTRONICS. At the time of transfer the FRAM I ships had SPS-37 and SPS-10 search radar antennas on forward tripod mast except *James E. Kyes* with SPS-40 and SPS-10 radars; *Dang Yang* had SPS-6 and SPS-10 radars. Fitted with SQS-23 sonar exept *Dang Yang* has SQS-29 series sonar.

DANG YANG (as USS *Lloyd Thomas*) *1970, United States Navy*

YUEH YANG—See following page *1973*

Destroyers—*continued*

1 Ex-US "GEARING" CLASS RADAR PICKET

Name	No.	Builder	Launched	US Comm	Transferred
FU YANG (ex-USS *Ernest G. Small*, DD 838)	DD 7	Bath Iron Works Corp	14 June 1945	21 Aug 1945	19 Feb 1971

Displacement, tons	2 425 standard; approx 3 500 full load
Length, feet (*metres*)	390·5 (*119·0*) oa
Beam, feet (*metres*)	40·8 (*12·4*)
Draught, feet (*metres*)	19 (*5·8*)
Guns	6—5 inch (*127 mm*) 38 calibre DP (twin)
A/S weapons	6—12·75 inch (*324 mm*) torpedo tubes (Mk 32 triple); 2 fixed hedgehogs
Main engines	2 geared turbines; (General Electric); 60 000 shp; 2 shafts
Boilers	4 (Babcock & Wilcox)
Speed, knots	34
Complement	approx 275

ELECTRONICS. At time of transfer the *Fu Yang* had SPS-37 and SPS-10 search radars on forward tripod mast, and large TACAN (tactical aircraft navigation) "beehive" antenna on second tripod mast. Fitted SQS-29 hull-mounted sonar and SQA-10 variable depth sonar.

Former US Navy radar picket destroyer of the "Gearing" class. Converted to a radar picket destroyer (DDR) during 1952 and subsequently modernised under the Fleet Rehabilitation and Modernisation (FRAM II) programme; redesignated as a "straight" destroyer (DD), but retained specialised electronic equipment. Not fitted with helicopter flight deck or hangar.

PHOTOGRAPHS. A photograph of the *Fu Yang* as the *Ernest D. Small* appears in the 1972-1973 edition.

6 Ex-US "ALLEN M. SUMNER" CLASS

Name	No.	Builder	Launched	US Comm	Transferred
HSIANG YANG (ex-USS *Brush*, DD 745)	DD 1	Bethlehem Steel (Staten Is)	28 Dec 1943	17 Apr 1944	Feb 1970
HENG YANG (ex-USS *Samuel N. Moore*, DD 747)	DD 2	Bethlehem Steel (Staten Is)	23 Feb 1944	24 June 1944	Feb 1970
HUA YANG (ex-USS *Bristol*, DD 857)	DD 3	Bethlehem Steel (San Pedro)	29 Oct 1944	17 Mar 1945	Feb 1970
YUEH YANG (ex-USS *Haynsworth*, DD 700)	DD 5	Federal SB & DD Co	15 Apr 1944	22 June 1944	May 1970
HUEI YANG (ex-USS *English*, DD 696)	DD 6	Federal SB & DD Co	27 Feb 1944	4 May 1944	Sep 1970
PO YANG (ex-USS *Maddox*, DD 731)	DD 10	Bath Iron Works Corp	19 Mar 1944	2 June 1944	July 1972

Displacement, tons	2 200 standard; 3 320 full load
Length, feet (*metres*)	376·5 (*114·8*) oa
Beam, feet (*metres*)	40·9 (*12·4*)
Draught, feet (*metres*)	19 (*5·8*)
Guns	6—5 inch (*127 mm*) 38 calibre DP (twin) up to 6—3 inch (*76 mm*) 50 calibre AA (2 twin, 2 single) in most ships, some; including *Heng Yang* and *Yueh Yang*, have 8—40 mm (1 quad, 2 twin).
A/S weapons	6—12·75 inch (*324 mm*) torpedo tubes (Mk 32 triple); 2 fixed hedgehogs; depth charges in some ships
Main engines	2 geared turbines (General Electric or Westinghouse); 60 000 shp; 2 shafts
Boilers	4 (Babcock & Wilcox)
Speed, knots	34
Complement	approx 275

Former US Navy destroyers of the "Allen M. Sumner" class. These ships have not been modernised under the FRAM programmes, but retain their original configurations with removal of original torpedo tubes, and 40 mm and 20 mm AA guns, and installation of improved electronic equipment. Secondary gun battery now varies; during the 1950s most of these ships were rearmed with six 3 inch AA guns (two single alongside forward funnel and two twin amidships); number retained apparently varies from ship to ship, with some ships retaining original 40 mm guns.

ELECTRONICS. These ships have SPS-6 and SPS-10 search radars on their tripod mast.

PHOTOGRAPHS. The *Fu Yang* can be distinguished from the other six-gun destroyers operated by Taiwan China by the former ship's additional space between funnels and tripod mast forward of her second funnel. In the above photograph the *Yueh Yang*'s 40 mm guns, their separate gun directors in "tubs" aft of the second funnel, and depth charge rack are clearly evident.

YUEH YANG 1973

HSIANG YANG 1971, United States Navy

4 Ex-US "FLETCHER" CLASS

Name	No.	Launched	US Comm	Transferred
KWEI YANG (ex-USS *Twining*, DD 540)	DD 8	11 July 1943	1 Dec 1943	Aug 1971
CHING YANG (ex-USS *Mullany*, DD 528)	DD 9	12 Oct 1942	23 Apr 1943	Oct 1971
AN YANG (ex-USS *Kimberly*, DD 521)	DD 18	4 Feb 1943	22 May 1943	June 1967
KUEN YANG (ex-USS *Yarnall*, DD 541)	DD 19	25 July 1943	30 Dec 1943	June 1968

Displacement, tons	2 100 standard; 3 050 full load
Length, feet (*metres*)	376·5 (*114·7*) oa
Beam, feet (*metres*)	35·9 (*11·9*)
Draught, feet (*metres*)	18 (*5·5*)
Guns	5—5 inch (*127 mm*) 38 calibre DP (single) except 4 guns in *Ching Yang* 6—3 inch (*76 mm*) 50 calibre AA (twin) in *Kwei Yang* and *Ching Yang*; 6—40 mm AA (twin) in *An Yang* and *Kuen Yang*
A/S weapons	2 fixed hedgehogs; depth charges 6—12·75 inch (*324 mm*) torpedo tubes (Mk 32 triple) in *Kwei Yang* and *Ching Yang*
Torpedo tubes	5—21 inch (*533 mm*) quintuple in *Kuen Yang*
Main engines	2 geared turbines (General Electric in *An Yang*, Allis Chalmers in *Kuen Yang*, Westinghouse in others); 60 000 shp; 2 shafts
Boilers	4 (Babcock & Wilcox)
Speed, knots	36
Complement	approx 250

Former US "Fletcher" class destroyers. Built by Bethlehem Steel Co, San Francisco, except *An Yang* by Bethlehem at Staten Island, New York. *An Yang* retains original pole mast; others have tripod mast. Only *Kuen Yang* retains anti-ship torpedo tubes.

AN YANG ***1971, courtesy Toshio Tamura***

Destroyers—*continued*

2 Ex-US "GLEAVES" CLASS

Name	No.	Launched	US Comm	Transferrec
HSUEN YANG (ex-*Hatakze*, ex-USS *Macomb*, DMS 23, ex-DD 458)	DD 16	22 Sep 1941	26 Jan 1942	Aug 19
NAN YANG (ex-USS *Plunkett*, DD 431)	DD 17	9 Mar 1940	16 July 1940	Feb 19

Displacement, tons	1 700 standard; 2 575 full load
Length, feet (*metres*)	341 (*104·0*) wl; 348·33 (*106·2*) oa
Beam, feet (*metres*)	36 (*11·0*)
Draught, feet (*metres*)	18 (*5·5*)
Guns	4—5 inch (*127 mm*) 38 calibre DP (single) in *Nan Yang*; 3 guns in *Hsien Yang* (see Gunnery notes) several 40 mm AA several 20 mm AA
A/S weapons	depth charges
Main engines	2 geared turbines (Westinghouse in *Hsuen Yang*, General Electric in *Nan Yang*); 50 000 shp; 2 shafts
Boilers	4 (Babcock & Wilcox)
Speed, knots	34
Complement	250

HSUEN YANG (ex-*Hatakze*) — *1970, Courtesy Toshio Tamura*

Former US destroyers of the "Gleaves" class. *Hsien Yang* built by Bath Iron Works Corp, and *Nan Yang* by Federal SB & DD Co.

The original *Hsien Yang* was the former USS *Rodman* (ex-DMS 21, ex-DD 456) transferred to Taiwan China in July 1955. After she ran aground and sustained severe damage two other ships of this class which had served with the Japanese Navy were transferred to Taiwan China for cannibalisation to repair the *Hsien Yang*. Subsequently, the ex-USS *Macomb* was judged in better condition than the damaged ship and was placed in service with the damaged ship's name and number.

Also acquired on 6 Aug 1970 for cannibalisation was the ex-Japanese *Asakaze*, ex-USS *Ellyson* (DMS 19, ex-DD 454). Both the ex-*Rodman* and ex-*Ellyson* are being scrapped in Taiwan.

GUNNERY. As built *Nan Yang* mounted five 5 inch guns; reduced during World War II to four guns wi removal of mount in "Q" position. The *Hsuen Yan* built with four guns but "Y" mount removed in 194 when converted to high-speed minesweeper (DMS In Japanese service the "Y" mount was again installe and the "B" 5 inch mounting was removed; 20 mm gur mounted in "B" position (see photograph).

2 Ex-US "BENSON" CLASS

Name	No.	Launched	US Comm	Transferred
HAN YANG (ex-USS *Hilary P. Jones*, DD 427)	DD 15	14 Dec 1939	7 Sep 1940	26 Feb 195
LO YANG (ex-USS *Benson*, DD 421)	DD 14	15 Nov 1939	25 July 1940	26 Feb 195

Displacement, tons	1 620 standard; 2 575 full load
Length, feet (*metres*)	347·8 (*105·9*) oa
Beam, feet (*metres*)	36·1 (*10·9*)
Draught, feet (*metres*)	18·0 (*5·5*)
Guns	4—5 inch (*127 mm*) 38 calibre DP (single) 4—40 mm AA (twin) several 20 mm AA
A/S weapons	depth charges
Main engines	2 geared turbines (Bethlehem); 50 000 shp; 2 shafts
Boilers	4 (Babcock & Wilcox in *Lo Yang*; Foster Wheeler in *Han Yang*)
Speed, knots	approx 34 (36·7 designed)
Complement	approx 230

Former US "Benson" class destroyers. *Lo Yang* built by Bethlehem Shipbuilding, Quincy, Massachusetts; *Han Yang* built by Charleston Navy Yard, South Carolina.

DISPOSALS

The destroyer **Tan Yan**, lately employed as a training ship, was scrapped in 1971. She is the former Japanese *Yukikaze* (see 1971-1972 and previous editions for descriptions).

HAN YANG — *Republic of China Navy*

FRIGATES

1 Ex-US "RUDDEROW" CLASS

Name	No.	Launched	US Comm	Transferred
TAI YUAN (ex-USS *Riley*, DE 579)	DE 27	29 Dec 1943	13 Mar 1944	10 July 1968

Displacement, tons	1 450 standard; approx 2 000 full load
Length, feet (*metres*)	300 (*91·4*) wl; 306 (*93·3*) oa
Beam, feet (*metres*)	37 (*11·3*)
Draught, feet (*metres*)	14 (*4·3*)
Guns	2—5 inch (*127 mm*) 38 cal DP 4—40 mm AA (twin) 4—20 mm AA (single)
A/S weapons	6—12·75 inch (*324 mm*) torpedo tubes (Mk 32 triple) 1 hedgehog depth charges
Main engines	Geared turbines (General Electric) with electric drive; 12 000 shp; 2 shafts
Boilers	2 (Foster Wheeler)
Speed, knots	24
Complement	approx 200

Former US Navy destroyer escort. Built by Bethlehem SB Co, Higham, Massachusetts. Refitted with tripod mast and platforms before bridge for 20 mm guns. (Hedgehog is on main deck, behind forward 5 inch mount). SPS-6 and SPS-10 search radars are installed.

DISPOSALS

The frigate **Tai Kang** DE 21 (ex-USS *Wyffel*, DE 6) of the so-called "short-hull" type was scrapped in 1972 (see 1971-1972 and previous editions for description).

TAI YUAN — *Iain G. B. Lovie*

FU SHAN—see following page — *Courtesy "Ships of the World"*

Frigates—*continued*

4 Ex-US "BOSTWICK" CLASS

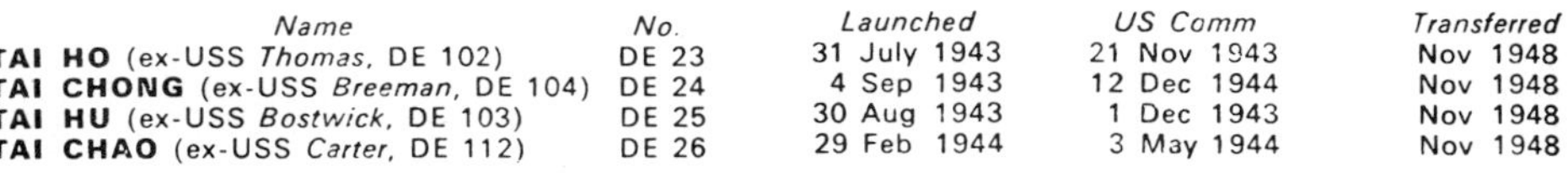

Name	No.	Launched	US Comm	Transferred
TAI HO (ex-USS *Thomas*, DE 102)	DE 23	31 July 1943	21 Nov 1943	Nov 1948
TAI CHONG (ex-USS *Breeman*, DE 104)	DE 24	4 Sep 1943	12 Dec 1944	Nov 1948
TAI HU (ex-USS *Bostwick*, DE 103)	DE 25	30 Aug 1943	1 Dec 1943	Nov 1948
TAI CHAO (ex-USS *Carter*, DE 112)	DE 26	29 Feb 1944	3 May 1944	Nov 1948

Displacement, tons	1 240 standard; 1 900 full load
Length, feet (*metres*)	300 (*91·4*) wl; 306 (*93·3*) oa
Beam, feet (*metres*)	36·6 (*11·2*)
Draught, feet (*metres*)	14 (*4·3*)
Guns	2—5 inch (*127 mm*) 38 cal DP 8—40 mm AA (2 twin, 4 single) 4—20 mm AA (single)
A/S weapons	6—12·75 inch (*324 mm*) torpedo tubes (Mk 32 triple); 1 hedgehog depth charges
Main engines	Diesel-electric (4 General Motors diesels); 6 000 bhp; 2 shafts
Speed, knots	21
Complement	approx 200

Former US Navy destroyer escorts. All built by Dravo Corp, Wilmington, Delaware, but first two units completed by Norfolk Navy Yard (Virginia).
These ships were expected to be decommissioned during 1973 and scrapped.

GUNNERY. The original main battery of three 3 inch 50 cal guns have been replaced by two 5 inch guns in open mounts.

TAI HO (5 inch guns, bridge refitted) *Toshio Tamura*

11 FRIGATES } Ex-US APD TYPE
1 TRANSPORT }

Name	No.	Launched	US Comm	Transferred
YU SHAN (ex-USS *Kinzer*, APD 91/DE 232)	PF 32	9 Dec 1943	1 Nov 1944	Apr 1965
HWA SHAN (*Donald W. Wolf*, APD 129/DE 713)	PF 33	22 July 1944	13 Apr 1945	May 1965
WEN SHAN (ex-*Gannert*, APD 42/DE 60)	PF 34	17 Apr 1943	23 July 1943	May 1966
FU SHAN (ex-*Truxtun*, APD 98/DE 282)	PF 35	9 Mar 1944	9 July 1954	Mar 1966
LU SHAN (ex-USS *Bull*, APD 78/DE 693)	PF 36	25 Mar 1943	12 Aug 1943	Aug 1966
SHOA SHAN (ex-*Kline*, APD 120/DE 687)	PF 37	27 June 1944	18 Oct 1944	Mar 1966
TAI SHAN (ex-*Register*, APD 92/DE 233)	PF 38	20 Jan 1944	11 Jan 1945	Oct 1966
HENG SHAN (*R. W. Herndon*, APD 121/DE 688)	PF 39	15 July 1944	3 Nov 1944	Oct 1966
KANG SHAN (*G. W. Ingram*, APD 43/DE 62)	PF 42	8 May 1943	11 Aug 1943	July 1967
CHUNG SHAN (ex-*Blessman*, APD 48/DE 69)	PF 43	19 June 1943	19 Sep 1943	July 1967
LUNG SHAN (ex-*Schmitt*, APD 76/DE 676)	PF 44	29 May 1943	24 July 1943	Feb 1969
TIEN SHAN (*Kleinsmith*, APD 132/DE 718)	APD 215	27 Jan 1945	12 June 1945	May 1960

Displacement, tons	1 400 standard; 2 130 full load
Length, feet (*metres*)	300 (*91·4*) wl; 306 (*93·3*) oa
Beam, feet (*metres*)	37 (*11·3*)
Draught, feet (*metres*)	12·6 (*3·2*)
Guns	2—5 inch (*127 mm*) 38 cal DP 6—40 mm AA (twin) 4—20 m AA (single) except *Hwa Shan* and possibly others have eight guns (twin mounts)
A/S weapons	6—12·75 inch (*324 mm*) torpedo tubes (Mk 32 triple) except *Heng Shan* and possibly others have two hedgehogs depth charges
Main engines	Geared turbines (General Electric) with electric drive; 12 000 shp; 2 shafts
Boilers	2 (Foster Wheeler)
Speed, knots	23·6
Complement	approx 200

Former US Navy high speed transports (APD) employed as frigates. All designated PF except *Tien Shan* which is designated APD.
All begun as destroyer escorts (DE), but converted during construction or after completion to high speed transports carrying 160 troops, commandos, or frogmen, PF 32 and 35 built by Charleston Navy Yard, South Carolina; PF 33, 36, and APD 215 by Defoe SB Co, Bay City, Michigan; PF 34, 42, and 43 by Bethlehem SB Co, Hingham, Massachusetts; PF 37, 39, and 44 by Bethlehem, Quincy, Mass.
The ex-USS *Walter B. Cobb* (APD 106/DE 596) transferred to Taiwan China in 1966 was lost at sea while under tow; replaced by ex-USS *Bull*.
Configurations differ: APD 37 class has high bridge; APD 87 class has low bridge. Radars and fire control equipment vary.

GUNNERY. All ships are now believed to have been refitted with a second 5 inch gun aft. One twin 40 mm gun mount is forward of bridge and two twin mounts are amid ships. Note after 5 inch mount and depth charge racks in photo of *Lung Shan*. Davits amidships can hold four LCVP-type landing craft.

HWA SHAN *1971, Iain G. B. Lovie*

LUNG SHAN *1973*

PATROL VESSELS

3 Ex-US MSF TYPE

WU SHENG	(ex-USS *Redstart*, MSF 378)	PCE 66	18 Oct 1944
CHU YUNG	(ex-USS *Waxwing*, MSF 389)	PCE 67	10 Mar 1945
MO LING	(ex-USS *Steady*, MSF 118)	PCE 70	6 June 1942

Displacement, tons	890 standard; 1 250 full load
Dimensions, feet	215 wl; 221·1 oa × 32·1 × 10·8
Guns	2—3 inch (*76 mm*) 50 cal AA (single); 4—40 mm AA (twin); 4—20 mm AA (twin)
A/S weapons	1 hedgehog; 3—12·75 inch (*324 mm*) torpedo tubes (Mk 32 triple); depth charges
Main engines	Diesel-electric (General Motors diesels); 3 530 bhp; 2 shafts = 18 knots
Complement	approx 80

Former US Navy minesweepers of the "Auk" class; originally designated AM. *Wu Sheng* built by Savannah Machine & Foundry Co, Georgia, others by American SB Co, Cleveland, Ohio, respectivly; launch dates above. *Wu Sheng* transferred to Taiwan China in July 1965, *Chu Yung* in Nov 1965 and *Mo LIng* in Mar 1968.
Minesweeping equipment removed and second 3 inch gun fitted aft in Taiwan service. *Chein Men* PCE 45 (ex-USS *Toucan*, MSF 387) sunk by Communist Chinese warships south of Quemoy Island on 6 Aug 1965; *Mo Ling* reported still in service (connection to previous edition).

Ex-US MSF TYPE (with 3 inch gun aft)

1 Ex-US PCE TYPE

WEI YUAN (ex-*Yung Hsiang*, PF 42, ex-USS PCE 869) PCE 68

Displacement, tons	640 standard; 940 full load
Dimensions, feet	180 wl; 184·5 oa × 33·1 × 9·8
Guns	2—3 inch (*76 mm*) 50 cal AA (single); 4—40 mm AA (twin); 5—20 mm AA (single)
A/S weapons	1 hedgehog; depth charges
Main engines	Diesels (General Motors); 1 800 bhp; 2 shafts = 15 knots
Complement	approx 120

Former US Navy submarine chaser—escort. Built by Albania Engine & Machinery Works, Portland, Oregon; launched 6 Feb 1943 and commissioned 19 Sep 1943. Transferred to Taiwan China in Feb 1946. Second 3 inch gun provided (aft) in 1955. *Yung Tai* PCE 62, ex-PF 41 (ex-USS PCE 867) damaged in action with Communist Chinese forces on 14 Nov 1965 and subsequently discarded.
The *Wei Yuan* was decommissioned in 1972 and is expected to be stricken in the near future.

Ex-US PCE TYPE (with 3 inch gun aft)

Ex-US 185-ft AM TYPE

All former US Navy 185-foot minesweepers of the "Admirable" class have been stricken or reclassified. One ship survives in the Taiwan Chinese Navy as a minelayer and two as auxiliaries. See 1971-1972 and previous editions for characteristics and ship lists.

Ex-US 173-ft PC/PGM TYPE

All former US Navy 173-foot submarine chasers and motor gunboats have been stricken. with two units now operated by the Customs Service (listed on later page). See 1971-1972 and previous editions for characteristics and ship lists.

Ex-US 110-ft SC TYPE

All former US Navy wood-hull, 110-foot submarine chasers have been stricken. See 1971-1972 and previous editions for characteristics and ship lists.

COASTAL MINELAYERS

1 Ex-US AM TYPE

YUNG FENG (ex-USS *Prime*, AM 279) MMC 50 22 Jan 1944

Displacement, tons	945 full load
Dimensions, feet	180 wl; 184·5 oa × 33 × 9·33
Guns	1—3 inch (*76 mm*) 50 cal AA; 2—40 mm AA (single); 4—20 mm AA (single)
Main engines	Diesel (Cooper Bessemer); 1 710 bhp; 2 shafts = 14 knots
Complement	approx 100

Former US Navy minesweeper of the "Admirable" class. Built Gulf SB Co, Chicasaw, Alabama; launch dates above; commissioned 12 Sep 1944. Transferred to Taiwan China in June 1949. Minesweeping equipment subseqently removed and mine rail fitted on port side aft. The ship may now have been decommisioned.

MINESWEEPERS

13 US MSC TYPE

YUNG PING	MSC 155 (ex-US MSC 140)
YUNG AN	MSC 156 (ex-US MSC 140)
YUNG NIEN	MSC 157 (ex-US MSC 277)
YUNG CHOU	MSC 158 (ex-US MSC 278)
YUNG HSIN	MSC 159 (ex-US MSC 302)
YUNG JU	MSC 160 (ex-US MSC 300)
YUNG LO	MSC 161 (ex-US MSC 306)
YUNG FU	MSC 162 (ex-*Diest*, ex-US AMS 77)
YUNG CHENG	MSC 165 (ex-*Maasieck*, ex-US AMS 78)
YUNG SHAN	MSC 164 (ex-*Lier*, ex-US AMS 63)
YUNG CHING	MSC 163 (ex-*Eekloo*, ex-US AMS 101)
YUNG LO	MSC 161 (ex-US MSC 306)
YUNG SUI	MSC 168 (ex-*Diksmude*, ex-US AMS 65)

Displacement, tons	approx 380 full load
Dimensions, feet	144 oa × 28 × 8·5
Guns	2—20 mm AA (twin) in MSC 155-161
Main engines	Diesels (General Motors); 880 bhp; 2 shafts = 13·5 knots
Complement	40 to 50

Non-magnetic, wood-hulled minesweepers built in the United States specifically fo transfer to allied navies. First seven units listed above transferred to Taiwan Chin upon completion: MSC 155 and 156 in June 1965, MSC 157 in Dec 1958, MSC 15 in July 1959, MSC 159 in Mar 1965 MSC 160 in Apr 1965, and MSC 161 in June 1966. The seven other units were transferred to Belgium upon completion in 1953 1955; retransferred to Taiwan China in Nov 1969. The *Yung Chi* MSC 166 (ex *Charleroi*, ex-US AMS 152) reportedly has been cannibalised for spare parts.
All are of similar design; the ex-Belgium ships have a small boom aft on a pole mast They carried a single 40 mm gun forward in Belgium service; current armament unknown (Photograph shows ex-Belgium *Lier* under tow to Taiwan late in 1969; note gun removed; short pole mast aft).

YUNG LO *1966*

YUNG SHAN (under tow) *1969*

YUNG NIEN *1963, Official*

MSB 12 (ex-US MSB 4)

Former US Army minesweeping boat; assigned hull number MSB 4 in US Navy and transferred to Taiwan China in Dec 1961.

MSML 1	**MSML 5**	**MSML 7**	**MSML 11**
MSML 3	**MSML 6**	**MSML 8**	**MSML 12**

Fifty-foot minesweeping launches built in the United States and transferred to Taiwan China in Mar 1961.

TORPEDO BOATS

2 79-ft TYPE

FUH KWO PT 515 **TIAN KWO** PT 516

Displacement, tons	46 light; 53 full load
Dimensions, feet	79 oa × 23·25 × 5·5
Guns	1—40 mm AA; 2—·05 cal MG (single)
Torpedo launchers	2
Main engines	3 gasoline engines; 3 shafts = 39 knots max; 32 knots cruising
Complement	12

Built by Huckins Yacht Corp, Jacksonville, Florida. Transferred to Taiwan China on 1 Sep 1957.

2 71-ft TYPE

FAAN KONG PT 513 **SAO TANG** PT 514

Displacement, tons	39 light; 46 full load
Dimensions, feet	71 oa × 19 × 5
Guns	1—20 mm AA 4—·50 cal MG (twin)
Torpedo launchers	2 (?)
Main engines	3 gasoline engines; 3 shafts = 42 knots max; 32 knots cruising
Complement	12

Built by Annapolis Yacht Yard, Annapolis, Maryland. Transferred to Taiwan China on 19 Aug 1957 and 1 Nov 1957, respectively.

2 JAPANESE TYPE

FUH CHOW PT 511 **HSUEH CHIH** PT 512

Displacement, tons	33 light; 40 full load
Dimensions, feet	69 oa × 19·9
Guns	1—40 mm AA; 2—20 mm AA (twin)
Torpedo launchers	2—18 inch (457 *mm*)
Main engines	3 gasoline engines; 3 shafts = 40 knots max; 27 knots cruising
Complement	12

Built by Mitsubishi SB Co. Transferred to Taiwan China on 1 June 1957 and 6 Nov 1957, respectively. The 40 mm gun is not mounted in the adjacent photograph (can be fitted forward of bridge).

PT 511

DOCK LANDING SHIPS

1 Ex-US "ASHLAND" CLASS

TUNG HAI (ex-USS *White Marsh*, LSD 8) LSD 191

Displacement, tons	4 790 standard; 8 700 full load
Dimensions, feet	454 wl; 457·8 oa × 72 × 18
Guns	12—40 mm AA
Main engines	Skinner Unaflow; 2 shafts; 7 400 ihp = 15·6 knots
Boilers	2, of 2-drum type
Complement	326 (total accommodation)

Built by Moore Dry Dock Co. Launched on 19 July 1943. Designed to serve as parent ship for landing craft and coastal craft. Transferred from the US Navy to the Chinese (Taiwan) Navy on 17 Nov 1960 at Long Beach, California.

TUNG HAI *1965*

AMPHIBIOUS FLAGSHIPS

2 Ex-US LST TYPE

KAO HSIUNG (ex-*Chung Hai*, LST 219 ex-USS *Dukes County*, LST 735) AGC 2 (ex-*Chung Chih*, LST 226, ex-USS *Sagadahoc County*, LST 1091) AGC 1

Former US Navy tank landing ships employed as flagships for amphibious forces. The ex-USS *Dukes County* was transferred to Taiwan China in May 1957 for service as an LST; modified to flagship and redesignated AGC 1 in 1964 (renamed); a second LST is reported to have been subsequently modified for use as an amphibious command and support ship. See characteristics below.

KAO HSIUNG (ex-*Chung Hai*) as LST

TANK LANDING SHIPS

21 Ex-US LST TYPE

LST	*Name*	*Transferred*
201	**CHUNG HAI** (ex-USS LST 755)	Apr 1946
203	**CHUNG TING** (ex-USS LST 537)	Mar 1946
204	**CHUNG HSING** (ex-USS LST 557)	Mar 1946
205	**CHUNG CHIEN** (ex-USS LST 716)	June 1946
206	**CHUNG CHI** (ex-USS LST 1017)	Dec 1946
208	**CHUNG SHUN** (ex-USS LST 732)	Mar 1946
209	**CHUNG LIEN** (ex-USS LST 1050)	Jan 1947
210	**CHUNG YUNG** (ex-USS LST 574)	Mar 1959
216	**CHUNG KUANG** (ex-USS LST 503)	June 1960
217	**CHUNG SUO** (ex-USS *Bradley County*, LST 400)	Sep 1958
218	**CHUNG CHIH** (ex-USS *Berkley County*, LST 279)	June 1960
221	**CHUNG CHUAN** (ex-LST 1030)	Feb 1948
222	**CHUNG SHENG** (ex-LST 211, ex-USS LST 1033)	Dec 1947
223	**CHUNG FU** (ex-USS *Iron County*, LST 840)	July 1958
224	**CHUNG CHENG** (ex-USS *Lafayette County*, LST 859)	Aug 1958
225	**CHUNG CHIANG** (ex-USS *San Bernadino County*, LST 1110)	Aug 1958
227	**CHUNG MING** (ex-USS *Sweetwater County*, LST 1152)	Oct 1958
228	**CHUNG SHU** (ex-USS LST 520)	Sep 1958
229	**CHUNG WAN** (ex-USS LST 535)	Sep 1958
230	**CHUNG PANG** (ex-USS LST 578)	Sep 1958
231	**CHUNG YEH** (ex-USS *Sublette County*, LST 1144)	Sep 1961

Displacement, tons	1 653 standard; 4 080 full load
Dimensions, feet	316 wl; 328 oa × 50 × 14
Guns	varies; up to 10—40 mm AA (2 twin, 6 single) with some modernised ships rearmed with 2—3 inch AA (single) and 6—40 mm AA (twin) several 20 mm AA (twin or single)
Main engines	Diesel (General Motors); 1 700 bhp; 2 shafts = 11·6 knots
Complement	varies: 100 to 125 in most ships

Former US Navy tank landing ships constructed during World War II. Dates transferred to Taiwan China are listed above. These ships have been extensively modernised with several ships having been essentially rebuilt. Additional landing craft davits added to modernised ship.
LST 211 ex-USS LST 1033 changed to LST 222 on 13 Nov 1957. Other Taiwan pennant numbers in the LST series may have been assigned to more than one ship.

Several LSTs have been stricken: ex-USS LST 717 (no name assigned; acquired in 1946 and reported sunk in 1948); *Chung Cheng* LST 207 ex-USS LST 1075, *Chung Hsun* LST 208 ex-USS LST 993, *Chung Kung* LST 213 ex-USS LST 945, *Chung Yu* LST 215 ex-USS LST 330. One of these ships is believed to have been sunk by Communist Chinese torpedo boats off Quemoy Island on 25 Aug 1958.
Chung Chuan LST 202 ex-USS LST 1030 converted to repair ship ARL 335; now stricken.

MEDIUM LANDING SHIPS

4 Ex-US LSM TYPE

Name	*No.*	*Transferred*
MEI CHIN (ex-USS LSM 155)	LSM 341	May 1946
MEI SUNG (ex-USS LSM 431)	LSM 347	June 1946
MEI PING (ex-USS LSM 471)	LSM 353	Nov 1956
MEI LO (ex-USS LSM 362)	LSM 356	May 1962

Displacement, tons	1 095 full load
Dimensions, feet	196·5 wl; 203·5 oa × 34·5 × 7·3
Guns	2—40 mm AA (twin); 4 or 8—20 mm AA (4 single or 4 twin)
Main engines	Diesels; 2 800 bhp; 2 shafts = 12·5 knots
Complement	65 to 75

Former US Navy medium landing ships constructed during World War II. Originally numbered in the 200-series in Taiwan Chinese service, but changed in 300-series as above. Some numbers may have been assigned to more than one ship.
Several LSMs have been stricken: *Mei Peng* LSM 344 ex-USS LSM 344, *Mei Lo* LSM 242 ex-USS LSM 157 (destroyed by Communist Chinese artillery and beached on Quemoy Island on 8 Sep 1958), *Mei I* LSM 343 ex-USS LSM 285, *Mei Heng* LSM 245 ex-USS LSM 456, *Mei Hung* LSM 246 ex-USS LSM 442, *Mei Ho* LSM 248/CMC 348 ex-USS LSM 13.

Mei Chien LSM 349 ex-USS LSM 76, *Mei Hwa* LSM 350 ex-USS LSM 256 (sunk 1969), *Mei Chen* LSM 351 ex-USS LSM 427, *Mei Kung* LSM 352 ex-USS LSM 478, *Mei Wen* LSM 354 ex-USS LSM 472, *Mei Ham* LSM 355 ex-LSM 474, *Mei Shen* LSM 249 ex-USS LSM 433 (sunk), *Me Hung* LSM 346 ex-USS LSM 442.

Medium Landing Ships—*continued*

MEI KUNG (now stricken) *1962, Republic of China Navy*

UTILITY LANDING CRAFT

22 Ex-US LCU TYPE

	LCU		*LCU*
HO CHUN (ex-LCU 892)	481	**HO CHUN** (ex-LCU 1225)	494
HO CH'UNG (ex-LCU 1213)	482	**HO YUNG** (ex-LCU 1271)	495
HO CHUNG (ex-LCU 849)	484	**HO CHIEN** (ex-LCU 1278)	496
HO CHANG (ex-LCU 512)	485	**HO CHI** (ex-LCU 1212)	501
HO CHENG (ex-LCU 1145)	486	**HO HOEI** (ex-LCU 1218)	502
HO SHAN (ex-LCU 1596)	488	**HO YAO** (ex-LCU 1244)	503
HO CHUAN (ex-LCU 489)	489	**HO DENG** (ex-LCU 1367)	504
HO SENG (ex-LCU 1598)	490	**HO FENG** (ex-LCU 1397)	505
HO MENG (ex-LCU 1599)	491	**HO CHAO** (es-LCU 1429)	506
HO MOU (ex-LCU 1600)	492	**HO TENG** (ex-LCU 1452)	507
HO SHOU (ex-LCU 1601)	493	**HO CHIE** (ex-LCU 700)	SB 1

21 Ex-US LCU TYPE

LCU 501 series:

Displacement, tons	158 light; 268 full load
Dimensions, feet	115·1 oa × 32 × 4·2
Guns	2—20 mm AA (single); some units also may have 2—·50 cal MG
Main engines	3 diesels; 675 bhp; 3 shafts = 10 knots
Complement	10 to 25 assigned

LCU 1466 series:

Displacment, tons	130 light; 280 full load
Dimensions, feet	115·1 oa × 34 × 4·1
Guns	3—20 mm AA (single); some units also have may 2—·50 cal MG
Main engines	3 diesels; 675 bhp; 3 shafts = 10 knots
Complement	15 to 25 assigned

The LCU 501 series formerly were built in the United States during World War II; initially designated LCT(6) series. LCU 1466 series built by Ishikowajima Heavy Industries Co, Tokyo, Japan, for transfer to Taiwan China; completed in 1955. All originally numbered in 200-series; subsequently changed to 400 and 500-series numbers.

LANDING SHIP INFANTRY AND SUPPORT SERIES

All former US Navy LSI(G), LSI(L), LSI(M), and LSS(L) ships transferred to Taiwan China have been stricken. See 1971-1972 and previous editions for ship lists and characteristics.

HO MOU (LCU 492 ex-LCU 292)

REPAIR SHIPS

1 Ex-US "LIBERTY" TYPE

PIEN TAI (ex-USS *Tutuila*, ARG 4)ARG 516

Displacement, tons	5 766 standard; 14 350 full load
Dimensions, feet	416 wl; 441·5 oa × 57 × 23
Guns	(current armament unknown)
Main engines	Triple expansion (General Machinery Corp); 2 500 ihp; 1 shaft = 12·5 knots
Boilers	2 (Babcock & Wilcox)

"Liberty" ship (EC2) built by Bethlehem Steel Co, Baltimore, Maryland; launched on 12 Sep 1943 and commissioned on 8 Apr 1944. Originally fitted to repair internal combustion engines, but capabilities subsequently expanded. Transferred from active US Fleet to Taiwan China on 21 Feb 1972.

Repair Ships—*continued*

PIEN TAI (as USS *Tutuila*) *United States Navy*

1 Ex-US LST TYPE

SUNG SHAN (ex-USS *Agenor*, ARL 3, ex-LST 490) ARL 236 (ex-ARL 336)

Displacement, tons	1 625 light; 4 100 full load
Dimensions, feet	316 wl; 328 oa × 50 × 11
Guns	8—40 mm AA (quad); 8—20 mm AA (single)
Main engines	Diesels (General Motors); 1 800 bhp; 2 shafts = 11·6 knots
Complement	216

Begun as an LST but completed as a repair ship for landing craft (ARL). Built by Kaiser Co, Vancouver, Washington; launched 3 Apr 1943; commissioned 20 Aug 1943. Transferred to France in 1951 for service in Indochina; subsequently returned to United States and retransferred to Taiwan China on 15 Sep 1957.

Hsing An ARL 335 ex-USS *Achillies* ARL 41/LST 455 burned and grounded in 1949; subsequently salvaged and refitted by Communist Chinese. Designation ARL 335 subsequently assigned to Taiwan LST 202 ex-USS LST 1013 converted to repair ship; now stricken.

SURVEYING SHIPS

1 Ex-US C1-M-AV1 TYPE

CHU HWA (ex-USNS *Sgt. George D. Keathley*, T-AGS 35, ex-T-APC 117) AGS 564

Displacement, tons	6 090 tons
Dimensions, feet	338·8 oa × 50·3 × 17·5
Guns	(current armament unknown)
Main engines	Diesel; 1 750 bhp; 1 shaft = 11·5 knots

Built in 1945 as merchant ship; subsequently acquired by US Army for use as transport, but assigned to Navy's Military Sea Transportation Service in 1950 and designated as coastal transport (T-APC 117). Refitted for oceanographic survey work in 1966-1967 and redesignated T-AGS 35. Transferred to Taiwan China on 29 Mar 1972.

1 Ex-US 185-ft AM TYPE

YANG MING (ex-*Yung Ting*, ex-USS *Lucid*, AM 259) AGS 562 (ex-MSF 45)

LCU 501 series:

Displacement, tons	945 full load
Dimensions, feet	184·5 oa × 33 × 9·8
Guns	(current armament unknown)
Main engines	Diesels (Cooper Bessemer); 1 710 bhp; 2 shafts = 14·8 knots

Former US Navy minesweeper of the "Admirable" class. Built by American SB Co, Lorain, Ohio; launched 5 June 1943 and commissioned 1 Dec 1943. Transferred to Taiwan China in Aug 1945 and employed as fleet minesweeper (MSF 45). Subsequently converted to surveying ship and renamed.

1 Ex-US AUXILIARY TUG

CHIU LIEN (ex-USS *Geronimo*, ATA 207) AGS 563

LCU 1466 series:

Displacement, tons	835
Dimensions, feet	143 oa × 33·9 × 13·2
Guns	(current armament unknown)
Main engines	Diesel (General Motors); 1 500 bhp; 1 shaft = 13 knots

Former US Navy auxiliary tug. Built by Gulfport Boiler & Welding Works, Port Arthur, Texas; launched 4 Jan 1945 and commissioned 1 Mar 1945. Transferred to Taiwan China in Feb 1969 and converted to surveying ship. Currently employed as maritime college training ship; Navy manned.

The surveying ship *Lien Chang* AGSC 466 ex-USS LSIL 1017 was stricken in 1972.

DEGAUSSING SHIPS

1 Ex-US 185-ft AM TYPE

YUNG HSIU (ex-USS *Pinnacle*, AM 274) ADG 152 (ex-MSF 48)

LCU 501 series:

Displacement, tons	945 full load
Dimensions, feet	184·5 oa × 33 × 9·8
Guns	(current armament unknown)
Main engines	Diesels (Cooper Bessemer); 1 710 bhp; 2 shafts = 14·8 knots

Former US Navy minesweeper of the "Admirable" class. Built by Gulf SB Corp; launched 11 Sep 1943 and commissioned 24 May 1944. Transferred to Taiwan China in Aug 1945 and employed as fleet minesweeper (MSF 48). Subseqently converted to degaussing ship. The *Yung Hsiu* has been decommissioned and is expected to be stricken in the near future.

OILERS

1 Ex-SOVIET MERCHANT TYPE

KUI CHI (ex-Soviet *Tuapse*) AOG 506 (ex-AOG 306)

Displacement, tons	**18 100 full load**
Dimensions, feet	**489·75 oa × 62·8 × 25·4**
Guns	**AA weapons fitted**
Main engines	**Diesel; 5 520 bhp; 1 shaft = 14·5 knots**
Cargo	**11 000 tons fuel**

Built by Burmeister & Wain, Copenhagen; completed in 1953 for Soviet merchant service. Seized by Taiwan China forces in Taiwan Straits in June 1954 and subsequently commissioned in naval service; commissioned 20 Oct 1955.

Oilers—*continued*

1 JAPANESE TYPE

WAN SHOU AOG 512

Displacement, tons	1 049 light; 4 150 full load
Dimensions, feet	283·8 oa × 54 × 18
Guns	2—40 mm AA (sing e); 2—20 mm AA
Main engines	Diesel; 2 100 bhp; 1 shaft = 13 knots
Complement	70
Cargo	73 600 gallons fuel; 62 000 gallons water

Built by Ujina Shipbuilding Co, Hiroshima, Japan for Taiwan China. Commissioned for naval service on 1 Nov 1969. Employed in resupply of offshore islands.

WAN SHOU *1969*

3 Ex-US 310-ft AOG TYPE

CHANG PEI (ex-USS *Pecatonica* AOG 57) AOG 307 17 Mar 1945
LUNG CHUAN (ex-HMNZS *Endeavour*, ex-USS *Namakagon*, AOG 53) AOG 515 4 Nov 1944
HSIN LUNG (ex-USS *Elkhorn* AOG 7) AOG 516 15 May 1943

Displacement, tons	1 850 light; 4 335 full load
Dimensions, feet	292 wl; 310·75 oa × 48·5 × 15·7
Guns	(current armament unknown)
Main engines	Diesels (General Motors); 3 300 bhp; 2 shafts = 14 knots

Former US gasoline tankers of the "Patapsco" class. Built by Cargill, Inc, Savage, Minnesota; launch dates above. The *Chang Pei* was transferred to Taiwan China on 24 Apr 1961. The ex-USS *Namakagon* was transferred to New Zealand on 5 Oct 1962 for use as an Antarctic resupply ship; strengthened for polar operations and renamed *Endeavour*; returned to the US Navy on 29 July 1971 and retransferred to Taiwan China the same date. The *Hsin Lung* was transferred to Taiwan China on 1 July 1972.
The smaller (220·5 ft) *Yu Chuan* AOG 303 ex-USS *Wantanga* AOG 22 stricken in 1959 after running aground; *Hsin Kao* AOG 502 (ex-AOG 302), ex-USS *Towalgia* AOG 42 stricken in 1973.

2 Ex-US YO TYPE

SZU MING (ex-USS YO 198) AOG 504 (ex-AOG 304)
TAI YUN (ex-USS YO 175) AOG 510

Displacement, tons	650 light; 1 595 full load
Dimensions, feet	174 oa × 32
Guns	*Szu Ming*: 1—40 mm AA; 5—20 mm AA (single)
Main engines	Diesel (Union); 560 bhp; 1 shaft = 10·5 knots
Complement	approx 65

Former US Navy self-propelled fuel oil barges. *Szu Ming* built by Manitowoc SB Co, Manitowoc, Wisconsin, in 1945; *Tai Yun* built by Albina Engine & Machinery Works, Portland, Oregon, in 1944. Transferred to Taiwan China in Dec 1949 and Mar 1968, respectively.

2 JAPANESE TYPE

Two small oilers of Japanese construction also are reported to be in service.

DISPOSALS

The *O Mei* AO 509 (ex-AO 309), formerly the USS *Maumee* AG 124 (ex-AO 2), was scrapped in 1967. The *Ho Lan* AO 305, formerly the Polish *Praca* was scrapped in 1964.

CARGO SHIPS

1 Ex-US AKL TYPE

YUNG KANG (ex-USS *Mark*, AKL12 ex-AG 143, ex-US Army FS 214) AKL 514

Displacement, tons	approx 700
Dimensions, feet	176·5 oa × 32·3 × 10
Guns	(current armament unknown)
Main engines	Diesel; 1 000 bhp; 1 shaft = 10 knots

Built by Higgins in 1944 as a small cargo ship (freight amd supply) for the US Army. Transferred to US Navy on 30 Sep 1947; operated in Indochina area from 1963 until transferred to Taiwan China on 1 July 1971.

TUGS

TA TUNG (ex-USS *Chickasaw*, ATF 83) ATF 548 23 July 1942

Displacement, tons	1 235 standard; 1 675 full load
Dimensions, feet	195 wl; 205 oa × 38·5 × 15·5
Guns	1—3 inch (*76 mm*) 50 cal AA; several light AA
Main engines	Diesel-electric drive; 3 000 bhp; 1 shaft = 15 knots

Former US Navy "Apache" class fleet tug. Built by United Engineering Co, Alameda, California; launch date above. Transferred to Taiwan China in Jan 1966.

TA SUFH (ex-USS *Tonkawa*, ATA 176) ATR 547 1 Mar 1944
TA TENG (ex-USS *Cahokia*, ATA 186) ATA 549 18 Sep 1944

Displacement, tons	435 standard; 835 full load
Dimensions, feet	134·5 wl; 143 oa × 33·9 × 13
Guns	1—3 inch (*76 mm*) 50 cal AA; several light AA
Main engines	Diesel-electric (General Motors diesels); 1 500 bhp; 1 shaft = 13 knots

Former US Navy auxiliary ocean tugs. Built by Levingston SB Co, Orange, Texas; launch dates above. *Ta Sufh* transferred to Taiwan China in Apr 1966. *Ta Teng* assigned briefly to US Air Force in 1971; transferred to Taiwan China on 14 Apr 1972. A third tug of this type serves as a surveying ship.

TA WU (ex-US Army LT 1) ATA 542
TA MING (ex-US Army LT 220) ATA 543
TA YU (ex-US Army LT 310) ATA 545
TA CHING (ex-US Army LT 355) ATA

Former US Army harbour tugs; first three ships transferred in 1949 originally numbered in 300-series.

YTL 3 (ex-US Army ST 846)
YTL 8 (ex-US Army ST 2002)
YTL 9 (ex-US Army ST 2004)
YTL 10 (ex-US Army ST 2003)

Former US Army 76-foot harbour tugs.

YTL 11 (ex-USN YTL 454) **YTL 12** (ex-USN TYL 584) **YTL 13** (ex-USN YTL 585)

Former US Navy 66-foot harbour tugs.

MISCELLANEOUS

5 Ex-US FLOATING DRY DOCKS

HAY TAN (ex-USN AFDL 36) AFDL 1
KIM MEN (ex-USN AFDL 5) AFDL 2
HAN JIH (ex-USN AFDL 34) AFDL 3
FO WU 5 (ex-USN ARD 9) ARD 5
FO WU 6 (ex-USS *Windsor*, ARD 22) ARD 6

Former US Navy floating dry docks; see United States section for characteristics.

SERVICE CRAFT

Approximately 25 non-self-propelled service craft are in use; most are former US Navy service craft.

CUSTOMS SERVICE

Several small ships and small craft are in service with the Customs Service of Taiwan China, an agency of the Ministry of Finance. The larger ships include two former submarine chasers, listed below.

2 Ex-US PC TYPE

Name	RCN No.	Launched
TUNG KIANG (ex-USS *Placerville*, PC 1087)	PC 119	21 Aug 1943
HSI KIANG (ex-USS *Susanville*, PC 1149)	PC 120	11 Jan 1944

Displacement, tons	450 full load
Dimensions, feet	173·66 oa × 23 × 10·8
Guns	1—3 inch (*76 mm*)) 50 cal AA; several lighter guns
Main engines	Diesels (General Motors); 2 880 bhp; 2 shafts = 20 knots

Former US Navy steel-hulled submarine chasers. Launch dates above. Originally transferred to Taiwan China for naval use; subsequently allocated to the Customs Service. Armament believed to have been retained.

TANZANIA

Mercantile Marine

Lloyd's Register of Shipping: 11 vessels of 18 218 tons gross

FAST GUN BOATS

6 Ex-CHINESE "SHANGHAI" CLASS

Displacement, tons	100 full load
Dimensions, feet	120·0 × 18·0 × 6·0
Guns	4—37 mm (twin fore and aft)
Main engines	4 diesels; 4 800 bhp = 28 knots

Transferred by the Chinese People's Republic in 1970-71.
There are reported to be four small patrol boats, two of 50 tons and two of 27 tons. It was officially stated in 1967 that the four *Küstenwachboote* loaned to the Tanzania Government by the Federal Republic of Germany, KW 4, KW 5, KW 9 and KW 10, shipped from West Germany on 8 Dec 1963, and renamed *Rafiki*, *Papa*, *Uhura* and *Salama*, respectively, see full particulars in the 1966-67 edition, had been handed over to the Southern Engineering Company of Mombasa, Kenya.

THAILAND

Administration

Commander-in-Chief of the Navy:
Admiral Thavil Rayananon

Deputy Commander-in-Chief:
Admiral Kamol Sitakalin

Chief of the Naval Staff:
Vice-Admiral Jit Sangkhadul

Diplomatic Representation

Naval Attaché in London:
Captain Sam-Arng Kresupon

Naval Attaché in Washington:
Captain Kasem Rakcharcon

Strength of the Fleet

1 Destroyer Escort
9 Frigates
7 Corvettes
10 Patrol Vessels
13 Coastal Gunboats
15 Patrol Boats
5 Coast Guard Vessels
2 Coastal Minelayers
4 Coastal Minesweepers
7 Landing Ships
9 Landing Craft
1 Survey Ship
1 MCS Support Ship
19 Auxiliaries

New Construction

1 General Purpose Frigate (New Yarrow Design)
2 Corvette Frigates

Personnel

1973: *Navy,* 20 000 (2 000 officers and 18 000 ratings)
Marine Corps: 6 400 (400 officers and 6 000 men)

Mercantile Marine

Lloyd's Register of Shipping:
69 vessels of 108 271 tons gross

FRIGATES

Name	*No.*	*Builders*	*Launched*	*Completed*
PIN KLAO (ex-USS *Hemminger DE* 746)	3 (ex-1)	Western Pipe & Steel Co	12 Sep 1943	30 May 1944

Displacement, tons	1 240 standard; 1 900 full load
Length, feet (*metres*)	306·0 (*93·3*) oa
Beam, feet (*metres*)	37·0 (*11·3*)
Draught, feet (*metres*)	14·1 (*4·3*)
Guns, dual purpose	3—3 in (*76 mm*) 50 cal
Guns, AA	6—40 mm
A/S weapons	8 DCT
Torpedo tubes	6 (2 triple) for A/S torpedoes
Main engines	GM diesels with electric drive; 2 shafts; 6 000 bhp
Speed, knots	20
Range, miles	11 500 at 11 knots
Oil fuel, tons	300
Complement	220

Ex-US "Cannon" class. Transferred from US Navy to Royal Thai Navy at New York Navy Shipyard in July 1959 under MDAP. The 3—21 in torpedo tubes were removed and the 4—20 mm AA guns were replaced by 4—40 mm AA. The six A/S torpedo tubes were fitted in 1966.

PIN KLAO — *1966, Royal Thai Navy*

1 YARROW TYPE

CHAO PHRAYA

Displacement, tons	1 780 official figure
Length, feet (*metres*)	320·0 (*97·6*)
Beam, feet (*metres*)	36·0 (*11·0*)
Draught, feet (*metres*)	18·0 (*5·5*)
Missile launchers	1 quadruple "Seacat" s-to-a
Guns, dual purpose	2—4·5 in (*114 mm*) single
Guns, AA	2—40 mm single
A/S weapons	1 triple barrelled "Limbo" mortar; 2 depth charge throwers
Main engines	1 Rolls-Royce "Olympus" gas Turbine; 24 000 shp; 1 Crossley-Pielstick 12 PC2V diesel; 6 000 bhp
Speed, knots	26 approx
Complement	140

An order was placed with Yarrow & Co Ltd, Scotstoun, Glasgow on 21 Aug 1969 for a general purpose frigate. A long range vessel of a new design, developed by Yarrow resulting in a comparative low cost ship with an armament displacement ratio superior to that of any comparable warship. The ship is fully automatic with a consequent saving in complement. Launched 18 Nov 1971 for delivery early 1973.

CHAO PHRAYA — *courtesy Yarrow (Shipbuilders) Ltd*

ELECTRONICS. HSA CIC system. Racal DF.

RADAR. LW 02 air surveillance amidships; M 20 series fire control system with co-mounted search and tracking radars in radome for guns; M 44 aft for Seacat.

3 US NEW CONSTRUCTION CORVETTE TYPE

TAPI PF 107 **KHIRIRAT** PF 108 + 1

Displacement, tons	900 standard; 1 135 full load
Length, feet (*metres*)	275 (*83·8*) oa
Beam, feet (*metres*)	33 (*10·0*)
Draught, feet (*metres*)	10 (*3·0*)
Guns, surface	2—3 in (*76 mm*)
Guns, AA	2—40 mm
A/S weapons	Torpedoes, DCs, Hedgehogs
Main engines	FM Diesels; 6 000 bhp
Speed, knots	20

Of similar design to the Iranian corvettes of the "Bayandor" class. *Tapi* was ordered from the American Shipbuilding Co, Toledo, Ohio on June 27 1969 laid down 1 Apr 1970 and launched 17 Oct 1970. *Khirirat* was ordered from Norfolk SB & DD Co on 25 June 1971 to be laid down 18 Feb 1972 for delivery in 1973. Third vessel laid down by Norfolk SB & DD Co late 1972.

PF Type

Frigates—*continued*

2 "PRASAE" CLASS

Name	*No.*	*Builders*	*Laid down*	*Launched*	*Completed*
PRASAE (ex-USS *Gallup, PF* 47)	2	Consolidated Steel Corpn, Los Angeles	18 Aug 1943	17 Sep 1943	29 Feb 1944
TAHCHIN (ex-USS *Glendale, PF* 36)	1	Consolidated Steel Corpn, Los Angeles	6 Apr 1943	28 May 1943	1 Oct 1943

Displacement, tons 1 430 standard; 2 100 full load
Length, feet (*metres*) 304·0 (*92·7*) oa
Beam, feet (*metres*) 37·5 (*11·4*)
Draught, feet (*metres*) 13·7 (*4·2*)
Guns, dual purpose 3—3 in (*76 mm*) 50 cal.
Guns, AA 2—40 mm; 9—20 mm
A/S weapons 8 DCT
Main engines Triple expansion; 2 shafts; 5 500 ihp
Speed, knots 19
Boilers 2 small water tube 3-drum type
Oil fuel, tons 685
Range, miles 7 800 at 12 knots
Complement 180

Former US patrol frigates of the "Tacoma" class. Delivered to the Royal Thai Navy on 29 Oct 1951. They were of similar design to the British frigates of the "River" class.

PRASAE 1971

1 Ex-BRITISH "FLOWER" CLASS

BANGPAKONG (ex-*Gondwana*, ex-HMS *Burnet*) PF 4

Displacement, tons 1 060 standard; 1 350 full load
Length, feet (*metres*) 193·0 (*58·8*) pp; 203·2 (*61·9*) oa
Beam, feet (*metres*) 33·0 (*10·0*)
Draught, feet (*metres*) 14·5 (*4·4*)
Guns, dual purpose 1—3 in (*76 mm*) 50 cal.
Guns, AA 1—40 mm; 6—20 mm
A/S weapons 4 DCT
Main engines Triple expansion; 2 880 ihp
Speed, knots 16
Boilers 2 three-drum type
Oil fuel, tons 282
Range, miles 4 800 at 12 knots
Complement 100

Built by Ferguson Bros, Port Glasgow as a "Flower" class corvette. Laid down on 2 Nov. 1942, launched on 31 May 1943, completed on 23 Sept 1943. Served in Indian Navy before transfer to Royal Thai Navy on 15 May 1947. The 3 inch replaced a 4 inch gun, and the 40 mm replaced a 20 mm gun in 1966. Sister ship *Prasae* (ex-*Sind*, ex-*Betony*) was lost in the Korean War on 13 Jan 1951.

BANGPAKONG *Royal Thai Navy*

1 SLOOP TYPE

MAEKLONG No. 3

Displacement, tons 1 400 standard; 2 000 full load
Length, feet (*metres*) 269·0 (*82·0*)
Beam, feet (*metres*) 34·0 (*10·4*)
Draught, feet (*metres*) 10·5 (*3·2*)
Guns, surface 4—4·7 in (*120 mm*)
Guns, AA 3—40 mm; 3—20 mm
Main engines Triple expansion; 2 shafts; 2 500 ihp
Speed, knots 14
Boilers 2 water tube
Oil fuel, tons 487
Range, miles 8 000 at 12 knots
Complement 155 as training ship

Built by Uraga Dock Co, Japan. Laid down in 1936, launched on 27 Nov 1936, completed in June 1937. Designed as dual-purpose sloop and torpedo boat. Employed as training ship. The 4—18 inch torpedo tubes were removed. Sister ship *Tachin*, heavily damaged on 1 June 1945, was scrapped.

MAEKLONG *1967, Royal Thai Navy*

1 Ex-BRITISH "ALGERINE" CLASS

PHOSAMTON (ex-HMS *Minstrel*) MSF 1

Displacement, tons 1 040 standard; 1 335 full load
Length, feet (*metres*) 225·0 (*68·6*) oa
Beam, feet (*metres*) 35·5 (*10·8*)
Draught, feet (*metres*) 10·5 (*3·2*)
Guns, surface 1—4 in (*102 mm*)
Guns, AA 6—20 mm
A/S weapons 4 DCT
Main engines Triple expansion; 2 shafts; 2 000 ihp
Speed, knots 16
Boilers 2 three-drum type
Oil fuel, tons 270
Range, miles 5 000 at 10 knots
Complement 103

Former British "Algerine" class ocean minesweeper capable of fleet sweeping and escort duties. Built by Redfern Construction Co. Laid down in 1943, launched on 5 Oct 1944, completed in 1945. Transferred in Apr 1947. The 20 mm guns were increased from 3 to 6, and the DCTs from 2 to 4 in 1966.

PHOSAMTON *1965, Royal Thai Navy*

CORVETTES

7 "TRAD" CLASS

CHANDHABURI 16 Dec 1936 No. 22
CHUMPORN 18 Jan 1937 No. 31
PATTANI 16 Oct 1936 No. 13
PUKET 28 Sep 1935 No. 12
RAYONG 11 Jan 1937 No. 23
SURASDRA 28 Nov 1936 No. 21
TRAD 26 Oct 1935 No. 11

Displacement, tons	318 standard; 470 full load
Dimensions, feet	219 pp; 223 oa × 21 × 7
Guns	2—3 in AA; 1—40 mm AA; 2—20 mm AA; *Chumporn, Puket* and *Trad* 2—40 mm
Tubes	4—18 in (2 twin); *Chumporn, Puket* and *Trad* 2—18 in (twin)
Main engines	Parsons geared turbines; 2 shafts; 9 000 hp = 31 knots
Boilers	2 Yarrow
Oil fuel, tons	102
Range, miles	1 700 at 15 knots
Complement	70

Designed as torpedo boats, *Puket* and *Trad* were laid down on 8 Feb 1935 by Cantieri Riuniti dell'Adriatico, Monfalcone, for delivery by end of 1935. Launch dates above. Armament was supplied by Vickers-Armstrongs Ltd. First boat reached 32-34 knots on trials with 10 000 hp. All delivered by summer 1937. The 2 single 18 inch torpedo tubes and the 4—8 mm guns were removed.

TRAD

LIGHT FORCES

3 "SATTAHIP" CLASS

KANTANG No. 7 **KLONGYAI** No. 5 **SATTAHIP** No. 8

Displacement, tons	110 standard; 135 full load
Dimensions, feet	131·5 × 15·5 × 4
Guns	1—3 in; 1—20 mm
Tubes	2—18 in
Main engines	Geared turbines; 2 shafts; 1 000 shp = 19 knots
Boilers	2 water-tube
Range, miles	480 at 15 knots
Oil fuel, tons	18
Complement	31

Sattahip was built by the Royal Thai Naval Dockyard, Bangkok, laid down on 21 Nov 1956, launched on 28 Oct 1957 and completed in 1958. The other two were built by Ishikawajima Co, Japan, both launched on 26 Mar 1937 and completed on 21 June 1937.

KANTANG 1971

7 "LIULOM" CLASS

LIULOM (ex-*PC* 1253) **LONGLOM** (ex-*PC* 570) **PHALI** (ex-*PC* 1185) **SARASIN** (ex-*PC* 495) **SUKRIP** (ex-*PC* 1218) **THAYANCHON** (ex-*PC* 575) **TONGPLIU** (ex-*PC* 616)

Displacement, tons	280 standard; 400 full load
Dimensions, feet	174 oa × 23·2 × 6
Guns	1—3 in AA; 1—40 mm AA; 5—20 mm AA
A/S weapons	2 ASW torpedo tubes (except *Sarasin*)
Main engines	Diesel; 2 shafts; 3 600 bhp = 19 knots
Oil fuel, tons	60
Range, miles	6 000 at 10 knots
Complement	62 to 71, *Sukeip* 69 (10 officers, 59 men)

Former US submarine chasers. Launched in 1941-43. Nos. PC 7, 8, 4, 1, 5, 2 and 6, respectively.

Light Forces—*continued*

THAYANCHON *1969, Royal Thai Navy*

T 91 **T 92** **T 93**

Displacement, tons	87·5 standard
Dimensions, feet	104·3 × 17·5 × 5·5
Guns	1—40 mm AA; 1—20 mm AA
Main engines	Diesels; 1 600 bhp = 25 knots
Complement	21

Fast patrol boat type. Built by the Royal Thai Naval Dockyard, Bangkok. Completed 1971.

T 91 *1970, Royal Thai Navy*

T 11 (ex-US *PGM* 71) **T 12** (ex-US *PGM* 79) **T 13** (ex-US *PGM* 107) **T 14** (ex-US *PGM* 116) **T 15** (ex-US *PGM* 117) **T 16** (ex-US *PGM* 115) **T 17** (ex-US *PGM 113*) **T 18** (ex-US *PGM 114*) **T 19** (ex-US *PGM* 123) **T 110** (ex-US *PGM* 124)

Displacement, tons	130 standard; 147 full load
Dimensions, feet	99·0 wl; 101·0 oa × 21·0 × 6·0
Guns	1—40 mm AA; 4—20 mm AA; 2—·50 cal
Main engines	Diesels; 2 shafts; 1 800 bhp = 18·5 knots
Range, miles	1 500 at 10 knots
Complement	30

T 11 was built by Peterson Builders Inc, launched on 5 May 1965 and transferred to the Royal Thai Navy on 1 Feb 1966. T 13 was transferred 28 Aug 1967, T 14, T 15 on 18 Aug 1969 and 2 Oct 1969, T 16, T 17 and T 19 on 12 Feb 1970, T 19 and T 110 on 25 Dec 1970.

T 12 *1969, Royal Thai Navy*

CGC 3 (ex 13) **CGC 4** (ex 14) **CGC 5** (ex 15) **CGC 6** (ex 16)

Displacement, tons	95
Dimensions, feet	95 × 20·2 × 5
Guns	1—20 mm AA
A/S weapons	2 D.C. racks; 2 mousetraps
Main engines	4 diesels; 2 shafts; 2 200 bhp = 21 knots
Range, miles	1 500 at 14 knots
Complement	15

U S coastguard cutters transferred in 1954. Similar to those built for U.S.C.G. by U S Coast Guard Yard, Curtis Bay, in 1953. Cost £475,000 each.

CGC 14 *Royal Thai Navy*

Light Forces—*continued*

CGC 11 **CGC 1** (ex 11)

Displacement, tons	44·5
Dimensions, feet	83·1 × 16 × 4·5
Guns	1—20 mm AA
A/S weapons	2 DC racks; 2 mousetraps
Main engines	2 Viking petrol engines; 1 300 bhp = 20·5 knots

Former US Coast Guard cutter of the YP class. Of wooden hulled construction. Sister ship CGC 12 reported as converted for survey duties.

SC 7 (ex *SC*-31, ex-US *SC* 1632) **SC 8** (ex *SC*-32, ex-US *SC* 1633)

Displacement, tons	110 light; 125 full load
Dimensions, feet	111 × 17 × 6
Guns	1—40 mm; 3—20 mm
A/S weapons	Depth Charges, Mousetrap
Main engines	High-speed diesel = 18 knots
Range, miles	2 000 at 10 knots

Former US wooden submarine chasers. Built by South Coast Co, Newport Reach, California, in 1954-55. SC 33 (ex-*SC* 1634) was scrapped 8 Mar 1962.

T 21 **T 22** **T 23** **T 24** **T 25** **T 26** **T 27**

Displacement, tons	20 standard; 22 full load
Dimensions, feet	50 × 13
Guns	2—0·50 cal (1 twin)
Main engines	Diesels; 2 shafts; 480 bhp = 25 knots
Complement	5

Swift class patrol craft transferred from USN; T22 in Oct 1968, T23-25 in Nov 1970. T21 and 27 still in commission.

T 31 **T 32** **T 33** **T 34** **T 35** **T 36**

Displacement, tons	10·4 standard; 13·05 full load
Dimensions, feet	35 × 10
Guns	2—0·50 cal (1 twin); 2—0·30 cal
Main engines	Diesels; 2 shafts; 225 bhp = 14 knots
Complement	7

Ten more of this type were transferred from the US by the end of 1972. USN RPC type.

ARMOURED GUNBOATS. Of the two armoured gunboats or coast defence monitors (1,000 tons with 6-inch guns) built by Vickers Armstrong in 1928-30, *Ratanakosindra* was withdrawn from service in 1968 and *Sukothai* was removed from the effective list in 1971.

MINEWARFARE FORCES

2 "BANGRACHAN" CLASS (COASTAL MINELAYERS)

BANGRACHAN (No. 1) **NHONG SARHAI** (No. 2)

Displacement, tons	368 standard; 408 full load
Dimensions, feet	160·8 × 25·9 × 7·2
Guns	2—3 in AA; 2—20 mm AA
Mines	142 capacity
Main engines	Burmeister & Wain diesels; 2 shafts; 540 bhp = 12 knots
Oil fuel, tons	18
Range, miles	2 700 at 10 knots
Complement	55

Launched by Cantiere dell'Adriatico, Monfalcone in 1936, *Nhong Sarhai* on 22 July.

BANGRACHAN

BANGKEO (ex-USS *MSC* 303) 6 **LADYA** (ex-USS *MSC* 297) 5
DONCHEDI (ex-USS *MSC* 313) 8 **TADINDENG** (ex-USS *MSC* 301) 7

Displacement, tons	330 standard; 362 full load
Dimensions, feet	145·3 oa × 27 × 8·5
Guns	2—20 mm AA
Main engines	4 GM diesels; 2 shafts; 1 000 bhp = 13 knots
Range, miles	2 500 at 10 knots
Complement	43 (7 officers, and 36 men)

Built by Peterson Builders Inc, Sturgeon Bay, Wisc, (*Ladya* and *Donchedi*), Tacoma Boat building Co Tacoma, Wash. (*Tadindeng*) and Dorchester Shipbuilding Corp, Camden (*Bangkeo*). *Ladya* was transferred on 14 Dec 1963, *Bangkeo* on 9 July 1965, *Tadindeng* on 26 Aug 1965, and *Donchedi* on 17 Sep 1965 (last three launched

Minewarfare Forces—*continued*

in 1964, 1 July, 11 Apr, 22 Dec). Of the ex-US *YMS* type, *Bangkeo* (ex-*YMS* 384), *Ladya* (ex-*YMS* 138) and *Tadindeng* (ex-*YMS* 21) were removed from the effective list in 1964 and 1965.

BANGKEO 1971

MINESWEEPER SUPPORT SHIP

RANG KWIEN MCS 11 (ex-*Umihari Maru*)

Displacement, tons	586 standard
Dimensions, feet	162·3 × 31·2 × 13·0 max
Main engines	Triple expansion steam; Speed = 10 knots

Built in 1944 by Mitsubishi Co as a tug. Acquired by Royal Thai Navy on 6 Sep 1967.

RANG KWIEN 1969, *Royal Thai Navy*

AMPHIBIOUS FORCES

4 Ex-US LST TYPE

ANGTHONG (ex-USS *LST* 294) LST 1
CHANG (ex-USS *Lincoln County LST* 898) LST 2
LANTA (ex-USS *Stone County LST* 1141) LST 4
PANGAN (ex-USS *Stark County LST* 1134) LST 3

Displacement, tons	1 625 standard; 4 080 full load
Dimensions, feet	316 wl; 328 oa × 50 × 14
Guns	6—40 mm; 4—20 mm
Main engines	GM diesels; 2 shafts; 1 700 bhp = 11 knots
Range, miles	9 500 at 9 knots
Complement	80

Angthong is employed as a transport. *Chang*, transferred to Thailand in 1962, was built by Dravo Corp, laid down on 15 Oct 1944, launched on 25 Nov 1944 and completed on 29 Dec 1944. *Pangan* was transferred on 16 May 1966 and *Lanta* on 12 Mar 1970.

CHANG **1965, *Royal Thai Navy***

3 Ex-US LSM TYPE

KRAM (ex-USS *LSM* 469) LSM 3 **KUT** (ex-USS *LSM* 338) LSM 1
PHAI (ex-USS *LSM* 333) LSM 2

Displacement, tons	743 standard; 1 095 full load
Dimensions, feet	196·5 wl; 203·5 oa × 34·5 × 8·3
Guns	2—40 mm AA
Main engines	Diesel direct drive; 2 shafts; 2 800 bhp = 12·5 knots
Range, miles	2 500 at 12 knots
Complement	55

Former United States landing ship of the LCM, later LSM (Medium Landing Ship), type. *Kram* was transferred to Thailand under MAP at Seattle, Wash, on 25 May 1962; she was built by Brown Shipbuilding Col, Houston, Tex, laid down on 27 Jan 1945, launched on 17 Feb 1945, and completed on 17 Mar 1945. A photograph of *Kut* appears in the 1956-57 to 1964-65 editions, and of *Kram* in the 1965-66 to 1969-70 editions.

Amphibious Forces—*continued*

NAKA LSSL 3 (ex-USS *LSSL* 102)

Displacement, tons	233 standard; 287 full load
Dimensions, feet	152 wl; 158 oa × 23 × 4·25
Guns	1—3 inch; 4—40 mm AA; 4—20 mm AA; 4—81 mm mortar
Main engines	Diesels; 2 shafts; 1 320 bhp = 15 knots
Range, miles	4 700 at 10 knots

Transferred in 1966. Acquired when Japan returned her to USA. Support gunboat.

2 Ex-US LCI TYPE

PRAB (ex-*LCI M* 670) *LCI* 1 **SATAKUT** (ex-*LCI M* 739) LCI 2

Displacement, tons	230 standard; 387 full load
Dimensions, feet	157 × 23 × 6
Guns	2—20 mm AA
Main engines	Diesel; 2 shafts; 1 320 bhp = 14 knots
Complement	54

Former United States landing craft of the LCI (Infantry Landing Craft) type. A photograph of *Prab* appears in the 1957-58 and earlier editions.

SATAKUT *Royal Thai Navy*

6 LCU Ex-US LCT (6) TYPE

ARDANG (LCU 3) **MATAPHON** (LCU 1) **RAWI** (LCU 2)
KOLUM (LCU 5) **PHETRA** (LCU 4) **TALIBONG** (LCU 6)

Displacement, tons	134 standard; 279 full load
Dimensions, feet	112 × 32 × 4
Guns	2—20 mm AA
Main engines	Diesel; 3 shafts; 675 bhp = 10 knots
Complement	37

Former United States landing craft of the LCT(6) type. Employed as transport ferries. A photograph of *Mataphon* appears in the 1950-51 to 1961-62 editions.

SURVEY SHIP

CHANDHARA

Displacement, tons	870 standard; 996 full load
Dimensions, feet	229·2 oa × 34·5 × 10
Guns	1—20 mm AA
Main engines	2 diesels; 2 shafts; 1 000 bhp = 13·25 knots
Range, miles	10 000 (cruising)
Complement	72

Built by C. Melchers & Co, Bremen, Germany. Laid down on 27 Sep 1960. Launched on 17 Dec 1960. Can also be used as training ship and yacht.

CHANTHARA *1962, Royal Thai Navy*

2 OCEANOGRAPHIC CRAFT

Of 90 tons, launched in 1955 with a crew of 8.

TRANSPORTS

SICHANG AKL 1

Displacement, tons	815 standard
Dimensions, feet	160 × 28 × 16
Main engines	Diesel; 2 shafts; 550 bhp = 16 knots
Complement	30

Built by Harima Co, Japan. *Sichang* was launched on 10 Nov 1937. Completed in Jan 1938. A photograph of this ship appears in the 1953-54 to 1959-60 editions. Sister ship *Pangan* was deleted from the list in 1962.

KLED KEO A 7

Displacement, tons	382 standard; 450 full load
Dimensions, feet	154·9 × 25·4 × 14
Guns	3—20 mm
Main engines	1 diesel; 600 hp = 12 knots max
Complement	54

OILERS

PROET

Displacement, tons	360 (official figure)
Dimensions, feet	122·7 × 19·7 × 8·7
Main engines	Diesels; 500 bhp = 9 knots

Built by the Royal Thai Naval Dockyard, Bangkok. Commissioned on 16 Jan 1970.

SAMED

Displacement, tons	360 standard; 485 full load
Dimensions, feet	120 × 20 × 10
Main engines	Diesel; 500 bhp = 9 knots

Built by Royal Thai Naval Dockyard, Bangkok. Launched on 8 July 1966. Commissioned on 15 Dec 1970.

CHULA AO 2

Displacement, tons	2 395 standard
Dimensions, feet	328 × 43·2 × 25 feet
Main engines	Steam turbine

This tanker and *Matra* (see below) were acquired for naval oiling and supply duties.

CHULA *1969, Royal Thai Navy*

MATRA AO 3

Displacement, tons	4 744
Dimensions, feet	328 × 45·2 × 20
Main engines	Steam turbine

Employed as a freighting and fleet replenishment tanker and naval supply ship.

SAMUI (ex-USS YOG 60) YO 4

Displacement, tons	422 standard
Dimensions, feet	174·5 × 32 × 15
Main Engines	Diesel; 2 shafts; 600 bhp = 8 knots
Complement	49

Small tanker of the ex-YOG type. Employed as a fleet auxiliary attendant oiler. A photograph appears in the 1956-57 to 1969-70 editions.

PRONG

Displacement, tons	150 standard
Dimensions, feet	95 × 18 × 7·5
Main engines	Diesel; 150 bhp = 10 knots
Complement	14

Launched in 1938. Employed as a small naval auxiliary servicing tanker.

WATER CARRIERS

CHUANG

Displacement, tons	305 standard; 485 full load
Dimensions, feet	98 × 18 × 7·2 (official figures)
Main engines	GM diesel; 500 bhp = 11 knots
Complement	29

Built by the Royal Thai Naval Dockyard, Bangkok. Launched on 14 Jan 1965.

CHAN YW 6

Displacement, tons	355 standard
Dimensions, feet	139·5 × 24 × 10
Main engines	Diesel; Speed = 6 knots

A photograph of this ship appears in the 1956-57 to 1959-60 editions.

TUGS

SAMAESAN (ex-*Empire Vincent*) YTB 7

Displacement, tons	503 full load
Dimensions, feet	105·0 × 26·5 × 13·0
Main engines	Triple expansion; 850 ihp = 10·5 knots
Complement	27

Built by Cochrane & Sons Ltd, Selby, Yorks, England. Photograph in 1957-58 and earlier editions.

KLUENG BADAN (ex-USN *YTL*) **RAD** (ex-USN *YTL*)
MARN VICHAI (ex-USN *YTL*)

Displacement, tons	63 standard (*Rad* 52 standard)
Dimensions, feet	64·7 × 16·5 × 6·0 (*Rad* 60·7 × 17·5 × 5·0)
Main engines	Diesels; speed = 8 knots (*Rad* 6 knots)

TRINIDAD AND TOBAGO

COAST GUARD

Administration

Commanding Officer, T. & T. Coast Guard: Captain D. F. A. Bloom MOM, GM

Personnel

1973; 196 (21 officers, 175 ratings)

Mercantile Marine

Lloyds' Register of Shipping: 23 vessels of 17 988 tons gross

PATROL CRAFT

2 LATER VOSPER TYPE

BUCCO REEF CG 4 **CHAGUARAMUS** CG 3

Displacement, tons	100 standard; 125 full load
Dimensions, feet	95·0 wl; 103·0 × 19·8 × 5·8
Guns	1—20 mm Hispano Suiza
Main engines	2 Paxman Ventura diesels; 2 900 bhp = 24 knots
Oil fuel, tons	20
Range, miles	2 000 at 13 knots
Complement	19 (3 officers, 16 ratings)

Chaguaramus was laid down on 1 Dec 1970 and launched on 29 Mar 1971. Both commissioned at Portsmouth on 18 Mar 1972. Fitted with modern navigational equipment, air-conditioning and roll-damping.

CHAGUARAMUS *1972, Wright & Logan*

2 VOSPER TYPE

COURLAND BAY CG 2 **TRINITY** CG 1

Displacement, tons	96 standard; 123 full load
Dimensions, feet	95·0 wl; 102·6 oa × 19·7 × 5·5
Guns	1—40 mm Bofors
Main engines	2 Vee-form 12 cyl Paxman Ventura YJCM turbo-charged diesels; 2 910 bhp = 24·5 knots (max)
Oil fuel, tons	18
Range, miles	1 800 at 13·5 knots
Complement	17 (3 officers, 14 ratings)

Designed and built by Vosper Limited, Portsmouth. Of steel construction with aluminium alloy superstructure. Up-to-date radar and navigation equipment is fitted, and the boats are air-conditioned throughout except the engine room. Vosper roll-damping equipment is fitted for improved sea-keeping and greater efficiency and comfort of the crews. Laid down Oct 1963. *Trinity* was launched on 14 Apr 1964. Both were commissioned at Portsmouth on 20 Feb 1965. *Trinity* is named after Trinity Hills, so named by Columbus on making his landfall in 1498, and *Courland Bay* after a bay in Tobago where a settlement was founded by the Duke of Courland in the 17th century.

COURLAND BAY *1972, Trinidad & Tobago Coast Guard*

TRINITY *1969, Trinidad & Tobago Coast Guard*

Patrol Craft—*continued*

1 60 ft TYPE

SEA HAWK

Dimensions, feet	60 × 17·3 × 3·5
Guns	1 machine gun
Main engines	2 Rolls Royce diesels; 250 hp = 14·5 knots
Radius, miles	400
Complement	6 (1 officer, 5 men)

Built by J. Taylor (Shipbuilders) Ltd, Shoreham-by-Sea. Extensively refitted in 1969; but taken out of service in Dec 1971 and placed in reserve.

SEA HAWK *1970, Trinidad & Tobago Coast Guard*

1 45ft TYPE

SEA SCOUT CG 5

Length, feet	45·0
Main engines	1 GM 671 diesel; speed = 12 knots

Built by J. Taylor (Shipbuilders) Ltd, Shoreham-by-Sea. Refitted in 1970 with a single GM 671 diesel in place of the former two Perkins diesels.

SEA SCOUT *1972, Trinidad & Tobago Coast Guard*

4 INSHORE TYPE

CG 6 **CG 7** **CG 8** **CG 9**

Three Glastron glass fibre runabouts and one locally built (also of glass fibre), all capable of 27 knots, are used for inshore patrol work, mainly in the Gulf of Paria.

CG 6 *1971, Trinidad & Tobago Coast Guard*

TOGO

PATROL BOATS

It was reported that Togo, which proclaimed independence on 27 April 1960, had acquired 3 steel 100 ft motor patrol boats and 1 steel 95 ft river gunboat and intended to acquire in the near future 1 steel 130 ft patrol vessel.

TUNISIA

Administration

Chief of Naval Staff: Capitaine de Fregate Jedidi Bechir

Personnel

1973; 1 900 officers and men

Mercantile Marine

Lloyds' Register of Shipping: 23 vessels of 28 268 tons gross

CORVETTE

1 FRENCH A-69 TYPE AVISO

Displacement, tons	950 standard; 1 260 full load
Dimensions, feet	262·5 oa × 33·8 × 9·8
Guns	1—3·9 in AA. 2—20 mm
A/S weapons	1 sextuple Mk 64 rocket launcher (375 mm) 4 fixed torpedo launchers for homing torpedoes
Main engines	2 SEMT Pielstick PC2V Diesels; 2 shafts; c-p propellers; 1 100 shp = 24 knots
Range, miles	4 500 at 15 knots
Complement	62

Ordered from France in 1972. (See Coastal minesweeper below).

COASTAL MINESWEEPER

COQUELICOT (ex-USN MSC 84)

French minesweeper of the "Acacia" class loaned to Tunisia for one year in 1973 until completion of the A69 Type Aviso ordered from France is completed.

LIGHT FORCES

2 "P 48" TYPE

BIZERTE P 301 **HORRIA** (ex-*Liberte*) P 302

Displacement, tons	250
Dimensions, feet	157·5 × 23·3 × 7
Guns	2—40 mm AA
Missiles	8 SS-12 M
Main engines	2 diesels; 4 800 bhp = 20 knots
Range, miles	2 000 at 16 knots

Built by Ch Franco-Belges (Villeneuve, la Garenne). *Bizerte* was launched on 20 Nov 1969 and completed 10 July 1970. *Horria* launched 12 Feb 1970 and completed Oct 1970.

HORRIA *1972. Tunisian Navy*

SAKIET SIDI YOUSSEF (ex-*UW 12*) P 303

Displacement, tons	325 standard; 400 full load
Dimensions, feet	170 pp × 23 × 6·5
Guns	1—40 mm; 2—20 mm
A/S weapons	1 hedgehog; 2 DCT; 2 DC racks
Main engines	4 Pielstick-SEMT diesels; 2 340 bhp = 19 knots
Range, miles	2 000 at 15 knots
Complement	4 officers, 59 men

Patrol vessel of the "Fougueux" type. Built in France by Dubigeon, Nantes, under US off-shore order. Purchased by Federal Germany in 1957 and served as A/S trials vessel. Transferred to Tunisia in Dec 1969.

SAKIET SIDI YOUSSEF *1971, Tunisian Navy*

AL JALA P 203 **JOUMHOURIA** P 202
ISTIKLAL (ex-*VC* 11, *P* 761) P 201 **REMADA** P 204

Displacement, tons	75 standard; 82 full load
Dimensions, feet	104·5 × 15·5 × 5·5
Guns	2—20 mm AA
Main engines	2 Mercedes-Benz diesels; 2 shafts; 2 400 bhp = 28 knots
Range, miles	1 400 at 15 knots
Complement	17

Light Forces—*continued*

Istiklal, seaward defence motor launch of the VC type, built by Lurssens in Germany, and completed in 1958, was transferred from the French Navy on 22 Sep 1959. Others of this class transferred as follows: *Joumhouria* Jan 1961, *Al Jala* Nov 1963 and *Remada* July 1967.

ISTIKLAL *1971, Tunisian Navy*

V 101 **V 102** **V 103** **V 104** **V 105** **V 106** **V 107** **V 108**

Displacement, tons	38
Dimensions, feet	83 × 15·6 × 4·1
Guns	1—20 mm
Main engines	2 twim GM diesels; 2 400 hp = 23 knots
Range, miles	900 at 16 knots
Complement	11

Officially rated as *Vedettes Cotiers*. In general duties in harbour and off the coast V 107 and V 108 were added to the flotilla in 1971.

V 104 *1970, Tunisian Navy*

TUG

RAS ADAR (ex-*Zeeland*, ex-*Pan American*, ex-*Ocean Pride*. ex-HMS *Oriana, BAT 1*)

Displacement, tons	540 standard
Dimensions, feet	144·4 × 33 × 13·5

Built by the Gulfport Boilerworks & Eng Co in 1942 and lend leased to the Royal Navy in that year as BAT 1 HMS *Oriana*, returned and sold in 1946 as Ocean *Pride*, then *Pan America* in 1947, then *Zeeland* in 1956.

RAS ADAR *1970, Tunisian Navy*

TURKEY

Administration

Chief of the Navy:
Admiral Kemal Kayacan

Chief of Staff, Turkish Naval Forces:
Vice Admiral Bülent Ulusu

Fleet Commander:
Vice-Admiral Hilmi Firat

Personnel

1973: 38 500 officers and ratings

Strength of the Fleet

12 Destroyers
2 Frigates (Building)
9 Corvettes
13 Submarines
6 Patrol Vessels
11 Torpedo Boats
43 Patrol Launches
9 Minelayers (6 Coastal)
16 Coastal Minesweepers
4 Inshore Minesweepers
41 LCTs
11 LCUs
20 LCM's
18 LCVP's
2 Submarine Depot Ships
2 Submarine Rescue Ships
2 Repair Ships
7 Oilers
11 Boom and Gate Vessels
1 Training Ship
2 Tugs

Diplomatic Representation

Naval Attaché in London:
Rear-Admiral E. Göksan (Defence Attaché)

Naval Attaché in Washington:
Captain Irfan Tinaz

Mercantile Marine

Lloyd's Register of Shipping:
340 vessels of 743 071 tons gross

DESTROYERS

3 MODIFIED "GEARING" CLASS

Name	*No.*	*Builders*	*Launched*	*Completed*
ADATEPE (ex-USS *Forest Royal*, DD 872)	D 353	Bethlehem (Staten Is.)	17 Jan 1946	28 June 1946
KOCATEPE (ex-USS *Harwood*, DD 861)	D 354	Bethlehem (San Pedro)	24 May 1945	28 Sep 1945
TINAZTEPE (ex-USS *Keppler*, DD 765)	D 355	Bethlehem (San Francisco)	24 June 1945	23 May 1947

Displacement, tons	2 425 standard; 3 500 full load
Length, feet (*metres*)	390·5 (*119·0*) oa
Beam, feet (*metres*)	40·9 (*12·5*)
Draught, feet (*metres*)	19·0 (*5·8*)
Guns	4—5 in (*127 mm*) 38 cal dual purpose (2 twin)
A/S weapons	*Adatepe:* 1 Asroc 8-tube launcher; 2 triple torpedo tubes (Mk 32); Facilities for small helo *Kocatepe:* 1 Trainable Hedgehog; 2 Triple torpedo tubes (Mk 32); 2 Fixed Torpedo tubes (Mk 28). Facilities for small Helo
Main engines	2 geared turbines; 2 shafts; 60 000 shp
Boilers	4 Babcock & Wilcox
Speed	34 knots
Oil fuel, tons	650
Range, miles	4 800 at 15 knots, 2 400 at 25 knots
Complement	275 (15 officers, 260 ratings)

GENERAL
Adatepe was a FRAM I conversion and *Kocatepe* and *Tinaztepe* FRAM II. They were transferred to Turkey on 27 Mar 1971 (*Adatepe*) 17 Dec 1971 (*Kocatepe*) and 30 June 1972 (*Tinaztepe*).

RADAR. *Adatepe*: SPS 40 long range air search; SPS 10 surface search; gun fire control Mk 68 radar. *Kocatepe* and *Tinaztepe*: SPS 6 long range S band air surveillance; SPS 10 surface search; Mk 68 as above.

SONAR. *Adatepe* SQS 23. *Kocatepe* and *Tinaztepe* SQS 29.

KOCATEPE (as Harwood) — *Added 1972, USN*

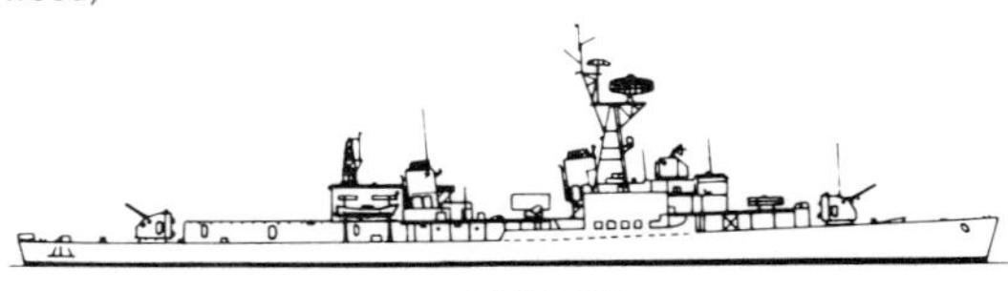
ADATEPE

2 MODIFIED "SUMNER" CLASS

Name	*No.*	*Builders*	*Launched*	*Completed*
MUAVENET (ex-USS *Gwin*, ex-DM 33, ex-DD 772)	D 357	Bethlehem (San Pedro)	9 Apr 1944	30 Sep 1944
ZAFER (ex-USS *Hugh, Purvis* ex-DD 709)	D 356	Federal SB and DD Co	17 Dec 1944	1 Mar 1945

Displacement, tons	2 250 standard; 3 375 full load
Length, feet (*metres*)	375·5 (*114·8*)
Beam, feet (*metres*)	40·9 (12·5)
Draught, feet (*metres*)	19·0 (*5·8*)
Guns	6—5 in 38 cal
A/S weapons	2 Triple torpedo launchers Mk 32 2 Hedgehogs, 2 DASH helicopters
Machinery	2 geared turbines; 2 shafts; 60 000 shp
Boilers	4 Babcock & Wilcox
Speed	34 knots
Oil fuel, tons	650
Range, miles	4 600 at 15 knots
Complement	275 (15 officers, 260 ratings)

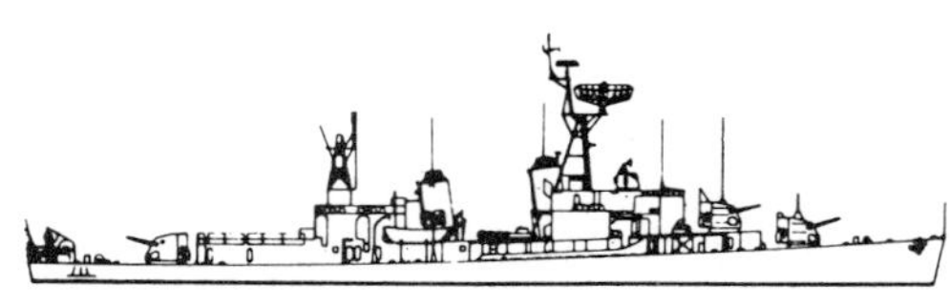
WALLACE L. LIND (DD 703) Allen M. Sumner Class FRAM II

GENERAL
Muavenet was of the "Smith" (modified "Allen M. Sumner") class of USN Destroyer Minelayers. After modernisation at Philadelphia she joined the Turkish Fleet in mid-1972 having been transferred from USN on 22 Oct 1971. *Zafer* is a standard FRAM II Sumner class.

RADAR. *Muavenet* SPS 6. Long range S-band air surveillance; Mk 68 radar director. *Zafer* SPS 40 long range air search and SPS 10 surface search.

MINES. *Muavenet* has retained a mine-laying ability.

SONAR. SQS 29.

Destroyers—*continued*

3 "I" CLASS
(Ex-US "FLETCHER" CLASS)

Name	No.	Builders	Launched	Completed
ICEL (ex-USS *Preston*, DD 795)	D 344	Bethlehem Company, San Pedro	12 Dec 1943	20 Mar 1944
ISKENDERUN (ex-USS *Boyd*, DD 544)	D 343	Bethlehem Company, San Pedro	29 Oct 1942	8 May 1943
IZMIT (ex-USS *Cogswell*, DD 651)	D 342	Bath Iron Works Corporation	5 June 1943	17 Aug 1943

Displacement, tons	2 050 standard; 3 000 full load
Length, feet (*metres*)	376·5 (*114·8*) oa
Beam, feet (*metres*)	39·5 (*12·1*)
Draught, feet (*metres*)	18·0 (*5·5*)
Guns, surface	4—5 in (*127 mm*) 38 cal
Guns, AA	6—3 in (*76 mm*)
A/S weapons	2 Hedgehogs
Torpedo tubes	5—21 in (*533 mm*) quintupled
Main engines	GE geared turbines; 2 shafts; 60 000 shp
Speed, knots	34
Boilers	4 Babcock & Wilcox
Oil fuel, tons	650
Range, miles	5 000 at 15 knots
Complement	250

TRANSFER. Transferred *Iskenderun* and *Ismit* on 1 Oct 1969, and *Icel* on 15 Nov 1969.

IZMIT 1972, *Turkish Navy*

RADAR. Search: SPS 6. Tactical: SPS 10. Fire Control: GFCS 68.

DISPOSALS. *Istanbul* (D 340) and *Izmir* (D 341) deleted 1973.

4 "G" CLASS
(Ex-US "GLEAVES" CLASS)

Name	No.	Builders	Laid down	Launched	Completed
GAZIANTEP (ex-USS *Lansdowne*, DD 486)	D 348 (ex-344)	Federal SB & DD Co, Port Newark	July 1941	20 Feb 1942	29 Apr 1942
GELIBOLU (ex-USS *Buchanan*, DD 484)	D 346	Federal SB & DD Co, Port Newark	11 Feb 1941	22 Nov 1941	21 Mar 1942
GEMLIK (ex-USS *Lardner*, DD 487)	D 347	Federal SB & DD Co, Port Newark	July 1941	20 Mar 1942	13 May 1942
GIRESUN (ex-USS *McCalla*, DD 488)	D 345	Federal SB & DD Co, Port Newark	July 1941	20 Mar 1942	27 May 1942

Displacement, tons	1 810 standard; 2 580 full load
Length, feet (*metres*)	341·0 (*103·9*)wl; 348·5 (*106·2*)oa
Beam, feet (*metres*)	36·0 (*11·0*)
Draught, feet (*metres*)	18·0 (*5·5*)
Guns, surface	*D345, D346*: 3—5 in (*127 mm*) 38 cal.; *D344, D347*: 4—5 in (*127 mm*) 38 cal.
Guns, AA	*D345, D346*: 4—3 in (*76 mm*); *D344, D347*: 4—40 mm
A/S weapons	2 Hedgehogs; homing torpedoes;
Torpedo tubes	5—21 in (*533 mm*)
Main engines	GE geared turbines; 2 shafts; 50 000 shp
Speed, knots	37 designed; 34 max
Boilers	4 Babcock & Wilcox
Oil fuel, tons	600
Range, miles	5 000 at 15 knots
Complement	250

GENERAL
Former US "Gleaves" class destroyers, acquired by Turkey early in 1949. *Gelibolu* and *Giresun* were formally taken over on 29 Apr 1949, and *Gaziantep* and *Gemlik* in 1950. Modernised in USA in 1957-58 and fitted with tripod instead of pole foremast and raised bridge.

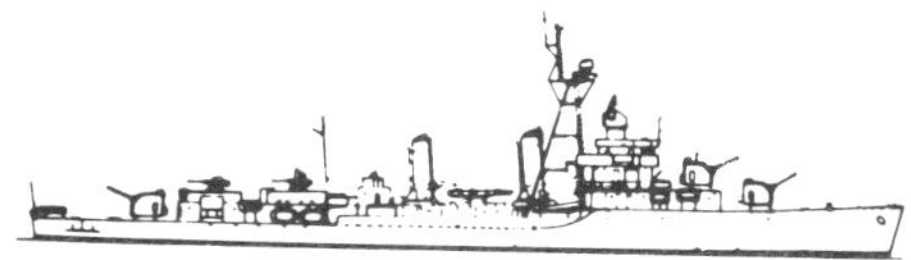
GELIBOLU, GIRESUN

GUNNERY. The 5 in gun in "X" position, 40 mm AA and 20 mm AA guns in *Gelibolu* and *Giresun* were replaced by four 3-in AA guns in two twin mountings.

GAZIANTEP (four 5-inch guns) 1970, *Stefan Terzibaschitsch*

GIRESUN (three 5-inch guns) 1972, *Dr. Giorgio Arra*

GAZIANTEP, GEMLIK
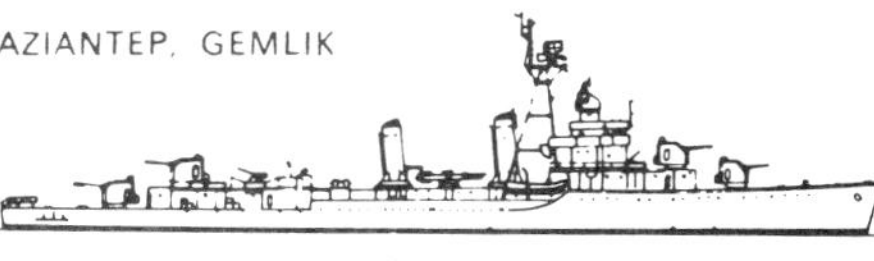

RADAR. Search: SPS 6. Tactical: SPS 10. Fire Control: GFCS 68.

FRIGATES

2 NEW CONSTRUCTION

Displacement, tons	1 450 standard; 1 950 full load
Length, feet (*metres*)	311·7 (*95·0*)
Beam, feet (*metres*)	38·7 (*11·8*)
Draught, feet (*metres*)	18·1 (*5·5*)
Guns	4—3 in (*76 mm*) 2 twin
Tubes	6—12·6 in (*320 mm*) 2 triple
Aircraft	1 helicopter
Main engines	4 Fiat diesels; 2 shafts; 24 000 bhp
Speed, knots	25

First warships built in Turkey. The prototype, *Berk*, was laid down in the Gölcük naval yard on 9 Mar 1967, and *Peyk* on 18 Jan 1968. *Berk* was launched on 25 June 1971 and *Peyk* in June 1972. Estimated completion dates are *Berk* 1973 and *Peyk* June 1974. Both are named after famous ships of the Ottoman Navy. Said to have been inspired by the destroyer escorts of the US "Claud Jones" class, but there is not a great deal of resemblance.

BERK 1972, *Turkish Navy*

CORVETTES

7 "CANDARLI" CLASS

CANDARLI (ex-*Frolic*, 22 July 1943) A 593 (ex-AGS 2)
CARDAK (ex-*Tourmaline*, 4 Oct. 1942) A 596
CARSAMBA (ex-*Tattoo*, 27 Jan 1943) A 594 (ex-AGS 1)
EDREMIT (ex-*Chance*) A 598
CESME (ex-*Elfreda*, 25 Jan 1943) A 595
EDINCIK (ex-*Grecian*, 22 Sep 1943) A 597 (ex-598)
EREGLI (ex-*Pique*, 26 Oct 1942) A 592

Displacement, tons	1 010 standard; 1 250 full load
Length, feet (*metres*)	215·0 (*61·4*) wl; 221·0 (*67·4*) oa
Beam, feet (*metres*)	32·0 (*9·8*)
Draught, feet (*metres*)	10·8 (*3·3*)
Guns	1—3 in (*76 mm*); 6—40 mm
Main engines	Diesel electric; 2 shafts; 3 500 bhp
Speed, knots	18

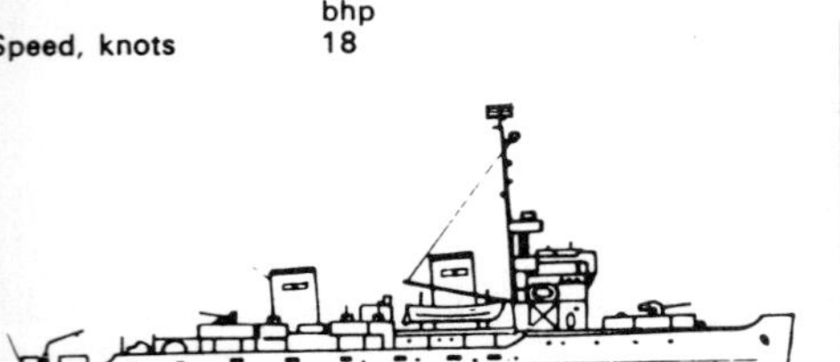

CANDARLI *Class*

CANDARLI — *1972, Dr Giorgio Arra*

Former US fleet minesweepers of the "Auk" type. Transferred to Great Britain while under construction. ansferred to Turkey in Apr 1947. Built by Associated Shipbuilders, Cleveland (*Carsamba, Cesme* and *Edincik*); General Engineering & DD Co, Alameda (*Candarli*) and Gulf Shipbuilding Corporation, Houston (*Cardak* and *Eregli*). Launch dates above. Named after Turkish ports. *Erdemli* (ex-*Catherine*) was withdrawn from active service in 1963. *Cesme* and *Cardak* are Headquarters Ships. *Eregli* is Logistic Support Ship, *Edincik* is training Ship, *Carsamba* and *Candarli* are Survey Ships.

2 "ALANYA" CLASS

Name	*No.*	*Builders*	*Launched*
ALANYA (ex-*Broome*)	A 589 (ex-M 501)	Evans Deakin, Brisbane	6 Oct 1941
AYVALIK (ex- *Antalya*, ex-*Geraldton*)	A 588 (ex-M 500)	Poole & Steele, Sydney	16 Aug 1941

Displacement, tons	790 standard; 1 025 full load
Length, feet (*metres*)	162·0 (*49·4*) pp; 186·0 (*56·7*) oa
Beam, feet (*metres*)	31·0 (*9·4*)
Draught, feet (*metres*)	8·5 (*2·6*)
Guns, surface	1—4 in (*102 mm*)
Guns, AA	1—40 mm; 4—20 mm
A/S weapons	2 DCT
Main engines	Triple expansion; 2 shafts; 1 800 ihp
Speed, knots	15
Boilers	2 water tube
Oil fuel, tons	170
Range, miles	4 500 at 10 knots
Complement	85

Both Australian built "Bathurst" class fleet minesweepers, 1940-42. Served in the Royal Navy. Acquired from Great Britain in Aug 1946. Named after Turkish ports. Both are now Logistic Support Ships. *Hamit Naci* (ex-*Ayancik*, ex-*Launceston*) was withdrawn from service in 1965, *Ayvalik* (ex-*Gawler*) in 1963 and *Amasra* (ex-*Pirie*) in 1971.

AYVALIK — *1968*

SUBMARINES

4 HOWALDS WERKE TYPE

Displacement, tons	1 000 surfaced; 1 290 dived
Dimensions, feet	183·4 × 20·5 ×
Torpedo tubes	8—21 in bow
Main engines	Diesel Electric; 1 shaft; 5 000 hp
Speed, knots	22 dived

Building at Kiel. First boat laid down 2 Aug 1972.

HOWALDS WERKE

13 Ex-US GUPPY I and IIA CLASS

Displacement, tons	1 850 standard; 2 440 submerged
Length, feet (*metres*)	308 (*94*)
Beam, feet (*metres*)	27·2 (*8·3*)
Draught, feet (*metres*)	17 (*5·2*)
Torpedo tubes	10—21 in (*533 mm*), 6 bow and 4 stern; 24 torpedoes carried
Main engines	3 GM 2-stroke diesels, total 4 800 hp, Electric motors, total 5 400 hp
Speed, knots	17 on surface; 15 submerged
Range, miles	12 000 at 10 knots
Oil fuel (tons)	330
Complement	85

Name	*Nato No.*	*Builders*	*Launched*	*Completed*
BIRINCI INÖNÜ (ex USS *Brill, SS 330*)	S 330	Electric Boat Co	25 June 1944	26 Oct 1944
CANAKKALE (ex-USS *Bumper, SS 333*)	S 333	Electric Boat Co	6 Aug 1944	9 Dec 1944
CERBE (ex-USS *Hammerhead, SS 364*)	S 341	Manitowoc SB Co	27 Oct 1943	1 Mar 1944
GÜR (ex-USS *Chub*, ex-*Bonat, SS 329*)	S 334	Electric Boat Co	7 May 1944	28 Apr 1945
IKINCI INÖNÜ (ex-USS *Blueback, SS 326*)	S 331	Electric Boat Co	21 May 1944	23 Sep 1944
MURAT REIS (ex-USS *Razorback, SS 394*)	S 336	Portsmouth Navy Yard	27 Jan 1944	3 Apr 1944
ORUC REIS (ex-USS *Pomfret, SS 391*)	S 337	Portsmouth Navy Yard	27 Oct 1943	19 Feb 1944
SAKARYA (ex-USS *Boarfish, SS 327*)	S 332	Electric Boat Co	18 June 1944	21 Oct 1944
ULUÇALI REIS (ex-USS *Thornback, SS 418*)	S 338	Portsmouth Navy Yard	7 July 1944	13 Oct 1944
DUMLUPINAR (ex-USS *Caiman, SS 233*)	S 339	Electric Boat Co	30 Mar 1944	17 July 1944
PREVEZE (ex-USS *Entemedor, SS 340*)	S 345	Electric Boat Co	17 Dec 1944	6 Apr 1945
CERBE (ex-USS *Trutta, SS 421*)	S 340	Portsmouth Navy Yard	18 Aug 1944	16 Nov 1944
—— (ex-USS *Threadfin, SS 410*)	S 346	Portsmouth Navy Yard	26 June 1944	30 Aug 1944

Former US submarines of the "Balao" type acquired by Turkey. Of all-welded construction. *Canakkale*, officially transferred in 1950, was semi-streamlined before delivery. *Dumlupinar* (ex-*Blower*) was lost in the Dardanelles on 4 Apr 1953. *Preveze* semi-streamlined and *Cerbe*, fully streamlined, were transferred on 7 Aug 1954 and Oct 1954 respectively. Their loan was extended for five years in 1959 and they were eventually paid off in 1971. *Sakarya* was overhauled by the Electric Boat Division of the General Dynamics Corporation (formerly known as the Electric Boat Company), Groton, in 1957. *Turgut Reis* was transferred in Oct 1958 and *Hizar Reis* and *Piri Reis* on 20 Apr 1960 and 18 Mar 1960 at San Francisco Naval Shipyard. *Murat Reis* and *Burak Reis* were transferred on 30 Nov 1970 and 15 Dec 1970 respectively and *Uluçali Reis* and *Oruç Reis* on 1 July 1971. All the last eight except *Dumlupinar* (GUPPY IA) are of the GUPPY IIA conversion.
Dumlupinar transferred 30 June 1972 *Preveze* and *Cerbe* on 31 July 1972, S346 on 18 Aug 1972.

ORUC REIS (as *Pomfret*) — *1972, Turkish Navy*

LIGHT FORCES

NOTE. It is reported that consideration is being given to the purchase of Missile Boats armed with Exocet.

1 Ex-US "ASHEVILLE" CLASS (PG)

BORA (ex-USS *Surprise* PG97)

Displacement, tons	225 standard; 245 full load
Dimensions, feet	164·5 oa × 23·8 × 9·5
Guns	1—3 in 50 cal
Main engines	CODAG; 2 Cummins Diesels; 1 450 hp = 16 knots 1 GE gas turbine; 13 300 shp = 42 knots
Complement,	25

Commissioned in USA 17 Oct 1969. Transferred on 28 Feb 1973. More are likely to be transferred in future.

6 "AKHISAR" CLASS (Pc's)

AKHISAR P 114 (ex-*PC* 1641)
DEMIRHISAR P 112 (ex-*PC* 1639)
KOCHISAR P 116 (ex-*PC* 1643)
SIVRIHISAR P 115 (ex-*PC* 1642)
SULTANHISAR P 111 (ex-*PC* 1638)
YARHISAR P 113 (ex *PC* 1640)

Displacement, tons	280 standard; 412 full load
Dimensions, feet	170 wl; 173·7 oa × 23 × 10·2
Guns	1—3 inch dp; 1—40 mm AA
A/S weapons	4 DCT
Main engines	2 FM Diesels; 2 shafts; 2 800 bhp = 19 knots
Range, miles	6 000 at 10 knots
Complement	65 (5 officers and 60 men)

Similar to US 173 ft class submarine chasers. Built by Gunderson Bros, Engineering Co, Portland, Oregon, except *Kochisar* built in Golcuk Dockyard, Turkey. Transferred on 3 Dec 1964, 22 Apr 1965, 22 Apr 1965, 2 May 1964, 24 Sep 1964 and 22 Apr 1965 respectively.

YARHISAR *1972, Turkish Navy*

9 "KARTAL" CLASS (TORPEDO BOATS)

ALBATROS P 327 (ex-P 325)
ATMACA P 322 (ex-P 335)
DENIZKUSU P 321 (ex-P 336)
KARTAL P 324 (ex-P 333)
KASIRGA P 329 (ex-P 338)
MELTEM P 325 (ex-P 330)
PELIKAN P 326
SAHIN P 323 (ex-P 334)
SIMSEK P 328 (ex-P 332)

Displacement, tons	160 standard; 180 full load
Dimensions, feet	140·5 × 23·5 × 7·2
Guns	2—40 mm AA
Tubes	4—21 inch
Main engines	4 Maybach diesels; 4 shafts; 12 000 bhp = 42 knots

Of the German "Jaguar" type. Built by Lürssen, Vegesack, in 1966-67 (P 321, 322, 323, 324, 329, ex-P 336, 335, 334, 333, 338, respectively) others in 1968.

SIMSEK *1972, Turkish Navy*

2 "NASTY" TYPE (TORPEDO BOATS)

DOGAN (ex-*Hugin*) P 327
MARTI (ex-*Munin*) P 328

Displacement, tons	70 standard; 75 full load
Dimensions, feet	75·5 pp; 80·3 oa × 24·5 × 6·8
Gun	1—40 mm AA
Tubes	2—21 inch
Main engines	2 Napier Deltic turbo blown diesels; 6 200 bhp = 43 knots
Range, miles	450 at 40 knots; 600 at 25 knots

Transferred under a German-Turkish war reparations plan from West Germany and renamed. "Nasty" type, built by Boat Services Ltd, A/S in 1959-60.

DOGAN *Turkish Navy*

AB 25 (P 1225)
AB 26 (P 1226)
AB 27 (P 1227)
AB 28 (P 1228)
AB 29 (P 1229)
AB 30 (P 1230)
AB 31 (P 1231)
AB 32 (P 1232)
AB 33 (P 1233)
AB 34 (P 1234)

Displacement, tons	170 (official figure)
Dimensions, feet	132 × 21 × 5·5
Guns	2—40 mm
Speed	22 knots

Officially stated to be newly designed patrol boats of the motor launch type. Built at Gölcük Naval Yard. First was launched on 9 Mar 1967. Six similar launches are operated by the Gendarmerie.

AB 28 *1970, Turkish Navy*

AB 21 (ex PGM-104)
AB 23 (ex PGM-106)
AB 22 (ex PGM-105)
AB 24 (ex PGM-106)

Displacement, tons	130 standard, 147 full load
Dimensions, feet	101 × 21 × 7
Guns	2—40 mm; 4—20 mm
Main engines	2 diesels; 2 shafts; 1 850 hp = 18·5 knots
Range, miles	1 500 at 10 knots
Complement	15

Patrol gunboat type supplied from the United States in 1967-68.

AB 23 *1970, Turkish Navy*

J 12 J 13 J 14 J 15 J 16 J 17 J 18 J 19 J 20 J 21

Guns	1—40 mm; 1—20 mm
Main engines	4 MB diesels; 2 shafts; 2 700 bhp = 29 knots

Cutters of U.S.C.G. type built in 1960-61 by Schweers, Bardenfleth.

J 21 *1972, Dr. Giorgio Arra*

AB 1 (ex-*ML* 386) P 1201 (ex-P 321)
AB 2 (ex-*ML* 584) P 1202 (ex-P 322)
AB 3 (ex-*ML* 836) P 1203 (ex-P 323)
AB 4 (ex-*ML* 837) P 1204 (ex-P 324)
AB 6 (ex-*ML* 842) P 1206 (ex-P 326)
AB 7 (ex-*ML* 862) P 1207 (ex-P 327)

Displacement, tons	85 standard; 115 full load
Dimensions, feet	112 × 17·8 × 4
Guns	1—3 pdr; 2—20 mm AA; 4 MG
Main engines	2 Hall-Scott engines; 1 120 bhp = 21 knots
Oil, fuel tons	12
Range, miles	1 600 at 12 knots
Complement	18

Fairmile B type. Launched in 1940-42. Transferred in 1947.

AB 6 *1970, Turkish Navy*

Light Forces—*continued*

LS 9 P 1209 (ex-P 339)
LS 10 P 1210 (ex-P 308)
LS 11 P 1211 (ex-P 309)
LS 12 P 1212 (ex-P 310)

Displacement, tons	63 standard
Dimensions, feet	83·0 × 14·0 × 5·0
Gun	1—20 mm AA
A/S weapons	2 A/S Rocket launchers
Main engines	2 Cummins diesels; 1 100 bhp = 20 knots

Ex-US type, transferred on 25 June 1953. Pennant numbers changed in 1970.

LS 9 — *1972, Turkish Navy*

MTB 1 P 311
MTB 2 P 312
MTB 3 P 313
MTB 4 P 314
MTB 6 P 316
MTB 7 P 317
MTB 8 P 318
MTB 9 P 319
MTB 10 P 320

Displacement, tons	70 standard
Dimensions, feet	71·5 × 13·8 × 8·5
Main engines	Diesel; 2 000 bhp

All launched in 1942. General purpose craft. MTB 5 (315) was scrapped.

MINEWARFARE FORCES

1 "SCANATO" TYPE (MINELAYER)

NUSRET N 110 (ex-N 108)

Displacement, tons	1 880 standard
Length, feet (*metres*)	246 (*75·0*) pp; 252·7 (*77·0*) oa
Beam, feet (*metres*)	41 (*12·6*)
Draught, feet (*metres*)	11 (*3·4*)
Guns, dual purpose	4—3 in (*76 mm*), 2 twin mountings
Mines	400 capacity
Main engines	GM diesels, 4 800 hp; 2 shafts
Speed, knots	18
Complement	130

A new type of minelayer of special Scandinavian-NATO design. Built at Frederikshaven Dockyard, Denmark. Laid down in 1962, launched in 1964, and completed in 1965. Commissioned on 16 Sep 1964 at Copenhagen. Similar to Danish "Falster" class.

RADAR. Search: RAN 7S. Fire Control: X Band Navigation Radar.

NUSRET — *1972, Turkish Navy*

NUSRET

2 Ex-US LST TYPE (MINELAYERS)

—— (ex-German *Bochum*, ex-USS *Rice County*)
—— (ex-German *Bottrop*, ex-USS *Saline County*)

Displacement, tons	1 653 standard; 4 080 full load
Dimensions, feet	328 oa × 50 × 14
Guns	6—40 mm (2 twin, 2 single)
Main engines	2 GM Diesels; 2 shafts; 1 700 bhp = 11 knots
Range, miles	15 000 at 9 knots

Formerly USN LST's, Transferred to Germany in 1961 and thence to Turkey in Nov 1972.

5 LSM TYPE (COASTAL MINELAYERS)

MARMARIS (ex-*LSM* 481) N 103 (ex-100)
MERIC (ex-*LSM* 490) N 102
MERSIN (ex-*LSM* 492) N 104 (ex-103)
MORDOGAN (ex-*LSM* 484) N 101
MUREFTE (ex-*LSM* 493) N 105 (ex-104)

Displacement, tons	743 standard; 1 100 full load
Dimensions, feet	196·5 wl; 203·2 oa × 34·5 × 8·5
Guns	2—40 mm AA; 2—20 mm AA
Main engines	Diesels; 2 shafts; 2 880 bhp = 12 knots
Oil fuel (tons)	60
Range, miles	2 500 at 12 knots
Complement	70

Ex-U.S. Landing Ships Medium. All launched in 1945, converted into coastal minelayers by the U.S. Navy in 1952 and taken over by the Turkish Navy (LSM 481, 484 and 490) and the Norwegian Navy (LSM 492 and 493) in Oct 1952 under MAP. LSM 492 (*Vale*) and LSM 493 (*Vidar*) were retransferred to the Turkish Navy on 1 Nov 1960 at Bergen, Norway.

MERSIN — *1969*

1 YMP TYPE (COASTAL MINELAYER)

MEHMETCIK (ex-USS *YMP* 3) N 115

Displacement, tons	540 full load
Dimensions, feet	130 × 35 × 6
Main Engines	Diesels; 2 shafts; 600 bhp = 10 knots
Complement	22

Former US motor mine planter. Built by Higgins Inc, New Orleans. Completed in 1958. Steel hulled. Transferred under MAP in 1958. For harbour defence.

MEHMETCIK

12 MSC TYPE (CMS)

SAMSUN M 510 (ex-USA *MSC* 268)
SAPANCA M 517 (ex-USS *MSC* 312)
SARIYER M 518 (ex-USS *MSC* 315)
SAROS M 515 (ex-USS *MSC* 305)
SEDDULBAHIR M 513 (ex-*MSC* 272)
SELÇUK M 508 (ex-USS *AMS* 124)
SEYHAN M 509 (ex-USS *AMS* 142)
SEYMEN M 507 (ex-USS *AMS* 131)
SIGACIK M 516 (ex-USS *MSC* 311)
SILIFKE M 514 (ex-USS *MSC* 304)
SINOP M 511 (ex-USS *MSC* 270)
SURMENE M 512 (ex USS *MSC* 271)

Displacement, tons	320 standard; 370 full load
Dimensions, feet	138·0 pp; 144·0 oa × 28·0 × 9·0
Guns	2—20 mm AA
Main engines	2 diesels; 2 shafts; 1 200 bhp = 14 knots
Oil fuel, tons	25
Range, miles	2 500 at 10 knots
Complement	38 (4 officers, 34 men)

Transferred on 30 Sep 1958, 26 July 1965, 8 Sep 1967, 8 Nov 1965, 9 July 1959, 24 Mar 1970, 24 Mar 1970, 19 Nov 1970, 29 May 1965, 25 Oct 1965, 30 Jan 1959, 27 Mar 1959, respectivly. *Pavot* (ex-AMS 124) and *Renoncule* (ex-AMS 142) were transferred from France (via USA) on 24 Mar 1970 and *Seymen* from UK (via USA) on 19 Nov 1970.

SAMSUN — *1969*

Mine Warfare Forces—*continued*

4 MCB TYPE (CMS)

TIREBOLU M 532 (ex-HMCS *Comax*) **TERME** M 531 (ex-HMCS *Trinity*)
TEKIRDAG M 533 (ex-HMCS *Ungava*) **TRABZON** M 533 (ex-HMCS *Gaspe*)

Displacement, tons	390 standard; 412 full load
Dimensions, feet	140·0 pp; 152·0 oa × 20·8 × 7·0
Gun	1—40 mm
Main engines	Diesels; 2 shafts; 2 400 bhp = 16 knots
Oil fuel, tons	52
Range, miles	4 500 at 11 knots
Complement	40

Ex-Canadian MCBs. Sailed from Sydney, Nova Scotia, to Turkey on 19 May 1958.

TIREBOLU *1970, Turkish Navy*

FATSA M 502 (ex-*MSI* 17) **FINIKE** M 503 (ex-*MSI* 18)
FETHIYE M 501 (ex-*MSI* 16) **FOCA** M 500 (ex-*MSI* 15)

Displacement, tons	180 standard; 235 full load (official figure)
Dimensions, feet	111·9 × 23·5 × 7·9
Guns	1—50 cal
Main engines	4 diesels; 2 shafts; 960 bhp = 13 knots
Complement	20

Built in USA and transferred under MAP at Boston, Mass, Aug-Sep 1967. *Finike* was delivered by Peterson Builders Inc. on 8 Nov 1967.

FOCA *1970, Turkish Navy*

AMPHIBIOUS FORCES

4 LCT's

C101-104

One pair was launched early 1971 and a further pair are under construction.

37 LCT's

C301-337

Built in Turkey.

4 Ex-US LCU 501 SERIES

C201-204

Displacement, tons	160 light; 320 full load
Dimensions, feet	119 oa × 32·7 × 5
Guns	2—20 mm
Main engines	3 diesels; 675 bhp = 10 knots

Transferred from USA July 1967.

7 TURKISH-BUILT LCUs

Marginally larger than the ex-US LCUs above.

20 Ex-US LCM 6 TYPE

Displacement, tons	55 full load
Dimensions, feet	56 × 14 × 4
Main engines	2 diesels; 2 shafts; 450 bhp = 9 knots
Carrying capacity	34 tons or 80 troops

18 LCVP's

Of 14 tons full load and capable of 9 knots.

SUBMARINE DEPOT SHIPS

DONATAN A 583 (ex-USS *Anthedon*, AS 24)

Displacement, tons	8 100 standard
Dimensions, feet	492 × 69·5 × 26·5
Main engines	Geared turbines; 1 shaft; 8 500 shp = 14·4 knots
Boilers	2

Former US submarine tender of the "Aegir" class transferred to Turkey on 7 Feb 1969.

DONATAN *1972, Turkish Navy*

ERKIN A 591 (ex-*Trabzon*, ex-*Imperial*)

Displacement, tons	10 990 (official figure)
Dimensions, feet	441 × 58·5 × 23

Built in 1938. Purchased in 1968 and placed on the Navy list in 1970. The tender *Isin* Y 1230 (ex-A 570), formerly *Imia Leyteri*, was phased out in 1972. The tenders *Akin* and *Dalgie* have been discarded.

SUBMARINE RESCUE SHIPS

KURTARAN (ex-*Bluebird*, ASR 19, ex-*Yurak*) A 584

Displacement, tons	1 294 standard; 1 675 full load
Dimensions, feet	205·0 oa × 38·5 × 12·0
Guns	1—3 inch; 2—40 mm AA
Main engines	Diesel-electric; 3 000 bhp × 16 knots

Former salvage tug adapted as a submarine rescue vessel in 1947. Transferred from the US Navy on 15 Aug 1950.

KURTARAN *1971, A. & J. Pavia*

AKIN (ex-Greenlet ASR 10) A585

Displacement, tons	1 653 standard; 2 290 full load
Dimensions, feet	251·5 oa × 42 × 14·9
Main engines	Diesel-electric; 1 shaft; 3 000 bhp = 15 knots
Complement	85

Submarine rescue vessel, ex-USN "Chanticleer" class built by Moore SB & DD Co., Oakland in 1942. Transferred 2 June 1970.

REPAIR SHIPS

BASARAN (ex-*Patroclus*, *ARL* 19, ex-*LST* 955) A 582
ONARAN (ex-*Alecto*, *AGP* 14, ex-*LST* 558) A 581

Displacement, tons	1 625 standard; 4 080 full load
Dimensions, feet	316 wl; 328 oa × 50 × 14
Guns	2—40 mm AA; 8—20 mm AA
Main engines	Diesel; 2 shafts; 1 700 bhp = 11 knots
Oil fuel (tons)	1 000
Range, miles	9 000 at 9 knots
Complement	80

Former US repair ship and MTB tender, respectively, of the LST type. *Basaran* was launched on 22 Oct 1944 by Bethlehem Hingham Shipyard, *Onaran* on 14 Apr 1944 by Missouri Valley Bridge & Iron Co. Acquired from the USA in 1952 and 1947, respectively.

Repair Ships—*continued*

ONARAN *1972, Turkish Navy*

BASARAN *1970, Turkish Navy*

BOOM DEFENCE VESSELS

AG 6 (ex-*Cerberus*) P 306 (ex-A 895)

Displacement, tons	780 standard; 902 full load
Dimensions, feet	165·0 × 33·0 × 10·0
Guns	1—3 in; 4—20 mm AA
Main engines	Diesel-electric; 1 shaft; 1 500 bhp = 12·8 knots

Netlayer built by Bethlehem Steel Co, Staten Island. Launched in May 1952 and completed on 10 Nov 1952. Transferred from USA to Netherlands in Dec 1952. Used first as a boom defence vessel and latterly as salvage and diving tender since 1961 but retained her netlaying capacity. Handed back to USN (formality) on 17 Sep 1970 but immediately turned over to the Turkish Navy.

AG 6

AG 5 P 305 (ex-P 306)

Displacement, tons	680 standard; 960 full load
Dimensions, feet	148·7 pp; 173·8 oa × 35·0 × 13·5
Guns	1—40 mm AA; 3—20 mm AA
Main engines	4 MAN diesels; 2 shafts; 1 450 bhp = 12 knots

Netlayer AN 104 built in US off-shore programme by Kröger, Rendsburg for Turkey. Launched on 20 Oct 1960. Delivered on 25 Feb 1961.

AG 4 (ex-*Larch*, ex-*AN* 21) P 304

Displacement, tons	560 standard; 805 full load
Dimensions, feet	146·0 wl; 163·0 oa × 30·5 × 10·5
Guns	1—3 inch AA
Main engines	Diesel-electric; 800 bhp = 12 knots

Former US netlayer of the "Aloe" class. Built by American S.B. Co, Cleveland. Laid down in 1940. Launched on 2 July 1941. Completed in 1941. Acquired in 1947.

Boom Defence Vessels— *continued*

AG 4 *1969*

3 "BAR" CLASS

AG 1 (ex-*Barbarian*, 21 Oct 1937) P 301
AG 2 (ex-*Barbette*, 15 Dec 1937) P 302
AG 3 (ex-*Barfair*, 21 May 1938) P 303

Displacement, tons	750 standard; 1 000 full load
Dimensions, feet	150·0 pp; 173·8 oa × 32·2 × 9·5
Guns	1—3 inch AA
Main engines	Triple expansion; 850 ihp = 11·5 knots
Boilers	2 SE

Former British boom defence vessels. First two were built by Blyth S.B. Co and the third by J. Lewis & Sons. Launch dates above.

AG 3 *1970, Turkish Navy*

KALDIRAY (ex-P 305)

Measurement, tons	732 gross
Main engines	Steam reciprocating; 500 ihp = 10 knots
Complement	97

Built in 1938. Former French vessel. Purchased in 1964.

GATE VESSELS

Y 1216

Displacement, tons	360 (official figure)
Dimensions, feet	102·7 × 34 × 4·7

The gate vessels YNG 45, 46 and 47 were built by US for transfer to Turkey under MAP, and numbered Y 1201, 1202 and 1203.

OILERS

ULABAT **VAN**

NOTE. One 4 600 ton tanker under construction.

Displacement, tons	1 200
Main engines	Designed for a speed of 14·5 knots

Two small tankers for the Turkish Navy built in the Gölcük Dockyard, Izmit, in 1968-70.

Oilers—*continued*

ALBAY HAKKI BURAK A 572

Displacement, tons	3 800 full load
Dimensions, feet	251·3 pp; 274·7 oa × 40·2 × 18
Main Engines	2 GM diesels; electric drive; 4 400 bhp = 16 knots
Complement	88

Built in 1964.

ALBAY HAKKI BURAK *1972, Turkish Navy*

YUZBASI TOLUNAY A 571 (ex-A 586)

Displacement, tons	2 500 standard; 3 500 full load
Dimensions, feet	260 × 41 × 19·5
Main Engines	Atlas Polar-diesels; 2 shafts; 1 920 bhp = 14 knots

Built at Taskizak by Haskoy Naval D.Y., Istanbul. Launched on 22 Aug 1950.

YUZBASI TOLUNAY *1972, Turkish Navy*

AKAR (ex-*Istambul*, ex-*Adour*) A 570 (ex- A580)

Displacement, tons	4 289 light; 13 200 full load
Dimensions, feet	433 × 52·7 × 27
Main engines	Parsons geared turbines; 5 200 shp = 15 knots
Range, miles	10 000 at 10 knots

Oilers—*continued*

AKAR *1970, Turkish Navy*

AKPINAR (ex-*Chiwaukum*) A 574

Displacement, tons	700 light; 2 700 full load
Measurement, feet	1 453 deadweight
Dimensions, feet	212·5 wl; 220·5 oa × 37 × 12·8
Main Engines	Diesel; 800 bhp = 10 knots

Formerly the United States oiler *AOG 26*. Built by East Coast S.Y. Inc., Bayonne. Laid down on 2 Apr 1944. Launched on 5 May 1944. Completed on 22 July 1944. Transferred to Turkey in 1949.

GOLCUK Y 1207 (ex-A 573)

Displacement, tons	1 255
Measurement, feet	750 deadweight
Dimensions, feet	185 × 31·1 × 10
Main Engines	B. & W. diesel; 700 bhp = 12·5 knots

Built by Gölcük Dockyard, Ismit. Launched on 4 Nov 1953.

TRANSPORTS

ÜLKÜ (ex-FDR *Angeln*)

Measurement, tons	2 101 gross
Dimensions, feet	296·9 × 43·6 × 20·3
Main engines	Pielstick Diesels; 1 shaft; 3 000 bhp = 14 knots
Complement	57

Transferred by W. Germany 22 March 1972.

TUGS

ÖNCU **ÖNDER**

Displacement, tons	500
Speed	12 knots

The US harbour tugs ex-YTL 155, 751 were transferred under MAP.

TRAINING SHIP

SAVARONA

Displacement, tons	5 100
Length, feet (*metres*)	349·5 (*106·5*)wl; 408·5 (*124·5*)oa
Beam, feet (*metres*)	53 (*16·2*)
Draught, feet (*metres*)	20·5 (*6·2*) mean
Guns, surface	4—3 in (*76 mm*)
Guns, AA	2—40 mm; 2—20 mm
Main engines	6 geared turbines; 2 shafts; 10 750 shp
Speed, knots	21 designed; about 18 now
Boilers	4 watertube; 400 psi
Oil fuel, tons	2 100
Radius, miles	9 000 at 15 knots
Complement	132 + 81 midshipmen

Built by Blohm & Voss, Hamburg. Launched on 28 Feb 1931. Formerly probably the most sumptuously fitted yacht afloat. Equipment includes Sperry gyro-stabilisers. Converted into a training ship in 1952, the saloons and dining rooms being adapted as classrooms, workshops and libraries for 120 midshipmen.

SAVARONA

UNITED KINGDOM

Chief of the Defence Staff:
Admiral of the Fleet Sir Peter Hill-Norton, GCB
(To be relieved in October by Field Marshal Sir Michael Carver, GCB, CBE, DSO, MC)

Admiralty Board

Secretary of State for Defence (Chairman):
The Right Honourable Lord Carrington, KCMG, MC
Minister of State, Ministry of Defence (Vice-Chairman) and Minister of State for Defence Procurement:
Mr Ian Gilmour, MP
Parliamentary Under-Secretary of State for Defence for the Royal Navy:
Mr Anthony Buck, MP
Chief of the Naval Staff and First Sea Lord:
Admiral Sir Michael Pollock, GCB, MVO, DSC
Chief of Naval Personnel and Second Sea Lord:
Admiral Sir Derek Empson, KCB
Controller of the Navy:
Admiral Sir Anthony Griffin, KCB
Chief of Fleet Support:
Vice-Admiral G. F. A. Trewby, CEng, FIMechE, MIMarE, FRINA
Vice-Chief of the Naval Staff:
Vice-Admiral Sir Terence Lewin, KCB, MVO, DSC
Chief Scientist (Royal Navy): Mr Basil Wilfred Lythall, CB, MA
Deputy Under Secretary of State (Navy): Mr. Sydney Redman, CB
Second Permanent Under-Secretary for Administration: Sir Arthur Drew KCB, JP
Second Permanent Under-Secretary for Equipment: Sir Martin Flett, KCB

Commanders-in-Chief

Commander-in-Chief, Naval Home Command:
Admiral Sir Andrew Lewis, KCB
Commander-in-Chief, Fleet:
Admiral Sir Edward Ashmore, KCB, DSC

Flag Officers

Flag Officer, 1st Flotilla
Vice-Admiral I. G. Raikes, CBE, DSC
Flag Officer, 2nd Flotilla:
Rear-Admiral R. P. Clayton

Flag Officer Naval Air Command:
Vice-Admiral J. D. Treacher
Flag Officer, Submarines:
Vice-Admiral J. A. R. Troup DSC & Bar
Flag Officer Carriers and Amphibious Ships:
Rear-Admiral R. D. Lygo
Flag Officer Scotland and Northern Ireland:
Rear-Admiral M. N. Lucey, CB, DSC
Flag Officer Medway:
Rear-Admiral C. C. H. Dunlop, CBE
Flag Officer Plymouth:
Vice-Admiral A. M. Power, MBE
Flag Officer Sea Training:
Rear-Admiral J. O. Roberts
Flag Officer Malta:
Rear-Admiral D. A. Loram, MVO
Flag Officer Gibraltar:
Rear-Admiral H. W. E. Hollins
Flag Officer Spithead:
Rear-Admiral S. L. McArdle MVO, GM

General Officers, Royal Marines

Commandant-General, Royal Marines:
Lieutenant-General Ian Gourlay, OBE, MC
Chief of Staff to Commandant-General, Royal Marines:
Major-General Patrick Kay, MBE
Major General Training Group, Royal Marines:
Major-General Robert Loudon, OBE
Major-General Commando Forces Royal Marines:
Major-General John Owen, OBE

Diplomatic Representation

British Naval Attaché in Washington:
Rear-Admiral L. R. Bell Davies

American Naval Attaché in London:
Rear-Admiral Fillmore B. Gilkeson, US Navy

British Naval Attaché in Moscow:
Captain G. Hayne, RN
British Naval Attaché in Paris:
Captain L. A. Bird, RN

1973-74
New Construction
Cruisers
It is hoped to place the contract for the first TDC with Vickers in 1973.
(ordered 17 April 1973)
Destroyers and Frigates
Type 21. I to join the fleet. 7 building.
Type 22. It is hoped to order the first ship in 1973.
Type 42. 6 building.

Submarines
Design for improved classes continues.
SSNs. 7th and 8th to join the fleet. 9th and 10th building. 11th to be ordered.

MCM vessels
Wilton to join the fleet.
Negotiation of contract with Vosper Thornycroft for new GRP MCM vessels.

Survey Ship
Herald to join the fleet.

Salvage vessels
Two to join the fleet.

Patrol Craft
Four building.

RFAs
Two fleet replenishment ships building.
Two small fleet tankers to join the fleet.

Conversions

LPH
Hermes to complete.

Frigates
Leander— Ikara conversions to continue.

Equipment
Mark 24 torpedoes for submarines to enter service. US Mark 46 torpedoes to enter service. Exocet SSM to be operational in a few ships in 1974. Martel ASM entering service in Buccaneers.

Navy Estimates

1969-70: £642 043 000
1970-71: £659 378 500
1971-72: £690 000 000
1972-73: £700 000 000

Personnel

1969-70: 95 500
1970-71: 89 000
1971-72: 87 000
1972-73: 83 000
1973-74: 84 000

Mercantile Marine

Lloyd's Register of Shipping: 3 700 vessels of 28 624 875 tons gross

Strength of the Fleet

1 Fixed Wing Aircraft Carrier
2 Commando Ships (Helicopter Carriers)
4 Nuclear Powered Ballistic Missile Submarines
8 Fleet Submarines
23 Patrol Submarines
2 Assault Ships (Amphibious Cruiser Type)
2 Cruisers (Command Helicopter Cruisers)
10 Guided Missile Armed Light Cruisers
64 Frigates
6 Logistic Landing Ships
1 Helicopter Support Ship
1 Ice Patrol Ship
1 Mine Countermeasures Support Ship
1 Heavy Repair Ship (ex-Aircraft Carrier)
1 Submarine Parent Ship
3 Maintenance Ships
5 Coastal Patrol Vessels (ex-Coastal Minesweepers)
38 Coastal Minesweepers (including 12 Hunters)
24 Inshore Minesweepers (18 Auxiliary Services)
3 Controlled Minelayers
8 Survey Ships (including 4 Coastal Vessels)
5 Inshore Survey Craft
1 Landing Ship (LST Type)
24 Landing Craft (LCT Type)
33 Minor Landing Craft
5 Experimental Vessels (2 new construction)
1 Sonar Trials Ship (ex-Destroyer)
1 Harbour Training Ship (ex-Destroyer)
6 Fast Training and Patrol Boats
2 Seaward Defence Boats
10 Fleet Support and Supply Ships
25 Fleet Oilers
20 Mooring, Salvage and Boom Vessels
1 Royal Yacht and Hospital Ship
1 Diving Trials Ship
2 Cable Vessels
10 Armament Carriers
14 Water Carriers
41 Fleet Tenders
95 Auxiliaries and Service Craft
91 Fleet and Berthing Tugs

LIST OF PENNANT NUMBERS

Aircraft Carriers

R 09 Ark Royal

Commando Carriers

R 08 Bulwark
R 12 Hermes

Submarines

S 01 Porpoise
S 02 Rorqual
S 03 Narwhal
S 04 Grampus
S 05 Finwhale
S 06 Cachalot
S 07 Sealion
S 08 Walrus
S 09 Oberon
S 10 Odin
S 11 Orpheus
S 12 Olympus
S 13 Osiris
S 14 Onslaught
S 15 Otter
S 16 Oracle
S 17 Ocelot
S 18 Otus
S 19 Opossum
S 20 Opportune
S 21 Onyx
S 22 Resolution
S 23 Repulse
S 26 Renown
S 27 Revenge
S 63 Andrew
S 67 Alliance
S 72 Aeneas
S 101 Dreadnought
S 102 Valiant
S 103 Warspite
S 104 Churchill
S 105 Conqueror
S 106 Courageous
S 107 Swiftsure
S 108 Sovereign
S 109 Superb

Assault Ships

L 10 Fearless
L 11 Intrepid

Cruisers

C 20 Tiger
C 34 Lion
C 99 Blake

Destroyers

D 02 Devonshire
D 06 Hampshire
D 12 Kent
D 16 London
D 18 Antrim
D 19 Glamorgan
D 20 Fife
D 21 Norfolk
D 23 Bristol
D 35 Diamond
D 43 Matapan

Frigates

F 10 Aurora
F 12 Achilles
F 14 Leopard
F 15 Euryalus
F 16 Diomede
F 18 Galatea
F 27 Lynx
F 28 Cleopatra
F 32 Salisbury
F 34 Puma
F 36 Whitby
F 37 Jaguar
F 38 Arethusa
F 39 Naiad
F 40 Sirius
F 42 Phoebe
F 43 Torquay
F 45 Minerva
F 47 Danae
F 48 Dundas
F 52 Juno
F 53 Undaunted
F 54 Hardy
F 56 Argonaut
F 57 Andromeda
F 58 Hermione
F 59 Chichester
F 60 Jupiter
F 61 Llandaff
F 63 Scarborough
F 65 Tenby
F 69 Bacchante
F 71 Scylla
F 72 Ariadne
F 73 Eastbourne
F 75 Charybdis
F 77 Blackpool
F 78 Blackwood
F 80 Duncan
F 83 Ulster
F 84 Exmouth
F 85 Keppel
F 88 Malcolm
F 94 Pallister
F 97 Russell
F 99 Lincoln
F 101 Yarmouth
F 103 Lowestoft
F 104 Dido
F 106 Brighton
F 107 Rothesay
F 108 Londonderry
F 109 Leander
F 113 Falmouth
F 114 Ajax
F 115 Berwick
F 117 Ashanti
F 119 Eskimo
F 122 Gurkha
F 124 Zulu
F 125 Mohawk
F 126 Plymouth
F 127 Penelope
F 129 Rhyl
F 131 Nubian
F 133 Tartar
F 138 Rapid
F 197 Grenville

Logistic Landing Ships

L 3004 Sir Bedivere
L 3005 Sir Galahad
L 3027 Sir Geraint
L 3029 Sir Lancelot
L 3036 Sir Percivall
L 3503 Sir Tristram

Minelayers

N 13 Miner III
N 21 Abdiel

Helicopter Support Ship

K 08 Engadine

Support Ships & Auxiliaries

A 00 Britannia
A 70 Echo
A 71 Enterprise
A 72 Egeria
A 75 Tidespring
A 76 Tidepool
A 77 Pearleaf
A 78 Plumleaf
A 79 Bayleaf
A 80 Orangeleaf
A 81 Brambleleaf
A 84 Reliant
A 85 Faithful
A 86 Forceful
A 87 Favourite
A 88 Agile
A 89 Advice
A 90 Accord
A 91 Griper
A 92 Grinder
A 93 Dexterous
A 94 Director
A 95 Typhoon
A 96 Tidereach
A 97 Tideflow
A 98 Tidesurge
A 108 Triumph
A 111 Cyclone
A 122 Olwen
A 123 Olna
A 124 Olmeda
A 127 Torrent
A 128 Torrid
A 130 Gold Ranger
A 133 Hecla
A 134 Rame Head
A 135 Nordenfelt
A 137 Hecate
A 144 Hydra
A 160 Fort Dunvegan
A 163 Black Ranger
A 169 Brown Ranger
A 171 Endurance
A 176 Bullfinch
A 179 Whimbrel
A 185 Maidstone
A 186 Fort Rosalie
A 187 Forth
A 191 Berry Head
A 194 Tyne
A 200 Vidal
A 204 Robert Dundas
A 207 Wave Prince
A 218 Samsonia
A 222 Spapool
A 223 Nimble
A 224 Spabrook
A 230 Fort Langley
A 231 Reclaim
A 232 Kingarth
A 240 Bustler
A 241 Robert Middleton
A 257 Spaburn
A 259 St. Margarets
A 260 Spalake
A 261 Eddyfirth
A 262 Hartland Point
A 264 Reward
A 265 Wave Chief
A 268 Green Rover
A 269 Grey Rover
A 270 Blue Rover
A 280 Resurgent
A 281 Kinbrace
A 288 Sea Giant
A 289 Confiance
A 290 Confident
A 293 Careful
A 316 Fort Sandusky
A 329 Retainer
A 332 Caldy
A 333 Coll
A 334 Bern
A 336 Lundy
A 338 Skomer
A 339 Lyness
A 340 Graemsay
A 342 Foulness
A 344 Stromness
A 345 Tarbatness
A 346 Switha
A 377 Maxim
A 378 Kinterbury
A 387 Girdle Ness
A 390 Samson
A 404 Bacchus
A 406 Hebe
A 480 Resource
A 482 Kinloss
A 486 Regent
A 494 Salvalour
A 497 Salveda
A 499 Salvestor
A 500 Salvictor
A 503 Sea Salvor
A 505 Succour
A 506 Swin
A 507 Uplifter
A 508 Capable

Seaward Defence Boats

P 3104 Dee (Beckford)
P 3113 Droxford

Boom Defence Vessels

P 190 Laymoor
P 191 Layburn
P 192 Mandarin
P 193 Pintail
P 194 Garganey
P 195 Goldeneye
P 201 Barbain
P 202 Barfoot
P 232 Barmond
P 284 Moorsman
P 294 Barfoil

Coastal Patrol Vessels

P 1107 Beachampton
P 1155 Monkton
P 1189 Wasperton
P 1193 Wolverton
P 1196 Yarnton

Fast Patrol Boats

P 271 Scimitar
P 274 Cutlass
P 275 Sabre
P 276 Tenacity
P 1011 Brave Borderer
P 1012 Brave Swordsman
P 1114 Dark Gladiator
P 1115 Dark Hero

Coastal Minesweepers

M 1103 Kilmorey (Alfriston)
M 1109 Killiecrankie (Bickington)
M 1110 Bildeston
M 1113 Brereton
M 1114 Brinton
M 1115 Bronington
M 1124 St. David (Crichton)
M 1125 Cuxton
M 1126 Dalswinton
M 1130 Highburton
M 1133 Bossington
M 1136 Curzon (Fittleton)
M 1140 Gavinton
M 1141 Glasserton
M 1146 Venturer (Hodgeston)
M 1147 Hubberston
M 1150 Invermoriston
M 1151 Iveston
M 1153 Kedelston
M 1154 Kellington
M 1157 Kirkliston
M 1158 Laleston
M 1164 Maddiston
M 1165 Maxton
M 1166 Nurton
M 1167 Clyde (Repton)
M 1173 Mersey (Pollington)
M 1174 Puncheston
M 1175 Quainton
M 1180 Shavington
M 1181 Sheraton
M 1182 Shoulton
M 1187 Upton
M 1188 Walkerton
M 1192 Wilkieston
M 1194 Thames (Woolaston)
M 1195 Wotton
M 1198 Ashton
M 1199 Belton
M 1200 Soberton
M 1204 Montrose (Stubbington)
M 1205 Northumbria (Wiston)
M 1208 Lewiston
M 1209 Chawton
M 1216 Solent (Crofton)

Inshore Minesweepers

M 304 Waterwitch (Powderham 2720)
M 2002 Aveley
M 2010 Isis (Cradley)
M 2603 Arlingham (ex-TRV, ex-PAS)
M 2611 Bottisham R
M 2614 Bucklesham TRV
M 2616 Chelsham R
M 2621 Dittisham (ex-TRV)
M 2622 Downham TRV
M 2624 Elsenham TRV
M 2626 Everingham PAS
M 2628 Flintham (ex-TRV)
M 2630 Fritham TRV
M 2635 Haversham TRV
M 2636 Lasham TRV
M 2716 Pagham RNXS
M 2717 Fordham DGV
M 2726 Shipham RNXS
M 2733 Thakeham RNXS
M 2735 Tongham PAS
M 2737 Warmingham DGV
M 2780 Woodlark (Yaxham)
M 2781 Portisham RNXS
M 2783 Odiham RNXS
M 2784 Puttenham RNXS
M 2785 Birdham RNXS
M 2790 Thatcham DGV
M 2793 Thornham

DGV = *Degaussing Vessels*
PAS = *Port Auxiliary Service*
RNXS = *Royal Naval Auxiliary Service*
TRV = *Torpedo Recovery Vessels*
R = Reserve (ex-RAF)

Note: A few of the above ships are scheduled for disposal, and several are not yet completed, but their pennant numbers are logged here for the record.

AIRCRAFT CARRIER

Name	*Deck Letter*	*No.*	*Builders*	*Laid down*	*Launched*	*Completed*	*Refitted*
ARK ROYAL (ex-*Irresistible*)	R	R 09	Cammell Laird, Birkenhead	3 May 1943	3 May 1950	25 Feb 1955	Mar 1967-Feb 1970

Displacement, tons	43 060 standard; 50 786 full load
Length, feet (*metres*)	720·0 (*219·5*)pp; 845·0 (*257·6*)oa
Beam, feet (*metres*)	112·8 (*34·4*) hull
Draught, feet (*metres*)	36·0 (*11·0*)
Width, feet (*metres*)	166·0 (*50·6*)
Catapults	2 improved steam
Aircraft	30 fixed wing + 6 helicopters
Missile launchers	Fitted for four quadruple "Seacat"
Armour	4·5 in belt; 4 in flight deck; 2·5 in hangar deck; 1·5 in hangar side
Main engines	Parsons single reduction geared turbines; 4 shafts; 152 000 shp
Speed, knots	31·5 designed max
Boilers	8 Admiralty 3-drum type; pressure 400 psi (*28·1 kg/cm²*); superheat 600°F (316°C)
Oil fuel, tons	5 500 capacity
Complement	260 officers (as Flagship) 2 380 ratings (with Air Staff)

GENERAL
First British aircraft carrier with steam catapults. Had first side lift in a British aircraft carrier, situated amidships on the port side and serving the upper hangar but in 1959 this was removed, the deck part provided by the angled deck having obviated its necessity, leaving her with two centre lifts. In 1961, the deck landing projector sight, "Hilo" long range guidance system, and more powerful steam catapults were installed. Ship originally cost £21 428 000. Due for disposal late 1970s.'

ARK ROYAL *1972*

MODERNISATION. A three-years "special refit" and modernisation costing £32 500 000, from Mar 1967 to Feb 1970, enables her to operate both Phantom and Buccaneer Mk 2 aircraft. A fully angled deck 8·5 degrees off the centre line was fitted, involving two large extensions to the flight deck, and the size of the island was increased. A new waist catapult with an increased launching speed allows her to operate aircraft at almost "nil" wind conditions. A new direct acting gear was installed to enable bigger aircraft to be landed on at greater speeds.

RADAR. Search: Type 965 (2 sets), Type 993. Aircraft Direction: Type 982 and Type 983 height finder. Miscellaneous: Carrier controlled Approach Radar.

GUNNERY. Originally mounted 16—4·5 inch guns in eight twin turrets, two on each beam forward and two on each beam aft but the four on port side forward were removed in 1956, the four on starboard side forward in 1959, four in two forward turrets on after sponsons in 1964 and the four aft in 1969.

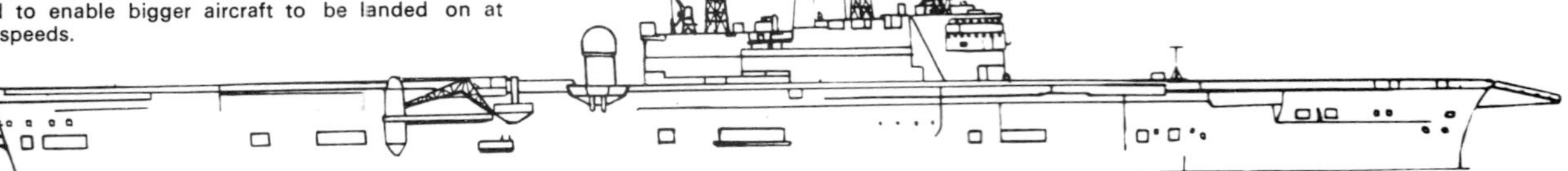

DRAWING. Starboard elevation and plan. Scale: 125 feet = 1 inch (1 : 1 500).

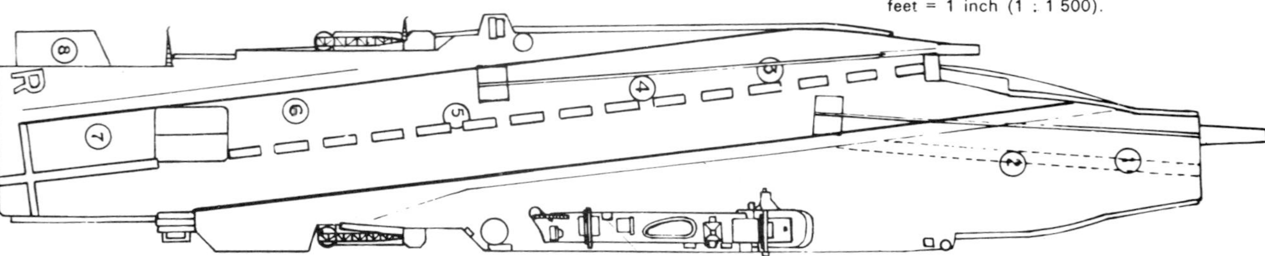

ARK ROYAL *1971*

ARK ROYAL *1971*

CRUISERS

1 PROJECTED THROUGH-DECK TYPE

INVINCIBLE

Displacement, tons	19 000 to 20 000 estimated
Length, feet (*metres*)	650·0 (*198·1*) approx
Beam, feet (*metres*)	84·0 (*25·6*) approx
Draught, feet (*metres*)	24·0 (*7·3*) approx
Aircraft	9 Sea King helicopters (could carry 6 Harriers)
Missile launchers	1 quadruple surface-to-surface; 2 twin "Sea Dart" surface-to-air
Main engines	"Olympus" gas turbines and "Tyne" gas turbines
Speed, knots	30 plus
Complement	1 200 (including aircrew)

First-of-class order from Vickers 17 April 1973 if follow-up orders are made, completion could be—first in 1978-79, second in 1980 and third in 1981-82.

She will be capable of providing a landing deck and hangar for helicopters, together with facilities for the command and control of naval and maritime air forces. The ship will be configured for a through deck, i.e. flight deck area, and approach will be unobstructed by superstructure, providing a limited run for V/STOL aircraft. With an angled deck she will virtually be a novel type of light fleet aircraft carrier. She will have two column masts and two funnels with an island bridge superstructure on the starboard side. Open forecastle head.

RADAR. As presently planned—Type 965 long range surveillance radar with double AKE-1 array; Type 992 Q general purpose radar; two Type 909 fire control and target radars for Sea Dart.

Through Deck Cruiser — *Vickers Shipbuilding 1973*

2 "TIGER" CLASS

Name	*No.*	*Builders and Engineers*	*Laid down*	*Launched*	*Completed*
BLAKE (ex-*Tiger*, ex-*Blake*)	C 99	Fairfield SB & Eng, Govan	17 Aug 42	20 Dec 45	8 Mar 61
TIGER (ex-*Bellerophon*)	C 20	John Brown, Clydebank	1 Oct 41	25 Oct 45	18 Mar 59

Displacement, tons	9 500 standard; 12 080 full load
Length, feet (*metres*)	538·0 (*164·0*) pp; 550·0 (*167·6*) wl 566·5 (*172·8*) oa
Beam, feet (*metres*)	64·0 (*19·5*)
Draught, feet (*metres*)	32·0 (*7·0*)
Aircraft	4 Sea King helicopters
Missile launchers	2 quadruple "Seacat"
Guns	2—6 in (*152 mm*) 1 twin; 2—3 in (*76 mm*) AA 1 twin
Armour	Belt 3·5 in—3·2 in (*89—83 mm*); deck 2 in (*51 mm*); turrets 3 in—1 in (*76—25 mm*)
Main engines	4 Parsons geared turbines; 4 shafts; 80 000 shp
Speed, knots	31·5 max
Boilers	4 Admiralty 3-drum type
Range, miles	2 000 at 30 knots; 4 000 at 20 knots; 6 500 at 13 knots
Oil fuel, tons	1 850
Complement	85 officers, 800 ratings

TIGER

Originally designed as orthodox cruisers. Work on the ships was stopped in July 1946, for eight years. The decision to complete them was announced on 15 Oct 1954. Dismantled for resumption to a new design in 1955. *Tiger* cost £13 113 000 and *Blake* £14 940 000. Helicopter conversion cost £5 500 000 for *Blake* and the astoniishng total of £13 250 000 for *Tiger*.

CONVERSION. *Blake* was converted to a command helicopter cruiser at HM Dockyard, Portsmouth from early 1965 until she recommissioned on 23 Apr 1969. *Tiger* was similarly converted during 1968 to 1972.

DRAWING. Starboard elevation and plan of *Blake*. Redrawn in 1972. Scale: 125 feet = 1 inch (1 : 1 500). *Tiger* starboard beam, redrawn 1972.

GUNNERY. The 6 inch fully automatic guns of advanced design are equally effective in surface and anti-aircraft roles. Rate of fire is 20 rpm, more than twice that of any previous cruiser. The 3 inch guns are capable of 90 rpm.

RADAR. Search: Type 965 and Type 992. Height Finder: Type 277. Fire control: 5 MRS 3 fire control directors.

ELECTRICAL. 4 turbo-generators provide 4 000 kW ac the first time this type power used in British cruisers.

ENGINEERING. Main machinery is largely automatic and can be remotely controlled. Steam conditions 400 psi pressure and 640°F. Propellers 11 ft dia, 285 rpm.

CLASS. It was announced in Feb 1972 that the unconverted sister ship *Lion* had been approved for disposal by scrapping. *Hawke* of this class, laid down in HM Dockyard, Portsmouth in Aug 1944, was cancelled in 1946 as was *Bellerophon* (ex-*Tiger*) a cruiser of enlarged design ordered from Vickers-Armstrongs.

BLAKE — *1972, Wright & Logan*

LIGHT CRUISERS

"TYPE 82"

Name	No.	Builders	Laid down	Launched	Commissioned
BRISTOL	D 23	Swan Hunter & Tyne Shipbuilders Ltd	15 Nov 1967	30 June 1969	31 Mar 1973

Displacement, tons	5 650 standard (approx) 6 750 full load
Length, feet (*metres*)	490·0 (*149·4*)wl; 507·0 (*154·5*)oa
Beam, feet (*metres*)	55·0 (*16·8*)
Draught, feet (*metres*)	22·5 (*6·9*)
Aircraft	Landing platform for 1 "Wasp" helicopter
Missile launchers	1 twin "Seadart" GWS 30 launcher aft
A/S weapons	1 "Ikara" single launcher forward; 1 "Limbo" three-barrelled depth charge mortar (Mark 10) aft
Guns	1—4·5 in (*115 mm*) Mark 8 forward; 4 saluting
Main engines	COSAG arrangement (combined steam and gas turbines) 2 sets Standard Range geared steam turbines, 30 000 shp; 2 Bristol-Siddeley marine "Olympus" gas turbines, 44 600 shp; 2 shafts; Total 74 600 shp
Speed, knots	30 approx estimated max
Boilers	2
Endurance, miles	Over 4 500 at 18 knots
Complement	433 (33 officers, 400 ratings)

BRISTOL on trials 1972

GENERAL.
Three funnels, one amidships and two aft abreast the mainmast.
Designed around a new weapons system. Fully stabilised to present a steady weapon platform. The gas turbines provide emergency power and high speed boost. The machinery is remotely controlled from a ship control centre. Automatic steering, obviating the need for a quartermaster. Many labour-saving items of equipment fitted to make the most efficient and economical use of manpower resulting in a smaller ship's company for tonnage than any previous warship. Fitted with Action Data Automation Weapon System. Started trials 10 April 1972.

MISSILES. The Seadart ship missile system, developed to meet the air threat of the 1970's and 1980's, also has a reasonable anti-ship capability. Its main advantages over the "Seaslug" system fitted in the "County" Class are; considerably improved surface-to-air performance, particularly at very high and very low levels. Quicker reaction time. Considerably improved target handling capacity. It is lighter and takes up less space.
Ikara is a long-range anti-submarine weapon system, developed in Australia, designed to deliver homing torpedoes to a position where they can attack submarine targets. It is propelled by rocket motor providing the missile with its long-range capability.

RADAR. Type 965 long range search radar with AKE double aerial outfit and IFF; Type 992 General-purpose radar; Type 909 fire control and target radar for Sea Dart.

COST. £22 500 000 (£27 000 000 overall). GEC-Marconi equipment for radar, weapons and communications cost over £3 000 000.

COMMUNICATIONS. By GEC-Marconi include SCOT satellite system compatible with both SKYNET and the US Defence satellites.

BRISTOL on trials 1972

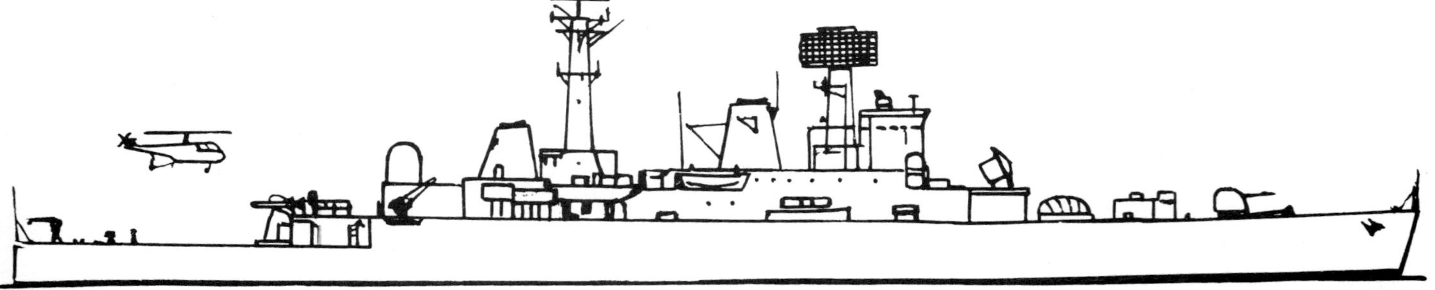
BRISTOL

Light Cruisers—*continued*

8 "COUNTY" CLASS

Name	No.	Builders	Laid down	Launched	Completed
ANTRIM	D 18	Fairfield SB & Eng Co Ltd, Govan	20 Jan 66	19 Oct 67	**14 July 70**
DEVONSHIRE	D 02	Cammell Laird & Co Ltd, Birkenhead	9 Mar 59	10 June 60	**15 Nov 62**
FIFE	D 20	Fairfield SB & Eng Co Ltd, Govan	1 June 62	9 July 64	**21 June 66**
GLAMORGAN	D 19	Vickers-Armstrongs Ltd, Newcastle-on-Tyne	13 Sep 62	9 July 64	**11 Oct 66**
HAMPSHIRE	D 06	John Brown & Co (Clydebank) Ltd, Glasgow	26 Mar 59	16 Mar 61	**15 Mar 63**
KENT	D 12	Harland & Wolff Ltd, Belfast	1 Mar 60	27 Sep 61	**15 Aug 63**
LONDON	D 16	Swan, Hunter & Wigham Richardson, Wallsend	26 Feb 60	7 Dec 61	**4 Nov 63**
NORFOLK	D 21	Swan, Hunter & Wigham Richardson, Wallsend	15 Mar 66	16 Nov 67	**7 Mar 70**

Displacement, tons	5 440 standard; 6 200 full load
Length, feet (*metres*)	505·0 (*153·9*) wl; 520·5 (*158·7*) oa
Beam, feet (*metres*)	54·0 (*16·5*)
Draught, feet (*metres*)	20·0 (*6·1*) max
Aircraft	1 "Wessex" helicopter
Missile launchers	Exocet in four ships (see *Missile* note) 1 twin "Seaslug" aft; 2 quadruple "Seacat" abaft after funnel; 2 sextuple 3 in, Mark 4
Guns	4—4·5 in (*115 mm*), 2 twin turrets forward; 2—20 mm, single (2—4·5 only in ships with Exocet)
Boilers	2 Babcock & Wilcox
Main engines	Combined steam and gas turbines. 2 sets geared steam turbines, 30 000 shp; 4 gas turbines, 30 000 shp. 2 shafts; Total 60 000 shp; (see *Engineering* notes)
Speed, knots	32·5 max
Complement	471 (33 officers and 438 men)

Kent and *London*, have mainmast stepped further aft. *Fife, Glamorgan, Antrim* and *Norfolk*, have the more powerful "Seaslug" II systems, later to be fitted in the first four. All fitted with stabilisers.

MISSILES. Exocet being fitted in *Devonshire, Hampshire* and two others in place of B turret.

GUNNERY. The 4—4·5 inch guns are radar controlled, fully automatic dual-purpose quick-firing. The 20 mm guns were added for picket duties in S.E. Asia, but have been retained for general close range duties.

ENGINEERING. These are the first ships of their size to have COSAG (combined steam and gas turbine machinery). This is of exceptionally compact and light design. Boilers work at a pressure of 700 psi and a temperature of 950 deg F. The steam and gas turbines are geared to the same shaft. Each shaft set consists of a high pressure and low pressure steam turbine of 15 000 shp combined output plus two G.6 gas turbines each of 7 500 shp. The gas turbines are able to develop their full power from cold within a few minutes, providing unprecedented mobility, and enabling ships lying in harbour without steam to get under way instantly in emergency.

ELECTRICAL. Two 1 000 kW turbo-alternators and three gas turbines alternators total 3 750 kW, at 440 V.a.c.

RADAR. Type 992 search radar; Height Finder Type 277; Type 901 fire control and Target radar aft for Seaslug; MRS 3 forward, port and starboard for gunnery fire control; Type 965 with double AKE-2 aerial outfit in *Norfolk, Glamorgan, Antrim* and *Fife* while the remainder have single AKE-1; IFF.

HABITABILITY. All vessels have the latest accommodation standards and are fully air-conditioned.

ANTRIM, NORFOLK

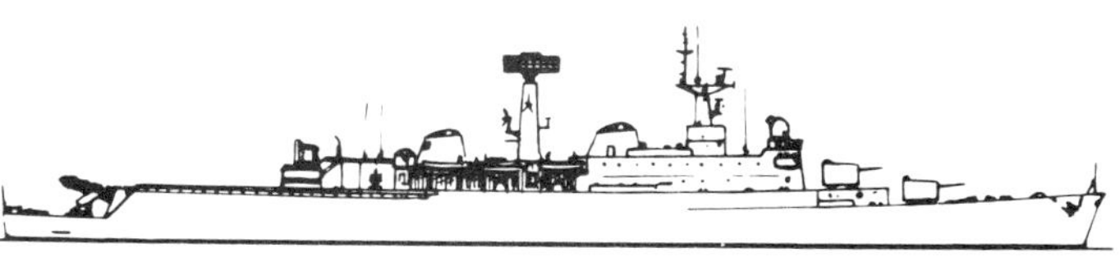

KENT, LONDON

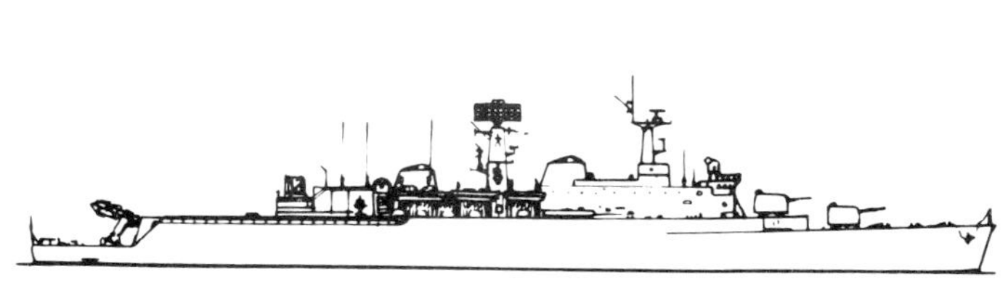

DEVONSHIRE, HAMPSHIRE

FIFE & GLAMORGAN

LONDON *1972*

DESTROYERS

3 + 3 "TYPE" 42

Name	Builders	Ordered	Laid down	Launched
SHEFFIELD	Vickers Ltd Shipbuilding Group, Barrow	14 Nov 1968	15 Jan 1970	10 June 1971
BIRMINGHAM	Cammell Laird & Co, Ltd, Birkenhead	21 May 1971		
COVENTRY	Cammell Laird & Co, Ltd, Birkenhead	21 May 1971		
CARDIFF	Vickers Ltd, Shipbuilding Group, Barrow	10 June 1971	3 Nov 1972	1974
05 (**SOUTHAMPTON**)	Swan Hunter & Tyne Shipbuilders, Ltd	11 Nov 1971		
06 (**MANCHESTER**)	Swan Hunter & Tyne Shipbuilders, Ltd	11 Nov 1971		

Displacement, tons	3 500 approx full load
Length, feet (*metres*)	392·0 (*119·5*)wl; 410·0 (*125·0*) oa
Beam, feet (*metres*)	47·0 (*14·3*)
Draught, feet (*metres*)	22·0 (*6·7*)
Aircraft	1 twin engined "Lynx" anti-submarine helicopter
Missile launchers	1 twin "Sea Dart" medium range surface-to-air (surface-to-surface capability)
Guns	1—4·5 in automatic, Mark 8, high rate of fire; 2—20 mm Oerlikon; 2 saluting
A/S weapons	Helicopter launched torpedoes
Main engines	COGOG arrangement of Rolls Royce Olympus gas turbines for full power; and 2 Rolls Royce Tyne gas turbines for cruising; reversible pitch propellers for manoeuvring; 2 shafts; 50 000 shp
Speed, knots	30 approx estimated max
Endurance	Over 4 000 miles at 18 knots
Complement	280 (20 officers and 260 ratings) (accommodation for 312)

SHEFFIELD

GENERAL
The first "Type 42" all gas-turbine propelled destroyer with the Sea Dart guided missile as her main armament is scheduled for service in 1973. The helicopter will carry an air-to-surface weapon for use against lightly defended surface ship targets such as fast patrol boats. The gas turbine installation is a development of that in the frigate *Exmouth*. Advantages include ability to reach maximum speed with great rapidity, reduction in space and weight and 25 per cent reduction in technical manpower. To cost £17 000 000 per ship. All to be in service by end 1977.

ELECTRONICS. Twin Scott Skyne satellite communication aerials; ADAWS.

RADAR. Type 965 with AKE-2 and IFF; Type 992Q General-purpose radar; Type 1006 navigation radar; Two Type 909 Sea Dart fire control and target radars; ECM; D/F.

SHEFFIELD, Artist's impression

1969, Vickers Limited

"DARING" CLASS. *Dainty* and *Defender* for disposal in 1969-70. *Delight* scrapped 1970, *Daring* 1971. *Decoy* (renamed *Ferré*) and *Diana* (*Palacios*) sold to Peru in 1969 and refitted by Cammell Laird Ltd, Birkenhead, for delivery in 1971-72. *Diamond* is engineering training ship. *Duchess* is lent to the Royal Australian Navy.

LATER "BATTLE" CLASS. Of the four radar pickets, *Aisne* was scrapped in 1970 and *Agincourt*, *Barrosa* and *Corunna* approved for disposal in 1971-72. Of the four standard destroyers, *Alamein* was scrapped in 1964, *Dunkirk* and *Jutland* in 1965 and *Matapan* has been converted into a Sonar Trials Ship, see later page.

"WEAPON" CLASS. Of the four radar pickets, *Battleaxe* was scrapped in 1964. *Broadsword* was expended as a target in 1968. *Crossbow* used as harbour training ship since 1967 (see particulars in 1965-66 edition). *Scorpion*, used for Naval Construction Research Establishment trials at Rosyth, scrapped 1971.

DIAMOND (training)

1971

FRIGATES

4 + 4 "TYPE 21" AMAZON CLASS

Displacement, tons	2 500 full load
Length, feet (*metres*)	360·0 (*109·7*)wl; 384·0 (*117·0*)oa
Beam, feet (*metres*)	41·8 (*12·7*) max
Draught, feet (*metres*)	12·3 (*3·7*) deep
Aircraft	1 twin engined "Lynx" anti-submarine helicopter
Missile launchers	1 quadruple "Seacat" surface-to-air (later ships will have "Seawolf"
Guns	1—4·5 in, Mark 8; 2—20 mm Oerlikon
A/S weapons	Helicopter launched torpedoes
Torpedo tubes	6 (2 triple)
Main engines	COGOG arrangement of 2 Rolls Royce "Olympus" gas turbines for speed; 2 Rolls Royce "Tyne" gas turbines for cruising; 2 shafts; 50 000 shp; controllable pitch propellers for astern
Speed, knots	34
Range, miles	4 500 at 18 knots
Complement	170 (11 officers and 159 ratings)

Name	*Builders*	*Laid down*	*Launched*	*Completion*
AMAZON	Vosper Thornycroft, Woolston	6 Nov 1969	26 Apr 1971	1974-75
ANTELOPE	Vosper Thornycroft, Woolston	23 Mar 1971	16 Mar 1972	
ACTIVE	Vosper Thornycroft, Woolston	23 July 1971	23 Nov 1972	
AMBUSCADE	Yarrow & Co, Ltd, Glasgow	June 1971	18 Jan 1973	
05	Yarrow & Co, Ltd, Glasgow	June 1972		
06	Yarrow & Co, Ltd, Glasgow	Oct 1972		
07	Yarrow & Co, Ltd, Glasgow			
08	Yarrow & Co, Ltd, Glasgow			

AMAZON

The Navy awarded Vosper Thornycroft, Portsmouth and Southampton, a contract on 27 Feb 1968 for the design of a patrol frigate to be prepared in full collaboration with Yarrow Ltd, Scotstoun. The resulting first "Type 21" all-gas-turbine powered frigate, *Amazon*, was for completion in summer 1972. This is the first custom built gas turbine frigate (designed and constructed as such from the keel up, as opposed to conversion) and the first warship designed by commercial firms for many years. All eight to be completed by end 1977.

RADAR. Type 992 Q general-purpose search radar; Type 978 navigation radar; GWS 24 fire control fore and aft for Seacat; Orion RTN-10X WSA-4 fire control system for guns; Cossor Type 1010 IFF interrogator; Plessey PTR 461 IFF transponder; CAAIS.

AMAZON model — *1969, Vosper Thornycroft Group*

"TYPE 22" PROJECTED

Displacement, tons	3 000 approx
Aircraft	1 "Lynx" helicopter
Missile launchers	"Sea Wolf" surface-to-air system; surface-to-surface system
Main engines	COGOG arrangement of Rolls Royce "Olympus" gas turbines and 2 Rolls Royce "Tyne" gas turbines driving 2 shafts
Speed, knots	30 approx estimated max

Designed as successors to the "Leander" class general purpose frigates the construction of which ceases with the completion of the scheduled programme of 26 ships. Order for first of class to be built by Yarrows expected during 1973.

ANTELOPE — *16 Mar 1972, Vosper Thornycroft Group*

AMAZON — *26 Apr, 1971*

Frigates—*continued*

16 "LEANDER" CLASS

Name	No.	Builders	Laid down	Launched	Completed
AJAX	F 114	Cammell Laird & Co Ltd, Birkenhead	12 Oct 59	16 Aug 62	10 Dec 63
DIDO	F 104	Yarrow & Co Ltd, Scotstoun, Glasgow	2 Dec 59	22 Dec 61	18 Sep 63
LEANDER	F 109	Harland & Wolff Ltd, Belfast	10 Apr 59	28 June 61	27 Mar 63
PENELOPE	F 127	Vickers-Armstrongs Ltd, Tyne	14 Mar 61	17 Aug 62	31 Oct 63
AURORA	F 10	John Brown & Co (Clydebank) Ltd	1 June 61	28 Nov 62	9 Apr 64
EURYALUS	F 15	Scotts' Shipbuilding & Eng, Greenock	2 Nov 61	6 June 63	16 Sep 64
GALATEA	F 18	Swan, Hunter & Wigham Richardson, Tyne	29 Dec 61	23 May 63	25 Apr 64
ARETHUSA	F 38	J. Samuel White & Co Ltd, Cowes	7 Sep 62	5 Nov 63	24 Nov 65
NAIAD	F 39	Yarrow & Co Ltd, Scotstoun, Glasgow	30 Oct 62	4 Nov 63	15 Mar 65
CLEOPATRA	F 28	HM Dockyard, Devonport	19 June 63	25 Mar 64	4 Jan 66
SIRIUS	F 40	HM Dockyard, Portsmouth	9 Aug 63	22 Sep 64	15 June 66
MINERVA	F 45	Vickers-Armstrongs Ltd, Tyne	25 July 63	19 Dec 64	14 May 66
PHOEBE	F 42	Alex Stephen & Sons Ltd, Glasgow	3 June 63	8 July 64	15 Apr 66
DANAE	F 47	HM Dockyard, Devonport	16 Dec 64	31 Oct 65	7 Sep 67
JUNO	F 52	John I. Thornycroft Ltd, Woolston	16 July 64	24 Nov 65	18 July 67
ARGONAUT	F 56	Hawthorn Leslie, Ltd, Hebburn-on-Tyne	27 Nov 64	8 Feb 66	17 Aug 67

Displacement, tons	2 450 standard; 2 860 full load
Length, feet (*metres*)	360 (*109·7*) wl; 372 (*113·4*) oa
Beam, feet (*metres*)	41 (*12·5*)
Draught, feet (*metres*)	18 (*5·5*) max (props)
Aircraft	1 Wasp helicopter armed with homing torpedoes
Missile launchers	1 or 2 quadruple "Seacat" and 2 sextuple 3" Mk 4 in later ships
Guns, dual purpose	2—4·5 in (*115 mm*), 1 twin
Guns, AA	2—40 mm, single; 2—20 mm, single in "Seacat" ships
A/S weapons	1 "Limbo" 3-barrelled DC mortar
Main engines	2 d.r. geared turbines; 2 shafts; 30 000 shp
Boilers	2
Speed, knots	30
Oil fuel, tons	460
Complement	251

GENERAL
An improvement on the Type "12". The main new features are long-range air warning radar, "Seacat" anti-aircraft missiles, improved anti-submarine detection equipment, and a lightweight helicopter armed with homing torpedoes.

ELECTRICAL. Alternating current, 440 volts, 60 cycles, 1 900 kW installation in early vessels and 2 500 kW in later vessels.

NOMENCLATURE. *Ajax*, *Dido* and *Leander* were originally to have been the last three frigates of the "Rothesay" class, *Fowey*, *Hastings* and *Weymouth*, respectively. *Penelope* was to have been the fifth frigate of the "Salisbury" class, *Coventry*.

GUIDED WEAPONS. *Naiad* was the first of the class to be completed with a "Seacat" missile launcher, followed by *Arethusa*, *Cleopatra*, *Phoebe*, *Minerva*, *Sirius*, *Juno*, *Argonaut*, and *Danae*. The 40 mm guns mounted in the earlier ships will be replaced by "Seacat".

IKARA. Special refits are being carried out to fit Ikara in place of the 4·5 mounting forward. *Leander* completed; *Galatea, Arethusa, Ajax, Aurora, Dido, Naiad* and probably *Euryalus* to be completed. Cost: original ships £5m—later ships £8-9 m.

RADAR. Search: Type 965 with single AKE aerial array, and Type 993 combined surface and air warning. Fire Control: X band. MRS.3/GWS-22 fire control directors. DF equipment. In Ikara conversions Type 965 aerial is removed to compensate for top-weight.

GUNNERY. 4·5 mounting removed in Ikara conversions. New bridge director. Sponsons to be fitted on shelter deck for additional 40 mm guns.

SONAR. VDS fitted in all ships except *Diomede*.

ACHILLES 1972

LEANDER *Class* with "Seacat"

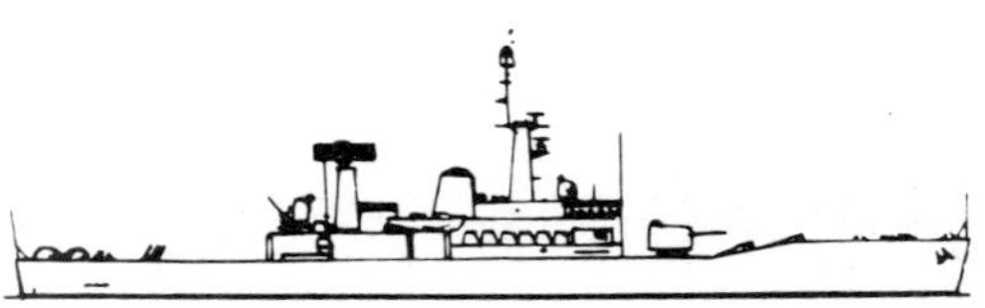
LEANDER *Class* with AA guns

LEANDER

10 IMPROVED "LEANDER" CLASS

Name	No.	Builders	Laid down	Launched	Completed
ANDROMEDA	F 57	HM Dockyard, Portsmouth	25 May 66	24 May 67	2 Dec 68
JUPITER	F 60	Yarrow & Co Ltd, Scotstoun, Glasgow	3 Oct 66	4 Sep 67	9 Aug 69
HERMIONE	F 58	Alex Stephen & Sons Ltd, Glasgow	6 Dec 65	26 Apr 67	11 July 69
BACCHANTE	F 69	Vickers Ltd, High Walker, Newcastle	27 Oct 66	29 Feb 68	17 Oct 69
SCYLLA	F 71	HM Dockyard, Devonport	17 May 67	8 Aug 68	12 Feb 70
CHARYBDIS	F 75	Harland & Wolff Ltd, Belfast	27 Jan 67	28 Feb 68	2 June 69
ACHILLES	F 12	Yarrow & Co Ltd, Scotstoun	1 Dec 67	21 Nov 68	9 July 70
DIOMEDE	F 16	Yarrow & Co Ltd, Scotstoun	30 Jan 68	15 Apr 69	2 Apr 71
APOLLO	F 70	Yarrow & Co Ltd, Scotstoun	1 May 69	15 Oct 70	28 May 72
ARIADNE	F 72	Yarrow & Co Ltd, Scotstoun	1 Nov 69	10 Sep 71	28 Dec 72

Displacement, tons	2 500 standard 2 962 full load
Length, feet (*metres*)	360 (*109·7*) wl; 372 (*113·4*) oa
Beam, feet (*metres*)	43 (*13·1*)
Draught, feet (*metres*)	18 (5·5)
Complement	263

All other details as above.

Frigates—*continued*

LEANDER (firing Ikara) *1973*

BACCHANTE *1970*

APOLLO *1972*

DIOMEDE *1972*

Frigates—*continued*

9 "ROTHESAY" CLASS

Name	No.	Builders	Laid down	Launched	Completed
BERWICK	F 115	Harland & Wolff Ltd, Belfast	16 June 1958	15 Dec 1959	1 June 1961
BRIGHTON	F 106	Yarrow & Co Ltd, Scotstoun	23 July 1957	30 Oct 1959	28 Sep 1961
FALMOUTH	F 113	Swan Hunter, Wigham Richardson	23 Nov 1957	15 Dec 1959	25 July 1961
LONDONDERRY	F 108	J. Samuel White & Co Ltd, Cowes	15 Nov 1956	20 May 1958	22 July 1960
LOWESTOFT	F 103	Alex Stephen & Sons Ltd, Govan	9 June 1958	23 June 1960	18 Oct 1961
PLYMOUTH	F 126	HM Dockyard, Devonport	1 July 1958	20 July 1959	11 May 1961
RHYL	F 129	HM Dockyard, Portsmouth	29 Jan 1958	23 Apr 1959	31 Oct 1960
ROTHESAY	F 107	Yarrow & Co Ltd, Scotstoun	6 Nov 1956	9 Dec 1957	23 Apr 1960
YARMOUTH	F 101	John Brown & Co Ltd, Clydebank	29 Nov 1957	23 Mar 1959	26 Mar 1960

Displacement, tons	2 380 standard; 2 800 full load
Length, feet (*metres*)	360·0 (*109·7*)wl; 370·0 (*112·8*)oa
Beam, feet (*metres*)	41·0 (*12·5*)
Draught, feet (*metres*)	17·3 (*5·3*) max (props)
Aircraft	1 "Wasp" helicopter armed with homing torpedoes
Missile launchers	1 quadruple for "Seacat"; 2 sextuple 3in Mark 4 rocket
Guns	2—4·5 in (*115 mm*) dp (1 twin) 2—20 mm AA single
A/S weapons	1 Limbo 3-barrelled DC mortar
Main engines	2 double reduction geared turbines; 2 shafts; 30 000 shp
Speed, knots	30 max
Boilers	2 Babcock & Wilcox
Oil fuel, tons	400 approx
Complement	235 (15 officers and 220 ratings)

Provided under the 1954-55 programme. Originally basically similar to the "Whitby" class but with modifications in layout as a result of experience gained.

MISSILES. The "Rothesay" class have been fitted with "Seacat" surface-to-air guided missile launchers as secondary armament in place of Bofors close range anti-aircraft guns.

MODERNISATION. *Rothesay* was reconstructed and modernised at HM Dockyard, Rosyth, in May 1966 to May 1968 during which she was equipped to operate a Wessex Wasp lightweight anti-submarine helicopter armed wtih homing torpedoes, and fitted with "dipping" sonar. A flight deck and hangar were built on aft, necessitating the removal of one of her anti-submarine mortars. A "Seacat" replaced the 40 mm gun. *Yarmouth, Plymouth, Londonderry, Lowestoft, Falmouth, Berwick, Rhyl* and *Brighton* in succession were similarly reconstructed as they came into dockyard for extended overhaul.

RADAR. Search: Some ships are fitted with Type 993 and others with Type 293. Fire Control: MRS.3. fire control: Type 978 air warning radar; optical Seacat director; DF.

ENGINEERING. Two Admiralty Standard Range turbines each rated at 15 000 shp. Propeller revolutions 220 rpm. Steam conditions 550 psi (*38·7 kg/cm²*) pressure and 850° F (450°C) temperature at boilers.

ELECTRICAL. Two turbo generators and two diesel generators in all ships. Total 1 140 kW. Alternating current, 440 volts, three phase, 60 cycles per second.

Modernised ROTHESAY *Class*

PLYMOUTH — *1970, Wright & Logan*

LOWESTOFT — *1971, Wright & Logan*

FALMOUTH — *1971*

Frigates—*continued*

4 "WHITBY" CLASS TYPE 12

Displacement, tons 2 150 standard; 2 560 full load
Length, feet (*metres*) 360·0 (*109·7*)wl; 369·8 (*112·7*)oa
Beam, feet (*metres*) 41·0 (*12·5*)
Draught, feet (*metres*) 17 (*5·2*) max (props)
Guns, dual purpose 2—4·5 in (*115 mm*) 1 twin
Guns, AA 2—40 mm Bofors (1 twin)
A/S weapons 2 Limbo 3-barrelled DC mortars
Boilers 2 Babcock & Wilcox
Pressure 550 psi (*38·7 kg/cm²*)
Temperature 850°F (454°C)
Main engines 2 sets d.r. geared turbines; 2 shafts; 30 430 shp
Speed, knots 31 (29 sea)
Oil fuel, tons 370
Complement 225 (12 officers and 213 ratings)

Name	*No.*	*Builders*	*Laid down*	*Launched*	*Completed*
BLACKPOOL*	F 77	Harland & Wolff Ltd, Belfast	20 Dec 1954	14 Feb 1957	13 Aug 1958
EASTBOURNE*	F 73	Vickers-Armstrongs Ltd Tyne	13 Jan 1954	29 Dec 1955	9 Jan 1958
TORQUAY*	F 43	Harland & Wolff Ltd, Belfast	11 Mar 1953	1 July 1954	10 May 1956
WHITBY*	F 36	Cammell Laird & Co Ltd, Birkenhead	30 Sep 1952	2 July 1954	19 July 1956

*(*Blackpool* was lent to the Royal New Zealand Navy until Apr 1971; her disposal is under review)

WHITBY *Class* for training

Ordered in 1951. Good sea-keeping qualities enable them to maintain their high speed in rough seas. Their twin-rudders improve manoeuvrability. They are all welded and were specially designed with the lightest possible structure.

ENGINEERING. Propelling machinery includes geared turbines of Y 100 design and high power. Double reduction gearing allows low propeller revolutions of 220 rpm at high power and the propeller efficiency is correspondingly high. This, with improvements in hull design, enables these frigates to achieve over 30 knots on only 75 per cent of the power required by older destroyers of comparable displacement.

RADAR. Search: Type 293 and Type 277 for surface search. Fire Control: X Band.

CAAIS. The first complete CAAIS (Computer Assisted Action Information System) to go to sea was installed in *Torquay* during her recent refit. Trials in 1972.

ELECTRICAL. System is alternating current, 440 volts; three phase, 60 cycles per second. Two turbo alternators and two diesel alternators. Total 1 140 kilowatts.

APPEARANCE. Later ships were completed with thicker, raked back funnel with dome cap (there are two stacks inside the funnel) and early ships of the class, which had vertical funnel, were similarly altered.

TRAINING. *Eastbourne*, and *Torquay*, Dartmouth Training Squadron, are now slightly different in appearance. They have only a single 40 mm.

WHITBY *1971, John Mortimer*

EASTBOURNE *1970, Wright & Logan*

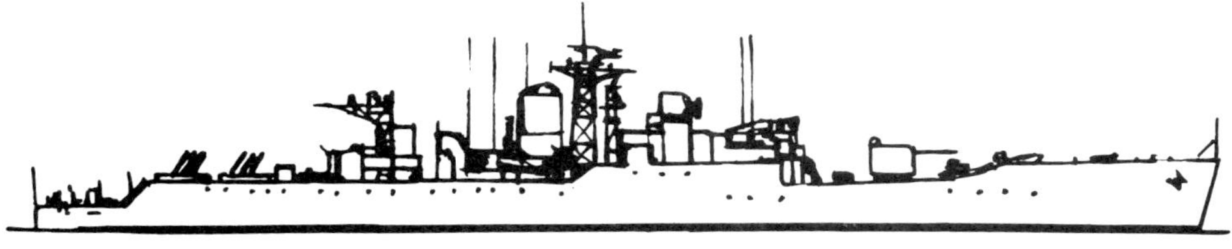

WHITBY

TORQUAY *1972*

Frigates—*continued*

6 "BLACKWOOD" CLASS TYPE 14

Name	No	Builders	Laid down	Launched	Completed
DUNDAS	F 48	J. Samuel White & Co Ltd, Cowes	17 Oct 1952	25 Sep 1953	16 Mar 1956
EXMOUTH	F 84	J. Samuel White & Co Ltd, Cowes	24 Mar 1954	16 Nov 1955	20 Dec 1957
HARDY	F 54	Yarrow & Co Ltd, Scotstoun	4 Feb 1953	25 Nov 1953	15 Dec 1955
KEPPEL	F 85	Yarrow & Co Ltd, Scotstoun	27 Mar 1953	31 Aug 1954	6 July 1956
PALLISER	F 94	Alex Stephen & Sons Ltd, Govan	15 Mar 1955	10 May 1956	13 Dec 1957
RUSSELL	F 97	Swan, Hunter & Wighan Richardson	11 Nov 1953	10 Dec 1954	7 Feb 1957

Displacement, tons	1 180 standard; 1 456 full load
Length, feet (*metres*)	300 (*91·4*) wl; 310 (*94·5*) oa
Beam, feet (*metres*)	33·0 (*10·1*)
Draught, feet (*metres*)	15·5 (*4·7*) max (props)
Guns, AA	2—40 mm Bofors (see *Gunnery*)
A/S weapons	2 "Limbo" 3-barrelled DC mortars
Boilers	2 Babcock & Wilcox Pressure 550 psi (*38·7 kg/cm²*) Temperature 850°F (454°C)
Main engines	1 set geared turbines; 1 shaft; 15 000 shp; (see *Machinery Conversion*)
Speed, knots	27·8 max; 24·5 sea
Radius, miles	4 000 at 12 knots
Oil fuel, tons	275
Complement	140 (8 officers and 132 ratings)

Anti-submarine utility type. Very lightly gunned. Of comparatively simple construction. Built in pre-fabricated sections. In 1958-59 their hulls were strengthened to withstand severe and prolonged sea and weather conditions on fishery protection in Icelandic waters.

RADAR. Equipped with Type 978 search radar.

GUNNERY. The original gun armament was three 40 mm Bofors AA guns, but one was removed.

TORPEDOES. 4—21 inch tubes (2 twin) mounted in *Blackwood, Exmouth, Malcolm* and *Palliser* were removed.

ENGINEERING. All engined by their builders, except *Pellew* and *Russell*, by Wallsend Slipway & Eng Co Ltd, and *Grafton* and *Malcolm* by Parsons Marine Steam Turbine Co Ltd, Wallsend-on-Tyne. The turbines were of advanced design. The propelling machinery of *Hardy* and *Keppel* included turbines of English Electric Co design. Four-bladed, 12 ft diameter propeller, 220 rpm.

FISHERY PROTECTION. *Duncan* (on completion as Leader in 1958), *Malcolm* (in 1959), *Palliser* (Apr 1958) and *Russell* (Jan 1958) originally formed the 1st Division of the Fishery Protection Squadron (now incorporated in the Fleet).

CLASS. Sister ship *Grafton* was officially approved for disposal in 1968-69 and *Murray* in 1969-70. *Pellew* was scrapped in 1971. *Duncan* was in reserve in 1972 and *Malcolm* in the sales list.

TRAINING. *Blackwood* was also for disposal in 1969 but it was officially stated in 1969 that she had arrived at Portsmouth to join *Crossbow* as harbour training ship for the shore establishments *Sultan* and *Collingwood*.

MACHINERY CONVERSION. Conversion of *Exmouth* to all-gas turbine propulsion at HM Dockyard, Chatham was completed on 20 July 1968. First major warship propelled entirely by gas turbines. One BSE Olympus for full power, with two Proteus engines for cruising. The Olympus engine develops 22 500 hp and the two Proteus engines 3 250 each = 6 500 hp, but only one system or the other will propel; they cannot be used together or for boost. Both these engines are marine versions of well-known and proven aircraft gas turbines and their use in warships benefits from extensive research and development already completed for aircraft use, and from which they have evolved. *Exmouth* enables the operational characteristics and benefits of all-gas turbine propulsion to be evaluated in the rigours of naval service. These benefits include reductions in weight and space of machinery and fuel, and in operating and maintenance staffs. Gas turbine machinery installations in *Exmouth* and in future ships will be operated and controlled from the bridge. Other new features in *Exmouth* are the use of a gas turbine developed by Centrax Ltd, Newton Abbot, Devon, for driving the main electric generator, and this incorporates a waste heat boiler to produce steam for auxiliary and domestic purposes. A controllable pitch propeller by Stone Manganese Marine Ltd, of Deptford, is fitted for astern operation. The installation for *Exmouth* was designed by the Yarrow-Admiralty Research Department in conjunction with Bristol Siddeley Engines Ltd, under the direction of the Navy Department.

RUSSELL — *1971, Wright & Logan*

HARDY — *1972, John G. Callis*

BLACKWOOD *Class*

EXMOUTH (Gas Turbines)

EXMOUTH (gas turbine propulsion) — *1971*

Frigates—*continued*

7 "TRIBAL" CLASS. TYPE 81

Name	No.	Builders	Laid down	Launched	Completed
ASHANTI	F 117	Yarrow & Co Ltd, Scotstoun	15 Jan 1958	9 Mar 1959	23 Nov 1961
ESKIMO	F 119	J. Samuel White & Co Ltd, Cowes	22 Oct 1958	20 Mar 1960	21 Feb 1963
GURKHA	F 122	J. I. Thornycroft & Co Ltd, Woolston	3 Nov 1958	11 July 1960	13 Feb 1963
MOHAWK	F 125	Vickers-Armstrongs Ltd, Barrow	23 Dec 1960	5 Apr 1962	29 Nov 1963
NUBIAN	F 131	HM Dockyard, Portsmouth	7 Sep 1959	6 Sep 1960	9 Oct 1962
TARTAR	F 133	HM Dockyard, Devonport	22 Oct 1959	19 Sep 1960	26 Feb 1962
ZULU	F 124	Alex Stephen & Sons Ltd, Govan	13 Dec 1960	3 July 1962	17 Apr 1964

Displacement, tons	2 300 standard; 2 700 full load
Length, feet (*metres*)	350·0 (*106·7*)wl; 360·0 (*109·7*)oa
Beam, feet (*metres*)	42·3 (*12·9*)
Draught, feet (*metres*)	17·5 (*5·3*) max (props)
Aircraft	1 "Wasp" helicopter
Missile launchers	2 quadruple "Seacat" in *Ashanti, Gurkha* and *Zulu* (which also has 2 sextuple 3" Mk 4 rockets and 2—20 mm AA guns
Guns	2—4·5 in (*115 mm*) dp single; 2—40 mm single
A/S weapons	1 "Limbo" 3-barrelled DC mortar
Main engines	Combined steam and gas turbine; Metrovick steam turbine; 12 500 shp. Metrovick gas turbine; 7 500 shp; 1 shaft; 20 000 shp
Speed, knots	28
Boilers	1 Babcock & Wilcox (plus 1 auxiliary boiler)
Oil fuel, tons	400
Complement	253 (13 officers and 240 ratings)

Ashanti, Eskimo and *Gurkha* were ordered under the 1955-56 Estimates, *Nubian* and *Tartar* 1956-57, and *Mohawk* and *Zulu* 1957-58. These versatile ships, designed as self-contained units for service in such areas as the Persian Gulf, are air-conditioned in all manned compartments. *Ashanti* cost £5 220 000.

RADAR. Type 969 with single AKE1 with IFF. Type 293 General-purpose air and surface warning; MRS 3 radar fire control for guns.

SONAR. *Ashanti* and *Gurkha* were fitted with variable depth sonar equipment in the counter well in 1970, see photographs.

ENGINEERING. These ships have COSAG (combined steam and gas) turbine propelling machinery. The engines are right aft. The principle employed is that of highly efficient steam turbines and gas turbines geared to the same propeller shaft. The gas turbines provide a high concentration of power in a very compact form and are used to boost the steam turbines for sustained bursts of high speed. They are also able to develop full power from cold within a few minutes, thus providing unprecedented mobility. The steam turbine provides power for normal cruising and manoeuvering. The gas turbine driving on the same propeller shaft provides additional power for high speed, and also enables the ship lying in harbour without steam up to get under way instantly in emergency. The machinery is remotely controlled at all powers. The main boiler works at a pressure of 550 psi and a temperature of 850 deg F. Five-bladed propeller, 11·75 ft diameter, 280 rpm. The machinery installations were designed by the Yarrow-Admiralty Research Department. Metropolitan-Vickers designed and manufactured the steam turbines, gas turbines, gearing and control gear. This lightweight and compact machinery enabled more fighting equipment to be carried than with orthodox machinery. The forward funnel serves the boiler, the after one the gas turbine.

OPERATIONAL. Totally enclosed bridge and air-conditioned operations room. Fitted with stabilisers. Twin rudders.

ELECTRICAL. Generator capacity of 1 500 kW. Fluorescent lighting in all living accommodation.

CONSTRUCTION. All-welded prefabrication. Robust hull with special emphasis on prevention of corrosion. Denny Brown stabilisers fitted to reduce rolling in heavy seas. Good seakeeping qualities facilitate speed in rough weather.

ANTI-SUBMARINE. The first frigates designed to carry a helicopter for anti-submarine reconnaissance. VDS fitted in *Mohawk, Gurkha, Ashanti, Nubian.*

HABITABILITY. High standard of living accommodation. All manned compartments air-conditioned.

NUBIAN 1972

MOHAWK John G. Callis, 1972

"TRIBAL" *Class*

"TRIBAL" *Class* with "Seacat"

ASHANTI (VDS in counter well) 1971

Frigates—*continued*

4 "LEOPARD" CLASS. TYPE 41

Name	*No.*	*Builders*	*Laid down*	*Launched*	*Completed*
JAGUAR	F 37	Wm Denny & Bros Ltd, Dumbarton	2 Nov 1953	30 July 1957	12 Dec 1959
LEOPARD	F 14	H.M. Dockyard, Portsmouth	25 Mar 1953	23 May 1955	30 Sep 1958
LYNX	F 27	John Brown & Co Ltd, Clydebank	13 Aug 1953	12 Jan 1955	14 Mar 1957
PUMA	F 34	Scotts' SB & Eng Co Ltd, Greenock	16 Nov 1953	30 June 1954	24 Apr 1957

Displacement, tons	2 300 standard, 2 520 full load
Length, feet (*metres*)	320 (*97·5*) pp; 330 (*100·6*) wl; 339·8 (*103·6*) oa
Beam, feet (*metres*)	40 (*12·2*)
Draught, feet (*metres*)	16 (*4·9*) max (props)
Guns, dual purpose	4—4·5 in (*115 mm*), 2 twin turrets
Guns, AA	1—40 mm
A/S weapons	1 Squid 3-barrelled DC mortar
Main engines	8 ASR 1 diesels in three engine rooms; 14 400 bhp; 2 shafts; 4 engines geared to each shaft.
Speed, knots	24
Radius, miles	2 300 at full power; 7 500 at 16 knots
Oil fuel (tons)	220
Complement	235 (15 officers, 220 ratings)

Designed primarily for anti-aircraft protection.

JAGUAR

CONSTRUCTION. All welded. *Jaguar, Lynx* and *Puma* were ordered on 28 June 1951. Fitted with stabilisers. The construction of another ship ordered under the 1956-57 Navy Estimates to have been named *Panther*, was cancelled in the 1957 defence economies.

RADAR. Search: Type 965 with single AKE 1 aerial and IFF and Type 993. Combined air and surface warning. Fire Control: Twin X-band fire control director unit. Type 975 nav radar. ECM and DF.

ENGINEERING. The propelling machinery comprises Admiralty Standard Range 1 diesels coupled to the propeller shafting through hydraulic gear boxes. These diesels are of light weight, about 17 lb/shp. *Jaguar* is the only ship of this class to be fitted with controllable pitch propellers, 12 ft diameter 200 rpm. The fuel tanks have a compensating system, so that sea water replaces oil fuel as it is used.

LEOPARD *1970, Wright & Logan*

RECONSTRUCTION. *Lynx* was extensively refitted in 1963 with new mainmast. *Puma* was similarly refitted in 1964, and *Leopard* in Oct 1964-Feb 1966, followed by *Jaguar*.

GUIDED MISSILES. "Seacat" missile launcher and director will replace the 40 mm gun mounting.

CLASS. A ship of this class, originally to have been named *Panther*, built by John Brown & Co Ltd, Clydebank, intended for the Royal Navy, was transferred to the Indian Navy and renamed *Brahmaputra*, see Indian section. Another *Panther* was projected to take her place, but this ship was not built as a unit of this class or under that name (see *Nomenclature* notes on following page).

JAGUAR, LEOPARD, LYNX, PUMA

LYNX

Frigates—*continued*

4 "SALISBURY" CLASS. TYPE 61

Name	No.	Builders	Laid down	Launched	Completed
CHICHESTER	F 59	Fairfield SB & Eng Co Ltd, Govan	25 Jan 1953	21 Apr 1955	16 May 1958
LINCOLN	F 99	Fairfield SB & Eng Co Ltd, Govan	20 May 1955	6 Apr 1959	7 July 1960
LLANDAFF	F 61	Hawthorn Leslie Ltd, Hebburn-on-Tyne	27 Aug 1953	30 Nov 1955	11 Apr 1958
SALISBURY	F 32	HM Dockyard, Devonport	23 Jan 1952	25 June 1953	27 Feb 1957

Displacement, tons: 2 170 standard; 2 408 full load
Length, feet (*metres*): 320·0 (*97·5*) pp; 330·0 (*100·6*) oa 339·8 (*103·6*) oa
Beam, feet (*metres*): 40·0 (*12·2*)
Draught, feet (*metres*): 15·5 (*4·7*) max (props)
Missile launchers: 1 quadruple "Seacat" in *Lincoln* and *Salisbury* which also have 2 sextuple 3 in rocket launchers
Guns, dual purpose: 2—4·5 in (*115 mm*)
Guns, AA: 2—40 mm; 2—20 mm in *Lincoln* and *Salisbury*
A/S weapons: 1 Squid triple-barrelled DC mortar
Main engines: 8 ASR 1 diesels in three engine rooms; 2 shafts; 14 400 bhp
Speed, knots: 24
Radius, miles: 2 300 at full power; 7 500 at 16 knots
Oil fuel, tons: 230
Complement: 237 (14 officers and 223 ratings)

Designed primarily for the direction of carrier-borne and shore based aircraft.

CONSTRUCTION. Ordered on 28 June 1951 except *Salisbury*, the prototype ship. Construction was all welded and largely prefabricated. The construction of the fifth ship, *Exeter*, ordered under the 1956-57 Navy Estimates, was cancelled in the 1957 defence economies. Fitted with stabilisers (except *Lincoln*).

ENGINEERING. *Salisbury* is powered by Admiralty Standard Range 1 heavy oil engines coupled to the propeller shafts through hydraulic couplings and oil operated reverse and reduction gear boxes. *Llandaff* is the only Type 61 frigate to have a 500 kW gas-turbine alternator and three diesel generators. *Lincoln* is fitted with controllable pitch propellers, rotating at 200 rpm, which are 12 feet in diameter, manufactured by Stone Marine & Engineering Co Ltd. The fuel tanks have a compensating system whereby sea water replaces oil fuel as it is consumed.

RECONSTRUCTION. In 1962 the after funnel and lattice mast combination in *Salisbury* was replaced by a single tall funnel with Type 965 aerial on top. *Chichester* in 1964 was refitted with both fore and main "macks". *Llandaff* completed similarly in 1966, and *Lincoln* in 1968. *Salisbury* also now has two "macks".

RADAR. Type 965 long-range surveillance with double AKE 2 with IFF; Type 993 combined air and surface warning; Type 277 Q height finder; Type 982 high definition target indicator; Twin radar fire control director; GWS-22 radar director aft for Seacat (*Salisbury* and *Lincoln* only); Type 975 nav radar.

CHICHESTER 1972

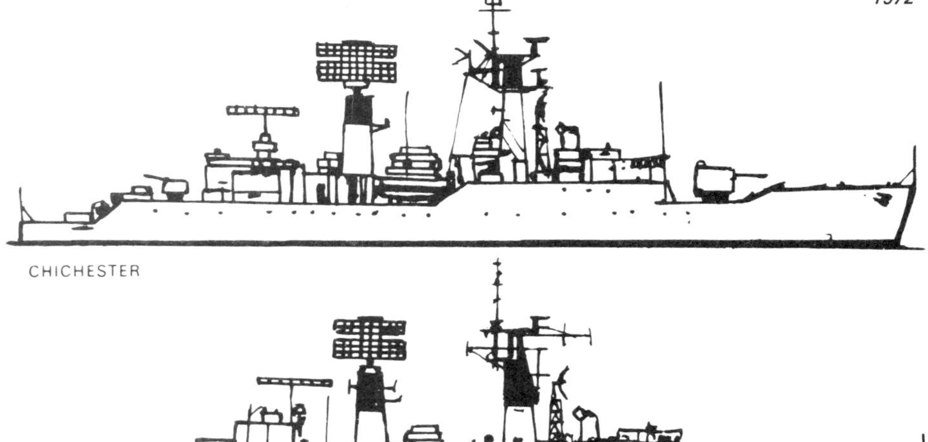

CHICHESTER

SALISBURY

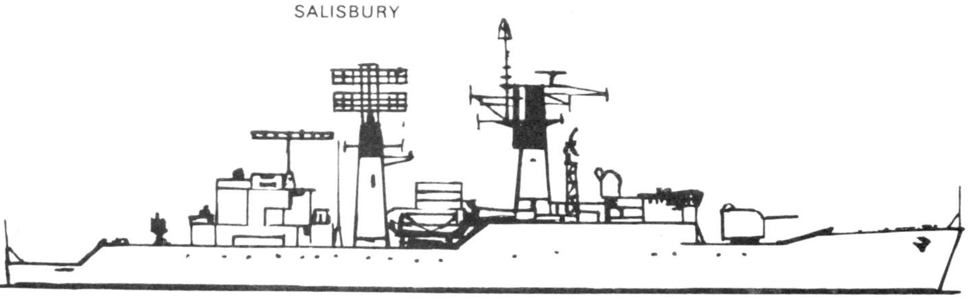

LINCOLN

LLANDAFF 1971

3 "TYPE 15" 1st RATE

Name	No.	Builders	Laid down	Launched	Completed
GRENVILLE	F 197	Swan, Hunter & Wigham Richardson, Ltd	1 Nov 41	12 Oct 42	27 May 43
RAPID	F 138	Cammell Laird & Co Ltd, Birkenhead	16 June 41	16 July 42	20 Feb 43
UNDAUNTED	F 53	Cammell Laird & Co Ltd, Birkenhead	8 Sep 42	19 July 43	3 Mar 44

Displacement, tons: 2 240 standard; 2 880 full load
Length, feet (*metres*): 339·5 (*103·5*) pp; 350·0 (*106·7*) wl; 362·8 (*110·6*) oa
Beam, feet (*metres*): 35·7 (*10·9*)
Draught, feet (*metres*): 17·0 (*5·2*)
Guns: 2—4 in (*102 mm*), 1 twin (in *Ulster*); 2—40 mm (1 twin) in *Grenville* and *Undaunted*
A/S weapons: *"U" class:* 2 Limbo 3-barrelled DC mortars (see notes)
Main engines: Parsons geared turbines; 2 shafts; 40 000 shp
Speed, knots: 36·75 designed; 31·25 sea
Boilers: 2 Admiralty 3 drum; Pressure 300 psi (*21·1 kg/cm²*) Superheat 640°F (*338°C*)
Range, miles: 1 300 at full power; 2 800 to 3 000 at 20 knots
Oil fuel, tons: 570 to 600
Complement: 195 (15 officers and 180 men)

Frigates—*continued*

RADAR. Search: Type 993 and Type 277 height finder (*Grenville* 978 on mainmast) ECM. DF. Nav radar 975.

"R" CLASS. Of the original flotilla of eight "R" class destroyers, *Racehorse* was scrapped in 1950 and *Raider*, *Redoubt*, and *Rotherham* (Leader) were transferred to the Indian Navy in 1949 and renamed *Rana*, *Ranjit* and *Rajput*, respectively. Of those converted into frigates *Rocket* was scrapped in 1967, *Roebuck* and *Relentless* in 1968. *Rapid* is seagoing training ship for marine engineer apprentices at HMS *Caledonia*, Rosyth. She was converted by Alex Stephen & Sons Ltd, Govan, in 1952-53.

"W" CLASS. Of the original flotilla of eight "W" class destroyers *Wessex* and *Whelp* were transferred to the South African Navy in 1950-52 and renamed *Jan van Riebeeck* and *Simon von Stel*, respectively, and *Kempenfelt* and *Wager* were sold to Yugoslavia in 1957 and renamed *Kotor* and *Pula*, respectively. Of those converted into frigates *Wrangler* was transferred to the South African Navy on 29 Nov 1956 and renamed *Vrystaat*, and *Whirlwind* scheduled for disposal in 1966, *Wizard* was scrapped in 1967 and *Wakeful* in 1971.

"V" CLASS. Of the original flotilla of eight "V" class destroyers, *Valentine* and *Vixen* were transferred to the Royal Canadian Navy in 1944 and renamed *Algonquin* and *Sioux*, respectively, and the leader *Hardy* was lost in the Second World War. Of those converted into frigates *Vigilant* and *Virago* were sold for scrap in 1965. *Venus* was sunk as a target in 1965, *Volage* was on the disposal list in 1966 (used as Harbour Training Ship, RM) and *Verulam* in 1971.

"U" CLASS. Converted in 1952-54, *Ulster* at HM Dockyard, Chatham, *Undaunted* by J. Samuel White & Co Ltd, Cowes. *Ulster* has a bowl-shaped sponson at the break and "Leopard" type bridge, *Undaunted* fitted with helicopter platform aft; she now has deckhouse in place of the twin 4 inch gun. *Grenville* has no 4 in, one "Limbo", two 40 mm, no helicopter platform; 2 417 tons standard; 13 officers, 190 men. In July 1966 the 20 × 30 ft section from the stern of *Urchin* was fitted to *Ulster*, damaged in May, at HM Dockyard, Devonport. Sister ships *Ulysses*, listed for disposal by scrapping in 1965 and *Ursa* in 1968. *Undine* was scrapped in 1965, *Urchin* in 1967 and *Urania* in 1971. *Ulster* paid off 29 Sept 1972.

GRENVILLE 1972

UNDAUNTED *1972, Wright & Logan*

"T" CLASS. *Troubridge* was officially approved for disposal in 1970.

"Z" CLASS. *Zest* was officially approved for disposal in 1969 and scrapped in 1970.

1 YARROW TYPE

MERMAID

Displacement, tons	2 300 standard; 2 520 full load
Dimensions	320 pp; 330 wl; 339·3 oa × 40 × 12
Guns	2—4 inch (twin). 4—40 mm
A/S weapons	1 Squid
Main engines	8 Diesels; 2 shafts; 2cp. propellers
Oil fuel, tons	230
Range, miles	4 800 at 15 knots

Some similarity in hull and machinery with "Leopard" class. Originally built for Ghana as a display ship for Nkrumah and called the *Black Star* at a cost of £5 m. but put up for sale after his departure. She was launched without ceremony on 29 Dec 1966 and completed in 1968. She was transferred to Portsmouth dockyard in April 1972 being acquired by the Royal Navy. Refit started October 1972 at Chatham.

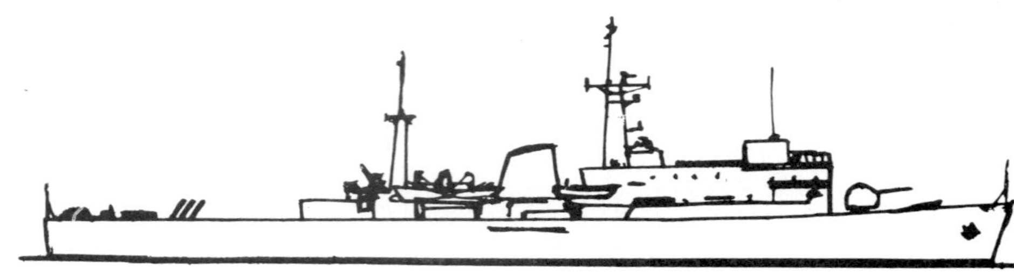

MERMAID

SONAR TRIALS SHIP

Name	*No.*	*Builders*	*Laid down*	*Launched*	*Completed*	*Converted*
MATAPAN	D 43	John Brown, Clydebank	11 Mar 1944	30 Apr 1945	5 Sep 1947	1971-1972

Displacement, tons	2 780 standard; 3 430 full load
Length, feet (*metres*)	355·0 (*108·2*) pp; 364·0 (*110·9*) wl; 379·0 (*115·5*) oa
Beam, feet (*metres*)	40·5 (*12·3*)
Draught, feet (*metres*)	18·0 (*5·5*)
Boilers	2 Admiralty 3-drum; 400 psi (*28·1 kg/cm²*); (650°F (*343°C*)
Main engines	Parsons geared turbines; 50 000 shp; 2 shafts
Speed, knots	35·75 designed; 30·5 sea
Radius, miles	1 300 at full power; 3 000 at 20 knots; 4 400 at 12 knots
Oil fuel, tons	680
Complement	268 (12 officers, and 256 men)

A former standard "Battle Class" destroyer which went into reserve almost immediately after being completed. Reconstructed at a cost of about £2 500 000. Attached to the Admiralty Underwater Weapons Establishment at Portland. Above particulars obtained before conversion.

CONVERSION. Taken in hand at HM Dockyard, Portsmouth in Jan 1971 for conversion into a Sonar Trials Ship. The rebuilding involved a new clipper bow, different bridge, remodelled superstructure, extension of the forecastle deck aft all the way to the counter, thus converting her into a flushdecker, adding a second funnel. Commissioned 2 Feb 1973 after a £2½m conversion.

MATAPAN *1972 MoD (UK)*

SUBMARINES

Nuclear Powered Ballistic Missile Submarines (SSBN)

4 "RESOLUTION" CLASS

Name	*No.*	*Builders*	*Laid down*	*Launched*	*Completion*
RENOWN	S 26	Cammell Laird & Co Ltd, Birkenhead	25 June 1964	25 Feb 1967	15 Nov 1968
REPULSE	S 23	Vickers-Armstrongs Ltd, Barrow-in-Furness	12 Mar 1965	4 Nov 1967	28 Sept 1968
RESOLUTION	S 22	Vickers-Armstrongs Ltd, Barrow-in-Furness	26 Feb 1964	15 Sep 1966	2 Oct 1967
REVENGE	S 27	Cammell Laird & Co Ltd, Birkenhead	19 May 1965	15 Mar 1968	4 Dec 1969

Displacement, tons	7 500 surface; 8 400 submerged
Length, feet (*metres*)	360 (*109·7*) pp; 425 (*129·5*) oa
Beam, feet (*metres*)	33 (*10·1*)
Draught, feet (*metres*)	30 (*9·1*)
Missiles, surface	16 tubes amidships for "Polaris" A—3's IRBM's, range 2 500 nautical miles
Torpedo tubes	6—21 in (*533 mm*) forward
Nuclear reactors	1 pressurised water cooled
Main engines	Geared steam turbines; 1 shaft
Speed, knots	20 on surface; 25 submerged
Complement	141 (13 officers, 128 ratings); 2 crews (see *Personnel*)

In Feb 1963 it was officially stated that it was intended to order four or five 7 000 ton nuclear powered submarines, each to carry 16 "Polaris" missiles, and it was planned that the first would be on patrol in 1968. Their hulls and machinery would be of British design. As well as building two submarines Vickers-Armstrongs would give lead yard service (ie act as the "parent" firm) to the builders of the other two. Four "Polaris" submarines were in fact ordered on 8 May 1963 (date of official announcement). The intention to build a fifth Polaris submarine was confirmed by the then Minister of Defence on 26 Feb 1964, but this intention was rescinded by a new Minister of Defence on 15 Feb 1965. Britain's first "Polaris" armed submarine. *Resolution*, put to sea on 22 June 1967 and completed 6 weeks trial in the Firth of Clyde and Atlantic on 17 Aug 1967.

RESOLUTION *1967*

DESIGN. These submarines, the largest ever built for the Royal Navy, differ in several respects from United States "Polaris" submarines, notably in having six torpedo tubes instead of four, and modified habitability.

SONAR AND RADAR. Fitted with a large sonar array mounted in the "forehead" position and an X band short range surveillance radar.

REFITS. Repulse completed July 1972.
Renown started Nov 1972.

PERSONNEL. Each submarine, which has accommodation for 19 officers and 135 ratings is manned on a two-crew basis, in order to get maximum operational time at sea on the pattern of the system in the United States "Polaris" submarines in which two complete crews relieve each other approximately every three months.

COST. £40 240 000, *Resolution*; £39 950 000, *Renown*; £37 500 000, *Repulse*; £38 600 000 *Revenge*; completed ships excluding missiles, £52 000 000 to £55 000 000 including weapon system.

REVENGE *1971*

REPULSE *1971*

Submarines—*continued*

Fleet Submarines
2 "VALIANT" CLASS (A)
3 "CHURCHILL" CLASS (B)
5 "SWIFTSURE" CLASS (C)

	Name	No.	Builder	Ordered	Laid down	Launched	Completed (Commissioned)
(A)	**VALIANT**	S 102	Vickers Ltd Shipbuilding Group, Barrow	31 Aug 1960	22 Jan 1962	3 Dec 1963	18 July 1966
	WARSPITE	S 103	Vickers Ltd Shipbuilding Group, Barrow	12 Dec 1962	10 Dec 1963	25 Sep 1965	18 Apr 1967
(B)	**CHURCHILL**	S 104	Vickers Ltd Shipbuilding Group, Barrow	21 Oct 1965	30 June 1967	20 Dec 1968	15 July 1970
	CONQUEROR	S 105	Cammell Laird & Co Ltd, Birkenhead	9 Aug 1966	5 Dec 1967	28 Aug 1969	9 Nov 1971
	COURAGEOUS	S 106	Vickers Ltd Shipbuilding Group, Barrow	1 Mar 1967	15 May 1970	7 Mar 1970	16 Oct 1971
(C)	**SWIFTSURE**	S 107	Vickers Ltd Shipbuilding Group, Barrow	3 Nov 1967	6 June 1969	7 Sep 1971	1973
	SOVEREIGN	S 108	Vickers Ltd Shipbuilding Group, Barrow	16 May 1969	18 Sep 1970	1972	
	SUPERB	S 109	Vickers Ltd Shipbuilding Group, Barrow	20 May 1970	Jan 1971		
	SCEPTRE	S 110	Vickers Ltd Shipbuilding Group, Barrow	Sep 1971			
		S 111	Vickers Ltd Shipbuilding Group, Barrow	1972			

Displacement, tons	3 500 standard; 4 500 submerged
Length, feet (*metres*)	285 (*86·9*); *Swiftsure* 272·0 (*82·9*)
Beam, feet (*metres*)	33·2 (*10·1*)
Draught, feet (*metres*)	27 (*8·2*)
Torpedo tubes	6—21 in (*533 mm*) homing; *Swiftsure* 5—21 in
Nuclear reactors	1 pressurised water-cooled
Main engines	EE Geared steam turbines; 1 shaft
Speed, knots	30 approx
Complement	103 (13 officers, 90 men) 97 (12 and 85) in *Swiftsure* class

It was announced on 31 Aug 1960 that the contract for a second nuclear powered submarine (*Valiant*) had been awarded to Vickers-Armstrong (Shipbuilders) Ltd, the principal sub-contractors being Vickers-Armstrong (Engineers) Ltd, for the machinery and its installation, and Rolls Royce and Associates for the nuclear steam raising plant. Her hull is broadly of the same design as that of *Dreadnought*, but she is slightly larger. She was originally scheduled to be completed in Sep 1965, but work was held up by the "Polaris" programme. All the above boats will be in service by end-1977 on present plans.

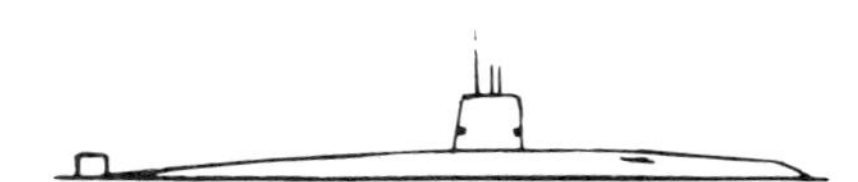
CHURCHILL, CONQUEROR, VALIANT, WARSPITE

SONAR AND RADAR. Fitted with a large sonar array mounted in the "forehead" position around the bow. Also fitted with X band short range surveillance radar.

ENDURANCE. On 25 Apr 1967 *Valiant* completed the 12,000-mile homeward voyage from Singapore, the record submerged passage by a British submarine, after 28 days non-stop.

ENGINEERING. *Valiant's* reactor core was made in Great Britain, with machinery of British design and manufacture similar to the shore prototype installed in the Admiralty Reactor Test Establishment at Dounreay. The main steam turbines and condensers were designed and manufactured by the English Electric Company, Rugby, and the electrical propulsion machinery and control gear by Laurence, Scott & Electromotors Ltd.

ANTI-SUBMARINE WARFARE. *Valiant* and her sister ships are equipped with sonar gear to detect at much greater ranges than that fitted in British patrol submarines.

CONQUEROR

VALIANT

Submarines—*continued*

1 PROTOTYPE NUCLEAR POWERED

Name	*No.*	*Builders*	*Engineers*	*Laid down*	*Launched*	*Commissioned*
DREADNOUGHT	S 101	Vickers-Armstrongs, Barrow	Rolls-Royce and Westinghouse	12 June 1959	21 Oct 1960	17 April, 1963

Displacement, tons	3 000 standard; 3 500 surface; 4 000 submerged
Length, feet (*metres*)	265·8 (*81·0*)
Beam, feet (*metres*)	32·2 (*9·8*)
Draught, feet (*metres*)	26 (*7·9*)
Torpedo tubes	6—21 in (*533 mm*) bow, all internal
Nuclear reactor	1 S5W pressurised water-cooled
Main engines	Geared steam turbines; 1 shaft
Speed, knots	30 approx
Complement	88 (11 officers, 77 men)

OFFICIAL STATEMENT. As originally planned *Dreadnought* was to have been fitted with a British designed and built nuclear reactor, but in 1958 an agreement was concluded with the United States Government for the purchase of a complete set of propulsion machinery of the type fitted in USS *Skipjack*. This agreement enabled the submarine to be launched far earlier. The supply of this machinery was made under a contract between the Westinghouse Electric Corporation and Rolls-Royce. The latter were also supplied with design and manufacturing details of the reactor and with safety information and set up a factory in this country to manufacture similar cores. *Dreadnought* has a hull of British design both as regards structural strength and hydrodynamic features, although the latter are based on the pioneering work of the US Navy in *Skipjack* and *Albacore*. From about amidships aft, the hull lines closely resemble *Skipjack* to accommodate the propulsion machinery. The forward end is wholly British in concept. In the Control Room and Attack Centre the instruments are fitted into consoles. Almost every electrical and mechanical part of the propulsion machinery is installed in duplicate to minimise the inconvenience of breakdowns. In addition, every control feature of the power plant and of the boat is duplicated. These innovations ensure an extremely high standard of reliability which, combined with the need to refuel at only very long intervals, give her the ability to undertake patrols of particularly long endurance at continued high underwater speeds.
Accommodation for her crew is of a standard impossible to attain in any previous submarine. The improved water distilling plant for the first time provides unlimited fresh water for shower baths and for washing machines in the fully equipped laundry. Separate mess spaces are provided for senior and junior ratings, arranged on either side of a large galley, equipped for serving meals on the cafeteria system. Particular attention was paid to the decoration and furnishing of living quarters and to recreational facilities which include cinema equipment, an extensive library and tape recordings, features which help to offset the monotony associated with prolonged underwater voyages.
She is fitted with an inertial navigation system and with means of measuring her depth below ice.

SONAR AND RADAR. Fitted with a large sonar array mounted in the "forehead" position around the bow. Also fitted with X band short range surveillance radar.

REFUELLING and REFIT. Announced on 30 Jan 1969 at Rosyth Dockyard that the first refuelling of a nuclear powered submarine had been completed in *Dreadnought*. Officially stated refit was completed in 1970.

DREADNOUGHT(with old side numbers)

Patrol Submarines

2 "A" CLASS

Name	*No*	*Builders*	*Laid down*	*Launched*	*Completed*
AENEAS	S 72	Cammell Laird & Co Ltd Birkenhead	10 Oct 1944	25 Oct 1945	31 July 1946
ANDREW	S 63	Vickers-Armstrongs Ltd. Barrow	13 Aug 1945	6 Apr 1946	16 Mar 1948

Displacement, tons	1 120 standard; 1 385 surface; 1 620 submerged
Dimensions, feet	283 × 22·2 × 17·1
Torpedo tubes	6—21 in (*533 mm*) internal, 4 bow 2 stern; 16 torpedoes carried External tubes removed (see notes)
Main engines	2 8-cyl diesels, 4 300 bhp 2 electric motors, 1 250 hp
Speed, knots	19 on surface, 8 submerged
Complement	60 to 68 (5 officers, 63 men)

These submarines were originally designed for service in the Pacific, Construction was entirely welded. Has "Snort" breathing equipment. *Aurochs*, the only one of the class not converted, broken up at Troon in Feb 1967. *Alderney* was listed in Feb 1968 for disposal *Artful* in Feb 1969, *Alcide* in Feb 1970, *Acheron* in Feb 1971 and *Artemis* and *Auriga* in Feb 1972. Actual scrapping dates: *Anchorite* and *Astute* 1970, *Alaric*, *Ambush* and *Amphion* 1971. *Alliance* deleted 1973.

SLAM. *Aeneas* was hired by Vickers in July 1972 for trials of SLAM anti-helicopter weapon.

SONAR AND RADAR. Fitted with sonar array on Fore casing. Fitted with X Band surveillance radar.

CONVERSION. The "A" class were rebuilt and streamlined with an enclosed fin conning tower 26·5 feet high.

ANDREW with gun *1972*

Submarines—*continued*

Patrol Submarines

13 "OBERON" CLASS
8 "PORPOISE" CLASS

Displacement, tons	1 610 standard; 2 030 surface; 2 410 submerged
Length, feet (*metres*)	241 (*73·5*) pp; 295·2 (*90·0*) oa
Beam, feet (*metres*)	26·5 (*8·1*)
Draught, feet (*metres*)	18 (*5·5*)
Torpedo tubes	8—21 in (*533 mm*) 6 bow 2 stern; 30 torpedoes carried
Main engines	2 ASR 1, 16 VMS diesels; 3 680 bhp; 2 electric motors; 6 000 shp; 2 shafts; electric drive
Speed, knots	12 surface, 17 submerged
Complement	68 (6 officers, 62 men) 71 (6 officers, 65 men) in "Porpoise" class

This class have improved detection equipment and are capable of high underwater speeds. They are able to maintain continuous submerged patrols in any part of the world and are equipped to fire homing torpedoes.

CONSTRUCTION. For the first time in British submarines plastic was used in the superstructure construction of the Oberon class. Before and abaft the bridge the superstructure is mainly of glass fibre laminate in most units of this class. The superstructure of *Orpheus* is of light alloy aluminium.

RCN. The submarine of the Oberon class laid down on 27 Sep 1962 at HM Dockyard, Chatham, as *Onyx* for the Royal Navy was launched on 29 Feb 1964 as *Ojibwa* for the Royal Canadian Navy. She was replaced by another "Oberon" class submarine named *Onyx* for the Royal Navy built by Cammell Laird, Birkenhead.

SONAR AND RADAR. Fitted with sonar with bow dome; and X Band surveillance radar.

GUNNERY. "O" class submarines serving in the Far East carried an Oerlikon gun during Indonesian Confrontation.

MODIFICATION. *Oberon* has been modified with deeper casing to house equipment for the initial training of personnel for nuclear powered submarines. Others of of this class are currently undergoing modification.

"OBERON" CLASS

Name	No.	Builders	Laid down	Launched	Completed
OBERON	S 09	H.M. Dockyard, Chatham	28 Nov 1957	18 July 1959	24 Feb 1961
OCELOT	S 17	H.M. Dockyard, Chatham	17 Nov 1960	5 May 1962	31 Jan 1964
ODIN	S 10	Cammell Laird & Co Ltd, Birkenhead	27 Apr 1959	4 Nov 1960	3 May 1962
OLYMPUS	S 12	Vickers-Armstrongs Ltd, Barrow	4 Mar 1960	14 June 1961	7 July 1962
ONSLAUGHT	S 14	H.M. Dockyard, Chatham	8 Apr 1959	24 Sep 1960	14 Aug 1962
ONYX	S 21	Cammell Laird & Co Ltd, Birkenhead	16 Nov 1964	18 Aug 1966	20 Nov 1967
OPOSSUM	S 19	Cammell Laird & Co Ltd, Birkenhead	21 Dec 1961	23 May 1963	5 June 1964
OPPORTUNE	S 20	Scotts' S.B. & Eng Co Ltd, Greenock	26 Oct 1962	14 Feb 1964	29 Dec 1964
ORACLE	S 16	Cammell Laird & Co Ltd, Birkenhead	26 Apr 1960	26 Sep 1961	14 Feb 1963
ORPHEUS	S 11	Vickers-Armstrongs Ltd, Barrow	16 Apr 1959	17 Nov 1959	25 Nov 1960
OSIRIS	S 13	Vickers-Armstrongs Ltd, Barrow	26 Jan 1962	29 Nov 1962	11 Jan 1964
OTTER	S 15	Scotts' S.B. & Eng Co Ltd, Greenock	14 Jan 1960	15 May 1961	20 Aug 1962
OTUS	S 18	Scotts' S.B. & Eng Co Ltd, Greenock	31 May 1961	17 Oct 1962	5 Oct 1963

"PORPOISE" CLASS

Name	No.	Builders	Laid down	Launched	Completed
CACHALOT	S 06	Scotts S.B. & Eng Co Ltd, Greenock	1 Aug 1955	11 Dec 1957	1 Sep 1959
FINWHALE	S 05	Cammell Laird & Co Ltd, Birkenhead	18 Sep 1956	21 July 1959	19 Aug 1960
GRAMPUS	S 04	Cammell Laird & Co Ltd, Birkenhead	16 Apr 1955	30 May 1957	19 Dec 1958
NARWHAL	S 03	Vickers-Armstrongs Ltd, Barrow	15 Mar 1956	25 Oct 1957	4 May 1959
PORPOISE	S 01	Vickers-Armstrongs Ltd, Barrow	15 June 1954	25 Apr 1956	17 Apr 1958
RORQUAL	S 02	Vickers-Armstrongs Ltd, Barrow	15 Jan 1955	5 Dec 1956	24 Oct 1958
SEALION	S 07	Cammell Laird & Co Ltd, Birkenhead	5 June 1958	31 Dec 1959	25 July 1961
WALRUS	S 08	Scotts' S.B. & Eng Co Ltd, Greenock	12 Feb 1958	22 Sep 1959	10 Feb 1961

PORPOISE — *1971, Wright & Logan*

WALRUS — *1971, Wright & Logan*

OBERON — *1973*

ORACLE — *1971, courtesy Godfrey H. Walker, Esq*

LIGHT FORCES

TENACITY *1973*

BRAVE SWORDSMAN and BRAVE BORDERER *1968*

1 VOSPER THORNYCROFT MISSILE TYPE

TENACITY P 276

Displacement, tons	165 standard; 220 full load
Dimensions, feet	130·0 wl; 142·0 deck, 144·5 oa × 26·6 × 7·8
Guns	2 MGs
Main engines	3 Rolls Royce Proteus gas turbines; 3 shafts; 12 750 bhp = 40 knots max 2 Paxman Ventura 6 cyl diesels on wing shafts for cruising = 16 knots
Range, miles	2 500 at 15 knots
Complement	32 (4 officers, 28 ratings)

Built as a private venture by Vosper Thornycroft Limited. Launched on 18 Feb 1969 at Camber Shipyard, Portsmouth. Steel hull and aluminium alloy superstructure. Fully air-conditioned quarters. Twice chartered by the Royal Navy in mid Mar 1971 and mid 1971 for NATO exercises with motor torpedo boats. Purchased outright by the Ministry of Defence (Navy) on 25 Jan 1972 (announced) for approximately £750 000 "as lying" and refitted with minor alterations and additions to meet naval requirements. To be used for exercises and fishery protection. Decca nav, radar. Commissioned Feb 1973.

2 "BRAVE" CLASS

BRAVE BORDERER P 1011 **BRAVE SWORDSMAN** P 1012

Displacement, tons	89 standard; 114 full load
Dimensions, feet	90·0 wl; 96·0 hull; 98·8 oa × 25·5 × 7·0 props
Armament	As MGB: 2—40 mm single guns in power operated mountings; 2—21 inch side launched torpedoes As MTB: 4—21 inch torpedoes; 1—40 mm gun
Main engines	3 Bristol Siddeley Proteus 1 250 gas turbines; 3 shafts; Fixed pitch propellers; 1 700 rpm; 10 500 shp = 52 knots max (46 knots continuous)
Fuel, tons	25 capacity
Complement	20 (3 officers, 17 ratings)

Designed as convertible and interchangeable torpedo boats and gunboats. Built by Vosper Ltd, Portsmouth. In reserve at Portsmouth.

3 FAST TRAINING BOATS

CUTLASS P 274 **SABRE** P 275 **SCIMITAR** P 271

Displacement, tons	102 full load
Dimensions, feet	90·0 wl; 100·0 oa × 26·6 × 6·4
Main engines	2 Rolls Royce Proteus gas turbines = 40 knots (2 Foden diesels for cruising in CODAG arrangement)
Range, miles	425 at 35 knots; 1 500 at 11·5 knots
Complement	12 (2 officers, 10 ratings)

No armament. Hull of glued laminated wood construction. Design developed from that of "Brave" class fast patrol boats. Completed July—December 1970. All built by Vosper Thornycroft Group, Portchester Shipyard.

SCIMITAR

MINEWARFARE FORCES

ABDIEL N 21

Displacement, tons	1 375 standard, 1 500 full load
Dimensions, feet	244·5 pp; 265 oa × 38·5 × 10
Mines	44 carried
Main engines	2 Paxman Ventura 16 cyl pressure charged diesels; 1 250 rpm; 2 690 bhp = 16 knots
Complement	123 (14 officers, 109 ratings)

Exercise minelayer for the Royal Navy ordered in June 1965 from John I. Thornycroft & Co Ltd, Woolston, Southampton. Laid down on 23 May 1966. Launched on 27 Jan 1967. Completed on 17 Oct 1967. Main machinery manufactured by Davey Paxman, Colchester. Main gearing supplied by Messrs Wisemans. Her function is to support mine countermeasure forces, maintain these forces when they are operating away from their shore bases, and lay exercise mines. Living accommodation is of a high standard. Cost £1 500 000.

ABDIEL *1970, courtesy Godfrey H. Walker, Esq*

NEW GRP MCM VESSELS

A new class of MCM Vessels is still in the design stage—a contract is being negotiated with Vosper-Thornycroft. The cost of these ships is likely to be in the region of £4-5 million.

GRP TYPE (CMS)

WILTON

Displacement, tons	450 standard
Dimensions, feet	153·0 oa × 28·8 × 8·5
Main engines	2 English Electric Deltic 18 diesels; 2 shafts; 3 000 bhp = 16 knots estimated max
Guns	1—40 mm Mark VII
Cost	£2 000 000
Complement	37 (5 officers and 32 ratings)

The world's first GRP warship. Contract signed on 11 Feb 1970. Launched on 18 Jan 1972. Prototype built of glass reinforced plastic to the existing minehunter design by Vosper Thornycroft at Woolston. Similar to the "Ton" class and fitted with reconditioned machinery and equipment from the scrapped *Derriton*. Completion 1973.

WILTON *1973, M.O.D.*

Mine Warfare Forces —*continued*

BOSSINGTON (minehunter) *1971*

MAXTON *1970*

37 "TON" CLASS (CMS)

ASHTON M 1198
BILDESTON M 1110
BOSSINGTON M 1133 (ex-*Embleton*)
BRERETON M 1113 (ex-*St. David*, ex-*Brereton*)
BRINTON M 1114
BRONINGTON M 1115 (ex-*Humber*, ex-*Bronington*)
CHAWTON M 1209
CLYDE M 1167 (ex-*Repton*, ex-*Ossington*)
CURZON M 1136 (ex-*Fittleton*)
CUXTON
GAVINTON M 1140
GLASSERTON M 1141
HIGHBURTON M 1130
HUBBERSTON M 1147
IVESTON M 1151
KEDLESTON M 1153
KELLINGTON M 1154
KILLIECRANKIE M 1109 (ex *Bickington*, ex-*Curzon*, ex-*Bickington*)
KILMOREY M 1103 (ex-*Alfriston*, ex-*Warsash*, ex-*Alfriston*)
KIRKLISTON M 1157 (ex-*Kilmorey*, ex-*Kirkliston*)
LALESTON M 1158
LEWISTON M 1208
MAXTON M 1165
MERSEY M 1173 (ex-*Pollington*)
MONTROSE M 1204 (ex-*Stubbington*)
NORTHUMBRIA M 1204 (ex-*Wiston*)
NURTON M 1166 (ex-*Montrose*, ex-*Nurton*)
ST. DAVID M 1124 (ex-*Crichton*, ex-*Clyde*, ex-*Crichton*)
SHERATON M 1181
SHOULTON M 1182
SOBERTON M 1200
SOLENT M 1216 (ex-*Crofton*)
THAMES M 1194 (ex-*Woolaston*)
UPTON M 1187
VENTURER M 1146 (ex-*Hodgeston*, ex-*Northumbria*, ex-*Hodgeston*)
WALKERTON M 1188
WOTTON M 1195

Displacement, tons	360 standard; 425 full load
Dimensions, feet	140·0 pp; 153·0 oa × 28·8 × 8·2
Guns	1—40 mm AA (removed in some ships); 2—20 mm AA (minehunters 2—40 mm)
Main engines	2 diesels; 2 shafts; 2 500 bhp (JVSS 12 Mirrlees), 3 000 bhp (18A-7A Deltic) = 15 knots (max); see *Engineering*
Oil fuel, tons	45
Radius, miles	2 300 at 13 knots
Complement	27 (36 in minehunters, 5 officers and 31 ratings)

Double mahogany hull and constructed of aluminium alloy and other materials with the lowest possible magnetic signature. John I. Thornycroft & Co Ltd, Southampton, was the parent firm for the group,which built this class of uniform design capable of sweeping both contact and influence type mines. The first, *Coniston*, was completed in Feb 1953. The last, *Lewiston*, in 1960. Vosper stabilisers. *Stubbington* and others have fibre-glass bottom sheathing.

ENGINEERING. Earlier vessels have Mirrlees diesels, but later units had Napier Deltic lightweight diesels. *Highburton*, the first with Deltic diesels, was accepted on 21 Apr 1955. Some earlier ships underwent conversion from Mirrlees to Deltic diesels. Generators for electrical power are in a separate engine room. Three-bladed propellers, 6 ft diameter, 400 rpm. *Shoulton*, refitted 1965-67 (recommissioned 5 Apr), has pump-jet propulsion.

MINEHUNTING. *Shoulton* was fitted with unique mine-hunting equipment, an all-British sonar development which enables her to locate and classify any mine-like objects on the sea bed with accuracy and range previously impossible. Since then *Bildeston, Bossington, Brereton, Brinton, Bronington, Gavinton, Hubberston, Iveston, Keddleston, Kellington, Kirkliston, Manton* and *Sheraton* have been refitted as minehunters, with active rudders incorporating electric motors for manoeuvring at slow speed. *Highburton* and *Glasserton* are fitted with Osbourne mine destroyer units.

APPEARANCE. *Ashton, Chawton, Lewiston, Mersey* (ex-*Pollington*), *Nurton, Sheraton, Soberton, Stubbington, Walkerton, Wiston* and others are fitted with an enclosed or frigate bridge.and tripod mast. *Shoulton* covered bridge.

TRANSFERS. *Dunkerton* and *Hazleton* were transferred to South Africa in 1955 and renamed *Pretoria* and *Kaapstad* respectively, *Durweston, Overton, Whitton* and *Wennington* to India in 1956, and renamed *Kakinada, Karwar, Cohnamore* and *Cuddalore*. respectively. *Castleton, Chilton, Dumbleton, Oakington, Packington* and *Stratton* to South Africa in 1958-59 and renamed *Johannesburg, East London, Port Elizabeth, Mosselbaai, Walvisbaai* and *Kimberley* respectively with *Durban* and *Windhoek*. *Darlaston* was sold to Malaysia in 1960 and renamed *Mahamiru, Hexton* in 1963 and renamed *Ledang; Dilston* and *Essington* in 1964 and renamed *Jerai* and *Kinabalu* respectively; and *Lullington* and *Thankerton* in 1966 and renamed *Tahan* and *Brinchang* respectively. *Alcaston, Chediston, Jackton, Singleton, Somerleyton* and *Swanston* were transferred to Australia in 1962, and renamed *Snipe, Curlew, Teal, Ibis, Hawk*, and *Gull*, respectively, *Aldington* to Ghana in 1964 and renamed *Ejura, Bevington. Hickleton, Ilmington, Rennington, Santon* and *Tarlton* to Argentina in 1968 and renamed *Tierra del Fuego, Neuquen, Formosa, Chaco, Chubut* and *Rio Negro*, respectively, *Mirmydon* (ex-*Edderton*) to Malasia in 1968; *Alvreton, Blaxton* and *Oulston* to Republic of Ireland in 1971 and renamed *Banba, Fola*, and *Grainne* respectively.

ROYAL NAVAL RESERVE. Eleven units were renamed and attached to Royal Naval Reserve Division Headquarters as follows (Division under *Name*):—

Thames	*Curzon*	*Solent*	*Venturer*	*St. David*	*Mersey*
London	Sussex	Solent	Severn	S. Wales	Mersey
Kilmorey	*Clyde*	*Montrose*	*Killiecrankie*	*Northumbria*	
Ulster	Clyde	Tay	Forth	Tyne	

(Humber Division disbanded in 1958 and HMS *Humber* reverted to original name *Bronington*.) The name *Warsash* was superseded by *Solent* in 1969.

KEDELSTON *1971, Wright & Logan*

PATROL CONVERSIONS. *Beachampton, Monkton, Wasperton, Wolverton* and *Yarnton* were converted into coastal patrol vessels late in 1971,

DIVING CONVERSION *Laleston* was converted into diving trials ship (recommissioned on 22 Mar 1967).

SURVEY CONVERSIONS. *Edderton* and *Sullington* of this class were converted into coastal survey ships in 1964 and renamed *Myrmidon* and *Mermaid*, respectively. (*Myrmidon* was sold to Malaysia and *Mermaid* approved for disposal in 1968-69).

CLASS. *Calton, Fenton, Floriston* and *Sefton* were officially approved for disposal by scrapping in 1966-67; *Badminton, Caunton* and *Lanton* an 1967-68, *Carhampton, Clarbeston, Derriton, Dufton, Flockton, Kemerton, Kildarton, Maryton, Penston, Picton* and *Roddington* in 1968-69, *Appleton, Boulston, Burnaston, Buttington, Chilcompton, Coniston, Dartington, Fiskerton* and *Letterston* in 1969-70, *Amerton, Houghton* and *Leverton* in 1970-71, *Belton, Dalswinton, Invermoriston, Puncheston*, and *Quainton* in 1971-72. *Maddiston* and *Wilkeston* were on the sales list in 1972. and *Shavington* in 1973.

21 "HAM" CLASS (IMS)

M 2601 M 2701 AND M 2777 SERIES

ARLINGHAM
DITTISHAM
FLINTHAM
THORNHAM (ABERDEEN)

RNXS
BIRDHAM
ODIHAM
PAGHAM
PORTISHAM
PUTTENHAM
SHIPHAM
THAKEHAM
TONGHAM

PAS
BUCKLESHAM
DOWNHAM
EVERINGHAM
FRITHAM
HAVERSHAM
LASHAM

DGV
FORDHAM
THATCHAM
WARMINGHAM

PAS FERRY
SANDRINGHAM (CLYDE)

Displacement, tons	120 standard; 159 full load
Dimensions, feet	2601 Series; 100 pp; 106·5 oa × 21·2 × 5·5 2701 Series; 100 pp; 107 oa × 21·7 × 5·7 2777 *et seq*: 100 pp; 107·5 oa × 22 × 5·8
Guns	1—40 mm Bofors AA or 1—20 mm Oerlikon AA forward (see *Gunnery*)
Main engines	2 Paxman diesels; 1 100 bhp = 14 knots max (9 knots sea speed) see *Engineering*
Oil fuel (tons)	15
Complement	15 (2 officers, 13 ratings)

MineWarfare Forces —*continued*

Designed to operate in shallow waters, rivers and estuaries. When built they were an entirely new type of vessel embodying novel features resulting from lessons learned during the war and in course of subsequent developments. Named after villages with the suffix "ham". The first inshore minesweeper, *Inglesham*, was launched by J. Samual White & Co Ltd, Cowes, on 23 Apr 1952. The 2701 series were of wooden construction, whereas the 2601 series were of composite construction. All the M 2701 series had a rubbing strake, unlike the M 2601 and M 2001 series.

GUNNERY. Most of the M 2601 series had the 40 mm gun replaced by a 20 mm gun. All the M 2701 series had a 20 mm gun (armament as minesweepers).

ENGINEERING. The main machinery was manufactured by Davey Paxman & Co Ltd. Colchester, or by Ruston & Hornsby Ltd, Lincoln, Foden Ltd, Sandbach, Cheshire, or Ransomes, Sims and Jeffries Ltd, Ipswich, under licence from Davey Paxman. Three-bladed propellers, 600 r.p.m.

NOMENCLATURE. *Fordham* was originally to have been named *Pavenham*.

SURVEY CONVERSIONS. *Powderham* and *Yaxham* were converted into inshore survey craft in 1964 and renamed *Waterwitch* and *Woodlark*, respectively.

DITTISHAM *1971*

TRANSFERS
Frettenham, Isham, Kingham, Mersham, Mileham, Petersham, Pineham, Rendlesham, Riplingham, Sparham, Stedham, Sulham, Tibenham, Wexham and *Whippingham* were transferred to France in 1954-55; *Hildersham* and *Littlesham* to India in 1955 and renamed *Bimlipitan* and *Bassein*, respectively; *Bassingham* to East Africa on 25 June 1958, but returned on 9 Oct 1961; *Bedham* to Malaysia in 1958 and renamed *Lanka Suka*, *Cardingham* and *Etchingham* to Hong Kong R.N.V.R. in 1959, but returned on 1 Apr 1966; *Altham, Asheldham* and *Brantingham* to Malaysia in 1959 and renamed *Sri Johar, Sri Perlis* and *Temasek*, respectively; *Malham* and *Ottringham* to Ghana at the end of 1959, and renamed *Yogoda* and *Afadzato* respectively; and *Harpham* and *Greetham* to Libya in 1963, and renamed *Brak* and *Zuara*, respectively; *Boreham* and *Felmersham* to Malaysia in 1966 and renamed *Jerong* and *Todak*, respectively; *Popham* and *Wintringham* to Australia on 9 June 1966 and renamed *Otter* and *Seal*, respectively; *Blunham, Bodenham* and *Elsenham* to South Yemen in 1967; *Neasham* to Australia in 1968.

2 "LEY" CLASS. M 2001 SERIES

AVELEY **ISIS** (ex-*Cradley*)

Displacement, tons	123 standard; 164 full load
Dimensions, feet	100 pp; 107 oa × 21·8 × 5·5
Guns	1—40 mm AA or 1—20 mm AA forward
Main engines	2 Paxman diesels; 700 bhp = 13 knots
Oil fuel (tons)	15
Complement	15 (2 officers, 13 ratings)

The "Ley" class differed from the "Ham" class. They were of composite (non-magnetic metal and wooden) construction, instead of all wooden construction. Their superstructure and other features also differed. They had no winch or sweeping gear, as they were mine hunters, not sweepers. They had smaller engines as less towing power was needed. *Aveley* is attached to Plymouth. *Cradley* was allocated to London Division R.N.R. in 1953 and renamed *Isis*.

AVELEY *1969*

AMPHIBIOUS WARFARE SHIPS

Name	*Deck Letter*	*No.*	*Builders*	*Laid down*	*Launched*	*Completed*
HERMES (ex-*Elephant*)	H	R 12	Vickers-Armstrongs, Barrow-in-Furness	21 June 1944	16 Feb 1953	18 Nov 1959

Displacement, tons	23 900 standard; 28 700 full load
Length, feet (*metres*)	650·0 (*198·1*) pp; 744·3) (*226·9*) oa
Beam, feet (*metres*)	90·0 (*27·4*) hull
Draught, feet (*metres*)	29·0 (*8·8*)
Width, feet (*metres*)	160·0 (*48·8*) overall
Aircraft	20 helicopters
Armour	Reinforced flight deck
Missile launchers	2 quadruple "Seacat" surface-to-air systems
Boilers	4 Admiralty 3-drum type
Main engines	Parsons geared turbines; 2 shafts; 76 000 shp
Speed, knots	28 designed max
Oil fuel, tons	3 880 furnace; 320 diesel; 1 000 avgas
Complement	1 830 (190 officers, 1 640 men) 2 100 with air squadrons

Originally name ship of a class including *Albion, Bulwark* and *Centaur*, but design was modified to a more advanced type, incorporating new equipment and improved arrangements, including five post-war developments—angled deck, steam catapult, landing sight, 3-D radar, and deck edge-lift. Air-conditioned. Embarked air squadrons and joined the Fleet summer 1960. Long refit 1964 to 1966, costing £10 000 000.
Two "Seacat" systems installed, and living accommodation improved. Refitted in 1969.

HERMES as fixed wing aircraft carrier *1971*

HERMES *1971*

Amphibious Warfare Ships—*continued*

CONVERSION. It was announced on 17 Feb 1971 that a start was to be made on the conversion of HMS *Hermes* to the commando ship role. She was taken in hand at HM Dockyard, Devonport on 1 Mar 1971. Completion as LPH is expected late 1973. Main features of conversion are:—Removal of steam catapults, arrester gear and fixed-wing aircraft facilities: Rearrangements to provide Commando accommodation and storage Changes to radar etc to meet the new role.

DRAWING. Port elevation and plan as fixed-wing aircraft carrier. Scale: 125 feet = 1 inch (1 : 1 500).

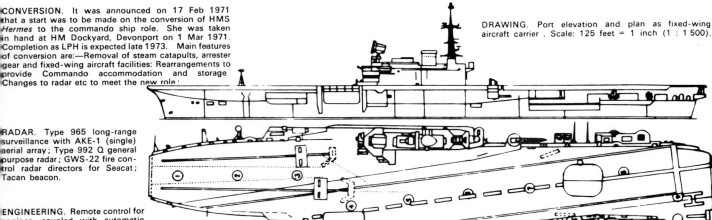

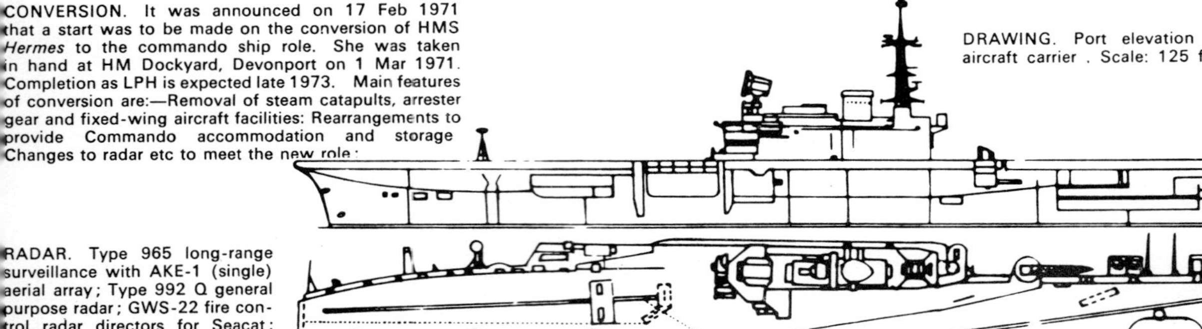

RADAR. Type 965 long-range surveillance with AKE-1 (single) aerial array; Type 992 Q general purpose radar; GWS-22 fire control radar directors for Seacat; Tacan beacon.

ENGINEERING. Remote control for engines, coupled with automatic feed for boilers, whereby with the entire complement of officers and men under cover and protected in "the citadel", a self-contained section proof against radio-active fall-out, the ship could be steamed through an atomic cloud.

FLIGHT DECK. Angled 6·5 deg off centre line of ship, the biggest angle that could be contrived in an aircraft carrier of the size. Strengthened to take Harrier aircraft.

ELECTRICAL. The plant is 440 volt, 3 phase, 60 cycle AC with a generating capacity of 5 440 kW.

Name	*Deck Letter*	*No.*	*Builders*	*Laid down*	*Launched*	*Completed*	*Converted*
BULWARK	B	R 08	Harland & Wolff Ltd, Belfast	10 May 1945	22 June 1948	4 Nov 1954	1959-60

Displacement, tons	23 300 standard; 27 705 full load
Length, feet (*metres*)	650 (*198·1*) pp; 737·8 (*224·9*) oa
Beam, feet (*metres*)	90 (*27·4*) hull
Draught, feet (*metres*)	28 (*8·5*)
Width, feet (*metres*)	123·5 (*37·7*) overall
Aircraft	20 helicopters
Landing craft	4 LCVP
Missiles	2 sextuple rocket launchers
Guns, AA	2 40 mm
Boilers	4 Admiralty 3 drum
Main engines	Parsons geared turbines 76 000 shp; 2 shafts
Speed, knots	28
Oil fuel, tons	3 880 furnace; 320 diesel
Complement	1 035 plus 900 Royal Marine Commando and troops

Former fixed-wing aircraft carrier. Converted into commando ship in Portsmouth Dockyard, Jan 1959 to Jan 1960. A full strength commando is available, which the ship can quickly transport and land with equipment. Their helicopters can disembark the commando's vehicles. The ship has sufficient stores and fuel to support the commandos in operations ashore. She can, at short notice, and entirely within her own resources, adapt the helicopters for anti-submarine work.

RADAR. Search: Type 965 in *Albion*, Type 293 in both ships. Aircraft Direction: Type 982 in *Bulwark*, Type 983 in both ships.

BULWARK 1971

GUNNERY. Eight 40 mm AA guns were removed during the initial conversion of *Bulwark* to provide space for four vehicle personnel landing craft carried at built-in gantries, leaving her with 18—40 mm AA. guns.

ENGINEERING. The three-bladed propeller in *Bulwark* was replaced by a four-bladed propeller. Propeller diameter 15·5 feet. At 28 knots the propellers work at 230 rpm.

CONVERSION. Basically *Bulwark* was not changed during her initial conversion, although the fixed wing capability, arrester wires and catapults were removed. Alterations and modifications were made to render the ship suitable as an all-helicopter troop carrier with 16 Westland Whirlwind aircraft, replaced at a later date by the Wessex, and four landing craft (vehicle or personnel).

DRAWING. Starboard elevation and plan of *Albion*. Drawn in 1972. Scale: 125 feet = 1 inch (1 : 1 500).

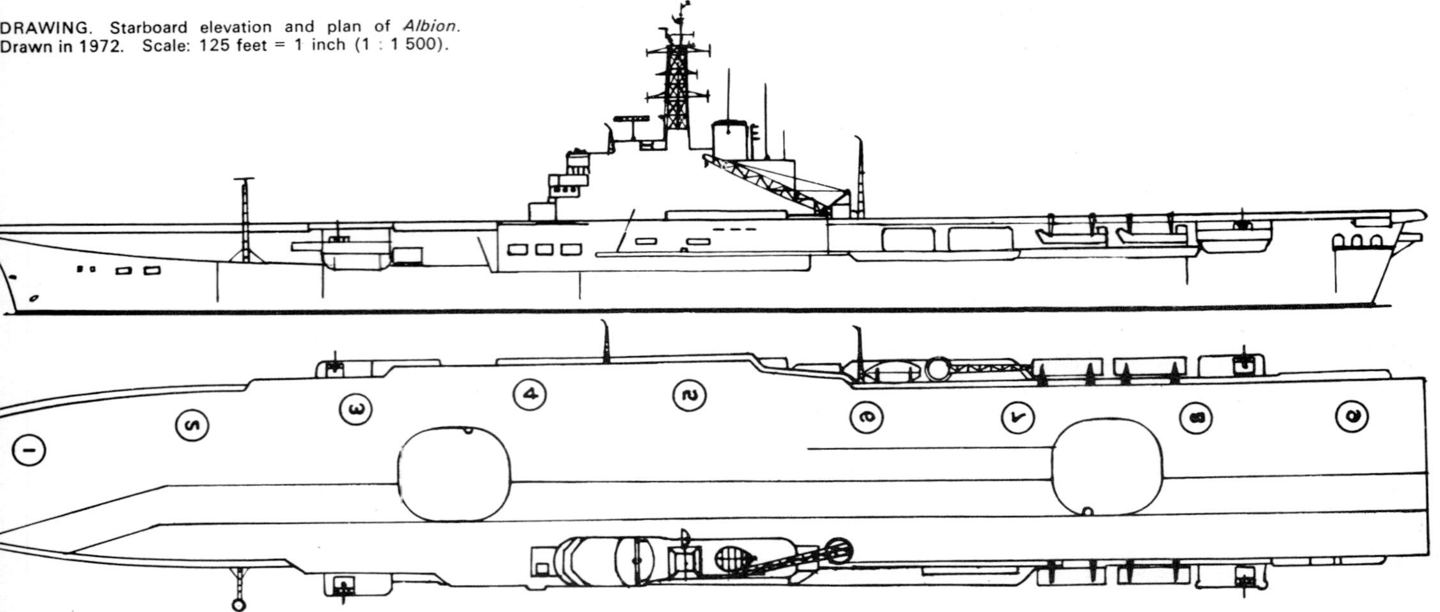

Amphibious Warfare Ships—*continued*

The ship was fitted with the most extensive air conditioning system in the Royal Navy. In 1963 *Bulwark* was further refitted to the same standard as *Albion*, with slight variation in air conditioning.

CLASS. It was announced in Feb 1971 that *Centaur*, fixed wing aircraft carrier, originally of this class, is for disposal. Of the other five of this class originally ordered *Arrogant*, original Hermes, *Monmouth* and *Polyphemus* were cancelled in 1945; and *Hermes* (ex-*Elephant*) was completed to a modified design (see previous page) *Albion* deleted on November 22 1972, being sold for scrap for £200 000.

BULWARK 1971

2 ASSAULT SHIPS (LPD)

Name	*No*	*Builders*	*Ordered*	*Laid down*	*Launched*	*Completed*
FEARLESS	L 10 (ex-L 3004)	Harland & Wolff Ltd, Belfast	1 Dec 1961	25 July 1962	19 Dec 1963	25 Nov 1965
INTREPID	L 11 (ex L 3005)	John Brown & Co. (Clydebank) Ltd	1 May 1962	19 Dec 1962	25 June 1964	11 Mar 1967

Displacement, tons	11 060 standard; 12 120 full load; 16 950 ballasted
Length, feet (*metres*)	500 (*152·4*) wl; 520 (*158·5*) oa
Beam, feet (*metres*)	80 (*24·4*)
Draught, feet (*metres*)	20·5 (*6·2*)
Draught, ballasted	32 (*9·8*) aft, 23 (*7·0*) fwd; 27·5 (*8·4*) mean
Landing craft	4 LCM(9) in dock; 4 LCVP at davits
Vehicles	*Specimen load*: 15 tanks, 7 three-ton and 20 quarter-ton trucks (20 three tonners on flight deck)
Aircraft	Flight deck facilities for 5 Wessex helicopters (6 operable)
Missiles, AA	4 "Seacat" systems
Guns, AA	2—40 mm Bofors
Boilers	2 Babcock & Wilcox
Main engines	2 EE turbines; 22 000 shp; 2 shafts
Speed, knots	21
Range, miles	5 000 at 20 knots
Complement	556 (36 officers, 520 men); 111 Royal Marines and Army

INTREPID 1972

FEARLESS 1972

These assault ships, with commando carriers, replace the former ships of the Amphibious Warfare Squadron. They carry landing craft which are floated through the open stern by flooding compartments of the ship and lowering her in the water; are able to deploy tanks, vehicles and men; have seakeeping qualities much superior to those of tank landing ships, and greater speed and range. Capable of operating independently. Another valuable feature is a helicopter platform which is also the deckhead of the dock from which the landing craft are floated out. Officially estimated building cost: *Fearless* £11 250 000; *Intrepid* £10 300 000.

TRAINING. In 1972 *Intrepid* will be used for the sea training of officers under training at the Britannia Royal Naval College, Dartmouth. When *Intrepid* is refitting *Fearless* will take over.

RADAR. Fitted with type 993 air and surface warning radar.

ENGINEERING. The two funnels are staggered across the beam of the ship, indicating that the engines and boilers are arranged *en echelon*, two machinery spaces having one turbine and one boiler installed in each space. The turbines were manufactured by the English Electric Co Rugby, the gearing by David Brown & Co, Huddersfield. Boilers work at a pressure of 550 lbs per sq in and a temperature of 850 deg F. Two 5-bladed propellers, 12·5 feet diameter, 200 rpm in *Fearless*.

ELECTRICAL. Power at 440V 60 c/s 3-phase a.c. is supplied by four 1 000 kW AEI turbo-alternators.

OPERATIONAL. Each ship is fitted out as a Naval Assault Group/Brigade Headquarters with an assault Operations Room from which naval and military personnel, can mount and control the progress of an assault operation.

SATELLITE SYSTEM. The Royal Navy fitted its first operational satellite communication system in *Intrepid* in 1969, the contract having been awarded to Plessey Radar.

TROOPS. Each ship can carry 380 to 400 troops at ship's company standards, and an overload of 700 marines and military personnel can be accommodated for short periods.

14 LCM (9) TYPE

LCM (9) 700	**LCM (9) 703**	**LCM (9) 706**	**LCM (9) 710**
LCM (9) 701	**LCM (9) 704**	**LCM (9) 707**	**LCM (9) 711**
LCM (9) 702	**LCM (9) 705**	**LCM (9) 708**	**LCM (9) 3507**
		LCM (9) 709	**LCM (9) 3508**

Displacement, tons	75 light; 176 loaded
Dimensions, feet	77 pp; 85 oa × 21·5 × 5·5
Capacity	2 battle tanks or 100 tons of vehicles
Main engines	2 Paxman 6 cyl. YHXAM diesels; 2 shafts; 624 bhp = 10 knots. Screws enclosed in Kort nozzles to improve manoeuvrability.

LCM (9) 3507 and LCM (9) 3508 were the first operational minor landing craft to be built since the Second World War. Ramped in the traditional manner forward, a completely enclosed radar-fitted wheelhouse is positioned aft. Upon completion they carried out familiarisation trials to perfect the new techniques required in launching and recovering LCMs from the flooded sterns of the parent assault ships. Four each of the 700 Series allocated to assault ships.

L 705 (F2) 1972, A. & J. Pavia

2 LCM (7) 7,000 SERIES (and NSB)

Displacement, tons	28 light; 63 loaded
Dimensions, feet	60·2 × 16 × 3·7
Main Engines	290 bhp = 9·8 knots

Nos. 7037, 7100. Three are employed as naval servicing boats and store carriers: 7037 (NSB 351), 7100 (NSB 359), 7104 (NSB 358). Some of the LCM (7) type were re-engined with Gray Marine diesels. 7087 and 7104 were removed from the list in 1968 and 7016 in 1969.

26 LCVP 100 SERIES

Displacement, tons	8·5 light; 13·5 full load; LCVP (ex-LCA (2)s 11·5 light 16 full load
Dimensions, feet	41·5 LCVP (2)s; 43 × 10 × 2·5
Main engines	130 bhp = 8 knots; LCVP (2)s: 2 Foden diesels, 200 bhp 10 knots

There are 12 LCVP (1)s Nos between Nos 102 and 136 and 14 LCVP (2)s, Nos 137 to 150. There were also a number of variations and prototypes of about the same length (43 feet).

Raiding Landing Craft, including LCR 5507 and 5508, and Navigational Landing Craft, including LCN 604 (ex-LCR 5505). LCA (1) 1275, 1330 1481, 1485, 1644 1678, 1705, 1712, 1733, 1745, 1779, and 1787 were for disposal in 1961, eleven more in 1963, and 1272, 1543, 1639, 1972 and 1891 in 1964, 1485 and 1700 in 1968. LCVP (2)s carried by *Intrepid* and *Fearless* can carry 35 troops or 2 Land Rovers. Crew 4. LCA (2)s were redesignated LCVPs (Landing Craft Vehicle and Personnel) in 1966.

2 LCP (L)3 500 SERIES

Displacement, tons	6·5 light; 10 loaded
Dimensions, feet	37 × 11 × 3·2
Main engines	225 bhp = 12 knots

There are two LCP (L) 3s Nos 501 and 503. Aurora gas turbines were installed in LCP (L) 3 No. 502. LCP (L) No. 556 was officially deleted from the list in 1969.

DESTROYER MAINTENANCE SHIPS

Name	*No.*	*Builders*	*Laid down*	*Launched*	*Completed*	*Converted*
TRIUMPH	A 108 (ex-*R* 16)	R & W Hawthorn Leslie, Hebburn	27 Jan 1943	2 Oct 1944	9 Apr 1946	HM Dockyard, Portsmouth 1 Jan 1958 to 7 Jan 1965

Displacement, tons	13 500 standard; 17 500 full load
Length, feet (*metres*)	630·0 (*192·0*)pp; 650·0 (*198·1*)wl 699·0 (*213·1*) oa
Beam, feet (*metres*)	80·0 (*24·4*)
Draught, feet (*metres*)	23·5 (*7·2*)
Width, feet (*metres*)	112·5 (*34·3*) overall
Aircraft	3 helicopters in flight deck hangar
Guns	4—40 mm AA; 3 saluting
Main engines	Parsons geared turbines; 2 shafts; 40 000 shp
Speed, knots	24·25
Boilers	4 Admiralty 3-drum type Pressure 400 psi (*28·1 kg/cm²*) Temperature 700°F (*371°C*)
Range, miles	10 000 at 14 knots; 5 500 at full speed
Oil fuel, tons	3 000
Complement	500 (27 officers, 473 men) plus 285 (15 officers, 270 men) of maintenance staff

TRIUMPH *1972, Wright & Logan*

Insulated for tropical service and partially air-conditioned.

CONVERSION. Cost of conversion: £10 200 000, including capital expenditure on the heavy repair plant carried and dockyard expenses over a protracted period.

CLASS. Of her original sister aircraft carriers, the *Venerable* (renamed *Karel Doorman*) was sold to the Royal Netherlands Navy on 1 Apr 1948 and renamed *Karel Doorman*, and again sold to Argentina on 15 Oct 1968 and renamed *25 de Mayo: Colossus* (renamed *Arromanches*) was sold to the French Navy in 1951; and two were completed as maintenance aircraft carriers, *Perseus* (scrapped in 1958) and *Pioneer* (scrapped in 1954). *Vengeance* was lent to the Royal Australian Navy early in 1953, but was returned to the Royal Navy in August 1955, and sold to the Brazilian Navy in 1956 (announced by Admiralty on 14 Dec); she was modernised in 1957-60 and commissioned in 1961 under the name *Minas Gerais*. *Warrior* was sold to the Argentine Navy in July 1958 and commissioned under the name *Independencia* in Jan 1959. *Glory* was broken up in 1961, and *Ocean* and *Theseus* in 1962. Of two half-sisters *Pioneer* was scrapped in 1954 and *Perseus* in 1958; *Unicorn* arrived at Dalmuir to be broken up on 15 June 1959.

MAINTENANCE SHIPS

1 "HEAD" CLASS

Name	*No.*	*Builders*	*Laid down*	*Launched*	*Completed*
BERRY HEAD	A 191	North Vancouver Ship Repairs	15 June 1944	21 Oct 1944	30 May 1945

Displacement, tons	9 000 standard; 11 270 full load
Length, feet (*metres*)	416·0 (*126·8*)pp; 441·5 (*134·6*)oa
Beam, feet (*metres*)	57·5 (*17·5*)
Draught, feet (*metres*)	22·5 (*6·9*)
Guns, AA	11—40 mm
Boilers	2 Foster Wheeler
Main engines	Triple expansion; 2 500 ihp
Speed, knots	10 approx
Oil fuel, tons	1 600 capacity
Complement	425

Escort Maintenance Ship. In reserve in 1972. *Berry Head* was refitted in 1968-69 to relieve HMS *Triumph* in the Far East, but returned in 1970.

DISPOSALS. *Duncansby Head* was returned to rhe Canadian Government in 1969 and scrapped. *Rame Head* deleted 1972.

"POINT" CLASS. *Dodman Point* deleted 1962, *Hartland Point* in 1972.

BERRY HEAD *1971*

SUBMARINE DEPOT SHIPS

2 "MAIDSTONE" CLASS

Name	*No.*	*Builders*	*Laid down*	*Launched*	*Completed*	*Reconstructed*
FORTH	A 187	John Brown, Clydebank	30 June 1937	11 Aug 1938	14 May 1939	1962-1966
MAIDSTONE	A 185	John Brown, Clydebank	17 Aug 1936	21 Oct 1937	5 May 1938	1958-1962

Displacement, tons	10 000 standard; 13 000 full load
Length, feet (*metres*)	497·0 (*151·5*)pp; 531·0 (*161·8*) oa
Beam, feet (*metres*)	73·0 (*22·3*)
Draught, feet (*metres*)	21·2 (*6·5*)
Guns, AA	5—40 mm Bofors (see *Gunnery*)
Boilers	4 Admiralty 3-drum type
Main engines	Geared turbines (Brown Curtis in *Forth*: Parsons in *Maidstone*) 2 shafts; 7 000 shp
Speed, knots	16
Oil fuel, tons	2 300
Complement	695 (45 officers and 650 men) Accommodation for 1 159 (119 officers and 1 040 men) normal; over 1 500 max

Equipment includes foundry, coppersmith's, plumbers', carpenters'; heavy and light machine, electrical and torpedo repair shops and plant for charging submarine batteries. Designed for maintaining nine operational submarines, and supplying over 140 torpedoes and a similar number of mines. Repair facilities on board for all material in attached submarines, and extensive diving and salvage equipment. There are steam laundry, hospital, chapel, two canteens, bakery, barber shops, operating theatre and dental surgery.

In Oct 1969, *Maidstone* was restored and recommissioned as an accommodation ship for 2 000 troops and sent to Belfast.

RECONSTRUCTION. *Maidstone* was extensively reconstructed in HM Dockyard, Portsmouth in 1958-62 as support ship for nuclear powered submarines with a lattice foremast and additional superstructure amidships. The conversion and modernisation included refitting as parent ship for the nuclear-powered submarine *Dreadnought*. *Forth* was similarly modernised and converted into a support ship for nuclear powered submarines in HM Dockyard Chatham, in 1962-63.

HMS. *Defiance* As the fleet Maintenance Base, Devonport and parent ship of the 2nd Submarine Squadron *Forth* became part of HMS *Defiance*.

DISPOSAL. The larger and younger submarine support ship *Adamant*, latterly in reserve at Plymouth, was disposed of in late 1970.

SURVEY SHIPS

3 "HECLA" CLASS

Name	No.	Builders	Laid down	Launched	Completed
HECATE	A 137	Yarrow & Co Ltd, Scotstoun	26 Oct 1964	31 Mar 1965	20 Dec 1965
HECLA	A 133	Yarrow & Co and Blythswood	6 May 1964	21 Dec 1964	9 Sep 1965
HYDRA	A 144	Yarrow & Co and Blythswood	14 May 1964	14 July 1965	5 May 1966

Displacement, tons	1 915 light; 2 733 full load
Measurement, tons	2 898 gross
Length, feet (*metres*)	235 (*71·6*) pp; 260·1 (*79·3*) oa
Beam, feet (*metres*)	49·1 (*15·0*)
Draught, feet (*metres*)	15·6 (*4·7*)
Aircraft	1 Wasp helicopter
Main engines	Diesel-electric drive; 1 shaft. 3 Paxman "Ventura" 12-cyl Vee turbocharged diesels; 3,840 bhp. 1 electric motor; 2 000 shp
Speed, knots	14·35 on trials
Range, miles	20 000 at 9 knots
Oil fuel, tons	450
Complement	118 (14 officers, 104 ratings)
Accommodation	123 (19 officers, 104 ratings)

The first to be designed with a combined oceanographical and hydrographical role. Of merchant ship design and similar in many respects to the Royal Research ship *Discovery*, they have range and endurance to fit them for their specialised work. The hull is strengthened for navigation in ice, and a propeller built into a transverse tunnel in the bow for good manoeuvrability. The fore end of the superstructure incorporates a Landrover garage and the after end a helicopter hanger with adjacent flight deck. Equipped with chartroom, drawing office and photographic studio; two laboratories, dry and wet; electrical engineering and shipwright workshops, and large storerooms. Capable of operating independently of shore support for long periods. Air-conditioned throughout.

HECATE, HECLA, HYDRA (Survey)

1 IMPROVED "HECLA" CLASS

HERALD

Displacement, tons	2 000 standard
Measurement, tons	2 900 gross
Aircraft	1 Wasp helicopter
Main engines	Diesel-electric drive; 1 shaft
Speed, knots	14 approx
Range, miles	20 000 at 9 knots
Complement	118

A later version of the "Hecla" class design. Ordered under the 1972-73 Supply (Ministry of Defence) Estimates. Being built by Robb Caledon, Leith, with main machinery manufactured by GEC/AEI Projects Ltd. Fitted with Hydroplot Satellite navigation system.

HECATE 1971

COASTAL SURVEY SHIPS

4 "FAWN" CLASS

BEAGLE A 319 **BULLDOG** A 317 **FAWN** A 325 **FOX** A 320

Displacement, tons	800 approx standard (official figure); 1 088 full load
Dimensions, feet	189 oa × 37·5 × 12
Main engines	4 Lister Blackstone ERS8M, 8 cyl. 4 str. diesels, coupled to 2 shafts, 2 000 bhp = 15 knots max designed, controllable pitch propellers
Range, miles	4 000 at 12 knots cruising
Complement	38 (4 officers, 34 ratings)

Designed for duty overseas, working in pairs. *Fawn* and *Fox* replaced the coastal minesweeper conversions. The first ship of the class launched was *Bulldog* on 12 July 1967 at Brooke Marine Ltd, Lowestoft, followed by *Beagle* on 7 Sep 1967, *Fox* on 6 Nov 1967 and *Fawn* on 29 Feb 1968. *Bulldog* was commissioned on 21 Mar 1968 and the others by the end of 1968. Built to commercial standards. Fitted with passive tank stabilizer to reduce rolling, most modern echo sounders, precision ranging radar, Decca "Hifix" system, automatic steering. Air-conditioned throughout. Carry 28·5 ft survey motor launch in davits.

FAWN 1969, *Wright & Logan*

FOX

Coastal Survey Ships—*continued*

Of the two coastal survey ships of the "Ton" class, modified coastal minesweepers, *Myrmidon* (ex-*Edderton*) was sold to Malaysia in 1968, and *Mermaid* (ex-*Sullington*) was officially approved for disposal by scrapping in 1968-69.

INSHORE SURVEY CRAFT

ENTERPRISE 1970

3 "E" CLASS

ECHO A 70 **EGERIA** A 72 **ENTERPRISE** A 71

Displacement, tons	120 standard; 160 full load
Dimensions, feet	100·0 pp; 106·8 oa × 22·0 × 6·8 max
Main engines	2 Paxman diesels; 2 shafts; controllable pitch propellers; 700 bhp = 14 knots max; 12 knots normal
Oil fuel, tons	15 capacity
Endurance, miles	1 600 at 10 knots
Complement	18 (2 officers, 16 ratings); accommodation for 22 (4 officers, 18 ratings)

Echo, the first Inshore Survey Craft, was built by J. Samuel White & Co Ltd, Cowes, launched on 1 May 1957, and commissioned on 12 Sep 1958. *Egeria* was built by Wm Weatherhead & Sons Ltd, Cockenzie, and *Enterprise* by M. W. Blackmore & Sons Ltd, Bideford. All built for coastal and harbour hydrographic surveys around the British Isles. Equipped with two echo sounding machines and sonar for wreck location, and survey equipment for triangulation ashore. Modern radar, wire sweep gear, echo sounding launch, and modern chart room.

2 "HAM" CLASS

MODIFIED INSHORE MINESWEEPERS

WATERWITCH (ex-*Powderham*) M 304 **WOODLARK** (ex-*Yaxham*) M 2780

Displacement, tons	120 standard; 160 full load
Dimensions, feet	107·5 oa × 22 × 5·5
Main engines	Diesels; 2 shafts; 1 100 bhp = 14 knots
Endurance, miles	1 500 at 12 knots
Complement	18 (2 officers, 16 ratings)

Inshore Survey Craft—*continued*

Former inshore minesweepers of the "Ham" class converted to replace the old survey motor launches *Meda* and *Medusa* for operation in inshore waters at home. *Waterwitch*, ex-M 2720, was seconded to Port Auxiliary Service in 1968.

WOODLARK *1971*

ICE PATROL SHIP

ENDURANCE (ex-*Anita Dan*) A 171

Displacement, tons	*circa* 3 600 (official)
Measurement, tons	2 641 gross
Length, feet (*metres*)	300 (*91·44*) oa; 305 (*92·96*) including helicopter deck extension
Beam, feet (*metres*)	46 (*14·02*)
Draught, feet (*metres*)	16·5 (*5·03*); 18 (*5·5*) max
Aircraft	2 Whirlwind Mk IX helicopters
Guns	2—20 mm
Main engines	B & W 550 VTBF diesels; 3 220 ihp; 1 shaft
Speed knots	14·5
Range, miles	12 000 at 14·5 knots
Complement	119 (13 officers, 106 men, including a small Royal Marine detachment) plus 12 spare berths for scientists

ENDURANCE *1972 MoD (UK)*

Purchased from J. Lauritzen Lines, Copenhagen (announced on 20 Feb 1967). Strengthened for operation in ice. Converted by Harland & Wolff, Belfast, into an ice patrol ship for southern waters to replace *Protector*, undertaking hydrographic and oceanographic surveys for the Royal Navy, as support ship and guard vessel. New name *Endurance* was announced 27 July, 1967. She was ready for deployment in the Antarctic for the 1968 season by Oct. Refitted May to Oct during the Antarctic winter.

An unusual feature for one of HM ships is her hull painted a vivid red for easy identification in the ice, particularly from the air. Her upperworks and funnel are the traditional white and buff of the naval surveying fleet. Another feature is that the ship can be controlled from the crow's nest so as to give her officers the furthest view of channels through the ice.

ENDURANCE (Ice Patrol Ship)

ROYAL YACHT

BRITANNIA A 00

Displacement, tons	**3 990 light; 4 961 full load**
Measurement, tons	**5 769 gross**
Dimensions, feet	**360·0 pp; 380·0 wl; 412·2 oa × 55·0 × 17·0 max**
Main engines	**Single reduction geared turbines; 2 shafts; 12 000 shp = 21 knots continuous cruising; 22·75 knots max (trials)**
Boilers	**2**
Radius, miles	**2 100 at 20 knots; 2 400 at 18 knots; 3 000 miles at 15 knots**
Oil fuel, tons	**330 (490 with auxiliary fuel tanks)**
Complement	**270**

Designed as a medium sized naval hospital ship for use by Her Majesty The Queen in peacetime as the Royal Yacht. Built by John Brown & Co Ltd, Clydebank. Completed on 14 Jan 1954. Construction conformed to mercantile practice. Fitted with Denny-Brown single fin stabilisers to reduce roll in bad weather from 20 deg to 6 deg. Cost £2 098 000. To pass under the bridges of the St. Lawrence Seaway when she visited Canada, the top 20 feet of her mainmast and the radio aerial on her foremast were hinged in Nov 1958 so that they could be lowered as required. Currently under refit at a cost of £2·1 million bringing her total cost to £12 million.

BRITANNIA *1972, John Mortimer*

HOVERCRAFT

1 "WINCHESTER" (SRN6) TYPE

Displacement, tons	10 normal gross weight
Dimensions, feet	48·4 × 23·0 × 15·0 oa (height) × 4·0 (skirt)
Main engines	1 Rolls Royce Gnome gas turbine; 900 shp = 50 knots
Range	200 miles

Modified with radar and military communications equipment for its primary role of a fast amphibious communication craft to support Royal Marine units.

1 "WELLINGTON" (BHN7) TYPE

Displacement, tons	50 max weight; 33 light
Dimensions, feet	78·33 × 45·5 × 34·0 oa (height) × 5·5 (skirt)
Main engines	1 Rolls Royce Proteus gas turbine; 4 250 shp = 60 knots
Complement	14 plus trials crew

First "hover warship" costing about £700 000, delivered to the inter-Service Hovercraft Trials Unit at the Royal Naval Air Station, Lee-on-Solent, in Apr 1970. She could be used as a missile armed fast patrol craft or amphibious assault craft. Winter trials in Swedish waters in Feb 1972. Records established: longest open sea voyage, furthest north, and sustained speeds of over 55 knots in the Baltic.

SRN6 *1971*

COASTAL PATROL VESSELS

5 MODIFIED "TON" CLASS

(FORMER COASTAL MINESWEEPERS)

BEACHAMPTON P 1007 (ex-M 1107)
MONKTON P 1055 (ex-M 1155)
WASPERTON P 1089 (ex-M 1189)
WOLVERTON P 1093 (ex-M 1193)
YARNTON P 1096 (ex-M 1196)

Displacement, tons	360 standard; 425 full load
Dimensions, feet	140·0 pp; 153·0 oa × 28·8 × 8·2
Guns	2—40 mm Bofors AA, single, 1 forward, 1 aft
Main engines	2 diesels; 2 shafts; 3 000 bhp = 15 knots max
Oil fuel, tons	45 bunkerage
Range, miles	2 300 at 13 knots
Complement	30 (5 officers and 25 ratings, but varies)

Former coastal minesweepers of the "Ton" class, refitted as gunboats at the end of 1971, re-designated as coastal patrol vessels and given "P" instead of "M" pennants in a "1 000" series instead of the former "1 100" series, but otherwise retaining the same numbers.

WOLVERTON 1972, *Michael D. J. Lennon*

SEAWARD DEFENCE BOATS

2 "FORD" CLASS

DEE (ex-*Beckford*) P 3104 (Mersey RNR) **DROXFORD** P 3113 (Clyde RNR)

Displacement, tons	120 standard; 142 full load
Dimensions, feet	110·0 wl; 117·2 oa × 20·0 × 7·0 props
Guns	1—40 mm Bofors AA
A/S weapons	DC rails; large and small DC
Main engines	Davey Paxman diesels. Foden engine on centre shaft. 1 100 bhp = 18 knots max; 15 knots sea
Oil fuel, tons	23
Complement	19

All built in 1953-57. Had modern electronic equipment, depth charge release gear and flares, and comprehensive electrical installations.

TRANSFERS. *Brayford* was sold to South African Navy in 1954 and *Glassford* in 1955. *Desford* was transferred to Ceylon in 1955. *Elmina* and *Komenda* were built for Ghana in 1962. *Axford*, *Hinksford* and *Montford* were sold to Nigeria 1 July 1966, *Dubford* and *Gifford* in 1968, and *Bryansford* in 1969. *Aberford* to Kenya in 1969.

Seaward Defence Boats—*continued*

CLASS. *Camberford, Greatford, Ickford, Marlingford, Mayford, Shalford* and *Tilford* were approved for disposal during 1966-67.

DROXFORD 1972, *Wright & Logan*

DIVING TRIALS SHIP

RECLAIM ((ex-*Salverdant*) A 231

Displacement, tons	1 200 standard; 1 800 full load
Dimensions, feet	200 pp; 217·8 oa × 38 × 15·5
Main engines	Triple expansion; 2 shafts; 1 500 ihp = 12 knots
Oil fuel, tons	310
Range, miles	3 000
Complement	84

Built by Wm. Simons & Co Ltd, Renfrew. Engined by Aitchison Blair Ltd. Laid down on 9 Apr 1946. Launched on 12 Mar 1948. Completed on Oct 1948. Construction based on the design of a "King Salvor" class naval ocean salvage vessel. First deep diving and submarine rescue vessel built as such for the Royal Navy. Fitted with sonar, radar, echo-sounding apparatus for detection of sunken wrecks, and equipped for submarine rescue work. Formerly tender to H.M.S. *Vernon* shore establishment, Portsmouth for deep diving experiments, and subsequently a deep diving vessel in the Portsmouth Squadron. Reclassified as Mine Countermeasures Support and Diving Trials Ship in 1960, and attached to HMS *Lochinvar*, the minesweeping base at Port Edgar, but her mine countermeasures functions were taken over in 1968 by the minelayer *Abdiel*. Carried out deep diving experiments in the Canary Islands in Jan to Mar 1961.

RECLAIM 1972

ROYAL FLEET AUXILIARY SERVICE
LARGE FLEET TANKERS

3 "OL" CLASS

OLMEDA (ex-*Oleander*) A 124
OLNA A 123
OLWEN (ex-*Olynthus*) A 122

Displacement, tons	10 890 light; 33 240 full load
Measurement, tons	22 350 deadweight; 18 600 gross
Dimensions, feet	611·1 pp; 648·0 oa × 84·0 × 34·0
Aircraft	2 Wessex helicopters (can carry 3)
Main engines	Pametrada double reduction geared turbines; 26 500 shp = 19 knots (21·2 on trials)
Boilers	2 Babcock & Wilcox, 750 lbs sq in, 950 deg F
Complement	87 (25 officers and 62 ratings)

Largest and fastest ships when they joined the Royal Fleet Auxiliary Service. *Olmeda* was launched on 19 Nov 1964 and completed on 18 Oct 1965 by Swan Hunter, Wallsend, with machinery by Wallsend Slipway & Eng Co Ltd, while *Olna* and *Olwen* were launched on 28 July 1965 and 10 July 1964 and completed on 1 Apr 1966 and 21 June 1965, respectively, by Hawthorn Leslie, Hebburn, engined by Hawthorn Leslie (Engineers) Ltd.

Designed for support of the Fleet, with handling gear for transferring fuels and stores by jackstay and derricks whilst steaming at speed A helicopter landing platform and hangar enable ships to collect stores by air. Specially strengthened for operations in ice. Accommodation of a high standard, fully air-conditioned. *Olna* has a transverse bow thrust unit for improved manoeuvrability in confined waters and a new design of replenishment at sea systems.

OLNA 1972, *Dr. Giorgio Arra*

2 LATER "TIDE" CLASS

TIDESPRING A 75 **TIDEPOOL** A 76

Displacement, tons	8 531 light; 25 931 full load
Measurement, tons	17 400 deadweight; 14 130 gross
Dimensions, feet	550·0 pp; 583·0 oa × 71·0 × 32·0
Main engines	Double reduction geared turbines; 15 000 shp = 17 knots
Boilers	2 Babcock & Wilcox
Complement	115 (30 officers and 85 ratings)

Built by Hawthorn Leslie, Hebburn with machinery by Hawthorn Leslie (Engineers) Ltd. Highly specialised ships for fuelling (13 000 tons cargo fuel) and storing naval vessels at sea and capable of high performance under rigorous service conditions. Their all-round capability is enhanced by a helicopter platform and hangar. *Tidespring* was laid down on 24 July 1961, launched on 3 May 1962, and accepted on 18 Jan 1963. *Tidepool* was laid down on 4 Dec 1961 and launched on 11 Dec 1962.

TIDEPOOL 1971

3 "TIDE" CLASS

TIDEFLOW (ex-*Tiderace*) A 97
TIDESURGE (ex-*Tiderange*) A 98
TIDEREACH A 96

Displacement, tons	9 040 light; 25 940 full load
Measurement, tons	16 900 deadweight; 13 700 gross
Dimensions, feet	550 pp; 583 oa × 71 × 32 max.
Main engines	Double reduction geared turbines; 15 000 shp = 17 knots

Large Fleet Tankers—*continued*

Tidereach, launched by Swan Hunter & Wigham Richardson Ltd, Wallsend-on-Tyne, on 2 June 1954, and completed on 30 Aug 1955, was the first of the new Fleet Replenishment Tankers. The main machinery was manufactured by the Wallsend Slipway Co. Designed for the support of the Fleet and replenishment under way at sea. Capacious (15 000 tons of fuel cargo). Oil cargo can be discharged at high rate to ships on either beam or astern. *Tiderange* (renamed *Tidesurge* in 1958) was launched at I. L. Thompson & Sons Ltd, Sunderland, on 30 Aug 1954, the main machinery of both being manufactured by North Eastern Marine Engineering Co Ltd, Wallsend. A fourth ship, *Tide Austral*, built for Australia, was renamed *Supply* on 7 Sep 1962.

TIDEFLOW — *1969, Wright & Logan*

TIDESURGE — *1970*

Name	*No.*	*Builders*	*Launched*
WAVE CHIEF (ex-*Empire Edgehill*)	A 265	Harland & Wolff, Ltd Govan, Glasgow	4 Apr 1946

Displacement, tons	4 750 light; 8 200 standard; 16 650 full load
Measurement, tons	11 900 deadweight; 8 447 gross
Dimensions, feet	465·3 pp; 492·5 oa × 64·5 × 28·5
Main engines	Double reduction geared turbines; 6 800 shp = 14·5 knots
Boilers	Three-drum type

Launch dates above. *Wave Baron*, *Wave Chief*, in service, and *Wave Ruler* fleet replenish-ment tankers, *Wave Prince* freighter. Turbines of Metrovick type in *Wave Baron*, *Wave Chief*, Parsons in *Wave Prince* and *Wave Ruler*. *Wave Baron* and *Wave Prince* were mod-ernised in 1961-62 but are in reserve. *Wave Ruler* is acting as the oiling depot ship at Gan, replacing *Wave Victor* which is up for sale in Singapore.

CLASS. *Wave Commander* and *Wave Liberator* were scrapped in 1959. *Wave Conquerer* and *Wave King* were sold in 1960. *Wave Emperor*, *Wave Governor*, *Wave Premier* and *Wave Regent* were scrapped in 1960. *Wave Monarch* was sold to foreign interests in 1961. *Wave Protector* was broken up in Italy in 1963. *Wave Knight* was broken up in Antwerp in 1964. *Wave Master* was scrapped in 1964. *Wave Sovereign* was sold in 1967, *Wave Duke* and *Wave Laird* were sold for scrap in 1970.

WAVE CHIEF — *1972, Wright & Logan*

SUPPORT TANKERS

BRAMBLELEAF (ex-*London Loyalty*) A 81

Measurement, tons	17 960 deadweight; 12 123 gross; 7 042 net
Dimensions, feet	526 pp; 556·7 oa × 71·3 × 30
Main engines	Doxford 6-cyl. diesel; 6 800 bhp = 14·5 knots (*Bayleaf*); 14 knots (*Brambleleaf*)
Oil fuel (tons)	1 470

Built by Furness S.B. Co Ltd. *Brambleleaf* was completed in Jan 1954. From London & Overseas Freighters Ltd, 22 May 1959. *Overseas Adventurer* is to be chartered in 1973 as *Cherryleaf*. Astern fuelling.

Support Tankers—*continued*

BRAMBLELEAF — *1969, Wright & Logan*

LIMITED REPLENISHMENT TANKERS

ORANGELEAF (ex-M.V. *Southern Satellite*) A 80

Measurement, tons	17 475 deadweight; 12 481 gross; 6 949 net
Dimensions, feet	525 pp; 556·5 oa × 71·7 × 30·5 mean
Main engines	Doxford 6-cyl. diesel; 6 800 bhp = 15 knots
Oil fuel (tons)	1 610

Built by Furness Shipbuilding Co Ltd. Haverton Hill on Tees. Launched on 8 Feb 1955. Completed June 1955. From South Georgia Co Ltd, 25 May 1959. Astern fuelling.

CLASS. The oiler *Cherryleaf*, A 82 (ex-MV *Laurelwood*) was returned to her original owners (Molasses & General Transport Co Ltd) in 1966 and sold to Greek interests. The oiler *Appleleaf*, A 83 (ex-MV *George Lyras*), the first of the "Leaf" class acquired by the Royal Navy, taken over in 1959, was returned to her original owners in Jan 1970.

ORANGELEAF — *1971*

PEARLEAF A 77

Displacement, tons	24 900 full load
Measurement, tons	18 045 deadweight; 12 139 gross; 7 216 net
Dimensions, feet	535 pp; 568 oa × 71·7 × 30
Main engines	Rowan Doxford 6-cyl. diesels; 8 800 bhp = 15·8 knots

Built by Scotstoun Yard of Blythswood Shipbuilding Co Ltd, for Jacobs and Partners Ltd, London. Launched on 15 Oct 1959 and completed in Jan 1960. Chartered by the Royal Navy on completion. Can carry three different grades of cargo. Astern and abeam fuelling.

PEARLEAF — *1966, Wright & Logan*

MOBILE RESERVE TANKERS

DERWENTDALE (ex-M.V. *Halcyon Breeze*)

Displacement, tons 88 555 full load
Measurement, tons 28 288 net; 42 343 gross; 72 550 deadweight
Dimensions, feet 761·0 pp; 799·0 oa × 117·8 × 42·3
Main engines B. & W. 9 cyl diesels; 1 shaft; 20 700 bhp = 15·5 knots
Complement 56

Commercial oil tanker built by Hitachi, Japan. Launched on 8 Jan 1964. Taken over by Great Britain in 1967. Chartered for Royal Fleet Auxiliary Service from the Court Line.

DEWDALE (ex-M.V. *Edenfield*)

Measurement, tons 21 542 net; 35 805 gross; 63 588 deadweight
Dimensions, feet 747·0 pp; 774·5 oa × 107·8 × 41·5
Main engines B. & W. 9 cyl diesels; 1 shaft; 17 000 bhp = 15 knots
Complement 51

The Ministry of Defence (Royal Navy) chartered three large tankers (announced on 13 July 1967) for service East of Suez, and renamed them, re-introducing traditional "Dale" class names. After limited modifications the ships operated in the Indian Ocean area. But *Ennerdale* sank on 1 June 1970 after striking a submerged hazard in the Indian Ocean.

DERWENTDALE *1972*

DEWDALE *1969, Wright & Logan*

SMALL FLEET TANKERS

PLUMLEAF A 78

Displacement, tons 24 920 full load
Measurement, tons 18 562 deadweight; 12 692 gross
Dimensions, feet 534 pp; 560 oa × 72 × 30
Main engines N.E. Doxford 6-cyl diesels; 9 350 bhp = 15·5 knots

Built by Blyth DD & Eng Co Ltd. Launched 29 Mar 1960. Completed July 1960 Astern and abeam fuelling.

PLUMLEAF *1972, Wright & Logan*

2 "RANGER" CLASS

Displacement, tons 6 630 full load
Measurement, tons 3 435 to 3 781 deadweight
Dimensions, feet 349·5 pp; 365·8 oa × 47·0 × 20·0
Main engines Burmeister & Wain diesels; 2 750 bhp = 12 knots

Built by Harland & Wolff Ltd, Govan, Glasgow. Launch dates above. The funnel is on the port side. All fitted with special derrick on the beam to facilitate fuelling at sea. *Gray Ranger* was lost during the Second World War. *Green Ranger* was deleted from the list in 1965. *Blue Ranger* in reserve, was on the disposal list in 1972, and *Gold Ranger* in 1973.

BLACK RANGER *1967, Courtesy Godfrey H. Walker, Esq.*

Small Fleet Tankers—*continued*

5 "ROVER" CLASS

GREEN ROVER A 268 **GREY ROVER** A 269 **BLUE ROVER** A 270

GOLD ROVER + 1 NEW CONSTRUCTION

Displacement, tons 11 522 full load
Measurement, tons 3 185 net; 7 060 deadweight; 7 510 gross
Dimensions, feet 461·0 × 63·0 × 24·0
Main engines 2 Ruston & Hornsby 16 cyl. uni-directional diesels; 1 shaft; controllable pitch propeller; 16 000 bhp = 19 knots (Pielstick diesels in new construction).
Complement 47 (16 officers and 31 men)

Small fleet tankers designed to replenish HM ships at sea with fuel, fresh water, limited dry cargo and refrigerated stores under all conditions while underway. *Blue Rover* is classified as "Fleet Replenishment Tanker". A helicopter landing platform is provided, served by a stores lift, to enable stores to be transferred at sea by helicopter. Built at Swan Hunter, Hebburn-on-Tyne, *Green Rover* was launched on 19 Dec 1968, *Grey Rover* on 17 Apr 1969, *Blue Rover* on 11 Nov 1969 and *Gold Rover* on 7 Mar 1973.

BLUE ROVER *1971, John G. Callis*

GREY ROVER *May, 1970, Wright & Logan*

1 "EDDY" CLASS

EDDYFIRTH A 261

Displacement, tons 1 960 light; 4 160 full load
Measurement, tons 2 300 gross; 2 200 deadweight
Dimensions, feet 270 pp; 286 oa × 44 × 17·2
Main engines 1 set triple expansion; 1 shaft; 1 750 ihp = 12 knots
Boilers 2 oil burning cylindrical

Built by Lobnitz & Co Ltd, Renfrew. Completed on 10 Feb 1954. Classed 100 A1 at Lloyd's for the carriage of petroleum in bulk. Cargo capacity: 1 650 tons oil.

CLASS. *Eddybay, Eddybeach, Eddycliffe, Eddycreek* and *Eddyreef* were disposed of in 1963 and 1964. *Eddyrock* was sold in 1967. *Eddyness* was sold for scrap in 1970.

EDDYFIRTH ***1971, John G. Callis***

HELICOPTER SUPPORT SHIP

ENGADINE K 08

Displacement, tons	8 000 to 9 000 full load
Measurement, tons	6 384 gross; 2 848 net
Dimensions, feet	424·0 oa × 58·4 × 22·1
Aircraft	4 Wessex and 2 Wasp or 2 Sea King helicopters
Main engines	1 Sulzer two stroke, 5 cyl turbo charged 5RD68 diesel; 5 500 bhp = 16 knots
Complement	RFA: 61 (15 officers, 46 men); RN: 14 (2 officers, 12 ratings) Accommodation for a further RN 113 (29 officers and 84 ratings)

Projected under the 1964-65 Navy Estimates. Built by Henry Robb Ltd, Leith. Ordered on 18 Aug 1964. Laid down on 9 Aug 1965. Officially named on 15 Sep 1966. Accepted into service on 15 Dec 1967. Largest ship then built by the company. Intended for the training of helicopter crews in deep water operations. Fitted with Denny Brown stabilisers to provide greater ship control during helicopter operations, the only RFA vessel so equipped.

ENGADINE *1972, Wright & Logan*

ENGADINE *1969*

LOGISTIC LANDING SHIPS

SIR GERAINT *1971, Royal Navy*

SIR LANCELOT L 3029 (ex-LSL 01)

Displacement, tons	3 370 light; 5 550 load
Measurement, tons	6 390 * gross; 2 180 deadweight
Dimensions, feet	366·3 pp; 412·1 oa × 59·8 × 12·8 mean draught
Main engines	2 Denny/Sulzer 12MD51 diesels; 9 520 bhp 8 250 bhp at 325 rpm = 17 knots service speed
Oil fuel, tons	811
Aircraft facilities	Wessex forward and aft
Guns	2—40 mm Bofors
Cranes	2 at 20 tons; 2 at 3 tons
Complement	Crew 68 (18 officers 50 ratings) Military passengers 340 (43 officers and warrant officers, 297 sergeants and other ranks)

CONSTRUCTION. Completed in Jan 1964 by the Fairfield Shipbuilding and Engineering Co to the order of the Ministry of Transport on behalf of the Ministry of Defence (Army). Transferred to the RFA on 3 Jan 1970.

LOGISTIC. Fitted for bow and stern loading with drive-through facility and deck to deck ramps, the ship is capable of discharging a full load of vehicles on to a beach. Facilities are provided for stowing and operating military pontoon equipment. On-board maintenance of vehicles and equipment and stowage of special military cargo are catered for.

ENGINEERING. Passive tank stabiliser system and bow thrust propulsion unit are fitted. All accommodation is air-conditioned and close circuit television fitted for entertainment and operational use.

AIRCRAFT FACILITIES. *Sir Lancelot* has full capability for operating Wessex helicopters from the after landing platform by day or night. The fore deck is suitable for operating helicopters by day only in favourable weather conditions and sheltered waters.

*Gross tonnage not yet remeasured.

Logistic Landing Ships—*continued*

5 PRODUCTION SERIES (LSL 02-06)

Displacement, tons	3 270 light; 5 674 load
Measurement, tons	4 473 gross; 2 404 deadweight
Dimensions, feet	366·3 pp; 412 oa × 59·8 × 13 mean draught
Main engines	2 Mirrlees National Monarch ALSSDM10 diesels; 9 400 bhp 8 460 bhp at 314 rpm = 17 knots service speed
Oil fuel, tons	816
Aircraft facilities	Wessex forward and aft
Guns	2—40 mm Bofors
Cranes	1 at 20 tons; 2 at 4¼/8½ tons
Complement	Crew 68 (18 officers, 50 ratings) Military passengers 340 (43 officers and warrant officers, 297 sergeants and other ranks)

Name	*No.*	*Laid down*	*Launched*	*Completed*	*Listed RFA*
SIR GALAHAD	L 3005 (ex-LSL 02)	Feb 1965	19 Apr 1966	17 Dec 1966	7 Mar 1970
SIR GERAINT	L 3037 (ex-LSL 04)	June 1965	26 Jan 1967	12 July 1967	5 Mar 1970
Built by Alexander Stephen & Sons Ltd Linthouse					
SIR BEDIVERE	L 3004 (ex-LSL 03)	Oct 1965	20 July 1966	18 May 1967	14 Jan 1970
SIR TRISTRAM	L 3505 (ex-LSL 05)	Feb 1966	12 Dec 1966	14 Sep 1967	30 Jan 1970
SIR PERCIVALE	L 3036 (ex-LSL 05)	Apr 1966	4 Oct 1967	23 Mar 1968	6 Mar 1970
Built by Hawthorn Leslie (Shipbuilders) Ltd, Hebburn-on-Tyne					

DESIGN. Similar in size and capacity to class prototype *Sir Lancelot* but layout modified following trials with prototype.

LOGISTIC. Vehicle deck provides increased vehicle stowage and improved flying facilities forward. Revision of military accommodation and services carried out.

ENGINEERING. Bridge control of main engines and machinery data-logging equipment fitted.

AIRCRAFT FACILITIES. These five ships have full capability for operating Wessex helicopters from both the after landing platform and the foredeck by day or night. Up to 20 Wessex helicopters can be carried (11 on the Tank Deck and 9 on the Vehicle Deck).

1"LST"(3) CLASS

EMPIRE GULL (ex-*Trouncer*)

Measurements, tons	4 257·9 gross
Dimensions, feet	347 × 54·1 × 12
Main engines	2 Triple Expansion; 2 shafts; 5 500 shp
Boilers	2 Water Tube
Oil fuel	950 Tons
Complement	63 officers and men
Troop accommodation	8 officers, 72 ORs

In commission until Oct 1974 at least.

STORE SUPPORT SHIPS

LYNESS A 339 **STROMNESS** A 344 **TARBATNESS** A 345

Displacement, tons	*circa* 16 500 laden (official figure)
Measurements, tons	12 359 gross; 4 744 net; 7 782 deadweight
Dimensions, feet	490 pp; 524 oa × 72 × 25·5
Aircraft	Facilities for helicopters
Main engines	Wallsend-Sulzer 8-cyl RD.76 diesel; 11 520 bhp = 17 knots
Complement	184

Designed and built by Swan Hunter & Wigham Richardson Ltd, Wallsend-on-Tyne. Lifts and mobile appliances provided for handling stores internally, and a new replenishment at sea system and a helicopter landing platform for transferring loads at sea. A novel feature of the ships is the use of close circuit television to monitor the movement of stores. All air-conditioned. *Lyness* was completed on 22 Dec 1966, *Stromness* on 21 Mar 1967, and *Tarbatness* Sept 1967. *Lyness* is an Air-Stores Support Ship.

LYNESS *1972*

AIR STORE SUPPORT SHIPS

(See Lyness above)

RELIANT (ex-*Somersby*) A 84

Displacement, tons	4 447 light as built; 13 737 full load
Measurement, tons	9 290 deadweight (summer), 8 460 gross
Dimensions, feet	440 pp; 468·8 oa × 61·5 × 26·2
Main engines	Doxford 6 cyl, diesel; 8 250 bhp = 18 knots
Complement	110 officers and men

Built by Sir James Laing & Sons Ltd, Sunderland. Engined by Hawthorne Leslie. Completed in 1954. Converted for her new role at North Shields. Sailed from Chatham on 4 Nov 1958 for the Far East as the Royal Navy's first air/victualling stores issuing ship capable of replenishing aircraft carriers at sea. Has an endurance of 50 days steaming at 16 knots, and carries 40 000 different patterns of aircraft spares and general naval stores. Fully air-conditioned for service in the tropics. Her conversion was based on the concept that aircraft carriers should be able to spend more time at sea, independant of shore bases. Originally named *Somersby*. Renamed *Reliant* in 1958. As refitted she has a helicopter pad aft for stores transfer. Soon reducing to reserve.

RELIANT *1970, Courtesy Godfrey H. Walker* Esq.

FLEET REPLENISHMENT SHIPS

REGENT A 486 **RESOURCE** A 480

Displacement, tons	19 000 full load (deep departure)
Measurement, tons	18 029 gross
Dimensions, feet	600·0 pp; 640·0 oa × 77·2 × 26·1
Aircraft	1 Wessex helicopter
Guns	2—40 mm Bofors (single)
Main engines	AEI steam turbines; 20 000 shp = 20 knots
Complement	119 R.F.A. service and Merchant Navy officers and ratings; 52 Navy Dept industrial and non-industrial civil servants; 11 Royal Navy (1 officer and 10 ratings) for helicopter flying and maintenance

Ordered on 24 Jan 1963. Built by Scott's Shipbuilding & Engineering Co, Greenock, and Harland & Wolff, Belfast. They have lifts for armaments and stores, and helicopter platforms for transferring loads at sea. Designed from the outset as Fleet Replenishment Ships (previous ships had been converted merchant vessels). Air-conditioned. *Resource* was launched at Greenock on 11 Feb 1966, *Regent* at Belfast on 9 Mar 1966. Official title is Ammunition, Food, Explosives, Stores Ship (AFES).

REGENT *1971*

RESURGENT (ex-*Changchow*) A 280 **RETAINER** (ex-*Chungking*) A 329

Displacement, tons	14 000 (approx)
Measurement, tons	*Resurgent* 9 511 gross; *Retainer* 9 301 gross
Dimensions, feet	451 pp; 477·2 oa × 62 × 29 max
Main engines	Doxford diesel; 1 shaft; 6 500 bhp = 15 knots
Oil fuel (tons)	925

Built by Scotts' Shipbuilding and Engineering Co Ltd, Greenock, and completed in 1951 and 1950, respectively. *Retainer* was purchased in 1952 and converted into a naval storeship during autumn 1954-April 1955 by Palmers Hebburn Co Ltd, where further conversion was carried out Mar-Aug 1957 to extend her facilities as a stores ship, including the fitting out of holds to carry naval stores, the installation of lifts for stores, the provision of extra cargo handling gear and new bridge wings. *Resurgent* was taken over on completion for employment as a fleet replenishment ship.

RESURGENT *1971, Dr. Giorgio Arra*

ARMAMENT SUPPORT SHIPS

2 "FORT" CLASS

FORT ROSALIE A 186 **FORT SANDUSKY** A 316

Displacement, tons	5 250 light; 9 788 normal (13 820 full load)
Measurement, tons	8 570 deadweight; 7 201 to 7 332 gross
Dimensions, feet	416 pp; 424·5 wl; 441·5 oa × 57 × 27
Main engines	Triple expansion; 2 500 ihp = 11 knots
Boilers	3 SE cylindrical

Both launched in 1944. *Fort Rosalie* and *Fort Sandusky* are Armament Support Ships. Both laid up at Rosyth ,1 May 1972. New "Ness" class due to replace them.

CLASS. *Fort Beauharnois* was scrapped in 1962, *Fort Constantine* was broken up at Hamburg im 1969. *Fort Charlotte* sold in 1968. *Fort Duquesne* was broken up in Holland in 1967. *Fort Dunvegan* in 1969. *Fort Langley* was returned to the Canadian Government, it was officially stated in 1970; she arrived at Bilbao, Spain, to be broken up on 21 July 1970.

FORT ROSALIE *1971*

STORE CARRIERS

2 "BACCHUS" CLASS

BACCHUS A 404 **HEBE** A 406

Displacement, tons	2 740 light; 7 958 full load
Measurement, tons	4 823 gross; 2 441 net; 5 218 deadweight
Dimensions, feet	350 pp; 379 oa × 55 × 22 max
Main engines	Swan Hunter Sulzer diesel; 1 shaft; 5 500 bhp 15 knots
Oil fuel, tons	720
Complement	57

Storecarriers—*continued*

Built by Henry Robb Ltd, Leith, for the British India Steam Navigation Co. Taken over by the Royal Navy on completion on long term "bare-boat" charter. *Bacchus* was completed in Sep 1962, *Hebe* in May 1962. Crew accommodation and engines aft as in tankers.

HEBE (see Col. 1) *1969*

ROBERT DUNDAS A 204 **ROBERT MIDDLETON** A 241

Displacement, tons	900 light; 1 900 full load
Measurement, tons	1 000 deadweight; 1 125 gross
Dimensions, feet	210 pp; 222·5 oa × 36 × 13·5 mean
Main engines	Atlas Polar Diesel; 1 shaft; 960 bhp = 10·5 knots
Oil fuel, tons	60
Complement	17

Coastal store carriers. Both built by Grangemouth Dockyard Co Ltd. Machinery by British Auxiliaries Ltd, Govan. Launched on 28 July and 29 June 1938, respectively. *Robert Dundas* laid up.

ROBERT MIDDLETON *1969, Courtesy Godfrey H. Walker Esq.*

ROYAL MARITIME AUXILIARY SERVICE AND PORT AUXILIARY SERVICE

NOTE. To avoid over complication the ships and vessels of the Royal Naval Auxiliary Service and some of the Royal Corps of Transport are included here.

MOORING SALVAGE AND BOOM VESSELS

4 "WILD DUCK" CLASS

RMAS
GARGANEY P 194
MANDARIN P 192
GOOSANDER
POCHARD

PAS
GOLDENEYE P 195
PINTAIL P 193

Displacement, tons	950
Measurement, tons	283 deadweight
Dimensions, feet	150 pp; 168·2 excluding horns × 36·5 × 10·8
Main engines	1 Davey Paxman 16 cyl diesel; 1 shaft; controllable pitch propeller; 550 bhp = 10 knots
Range, miles	3 000 at 10 knots
Complement	24 (6 officers, 6 petty officers, 12 ratings)

GARGANEY *1969*

Mandarin was the first of a new class of marine service vessels. Launched on 17 Sep 1963 and handed over on 5 Mar 1964. *Pintail* was launched on 3 Dec 1963. Both built by Cammell Laird & Co Ltd, Birkenhead. Designed to be used for mooring, salvage and boom work. Previously these three tasks were separately undertaken by specialist vessels, but the new type is able to give all three services. Capable of laying out and servicing the heaviest moorings used by the Fleet and also maintaining booms for harbour defence. Heavy lifting equipment enables a wide range of salvage operations to be performed, especially in harbour clearance work. The special heavy winches have an ability for tidal lifts over the apron of 200 tons. *Gargeney* and *Goldeneye* were built in 1965-66 by Brooke Marine Ltd, Lowestoft. *Goosander* and *Pochard* are building.

MANDARIN *1969*

Mooring, Salvage and Boom Vessels—*continued*

LAYBURN P 191 RMAS **LAYMOOR** P 190 RN

Displacement, tons	800 standard; 1 050 full load
Dimensions, feet	160 pp; 192·7 oa × 34·5 × 11·5 feet
Main engines	Triple expansion; 1 shaft; 1 300 ihp = 10 knots
Boilers	2 Foster Wheeler "D" type; 200 psi
Complement	2 officers; 29 to 34 ratings

Both built by Wm, Simons & Co Ltd (Simons-Lobnitz Ltd). *Layburn*, which cost £565 000 was completed on 7 June 1960. *Laymoor* was accepted on 9 Dec 1959. Designed for naval or civilian manning. Lifting capacity is greater than that of predecessors; improvement in accommodation enables them to be operated in any climate.

LAYBURN *1970*

MOORSMAN P 284 RMAS

Displacement, tons	1 040 light; 1 510 full load
Dimensions, feet	196·9 oa × 35·5 × 13·5
Main engines	1 000 hp = 10 knots

Fitted with salvage pumps, air compressors and diving equipment. *Moorsman* is of the larger type built by H.M. Dockyard, Chatham. *Moorsman*, at Greenock, is civilian manned.

CLASS. *Moordale* was sold in 1961. *Moorburn* for disposal in 1962, *Mooress* and *Moorfowl* in 1963. In 1963 *Moorcock* was broken up at Troon, *Moorfield* was sold to Pounds, *Moorfire* was broken up at the Forth, *Moorfly* was sold as Sophia G. *Moorgrass* was broken up at Troon, *Moorgrieve* was sold and became *Octopus* in 1965. *Moorhill* was sold as Portuguese mercantile, *Moormyrtle* was broken up at Cork and *Moorside* was broken up on the Forth. *Moorpout* was for disposal in 1968, *Moorhen* and *Moorland* in 1970.

MOORHEN *1967, Wright & Logan*

BARFOOT P 202 **BARMOND** P 232

Displacement, tons	750 standard; 1 000 full load
Dimensions, feet	150 pp; 173·8 oa; 182 over horns × 23·2 × 11·5
Main engines	Triple expansion; 850 ihp = 11 knots (Sea speed 9 knots)
Boilers	2 single ended (200 lbs per sq in)
Fuel, tons	214 coal (*Barfoam* and *Barmond* converted to oil in 1966)
Radius, miles	3 000
Complement	32

Launched by Blyth DD & SB Co on 8 Jan 1940, John Lewis & Sons Ltd, Aberdeen on 25 Sep 1942, Philip & Son Ltd, Dartmouth on 18 July 1942, and Wm Simons & Co Ltd, Renfrew on 24 Dec 1942, respectively.
Bow lift of 27 to 70 tons. *Barhill* and *Barndale* were Port Auxiliary Service Craft. *Barfoot* and *Barmond* are also civilian manned.

TRANSFERS. *Barbrake* and *Barcross* were transferred to South Africa, *Barbarian*, *Barbette* (first of this name in the class, launched on 15 Dec 1937) and *Barfair* to Turkey, *Baron* to Ceylon in 1958 (purchased by the Colombo Port Commission).

BARFOOT

7 "KIN" CLASS RMAS

DISPENSER 22 Apr 43
KINBRACE A 281 17 Jan 45 (PAS)
KINGARTH A 232 22 May 44
KINLOSS A 482 14 Apr 45
UPLIFTER A 507 29 Nov 43

Mooring, Salvage and Boom Vessels—*continued*

Displacement, tons	950 standard; 1 050 full load
Measurement, tons	775 gross; 262 deadweight
Dimensions, feet	150·0 pp; 179·2 oa × 35·2 × 9·5 mean; 12·0 max
Main engines	*Kinbrace, Kingarth, Kinloss, Uplifter:* 1 British Polar Atlas M44M diesel; 630 bhp = 9 knots; Others: Triple expansion; 1 shaft; 600 ihp = 9 knots
Boilers	1 return tube cylindrical (30 ton) in others
Complement	34

Originally classified as Coastal Salvage Vessels, but re-rated Mooring, Salvage and Boom Vessels in 1971. Launch dates above. Equipped with horns and heavy rollers. Can lift 200 tons dead weight over the bow. *Kinbrace, Kingarth, Kinloss* and *Swin* were built by A. Hall, Aberdeen, *Succour* and *Uplifter* by Smith's Dock Co Ltd. *Uplifter* was the only salvage vessel wearing the White Ensign. She was laid down on 13 Feb 1943, and completed on 6 Apr 1944. (*Kingarth* wore the White Ensign in 1957). *Dispenser* was on charter to Liverpool & Glasgow Salvage Association, but returned in 1971. *Succour* and *Swin* were Royal Fleet Auxiliaries wearing the Blue Ensign. *Kinloss* is in the Port Auxiliary Service as a mooring vessel. *Kinbrace, Kingarth* and *Uplifter* were refitted with diesel engines in 1966-67, and *Kinloss* in 1963-64.
A photograph of *Kingarth* appears in the 1959-60 and earlier editions, of *Swin* in the 1956-57 and earlier editions, and of *Uplifter* in the 1960-61 to 1962-63 editions.

CLASS. *Lifeline* was on the disposal list in 1960. Sister ship *Help* was broken up in Holland in 1968.

KINLOSS *1966, Wright & Logan*

OILERS

6 "OILPRESS" CLASS

OILBIRD Y 25
OILFIELD Y 24
OILMAN Y 26
OILPRESS Y 21
OILSTONE Y 22
OILWELL Y 23

Displacement, tons	280 standard; 530 full load
Dimensions, feet	130·0 wl; 139·5 oa × 30·0 × 8·3
Main engines	1 Lister Blackstone ES6 diesel; 1 shaft; 405 shp at 900 rpm
Complement	11 (4 officers and 7 ratings)

Coastal tankers. Ordered on 10 May 1967 from Appledore Shipbuilders Ltd. Three are diesel oil carriers and three FFO carriers.

OILWELL *1972, Dr. Giorgio Arra*

TRIALS SHIP

1 NEW CONSTRUCTION

WHITEHEAD ETV 01

Displacement, tons	3 040 full load (official figures)
Dimensions, feet	291·0 wl; 319·0 oa × 48·0 × 17·0
Main engines	2 Paxman 12 YLCM diesels; 1 shaft; 3 400 bhp = 15·5 knots
Endurance, miles	4 000 nautical at 12 knots
Complement,	10 officers, 32 ratings, 15 trials and scientific staff

Designed to provide mobile preparation, firing and control facilities for weapons and research vehicles. Built by Scotts, Shipbuilding Co Ltd, Greenock. Launched on 5 May 1970. Named after Robert Whitehead, the torpedo development pioneer and engineer. Fitted with equipment for tracking weapons and targets and for analysing the results of trials.

WHITEHEAD *1972*

CONTROLLED MINELAYERS

3 "MINER" CLASS

MINER III (RMAS) **BRITANNIC** **STEADY** (PAS)

Displacement, tons: 300 standard; (355 full load)
Dimensions, feet: 110·2 × 26·5 × 8·0
Main engines: Ruston & Hornsby diesels; 2 shafts; 360 bhp = 10 knots

All built by Philip & Son Ltd, Dartmouth, and engined by Ruston & Hornsby Ltd, Lincoln. *Miner V* was converted into a cable lighter and renamed *Britannic* in 1960 with PAS as store carrier. A photograph of *Britannic* appears in the 1969-70 to 1971-72 editions. *Miner VII* was adapted as a stabilisation trials ship at Portsmouth and renamed *Steady* in 1960 with PAS. *Miner III* was a tender for Clearance Diving Teams attached to HMS *Vernon* shore establishment but was relieved by the coastal minesweeper *Laleston* as diving trials ship in 1967. *Miner III* is now RMAS diving tender at Pembroke Dock. *Miner IV* and *Mindful* (ex-*Miner VIII*) were sold in 1965, *Minstrel* (ex-*Miner I*) was for disposal in 1965 and *Miner VI* in 1968. *Gossamer* (ex-*Miner II*) was damaged as a target and sunk by Iranian destroyer *Artemiz* off the Dorset coast in 1970. The coastal minelayer *Plover* was scrapped in 1968.

MINER III — *1972, Wright & Logan*

TORPEDO RECOVERY VESSELS

TORRENT A 127 **TORRID** A 128

Measurement, tons: 550 gross
Length, feet: 151·0
Main engines: Paxman diesels; 700 bhp = 12 knots

Torrent was completed in Sept 1971 and *Torrid* in Jan 1972.

TORRENT — *1972*

THOMAS GRANT PAS

Displacement, tons: 209 light; 461 full load
Measurement, tons: 252 deadweight; 218 gross
Dimensions, feet: 113·5 × 25·5 × 8·8
Main engines: 2 diesels; Speed = 9 knots

Built as a local store carrier by Charles Hill & Sons Ltd, Bristol. Launched on 11 May 1953 and completed in July 1953. Converted into a torpedo recovery vessel in 1968.

THOMAS GRANT — *Added 1969*

LANDING CRAFT

9 LCT (8) TYPE (RCT)

AACHEN L 4062 **ABBEVILLE** L 4041 **AGHEILA** L 4002 **AKYAB** (ex-*Rampart*) L 4037 **ANDALNES** L 4097 **ANTWERP** L 4074 **AREZZO** L 4128 **ARAKAN** L 4164 **AUDEMER** L 4061

Displacement, tons: 657 light; 895 to 1 017 loaded
Dimensions, feet: 225 pp; 231·2 oa × 39 × 3·2 forward; 5 aft
Beaching draughts
Main engines: 4 Paxman engines; 1 840 bhp 12·6 knots (9 knots cruising)
Complement: 33 to 37

Akyab has lattice mast aft and deckhouse forward. *LCT* (8) 4002 (*Agheila*), 4037 (*Akyab*, ex-*Rampart*), 4041 (*Abbeville*), 4061 (*Audemer*), 4062 (*Aachen*), 4073 (*Ardennes*), 4074 (*Antwerp*), 4085 (*Agedabia*), 4086 (*Arromanches*), which has a large lattice mast forward, 4097 (*Andalnes*), 4182 (*Arezzo*) and 4164 (*Arakan*) were transferred from the Royal Navy to the Army.

CLASS. *LCT* (8) 4042, 4045, 4050, 4148, 4156 and 4165 were stricken from the list in 1958, and 4025, 4049, 4063 and 4098 in 1960. *LCT* (8) 4063, *Jawada*, on loan to a commercial company, was for disposal at Bahrein. *Redoubt*, L 4001, was sold in 1966 as *Dimitris* 9, and *Sallyport*, L 4064, was sold in 1967 as *Fedra*. *Counterguard*, L 4043 was sold to Malaysia in 1965 and renamed *Sri Langkawi*. *Buttress*, L 4099, was sold to France, in July 1965 and renamed L 9061. *Parapet*, L 4039, was sold to La Société Maseline Ltd (Merchants), Sark, in 1966. *Bastion*, L 4040, was sold to Zambia on 15 Sep 1966. *Citadel*, L 4038, and *Portcullis*, L 4044, which were to have been converted into fleet degaussing vessels, were deleted from the Navy List in 1969. *Agedabia* L 4085 was sold and *Ardennes* L 4073 and *Arromanches* L 4086 were acquired by Singapore in 1970.

AUDEMER — *1968, Skyfotos*

ANDALNES — *1969, Skyfotos*

CABLE SHIPS

RMAS

BULLFINCH (19 Aug 1940) A 176 **ST. MARGARETS** (13 Oct 1943) A 259

Displacement, tons: 1 300 light; 2 500 full load
Measurement, tons: 1 524 gross; 1 200 deadweight
Dimensions, feet: 228·8 pp; 252 oa × 36·5 × 16·3 mean
Main engines: Triple expansion; 2 shafts; 1 250 ihp = 12 knots

Both built by Swan, Hunter & Wigham Richardson Ltd. Launch dates above. *Bullfrog* and *Bullhead* of this type were transferred to Cable and Wireless service in 1947. Provision was made for mounting one 4 inch gun and four 20 mm AA guns but no armament is fitted. A photograph of *St Margarets* appears in the 1967-68 to 1971-72 editions.

BULLFINCH — *1970*

EXPERIMENTAL TRIALS VESSELS

1 NEW CONSTRUCTION

CRYSTAL RDV 01 Dockyard control

Displacement, tons	3 040 deep
Dimensions, feet	410·0 wl; 413·5 × 56·0 × 5·5
Complement	60, including scientists

Unpowered floating platform for Sonar Research and Development. Built at H.M. Dockyard, Devonport. Ordered in Dec 1969. Begun in Mar 1970 for completion in Sep 1971. A harbour-based laboratory without propulsion machinery or steering which will provide the Admiralty Underwater Weapons Establishment at Portland with a stable platform on which to carry out acoustic tests and other research projects.

CRYSTAL 1972

WHIMBREL (ex-*NSC* (E) 1012) PAS

Displacement, tons	300
Dimensions, feet	190 × 30 × 4·5

Experimental Trials Vessel. Basically of the tank landing craft LCT (3) Type.

WHIMBREL *1968, A. & J. Pavia*

ICEWHALE PAS

Displacement, tons	289 standard; 350 full load
Dimensions, feet	120 × 24 × 9
Main engines	Speed = 9 knots
Complement	12 (Master, Mate and 10 ratings)

Experimental Trials Vessel for the Underwater Weapons Establishment, Portland.

ICEWHALE *1968, John G. Callis*

ARMAMENT CARRIERS

KINTERBURY A 378 **THROSK**

Displacement, tons	1 490 standard; 1 770 full load
Measurement, tons	600 deadweight
Dimensions, feet	185 pp; 199·8 × 34·3 × 13
Main engines	Triple expansion; 1 shaft; 900 ihp = 11 knots
Coal, tons	154

Launched on 14 Nov 1942 and in 1943 and completed on 4 Mar 1943 and 22 Dec 1943, respectively. Both built by Philip & Son Ltd. Rated as naval armament carriers Converted in 1959 with hold stowage and a derrick for handling guided missiles for attending and servicing the guided weapons trials ship *Girdle Ness.*

Armament Carriers—*continued*

KINTERBURY *1972, Wright & Logan*

BOWSTRING **CATAPULT** **FLINTLOCK**

Of various displacements and data. *Blowpipe* and *Obus* sold. *Ballista, Matchlock* and *Spear* deleted.

MAXIM A 377

Displacement, tons	604 to 663
Measurement, tons	340 deadweight
Dimensions, feet	144·5 × 25 × 8
Main engines	Reciprocating; 500 ihp = 9 knots
Complement	13

Built by Lobnitz & Co Ltd, Renfrew. Launched on 6 Aug 1945. *Chattenden* was reduced in 1961 to a dumb derrick lighter. *Snider* was disposed of in 1968. *Enfield* was sold in 1969. *Gatling* was broken up at Cork in 1970. *Nordenfelt* deleted.

WATER CARRIERS

4 "WATER" CLASS

WATERFALL Y 17
WATERSHED Y 18
WATERSIDE Y 20
WATERSPOUT Y 19

Measurement, tons	285 gross
Dimensions, feet	123 pp, 131·5 oa × 24·8 × 8
Main engines	Diesels; 1 shaft; 1 100 bhp = 11 knots

Built by Drypool Engineering & Drydock Co, Hull. Launched on 30 Mar 1966, 3 Aug 1966, 20 June 1967 and 29 Dec 1966, respectively. A photograph of *Watershed* appears in the 1969-70 to 1971-72 editions.

WATERFALL *1972, Wright & Logan*

4 "SPA" CLASS

SPALAKE (10 Aug 1946) A 260
SPAPOOL (28 Feb 1946) A 222
SPABROOK (24 Aug 1944) A 224
SPABURN (5 Jan 1946) A 257

Displacement, tons	1 219 full load
Measurement, tons	630 deadweight; 672 to 719 gross
Dimensions, feet	160 pp; 172 oa × 30 × 12
Main engines	Triple expansion; 675 ihp = 9 knots
Coal, tons	90

Spalake and *Spapool* were built by Charles Hill & Sons Ltd, Bristol and *Spabrook* and *Spaburn* by Philip & Son Ltd, Dartmouth. *Spabeck*, high test peroxide carrier for the experimental submarine *Explorer*, was disposed of in May 1966. *Spapool* in Mombasa.

SPAPOOL **1971**

Water Carriers—*continued*

6 "FRESH" CLASS

FRESHBURN **FRESHLAKE** **FRESHMERE** **FRESHPOND** **FRESHPOOL** **FRESHSPRING**

Displacement, tons: 594
Dimensions, feet: 126·2 × 25·5 × 10·8 max
Main engines: Triple expansion; 450 ihp = 9 knots

Freshspring was converted from coal to oil fuel, in 1961. A photograph of *Freshpond* appears in the 1951-52 to 1953-54 editions and of *Freshlake* in the 1963-64 to 1965-66 editions. *Freshbrook* and *Freshnet* were stricken in 1963, *Freshwater* and *Freshwell* sold in 1968, and *Freshford, Freshspray* and *Freshtarn* in 1969. *Freshener* was for disposal in 1971. *Freshpool* is in reserve.

FRESHPOOL — *1966, courtesy Dr. Giorgio Arra*

TUGS

ROYSTERER

3 NEW CONSTRUCTION OCEAN TUGS RMAS

ROBUST PAS **ROLLICKER** **ROYSTERER**

Displacement, tons: 1 630 full load
Dimensions, feet: 162·0 pp; 178·0 oa × 38·5 × 21·3
Main engines: 2 Mirrlees KMR 6 diesels (by Lister Blackstone Mirrlees Marine Ltd); 2 shafts; 4 500 bhp at 525 rpm = 15 knots
Endurance, miles: 13 000 nautical at 12 knots
Complement: 31 (10 officers and 21 ratings) (and able to carry salvage party of 10 RN officers and ratings)

These are the biggest and most powerful ocean tugs ever built for the Royal Navy. Built by Charles D. Holmes at Beverley Shipyard, Hull. Designed principally for salvage and long range towage but can be used for general harbour duties. Cost over £2 million apiece.

TYPHOON A 95

Displacement, tons: 800 standard; 1 380 full load
Dimensions, feet: 181·0 pp; 200·0 oa × 40·0 × 13·0
Main engines: 2 turbocharged vee type 12-cyl diesels; 1 shaft; 2 750 bhp = over 16 knots

Built by Henry Robb & Co Ltd, Leith. Launched on 14 Oct 1958. Completed in 1960. Diesels manufactured by Vickers-Armstrongs Ltd, Barrow-in-Furness. The machinery arrangement of two diesels geared to a single shaft was an innovation for naval ocean tugs. Controllable pitch propeller, 150 rpm. Fitted for fire fighting, salvage and ocean rescue, with a heavy mainmast and derrick attached. Bollard pull 32 tons.

TYPHOON — *1970*

5 "CON" CLASS RMAS

ACCORD **ADVICE** **AGILE** **CONFIANCE** (15 Nov 1955) A 289 PAS **CONFIDENT** (17 Jan 1956) A 290 PAS

Displacement, tons: 760 full load
Dimensions, feet: 140·0 pp; 154·8 oa × 35·0 × 11·0
Main engines: 4 Paxman HAXM diesels; 2 shafts; 1 800 bhp = 13 knots
Complement: 29 plus 13 salvage party

Confiance and *Confident* were built by A. & J. Inglis Ltd, Glasgow. Launch dates above. *Confiance* was completed on 27 Mar 1956. Fitted with 2·50 m diam Stone Kamewa controllable pitch propellers. *Accord, Advice* and *Agile*, formerly rated as dockyard tugs' were officially added to the "Confiance "class in 1971 as part of the Royal Maritime Auxiliary Service ocean towing force. Fitted for 1—40 mm AA.

Tugs—*continued*

AGILE — *1972, John G. Callis*

3 "SAMSON" CLASS PAS

SAMSON (14 May 1953) A 390 **SEA GIANT** (2 June 1954) A 288 **SUPERMAN** (23 Nov 1953)

Displacement, tons: 1 200 full load
Measurement, tons: 850 gross
Dimensions, feet: 165 pp; 180 oa × 37 × 14
Main engines: Triple expansion; 2 shafts; 3 000 ihp = 15 knots

All built and engined by Alexander Hall & Co Ltd, Aberdeen. Launch dates above. A photograph of *Superman* appears in the 1969-70 to 1971-72 editions.

SEA GIANT — *1972, John G. Callis*

2 "BUSTLER" CLASS

CYCLONE (ex-*Growler*, 10 Sep 1942) A 111 **REWARD** (13 Oct 1944) A 264

Displacement, tons: 1 118 light; 1 630 full load
Dimensions, feet: 190·0 pp; 205·0 oa × 40·2 × 16·8
Main engines: 2 Atlas Polar 8-cyl diesels; 1 shaft; 4 000 bhp = 16 knots
Oil fuel, tons: 405
Range, miles: 17 000
Complement: 42

All built by Henry Robb Ltd, Leith.

6 FLEET SERVICING TUGS PAS

EMPIRE ACE **EMPIRE ROSA** **EMPIRE DEMON** **FRISKY** **EMPIRE FRED** **RESOLVE**

All slightly different.

BOMSHELL CLASS PAS

CANNON	**EMINENT**	**HANDMAID**	**SECURITY**
CHAINSHOT	**FIDGET**	**IMPETUS**	**TAMPEON**
DIVER	**FOREMOST**	**INTEGRITY**	**TRUNNION**
DRIVER	**FREEDOM**	**PROMPT**	**VAGRANT**
	GRAPESHOT	**RESOLVE**	**WEASEL**

Harbour diesel tugs.

7 DIRECTOR CLASS PAS

DEXTROUS A93 **DIRECTOR** A94 **FAITHFUL** A85 **FORCEFUL** A86 **FAVORITE** A87 **GRIPER** A91 **GRINDER** A92

Displacement, tons: 710 full load
Dimensions, feet: 157·2 oa × 30 (60 over paddle boxes) × 10
Main engines: Paxman diesels and BTH motors; diesel electric; 2 shafts; 2 paddle wheels; 2 000 bhp = 13 knots
Complement: 21

Modern paddlers.

FORCEFUL — *1969, courtesy Dr. Giorgio Arra*

Tugs—*continued*

20 "DOG" CLASS PAS

AIREDALE
ALSATIAN
BASSET
BEAGLE
BOXER
CAIRN
COLLIE
CORGI
DALMATIAN
DEERHOUND
ELKHOUND
HUSKY
LABRADOR
MASTIFF
POINTER
SALUKI
SEALYHAM
SETTER
SHEEPDOG
SPANIEL

Medium berthing tugs.

SEALYHAM ("Dog" Class) *1972, Michael D. J. Lennon*

8 "GIRL" CLASS
10 "IMPROVED GIRL" CLASS PAS

AGATHA
AGNES
ALICE
AUDREY
BARBARA
BETTY
BRENDA
BRIDGET
CELIA
CHARLOTTE
CHRISTINE
CLARE
DAISY
DAPHNE
DORIS
DOROTHY
EDITH
FELICITY

Harbour berthing tugs. What comes after an "Improved Girl" is not mentioned officially.

FLEET TENDERS

BEE **CICADA** **CRICKET** **GNAT** **LADYBIRD** **SCARAB** (RMAS)

Displacement, tons	450 full load
Dimensions, feet	111·8 oa × 28 × 11
Main engines	Lister-Blackstone Diesels; 1 shaft; 660 bhp = 10·5 knots
Complement	10

All built by C. D. Holmes Ltd, Beverley, Yorks in 1970-71, first three as stores carriers, two as armament carriers and *Scarab*, as mooring vessel.

BEE *1971, John G. Callis*

12 "ABERDOVEY" CLASS

ABERDOVEY
ABINGER
ALNESS
ALNMOUTH
APPLEBY
ASHCOTT
BEAULIEU
BEDDGELERT
BEMBRIDGE
BIBURY
BLAKENEY
BRODICK

Displacement, tons	117·5 full load
Dimensions, feet	79·8 oa × 18 × 5·5
Main engines	1 Lister-Blackstone Diesel; 1 shaft; 225 bhp = 10·5 knots
Complement	6

"A" names built by Isaac Pimblott & Sons, Northwich. "B" names by J. S. Doig, Grimsby 1963-71. Sixty fleet tenders are planned to replace the ageing MFV's. Multi-purpose for stores (25 tons), passengers (200 standing) plus a couple of torpedos

APPLEBY *1971, Wright & Logan*

Fleet Tenders—*continued*

23 "CARTMEL" CLASS

CARTMEL
CAWSAND
CLOVELLY
CRICCIETH
CRICKLADE
CROMARTY
DATCHET
DENMEAD
DORNOCH
DUNSTER
ELKSTONE
ELSING
EPWORTH
ETTRICK
FELSTED (RMAS)
FINTRY
FOTHERBY
FROXFIELD
FULBECK
GLENCOVE
GRASMERE
HOLMWOOD
HORNING

Displacement, tons	143 full load
Dimensions, feet	80 oa × 21 × 6·5
Main engines	1 Lister-Blackstone diesel; 1 shaft; 320 bhp = 10·5 knots
Complement	6

All fleet tenders as *"Aberdovey"* class except *Datchet*, diving tender with Gray diesels, 2 shafts, 450 bhp = 12 knots and *Felsted* with RMAS. Builders — first 4 "C"s and *Glencove* by Pimblott; *Cricklade, Denmead* and *Fulbeck* by C. D. Holmes, Beverley; *Cromarty, Dornoch, Fintry* and *Grasmere* by J. Lewis, Aberdeen; four "E"s by J. Cook Wivenhoe; *Datchet* by Vospers; remainder by R. Dunston, Thorne.

4 "LOYAL" CLASS

LOYAL FACTOR A 382
LOYAL GOVERNOR A510
LOYAL CHANCELLOR
LOYAL PROCTOR

Details as for "Cartmel" class. All employed by RNXS.

61 MFV TYPES

MFV 2, 7, 15, 63, 93, 96, 119, 139, 140, 175, 205, 256, 278, 289,
Length: 61·5 feet
MFV 642, 658, 686, 715, 740, 767, 775, 816, 911,
Length: 45 feet
MFV 1021, 1033, 1037, 1048, 1051, 1062, 1077, 1151, 1190, 1255
Length: 75 feet
MV 1527 Length: 90 feet

MFV 1151, Squirrel and *MVF 1080, Watchful* were used as Fishery Protection Gunboats until replaced. *MFVs* 105, 1021 and 1528 were deleted from the list in 1969, 7, 43, 45, 64, 65, 627, 657, 673 and 1254 in 1970, and 1015 in 1971.

TANK CLEANING VESSELS

7 "ISLES" CLASS

2 *Ardrossan Dockyard Co Ltd, Ardrossan*	
COLL A 333	7 Apr 1942
GRAEMSAY A 340	3 Aug 1942
2 *Cook, Welton & Gemmell Ltd, Beverley*	
BERN	2 May 1942
LUNDY A 366	29 Aug 1942
1 *A. & J. Inglis Ltd, Glasgow*	
SWITHA A 346	3 Apr 1942
3 *John Lewis & Sons Ltd, Aberdeen*	
CALDY A 332	31 Aug 1943
SKOMER A 338	17 June 1943

Displacement, tons	560 standard; 770 full load
Dimensions, feet	150 pp; 164 oa × 27·5 × 14
Main engines	Triple expansion; 1 shaft; 850 ihp = 12 knots
Boilers	1 cylindrical
Coal, tons	183

Launch dates above. Former minesweeping trawlers converted to tank cleaning vessels. Classed as port auxiliary service craft and have "A" pennant numbers. Sister ship *Bardsey*, also converted, was taken over by Malta Dockyard. For transfers, disposals and other particulars of "Isles" class trawlers see 1961-62 edition.

SWITHA *1967, J. W. Kennedy*

NUCLEAR DECONTAMINATION VESSEL

MAC 1012

New construction. Launched at Chatham early in 1971. Length 180 feet, beam 30 feet. To be used in connection with the disposal of radio active waste from the Chatham nuclear powered submarine refitting complex.

UNITED STATES OF AMERICA

Compiled and Edited by Norman Polmar

ADMINISTRATION

ecretary of the Navy:
John W. Warner

PRINCIPAL FLAG OFFICERS

'hairman, Joint Chiefs of Staff:
Admiral Thomas H. Moorer, USN

'hief of Naval Operations:
Admiral Elmo R. Zumwalt, Jnr, USN

ice Chief of Naval Operations:
Admiral Maurice F. Weisner, USN (to fall 1973)
Vice Admiral James K. Holloway, III, USN (from fall 1973)

eputy Chief of Naval Operations (Manpower and Naval Reserve):
Vice Admiral David H. Bagley, USN

eputy Chief of Naval Operations (Submarine Warfare):
Vice Admiral Eugene P. Wilkinson, USN

eputy Chief of Naval Operations (Surface Warfare):
Vice Admiral Robert E. Adamson, Jnr, USN

eputy Chief of Naval Opreations (Air Warfare):
Vice Admiral William D. Houser, USN

eputy Chief of Naval Operations (Logistics):
Vice Admiral Charles S. Minter, Jnr, USN

eputy Chief of Naval Operations (Plans and Policy):
Vice Admiral Frank W. Vannoy, USN

* **Commander-in-Chief Atlantic and Commander-in-Chief Atlantic Fleet:*
Admiral Ralph W. Cousins, USN

**Commander-in-Chief Pacific:*
Admiral Noel A. M. Gayler, USN

ommander-in-Chief Pacific Fleet:
Admiral Bernard A. Clarey, USN (to fall 1973)
Admiral Maurice F. Weisner, USN (from fall 1973)

ommander Third Fleet (Eastern Pacific):
Vice Admiral William T. Rapp, USN

ommander Second Fleet (Atlantic):
Vice Admiral John G. Finneran, USN

ommander Sixth Fleet (Mediterranean):
Vice Admiral Daniel J. Murphy, USN

ommander Seventh Fleet (Western Pacific):
Vice Admiral James K. Holloway, III, USN

ommander Military Sealift Command:
Rear Admiral John D. Chase, USN

hief of Naval Training:
Vice Admiral Malcolm W. Cagle, USN

hief of Naval Reserve:
Vice Admiral Damon W. Cooper, USN

ceanographer of the Navy:
Rear Admiral Joseph E. Snyder, Jnr, USN

MARINE CORPS

ommandant of the Marine Corps:
General Robert E. Cushman, Jnr, USMC

ssistant Commandant of the Marine Corps:
General Earl E. Anderson, USMC

hief of Staff:
Lieutenant General Foster C. Lahue, USMC

MATERIÉL

Chief of Naval Material:
Admiral Isaac C. Kidd, Jnr, USN

ommander Naval Air Systems Command:
Vice Admiral Kent L. Lee, USN

ommander Naval Electronic Systems Command:
Rear Admiral R. J. Schneider (ED), USN

ommander Naval Facilities Engineering Command:
Rear Admiral Albert R. Marschall, (CEC), USN

ommander Naval Ordnance Systems Command:
Rear Admiral Roger E. Spreen, USN

ommander Naval Ship Systems Command:
Rear Admiral Robert C. Gooding, (ED), USN

ommander Naval Supply Systems Command:
Rear Admiral Wallace R. Dowd, Jnr (SC), USN

DIPLOMATIC

Naval Attache and Naval Attaché for Air in London:
Rear Admiral Filmore B. Gilkeson, USN

Naval Attaché and Naval Attaché for Air in Moscow:
Rear Admiral James Mayo, USN

Naval Attaché and Naval Attaché for Air in Paris:
Captain Peter P. Cummins, USN

NOTE: *Unified Command with the Commander-in-Chief directing all US Army, Navy, and Air Force activities in the area. Only naval officers serving as Unified Commanders-in-Chief are listed. **In addition to Unified Commander, also Supreme Allied Commander Atlantic.

STRENGTH OF THE FLEET AND INDEX

The following table provides a tabulation of the ship strength of the United States Navy and an index to the ship listings within the United States section of this edition. Ship arrangement is based on function and employment; the official arrangement of ship types is contained in the "List of classifications of naval ships and service craft" which appears on a later page in this section. Numbers of ships listed in the table are estimated as of 1 July 1973 based on official and unofficial sources.

	Category-Type	*Active* a	*Building* b	*Reserve*
STRATEGIC MISSILE SUBMARINES				
SSBN	Ballistic Missile Submarines	41	—	—
SUBMARINES				
SSN	Attack Submarines (nuclear)	58	23	1
SSN	Research Submarines (nuclear)	2	—	—
SS	Attack Submarines (diesel post-war)	10	—	—
SS	Attack Submarines (diesel war-built)	10	—	6
SSG	Guided Missile Submarines (diesel)	—	—	1
LPSS	Transport Submarines	1	—	1
AGSS	Research Submarines	2	—	1
SST	Training Submarines	1	—	—
AIRCRAFT CARRIERS				
CVAN	Attack Carriers (nuclear)	1	2	—
CVA	Attack Carriers	13	—	1
CVS	Anti-Submarine Carriers	—	—	5
CVT	Training Carriers	1	—	—
SURFACE COMBATANTS				
	Sea Control Ships	1	—	—
CG	Missile Cruisers	3	—	—
CGN	Missile Cruisers (nuclear)	1	—	—
CLG	Light Missile Cruisers	4	—	2
DLGN	Missile Frigates (nuclear)	2	5	—
DLG	Missile Frigates	28	—	—
DL	Frigates (all-gun)	—	—	2
DDG	Missile Destroyers	29	—	—
DD	Destroyers (all-gun)	94	16	50
OCEAN ESCORTS				
PF	Patrol Frigates	—	1	—
DEG	Missile Escort Ships	6	—	—
DE-AGDE	Escort Ships (all-gun)	64	5	—
DE-DER	Escort Ships (war-built)	2	—	33
FIRE SUPPORT SHIPS				
BB	Battleships	—	—	4
CA	Heavy Cruisers	1	—	12
COMMAND AND COMMUNICATION SHIPS				
AGF	Miscellaneous Flagships	1	—	—
CC	National Command Ships	—	—	2
AGMR	Communication Relay Ships	—	—	2
AMPHIBIOUS WARFARE SHIPS				
LCC	Amphibious Command Ships	2	—	4
LHA	Amphibious Assault Ships	—	5	—
LPH	Amphibious Assault Ships	6	—	—
LKA	Amphibious Cargo Ships	6	—	12
LPA	Amphibious Transports	2	—	10
LPR	Amphibious Transports (small)	—	—	10
LPD	Amphibious Transport Docks	14	—	—
LSD	Dock Landing Ships	13	—	11
LST	Tank Landing Ships	20	—	27
LANDING CRAFT				
PATROL SHIPS AND CRAFT				
PG	Patrol Gunboats/Missile Boats	14	—	—
PHM	Patrol Hydrofoil Missile Boats	—	2	—
PGH	Patrol Gunboats (hydrofoil)	2	—	—
PCH	Patrol Craft (hydrofoil)	1	—	—
PTF	Fast Patrol Craft	17	—	—
RIVERINE WARFARE CRAFT				
SEAL SUPPORT CRAFT				
MINE WARFARE SHIPS				
MSO	Ocean Minesweepers	25	—	18
MSC	Coastal Minesweepers	11	—	2
MCS	Mine Countermeasure Ships	—	—	1
MINE WARFARE CRAFT				
UNDERWAY REPLENISHMENT SHIPS		61	1	20
FLEET SUPPORT SHIPS		83	5	48
LOGISTIC SUPPORT SHIPS		29	—	7
EXPERIMENTAL, RESEARCH AND SURVEYING SHIPS		44	2	5

Category-Type	Active a	Building b	Reserve
SERVICE CRAFT			
FLOATING DRY DOCKS			
DEEP SUBMERGENCE VEHICLES			

NOTES: (a) Includes ships undergoing overhaul and refuelling in the case of nuclear-powered ships; also includes approximately 30 destroyers, four ocean escorts, and 20 minesweepers (MSO-MSC) assigned to the Naval Reserve Force. (b) Generally includes ships authorised through Fiscal Year 1973 new construction programme although construction may not have begun.

Mercantile Marine

US Maritime Administration: 622 vessels of 8 782 000 tons gross active as of 1 Jan 1973 approx 575 additional vessels inactive of which half are to be scrapped.

Lloyd's Register of Shipping: 3 687 vessels of 15 024 148 tons gross.

Fiscal Year 1974 New Construction Programme

1 Nuclear-Powered FBM Submarine (Trident)
5 Nuclear-Powered Attack Submarines (SSN 688 class)
1 Nuclear-Powered Aircraft Carrier (CVAN 68 Class)
7 Destroyers (DD 963 Class)

Fiscal Year 1974 Conversion Programme

5 Nuclear-Powered FBM Submarines (SSBN) to Poseidon
1 Nuclear-Powered GM Frigate (DLGN) to improve AAW capability
2 Guided Missile Frigates (DLG) to improve AAW capability

Fiscal Year 1973 New Construction Programme

6 Nuclear-Powered Attack Submarines (SSN 688 class)
7 Destroyers (DD 963 class)
1 Patrol Frigate (PF)
2 Guided Missile Patrol Hydrofoils (PHM)
1 Destroyer Tender (AD 37 class)
1 Submarine Tender (AS 36 class)
2 Salvage and Rescue Tugs (ATS 1 class)

Fiscal Year 1973 Conversion Programme

2 Guided Missile Frigates (DLG) to improve AAW capability
6 Nuclear-Powered FBM Submarines (SSBN) to Poseidon
1 Submarine Tender (AS) to Poseidon support capability

Fiscal Year 1972 New Construction Programme

5 Nuclear-Powered Attack Submarines (SSN 688 class)
1 Nuclear-Powered Guided Missile Frigate (DLGN 38 class)
7 Destroyers (DD 963 class)
1 Replenishment Oiler (AOR 1 class)
1 Submarine Tender (AS 36 class)
1 Salvage and Rescue Tug (ATS 1 class)

Fiscal Year 1972 Conversion Programme

2 Guided Missile Frigates (DLG) to improve AAW capability
6 Nuclear-Powered Fleet Ballistic Missile Submarines (SSBN) to Poseidon

Fiscal Year 1971 New Construction Programme

1 Nuclear-Powered Guided Missile Frigate (DLGN)
4 Nuclear-Powered Attack Submarines (SSN)
6 Destroyers (DD)
2 Amphibious Assault Ships (LHA)
2 Oceanographic Research Ships (AGOR)

Fiscal Year 1971 Conversion Programme

6 Nuclear-Powered Fleet Ballistic Missile Submarines (SSBN) to Poseidon
4 Guided Missile Frigates (DLG) to improve AAW capability

The original FY 1971 programme has been modified as reflected above.

Fiscal Year 1970 New Construction Programme

1 Nuclear-Powered Attack Carrier (CVAN)
1 Nuclear-Powered Guided Missile Frigate (DLGN)
3 Destroyers (DD)
3 Nuclear-Powered Attack Submarines (SSN)
2 Amphibious Assault Ships (LHA)

Fiscal Year 1970 Conversion Programme

4 Nuclear-Powered Fleet Ballistic Missile Submarines (SSBN) to Poseidon
1 Guided Missile Frigate (DLG) to improve AAW capability
5 Ocean Minesweepers (MSO)

The original FY 1970 programme has been modified to reflect the above data.

Fiscal Year 1969 New Construction Programme

5 Destroyers, DD
2 Nuclear-Powered Attack Submarines, SSN
1 Amphibious Assault Ship, LHA
4 Fast Deployment Logistic Ships, FDL

Fiscal Year 1969 Conversion Programme

2 Nuclear-Powered Fleet Ballistic Missile Submarines, SSBN, to Poseidon
1 Guided Missile Frigate, DLG, to Terrier HT
1 Submarine Tender, AS, to Poseidon support
1 Cargo Ship, T-AK, to Poseidon support
1 Range Instrumentation Ship, T-AGM, to support Poseidon

Of the original FY 1969 programmes, the following ships were either deferred or cancelled, new construction 5 destroyers (DX), 1 All-Weather Patrol Boat (PB) 1 Destroyer Tender (AD), 1 Submarine Tender (AS), 4 Fast Deployment Logistic Ships (FDL), conversions 4 Fleet Ballistic Missile Submarines (SSBM) to Poseidon capability, 10 Ocean Minesweepers (MSO)

SPECIAL NOTES

United States Navy Ships that are in active commission are indicated by an asterisk next to the particular ship's name. It should be noted that this marking for active ships applies ONLY to the United States section of *Jane's Fighting Ships*.

The introductory passages in the United States section of this edition are based primarily on official United States Government statements and congressional hearings on the Fiscal Year 1974 Defense Budget. Any interpretation of these statements and hearings is solely the responsibility of the Compiler and Editor of the United States section, Mr. Norman Polmar.

PERSONNEL

	30 June 1972 (Actual)	30 June 1973 (Planned)	30 June 1974 (Planned)
Navy			
Officers	72 929	70 750	69 775
Enlisted men	511 789	498 686	492 282
Marine Corps			
Officers	19 249	19 053	18 945
Enlisted men	198 238	197 121	196 419

NAVAL AVIATION

US Naval Aviation currently consists of approx 5 500 aircraft flown by the Navy and Marine Corps. The principal naval aviation organisations are 14 carrier air wings, 24 maritime reconnaissance/patrol squadrons, and three Marine aircraft wings.
Fighters: approx 750 flown by 28 Navy carrier-based squadrons and 12 Marine squadrons. The Navy flies F-4 Phantoms from larger carriers, F-8 Crusaders from "Hancock" class carriers, and two squadrons are being equipped with F-14 Tomcats for assignments to the *Nimitz*. The Marine Corps has 12 squadrons with F-4 Phantoms.
Attack Aircraft: approx 1 270 flown by 42 Navy carrier-based squadrons and 13 Marine squadrons. The Navy flies A-6 Intruders and A-7 Corsairs from larger carriers, A-7 Corsairs or A-4 Skyhawks from "Hancock" class carriers, while the Marines fly A-6 Intruders and A-4 Skyhawks, except two Marine squadrons with AV-8A Harrier V/STOL aircraft.
(In addition to fighter and attack aircraft, carrier air wings have various combinations of E-1B Tracer or E-2A Hawkeye early warning aircraft, EA-6 Prowler or EKA-3 Skywarrior electronic warfare aircraft, RA-5C Vigilante or RF-8 Crusader reconnaissance aircraft, KA-6 Intruder tanker aircraft, S-2E Tracker anti-submarine aircraft, SH-3 Sea King anti-submarine aircraft, and utility aircraft and helicopters; Marine aircraft wings also have electronic warfare, reconnaissance, cargo, tanker, and utility aircraft and helicopters. Aircraft of these and other combat types also are assigned to readiness training, research, and developement squadrons.)
Patrol Aircraft: approx 400 P-3 Orion aircraft flown by 24 Navy patrol squadrons plus detachments and squadrons using special-mission EP-3, RP-3, and WP-3 aircraft for reconnaissance, weather reporting, and research.
Training Aircraft: approx 1 300 assigned to 27 Navy training squadrons.
Helicopters: approx 1 000 of all types used by Navy and Marine Corps.
Cargo, Transport, and Utility Aircraft: approx 450 of all types used by Navy and Marine Corps.
In addition to the above aircraft, the Naval Air Reserve Force has two carrier attack air wings (with F-8 Crusaders and A-4 Skyhawks), two anti-submarine carrier air groups (with S-2 Trackers and SH-3 Sea Kings), 12 patrol squadrons (with SP-2H Neptunes and P-3A Orions), and two transports quadrons. The Marine Reserve aircraft wing operates F-8 Crusaders, A-4 Skyhawks, and cargo and utility aircraft and helicopters.

MAJOR SHIPYARDS

Naval Shipyards

Boston Naval Shipyard, Boston, Massachusetts; being closed in 1973
Charleston Naval Shipyard, Charleston, South Carolina
Hunters Point Naval Shipyard, San Francisco, California (formerly a division of the San Francisco Bay Naval Shipyard and before that the San Francisco Naval Shipyard)
Long Beach Naval Shipyard, Long Beach, California
Mare Island Naval Shipyard, Vallejo, California (formerly a division of the San Francisco Bay Naval Shipyard); being closed in 1973
Norfolk Naval Shipyard, Norfolk, Virginia
Pearl Harbour Shipyard, Pearl Harbour, Hawaii
Philadelphia Naval Shipyard, Philadelphia, Pennsylvania
Portsmouth Naval Shipyard, Portsmouth, New Hampshire (located in Kittery, Maine)
Puget Sound Naval Shipyard, Bremerton, Washington

(Note: None of the above shipyards now is engaged in new construction, but are used for the overhaul and conversion of warships and auxiliaries.)

Commercial Shipyards

Avondale Shipyards, Inc, New Orleans, Louisiana
Bath Iron Works Corp, Bath, Maine
Bethlehem Steel Corp, Sparrows Point, Maryland
General Dynamics Corp, Electric Boat Division, Groton, Connecticut (formerly Electric Boat Company)
General Dynamics Corp, Quincy Shipbuilding Division, Quincy, Massachusetts (formerly Bethlehem Steel Corp Yard)
Ingalls Shipbuilding Corp (Litton Industries), East Bank Yard, Pascagoula, Mississippi
Ingalls Shipbuilding Corp (Litton Industries), West Bank Yard, Pascagoula, Mississippi
Lockheed Shipbuilding & Construction Co, Seattle, Washington
National Steel & Shipbuilding Co, San Diego, California
Newport News Shipbuilding & Dry Dock Co, Newport News, Virginia
Todd Shipyards Corp, San Pedro, California
Todd Shipyards Corp, Seattle, Washington

(Note: All of the above yards are engaged in naval and commercial shipbuilding, overhaul, and modernisation except for the General Dynamics/Electric Boat yard which is engaged only in submarine work.)

CLASSIFICATION OF NAVAL SHIPS AND SERVICE CRAFT

The following is the official US Navy list of classifications of naval ships and service craft as promulgated by the Secretary of the Navy. In actual usage, symbols preceded by the letter "E" indicate that the ship or craft is a prototype in an experimental or developmental status; the prefix "T" indicates that the ship is assigned to the Navy's Military Sealift Command and is civilian manned; and the prefix "F" indicates a ship being constructed by the United States for a foreign government.

COMBATANT SHIPS

(1) Warships

Aircraft Carriers:	
Attack Aircraft Carrier	CVA
Attack Aircraft Carrier (nuclear propulsion)	CVAN
ASW Aircraft Carrier	CVS
Surface Combatants:	
Battleship	BB
Heavy Cruiser	CA
Guided Missile Cruiser	CG
Guided Missile Cruiser (nuclear propulsion)	CGN
Light Cruiser	CL
Guided Missile Light Cruiser	CLG
Destroyer	DD
Guided Missile Destroyer	DDG
Radar Picket Destroyer	DDR
Frigate	DL
Guided Missile Frigate	DLG
Guided Missile Frigate (nuclear propulsion)	DLGN
Ocean Escorts:	
Escort Ship	DE
Guided Missile Escort Ship	DEG
Radar Picket Escort Ship	DER
Command Ship	CC
Submarines:	
Submarine	SS
Submarine (nuclear propulsion)	SSN
Guided Missile Submarine	SSG
Fleet Ballistic Missile Submarine (nuclear propulsion)	SSBN
Patrol Ships:	
Patrol Escort	PCE
Patrol Rescue Escort	PCER
Patrol Gunboat	PG

(2) Amphibious Warfare Ships

Amphibious Command Ship	LCC
Inshore Fire Support Ship	LFR
Amphibious Fire Support Ship	LFS
Amphibious Assault Ship (general purpose)	LHA
Amphibious Cargo Ship	LKA
Amphibious Transport	LPA
Amphibious Transport Dock	LPD
Amphibious Assault Ship	LPH
Amphibious Transport (small)	LPR
Amphibious Transport Submarine	LPSS
Dock Landing Ship	LSD
Tank Landing Ship	LST

(3) Mine Warfare Ships

Mine Countermeasures Ship	MCS
Minesweeper, Coastal (non-magnetic)	MSC
Minesweeper, Fleet (steel hulled)	MSF
Minesweeper, Ocean (non-magnetic)	MSO

COMBATANT CRAFT

(1) Patrol Craft

Patrol Craft (hydrofoil)	PCH
Patrol Gunboat (hydrofoil)	PGH
Fast Patrol Craft	PTF

(2) Landing Craft

Landing Craft, Assault	LCA
Landing Craft, Mechanised	LCM
Landing Craft, Personnel, Large	LCPL
Landing Craft, Personnel, Ramped	LCPR
Landing Craft, Utility	LCU
Landing Craft, Vehicle, Personnel	LCVP
Amphibious Warping Tug	LWT

(3) Mine Countermeasures Craft

Minesweeping Boat	MSB
Minesweeper, Drone	MSD
Minesweeper, Inshore	MSI
Minesweeping Launch	MSL
Minesweeper, River	MSM
Minesweeper, Patrol	MSR
Minesweeper, Special (Device)	MSS

(4) Riverine Warfare Craft

Assault Support Patrol Boat	ASPB
Armoured Troop Carrier	ATC
Command and Control Boat	CCB
Monitor	MON
River Patrol Boat	PBR
Patrol Craft, Inshore	PCF
Quiet Fast Boat	QFB
Riverine Utility Craft	RUC
Strike Assault Boat	STAB

(5) SEAL Support Craft

Landing Craft Swimmer Reconnaissance	LCSR
Light SEAL Support Craft	LSSC
Medium SEAL Support Craft	MSSC
Swimmer Delivery Vehicle	SDV

(6) Mobile Inshore Underseas Warfare (MIUW) Craft

MIUW Attack Craft	MAC

AUXILIARY SHIPS

Destroyer Tender	AD
Degaussing Ship	ADG
Ammunition Ship	AE
Store Ship	AF
Combat Store Ship	AFS
Miscellaneous	AG
Escort Research Ship	AGDE
Hydrofoil Research Ship	AGEH
Environmental Research Ship	AGER
Miscellaneous Command Ship	AGF
Missile Range Instrumentation Ship	AGM
Major Communications Relay Ship	AGMR
Oceanographic Research Ship	AGOR
Patrol Craft Tender	AGP
Radar Picket Ship	AGR
Surveying Ship	AGS
Auxiliary Submarine	AGSS
Technical Research Ship	AGTR
Hospital Ship	AH
Cargo Ship	AK
Cargo Ship Dock	AKD
Light Cargo Ship	AKL
Vehicle Cargo Ship	AKR
Stores Issue Ship	AKS
Cargo Ship and Aircraft Ferry	AKV
Net Laying Ship	ANL
Oiler	AO
Fast Combat Support Ship	AOE
Gasoline Tanker	AOG
Replenishment Oiler	AOR
Transport	AP
Self-propelled Barracks Ship	APB
Repair Ship	AR
Battle Damage Repair Ship	ARB
Cable Repairing Ship	ARC
Internal Combustion Engine Repair Ship	ARG
Landing Craft Repair Ship	ARL
Salvage Ship	ARS
Salvage Lifting Ship	ARSD
Salvage Craft Tender	ARST
Aircraft Repair Ship (Aircraft)	ARVA
Aircraft Repair Ship (Engine)	ARVE
Aircraft Repair Ship (Helicopter)	ARVH
Submarine Tender	AS
Submarine Rescue Ship	ASR
Auxiliary Ocean Tug	ATA
Fleet Ocean Tug	ATF
Salvage and Rescue Ship	ATS
Auxiliary Training Submarine	ATSS
Seaplane Tender	AV
Guided Missile Ship	AVM
Aviation Supply Ship	AVS
Auxiliary Aircraft Transport	AVT
Distilling Ship	AW
Training Aircraft Carrier	CVT
Fast Deployment Logistic Ship	FDL

SERVICE CRAFT*

Large Auxiliary Floating Dry Dock	AFDB
Small Auxiliary Floating Dry Dock	AFDL
Medium Auxiliary Floating Dry Dock	AFDM
Barracks Craft	APL
Auxiliary Repair Dry Dock	ARD
Medium Auxiliary Repair Dry Dock	ARDM
Deep Submergence Rescue Vehicle	DSRV
Deep Submergence Vehicle	DSV
Unclassified Miscellaneous	IX
Unclassified Miscellaneous Submarine	IXSS
Submersible Research Vehicle (nuclear propulsion)	NR
Target and Training Submarine (self-propelled)	SST
Submersible Craft (self-propelled)	X
Miscellaneous Auxiliary (self-propelled)	YAG
Open Lighter	YC
Car Float	YCF
Aircraft Transportation Lighter	YCV
Floating Crane	YD
Diving Tender	YDT
Covered Lighter (self-propelled)	YF
Ferryboat or Launch (self-propelled)	YFB
Yard Floating Dry Dock	YFD
Covered Lighter	YFN
Large Covered Lighter	YFNB
Dry Dock Companion Craft	YFND
Lighter (special purpose)	YFNX
Floating Power Barge	YFP
Refrigerated Covered Lighter (self-propelled)	YFR
Refrigerated Covered Lighter	YFRN
Covered Lighter (Range Tender) (self-propelled)	YFRT
Harbour Utility Craft (self-propelled)	YFU
Garbage Lighter (self-propelled)	YG
Garbage Lighter (non-self-propelled)	YGN
Salvage Lift Craft, Heavy	YHLC
Salvage Lift Craft, Light (self-propelled)	YLLC
Dredge (self-propelled)	YM
Salvage Lift Craft, Medium	YMLC
Gate Craft	YNG
Fuel Oil Barge (self-propelled)	YO
Gasoline Barge (self-propelled)	YOG
Gasoline Barge (non-self-propelled)	YOGN
Fuel Oil Barge (non-self-propelled)	YON
Oil Storage Barge	YOS
Patrol Craft (self-propelled)	YP
Floating Pile Driver	YPD
Floating Workshop	YR
Repair and Berthing Barge	YRB
Repair, Berthing and Messing Barge	YRBM
Floating Dry Dock Workshop (Hull)	YRDH
Floating Dry Dock Workshop (Machine)	YRDM
Radiological Repair Barge	YRR
Salvage Craft Tender	YRST
Seaplane Wrecking Derrick (self-propelled)	YSD
Sludge Removal Barge	YSR
Large Harbour Tug (self-propelled)	YTB
Small Harbour Tug (self-propelled)	YTL
Medium Harbour Tug (self-propelled)	YTM
Water Barge (self-propelled)	YW
Water Distilling Barge	YWDN
Water Barge (non-self-propelled)	YWN

*Self-propelled barges are indicated in parenthesis.

CLASSIFICATION OF MARITIME COMMISSION SHIP DESIGNS

Ships constructed under the jurisdiction of the US Maritime Commission by private shipyards are assigned Maritime Commission design classifications. These classifications consist of three groups of letters and numbers.

First group letter(s) indicate type of ship and number indicates size class. The letters of Maritime Commission ship classifications now on the US Navy List are:

Cargo	C
Emergency Cargo (Liberty)	EC
Passenger	P
Refrigerator	R
Special Purpose	S
Tanker	T
Victory Cargo	VC

Second group letter(s) indicate type of propulsion and number "2" indicates twin shaft ship and "4" quadruple shaft ship.

Motor (diesel)	M
Motor (diesel) Electric	ME
Steam (reciprocating or turbine)	S
Steam (turbine) Electric	SE

Third group of letters and numbers indicates the design of a particular type of ship, beginning with A1.

Fleet Ballistic Missile Submarines

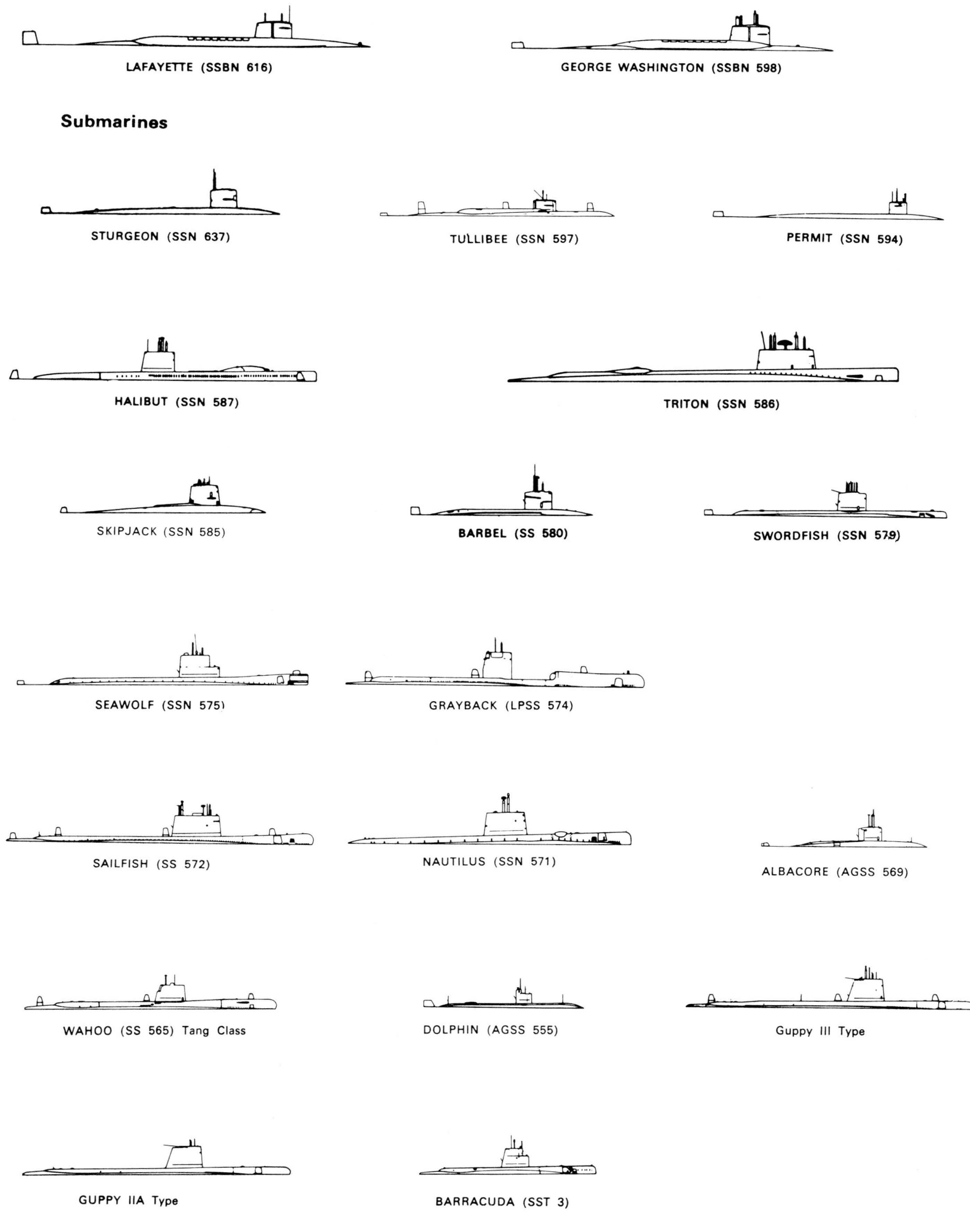

Scale: 1 inch = 150 feet (1 : 1 800)

Drawings by A. D. Baker

Aircraft Carriers

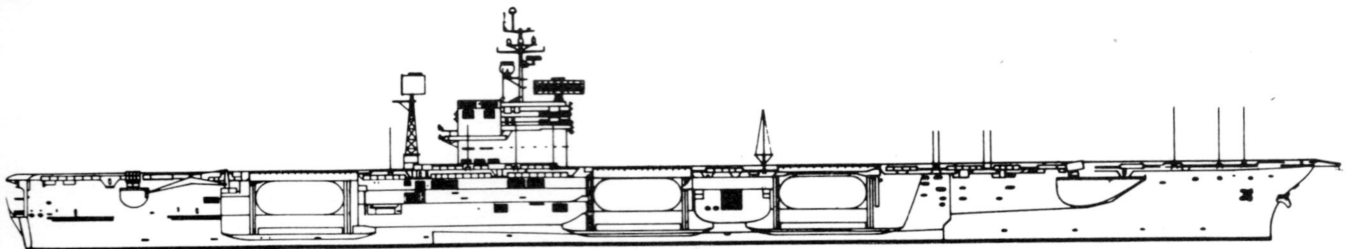

JOHN F. KENNEDY (CVA 67)

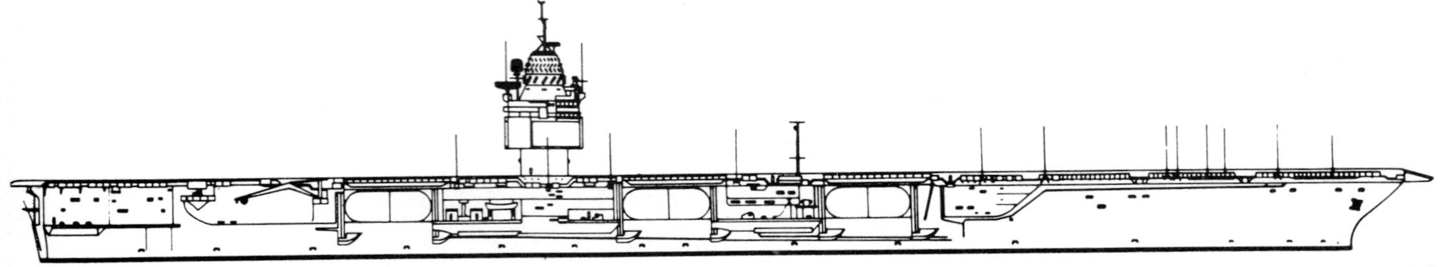

ENTERPRISE (CVAN 65)

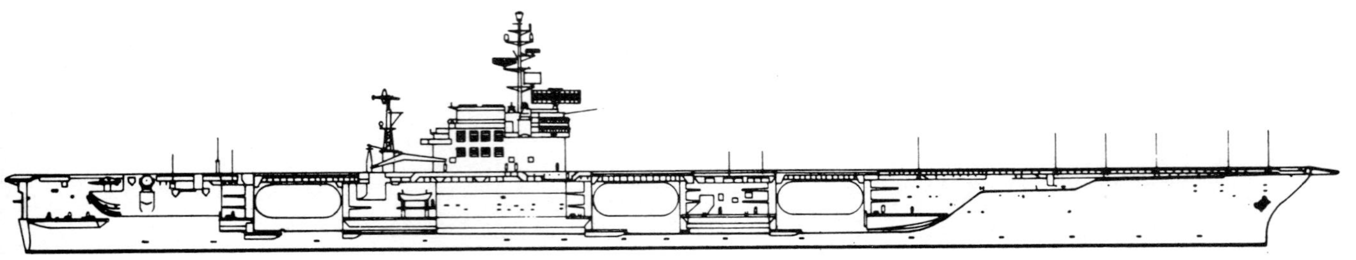

KITTY HAWK (CVA 63)

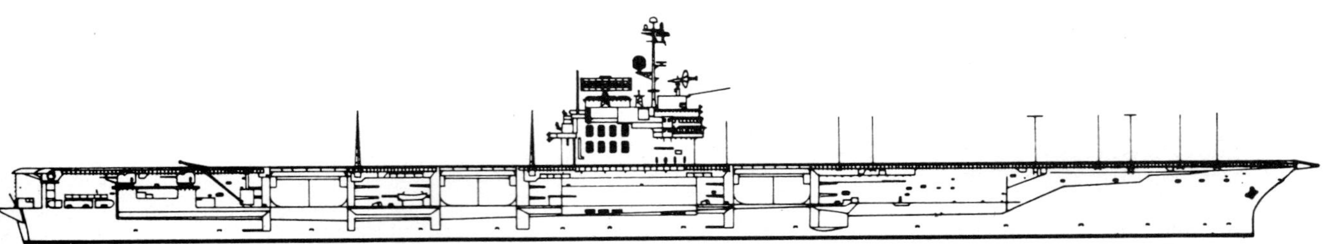

SARATOGA (CVA 60) Forrestal Class

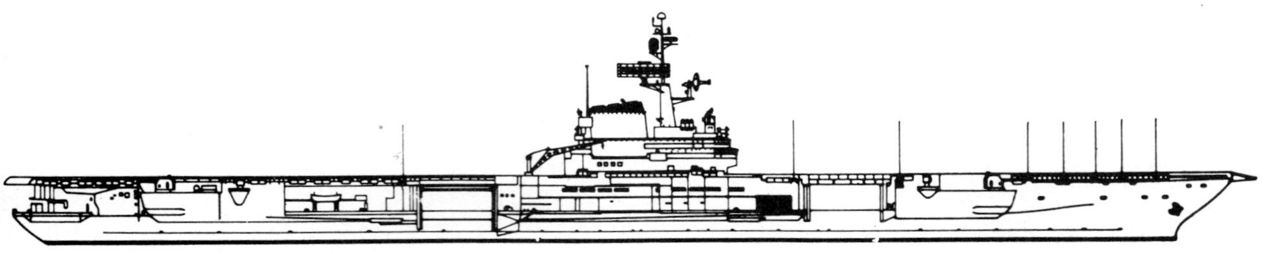

CORAL SEA (CVA 43) Midway Class (ROOSEVELT similar)

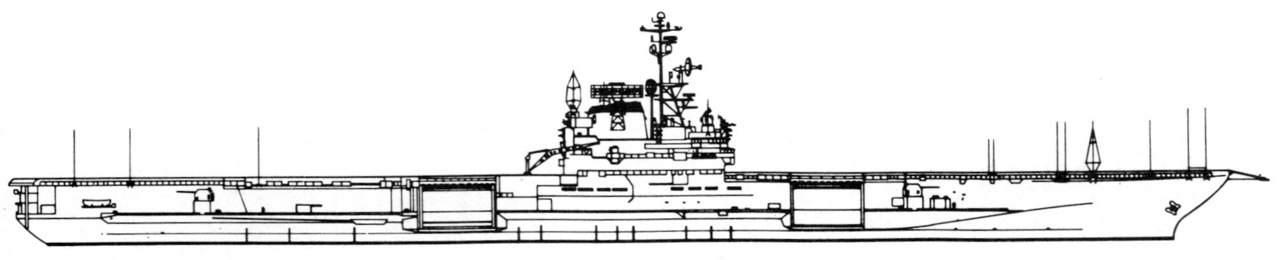

MIDWAY (CVA 41)

Scale: 1 inch = 150 feet (1 : 1 800)

Aircraft Carriers—*continued*

HANCOCK (CVA 19)

Guided Missile Cruisers

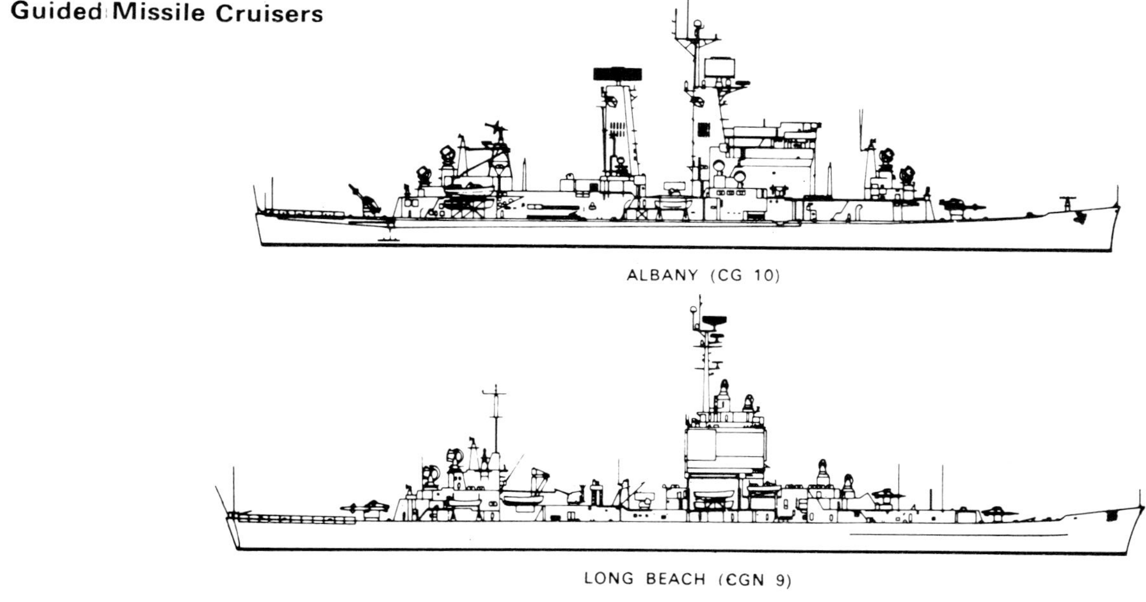

ALBANY (CG 10)

LONG BEACH (CGN 9)

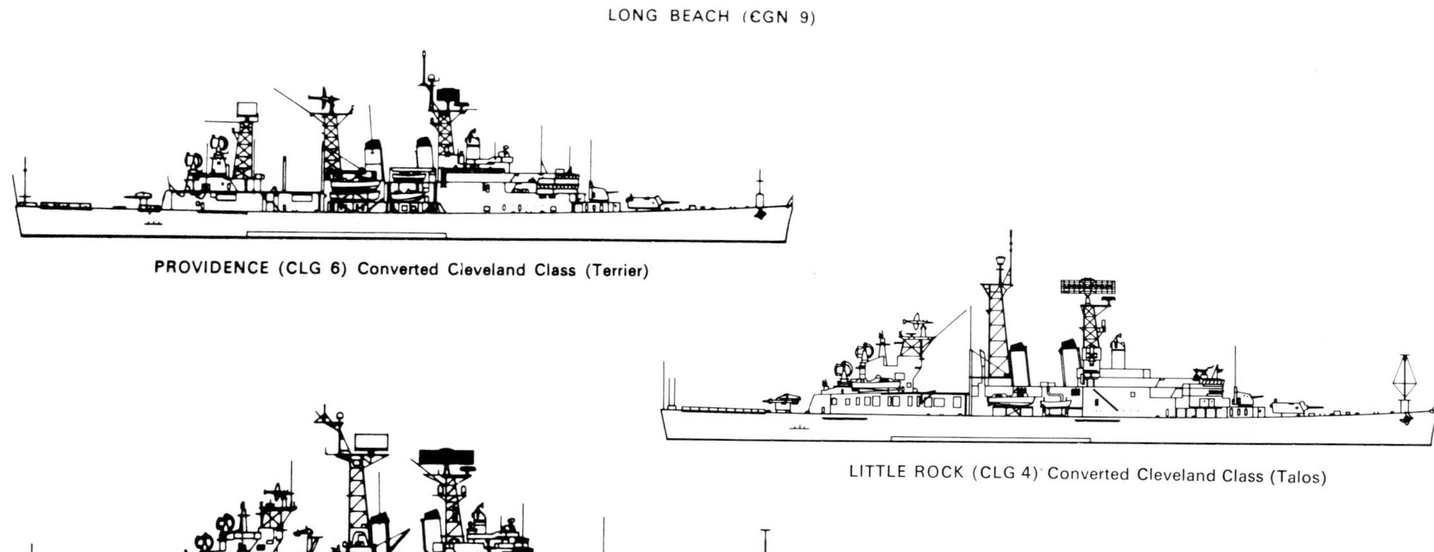

PROVIDENCE (CLG 6) Converted Cleveland Class (Terrier)

LITTLE ROCK (CLG 4) Converted Cleveland Class (Talos)

GALVESTON (CLG 3) Converted Cleveland Class (Talos)

Guided Missile Frigates

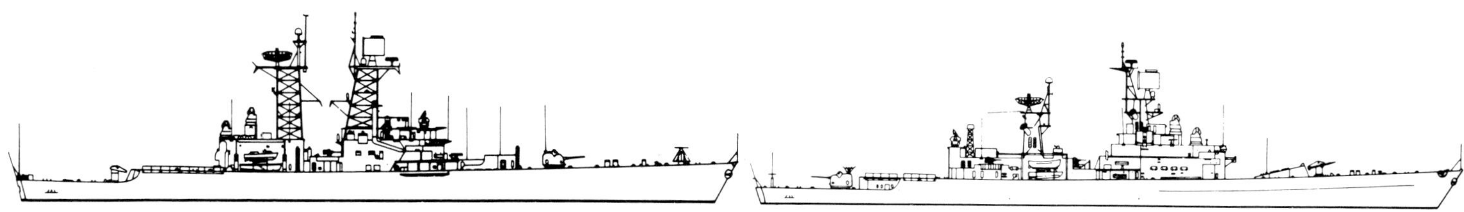

TRUXTUN (DLGN 35)

FOX (DLG 33) Belknap Class

Scale: 1 inch = 150 feet (1 : 1 800)

Guided Missile Frigates—*continued*

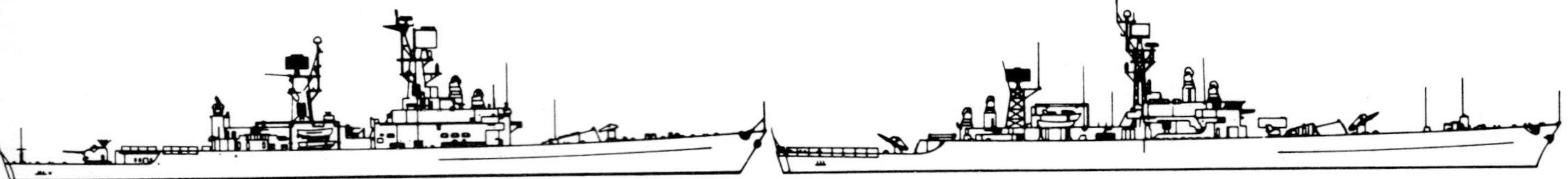

WAINWRIGHT (DLG 28) Belknap Class

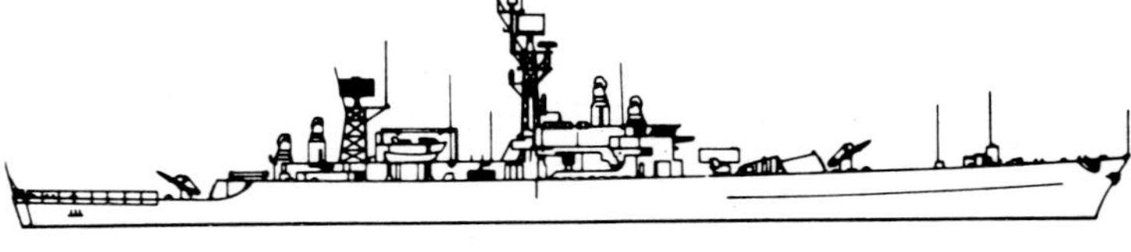

BAINBRIDGE (DLGN 25)

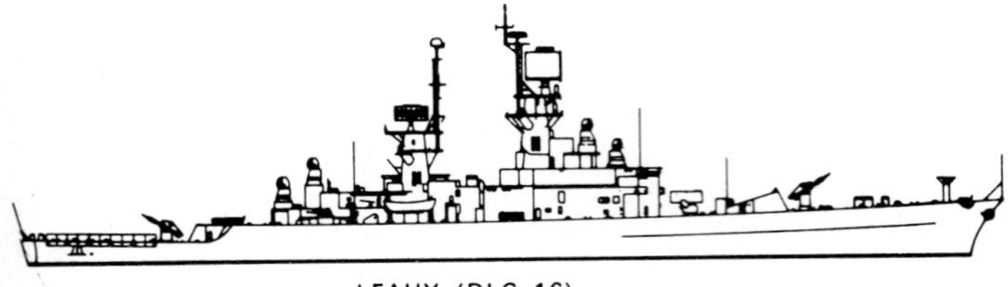

LEAHY (DLG 16)

MAHAN (DLG 11) Coontz Class

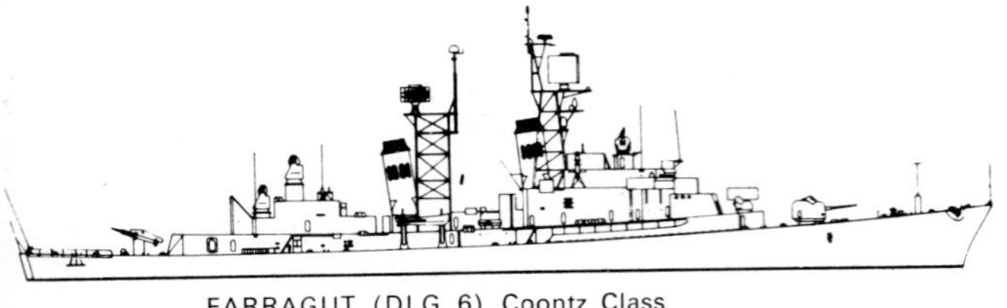

FARRAGUT (DLG 6) Coontz Class

Guided Missile Destroyers—*continued*

MITSCHER (DDG 35)

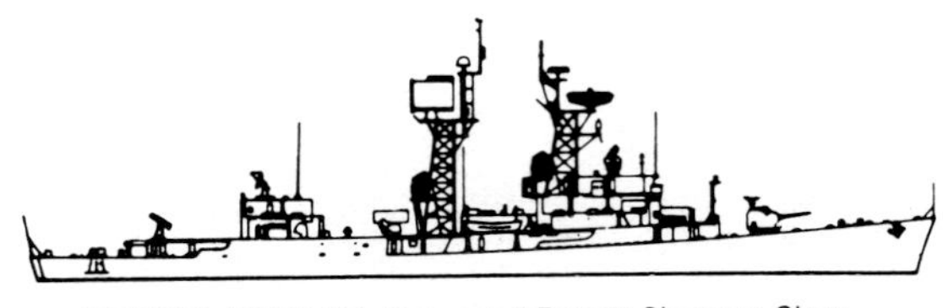

SOMERS (DDG 34) Converted Forrest Sherman Class

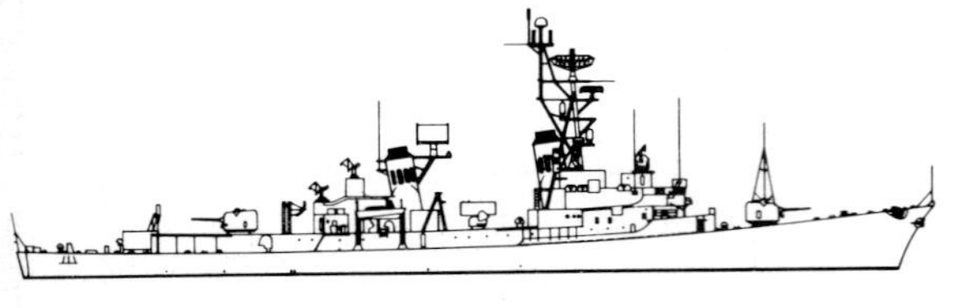

WADDELL (DDG 24) Charles F. Adams Class

BARNEY (DDG 6) Charles F. Adams Class

Destroyers

MANLEY (DD 940) Forrest Sherman Class

JONAS INGRAM (DD 938) Forrest Sherman Class (ASW)

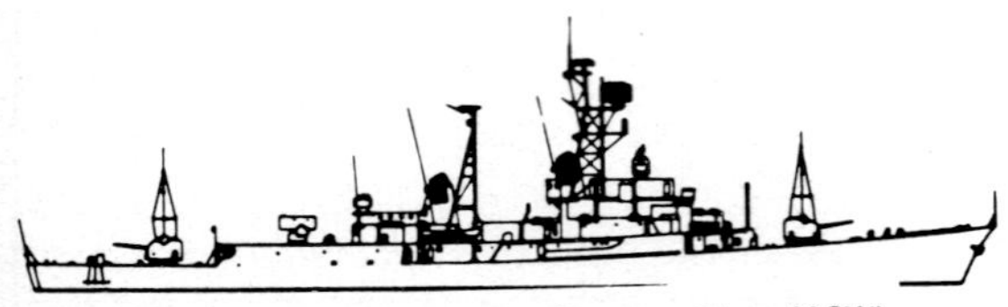

BARRY (DD 933) Forrest Sherman Class (ASW)

MEREDITH (DD 890) Gearing Class FRAM I

Scale: 1 inch = 150 feet (1 : 1 800)

Destroyers—*continued*

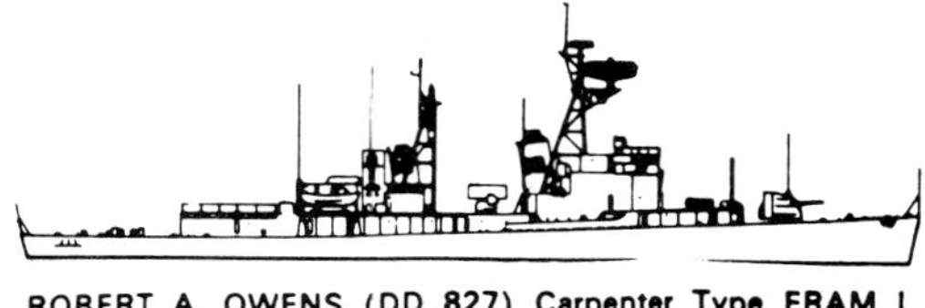
ROBERT A. OWENS (DD 827) Carpenter Type FRAM I

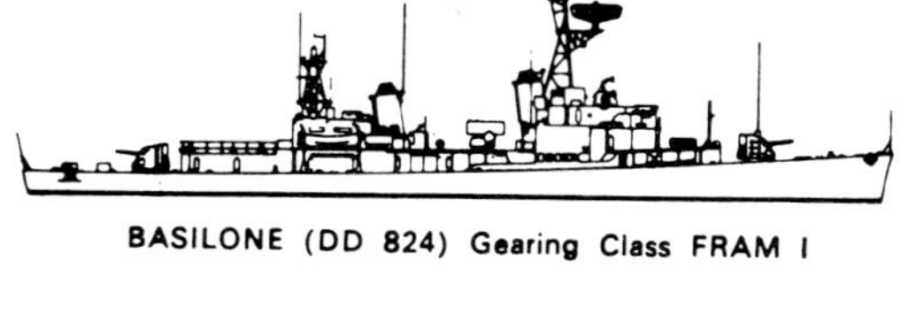
BASILONE (DD 824) Gearing Class FRAM I

NORRIS (DD 859) Gearing Class ex-Escorts

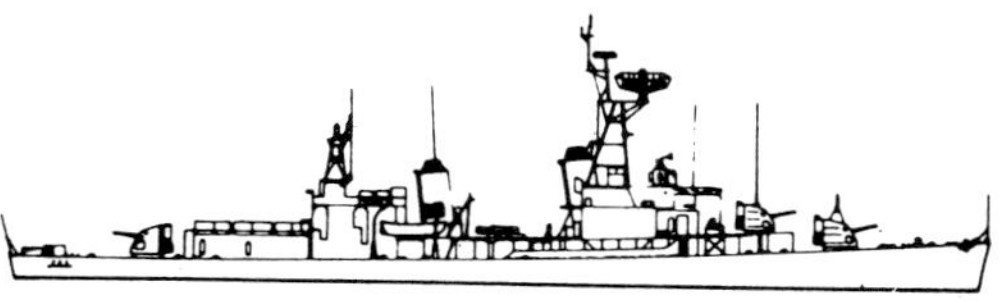
BENNER (DD 807) Gearing Class ex-Radar Pickets

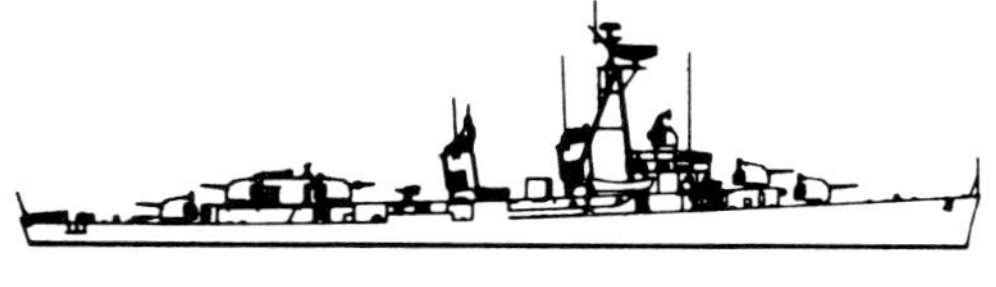
GOODRICH (DD 831) Gearing Class Radar Pickets

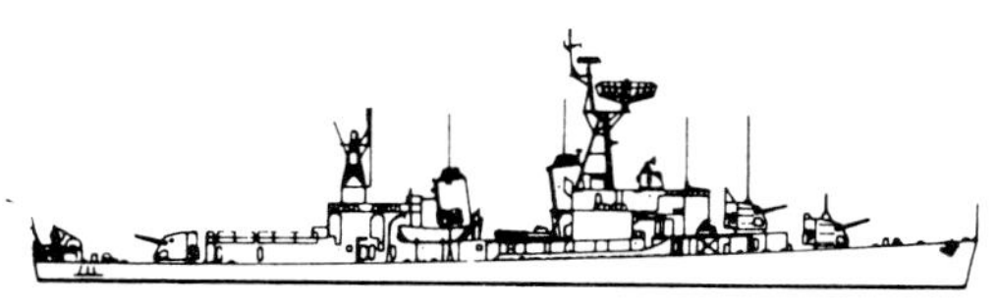
WALLACE L. LIND (DD 703) Allen M. Sumner Class FRAM II

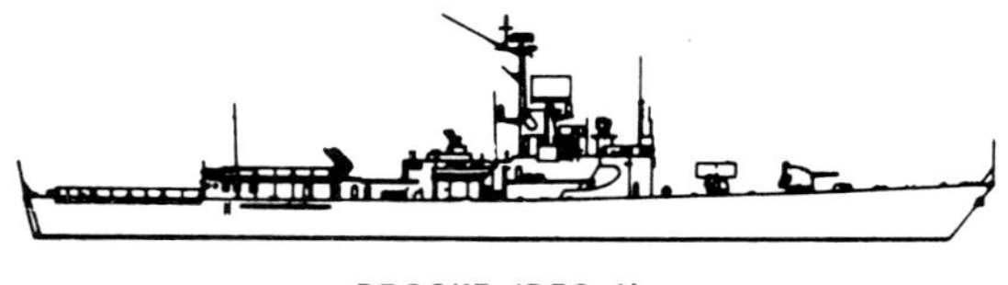
FLETCHER Class (5 guns)

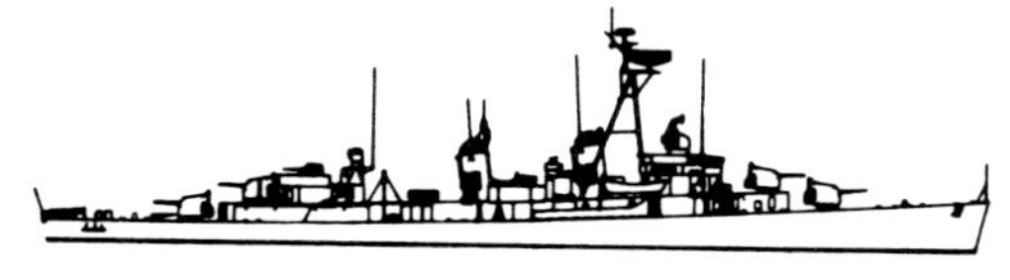
FLETCHER Class (4 guns)

Escort Ships

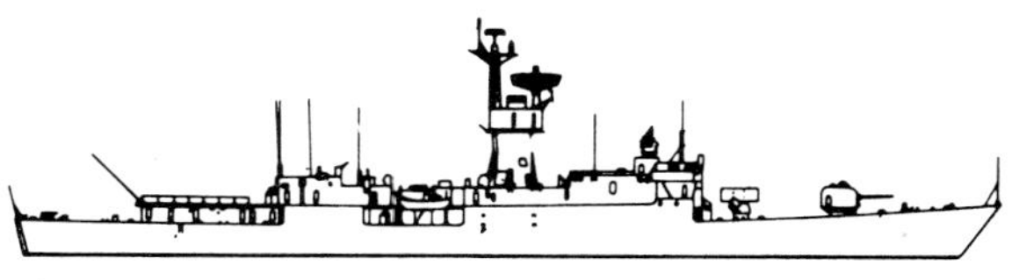
BROOKE (DEG 1)

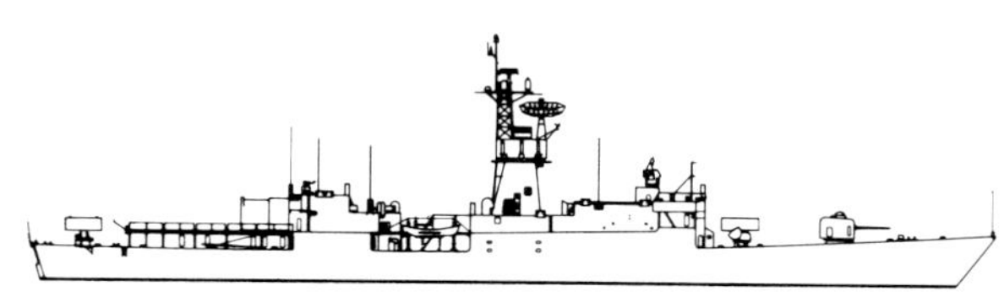
KNOX Class (DE 1052) improved

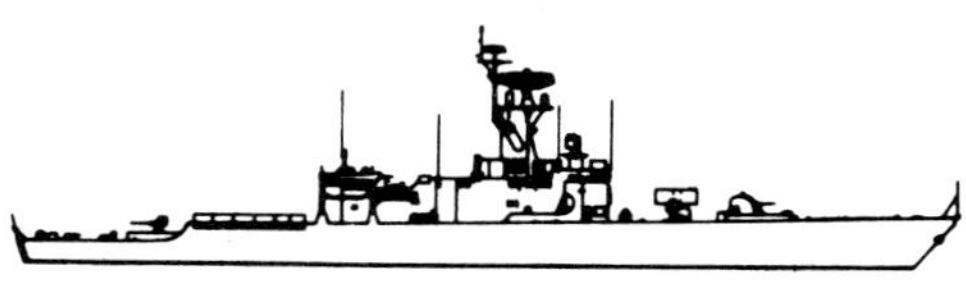
KNOX Class (DE 1052)

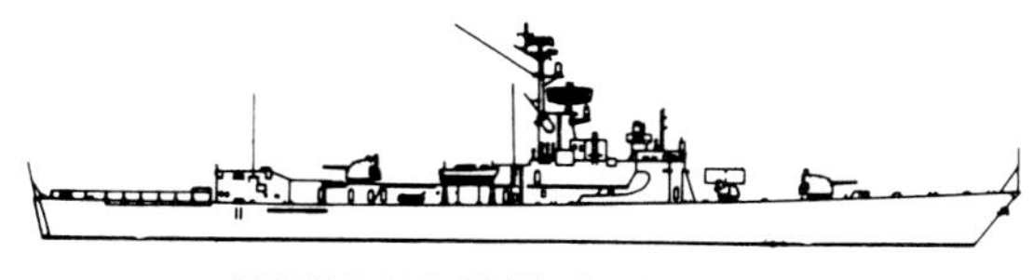
SAMPLE (DE 1048) Garcia Class

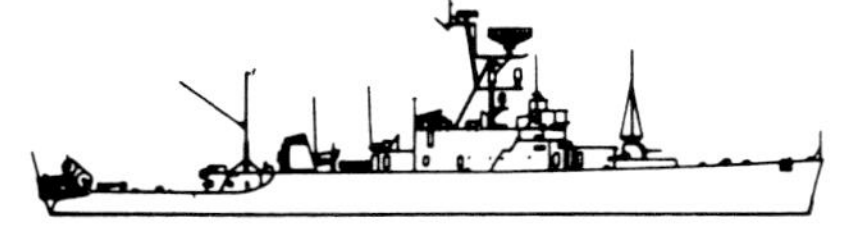
BRONSTEIN (DE 1037)

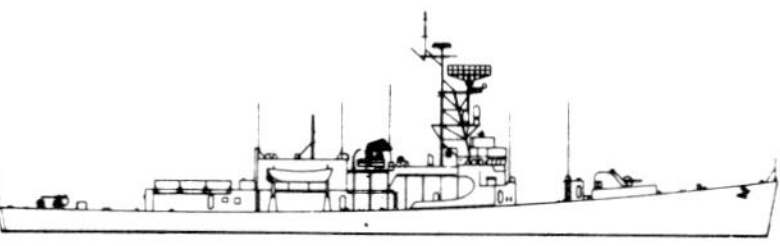
CHARLES D. BERRY (DE 1035) Claude Jones Class.

BRIDGET (DE 1024) Courtney Class

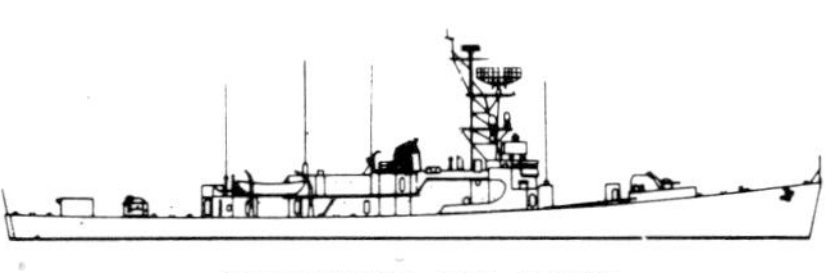
COURTNEY (DE 1021)

CALCATERRA (DER 390) Edsall Class Radar Pickets

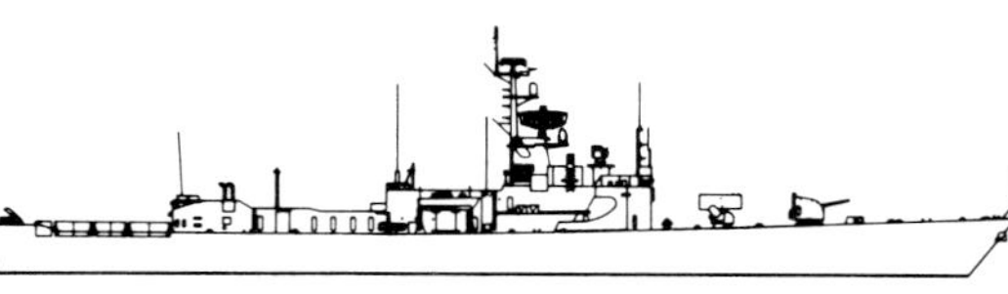
GLOVER (AGDE 1)

Scale: 1 inch = 150 feet (1 : 1 800)

Fire Support Ships/ Cruisers

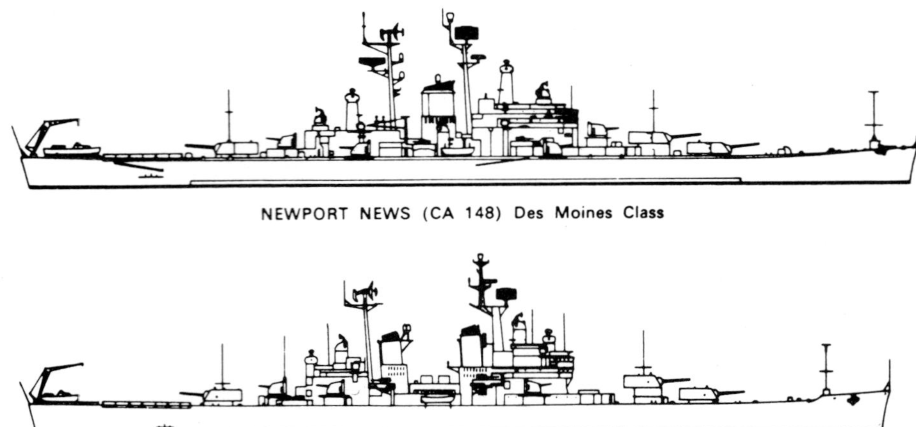

NEWPORT NEWS (CA 148) Des Moines Class

ST. PAUL (CA 73) Baltimore Class

Command Ships

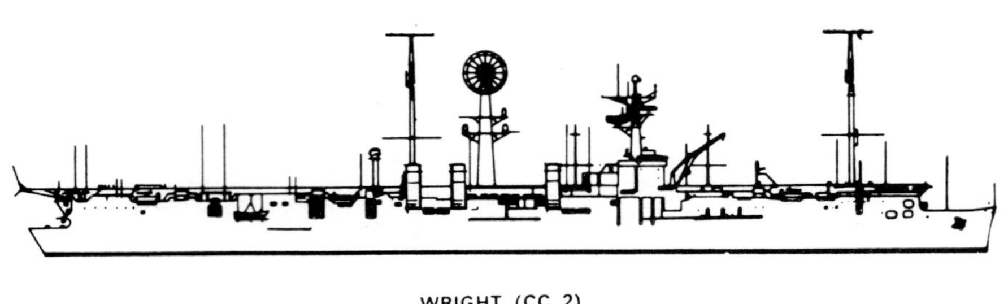

WRIGHT (CC 2)

Amphibious Warfare Ships

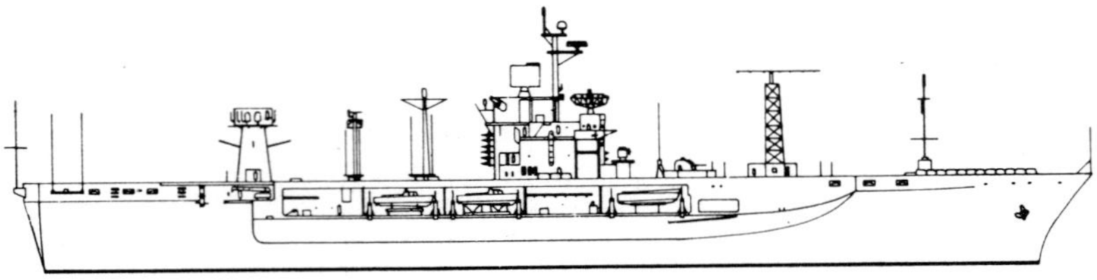

BLUE RIDGE (LCC 19)

NASHVILLE (LPD 13)

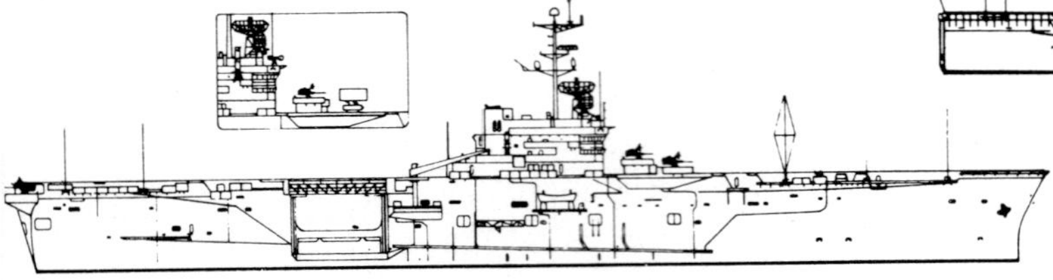

TRIPOLI (LPH 10) Iwo Jima Class (OKINAWA inset)

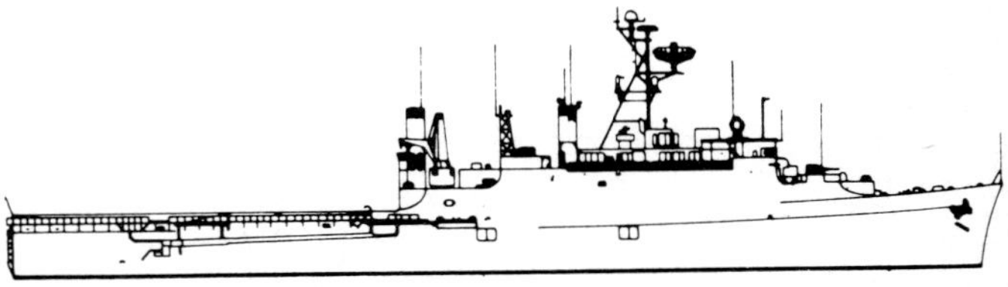

RALEIGH (LPD 1)

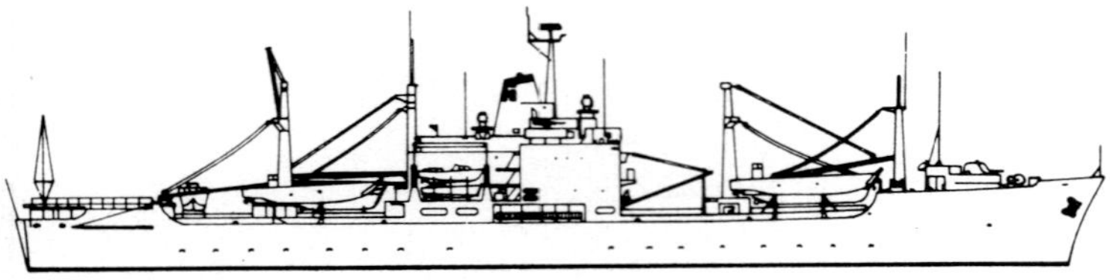

CHARLESTON (LKA 113)

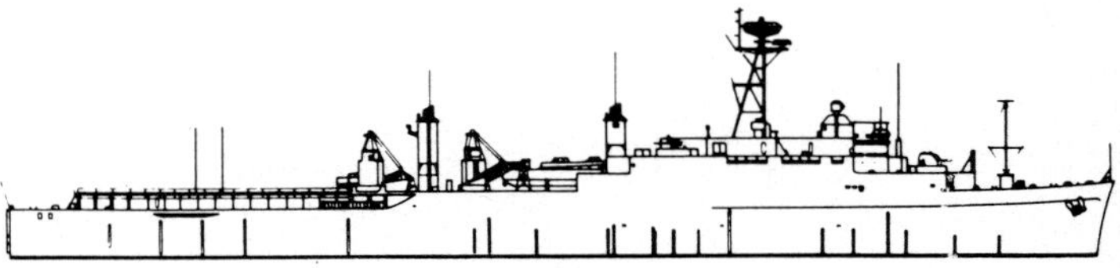

ANCHORAGE (LSD 36)

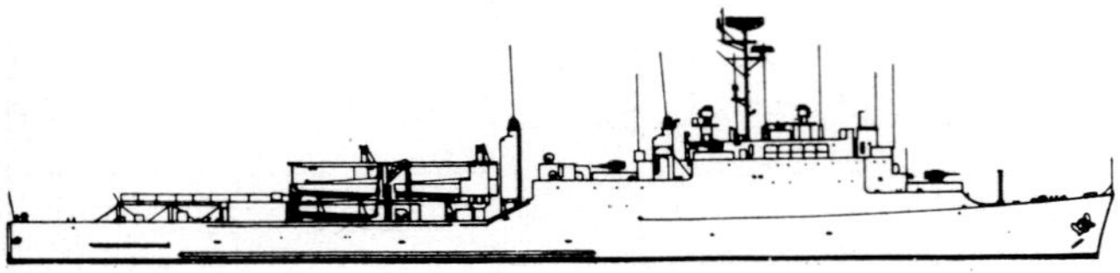

HERMITAGE (LSD 34) Thomaston Class

Scale: 1 inch = 150 feet (1 : 1 800)

Amphibious Warfare Ships—*continued*

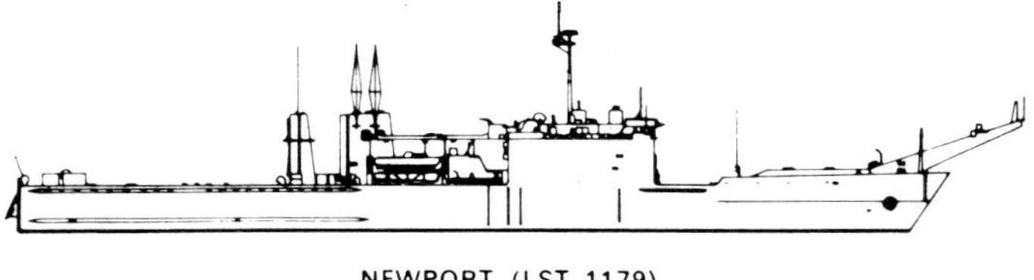

NEWPORT (LST 1179)

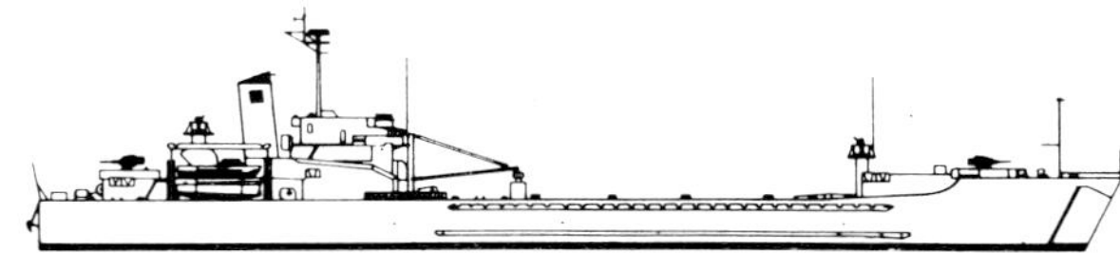

SUFFOLK COUNTY Class (LST 1171)

Auxiliary Ships

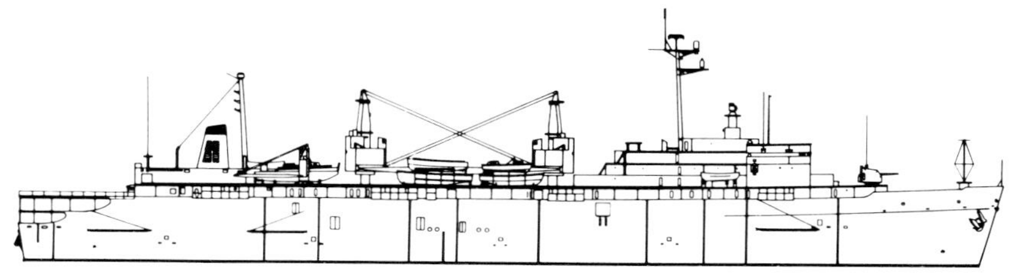

SAMUEL GOMPERS Class (AD 37)

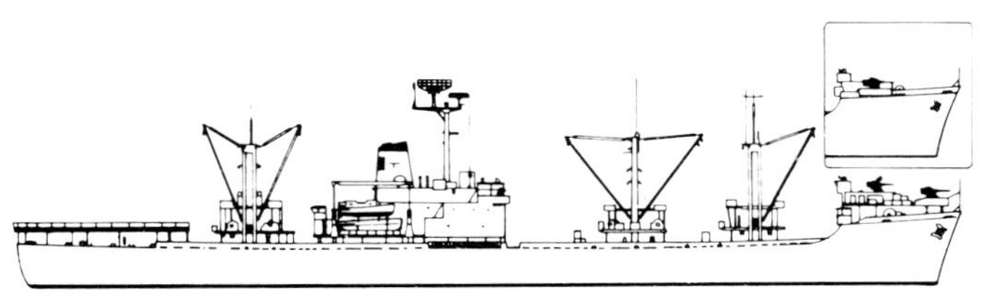

MAUNA KEA (AE 22) Suribachi Class
(inset shows gun variation)

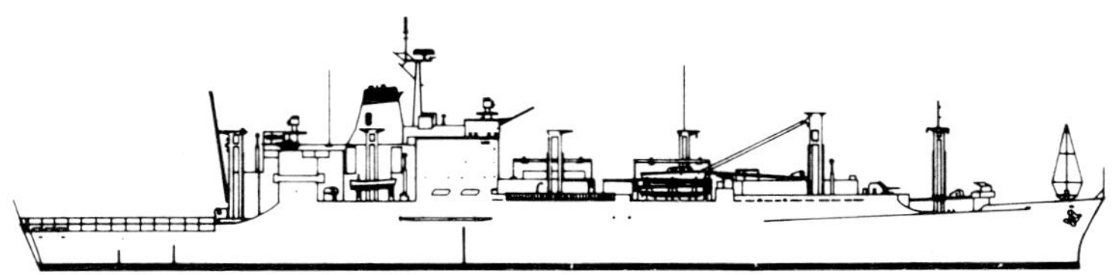

SANTA BARBARA (AE 28) Kilauea Class

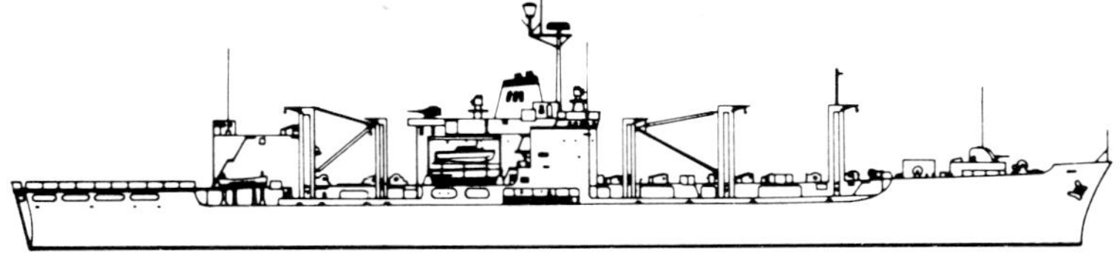

SAN JOSE (AFS 7) Mars Class

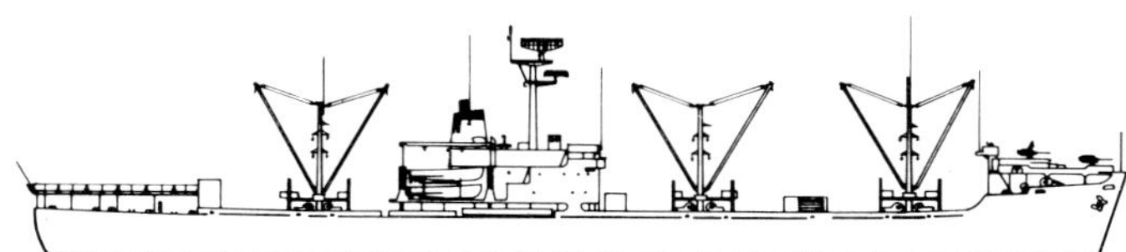

RIGEL (AF 58) R3-S-4A Type

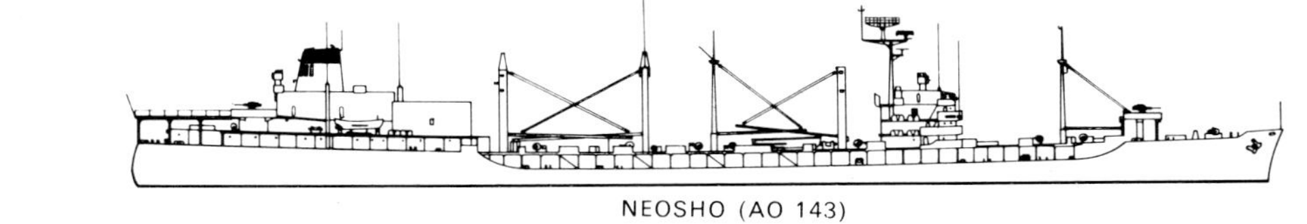

NEOSHO (AO 143)

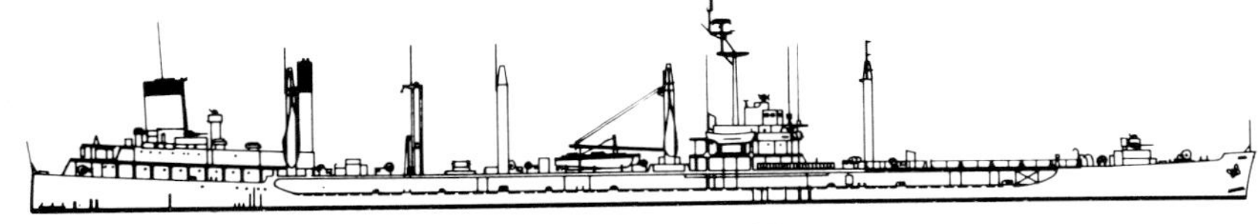

MISPILLION (AO 105) Jumboised T3-S2-A3

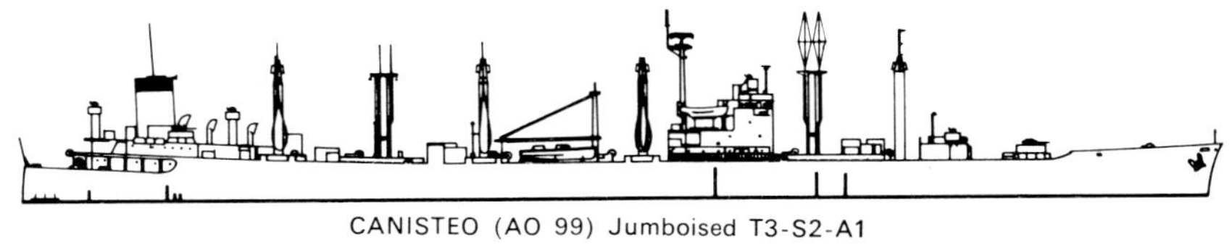

CANISTEO (AO 99) Jumboised T3-S2-A1

Scale: 1 inch = 150 feet (1 : 1 800)

Auxiliary Ships—*continued*

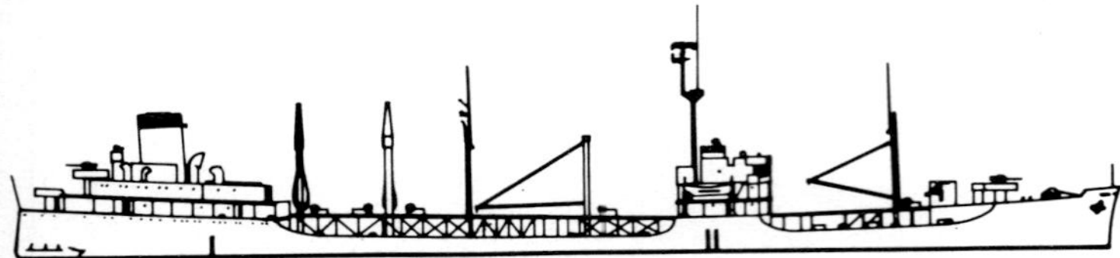
GUADALUPE (AO 32) T3-S2-A1 Type

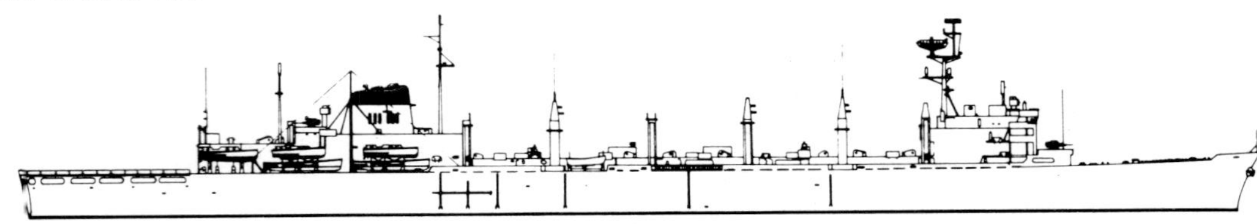
CAMDEN (AOE 2) Sacramento Class

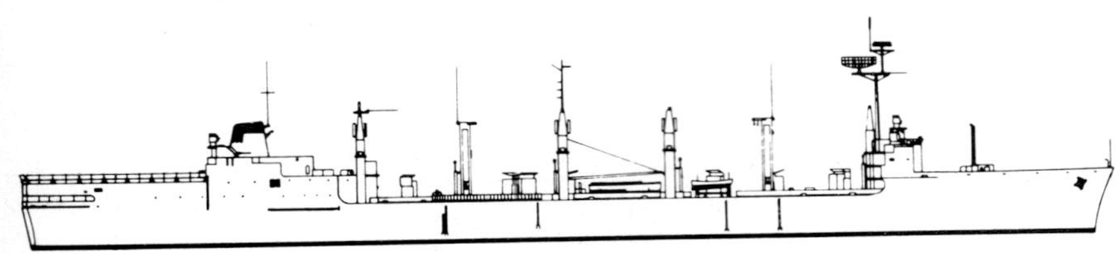
WABASH (AOR 5) Wichita Class

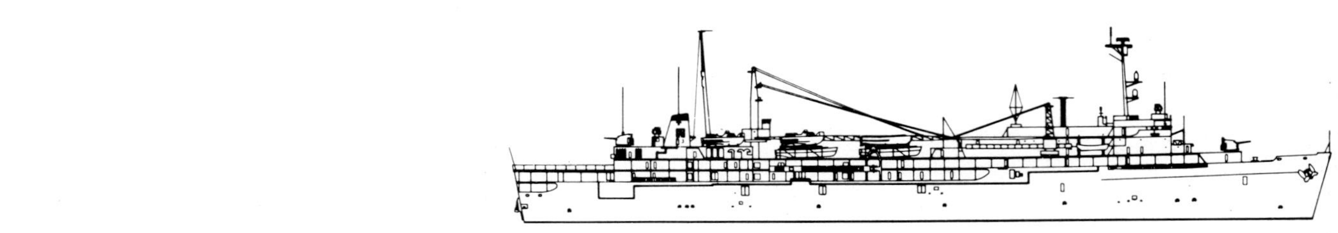
L. Y. SPEAR (AS 36)

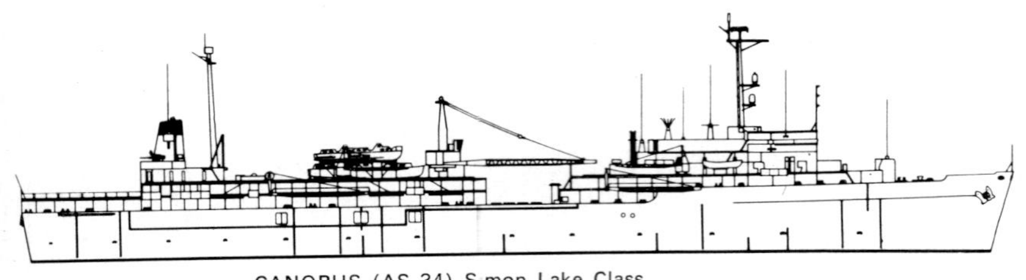
CANOPUS (AS 34) Simon Lake Class

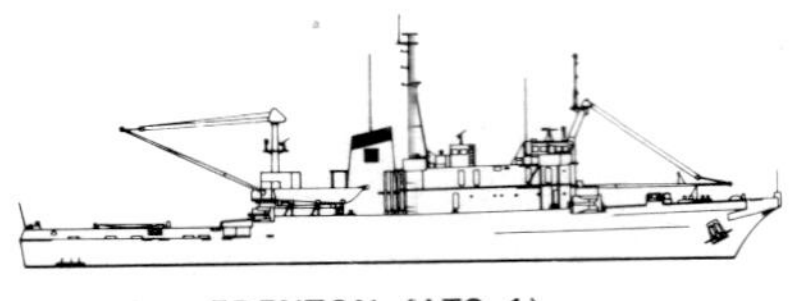
EDENTON (ATS 1)

PIGEON (ASR 21)

Scale: 1 inch = 150 feet (1 : 1 800)

Patrol Ships and Craft

ANTELOPE (PG 86) Asheville Class

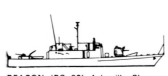

BEACON (PG 99) Asheville Class

Mine Warfare Ships

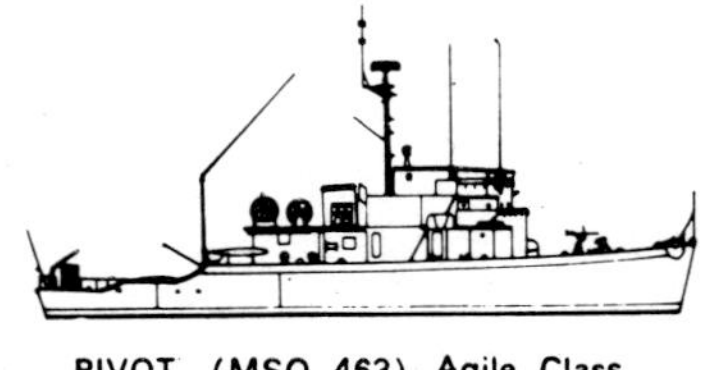
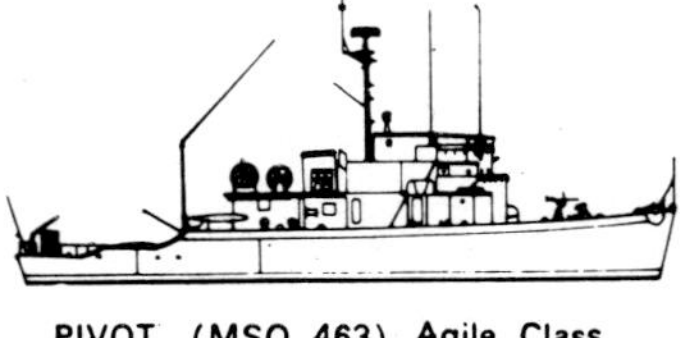
PIVOT (MSO 463) Agile Class

BLUEBIRD (MSC 121) Bluebird Class

Scale: 1 inch = 100 feet (1 : 1 200)

UNITED STATES SHIP HULL NUMBERS

(Type designations in order of arrangement within this volume; ships in numerical sequence)

Strategic Missile Submarines

SSBN—Fleet Ballistic Missile Submarines

"Geo. Washington" Class
598 George Washington
599 Patrick Henry
600 Theodore Roosevelt
601 Robert E. Lee
602 Abraham Lincoln

"Ethan Allen" Class
608 Ethan Allen
609 Sam Houston
610 Thomas A. Edison
611 John Marshall

"Lafayette" Class
616 Lafayette
617 Alexander Hamilton

"Ethan Allen" Class (Cont'd)
618 Thomas Jefferson

"Lafayette" Class (Cont'd)
619 Andrew Jackson
620 John Adams
622 James Monroe
623 Nathan Hale
624 Woodrow Wilson
624 Henry Clay
626 Daniel Webster
627 James Madison
628 Tecumseh
629 Daniel Boone
630 John C. Calhoun
631 Ulysses S. Grant
632 Von Steuben
633 Casimir Pulaski
634 Stonewall Jackson
635 Sam Rayburn
636 Nathanael Greene
640 Benjamin Franklin
641 Simon Bolivier
642 Kamehameha
643 George Bancroft
644 Lewis and Clark
645 James K. Polk
654 George C. Marshall
655 Henry L. Stimson
656 George Washington Carver
657 Francis Scott Key
658 Mariano G. Vallejo
659 Will Rogers

Submarines

SS SSN—Attack Submarines
AGSS—Auxiliary Submarines
LPSS—Amphibious Transport Submarines
SSG—Guided Missile Submarines

"Sealion" Type
315 Sealion LPSS

GUPPY IA Type
319 Becuna
324 Blenny

GUPPY III Type
343 Clamagore
344 Cobbler
346 Corporal
351 Greenfish

GUPPY IIA Type
377 Menhaden

GUPPY IA Type (Cont'd)
403 Atule
406 Sea Poacher

GUPPY IIA Type (Cont'd)
410 Threadfin

GUPPY III Type (Cont'd)
416 Tiru

GUPPY IA Type (Cont'd)
417 Tench

"Tigrone" Type
419 Tigrone AGSS

GUPPY IIA Type (Cont'd)
420 Tirante

GUPPY III Type (Cont'd)
425 Trumpetfish
487 Remora

GUPPY II Type
522 Amberjack
525 Grenadier

"Dolphin" Type
555 Dolphin AGSS

"Tang" Class
563 Tang
564 Trigger

TANG CLASS—*Continued*

565 Wahoo
566 Trout
567 Gudgeon
568 Harder

"Albacore" Type
569 Albacore AGSS

"Nautilus" Type (SSN)
571 Nautilus

"Sailfish" Class
572 Sailfish
573 Salmon

"Grayback" Type
574 Grayback LPSS

"Seawolf" Type (SSN)
575 Seawolf

"Darter" Type
576 Darter

"Grayback" Type
577 Growler SSG

"Skate" Class (SSN)
578 Skate
579 Swordfish

"Barbel" Class
580 Barbel
581 Blueback
582 Bonefish

"Skate" Class (SSN) (Cont'd)
583 Sargo
584 Seadragon

"Skipjack" Class (SSN)
585 Skipjack

"Triton" Type (SSN)
586 Triton

"Halibut" Type (SSN)
587 Halibut

"Skipjack" Class (SSN) (Cont'd)
588 Scamp
590 Sculpin
591 Shark
592 Snook

"Permit" Class (SSN)
594 Permit
595 Plunger
596 Barb

"Tullibee" Type (SSN)
597 Tullibee

"Permit" Class (SSN) (Cont'd)
603 Pollack
604 Haddo
605 Jack
606 Tinosa
607 Dace
612 Guardfish
613 Flasher
614 Greenling
615 Gato
621 Haddock

"Sturgeon" Class (SSN)
637 Sturgeon
638 Whale
639 Tautog
646 Grayling
647 Pogy
648 Aspro
649 Sunfish
650 Pargo
651 Queenfish
652 Puffer
653 Ray
660 Sand Lance
661 Lapon
662 Gurnard
663 Hammerhead
664 Sea Devil
665 Guitarro
666 Hawkbill
667 Bergall
668 Spadefish
669 Seahorse
670 Finback
671 Narwhal
672 Pintado
673 Flying Fish
674 Trepang
675 Bluefish
676 Billfish

"Sturgeon" Class (SSN) (Cont'd)
667 Drum
678 Archerfish
679 Silversides
680 William H. Bates
681 Batfish
682 Tunny
683 Parche
684 Cavalla

"Lipscomb" Type (SSN)
685 Glenard P. Lipscomb

"Sturgeon" Class (SSN) (Cont'd)
686 L. Mendel Rivers
687 Richard B. Russell

"Los Angeles" Class (SSN)
688 Los Angeles
689 Baton Rouge
690 Philadelphia
691
692 Omaha

SST—Training Submarines

"Barracuda" Type
3 Barracuda

Aircraft Carriers

CV CVA CVAN CVN—Attack Aircraft Carriers
CVS—ASW—Aircraft Carriers
CVT—Training Aircraft Carriers

"Hancock" Class
11 Intrepid CVS

Modernised "Essex" Class
12 Hornet CVS

"Hancock" class (Cont'd)
14 Ticonderoga CVS
16 Lexington CVT
19 Hancock

Modernised "Essex" Class (Cont'd)
20 Bennington CVS

"Hancock" Class (Cont'd)
31 Bon Homme Richard
34 Oriskany
38 Shangri-La CVS

"Midway" Class
41 Midway
42 Franklin D. Roosevelt
43 Coral Sea

"Forrestal" Class
59 Forrestal
60 Saratoga
61 Ranger
62 Independance

"Kitty Hawk" Class
63 Kitty Hawk
64 Constellation

"Enterprise" Type (CVAN)
65 Enterprise

"Kitty Hawk" Class (Cont'd)
66 America
67 John F. Kennedy

"Nimitz" Class (CVAN)
68 Nimitz
69 Dwight D. Eisenhower

Surface Combatants

Sea Control Ships

9 Guam LPH

CG CGN—Guided Missile Cruisers

"Long Beach" Type (CGN)
9 Long Beach

"Albany" Class
10 Albany
11 Chicago
12 Columbus

CLG—Guided Missile Light Cruisers

Converted "Cleveland" Class
3 Galveston
4 Little Rock
5 Oklahoma City
6 Province
7 Springfield
8 Topeka

DLG DLGN—Guided Missile Frigates

"Coontz" Class
6 Farragut
7 Luce
8 MacDonough
9 Coontz
10 King
11 Mahan
12 Dahlgren
13 William V. Pratt
14 Dewey
15 Preble

"Leahy" Class
16 Leahy
17 Harry E. Yarnell
18 Worden
19 Dale
20 Richmond K. Turner
21 Gridley
22 England
23 Halsey
24 Reeves

"Bainbridge" Type (DLGN)
25 Bainbridge

"Belknap" Class
26 Bellknap
27 Josephus Daniels
28 Wainwright
29 Jouett
30 Horne
31 Sterett
32 William H. Standley
33 Fox
34 Biddle

"Truxtun" Type (DLGN)
35 Truxtun

"California" Class (DLGN)
36 California
37 South Carolina

"Virginia" Class (DLGN)
38 Virginia
39 Texas

DL—Frigates

"Norfolk" Type
1 Norfolk

"Mitscher" Class
5 Wilkinson

DDG—Guided Missile Destroyers

"Chas F. Adams" Class
2 Charles F. Adams
3 John King
4 Lawrence
5 Claude V. Ricketts
6 Barney
7 Henry B. Wilson
8 Lynde McCormick
9 Towers
10 Sampson
11 Sellers
12 Robinson
13 Hoel
14 Buchanan
15 Berkeley
16 Joseph Strauss
17 Conyngham
18 Semmes
19 Tattnall
20 Goldsborough
21 Cochrane
22 Benjamin Stoddert
23 Richard E. Byrd
24 Waddell

Converted "Sherman" Class
31 Decatur
32 John Paul Jones
33 Parsons
34 Somers

Converted "Mitscher" Class
35 Mitscher
36 John S. McCain

DD—Destroyers

"Fletcher" Class
448 La Vallettee
499 Renshaw
502 Sigsbee
507 Conway
513 Terry
519 Daly
531 Hazelwood
537 Sullivans
562 Robinson
563 Ross
564 Rowe
566 Stoddard
567 Watts

FLETCHER CLASS—*Continued*

568 Wren
575 McKee
589 Izard
596 Shields
629 Abbott
630 Braine
643 Sigourney

Later "Fletcher" Class
649 Albert W. Grant
650 Caperton
651 Cogswell
652 Ingersoll
653 Knapp
654 Bearss
657 Charles J. Badger
659 Dashiell
661 Kidd
665 Bryant
666 Balck
669 Cotton
671 Gatling
672 Healy
674 Hunt
679 McNair
680 Melvin
682 Porterfield
683 Stockholm
684 Wedderburn
685 Picking
688 Remey
691 Mertz

"Allen M. Sumner" Class
692 Allen M. Sumner
693 Moale
697 Charles S. Sperry
698 Ault
699 Waldron
702 Hank
703 Wallace L. Lind
707 Soley
708 Harlan R. Dickson

"Gearing" Class
710 Gearing
713 Kenneth D. Bailey
714 William R. Rush
715 William M. Wood
716 Wiltsie
717 Theo E. Chandler
718 Hammer
719 Epperson

"Allen M. Sumner" Class (Cont'd)
723 Walke
724 Laffey
727 De Haven
728 Mansfield
729 Lyman K. Swenson
730 Collett
732 Hyman
734 Purdy

"Gearing" Class (Cont'd)
743 Southerland

"Allen M. Sumner" Class (Cont'd)
744 Blue
746 Taussig
752 Alfred A. Cunningham
753 John R. Pierce
755 John A. Bole
756 Beatty
757 Putnam
758 Strong
759 Lofberg
760 John W. Thomason
761 Buck
762 Henley
"Gearing" Class (Cont'd)
763 William C. Lawe

"Allen M. Sumner" Class (Cont'd)
770 Lowry
775 Willard Keith
775 James C, Owens
778 Massey
779 Douglas H. Fox
781 Robert K. Huntington

"Gearing" Class (Cont'd)
782 Rowan
783 Gurke
784 McKean
785 Henderson
786 Richard B. Anderson
788 Hollister
789 Eversole

Later "Fletcher" Class (Cont'd)
793 Cassin Young

"Gearing" Class (Cont'd)
805 Chevalier
806 Highbee
807 Benner
808 Dennis J. Buckley
817 Corry

GEARING CLASS—*Continued*

818 New
819 Holder
820 Rich
821 Johnson
822 Robert H. McCard
824 Basilone

"Carpenter" Type
825 Carpenter
"Gearing" Class (Cont'd)
826 Agerholm

"Carpenter" Type (Cont'd)
827 Robert A. Owens

"Gearing" Class (Cont'd)
829 Myles C. Fox
831 Goodrich
833 Herbert J. Thomas
835 Charles P. Cecil
836 George K. Mackenzie
837 Sarsfield
839 Power
840 Glennon
841 Noa
842 Fiske
844 Perry
845 Bausell
846 Ozbourn
847 Robert L. Wilson
849 Richard E. Kraus
850 Joseph P. Kennedy Jr.
851 Rupertus
852 Leonard F. Mason
853 Charles H. Roan
858 Fred T. Berry
859 Norris
860 McCaffery
862 Vogelgesang
863 Steinaker
864 Harold J. Ellison
865 Charles R. Ware
866 Cone
867 Stribling
868 Brownson
869 Arnold J. Isbell
871 Damato
873 Hawkins
874 Duncan
875 Henry W. Tucker
876 Rogers
877 Perkins
878 Vesole
879 Leary
880 Dyess
881 Bordelon
883 Newman K. Perry
884 Floyd B. Parkes
885 John F. Craig
886 Orleck
887 Brinkley Bass
888 Stickell
889 O'Hare
890 Meredith

"Forrest Sherman" Class
931 Forrest Sherman
933 Barry
937 George F. Davis
938 Jonas Ingram
940 Manley
941 Dupont
942 Bigelow
943 Blandy
944 Mullinnix
945 Hull
946 Edson
948 Morton
950 Richard S. Edwards
951 Turner Joy

"Spruance" Class
963 Spruance
964 Paul F. Foster

DEG—Guided Missile Escort Ships

"Brooke" Class
1 Brooke
2 Ramsey
3 Schofield
4 Talbot
5 Richard L. Page
6 Julius A. Furer

AGDE—Escort Research Ship

1 Glover

DE—Escort Ships/DER—Radar Picket Escort Ships

"Edsall" Class
130 Jacob Jones
134 Pope
140 J.R.Y. Blakeley
145 Huse
149 Chatelain
151 Poole
152 Peterson

"Bostwick" Class
162 Levy
163 McConnell
180 Trumpeter
181 Straub

"Edsall" Class (Cont'd)
240 Moore
244 Otterstetter/DER
245 Sloat
247 Stanton
249 Marchand
250 Hurst
253 Pettit
318 Kirkpatrick/DER
320 Menges
321 Mosley
323 Pride
342 Falgout/DER
326 Thomas J. Gary/DER
328 Finch/DER
329 Kretchmer/DER
330 O'Reilly
332 Price/DER
335 Daniel
336 Roy O. Hale/DER
337 Dale W. Peterson

"John C. Butler" Class
357 George E. Davis
367 French

"Edsall" Class (Cont'd)
382 Ramsden/DER
383 Mills/DER
384 Rhodes/DER
386 Savage/DER
387 Vance/DER
388 Lansing/DER
389 Durant/DER
390 Calcaterra/DER
391 Chambers/DER
392 Merrill
398 Cockrill
400 Hissem/DER

"John C. Butler" Class (Cont'd)
406 Edmonds
414 Le Ray Wilson
421 Chester T, O'Brien
531 Edward H. Allen
533 Howard F. Clark
539 Wagner/DER
540 Vandivier/DER

"Buckley" Class (Cont'd)
577 Alexander J. Luke

"Rudderow" Class (Cont'd)
581 McNulty
589 Tinsman

"Buckley" Class (Cont'd)
639 Gendreau
640 Fieberling
641 William C. Cole
643 Damon M. Cummings
667 Wiseman
696 Spangler
699 Marsh
704 Cronin

"Rudderow" Class (Cont'd)
707 Jobb

"Buckley" Class (Cont'd)
795 Gunason
798 Varian

"Dealey" Class
1015 Hammerberg

"Courtney" Class
1021 Courtney
1022 Lester
1023 Evans
1024 Bridget
1025 Bauer
1026 Hopper

"Claud Jones" Class
1033 Claud Jones
1035 Charles Berry
1036 McMorris

"Bronstein" Class
1037 Bronstein
1038 McCloy

"Garcia" Class
1040 Garcia
1041 Bradley
1043 Edward McDonnell
1044 Brumby
1045 Davidson
1047 Voge
1048 Sample
1049 Koelsch
1050 Albert David
1051 O'Callahan

"Knox" Class
1052 Knox
1053 Roark
1054 Gray
1055 Hepburn
1056 Connole
1057 Rathburne
1058 Mayerkord
1059 W. S. Sims
1060 Lang
1061 Patterson
1062 Whipple
1063 Reasoner
1064 Lockwood
1065 Stein
1066 Marvin Shields
1067 Francis Hammond
1068 Vreeland
1069 Bagley
1070 Downes
1071 Badger
1072 Blakely
1073 Robert E. Peary
1074 Harold E. Holt
1075 Trippe
1076 Fanning
1077 Ouellet
1078 Joseph Hewes
1079 Bowen
1080 Paul
1081 Aylwin
1082 Elmer Montgomery
1083 Cook
1084 McCandless
1085 Donald B. Beary
1086 Brewton
1087 Kirk
1088 Barbey
1089 Jesse L. Brown
1090 Ainsworth
1091 Miller
1092 Thomas C. Hart
1093 Capodanno
1094 Pharris
1095 Truitt
1096 Valdez
1097 Moinester

Fire Support Ships

BB—Battleships

"Iowa" Class
61 Iowa
62 New Jersey
63 Missouri
64 Wisconsin

CA—Heavy Cruisers

"Baltimore" Class
68 Baltimore
69 Boston
70 Canberra
71 Quincy
72 Pittsburgh
73 St. Paul
75 Helena

"Oregon City" Class
122 Oregon City
124 Rochester

"Baltimore" Class (Cont'd)
130 Bremerton
131 Fall River
133 Toledo

"Salem" Class
134 Des Moines

"Baltimore" Class (Cont'd)
135 Los Angeles

"Salem" Class (Cont'd)
139 Salem
148 Newport News

AGF—Miscellaneous Flagships

3 La Salle

CC—Command Ships

1 Northampton
2 Wright

AGMR—Major Communication Relay Ships

1 Annapolis
2 Arlington

Amphibious Warships

LCC—Amphibious Command Ships (ex-AGC)

"Mount McKinley" Class
7 Mount McKinley
12 Estes
16 Pocono
17 Taconic

"Blue Ridge" Class
19 Blue Ridge
20 Mount Whitney

LHA—Amphibious Assault Ships

1 Tarawa
2 Saipan
3 Philippine Sea
4 Leyte Gulf
5 Khe Sanh

LPH—Amphibious Assault Ships

"Iwo Jima" Class
2 Iwo Jima
3 Okinawa
7 Guadalcanal
9 Guam
11 New Orleans
12 Inchon

LKA—Amphibious Cargo Ships

"Andromeda" Class
54 Algol
57 Capricornus
61 Muliphen
88 Uvalde
93 Yancey
94 Winston
97 Merrick

"Rankin" Class
103 Rankin
104 Seminole
105 Skagit
106 Union
107 Vermilion
108 Washburn

"Tulare" Type
112 Tulare

"Charleston" Class
113 Charleston
114 Durham
115 Mobile
116 St. Louis
117 El Paso

LPA—Amphibious Transports

"Bayfield" Class
36 Cambria
44 Fremont
45 Henrico

"Haskell" Class
194 Sandoval
199 Maggoffin
208 Talladega
213 Mountrail
215 Navarro
220 Okanogan
222 Pickaway
237 Bexar

"Paul Revere" Class
248 Paul Revere
249 Francis Marion

LPR—Amphibious Transports (Small)

55 Laning
86 Hollis
90 Kirwin
100 Ringness
119 Beverley W. Reid
123 Diachenko
124 Horace A. Bass
127 Begor
132 Balduck
135 Weiss

LPD—Amphibious Transport Docks

"Raleigh" Class
1 Raleigh
2 Vancouver

"Austin" Class
4 Austin
5 Ogden
6 Duluth
7 Cleveland
8 Dubuque
9 Denver
10 Juneau
11 Coronado
12 Shreveport
13 Nashville
14 Trenton
15 Ponce

LSD—Dock Landing Ships

"Casa Grande" Class
13 Casa Grande
14 Rushmore
15 Shadwell
16 Cabildo
17 Catamount
18 Colonial
19 Comstock

CASA GRANDE CLASS—*Continued*
20 Donner
22 Fort Marion
26 Tortuga
27 Whetstone

"Thomaston" Class
28 Thomaston
29 Plymouth Rock
30 Fort Snelling
31 Point Defiance
32 Speigel Grove
33 Alamo
34 Hermitage
35 Monticello

"Anchorage" Class
36 Anchorage
37 Portland
38 Pensacola
39 Mt. Vernon
40 Fort Fisher

LST—Tank Landing Ships

1—510 series
344 Blanco County

511-1152 series

525 Caroline County
533 Cheboygan County
583 Churchill County
722 Dodge County
758 Duval County
762 Floyd County
819 Hampshire County
854 Kemper County
901 Litchfield County
980 Meeker County
983 Middlesex County
1082 Pitkin County
1084 Polk County
1096 St. Clair County
1123 Sedgwick County
1148 Sumner County
1150 Sutter County

"Talbot County" Type
1153 Talbot County

"Terrebonne Parish" Class
1157 Terrell County
1161 Vernon County
1166 Washtenaw County
1167 Westchedter County
1169 Whitfield County
1170 Windham County

"Suffolk County" Class
1173 Suffolk County
1174 Grant County
1177 Lorain County
1178 Wood County

"Newport" Class
1179 Newport
1180 Manitowac
1181 Sumter
1182 Fresno
1183 Peroria
1184 Frederick
1185 Schenectady
1186 Cayuga
1187 Tuscaloosa
1188 Saginaw
1189 San Bernadino
1190 Boulder
1191 Racine
1192 Spartanburg County
1193 Fairfax County
1194 Lamour County
1195 Barbour County
1196 Harlan County
1197 Barnstaple County
1198 Bristol County

LFR—Inshore Fire Support Ships

"Carronade" Type
1 Carronade

LSMR Type
401 Big Black River
405 Broadkill River
409 Clarion River
512 Lamoille River
513 Laramie River
515 Owyhee River
522 Red River
525 St Francis River
531 Smokey Hill River

ADVANCED SHIPBOARD SYSTEMS

ASROC (Anti-Submarine Rocket)
Anti-submarine missile launched from surface ships with homing torpedo or nuclear depth charge as warhead. Launcher is Mk 10 or Mk 26 combination ASROC/surface-to-air missile launcher or Mk 16 eight-cell "pepper box". Installed in US Navy cruisers (CG, CGN), frigates (DLG, DLGN), destroyers (DD,DDG), and escort ships (DE, DEG); Japanese, Italian, West German, and Canadian destroyer-type ships.
Weight of missile approximately 1 000 lbs; length 15 ft; diameter 1 ft; span of fins 2·5 ft; payload: Mk 44 or Mk 46 acoustic-homing torpedo or nuclear depth charge; range one to six miles.
Prime Contractors: Honeywell. Designation: RUR-5. Status: Operational.

AEGIS **(formerly Advanced Surface Missile System)**
Advanced surface-to-air missile system intended for use in US Navy frigates and destroyers to be built during the 1970s and 1980s. To have a capability against high-performance aircraft and air-launched, anti-ship missiles. Launcher is Mk 26 with combined surface-to-air and ASW missile capability. Aegis will have an electronic scanning radar with fixed antennae, and will be capable of controlling friendly aircraft as well as detection. Additional components will include the UYK-7 computer (a component of the Naval Tactical Data System) and "illuminators" for missile guidance. Prime contractor: RCA. Status: Development (radars only; initially to use Standard missile).

BPDMS (Basic Point Defence Missile System)
Close-in air defence system employing the Sparrow AIM-7E or 7F series missile (designated Sea Sparrow) and a modified ASROC-type "pepper box" launcher. Installed in several aircraft carriers, ocean escorts, one amphibious assault ship, and experimental ship *Norton Sound*. Status: Operational.

CAPTOR (Encapsuled Torpedo). Mk 46 torpedo inserted in mine casing. Prime contractor: Goodyear. Status: Production

CHAPARRAL Close-in Weapon System for defence against anti-ship missile and aircraft firing the Sidewinder AIM-9C missile. Adapted from Army MIM-72 Chaparral system.

CIWS (Close-in Weapon System) "Family" of advanced gun and missile systems to provide close-in or "point" defence for ships against anti-ship missiles and aircraft. Specific weapons being developed or evaluated under this programme include the Chaparral, Hybrid launcher, Pintle, Vulcan Air Defence, and Vulcan/Phalanx described on this page as well as the OTO Melara 35 mm twin gun mount.

HARPY **Advanced shipboard UHF tactical communications system.**

HYBRID Close-in Weapon System consisting of a launcher capable of firing different missiles against anti-ship missiles and aircraft, providing the opportunity of engaging a target at different ranges and aspects. Missiles being considered for the launcher include various Sidewinder and Sparrow modes, the Redeye (FIM-43) missile, and Hornet (AGM-64) missile.
Status: Development.

LAMPS (Light Airborne Multi-Purpose System)
Ship-launched helicopter intended for anti-submarine and missile-defence missions, with secondary roles of search-and-rescue and utility (e.g., parts and personnel transfer) For use aboard destroyer-type ships with hangars and certain amphibious warfare ships. Sensors include dipping sonar, magnetic airborne detection (MAD), and sonobuoys with digital relays to permit control and attack direction by launching ship. Radar provided to extend detection range vis-a-vis hostile surface missile ships. Weapons: 2 Mk 46 ASW torpedoes. Crew: pilot and 2 operators.
Status: Approximately 100 Kaman Seasprite helicopters being modified to SH-2D configuration as interim LAMPS. Initially being deployed on frigates and escort ships.

NTDS (Naval Tactical Data System)
Combination of digital computers, displays, and transmission links to increase an individual ship commander's capability to assess tactical data and take action by integrating input from various sensors (e.g., radars) and providing display of tactical situation and the defence or offence options available. Data can be transmitted among NTDS-equipped ships. An automatic mode initiates action to respond to greatest threats in a tactical situation. Also can be linked to Airborne Tactical Data System (ATDS) in E-2 Hawkeye aircraft.
Fitted in all US Navy aircraft carriers, missile-armed cruisers and frigates, new amphibious command ships, and two escort ships (*Voge* and *Koelsch*).
Status: Operational

PDSMS **(Point Defence Surface Missile System). Follow-on to BPDMS with a Target Acquisition System (TAS), powered director, smaller launcher, and control console combined with the Sea Sparrow missile.**
Status: Under development; also a NATO co-operative programme (less TAS) with Belgium, Denmark, Italy, Netherlands and Norway. Intended for ships without larger missile capability.

PINTLE Rapid-fire, close-in gun system similar to Vulcan/Phalanx weapon but firing 20 mm ammunition from a three-barrel, light-weight "Gatling" gun.
Status: Development.

SAMID (Ship Anti-Missile Integrated Defence)
An immediate effort to provide ships with defence against anti-ship attack missiles (e.g., Styx). SAMID integrates existing shipboard weapons, electronic warfare equipment, and passive and active sensors into a co-ordinated system. Data processing in larger ships will be compitable with NTDS. Effect will be to reduce reaction time from detection of missile to ships' response. (with deceptive electronic warfare and/or weapons). To be installed initially in frigates and aircraft carriers.
Status: Under evaluation.

SECT (Submarine Emergency Communications Transmitter)
Alarm device to warn if a submarine is disabled or sunk. One SECT buoy is to be installed in each US Navy nuclear attack submarine (SSN) and two in each ballistic missile submarine (SSBN), so arranged in the latter submarine that at least one buoy would survive the submarine being hit by a torpedo at any point. The system would release the buoy when (1) the water depth exceeds that of safe submarine operation, (2) subject to an internal pressure that exceeds certain limits, or (3) a "dead-man's switch" is not reset by the crew at two hour intervals. Upon release the buoy would float freely to the surface and transmit pre-set messages on four high frequencies to automatic receivers ashore; it could serve as a homing beacon to locate the *general* area of a submarine in distress.
Status: Advanced development. Prime contractor: Collins Radio.

SHORTSTOP
Advanced shipboard electronic system for anti-ship missile defence. Essentially a follow-on to the SAMID programme, SHORTSTOP is based on an advanced electronic-warfare system with electronically scanned passive receivers, computerised threat recognition, and computer-assisted reactive countermeasure control against anti-ship attack missiles. Officially described as "the most ambitious shipboard electronic warfare project yet undertaken". Initially to be fitted in the frigates. A SHORTSTOP JUNIOR system is being developed for smaller ships.

SINS (Ships' Inertial Navigation System) Navigation system providing exact navigation information without active input from terrestrial sources. Prime components are gyroscopes and accelerometers that relate movement of the ship in all directions, ship speed through water and over ocean floor, and true north to give a continuous report of the ship's position.
Status: Operational

SUBROC (Submarine Rocket)
Anti-submarine missile launched from submarines with nuclear warhead. Launched from 21-inch torpedo tube. Carried in US Navy submarines of "Permit" and later classes with amidships torpedo tubes, BQQ-2 sonar and Mk 113 torpedo fire control systems. The missile is fired from the submerged submarine, rises up through the surface, travels through air toward the hostile submarine, and then re-enters the water to detonate.
Weight of missile approximately 4 000 lbs; length 21 ft; diameter 1·75 ft (maximum); estimated range 25 to 30 miles.
Prime contractor: Goodyear. Designation: UUM-44A. Status: Operational.

VULCAN AIR DEFENCE SYSTEM Vulcan six-barrel 20 mm gun of Vulcan/Phalanx system employed with existing shipboard fire control director (vice Phalanx fire control) Status: Evaluation (in frigate *Coontz*).

VULCAN/PHALANX Rapid-fire, close-in gun system being developed to provide "last-ditch" defence against anti-ship missiles. Fires 20 mm ammunition from six-barrel "gatling" gun with "dynamic gun aiming" with fire control radar tracking projectiles and target(s). Initially to be installed in aircraft carriers. Status: Production (prototype in escort ship *Lockwood*.

TORPEDOES

Designation	*Launch Platforms*	*Weight (pounds)*	*Length (feet)*	*Diameter (inches)*	*Propulsion*	*Guidance*	*Notes*
Mk 37 Mod 2	Submarines	1 690	13·5	19	Electric	Wire	Anti-submarine
Mk 37 Mod 3	Submarines	1 400	11·3	19	Electric	Active-passive acoustic homing	Anti-submarine
Mk 44 Mod 1	Surface ships (Mk 32 tubes and ASROC); aircraft	433	8·5	12·75	Electric	Active acoustic homing	Anti-submarine
Mk 45 Mod 1 & Mod 2 (ASTOR)	Submarines	2 400	19·9	19	Electric	Wire	Anti-submarine; nuclear warhead; 10+ mile range
Mk 46 Mod 0	Surface ships (Mk 32 tubes and ASROC); aircraft	580	8·4	12·75	Solid-propellant	Active-passive acoustic homing	Anti-submarine; successor to Mk 44
Mk 46 Mod 1	Surface ships (Mk 32 tubes and ASROC); aircraft	512	8·4	12·75	Liquid mono-propellant	Active-passive acoustic homing	Anti-submarine; successor to Mk 44
Mk 48 Mod 0	Submarines	Approx 3 600	19	21	Liquid mono-propellant	Wire/terminal acoustic homing	Anti-submarine; development only; some will convert to Mod 2; approx 25 mile range; Westinghouse
Mk 48 Mod 1	Submarines	approx 3 600	19	21	Liquid mono-propellant	Wire/terminal acoustic homing	Anti-submarine and anti-shipping; larger warhead than Mod 0; in production by Clevite
Mk 48 Mod 2	Submarines	approx 3 600	19	21	Liquid mono-propellant	Wire/terminal acoustic homing	Anti-submarine and anti-shipping; version of Mod 0; Westinghouse

STRATEGIC MISSILE SUBMARINES

The United States is proceeding with development of an advanced strategic missile submarine programme known as "Trident" (previously designated ULMS for Underwater Long-range Missile System). In requesting almost $2 *billion* from the Congress for Trident in the Fiscal Year 1974 budget, Secretary of Defense Elliot L. Richardson stated: "The sea-based missile force is the most survivable element of our strategic retaliatory capability and the Trident programme provides confidence that it will remain so for the foreseeable future".

The US strategic offensive forces now are composed of 1 054 land-based ICBMs, approximately 450 B-52 and FB 111 bombers, and 41 Polaris-Poseidon submarines carrying 656 missiles. The number of ICBMs will be reduced by 54 and the number of bombers will be reduced by about half during the next few years. However, the number of deliverable warheads will increase as 550 Minutemen III missiles and 496 Poseidon missiles are fitted with Multiple Independently Targeted Re-entry Vehicles (MIRV), three per Minuteman and ten per Poseidon. The MIRV concept permits a single missile to deliver small warheads against several separated targets.

With the completion of the Minuteman III and Poseidon programmes in the mid-1970s the United States will have some 8 000 strategic offensive warheads of which 5 120 or approximately two-thirds will be carried by Polaris and Poseidon submarines. (This calculation does not consider the three re-entry vehicles per Polaris A-3 missile in ten remaining Polaris submarines as separate warheads because they cannot be directed to different targets, but are "shot-gunned" at the same target to increase damage and overcome possible defences.)

The number of warheads is only one measure of strategic offensive forces. The other principal measures are a number of launch vehicles (the actual missiles or bombers) and megatonnage. In both of these respects US land-based ICBMs and strategic bombers have a quantitative superiority over the Polaris/Poseiden submarine force. Ironically, in *both* of these measures the Soviet Union has a quantitative superiority over the United States.

TRIDENT. The President in January 1972 directed the Department of Defense to "develop a programme to build additional missile launching submarines carrying a new and far more effective missile". This advanced submarine is part of the Underwater Long-range Missile System (ULMS) named Trident in May 1972.

According to official statements, Trident is being developed at an accelerated rate because of "the continuing Soviet strategic offensive force build up, with its long-term implications".

Elaborating on this decision, in February 1972, the then Secretary of Defense Melvin R. Laird said: "I have carefully reviewed all alternatives for new strategic initiatives and have decided that acceleration of the ULMS programme is the most appropriate alternative, since the at sea portion of our sea-based strategic forces has the best long term prospect for high pre-launch survivability".

The Trident programme has essentially two phases: Trident I provides for the development of a long-range missile that could be fitted into the "Lafayette" class FBM submarines in the late 1970s or early 1980s. This missile would, in some respects, be an improved Poseidon missile with more range. This plan would, however, limit the flexibility of design of the advanced missile and submarine developed under the Trident phase of the programme. Thus, as now proposed, the programme would force the Trident submarines constructed in the late 1970s and 1980s to have internal, vertical missile tubes and other missile submarine features developed during the 1950s which were the basis for the Polaris/Poseidon programmes.

Trident II provides for the development of a new nuclear-propelled missile submarine (described on the following page) and a longer-range missile with a range of approximately 6 000 miles. The missile would have or be capable of being fitted with multiple warheads (MIRV), and decoys and jamming devices for penetrating ballistic missile defences.

SURFACE SHIPS. Navy proposals for a Ballistic Missile Ship (BMS) as a means of rapidly increasing US strategic offensive capabilities has, for all practical purposes, been abandoned. There was considerable opposition to this concept both from within and outside the Navy. One BMS option was to fit the ships with modularised support and launch facilities to carry Minuteman III missiles now assigned to the Air Force and deployed in underground silos in the United States (see 1971-1972 edition for details).

STRATEGIC CRUISE MISSILE. The US Navy is studying the feasibility of a strategic cruise missile, a submarine-launched weapon with ram-jet propulsion that could deliver nuclear warheads on urban targets.

According to a 1972 statement by the Director Defense Research & Engineering: "Informal Navy studies with respect to the development or sea-based strategic cruise missiles have led us to the conclusion that such a missile could effectively diversify our strategic forces. Development of a strategic cruise missile system is within the state of the art and is technically feasible without major new developments".

At this time there are no proposals for construction of strategic cruise missile submarines; rather, if such a weapon is developed the Navy's older Polaris missile submarines would be refitted to launch the new missile or possibly some attack submarines would be adopted to that role.

The strategic cruise missile would have a low-level, terrain following flight path over land, much like that of a manned bomber in contrast to the ballistic trajectory of a Polaris/Poseidon missile.

BALLISTIC MISSILE DEFENCE. Also abandoned at this time is the concept of a Sea-based Ballistic Missile Intercept System (SABMIS) as a supplement or alternative to land-based Anti-Ballistic Missile (ABM) systems. Instead, the United States is proceeding with the development of the land-based Safeguard ABM in an effort to increase the survivability of a limited number of Minuteman ICBMs. However, recent official statements indicate that the Safeguard ABM cannot adequately perform the task and additional "terminal" or "point defence" ABM systems are being proposed for this role (see 1971-1972 edition for details).

POLARIS. As initially completed, the US Navy's 41-submarine fleet ballistic missile force consisted of five submarines armed with the 1 370-statute-mile Polaris UGM-27A (A-1) missile, 13 submarines with the 1 700-mile Polaris UGM-27B (A-2) missile, and 23 with the 2 875-mile Polaris UGM-27C (A-3) missile. The five "George Washington" class submarines armed with the A-1 missile have been converted to fire the A-3 version as will the five "Ethan Allen" class submarines built with an A-2 capability. The remaining 31 submarines of the "Lafayette" class (with A-2 or A-3 missiles) all are being rearmed with the improved Poseidon missile.

Of the 41 submarine FBM force, about half is on deterrent patrol at any given time. The remaining operational submarines are either undergoing replenishment and refit between deterrent patrols or are undergoing overhaul or conversion.

FLEET BALLISTIC MISSILE SUBMARINES: TRIDENT PROJECT

Displacement, tons	approx 8 000 to 12 000 surface approx 15 000 submerged
Length, feet	approx 450 to 500 oa
Main engines	steam turbines, 1 shaft
Reactors	1 pressurised-water cooled
Missiles	24 tubes for Trident I submarine-launched ballistic missiles

Development of the Trident strategic missile submarine is underway with the lead "ship" requested in the Fiscal Year 1974 new construction programme. The submarine probably will be built by General Dynamics/Electric Boat and is scheduled for completion in 1979.

The number of submarines to be built has not yet been determined ; factors known to be under consideration include total US strategic weapon requirements in the 1980s and beyond, the need to replace the 'George Washington" and "Ethan Allen" class Polaris submarines which will be approaching their second decade of service when the first Trident submarine is completed and the influence of the Strategic Arms Limitation Talks (SALT) between the United States and Soviet Union. An initial "buy" of ten Trident submarines is being considered.

The above characteristics are unofficial estimates based on the discussion of Navy officials before Congressional committees. (See *Design* notes) Detailed dimensions and particulars of the submarine have not yet been determined.

The principal characteristics of the Trident concept as proposed were: (1) long-range missile (circa 6 000 miles) to permit targeting the Soviet Union while the submarine cruises in the South Atlantic, South Pacific or Indian Oceans, making effective ASW virtually impossible, (2) extremely quiet submarines, (3) a high at-sea to in-port ratio, (4) high systems reliability, (5) dedicated systems design to provide the most effective submarine, and (6) underwater launch capability. Modular construction techniques would greatly facilitate maintenance, overhaul and subsequent modernisation.

DESIGN. The size of the ULMS submarine is dictated primarily by the larger missile required for the estimated 6 000-mile range and the larger reactor plant to drive the ship. The submarine will have 24 tubes for the long-range missiles (compared to 16 tubes for US, British, French and Soviet strategic missile submarines, except the Soviet "Delta" class which has only 12 tubes). The Trident missile tubes will be in a vertical position penetrating the main submarine pressure hull. Early studies had indicated several advantages would accrue from advanced design concepts such as housing the missiles in a horizontal position external to the main pressure hull.

FISCAL. No official cost estimates for the Trident programme have been published at this time. Unofficial cost estimates are approximately $1 *billion* per submarine, including missiles and ten-year operational costs. Construction costs are expected to be $300 000 000 to $500 000 000 per submarine, dependent in part on the number of submarines and construction schedule.

The Fiscal Year 1969 budget provided $5 400 000 for Trident development; $10 000 000 provided in FY 1970 $44 000 000 in FY 1971; $110 000 in FY 1972. A Department of Defense request in January 1972 to increase the FY 1972 allocation to Trident by $35 000 000 was rejected by the Congress.

The FY 1973 budget requested $942 000 000 for the Trident programme and $1 712 000 000 is requested in the FY 1974 budget.

MISSILES. The Trident submarine initially will be armed with the Trident I missile, scheduled to be operational early in 1979. This missile is expected to have a range of 4 000 miles, a range already exceeded by the SS-N-8 missile in Soviet "Delta" class submarines. However, the US missile will have a MIRV warhead while *at this writing* no statements by US officials have indicated the Soviet submarine missile has a multiple warhead. Subsequently the longer-range Trident II missile would be fitted in these submarines.

JAMES MONROE (SSBN 662) *1972, United States Navy*

31 FLEET BALLISTIC MISSILE SUBMARINES (FBM): "LAFAYETTE" CLASS

Name	No.	Builder	Laid down	Launched	Commissioned
*LAFAYETTE	SSBN 616	General Dynamics (Electric Boat Div)	17 Jan 1961	8 May 1962	23 Apr 1963
*ALEXANDER HAMILTON	SSBN 617	General Dynamics (Electric Boat Div)	26 June 1961	18 Aug 1962	27 June 1963
*ANDREW JACKSON	SSBN 619	Mare Island Naval Shipyard	26 Apr 1961	15 Sep 1962	3 July 1963
*JOHN ADAMS	SSBN 620	Portsmouth Naval Shipyard	19 May 1961	12 Jan 1963	12 May 1964
*JAMES MONROE	SSBN 622	Newport News Shipbuilding & DD Co	31 July 1961	4 Aug 1962	7 Dec 1963
*NATHAN HALE	SSBN 623	General Dynamics (Electric Boat Div)	2 Oct 1961	12 Jan 1963	23 Nov 1963
*WOODROW WILSON	SSBN 624	Mare Island Naval Shipyard	13 Sep 1961	22 Feb 1963	27 Dec 1963
*HENRY CLAY	SSBN 625	Newport News Shipbuilding & DD Co	23 Oct 1961	30 Nov 1962	20 Feb 1964
*DANIEL WEBSTER	SSBN 626	General Dynamics (Electric Boat Div)	28 Dec 1961	27 Apr 1963	9 Apr 1964
*JAMES MADISON	SSBN 627	Newport News Shipbuilding & DD Co	5 Mar 1962	15 Mar 1963	28 July 1964
*TECUMSEH	SSBN 628	General Dynamics (Electric Boat Div)	1 June 1962	22 June 1963	29 May 1964
*DANIEL BOONE	SSBN 629	Mare Island Naval Shipyard	6 Feb 1962	22 June 1963	23 Apr 1964
*JOHN C. CALHOUN	SSBN 630	Newport News Shipbuilding & DD Co	4 June 1962	22 June 1963	15 Sep 1964
*ULYSSES S. GRANT	SSBN 631	General Dynamics (Electric Boat Div)	18 Aug 1962	2 Nov 1963	17 July 1964
*VON STEUBEN	SSBN 632	Newport News Shipbuilding & DD Co	4 Sep 1962	18 Oct 1963	30 Sep 1964
*CASIMIR PULASKI	SSBN 633	General Dynamics (Electric Boat Div)	12 Jan 1963	1 Feb 1964	14 Aug 1964
*STONEWALL JACKSON	SSBN 634	Mare Island Naval Shipyard	4 July 1962	30 Nov 1963	26 Aug 1964
*SAM RAYBURN	SSBN 635	Newport News Shipbuilding & DD Co	3 Dec 1962	20 Dec 1963	2 Dec 1964
*NATHANAEL GREENE	SSBN 636	Portsmouth Naval Shipyard	21 May 1962	12 May 1964	19 Dec 1964
*BENJAMIN FRANKLIN	SSBN 640	General Dynamics (Electric Boat Div)	25 May 1963	5 Dec 1964	22 Oct 1965
*SIMON BOLIVAR	SSBN 641	Newport News Shipbuilding & DD Co	17 Apr 1963	22 Aug 1964	29 Oct 1965
*KAMEHAMEHA	SSBN 642	Mare Island Naval Shipyard	2 May 1963	16 Jan 1965	10 Dec 1965
*GEORGE BANCROFT	SSBN 643	General Dynamics (Electric Boat Div)	24 Aug 1963	20 Mar 1965	22 Jan 1966
*LEWIS AND CLARK	SSBN 644	Newport News Shipbuilding & DD Co	29 July 1963	21 Nov 1964	22 Dec 1965
*JAMES K. POLK	SSBN 645	General Dynamics (Electric Boat Div)	23 Nov 1963	22 May 1965	16 Apr 1966
*GEORGE C. MARSHALL	SSBN 654	Newport News Shipbuilding & DD Co	2 Mar 1964	21 May 1965	29 Apr 1966
*HENRY L. STIMSON	SSBN 655	General Dynamics (Electric Boat Div)	4 Apr 1964	13 Nov 1965	20 Aug 1966
*GEORGE WASHINGTON CARVER	SSBN 656	Newport News Shipbuilding & DD Co	24 Aug 1964	14 Aug 1965	15 June 1956
*FRANCIS SCOTT KEY	SSBN 657	General Dynamics (Electric Boat Div)	5 Dec 1964	23 Apr 1966	3 Dec 1966
*MARIANO G. VALLEJO	SSBN 658	Mare Island Naval Shipyard	7 July 1964	23 Oct 1965	16 Dec 1966
*WILL ROGERS	SSBN 659	General Dynamics (Electric Boat Div)	20 Mar 1965	21 July 1966	1 Apr 1967

Displacement, tons	6 650 light surface; 7 320 standard surface; 8 250 submerged
Length, feet (*metres*)	425 (*129·5*) oa
Beam, feet (*metres*)	33 (*10·1*)
Draft, feet (*metres*)	31·5 (*9·6*)
Missile launchers	16 tubes for Polaris A-3 except those submarines converted to Poseidon missiles (see *Missile* notes)
Torpedo tubes	4—21 inch (*533 mm*) forward
Main engines	2 geared turbines 15 000 shp; 1 shaft
Nuclear reactor	1 pressurised-water cooled S5W (Westinghouse)
Speed, knots	20 surface; approx 30 submerged
Complement	140 (14 officers, 126 enlisted men)

These Fleet Ballistic Missile (FBM) submarines are the largest undersea craft ever built in the West. The first four submarines (SSBN 616-620) of this class were authorised in the Fiscal Year 1961 shipbuilding programme with five additional submarines (SSBN 622-626) authorised in a supplemental FY 1961 programme; SSBN 627-636 (ten) in FY 1962, SSBN 640-645 (six) in FY 1963, and SSBN 654-659 (six) in FY 1964. Cost for the earlier ships of this class was approximately $109 500 000 per submarine.

CLASSIFICATION. The *Benjamin Franklin* and later submarines officially are considered a separate class; however, differences are minimal (eg. quieter machinery) and all 31 submarines generally are considered as a single class.

DANIEL WEBSTER (SSBN 626) *United States Navy*

DESIGN. The *Daniel Webster* has diving planes mounted on bow in lieu of sail-mounted planes, the only "16-tube" FBM submarine of any navy with this configuration. (Note photograph on the previous page)

ENGINEERING. The *Benjamin Franklin* and subsequent submarines of this class have been fitted with quieter machinery. All SSBNs have diesel-electric stand-by machinery, snorkels, and "outboard" auxiliary propeller for emergency use.
The nuclear cores inserted in refuelling these submarines during the late 1960s and early 1970s cost approximately $3 500 000 and provide energy for approximately 400 000 miles.

MISSILES. The first eight ships of this class were fitted with the Polaris A-2 missile (1 725 statute mile range) and the 23 later ships with the Polaris A-3 missile (2 880 statute mile range).
The SSBN 620 and SSBN 622-625 (5 ships) were re-armed with the Polaris A-3 missile during overhaul-refuellings from 1968- to 1970. It is planned to subsequently convert these ships to carry the Poseidon missile.
The *James Madison* was the first submarine to undergo conversion to carry the Poseidon missile. She began conversion in February 1969 and was completed in June 1970; ship and missile-firing trials followed, and the submarine began the first deterrent patrol with Poseidon missiles on 31 March 1971.

Poseidon conversion, overhaul, and reactor refuelling are conducted simultaneously. In addition to changes in missile tubes to accommodate larger Poseidon, the conversion provides replacement of Mk 84 fire control system with Mk 88 system. The Poseidon conversion schedule as given below should be completed by 1976. Some of the options for the Trident missile programme include the rearming submarines of this class with an advanced missile, providing a longer range capability than available with the Poseidon missile.

DANIEL BOONE (SSBN 629) *United States Navy*

Strategic Missile Submarines—*Continued*

DANIEL BOONE (SSBN 629)

1970, United States Navy

"LAFAYETTE" CLASS *continued*

NAVIGATION. FBM submarines are equipped with an elaborate Ship's Inertial Navigation System (SINS), a system of gyroscopes and accelerometers which relates movement of the ship in all directions, true speed through the water and over the ocean floor, and true north to give a continuous report of the submarine's position. The system includes the capability of both optical and electronic checks. Navigation data produced by SINS can be provided to each missile's guidance package until the instant the missile is fired.
The first 19 submarines have three Mk 2 SINS and the 12 later submarines have two Mk 2 SINS; all have navigational satellite receivers.

NOMENCLATURE. FBM submarines are named for "famous Americans", including South American and Hawaiian leaders as well as Europeans who aided the United States war for independence. The lead ship of the class is named after the French aristocrat who served with George Washington in the American Revolution.

OPERATIONAL. The *Andrew Jackson* launched the first Polaris A-3 missile from a submarine on 26 Oct 1963. The *Daniel Webster* was the first submarine to deploy with the A-3 missile, beginning her first patrol on 28 Sep 1964. The *Daniel Boone* was the first Polaris submarine to deploy to the Pacific, beginning her first patrol with the A-3 missile on 25 Dec 1964.

PERSONNEL. Each FBM submarine is assigned two alternating crews designated "Blue" and "Gold". Each crew mans the submarine during a 60-day patrol and partially assists during the intermediate 28-day refit alongside a Polaris tender. The "off-duty" crew is undergoing training or is on leave. All FBM submarines are fully air conditioned and the newer ships have elaborate crew study and recreation facilities.

PHOTOGRAPHS. Fleet ballistic missile submarines converted to Poseidon are virtually indistinguishable from pre-conversion appearance. FBM submarines rarely operate on the surface and photographs are difficult to obtain. Note that the *John C. Calhoun*, shown below entering Holy Loch, Scotland, has her sail number painted out.

POSEIDON CONVERSION SCHEDULE

No.	*Programme*	*Conversion Yard*	*Start*	*Complete*
SSBN 616	FY 1973	General Dynamics Corp (Electric Boat)	Oct 1972	Apr 1974
SSBN 617	FY 1973	Newport News SB & DD Co	Jan 1973	June 1974
SSBN 627	FY 1968	General Dynamics Corp (Electric Boat)	Feb 1969	June 1970
SSBN 628	FY 1970	Newport News SB & DD Co	Nov 1969	Feb 1971
SSBN 629	FY 1968	Newport News SB & DD Co	May 1969	Aug 1970
SSBN 630	FY 1969	Mare Island Naval Shipyard	Aug 1969	Feb 1971
SSBN 631	FY 1970	Puget Sound Naval Shipyard	Oct 1969	Dec 1970
SSBN 632	FY 1969	General Dynamics Corp (Electric Boat)	July 1969	Nov 1970
SSBN 633	FY 1970	General Dynamics Corp (Electric Boat)	Jan 1970	Apr 1971
SSBN 634	FY 1971	General Dynamics (Electric Boat)	July 1970	Oct 1971
SSBN 635	FY 1970	Portsmouth Naval Shipyard	Jan 1970	Sep 1971
SSBN 636	FY 1971	Newport News SB & DD Co	July 1970	Sep 1971
SSBN 640	FY 1971	General Dynamics Corp (Electric Boat)	Feb 1971	May 1972
SSBN 641	FY 1971	Newport News SB & DD Co	Feb 1971	May 1972
SSBN 642	FY 1972	General Dynamics Corp (Electric Boat)	July 1971	Oct 1972
SSBN 643	FY 1971	Portsmouth Naval Shipyard	Apr 1971	Aug 1972
SSBN 644	FY 1971	Puget Sound Naval Shipyard	Apr 1971	July 1972
SSBN 645	FY 1972	Newport News SB & DD Co	July 1971	Nov 1972
SSBN 654	FY 1972	Puget Sound Naval Shipyard	Sep 1971	Feb 1973
SSBN 655	FY 1972	Newport News SB & DD Co	Nov 1971	Mar 1973
SSBN 656	FY 1972	General Dynamics Corp (Electric Boat)	Nov 1971	Mar 1973
SSBN 657	FY 1972	Puget Sound Naval Shipyard	Feb 1972	Apr 1973
SSBN 658	FY 1973	Newport News SB & DD Co	Aug 1972	Nov 1973
SSBN 659	FY 1973	Portsmouth Naval Shipyard	Oct 1972	Jan 1974

JOHN C CALHOUN (SSBM 630)

1970, United States Navy, PH1 T. Milton Putray

Strategic Missile Submarines —*continued*

5 FLEET BALLISTIC MISSILE SUBMARINES (SSBN): "ETHAN ALLEN" CLASS

Name	No.	Builder	Laid down	Launched	Commissioned
*ETHAN ALLEN	SSBN 608	General Dynamics (Electric Boat Div, Groton)	14 Sep 1959	22 Nov 1960	8 Aug 1961
*SAM HOUSTON	SSBN 609	Newport News Shipbuilding & DD Co	28 Dec 1959	2 Feb 1961	6 Mar 1962
*THOMAS A. EDISON	SSBN 610	General Dynamics (Electric Boat Div, Groton)	15 Mar 1960	15 June 1961	10 Mar 1962
*JOHN MARSHALL	SSBN 611	Newport News Shipbuilding & DD Co	4 Apr 1960	15 July 1961	21 May 1962
*THOMAS JEFFERSON	SSBN 618	Newport News Shipbuilding & DD Co	3 Feb 1961	24 Feb 1962	4 Jan 1963

Displacement, tons	6 900 standard surface; 7 900 submerged
Length, feet (*metres*)	410·5 (*125·1*) oa
Beam, feet (*metres*)	33 (*10·1*)
Draft, feet (*metres*)	30 (*9·4*)
Missile launchers	16 tubes for Polaris A-2 (see *Missile* notes)
Torpedo tubes	4—21 inch (*533 mm*) forward
Main engines	2 geared turbines (General Electric); 15 000 shp; 1 shaft
Nuclear reactor	1 pressurised-water cooled S5W (Westinghouse)
Speed, knots	20 surface; approx 30 submerged
Complement	112 (12 officers, 100 enlisted men)

These submarines were designed specifically for the FBM role and are larger and better arranged than the earlier "George Washington" class submarines. The first four ships of this class were authorised in the Fiscal Year 1959 programme; the *Thomas Jefferson* (which is out of numerical sequence) was in the FY 1961 programme. These submarines and the previous "George Washington" class will not be converted to carry the Poseidon missile because of material limitations and the age they would be after conversion. Also the "George Washington" class submarines are depth limited compared to the later FBM classes which, according to official statements, are based on the "Permit" SSN design.

DESIGN. These submarines and the subsequent "Lafayette" class are deep-diving submarines with a depth capability similar to the "Permit" class attack submarines; pressure hulls of HY-80 steel.

MISSILES. These ships were initially armed with the Polaris A-2 missile (1 725 statute mile range). The *Ethan Allan* launched the first A-2 missile fired from a submarine on 23 Oct 1961. She was the first submarine to deploy with the A-2 missile, beginning her first patrol on 26 June 1962. The *Ethan Allan* fired a Polaris A-2 missile in the Christmas Island Pacific Test Area on 6 May 1962 in what was the first complete US test of a ballistic missile including detonation of the nuclear warhead. All five of these ships are scheduled for modification to fire the A-3 missile (2 880 statute mile range). They will not be fitted with the advanced Poseidon missile.

Fitted with Mk 80 fire control system and compressed air missile ejectors; to have Mk 84 fire control systems and gas-steam missile ejectors with A-3 missile.

NAVIGATION. Fitted with two Mk 2 Ship's Inertial Navigation Systems (SINS) and navigational satellite receiver.

PERSONNEL. Alternating "Blue" and "Gold" crews are assigned to these submarines as in "Lafayette" class submarines.

PHOTOGRAPHS. Note sail number is painted out in view of *Ethan Allen* underway off Rota, Spain.

JOHN MARSHALL (SSBN 611) *1967, United States Navy*

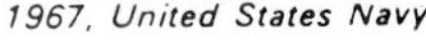

SAM HOUSTON (SSBN 609) *1967, United States Navy*

ETHAN ALLEN (SSBN 608) *1971, United States Navy, PH3 P. J. Roberts*

Strategic Missile Submarines—*Continued*

5 FLEET BALLISTIC MISSILE SUBMARINES (SSBN): "GEORGE WASHINGTON" CLASS

Name	*No.*	*Builder*	*Laid down*	*Launched*	*Commissioned*
***GEORGE WASHINGTON**	SSBN 598	General Dynamics (Electric Boat Div, Groton)	1 Nov 1957	9 June 1959	30 Dec 1959
***PATRICK HENRY**	SSBN 599	General Dynamics (Electric Boat Div, Groton)	27 May 1958	22 Sep 1959	9 Apr 1960
***THEODORE ROOSEVELT**	SSBN 600	Mare Island Naval Shipyard	20 May 1958	3 Oct 1959	13 Feb 1961
***ROBERT E. LEE**	SSBN 601	Newport News Shipbuilding & DD Co	25 Aug 1958	18 Dec 1959	16 Sep 1960
***ABRAHAM LINCOLN**	SSBN 602	Portsmouth Naval Shipyard	1 Nov 1958	14 May 1960	11 Mar 1961

Displacement, tons	5 900 standard surface; 6 700 submerged
Length, feet (*metres*)	381·7 (*115·8*) oa
Beam, feet (*metres*)	33 (*10·1*)
Draft, feet (*metres*)	29 (*8·8*)
Missile launchers	16 tubes for Polaris A-3
Torpedo tubes	6—21 inch (*533 mm*) forward
Main engines	2 geared turbines (General Electric); 15 000 shp, 1 shaft
Nuclear reactor	1 pressurised-water cooled S5W (Westinghouse)
Speed, knots	20 surface; approx 30 submerged
Complement	112 (12 officers, 100 enlisted men)

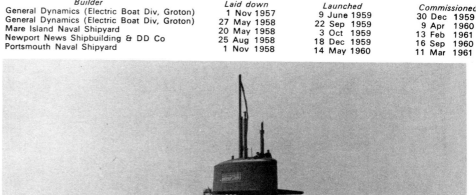

The *George Washington* was the West's first ship to be armed with ballistic missiles. A supplement to the Fiscal Year 1958 new construction programme signed on 11 Feb 1958 provided for the construction of the first three Fleet Ballistic Missile (FBM) submarines. The Navy had already ordered the just-begun attack submarine *Scorpion* (SSN 589) to be completed as a missile submarine on 31 Dec 1957; the hull was redesignated SSBN 598 and completed as the *George Washington*. The *Patrick Henry* similarly was reordered on the last day of 1957, her materials having originally been intended for the not-yet-started SSN 590. These submarines and three sister ships (two authorised in FY 1959) were built to a modified "Skipjack" class design with almost 130 feet being added to the original design to accommodate two rows of eight missile tubes, fire control and navigation equipment, and auxiliary machinery.

GEORGE WASHINGTON (SSBN 598)

United States Navy

ENGINEERING. The *George Washington* was the first FBM submarine to be overhauled and "refuelled". During her 4½ years of operation on her initial reactor core she carried out 15 submerged missile patrols and steamed more than 100 000 miles.

MISSILES. These ships were initially armed with the Polaris A-1 missile (1 380 statute mile range). The *George Washington* successfully fired two Polaris A-1 missiles while submerged off Cape Canaveral (Kennedy) on 20 July 1960 in the first underwater launching of a ballistic missile from a US submarine. She departed on her initial patrol on 15 Nov 1960 and remained submerged for 66 days, 10 hours. All five submarines of this class have been refitted to fire the improved Polaris A-3 missile (2 880 statute mile range). Missile refit and first reactor refuelling were accomplished simultaneously during overhaul: *George Washington* from 20 June 1964 to 2 Feb 1966, *Patrick Henry* from 4 Jan 1965 to 21 July 1966, *Theodore Roosevelt* from 28 July 1965 to 14 Jan 1967, *Robert E. Lee* from 23 Feb 1965 to 2 July 1966, and *Abraham Lincoln* from 25 Oct 1965 to 3 June 1967; four at Electric Boat yard in Groton, Connecticut, and *Robert E. Lee* at Mare Island Naval Shipyard (California).

These submarines all have Mk 84 fire control systems and gas-steam missile ejectors (originally fitted with Mk 80 fire control systems and compressed air missile ejectors, changed during A-3 missile refit).

These submarines will not be modified to carry and launch the advanced Poseidon ballistic missile.

ABRAHAM LINCOLN (SSBN 602) *United States Navy*

NAVIGATION. Fitted with three Mk 2 Ship's Inertial Navigation Systems (SINS) and navigational satellite receiver.

PERSONNEL. Alternating "Blue" and "Gold" crews are assigned to these submarines as in "Lafayette" class submarines.

PHOTOGRAPHS. Note that "hump" of hull extension for housing missile tubes is more pronounced in these submarines than later classes. Note the bitts and capstans visible in view of *Abraham Lincoln* while mooring; as in SSNs, most hull projects are removable or retractable to provide a "clean" hull and reduce noise as submarine passes through water.

ROBERT E. LEE (SSBN 601) ***1966, United States Navy***

SUBMARINES

The US Navy's submarine forces consist of two principal categories: fleet ballistic missile submarines (SSBN), listed in the previous section on Strategic Missile Submarines , and attack submarines (SS and SSN).

During 1973 the number of attack submarines in commission continued to decline as part of the overall reduction of the US Navy. However, this reduction was mitigated somewhat by the delivery of several nuclear-propelled submarines. Still, the US nuclear submarine production is about one-half that of the Soviet Union; similarly, the Soviets have developed several more classes of submarines in the past few years than has the US Navy. Concern also is being voiced about the increasing size and cost of US nuclear submarines, and delays in construction programmes.

As of June 1973 the US submarine forces contained 53 first-line nuclear attack submarines, eight second-line nuclear submarines, 10 modern diesel attack submarines, and a few modernised World War II-built submarines (GUPPY types). In addition, two research submarines, one transport submarine, and one training submarine are active. Thus, an estimated 85 submarines were active in the US Navy in addition to 41 nuclear-propelled strategic missile submarines.

Construction continues of the relatively large "Los Angeles" class attack submarines (SSN 688). Some dissatisfaction has been expressed with the SSN 688 design because of its large size, high cost, and reported minimal increase in performance over the previous "Sturgeon" class (SSN 637). The estimated US nuclear powered-attack submarine strength in 1974 when the *Los Angeles* will be commissioned is 66 submarines. At that time the pioneer *Nautilus* will be 20 years of age, thus an *increase* in SSN strength will be retarded slightly because of the older submarines being phased out of service and the seemingly inevitable delay in US nuclear submarine construction programmes.

ELECTRONICS. Programmes are underway to increase the capabilities of sonars installed in attack submarines. The BQQ-2 sonars of the "Permit"/"Sturgeon"/"Narwhal" classes will receive the search sonar which provides a digital multi-beam modification with a wide/narrow band, processing options, and accelerated active search radar. These submarines also will recieve Sub Close Contact Sonar, a mine detection sonar. The BQR-2 passive detecting sonar installed in pre-"Permit" nuclear attack submarines will receive a Digital Multi-Beam Steering (DIMUS) modification to provide a multi-target, automatic track capability and wide/narrow band signal processing option.

SSN loading Mk 48 torpedo — *1972, United States Air Force*

NOMENCLATURE. US submarines generally have been named for fish and other marine life except that fleet ballistic missile submarines have been named for famous Americans. The tradition of naming "fleet" and "attack" submarines for fish was broken in 1971 when three submarines of the "Sturgeon" class and the one-of-a-kind SSN 685 were named for deceased members of the Congress. Previously US destroyer-type ships have honoured members of the Congress.

Later in 1971 the SSN 688, lead ship for a new class of attack submarines, was named *Los Angeles*, introducing "city" names to US submarines. This was the third name source applied to US submarines within a year, indicating the considerable confusion in ship nomenclature within the Navy.

(Of late, several types of auxiliary ships also have been named for cities, a name source traditionally applied to cruisers in the US Navy)

TACTICAL CRUISE MISSILE SUBMARINES: PROPOSED

The Navy is planning to construct a class of nuclear-propelled submarines armed with anti-ship tactical "cruise" missiles to provide an improved capability for attacking advanced Soviet surface warships. Conceptual design work on this class is underway with construction proposed in the mid-1970s as follow-on to the "Los Angeles" class.

According to Vice Admiral H. G. Rickover, head of the US Navy's nuclear propulsion programme: "Modern high-speed US nuclear attack submarines (SSN) armed with long-range tactical cruise missiles could successfully engage and neutralise typical Soviet task forces. In neutralising such a force, the US submarine need never approach within range of the enemy's ASW capability because the cruise missile extends the SSN attack range beyond any foreseeable surface ASW sonar range. Consequently, the cruise missile firing submarine survivability is significantly greater than any other platform that could engage a modern Soviet task force".

In addition to the anti-ship missile capabilities, the tactical cruise missile submarine would have approximately the same anti-submarine sensors and weapons as a "Los Angeles" class submarine. The submarines would be large even in comparison with the "Los Angeles" class because of the requirement for cruise missile launching tubes and missile control equipment in addition to the existing submarine systems. In view of the size of the "Los Angeles" class great concern is being voiced about the potential size and costs of the tactical cruise missile submarine. A range of 1 500 miles has been mentioned for such a missile.

18 + 5 NUCLEAR-POWERED ATTACK SUBMARINES (SSN): "LOS ANGELES" CLASS

Displacement, tons	6 900 submerged
Length, feet	360 oa
Beam, feet	33
Draft, feet	32 max
Torpedo tubes	4—21 in (*533 mm*) amidships
A/S weapons	SUBROC and Mk 48 A/S torpedoes
Main engines	2 geared turbines; 1 shaft
Nuclear reactor	1 pressurised-water cooled
Speed, knots	30+ submerged

Name	No.	Builder	Laid down	Launch	Commission
LOS ANGELES	**SSN 688**	Newport News SB & DD Co	8 Jan 1972	June 1973	Late 1974
BATON ROUGE	**SSN 689**	Newport News SB & DD Co	18 Nov 1972	Apr 1974	1975
PHILADELPHIA	**SSN 690**	General Dynamics (Electric Boat)	12 Aug 1972	Mar 1974	1975
MEMPHIS	**SSN 691**	Newport News SB & DD Co	June 1973	Aug 1974	1975
OMAHA	**SSN 692**	General Dynamics (Electric Boat)	27 Jan 1973	Aug 1974	1975
	SSN 693	Newport News SB & DD Co	July 1973	1975	1976
GROTON	**SSN 694**	General Dynamics (Electric Boat)	Apr 1973	Dec 1974	1976
	SSN 695	Newport News SB & DD Co			
	SSN 696	General Dynamics (Electric Boat)			
	SSN 697	General Dynamics (Electric Boat)			
	SSN 698	General Dynamics (Electric Boat)			1976-1978
	SSN 699	General Dynamics (Electric Boat)			
Six submarines	**SSN 700-705**	Fiscal Year 1973 programme			
Five submarines	**SSN 706-710**	Proposed Fiscal Year 1974 programme			

These are "high-speed" attack submarines intended to counter the new Soviet classes of submarines that went to sea during the late 1960s and early 1970s.

The SSN 688-690 (3 ships) were authorised in the Fiscal Year 1970 new construction programme, SSN 691-694 (4 ships) in FY 1971, and SSN 695-699 (5 ships) in FY 1972. Contracts for the construction of these 12 submarines were awarded on 8 Jan 1971 (prior to authorisation of the FY 1972 programme). SSN 700-705 (6 ships) authorised in FY 1973 and fire submarines requested in FY 1974 new construction programme. See *Fiscal* notes for cost data.

Approximately 30 submarines of this design will be constructed under FY 1970-1975 programmes.

Detailed design of the SSN 688 class as well as construction of the lead submarine was contracted to the Newport News Shipbuilding & Dry Dock Company, Newport News, Virginia; the follow-on ships were awarded to Newport News and to the General Dynamics Electric Boat Division yard at Groton, Connecticut.

DESIGN. These submarines will be considerably larger than the previous "Sturgeon" class. All construction features, including sail size, hull shape, propulsion plant design, machinery mounting technique, auxiliary machinery, etc, will be designed to provide the maximum degree of quietness possible. Their sound level will be similar to the "Sturgeon" class when both submarines are travelling at comparable speeds.

ELECTRONICS. Electronic equipment planned for these submarines includes BQX-5 (formerely BQS-13DNA) long-range detection sonar, BQS-15 close contact avoidance sonar, and BPS-15 surface search radar. UYK-7 computer will be installed to assist command and control functions.

ENGINEERING. Unofficial sources indicate that a modified surface ship nuclear reactor plant may be used in this class. The "smallest" surface ship reactor now available for submarine use is the D2G type used in the frigates *Bainbridge* and *Truxtun*; these reactors each produce approximately 30 000 shp.

FISCAL. The FY 1970 shipbuilding programme provided $504 500 000 for the construction of the SSN 688-690 plus $110 000 000 for procurement of long-lead time equipment (primarily reactor components) for five additional submarines. However, the Nixon Adminstration requested only three SSN-688 class submarines in FY 1971. The congress subsequently voted four submarines in FY 1971 and appropriated $662 000 000 for their construction plus long-lead time equipment for the FY 1972 programme. The FY 1972 budget provided $904 000 000 for SSN 695-699 plus advance procurement for six additional submarines. The FY 1973 budget requested $1·042 *billion* to fund the full construction of six additional submarines plus long-lead components for later submarines. The FY 1974 budget requests $921 600 000 for five submarines.

Initial cost estimates for the first 12 submarines prior to start of construction was $2 *billion* or an average of $166 000 000 per ship; however, revised estimates indicate that later submarines of this class probably will cost in excess of $200 000 000 per ship.

Submarines—*continued*

1 NUCLEAR POWERED ATTACK SUBMARINE (SSN): QUIET DESIGN

Displacement, tons	over 5 000 submerged
Length, feet	over 300 oa
Torpedo tubes	4—21 inch (*533 mm*) amidships
A/S weapons	SUBROC and A/S torpedoes
Main engines	Turbine-electric drive (General Electric); 1 shaft
Nuclear reactor	1 pressurised-water cooled S5WA (Westinghouse)
Speed, knots	approx 25 submerged
Complement	over 100

Name	*No.*	*Builder*	*Laid down*	*Launch*	*Commission*
GLENARD P LIPSCOMB	SSN 685	General Dynamics	5 June 1971	June 1973	June 1974

The Turbine-Electric Drive Submarine (TEDS) is being built to test "a combination of advanced silencing techniques" involving "a new kind of propulsion system, and new and quieter machinery of various kinds", according to the Department of Defense. The noise level produced by an operating submarine is an important factor in its ability to remain undetected by an opponent's passive listening devices and its own ability to detect the opponent. The TEDS project will permit an at-sea evaluation of improvements in ASW effectiveness due to noise reduction. The SSN 685 will be slightly larger than "Sturgeon" class submarines and somewhat slower.

No class of turbine-electric nuclear submarines is planned at this time. Rather, quieting features developed in the SSN 685 which do not detract from speed probably will be incorporated in the SSN 688 design and subsequent SSN classes. (The TEDS design is several years ahead of the SSN 688 design)

Authorised in the Fiscal Year 1968 new construction programme; estimated construction cost will be between $150 000 000 and $200 000 000.

Design of an advanced submarine specifically intended for quiet operation began with Navy studies which commenced in October 1964. Approval to construct the submarine was revoked on at least one occasion by the Department of Defense in an effort to combine several desired characteristics in a single submarine design. However, high speed and silent operation apparently are not compatible with available technolgy.

Final Department of Defense approval for construction of the turbine-electric drive submarine was announced on 25 Oct 1968. A contract was awarded to GD/EB for construction of the SSN 685 on 16 Dec 1968.

ENGINEERING. Turbine-electric drive eliminates the noisy reduction gears of standard steam turbine power plants, the major source of noise in a nuclear-powered submarine. The turbine-electric power plant is larger and heavier than comparable steam turbine submarine machinery.

The *Tullibee* (SSN 597) was an earlier effort at noise reduction through a turbine-electric nuclear plant.

1 NUCLEAR POWERED ATTACK SUBMARINE (SSN): "NARWHAL" TYPE

Displacement, tons	4 450 standard; 5 350 submerged
Length, feet (*metres*)	314 (*95·7*) oa
Beam, feet (*metres*)	38 (*11·5*)
Draft, feet (*metres*)	26 (*7·9*)
Torpedo tubes	4—21 inch (*533 mm*) amidships
A/S weapons	SUBROC and A/S torpedoes
Main engines	2 steam turbines; approx 17 000 shp; 1 shaft
Nuclear reactor	1 pressurised water-cooled S5G (General Electric)
Speed, knots	approx 20 surface; approx 30 submerged
Complement	107 (12 officers, 95 enlisted men)

Name	*No*	*Builder*	*Laid down*	*Launched*	*Commissioned*
*NARWHAL	SSN 671	General Dynamics (Electric Boat)	17 Jan 1966	9 Sep 1967	12 July 1969

NARWHAL (SSN 671) *1969, General Dynamics, Electric Boat Division*

The *Narwhal* is a large attack submarine with an improved propulsion system. She is the largest "straight" nuclear-powered attack submarine yet built by the US Navy (slightly shorter than the pioneers *Nautilus* and *Seawolf*, but wider, deeper, and heavier). Authorised in the Fiscal Year 1964 new construction programme.

DESIGN. The *Narwhal* is similar to the "Sturgeon" class submarines in design.

ELECTRONICS. Fitted with BQQ-2 sonar system. See "Sturgeon" and "Permit" classes for general notes.

ENGINEERING. The *Narwhal* is fitted with the prototype sea-going S5G Natural Circulation Reactor. According to Vice Admiral H. G. Rickover, the Natural Circulation Reactor "offers promise of increased reactor plant reliability, simplicity, and noise reduction due to the elimination of the need for large reactor coolant pumps and associated electrical and control equipment by taking maximum advantage of natural convection to circulate the reactor coolant".

Natural circulation eliminates the requirement for primary coolant pumps, the second noisiest component of a pressurised-water propulsion system after the steam turbines.

The Atomic Energy Commission's Knolls Atomic Power Laboratory was given prime responsibility for development of the power plant. Construction of a land-based prototype plant began in May 1961 at the National Reactor Testing Station in Idaho. The reactor achieved initial criticality on 12 Sep 1965.

NARWHAL (SSN 671) ***1969, General Dynamics, Electric Boat Division***

Submarines—*continued*

37 NUCLEAR-POWERED ATTACK SUBMARINES (SSN): "STURGEON" CLASS

Displacement, tons	3 860 standard; 4 630 submerged
Length, feet (*metres*)	292·2 (*89·0*) oa
Beam, feet (*metres*)	31·7 (*9·5*)
Draft, feet (*metres*)	26 (*7·9*)
Torpedo tubes	4—21 inch (*533 mm*) amidships
A/S weapons	SUBROC and A/S torpedoes
Main engines	2 steam turbines; approx 15 000 shp; 1 shaft
Nuclear reactor	1 pressurised-water cooled S5W (Westinghouse)
Speed, knots	approx 20 surface; approx 30 submerged
Complement	107 (12 officers, 95 enlisted men)

Name	*No.*	*Builder*	*Laid down*	*Launched*	*Commissioned*
***STURGEON**	SSN 637	General Dynamics (Electric Boat)	10 Aug 1963	26 Feb 1966	3 Mar 1967
***WHALE**	SSN 638	General Dynamics (Quincy)	27 May 1964	14 Oct 1966	12 Oct 1968
***TAUTOG**	SSN 639	Ingalls Shipbuilding Corp	27 Jan 1964	15 Apr 1967	17 Aug 1968
***GRAYLING**	SSN 646	Portsmouth Naval Shipyard	12 May 1964	22 June 1967	11 Oct 1969
***POGY**	SSN 647	Ingalls Shipbuilding Corp	4 May 1964	3 June 1967	15 May 1971
***ASPRO**	SSN 648	Ingalls Shipbuilding Corp	23 Nov 1964	29 Nov 1967	20 Feb 1969
***SUNFISH**	SSN 649	General Dynamics (Quincy)	15 Jan 1965	14 Oct 1966	15 Mar 1969
***PARGO**	SSN 650	General Dynamics (Electric Boat)	3 June 1964	17 Sep 1966	5 Dec 1967
***QUEENFISH**	SSN 651	Newport News SB & DD Co	11 May 1965	25 Feb 1966	6 Dec 1966
***PUFFER**	SSN 652	Ingalls Shipbuilding Corp	8 Feb 1965	30 Mar 1968	9 Aug 1969
***RAY**	SSN 653	Newport News SB & DD Co	1 Apr 1965	21 June 1966	12 Apr 1967
***SAND LANCE**	SSN 660	Portsmouth Naval Shipyard	15 Jan 1965	11 Nov 1969	25 Sep 1971
***LAPON**	SSN 661	Newport News SB & DD Co	26 July 1965	16 Dec 1966	14 Dec 1967
***GURNARD**	SSN 662	San Francisco NSY (Mare Island)	22 Dec 1964	20 May 1967	6 Dec 1968
***HAMMERHEAD**	SSN 663	Newport News SB & DD Co	29 Nov 1965	14 Apr 1967	28 June 1968
***SEA DEVIL**	SSN 664	Newport News SB & DD Co	12 Apr 1966	5 Oct 1967	30 Jan 1969
***GUITARRO**	SSN 665	San Francisco NSY (Mare Island)	9 Dec 1965	27 July 1968	9 Sep 1972
***HAWKBILL**	SSN 666	San Francisco NSY (Mare Island)	12 Sep 1966	12 Apr 1969	4 Feb 1971
***BERGALL**	SSN 667	General Dynamics (Electric Boat)	16 Apr 1966	17 Feb 1968	13 June 1969
***SPADEFISH**	SSN 668	Newport News SB & DD Co	21 Dec 1966	15 May 1968	31 July 1969
***SEAHORSE**	SSN 669	General Dynamics (Electric Boat)	13 Aug 1966	15 June 1968	19 Sep 1969
***FINBACK**	SSN 670	Newport News SB & DD Co	26 June 1967	7 Dec 1968	4 Feb 1970
***PINTADO**	SSN 672	San Francisco NSY (Mare Island)	27 Oct 1967	16 Aug 1969	29 Apr 1971
***FLYING FISH**	SSN 673	General Dynamics (Electric Boat)	30 June 1967	17 May 1969	29 Apr 1970
***TREPANG**	SSN 674	General Dynamics (Electric Boat)	28 Oct 1967	27 Sep 1969	14 Aug 1970
***BLUEFISH**	SSN 675	General Dynamics (Electric Boat)	13 Mar 1968	10 Jan 1970	8 Jan 1971
***BILLFISH**	SSN 676	General Dynamics (Electric Boat)	20 Sep 1968	1 May 1970	11 Sep 1971
***DRUM**	SSN 677	San Francisco NSY (Mare Island)	20 Aug 1968	23 May 1970	15 Apr 1972
***ARCHERFISH**	SSN 678	General Dynamics (Electric Boat)	19 June 1969	16 Jan 1971	17 Dec 1971
***SILVERSIDES**	SSN 679	General Dynamics (Electric Boat)	13 Oct 1969	4 June 1971	5 May 1972
***WILLIAM H. BATES**	SSN 680	Ingalls Shipbuilding (Litton)	4 Aug 1969	11 Dec 1971	12 Apr 1973
***BATFISH**	SSN 681	General Dynamics(Electric Boat)	9 Feb 1970	9 Oct 1971	1 Sep 1972
TUNNY	SSN 682	Ingalls Shipbuilding (Litton)	22 May 1970	10 June 1972	Sep 1973
PARCHE	SSN 683	Ingalls Shipbuilding (Litton)	10 Dec 1970	13 Jan 1973	Mar 1974
***CAVALLA**	SSN 684	General Dynamics (Electric Boat)	4 June 1970	19 Feb 1972	9 Feb 1973
L. MENDEL RIVERS	SSN 686	Newport News SB & DD Co	26 June 1971	May 1973	mid 1974
RICHARD B. RUSSELL	SSN 687	Newport News SB & DD Co	19 Oct 1971	Jan 1974	early 1975

The 37 "Sturgeon" class attack submarines comprise the largest US Navy group of nuclear-powered ships built to the same design (followed by the 31 "Lafayette" class ballistic missile submarines).
These submarines are intended to seek out and destroy enemy submarines. They are similar in design to the previous "Permit" (ex-"Thresher") class but are slightly larger. SSN 637-639 (3 ships) were authorised in the Fiscal Year 1962 new construction programme. SSN 646-653 (8 ships) in FY 1963, SSN 660-664 (5 ships) in FY 1964, SSN 665-670 (6 ships) in FY 1965, SSN 672-677 (6 ships) in FY 1966, SSN 678-682 (5 ships) in FY 1967, SSN 683-684 (2 ships) in FY 1968, and SSN 686 and SSN 687 in FY 1969.
Some of these ships are requiring *seven* years for construction (keel laying to completion).

CONSTRUCTION. The *Pogy* was begun by the New York Shipbuilding Corp (Camden, New Jersey), but was towed to Ingalls Shipbuilding Corp for completion; contract with the New York Shipbuilding Corp was terminated on 5 June 1967; contract for completion awarded to Ingalls Shipbuilding Corp on 7 Dec 1967.
The *Guitarro* sank in 35 feet of water on 15 May 1969 while being fitted out at the San Francisco Bay Naval Shipyard. According to a congressional report, the sinking, caused by shipyard workers, was "wholly avoidable". Subsequently raised; damage estimated at $25 000 000 to repair damage due to interior flooding. Completion delayed more than two years.

DESIGN. These submarines are slightly larger than the previous "Permit" (ex-"Thresher") class and can be identified by their taller sail structure and the lower position of their diving planes on the sail (to improve control at periscope depth). Sail height is 20 feet, 6 inches above deck. Sail-mounted diving planes rotate to vertical for breaking through ice when surfacing in arctic regions.
These ships incorporate modifications of the submarine safety (SUBSAFE) programme established after the loss of the *Thresher*. These submarines probably are slightly slower than the previous "Permit" and "Skipjack" classes because of their increased size with the same propulsion system as in the earlier classes.

ELECTRONICS. These submarines are fitted with the advanced BQQ-2 sonar system. Principal components of the BQQ-2 include the BQS-6 active sonar, with transducers mounted in a 15-foot diameter sonar sphere, and BQR-7 passive sonar, with hydrophones in a conformal array on sides of forward hull. The active sonar sphere is fitted in the optimum bow position, requiring placement of torpedo tubes amidships. These submarines also have BQS-8 and BQS-13 active passive sonars; transducers for the former are in two small domes aft of sail structure. BQS-8 sonar is intended primarily for under-ice-navigation. Sonar suite of *Guitarro* is of an improved design. BPS-14 surface search radar fitted. These submarines have the Mk 113 torpedo fire control director.

MISSILES. Compatability tests were conducted during 1972-1973 with several submarines of this class and the Harpoon anti-ship missile.

NOMENCLATURE. *William H. Bates* ex-*Redfish*, renamed 25 June 1971 to honour deceased member of Congress.

OPERATIONAL. The *Whale*, *Pargo*, and older nuclear submarine *Sargo* conducted exercises in the Arctic ice pack during March-April 1969. The *Whale* surfaced at the geographic North Pole on April 6, the 60th anniversary of Rear Admiral Robert E. Peary reaching the North Pole. This was believed the first instance of single-screw US nuclear submarines surfacing in the Arctic ice.
The *Hammerhead* and the older nuclear submarine *Skate* conducted exercises in the Arctic during November-December 1970, with the *Hammerhead* surfacing at the North Pole on Nov. 20.
The *Trepang* operated in the Arctic with the *Skate* during the spring of 1971.

SUBMERSIBLES. The *Hawkbill* has been modified to carry and support the Navy's Deep Submergence Rescue Vehicles (DSRV). The *Hawkbill* can transport a 50-foot DSRV "piggyback" on her after deck and while submerged can launch and recover the DSRV. The DSRV also can "land" on the submarine's forward hatch as well as the after hatch to transfer personnel. See section on Deep Submergence Vehicles for additional DSRV details.
The research submarine *Halibut* (SSN 587) also is fitted to carry the DSRV. The modifications do not affect the *Hawkbill's* combat capabilities.

ARCHERFISH (SSN 678) *1971, General Dynamics Corp*

POGY (SSN 647) *1971, Ingalls Shipbuilding*

Submarines—*continued*

PHOTOGRAPHS. These submarines have streamlined hulls with few deck projections to interrupt their clean lines; the two small domes on the main deck aft of the sail structure are BQS-8 sonar transducers and the darker "windows" on the sail structure (forward of diving planes) are BQS-8 hydrophones. Capstans and cleats are retractable.

The *Hawkbill* is shown carrying the submersible DSRV-1 The markings on the submarines' sail and around her forward hatch are luminescent to assist underwater "mating" operations.

A photograph of the *Whale* surfaced through ice at the North Pole, with her diving planes rotated to the vertical position, appears in the 1971-1972 and 1972-1973 editions.

BLUEFISH (SSN 675) — *1970, General Dynamics, Electric Boat Division*

POGY (SSN 647) — *1971, Ingalls Shipbuilding*

HAWKBILL (SSN 666) with DSRV-1 — *1971, United States Navy*

Submarines—*continued*

13 NUCLEAR-POWERED ATTACK SUBMARINES (SSN): "PERMIT" CLASS

Displacement, tons	3 750 standard, *Flasher, Greenling*, and *Gato* 3 800 tons; 4 300 submerged except *Jack* 4 500, submerged, *Flasher, Greenling*, and *Gato* 4 600 submerged
Length, feet (*metres*)	278·5 (*84·9*) oa except *Jack* 295·7 (*89·5*), *Flasher, Greenling* and *Gato* 292·2 (*89·1*)
Beam, feet (*metres*)	31·7 (*9·6*)
Draft, feet (*metres*)	25·2 (*7·6*)
Torpedo tubes	4—21 in (*533 mm*) amidships
A/S weapons	SUBROC and A/S torpedoes
Main engines	2 steam turbines, approx 15 000 shp; 1 shaft
Nuclear reactor	1 pressurised-water cooled S5W (Westinghouse)
Speed, knots	approx 20 surface; approx 30 submerged
Complement	107 (12 officers, 95 enlisted men)

Name	*No*	*Builder*	*Laid down*	*Launched*	*Commissioned*
*PERMIT	SSN 594	Mare Island Naval Shipyard	16 July 1959	1 July 1961	29 May 1962
*PLUNGER	SSN 595	Mare Island Naval Shipyard	2 Mar 1960	9 Dec 1961	21 Nov 1962
*BARB	SSN 596	Ingalls Shipbuilding Corp	9 Nov 1959	12 Feb 1962	24 Aug 1963
*POLLACK	SSN 603	New York Shipbuilding Corp	14 Mar 1960	17 Mar 1962	26 May 1964
*HADDO	SSN 604	New York Shipbuilding Corp	9 Sep 1960	18 Aug 1962	16 Dec 1964
*JACK	SSN 605	Portsmouth Naval Shipyard	16 Sep 1960	24 Apr 1963	31 Mar 1967
*TINOSA	SSN 606	Portsmouth Naval Shipyard	24 Nov 1959	9 Dec 1961	17 Oct 1964
*DACE	SSN 607	Ingalls Shipbuilding Corp	6 June 1960	18 Aug 1962	4 Apr 1964
*GUARDFISH	SSN 612	New York Shipbuilding Corp	28 Feb 1961	15 May 1965	20 Dec 1966
*FLASHER	SSN 613	General Dynamics (Electric Boat)	14 Apr 1961	22 June 1963	22 July 1966
*GREENLING	SSN 614	General Dynamics (Electric Boat)	15 Aug 1961	4 Apr 1964	3 Nov 1967
*GATO	SSN 615	Ingalls Shipbuilding Corp	15 Dec 1961	14 May 1964	25 Jan 1968
*HADDOCK	SSN 621	Ingalls Shipbuilding Corp	24 Apr 1961	21 May 1966	22 Dec 1967

These submarines were the first of a series of advanced attack submarines intended to seek out and destroy enemy submarines. They have a greater depth capability than previous nuclear-powered submarines and are the first to combine the SUBROC anti-submarine missile capability with the advanced BQQ-2 sonar system. The lead ship of the class, the ill-fated *Thresher* (SSN 593), was authorised in the Fiscal Year 1957 new construction programme, the SSN 594-596 (3 ships) in FY 1958, SSN 603-607 (5 ships) in FY 1959, SSN 612-615 (4 ships) in FY 1960, and SSN 621 in FY 1961.

The *Thresher* (SSN 593) was lost off the coast of New England on 10 Apr 1963 while on post-overhaul trials. She went down with 129 men on board (108 crewmen plus four naval officers and 17 civilians on board for trials).

Later submarines of this class were delayed because of the Submarine Safety (SUBSAFE) program modifications, increased quality control of submarine construction, and specific problems at shipyards.

CLASS. These submarines were originally listed as belonging to the "Thresher" class; now referred to as the "Permit" class after loss of the *Thresher* in 1963.

CONSTRUCTION. *Greenling* and *Gato* were launched by the Electric Boat Division of the General Dynamics Corp (Groton, Connecticut); towed to Quincy Division (Massachusetts) for lengthening and completion.

PLUNGER (SSN 595) *United States Navy*

DESIGN. The *Plunger, Barb, Pollack*, and *Dace* were ordered as guided missile submarines (SSGN) and were to each carry four Regulus II missiles. They were re-ordered as "Thresher" class attack submarines after the Regulus II programme was cancelled on 18 Dec 1958 (retaining numerical sequence in the submarine series). The *Jack* was built to a modified design to test a different power plant (see *Engineering* notes).

The *Flasher, Gato*, and *Greenling* were modified during construction; fitted with SUBSAFE features, heavier machinery, and larger sail structures.

These submarines have a modified "tear-drop" hull design. Their bows are devoted to sonar and their four torpedo tubes are amidships, angled out, two to port and two to starboard.

The sail structure height of these submarines is 13 feet, 9 inches to 15 feet above the deck, with later submarines of this class having a sail height of 20 feet.

ELECTRONICS. These submarines are fitted with the advanced BQQ-2 sonar system (first installed in the *Tullibee*, SSN 597). Principal components of the BQQ-2 include the BQS-6 active sonar, with transducers mounted in a 15-foot diameter sonar sphere, and BQR-7 passive sonar, with hydrophones in a conformal array along sides of forward hull. The active sonar sphere is fitted in the optimum bow position, requiring placement of torpedo tubes amidships. The advanced BQS-13DNA active/passive sonar will be fitted in these submarines.

These submarines have the Mk 113 torpedo fire control director.

ENGINEERING. The *Jack* is fitted with two propellers on essentially one shaft (actually a single shaft within a sleeve-like shaft) and a counter-rotating turbine without a reduction gear. Both innovations are designed to reduce operating noises. To accommodate the larger turbine the engine spaces were lengthened ten feet and the shaft structure was lengthened seven feet to mount the two propellers. The propellers are of different size and are smaller than in the other submarines of this class. Also eliminated in *Jack* was a clutch and secondary-propulsion electric motor.

The *Jack's* propulsion arrangement provides a ten per cent increase in power efficiency, but no increase in speed.

NOMENCLATURE. Names changed during construction: *Plunger* ex-*Pollack*: *Barb* ex-*Pollack*: ex-*Plunger*: *Pollack* ex-*Barb*.

GUARDFISH (SSN 612) *1968, United States Navy*

TULLIBEE (SSN 597)—See following page *1968, United States Navy*

Submarines—*continued*

1 NUCLEAR-POWERED ATTACK SUBMARINE (SSN): "TULLIBEE" TYPE

Name	No	Builder	Laid down	Launched	Commissioned
*TULLIBEE	SSN 597	General Dynamics (Electric Boat)	26 May 1958	27 Apr 1960	9 Nov 1960

Displacement, tons	2 317 standard; 2 640 submerged
Length, feet (*metres*)	273 (*83·2*) oa
Beam, feet (*metres*)	23·3 (*7·1*)
Draft, feet (*metres*)	21 (*6·4*)
Torpedo tubes	4—21 in (*533 mm*) amidships
A/S weapons	A/S torpedoes
Main engines	Turbo-electric drive with steam turbine (Westinghouse) 2 500 shp; 1 shaft
Nuclear reactor	1 pressurised water cooled S2C (Combustion Engineering)
Speed, knots	approx 15 surface; 15+ submerged)
Complement	56 (6 officers, 50 enlisted men)

The *Tullibee* was designed specifically for anti-submarine operations and was the first US submarine with the optimum bow position devoted entirely to sonar. No additional submarines of this type were constructed because of the success of the larger, more-versatile "Permit" class. The *Tullibee* was authorised in the Fiscal Year 1958 new construction programme. She is no longer considered a "first line" submarine.

DESIGN. The *Tullibee* has a modified, elongated "tear-drop" hull design. Originally she was planned as a 1 000-ton craft, but reactor requirements and other considerations increased her size during design and construction.

The *Tullibee* has four amidships torpedo tubes angled out from the centreline, two to port and two to starboard. However, she is not fitted to fire the SUBROC anti-submarine missile. She cannot match the "Thresher" and later SSN classes in underwater speed or manoeuvrability.

ELECTRONICS. The *Tullibee* was the first submarine fitted with the advanced BQQ-2 sonar system (see "Permit" class listing for details). The fin-like sonar domes are PUFFs for BQG-4 passive fire control sonar; in the earlier photograph only two PUFF domes are installed (not to be confused with fin-like rudder); later photograph shows three PUFF domes with second dome (aft of sail structure) painted light color.

PUFF is an acronym for Passive Underwater Fire-control Feasibility system. Fitted with Mk 112-1 torpedo fire control system.

ENGINEERING. The *Tullibee* has a small nuclear power plant designed and developed by the Combustion Engineering Company.

The *Tullibee* propulsion system features turbo-electric drive rather than conventional steam turbines with reduction gears in an effort to reduce operating noises.

NAVIGATION. The *Tullibee* is fitted with Ships Inertial Navigation System (SINS).

TULLIBEE (SSN 597) *1960, United States Navy*

5 NUCLEAR-POWERED ATTACK SUBMARINES (SSN): "SKIPJACK" CLASS

Name	No	Builder	Laid down	Launched	Commissioned
*SKIPJACK	SSN 585	General Dynamics (Electric Boat)	29 May 1956	26 May 1958	15 Apr 1959
*SCAMP	SSN 588	Mare Island Naval Shipyard	23 Jan 1959	8 Oct 1960	5 June 1961
*SCULPIN	SSN 590	Ingalls Shipbuilding Corp	3 Feb 1958	31 Mar 1960	1 June 1961
*SHARK	SSN 591	Newport News SB & DD Co	24 Feb 1958	16 Mar 1960	9 Feb 1961
*SNOOK	SSN 592	Ingalls Shipbuilding Corp	7 Apr 1958	31 Oct 1960	24 Oct 1961

Displacement, tons	3 075 standard; 3 500 submerged
Length, feet (*metres*)	251·7 (*76·7*) oa
Beam, feet (*metres*)	31·5 (*9·6*)
Draft, feet (*metres*)	28 (*8·5*)
Torpedo tubes	6—21 in (*533 mm*) forward
A/S weapons	A/S torpedoes
Main engines	2 steam turbines (Westinghouse in *Skipjack*; General Electric in others); approx 15 000 shp; 1 shaft
Nuclear reactor	1 pressurised-water cooled S5W (Westinghouse)
Speed, knots	approx 20 surface; 30+ submerged
Complement	93 (8 officers, 85 enlisted men)

The "Skipjack" class combines the high-speed endurance of nuclear propulsion with the high-speed "tear-drop" hull design tested in the conventionally powered submarine *Albacore* (AGSS 569). (See *Design* and *Engineering* notes). The *Skipjack* was authorised in the Fiscal Year 1956 new construction programme; the five other submarines of this class were authorised in FY 1957. Although they are now nearing their first decade of service, these submarines are still considered suitable for "first line" service. Officially described as fastest US nuclear submarines in service.

Each cost approximately $40 000 000.

The *Scorpion* (SSN 589) of this class was lost some 400 miles southwest of the Azores while en route from the Mediterranean to Norfolk, Virginia, in May 1968. She went down with 99 men on board.

CONSTRUCTION. The *Scorpion's* keel was laid down twice: the original keel laid down on 1 Nov 1957 was renumbered SSBN 598 and became the Polaris submarine *George Washington*; the second SSN 589 keel became the *Scorpion*. The *Scamp's* keel laying was delayed when material for her was diverted to the SSBN 599. This class introduced the Newport News Shipbuilding and Dry Dock Company and the Ingalls Shipbuilding Corporation to nuclear submarine construction. Newport News had not previously built any submarine since before World War I; Ingalls previously had built only one submarine, the *Blueback* (SS 581), launched in 1959.

DESIGN. The *Skipjack* was the first US nuclear submarine built to the "tear-drop" or modified spindle hull design for improved underwater performance. These submarines have a single propeller shaft (vice two in earlier nuclear submarines) and their diving planes are mounted on sail structures to improve underwater manoeuvrability. No after torpedo tubes are fitted because of their tapering sterns.

SNOOK (SSN 592) *1964, United States Navy*

Submarines—*continued*

"SKIPJACK" CLASS —*continued*

ELECTRONICS. Original sonar equipment was modified to provide improved ASW capabilities.
Mk 112 torpedo fire control director.

ENDURANCE. The *Scorpion* set an endurance record in 1962 when she maintained a sealed atmosphere for 70 consecutive days.

ENGINEERING. The "Skipjack" class, introduced the S5W fast attack submarine-propulsion plant which has been used in all subsequent attack and missile submarines until the "Los Angeles" (SSN 688) class except the *Narwhal*. The plant was developed by the Bettis Atomic Power Laboratory.

PHOTOGRAPHS. Note streamlined shape and lack of projections; all equipment outside of the hull is either recessed or retractable.

SHARK (SSN 591)—See previous page *1968, United States Navy*

1 NUCLEAR-POWERED RESEARCH SUBMARINE (SSN): "HALIBUT" TYPE

Name	*No.*	*Builder*	*Laid down*	*Launched*	*Commissioned*
***HALIBUT**	SSN 587 (ex-SSGN 587)	Mare Island Naval Shipyard, Vallejo, Calif	11 Apr 1957	9 Jan 1959	4 Jan 1960

Displacement, tons	3 850 standard; 5 000 submerged
Length, feet (*metres*)	350 (*106·6*) oa
Beam, feet (*metres*)	29.5 (*8·9*)
Draft, feet (*metres*)	21·5 (*6·5*)
Torpedo tubes	6—21 in (*533 mm*) 4 fwd; 2 aft
Main engines	2 steam turbines (Westinghouse), approx 6 000 shp; 2 shafts
Nuclear reactor	1 pressurised-water cooled S3W (Westinghouse)
Speed, knots	15·5 surface; 15+ submerged
Complement	97 (9 officers, 88 enlisted men)

The *Halibut* is believed to have been the first submarine designed and constructed specifically to fire guided missiles. The Soviet "Juliett" class guided missile submarines with diesel-electric propulsion were constructed after the *Halibut*.

She was originally intended to have diesel-electric propulsion but on 27 Feb 1956 the Navy announced she would have nuclear propulsion. She was the US Navy's only nuclear powered *guided* missile submarine (SSGN) to be completed. Authorised in the Fiscal Year 1956 new construction programme and built for an estimated cost of $45 000 000.

The *Halibut* was reclassifed as an attack submarine on 25 July 1965 after the Navy discarded the Regulus submarine-launched missile force. Her missile equipment was removed; she is no longer considered a "first line" submarine and is employed in experimental work. The submarine's large missile compartment makes her an excellent ship for underwater projects.

The Navy has stated that the *Halibut* and earlier *Seawolf* have been designated as "mother" submarines for the deep submergence research programmes. Reportedly the *Halibut* has been fitted with a ducted bow thruster to permit precise control and manoeuvering.
She can carry the 50-foot Deep Submergence Rescue Vehicle (DSRV) and other submersibles on her after deck; the submersibles can "take off" from and land" on" the *Halibut* while the larger craft is submerged.

DESIGN. The *Halibut* was built with a large missile hangar faired into her bow. Her hull was intended primarily to provide a stable surface launching platform rather than for speed or manoeuvrability.

ENGINEERING. Fitted with same reactor propulsion plant as *Skate* and *Sargo*. Submerged speed of *Halibut* is less than "Skate" class because of larger hull volume and shape.

MISSILES. The *Halibut* was designed to carry two Regulus II surface-to-surface missiles. The Regulus II was a transonic missile which could carry a nuclear warhead and had a range of 1 000 miles. The Regulus II was cancelled before becoming operational and the *Halibut* operated from 1960 to 1964 carrying five Regulus I missiles, subsonic cruise missiles which could deliver a nuclear warhead on targets 500 miles from the launching ship or submarine.
During this period the US Navy operated a maximum of five Regulus "guided" (cruise) missile submarines, the *Halibut*, the post-war constructed *Grayback* (SSG 574 now LPSS 574) and *Growler* (SSG 577), and the World War II-built *Tunny* (SSG 282 subsequently LPSS 282) and *Barbero* (SSG 317). The *Grayback* and *Growler* each could carry four Regulus I missiles and the older submarines each carried two missiles.
As SSGN carried a complement of 11 officers and 108 enlisted men.

NAVIGATION. The *Halibut* is fitted with Ship's Inertial Navigation System (SINS).

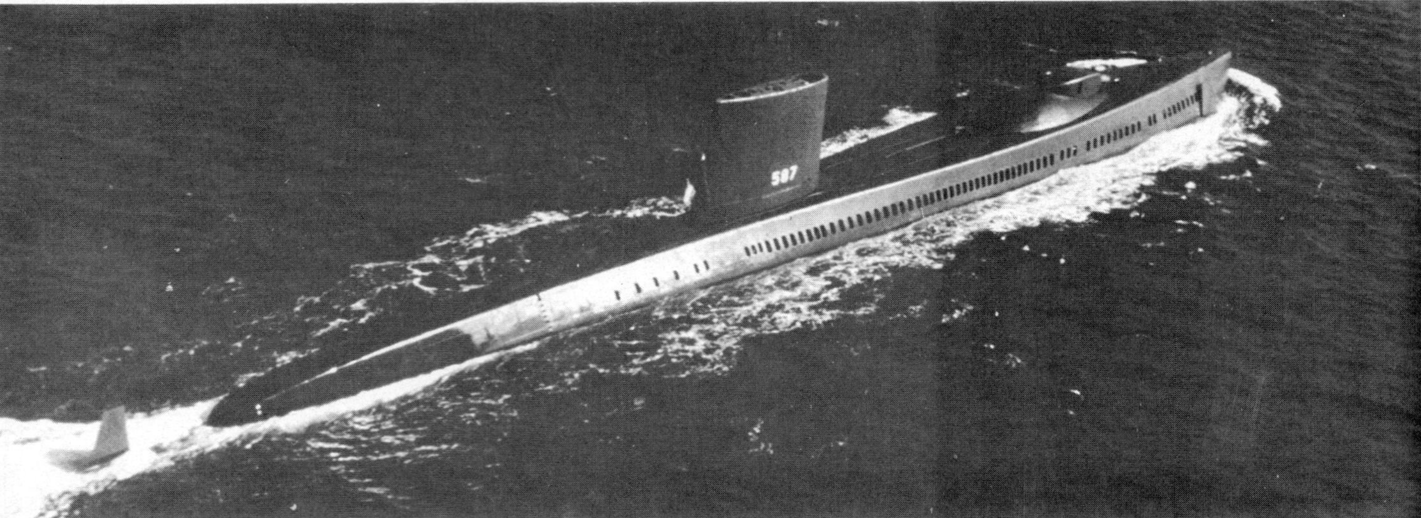

HALIBUT (SSN 587) *1968, United States Navy*

HALIBUT (SSN 587) *1968, United States Navy*

Submarines—*continued*

1 NUCLEAR-POWERED ATTACK SUBMARINE (SSN): "TRITON" TYPE

Name	*No.*	*Builder*	*Laid down*	*Launched*	*Commissioned*
TRITON	SSN 586 (ex-SSRN 586)	General Dynamics Corp (Electric Boat), Groton, Conn	29 May 1956	19 Aug 1958	10 Nov 1959

Displacement, tons	5 940 standard; 7 780 submerged
Length, feet (*metres*)	447·5 (*136·3*) oa
Beam, feet (*metres*)	37 (*11·3*)
Draft, feet (*metres*)	24 (*7·3*)
Torpedo tubes	6—21 in (*533 mm*) 4 fwd; 2 aft
Main engines	2 steam turbines (General Electric); approx 34 000 shp; 2 shafts
Nuclear reactors	2 pressurised-water cooled S4G (General Electric)
Speed, knots	27 surface; 20+ submerged
Complement as SSRN	172 (16 officers, 156 men enlisted

The *Triton* was designed and constructed to serve as a radar picket submarine to operate in conjunction with surface carrier task forces. She is the longest submarine ever constructed and is exceeded in displacement only by the later Polaris missile submarines. Authorised in the Fiscal Year 1956 new construction programme and built for an estimated cost of $109 000 000.

The *Triton* circumnavigated the globe in 1960, remaining submerged except when her sail structure broke the surface to enable an ill sailor to be taken off near the Falkland Islands. The 41 500-mile cruise took 83 days and was made at an average speed of 18 knots.

The underwater giant was reclassified as an attack submarine (SSN) on 1 Mar 1961 as the Navy dropped the radar picket submarine programme. She is no longer considered a "first line" submarine and was decommissioned on 3 May 1969 to become the first US nuclear submarine to be relegated to the "mothball fleet". There had been proposals to operate the *Triton* as an underwater national command post afloat, but no funds were provided.

DESIGN. The *Triton* was designed to operate as a surface radar picket, submerging when in danger of enemy attack. She was fitted with an elaborate combat information centre and large radar antenna which retracted into the sail structure.

ENGINEERING. The *Triton* is the only US submarine with two nuclear reactors. The Atomic Energy Commission's Knolls Atomic Power Laboratory was given prime responsibility for development of the power plant. After 2½ years of operation, during which she steamed more than 110 000 miles, the *Triton* was overhauled and refuelled from July 1962 to March 1964.

TRITON (SSN 586) *United States Navy*

SWORDFISH (SSN 579)—See following page *1970, United States Navy, PH1 John D. Osborne*

SKATE (SSN 578)—See following page *United States Navy*

Submarines—*continued*

4 NUCLEAR-POWERED ATTACK SUBMARINES (SSN): "SKATE" CLASS

Name	*No.*	*Builder*	*Laid down*	*Launched*	*Commissioned*
***SKATE**	SSN 578	General Dynamics (Electric Boat)	21 July 1955	16 May 1957	23 Dec 1957
***SWORDFISH**	SSN 579	Portsmouth Naval Shipyard	25 Jan 1956	27 Aug 1957	15 Sep 1958
***SARGO**	SSN 583	Mare Island Naval Shipyard	21 Feb 1956	10 Oct 1957	1 Oct 1958
***SEADRAGON**	SSN 584	Portsmouth Naval Shipyard	20 June 1956	16 Aug 1958	5 Dec 1959

Displacement, tons	2 570 standard; 2 861 submerged
Length, feet (*metres*)	267·7 (*81·5*) oa
Beam, feet (*metres*)	25 (*7·6*)
Draft, feet (*metres*)	21 (*6·4*)
Torpedo tubes	8—21 in (*533 mm*) 6 forward; 2 aft (short)
Main engines	2 steam turbines (Westinghouse) approx 6 600 shp; 2 shafts
Nuclear reactor	1 pressurised-water cooled S3W (Westinghouse) in *Skate* and *Sargo*; 1 pressurised-water cooled S4W (Westinghouse) in *Swordfish* and *Seadragon*
Speed, knots	15·5 surface; 20+ submerged
Complement	95 (8 officers, 87 enlisted men)

The "Skate" class submarines were the first production model nuclear-powered submarines. They are similar in design to the *Nautilus*, but smaller. The *Skate* and *Swordfish* were authorised in the Fiscal Year 1955 new construction programme, and the *Sargo* and *Seadragon* in FY 1956.

The *Skate* was the first submarine to make a completely submerged transatlantic crossing; in 1958 she established a (then) record of 31 days submerged with a sealed atmosphere; on 11 Aug 1958 she passed under the North Pole during a polar cruise; and on 17 Mar 1959 she became the first submarine to surface at the North Pole. The *Sargo* undertook a polar cruise during January-February 1960 and surfaced at the North Pole on 9 Feb 1960. The *Seadragon* transited from the Atlantic to the Pacific via the Northwest Passage (Lancaster Sound, Barrow and McClure Straits) in August 1960. The *Skate* operating from New London, Connecticut, and the *Seadragon*, based at Pearl Harbour, rendezvoused under the North Pole on 2 Aug 1962 and then conducted anti-submarine exercises under the polar ice pack and surfaced together at the North Pole.

The *Skate* also operated in the Arctic Ocean during April-May 1969, conducting exercises under the Arctic ice pack with the later nuclear-powered attack submarines *Pargo* and *Whale*; and again during the spring of 1971 with the nuclear attack submarine *Trepang*.

DESIGN. The "Skate" design is similar to the *Nautilus-Seawolf* design with GUPPY hull, bow diving planes, and twin propellers.

SEADRAGON (SSN 584) *1965, United States Navy*

ENGINEERING. The reactors for this class were developed by the Atomic Energy Commission's Bettis Atomic Power Laboratory, the new propulsion system was similar to that of the *Nautilus* but considerably simplified with improved operation and maintenance. The propulsion plant developed under this programme had two arrangements, the S3W configuration in the *Skate*, *Sargo* and *Halibut* and the S4W configuration in the *Swordfish* and *Seadragon*. Both arrangements have proven satisfactory. The *Skate* began her first overhaul and refuelling in January 1961 after steaming 120 862 miles on her initial reactor core during three years of operation. The *Swordfish* began her first overhaul and refuelling in early 1962 after more than three years of operation in which time she steamed 112 000 miles.

1 NUCLEAR-POWERED RESEARCH SUBMARINE (SSN): "SEAWOLF" TYPE

Name	*No.*	*Builder*	*Laid down*	*Launched*	*Commissioned*
***SEAWOLF**	SSN 575	General Dynamics (Electric Boat), Groton, Connecticut	15 Sep 1953	21 July 1955	30 Mar 1957

Displacement, tons	3 720 standard; 4 280 submerged
Length, feet (*metres*)	337·5 (*102·9*) oa
Beam, feet (*metres*)	27·7 (*8·4*)
Draft, feet (*metres*)	22 (*6·7*)
Torpedo tubes	6—21 in (*533 mm*) forward
Main engines	2 steam turbines (General Electric), approx 15 000 shp; 2 shafts
Nuclear reactor	1 pressurised-water cooled S2Wa (Westinghouse)
Speed, knots	19 surface; 20+ submerged
Complement	105 (10 officers, 95 enlisted men)

The *Seawolf* was the world's second nuclear-propelled vehicle; she was constructed almost simultaneously with the *Nautilus* to test a competitive reactor design. Funds for the *Seawolf* were authorised in the Fiscal Year 1952 new construction programme.

The *Seawolf* established a submerged endurance record in 1958 when she remained submerged for 60 consecutive days, travelling a distance of 13 761 miles with a completely sealed atmosphere. She is no longer considered a "first line" submarine and has been engaged primarily in research work since 1969.

ENGINEERING. Initial work in the development of naval nuclear propulsion plants investigated a number of concepts, two of which were of sufficient interest to warrant full development: the pressurised water and liquid metal (sodium). The *Nautilus* was provided with a pressurised-water reactor plant and the *Seawolf* was fitted initially with a liquid-metal reactor.

Originally known as the Submarine Intermediate Reactor (SIR), the liquid metal-plant was developed by the Atomic Energy Commission's Knolls Atomic Power Laboratory.

The SIR Mark II/S2G reactor in the *Seawolf* achieved initial criticality on 25 June 1956. Steam leaks developed during the dockside testing. The plant was shut down and it was determined that the leaks were caused by sodium-potassium alloy which had entered the superheater steam piping. After repairs and testing the *Seawolf* began sea trials on 21 Jan 1957. The trials were run at reduced power and after two years of operation the *Seawolf* entered the Electric Boat yard for removal of her sodium-cooled plant and installation of a pressurised-water plant similar to that installed in the *Nautilus* (designated S2Wa). When the original *Seawolf* plant was shut down in December 1958 the submarine had steamed a total of 71 611 miles. She was recommissioned on 30 Sep 1960. The pressurised-water reactor was refuelled for the first between May 1965 and August 1967, having propelled the *Seawolf* for more than 161 000 miles on its initial fuel core.

SEAWOLF (SSN 575) *1967, United States Navy*

Submarines—*continued*

3 ATTACK SUBMARINES (SS): "BARBEL" CLASS

Name	*No.*	*Builder*	*Laid down*	*Launched*	*Commissioned*
***BARBEL**	SS 580	Portsmouth Naval Shipyard	18 May 1956	19 July 1958	17 Jan 1959
***BLUEBACK**	SS 581	Ingalls Shipbuilding Corporation	15 Apr 1957	16 May 1959	15 Oct 1959
***BONEFISH**	SS 582	New York Shipbuilding Corp	3 June 1957	22 Nov 1958	9 July 1959

Displacement, tons	2 145 surface; 2 895 submerged
Length, feet (*metres*)	219·5 (*66·8*) oa
Beam, feet (*metres*)	29 (*8·8*)
Draft, feet (*metres*)	28 (*8·5*)
Torpedo tubes	6—21 in (*533 mm*) forward
Main engines	3 diesels 4 800 bhp (Fairbanks Morse); 2 electric motors (General Electric) 3 150 shp; 1 shaft
Speed, knots	15 on surface; 25 submerged
Complement	79 (10 officers, 69 men)

These submarines were the last non-nuclear combatant submarines built by the US Navy. All three were authorised in the Fiscal Year 1956 new construction programme.

CONSTRUCTION. The *Blueback* was the first submarine built by the Ingalls Shipbuilding Corp at Pascagoula, Mississippi, and the *Bonefish* was the first constructed at the New York Shipbuilding Corp yard in Camden, New Jersey.

DESIGN. These submarines have the "tear-drop" or modified spindle hull design which was tested in the experimental submarine *Albacore*. As built their diving planes were bow-mounted; subsequently relocated to the sail structure.
These submarines introduced a new concept in centralised arrangement of controls in an "attack centre" to increase efficiency; the concept has been adapted for all later US combat submarines.

PHOTOGRAPHS. Note forward position of diving planes on sail structure, bow configuration for maximum underwater performance, and clear decks that are void of projections.

BLUEBACK (SS 581) *1967, United States Navy*

BONEFISH (SS 582) *1969, United States Navy*

1 NUCLEAR POWERED ATTACK SUBMARINE (SSN): "NAUTILUS" TYPE

Name	*No.*	*Builder*	*Laid down*	*Launched*	*Commissioned*
***NAUTILUS**	SSN 571	General Dynamics (Electric Boat) Groton, Connecticut	14 June 1952	21 Jan 1954	30 Sep 1954

Displacement, tons	3 530 standard; 4 040 submerged
Length, feet (*metres*)	323·7 (*98·6*) oa
Beam, feet (*metres*)	27·6 (*8·4*)
Draft, feet (*metres*)	22 (*6·7*)
Torpedo tubes	6—21 in (*533 mm*) forward
Main engines	2 steam turbines (Westinghouse), approx 15 000 shp; 2 shafts
Nuclear reactor	1 pressurised-water cooled S2W (Westinghouse)
Speed, knots	18 surface; 20+ submerged
Complement	105 (10 officers, 95 enlisted men)

The *Nautilus* was the world's first nuclear-propelled vehicle. She predated the first Soviet nuclear-powered submarine by an estimated five years.

The Chief of Naval Operations initially established a requirement for a nuclear-propelled submarine in August 1949 and specified a "ready-for-sea" date of January 1955. The funds for construction of the *Nautilus* were authorised in the Fiscal Year 1952 budget. The *Nautilus* put to sea for the first time on 17 Jan 1955 and signalled the historic message: "Underway on nuclear power".
On her shakedown cruise in May 1955 the *Nautilus* steamed submerged from London, Connecticut, to San Juan, Puerto Rico, travelling more than 1 300 miles in 84 hours at an average speed of almost 16 knots; she later steamed submerged from Key West, Florida, to New London, a distance of 1 397 miles, at an average speed of more than 20 knots.

During 1958 the *Nautilus* undertook extensive operations under the Arctic ice pack and in August she made history's first polar transit from the Pacific to the Atlantic, steaming from Pearl Harbour to Portland, England. She passed under the geographic North Pole on 3 Aug 1958.

The *Nautilus* is no longer considered a "first line" submarine and can be expected to be decommissioned in the near future.

DESIGN. The *Nautilus* and *Seawolf* have GUPPY-type hull configurations. The *Seawolf* has a stepped sail and a slight rise at the bow.

ENGINEERING. In January 1948 the Department of Defense requested the Atomic Energy Commission to undertake the design, development, and construction of a nuclear reactor for submarine propulsion. Initial research and conceptual design of the Submarine Thermal Reactor (STR) was undertaken by the Argonne National Laboratory. Subsequently the Atomic Energy Commission's Bettis Atomic Power Laboratory, operated by the Westinghouse Electric Corporation, undertook development of the first nuclear propulsion plant.

The *Nautilus* STR Mark II nuclear plant (redesignated S2W) was first operated on 20 Dec 1954 and first developed full power on 3 Jan 1955.

After more than two years of operation, during which she steamed 62 562 miles, the *Nautilus* began an overhaul which included refuelling in April 1957. She was again refuelled in 1959 after steaming 91 324 miles on her second fuel core, and again in 1964 after steaming approximately 150 000 miles on her third fuel core. (The prototype Mark I/S1W plant was refuelled in 1955, 1958, 1960, and 1967; it remains in operation as an experimental and training facility)

PHOTOGRAPH. Two light areas on deck are emergency, tethered marker buoys (fitted to all US submarines) for localisation of sunken submarine and to winch down McCann submarine rescue chamber.

Submarines—*continued*

NAUTILUS (SSN 571) *United States Navy*

1 GUIDED MISSILE SUBMARINE (SSG): "GROWLER" TYPE

Name	*No.*	*Builder*	*Laid down*	*Launched*	*Commissioned*
GROWLER	SSG 577	Portsmouth Naval Shipyard	15 Feb 1955	5 Apr 1959	30 Apr 1958

Displacement, tons	2 540 standard; 3 515 submerged
Length, feet (*metres*)	317·6 (*96·8*) oa
Beam, feet(*metres*)	27·2 (*8·2*)
Draft, feet (*metres*)	19 (*5·8*)
Torpedo tubes	6—21 inch (*533 mm*) 4 fwd; 2 aft
Main engines	3 diesels (Fairbanks Morse); 4 600 bhp/2 electric motors (Elliott); 5 600 shp; 2 shafts
Speed, knots	20 surface; 17 submerged
Complement	84 officers and enlisted men

The *Growler* was authorised in tne Fiscal Year 1955 new construction programme; completed as a guided missile submarine to fire the Regulus surface-to-surface cruise missile (see *Halibut*, SSN 587, for *Missile* notes). When the Regulus submarine missile programme ended in 1964 the *Growler* and her near-sister submarine *Grayback* were withdrawn from service; the *Grayback* subsequently converted to an amphibious transport submarine (LPSS). The *Growler* was scheduled to undergo a similar conversion when the *Grayback* was completed, but the second conversion was deferred late in 1968 because of rising ship conversion costs. The *Growler* is in reserve as an SSG.

DESIGN. The *Grayback* and *Growler* initially were designed as attack submarines similar to the *Darter*. Upon redesign as missile submarines they were cut in half on the building ways and were lengthened approximately 50 feet, two cylindrical hangars, each 11 feet high and 70 feet long, were superimposed on their bows, a missile launcher was installed between the hangars and sail structure, and elaborate navigation and fire control systems were fitted. The height of the sail structure on the *Growler* is approximately 30 feet above the deck; the *Grayback's* lower sail structure was increased during LPSS conversion.

GRAYBACK (left), GROWLER (right) *1964, United States Navy*

1 ATTACK SUBMARINE (SS): "DARTER" TYPE

Name	*No.*	*Builder*	*Laid down*	*Launched*	*Commissioned*
***DARTER**	SS 576	General Dynamics Corp (Electric Boat)	10 Nov 1954	28 May 1956	20 Oct 1956

Displacement, tons	1 720 surface; 2 388 submerged
Length, feet (*metres*)	268·6 (*81·9*) oa
Beam, feet (*metres*)	27·2 (*8·3*)
Draft, feet (*metres*)	19 (*5·8*)
Torpedo tubes	8—21 in (*533 mm*) 6 fwd; 2 aft
Main engines	3 diesels (Fairbanks Morse); 4 500 bhp electric motors (Elliott); 2 shafts
Speed, knots	19·5 surface; 14 submerged
Complement	83 (8 officers, 75 men)

Designed for high submerged speed with quiet machinery. Planned sister submarines *Growler* and *Grayback* were completed to missile-launching configuration.

Basic design of the *Darter* is similar to the "Tang" class described on a later page.

Authorised in Fiscal Year 1954 shipbuilding programme. No additional submarines of this type were built because of shift to high-speed hull design and nuclear propulsion.

DARTER (SS 576) *United States Navy*

Submarines—*continued*

1 AMPHIBIOUS TRANSPORT SUBMARINE (LPSS): "GRAYBACK" TYPE

Name	*No.*	*Builder*	*Laid down*	*Launched*	*Commissioned*	*LPSS Comm.*
***GRAYBACK**	LPSS 574 (ex-SSG 574)	Mare Island Naval Shipyard	1 July 1954	2 July 1957	7 Mar 1958	9 May 1969

Displacement, tons	2 670 standard; 3 650 submerged
Length, feet (*metres*)	334 (*101·8*) oa
Beam, feet (*metres*)	30 (*9·0*)
Draft, feet (*metres*)	19 (*5·8*)
Torpedo tubes	8—21 inch (*533 mm*) 6 fwd; 2 aft
Main engines	3 diesels (Fairbanks Morse); 4 500 bhp/2 electric motors (Elliott); 5 600 shp; 2 shafts
Speed, knots	20 surface; 17 submerged
Complement	87 (9 officers, 78 enlisted men)
Troops	67 (7 officers, 60 enlisted men)

The *Grayback* has been fully converted to a transport submarine and is officially classified as an amphibious warfare ship. She was originally intended to be an attack submarine, being authorised in the Fiscal Year 1953 new construction programme, but redesigned in 1956 to provide a Regulus missile launching capability; completed as SSG 574 in 1958, similar in design to the *Growler* (SSG 577). See *Growler* listing for basic design notes.

CONVERSION. The *Grayback* began conversion to a transport submarine at the San Francisco Bay Naval Shipyard (Mare Island) in November 1967. The conversion was originally estimated at $15 200 000 but was actually about $30 000 000. She was reclassified from SSG to LPSS on 30 Aug 1968 (never officially designated APSS).

During conversion the *Grayback* was fitted to berth and mess 67 troops and carry their equipment including landing craft or swimmer delivery vehicles (SDV). Her torpedo tubes and hence attack capability are retained. As completed (SSG) the *Grayback* had an overall length of 322 ft 4 in; lengthened 12 ft during LPSS conversion. Conversion was authorised in Fiscal Year 1965 programme and completed in June 1969; delayed because of higher priorities being allocated to other submarine projects.

ELECTRONICS. **Fitted with BQG-4 passive fire control sonar (note three fin-like PUFF sonar domes).**

PHOTOGRAPHS. Bow and stern views of the *Grayback* appear in the 1972-1973 edition.

GRAYBACK (LPSS 574) ***1969, United States Navy***

2 ATTACK SUBMARINES (SS): "SAILFISH" CLASS

Name	*No.*	*Builder*	*Laid down*	*Launched*	*Commissioned*
***SAILFISH**	SS 572 (ex-SSR 572)	Portsmouth Naval Shipyard	8 Dec 1953	7 Sep 1955	14 Apr 1956
***SALMON**	SS 573 (ex-AGSS 573, ex-SSR 573)	Portsmouth Naval Shipyard	10 Mar 1954	25 Feb 1956	25 Aug 1956

Displacement, tons	2 625 surface; 3 168 submerged
Length, feet (*metres*)	350·4 (*106·8*) oa
Beam, feet (*metres*)	28·4 (*8·8*)
Draft, feet (*metres*)	18 (*5·5*) max
Torpedo tubes	6—21 in (*533 mm*) forward
Main engines	4 diesels (Fairbanks Morse); 6 000 bhp/2 electric motors (Elliott); 8 200 shp; 2 shafts
Speed, knots	19·5 on surface; 14 submerged
Complement	95 (12 officers, 83 enlisted men)

Largest non-nuclear submarines built by the US Navy since the *Narwhal* (SS 167) and *Nautilus* (SS 168) completed in 1930. The *Sailfish* and *Salmon* were built as radar picket submarines (SSR) with air search radar antennas on deck and elaborate air control centres. Authorised in Fiscal Year 1952 programme. Both submarines underwent FRAM II modernisation.
These are believed to be the largest non-nuclear submarines in service with any navy.

CLASSIFICATION. Reclassified from radar picket submarines (SSR) to SS on 1 Mar 1961; *Salmon* reclassified AGSS on 29 June 1968 to serve at test and evaluation submarine for Navy's Deep Submergence Rescue Vehicle (DSRV). However, the DSRV programme was delayed and the *Salmon* reverted to the SS designation on 30 June 1969.

All ten of the World War II-built submarines that had been converted to radar picket configurations have been stricken except for the *Tigrone* (AGSS 419), which survives as a research submarine (described on a later page in this section).

Radar picket submarines were to operate ahead of carrier task forces to provide early warning of air attack; upon coming under attack themselves they would submerge for safety. The Soviet Navy operate several modified "W" class submarine in the radar picket role.

ELECTRONICS. Fitted with BQG-4 passive fire control sonar (note three fin-like PUFF sonar domes). The fourth "fin" at stern is the upper rudder.

PHOTOGRAPHS. **Note size of PUFF fins in comparison to men in photograph of the** ***Salmon*****.**

SAILFISH (SS 572) *1966, United States Navy*

SALMON (SS 573) *United States Navy*

Submarines—*continued*

4 ATTACK SUBMARINES (SS): "TANG" CLASS

isplacement, tons 2 100 surface; 2 700 submerged
ength, feet (*metres*) 287 (*87·4*) oa
eam, feet (*metres*) 27·3 (*8·3*)
raft, feet (*metres*) 19 (*6·2*)
orpedo tubes 8—21 in (*533 mm*) 6 fwd, 2 aft
ain engines 3 diesels (Fairbanks-Morse); 4 500 bhp/2 electric motors; 5 600 shp; 2 shafts
peed, knots 16 surface; 16 submerged
omplement 83 (8 officers, 75 men)

Name	*No.*	*Builder*	*Laid down*	*Launched*	*Commissioned*
•**TANG**	SS 563	Portsmouth Naval Shipyard	18 Apr 1949	19 June 1951	25 Oct 1951
•**WAHOO**	SS 565	Portsmouth Naval Shipyard	24 Oct 1949	16 Oct 1951	30 May 1952
•**TROUT**	SS 566	Electric Boat Co, Groton	1 Dec 1949	21 Aug 1951	27 June 1952
•**GUDGEON**	SS 567	Portsmouth Naval Shipyard	20 May 1950	11 June 1952	21 Nov 1952

his design embodied various improvements to provide igh submerged speed, based largely on German Vorld War II submarine developments.
rigger was the first US Navy submarine of the post-war rogramme to be laid down. *Tang* was the first of the ew class to be completed. *Tang* and *Trigger* authorised n Fiscal Year 1947 new construction programme. *Wahoo* nd *Trout* in FY 1948, and *Gudgeon* and *Harder* in FY 1949. he *Gudgeon* was the first United States submarine to ircumnavigate the world during Sep 1957-Feb 1958. ll of these submarines are active.

LECTRONICS. BQG-4 PUFF sonar domes installed n some of these submarines. See GUPPY III submarine sting for details.

NGINEERING. *Tang, Trigger, Trout* and *Wahoo* were riginally powered by a compact, radial type engine roduced after five years of development work, comprising 16-cylinder 2-cycle plant, mounted vertically with four ows of cylinders radially arranged. These new engines vere half the weight and two-thirds the size of the engines reviously available for submarines. They proved to be nsatisfactory and were replaced by machinery similar o that in *Gudgeon* and *Harder* which have a Fairbanks-Morse high speed lightweight engine mounted horizontally. The electric motors are Elliott in *Tang* and *Trigger* General Electric in *Wahoo* and *Trout,* Westinghouse in *Gudgeon* and *Harder.*
norkel fitted as in all later US nuclear and conventionally propelled submarines.

RECONSTRUCTION. All six submarines of this class were built with an overall length of 269 ft 2 in. The *Tang, Trigger, Trout* and *Wahoo* had their original diesel engines replaced during the late 1950 s. During the process they were cut in half and a 9 ft section inserted amidships. All six submarines were modernised during the 1960 s with the installation of improved electronics equipment and other features; additional sections were added to give an overall length of 287 ft.

PHOTOGRAPHS. Note that the *Trigger,* shown at Malta in November 1969, does not have PUFF domes. Her antennas and periscopes are raised.

DISPOSALS

Trigger (SS 564) stricken on 2 July; **Harder** (SS 568) stricken on 19 July 1973.

GUDGEON (SS 567) *1970, US Navy, PH3 J. B. Land*

WAHOO (SS 565) *1968, United States Navy.*

TRIGGER (SS 564) ***1969, Anthony & Joseph Pavia***

DOLPHIN (AGSS 555) **See following page** *United States Navy*

Submarines—*continued*

1 RESEARCH SUBMARINE (AGSS): "DOLPHIN" TYPE

Name	No.	Builder	Laid down	Launched	Commissioned
*DOLPHIN	AGSS 555	Portsmouth Naval Shipyard	9 Nov 1962	8 June 1968	17 Aug 1968

Displacement, tons	800 standard; 930 full load
Length, feet	152
Beam, feet	19·3
Diameter, feet	18 (maximum)
Torpedo tubes	Removed
Main engines	Diesel/electric (2 Detroit 12V71 diesels), 1 500 hp; 1 shaft
Speed, knots	12+ submerged
Complement	23 (3 officers, 20 enlisted men) plus 4 to 7 scientists

The *Dolphin* is an auxiliary submarine specifically designed for deep-diving operations. Authorised in Fiscal Year 1961 new construction programme, but delayed because of changes in mission and equipment coupled with higher priorities being given to other submarine projects The *Dolphin* is fitted for deep-ocean sonar and oceanographic research. She is highly automated and has three computer-operated systems, a safety system, hovering system, and one that is classified. The digital-computer submarine safety system monitors equipment and provides data on closed-circuit television screens; malfunctions in equipment or trends towards potentially dangerous situations set off an alarm and if they are not corrected within the prescribed time the system, unless overridden by an operator, automatically brings the submarine to the surface. There are several research stations for scientists in the *Dolphin* and she is fitted to take water samples down to her operating (test) depth. The single, experimental torpedo tube was removed in 1970.
Underwater endurance is limited (endurance and habitability were considered of secondary importance in design). On 24 Nov 1968 the *Dolphin* "descended to a depth greater than that recorded by any other operational submarine "according to official statements.

DOLPHIN (AGSS 555) *United States Navy*

CLASSIFICATION. The *Dolphin*'s number was taken from a block (551-562) authorised but cancelled late in World War II with no construction being assigned (Submarines built in Norway and Denmark were assigned the hull numbers SS 553 and SS 554, respectively, for financial accounting purposes, hull numbers SS 551 and SS 552 in this series were assigned to the late hunter-killer submarines *Bass*, ex-SSK 2, and *Bonita* ex-SSK 3 respectively)

DESIGN. The *Dolphin* has a constant diameter, cylindrical pressure hull approximately 15 feet in outer diameter closed at both ends with hemispherical heads. Pressure hull fabricated of HY-80 steel with aluminium and fibre glass used in secondary structures to reduce weight, a critical factor in retaining buoyancy at deep depths. No conventional diving planes are mounted; improved rudder design and other features provide manoeuvring control and hovering capability. Access is through a single hatch in the pressure hull (opening into sail structure).

ENGINEERING. Fitted with 330 cell silver zinc battery. Submerged endurance is approximately 24 hours with an at-sea endurance of 14 days.

STATUS. Completed in early 1969, approximately five years behind official schedule at time of keel laying. The *Dolphin* is in commission and has a commanding officer.

PHOTOGRAPHS. Note the *Dolphin's* rounded, constant-diameter hull configuration in the above photograph; note her small deck area, narrow sail structure, raised periscope. A photograph of the *Dolphin* being launched, showing her stern configuration, appeared in the 1970-1971 edition and a photograph of the *Dolphin* design model appeared in the 1969-1970 edition.

1 RESEARCH SUBMARINE (AGSS): "ALBACORE" TYPE

Name	No.	Builder	Laid down	Launched	Commissioned
ALBACORE	AGSS 569	Portsmouth Naval Shipyard	15 Mar 1952	1 Aug 1953	5 Dec 1953

Displacement, tons	1 500 surface; 1 850 submerged
Length, feet (*metres*)	210·5 (*63·6*) oa
Beam, feet (*metres*)	27·5 (*8·4*)
Draft, feet (*metres*)	18·5 (*5·6*)
Torpedo tubes	None
Main engines	2 diesels, radial pancake type (General Motors) electric motor (Westinghouse) 15 000 shp; 1 shaft
Speed, knots	25 on surface; 33 submerged
Complement	52 (5 officers, 47 men)

High speed experimental submarine. Conventionally powered submarine of radical design with new hull form which makes her faster and more manoeuverable than any other conventional submarine. Officially described as a hydrodynamic test vehicle. Streamlined, whale shaped without the naval flat-topped deck. Conning tower resembles a fish's dorsal fin.

The *Albacore* was decommissioned and placed in reserve on 1 Sep 1972.

EXPERIMENTAL. The *Albacore* has been extensively modified to test advanced submarine design and engineering concepts.
Phase I modifications were made from July 1954 to February 1955 to eliminate the many "bugs" inherent with completely new construction and equipment.
Phase II modifications from Dec 1955 to Mar 1956 during which conventional propeller-rudder-stern diving plane arrangement was modified; the new design provided for the propeller to be installed *aft* of the control surfaces. (At this time a small auxiliary rudder on the sail was removed)
A concave bow sonar dome was fitted for tests in 1960.
Phase III modifications from Nov 1960 to Aug 1961 during which an entirely new stern was installed featuring the stern planes in an "X" configuration, a system of ten hydraulic operated dive brakes around the hull amidships, a dorsal rudder, and a new bow sonar dome. Phase IV modifications from Dec 1962 to Mar 1965 during which a silver-zinc battery was installed and counter-rotating stern propellers rotating around the same axis were fitted.
The *Albacore* conducted trials with towed sonar arrays from May to July 1966.
All modifications were made at the Portsmouth Naval Shipyard.

PHOTOGRAPH. Note stern rudder configuration; rounded hull without superstructure deck common to previous and contemporary submarines. Round electronic "ball" antenna on sail structure. Deck cleats and other equipment are recessed into hull.

ALBACORE (AGSS 569) *United States Navy*

Submarines—*continued*

7 ATTACK SUBMARINES (SS): GUPPY III TYPE

isplacement, tons 1 975 standard; 2 450 submerged
ength, feet (*metres*) 326·5 (*99·4*) oa
eam, feet (*metres*) 27 (*8·2*)
raft, feet (*metres*) 17 (*5·2*)
orpedo tubes 10—21 in (*533 mm*), 6 fwd, 4 aft
lain engines 4 diesels; 6 400 bhp/2 electric motors; 5 400 shp; 2 shafts
peed, knots 20 surface; 15 submerged
omplement approx 85

Name	*No*	*Builder*	*Laid down*	*Launched*	*Commissioned*
***CLAMAGORE**	SS 343	Electric Boat Co	16 Mar 1944	25 Feb 1945	21 Oct 1944
***COBBLER**	SS 344	Electric Boat Co	3 Apr 1944	1 Apr 1945	8 Aug 1945
***CORPORAL**	SS 346	Electric Boat Co	27 Apr 1944	10 June 1945	9 Nov 1945
***GREENFISH**	SS 351	Electric Boat Co	29 June 1944	21 Dec 1945	7 June 1946
***TIRU**	SS 416	Mare Island Navy Yard	17 Apr 1944	16 Sep 1947	1 Sep 1948
***TRUMPETFISH**	SS 425	Cramp Shipbuilding Co	23 Aug 1943	13 May 1945	29 Jan 1946
***REMORA**	SS 487	Portsmouth Navy Yard	5 Mar 1945	12 July 1945	3 Jan 1946

ine submarines of the "Balao" and "Tench" classes were odernised under the GUPPY III programme in 1960-962 (see *Design* notes). All previously were GUPPY submarines. Plans for 15 additional GUPPY III odernisations were dropped in favour of new con-ruction, nuclear-powered submarines.

ESIGN. The Greater Underwater Propulsion Pro-amme (GUPPY) evolved after World War II as a method improve underwater performance of existing US ubmarines. The GUPPY concept was based on the erman Type XXI submarines which were mass produced 1944-1945. The Type XXI characteristics included a streamlined hull and superstructure, snorkel, and increased battery power.

The US Navy's GUPPY conversions have similar features with resulting increases in underwater speed and endurance, plus improved fire control and electronic equipment over their unmodernised sister submarines.

ELECTRONICS. GUPPY submarines are fitted with BQR-2 array sonar. GUPPY III submarines all have BQG-4 sonar (see *Photograph* notes).

ENGINEERING. The GUPPY III submarines have two increased capacity, 126-cell electric batteries as do GUPPY IIA and IA submarines. All GUPPY submarines are fitted with snorkel to permit operation of diesel engines to charge batteries and for propulsion while at periscope depth. The *Tiru* has only three diesel engines (4 800 hp).

PHOTOGRAPHS. Small, fin-like structures on submarines are antenna domes for BQG-4 fire control sonar (referred to as PUFFS—acronym for Passive Underwater Fire control Feasibility System, an anti-submarine targeting system). GUPPY conversions have rounded bows as opposed to "ship" bows in streamlined fleet-type submarines.

DISPOSALS AND TRANSFERS

Volador (SS 490), **Pickerel** (SS 524) transferred to Italy on 18 Aug 1972;

COBBLER (SS 344) *1970, Anthony & Joseph Pavia*

GREENFISH (SS 351) ***1969, United States Navy***

1 ATTACK SUBMARINE (SS): GUPPY II TYPE

isplacement, tons 1 870 standard; 2 420 submerged
ength, feet (*metres*) 307·5 (*93·6*) oa
eam, feet (*metres*) 27·2 (*8·3*)
raft, feet (*metres*) 18 (*5·5*)
orpedo tubes 10—21 in (*533 mm*); 6 fwd, 4 aft
lain engines 3 diesels; 4 800 bhp/2 electric motors; 5 400 shp; 2 shafts
peed, knots 18 surface; 15 submerged
omplement Approx 80

Name	*No.*	*Builder*	*Laid down*	*Launched*	*Commissioned*
***AMBERJACK**	SS 522	Boston Navy Yard	8 Feb 1944	15 Dec 1944	4 Mar 1946

eventeen submarines of the "Balao" and "Tench" asses were modernised under the GUPPY II programme 1948-1951, including two submarines earlier mod-nised to GUPPY I standards. General GUPPY notes e found in the GUPPY III listing.

The *Cochino* (SS 345) of this type was lost off Norway on a training cruise on 26 Aug 1949.

One submarine of this type remains active.

ENGINEERING. The GUPPY II submarines have four 126-cell electric batteries; fitted with snorkel.

DISPOSALS AND TRANSFERS

Pomodon (SS 486) stricken on 1 Aug 1970, **Diodon** (SS 349) stricken on 15 Jan 1971; **Halfbeak** (SS 352) stricken on 1 July 1971; **Catfish** (SS 339) transferred to Argentina on 1 July 1971; **Cubera** (SS 347) transferred to Venezuela on 5 Jan 1972; **Grampus** (SS 523) to Brazil 13 May 1972; **Sirago** (SS 485) stricken on 1 June 1972; **Odax** (SS 484) transferred to Brazil on 8 July 1972; **Dogfish** (SS 350) to Brazil on 28 July 1972; **Sea Leopard** (SS 483) transferred to Brazil on 27 Mar 1973; **Cutlass** (SS 478) transferred to Taiwan China on 12 Apr 1973; **Grenadier** (SS 525) transferred to Venezuela on 15 May 1973; **Tusk** (SS 426) decommissioned for transfer to Taiwan China.

GRENADIER (SS 525) stricken in 1973

Submarines—*continued*

3 ATTACK SUBMARINES (SS): GUPPY IIA TYPE

Displacement, tons	1 840 standard; 2 445 submerged
Length, feet (*metres*)	306 (*93·2*) oa
Beam, feet (*metres*)	27 (*8·2*)
Draft, feet (*metres*)	17 (*5·2*)
Torpedo tubes	10—21 inch (*533 mm*); 6 fwd; 4 aft
Main engines	3 diesels 4 800 bhp/2 electric motors; 5 400 shp; 2 shafts
Speed, knots	17 surface; 15 submerged
Complement	Approx 85

Name	*No.*	*Builder*	*Laid down*	*Launched*	*Commissioned*
***JALLAO**	SS 368	Manitowoc Shipbuilding Co	29 Sep 1943	12 Mar 1944	8 July 1944
MENHADEN	SS 377	Manitowoc Shipbuilding Co	21 June 1944	20 Dec 1944	22 June 1945
***TIRANTE**	SS 420	Portsmouth Navy Yard	28 Apr 1944	9 Aug 1944	6 Nov 1944

Sixteen submarines of the "Balao" and "Tench" classes were modernised under the GUPPY IIA programme in 1952-54. The *Stickleback* (SS 514) of this type was rammed by the US escort ship and sunk off Hawaii on 29 May 1958. General GUPPY conversion notes are found in the GUPPY III listing.
Menhaden decommissioned in 1971 and placed in reserve. Two submarines of this type remain active.

PHOTOGRAPHS. Note that virtually all GUPPY submarines have had their older "stepped" superstructures replaced by streamlined superstructures constructed of light-weight material. *Threadfin* is one of the few with a "stepped" structure.

DISPOSALS AND TRANSFERS
Razorback (SS 394) transferred to Turkey on 30 Nov 1970, **Sea Fox** (SS 402) transferred to Turkey on 15 Dec 1970, **Ronquil** (SS 396) transferred to Spain on 1 July 1971, **Pomfret** (SS 391) and **Thornback** (SS 418) transferred to Turkey on 1 July 1971; **Hardhead** (SS 365) transferred to Greece on 26 July 1972; **Entemedor** (SS 340) and **Trutta** (SS 421) to Turkey on 31 July 1972; **Threadfin** (SS 410) to Turkey on 18 Aug 1972; **Picuda** (SS 382) and **Bang** (SS 385) transferred to Spain on 1 Oct 1972, **Quillback** (SS 424) stricken on 23 Mar 1973.

THREADFIN (SS 410) —to Turkey *1967, United States Navy*

5 ATTACK SUBMARINES (SS): GUPPY IA TYPE

Displacement, tons	1 870 standard, 2 440 submerged
Length, feet (*metres*)	308 (*93·8*) oa
Beam, feet (*metres*)	27 (*8·2*)
Draft, feet (*metres*)	17 (*5·2*)
Torpedo tubes	10—21 in (*533 mm*), 6 fwd, 4 aft
Main engines	3 diesels; 4 800 bhp/2 electric motors; 5 400 shp; 2 shafts
Speed, knots	17 surface; 15 submerged
Complement	approx 85

Name	*No.*	*Builder*	*Laid down*	*Launched*	*Commissioned*
BECUNA	SS 319	Electric Boat Co	29 Apr 1943	30 Jan 1944	27 May 1944
BLENNY	SS 324	Electric Boat Co	8 July 1943	9 Apr 1944	27 July 1944
ATULE	SS 403	Portsmouth Navy Yard	2 Dec 1943	6 Mar 1944	21 June 1944
SEA POACHER	SS 406	Portsmouth Navy Yard	23 Feb 1944	20 May 1944	31 July 1944
TENCH	SS 417	Portsmouth Navy Yard	1 Apr 1944	7 July 1944	6 Oct 1944

Ten submarines of the "Balao" and "Tench" classes were modernised under the GUPPY IA programme in 1951 General GUPPY conversion notes are found in the GUPPY III listing.
Becuna, Blenny, Atule, Sea Poacher and *Tench* all were decommissioned late in 1969 and placed in reserve; redesignated as AGSS on 1 Oct 1969 while being decommissioned. All redesignated SS on 30 June 1971.

PHOTOGRAPHS. *Blenny* has later sail structure and three PUFF sonar antennas for BQG-4 sonar.

BLENNY (SS 324) *1966, United States Navy*

DISPOSALS AND TRANSFERS
Sea Robin (SS 407) stricken on 1 Oct 1970; **Chivo** (SS 341) transferred to Argentina on 1 July 1971; **Chopper** (IXSS 342/AGSS 342/SS 342) stricken on 1 Oct 1971; **Caiman** (SS 323) transferred to Turkey on 30 June 1972; **Blackfin** (SS 322) stricken on 15 Sep 1972 (target; not transferred).

All submarines of the World War II-built "Tench", "Balao", and "Gato" classes have been stricken from the Navy List except those converted to GUPPY configurations and the two specialised submarines described on the following page. See 1971-1972 edition for lists of transfers, disposals, and losses.

Disposal of the research submarine *Baya* (AGSS 318) was delayed one year; stricken in mid-1972.

The submarine reserve training programme has bee reorganised. The 16 immobilised submarines assigne to the Naval Reserve all were stricken in December 197' The *Chopper* (late IXSS 342) has replaced the *Hak* (SS 256) as salvage hulk for training in submarin rescue and salvage; periodically towed to sea and sun off Norfolk, Virginia.

TENCH (SS 417) *1968, United States Navy*

Submarines—*continued*

1 RESEARCH SUBMARINE (AGSS): "TIGRONE" TYPE

Name	No.	Builder	Laid down	Launched	Commissioned
*TIGRONE	AGSS 419	Portsmouth Navy Yard	8 May 1944	20 July 1944	25 Oct 1944

Displacement, tons	1 840 standard; 2 400 submerged
Length, feet (*metres*)	312 (*95·1*) oa
Beam, feet (*metres*)	27·2 (*8·3*)
Draft, feet (*metres*)	16·5 (*5·0*)
Torpedo tubes	10—21 in (*533 mm*); 6 fwd, 4 aft
Main engines	4 diesels (Fairbanks Morse); 5 400 bhp/4 electric motors (General Electric); 2 shafts
Speed, knots	20 surface; 10 submerged
Complement	approx 85

Originally a "Tench" class submarine refitted as a radar picket submarine in 1947-1948, being provided with elaborate air search radar and air control centre. Reverted to attack submarine status in 1959 with end of submarine radar picket programme. Subsequently fitted with large bow sonar installation and used for research and experimental work.

CLASSIFICATION. *Tigrone* changed from SS to radar picket submarine (SSR) on 31 Mar 1948, reverted to SS designation on 15 Aug 1959; changed to auxiliary submarines (AGSS) on 1 Dec 1963.

ENGINEERING. Fitted with snorkel installation.

PHOTOGRAPH. Note large bow structure housing surface ship sonar installed for research. Two "ball" electronic antennas are fitted atop the sonar structure. Similar antennas are found on the bows of late US nuclear powered submarines and have been seen on a Soviet "W" class submarine.

TIGRONE (AGSS 419) *1968, United States Navy*

1 AMPHIBIOUS TRANSPORT SUBMARINE (LPSS): "SEALION" TYPE

Name	No.	Builder	Laid down	Launched	Commissioned
SEALION	LPSS 315	Electric Boat Company, Groton	25 Feb 1943	31 Oct 1943	8 Mar 1944

Displacement, tons	2 145 surface; 2 500 submerged
Length, feet (*metres*)	311·5 (*95·0*)
Beam, feet (*metres*)	27 (*8·2*)
Draft, feet (*metres*)	17 (*5·2*)
Torpedo tubes	Removed
Guns	Removed
Main engines	2 diesels (General Motors), 2 305 bhp/4 electric motors (General Electric); 2 shafts
Speed, knots	13 surface; 10 submerged
Complement	74 (6 officers, 68 men)
Troops	160

Originally a "Balao" class submarine converted to underwater transport for carrying Marines, commandos or frogmen in covert operations where surface ships would be too vulnerable. The *Sealion* was to have been replaced by conversion of the *Growler* (SSG 577) to a transport submarine; however, conversion of *Growler* was cancelled.
The *Sealion* was decommissioned and placed in reserve in Feb 1970.

CLASSIFICATION. *Sealion* changed from SS to transport submarine (SSP) in March 1948; changed to auxiliary transport submarine (ASSP) in January 1950; changed to APSS in October 1956; changed again to amphibious transport submarine (LPSS) on 1 Jan 1969

CONVERSION. The *Sealion* was converted to a transport submarine at the San Francisco Naval Shipyard in 1948. All torpedo tubes and half of her diesel propulsion plant were removed to provide berthing for 160 troops; stowage provided for rubber rafts and other equipment in enlarged superstructure deck aft of conning tower.

ENGINEERING. Fitted with snorkel installation.

STATUS. In 1960 the *Sealion* was assigned to operational reserve training duties; recommissioned late in 1961 with increase of US conventional warfare capabilities.

SEALION (LPSS 315) *1965, United States Navy*

See 1971-1972 edition for disposals of earlier transport submarines.

1 TRAINING SUBMARINE (SST): "BARRACUDA" TYPE

Name	No.	Builder	Laid down	Launched	Commissioned
*BARRACUDA (ex-*K 1*)	SS-T3 (ex-SST 3, ex-SSK 1)	Electric Boat Company, Groton	1 July 1949	2 Mar 1951	10 Nov 1951

Displacement, tons	756 surface; 1 160 submerged
Length, feet (*metres*)	196 (*59·7*) oa
Beam, feet (*metres*)	24·8 (*7·5*)
Draft, feet (*metres*)	16 (*4·9*)
Torpedo tubes	4—21 inch (*533 mm*), 2 fwd, 2 aft
Main engines	3 diesels (General Motors); 1 050 bhp; 2 electric motors (General Electric); 2 shafts
Speed, knots	10 surface; 8 submerged
Complement	50 (5 officers, 45 enlisted men)

Authorised in Fiscal Year 1948 shipbuilding programme. Medium-size, quiet, and highly manoeuverable design intended specifically for anti-submarine operations. Originally had an ungainly bow housing large BQR-4 passive detection sonar.
By 1959 this design was considered to be unsuitable for the anti-submarine role, lacking endurance, speed, and range for effective ASW; assigned as target submarine for ASW training and redesignated SST 3 on 15 July 1959. The *Barracuda* was redesignated SS-T3 on 1 Aug 1972 reflecting assignment as an "attack submarine"; the change was administrative to increase attack submarine force levels and no changes were made to the craft.

Official status is "in service" vice in commission.

BARRACUDA (SST 3) *United States Navy*

DISPOSALS

The two target and training submarines of the "Mackerel" class, **Mackerel** (SST 1, ex-AGSS 570) and **Marlin** (SST 2), were stricken on 31 Jan 1973.
See 1972-1973 and previous editions for characteristics.

AIRCRAFT CARRIERS

The US Navy currently operates 14 attack aircraft carriers (CVA/CV)
This is a reduction of nine carriers from the Navy's peak Vietnam War strength of 1968-1969 when 15 attack carriers and eight A/S carriers were in service, with one of the latter actually operating as a "limited CVA" Two large, nuclear-powered aircraft carriers are under construction, with the first scheduled to become operational during 1974. At that time the Navy's oldest attack carrier, the *Hancock*, will be 30 years old.

The long-delayed third "Nimitz" class nuclear carrier, now designated CVN 70, is being proposed for construction in the Fiscal Year 1973-1974 budgets. This ship would provide the Navy with 12 large carriers of post-war construction by 1981, four of them nuclear-propelled. By the end of this decade none of the World War II-built "Essex-Hancock" or "Midway" class aircraft carriers would be suitable for first-line operations.

It is considered unlikely that additional large attack carriers will be constructed. Despite their great mobility, flexibility, and striking power, they have been severely criticised of late as being too expensive and too vulnerable although (no less expensive or less vulnerable weapon systems have been put forward as replacements for their non-nuclear war capabilities). Instead, it is likely that the Navy will propose a smaller, less-capable but politically more-acceptable "aircraft carrier" for construction during the late 1970s and 1980s. This latter ship could be an improved (and enlarged) version of the proposed sea control ship; see description under Surface Combatants on a later page.

Continued reductions in the number of active carriers has forced the Navy to undertake a new carrier-basing programme, and the budget constraints coupled with the changing Soviet naval capabilities has resulted in development of the so-called "CV" concept of carrier operations.

Heretofore all US aircraft carriers were based at ports in the United States, periodically deploying overseas to maintain carriers at all times in the Mediterranean and Western Pacific, and elsewhere as circumstances warranted. At this writing one US carrier will be based at Piraeus, Greece, and one at Yokosuka, Japan. This action will make more "carrier days" available in each area by reducing trans-ocean transits. (Previously the largest US warships based overseas were a cruiser flagship in the Mediterranean and one in the Western Pacific)

The "CV" concept provide for both "tactical air" (eg, fighter, attack, special mission) and anti-submarine aircraft to be based on the same aircraft carrier simultaneously. For the past two decades the Navy had segregated these aircraft on attack carriers (CVA) and anti-submarine carriers (CVS). The reduced number of carriers in service and the increasing number of Soviet nuclear-propelled submarines, and missile-armed surface warships and submarines have required that a single task force be capable of countering more varied threats. The carrier *Saratoga* evaluated the CV concept during operations in the Atlantic and Mediterranean during 1971, carrying various mixes of tactical and anti-submarine aircraft. On a regular basis the other large carriers will be fitted to operate anti-submarine fixed-wing aircraft (S-2 Tracker and later S-3 Viking) as well as SH-3 helicopters. The principal changes are provisions for an anti-submarine attack coordination centre and the required maintenance facilities.

Under the CV concept a carrier *may* offload some of the attack and reconnaissance aircraft normally assigned to an attack air wing and replace them with varying numbers of fixed-wing A/S aircraft. Helicopters configured for A/S normally will be embarked in most carriers. Then, as the tactical situation changes the carrier can be provided with more attack or A/S aircraft as required The total number of aircraft assigned to a carrier also would vary because the different aircraft types are not interchangeable on a one-for-one basis, and the aircraft capacities of the carriers differ.

Two nuclear-propelled carriers are under construction, the *Nimitz* and *Dwight D. Eisenhower*. The long-delayed third ship of this class is proposed in the Fiscal Year 1973-1974 new construction programmes (see below).

CVN 70 PROGRAMME. The proposal for this ship, the US Navy's fourth nuclear-propelled aircraft carrier, dates back to late 1966 when then-Secretary of Defense Robert S. McNamara approved a programme of constructing three nuclear carriers, to be started in alternate years. The lead ship (*Nimitz*) was authorised in the Fiscal Year 1967 new construction programme; however, the second (*Dwight D. Eisenhower*) was not authorised until FY 1970. Also in that budget the Navy requested long-lead time components for the third ship to restore the timing of the original plan. No funds were voted for the ship and instead a Congressional resolution called for a "comprehensive study and investigation" of carrier costs, effectiveness and numbers.

The FY 1971 budget request asked long-lead time funds for the ship, but Congress deferred action, pending its own study and an alleged review of carriers by the National Security Council. The Congressional study group reported 8-to-1 in favour of constructing the carrier; the National Security Council study did not address the carrier question.

There was no request for funding of CVN 70 in the FY 1972 budget. Secretary of Defense Melvin Laird did state that the U.S. commitments eventually would require construction of another nuclear carrier. Accordingly, the FY 1973 budget provided funding of advanced components for the CVN 70 with full funding requested in the FY 1974 budget.

ATTACK AIR WINGS. Each post-war attack carrier normally operates an air wing of 85 to 95 aircraft comprised of two fighter squadrons with 24 Phantoms, two or three light attack squadrons with 24 or 36 A-7 Corsairs, one attack squadron with 12 A-6 Intruders, and small squadrons or detachments with four RA-5C Vigilantes for reconnaissance, four EA-6A Prowlers for electronic warfare, four E-2A Hawkeyes for early warning, and four KA-6 Intruder tankers.

The smaller "Essex/Hancock" class attack carriers that remain in CVA status operate F-8 Crusader fighters, A-7 Corsair and A-4 Skyhawk attack planes, RF-8G Crusader photo-recce planes, EKA-3B Skywarrior tanker/electronic warfare aircraft, and E-1B Tracers in the airborne early warning role.

All attack carriers also have C-1 Trader carrier on-board delivery (COD) cargo aircraft and UH-2 utility helicopters assigned.

2 + 1 NUCLEAR-POWERED ATTACK AIRCRAFT CARRIERS (CVAN/CVN): "NIMITZ" CLASS

Name	*No.*	*Builder*	*Laid down*	*Launch*	*Commission*
NIMITZ	CVAN 68	Newport News	22 June 1968	13 May 1972	Dec 1973
DWIGHT D. EISENHOWER	CVAN 69	Newport News	15 Aug 1970	Jan 1974	mid 1975
(Proposed FY 1973-1974)	**CVN 70**	Newport News	Nov 1975		early 1981

Displacement, tons	91 400 full load
Length, feet (*metres*)	1 040 (*317·0*) wl; 1 092 (*332·0*) oa
Beam, feet (*metres*)	134 (*40·8*)
Draft, feet (*metres*)	37 (*11·3*)
Flight deck width, feet (*metres*)	252 (*76·8*)
Catapults	4 steam
Aircraft	approx 90
Missiles	3 Basic Point Defence Missile System (BPDMS) launchers with Sea Sparrow missiles
Main engines	Geared steam turbines; 260 000 shp; 4 shafts
Nuclear reactors	2 pressurised-water cooled
Speed, knots	30+
Complement	3 300 plus approx 2 800 assigned to air wing for a total of 6 100 per ship

The lead ship for this class and the world's second nuclear-powered aircraft carrier was ordered $9\frac{1}{2}$ years after the first such ship, the USS *Enterprise*. The *Nimitz* was authorised in the Fiscal Year 1967 new construction programme and the *Dwight D. Eisenhower* in the FY 1970 programme. Both ships are being built by the Newport News Shipbuilding & Dry Dock Co, Newport News, Virginia, the only US shipyard now capable of constructing large, nuclear-powered aircraft carriers.

Estimated construction costs are $594 000 000 for the *Nimitz* and $616 000 000 for the *Dwight D. Eisenhower* (revised 1971 estimates).

The CVN 70 is proposed in the FY 1973 and 1974 programme with $299 000 000 requested for advanced components in the FY 1973 budget and $657 000 000 in the FY 1974 new construction programme to complete funding. Estimated total construction cost is $1 *billion*.

The completion of the first two ships has been delayed approximately one year because of delays in the delivery of nuclear plant components.

NIMITZ (CVAN 68) at launching — *1972, United States Navy, PH1 T. Hilton Putnam*

DESIGNATION. The third ship of this class is designated an "aircraft carrier" (CV) because she will carry fighter, attack, and anti-submarine aircraft; the other ships will be modified to CV status after completion.

ELECTRONICS. These ships will have the Naval Tactical Data System (NTDS) and the following radars: SPS-10 surface search, SPS-43A two-dimensional air search, and SPS-48 three-dimensional air search, and SPN-42, SPN-43, and SPN-44 navigation equipment. These ships will not have sonar.

ENGINEERING. These carriers will each have only two nuclear reactors compared to the eight reactors required for the carrier *Enterprise*. The nuclear cores for the reactors in these ships are expected to provide sufficient energy for the ships to each steam for at least 13 years, an estimated 800 000 to 1 million miles between "refuelling"

FISCAL. Reportedly, US Navy ship construction funding for attack carriers since FY 1965 has been: $12 100 000 in 1965, $191 900 000 in 1966, $535 900 000 in 1967, $48 500 000 in 1968, $121 700 000 in 1969, and $377 100 000 in 1970.

No CVAN funding was provided in FY 1971. The FY 1972 budget provided $164 000 000 in additional funding for the CVAN 68 and CVAN 69. The CVN 70 funding is described above.

NOMENCLATURE. The *Nimitz* honours Fleet Admiral Chester W. Nimitz who was Commander-in-Chief Pacific Fleet and Commander-in-Chief Pacific Ocean Areas during World War II, and Chief of Naval Operations from December 1945 to December 1947.

The *Dwight D. Eisenhower* is believed the first major US surface warship to be named for an Army officer; General of the Army Eisenhower commanded Allied Forces in Western Europe in 1944-45, subsequently was first Supreme Allied Commander in NATO, and President of the United States from January 1953 to January 1961. The CVAN 69 was named *Eisenhower* on 21 Feb 1970; renamed *Dwight D. Eisenhower* on 25 May 1970, but Secretary of Defense Laird dedicated the ship as the "USS *Eisenhower*" at the keel laying on 15 Aug 1970. The third ship is expected to be named for the late Harry S. Truman or Lyndon B. Johnson.

PHOTOGRAPHS. The *Nimitz* is shown above at "launching" (flooding of building dock).

Aircraft Carriers—*Continued*

4 ATTACK AIRCRAFT CARRIERS (CVA CV): "KITTY HAWK" CLASS

Name	*No.*	*Builder*	*Laid down*	*Launched*	*Commissioned*
***KITTY HAWK**	CV 63	New York Shipbuilding Corp, Camden, NJ	27 Dec 1956	21 May 1960	29 Apr 1961
***CONSTELLATION**	CVA 64	New York Naval Shipyard	14 Sep 1957	8 Oct 1960	27 Oct 1961
***AMERICA**	CVA 66	Newport News Shipbuilding & Dry Dock Co	9 Jan 1961	1 Feb 1964	23 Jan 1965
***JOHN F. KENNEDY**	CVA 67	Newport News Shipbuilding & Dry Dock Co	22 Oct 1964	27 May 1967	7 Sep 1968

Displacement, tons	
Kitty Hawk	60 100 standard; 80 800 full load
Constellation	60 100 standard; 80 800 full load
America	60 300 standard; 80 800 full load
John F. Kennedy	61 000 standard; 87 000 full load
Length, feet (*metres*)	990 (*301·8*) wl
Kitty Hawk	1 062·5 (*323·9*) oa
Constellation	1 072·5 (*326·9*) oa
America J.F.K.	1047·5 (*319·3*) oa
Beam, feet (*metres*)	
Kitty Hawk, Constellation	129·5 (*38·5*)
America, J.F.K.	130 (*39·6*)
Draft, feet (*metres*)	35·9 (*10·9*)
Flight deck width, feet, (*metres*)	
J.F.K.	252 (*76·9*) maximum
Others	249 (*76·0*) maximum
Catapults	4 steam
Aircraft	approx 85 in *Kitty Hawk* and *Constellation*; approx 95 in *America* and *John F. Kennedy*
Missile launchers	2 twin Terrier surface-to-air launchers (Mk 10) in *Kitty Hawk, Constellation, America* 3 Basic Point Defence Missile System (BPDMS) launchers with Sea Sparrow missiles in *John F. Kennedy*
Main engines	4 geared turbines (Westinghouse); 280 000 shp; 4 shafts
Boilers	8—1 200 psi (*83·4 kg/cm²*) (Foster Wheeler)
Speed	35 knots
Complement	2 795 (150 officers, approx 2 645 enlisted men) plus approx 2 150 assigned to attack air wing for a total of 4 950 officers and enlisted men per ship

AMERICA (CVA 66) *1970, United States Navy, PH3 L. J. Lafeir*

These ships were built to an improved "Forrestal" design and are easily recognised by their smaller island structure which is set further aft than the superstructure in the four "Forrestal" class ships. Lift arrangement also differs (see design notes). The *Kitty Hawk* was authorised in Fiscal Year 1956 new construction programme, the *Constellation* in FY 1957, the *America* in FY 1961, and the *John F. Kennedy* in FY 1963. Completion of the *Constellation* was delayed because of a fire which ravaged her in the New York Naval Shipyard in December 1960. Construction of the *John F. Kennedy* was delayed because of debate over whether to provide her with conventional or nuclear propulsion.

Construction costs were $265 200 000 for *Kitty Hawk*, $264 500 000 for *Constellation*, $248 800 000 for *America*, and $277 000 000 for *John F. Kennedy*.

CLASSIFICATION. Officially known as the "Kitty Hawk" class; generally referred to as improved "Forrestals". The *John F. Kennedy* is officially a separate one-ship class.

KITTY HAWK changed from CVA 63 to CV 63 on 29 Apr 1973.

DESIGN. These ships are officially considered to be of a different design than the "Forrestal" class. The island structure is smaller and set farther aft in the newer ships with two deck-edge lifts forward of the superstructure, a third lift aft of the structure, and the port-side left on the after quarter (compared with two lifts aft of the island and the port-side lift at the forward end of the angled deck in the earlier ships). This lift arrangement considerably improves flight deck operations. All four of these ships also have a small radar mast aft of the island structure. The *John F. Kennedy* and *America* have stem anchors because of their bow sonar dome.

ELECTRONICS. All four ships of this class have highly sophisticated electronic equipment including the Naval Tactical Data System (NTDS). The *America* and *John F. Kennedy* have bow-mounted SQS-23 sonar, the first US attack carriers with anti-submarine sonar (several ASW carriers have been fitted with sonar during modernisations).

All four ships have SPS-43 search radar antenna on island structure; three ships also have a three-dimensional SPS-52 search radar antenna on island and an SPS-30 search radar antenna on second mast while the *John F. Kennedy* has SPS-48 antenna on second mast; being fitted with SPS-58 radar to detect low-flying aircraft and missiles. All ships have TACAN navigation pods or "bee-hives".

MISSILES. The three Terrier-armed ships have an Mk10 Mod 3 launcher on the starboard quarter and a Mod 4 launcher on the post quarter.

NOMENCLATURE. US aircraft carriers are generally named after battles and historic ships. However, the *Kitty Hawk* better honours the site where the Wright brothers made their historic flights than the converted aircraft ferry of that name which served in World War II. The *Constellation* remembers a frigate built in 1797 and a later ship still afloat at Baltimore, Maryland, although no longer in Navy commission. The name "America" was previously carried by a 74-gun ship of the line launched in 1782, and presented to France, by the racing schooner which gave her name to the America's Cup, and by the German liner *Amerika* which was taken over by the US Navy in World War I, renamed, and used as a troop transport. The *John F. Kennedy* remembers the martyred president who was assassinated in 1963. The destroyer *Joseph P. Kennedy Jr.* (DD 850) honours his older brother who was killed in a bomber explosion over England in World War II.

PHOTOGRAPHS. In the above photograph of the *America* E-2 Hawkeye and EKA-3 Skywarrior electronic aircraft are on the ship's forward catapults; below an E-2 (over the bow) has just been launched from a catapult on the angled deck. On the following page note the *John F. Kennedy's* angled funnel.

AMERICA (CVA 66) *1972, United States Navy, PH3 G. R. Stromquist*

Aircraft Carriers—*continued*

JOHN F. KENNEDY (CVA 67) *1969, United States Navy*

JOHN F. KENNEDY (CVA 67) *1973, United States Navy, PH1 D. D. Deverman*

AMERICA (CVA 66)
Drawing by A. D. Baker

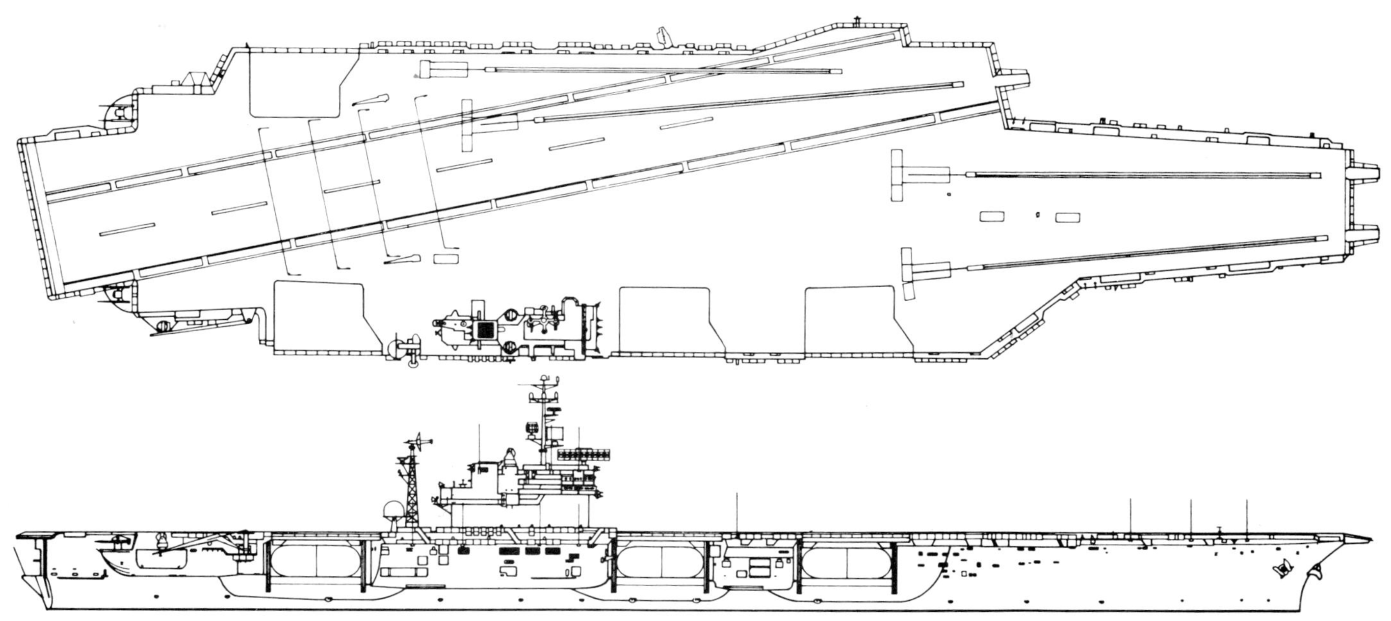

Aircraft Carriers—*continued*

1 NUCLEAR-POWERED ATTACK AIRCRAFT CARRIER (CVAN): "ENTERPRISE" TYPE

Name	*No.*	*Builder*	*Laid down*	*Launched*	*Commissioned*
*ENTERPRISE	CVAN 65	Newport News Shipbuilding & Dry Dock Co	4 Feb 1958	24 Sep 1960	25 Nov 1961

Displacement, tons	75 700 standard; 89 600 full load
Length, feet (*metres*)	1 040 (*317·0*) wl; 1 123 (*341·3*) oa
Beam, feet (*metres*)	133 (*40·5*)
Draft, feet (*metres*)	35·8 (*10·8*)
Flight deck width, feet (*metres*)	257 (*78·3*) maximum
Catapults	4 Steam
Aircraft	approx 95
Missile launchers	3 Basic Point Defence Missile System (BPDMS) launchers with Sea Sparrow missiles (see *Armament* notes)
Main engines	4 geared steam turbines (Westinghouse); approx 280 000 shp; 4 shafts
Nuclear reactors	8 pressurised-water cooled A2W (Westinghouse)
Speed, knots	35
Complement	3 100 (162 officers, approx 2 940 enlisted men) plus 2 400 assigned to attack air wing for a total of 5 500

ENTERPRISE (CVAN 65) — *1969, United States Navy*

The *Enterprise* was the largest warship ever built at the time of her construction and will be rivalled in size only by the nuclear-powered "Nimitz" class ships. The *Enterprise* was authorised in the Fiscal Year 1958 new construction programme. She was launched only 19 months after her keel was laid down.

The *Enterprise* was flagship of Task Force One during Operation Sea Orbit when the carrier, the nuclear-powered cruiser *Long Beach* (CGN 9), and the nuclear-powered frigate *Bainbridge* (DLGN 25) circumnavigated the world, in 1964, cruising more than 30 000 miles in 64 days (underway 57 days) without refuelling.

The cost of the *Enterprise* was $451 300 000.

The Fiscal Year 1960 budget provided $35 000 000 to prepare plans and place orders for components of a second nuclear-powered carrier, but the project was deferred.

ARMAMENT. The *Enterprise* — "the world's largest warship"—was completed without any armament in an effort to hold down construction costs. Space for Terrier missile system was provided. Short-range Sea Sparrow BPDMS subsequently was installed.

DESIGN. Built to a modified "Forrestal" Class design The most distinctive feature is the island structure. Nuclear propulsion eliminated requirement for smoke stack and boiler air intakes, reducing size of superstructure, and reducing vulnerability to battle damage, radioactivity and biological agents. Rectangular fixed-array radar antennas ("billboards") are mounted on sides of island; electronic countermeasures (ECM) antennas ring cone-shaped upper levels of island structure. Fixed antennas have increased range and performance (see listing for cruiser *Long Beach*). The *Enterprise* has four deck-edge lifts, two forward of island and one aft on starboard side and one aft on port side (as in "Kitty Hawk" class).

ELECTRONICS. Fitted with the Naval Tactical Data System (NTDS). In addition to SPS-32 and SPS-33 "billboard" radar systems, the *Enterprise* has SPS-10 and SPS-12 search radars and various navigation radar antennas atop her island structure; SPS-58 radar fitted to detect low-flying aircraft and missiles. TACAN navigation pod caps mast.

ENGINEERING. The *Enterprise* is the world's second nuclear-powered warship (the cruiser *Long Beach* was completed a few months earlier). Design of the first nuclear powered aircraft carrier began in 1950 and work continued until 1953 when the programme was deferred pending further work on the submarine reactor programme. The large ship reactor project was reinstated in 1954 on the basis of technological advancements made in the previous 14 months. The Atomic Energy Commission's Bettis Atomic Power Laboratory was given prime responsibility for developing the nuclear power plant.

The first of the eight reactors installed in the *Enterprise* achieved initial criticality on 2 Dec 1960, shortly after the carrier was launched. After three years of operation during which she steamed more than 207 000 miles, the *Enterprise* was overhauled and refuelled from November 1964 to July 1965. Her second set of cores provided

ENTERPRISE (CVAN 65)
Drawing by A. D. Baker

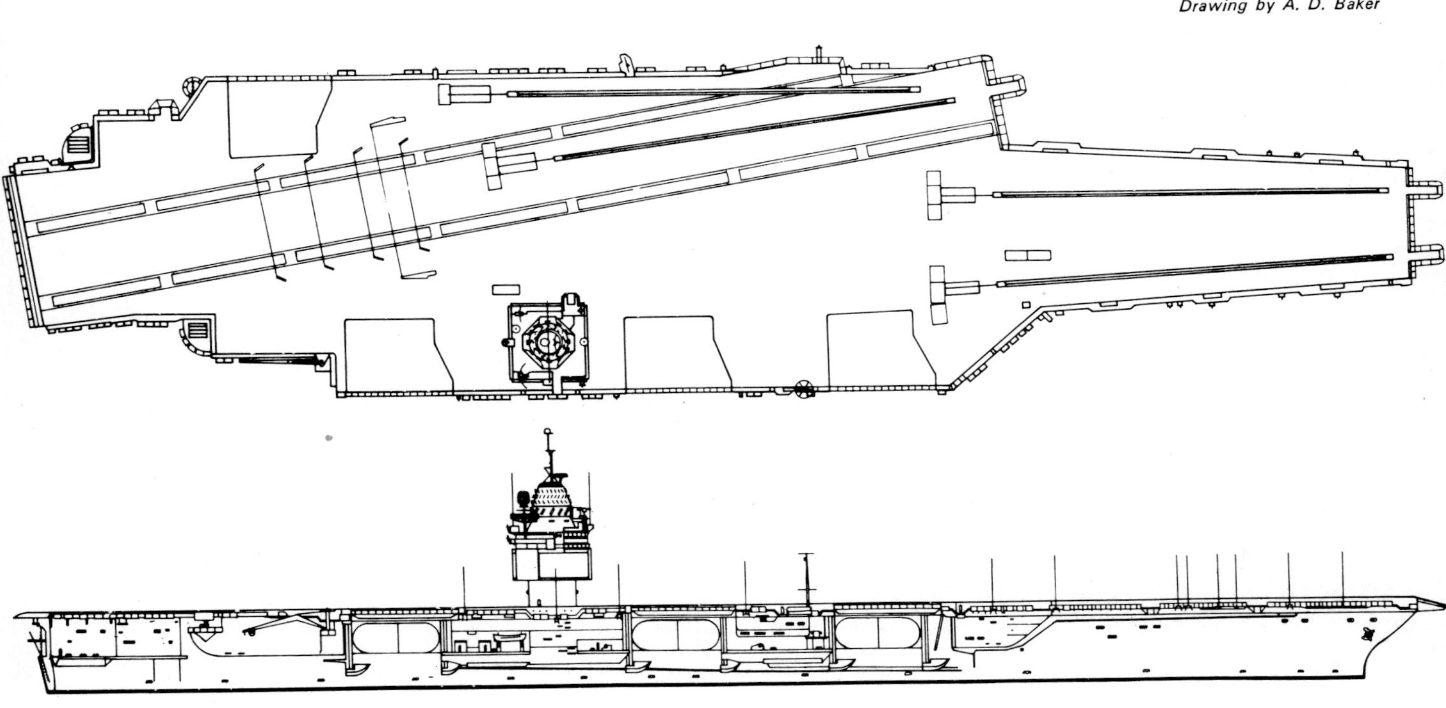

Aircraft Carriers—*continued*

"ENTERPRISE" TYPE—*continued*

about 300 000 miles steaming. The eight cores initially installed in the *Enterprise* cost $64 000 000; the second set cost about $20 000 000.

The *Enterprise* underwent an extensive overhaul from October 1969 to January 1971, which included installation of a new set of uranium cores in the ship's eight nuclear reactors. The overhaul and refuelling took place at the Newport News shipyard. Estimated cost of the overhaul was approximately $30 000 000, with $13 000 000 being for non-nuclear repairs and alterations, and $17 000 000 being associated with installation of the new nuclear cores (the latter amount being in addition to the $80 000 000 cost of the eight cores). This third set of cores is expected to fuel the ship for 10 to 13 years, according to Vice Adm H. G. Rickover.

In addition to virtually unlimited high-speed endurance nuclear propulsion for aircraft carriers provides additional space for aviation fuels and ordnance, elimination of stack gases and smoke which have corrosive effects on electronic antennas and aircraft, virtually unlimited electrical power, and the ability to quickly change speed without affecting the number of personnel on watch in the engineering spaces.

There are two reactors for each of the ship's four shafts. The eight reactors feed 32 heat exchangers. The *Enterprise* developed more horsepower during her propulsion trials than any other ship in history (officially "in excess of 200 000 shaft horsepower"; subsequently Navy officials stated that she can generate 280 000 hp).

NOMENCLATURE. Eight US Navy ships have carried the name *Enterprise*. The first was a British supply sloop captured in 1775 and armed for use on Lake Champlain. The seventh *Enterprise* (CV 6) was the most famous US carrier of World War II. She earned 20 battle stars. That "Big E" was sold in 1958 and scrapped.

PHOTOGRAPHS. In the above photograph note the Sea Sparrow missile launcher at near full elevation on a sponson on the ship's port quarter. In the bottom photograph on this page an A-6 Intruder with wings folded is on the ship's forward starboard deck-edge elevator.

ENTERPRISE (CVAN 65) *1968, United States Navy*

ENTERPRISE (CVAN 65) *1969, United States Navy*

ENTERPRISE (CVAN 65) *1968, United States Navy*

Aircraft Carriers—*continued*

4 ATTACK AIRCRAFT CARRIERS (CVA/CV): "FORRESTAL" CLASS

Name	*No.*	*Builder*	*Laid down*	*Launched*	*Commissioned*
*FORRESTAL	CVA 59	Newport News SB & DD Co	14 July 1952	11 Dec 1954	1 Oct 1955
*SARATOGA	CV 60	New York Naval Shipyard	16 Dec 1952	8 Oct 1955	14 Apr 1956
*RANGER	CVA 61	Newport News SB & DD Co	2 Aug 1954	29 Sep 1956	10 Aug 1957
*INDEPENDENCE	CV 62	New York Naval Shipyard	1 July 1955	6 June 1958	10 Jan 1959

Displacement, tons	
Forrestal	59 650 standard; 78 000 full load
Others	60 000 standard; 78 000 full load
Length, feet (*metres*) *Forrestal, Saratoga*	990 (*301·8*) wl
Ranger	1 039 (*316·7*) oa
Independence	1 046·5 (*319·0*) oa
Beam, feet (*metres*)	129·5 (*38·5*)
Draft, feet (*metres*)	37 (*11·3*)
Flight deck width, feet (*metres*)	
Ranger	260 (*79·2*) maximum
Others	252 (*76·8*) maximum
Catapults	4 Steam
Aircraft	approx 85
Guns	4—5 inch (*127 mm*) 54 cal DP (single) removed from *Forrestal* (see *Gunnery* notes)
Missile launchers	1 Basic Point Defence Missile System (BPDMS) launcher with Sea Sparrow missiles in *Forrestal*
Main engines	4 geared turbines (Westinghouse) 4 shafts 260 000 shp in *Forrestal* 280 000 shp in others
Boilers	8—615 psi (*42·7 kg/cm²*) in *Forrestal* 1 200 psi (*83·4 kg/cm²*) in others (all Babcock & Wilcox)
Speed, knots	
Forrestal	33
Others	35
Complement	2 790 (145 officers, approx 2 645 enlisted men) plus approx 2 150 assigned to attack air wing for a total of 4 940+ per ship

SARATOGA (CV 60) *1969, United States Navy*

The *Forrestal* was the world's first aircraft carrier designed and built after World War II. The *Forrestal* design drew heavily from the aircraft carrier *United States* (CVA 58) which was cancelled immediately after being laid down in April 1949. The *Forrestal* was authorised in the Fiscal Year 1952 new construction programme; the *Saratoga* followed in the FY 1953 programme, the *Ranger*. Construction costs were $188 900 000 for *Forrestal*, $213 900 000 for *Saratoga*, $173 300 000 for *Ranger*, and $225 300 000 for *Independence*.

AIRCRAFT. During 1971 the *Saratoga* was modified to serve as a "CV" combining both attack carrier and anti-submarine carrier capabilities in one ship; provided with anti-submarine attack coordination centre, maintenance facilities for S-2E Tracker A/S aircraft, and ship's fuel system modified to support piston-engine Trackers as well as turbojet and turboprop aircraft normally embarked. Thus modified she operated ten S-2E Trackers and eight SH-3 Sea King helicopters with her RA-5C Vigilante reconnaissance aircraft removed to provide space. Other ships to be similarly modified.

CLASSIFICATION. The *Forrestal* and *Saratoga* were initially classified as Large Aircraft Carriers CVB 59 and 60, respectively; reclassified as Attack Aircraft Carriers (CVA) in October 1952 to reflect their purpose rather than size. The ill-fated *United States* was a "heavy" carrier (CVA).

Saratoga redesignated CV 60 vice CVA 60 on 30 June 1972; *Independence* to CV 62 on 28 Feb 1973.

DESIGN. The "Forrestal" Class ships were the first aircraft carriers designed and built specifically to operate jet-propelled aircraft. The *Forrestal* was redesigned early in construction to incorporate British-developed angled flight deck and steam catapults. These were the first US aircraft carriers built with an enclosed flight deck to improve seaworthiness. Four large deck-edge lifts are fitted, one forward of island structure to starboard, two aft of island structure to starboard and one at forward edge of angled flight deck to port. Other features include armoured flight deck and advanced underwater protection and internal compartmentation to reduce effects of conventional and nuclear attack. Mast configurations differ; the *Forrestal* originally had two masts, one of which was removed in 1967.

ELECTRONICS. The primary radars installed in these ships are SPS-43, SPS-30, and SPS-10 search radars, and SPN-10 navigation radar. Small TACAN navigation pods top the masts of these ships.
SPS-58 radar being installed to detect low-flying aircraft and missiles.
Naval Tactical Data System (NTDS) is installed in all four ships.

ENGINEERING. The *Saratoga* and later ships have an improved steam plant; increased machinery weight of the improved plant is more than compensated by increased performance and decreased fuel consumption.

GUNNERY. All four ships initially mounted 8—5 inch guns in single mounts, two mounts on each quarter. The forward sponsons carrying the guns interfered with ship operations in rough weather, tending to slow the ships down. The forward sponsons and guns were subsequently removed (except in *Ranger*), reducing armament to four guns per ship. The guns are 5 inch/54 calibre, rapid-fire, dual-purpose weapons.
The four after 5 inch guns were removed from the *Forrestal* late in 1967 and a single BPDMS launcher for Sea Sparrow missiles was installed forward on the starboard side. Two additional launchers will be installed.

NOMENCLATURE. The *Forrestal* honours James V. Forrestal, Secretary of the Navy from 1944 until he was appointed the first US Secretary of Defense in 1947, a post he held until shortly before his death in 1949. The *Saratoga* commemorates the battle at Saratoga, New York, in the American Revolution and five earlier US warships including a carrier of World War II fame (CV 3). The first USS *Ranger* was a sloop built in 1777 and a later ship of that name was the first US built-for-the-purpose carriers (CV 4). The first USS *Independence* was a sloop built in 1775 and a later ship of that name was a light carrier (CVL 22) that saw extensive combat in World War II.

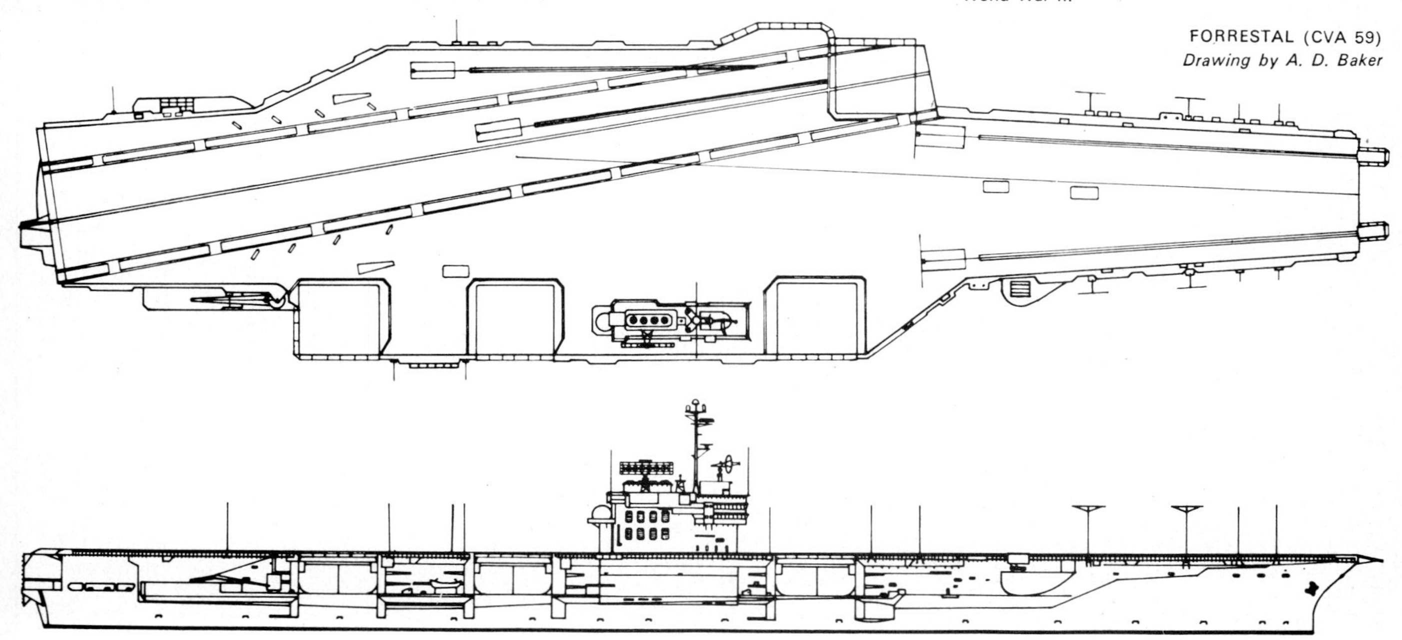

FORRESTAL (CVA 59)
Drawing by A. D. Baker

Aircraft Carriers—*continued*

SARATOGA (CV 60) *1970, United States Navy, PH1 R. D. Williams*

RANGER (CVA 61) *1968, United States Navy*

FORRESTAL (CVA 59) *1971, United States Navy*

INDEPENDENCE (CV 62) *1970, United States Navy*

Aircraft Carriers—*continued*

3 ATTACK AIRCRAFT CARRIERS (CVA): "MIDWAY" CLASS

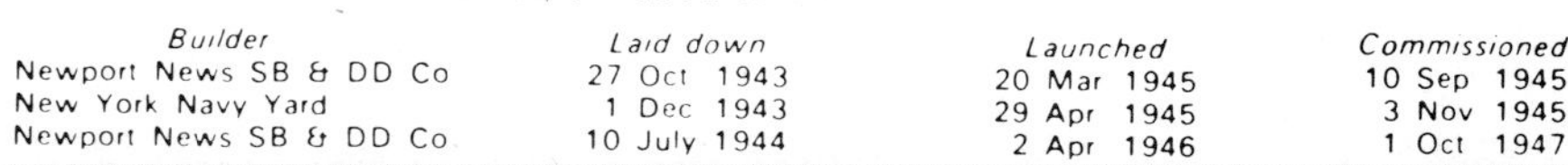

Name	*No*	*Builder*	*Laid down*	*Launched*	*Commissioned*
*MIDWAY	CVA 41	Newport News SB & DD Co	27 Oct 1943	20 Mar 1945	10 Sep 1945
*FRANKLIN D. ROOSEVELT	CVA 42	New York Navy Yard	1 Dec 1943	29 Apr 1945	3 Nov 1945
*CORAL SEA	CVA 43	Newport News SB & DD Co	10 July 1944	2 Apr 1946	1 Oct 1947

Displacement, tons	
Midway	51 000 standard
F. D. Roosevelt	51 000 standard
Coral Sea	52 500 standard
	all approx 64 000 full load
Length, feet (*metres*)	900 (*274·3*) wl; 979 (*298·4*) oa
Beam, feet (*metres*)	121 (*36·9*)
Draft, feet (*metres*)	35·3 (*10·8*)
Flight deck width, feet (*metres*)	238 (*72·5*) maximum
Catapults	2 steam except 3 in *Coral Sea*
Aircraft	approx 75
Guns	4—5 inch (*127 mm*) 54 cal DP in *F. D. Roosevelt*; three guns in *Midway* and *Coral Sea* (see *Gunnery* notes)
Main engines	4 geared turbines (Westinghouse in *Midway* and *Coral Sea*; General Electric in *F. D. Roosevelt*); 212 000 shp; 4 shafts
Boilers	12—615 psi (*41·7 kg/cm²*) (Babcock & Wilcox)
Speed, knots	33
Complement	2 615 (140 officers, approx 2 475 enlisted men) except *Coral Sea* 2 710 (165 officers, approx 2 545 enlisted men) plus approx 1 800 assigned to attack air wing for a total of 4 400 to 4 500 per ship

These carriers were the largest US warships constructed during World War II. Completed too late for service in that conflict, they were the backbone of US naval strength for the first decade of the Cold War. Beginning in 1949 they were modified to store, assemble, and load nuclear weapons, making them the world's first warships with a nuclear strike capability. (P2V-3C Neptunes and AJ-1 Savages were the first delivery aircraft.) All three ships operated in the Atlantic and Mediterranean during the Korean War, but subsequently they have operated in the Pacific. The entire class has been in active service (except for overhaul and modernisation) since the ships were completed more than 25 years ago.
Construction cost of *Midway* was $85 600 000, *F. D. Roosevelt* $85 700 000, and *Coral Sea* $87 600 000.

CLASSIFICATION. These ships were initially classified as Large Aircraft Carriers CVB 41-43, respectively, reclassified as Attack Aircraft Carriers (CVA) in October 1952.

DESIGN. These ships were built to the same design with a standard displacement of 45 000 tons, full load displacement of 60 100 tons, and an overall length of 968 feet. They have been extensively modified since completion (see notes below). These ships were the first US aircraft carriers with an armoured flight deck and the first US warships with a designed width too large to enable them to pass through the Panama Canal.
The unnamed CVB 44, 56 and 57 of this class were cancelled prior to the start of construction.

ELECTRONICS. Naval Tactical Data System (NTDS) in *Midway* and *Coral Sea*.

The principal radars installed on these ships are SPS-10, SPS-30, SPS-43, SPN-6, and SPN-10. *Midway* fitted with SPS-58 radar to detect low-flying aircraft and missiles. Note that *Coral Sea* retains large TACAN (Tactical Air Navigation) "bee hive" antenna atop mast compared to smaller antenna pods on *Midway* and *Franklin D. Roosevelt*.

GUNNERY. As built these ships mounted 18—5 inch guns (14 in *Coral Sea*), 84—40 mm guns, and 28—20 mm guns. Armament reduced periodically with 3 inch guns replacing lighter weapons. Minimal 5 inch armament remains. The 5 inch guns are 54 calibre Mk 39, essentially modified 5 inch/38 calibre with a longer barrel for greater range; not to be confused with rapid-fire 5 inch 54s of newer US warships.

MIDWAY (CVA 41) — *1971, United States Navy*

CORAL SEA (CVA 43) — *1970, United States Navy, PH2 George W. Estaver*

MODERNISATION. All three "Midway" Class carriers have been extensively modernised. Their most extensive conversion "package" gave them angled flight decks, steam catapults, enclosed "hurricane" bows, new electronics, and new lift arrangement (*Franklin D. Roosevelt* from 1953 to 1956, *Midway* from 1954 to 1957, and *Coral Sea* from 1956 to 1960; all at Puget Sound Naval Shipyard). Lift arrangement was changed in *Franklin D. Roosevelt* and *Midway* to one centreline lift forward, one deck-edge list aft of island on starboard side, and one deck-edge lift at forward end of angled deck on port side. The *Coral Sea* has an improved arrangement with one lift forward and one aft of island on starboard side and third lift outboard on port side aft.
The *Midway* began another extensive modernisation at the San Francisco Bay Naval Shipyard in February 1966; she was recommissioned on 31 Jan 1970 and went to sea in March 1970.
Her modernisation included provisions for handling newer aircraft, new catapults, new lifts (arranged as in *Coral Sea*), and new electronics. A similar modernisation planned for the *Franklin D. Roosevelt*, to have begun in Fiscal Year 1970, has been cancelled because the *Midway* modernisation is taking longer and costing more than originally estimated (24 months and $88 000 000 was planned; actual work required approximately 52 months and $202 300 000). The *Franklin D. Roosevelt* completed an austere overhaul in June 1969 which enables her to operate the new A-6 Intruder and A-7 Corsair II attack aircraft; cost of overhaul was $46 000 000.
The *Midway* is now the most capable of the three ships (for example, her lifts can handle aircraft weights to 100 000 pounds compared to 74 000 pounds for the *Coral Sea* and *Franklin D. Roosevelt*).

Aircraft Carriers—*continued*

FRANKLIN D. ROOSEVELT (CVA 42) *1970, United States Navy*

CORAL SEA (CVA 43) *1971, United States Navy*

MIDWAY (CVA 41) *1970, United States Navy*

FRANKLIN D. ROOSEVELT (CVA 42)
Drawing by A. D. Baker

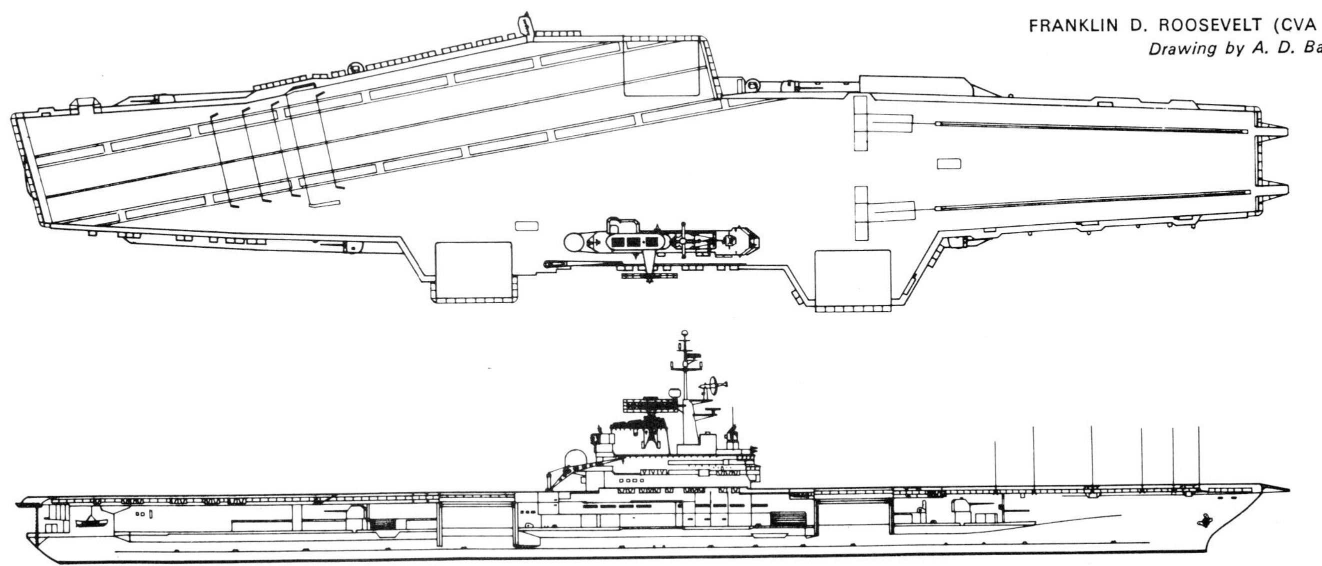

Aircraft Carriers—*Continued*

3 ATTACK AIRCRAFT CARRIERS (CVA)
3 ASW AIRCRAFT CARRIERS (CVS) "HANCOCK" CLASS
1 TRAINING CARRIER (CVT)

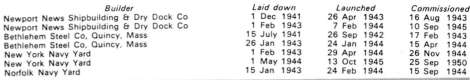

Name	*No.*	*Builder*	*Laid down*	*Launched*	*Commissioned*
*INTREPID	CVS 11	Newport News Shipbuilding & Dry Dock Co	1 Dec 1941	26 Apr 1943	16 Aug 1943
TICONDEROGA	CVS 14	Newport News Shipbuilding & Dry Dock Co	1 Feb 1943	7 Feb 1944	10 Sep 1945
*LEXINGTON	CVT 16	Bethlehem Steel Co, Quincy, Mass	15 July 1941	26 Sep 1942	17 Feb 1943
*HANCOCK	CVA 19	Bethlehem Steel Co, Quincy, Mass	26 Jan 1943	24 Jan 1944	15 Apr 1944
BON HOMME RICHARD	CVA 31	New York Navy Yard	1 Feb 1943	29 Apr 1944	26 Nov 1944
*ORISKANY	CVA 34	New York Navy Yard	1 May 1944	13 Oct 1945	25 Sep 1950
SHANGRI-LA	CVS 38	Norfolk Navy Yard	15 Jan 1943	24 Feb 1944	15 Sep 1944

Displacement, tons	approx 32 800 standard, except *Oriskany* 33 250
CVA type	approx 44 700 full load
Others	approx 42 000 full load except *Lexington* 39 000
Length, feet (*metres*)	894·5 (*272·6*) oa except *Oriskany* 890 (*271·3*); 820 (*249·9*) wl
Beam, feet (*metres*)	103 (*30·8*) except *Oriskany* 106·5 (*32·5*)
Draft, feet (*metres*)	31 (*9·4*)
Flight deck width feet (*metres*)	192 (*58·5*) maximum except *Oriskany* 195 (*59·5*)
Catapults	2 steam
Aircraft	70 to 80 for CVA type; approx 45 for CVS type; none assigned to *Lexington*
Guns	4—5 inch (*127 mm*) 38 cal dual-purpose (single); removed from *Lexington*
Main engines	4 geared turbines (Westinghouse); 150 000 shp; 4 shafts
Boilers	8—600 psi (*41·7 kg/cm²*) (Babcock & Wilcox)
Speed, knots	30+
Complement CVA type	2 130 (130 officers, approx 2 000 enlisted men) plus approx 1 500 assigned to attack air wing for a total of 3 630 per ship
CVS type	1 615 (115 officers, approx 1 500 enlisted men) plus approx 800 assigned to ASW air group for a total of 2 400 per ship
Lexington	1 440 (75 officers, 1 365 enlisted men); no air unit assigned

ORISKANY (CVA 34) — *1970, United States Navy*

These ships originally were "Essex" class aircraft carriers; extensively modernised during 1950s, being provided with enclosed, hurricane-bow, angled flight deck, improved elevators, increased aviation fuel storage, and steam catapults (last feature permits operation of more-advanced aircraft that can be flown from modernised "Essex" class). Construction of *Oriskany* suspended after World War II and she was completed in 1950 to a modified "Essex" design. See "Essex" class listing for additional notes.

Bon Homme Richard decommissioned on 2 July 1971 and *Shangri-La* on 30 July 1971, both placed in reserve. *Ticonderoga* decommissioned in 1973.

The *Hancock* had been scheduled for decommissioning in late 1971, but is retained in commission to provide 14-ship CVA / CV force level.

Intrepid taken ont of active service in June 1973.; she was the US Navy's last "dedicated" ASW Carrier.

CLASSIFICATION. All "Essex" class ships originally were designated as Aircraft Carriers (CV); reclassified as Attack Aircraft Carriers (CVA) in Oct 1952. *Intrepid* reclassified as ASW Support Aircraft Carrier (CVS) on 31 Mar 1962, *Lexington* on 1 Oct 1962, *Shangri-La* on 30 June 1969, *Ticonderoga* on 21 Oct 1969. The *Lexington* became the Navy's training aircraft carrier in the Gulf of Mexico on 29 Dec 1962 (correction from previous edition); reclassified CVT on 1 Jan 1969.

ELECTRONICS. The *Oriskany* and the frigates *King* (DLG 10) and *Mahan* (DLG 11) conducted the initial sea trials of the Naval Tactical Data System (NTDS) in 1961-1962.

The principal radars in these ships are SPS-43, SPS-30, and SPS-10 search radars, and SPN-10 navigation radar, except *Lexington* has SPS-43 SPS-12, SPS-10, and SPN-10 (the SPS-8 formerly mounted has been removed). TACAN aircraft navigation pods stop their masts.

MODERNISATION. These ships have been modernised under several programmes to increase their ability to operate more-advanced aircraft. The *Oriskany* was completed with some post-war ("jet age") features incorporated. The most prominent difference from their original configuration is angled flight deck and removal of twin 5-inch gun mounts from flight deck forward and aft of island structure. Three elevators fitted: "Pointed" centreline lift forward between catapults, deckedge lift on portside at leading edge of angled deck, and deckedge lift on starboard side aft of island structure. Minimal gun battery retained (see description of original armament under "Essex" class listings). Remaining guns removed from *Lexington* in 1969.

OPERATIONAL. The *Shangri-La* while designated as an anti-submarine carrier operated as a "limited attack carrier" off Vietnam during 1969-1970, carrying an air wing of A-4 Skyhawk and A-1 Skyraider attack planes, with the latter being phased out of the Navy during that period, and later F-8 Crusader fighters.

As of 1 Jan 1972 the *Lexington* had recorded 293 000 arrested aircraft landings during her operational career (1943-1947, 1955-present).

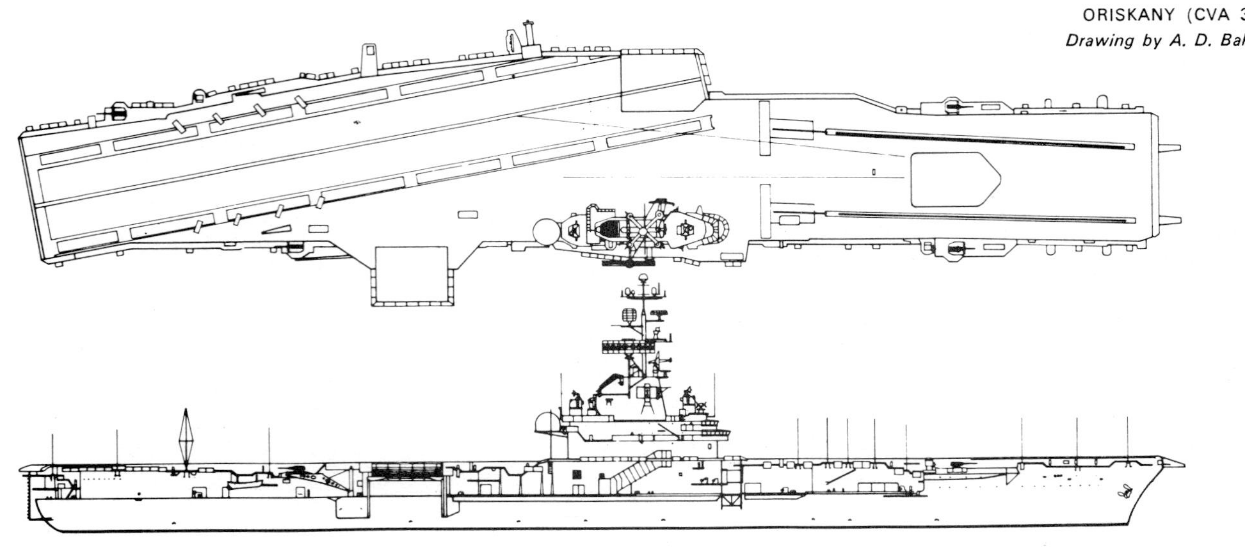

ORISKANY (CVA 34)
Drawing by A. D. Baker

Aircraft Carriers—*Continued*

"HANCOCK" CLASS—*continued*

NOMENCLATURE. All 24 "Essex" class carriers are named for early American ships or battles except for *Shangri-La*, which is named for the imaginary locale in James Hilton's novel which President Roosevelt told the press was the base for the Doolittle-Halsey raid against Japan in 1942. Several ships renamed during construction to carry on names of carriers lost in battle. The *Hancock* and *Ticonderoga* exchanged names during construction.

PHOTOGRAPHS. The carrier *Oriskany* is shown in the Gulf of Tonkin with an E-1B Tracer early warning aircraft being prepared for launch on her starboard catapult forward of the island; the *Intrepid* has sub-hunting S-2E Trackers and SH-3 Sea kings on her flight deck. She also carries E-1B early warning aircraft and a utility helicopter; the *Hancock* is shown with more than 50 aircraft on her flight deck.

DISPOSALS

Nine "straight-deck" carriers of this class have been stricken: **Franklin** (AVT 8, ex-CVS 13) stricken on 1 Oct 1964; **Bunker Hill** (AVT 8, ex-CVS 17) stricken on 1 Nov 1966, but retained as moored electronic test ship at San Diego, California, until Nov 1972; **Tarawa** (AVT 12, ex-CVS 40) stricken on 1 June 1967; **Leyte** (AVT 10, ex-CVS 32) stricken on 1 June 1969; **Philippine Sea** (AVT 11, ex-CVS 47), **Lake Champlain** (CVS 39), and **Boxer** (LPH 4, ex-CVS 21) stricken on 1 Dec 1969; **Princeton** (LPH 5, es-CVS 37) stricken on 30 Jan 1970; **Valley Forge** (LPH 8, ex-CVS 45) stricken on 15 Jan 1970.

Of the "Essex" class ships modernised to an angled-deck configuration: **Wasp** (CVS 18) stricken on 1 July 1972; **Essex** (CVS 9), **Yorktown** (CVS 10), **Randolph** (CVS 15), **Kearsarge** (CVS 33), **Antietam** (CVS 36) stricken in 1973.

ORISKANY (CVA 34) — *1970, United States Navy*

HANCOCK (CVA 19) — *1971, United States Navy, PH2 M. E. Mowbray*

INTREPID (CVS 11) — *1969, United States Navy*

Aircraft Carriers—*Continued*

2 ASW AIRCRAFT CARRIERS (CVS): MODERNISED "ESSEX" CLASS

Name	*No.*	*Builder*	*Laid down*	*Launched*	*Commissioned*
ORNET	CVS 12	Newport News Shipbuilding & Dry Dock Co	3 Aug 1942	29 Aug 1943	29 Nov 1943
ENNINGTON	CVS 20	New York Navy Yard	15 Dec 1942	26 Feb 1944	6 Aug 1944

Displacement, tons	approx 33 000 standard; approx 40 060 full load
Length, feet (*metres*)	820 (*249·9*) wl; 8900 (*271·3*) oa
Beam, feet (*metres*)	102 (*31*); 93 (*28·4*)
Draft, feet (*metres*)	31 (*9·4*)
Flight deck width feet (*metres*)	196 (*59·7*) maximum
Catapults	2 hydraulic
Aircraft	approx 45 (including 16 to 18 helicopters)
Guns	4—5 inch (*127 mm*) 38 cal dual-purpose (single)
Main engines	4 geared turbines (Westinghouse); 150 000 shp; 4 shafts
Boilers	8—600 psi (*41·7 kg/cm²*) (Babcock & Wilcox)
Speed, knots	30+
Complement	1 615 (115 officers, approx 1 500 enlisted men) plus approx 800 assigned to ASW air group for a total of 2 400 per ship.

The two above ships and the previously listed "Hancock" class are the survivors of the 24 "Essex" class fleet carriers built during the World War II (with one ship, *Oriskany*, not completed until 1950). Both of the above ships were extensively modernised during the 1950s; however, they lack the steam catapults and other features of the "Hancock" class.
The late *Antietam* of this class was the world's first aircraft carrier to be fitted with an angled flight deck to increase efficiency and safety of high-performance aircraft operations aboard carriers.
The *Bennington* was decommissioned on 15 Jan 1970 and the *Hornet* on 26 June 1970; both ships are in reserve.

CLASSIFICATION. These ships originally were designated as Aircraft Carriers (CV); reclassified as Attack Carriers(CVA) in Oct 1952. Subsequently they became ASW Support Aircraft Carriers (CVS): *Hornet* on 27 June 1958, and *Bennington* on 30 June 1959.

DESIGN. All 24 "Essex" class ships were built to the same basic design except for the delayed *Oriskany*. Standard displacement as built was 27 100 tons, full load displacement was 36 380 tons, and overall length 888 or 972 feet. Two additional ships of this class were cancelled while under construction, the *Reprisal* (CV 35) and *Iwo Jima* (CV 46), and six others were cancelled prior to keel laying, the unnamed CV 50-55. See 1971-1972 and previous editions for notes on armament as originally completed and ship nomenclature.

ELECTRONICS. The primary radars in these ships are SPS-43, SPS-30, and SPS-10 search radars, and SPN-10 navigation radars; TACAN aircraft navigation pods top masts. Both ships have SQS-23 bow-mounted sonar.

MODERNISATION. These ships have been modernised under several programmes to increase their ability to operate advanced aircraft and to improve sea keeping. Also modernised to improve anti-submarine capabilities under the Fleet Rehabilitation and Modernisation (FRAM II) programme.

LIGHT AIRCRAFT CARRIERS (CVL)

All light aircraft carriers have been stricken from the Navy List, transferred or reclassified.

Of the nine ships of the "Independence" class converted during construction from light cruisers: **Independence** (CVL 22) used in atomic bomb and radiological experiments from July 1946 until sunk on 29 Jan 1951; **Princeton** (CVL 23) sunk in World War II; **Belleau Wood** (CVL 24) to France on 5 Sep 1953 (scrapped); **Cowpens** (AVT 1, ex-CVL 25) stricken on 1 Nov 1959; **Monterey** (AVT 2, ex-CVL 26) stricken on 1 June 1970; **Langley** (CVL 27) to France on 8 Jan 1951 (scrapped); **Cabot** (AVT 3, ex-CVL 28) to Spain on 30 Aug 1967; **Bataan** (AVT 4, ex-CVL 29) stricken on 1 Sep 1959; **San Jacinto** (AVT 5, ex-CVL 30) stricken on 1 June 1970.

The larger, built-for-the-purpose light carriers of the "Saipan" class have been converted to other roles: *Saipan* (AVT 6, ex-CVL 48) converted to major communications relay ship (AGMR 2) and *Wright* (AVT 7, ex-CVL 49) converted to command ship (CC 2).

BENNINGTON (CVS 20) *1968, United States Navy*

HORNET (CVS 12) *1968, United States Navy*

SURFACE COMBATANTS

The US Navy has established the category of Surface Combatants to include battleships, cruisers, frigates, and destroyers. The various types of escort ships (DE/DEG/DER) previously addressed within the context of destroyer-type ships now are listed separately in the official category of Ocean Escorts. Also, within *Jane's Fighting Ships* the battleships and non-missile cruisers (CA/CL) are listed as Fire Support Ships because of their limited capabilities for anti-air, anti-submarine, and surface warfare in the context of modern naval operations. The planned Surface Combatant strength during 1973 was to be approximately 135 ships: six missile-armed cruisers (one nuclear powered) plus two ships being de-commissioned; 30 missile-armed frigates (two nuclear powered); 29 missile-armed destroyers; and 70 all-gun destroyers.

In addition, 20-odd destroyers are assigned to the Naval Reserve Force and are manned by joint active-Naval Reserve crews. The above strength compares to some 250 active ships in the cruiser-frigate-destroyer categories at the peak of the Navy's Vietnam War strength in 1968-1969.

During the 1970s new construction programmes are expected to provide the US Navy with five nuclear-powered, missile-armed frigates (the size of World War II-era cruisers) and 30 essentially all-gun destroyers of the controversial "Spruance" class. Anticipating the retirement of seven war-built missile cruisers and 60 war-built destroyers during this period, by the end of the decade the Navy's surface combatant strength will be about 110 ships. Although nine ships will be nuclear powered (giving the Navy two all-nuclear carrier task groups), on balance the oldest of the post-war "Forrest Sherman" class destroyers will be 25 years old.

Thus, it appears that in view of anticipated US commitments about 1980, missions heretofore considered within the purview of destroyers will be given to the less-capable but numerous escort ships and possibly the proposed advanced-design patrol ships. A final factor to be considered in the Surface Combatant equation is the sea control ship, described below.

SEA CONTROL SHIPS: PROPOSED

Displacement, tons	approx 14 000 full load
Length, feet	630 wl; approx 650 oa
Beam, feet	76
Draft, feet	21
Aircraft	3 AV-8 Harrier V/STOL strike aircraft (or successor) 14 SH-3 Sea King helicopters (or successor)
Guns	several 20 mm Vulcan-Phalanx rapid-fire guns
Main engines	gas turbines (LM 2500); probably 1 shaft
Speed, knots	approx 26 knots

The Navy has proposed the sea control ship to operate V/STOL fixed-wing aircraft and helicopters in defence of underway replenishment groups, amphibious task forces, and merchant convoys. Because of the limited capabilities of the ships and their embarked aircraft they could operate only in areas of limited enemy threat. The sea control ship will have minimum sensors and weapons, relying instead upon embarked aircraft and the capabilities of escorting warships. In addition to operating and maintaining its embarked aircraft, the sea control ship would provide maintenance to helicopters on destroyers and escort ships.

The Fiscal Year 1973 budget provided $10 000 000 for design efforts. It had been expected that construction of the first ship would be funded in the FY 1974 budget; however, only $29 300 000 provided for continuation of studies and design.
If authorised in the FY 1975 budget, the first ship could be completed in 1979 with all eight ships now proposed being at sea by the early 1970s. Planned cost per ship is $100 000 000 maximum.
The National Steel and Shipbuilding Co of San Diego, California, has been awarded a contract for detailed design of the ship; it is anticipated that the sea control ships will be built by National Steel and at least one other shipyard.

AIRCRAFT. Aircraft capacity is based on one radar warning and up to two anti-submarine helicopters being airborne at all times and at least one V/STOL aircraft and another A/S helicopter on deck ready for immediate launch.

DESIGN. Preliminary designs provide for a ship resembling World War II-era escort carriers or the "Iwo Jima" class amphibious assault ships with a clear flight deck and "island" structure to starboard. Two aircraft elevators are planned, but no catapult or arresting wires.

DESIGNATION. As originally conceived this ship was known as an "air capable ship" and given the tentative designation DH indicating it would be a "destroyer type" warship with helicopter capability. However, on 8 May 1971 Admiral Zumwalt, the Chief of Naval Operations, said that the ship would be designated as the "sea control ship" in an apparent move to arouse interest and support for the programme. The initials SCS are being used in official documentation.

ELECTRONICS. The sea control ship will have austere electronics equipment with helicopters serving in the Airborne Early Warning (AEW) role to provide long-range detection and warning of hostile ships and aircraft.

GUNNERY. The 20 mm Close-In Weapon System (CIWS) will provide minimum defence against enemy anti-ship missiles that penetrate "area defence" missile systems of accompanying warships or possibly friendly aircraft.

1 INTERIM SEA CONTROL SHIP: "IWO JIMA" CLASS

Name	*No.*	*Builder*	*Laid down*	*Launched*	*Commissioned*
***GUAM**	LPH 9	Philadelphia Naval Shipyard	15 Nov 1962	22 Aug 1964	16 Jan 1965

Displacement, tons	18 300 full load
Length, feet (*metres*)	592 (*180·0*) oa
Beam, feet (*metres*)	84 (*25·6*)
Draft, feet (*metres*)	26 (*7·9*)
Flight deck width, feet (*metres*)	105 (*31·9*) maximum
Aircraft	AV-8A Harrier V/STOL strike aircraft SH-2F Sea Sprite A/S helicopters SH-3H Sea King A/S helicopters
Guns	8—3 inch (*76 mm*) 50 calibre AA (twin)
Main engines	1 geared turbine; 23 000 shp; 1 shaft
Boilers	2 (Babcock & Wilcox)
Speed, knots	20 (sustained)
Complement	approx 600

The amphibious assault ship *Guam* (LPH 9) is being employed as an interim sea control ship to develop operational concepts and tactics for the planned new construction ships described above.
The *Guam* was modified from Oct 1971 to Jan 1972, receiving improved aircraft maintenance capabilities, new deck markings, modified deck lighting and aircraft control/direction facilities, and being provided with an anti-submarine sensor analysis centre.

The ship began operations as an interim sea control ship early in 1972. She now operates various combinations of SH-2F Seasprite and SH-3H Sea King helicopters from Helicopter A/S Squadron 15 (HS-15) and AV-8A Harrier V/STOL aircraft from Marine Attack Squadron 513 (VMA-513). See "Iwo Jima" class listing under Amphibious Warfare Ships for additional notes.

ELECTRONICS. The *Guam* has SPS-10 and SPS-40 search radar antennas, SPN-10 navigation radar, and Carrier-Control Approach (CCA) radar; small TACAN (Tactical Air Navigation) pod atop mast.

PHOTOGRAPHS. The photograph below shows the *Guam* with an AV-8A Harrier about to touch down on her flight deck while two other Harriers are parked forward. A UH-46 Sea Knight helicopter hovers off the ship's starboard side. Note that the *Guam's* starboard deck-edge lift is raised to flight deck level (above hangar bay opening).

GUAM (LPH 9) *1972, United States Navy PH2 John E. Koppari*

Surface Combatants—*continued*

3 GUIDED MISSILE CRUISERS (CG): "ALBANY" CLASS

Name	No.	Builder	Laid down	Launched	Commissioned	CG Comm.
* ALBANY	CG 10 (ex-CA 123)	Bethlehem Steel Co (Quincy)	6 Mar 1944	30 June 1945	15 June 1946	3 Nov 1962
* CHICAGO	CG 11 (ex-CA 136)	Philadelphia Navy Yard	28 July 1943	20 Aug 1944	1 Jan 1945	2 May 1964
* COLUMBUS	CG 12 (ex-CA 74)	Bethlehem Steel Co (Quincy)	28 June 1943	30 Nov 1944	8 June 1945	1 Dec 1962

Displacement, tons	13 700 standard; 17 500 full load
Length, feet (*metres*)	664 (*202.4*) wl; 673 (*205.3*) oa
Beam, feet (*metres*)	70 (*21.6*)
Draft, feet (*metres*)	27 (*8.2*)
Missile launchers	2 twin Talos surface-to-air launchers; 2 twin Tartar surface-to-air launchers
Missile launchers	2 twin Talos surface-to-air launchers 2 twin Tartar surface-to-air launchers
Guns	2—5 in (*127 mm*) 38 calibre dual-purpose (see *Gunnery* notes)
A/S weapons	1 ASROC 8-tube launcher 2 triple torpedo tubes (Mk 32)
Helicopter	utility helicopter carried
Main engines	4 geared turbines (General Electric); 120 000 shp; 4 shafts
Boilers	4 (Babcock & Wilcox)
Speed, knots	33
Complement	1 000 (60 officers, approx 940 enlisted men)

These ships were fully converted from heavy cruisers, the *Albany* having been a unit of the "Oregon City" class and the *Chicago* and *Columbus* of the "Baltimore" class. Although the two heavy cruiser classes differ in appearance (see Fire Support Ships), they have the same hull dimensions and machinery. These three missile ships now form a new, homogeneous class.

The cruiser *Fall River* (CA 131) was originally scheduled for missile conversion, but was replaced by the *Columbus*.

Proposals to convert two additional heavy cruisers (CA 124 and CA 130) to missile ships (CG 13 and CG 14) were dropped, primarily because of high conversion costs and improved capabilities of newer missile-armed frigates.

CONVERSION. During conversion to missile configuration these ships were stripped down to their main hulls with all cruiser armament and superstructure being removed. New superstructures make extensive use of aluminium to reduce weight and improve stability. Former masts and stacks were replaced by "macks" which support electronic antennas and have machinery exhausts vented from sides near top. The *Albany* was converted at the Boston Naval Shipyard between January 1959 and November 1962; the *Columbus* at Puget Sound Naval Shipyard from June 1959 to March 1963; and *Chicago* at San Francisco Naval Shipyard from July 1959 to September 1964.

Helicopter landing area on fantail, but no hangar or support facilities.

ELECTRONICS. These ships are fitted with SQS-23 sonar which is linked to the ASROC fire control system. The Naval Tactical Data System (NTDS) is fitted in the *Albany* and *Chicago*.

The radar arrangements differ slightly: the *Albany* has SPS-48 three-dimensional and SPS-10 search radars on her forward "mack", an SPS-43 radar on her second "mack", and an SPS-30 on the after platform (no SPS-30 atop bridge structure); the *Chicago* has SPS-30 forward and aft, SPS-52 and SPS-10 on her forward "mack", and an SPS-43 on her after "mack"; the *Columbus* has SPS-30 forward and aft, an SPS-39 three-dimensional and SPS-10 search radar on her forward "mack", and an SPS-43 on her after "mack".

GUNNERY. No guns were fitted when these ships were converted to missile cruisers. Two single, *open-mount* 5 inch guns were fitted subsequently to provide minimal defence against low-flying, subsonic aircraft or torpedo boat attacks.

Two Mk 56 directors installed for gun control.

MISSILES. One twin Talos launcher is forward and one aft; a twin Tartar launcher is on each side of the main bridge structure. During conversion space was allocated amidships for installation of eight Polaris missile tubes, but the plan to install ballistic missiles in cruisers was cancelled in mid-1959. Reportedly, 92 Talos and 80 Tartar missiles are carried.

MODERNISATION. The *Albany* underwent an extensive anti-air warfare modernisation at the Boston Naval Shipyard; "conversion" began in February 1967 and was completed in August 1969. She was formally recommissioned on 9 Nov 1968. The *Chicago* and *Columbus* will not have AAW modernisations.

The *Albany's* AAW conversion included installation of NTDS, a digital Talos fire-control system which provides faster and more-reliable operation, and improved SPS-48 and SPS-30 air search radars (the *Albany* also has an SPS-43 long-range and SPS-10 short-range search radars, and SPG-51C fire-control radar).

PHOTOGRAPHS. A broadside view of the *Chicago* and other views of this class appear in the 1972-1973 edition.

The single 5 inch gun mounts are alongside after "mack" structure.

ALBANY (CG 10) — *1970, Anthony & Joseph Pavia*

COLOMBUS (CG 12) — *1972, Giorgio Arra*

COLOMBUS (CG 12) — *1972, Giorgio Arra*

Surface Combatants—*continued*

1 NUCLEAR-POWERED GUIDED MISSILE CRUISER (CGN): "LONG BEACH" TYPE

Name	*No.*	*Builder*	*Laid down*	*Launched*	*Commissioned*
•**LONG BEACH**	CGN 9 (ex-CGN 160, CLGN 160)	**Bethlehem Steel Co, (Quincy, Massachusetts)**	2 Dec 1957	14 July 1959	**9 Sep 1961**

Displacement, tons	14 200 standard; 17 350 full load
Length, feet (*metres*)	721·2 (*220*) oa
Beam, feet (*metres*)	73·2 (*22·3*)
Draft, feet (*metres*)	29 (*8·8*)
Missile launchers	1 twin Talos surface-to-air launcher (Mk 12 Mod 0) 2 twin Terrier surface-to-air launchers (Mk 10 Mod 1 and 2)
Guns	2—5 in (*127 mm*) 38 calibre dual-purpose (see *Gunnery* notes)
A/S weapons	1 ASROC 8-tube launcher 2 triple torpedo tubes (Mk 32)
Helicopter	utility helicopter carried
Main engines	2 geared turbines (General Electric); approx 80 000 shp; 2 shafts
Reactors	2 pressurised-water cooled C1W (Westinghouse)
Speed, knots	approx 35
Complement	1 000 (60 officers, approx 950 enlisted men)

The *Long Beach* was the first ship to be designed and constructed from the keel up as a cruiser for the United States since the end of World War II. She is the world's first nuclear-powered surface warship and the first warship to have a guided missile main battery. She was authorised in the Fiscal Year 1957 new construction programme. Estimated construction cost was $332 850 000. Construction was delayed because of shipyard strike.
No additional new-construction cruisers are planned because of the capabilities of new guided-missile frigates (DLG and DLGN), which are approaching the size of World War II-era light cruisers.

CLASSIFICATION. The *Long Beach* was ordered as a Guided Missile Light Cruiser (CLGN 160) on 15 Oct 1956; reclassified as a Guided Missile Cruiser (CGN 160) early in 1957 and renumbered (CGN 9) on 1 July 1957.

DESIGN. The *Long Beach* was initially planned as a large destroyer or "frigate" of about 7 800 tons (standard displacement) to test the feasibility of a nuclear powered surface warship. Early in 1956 the decision was made to capitalise on the capabilities of nuclear propulsion and her displacement was increased to 11 000 tons and a second Terrier missile launcher was added to the design. A Talos missile launcher was also added to the design which, with other features, increased displacement to 14 000 tons by the time the contract was signed for her construction on 15 October 1956.

ELECTRONICS. The *Long Beach* has fixed-array ("billboard") radar which provides increased range over rotating antennas. Horizontal antennas on bridge superstructure are for SPS-32 bearing and range radar; vertical antennas are for SPS-33 target tracking radar. The SPS-33 uses an "S" band frequency and the SPS-32 is VHF; both frequency scan in elevation. Developed and produced by Hughes Aircraft, they are believed the first operational fixed-array radar systems in the Western world. Also installed in the nuclear-powered aircraft carrier *Enterprise* (CVAN 65).
SPS-12 and SPS-10 search radars are mounted on the forward mast.

The SPS-32/33 "Scanfar" radars and the associated computers were modified in 1970 to improve performance. She is equipped with Naval Tactical Data System (NTDS) and SQS-23 sonar.

LONG BEACH (CGN 9) *1968, United States Navy*

ENGINEERING. The reactors are similar to those of the nuclear-powered aircraft carrier *Enterprise* (CVAN 65). The *Long Beach* first got underway on nuclear power on 5 July 1961. After four years of operation and having steamed more than 167 000 miles she underwent her first overhaul and refuelling at the Newport News Shipbuilding and Dry Dock Company from August 1965 to February 1966.

GUNNERY. Completed with an all-missile armament. Two single 5 inch mounts were fitted during 1962-1963 yard period to provide defence against low-flying, subsonic aircraft and torpedo boats.

MISSILES. Initial plans provided for installation of the Regulus II surface-to-surface missile, a transonic missile which carried a nuclear warhead and had a 1 000-mile range. Upon cancellation of the Regulus II programme, provision was made for providing eight Polaris missile tubes, but they were never installed. Plans to provide Polaris were dropped early in 1961 in an effort to reduce construction costs.
Reportedly, the *Long Beach* carries 40 Talos and 240 Terrier missiles.

NOMENCLATURE. Cruisers are named for American cities. Since 1971 the Navy also has named attack submarines for cities, beginning with the SSN 688 (*Los Angeles*).

OPERATIONAL. Talos missiles fired from the *Long Beach* have downed Communist aircraft in what are believed to have been the first surface-to-air "kills" in combat with ship-launched missiles.
While operating in the Tonkin Gulf, the ship's Talos missiles shot down one supersonic MiG fighter on May 23, 1968, and a second MiG in June 1968; both aircraft were over North Vietnam at the time of their destruction.

LONG BEACH (CGN 9) *1968, United States Navy*

Surface Combatants—*continued*

6 GUIDED MISSILE LIGHT CRUISERS (CLG): CONVERTED "CLEVELAND" CLASS

Name	*No.*	*Builder*	*Laid down*	*Launched*	*Commissioned*	*CLG Comm.*
GALVESTON	CLG 3 (ex-CL 93)	Cramp Shipbuilding (Philadelphia)	20 Feb 1944	22 Apr 1945	(see notes)	28 May 1958
***LITTLE ROCK**	CLG 4 (ex-CL 92)	Cramp Shipbuilding (Philadelphia)	6 Mar 1943	27 Aug 1944	17 June 1945	3 June 1960
***OKLAHOMA CITY**	CLG 5 (ex-CL 91)	Cramp Shipbuilding (Philadelphia)	8 Mar 1942	20 Feb 1944	22 Dec 1944	7 Sep 1960
***PROVIDENCE**	CLG 6 (ex-CL 82)	Bethlehem Steel Co (Quincy)	27 July 1943	28 Dec 1944	15 May 1945	17 Sep 1959
***SPRINGFIELD**	CLG 7 (ex-CL 66)	Bethlehem Steel Co (Quincy)	13 Feb 1943	9 Mar 1944	9 Sep 1944	2 July 1960
TOPEKA	CLG 8 (ex-CL 67)	Bethlehem Steel Co (Quincy)	21 Apr 1943	19 Apr 1944	23 Dec 1944	26 Mar 1960

Displacement, tons 10 670 standard; 14 600 full load
Length, feet (*metres*) 600 (*182·9*) wl; 610 (*185·9*) oa
Beam, feet (*metres*) 66·3 (*20·2*)
Draft, feet (*metres*) 25 (*7·6*)
Missile launchers:
CLG 3, 4, 5: 1 twin Talos surface-to-air launcher (Mk 7 Mod 0)
CLG 6, 7, 8: 1 twin Terrier surface-to-air launcher (Mk 9 Mod 1)
Guns CLG 4-7: 3—6 in (*152 mm*) 47 cal; 2—5 in (*127 mm*) 38 cal dual-purpose
CLG 3, 8: 6—6 in (*152 mm*) 47 cal; 6—5 in (*127 mm*) 38 cal dual-purpose
Helicopters utility helicopter carried
Main engines 4 geared turbines (General Electric); 100 000 shp; 4 shafts
Boilers 4 (Babcock & Wilcox)
Speed 31·6 knots
Complement CLG 4-7: 1 680 officers and enlisted men (including fleet staff)
CLG 3, 8: 1 200 officers and enlisted men

GALVESTON (CLG 3) *1967, United States Navy*

These ships were converted from light cruisers of the "Cleveland" class (see Fire Support Ships). Although generally similar, the six ships are of four distinct designs: the *Galveston* armed with Talos missiles; the *Little Rock* and *Oklahoma City* armed with Talos and fitted as fleet flagships; the *Providence* and *Springfield* armed with Terrier and fitted as fleet flagships; and the *Topeka* armed with Terrier. The flagships normally rotate as flagships of the Sixth Fleet in the Mediterranean and the Seventh Fleet in the Western Pacific.
The *Topeka* was decommissioned on 5 June 1969, the *Galveston* was decommissioned on 25 May 1970; both are in reserve. The *Providence* and *Springfield* were to be decommissioned in the latter part of 1973 and placed in reserve.
The *Little Rock* is active in the Mediteranean and the *Oklahoma City* in the Pacific.

CLASSIFICATION. The *Galveston* was reclassified CLG 93 on 4 Feb 1956 and CLG 3 on 23 May 1957. All US Navy guided missile cruisers were numbered in a single series, the CAG 1 and CAG 2 having been the *Boston* (now CA 69) and *Canberra* (CA 70) respectively.

CONSTRUCTION. The construction of the *Galveston* was suspended on 24 June 1946 when nearly complete; placed in reserve until 1956 when taken in hand for conversion to a missile ship. She got underway for the first time on 30 June 1958.

CONVERSION. All six of these ships had their two after 6 inch gun turrets replaced by a twin surface-to-air missile launcher, superstructure enlarged to support missile fire control equipment, lattice masts fitted to carry antennas, 5 inch battery reduced (from original 12 guns), and all 40 mm and 20 mm light anti-aircraft guns removed. The four ships fitted as fleet flagships additionally had their No. 2 turret of 6 inch guns removed and their forward superstructure enlarged to provide command and communications spaces for the flag staff.
The *Galveston* began conversion at the Philadelphia Naval Shipyard in August 1956 and was completed in September 1958; the *Little Rock* began conversion at the New York Shipbuilding Corp (Camden, New Jersey) in January 1957 and was completed in June 1960; the *Oklahoma City* began conversion at the Bethlehem Steel shipyard in San Francisco in May 1957 and was completed in September 1960; the *Providence* began conversion at the Boston Naval Shipyard in June 1957 and was completed in September 1959; the *Springfield* began conversion at the Bethlehem Steel shipyard in Quincy, Massachusetts, in August 1957, but was moved to the Boston Naval Shipyard in March 1960 for completion in July 1960; and the *Topeka* was converted at the New York Naval Shipyard between August 1957 and March 1960.

PROVIDENCE (CLG 6) *1969, United States Navy*

There is a helicopter landing area on the fantail, but only limited support facilities are provided; no hangar.

ELECTRONICS. The Terrier-armed ships have SPS-43 and SPS-10 radars on their forward mast, an SPS-30 radar on the second mast, and an SPS-52 or SPS-39 three-dimensional radar on the third mast; the Talos-armed ships have SPS-43 and SPS-10 radars on their forward mast, an SPS-52 or SPS-39 three-dimensional radar on their after mast, and an SPS-30 on the after platform.

The *Little Rock* has had her SPS-39 three-dimensional search radar removed.
These ships have no ASW sonar.

GUNNERY. As converted to missile-gun cruisers these ships each retained one Mk 37 and one Mk 39 gunfire control directors forward; the Mk 39 director has been removed from the *Oklahoma City*.

MISSILES. Reportedly, the three ships armed with Terrier each carry 120 missiles and the three ships armed with Talos each carry 46 missiles.

SPRINGFIELD (CLG 7) *1972, Giorgio Arra*

Surface Combatants—*continued*

3 NUCLEAR-POWERED GUIDED MISSILE FRIGATES (DLGN): "VIRGINIA" CLASS

Name	*No.*	*Builder*	*Laid down*	*Launch*	*Commission*
VIRGINIA	DLGN 38	Newport News SB & DD Co	19 Aug 1972	Dec 1973	1975
TEXAS	**DLGN 39**	Newport News SB & DD Co	Apr 1973	late 1974	1976
	DLGN 40	Newport News SB & DD Co	Dec 1973	1975	1976

Displacement, tons	approx 10 000 full load
Length, feet (*metres*)	585 (*177·3*) oa
Beam, feet (*metres*)	61 (*18·5*)
Draft, feet (*metres*)	29·5 (*9·0*)
Helicopters	2 (see *Helicopter* notes)
Missile launchers	2 combination twin Tartar-D/ASROC launchers firing Standard MR surface-to-air missile (Mk 26)
Guns	2—5 inch (*127 mm*) 54 calibre dual-purpose (Mk 45) (single)
A/S weapons	ASROC (*see above*) 2 triple torpedo tubes (Mk 32)
Main engines	2 geared turbines; 2 shafts
Reactors	2 pressurised-water cooled D2G (General Electric)
Speed, knots	30+
Complement	approx 500 officers and enlisted men

The Navy planned to construct at least eight ships of this class to provide all-nuclear escorts for two nuclear-powered attack carriers. However, in May 1971 the Department of Defense announced that two ships proposed for the FY 1973 programme would not be built because of cost increases.
The DLGN 38 was authorised in the Fiscal Year 1970 new construction programme, the DLGN 39 in FY 1971, and the DLGN 40 in FY 1972.

DESIGN. The principal differences between the DLGN 38 class and the "California" class will be the improved anti-air warfare capability, electronic warfare equipment, anti-submarine fire control system, and the combat information centre (CIC) facilities. The deletion of the ASROC "pepper-box" launcher permitted the later ships to be ten feet shorter.

ELECTRONICS. The DLGN 40 and later ships were to have the advanced radar systems associated with the "Aegis" advanced surface missile system. (The radars for this system now are under development; the development of the associated missile-launching equipment has been deferred.)
These ships will have the Naval Tactical Data System (NTDS) with the UYK-7 computer, Mk 116 underwater fire control system, Mk 86 gunfire control system, SQS-26CX sonar, SPS-48 three-dimensional search radar, and SPS-40 search radar.

FISCAL. The FY 1969 budget provided $52 000 000 for long-lead time components (primarily electronics and propulsion plant) for the DLGN 38 and DLGN 39. The FY 1970 budget provided $196 000 000 to complete the DLGN 38 plus $58 000 000 for long-lead time components for the DLGN 40 and DLGN 41 and $9 900 000 for fire control radars for the DLGN 39 and DLGN 40. The FY 1971 budget povided $182 800 000 to complete funding the DLGN 39 plus $28 000 000 for advanced procurement. The FY 1972 budget provided $195 000 000 for the DLGN 40.
The estimated cost of the DLGN 38 is $222 000 000 and $213 800 000 for the DLGN 39, with subsequent ships costing an estimated average of $208 000 000 per ship. Unofficial estimates for these ships are approximately $250 000 000 each.

GUNNERY. These ships will have the 5 inch Light Weight Gun System (LWGS) of the Mk 45 type also being installed in the "Spruance" class destroyers.

HELICOPTERS. A hangar for helicopters is installed beneath the fantail flight deck with a telescoping hatch cover and an electro-mechanical elevator provided to transport helicopters between the main deck and hangar. These are the first US post-World War II destroyer/cruiser ships with a hull hangar.

MISSILES. The initial design for this class provided for a single surface-to-air missile launcher; revised in 1969 to provide two Mk 26 launchers that will fire the Standard-Medium Range (MR) surface-to-air missile and the ASROC anti-submarine missile. "Mixed" Standard/ASROC magazines are planned for each launcher. The digital ASW fire control system will simplify weapon system interfaces compared to previous US missile-armed warships.

DRAWING. Chaff-rocket (CHAFROC) launchers are shown forward of bridge and aft of boat davits with triple anti-submarine torpedo tubes also aft of boat davits; "California" design on the previous page has the torpedo tubes built into superstructure.

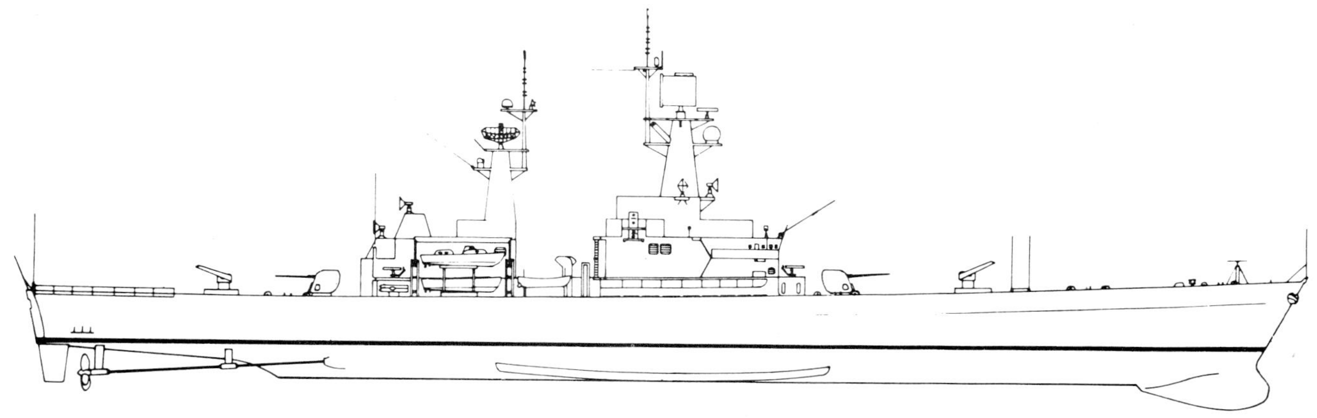

Drawing by A. D. Baker

OKLAHOMA CITY (CLG 5) *1972, United States Navy*

Surface Combatants—*continued*

2 NUCLEAR-POWERED GUIDED MISSILE FRIGATES (DLGN): "CALIFORNIA" CLASS

Name	*No.*	*Builder*	*Laid down*	*Launch*	*Commission*
CALIFORNIA	DLGN 36	Newport News Shipbuilding & Dry Dock Co	23 Jan 1970	22 Sep 1971	Dec 1973
SOUTH CAROLINA	DLGN 37	Newport News Shipbuilding & Dry Dock Co	1 Dec 1970	1 July 1972	late 1974

Displacement tons	10 150 full load
Length, feet (*metres*)	596 (*181·7*) oa
Beam, feet (*metres*)	61 (*18·6*)
Missile launchers	2 single Tartar-D surface-to-air launchers firing Standard MR (Mk 13 Mod 3)
Guns	2—5 inch (*127 mm*) 54 calibre dual-purpose (Mk 45) (single)
A/S weapons	torpedo tubes 1 ASROC 8-tube launcher
Main engines	2 geared turbines; 2 shafts
Reactors	2 pressurised-water cooled D2G (General Electric)
Speed, knots	30+
Complement	approx 550 officers and enlisted men

These are large, multi-purpose warships intended primarily to operate with fast carrier forces. Their high-speed and endurance capabilities also makes them suitable for independent operations.
The *California* was authorised in the Fiscal Year 1967 new construction programme and the *South Carolina* in the FY 1968 programme. The construction of a third ship of this class (DLGN 38) also was authorised in FY 1968, but the rising costs of these ships and development of the DXGN/DLGN 38 design caused the third ship to be deferred.

The contract for both ships was awarded on 13 June 1968. **The frigate *California* together with the three previously built nuclear escort ships (*Long Beach, Bainbridge, Truxtun*) will provide one all-nuclear carrier task group consisting of one attack aircraft carrier and four escorts.**

ELECTRONICS. Fitted with bow-mounted SQS-26 sonar and the Naval Tactical Data Stysem (NTDS). These ships will have SPS-48 three-dimensional, SPS-10, and SPS-40 search radar antennas.

ENGINEERING. Estimated nuclear core life for these ships will provide 700 000 miles "range"; estimated cost is $11 500 000 for the two initial nuclear cores.

FISCAL. Estimated cost is $200 000 000 for *California* and $180 000 000 for *South Carolina*. See 1971-1972 edition for funding history.

GUNNERY. These ships are the heaviest gunned missile frigates yet built. Fitted with improved Mk 86 gunfire control system.

MISSILES. Reportedly, these ships will carry some 80 surface-to-air missiles divided equally between a magazine beneath each launcher. The launchers will fire the Standard-MR missile.

NOMENCLATURE. Destroyer-type ships in the US Navy have traditionally been named for officers and enlisted personnel of the Navy and Marine Corps, Secretaries of the Navy, members of Congress who have influenced naval affairs, and inventors. The frigates generally honour admirals and commodores of the Navy; however, in January 1970 it was announced that henceforth frigates would be named for states of the Union with the first frigate so named honouring California, home state of the incumbant president. The DLGN 37 honours the home state of the late L. Mendel Rivers, chairman of the House of Representatives Committee on Armed Services from 1965 until his death in 1971. The "Sturgeon" class submarine SSN 686 was renamed while under construction to honour the late representative.

PHOTOGRAPHS. The photograph at right shows the *California* at launching. Views of nuclear-propelled ships while under construction or fitting-out rarely are released to the press.
The "California" class can be distinguished from the subsequent "Virginia" class frigates by the ASROC launcher and "reload house" forward of the bridge and the after 5 inch gun being one level above the main deck in the earlier ships. Note the tower-like mast structures in both US classes; similar to the Soviet missile cruiser designs.

CALIFORNIA (DLGN 36) launching
1971, Newport News

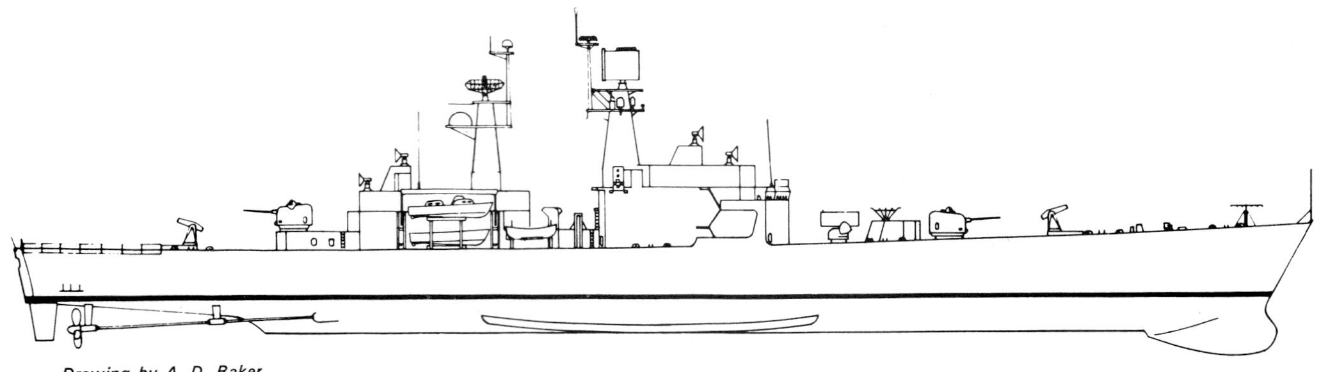
Drawing by A. D. Baker

TRUXTUN (DLGN 35)—see following page
1970, United States Navy, PH1 E. L. Goligoski

Surface Combatants—*continued*

1 NUCLEAR-POWERED GUIDED MISSILE FRIGATE (DLGN): "TRUXTUN" TYPE

Name	*No.*	*Builder*	*Laid down*	*Launched*	*Commissioned*
***TRUXTUN**	DLGN 35	New York Shipbuilding Corp (Camden)	17 June 1963	19 Dec 1964	27 May 1967

Displacement, tons	8 200 standard; 9 200 full load
Length, feet (*metres*)	564 (*171·9*) oa
Beam, feet (*metres*)	58 (*17·7*)
Draft, feet (*metres*)	31 (*9·4*)
Missile launchers	1 twin Terrier/ASROC launcher (Mk 10 Mod 7)
Guns	1—5 inch (*127 mm*) 54 calibre dual-purpose; 2—3 in (*76 mm*) 50 calibre anti-aircraft (single)
A/S weapons	ASROC (see above); 4 fixed torpedo tubes (Mk 32)
Helicopters	facilities for helicopter
Main engines	2 geared turbines; approx 60 000 shp; 2 shafts
Reactors	2 pressurised water-cooled D2G (General Electric)
Speed, knots	30+
Complement	approx 500 (35 officers, 465 enlisted men)

The *Truxtun* was the US Navy's fourth nuclear-powered surface warship. The Navy has requested seven oil-burning frigates in the Fiscal 1962 shipbuilding programme; the Congress authorised seven ships, but stipulated that one must be nuclear powered. Construction cost was $138 667 000.

ELECTRONICS. The *Truxtun* has bow-mounted SQS-26 sonar and the Naval Tactical Data System (NTDS). Fitted with SPS-48 three-dimensional and SPS-10 search radars on forward mast and an SPS-40 search radar and TACAN (Tactical Aircraft Navigation) "pod" on after mast.

TRUXTUN (DLGN 35) — *1970, United States Navy*

ENGINEERING. Power plant is identical to that of the frigate *Bainbridge*.

MISSILES. The twin missile launcher aft can fire both Terrier anti-aircraft missiles and ASROC anti-submarine rockets.

NOMENCLATURE. The *Truxtun* is the fifth ship to be named for Commodore Thomas Truxton (sic) who commanded the frigate *Constellation* (38 guns) in her successful encounter with the French frigate *L'Insurgente* (44) in 1799.

TORPEDOES. Fixed Mk 32 tubes are below 3-inch gun "tubs", built into superstructure. The two Mk 25 torpedo tubes built into her stern are not used.

PHOTOGRAPHS. The *Truxtun* can be readily identified by her squared lattice radar masts, empty "B" gun position and lack of funnel. Two chaff rocket (CHAFROC) launchers subsequently have been fitted in the "B" position.

1 NUCLEAR-POWERED GUIDED MISSILE FRIGATE (DLGN): "BAINBRIDGE" TYPE

Name	*No.*	*Builder*	*Laid down*	*Launched*	*Commissioned*
***BAINBRIDGE**	DLGN 25	Bethlehem Steel Co (Quincy)	15 May 1959	15 Apr 1961	6 Oct 1962

Displacement, tons	7 600 standard; 8 580 full load
Length, feet (*metres*)	550 (*167·6*)wl; 565 (*172·5*) oa
Beam, feet (*metres*)	57·9 (*17·6*)
Draft, feet (*metres*)	29 (*7·9*)
Missile launchers	2 twin Terrier surface-to-air launchers
Guns	4—3 inch (*76 mm*) 50 calibre anti-aircraft (twin)
A/S weapons	1 ASROC 8-tube launcher; 2 triple torpedo tubes (Mk 32)
Main engines	2 geared turbines; approx 60 000 shp; 2 shafts
Reactors	2 pressurised-water cooled D2G (General Electric)
Speed, knots	30+
Complement	approx 450 (26 officers, approx 425 enlisted men)

The *Bainbridge* was the US Navy's third nuclear-powered surface warship and the world's first "destroyer type" ship to have nuclear propulsion. She is larger than the light anti-aircraft cruisers the United States built during World war II. Authorised in Fiscal Year 1956 shipbuilding programme. Construction cost was $163 610 000.

DESIGN. Two heavy lattice radar masts are fitted in place of conventional masts and funnels.

ELECTRONICS. Fitted with SQS-23 bow-mounted sonar.
The *Bainbridge* has SPS-52 three-dimensional search radar and SPS-10 search radar on her forward mast, and an SPS-37 search radar antenna on her after mast.

ENGINEERING. Development of a nuclear power plant suitable for use in a large "destroyer type" warship began in 1957. The Atomic Energy Commission's Knolls Atomic Power Laboratory undertook development of the destroyer power plant (designated D1G/D2G).

MISSILES. Reportedly, 80 missiles are carried divided between the forward and after Terrier magazines.
The *Bainbridge* has a Terrier Mk 10 Mod 5 launcher forward and Mk 10 Mod 6 aft.

MODERNISATION. The *Bainbridge* is scheduled to undergo an anti-air warfare (AAW) modernisation to improve capabilities. The Naval Tactical Data System (NTDS) will be fitted.

BAINBRIDGE (DLGN 25) — *1971, United States Navy*

Surface Combatants—*continued*

9 GUIDED MISSILE FRIGATES (DLG): "BELKNAP" CLASS

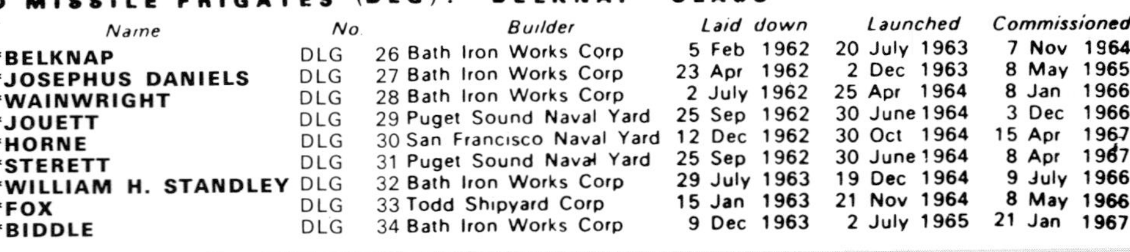

Name	No.	Builder	Laid down	Launched	Commissioned
*BELKNAP	DLG 26	Bath Iron Works Corp	5 Feb 1962	20 July 1963	7 Nov 1964
*JOSEPHUS DANIELS	DLG 27	Bath Iron Works Corp	23 Apr 1962	2 Dec 1963	8 May 1965
*WAINWRIGHT	DLG 28	Bath Iron Works Corp	2 July 1962	25 Apr 1964	8 Jan 1966
*JOUETT	DLG 29	Puget Sound Naval Yard	25 Sep 1962	30 June 1964	3 Dec 1966
*HORNE	DLG 30	San Francisco Naval Yard	12 Dec 1962	30 Oct 1964	15 Apr 1967
*STERETT	DLG 31	Puget Sound Naval Yard	25 Sep 1962	30 June 1964	8 Apr 1967
*WILLIAM H. STANDLEY	DLG 32	Bath Iron Works Corp	29 July 1963	19 Dec 1964	9 July 1966
*FOX	DLG 33	Todd Shipyard Corp	15 Jan 1963	21 Nov 1964	8 May 1966
*BIDDLE	DLG 34	Bath Iron Works Corp	9 Dec 1963	2 July 1965	21 Jan 1967

Displacement, tons	6 570 standard; 7 930 full load
Length, feet (*metres*)	547 (*166·7*) oa
Beam, feet (*metres*)	54·8 (*16·7*)
Draft, feet (*metres*)	28·8 (*8·7*)
Missile launchers	1 twin Terrier/ASROC launcher (Mk 10 Mod 7)
Guns	1—5 inch (*127 mm*) 54 cal dual-purpose 2—3 inch (*76 mm*) 50 cal anti-aircraft (single)
A/S weapons	ASROC (see above) 2 triple torpedo tubes (Mk 32)
Helicopters	1 SH-2D LAMPS helicopter
Main engines	2 geared turbines (General Electric in DLG 26-28, 32, 34; De Laval in DLG 29-31, 33); 85 000 shp; 2 shafts
Boilers	4 (Babcock & Wilcox in DLG 26-28, 32, 34; Combustion Engineering in DLG 29-31, 33)
Speed, knots	34
Complement	418 (31 officers, 387 enlisted men) including squadron staff

These ships are considered excellent anti-submarine and anti-air warfare ships, intended to screen fast carrier task forces. The DLG 26-28 were authorised in the Fiscal Year 1961 new construction programme; the DLG 29-34 in FY 1962 programme.

DESIGN. These ships are distinctive by having their single missile launcher forward and 5 inch gun mount aft. This arrangement allowed missile stowage in the larger bow section and provided space aft of the superstructure for a helicopter hangar and platform. The reverse gun-missile arrangement preferred by some commanding officers, is found in the *Truxtun*. The "Belknap" class ships have their masts and stacks combined into "mack" structures.

ELECTRONICS. SQS-26 bow-mounted sonar installed. These ships have the Naval Tactical Data System (NTDS). Fitted with SPS-48 three-dimensional and SPS-10 search radars on their forward "mack" and an SPS-37 (first three ships) or SPS-40 search radar on their after "mack".

GUNNERY. The 5 inch guns were installed previously on forward sponsons of the "Forrestal" class carriers. They are rapid fire-Mk 42 single 5 inch guns and the single 3 inch guns are Mk 34.

HELICOPTERS. These ships and the nuclear-powered *Truxtun* are the only US frigates now operational that have a full helicopter support capability.

MISSILES. The *Truxtun* and "Belknap" class ships have a twin Terrier/ASROC Mk 10 missile launcher. A "triple-ring" rotating magazine stocks both Terrier anti-aircraft missiles and ASROC anti-submarine rockets, feeding either weapon to the launcher's two firing arms. The rate of fire and reliability of the launcher provide a potent AAW/ASW capability to these ships.

TORPEDOES. As built, these ships each had two 21 inch tubes for anti-submarine torpedoes installed in the structure immediately forward of the 5 inch mount, one tube angled out to port and one to starboard; subsequently removed.

STERETT (DLG 31) — *1972, United States Navy, PHAN Delvin D. Bren*

JOSEPHUS DANIELS (DLG 27) — *1972, Giorgio Arra*

WILLIAM H. STANDLEY (DLG 32) — *1972, Giorgio Arra*

Surface Combatants—*continued*

9 GUIDED MISSILE FRIGATES (DLG) "LEAHY" CLASS

Displacement, tons	5 670 standard; 7 800 full load
Length, feet (*metres*)	533 (*162·5*) oa
Beam, feet (*metres*)	54·9 (*16·6*)
Draft, feet (*metres*)	24·5 (*7·4*)
Missile launchers	2 twin Terrier surface-to-air launchers (Mk 10 Mod 5)
Guns	4—3 inch (*76 mm*) 50 cal anti-aircraft (twin)
A/S weapons	1 ASROC 8-tube launcher 2 triple torpedo tubes (Mk 32)
Main engines	2 geared turbines (see *Engineering* notes); 85 000 shp; 2 shafts
Boilers	4 (Babcock & Wilcox in DLG 16-18; Foster Wheeler in DLG 19-24)
Speed, knots	34
Complement	396 (31 officers, 365 enlisted men) including squadron staff

Name	*No*	*Builder*	*Laid down*	*Launched*	*Commissioned*
*LEAHY	DLG 16	Bath Iron Works Corp	3 Dec 1959	1 July 1961	4 Aug 1962
*HARRY E YARNELL	DLG 17	Bath Iron Works Corp	31 May 1960	9 Dec 1961	2 Feb 1963
*WORDEN	DLG 18	Bath Iron Works Corp	19 Sep 1960	2 June 1962	3 Aug 1963
*DALE	DLG 19	New York SB Corp	6 Sep 1960	28 July 1962	23 Nov 1963
*RICHMOND K TURNER	DLG 20	New York SB Corp	9 Jan 1961	6 Apr 1963	13 June 1964
*GRIDLEY	DLG 21	Puget Sound B & D Co	15 July 1960	31 July 1961	25 May 1963
*ENGLAND	DLG 22	Todd Shipyards Corp	4 Oct 1960	6 Mar 1962	7 Dec 1963
*HALSEY	DLG 23	San Francisco Naval Yard	26 Aug 1960	15 Jan 1962	20 July 1963
*REEVES	DLG 24	Puget Sound Naval Yard	1 July 1960	12 May 1962	16 May 1964

These ships are "double-end" missile frigates especially designed to screen fast carrier task forces. They are limited in only having 3 inch guns in comparision wth 5 inch guns on other DLG classes. The DLG 16-18 authorised in the Fiscal Year 1958 new construction programme; DLG 19-24 in the FY 1959 programme.

DESIGN. These ships are distinctive in having twin missile launchers forward and aft with ASROC "pepper box" launcher between the forward missile launcher and bridge on main deck level. Masts and stacks are combined into "macks".
There is a helicopter landing area aft but only limited support facilities are provided; no hangar.

ELECTRONICS. These ships were fitted with the Naval Tactical Data System (NTDS) during AAW modernisation. SQS-23 bow mounted sonar installed. These ships have SPS-10 and SPS-48 search radars on forward mast (the latter replacing SPS-39 or SPS-52 in some ships) and an SPS-37 search radar on their after mast.
Halsey, *Worden*, *Richard K. Turner* and *Reeves* were completed with only two missile directors; four directors (Mk 76) carried after AAW modernisation.

ENGINEERING. General Electric turbines in DLG 16-18; De Laval turbines in DLG 19-22; and Allis-Chalmers turbines in DLG 23 and DLG 24.

MISSILES. Reportedly, each ship carries 80 missiles divided between the two Terrier magazines.

MODERNISATION. These ships have undergone an anti-air warfare (AAW) modernisation to improve the effectiveness of their electronic and missile systems. The modernisation included enlarging superstructure to provide space for electronic equipment, installation of NTDS, the Mk 76 fire control system for Terrier and Standard missiles (including SPG-55B radar and Mk 119 computer), and larger ships' service turbo generators. The *Leahy* was modernised et the Philadelphia Naval Shipyard; others at Bath Iron Works, Bath, Maine; the *Leahy* from Feb 1967 to Aug 1968, *Yarnell* from Feb 1968 to May 1969, *Gridley* from Sep 1968 to Jan 1970, *Reeves* from Apr 1969 to May 1970, *Worden* from Nov 1969 to Jan 1971, *England* from Apr 1970 to June 1971, *Dale* from Nov 1970 to Nov 1971, *Richmond K. Turner* from Jay 1971 to May 1972, and *Halsey* from Nov 1971 to Dec 1972.
Cost of *Leahy* modernisation was $36 100 000.

NOMENCLATURE. The *England* is the second US warship to honour a sailor killed at Pearl Harbour on 7 Dec 1941; the first *England* (DE 635) sank six Japanese submarines in just 12 days during May of 1944.

HARRY E. YARNELL (DLG 17) — *1972, Giorgio Arra*

GRIDLEY (DLG 21) — *1970, United States Navy*

HARRY E. YARNELL (DLG 17) — *1972, Giorgio Arra*

Surface Combatants—*continued*

DALE (DLG 19) *1972, United States Navy*

MacDONOUGH (DLG 8)—see following page *1971, United States Navy, PH1, John P. Francavillo*

PREBLE (DLG 15)—see following page *1970, United States Navy, Joseph F. Garfinkel*

Surface Combatants—*continued*

10 GUIDED MISSILE FRIGATES (DLG): "COONTZ" CLASS

Displacement, tons	4 700 standard; 5 800 full load
Length, feet (*metres*)	512·5 (*156·2*) oa
Beam, feet (*metres*)	52·5 (*15·9*)
Draft, feet (*metres*)	25 (*7·6*)
Missile launchers	1 twin Terrier surface-to-air launcher (Mk 10 Mod 0)
Guns	1—5 inch (*127 mm*) 54 cal dual purpose; 4—3 in (*76 mm*) 50 cal anti-aircraft (twin) (removed in modernised ships)
A/S weapons	1 ASROC 8-tube launcher 2 triple torpedo tubes (Mk 32)
Main engines	**2 geared turbines (see *Engineering* notes); 85 000 shp; 2 shafts**
Boilers	4 (Foster Wheeler in DLG 6-8; Babcock & Wilcox in DLG 9-15)
Speed, knots	34
Complement	**370 (22 officers, 348 enlisted men); 377 in modernised ships (21 officers, 356 enlisted men)**
Flag Staff	**19 (7 officers, 12 enlisted men)**

Name	*No*	*Builder*	*Laid down*	*Launched*	*Commissioned*
*FARRAGUT	DLG 6	Bethlehem Co, Quincy	3 June 1967	18 July 1958	10 Dec 1960
*LUCE	DLG 7	Bethlehem Co, Quincy	1 Oct 1957	11 Dec 1958	20 May 1961
*MACDONOUGH	DLG 8	Bethlehem Co, Quincy	15 Apr 1958	9 July 1959	4 Nov 1961
*COONTZ	DLG 9	Puget Sound Naval Yard	1 Mar 1957	6 Dec 1958	15 July 1960
*KING	DLG 10	Puget Sound Naval Yard	1 Mar 1957	6 Dec 1958	17 Nov 1960
*MAHAN	DLG 11	San Francisco Naval Yard	31 July 1957	7 Oct 1959	25 Aug 1960
*DAHLGREN	DLG 12	Philadelphia Naval Yard	1 Mar 1958	16 Mar 1960	8 Apr 1961
*WILLIAM V PRATT	DLG 13	Philadelphia Naval Yard	1 Mar 1958	16 Mar 1960	4 Nov 1961
*DEWEY	DLG 14	Bath Iron Works, Maine	10 Aug 1957	30 Nov 1958	7 Dec 1959
*PREBLE	DLG 15	Bath Iron Works, Maine	16 Dec 1957	23 May 1959	9 May 1960

These ships are "single-end" missile frigates intended to screen fast carrier task forces. Their design is based on the "Mitscher" class (DL/DDG). The DLG 6-11 were authorised in the Fiscal Year 1956 shipbuilding programme; the DLG 12-15 in FY 1957 programme. Average cost per ship was $52 000 000.

CLASSIFICATION. The *Farragut*, *Luce* and *McDonough* initially were classified as DL 6-8, respectively; changed to DLG on 14 Nov 1956. These ships are known officially as the "Coontz" class as that ship was the first to be ordered as a DLG (DLG 9-11 ordered on 18 Nov 1955; DLG 6-8 ordered on 27 Jan 1956).

DESIGN. These ships are the only US guided missile "frigates" with separate masts and funnels. They have aluminium superstructures to reduce weight and improve stability. Early designs for this class had a second 5 inch gun mount in the "B" position; design revised when ASROC "pepper box" launcher was developed.
Helicopter landing area on stern, but no hangar and limited support capability.

ELECTRONICS. The *King* and *Mahan* along with the aircraft carrier *Oriskany* (CVA 34) were the first ships fitted with the Naval Tactical Data System (NTDS), conducting operational evaluation of the equipment in 1961-1962.
As completed these ships had an SPS-10 and three-dimensional SPS-39 search radars on their forward mast, and an SPS-37 search radar and TACAN (Tactical Aircraft Navigation) "bee hive" antenna on second mast. Prior to AAW modernisation some ships had the SPS-39 replaced with the SPS-52 radar. During modernisation the SPS-48 three-dimensional search radar is fitted on the forward mast, an improved TACAN "pod" is fitted on the second mast, and NTDS installed. These ships have SQS-23 sonar.
The *Coontz* was fitted with the SSM-5 Test Evaluation and Monitoring System (TEAMS) in 1968 for operational evaluation of the electronic check-out system, subsequently removed. See *Knox* (DE 1052) for details.

ENGINEERING. De Laval turbines in DLG 6-8 and DLG 15; Allis-Chalmers turbines in DLG 9-14.

GUNNERY. These ships have Mk 42 single 5 inch guns and Mk 33 twin 3 inch guns (latter removed during modernisation).

MISSILES. The first five ships of this class were built with Terrier BW-1 beam-riding missile systems; five later ships built with Terrier BT-3 homing missile systems. See *Modernisation* notes for conversion of earlier ships to improved missile capability. Reportedly, each ship carries 40 missiles.

MODERNISATION. These ships are all undergoing anti-air warfare (AAW) modernisations to improve the effectiveness of their electronic and missile system. All modernised at the Philadelphia Naval Shipyard: *Farragut* from May 1968 to Feb 1970, *Preble* from Jan 1969 to Apr 1970, *Dewey* from Nov 1969 to Mar 1971, *Luce* from Feb 1970 to May 1971, *Coontz* from Feb 1971 to Apr 1972, *Dahlgren* from Feb 1972 to Mar 1973, *William V. Pratt* from Oct 1972 to late 1973, *MacDonough* from Apr 1973 to mid 1974.
The modernisation includes enlarging superstructure to provide space for electronic equipment, installation of NTDS and improved TACAN, converting first five ships to improve guidance capability for Terrier and, Standard missiles (Mk 76 fire control system), provision of larger ships service turbo generators, and removal of twin 3 inch gun mounts.
The *Farragut* also had improved ASROC reload capability provided and second mast increased in height. These modifications are not anticipated for the other ships. Cost of modernisation was $39 000 000 per ship in FY 1970 conversion programme.

NOMENCLATURE. The DLG 7 was to have been named *Dewey*, named *Luce* in 1957.

PRATT (DLG 13) — *1972, Giorgio Arra*

FARRAGUT (DLG 6) — *1970, United States Navy, PHC F. W. Gotavco*

LUCE (DLG 7) — *1971, United States Navy, D. V. Angelucci*

Surface Combatants—*continued*

1 FRIGATE (DL): "MITSCHER" CLASS

Name	*No.*	*Builder*	*Laid down*	*Launched*	*Commissioned*
WILKINSON	DL 5 (ex-DD 930)	Bethlehem Steel Co (Quincy)	1 Feb 1950	23 Apr 1952	3 Aug 1954

Displacement, tons	3 675 standard; 4 730 full load
Length, feet (*metres*)	493 (*150·3*) oa
Beam, feet (*metres*)	50 (*15·2*)
Draft, feet (*metres*)	26 (*7·9*)
Guns	2—5 inch (*127 mm*) 54 calibre dual-pupose (single)
A/S weapons	2 triple torpedo tubes (Mk 32) 4 torpedo tubes (Mk 23)
Helicopters	facilities for helicopter
Main engines	2 geared turbines (Westinghouse) 80 000 shp; 2 shafts
Boilers	4—1 200 psi (*84·4 kg/cm²*) (Foster Wheeler)
Speed, knots	35
Complement	389 (34 officers, 355 enlisted men)

Four ships of this classs of "destroyer leader" were completed in 1953-1954; two ships subsequently were converted to guided missile destroyers: *Mitscher* (DL 2/DDG 35) and *John S. McCain* (DL 3/DDG 36). Plans to convert the two other ships to a DDG configuration were dropped; one all-gun ship has been stricken (see below).

The *Wilkinson* was decommissioned in Dec 1969 and placed in reserve. Although fitted with the large SQS-26 sonar, the ship lacked advanced anti-submarine weapons and fire control system for combatting modern submarines.

CLASSIFICATION. Originally classified as a destroyer (DD 930); reclassified as a destroyer leader (DL 5) on 9 Feb 1951 while under construction. The DL symbol was changed to "frigate" on 1 Jan 1955.

ELECTRONICS. SQS-26 bow-mounted sonar installed, but a prototype system and not integrated with an advanced A/S fire control system.

The *Wilkinson's* final electronic configuration included SPS10 and SPS-29 search radar antennas on forward tripod mast, with a large TACAN pod topping the mast; large SPS-8 height-finding radar on after deckhouse. (Note unusual lattice mast on second funnel in the photograph below).

GUNNERY. As built the *Wilkinson* and other ships of this class each had two Mk 42 single 5 inch/54 calibre guns and four 3 inch/50 calibre guns (plus two 12·75 inch Weapon Able A/S rocket launchers and four fixed 21 inch A/S torpedo tubes). Rapid-fire Mk 23 twin 3 inch/70 calibre guns were installed in place of the original 3 inch guns in 1957-1958. After 3 inch mount subsequently removed to provide helicopter deck; forward 3 inch mount later deleted, leaving only 5 inch gun armament.

DISPOSAL

Willis A. Lee (DL 4) stricken on 15 May 1972 (in reserve since Dec 1969).

WILKINSON (DL 5) *1968, United States Navy*

1 FRIGATE (DL): "NORFOLK" TYPE

Displacement, tons	5 600 standard; 7 300 full load
Length, feet (*metres*)	540·2 (*164·6*) oa
Beam, feet (*metres*)	54·2 (*16·5*)
Draft, feet (*metres*)	26 (*7·9*)
Guns	8—3 inch (*76 mm*) 70 calibre dualpurpose (twin)
A/S weapons	1 ASROC 8-tube launcher 2 triple torpedo tubes (Mk 32)
Main engines	2 geared turbines (General Electric); 80 000 shp; 2 shafts
Boilers	4—1 200 psi (*84·4 kg/cm²*) (Babcock & Wilcox)
Speed, knots	32
Complement	411 (26 officers, 385 enlisted men)

Name	*No.*	*Builder*	*Laid down*	*Launched*	*Commissioned*
NORFOLK	DL 1 (ex-CLK 1)	New York Shipbuilding Corp	1 Sep 1949	29 Dec 1951	4 Mar 1953

NORFOLK (DL 1) *1968, United States Navy*

The Norfolk was one of two cruiser-size anti-submarine ("killer") ships authorised in 1948. Their size was to provide a rough-weather, long-range ASW capability. Construction of the CLK 2 was deferred on 2 Mar 1949 and cancelled on 9 Feb 1951; her keel was not laid down. She was to have been named *New Haven*.

The *Norfolk* was decommissioned on 15 Jan 1970 and placed in reserve.

A/S WEAPONS. The *Norfolk* was originally armed with four Weapon Alfa (formerly Weapon able) rocket launchers. The two launchers aft of the second funnel have been replaced by an ASROC rocket launcher. The *Norfolk* has served as test ship for ASW equipment and was the primary test ship for ASROC. (Original armament included fixed torpedo tubes, but not the two triple torpedo launchers now installed on the main deck alongside the bridge structure.)

CLASSIFICATION. The *Norfolk* was reclassified as a Destroyer Leader (DL 1) on 9 Feb 1951 while under construction; the symbol DL having been changed to Frigate on 1 Jan 1955. While engaged in experimental work she was designated EDL 1.

DESIGN. The *Norfolk* was the first ship fully designed and built by the US Navy after World War II. She has a cruiser hull similar in size to the anti-aircraft cruisers (CLAA) but with a distinctive design including a clipper bow.

ELECTRONICS. An SQS-23 anti-submarine sonar was installed in 1958, the first ship so fitted.

The *Norfolk* had SPS-10 and SPS-29 search radar antennas on forward mast when decommissioned.

ENGINEERING. The *Norfolk* was the first US Navy ship with a 1 200 pounds-per-square inch steam propulsion plant. Fitted with six-bladed propellers. The *Norfolk* reached 35 knots on sea trials.

GUNNERY. Original gun armament consisted of eight 3 inch/50 calibre guns in twin open mounts and eight 20 mm guns. Faster-firing 3 inch/70s in enclosed mounts were fitted and the lighter weapons were removed.

The 3 inch guns are Mk 23 weapons, of a type previously installed in the "Mitscher" class frigates and "Carpenter" class destroyers. They are credited with a rate of fire of 95 rounds per barrel per minute.

NOMENCLATURE. The *Norfolk* retains her cruiser name; the only ship in the destroyer "family" named for a city.

Surface Combatants—*continued*

2 GUIDED MISSILE DESTROYERS (DDG): CONVERTED "MITSCHER" CLASS

Name	*No.*	*Builder*	*Laid down*	*Launched*	*DL Comm.*	*DDG Comm*
*MITSCHER	DDG 35 (ex-DL 2, ex-DD 927)	Bath Iron Works	3 Oct 1949	26 Jan 1952	15 May 1953	29 June 1968
*JOHN S. McCAIN	DDG 36 (ex-DL 3, ex-DD 928)	Bath Iron Works	24 Oct 1949	12 July 1952	12 Oct 1953	21 June 1969

Displacement, tons	5 200 full load
Length, feet (*metres*)	493 (*150·3*) oa
Beam, feet (*metres*)	50 (*15·2*)
Draft, feet (*metres*)	21 (*6·7*)
Missile launchers	1 single Tartar surface-to-air launcher (Mk 13 Mod 2)
Guns	2—5 inch (*127 mm*) 54 calibre dual-purpose (single)
A/S weapons	1 ASROC 8-tube launcher 2 triple torpedo tubes (Mk 32)
Main engines	2 geared turbines (General Electric); 80 000 shp; 2 shafts
Boilers	4 (Combustion Engineering)
Speed, knots	35
Complement	377 (28 officers, 349 enlisted men)

These ships are former "Mitscher" class all-gun frigates which have been converted to a guided missile and improved ASW configuration. They were reclassified as guided missile "destroyers" rather than frigates because of Tartar armament. The *Mitscher* and *John S. McCain* were reclassified as DDG on 15 Mar 1967. See "Mitscher" class for additional notes.

CONVERSION. Both ships were converted to DDG at the Philadelphia Naval Shipyard. The *Mitscher* began conversion in March 1966 and the *John S. McCain* in June 1966. Superstructure was modified with ASROC launcher installed forward of the bridge in "B" position; two heavy lattice masts fitted; triple Mk 32 torpedo tubes retained amidships; and single Tartar Mk 13 launcher installed aft (system weighs approximately 135 000 pounds).

ELECTRONICS. SQS-23 sonar installed; SPS-10 and SPS-37 search radars on forward mast and SPS-48 three-dimensional search radar and "bee hive" TACAN on after mast.

GUNNERY. The original Mk 42 gun mounts have been replaced by modified Mk 42 mounts with local anti-aircraft controls deleted (starboard "bubble" or "frog-eye" on mount removed; port dome is for local anti-surface control).

MISSILES. Tartar magazine capacity is reportedly 40 missiles.

NOMENCLATURE. Vice Admirals Marc A. Mitscher and John S. McCain commanded the US Navy's fast carrier task forces in the Pacific War during 1943-1945 (Task Forces 38 and 58 of the US Third and Fifth Fleets).

PHOTOGRAPHS. Note rounded bridge facings. These ships can be distinguished from the "Forrest Sherman" class DDG conversions at a distance by the larger ships' ASROC launcher in the "B" position and the second 5 inch gun aft. Note old-style TACAN "bee-hive" antenna.

JOHN S. McCAIN (DDG 36) — *1969, United States Navy*

JOHN S. McCAIN (DDG 36) — *1969, United States Navy*

MITSCHER (DDG 35) — *1969, United States Navy*

DG DESTROYER PROGRAMME

Long-range planning has begun on a new class of missile-armed destroyers, tentatively designated as the DG design. These ships would not be constructed until completion of the "Spruance" (DD 963) and patrol frigate (PF) programmes in the early 1980s. The DG ships probably would be armed with both anti-aircraft and anti-ship missiles as their "main battery" in addition to close-in weapons for terminal defence against hostile anti-ship missiles. Anti-submarine capabilities can be expected to include a medium-size sonar vice the large SQS-26 sonar of the "Spruance" class destroyers.

DXG DESTROYER DESIGN

These ships were a planned variation of the DD 963 class all-gun destroyers but with an improved anti-aircraft capability afforded by a Tartar-D surface-to-air missile system.
Initial Department of Defense planning called for 28 ships of this design. However, construction of these ships was not proposed in the Fiscal Year 1971 shipbuilding programme as previously anticipated. In view of the increasing cost estimates of the non-missile DD 963 class ships *prior* to the start of their construction, and probable new destroyer concepts, this class apparently will not be built. (The missile-armed DDG ships would, of course have been more expensive than the "straight" DD ships.)
The planned DDG/DXG programme provided for a ship similar in many respects to the DD 963 class ships to reduce design and construction costs. The missile-armed design would be similar to the DD type, but somewhat larger.

ELECTRONICS. The Aegis advanced detection and missile guidance radars tentatively were planned for these ships (formerly designated ASMS for Advanced Surface Missile System). Development of the advanced surface-to-air missile component of Aegis has been deferred. The nuclear-powered guided missile frigate DLGN 40 is planned for Aegis radar installation.

Surface Combatants—*continued*

4 GUIDED MISSILE DESTROYERS (DDG): CONVERTED "FORREST SHERMAN" CLASS

Name	No.	Builder	Laid down	Launched	DD Comm.	DDG Comm
*DECATUR	DDG 31 (ex-DD 936)	Bethlehem Steel Co (Quincy)	13 Sep 1954	15 Dec 1955	7 Dec 1956	29 Apr 1967
*JOHN PAUL JONES	DDG 32 (ex-DD 932)	Bath Iron Works	18 Jan 1954	7 May 1955	5 Apr 1956	23 Sep 1967
*PARSONS	DDG 33 (ex-DD 949)	Ingalls Shipbuilding Corp	17 June 1957	19 Aug 1958	29 Oct 1959	3 Nov 1967
*SOMERS	DDG 34 (ex-DD 947)	Bath Iron Works	4 Mar 1957	30 May 1958	3 Apr 1959	10 Feb 1968

Displacement, tons	4 150 full load
Length, feet (*metres*)	
DDG 31-32	418·4 (*127·5*) oa
DDG 33-34	418 (*127·4*) oa
Beam, feet (*metres*)	
DDG 31-32	45·2 (*13·8*)
DDG 33-34	45 (*13·7*)
Draft, feet (*metres*)	20 (*6·1*)
Missile launchers	1 single Tartar surface-to-air launcher (Mk 13 Mod 1)
Guns	1—5 inch (*127 mm*) 54 calibre dual-purpose)
A/S weapons	1 ASROC 8-tube launcher 2 triple torpedo tubes (Mk 32)
Main engines	2 geared turbines (Westinghouse in *John Paul Jones*; General Electric in others); 70 000 shp; 2 shafts
Boilers	4 (Foster Wheeler in *Decatur* and *Parsons*; Babcock & Wilcox in *John Paul Jones* and *Somers*)
Speed	33 knots
Complement	335 (22 officers, 313 enlisted men)

These four ships are former "Forrest Sherman" class destroyers that have been converted to a guided missile and improved ASW configuration. Plans for additional DDG conversions of this class were dropped (the *Turner Joy*, DD 951, was to have been the fifth missile ship of this type). The *Decatur* was reclassified as DDG 31 on 15 Sep 1966; the *John Paul Jones, Somers*, and *Parsons* became DDG on 15 Mar 1967. See "Forrest Sherman" class for additional notes.

CONVERSION. The *Decatur* began conversion to a DDG at the Boston Naval Shipyard on 15 June 1965, the *John Paul Jones* at the Philadelphia Naval Shipyard on 2 Dec 1965, the *Parsons* at the Long Beach (California) Naval Shipyard on 30 June 1965, and the *Somers* at the San Francisco Bay Naval Shipyard on 30 Mar 1966.
During conversion all existing armament was removed except the forward 5 inch gun; two triple ASW torpedo tubes were installed forward of the bridge; two heavy lattice masts fitted; ASROC launcher mounted aft of second stack; single Tartar Mk 13 launcher installed aft (on 01 level; system weighs approximately 135 000 pounds).
Original DDG conversion plans provided for Drone Anti-Submarine Helicopter (DASH) facilities; however, ASROC was substituted in all four ships as DASH lost favour in the Navy.

ELECTRONICS. SQS-23 sonar installed. SPS-10 and SPS-37 search radars on forward mast except *Somers* has SPS-40 in lieu of SPS-37; all have SPS-48 three-dimensional search radar on after mast.

GUNNERY. The original Mk 42 forward gun mount has been replaced by a modified Mk 42 mount with the local anti-aircraft control deleted (starboard "bubble" or "frog-eye" on mount removed; port dome is for local anti-surface control).

MISSILES. Reportedly Tartar magazine capacity is 40 missiles.

NOMENCLATURE. The *John Paul Jones* honours the Scottish-born father of the American Navy who later served as a rear-admiral in the Russian Navy (1788).

DECATUR (DDG 31) — *1972, United States Navy, PH3 D. L. Pierce*

PARSONS (DDG 33) — *1968, United States Navy*

PARSONS (DDG 33) — *1972, United States Navy*

Surface Combatants—*continued*

23 GUIDED MISSILE DESTROYERS (DDG): "CHARLES F. ADAMS" CLASS

Displacement, tons	3 370 standard; 4 500 full load
Length, feet (*metres*)	437 (*132·8*) oa
Beam, feet (*metres*)	47 (*14·3*)
Draft, feet (*metres*)	20 (*6·1*)
Missile launchers	
DDG 2-14	1 twin Tartar surface-to-air launcher (Mk 11 Mod 0)
DDG 15-24	1 single Tartar surface-to-air launcher (Mk 13 Mod 0)
DDG 4 and 13	1 multiple launcher for Chaparral (see *Missile* notes)
Guns	2—5 inch (*127 mm*) 54 cal dual-purpose
A/S weapons	1 ASROC 8-tube launcher; 2 triple torpedo tubes (Mk 32)
Main engines	2 geared steam turbines (General Electric in DDG 2, 3, 7, 8, 10-13, 15-22; Westinghouse in DDG 4-6, 9, 14, 23, 24,); 70 000 shp; 2 shafts
Boilers	4 (Babcock & Wilcox in DDG2. 3. 7. 8. 10-13, 20-22; Foster Wheeler in DDG 4-6, 9, 14; Combustion Engineering in DDG 15-19)
Speed, knots	35
Complement	354 (24 officers, 330 enlisted men)

Name	*No.*	*Builder*	*Laid down*	*Launched*	*Commissioned*
*CHARLES F. ADAMS	DDG 2	Bath Iron Wotks	16 June 1958	8 Sep 1959	10 Sep 1960
*JOHN KING	DDG 3	Bath Iron Works	25 Aug 1958	30 Jan 1960	4 Feb 1961
*LAWRENCE	DDG 4	New York Shipbuilding Corp	27 Oct 1958	27 Feb 1960	6 Jan 1962
*CLAUDE V. RICKETTS	DDG 5	New York Shipbuilding Corp	18 May 1959	4 June 1960	6 Jan 1962
*BARNEY	DDG 6	New York Shipbuilding Corp	18 May 1959	10 Dec 1960	11 Aug 1962
*HENRY B. WILSON	DDG 7	Defoe Shipbuilding Co	28 Feb 1958	23 Apr 1959	17 Dec 1960
*LYNDE McCORMICK	DDG 8	Defoe Shipbuilding Co	4 Apr 1958	9 Sep 1960	3 June 1961
*TOWERS	DDG 9	Todd Shipyards Inc, Seattle	1 Apr 1958	23 Apr 1959	6 June 1961
*SAMPSON	DDG 10	Bath Iron Works	2 Mar 1959	9 Sep 1960	24 June 1961
*SELLERS	DDG 11	Bath Iron Works	3 Aug 1959	9 Sep 1960	28 Oct 1961
*ROBISON	DDG 12	Defoe Shipbuilding Co	23 Apr 1959	27 Apr 1960	9 Dec 1961
*HOEL	DDG 13	Defoe Shipbuilding Co	1 June 1960	4 Aug 1960	16 June 1962
*BUCHANAN	DDG 14	Todd Shipyards Inc, Seattle	23 Apr 1959	11 May 1960	7 Feb 1962
*BERKELEY	DDG 15	New York Shipbuilding Corp	1 June 1960	29 July 1961	15 Dec 1962
*JOSEPH STRAUSS	DDG 16	New York Shipbuilding Corp	27 Dec 1960	9 Dec 1961	20 Apr 1963
*CONYNGHAM	DDG 17	New York Shipbuilding Corp	1 May 1961	19 May 1962	13 July 1963
*SEMMES	DDG 18	Avondale Marine Ways Inc	18 Aug 1960	20 May 1961	10 Dec 1962
*TATTNALL	DDG 19	Avondale Marine Ways Inc	14 Nov 1960	26 Aug 1961	13 Apr 1963
*GOLDSBOROUGH	DDG 20	Puget Sound B & DD Co	3 Jan 1961	15 Dec 1961	9 Nov 1963
*COCHRANE	DDG 21	Puget Sound B & DD Co	31 July 1961	18 July 1962	21 Mar 1964
*BENJAMIN STODDERT	DDG 22	Puget Sound B & DD Co	11 June 1962	8 Jan 1963	12 Sep 1964
*RICHARD E. BYRD	DDG 23	Todd Shipyards Inc, Seattle	12 Apr 1961	6 Feb 1962	7 Mar 1964
*WADDELL	DDG 24	Todd Shipyards Inc, Seattle	6 Feb 1962	26 Feb 1963	28 Aug 1964

These destroyers are considered excellent multi-purpose ships. The DDG 2-9 were authorised in the Fiscal Year 1957 new construction programme, DDG 10-14 in FY 1958, DDG 15-19 in FY 1959, DDG 20-22 in FY 1960, DDG 23 and DDG 24 in FY 1961. Three additional ships of this design have been built in US shipyards for Australia (DDG 25-27) and three for West Germany (DDG 28-30).

CLASSIFICATION. The first eight ships were initially assigned hull numbers in the standard DD series (DDG 952-959); renumbered while under construction. The DDG 1 was the *Gyatt* (ex-DD 712), which operated as a missile destroyer from 1956 to 1962.

DESIGN. These ships were built to an improved "Forrest Sherman" class design with aluminium superstructures and a high level of habitability including air conditioning in all living spaces. They do not have the second radar trellis mast nor secondary gun battery of the earlier class. DDG 20-24 have stem anchors because of sonar arrangements.
Several ships have been modified with an extension of the bridge structure on the starboard side on the 02 level, providing additional space for storage (DDG 2, 6, 10, 18, and other ships).

ELECTRONICS. DDG 20-24 have bow-mounted SQS-23 sonar; earlier ships have SQS-23 sonar with hull domes.
DDG 2-14 have SPS-37 and SPS-10 search radars on tripod mast; DDG 15-24 have SPS-40 and SPS-10. All ships apparently being fitted with antenna associated with SPS-52 radar, but the ships retain SPS-39 system (three-dimensional search antenna on second stack); these ships were completed with SPS-39 radar antenna aft.
Mk-74 guided missile fire control system is provided. The *Towers* is the first US Navy ship to be fitted with the Ship Anti-Missile Integrated Defence (SAMID) to counter the Soviet cruise missile threat (Styx, etc); this system integrates existing electronic equipment and weapons to reduce reaction time when under attack. Also fitted with chaff rockets (CHAFFROC).

GUNNERY. These ships have rapid-fire Mk 42 guns. The *Charles F. Adams* has modified mounts with local anti-aircraft controls deleted (starboard "bubble" or "frog-eye" on mounts removed; port dome is for local anti-surface control).

BARNEY (DDG 6) — *1971, United States Navy*

CONYNGHAM (DDG 17) — *1971, US Navy, PH1 Robert L. Varney*

SOMERS (DDG 34)—see previous page — *1971, United States Navy, PH2 Kenneth R. Deam*

Surface Combatants—*continued*

'C.F. ADAMS" CLASS *continued*

ЛISSILES. The DDG 2-14 have a twin Mk.11 Tartar ıissile launcher while the DDG 15-24 have a single Лk 13 Tartar launcher. The Mk 11 launcher installation veighs 165 240 pounds while the Mk 13 weighs only 32 561 pounds. Reportedly, their magazine capacities ıre 42 and 40 missiles, respectively, and ships equipped vith either launcher can load, direct, and fire about six nissiles per minute. (The twin Mk 11 launcher is nstalled in the cruisers CG 10-12; the "Mitscher" and 'Forrest Sherman" DDG conversions have a similar Лk 13 launcher which weighs approximately 135 000 ›ounds.)

.*awrence* and *Hoel* fitted in 1972-1973 with multiple auncher for Chaparral (MIM-72A) and other point-lefence missiles.

ЈOMENCLATURE. The DDG 5 was originally named *Biddle*; renamed *Claude V. Ricketts* on 28 July 1964 to ıonour the late Vice Chief of Naval Operations who had supported multi-national NATO manning of ballistic nissile surface ships. (The name *Biddle* subsequently was assigned to the DLG 34.) The DDG 23 honours the famed polar explorer and naval aviator.

PHOTOGRAPHS. Note difference in radars on tripod mast and missile launchers on DDG 2-14 and DDG 15-24 series of this class.

HENRY B. WILSON (DDG 7) — *1969, United States Navy*

CLAUDE V. RICKETTS (DDG 5) — *1971, United States Navy, PH2 W. Striegel*

BUCHANAN (DDG 14) — *United States Navy*

RICHARD E. BYRD (DDG 23) — *1970, Anthony & Joseph Pavia*

Surface Combatants—*continued*

16 + 7 DESTROYERS (DD): "SPRUANCE" CLASS (FORMERLY DX TYPE)

Displacement, tons	6 900 full load
Length, feet (*metres*)	560 (*171·0*)
Beam, feet (*metres*)	54 (*16·4*)
Draft, feet (*metres*)	28 (*8·6*)
Helicopters	Light Airborne Multi-Purpose System (LAMPS) helicopter
Missile launchers	1 Basic Point Defence Missile System (BPDMS) multiple-launcher for Sea Sparrow missiles
Guns	2—5 inch (*127 mm*) 54 calibre dual-purpose (Mk 45) (single)
A/S weapons	1 ASROC 8-tube launcher fixed torpedo tubes (Mk 32)
Main engines	4 gas turbines (General Electric) approx 80 000 shp; 2 shafts
Speed, knots	30+
Complement	approx 270

Name	*No.*	*Start Erection*	*Launch*	*Commission*
SPRUANCE	DD 963	27 Nov 1972	Nov 1973	late 1974
PAUL F. FOSTER	DD 964	6 Feb 1973	1974	1975
	DD 965	Apr 1973	1974	1975
	DD 966	July 1973	1974	1975
	DD 967	Oct 1973	1974	1975

No.	*Commission*	*No.*	*Commission*	*No.*	*Commission*
DD 968	early 1976	**DD 972**	1976	**DD 976**	1977
DD 969	1976	**DD 973**	1977	**DD 977**	1977
DD 970	1976	**DD 974**	1977	**DD 978**	1978
DD 971	1976	**DD 975**	1977		

7 ships **DD 979-985** Proposed FY 1974 programme.

These ships were intended as replacements for the large number of World War II-built destroyers that have undergone extensive modernisation (FRAM) to enable them to serve into the 1970s. According to official statements: "The primary mission of these ships is anti-submarine warfare including operations as an integral part of attack carrier task forces. They also have the capability for shore bombardment and for surface warfare, and will have short range missiles for defense against airborne threats, including enemy missiles. Their effectiveness against submarines is expected to be far greater, particularly at high speeds, than that of current Navy ships due to ship silencing techniques and improved sea-keeping capabilities."

These ships are believed the worlds largest surface warships now under construction except for aircraft carriers without a major guided missile system. The Sea Sparrow weapon in these ships provides a close-in, terminal defence capability.

The Fiscal Year 1969 new construction programme proposed by the Department of Defense requested funding for the first five ships of this class; however; funds were denied by the Congress because of the design status. In the FY 1970 programme the Congress approved funds for five ships, but increasing costs forced the Department of Defense to construct only three ships under the FY 1970 programme (DD 963-965); six ships were authorised in the FY 1971 programme (DD 966-971); seven ships (DD 972-978) in the FY 1972 programme and seven ships (DD 979-985) were requested in the FY 1973 programme but were not approved; again requested in FY 1974 budget.

There have been technical criticisms voiced about these ships (see *Status* notes) and congressional opposition to construction of the entire 30-ship class in one shipyard. In conjunction with shipyard difficulties encountered with the first commercial ships built at the yard and delays in constructing the *Tarawa* class assault ships (LHA) at the same yard, some observers believe that only part of the class will be built, possibly only the 16 ships in the FY 1970-1972 programmes.

CONSTRUCTION. All ships of this class will be constructed by the Litton Ship Systems Division of Litton Industries in Pascagoula, Mississippi. The "production facility" is a new shipyard which launched its first ship (a commercial freighter) in 1971. Advanced production techniques including modular assembly of large ship components is featured. A contract for the development and production of the entire DD 963 class was awarded to Litton on 23 June 1970; that award also provided go-ahead for the first three ships.

CLASSIFICATION During the early proposal stage these ships were designated as the DX project, the letter "X" signifying that the characteristics were not fully defined.

DESIGN. Extensive use of the modular concept is used to facilitate initial construction and bloc modernisation of the ships.

The ships will be highly automated, resulting in about 20 per cent reduction in personnel over a similar ship with conventional systems.

ELECTRONICS. These ships will have SQS-26 sonar and will be the first US warships with a completely digital command and control system, which will reduce complexity and speed up production. (Most existing systems have a mixture of digital and analog components.)

To be fitted with SPS-40A and SPS-55 radars, SQS-26CX sonar, and Mk 116 underwater fire control system. Advanced electronic countermeasure (ECM) equipment, will be fitted.

The Combat Information Centre (CIC) will provide a centralised location for information and displays for all sensor and weapon systems.

Provision in stern for eventual installation of SQS-35 Independent Variable Depth Sonar (IVDS).

Fire control system for guns is Mk 86.

GUNNERY. These ships will have the 5 inch 54 calibre, light-weight Mk 45 gun. An improved 5 inch 54 calibre Mk 65 gun is being considered for use on later ships in this series.

ENGINEERING. These ships will be the first large US warships to employ gas turbine propulsion. Each ship will have four General Electric LM2500 marine gas turbine engines, a shaft-power version of the TF39 turbofan aircraft engine. The LM2500 is rated at approximately 20 000 horsepower. The gas turbine was selected because of comparatively low operating costs, smaller space requirements, rapid replacement capability, and cold-start capability (the engines can go from "cold iron" to full power in 12 minutes).

These ships will have controllable-pitch propellers because gas turbine engines cannot use a reversible shaft; to be fitted with advanced self-noise reduction features.

During normal operations these ships will "steam" on two engines, going to three and then four engines for higher speeds. Range is estimated at 6 000 miles at 20 knots.

FISCAL. The proposed FY 1973 defence budget requested $612 000 000 for the DD 979-985 (seven ships). Only $247 000 000 was approved in FY 1973 for long-lead time components. The FY 1974 budget requests $590 900 000 to complete funding of the ships.

The average cost per ship of this class is officially estimated at $85 000 000, but more likely will be in excess of $100 000 000 per ship. See 1971-1972 edition for additional fiscal data.

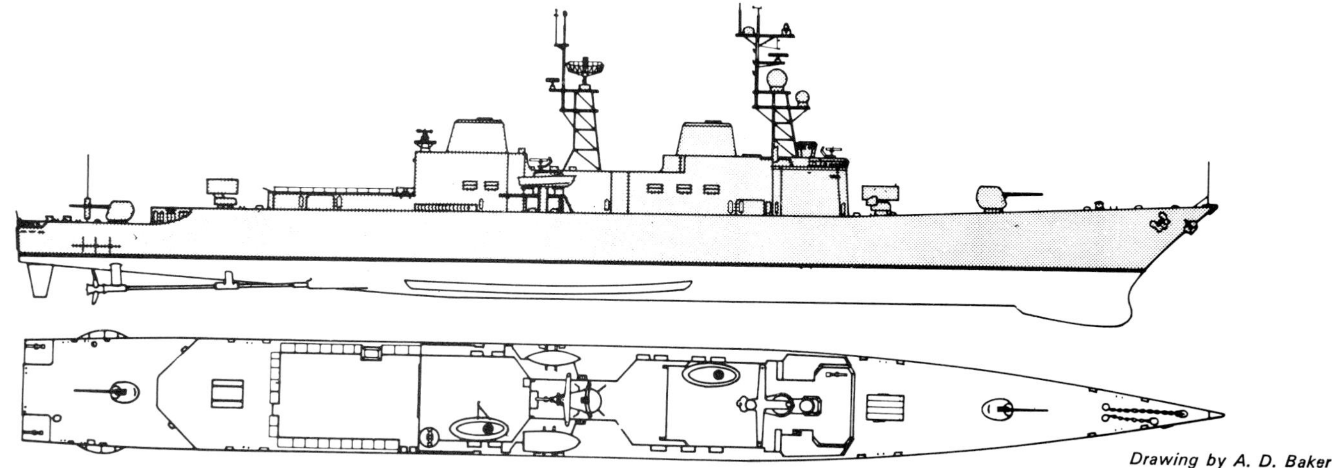

Drawing by A. D. Baker

SPRUANCE (DD 963) *Litton Industries Artist's Concept*

Surface Combatants—*continued*

"SPRUANCE" CLASS —*continued*

NOMENCLATURE. The *Spruance* is named for Admiral Raymond A. Spruance, who had tactical command of the US carriers in the Battle of Midway (June 1942) and of the US fleet in the Battle of the Marianas (June 1954), two of the major engagements of the Pacific War. He also was considered one of the leading intellectuals of the US Navy.

PHOTOGRAPH. Artist's concept has been "reversed" with funnels being placed starboard and port going from bow to stern; drawings are based on official design model.

14 DESTROYERS (DD) "FORREST SHERMAN" CLASS

Displacement, tons	approx 2 800 standard approx 4 050 standard
Length, feet (*metres*)	
DD 931-944	418·4 (*127·5*) oa
except DD 933	425
DD 945-951	418 (*127·4*) oa
Beam, feet (*metres*)	
DD 931-944	**45·2 (*13·8*)**
DD 945-951	**45 (*13·7*)**
Draft, feet (*metres*)	**20 (*6·1*)**
Guns A/S Mod	2—5 in (127 *mm*) 54 calibre dual-purpose (single)
Others	3—5 in (*127 mm*) 54 calibre dual-purpose (single) 2—3 in (*76 mm*) 50 calibre anti-aircraft (twin) in DD 931, 944, 945, 946
A/S weapons	
A/S Mod	1 ASROC 8-tube launcher 2 triple torpedo tubes (Mk 32)
Others	2 hedgehogs; depth charges retained in a few ships 2 triple torpedo tubes (Mk 32)
Main engines	2 geared turbines (Westinghouse in DD 931 and 933; General Electric in others); 70,000 shp; 2 shafts
Boilers	4 (Babcock & Wilcox in DD 931 and 933, 940-942, 945, 946, 950, 951; Foster Wheeler in others)
Speed	33 knots
Complement	292 (17 officers, 275 enlisted men) in unmodified ships; 304 (17 officers, 287 enlisted men) in A/S Mod ships

Name	No	Builder	Laid down	Launched	Commissioned
*FORREST SHERMAN	DD 931	Bath Iron Works	27 Oct 1953	5 Feb 1955	9 Nov 1955
*BIGELOW	DD 942	Bath Iron Works	6 July 1955	2 Feb 1957	8 Nov 1957
*MULLINNIX	DD 944	Bethlehem Steel Co (Quincy)	5 Apr 1956	18 Mar 1957	7 Mar 1958
*HULL	DD 945	Bath Iron Works	12 Sep 1956	10 Aug 1957	3 July 1958
*EDSON	DD 946	Bath Iron Works	3 Dec 1956	1 Jan 1958	7 Nov 1958
*TURNER JOY	DD 951	Puget Sound Bridge & DD	30 Sep 1957	5 May 1958	3 Aug 1959

ANTI-SUBMARINE MODIFIED

Name	No	Builder	Laid down	Launched	Commissioned
*BARRY	DD 933	Bath Iron Works	15 Mar 1954	1 Oct 1955	31 Aug 1956
*DAVIS	DD 937	Bethlehem Steel Co (Quincy)	1 Feb 1955	28 Mar 1956	28 Feb 1957
*JONAS INGRAM	DD 938	Bethlehem Steel Co (Quincy)	15 June 1955	8 July 1956	19 July 1957
*MANLEY	DD 940	Bath Iron Works	10 Feb 1955	12 Apr 1956	1 Feb 1957
*DU PONT	DD 941	Bath Iron Works	11 May 1955	8 Sep 1956	1 July 1957
*BLANDY	DD 943	Bethlehem Steel Co (Quincy)	29 Dec 1955	19 Dec 1956	26 Nov 1957
*MORTON	DD 948	Ingalls Shipbuilding Corp	4 Mar 1957	23 May 1958	26 May 1959
*RICHARD S. EDWARDS	DD 950	Puget Sound Bridge & DD	20 Dec 1956	24 Sep 1957	5 Feb 1959

These ships were the first US destroyers of post-World War II design and construction. Four have been converted to a guided missile configuration and are listed separately. They were authorised in the Fiscal Year 1952-1956 new construction programmes. These ships each cost approximately $26 000 000.
All of these ships are active.

ARMAMENT. As built all 18 ships of this class had three single 5 inch guns, two twin 3 inch mounts, four fixed 21 inch ASW torpedo tubes (amidships); two ASW hedgehogs (forward of bridge), and depth charge racks.

DESIGN. The entire superstructures of these ships are of aluminium to obtain maximum stability with minimum displacement. All living spaces are air conditioned. The *Decatur* and later ships have higher bows; the *Hull* and later ships have slightly different bow designs. The *Barry* had her sonar dome moved forward in 1959 and a stem anchor fitted.

ELECTRONICS. SQS-23 sonar installed with the *Barry* being the first US warship fitted with bow mounted sonar. Variable depth sonar installed on stern of A/S modified ships.
These ships have SPS-10 and SPS-37 or SPS-40 search radar antennas; the A/S modified ships have SPS-40 except *Barry* and *Davis* which retain SPS-37. The *Mullinnix* has SPS-10 and SPS-6 radar antennas.
Several ships fitted with improved electronic warfare equipment.

GUNNERY. With original armament of one 5 inch mount forward and two 5 inch mounts aft, these were the first US warships with more firepower aft than forward. Note that *Barry* and later ships have their Mk 68 gunfire control director forward and Mk 56 director aft; positions reversed in earlier ships.

MODERNISATION. Eight ships of this class were extensively modified in 1967-1971 to improve their anti-submarine capabilities: *Barry, Davis, Du Pont* at the Boston Naval Shipyard; *Jonas Ingram, Manley, Blandy* at the Philadelphia Naval Shipyard; and *Morton, Richard S. Edwards* at the Long Beach (California) Naval Shipyard. During modernisation the anti-submarine torpedo tubes installed forward of bridge (on 01 level), deckhouse aft of second funnel extended to full width of ship, ASROC launcher installed in place of after gun mounts on 01 level, and variable depth sonar fitted at stern. Six ships of this class were not provided improved A/S capabilities because of increased costs.

MORTON (DD 948) *1972, United States Navy, PH1 E. L. Goligoski*

DUPONT (DD 941) *1972, United States Navy, PH1 Jerry W. Cook*

Surface Combatants—*continued*

DAVIS (DD 937) *1972, United States Navy*

JONAS INGRAM (DD 938) (ASW Mod.) *1970, United States Navy*

MULLINNIX (DD 944) *1970, Anthony & Joseph Pavia*

TURNER JOY (DD 951) ***1970, United States Navy, PH3 Dennis McClosky***

Surface Combatants—*continued*

67 DESTROYERS (DD): MODERNISED "GEARING" CLASS (FRAM I)

Displacement, tons	2 425 standard; 3 480 to 3 520 full load
Length, feet (*metres*)	390·5 (*119·0*) oa
Beam, feet (*metres*)	40·9 (*12·4*)
Draft, feet (*metres*)	19 (*5·8*)
Missile launchers	Chaparral surface-to-air missile launcher in *Floyd B. Parks*
Guns	4—5 in (*127 mm*) 38 calibre dual-purpose (twin)
A/S weapons	1 ASROC 8-tube launcher 2 triple torpedo tubes (Mk 32) facilities for small helicopter
Main engines	2 geared turbines (General Electric or Westinghouse); 60 000 shp 2 shafts
Boilers	4 (Babcock & Wilcox or combination Babcock & Wilcox and Foster-Wheeler)
Speed, knots	34
Complement	274 (14 officers, 260 enlisted men)

Name	*No.*	*Builder*	*Launched*	*Commissioned*
*GEARING	DD 710	Federal SB & DD Co	18 Feb 1945	3 May 1945
*WILLIAM R. RUSH	DD 714	Federal SB & DD Co	8 July 1945	21 Sep 1945
*WILLIAM M. WOOD	DD 715	Federal SB & DD Co	29 July 1945	24 Nov 1945
*WILTSIE	DD 716	Federal SB & DD Co	31 Aug 1945	12 Jan 1946
*THEODORE E. CHANDLER	DD 717	Federal SB & DD Co	20 Oct 1945	22 Mar 1946
*HAMNER	DD 718	Federal SB & DD Co	24 Nov 1945	11 July 1946
*EPPERSON	DD 719	Federal SB & DD Co	22 Dec 1945	19 Mar 1949
*SOUTHERLAND	DD 743	Bath Iron Works Corp	5 Oct 1944	22 Dec 1944
*WILLIAM C. LAWE	DD 763	Bethlehem (San Francisco)	21 May 1945	18 Dec 1946
*ROWAN	DD 782	Todd Pacific Shipyards	29 Dec 1944	31 Mar 1945
*GURKE	DD 783	Todd Pacific Shipyards	15 Feb 1945	12 May 1945
*McKEAN	DD 784	Todd Pacific Shipyards	31 Mar 1945	9 June 1945
*HENDERSON	DD 785	Todd Pacific Shipyards	28 May 1945	4 Aug 1945
*RICHARD B. ANDERSON	DD 786	Todd Pacific Shipyards	7 July 1945	26 Oct 1945
*HOLLISTER	DD 788	Todd Pacific Shipyards	9 Oct 1945	26 Mar 1946
*EVERSOLE	DD 789	Todd Pacific Shipyards	8 Jan 1946	10 July 1946
*HIGBEE	DD 806	Bath Iron Works Corp	12 Nov 1944	27 Jan 1945
*DENNIS J. BUCKLEY	DD 808	Bath Iron Works Corp	20 Dec 1944	2 Mar 1945
*CORRY	DD 817	Consolidated Steel Corp	28 July 1945	26 Feb 1946
*NEW	DD 818	Consolidated Steel Corp	18 Aug 1945	5 Apr 1946
*HOLDER	DD 819	Consolidated Steel Corp	25 Aug 1945	18 May 1946
*RICH	DD 820	Consolidated Steel Corp	5 Oct 1945	4 July 1946
*JOHNSTON	DD 821	Consolidated Steel Corp	19 Oct 1945	10 Oct 1945
*ROBERT H. McCARD	DD 822	Consolidated Steel Corp	9 Nov 1945	26 Oct 1946
*BASILONE	DD 824	Consolidated Steel Corp	21 Dec 1945	26 July 1949
*AGERHOLM	DD 826	Bath Iron Works Corp	30 Mar 1946	20 June 1946
*MYLES C. FOX	DD 829	Bath Iron Works Corp	13 Jan 1945	20 Mar 1945
HERBERT J. THOMAS	DD 833	Bath Iron Works Corp	25 Mar 1945	29 May 1945
*CHARLES P. CECIL	DD 835	Bath Iron Works Corp	22 Apr 1945	29 June 1945
*GEORGE K. MacKENZIE	DD 836	Bath Iron Works Corp	13 May 1945	13 July 1945
*SARSFIELD	DD 837	Bath Iron Works Corp	27 May 1945	31 July 1945
*POWER	DD 839	Bath Iron Works Corp	30 June 1945	13 Sep 1945
*GLENNON	DD 840	Bath Iron Works Corp	14 July 1945	4 Oct 1945
*NOA	DD 841	Bath Iron Works Corp	30 July 1945	2 Nov 1945
*FISKE	DD 842	Bath Iron Works Corp	8 Sep 1945	28 Nov 1945
PERRY	DD 844	Bath Iron Works Corp	25 Nov 1945	17 Jan 1946
*BAUSELL	DD 845	Bath Iron Works Corp	19 Nov 1945	7 Feb 1947
*OZBOURN	DD 846	Bath Iron Works Corp	22 Dec 1945	5 Mar 1946
*ROBERT L. WILSON	DD 847	Bath Iron Works Corp	5 Jan 1946	28 Mar 1946
*RICHARD E. KRAUS (ex-AG 151)	DD 849	Bath Iron Works Corp	2 Mar 1946	23 May 1946
JOSEPH P. KENNEDY Jr	DD 850	Bethlehem (Quincy)	26 July 1945	15 Dec 1945
*RUPERTUS	DD 851	Bethlehem (Quincy)	21 Sep 1945	8 Mar 1946
*LEONARD F. MASON	DD 852	Bethlehem (Quincy)	4 Jan 1946	28 June 1946
*CHARLES H. ROAN	DD 853	Bethlehem (Quincy)	15 Mar 1945	12 Sep 1946
*VOGELGESANG	DD 862	Bethlehem (Staten Island)	15 Jan 1945	28 Apr 1945
*STEINAKER	DD 863	Bethlehem (Staten Island)	13 Feb 1945	26 May 1945
*HAROLD J. ELLISON	DD 864	Bethlehem (Staten Island)	14 Mar 1945	23 June 1945
CHARLES R. WARE	DD 865	Bethlehem (Staten Island)	12 Apr 1945	21 July 1945
*CONE	DD 866	Bethlehem (Staten Island)	10 May 1945	18 Aug 1945
*STRIBLING	DD 867	Bethlehem (Staten Island)	8 June 1945	29 Sep 1945
*BROWNSON	DD 868	Bethlehem (Staten Island)	15 Mar 1945	17 Nov 1945
*ARNOLD J. ISBELL	DD 869	Bethlehem (Staten Island)	6 Aug 1945	17 Nov 1945
*DAMATO	DD 871	Bethlehem (Staten Island)	21 Nov 1945	27 Apr 1946
*HAWKINS	DD 873	Consolidated Steel Corp	7 Oct 1944	10 Feb 1945
*HENRY W. TUCKER	DD 875	Consolidated Steel Corp	8 Nov 1944	12 Mar 1945
*ROGERS	DD 876	Consolidated Steel Corp	20 Nov 1944	26 Mar 1945
*VESOLE	DD 878	Consolidated Steel Corp	29 Dec 1944	23 Apr 1945
*LEARY	DD 879	Consolidated Steel Corp	20 Jan 1945	7 May 1945
*DYESS	DD 880	Consolidated Steel Corp	26 Jan 1945	21 May 1945
*BORDELON	DD 881	Consolidated Steel Corp	3 Mar 1945	5 June 1945
*NEWMAN K. PERRY	DD 883	Consolidated Steel Corp	17 Mar 1945	26 July 1945
*FLOYD B. PARKS	DD 884	Consolidated Steel Corp	31 Mar 1945	31 July 1945
*JOHN R. CRAIG	DD 885	Consolidated Steel Corp	14 Apr 1945	20 Aug 1945
*ORLECK	DD 886	Consolidated Steel Corp	12 May 1945	15 Sep 1945
*BRINKLEY BASS	DD 887	Consolidated Steel Corp	26 May 1945	1 Oct 1945
*O'HARE	DD 889	Consolidated Steel Corp	22 June 1945	29 Nov 1945
*MEREDITH	DD 890	Consolidated Steel Corp	28 June 1945	31 Dec 1945

These ships are enlarged versions of the "Allen M. Sumner" class with an additional 14-foot section amidships for additional fuel tanks. All of the above listed ships have been extensively modernised under the FRAM I programme (see *Modernisation* notes). The *Richard E. Kraus* (ex-AG 151) and *Sarsfield* are used for experimental work (EDD). (The former ship was designated AG 151 from 24 Aug 1949 to 11 Dec 1953). The following ships are assigned to Naval Reserve training; manned with crews composed jointly of active and reserve personnel: *Arnold J. Isbell, Bass, Damato, Dyess, Ellison, Gearing, Holder, Johnston, McCard, McKean, Wiltsie.* All "Gearing" class FRAM I ships are active except for the *Herbert J. Thomas* decommissioned in 1970; *Perry, Charles R. Ware, Joseph P. Kennedy, Jr*, were to decommission in 1973.
Several additional ships of this class were to be stricken/transferred or assigned to Naval Reserve training during 1973-1974.

The "Gearing" class initially covered hull numbers DD 710-721, 742, 743, 763-769, 782-791, 805-926. Forty-nine of these ships were cancelled in 1945 (DD 768, 769, 809-816, 854-856, and 891-926); four ships were never completed and were scrapped in the 1950s: *Castle* (DD 720), *Woodrow R. Thompson* (DD 721), *Lansdale* (DD 766), and *Seymour D. Owens* (DD 767).

After World War II several "Gearing" class destroyers were completed to specialised anti-submarine configurations (DDK "hunter-killer"); otherr ships were converted to escort (DDE) and radar picket (DDR) configurations. Subsequently all surviving ships modernised under FRAM I and FRAM II programmes. Two ex-DDK ships (FRAM II) and the various FRAM II "Gearing" class destroyers are listed on subsequent pages.

ARMAMENT-DESIGN. As built these ships had a pole mast and carried an armament of six 5 inch guns (twin mounts), 12 40 mm AA guns (2 quad, 2 twin), 11 20 mm AA guns (single), and 10 21 inch torpedo tubes (quin). After World War II the after bank of tubes was replaced by an additional quad 40 mm mount. All 40 mm and 20 mm guns were replaced subsequently by six 3 inch guns (2 twin, 2 single) and a tripod mast was installed to support heavier radar antennas. The 3 inch guns and remaining torpedo tubes were removed during FRAM conversion.

ELECTRONICS. These ships have SPS-10 and SPS-40 or SPS-37 search radars on their forward tripod mast; advanced electronic warfare equipment fitted to most ships with an enlarged electronic "stack" atop the helicopter hangar-ASROC magazine structure. Fitted with SQS-23 sonar. *Brownson* fitted with SQQ-23 (modified SQS-23) for evaluation.

ENGINEERING. Range is 5 800 miles at 15 knots.

HELICOPTERS. These ships no longer operate drone helicopters, but rely on ASROC and tube-launched torpedoes. for anti-submarine weapons. They had been fiited to operate the Drone Anti-Submarine Helicopter (DASH) during FRAM modernisation.

MISSILES. *Floyd B. Parks* fitted with Chaparral point defense missile system in 1972. See "Charles F. Adams" class for details.

MODERNISATION. All of these ships have undergone extensive modernisation under the Fleet Rehabilitation and Modernisation (FRAM I) programme They were

HAROLD J. ELLISON (DD 864) — *1972, US Navy, PHC Roger E. Barnes*

Surface Combatants—*continued*

"GEARING" CLASS FRAM I—*continued*

stripped of all armament except two 5 inch mounts. new anti-submarine weapons were installed including facilities for operating ASW helicopters. new electronic equipment was installed. machinery was overhauled. living and working spaces were rehabilitated. For budgeting reasons FRAM I work was officially considered a "conversion". The *Perry* was the first ship to undergo FRAM I conversion. the work being accomplished at the Boston Naval Shipyard from May 1959 to April 1960; her FRAM I cost an estimated $7 700 000

There are two basic FRAM I configurations: the DD 786, 790, 826, 841, 844, 845, 847, and 890 (eight ships)6 have twin 5 inch mounts in "A" and "B" positions and Mk 32 torpedo launchers abaft second funnel; others have twin 5 inch mounts in "A" and "Y" positions and Mk 32 launchers on 01 level in "B" position.

The *Herbert J. Thomas* was additionally modified for protection against biological, chemical, and atomic attack; the ship is fully "sealed" with enclosed lookout and control positions, special air conditioning provisions, *et cetera*. (Modified at Mare Island Naval Shipyard from July 1963 to July 1964.)

DISPOSALS AND TRANSFERS (since 1 Jan 1970)
Fechteler (DD 870) stricken on 11 Sep 1970; **Samuel B. Roberts** (DD 823) stricken on 2 Nov 1970; **Forrest Royal** (DD 872) transferred to Turkey on 27 Mar 1971; **Stickell** (DD 888) transferred to Greece on 1 July 1972; **Eugene A. Greene** (DD 711), **Furse** (DD 882) transferred to Spain on 31 Aug 1972; **Warrington** (DD 843) stricken on 1 Oct 1972; **Shelton** (DD 790) transferred to Spain on 15 Mar 1973; **James E. Kyes** (DD 787), **Hanson** (DD 832) to Spain on 31 Mar 1973; (**Warrington** heavily damaged by mine off North Vietnam).

CHARLES H. ROAN (DD 853) — *1971, Anthony & Joseph Pavia*

WILLIAM R. RUSH (DD 714) — *1970, United States Navy*

WILLIAM M. WOOD (DD 715) — *1971, Anthony & Joseph Pavia*

BORDELON (DD 881) and TRUMPETFISH (SS 425) — ***1971, United States Navy, PH1 John Francavillo***

Surface Combatants—*continued*

2 DESTROYERS (DD): "CARPENTER" TYPE (FRAM I)

Displacement, tons	2 425 standard; 3 410 full load
Length, feet (*metres*)	390·5 (*119·0*) oa
Beam, feet (*metres*)	40·9 (*12·4*)
Draft, feet (*metres*)	19 (*5·8*)
Guns	2—5 in (*127 mm*) 38 calibre dual-purpose (twin)
A/S weapons	1 ASROC 8-tube launcher; 2 triple torpedo tubes (Mk 32); facilities for small helicopter
Main engines	2 geared turbines (Westinghouse in *Carpenter*, General Electric in *Robert A. Owens*); 60 000 shp; 2 shafts
Boilers	4 (Babcock & Wilcox)
Speed, knots	34
Complement	264 (14 officers, 250 enlisted men)

Name	*No.*	*Builder*	*Launched*	*Commissioned*
***CARPENTER**	DD 825	Consolidated Steel Corp	30 Dec 1945	15 Dec 1946
***ROBERT A. OWENS**	DD 827	Bath Iron Works Corp	15 July 1946	5 Nov 1949

These ships were laid down as units of the "Gearing" class. Their construction was suspended after World War II until 1947 when they were towed to the Newport News Shipbuilding and Drydock Co for completion as "hunter-killer" destroyers (DDK). As specialised ASW ships they mounted 3 inch (76 mm) guns in place of 5 inch mounts and were armed with improved ahead-firing anti-submarine weapons (hedgehogs and Weapon Able/Alfa); special sonar equipment installed. The DDK and DDE classifications were merged in 1950 with both of these ships being designated DDE on 4 March 1950. Upon being modernised to the FRAM I configuration they were reclassified DD on 30 June 1962.

The *Carpenter* is assigned to Naval Reserve training; the *Robert A. Owens* is active.

ELECTRONICS. These ships have SPS-10 and SPS-40 search radars on their forward tripod mast and electronic warfare "pods" on a smaller tripod mast forward of their second funnel.

PHOTOGRAPHS. The *Carpenter* and *Robert A. Owens* are distinguished as the only US destroyers with one twin 5 inch gun mount.

ROBERT A. OWENS (DD 827) *1969, A. & J. Pavia*

2 DESTROYERS (DD): "GEARING" CLASS (FRAM II) ex-ESCORTS

Displacement, tons	2 425 standard; approx 3 500 full load
Length, feet (*metres*)	390·5 (*119·0*) oa
Beam, feet (*metres*)	40·9 (*12·4*)
Draft, feet (*metres*)	19 (*5·8*)
Guns	4—5 inch (*127 mm*) 38 calibre DP (twin)
A/S weapons	1 trainable hedgehog (Mk 15); 2 triple torpedo tubes (Mk 32); facilities for small helicopter
Main engines	2 geared turbines (Allis-Chalmers and Westinghouse, respectively); 60 000 shp; 2 shafts
Boilers	4 (Babcock & Wilcox)
Speed, knots	34
Complement	275 (15 officers, 260 enlisted men)

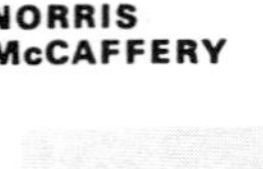

Name	*No.*	*Builder*	*Launched*	*Commissioned*
NORRIS	DD 859	Bethlehem Steel (San Pedro)	25 Feb 1945	9 June 1945
***McCAFFERY**	DD 860	Bethlehem Steel (San Pedro)	12 Apr 1945	26 July 1945

These ships are "Gearing" Class destroyers. They were modified for anti-submarine warfare specialisation in 1949-1950 with trainable hedgehog installed in "B" position and classification changed to "hunter-killer" destroyers (DDK); changed to "escort" destroyers (DDE) on 4 March 1950. Again classified as "straight" destroyers (DD) on 30 June 1962 with FRAM II modernisation. No ASROC provided.
The *McCaffery* remains in active commission (correction to previous edition); the *Norris* is in reserve.

ELECTRONICS. These ships have SPS-6 and SPS-10 search radars on their tripod mast Fitted with SQS-29 series hull mounted sonar.

McCAFFERY (DD 860) *1969, United States Navy*

PHOTOGRAPHS. The *McCaffery* has the Mk 15 hedgehog covered in this photograph. Note unusual configuration of electronic warfare mast.

DISPOSALS AND TRANSFERS
Fred T. Berry (DD 858) stricken on 15 Sep 1970; **Harwood** (DD 861) transferred to Turkey on 17 Dec 1971; **Keppler** (DD 765) transferred to Turkey on 30 June 1972; **Lloyd Thomas** (DD 764) transferred to Taiwan China on 30 Oct 1972.

Surface Combatants—*continued*

1 DESTROYER (DD): "GEARING" CLASS (FRAM II) ex-RADAR PICKET

Displacement, tons	2 425 standard; approx 3 500 full load
Length, feet (*metres*)	390·5 (*119·0*) oa
Beam, feet (*metres*)	40·9 (*12·4*)
Draft, feet (*metres*)	19 (*5·8*)
Guns	6—5 inch (*127 mm*) 38 calibre DP (twin)
A/S weapons	2 fixed hedgehogs 2 triple torpedo tubes (Mk 32) facilities for small helicopter
Main engines	2 geared turbines (General Electric except Westinghouse in *Perkins*) 60 000 shp; 2 shafts
Boilers	4 (Babcock & Wilcox)
Speed, knots	34
Complement	275 (15 officers, 260 enlisted men)

Name	*No.*	*Builder*	*Launched*	*Commissioned*
BENNER	DD 807	Bath Iron Works Corp	20 Nov 1944	13 Feb 1945

This ship is a "Gearing" class destroyer, originally modified to serve as a radar picket destroyer and reclassified DDR on 18 March 1949. Subsequently modernised under the 'Gearing" FRAM II programme with special electronics equipment removed; reclassified as a "straight" destroyer (DD) on 30 June 1962. Fitted with helicopter hangar and flight deck but no ASROC, thus considered a FRAM II modernisation.
The *Benner* is in reserve.

ELECTRONICS. The *Benner* has SPS-40 and SPS-10 search radar antennas on her tripod mast; electronic warfare equipment on "stack" atop hangar structure. Fitted with SQS-29 series hull-mounted sonar. No variable depth sonar as in former DDRs listed below.

BENNER (DD 807) *1969, United States Navy*

3 DESTROYERS (DD): "GEARING" CLASS (FRAM II) RADAR PICKETS

Displacement, tons	2 425 standard; approx 3 500 full load
Length, feet (*metres*)	390·5 (*119·0*) oa
Beam, feet (*metres*)	40·9 (*12·4*)
Draft, feet (*metres*)	19 (*5·8*)
Guns	6—5 inch (*127 mm*) 38 calibre DP (twin)
A/S weapons	2 fixed hedgehogs 2 triple torpedo tubes (Mk 32)
Main engines	2 geared turbines (General Electric); 60 000 shp; 2 shafts
Boilers	4 (Babcock & Wilcox)
Speed, knots	34
Complement	275 (15 officers, 260 enlisted men)

Name	*No.*	*Builder*	*Launched*	*Commissioned*
KENNETH D. BAILEY	DD 713	Federal SB & DD Co	17 June 1945	31 July 1945
GOODRICH	DD 831	Bath Iron Works	25 Feb 1945	24 Apr 1945
DUNCAN	DD 874	Consolidated Steel Corp	27 Oct 1944	25 Feb 1945

These ships were "Gearing" class destroyers, modified to serve as radar picket destroyers and reclassified (DDR) on 18 March 1949, except *Kenneth D. Bailey* on 9 April 1953. Subsequently modernised under "Gearing" FRAM II programme, but retained special electronic equipment and were not provided with drone helicopter (DASH) facilities; classified as "straight" destroyers (DD) on 1 January 1969.
The three surviving ships of this type were decommissioned in 1969-1971.

ELECTRONICS. These ships have SPS-37 and SPS-10 search radars on forward mast, TACAN (tactical air navigation) "beehive" antenna on short tripod mast forward of second funnel, and SPS-30 search radar atop after deckhouse (except SPS-8 in *Duncan*). During FRAM process these ships were fitted with SQS-29 series hull-mounted sonar; variable depth sonar fitted in all except *Duncan*.

DISPOSALS AND TRANSFERS (ex-DDR types)
Turner (DD 834) stricken on 26 Sep 1969; **Frank Knox** (DD 742) transferred to Greece on 23 Jan 1971; **Ernest G. Small** (DD 838) transferred to Taiwan China on 19 Feb 1971; **Chevalier** (DD 805) transferred to South Korea on 5 July 1972; **Everett F. Larson** (DD 830) to South Korea on 30 Oct 1972; **Perkins** (DD 877) transferred to Argentina on 15 Jan 1973.

KENNETH D. BAILEY (DD 713) *1968, United States Navy*

Surface Combatants—*continued*

24 DESTROYERS (DD) MODERNISED "ALLEN M. SUMNER" CLASS (FRAM II)

Displacement, tons	2 200 standard; 3 320 full load
Length, feet (*metres*)	376·5 (*114·8*) oa
Beam, feet (*metres*)	40·9 (*12·4*)
Draft, feet (*metres*)	19 (*5·8*)
Guns	6—5 in (*127 mm*) 38 calibre DP (twin)
A/S Weapons	2 triple torpedo tubes (Mk 32) 2 ahead-firing hedgehogs facilities for small helicopter
Main engines	2 geared turbines; 60 000 shp; 2 shafts
Boilers	4
Speed, knots	34
Complement	274 (14 officers, 260 enlisted men)

Name	*No.*	*Builder*	*Launched*	*Commissioned*
*ALLEN M SUMNER	DD 692	Federal SB & DD Co	15 Dec 1943	26 Jan 1944
*MOALE	DD 693	Federal SB & DD Co	16 Jan 1944	26 Feb 1944
*CHARLES S. SPERRY	DD 697	Federal SB P DD Co	13 Mar 1944	17 May 1944
*AULT	DD 698	Federal SB & DD Co	26 Mar 1944	31 May 1944
*WALDRON	DD 699	Federal SB & DD Co	26 Mar 1944	8 June 1944
*WALLACE L. LIND	DD 703	Federal SB & DD Co	14 June 1944	8 Sep 1944
WALKE	DD 723	Bath Iron Works Corp	27 Oct 1943	21 Jan 1944
*LAFFEY	DD 724	Bath Iron Works Corp	21 Nov 1943	8 Feb 1944
*DE HAVEN	DD 727	Bath Iron Works Corp	9 Jan 1944	31 Mar 1944
MANSFIELD	DD 728	Bath Iron Works Corp	29 Jan 1944	14 Apr 1944
LYMAN K. SWENSON	DD 729	Bath Iron Works Corp	12 Feb 1944	2 May 1944
COLLETT	DD 730	Bath Iron Works Corp	5 Mar 1944	16 May 1944
BLUE	DD 744	Bethlehem (Staten Island)	28 Nov 1943	20 Mar 1944
TAUSSIG	DD 746	Bethlehem (Staten Island)	25 Jan 1944	20 May 1944
ALFRED A. CUNNINGHAM	DD 752	Bethlehem (Staten Island)	3 Aug 1944	23 Nov 1944
JOHN A. BOLE	DD 755	Bethlehem (Staten Island)	1 Nov 1944	3 Mar 1945
*PUTNAM	DD 757	Bethlehem (San Francisco)	26 Mar 1944	12 Oct 1944
*STRONG	DD 758	Bethlehem (San Francisco)	23 Apr 1944	8 Mar 1945
LOFBERG	DD 759	Bethlehem (San Francisco)	12 Aug 1944	26 Apr 1945
JOHN W. THOMASON	DD 760	Bethlehem (San Francisco)	30 Sep 1944	11 Oct 1945
*LOWRY	DD 770	Bethlehem (San Pedro)	6 Feb 1944	23 July 1944
*MASSEY	DD 778	Todd Pacific Shipyards	19 Aug 1944	24 Nov 1944
*DOUGLAS H. FOX	DD 779	Todd Pacific Shipyards	30 Sep 1944	26 Dec 1944
STORMES	DD 780	Todd Pacific Shipyards	4 Nov 1944	27 Jan 1945
*ROBERT K. HUNTINGTON	DD 781	Todd Pacific Shipyards	5 Dec 1944	3 Mar 1945

These destroyers have been extensively modernised under the FRAM II programme.
Frank E. Evans (DD 754) cut in half by Australian carrier *Melbourne* on 2 June 1969; bow section sank with loss of 74 crew. Officially stricken from the Navy List on 1 July 1969; stern section sunk as target on 10 Oct 1969.
All ships of this class remaining in commission (indicated by asterisks) are operational Naval Reserve training ships; manned by joint crews of active and reserve personnel.

ELECTRONICS. These ships have SQS-29 series hull-mounted sonar (SQS-29 to -31 designation, depending upon frequency); variable depth sonar in most ships; fitted with SPS-40 or SPS-37 and small SPS-10 search radars on tripod mast.

MODERNISATION. All of these ships have been modernised under the fleet Rehabilitation and Modernisation (FRAM II) programme. New ASW torpedo tubes were installed as were facilities for operating drone ASW helicopters and variable depth sonar (VDS). Machinery was overhauled, new electronic equipment was installed, and living and working spaces were rehabilitated.

TORPEDOES. All ships have two Mk 32 triple tubes for ASW torpedoes on 01 level between funnels.

PHOTOGRAPHS. The *Moale* at right has an SPS-40 radar antenna on her tripod mast and a variable depth sonar installation on her stern; the *Lyman K. Swenson* below has an older SPS-37 search radar antenna and no VDS. Note hedgehogs alongside bridge, small platform and hangar for unmanned helicopter, and Mk 32 torpedo tubes between funnels. The larger "Gearing" class ships can be identified by additional spacing between funnels.

MOALE (DD 693) — *1970, United States Navy*

DISPOSALS AND TRANSFERS
Zellars (DD 777) transferred to Iran on 19 Mar 1971; **Ingraham** (DD 694) to Greece on 16 July 1971; **Stormes** (DD 780) to Iran on 16 Feb 1972; **O'Brien** (DD 725) stricken on 18 Feb 1972; **Borie** (DD 704) transferred to Argentina on 1 July 1972; **Hugh Purvis** (DD 709) transferred to Turkey on 1 July 1972. **Buck (DD 761); James C. Owens** (DD 776), transferred to Brazil in July 1973. Other planned transfers cancelled.

"ALLEN M. SUMNER" CLASS

All non-modernised destroyers of the "Allen M. Sumner" class were to have been stricken or transferred by 1973. See 1972-1973 and previous editions for characteristics. A photograph of the *Purdy* (DD 724) appears on the following page; note absence of secondary gun battery; six 5 inch guns as in ships of this type modernised under the FRAM II programme.

DISPOSALS AND TRANSFERS since 1 Jan 1970: **Soley** (DD 707) stricken on 13 Feb 1970; **Haynsworth** (DD 700) transferred to Taiwan China on 12 May 1970; **English** (DD 696) to Taiwan China on 11 Aug 1970; **John W. Weeks** (DD 701) stricken on 12 Aug 1970; **Gainard** (DD 706) transferred to Iran on 19 Mar 1971; **Harlan R. Dickson** (DD 708) stricken on 1 July 1972; **Hank** (DD 702) transferred to Argentina on 1 July 1972; **Willard Keith** (DD 775) transferred to Colombia on 1 July 1972; **Maddox** (DD 731) transferred to Taiwan China on 6 July 1972; **Beatty** (DD 756) transferred to Venezuela on 14 July 1972; **Compton** (DD 705) transferred to Brazil on 27 Sep 1972; **Purdy** (DD 734), **John R. Pierce** (DD 753), **Henley** (DD 762) were to be stricken in 1973.

LYMAN K. SWENSON (DD 729) — *1970, United States Navy, PHC T. J. Taylor*

Surface Combatants—*continued*

17 DESTROYERS (DD): LATER "FLETCHER" CLASS

Name	No.	Builder	Launched	Commissioned
BEARSS (4 guns)	DD 654	Gulf SB Corpn	25 July 1943	12 Apr 1944
CAPERTON (4)	DD 650	Bath Iron Works Corpn	24 July 1943	30 July 1943
CASSIN YOUNG	DD 793	Bethlehem Co San Pedro	12 Sep 1943	31 Dec 1943
CHARLES J. BADGER	DD 657	Bethlehem Co Staten Island	3 Apr 1943	23 July 1943
COTTEN (4)	DD 669	Federal SB & DD Co	12 June 1943	24 July 1943
DASHIELL (4)	DD 659	Federal SB & DD Co	6 Feb 1943	20 Mar 1943
HEALY (4)	DD 674	Federal SB & DD Co	1 Aug 1943	22 Sep 1943
HUNT (4)	DD 672	Federal SB & DD Co	4 July 1943	3 Sep 1943
JOHN HOOD (4)	DD 655	Gulf SB Corpn	23 Oct 1943	7 June 1944
KIDD	DD 661	Federal SB & DD Co	28 Feb 1943	23 Apr 1944
KNAPP	DD 653	Bath Iron Works Corpn	10 July 1943	16 Sep 1943
McNAIR (4)	DD 679	Federal SB & DD Co	14 Nov 1943	30 Dec 1943
MELVIN	DD 680	Federal SB & DD Co	17 Oct 1943	24 Nov 1943
PICKING (4)	DD 685	Bethlehem Co Staten Island	31 May 1943	21 Sep 1943
PORTERFIELD	DD 682	Bethlehem Co San Pedro	13 June 1943	30 Oct 1943
REMEY	DD 688	Bath Iron Works Corpn	24 July 1943	30 Sep 1943
STOCKHAM	DD 683	Bethlehem Co, San Francisco	25 June 1943	11 Feb 1944

Displacement, tons	2 050 standard; 3 500 full load
Length, feet (*metres*)	376·5 (*114·7*) oa
Beam, feet (*metres*)	39·5 (*11·9*)
Draft, feet (*metres*)	18 (*5·5*)
Guns	4 or 5—5 inch (*127 mm*) 38 calibre DP (single); 10—40 mm AA (twin) or 6—3 in (*76 mm*) AA (twin) see *Armament* notes
A/S weapons	depth charges; 2 fixed hedgehogs; 2 triple torpedo tubes (Mk 32) in some ships.
Torpedo tubes	5 or 10—21 inch (*533 mm*) quintuple (removed from some ships)
Main engines	2 geared turbines; 60 000 shp; 2 shafts
Boilers	4
Speed, knots	35
Complement	250 (14 officers, 236 enlisted men) (designed wartime 329)

Fifty-six destroyers of this class were completed in 1943-1944. They are essentially the same as the original "Fletcher" class. All surviving ships of this class are in reserve.

ARMAMENT-DESIGN. As built, these ships each mounted five 5 inch guns, ten 40 mm AA guns, several 20 mm guns, and ten 21 inch torpedo tubes. The twin 40 mm gun mounts were installed just forward of and below the bridge, alongside the second funnel, and atop the after deckhouse.
All secondary guns have been removed from some ships (see photograph of *Porterfield*).
After World War II a large number of these ships had their pole mast replaced by a tripod mast and five torpedo tubes between funnels were removed. All 20 mm guns also were removed. Twenty ships had their No. 3 ("Q") 5 inch mount removed and the 40 mm guns replaced by six 3 inch guns (twin), the latter installed between funnels and atop after deckhouse.
All ships active during the 1960s were fitted with triple Mk 32 tubes for ASW torpedoes.

TRANSFERS. Ships of this class serve in the navies of Argentina, Brazil, Chile, South Korea, Japan, Peru, Spain and Turkey.

DISPOSALS AND TRANSFERS (since 1 Jan 1970)
Hopewell (DD 681) stricken on 2 Jan 1970; **Mertz** (DD 691) stricken on 1 Oct 1970; **Albert W. Grant** (DD 649) stricken on 14 Apr 1971; **Bennion** (DD 662) stricken on 15 Apr 1971; **Uhlmann** (DD 687) stricken on 15 July 1972; **Chauncey** (DD 667); **Porter** (DD 800) stricken on 1 Oct 1972; **Bullard** (DD 660) stricken on 1 Dec 1972; **Norman Scott** (DD 690) on 15 Apr 1973.

PICKING (DD 685) — *1964, United States Navy*

PORTERFIELD (DD 682) — *1965, United States Navy*

PURDY (DD 734)—See previous page — *1971, US Navy, PHC Frederick W. Gotauco*

Surface Combatants—*continued*

15 DESTROYERS (DD): "FLETCHER" CLASS

Displacement, tons	2 100 standard; 3 050 full load
Length, feet (*metres*)	376·5 (*114·7*) oa
Beam, feet (*metres*)	39·5 (*11·9*)
Draft, feet (*metres*)	18 (*5·5*)
Guns	4 or 5—5 inch (*127 mm*) 38 calibre DP (single) except 3 guns in *Hazelwood* 6—40 mm AA (twin) or 6—3 inch (*76 mm*) AA (twin) (see *Armament* notes)
A/S weapons	depth charges 2 fixed hedgehogs 2 triple torpedo tubes (Mk 32) in some ships
Torpedo tubes	5 or 10—21 inch (*533 mm*) quintuple (removed from some ships)
Main engines	2 geared turbines; 60 000 shp; 2 shafts
Boilers	4
Speed, knots	35
Complement	249 (14 officers, 235 enlisted men) (designed wartime 329)

Name	*No*	*Builder*	*Laid down*	*Launched*	*Commissioned*
ABBOT (4 guns)	DD 629	Bath Iron Works Corpn	21 Sep 1942	17 Feb 1943	23 Apr 1943
DALEY (4)	DD 519	Bethlehem Co, Staten Island	29 Apr 1942	24 Oct 1942	10 Mar 1943
HAZELWOOD (3)	DD 531	Bethlehem Co, San Francisco	11 Apr 1942	20 Nov 1942	18 June 1943
LA VALLETTE	DD 448	Federal SB & DD Co	27 Nov 1941	21 June 1942	12 Aug 1942
McKEE	DD 575	Consolidated Steel Corpn	2 Mar 1942	2 Aug 1942	31 Mar 1943
ROBINSON	DD 562	Seattle-Tacoma SB Corpn	12 Aug 1942	28 Aug 1943	31 Jan 1944
ROSS (4)	DD 563	Seattle-Tacoma SB Corpn	7 Sep 1942	10 Sep 1943	21 Feb 1944
ROWE (4)	DD 564	Seattle-Tacoma SB Corpn	7 Dec 1942	30 Sep 1943	13 Mar 1944
SIGOURNEY	DD 643	Bath Iron Works Corpn	7 Dec 1942	24 Apr 1943	29 June 1943
SIGSBEE	DD 502	Federal SB & DD Co	22 July 1942	7 Dec 1942	23 Jan 1943
STODDARD (4)	DD 566	Seattle-Tacoma SB Corpn	10 Mar 1943	19 Nov 1943	15 Apr 1944
TERRY	DD 513	Bath Iron Works Corpn	8 June 1942	22 Nov 1942	26 Jan 1943
THE SULLIVANS (4)	DD 537	Bethlehem Co, San Francisco	10 Oct 1942	4 Apr 1943	30 Sep 1943
WATTS	DD 567	Seattle-Tacoma SB Corpn	26 Mar 1943	31 Dec 1943	29 Apr 1944
WREN	DD 568	Seattle-Tacoma SB Corpn	24 Apr 1943	29 Jan 1944	22 May 1944

One hundred nineteen ships of this class were completed in 1942-1945.
Eleven ships of this class were cancelled: DD 505, 506, 523-525, 542, 543, 548, 549, *Percival* (DD 542), and *Watson* (DD 482). The last two were to have been 2 100-ton destroyers with experimental power plants. (The experimental ships DD 503 and DD 504, of an unspecified type, were cancelled in 1941.)
All surviving ships of this class are in reserve. The last active ship was the *Shields* (DD 596), in continuous commission from 1945 to 1972.

ARMAMENT-DESIGN. These ships marked reversion to flush-deck destroyers by the US Navy after several broken-deck designs built during the 1930s and early 1940s. This design was extremely successful and 56 additional ships of this class were constructed (listed separately).
As built, these ships mounted five 5 inch guns, six to ten 40 mm AA guns, several 20 mm AA guns, and ten 21 inch torpedo tubes. The twin 40 mm gun mounts were installed on each side of the second funnel and atop the after deckhouse.
After World War II a large number of these ships had their pole mast replaced by a tripod mast and the five torpedo tubes between funnels were removed. All 20 mm guns also removed. Twenty-one ships had their No. 3 ("Q") 5 inch mount removed and the 40 mm guns replaced by six 3 inch guns (twin), the latter installed between funnels and atop after deckhouse.
Ships in commission during the 1960s were fitted with triple Mk 32 launchers for ASW torpedoes.

HELICOPTERS. The *Hazelwood* was extensively modified to serve as test ship for the Drone Anti-Submarine Helicopter (DASH) programme.

NOMENCLATURE. Ships renamed while building: DD 537 ex-*Putnam*, DD 594 ex-*Mansfield*.
The DD 535 was renamed *James Miller* on 5 Aug 1971 to permit the name *Miller* to be assigned to DE 1091.

TRANSFERS. Ships of this class serve in the navies of Argentina, Brazil, Colombia, West Germany, Greece, Italy, South Korea, Mexico, Peru, Spain, and Taiwan China.

DISPOSALS AND TRANSFERS (since 1 Jan 1970)
Pritchett (DD 561) transferred to Italy on 10 Jan 1970; **Stanley** (DD 478) stricken on 1 Dec 1970; **Metcalf** (DD 595) stricken on 2 Jan 1971; **Twining** (DD 540) transferred to Taiwan China on 1 July 1971; **Cowell** (DD 547), **Braine** (DD 630) transferred to Argentina on 17 Aug 1971; **Mullany** (DD 528) transferred to Taiwan China on 6 Oct 1971; **Shields** (DD 596) transferred to Brazil on 6 July 1972; **Schroeder** (DD 501), **Foote** (DD 511), **McCord** (DD 534), **Miller** (DD 535) stricken on 1 Oct 1972; **Trathen** (DD 530), **Wickes** (DD 578), **Haraden** (DD 585), **Bell** (DD 587), **Burns** (DD 588) stricken on 1 Nov 1972 (all targets); **Hudson** (DD 475), **Stevens** (DD 479), **Stephen Potter** (DD 538), **Franks** (DD 554) stricken on 1 Dec 1972; **Owen** (DD 536), **Laws** (DD 558) **Hart** (DD 594) stricken on 15 Apr 1973.

"BENSON" AND "GLEAVES" CLASSES

All destroyers of the "Benson" and "Gleaves" classes completed 1940-1943 have been stricken or transferred to other navies. See 1971-1972 and previous editions for characteristics. Several ships of these classes serve in the navies of Greece, Italy, Taiwan China, and Turkey. The **Niblack** (DD 424) stricken in 1968, has been retained as a test hull for floating dry dock experiments at Davisville, Rhode Island.

THE SULLIVANS (DD 537) — *United States Navy*

HAZELWOOD (DD 531) — *United States Navy*

ABBOT (DD 629) — *United States Navy*

OCEAN ESCORTS

The US Navy is completing the last ships of the controversial "Knox" class ocean escorts. These ships will provide the Navy with 65 "first-line" ocean escorts in the mid-1970s (ie, ships with long-range SQS-26 sonar and ASROC anti-submarine rocket launcher): 45 "Knox" class, 6 "Brook" class, 10 "Garcia" class, 2 "Bronstein" class, and the escort research ship *Glover*.

These 65 ocean escorts represent 20 per cent of the Navy's 1974 warship strength, the highest ratio of ocean escort ships to warships since the end of World War II almost three decades ago.

A new escort ship programme is being initiated. Now known as the Patrol Frigate (PF), the new ship will emphasise anti-missile and anti-ship defences with some reduction in anti-submarine capabilities (SQQ-23 sonar vice larger SQS-26 and no ASROC). The PF programme provides for 50 ships to be completed between 1977 and 1985.

Despite its P-series designation, the PF is actually an ocean escort or destroyer escort on the basis of recent US Navy classifications, although in virtually all other navies this type of ship is referred to as a "frigate". The PF is larger than all previous US Navy DE-type ships. Although comparable in displacement to the Soviet "Krivak" class destroyer, which is considerably shorter, the PF has the speed and armament normally associated with an escort ship/frigate.

The approximately 35 World War 11-built escort ships that remain on the Navy list have no practical anti-submarine capability against undersea craft constructed during the past 25 years. Some were employed successfully in the Vietnam War as Coastal patrol ships for interdicting attempts to send men and supplies into South Vietnam by sea. This mission can be better accomplished by other ships now available to the US Navy.

Two war-built escort ships, both of the DER radar picket configuration, remain in service, employed primarily in the surveillance of Soviet activities.

HAROLD E. HOLT (DE 1074) landing SH-2D — *1972, US Navy, PHC L. B. Moran*

HELICOPTERS. The "Brooke", "Knox", and "Garcia" class ships are scheduled to be provided with the Light Airborne Multi-Purpose System (LAMPS), the SH-2D helicopter. The first ship to be modified to operate the SH-2D was the *Harold E. Holt* (DE 1074), completed in February 1972. Others are to follow at a regular rate during the next few years. Hangars will be enlarged with an extending section added; in addition, the "Knox" class ships require enlargement of their flight deck.

MISSILES. ASROC anti-submarine missile launchers in several "Knox" class ships have been modified to permit firing of the Standard surface-to-surface missile. This is an anti-ship variant of the Standard-ARM air-launched, anti-radiation missile (AGM-78) and ship-launched, anti-aircraft missile (RIM-66/67 series).

NOMENCLATURE. Escort ships generally are named for US Navy, Marine Corps, and Coast Guard personnel.

PHOTOGRAPHS. In the adjacent photograph the *Harold E. Holt* lands an SH-2D Seasprite helicopter during operations off the coast of Southern California. Note the partially raised hangar door on the DE, the helicopter control compartment on the starboard side of the hangar, Sea Sparrow missile launched aft of helicopter deck, and stern opening for variable depth sonar.

PATROL FRIGATE (PF)

PATROL FRIGATES (PF): PROPOSED

Displacement, tons	3 400 full load
Length, feet (*metres*)	450 (*137*)
Beam, feet (*metres*)	45 (*13·7*)
Draft, feet (*metres*)	23 (*7·2*)
Missile launchers	1 single launcher for standard Harpoon missiles (Mk 13 Mod 4) (see *Missile* notes)
Guns	(tentatively) 2—35 mm AA (twin) or 1—76 mm AA
A/S weapons	2 SH-2D LAMPS helicopters 2 triple torpedo tubes (Mk 32)
Main engines	Gas turbines; 40 000 shp; 1 shaft = approx 28 knots
Complement	185

The Navy has proposed a class of 50 ships of this type for the escort of amphibious forces, underway replenishment groups, and convoys. They are follow-on ships to the large classes of ocean escorts (DE) built in the 1960s and early 1970s, but with emphasis on anti-missile/anti-ship defences to complement the ocean escorts which emphasise anti-submarine capabilities (eg, large SQS-26 sonar, ASROC).

The lead ship of this class was authorised in the Fiscal Year 1973 new construction programme with completion scheduled for 1977. There would be a delay of about 18 months between the lead and follow-on ships; subsequently, the additional ships would be constructed at the rate of about 12 per year.

Contracts were awarded to Bath Iron Works, Bath, Maine, for $3 000 000, and to Todd Shipyards Corp, Seattle, Washington, for $1 800 000, on 12 Apr 1972 to undertake design work on the PF. This places the firms in a preferred position with respect to construction contracts for these ships.

DESIGNATION. These ships officially are referred to as "patrol frigates" with the designation PF. However, according to an official statement this "is not necessarily the designation these ships will be assigned when they become reality".

These ships are similar in size and mission to US ocean escorts (DE). For the past two decades the term "frigates (DL/DLG) has been applied by the US Navy to ships of destroyer leader/cruiser size. Previously, the US Navy used the term "frigate" for a series of World War II-built escort ships (PF 1-102) and subsequently for ships built specifically for transfer to allied navies (PF 103-108).

ELECTRONICS. SQG-23 PAIR (modified SQS-23) hull-mounted sonar is planned for these ships.

They will be fitted with "austere" electronic warfare equipment in an effort to help hold down construction costs. This could inhibit the ships' defence against advanced Soviet anti-ship missiles. Mk 92 fire control system (Americanised version of the WM-28 system developed by N. V. Hollandse Signallapparaten), and SPS-49 and SPS-55 search radars will be fitted.

ENGINEERING. Each ship will be powered by two General Electric LM2500 marine gas turbine engines. See "Spruance" class (DD 963) listing for additional data. Range is unofficially reported at 4 500 miles at 20 knots.

FISCAL. The Navy requested reallocation of $51 600 000 of FY 1972 funds on 30 July 1971 for initiation of this programme; however, the Congress did not act on the request. Approximately $12 000 000 has been spent in FY 1971-1972 for studies and preliminary design.

The FY 1973 new construction programme provided $193 000 000 to complete the design, fund "start-up" efforts for ship equipment, and fund the lead ship. Estimated cost per follow-on ship is $45 000 000 to $55 000 000.

GUNNERY. Tentative candidates for the PF gun are adaptions of the twin 35 mm OTO Melara or the single 76 mm/62 calibre OTO Melara, with 1 100 and 90 rounds per-minute rates of fire, respectively. The larger gun has been designated Mk 75 in US service. These guns are intended primarily for defence against enemy anti-ship missiles that "leak" through the ships' Standard missile system.

HELICOPTERS. These ships will have landing area at stern and hangar for operating two SH-2D Seasprite or follow-on helicopters in anti-submarine and limited anti-ship missile defence roles.

MISSILES. The single-arm Tartar-type missile launcher will be capable of firing both Standard surface-to-air and Harpoon surface-to-surface missiles, according to current plans. "Mixed" missile magazines will be provided.

DRAWING. The PF arrangement has been extensively changed; a new view was not available when this page closed.

Ocean Escorts—*continued*

6 GUIDED MISSILE ESCORT SHIPS (DEG): "BROOKE" CLASS

isplacement, tons	2 640 standard; 3 425 full load
ength, feet (*metres*)	414·5 (*126·3*) oa
eam, feet (*metres*)	44·2 (*13·5*)
raft, feet (*metres*)	24 (*7·3*)
issile launchers	1 single Tartar surface-to-air launcher
uns	1—5 inch (*127 mm*) 38 calibre dual-purpose
/S weapons	1 ASROC 8-tube launcher 2 triple torpedo tubes (Mk 32) 2 fixed torpedo tubes (stern) (Mk 25) facilities for small helicopter
Main engines	1 geared turbine (Westinghouse); 35 000 shp; 1 shaft
Boilers	2—1 200 psi (*83·4 kg/cm²*) (Foster Wheeler)
Speed, knots	27
Complement	241 (16 officers, 225 enlisted men)

Name	*No.*	*Builder*	*Laid down*	*Launched*	*Commissioned*
***BROOKE**	DEG 1	Lockheed SB & Construction Co	10 Dec 1962	19 July 1963	12 Mar 1966
***RAMSEY**	DEG 2	Lockheed SB & Construction Co	4 Feb 1963	15 Oct 1963	3 June 1967
***SCHOFIELD**	DEG 3	Lockheed SB & Construction Co	15 Apr 1963	7 Dec 1963	20 Apr 1968
***TALBOT**	DEG 4	Bath Iron Works Corp	4 May 1964	6 Jan 1966	22 Apr 1967
***RICHARD L. PAGE**	DEG 5	Bath Iron Works Corp	4 Jan 1965	4 Apr 1966	5 Aug 1967
***JULIUS A. FURER**	DEG 6	Bath Iron Works Corp	12 July 1965	22 July 1966	11 Nov 1967

hese ships are identical to the "Garcia" class escorts except for the Tartar missile system in lieu of a second inch gun mount and different electronic equipment. DEG 1-3 were authorised in the Fiscal Year 1962 new construction programme and the DEG 4-6 in the FY 1963 programme. Plans for ten additional DEGs in FY 1964 and possibly three more DEGs in a later programme were dropped because of the $11 000 000 additional cost of a DEG over DE. See "Garcia" class for additional notes.

CLASSIFICATION. DEG 7-11 are guided missile "frigates" built in Spain with US assistance.

LECTRONICS. SQS-26AX bow mounted sonar installed. SPS-52 three-dimensional search radar is mounted on the "mack" (combination mast and stack) and SPS-10 search radar is installed on the mast. SPG-2 missile fire control radar is installed aft of the "mack".

HELICOPTERS. These ships were designed to operate Drone Anti-Submarine Helicopters (DASH), but the programme was cut back before helicopters were provided to these ships. Small hangar aft.
These ships are scheduled to be fitted to operate the Light Airborne Multi-Purpose System (LAMPS), now the SH-2D helicopter.

MISSILES. These ships have a single Tartar Mk 22 launching system which weighs 92 395 pounds. Reportedly, the system has a rate of fire similar to the larger Mk 11 and Mk 13 systems installed in guided missile destroyers, but the DEG system has a considerably smaller magazine capacity (16 missiles according to unofficial sources).

The DEGs have a single Mk 74-2 missile fire control system whereas the larger DDGs have two such systems, providing a considerably greater anti-air warfare capability. The DEG 4-6 have automatic ASROC loading system (note angled base of bridge structure aft of ASROC "pepper box" in these ships).

PHOTOGRAPHS. Note stem anchor and second anchor on port side near 5 inch gun, stern tube openings in *Brooke*.

BROOKE (DEG 1) *1969, United States Navy,*

SCHOFIELD (DEG 3) *1969, US Navy,*

BROOKE (DEG 1) *United States Navy*

Ocean Escorts—*continued*

46 ESCORT SHIPS (DE): "KNOX" CLASS

Displacement, tons	3 011 standard; 4 100 full load
Length, feet (*metres*)	438 (*133·5*) oa
Beam, feet (*metres*)	46·75 (*14·25*)
Draft, feet (*metres*)	24·75 (*7·55*)
Guns	1—5 inch (*127 mm*) 54 calibre dual purpose; 1—20 mm Vulcan/Phalanx CIWS in *Lockwood*; see note
Missile launchers	1 Sea Sparrow BPDMS multiple launcher (being installed); see notes
A/S weapons	1 ASROC 8-tube launcher; 4 fixed torpedo tubes (Mk 32); 1 SH-2D LAMPS helicopter being provided (see notes)
Main engines	1 geared turbine (Westinghouse) 35 000 shp; 1 shaft
Boilers	2—1 200 psi (*83·4 kg/cm²*)
Speed, knots	27+
Complement	245 (17 officers, 228 enlisted men); increased to 283 (22 officers, 261 enlisted men) with BPDMS and LAMPS installation; as built 12 ships had accommodations for 2 staff officers

Name	*No.*	*Builder*	*Laid down*	*Launched*	*Commissione*
***KNOX**	DE 1052	Todd Shipyards (Seattle)	5 Oct 1965	19 Nov 1966	12 Apr 196
***ROARK**	DE 1053	Todd Shipyards (Seattle)	2 Feb 1966	24 Apr 1967	22 Nov 196
***GRAY**	DE 1054	Todd Shipyards (Seattle)	19 Nov 1966	3 Nov 1967	4 Apr 197
***HEPBURN**	DE 1055	Todd Shipyards (San Pedro)	1 June 1966	25 Mar 1967	3 July 196
***CONNOLE**	DE 1056	Avondale Shipyards	23 Mar 1967	20 July 1968	30 Aug 196
***RATHBURNE**	DE 1057	Lockheed SB & Constn Co	8 Jan 1968	2 May 1969	16 May 197
***MEYERKORD**	DE 1058	Todd Shipyards (San Pedro)	1 Sep 1966	15 July 1967	28 Nov 196
***W. S. SIMS**	DE 1059	Avondale Shipyards	10 Apr 1967	4 Jan 1969	3 Jan 197
***LANG**	DE 1060	Todd Shipyards (San Pedro)	25 Mar 1967	17 Feb 1968	28 Mar 197
***PATTERSON**	DE 1061	Avondale Shipyards	12 Oct 1967	3 May 1969	14 Mar 197
***WHIPPLE**	DE 1062	Todd Shipyards (Seattle)	24 Apr 1967	12 Apr 1968	22 Aug 197
***REASONER**	DE 1063	Lockheed SB & Constn Co	6 Jan 1969	1 Aug 1970	31 July 197
***LOCKWOOD**	DE 1064	Todd Shipyards (Seattle)	3 Nov 1967	5 Sep 1964	5 Dec 197
***STEIN**	DE 1065	Lockheed SB & Constn Co	1 June 1970	19 Dec 1970	8 Jan 197
***MARVIN SHIELDS**	DE 1066	Todd Shipyards (Seattle)	12 Apr 1968	23 Oct 1969	10 Apr 197
***FRANCIS HAMMOND**	DE 1067	Todd Shipyards (San Pedro)	15 July 1967	11 May 1968	25 July 197
***VREELAND**	DE 1068	Avondale Shipyards	20 Mar 1968	14 June 1969	13 June 197
***BAGLEY**	DE 1069	Lockheed SB & Constn Co	22 Sep 1970	24 Apr 1971	6 May 197
***DOWNES**	DE 1070	Todd Shipyards (Seattle)	5 Sep 1968	13 Dec 1969	28 Aug 197
***BADGER**	DE 1071	Todd Shipyards (Seattle)	17 Feb 1968	7 Dec 1968	1 Dec 197
***BLAKELY**	DE 1072	Avondale Shipyards	3 June 1968	23 Aug 1969	18 July 197
***ROBERT E. PEARY**	DE 1073	Lockheed SB & Constn Co	20 Dec 1970	23 June 1971	23 Sep 197
***HAROLD E. HOLT**	DE 1074	Todd Shipyards (San Pedro)	11 May 1968	3 May 1969	26 Mar 197
***TRIPPE**	DE 1075	Avondale Shipyards	29 July 1968	1 Nov 1969	19 Sep 197
***FANNING**	DE 1076	Todd Shipyards (San Pedro)	7 Dec 1968	24 Jan 1970	23 July 197
***OUELLET**	DE 1077	Avondale Shipyards	15 Jan 1969	17 Jan 1970	12 Dec 197
***JOSEPH HEWES**	DE 1078	Avondale Shipyards	15 May 1969	7 Mar 1970	27 Feb 197
***BOWEN**	DE 1079	Avondale Shipyards	11 July 1969	2 May 1970	22 May 197
***PAUL**	DE 1080	Avondale Shipyards	12 Sep 1969	20 June 1970	14 Aug 197
***AYLWIN**	DE 1081	Avondale Shipyards	13 Nov 1969	29 Aug 1970	18 Sep 197
***ELMER MONTGOMERY**	DE 1082	Avondale Shipyards	23 Jan 1970	21 Nov 1970	30 Oct 197
***COOK**	DE 1083	Avondale Shipyards	20 Mar 1970	23 Jan 1971	18 Dec 197
***McCANDLESS**	DE 1084	Avondale Shipyards	4 June 1970	20 Mar 1971	18 Mar 197
***DONALD B. BEARY**	DE 1085	Avondale Shipyards	24 July 1970	22 May 1971	22 July 197
***BREWTON**	DE 1086	Avondale Shipyards	2 Oct 1970	24 July 1971	8 July 197
***KIRK**	DE 1087	Avondale Shipyards	4 Dec 1970	25 Sep 1971	9 Sep 197
***BARBEY**	DE 1088	Avondale Shipyards	5 Feb 1971	4 Dec 1971	11 Nov 197
***JESSE L. BROWN**	DE 1089	Avondale Shipyards	8 Apr 1971	18 Mar 1972	17 Feb 197
***AINSWORTH**	DE 1090	Avondale Shipyards	11 June 1971	15 Apr 1972	31 Mar 197
MILLER	DE 1091	Avondale Shipyards	6 Aug 1971	3 June 1972	June 197
THOMAS C. HART	DE 1092	Avondale Shipyards	8 Oct 1971	12 Aug 1972	June 197
CAPODANNO	DE 1093	Avondale Shipyards	12 Oct 1971	21 Oct 1972	Aug 197
PHARRIS	DE 1094	Avondale Shipyards	11 Feb 1972	16 Dec 1972	Oct 197
TRUETT	DE 1095	Avondale Shipyards	27 Apr 1972	3 Feb 1973	Dec 197
VALDEZ	DE 1096	Avondale Shipyards	30 June 1972	4 Mar 1973	Feb 197
MOINESTER	DE 1097	Avondale Shipyards	25 Aug 1972	June 1973	Apr 197

The 46 "Knox" class escort ships comprise the largest group of destroyer-type warships built to the same design in the West since the end of World War II. These ships are almost identical in design to the previous "Garcia" and "Brooke" classes, but slightly larger primarily because of use of non-pressure-fired boilers. DE 1052-1061 (10 ships) were authorised in the Fiscal Year 1964 new construction programme, DE 1062-1077 (16 ships) in FY 1965, DE 1078-1087 (10 ships) in FY 1966, DE 1088-1097 (10 ships) in FY 1967, and DE 1098-1107 (10 ships) in FY 1968. However, construction of six ships (DE 1102-1107) was deferred in 1968 as US Navy emphasis shifted to the more versatile and faster DX DXG ships; three additional ships (DE 1099-1101) were deferred late in 1968 to finance cost overruns of FY 1968 nuclear-powered attack submarines and to comply with a Congressional mandate to reduce expenditures; the last ship of the FY 1968 programme (DE 1098) was deferred early in 1969.

These ships have cost considerably more than originally estimated. Contract cost of early ships was $10 800 000 each; actual cost unofficially estimated at almost $18 000 000 per ship.

The DEG 7-11 guided missile "frigates" being built in Spain are similar to this design.

CONSTRUCTION. The ships built at Avondale Shipyards in Westwego, Louisiana, are constructed with a mass production technique of fabricating the hulls by using structural carbon steel tees split from wide-flange beams as longitudinal members. The hulls are built keel-up to permit downhand welding with the force of gravity allowing the molten weld to follow the contour of the hull and flow more easily between hull plates. Prefabricated, inverted hull modules first are assembled on a permanent platen, then lifted by hydraulic units and moved laterally into giant turning rings which rotate the hull into an upright position. Avondale, which also builds the "Hamilton" class cutters for the Coast Guard, side launches these ships.

DESIGN. These ships have a very large superstructure and a distinctive, cylindrical "mack" structure combining masts and engine exhaust stacks.

ELECTRONICS. SQS-26CX bow-mounted sonar; installation of SQS-13 Independent Variable Depth Sonar (IVDS) on 36 ships began in 1971.

These ships have SPS-40 and SPS-10 search radar antennas on their "mack" structures.

The DE 1078-1097 (20 ships) are being fitted with

HAROLD E. HOLT (DE 1074)—with BPDMS and LAMPS *1972, US Navy*

BOWEN (DE 1079) with BPDMS and LAMPS *1972, United States Navy*

Ocean Escorts—*continued*

ROBERT E. PEARY (DE 1073) *1972, United States Navy*

KNOX" CLASS—*continued*

SM-5 Test Evaluation and Monitoring System (TEAMS) hich continuously checks shipboard radar and sonar ystems. If TEAMS detects a malfunction an automatic earch will be conducted throughout the subsystems ntil the fault is found and the defective component lentified for repair or replacement.

NGINEERING. DE 1101 was to have had gas turbine ropulsion; construction of the ship was cancelled when ecision was made to provide gas turbine propulsion in Spruance" class (DD 963).
he *Peterson* is fitted with Baldwin-Lima-Hamilton ontrollable-pitch propellers for evalution for possible se in the "Spruance" class destroyers; her shafts are on-reversible.

UNNERY. Gun armament for these ships consists of single 5 inch/54 calibre Mk 42 mount forward with ocal anti-surface control (portside "bubble" or "frog-eye") ut no local anti-aircraft control capability.
ockwood fitted with 20 mm rapid-fire Close In Weapon ystem (CIWS) in 1972 for operational evaluation.

HELICOPTERS. These ships were designed to operate he now-discarded DASH unmanned helicopter. eginning in 1972 they are being modified to accommo-late the Light Airborne Multi-Purpose System, the H-2D anti-submarine helicopter; hangar and flight deck re enlarged. Cost is approximately $1 000 000 per ship or LAMPS modification.

MISSILES. Installation of Sea Sparrow Basic Point Defence Missile System (BPDMS) launcher on all ships f this class began in 1971. This provides a close-range, nti-aircraft missile capability. In addition, some ships re being fitted to fire the Standard interim surface-to-urface missile from the ASROC launcher fitted forward f the bridge structure. Two of the eight "cells" in the ASROC launcher are modified to fire a single Standard. Cost is approximately $400 000 per ship for BPDMS and $750 000 for Standard missile modification.
hrough 1973 the BPDMS installed in DE 1062, 1064, 067, 1071, 1072, 1075, and 1077; modified NATO BPDMS installed for evaluation in *Downes.*

NOMENCLATURE. The lead ship of this class is named or naval historian Dudley W. Knox (the DD 742 was named for Frank Knox who was secretary of the Navy rom 1940 to 1944). The *Harold E. Holt* honours the ate Prime Minister of Australia, a firm supporter of U.S. policy in Southeast Asia during the Vietnam War. The *Jesse L. Brown* remembers the first US naval aviator of the Negro race; he was killed in action during the Korean War.
The DE 1073 originally was named *Conolly*; changed on 12 May 1971.

BAGLEY (DE 1069) *1972, United States Navy*

STATUS. These ships are considerably behind schedule partially because of shipyard labour strikes and delays in Navy acceptance. The Fiscal Year 1964 ships are taking $2\frac{1}{2}$ to 4 years to build; some FY 1965 ships were not laid down until 1970, more than four years after the FY 1964 ships.
These ships have been criticised by some authorities as being inferior to their foreign contemporaries. Critics note the delay in providing variable depth sonar and a helicopter capability, the minimal gun armament, and the use of conventional propulsion vice gas turbines or combination diesel-gas turbines.

TORPEDOES. Improved ASROC-torpedo reloading capability as in some ships of previous "Garcia" class (note slanting face of bridge structure immediately behind ASROC "pepper box"). Four Mk 32 torpedo tubes are fixed in the amidships structure, two to a side angled out at 45 degrees. The arrangement provides improved loading capability over exposed triple Mk 32 torpedo tubes.

AYLWIN (DE 1081) *PH1 James A. Warren* *1972, United States Navy*

Ocean Escorts—*continued*

10 ESCORT SHIPS (DE): "GARCIA" CLASS

Name	*No*	*Builder*	*Laid down*	*Launched*	*Commissioned*
*GARCIA	DE 1040	Bethlehem Steel (San Francisco)	16 Oct 1962	31 Oct 1963	21 Dec 1964
*BRADLEY	DE 1041	Bethlehem Steel (San Francisco)	17 Jan 1963	26 Mar 1964	15 May 196
*EDWARD McDONNELL	DE 1043	Avondale Shipyards	1 Apr 1963	15 Feb 1964	15 Feb 196
*BRUMBY	DE 1044	Avondale Shipyards	1 Aug 1963	6 June 1964	5 Aug 196
*DAVIDSON	DE 1045	Avondale Shipyards	30 Sep 1963	2 Oct 1964	7 Dec 196
*VOGE	DE 1047	Defoe Shipbuilding Co	21 Nov 1963	4 Feb 1965	25 Nov 196
*SAMPLE	DE 1048	Lockheed SB & Construction Co	19 July 1963	28 Apr 1964	23 Mar 196
*KOELSCH	DE 1049	Defoe Shipbuilding Co	19 Feb 1964	8 June 1965	10 June 196
*ALBERT DAVID	DE 1050	Lockheed SB & Construction Co	29 Apr 1964	19 Dec 1964	19 Oct 196
*O'CALLAHAN	DE 1051	Defoe Shipbuilding Co	19 Feb 1964	20 Oct 1965	13 July 196

Displacement, tons	2 620 standard; 3 400 full load
Length, feet (*metres*)	414·5 (*126·3*) oa
Beam, feet (*metres*)	44·2 (*13·5*)
Draft, feet (*metres*)	24 (*7·3*)
Guns	2—5 in (*127 mm*) 38 calibre dual-purpose
A/S weapons	1 ASROC 8-tube launcher 2 triple torpedo tubes (Mk 32) facilities for small helicopter
Main engines	1 geared turbine (Westinghouse); 35 000 shp; 1 shaft
Boilers	2—1 200 psi (*83·4 kg/cm²*) (Foster Wheeler)
Speed, knots	27
Complement	247

These ships exceed many of the world's destroyers in size and ASW capability, but are designated escort ships by virtue of their single propeller shaft and limited speed. The DE 1040 and DE 1041 were authorised in the Fiscal Year 1961 new construction programme DE 1043-1045 in FY 1962, and DE 1047-1051 in FY 1963.
All ten ships are active.

CLASSIFICATION. Hull numbers DE 1039, DE 1042, and 1046 were assigned to frigates built overseas for Portugal.

DESIGN. These ships are an enlargement of the previous "Bronstein" design. They have a flush deck, radically raked stem, stem anchor, and mast and stack combined into a "mack" structure. Anchors are mounted at stem and on portside, just forward of 5 inch gun. Fitted with gyrostabilising fins.

ELECTRONICS. Bow-mounted SQS-26 AXR sonar in DE 1040-1045; SQS-26 BX sonar in DE 1046-1051. SPS-40 and SPS-10 search radar antennas on "mack". The *Voge* and *Koelsch* have been fitted with a specialised ASW Naval Tactical Data System (NTDS).

ENGINEERING. These ships have an advanced "pressure-fired steam generating plant" which generates 70 percent more power than previous steam plants of the same size and weight. Each boiler has an integrated supercharger and associated control system which provides automatic regulation of fuel, air, and water. The boilers can use JP-5 jet fuel or diesel oil which facilitates boiler maintenance and cleaning, and ballasting empty fuel tanks with sea water. Finally, fewer engineering personnel are required to operate the plant.
A small auxiliary boiler is provided to supply steam when in port. Special noise-reduction features are provided.

HELICOPTERS. The Drone Anti-Submarine Helicopter (DASH) programme was cut back before these ships were provided with helicopters. Reportedly, only the *Bradley* actually operated with DASH.
These ships are scheduled to be eventually fitted to operate the Light Airborne Multi-Purpose System (LAMPS), now the SH-2D helicopter.

MISSILES. The *Bradley* was fitted with a Sea Sparrow Basic Point Defense Missile System (BPDMS) in 1967-1968; removed for installation in the carrier *Forrestal*. The BPDMS "pepperbox" was fitted between funnel and after 5 inch mount.

TORPEDOES. Most of these ships were built with two Mk 25 torpedo tubes built into their transom for launching wire-guided ASW torpedoes. However, they have been removed from the earlier ships and deleted in the later ships. The *Voge* and later ships have automatic ASROC reload system (note angled base of bridge structure behind ASROC "pepper box" in these ships).

O'CALLAHAN (DE 1051) — *1970, United States Navy, PHC T. J. Taylor*

EDWARD McDONNELL (DE 1043) — *1970, United States Navy, PHC Frederick Gotauco*

SAMPLE (DE 1048) — *1970, United States Navy*

Ocean Escorts—*continued*

1 ESCORT RESEARCH SHIP (AGDE): "GLOVER" TYPE

·isplacement, tons	2 643 standard; 3 426 full load
·ength, feet (*metres*)	414·5 (*126·3*) oa
·eam, feet (*metres*)	44·2 (*13·5*)
·raft, feet (*metres*)	14·5 (*4·3*)
·uns	1—5 in (*127 mm*) 38 calibre dual purpose
·/S weapons	1 ASROC 8-tube launcher 2 triple torpedo tubes (Mk 32) facilities for small helicopter
·ain engines	1 geared turbine (Westinghouse); 35 000 shp; 1 shaft
·oilers	2—1 200 psi (*83·4 kg/cm²*) (Foster Wheeler)
·peed, knots	27
·omplement	227 (14 officers, 213 enlisted men) plus 38 civilian technicians

Name	No.	Builder	Laid down	Launched	Commissioned
·**GLOVER**	AGDE 1 (ex-AG 163)	Bath Iron Works	29 July 1963	17 Apr 1965	13 Nov 1965

·he *Glover* was built to test an advanced hull design and ·ropulsion system, much the same as the *Albacore* ·AGSS 569) embodied advanced submarine design ·oncepts. However, unlike the *Albacore* the *Glover* has full combat capability.

·he ship was originally authorised in the Fiscal Year 1960 ·ew construction programme, but was postponed and ·- introduced in the FY 1961 programme. Estimated ·onstruction cost was $29 330 000.

·ESIGN. The *Glover* has a massive bow sonar dome ·ntegral with her hull and extending well forward ·nderwater; another "pod" or "nacelle" aft supports ·ounter-rotating propellers mounted on a single shaft. ·bove the waterline the *Glover* is almost identical to the ·Garcia" class escort ships.

·o reload capability for ASROC because of space ·equirements for equipment and technical personnel.

·LECTRONICS. The *Glover* has bow-mounted SQS-26 ·XR active sonar, hull-mounted SQR-13 Passive/Active ·etection and Location (PADLOC) sonar, and SQS-35 Independent Variable Depth Sonar (IVDS) lowered from the stern.

SPS-40 and SPS-10 search radars are fitted on the "mack" structure.

The ship has a prototype tactical assignment console that integrates signals from the three sonars and radars to present combined and coordinated tactical situation presentations in the Combat Information Centre (CIC). Reportedly, the tactical assignment console increases the combat effectiveness of the ship to a considerable extent.

PHOTOGRAPH. Stern configuration differs from "Garcia" class escort ships.

GLOVER (AGDE 1) — *1969, United States Navy PHAN T. R. Hearsum*

GLOVER (AGDE 1) — *1968, United States Navy*

2 ESCORT SHIPS (DE): "BRONSTEIN" CLASS

·isplacement, tons	2 360 standard; 2 650 full load
·ength, feet (*metres*)	371·5 (*113·2*) oa
·eam, feet (*metres*)	40·5 (*12·3*)
·raft, feet (*metres*)	23 (*7·0*)
·uns	3—3 inch (*76 mm*) 50 calibre AA (twin forward, single aft)
·/S weapons	1 ASROC 8-tube launcher 2 triple torpedo tubes (Mk 32) facilities for small helicopter
Main engines	1 geared turbine (De Lavel); 20 000 shp; 1 shaft
Boilers	2 (Foster Wheeler)
Speed, knots	26
Complement	220

Name	No.	Builder	Laid down	Launched	Commissioned
·**BRONSTEIN**	DE 1037	Avondale Shipyards	16 May 1961	31 Mar 1962	15 June 1963
·**McCLOY**	DE 1038	Avondale Shipyards	15 Sep 1961	9 June 1962	21 Oct 1963

These two ships may be considered the first of the "second generation" of post-World War II escort ships which are comparable in size and ASW capabilities to conventional destroyers. The *Bronstein* and *McCloy* have several features such as hull design, large sonar, and ASW weapons that subsequently were incorporated into the mass-produced "Garcia", "Brooke", and "Knox" classes.

Both ships were built under the Fiscal Year 1960 new construction programme by Avondale Shipyards in Westwego, Louisiana.

DESIGN. These ships have a sharply raked stem, stem anchor, and mast and stacks combined in a "mack" structure. Position of stem anchor and portside anchor (just forward of gun mount) necessitated by large bow sonar dome. Note the deckhouse adjacent to "mack" in photograph of *McCloy*.

ELECTRONICS. SQS-26 bow-mounted sonar installed. SPS-40 and SPS-10 search radars mounted on "mack".

McCLOY (DE 1038) — *1971, United States Navy, PHC F. W. Gotauco*

Ocean Escorts—*continued*

USS McCLOY (DE 1038) — *1972, United States Navy*

BRONSTEIN (DE 1037) — ***United States Navy***

3 ESCORT SHIPS (DE): "CLAUD JONES" CLASS

Displacement, tons	1 450 standard; 1 750 full load
Length, feet (*metres*)	310 (*95·0*) oa
Beam, feet (*metres*)	37 (*11·3*)
Draft, feet (*metres*)	18 (*5·5*)
Guns	1 or 2—3 inch (*76 mm*) 50 cal AA see *Armament* notes
A/S weapons	2 triple torpedo tubes (Mk 32)
Main engines	4 diesels (Fairbanks Morse); 9 200 bhp; 1 shaft
Speed, knots	22
Complement	175 (15 officers, 160 enlisted men)

Name	*No.*	*Builder*	*Laid down*	*Launched*	*Commissioned*
***CLAUD JONES**	DE 1033	Avondale Marine Ways, Inc	1 June 1957	27 May 1958	10 Feb 195
***CHARLES BERRY**	DE 1035	Avondale Marine Ways, Inc	29 Oct 1958	17 Mar 1959	25 Nov 195
***McMORRIS**	DE 1036	Avondale Marine Ways, Inc	5 Nov 1958	26 May 1959	4 Mar 196

These diesel-powered escorts were built in an effort to develop an economical DE suitable for mass production, however, they cannot carry the sonar and weapons necessary to cope with modern submarines.

The *Claud Jones* was authorised in the Fiscal Year 1956 shipbuilding programme and the *Charles Berry* and *McMorris* in the FY 1957 programme. The two later ships originally were ordered from the American Shipbuilding Co (Lorain, Ohio) but were completed by Avondale Marine Ways.

ARMAMENT. **As built these ships each had two 3 inch guns (single closed mount forward and open mount aft), two ahead-firing hedgehog launchers, two torpedo tubes (Mk 32), and one depth charge rack. The *Charles Berry* and *McMorris* had their hedgehogs removed and were fitted with the Norwegian-developed Terne III ASW missile launcher from 1961 to 1964. Fixed torpedo tubes removed from all ships and triple torpedo launchers installed. After 3 inch gun and depth charge rack** removed from *Charles Berry* to compensate for weight o variable depth sonar.

DESIGN. These are the only diesel-powered destroyer-type ships built by the US Navy since World War II. They have aluminium superstructure tripod mast forward and pole mast amidships, and two funnels. Note that *McMorris* has a deckhouse between funnels.

ELECTRONICS. These ships have SPS-10 and SPS-6 or SPS-12 search radars. SQS-29/32 hull-mounted sonars; variable depth sonar has been removed.

CLAUD JONES (DE 1033) — *1971, United States Navy, PH1 D. M. Dreher*

TRANSFER

John R. Perry (DE 1034) transferred to Indonesia on 20 Feb 1973.

PHOTOGRAPHS. Note unusual twin stack configuration, unique to US ocean escort ships. The *Charles Berry* retains the deckhouse between the forward gun and bridge. All now have built-up section between funnels as in *McMorris*. Note small after mast and the electronic antenna between funnels.

Ocean Escorts—*continued*

CHARLES BERRY (DE 1035) *1971, United States Navy*

McMORRIS (DE 1036) ***1969, United States Navy by PH2 B. M. Laurich***

7 ESCORT SHIPS (DE): "DEALEY" AND "COURTNEY" CLASSES

Displacement, tons	1 450 standard; approx 1 900 full load
Length, feet (*metres*)	314·5 (*95·9*) oa
Beam, feet (*metres*)	36·8 (*11·2*)
Draft, feet (*metres*)	13·6 (*4·2*)
Guns	2—3 inch (*76 mm*) 50 calibre AA (twin)
A/S weapons	2 triple torpedo tubes (Mk 32) helicopter facilities in DE 1021-1026
Main engines	1 geared turbine (De Laval); 20 000 shp; 1 shaft
Boilers	2 (Foster Wheeler)
Speed, knots	25
Complement	approx 165 (15 officers, 150 enlisted men)

Name	*No.*	*Builder*	*Laid down*	*Launched*	*Commissioned*
***HAMMERBERG**	DE 1015	Bath Iron Works Corpn	12 Nov 1953	20 Aug 1954	2 Mar 1955
***COURTNEY**	DE 1021	Defoe SB Co, Bay City, Mich	2 Sep 1954	2 Nov 1955	24 Sep 1956
***LESTER**	DE 1022	Defoe SB Co, Bay City, Mich	2 Sep 1954	5 Jan 1956	14 June 1957
***EVANS**	DE 1023	Puget Sound B & D Co	8 Apr 1955	14 Sep 1955	14 June 1957
***BRIDGET**	DE 1024	Puget Sound B & D Co	19 Sep 1955	25 Apr 1956	24 Oct 1957
***BAUER**	DE 1025	Bethlehem, San Francisco	1 Dec 1955	4 June 1957	21 Nov 1957
***HOOPER**	DE 1026	Bethlehem, San Francisco	4 Jan 1956	1 Aug 1957	18 Mar 1958

These ships, originally two similar classes totalling 13 units, were the US Navy's first post-World War II escort ships.
DE 1006 authorised in the Fiscal Year 1952 shipbuilding programme; DE 1015 in FY 1953; DE 1021 and DE 1022 in FY 1954; DE 1023-1027 in FY 1955. The *Dealey* cost an estimated $15 000 000.
The *Evans*, *Bridget*, *Bauer* and *Hooper* are operational Naval Reserve training ships. The others are in commission.

ARMAMENT. As built each ship mounted four 3 inch guns (twin closed mount forward, twin open mount aft), one weapon Able/Alfa rocket launcher two torpedo tubes (Mk 32), and depth charge racks and projectors. Fixed torpedo tubes have been replaced in all ships by two triple torpedo launchers; depth charge racks removed from most ships. Weapon Alfa rocket launcher removed in late 1960s.

CLASSIFICATION. Hull numbers DE 1007-1013 were assigned to "Le Normand" class (Type E-52)) frigates built in French shipyards with US funds; DE 106-1019 were "Le Corse" class (Type E-50) frigates built in France with US funds; DE 1020 and DE 1031 "Centauro" class frigates built in Italian yards with US funds; DE 1032 was built in an Italian yard for Portugal (*Pero Escobar*). The ships were officially transferred to foreign navies upon completion.

DESIGN. These ships differ radically from the "destroyer escorts" (DE) built by the US Navy during World War II They have all aluminium superstructures, lattice masts to support extensive electronic antennas, and are single-screw ships. Originally intended for mass production in wartime. Light displacement is 1 280 tons.

ELECTRONICS. These ships have SPS-6 and SPS-10 search radars on their lattice mast.
Hull mounted sonars differ; the *Courtney*, *Lester*, and *Hammerberg* have variable depth sonar (note stern equipment in photographs).

MODERNISATION. These ships have been extensively modernised since completion. Three basic configurations remain: (1) ships with accommodation for escort division or squadron staff without helicopter deck (as *Courtney*); (2) ships with staff provisions and helicopters hangar and flight deck (as *Hammerberg* and *Lester*); and (3) ships with no staff spaces but with helicopter hangar and flight deck (as *Bauer*). Note level of triple Mk 32 torpedo tubes in *Bauer*.

NOMENCLATURE. *Hooper* ex-*Gatch*, was renamed on 19 July 1956.

DISPOSALS AND TRANSFERS
Van Voorhis (DE 1028), **Joseph K. Taussig** (DE 1030) stricken on 1 July 1972; **Cromwell** (DE 1014) stricken on 5 July 1972; **Dealey** (DE 1006) transferred to Uruguay on 5 July 1972; **John Willis** (DE 1027) stricken on 7 July 1972; **Hartley** (DE 1029) transferred to Colombia on 8 July 1972.

Ocean Escorts—*continued*

HAMMERBERG (DE 1015) *1972, United States Navy*

COURTNEY (DE 1021) *1970, US Navy, PHCS Walter H. Long*

LESTER (DE 1022) *1970, US Navy, J. R. Andrews*

BAUER (DE 1025) *1969, US Navy, PH1 D. Nichols*

Ocean Escorts—*continued*

18 RADAR PICKET ESCORT SHIPS (DER): CONVERTED "EDSALL" CLASS

Displacement, tons: 1 590 standard; 1 850 full load
Length, feet (*metres*): 306 (*93·3*) oa
Beam, feet (*metres*): 36·6 (*11·1*)
Draft, feet (*metres*): 14 (*4·3*)
Guns: 2—3 inch (*76 mm*) 50 cal AA (single) 2—20 mm AA in *Calcaterra* and *Thomas J. Gary*
A/S weapons: 2 triple torpedo tubes (Mk 32) in most ships; 1 trainable hedgehog (Mk 15) depth charge tack (depth charge rack removed from *Calcartera* and *Thomas J. Gary*; hedgehog removed from *Calcaterra*).
Main engines: 4 diesels (Fairbanks Morse), 6 000 bhp; 2 shafts
Speed, knots: 21
Complement: 169 (19 officers, 150 enlisted men)

Name	No.	Builder	Launched	Commissioned
*CALCATERRA	DER 390	Brown SB Co, Houston	16 Aug 1943	17 Nov 1943
CHAMBERS	DER 391	Brown SB Co, Houston	17 Aug 1943	22 Nov 1943
DURANT	DER 389	Brown SB Co, Houston	3 Aug 1943	16 Nov 1943
FALGOUT	DER 324	Consolidated Steel Corpn	24 July 1943	15 Nov 1943
FINCH	DER 328	Consolidated Steel Corpn	28 Aug 1943	13 Dec 1943
HISSEM	DER 400	Brown SB Co, Houston	26 Dec 1943	13 Jan 1944
KIRKPATRICK	DER 318	Consolidated Steel Corpn	5 June 1943	23 Oct 1943
KRETCHMER	DER 329	Consolidated Steel Corpn	31 Aug 1943	13 Dec 1943
LANSING	DER 388	Brown SB Co, Houston	3 Aug 1943	10 Nov 1943
MILLS	DER 383	Brown SB Co, Houston	26 May 1943	12 Oct 1943
OTTERSTETTER	DER 244	Brown SB Co, Houston	19 Jan 1943	6 Aug 1943
PRICE	DER 332	Consolidated Steel Corpn	30 Oct 1943	12 Jan 1944
RAMSDEN	DER 382	Brown SB Co, Houston	24 May 1943	19 Oct 1943
RHODES	DER 384	Brown SB Co, Houston	29 June 1943	25 Oct 1943
ROY O. HALE	DER 336	Consolidated Steel Corpn	20 Nov 1943	3 Feb 1944
SAVAGE	DER 386	Brown SB Co, Houston	15 July 1943	29 Oct 1943
*THOMAS J. GARY	DER 326	Consolidated Steel Corpn	21 Aug 1943	27 Nov 1943
VANCE	DER 387	Brown SB Co, Houston	16 July 1943	1 Nov 1943

Thirty-six ships of this type were converted to radar picket ships between 1951 and 1958; redesignated DER (See *Conversion* notes). Eleven of these ships were on loan to the US Coast Guard from 1951 to 1954 (they retained Navy names and were designated WDE with hull numbers upped by one hundred to avoid confusion with Coast Guard numbering series: DE 322-325, 328, 331, 334, 382, 387-389 and 391.)

Several ships were used in Operation MARKET TIME in the South China Sea and Gulf of Tonkin to halt Communist infiltration of men and arms to South Vietnam; while engaged in MARKET TIME several ·50 calibre machineguns are mounted.

All in reserve except *Kretchmer* and *Thomas J. Gary* which are active; *Calcaterra* was to decommission in 1973.

ARMAMENT. Upon conversion to radar picket ships these ships were fitted with six 20 mm guns; subsequently removed. See "Edsall" class listing for details of original DE configuration.
Forward 3 inch mount is enclosed; after mount open or enclosed, depending upon availability.

CONVERSION. Conversion to radar picket escorts included removal of conventional torpedo tubes and 40 mm guns; installation of mess compartment on main deck and other habitability improvements; fitting of two tripod masts to support radar antennas and TACAN navigation "bee-hive" antenna; installation of SPS-8 height-finding radar antenna atop after deckhouse; combat information centre (CIC) expanded and improved; and aluminium superstructure installed. Note trainable hedgehog fitted in "B" position in place of second 3 inch mount. TACAN and SPS-8 removed from active ships when seaward radar picket barrier was ended in 1965. (Photograph of *Mills* shows full-array configuration). The DERs in service during the latter 1960s had SPS-28 and SPS-10 or SPS-8 radar antennas on their forward mast; and electronic warfare "pods" on after mast.

ENGINEERING. Maximum operational speed for remaining ships is about 19 knots.

DISPOSALS AND TRANSFERS (since 1 Jan 1970)
Camp (DER 251) transferred to South Vietnam on 13 Feb 1971; **Forster** (DER 334) transferred to South Vietnam on 25 Sep 1971. **Blair** (DER 317), **Sturtevant** (DER 239), **Joyce** (DER 317), **Strickland** (DER 313) stricken on 1 Dec 1972.

CALCATERRA (DER 390) — *1970, US Navy.*

MILLS (DER 383) — *1964, United States Navy*

2 RADAR PICKET ESCORT SHIPS (DER): CONVERTED "JOHN C. BUTLER" CLASS

Displacement, tons: 1 745 standard; 2 100 full load
Length, feet (*metres*): 306 (*93·3*) oa
Beam, feet (*metres*): 36·6 (*11·2*)
Draft, feet (*metres*): 11 (*3·4*)
Guns: 2—5 in (*127 mm*) 38 cal DP
A/S weapons: 1 trainable hedgehog (Mk 15) depth charge rack
Main engines: 2 geared turbines (Westinghouse) 12 000 shp; 2 shafts
Boilers: 2 (Babcock & Wilcox)
Speed, knots: 24
Complement: 187

Name	No	Builder	Laid down	Launched	Commissioned
VANDIVIER	DER 540	Boston Naval Shipyard	8 Nov 1943	27 Dec 1943	1 Dec 1955
WAGNER	DER 539	Boston Naval Shipyard	8 Nov 1943	27 Dec 1943	31 Dec 1955

These two ships were begun as standard Destroyer Escorts (DE); construction suspended in 1946. Work resumed in 1954 and they were completed as Radar Picket Escort Ships (DER) at the Boston Naval Shipyard. Light displacement 1 260 tons. Both ships are in reserve.

ENGINEERING. These are the US Navy's only steam-driven radar picket escort ships; all others have diesel propulsion.

PHOTOGRAPH. Note tripod masts, TACAN navigation "bee-hive" antenna on after mast and SPS-8 height-finding radar antenna atop after deckhouse.

VANDIVIER (DER 540) — *United States Navy*

Ocean Escorts—*continued*

5 ESCORT SHIPS (DE): "JOHN C. BUTLER" CLASS

Displacement, tons	1 350 standard; 2 100 full load
Length, feet (*metres*)	306 (*93·3*) oa
Beam, feet (*metres*)	36·6 (*11·3*)
Draft, feet (*metres*)	11 (*3·4*)
Guns	2—5 inch (*127 mm*) 38 cal DP (single); 2 to 8—40 mm AA (twin)
A/S weapons	1 hedgehog, depth charge racks
Main engines	2 geared turbines (General Electric or Westinghouse); 12 000 shp; 2 shafts
Boilers	2 (Babcock & Wilcox or Combustion Engineering)
Speed, knots	24
Complement	190

Name	*No.*	*Builder*	*Launched*	*Commissioned*
DUFILHO	DE 423	Brown SB Co, Houston	9 Mar 1944	21 July 1944
EDMONDS	DE 406	Brown SB Co, Houston	17 Dec 1943	3 Apr 1944
FRENCH	DE 367	Consolidated Steel Corpn, Orange	17 June 1944	9 Oct 1944
HOWARD F. CLARK	DE 533	Boston Naval Shipyard	8 Nov 1943	25 May 1944
LE RAY WILSON	DE 414	Brown SB Co, Houston	28 Jan 1944	10 May 1944

EDMONDS (DE 406) *1959, United States Navy*

These ships were originally rated as Destroyer Escorts (DE). All surviving ships of this type are in reserve.

ARMAMENT. Designed armament for this class was two 5 inch guns, ten 40 mm guns (one quad, three twin), six 20 mm guns, and one bank of three 21 inch torpedo tubes. (With full armament the designed wartime complement was 15 officers and 207 enlisted men.)

CONVERSIONS. The *Wagner* (DE 539) and *Vandivier* (DE 540) of this type were completed as radar picket ships and are listed separately.

DESIGN. This class is officially the WGT design group, the WGT symbol indicating geared turbine drive.

DISPOSALS (since 1 Jan 1970)
John C. Butler (DE 339), **Joseph E. Connolly** (DE 450) stricken on 1 June 1970; **John L. Williamson** (DE 370) stricken on 15 Sep 1970; **Conklin** (DE 439) stricken on 1 Oct 1970; **Gentry** (DE 349), **Lloyd E. Acree** (DE 356), **La Prade** (DE 409), **Kendall C. Campbell** (DE 443) stricken on 15 Jan 1972; **Key** (DE 348), **Rombach** (DE 364), **Goss** (DE 444), **Gilligan** (DE 508) stricken on 1 Mar 1972; **Richard W. Suesens** (DE 342), **Mack** (DE 358), **Pratt** (DE 363), **Stafford** (DE 411), **Oliver Mitchell** (DE 417) stricken on 15 Mar 1972.
Raymond (DE 341), **Kenneth Willett** (DE 354), **Johnnie Hutchins** (DE 360), **Melvin Norman** (DE 416), **Tabberer** (DE 418), **Robert F. Keller** (DE 419), **Chester T. O'Brien** (DE 421), **Edward H. Allen** (DE 531), stricken on 1 July 1972; **Rizzi** (DE 537), **Osberg** (DE 538), stricken on 1 Aug 1972; **O'Flaherty** (DE 340), **Edwin A. Howard** (DE 346), **Doyle C. Barnes** (DE 353), **George E. Davies** (DE 357), **Rolf** (DE 362), **Dennis** (DE 405), **Lawrence C. Taylor** (DE 415), **Leland E. Thomas** (DE 420), **Corbesier** (DE 438), **William Seiverling** (DE 441), **Hanna** (DE 449), **Silverstein** (DE 534), stricken on 1 Dec 1972.

ESCORT SHIPS (DE): "RUDDEROW" CLASS

All escort ships of the "Rudderow" (TEV) class have been stricken. See 1972-1973 and previous editions for characteristics. Ships of this class serve in the navies of South Korea and Taiwan China.

DISPOSALS (since 1 Jan 1970)
Coates (DE 685) stricken on 30 Jan 1970; **Parle** (DE 708) stricken on 1 July 1970; **Leslie L. B. Knox** (DE 580) stricken on 15 Jan 1972; **McNulty** (DE 581) stricken on 11 Feb 1972; **Tinsman** (DE 589) stricken on 15 May 1972; **Hodges** (DE 231), **Thomas F. Nickel** (DE 587) stricken on 1 Dec 1972.

3 ESCORT SHIPS (DE): "BOSTWICK" CLASS

Displacement, tons	1 240 standard; 1 900 full load
Length, feet (*metres*)	306 (*93·3*) oa
Beam, feet (*metres*)	36·6 (*11·2*)
Draft, feet (*metres*)	14 (*4·3*)
Guns	3—3 inch (*76 mm*) 50 cal AA (single); up to 6—40 mm AA (twin); several 20 mm AA
A/S weapons	1 hedgehog; depth charges
Main engines	Diesel-electric (4 General Motors diesels); 6 000 bhp; 2 shafts
Speed, knots	21
Complement	150

Name	*No*	*Builder*	*Launched*	*Commissioned*
LEVY	DE 162	Federal SB & DD Co, Pt Newark	28 Mar 1943	13 May 1943
STRAUB	DE 181	Federal SB & DD Co, Pt Newark	18 Sep 1943	25 Oct 1943
TRUMPETER	DE 180	Federal SB & DD Co, Pt Newark	18 Sep 1943	25 Oct 1943

ACREE (DE 167) stricken in 1972 *United States Navy*

These ships originally were rated as Destroyer Escorts (DE). When built they were known as the "Cannon" class, but after the first three ships (DE 99-101) were transferred to Brazil upon completion in 1944-1945 and the fourth ship (DE 102) went to China in 1948 the design has been referred to as the "Bostwick" class for the DE 103, the "first" US Navy ship.
All surviving ships of this class in the US Navy are in reserve. See "Transfer" notes for the several navies that now operate ships of this class. See 1971-1972 and previous editions for disposals.

ARMAMENT. Designed armament for this class was three 3 inch guns, six 40 mm guns (three twin), several 20 mm guns, and a bank of three 21 inch torpedo tubes. Torpedo tubes removed and light AA guns reduced. (With full armament the designed wartime complement was 15 officers and 201 enlisted men.)

DESIGN. This class is officially the DET design group the DET symbol indicating diesel-electric tandem motor drive.

TRANSFERS. Ships of this class currently serve in the navies of Brazil, France, Greece, Italy, Japan, South Korea, Peru, the Philippines, Taiwan China, Thailand, and Uruguay.

PHOTOGRAPH. The *Acree* is shown with her triple torpedo tube mount, and two 40 mm AA guns and eight 20 mm AA guns in addition to her main battery of three 3 inch AA guns. This was her World War II armament as the ship was decommissioned on Apr 1, 1946; the ship has been in reserve since that time.

DISPOSALS (since 1 Jan 1970)
Parks (DE 165), **Acree** (DE 167), **Cooner** (DE 172), **Coffman** (DE 191) stricken on 1 July 1972; **McConnell** (DE 163) stricken on 1 Oct 1972; **Osterhaus** (DE 164) stricken on 1 Nov 1972.

Ocean Escorts—*continued*

4 ESCORT SHIPS (DE): "BUCKLEY" CLASS

Displacement, tons	1 400 standard; 2 170 full load
Length, feet (*metres*)	306 (*93·3*) oa
Beam, feet (*metres*)	37 (*11·3*)
Draft, feet (*metres*)	14 (*4·3*)
Guns	2 or 3—3 inch (*76 mm*) 50 cal AA (single); up to 8—40 mm AA per ship (removed entirly from some ships)
A/S weapons	1 hedgehog; depth charge racks
Main engines	Turbo-electric drive (General Electric turbines); 12 000 shp; 2 shafts
Boilers	2
Speed, knots	23·5
Complement	180

Name	*No.*	*Builder*	*Launched*	*Commissioned*
GENDREAU	DE 639	Bethlehem, San Francisco	12 Dec 1943	17 Mar 1944
GUNASON	DE 795	Consolidated Steel Corpn, Orange	16 Oct 1943	1 Feb 1944
MARSH	DE 699	Defoe Co, Bay City, Mich	29 Jan 1943	12 Jan 1944
WISEMAN	DE 667	Dravo Corpn, Pittsburgh	6 Nov 1943	4 Apr 1944

These ships were originally rated as Destroyer Escorts (DE). Forty-six ships of this type were transferred to the Royal Navy in 1944 under the Lend-Lease where they served as frigates; six of these ships were lost and the remainder were returned to the United States and scrapped.
All surviving ships of this class are in reserve.

ARMAMENT. Designed armament for this class was three 3 inch guns, six 40 mm guns (three twin), several 20 mm guns, and one bank of three 21 inch torpedo tubes. During 1945, 11 ships were fitted with a 5 inch main battery in lieu of 3 inch guns. Torpedo tubes removed and 40 mm and 20 mm weapons reduced. (With full armament the designed wartime complement was 15 officers and 198 enlisted men).
All surviving ships have 3 inch guns.

CONVERSIONS. Fifty ships of this type were converted to high speed transports (see Amphibious Warfare ships).

DESIGN. This class is officially the TE design group, the TE symbol indicating turbine-electric drive with 3 inch guns.

ENGINEERING. The *Marsh* and *Wiseman*, have been modified to provide electrical power to shore activities and each has two large reels for power cables amidships.

MARSH (DE 699) (Power transmission) *United States Navy*

DISPOSALS (since 1 Jan 1970)
J. Douglas Blackwood (DE 219) stricken on 30 Jan 1970; **Alexander J. Luke** (DE/DER 577) stricken on 1 May 1970 (target); **Cronin** (DE 704) stricken on 1 June 1970 (target); **Fieberling** (DE 640), **William C. Cole** (DE 641), **Damon M. Cummings** (DE 643), **Splanger** (DE 696) stricken on 1 Mar 1972; **Coolbaugh** (DE 217), **Frank M. Robinson** (DE 220) stricken on 1 July 1972; **Jack W. Wilke** (DE 800) stricken on 1 Aug 1972; **Holton** (DE 703) stricken on 1 Nov 1972; **Eichenberger** (DE 202), **Gillette** (DE 681), **Osmus** (DE 701), **Frybarger** (DE 705), **Major** (DE 796), **Varian** (DE 798) stricken on 1 Dec 1972.

6 ESCORT SHIPS (DE): "EDSALL" CLASS

Displacement, tons	1 200 standard; 1 850 full load
Length, feet (*metres*)	306 (*93·3*) oa
Beam, feet (*metres*)	36·6 (*11·3*)
Draft, feet (*metres*)	11 (*3·4*)
Guns	3—3 inch (*76 mm*) 50 cal AA (2 guns in *Peterson*) (single); up to 8—40 mm AA (removed entirely from some ships)
A/S weapons	1 hedgehog; depth charge rack (see *Conversion* notes)
Main engines	4 diesels (Fairbanks Morse); 6 000 shp; 2 shafts
Speed, knots	21
Complement	149

Name	*No.*	*Builder*	*Launched*	*Commissioned*
CHATELAIN	DE 149	Consolidated Steel Corpn	21 Aug 1943	22 Sep 1943
COCKRILL	DE 398	Brown SB Co, Houston	29 Oct 1943	24 Dec 1943
HUSE	DE 145	Consolidated Steel Corpn	23 Mar 1943	30 Aug 1943
MOORE	DE 240	Brown SB Co, Houston	21 Dec 1942	1 July 1943
PETERSON	DE 152	Consolidated Steel Corpn	15 May 1943	29 Sep 1943
PETTIT	DE 253	Brown SB Co, Houston	28 Apr 1943	23 Sep 1943

These ships were originally rated as Destroyer Escorts. Thirty-six ships of this type have been converted to radar picket ships (DER) and are listed separately.
None of these ships are in commission, all in reserve.

ARMAMENT. Designed armament for this class was three 3 inch guns, eight 40 mm guns (one quad, two twin) several 20 mm guns, and a bank of three 21 inch torpedo tubes. Rearmament with two 5 inch guns in place of the 3 inch battery was planned but not carried out. Torpedo tubes removed after World War II and anti-aircraft guns reduced in some ships. (With full armament the designed wartime complement was 15 officers and 201 enlisted men).

CONVERSIONS. The *Peterson* was modified to a special ASW configuration in 1951-1952; two trainable hedgehogs fitted in the "B" position forward of the bridge, additional sonar installed, and a short second mast fitted; all light AA guns were removed. She was decommissioned in April 1965.

DESIGN. This class is officially the FMR design group, the FMR symbol indicating Fairbanks Morse diesel with reverse gear drive.

DISPOSALS (since 1 Jan 1970)
Stanton (DE 247) stricken on 1 Dec 1970; **Jacob Jones** (DE 130), **Pope** (DE 134), **J. R. Y. Blakeley** (DE 140), **Poole** (DE 151), **J. Richard Ward** (DE 243), **Sloat** (DE 245), **Marchland** (DE 249), **Menges** (DE 320), **Mosley** (DE 321), **Pride** (DE 323), **Dale W. Peterson** (DE 337) stricken on 2 Jan 1971; **O'Reilly** (DE 330), **Daniel** (DE 335) stricken on 15 Jan 1971; **Merrill** (DE 392) stricken on 2 Apr 1972; **Herbert C. Jones** (DE 137), **Neunzer** (DE 150), **Swenning** (DE 394(, **Willis** (DE 395), **Janssen** (DE 396), **Stockdale** (DE 399 stricken on 1 July 1972; **Hammann** (DE 131), **Douglas L. Howard** (DE 138), **Farquhar** (DE 139), **Hill** (DE 141), **Inch** (DE 146), **Stewart** (DE 238), stricken on 1 Oct 1972; **Keith** (DE 241), **Tomich** (DE 242), **Swasey** (DE 248), **Ricketts** (DE 254) stricken on 1 Nov 1972; **Hurst** (DE 250) stricken on 1 Dec 1972.

HUSE (DE 145) *Skyphotos*

PETERSON (DE 152) *United States Navy*

FIRE SUPPORT SHIPS

The ships listed in this section are those suitable only for gunfire and rocket support of amphibious landings and other coastal operations because of their lack of advanced anti-aircraft, anti-submarine, and command and control capabilities. Under the official (administrative) classification list the battleships and cruisers are rated as Surface Combatants.

As of mid-1973 only one fire support ship remained in commission, the heavy cruiser *Newport News*. Plans to decommission *Newport News* have been postponed. There now are no plans to provide the active Fleet with additional ships armed with guns larger than 5 inch calibre and the two active 6 inch gunned cruiser-flagships, carrying a total of six guns (half of the armament of one Soviet "Sverdlov" class cruiser), are expected to be decommissioned during the later 1970s.

BATTLESHIPS. The battleship *New Jersey* was decommissioned in 1969 after making one deployment to the Western Pacific in the role of fire support ship. She remains on the Navy List in reserve, moored near her sister ship *Missouri* at the Puget Sound Naval Shipyard Bremerton, Washington. The two other battleships of the "Iowa" class, the *Iowa* and *Wisconsin*, remain in reserve at the Philadelphia Naval Shipyard.

CRUISERS. Several all-gun cruisers armed with 8 inch guns remain in reserve in addition to the gun-missile cruisers *Boston* and *Canberra*. These ships are listed here because of their limited capabilities for performing missions other than gunfire support. The *Boston* and *Canberra* have been reclassified as heavy cruisers (CA vice CAG) because of the limited effectiveness of their Terrier BW missiles for task force defence.

FIRE SUPPORT SHIPS. Plans developed during the mid-1960s to design and construct a new class of landing force support ships (designated LFS) have been deferred indefinitely. A request for funding of contract definition under the Fiscal Year 1970 budget was denied by the Congress.

The proposed LFS would have combined in one hull an armament of large calibre guns and possibly rocket launchers. The guns were to provide long-range, accurate, and high destructive fire while the rockets would provide saturation fire. The LFS main battery would be three 8 inch Major Calibre Light Weight Guns (MCLWG) that would fire conventional and rocket-assisted projectiles, the latter expected to have a range of more than 50 miles. The ship would have had a relatively large magazine capacity, probably 750 to 800 rounds per 8 inch gun barrel. Secondary gun armament was to be two 5 inch rapid fire guns for close-in support missions and self-defence (possibly supplemented in the latter role by point-defence missiles).

Detailed characteristics of the ship had not been developed; however, Navy officials told *Jane's Fighting Ships* that they expected the ship to displace about 8 000 tons full load, have an overall length of 400 to 500 feet, and be capable of speeds in excess of 20 knots to permit an LFS to accompany post-war amphibious assault ships. The inshore fire support ships (LFR), former medium landing ships—rocket (LSMR), are listed with Amphibious warfare ships (L-designation).

PHOTOGRAPHS. The photograph below shows the *New Jersey* in action off the coast of South Vietnam in April 1969, firing some of the last rounds to be fired by a battleship. At bottom are two sister dreadnoughts mothballed at Philadelphia. Prior to 1967 the *New Jersey* had been anchored between them. The carrier *Antietam* (CVS 36) is at far left.

4 BATTLESHIPS (BB): "IOWA" CLASS

Name	*No.*	*Builder*	*Laid down*	*Launched*	*Commissioned*
IOWA	BB 61	New York Navy Yard	27 June 1940	27 Aug 1942	22 Feb 1943
NEW JERSEY	BB 62	Philadelphia Navy Yard	16 Sep 1940	7 Dec 1942	23 May 1943
MISSOURI	BB 63	New York Navy Yard	6 Jan 1941	29 Jan 1944	11 June 1944
WISCONSIN	BB 64	Philadelphia Navy Yard	25 Jan 1941	7 Dec 1943	16 Apr 1944

Displacement, tons	45 000 standard; 59 000 full load
Length, feet (*metres*)	860 (*262·1*) wl; 887·2 (*270·4*) oa except *New Jersey* 887·6 (*270·5*)
Beam, feet (*metres*)	108·2 (*33·0*)
Draft, feet (*metres*)	38 (*11·6*)
Guns	9—16 inch (*406 mm*) 50 cal. 20—5 inch (*127 mm*) 38 cal. dual purpose. several 40 mm guns in all except *New Jersey*
Main engines	4 geared turbines (General Electric in BB 61 and BB 63; Westinghouse in BB 62 and BB 64; 212 000 shp; 4 shafts
Boilers	8 (Babcock & Wilcox)
Speed, knots	33 (all have reached 35 knots in service)
Complement	designed complement varied, averaging 169 officers and 2 689 enlisted men in wartime; *New Jersey* was manned by 70 officers and 1 556 enlisted men (requirements reduced with removal of all light anti-aircraft weapons, floatplanes, and reduced operational requirements) in 1968-1969

These ships were the largest battleships ever built except for the Japanese *Yamato* and *Musashi* (64 170 tons standard, 863 feet overall, 9—18·1 inch guns.) All four "Iowa" class ships were in action in the Pacific during World War II, primarily screening fast carriers and bombarding amphibious invasion objectives. Three were mothballed after the war with the *Missouri* being retained in service as a training ship. All four ships again were in service during the Korean War (1950-1953) as shore-bombardment ships; all mothballed 1954-1958.

The *New Jersey* began reactivation in mid-1967 at a cost of approximately $21 000 000; recommissioned on 6 Apr 1968. The *Iowa* and *Wisconsin* remained in reserve at the Philadelphia Naval Shipyard where the *New Jersey* had been berthed and reactivated; and the mothballed *Missouri* at the Puget Sound Naval Shipyard, Bremerton, Washington.

The *New Jersey* was again decommissioned on 17 Dec 1969 and mothballed at Bremerton with the *Missouri*. Two additional ships of this class were laid down, but never completed: *Illinois* (BB 65), laid down 15 Jan 1945, and *Kentucky* (BB 66), laid down 6 Dec 1944. The *Illinois* was 22 percent complete when cancelled on 11 Aug 1945. The *Kentucky* was 69·2 percent complete when construction was suspended late in the war; floated from its building dock on 20 Jan 1950. Conversion to a missile ship (BBG) was proposed, but no work was undertaken and she was stricken on 9 June 1958 and broken up for scrap.

Approximate construction cost was $114 485 000 for *Missouri*; other ships cost slightly less.

AIRCRAFT. As built, each ship carried three floatplanes for scouting and gunfire spotting and had two quarterdeck catapults. Catapults removed and helicopters carried during the Korean War.

ARMOUR. These battleships are the most heavily armoured US warships ever constructed, being designed to survive ship-to-ship combat with enemy ships armed with 16 inch guns. The main armour belt consists of Class A steel armour 12·1 inches thick tapering vertically to 1·62 inches; a lower armour belt aft of Turret No. 3 to protect propeller shafts is 13·5 inches; turret faces are 17 inches; turret tops are 7·25 inches; turret backs are 12 inches; barbetts have a maximum of 11·6 inches of armour; second deck armour is 6 inches; and the three-level conning tower sides are 17·3 inches with an armoured roof 7·25 inches (the conning tower levels are pilot house, navigation bridge, and flag-signal bridge).

NEW JERSEY (BB 63) *1969, United States Navy*

WISCONSIN (BB 64), IOWA (BB 61) *United States Navy*

Fire Support Ships—*continued*

"IOWA" CLASS *continued*

DESIGN. These ships carried heavier armament than previous US battleships and had increased protection and larger engines accounting for additional displacement and increased speed. Design includes clipper bow and long foredeck, with graceful sheer (see photographs). All fitted as fleet flagships with additional accommodations and bridge level for admiral and staff.

ELECTRONICS. During 1968-1969 the *New Jersey* was fitted with SPS-10 and SPS-12 search radars.

GUNNERY. The Mk VII 16 inch guns in these ships fire projectiles weighing up to 2 700 pounds (*1 225 kg*) (armour piercing) a maximum distance of 23 miles (*39 km*). As built, these ships had 80—40 mm and 49 to 60—20 mm anti-aircraft guns (except *Iowa*, only 19 quad 40 mm mounts); all 20 mm guns removed and a reduced number of 40 mm weapons remain on the mothballed ships. During 1968-1969 the *New Jersey* was fitted with two Mk 34 fire control directors in addition to the two Mk 56 and four Mk 37 previously installed. Mk 48 shore bombardment computer installed when reactivated.

NOMENCLATURE. US battleships are generally named for states; the exception was the *Kearsarge*, BB 5 launched in 1899 (later *Crane Ship No. 1*, AB 1). Beginning in 1969 the Navy has named frigates for states.

OPERATIONAL. The *New Jersey* made one deployment to the Western Pacific during her third (1968-1969) commission.
During the deployment she was on the "gun line" off South Vietnam for a total of 120 days with 47 days being the longest sustained period at sea.
While on the "gun line" the *New Jersey* fired 5 688 rounds of ammunition from her 16 inch main battery guns and a total of 6 200 rounds during the commission, the additional firings being for tests and training. While off Vietnam she also fired some 15 000 rounds from her 5 inch secondary battery guns.
(In comparison, during World War II the *New Jersey* fired 771 main battery rounds and during two deployments in the Korean War and midshipmen training cruises she fired 6 671 main battery rounds.)

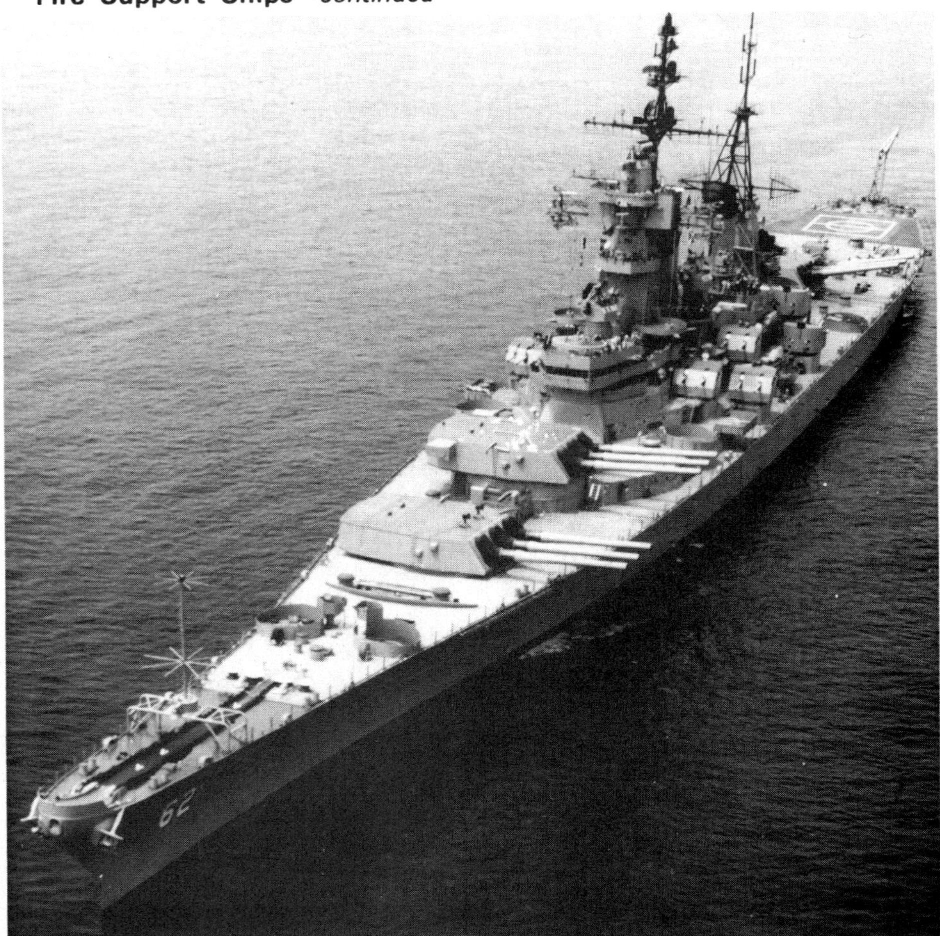

NEW JERSEY (BB 62) *1968, United States Navy*

NEW JERSEY (BB 62) *1968, United States Navy*

BOSTON (CA 69)—See following page *1968, United States Navy*

Fire Support Ships—*continued*

2 HEAVY CRUISERS (CA): "BOSTON-CANBERRA" TYPE (ex-CAG)

Name	*No.*	*Builder*	*Laid down*	*Launched*	*Commissioned*	*CAG Comm.*
BOSTON	CA 69 (ex-CAG 1)	Bethlehem Steel Co (Quincy)	30 June 1941	26 Aug 1942	30 June 1943	1 Nov 1955
CANBERRA	CA 70 (ex-CAG 2)	Bethlehem Steel Co (Quincy)	3 Sep 1941	19 Apr 1943	14 Oct 1943	15 June 1956

Displacement, tons	13 300 standard; 17 500 full load
Length, feet (*metres*)	664 (*222·3*) wl; 673·5 (*205·3*) oa
Beam, feet (*metres*)	70·8 (*21·6*)
Draft, feet (*metres*)	26 (*7·9*)
Missile launchers	2 twin Terrier launchers
Guns	6—8 inch (*203 mm*) 55 cal (triple) 10—5 inch (*127 mm*) 38 DP (twin) 8—3 inch (*76 mm*) 50 cal AA (twin)
Main engines	4 geared turbines (General Electric), 120 000 shp; 4 shafts
Boilers	4 (Babcock & Wilcox)
Speed, knots	33
Complement	1 273 (73 officers; 1 200 enlisted men)

These were the US Navy's first guided missile warships. Originally heavy cruisers (CA) of the "Baltimore" class. Converted 1952-1956 to combination gun-missile configuration and reclassified CAG on 4 Jan 1952. Subsequently reclassified as CA on 1 May 1968, reverting to original hull numbers. They both retained Terrier missile armament but their early BW-1 missile systems were no longer considered suitable for task force defence against high-performance aircraft.
Retention of 8 inch guns forward made these ships valuable in the fire support role during the Vietnamese conflict.

The *Boston* was decommissioned on 5 May 1970 and placed in reserve and the *Canberra* was decommissioned on 16 Feb 1970 and placed in reserve.

CONVERSION. Both ships were converted to a missile configuration at the New York Shipbuilding Corp. Camden, New Jersey. *Boston* conversion ordered on 4 Dec 1951 and *Canberra* on 28 Jan 1952. Conversion included removal of after 8-inch gun turret (143 tons) and after twin 5-inch mount; all 40 mm and 20 mm guns replaced by six 3-inch twim mounts (subsequently reduced to four mounts). Superstructure modified and twin funnels replaced by single large funnel (as in "Oregon City" class cruisers). Forward pole mast replaced by lattice radar mast and radar platform fitted aft of second polemast. Missile system installation includes rotating magazines below decks, loading and check-out equipment, and two large directors aft. Estimated conversion cost was $30 000 000 for the two ships.

ELECTRONICS. The *Boston* has exnerimental, three-dimensional air search radar on forward mast (topped by TACAN); a similar antenna was removed from the *Canberra* in mid-1968. Both ships have an SPS-43 search radar antenna atop pole mast and an SPS-30 antenna on platform aft of pole mast.

BOSTON (CA 69) *1968, United States Navy*

MISSILES. Reportedly, each ship carries 144 missiles in two rotating magazines. Each launcher can load and fire two missiles every 30 seconds; loading is completely automatic with missiles sliding onto launchers in the vertical position.

NOMENCLATURE. The *Canberra* was originally named *Pittsburgh*; she was renamed while under construction to honour an Australian cruiser of that name which was sunk with several US Navy Ships in the Battle of Savo Island in August 1942. She is the only US warship named for a foreign capital city.

PHOTOGRAPHS. Twin 3-inch gun mounts abaft missile directors have been removed from both ships. The photographs of the *Boston*, taken in 1968, show her still carrying the "1" of her late CAG 1 designation. Note only the *Canberra* has a helicopter "platform" (angled in on starboard side to provide for boat stowage). The photograph of the *Boston* on the previous page shows her firing away from camera at North Vietnamese coastal craft.

CANBERRA (CA 70) *1968 United States Navy*

DES MOINES (CA 134)—see following page *United States Navy*

Fire Support Ships—*continued*

3 HEAVY CRUISERS (CA): "SALEM" CLASS

Displacement, tons	17 000 standard; 21 500 full load
Length, feet (*metres*)	700 (*213·4*) wl; 716·5 (*218·4*) oa
Beam, feet (*metres*)	76·3 (*23·3*)
Draft, feet (*metres*)	26 (*7·9*)
Guns	9—8 inch (*203 mm*) 55 cal (triple) 12—5 inch (*127 mm*) 38 cal DP (twin) 4—3 inch (*76 mm*) 50 cal AA (twin) in *Newport News*; 20—3 inch guns in others (see *Gunnery* notes)
Main engines	4 geared turbines (General Electric); 120 000 shp; 4 shafts
Boilers	4 (Babcock & Wilcox)
Speed, knots	33
Complement CA 148	approx 1 200

Name	*No.*	*Builder*	*Laid down*	*Launched*	*Commissioned*
DES MOINES	CA 134	Bethlehem Steel Co (Quincy)	28 May 1945	27 Sep 1946	17 Nov 1948
SALEM	CA 139	Bethlehem Steel Co (Quincy)	4 June 1945	25 Mar 1947	9 May 1949
***NEWPORT NEWS**	CA 148	Newport News SB & DD Co	1 Oct 1945	6 Mar 1947	29 Jan 1949

NEWPORT NEWS (CA 148) *1967, United States Navy,*

NEWPORT NEWS (CA 148) *1967, United States Navy*

These ships were the largest and most powerful 8 inch-gun cruisers ever built. Completed too late for World War II, they were employed primarily as flagships for the Sixth Fleet in the Mediterranean and the Second Fleet in the Atlantic. The *Salem* was decommissioned on 30 Jan 1959 and the *Des Moines* on 14 July 1961. The *Newport News*, normally flagship of the second Fleet was employed as a fire support ship off Vietnam in 1967-1968; with the Spanish *Canarias* this is the only heavy cruiser in service in any Western navy.

Periodic plans to decommission the *Newport News* during the past few years have been delayed to retain the ship's "big gun" capability in the Fleet.

The ship's No. 2 main battery was damaged in an accidental explosion in 1972; not repaired, giving the ship only six useable 8-inch guns.

AIRCRAFT. As completed the *Des Moines* had two stern catapults and carried four floatplanes; catapults removed.

DESIGN. These ships are an improved version of the previous "Oregon City" class. The newer cruisers have automatic main batteries, larger main turrets, taller fire control towers, and larger bridges. The *Des Moines* and *Newport News* are fully air conditioned.

Nine additional ships of this class were cancelled: the *Dallas* (CA 140) and the unnamed CA 141-142, CA 149-153.

ELECTRONICS. The *Newport News* has an SPS-37 search radar antenna and TACAN on her forward mast, and SPS-8 and SPS-6 antennas on her after mast. (The small antenna on the forward mast is an SPS-10).

GUNNERY. These cruisers were the first ships to be armed with fully automatic 8 inch guns firing cased ammunition. The guns can be loaded at any elevation from —5 to +41 degrees; rate of fire is four times faster than earlier 8 inch guns. Mk XVI 8-inch guns in these ships; other heavy cruisers remaining on Navy List have Mk XV guns.

As built these ships mounted 12 5 inch guns, 24 3 inch guns (in twin mounts), and 12 20 mm guns (single mounts). The 20 mm guns were removed almost immediately and the 3 inch battery was reduced gradually as ships were overhauled. (With full armament the designed wartime complement was 1 860).

MODERNISATION. The *Newport News* has been extensively modified to provide improved flagship facilities; note elaborate antennas on masts, forecastle, atop turrets, and on stern crane; superstructure extended outwards on both sides between forward 3 inch twin mounts and secondary battery directors; only two 3 inch twin mounts remain (alongside bridge).

1 HEAVY CRUISER (CA): "OREGON CITY" CLASS

Displacement, tons	13 700 standard; 17 500 full load
Length, feet (*metres*)	664 (*202·4*) wl; 673·5 (*205·3*) oa
Beam, feet (*metres*)	70·9 (*21·6*)
Draft, feet (*metres*)	26 (*7·8*)
Guns	9—8 inch (*203 mm*) 55 cal (triple) 12—5 inch (*127 mm*) 38 cal DP (twin) 20—3 inch (*127 mm*) 50 cal AA (twin)
Main engines	4 geared turbines (General Electric); 120 000 shp; 4 shafts
Boilers	4 (Babcock & Wilcox
Speed, knots	33
Complement	1 700 (designed wartime)

Name	*No.*	*Builder*	*Laid down*	*Launched*	*Commissioned*
ROCHESTER	CA 124	Bethlehem Steel Co (Quincy)	29 May 1944	28 Aug 1945	20 Dec 1946

ROCHESTER (CA 124) *United States Navy*

This ship is similar in design to the earlier "Baltimore" class but with a single funnel and a more compact superstructure. Three ships of this class were completed the *Albany* (CA 123) was converted to guided missile cruiser (CG 10) in 1958-1962; the *Oregon City* (CA 122) has been stricken; the *Rochester* has been in mothballs since 1961.

AIRCRAFT. As completed the *Rochester* had two stern catapults and carried four floatplanes; catapults removed.

DESIGN. This cruiser is almost identical in design to the "Baltimore" class except for the superstructure.

Seven additional ships of this class were cancelled; the *Northampton* (CA 125) *Cambridge* (CA 126) *Bridgeport* (CA 127), *Kansas* (CA 128), *Tulsa* (CA 129), *Norfolk* (CA 137) and *Scranton* (CA 138); the *Northampton* was later re-ordered as a command ship (CLC 1, now CC 1).

GUNNERY. This class was designed to mount nine 8 inch guns, 12 5 inch guns, 48 40 mm guns (11 quad and two twin mounts), and 24 20 mm guns. Lighter weapons replaced by twin 3 inch mounts in *Rochester*

DISPOSAL

Oregon City (CA 122) stricken on 1 Nov 1970.

Fire Support Ships—*continued*

7 HEAVY CRUISERS (CA): "BALTIMORE" CLASS

Displacement, tons	13 600 standard; 17 200 full load
Length, feet (*metres*)	664 (*204·4*) wl; 673·5 (*205·3*) oa
Beam, feet (*metres*)	70·9 (*21·6*)
Draft, feet (*metres*)	26 (*7·9*)
Guns	9—8 inch (*203 mm*) 55 cal (triple) 12—5 inch (*127 mm*) 38 cal DP (twin) except 10 guns in *Saint Paul* up to 20—3 inch (*76 mm*) 50 cal DP (twin) (see *Gunnery* notes) except 48—40 mm AA in *Quincy*
Main engines	4 geared turbines (General Electric); 120 000 shp; 4 shafts
Boilers	4 (Babcock & Wilcox)
Speed, knots	33
Complement	1 146 (61 officers, 1 085 enlisted men) in *Saint Paul*; designed wartime complement 1 772 in *Quincy*; 1 969 in later ships

Name	*No.*	*Builder*	*Laid down*	*Launched*	*Commissioned*
QUINCY	CA 71	Bethlehem Steel Company, Quincy	9 Oct 1941	23 June 1943	15 Dec 1943
PITTSBURG	CA 72	Bethlehem Steel Company, Quincy	3 Feb 1943	22 Feb 1944	10 Oct 1944
ST. PAUL	CA 73	Bethlehem Steel Company, Quincy	3 Feb 1943	16 Sep 1944	17 Feb 1945
HELENA	CA 75	Bethlehem Steel Company, Quincy	9 Sep 1943	28 Apr 1945	4 Sep 1945
BREMERTON	CA 130	New York Shipbuilding Corporation	1 Feb 1943	2 July 1944	29 Apr 1945
TOLEDO	CA 133	New York Shipbuilding Corporation	13 Sep 1943	6 May 1945	27 Oct 1946
Ex-LOS ANGELES	CA 135	Philadelphia Naval Shipyard	28 July 1943	20 Aug 1944	22 July 1945

Fourteen ships of this class were completed; four of the ships have been converted to guided missile cruisers: the *Boston* (CA 69/CAG 1), *Canberra* (CA 70/CAG 2), *Columbus* (CA 74, now CG 12), and *Chicago* (CA 136, now CG 11). The remaining all-gun cruisers were phased out of the active fleet as missile ships became available. The *Quincy* in 1954, *Pittsburg* in 1955, *Helena* in 1963, *Bremerton* in 1960, *Toledo* in 1960, *Los Angeles* in 1966, and *Saint Paul* in 1971.

AIRCRAFT. As completed these ships had two stern catapults and carried four floatplanes; catapults removed after World War II.

GUNNERY. These ships were completed with nine 8 inch guns, 12—5 inch guns, 48—40 mm guns (12 quad mounts in CA 68-71, 11 quad and two twin mounts in later ships), and 23—20 mm guns. All 20 mm weapons were removed and the 40 mm guns were replaced by 20—3 inch guns (twin mounts) in all above ships but the *Quincy*. The number of 3 inch guns was reduced subsequently in some ships before they were mothballed. (The *Helena* had only 14—3 inch guns when decommissioned; the *Saint Paul* retained only 12). The *Saint Paul* also lost the twin 5 inch mount forward of her bridge. Prior to being decommissioned the *Saint Paul* used rocket-assisted 8 inch projectiles during shore bombardment firing in the Vietnam conflict; reportedly, her guns attained a range of 34 miles (approx 60 000 yards), believed to be the longest distance ever fired by a naval gun. It can not be ascertained if this is the maximum range possible with the ship's guns that have been modified to fire the rocket-assisted projectiles that weigh some 113 pounds.

MODERNISATION. The *Saint Paul*, *Helena*, and *Los Angeles* have been modified to improve their flagship facilities; advanced electronic equipment fitted and pole foremast replaced by a pylon mast to support additional antennae including "bee-hive" TACAN (Tactical Air Navigation system to guide aircraft). The *Saint Paul's* main radar antennae are an SPS-37 forward and an SPS-8 aft; the *Helena* had a large SPS-43 antenna forward when decommissioned.

NOMENCLATURE. Ships renamed during construction were *Quincy*, ex-*Saint Paul*; *Pittsburg*, ex-*Albany*; *Saint Paul*, ex-*Rochester*; and *Helena*, ex-*Des Moines*.
CA 135 name cancelled on 25 May 1971 to permit assignment to SSN 688.

DISPOSALS
Macon (CA 132) stricken on 1 Nov 1969; **Baltimore** (CA 68) stricken on 15 Feb 1971; **Fall River** (CA 131) stricken on 19 Feb 1971.

All US heavy cruisers of pre-World War II construction and all light cruisers (CL) and light anti-aircraft cruisers (CLAA) have been stricken. See 1971-1972 edition for compilation of strike dates of CL-CLAA ships retained into the post-war era. Six "Cleveland" class light cruisers converted to hermaphrodite gun-missile ships (CLG) are listed in this edition as Surface Combatants. Several light crusiers of the pre-World War II "Brooklyn" and "St. Louis" classes remain in service with Argentina, Brazil, and Chile.

SAINT PAUL (CA 73) — *1967, United States Navy*

SAINT PAUL (CA 73) — *1966, United States Navy*

HELENA (CA 75) — *United States Navy*

COMMAND AND COMMUNICATION SHIPS

This category consists of the command and communication ships operated in support of national and joint US commands. These are different functions than fleet and amphibious command ships that support essentially Navy or Navy-Marine Corp activities.

The only joint command flagship now in commission is the *La Salle* which serves as flagship for the Commander. US Middle East Force who represents US military interests "East of Suez" to the Straits of Malacca. The Commander US Middle East Force is generally a Rear Admiral.

In reserve are two ships configured to serve as afloat command posts for the President or other national authorities and two communication relay ships. The command ships *Northampton* and *Wright* were designated as National Emergency Command Posts Afloat (NECPA) and operated off the Atlantic coast of the United States, prepared to receive the President or other national authorities.

The major communication relay ships *Arlington* and *Annapolis* were operated by the Navy to provide mobile communication facilities for Navy and other service commanders where shore-based communication facilities were inadequate or did not exist. While the command ships *Northampton* and *Wright* are floating command headquarters and their communication facilities are for transmitting and receiving large volumes of voice and teletype communications (as well as electronic data), the communication relay ships *Annapolis* and *Arlington* are equipped to relay large volumes of teletype communications. Further, the two radio relay ships do not have the command centres, theatres, data display facilities, message centres, and staff accommodations that are the keys to the command ships' capabilities.

1 MISCELLANEOUS FLAGSHIP (AGF): CONVERTED AMPHIBIOUS TRANSPORT DOCK

Name	*No.*	*Builder*	*Laid down*	*Launched*	*Commissioned*
***LA SALLE**	AGF 3 (ex-LPD 3)	New York Naval Shipyard	2 Apr 1962	3 Aug 1963	22 Feb 1964

Displacement, tons	8 040 light; 13 900 full load
Length, feet (*metres*)	500 (*152·0*) wl; 521·8 (*158·4*) oa
Beam, feet (*metres*)	84 (*25·6*)
Draft, feet (*metres*)	21 (*6·4*)
Guns	8—3 inch (*76 mm*) 50 cal AA (*twin*)
Main engines	Steam turbines; 24 000 shp; 2 shafts
Boilers	2
Speed, knots	20 sustained; 23 maximum
Complement	387 (18 officers, 369 enlisted men)
Flag accommodations	59 (12 officers, 47 enlisted men)

The *La Salle* serves as flagship for the US Commander Middle East Force, operating in the Persian Gulf, Arabian Sea, and Indian Ocean; the ship is based at Bahrain. She replaced the *Valcour* (AGF 1) in 1972.

Converted in 1972 with elaborate command and communications facilities being installed; accommodations provided for admiral and staff; additional air conditioning fitted; painted white to help retard heat of Persian Gulf area. Reclassified as a flagship and designated AGF 3 on 1 July 1972 (the designation AGF 2 not used because of ship's previous "3" hull number).

DESIGN. The *La Salle* is a former amphibious transport dock (LPD) of the "Raleigh" class. Authorised in Fiscal Year 1961 new construction programme she served as an amphibious ship from completion until 1972.

DISPOSAL

Valcour (AGF 1, ex-AVP 55) stricken in 1972. All other AVP-type ships stricken from Navy List (see 1971-1972 and previous editions for description and disposals); two ships of this type remain in service with the US Coast Guard.

LA SALLE (AGF 3) *1972, United States Navy*

LA SALLE (AGF 3) *1972, United States Navy*

1 COMMAND SHIP (CC): CONVERTED HEAVY CRUISER

Name	*No.*	*Builder*	*Laid down*	*Launched*	*Commissioned*
NORTHAMPTON	CC 1 (ex-CLC 1, ex-CA 125)	Bethlehem Steel Co (Quincy)	31 Aug 1944	27 Jan 1951	7 Mar 1953

Displacement, tons	14 700 standard; 17 200 full load
Length, feet (*metres*)	664 (*202·4*) wl; 676 (*206·0*) oa
Beam, feet (*metres*)	71 (*21·6*)
Draft, feet (*metres*)	29 (*8·8*)
Guns	1—5 in (*127 mm*) 54 cal dual-purpose (see *Gunnery* notes)
Helicopters	2 normally carried
Armour	Side 6 in (*152 mm*); Decks 3 in + 2 in (*76 + 51 mm*)
Main engines	4 geared turbines (General Electric); 120 000 shp; 4 shafts
Boilers	4 (Babcock & Wilcox)
Speed, knots	33
Complement	1 191 (68 officers, 1 123 enlisted men)
Flag accommodations	approx 450

The *Northampton* was begun as a heavy cruiser of the "Oregon City" class, numbered CA 125. She was cancelled on 11 Aug 1945 when 56·2 per cent complete. She was re-ordered as a command ship on 1 July 1948 and designated CLC 1 (Task Force Command Ship and later Tactical Command Ship). As CLC 1 she was configured for use primarily by fast carrier force commanders and fitted with an elaborate combat information centre (CIC), electronic equipment, and flag accommodations. She was largely employed as flagship for Commander Second Fleet in the Atlantic prior to her being made available for use by national authorities. Her designation was changed to CC (Command Ship) on 15 April 1961 and she was relieved as Second Fleet flagship on October 1961.

Decommissioned on 8 April 1970 and placed in reserve.

DESIGN. The *Northampton* is one deck higher than other US heavy cruisers to provide additional office and equipment space. Her foremast is the tallest unsupported mast afloat (125 feet). All living and working spaces are air-conditioned. Helicopter landing area aft, but no hangar.

ELECTRONICS. Advanced communications, electronic data processing equipment, and data displays are installed; tropospheric scatter and satellite relay communications facilities. As CLC 1 the *Northampton* carried what was believed the largest radar antenna afloat (see 1968-69 and earlier editions); designated SPS-2; removed in 1963. SPS-37 and SPS-8A search radar antennas on after tower.

Command and Communication Ships—*continued*

"NORTHAMPTON" Type—*continued*

GUNNERY. As built the *Northampton* mounted 4—5 inch and 8—3 inch weapons. The 5 inch guns were Mk 16 54 calibre weapons capable of firing up to 45 rounds per minute. (Similar weapons are installed in US destroyer-type ships built since World War II.) The original 3 inch 50 calibre guns in open twin mounts were replaced by twin 3 inch/70 calibre rapid-fire guns in closed mounts. The latter were removed in 1962 because of high maintenance requirements; removal of the guns and their ammunition hoists, *et cetera*, provided additional space for berthing, offices, and electronic equipment. When decommissioned she was armed with only one 5 inch gun in the "X" position.

OPERATIONAL. The *Northampton* served as flagship of the US Sixth Fleet in the Mediterranean in 1954-1955, and as flagship of the US Second Fleet in the Western Atlantic from 1955 to 1961.

PHOTOGRAPHS. Penultimate configuration shown below; forward 5 inch gun and gun director above bridge subsequently removed. See 1972-1973 edition for later photograph.

NORTHAMPTON (CC 1) *United States Navy*

1 COMMAND SHIP (CC)
1 MAJOR COMMUNICATIONS RELAY SHIP (AGMR) } CONVERTED AIRCRAFT CARRIERS

Name	*No.*	*Builder*	*Laid down*	*Launched*	*CVL Comm*	*CC-AGMR Comm.*
WRIGHT	CC 2 (ex-AVT 7, ex-CVL 49)	New York SB Corp	21 Aug 1944	1 Sep 1945	9 Feb 1947	11 May 1963
ARLINGTON (ex-*Saipan*)	AGMR 2 (ex-CC 3, ex-AVT 6, ex-CVL 48)	New York SB Corp	10 July 1944	8 July 1944	14 July 1945	27 Aug 1966

Displacement, tons	14 500 standard; 19 600 full load
Length, feet (*metres*)	664 (*202·4*) wl; 683·6 (*208·4*) oa
Beam, feet (*metres*)	76·8 (*23·6*)
Draft, feet (*metres*)	28 (*8·5*)
Flight deck width, feet (*metres*)	109 (*33·2*)
Guns	*Wright* 8—40 mm anti-aircraft (twin); *Arlington* 8—3 in (*76 mm*) 50 calibre (twin)
Helicopters	5 or 6 carried by *Wright*
Main engines	4 geared turbines (General Electric); 120 000 shp; 4 shafts
Boilers	4 (Babcock & Wilcox)
Speed, knots	33
Complement	746 plus approx 1 000 on command or communications staff

These ships were built as the light carriers *Saipan* (CVL 48) and *Wright* (CVL 49), respectively. They served as experimental and training carriers for a decade before being mothballed in 1967. Both were reclassified as Auxiliary Aircraft Transports on 15 May 1959, being designated AVT 6 (*Saipan*) and AVT 7 (*Wright*). The *Wright* was converted to a command ship at the Puget Sound Naval Shipyard, 1962-1963; the *Saipan* was to have been similarly converted, but the requirement for an additional ship of this category was cancelled. The *Saipan* subsequently was converted to a major communications relay ship at the Alabama Drydock and Shipbuilding Company in 1953-1965, and renamed *Arlington*. See Conversion and Nomenclature notes. The *Arlington* was decommissioned on 14 Jan 1970 and placed in reserve; the *Wright* was similarly decommissioned on 22 May 1970 and placed in reserve.

CONVERSION. The *Wright* was converted to a command ship under the Fiscal Year 1962 authorisation at a cost of $25 000 000. Like the *Northampton*, she is fitted with elaborate communications, data processing, and display facilities for use by national authorities. The command spaces include presentation theatres similar to those at command posts ashore. The *Wright* has the most powerful transmitting antennas ever installed on a ship. They are mounted on plastic-glass masts to reduce interference with electronic transmissions. The tallest mast is 83 feet high and is designed to withstand 100-mph winds. She was reclassified from AVT 7 to CC 2 on 1 Sep 1962.

The *Saipan* was converted to a major communications relay ship at a cost of $26 886 424. She actually began conversion to a command ship (CC 3) and work was halted in February 1964. Work was resumed for her conversion to a communications ship later that year. She is fitted with elaborate communications relay equipment for the support of major commands afloat or ashore. The *Saipan* was reclassified from AVT 6 to CC 3 on 1 Jan 1964, and to AGMR 2 on 3 Sep 1964; she was renamed *Arlington* in April 1965.

WRIGHT (CC 2) *1968, United States Navy*

The flat unencumbered deck of an aircraft carrier-type ship facilitates antenna placement for optimum electro-magnetic wave propagation. The new "Blue Ridge" class of amphibious command ships has a similar appearance.

NOMENCLATURE. The Navy's two communications ships are named for the naval radio stations at Arlington, Virginia, and Annapolis, Maryland.

Command and Communication Ships—*continued*

ARLINGTON (AGMR 2)—See previous page *1967, United States Navy*

1 MAJOR COMMUNICATIONS RELAY SHIP (AGMR): CONVERTED ESCORT CARRIER

Name	*No.*	*Builder*	*Laid down*	*Launched*	*CVE Comm.*	*AGMR Comm*
ANNAPOLIS	AGMR 1 (ex-AKV 39, ex-CVE 107)	Todd Shipyards (Tacoma)	29 Nov 1943	20 July 1944	5 Feb 1945	7 Mar 1964

Displacement, tons	11 473 standard; 22 500 full load
Length, feet (*metres*)	525 (*160·0*) wl; 563 (*171·6*) oa
Beam, feet (*metres*)	75 (*22·9*)
Draft, feet (*metres*)	30·6 (*9·3*)
Flight deck width, feet (*metres*)	106 (*32·5*)
Guns	8—3 in (*76 mm*) 50 calibre anti-aircraft (twin)
Main engines	2 turbines (Allis Chalmers); 16 000 shp; 2 shafts
Boilers	4 (Combustion Engineering)
Speed, knots	18
Complement	710 (44 officers, 666 enlisted men)

The *Annapolis* was built as the escort aircraft carrier *Gilbert Islands* (CVE 107). She was decommissioned on 21 May 1946 and placed in reserve; again active as a CVE from Sep 1951 to Jan 1955 when she was again decommissioned. While in reserve, on 7 May 1959 she was reclassified as a Cargo Ship and Aircraft Ferry (AKV 39). Converted into a communications ship by the New York Naval Shipyard, 1962-1964.
Decommissioned on 20 Dec 1969 and placed in reserve.

CONVERSION. During conversion the ship was fitted with elaborate communications relay equipment including approximately 30 transmitters providing frequency band coverage from low frequency to ultra-high frequency. The power outputs of the transmitters vary from 10 to 10 000 watts. Numerous radio receivers also were installed as were five large antenna towers. The ship was renamed *Annapolis* and reclassified AGMR 1 on 1 June 1963.
The former escort carrier *Vella Gulf* (AKV 11, ex-CVHE 111, ex-CVE 111) was to have been converted to the AGMR 2; her conversion never began because of the availability of the larger carrier *Saipan* for use in this role.

DESIGN. The *Gilbert Islands* was one of 19 "Commencement Bay" class escort carriers built during the latter part of World War II. This ship is the last escort or "jeep" aircraft carrier on the Navy List.

ANNAPOLIS (AGMR 1) *1964 United States Navy*

PHOTOGRAPHS. Note enclosed "hurricane bow" installed during conversion to AGMR to improve rough-sea operation. She has a small helicopter landing area on the port side of the former flight deck.

ANNAPOLIS (AGMR 1) *1966, United States Navy*

AMPHIBIOUS WARFARE SHIPS

The US Navy's amphibious lift capability continues to be reduced although it has been extensively modernised. From a peak Vietnam War strength of about 165 ships of this category three years ago, the US Navy now operate just over 60 ships in this category. These ships are capable of lifting slightly more than three brigade/air group assault teams (about nine rifle battalions plus support, air and logistics element).
All active amphibious ships are of post-World War II construction and capable of a sustained speed of 20 knots. With respect to helicopter assault, all US Navy amphibious ships now have a helicopter platform and many also have hangar and maintenance facilities. Assault, gunship, cargo and medical evacuation ("medevac") helicopters regularly come to roost on their decks. In addition, minesweeping helicopters (RH-53 Sea Stallion) and VSTOL strike aircraft (AV-8A Harrier) will be seen more frequently aboard these ships. The twin-engine, STOL counter-insurgency OV-10A Bronco did conduct "carrier qualification" landings and takeoffs with one of the late "Essex" class assault ships, but the lack of arresting gear and the take-off run required for these planes make regular LPH/LHA operations unlikely.
The amphibious assault ship *Guam* (LPH 9) was modified late in 1971 to serve as an interim sea control ship. The *Guam* began operations to develop sea control ship techniques and doctrine in January 1972. The ship is listed in the section on Surface Combatants.

FIRE SUPPORT SHIPS. The various Surface Combatant Ships (battleships and heavy cruisers) suitable only for gunfire support are listed in a previous section of this edition (Fire Support Ships). The rocket support ships (LFR) are listed in this section because of their L-designations.

TRANSPORT SUBMARINES. The transport submarines of the US Navy are listed in the Submarine section of this edition, in their normal place in the Navy's sequence of hull numbers.

BLUE RIDGE (LCC 19) and MOUNT WHITNEY (LCC 20) *1971, United States Navy, PH1 Claude V. Sneed*

2 AMPHIBIOUS COMMAND SHIPS (LCC): "BLUE RIDGE" CLASS

Displacement, tons	19 290 full load
Length, feet (*metres*)	620 (*188·5*) oa
Beam, feet (*metres*)	82 (*25·3*)
Main deck width, feet (*metres*)	108 (*33*)
Draft, feet (*metres*)	27 (*8·2*)
Guns	4—3 in (*76 mm*) 50 cal AA (twin)
Helicopters	Utility helicopter carried
Main engines	1 geared turbine (General Electric); 22 000 shp; 1 shaft
Boilers	2 (Foster Wheeler)
Speed, knots	20
Complement	732 (52 officers, 680 enlisted men)
Flag accommodation	688 (217 officers, 471 enlisted men)

Name	*No.*	*Builder*	*Laid down*	*Launched*	*Commissioned*
* **BLUE RIDGE**	LCC 19	Philadelphia Naval Shipyard	27 Feb 1967	4 Jan 1969	14 Nov 1970
* **MOUNT WHITNEY**	LCC 20	Newport News SB & DD Co	8 Jan 1969	8 Jan 1970	16 Jan 1971

These are the first amphibious force flagships of post-World War II design. They can provide integrated command and control facilities for sea, air and land commanders in amphibious operations. The *Blue Ridge* was authorised in the Fiscal Year 1965 new construction programme, the AGC 20 in FY 1966. An AGC 21 was planned for the FY 1970 programme but cancelled late in 1968. It was proposed that the last ship combine fleet as well as amphibious force command-control facilities.

CLASSIFICATION. Originally designated Amphibious Force Flagships (AGC); redesignated Amphibious Command Ships (LCC) on 1 Jan 1969.

DESIGN. General hull design and machinery arrangement are similar to the "Iwo Jima" class assault ships.

BLUE RIDGE (LCC 19) *1971, United States Navy*

ELECTRONICS. Fitted with SPS-48 three-dimensional search radar, SPS-40 and SPS-10 search radar, 3 are on "island" structure. After "tower" does not have large antenna sphere originally intended for these ships. (See model photo in 1970-1971 edition.) Tactical Aircraft Navigation (TACAN) pod tops mast.
Both ships fitted with Naval Tactical Data System (NTDS). Antennas adjacent to helicopter landing area swing out for flight operations.

GUNNERY. At one stage of design two additional twin 3 inch mounts were provided on forecastle; subsequently deleted from final designs. Antennas and their supports severely restrict firing arcs of guns.

MOUNT WHITNEY (LCC 20) *1970, Newport News Shipbuilding & Dry Dock Co.*

Amphibious Warfare Ships—*continued*

4 AMPHIBIOUS COMMAND SHIPS (LCC): "MOUNT McKINLEY" CLASS

[D]isplacement, tons	7 510 light; 12 560 full load
[L]ength, feet (*metres*)	435 (*132·2*) wl; 495·3 (*150·5*) oa
[B]eam, feet (*metres*)	63 (*19·2*)
[D]raft, feet (*metres*)	28·2 (*8·5*)
[D]raft, feet (*metres*)	28·2 (*8·5*)
[G]uns	1—5 inch (*127 mm*) 38 cal DP 4—40 mm AA (twin)
[H]elicopters	Utility helicopter carried
[M]ain engines	**1 turbine (General Electric) 6 000 shp; 1 shaft**
[B]oilers	2 (Babcock & Wilcox in AGC 7; Combustion Engineering in others)
[S]peed, knots	16·4
[C]omplement (ship)	517 (36 officers, 486 enlisted men)

Name	No.	Builder	Launched	Commissioned
MOUNT McKINLEY	LCC 7	North Carolina SB Co	27 Sep 1943	1 May 1944
ESTES	LCC 12	North Carolina SB Co	1 Nov 1943	9 Oct 1944
POCONO	LCC 16	North Carolina SB Co	25 Jan 1945	29 Dec 1945
TACONIC	LCC 17	North Carolina SB Co	10 Feb 1945	17 Jan 1946

[A]cquired by the Navy in 1943-1944 while under con[s]truction to Maritime Commission C2-S-AJ1 design. [A]fter 5 inch gun and two twin 40 mm mounts replaced [b]y helicopter platform. The *Pocono* and *Taconic* have [a] single mast aft in lieu of after king post in earlier ships. [A]ll survivors transferred to Maritime Administration [r]eserve (remain on Navy List).

[C]LASSIFICATION. Originally referred to as Auxiliary [C]ombined Operations and Communications Headquarters [S]hips, but designated Amphibious Force Flagships [(]AGC); five surviving ships redesignated Amphibious [C]ommand Ships (LCC) on 1 Jan 1969.

[E]LECTRONICS. The *Mount McKinley* and *Estes* had [a]n SPS-37 search radar antenna on the forward king post [S]PS-30 and SPS-10 antennas on the lattice mast atop [t]he superstructure, and a TACAN antenna installed on [t]he after king post; the *Pocono* and *Taconic* had a TACAN [a]ntenna on the forward king post, SPS-30 and SPS-10 [a]ntennas on the lattice mast atop the superstructure, and [a]n SPS-37 antenna on the after pole mast.

ESTES (LCC 12) *1969, United States Navy*

[D]ISPOSALS
[F]ourteen World War II amphibious force flagships [h]ave been stricken from the Navy List: **Appalachian** [(]AGC 1) on 1 Mar 1959; **Blue Ridge** (AGC 2), **Rocky [M]ount** (AGC 3) on 1 Jan 1960; **Ancon** (AGC 4) on 25 [F]eb 1946; **Catoctin** (AGC 5) on 1 Mar 1959; **Mount [O]lympus** (AGC 8) in 1961; **Wasatch** (AGC 9) on 1 [J]an 1960; **Auburn** (AGC 10), **Panamint** (AGC 13) [i]n late 1960; **Teton** (AGC 14), **Adirondack** (AGC 15) in 1961; **Biscayne** (AGC 18, ex-AVP 11) transferred to US Coast Guard on 19 July 1946. **Eldorado** (AGC/LCC 11) stricken on 16 Nov 1972.
The **Duane** (AGC 6) was retained by the Coast Guard. All except the **Ancon, Duane,** and **Biscayne** were converted C2 merchants hull. Several other Coast Guard cutters served as amphibious command ships with WAGC designations (see "Campbell" class).
The yacht **Williamsburg** (ex-*Aras*, ex-PG 56) was designated AGC 369 in 1945, served as presidential yacht until stricken in 1962 (converted to oceanographic research ship, renamed *Anton Bruun*).

MOUNT WHITNEY (LCC 20)—See previous page *1970, United States Navy*

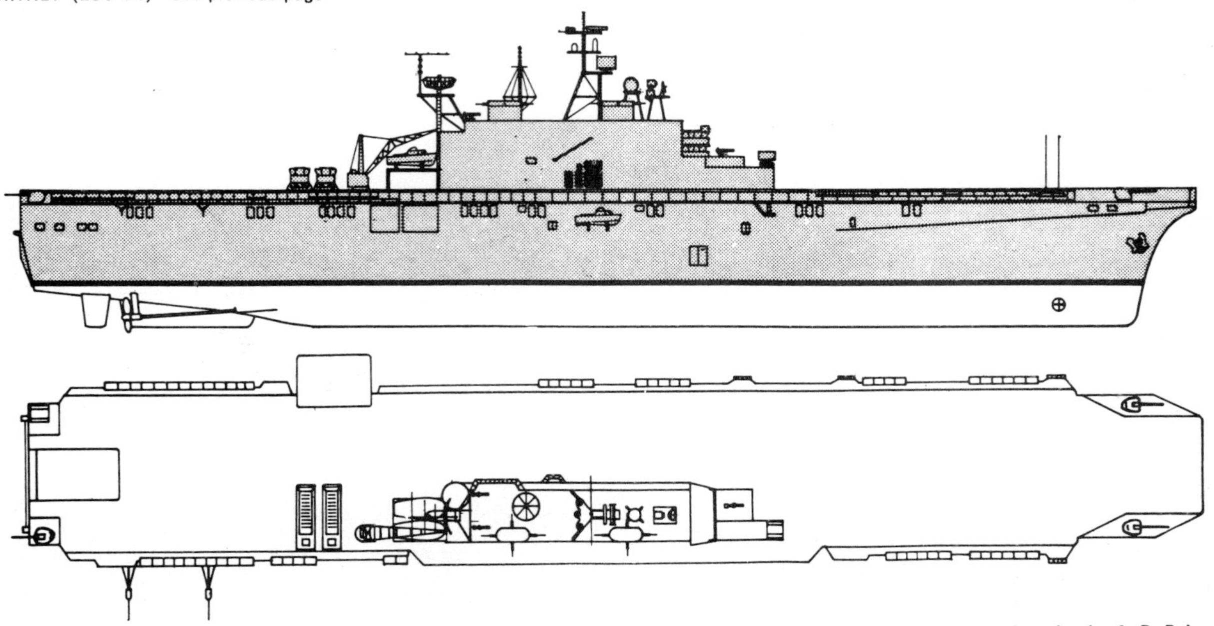

TARAWA Class LHA —See following page

Drawing by A. D. Baker

Amphibious Warfare Ships—*continued*

5 AMPHIBIOUS ASSAULT SHIPS (LHA): "TARAWA" CLASS

Displacement, tons	39 300 full load
Length, feet	820 oa
Beam, feet	106
Draft, feet	27·5
Guns	3—5 inch (*127 mm*) 54 cal DP (single) 6—20 mm AA (single)
Missile launchers	2 Basic Point Defence Missile System (BPDMS) launchers
Aircraft	approx 30 troop helicopters; possibly AV-8 V/STOL close support aircraft in place of some helicopters
Main engines	Geared turbines; 70 000 shp; 2 shafts
Boilers	2
Speed, knots	approx 22 sustained; approx 24 max
Troops	1 825 (163 officers, 1 662 enlisted men)

Name	*No.*	*Start**	*Launch*	*Commission*
TARAWA	LHA 1	15 Nov 1971	Dec 1973	1975
SAIPAN	LHA 2	21 July 1972	mid 1974	1975
PHILIPPINE SEA	LHA 3	July 1973	late 1974	1975
LEYTE GULF	LHA 4	late 1973	1975	1976
KHE SANH	LHA 5	mid 1974	1975	1976

***Erection of first module**

This is a new class of large amphibious warfare ships combining the characteristics of several previous designs including a full-length flight deck, a landing craft docking well, a large garage for trucks and armoured vehicles, and troop berthing for a reinforced battalion. The LHA 1 was authorised in the Fiscal Year 1969 new construction programme, the LHA 2 and LHA 3 in FY 1970, with two additional ships being authorised in FY 1971. The Navy announced on Jan 20, 1971 that four additional ships of this type previously planned would not be constructed. When the contract was awarded for the LHA programme it included a provision that if the last four ships were not built the government would be charged "cancellation fees" of $109 700 000; this charge—more than half the cost of an LHA—was provided in the FY 1972 budget.

Through 1972 approximately $960 000 000 had been appropriated for the five-ship programme (including the $109 000 000 cancellation fee); early in 1973 the Department of Defense requested an additional $192 000 000 for the LHA programme. *Discounting* the cancellation fee, this results in an average cost of approximately $210 000 000 per ship.

All ships of this class are under construction by Litton Systems Inc at a new ship production facility known as "Ingalls West". The new yard, located at Pasagoula, Mississippi, was developed specifically for multi-ship construction of the same design.

Late in 1971 the Navy announced that the LHA design work was behind schedule. Subsequently the Secretary of Defense announced that the ships would be delayed 12 to 16 months.

AMPHIBIOUS ASSAULT SHIP *Artist's concept by G. Meyer*

CONTRACT. These were the first ships to be procured by the US Navy with the acquisition processes known as Concept Formulation, Contract Definition, and Total Package Procurement. The proposals of Litton Systems Inc and two other shipbuilding firms were submitted in response to specific performance criteria related to the ships' mission. The firms submitted detailed designs and cost estimates for series production of not less than five ships of this type. This procurement process subsequently has been abandoned.

DESIGN. The LHA is intended to combine the features of an amphibious assault ship (LPH), amphibious cargo ship (LKA), and amphibious transport dock (LPD) into a single hull. Beneath the flight deck is a half-length hangar deck, the two being connected by an elevator amidships on the port side and a stern lift; beneath the hangar deck is a docking well capable of accommodating four LCU-1610 type landing craft.

Bow thruster provided for holding position while off-loading landing craft.

ELECTRONICS. Radars planned for these ships are the SPS-52 three-dimensional search, and SPS-10 and SPS-40; advanced communications and helicopter navigation equipment provided. Each ship also will have an Integrated Tactical Amphibious Warfare Data System (ITAWDS) to provide computerised support in control of helicopters and aircraft, shipboard weapons and sensors, navigation, landing craft control, and electronic warfare. SPN 35-aircraft navigation radar fitted on after end of "island" structure.

Chaff Rocket (CHAFROC) launchers fitted on super structure.

GUNNERY. These ships will be armed with three inch/54 calibre Mk 45 light-weight, rapid-fire guns. S 20 mm guns will be fitted for close-in defense (n Close-in Weapon System).

MEDICAL. These ships are to be fitted with extensiv medical facilities including operating rooms, X-ray room hospital ward, isolation ward, laboratories, pharmacy dental operating room and medical store rooms.

NOMENCLATURE. Announced names for these ship remember four major naval actions of World War II ar the 1968 battle at Khe Sanh, South Vietnam, where U Marines held a position against sustained attacks b North Vietnamese forces. The first four names previous were carried by aircraft carriers.

TRIPOLI (LPH 10) *United States Navy*

Amphibious Warfare Ships—*continued*

6 AMPHIBIOUS ASSAULT SHIPS (LPH): "IWO JIMA" CLASS

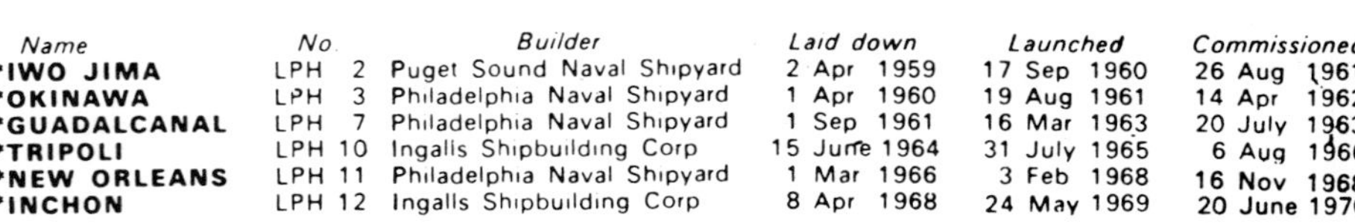

Name	*No*	*Builder*	*Laid down*	*Launched*	*Commissioned*
*IWO JIMA	LPH 2	Puget Sound Naval Shipyard	2 Apr 1959	17 Sep 1960	26 Aug 1961
*OKINAWA	LPH 3	Philadelphia Naval Shipyard	1 Apr 1960	19 Aug 1961	14 Apr 1962
*GUADALCANAL	LPH 7	Philadelphia Naval Shipyard	1 Sep 1961	16 Mar 1963	20 July 1963
*TRIPOLI	LPH 10	Ingalls Shipbuilding Corp	15 June 1964	31 July 1965	6 Aug 1966
*NEW ORLEANS	LPH 11	Philadelphia Naval Shipyard	1 Mar 1966	3 Feb 1968	16 Nov 1968
*INCHON	LPH 12	Ingalls Shipbuilding Corp	8 Apr 1968	24 May 1969	20 June 1970

)isplacement, tons	17 000 light; 18 300 full load
.ength, feet (*metres*)	592 (*180·0*) oa
eam, feet (*metres*)	84 (*25·6*)
)raft, feet (*metres*)	26 (*7·9*)
light deck width, feet (*metres*)	105 (*31·9*) maximum
lelicopters	20-24 medium (CH-46) 4 heavy (CH-53) 4 observation (HU-1)
uns	8—3 in (*76 mm*) 50 cal AA (twin) except 6 guns in *Okinawa*
lissile launchers	1 Basic Point Defence Missile System (BPDMS) launcher firing Sea Sparrow missiles in *Okinawa*
lain engines	1 geared turbine, 23 000 shp; 1 shaft
oilers	2—655 psi (Combustion Engineering Babcock & Wilcox)
;peed, knots	20 (sustained)
:omplement	528 (48 officers, 480 enlisted men)
roops	2 090 (190 officers, 1 900 enlisted men)

he *Iwo Jima* was the world's first ship designed and onstructed specifically to operate helicopters. These hips correspond to Commando Ships in the Royal Navy, xcept that the US ships do not carry landing craft ave for the *Inchon* which has davits aft for two LCVPs. ach LPH can carry a Marine battalion landing team, its uns, vehicles, and equipment, plus a reinforced squadron f transport helicopters and various support personnel. he *Iwo Jima* was authorised in the Fiscal Year 1958 ew construction programme, the *Okinawa* in FY 1959, *uadalcanal* in FY 1960, *Guam* in FY 1962, *Tripoli* in FY 963, *New Orleans* in FY 1965, and *Inchon* in FY 1966. stimated cost of the *Iwo Jima* is $40 000 000.

'he *Guam* was modified late in 1971 and began operations ı January 1972 as an interim sea control ship. See ection on Surface Combatant section for details. She etains her LPH designation.

ESIGN. These ships resemble World War II-era escort arriers in size but have massive bridge structures, hull ontinued up to flight deck providing enclosed bows, d rounded flight decks. Each ship has two deck-edge s, one to port opposite the bridge and one to starboard of island. Full hangars are provided; no arresting ires or catapults. Two small elevators carry cargo om holds to flight deck.

LECTRONICS. These ships have SPS-40 and SPS-10 arch radars, and SPN-10 navigation radar; TACAN od tops mast; advanced electronic warfare equipment ted.

UNNERY. Guns are in four twin mounts, two forward island structure and two at stern, "notched" into flight eck. The *New Orleans* and *Inchon* have closed gun ounts forward of their islands.

EDICAL. These ships are fitted with extensive medical cilities including operating room, X-ray room, hospital ard, isolation ward, laboratory, pharmacy, dental erating room, and medical store rooms.

ISSILES. *Okinawa* fitted with BPDMS launcher ward of island structure in early 1970.

OMENCLATURE. Amphibious assault ships are named r battles in Marine Corps history. Iwo Jima, Okinawa, uadalcanal, and Guam were World War II campaigns; e Marines fought Barbary pirates at Tripoli in 1801 and elped stop the British at New Orleans in 1814. There as also a naval battle at New Orleans during the nerican Civil War. *Inchon* was the near-perfect 1950 nphibious assault in Korea.

HOTOGRAPHS. Note Sea Sparrow launcher "box" rward of bridge on *Okinawa*. The photographs of e *Inchon* show her port-side elevator folded against ull; note LCVP davit at stem and large, CH-53 Sea tallion helicopters.

ISPOSALS

ıe **Thetis Bay** (LPH 6, ex-CVHA 1, ex-CVE 90) was ricken on 1 Mar 1964. The **Block Island** (originally VE 106) was reclassified LPH 1 on 22 Dec 1957 but conersion was cancelled and she reverted to CVE status ı 17 Jan 1959; subsequently stricken (as AKV 38) and rapped.

"ESSEX" CLASS

ll three "Essex" class fast carriers employed as amphibus assault ships have been discarded: **Boxer** (LPH 4, -CVS 21) stricken on 1 Dec 1969, **Princeton** (LPH 5, -CVS 37) stricken on 30 Jan 1970, and **Valley Forge** PH 8, ex-CVS 45) stricken on 15 Jan 1970.

OKINAWA (LPH 3) *1970, United States Navy, PH3 De Varold Bengston*

INCHON (LPH 12) *1972, Stefan Terzibaschitsch*

INCHON (LPH 12) *1972, Stefan Terzibaschitsch*

Amphibious Warfare Ships—*continued*

5 AMPHIBIOUS CARGO SHIPS (LKA): "CHARLESTON" CLASS

Name	No.	Laid down	Launched	Commissioned
***CHARLESTON**	LKA 113	5 Dec 1966	2 Dec 1967	14 Dec 1968
***DURHAM**	LKA 114	10 July 1967	29 Mar 1968	24 May 1969
***MOBILE**	LKA 115	15 Jan 1968	19 Oct 1968	20 Sep 1969
***ST. LOUIS**	LKA 116	3 Apr 1968	4 Jan 1969	22 Nov 1969
***EL PASO**	LKA 117	22 Oct 1968	17 May 1969	17 Jan 1970

Displacement, tons	20 700 full load
Dimensions, feet	575·5 oa × 82 × 25·5
Guns	8—3 inch (*76 mm*) 50 cal AA (twin)
Main engines	1 steam turbine; 22 000 shp; 1 shaft = 20+ knots
Boilers	2 (Combustion Engineering)
Complement	334 (24 officers, 310 enlisted men)
Troops	226 (15 officers, 211 enlisted men)

These ships are designed specifically for the attack cargo ship role; they carry 18 landing craft (LCM) and supplies for amphibious operations. Design includes two heavy-lift cranes with a 78·4-ton capacity, two 40-ton capacity booms, and eight 15-ton capacity booms; helicopter deck aft.
The LKA 113-116 were authorised in the Fiscal Year 1965 shipbuilding programme; LKA 117 in FY 1966 programme.
All built by Newport News Shipbuilding and Dry Dock Co, Virginia. Cost is approximately $21 000 000 per ship.

CLASSIFICATION. Originally designated Attack Cargo Ship (AKA). *Charleston* redesignated Amphibious Cargo Ship (LKA) on 14 Dec 1968; others to LKA on 1 Jan 1969.

ENGINEERING. These are among the first US Navy ships with a fully automated main propulsion plant; control of plant is from bridge or central machinery space console. This automation permitted a 45-man reduction in complement.

NOMENCLATURE. Amphibious cargo ships are named for counties.

ST. LOUIS (LKA 116) *1969, Newport News SB & DD Co*

ST. LOUIS (LKA 116) *1969, Newport News SB & DD Co*

1 AMPHIBIOUS CARGO SHIP (LKA): "TULARE" TYP

*** TULARE** (ex- *Evergreen Mariner*) LKA 112

Displacement, tons	12 000 light; 16 800 full load
Dimensions, feet	564 oa × 76 × 26
Guns	12—3 inch 50 cal AA (twin)
Main engines	Turbine (De Laval); 22 000 shp; 1 shaft = 23 knots
Boilers	2 (Combustion Engineering)
Complement	437 (38 officers, 399 enlisted men)
Troops	319 (18 officers, 301 enlisted men)

Built by Bethlehem, San Fracisco. Laid down on 16 Feb 1953, launched on Dec 1953: Acquired by Navy during construction. Commissioned on 13 Jan 19 C4-S-1 type. Has helicopter landing platform and booms capable of lifting 60-t landing craft. Carries 9 LCM-6 landing craft. Designation changed from AKA 1 to LKA 112 on 1 Jan 1969.

CLASS. Thirty-five "Mariner" design C4-S-1 merchant ships built during the ea 1950s; five acquired by Navy, three for conversion to amphibious ships (AKA-AP and two for support of Polaris-Poseidon programme (designated AG).

TULARE (LKA 112) *1969, US Navy,*

5 AMPHIBIOUS CARGO SHIPS (LKA): "RANKIN" CLASS

Name	No.	Launched	Commissione
RANKIN	LKA 103	22 Dec 1944	25 Feb 194
SEMINOLE	LKA 104	28 Dec 1944	8 Mar 194
UNION	LKA 106	23 Nov 1944	25 Apr 194
VERMILION	LKA 107	12 Dec 1944	23 June 194
WASHBURN	LKA 108	12 Dec 1944	17 May 194

Displacement, tons	6 456 light; 14 160 full load
Dimensions, feet	459·2 oa × 63 × 26·3
Guns	1—5 inch 38 cal DP (removed from some ships); 8—40 mm AA (twin)
Main engines	Geared turbine (General Electric); 1 shaft; 6 000 shp = 16·5 knots
Boilers	2 (Combustion Engineering)
Complement	247
Troops	138

All built by North Carolina SB Co, Wilmington, North Carolina. Maritime Commissi C2-S-AJ3 type. Ten 20 mm AA guns removed. Designation changed from AKA LKA on 1 Jan 1969.
All of the above ships are in Maritime Administration reserve (remain on the Navy Lis

VERMILION LKA 107) *1970, United States Nav*

MOBILE (LKA 115) *1960, United States Navy*

Amphibious Warfare Ships—*continued*

7 AMPHIBIOUS CARGO SHIPS (LKA): "ANDROMEDA" CLASS

Name	*No.*	*Launched*	*Commissioned*
THUBAN (ex-AK 68)	LKA 19	26 Apr 1943	10 June 1943
ALGOL (ex-*James Baines*)	LKA 54	17 Feb 1943	21 July 1944
CAPRICORNUS (ex-*Spitfire*)	LKA 57	14 Aug 1943	31 May 1944
MULIPHEN	LKA 61	26 Aug 1944	23 Oct 1944
YANCEY	LKA 93	8 July 1944	11 Oct 1944
WINSTON	LKA 94	30 Nov 1944	19 Jan 1945
MERRICK	LKA 97	28 Jan 1945	31 Mar 1945

Displacement, tons	7 430 light; 14 000 full load
Dimensions, feet	435 wl; 495·2 oa × 63 × 24 max
Guns	1—5 inch, 38 cal (removed from some ships); 8—40 mm AA (twin) except *Thuban* 4—3 inch 50 cal AA in lieu of 40 mm
Main engines	Geared turbines (General Electric); 1 shaft; 6 000 shp = 16·5 knots
Boilers	2 (Foster Wheeler)
Complement	247
Troops	414

Algol, Capricornus, and *Yancey* built by Moore DD Co, Oakland, California; others by Federal SB & Co, DD Kearney, New Jersey. C2-S-B1 type. Can carry over 5 200 tons of cargo and 2 200 tons of tanks. *Wyandot,* AK A92, assigned to the Navy's Military Sea Transportation Service and manned by a civilian crew since 1963, was redesignated T-AK 283 on 1 Jan 1969. Designation of other ships remaining on Navy List changed from AKA to LKA on 1 Jan 1969.
All of the above ships are in Maritime Administration reserve (remain on the Navy List).

DISPOSALS (since 1 Jan 1970()
Arneb LKA 56 stricken on 13 Aug 1971.

MULIPHEN (LKA 61) *1968, United States Navy*

MULIPHEN (LKA 61) *1968, United States Navy*

2 AMPHIBIOUS TRANSPORTS (LPA): "PAUL REVERE" CLASS

Name	*No.*	*Launched*	*Commissioned*
***PAUL REVERE** (ex-*Diamond Mariner*)	LPA 248	13 Feb 1954	3 Sep 1958
***FRANCIS MARION** (ex-*Prairie Mariner*)	LPA 249	11 Apr 1953	6 July 1961

Displacement, tons	10 709 light; 16 838 full load
Dimensions, feet	563·5 oa × 76 × 27
Guns	8—3 inch 50 cal AA (twin)
Main engines	geared turbines (General Electric); 22 000 shp; 1 shaft = 22 knots
Boiler	2 (Foster Wheeler)
Complement	414 (35 officers, 379 enlisted men)
Troops	1 657 (96 officers, 1 561 enlisted men)

Paul Revere is a C4-S-1 type cargo vessel converted into an Attack Transport by Todd Shipyard Corp, San Pedro, Calif, under the Fiscal Year 1957 Conversion programme. Fitted with helicopter platform. *Francis Marion* was a similar "Mariner" type hull converted into an APA by Bethlehem Steel, Key Highway Yard, Baltimore, Md, under the Fiscal Year 1959 programme. Both ships were built by New York Shipbuilding Corporation, Camden, New Jersey. Designation changed from APA to LPA on 1 Jan 1969.
These are the only attack transports in active US service. Fitted to serve as force flagship.

PAUL REVERE (LPA 248) *1969, US Navy*

FRANCIS MARION (LPA 249) *1969, Anthony and Joseph Pavia*

8 AMPHIBIOUS TRANSPORTS (LPA): "HASKELL" CLASS

Name	*No.*	*Launched*	*Commissioned*
SANDOVAL	LPA 194	11 Sep 1944	7 Oct 1944
MAGODFFIN	LPA 199	4 Oct 1944	25 Oct 1944
TALLADEGA	LPA 208	17 Aug 1944	31 Oct 1944
MOUNTRAIL	LPA 213	20 Sep 1944	6 Nov 1944
NAVARRO	LPA 215	3 Oct 1944	15 Nov 1944
OKANOGAN	LPA 220	22 Oct 1944	3 Dec 1944
PICKAWAY	LPA 222	5 Nov 1944	12 Dec 1944
BEXAR	LPA 237	25 July 1945	9 Oct 1945

Displacement, tons	6 720 light; 10 470 full load
Dimensions, feet	436·5 wl; 455 oa × 62 × 24
Guns	12—40 mm AA (1 quad, 4 twin) forward quad 40 mm mount removed from some ships
Main engines	Geared turbine; 1 shaft; 8 500 shp = 17·7 knots
Boilers	2 (Babcock & Wilcox)
Complement	536
Troops	1 560

VC2-S-AP5 "Victory" type, all launched in 1944-1945. All have county names. 3 000 tons cargo. All in Maritime Administration reserve (on Navy List). Designation of ships remaining on Navy List changed from APA to LPA on 1 Jan 1969.
The 5-inch gun was removed. *Shelburne* APA 205 converted to missile range instrumentation ship for Poseidon programme; redesignated AGM 22.

OKANOGAN (LPA 220) *1967, United States Navy*

SANDOVAL (LPA 194) *1970, United States Navy*

2 AMPHIBIOUS TRANSPORTS (LPA): "BAYFIELD CLASS"

FREMONT (ex-*Sea Corsair*)	LPA 44 (ex-AP 89)	31 Mar 1943	23 Nov 1943
HENRICO (ex-*Sea Darter*)	LPA 45 (ex-AP 90)	31 Mar 1943	24 June 1943

Displacement, tons	8 100 light; 15 200 full load
Dimensions, feet	465 wl; 492 oa × 69·5 × 26·5
Guns	1—5 inch (*127 mm*) DP 8—40 mm AA (twin) in *Henrico* 8—40 mm AA (2 twin and 1 quad) in *Fremont*
Main engines	Geared turbine (General Electric); 8 500 shp 1 shaft; = 18·4 knots

Amphibious Warfare Ships—*continued*

"BAYFIELD" class—*continued*

Boilers	2 Foster Wheeler
Complement	504 to 581
Troops	1 212 to 1 600
Flag accommodation	151

C3-S-A2 type. Built by Ingalls Shipbuilding Corp, Pascagoula, Mississippi. Designation changed from APA to LPA on 1 Jan 1969.

DISPOSALS (since 1 Jan 1970)
Cambria LPA 36 stricken on 14 Sep 1970; **Chilton** LPA 38 stricken on 1 July 1972.

FREMONT (LPA 44) *1966, United States Navy*

FREMONT (LPA 44) *1966, United States Navy*

10 AMPHIBIOUS TRANSPORTS (SMALL) (LPR): CONVERTED DE TYPE

Name	*No.*	*Launched*	*Commissioned*
LANING	LPR 55 ex-DE 159	4 July 1943	1 Aug 1943
HOLLIS	LPR 86 ex-DE 794	11 Sep 1943	24 Jan 1943
KIRWIN	LPR 90 ex-DE 229	16 June 1944	4 Nov 1945
RINGNESS	LPR 100 ex-DE 590	5 Feb 1944	25 Oct 1944
BEVERLY W. REID	LPR 119 ex-DE 722	4 Mar 1944	25 June 1945
DIACHENKO	LPR 123 ex-DE 690	15 Aug 1944	8 Dec 1944
HORACE A. BASS	LPR 124 ex-DE 691	12 Sep 1944	21 Dec 1944
BEGOR	LPR 127 ex-DE 711	25 May 1944	14 Mar 1945
BALDUCK	LPR 132 ex-DE 716	27 Oct 1944	7 May 1945
WEISS	LPR 135 ex-DE 719	17 Feb 1945	7 July 1945

Displacement, tons	1 400 standard; 2 130 full load
Dimensions, feet	300 wl; 306 oa × 37 × 12·6
Guns	1—5 in (*127 mm*) 38 cal DP; 4—40 mm AA (twin) in modernised ships; 8—40 mm AA (twin) in others
ASW weapons	2 triple torpedo launchers (Mk 32) in modernised ships; depth charges in others.
Main engines	Geared turbines (General Electric) with electric drive; 12 000 shp; 2 shafts = 23·6 knots
Boilers	2 ("D" Express)
Complement	204 (designed wartime; 12 or 15 officers, 189 or 192 enlisted men, depending upon DE type)
Troops	162 (12 officers, 150 enlisted men)

These ships are former Destroyer Escorts (DE) converted or completed during World War II to transports for carrying commandoes, reconnaissance troops or frogmen. Fifty-six DEs were completed to this configuration and an additional 38 ships were converted after service as destroyer escorts; nine planned conversions were cancelled (APD 41, 58, 64, 67, 68, 82, 83, 137, 138). Originally designated as High Speed Transports (APD); designation of 13 ships remaining on Navy List as of 1 Jan 1969 changed to Amphibious Transports (Small) (LPR). Converted from TE and TEV type destroyer escorts with troop quarters being provided, single 5 inch gun and six to eight 40 mm guns (twin) replacing previous armament, davits installed amidships for four LCVPs, and 10-ton capacity boom placed aft.
All surviving ships of this type in the US Navy are in reserve, the last to be decommissioned being the *Beverly W. Reid*, *Diechenko*, and *Weiss*, all in 1969.
See 1971-1972 edition for detailed disposal and transfer notes.

MODERNISATION. All except *Ringness* and *Begor* were modernised during the 1960s as part of the FRAM II programme. They have new bridge configurations, additional electronic equipment, tripod mast (in some ships place of forward pole mast), improved habitability, ASW torpedo launchers, and retain only two 40 mm twin mounts (aft).

TRANSFERS. Ships of this class serve in the navies of Chile, Colombia, Ecuador, South Korea, Mexico and Taiwan China.

CONVERTED DE TYPE—*continued*

PHOTOGRAPHS. The *Beverly W. Reid* and *Kirwin* have undergone Fleet Rehabilitation and Modernisation (FRAM) process; note enlarged structure between 5 inch gun mount and bridge, modified bridge, additional whip antennas. Both ships retain pole mast (see 1970-1971 edition for photographs of *Ruchamkin* with tripod mast). Neither of these ships has Mk 32 anti-submarine torpedo tubes in these views; normally installed in FRAM transports just forward of boat davits.

DISPOSALS (since 1 Jan 1970)
Knudson LPR 101 stricken on 15 July 1972.

BEVERLY W. REID (LPR 119)—Modernised *1968, United States Navy*

KIRWIN (LPR 90)—Modernised *1963, United States Navy*

12 AMPHIBIOUS TRANSPORT DOCKS (LPD): "AUSTIN" CLASS

Name	*No.*	*Laid down*	*Launched*	*Commissioned*
***AUSTIN**	LPD 4	4 Feb 1963	27 June 1964	6 Feb 1965
***OGDEN**	LPD 5	4 Feb 1963	27 June 1964	19 June 1965
***DULUTH**	LPD 6	18 Dec 1963	14 Aug 1965	12 Apr 1966
***CLEVELAND**	LPD 7	30 Nov 1964	7 May 1966	21 Apr 1967
***DUBUQUE**	LPD 8	25 Jan 1965	6 Aug 1966	1 Sep 1967
***DENVER**	LPD 9	7 Feb 1964	23 Jan 1965	26 Oct 1968
***JUNEAU**	LPD 10	23 Jan 1965	12 Feb 1966	12 July 1969
***CORONADO**	LPD 11	3 May 1965	30 July 1966	23 May 1970
***SHREVEPORT**	LPD 12	27 Dec 1965	22 Oct 1966	12 Dec 1970
***NASHVILLE**	LPD 13	14 Mar 1966	7 Oct 1967	14 Feb 1970
***TRENTON**	LPD 14	8 Aug 1966	3 Aug 1968	6 Mar 1971
***PONCE**	LPD 15	31 Oct 1966	20 May 1970	10 July 1971

Displacement, tons	10 000 light; 16 900 full load
Length, feet (*metres*)	570 (*173·3*) oa
Beam, feet (*metres*)	84 (*25·6*)
Draft, feet (*metres*)	23 (*7·0*)
Guns	8—3 in (*76 mm*) 50 cal AA (twin)
Helicopters	Up to 6 UH-34 or CH-46 (see *Helicopter* notes)
Main engines	2 steam turbines (De Laval); 24 000 shp; 2 shafts = 20 knots sustained
Boilers	2 (Babcock & Wilcox)
Complement	490 (30 officers, 460 enlisted men)
Troops	930 in LPD 4-6 and LPD 14-16; 840 in LPD 7-13
Flag accommodations	Approx 90 in LPD 7-13

These ships are enlarged versions of the previous "Raleigh" class; most notes for the "Raleigh" class apply to these ships. All 12 of these ships are officially considered in a single class; earlier references to separate classes were based on contract awards to builders.
The LPD 4-6 were authorised in the Fiscal Year 1962 new construction programme, LPD 7-10 in FY 1963, LPD 11-13 in FY 1964, LPD 14 and LPD 15 in FY 1965, and LPD 16 in FY 1966. LPD 16 was deferred in favour of LHA programme; formerly cancelled in Feb 1969. No additional ships of this type are planned in view of the LHA capabilities.
LPD 4-6 built by New York Naval Shipyard; LPD 7-8 built by Ingalls Shipbuilding Corp; LPD 9-15 built by Lockheed Shipbuilding & Construction Co, Seattle, Washington. Completion of later ships has been delayed.

Amphibious Warfare Ships—*continued*

"AUSTIN" CLASS—*continued*

DESIGN. These ships are 48 feet longer than the previous "Raleigh" class with the additional space used to carry more cargo, especially vehicles, and more fuel oil. The *Cleveland* and six later ships differ from the first three and last three in detail (eg, flagship facilities for amphibious squadron commander in LPD 7-13).
Austin has only one bridge level; LPD 7-13 have two bridge levels.

HELICOPTERS. These ships do not have integral hangars or aircraft maintenance facilities. All have been fitted with small hangars that telescope open (from 25 feet to 62 feet) to provide limited shelter for helicopter maintenance. Note photographs on following page.

NOMENCLATURE. Amphibious transport docks are named for United States cities the namesake of which were explorers and developers of America. Some of the names previously were borne by cruisers.

TRENTON (LPD 14) *1971, Lockheed SB & Constn Co.*

2 AMPHIBIOUS TRANSPORT DOCKS (LPD): "RALEIGH" CLASS

Name	*No.*	*Laid down*	*Launched*	*Commissioned*
•**RALEIGH**	LPD 1	23 June 1960	17 Mar 1962	8 Sep 1962
•**VANCOUVER**	LPD 2	19 Nov 1960	15 Sep 1962	11 May 1963

Displacement, tons	8 040 light; 13 900 full load
Length, feet (*metres*)	500 (*152·0*) wl 521·8 (*158·4*) oa
Beam, feet (*metres*)	84 (*25·6*)
Draft, feet (*metres*)	21 (*6·4*)
Guns	8—3 in (*76 mm*) 50 cal AA
Helicopters	up to 6 UH-34 or CH-46 (see *Helicopter* notes)
Main engines	2 steam turbines; (De Laval); 24 000 shp; 2 shafts = 20 knots sustained
Boilers	2 (Babcock & Wilcox)
Complement	490 (30 officers, 460 enlisted men)
Troops	930

The amphibious transport dock was developed from the dock landing ship (LSD) concept but provides more versatility. The LPD replaces the Amphibious Transport (LPA) and, in part, the Amphibious Cargo Ship (LKA) and dock landing ship. The LPD can carry a "balanced load" of assault troops and their equipment, has a docking well for landing craft, a helicopter deck, cargo holds and vehicle garages. The *Raleigh* was authorised in the Fiscal Year 1959 new construction programme, the *Vancouver* in FY 1960. Built by New York Naval Shipyard. Approximate construction cost was $29 000 000 per ship.
A third ship of this class, *La Salle* (LPD 3), was reclassified as a command ship (AGF 3) on 1 July 1972.

DESIGN. These ships resemble dock landing ships (LSD) but have fully enclosed docking well with the roof forming a permanent helicopter platform. The docking well is 168 feet long and 50 feet wide, less than half the length of wells in newer LSDs; the LPD design provides more space for vehicles, cargo, and troops. Ramps allow vehicles to be driven between helicopter deck, parking area, and docking well; side ports provide roll-on/roll off capability when docks are available. An overhead monorail in the docking well with six cranes facilitates loading landing craft.

HELICOPTERS. These ships are not normally assigned helicopters because they lack integral hangars and maintenance facilities. It is intended that helicopters from a nearby amphibious assault ship (LHA or LPH) would provide helicopters during an amphibious operation. Hangars have been fitted (see "Austin" class notes).

LANDING CRAFT. The docking well in these ships can hold one LCU and three LCM-6s or four LCM-8s or 20 LVTs (amphibious tractors). In addition, two LCM-6s or four LCPLs are carried on the boat deck which are lowered by crane.

PHOTOGRAPHS. There are four LCPLs nested on the *Raleigh* between her superstructure and helicopter deck on the 02 level. LPD flight decks extend to stern counter while LSDs have a significant opening where flight deck ends short of stern.

NASHVILLE (LPD 13) *1969, Lockheed SB & Constn Co*

AUSTIN (LPD 4) *1969, United States Navy*

PONCE (LPD 15) *1971, Lockheed Shipbuilding & Construction*

Amphibious Warfare Ships—*continued*

RALEIGH (LPD 1)

1969, United States Navy

5 DOCK LANDING SHIPS (LSD): "ANCHORAGE" CLASS

Name	*No.*	*Laid down*	*Launched*	*Commissioned*
***ANCHORAGE**	LSD 36	13 Mar 1967	5 May 1968	15 Mar 1969
***PORTLAND**	LSD 37	21 Sep 1967	20 Dec 1969	3 Oct 1970
***PENSACOLA**	LSD 38	12 Mar 1969	11 July 1970	27 Mar 1971
***MOUNT VERNON**	LSD 39	29 Jan 1970	17 Apr 1971	13 May 1972
***FORT FISHER**	LSD 40	15 July 1970	22 Apr 1972	9 Dec 1972

Displacement, tons	8 600 light; 13 700 full load
Dimensions, feet	553·33 oa × 84 × 18·66
Guns	8—3 in (*76 mm*) 50 cal AA (twin)
Main engines	Geared turbines (De Laval); 24 000 shp; 2 shafts = 20 knots sustained
Boilers	2 (Foster Wheeler except Combustion Engineering in *Anchorage*)
Complement	397 (21 officers, 376 enlisted men)
Troops	376 (28 officers, 348 enlisted men)

Improved dock landing ships, slightly larger than previous class; designed to replace earlier LSDs which are unable to meet 20-knot amphibious lift requirement. Similar in appearance to earlier classes but with a tripod mast. Helicopter platform aft with docking well partially open; helicopter platform can be removed. Docking well approximately 430 × 50 feet can accommodate three LCU-type landing craft. Space on deck for one LCM, and davits for one LCPL and one LCVP. Two 50-ton capacity cranes.

LSD 36 was authorised in Fiscal Year 1965 shipbuilding programme; LSD 37-39 in FY 1966 programme; LSD 40 in FY 1967 programme. *Anchorage* built by Ingalls Shipbuilding; LSD 37-40 by General Dynamics (Quincy).
Estimated construction cost is $11 500 000 per ship.

CLEVELAND (LPD 7) loading LCMs and LCVP *US Navy*

PENSACOLA (LSD 38) *1971, General Dynamics Corp*

PORTLAND (LSD 37) *1971, United States Navy, PH1 Robert L. Varney*

Amphibious Warfare Ships—*continued*

PENSACOLA (LSD 38) *1971, General Dynamics Corp*

8 DOCK LANDING SHIPS (LSD): "THOMASTON" CLASS

Name	*No.*	*Launched*	*Commissioned*
***THOMASTON**	LSD 28	9 Feb 1954	17 Sep 1954
***PLYMOUTH ROCK**	LSD 29	7 May 1954	24 Jan 1955
***FORT SNELLING**	LSD 30	16 July 1954	24 Jan 1955
***POINT DEFIANCE**	LSD 31	28 Sep 1954	31 Mar 1955
***SPIEGEL GROVE**	LSD 32	10 Nov 1955	8 June 1956
***ALAMO**	LSD 33	20 Jan 1956	24 Aug 1956
***HERMITAGE**	LSD 34	12 June 1956	17 Dec 1956
***MONTICELLO**	LSD 35	10 Aug 1956	29 Mar 1957

Displacement, tons	6 880 light; 11 270 full load, *Alamo, Hermitage, Monticello, Spiegel Grove:* 12 150 full load
Dimensions, feet	510 oa × 84 × 19 max
Guns	12—3 inch (76 mm) 50 cal AA (twin)
Main engines	Steam turbines (General Electric); 24 000 shp; 2 shafts = 22·5 knots
Boilers	2 (Babcock & Wilcox)
Complement	400
Troops	340

Built by Ingalls Shipbuilding Corp, Pascagoula, Mississippi. Constructed to provide 20-knot LSD capability. Fitted with helicopter platform over docking well; two 5-ton capacity cranes; can carry 21 LCM(6) or 3 LCU and 6 LCM landing craft or approximately 50 LVTs (amphibious tractors) in docking well plus 30 LVTs on mezzanine and super decks (with helicopter landing area clear).
As built each ship had 16—3 inch AA guns; twin mount on each side wall (aft of boats davits) has been removed.
Note pole mast compared to tripod mast of subsequent "Anchorage" class for rapid identification; later class has enclosed 3 inch gun mounts forward of bridge.

NOMENCLATURE. Dock landing ships are named for historic sites in the United States except that the *Anchorage, Portland,* and *Pensacola* primarily honour cities.

SPIEGEL GROVE (LSD 32) *1968, United States Navy*

SPIEGEL GROVE (LSD 32) *1968, United States Navy*

11 DOCK LANDING SHIPS (LSD): "CASA GRANDE" CLASS

Name	*No.*	*Launched*	*Commissioned*
CASA GRANDE	LSD 13	11 Apr 1944	5 June 1944
RUSHMORE	LSD 14	10 May 1944	3 July 1944
SHADWELL	LSD 15	24 May 1944	24 July 1944
CABILDO	LSD 16	28 Dec 1944	15 Mar 1945
CATAMOUNT	LSD 17	27 Jan 1945	9 Apr 1945
COLONIAL	LSD 18	28 Feb 1945	15 May 1945
COMSTOCK	LSD 19	28 Apr 1945	2 July 1945
DONNER	LSD 20	6 Apr 1945	31 July 1945
FORT MARION	LSD 22	22 May 1945	29 Jan 1946
TORTUGA	LSD 26	21 Jan 1945	8 June 1945
WHETSTONE	LSD 27	18 July 1945	12 Feb 1946

Displacement, tons	4 790 standard; 9 375 full load
Dimensions, feet	475·4 oa × 76·2 × 18 max
Guns	8— or 12—40 mm AA (2 quad plus 2 twin in some ships)
Main engines	Geared turbines (Newport News except Westinghouse in *Fort Marion*); 2 shafts; 7 000 shp except 9 000 in *Fort Marion* = 15·4 knots except 15·6 knots in *Fort Marion*
Boilers	2
Complement	265 (15 officers, 250 men)

LSD 13-19 built by Newport News SB & DD Co, Virginia; LSD 20, 26, 27 built by Boston Navy Yard; LSD 22 by Gulf SB Corp, Chickasaw, Alabama; *Fort Snelling*, LSD 23, and *Point Defiance*, LSD 24, cancelled in 1945; former ship completed for merchant service, reacquired by Navy as cargo ship *Taurus*, T-AK 273, T-AKR 8 (stricken in 1968). LSD 9-12 of this class transferred to Britain in 1943-1944.
Docking well is 392 × 44 feet; can carry 3 LCUs or 18 LSMs or 32 LVTs (amphibious tractors) in docking well. All ships are fitted with helicopter platform.
Catamount, Colonial, Donner and *Fort Marion*, were modernised under the FRAM II programme in 1960-1962.
All surviving ships of this class are in Navy or Maritime Administration reserve (the latter ships remain on the Navy List).

ARMAMENT. Arrangement differs; all ships have two quad 40 mm mounts on forward superstructure; some have two twin 40 mm mounts on dock walls aft.
As built, each ship had a single 5 inch DP gun, 12—40 mm AA guns, and several 20 mm AA guns.

TRANSFERS
Fort Mandan LSD 21 to Greece on 23 Jan 1971, **San Marcos** LSD 25 to Spain on 1 July 1971.

DOCK LANDING SHIPS (LSD): "ASHLAND" CLASS

All ships of this class have been stricken or transferred to foreign navies; see 1972-1973 and previous editions for characteristics.

DONNER (LSD 20) *1968, United States Navy*

COMSTOCK (LSD 19) *1965, United States Navy*

Amphibious Warfare Ships—*continued*

20 TANK LANDING SHIPS (LST): "NEWPORT" CLASS

Name	No.	Laid down	Launched	Commissioned
*NEWPORT	LST 1179	1 Nov 1966	3 Feb 1968	7 June 1969
*MANITOWOC	LST 1180	1 Feb 1967	4 June 1969	24 Jan 1970
*SUMTER	LST 1181	14 Nov 1967	13 Dec 1969	20 June 1970
*FRESNO	LST 1182	16 Dec 1967	28 Sep 1968	22 Nov 1969
*PEORIA	LST 1183	22 Feb 1968	23 Nov 1968	21 Feb 1970
*FREDERICK	LST 1184	13 Apr 1968	8 Mar 1969	11 Apr 1970
*SCHENECTADY	LST 1185	2 Aug 1968	24 May 1969	13 June 1970
*CAYUGA	LST 1186	28 Sep 1968	12 July 1969	8 Aug 1970
*TUSCALOOSA	LST 1187	23 Nov 1968	6 Sep 1969	24 Oct 1970
*SAGINAW	LST 1188	24 May 1969	7 Feb 1970	23 Jan 1971
*SAN BERNARDINO	LST 1189	12 July 1969	28 Mar 1970	27 Mar 1971
*BOULDER	LST 1190	6 Sep 1969	22 May 1970	30 Apr 1971
*RACINE	LST 1191	13 Dec 1969	15 Aug 1970	9 July 1971
*SPARTANBURG COUNTY	LST 1192	7 Feb 1970	11 Nov 1970	1 Sep 1971
*FAIRFAX COUNTY	LST 1193	28 Mar 1970	19 Dec 1970	16 Oct 1971
*LA MOURE COUNTY	LST 1194	22 May 1970	13 Feb 1971	18 Dec 1971
*BARBOUR COUNTY	LST 1195	15 Aug 1970	15 May 1971	12 Feb 1972
*HARLAN COUNTY	LST 1196	7 Nov 1970	24 July 1971	8 Apr 1972
*BARNSTABLE COUNTY	LST 1197	19 Dec 1970	2 Oct 1971	27 May 1972
*BRISTOL COUNTY	LST 1198	13 Feb 1971	4 Dec 1971	5 Aug 1972

Displacement, tons	8 342 full load
Dimensions, feet (*metres*)	522·3 (*158·7*) oa × 69·5 (*21·0*) × 15 (*4·5*) (aft)
Guns	4—3 inch (*76 mm*) 50 cal AA (twin)
Main engines	6 diesels (Alco); 2 shafts, 16 000 hp = 20 knots (sustained)
Complement	213 (11 officers, 202 enlisted men)
Troops	379 (20 officers, 359 enlisted men)

These ships are of an entirely new design larger, and faster than previous tank landing ships. They operate with 20-knot amphibious squadrons to transport tanks, other heavy vehicles, engineer equipment, and supplies which cannot be readily landed by helicopters or landing craft.
The *Newport* was authorised in the Fiscal Year 1965 new construction programme. LST 1180-1187 (8 ships) in FY 1966, and LST 1188-1198 (11 ships) in FY 1967. LST 1179-1181 built by Philadelphia Naval Shipyard, LST 1182-1198 built by National Steel & Shipbuilding Co, San Diego, California. Seven additional ships of this type that were planned for the Fiscal Year 1971 new construction programme have been deferred.

DESIGN. These ships are the first LSTs to depart from the bow-door design developed by the British early in World War II. The hull form required to achieve 20 knots would not permit bow doors, thus these ships unload by a 112-foot ramp over their bow.

"NEWPORT" CLASS —*continued*

The ramp is supported by twin derrick arms. A ramp just forward of the superstructure connects the lower tank deck with the main deck and a vehicle passage through the superstructure provides access to the parking area amidships. A stern gate to the tank deck permits unloading of amphibious tractors into the water, or unloading of other vehicles into an LCU or onto a pier. Vehicle stowage is rated at 500 tons and 19 000 square feet (5 000 sq ft more than previous LSTs). Full load draft is 15 feet aft and six feet forward.

NOMENCLATURE. LSTs are named for counties and parishes.

PHOTOGRAPHS. Note uneven, staggered funnels, bow opening when ramp is lowered, anchors on starboard side forward and at stern, tunnel opening in superstructure, and helicopter spots marked aft of funnels. Twin 3 inch closed gun mounts are difficult to distinguish in clutter atop superstructure.

NEWPORT (LST 1179) *1969, US Navy,*

RACINE (LST 1191) *1971, United States Navy, PH3 D. W. Read*

NEWPORT (LST 1179) *1969, United States Navy*

NEWPORT (LST 1179) *1970, United States Navy*

Amphibious Warfare Ships—*continued*

3 TANK LANDING SHIPS (LST): "SUFFOLK COUNTY" CLASS

Name	*No.*	*Builder*	*Launched*
SUFFOLK COUNTY	LST 1173	Boston Navy Yard	5 Sep 1956
LORAIN COUNTY	LST 1177	American SB Co, Lorrain, Ohio	22 June 1957
WOOD COUNTY	LST 1178	American SB Co, Lorrain, Ohio	14 Dec 1957

Displacement, tons	4 164 light; 8 000 full load
Dimensions, feet	445 oa × 62 × 16·5
Guns	6—3 inch, 50 cal AA (twin)
Main engines	Diesels; 14 400 bhp; 2 shafts; (controllable pitch propellers) = 17·5 knots
Complement	184 (10 officers, 174 men)
Troops	approx 575

Originally a class of seven tank landing ships (LST 1171, 1173-1178 with LST 1172 not built). They were faster and had a greater troop capacity than earlier LSTs; considered the "ultimate" design attainable with the traditional LST bow-door configuration. *Suffolk County* commissioned on 15 Aug 1957, *Lorain County* on 3 Oct 1859, and *Wood County* on 5 Aug 1969.
The surviving ships were decommissioned in 1972 and are in reserve; they probably will be transferred to foreign navies or assigned to the Military Sealift Command for use as cargo ships.
The *Graham County* (LST 1176) has been converted to a gunboat support ship (AGP); see description under Fleet Support Ships.

DESIGN. High degree of habitability with all crew and troop living spaces air conditioned. Can carry 23 medium tanks or vehicles up to 75 tons on 288-foot-long (lower) tank deck. Davits for four LCVP-type landing craft. Liquid cargo capacity of 170 000 gallons (US) diesel or jet fuel plus 7 000 gallons (US) of petrol for embarked vehicles; some ships have reduced troop spaces and carry additional 250 000 gallons (US) of aviation petrol for pumping ashore or to other ships.

ENGINEERING. All built with six Nordburg diesels. First four ships now have six Fairbanks Morse diesels, electric couplings and reduction gears (14 400 bhp = 17·5 knots). *Lorain County* and *Wood County* now have six Cooper Bessemer diesels, electric couplings and reduction gears (14 400 bhp = 17·5 knots).

TRANSFERS
De Soto County LST 1171, **York County** LST 1175 transferred to Italy on 17 July 1972; **Grant County** LST 1174 transferred to Brazil on 15 Jan 1973.

PHOTOGRAPHS. The "Suffolk County" class LSTs are identified by their twin fire control towers forward.

WOOD COUNTY (LST 1178) *1971, J. S. Kinross*

4 TANK LANDING SHIPS (LST): "TERREBONNE PARISH" CLASS

Name	*No.*	*Launched*	*Commissioned*
TERRELL COUNTY	LST 1157	6 Dec 1952	19 Mar 1953
***WASHTENAW COUNTY**	MSS 2 (ex-LST 1166)	22 Nov 1952	29 Oct 1953
WESTCHESTER COUNTY	LST 1167	18 Apr 1953	10 Mar 1954
WHITFIELD COUNTY	LST 1169	22 Aug 1953	14 Sep 1954

Displacement, tons	2 590 light; 5 800 full load
Dimensions, feet	384 oa × 55 × 17
Guns	6—3 inch, 50 cal AA (twin)
Main engines	4 General Motors; diesels; 6 000 bhp 2 shafts; (controllable pitch propellers;) = 15 knots
Complement	115
Troops	395

Originally a class of 15 tank landing ships (LST 1156-1170). *Terrell County* built by Bath Iron Works Corp, Bath Maine; others by Christy Corp.

Six ships were transferred from reserve to the Military Sealift Command in 1972 for use as cargo ships: *Tioga County* LST 1158, *Traverse County* LST 1160, *Wahkiakum County* LST 1162, *Waldo County* LST 1163, *Walworth County*, LST 1164 and *Washoe County* LST 1965. Four of the ships listed above were to transfer to the Military Sealift Command during 1973 but transfer delayed and they were decommissioned. (See Military Sealift Ships).
Washtenaw County redesignated as a special minesweeper (MSS) on 1 Feb 1972 to support US minesweeping operations off North Vietnam; minimum modifications. Her future is uncertain.

TRANSFERS
Terrebonne Parish LST 1156, **Wexford County** LST 1168 transferred to Spain on 29 Oct 1971; **Tom Green County** LST 1159 transferred to Spain on 6 Jan 1972.

TERRELL COUNTY (LST 1157) *1969, United States Navy*

1 TANK LANDING SHIP (LST): "TALBOT COUNTY" TYPE

TALBOT COUNTY LST 1153

Displacement, tons	2 324; 6 000 full load
Dimensions, feet	368 wl; 382 oa × 54 × 17
Guns	2—5 in, 38 cal DP (single); 4—40 mm AA (twin)
Main engines	Geared turbines (Westinghouse); 2 shafts; 6 000 shp = 14 knots
Boilers	2
Complement	190
Troops	197

The *Talbot County* and her sister ship *Tallahatchie County* (LST 1154) were the only steam-driven LSTs built for the US Navy. Built by Boston Navy Yard; *Talbot County* launched on 24 Apr 1947 and commissioned on 3 Sep 1947. Improved arrangements and greater cargo capacity than the war-built LSTs. The *Talbot County* was decommissioned in Apr 1970; in reserve.

CONVERSION. *Tallahatchie County* converted to an advance aviation base ship (AVB 2); stricken in 1970.

TALBOT COUNTY (LST 1153) *A. & J. Pavia*

17 TANK LANDING SHIPS (LST): 511-1152 SERIES

Name	*No.*	*Launched*	*Commissioned*
CAROLINE COUNTY	LST 525	20 Dec 1943	14 Feb 1944
CHEBOYGAN COUNTY	LST 533	1 Dec 1943	27 Jan 1944
CHURCHILL COUNTY	LST 583	5 July 1944	2 Aug 1944
DODGE COUNTY	LST 722	21 Aug 1944	13 Sep 1944
DUVAL COUNTY	LST 758	25 July 1944	19 Aug 1944
FLOYD COUNTY	LST 762	1 Aug 1944	5 Sep 1944
HAMPSHIRE COUNTY	LST 819	21 Oct 1944	14 Nov 1944
KEMPER COUNTY	LST 854	20 Nov 1944	14 Dec 1944
LITCHFIELD COUNTY	LST 901	9 Dec 1944	11 Jan 1945
MEEKER COUNTY	LST 980	27 Jan 1944	26 Feb 1944
MIDDLESEX COUNTY	LST 983	10 Feb 1944	25 Mar 1944
PITKIN COUNTY	LST 1082	26 Jan 1945	7 Feb 1954
POLK COUNTY	LST 1084	19 Jan 1945	19 Feb 1945
ST. CLAIR COUNTY	LST 1096	10 Jan 1945	2 Feb 1945
SEDGWICK COUNTY	LST 1123	29 Jan 1945	19 Feb 1945
SUMNER COUNTY	LST 1148	23 May 1945	9 June 1945
SUTTER COUNTY	LST 1150	30 May 1945	20 June 1945

Displacement, tons	1 653 standard; 2 366 beaching; 4 080 full load
Dimensions, feet	316 wl; 328 oa × 50 × 14
Guns	6—40 mm AA (2 twin and 2 single) reduced in some ships
Main engines	GM diesels; 2 shafts; 1 700 bhp = 11·6 knots
Complement	119
Troops	147

The US Navy built 1 052 LSTs during World War II in two series: LST 1-150 and LST 511-1152; an even 100 ships were cancelled: LST 85-116, 142-156, 182-196, 232-236, 248-260, 296-300, 431-445. Forty-one were lost during the war. Hundreds of these ships have been transferred to foreign navies or converted to auxiliary configurations.
County or Parish names were assigned to 158 LSTs on the Navy List as of 1 July 1955; 36 Japanese-manned LSTs assigned to the Military Sea Transportation Service (MSTS) at that time were not named.
All of the surviving ships of this series are in reserve except for those operated by the Military Sealift Command (listed separately). The latter ships are used as cargo carriers and are no longer suitable for amphibious operations.

Amphibious Warfare Ships—*continued*

LST 511-1152 SERIES *Continued*

DESIGN. These ships are of the classical LST design developed early in World War II by the British; fitted with bow doors, tunnel-like tank deck with trucks, cargo, or landing craft carried on upper deck; small "island" structure aft with davits for two LCVP-type landing craft. Cargo capacity 2 100 tons. Fitted with tripod masts during postwar period.

TRANSFERS. Ships of this class serve in the navies of Brazil, Greece, Indonesia, Japan, South Korea, Malaysia, Mexico, Philippines, Singapore, Spain, Thailand, Taiwan China, Mainland China, and South Vietnam.

DISPOSALS AND TRANSFERS (Since 1 Jan 1970)

Jerome County LST 848 to South Vietnam on 1 Apr 1970; **Snohomish County** LST 1126 stricken on 1 July 1970; **Clarke County** LST 601, **Iredell County** LST 839 to Indonesia on 15 July 1970; **Luzerne County** LST 902, **Monmouth County** LST 1032 stricken on 12 Aug 1970; **Jennings County** LST 846 stricken on 25 Sep 1970; **Harnett County** LST/AGP 821 to South Vietnam on 12 Oct 1970; **Summit County** LST 1146 transferred to Maritime Administration reserve on 16 Mar 1970. **Page County** LST 1076 to Greece on 5 Mar 1971; **Holmes County** LST 836 to Singapore on 1 July 1971; **Outagamie County** LST 1073 to Brazil on 24 May 1971; **Garrett County** LST/AGP 786 to South Vietnam on 24 April 1971; **Hunterdon County** LST/AGP 838 to Malaysia on 1 July 1971; **Park County** LST 1077 to Mexico on 20 Sep 1971; **San Jaoquin County** LST 1122 stricken on 1 May 1972.

SUMNER COUNTY (LST 1148) *1968, United States Navy*

1 TANK LANDING SHIP (LST): 1-510 SERIES

BLANCO COUNTY LST 344

Displacement, tons	1 625 light; 2 366 beaching; 4 050 full load
Dimensions, feet	328 oa × 50 × 14·3
Guns	8—40 mm AA (2 twin and 4 single)
Main engines	diesels; (General Motors); 1 700 bhp; 2 shafts = 11·6 knots
Complement	119
Troops	147

Built by Norfolk (Virginia) Navy Yard; launched on 15 Oct 1942; commissioned on 29 Nov 1942.

TRANSFERS (since 1 Jan 1970)
Bulloch County LST 509 transferred to South Vietnam on 1 Apr 1970.

BLANCO COUNTY (LST 344) *courtesy "Our Navy"*

INSHORE FIRE SUPPORT SHIP (LFR): "CARRONADE" TYPE

Name	*No.*	*Builder*	*Commisioned*
CARRONADE	LFR 1 (ex-IFS 1)	Puget Sound Bridge	25 May 1955

Displacement, tons	1 040 standard; 1 500 full load
Dimensions, feet	245 oa × 38·5 × 10
Guns	1—5 inch 28 cal dual-purpose 4—40 mm AA (twin) 2—20 mm AA (single)
Rocket launchers	8 rapid-fire launchers for 5 inch rockets
Main engines	2 diesels (Fairbanks-Morse); 3 100 bhp; 2 shafts = 15 knots
Complement	139 (9 officers, 130 enlisted men)

The *Carronade* was specifically designed to provide fire support for amphibious landings; she is an improvement over the World War II-era LSMR but lacks big-gun firepower. Built by Puget Sound Bridge & Dredging Co; laid down on 19 Nov 1952; launched on 26 May 1953. Placed in reserve and mothballed from 1960 to 1965 when re-commissioned for duty in Vietnam conflict. Subsequently decommissioned and again mothballed on 24 July 1970.
Designation changed from IFS 1 to LFR 1 on 1 Jan 1969 (both Inshore Fire Support Ship).The Carronade was stricken May 1973.

ENGINEERING. Fitted with controllable-pitch propellers.

NOMENCLATURE. The *Carronade* is named for the short-range, highly effective weapon developed by the ironworks of the Carron Company, Scotland, and introduced first in the Royal Navy in 1779.

CARRONADE (LFR 1) *1966, United States Navy*

CARRONADE (LFR 1) *1967, United States Navy*

INSHORE FIRE SUPPORT SHIPS (LFR): FORMER LSMR

Name	*No.*	*Builder*	*Commissioned*
BIG BLACK RIVER	LFR 401	Charleston Navy Yard	7 Apr 1945
BROADKILL RIVER	LFR 405	Charleston Navy Yard	2 May 1945
LAMOILLE RIVER	LFR 512	Brown Shipbuilding	5 July 1945
LARAMIE RIVER	LFR 513	Brown Shipbuilding	9 July 1945
OWYHEE RIVER	LFR 515	Brown Shipbuilding	16 July 1945
RED RIVER	LFR 522	Brown Shipbuilding	6 Aug 1945
SMOKEY HILL RIVER	LFR 531	Brown Shipbuilding	25 Sep 1945

Displacement, tons	994 standard; 1 084 full load
Dimensions, feet	LSMR 401 and 405 197·2 wl; 203·5 oa × 34·5 × 10 others 204·5 wl; 206·2 oa × 34.5 × 10
Guns	1—5 inch 38 calibre dual-purpose 4—40 mm AA (twin)
Rocket launchers	8 twin launchers for 5 inch rockets
Main engines	2 diesel (General Motors); 2 800 bhp; 2 shafts = 12·6 knots
Complement	137 (7 officers, 130 enlisted men)

These ships were redesigned during construction to provide fire support for amphibious landings. They have pointed bows, bridge structure aft, and 5 inch mount forward of bridge (earlier LSMRs had 5 inch gun aft of bridge). Built by Charleston Navy Yard and Brown Shipbuilding Company, Houston, Texas; originally 48 ships in these series (LSMR 401-412 and LSMR 501-536); all launched 1945; completed 1945-1946. Most mothballed after World War II; LSMR 401, 403, 409, and 412 served in Korean conflict of 1950-1953; the LSMR 612 was active from 1945 to 1955, serving as a training ship during Korean conflict; these ships were named for rivers on 1 Oct 1955.
Original designation of Medium Landing Ship—Rocket (LSMR) changed to Inshore Fire Support Ship (LFR) for 11 surviving ships on 1 Jan 1969.
LFR 409, 525, and 536 recommissioned in 1965 for duty off Vietnam; all decommissioned in 1970 and subsequently stricken. With the *Carronade* these ships formed Inshore Fire Support Division 93 for service in the Vietnam conflict.
All seven of these ships were stricken in May 1973.

ROCKETS. The automatic rocket launchers each fire 30 spin-stabilised rockets per minute.

DISPOSALS (since 1 Jan 1970)
Full list of stricken ships in 1967-68 edition; one ship remains on Navy List with other designation; *Elk River* (ex-LSMR 501) as ocean engineering range support ship (IX 501).
Clarion River (LSMR/LFR 409) stricken on 8 May 1970; **White River** (LSMR/LFR 536) stricken on 22 May 1970; **St. Francis River** (LSMR/LFR 525) stricken on 17 Apr 1970; **Des Plaines River** (LSMR/LFR 412) stricken on 1 Sep 1972.

LAMOILLE RIVER (LSMR 512) *1950, United States Navy*

LANDING CRAFT

2 AMPHIBIOUS ASSAULT LANDING CRAFT: AEROJET-GENERAL DESIGN

Weight, tons	85·8 empty; 166·4 gross
Dimensions, feet	99 oa × 48 × (height) 23
Main engines	4 gas turbines (Avco-Lycoming T40); 11 200 hp; 4 aircraft type propellers in rotating shrouds for propulsive thrust = approx 50 knots cruise
Lift engines	2 gas turbines (Avco-Lycoming T40); 5 600 hp; 8 horizontal fans (2 sets) for cushion lift
Complement	6

These are air cushion vehicle (ACV) landing craft being developed by the Aerojet-General Corp, and being built by Tacoma Boatbuilding Co, Tacoma, Washington, under Navy contract. Both craft will complete early in 1974. They will be evaluated in competition with the Bell design described below.
Above dimensions are for craft on air cushion; when at rest dimensions are 97 × 44 × 19.
Design features include aluminium construction, bow and stern ramps, 75-ton cargo capacity on deck area of 2 100 square feet; sound-insulated compartments each holding four crew or passengers and three engines housed in each side structure; rotating shrouds provide propulsion and steering.
Performance parameters include four-hour endurance (200-n mile range), four-foot obstance clearance, and ability to maintain cruise speed in Sea State 2 with 25-knot headwind.

PROJECT. Aerojet-General and Bell Aerosystems were awarded contracts in January 1969 to design competitive assault landing craft employing ACV technology. Subsequently, awards were made to both companies in March 1971 to build and test two craft per company.
These are air cushion or bubble craft, supported above the land or water surface by a continuously generated cushion or bubble of air held by flexible "skirts" that surround the base of the vehicle. According to US Navy usage, they differ from surface effect ships (SES) which have rigid sidewalls that penetrate the water surface to help hold the cushion or bubble. Official designation of these craft is Amphibious Assault Landing Craft (AALC), with the Aerojet-General design being referred to as AALC—Jeff(A) and the Bell Aerosystems craft as AALC—Jeff(B)
The two SES constructed for the US Navy are listed with Experimental, Research, and Surveying Ships; also see listing for Patrol Ships and Craft in this edition for additional SES programme details.

2 AMPHIBIOUS ASSAULT LANDING CRAFT: BELL DESIGN

Weight, tons	162·5 gross
Dimensions, feet	86·75 oa × 47 × (height) 23·5
Main/lift engines	6 gas turbines (Avco-Lycoming T40); 16 800 hp; interconnected with 2 aircraft-type propellers in rotating shrouds for propulsive thrust and 4 horizontal fans for cushion lift = approx 50 knots cruise
Complement	6

ACV landing craft being built by Bell Aerosystems. Scheduled for completion in 1974.
Above dimensions are for craft on air cushion; when at rest dimensions are 80 × 43 × 19.
Aluminium construction, bow and stern ramps, 75-ton cargo capacity on deck area of 1 738 square feet; sound-insulated compartments for crew or passengers and three engines houscd in each side structure (with raised compartment on starboard side to provide two helmsmen with 360-degree field of vision). Performance parameters similar to Aerojet-General craft.
Distinguished from Aerojet-General craft by having only two shrouded propellers for thrust and steering.

AEROJET-GENERAL DESIGN (MODEL)

47 UTILITY LANDING CRAFT: LCU 1610 SERIES

LCU 1613	**LCU 1627**	**LCU 1641**	**LCU 1651**	**LCU 1661**
LCU 1614	**LCU 1628**	**LCU 1642**	**LCU 1651**	**LCU 1662**
LCU 1616	**LCU 1629**	**LCU 1644**	**LCU 1653**	**LCU 1663**
LCU 1617	**LCU 1630**	**LCU 1645**	**LCU 1654**	**LCU 1664**
LCU 1618	**LCU 1631**	**LCU 1646**	**LCU 1655**	**LCU 1665**
LCU 1619	**LCU 1632**	**LCU 1647**	**LCU 1656**	**LCU 1666**
LCU 1621	**LCU 1633**	**LCU 1648**	**LCU 1657**	**LCU 1667**
LCU 1623	**LCU 1634**	**LCU 1649**	**LCU 1658**	**LCU 1668**
LCU 1624	**LCU 1637**	**LCU 1650**	**LCU 1659**	**LCU 1669**
			LCU 1660	**LCU 1670**

Displacement, tons	200 light; 375 full load
Dimensions, feet	134·9 oa × 29 × 6·1
Guns	2—50 cal machine guns
Main engines	Diesels (Detroit); 1 000 bhp; 2 shafts = 11 knots (see *Engineering* notes)
Complement	12 to 14 (enlisted men)

LCU 1610 SERIES—*continued*

Improved landing craft, larger than previous series; can carry three M-103 or M-48 tanks (approx 64 tons and 48 tons respectively). Cargo capacity 170 tons.
LCU 1610-1612 built by Christy Corp, Sturgeon Bay, Wisconsin; LCU 1613-1619, 1623, 1624 built by Gunderson Bros Engineering Corp, Portland, Oregon; LCU 1620, 1621,1625,1626,1629,1630 built by Southern Shipbuilding Corp, Slidell, Louisiana; LCU 1622 built by Weaver Shipyards, Texas; LCU 1627, 1628, 1631-1636 built by General Ship and Engine Works (last six units completed in 1968). LCU 1638-1645 built by Marinette Marine Corp, Marinette, Wisconsin (completed 1969-1970); LCU 1646-1666 built by Defoe Shipbuilding Co, Bay City, Michigan (completed 1970-1791). The one-of-a-kind aluminium hull, 133·8 ft LCU 1637 built by Pacific Coast Engineering Co, Alameda, California. LCU 1667-1670 built by General Ship & Engine Works, East Boston, in 1973-1974.
LCU 1636, 1638, 1639, 1640 reclassified as YFB 88-91 in October 1969 LCU 1620 and 1625 to YFU 92 and 93 respectively, in April 1971; LCU 1611. 1615 1622 to YFU 97-99 in Feb 1972; LCU 1610,1612 to YFU 100 and 101 respectively, in Aug 1972.

**ENGINEERING. These landing craft have four 250 bhp diesel engines with Kort-nozzle propellers on twin shafts except for the LCU 1620, 1621, and 1625 which have two 500-bhp diesel engines on vertical shafts fitted with vertical-axis, cycloidal six-bladed propellers. The cycloidal propellers provide thrust in any horizontal direction alleviating the need for rudders. The LCU 1622 was to have been fitted with gas-turbine propulsion machinery, but this project was cancelled.
Endurance is 1 200 miles at eight knots.**

TRANSFERS. **LCU 1626 was transferred to Burma in 1967.**

PHOTOGRAPHS. Note amidships, right-side "Island" structure of LCU 1649; LCU 1625 differs with built up-structure aft. All except LCU 1621, and 1625 have bow and stern ramps.

LCU 1649 — *1970, Defoe Shipbuilding*

LCU 1649 — *1970, Defoe Shipbuilding*

25 UTILITY LANDING CRAFT: LCU 1466 SERIES

LCU 1466	**LCU 1472**	**LCU 1485**	**LCU 1490**	**LCU 1537**
LCU 1467	**LCU 1473**	**LCU 1486**	**LCU 1492**	**LCU 1539**
LCU 1468	**LCU 1477**	**LCU 1487**	**LCU 1525**	**LCU 1547**
LCU 1469	**LCU 1482**	**LCU 1488**	**LCU 1535**	**LCU 1548**
LCU 1470	**LCU 1484**	**LCU 1489**	**LCU 1536**	**LCU 1559**

Displacement, tons	180 light; 360 full load
Dimensions, feet	115 wl; 119 oa × 34 × 6 max
Guns	2—20 mm
Main engines	3 diesels (Gray Marine); 675 bhp; 3 shafts = 18 knots
Complement	14

These are enlarged versions of the World War II-built LCTs; constructed during the early 1950s. LCU 1608 and 1609 have modified propulsion systems; LCU 1582 and later craft have Kort nozzle propellers. LCU 1496 reclassified as YFU 70 on 1 Mar 1966; LCU 1471 to YFU 88 in May 1968; LCU 1576, 1582 and 1608 to YFU 89-91, respectively, in June 1970; LCU 1488, 1491, and 1609 to YFU 94-96 on 1 June 1971; YFU 94 reverted to LCU 1488 on 1 Feb 1972.

CLASSIFICATION. The earlier craft of this series were initially designated as Utility Landing Ships (LSU); redesignated Utility Landing Craft (LCU) on 15 Apr 1952 and classified as sevice craft.

DISPOSALS, TRANSFERS AND LOSSES

LCU 1478 was transferred to Norway and **LCU 1479, 1480, 1501, 1502** were transferred to South Vietnam upon completion; **LCU 1504-1593** were built under US Navy contract for US Army; **LCU 1594-1607** were built in Japan for the Japanese and Nationalist Chinese navies; **LCU 1503** lost accidentally in Aug 1953; **LCU 1476, 1483, 1495, 1497. 1499** to Department of the Interior in 1960-1979; **LCU 1475** to South Vietnam in 1969; **LCU 1493 1494** to South Vietnam in 1970; **LCU 1500** sunk in Vietnam in Mar 1969; **LCU 1481. 1498** to South Vietnam in 1972.

Landing Craft—*continued*

LCU 1468 with mast lowered *1969, US Navy, PH1 A. A. Clemons*

LCU 1488 *1965, United States Navy*

23 UTILITY LANDING CRAFT: LCU 501 SERIES

LCU 539	**LCU 660**	**LCU 768**	**LCU 1124**	**LCU 1430**
LCU 588	**LCU 666**	**LCU 803**	**LCU 1241**	**LCU 1451**
LCU 599	**LCU 667**	**LCU 871**	**LCU 1348**	**LCU 1462**
LCU 608	**LCU 674**	**LCU 893**	**LCU 1348**	
LCU 654	**LCU 742**	**LCU 1045**	**LCU 1387**	

Displacement, tons	143 160 light; 309 to 320 full load
Dimensions, feet	105 wl; 119 oa × 32·7 × 5 max
Guns	2—20 mm
Main engines	Diesels (Gray Marine); 675 bhp; 3 shafts = 10 knots
Complement	13 (enlisted men)

Formerly LCT(6) 501-1465 series; built in 1943-1944. Can carry four tanks or 200 tons of cargo. LCU 524, 529, 550, 562, 592, 600, 629, 664, 666, 668, 677, 686, 742, 764, 776, 788, 840, 869, 877, 960, 973, 974, 979, 980, 1056, 1082, 1086, 1124, 1136, 1156, 1159, 1162, 1195, 1224, 1236, 1250, 1283, 1286, 1363, 1376, 1378, 1384, 1386, 1398, 1411, and 1430 reclassified as YFU 1 through 46, respectively, on 18 May 1958; LCU 1040 reclassified YFB 82 on 18 May 1958; LCU 1446 reclassified YFU 53 in 1964; LCU 509, 637, 646, 709, 716, 776, 851, 916, 973, 989, 1126, 1165, 1203, 1232, 1385, and 1388 reclassified as YFU 54 through 69, respectively, on 1 Mar 1966; LCU 780 reclassified as YFU 87. YFU 9 reverted to LCU 666 on 1 Jan 1962; LCU 1459 converted to YLLC 4; changes reflect employment as general cargo craft assigned to shore commands (see section on Service Craft).

CLASSIFICATION. Originally rated as Landing Craft, Tank (LCT(6)); redesignated Utility Landing Ships (LSU) in 1949 to reflect varied employment; designation changed to Utility Landing Craft (LCU) on 15 Apr 1952 and classified as service craft.

See 1970-1971 edition for war losses, disposals, and transfers prior to 1965.

MECHANISED LANDING CRAFT: LCM 8 TYPE

Displacement, tons	115 full load (steel) or 105 full load (aluminium)
Dimensions, feet	75·6 × 73·7 oa or 21 × 5·2
Main engines	2 diesels(Detroit or General Motors); 650 bhp; 2 shafts = 9 knots
Complement	5 (enlisted men)

Constructed of welded-steel and (later units) aluminium. Can carry one M-48 or M-60 tank (both approx 48 tons) or 60 tons cargo; range is 150 nautical miles at full load. Also operated in large numbers by the US Army.

LCM-8 carrying M-48 tank ***1970, US Navy, PH1 Robert Woods***

MECHANISED LANDING CRAFT: LCM 6 TYPE

Displacement, tons	60 to 62 full load
Dimensions, feet	56·2 oa × 14 × 3·9
Main engines	2 diesels; 450 bhp; 2 shafts = 9 knots

Welded-steel construction. Cargo capacity is 34 tons or 80 troops.

LANDING CRAFT VEHICLE AND PERSONNEL (LCVP)

Displacement, tons	13·5 full load
Dimensions, feet	35·8 oa × 10·5 × 3·5
Main engines	diesel; 1 shaft; 325 bhp = 9 knots

Constructed of wood or fibreglass-reinforced plastic. Fitted with 30-calibre machine guns when in combat areas. Cargo capacity, 8 000 lbs; range, 110 nautical miles at full load.

LCVP from LST 1157 *1969, United States Navy*

2 WARPING TUGS (LWT); NEW CONSTRUCTION

LWT 1 **LWT 2**

Displacement, tons	61 (hoisting weight)
Dimensions, feet	85 oa × 22 × 6·75
Main engines	2 diesels (Harbourmaster); 420 bhp; 2 steerable shafts = 9 knots
Complement	6 (enlisted men)

These craft are employed in amphibious landings to handle pontoon causeways. The LWT 1 and 2 are prototypes of a new, all-aluminium design completed in 1970. A collapsable A-frame is fitted forward to facilitate handling causeway anchors and ship-to-shore fuel lines. They can be "side loaded" on the main deck of an LST 1179 class ship or carried in an LPD/LSD type ship.
The propulsion motors are similar to outboard motors, providing both steering and thrust, alleviating the need for rudders.
Built by Campbell Machine, San Diego, California.

LWT 2 *United States Navy*

WARPING TUGS (LWT)

Displacement, tons	approx 120
Dimensions, feet	92·9 oa × 23 × 6·5
Main engines	2 outboard propulsion units = 6·5 knots

These craft are fabricated from pontoon sections and are assembled by the major amphibious commands as required.

LWT 85 ***United States Navy***

PATROL SHIPS AND CRAFT

he US Navy has several programmes underway to evelop advanced patrol ships and craft. Illustrated on is page are two of the types being developed, the ocean-oing surface effect ship and hydrofoil craft. In ad-ition, several types of inshore/coastal/riverine combat raft are being designed although at this time no pro-urement is anticipated for the US Navy until further tudies of requirements have been conducted.

he PF-type ships previously described in this section ow are listed with Ocean Escorts because of their size nd missions which are more akin to the Navy's DE-eries warships.

)fficially the US Navy's classification Patrol Ships ncludes patrol gunboats (PG) and the now-discarded atrol escorts (PCE) and patrol rescue escorts (PCER). he Patrol Craft officially listed are patrol craft (hydrofoil) PCH), patrol gunboat (hydrofoil) (PGH), and fast atrol craft (PTF). In addition, there are some "patrol" ypes in the Riverine Warfare Craft category. The designations now being used for the proposed patrol rigate (PF) and patrol hydrofoil missile boat (PHM) do not officially "exist", although they are common US Navy usage.

SURFACE EFFECT SHIPS. The Navy is developing reliminary designs for large, ocean-going surface effect hips (SES) with a primary role of anti-submarine warfare. his concept differs from the air cushion vehicle (ACV) n that the SES has rigid sidewalls that penetrate the vater surface as the craft rides on a cushion or bubble f air.

hese craft will be "in part" an outgrowth of the smaller urface effect ships now being developed for the Navy y Aerojet-General and Textron's Bell Aerospace Division (see description under Experimental, Research, nd Surveying Ships).

TUCUMCARI (PGH 2) *1971, US Navy, PH1 Claude V. Sneed*

According to Admiral Zumwalt: "We have placed a very high priority on the surface effect ship on the premise that this offers the potential for destroyer-size ships to conduct anti-submarine warfare on top of the water at speeds two or three times greater than the fastest sub-marines. "This will not only complicate the submarine's detection, evasion and weapons solution problems, but will make the surface effect ship much less vulnerable to torpedo attack".

COASTAL AND RIVERINE CRAFT. **Beginning in 1965 the US Navy built up a force of approximately 650 coastal and riverine craft for use in the Vietnam War. These craft were most successful in their efforts to halt Communist infiltration of men and arms into South Vietnam by sea and river, and in support South Vietnamese and US military operations on inland waterways. "Vietnamisation" of the coastal and riverine forces began in June 1968 and by 1972 virtually all of these small craft had been transferred to the South Vietnamese forces (including 26 patrol boats from the US Coast Guard).**

The US Navy has retained a few riverine craft of various types, primarily for research.

(Several of these craft also have been transferred to the Thai, Philippine, and South Korean navies).

Several new designs are being developed for use by US and allied navies.

AIR CUSHION VEHICLES. **The US Navy conducted two six-month evaluations of three SK-5 type air cushion vehicles in Vietnam. Designated Patrol Air Cushion Vehicle (PACV) in Navy service, the three vehicles encountered varied success. With a general lack of enthusiasm for such craft, especially in view of armed helicopter capabilities, and the reduction of US Navy inshore/riverine forces, the three PACVs have been transferred to the US Coast Guard and are listed in that section of this edition.**

MILITARY ASSISTANCE PROGRAMME. The United States has provided four principal patrol craft designs to foreign navies under the Military Assistance Programme (MAP) in recent years. These craft are the PGM 59 class, a 100-foot, relatively slow but seaworthy craft of about 145 tons; the Sewart 85-foot and 65-foot motor gun-boats, armed only with 50 calibre MGs; and the 40 foot Sewart aluminium launch. Bertram 31-foot "Enforcers" with fibreglass hulls also have been provided as local police craft.

2 000-ton SURFACE EFFECT SHIPS (SES): PROPOSED

Weight, tons	2 000 gross
Dimensions, feet	approx 240 × 100
Helicopters	1 or 2 (SH-2 or SH-3 series) helicopters
Missile launchers	(tentatively) Harpoon surface-to-surface launchers
Guns	(tentatively) 20 mm Vulcan/Phalanx Close-in Weapon System
Main engines	gas turbines = 80+ knots

The Navy has awarded contracts for the preliminary design of a 2 000-ton Surface Effect Ship (SES). The ship will be primarily a test and evaluation platform for large SES technology; however, the ship will be armed with state-of-the-art weapons and will be capable of operating helicopters.

Contracts were awarded on 10 Nov 1972 for prelimary of the ship to: Aerojet-General ($2 900 000), Bell Aerospace ($3 000 000), Litton Industries ($2 700 000), and Lockheed ($2 300 000).

Construction of the prototype ship of this design can be expected to begin in the mid-1970s.

2 000-ton SES DESIGN *Bell Aerospace*

HELICOPTERS. The 2 000-ton SES probably will carry one or two large multi-mission helicopters of the SH-3 OR SH-2 D/F type. The above artist's concept shows one configuration under consideration that provides helicopter landing spaces forward and aft and helicopter hangars on either side of the bridge structure. Final configuration probably will have landing area aft only.

Patrol Ships and Craft—*continued*

13 PATROL GUNBOATS (PG) / 2 PATROL MISSILE BOATS — "ASHEVILLE" CLASS

Name	No.	Builder	Commissioned
* **ASHEVILLE**	PG 84	Tacoma Boatbuilding	6 Aug 1966
* **GALLUP**	PG 85	Tacoma Boatbuilding	22 Oct 1966
* **ANTELOPE**	PG 86	Tacoma Boatbuilding	4 Nov 1967
* **READY**	PG 87	Tacoma Boatbuilding	6 Jan 1968
* **CROCKETT**	PG 88	Tacoma Boatbuilding	24 June 1967
* **MARATHON**	PG 89	Tacoma Boatbuilding	11 May 1968
* **CANON**	PG 90	Tacoma Boatbuilding	26 July 1968
* **TACOMA**	PG 92	Tacoma Boatbuilding	14 July 1969
* **WELCH**	PG 93	Peterson Builders	8 Sep 1969
* **CHEHALIS**	PG 94	Tacoma Boatbuilding	11 Aug 1969
* **DEFIANCE**	PG 95	Peterson Builders	24 Sep 1969
* **GRAND RAPIDS**	PG 98	Tacoma Boatbuilding	5 Sep 1970
* **BEACON**	PG 99	Peterson Builders	21 Nov 1969
* **DOUGLAS**	PG 100	Tacoma Boatbuilding	6 Feb 1971
* **GREEN BAY**	PG 101	Peterson Builders	5 Dec 1969

READY (PG 87) *1973, Giorgio Arra*

Displacement, tons	225 standard; 245 full load
Dimensions, feet	164·5 oa × 23·8 × 9·5
Missile launchers	2 launchers for Standard surface-to-surface missile in *Antelope* and *Ready*
Guns	1—3 in (*76 mm*) 50 cal (forward); 1—40 mm (aft); 4—50 cal MG (twin) except 40 mm gun removed from *Antelope* and *Ready*
Main engines	CODAG: 2 diesels (Cummins); 1 450 shp; 2 shafts = 16 knots; 1 gas turbine (General Electric); 13 300 shp; 2 shafts = 40+ knots
Complement	24 to 27 (3 officers, 21 to 24 enlisted men)

Originally a class of 17 patrol gunboats (PG ex-PGM) designed to perform patrol, blockade, surveillance, and support missions. No anti-submarine capability. Requirement for these craft was based on the volatile Cuban situation in the early 1960s. They are the largest patrol-type craft built by the US Navy since World War II and the first US Navy ships with gas-turbine propulsion.
Several of these gunboats were used by the US Navy for coastal patrol operations in the Vietnam War; the *Surprise* and *Defiance* deployed to the Mediterranean in November 1970, the first of the class to operate in the Atlantic and Med areas.
Built by Tacoma Boatbuilding Co of Tacoma, Washington, and Petersen Builders of Sturgeon Bay, Wisconsin. PG 84 and PG 85 authorised in Fiscal Year 1963 new construction programme; PG 86 and PG 87 in FY 1964; PG 88-90 in FY 1965; PG 92-101 in FY 1966. *Asheville* was laid down on 15 Apr 1964 and launched on 1 May 1965; later ships approximately 18 months from keel laying to completion. Cost per ship approximately $5 000 000.

ANTELOPE (PG 86) *1973, Giorgio Arra*

CLASSIFICATION. These ships originally were classified as motor gunboats (PGM); reclassified as patrol boats (PG) with same hull numbers on 1 Apr 1967. This created a duplication of hull numbers used by the US Navy during World War II for designating ex-British "Arabis" or "Flower" class corvettes acquired under "reverse" lend lease in early 1942 and similar ships built in Canada with US funds (the Canadian-built ships serving in the US or Royal Navy); the first PG 101 was the Canadian-built *Asheville* the first of the US Navy's World War II "frigates" (subsequently redesignated PF 1).
PGM 1-32 were submarine chasers modified during World War II with additional guns; PGM 33-83, 91, 102-121 assigned to gunboats built since 1955 for transfer to foreign navies.

DESIGN. All-aluminium hull and aluminium-fibreglass superstructure. Because of the heat-transmitting qualities of the aluminium hull and the amount of waste heat produced by a gas turbine engine the ships are completely air conditioned.

ANTELOPE (PG 86) firing standard missile *1972, United States Navy*

ENGINEERING. These ships have a Combination Diesel and Gas Turbine (CODAG) propulsion system with twin diesel engines for cruising and a gas turbine for high-speed operations. The gas turbine is an LM1500 with the gas generator essentially the same as the J-79-8 aircraft engine (used in the F-4 Phantom and other aircraft). The transfer from diesel to gas turbine propulsion (or vica versa) can be accomplished while underway with no loss of speed. From full stop these ships can attain 40 knots in one minute; manoeuvrability is exellent due in part to controllable pitch-propellers. Speed and propeller pitch is controlled directly from the pilot house console. Either JP-5 or diesel fuel can be used for both the gas turbine and diesels.
Arrangement of gas turbine intake differs on later ships.

GUNNERY. The *Antelope* and *Ready* have the Mk 87 weapons control system for rapid acquisition and tracking of fast-moving targets; the system can also direct and fire appropriate weapons automatically. The Mk 87 can operate in a radar mode or with a stabilised optical sight on the weather decks. No further procurement of this advanced fire control system is planned in the Navy although it is being fitted to a number of foreign warships.
(The Mk 87 is an American-produced copy of the Hollandse Signaalapparaten M22 weapons control system).
Other ships have Mk 63 Mod 29 Gunfire Control System with SPG-50 fire control radar.

GRAND RAPIDS (PG 98) *1970, Tacoma Boatbuilding*

MISSILES. The *Benica* (PG 96) was experimentally fitted with a single launcher aft for the Standard interim anti-ship missile in 1971; removed prior to transfer to South Korea later that year.
During the latter part of 1971 the *Antelope* and *Ready* were provided with two standard missile launchers. The box-like missile launchers are fitted at the stern (40 mm gun removed); a reload is provided in an adjacent magazine for each launcher.

NOMENCLATURE. Patrol gunboats are named for small American cities; however, the *Surprise* remembers several earlier US naval ships.

TRANSFERS
Benecia (PG 96) transferred to South Korea on 2 Oct 1971; **Surprise** (PG 97) transferred to Turkey on 28 Feb 1973. Additional transfers from this class to Turkey are antcipated.

PHOTOGRAPHS. Note Mk 87 antenna sphere on the *Ready*. The gas turbine air intake is immediately aft of the bridge structure; the adjacent large funnel is the turbine exhaust with a smaller diesel exhaust stack to either side. The *Antelope* and *Ready* are shown at Monaco and the *Antelope* firing an RIM-66A Standard missile.

MARATHON (PG 89) *1968, United States Navy*

Patrol Ships and Craft—*continued*

2 PATROL HYDROFOIL MISSILE BOATS (PHM)

PHM 1 **PHM 2**

Displacement, tons	220 tons
Dimensions, feet	approx 130 × 25 × 18 (with foils down)
Missile launchers	4 launchers for Harpoon Surface to-surface-missile
Guns	1—76 mm/62 calibre AA (see *Gunnery* notes)
Main engines	foil borne; 1 gas turbine (General Electric LM 2 500); water-jet propulsion = 40 + knots hull borne; 2 diesels (Mercedes-Benz); water-jet propulsion =
Complement	approx 21 (accomodation for 5 officers and 18 enlisted men)

The US Navy plans a class of approximately 30 missile boats of this design for "shadowing" Soviet naval forces in restricted sea areas and defence of amphibious landing areas, in both roles relieving larger destroyers and escort ships currently employed for those puposes.
The PHM is being developed in conjunction with other NATO navies in an effort to develop a basic design that would be universally acceptable with minor modifications. At this writing Germany and Italy have joined in the PHM effort with financial support of the craft's developement.
The Navy awarded a contract to the Boeing Company, Seattle, Washington, in December 1971 to design the PHM based on a modified *Tucumcari* plan, and to procure long-lead time components for the first two boats; subsequently Boeing was awarded a construction contract in March 1973 for PHM 1 and PHM 1 authorised in the Fiscal Year 1973 new constructional programme. Estimated cost of the PHM 1 and PHM 2 is $77 000 000; the subsequent boats are estimated to cost $18 000 000 each.
Both PHMs were to be launched in 1974.

DESIGN. The PHM design provides for fully submerged foils; the forward foil assembly provides steering by rotating the strut about its vertical axis. The foil-borne operation is automatic with a wave-height sensing system to maintain the hull clear of the seas. For displacement operation the forward foil rotates forward and the after foil back and up over the stern (the after foils are joined together, unlike those of the *Tucumcari* that can swing outboard and up). Aluminium construction. Designed for foilborne operations at speeds in excess of 40 knots in 8- to 12- foot seas; range is over 500 nautical miles at 40 knots.

ELECTRONICS. The Mk 92 fire control system will be fitted (Americanised version of the WM-28 radar and weapon control system developed by N. V. Hollandse Signallapparaten).

GUNNERY. Gun armament will be a single 76 mm/62 calibre OTO Melara rapid-fire weapon (designated Mk 75 in US service). No secondary gun armament is planned for the US units; the German and Italian navies are planning to provide their units with two 20 mm single gun mounts on the 01 level aft of the spherical fire control radar antenna.

PHOTOGRAPHS. Note light-weight cannister launchers for Harpoon missile on fantail in artist's concept of PHM.

PHM DESIGN *Boeing Company*

1 HYDROFOIL GUNBOAT (PGH): "TUCUMCARI" TYPE

***TUCUMCARI** PGH 2

Displacement, tons	58 full load
Dimensions, feet	71·75 oa × 19·5 × 4·5 (hull borne) or 13·9 (foils down)
Guns	1—40 mm AA; 2—20 mm AA (twin) 4—·50 cal MG (twin)
Main engines	foil borne: 1 gas turbine (Proteus); 3 040 hp; water-jet propulsion = 40+ knots hull borne: 1 diesel (General Motors); 150 bhp; water-jet propulsion
Complement	13 (1 officer, 12 enlisted men)

The *Tucumcari* is one of two hydrofoil gunboats built by the US Navy as competitive prototypes. Built by Boeing Company in Seattle, Washington, with hull fabricated by Gunderson Brothers of Portland, Oregon. Laid down on 1 Sep 1966, launched on 15 July 1967, placed in service on 7 Mar 1968. Construction cost was $4 000 000. Hydrofoil gunboats are "in service" rather than being in commission.

During the latter half of 1971 the *Tucumcari* operated in European waters in a series of most successful demonstrations for NATO naval officials; subsequently she was severely damaged in running aground on 15 Nov 1972.

DESIGN. The *Tucumcari* has the canard foil configuration with approximately 30 per cent of the boat's weight supported by the forward foil and 70 per cent by the aft set of foils. The forward foil assembly provides steering by means of rotating the strut about its vertical axis. The foil-borne operation is automatic with a wave-height sensing system to maintain the hull clear of the sea. The foils are fully retractable for hull borne-operations. Aluminuim construction.

"TUCUMCARI" TYPE—*Continued*

ENGINEERING. During foil-borne operations the craft's gas turbines drive a water-jet pump instead of a propeller. Water is taken in from the sea through openings in the main pods and carried in ducts within the foil struts to the pump inlet. The water—at the rate of approximately 27 000 gallons (100 tons) per minute—is then pumped out through nozzles under the craft's stern to obtain thrust. The jet pump has a thrust rating comparable to the 18 000-pound thrust of commercial aircraft engines. Hull-borne operation is by means of a diesel-driven water-jet pump.

GUNNERY. Prior to early 1971 deployment to the Mediterranean the *Tucumcari's* 81 mm mortar was replaced by a twin 20 mm "turret". The after 20 mm "turret" can be easily removed to provide more deck space (see photograph of craft with foils raised.)

PHOTOGRAPHS. The *Tucumcari* can be distinguished from the *Flagstaff* by the former's larger deckhouse structure and bow foil strut; the *Flagstaff* has a stern strut and short funnel aft. The twin 20 mm "turret" on the fantail is easily removed to provide additional deck space. The photographs below shows the *Tucumcari* in Copenhagen harbour on her NATO demonstration.

TUCUMCARI (PGH 2) *1971 US Navy, PHC B. M. Anderson*

TUCUMCARI (PGH 2) *1971, US Navy, PHC B. M. Anderson*

TUCUMCARI (PGH 2) *Boeing*

Patrol Ships and Craft—*continued*

1 HYDROFOIL GUNBOAT (PGH): "FLAGSTAFF" TYPE

***FLAGSTAFF** PGH 1

Displacement, tons	56·8 full load
Dimensions, feet	74·4 oa × 21·4 × 4·5 (hull borne) or 13·5 (foils down)
Guns	1—40 mm AA
Main engines	foil borne: 1 gas turbine (Rolls-Royce); 3 620 hp; controllable pitch propeller = 40+ knots hull borne; 2 diesels (General Motors); 300 bhp water-jet propulsion
Complement	13 (1 officer, 12 enlisted men)

The *Flagstaff* is a competitive prototype being evaluated with the *Tucumcari*. Built by Grumman Aircraft Corporation in Stuart, Florida. Laid down on 15 July 1966, launched on 9 Jan 1968, placed in service in July 1968. Construction cost was $3 600 000. The *Flagstaff* has conducted sea trials with a 152 mm howitzer (see *Gunnery* notes), foil-mounted sonars, and towed shapes representing variable depth sonar (VDS).

DESIGN. The *Flagstaff* has a conventional foil arrangement with 70 per cent of the craft's weight supported by the forward set of foils and 30 per cent of the weight supported by the stern foils. Steering is accomplished by movement of the stern strut about its vertical axis. Foil-borne operation is automatically controlled by a wave-height sensing system. The foils are fully retractable for hull-borne operations. Aluminium construction.

ENGINEERING. During foil-borne operations the propeller is driven by a geared transmission system contained in the tail strut and in the pod located at the strut-foil connection. During hull-borne operation two diessel engines drive a water-jet propulsion system. Water enters the pump inlets through openings in the hull and the thrust is exerted by water flow through nozzles in the transome. Steering in the hull-borne mode is by deflection vanes in the water stream. Rolls-Royce Tyne Mk 621 gas turbine engine.

GUNNERY. Originally armed with one 40 mm gun forward, four ·50 cal MG amidships, and an 81 mm mortar aft.

Rearmed in 1971 with a 152 mm gun forward. The weapon was the same used on the Army's Sheridan armoured reconnaissance vehicle; low-velocity firing a fully combustible cartridge. After firing trials in 1971 the gun was removed. See page 706 of 1971-1972 edition for view of *Flagstaff* underway with 152 mm gun.

FLAGSTAFF (PGH 1) — *1968, United States Navy*

FLAGSTAFF (PGH 1) with 152 mm howitzer — *1971, US Navy*

FLAGSTAFF (PGH 1) — *Grumman*

1 EXPERIMENTAL HYDROFOIL (PCH): "HIGH POINT" TYPE

***HIGH POINT** PCH 1

Displacement, tons	110 full load
Dimensions, feet	115 oa × 31 × 6 (hull borne) or 17 (foils down)
Guns	2—50 cal MG (twin). See *Gunnery* notes
A/S weapons	4 torpedo launchers (twin)
Main engines	foil borne; 2 gas turbines (Bristol Siddeley Marine Proteus); 6 200 shp; 2 paired counter-rotating propellers = 48 knots hull borne; diesel (Curtis Wright); 600 bhp; retractable outdrive with 1 propeller = 12 knots
Complement	13 (1 officer, 12 enlisted men)

Experimental hydrofoil submarine chaser. Authorised under Fiscal Year 1960 programme. Built jointly by Boeing Aircraft Corpn, Seattle, Washington, and J. M. Martinac, Tacoma, Washington, at Martinac's Tacoma Yard. Laid down on 27 Feb 1961. Launched on 17 Aug 1962. Completed and placed in service on 3 Sep 1963. Employed in experimental hydrofoil work.

GUNNERY. A single 40 mm gun was mounted forward in 1968; subsequently removed. Machine guns are not normally mounted.

No 9 Recently used in various component tests for PHM programme.

HIGH POINT (PCH 1) — *Boeing*

HIGH POINT (PCH 1) — *Boeing*

4 FAST PATROL BOATS (PTF): PTF 23 TYPE

***PTF 23** ***PTF 24** ***PTF 25** ***PTF 26**

Displacement, tons	105 full load
Dimensions, feet	94·66 oa × 23·2 × 7
Guns	1—81 mm mortar; 1—50 cal MG (mounted over mortar); 1—40 mm (aft); 2—20 mm (single)
Main engines	2 diesels (Napier Deltic); 6 200 bhp; 2 shafts = approx 40 knots
Complement	approx 20

PTF 23-26 built by Sewart Seacraft Division of Teledyne Inc of Berwick, Louisiana. First unit completed in 1967, others in 1968. Aluminium hulls. Commercial name is "Osprey".

All four units are in service.

PTF 23 TYPE — *United States Navy*

Patrol Ships and Craft—*continued*

PTF 23 TYPE *United States Navy*

6 FAST PATROL BOATS (PTF): PTF 17 TYPE

* PTF 17	* PTF 19	* PTF 21
* PTF 18	* PTF 20	* PTF 22

Displacement, tons: 85 full load
Dimensions, feet: 80·3 oa × 24·5 × 6·8
Guns (may vary): 1—81 mm mortar; 1—40 mm; 2—20 mm (single); 1—50 cal MG (mounted over mortar)
Main engines: 2 diesels (Napier-Deltic); 6 200 bhp; 2 shafts = approx 45 knots
Complement: 19 (3 officers, 16 enlisted men)

PTF 17-22 built by John Trumpy & Sons, Annapolis, Maryland; lead boat completed in late 1967, others 1968-1970. Based on "Nasty" design.
All six units are in service (PTF 21 and 22 were given "commissioned" status on 14 May 1969 but subsequently returned to "in service" on 23 Sep 1970).

7 FAST PATROL BOATS (PTF): "NASTY" TYPE

* PTF 3	* PTF 6	* PTF 10	* PTF 12
* PTF 5	* PTF 7	* PTF 11	

Displacement, tons: 85 full load
Dimensions, feet: 80·3 oa × 24·5 × 6·8
Guns (may vary): 1—81 mm mortar; 1—40 mm; 2—20 mm (single); 1—50 cal MG (mounted over mortar)
Main engines: 2 diesels (Napier-Deltic); 6 200 bhp; 2 shafts = 45 knots
Complement: 19 (3 officers, 16 enlisted men)

PTF 3-16 of the "Nasty" type were built by Boatservice Ltd A/S of Mandal, Norway. Same design as the Norwegian Navy's "Tjeld" class torpedo boats. PTF 3 and PTF 4 delivered to USA in December 1962, PTF 5-8 in April 1964, and PTF 9-16 in September 1964. Hulls made of two layers of mahogany which sandwich a layer of fibreglass. British engines. Endurance is 450 miles at 41 knots or 600 miles at 25 knots.

DISPOSALS AND LOSSES
PTF 1 (ex-PT 810) and **PTF 2** (ex-PT 811) stricken from the Navy list on 1 Aug 1955 (sunk as targets). Sunk in Vietnam: **PTF 4** on Nov 4 1965, **PTF 8** on 16 June 1966, **PTF 9** on 7 Mar 1966, **PTF 14** on 22 Apr 1966, **PTF 15** on 22 Apr 1966, and **PTF 16** on 19 Aug 1966; **PTF 13** stricken in 1972.

PTF "NASTY" TYPE *1970, United States Navy*

PTF "NASTY" TYPE *1970, US Navy, Ensign Rodney Moen*

COASTAL PATROL AND INTERDICTION CRAFT

Displacement, tons: 71·25 full load
Dimensions, feet: 99·2 oa × 18 × 6
Guns: 4—30 mm MG (twin) basic
Main engines: 3 gas turbines (Avco-Lycoming TF-25); 5 400 hp; water-jet propulsion = 45 knots
2 auxiliary outboard drive diesels; 300 bhp
Complement: approx 15 (varies with armament)

The US Navy has developed the Coastal Patrol and Interdiction Craft (CPIC) for coastal/inshore operations, succeeding the PTF types. The CPIC is capable of operating in rougher water than the PTFs and is more adaptable for cold and hot weather operating areas.
The prototype CPIC was built by Tacoma Boatbuilding Co, Tacoma, Washington, for transfer to South Korea during 1973. Additional units may be built in South Korea. US Navy requirements for these craft are being studied.
Basic CPIC design provides for two 30 mm twin gun mounts, one forward and one amidships on 01 deck level aft of bridge. Other weapons may be carried as required for specific operations including possibly Harpoon missile in light-weight canister launcher.

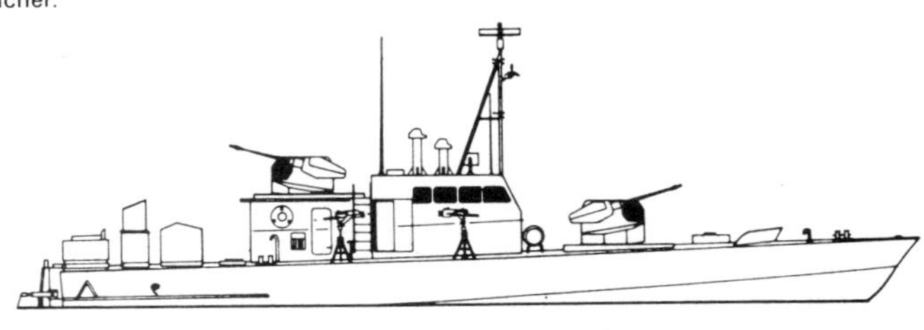

SPECIAL WARFARE CRAFT

The US Navy is developing the technologies necessary to produce a number of small craft designs suitable for inshore and coastal warfare missions of the US Navy and allied navies.
Specific designs being considered are the coastal Patrol and interdiction Craft (CPIC), described above; Coastal Patrol Craft (CPC); Shallow Water Attack craft, Medium (SWAM); and Shallow Water Attack craft, Light (SWAL).

SWIMMER SUPPORT CRAFT

The US Navy operates several specialised craft in support of "frogmen" (combat swimmers) assigned to SEAL (Sea-Air-Land) teams, Underwater Demolition Teams (UDT), and explosive Ordenance Disposal (EOD) teams. Most of the craft listed in previous editions have been discarded and the primary craft in service today is the 36-foot Medium SEAL Support Craft (MSSC). A new craft for this role probably will be developed in the near future.

MEDIUM SEAL SUPPORT CRAFT(MSSC) *United States Navy*

RIVERINE WARFARE CRAFT

5 INSHORE PATROL CRAFT (PCF): "SWIFT" TYPE

5 PCF Mark 1 series

Displacement, tons: 22·5 full load
Dimensions, feet: 50·1 oa × 13 × 3·5
Guns: 1—81 mm mortar, 3—50 cal MG (twin MG mount atop pilot house and single MG mounted over mortar)
Main engines: 2 geared diesels (General Motors); 960 shp; 2 shafts = 28 knots
Complement: 6 (1 officer, 5 enlisted men)

The "Swift" design is adapted from the all-metal crew boat which is used to support off-shore drilling rigs in the Gulf of Mexico. Approximately 125 built since 1965. Most transferred to South Vietnam (see below).
Designation changed from Fast Patrol Craft (PCF) to Inshore Patrol Craft on 14 Aug 1968.

TRANSFERS. PCF 33, 34, and 83-86 transferred to the Philippines in 1966. Additional PCFs of this type constructed specifically for transfer to Thailand, the Philippines, and South Korea; not assigned US hull numbers in the PCF series. 104 PCFs formerly manned by US Navy personnel transferred to South Vietnam in 1968-1970.

PCF MARK 1 TYPE *1969, United States Navy*

Riverine Warfare Craft—*continued*

35 RIVER PATROL BOATS (PBR)

15 **PBR** Mk II series 20 **PBR** Mk III series

Displacement, tons	8
Dimensions, feet	32 oa × 11 × 2·6
Guns	3—·50 cal MG (twin mount forward; single aft); 1—40 mm grenade launcher; 1—60 mm mortar in some boats
Main engines	2 geared diesels (General Motors); water jets = 25+ knots
Complement	4 or 5 (enlisted men)

Fibreglass hull river patrol boats. Approximately 425 built 1967-1970; most transferred to South Vietnam. Twenty Mk III type built for US Navy 1972-1973.

PBR Mk II Type *United States Navy*

2 ASSAULT SUPPORT PATROL BOATS (ASPB)

Dimensions, feet	50 oa × 20
Guns	1—105 mm howitzer; 2—30 mm; 2—7·62 mm MG; 1—40 mm grenade launcher (see notes)
Main engines	3 gas turbines (United Aircraft of Canada); water-jet propulsion = approx 40 knots (designed)

The Sikorsky Aircraft Division of United Aircraft Corp, and the Sewart Seacraft Division of Teledyne, Inc, have developed prototype advanced ASPBs for the Navy (designated Mark 2). The Sikorsky craft is described above and shown on trials during March-April 1969 in Long Island Sound. It has a light-weight 105 mm howitzer and two 20 mm cannon mounted in a tank-like turret which has a 360 degree field of fire. The smaller, forward mount is remote controlled and initially contains two 7·62 mm MG and a 40 mm grenade launcher, but Sikorsky has proposed replacing the machine-guns with two 20 mm cannon. Also fitted for minesweeping; note position of radar on tripod mast aft. The Sewart Seacraft ASPB is similar, but initially has an 81 mm mortar in lieu of the 105 mm howitzer. Both craft are heavily armoured with the main turret and engines on shock springs to reduce effects of mine explosions.

No production will be undertaken at this time; reportedly the designed speed has not been achieved.

ASPB Mk 2 *1969, Sikorsky United Aircraft*

3 ASSAULT SUPPORT PATROL BOATS (ASPB)

Displacement, tons	36·25 full load
Dimensions, feet	50 oa × 15·6 × 3·75
Guns (varies)	1 or 2—20 mm (with 2—·50 cal MG in boats with one 20 mm) 2—30 cal MG; 2—40 mm high-velocity grenade launchers
Main engines	2 diesels (General Motors); 2 shafts = 14 knots sustained
Complement	6 (enlisted)

The ASPB was designed specifically for riverine operations to escort other river craft, provide mine countermeasures during river operations, and interrupt enemy river traffic. Welded-steel hulls. Armament changed to above configuration in 1968; some boats have twin—50 cal MG "turret" forward in place of single 20 mm gun.

Note that open stern well is plated over in the ASPB pictured here (A-131-2); a view of an ASPB with 81 mm mortar/·50 cal MG aft appears in the 1968-1969 editions.

ASSAULT SUPPORT PATROL BOAT (ASPB) *1968, United States Navy*

2 MONITORS (MON)

Displacement, tons	80 to 90 full load
Dimensions, feet	60·5 oa × 17·5 × 3·5
Guns	1—105 mm howitzer; 2—20 mm; 3—·30 cal MG; 2—40 mm high-velocity grenade launchers (see notes)
Main engines	2 diesels; 2 shafts = 8 knots
Complement	11 (enlisted)

These craft designed to provide fire support for riverine operations as well as security for afloat bases. Heavily armoured. One of the remaining US monitors has 105 mm gun; other has two Army M10-8 flame throwers and only one 20 mm gun—dubbed "zippo" monitor.

MONITOR (MON) with howitzer *1968, United States Navy*

15 "MINI" ARMOURED TROOP CARRIERS (ATC)

Dimensions feet	36 oa × 12·66 × 3·5
Main engines	2 diesels (General Motors); water-jet propulsion = 28 knots except one unit with gas turbines.
Complement	2
Troops	15 to 20

A smaller ATC for riverine and swimmer delivery operations; aluminium hull; ceramic armour. Draft is one foot when underway at high speed.

"MINI" ARMOURED TROOP CARRIER (36-ft)

6 ARMOURED TROOP CARRIERS (ATC)

Displacement, tons	66 full load
Dimensions, feet	65·5 oa × 17·5 × 3·25
Guns	1 or 2—20 mm; 2—·50 cal MG; 2 to 6—·30 cal MG; 1—40 mm high-velocity grenade launcher; 2—40 mm low-velocity grenade launchers
Main engines	2 diesels (General Motors); 2 shafts = 8·5 knots max (6 knots sustained)

These craft were converted from LCM-6 landing craft to transport troops, small vehicles field artillery, and supplies. Heavily armoured. Several have been fitted with light steel helicopter platforms to facilitate evacuation of wounded personnel. Armament changed to the above configuration in 1968.

ARMOURED TROOP CARRIER (ATC) *1968, United States Navy*

1 COMMAND AND CONTROL BOAT (CCB)

Displacement, tons	80 full load
Dimensions, feet	61 oa × 17·5 × 3·4
Guns	3—20 mm; 2—·30 cal MG; 2—40 mm high velocity-grenade launchers
Main engines	2 diesels (Detroit); 2 shafts = 8·5 knots max (6 knots sustained)
Complement	11

These craft serve as afloat command posts providing command and communications facilities for ground force and boat group commanders. Heavily armoured. Armament changed to above configuration in 1968. Converted from LCM-6 landing craft.

MINE WARFARE SHIPS

ıe mining of Haiphong harbour and other North Vietnam-ıe ports in April of 1972 has caused a revival of interest mine warfare in the United States. The mining ›erations, conducted by Navy carrier-based aircraft, considered the beginning of that phase of US military ›erations against North Vietnam which culminated in ›e cease-fire agreement of January 1973.
ubsequently, US minesweeping operations have been ›nducted to clear North Vietnamese waters. These ›erations were carried out by Navy- and Marine-piloted H-53 Sea Stallion helicopters, and the few ocean mine-weepers (MSO) remaining in active service.

oth the mining and minesweeping operations provided ›pportunities for the Navy to test and practice mine arfare techniques that had been developed during the vo decades since the Korean War of 1950-1953. owever, it appears unlikely that the Vietnam War will ause any change in the downward trend of mine warfare *hip* strength. During 1973-1974 the active Navy mine-weeping fleet consists of ten active ocean minesweepers us 26 ocean and coastal "sweeps" manned by combined active and reserve crews and assigned to the Naval Reserve Force. This compares to 63 ocean minesweepers in active service during the mid-1960s. Similarly, the US Navy has no surface warships capable of laying mines and the number of submarines capable of planting mines is declining.
The only large mine warfare ship remaining on the Navy list is the mothballed mine countermeasures ship *Oark* (MCS 2), described on a later page. She cannot operate the large CH-53/RH-53 helicopters required for effective "airborne" minesweeping.
The Navy has established a Helicopter Mine Countermeasures Squadron (HM-12) to operate RH-53 Sea Stallion helicopters in the mine countermeasure role. These helicopters tow acoustic and magnetic minesweeping devices. Deliveries of the RH-53 began in April 1973, replacing modified CH-53 helicopters in use since early 1972. These helicopters can operate from bases or amphibious ships such as amphibious assault ships (LPH) and amphibious transport docks (LPD). In addition, they can be deployed rapidly in Air Force C-5A long-range transports, providing more mobility and flexibility than the existing 14-knot minesweepers.
Planning continues for development of future mine hunting/sweeping concepts. At this time there are no construction plans. Although conventional displacement hulls are currently being considered for the mine hunting/sweeping role, future developments in the category of surface platforms could include surface effect ships (SES) or hydrofoil craft. These ships would have a rapid deployment capability, be highly automated to reduce personnel requirements, and be capable of sweeping or destroying advanced-technology mines.
In addition to the ships described in this section, two "Terrebonne Parish" class tank landing ships have been temporarily assigned to support minesweeping operations in Vietnam (in addition to the amphibious ships serving as afloat bases for the minesweeping helicopters). The *Washtenaw County* (LST 1166), redesignated MSS 2 on 1 Feb 1973, and the *Westchester County* (LST 1167) were to revert to their LST role upon completion of the Vietnam operation (code name END SWEEP); see Amphibious Warfare Ships for additional information on these ships.

OCEAN MINESWEEPER (MSO): "ABILITY" CLASS

he two surviving minesweepers of this class, **Alacrity** (MSO 520) and **Assurance** MSO 521), have been allocated to sonar test programmes and redesignated as auxiliary hips AG 520 and AG 521, respectively. See listing under Experimental, Research, nd Surveying Ships. **Ability** (MSO 519) of this class stricken on 1 Feb 1971.

4 OCEAN MINESWEEPERS (MSO): "ACME" CLASS

Name	*No.*	*Launched*	*Commissioned*
ACME	MSO 508	23 June 1955	27 Sep 1956
***ADROIT**	MSO 509	20 Aug 1955	4 Mar 1957
ADVANCE	MSO 510	12 July 1957	16 June 1958
***AFFRAY**	MSO 511	18 Dec 1956	8 Dec 1958

Displacement, tons	720 light; 780 full load
Dimensions, feet	173 oa × 35 × 10
Guns	1—40 mm AA; 2—50 cal MG
Main engines	4 Packard diesels; 2 shafts; 2 800 bhp = 14 knots
Complement	70 peacetime; 68 wartime

his class is different from the "Agile" type but has similar basic particulars. All built y Frank L. Sample, Jnr, Inc, Boothbay Harbour, Maine. Plans to modernise these hips were cancelled (see notes under "Agile" class).

wo ships were decommissioned and placed in reserve late in 1970. *Adroit* and *Affray* re assigned to Naval Reserve training, manned partially by active and partially by reserve ersonnel (see notes under "Agile" class).

AFFRAY (MSO 511) *1969, United States Navy*

ADVANCE (MSO 510) *1968, United States Navy*

40 OCEAN MINESWEEPERS (MSO): "AGILE" CLASS

Name	*No.*	*Launched*	*Commissioned*
AGILE	MSO 421	19 Nov 1955	21 June 1956
AGGRESSIVE	MSO 422	4 Oct 1952	25 Nov 1953
BOLD	MSO 424	14 Mar 1953	25 Sep 1953
BULWARK	MSO 425	14 Mar 1953	12 Nov 1953
***CONSTANT**	MSO 427	14 Feb 1952	8 Sep 1954
***DASH**	MSO 428	20 Sep 1952	14 Aug 1953
***DETECTOR**	MSO 429	5 Dec 1952	26 Jan 1954
***DIRECT**	MSO 430	27 May 1953	9 July 1954
***DOMINANT**	MSO 431	5 Nov 1953	8 Nov 1954
***ENGAGE**	MSO 433	18 June 1953	29 June 1954
EMBATTLE	MSO 434	27 Aug 1953	16 Nov 1954
***ENHANCE**	MSO 437	11 Oct 1952	16 Apr 1955
***ESTEEM**	MSO 438	20 Dec 1952	10 Sep 1955
***EXCEL**	MSO 439	25 Sep 1953	24 Feb 1955
***EXPLOIT**	MSO 440	10 Apr 1953	31 Mar 1954
***EXULTANT**	MSO 441	6 June 1953	22 June 1954
***FEARLESS**	MSO 442	17 July 1953	22 Sep 1954
***FIDELITY**	MSO 443	21 Aug 1953	19 Jan 1955
FIRM	MSO 444	15 Apr 1953	12 Oct 1954
***FORTIFY**	MSO 446	14 Feb 1953	16 July 1954
***ILLUSIVE**	MSO 448	12 July 1952	14 Nov 1953
***IMPERVIOUS**	MSO 449	29 Aug 1952	15 July 1954
***IMPLICIT**	MSO 455	1 Aug 1953	10 Mar 1954
***INFLICT**	MSO 456	6 Oct 1953	11 May 1954
LUCID	MSO 458	14 Nov 1953	4 May 1955
NIMBLE	MSO 459	6 Aug 1954	11 May 1955
OBSERVER	MSO 461	19 Oct 1954	31 Aug 1955
PINNACLE	MSO 462	3 Jan 1955	21 Oct 1955
***PLUCK**	MSO 464	6 Feb 1954	11 Aug 1954
PRIME	MSO 466	27 May 1954	11 Oct 1954
REAPER	MSO 467	25 June 1954	10 Nov 1954
SKILL	MSO 471	23 Apr 1955	7 Nov 1955
VITAL	MSO 474	12 Aug 1953	9 June 1955
***CONQUEST**	MSO 488	20 May 1954	20 July 1955
***GALLANT**	MSO 489	4 June 1954	14 Sep 1955
***LEADER**	MSO 490	15 Sep 1954	16 Nov 1955
***PLEDGE**	MSO 492	20 July 1955	20 Apr 1956
STURDY	MSO 494	28 Jan 1956	23 Oct 1957
SWERVE	MSO 495	1 Nov 1955	27 July 1957
VENTURE	MSO 496	27 Nov 1956	3 Feb 1958

Displacement, tons	665 light; 750 full load
Dimensions, feet	165 wl; 172 × 36 × 13·6
Guns	1—40 mm AA; 2—·50 cal MG (replaced by 2—20 mm AA in several ships); some modernised ships are unarmed
Main engines	4 Packard diesels; 2 shafts; controllable pitch propellers; 2 280 bhp = 15·5 knots; *Dash, Detector, Direct* and *Dominant*, have 4 GM diesels; 1 520 bhp (see *Modernisation* notes)
Complement	70 peacetime; 68 wartime (see *Status* notes.)

These ships were built on the basis of mine warfare experience in the Korean War (1950-1953); they have wooden hulls and non-magnetic equipment. *Bold* and *Bulwark* were built by the Norfolk (Virginia) Naval Shipyard; others by private yards.

Thirty-six ships of this class transferred to NATO navies upon completion.
Initially designated as minesweepers (AM); reclassified as ocean minesweepers (MSO) in Feb 1955. Originally fitted with UQS-1 mine detecting sonar.

Beginning in 1970 a number of these ships were decommissioned and placed in reserve or assigned to Naval Reserve training; see *Status* notes.

ENGINEERING. Diesel engines are fabricated of non-magnetic stainless steel alloy to help reduce possibility of detonating magnetic mines. Range is 2 400 miles at ten knots.

MODERNISATION. The 62 ocean minesweepers in commission during the mid-1960s all were to have been modernised; estimated cost and schedule per ship were $5 000 000 and ten months in shipyard. However, some of the early modernisations took as long as 26 months which, coupled with changes in mine countermeasure techniques, led to cancellation of programme after 13 ships were modernised: MSO 433, 437, 438, 441-443, 445, 446, 448, 449, 456, 488, and 490.

The modernisation provided improvements in mine detection, engines, communications, and habitability: four Waukesha Motor Co diesel engines installed (plus two or three

Mine Warfare Ships—*continued*

"AGILE" CLASS *continued*

diesel generators for sweep gear), SQQ-14 sonar with mine classification as well as detection capability provided, twin 20 mm AA in some ships (replacing single 40 mm because of space requirements for sonar hoist mechanism), habitability improved, and advanced communications equipment fitted; bridge structure in modernised ships extended around mast and aft to funnel. Complement in active modernised ships is 6 officers and 70 enlisted men.
Some MSOs have received SQQ-14 sonar but not full modernisation.

STATUS. Of the surviving ships of this class, ten are in active commission (MSO 433, 437 442, 443, 445, 446, 448, 449, 456, 490), 14 are employed in Naval Reserve training (MSO 427-431, 438-441, 455, 464, 488, 489, 492), and 16 are decommissioned in reserve ("mothballs"). The active ships are manned by crews of 72 to 76 officers and enlisted men; the reserve training ships generally have a crew of 3 officer and 36 enlisted active Navy personnel plus 2 officer and 29 enlisted reserve personnel. Wartime ("mobilisation") complement is 6 officers and 80 enlisted men for MSOs.

TRANSFERS. Ships of this class serve in the navies of Belgium, France, Italy, Netherlands, Norway, Philippines, Portugal, Spain and Uruguay.

DISPOSALS AND TRANSFERS (since 1 Jan 1970)
Avenge MSO 423 stricken on 1 Feb 1970 (fire); **Sagacity** MSO 469 stricken on 1 Oct 1970 (grounding); **Notable** MSO 460, **Rival** MSO 468, **Salute** MSO 470, **Valor** MSO 472 stricken on 1 Feb 1971; **Vigor** MSO 473 transferred to Spain on 5 Apr 1972; **Conflict** MSO 426, **Guide** MSO 447 stricken on 9 June 1972; **Dynamic** MSO 432; **Pivot** MSO 463, **Persistent** MSO 491 to Spain on 1 July 1972; **Endurance** MSO 435, **Loyalty** MSO 457 stricken on 1 July 1972; **Energy** MSO 436, **Firm** MSO 444 transferred to the Philippines on 5 July 1972; **Force** MSO 445 sunk 24 April 1973 (Fire).

LEADER (MSO 490) no gun *1972, Harbor Boat Building Co*

EXCEL (MSO 439) no gun *1971, United States Navy*

EXPLOIT (MSO 440) with 40 mm gun *1969, United States Navy*

ENHANCE (MSO 437) no guns *1971, Harbor Boat Building Co*

13 COASTAL MINESWEEPERS (MSC): "BLUEBIRD" CLASS

Name	*No.*	*Launched*	*Commissioned*
BLUEBIRD	MSC 121	11 May 1953	24 July 1953
CORMORANT	MSC 122	8 June 1953	14 Aug 1953
***PARROT**	MSC 197	27 Nov 1954	28 June 1955
***PEACOCK**	MSC 198	19 June 1954	7 Feb 1955
***PHOEBE**	MSC 199	21 Aug 1954	29 Apr 1955
***SHRIKE**	MSC 201	21 July 1954	21 Mar 1955
***THRASHER**	MSC 203	6 Oct 1954	16 Aug 1955
***THRUSH**	MSC 204	5 Jan 1955	8 Nov 1955
***VIREO**	MSC 205	30 Apr 1954	7 June 1955
***WARBLER**	MSC 206	18 June 1954	16 July 1955
***WHIPPOORWILL**	MSC 207	13 Aug 1954	20 Oct 1955
***WIDGEON**	MSC 208	15 Oct 1954	28 Nov 1955
***WOODPECKER**	MSC 209	7 Jan 1955	3 Feb 1956

Displacement, tons	320 light; 370 full load
Dimensions, feet	138 pp; 144 oa × 28 × 8·2
Guns	2—20 mm AA (twin)
Main engines	2 GM diesels; 2 shafts; 880 bhp = 12 knots (MSC 200-209) Packard engines; 2 shafts; 1 200 bhp = 12·5 knots; (MSC 121, 122, 190-199)
Complement	26 peacetime; 38 wartime (see notes)

Constructed throughout of wood and other materials with the lowest possible magnetic attraction to attain the greatest possible safety factor when sweeping for magnetic mines. Fitted with UQS-1 sonar. Range is 2 500 miles at ten knots.

Only named vessels AMS 121, 122, 190-209 were commissioned into US Navy with MSC 200 and 202 being transferred to Spain in 1959 (replaced by MSC 298 and 290 in US Navy)
An additional 167 coastal minesweepers of this design were built in US private shipyards for NATO and other allied navies (see *Transfers*).
Bluebird decommissioned in 1971 and *Cormorant* in 1970 and placed in reserve. The 11 other ships are manned jointly by active and reserve crews and assigned to Naval Reserve training/Naval Reserve Force. These ships are manned by crews of 1 officer and 11 enlisted active navy personnel plus 3 officers and 11 enlisted reserve personnel. Wartime ("mobilisation") complement is 5 officers and 33 enlisted men.

TRANSFERS. Minesweepers of this class serve in the navies of Belgium, Denmark, France, Greece, Indonesia, Japan, South Korea, Netherlands, Norway, Pakistan, Philippines, Portugal, Spain, Taiwan China, Thailand, Tunisia, Turkey, and South Korea. (See 1971-1972 and previous editions for details of earlier transfers).

DISPOSALS AND TRANSFERS (since 1 Jan 1970)
Jacana MSC 193, **Meadow Lark** MSC 196 transferred to Indonesia on 7 Apr 1971; **Falcon** MSC 190, **Limpkin** MSC 195 to Indonesia on 24 June 1971; **Hummingbird** MSC 192 to Indonesia on 12 July 1971; **Frigate Bird** MSC 191 to Indonesia on 11 Aug 1971; **Kingbird** MSC 194 stricken on 1 July 1972 (collision); **Parrot** MSC 197 stricken in Aug 1972.

Albatross MSC 289 and **Gannet** MSC 290 of a modified design were stricken on 1 Apr 1970.

PEACOCK (MSC 198) *United States Navy*

Mine Warfare Ships—*continued*

BLUEBIRD (MSC 121) *1967, United States Navy*

FLEET MINESWEEPERS (MSF): "AUK" AND "ADMIRABLE" CLASSES

The 29 surviving fleet minesweepers (MSF) of the "Auk" and "Admirable" classes were stricken by the US Navy on 1 July 1972. See 1972-1973 and previous editions for names, hull numbers, and characteristics. Subsequently, 21 of these ships were transferred to Mexico on 19 Sep 1972 and in Feb 1973, with 10 ships intended for active service and the remainder for parts cannibalisation; units transferred were: MSF 64, 101, 104, 105, 111, 120, 123, 124, 128, 306, 311, 314-319, 322, 340, 379, and 381 (all "Auk" class except *Specture* MSF 306 and *Superior* MSF 311 of "Admirable" class).

TRANSFERS. Ships of the "Auk" class serve in the navies of South Korea, Mexico, Norway, Peru, Philippines, Taiwan China, and Uruguay; ships of the "Admirable" class serve in the navies of Burma, Dominican Republic, Mexico, Taiwan China, and South Vietnam.

Bittern MHC 43, a prototype coastal mine hunter built in 1955-1957, has been on loan to a commercial operator since July 1966; officially stricken by US Navy on 1 Feb 1972.

1 MINE COUNTERMEASURES SHIP (MCS): "CATSKILL" CLASS

Name	*No.*	*Builder*	*Laid down*	*Launched*	*LSV Comm*	*MCS Comm*
OZARK	MCS 2 (ex-LSV 2, ex-CM 7, ex-AP 107)	Willamette Iron & Steel	12 July 1941	15 June 1942	23 Sep 1944	24 June 1966

Displacement, tons	5 875 standard; 9 040 full load
Length, feet (*metres*)	440 (*134·1*) wl; 455·5 (*138·8*) oa
Beam, feet (*metres*)	60·2 (*18·4*)
Draft, feet (*metres*)	20 (*6·1*)
Guns	2—5 inch (*127 mm*) 38 cal DP (single)
Helicopters	2 RH-3A minesweeping helicopters
Main engines	2 geared turbines (General Electric); 11 000 shp; 2 shafts
Boilers	4 (Combustion Engineering "D" type)
Speed, knots	20·3
Complement	586 (47 officers and 539 enlisted men)

The *Ozark* was one of two similar ships converted to carry and support minesweeping launches and helicopters. Sister ship *Catskill* (MSC 1) has been stricken.

Although extensively converted for the mine warfare role, the *Ozark* was not considered suitable for advanced mine countermeasures operations (she cannot operate the large RH-53D minesweeping helicopters); decommissioned on 6 Feb 1970 and transferred to Maritime Administration reserve (remains on Navy List).

CLASSIFICATION. Designed as a large minelayer (CM), redesignated as a troop transport (AP), and initially completed as a vehicle landing ship (LSV). Reclassified as a mine warfare command and support ship (MCS) in 1955, changed to mine countermeasures and support ship (MCS) in 1958, to mine countermeasures support ship (MCS) on 25 Aug 1960, and to mine countermeasures ship (MCS) on 14 Aug 1968.
The *Ozark* was decommissioned and placed in reserve on 29 June 1946; stricken from the Navy List on 1 Sep 1961 but reinstated on 1 Oct 1963 for conversion to MCS configuration.

CONVERSION. Converted to a mine countermeasures ship under the Fiscal Year 1963 shipbuilding and conversion programme at Norfolk Shipbuilding & Dry Dock Corp, Norfolk, Virginia, from Sep 1963 to June 1966. Converted to carry and support 20 minesweeping launches (MSL) and two RH-3A minesweeping helicopters. Maintenance shops, minesweeping equipment stowage, and accommodation for minesweeping crews provided.

DESIGN. In the LSV role the *Ozark* could carry amphibious tractors and tanks, unloaded into the water by a stern ramp. Original armament consisted of two 5 inch DP guns and eight 40 mm AA guns.

OZARK (MCS 2) *1969, United States Navy*

DISPOSALS
Five additional ships were built to this basic design: **Saugus** MCS 4 (ex-LSV 4, ex-AN 4) stricken from the Navy List on 1 July 1961; **Monitor** MCS 5 (ex-LSV 5, ex-AN 5) and **Osage** MCS 3 (ex-LSV 3, ex-AN 3) stricken on 1 Sep 1961; **Galilea** (ex-*Montauk*) AKN 6 (ex-LSV 6, ex-AN 2, ex-AP 161) stricken on 1 Sep 1960; **Catskill** MCS 1 (ex-LSV 1, ex-CM 6, ex-AP 106) stricken on 1 July 1961, reinstated on Navy List on 1 June 1964, and again stricken (after conversion) on 20 Nov 1970.
Epping Forest MCS 7 (ex-LSD 4) stricken on 1 Nov 1968.
Orleans Parish MCS 6 (ex-LST 1069) redesignated as LST on 1 June 1966 (listed with Military Sealift Ships).

FLEET MINELAYER (MMF)

The cruiser-type fleet minelayer **Terror** (MMF 5, ex-MM 5, ex-CM 5) stricken on 1 Nov 1970. (See 1970-1971 and previous editions for characteristics).

FAST MINELAYERS (MMD)

Fast minelayers converted during construction from "Allen M. Sumner" class destroyers: **Robert H. Smith** (MMD/DM 23, ex-DD 735) stricken on 26 Feb 1971; **Thomas E. Fraser** (MMD/DM 24, ex-DD 736), **Shannon** (MMD/DM 25, ex-DD 737) stricken on 1 Nov 1970; **Harry F. Bauer** (MMD/DM 26, ex-DD 738 stricken on 15 Aug 1971.
Adams (MMD/DM 27, ex-DD 739), **Tolman** (MMD/DM 28, ex-DD 740) stricken on 1 Dec 1970; **Henry A. Wiley** (MMD/DM 29, ex-DD 749) stricken on 15 Oct 1970; **Shea** (MMD/DM 30, ex-DD 750) expected to be stricken during 1973. **J. William Ditter** (DM 31), ex-DD 751), stricken on 11 Oct 1945 (battle damaged); **Lindsey** (MMD/DM 32, ex-DD 771) stricken on 1 Oct 1970; **Gwin** (MMD/DM 33, ex-DD 772) stricken on 15 Aug 1971 and transferred to Turkey on 22 Oct 1971. **Aaron Ward** (DM 34, ex-DD 773) stricken on 11 Oct 1945 (battle damaged).

OZARK (MCS 2) *1966, United States Navy*

MINE COUNTERMEASURES CRAFT

1 SPECIAL MINESWEEPER (MSS)

***MSS 1** (ex-*Harry L. Gluckman*)

Displacement, tons	15 000 full load
Dimensions, feet	441·5 oa × 57 ×28
Main engines	5 outboard deck mounted diesels = 10 knots
Complement	9 (1 officer, 8 enlisted men)

A "Liberty" ship converted to explode pressure mines. Specially modified to withstand mine explosions and remain afloat and underway. Conversion authorised in Fiscal Year 1966 and work began at American Shipbuilding Co, Lorain, Ohio, in Aug 1966; completed on 16 June 1969. EC-2S-C1 design originally completed in 1943. The MMS 1 placed in reserve on 15 Mar 1973.

(Ten "Liberty" ships were partially modified in 1952-1953 to explode pressure mines. Only one ship placed in service, the ex-*John L. Sullivan* as YAG-37. Fitted with four T-34 turbo-prop aircraft engines on deck and stuffed with buoyancy material. She was employed in mine countermeasures experiments until reduced to a floating wreck; scrapped in 1958).

16 MINESWEEPING BOATS (MSB)

MSB 6	**MSB 16**	**MSB 28**	**MSB 40**
MSB 7	**MSB 17**	**MSB 29**	**MSB 41**
MSB 13	**MSB 25**	**MSB 35**	**MSB 51**
MSB 15	**MSB 26**	**MSB 36**	**MSB 52**

Displacement, tons	30 light; 39 full load except MSB 29, 80 full load
Dimensions, feet	57·2 × 15·5 × 4 except MSB 29, 82 × 19 × 5·5
Guns	several MG (Vietnam configuration)
Main engines	2 geared diesels (Packard); 2 shafts; 600 bhp = 12 knots
Complement	6 (enlisted)

Wooden-hull minesweepers intended to be carried to theatre of operations by large assault ships; however, they are too large to be easily handled by cranes and assigned to sweeping harbours. From 1966 to Sep 1970 they were used extensively in Vietnam for river operations.

Of 49 minesweeping boats of this type built only 16 remain in active service all based at Charleston, South Carolina. (See 1971-1972 and previous editions for details of earlier disposals and additional data).

MSB 1-4 were ex-Army minesweepers built in 1946 (since discarded), MSB 5-54 (less MSB 24) were completed in 1952-1956. MSB 24 was not built. MSB 29 built to enlarged design by John Trumpy & Sons, Annapolis, Maryland in an effort to improve seakeeping ability.

Normally commanded by chief petty officer or petty officer first class.

ENGINEERING. MSB 5 was the first vessel built for the US Navy with gas turbine engines (to provide power for the boat's generators). 48 MSBs fitted with gas turbine generators.

GUNNERY. MSBs serving in South Vietnam were fitted with several machineguns and removable fibreglass armour. Note machineguns in tub amidships and on bow of MSB 17; shown below sweeping on the Long Tao river in South Vietnam.

MSB 17 — *1966, United States Navy*

1 INSHORE MINESWEEPER (MSI): "COVE" CLASS

***CAPE** MSI 2

Displacement, tons	120 light; 240 full load
Dimensions, feet	105 × 22 × 10
Main engines	2 GM diesels; 1 shaft; 650 bhp = 12 knots
Complement	21 (3 officers, 18 men)
Guns	(removed)

The *Cape* and a sister ship *Cove* (MSI 1) were prototype inshore minesweepers authorised under the Fiscal Year 1956 new construction programme. Both built at Bethlehem Shipyards Co, Bellingham, Washington. *Cape* laid down on 1 May 1957, launched on 5 Apr 1968, and placed in service on 27 Feb 1959.

The *Cape* is operated by the Naval Undersea Research Development Center, San Diego, California; neither in service nor in commission.

Cove MSI 1 transferred to Johns Hopkins Applied Physics Laboratory on 31 July 1970; technically she remains on the Navy List.

MSI 3-10 were built in the Netherlands for the Dutch Navy under US Military Assistance Programme; MSI 11 and MSI 12 built in Denmark under MAP; MSI 13 and MSI 14 built in United States for Iran; MSI 15-19 built in United States for Turkey.

CAPE MSI 2 — *1968, United States Navy*

16 MINESWEEPING LAUNCHES (MSL)

Displacement, pounds	23 100 full load
Hoisting weight, pounds	18 500
Dimensions, feet	36 oa × 11·6 × 3·7
Main engines	Gas turbine; 1 shaft; 200 shp = 12 knots or geared diesel; 1 shaft; 160 bhp = 10 knots
Complement	4 to 6 (enlisted men)

Versatile minesweeping craft intended to sweep for acoustic, magnetic, and moored mines in inshore waters and in advance of landing craft. They are carried by large amphibious ships to assault areas. 16 of these craft remain; all based at Charleston, South Carolina.

CONSTRUCTION. MSL 1-4 completed in 1946 (wood hull, gas turbine); MSL 5-29 completed in 1948 (wood hull, gas turbine); MSL 30 completed in 1948 (plastic hull, gas turbine); MSL 31-56 completed in 1966 (plastic hull; geared diesel); three wood hull boats converted to geared diesel in 1967.

MSL 11, MSL 17, MSL 14 — *1967, United States Navy*

RIVERINE MINECOUNTERMEASURE CRAFT

None of the riverine minecountermeasure craft developed by the US Navy during the Vietnam War remain in service; they have been transferred to South Vietnam or scrapped, except for a few laid up in reserve. These craft were patrol minesweepers (MSR), modified ASPB patrol craft; river minesweepers (MSM), converted from LCM-6 landing craft; and small drone minesweepers (MSD). See 1972-1973 and previous editions for characteristics and photographs.

MSS 1 — *1969, United States Navy*

UNDERWAY REPLENISHMENT SHIPS

Underway replenishment (UNREP) ships provide fuel, munitions, provisions, spare parts, and other materiel to warships in forward areas. Replenishment normally is conducted while the ships steam on parallel courses about one hundred feet apart.

In addition, most US Navy replenishment ships are fitted with helicopter platforms to permit helicopters to transfer supplies by vertical replenishment (VERTREP). Virtually all materiel except fuel oil can be transferred by helicopter, reducing, or if fuel oil is not required alleviating, the need for the replenishment ship and warship to steam in close company. Helicopters are carried specifically for this purpose by the newer ammunition ships (AE), the combat store ships (AFS), and the fast combat support ships (AOE). Carrier-based helicopters are sometimes employed in this role when an aircraft carrier is in the area.

All underway replenishment ships are Navy manned with one recent exception, and most are armed with guns for limited self-defence. The logistic ships operated by the Military Sealift Command (MSC) are listed separately under the category of Military Sealift Ships. They normally are not equipped for underway replenishment of other ships, but carry cargo for all of the US armed services from port to port.

A number of concepts are being examined in an effort to improve replenishment capabilities within the current constrained defense budgets: (1) Early in 1972 a civilian-manned merchant tanker under charter to the Military Sealift Command conducted experimental underway replenishments with warships; (2) the complement of the Navy oiler *Marias* (AO 57) has been reduced to just over 100 men on an experimental basis in an effort to reduce operating costs, albeit at the expense of some ship capabilities and readiness; and (3) the oiler *Taluga* (AO 62) was transferred in May 1972 to the Military Sealift Command for operation with a civilian view as an underway replenishment ship on a trial basis. She now is designated T-AO and has the prefix USNS (United States Naval Ship) vice USS.

8 AMMUNITION SHIPS (AE): "KILAUEA" CLASS

Name	*No.*	*Laid down*	*Launched*	*Commissioned*
***KILAUEA**	AE 26	10 Mar 1966	9 Aug 1967	10 Aug 1968
***BUTTE**	AE 27	21 July 1966	9 Aug 1967	29 Nov 1968
***SANTA BARBARA**	AE 28	20 Dec 1966	23 Jan 1968	11 July 1970
***MOUNT HOOD**	AE 29	8 May 1967	17 July 1968	1 May 1971
***FLINT**	AE 32	4 Aug 1969	9 Nov 1970	20 Nov 1971
***SHASTA**	AE 33	10 Nov 1969	3 Apr 1971	26 Feb 1972
***MOUNT BAKER**	AE 34	10 May 1970	23 Oct 1971	22 July 1972
***KISKA**	AE 35	4 Aug 1971	11 Mar 1972	16 Dec 1972

Displacement, tons	20 500 full load
Dimensions, feet	564 oa × 81 × 25·7
Guns	8—3 inch (*76 mm*) 50 cal AA (twin)
Helicopters	2 UH-46 Sea Knight cargo helicopters normally assigned
Main engines	Geared turbines (General Electric); 22 000 shp; 1 shaft = 20 knots
Boilers	3 (Foster Wheeler)
Complement	401 (28 officers, 373 enlisted men)

Ammunition ships of an advanced design. Fitted for rapid transfer of missiles and other munitions to ships alongside or with helicopters in vertical replenishment operations (VERTREP). Helicopter platform and hangar aft. AE 26 and 27 authorised in Fiscal Year 1965 new construction programme, AE 28 and 29 in FY 1966, AE 32 and 33 in FY 1967, and AE 34 and 35 in FY 1968. AE 26 and 27 built by General Dynamics Corp, Quincy, Massachusetts; AE 28 and 29 Bethlehem Steel Corp, Sparrows Point, Maryland; and AE 32-35 by Ingalls Shipbuilding Corp, Pascagoula, Mississippi.

The 3 inch guns are arranged in twin closed mounts forward and twin open mounts aft, atop superstructure, between funnel and after booms.
All of these ships are active.

KISKA (AE 35) — *1972, Ingalls Shipbuilding*

BUTTE (AE 27) — *1972, Giorgio Arra*

5 AMMUNITION SHIPS (AE): "SURIBACHI" CLASS

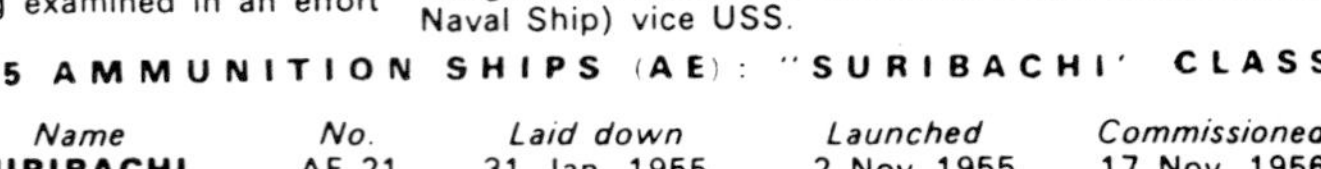

Name	*No.*	*Laid down*	*Launched*	*Commissioned*
***SURIBACHI**	AE 21	31 Jan 1955	2 Nov 1955	17 Nov 1956
***MAUNA KEA**	AE 22	16 May 1955	3 May 1956	30 Mar 1957
***NITRO**	AE 23	20 May 1957	25 June 1958	1 May 1959
***PYRO**	AE 24	21 Oct 1957	5 Nov 1958	24 July 1959
***HALEAKALA**	AE 25	10 Mar 1958	17 Feb 1959	3 Nov 1959

Displacement, tons	7 470 light; 10 000 standard; 17 500 full load
Dimensions, feet	512 oa × 72 × 29
Guns	4—3 inch (*76 mm*) 50 cal AA (twin)
Main engines	Geared turbines (Bethlehem); 16 000 shp; 1 shaft = 20·6 knots
Boilers	2 (Combustion Engineering)
Complement	316 (18 officers, 298 enlisted men)

Ammunition ships designed specifically for underway replenishment. All built by Bethlehem Steel Corp, Sparrows Point Maryland. A sixth ship of this class to have been built under the FY 1959 programme was cancelled.
All ships modernised in 1960s, being fitted with high-speed transfer equipment, three holds configured for stowage of missiles up to and including the 33-foot Talos, and helicopter platform fitted aft (two after twin 3 inch gun mounts removed).
Arrangements of twin 3 inch gun mounts differ, some ships have them in tandem and and others side-by-side.
All of these ships are active.

NOMENCLATURE. Ammunition ships are named for volcanoes and explosives (eg *Nitro* for nitroglycerine and *Pyro* for pyrotechnic).

PYRO (AE 24) — *1971, US Navy, PH 2, Brian L. Chandler*

HALEAKALA (AE 25) — *1968, United States Navy*

FLINT (AE 32) — *1971, Ingalls Shipbuiding*

Underway Replenishment Ships—*continued*

6 AMMUNITION SHIPS (AE): "WRANGELL" CLASS

Name	No.	Launched	Commissioned
WRANGELL (*ex-Midnight*)	AE 12	14 Apr 1944	28 May 1944
FIREDRAKE (*ex-Winged Racer*)	AE 14	12 May 1944	27 Dec 1944
***VESUVIUS** (*ex-Gamecock*)	AE 15	26 May 1944	3 July 1944
***MOUNT KATMAI**	AE 16	6 Jan 1945	21 July 1945
GREAT SITKIN	AE 17	20 Jan 1945	11 Aug 1945
PARICUTIN	AE 18	30 Jan 1945	25 July 1945

Displacement, tons	6 350 light; 15 295 full load
Dimensions, feet	435 wl; 459·2 oa × 63 × 28·2
Guns	2 or 4—3 inch (*76 mm*) 50 cal AA (single)
Main engines	Geared turbine (General Electric); 6 000 shp; 1 shaft = 16·4 knots
Boilers	2 (Babcock & Wilcox or Combustion Engineering)
Complement	approx 265

C2 type cargo ships built by North Carolina Shipbuilding Co, Wilmington, NC. Officially the "Mount Hood" class, the *Mount Hood* AE 11 of this type being sunk in World War II. One 5 inch gun and four 40 mm AA guns removed; the *Firedrake, Mount Katmai,* and *Paricutin* have a helicopter platform installed aft in place of two after 3 inch guns. Four ships decommissioned and placed in reserve 1970-1973.

DISPOSALS
Diamond Head AE 19 stricken on 1 Mar 1973.

WRANGELL (AE 12) *1968, United States Navy*

FIREDRAKE (AE 14) *1969, United States Navy*

1 AMMUNITION SHIP (AE): "LASSEN" CLASS

Name	No.	Launched	Commissioned
MAUNA LOA	AE 8	14 Apr 1943	27 Oct 1943

Displacement, tons	5 220 light; 14 225 full load
Dimensions, feet	435 wl; 459 oa × 63 × 26·5
Guns	2—3 inch (*76 mm*) 50 cal AA (single)
Main engines	Diesel (Nordberg); 6 000 bhp; 1 shaft = 15·3 knots
Complement	281

Built by the Tampa Shipbuilding Co, Tampa, Florida. Modified C2 type, converted by Navy. Original armament was one 5 inch gun, four 3 inch guns, and four 40 mm AA AA guns. *Mauna Loa* transferred to Maritime Administration reserve in 1960; re-acquired and returned to the Navy in Sep 1961 and recommissioned on 27 Nov 1961; fitted with helicopter platform aft. Decommissioned and placed in reserve in 1970.

PHOTOGRAPHS. Note helicopter platform in photograph of *Mauna Loa*; shadow from overhang of forward 3 inch gun "tubs".

DISPOSALS
Akutan AE 13 stricken in 1961, **Lassen** AE 3 stricken on 1 July 1961, **Mount Baker** AE 4 stricken on 2 Dec 1969, **Shasta** AE 6 stricken on 1 July 1969, **Rainier** AE 5 stricken on 7 Aug 1970, **Mazama** AE 9 stricken on 1 Sep 1970.
"Sangay" class: **Sangay**, AE 10, stricken in 1961 and **Formalhaut**, AE 20 ex-AK 22 transferred to Maritime Administration in Sep 1962.
Converted AKA type: **Virgo** AE 30 ex-AKA 20, ex-AK 69, stricken on 18 Feb 1971; **Chara** AE 31 ex-AKA 58 stricken on 10 Mar 1972.

MAUNA LOA (AE 8) *1965 United States Navy*

5 STORE SHIPS (AF): R2-S-BV1 TYPE

Name	No.	Launched	Commissioned
ZELIMA (*ex-Golden Rocket*)	AF 49	2 Mar 1945	27 July 1946
ARCTURUS (*ex-Golden Eagle*)	AF 52	15 Mar 1942	18 Nov 1961
PICTOR (*ex-Great Republic*)	AF 54	4 June 1942	13 Sep 1950
ALUDRA (*ex-Matchless*)	AF 55	14 Oct 1944	7 July 1952
PROCYON (*ex-Flying Scud*)	AF 61	1 July 1942	24 Nov 1961

Displacement, tons	6 914 light; 15 500 full load
Dimensions, feet	459·2 oa × 63 × 28
Guns	8—3 inch (*76 mm*) 50 cal AA (twin) in *Aludra*; most of others are unarmed
Main engines	Geared turbine; 6 000 shp; 1 shaft = 16 knots
Boilers	2

All built by Moore Dry Dock Co, Oakland, California. R2-S-BV1 type refrigerated cargo ships; similar to C2-S-B1 design but built as "reefers".
Arcturus is formerly USNS *Golden Eagle*, transferred from Military Sea Transportation Service to active Navy; renamed on 13 Sep 1961 and commissioned as USS on 18 Nov 1961 after modification for underway replenishment at the New York Naval Shipyard. These ships have been fitted with helicopter platforms.
All have been decommissioned and are in Navy or Maritime Administration reserve fleets; last active ship was *Arcturus*, decommissioned in 1973.

DISPOSALS
Sirius AF 60 stricken in 1965, **Bellatrix** AF 62 stricken on 1 Oct 1968, **Alstede** AF 48 stricken on 31 Oct 1969.

NOMENCLATURE. Store ships are named for stars and constellations.

PROCYON (AF 61) *1970, United States Navy*

ALUDRA (AF 55) *1967, United States Navy*

ARCTURUS (AF 52) *United States Navy*

Underway Replenishment Ships—*continued*

2 STORE SHIPS (AF): R3-S-4A TYPE

Name	No.	Launched	Commissioned
*RIGEL	AF 58	15 Mar 1955	2 Sep 1955
*VEGA	AF 59	26 Apr 1955	10 Nov 1955

Displacement, tons	7 950 light; 15 540 full load
Dimensions, feet	475 wl; 502 oa × 72 × 29 max
Guns	4—3 inch (*76 mm*) 50 cal AA (twin)
Main engines	Geared turbine (General Electric); 16 000 shp; 1 shaft = 20 knots
Boilers	2 (Combustion Engineering)
Complement	approx 350

Built by Ingalls Shipbuilding Co, Pascagoula. R3-S-4A type. Helicopter platform fitted (two after twin 3 inch mounts removed). Both of these ships are active.

RIGEL (AF 58) *1968, United States Navy*

1 STORE SHIP (AF): "VICTORY" TYPE

Name	No.	Launched	Commissioned
*DENEBOLA (ex-*Hibbing Victory*)	AF 56	10 June 1944	20 Jan 1954

Displacement, tons	6 700 light; 12 130 full load
Dimensions, feet	455·2 × 62 × 28·5
Guns	4—3 inch (*76 mm*) 50 cal AA (twin)
Main engines	Geared turbine (Westinghouse); 8 500 shp; 1 shaft = 18 knots
Boilers	2 (Combustion Engineering)
Complement	225

Built by Oregon Shipbuilding Co, Portland, Oregon. Originally VC2-S-AP3 "Victory" type. Acquired by the Navy on 1 May 1952 and converted to underway replenishment ship at New York Naval Shipyard.
Two after twin 3 inch gun mounts removed and helicopter platform fitted.

DENEBOLA (AF 56) *1964, United States Navy*

1 STORE SHIP (AF): C2-S-E1 TYPE

Name	No.	Launched	Commissioned
HYADES (ex-*Iberville*)	AF 28	12 June 1943	30 Sep 1943

Displacement, tons	6 313 light; 15 300 full load
Dimensions, feet	468·66 oa × 63 × 28
Guns	2—3 inch (*76 mm*) 50 cal AA (single)
Main engines	Geared turbine (General Electric); 6 000 shp; 1 shaft = 15·5 knots
Boilers	2 (Babcock & Wilcox)
Complement	252

Built by Gulf Shipbuilding Co, Chickensaw, Alabama. Original armament included one 5 inch gun. Helicopter deck fitted aft in place of two single 3 inch guns during 1962. Decommissioned and placed in reserve in 1969.

DISPOSALS
Graffias AF 29 stricken on 19 Dec 1969.

HYADES (AF 28) *Ing Augusti Nani*

7 COMBAT STORE SHIPS (AFS): "MARS" CLASS

Name	No.	Laid down	Launched	Commissioned
*MARS	AFS 1	5 May 1962	15 June 1963	21 Dec 1963
*SYLVANIA	AFS 2	18 Aug 1962	15 Aug 1963	11 July 1964
*NIAGARA FALLS	AFS 3	22 May 1965	26 Mar 1966	29 Apr 1967
*WHITE PLAINS	AFS 4	2 Oct 1965	23 July 1966	23 Nov 1968
*CONCORD	AFS 5	26 Mar 1966	17 Dec 1966	27 Nov 1968
*SAN DIEGO	AFS 6	11 Mar 1965	13 Apr 1968	24 May 1969
*SAN JOSE	AFS 7	8 Mar 1969	13 Dec 1969	23 Oct 1970

Displacement, tons	16 500 full load
Dimensions, feet	581 oa × 79 × 24
Guns	8—3 in, 50 cal AA (twin)
Helicopters	2 UH-46 Sea Knight helicopters normally assigned
Main engines	Steam turbines; 22 000 shp; 1 shaft = 20 knots
Boilers	3 (Babcock & Wilcox) (one spare)
Complement	430 (30 officers, 400 enlisted men)

All built by National Steel & Shipbuilding, San Diego, California. Of a new design with a completely new replenishment at sea system. "M" frames replace conventional king posts and booms, which are equipped with automatic tensioning devices to maintain transfer lines taut between the ship and the warships being replenished despite rolling and yawing. Computers provide up-to-the-minute data on stock status with data displayed by closed-circuit television. Five holds (one refrigerated). Cargo capacity 2 625 tons dry stores and 1 300 tons refrigerated stores (varies with specific loadings).

Automatic propulsion system with full controls on bridge. SPS-40 radar fitted in *Mars* and *Sylvania*, later ships smaller radar; some ships have TACAN (tactical aircraft navigation radar).
Mars authorised in Fiscal Year 1961 shipbuilding programme. *Sylvania* in FY 1962. *Niagara Falls* in FY 1964. *White Plains* and *Concord* in FY 1965. *San Diego* in FY 1966. *San Jose* in FY 1967.

NOMENCLATURE. Combat store ships are named for American cities.

SYLVANIA (AFS 2) *1972, Giorgio Arra*

Underway Replenishment Ships—*continued*

MARS Class—*continued*

PHOTOGRAPHS. The *Niagara Falls* is shown in the Gulf of Tonkin as the aircraft carrier *Bon Homme Richard* (CVA 31) makes an approach to take on stores during an underway replenishment operation. Note the store ship's two-door hangar, capable of accommodating two UH-46 Sea Knight cargo helicopters. A large TACAN "bee hive" antenna tops her mast, facilitating night helicopter flights.

SAN JOSE (AFS 7) *1971, US Navy, PH1 John Lucas*

NIAGARA FALLS (AFS 3) *1970, US Navy, PH2 G. R. Dahlberg*

1 STORES ISSUE SHIP (AKS): "VICTORY" TYPE

Name	No.	Commissioned
ALTAIR (ex-*Aberdeen Victory*)	AKS 32 (ex-AK 257)	31 Jan 1952

Displacement, tons	4 420 light; 15 580 full load
Dimensions, feet	455·2 oa × 62 × 28·5
Guns	4—40 mm AA (twin)
Main engines	Geared turbine; 8 500 shp; 1 shaft = 16·5 knots
Boilers	2
Complement	320 (17 officers, 213 enlisted men)

VC2-S-AP 3 type. Built by Oregon Shipbuilding Corp, Portland, Ore; launched on 30 May 1944; transferred to Navy on 7 July 1951, operating briefly as cargo ship (AK 257) until converted Jan-Dec 1953 to stores issue ship (AKS) at Norfolk Naval Shipyard. Fitted to carry spare parts and dry stores for combatant ships. Fitted with helicopter platform on fantail for "vertical replenishment" (VERTREP) operations. Decommisisoned on 2 May 1969 and placed in reserve.

6 OILERS (AO): "NEOSHO" CLASS

Name	No	Launched	Commissioned
NEOSHO	AO 143	10 Nov 1953	24 Sep 1954
MISSISSINEWA	AO 144	12 June 1954	18 Jan 1955
HASSAYAMPA	AO 145	12 Sep 1954	19 Apr 1955
KAWISHIWI	AO 146	11 Dec 1954	6 July 1955
TRUCKEE	AO 147	10 Mar 1955	23 Nov 1955
PONCHATOULA	AO 148	9 July 1955	12 Jan 1956

Displacement, tons	11 600 light; 38 000 to 40 000 full load
Dimensions, feet	640 wl; 655 oa × 86 × 35
Guns	8 or 12—3 inch (*76 mm*) 50 cal AA (twin)
Main engines	Geared turbines (General Electric); 28 000 shp; 2 shafts = 20 knots
Boilers	2 (Babcock & Wilcox)
Complement	approx 360 (30 officers and 330 enlisted men including staff)

Neosho built by Bethlehem Steel Co, Quincy, Massachusetts; others by New York Shipbuilding Corp, Camden, New Jersey. These are the largest "straight" oilers (AO) constructed for the Navy. Cargo capacity is approximately 180 000 barrels of liquid fuels.
Original armament was two 5 inch DP guns and 12 3 inch AA guns; former removed in 1969. Two twin 3 inch gun mounts removed from *Neosho, Mississinewa,* and *Truckee* and helicopter platform installed. Those ships also have additional superstructure installed forward of after "island" structure. All fitted to carry a service force commander and staff (12 officers). All of these ships are active.

NOMENCLATURE. Oilers are named after American rivers with Indian names.

PONCHATOULA (AO 148) *1970, US Navy, PH1 E. L. Goligoski*

5 OILERS (AO): "JUMBOISED" T3-S2-A3

Name	No	Launched	Commissioned
***MISPILLION**	AO 105	10 Aug 1945	29 Dec 1945
***NAVASOTA**	AO 106	30 Aug 1945	27 Feb 1946
***PASSUMPSIC**	AO 107	31 Oct 1945	1 Apr 1946
***PAWCATUCK**	AO 108	19 Feb 1945	10 May 1946
***WACCAMAW**	AO 109	30 Mar 1946	25 June 1946

Displacement, tons	11 000 light; 34 750 full load
Dimensions, feet	646 oa × 75 × 35·5
Guns	4—3 inch (*76 mm*) 50 cal AA (single)
Main engines	Geared turbines (Westinghouse); 13 500 shp; 2 shafts = 16 knots
Boilers	4 (Babcock & Wilcox)
Complement	290 (16 officers, 274 men)

All built by Sun Shipbuilding & Dry Dock Co, Chester, Pennsylvania. Originally T3-S2-A-3 oilers; converted during mid-1960s under "jumbo" programme. Enlarged midsections added to increase cargo capacity to approximately 150 000 barrels. Helicopter platform fitted *forward*. All of these ships are active.

WACCAMAW (AO 109) *1966, United States Navy*

3 OILERS (AO): "JUMBOISED" T3-S2-A1 TYPE

Name	No.	Launched	Commissioned
***ASHTABULA**	AO 51	22 May 1943	7 Aug 1943
***CALOOSAHATCHEE**	AO 98	2 June 1945	10 Oct 1945
***CANISTEO**	AO 99	6 July 1945	3 Dec 1945

Displacement, tons	34 750 full load
Dimensions, feet	644 oa × 75 × 31·5
Guns	4—3 inch (*76 mm*) 50 cal AA (single)
Main engines	Geared turbines; 13 500 hp; 2 shafts = 18 knots
Boilers	4 (Foster Wheeler)
Complement	300 (13 officers and 287 enlisted men)

All built by Bethlehem Steel Co, Sparrows Point, Maryland. Originally T3-S2-A1 oilers; converted during mid-1960s under "jumbo" programme. Enlarged midsections added to increase cargo capacity to approximately 143 000 barrels plus 175 tons of munitions and 100 tons refrigerated stores. No helicopter platform fitted.

ASHTABULA (AO 51) *1970, US Navy, PH1 B. L. Kuykendall*

Underway Replenishment Ships—*continued*

CALOOSAHATCHEE (AO 98) *1970, US Navy, PH3 T. R. Hearsum*

3 OILERS (AO): T2-A TYPE

Name	*No.*	*Launched*	*Commissioned*
KENENBEC (ex-*Corsicana*)	AO 36	19 Apr 1941	4 Feb 1942
KANKAKEE (ex-*Colina*)	AO 39	24 Jan 1942	4 May 1942
TAPPAHANNOCK (ex-*Jorkay*)	AO 43	18 Apr 1942	22 June 1942

Displacement, tons	21 580 full load
Dimensions, feet	501·4 oa × 68 × 30·75
Guns	2 or 4—3 inch (*76 mm*) 50 cal AA (single)
Main engines	Geared turbine (Westinghouse except General Electric in *Kanakee*); 12 000 shp; = 16·7 knots
Boilers	2 (Foster Wheeler except Babcock and Wilcox in *Tappahannock*)

Fleet oilers of World War II construction but smaller and less capable than the contemporary T-3 series. *Tappahannock* built by Sun Shipbuilding and Dry Dock Co, Chester, Pennsylvania; others by Bethlehem Steel Co, Sparrows Point, Maryland. Cargo capacity approximately 130 000 barrels.

Original armament for this class was one 5 inch DP gun, four 3 inch AA guns, and eight 40 mm AA guns; subsequently reduced as above.

The *Tappahannock* is in Navy reserve; the *Kankakee* and *Kenebec* are in Maritime Administration reserve fleets but remain on the Navy List.

CACAPON (AO 52) *1972, United States Navy, PH1 R. W. Milton*

TRUCKEE (AO 147) *1972, United States Navy*

MISPILLION (AO 105) *1970, United States Navy, PH2 Brian L. Chandler*

Underway Replenishment Ships—*continued*

13 OILERS (AO): T3-S2-A1 TYPE

Name	*No.*	*Launched*	*Commissioned*
SABINE (ex-*Esso Albany*)	AO 25	27 Apr 1940	25 Sep 1940
***GUADALUPE** (ex-*Esso Raleigh*)	AO 32	26 Jan 1940	5 June 1941
***CACAPON**	AO 52	6 June 1943	21 Sep 1943
***CALIENTE**	AO 53	26 Aug 1943	22 Oct 1943
CHIKASKIA	AO 54	2 Oct 1943	10 Nov 1943
AUCILLA (ex-*Escanaba*)	AO 56	20 Nov 1943	22 Dec 1943
***MARIAS**	AO 57	21 Dec 1943	12 Feb 1944
***MANATEE**	AO 58	19 Feb 1944	6 Apr 1944
***SEVERN**	AO 61	31 May 1944	19 July 1944
***TALUGA**	T-AO 62	10 July 1944	25 Aug 1944
***CHIPOLA**	AO 63	21 Oct 1944	30 Nov 1944
***TOLOVANA**	AO 64	6 Jan 1945	24 Feb 1945
ALLAGASH	AO 97	14 Apr 1945	21 Aug 1945

Displacement, tons	25 525 full load
Dimensions, feet	553 oa × 75 × 31·5
Guns	4—3 inch (*76 mm* 50 cal AA (single) in most ships; a few ships retain 5 inch guns of original armament (see notes below)
Main engines	Geared turbines; 13 500 shp; 2 shafts = 18 knots
Boilers	4 (Foster/Wheeler)
Complement	274 (14 officers, 260 enlisted men)

All built by Bethlehem Steel Co, Sparrows Point, Maryland, except *Guadalupe* by Newport News Shipbuilding & Dry Dock Co, Virginia. Original armament varied from one to four 5 inch DP guns; up to four 3 inch AA guns, and eight 40 mm AA guns. Cargo capacity approximately 145 000 barrels.
Several of these ships have been enlarged through "jumbo" conversion programme and are listed on a previous page. The *Marias* is operated by the Military Sealift Command with a civilian crew; the eight other active oilers of this type are Navy manned; four ships are on Maritime Administration reserve but remain on Navy list.

DISPOSALS

"T3-S2-A1" type: **Salamonie** AO 26 stricken on 2 Sep 1969, **Kaskaskia** AO 27 stricken on 19 Dec 1969, **Platte** AO 24 stricken 25 Sep 1970, **Chemung** AO 30 stricken 18 Sep 1970, **Elokomin** AO 55 stricken Mar 1970, **Nantahala** AO 60 stricken on 1 July 1973.
"T3-S-A1" type: **Enoree** AO 69 and **Niobrara** AO 72 were stricken in Dec 1958.
"T2-A" type: **Merrimack** AO 37 and **Monagahela** AO 42 were stricken in Dec 1958.
Distilling ships, ex-oilers, of the "Pasig" class **Abatan** AW 4 (ex-*Mission San Lorenzo* AO 92) and **Pasig** AW 3 (ex-*Mission San Xavier* AO 91) transferred to the Maritime National Defence Reserve Fleet in 1960-61, but **Abatan** was reacquired in Sep 1962 stricken 1 June 1970 but retained as water storage hulk at Guatonamo Bay, Cuba; **Cimarron**, AO 22, stricken on 1 Oct 1968 (scrapped); **Mattaponi** AO 41 stricken 15 Oct 1970, **Neches** AO 47 stricken 1 Oct 1970, **Chukawan** AO 100 stricken on 1 July 1972.

CHIPOLA (AO 63) *1969, United States Navy*

MANATEE (AO 58) *1968, United States Navy*

4 FAST COMBAT SUPPORT SHIPS (AOE): "SACRAMENTO" CLASS

Name	*No.*	*Laid down*	*Launched*	*Commissioned*
• **SACRAMENTO**	AOE 1	30 June 1961	14 Sep 1963	14 Mar 1964
• **CAMDEN**	AOE 2	17 Feb 1964	29 May 1965	1 Apr 1967
• **SEATTLE**	AOE 3	1 Oct 1965	2 Mar 1968	5 Apr 1969
• **DETROIT**	AOE 4	29 Nov 1966	21 June 1969	28 Mar 1970

Displacement, tons	19 200 light; 53 600 full load
Dimensions, feet	793 oa × 107 × 39·3
Guns	8—3 inch (*76 mm*) 50 cal AA (twin)
Helicopters	2 UH-46 Sea Knight helicopters normally assigned
Main engines	Geared turbines (General Electric); 100 000 shp; 2 shafts = 26 knots
Boilers	4 (Combustion Engineering)
Complement	600 (33 officers, 567 enlisted men)

These ships operate primarily with fast carrier task forces to provide rapid replenishment at sea of petroleum, munitions, provisions, and fleet freight. Fitted with helicopter platform, internal arrangements, and large hangar for vertical replenishment operations (VERTREP). Cargo capacity 177 000 barrels plus 2 150 tons munitions, 500 tons dry stores, 250 tons refrigerated stores (varies with specific loadings).
Built by Puget Sound Naval Shipyard except *Camden* by New York Shipbuilding Corp, Camden, New Jersey. *Sacramento* authorised in Fiscal Year 1961 new construction programme; *Camden* in FY 1963, *Seattle* in FY 1965, and *Detroit* in FY 1966. Construction of AOE 5 in FY 1968 was deferred and then cancelled in November 1969. No additional ships of this type are planned because of high cost, the availability of new-construction ammunition ships, and the great success of the smaller "Wichita" class replenishment oilers. Approximate cost of the *Camden* was $70 000 000.

ENGINEERING. *Sacramento* and *Camden* have machinery intended for the cancelled battleship *Kentucky* (BB 66).

PHOTOGRAPHS. Note large, triple-door helicopter hangars on *Seattle*; fork-lift trucks manoeuver cargo on her helicopter deck. Replenishment equipment is primarily on port side for transfer to carriers; ship's boats are on starboard side of hangar.
These ships can be distinguished from the smaller "Wichita" class replenishment oilers by their larger superstructures and funnel, helicopter deck at higher level, and hangar structure aft of funnel.

NOMENCLATURE. Fast combat support ships are named for American cities.

SEATTLE (AOE 3) *1970, United States Navy*

DETROIT (AOE 4) *1972, US Navy, J. R. Andrews*

Underway Replenishment Ships—*continued*

SEATTLE (AOE 3) *1970, United States Navy, PH2 T. M. Staley*

5 GASOLINE TANKERS (AOG): "PATAPSCO" CLASS

Name	*No.*	*Launched*	*Commissioned*
PATAPSCO	AOG 1	18 Aug 1942	4 Feb 1943
KISHWAUKEE	AOG 9	24 July 1943	27 May 1944
***CHEWAUCAN**	AOG 50	22 July 1944	19 Feb 1945
***NESPELEN**	AOG 55	10 Apr 1945	9 Aug 1945
***NOXUBEE**	AOG 56	3 Apr 1945	19 Oct 1945

Displacement, tons	1 850 light; 4 570 full load
Dimensions, feet	292 wl; 310·8 oa × 48·5 × 15·7 max
Guns	2 or 3—3 inch (*76 mm*) 50 cal AA (single)
Main engines	Diesel-electric; 3 100 bhp; 2 shafts = 14 knots
Complement	81 (6 officers, 75 enlisted men)

Navy designed small fuel ships originally intended to carry diesel and aviation fuels. All built by Cargill Inc, Savage, Minnesota. Cargo capacity 17 775 barrels. *Kishwaukee Noxubee* and *Patapsco* were reacquired from the Maritime Administration and re-commissioned in 1966. Three ships remain active.

DISPOSALS
Maquoketa T-AOG 51 was stricken, **Kern** AOG 2, **Wabash** AOG 4, and **Maquoketa** AOG 51 were transferred to Maritime Administration in 1958 and **Susquehanna** AOG 5 in 1959-60. **Ontonagon** AOG 36 was stricken from the Navy List and returned to Maritime Administration on 13 Nov 1957. **Agawam** AOG 6, **Nemasket** AOG 10, and **Rio Grande** AOG 3 were disposed of in 1961. **Chestatee** AOG 49 and **Wacissa** AOG 59 were stricken in 1963 and scrapped. **Mattabesset**, AOG 52, stricken on 1 Oct 1968 and transferred to Maritime Administration.

TRANSFERS. *Natchoug* AOG 54 was transferred to Greece under the MDAP on 1 Aug 1959. *Pinnebog* AOG 58 is on loan to the US Air Force, *Pecatonica* AOG 57 was transferred to Taiwan China in Apr 1962. *Namakagon* AOG 53 was loaned to New Zealand in 1963; returned and retransferred to Taiwan China on 29 June 1971; *Elkhorn* AOG 7 transferred to Taiwan China on 1 July 1972, *Genesee* AOG 8 transferred to Chile on 1 July 1972, *Tombigbee* AOG 11 transferred to Greece on 7 July 1972.

7 REPLENISHMENT OILERS (AOR): "WICITA" CLASS

Name	*No.*	*Laid down*	*Launched*	*Commissioned*
***WICHITA**	AOR 1	18 June 1966	16 Mar 1968	7 June 1969
***MILWAUKEE**	AOR 2	29 Nov 1966	17 Jan 1969	1 Nov 1969
***KANSAS CITY**	AOR 3	20 Apr 1968	28 June 1969	6 June 1970
***SAVANNAH**	AOR 4	22 Jan 1969	25 Apr 1970	5 Dec 1970
***WABASH**	AOR 5	21 Jan 1970	6 Feb 1971	20 Nov 1971
KALMAZOO	AOR 6	28 Oct 1970	11 Nov 1972	July 1973
	AOR 7	Jan 1974	1974	1976

Displacement, tons	38 100 full load
Dimensions, feet	659 oa × 96 × 33·3
Guns	4—3 inch (*76 mm*) 50 cal AA (twin)
Main engines	Geared turbines; 32 000 shp; 2 shafts = 20 knots (18 knots on 2 boilers)
Boilers	3 (Foster Wheeler)
Complement	345 (20 officers, 325 enlisted men)

These ships provide rapid replenishment at sea of petroleum and munitions with a limited capacity for provision and fleet freight. Fitted with helicopter platform and internal arrangement for vertical replenishment operations (VERTREP), but no hangar. Cargo capacity 175 000 barrels plus 600 tons munitions, 425 tons dry stores, 150 tons refrigerated stores.
All built by General Dynamics Corp, Quincy, Massachusetts, except AOR 7 by National Steel and Shipbuilding Co, San Diego, California. *Wichita* and *Milwaukee* authorised in Fiscal Year 1965 new construction programme *Kansas City* and *Savannah* in FY 1966, *Wabash* and *Kalamazoo* in FY 1967, and AOR 7 in FY 1972. Approximate cost of *Milwaukee* was $27 700 000.

NOMENCLATURE. Replenishment oilers are named after American cities. The port city of Savannah, Georgia, also is honoured by the world's first nuclear-propelled merchant ship, the NS *Savannah*, which is now laid up out of service at that city.

PATAPSCO (AOG 1) *1966, United States Navy*

MILWAUKEE (AOR 2) *1972, Giorgio Arra*

WICHITA (AOR 1) *1970, United States Navy*

FLEET SUPPORT SHIPS

Fleet support ships provide primarily maintenance and related towing and salvage services at advanced bases and at ports in the United States. These ships normally not provide fuel, munitions, or other supplies except when ships are alongside for maintenance. A notable exception are the self-propelled barrack ships (APB) that serve as semi-autonomous advanced bases for small landing craft or riverine craft in advanced areas.

Most ships are Navy manned and armed; a few are operated by the Military Sealift Command. The latter are civilian manned and have T-designations.

3 DESTROYER TENDERS (AD): "GOMPERS" CLASS

Name	*No.*	*Laid down*	*Launched*	*Commissioned*
• **SAMUEL GOMPERS**	AD 37	9 July 1964	14 May 1966	1 July 1967
• **PUGET SOUND**	AD 38	15 Feb 1965	16 Sep 1966	27 Apr 1968

AD 40 (Fiscal year 1973 programme)

Displacement, tons	22 260 full load
Dimensions, feet	643 oa × 85 × 22·5
Guns	1—5 inch (*127 mm*) 38 cal DP in *Samuel Gompers* and *Puget Sound*
Missile launchers	1 Basic Point Defence Missile System (BPDMS) launcher firing Sea Sparrow missiles planned for AD 40
Main engines	Geared turbines (De Laval); 20 000 shp; 1 shaft = 20 knots
Boilers	2 (Combustion Engineering)
Complement	1 806 (135 officers, 1 671 enlisted men)

These are the first US destroyer tenders of post-World War II design; capable of providing repair and supply services to new destroyer-type ships which have advanced missile, anti-submarine, and electronic systems. The tenders also have facilities for servicing nuclear power plants. Services can be provided simultaneously to six guided-missile destroyers moored alongside. Basic hull design similar to "L. Y. Spear" and "Simon Lake" submarine tenders. Provided with helicopter platform and hangar; two 7 000-pound capacity cranes.
Samuel Gompers authorised in Fiscal Year 1964 new construction programme and *Puget Sound* in FY 1965 programme. Both ships built by Puget Sound Naval Shipyard, Bremerton, Washington.
AD 39 of FY 1969 programme cancelled prior to start of construction to provide funds for overruns in other new ship programmes.
AD 40 of this class authorised in FY 1973 new construction programme; estimated cost of this ship $86 900 000. NATO Sea Sparrow missile system planned for AD 40.

NOMENCLATURE. Destroyer tenders generally are named for geographic areas. Samuel Gompers was an American labour leader.

SAMUEL GOMPERS (AD 37) — *1968, United States Navy*

6 DESTROYER TENDERS (AD): "KLONDIKE" CLASS

Name	*No.*	*Launched*	*Commissioned*
ARCADIA	AD 24	19 Nov 1944	13 Sep 1951
EVERGLADES	AD 24	28 Jan 1945	25 May 1951
***SHENANDOAH**	AD 26	29 Mar 1945	13 Aug 1945
***YELLOWSTONE**	AD 27	12 Apr 1945	15 Jan 1946
ISLE ROYAL	AD 29	19 Sep 1945	9 June 1962
***BRYCE CANYON**	AD 36	7 Mar 1946	15 Sep 1950

Displacement, tons	8 165 standard; 16 635 to 16 900 full load
Dimensions, feet	465 wl; 492 oa × 69·5 × 27·2
Guns	1—5 inch (*127 mm*) 38 cal DP
Main engines	Geared turbines; 8 500 shp 1 shaft = 18·4 knots
Boilers	2 (Foster-Wheeler or Babcock & Wilcox)
Complement	778 to 918

These ships are of modified C-3 design completed as destroyer tenders. Officially considered two classes (see below). *Arcadia*, *Shenandoah*, *Yellowstone* built by Todd Shipyards, Los Angeles, Calif; *Bryce Canyon* by Charleston Navy Yard; *Everglades* by Los Angeles SB & DD Co; and *Isle Royal* by Todd Pacific Shipyards, Seattle, Wash. *Isle Royal* first commissioned on 26 Mar 1946 and placed in reserve before being completely outfitted; recommissioned for service on 9 June 1962 and commenced operations in January 1963.
Originally 14 ships of two similar designs, the "Klondike" class of AD 22-25 and "Shenandoah" class of AD 26-33, 35, and 36. *Great Lakes* (AD 30), *New England* (AD 32), *Canopus* (AD 33, ex-AS 27), *Arrow Head* (AD 35, ex-AV 19) cancelled before completion; *Klondike* (AD 22) reclassified AR 22; *Grand Canyon* (AD 28) reclassified AR 28. Also see *Disposals* and *Transfers*.
Three ships remain in active service; others in reserve. (*Arcadia* remains on Navy List in Maritime Administration reserve fleet).

ARMAMENT. Original armament for "Klondike" class was 1—5 in gun, 4—3 in guns, and 4—40 mm guns; for "Shenandoah" class was 2—5 in guns and 8—40 mm guns.

MODERNISATION. Most of these ships have been modernised under the FRAM II programme to service modernised destroyers fitted with ASROC, improved electronics, helicopters, etc.

DISPOSALS AND TRANSFERS
Tidewater AD 31 transferred to Indonesia in Jan 1971 for use as tender to off-shore oil operations (Navy manned); **Frontier** AD 25 stricken on 1 Dec 1972.

ISLE ROYAL (AD 29) — *1970, United States Navy*

PUGET SOUND (AD 38) — *1972, United States Navy*

Fleet Support Ships—*continued*

SHENANDOAH (AD 26) *1964, United States Navy*

ISLE ROYAL (AD 29) *1970, United States Navy*

1 DESTROYER TENDER (AD): "CASCADE" TYPE

Name	*No.*	*Launched*	*Commissioned*
CASCADE	AD 16	7 June 1942	12 Mar 1943

Displacement, tons	9 800 standard; 16 600 full load
Dimensions, feet	492 oa × 69·5 × 27·2
Guns	1—5 inch (*127 mm*) 38 cal DP
Main engines	Turbines (General Electric); 1 shaft; 8 500 shp = 18·4 knots
Boilers	2 (Foster-Wheeler)
Complement	857

Built by Western Pipe & Steel Co, San Francisco, C3-S1-N2 type. Modernised to service FRAM destroyers.
The *Cascade* is in active service.

CASCADE (AD 16) *1971, United States Navy*

5 DESTROYER TENDERS (AD): "DIXIE" CLASS

Name	*No.*	*Launched*	*Commissioned*
* **DIXIE**	AD 14	27 May 1939	25 Apr 1940
* **PRAIRIE**	AD 15	9 Dec 1939	5 Aug 1940
* **PIEDMONT**	AD 17	7 Dec 1942	5 Jan 1944
* **SIERRA**	AD 18	23 Feb 1943	20 Mar 1944
* **YOSEMITE**	AD 19	16 May 1943	25 May 1944

Displacement, tons	9 450 standard; 17 176 full load
Dimensions, feet	520 wl; 530·5 oa × 73·3 × 25·5
Guns	1 or 2—5 inch (*127 mm*) 38 cal DP
Main engines	Geared turbines; 2 shafts; 11 000 shp = 19·6 knots
Boilers	4 (Babcock & Wilcox "A")
Complement	1 076 to 1 698 (total accommodation)

Dixie and *Prairie* built by New York Shipbuilding Corp, Camden, New Jersey; others by Tampa Shipbuilding Co, Florida. All five ships are active. The two after 5 inch guns and the eight 40 mm AA guns were removed.
All five ships are active, amongst the oldest ships remaining in service with the US Navy.

"DIXIE" Class—*continued*

MODERNISATION. All of these ships have been modernised under the FRAM II programme to service destroyers fitted with ASROC, improved electronics, helicopters, etc. Two or three 5 inch guns and eight 40 mm guns removed during modernisation.

PIEDMONT (AD 17) *1970, United States Navy*

YOSEMITE (AD 19) *1968, United States Navy*

YOSEMITE (AD 19) *1968, United States Navy*

1 DEGAUSSING SHIP (ADG): Ex-MINESWEEPER

Name	*No.*	*Launched*	*Commissioned*
SURFBIRD	ADG 383 (ex-MSF 383)	31 Aug 1944	25 Nov 1944

Displacement, tons	890 standard; 1 250 full load
Dimensions, feet	215 wl; 221·2 oa × 32·2 × 10·8
Main engines	Diesel electric; 2 shafts; 3 532 bhp = 18 knots
Complement	70

Built by American Shipbuilding Co, Lorain, Ohio. Laid down on 15 Feb 1944. Former Fleet Minesweeper of the steel-hulled type, MSF (ex-AM), reclassified as ADG on 18 May 1957. Decommissioned on 18 Dec 1970 and placed in reserve.

SURFBIRD (ADG 383) *United States Navy*

Fleet Support Ships—*continued*

3 DEGAUSSING SHIPS (ADG): Ex-PCE

Name	*No.*	*Launched*
LODESTONE (ex-*PCE* 876)	ADG 8	30 Sep 1943
MAGNET (ex-*PCE* 879)	ADG 9	1 Sep 1943
DEPERM (ex-*PCE* 883)	ADG 10	14 Jan 1944

Displacement, tons	640 standard; 900 full load
Dimensions, feet	184·5 oa × 33 × 9·5
Main engines	Diesels (General Motors); 1 800 bhp except 2 000 bhp in *Deperm*; 2 shafts = 15·7 knots

Patrol Vessels—Escort (PCE) completed as degaussing craft YDG 8-10; changed to ADG on 1 Nov 1947; named on 1 Feb 1955. In reserve since 1946-1947.

REPOSE (AH 16) *1970, US Navy, PH2 Wayne Massie*

1 GUNBOAT SUPPORT SHIP (AGP): CONVERTED LST

Name	*No.*	*Launched*	*Commissioned*
***GRAHAM COUNTY**	AGP 1176 (ex-LST 1176)	19 Sep 1957	17 Apr 1958

Displacement, tons	approx 8 000 full load
Dimensions, feet	445 oa × 62 × 16·5
Guns	6—3 inch (*76 mm*) 50 cal AA (twin)
Main engines	Diesels (Fairbanks-Morse); 9 600 bhp; 2 shafts (controllable-pitch-propellers) = 14·5 knots

Originally an LST of the "Suffolk" County class built by Newport News SB & DD Co, Newport News, Virginia. Converted in 1972 to support US patrol gunboats (PG) and hydrofoil gunboats (PHM) deployed to Mediterranean area. Redesignated gunboat support ship (AGP) on 1 Aug 1972. Fitted with repair shops and spare parts storage.

Four earlier LSTs modified to support riverine craft in Vietnam also were designated AGP (with LST hull numbers); see listing for Amphibious Warfare Ships in 1971-1972 and previous editions. AGP 1-20 were converted yachts, seaplane tenders, cargo ships, and LSTs employed during World War II to service motor torpedo boats.

GRAHAM COUNTY *1973, Giorgio Arra*

2 HOSPITAL SHIPS (AH): "HAVEN" CLASS

Name	*No.*	*Launched*	*Commissioned*
REPOSE (ex-*Marine Beaver*)	AH 16	8 Aug 1944	26 May 1945
***SANCTUARY** (ex-*Marine Owl*)	AH 17	15 Aug 1944	20 June 1945

Displacement, tons	11 141 standard; 15 400 full load
Dimensions, feet	496 wl; 529 oa × 71·5 × 24
Main engines	Geared turbines (General Electric); 1 shaft; 9 000 shp = 18·33
Boilers	2 (Babcock & Wilcox)
Complement	530 (70 officers, 460 enlisted) in *Sanctuary*)

Floating hospital complexes built into C4-S-B2 merchant hulls. Built by Sun Shipbuilding & Dry Dock Co, Chester, Pennsylvania. Originally fitted with beds for approximately 700 patients.

Repose reacquired from Maritime Administration reserve in 1965 and *Sanctuary* in 1966 for service off Vietnam; modernised and medical facilities updated. *Repose* decommissioned on 15 Aug 1970 and assigned as station hospital annex at Long Beach, California, until new shore facilities are completed. Her machinery is shut down and closed off; electric power and fresh water are provided from land.

Sanctuary decommissioned as hospital ship on 15 Dec 1971. Subsequently converted during 1972 to "dependent support ship" at Hunter's Point Naval Shipyard, San Francisco California; recommissioned on 18 Nov 1972. First US Navy ship with mixed male-female crew (although previously female nurses assigned to hospital ships and transports) complement includes two women officers and 60 women enlisted. Special facilities provided for obstretrics, gynecology, maternity, and nursery services; beds for 120 patients under normal conditions and 300 in emergency.

Sanctuary stationed at Pireaus, Greece, to provide support for dependents of crews of US warships based in Pireaus. Photograph shows *Sanctuary* at anchor in Danang harbour, South Vietnam. Note TACAN electronic pod on forward kingpost and helicopter platform aft for helicopter delivery of casualties.

Consolation (AH 15) of this class has been chartered by a private group and has operated under the name *Hope* as a floating hospital, laboratory, and medical school since 1961.

SANCTUARY (AH 17) *1970, US Navy, PH3 Dennis McClosky*

NET LAYING SHIPS

All US Navy net laying ships (ANL) have been discarded except for the *Naub* (ex-AN 84), in service as a salvage craft tender (designated YRST 4); see listing unc Service Craft. *Naubuc* is a former "Cohoes" class net laying ship.
Cohoes (ANL 78, ex-AN 78) stricken on 30 June 1972. See 1972-1973 edition characteristics and photograph.
All net laying ships of the "Tree" class have been stricken; last unit in US Navy servi was *Butternut* (ex-ANL 9, ex-AN 9, ex-YN 4), lately employed in experimental wc as YAG 60 until stricken on 1 July 1971.

6 SELF-PROPELLED BARRACKS SHIPS (APB)

Name	*No.*	*Launched*
COLLETON	APB 36 (ex-APL 36)	30 July 19
ECHOLS	APB 37 (ex-APL 37)	30 July 19
MERCER	APB 39 (ex-APL 39)	17 Nov 19
NUECES	APB 40 (ex-APL 40)	6 May 19
DORCHESTER	APB 46 (ex-AKS 17, ex-LST 1112)	12 Apr 19
KINGMAN	APB 47 (ex-AKS 18, ex-LST 1113)	17 Apr 19

Displacement, tons	2 189 light; 4 080 full load
Dimensions, feet	136 wl; 328 oa × 50 × 11
Guns	Vary (see notes)
Main engines	Diesels (General Motors); 1 600 to 1 800 bhp 2 shafts; = 1 (*APB* 41-50); or 10 knots (*APB* 35-40)
Complement	193 (13 officers, 180 enlisted men)
Troops	1 226 (16 officers, 1 200 enlisted men)

Self-propelled barracks ships (APB) that provide support and accommodations f small craft and riverine forces. All ex-LST type ships of the same basic characteristic *Benewah* and *Colleton* recommissioned on 28 Jan 1967 for service in Vietnam; *Merc* and *Nueces* recommissioned in 1968 for service in Vietnam. All four decommissione in 1969-1971 as US riverine forces in South Vietnam were reduced.
Benewah (APB 35) reclassified as IX 311 on 26 Feb 1971 for use as barracks shi at Subic Bay, Philippines; to be transferred to South Vietnam.
These most useful ships supported the joint Army-Navy Mobile Riverine Force in th Mekong Delta region of South Vietnam (Navy River Assault Flotilla 1/Task Force 11 River Support Squadron 7). Complement of each ship in this role was 12 officers an 186 enlisted men, and 900 troops and boat crew personnel were carried. These fo ships have an armament of two 3 inch guns (single) eight 40 mm guns (two qua mounts), eight ·50 cal MG, and ten ·30 cal MG. They each have troop berthing ar messing facilities, evaporators which produce up to 40 000 gallons of fresh water p day, a 16-bed hospital, X-ray room, dental room, bacteriological laboratory, pharmac laundry, library, and tailor shop; living and most working spaces are air conditione Most ships not activated for Vietnam have eight 40 mm AA guns (quad).
Colleton shown below with 12 riverine craft alongside; ships reactivated for Vietna provide with helicopter platform; 3 inch guns installed at after end of helicopter platfor with quad 40 mm mounts at bow and stern.

DISPOSALS (since 1 Jan 1970)
Vandenburgh APB 48 (ex-AKS 19, ex-LST 1114) stricken on 1 Apr 1972.

MERCER (APB 39) *1968, United States Navy*

COLLETON (APB 36) *1967, United States Navy*

Fleet Support Ships—*continued*

2 REPAIR SHIPS (AR): Ex-DESTROYER TENDERS

Name	*No.*	*Launched*	*Commissioned*
KLONDIKE	AR 22 (ex-AD 22)	12 Aug 1944	30 July 1945
GRAND CANYON	AR 28 (ex-AD 28)	27 Apr 1945	5 Apr 1946

Displacement, tons	8 165 standard; 16 635 full load
Dimensions, feet	465 wl; 492 oa × 69·5 × 27·2
Guns	2—3 inch (*76 mm*) 50 cal AA (single) in *Klondike* 1—5 inch (*127 mm*) 38 cal DP in *Grand Canyon*
Main engines	Geared turbines (General Electric in *Klondike* Westinghouse in *Grand Canyon*); 8 500 shp; 1 shaft = 18·4 knots
Boilers	2 (Babcock & Wilcox in *Klondike;* Foster-Wheeler in *Grand Canyon*)
Complement	826 (48 officers, 778 enlisted men) and 977 (59 officers, 918 enlisted men) designed wartime for *Klondike* and *Grand Canyon* respectively

hese ships are modified C-3 designs completed as destroyer tenders and subsequently classified as repair ships, the *Klondike* being redesignated AR 22 on 20 Feb 1960 nd the *Grand Canyon* on 10 Mar 1971.
londike built by Los Angeles Shipbuilding Corp and *Grand Canyon* by Todd Shipards, also Los Angeles, Calif. These ships differ in detail, being of slightly different esigns; note mast and kingpost arrangements. The *Grand Canyon* has been modernized; note helicopter platform and hangar aft. *Klondike's* designed armament was —5 in gun, 4—3 in guns, and 4—40 mm guns; *Grand Canyon's* designed armament as 2—5 in guns and 8—40 mm guns.
londike decommissioned on 15 Dec 1970 and placed in service in reserve as station hip at San Diego, Calif; *Grand Canyon* is active.

OMENCLATURE. Repair ships normally are named for mythological characters.

KLONDIKE (AR 22) — *1969, United States Navy*

GRAND CANYON (AR 28) — *1968, United States Navy*

1 REPAIR SHIP (AR): Ex-DESTROYER TENDER

Name	*No.*	*Commissioned*
ARKAB (ex-*Mormacpenn*)	AR 23 (ex-AD 21, ex-AK 31)	15 June 1941

Displacement, tons	8 560 standard; 14 800 full load
Dimensions, feet	465 wl; 492·5 oa × 69·8 × 24·8
Guns	4—3 inch (*76 mm*) 50 cal AA (single)
Main engines	Geared turbines (General Electric); 8 500 shp; 1 shaft; 18·4 knots
Boilers	2 (Foster-Wheeler)

uilt by Ingalls SB Co, Pascagoula, Miss; launched on 21 Dec 1940. Former destroyer ender, reclassified as repair ship on 15 Apr 1960 and designation changed from AD to R. One 5 inch gun and 4—40 mm guns were removed. The *Markab* was deommissioned on 19 Dec 1969 but remains in service in reserve as station ship at Mare sland, Calif.

MARKAB (AR 23) — *United States Navy*

1 REPAIR SHIP (AR): "AMPHION" CLASS

Name	*No.*	*Launched*	*Commissioned*
CADMUS	AR 14	5 Aug 1945	23 Apr 1946

Displacement, tons	7 826 standard; 14 490 full load
Dimensions, feet	456 wl; 492 oa × 70 × 27·5
Guns	1—5 inch (*127 mm*) 38 cal DP
Main engines	Turbines (Westinghouse); 8 500 shp; 1 shaft = 16·5 knots
Boilers	2 (Foster-Wheeler)
Complement	921 (67 officers, 854 enlisted men) designed wartime

Built by Tampa Shipubilding Co. C 3 cargo type. Designed armament was two 5 inch guns and eight 40 mm guns (quad). *Cadmus* decommissioned and placed in reserve in 1971.

The *Amphion* (AR 13) of this class was transferred to Iran in Oct 1971.

CADMUS (AR 14) — *1964, United States Navy*

2 REPAIR SHIPS AR): "DELTA" CLASS

Name	*No.*	*Commissioned*
DELTA (ex-*Hawaiian Packer*)	AR 9 (ex-AK 29)	16 June 1941
BRIAREUS (ex-*Hawaiian Planter*)	AR 12	16 Nov 1943

Displacement, tons	8 975 standard; 14 500 full load
Dimensions, feet	465·5 wl; 490·5 oa × 69·5 × 24·3
Guns	4—3 inch (*76 mm*) 50 cal AA (single)
Main engines	Geared turbines (Newport News); 8 500 shp; 1 shaft = 17 knots
Boilers	2 (Foster-Wheeler and Babcock & Wilcox, respectively)
Complement	688 (29 officers, 559 enlisted men); 903 and 924, respectively, designed wartime

C-3 type built by Newport News SB & DD Co, Newport News, Va. Both launched in 1941 with *Briareus* serving as a merchant ship before being acquired by the Navy. The 5 inch and 4—40 mm guns removed. *Briareus* decommissioned in 1955 and placed in reserve; *Delta* decommissioned in 1970 remains in service in reserve as station ship at Bremerton, Wash.

DELTA (AR 9) — *1969, United States Navy*

AJAX (AR 6) — *1970, US Navy, PH2 Benjamin Startt*

Fleet Support Ships—*continued*

4 REPAIR SHIPS (AR): "VULCAN" CLASS

Name	No.	Launched	Commissioned
***VULCAN**	AR 5	14 Dec 1940	16 June 1941
***AJAX**	AR 6	22 Aug 1942	30 Oct 1942
***HECTOR**	AR 7	11 Nov 1942	7 Feb 1944
***JASON**	AR 8	3 Apr 1943	19 June 1944

Displacement, tons	9 140 standard; 16 200 full load
Dimensions, feet	520 wl; 529·3 oa × 73·3 × 23·3
Guns	4—5 inch (*127 mm*) 38 cal DP (single)
Main engines	Geared turbines; 11 000 shp; 2 shafts = 19·2 knots
Boilers	4 (Babcock & Wilcox 3-drum)
Complement	715 (23 officers, 692 enlisted men); 950 designed wartime

Vulcan was built by New York SB Corpn under the 1939 programme and the other three by Los Angeles SB & DD Corpn under the 1940 Programme. All carry a most elaborate equipment of machine tools to undertake repairs of every description. *Jason*, originally designated ARH 1 and rated as heavy hull repair ship, was reclassified AR 8 on 9 Sep 1957. Eight 40 mm AA guns (twin) have been removed.
All of these ships are active.

AJAX (AR 6) *1970, US Navy, PH2 Benjamin Startt*

2 CABLE SHIPS (ARC): "AEOLUS" CLASS

Name	No.	Commissioned
***AEOLUS** (ex-*Turandot*)	T-ARC 3 (ex-AKA 47)	18 June 1945
***THOR** (ex-*Vanadis*)	T-ARC 4 (ex-AKA 49)	9 July 1945

Displacement, tons	7 040 full load
Dimensions, feet	400 wl; 438 oa × 58·2 × 19·25
Guns	None
Main engines	Turbo-electric (Westinghouse); 6 000 shp; 2 shafts = 16·9 knots
Boilers	2 (Wickes)

Built as S4-SE2-BE1 attack cargo ships by Walsh-Kaiser Co, Providence, Rhode Island. Transferred to Maritime Administration and laid up in reserve from 1946 until reacquired by Navy for conversion to cable ships in 1955-1956. Converted to cable ships at the Key Highway Plant of Bethlehem Steel Corp, Baltimore, Maryland, being recommissioned on 14 May 1955 and 3 Jan 1956, respectively. Fitted with cable-laying bow sheaves, cable stowage tanks, cable repair facilities, and helicopter platform aft.
Both ships are employed in hydrographic and cable operations. They were both Navy manned until 1973 when transferred to Military Sealift Command and provided with civilian crews.

AEOLUS (T-ARC 3) *1970, US Navy, PH1 E. L. Goligoski*

AEOLUS (T-ARC 3) *United States Navy*

THOR (T-ARC 4) *1964, United States Navy*

2 CABLE SHIPS (ARC): "NEPTUNE" CLASS

***NEPTUNE** (ex-*William H. G. Bullard*)	T-ARC 2
***ALBERT J. MYER**	T-ARC 6

Displacement, tons	7 400 full load
Dimensions, feet	322 wl; 370 oa × 47 × 18
Guns	4—20 mm AA (twin) in *Neptune*
Main engines	Reciprocating (Skinner); 4 800 ihp; 2 shafts = 14 knots
Boilers	2 (Combustion Engineering)

Built as S3-S2-BP1 type cable ships for Maritime Administration. Both ships bui by Pisey & Jones Corp, Wilmington, Delaware, completed 1945-1946.
Neptune acquired by Navy from Maritime Administration in 1953 and sister sh *Albert J. Myer* from US Army in 1966, latter ship for operation by Military Sea Trans portation Service (now Military Sealift Command). They have been fitted wi electric cable handling machinery (in place of steam equipment) and precision naviga tion equipment; helicopter platform in *Neptune*.
Both ships are operated by the Military Sealift Command with civilian crews; *Neptun* was Navy manned until 1973 when transferred to MSC.
The USNS *Neptune* (T-ARC 2) should not be confused with the commercial cable sh *Neptun* of the United States Undersea Cable Corp.

See 1971-1972 edition for disposals of other cable ships.

NEPTUNE (T-ARC 2) *United States Navy*

ALBERT J. MYER (T-ARC 6) *United States Navy*

CHLORIS (ARVE 4) *United States Navy*

Fleet Support Ships—*continued*

13 REPAIR SHIPS: CONVERTED LST TYPE

(Battle damage Repair Ships)

ZEUS	ARB 4 (ex-LST 132)	**SARPEDON**	ARB 7 (ex-LST 956)
MIDAS	ARB 5 (ex-LST 524)	**TELAMON**	ARB 8 (ex-LST 957)

(Landing Craft Repair Ships)

ACHELOUS	ARL 1 (ex-LST 10)	**SATYR**	ARL 23 (ex-LST 852)
AMYCUS	ARL 2 (ex-LST 489)	**SPHINX**	ARL 24 (ex-LST 963)
EGERIA	ARL 8 (ex-LST 136)	**INDRA**	ARL 37 (ex-LST 1147)

(Aircraft Repair Ships—Aircraft)

FABIUS	ARVA 5 (ex-LST 1093)	**MEGARA**	ARVA 6 (ex-LST 1095)

(Aircraft Repair Ship—Engine)

CHLORIS ARVE 4 (ex-LST 1094)

Displacement, tons	1 625 light; 4 100 full load
Dimensions, feet	316 wl; 328 oa × 50 × 11
Guns	8—40 mm AA (quad); several 20 mm AA in some ships
Main engines	Diesels (General Motors); 1 800 bhp; 2 shafts = 11·6 knots
Complement	251 to 286

All launched in 1942-1945. Modified from basic LST design with several machine shops, material and ports storage, lifting gear, etc; ARLs cater to small amphibious, riverine, and minesweeping craft.
Photographs of ARLs active in Vietnam waters appear in the 1972-1973 and previous editions.

DISPOSALS AND TRANSFERS (since 1 Jan 1965)

Pandemus ARL 18 stricken on 1 Oct 1968 (target). **Amycus** ARL 2 stricken on 1 June 1970; **Askari** ARL 30 to Indonesia on 31 Aug 1971, **Krishna** ARL 38 to Philippines on 30 Oct 1971. **Atlas** ARL 7 and **Endymion** ARL 9 stricken on 1 June 1972.
Liberty EC-2 type **Tutuila** ARG 4 transferred to Taiwan China on 21 Feb 1972.

SPHINX (ARL 24) *1968, United States Navy*

FABIUS (ARVA 5) *United States Navy*

14 SALVAGE SHIPS (ARS): "DIVER" CLASS

Name	*No.*	*Launched*	*Commissioned*
***ESCAPE**	ARS 6	22 Nov 1942	20 Nov 1943
***GRAPPLE**	ARS 7	31 Dec 1942	16 Dec 1943
***PRESERVER**	ARS 8	1 Apr 1943	11 Jan 1944
CURRENT	ARS 22	25 Sep 1943	14 June 1944
***DELIVER**	ARS 23	25 Sep 1943	18 July 1944
***GRASP**	ARS 24	31 July 1943	22 Aug 1944
***SAFEGUARD**	ARS 25	20 Nov 1943	31 Oct 1944
***GEAR**	ARS 34	24 Oct 1942	24 Sep 1943
***BOLSTER**	ARS 38	23 Dec 1944	1 May 1945
***CONSERVER**	ARS 39	27 Jan 1945	9 June 1945
***HOIST**	ARS 40	31 Mar 1945	21 July 1945
***OPPORTUNE**	ARS 41	31 Mar 1945	5 Oct 1945
***RECLAIMER**	ARS 42	25 June 1945	20 Dec 1945
***RECOVERY**	ARS 43	4 Aug 1945	15 May 1946

Displacement, tons	1 530 standard; 1 900 full load
Dimensions, feet	207 wl; 213·5 oa × 39 × 13
Guns	1—40 mm AA (removed from some ships); 2—·50 cal MG or 2—20 mm guns fitted in some ships
Main engines	Diesel-electric; 2 shafts; 2 440 shp = 14 knots
Complement	85 (120 designed wartime)

These ships are fitted for salvage and towing; equipped with compressed air diving gear. All built by Basalt Rock Co, Napa Calif. Note position of 20 mm guns at bridge level on *Recovery*.
The *Gear* is operated by a commercial firm in support of Navy activities; two additional ships are on loan to private salvage firms, the *Cable* ARS 19 and *Curb* ARS 21, and support naval requirements as needed. All others are active with Navy crews expect *Current* decommissioned in 1972.

CONVERSIONS. *Chain* ARS 20 and *Snatch* ARS 27 converted to oceanographic research ships, designated AGOR 17 and AGOR 18, respectively.

DISPOSALS
Clamp (ex-*Atlantic Salvor*) ARS 33 stricken in July 1963.

NOMENCLATURE. Salvage ships are named for words relating to salvage activities.

RECOVERY (ARS 43) *1969, United States Navy*

HOIST (ARS 40) *United States Navy*

GRAPPLE (ARS 7) *1970, US Navy, PH3 C. P. Weston*

2 SALVAGE LIFTING SHIPS (ARSD): CONVERTED LSM

GYPSY ARSD 1 (ex-*LSM* 549) **MENDER** ARSD 2 (ex-*LSM* 550)

Displacement, tons	740 standard; 1 095 full load
Dimensions, feet	224 2 × 34 × 7
Guns	2—20 mm AA
Main engines	Diesel; 2 shafts; 2 800 bhp = 13 knots
Complement	65

Former medium landing ships used as diving tenders. Built by Brown SB Co, Houston, Texas; both launched on 7 Dec 1945. In reserve.
Sister ships *Salvager* (ex-LSM 551) ARSD 3 and *Windlass* (ex-LSM 552) ARSD 4 were reclassified as YMLC 3 and YMLC 4, respectively, on 1 Nov 1967.

2 SALVAGE TENDERS (ARST): CONVERTED LST

LAYSAN ISLAND ARST 1 (ex-*LST* 1098) **PALMYRA** ARST 3 (ex-*LST* 1100)

Displacement, tons	1 653 standard; 4 080 full load
Dimensions, feet	328 × 50 × 11 × 14·3 max
Guns	8—40 mm AA (quad)
Main engines	Diesel; 1 800 bhp; 2 shafts = 11·6 knots
Complement	289

Former tank landing ships. Built by Jeffersonville Bridge & Machinery Co, Jeffersonville, Ind; launched on 27 Jan 1945 and 20 Feb 1945, respectively. In reserve.

Fleet Support Ships—*continued*

1 HELICOPTER REPAIR SHIP (ARVH): CONVERTED SEAPLANE TENDER

***CORPUS CHRISTI BAY** (ex-*Albermarle*) T-ARVH 1 (ex-AV 5)

Displacement, tons	8 671 standard; 13 475 full load
Dimensions, feet	508 wl; 537 oa × 69·2 × 21·3
Guns	None
Main engines	Geared turbines (Parsons); 12 000 shp; 2 shafts = 19·7 knots
Boilers	4 (Babcock & Wilcox)
Complement	130 (25 officers, 105 men) plus 310 Army personnel

Built as a large seaplane tender by the New York Shipbuilding Corp, Camden, New Jersey, under the Fiscal Year 1937 shipbuilding Programme; laid down on 12 June 1939, launched on 13 July 1940, commissioned on 20 Dec 1940. She was modernised in 1956-1957 and subsequently converted to a helicopter repair ship in 1964-1965 (see *Conversion* notes).

All other US Navy seaplane tenders have been stricken or transferred to foreign navies; see 1972-1973 and previous editions for ship lists, descriptions, and dispositions.

The *Corpus Christi Bay* is in service, operated by the Military Sealift Command (formerly MSTS) and manned by a civilian operating crew and army helicopter maintenance battalion. Placed in ready reserve in 1973.

CONVERSION. The *Albermarle* was converted under the Fiscal Year 1956 programme at the Philadelphia Naval Shipyard to support the P6M Seamaster jet-propelled seaplane. Recommissioned on 21 Oct 1957. Decommissioned in 1960 and placed in the Maritime Administration Reserve Fleet. Stricken from the Navy List in Sep 1962. Reacquired by the Navy in Aug 1964 for conversion to a helicopter repair ship. The *Albermarle* was converted to an aircraft repair ship (helicopter) at the Charleston Naval Shipyard in 1964-1965; fitted with 33 maintenance shops specialising in helicopter repairs, closed-circuit television provided for rapid transmission of drawings and blueprints from central technical library, automatic boiler controls to reduce operating crew, flight control tower (installed on flying bridge), and improved habitability features; amidships hangar structure extended aft and topped with a 50 × 150 ft helicopter platform with four-part steel hatch to permit helicopters to be lowered into hangars; two 20-ton capacity cranes installed aft of second funnel; smaller helicopter deck installed forward. All armament removed. Renamed *Corpus Christi Bay* and designated T-ARVH 1 on 27 Mar 1965. Deployed to South Vietnam to repair Army light fixed-wing aircraft and helicopters.

DESIGN. As built the *Albermarle* and her sister ship *Curtiss* (AV 4) resembled the "Currituck" class configuration, but with twin funnels. Both of these large seaplane tender designs provided extensive maintenance shops and spare parts, munition, and petrol stowage to support seaplane squadrons; space provided for squadron flight crews and Fleet Air Wing staff; aircraft hangar amidships, open deck aft, and two large aircraft cranes (20-ton capacity in "Curtiss" class; 30-ton capacity in "Currituck" class). As built the *Albermarle* had an armament of 4 5 inch DP guns and 16 40 mm AA guns.

NOMENCLATURE. Seaplane tenders were named after bays and harbours.

CORPUS CHRISTI BAY (T-ARVH 1) *United States Navy*

CORPUS CHRISTI BAY (T-ARVH 1)

4 SUBMARINE TENDERS (AS): "L. Y. SPEAR" CLASS

Name	No.	Laid down	Launched	Commissioned
***L. Y. SPEAR**	AS 36	5 May 1966	7 Sep 1967	28 Feb 1970
***DIXON**	AS 37	7 Sep 1967	20 June 1970	7 Aug 1971
	AS 39	(Fiscal Year 1972 programme)		
	AS 40	(Fiscal Year 1973 programme)		

Displacement, tons	13 000 standard; AS 36 and AS 37 23 350 full load; AS 39 and AS 40 24 000 full load
Dimensions, feet	643·6 oa × 85 × 25·3 (AS 39 and AS 40 28·6)
Guns	2—5 inch (*127 mm*) 38 cal DP in *L. Y. Spear* and *Dixon*, 4—20 mm AA planned for AS 39 and AS 40
Missile launchers	1 Basic Point Defence Missile System (BPDMS) launcher firing Sea Sparrow missiles planned for AS 39 and AS 40
Main engines	Geared turbines (General Electric); 20 000 shp; 1 shaft = 20 knots
Boilers	2 (Foster Wheeler)
Complement	1 072 (42 officers, 1 030 enlisted men)

These ships are the first US submarine tenders designed specifically for servicing nuclear-propelled attack submarines with latter ships built to a modified design to support SSN-688 class submarines. (Four previous submarine tenders of post-World War II construction are configured to support ballistic missile submarines.) Basic hull design similar to "Samuel Gompers" class destroyer tenders. Provided with helicopter deck but no hangar. Each ship can simultaneously provide services to four submarines moored alongside.

L. Y. Spear authorised in Fiscal Year 1965 new construction programme and *Dixon* in FY 1966 programme. Both ships built by General Dynamics Corp, Quincy, Massachusetts.

AS 38 of FY 1969 programme cancelled prior to start of construction to provide funds for overruns in other new ship programmes.

AS 39 authorised in FY 1972 new construction programme and AS 40 in FY 1973 programme; estimated cost of latter ship $79 900 000. Later ships will have NATO Sea Sparrow missile system.

NOMENCLATURE. Submarine tenders generally are named after pioneers in submarine development and mythological characters.

DIXON (AS 37) *1971, US Navy, PH1 Robert L. Varney*

L. Y. SPEAR (AS 36) *1969, General Dynamics (Quincy)*

2 SUBMARINE TENDERS (AS): "SIMON LAKE" CLASS

Name	No.	Laid down	Launched	Commissioned
***SIMON LAKE**	AS 33	7 Jan 1963	8 Feb 1964	7 Nov 1964
***CANOPUS**	AS 34	2 Mar 1964	12 Feb 1965	4 Nov 1965

Displacement, tons	21 450 to 22 250 full load
Dimensions, feet	643·7 × 85 × 30
Guns	4—3 inch (*76 mm*) 50 cal AA (twin)
Main engines	Geared turbines; 20 000 shp; 1 shaft = 18 knots
Boilers	2 (Combustion Engineering)
Complement	1 075 (55 officers, 1 020 men)

These ships are designed specifically to service Fleet Ballistic Missile Submarines (SSBN), with as many as three submarines alongside being supported simultaneously. The *Simon Lake* was authorised in the Fiscal Year 1963 new construction programme and built by the Puget Sound Naval Shipyard; the *Canopus* was authorised in FY 1964 and built by Ingalls Shipbuilding Corp. AS 35 was authorised in FY 1965 programme, but her construction was deferred. The last ship would have permitted one tender to be assigned to each of five FBM submarine squadrons with a sixth ship available to rotate when another was in overhaul; however, only four SSBN squadrons were established.

Note cranes amidships, funnel location (flanked by gun mounts, and helicopter platform).

Fleet Support Ships—*continued*

HUNLEY (AS 31) *United States Navy*

L. Y. SPEAR (AS 36) *1970, United States Navy*

PROTEUS (AS 19) *1963, United States Navy*

NEREUS (AS 17) *United States Navy*

Fleet Support Ships—*continued*

CANOPUS (AS 34) servicing SSBN *1970, US Navy, PH1 Robert Woods*

SIMON LAKE (AS 33) *1965 United States Navy*

2 SUBMARINE TENDERS (AS): "HUNLEY" CLASS

Name	*No*	*Laid down*	*Launched*	*Commissioned*
***HUNLEY**	AS 31	28 Nov 1960	28 Sep 1961	16 June 1962
***HOLLAND**	AS 32	5 Mar 1962	19 Jan 1963	7 Sep 1963

Displacement, tons	10 500 standard; 18 300 full load
Dimensions, feet	599 × 83 × 24
Guns	4—3 inch (*76 mm*) 50 cal AA (twin)
Main engines	Diesel-electric (10 Fairbanks-Morse diesels); 15 000 bhp; 1 shaft = 19 knots
Complement	1 081 (58 officers, 1 023 men) plus accommodation for 30 officers and 270 men from submarines

These ships are the first US submarine tenders of post-World War II construction; designed specifically to provide repairs and supply services to fleet ballistic missile submarines (SSBN). Provided with 52 separate workshops to provide complete support to nuclear plants, electronic and navigation systems, missiles, and other submarine systems. Helicopter platform fitted aft but no hangar. Both ships originally fitted with a 32-ton-capacity hammerhead crane (see 1972-1973 and previous editions for photographs); subsequently refitted with two amidships cranes as in "Simon Lake" class (see accompanying photographs).

Hunley authorised in Fiscal Year 1960 shipbuilding programme and built by Newport News Shipbuilding & Dry Dock Co, Virginia; *Holland* authorised in FY 1962 programme and built by Ingalls Shipbuilding Corp, Pascagoula, Mississippi. Former ship cost $24 359 800.

NOMENCLATURE. *Holland* is named after John Philip Holland, an Irish emigrant to the United States, and submarine designer and builder. One of his submarines was accepted by the US Navy in 1900 and became Submarine Torpedo Boat No 1, named *Holland*, the first officially accepted US Navy submarine.

HOLLAND (AS 32) *United States Navy*

7 SUBMARINE TENDERS (AS): "FULTON" CLASS

Name	*No.*	*Launched*	*Commissioned*
***FULTON**	AS 11	27 Dec 1940	12 Sep 1941
***SPERRY**	AS 12	17 Dec 1941	1 May 1942
BUSHNELL	AS 15	14 Sep 1942	10 Apr 1943
***HOWARD W. GILMORE**	AS 16	16 Sep 1943	24 May 1944
NEREUS (ex-*Neptune*)	AS 17	12 Feb 1945	27 Oct 1945
***ORION**	AS 18	14 Oct 1942	30 Sep 1943
***PROTEUS**	AS 19	12 Nov 1942	31 Jan 1944

Displacement, tons	9 734 standard; 18 000 full load *Proteus:* 10 234 standard; 18 500 full load
Dimensions, feet	530·5; *Proteus* 574·5 oa × 73·3 × 25·5
Guns	2—5 inch (*127 mm*) 38 cal DP except one gun in *Proteus*
Main engines	Diesel-electric (General Motors); 11 200 to 11 800 bhp; 2 shafts = 15·4 knots
Complement	917 (34 officers, 883 enlisted men); except *Proteus* 1 121 (51 officers, 1 070 enlisted men)

CONVERSION. *Proteus* AS 19 was converted at the Charleston Naval Shipyard, under the Fiscal Year 1959 conversion programme, at a cost of $23 000 000 to service nuclear-powered fleet ballistic missile submarines (SSBN). Conversion was begun on 19 Jan 1959 and she was recommissioned on 8 July 1960. She was lengthened by adding a section amidships 44 feet in length, and the bare hull weight of this 6-deck high insertion was approximately 500 tons. Three 5 inch guns were removed and her upper decks extended aft to provide additional workshops. Storage tubes for Polaris missiles installed; bridge crane amidships loads and unloads missiles for alongside submarines.

MODERNISATION. *Bushnell, Fulton, Howard W. Gilmore, Nereus, Orion* and *Sperry* have undergone FRAM II modernisation to service nuclear powered attack submarines. Additional maintenance shops provided to service nuclear plant components and advanced electronic equipment and weapons. After two 5 inch guns and eight 40 mm guns (twin) removed.

DISPOSALS AND TRANSFERS

C-3 type: **Pelias** AS 14 stricken on 1 Aug 1971, **Griffin** AS 13 stricken on 1 Aug 1972. C3-S-A2 type: **Anthendon** AS 24 and **Clytie** AS 26 stricken on 1 Sep 1961 (former ship subsequently transferred on 7 Sep 1969 from Maritime Administration reserve to Turkey), **Apollo** AS 25 stricken on 1 July 1963, **Aegir** AS 23 stricken on 25 Jan 1971. Modified C-3 type: **Euryale** AS 22 stricken on 1 Dec 1971.

HOWARD W. GILMORE (AS 16) *1971, United States Navy*

FULTON (AS 11) *1971, US Navy, Joseph R. Andrews*

2 SUBMARINE RESCUE SHIPS (ASR): "PIGEON" CLASS

Name	*No.*	*Builder*	*Launched*	*Comm.*
***PIGEON**	ASR 21	Alabama DD & SB Co (Mobile)	13 Aug 1969	28 Apr 1973
***ORTOLAN**	ASR 22	Alabama DD & SB Co (Mobile)	10 Sep 1969	June 1973

Displacement, tons	4 200 full load
Dimensions, feet	251 oa × 86 (see *Design* notes) × 21·25
Guns	2—3 inch (*76 mm*) 50 cal AA (single); 4—·50 cal MG
Main engines	4 diesels; 6 000 bhp; 2 shafts = 15 knots
Complement	115 (6 officers, 109 enlisted men)
Staff accommodation	14 (4 officers, 10 enlisted men)
Submersible operators	24 (4 officers, 20 enlisted men)

Fleet Support Ships—*continued*

"PIGEON" Class—*continued*

These are the world's first ships designed specifically for this role, all other ASR designs being adaptations of tug types. The ASR 21 class ships will serve as (1) surface support ships for the Deep Submergence Rescue Vehicles (DSRV), (2) rescue ships employing the existing McCann rescue chamber, (3) major deep-sea diving support ships, and (4) operational control ships for salvage operations.

The Navy had planned in the 1960s to replace the 10-ship ASR force with new construction ASRs. However, only two ships have been funded with procurement of others deferred.

ASR 21 authorised in Fiscal Year 1967 new construction programme and ASR 22 in FY 1968 programme. Both ships built by Alabama Dry Dock and Shipbuilding Co, Mobile, Alabama; they have been delayed more than two years by a shipyard strike and technical difficulties.

DESIGN. These ships have twin, catamaran hulls, the first ocean-going catamaran ships to be built for the US Navy since Robert Fulton's steam gunboat *Demologus* of 1812. The design provides a large deck working area, facilities for raising and lowering submersibles and underwater equipment, and improved stability when operating equipment at great depths. Each of the twin hulls is 251 feet long and 26 feet wide. The well between the hulls is 34 feet across, giving the ASR a maximum beam of 86 feet. Fitted with helicopter platform.

DIVING. These ships have been fitted with the Mk II Deep Diving System to support conventional or saturation divers operating at depths to 850 feet. The system consists of two decompression chambers, two personnel transfer capsules to transport divers between the ship and ocean floor, and the associated controls, winches, cables, gas supplies, *et cetera*. Submarine rescue ships are the US Navy's primary diving ships and the only ones fitted for helium-oxygen diving.

ELECTRONICS. Fitted with precision three-dimensional sonar system for tracking submersibles.

ENGINEERING. Space and weight are reserved for future installation of a ducted thruster in each bow to enable the ship to maintain precise position while stopped or at slow speeds. Range is 8 500 miles at 13 knots.

NOMENCLATURE. Submarine rescue ships traditionally have carried bird names (the US Navy's first six ASRs were converted "Bird" class minesweepers).

SALVAGE. During major salvage operations the ASR can serve as a command post for the salvage master. Note two mooring buoys ("spuds") forward of bridge in artist's concept; there are two additional buoys aft. (Precise mooring is required in diving and salvage work, and for operating McCann submarine rescue chamber).

SUBMERSIBLES. Each ASR is capable of transporting, servicing, lowering, and raising two Deep Submergence Rescue Vehicles (DSRV) (see section on Deep Submergence Vehicles).

PIGEON (ASR 21) *1971, Alabama DD & SB Co*

PIGEON (ASR 21) *1972, Alabama DD & SB Co*

1 SUBMARINE RESCUE SHIP (ASR): "PENGUIN" TYPE

Name	*No.*	*Launched*
***SKYLARK** (ex-*Yustaga*)	ASR 20 (ex-ATF 165)	19 Mar 1946

Displacement, tons	1 235 standard; 1 740 full load
Dimensions, feet	195 wl; 205 oa × 38·5 × 15·3
Guns	Removed
Main engines	Diesel-electric (General Motors diesel); 1 shaft; 3 000 bhp = 14 knots
Complement	85 (106 designed wartime)

Former fleet tug converted to ASR in 1957. Built by Charleston SB & DD Co.
The *Skylark* is equipped with powerful pumps, heavy air compressors, and submarine rescue chamber. Fitted for helium-oxygen diving. Guns removed; formerly armed with one 3 inch gun. See "Chanticleer" class for additional notes applicable to this class. *Syklark* decommissioning delayed to 1973 or 1974.

DISPOSALS AND TRANSFERS

Bluebird ASR 19 transferred to Turkey on 15 Aug 1950; **Penguin** ASR 12 stricken on 30 June 1970 (scrapped).

6 SUBMARINE RESCUE SHIPS (ASR):

	ASR	*Launched*		ASR	*Launched*
***COUCAL**	8	29 May 1942	***PETREL**	14	26 Sep 1945
***FLORIKAN**	9	14 June 1942	***SUNBIRD**	15	3 Apr 1945
***KITTIWAKE**	13	10 July 1945	***TRINGA**	16	25 June 1945

Displacement, tons	1 653 standard; 2 290 full load
Dimensions, feet	240 wl; 251·5 oa × 42 × 14·9
Guns	2—20 mm AA in some ships
Main engines	Diesel-electric (Alco in first 4 ships, GM in others); 1 shaft; 3 000 bhp = 14·9 knots
Complement	85 (102 designed wartime)

Large tug-type ships equipped with powerful pumps, heavy air compressors, and rescue chambers for submarine salvage and rescue operations. ASR 7-9 built by Moore SB & DD Co, Oakland, Calif, and ASR 13-16 by Savannah Machine & Foundry Co, Savannah, Ga. Fitted for helium-oxygen diving equipment (submarine rescue ships are the principal deep-sea diving ships in the Navy and the only ones with a built-in helium capability).

As built each ship was armed with two 3 inch AA guns; removed 1957-1958. Some ships subsequently fitted with two 20 mm AA guns.

One ASR normally is deployed to the Western Pacific and one in the Mediterranean with the others at US submarine bases in the continental United States and Hawaii.

DISPOSALS AND TRANSFERS

Greenlet ASR 10 transferred to Turkey on 12 June 1970; **Chanticleer** ASR 7 stricken 1 June 1973 (delayed from 1972).

FULTON (AS 11), SKYLARK (ASR 20), five SSNs at New London, Connecticut *United States Navy*

Fleet Support Ships—*continued*

FLORIKAN (ASR 9) *1970, US Navy, PH2 Leroy Palmer*

FLORIKAN (ASR 9) *1971, United States Navy*

ACCOKEEK (ATA 181) *1970, United States Navy*

6 AUXILIARY TUGS (ATA): "MARICOPA" CLASS

	ATA	Launched		ATA	Launched
ACCOKEEK	181	27 July 1944	**TATNUCK**	195	14 Dec 1944
PENOBSCOT	188	12 Oct 1944	**STALLION**	193	24 Nov 1944
SAMOSET	190	26 Oct 1944	**KEYWADIN**	213	9 Apr 1945

Displacement, tons	534 standard; 835 full load
Dimensions, feet	134·5 wl; 143 oa × 33·9 × 13
Guns	1—3 inch (*76 mm*) 50 cal AA or 4—20 mm AA (twin); all guns removed from some ships
Main engines	Diesel-electric (General Motors diesels); 1 500 bhp; 1 shaft = 13 knots
Complement	45 (5 officers, 40 enlisted men)

Steel-hulled tugs formerly designated as rescue tugs (ATR); renumbered in same series as larger fleet tugs (ATF) when designation changed to ATA in 1944. All above ships built by Livingston SB Corp, Orange, Texas, or Gulfport Boiler & Welding Works, Port Arthur, Texas. During 1948 they were assigned names that had been carried by discarded fleet and yard tugs.
All of the surviving ships were decommissioned in 1970-1971 and placed in reserve. Two ships of this class serve in the Coast Guard.

"HARICOPA" Class—*continued*

NOMENCLATURE. US tugs of World War II construction and previous classes were named for Indian tribes and words.

TRANSFERS. *Bagaduce* ATA 194 and *Wampanoag* ATA 202 to Coast Guard in 1959, *Wateree* ATA 174 to Peru in 1961, *Tankowa* ATA 176 to Nationalist China in 1962, *Sotoyomo* ATA 121 to Mexico in 1963, *Undaunted* ATA 199 to Bureau of Commercial Fisheries, Department of Interior in 1964, *Geronimo* ATA 207 (on loan to Bureau of Commercial Fisheries from 1962 to 1968) to Taiwan China on 8 Feb 1969, *Kalmia* ATA 184, *Koka* ATA 185, *Umpqua* ATA 209 Colombia on 1 July 1971, *Mahopac* ATA 196 to Taiwan China on 1 July 1971; *Tillamook* ATA 192 to South Korea on 25 July 1971, *Sagamore* ATA 208 to Dominican Republic on 1 Feb 1972, *Salish* ATA 187, *Catawba* ATA 210 to Argentina on 10 Feb 1972, *Cahokia* ATA 186 (loan to US Air Force in 1971) to Taiwan China on 29 Mar 1972, *Wandank* ATA 204 to Department of Interior.

DISPOSALS (since 1 Jan 1965)
Allegheny ATA 179 stricken on 14 Dec 1968, **Sunnadin** ATA 197 stricken on 20 Nov 1969.
Army LT-type **ATA 204** (ex-US Army LT 455) stricken on 30 July 1971. See 1971-1972 and previous editions for characteristics.

25 FLEET TUGS (ATF): "APACHE" CLASS

	ATF	Launched		ATF	Launched
***APACHE**	67	8 May 1942	***PAKANA**	108	3 Mar 1943
***UTE**	76	24 June 1942	***QUAPAW**	110	15 May 1943
***CREE**	84	17 Aug 1942	***TAKELMA**	113	18 Sep 1943
***LIPAN**	85	17 Sep 1942	***TAWAKONI**	114	28 Oct 1943
***MATACO**	86	14 Oct 1942	***ATAKAPA**	149	11 July 1944
SENECA	91	2 Feb 1943	***LUISENO**	156	17 Mar 1945
***TAWASA**	92	22 Feb 1943	***NIPMUC**	157	12 Apr 1945
***ABNAKI**	96	22 Apr 1943	***MOSOSPELEA**	158	7 Mar 1945
***CHOWANOC**	100	20 Aug 1943	***PAIUTE**	159	4 June 1945
***COCOPA**	101	5 Oct 1943	***PAPAGO**	160	21 June 1945
***HITCHITI**	103	29 Jan 1944	***SALINAN**	161	20 July 1945
***MOCTOBI**	105	25 Mar 1944	***SHAKORI**	162	9 Aug 1945
***MOLALA**	106	23 Dec 1942			

Displacement, tons	1 235 standard; 1 675 full load
Dimensions, feet	195 wl; 205 oa × 38·5 × 15·5 max
Guns	1—3 inch (*76 mm*) 50 cal AA; some ships in forward areas have machine guns in "tubs" aft of bridge
Main engines	Diesel-electric drive; 1 shaft; 3 000 bhp = 15 knots
Complement	75 (5 officers, 70 enlisted men; 85 wartime)

Large ocean tugs fitted with powerful pumps and other salvage equipment. ATF 96 and later ships ("Abnaki" class) have smaller funnel. As built these ships mounted 2—40 mm guns in addition to 3 inch gun. All surviving ships built by Charleston SB & DD Co, or United Engineering Co, Alameda, Calif, except *Seneca* built by Cramp SB Co, Philadelphia, Pa, and *Tawasa* by Commercial Iron Works, Portland, Oreg. *Pakana* stricken in 1963 but reinstated on Navy List in 1963. *Lipan* and *Mosospelea* transferred to Military Sealift Command in 1973; redesignated T-ATF and civilian manned.
Three ships of this class serve in the Coast Guard.

CONVERSIONS. *Chetco* ATF 99, *Yurok* ATF 164, and *Yustaga* ATF 165 converted to submarine rescue ships ASR 12, 19, and 20, respectively; *Serrano* ATF 112 converted to surveying ship AGS 24.

TRANSFERS. *Avoyel* ATF 150 and *Chilula* ATF 152 to Coast Guard in 1956, *Yuma* ATF 94 to Pakistan in 1959, *Tekesta* ATF 93 to Chile in 1960, *Cusabo* ATF 155 to Ecuador in 1960, *Choctaw* ATF 70 to Columbia in 1961, *Menominee* ATF 73 to Indonesia in 1961, *Pinto* ATF 90 to Peru in 1961, *Arapaho* ATF 68 and *Cahuilla* ATF 152 to Argentina in 1961, *Tolowa* ATF 116 to Venezuela in 1962. *Potawatomii* ATF 109 to Chile in 1963, *Bannock* ATF 81 to Italy in 1954, *Chickasaw* ATF 83 to Taiwan China in 1966; *Utina* ATF 163 to Venezuela on 30 Sep 1971; *Arikara* ATF 98 to Chile on 1 July 1972, *Kiowa* ATF 72 to Dominican Republic on 16 Oct 1972, *Sioux* ATF 75 to Turkey on 30 Oct 1972.

DISPOSALS (since 1 Jan 1965)
Munsee ATF 107 stricken on 3 Nov 1969.

MOSOSPELEA (T-ATF 158) *1968, United States Navy*

Fleet Support Ships—*continued*

COCOPA (ATF 101)—no funnel type *1970, USN, PH2 Donna M. Young*

BEAUFORT (ATS 2) *1971, Brooke Marine*

CREE (ATF 84) *1970, US Navy, PH2 Leroy Palmer*

EDENTON (ATS 1) *1971, US Navy, PH 2 Brian Erb*

BEAUFORT (ATS 2) *1971, Brooke Marine*

5 SALVAGE AND RESCUE SHIPS (ATS): "EDENTON" CLASS

Name	*No.*	*Laid down*	*Launched*	*Commission*
***EDENTON**	ATS 1	1 Apr 1967	15 May 1968	23 Jan 1971
***BEAUFORT**	ATS 2	19 Feb 1968	20 Dec 1968	22 Jan 1972
BRUNSWICK	ATS 3	5 June 1968	14 Oct 1969	10 Dec 1972
	ATS 4	Fiscal Year 1972 programme		
	ATS 5	Fiscal Year 1973 programme		

Displacement, tons	3 117 full load
Dimensions, feet	282·66 oa × 50 × 15·1
Guns	2—20 mm AA; 4—·50 cal MG
Main engines	4 diesels (Paxman); 6 000 bhp; 2 shafts = 16 knots
Complement	102 (9 officers and 93 enlisted men)

These tugs are designed specifically for salvage operations and are capable of (1) ocean towing, (2) supporting diver operations to depths of 850 feet, (3) lifting submerged objects weighing as much as 600 000 pounds from a depth of 120 feet by static tidal lift or 30 000 pounds by dynamic lift, (4) fighting ship fires, and (5) performing general salvage operations.
The ATS 1 was authorised in the Fiscal Year 1966 shipbuilding programme; ATS 2 and ATS 3 in the FY 1967 programme. All three ships constructed by Brooke Marine, Lowestoft, England. ATS 4 and ATS 5 planned for FY 1970 programme were deferred with ATS 4 being authorised in the FY 1972 programme and ATS 5 and 6 being requested in FY 1973 with only one ship approved.
Designation changed from salvage tug (ATS) to salvage and rescue ship (ATS) on 16 Feb 1971.

DIVING. **These ships can carry the air-transportable Mk I Deep Diving System to support four divers working in two-man shifts at depths to 850 feet. The system** consists of a double-chamber decompression chamber, a personnel transfer capsule to transport divers between the ships and ocean floor, and the associated controls, winches, cables, gas supplies, *et cetera*. The ships organic diving capability is compressed air.

ENGINEERING. **Fitted with controllable-pitch propellers and tunnel bow thruster for precise manoeuvering.**

NOMENCLATURE. Salvage tugs are being named for small American cities.

EDENTON (ATS 1) *1971, United States Navy*

SEAPLANE TENDERS (AV) AND ADVANCED AVIATION BASE SHIPS (AVB)

All US Navy seaplane tenders and aviation base ships have been stricken or transferred except for the ex-*Albermarle* AV 5 which remains in service as a helicopter repair ship, renamed *Corpus Christi Bay* ARVH 1.
See 1972-1973 edition for final disposal and transfer notes for these ship types.

SEALIFT SHIPS

Military Sealift Ships provide ocean transportation for all components of the Department of Defense. These ships are operated by the Navy's Military Sealift Command, renamed on 1 Aug 1970 from Military Sea Transportation Service (MSTS).

The cargo ships, tankers, troop transports and landing ships, listed below carry military cargo and personnel from port to port except that Military Sealift Command tankers do transfer petroleum to Navy oilers in overseas areas. In addition, the Military Sealift Command directs the chartering of merchantmen owned by shipping lines or private parties to carry government cargo.

The Commander, Deputy Commander, and Area Commanders (Atlantic, Pacific, and Far East) are flag officers of the Navy on active duty. All ships are civilian manned with most of their crews being Civil Service employees of the Navy. However, the tankers are operated under contract to commercial tanker lines and are manned by merchant seamen and some ships are manned by Japanese and Korean merchant seamen under the command of US personnel (see notes for specific ships). In addition to the ships listed in this section, the Military Sealift Command also operates a number of Special Project ships that support other defence-related activities, mostly research, surveying, and missile-range support ships (see Experimental, Research and Surveying Ships listing). Other Special Project ships are the cable ships, a few tugs, and helicopter repair ship *Corpus Christi Bay* (T-ARVH 1) listed in the section on Fleet Support Ships. A few Navy-manned logistic ships are included in this section although they are not under the control of the Military Sealift Command.

ARMAMENT. No ships of the Military Sealift Command are armed.

CLASSIFICATION. Military Sealift Command ships are assigned standard US Navy hull designations with the added designation prefix "T". Ships in this category are referred to as "USNS" (United States Naval Ship) vice "USS" (United States Ship) which is used for Navy-manned ships.

NEW SHIPS. Proposals by the Military Sealift Command to construct new ships specifically for MSC use have been rejected, primarily because of Congressional opposition. These projects included a series of fast deployment logistic ships (FDL) which would have been based overseas with arms, munitions, and equipment for US troops that would be airlifted overseas, and a class of multi-purpose cargo ships. The latter are described in the 1971-1972 edition of *Jane's Fighting Ships*.

The Military Sealift Command now plans to sponsor the construction of nine 25 000 deadweight-ton tankers which would be built by private industry and operated by commercial shipping firms under long-term charter to the government. With this charter security private financing would be encouraged and the ships would be largely amortised after the minimum government use, after which they could be used in private service or purchased outright by the government. This concept has already financed the roll-on/roll-off vehicle cargo ship *Admiral William M. Callaghan*, an advanced gas-turbine-propelled ship completed in 1968.

The Military Sealift Command cargo fleet is being modernised by the transfer of several Navy LSTs constructed in the 1950s. These ships will be employed in cargo operations and are no longer considered suitable for amphibious assault operations. (See the specific class listings).

All aircraft transports (AVT) and cargo and aircraft ferry ships (AKV) have been stricken from the Navy List. See 1971-1972 edition for characteristics of the last AKVs in service. Disposals since 1 Jan 1970 are listed on a subsequent page of this listing.

STORE SHIPS (AF)

All refrigerated store ships (AF) operated by the Military Sealift Command have been stricken from the Navy List:

VC2-S-AP3 "Victory" type: **Asterion** T-AF 63 and **Perseus** T-AF 64 transferred to Maritime Administration in 1973 for scrapping.
R1-M-AV3 "Adria" class: **Bondia** T-AF 42 transferred to Maritime Administration in 1973 for scrapping.
C2-S-B1 "Eagle" class: **Bald Eagle** T-AF 50 and **Blue Jacket** T-AF 51 stricken on 19 Oct 1971 and transferred to Maritime Administration reserve fleet.

CARGO SHIP: Ex-LANDING SHIP MEDIUM

The unnamed cargo ship AG 335 (hull number T-AG 335), formerly LSM 335, was stricken on 21 Dec 1970 and transferred to the Department of the Interior. See 1970-1971 and previous editions for description and data on LSM disposals.

Of 558 LSMs constructed during World War II, only 10 remain on the US Navy List: seven inshore fire support ships (LFR), two salvaging lifting ships (ARSD), and one test range support ship (IX). Other LSMs now serve the navies of Argentina, Chile, Mainland China, Taiwan China, Denmark, Dominican Republic, Ecuador, West Germany, Greece, Japan, South Korea, Peru, Philippines, Spain, Thailand, Venezuela, North Vietnam, South Vietnam.

3 CARGO SHIPS (AG): FORMER DEPOT SHIPS

***PHOENIX** (ex-*Arizona*, ex-*Capitol Victory*)	T-AG 172
***PROVO** (ex-*Utah* ex-*Drew Victory*)	T-AG 173
***CHEYENNE** (ex-*Wyoming*, ex-*Middlesex Victory*)	T-AG 174

Displacement, tons	6 700 light; 2 400 full load
Dimensions, feet	455 × 62
Main engines	Geared turbines; 6 000 bhp ; 1 shaft = 15·5 knots
Boilers	2

These ships were acquired in 1963 from the Maritime Administration. Initially they were employed as forward depot ships; now used as general cargo ships. Korean manned.

CANCELLATION. The 12 "Victory" ships planned as forward depot ships were not acquired from the Maritime Admimistration Reserve Fleet on 1 Feb 1966 as requested. They were to have been redesignated T-AG 179 to 190 and given new Navy names (see complete list in the 1966-1967 edition) but were chartered to and operated by commercial shipping companies in Vietnam service under their original "Victory" names.

PROVO (T-AG 173) *United States Navy*

2 HEAVY LIFT SHIPS (AK): "BROSTROM" TYPE

* **PVT. LEONARD C. BROSTROM** (ex-*Marine Eagle*)	T-AK 255
MARINE FIDDLER	T-AK 267

Displacement, tons	13 865 deadweight
Dimensions, feet	520 oa × 71·5 × 33
Main engines	Geared turbine; 9 000 shp ; 1 shaft = 15·8 knots
Boilers	2
Complement	57 (14 officers, 43 men)

These ships have 150-ton-capacity booms, the most powerful lift capacity of any US ships. C4-S-B1 type. *Marine Fiddler* being decommissioned in 1973 for transfer to Maritime Administration reserve; eventual fate unknown.

MARINE FIDDLER (T-AK 267) *United States Navy*

5 FBM CARGO SHIPS (AK): "VICTORY" TYPE

BETELGEUSE (ex-*Colombia Victory*)	AK 260
***NORWALK** (ex-*Norwalk Victory*)	T-AK 279
***FURMAN** (ex-*Furman Victory*)	T-AK 280
***VICTORIA** (ex-*Ethiopia Victory*)	T-AK 281
***MARSHFIELD** (ex-*Marshfield Victory*)	T-AK 282

Displacement, tons	6 700 light; *Betelgeuse* 15 580 full load; others 11 150 full load
Dimensions, feet	455·25 oa × 62 × 24 except *Betelgeuse* 28·5
Guns	8—40 mm AA (twin) in *Betelgeuse*; others unarmed
Main engines	geared turbine; 8 500 shp; 1 shaft = 17 knots
Boilers	2
Complement	T-AK type 80 to 90 plus Navy detachment

Former merchant ships of the VC2-S-AP3 "Victory" type built during World War II. Extensively converted to supply supply tenders for Fleet Ballistic Missile (FBM) submarines. Fitted to carry torpedoes, spare parts, packaged petroleum products, bottled gas, black oil and diesel fuel, frozen and dry provisions, and general cargo as well as missiles. No. 3 hold converted to carry 16 Polaris missiles in vertical position; tankage provided for 355 000 gallons of diesel oil and 430 000 gallons of fuel oil (for submarine tenders).

Betelgeuse was Navy manned; others civilian manned by Military Sealift Command with small Navy detachments for security and technical services. Active ships being modified to carry Poseidon missile in lieu of Polaris.
Betelgeuse reactivated by the Navy in 1951 from Maritime Administration reserve fleet. Decommissioned in 1971 and placed in reserve.
Norwalk converted to FBM cargo ship by Boland Machine & Manufacturing Co, and accepted for service on 30 Dec 1963.
Furman converted by American Shipbuilding Co, and accepted in Oct 1964.
Victoria converted by Philadelphia Naval Shipyard, and accepted in Oct 1965.
Marshfield converted by Boland Machine & Manufacturing Co, and accepted in June 1970.

MARSHFIELD (T-AK 282) *1970, United States Navy, Nancy Chutz*

Sealift Ships—*continued*

BETELGEUSE (AK 260) as "mothballed" in reserve status under a new concept in which a nylon and neoprene cover is drawn over the ship; the covering is inflated with dehumidified air.

1 CARGO SHIP (AK): "BLAND" TYPE

***SCHUYLER OTIS BLAND** T-AK 277

Displacement, tons	15 910 full load
Dimensions, feet	478 × 66 × 30
Main engines	Geared turbine; 13 750 shp; 1 shaft; = 18·5 knots
Boilers	2

Acquired from the Maritime Administration by the Military Sea Transportation Service in July 1961. The only ship of the type (C3-S-DX1).

SCHUYLER OTIS BLAND (T-AK 277) *United States Navy*

6 CARGO SHIPS (AK): O'BRIEN" CLASS

***FENTRESS** (ex-V 206)	T-AK 180
***HERKIMER** (ex-V 203)	T-AK 188
***MUSKINGUM** (ex-V 208)	T-AK 198
***COLONEL WILLIAM J. O'BRIEN** (ex-*Maiden's Eye*)	T-AK 246
***SHORT SPLICE**	T-AK 249
***PRIVATE FRANK J. PETRARCA** (ex-*Long Splice*)	T-AK 250

Displacement, tons	2 460 light; 7 450 full load
Dimensions, feet	338·7 × 50 × 21
Main engines	Diesel; 1 750 bhp; 1 shaft = 11·5 knots

C1-M-AV1 Type. *Colonel William J. O'Brien* and *Short Splice* were converted to heavy lift ships and have two 80-ton capacity cranes.

HERKIMER (T-AK 188) *United States Navy*

SHORT SPLICE (T-AK 249) *United States Navy*

1 CARGO SHIP (AK): "ELTANIN" TYPE

***MIRFAK** T-AK 271

Displacement, tons	2 036 light; 4 942 full load
Dimensions, feet	256·8 wl; 262·2 oa × 51·5 × 18·7
Main engines	Diesel-electric (ALCO diesels with Westinghouse electric motors); 3 200 bhp; 2 shafts = 13 knots

Built for MSTS by Avondale Marine Ways, New Orleans, La. Designed for Arctic operation with hull strengthened against ice. C1-M E2-13a type. Launched on 5 Aug 1957. Note icebreaking prow in photo.

CONVERSION. Two other ships of this class converted for oceanographic research: *Eltanin*, reclassified from T-AK 270 to T-AGOR 8 on 15 Nov 1962; *Mizar* T-AK 272 was reclassified T-AGOR 11 on 15 Apr 1964 (see Experimental, Research and Surveying Ships).

MIRFAK (T-AK 271) *United States Navy*

11 CARGO SHIPS (AK): "VICTORY" TYPE

***GREENVILLE VICTORY**	T-AK 237
***PVT. JOHN R. TOWLE** (ex-*Appleton Victory*)	T-AK 240
***PVT. FRANCIS X. McGRAW** (ex-*Wabash Victory*)	T-AK 241
***SGT. ANDREW MILLER** (ex-*Radcliffe Victory*)	T-AK 242
***SGT. MORRIS E. CRAIN** (ex-*Mills Victory*)	T-AK 244
***LIEUT. GEORGE W. G. BOYCE** (ex-*Waterville Victory*)	T-AK 251
***LIEUT. ROBERT CRAIG** (ex-*Bowling Green Victory*)	T-AK 252
***SGT. TRUMAN KIMBRO**	T-AK 254
***LIEUT. JAMES E. ROBINSON** (ex-T-AG 170, ex-T-AK 274, ex-AKV 3, ex-*Czechoslovakia Victory*)	T-AK 274
***PVT. JOSEPH F. MERRELL** (ex-AKV 4, ex-*Grange Victory*)	T-AK 275
***SGT. JACK J. PENDLETON** (ex-AKV 5)	T-AK 276

Displacement, tons	6 700 light; 12 450 full load
Dimensions, feet	455·25 oa × 62 × 28·5
Main engines	Geared turbine; 8 500 shp ; 1 shaft = 15 or 17 knots (see notes)
Boilers	2

Former merchant ships of the "Victory" type built during World War II. VC2-S-AP3 type capable of 17 knots except T-AK 251, 252, and 254 are VC2-S-AP2 type capable of 15 knots.
Three ships originally acquired by Navy from Maritime Administration as aircraft cargo and ferry ships (AKV); reclassified as "straight" cargo ships (AK) on 7 May 1959. *Lieut. James E. Robinson* modified for special project work and designated T-AG in 1963; reverted to T-AK 274 on 1 July 1964.
Several other "Victory" cargo ships transferred to Navy after World War II have been converted to research (AG) and space/missile support ships (AGM). "Victory" type cargo ships initially configured as forward depot ships and as Fleet Ballistic Missile (FBM) cargo ships are listed separately.
These ships are unarmed and civilian manned by the Military Sealift Command.

RECLASSIFICATION. The former Military Sea Transportation Service Aircraft Cargo and Ferry Ships *Lieut, James E. Robinson, Private Joseph F. Merrel* and *Sergeant Jack J. Pendleton*, AKV 3, AKV 4, and AKV 5, respectively, were reclassified as Cargo Ships, Ak 274, AK 275 and AK 276 on 7 May 1959. *Kingsport Victory* T-AK 239, was renamed and reclassified *Kingsport* T-AG 164 in 1962 (see Experimental, Research and Surveying ships).
Lieut James E. Robinson T-AK 274, was to have been transferred to the Maritime Administration, but was modified for special project work and reclassified as T-AG 170 in 1963, and reverted to the original classification T-AK 274 on 1 July 1964.
Haiti Victory T-AK 238 and *Dalton Victory* T-AK 256 converted to satellite tracking and recovery ships, reclassified and renamed, *Longview* T-AGM 3 and *Sunnyvale* T-AGM 5, respectively.
Pvt. Joe E. Mann T-AK 253, ex-*Owensboro Victory*, was fitted out as a range instrumentation and telemetry ship for the Pacific Missile Range in Oct 1958 and renamed *Richfield* T-AGM 4.
The ship intended for designation AK 278 became the *Sea Lift*, T-LSV 9, subsequently changed to T-AKR 9.

DISPOSALS
Sgt. Archer T. Gammon T-AK 243 transferred to Maritime Administration in 1973 for scrapping.
C2-S-B1 "Andromeda" class: **Wyandot** T-AK 283 ex-AKA 92 transferred to Maritime Administration in 1973 for scrapping.

PVT JOSEPH F. MERRELL (T-AK 275) *United States Navy*

Sealift Ships—*continued*

LT ROBERT CRAIG (T-AK 252) *United States Navy*

PVT JOHN R. TOWLE (T-AK 240) in Antarctic *1961, US Navy*

SGT MORRIS E CRAIN (T-AK 244) *United States Navy*

1 DOCK CARGO SHIP (AKD): "POINT BARROW" TYPE

***POINT BARROW** T-AKD 1

Displacement, tons	5 940 light; 9 415 standard; 14 094 full load
Measurement, tons	12 000 gross; 4 020 deadweight
Dimensions, feet	475 wl; 492 oa × 78 × 22
Main engines	Turbine; 2 shafts; 6 000 shp = 18 knots
Boilers	2
Complement	66
Passengers	42

Built for MSTS by Maryland Shipbuilding & Dry Dock Co. Laid down on 18 Sep 1956, launched on 25 May 1957 and commissioned on 28 Feb 1958. Delivered to MSTS on 29 May 1958. S2-ST-23A type. Originally a roll-on / roll-off ship to load vehicles on ramp. Winterised for Arctic service. Ballasting arrangements permit embarking and debarking landing craft as in dock landing ships.

Subsequently refitted with hangar over docking well and employed in transport of large booster rockets to Cape Kennedy space centre. Primarily used to carry the second stage of the Saturn V moon rocket and Lunar Modules.

Placed out of service in reserve on 1 Jan 1971; subsequently reactivated in mid-1972 for use as transport for booster rockets.

POINT BARROW (T-AKD 1) *1970, United States Navy*

POINT BARROW (T-AKD 1) *1970, United States Navy*

LIGHT CARGO SHIPS (AKL)

The last light cargo ships (AKL) employed by Navy/Military Sealift Command in coastal cargo operations have been stricken: **Redbud** T-AKL 398 ex-US Coast Guard WAGL 398 returned to Coast Guard on 20 Nov 1970 as WLB 398 and transferred to Philippines on 1 Mar 1972; **Mark** AKL-12 ex-AG 143, ex-US Army FS 214 transferred to Taiwan China on 1 July 1972; **Brule** AKL 28 ex-US Army FS 370 transferred to South Korea on 1 Nov 1971.

See 1971-1972 and previous editions for characteristics and other AKL disposals and transfers.

1 VEHICLE CARGO SHIP (AKR): "SEA LIFT" TYPE

SEA LIFT T-AKR 9 (ex-T-LSV 9)

Displacement, tons	11 130 light; 16 940 standard; 21 700 full load
Measurement, tons	15 750 gross; 12 100 deadweight
Dimensions, feet	540 oa × 83 × 29
Main engines	Geared steam turbines; 2 shafts; 19 400 shp = 20 knots
Boilers	2
Complement	62 plus 12 Passengers

Improved roll-on/roll-off vehicle cargo ship. Maritime Administration C4-ST-67a type. Built by the Puget Sound Bridge & Dry Dock Co, (now Lockheed Shipbuilding and Construction Co), Seattle, Wash, at a cost of $15 895 500. Authorised under the Fiscal Year 1963 programme. Laid down on 19 May 1964 and launched on 18 Apr 1965. Delivered to Navy on 25 Apr 1967 and to MSTS on 19 May 1967. Designed for point-to-point sea transportation of Department of Defense self-propelled, fully loaded, wheeled, tracked and amphibious vehicles and general cargo. Internal ramps, stern ramp and side openings provide for quick loading and unloading. Designation changed from T-LSV to T-AKR on 1 Jan 1969.

SEA LIFT (T-AKR 9) *1966, Lockheed Shipbuilding*

SEA LIFT (T-AKR 9) *1966, Lockheed Shipbuilding*

1 VEHICLE CARGO SHIP (AKR): "COMET" TYPE

***COMET** T-AKR 7 (ex-T-LSV 7, ex-T-AK 269)

Displacement, tons	7 605 light; 18 150 full load
Measurement, tons	12 750 gross; 6 500 deadweight
Dimensions, feet	465 pp; 499 oa × 78 × 28·8
Main engines	Geared turbines (General Electric); 2 shafts; 13 200 shp = 18 knots
Boilers	2 (Babcock & Wilcox)
Complement	73

Roll-on/roll-off vehicle carrier built for MSTS by Sun Shipbuilding & Dry Dock Co. C3-ST-14A type. Laid down on 15 May 1956. Launched on 31 July 1957. Completed on 27 Jan 1958. Has ramp system for loading and discharging. The hull is strengthened against ice. Can accommodate 700 vehicles in two after holds; the forward holds are for general cargo. Equipped with Denny-Brown Stabilisers. Reclassified from T-AK to T-LSV on 1 June 1963, and changed to T-AKR on 1 Jan 1969. LSV 1-6 were World War II-built amphibious ships; subsequently redesignated as mine warfare ships (MCS) and net cargo ship (AKN).

Sealift Ships—*continued*

COMET (T-AKR 7) *United States Navy*

DISPOSALS

Taurus (T-AKR 8, ex-T-LSV 8, ex-AK 273, ex-LSD 23) deactivated in 1968 and subsequently scrapped; officially stricken on 22 June 1971 (almost two years after being sold for scrap).

Galilea AKN 6, ex-LSV 6, ex-AP 161 stricken from the Navy List on 1 Sep 1961 and transferred to Maritime Administration.

CARGO AND AIRCRAFT FERRY SHIPS (AKV)

All escort carrier-type ships designated as cargo and aircraft ferry ships (AKV) have been stricken; disposals since 1 Jan 1970:
Siboney AKV 12 ex-CVE 112, **Tinian** AKV 23 ex-CVE 123 stricken on 1 June 1970; **Kula Gulf** T-AKV 8 ex-CVE 108, **Point Cruz** T-AKV 19, ex-CVE 119, **Card** T-AKV 40 ex-CVU 11, ex-CVE 11, **Core** T-AKV 41 ex-CVU 13, ex-CVE 13, **Croatan** T-AKV 43 ex-CVU 25, ex-CVE 25 stricken on 15 Sep 1970; **Vella Gulf** AKV 11 ex-CVE 111, **Badoeng Strait** AKV 16 ex-CVE 116, **Saidor** AKV 17 ex-CVE 117 stricken on 1 Dec 1970; **Commencement Bay** AKV 37 ex-CVE 105, **Cape Gloucester** AKV 9 ex-CVE 109, **Rendova** AKV 14 ex-CVE 114 stricken on 1 Apr 1971; **Rabaul** AKV 21 ex-CVE 121 stricken on 1 Sep 1971; **Breton** T-AKV 42 ex-CVU 23, ex-CVE 23 stricken on 29 Feb 1972.

See 1971-1972 and previous editions for characteristics and earlier disposals.

AIRCRAFT TRANSPORTS (AVT)

All former "Essex" class fast carriers and "Independence" class light carriers designated as aircraft transports (AVT) have been stricken except for the **Cabot** AVT 3 ex-CVL 28 transferred to Spain on 30 Aug 1967. See Aircraft Carrier listing for details of disposals. The two "Saipan" class light carriers have been converted to other roles: *Wright* AVT 7 ex- CVL 49 converted to national command ship CC 2; *Saipan* AVT 6 ex-CVL 48 converted to communications ship AGMR 2, renamed *Arlington*.
Whereas several cargo and aircraft ferry ships have been in active service since World War II (operated by Military Sea Transportation Service/Military Sealift Command), none of the larger aircraft transports has been in service in the AVT role. Since the Korean War (1950-1953) the larger ships (AVT) were not considered "aircraft carriers" because of their inability to operate modern fixed-wing aircraft without extensive reconstruction. The last US "straight-deck" carrier (non-angled flight deck) to operate fixed-wing aircraft was the *Lake Champlain* (CVS 39), decommissioned in 1965 and subsequently stricken on 1 Sep 1971.

1 TANKER (AO): "EXPLORER" TYPE

*** AMERICAN EXPLORER** T-AO 165

Displacement, tons	16 500 gross; 22 525 deadweight
Dimensions, feet	615 oa × 80 × 44·5
Main engines	Steam turbines; 22 000 shp; 1 shaft = 20 knots

T5-S-RM2a type. Laid down on 9 July 1957; launched on 11 Apr 1958. Built by Ingalls Shipbuilding Corporation, Pascagoula, for the Maritime Administration, but acquired by Military Sea Transportation Service. Cargo capacity 190 300 barrels. Operated for Military Sealift Command by commercial firm.

AMERICAN EXPLORER (T-AO 165) *United States Navy*

3 TANKERS (AO): "MAUMEE" CLASS

		Launched
***MAUMEE**	T-AO 149	16 Feb 1956
***SHOSHONE**	T-AO 151	17 Jan 1957
***YUKON**	T-AO 152	16 Mar 1956

Displacement, tons	25 000 deadweight
Measurement, tons	16 500 gross; 25 000 deadweight
Dimensions, feet	591 wl; 620 oa × 83·5 × 32
Main engines	Geared turbine; 20 460 shp; 1 shaft = 18 knots

Yukon laid down 16 May 1955 by Ingalls, Pascagoula, delivered May 1957. *Maumee* laid down 8 Mar 1955, delivered Dec 1956. *Shoshone* laid down 15 Aug 1955 by Sun Shipbuilding, Chester, delivered Apr 1957. T5-S-12A type. *Potomac* T-AO 150 sank at Morehead, North Carolina, after explosion on 26-27 Sep 1961, but was rebuilt in 1963-1964, renamed SS *Shenandoah* and chartered to MSTS. Cargo capacity 203 216 barrels.
Maumee provided with ice-strengthened bow during 1969-1970 modification at Norfolk SB & DD Co; employed in transporting petroleum products to Antarctica in support of US scientific endeavours.
These ships are operated for the Military Sealift Command by commercial firms.

8 TANKERS (AO): "MISSION" CLASS

		Launched	Commissioned
***SUAMICO** (ex-*Harlem Heights*)	T-AO 49	30 May 1942	10 Aug 1942
***TALLULAH** (ex-*Valley Forge*)	T-AO 50	25 June 1942	5 Sep 1942
***PECOS** (ex-*Corsicana*)	T-AO 65	17 Aug 1942	5 Oct 1942
***MILLICOMA** (ex-*Conastoga*, ex-*King's Mountain*)	T-AO 73	21 Jan 1943	5 Mar 1943
***SAUGATUCK** (ex-*Newton*)	T-AO 75	7 Dec 1942	19 Feb 1943
***SCHUYLKILL** (ex-*Louisburg*)	T-AO 76	16 Feb 1943	9 Apr 1943
***COSSATOT** (ex-*Fort Necessity*)	T-AO 77	28 Feb 1943	20 Apr 1943
***MISSION SANTA YNEZ**	T-AO 134	19 Dec 1943	(see notes)

Displacement, tons	5 730 light; 22 380 full load
Dimensions, feet	503 wl; 523·5 oa × 68 × approx 30
Main engines	Turbo-electric drive; 6 000 shp (except *Mission Santa Ynez* 10 000 shp); 1 shaft = 15 knots (except *Mission Santa Ynez* 16 knots)
Boilers	2 (Babcock & Wilcox)

T2-SE-A1 tankers begun as merchant ships but acquired by Navy and completed as fleet oilers (AO) except the *Mission Santa Ynez* of T2-SE-A2 type delivered as merchant tanker on 13 March 1944 and subsequently acquired by Navy on 22 Oct 1947. During the post World War II period all of these ships were employed in the tanker role, carrying petroleum point-to-point.
All built by Sun Shipbuilding & Dry Dock Co, Chester, Pennsylvania, except *Mission Santa Ynez* built by Marine Ship Corp, Sausalito, California. Cargo capacity approximately 134 000 barrels.

DISPOSALS AND TRANSFERS (since 1 Jan 1970)

Mission San Rafael T-AO 130 stricken on 28 Apr 1970, **Mission Santa Cruz** T-AO 133 stricken on 15 Sep 1970, **Shawnee Trail** T-AO 142 stricken on 29 Feb 1972, **Chepachet** T-AO 78 stricken on 13 Mar 1972, **Mission Buenaventura** T-AO 111 stricken on 31 Mar 1972, **Cache** T-AO 67 stricken on 6 May 1972, **Cowanesque** T-AO 67 stricken on 1 June 1972, **Pioneer Valley** T-AO 140 stricken on 15 Aug 1972 (not transferred to Columbia). Some ships technically remain on the Navy List but have been "permanently" transferred to Maritime Administration reserve fleet and are expected to be disposed of in the near future.

SCHUYLKILL (T-AO 76) *United States Navy*

SHOSHONE (T-AO 151) *United States Navy*

Sealift Ships—*continued*

4 GASOLINE TANKERS (AOG): "PECONIC" CLASS

		Launched
***RINCON**	T-AOG 77	5 Jan 1945
***NODAWAT** (ex-*Belridge*)	T-AOG 78	15 May 1945
***PETALUMA** (ex-*Raccoon Bend*, ex-*Tavispan*)	T-AOG 79	9 Aug 1945
***PISCATAQUA** (ex-*Cisne*, ex-*Taveta*)	T-AOG 80	10 Sep 1945

Displacement, tons 2 060 light; 6 000 full load
Dimensions, feet 325·2 oa × 48·2 × 19·1
Main engines diesel; 1 400 bhp; 1 shaft = 10 knots

T1-M-BT2 gasoline tankers built by Todd Shipyards Corp, Houston, Texas, as merchant tankers. All acquired by Navy in 1950 and assigned to Military Sea Transportation Service and employed in point-to-point carrying of petroleum. Cargo capacity approximately 30 000 barrels.

DISPOSALS
T1-MET-24a type: **Chattahooche** T-AOG 82 stricken on 22 Feb 1972, **Alatna** T-AOG 81 permanently transferred to Maritime Administration reserve fleet on 8 Aug 1972.

RINCON (T-AOG 77) *United States Navy*

PETALUMA (T-AOG 79) *United States Navy*

1 TRANSPORT (AP): "BARRETT" CLASS

		Launched	Completed
***BARRETT** (ex-*President Jackson*)	T-AP 196	27 June 1950	15 Dec 1951

Displacement, tons 17 600 standard; 19 600 full load
Measurement, tons 12 660 gross; 10 600 deadweight
Dimensions, feet 533 oa × 73 × 27
Main engines Geared turbines; 1 shaft; 13 750 shp = 19 to 20 knots (cruising), see *Engineering*
Troops 1 900 (400 officers, 1 500 men)

Maritime Administration type P2-S1-DN1. Three sister ships built by the New York Shipbuilding Corporation, New Jersey. Originally laid down as passenger ships for the American President Lines but taken over by the Navy to be completed as troop transports. Troop carrying capacity of 1 500 plus 396 cabin berths for officers and dependents. Troop lift can be increased by at least 1 000 men if necessary by converting recreation areas into berthing spaces. All spaces are air-conditioned except the engine room and bridge. The *Barret* is the only US Navy troop transport in service. On sea trials *Barrett* attained a speed of 21·5 knots at full power.

DISPOSALS
Geiger T-AP 197 stricken from Navy List (Military Sealift Command) and transferred to Maritime Administration reserve fleet on 27 Apr 1971; **Upshur** T-AP 198 was stricken and transferred on 2 Apr 1973 to the state of Maine as a training ship.

UPSHUR (T-AP 198) *Skyfotos*

BARRETT (T-AP 196) *United States Navy*

6 CARGO SHIPS: LST TYPE

Name	No.	Launched
***TIOGA COUNTY**	T-LST 1158	11 Apr 1953
***TRAVERSE COUNTY**	T-LST 1160	3 Oct 1953
***WAHKIAKUM COUNTY**	T-LST 1162	23 Jan 1953
***WALDO COUNTY**	T-LST 1163	17 Mar 1953
***WALWORTH COUNTY**	T-LST 1164	18 May 1953
***WASHOE COUNTY**	T-LST 1165	14 July 1953

Displacement, tons 2 590 light; 5 800 full load
Dimensions, feet 384 oa × 55 × 17
Main engines diesels (4 General Motors); 6 000 bhp; 2 shafts (controllable pitch propellers) = 15 knots
Complement approx 45

"Terrebonne Parish" class tank landing ships completed in 1953; first two built ships by Bath Iron Works, Bath, Maine; remainder by Ingalls Shipbuilding Corp, Pascagoula, Mississippi. Transferred to Military Sealift Command in 1972 for operations as cargo ships; five additional ships of this class were scheduled to be acquired by MSC in 1973 but their transfer has been delayed (see Amphibious Warfare Ships).
In MSC service they have been modified to handle bulk cargo as well as vehicles; all guns removed; living spaces modified to higher standard for civilian crews. No longer considered available for amphibious assault.

TRAVERSE COUNTY (LST 1160) in Navy service *1970, US Navy*

33 CARGO SHIPS: LST TYPE

***LST 47**	T-LST 47	***LST 607**	T-LST 607
***LST 117**	T-LST 117	***LST 613**	T-LST 613
LST 176	T-LST 176	***LST 623**	T-LST 623
***LST 230**	T-LST 230	***LST 629**	T-LST 629
***LST 276**	T-LST 276	***LST 630**	T-LST 630
***LST 287**	T-LST 287	**LST 643**	T-LST 643
LST 399	T-LST 399	***LST 649**	T-LST 649
***LST 456**	T-LST 456	***LST 664**	T-LST 664
***LST 491**	T-LST 491	**DAVIESS COUNTY**	T-LST 692
LST 530	T-LST 530	**DE KALB COUNTY**	T-LST 715
***CHASE COUNTY**	T-LST 532	***HARRIS COUNTY**	T-LST 822
***LST 550**	T-LST 550	***NEW LONDON COUNTY**	T-LST 1066
LST 566	T-LST 566	***NYE COUNTY**	T-LST 1067
LST 572	T-LST 572	***ORLEANS PARISH** (ex-MCS 6)	T-LST 1069
***LST 579**	T-LSR 579	***LST 1072**	T-LST 1072
LST 587	T-LST 587	**PULASKI COUNTY**	T-LST 1088
LST 590	T-LST 590		

Displacement, tons LST 511-1152; 1 653 standard; 4 080 full load
LST 1-510; 1 625 light; 4 050 full load
Dimensions, feet 328 oa × 50 × 14
Main engines Diesels (General Motors); 1 700 bhp; 2 shafts = 11·6 knots
Complement approx 40

Former Navy-manned tank landing ships now employed to carry cargo in the Western Pacific. T-LST 287, 532, 590, 664, 692, 822, 1066, 1067, 1069, 1072, and 1088 (11 ships) are manned by South Korean civilian personnel; all others by Japanese personnel. These ships have been modified for cargo operations in the Western Pacific; main deck hatch enlarged, cargo booms provided in some ships, all guns removed. No longer considered suitable for amphibious assault role. All of these ships are expected to be decommissioned in 1973-1974 as newer LSTs become available to Military Sealift Command.

RECLASSIFICATION. The *Orleans Parish* was fitted to support minesweepers and reclassified a Mine Countermeasures Support Ship (MCS 6) on 19 Jan 1959; subsequently reclassified T-LST on 1 June 1966 and assigned to Military Sealift Command.

DISPOSALS AND TRANSFERS (MSC ships only)
LST 600 stricken on 1 June 1969, **Chesterfield County** LST 551 stricken on 1 June 1970, **Clearwater County** LST 602 (operated by US Air Force) transferred to Mexico on 25 May 1972, **LST 581**, **626**, **Plumas County** T-LST 1083 stricken on 1 June 1972, **LST 222**, **488**, **546** transferred to Philippines on 15 July 1872.

LST 287 (T-LST 287) *United States Navy*

SHOSHONE (T-AO 151) *United States Navy*

EXPERIMENTAL, RESEARCH AND SURVEYING SHIPS

1 EXPERIMENTAL SURFACE EFFECT SHIP: AEROJET-GENERAL DESIGN

SES-100A

Weight, tons	100 gross
Dimensions, feet	81·9 oa × 41·9 × 18·3 (height)
Main lift engines	4 gas turbines; 12 000 hp; three fans for lift and two water-jet propulsion systems = 80+ knots

Surface effects ship developed by Aerojet-General Corp, and built by Tacoma Boatbuilding Co, Tacoma, Washington, to test feasibility of large SES for naval missions. Christened in July 1971; underway in mid-1972 in competition with the Bell design described below. Aluminium construction with rigid sidewalls to hold cushion or bubble of air. Cargo capacity ten tons (instrumentation during evaluation); provision for crew of four and six observers.

A photograph of the SES-100A on a platform appears in the 1972-1973 edition. Initially the large SES project was a joint Navy-Maritime Administration effort; however, the Maritime Administration was forced to withdraw financial support in 1970.

PROGRAMME. Two other types of ocean-going "air support" platforms are being developed for the US Navy at this time; air cushion vehicle (ACV) landing craft described in the section on Landing Craft and an armed SES design listed with Patrol Ships and Craft.

SES-100A *1972, Aerojet General*

1 EXPERIMENTAL SURFACE EFFECT SHIP: BELL AEROSYSTEMS DESIGN

SES-100B

Weight, tons	100 gross
Dimensions, feet	78 oa × 35
Main engines	3 gas turbines (Pratt & Whitney FT12A-6); 13 500 hp; 2 semi-submerged, super-cavitating propellers = 80+ knots
Lift engines	3 gas turbines (United Aircraft of Canada ST6J-70); 1 500 hp; eight lift fans

Surface effects ship developed by Bell Aerospace Division of the Textron Corp; built Bell facility in Michoud, Louisiana. Christened on March 6, 1971; underway in Feb 1972 as competitive development platform for Navy.

Aluminium hull with rigid sidewalls to hold cushion or bubble of air. Cargo capacity ten tons (instrumentation during evaluation); provision for crew of four and six observers.

The SES-100B is credited with having set an SES speed record of more than 70 knots during trials in March 1973.

SES-100B *1973, Bell Aerosystems*

2 SONAR TEST SHIPS (AG): Ex-MINESWEEPERS

Name	*No.*	*Launched*	*Commissioned*
***ALACRITY**	AG 520 (ex-MSO 520)	8 June 1957	2 Oct 1958
***ASSURANCE**	AG 521 (ex-MSO 521)	31 Aug 1957	22 Nov 1958

Displacement, tons	810 light; 934 full load
Dimensions, feet	190 oa × 36 × 14·5
Guns	1—40 mm AA (as MSO)
Main engines	2 diesels (General Motors); 2 700 bhp; 2 shafts (controllable pitch propellers) = 15 knots

Former ocean minesweepers. Both built by Peterson Builders Inc., Sturgeon Bay, Wisconsin. Wood-hulled with non-magnetic engines and fittings. Both ships modified for sonar test activities and redesignated as miscellaneous auxiliaries (AG) on 1 June 1973 and 1 Mar 1973, respectively.

DISPOSALS
Ability MSO 519 stricken in 1 Feb 1971

ALACRITY (AG 520) *1969, United States Navy*

1 HYDROGRAPHIC RESEARCH SHIP (AG)

***FLYER** (ex-*American Flyer*, ex-*Water Witch*) T-AG 178

Displacement, tons	7 360 light; 11 000 full load
Dimensions, feet	459·2 oa × 63 × 28
Main engines	Turbines; 6 000 shp; 1 shaft = 17 knots
Boilers	2
Complement	55 (14 officers, 41 men)

Acquired from Maritime Administration on 9 Feb 1965. C2-S-B1 type. Operated by Military Sealift Command for Naval Electronic Systems Command, civilian manned.

FLYER (T-AG 178) *United States Navy*

1 HYDROGRAPHIC RESEARCH SHIP (AG): "VICTORY" TYPE

***KINGSPORT** (ex-*Kingsport Victory*) T-AG 164

Displacement, tons	7 190 light; 10 680 full load
Dimensions, feet	455 oa × 62 × 22
Main engines	Geared turbines; 8 500 shp; 1 shaft = 15·2 knots
Boilers	2
Complement	73 (13 officers, 42 men, 15 technicians)

VC2-S-AP3. Built in 1944 by the California Shipbuiding Corp, Los Angeles. Former cargo ship in the MSTS fleet. Name shortened, ship reclassified and converted in 1961-1962 by Willamette Iron & Steel Co, Portland, Oregon, into the world's first satellite communications ship, for Project Advent, involving the promotion of a terminal to meet the required military capability for high capacity, world-wide radio communications using high altitude hovering satellites, and the installation of ship-to-shore communications, facilities, additional electric power generating equipment, a helicopter landing platform, aerological facilities, and a 30-foot parabolic communication antenna housed in a 53-ft diameter plastic radome abaft the superstructure. Painted white for operations in the tropics. Project Advent Syncom satellite relay operations were completed in 1966, and *Kingsport* was reassigned to hydrographic research. Antenna sphere now removed.

Operated by Military Sealift Command for naval Electronic Systems Command; civilian manned.

Broadside view appears in 1968-1969 edition; note antenna mast on helicopter platform in photograph; exhaust ducts fitted to funnel.

KINGSPORT (T-AG 164) *United States Navy*

Experimental, Research and Surveying Ships—*continued*

1 POSEIDON TEST SHIP (AG): "MARINER" TYPE

OBSERVATION ISLAND (ex-*YAG* 57, ex-*Empire State Mariner*) AG 154

Displacement, tons	17 600 full load
Dimensions, feet	529·5 wl; 563 oa × 76·2 × 29
Main engines	Geared turbines (General Electric); 19 250 shp; 1 shaft = 20 knots
Boilers	2
Complement	350

Built as a "Mariner" class merchant ship (C4-S-1a type) built by New York Shipbuilding Corp, Camden, New Jersey; launched on 15 Aug 1953; acquired by the Navy on 10 Sep 1956 for use as a Fleet Ballistic Missile (FBM) test ship. Converted at Norfolk Naval Shipyard; commissioned on 5 Dec 1958.

Employed to test fire Polaris and later Poseidon missiles. Navy manned. Decommissioned on 25 Sep 1972 and placed in Maritime Administration reserve; remains on Navy List.

MISSILE TESTING. The ship is fitted with complete missile testing, servicing and firing systems. She fired the first ship-launched Polaris missile at sea on 27 Aug 1959. Refitted to fire the improved Poseidon missile in 1969 and launched the first Poseidon test missile fired afloat on 16 Dec 1969.

OBSERVATION ISLAND (AG 154) *1971, US Navy, PH1 J. R. Hobbs*

1 EXPERIMENTAL NAVIGATION SHIP (AG): "MARINER" TYPE

***COMPASS ISLAND** (ex-*YAG* 56, ex-*Garden Mariner*) AG 153

Displacement, tons	16 076 full load
Dimensions, feet	529·5 pp; 563 oa × 76·3 × 29
Main engines	Geared turbines (General Electric); 19 250 shp; 1 shaft = 20 knots
Boilers	2

Originally a Mariner class merchant ship (C4-S-1a type); built by New York Shipbuilding Corp, Camden, New Jersey; launched on 24 Oct 1953 and acquired by the Navy on 29 Mar 1956.

Converted by New York Naval Shipyard; commissioned on 3 Dec 1956 for the development of the Fleet Balistic Missile guidance and ship navigation systems. Her mission is to assist in the development and valuation of a navigation system independant of shore-based aids. Navy manned.

COMPASS ISLAND (AG 153) *United States Navy*

DISPOSALS AND RECLASSIFICATIONS

Acquisition of **AG 155** (C-4 cargo ship) was cancelled; **Hunting** AG 156 (ex-EAG 398, ex-LSM 398) sonar test ship, strcken in 1962; **King County** AG 157 (ex-LST 857) Regulus missile test ship, stricken in 1961; acquisition of research ship **AG 158** was cancelled; **Oxford** AG 159 reclassified AGTR 1; **AG 160** and **AG 161** reclassified AGM 1 and AGM 22, respectively; **Mission Capistrano** AG 162 (ex-AO 112) sound test ship stricken on 19 Oct 1971; **Glover** AG 163 reclassified AGDE 1.

AG 165-168 reclassified AGTR 2-5, respectively; **Private J. E. Valdez** AG 169 (ex-APC 119) special mission ship, stricken in 1970; **Lieutenant J. E. Robinson** AG 170 (ex-AK 274) reclassified AK-274; **Seargent Joseph E. Muller** AG 171 (ex-APC 118) special mission ship, stricken in 1970; **AG 172-174** are in service as cargo ships.

Sergeant Curtis F. Shoup AG 175, survey support ship, stricken in 1970; **Peregine** AG 176 (ex-MSF 373) experimental ship, stricken in 1969; **Shearwater** AG 177 (ex-FS 411) special mission ship, returned to US Army in 1967. **AG 179-190** assigned to 12 "Victory" cargo ship to have been used as floating depot ships; project cancelled; **Spokane** AG 191 (ex-CLAA 120) was to be converted to sonar test ship; project cancelled and ship stricken 15 Apr 1972 (see 1970-1971 edition for details).

1 HYDROFOIL RESEARCH SHIP (AGEH)

***PLAINVIEW** AGEH 1

Displacement, tons	320 full load
Dimensions, feet	212 oa × 40·5 × 10 (hull borne) or 26 (with foils down)
A/S weapons	2 triple torpedo tubes (Mk 32)
Main engines	2 gas turbines (General Electric); 30 000 hp; 2 diesels; 1 200 = 50 knots
Complement	20 (6 officers, 14 men)

Aluminium hull experimental hydrofoil. Three retractable foils, 25 ft in height, each weighing 7 tons, fitted port and starboard and on stern, and used in waves up to 15 feet. Initial maximum speed of about 50 knots, with later modifications expected to raise the speed to 80 knots. Fitted with the largest titanium propellers made. The two 15 000 hp gas turbines are General Electric J-79 jet aircraft engines modified for marine use. Power plant and transmission designed to permit future investigation of various types of foils. Built by Lockheed Shipbuilding & Construction Co, Seattle, Washington. Laid down on 8 May 1964, launched on 28 June 1965, and placed in service on 1 May 1969. Delayed because of engineering difficulties. In service vice being in commission.

DISPOSALS

The hydrofoil test craft **Denison**, briefly operated by the Navy, has been returned to the Maritime Administration and subsequently sold commercially. Photographs and description appear in the 1970-1971 edition.

PLAINVIEW (AGEH 1) *1972, United States Navy*

ENVIRONMENTAL RESEARCH SHIPS (AGER)

The Navy has stricken the two surviving intelligence collection ships classified as environmental research ships; the **Banner** (AGER 1, ex-AKL 25 ex-FS 345) on 14 Nov 1969, and the **Palm Beach** (AGER 3, ex-AKL 45, ex-FS 217) on 1 Dec 1969. The third ship of this type, the *Pueblo* (AGER 2, ex-AKL 44, ex-FS 344), was boarded and captured by North Korean forces in what were believed international waters off the port of Wonsan in January 1968. Her crew of 80 naval personnel and two civilians were interned for a year (one sailor was killed in the capture). At this writing the ship still was interned by North Korea; her name remains on the US Navy List. These ships are described in the 1969-1970 and previous editions.

1 RANGE INSTRUMENTATION SHIP (AGM): "VICTORY" TYPE

***RANGE SENTINEL** (ex-*Sherburne*) T-AGM 22 (ex-APA 205)

Dimensions, feet	455 oa × 62 × 24
Main engines	Turbine (Westinghouse); 8 500 hp; 1 sha t = 17·7 knots
Boilers	2 (Combustion Engineering)
Complement	78 (14 officers, 54 men, 10 technical personnel)

Former attack transport converted specifically to serve as a range instrumentation ship in support of the Poseidon Fleet Ballistic Missile (FBM) programme. Built by Permanente Metals Corp, Richmond, California; commissioned on 20 Sep 1944. VC2-S-AP5 type.

Stricken from the Navy List on 1 Oct 1958 and transferred to Maritime Administration reserve fleet; reacquired by the Navy on 22 Oct 1969 for AGM conversion. Converted from Oct 1969 to Oct 1971; operated by Military Sealift Command and civilian manned.

2 RANGE INSTRUMENTATION SHIPS (AGM): "JUMBOISED" T2-SE-A2 TYPE

***VANGUARD** (ex-*Mussel Shoals*, ex-*Mission San Fernando*) T-AGM 19 (ex-T-AO 122)
***REDSTONE** (ex-*Johnstown*, ex-*Mission de Pala*) T-AGM 20 (ex-T-AO 114)

Displacement, tons	21 626 full load
Dimensions, feet	595 oa × 75 × 25
Main engines	Turbine-electric; 1 shaft; 10 000 shp = 16 knots
Boilers	2 (Babcock & Wilcox)
Complement	*Vanguard* 19 officers, 71 enlisted men, 108 technical personnel; *Redstone* 20 officers, 71 enlisted men, 120 technical personnel.

Former "Mission" class tankers converted in 1964-1966 to serve as mid-ocean communications and tracking ships in support of the Apollo manned lunar flights. A third ship of this type has been stricken (see *Disposal* notes below).

All built in 1944 by Marinship, Sausalito, California, as tankers. T2-SE-A2 type. Converted to Range Instrumentation Ships (RIS) by General Dynamics, Quincy Division, Massachusetts; each ship was cut in half and a 72-foot mid-section was inserted, increasing length, beam, and displacement; approximately 450 tons of electronic equipment installed for support of lunar flight operations, including communications and tracking systems; balloon hangar and platform fitted aft. Cost of converting the three ships was $90 000 000. Operated by Military Sealift Command for Air Force Eastern Test Range in Atlantic (*Vanguard*) and for NASA Goddard Space Flight Centre (*Redstone*). Civilian crews.

DISPOSALS

Mercury (ex-*Flagstaff, Mission San Juan*) T-AGM 21 (ex-T-AO 126) transferred to Maritime Administration in 1969 (converted to merchant configuration).

Experimental, Research and Surveying Ships—*continued*

VANGUARD (T-AGM 19) *1966, General Dynamics*

REDSTONE (T-AGM 20) *1970, United States Air Force*

2 RANGE INSTRUMENTATION SHIPS (AGM): C4-S-A1 TYPE

***GENERAL H. H. ARNOLD** (ex-USNS *General R. E. Collan*) T-AGM 9 (ex-T-AP 139)
***GENERAL HOYT S. VANDENBERG** (ex-USNS *General Harry Taylor*) T-AGM 10 (ex-T-AP 145)

Displacement, tons	16 600 full load
Dimensions, feet	552·9 oa × 71·5 × 26·3
Main engines	Geared turbines (Westinghouse); 9 000 shp; 1 shaft = 15 knots
Boilers	2 (Babcock & Wilcox)
Complement	205 (21 officers, 71 men, 113 technical personnel)

Former transports converted in 1962-1963 for monitoring Air Force missiles firing and satellite launches. Both ships built in 1944 by Kaiser Co. Richmond, California, as large troop transports. C4-S-A1 type. Upon conversion to Range Instrumentation Ships (RIS) they were placed in service in 1963 under Air Force operation, however assigned to MSTS for operation on 1 July 1964 (*Arnold*) and 13 July 1964 (*Vandenberg*).
Both ships are operated by Military Sealift Command for Air Force Eastern Test Range in Atlantic. Civilian manned.

DISPOSALS
C1-M-AV1 type: **Sword Knot** T-AGM 13 stricken on 1 Apr 1971, **Rose Knot** T-AGM 14 stricken on 26 Mar 1968, **Coastal Sentry** T-AGM 15 ex-AK 212 stricken on 11 July 1968, **Timber Hitch** T-AGM 17 stricken on 5 Feb 1968, **Sampan Hitch** T-AGM 18 stricken on 24 June 1968.
EC2 "Liberty" type: **American Mariner** T-AGM 12 stricken on 1 July 1965; employed as target hulk on Chesapeake Bay.

5 RANGE INSTRUMENTATION SHIPS (AGM): "VICTORY" TYPE

***LONGVIEW** (ex-*Haiti Victory*)	T-AGM 3 (ex-T-AK 238)
***SUNNYVALE** (ex-*Dalton Victory*)	T-AGM 5 (ex-T-AK 256)
WATERTOWN (ex-SS *Niantic Victory*)	T-AGM 6
HUNTSVILLE (ex-SS *Knox Victory*)	T-AGM 7
***WHEELING** (ex-*Seton Hall Victory*)	T-AGM 8

Displacement, tons	10 680 full load
Dimensions, feet	T-AGM 6, 7: 455·8 oa × 62 × 28·6 T-AMG 3, 5, 8: 455·3 oa × 62·2 × 28 (draft varies)
Main engines	geared turbines; 8 500 shp; 1 shaft = 16·2 knots for T-AGM 6 and 7; 17 knots for others
Boilers	2

All VC2-S-AP3 type; details vary. All extensively modified to serve as Range Instrumentation Ships (RIS) in support of American military and National Aeronautics and Space Administration (NASA) missile and space programmes.
Longview built in 1944 by Permanente Metals Corp, Richmond, California. Assigned to MSTs on 1 Mar 1950 (as T-AK 238); operated in support of Air Force Western Test Range in Pacific; civilian crew of 12 officers, 41 men, plus 20 technical personnel. Fitted with helicopter hangar and platform aft.
Sunnyvale built in 1944 by California SB Corp, Los Angeles. Assigned to MSTS on 6 Aug 1950 (as T-AK 256); operated in support of Air Force Western Test Range in Pacific; civilian crew of 12 officers, 41 men, plus 20 technical personnel. Fitted with helicopter hangar and platform aft.
Watertown built in 1944 by Oregon SB Corp, Portland, Oregon. Assigned to MSTS on 11 Aug 1960; operated in supoprt of Air Force Western Test Range in Pacific and NASA until removed from service and placed in reserve in 1972. The ship had been operated by a civilian crew of 14 officers, 55 men, plus 72 technical personnel.
Huntsville built in 1954 by Oregon SB Corp, Portland, Oregon. Assigned to MSTS on 1 Mar 1960; operated in support of Air Force Western Test Range in Pacific and NASA until taken out of service in Jan 1973; will be stricken in the near future. Civilian crew of 14 officers, 55 men, plus 72 technical personnel.
Wheeling built in 1954 by Oregon SB Corp, Portland Oregon. Assigned to MSTS on 28 May 1964; operated in support of Navy Pacific Missile Range; civilian crew of 13 officers, 46 men, plus 48 technical personnel (accomodation for 64). Fitted with helicopter hangar and platform aft.

HELICOPTERS. These ships fitted with helicopter platforms and hangars periodically carry helicopters

DISPOSALS
Richfield T-AGM 4, ex-T-AK 253, **Range Tracker** T-AGM 1, ex-T-AG 160, stricken on 28 Apr 1970.

Twin Falls T-AGM II of this type stricken on 28 Apr 1960 but subsequently reacquired by Navy for conversion to surveying ship (T-AGS 37); conversion subsequently cancelled and again stricken on 1 Sep 1972.

AKL type *Range Recoverer* T-AGM 2 ex-T-AG 161 ex-FS 278 redesignated YFRT 524 on 16 May 1972; see listing under Service Craft section.

GEN. HOYT S. VANDENBERG (T-AGM 10) *United States Navy*

HUNTSVILLE (T-AGM 7) ***1967, NASA***

LONGVIEW (T-AGM 3) ***1970, United States Navy, PH3 J. B. Land***

Experimental, Research and Surveying Ships—*continued*

SUNNYVALE (T-AGM 5) *United States Navy*

WATERTOWN (T-AGM 6) *United States Navy*

WHEELING (T-AGM 8) *United States Navy*

2 UTILITY RESEARCH SHIPS (AGOR)

Name	*No.*	*Laid down*	*Launched*	*Delivered*
GYRE	AGOR 21	9 Oct 1972	May 1973	Aug 1973
MOANA WAVE	AGOR 22	10 Oct 1972	May 1973	Sep 1973

Displacement, tons	950 full load
Dimensions, feet	165 oa × 36 × 10
Main engines	2 turbo-charged diesels; 1 700 bhp; 2 shafts (controllable pitch propellers) = 13 knots maximum; 12 knots cruising
Complement	21 (including scientific personnel)

Both ships built by Halter Marine Services Inc, New Orleans, Louisiana. They are based on a commercial ship design. Fitted with a 150 hp retractable propeller pod for low-speed or station keeping with main machinery shut down.
The Navy plans to construct several of these small, "utility" oceanographic research ships to replace older and obsolescent ships now operated by civilian research and educational institutions in support of Navy programmes. The above ships will be assigned to Texas A & M University and the University of Hawaii, respectively.

CANCELLATION. The planned AGOR 19 and AGOR 20 of a larger design were cancelled in Feb 1969.

1 OCEANOGRAPHIC RESEARCH SHIP (AGOR): "HAYES" TYPE

***HAYES** T-AGOR 16

Displacement, tons	3 080 full load
Dimensions, feet	220 wl; 246·5 oa × 75 (see *Design* notes) × 18·8
Main engines	Geared diesels; 5 400 bhp; 2 shafts = 15 knots
Complement	74 (11 officers, 33 men, 30 scientists)

Authorised in Fiscal Year 1967 new construction programme. The T-AGOR 16 is one of two classes of modern US naval ships to have a catamaran hull, the other being the ASR 21 class submarine rescue ships. Built by Todd Shipyards, Seattle, Washington; completed in late 1971. Estimated cost is $15 900 000. Laid down 12 Nov 1969; launched 2 July 1970.
Operated by the Military Sealift Command for the Office of Naval Research under the technical control of the Oceanographer of the Navy; civilian crew.

DESIGN. Catamaran hull design provides large deck working area, centre well for operating equipment at great depths, and removes laboratory areas from main propulsion machinery. Each hull is 246·5 feet long and 24 feet wide (maximum). There are three 36-inch diameter instrument wells in addition to the main centre well.

The T-AGOR 16 differs in appearance from the ASR 21 class ships by the oceanographic ship having a small deck working space aft of the bridge structure and the absence of stern helicopter platform of the rescue ships.

"HAYES"—*continued*

ENGINEERING. Fitted with controllable pitch propellers. An auxiliary 165-shp diesel is fitted in each hull to provide "creeping" speed of 2 to 4 knots.
Separation of controllable pitch propellers by catamaran hull separation provides high degree of manoeuverability eliminating the need for bow thrusters.
Range is 6 000 miles at 13·5 knots.

NOMENCLATURE. Oceanographic research ships and surveying ships generally are named for naval oceanographers, hydrographers, and explorers. (Converted ships generally retain original names).
The AGOR 16 is named for Dr. Harvey C. Hayes of the Naval Research Laboratory, known as the "father of sonar in the US Navy".

TRANSFERS
Josiah Willard Gibbs T-AGOR 1 ex-AVP 51 transferred to Greece on 7 Dec 1971.

PHOTOGRAPHS. Note widely spaced side-by-side funnels, after mast atop king post-like structure offset to starboard.

HAYES (T-AGOR 16) *1971, Todd Shipyards Corp*

HAYES (T-AGOR 16) *1971, Camera Craft*

HAYES (T-AGOR 16) *1971, Todd Shipyards Corp*

MELVILLE (AGOR 14) *1969, Defoe Shipbuilding*

Experimental, Research and Surveying Ships—*continued*

2 OCEANOGRAPHIC RESEARCH SHIPS (AGOR): "MELVILLE" CLASS

Name	*No.*	*Laid down*	*Launched*	*Delivered*
***MELVILLE**	AGOR 14	12 July 1967	10 July 1968	27 Aug 1969
***KNORR**	AGOR 15	9 Aug 1967	21 Aug 1968	14 Jan 1970

Displacement, tons	1 915 standard; 2 080 full load
Dimensions, feet	244·9 × 46·3 × 15
Main engines	Diesel 2 500 bhp; 2 cycloidal propellers = 12 knots
Complement	50 (9 officers, 16 men, 25 scientists)

Oceanographic research ships of an advanced design. AGOR 14 and AGOR 15 authorised in Fiscal Year 1966 new construction programme; AGOR 19 and AGOR 20 of this type in FY 1968 programme, but construction of the latter ships was cancelled. The *Melville* and *Knorr* built by Defoe Shipbuilding Co, Bay City, Michigan. *Melville* operated by Scripps Institution of Oceanography and *Knorr* by Woods Hole Oceanography Institution for the Office of Naval Research; under technical control of the Oceanographer of the Navy.

DESIGN. Fitted with internal wells for lower equipment; underwater lights and observation ports. Facilities for handling small research submersibles.

ENGINEERING. First US Navy ocean-going ships with cycloidal propellers permitting the ships to turn 360 degrees in their own length. One propeller is fitted at each end of the ship, providing movement in any direction and optimum station keeping without use of thrusters. They have experienced engineering difficulties.

8 OCEANOGRAPHIC RESEARCH SHIPS (AGOR): "CONRAD" CLASS

Name	*No.*	*Laid down*	*Launched*	*Delivered*
***ROBERT D. CONRAD**	AGOR 3	19 Jan 1961	26 May 1962	29 Nov 1962
***JAMES M. GILLISS**	T-AGOR 4	31 May 1961	19 May 1962	5 Nov 1962
***SANDS**	T-AGOR 6	23 Aug 1962	14 Sep 1963	8 Feb 1965
***LYNCH**	T-AGOR 7	7 Sep 1962	17 Mar 1964	22 Oct 1965
***THOMAS G. THOMPSON**	AGOR 9	12 Sep 1963	18 July 1964	4 Sep 1965
***THOMAS WASHINGTON**	AGOR 10	12 Sep 1963	1 Aug 1964	17 Sep 1965
***DE STEIGUER**	T-AGOR 12	12 Nov 1965	21 Mar 1966	28 Feb 1969
***BARTLETT**	T-AGOR 13	18 Nov 1965	24 May 1966	15 Apr 1969

Displacement, tons	varies; approx 1 200 standard; 1 380 full load
Dimensions, feet	191·5 wl; 208·9 oa × 37·4 × 15·3
Main engines	Diesel-electric (Caterpillar Tractor Co diesels); 10 000 bhp; 1 shaft = 13·5 knots
Complement	41 (9 officers, 17 men, 15 scientists except *De Steigeur* and *Bartlett*, 8 officers, 18 men)

This is the first class of ships designed and built by the US Navy for oceanographic research. Fitted with instrumentation and laboratories to measure the earth's gravity and magnetic fields, water temperature, sound transmission in water, and the geological profile of the ocean floor.
Special features include 10 ton capacity boom and winches for handling over-the-side equipment; bow thruster propulsion unit for precise manoeuvrability and station keeping; 620 hp gas turbine (housed in funnel structure) for providing "quiet" power when conducting operations in which use of main engines would generate too high a noise level (gas turbine also can drive the ship at 6·5 knots); endurance of 12 000 miles at 12 knots.

Robert D. Conrad built by Gibbs Corp, Jacksonville, Florida. Operated by Lamont Geological Observatory of Columbia University under technical control of the Oceanographer of the Navy.
James H. Gilliss built by Christy Corp, Sturgeon Bay, Wisconsin. Operated by the University of Miami (Florida) since 1970 in support of Navy programmes.
Sands and *Lynch* built by Marietta Manufacturing Co, Point Pleasant, West Virginia. Operated by Military Sealift Command under the technical control of the Oceanographer of the Navy. Civilian crew.
Thomas G. Thompson built by Marinette Marine Corp, Marinette, Wisconsin. Operated by University of Washington (state) under technical control of the Oceanographer of the Navy; civilian crew.
Thomas Washington built by Marinette Marine Corp, Marinette, Wisconsin. Operated by Scripps Institution of Oceanography (University of California) under technical control of the Oceanographer on the Navy; civilian crew.
De Steiguer and *Bartlett* built by Northwest Marine Iron Works, Portland, Oregon Operated by Military Sealift Command under the technical control of the Oceanographer of the Navy; civilian crew.

Charles H. Davis AGOR 5 of this type was transferred to New Zealand on 10 Aug 1970.

PHOTOGRAPHS. Note built-up structure amidships on *De Steiguer*; the *Thomas D. Thompson* has side structure built up amidships.

SANDS (T-AGOR 6) *United States Navy*

THOMAS G. THOMPSON (AGOR 9) *United States Navy*

DE STEIGUER (T-AGOR 12) *United States Navy*

BARTLETT (T-AGOR 13) *United States Navy*

1 OCEANOGRAPHIC RESEARCH SHIP (AGOR): Ex-SALVAGE SHIP

Name	*No.*	*Launched*	*Commissioned*
***CHAIN**	AGOR 17 (ex-ARS 20)	3 June 1943	31 Mar 1944

Displacement, tons	2 100 full load
Dimensions, feet	207 wl; 213·5 oa × 39 × 15
Main engines	Diesel electric (4 Cooper Bessemer diesels); approx 3 000 bhp; 2 shafts = 14 knots
Complement	29 + 26 scientists

Converted from a salvage ship for oceanographic research. Built by Basalt Rock Co, Napa, California. Commission date as ARS. Converted to an oceanographic research ship by Savannah Machine & Foundry in 1958. The *Chain* is operated by the Woods Hole Oceanographic Institution for the Office of Naval Research under the technical control of the Oceanographer of the Navy. Civilian crew.

ENGINEERING. Fitted with an auxiliary 250 hp outboard propulsion unit for manoeuvering at low speeds (up to 4·5 knots).

DISPOSALS
Argo AGOR 18 (ex-*Snatch*, ARS 27) similarly converted; stricken on 1 May 1970. 1970.

2 OCEANOGRAPHIC RESEARCH SHIPS (AGOR): Ex-CARGO SHIPS

Name	*No.*	*Launched*	*Delivered*
ELTANIN	T-AGOR 8 (ex-T-AK 270)	16 Jan 1957	2 Aug 1957
*** MIZAR**	T-AGOR 11 (ex-T-AK 272)	7 Oct 1957	22 Nov 1957

Displacement, tons	2 036 light; 4 942 full load
Dimensions, feet	256·8 wl; 262·2 oa × 51·5 × 18·7; (*Mizar* 22·8)
Main engines	Diesel-electric (ALCO diesels, Westinghouse electric motors) 3 200 bhp; 2 shafts = 12 knots
Complement	*Eltanin:* 12 officers, 36 men, 38 scientists *Mizar:* 11 officers, 30 men, up to 15 scientists

Built for Military Sea Transportation Service by Avondale Marine Ways, New Orleans, La. Designed for Arctic operation with hull strengthened against ice. C1-ME2-13a type. Delivered as cargo ships to MSTS (now Military Sealift Command) and subsequently converted to oceanographic research ships.
As research ships the *Eltanin* is operated by Military Sealift Command for National Science Foundation, *Mizar* by Military Sealift Command for Naval Research Laboratory, latter ship under technical control of the Oceanographer of the Navy; civilian crews. *Eltanin* taken out of service in Feb 1973; expected to be decommissioned and placed in reserve.

CONVERSION. *Eltanin* was converted in 1961 into a scientific labotarory for Antarctic research programme for the National Science Foundation. Equipped to study meteorology, the upper atmosphere, marine and terresrtial biology, physical oceanography, submarine geology, and geomagnetic conditions.
Mizar converted in 1962 into deep sea research ship. Equipped with centre well for lowering oceanographic equipment including towed sensor platforms, fitted with laboratories and elaborate photographic facilities, hydrophone system and computer for seafloor navigation and tracking towed vehicles. The *Mizar* had key roles in the searches for the US nuclear submarines *Thresher* and *Scorpion*; the French submarine *Eurydice*: and recovery of the H-bomb lost at sea off Palomares, Spain.

Experimental, Research and Surveying Ships—*continued*

MIZAR (T-AGOR 11) *United States Navy*

ELTANIN (T-AGOR 8) *United States Navy*

OCEANOGRPAHIC RESEARCH CRAFT

The Navy also owns a number of smaller oceanographic research craft that are operated by various educational and research institutions in support of Navy programmes; under technical control of the Oceanographer of the Navy; no Navy hull numbers are assigned; all are 100 feet in length or smaller except for the *Lamb*, a converted 136-foot minesweeper (YMS/AMS type) operated by the Lamont Geophysical Laboratory.

HYDROGRAPHIC SURVEYING SHIPS (AGS): PROJECT HYSURCH

An advanced class of hydrographic surveying ships is planned which will be capable of surveying 1 000 square miles and produce finished charts within a five-day period. Each ship would serve as a "mother" ship for several 20-foot launches to provide capability of mapping 50 square miles of ocean floor in two days. HYSURCH stands for Hydrographic Survey and Mapping System.

Ship construction tentatively is planned for late 1970s new construction programmes.

DISPOSALS

All Navy-manned surveying ships have been stricken:
Pursuit (AGS 17, ex-AM 108) stricken in 1960, **Prevail** (AGS 20, ex-AM 107), **Requisite** (AGS 18, ex-AM 109) stricken in 1964, **Towhee** (AGS 28, ex-AM 388) stricken on 1 May 1969, **San Pablo** (AGS 30, ex-AVP 30) stricken on 1 June 1969, **Tanner** (AGSS 15, ex-AKA 34) stricken on 1 Aug 1969, **Maury** (AGS 16, ex-AKA 36) stricken on 19 Dec 1969, **Serrano** (AGS 24, ex-ATF 112) stricken on 2 Jan 1970, **Rehoboth** (AGS 50, ex-AVP 50) stricken on 15 Apr 1970, **Sheldrake** (AGS 19, ex-AM 62) stricken on 30 June 1968.
Littlehales (AGSC 15, ex-YF 854), the Navy's last coastal surveying ship, was stricken on 20 Feb 1968 (but not decommissioned until 1 Apr 1968, more than a month after she was struck.

TWIN FALLS former "Victory" type merchant ship *Twin Falls Victory*, in service as missile range instrumentation ship (RIS) from 1964 to 1970 (designated T-AGM 11); stricken from Navy List on 28 Apr 1970 and placed in Maritime Administration reserve fleet; Navy planned to reacquire in 1972 for conversion to surveying ship (T-AGS 37), but project cancelled and ship transferred to New York City on 6 Nov 1972 for use as trade school facility.

COASTAL CRUSADER (T-AGS 36 as T-AGM 16) *United States Navy*

1 SURVEYING SHIP (AGS): C1-M-AV1 TYPE

COASTAL CRUSADER T-AGS 36 (ex-T-AGM 16)

Dimensions, feet	338·8 oa × 50·3 × 12
Main engines	Diesel; 1 750 bhp; 1 shaft = 11·5 knots

C1-M-AV1 TYPE

Built in 1945 by Leatham D. Smith SB Co, Sturgeon Bay, Wisconsin. Acquired fo conversion to a missile range tracking ship by US Air Force; transferred to Militar Sea Transportation service as T-AGM 16 on 1 July 1964.
Reclassified as a surveying ship (T-AGS 36) on 1 Dec 1969 but taken out of servic and placed in reserve prior to operation as an AGS.

DISPOSALS

Sgt. George D. Keathley T-AGS 35 ex-T-APC 117 of this type transferred to Taiwan China on 29 Mar 1972.

1 SURVEYING SHIP (AG): "S. P. LEE" TYPE

Name	*No.*	*Launched*	*Delivered*
***S. P. LEE**	T-AG 192 (ex-T-AGS 31)	19 Oct 1967	13 Dec 1968

Displacement, tons	1 200 standard; 1 400 full load
Dimensions, feet	191·5 wl; 209 oa × 39 × 15
Main engines	Diesel-electric; 1 shaft; 1 200 hp = 15 knots
Complement	41 (9 officers, 19 men, 13 scientists)

This is the first class of ships designed and built for the US Navy for surveying operation Same design as the "Conrad" class oceanographic research ships with different instru mentation and equipment. Special features include bow propulsion unit for precis manoeuvrability and station keeping; endurance of 12 000 miles at 12 knots.
Built by Defoe SB Co, Bay City, Michigan. Authorised in Fiscal Year 1965 shipbuildin programme; laid down on 27 June 1966. Configured for ocean surveying, but re designated as a research ship (AG 192) on 25 Sep 1970 and assigned to the Nava Undersea Research & Development Center, San Diego, California. Operated b Military Sealift Command with a civilian crew. Note equipment on stern in 197 photograph of ship operating in Mediterranean.

DISPOSALS

Kellar T-AGS 25 of this design transferred to Portugal on 21 Jan 1972.

S. P. LEE (T-AG 192) *1970, A. & J. Pavia*

2 SURVEYING SHIPS (AGS): "CHAUVENET" CLASS

Name	*No.*	*Laid Down*	*Launched*	*Delivered*
***CHAUVENET**	T-AGS 29	24 May 1967	13 May 1968	13 Nov 197
***HARKNESS**	T-AGS 32	30 June 1967	12 June 1968	29 Jan 197

Displacement, tons	4 200 full load
Dimensions feet,	393·2 oa × 54 × 16
Main engines	Diesel (Westinghouse); 3 600 bhp; 1 shaft = 15 knot
Complement	175 (13 officers, approx 150 men and technical personne 12 scientists)

A class of large research ships capable of extensive military hydrographic and oceano graphic surveys, supporting coastal surveying craft, amphibious survey teams an helicopters. Fitted with heplicoter hangar and platform.
Chauvenet authorised in Fiscal Year 1965 new construction programme; *Harkness* in FY 1966 programme. Both ships built by Upper Clyde Shipbuilders, Govan Division Glasgow, Scotland.
These ships are operated by the Military Sealift Command for the Oceanographer o the Navy with Navy detachments on board. Civilian crews.

HARKNESS (T-AGS 32) *United States Navy*

Experimental, Research, and Surveying Ships—*continued*

4 SURVEYING SHIPS (AGS): "BENT" CLASS

Name	No.	Laid down	Launched	Delivered
*SILAS BENT	T-AGS 26	2 Mar 1964	16 May 1964	23 July 1965
*KANE	T-AGS 27	19 Dec 1964	20 Nov 1965	19 May 1967
*WILKES	T-AGS 33	18 July 1968	31 July 1969	28 June 1971
*WYMAN	T-AGS 34	18 July 1968	30 Oct 1969	3 Nov 1971

Displacement, tons	1 935 standard; *Silas Bent* and *Kane* 2 558 full load; *Wilkes* 2 540 full load; *Wyman* 2 420 full load
Dimensions, feet	285·3 oa × 48 × 15·1
Main engines	Diesel-electric (Westinghouse diesels); 3 600 bhp; 1 shaft = 14 knots
Complement	77 to 79 (12 or 13 officers, 35 or 36 men, 30 scientists)

Designed specifically for surveying operations. Special features include seafloor mapping equipment; bow propulsion unit for precise manoeuvrability and station keeping. All four ships operated by Military Sealift Command for the Oceanographer of the Navy; civilian crews.
Silas Bent **built by American SB Co, Lorain, Ohio;** ***Kane*** **built by Christy Corp, Sturgeon Bay, Wisconsin;** ***Wilkes*** **and** ***Wyman*** **built by Defoe SB Co, Bay City, Michigan.**

WILKES (T-AGS 33) *1971, United States Navy*

WYMAN (T-AGS 34) *1971, United States Navy*

3 SURVEYING SHIPS (AGS): "VICTORY" TYPE

***BOWDITCH** (ex-SS *South Bend Victory*)	T-AGS 21
***DUTTON** (ex-SS *Tuskegee Victory*)	T-AGS 22
***MICHELSON** (ex-SS *Joliet Victory*)	T-AGS 23

Displacement, tons	4 512 full load
Dimensions, feet	455·2 oa × 62·2 × 25
Main engines	Turbine; 8 500 shp; 1 shaft = 15 knots
Boilers	2
Complement	100 to 101 (13 or 14 officers, 47 men, approx 40 technical personnel)

VC2-S-AP3 type built in 1945, *Bowditch* and *Michelson* by Oregon Shipbuilding Co; *Dutton* by South Coast Co. Newport Beach, California. All converted to support the Fleet Ballistic Missile Programme, *Dutton* and *Michelson* at Philadelphia Naval Shipyard 8 Nov 1957 to 16 Nov 1958 and 1 Mar 1958 to 31 Dec 1968, respectively, and *Bowditch* at Charleston Naval Shipyard 10 Oct 1957 to 30 Sep 1958.
Designed to chart the ocean floor and to record magnetic fields and gravity.
Operated by Military Sealift Command for the Oceanographer of the Navy; civilian crews.

MICHELSON (T-AGS 23) *United States Navy*

TECHNICAL RESEARCH SHIPS (AGTR)

The Navy has stricken the intelligence collection ships that were designated as technical research ships.
The Oxford (AGTR 1, ex-AG 159), Georgetown (AGTR 2, ex-AG 165), and Jamestown (AGTR 3, ex-AG 166) stricken on 19 Dec 1969, Belmont (AGTR 4, ex-AG 167) stricken on 16 Jan 1970.
The Liberty (AGTR 5, ex-AG 168) was severely damaged by Israeli aircraft and torpedo boat attack in the Eastern Mediterranean on 8 June 1967. She subsequently was decommissioned and placed in reserve until stricken on 1 June 1970. These ships are described in the 1969-1970 edition.

DISPOSALS AND RECLASSIFICATIONS

Target ship **Atlanta** IX 304 (ex-CL 104), a converted light cruiser employed in explosive tests, was stricken from the Navy List on 1 Apr 1970 (sunk as target).
Mobile listening barge **MONOB I** IX 309 (ex-YW 87) reclassified as YAG 61 on 1 July 1970 (see Service Craft listing).
Hydrographic research ships **Rexburg** PCER 855 and **Marysville** PCER 857 stricken on 7 Mar 1970 and 15 July 1970, respectively.
Ex-aircraft carrier **Bunker Hill** AVT 9 (ex-CVS 17) stricken on 1 Nov 1966 served as a stationary electronic test ship from 1965 until late 1972. (See 1971-1972 edition for characteristics and photographs).
(The research ships *George Eastman* YAG 39 and *Granville S. Hall* YAG 40 are listed with service Craft; the experimental hydrofoil ships *Plainview* AGEH 1 and *High Point* PCH 1 are listed with Patrol Ships and Craft; the research escort ship *Glover* AGDE 1 is listed with Ocean Escorts).

1 GUNNERY AND GUIDED MISSILE TEST SHIP (AVM): CONVERTED SEAPLANE TENDER

***NORTON SOUND** AVM 1 (ex-AV 11)

Displacement, tons	9 106 standard; 15 170 full load
Length, feet (*metres*)	543·25 (*165·2*) oa
Beam, feet (*metres*)	71·6 (*21·5*)
Draft, feet (*metres*)	23·5 (*7·15*)
Guns	1—5 inch (*127 mm*) 54 calibre DP experimental (see *Gunnery* notes)
Missile launchers	1 twin launcher for Standard testing 1 Basic Point Defence Missile System (BPDMS) launcher for Sea Sparrow missiles (see *Missile* notes)
Main engines	2 geared turbines (Allis-Chalmers) 12 000 shp; 2 shafts
Boilers	4 (Babcock & Wilcox)
Speed, knots	19·2
Complement	292 (22 officers, 270 enlisted men)

The *Norton Sound* serves as a seagoing weapons laboratory and test centre under the operational control of Commander, Cruiser-Destroyer Force, Pacific Fleet. She was originally a seaplane tender (AV 11) of the "Currituck" class.
Assigned to Operational Development Force as experimental rocket ship on 28 Nov 1947; modified at Philadelphia Naval Shipyard Mar-Sep 1948 and fitted with helicopter platform forward and missile launching ramp aft during late 1940s and reclassified as guided missile test ship (AVM 1) on 8 Aug 1951. Subsequently served as test ship for several guided missile systems and, lately, for advanced gun systems.

NORTON SOUND (AVM 1) *1969, United States Navy*

CONSTRUCTION. Built by Los Angeles Shipbuilding & Dry Dock Co, San Pedro, Calif. Laid down 7 Sep 1942; launched 28 Nov 1943; commissioned 8 Jan 1945. As built the *Norton Sound* had a 30-ton capacity boom atop her large, amidships aircraft hangar and a second 30-ton boom on her fantail; second boom removed when fitted with missile launching ramp. Original armament consisted of four 5 inch guns, two in single mounts forward and two in single mounts atop hangar, and 20 40 mm AA guns; forward 5 inch guns removed to make space for helicopter platform; all other original armament subsequently removed.

GUNNERY. Fitted in 1969 with light-weight 5 inch 54 cal gun and associated Mark 86 Gunfire Control System for operational test and evaluation. The light weight Mark 45 gun is intended for new-construction ships.

MISSILES. The *Norton Sound* has served as a test platform for several ship-launched rockets and missiles. Currently a twin surface-to-air missile launcher is installed aft for tests of the Standard missile as is a "pepper box" BPDMS launcher for the Sea Sparrow missile.

Experimental, Research and Surveying Ships—*continued*

1 TEST RANGE SUPPORT SHIP (IX): CONVERTED LSMR

Name	*No.*	*Launched*	*Commissioned*
***ELK RIVER**	IX 501 (ex-LSMR 501)	21 Apr 1954	27 May 1945

Displacement, tons	1 100 full load
Dimensions, feet	225 oa × 50 × 9·2
Main engines	Diesels; 1 400 bhp; 2 shafts = 11 knots
Complement	25 + 20 technical personnel

The *Elk River* is a former rocket landing ship specifically converted to support Navy deep submergence activities on the San Clemente Island Range off the coast of Southern California. Built by Brown Shipbuilding Co, Houstan, Texas
The ship is capable of supporting the following activities: (1) deep diving for man-in-the-sea programmes, (2) deep diving for salvage programmes, (3) submersible test and evaluation, (4) underwater equipment testing, and (5) deep mooring operations. Operated by combined Navy-civilian crew.

CONVERSION. The *Elk River* was withdrawn from the Reserve Fleet and converted to a range support ship in 1967-1968 at Avondale Shipyards Inc, Westwego, Louisiana, and the San Francisco Bay Naval Shipyard.
The basic LSMR hull was lengthened and eight-foot sponsons were added to either side to increase deck working space and stability; superstructure added forward. An open centre well was provided to facilitate lowering and raising equipment; also fitted with 65-ton-capacity gantry crane (on tracks) to handle submersibles and active positioning mooring system to hold ship in precise location without elaborate mooring and permit shifting within the moor. Five anchors including bow anchor.

DIVING. Fitted with prototype Mk 2 Deep Diving System (see "Pigeon class" submarine rescue ships).

ELK RIVER (IX 501) — *1968, United States Navy*

1 TORPEDO TEST SHIP (IX)

***NEW BEDFORD** IX 308 (ex-AKL 17, ex-FS 289)

Displacement, tons	approx 700
Dimensions, feet	176·5 oa × 32·8 × 10
Main engines	Diesel; 1 000 bhp; 1 shaft = 10 knots

Small Army cargo ship (freight and supply) acquired by Navy on 1 Mar 1950 for cargo work and subsequently converted to support torpedo testing. Operated by Naval Torpedo Station, Keyport, Washington. Other craft serving in this role are described in the section on Service Craft (YFRT type).

NEW BEDFORD (IX 308) — *1966, United States Navy*

1 INSTRUMENTATION PLATFORM (IX)

***BRIER** IX 307 (ex-WLI 299)

Displacement, tons	178
Dimensions, feet	100 × 24 × 4·5
Machinery	Diesel with electric drive; 300 bhp; 2 shafts = 8·5 knots

Former Coast Guard buoy tender built in 1943; acquired by Navy on 10 Mar 1969 for use as instrument platform for explosive testing; redesignated IX 307 on 29 Aug 1970.

1 WEAPON TEST SHIP (IX)

***IX 306** (ex-FS 221)

Displacement, tons	906 full load
Dimensions, feet	179 oa × 33 × 10
Main engines	Diesel; 1 shaft = 12 knots

Former Army cargo ship (freight and supply) acquired by the Navy in January 1966 and subsequently converted to a weapon test ship, being placed in service late in 1969. Conducts research for the Naval Underwater Weapons Research and Engineering Station, Newport, Rhode Island; operates in Atlantic Underwater Test and Evaluation Centre (AUTEC) range in Caribbean. Manned by Navy and civilian RCA personnel. Note white hull with blue bow and torpedo tube opening on starboard side just aft of hull number.

IX 306 — *1969, United States Navy*

MISCELLANEOUS

1 PRESIDENTIAL YACHT

***SEQUOIA** AG 23

Displacement, tons	approx 110
Dimensions, feet	99 wl; 104 oa × 18·2
Main engines	2 diesels; 450 bhp; 2 shafts = 11·5 knots
Complement	21 (1 officer, 20 enlisted men; accommodation for only 14 of crew)
Passengers	accommodation for 7 under normal conditions

Built by Mathis Yacht & Shipbuilding Co, Camden, New Jersey, in 1925. Acquired by Navy and placed in commission on 25 Mar 1933; no longer in commission but remains in service. Assigned as presidential yacht in 1968; previously assigned to the Secretary of the Navy. Based in Washington, DC.

SEQUOIA (AG 23) — *United States Navy*

1 SAIL FRIGATE

***CONSTITUTION** IX 21 launched 21 Oct 1797

The oldest ship of the US Navy remaining on the Navy List. "In service" status as a relic at Boston. Periodically she is taken out into Boston Harbour and "turned around". The *Constitution* began an extensive, $4 200 000 overhaul in April 1973 at the Boston Naval Shipyard; to complete in early 1975.
Characteristics and photograph appear in the 1970-1971 edition.

The self-propelled barracks ship **Benewah** (APB 35) was reclassified IX 311 on 1 Apr 1971 pending later transfer to South Vietnam; she is now at Subic Bay, Philippines. The classification **IX 310** has been assigned to a group of barges used at the Naval Underwater Sound Laboratory, Newport, Rhode Island.
The former PT 809 is employed as guard boat for the presidential Yacht; named **Guardian.** Not officially on Navy List, but Navy manned with Secret Service personnel carried. Based at the Navy Yard in Washington, D.C.

SERVICE CRAFT

The US Navy operates several hundred service craft, primarily small craft that provide services to the Fleet in harbours and ports. Only the self-propelled craft are listed here. In addition, there are hundreds of non-self-propelled barge-like craft for carrying cargo, floating cranes, dredges, workshops, power barges, berthing barges, water and fuel barges, garbage scows, *et cetera*. In addition, a few "ships", a training submarine, (SST), and the nuclear-propelled research submersible NR-1 officially are designated as service craft. Only the Y-prefix ships and craft are listed in this section (the "Y" originally indicating yardcraft).

The specific type strengths are as of 1 Jan 1973. Asterisks are used to indicate only those active service craft with names.

1 MOBILE LISTENING BARGE (YAG)

***MONOB I** YAG 61 (ex-IX 309, ex-YW 87)

Displacement, tons	1 390 full load
Dimensions, feet	174 oa × 33

The *Monob I* is a mobile listening barge converted from a self-propelled water barge. Built in 1943 and converted for acoustic research in 1969, being placed in service in May 1969. Conducts research for the Naval Ship Research and Development Centre; based at Port Everglades, Florida.
Designation changed from IX 301 to YAG 61 on 1 July 1970.

MONOB I — *United States Navy*

1 RESEARCH SHIP (YAG): "LIBERTY" TYPE

GEORGE EASTMAN YAG 39

Displacement, tons	6 000 light; 11 600 full load
Dimensions, feet	422·7 oa × 57 × 34·7
Main engines	Steam reciprocating; 2 500 ihp; 1 shaft = 11 knots
Boilers	2
Accommodation	169 (19 officers, 150 enlisted men)

EC2-S-C1 "Liberty" ship built by Permanente Metals Corp, Richmond, California; launched on 20 Apr 1943 and delivered as merchant ship on 5 May 1943. The ship was acquired by the Navy on 2 Apr 1953 for use as a nuclear effects research ship (designated YAG 39); not employed as minesweeping ship as were other "Liberty" type ships. The now-stricken *Granville S. Hall* was employed in a similar role.
As a research ship the *George Eastman* was fitted with instrumentation to detect nuclear fallout and radiation; ship controls enclosed in a specially protected compartment; also equipped for remote control for unmanned operation in contaminated areas. Also used in ship biological and chemical defence research. Now in reserve.

DISPOSALS
Granville S. Hall YAG 40 of the "Liberty" type was stricken in 1971.
1972 edition).
The experimental minefield sweeper **YAG 37** (ex-*John L. Sullivan*) was scrapped in 1958, **YAG 36** (ex-*Floyd W. Spencer*) and **YAG 38** (ex-*Edward Kavanagh*) were stricken in 1960. The Fleet X-ray examination ship **Whidbey** AG 141, was stricken on 1 May 1959.
The former netlaying ship **Butternut** (ex-ANL 9, ex-AN 9, ex-YN 4) was reinstated on the Navy List as YAG 60 on 28 Oct 1969; after brief service in support of the Pacific Missile Range, she was taken out of service in late 1970 and stricken on 1 July 1971.

GEORGE EASTMAN (YAG 39) — *1966, United States Navy*

1 RESEARCH YACHT (YAG)

***SALUDA** (ex-*Odyssey*) YAG 87 (ex-IX 87)

Dimensions, feet	73·6 wl; 88·6 oa × 18

Wood-hulled sailing yacht; yawl rigged. Employed in acoustic research at San Diego, California. Auxiliary diesel.
Built in 1938 by H. B. Nevins, City Island, New York. Acquired by Navy in 1943.

3 DIVING TENDERS (YDT)

Tenders used to support shallow-water diving operations. Three self-propelled diving tenders are on the Navy List: YDT 9 ex-LCU 854, *Phoebus* YDT 14 ex-YF 294, and *Suitland* YDT 15 ex-YF 336. (Two non-self-propelled YDTs are in service.)

23 COVERED LIGHTERS (YF)

Lighters used to transport material in harbours; self-propelled; 23 are on the Navy List, six of which are named: **Lynnhaven** (YF 328), **Little Compton** (YF 864), **Keyport** (YF 885), and **Kodiak** (YF 886).

7 FERRYBOATS (YFB)

Ferryboats used to transport personnel and vehicles in large harbours; self-propelled; one is under construction and seven are on the Navy List, one of which is named; **Aquidneck** (YFB 14). The YFB 88-91 are the former LCU 1636, 1638-1640, all reclassified on 1 Sep 1969.

YFB 88 (ex-LCU 1636) — *United States Navy*

YFB 87 — *1970, US Navy, Kenneth Ollar*

1 REFRIGERATED COVERED LIGHTER (YFR)

Lighter used to store and transport food and other materials which require refrigeration; one remains on the Navy List.

11 COVERED LIGHTERS (RANGE TENDER) (YFRT)

Lighters used for miscellaneous purposes; 11 are on the Navy List. The YFRT 520 is employed in torpedo testing and is fitted with a triple Mk 32 launcher. The **Range Recoverer** YFRT 521 (ex-T-AGM 2, ex-T-AG 161, ex-US Army FS 278), is a former missile range instrumentation ship (RIS); redesignated YFRT 521 on 16 May 1972; see description under Experimental, Research and Surveying Ships in 1972-1973 edition.

YFRT 520 — *1969, United States Navy*

RANGE RECOVERER (YFRT 21) — *United States Navy*

Service Craft—*continued*

10 HARBOUR UTILITY CRAFT (YFU)

YFU 71 **YFU 72** **YFU 73** **YFU 74** **YFU 75** **YFU 76** **YFU 77** **YFU 80** **YFU 81** **YFU 82**

Dimensions, feet	125 oa × 36 × 7·5
Main engines	diesels = 8 knots
Guns	2—50 cal MG

Militarised versions of a commercial lighter design. Used for off-loading large ships in harbours and ferrying cargo from one coastal port to another. Built by Pacific Coast Engineering Co. Alameda, California; completed 1967-1968. Can carry more than 300 tons cargo; considerable cruising range.

TRANSFERS AND LOSSES
YFU 79 transferred to South Vietnam in Nov 1968; YFU 78 sunk in Vietnam in March 1969.
YFU 71-77 and YFU 80-82 loaned to US Army in 1970 for use in South Vietnam.

YFU 75 *1968, United States Navy*

YFU 74 *1969, United States Navy*

26 HARBOUR UTILITY CRAFT (YFU): FORMER LANDING CRAFT

YFU 4 (ex-LCU 562)	**YFU 53** (ex-LCU 1446)	**YFU 91** (ex-LCU 1608)
YFU 24 (ex-LCU 980)	**YFU 55** (ex-LCU 637)	**YFU 93** (ex-LCU 1625)
YFU 25 (ex-LCU 1056)	**YFU 57** (ex-LCU 709)	**YFU 95** (ex-LCU 1491)
YFU 39 (ex-LCU 1363)	**YFU 59** (ex-LCU 776)	**YFU 96** (ex-LCU 1609)
YFU 44 (ex-LCU 1398)	**YFU 61** (ex-LCU 916)	**YFU 97** (ex-LCU 1611)
YFU 45 (ex-LCU 1411)	**YFU 62** (ex-LCU 973)	**YFU 98** (ex-LCU 1615)
YFU 50 (ex-LCU 1486)	**YFU 67** (ex-LCU 1232)	**YFU 99** (ex-LCU 1622)
YFU 52 (ex-LCU 743)	**YFU 69** (ex-LCU 1388)	**YFU 100** (ex-LCU 1610)
	YFU 83 (new; see notes)	**YFU 101** (ex-LCU 1612)

Former utility landing craft employed primarily as harbour and coastal cargo craft (see section on Landing Craft for basic data). YFU 39 is assigned to Mine Force, Pacific Fleet, and is based at Long Beach, California, to support and sow practice mines for MSBs; YFU 44 is assigned to Naval Undersea Research and Development Centre at Long Beach and is fitted with an open centre well for lowering equipment; YFU 53 also is assigned to the Centre and has an open centre well for handling the CURV tethered torpedo recovery device.
YFU 83 built by Defoe Shipbuilding Co (same design as LCU 1646). YFU 54, 56, 61, 64, 67-70 loaned to US Army in April 1970 for use in South Vietnam. YFU 78 sunk in Vietnam in 1969.

CLASSIFICATIONS. YFU 1-70 and 84-101 all were former utility landing craft. Several reverted to LCU designations at various times and three were modified for salvage work: YFU 2, 16, and 33 to YLLC 5, 2, and 3 respectively.

DISPOSALS, TRANSFERS AND LOSSES
Recent YFU/LCU disposals include **YFU 12** (ex-LCU 686) sunk in Vietnam in 1968; **YFU 78** sunk in Vietnam in 1969.
YFU 84-86 formerly on loan to Denmark as LCUs returned and stricken in 1971; **YFU 5, 7, 20, 36, 37** stricken in 1970, **YFU 8, 47, 58, 60, 92** stricken in 1971; **YFU 90** transferred to South Vietnam in 1971; **YFU 87** stricken in 1972; **YFU 56, 68,** transferred to Khmer Republic (Cambodia) on 19 May 1972; **YFU 88, 95** transferred to Spain on 28 June 1972.

YFU 83 *1971, Defoe Shipbuilding*

YFU 39 *1970, United States Navy*

15 GARBAGE LIGHTERS (YG)

Lighters used to collect garbage and refuse from ships in port, especially those not moored to a pier; popularly known as "honey barges"; self-propelled; 15 are on the Navy List.

LIGHT SALVAGE LIFT CRAFT (YLLC)

YLLC 1 (ex-LCU 1388), **YLLC 3** (ex-LCU 1195), **YLLC 5** (ex-LCU 529) transferred to South Vietnam; **YLLC 2** (ex-YFU 16, ex-LCU 788) stricken on 1 May 1972 for sale to commercial firms; **YLLC 4** (ex-LCU 1459) sunk in Vietnam on 15 Nov 1968.

10 GATE CRAFT (YHG)

Specialised craft intended to tend anti-submarine and anti-torpedo nets in harbours; self-propelled; 10 are on the Navy List.

70 FUEL BARGES (YO)

Small liquid fuel carriers intended to fuel ships where no pierside fueling facilities are available; self-propelled; 70 are on the Navy List. Four are named: **Casing Heap** YO 47, **Crownbrock** YO 48, **Whipstock** YO 49, **Gauger** YO 55.

YO 130 *1970, United States Navy*

20 GASOLINE BARGES (YOG)

Similar to the fuel barges (YO), but carry gasoline and aviation fuels; self-propelled; 20 are on the Navy List. One is named: **Lieut. Thomas W. Fowler** YOG 107.

26 SEAMANSHIP TRAINING CRAFT (YP)

YP 584 **YP 585** **YP 586** **YP 587** **YP 589** **YP 590** **YP 591** **YP 654** **YP 655** **YP 656** **YP 657** **YP 658** **YP 659** **YP 660** **YP 661** **YP 662** **YP 664** **YP 664** **YP 665** **YP 666** **YP 667** **YP 668** **YP 669** **YP 670** **YP 671** **YP 672**

YP 584 series:

Displacement, tons	50
Dimensions, feet	75 oa × 16 × 4·5
Main engines	2 diesels (Superior); 400 bhp; 2 shafts = 12 knots

YP 654 series:

Displacement, tons	69·5 full load
Dimensions, feet	80·4 oa × 18·75 × 5·3
Main engines	4 diesels (General Motors); 660 bhp; 2 shafts = 13·5 knots

These craft are used for instruction in seamanship and navigation at the Naval Academy, Annapolis, Maryland, and Naval Officer Candidate School, Newport, Rhode Island. Fitted with surface search radar, Fathometer, gyro compass, and UHF and MF radio; the YP 655 additionally fitted for instruction in oceanographic research.
YPs numbered below 654 are older craft of a once-numerous type employed for training and utility work. YP 654-663 built by Stephens Bros, Inc, Stockton, Calif. completed in 1958; YP 664 and 665 built by Elizabeth City Shipbuilders, Inc, Elizabeth City, North Carolina; YP 666 and 667 built by Stephens Bros; YP 668 built by Peterson Boatbuilding Co, Tacoma, Washington, completed in 1968; YP 669-672 built by Peterson completed in 1971-1972.
These craft are of wooden construction with aluminium deck houses.
YP 588 stricken in 1972.

Service Craft—*continued*

YP 654 type — *United States Navy*

YP 669 — *1971, Peterson Builders*

1 SALVAGE CRAFT TENDER (YRST): CONVERTED NET LAYER

***NAUBUC** YRST 4 (ex-AN 84)

Former "Cohoes" class net layer converted to a self-propelled salvage craft tender for coastal cable laying and salvage support. Launched on 15 Apr 1944 and commissioned on 15 Mar 1945; stricken from the Navy List in Sep 1962, but reacquired in 1967 and converted to YRST. She is the only self-propelled YRST.

NAUBUC (YRST 4) — *1968, United States Navy*

74 LARGE HARBOUR TUGS (YTB)

Name	No.
EDENSHAW	YTB 752
MARIN	YTB 753
PONTIAC	YTB 756
OSHKOSH	YTB 757
PADUCAH	YTB 758
BOGALUSA	YTB 759
NATICK	YTB 760
OTTUMWA	YTB 761
TUSCUMBIA	YTB 762
MUSKEGON	YTB 763
MISHAWAKA	YTB 764
OKMULGEE	YTB 765
WAPAKINETA	YTB 766
APALACHICOLA	YTB 767
ARCATA	YTB 768
CHESANING	YTB 769
DAHLONEGA	YTB 770
KEOKUK	YTB 771
NASHUA	YTB 774
WAUWATOSA	YTB 775
WEEHAWKEN	YTB 776
NOGALES	YTB 777
APOPKA	YTB 778
MANHATTAN	YTB 779
SAUGUS	YTB 780
NIANTIC	YTB 781
MANISTEE	YTB 782
REDWING	YTB 783
KALISPELL	YTB 784
WINNEMUCCA	YTB 785
TONKAWA	YTB 786
KITTANNING	YTB 787
WAPATO	YTB 788
TOMAHAWK	YTB 789
MENOMINEE	YTB 790
MARINETTE	YTB 791
ANTIGO	YTB 792
PIQUA	YTB 793
MANDAN	YTB 794
KETCHIKAN	YTB 795
SACO	YTB 796
TAMAQUA	YTB 797
OPELIKA	YTB 789
NATCHITOCHES	YTB 799
EFAULA	YTB 800
PALATKA	YTB 801
CHERAW	YTB 802
NANTICOKE	YTB 803
AHOSKIE	YTB 804
OCALA	YTB 805
TUSKEGEE	YTB 806
MASSAPEQUA	YTB 807
WENATCHEE	YTB 808
AGAWAN	YTB 809
ANOKA	YTB 810
HOUMA	YTB 811
ACCONAC	YTB 812
POUGHKEEPSIE	YTB 813
WAXAHATCHIE	YTB 814
NEODESHA	YTB 815
CAMPTI	YTB 816
HAYANNIS	YTB 817
MECOSTA	YTB 818
IUKA	YTB 819
WANAMASSA	YTB 820
TONTOGANY	YTB 821
PAWHUSKA	YTB 822
CANONCHET	YTB 823
SANTAQUIN	YTB 824
WATHENA	YTB 825
WASHTUCNA	YTB 826
CHETEK	YTB 827

Basic YTB design:

LARGE HARBOUR TUGS—*continued*

Displacement, tons	350 full load
Dimensions, feet	109 oa × 30 × 13·8
Machinery	2 diesels; 2 000 bhp; 2 shafts
Complement	10 to 12 (enlisted)

Large harbour tugs; 74 are in service or under construction. YTB 752 completed in 1959, YTB 753 in 1960, YTB 756-762 in 1961, YTB 763-766 in 1963, YTB 770 and YTB 771 in 1964, YTB 767-769, 776 in 1965, YTB 774, 775, 777-789 in 1966, YTB 790-793 in 1967, YTB 794 and 795 in 1968, YTB 796-803 in 1969, and YTB 804-815 completed in 1970-1972, YTB 816-827 completed 1972-1973.

TUSKEGEE (YTB 806) — *1970, Peterson Builders*

PADUCAH (YTB 758) — *United States Navy*

14 SMALL HARBOUR TUGS (YTL)

Fourteen of these craft are on the Navy List; unnamed.

121 MEDIUM HARBOUR TUGS (YTM)

Numbered in YTM 128-779 series; several formerly designated YTB or are former US Army tugs. Most have names.

MASCOUTAN (YTM 760) — *1971, US Navy, PH2 C. Velasquez*

31 WATER BARGES (YW)

Barges modified to carry water to ships in harbour; self-propelled; 31 of these craft are on the Navy List.

FLOATING DRY DOCKS

The US Navy operates a number of floating dry docks to supplement dry dock facilities at major naval activities, to support fleet ballistic missile submarines (SSBN) at advanced bases, and to provide repair capabilities in forward combat areas.

The larger floating dry docks are made sectional to facilitate movement overseas and to render them self docking. The ARD-type docks have the forward end of their docking well closed by a structure resembling the bow of a ship to facilitate towing. Berthing facilities, repair shops, and machinery are housed in sides of larger docks. None is self-propelled.

Twenty-four floating dry docks are in Navy service (including two partial docks), 15 are out of service in reserve (including two partial docks), 29 are on lease to commercial firms for private use, and 24 are on loan to other US services and foreign navies (including one partial dock). Asterisks indicate docks in active US service.

LARGE AUXILIARY FLOATING DRY DOCKS

Name-No.	Capacity	Construction	Notes
***AFDL 1**	1 000 tons	Steel	Guantanamo Bay, Cuba
AFDL 2	1 000 tons	Steel	Reserve
***AFDL 6**	1 000 tons	Steel	Little Creek, Virginia
AFDL 7	1 900 tons	Steel	Reserve
AFDL 8	1 000 tons	Steel	Commercial lease
AFDL 9	1 000 tons	Steel	Commercial lease
***AFDL 10**	1 000 tons	Steel	Subic Bay, Philippines
AFDL 12	1 000 tons	Steel	Reserve
AFDL 15	1 000 tons	Steel	Commercial lease
AFDL 16	1 000 tons	Steel	Commercial lease
AFDL 19	1 000 tons	Steel	Commercial lease
***AFDL 21**	1 000 tons	Steel	Guam, Marianas
***AFDL 23**	1 900 tons	Steel	Danang, South Vietnam
AFDL 25	1 000 tons	Steel	Reserve
AFDL 29	1 000 tons	Steel	Commercial lease
AFDL 30	1 000 tons	Steel	Commercial lease
AFDL 35	2,800 tons	Concrete	Reserve
AFDL 37	2 800 tons	Concrete	Commercial lease
AFDL 38	2 800 tons	Concrete	Commercial lease
AFDL 40	2 800 tons	Concrete	Commercial lease
AFDL 41	2 800 tons	Concrete	Commercial lease
***AFDL 42**	2 800 tons	Concrete	Long Beach Nav Shipyard
AFDL 43	2 800 tons	Concrete	Commercial lease
AFDL 45	2 800 tons	Concrete	Commercial lease
AFDL 47	6 500 tons	Steel	Commercial lease
***AFDL 48**	4 000 tons	Concrete	Long Beach Nav Shipyard

AUXILIARY REPAIR DRY DOCKS AND MEDIUM AUXILIARY REPAIR DRY DOCKS

***ARD 5**	3 000 tons	Steel	New London, Connecticut
***ARD 7**	3 000 tons	Steel	New London, Connecticut
***ARD 11**	3 000 tons	Steel	Key West, Florida
ARD 16	3 000 tons	Steel	Reserve
ARDM 3 (ex ARD 18)	3 000 tons	Steel	Reserve
***OAK RIDGE** ARDM 1 (ex-ARD 19)		Steel	Rota, Spain
***WHITE SANDS** ARD 20	3 000 tons	Steel	San Diego, California
ARD 24	3 000 tons	Steel	Reserve
ARD 25	3 000 tons	Steel	Reserve
***ALAMAGORDO** ARDM 2 (ex-ARD 26)		Steel	Charleston South Carolina
ARD 27	3 000 tons	Steel	Reserve
***ARCO** ARD 29	3 000 tons	Steel	Guam, Marianas
***ARD 30**	3 000 tons	Steel	Pearl Harbour Nav Shipyard
***ARD 31**	3 000 tons	Steel	US Air Force

YARD FLOATING DRY DOCKS

YFD 7	18 000 tons	Steel (3)	Commercial lease
YFD 8	20 000 tons	Wood	Commercial lease
YFD 9	16 000 tons	Wood	Commercial lease
YFD 23	10 500 tons	Wood	Commercial lease
YFD 54	5 000 tons	Wood	Commercial lease
YFD 68	14 000 tons	Steel (3)	Commercial lease
YFD 69	14 000 tons	Steel (3)	Commercial lease
YFD 70	14 000 tons	Steel (3)	Commercial lease
YFD 71	14 000 tons	Steel (3)	Commercial lease
***YFD 83** (ex-AFDL 31)	1 000 tons	Steel	US Coast Guard

LARGE AUXILIARY FLOATING DRY DOCKS

***AFDB 1** (partial)	40 000 tons	Steel (4)	Subic Bay, Philippines
AFDB 1 (partial)	60 000 tons	Steel (6)	Reserve
AFDB 2	90 000 tons	Steel (10)	Reserve
AFDB 3	81 000 tons	Steel (9)	Reserve
AFDB 4	55 000 tons	Steel (7)	Reserve
AFDB 5	55 000 tons	Steel (7)	Reserve
AFDB 6	55 000 tons	Steel (7)	Reserve
AFDB 7 (partial)		Steel (2)	Reserve
***AFDB 7** (partial)	10 000 tons	Steel (1)	US Army
***LOS ALAMOS** AFDB 7 (partial)	40 000 tons	Steel (4)	Holy Loch, Scotland

MEDIUM AUXILIARY FLOATING DRY DOCKS

AFDM 1 (ex-YFD 3)	15 000 tons	Steel (3)	Commercial lease
AFDM 2 (ex-YFD 4)	15 000 tons	Steel (3)	Commercial lease
AFDM 3 (ex-YFD 6)	18 000 tons	Steel (3)	Commercial lease
***AFDM 5** (ex-YFD 21)	18 000 tons	Steel (3)	Subic Bay, Philippines
***AFDM 6** (ex-YFD 62)	18 000 tons	Steel (3)	Subic Bay, Philippines
***AFDM 7** (ex-YFD 63)	18 000 tons	Steel (3)	Davisville, Rhode Island
***RICHLAND** AFDM 8 (YFD ex-64)	18 000 tons	Steel (3)	Guam, Marianas
AFDM 9 (ex-YFD 65)	18 000 tons	Steel (3)	Commercial lease
AFDM 10	18 000 tons	Steel (3)	Commercial lease

Figures in parenthesis indicate the number of sections for sectional docks. Each section of the AFDB docks has a lifting capacity of about 10 000 tons. Four sections of the AFDB 7 form the floating dry dock *Los Alamos* at Holy Loch, Scotland, one section is used at Kwajalein atoll by the US Army in support of the Nike-X missile project and two sections are in reserve. (The AFDB sections each are 256 feet long 80 feet in width, with wing walls 83 feet high; the wing walls, which contain compartments, fold down when the sections are towed).
The *White Sands* (ARD 20) is employed in support of the deep-diving bathyscaph *Trieste II* (see section on Deep Submergence Vehicles). Early in 1969 the *White Sands*, with *Trieste II* on board, was towed to the Azores to support investigation of the remains of the nuclear-powered submarine *Scorpion* (SSN 589).
All floating dry docks were built during World War II except the YFD 82 (ex-ARD 1). All remaining floating dry docks were built during World War II.

TRANSFERS. The following floating dry docks are on foreign loan: ARD 23 to Argentina; AFDL 39, ARD 14 to Brazil; ARD 32 to Chile; ARD 28 to Columbia; ARD 1 to Ecuador; AFDL 11 to Khmer Republic (Cambodia); ARD 15, AFDL 28 to Mexico; ARD 6 to Pakistan; AFDL 26 to Paraguay; AFDL 33, ARD 8 to Peru; AFDL 20, AFDL 4 to Philippines; ARD 9, *Windsor* (ARD 22) to Taiwan China; ARD 13 to Venezuela; AFDL 22 to South Vietnam; ARD 12 to Turkey; *Arco* (ARD 29) to Iran.

AFDL 21 under tow — *1965, United States Navy*

SSBN in OAK RIDGE (ARDM 1) — *1964, United States Navy*

DEEP SUBMERGENCE VEHICLES

The US Navy operates several deep submergence vehicles for scientific, military research, and operational military missions.

The US Navy acquired its first deep submergence vehicle with the purchase of the bathyscaph *Trieste* in 1958. The *Trieste* was designed and constructed by Professor Auguste Piccard, the noted Swiss physicist and aeronaut. The US Navy sponsored research dives in the Mediterranean Sea with the *Trieste* in 1957 after which the bathyscaph was purchased outright and brought to the United States.
The *Trieste* reached a record depth of 35 800 feet (*10 910 metres*) in the Challenger Deep off the Marianas on 23 Jan 1960, being piloted by Lieutenant Don Walsh, USN, and Jacques Piccard (son of Auguste). Rebuilt and designated *Trieste II*, the craft was subsequently used in the search for wreckage of the nuclear-powered submarine *Thresher* (SSN 593) was lost in 1963 and the *Scorpion* (SSN 589) lost in 1968.
During this period the US Navy sponsored development of the *Alvin*, a deep submergence research vehicle, which served as prototype for the later *Turtle* and *Sea Cliff* submersibles. The *Alvin* subsequently was accidentally lost at sea on 16 Oct 1968, but was salvaged on 30 Aug 1969. She has been rebuilt.

After the loss of the *Thresher* the US Navy initiated an extensive deep submergence programme that led to construction of two Deep Submergence Rescue Vehicles (DSRV); however, other vehicles proposed in the recommended programme were not built because of a lack of interest, changing operational concepts, and funding limitations.

The final "approved" programme of the post-*Thresher* Deep Submergence Systems Project included six DSRV rescue submersibles and two DSSV search submersibles, plus several unmanned underwater devices.

Several of these deep submergence vehicles and other craft and support ships are operated by Submarine Development Group One at San Diego, California. The Group is a major operational command that includes advanced diving equipment; divers trained in "saturation" techniques; the DSVs *Trieste II*, *Turtle*, *Sea Cliff*, DSRV-1, DSRV-2; the submarine *Dolphin* (AGSS 555); several submarine rescue ships; the floating dry dock *White Sands* (ARD 20); and tug *Apache* (ATF 67).
The hull of the original *Trieste* is rusting on blocks at the Navy Yard in Washington, DC.

MIDGET SUBMARINES

The US Navy's only "Midget" submarine, the 50-foot long **X-I** was stricken on 16 Feb 1973. See 1972-1973 edition for characteristics and photographs.

NUCLEAR POWERED RESEARCH VEHICLE: PROPOSED

A second nuclear-powered submersible research vehicle has been proposed by Vice Adm, H. G. Rickover, US Navy (Retired), Deputy Commander for Nuclear Propulsion, Naval Ship Systems Command. The craft would have a greater depth capability than the NR-1 (described below) and would employ a nuclear plant similar to that of the earlier craft.

Reportedly, Adm, Rickover began development of the so-called "NR-2" in 1971. Estimated construction time would be 2½ years; however, construction has not yet been approved.

NR-1 — *1969, General Dynamics, Electric Boat*

1 NUCLEAR POWERED OCEAN ENGINEERING AND RESEARCH VEHICLE

Name	*Builder*	*Launched*
NR-1	General Dynamics (Electric Boat)	25 Jan 1969

Displacement, tons	400 submerged
Length, feet	136·4 oa × 12·4 × 14·6
Diameter, feet	12 maximum
Machinery	Electric motors, 2 propellers; four ducted thrusters
Reactor	1 pressurised-water cooled
Complement	3 officers, 2 enlisted men, 2 scientists

The NR-1 was built primarily to serve as a test platform for a small nuclear propulsion plant; however, the craft additionally provides an advanced deep submergence ocean engineering and research capability. Vice Admiral Rickover conceived and initiated the NR-1 in 1964-1965 (the craft was not proposed in a Navy research or shipbuilding budget).
Built by Electric Boat Division of General Dynamics Corp, Groton, Connecticut; laid down on 10 June 1967; launched on 25 Jan 1969; completed late in 1969. Commanded by an officer-in-charge vice commanding officer.

Describing the craft Vice Adm Rickover has stated: "The (NR-1) will be able to perform detailed studies and mapping of the ocean bottom, temperature, currents, and other oceanographic parameters for military, commercial, and scientific use. The development of a nuclear propulsion plant for an oceanographic research vehicle will result in greater independence from surface support ships and essentially unlimited endurance of propulsion and auxiliary power for detailed exploration of the ocean.
"The submarine (NR-1) will have viewing ports for visual observation of its surroundings and the ocean bottom. In addition, a remote grapple will be installed to permit collection of marine samples and other items. With its depth capability, the NR-1 is expected to be capable of exploring areas of the Continental Shelf, an area which appears to contain most accessible wealth in mineral and food resources in the seas. Such exploratory charting may also help the United States in establishing sovereignty over parts of the Continental Shelf".

CONSTRUCTION. Vice Adm Rickover originally planned to construct the NR-1 using "state of the art" equipment, with the cost of such a vehicle estimated to be $30 000 000 in March 1965. During detailed design of the NR-1 the Navy determined that improved equipment had to be developed and a larger hull than originally planned would be required. Consequently, in July 1967 the Navy obtained Congressional approval to proceed with construction of the NR-1 at an estimated cost of $58 000 300. The final estimated ship construction cost at time of launching was $67 500 000 plus $19 900 000 for oceanographic equipment and sensors, and $11 800 000 for research and development (mainly related to the nuclear propulsion plant), for a total estimated cost of $99 200 000.

DESIGN. The NR-1 is fitted with wheels beneath the hull to permit "bottom crawling". This will obviate the necessity of hovering while exploring the ocean floor. Submarine wheels, a concept proposed as early as the first decade of this century by submarine inventor Simon Lake, were tested in the small submarine *Mackerel* (SST 1).
The NR-1 is fitted with external lights, external television cameras, a remote-controlled manipulator, and various recovery devices. No periscopes, but fixed television mast. Credited with a 30 day endurance.

ENGINEERING. The NR-1 reactor plant was designed by the Atomic Energy Commission's Knolls Atomic Power Laboratory. She is propelled by two propellers driven by electric motors outside the pressure hull with power provided by a turbine generator within the pressure hull. Four ducted thrusters, two horizontal and two vertical, are provided for precise manoeuvring.

PHOTOGRAPHS. No photographs of the NR-1 have been released for publication since the craft's sea trials in 1969. Note fixed TV mast at after end of sail structure.

NR-1 — *1969, General Dynamics Electric Boat*

2 DEEP SUBMERGENCE RESCUE VEHICLES

No.	*Builder*	*Launched*
DSRV-1	Lockheed Missiles and Space Co. (Sunnyvale, Calif)	**24 Jan 1970**
DSRV-2	Lockheed Missiles and Space Co. (Sunnyvale, Calif)	**1 May 1971**

Weight in air, tons	35
Length, feet	49·2 oa
Diameter, feet	8
Propulsion	Electric motors, propeller mounted in control shroud and four ducted thrusters
Speed, knots	5 (maximum)
Endurance	12 hours at 3 knots
Operating depth, feet	5 000
Complement	3 (pilot, co-pilot, rescue sphere operator) + 24 rescuees

The Deep Submergence Rescue Vehicle is intended to provide a quick-reaction, world-wide, all-weather capability for the rescue of survivors in a disabled submarine. The DSRV will be transportable by road, aircraft (in C-141 and C-5 jet cargo aircraft), surface ship (on ASR 21 class submarine rescue ships), and specially modified submarines (SSN type).
Upon notification that a submarine is disabled on the ocean floor the DSRV and its support equipment (all necessary check-out equipment and spare parts being housed in a mobile van) will be loaded in cargo aircraft and flown to a port near the disabled submarine. The DSRV and van will then be towed to a pier and loaded aboard a "mother" submarine, which had proceeded to the port upon notification that a submarine was disabled.
The mother submarine, with the DSRV attached to her main deck (aft of the sail structure), will then proceed to the disabled submarine and serve as an underwater base for the DSRV which will shuttle back and forth between the disabled submarine and the mother submarine. On each trip the DSRV will carry up to 24 survivors from the disabled submarine. The mother submarine will launch and recover the DSRV while submerged and, if necessary, while under ice. A total of six DSRVs were planned, but only two have been funded.
The operational effectiveness of the craft is limited severely by the lack of large numbers of ships and submarines that air transport and support the craft.
DSRV-2 placed in service on 7 Aug 1972.

Deep Submergence Vehicles—*continued*

DEEP SUBMERGENCE RESCUE VEHICLES—*Continued*

COST. The estimated construction cost for the DSRV-1 is $41 000 000 and for the DSRV-2 $23 000 000. The development, construction, test, and support of both vehicles through Fiscal Year 1975 is now estimated at $220 000 000. This expenditure includes the design and construction of both vehicles, specific research and development associated with the rescue programme, surface support equipment, modifications to "mother" submarines, test and evaluation programmes, procurement of replacement and spare parts, and training of the DSRV operators and support personnel. The DSRV programme has been forced to support research and development into deep-ocean materials equipment, and other technology-related areas not envisioned in earlier programme cost estimates.

DESIGN. The DSRV outer hull is constructed of formed fibreglass. Within this outer hull are three interconnected spheres which form the main pressure capsule. Each sphere is 7·5 feet in diameter and is constructed of HY-140 steel. The forward sphere contains the vehicle's control equipment and is manned by the pilot and co-pilot, the centre and after spheres accommodate 24 passengers and a third crewman. Under the DSRVs centre sphere is a hemispherical protrusion or "skirt" which seals over the disabled submarine's hatch. During the mating operation the skirt is pumped dry to enable personnel to transfer between the DSRV and disabled or mother submarine.

ELECTRONICS. Elaborate search and navigational sonar, and closed-circuit television (supplemented by optical devices) are installed in the DSRV to determine the exact location of a disabled submarine within a given area and for pinpointing the submarine's escape hatches. Side-looking sonar will be fitted for search missions.

ENGINEERING. Propulsion and control of the DSRV are achieved by a stern propeller in a movable control shroud and four ducted thrusters, two forward and two aft. These, plus a mercury trim system, permit the DSRV to manoeuvre and hover with great precision, and to mate with submarines lying at angles up to 45 degrees from the horizontal. An elaborate Integrated Control and Display (ICAD) system employs computers to present sensor data to the pilots and transmit their commands to the vehicle's control and propulsion system.

OPERATIONAL. The DSRV-1 and DSRV-2 were to undergo extensive sea trials through 1971, during which time they could be made available for emergency submarine rescue. However, long-range rapid-reaction rescue requires the use of shore facilities support ships, aircraft, and other related equipment that are not yet available.
The first nuclear-powered submarines to be fitted as "mother" submarines to carry and support a DSRV are the *Halibut* (SSN 587), *Finback* (SSN 670) and *Hawkbill* (SSN 666).
If a six-vehicle DSRV force is completed two vehicles would be based at each Rescue Unit Home Port (RUHP) in San Diego, California; Charleston, South Carolina; and New London, Connecticut.

PHOTOGRAPHS. An artist's concept of a DSRV "landing" on a submarine hatch appears in the 1971-1972 edition; a view of the DSRV-1 being assembled appears in the 1970-1971 edition.

DSRV-1 on Hawkbill (SSN 666) *1971, US Navy*

DSRV-1 on trailer ("mating skirt" removed) *1970, United States Navy*

2 RESEARCH VEHICLES: MODIFIED "ALVIN" TYPE

Name	*No.*	*Launched*
SEA CLIFF (ex-*Autec I*)	DSV 4	11 Dec 1968
TURTLE (ex-*Autec II*)	DSV 3	11 Dec 1968

Weight, tons	21
Length, feet	25 oa
Beam, feet	8
Propulsion	Electric motors, trainable stern propeller; 2 rotating propeller pods
Speed, knots	2·5
Endurance	8 hours at 22 knots
Operating depth, feet	6 500
Complement	2 (pilot, observer)

Both submersibles built by Electric Boat Division of General Dynamic Corp, Groton Connecticut. Intended for deep submergence research and work tasks. Designated *Autec I* and *Autec II* during construction, but assigned above names in dual launching on 11 Dec 1968. Completed in 1969.
Designated DSV 4 and DSV 3, respectively, on 1 June 1971.

CONSTRUCTION. Three pressure spheres were fabricated for the *Alvin* submersible programme, one for installation in the *Alvin*, a spare, and one for testing. The second and third spheres subsequently were allocated to these later submersibles.

DESIGN. Twin-arm manipulator fitted to each submersible. Propulsion by stem propeller and two smaller, manoeuvering propeller "pods" on sides of vehicles; no thrusters.

PHOTOGRAPHS. Note different "nose" and "tail" configurations in side views of *Sea Cliff*.

SEA CLIFF *1968, General Dynamics, Electric Boat*

SEA CLIFF stern view *1970, General Dynamics, Electric Boat*

SEA CLIFF *United States Navy*

1 RESEARCH VEHICLE: "ALVIN" TYPE

ALVIN DSV 2

The research submersible *Alvin* accidentally sank in 5 051 feet of water some 120 miles south of Cape Cod, Massachusetts, on 16 Oct 1968 when a cable broke on her catamaran support ship *Lulu*. Her access hatch was open and the submersible flooded; there were no casualties. She was salvaged on 28 Aug 1969 by the oceanographic research ship *Mizar* (T-AGOR 11) and the commercial submersible *Aluminaut*.
The *Alvin* was operated by the Woods Hole Oceangraphic Institution for the Office of naval research which designed and funded construction of the *Alvin*. The *Alvin* was built in 1964. See 1968-1969 edition (pp 471-472) for additional details. A photograph of the smashed *Alvin* after salvage appears in the 1970-1971 edition. The *Alvin* is being fitted with the world's first submersible titanium pressure hull; scheduled for completion in mid-1973. Her new operating depth will be 12 000 feet. The *Alvin* was designated DSV 2 on 1 June 1971.

Deep Submergence Vehicles—*continued*

1 BATHYSCAPH RESEARCH VEHICLE: "TRIESTE" TYPE

Name	*No.*
TRIESTE II	DSV 1 (ex-X-2)

Weight in air, tons	84
Displacement, tons	303 submerged
Length, feet	78·6
Beam, feet	15·3
Propulsion	Electric motors, 3 propellers aft, ducted thruster forward (see *Design* notes)
Speed, knots	2
Endurance	10-12 hours at 2 knots
Operating depth, feet	12 000 (see *Design* notes)
Complement	3 (2 operators, 1 observer)

The *Trieste II* is the extensively rebuilt *Trieste I* which the US Navy purchased in 1958 from professor Auguste Piccard. Several "modernisations" have resulted in the current vehicle being essentially a "new" craft, the third to be named *Trieste*, (The original *Trieste* was built at Castellammare, Italy; launched on 1 Aug 1953).
The vehicle is operated by Submarine Development Group One at San Diego, California, and is used primarily as a test bed for underwater equipment and to train deep submergence vehicle operators (hydronauts).
Designated as a "submersible craft" and assigned the designation X-2 on 1 Sep 1969; subsequently changed to DSV 1 on 1 June 1971.

DESIGN. The *Trieste II* is essentially a large float with a small pressure sphere attached to the underside. The float, which is filled with aviation petrol, provides buoyancy. Designed operating depth is 20 000 feet but dives have been limited to approximately 12 000 feet. (The record-setting Challenger Deep dive was made with a Krupp sphere which has a virtually unlimited depth capability).
The bathyscaph was essentially rebuilt for a second time at the Mare Island Naval Shipyard in Sep 1965-Aug 1966 with a modified float, pressure sphere, propulsion system, and mission equipment being fitted. In the broadside view the sphere is now largely hidden by protective supports to keep the sphere clear of the welldeck when the craft rests in a floating dry dock. (Compare with photographs of the earlier *Trieste II* configuration in the 1969-1970 edition).
Fitted with external television cameras and mechanical manipulator; computerised digital navigation system installed.
During 1973 the *Trieste II* was fitted with a fuel-cell powerplant for operational evaluation. The plant was developed by Pratt & Whitney; designated Powercel 15A.

PHOTOGRAPHS. Note forward "Legs" to prevent pressure sphere from sinking into ocean floor when craft is resting on the bottom. Lights, manipulators, cameras, and and other devices are mounted forward of the sphere, partially in view of sphere's viewpoint.

TRIESTE II — *1970, United States Navy*

NEMO DSV 5

A deep submergence vehicle built by the Naval Civil Engineering Laboratory, Port Hueneme, California, in 1970. Fabricated of acrylic (plastic); depth capability 600 feet. Normal mode of operation is to lower an anchor to the seafloor and then winch itself down. One or two operators.

DEEP VIEW

Weight in air, tons	5·75
Length, feet	16·5
Width, feet	6
Propulsion	4 electric motors (5 hp each), 2 propellers aft, 1 lateral propeller, 1 vertical propeller
Speed, knots	1—2 sustained; 4 maximum
Endurance, hours	4—6
Operating depth, feet	1 500
Complement	2

Designed and built by the Naval Undersea Research and Development Centre, San Diego, California. The *Deep View* is the first submersible that incorporates glass (borosillicate) in the pressure capsule structure with a glass hemisphere capping the forward end of the craft, the remainder of the pressure capsule is fabricated of HY-100 steel. The Glass is 1·125 inches thick. Built in 1971.
The power source consists of 20 lead-acid batteries in two pods that can be jettisoned in an emergency to provide the craft with additional buoyancy. Normal and emergency ballast also consists of droppable weights.
The craft is operated by Naval Undersea Research and Development Centre.

DEEP VIEW — *1971, United States Navy*

TRIESTE II — *1970, United States Navy*

MAKAKAI

A deep submergence vehicle built by the Naval Undersea Research and Development Centre's Hawaiian laboratory in 1971. Pressure capsule is a fully transparent acrylic (plastic) sphere which is mounted on an aluminium frame secured to two pontoons; depth capability 600 feet. One or two operators.

MAKAKAI — *United States Navy*

DEEP SUBMERGENCE SEARCH VEHICLE (STUDY)

The Deep Submergence Search Vehicle was intended to perform object location and small object recovery missions on the ocean floor to depths of 20 000 feet (an area which encompasses some 80 per cent of the ocean floor). The DSSV was to have been transportable by aircraft (in C-5 jet cargo aircraft), surface ships, and specially configured support submarines.
Two Search and Recovery Forces had been proposed, each to consist of one DSSV, one set of Unmanned Instrument Platforms (UIP), a specially configured "Mother" submarine, and a surface support ship.
A contract for final design and construction of the DSSV-1 was awarded to the Lockheed Missile and Space Company, Sunnyvale, California.
However, subsequent budget limitations have halted all procurement of DSSV components and, since January 1970, only studies into advanced pressure hull materials, buoyancy materials, and fuel cells are being funded. See 1971-1972 edition for detailed characteristics.

COAST GUARD

Command

Commandant, United States Coast Guard: Admiral Chester R. Bender
Assistant Commandant: Vice Admiral Thomas R. Sargent III
Chief of Staff: Rear Admiral Edward D. Scheiderer
Commander, Atlantic Area: Vice Admiral Benjamin F. Engel
Commander, Pacific Area: Vice Admiral Mark A. Whalen

Establishment

The United States Coast Guard was established by an Act of Congress approved Jan 28, 1915, which consolidated the Revenue Cutter Service (founded in 1790) and the Life Saving Service (founded in 1878). The act of establishment stated the Coast Guard "shall be a military service and branch of the armed forces of the United States at all times. The Coast Guard shall be a service in the Treasury Department except when operating as a service in the Navy".
The Congress further legislated that in time of national emergency or when the President so directs, the Coast Guard operates as a part of the Navy. The Coast Guard did operate as a part of the Navy during the First and Second World Wars.
The Lighthouse Service (founded in 1789) was transferred to the Coast Guard on July 1, 1939.
The Coast Guard was transferred to the newly established Department of Transportation on April 1, 1967.

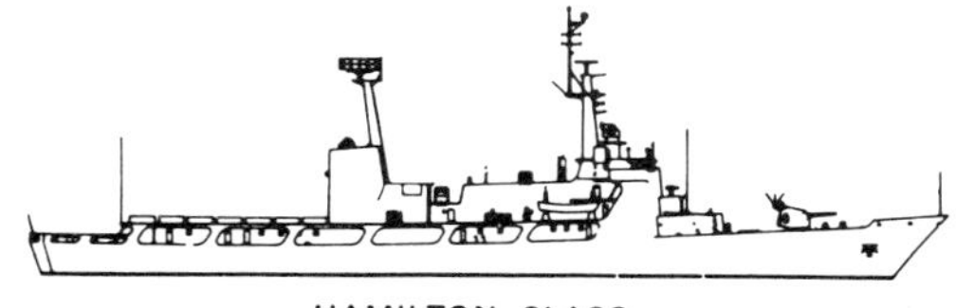

HAMILTON CLASS

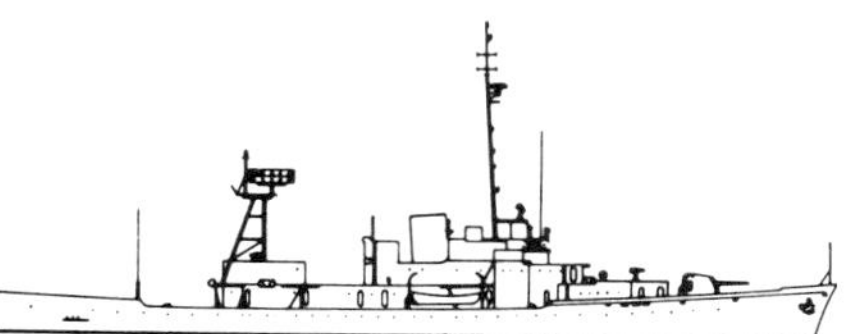

CAMPBELL CLASS

Missions

The current missions of the Coast Guard are to (1) enforce or assist in the enforcement of applicable Federal laws upon the high seas and waters subject to the jurisdiction of the United States; (2) administer all Federal laws regarding safety of life and property on the high seas and on waters subject to the jurisdiction of the United States, except those laws specifically entrusted to other Federal agencies; (3) develop, establish, maintain, operate, and conduct aids to maritime navigation, ocean stations, icebreaking activities, oceanographic research, and rescue facilities; and (4) maintain a state of readiness to function as a specialised service in the Navy when so directed by the President.

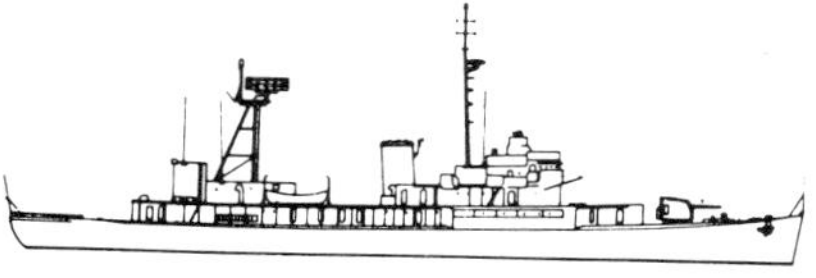

CASCO CLASS

Cutters

All Coast Guard vessels are referred to as "cutters". Cutter names are preceded by USCGC. Cutter serial numbers are prefixed with letter designations, the first letter being "W". The first two digits of serial numbers for cutters less than 100 feet in length indicate their approximate length over all. All Coast Guard cutters are active unless otherwise indicated.

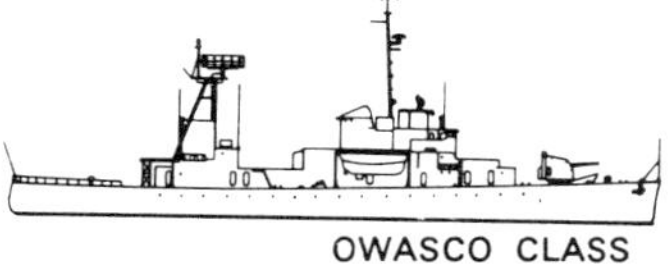

OWASCO CLASS

Cutter Strength

27 High Endurance Cutters
16 Medium Endurance Cutters
1 Meteorological Cutter
79 Patrol Boats
2 Hovercraft (being stricken)
29 Harbour Tugs
9 Icebreakers
4 Training Cutters
35 Seagoing Buoy Tenders
73 Coastal River-Inland Tenders
7 Oceangoing Tugs
(classified as Medium Endurance Cutters

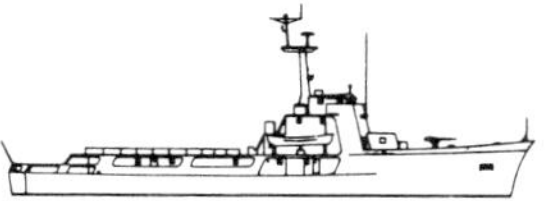

RELIANCE CLASS

Personnel

July 1973 (planned): 4 588 officers, 1 270 warrant officers, 30 665 enlisted men.

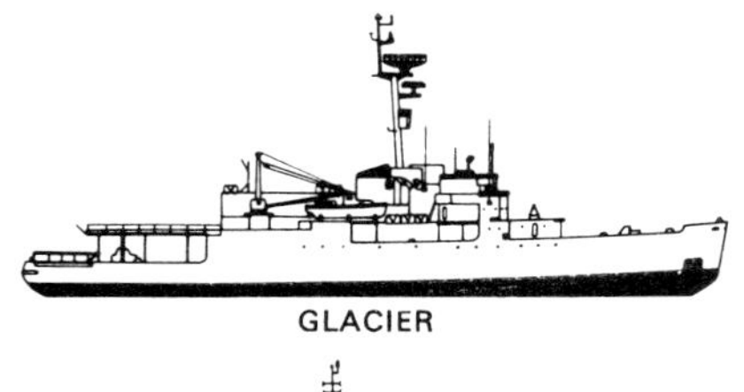

GLACIER

Aviation

The Coast Guard operates a small air arm to support Coast Guard operations. As of June 30, 1973, the Coast Guard operated 16 HC-130 Hercules, 35 HU-16 Albatross, 1 VC-4A Gulfstream I, and 1 VC-11A Gulfstream II fixed wing aircraft; 35 HH-3F and 71 HH-52A helicopters.

Vietnam Operations

Several Coast Guard cutters were deployed to Southeast Asia to supplement US Naval forces during the Vietnam War. These cutters remained under Coast Guard colours, but were under Navy operational control and assigned to the Commander, Coastal Surveillance Force (Task Force 115). During the peak of the Coast Guard involvement five high-endurance cutters and 26 82-foot patrol boats were committed to Vietnam operations.
Subsequently, seven high endurance cutters and all 26 of the patrol boats were transferred to the Vietnam Navy between 16 May 1969 and 21 Dec 1971.

BURTON ISLAND

MIDGETT (WHEC 726) with HH-3F and Hovercraft

1972, United States Coast Guard

High Endurance Cutters — *continued*

12 HIGH ENDURANCE CUTTERS (WHEC): "HAMILTON" (378) CLASS

)isplacement, tons	2 716 standard; 3 050 full load
.ength, feet	350 wl; 378 oa
eam, feet	42·8
)raft, feet	20
iuns	1—5 inch (*127 mm*) 38 cal dual-purpose 2—81 mm mortars 4—·50 cal MG
/S weapons	2 fixed hedgehogs (removed from some ships, see *ASW* notes) 2 triple torpedo tubes (Mk 32)
elicopters	1 HH-52 or HH-3 helicopter
ain engines	Combined Diesel and Gas turbine (CODAG): 2 diesels (Fairbanks-Morse) 7 000 hp; 2 gas turbines (Pratt & Whitney), 28 000 hp; aggregate 35 000 hp; 2 shafts
peed	29
omplement	155 (15 officers, 140 enlisted men)

Name	*No.*	*Laid down*	*Launched*	*Completed*
HAMILTON	WHEC 715	Jan 1965	18 Dec 1965	20 Feb 1967
DALLAS	WHEC 716	7 Feb 1966	1 Oct 1966	1 Oct 1967
MELLON	WHEC 717	25 July 1966	11 Feb 1967	22 Dec 1967
CHASE	WHEC 718	15 Oct 1966	20 May 1967	1 Mar 1968
BOUTWELL	WHEC 719	12 Dec 1966	17 June 1967	14 June 1968
SHERMAN	WHEC 720	13 Feb 1967	23 Sep 1967	23 Aug 1968
GALLANTIN	WHEC 721	17 Apr 1967	18 Nov 1967	20 Dec 1968
MORGENTHAU	WHEC 722	17 July 1967	10 Feb 1968	14 Feb 1969
RUSH	WHEC 723	23 Oct 1967	16 Nov 1968	3 July 1969
MUNRO	WHEC 724	18 Feb 1970	5 Dec 1970	10 Sep 1971
JARVIS	WHEC 725	9 Sep 1970	24 Apr 1971	30 Dec 1971
MIDGETT	WHEC 726	5 Apr 1971	4 Sep 1971	17 Mar 1972

These are large, attractive, multi-purpose cutters. All built by Avondale Shipyards, Inc, New Orleans, Louisiana. All these ships are in active service.

ASW ARMAMENT. Hedgehog anti-submarine weapons are being removed from earlier ships during overhaul and Mk 309 fire control system for Mk 32 torpedo launchers installed. Hedgehogs deleted in later ships. *Hamilton* was first to drop hedgehogs and receive Mk 309 during 1970 overhaul.

DESIGN. These ships have clipper bows, twin funnels enclosing a helicopter hangar, helicopter platform aft. All are fitted with oceanographic laboratories, elaborate communications equipment, and meteorological data gathering facilities. Superstructure is largely of aluminium construction. Bridge control of manoeuvring is by aircraft-type "joy stick" rather than wheel.

ELECTRONICS. Fitted with SQS-36 sonar. Closed-circuit television permits bridge personnel to monitor displays in the Combat Information Centre (CIC). Fitted with SPS-29 and SPS-51 radars.

ENGINEERING. The *Hamiltons* are the largest US 'military' ships with gas turbine propulsion pending completion of the Navy's DD963 class destroyers.
The Pratt & Whitney gas turbines are FT-4A, marine variant of the J75 aircraft engine used in the Boeing 707 transport and F-105 fighter-bomber; the Fairbanks Morse diesels are 12 cylinder; variable pitch propellers fitted. Engine and propeller pitch consoles are located in wheelhouse and at bridge wing stations as well as engine room control booth.
A retractable bow propulsion unit is provided for station keeping and precise manoeuvring. (Unit is located directly below hedgehogs, immediately aft of sonar dome).
Range is 14 000 miles at 11 knots on diesels and 2 400 miles at 29 knots on gas turbines.

NOMENCLATURE. The first nine ships of this class were named for secretaries of the Treasury Department, reflecting the Coast Guard being a part of that department from 1915 to 1967, when it was transferred to the newly formed Department of Transportation. Subsequent ships of this class honour Coast Guard heroes.
Later ships are referred to as "Hero" class.

PHOTOGRAPHS. Coast Guard cutters are often seen in "troubled waters": the *Rush* was photographed in Southeast Asia and the *Sherman* off Cuba. The *Boutwell* is shown in more tranquil waters off Genoa, Italy. The *Sherman* and *Boutwell* have hedgehogs in "B" position; Mk 32 torpedo tubes amidships.

RUSH (WHEC 723) — *1970, United States Navy*

SHERMAN (WHEC 720) — *1970, US Navy, PH3 L. J. Lafeir Jnr.*

BOUTWELL (WHEC 719) — *1971, Giorgio Arra*

High Endurance Cutters —*continued*

6 HIGH ENDURANCE CUTTERS (WHEC): "CAMPBELL" (327) CLASS

Name	*No.*	*Builder*	*Laid down*	*Launched*	*Completed*
BIBB (ex-*George M. Bibb*)	WHEC 31	Charleston Navy Yard	18 May 1935	14 Jan 1937	19 Mar 1937
CAMPBELL (ex-*George W. Campbell*)	WHEC 32	Philadelphia Navy Yard	1 May 1935	3 June 1936	22 Oct 1936
DUANE (ex-*William J. Duane*)	WHEC 33	Philadelphia Navy Yard	1 May 1935	3 June 1936	16 Oct 1936
INGHAM (ex-*Samual D. Ingham*)	WHEC 35	Philadelphia Navy Yard	1 May 1935	3 June 1936	6 Nov 1936
SPENCER (ex-*John C. Spencer*)	WHEC 36	New York Navy Yard	11 Sep 1935	6 Jan 1936	13 May 1937
TANEY (ex-*Roger B. Taney*)	WHEC 37	Philadelphia Navy Yard	1 May 1935	3 June 1936	19 Dec 1936

Displacement, tons	2 216 standard; 2 414 full load
Length, feet	308 wl; 327 oa
Beam, feet	41
Draft, feet	15
Guns	1—5 inch (*127 mm*) 38 cal dual-purpose; 2—81 mm mortars several ·50 cal MG
A/S weapons	Removed
Main engines	Geared turbines (Westinghouse); 6 200 shp; 2 shafts
Boilers	2 (Babcock & Wilcox)
Speed, knots	19·8
Complement	143 (13 officers, 130 enlisted men.

Rated as 327-foot cutters. These were the Coast Guard's largest cutters until the *Hamilton* was completed in 1967.

The *Duane* served as an amphibious force flagship during the invasion of Southern France in August 1944 and was designated AGC 6 (Coast Guard manned); the other ships of this class, except the lost *Alexander Hamilton* (PG 34), similarly employed but retained Coast Guard number with WAGC prefix (amidships structure built up and one or two additional masts installed); all reverted to gunboat configuration after war (WPG designation). All of these cutters remain in active service. *Spencer* was scheduled to be decommissioned early in 1974.

ASW ARMAMENT. During the 1960s these ships each had an ASW armament of one ahead-firing fixed hedgehog and two Mk 32 triple torpedo launchers; subsequently removed from all ships.

DESIGNATION. These ships were desginated as high endurance cutters (WHEC) on 1 May 1966; previously WPG.

GUNNERY. As built these ships had two 5-inch 51 cal guns (single mounts forward) and several smaller guns; rearmed during World War II with an additional single 5 inch 51 cal gun installed aft plus two or three 3 inch 50 cal anti-aircraft guns, and several 20 mm anti-aircraft guns (depth charge racks installed); *Taney* was experimentally armed with four 5 inch 38 cal guns in single mounts. Armament of all ships after World War II reduced to one 5 inch 38 cal gun and two 40 mm guns.

ENGINEERING. Range is 4 000 miles at 20 knots and 8 000 miles at 10·5 knots.

NOMENCLATURE. Named for secretaries of the Department of Treasury; names shortened to surnames only in 1942.

INGHAM (WHEC 35) *United States Coast Guard*

DUANE (WHEC 33) ***1968, United States Navy***

1 TRAINING CUTTER (WTR) / 1 METEOROLOGICAL CUTTER (WAGW) — "CASCO" (311) CLASS

Name	*No.*	*Builder*	*Laid down*	*Launched*	*Navy Comm.*
UNIMAK	WTR 379 (ex-WHEC 379, ex-AVP 31)	Associated Shipbuilders	15 Feb 1942	15 Feb 1942	31 Dec 1943
GRESHAM (ex-*Willoughby*)	WAGW 387 (ex-WHEC 387, ex-AGP 9, AVP 57)	Lake Washington Shipyard	15 Mar 1943	21 Aug 1943	18 June 1944

Displacement, tons	1 766 standard; 2 800 full load
Length, feet	300 wl; 310·75 oa
Beam, feet	41
Draft, feet	13·5
Guns	1—5 inch (*127 mm*) 38 cal dual-pupose in *Unimak* (removed from *Gresham*)
A/S weapons	Removed
Main engines	Diesels (Fairbanks Morse), 6 080 bhp; 2 shafts
Speed, knots	18 2
Complement	*Gresham* 136 (14 officers, 122 enlisted men) *Unimak* 101 (12 officers, 89 unlisted men)

Rated as 311-foot cutters. These are the survivors of 18 former seaplane tenders transferred from the Navy in 1946-1948 (WAVP/WMEC 370-384 initially on loan and WAVP/WMEC 385-387 on permanent transfer). *Gresham*, modified for ocean station-meterological work; she was decommissioned in 1973. The *Unimak* is a reserve training ship.

DESIGNATION. These ships were designated WAVP in Coast Guard service until changed to high endurance cutters (WHEC) on 1 May 1966. *Unimak* changed to WTR on 28 Nov 1969.

UNIMAK (WTR 379) *United States Coast Guard*

High Endurance Cutters —*continued*

CASCO" CLASS — *Continued*

NGINEERING. Range is 22 000 miles at 11 knots nd 8 000 miles at 19 knots.

ISPOSALS AND TRANSFERS
oos Bay (WHEC376, ex-AVP 36) returned to Navy 1967 and sunk as target; **Dexter** (WHEC 385, ex-GC 18, ex-AVP 11), **Mackinac** (WHEC 371, ex-AVP 3), and **Matagorda** (WHEC 373, ex-AVP 22) returned Navy in 1968 and sunk as targets; **Casco** (WHEC 370, x-AVP 12) returned to Navy in 1969 and sunk as target; **umboldt** (WHEC 372, ex-AVP 21) and **Half Moon** WHEC 378, ex-AVP 26) stricken in 1970; **Yakutat** WHEC 380, ex-AVP 32) and **Bering Strait** (WHEC 82, ex-AVP 34) transferred to South Vietnam on 1 an 1971; **Castle Rock** (WHEC 383, ex-AVP 35) and **ook Inlet** (WHEC 384, ex-AVP 36) transferred to outh Vietnam on 21 Dec 1971; **Chincoteague** (WHEC 75, ex-AVP 48) and **McCulloch** (WHEC 186, ex-AGP , ex-AVP 50) transfererd to South Vietnam on 21 June 972; **Absecon** (WHEC 374, ex-AVP 23) to South ietnam on 15 July 1972; **Rockaway** (WAGO/WHEC 77, ex-AVP 29) and **Barataria** (WHEC 381, ex-AVP 33) ecommissioned in 1972 and 1969, respectively, and waiting disposal.

GRESHAM (WAGW 387 as WHEC) *United States Coast Guard*

11 HIGH ENDURANCE CUTTERS: (WHEC): "OWASCO" (255) CLASS

isplacement, tons	1 563 standard; 1 913 full load
ength, feet	254 oa
eam, feet	43
raft, feet	17
uns	1—5 inch (*127 mm*) 38 cal dual-purpose; 2—81 mm mortars; Several ·50 cal MG
/S weapons	Removed
lain engines	Geared turbines (Westinghouse) with electric drive; 4 000 shp; 1 shaft
oilers	2
peed, knots	18·4
omplement	139 (13 officers, 126 enlisted men)

Name	*No.*	*Laid down*	*Launched*	*Completed*
OWASCO	WHEC 39	17 Nov 1943	18 June 1944	18 May 1945
WINNEBAGO	WHEC 40	1 Dec 1943	2 July 1944	21 June 1945
CHAUTAUQUA	WHEC 41	22 Dec 1943	14 May 1944	4 Aug 1945
WACHUSETT (ex-*Huron*)	WHEC 44	3 July 1944	5 Nov 1944	23 Mar 1946
ESCANABA (ex-*Otsego*)	WHEC 64	25 Oct 1944	25 Mar 1945	20 Mar 1946
WINONA	WHEC 65	8 Nov 1944	22 Apr 1945	15 Aug 1946
KLAMATH	WHEC 66	13 Dec 1944	2 Sep 1945	5 Sep 1946
MINNETONKA (ex-*Sunapee*)	WHEC 67	26 Dec 1944	21 Nov 1945	20 Sep 1946
ANDROSCOGGIN	WHEC 68	30 Dec 1944	16 Sep 1945	20 Sep 1946
MENDOTA	WHEC 69	1 June 1943	29 Feb 1944	2 June 1946
PONTCHARTRAIN (ex-*Okeechobee*)	WHEC 70	1 July 1943	29 Apr 1944	28 July 1945

ated as 255-foot cutters. All built by Western Pipe & eel Company, San Pedro, California, except for the *Mendota* and *Pontchartrain*, built by Coast Guard yard, urtis Bay, Maryland.
ll of these cutters were scheduled to be decommissioned uring 1973 except *Minnetonka* and *Winona* scheduled or mid-1974.

SW ARMAMENT. During the 1960s these ships each ad an ASW armament of one ahead-firing fixed edgehog and two Mk 32 triple torpedo launchers; ubsequently removed from all ships.

ESIGNATION. These ships originally were designated s gunboats (WPG); changed to high endurance cutters WHEC) on 1 May 1966.

NGINEERING. Range is 12 000 miles at 10 knots.

UNNERY. As built these ships each mounted four -inch guns (twin), four 40-mm anti-aircraft guns (twin), nd four 20 mm anti-aircraft guns; subsequently reduced. Original depth charge racks also removed).

ISPOSALS
roquois (WPG 43) was stricken in 1965; **Sebago** WHEC 42) decommissioned in 1972 for disposal.

WACHUSETT (WHEC 44) *1970, United States Coast Guard*

WASCO (WHEC 39) *United States Coast Guard*

SPENCER (WHEC 36)—see previous page *1970, US Coast Guard*

MEDIUM ENDURANCE CUTTERS

16 MEDIUM ENDURANCE CUTTERS (WMEC): "RELIANCE" (210) CLASS

Name	No.	Launched	Completed
RELIANCE	WMEC 515	25 May 1963	20 June 1964
DILIGENCE	WMEC 616	20 July 1963	26 Aug 1964
VIGILANT	WMEC 617	24 Dec 1963	3 Oct 1964
ACTIVE	WMEC 618	31 July 1965	17 Sep 1966
CONFIDENCE	WMEC 619	8 May 1965	19 Feb 1966
RESOLUTE	WMEC 620	30 Apr 1966	8 Dec 1966
VALIANT	WMEC 621	14 Jan 1967	28 Oct 1967
COURAGEOUS	WMEC 622	18 Mar 1967	10 Apr 1968
STEADFAST	WMEC 623	24 June 1967	25 Sep 19
DAUNTLESS	WMEC 624	21 Oct 1967	10 June 19
VENTUROUS	WMEC 625	11 Nov 1967	16 Aug 19
DEPENDABLE	WMEC 626	16 Mar 1968	22 Nov 19
VIGOROUS	WMEC 627	4 May 1968	2 May 19
DURABLE	WMEC 628	29 Apr 1967	8 Dec 19
DECISIVE	WMEC 629	14 Dec 1967	23 Aug 19
ALERT	WMEC 630	19 Oct 1968	4 Aug 19

Displacement, tons	950 standard; 1 000 full load except WMEC 615-619 970 full load
Dimensions, feet	210·5 oa × 34 × 10·5
Guns	1—3 inch (*76 mm*) 50 calibre AA; 2—50 cal MG
Helicopters	1 HH-52 or HH-3 helicopter embarked for missions
Main engines	2 turbo-charged diesels; 2 shafts; 5 000 hp = 18· knots; WMEC 615-619 also have 2 gas turbines (2 000 hp); no speed increase
Complement	61 (7 officers, 54 enlisted men)

Rated as 210-foot cutters. Designed for search and rescue duties. Design features include 360-degree visibility from wheelhouse; helicopter flight deck (no hangar); and engine exhaust vent at stern in place of conventional funnel. Capable of towing ships up to 10 000 tons. Air conditioned throughout except engine room; high degree of habitability.

WMEC 615-617 built by Todd Shipyards; WMEC 618 built by Christy Corp; WMEC 619, 625, 628, 629 built by Coast Guard Yard, Curtis Bay, Baltimore, Maryland; WMEC 620-624, 626, 627, 630 by American Ship-building Co.

All of these cutters are active.

AIRCRAFT. The *Alert* was the first US ship fitted with the Canadian-developed "Beartrap" helicopter hauldown system. An HH-52A helicopter conducted trials late in 1969, making 30 successful landings despite winds over 40 mph.

No further procurement of this system has been funded.

DESIGNATION. These ships were originally designated as patrol craft (WPC); changed to WMEC on 1 May 1966.

ENGINEERING. Fitted with controllable-pitch propellers. The first five ships have twin Solar, 2 000 hp gas turbines in addition to the diesels common to all ships, of this class.

Diesels are ALCO model 251-B.

Range is 6 100 miles at 13 knots for WMEC 615-619 and 6 100 miles at 14 knots for later ships.

DILIGENCE (WMEC 616) landing HH-52A — *1969, United States Coast Guard*

VIGILANT (WMEC 617)

Endurance is 1 500 miles at 9 knots.

"ACTIVE" CLASS

All 33 of the steel patrol cutters of the 125-foot "Active" class have been stricken except the *Cuyahoga*, employed as a training ship and listed on a later page. The "Active" class boats were number WPC/WMEC 125-157; completed in 1926-1927.

TUG TYPE

Several tug-type cutters officially are listed as Medium Endurance Cutters. These ships are described on a later page under the heading Oceangoing Tugs.

PATROL BOATS

26 PATROL BOATS (WPB): 95 ft CLASS

CAPE CARTER	95309	**CAPE HORN**	95322
CAPE CORAL	95301	**CAPE JELLISON**	95317
CAPE CORWIN	95326	**CAPE KNOX**	95312
CAPE CROSS	95321	**CAPE MORGAN**	95313
CAPE CURRENT	95307	**CAPE NEWAGEN**	95318
CAPE FAIRWEATHER	95314	**CAPE ROMAIN**	95319
CAPE FOX	95316	**CAPE SHOALWATER**	95324
CAPE GEORGE	95306	**CAPE SMALL**	95300
CAPE GULL	95304	**CAPE STARR**	95320
CAPE HATTERAS	95305	**CAPE STRAIT**	95308
CAPE HEDGE	95311	**CAPE UPRIGHT**	95303
CAPE HENLOPEN	95328	**CAPE WASH**	95310
CAPE HIGGON	95302	**CAPE YORK**	95332

CG 95321—95335	**CG 95312—95314, 95316—95320**	**CG 95300—95311**
"C" Class (built 1958-59)	"B" Class (built 1955-56)	"A" Class (built 1953)

Displacement, tons	106 (B); 105 (A); 98 (C))
Dimensions, feet	95 oa × 19 × 6
Guns	16 cutters have 1—81 mm mortar and 2—50 cal MG; 10 cutters have 2—50 cal MG
Main engines	4 diesels; 2 shafts (2 engines in tandam each shaft); 2 200 bhp = 20 knots max
Endurance, miles	1 500 cruising range
Complement	14 (1 officer, 13 enlisted men)

Rated as 95 ft Cutters. Designed and built at Coast Guard Yard, Curtis Bay, Marylan for port security, search and rescue. Steel hulled, twin screws. "C" class boats for search and rescue, have less electronics.

ENGINEERING. Diesels are Cummings VT12-600M. Range is 2 600 miles for "A" class, 3 000 miles for "B" class, and 2 800 miles for "C" class, all at 9 knots.

TRANSFERS. Nine boats of this type were transferred to the South Korean Navy i 1968: *Cape Falcon* (95330), *Cape Providence* (95335), *Cape Rosier* (95333), *Cap Sable* (95334), *Cape Trinity* (95331), *Cape Darby* (95323), *Cape Florida* (95325, *Cape Kiwanda* (95329), and *Cape Porpoise* (95327).

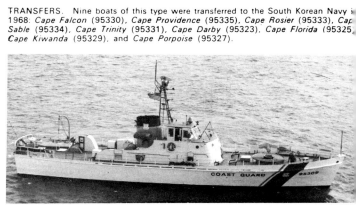

CAPE CARTER (WPB 95309) — *1968 U.S. Coast Guard*

Patrol Boats—*continued*

CAPE CROSS (WPB 95321) *1969, US Coast Guard*

53 PATROL BOATS (WPB): 82ft CLASS

Name	No.	Name	No.
POINT ARENA	82346	POINT LOBOS	82366
POINT BAKER	82342	POINT LOOKOUT	82341
POINT BARROW	82348	POINT MONROE	82353
POINT BATAN	82340	POINT NOWELL	82363
POINT BENNETT	82351	POINT RICHMOND	82370
POINT BONITA	82347	POINT ROBERTS	82332
POINT BRIDGE	82338	POINT SAL	82352
POINT BROWN	82362	POINT SPENCER	82349
POINT CHARLES	82361	POINT STEELE	82359
POINT CHICO	82339	POINT STUART	82358
POINT COUNTESS	82335	POINT SWIFT	82312
POINT DIVIDE	82337	POINT THATCHER	82314
POINT ESTERO	82344	POINT TURNER	82365
POINT EVANS	82354	POINT VERDE	82311
POINT FRANCIS	82356	POINT WARDE	82368
POINT FRANKLIN	82350	POINT WELLS	82343
POINT GLASS	82336	POINT WHITEHORN	82364
POINT HANNON	82355	POINT WINSLOW	82360
POINT HERRON	82318	POINT BARNES	82371
POINT HEYER	82369	POINT BROWER	82372
POINT HIGHLAND	82333	POINT CAMDEN	82373
POINT HOPE	82302	POINT CARREW	82374
POINT HURON	82357	POINT DORAN	82375
POINT JUDITH	82345	POINT HARRIS	82376
POINT KNOLL	82367	POINT HOBART	82377
POINT LEDGE	82334	POINT JACKSON	82378
		POINT MARTIN	82379

CG 82332—82370
"C" class (built 1962-63 and 1965-67)

CG 82371—82379
"D" Class (built 1969-70)

Displacement, tons	64 standard; 67 full load
Dimensions, feet	78·1 wl; 83 oa × 17·2 × 5·8
Guns	C Class: 1—81 mm mortar and 1—50 cal MG or 2—·50 cal MG (except *Point Steele* unarmed) D Class: 2—·50 cal MG
Main engines	2 diesels; 2 shafts; 1 600 bhp = 20 knots
Complement	8 (enlisted men)

Rated as 82 ft Cutters. Designed and built at Coast Guard Yard, for law enforcement, search and rescue. Steel hulls, unmanned engine room controlled from the bridge, power steering and air conditioning. "C" class modifications (also 82318) include increase in bhp to 1 600 and speed to 20 knots. In 1965 26 of these craft were deployed with the Navy and transferred to duty in Vietnam (subsequently transferred to South Vietnamese Navy). As a result 17 replacement cutters were added to the construction programme plus nine already planned. Of the latter, *Point Arena, Point Barrow, Point Bonita, Point Franklin, Point Judith* and *Point Spencer* were built under the Fiscal Year 1965 Programme by Martinac SB, Tacoma, Wash, and 82351 to 82370 in the 1966 programme. Nine "D" class cutters built by Coast Guard Yard with first, *Point Barnes*, completed on 19 Dec 1969.

Range is 1 500 miles at 9 knots.

NOMENCLATURE. CG 82301-82344 were assigned "Point" names in Jan 1964.

TRANSFERS. All 26 boats of this class that comprised Coast Guard Squadron One in Vietnam have been transferred to the South Vietnamese Navy: *Point League* (82304) *Point Garnet* (82310, *Point Clear* (82315), *Point Gammon* (82328), *Point Comfort*, (82317), *Point Ellis* (82330), *Point Slocum* (82313), *Point Hudson* (82322) transferred in 1969; *Point Arden* (82309), *Point Banks* (82 327), *Point Caution* (82301), *Point Cypress* (82326), *Point Dume* (82325), *Point Glover* (82307), *Point Grace* (82323), *Point Grey* (82324), *Point Jefferson* (82306), *Point Kennedy* (82320), *Point Lomas* (82321), *Point Mást* (82316), *Point Monroe* (82331), *Point Orient* (82319), *Point Partridge* (82305), *Point Welcome* (82329), *Point White* (82308) *Point Young* (82303) in 1970.

POINT BENNETT (WPB 82351) *1969, United States Coast Guard*

AIR CUSHION VEHICLES

2 AIR CUSHION VEHICLES (ACV): SK-5 TYPE

HOVER 01 **HOVER** 03

Weight, tons	8·5 normal gross; 10 overload gross
Dimensions, feet	38·8 oa × 23·8 × 16 (height)
Guns	Removed
Main engines	1 gas turbine (General electric); 1 150 shp; 1 three-bladed, variable-pitch aircraft propeller = 60 knots
Complement	3+ (enlisted men)

These are Americanised versions of the British-developed SR.N5 hovercraft. Built as the SK-5 by Bell Aerosystems of Buffalo, New York, under licence from Saunders-Roe Division of Westland Aircraft Limited. Delivered to US Navy late in 1965 and designated Patrol Air Cushion Vehicles (PACV) 1 and 3; transferred to the US Coast Guard in Oct 1969 for evaluation in search, rescue, support of navigation aids, and possibly law enforcement missions.

The PACV 1-3 were twice deployed to South Vietnam in 1966-1969. The craft encountered mixed success in their two combat deployments they were found lacking in coastal operations but were highly successful in the marshy Plain of Reeds during the wet season.

In overhaul from July 1970 to October 1970, with operational evaluation commencing in January 1971. Both were to be discarded during 1973.

In Coast Guard service the craft are unarmed and can normally carry 15 to 18 passengers in cabin in addition to minimum three-man crew.

DESIGN. The hard bottom of the ACVs travels on a cushion of air more than four feet thick. Flexible, air-actuated trunks provide obstacle clearance and ditch crossing capability over land and improved riding qualities over water. A large buoyancy chamber subdivided into watertight compartments, provides flotation on water.

ENGINEERING. A General Electric 7LM-100 marine gas turbine engine drives both the lift fan, which forces air downward to create the air cushion beneath the craft, and the aft-mounted propeller which provides propulsion. This is a marine version of the T58-8 aircraft engine.

GUNNERY. Armament in Navy service modified to various combinations; official armament during 1968-1969 deployment was 2—·50 calibre MG in a twin mount over the cabin (see photograph), 2—7·62 mm MG (single), and 2 grenade launchers. Unarmed in Coast Guard service.

LOSS. Hover 2 of this type sunk in Lake Michigan on 23 Nov 1971; no loss of life.

HOVER 01 *1970, US Coast Guard, PHC Ralph Sunderlin*

HOVER 02 (accidentally lost) *1970, United States Coast Guard*

POINT THATCHER (WPB 82314) *1971, United States Coast Guard*

ICEBREAKERS

2 ICEBREAKERS (WAGB): NEW CONSTRUCTION

Name	No.	Builder	Laid down	Completed
POLAR STAR	WAGB 10	Lockheed Shipbuilding Co	15 May 1972	Aug 1975
POLAR SEA	WAGB 11	Lockheed Shipbuilding Co.		

Displacement, tons	12 200 full load
Length, feet	185 oa × 78 × 28
Main engines	Diesels supplemented by gas turbines; 66 000 hp; 3 shafts = 17 knots
Complement	138 plus 10 scientists

The Fiscal Year 1971 budget for the department of Transportation provides $59 000 000 for construction of a new Coast Guard icebreaker, the first ship in a programme to replace the "Wind" class ships. A second ship was provided in the Fiscal Year 1973 budget.

The new icebreaker will be the largest Coast Guard-operated ship. The icebreaking capability of this ship with diesel power alone will exceed that of the US icebreaker *Glacier* and approach that of the Soviet *Moskva* and the Canadian *St. Laurent*; with the gas turbines operating, the new US icebreaker's available shaft horsepower will exceed that of any icebreaker afloat including the Soviet nuclear-powered ship *Lenin*. Both ships are under construction at the Lockheed Shipbuilding & Construction Co, Seattle, Washington.

ENGINEERING. This new WAGB design provides for conventional diesel engines for normal cruising and gas turbines for maximum power situations. The diesel engines will drive generators producing AC power; the main propulsion DC motors will draw power through rectifiers permitting absolute flexibility in the delivery of power from alternate sources. The use of controllable-pitch propellers on three shafts will permit manoeuvering in heavy ice without the risk to propeller blades caused by stopping the shaft while going from ahead to astern.
The Coast Guard had given consideration to the use of nuclear power for an icebreaker, however, at this time the gas turbine-diesel combination can achieve the desirable power requirements without the added cost and operating restrictions of a nuclear powerplant.

POLAR SEA *1971, United States Coast Guard*

1 ICEBREAKER (WAGB): "GLACIER" TYPE

Name	No.	Launched	Commissioned
GLACIER	WAGB 4 (ex-AGB 4)	27 Aug 1954	27 May 1955

Displacement, tons	8 449 full load
Dimensions, feet	309·6 oa × 74 × 29
Guns	4—·50 cal MG (see *Gunnery* notes)
Helicopters	2 helicopters normally embarked
Main engines	Diesel-electric (10 Fairbanks-Morse diesels and 2 Westinghouse electric motors); 2 shafts; 21 000 hp = 17·6 knots
Complement	229 (14 officers, 215 enlisted men)

The largest icebreaker in US service; designed and built by Ingalls Shipbuilding Corp, Pascagoula, Mississippi laid down on 3 Aug 1953. Transferred from Navy (AGB 4) to Coast Guard on 30 June 1966. During 1972 the *Glacier* and assigned helicopters were painted red to improve visibility in Arctic regions. All other icebreakers painted red during 1973.

ENGINEERING. When built the *Glacier* had the largest capacity single-armature DC motors ever built and installed in a ship. Range is 29 200 miles at 12 knots or 12 000 miles at 17·6 knots.

GUNNERY. As built the *Glacier* was armed with two 5 inch AA guns (twin), six 3 inch AA guns (twin), and four 20 mm AA guns; lighter weapons removed prior to transfer to Coast Guard; 5 inch guns removed in 1969.

GLACIER (WAGB 4) *1968, US Coast Guard*

6 ICEBREAKERS (WAGB): "WIND" CLASS

Name	No.	Launched
STATEN ISLAND (ex-*Northwind*)	WAGB 278 (ex-AGB 5)	28 Dec 1942
SOUTHWIND	WAGB 280 (ex-AGB 3)	8 Mar 1943
WESTWIND	WAGB 281	31 Mar 1943
NORTHWIND	WAGB 282	25 Feb 1945
BURTON ISLAND	WAGB 283 (ex-AGB 1, ex-AG 88)	30 Apr 1946
EDISTO	WAGB 284 (ex-AGB 2, ex-AG 89)	29 May 1946

Displacement, tons	3 500 standard; 6 515 full load
Dimensions, feet	250 pp; 269 oa × 63·5 × 29
Helicopters	2 helicopters normally embarked
Guns	4—·50 cal MG (see *Gunnery* notes)
Main engines	Diesel-electric (6 diesels); 2 shafts; 10 000 hp = 16 knots
Complement	181 (14 officers, 167 enlisted men)

Originally seven ships in this class built by Western Pipe & Steel Co, San Pedro, California. Five ships were delivered to the US Coast Guard during World War II and two to the US Navy in 1956.
Three of the Coast Guard ships were transferred to the Soviet Navy in 1945: *Northwind* (first of name, WAGB 278) renamed *Severni Veter* and returned to US Navy in 1951 and commissioned as *Staten Island* (AGB 5); *Southwind* renamed *Kapitan Belusov* and returned to US Navy in 1950 and commissioned as *Atka* (AGB 3); *Westwind* renamed *Severni Polius* and returned to US Coast Guard in 1951.
The four "Wind" class ships in the US Navy were transferred to the Coast Guard: *Edisto* on 20 Oct 1965, *Staten Island* on 1 Feb 1966, *Atka* on 20 Oct 1966 (renamed *Southwind* in January 1967), and *Burton Island* on 15 Dec 1966.
The *Edisto* operates on the Great Lakes.

AIRCRAFT. All of these ships have telescoping hangars to protect helicopters and permit maintenance at night and in inclement weather.

ENGINEERING. These ships were built with a bow propeller shaft in addition to the two stern shafts; bow shaft removed from all units because it would continually break in hard storis ice. Main engines are Fairbanks Morse 38D81/8. Range is 38 000 miles at 10·5 knots or 16 000 miles at 16 knots.

GUNNERY. As built the five Coast Guard ships each mounted four 5 inch guns (one twin mount forward and one twin mount aft on 01 level) and 12 40 mm anti-aircraft guns (quad); the two Navy Ships were completed with only forward twin 5 inch mount (as built a catapult and cranes were fitted immediately behind the funnel and one floatplane was carried). Armament reduced after war and helicopter platform eventually installed in all ships.

During the 1960s the *Eastwind* carried two 3 inch guns (twin), the *Northwind* two 5 inch guns (twin), and the three other ships each mounted one 5 inch gun; all armament removed in 1969-1970.

DISPOSALS
Eastwind WAGB 279 stricken in 1972.

BURTON ISLAND (WAGB 283) *US Coast Guard*

NORTHWIND (WAGB 282) *1969, US Coast Guard*

Icebreakers—*continued*

BURTON ISLAND (WAGB 283) *1971, US Navy, PH2 J. J. Carmerrale*

1 ICEBREAKER (WAGB): "MACKINAW" TYPE

MACKINAW (ex-*Manitowac*) WAGB 83

Displacement, tons	5 252
Dimensions, feet	290 oa × 74 × 19
Helicopters	1 helicopter
Main engines	Diesel; with electric drive; 3 shafts (1 forward, 2 aft); 10 000 bhp = 18·7 knots
Complement	127 (10 officers, 117 enlisted men)

Built by Toledo Shipbuilding Co, Ohio. Laid down on 20 Mar 1943. Launched on 6 Mar 1944. Commissioned on 20 Dec 1944. Completed in Jan 1945. Specially designed and constructed with 1·6 in. plating for service as icebreaker on the great Lakes. Equipped with two 12-ton cranes. Clear area for helicopter is provided on the quarter deck.

Range is 60 000 miles at 12 knots.

MACINAW (WAGB 83) *United States Coast Guard*

1 ICEBREAKER (WAGB): "STORIS" TYPE

STORIS (ex-*Eskimo*) WAGB 38

Displacement, tons	1 715 standard; 1 925 full load
Dimensions, feet	230 oa × 43 × 15
Guns	1—3 in, 50 cal; 2—·50 cal MG
Main engines	Diesel-electric; 1 shaft; 1 800 bhp = 14 knots
Complement	106 (10 officers, 96 enlisted men)

Built by Toledo Shipbuilding Co, Ohio. Laid down 14 July 1941; launched on 4 Apr 1942; completed on 30 Sep 1942. Ice patrol tender. Strengthened for ice navigation. Employed on Alaskan service. Search, rescue and law enforcement are primary duties. Makes supply runs to isolated Coast Guard installations within her patrol area. Her designation was changed from WAG to WAGB on 1 May 1966.
Range is 22 000 miles at 8 knots or 12 000 miles at 4 knots.

STORIS (WAGB 38) *1968 US Coast Guard*

TRAINING CUTTERS

The Coast Guard operates two training cutters and two reserve training cutters, one of the latter being the *Unimak*, listed earlier with the high endurance cutters. In addition, the former training cutter *Tanager* is in reserve.
The *Eagle*, employed to train cadets at the Coast Guard Academy, is the only sail training ship operated by any US service.

1 TRAINING CUTTER (WTR): Ex-RADIO SHIP

(ex-*Coastal Messenger*, ex-USS *Doddridge*, *AK* 176)

COURIER WTR 410 (ex-WAGR)

Displacement, tons	5 800 standard; 7 500 full load
Dimensions, feet	338·5 × 50·3 × 18
Armament	None
Main engines	Diesel direct drive (Nordberg 82D diesel); 1 700 bhp = 11 knots
Complement	55 (10 officers, 45 enlisted men)

CI-M-AVI type, launched in 1945. Built as a naval cargo ship but not used by the Navy. Acquired by the US Coast Guard from the US Maritime Commission in 1951, fitted out as an overseas radio relay base, manned by the Coast Guard and operated for the United States Information Agency as a relay station for the "Voice of America" broadcasts from 7 Sep 1952 until 17 May 1964. She was virtually a seagoing radio broadcasting station with transmitting equipment the most powerful of its kind ever installed in any vessel. She commissioned on 15 Feb 1952 and began broadcasts on 7 Sep 1952, being stationed at Island of Rhodes, Greece. She returned to the USA in 1964 and was decommissioned on 25 Aug 1964, but was converted and recommissioned on 1 July 1965 and employed as a training "cutter" for the reserve at Yorktown, Va. Her special communication equipment has been removed.
The *Courier* has been decommissioned and is in reserve.

DISPOSALS
Lamar WTR 899 ex-PCE 899 stricken in 1971 (see 1971-1972 edition for description and photograph).

COURIER (WTR 410) *1968, United States Coast Guard*

1 TRAINING CUTTER (WTR): Ex-MINESWEEPER

TANAGER WTR 885 (ex-WTR 385, ex-MSF 385)

Displacement, tons	890 standard; 1 077 full load
Dimensions, feet	215 wl; 221 oa × 32·3 × 14
Guns	removed
Main engine	Diesel-electric; 2 shafts; 3 474 bhp = 17·5 knots
Complement	47 (6 officers, 41 men) plus 80 reserve trainee

Former fleet minesweeper, large steel-hulled type, acquired from the US Navy in 1964 as a Coast Guard Reserve training ship, at Yorktown, Va. Her minesweeping equipment was removed and a living compartment added. Built by American Shipbuilding Co, Lorain, Ohio. Laid down on 29 Mar 1944. Launched on 9 Dec 1944
Endurance is 7 200 miles at 9 knots.
Armament of single 3 inch gun and ASW hedgehog have been removed.
The *Tanager* was decommissioned on 1 Feb 1972 and may be stricken in near future.

TANAGER (WTR 885) *1970, United States Coast Guard*

Training Cutters —*continued*

1 TRAINING CUTTER (IX): "ACTIVE" CLASS

CUYAHOGA WIX 157 (ex-WMEC 157, ex-WPC 157, ex-WAG 26)

Dimensions, feet	215 oa × 24 × 8
Guns	Removed
Main engines	Diesel; 2 shafts; 800 bhp = 13·2 knots
Complement	11 (1 officer, 10 enlisted men)

Built in 1926 as one of the 33 "Active" class steel patrol boats. The *Cuyahoga* is the only cutter of this type remaining on the Coast Guard list. She is based at Yorktown, Virginia.

CUYAHOGA (WIX 157) *1966, United States Coast Guard*

1 TRAINING BARK (IX)

EAGLE (ex-*Horst Wessel*) WIX 327

Displacement, tons	1 634; 1 816 full load
Dimensions, feet	265·8 pp; 295·2 oa × 39·3 × 17
Sail area, sq ft	21 351
Height of masts, feet	150
Main engines	Auxiliary diesel; 740 bhp 1 shaft; = 10·5 knots (as high as 18 knots under full sail alone)
Oil fuel, tons	**48**
Endurance, miles	**3 500 at 10 knots with diesel**
Complement	280

Former German training ship for 200 naval cadets. Built by Blohm & Vos, Hamburg. Launched on 13 June 1936. Taken by the United States as part of reparations after the Second World War for employment in US Coast Guard Practice Squadron. Taken over at Bremerhaven in Jan 1946; arrived at home port, New London, Connecticut, in July 1946. She has made several cruises to European waters to train Coast Guard cadets.

CLASS. Sister ship, *Albert Leo Schlageter*, was also taken by the United States in 1945 but was sold to Brazil in 1948 and re-sold to Portugal in 1962. Another ship of similar design, the *Gorch Foch*, transferred to the Soviet Union in 1946 and survives as the *Tovarisch*.

EAGLE (WIX 327) *United States Coast Guard*

SEAGOING TENDERS

35 SEAGOING TENDERS (WLB) / 1 OCEANOGRAPHIC CUTTER (WAGO) — "BALSAM" CLASS

Name	No.	Launched	Name	No.	Launched
BALSAM *	WLB 62	1942	**BITTERSWEET**	WLB 389	1944
COWSLIP	WLB 277	1942	**BLACKHAW***	WLB 390	1944
GENTIAN	WLB 290	1942	**BLACKTHORN**	WLB 391	1944
LAUREL	WLB 291	1942	**BRAMBLE** *	WLB 392	1944
CLOVER	WLB 292	1942	**FIREBUSH**	WLB 393	1944
EVERGREEN	WAGO 295	1943	**HORNBEAM**	WLB 394	1944
SORREL *	WLB 296	1943	**IRIS**	WLB 395	1944
IRONWOOD	WLB 297	1944	**MALLOW**	WLB 396	1944
CITRUS *	WLB 300	1943	**MARIPOSA**	WLB 397	1944
CONIFER	WLB 301	1943	**SAGEBRUSH**	WLB 399	1944
MADRONA	WLB 302	1943	**SALVIA**	WLB 400	1944
TUPELO	WLB 303	1943	**SASSAFRAS**	WLB 401	1944
MESQUITE	WLB 305	1943	**SEDGE** *	WLB 402	1944
BUTTONWOOD	WLB 306	1943	**SPAR** *	WLB 403	1944
PLANETREE	WLB 307	1943	**SUNDEW** *	WLB 404	1944
PAPAW	WLB 308	1943	**SWEETBRIER**	WLB 405	1944
SWEETGUM	WLB 309	1943	**ACACIA**	WLB 406	1944
BASSWOOD	WLB 388	1944	**WOODRUSH**	WLB 407	1944

Displacement, tons	935 standard; 1 025 full load
Dimensions, feet	180 oa × 37 × 13
Guns	1—3 inch 50 calibre in *Citrus, Cowslip, Hornbeam, Sedge,* and *Sorrel* (original armament); replaced by ·50 calibre MG in others; six are unarmed
Main engines	Diesel electric;-1 shaft; 1 000 hp in tenders numbered in WLB 62-303 series except *Ironwood* = 12·8 knots; others 1 200 hp = 13 knots except *Sundew* 1 800 hp = 15 knots
Complement	53 (6 officers, 47 enlisted men)

Seagoing buoy tenders. *Ironwood* built by Coast Guard yard at Curtis Bay, Baltimore, Maryland; others by Marine Iron & Shipbuilding Co, Duluth, Minnesota or Zeneth Dredge Co, Duluth, Minnesota.

The *Evergreen* has been refitted as an oceanographic cutter (WAGO) and is painted white.

Eight ships indicated by asterisks are strengthened for icebreaking.

Three ships, *Cowslip, Bittersweet,* and *Hornbean,* have controllable pitch, bow-thrust propellers to assist in manoeuvring. All WLBs have a 20-ton capacity boom.

DISPOSALS AND TRANSFERS

Redbud WLB 398 (ex-US Navy T-AKL 398, ex-Coast Guard WAGL 398) transferred to Philippines on 1 Mar 1972; **Cactus** WLB 270, **Woodbine** WLB 289 stricken in 1972.

Ex-Army mineplanter type: **Magnolia** WLB 328 (ex-ACM 3) stricken in 1971; **Ivy** WLB 329 (ex-ACM 5), **Jonquil** WLB 330 (ex-ACM 6), **Willow** WLB 332 (ex-ACM 8) stricken in 1968, last transferred to Philippines in 1971; **Heather** WLB 331 (ex-ACM 7) stricken in 1967.

BITTERSWEET (WLB 389) no gun *US Coast Guard*

HORNBEAM (WLB 394) gun aft of funnel ***1969, US Coast Guard***

EAGLE (WIX 327) *United States Navy*

COASTAL TENDERS

5 COASTAL TENDERS (WLM): "RED" CLASS

Name	No.	Launched	Name	No.	Launched
RED WOOD	WLM 685	1964	**RED CEDAR**	WLM 688	1970
RED BEECH	WLM 688	1964	**RED OAK**	WLM 689	1971
RED BIRCH	WLM 687	1965			

Displacement, tons: 471 standard; 512 full load
Dimensions, feet: 157 oa × 33 × 6
Main engines: 2 diesels; 2 shafts; 1 800 hp = 12·8 knots
Complement: 31 (4 officers, 27 enlisted men)

All built by Coast Guard yard, Curtis Bay, Baltimore, Maryland. *Red Cedar* completed late in 1970 and *Red Oak* late in 1971.
Fitted with controllable-pitch propellers and bow thrusters; steel hulls strengthened for light icebreaking. Steering and engine controls on each bridge wing as well as in pilot house. Living spaces are air conditioned. Endurance is 3 000 miles at 11·6 knots. Fitted with 10-ton capacity boom.

RED BIRCH (WLM 687) — *1968, U.S. Coast Guard*

3 COASTAL TENDERS (WLM): "HOLLYHOCK" CLASS

FIR WLM 212 **HOLLYHOCK** WLM 220 **WALNUT** WLM 252

Displacement, tons: 989
Dimensions, feet: 175 × 34 × 12
Main engines: Diesel reduction; 2 shafts; 1 350 bhp = 12 knots
Complement: 40 (5 officers, 35 enlisted men)

Launched in 1937 (*Hollyhock*) and 1939 (*Fir* and *Walnut*). *Walnut* was re-engined by Willamette Iron & Steel Co, Portland, Oregon, in 1958. Redesignated Coastal Tenders, WLM, instead on Buoy Tenders, WAGL on 1 Jan 1965. Fitted with 20-ton capacity boom.

WALNUT (WLM 252) — *1963, United States Coast Guard*

1 COASTAL TENDER (WLM): "JUNIPER" TYPE

JUNIPER WLM 224

Displacement, tons: 794
Dimensions, feet: 177 × 33 × 9·2
Main engines: Diesel, with electric drive; 2 shafts; 900 bhp = 10·8 knots
Complement: 38 (4 officers, 34 enlisted men)

Launched on 18 May 1940. Redesignated WLM vice WALG on 1 Jan 1965. Fitted with 20-ton capacity boom.

DISPOSALS

Several coastal tenders of various types have been stricken. **Hemlock** (WAGL 217) in 1958, **Violet** (WAGL 250) in 1962, **Arbutus** (WLM 203, ex-WAGL 203) in 1967, **Mistletoe** (WLM 237, ex-WAGL 237) in 1968, **Lilac** (WLM 277) in 1972.

Of the two "Hawthorne" class coastal tenders, **Hawthorne** WLM 215 (ex-WAGL 215) was decommissioned on 24 July 1964, and **Oak** WLM 239 (ex-WAGL 239) on 1 Sep **1964. Both were officially deleted from the list in 1965. The larger but older Cedar was sold in June 1955.**

Coastal Tenders—*continued*

JUNIPER (WLM 224) — *United States Coast Guard*

7 COASTAL TENDERS (WLM): "WHITE" CLASS

WHITE BUSH WLM 542
WHITE HEATH WLM 545
WHITE HOLLY WLM 543
WHITE LUPINE WLM 546
WHITE PINE WLM 547
WHITE SAGE WLM 544
WHITE SUMAC WLM 540

Displacement, tons: 435 standard; 600 full load
Dimensions, feet: 133 oa × 31 × 9
Main engines: Diesel; 2 shafts; 600 bhp = 9·8 knots
Complement: 21 (1 officer, 20 enlisted men)

All launched in 1943. All seven ships are former US Navy YFs, adapted for the Coast Guard. The *White Alder* (WLM 541) was sunk in a collision on 7 Dec 1968. Fitted with 10-ton capacity boom.

WHITE HOLLY (WLM 543) — *1968, U S Coast Guard*

INLAND TENDERS

TERN WLI 80801

Displacement, tons: 168 full load
Dimensions, feet: 80 oa × 25 × 5
Main engines: Diesels; 2 shafts; 450 hp = 10 knots
Complement: 7 (enlisted men)

The *Tern* is prototype for a new design of inland buoy tenders. A cutaway stern and gantry crane (the first installed in a Coast Guard tender) permit lifting buoys aboard from the stern. The crane moves on rails that extend forward to the deck house. Fitted with 125 hp bow thruster to improve manoeuvrability. Air conditioned.
Built by Coast Guard yard at Curtis Bay, Baltimore, Maryland. Launched on 15 June 1968 and placed in service on 7 Feb 1969. She will undergo extensive evaluation to determine if design advantage justifies further craft of this type.

TAMARACK WLI 248

Displacement, tons: 400 full load
Dimensions, feet: 124 oa × 30 × 8
Main engines: Diesels; 1 shaft; 520 hp = 10 knots

Launched in 1934. Fitted with 10-ton capacity boom. Out of service.

MAPLE WLI 234 **NARCISSUS** WLI 238 **ZINNIA** WLI 255

Displacement, tons: 370 full load
Dimensions, feet: 122 oa × 28 × 8
Main engines: Diesels; 2 shafts; 980 hp (800 in *Maple*) = 10·3 knots except *Maple* 10 knots
Complement: 30 (1 officer, 19 enlisted men)

All launched in 1939. The *Maple* has a 6½-ton capacity boom; others have a 10-ton capacity boom. *Narcissus* decommissioned in 1971 and *Zinnia* in 1972.

COSMOS WLI 293
BARBERRY WLI 294
RAMBLER WLI 298
BLUEBELL WLI 313
SMILAX WLI 315
PRIMROSE WLI 316
VERBENA WLI 317

Displacement, tons: 178 full load
Dimensions, feet: 100 oa × 24 × 5
Main engines: Diesels; 2 shafts 600; hp = 10·5 knots except *Barberry* 11 knots
Complement: 15 (1 officer, 14 enlisted men)

Cosmos launched in 1942, *Barberry* in 1943, *Bluebell* in 1945, others in 1944. The *Barberry* has controllable-pitch propellers. The *Barberry* and *Verbena* are fitted with pile drivers. *Barberry* decommissioned in 1970.

AZALEA WLI 641

Displacement, tons: 200 full load
Dimensions, feet: 100 oa × 24 × 5
Main engines: Diesels; 2 shafts; 440 hp = 9 knots
Complement: 14 (1 officer, 13 enlisted men)

Launched in 1958. Fitted with pile driver.

Inland Tenders—*continued*

BUCKTHORN WLI 642

Displacement, tons 200 full load
Dimensions, feet 100 oa × 24 × 4
Main engines Diesels; 2 shafts; 600 hp = 7·3 knots
Complement 14 (1 officer, 13 enlisted men)

Launched in 1963.

CLEMATIS WLI 74286 **SHADBUSH** WLI 74287

Displacement, tons 93 full load
Dimensions, feet 74 oa × 19 × 4
Main engines Diesels; 2 shafts; 330 hp = 8 knots
Complement 9 (enlisted men)

Launched in 1944.

BLUEBERRY WLI 65302

Displacement, tons 45 full load
Dimensions, feet 65 oa × 17 × 14
Main engines Diesels; 2 shafts; 330 hp = 10·5 knots
Complement 5 (enlisted men)

Launched in 1942.

BLACKBERRY WLI 65303 **CHOKEBERRY** WLI 65304 **LOGANBERRY** WLI 65305

Displacement, tons 68 full load
Dimensions, feet 65 oa × 17 × 4
Main engines Diesels; 1 shaft; 220 hp = 9 knots
Complement 5 (enlisted men)

Launched in 1946.

BAYBERRY WLI 65400 **ELDERBERRY** WLI 65401

Displacement, tons 68 full load
Dimensions, feet 65 oa × 17 × 4
Main engines Diesels; 2 shafts; 400 hp = 11·3 knots
Complement 5 (enlisted men)

Launched in 1954.

TERN (WLI 80801) *1969, United States Coast Guard*

BUCKTHORN (WLI 642) *1966, United States Coast Guard*

BAYBERRY (WLI 65400) *US Coast Guard*

CONSTRUCTION TENDERS

ANVIL WLIC 75301 **HAMMER** WLIC 75302 **SLEDGE** WLIC 75303 **MALLET** WLIC 75304 **VISE** WLIC 75305 **CLAMP** WLIC 75306 **WEDGE** WLIC 75307 **SPIKE** WLIC 75308 **HATCHET** WLIC 75309 **AXE** WLIC 75310

Displacement, tons 145 full load
Dimensions, feet 75 oa (WLIC 75306-75310 are 76 oa) × 22 × 4
Main engines Diesels; 2 shafts; 600 hp = 10 knots
Complement 9 or 10 (1 officer in *Mallet, Sledge* and *Vise*; 9 enlisted men in all)

Launched 1962-1965

SLEDGE (WLIC 75303) Pushing barge *US Coast Guard*

RIVER TENDERS

SUMAC WLR 311

Displacement, tons *Sumac* 404 full load
Dimensions, feet 115 oa × 30 × 6
Main engines Diesels; 3 shafts; 960 hp = 10·6 knots
Complement 23 (1 officer, 22 enlisted men)

Built in 1943. **Fern** WLR 304 stricken.

DOGWOOD WLR 259 **FORSYTHIA** WLR 63 **SYCAMORE** WLR 268

Displacement, tons 230 full load, except *Forsythia* 280
Dimensions, feet 114 oa × 26 × 4
Main engines Diesels; 2 shafts; 2 800 hp = 11 knots
Complement 21 (1 officer, 20 enlisted men)

Dogwood and *Sycamore* built in 1940; *Forsythia* in 1943.

FOXGLOVE WLR 285.

Displacement, tons 350 full load
Dimensions, feet 114 oa × 30 × 6
Main engines Diesels; 3 shafts; 8 500 hp = 13·5 knots
Complement 21 (1 officer, 20 enlisted men)

Built in 1945.

GOLDENROD WLR 213 **POPLAR** WLR 241

Displacement, tons 235 full load
Dimensions, feet 104 oa × 24 × 4
Main engines Diesels; 2 shafts; 800 hp = 11·5 knots
Complement 17 (1 officer, 16 enlisted men)

Built in 1938 and 1939, respectively.

LANTANA WLR 80310

Displacement, tons 235 full load
Dimensions, feet 80 oa × 30 × 6
Main engines Diesels; 3 shafts; 10 000 hp = 10 knots
Complement 20 (1 officer, 19 enlisted men)

Built in 1943.

GASCONADE WLR 75401 **MUSKINGUM** WLR 75402 **WYACONDA** WLR 75403 **CHIPPEWA** WLR 75404 **CHEYENNE** WLR 75405 **KICKAPOO** WLR 75406 **KANAWHA** WLR 75407 **PATOKA** WLR 75408 **CHENA** WLR 75409

Displacement, tons 145 full load
Dimensions, feet 75 oa × 22 × 4
Main engines Diesel; 2 shafts; 600 hp = 10·8 knots
Complement 12 (enlisted men)

Built 1964-1971.

OLEANDER WLR 73264

Displacement, tons 90 full load
Dimensions, feet 73 oa × 18 × 5
Main engines Diesel; 2 shafts; 300 hp = 12 knots
Complement 10 (enlisted men)

Built in 1940.

River Tenders—*continued*

OSAGE (WLR 65505) *US Coast Guard*

OUACHITA	WLR 65501	**SCIOTO**	WLR 65504
CIMARRON	WLR 65502	**OSAGE**	WLR 65505
OBION	WLR 65503	**SANGAMON**	WLR 65506

Displacement, tons	139 full load
Dimensions, feet	65·6 oa × 21 × 5
Main engines	Diesel; 2 shafts; 600 hp = 12·5 knots
Complement	10 (enlisted men)

Built in 1960-1962.

OCEANGOING TUGS

1 MEDIUM ENDURANCE CUTTER (WMEC) } ARS TYPE
1 OCEANOGRAPHIC CUTTER (WAGO)

Name	No.	Launched	Navy Comm.
ACUSHNET (ex-*Shackle*)	WAGO 167 (ex-WAT 167, ARS 9)	1 Apr 1943	5 Feb 1944
YOCONA (ex-*Seize*)	WMEC 168 (ex-WAT 168, ARS 26)	8 Apr 1944	3 Nov 1944

Displacement, tons	1 557 standard; 1 745 full load
Dimensions, feet	213·5 oa × 39 × 15
Main engines	Diesels; 2 shafts; 3 000 hp = 15·5 knots
Complement	*Acushnet* 64 (7 officers, 57 enlisted men) *Yacona* 72 (7 officers, 65 enlisted men)

Large, steel-hulled tugs transferred from the Navy to the Coast Guard after World War II. Both by Basalt Rock Co, Napa, California. *Acushnet* modified for handling environmental data buoys and reclassified WAGO in 1969; *Yocona* reclassified as WMEC in 1969. Armament removed.

YOCONA (WMEC 168) *1970, United States Coast Guard*

3 MEDIUM ENDURANCE CUTTERS (WMEC): ATF TYPE

Name	No.	Launched	Navy Comm.
CHILULA	WMEC 153 (ex-WAT 153, ATF 153)	1 Dec 1944	5 Apr 1945
CHEROKEE	WMEC 165 (ex-WAT 165, ATF 66)	10 Nov 1939	26 Apr 1940
TAMOROA (ex-*Zuni*)	WMEC 166 (ex-WAT 166, ATF 95)	13 July 1943	9 Oct 1943

Displacement, tons	1 731 full load
Dimensions, feet	205 oa × 38·5 × 17
Guns	1—3 inch 50 calibre; 2—·50 cal MG
Main engines	Diesel electric (General Motors diesel); 1 shaft; 3 000 hp = 16·2 knots
Complement	72 (7 officers, 65 enlisted men)

Steel-hulled tugs transferred from the Navy to the Coast Guard after World War II; *Chilula* officially on loan since 9 July 1956 until stricken from the Navy List on 1 June 1969. Classification of all three ships changed to WMEC in 1969. *Chilula* built by Charleston Shipbuilding & Dry Dock Co, Charleston, South Carolina; *Cherokee* built by Bethlehem Steel Co, Staten Island, New York; *Tamaroa* built by Commercial Iron Works, Portland, Oregon.

DISPOSALS

Avoyel (WMEC 150, ex-WAT 150, ex-ATF 150) stricken in 1970.

Oceangoing Tugs—*continued*

TAMAROA (WMEC 166) *1970, United States Coast Guard*

2 MEDIUM ENDURANCE CUTTERS (WMEC): ATA TYPE

Name	No.	Launched	Navy Comm.
MODOC (ex-*Bagaduce*)	WMEC 194 (ex-WATA 194, ATA 194)	4 Dec 1944	14 Feb 1945
COMANCHE (ex-*Wampanoag*)	WMEC 202 (ex-WATA 202, ATA 202)	10 Oct 1944	8 Dec 1944

Displacement, tons	534 standard; 860 full load
Dimensions, feet	143 oa × 33·8 × 14
Armament	2—·50 cal MG
Main engines	Diesel electric (General Motors diesel); 1 shaft; 1 500 hp = 13·5 knots
Complement	47 (5 officers, 42 enlisted men)

Steel-hulled tugs. The *Modoc* was stricken from the Navy List after World War II and transferred to Maritime Administration; transferred to Coast Guard on 15 Apr 1959. *Comanche* transferred on loan from Navy to Coast Guard from 25 Feb 1959 until stricken from Navy List on 1 June 1969. Both ships reclassified as WMEC in 1969. *Modoc* built by Levingston Shipbuilding Co, Orange, Texas; *Comanche* built by Gulfport Boiler & Welding Works, Port Arthur, Texas.

COMANCHE (WMEC 202) *1969, United States Coast Guard*

HARBOUR TUGS

MANITOU	WYTM 60	**MOHICAN**	WYTM 73	**CHINOOK**	WYTM 96
KAW	WYTM 61	**ARUNDEL**	WYTM 90	**OJIBWA**	WYTM 97
APALACHEE	WYTM 71	**MAMONING**	WYTM 91	**SNOHOMISH**	WYTM 98
YANKTON	WYTM 72	**NAUGATUCK**	WYTM 92	**SAUK**	WYTM 99
		RARITAN	WYTM 93		

Displacement, tons	370 full load
Dimensions, feet	110 oa × 27 × 11
Main engines	Diesel-electric; 1 shaft; 1 000 hp = 11·2 knots
Complement	20 (1 officer, 19 enlisted men)

Built in 1943 except WYTM 90-93 built in 1939.

MESSENGER WYTM 85009

Displacement, tons	230 full load
Dimensions, feet	85 oa × 23 × 9
Main engines	Diesel; 1 shaft; 700 hp = 9·5 knots
Complement	10 (enlisted)

Built in 1944.

CAPSTAN	WYTL 65601	**CATENARY**	WYTL 65606	**LINE**	WYTL 65611
CHOCK	WYTL 65602	**BRIDLE**	WYTL 65607	**WIRE**	WYTL 65612
SWIVEL	WYTL 65603	**PENDANT**	WYTL 65608	**BITT**	WYTL 65613
TACKLE	WYTL 65604	**SHACKLE**	WYTL 65609	**BOLLARD**	WYTL 65614
TOWLINE	WYTL 65605	**HAWSER**	WYTL 65610	**CLEAT**	WYTL 65615

Displacement, tons	72 full load
Dimensions, feet	65 oa × 19 × 7
Main engines	Diesel; 1 shaft; 400 hp = 9·8 knots except WYTL 65601-65606 10·5 knots
Complement	10 (enlisted men)

Built from 1961 to 1967.

SUPPLY SHIPS (WAK)

All Coast Guard supply ships (WAK) have been stricken: **Kukui** WAK 186 ex-AK 174 transferred to Philippines on 1 Mar 1972; see "Balsam" class seagoing tenders for transfer of **Redbud** to Philippines.

NATIONAL OCEANIC AND ATMOSPHERIC ADMINISTRATION

Command

Director, National Ocean Survey: Rear Admiral Allen L. Powell

Associate Director, Office of Fleet Operations: Rear Admiral Eugene A. Taylor

Director, Atlantic Marine Center: Rear Admiral Alfred C. Holmes

Director, Pacific Marine Center: Rear Admiral Herbert R. Lippold Jnr.

Missions

The National Ocean Survey operates the ships of the National Oceanic and Atmospheric Administration (NOAA), a federal agency created in 1970. During 1972-1973 the National Marine Fisheries Service (formerly the Bureau of Commercial Fisheries of the Department of Interior) was consolidated into the NOAA fleet which is operated by the National Ocean Survey. Approximately 15 small ships and craft 65 feet or longer are counted in the National Marine Fisheries Service. The former National Marine Fisheries vessels are not described because of the specialised, non-military nature of their work.

The National Ocean Survey prepares nautical and aeronautical charts; conducts geodetic, geophysical, oceanographic, and marine surveys; predicts tides and currents; tests, evaluates, and calibrates sensing systems for ocean use; and conducts the development and eventually will operate a national system of automated ocean buoys for obtaining environmental information.

The National Ocean Survey is a civilian agency that supports national civilian and military requirements. During time of war the ships and officers of NOAA, can be expected to operate with the Navy, either as a separate service or integrated into the Navy.

Establishment

The "Survey of the Coast" was established by an act of Congress on Feb 10, 1807. Renamed US Coast Survey in 1834 and again renamed Coast and Geodetic Survey in 1878. The commissioned officer corps was established in 1917. The Coast and Geodetic Survey was made a component of the Environmental Science Services Administration on July 13, 1965, when that agency was established within the Department of Commerce. The Environmental Science Services Administration subsequently became the National Oceanic and Atmospheric Administration in October 1970 with the Coast and Geodetic Survey being renamed National Ocean Survey and its jurisdiction expanded to include the US Lake Survey, formerly a part of the US Army Corps of Engineers; the Coast Guard's national data buoy development project; and the Navy's National Oceanographic Instrumentation Centre.

Ships

National Ocean Survey ship designations are: OSS for Ocean Survey Ship, MSS for Medium Survey Ship, CSS for Coastal Survey Ship, and ASV for Auxiliary Survey Vessel. No National Ocean Survey Ships are armed. All ships are active except where noted with specific ships.

Personnel

1973: approx 345 commissioned officers and approx 2 000 civil service personnel. (In addition to commissioned officers of the NOAA, several naval officers are assigned to NOAA, the most senior being Vice Admiral William W. Behrens, Jnr, US Navy, Associate Administrator (NOAA) for Interagency Relations).
ASSOCIATE

Aviation

The National Ocean Survey's Coastal Mapping Division operates two aircraft for aerial photographic missions, a twin-engine de Havilland Canada Buffalo and a twin-engine North American Rockwell Aero Commander.

SURVEY SHIPS

1 OCEANOGRAPIC SURVEY SHIP (OSS): "RESEARCHER" TYPE

Name	*No.*	*Launched*	*Commissioned*
RESEARCHER	OSS 03	5 Oct 1968	8 Oct 1970

Displacement, tons	2 875 light
Dimensions, feet	278·25 oa × 51 × 16·25 (*84·7 m × 15·5 m × 4·9 m*)
Main engines	2 geared diesels; 3 200 hp; 2 shafts = 16 knots
Complement	13 officers, 54 crewmen
Scientists	10 to 13

The *Researcher* was designed specifically for deep ocean research; she is ice strengthened. Estimated cost $10 000 000. Fitted with 20-ton capacity crane, 5-ton capacity crane, four 2½-ton capacity cranes, and an A-frame with 10-ton lift capacity. Built by American Shipbuilding Co, Lorain, Ohio.

DESIGN. Fitted with computerised data acquisition system that automatically samples, processes, and records oceanographic, geophysical, hydrographic, and meteorological data. The 20-ton telescoping crane is designed to handle special sampling equipment and small submersible vehicles as well as small boats. S2-MT-MA74a type.

ENGINEERING. Controllable pitch propellers. A 450-horsepower, 360-degree retractable bow thruster provides sustained low speeds up to seven knots and permits precise positioning. Cruising speed is 14·5 knots with a range of 13000 nautical miles.

2 OCEANOGRAPHIC SURVEY SHIPS (OSS): "OCEANOGRAPHER" CLASS

Name	*No.*	*Launched*	*Commissioned*
OCEANOGRAPHER	OSS 01	18 Apr 1964	13 July 1966
DISCOVERER	OSS 02	29 Oct 1964	29 Apr 1967

Displacement, tons	3 959 light
Dimensions, feet	303·3 oa × 52 × 18·5 (*92·4 m × 15·8 m × 5·6 m*)
Main engines	4 diesels with electric drive; 5 000 bhp; 2 shafts = 16+ knots
Complement	13 officers, 80 crewmen
Scientists	20 to 22

Ice strengthened construction. Fitted with a 5-ton capacity crane and a a 3½-ton capacity crane. Built by Aerojet-General Corp, Jacksonville Shipyard, Jacksonville, Florida. *Discoverer* deactivated in 1973 and placed in reserve.

DESIGN. Fitted with computerised data acquisition system. Center well 8 × 6 feet provides sheltered access to sea for SCUBA divers and for lowering research equipment Six ports in submerged bow observation chamber. S2-MET-MA62a type.

ENGINEERING. A 400-horsepower, through-hull bow thruster provides precise manoeuvring. Not equipped for silent operation. Cruising speed is 16 knots with a range of 15 200 nautical miles.

RESEARCHER (OSS 03) *National Ocean Survey*

OCEANOGRAPHER (OSS 01) *National Ocean Survey*

DISCOVERER (OSS 02) *National Ocean Survey*

Survey Ships—*continued*

DISCOVERER (OSS 02) *National Ocean Survey*

1 HYDROGRAPHIC SURVEY SHIP (OSS): "SURVEYOR" TYPE

Name	*No.*	*Launched*	*Commissioned*
SURVEYOR	OSS 32	25 Apr 1959	30 Apr 1960

Displacement, tons	3 150 light
Dimensions, feet	292·3 oa × 46 × 18 (*88·8 m × 14·0 m × 5·5 m*)
Main engines	1 steam turbine (De Laval); 3 520 shp; 1 shaft = 15+ knots
Complement	14 officers, 76 crewmen
Scientists	8

Specially designed for marine charting and geophysical surveys. Fitted with helicopter platform aft. Ice strenghtened. Twin telescoping 2½-ton capacity cargo booms (forward) and 12½-ton capacity crane. Estimated cost $6 000 000. Built by National Steel & Co, San Diego, California. The *Surveyor* was deactivated in 1973 and placed in reserve.

DESIGN. Large bilge keel (18 inches × 70 feet) permits oceanographic observations to be performed up to Sea State 6. S2-S-RM28a type.

ENGINEERING. Retractable outboard motor mounted to stern for precision manoeuvring. Cruising speed is 15 knots with a range of 10 500 nautical miles.

DISPOSALS

Pathfinder OSS 30, ex-US Navy AGS 1 decommissioned in 1972 and stricken. See 1972-1973 edition for description and photograph.

SURVEYOR (OSS 32) *National Ocean Survey*

3 HYDROGRAPHIC SURVEY SHIPS (MSS): "FAIRWEATHER" CLASS

Name	*No.*	*Launched*	*Commissioned*
FAIRWEATHER	MSS 20	15 Mar 1967	2 Oct 1968
RAINIER	MSS 21	15 Mar 1967	2 Oct 1968
MT. MITCHELL	MSS 22	29 Nov 1966	23 Mar 1968

Displacement, tons	1 798 light
Dimensions, feet	231 oa × 42·07 × 13·9 (*70·2 m × 12·8 m × 4·2 m*)
Main engines	2 diesels; 2 400 bhp; 2 shafts = 13+ knots
Complement	12 officers, 62 crewmen
Scientists	

Ice strengthened. Built by Aeroiet-General Corp, Jacksonville Shipyard, Jacksonville, Fla. SI-MT-MA72a type.

ENGINEERING. Fitted with a 200-horsepower, through-bow thruster for precise manoeuvring. Controllable-pitch propellers. Cruising speed is 13 knots with a range of 9 000 nautical miles.

MT MITCHELL (MSS 22) *National Ocean Survey*

RAINIER (MSS 21) *National Ocean Survey*

FAIRWEATHER (MSS 20) *National Ocean Survey*

DAVIDSON (CSS 31) *National Ocean Survey*

2 HYDROGRAPHIC SURVEY SHIPS (CSS): "McARTHUR" CLASS

Name	*No.*	*Launched*	*Commissioned*
McARTHUR	CSS 30	15 Nov 1965	15 Dec 1966
DAVIDSON	CSS 31	7 May 1966	10 Mar 1967

Displacement, tons	995 light
Dimensions, feet	175 oa × 38 × 11·5 (*53·0 m × 11·5 m × 3·5 m*)
Main engines	2 diesels; 1 600 bhp; 2 shafts = 13·5+ knots
Complement	6 officers, 30 crewmen

Designed for nearshore operations. Ice strengthened. Built by Norfolk SB & DD Co, Norfolk, Virginia. SI-MT-MA70a type.

ENGINEERING. Controllable-pitch propellers. Cruising speed is 13·5 knots with a range of 4 500 nautical miles.

Survey Ships—*continued*

McARTHUR (CSS 30) *National Ocean Survey*

2 HYDROGRAPHIC SURVEY SHIPS (CSS): "PEIRCE" CLASS

Name	*No.*	*Launched*	*Commissioned*
PEIRCE	CSS 28	15 Oct 1962	6 May 1963
WHITING	CSS 29	20 Nov 1962	8 July 1963

Displacement, tons	760 light
Dimensions, feet	164 oa × 33 × 10·1 (*50·0 m × 10·0 m × 3·1 m*)
Main engines	2 diesels; 1 600 bhp; 2 shafts = 12·5+ knots
Complement	6 officers, 30 crewmen

Designed for nearshore operations. Ice strengthened. Built by Marietta Manufacturing Co, Point Pleasant, West Virginia. SI-MT-59a type.

ENGINEERING. Controllable pitch-propellers. Cruising speed is 12·5 knots with a range of 4 500 nautical miles.

PEIRCE (CSS 28) *National Ocean Survey*

WHITING (CSS 29) *National Ocean Survey*

COASTAL VESSELS

2 WIRE DRAG VESSELS (ASV); "RUDE" CLASS

Name	*No.*	*Launched*	*Commissione*
RUDE	ASV 90	17 Aug 1966	29 Mar 196
HECK	ASV 91	1 Nov 1966	29 Mar 196

Displacement, tons	214 light
Dimensions, feet	90 oa × 22 × 7 (*27·4 m × 6·7 m × 2·1 m*)
Main engines	2 diesels; 800 bhp; 2 shafts = 11·5+ knots
Complement	2 officers, 9 crewmen

Designed to search out underwater navigational hazards along the coast using wir drags. Built by Jacobson Shipyard Inc, Oyster Bay, New York. SI-MT-MA71a type A single commanding officer is assigned to both vessels; normally he rides one shi and the executive officer the other.

ENGINEERING. Propellers are guarded by shrouds similar to Kort nozzles. Auxiliary propulsion provides 50 horsepower to each propeller for dragging operations. Cruising speed is 11·5 knots with a range of 740 nautical miles (provisions carried for eight days.)

RUDE (ASV 90) *National Ocean Survey*

1 CURRENT SURVEY VESSEL (ASV); "FERREL" TYPE

Name	*No.*	*Launched*	*Commissione*
FERREL	ASV 92	4 Apr 1968	4 June 196

Displacement, tons	363 light
Dimensions, feet	133·25 × 32 × 7 (*40·5 m × 9·7 m × 2·1 m*)
Main engines	2 diesels; 820 bhp; 2 shafts = 10+ knots
Complement	3 officers, 13 crewmen

Specially designed to conduct nearshore and estuarine current surveys. Limite surface meteorological observations also are made. Buoy workshop provided in 450 square feet of enclosed deck area with buoy stowage on open after deck. Built b Zeigler Shipyard, Jennings, Louisiana. SI-MT-MA83a type.

ENGINEERING. Fitted with 100-horsepower, electric-driven bow thruster. Cruisin speed is 10 knots (provisions for 15 days carried).

FERREL (ASV 92) *National Ocean Survey*

FERREL (ASV 92) *National Ocean Survey*

UNION OF SOVIET SOCIALIST REPUBLICS

Administration	Flag Officers Soviet Navy
Commander-in-Chief of the Soviet Navy and First Deputy Minister of Defence:	Admiral of the Fleet of the Soviet Union Sergei Georgiyevich Gorshkov
First Deputy Commander-in-Chief of the Soviet Navy:	Admiral of the Fleet Vladimir Afanasevich Kasatonov
Assistant Chief of the General Staff of the Armed Forces:	Admiral of the Fleet S. M. Lobov
Deputy Commander-in-Chief:	Admiral N. N. Amelko
Deputy Commander-in-Chief:	Engineer Admiral P. G. Kotov
Deputy Commander-in-Chief:	Engineer Vice Admiral V. G. Novikov
Commander of Naval Aviation:	Marshall Ivan I. Borzov
Chief of the Political Directorate:	Admiral V. M. Grishanov
Chief of Rear Services:	Admiral G. G. Oleynik
Chief of Naval Training Establishments:	Vice-Admiral I. M. Kuznetsov
Chief of Main Naval Staff:	Admiral of the Fleet N. D. Sergeyev
1st Deputy Chief of the Main Naval Staff:	Admiral V. N. Alekseyev
Chief of the Hydrographic Service:	Vice-Admiral A. I. Rassokho
Northern Fleet	
Commander-in-Chief:	Admiral G. M. Yegorov
1st Deputy Commander-in-Chief:	Vice-Admiral N. I. Khovrin
Chief of Staff:	Vice-Admiral V. G. Kichev
In Command of the Political Department:	Admiral F. Ya Sizov
Pacific	
Commander-in-Chief:	Admiral N. I. Smirnov
1st Deputy Commander-in-Chief:	Vice-Admiral V. P. Maslov
Chief of Staff:	Vice-Admiral G. A. Bondarenko
In Command of the Political Department:	Rear-Admiral S. S. Bevz
Black Sea	
Commander-in-Chief:	Admiral V. S. Sysoyev
1st Deputy Commander-in-Chief:	Vice-Admiral N. M. Baranov
Chief of Staff:	Vice-Admiral B. Yamkovoy
In Command of the Political Department:	Vice-Admiral I. S. Rudnev
Baltic	
Commander-in-Chief:	Admiral V. V. Mikhaylin
1st Deputy Commander-in-Chief:	Vice-Admiral L. V. Mizin
Chief of Staff:	Rear-Admiral A. Kosov
In Command of the Political Department:	Rear-Admiral N. I. Shablikov
Caspian Flotilla	
Commander-in-Chief:	Rear-Admiral Ya M. Kudelkin
In Command of the Political Department:	Rear-Admiral P. D. Burlachenko
Leningrad Naval Base	
Commanding Officer:	Vice-Admiral V. M. Leonenkov
In Command of the Political Department:	Rear-Admiral A. A. Plekhanov
Head of the Order of Lenin Naval Academy:	Admiral A. Ya Orel
Head of Frunze Naval College:	Vice-Admiral V. A. Khrenov

SOVIET NAVAL AVIATION

The Soviet Navy operates 1 200 fixed-wing aircraft and helicopters in *Morskaya Aviatsiya*, the world's second largest naval air arm. The primary combat components are
(1) Long range and medium bombers employed in the maritime reconnaissance role
(2) Medium bombers mostly equipped with air-to-surface missiles in the anti-ship strike role.
(3) Land based patrol aircraft, amphibians and helicopters in the anti-submarine role.
The Soviet Navy flies no fixed-wing aircraft from ships, but several medium classes of destroyers and all modern missile armed cruisers, and the cruiser-helicopter ships *Moskva* and *Leningrad* can carry helicopters. The two helicopter ships are the largest built to date by any navy specifically for anti-submarine operations and are the first Soviet warships intended primarily for aviation activities. (A third ship possibly of an improved design is believed to be under construction according to some reports)

Bombers. The Soviet naval air arm has about 50 heavy and 450 medium bombers in the anti-shipping, strike, tanker and reconnaissance roles. The main strike force comprises about 300 "Badger" equipped with "Kipper" and "Kelt" air-to-surface missiles. The reconnaissance aircraft are about 50 "Bear D" (long range recce); 50 "Badger" and a similar number of "Blinder A". The latter and some of the "Badger" have a bombing capability. About 50 "Beagle" light bombers remain in service.

ASW Helicopters. Over 100 anti-submarine helicopters are believed to be in the naval air arm, mostly Ka-25 "Hormone" (a twin-turbine craft known as the "Harp" in the prototype stage) and some of the older Mi-4 "Hound" helicopters. The "Hormone" anti-submarine helicopters, armed with torpedoes or other ASW weapons operate from the large helicopter cruisers *Moskva* and *Leningrad* which can each operate some 15 to 20 helicopters, servicing them in a hangar below the flight deck. They have also been seen in the "Kara", "Kresta" I and "Kresta II" class cruisers which are the first Soviet ships of this type to be fitted with a helicopter hangar. In some of these ships the radar fitted helicopter may also have a reconnaissance role associated with the surface-to-surface missile system. The older MI-4 "Hound" and other "Hormone" helicopters are used in the ASW role from shore bases. Other types of helicopter are also used in the transport role ashore.

ASW Patrol Aircraft. The Soviet Union is the only nation other than Japan maintaining modern military flying boats, about 80 Be-12 "Mail" (turboprop) air caft of this type being operational. The latter aircraft, an amphibian often photographed on runways, has an advanced anti-submarine capability evidenced by a radome extending forward, a Magnetic Anomaly Detector (MAD) boom extending aft and a weapons bay in the rear fuselage. The numbers of the shore based ASW patrol aircraft IL 38 "May" are growing, some 30 are now in service. They have been seen in northern waters and reported in service with Soviet Units based in Egypt.

The "May" is a militarised version of the four-turboprop commercial air freighter (code name "Coot") in wide commercial service. The patrol/anti-submarine version has been lengthened and fitted wtih a MAD boom as well as other electronic equipment and a weapons capability similar to the US Navy's conversion of the Lockheed Electra into the P-3 "Orion" patrol aircraft.

Transports/Training Aircraft. There are also a few hundred transports, utility, and training fixed-wing aircraft and helicopters under Navy control.

*Aircraft names are NATO code names; "B" names indicate bombers, "H" names for helicopters, and "M" names for miscellaneous aircraft.

SOVIET NAVAL RADARS

Code Name	*Freq. Band*	*Function*	*Ship Application*
Big Net	S or L	Long-range air warning	Kresta I, Kashin (some) Dzerzhinski
Boat Sail	S or L	Surveillance	Whisky Canvas Bag
Dead Duck	C	IFF	General
Drum Tilt	X	Short-range armament Control	General with 30 mm guns
Fan Song E	C	Control for SA-N-2	Dzerzhinski
Flat Spin	L or S	Air surveillance	Some destroyers
Hair Net		Search & surveillance	Older cruisers and destroyers
Half Bow		Torpedo fire control	Older destroyers
Hawk Screech/ Owl Screech	C	Acquisition and fire control for main armament	Ships mounting 57—100 mm guns
Head Light	X and C	Missile control	Most modern major surface ships
Head Net A	S	Air surveillance	Kynda, Kashin, Krupny and other destroyers
Head Net B	S	Air surveillance	Krupny (some)
Head Net C	S	Air surveillance and Height Finder	Kiev, Moskva, Kara, Kresta I and II and SAM fitted destroyers
High Lune	S	Height finder	Dzerzhinski (with FanSong E)
High Pole	C	IFF	General
Horn Spoon		Navigation	General
Knife Rest		Air warning	Sverdlov's
Long Bow		Torpedo fire control	Destroyers
Muff Cob	C or X	Fire control	Moskva, Kresta I & II, Ugra, Lama, Poti, T58, Polnocny, Light Forces
Owl Screech (see Hawk Screech)			
Peel Group	X	SA-N-1 fire control	Kresta I, Kashin, Kynda, SAM Kotlin, Kanin
Plinth Net		Surface search	Obsolete
Pot Drum	X	Surface search	Some Light Forces and Kronstadts
Pot Head	X	Surface search	Some Light Forces and Kronstadts
Round Top		Fire control system	Older destroyers
Scoop Pair	E	SS-N-3 guidance	Kresta I and Kynda
Ship Globe	E	Missile Tracking	Instrumentation ships
Skin Head	X	Surface search	Some Light Forces & Krupny
Slim Net	S	Surface search	Some destroyers and frigates
Snoop Plate	X	Surveillance	Submarines
Snoop Slab	X	Surveillance	Submarines
Snoop Tray	X	Surveillance	Submarines
Square Head	C	IFF interrogator	Osa, Kotlin and Skory
Square Tie	X	Surface search	Osa
Strut Curve	S	Medium range search	Poti, Support ships
Top Bow	X	Fire control	Some cruisers and destroyers
Top Sail	L	Air surveillance	Moskva, Kiev, Kara, Kresta II
Top Trough	S	Surface Search	Sverdlov's
Wasp Head		Fire control system	Older destroyers
Witch Five	C	IFF	Some cruisers and destroyers

SOVIET NAVAL MISSILES

Type	System	Missile Code-Name	Launch Platform/	No. Of Tubes/ Launchers	Mach. speed	Max. Range (n. miles)	Notes
SSM (cruise)	SS-N-1	Scrubber	4 "Kildin" destroyers	1.	1·0	130	Subsonic and obsolescent. Six other "KRUPNY" class were converted to carry SA-N-1 missiles and became "KANIN" class. Operational in 1958.
			2 "Krupny" destroyers	2			
SSM (cruise)	SS-N-2	Styx	25 "Komar" missile boats	2	0·9	23	Two versions—A and B. It seems likely that the former is an export version. Probably has an active radar homing capability. Operational in 1960.
			65 "Osa I" missile boats	4			
SSM (cruise)	SS-N-3	Shaddock	4 "Kynda" cruisers	8	1·5	300	Requires external guidance from aircraft. Operational in 1961-62.
			4 "Kresta I" cruisers	4			
			16 "Juliet" submarines	4			
			3 "Echo I" submarines	6			
			27 "Echo II" submarines	8			
			7 "Whisky Long Bin" submarines	4			
			5 "Whisky Twin Cylinder" submarines	2			
Strat	SS-N-4	Sark	11 "Golf I" submarines	3	—	350	An obsolescent system now being phased-out with the submarines carrying it. Operational in 1958-60
			2 "Zulu V" submarines	2			
Strat	SS-N-5	Serb	11 "Golf II" submarines	3	—	650	Development of SS-N-4 system. Operational in 1963.
			9 "Hotel II" submarines	3			
Strat	SS-N-6	Sawfly	32 "Yankee" submarines	16	—	1 350	Dived launch. Operational in 1969.
SSM (dived cruise)	SS-N-7		11 "Charlie" submarines	8	1.5	30	Dived launch. Operational in 1969-70.
Strat	SS-N-8		4 "Delta" submarines	12	—	4 000	Dived launch. Operational in 1973.
SSM	SS-N-9		6 "Nanuchka" missile boats	6	1·0+	150	Operational in 1968-69.
SSM	SS-N-10		1+2 "Kara" cruisers	8	1·2	29	Operational in 1968.
			6 "Kresta II" cruisers	8			
			5 "Krivak" destroyers	4			
SSM	SS-N-11		55 "Osa II" missile boats	4	0·9	29	Probably modified Styx with folding wings. Low altitude capability.
						S/Slant Range	
SAM	SA-N-1	Goa	8 SAM "Kotlin" destroyers	2 (1 twin)	2	15	
			6 "Kanin" destroyers	2 (1 twin)			
			19 "Kashin" destroyers	4 (2 twin)			
			4 "Kynda" cruisers	2 (1 twin)			
			4 "Kresta I" cruisers	4 (2 twin)			
SAM	SA-N-2	Guideline	1 "Dzerzhinski" cruiser	2 (1 twin)		25	
SAM	SA-N-3	Goblet	2 'Moskva" cruisers	4 (2 twin)		20	
			6 "Kresta II" cruisers	4 (2 twin)			
			1 + 2 "Kara" cruisers	4 (2 twin)			
SAM	SA-N-4		2 "Sverdlov conversion" cruisers	1		20	
			1 + 2 "Kara" cruisers	2			
			5 "Krivak" destroyers	2			
			6 "Nanuchka" missile boats	1			
			11 "Grisha" corvettes	1			
						Max. Range (n. miles).	
ASM	AS-1	Kennel	c50 "Badger B" bomber	2	0·9	55	Obsolete.
ASM	AS-2	Kipper	c150 "Badger C" bomber	1	1·2	115	Obsolescent
ASM	AS-3	Kangaroo	c20 "Bear B" and "C" bomber	2	2	400	
ASM	AS-4	Kitchen	? "Blinder B" bomber	1	2+	185	Inertial Guided.
ASM	AS-5	Kelt	c150 "Badger G"	2	0·9	100	Replacing AS-1 Active homer.
ASM	AS-6	—	c50 "Badger modified" bombers	2	3	150	Possibly also to be used in "Backfire"

NOTE: Numbers of aircraft under AS-1 to AS-6 are approximate.

MISSILE LAUNCHERS—TOTALS

Cruise Missiles (SSM's)

Long Range (50 nm+)	Surface launchers	92
	S/M launchers	336
Short Range (less than 50 nm)	Surface launchers	606
	S/M launchers	88

Strategic Missiles (SLBM's)

(all submarine launched)	
Medium Range	97
Long Range ("Yankees" and "Deltas")	560
Surface-to-Air (SAM's)	
(all surface launched)	197
Air-to-Surface (ASM's)	690

NOTES:—

a). SAM's are now frequently fitted in SSM-carrying ships.

b). Total of ASM's very approximate.

c). Total of missiles carried by surface ships not listed owing to lack of reliable information.

SOVIET NAVAL STRENGTHS

Class	North	Baltic	Black Sea (incl. Caspian)	Pacific	Total
Fleet Submarines					
Delta	4	—	—	—	4
Yankee	24	—	—	8	32
Hotel II	6	—	—	3	9
Charlie	11	—	—	—	11
Echo II	15	—	—	12	27
Echo I	1	—	—	2	3
Victor	12	—	—	—	12
November	9	—	—	4	13
Golf I & II	14	—	—	8	22 (11 of each type)
Zulu V	2	—	—	—	2
Juliet	10	—	—	6	16
W Twin Cylinder					5
}	6	2	—	4	
W Long Bin					7
Alpha	1	—	—	—	1
Bravo	1	2	1	—	4
Foxtrot	31	14 (varying)	—	11	56
Romeo	—	5	9	—	14
Quebec	—	11	11	—	22
Zulu	12	5	—	5	22
Whisky	25	44	27	34	130
Whisky Canvas Bag	3	—	—	2	5

Class	North	Baltic	Black Sea (incl. Caspian)	Pacific	Total
Surface Ships					
Kiev	—	—	1+1	—	1+1
Kara	—	—	1+2	—	1+2
Moskva	—	—	2	—	2
Sverdlov	2	3	4	3	12
Chapaev	1	1	—	—	2
Kirov	—	1	1	—	2
Kresta II	3	2	1	—	6
Kresta I	3	—	—	1	4
Kynda	—	—	2	2	4
Krivak	2	3	—	—	5
Kashin	6	3	5	5	19
Kanin	3	2	—	1	6
Krupny	—	—	—	2	2
SAM Kotlin	2	1	3	2	8
Kildin	—	—	2	2	4
Kotlin	3	5	3	7	18
Tallin	—	1	—	—	1
Skory	7	12	10	16	45
Nanuchka	—	3	3	—	6
Mirka I and II	5	4	12	4	25
Petya I and II	12	10	11	12	45
Kola	2	1	3	—	6
Riga	14	5	15	14	48
Ugra	4	2	—	2	6
Lama	2	—	1	2	5
Don	3	—	—	3	6
Grisha	3	2	4	2	11

Class	North	Baltic	Black Sea (incl. Caspian)	Pacific	Total
Stenka	—	19	4	7	30
Poti	25	25	5	15	70
SO 1	—	45	40	15	100
Kronstadt	5	20	8	7	40
Fleet Sweepers	45	60	40	50	10 Natya
					45 Yurka
					20 T 58
					120 T 43
Coastal Sweepers	30	45	25	25	70 Vanya
					35 Sasha
					20 T 301
Pchela	—	10	15	—	25
Komar	—	5	15	5	25
Osa	25	35	25	35	120
					65 Type I
					55 Type II
Torpedo Boats	20	80	45	45	190
					40 Shershen
					130 P6, 8 & 10
					20 P4
Alligator	1	4	3	3	11
Polnocny	12	15	18	15	60
Landing Craft	20	30	45	40	135
					10 MP 8
					25 MP 4
					30 Vydra
					70 MP 10
Intelligence Ships (AIGs)	15	8	15	15	53

AIRCRAFT CARRIERS

1+1 KIEV CLASS (AIRCRAFT CARRIERS)

KIEV +1

Displacement, tons	45 000
Length, feet (*metres*)	925 (*282*) oa. 880 (*268*) wl.
	100 (*30·5*) (hull)
Beam, feet (*metres*)	200 (*61*) (overall, including flight deck and sponsons)
Aircraft	35 fixed wing (? Freehand type)
	35 Hormone A helicopters
Missile Launchers	2 twin SA-N-3 for Goblet missiles
	1 unidentified twin launcher
Guns	28—57 mm
A/S Weapons	2—12 tube launchers forward
Speed, knots	At least 30

The *Kiev,* now fitting out at Nikolayev, and what is presumed to be her sister building at the same yard, mark an impressive and logical advance by the Soviet Navy. The arrival of these ships has been heralded by Admiral Gorshkov's support for embarked tactical air as a necessity for navies employed in extending political influence far abroad, and by a softening of previous Soviet criticisms of this class of ship.

As forecast in last year's edition of "Fighting Ships" *Kiev* appears to be a carrier designed for VTOL aircraft and helicopter operations. There is at present no sign of steam catapults, arrester gear, mirror-landing-sights, and all the expensive gear required for fixed-wing operations. Nor is there yet any evidence of the existence of a fixed-wing aircraft suitable for carrier operations. On the other hand, as was said last year, the Freehand VTOL aircraft or its derivative, and the Hormone A helicopter could both be embarked. Two examples of the former, designed by Yakovlev, appeared at the 1967 Domodedovo air show, were clearly subsonic and mounted 16-round rocket packs under each wing in one aircraft. They were powered by twin Turbojet engines, had a wide fuselage to accommodate these and short delta wings of about 27 ft wing-span. The overall length of the aircraft was about 58 ft. Since 1967 further trials of what is apparently an improved version of Freehand have continued at Ramenskoye airfield near Moscow, culminating in sea-trials from a specially fitted pad on the flight-deck of *Moskva.* These were primarily in the Black Sea—her subsequent deployment to the Mediterranean may have indicated stage two in these trials.

So there are aircraft available for this carrier in the Soviet Naval Air Force and a rough estimate of her hangar capacity suggests that *Kiev* could carry 35 of each type simultaneously. Her forward lift appears to be adequate to accommodate a Freehand type but until more detailed evidence is available this, with many other deductions, must remain conjectural.

Her armament is of interest, her missiles being, if present estimates are correct, similar to those in *Moskva* whilst she may carry a heavy armament of medium calibre guns. The missile-systems SAN-3, using Goblet missiles with a slant range of some 20 miles, are possibly to balance the lack of embarked high-performance fighters and are of longer range than the BPDMS's with Sea Sparrow which are fitted in the latest U.S. carriers. The heavy gun armament is a complete break with the latter's armament—neither *Nimitz* nor *Enterprise* carry any guns. But provision of an increasingly heavy conventional gun-armament can be seen throughout the Soviet surface fleet and this class could be a prime example of this trend.

If *Kiev* turns out to have similar A/S weapons to *Moskva* (Twin A/S rocket launchers foreward and a possible A/S weapon launcher) another radical change in carrier practice will have been seen. The A/S rocket launchers would presuppose a sonar fit of a hull mounted set and/or VDS, showing the Soviets have taken the submarine threat seriously. It could be argued that if a submarine had reached the range of such weapons system would the carrier not be a sitting-duck? This depends very largely on the speed and handling of that ship and the efficiency of the A/S helicopters which, presumably, would work with the weapon-launcher. It is as yet far too early to say.

Finally, can we estimate the future of this class and its tasks? The building of only two Moskvas is an enigma unless they are considered as fore-runners of *Kiev.* With world-wide Soviet deployments a pair of ships is clearly insufficient, allowing for maintenance and any refitting required. The design of the carrier must have been on the drawing-board before *Moskva* was commissioned in 1967. Perhaps the decision to build more of the latter was delayed until after the extensive heavy-weather operations which *Moskva* and *Leningrad* carried out. It seems most likely that these were sufficiently successful to encourage the Soviet navy to proceed with the larger ships. On the other hand there may have been deficiencies which could be met only in a bigger vessel. The reasons are academic—the result is only two Moskva's and the probability of a steadily increasing number of Kievs. How many? This is for the Soviets to decide but a minimum of six would be not unlikely.

What of the tasks? Just as Admiral Gorshkov intimated—a powerful addition to the political impact of the Soviet fleet in peacetime. With ships capable of operating VTOL strike aircraft and troop-lift helicopters their credibility in the intervention role would be increased, and their fleet would be that much more prepared for hostilities. Such ships roles could be changed merely by alterations in the number and type of aircraft enbarked. They are clearly not as enormously expensive as the US nuclear-powered carriers but will greatly enhance the manifest capability of the Soviet fleet to operate effectively world-wide in both peace and war.

1973, USN Artists Impression

KIEV

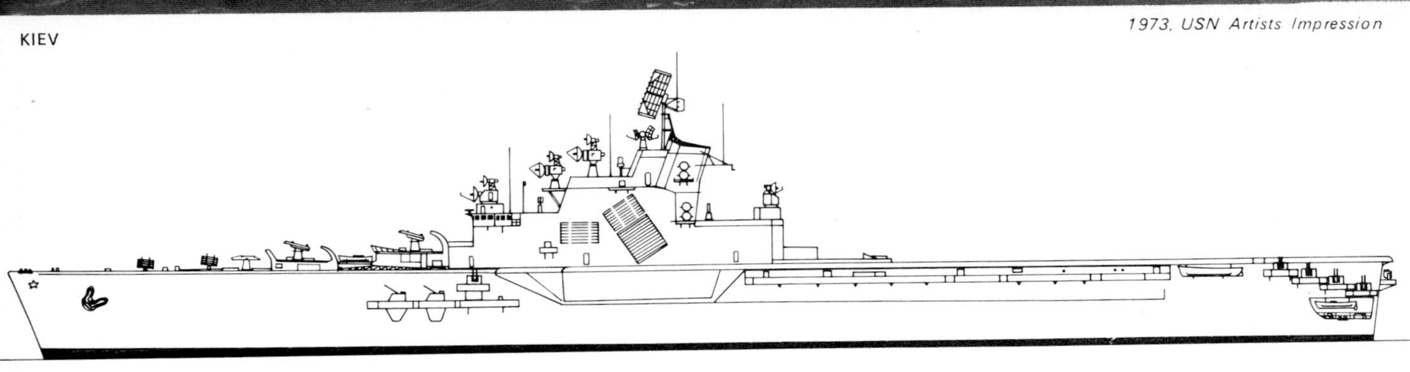

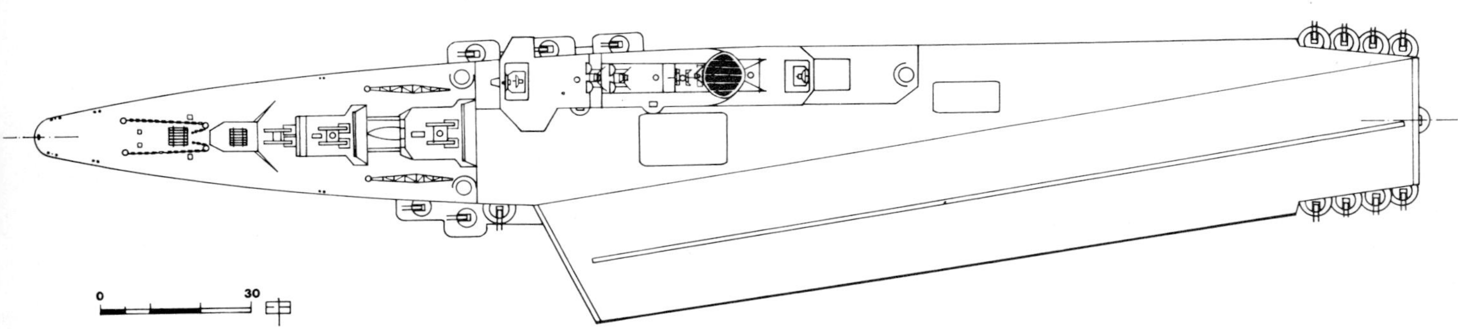

HELICOPTER CRUISERS

2 "MOSKVA" CLASS

LENINGRAD **MOSKVA**

Displacement, tons	15 000 standard; 18 000 full load
Length, feet (*metres*)	624·8 (*190·5*); 644·8 oa (*196·6*)
Flight deck, feet (*m*)	295·3 (*90·0*) aft of superstructure
Width, feet (*metres*)	115·0 (*35·0*)
Beam, feet (*metres*)	75·9 (*23*)
Draught, feet (*metres*)	24·9 (*7·6*)
Aircraft	18 Hormone A ASW helicopters
Missile launchers	2 surface-to-air "SA-N-3" systems of twin launchers and 1 twin launcher possibly for anti-submarine missiles
Guns, dual purpose	4—57 mm (2 twin mountings)
A/S weapons	2—12 tube mortars on forecastle
Torpedo tubes	2 quintuple 21 inch
Main engines	Geared turbines; 2 shafts; 100 000 shp
Boilers	4 watertube
Speed, knots	30 max
Complement	800

GENERAL
Both built at Nikolayev, *Moskva* probably being laid down in 1962-3 as she carried out sea-trials in mid-1967. This class represented a radical change of thought in the Soviet fleet. The design must have been completed while the *"November"* class submarines were building and with her heavy A/S armament and efficient sensors (helicopters and VDS) suggests an awareness of the problem of dealing with nuclear submarines. Alongside what is apparently a primary A/S role these ships have a capability ror A/A warning and self-defence as well as a command function. With a full fit of radar and ECM equipment they clearly represent good value for money. Both ships handle well in heavy weather and are capable of helicopter-operations under adverse conditions. Why only two were built is discussed earlier in the notes on the *"Kiev"* class aircraft carriers.

RADAR. Search: Top Sail 3-D and Head Net C 3-D. Fire control: Head Light (2). Muff Cob. Miscellaneous: Electronic warfare equipment.

SONAR. VDS and, probably, hull mounted set.

MOSKVA (different pennant number) *1972*

MOSKVA *1968, US Navy*

MOSKVA *1968, USNFE*

Helicopter Cruisers—*continued*

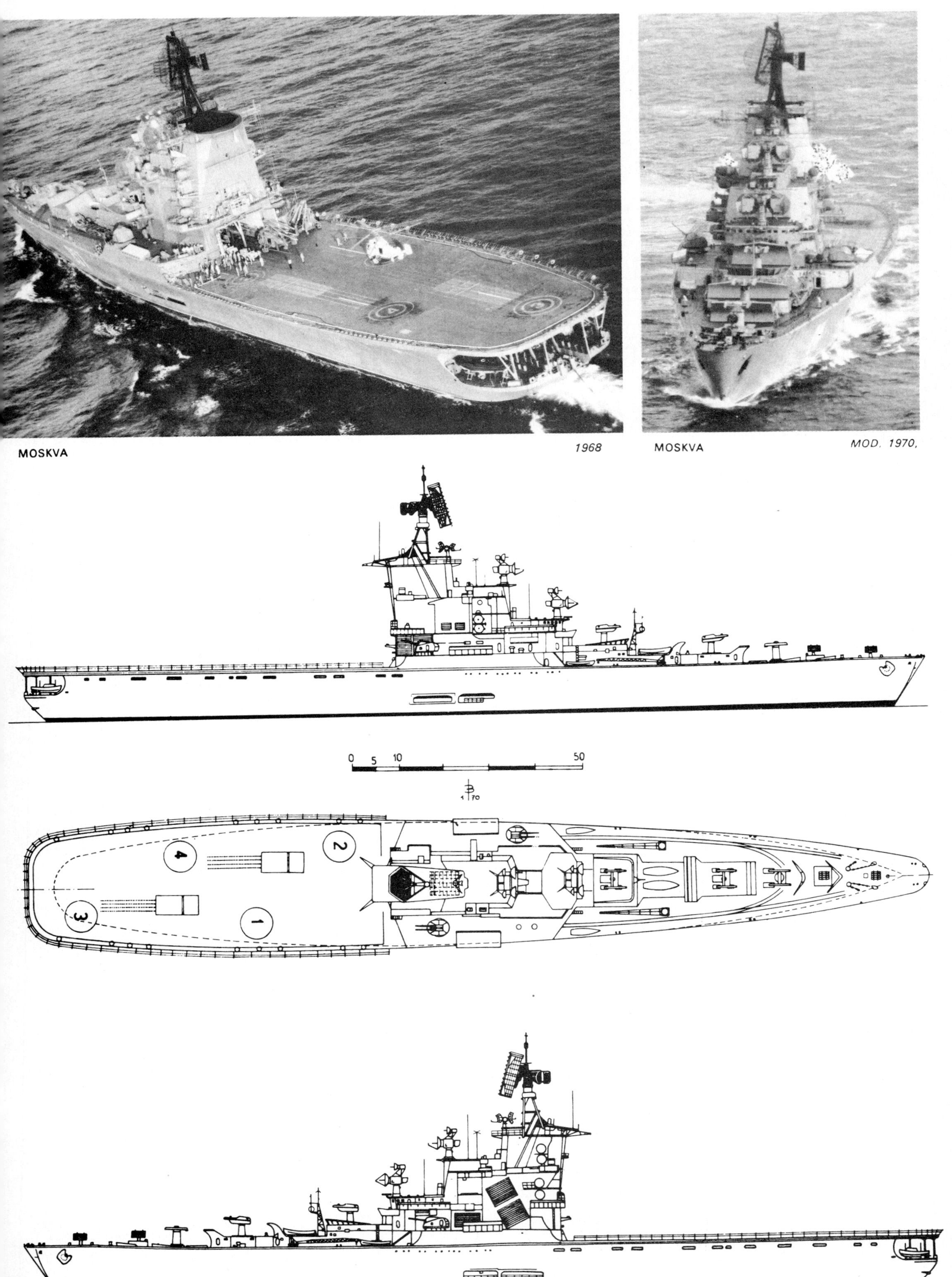

MOSKVA 1968

MOSKVA MOD. 1970,

SUBMARINES

Ballistic Missile classes

4 "DELTA" CLASS

(BALLISTIC MISSILE SUBMARINES SSBN's)

Displacement, tons	8 000 surfaced; 9 000 dived
Length, feet (*metres*)	426·5 (*130·0*)
Beam, feet (*metres*)	34·8 (*10·6*)
Draught, feet (*metres*)	32·8 (*10·0*)
Missile launchers	12 SSN-8 tubes
Torpedo tubes	8—21 in
Main engines	Nuclear reactor; Steam turbines; 2 screws; 24 000 shp
Speed, knots	25
Complement	About 120

"Delta" Class

This adaptation of the "Yankee" class SSBN's was announced at the end of 1972. The missile armament is twelve SSN-8's with a range of 4000 nautical miles, presumably armed with single heads, rather than MRV's. Otherwise the details of this class are similar to the "Yankee" class although with only twelve tubes containing longer range missiles the silhouette must be similar to that illustrated. The longer-range SSN-8 missiles can be assumed to be of greater length than the SSN-6's and, as this length could not be accommodated below the keel, they must stand several feet proud of the after-casing of the "Yankee" class. At the same time their presumed greater diameter and the need to compensate for the additional top-weight would seem to be the reasons for the reduction to twelve missiles.

So far as the "Delta" class building programme is concerned this must be viewed in the light of the SALT agreement signed on May 26 1972 by Mr. Brezhnev and President Nixon. This agreement, once various substitution sums for pre-1964 ICBMs and older submarine-launched missiles have been done, would allow the USSR to maintain 62 SSBNs and a total of 950 missiles in their fleet. On previous form it is unlikely that only 1 of the 45 "Delta" and "Yankee" submarines completed or under construction at the beginning of 1973 was, in fact, a "Delta". Allowing for a building rate of 6-7 SSBN's per year a total of 32 appears likely for the "Yankees This means that 13 "Deltas" were built or building i January which, with a building time of about two yea fits the present rate. Therefore, 4 "Deltas" are assume complete and in commission or under trials by mid-197 and the total of 30 (62 minus the "Yankees") allowed b SALT could be reached by 1978, provided all "Hotels and "Golfs" were phased-out by then. This would mea that only 872 of the allowed 950 missiles would be aflo but this is presumably acceptable.

It is, however, possible that a completely new class whic could mount 16 SSN-8 missiles may increase this numbe though there is no evidence for this.

32 "YANKEE" CLASS

(BALLISTIC MISSILE SUBMARINES SSBN's)

Displacement, tons	8 000 surface; 9 000 submerged
Length, feet (*metres*)	426·5 (*130·0*)
Beam, feet (*metres*)	34·8 (*10·6*)
Draught, feet (*metres*)	32·8 (*10·0*)
Missile launchers	16 SS-N-6 tubes
Torpedo tubes	8—21 in
Main engines	Nuclear reactors; steam turbines; 24 000 shp
Speed, knots	25
Complement	About 120

The first units of this class were reported in 1968. The vertical launching tubes are arranged in two rows of eight, and the missiles have a range of 1 500 nautical miles.

At about the time that the USS *George Washington* was laid down (1 Nov 1957) as the world's first SSBN it is likely that the Soviet Navy embarked on its own major SSBN programme. With experience gained from the diesel-propelled "Golf" class and the nuclear-propelled "Hotel" class, both originally carrying three SS-N4 (350 mile) missiles in the fin, the "Yankee" design was completed mounting 16 SSN-6 (1350 miles) missiles in the hull in two banks of 8. The first of the class was delivered late-1967 and the programme then accelerated from 4 boats in 1968 to 8 in 1971. The original deployment of this class was to the Eastern seaboard of the US giving a coverage at least as far as the Mississippi. Increase in numbers allowed a Pacific patrol to be established off California extending coverage at least as far as the Rockies. To provide greater coverage and more flexible operations a longer range missile system was needed and this is now at sea in the "Delta" class.

"Yankee" Class *1970*

"Yankee" Class *1970 S. Breyer*

Submarines— *continued*

Ballistic Missile classes

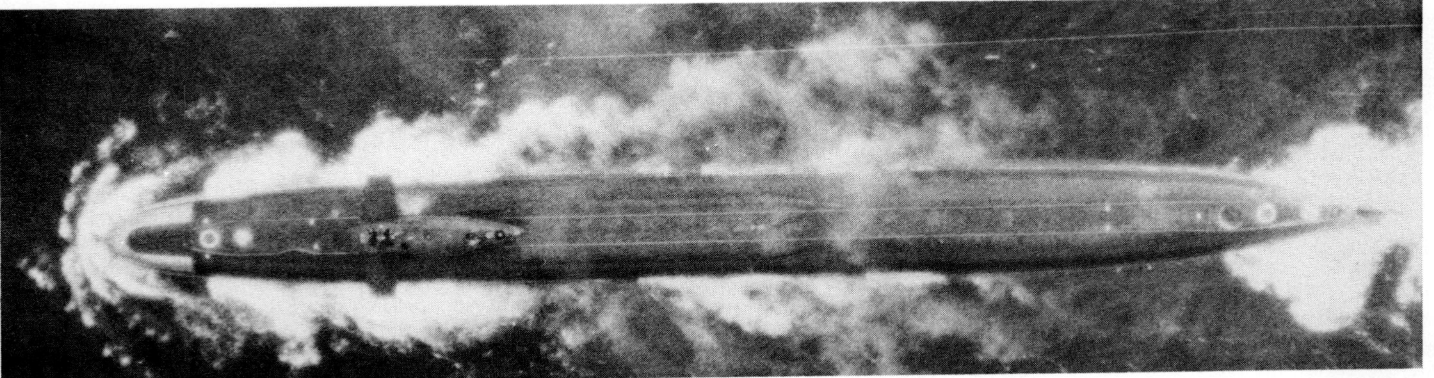
"Yankee" Class 1972

9 "HOTEL" II CLASS

(BALLISTIC MISSILE SUBMARINES SSBNs)

Displacement, tons	3 700 surface; 4 100 submerged
Length, feet (*metres*)	377·2 (*115·2*)
Beam, feet (*metres*)	28·2 (*8·6*)
Draught, feet (*metres*)	25 (*7·6*)
Missile launchers	3 SS-N-5 tubes
Torpedo tubes	6—21 in (bow); 4—16 in (aft) (anti-submarine)
Main engines	Nuclear reactor, steam turbines; 22 500 shp
Speed, knots	20 (dived)
Complement	90

Long range submarines with three vertical ballistic missile tubes in the large fin. All this class were completed between 1958 and 1962. Originally fitted with SS-N-4 system with "Sark" missiles (350 miles). Between 1963 and 1967 this system was replaced by the SS-N-5 system with "Serb" missiles capable of 650 mile range. Since then these boats have been deployed off both coasts of the USA and Canada. As the limitations of SALT are felt the "Hotel II's" will probably be phased-out to allow the maximum number of "Delta" class to be built. The earlier boats of this class, which was of a similar hull and reactor design to the "Echo" class, will, by the late 1970's, be reaching their twentieth year in service.

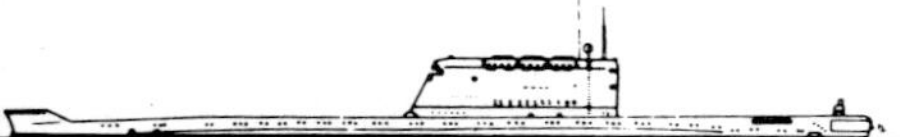
"Hotel" Class

"Hotel II" Class 1972

"Hotel" *Class* 1971

Submarines—*continued*

Ballistic Missile classes

22 "GOLF I and II" CLASS

(BALLISTIC MISSILE SUBMARINES SSB)

Displacement, tons	2 350 surface; 2 800 submerged
Length, feet (*metres*)	320·0 (*97·5*)
Beam, feet (*metres*)	25·1 (*7·6*)
Draught, feet (*metres*)	22·0 (*6·7*)
Missile launchers	3 SS-N-4 (G 1); 3 SS-N-5 (G II)
Torpedo tubes	10—21 in (bow)
Main engines	3 diesels; 3 shafts; 6 000 hp; Electric motors; 6 000 hp
Speed, knots	17·6 surface; 17 submerged
Range, miles	22 700 surface cruising
Complement	86 (12 officers, 74 men)

This type has a very large fin fitted with three vertically mounted tubes and hatches for launching ballistic missiles. Built at Komsomolsk and Severodvinsk. Building started in 1958 and finished in 1961-62. After the missile conversion of the "Hotel" class was completed in 1967 about half this class was converted to carry the SS-N-5 system with 650 mile Serb missiles in place of the shorter range (350 mile) Sarks. One of this class has been built by China, although apparently lacking missiles.

"Golf I" Class *1962, US Navy*

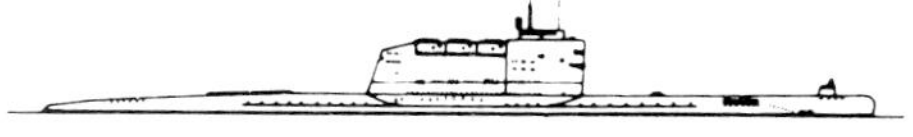
"Golf" *Class*

"Golf I" Class missile Type (side opening hatches open) *1962, US Navy*

2 "ZULU V" CLASS

(Ex-BALLISTIC MISSILE SUBMARINES SSB)

Displacement, tons	2 100 surface; 2 600 submerged
Length, feet (*metres*)	295·3 (*90·0*)
Beam, feet (*metres*)	24·1 (*7·3*)
Draught, feet (*metres*)	19·0 (*5·8*)
Missile launchers	2 tubes for SS-N-4 missiles
Torpedo tubes	10—21 in
Main engines	3 diesels; 3 shafts; 10 000 bhp; 3 electric motors; 3 500 hp
Speed, knots	18 surface; 15 submerged
Complement	85

These were basically of "Z" class design but converted in 1955-57 to ballistic missile submarines with larger fins and two vertical tubes for launching Sark (350 mile) missiles on the surface. These were the first Soviet ballistic missile submarines. Of the seven converted only two remain and these are probably used only for scientific and fishery research being no longer operational.

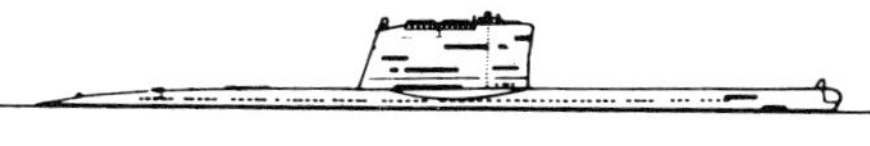
"Zulu V" Class

"Zulu V" *Class* *1972*

Submarines—*continued*

Cruise Missile classes

1 + ? "PAPA" CLASS

A new class of nuclear submarine, named "Papa", with a cruise-missile armament is building and some units may already be in service. Details are not yet available but it is unlikely that she would be any less efficient than the "Charlie" class. This suggests an armament of at least eight missiles although whether these are of the SS-N-7 type has yet to be discovered.

11 "CHARLIE" CLASS

(CRUISE MISSILE SUBMARINE SSGN)

Displacement, tons	4 300 surface; 5 100 submerged
Length, feet (*metres*)	295 (*90·0*)
Beam, feet (*metres*)	32·8 (*10·0*)
Draught, feet (*metres*)	24·6 (*7·5*)
Missile launchers	8 tubes for SS-N-7 missile system
Torpedo tubes	8—21 in
Main engines	Nuclear reactor; steam turbines; 24 000 shp
Speed, knots	30 approx, submerged, 20 surface
Complement	100

A new type of cruise-missile submarine building at Gorky at a rate of about 3 per year. The first of class was delivered in 1968, representing a very significant advance in the cruise-missile submarine field. With a speed of at least 30 knots and mounting eight missile tubes for the SSN-7 system (30 miles range) which has a dived launch capability, this is a great advance on the "Echo" class. Having an improved hull and reactor design these boats must be assumed to have an organic control for their missile system and therefore pose a notable threat to any surface force. Their deployment to the Mediterranean, the area of the US 6th Fleet, suggests their probable employment. The only strange thing about them is their comparatively low building rate. If they were failures presumably the programme would have stopped but this is not so.

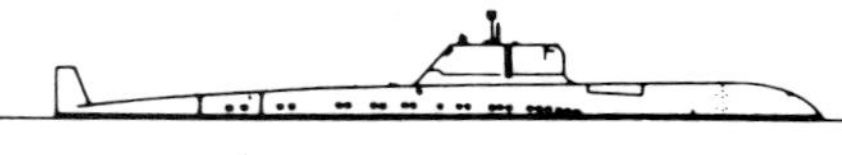

"Charlie Class"

"Charlie" Class *1970*

"Charlie" *Class* *1972*

"Charlie" Class *1970, S. Breyer*

Submarines—*continued*
Cruise Missile classes

3 "ECHO I" CLASS
(CRUISE MISSILE SUBMARINES SSGN)

Displacement, tons	4 600 surface; 5 000 submerged
Length, feet (*metres*)	380·9 (*116·0*)
Beam, feet (*metres*)	28·4 (8·6)
Draught, feet (*metres*)	25·9 (*7·9*)
Missile launchers	6 SS-N-3 launching tubes
Torpedo tubes	6—21 in (bow); 4—16 in (aft) anti-submarine
Main engines	Nuclear reactors, steam turbines; 22 500 shp
Speed, knots	20 max; 12 cruising
Complement	92 (12 officers, 80 men)

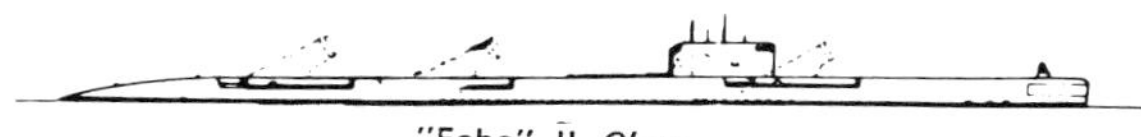

"Echo" II *Class*

Completed in 1960-62. The six SSN-3 launchers for Shaddock missiles are hinged within either side of the casing requiring the submarine to surface for launch.

The hull of this class is very similar to the "Hotel"/"November" type and it is probably powered by similar nuclear plant. This class was started at about the same time as the "Juliet" diesel-driven SSG's, and may have been intended as a nuclear prototype using the same SS-N-3 system. Only five "Echo I's" were built, probably an adequate test for a new weapon system, being followed immediately by the "Echo II's". The Soviet fleet now had a continuing production of SSGN's which, although the 300 mile range SS-N-3 system requires external guidance, nevertheless presented a powerful threat to any task force.

27 "ECHO II" CLASS
(CRUISE MISSILE SUBMARINES SSGN)

Displacement, tons	5 000 surface; 5 600 submerged
Length, feet (*metres*)	387·4 (*118*)
Beam, feet (*metres*)	28·4 (*8·6*)
Draught, feet (*metres*)	25·9 (*7·9*)
Missiles, launchers	8 SS-N-3 launching tubes
Torpedo tubes	6—21 in (bow); 4—16 in (aft) A/S
Main engines	Nuclear reactor, steam turbines; 22 500 shp
Speed, knots	20 max; 12 to 14 cruising
Complement	100

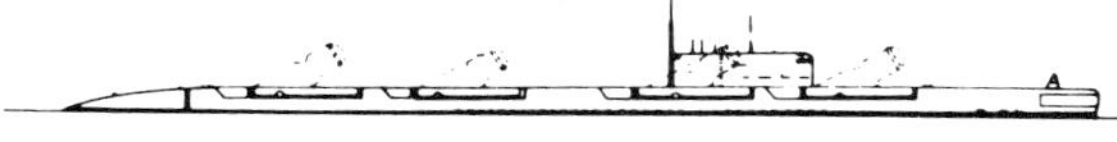

"Echo" II *Class*

The "Echo II" was the natural development of the "Echo I". With a slightly lengthened hull, a fourth pair of launchers was installed and between 1963 and 1967 twenty-seven of this class were built. They are now deployed evenly between the Pacific and Northern fleets and still provide a useful group of boats for operations such as those of the mixed task force which was in the South China Sea in June 1972. As well as surface ships this included 3 "Echo II's" and an "Echo I".

"Echo II" Class *1972*

"Echo II" Class *1971*

Submarines—*continued*
Cruise Missile classes

16 "JULIET" CLASS

(CRUISE MISSILE SUBMARINES SSG)

Displacement, tons	2 200 surface; 2 500 submerged
Length, feet (*metres*)	280·5 (*85·5*)
Beam, feet (*metres*)	31·4 (*9·5*)
Draught, feet (*metres*)	20·0 (*6·1*)
Missile launchers	4 SS-N-3 tubes; 2 before and 2 abaft the fin
Torpedo tubes	6—21 in (bow); 2 or 4—16 in (aft) for A/S
Main engines	Diesels; 6 000 bhp Electric motors; 6 000 hp
Speed, knots	16 surface; 16 submerged

Completed between 1962 and 1967. An unmistakable class with a high casing to house the 4 SS-N-3 launchers, one pair either end of the fin which appears to be comparatively low. This class was the logical continuation of the "Whisky" class conversions but was overtaken by the "Echo" class SSGN's. A number of this class has in the past been deployed to the Mediterranean.

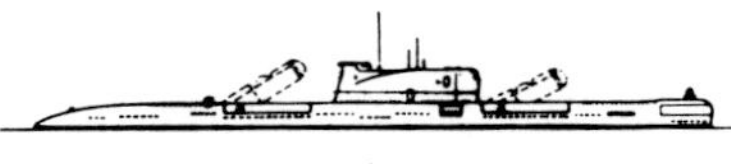

"Juliet" *Class*

"Juliet" Class *1972*

"Juliet" *Class* *1972*

"Juliet" Class *1972, US Navy*

Submarines—*continued*
Cruise Missile classes

7 "WHISKY LONG-BIN" CLASS

(CRUISE MISSILE SUBMARINES SSG)

Displacement, tons	1 300 surface; 1 800 submerged
Length, feet (*metres*)	272·3 (*83·0*)
Beam, feet (*metres*)	19·8 (*6·0*)
Draught, feet (*metres*)	15·7 (*4·8*)
Missile launchers	4 SS-N-3 tubes
Torpedo tubes	4—21 in
Main engines	Diesels; 4 000 bhp; Electric motors; 2 500 hp
Speed, knots	17 surface; 15 submerged

A more efficient modification of the "Whisky" class than the Twin-Cylinder with four SSN-3 launchers built into a remodelled fin on a hull lengthened by 26 feet. Converted between 1960-63—no organic guidance and therefore reliance must be made on aircraft or surface-ship cooperation. Must still be a very noisy boat when dived.

"Whisky" *Class* Long Bin

"Whisky Long-bin" Class *1970, Niels Gartig*

"Whisky Long-Bin" Class *1968, S. Breyer*

5 "WHISKY TWIN CYLINDER" CLASS

(CRUISE MISSILE SUBMARINES SSG)

Displacement, tons	1 100 surface; 1 600 submerged
Length, feet (*metres*)	247 (*75·3*)
Beam, feet (*metres*)	19 (*5·8*)
Draught, feet (*metres*)	15·1 (*4·6*)
Missile launchers	2 cylinders for SS-N-3
Torpedo tubes	6—21 in (4 bow, 2 stern)
Main engines	Diesels; 4 000 bhp; Electric motors; 2 500 hp
Speed, knots	17 surface; 15 submerged

A 1958-60 modification of the conventional "Whisky" class designed to test out the SSN-3 system at sea. Probably never truly operational being a thoroughly messy conversion which must make a noise like a train if proceeding at any speed above dead slow when dived. The modification consisted of fitting a pair of launchers abaft the fin.

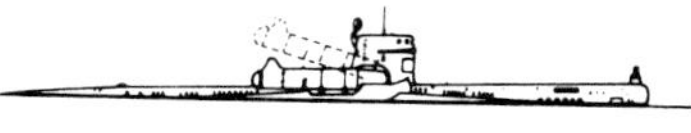

"Whisky" *Class* Twin Cylinder

"Whisky" Twin Cylinder Class *1970, Col Borg*

Submarines—*continued*

Fleet Submarine classes

1 "ALPHA" CLASS (FLEET SUBMARINE)

Displacement, tons	3 000 surface
Length, feet (*metres*)	260 (*79·3*)
Main engines	Probably nuclear

One unit only of this class was completed in 1970. Her form of propulsion is by no means certain nor is her purpose.

12 "VICTOR" CLASS

(FLEET SUBMARINES)

Displacement, tons	3 600 surface; 4 200 submerged
Length, feet (*metres*)	285·4 (*87·0*)
Beam, feet (*metres*)	32·8 (*10·0*)
Draught, feet (*metres*)	26·2 (*8·0*)
Torpedo tubes	8—21 in
Main engines	Nuclear reactors; steam turbines; 24 000 shp
Speed, knots	26 surface; 30 plus submerged

This appears to be a class with great possibilities. Designed purely as a torpedo carrying submarine its much increased speed makes it a menace to all but the fastest ships. The first of class entered service in 1967-8 with a subsequent building rate of about two per year.

"Victor" Class

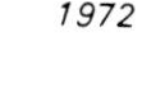

1972

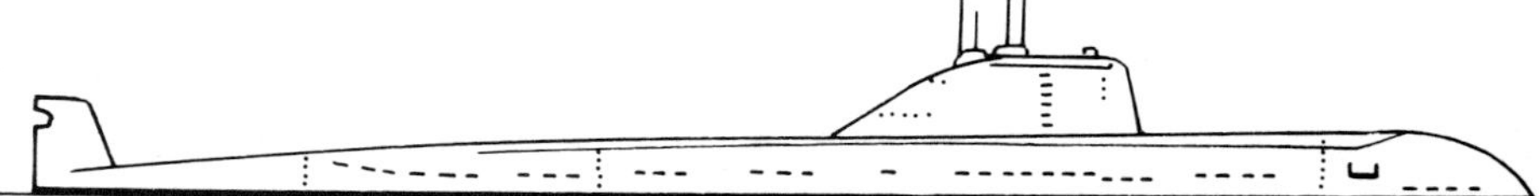

"Victor" Class

"Victor" Class

1972

Submarines—*continued*

Fleet Submarine classes

13 "NOVEMBER" CLASS

(FLEET SUBMARINES)

Displacement, tons	3 500 surface; 4 000 submerged
Length, feet (*metres*)	360·9 (*110·0*)
Beam, feet (*metres*)	32·1 (*9·8*)
Draught, feet (*metres*)	24·3 (*7·4*)
Torpedo tubes	6—21 in (bow); 4—16 in (aft) A/S
Main engines	Nuclear reactor, steam turbines; 22 500 shp
Speed, knots	20 surface; 25 submerged
Complement	88

The first class of Soviet Fleet Submarines which entered service between 1958 and 1963. The hull form with the great number of free-flood holes in the casing suggests a noisy boat and it is surprising that greater efforts have not been made to supersede this class with the "Victors". In 1970 one of this class sank south-west of the United Kingdom.

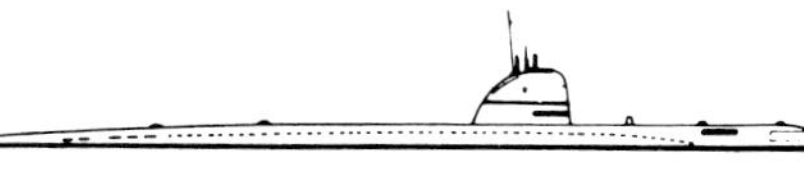

"November" Class

"November" *Class* *1965 USSR*

"November" *Class*

Patrol Submarine classes

4 "BRAVO" CLASS (PATROL SUBMARINES)

Displacement, tons	2 500 surface; 2 800 submerged
Length, feet (*metres*)	229·6 (*70*)
Beam, feet (*metres*)	24·8 (*7·5*)
Draught, feet (*metres*)	14·8 (*4·5*)
Torpedo tubes	6—21 in
Main engines	Diesel-Electric
Speed, knots	16

"BRAVO" Class

A class of conventional submarine whose purpose remains unclear. Only a few have been built since 1968 and the drawing is merely an indication of the general form which this class may be expected to have. The beam-to-length ratio is larger than normal in a diesel submarine which would account in part for the large displacement for a comparatively short hull.

Submarines—*continued*

56 "FOXTROT" CLASS

(PATROL SUBMARINES)

Displacement, tons	2 000 surface; 2 300 submerged
Length, feet (*metres*)	296·8 (*90·5*)
Beam, feet (*metres*)	24·1 (*7·3*)
Draught, feet (*metres*)	19·0 (*5·8*)
Torpedo tubes	10—21 in (6 bow, 4 aft) (20 torpedoes carried)
Main engines	Diesels; 3 shafts; 6 000 bhp; 3 electric motors; 6 000 hp
Speed, knots	20 surface; 15 submerged
Complement	70
Range	20 000 miles surface cruising

Built between 1958 and 1967 at Sudomekh and Leningrad. A follow-on of the "Zulu" class with similar propulsion to the "Golf" class. A most successful class which has been deployed world-wide, forming the bulk of the Soviet submarine force in the Mediterranean. Four transferred to India in 1968-69.

"Foxtrot" Class

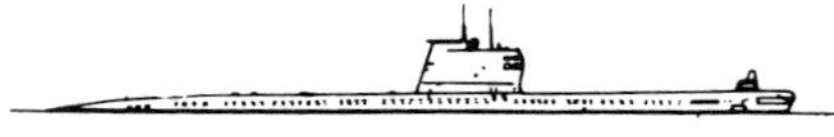
"Foxtrot" *Class*

"Foxtrot" Class 1971

"Foxtrot" *Class* 1972

14 "ROMEO" CLASS

(PATROL SUBMARINES)

Displacement, tons	1 100 surface; 1 600 submerged
Length, feet (*metres*)	246·0 (*75·0*)
Beam, feet (*metres*)	24·0 (*7·3*)
Draught, feet (*metres*)	14·5 (*4·4*)
Torpedo tubes	6—21 in bow
Main engines	Diesels; 4 000 bhp; Electric motors; 4 000 hp; 2 shafts
Speed, knots	17 surface; 14 submerged
Complement	65

These are a medium range type of an improved "W" class design with modernised superstructure, conning tower, and sonar installation. All built in 1958 to 1961. It is probable that this would have been a much larger class had it not been for the advent of the nuclear submarines. Six of this class transferred to Egypt in 1966 and the Chinese are building a considerable force of the same type of submarines.

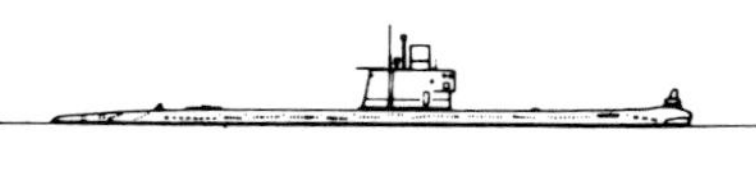
"Romeo" *Class*

"Romeo" Class 1972

Submarines—*continued*

22 "QUEBEC" CLASS

(PATROL SUBMARINES)

Displacement, tons	650 surface; 740 submerged
Length, feet (*metres*)	185·0 (*56·4*)
Beam, feet (*metres*)	18·0 (*5·5*)
Draught, feet (*metres*)	13·2 (*4·0*)
Torpedo tubes	4—21 in bow
Main engines	1 diesel; 3 shafts; 3 000 bhp 3 electric motors; 2 500 hp
Speed, knots	18 surface; 16 submerged
Oil fuel, tons	50
Range, miles	7 000 cruising
Complement	40

Short range, coastal submarines. Built from 1954 to 1957. Thirteen were constructed in 1955 by Sudomekh Shipyard, Leningrad. The earlier boats of this class were fiitted wth what was possibly a closed-cycle propulsion, probably on the third shaft. This may however, have been a Walther HTP turbine but, whatever it was, it is believed to have been unsuccessful and subsequently removed.

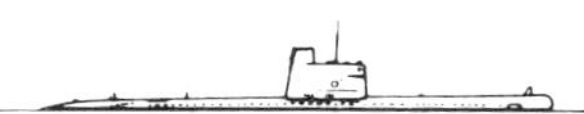
"Quebec" *Class*

"Quebec" Class — *1965, S. Breyer*

"Zulu IV" Class with extended fin — *1972*

22 "ZULU IV" CLASS

(PATROL SUBMARINES)

Displacement, tons	1 900 surface; 2 200 submerged
Length, feet (*metres*)	259·3 (*90·0*)
Beam, feet (*metres*)	23·9 (*7·3*)
Draught, feet (*metres*)	19·0 (*5·8*)
Torpedo tubes	10—21 in (6 bow, 4 stern); 24 torpedoes carried (or 40 mines)
Main engines	Diesel-electric; 3 shafts 3 diesels; 10 000 bhp 3 electric motors; 3 500 hp
Speed, knots	18 surface; 15 submerged
Radius, miles	20 000 to 26 000
Complement	70

The first large post-war patrol submarines built by USSR. Completed from late 1951 to 1955. General appearance is streamlined with a complete row of free-flood holes along the casing. Eighteen were built by Sudomekh Shipyard, Leningrad, in 1952-55 and others at Severodvinsk. The general external similarity to the later German U-boats of WW II suggests that this was not an entirely indigenous design. All now appear to be of the "Zulu" IV type. A recent deployment of six of these boats to the Mediterranean shows them still to be in active service, possibly as first-command boats.

The "Zulu V" conversions of this class provided the first Soviet ballistic missile submarines with SS-N-4 systems.

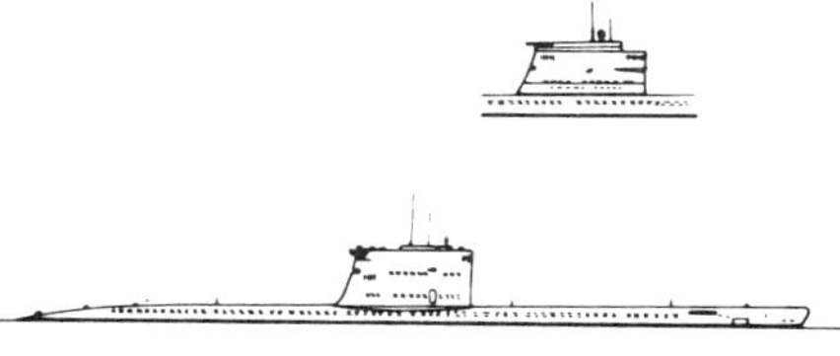
"Zulu IV" Class

"Zulu IV" *Class* — *1969, MOD*

Submarines—*continued*

130 "WHISKY" CLASS

(PATROL SUBMARINES)

Displacement, tons	1 030 surface; 1 180 submerged
Length, feet (*metres*)	240·0 (*73·2*)
Beam, feet (*metres*)	22·0 (*6·7*)
Draught, feet (*metres*)	15·0 (*4·6*)
Torpedo tubes	6—21 in (4 bow, 2 stern); 18 torpedoes carried (or 40 mines)
Main engines	Diesel-electric; 2 shafts; Diesels: 4 000 bhp Electric motors: 2 500 hp
Speed, knots	17 surface, 15 submerged
Radius, miles	13 000 to 16 500
Complement	60

"Whisky" *Class*

This was the first post-war Soviet design for a medum-range submarine. Like its larger contemporary the "Zulu", this class shows considerable German influence. About 240 of the "Whisky s" were built between 1951 and 1957 at yards throughout the USSR. Became for for a number of years the work-horse of the Soviet submarine fleet and is still deployed out-of-area from time to time. Now being paid-off at an accelerating rate, possibly currently 15-20 per year. Has been the most popular export model; currently in service in Albania (4) Bulgaria (2), China (21), Egypt (6), Indonesia (10), North Korea (4) and Poland (4).

"Whisky" Class *1970, Niels Gartig*

"Whisky" Class *1972*

"Whisky" Class *1970, MOD (UK)*

5 "WHISKY CANVAS-BAG" CLASS

(RADAR PICKET SUBMARINES)

Displacement, tons	1 100 surface; 1 200 submerged
Length, feet (*metres*)	240·0 (*73·2*)
Beam, feet (*metres*)	22·0 (*6·7*)
Draught, feet (*metres*)	15·0 (*4·6*)
Torpedo tubes	6—21 in (4 bow, 2 stern)
Main engines	Diesels: 4 000 bhp Electric motors: 2 500 hp
Speed, knots	17 surface; 15 submerged

Basically of same design as the "Whisky" class but with long-range Boat-Sail radar aerial mounted on the fin. The coy way in which this is normally covered prompted the title "Canvas Bag". Converted in 1959 to 1963.

Whisky Canvas Bag *1972, S. Breyer*

CRUISERS

12 "SVERDLOV" CLASS

ADMIRAL LAZAREV
ADMIRAL SENYAVIN
ADMIRAL USHAKOV
ALEKSANDR NEVSKI
ALEKSANDR SUVOROV
DMITRI POZHARSKI
DZERZHINSKI
MIKHAIL KUTUSOV
MURMANSK
OKTYABRSKAYA REVOLUTSIYA
SVERDLOV
ZHDANOV

Displacement, tons	15 450 standard; 19 200 full load
Length, feet (*metres*)	656·2 (*200·0*)pp; 689·0 (*210·0*)oa
Beam, feet (*metres*)	72·2 (*22·0*)
Draught, feet (*metres*)	24·5 (*7·5*) max
Armour	Belts 3·9—4·9 in (*100—125 mm*); fwd and aft 1·6—2 in (*40—50 mm*); turrets 4·9 in (*125 mm*); C.T. 5·9 in (*150 mm*); decks 1—2 in (*25—50 mm*) and 2—3 in (*50—75 mm*)
Missile launchers	Twin "SA-N-2" aft in *Dzerzhinski* (see conversions)
Guns, surface	12—6 in (*152 mm*), 4 triple (3 Twins in *Dzerzhinski*)
Guns, dual purpose	12—3·9 in (*100 mm*), 6 twin
Guns, AA	22 to 32—37 mm (11 to 16 twin mounts), see *Gunnery*
Torpedo tubes	10—21 in (*533 mm*) 2 quintuple (see *Torpedoes*)
Mines	140 to 250 capacity
Boilers	6 watertube
Main engines	Geared turbines; 2 shafts; 130 000 shp
Speed, knots	34
Range, miles	8 700 at 18 knots
Oil fuel, tons	3 800
Complement	1 000 average

GENERAL

Of the 24 cruisers of this class originally projected, 20 keels were laid and 17 hulls were launched from 1951 onwards, but only 14 ships were completed by 1956. There were two slightly different types. *Sverdlov* and sisters had the 37 mm AA guns near the fore-funnel one deck higher than in later cruisers. All ships are fitted for minelaying. Mine stowage is on the second deck.

CONVERSIONS. *Dzerzhinski* has been fitted with an SA-N-2 launcher aft replacing one X-Turret. In 1972 *Admiral Senyavin* returned to service with both X and Y turrets removed and replaced by a helicopter pad and a hangar surmounted by four 30 mm mountings and an SA-N-4 mounting. At about the same time *Zhdanov* appeared on the scene with a different outfit. She has had only X-turret removed and replaced by a high deckhouse mounting an SA-N-4 launcher. Radar, in all cases, to suit.

ELECTRONICS. Fitted with a large amount of electronic equipment. A long range air surveillance radar antenna is mounted high up on the forward side of the mainmast, and what appears to be a height finder antenna aft of the forward funnel in the *Dzerzhinski*.
A "cheese" antenna for a surface search radar is mounted at the top of the mainmast, and what may be an antenna for a low coverage and "Sea skimmer" detection radar at the top of the foremast. Four parabolic antennae are mounted on the guided missile director.
Navigation radar antennae are mounted before the superstructure. Other electronic detection equipment is fitted and probably active jamming equipment. Earlier ships of the class noticeably carry considerably less electronic gear than *Dzerzhinski*.

RADAR. Search: Head Net A, Strut Curve and some ships fitted with Big Net and Top Trough. *Dzerzhinski* only.—Fire control: with Peel Group and Drum Tilt. High Lune and Fan Song E for SA-N-2 system.

TORPEDOES. *Oktyabrskaya Revolutsya* and *Murmansk* no longer have tubes.

NAMES. The ship first named *Molotovsk* was renamed *Oktyabrskaya Revolutsiya* in 1957.

DISPOSAL AND TRANSFER. *Admiral Nakhimov* was deleted from the list in 1969. *Ordzhonikidze* was transferred to the Indonesian Navy in Oct 1962 and renamed *Irian*. Now scrapped.

MURMANSK (ex-*Zhdanov*) 1967

ZHDANOV (after conversion) 1972

DRAWING. Starboard elevation and plan of *Dzerzhinski*.
Scale: 125 feet = 1 inch (1 : 1 500).

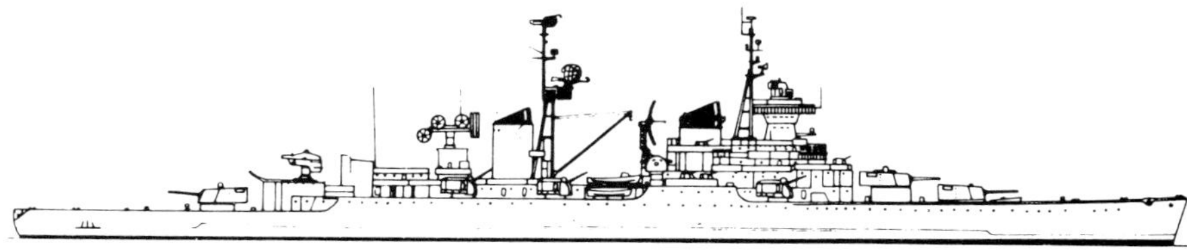

DZERZHINSKI. Twin missile launcher in place of "X" turret

SVERDLOV *Class*

Cruisers—*continued*

DZERZHINSKI with twin SA-N-2 launcher in place of "X" turret *1972*

MIKHAIL KUTUZOV with "Top Trough" radar on mainmast *1970*

ADMIRAL SENYAVIN (after conversion showing hangar and SA-N-4) *1972*

Cruisers—*continued*

2 "CHAPAEV" CLASS

KOMSOMOLETS (ex-*Chkalov*) **ZHELEZNYAKOV**

Displacement, tons	11 500 standard; 15 000 full load
Length, feet (*metres*)	659·5 (*201·0*)
Beam, feet (*metres*)	62 (*18·9*)
Draught, feet (*metres*)	24 (*7·3*)
Guns, surface	**12—6 in (*152 mm*), 4 triple**
Guns, dual purpose	**8—3·9 in (*100 mm*), 4 twin**
Guns, AA	**24—37 mm (12 twin)**
Mines	**100 to 200 capacity**
Boilers	**6 watertube**
Main engines	**Geared turbines, with diesels for cruising speeds; 4 shafts; 120 000 shp**
Speed, knots	**34**
Range, miles	5 400 at 15 knots
Oil fuel, tons	2 500
Complement	900

Laid down in 1939-40. Launched during 1941-47. All work on these ships was stopped during the war, but was resumed in 1946-47. Completed in 1948-50. Catapults were removed from all ships of this type. Both remaining ships serve as training cruisers.

RADAR. These ships do not appear to have been fitted with modern electronic equipment. It is reasonable to assume that they have long range surveillance radars and Gunfire Control tracking radar.

GUNNERY. Turret guns are in separate sleeves allowing independent elevation to at least 50 degrees.

APPEARANCE. Heavy director on control tower, pole foremast and tripod mainmast forward of after funnel. Vertical funnels. Higher freeboard and funnels than "Kirov" class. Resemble "Sverdlov" class but forecastle deck breaks abreast forefunnel instead of at quarter deck.

DRAWING. Starboard elevation and plan. Scale: 125 feet = 1 inch (1 : 1 500).

DISPOSALS. *Chapaev, Frunse* and *Kuibyshev* of this class were discarded; and the remaining two ships are obsolescent and will probably be laid up in the near future.

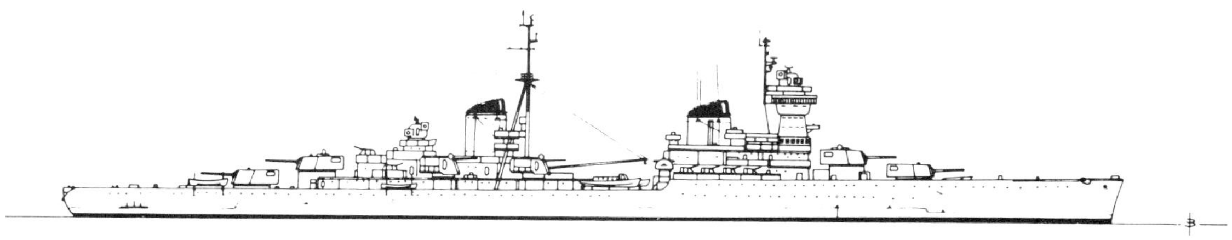

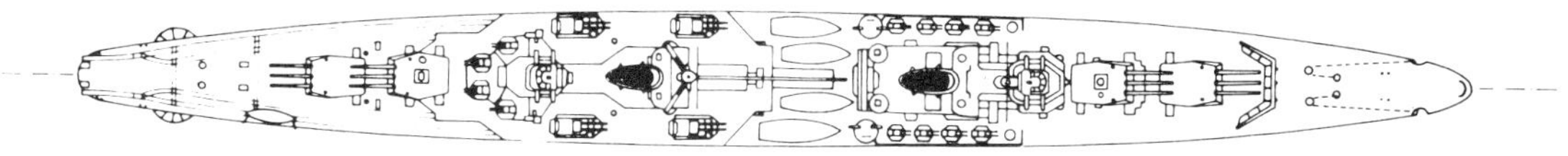

KOMSOMOLETS *1970, Niels Gartig*

ZHELEZNYAKOV *1959, Antonov Rogov*

Cruisers—*continued*

2 "KIROV" CLASS

Displacement, tons	8 500 standard; 10 000 full load
Length, feet (*metres*)	613·5 (*178·0*)pp; 626·7 (*191·0*)oa
Beam, feet (*metres*)	56·3 (*17·6*)
Draught, feet (*metres*)	**20·7 (*6·3*)**
Armour	**Side 3 in (*75 mm*); deck 2 in (*50 mm*); C.T. and gunhouses 3·9 in (*100 mm*)**
Guns, surface	**9—7·1 in (*180 mm*)**
Guns, dual purpose	**6—3·9 in (*100 mm*)**
Torpedo tubes	**6—21 in (*533 mm*) removed**
Mines	**60—90 capacity**
Main engines	**Geared turbines, with diesels for cruising speeds; 2 shafts; 113 000 shp**
Boilers	**6 Yarrow**
Speed, knots	**34**
Range, miles	4 000 at 15 knots
Oil fuel, tons	2 500
Complement	734

Name	*Builders*	*Laid down*	*Launched*	*Completed*
KIROV	Putilov DY	**1934**	**1 Dec 1936**	**28 Sep 1938**
SLAVA (ex-*Molotov*)	Marti Yard, Nikolaye	**1935**	**23 Feb 1939**	**1944**

Design and technical direction of construction by Ansaldo. Of this class *Ordzhonikidze* under construction at Nikolayev, was wrecked by high explosives before the enemy occupied that port in Aug 1941.

APPEARANCE. ***Kirov*** **has very long forecastle, heavy tripod mast stepped abaft forebridge, light tripod stepped abaft second funnel, very large funnels.** ***Slava*** **has high director tower on forebridge, light tripod foremast abaft bridge, heavy tripod mainmast stepped abaft second funnel and generally lighter appearance.**

RADAR. Search: Head Net A and Strut Curve. Fire Control: Probably Drum Tilt. Hairnet.

GUNNERY. Triple guns are mounted in one sleeve and are incapable of individual elevation. Maximum elevation 40 degrees. For her role as a training ship *Kirov* has 9—7·1 inch, 6—3·9 inch, 8—37 mm and 2 older guns and no torpedo tubes.

DISPOSALS. *Kaganovich*, *Kalinin* and *Maksim Gorki* of this class are reported to have been scrapped. *Voroshilov* was the sixth cruiser of this group.

DRAWING. Starboard elevation and plan of ***Kirov.*** **Drawn in 1970. Scale: 125 feet = 1 inch (1 : 1 500).**

NAMES. *Molotov* was reported to have been renamed *Slava* in 1962.

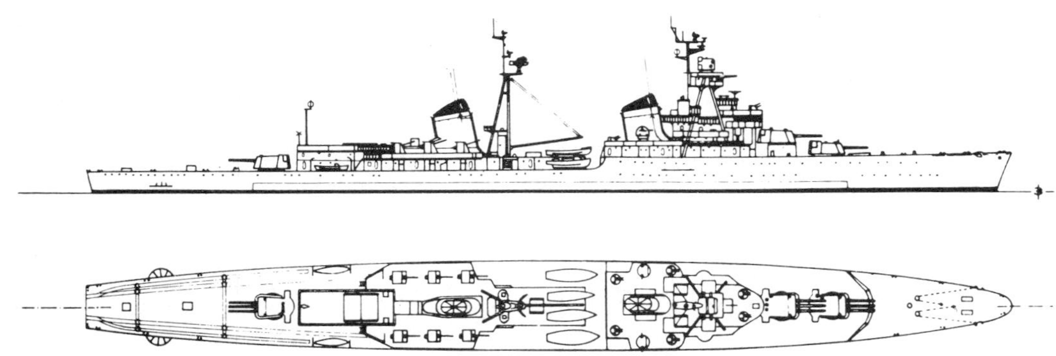

SLAVA *1971, MOD, (UK)*

KIROV *1970, Bertil Gard*

"KARA" CLASS (CLGM)

NIKOLAYEV + 2 building

Displacement, tons	10 000
Length, feet (*metres*)	560 (*170·7*)
Beam, feet (*metres*)	62 (*18·9*)
Draught, feet (*metres*)	20 (*6·2*)
Aircraft	1 Hormone A helicopter. (Hangar aft)
Missile Systems	8—SS-N-10 (Two mounts abreast bridge) 2—SA-N-4 (either side of mast) 2—SA-N-3 (Twins for'd and aft)
Guns	4—76 mm (2 Twins abaft bridge) 8—30 mm (4 Twins abreast funnel)
A/S Weapons	2—16 barrelled MBU rocket launchers (forward) 2—6 barrelled MBU rocket launchers (aft)
Torpedo tubes	10—21 in (2 pentad mountings abaft funnel)
Main Engines	Probably gas-turbine
Speed, knots	Approximately 34

GENERAL
Apart from the specialised "Moskva" class this is the first large cruiser to join the Soviet navy since the "Sverdlov's". Built at Nikolayev, she was first seen in public when she entered the Mediterranean from the Black Sea on 2 March 1973. Clearly capable of prolonged operations overseas she has yet to prove her seakeeping qualities. However on past experience these will presumably be up to the high standard set by her predecessors.

RADAR. Topsail and Headnet C; Headlight for SA-N-3 system; Owl Screech for 76 mm guns; separate systems for SA-N-4; Drum Tilt for 30 mm guns.

ECM. A full outfit appears to be housed on the bridge and mast.

MISSILES. In addition to the "Kresta II" armament of eight tubes for the SS-N-10 (29 mile) surface-to-surface system and the pair of twin launchers for SA-N-3 system with Goblet missiles, "Kara" mounts the new SA-N-4 system in two silos, either side of the mast. The combination of such a number of systems presents a formidable capability, matched by no other ship.

GUNNERY. The sighting of both main and secondary armament on either beam in the waist follows the precedent of both "Kresta" classes, although the weight of the main armament is increased.

SONAR AND A/S. VDS is mounted below the helicopter pad and is presumably complementary to a hull-mounted set or sets. The presence of the helicopter with dipping-sonar and an A/S weapon load adds to her long-range capability.

NIKOLAYEV *1973*

NIKOLAYEV *1973, MOD (UK)*

Cruisers—*continued*

ACCOMMODATION. It is interesting to speculate on conditions below decks which are presumably fairly spartan but certainly must have some form of air-conditioning. However the demands on space for the great number of radar offices and heat-generating machinery—spaces must be less, even, than that for magazines. From forward to aft this will include:—
a) one amidships for forward MBUs.
b) one amidships for forward SA-N-3.
c) one on either beam for SS-N-10.
d) one on either beam for 76 mm ammunition.
e) one on either beam for SA-N-4.
f) one on either beam for 30 mm ammunition.
g) presumably one on either beam for reload torpedoes.
h) one amidships for after SA-N-3.
i) one on either beam for after MBUs.

NIKOLAYEV — *1973*

6 "KRESTA II" CLASS (CLGM)

ADMIRAL MAKAROV
ADMIRAL NANAKHIMOV
KRONSTADT
+3

Displacement, tons	6 000 standard; 7 500 full load
Length, feet (*metres*)	519·9 (*158·5*)
Beam, feet (*metres*)	55·1 (*16·8*)
Draught, feet (*metres*)	19·7 (*6·0*)
Aircraft	1 Hormone A
Missile launchers	2 quadruple for SS-N-10; 2 twin for SA-N-3
A/S weapons	2—12 barrelled forward and 2—6 barrelled aft for rocket launchers
Torpedo tubes	10—21 in (two quintuple)
Guns	4—57 mm (2 twin) dual purpose; 8—30 mm (4 twin) anti-aircraft
Main engines	Steam turbines; 2 shafts 100 000 shp
Boilers	4 watertube
Speed, knots	33
Range, miles	5 000 at 18 knots
Complement	500

KRESTA II Class — *1969, S. Breyer*

GENERAL

Multi-purpose guided missile armed, anti-submarine and helicopter cruisers. The design was developed from that of the "Kresta I" class, but the layout is more sophisticated and the missile and director and radar complex presents a bristling appearance. The missile armament shows an advance on the "Kresta I" SAM armament and a complete change of practice in the fitting of the SS-N-10 system with 29 mile range missiles. This is a mach 1·2 missile and the fact that it has subsequently been fitted in the "Kara" and "Krivak" classes indicates a possible change in tactical thought. Building of this class is continuing. Built at Leningrad from 1968 onwards.

FLIGHT. A flight of two helicopters could be operated, although the normal would appear to be one on the apron aft with adjacent low hangar.

ELECTRONICS. The electronic installation appears to have exploited in a smaller compass that fitted in the helicopter missile cruisers *Moskva* and *Leningrad* and is a logical improvement on that in the "Kresta" I class.

RADAR. The radar installation seems to be similar to that in the "Moskva" class with the same "Top Sail" 3 D and Head Net C 3D for search radar and the Head Light and "Peel Group" (2) fire control radar for surface to air missiles and "Drum Tilt" (2) for guns. Muff Cob also fitted.

KRESTA II Class — *1971*

KRESTA II Class — *1971, S. Breyer*

Cruisers—*continued*

4 "KRESTA I" CLASS (CLGM)

ADMIRAL DROZD | **SEVASTOPOL**
ADMIRAL ZOZULYA | **VLADIVOSTOK**

Displacement, tons	5 140 standard; 6 500 full load
Length, feet (*metres*)	510 (*155·5*)
Beam, feet (*metres*)	55·1 (*16·8*)
Draught, feet (*metres*)	18·0 (*5·5*)
Aircraft	1 Hormone A helicopter with hangar aft
Missile launchers	2 twin SS-N-3 for Shaddock 2 twin SA-N-1 for Goa
A/S weapons	2—12-barrelled launchers forward 2—6-barrelled launchers aft
Torpedo tubes	10 (two quintuple) 21 in
Guns	4—57 mm (2 twin)
Main engines	Steam turbines; 2 shafts; 100 000 shp
Boilers	4 watertube
Speed, knots	34
Range, miles	4 500 at 18 knots
Complement	400

GENERAL
Provided with a helicopter hangar and flight apron aft for the first time in a Soviet ship. This could give an enhanced A/S capability and could certainly provide carried-on-board target-location facilities for the 300 mile SB-N-3 system at a lower, possibly optimum, range. The "Kresta I" was, therefore the first Soviet missile cruiser free to operate alone and distant from own aircraft.

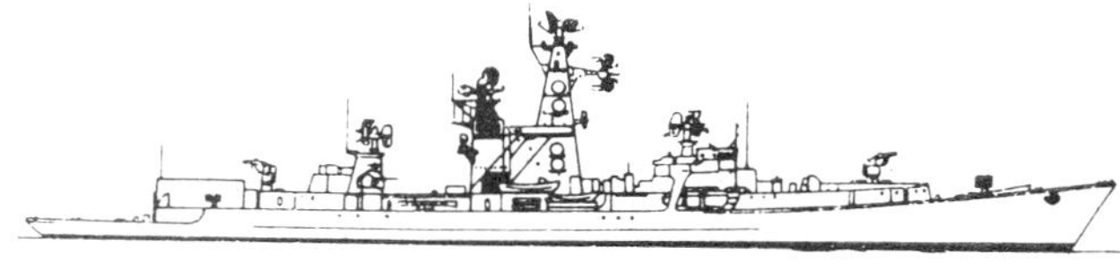
KRESTA I *Class*

Two ships of the class were reported building at the Zhdanov Shipyard, Leningrad. The prototype ship was laid down in Sep 1964, launched in 1965 and carried out sea trials in the Baltic in Feb 1967. The second ship was launched in 1966 and the others in 1967-68.

RADAR. These vessels illustrate the greatly increased use of electronic equipment in the USSR navy. A long range air surveillance radar antenna is mounted above the funnel, whilst a V beam, 3-D radar antenna is mounted at the top of the superstructure. This radar is probably used to provide acquisition data for the surface to air missile systems. A pair of what appear to be surface surveillance radar antennae are mounted on a sponson of the superstructure. These are probably used for surface tactical data acquisition and for surface fire control in a "track-while-scan" mode. The two missile directors each carry antennae of a type seen in "Precision Approach Radar Systems" where target position is obtained in the horizontal and vertical planes separately, unlike the more orthodox conical scan or monopulse tracking radar systems which employ a circular parabolic antenna. Four pods, or radomes, are fitted to the sides of the superstructure. These are similar to those fitted in the "Moskva" class helicopter missile cruisers and probably contain passive detection and active jamming equipment. Search: Head Net C 3D and Big Net. Fire Control: Scoop Pair for "Shaddock" system and Peel Group (2) for "Goa" system. Muff Cob.

The all-round radar on top of the mast is known as "Head Net-C" and the fire control radar for the "SA-N-1" missiles forward and aft is known as "Peel Group".

KRESTA I Class — *1969, MOD (UK)*

KRESTA I Class No. 546 — *1971, US Navy*

Cruisers—*continued*

KRESTA I Class *1971, USN*

KRESTA I Class *1971, Canadian Armed Forces*

Cruisers—*continued*

4 "KYNDA" CLASS (CLGM)

ADMIRAL FOKIN
ADMIRAL GOLOVKO
GROZNY
VARYAG

Displacement, tons	4 500 standard; 6 000 full load
Length, feet (*metres*)	465·8 (*142·0*)
Beam, feet (*metres*)	51·8 (*15·8*)
Draught, feet (*metres*)	17·4 (*5·3*)
Aircraft	Pad for helicopter on stern
Missile launchers	2 quadruple mounts, 1 fwd, 1 aft for SS-N-3 system 1 twin mount on forecastle for SA-N-1 system
A/S weapons	2—12 barrelled rocket launchers on forecastle
Guns, AA	4—3 in (*76 mm*) 2 twin
Torpedo tubes	6—21 in (*533 mm*) 2 triple ASW amidships.
Main engines	2 sets geared turbines; 2 shafts; 100 000 shp
Boilers	4 high pressure
Speed, knots	35
Complement	390

KYNDA Class

GENERAL
The first light cruiser of this class was laid down in June 1960, launched in Apr 1961 at Zhdanov Shipyard, Leningrad, and completed in June 1962. The second ship was launched in Nov 1961 and fitted out in Aug 1962. The others were completed by 1965. Two enclosed towers, instead of masts, are stepped forward of each raked funnel. Two screws and two rudders. In this class there is no helicopter embarked, so some form of external target-location and, possibly, mid-course guidance, would be required for the SS-N-3 system. She will therefore be constrained in her operations compared with the "Kresta I" with her own helicopter.

RADAR. Equipped with a very comprehensive and generous electronics installation. Fitted with duplicated combined air and surface search radars, with duplicated antennae at the foremast and mainmast heads. The reason for the duplication may be for reserves in the event of action damage. The antennae, mounted in pairs on the sponsons extending forward from the foremast and aft from the mainmast are probably used for surface tracking of targets to be engaged by the "Shaddock" surface-to-surface missiles. The use of four separate antennae for this purpose seems to be because the techniques of Track-while-scan may not be trusted, or yet developed by the Soviet Navy. The "Goa" surface to air missiles, launched from the forward mounting are controlled by the radar, whose antennae are mounted on the director above the bridge, whilst the guns are radar controlled from the antenna mounted abaft the after funnel. Search: Head Net A. Fire Control: Scoop Pair (2) for "Shaddock" systems, Peel Group for "Goa" systems and Owl Screech for gun.

KYNDA Class No. 854 *1972*

KYNDA Class No. 810 *1972*

DESTROYERS

5 "KRIVAK" CLASS (DDGSP)

BODRY **SVIREPY**
DOSTOYNY **+ 2**

KRIVAK *Class*

KRIVAK Class 1972

Displacement, tons	4 800 standard; 5 200 full load
Length, feet (*metres*)	404·8 (*123·4*)
Beam, feet (*metres*)	45·9 (*14·0*)
Draught, feet (*metres*)	16·4 (*5·0*)
Missile launchers	4 (in an angled quadruple bank) for SS-N-10 surface-to-surface missiles, in "A" position; 2 for SA-N-4 surface-to-air missiles
A/S weapons	2 twelve-barrelled launchers forward for rocket missiles in "B" position
Torpedo tubes	8—21 in (*533 mm*) in two quadruple banks on port and starboard sides amidships
Guns	4—3 in (*76 mm*) dual purpose automatic (2 twin) in "X" and "Y" positions; 4—30 mm
Main engines	8 sets Gas turbines; 2 shafts; 112 000 shp
Speed, knots	38

GENERAL
This handsome class, the first ship of which appeared in 1971, appears to be a most successful design incorporating surface and anti-air capability, a VDS with associated MBUs, two banks of tubes, all in a hull designed for both speed and sea-keeping. The use of gas-turbines gives "Krivak" a rapid acceleration and an availability which cannot be matched by steam driven ships.

RADAR. Head Net C. Drum Tilt and Head Light.

MISSILES. The surface-to-surface missiles of the SS-N-10 system have a range of 29 miles, continuing the short-range trend of the "Kresta II" class and followed by the "Kara" class. The SA-N-4 SAMs are of a new design which is now mounted also in the "Kara", "Nanuchka" and "Grisha" classes. The launcher retracts into the mounting for stowage and protection, rising to fire and retracting to reload. The two mountings are forward of the bridge and abaft the funnel.

KRIVAK Class 1972

KRIVAK Class 1972

Destroyers—*continued*

KRIVAK Class

1971

19 "KASHIN" CLASS (DLG)

KRASNY-KAVKAZ	**SMETLIVY**
KRASNY-KRIM	**SOOBRAZITELNY**
OBRAZTSOVY	**SPOSOBNY**
OTVAZHNY	**STEREGUSHCHY**
PROVORNY	**STROGNY**
SLAVNY	**STROYNY**
SMELY	+ 6

KASHIN Class

Displacement, tons	4 300 standard; 5 200 full load
Length, feet (*metres*)	470·9 (*143·3*)
Beam, feet (*metres*)	52·5 (*15·9*)
Draught, feet (*metres*)	19 (*5·8*)
Missile launchers	4 (2 twin) SA-N-1 mounted in "B" and "X" positions for surface-to-air missiles
Guns, AA	4—3 in (*76 mm*), 2 twin, in "A" and "Y" positions
A/S weapons	2—12 barrelled ASW rocket launchers forward; 2—6 barrelled ASW rocket launchers aft
Torpedo tubes	5—21 in (*533 mm*) quintuple, amidships for ASW torpedoes
Main engines	8 sets gas turbines; each 12 000 hp; 2 shafts; 96 000 shp
Speed, knots	35

GENERAL
The first class of warships in the world to rely entirely on gas turbine-propulsion giving them the quick get-away and acceleration necessary for modern tactics. These ships were delivered from 1962 onwards from the Zhdanov Yard, Leningrad and the Nosenko Yard, Nikolayev. Despite their comparative youth the "Kashin's" with a somewhat dated SAM system, no SSM, and neither helicopter nor VDS, have been rapidly out-dated by later classes.

RADAR. Search: Head Net C and Big Net in some ships; Head Net A (2) in others. Fire control: Peel Group (2) for "Goa" system and Owl Screech (2) for guns.
There are differing radars atop the mainmast in some ships, see photographs below.

KASHIN Class with HEAD NET A radar

1971

Destroyers—*continued*

6 "KANIN" CLASS (DDG)

BOYKY	**ZHGUCHY**
DERZKY	**ZORKY**
GREMYASHCHYI	+ 1

Displacement, tons	3 700 standard; 4 600 full load
Length, feet (*metres*)	456·9 (*139·3*)
Beam, feet (*metres*)	48·2 (*14·7*)
Draught, feet (*metres*)	16·4 (*5·0*)
Aircraft	Helicopter pad
Missile launchers	1 twin "SA-N-1" mounted aft for surface-to-air missiles
A/S weapons	Three 12-barrelled rocket launchers for ASW
Guns	8—57 mm (2 quadruple forward) or 8—30 mm (twin)
Torpedo tubes	10—21 in (*533 mm*) A/S (2 quintuple)
Main engines	2 sets geared steam turbines; 2 shafts; 80 000 shp
Boilers	4 watertube
Oil fuel, tons	900
Speed, knots	34
Complement	350

KANIN Class

GENERAL
All ships of this class have been converted from "Krupny's" at Zhdanov Yard, Leningrad from 1967 onwards, being given a SAM capability instead of the latter's SSM armament.

APPEARANCE. As compared with the "Krupny" class these ships have enlarged bridge, converted bow (probably for a new sonar) and larger helicopter platforms.

RADAR. Search: Head Net C or Head Net A. Fire Control: Peel Group for "Goa", Hawk Screech for guns.

KANIN SAM Class No. 911 — *1972*

KANIN SAM Class — *S. Breyer*

KANIN Class, Hull 2, No. 557, single saluting gun forward — *1972*

Destroyers—*continued*

2 "KRUPNY" CLASS (DDGS)

GNEVNY	GORDY

Displacement, tons	3 650 standard; 4 650 full load
Length, feet (*metres*)	452 (*137·8*)
Beam, feet (*metres*))	48·2 (*14·7*)
Draught, feet (*metres*)	16·5 (*5·0*)
Missile launchers	2 mountings; 1 forward, 1 aft for "SS-N-1" system
Guns, AA	16—57 mm, (4 quadruple; 2 amidships, 1 forward, 1 aft)
Torpedo launchers	6 (2 triple) for 21 in A/S torpedoes
Main engines	Geared steam turbines; 2 shafts 80 000 shp
Boilers	4 high pressure water tube
Speed, knots	34
Complement	360

KRUPNY *Class*

Flush-decked destroyers designed to carry surface-to-surface guided missiles. Helicopter spot landing apron on the stern. Initial construction started in 1958 at Leningrad. Four ships of this class were converted to to carry surface-to-air missiles in 1967 to 1971 and are known as the "Kanin" class, two more subsequently converted.

RADAR. Search: Either Head Net C 3D or Head Net A. Fire Control: Hawk Screech (2) for guns, and, probably surface missiles. Skinhead.

GNEVNY — *1969, MOD, UK*

KRUPNY Class — *1971, USN*

KRUPNY Class No. 703 with HEAD NET A on foremast — *1972*

Destroyers—*continued*

8 "SAM KOTLIN" CLASS (DDG)

BRAVY
NAKHODCHIVY
NASTOYCHIVY
SKROMNY
SKRYTNY
SOZNATELNY
+ 2

Displacement, tons	2 850 standard; 3 885 full load
Length, feet (*metres*)	414·9 (*126·5*)
Beam, feet (*metres*)	42·6 (*13·0*)
Draught, feet (*metres*)	16·1 (*4·9*)
Missile launchers	1 twin SA-N-1 mounted aft
Guns	2—3·9 in (100 *mm*) dp (1 twin) 4—57 mm AA (1 quadruple) 4—30 mm in later ships
A/S weapons	6 side thrown DC projectors or 2—12 barrelled ASW rocket launchers
Main engines	Geared turbines; 2 shafts 72 000 shp
Boilers	4 high pressure
Speed, knots	36
Range, miles	5 500 at 16 knots
Complement	285

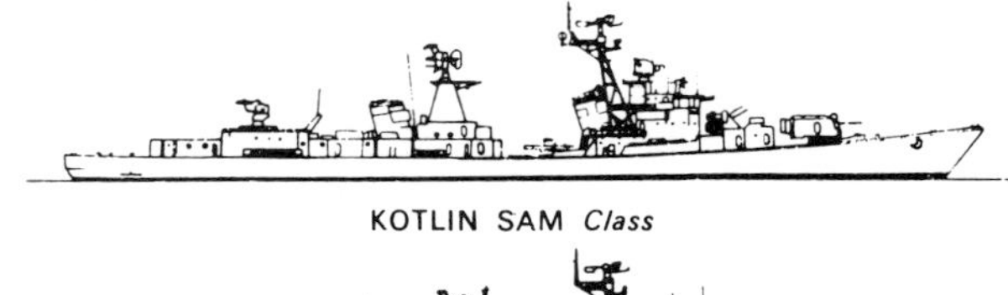

KOTLIN SAM *Class*

KOTLIN SAM PROTOTYPE *Class*

Converted "Kotlin" class destroyers with a surface-to-air missile launcher in place of the main twin turret aft and anti-aircraft guns reduced to one quadruple mounting.

The prototype conversion was completed about 1962 and the others since 1966. One ship transferred to Poland.

APPEARANCE. The prototype "Kotlin" SAM class has a different after funnel and different electronic pedestal to those in the standard "Kotlin" SAM class.

RADAR. Search: Head Net C 3D or Head Net A. Fire Control: Peel Group for "Goa" system, Hawk Screech for guns. Drum Tilt for 30 mm in later ships.

SAM KOTLIN Class — *1971, USN*

Later SAM KOTLIN (with 2 extra Drum Tilt and 4—30 mm by after funnel) — *1973*

SAM KOTLIN Class (with different design of midship radar pedestal and after funnel from the prototype). — *1971 MOD (UK)*

Destroyers— *continued*

4 "KILDIN" CLASS (DDGS)

BEDOVY **NEULOVIMY**
+ 2

Displacement, tons	3 000 standard; 4 000 full load
Length, feet (*metres*)	414·9 (*126·5*)
Beam, feet (*metres*)	42·6 (*13·0*)
Draught, feet (*metres*)	16·1 (*4·9*)
Missile launchers	1 for "SS-N-1" system
A/S weapons	2—16 barrel rocket launchers on forecastle
Guns, AA	16—57 mm, 4 quadruple
Torpedo tubes	4—21 in (2 twin)
Main engines	Geared turbines; 2 shafts 72 000 shp
Boilers	4 high pressure
Speed, knots	36 max
Range, miles	5 500 at 16 knots
Complement	350 officers and men

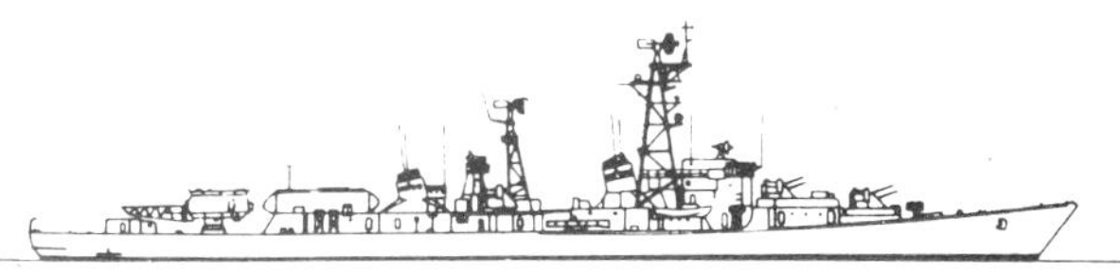

KILDIN *Class*

Large destroyers with the "Kotlin" type hull, but re-designed as guided missile armed destroyers with a launcher installed in place of the after gun mountings.

Bedovyj was rebuilt in 1957-58 in Nikolaev. Only *Bedovyj* had 16—45 mm AA (4 quadruple), other three 16—57 mm AA (4 quadruple). *Bedovy* has a different foremast and funnels from her three sister ships and retains gunnery director on top of bridge. (See photographs).

RADAR. Search: Head Net A and Slim Net. Fire Control: Hawk Screech (2) for guns and probably, surface missiles. Flat Spin in some.

BEDOVY (with KOTLIN type director) *1970*

KILDIN Class *1969, S. Breyer*

BEDOVYJ *1971*

Destroyers— *continued*

18 "KOTLIN" CLASS (DD)

BESSLEDNYJ	SVETLYIJ
BLAGORODNYJ	VDOKHNOVENNYJ
BLESTYASHCHYJ	VDUMCHIVYJ
BURLIVYJ	VOZBUZHDENNYJ
NAPORISTYJ	VOZMUSHCHENNYJ
PLAMENNYJ	VYDERZHANNYJ

KOTLIN HELO *Class*

KOTLIN *Class* (KOTLIN MOD *Class* after TT replaced by deckhouse)

Displacement, tons	2 850 standard; 3 885 full load
Length, feet (*metres*)	414·9 (*126·5*)
Beam, feet (*metres*)	42·6 (*13·0*)
Draught, feet (*metres*)	16·1 (*4·9*) max
Guns	4—5·1 in (*130 mm*) dp (2 twin) 16—45 mm AA (4 quadruple)
A/S weapons	6 side thrown DC projectors or 2—16 barrelled rocket launchers
Torpedo tubes	10—21 in (*533 mm*)
Mines	80 capacity
Main engines	Geared turbines; 2 shafts; 72 000 shp
Boilers	4 high pressure
Speed, knots	36
Range, miles	5 500 at 16 knots
Complement	285

GENERAL
These destroyers, built in 1954-57, were designed for mass production. The last four hulls were converted to "Kildin's".

ANTI-SUBMARINE WARFARE. The six depth charge throwers are welded to the deck, three on each beam at the stern, affording only transverse throw. They are apparently charged from deck magazines. Some ships of the class were modified with deckhouse replacing the after torpedo tubes and a pair of ASW rocket launchers added forward and aft.

MODERNISATION. Several of this class were modernised, with extensive modifications in anti-submarine and anti-aircraft armament. Some, including *Svetlyj* were fitted with helicopter platform abaft the after mounting. Seven more were converted with surface-to-air twin missile launcher aft, installed atop a deckhouse in place of the after guns; with missile radar and tower fitted before the after funnel, see previous page.

RADAR. Search: Slim Net and Strut Curve. Fire Control: Hawk Screech (2). Hair Net. Square Head. Flat Spin in some.

KOTLIN Class — *1970, S. Breyer*

KOTLIN Class — *1972*

KOTLIN Class (helicopter platform aft) — *1969, MOD, (UK)*

Destroyers—*continued*

45 "SKORY" CLASS (DD)

BESSMENNY	**BEZUKORIZNENNY**
OTCHAYANNY	**OZHESTOCHENNY**
OTVETSTVENNY	**OZHIVLENNY**
SERDITY	**STATNY**
SERIOZNY	**STEPENNY**
SMOTRYASHCHI	**STOJKY**
SOKRUSHITELNY	**STREMITELNY**
SOLIDNY	**SUROVY**
SOVERSHENNY	**SVOBODNY**
VDUMCHIVY	**VRAZUMITELNYI**

Displacement, tons	2 600 standard; 3 500 full load
Length, feet	395·2 (*120·5*)
Beam, feet (*metres*)	38·9 (*11·8*)
Draught, feet (*metres*)	15·1 (*4·6*)
Guns, surface	4—5·1 in (*130 mm*), 2 twin
Guns, AA	2—3·4 in (*85 mm*), 1 twin; 8—37 mm (4 twin), formerly 7—37 mm single see *Modernisation* and *Armament*
A/S weapons	4 DCT
Torpedo tubes	10—21 in (*533 mm*)
Mines	80 capacity
Main engines	Geared turbines; 2 shafts; 60 000 shp
Boilers	4 high pressure
Speed, knots	33
Range, miles	3 900 at 13 knots
Complement	260

There were to have been 85 destroyers of this class, but construction beyond 75 units was discontinued in favour of later types of destroyers, and the number has been further reduced to 45 by transfers to other countries, translations to other types and disposals.

MODERNISATION. Six or so ships of the "Skory" class were modified from 1959 onwards under the fleet rehabilitation and modernisation programme, including extensive alterations to anti-aircraft armament, electronic equipment and anti-submarine weapons.

APPEARANCE. There were three differing types in this class, the anti-aircraft guns varying with twin and single mountings; and two types of foremast, one vertical with all scanners on top and the other with one scanner on top and one on a platform half way.

SVOBODNYJ *1968*

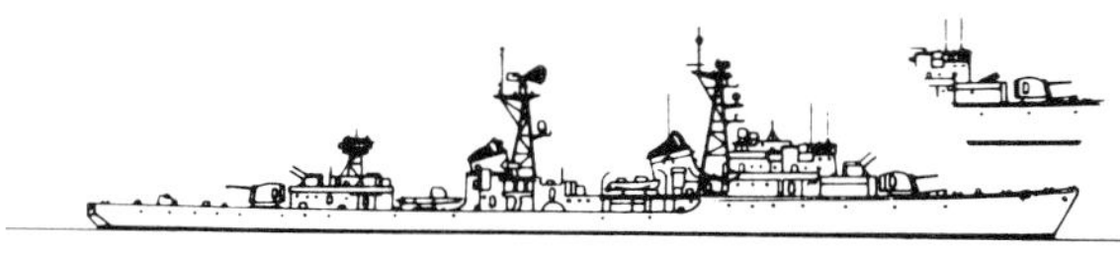

SKORY Modified *Class*

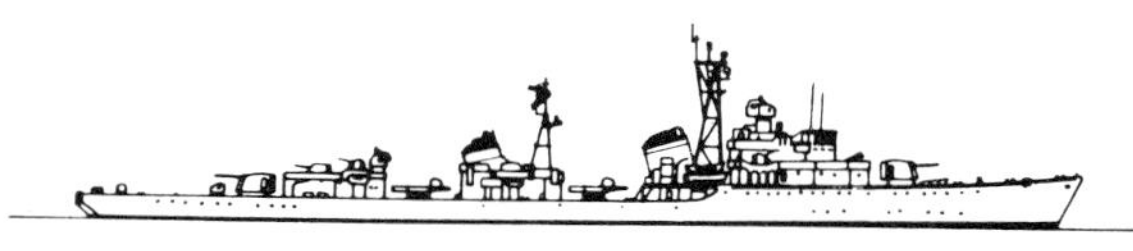

SKORY Original *Class*

RADAR. Search: Strut Curve and unknown S Band. Fire Control: Obsolescent X Band. Square Head.

ARMAMENT. Modernised ships have five 57 mm single, five torpedo tubes and two 16-barrelled ASW rocket launchers.

TRANSFERS. Of this class *Skory* and *Smeriivy* were transferred to the Polish Navy in 1957-58, two to the Egyptian Navy in 1956, four to the Indonesian Navy in 1959, and two (modernised) to Egypt in 1968.

1 "TALLIN" CLASS (DD)

NEUSTRASHIMYJ

Displacement, tons	3 200 standard; 4 300 full load
Length, feet (*metres*)	440·0 (*134·0*) oa
Beam, feet (*metres*)	44·9 (*13·7*)
Draught, feet (*metres*)	16·1 (*4·9*)
Guns, dual purpose	4—5·1 in (*130 mm*) semi-automatic (2 twin)
Guns, AA	16—45 mm (4 quadruple)
A/S weapons	2—16 barrelled ASW rocket launchers and 2 DC rocket launchers
Torpedo tubes	10—21 in (*533 mm*), 2 quintuple
Mines	70 to 90 according to size
Main engines	Geared turbines; 2 shafts; 80 000 shp
Boilers	4 water tube
Speed, knots	38
Range, miles	2 500 at 18 knots
Oil fuel, tons	850
Complement	340

Built in 1952-54.

TALLIN *Class*

GUNNERY. The 5·1 inch (*130 mm*) guns in two twin turrets, including firing directors, are fully stabilised.

RADAR. Search: Slim Net and Strut Curve. Fire Control: Hawk Screech (2).

NEUSTRASHIMYJ ("Tallin" Class) *Skyfotos*

FRIGATES

6 "KOLA" CLASS

Displacement, tons	1 500 standard; 1 900 full load
Length, feet (*metres*)	315·0 (*96·0*) oa
Beam, feet (*metres*)	35·4 (*10·8*)
Draught, feet (*metres*)	11·5 (*3·5*)
Guns, dual purpose	4—3·9 (*100 mm*) single
Guns, AA	4—37 mm (2 twin)
A/S weapons	DCT's and racks
Torpedo tubes	3—21 in (*533 mm*)
Main engines	Geared turbines; 2 shafts; 30,000 shp
Boilers	2
Speed, knots	31
Complement	190

KOLA *Class*

Built in 1950-52. In design this class of flushdecked destroyer escort appears to be a combination of the former German "Elbing" type torpedo boat destroyers, with a similar hull form, and of the earlier Soviet "Birds" class escorts.

GUNNERY. The four 3·9 inch guns were mounted as in the "Gordy" class destroyers.

RADAR. Navigational and obsolescent type for control.

"Kola" Class

48 "RIGA" CLASS

Displacement, tons	1 200 standard; 1 600 full load
Length, feet (*metres*)	298·8 (*91·0*)
Beam, feet (*metres*)	33·7 (10·2)
Draught, feet (*metres*)	11 (*3·4*)
Guns, dual purpose	3—3·9 in (*100 mm*) single
Guns, AA	4—37 mm (2 twin)
A/S weapons	2—16 barrelled rocket launchers; 4 DC projectors
Torpedo tubes	3—21 in (*533 mm*)
Main engines	Geared turbines; 2 shafts; 25 000 shp
Boilers	2
Speed, knots	28
Range, miles	2 500 at 15 knots
Complement	150

Built from 1952 to 1959. Successors to the "Kola" class escorts, of which they are lighter and less heavily armed but improved versions. Fitted with mine rails.

ANTI-SUBMARINE. The two 16-barrelled rocket launchers are mounted just before the bridge abreast "B" gun.

RADAR. Search: Slim Net. Fire Control: Obsolescent type.

TRANSFERS. Bulgaria (2), China (4), East Germany (2), Finland (2), Indonesia (6).

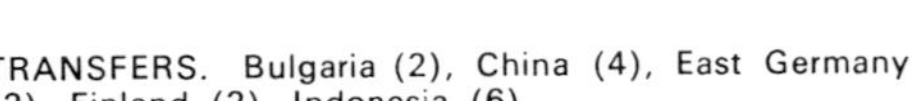

RIGA *Class*

RIGA Class — *1971, MOD (UK)*

25 "MIRKA I AND II" CLASS

Displacement, tons	950 standard; 1 100 full load
Length, feet (*metres*)	269·9 (*82·3*)
Beam, feet (*metres*)	29·9 (*9·1*)
Draught, feet (*metres*)	9·8 (*3·0*)
A/S weapons	4—12 barrel rocket launchers (2 forward, 2 aft) (1); 2—16 barrel rocket launchers (II)
Guns, AA	4—3 in (*76 mm*) (2 twin) (I)
Torpedo tubes	5—16 in anti-submarine (I) 10—16 in (II)
Main engines	2 diesels; total 6 000 hp; 2 gas turbines, total 31 000 hp; 2 shafts
Speed, knots	33
Complement	100

This class of ships was built in 1964-69 as improved "Petya" class. Some units have the after anti-submarine rocket launchers removed and an additional quintuple 16-inch torpedo mounting fitted between the bridge and the mast. At least one mounts VDS.

MIRKA II Class (with two torpedo mountings) — *1968*

RADAR. Search: Slim Net. Fire Control: Hawk Screech.

MIRKA *Class*

MIRKA II Class No. 876 (with two torpedo mountings) — *1972*

Frigates—*continued*

20 "PETYA I" CLASS
25 "PETYA II" CLASS

Displacement, tons	950 standard; 1 150 full load
Length, feet (*metres*)	270 (*82·3*)
Beam, feet (*metres*)	29·9 (*9·1*)
Draught, feet (*metres*)	10·5 (*3·2*)
Guns, dual purpose	4—3 in (*76 mm*), (2 twin)
A/S weapons	4—16 barrelled rocket launchers (I) 2—12 barrelled rocket launchers (II)
Torpedo tubes	5—16 in (*406 mm*) (I) 10—16 in (*406 mm*) (II)
Main engines	2 diesels, total 6 000 hp; 2 gas turbines; total 30 000 hp; 2 shafts
Speed, knots	34
Complement	100

Petya I with VDS *1973, S. Breyer*

PETYA *Class*

Small freeboard with a low wide funnel. The first ship reported to have been built in 1960-61 by Kalinigrad. Construction continued until about 1964. Fitted with two mine rails. "Petya II's" sacrifice rocket launchers for extra tubes whilst two of the "Petya II's" have lost the after 3 in turret to compensate for VDS.

RADAR. Search: Slim Net. Fire Control: Hawk Screech.

PETYA II Class *1970 ,MOD (UK)*

CORVETTES

11 "GRISHA" CLASS

Displacement, tons	750 full load
Dimensions, feet	234·8 × 32·8 × 9·2
Missile launchers	SA-N-4 surface-to-air
Guns	2—57 mm dual purpose (1 twin)
Torpedo tubes	4—16 in anti-submarine
A/S weapons	2—12 barrelled rocket launchers
Main engines	2 gas turbines; 2 diesels = 30 knots

This new class is probably the successors to the "Poti". The "Grisha" class is reported to have started series production in the late 1969-70 period. Five built by end of 1972, with a continuing programme of 3 a year. SA-N-4 launcher mounted forward.

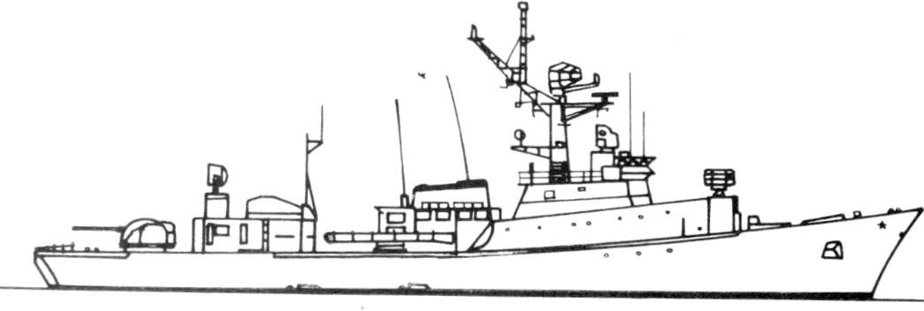

GRISHA Class

GRISHA Class *1972*

GRISHA Class *1972*

CORVETTES

70 "POTI" CLASS

Displacement, tons	550 standard; 650 full load
Dimensions, feet	195·2 × 26·2 × 9·2
Guns	2—57 mm AA (1 twin mounting)
Tubes	4—16 in anti-submarine
A/S weapons	2—12 barrelled rocket launchers
Main engines	2 gas turbines; 2 diesels; 4 shafts; total 20 000 hp=28 knots

This class of coastal escort vessels was under series construction from 1961 to 1968. Strut Curve and Muff Cob Radars.

"Poti" Class 1971

"Poti" Class 1970, S. Breyer

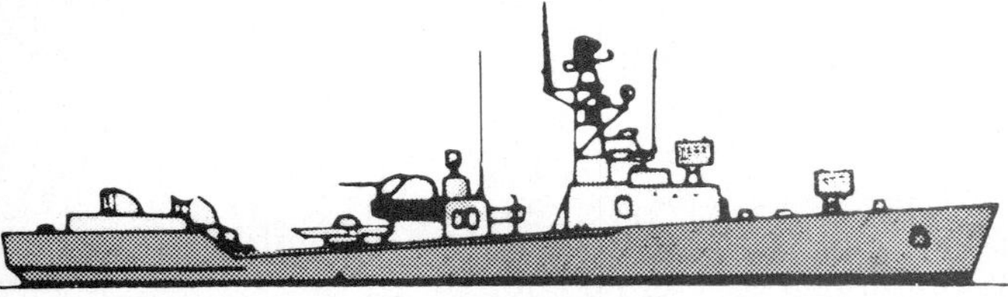
POTI *Class*

40 "KRONSTADT" CLASS

Displacement, tons	310 standard; 380 full load
Dimensions, feet	170·6 × 21·5 × 9·0
Guns	1—3·9 in; 2—37 mm AA
A/S weapons	Depth charge projectors
Main engines	3 diesels; 3 shafts; 3 300 hp = 24 knots
Range, miles	1 500 at 12 knots
Complement	65

Built in 1948-56. Flush-decked with large squat funnel, slightly raked, and massive block bridge structure. Pot Drum radar. Now being phased out of service due to age. About 20 boats were rebuilt as communications relay ships of the "Libau" class.

TRANSFERS. Bulgaria (2), China (24), Cuba (18), Indonesia (14), Poland (8), Romania (3).

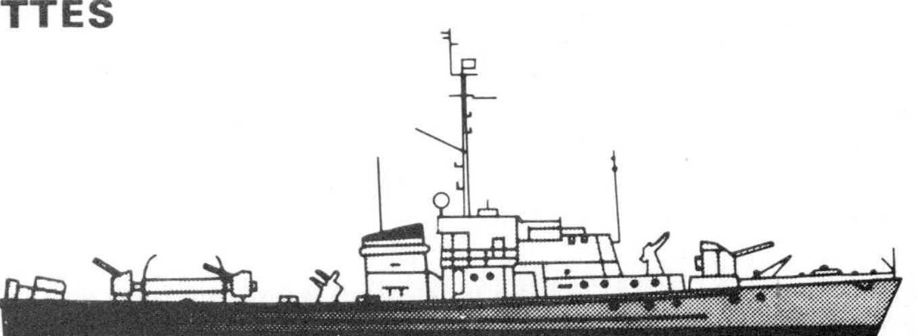
KRONSTADT Class

"Kronstadt" Class

"Kronstadt" Class 1970, courtesy, Godfrey H. Walker Esq.

100 "SO-I" CLASS

Displacement, tons	215 light; 250 normal
Dimensions, feet	138·6 × 20·0 × 9·2
Guns	4—25 mm AA (2 twin mountings) see notes
A/S weapons	4 five-barrelled ahead throwing rocket launchers
Main engines	3 diesels; 6 000 bhp = 29 knots
Range, miles	1 100 at 13 knots
Complement	30

Built since 1957. Steel hulled. Modernised boats of this class have only two 25 mm AA guns but also have four 16 in anti-submarine torpedo tubes.

"SO I" Class 1968

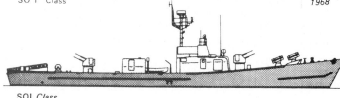

SOI *Class*

LIGHT FORCES

6 "NANUCHKA" CLASS (MISSILE BOATS)

Displacement, tons	800 normal (approx)
Length, feet (*metres*)	196·8 (*60·0*)
Beam, feet (*metres*)	39·6 (*12·0*)
Draught, feet (*metres*)	9·9 (*3·0*)
Missile launchers	6 (2 triple) for SS-N-9 surface-to-surface system; SA-N-4 surface-to-air system forward
Guns	2—57 mm AA (1 twin)
A/S weapons	1 or 2 A/S rocket launchers
Main engines	Diesels
Speed, knots	32

A new class of diesel powered craft with SSM launchers as the main armament probably mainly intended for deployment in coastal waters. Reported to have a very high beam to length ratio making her a much steadier firing platform than the *Osas* and *Komars*. Built from 1969 onwards.

RADAR. Search: Slim Net. Fire Control: Hawk Screech.

NANUCHKA Class No. 968 S. Breyer

LIGHT FORCES—*continued*

120 "OSA I and II" CLASS (65 I and 55 II) (MISSILE BOATS)

Displacement, tons	165 standard; 200 full load
Dimensions, feet	128·7 × 25·1 × 5·9
Missile launchers	4 in two pairs abreast for "SS-N-2A"
Guns	4—30 mm; (2 twin, 1 forward, 1 aft)
Main engines	3 diesels; 13 000 bhp = 32 knots
Range, miles	800 at 25 knots
Complement	25

These boats, built since 1959, have a larger hull and four launchers in two pairs as compared with one pair in the "Komar" class. They have a surface-to-surface missile range of up to 23 miles. Later boats have cylindrical missile launchers, comprising the "Osa II" class.

This class was a revolution in naval shipbuilding. Although confined by their size and range to coastal operations the lethality and accuracy of the Styx missile have already been proved by the sinking of the Israeli destroyer *Eilat* on 21 Oct 1967 by an Egyptian "Komar". The operations of the Indian "Osa's" in the war with Pakistan in December 1971 were equally successful against merchant vessels by night. These operations surely represent a most important lesson in naval operations and, in light of this, the list of transfers should be noted.

TRANSFERS. China (17), Cuba (2), Egypt (12), East Germany (12), India (8), Poland (12), Romania (5), Syria (2), Yugoslavia (10).

"OSA" Class firing missile 1972

"Osa" I Class 1970

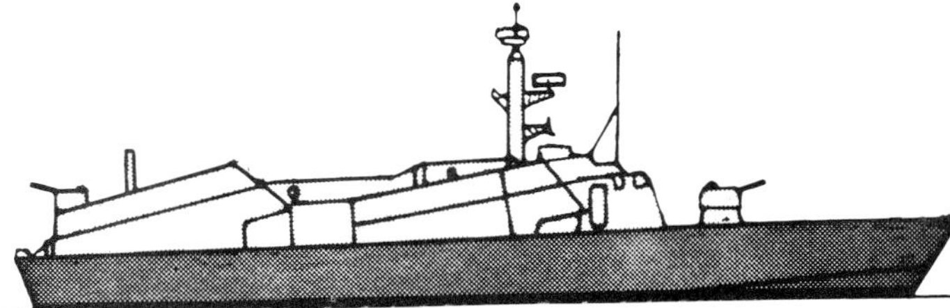

OSA *Class*

"Osa" II Class *1970, courtesy Godfrey H. Walker, Esq.*

25 "KOMAR" CLASS (MISSILE BOATS)

Displacement, tons	70 standard; 80 full load
Dimensions, feet	83·7 × 19·8 × 5·0
Missile launchers	2 for "SS-N-2 A" system
Guns	2—25 mm AA (1 twin forward)
Range, miles	400 at 30 knots
Main engines	4 diesels; 4 shafts; 4 800 bhp = 40 knots

A smaller type of boat converted from "P 6" class torpedo boats. Fitted with two surface-to-surface launchers aft in a hooded casing approximately 45 degrees to the deck line with a range of 23 miles. First units completed 1961.

TRANSFERS. China (total of 13 including home grown variety), Cuba (18), Egypt (7), Indonesia (12), Syria (6).

"Komar" Class ***1968***

30 "STENKA" CLASS

Displacement, tons	170 standard; 210 full load
Dimensions, feet	130·7 × 25·1 × 6·0
Guns	4—30 mm AA (2 twin)
Torpedo tubes	4—16 in (*406 mm*) anti-submarine
A/S weapons	2 depth charge racks
Main engines	3 diesels; 10 000 bhp = 40 knots
Complement	25

Based on the hull design of the guided missile boats of the "Osa" class. Built from 1967-68 onwards.

RADAR. Search: Square Tie. Fire Control: Drum Tilt. Pot Drum.

"STENKA" Class *1972*

Stenka Class *1973, S. Breyer*

STENKA *Class*

15 "MO VI" CLASS (A/S CRAFT)

Displacement, tons	64 standard; 73 full load
Dimensions, feet	83·6 × 19·7 × 4·0
Guns	4—25 mm AA (2 twin)
A/S weapons	2 depth charge mortars; 2 depth charge racks
Main engines	4 diesels; 4 shafts; 4 800 bhp = 40 knots

Built in 1956 to 1960. Based on the hull design of the "P-6" class motor torpedo boats.

"MO VI" Class No. 997 *1972*

LIGHT FORCES *—Continued*

25 "PCHELA" CLASS (HYDROFOILS)

Displacement, tons	70 standard; 80 full load
Dimensions, feet	82·0 × 19·7 × ?
Guns	4 MG (2 twin)
Main engines	2 diesels; 6 000 bhp = 50 knots

This class of hydrofoils, is reported to have been built since 1964-65. Also carry depth charges.

"Pchela" Class 1970

40 "SHERSHEN" CLASS (TORPEDO BOATS)

Displacement, tons	150 standard; 160 full load
Dimensions, feet	115·5 × 23·1 × 5·0
Guns	4—30 mm AA (2 twin)
Tubes	4—21 in (single)
A/S weapons	12 DC
Main engines	Diesels; 3 shafts; 13 000 bhp = 41 knots
Complement	16

These large torpedo boats have basically the same hull and layout as the "Osa" class missile boats, but with the torpedo tubes in the launcher positions. Built from 1962 onwards.

TRANSFERS. East Germany (15), Egypt (6), Yugoslavia (13).

"Shershen" Class *1966, S. Breyer*

"Shershen" Class *1970, S. Breyer*

130 "P 6" "P 8" "P 10" CLASSES (TORPEDO BOATS)

Displacement, tons	66 standard; 75 full load
Dimensions, feet	84·2 × 20·0 × 6·0
Guns	4—25 mm AA
Tubes	2—21 in (or mines, or depth charges)
Main engines	4 diesels; 4 shafts; 4 800 bhp = 43 knots
Range, miles	450 at 30 knots
Complement	25

The "P 6" class was of a standard medium sized type running into series production. Launched during 1951 to 1960. Known as "MO VI" class in the submarine chaser version. The later versions, known as the "P 8" and "P 10" classes, are powered with gas turbines, and have different bridge and funnel, "P 8" boats have hydrofoils.

TRANSFERS. China (80, indigenous construction), Cuba (12), Egypt (24), East Germany (18), Guinea (4), Indonesia (14), Iraq (12), Nigeria (3), Poland (20), North Vietnam (6).

"P 6" Class

" P 6" Class after modernisation *1972, S. Breyer*

"P 8" Class *en flotille* *1969, S. Breyer*

"P 10" Class *1968, Col Breyer*

20 "P 4" CLASS (TORPEDO BOATS)

Displacement, tons	25
Dimensions, feet	62·7 × 11·6 × 5·6
Guns	2 MG (1 twin)
Tubes	2—18 in
Main engines	2 Diesels; 2 shafts; 2 200 bhp = 50 knots

Originally a numerically large class of boats with aluminium alloy hulls. Launched in 1951-58. The earlier units are being discarded.

TRANSFERS. Albania (12), Bulgaria (8), China (70), Cuba (12), Cyprus (6), North Korea (40), Romania (8), Somalia (4), Syria (17).

"P 4" Class

MINEWARFARE FORCES

10 "NATYA" CLASS (MSF)

Displacement, tons	650
Dimensions, feet	200·1 × 34·1 × 7·2
Guns	4—30 mm AA (2 twin); 4—25 mm AA (2 twin)
A/S weapons	2 rocket launchers
Main engines	2 diesels; 5 000 bhp = 18 knots

A new class of fleet minesweepers first reported in 1971, evidently intended as successors of the "Yurka" class. Building rate of 3 a year.

"YURKA" Class 1972

45 "YURKA" CLASS

Displacement, tons	500 standard; 550 full load
Dimensions, feet	171·9 × 31 × 8·9
Guns	4—30 mm AA (2 twin)
Main engines	2 diesels; 4 000 bhp = 18 knots

A class of medium fleet minesweepers with steel hull. Built from 1963 to the late 1960s. Reportedly powered with diesels.

Yurka Class 1973, S. Breyer

20 "T 58" CLASS (MSF)

Displacement, tons	790 standard; 900 full load
Dimensions, feet	229·9 × 29·5 × 7·9
Guns	4—57 mm AA (2 twin)
Main engines	2 diesels; 2 shafts; 4 000 bhp = 18 knots

Built from 1957 to 1964. Of this class 14 were converted to submarine rescue ships with armament and sweeping gear removed, see later page ("Valdai" class).

"T 58" with "Muff Cob" fire control radar on bridge 1968

120 "T 43" CLASS (MSL)

Displacement, tons	500 standard; 610 full load
Dimensions, feet	190·2 × 28·2 × 6·9
Guns	4—37 mm AA (2 twin); 4—25 mm AA (2 twin)
Main engines	2 diesels; 2 shafts; 2 000 bhp = 17 knots
Range, miles	1 600 at 10 knots
Complement	40

A handy type built in 1948-57 in shipyards throughout the Soviet Union. A number of this class was converted into radar pickets (see photograph of No. 55 in the 1965-66 to 1967-68 editions) and into rescue ships with no armament. The remainder is gradually being replaced by newer types of fleet minesweepers.

TRANSFERS. Albania (2), Bulgaria (2), China (20), Egypt (6), Indonesia (6), Poland (12), Syria (2).

"T 43" Class 1972

6 "ZHENYA" CLASS (CMS)

Displacement, tons	320
Dimensions, feet	141 × 25 × 7
Guns	2—30 mm (twin)
Main engines	2 diesels = ? 18 knots

A recent design presumably the successors of the "Vanya's".

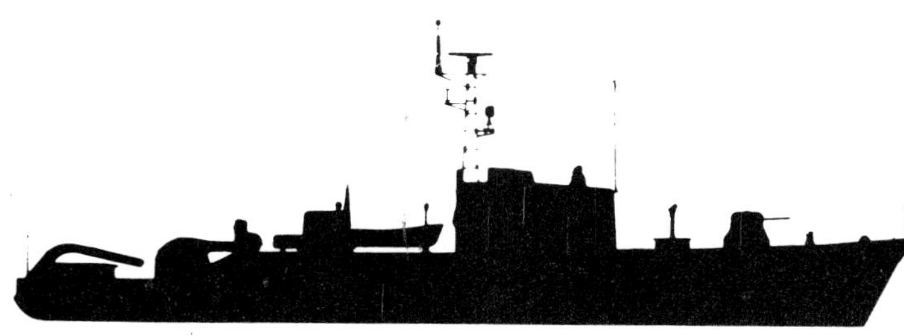

ZHENYA Class MSM

70 "VANYA" CLASS (CMS)

Displacement, tons	250 standard; 275 full load
Dimensions, feet	130·7 × 24 × 6·9
Guns	2—30 mm AA (1 twin)
Main engines	2 diesels; 2 200 bhp = 18 knots
Complement	30

A coastal class with wooden hulls of a type suitable for series production built from 1961 onwards. Basically similar to NATO type coastal minesweepers.

"Vanya" Class 1970, S. Breyer

35 "SASHA" CLASS (CMS)

Displacement, tons	245 standard; 280 full load
Dimensions, feet	150·9 × 20·5 × 6·6
Guns	1—57mm dp; 4—25 mm AA (2 twin)
Main engines	2 diesels; 2 200 bhp = 18 knots
Complement	25

Basically similar to NATO coastal minesweepers, but of steel construction. This series did not run into the number at first projected, construction having been discontinued in favour of later types.

"Sasha" Class 1968, S. Breyer

20 "T 301" CLASS (CMS)

Displacement, tons	150 standard; 180 full load
Dimensions, feet	128·0 × 18·0 × 4·9
Guns	2—37 mm AA; 2 MG
Main engines	2 diesels; 2 shafts; 1 440 bhp = 17 knots

Built from 1946 to 1956. Several were converted to survey craft, and many adapted for other purposes or used for port duty and auxiliary service. Now being withdrawn from service due to age.

"T 301" Class

"TR 40" CLASS (IMS)

Displacement, tons	40 standard; 60 full load
Dimensions, feet	55·8 × 11·5 × 4·0
Guns	2 MG (1 twin)
Main engines	Diesels; speed 18 knots

"K 8" CLASS (IMS)

Displacement, tons	50 standard; 70 full load
Dimensions, feet	92·0 × 13·5 × 2·3
Guns	2—25 mm forward; 2 MG (twin) aft
Main engines	Diesels; 600 bhp = 14 knots

Auxiliary motor minesweeping boats of the inshore ("TR 40") and river ("K 8") types. A total of about 100 of both classes in service.

AMPHIBIOUS VESSELS

11 "ALLIGATOR" CLASS

Displacement, tons	4 100 standard; 5 800 full load
Dimensions, feet	374·0 × 50·9 × 12·1
Guns	2—57 mm AA
Main engines	Diesels; 8 000 bhp = 15 knots

Largest type of Soviet landing ship built in the USSR to date. LST type. First ship built in 1965-66 and commissioned in 1966. These ships have ramps on the bow and stern. Carrying capacity 1 700 tons. There are three variations of rig. In earlier type two or three cranes are carried—later types have only one crane. In the third type the bridge structure has been raised and the forward deck house has been considerably lengthened.

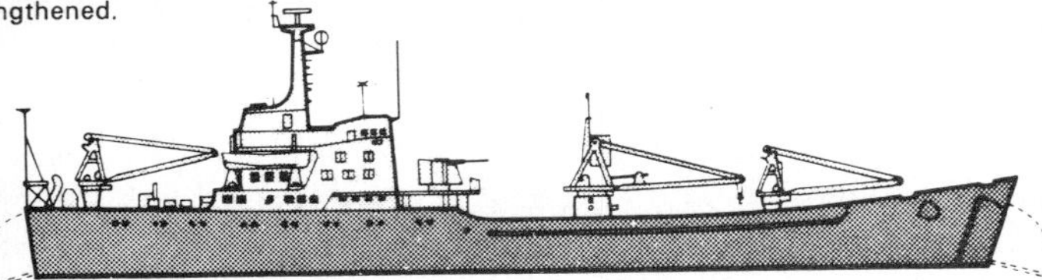

ALLIGATOR Class

ALLIGATOR Class *1972*

ALLIGATOR Class II *1972, H W. Van Boeijen*

60 "POLNOCNY" CLASS

Displacement, tons	780 standard; 1 000 full load (Type IX 1 300)
Dimensions, feet	246·0 × 29·5 × 9·8 (Type IX 265 × 27·7 × 9·8)
Guns	1 twin 30 mm turret in all but earliest ships
A/S weapons	2—18 barrelled rocket projectors
Main engines	2 diesels; 5 000 bhp = 18 knots

A type of amphibious vessel basically similar to the US medium landing ship, rocket (LSMR) type. Can carry 6 tanks. Up to 9 types of this class have been built. In I to IV the mast and funnel are combined—in V onwards the mast is stepped on the bridge—in VI to VIII there is a redesign of the bow-form—IX is a completely new design of 40 ft greater length and corresponding increase in tonnage. Muff Cob radar.

POLNOCNY Class with 2—30 mm AA before bridge and fire control radar on bridge

POLNOCNY Class

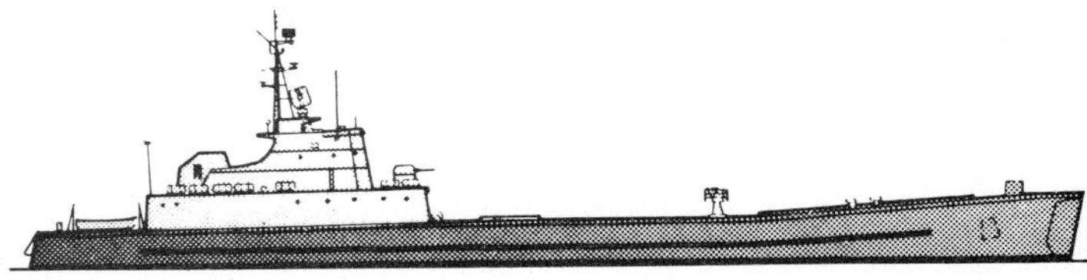

POLNOCNY Class

POLNOCNY Class *1972*

Amphibious Vessels—*continued*

10 "MP 8" TYPE

Displacement, tons 800 standard; 1 200 full load
Dimensions, feet 239·5 × 34·8 × 15·1
Guns 4—57 mm (2 twin)
Main engines Diesels; 4 000 bhp = 15 knots

Old type of landing ship with a short and low quarter deck abaft the after castle and a waist between the gun mounting before the bridge and gun mounting on the high forecastle. Can carry 6 tanks. Carrying capacity 400 tons.
The twelve tank landing ships of the "MP 2" type were deleted from the list in 1972.

"MP 8" Type *1970, S. Breyer*

25 "MP 4" TYPE

Displacement, tons 800 full load
Dimensions, feet 183·7 × 26·2 × 8·9
Guns 4—25 mm (2 twin)
Main engines Diesels; 2 shafts; 1 100 bhp = 12 knots

Built in 1956-58. Of the small freighter type in appearance. Two masts, one abaft the bridge and one in the waist. Gun mountings on poop and forecastle. Can carry 6 to 8 tanks. Several ships now serve as transports. Carrying capacity 500 tons.

"Vydra" Type *1971*

30 "VYDRA" CLASS (LCU)

Displacement, tons 300 standard; 500 full load
Dimensions, feet 157·4 × 24·6 × 7·2
Main engines 2 diesels; 2 shafts; 400 hp = 15 knots

A new class of landing craft of the LCU type. Built from 1967 onwards. No armament.

MP 10/SMB 1 Type *1971*

70 "MP 10" CLASS (LCU)

Displacement, tons 200 standard; 420 full load
Dimensions, feet 157·5 × 21·3 × 6·5
Main engines 2 diesels; 2 shafts; 400 hp = 11 knots

A type of landing craft basically similar to the British LCT (4) type in silhouette and layout. Can carry 4 tanks. Loading capacity about 150 tons.

"T 4" CLASS (LCM)

Displacement, tons 80 full load
Dimensions, feet 65·6 × 18·4 × 3·3

Small landing craft of the LCM type with a loading capacity of one tank.

COMMUNICATIONS RELAY SHIPS

20 "LIBAU" CLASS

Displacement, tons 310 standard; 380 full load
Dimensions, feet 170·6 × 21·5 × 9·0
Main engines 3 diesels; 2 shafts; 3 300 bhp = 24 knots
Range, miles 1 500 at 12 knots

Formerly submarine chasers of the "Kronstadt" class rebuilt in 1955-56. Circa 20 units. No armament.

CABLE SHIPS

5 "KLASMA" CLASS

DONETZ INGUL TSNA YANA ZEYA

Displacement, tons 6 900
Measurement, tons 3 400 deadweight; 6 000 gross
Dimensions, feet 427·8 × 52·5 × 17
Main engines 5 Wärtsilä Sulzer diesels; 4 950 shp = 14 knots
Complement 118

Ingul and *Yana* were built by Wärtsilä, Helsingforsvarvet, Finland, laid down on 10 Oct 1961 and 4 May 1962 and launched on 14 Apr 1962 and 1 Nov 1962 respectively. *Donetz* and *Tsna* were built at the Wärtsilä, Abovarvet, Abo. *Donetz* was launched on 17 Dec 1968 and completed 3 July 1969. *Tsna* was completed in summer 1968. *Zeya* was delivered on 20 Nov 1970. *Donetz*, *Tsna* and *Zeya* are of slightly modified design.

TSNA (modified "Klasma" Class) *1970*

INGUL *1972*

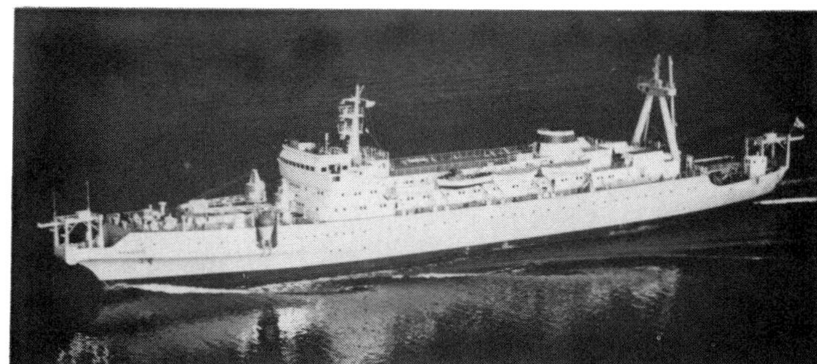

DONETZ (modified "Klasma" Class) *1972, Oy Wärtsilä Ab*

ZEYA (modified "Klasma" Class) *1972, Bjorn Borg*

TORPEDO RECOVERY/PATROL BOATS

"POLUCHAT I" CLASS

Displacement, tons	100 standard
Dimensions, feet	98·4 × 19·7 × 5·9
Guns	2—25 mm (1 twin) or 2 MG (1 twin)

Employed as specialised or dual purpose torpedo recovery vessels and/or patrol boats. Number reported up to 100. They have a stern slipway.

TRANSPORTS

2 "LAKE" CLASS

KAMCHATKA **MONGOL**

Former pennant numbers were P-380 and P-242, respectively. The former Japanese cargo ships and military transports, ex-*Hayasaki*, ex-*No. 13*, and ex-*No. 137*, and the former Italian supply ship, ex-*Montecucco*, ex-KT 32, were deleted from the list in 1968, having been discarded on account of age or obsolescence.

6 COASTAL TYPE

SHIM **OLGA** **USSURIJ** (ex-*Okhotsk*)
OB **SHILKA** **VISHERA**

Former pennant Nos. were P-247 (*Ob*), P 274 (*Shilka*), P 365 (*Ussurij*), P-379 (*Vishera*). *Olga* and *Ishim* are Coast Guard transports. *Ob* is 1 194 ton diesel electric Antarctic support ship.

RADAR PICKETS

5 "T 43"/AGR CLASS

Displacement, tons	500 standard; 610 full load
Dimensions, feet	190·2 × 28·2 × 6·9
Guns	4—37 mm AA; 2—25 mm AA
Main engines	2 diesels; 2 shafts; 2 000 bhp = 17 knots
Range, miles	1 600 at 10 knots
Complement	77

Former fleet minesweepers of the "T 43" class converted into radar pickets with comprehensive electronic equipment. It is reported that there may be a dozen vessels of this type. A large "Big Net"-like radar is mounted on the mainmast.

T45/AGR Class — *1973, S. Breyer*

MISCELLANEOUS

ZARJA

Measurement, tons 71 net; 333 gross

Auxiliary vessel built in 1952. One of some 50 or so similar schooners built in Finland. Constructed almost entirely of wood. Classed as a research vessel.

NEREY **NOVATOR** **VLADIMIR OBRUCHEV**

All three of these ships are former fleet tugs converted to survey vessels.

PETRODVORETSK

Reported to be a former ferry ship converted for special surveying duties.

ANGARA (ex-*Hela*)

Displacement, tons	2 115 standard; 2 500 full load
Dimensions, feet	323 × 42·5 × 11
Guns	2—4·1 in; 1—37 mm AA; 2—20 mm AA
Main engines	4 MAN diesels; 2 shafts; 6 300 bhp = 18 knots
Range, miles	2 000 at 15 knots

Former yacht built by Stülcken, Hamburg. Launched in 1939. In the Black Sea.

DISTILLATION SHIPS

10 "VODA" CLASS

Displacement, tons	2 100 standard
Dimensions, feet	267·3 × 37·7 × 14
Main engines	Diesels; speed = 12 knots

Water distillation ships built in 1956 onwards. No armament.

TRAINING SHIPS

ZENIT — *1970, Michael D. J. Lennon*

3 "ZENIT" CLASS

GORIZONT **MERIDIAN** **ZENIT**

Measurements, tons	4 374 gross; 986 net
Length, feet	352·6
Beam, feet	47·2
Main engines	Two 8-cylinder diesels geared to one shaft

All were built in East Germany at Rostock by Schiffswerft Neptune in 1961-62. Mercantile Cadet Training but produces officers for the Navy. Not on the Navy List.

2 "SEDOV" TYPE

KRUZENSTERN **SEDOV**

Measurement, tons 3 064 gross

Barques. Built in 1921. Employed as sail training ship for midshipmen, cadets and junior seamen. Not on the Navy List. A photograph of *Sedov* appears in the 1968-69 edition.

1 Ex-GERMAN TYPE

TOVARISCH (ex-*Gorch Foch*)

Displacement, tons	1 350
Dimensions, feet	242·8 × 39·3 × 15
Sail area	19 350 sq ft
Guns	2—20 mm AA
Main engines	MAN diesel; 1 shaft; 520 bhp = 8 knots
Oil fuel, tons	25
Radius, miles	3 500 at 8 knots
Complement	260

Barque. Ex-German training ship. Built by Blohm & Voss, Hamburg. Launched in 1933. Of mercantile attachment but produces personnel for the Navy. Sail area: 2 150 sq yds. Not on the Navy List.

TOVARISCH — *1972*

10 SCHOONER TYPE

ENISEJ **PRAKTIKA** (ex-*Passat*) **TOBOL** **UCHEBA** (ex-*Mousson*)

Displacement, tons 300 approximately (ships vary)

Three masts. In the Baltic. Sailing vessels for training cadets, boys and volunteers. There are about ten three-masted schooners of 300 tons with one square sail on the foremast of the same class as the *Pratika* and *Ucheba*, built in Finland. They are described as very nice little ships. Not on the Navy List.

None of the above training ships are officially recognised as naval ships.
The old nominal training ship *Aurora* was deleted in 1963 as although she still exists as a prestige tourist relic (famous to the USSR as the cruiser from which the first round of the October Revolution was fired) she is a museum ship and no longer of military value.
There are also the engineering training ships *Professor Kudrevitch*, *Professor Shchyogolev*, *Professor Yushchenko* and *Professor Aruchkov*, all built in 1970-71.
The training ships *Nyeman* (ex-*Isar*, ex-*Puma*) and *Cristoforo Colombo* (ex-Z 18) were in 1971 reported discarded.

SUPPORT AND DEPOT SHIPS

8 "UGRA" CLASS (SUBMARINE SUPPORT)

TOBOC + 7

Displacement, tons 6 750 standard; 9 500 full load
Length, feet (*metres*) 463·8 (*141·4*)
Beam, feet (*metres*) 57·6 (*17·6*)

Range, miles 10 000 at 12 knots

Improved versions of the "Don" class. Built from 1961 onwards, all in Nikolayev. Built on warship lines. Equipped with workshops. Provided with a helicopter plaftorm. Carries a large derrick to handle torpedoes. Has mooring points in hull about 100 feet apart, and has baggage ports possibly for coastal craft and submarines. The last pair of this class mount a large superstructure from the mainmast to quarter-deck and are used for training.

RADAR. Search Slim Net. Fire Control: Hawk Screech (2). Strut Curve. Muff Cob.

TRANSFER. The ninth ship, *Amba*, which had four 76 mm guns, was transferred to India.

"Ugra" Class No. 82 *Skyfotos*

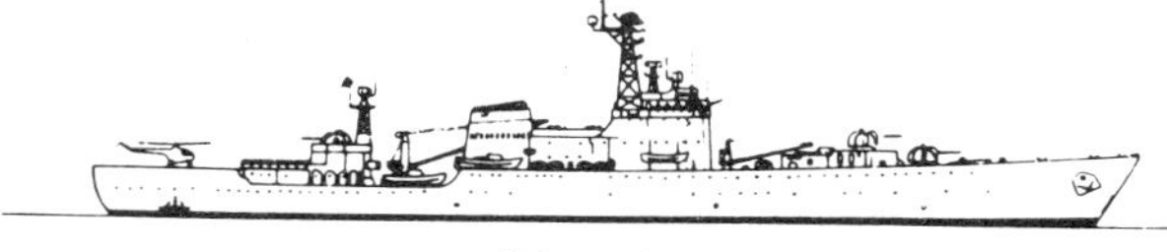

UGRA *Class*

UGRA Class *1971, USN*

"Ugra" Class *1970, Niels Gartig*

UGRA Class No. 913 *1972*

Support and Depot Ships—*continued*

6 "DON" CLASS (SUBMARINE SUPPORT)

DMITRI GALKIN **MIKHAIL TUKAEVSKY**
FEDOR VIDYAEV **NIKOLAY STOLBOV**
MAGOMED GADZHIEV **VIKTOR KOTELNIKOV**

Displacement, tons	6 700 standard; 9 000 full load
Length, feet (*metres*)	458·9 (139·9)
Beam, feet (*metres*)	57·7 (*17·6*)
Draught, feet (*metres*)	22·3 (*6·8*)
Aircraft	Provision for helicopter in two ships
Guns, dual purpose	4—3·9 (*100 mm*)
Guns, AA	8—57 mm (4 twin)
Main engines	4 or 6 diesels; 14 000 bhp
Speed, knots	21
Complement	300

MAGOMED GADZHIEV *1970*

Support ships, all named after officers lost in WW II. Built in 1957 to 1962. Originally seven ships were built, all in Nikolaev. One was transferred to Indonesia in 1962. Quarters for about 450 submariners.

RADAR. Search: Slim Net and probably Strut Curve. Fire Control: Hawk Screech (2).

DON HELO *Class*

DON *Class*

DON Class *1972*

1 "PURGA" CLASS

Displacement, tons	2 250 standard; 3 000 full load
Length, feet (*metres*)	324·8 (*99·0*)
Beam, feet (*metres*)	44·3 (*13·5*)
Draught, feet (*metres*)	17·1 (*5·2*)
Guns, dual purpose	4—3·9 in (*100 mm*) singles
Mines	50 capacity
Main engines	Diesels
Speed, knots	18
Complement	250

Laid down in 1939 in Leningrad and completed in 1948. Sturdy oceangoing general purpose ship equipped as icebreaker, escort, training ship and tender. Fitted with directors similar to those in the "Riga" class frigates. Modernised in 1958-60.

"Purga" Class

Support and Depot Ships—*continued*

"Lama" Class

5 "LAMA" CLASS (MISSILE SUPPORT)

Displacement, tons	5 000 standard; 7 000 full load
Length, feet (*metres*)	370·0 (*112·8*) oa
Beam, feet (*metres*)	47·2 (*14·4*)
Draught, feet (*metres*)	19·0 (*5·8*)
Guns, dual purpose	8—57 mm, 2 quadruple, 1 on the forecastle; 1 on the break of the quarter deck
Main engines	Diesels; 2 shafts; 5 000 shp
Speed, knots	15

Support and repair ships of the depot and freighting type. Their features indicate a possible missile armed surface ship supply role. The engines are sited aft to allow for a very large and high hangar or hold amidships for carrying missiles or weapons spares. The amidships hold or hangar structure is about 12 feet high above the main deck. There are doors at the forward end with rails leading in. This is surmounted by a turntable gantry or travelling cranes for transferring armaments to combatant ships.
There are mooring points along the hull for low vessels such as submarines to come alongside. The turntable amidships is built up 2 feet above the upper deck. The two cranes are in the stowed position and there appear to be pulleyed lifting arrangements, apparently intended to service the well deck and overside. The well deck is about 40 feet long, enough for a missile to fit horizontally before being lifted vertically for loading in submarines. The ships can apparently be used for salvage and towing.

RADAR. Search: Slim Net and Strut Curve. Fire Control: Hawk Screech. (2).

"Lama" Class *Skyfotos*

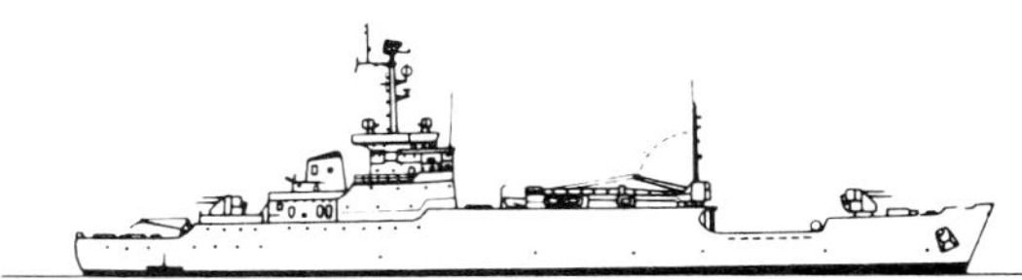
LAMA *Class*

ALESHA Class *1972*

2 "ALESHA" CLASS

075 083

Displacement, tons	3 600 standard; 4 300 full load
Dimensions, feet	337·9 × 47·6 × 15·7
Guns	4—57 mm AA (1 quadruple forward)
Main engines	4 diesels; 2 shafts; 8 000 bhp = 20 knots
Complement	150

Multi-purpose support ship type: minelayer, barrage vessel, rescue ship and tender. 075 has been in service since 1965. Originally reported to have a capacity for 400 mines below decks, with four mine tracks to provide stern launchings for exercises, but this class may well not be minelayers, although, like many other Soviet ships they may have been built with this capability.

2 " WILHELM BAUER" CLASS

KUBAN (ex-*Waldemar Kophamel*) **PECHORA** (ex-*Otto Wünche*)

Displacement, tons	4 726 standard; 5 600 full load
Dimensions, feet	446·0 × 52·5 × 14·5
Main engines	4 MAN diesels; 2 shafts; 12 400 bhp = 20 knots

Former German. Launched in 1939. Submarine tenders. *Kuban* was salvaged in 1950-51 after being sunk in shallow water by bombing in WW II and was rehabilitated in 1951-57.
The depot ships ex-*Adolf Luderitz*; *Volga* (ex-*Juan Sebastian de Elcano*) and ex-*Donetz* (ex-*Weichdes*, ex-*Syra*) are reported probably scrapped. The submarine tenders *Terek* (ex-*Elbe*), *Irtysh* (ex-*Kronstadt*), and *Saratov* were in 1971 reported to have been discarded.

Support and Depot Ships—*continued*

8 "AMUR" CLASS

Displacement, tons	6 500 full load
Dimensions, feet	377·3 × 57·4 × 18·0
Main engines	Diesels; 2 shafts

A new class of general purpose tenders or depot ships built since circa 1969. Successors to the "Oskol'" class.

AMUR Class (6th of class) 1973

10 "OSKOL" CLASS

Displacement, tons	2 500 standard; 3 000 full load
Dimensions, feet	295·2 × 39·4 × 14·8
Main engines	2 diesels; 2 shafts; speed = 16 knots

Three series: "Oskol I" class, well-decked hull, no armament; "Oskol II" Class, well-decked hull, armed with 2—57 mm guns (1 twin) and 4—25 mm guns (2 twin); "Oskol III" class, flush-decked hull. General purpose tenders and repair ships. Built from 1963 to 1970 in Poland.

AMUR Class 1972, *H. W. Van Boeijen*

AMUR Class 1972

6 "ATREK" CLASS

ATREK AYAT BAKHMUT DVINA MURMATS OSIPOV

Displacement, tons	3 500 standard; 6 700 full load
Measurement, tons	3 258 gross
Dimensions, feet	336 × 49 × 20
Main engines	Expansion and exhaust turbines; 1 shaft; 2 450 hp = 13 knots
Boilers	2 water tube
Range, miles	3 500 at 13 knots

Built in 1956-58, and converted to naval use from "Kolomna" class freighters. There are six of these vessels employed as submarine tenders and replenishment ships.

ATREK V(B)-272 *1959, Sergei Romanov*

5 "DNEPR" CLASS

PM 17

Displacement, tons	4 500 standard; 5 250 full load
Dimensions, feet	370·7 × 54·1 × 14·4
Main engines	Diesels; 2 000 bhp = 12 knots

Bow lift repair and depot ships for fleet support and maintenance. Built in 1957-66 as repair ships, equipped with workshops and servicing facilities. The last two ships of this class are flushdecked ("Dnepr II" class).

PM 17 ("Dnepr I" Class) *1965*

2 "TOVDA" CLASS

INZA (ex-*Novoshaktinsk*) **TOVDA**

Displacement, tons	3 000 standard; 4 000 full load
Dimensions, feet	282·1 × 39·4 × 16·0
Guns	6—57 mm AA (3 twin mountings)
Main engines	Triple expansion; 1 300 ihp = 11 knots

Polish built ex-tankers converted in 1958 to 1960. Depot and repair ships. Also known as the "Soldek" class, but the NATO designation is "Tovda" class.

"Tovda" Class *1959*

2 "DESNA" CLASS

CHAZHMA CHUMIKAN

Displacement, tons	5 300 light; 14 065 full load
Dimensions, feet	457·7 × 59·0 × 25·9
Aircraft	1 helicopter
Main engines	Triple expansion; 4 000 ihp = 18 knots

Formerly freighters of the "Dzankoy" class (7 265 tons gross). Soviet Range Instrumentation Ships (SRIS). The "Desna" class have a larger hull than the "Sibir" class and are better equipped. Active since 1963. Large radome on the bridge.

53 INTELLIGENCE COLLECTORS (AGI's)

6 "PRIMORYE" CLASS

PRIMORYE **KAVKAZ** **KRYM** **ZABAIKALYE** **ZAPOROZYE** **ZAKARPATYE**

Displacement, tons 5 000
Dimensions, feet 274 × 45 × 26·2

The most modern intelligence collectors in the world, apparently with built-in processing and (?) analysis.

PRIMORYE Class

15 "OKEAN" CLASS

ALIDADA **AMPERMETR** **BAROGRAF** **BAROMETR** **DEFLEKTOR** **EKHOLOT** **GIDROFON** **KRENOMETR** **LINZA** **LOTLIN** **REDUKTOR** **REPITER** **TEODOLIT** **TRAVERZ** **ZOND**

REDUKTOR, "Okean" Class AGI — *1972, H. W. van Boeijen*

8 "LENTRA" CLASS

GS 34 **GS 36** **GS 41** **GS 43** **GS 46** **GS 47** **GS 55** **GS 59**

"LENTRA" CLASS — *1968, Mr Michael D. J. Lennon*

8 "MAYAK" CLASS

ANEROID **GIRORULEVOY** **KHERSONES** **KURS** **KURSOGRAF** **LADOGA** **GS 239** **GS 242**

"MAYAK" Class — *1972*

GIRORULEVOY, "Mayak" Class — *1972*

4 "MIRNY" CLASS

BAKAN **LOTSMAN** **VAL** **VERTIKAL**

BAKAN "Mirny" Class AGI — *1972*

5 "MOMA" CLASS

ARKEPELAG **ILMEN** **NAKHODKA** **PELORUS** **SELIGER**

ARKCHIPELAG, "Moma" Class AGI — *1972*

2 "PAMIR" CLASS

GIDROGRAF **PELENG**

2 "DNEPR" CLASS

IZMERITEL **PROTRAKTOR**

1 "T 58" CLASS

GIDROLOG

2 "ZUBOV" CLASS

G. SARYCHEV **K. LAPTEV**

NIKOLAI ZUBOV

SURVEY SHIPS

21 "MOMA" CLASS (+5 AGI's)

ANADIR **ARTIKA** **ASKOLD** **BEREZAN** **CHELEKEN** **EKVATOR** **KILDIN** **KRILON** **KOLGUEV** **OKEAN** **TAYMYR** **ZAPOLARA**

Displacement, tons	1 240 standard; 1 800 full load
Dimensions, feet	219·8 × 32·8 × 13·2
Main engines	Diesels; speed 16 knots

Eight ships of this class were reported to have been built from 1967 to 1970 and the remainder since.

CHELEKEN, "Moma" Class AGS *1972*

8 "KAMENKA" CLASS

Displacement, tons	1 000 standard
Dimensions, feet	180·5 × 31·2 × 11·5
Main engines	Diesels; speed 16 knots

The ships of this class are not named but have a number with the prefix letters "GS". All reported to have been built since *circa* 1967-68. The "Shalanda" class shallow draught small surveying craft were deleted from the list in 1972.

2 "TELNOVSK" CLASS

AYTADOR **SVIYAGA**

Displacement, tons	1 200 standard
Measurement, tons	1 217 gross, 448 net
Dimensions, feet	229·6 × 32·8 × 13·1
Main engines	Diesels; speed 10 knots

Formerly coastal freighters. Built in Bulgaria and Hungary. Refitted and modernised for naval supply and surveying duties.

AYTADOR *1965, Mr Michael D. J. Lennon*

3 "POLYUS" CLASS

BAIKAL **BALKHASH** **POLYUS**

Displacement, tons	6 900 standard
Dimensions, feet	365·8 × 47·2 × 20·7
Main engines	Diesel-electric; 3 400 hp = 14 knots

These ships of the "Polyus" class were built in East Germany in 1961-64.

POLYUS *1972*

VITYAZ (ex-*Mars*)

Displacement, tons	5 700 standard
Main engines	Diesels; 3 000 bhp = 14·5 knots
Range, miles	18 400 at 14 knots
Complement	137 officers and men including 73 scientists

Oceanographic research ship. Formerly a German freighter built at Bremen in 1939 Equipped with 13 laboratories.

VITYAZ *1972, Michael D. J. Lennon*

Survey Ships—*continued*

MICHAIL LOMONOSOV

Displacement, tons	5 960 normal
Measurement, tons	3 897 gross; 1 195 net
Dimensions, feet	336·0 × 47·2 × 14·0
Main engines	Triple expansion; 2 450 ihp = 13 knots

Built by Neptune, Rostock, in 1957 from the hull of a freighter of the "Kolomna" class. Operated not by the Navy but by the Academy of Science. Equipped with 16 laboratories. Carries a helicopter for survey.

MICHAIL LOMONOSOV *1970, Michael D. J. Lennon*

11 "NIKOLAI ZUBOV" CLASS

A. CHIRIKOV
A. VILKITSKIJ
BORIS DAVIDOV
F. LITKE
KHARITON LAPTEV
NIKOLAI ZUBOV
S. CHELYUSKIN
SEJMEN DEZHNEV
T. BELLINSGAUSEN
V. GOLOVNIN

Displacement, tons	2 674 standard; 3 021 full load
Dimensions, feet	295·2 × 42·7 × 15
Main engines	2 diesels; speed = 16·7 knots
Complement	108 to 120, including 70 scientists

Oceanographic research ships built at Szczecin Shipyard, Poland in 1964. *Nikolai Zubov* visited London in 1965. Employed on survey in the Atlantic.

NIKOLAI ZUBOV

GAVRIL SARITSHEV *1966, Michael D. J. Lennon*

3 "MURMAN" CLASS

MURMAN **OKEAN** **OKHOTSK**

Displacement, tons	1 500 standard; 3 200 full load
Dimensions, feet	265·8 × 42·5 × 18·2
Guns	3—5·1 in; 2—3 in; 2 MG
Main engines	Triple expansion; 2 shafts; 2 400 ihp = 14 knots
Complement	160

Launched in 1937-38. In the Far East. Former minelayers converted into survey ships. *Murman* was fitted with a helicopter platform in 1962. A photograph of *Okhotsk* appears in the 1955-56 to 1965-66 editions.

Measurement, tons	10 826 deadweight; 5 419 gross, 2 946 net
Dimensions, feet	456·0 × 58·0 × 15·5
Main engines	2 diesels

Built at Abo in Finland in 1959. Converted for surveying. Fitted with directional aerial between bridge and funnel.

DOLINSK (ex-ARKHANGELSK) *1972, Michael D. J. Lennon*

IZUMRUD

Measurement, tons	3 862 gross; 465 net
Main engines	Powered by diesel-electric machinery

A new type of research and survey ship built in 1970.

IZUMRUD *1972, Michael D. J. Lennon*

16 "SAMARA" CLASS

AZIMUT
DEVIATOR
GIDROLOG
GIGROMETR
GLOBUS
GLUBOMER
GORIZONT
GRADUS
KOMPAS
PAMYAT MERKURYIA
RUMB
TROPIK
ZENIT
VAGACH
VOSTOK
YUG

Displacement, tons	800 standard; 1 000 full load
Measurement, tons	1 276 gross; 1 000 net
Dimensions, feet	180·4 × 32·8 × 11·5
Main engines	Diesels; speed 16 knots

Built at Gdansk, Poland since 1962 for hydrographic surveying and research.

KOMPAS *1970, Michael D. J. Lennon*

GLOBUS *1972, Michael D. J. Lennon*

AZIMUT *1972, Michael D. J. Lennon*

2 "MALYGIN" CLASS

STEFAN MALYGIN
NICOLAI KOLOMEITEY

Both built by Turku, Finland Launched 16 Nov 1970 and 16 Nov 1971 respectively.

RESEARCH SHIPS

2 "ORBELI" CLASS

AKADEMIK IOSIF ORBELI
PROFESSOR NIKOLAI BARABSKI

Both of 9 727 tons gross built in Warnemünde 1969-71.

7 "AKADEMIK KURCHATOV" CLASS

AKADEMIK KOROLEV (1967)
AKADEMIK KURCHATOV (1965)
AKADEMIK SHIRSHOV (1967)
AKADEMIK VERBADSKIJ (1967)
DMITRI MENDELEYEV (1968)
PROFESSOR ZUBOV (1967)
PROFESSOR VIZE (1967)

Displacement, tons	6 681 full load
Measurement, tons	1 387 net; 1 986 deadweight; 5 460 gross
Dimensions, feet	400·3 to 406·8 × 56·1 × 15·0
Main engines	2 Halberstadt 6-cylinder diesels; 2 shafts; 8 000 bhp = 18 to 20 knots

All built by Mathias Thesen Werft at Wisman, East Germany. Launch dates above.

PROFESSOR VIZE *1972, H. W. van Boeijen*

AKADEMIK SHIRSHOV *1972, Michael D. J. Lennon*

AKADEMIK VERNADSKIJ *1970, Mr. Michael D. L. Jennon*

9 "PASSAT" CLASS

MUSSON
OKEAN
PASSAT
PRIBOJ
PORIV
PRILIV
SHKVAL
VIKHR
VOLNA

Research or weather ships built at Szczecin, Poland, since 1968. Aerials differ in certain ships.

OKEAN *1972, Michael D. J. Lennon*

PASSAT *1970, Michael D. J. Lennon*

2 "LEBEDEV" CLASS

PETR LEBEDEV **SERGEI VAVILOV**

Measurement, tons	1 180 net; 3 561 gross
Main engines	Diesels

Research vessels with comprehensive equipment and accommodation. Both built in 1954.

PETR LEBEDEV *1970, Michael D. J. Lennon*

PROFESSOR DERYUGIN
AKADEMIK BERG
AKADEMIK KNIPOUITCH

Fishery research ships of 1 166 tons net; 3 165 gross. Built in the USSR at Nikolajv between 1964 and 1968.

AYSBERG **ISSLEDOVATEL** **OKEANOGRAF** **POLIARNIK** **TAMANGO**

Converted trawlers of 265 tons gross; 93 net for research. All M-Research. *Aysberg, Okeanograf* and *Poliarnik* have visited the United Kingdom. Built in 1952 to 1970.

OKEANOGRAF *1970, Michael D. J. Lennon*

SPACE ASSOCIATED SHIPS

4 "SIBIR" CLASS

CHUKOTKA **SAKHALIN** **SIBIR** **SUCHAN**

Displacement, tons	4 000 standard; 5 000 full load
Measurement, tons	3 767 gross (*Chukotka* 3 800, *Suchan* 3 710)
Dimensions, feet	354 × 49·2 × 20
Guns	6—45 mm AA; 2 MG
Main engines	Triple expansion; 2 shafts; 3 300 ihp = 15 knots
Range, miles	3 300 at 12 knots

Converted bulk ore carriers employed as Missile Range Ships in the Pacific. *Sakhalin* and *Sibir* have three radomes forward and aft, and carry helicopters. *Suchan* is also equipped with a helicopter flight deck. Launched in 1957-59. Formerly freighters of the Polish "B 31" type. Rebuilt in 1958-59 as missile range ships in Leningrad.

1 "GAGARIN" CLASS

KOSMONAUT YURIY GAGARIN

Displacement, tons	45 000
Measurement, tons	32 291 gross; 5 247 net
Dimensions, feet	757·9; 773·3oa × 101·7 × 30·0
Main engines	2 geared steam turbines; 1 shaft; 19 000 shp = 17 knots max

Design based on the "Sofia" or "Akhtubu" (ex-"Hanoi") class steam tanker. Built at Leningrad in 1970, completing in 1971. Used for investigation into conditions in the upper atmosphere, and the control of space vehicles. She is the largest Soviet research vessel. Has bow and stern thrust units for ease of berthing.

KOSMONAUT YURIY GAGARIN — *1972, Michael D. J. Lennon*

1 "KOMAROV" CLASS

KOSMONAUT VLADIMIR KOMAROV (ex-*Genichesk*)

Displacement, tons	17 500 full load
Measurement, tons	8 000 approximately
Dimensions, feet	510·8 × 75·5 × 29·5
Main engines	Diesels; 2 shafts; 24 000 bhp = 22 knots

Former freighter of the "Poltava" class, *Kosmonaut Vladimir Komarov* was launched in 1966. Built at the Leningrad Shipyard. Designed for the Soviet Academy of Science as a research vessel to study higher layers of atmosphere in the tropical zone of the western part of the Atlantic Ocean. Prominent features of the ship are the unusual hull sponsons and the radomes, massive plastic spheres enclosing radar arrays. The ship is named in honour of the Soviet astronaut who died when his space craft crashed in 1967.

KOSMONAUT VLADIMIR KOMAROV — *1969, Skyfotos*

1 "KOROLEV" TYPE

AKADEMIK SERGEI KOROLEV

Displacement, tons	21 250
Measurement, tons	17 114 gross; 2 185 net
Dimensions, feet	597·1 × 82·0 × 30·0

Built at Nikolaev in 1970, completing in 1971. Equipped with the smaller type radome and two "saucers"

8 "BASKUNCHAK" (ex-VOSTOK) CLASS

APSHERON **BASKUNCHAK** **DAURIYA** **DIKSON** **DONBASS** **SEVAN** **TAMAN** **YAMAL**

Measurement, tons	2 215 net; 6 450 deadweight; 4 896 gross
Dimensions, feet	400·3 × 55·1 × 14·0
Main engines	B & W 9-cylinder diesels; speed 15 knots

Standard timber carriers modified with helicopter flight decks. Built at Leningrad between 1963 and 1966. Entirely manned by naval personnel.

BASKUNCHAK — *1970, Michael D. J. Lennon*

7 "MORZHOVETS" (ex-VOSTOK *) CLASS

BOROVICHI * **BEZHITSA** **DOLINSK** **KEGOSTROV** * **MORZHOVETS** * **NEVEL** *

Former timber carriers but completely modified with a comprehensive array of tracking, direction finding and directional aerials. Additional laboratories built above the forward holds. Same measurements as the "Baskunchak" class, but tonnage increased to 5 277 gross and 967 net. *Bezhitsa* is ex-"Poltava" class, *Dolinsk* is ex-*Arkhangelsk* class and remainder (starred) "Vostok" class.

BEZHITSA — *1972, Michael D. J. Lennon*

MORZHOVETS — *1970, Michael D. J. Lennon*

Ex-"POVOLETS CLASS

RISTNA

Measurement, tons	1 819 net; 4 200 deadweight; 3 724 gross
Dimensions, feet	347·8 × 47·9 × 14·0
Main engines	MAN 6-cylinder diesels; speed = 15 knots

Classed as M Research. Converted from a timber carrier. Built in East Germany at Rostok by Schiffswerft Neptun in 1963. Painted white. Fitted with directional aerials on top of bridge wings. Served as Missile Detection Ship. In the same group as the "Morzhovets" class, see above.

RISTNA (ex-"Povolets" class) — *1970, Michael D. J. Lennon*

Space Associated Ships—*continued*

KOSMONAUT YURIY GAGARIN *1972*

KOSMONAUT VLADIMIR KOMAROV *1972, Michael D. J. Lennon*

AKADEMIK SERGEI KOROLEV *1972, Michael D. J. Lennon*

REPLENISHMENT SHIPS AND TANKERS

NOTE: With the Soviet merchant fleet under State control any of whose ships, including tankers, may be diverted to a fleet support role at any time.

1+1 "CHILIKIN" CLASS

BORIS CHILIKIN + 1

Displacement, tons	20 500 full load
Dimensions, feet	531·5 × 70·2 × 28·1 loaded
Guns	4—57 mm (2 twin)

Based on the "Velikij Oktyabr" merchant ship tanker design and built at Leningrad completing in 1971. This is the first Soviet Navy purpose built underway fleet replenishment ship for the supply of both liquids and solids, indicating a growing awareness of the need for afloat support for a widely dispersed fleet.

BORIS CHILIKIN *1972*

BORIS CHILIKIN *1972*

1 "MANYCH" CLASS

Displacement, tons	7 500
Guns	4—57 mm (2 twin) with Muff Cob radar

Completed 1972, probably in Finland. A smaller edition of the "Boris Chilikin" but showing the new interest in custom built replenishment ships. The height point on the single gantry is very similar to that on "Chilikin's" third gantry.

MANYCH *1973*

MANYCH *1973*

1 "SOFIA" CLASS

AKHTUBA (ex-*Khanoy*)

Displacement, tons	45 000 full load
Measurement, tons	62 000 deadweight, 32 840 gross, 16 383 net
Dimensions, feet	757·9 × 101·7 × 32·8

AKHTUBA *1972, Michael D. J. Lennon*

Built as the merchant tanker *Khanoy* in 1963 at Leningrad, she was taken over by the Navy in 1969 and renamed *Akhtuba*. The hull type was used in the construction of the space associated ship *Kosmonaut Yuriy Gagarin.*

7 "KAZBEK" CLASS

ALATYR **ANDREY** **DESNA** **KERCH** **SLAVGOROD** **VISHINSKY** **VOLKHOV**

Displacement, tons	16 250 full load
Measurement, tons	16 250 deadweight; 3 942 gross; 8 229 net
Dimensions, feet	479·0 × 63·0 × 23·0
Main engines	2 diesels driving single screw

Former "Leningrad" class merchant fleet tankers taken over by the Navy as oilers. All built at Leningrad from 1954 to 1957. Sister ship *Kazbec* was returned to the mercantile marine in 1970.

4 "ALTAY" CLASS

ELYENYA **IZHORA** **KOLA** **YEGORLIK**

Displacement, tons	5 500 standard
Dimensions, feet	344·5 × 49·2 × 19·7
Main engines	Diesels; speed = 14 knots

ALTAY Class *1972*

Built from 1967 onwards. Naval oilers with no armament.

6 "UDA" CLASS

DUNAY **KOIDA** **LENA** **SHEKSNA** **TEREK** **VISHERA**

Displacement, tons	5 500 standard; 7 200 full load
Dimensions, feet	400·3 × 51·8 × 20·3
Main engines	Diesels; 2 shafts; 8 000 bhp = 17 knots

UDA Class *1966, Col Breyer*

A medium type of Soviet supply ships. Built since 1961.

2 "PEVEK" CLASS

PEVEK **ZOLOTOY ROG**

Displacement, tons	4 000 standard
Measurement, tons	4 500 deadweight
Dimensions, feet	344·5 × 47·9 × 20·0
Main engines	Diesels; 2 900 bhp = 14 knots

A type similar to the United States AOG gasolene carriers. Built in Finland in 1960.

2 "OLEKMA" CLASS

IMAN **OLEKMA**

Displacement, tons	3 300
Dimensions, feet	344·5 × 49·2 × 20·0

Replenishment Ships and Tankers—*continued*

OLEKMA Class *1972*

Built in Finland in the mid 1960s. Similar to the "Pevek" class.

4 "KONDA" CLASS

KONDA **ROSSOSH** **SOYANNA** **YAKHROMA**

Displacement, tons	1 178 standard
Dimensions, feet	226·4 × 32·8 × 13·8
Main engines	1 100 bhp = 13 knots

CRYPTON

Measurement, tons 1 769 gross; 559 net

Naval fuel tanker of the "Baskunchak" class. Built in 1965 when she went into Atlantic service. It was reported in 1972 she is reverting to mercantile service. A photograph appears in the 1965-66 to 1971-72 editions.

20 "KHOBI" CLASS

CHEREMSHAN **INDIGA** **KHOBI** **METAN** **LOVAT** **ORSHA** **SEIMA** **SHACHA** **SHELON** **SOSVA** **TUNGUSKA**

Displacement, tons	800 light; 2 000 approx full load
Main engines	Speed 12 to 14 knots

Of this class numerous units are reported to have been built from 1957 to 1959.

SALVAGE VESSELS

"NEPA" CLASS

Displacement, tons	3 500 light; 5 000 standard
Dimensions, feet	410·1 × 52·5 × 16·4
Main engines	Diesels; 2 shafts

New type of submarine rescue and salvage ships similar to the "Prut" class but improved and enlarged and with a special high stern which extends out over the water for rescue manoeuvres. Built since 1969.

"Prut" Class SS 87 *1970, S. Breyer*

9 "PRUT" CLASS

ALTAI **BRESHTAU** **ZHIGULI**

Displacement, tons	2 120 standard; 3 500 full load
Dimensions, feet	296·0 × 36·1 × 13·1
Main engines	Diesels; 4 200 bhp = 18 knots

Large rescue vessels with raked down flush deck and mainmast derrick. Built since 1960.

"Prut" Class MB 23 *1965*

8 "SURA" CLASS

Displacement, tons	3 150 full load
Dimensions, feet	285·4 × 48·6 × 16·4
Main engines	Diesels; 1 770 bhp = 13·2 knots

Large salvage and rescue ships built since 1965 in East Germany. Six built by 1972.

Salvage Vessels—*continued*

KHL 21 "SURA" Class ARSD *1972*

"OKHTENSKIY" CLASS

MB 24 **MB 42** **MB 52**

Displacement, tons	835
Dimensions, feet	134·5 wl; 143 oa × 34 × 15
Guns	1—3 in dp; 2—20 mm AA
Main engines	2 BM diesels; 2 electric motors. 2 shafts; 1 875 bhp = 14 knots
Oil fuel, tons	187
Complement	34

Oceangoing salvage and rescue tugs. In addition to the above numbers there are many other units of this large class. Fitted with powerful pumps and other apparatus for salvage. Other numbers reported are A 2, 480, 481, 490, 495, 515, 525, 580, 610 612, 621, and 663.

MB 52 *1971, MOD, DPR(N), Official*

SUBMARINE RESCUE SHIPS

14 "T 58" CLASS ("VALDAY" TYPE)

Displacement, tons	725 standard; 850 full load
Dimensions, feet	222·1 × 29·9 × 7·5
Main engines	2 diesels; 2 shafts; 5 000 bhp = 20 knots

Basically of similar design to that of the "T 58" class larger fleet minesweepers, but the hulls were completed as emergency salvage vessels and submarine rescue ships at Leningrad. Equipped with diving bell, decompression chamber, lifting gear and emergency medical ward. Known as the "Valday" type. It has been reported that there may be 15 of the "T 58" hull type and six of the "T 43" hull design. One transferred to India (*Nistar*).

VALDAY Type *1970, S. Breyer*

LIFTING VESSELS

15 "NEPTUN" TYPE

Displacement, tons	700 light; 1 230 standard
Dimensions, feet	170·6 × 36·1 × 12·5
Main engines	Oil fuel; speed = 12 knots

Similar to western boom defence vessels or netlayers. Built in 1957-60 by Neptun, Rostok. Have a crane of 75 tons lifting capacity on the bow.

"Neptun" Class No. 13

ICEBREAKERS

1 PROJECTED. LARGE NUCLEAR POWERED

Main engines	Nuclear reactors; steam turbines; 80 000 hp

According to the Wärtsilä yard the most powerful icebreaker in the world is planned to be built by the Soviet Union.

2 NUCLEAR POWERED

IVAN MOSKVITIN
SEMYON DESHNEV

Similar to *Lenin* but of 15 000 tons and with two reactors and 30 000 shp. Both completed in Admiralty Yard, Leningrad—25 Mar 1971 and 3 Sept 1971 respectively.

2 NUCLEAR POWERED

ARKTIKA

Displacement, tons	25 000 standard;
Dimensions, feet	524·9 × 82·0 × 33·5
Aircraft	10 helicopters served by hangar
Main engines	2 nuclear reactors; steam turbines; 30 000 shp = 25 knots

ARKTIKA (Sketch) 1967

1 LARGE NUCLEAR POWERED TYPE

LENIN

Displacement, tons	16 000
Dimensions, feet	440 × 90·5 × 25
Aircraft	2 helicopters
Main engines	3 pressurised water-cooled nuclear reactors. 4 steam turbines; 3 shafts (no shaft in bow); 44 000 shp = 18 knots max
Complement	230

The world's first nuclear powered surface ship to put to sea. Reported to have accommodation for 1 000 personnel.

CONSTRUCTION. Built at the Admiralty Yard, Leningrad. Launched on 5 Dec 1957. Completed and commissioned on 15 Sep 1959.

ENGINEERING. The nuclear reactors enable her to steam for 18 months without refuelling. Fuel consumption is reported to be only five ounces daily. The turbines were manufactured by the Kirov plant in Leningrad. Three propellers aft, but no forward screw.

OPERATION. With her reinforced prow she is able to force a 100 ft wide ice-free swath and move continually through solid pack ice 8 feet thick at 3 to 4 knots.

LENIN 1972

Icebreakers—*continued*

3 DIESEL POWERED

Displacement, tons	21 100
Dimensions, feet	445·4 × 85·3 × 36·0
Aircraft	Helicopters
Main engines	9 Wärtsilä-Sulzer 12 cyl 2H 40/48 diesels with Oy Stromberg Ab generators; 3 shafts; 23 000 shp (41 400 bhp main diesel effect = 21 knots max)
Endurance	40 000 miles at 15 knots
Complement	115

The Soviet Union ordered three large and powerful icebreakers on 29 Apr 1970 from Wärtsilä, Helsinki, for delivery in 1974, 1975 and 1976. These will be the largest diesel icebreakers in the world. Seven Wärtsilä 814 TK auxiliary diesels, 8 520 bhp. Propelling and auxiliary machinery controlled electronically.

VLADIVOSTOK 1972, B. Borg

5 "MOSKVA" CLASS

VLADIVOSTOCK KIEV LENINGRAD MOSKVA MURMANSK

Displacement, tons	12 840 standard; 15 360 full load
Dimensions, feet	368·8 wl; 400·7 oa × 80·3 × 31 (normal); 34·5 max
Aircraft	2 helicopters
Main engines	8 Sulzer diesel-electric; 3 shafts; 22 000 shp = 18 knots
Oil fuel, tons	3 000
Radius, miles	20 000
Complement	145

DESIGN. Designed to stay at sea for a year without returning to base. The concave embrasure in the ship's stern is a housing for the bow of a following vessel when additional power is required. There is a landing deck for helicopters and hangar space for two machines.

CONSTRUCTION. Built by Wärtsilä-Koncernen A/B Sandvikens Skeppsdocka, Helsinki. *Moskva* was launched on 10 Jan 1959 and completed in June 1960. *Leningrad* was laid down in Jan 1959. Launched on 24 Oct 1959, and completed in 1962. *Kiev* was completed in 1966. *Murmansk* was launched on 14 July 1967 and *Vladivostok* on 28 May 1968.

ENGINEERING. Eight generating units of 3 250 bhp each comprising eight main diesels of the Wärtsilä-Sulzer 9 MH 51 type which together have an output of 26.000 electric hp. Four separate machinery compartments. Two engine rooms, four propulsion units in each. Three propellers aft. No forward propeller. Centre propeller driven by electric motors of 11 000 hp and each of the side propellers by motors of 5 500 hp. Two Wärtsilä-Babcock & Wilcox boilers for heating and donkey work.

OPERATION. *Moskva* has four pumps which can move 480 metric tons of water from one side to the other in two minutes to rock the icebreaker and wrench her free of thick ice.

MOSKVA *1960, Wärtsilä-Koncernen A/B Sandvikens Skeppsdocka*

Icebreakers—*continued*

3 "KAPITAN" CLASS

Name	*Measurement*	*Launched*	*Completed*
KAPITAN BELOUSOV	5 360 tons gross	1954	1955
KAPITAN MELECHOV	4 000 tons gross	19 Oct 1956	1957
KAPITAN VORONIN	3 416 tons gross	1955	1956

Displacement, tons 4 375 to 4 415 standard; 5 350 full load
Dimensions, feet 265 wl; 273 oa × 63·7 × 23
Main engines Diesel-electric; 6 Polar 8 cyl; 10 500 bhp = 14·9 knots
Oil fuel, tons 740
Complement 120

Kapitan Belousov was laid down at the end of 1952 and completed in Sep 1954. All built by Wärtsilä-Koncernen A/B, Sandvikens Skeppsdocka, Helsinki. The ships have four screws, two forward under the forefoot and two aft.

KAPITAN BELOUSOV *1970, Michael D. J. Lennon*

ALESCHA POPOVICH (ex-German *Eisvogel*)

Displacement, tons 2 090
Dimensions, feet 200·1 × 49·2 × 21·7
Main engines 2 Triple expansion; 3 200 ihp = 13 knots
Boilers 1

Former German icebreaker. Built by Aalborgs. Launched in 1941. In the White Sea. The icebreakers *Polluks* (ex-German *Pollux*) and *Iliya Muromets* (ex-German *Eisbar*) were deleted from the list in 1972.

PERESVET (ex-*Castor*)

Displacement, tons 5 150
Dimensions, feet 245·3 × 68·9 × 19·7
Main engines Triple expansion; 3 shafts; 9 600 ihp = 15 knots
Boilers 4 Wagner

Former German icebreaker. Built by Schichau, Danzig. Launched in 1939. In 1962-63 she was fitted with a helicopter platform.

21 "DIBRONYA NIKITICH" ("LEDOKOL") CLASS

AFANASIJ NIKITIN	**IVAN MOSKVITIN**	**SEMYON DEZHNEV**
BURAN	**IVAN KRUZENSHTERN**	**SEMEN CHELYUSHKIN**
DOBRINYA NIKITICH	**KHARITON LAPTEV**	**VASILIJ POYARKOV**
EROFFREY KHABAROV	**PERESVET**	**VASILIJ PRONCHISHCHEV**
FEDOR LITKE	**PETR PAKHTUSOV**	**VLADIMIR RUSANOV**
GEORGIJ SEDOV	**PLUG**	**YIRIY LISYANSKIJ**
ILYA MUROMETS	**SADKO**	**VYUGA**

Displacement, tons 2 500 standard (average)
Measurements, tons 2 305 gross (ships vary)
Dimensions, feet 223·1 × 59·1 × 18·1
Main engines 3 shafts; speed = 13·8 knots

All built at Leningrad between 1961 and 1965. Divided between the Baltic, Black Sea and Far East. Formerly known as *Ledokol* 1 onwards in a numerical series.

DOBRINYA NIKITICH *1972*

VLADIMIR RUSANOV (ex-LEDOKOL 7) *Michael D. J. Lennon*

2 "ADMIRAL" CLASS

Name	*Builders*	*Launched*	*Completed*
ADMIRAL LAZAREV (ex-*Yosif Stalin*)	Baltic Works, Leningrad	14 Aug 1937	1939
MIKOYAN (ex-*Otto Schmidt*)	Nikolayev	1938	1939

Displacement, tons 11 000
Measurement, tons 4 866 gross
Dimensions, feet 335·8 pp; 351 oa × 75·5 × 22
Aircraft 1 helicopter
Main engines Triple expansion with diesel-electric propulsion for cruising; 3 shafts; 10 050 hp = 15·5 knots
Boilers 9
Fuel, tons 4 000 coal; and diesel oil
Complement 142

3 aircraft and 1 catapult were included in the design. All in the White Sea. Of two sister ships, *Admiral Makarov* (ex-*Vyacheslav Molotov*, was reported in 1967 being scrapped in Spain, and *Lazar Kaganovich* was deleted from the list in 1972.

MIKOYAN after refit *1965, col Breyer*

Most of the above icebreakers are immensely strong in framing and scantlings, with exceptionally thick plating, and decks strengthened for mounting guns in wartime.

Of older icebreakers, *Davidov* (ex-*Krasnyi Oktyabr*, ex-*Nadyazhnyi*) was discarded in 1959 when *Fedor Litke* (ex-*Kanada*, ex-*Earl Grey*) was also scrapped, *Vladimir Rusanov* (ex-*Bonaventure*) was scrapped about 1963, and *Yermak* in 1965. *Sevmorput, Stepan Makarov, Tamyr, Montcalm*, and ex-*Krisjans Valdemaras* were deleted from the list in 1969 as no longer operational or unfit for further service on account of age or obsolescence. The old (1916-built) *Dobrinya Nikitich* was in 1971 reported to have been discarded and her name given to an icebreaker of the "Ledokol" class. In 1972 *Vladimir Ilyich* (ex-*Lenin*, ex-*Aleksandr Nevskii*) built in 1917 was reported out of service since 1968, and *Malygin* (ex-*Voima*) built in 1917 was deleted from the list with *Sadko* (ex-*Lintrose*) built in 1913 and *Georgij Sedov* (ex-*Beothic*) built in 1909.

FLEET TUGS

4 "PAMIR" CLASS

AGATAN **ALDAN** **ARBAN** **PAMIR**

Measurement, tons 1 443 to 2 032 gross
Dimensions, feet 256 oa × 42 × 13·5
Main engines Two 10 cyl 4 str diesels; 2 shafts; 4 200 bhp = 17 knots

Salvage tugs built at AB Gävie, Varv, Sweden, in 1959-60. Equipped with strong derricks, powerful pumps, air compressors, diving gear, fire fighting apparatus and electric generators.

"Pamir" Class *1970, S. Breyer*

There are many other tugs in the Fleet, see under Salvage Vessels on previous page, but numbers of tugs formerly listed have been deleted as they change or are suppressed from time to time.

"Okhtenskiy" Class No. SB 3 ***1968***

UGANDA

Mercantile Marine

Lloyd's Register of Shipping:
1 vessel of 5 510 tons

President Amin has said that Uganda will acquire a navy. No details of building or funding have been given. As Uganda's coastline is contiguous to those of Tanzania and Kenya on Lake Victoria it is not clear how the Ugandan Navy would operate. Previous armed vessels on the Lake were either converted from civil craft or transported overland in sections from the East Coast by the British and Germans during World War I.

URUGUAY

Administration

Inspector General of the Navy:
Rear Admiral Pedro Torres Negreira

Diplomatic Representation

Naval Attache in Washington:
Captain Ademar Torres

Mercantile Marine

Lloyd's Register of Shipping:
39 vessels of 142 828 tons gross

Personnel

1973: Total: 1 800 officers and men

FRIGATE

2 Ex-US "BOSTWICK" CLASS

Name	*No.*	*Builders*	*Launched*	*Completed*
ARTIGAS (ex-USS *Bronstein DE* 189)	DE 2	Federal SB & DD Co, Pt. Newark	14 Nov 1943	13 Dec 1943
URUGUAY (ex-USS *Baron, DE* 166)	DE 1	Federal SB & DD Co Pt. Newark	9 May 1943	5 July 1943

Displacement, tons: 1 240 standard; 1 900 full load
Length, feet (*metres*): 306·0 (*93·3*) oa
Beam, feet (*metres*): 37·0 (*11·3*)
Draught, feet (*metres*): 17·1 (*5·2*)
Guns, dual purpose: 3—3 in (*76 mm*) single
Guns, AA: 2—40 mm (see *Gunnery* notes)
A/S weapons: Hedgehog; 8 DCT; 1 DCR (see *Torpedo Tubes* notes)
Main engines: Diesel-electric; 2 shafts; 6 000 bhp
Speed, knots: 19
Range, miles: 8 300 at 14 knots
Oil fuel, tons: 315 (95 per cent)
Complement: 160

Former United States destroyer escorts of the "Bostwick" class, transferred to Uruguay in 1952.

RADAR. Equipped with SPS 6 search and tactical radar.

GUNNERY. Formerly also mounted ten 20 mm anti-aircraft guns, but these have been removed.

TORPEDO TUBES. The three 21-inch torpedo tubes in a triple mounting, originally carried, were suppressed.

APPEARANCE. Practically identical, but *Uruguay* can be distinguished by the absence of a mainmast, whereas *Artigas* has a diminutive pole mast aft.

ARTIGAS *1971*

MONTEVIDEO (ex-HMCS *Arnprior*, ex-HMS *Rising Castle*) PF 1

Displacement, tons: 1 010 standard; 1 600 full load
Length, feet (*metres*): 251·8 (*76·7*)
Beam, feet (*metres*): 36·7 (*11·2*)
Draught, feet (*metres*): 17·5 (*5·3*) max
Guns: 1—3 in (*76 mm*) dp; 2—40 mm AA; 4—20 mm AA
A/S weapons: Hedgehog; 4 DCT; 1 DCR
Main engines: Triple expansion; 190 rpm; 2 750 ihp
Speed, knots: 17
Boilers: 2 water tube
Range, miles: 5 400 at 9·5 knots
Oil fuel, tons: 480 max
Complement: 90

Former successively British and Canadian "Castle" class corvette (frigate). Employed as a training ship.

MONTEVIDEO *1971*

1 Ex-US "DEALEY" CLASS

18 DE JULIO (ex-USS *Dealey*) DE 3

Displacement, tons: 1 450 standard; 1 900 full load
Length, feet (*metres*): 314·5 (*95·9*) oa
Beam, feet (*metres*): 36·8 (*11·2*)
Draught, feet (*metres*): 13·6 (*4·2*)
Guns: 4—3 in (*76 mm*)
A/S weapons: 2 triple torpedo tubes (Mk 32)
Main engines: 1 De Laval geared turbine; 20 000 shp; 1 shaft
Boilers: 2 Foster Wheeler
Speed, knots: 25
Complement: 165

Purchased 28 July 1972. *Dealey* was the first post-war US escort ship. A second ship is to be purchased.

ESCORT

COMANDANTE PEDRO CAMPBELL, MSF 1 (ex-USS *Chickadee*, *MSF* 59)

Displacement, tons	890 standard; 1 250 full load
Dimensions, feet	215 wl; 221·2 oa × 32·2 × 10·8
Guns	1—3 in. 50. cal dp; 2—40 mm AA
Main engines	Diesel electric; 2 shafts; 3 118 bhp = 18 knots
Complement	105

Former United States fleet minesweeper of the "Auk" class. Built by Defoe B. & M. Works. Launched on 20 July 1942. Transferred on loan and commissioned at San Diego, Calif. on 18 Aug 1966. Employed as PCE, escort patrol vessel, or corvette.

COMANDANTE PEDRO CAMPBELL *1971*

PATROL VESSELS

1 Ex-US MSO TYPE

MALDONADO (ex-*Bir Hakeim* M 614, ex-USS *AM* 451)

Displacement, tons	700 standard; 795 full load
Dimensions, feet	165·0 wl; 171·0 oa × 35·0 × 10·3
Guns	1—40 mm AA
Main engines	2 GM diesels; 2 shafts; 1 600 bhp = 13·5 knots
Range, miles	3 000 at 10 knots
Complement	54

Former US ocean minesweeper transferred to France in Feb 1954. Returned to the US Navy and transferred to Uruguay on 9 April 1970.

1 "PAYSANDU" CLASS

SALTO PR 2

Displacement, tons	150 standard; 180 full load
Dimensions, feet	137 × 18 × 10
Guns	1—40 mm AA
Main engines	2 Germania diesels; 1 000 bhp = 17 knots
Oil fuel, tons	18
Range, miles	4 800 at 10·7 knots
Complement	26

Training ship. Built by Cantieri Navali Riuniti, Ancona, Italy. Launched on 11 Aug 1935. Of two sister ships, *Paysandu* was deleted in 1963 and *Rio Negro* in 1969.

SALTO *1971*

PATROL CRAFT

PR 11

Displacement, tons	70
Dimensions, feet	93·0 × 19·0 × 7·0
Speed, knots	25

Built by Lurssen in 1957.

PAYSANDU PR 12

Displacement, tons	60
Dimensions, feet	83·0 × 18·0 × 6·0
Speed, knots	22

Built by Sewart, USA in 1968.

COASTAL MINESWEEPERS

RIO NEGRO (ex-*Marguerite*, ex-USS *AMS 94*)

Displacement, tons	370 standard; 405 full load
Dimensions, feet	136·2 pp; 141·0 oa × 26·0 × 8·3
Guns	2—20 mm AA
Main engines	2 GM diesels; 2 shafts; 1 200 bhp 13 knots
Oil fuel, tons	40
Range, miles	2 500 at 10 knots
Complement	38

Ex-US coastal minesweeper built for France under MDAP. Stricken from the French Navy in 1969 and returned to US ownership. She was transferred to Uruguay at Toulon on 10 Nov 1969.

SURVEY SHIP

CAPITAN MIRANDA CS 10

Displacement, tons	516 standard; 549 full load
Dimensions, feet	148 pp; 179 oa × 26 × 10·5
Main engines	1 MAN diesel; 500 bhp = 11 knots
Oil fuel, tons	37
Complement	52

Built by Sociedad Espanola de Construccion Naval, Matagorda, Cadiz. Launched in 1930. Used as general utility tender.

CAPITAN MIRANDA *1971*

SALVAGE VESSEL

HURACAN (ex-USS *Nahaut, AN* 83)

Displacement, tons	560 standard; 760 full load
Dimensions, feet	146 wl; 163 oa × 30·5 × 11·8
Guns	4—20 mm single
Main engines	Diesel electric; 1 shaft; 1 000 bhp = 11·5 knots
Complement	48

Former US netlayer, purchased in April 1969 for salvage services.

RESCUE LAUNCH

AR 1

Displacement, tons	25 standard; 30 full load
Dimensions, feet	63·0 × 15·0 × 3·8
Guns	4 MG
Main engines	2 Hall-Scott Defender; 1 260 bhp = 33·5 knots
Range, miles	600 at 15 knots
Complement	8

British type rescue launch. Rated as *Lancha de Rescate*. Launched on 4 July 1944. A photograph of AR 1 appears in the 1953-54 to 1957-58 editions.

OILERS

PRESIDENTE ORIBE AO 9

Measurement, tons	17 920 gross; 28 267 deadweight
Dimensions, feet	587·2 pp; 620 oa × 84·3 × 33
Main engines	1 Ishikawajima turbine; 12 500 shp = 16·75 knots
Boilers	2 Ishikawajima-Harima Foster Wheeler type
Range, miles	16 100 at 16 knots
Complement	76

Built by Ishikawajima-Harima Ltd, Japan. Delivered to the Uruguayan Navy on 22 Mar 1962.

PRESIDENTE ORIBE *1971*

PRESIDENTE RIVERA

Measurement, tons	19 350

Reported as built in Spain, completing in 1971.

VENEZUELA

Administration

Commander General of the Navy (Chief of Naval Operations):
Rear-Admiral Armando Perez Leefmans

Chief of Naval Staff:
Rear-Admiral Enrique Dominauez Garcia

Personnel

1973: 7 500 officers and men including 4 000 of the Marine Corps

Strength of the Fleet

4 Destroyers
6 Frigates
4 Submarines (2 building)
12 Missile Boats/FPBs (all building)
10 Patrol Craft
4 Medium Landing Ships
1 Transport Landing Ship
2 Transports
12 Coast Guard Vessels
3 Surveying Vessels
5 Tugs
5 Harbour Tugs
1 Floating Dock

Diplomatic Representation

Naval Attaché in London:
Vacant

Naval Attaché in Washington:
Rear Admiral Luis Ramirez Aranda

Mercantile Marine

Lloyd's Register of Shipping:
113 vessels of 4 111 242 tons gross

DESTROYERS

3 "ARAGUA" CLASS

Name	*No.*	*Builders*	*Laid down*	*Launched*	*Completed*
ARAGUA	D 31	Vickers Ltd, Barrow	29 June 1953	27 Jan 1955	14 Feb 1956
NUEVA ESPARTA	D 11	Vickers Ltd, Barrow	24 July 1951	19 Nov 1952	8 Dec 1953
ZULIA	D 21	Vickers Ltd, Barrow	24 July 1951	29 June 1953	15 Sep 1954

Displacement, tons	2 600 standard; 3 670 full load
Length, feet (*metres*)	384·0 (*117·0*)wl; 402·0 (*122·5*)oa
Beam, feet (*metres*)	43·0 (*13·1*)
Draught, feet (*metres*)	19·0 (*5·8*)
Missiles	2 quadruple "Seacat" in D 11
Guns, dual purpose	6—4·5 (*114 mm*), 3 twin
Guns, AA	16—40 mm (8 twin) 4—40 mm (2 twin) in D 11 only
A/S weapons	2 DCT; 2 DC racks ("Squids" in D 11 and D 21)
Torpedo tubes	3—21 in (*533 mm*) triple (none in D 11)
Boilers	2 Yarrow
Main engines	Parsons geared turbines; 2 shafts; 50 000 shp
Speed, knots	34
Range, miles	5 000 at 10 knots
Complement	256 (20 officers, 236 men)

ARAGUA — *1969, Venezuelan Navy, Official*

All built in Great Britain. *Nueva Esparta* and *Zulia* were ordered in 1950. Air conditioned. Two engine rooms and two boiler rooms served by a single uptake. The 4·5 inch guns are fully automatic. *Nueva Esparta* and *Zulia* refitted at Palmers Hebburn Works, Vickers in 1959, and at New York Navy Yard in 1960 to improve anti-submarine and anti-aircraft capabilities. *Aragua* refitted by Palmers Hebburn in 1964-65, *Nueva Esparta* at Cammell Laird in 1968-69 when "Seacat" launchers were fitted and some 40 mm and the torpedo tubes removed.

RADAR. Search: AWS 2 and (*Nueva Esparta*) SPS 6. Fire Control: X Band.

NUEVA ESPARTA — *1970, Venezuelan Navy,*

1 Ex-US "ALLEN M. SUMNER" CLASS

Name	
CARABOBO	(ex-USS *Beatty* DD 756)

Builders	*Launched*	*Commissioned*
Bethlehem, Staten Is.	30 Nov 1944	31 Mar 1945

Displacement, tons	1 000 surface; 1 290 dived
Length, feet (*metres*)	183·4 (*55·9*)
Beam, feet (*metres*)	20·5 (*6·25*)
Draught, feet (*metres*)	19·8 (*6·0*)
Torpedo tubes	8—21 inch
Main engines	Diesel-electric, 5 000 hp 1 shaft
Speed, knots	22 Dived
Complement	32

Transferred from USN 14 July 1972.

ALLEN M. SUMNER *Class*

FRIGATES

6 "ALMIRANTE CLEMENTE" CLASS

Displacement, tons	1 300 standard; 1 500 full load
Length, feet (*metres*)	325·11 (*99·1*) oa
Beam, feet (*metres*)	35·5 (*10·8*)
Draught, feet (*metres*)	12·2 (*3·7*)
Guns, dual purpose	4—4 in (*102 mm*) 2 twin
Guns, AA	4—40 mm; 8—20 mm (modified group 40 mm only)
A/S weapons	2 "Squids", 4 DCT and 2 DC racks in original group; 1 "Hedgehog" 4 DCT and 2 DC racks in modified group
Torpedo tubes	3—21 in (*533 mm*) triple (original group only)
Boilers	2 Foster Wheeler
Main engines	2 sets geared turbines; 2 shafts; 24 000 shp
Speed, knots	32 max, 28 in service
Range, miles	3 500 at 15 knots
Oil, fuel tons	350
Complement	162 (12 officers, 150 men)

Name	*No.*	*Laid down*	*Launched*	*Completed*
ALMIRANTE CLEMENTE	D 12	5 May 1954	12 Dec 1954	1956
ALMIRANTE JOSE GARCIA	D 33	12 Dec 1954	12 Oct 1956	1957
ALMIRANTE BRION	D 23	12 Dec 1954	4 Sep 1955	1957
GENERAL JOSÉ DE AUSTRIA	D 32	12 Dec 1954	15 July 1956	1957
GENERAL JOSÉ TRINIDAD MORAN	D 22	5 May 1954	12 Dec 1954	1956
GENERAL JUAN JOSÉ FLORES	D 13	5 May 1954	7 Feb 1955	1956

All built by Ansaldo, Leghorn. The first three were ordered in 1953. Three more were ordered in 1954. Aluminium alloys were widely employed in the building of all superstructure. All six ships are fitted with Denny-Brown fin stabilisers and air conditioned throughout the living and command spaces.

MODERNISATION. *Almirante José Garcia, Almirante Brion* and *General José de Austria* were refitted by Ansaldo, Leghorn, in 1962 to improve their anti-submarine and anti-aircraft capabilities: this group are known as "Modified Almirante Clemente" type. *Almirante Clemente* and *General José Trinidad Moran* were refitted by the Cammell Laird/Plessey group during 1969.

GUNNERY. The 4 inch anti-aircraft guns are fully automatic and radar controlled.

RADAR. Search: MLA 1. Fire Control: X Band.

GENERAL JOSE TRINIDAD MORAN *1972, Venezuelan Navy,*

GENERAL JOSE DE AUSTRIA (modified group) *1972, Venezuelan Navy, Official*

SUBMARINES

2 Ex-US "GUPPY II" TYPE

CARITE S 11 (ex-USS *Tilefish*, SS 307)
TIBERON S 12 (ex-USS *Cubera* SS 347)

Displacement, tons	1 870 surface; 2 420 submerged
Length, feet (*metres*)	307·5 (*93·8*)
Beam, feet (*metres*)	27·0 (*8·2*)
Draught, feet (*metres*)	18·0 (*5·5*)
Torpedo tubes	10—21 in (*533 mm*), 6 bow, 4 stern
Main engines	3 diesels; 4 800 shp; 2 electric motors, 5 400 shp 2 shafts
Speed, knots	18 on surface; 15 submerged
Range, miles	12 000 at 10 knots
Oil fuel, tons	300
Complement	80

Carite built by Mare Island Navy Shipyard, California. Launched on 25 Oct 1943. Commissioned on 28 Dec 1943. Purchased by Venezuela in 1960 after a four months overhaul in the United States. Transferred from the US Navy at San Francisco on 4 May 1960. Overhauled in San Francisco Navy Yard in 1962 to Guppy II standards. *Tiberon* built by Electric Boat Co, Groton, launched 17 June 1945, commissioned 19 Dec 1945. Transferred to Venezuela 5 Jan 1972.

CARITE *1969, Venezuelan Navy, Official*

2 HOWALDTSWERKE TYPE

Displacement, tons	2 200 standard; 3 320 full load
Length, feet (*metres*)	376·5 (*114·8*)
Beam, feet (*metres*)	40·9 (*12·4*)
Draught, feet (*metres*)	19·0 (*5·8*)
Guns	6—5 in dual purpose (twins)
A/S weapons	2 Fixed Hedgehogs. DCs 2 triple torpedo launchers (Mk 32)
Main engines	2 geared turbines, 60 000 shp 2 shafts
Speed, knots	34
Complement	274

Building in Germany for completion in 1974-75.

GLAVKOS *Class*

LIGHT FORCES

6 VOSPER-THORNYCROFT 121 FT CLASS (MISSILE BOATS AND FPBs)

Displacement, tons	150 (approx)
Length, feet (*metres*)	121·3 (*37*)
Missiles	3 to be armed with Otomat
Guns	Second 3 to be armed with Oto Melara 3 in
Main engines	MTU diesels; 3 600 hp 2 shafts
Speed, knots	30

A £6m. order, the first laid down in Jan 1973 for completion in autumn 1974. A new design of steel-hulled FPBs and missile boats, fitted with Elsag fire-control system NA 10 mod 1 and Selenia radar.

Vosper Thornycroft 37 m FPB (with missiles) *1973, Vosper Thornycroft*

10 Ex-US PC TYPE (PATROL CRAFT)

ALBATROS	(ex-USS PC 582)	P-04
ALCATRAZ	(ex-USS PC 565)	P-03
CALAMAR	(ex-USS PC 566)	P-02
CAMARON	(ex-USS PC 483)	P-08
CARACOL	(ex-USS PC 1077)	P-06
GAVIOTA	(ex-USS PC 619)	P-10
PETREL	(ex-USS PC 1176)	P-05
PULPO	(ex-USS PC 465)	P-07
MEJILLON	(ex-USS PC 487)	P-01
TOGOGO	(ex-USS PC 484)	P-09

Displacement, tons	280 standard; 430 full load
Dimensions, feet	170·0 wl; 173·7 oa × 23·0 × 10·8
Guns	1—3 in dp; 2—40 mm AA (1 twin); 2—20 mm AA
A/S weapons	Provision for 4 DCT
Main engines	2 Fairbanks-Morse diesels; 2 shafts; 2 800 bhp = 19 knots
Complement	65

Mejillon was refitted and overhauled by Diques y Astilleros Nacionalis, Venezuela, prior to commissioning in the Venezuelan Navy, and from 1962 onwards more ships of this type underwent similar preparation to join the fleet. Altogether twelve of these former United States submarine chasers of the steel-hulled "173-ft" type were purchased from the USA in Oct 1960 for anti-smuggling patrols, namely:—*Cooperstown* PC 484, *Dalhart* PC 619, *Edenton* PC 1077, *Gilmer* PC 565, *Honesdale* PC 566, *Larchmont* PC 487, *Lenoir* PC 582, *Minden* PC 1176, *Paragould* PC 465, *Rolla* PC 483, *Tarrytown* PC 1252 and *Tooell* PC 572, and with these the Navy assumed Coast Guard functions. The latter two ships were not refitted and were discarded. *Camaron*, *Pulpo* and *Gaviota* were placed in reserve 1968-70.

ALBATROS *1972, Venezuelan Navy*

8 "RIO" CLASS

RIO APURE **RIO CABRIALES** **RIO GUARICO** **RIO NEVERI**
RIO ARAUCA **RIO CARONI** **RIO NEGRO** **RIO TUY**

Displacement, tons	38
Dimensions, feet	82 × 15 × 4
Main engines	2 Mercedes-Benz MB 820 Bb diesels; 1 400 rpm; 1 350 bhp = 27 knots; 24—25 knots cruising

All built by the Chantiers Navales de l'Estereles, Cannes, during 1954-56.

RIO NEGRO *1972, Venezuelan Navy,*

RIO SANTO DOMINGO

Displacement, tons	40
Dimensions, feet	70 × 15 × 6
Main engines	2 GM diesels; 1 250 bhp = 24 knots

RIO TURBIO

Displacement, tons	40
Dimensions, feet	81·3 × 15 × 7·5
Main engines	4 GM diesels; 880 bhp = 20 knots

GOLFO DE CARIACO

Displacement, tons	37
Dimensions, feet	65 × 18 × 9
Main engines	Diesels; speed = 19 knots

TORBES (ex-*Felipe Santiago Esteves*, LC 12, ex-*Brion* CS 2) LA 12

Displacement, tons	47
Dimensions, feet	83 × 16 × 4
Guns	1—20 mm; 4 DCT
Main engines	2 petrol engines; 2 shafts; 1 200 bhp = 15 knots
Complement	10

Launched in 1937. Ex-US Coast Guard cutter 56196. Acquired in 1944. Of wooden construction. *Brion* was renamed *Felipe Santiago Esteves* in 1957 when LC pennant number was allocated and renamed *Torbes* No. LA 12, in 1962.

The survey launch *Torbes*, and the repair launch BT 1 were deleted from the list in 1962. *Caribe* was scrapped in 1956.

Antonio Diaz LC 11 (ex-CS 1, ex-56193), *Arismendi* LC 14 (ex-CS 4, ex-56194) and *Briceno Mendez* LC 13 (ex-CS 3, ex-56195) were deleted in 1960.

LANDING SHIPS

4 Ex-US LSM TYPE

LOS FRAILES T 15 (ex-USS *LSM* 544) **LOS ROQUES** T 14 (ex-USS *LSM* 543)
LOS MONJES T 13 (ex-USS *LSM* 548) **LOS TESTIGOS** T 16 (ex-USS *LSM* 545)

Displacement, tons	743 beaching; 1 095 full load
Dimensions, feet	196·5 wl; 203·5 oa × 34·5 × 8·3
Guns	1—40 mm AA; 4—20 mm AA
Main engines	Direct drive diesels; 2 shafts; 2 800 bhp = 12 knots
Range, miles	9 000 at 11 knots
Complement	59

All built by Brown Shipbuilding Co, Houston, Texas, in 1945. The former United States medium landing ships LSM 370, LSM 542, LSM 543, LSM 544, LSM 545 and LSM 548 were sold to Venezuela under MAP in Aug 1958, but only the latter four have been commissioned in the Venezuelan Navy. Ex-370 and 542 are employed on mercantile duties.

LOS MONJES *1970, Venezuelan Navy,*

TRANSPORT LANDING SHIP

GUAYANA T 18 (ex-USS *Quirinus*, ARL 39, ex-*LST* 1151)

Displacement, tons	1 625 light; 3 960 trials; 4 100 full load
Dimensions, feet	316 wl; 328 oa × 50 × 11·2 max
Guns	8—40 mm AA (two quadruple mountings)
Main engines	GM diesels; 2 shafts; 1 800 bhp = 11·6 knots
Complement	81 (11 officers 70 men)

Former US Navy landing craft repair ship. Built by Chicago Bridge and Iron Co, Seneca, Illinois. Laid down on 3 Mar 1945. Loaned to Venezuela in June 1962 and now used as a transport in the Venezuelan Navy.

GUAYANA *1970, Venezuelan Navy,*

TRANSPORTS

PUNTA CABANA T 17 **T 18** **T 19**

Three small troop carriers of about 3 000 tons with a speed of 17 knots for troops.

LAS AVES (ex-*Dos de Diciembre*) T 12

Displacement, tons	944
Dimensions, feet	234·2 × 33·5 × 10
Guns	4—20 mm (2 twin)
Main engines	2 diesels; 2 shafts; 1 600 bhp = 15 knots
Radius, miles	2 600 at 11 knots

Launched by Chantiers Dubigeon, Nantes-Chantenay, France in Sept. 1954. Light transport for naval personnel. Originally named *Dos de Diciembre*. Redesignated T 12 in 1958. Renamed *Las Aves* in 1961.

LAS AVES *1970, Venezuelan Navy,*

SURVEY SHIPS

3 "PUERTO" CLASS

PUERTO DE NUTRIAS (ex-USS *Tunxis*, AN 90) H 02
PUERTO MIRANDA (ex-USS *Waxsaw*, AN 91) H 03
PUERTO SANTO (ex-USS *Marietta*, AN 82) H 01

Displacement, tons	650 standard; 785 full load
Dimensions, feet	146 wl; 168·5 oa × 33·9 × 10·2 max
Guns	1—20 mm AA
Main engines	Bush-Sulzer diesel-electric; 1 shaft; 1 500 bhp = 12 knots
Complement	46

Survey Ships—*continued*

Former US netlayers of the "Cohoes" class. *Puerto Santo* was built by Commercial Iron Works, Portland, Oregon. Laid down on 17 Feb 1945, launched on 27 Apr 1945. Loaned from USA in Jan 1961 under MAP and converted into hydrographic survey vessel and buoy tender by US Coast Guard Yard, Curtis Bay, Maryland, in Feb 1962. All ships originally carried one 3-inch 50 cal dp gun. *Puerto du Nutrias* and *Puerto Miranda*, built by Zenith Bridge Co, Duluth, Minn, launched in 1944, completed in 1945, were loaned to Venezuela in 1963 under MAP and have remained in reserve ever since.

PUERTO SANTO *1970, Venezuelan Navy,*

TUGS

FELIPE LARRAZABAL R 21 (ex-USS *Utina*, ATF 163)

Displacement, tons	1 235 standard; 1 675 full load
Dimensions	205 oa × 38·5 × 15·5
Gun	1—3 in 50 cal AA
Main engines	Diesel-electric; 3 000 bhp; 1 shaft
Speed, knots	15
Complement	85

Transferred 3 Sept 1972. This is the third tug of this name. The first (ex-USS *Discoverer*, (ex-USCG *Auk*, AM 38 was deleted in 1962. The second (ex-USS *Tolowa*, ATF 116) was deleted in 1972 after damage when grounded.

FERNANDO GOMEZ (ex-USS *Dudley*, YTM 744, ex-*Diana*, ex-US Army ST 873) R 12.

Displacement, tons	161
Dimensions, feet	80 × 19 × 8
Main engines	Clark diesel, 6-cyl, 315 rpm; 380 bhp= 15 knots
Complement	10

GENERAL JOSE FELIX RIBAS R 13 (ex-USS *Oswegatchie*, YTM 778, ex-YTB 515)

Large harbour tug. Transferred on 4 June 1965 at San Diego, Calif.

NOTE. Tugs *Esteban Rojas*, *Dina* and *Caracas* were deleted in 1958. In Jan 1963 five small YTL harbour tugs were leased from USN and since then the medium tugs ex-*Wannalancet*, YTM 385 and ex-*Sassacus*, YTM 193 have been leased.

FLOATING DOCK

DF 1 (ex-USS *ARD* 13)

The ex-USN ARD 13 of 3 000 tons and built of steel was transferred on loan to Venezuela in Feb 1962 as DF 1.

VIETNAM (REPUBLIC OF)

Principal Flag Officers

Commander-in-Chief and Chief of Naval Operations:
Rear Admiral Tran Van Chon

Vice Chief of Naval Operations:
Commodore Larn Nquồn Tanh

Fleet Commander:
Captain Nguyen Thanh Chau

Diplomatic Representation

Defence Attaché in Washington D.C.:
Colonel Nguyen Linh Chieu

Defence Attaché in London:
Colonel Cao Xuan Ve

Strength of the Fleet

7 Frigates (High Endurance Cutters)
2 Frigates (Radar Picket Type)
8 Escorts (Including 5 Fleet Minesweepers)
1 Patrol Vessel (Submarine Chaser Type)
2 Coastal Minesweepers
20 Coastal Gunboats (Patrol Type)
25 Landing Ships (LST, LSM, LSSL, LSIL)
6 Oilers
26 Coast Guard Launches
850 Patrol, Coastal and Riverine Craft
165 Auxiliaries

Personnel

1972: 40 275 officers and enlisted men plus 13 800 marines.

Ships

All South Vietnamese Navy ships are prefixed by HQ for Hai Quan, meaning "navy".
Some of the patrol, coastal, and riverine craft are believed inoperative because of maintenance and support limitations.

Mercantile Marine

Lloyd's Register of Shipping:
39 vessels of 31 979 tons gross

FRIGATES

7 Ex-US 311-ft COAST GUARD CUTTERS

Name	*No.*	*Builder*	*Launched*	*US Navy Comm*	*Transferred*
TRAN QUANG KHAI (ex-USCGC *Bering Strait*, WHEC 382 ex-AVP 34)	HQ 02	Lake Washington SY	15 Jan 1944	19 July 1944	1 Jan 1971
TRAN NHAT DUAT (ex-USCGC *Yakutat*. WHEC 380 ex-AVP 32)	HQ 03	Associated Shipbuilders	2 July 1942	31 Mar 1944	1 Jan 1971
TRAN BINH TRONG (ex-USCGC *Castle Rock*, WHEC 383, ex-AVP 35)	HQ 05	Lake Washington SY	11 Mar 1944	8 Oct 1944	21 Dec 1971
TRAN QUOC TOAN (ex-USCGC *Cook Inlet*, WHEC 384, ex-AVP 36)	HQ 06	Lake Washington SY	13 May 1944	5 Nov 1944	21 Dec 1971
THAM NGU LAO (ex-USCGC *Absecon*, WHEC 374, ex-AVP 23)	HQ 15	Lake Washington SY	8 Mar 1942	28 Jan 1943	15 July 1972
LY THOUNG KIET (ex-USCGC *Chincoteague*, WHEC 375, ex-AVP 24)	HQ 16	Lake Washington SY	15 Apr 1942	12 Apr 1943	21 June 1972
NGO KUYEN (ex-USCGC *McCulloch*, WHEC 386, ex-USS *Wachapreague*, AGP 8, AVP 56)	HQ 17	Lake Washington SY	10 July 1943	17 May 1944	21 June 1972

Displacement, tons	1 766; standard 2 800 full load
Length, feet	300 wl; 310·75 oa
Beam, feet	41·1
Draught, feet	13·5
Guns	1—5 inch (*127 mm*) .38 cal DP 1 or 2—81 mm mortars in some ships; several MG
Main engines	Diesels (Fairbanks Morse); 6 080 bhp; 2 shafts
Speed, knots	approx 18
Complement	approx 200

Built as seaplane tenders of the "Barnegat" class for the US Navy; *Tran Nhat Duat* by Associated Shipbuilders, Seattle, Washington; others by Lake Washington Shipyard, Houghton, Washington.
All transferred to US Coast Guard in 1946-1948, initially on loan designated WAVP and then on permanent transfer except ex-*McCulloch* transferred outright from US Navy to Coast Guard; subsequently redesignated as high endurance cutters (WHEC). Transferred from US Coast Guard to South Vietnamese Navy in 1971-1972.
These ships are the largest combatants in the South Vietnamese Navy and the only ones to mount a 5 inch gun battery. All anti-submarine weapons are believed to have been removed prior to transfer.

PHOTOGRAPHS. These ships are distinguished from the former US Navy radar picket escorts of similar size by their pole masts forward, open side passages amidships, and radar antenna on second mast. Note combination ·50 cal MG/81 mm mortar forward of bridge in "B" position.

TRAN NHAT DUAT — *1971, Vietnamese Navy*

TRAN QUANG KHAI — *1971, Vietnamese Navy*

2 Ex-US DER TYPE

Name	*No.*	*Launched*	*US Navy Comm.*	*Transferred*
TRAN HUNG DAO (ex-USS *Camp*, DER 251)	HQ 01	16 Apr 1943	16 Sep 1943	6 Feb 1971
TRAN KHANH DU (ex-USS *Forster*, DER 334)	HQ 04	13 Nov 1943	25 Jan 1944	25 Sep 1971

Displacement, tons	1 590 standard; 1 850 full load
Length, feet	300 wl; 306 oa
Beam, feet	36·6
Draught, feet	14
Guns	2—3 inch (*76 mm*) 50 cal AA (single)
A/S weapons	6—12·75 inch (*324 mm*) torpedo tubes (Mk 32 triple) 1 trainable hedgehog (Mk 15) depth charge rack
Main engines	Diesel (Fairbank Morse); 6 000 bhp; 2 shafts
Speed, knots	21
Complement	approx 170

Former US Navy destroyer escorts, of the FMR design group. *Tran Hung Dao* built by Brown SB Co, Houston, Texas; *Tran Khanh Du* built by Consolidated Steel Corp, Orange, Texas.

TRAN KHANH DU — *1971, Vietnamese Navy*

Frigates—*continued*

2 Ex-US DER TYPE —*continued*

After World War II both ships were extensively converted to radar picket configuration to serve as seaward extension of US aircraft attack warning system; redesignated DER with original DE hull numbers. Large SPS-8 search radar and TACAN (tactical aircraft navigation) "pod" removed after radar picket barrier ended in 1965, but ships retained DER designation. Subsequently employed during 1960s in Indochina for coastal patrol and interdiction by US Navy (Operation MARKET TIME). Transferred to South Vietnamese Navy in 1971.

These ships are second in firepower in the South Vietnamese Navy only to the ex-US Coast Guard cutters with respect to gun calibre; however, these ships each mount two guns (forward mount enclosed, after mount open). Also, they are the most-capable anti-submarine ships of the Navy.

ELECTRONICS. SPS-28 and SPS-10 search radars on forward tripod mast. Apparently most electronic warfare equipment was removed prior to transfer (compare after masts with "pods" in photographs of US ships of this class in the United States section.)

THAN HUNG DAO *Vietnamese Navy*

PATROL VESSELS

3 Ex-US PCE TYPE

DONG DA II (ex-USS *Crestview, PCE* 895)	HQ 07	18 May 1943
NGOC HOI (ex-USS *Brattleboro, EPCER* 852)	HQ 12	1 Mar 1944
VAN KIEP II (ex-USS *Amherst, PCER* 853)	HQ 14	18 Mar 1944

Displacement, tons	640 standard; 903 full load
Dimensions, feet	180 wl; 184·5 oa × 33·1 × 9·5
Guns	1—3 inch (*76 mm*) 50 cal AA; 2—40 mm AA (single); 8—20 mm AA (twin)
A/S weapons	1 fixed hedgehog; depth charges
Main engines	Diesel (General Motors); 2 000 bhp; 2 shafts = 15 knots
Complement	approx 90

Former US Navy patrol vessels—escort (PCE), two of which were fitted as rescue ships (PCER) to pickup survivors of convoy sinkings. *Dong Da II* built by Willamette Iron & Steel Corp, Portland, Oregon; others by Pullman Standard Car Manufacturing Co, Chicago, Illinois; launch dates above. After World War II the *Ngoc Hoi* was employed as an experimental ship (designation given "E" prefix); others used for Naval Reserve training.

Dong Da II transferred to South Vietnam on 29 Nov 1961, *Ngoc Hoi* on 11 July 1966, and *Van Kiep II* in June 1970.

These ships are similar in design to the former minesweepers listed below.

NHUT TAO *Vietnamese Navy*

NGOC HOI *1971, Vietnamese Navy,*

5 Ex-US MSF TYPE

CHI LANG II (ex-USS *Gayety, MSF* 239)	HQ 08	19 Mar 1944
KY HOA (ex-USS *Sentry, MSF* 299)	HQ 09	15 Aug 1943
NHUT TAO (ex-USS *Serene, MSF* 300)	HQ 10	31 Oct 1943
CHI LINH (ex-USS *Shelter, MSF* 301)	HQ 11	14 Nov 1943
HA HOI (ex-USS *Prowess*, IX 305, ex-MSF 280)	HQ 13	17 Feb 1944

Displacement, tons	650 standard; 945 full load
Dimensions, feet	180 wl; 184·5 oa × 33 × 9·75
Guns	1—3 inch (*76 mm*) 50 cal AA; 2—40 mm AA (single); up to 8—20 mm AA (twin)
A/S weapons	1 fixed hedgehog; depth charges
Main engines	Diesel (Cooper Bessemer); 1 710 bhp; 2 shafts = 14 knots
Complement	approx 80

Former US Navy minesweepers of the "Admirable" class (originally designated AM). Built by Winslow Marine Railway & SB Co, Winslow, Washington, except *Ha Hoi* built by Gulf SB Corp, Chicasaw, Alabama; launch dates above. *Ha Hoi* served as a Naval Reserve training ship from 1962 to 1971 (redesignated as an unclassified auxiliary IX 305 on 1 Mar 1966).

Chi Lang II transferred to South Vietnam in Apr 1962, *Ky Hoa* transferred in Aug 1962, *Nhut Tao* and *Chi Linh* transferred in Jan 1964, and *Ha Hoi* transferred on 4 June 1970. Minesweeping equipment has been removed and two depth charge racks fitted on fantail; employed in patrol and escort roles. All of these ships are believed to have two 20 mm twin mounts at after end of bridge and one or two 20 mm twin mounts on fantail.

CHI LANG II *1962, Vietnamese Navy*

1 Ex-US PC TYPE

VAN DON (ex-USS *Anacortes, PC* 1569)	HQ 06	9 Dec 1944

Displacement, tons	280 standard; 450 full load
Dimensions, feet	170 wl; 173·7 oa × 3 × 10·8
Guns	1—3 inch (*76 mm*) 50 cal AA; 1—40 mm AA; 4—20 mm AA (single)
A/S weapons	2 mousetrap launchers; depth charges
Main engines	Diesel; 2 800 bhp; 2 shafts = 19 knots
Complement	approx 50

Van Don was built by Leathem D. Smith SB Co. Launch date above. Laid down on 26 Sep 1944 and completed on 14 Mar 1945. *Van Don* was transferred at Seattle, Washington on 23 Nov 1960. *Dong Da* ex-French *Ardent*, ex-USS PC 1167) was officially stricken from the list in 1961 and *Chi Lang* (ex-French *Mousquet* P 633, ex-USS PC 1144) in 1961, the names allocated to larger vessels, *Tay Ket* HQ 05 (ex-French *Glaive*, ex-USS PC 1146 and *Van Kiep* HQ 02 (ex-French *Intrepide*, ex-USS

1 Ex-US PC TYPE —*continued*

PC 1130)on 10 July 1965 and July 1965 respectively, and *Tuy Dong* (ex-*Trident*, ex-USS PC 1143) HQ 04, former French *escorteur cotier* transferred in 1956 was officially deleted in 1971.
Reportedly the *Van Don* remains on the Navy List as HQ 06 despite the assignment of that number to a former US 311-ft Coast Guard Cutter.

VAN DON — *1971, Vietnamese Navy*

PATROL GUNBOATS

20 100-ft PGM TYPE

Name	*No.*	*Transferred*
PHU DU	HQ 600 (PGM 64)	Feb 1963
TIEN MOI	HQ 601 (PGM 65)	Feb 1963
MINH HOA	HQ 602 (PGM 66)	Feb 1963
KIEN VANG	HQ 603 (PGM 67)	Feb 1963
KEO NGUA	HQ 604 (PGM 68)	Feb 1963
KIM QUI	HQ 605 (PGM 60)	May 1963
MAY RUT	HQ 606 (PGM 59)	May 1963
NAM DU	HQ 607 (PGM 61)	May 1963
HOA LU	HQ 608 (PGM 62)	July 1963
TO YEN	HQ 609 (PGM 63)	July 1963
DINH HAI	HQ 610 (PGM 69)	Feb 1964
TRUONG SA	HQ 611 (PGM 70)	Apr 1964
THAI BINH	HQ 612 (PGM 72)	Jan 1966
THI TU	HQ 613 (PGM 73)	Jan 1966
SONG TU	HQ 614 (PGM 74)	Jan 1966
TAT SA	HQ 615 (PGM 80)	Oct 1966
HOANG SA	HQ 616 (PGM 82)	Apr 1967
PHU QUI	HQ 617 (PGM 81)	Apr 1967
HON TROC	HQ 618 (PGM 83)	Apr 1967
THO CHAU	HQ 619 (PGM 91)	Apr 1967

Displacement, tons	117 full load
Dimensions, feet	100·33 oa × 21·1 × 6·9
Guns	1—40 mm AA; 2 or 4—20 mm AA (twin); 2—MG
Main engines	Diesel; 1 900 bhp; 2 shafts = 17 knots
Complement	approx 15

Welded-steel patrol gunboats built in the United States specifically for foreign transfer; assigned PGM numbers for contract purposes. Enlarged version of US Coast Guard 95-foot patrol boats with commercial-type machinery and electronic equipment. HQ 600-605 built by J. M. Martinac SB Corp, Tacoma, Washington; HQ 606-610 built by Marinette Marine Corp, Wisconsin.
All ships have a 20 mm twin mount on after end of deckhouse and some apparently have a second 20 mm mount aft; machineguns are atop deckhouse immediately behind low funnel and forward of 20 mm mount.

DINH HAI — *1967, United States Navy*

KIM QUI — *1970, Vietnamese Navy*

Patrol Gunboats—*continued*

26 Ex-USCG 82-ft "POINT" CLASS

LE PHUOC DUI	HQ 700 (ex-*Point Garnet* 82310)
LE VAN NGA	HQ 701 (ex-*Point League* 82304)
HUYNH VAN CU	HQ 702 (ex-*Point Clear* 82315)
NGUYEN DAO	HQ 703 (ex-*Point Gammon* 82328)
DAO THUC	HQ 704 (ex-*Point Comfort* 82317)
LE NGOC THANH	HQ 705 (ex-*Point Ellis* 82330)
NGUYEN NGOC THACH	HQ 706 (ex-*Point Slocum* 82313)
DANG VAN HOANH	HQ 707 (ex-*Point Hudson* 82322)
LE DINH HUNG	HQ 708 (ex-*Point White* 82308)
THUONG TIEN	HQ 709 (ex-*Point Dume* 82325)
PHAM NGOC CHAU	HQ 710 (ex-*Point Arden* 82309)
DAO VAN DANG	HQ 711 (ex-*Point Glover* 82307)
LE DGOC AN	HQ 712 (ex-*Point Jefferson* 82306)
HUYNH VAN NGAN	HQ 713 (ex-*Point Kennedy* 82320)
TRAN LO	HQ 714 (ex-*Point Young* 82303)
BUI VIET THANH	HQ 715 (ex-*Point Patrige* 82305)
NGUYEN AN	HQ 716 (ex-*Point Caution* 82301)
NGUYEN HAN	HQ 717 (ex-*Point Welcome* 82329)
NGO VAN QUYEN	HQ 718 (ex-*Point Banks* 82327)
VAN DIEN	HQ 719 (ex-*Point Lomas* 82321)
HO DANG LA	HQ 720 (ex-*Point Grace* 82323)
DAM THOAI	HQ 721 (ex-*Point Mast* 82316)
HUYNH BO	HQ 722 (ex-*Point Grey* 82324)
NGUYEN KIM HUNG	HQ 723 (ex-*Point Orient* 82319)
HO DUY	HQ 724 (ex-*Point Cypress* 82326)
TROUNG BA	HQ 725 (ex-*Point Maromc* 82331)

Displacement, tons	64 standard; 67 full load
Dimensions, feet	83 oa × 17·2 × 5·8
Guns	1—81 mm/50 cal MG (combination)plus 2 to 4—50 ca MG (single) or 1—20 mm
Main engines	2 diesels; 1 200 bhp; 2 shafts = 16·8 knots
Complement	8 to 10

Former US Coast Guard 82-ft patrol boats (designated WPB); actual length is 83 fee overall. All served in Vietnamese waters, manned by US personnel, comprisin Coast Guard Squadron One. HQ 700-707 transferred to South Vietnamese Navy i 1969, HQ 708-HQ 725 in 1970.
Numerous units of this type are in service with the US Coast Guard.

POINT CLASS — *1970, Vietnamese Navy*

COASTAL MINESWEEPERS

2 Ex-US MSC TYPE

HAM TU (ex-*MSC* 282)	HQ 114
CHUONG DUONG II (ex-*MSC* 282)	HQ 115

Displacement, tons	320 standard; 370 full load
Dimensions, feet	144 oa × 28 × 9
Guns	2—20 mm AA
Main engines	2 diesels; 2 shafts; 1 200 bhp = 12·5 knots
Complement	45

United States coastal motor minesweepers of the "Bluebird" class, non-magnetic type of wooden construction, constructed under the Mutual Defence Assistance Programm transferred to South Vietnam in Sep 1959 and Dec 1959, respectively. Sister shi *Bach Dang II* (ex-MSC 283) HQ 116 grounded on 9 Oct 1970; stripped and destroyed

DISPOSALS
Of the three coastal minesweepers of the ex-US YMS type transferred from the Frencl Navy on 11 Feb 1954, *Ham Tu* HQ 211 (ex-*Aubepine*, ex-D 315, ex-TMS 28) wa removed from the effective list in 1958. *Bach Bang* HQ 113, (ex-*Belledone*, ex-D 318 ex-YMS 78) in 1963, and *Chu'o'ng-Du'o'ng* HQ 112 (ex-*Digitale*, ex-D 326, ex-YMS 83)in 1964.

CHUONG DUONG II — *1971, Vietnamese Navy*

Coastal Minesweepers—*continued*

HAM TU—see previous page *1960, Vietnamese Navy*

LANDING SHIPS

6 Ex-US LST TYPE

CAM RANH (ex-USS *Marion County, LST* 975)	HQ 500	6 Jan 1945
DA NANG (ex-USS *Maricopa County, LST* 938)	HQ 501	15 Aug 1944
THI NAI (ex-USS *Cayuga County, LST* 529)	HQ 502	17 Jan 1944
VUNG TAU (ex-USS *Cochino County, LST* 603)	HQ 503	14 Mar 1944
QUI NHON (ex-USS *Bullock County, LST* 509)	HQ 504	23 Nov 1943
HNA TRANG (ex-USS *Jerome County, LST* 848)	HQ 505	2 Jan 1943

Displacement, tons	2 366 beaching; 4 080 full load
Dimensions, feet	316 wl; 328 oa × 50 × 14
Guns	7 or 8—40 mm AA (1 or 2 twin; 4 or 5 single); several 20 mm AA
Main engines	Diesel (General Motors); 1 700 bhp; 2 shafts = 11 knots
Complement	110

Former US Navy tank landing ships; launch dates above. HQ 500 and 501 built by Bethlehem Steel Co, Hingham, Massachusetts; HQ 502 and 504 by Jeffersonville B & M Co, Jeffersonville, Indiana; HQ 3 by Chicago Bridge & Iron Co. Illinois; HQ 5 by Kaiser Co, Richmond, California. HQ 500 and 502 have pole masts; others have lattice tripod masts.

QUI NHON *1971, Vietnamese Navy*

THI NAI *Vietnamese Navy*

DA NANG *1962, Vietnamese Navy*

Landing Ships —*continued*

6 Ex-US LSM TYPE

HAT GIANG (ex-LSM 9011, ex-USS LSM 335)	HQ 400	10 Nov 1944
HAN GIANG (ex-LSM 9012, ex-USS LSM 110)	HQ 401	28 Oct 1944
LAM GIANG (ex-USS LSM 226)	HQ 402	4 Sep 1944
NINH GIANG (ex-USS LSM 85)	HQ 403	15 Sep 1944
HUONG GIANG (ex-USS *Oceanside*, LSM 176)	HQ 404	12 Aug 1944
TIEN GIANG (ex-USS LSM 313)	HQ 405	24 May 1944
HAU GIANG (ex-USS LSM 276)	HQ 406	20 Sep 1944

Displacement, tons	743 beaching; 1 095 full load
Dimensions, feet	196·5 wl; 203·5 oa × 34·5 × 8·3
Guns	2—40 mm AA; 4—20 mm AA
Main engines	Diesel; 2 shafts; 2 800 bhp = 12 knots
Complement	73

Former US Navy medium landing ships; launch dates above.
Designed primarily to carry assault troops. First four transfreed to French Navy for use in Indo-China, Jan 1954. *LSM* 9011, 9012 transferred to Vietnam Navy, Dec 1955. LSM 9014, 9017, 9018, returned to USA in 1955. *Oceanside LSM* 175 transferred at Los Angeles on 1 Aug 1961, LSM 313 in 1962, *Hau Giang* (ex-LSM 276) on 10 June 1965.
Hat Giang and *Han Giang* are hospital ships (LSM-H); refitted for treating casualties and assigned political warfare personnel (in addition to normal complement). All are armed.

LAM GIANG *Vietnamese Navy*

HAT GIANG (LSM-H) *Vietnamese Navy*

4 Ex-US LSSL TYPE

DOAN NGOC TANG (ex-USS LSSL 9)	HQ 228	17 Aug 1944
LULU PHU THO (ex-USS LSSL 101)	HQ 229	27 Jan 1945
NGUYEN NGOC LONG (ex-USS LSSL 96)	HQ 230	6 Jan 1945
NIGUYEN DUC BONG (ex-USS LSSL 129)	HQ 231	13 Dec 1944

Displacement, tons	227 standard; 383 full load
Dimensions, feet	158 × 23·7 × 5·7
Guns	1—3 inch; 4—40 mm AA; 4—20 mm AA; 4 MG
Main engines	Diesel; 2 shafts; 1 600 bhp = 14 knots
Complement	60

Former US Navy landing ships support; designed to provide close-in-fire support for amphibious assaults, but suitable for general gunfire missions. Launch dates above.

The *Doan Ngoc Tang* was transferred to France in 1951 (*Hallebarde* L. 9023); transferred to Japan 1956-1964; returned and transferred to South Vietnam in 1965. Three other ships served in Japanese Navy 1953 to 1964; retransfered to South Vietnam in 1965 and 1966.

Three ships of this type sunk; *Le Van Binh* HQ 227, ex-French *Javeline* L 9024, ex-USS LSSL 10 sunk in 1966; *Neuyen Van Tru* HQ 225, ex-French *Framee*, ex-USS LSSL 105 sunk in 1970; *Le Trong Dam* HQ 226, ex-French *Arquesbusei* L 9022, ex-USS LSSL 4 sunk in 1970.

NIGUYEN DUC BONG *Vietnamese Navy*

Landing Ships—*continued*

LE TRONG DAM—sunk in 1970 *Vietnamese Navy*

5 Ex-US LSIL TYPE

LONG DAO (ex-French L 9029, ex-USS LSIL 698)	HQ 327	17 June 1944
THAN TIEN (ex-French L 9035, ex-USS LSIL 702)	HQ 328	28 June 1944
THIEN KICH (ex-French L 9038, ex-USS LSIL 872)	HQ 329	4 Oct 1944
LOI CONG (ex-French L 9034, ex-USS LSIL 699)	HQ 330	21 June 1944
TAM SET (ex-French L 9033, ex-USS LSIL 871)	HQ 331	3 Oct 1944

Displacement, tons	227 standard; 383 full load
Dimensions, feet	158 × 22·7 × 5·3
Guns	1—3 inch; 1—40 mm AA; 2—20 mm AA; 4 MG; and up to 4 army mortars (2—81 mm; 2—60 mm)
Main engines	Diesel; 2 shafts; 1 600 bhp = 14·4 knots
Complement	55

Former US Navy landing ships infantry; launch dates above. Designed to carry 200 troops. *Tam Set* originally transferred to France in 1951 and others in 1953 for use in Indochina; subsequently retransferred in 1956 to South Vietnam.

LONG DAO *1971, Vietnamese Navy*

UTILITY LANDING CRAFT

19 Ex-US LCU TYPE

HQ 533 (ex-US LCU 1479)
HQ 534 (ex-US LCU 1480)
HQ 535 (ex-US LCU 1221)
HQ 536 (ex-US LCU 1446)
HQ 537 (ex-US LCU 1501)
HQ 538 (ex-US LCU 1594)
HQ 539 (ex-US LCU 1502)
HQ 540 (ex-US LCU 1475)
HQ 541 (ex-US LCU 1477)
HQ 542 (ex-US LCU 1494)
HQ 543 (ex-US LCU 1493)
HQ 544 (ex-US LCU 1485)
HQ 545 (ex-US LCU 1484)
HQ 546 (ex-US YFU 90, ex-LCU 1582)
HQ 547 (ex-US LCU 1481)
HQ 548 (ex-US LCU 1498)
HQ 560 (ex-US YLLC 1, LCU 1348)
HQ 561 (ex-US YLLC 5, YFU 2, LCU 529)
HQ 562 (ex-US YLLC 3, YFU 33, LCU 1195)

LCU 501 series

Displacement, tons	309 to 320 full load
Dimensions, feet	105 wl; 119 oa × 32·7 × 5
Main engines	Diesels (Gray Marine); 675 bhp; 3 shafts = 10 knots

LCU 1466 series

Displacement, tons	360 full load
Dimensions, feet	115 wl; 119 oa × 34 × 5·25
Main engines	Diesels (Gray Marine); 675 bhp; 3 shafts = 8 knots

Former US Navy utility landing craft; 501 series built during World War II with LCT (6) designation; 1466 series built during the early 1950s. Transferred to South Vietnam from 1954 to 1971, with some of the earlier craft serving briefly in French Navy in Indichina waters.
Three units (ex-YLLC) converted while in US Navy service for use as salvage lifting craft; fitted with 20-ton capacity "A" frame derrick, special anchors, diver's air compressors, welding equipment, and salvage pumps.
Most units armed with two 20 mm AA guns; armament varies with assignment.

HQ 538 *1971, Vietnamese Navy*

Utility Landing Craft—*continued*

HQ 561 (as YLLC 5) *United States Navy*

RIVERINE CRAFT

The US Navy has transferred approximately 700 armed small craft to South Vietnam since 1965 for use in riverine and coastal areas of Indochina. A few former French riverine craft also survive. The exact number of these craft now in service is not known. The following totals are the offical South Vietnamese Navy listings for 1972.

Some of these craft may not be operational because of maintenance limitations of the South Vietnamese Navy and some are believed to have been lost during the April-May 1972 invasion of South Vietnam by regular forces of the Democratic Republic of (North) Vietnam.
In addition to the armed craft grouped here under the category of Riverine (Warfare) Craft, there are numerous small landing craft which are armed.

107 Ex-US "SWIFT" TYPE

Displacement, tons	22·5 full load
Dimensions, feet	50 oa × 13 × 3·5
Guns	1—81 mm mortar/1—·50 cal mG combination Mount: 2—·50 cal MG (twin)
Main engines	2 geared diesels (General Motors); 960 bhp; 2 shafts = 28 knots
Complement	6

All-metal inshore patrol craft (PCF). Transferred to South Vietnam from 1968 to 1970. Numbered in HQ 3800-3887 and later series.

HQ 3825 *1970, Vietnamese Navy*

293 Ex-US PBR TYPE

Displacement, tons	PBR I series: 7·5 PBR II series: 8
Dimensions, feet	PBR I series: 31 oa × 10·5 × 2·5 PBR II series: 32 oa × 11 × 2·6
Guns	3—·50 cal MG (twin mount forward; single gun aft)
Main engines	2 geared diesels; 440 bhp; water-jet propulsion = 25+ knots
Complement	4 or 5

River patrol boats (PBR) with fibreglass (plastic) hulls. Transferred to South Vietnam from 1968 to 1970. Numbered in HQ 7500-7749 and 7800 series.

PBR TYPE *1970, Vietnamese Navy*

Riverine Craft—*continued*

27 Ex-US RPC TYPE

Displacement, tons	15·6
Dimensions, feet	35·75 *oa* × 10·3 × 3·6
Guns	varies: 2—·50 cal MG (twin); 3—·30 cal MG (twin mount aft and single gun at conning station); some units have additional twin ·30 cal mount in place of ·50 cal MH
Main engines	2 geared diesels; 2 shafts = 14 knots

River patrol craft (RPC); predecessor to PBR type. Welded-steel hulls. Few used by US Navy as minesweepers, but most of the 34 units built were transferred to South Vietnam upon completion in 1965; others in 1968-1969. Numbered HQ 7000-7028.

RPC TYPE *1970, Vietnamese Navy*

84 Ex-US ASPB TYPE

Displacement, tons	36·25 full load
Dimensions, feet	50 *oa* × 15·6 × 3·75
Guns	varies: 1 or 2—20 mm (with 2—·50 cal MG in boats with one 20 mm); 2—·30 cal MG; 2—40 mm grenade launchers
Main engines	2 geared diesels; 2 shafts = 14 knots sustained
Complement	6

Assault support patrol boats (ASPB) with welded-steel hulls. Transferred to South Vietnam from 1969 to 1970. Numbered in HQ 5100 series. These craft operate in escort, river interdiction, and minesweeping roles.

ASPB TYPE *1970, Vietnamese Navy*

42 Ex-US MONITORS

Displacement, tons	80 to 90 full load
Dimensions, feet	60·5 *oa* × 17·5 × 3·5
Guns	1—105 mm howitzer; 2—20 mm; 3—·30 cal MG; 2—40 mm grenade launchers
Main engines	2 geared diesels; 2 shaft = 9 knots
Complement	11

River monitors (MON). Transferred to South Vietnam in 1969-1970. Numbered in HQ 6500 series.

MONITOR *1970, Vietnamese Navy*

22 Ex-US LCM MONITORS

Displacement, tons	75 full load
Dimensions, feet	60 *oa* × 17·
Guns	varies: 1—81 mm mortar or 2 M10-8 flame throwers; 1—40 mm; 1—20 mm; 2—·50 cal MG; possibly 2 to 4—·30 cal MG
Main engines	2 geared diesels; 2 shafts = 8 knots
Complement	approx 10

Twenty-four LCM-6 landing craft converted to this configuration from 1964 to 1967. Predecessor to the "monitor" listed above. Transferred to South Vietnam from 1965 to 1970. Numbered in HQ 1800 series.

LCM MONITOR *1970, Vietnamese Navy*

100 Ex-US ATC TYPE

Displacement, tons	66 full load
Dimensions, feet	65·5 *oa* × 17·5 × 3·25
Guns	varies: 1 or 2—20 mm; 2—·50 cal MG; several ·30 cal MG; 2—40 mm grenade launchers
Main engines	2 geared diesels; 2 shafts = 8·5 knots (6 knots sustained)

Armoured troop carriers(ATC). Some fitted with steel helicopter platforms or evacuation of wounded. Transferred to South Vietnam in 1969. Numbered in HQ 1200 series. A few additional units of this design are fitted with extra fuel tanks and serve as refuelers.

ATC TYPE *1970, Vietnamese Navy*

9 Ex-US CCB TYPE

Displacement, tons	80 full load
Dimensions, feet	61 *oa* × 17·5 × 3·4
Guns	3—20 mm; 2—·30 cal MG; 2—40 mm grenade launchers
Main engines	2 geared diesels; 2 shafts = 8·5 knots maximum (6 knots sustained)
Complement	11

Command and control boats (CCB) to provide command and communication facilities for riverine commanders. Transferred to South Vietnam in 1969-1970. Numbered HQ 6100-6108.

4 Ex-US CSB TYPE

Dimensions, feet	56 *oa* × 18·75 × 6
Guns	4—·50 cal MG (twin)
Main engines	2 geared diesels; 2 shafts = 6 knots
Complement	6

Combat salvage boats (CSB) converted from LCM-6 landing craft; configured for river salvage and to support diving operations. Ten-ton capacity "A" frame forward.

Ex-FRENCH CRAFT

The Vietnamese Navy still lists 43 ex-French STCAN/FOM and 14 LCM Commandament as being in service. The latter are converted LCM-3 landing craft.

STCAN/FOM *Vietnamese Navy*

LCM-COMMANDAMENT *Vietnamese Navy*

Riverine Craft—*continued*

MINESWEEPING LAUNCHES

The Vietnamese Navy lists 24 minesweeping launches; ten MLMS 50-foot type transferred in 1963 from US Navy (numbered HQ 150-155, 157-160; HQ 156 and 161 stricken in 1971); eight MSM 56-foot type transferred in 1970 (numbered HQ 1700-1707); six MSR 50-foot type transferred in 1970 (numbered HQ 1900-1905). Other riverine craft had a minesweeping capability (see photograph of ATC type).

MLMS — *1971, Vietnamese Navy*

SUPPORT SHIPS

3 Ex-US MODIFIED LST TYPE

MY THO (ex-USS *Harnett County*, AGP 821, ex-LST 821)	HQ 800	27 Oct	1944
CAN THO (ex-USS *Garrett County*, AGP 786, ex-LST 786)	HQ 801	22 July	1944
VINH LONG (ex-USS *Satyr*, ARL 23, ex-LST 852)	HQ 802	13 Nov	1944

Displacement, tons	AGP type: 4 080 full load ARL type: 4 100 full load
Dimensions, feet	316 wl; 328 oa × 50 × 14
Guns	AGP type: 8—40 mm AA (2 twin, 4 single) ARL type: 8—40 mm AA (2 quad)
Main engines	Diesels (General Motors); 1 700 bhp except *Vinh Long* 1 800 bhp; 2 shafts = 11·6 knots

Former US Navy ships of LST design employed in support of coastal and riverine craft. Launch dates above. *Vinh Long* converted during construction to landing craft repair ship (ARL); others completed as standard LSTs but were modified in late 1960 s to support US Navy small craft in Vietnamese waters; redesignated as patrol craft tenders (AGP) on 25 Sep 1970. The *Vinh Long* has more extensive repair facilities.
My Tho transferred to South Vietnam on 12 Oct 1970, *Can Tho* on 23 Apr 1971, and *Vinh Long* on 15 Oct 1971.
A photograph of the *Garrett County* supporting PBRs and UH-1B helicopters in Vietnamese waters appears in the 1970-1971 edition.

VINH LONG — *Vietnamese Navy*

MY THO — *1971, Vietnamese Navy*

TRAINING SHIP

1 Ex-US FS TYPE

HOA GIANG (ex-*Dinh An*, ex-*Ingenieur en Chef Griod*, ex-US Army *FS* 287, ex-*Governor Wright*) HQ 451

Displacement, tons	950
Dimensions, feet	176 × 32·3 × 10·2
Main engines	2 GM diesels; 1 shaft; 1 000 bhp = 10 knots
Complement	4 officers, 36 men

Former French survey vessel (ex-US Army freighter), sold to Vietnam in Dec 1955. Formerly rated as a light cargo ship (AKL), or supply vessel, but adapted and reclassified as training ship in 1966.

Training Ships—*continued*

HOA GIANG — *1971, Vietnamese Navy*

OILERS

6 Ex-US YOG TYPE

HQ 470 (ex-*L'Aulne*, ex-US YOG 80)
HQ 471 (ex-*YOG* 33)
HQ 472 (ex-US *YOG* 67)
HQ 473 (ex-US *YOG* 71)
HQ 474 (ex-*YOG* 131)
HQ 475 (ex-*YOG* 56)

Displacement, tons	450 light; 1 253 full load
Dimensions, feet	174·0 × 32·0 × 10·9
Main engines	Diesels; 1 shaft = 10 knots
Cargo capacity	6 570 barrels

Former US Navy small gasoline tankers. HQ 470 transferred to South Vietnam in Jan 1951, HQ 471 in Aug 1963, HQ 472 in July 1967, HQ 473 in Mar 1970; HQ 474 in Apr 1971, and HQ 475 in June 1972. No Vietnamese names.

HQ 470 — *1971, Vietnamese Navy*

HQ 471 — *Vietnamese Navy*

WATER CARRIER

2 Ex-US YW TYPE

HQ 9118 (ex-US YW 152)
HQ 9113 (ex-US YW 153)

Former US Navy self-propelled water carriers. Transferred to South Vietnam in 1956. No Vietnamese name assigned.

HARBOUR TUGS

9 Ex-US YTL TYPE

HQ 9500 (ex-US YTL 152)
HQ 9501 (ex-US YTL 245)
HQ 9503 (ex-US YTL 200)
HQ 9504 (ex-US YTL 206)
HQ 9507 (ex-US YTL 423)
HQ 9508 (ex-US YTL 452)
HQ 9509 (ex-US YTL 456)
HQ 9510 (ex-US YTL 586)
HQ 9511 (ex-US YTL 457)

Former US Navy harbour tugs. HQ 9500 transferred to South Vietnam in 1955; HQ 9501, 9503, 0954 in 1956; others from 1968 to 1970.

JUNK FORCE

There are approximately 250 motor-propelled junks in naval service. The breakdown as of January 1972 included 62 command junks, 31 Kien Giang junks, and 153 Yabuta junks. Some of the Yabuta junks are fabricated of ferrous cement. The Yabuta junk illustrated below has two ·50 cal MG; some also have a 60 mm mortar. Diesel propulsion permits them to overtake and search some of the thousands of coastal sailing craft in Indochina waters. The Vietnamese Navy has discarded the armed sailing junks previously employed in this role.

Junk Forces—*continued*

YABUTA JUNK *1971, Vietnamese Navy*

FERROUS CEMENT JUNK *Vietnamese Navy*

MISCELLANEOUS

Numerous craft are operated by the Vietnamese Navy in addition to those described above. However, details are not available.

The former US Coast Guard lightship WLV-523 was transferred to South Vietnam on 25 Sep 1971 for use as an offshore radar station to supplement 16 coastal radar stations on shore which are operated to detect seaborne infiltration effort; renamed *Da Bong* (304). The shore stations are manned by naval personnel.

VIETNAM (North)

Administration

Commander-in-Chief of the Navy: Rear Admiral Ta Xuan Thu

Strength of the Fleet

5 Landing Craft	3 Corvettes
4 Minesweeping Boats	18 Torpedo Boats
30 Patrol Craft (Launches)	28 Gunboats
100 Junks and Auxiliaries	7 Landing Ships

Personnel

1973: Total 5 000 officers and ratings

Mercantile Marine

Lloyd's Register of Shipping: 5 vessels of 713 tons

CORVETTES

3 USSR "SOI" TYPE

Displacement, tons	215 light; 250 normal
Dimensions, feet	138·0 pp; 147·0 oa × 20 × 10 max
Guns	4—25 mm (2 twin mountings)
A/S weapons	4 ahead throwing rocket launchers; 2 DCT
Range, miles	1 100 at 13 knots
Complement	30

Four submarine chasers of Soviet "SOI" type were originally transferred to North Vietnam, two in 1960-61 and two in 1964-65, but one was sunk by US Navy aircraft on 1 Feb 1966.

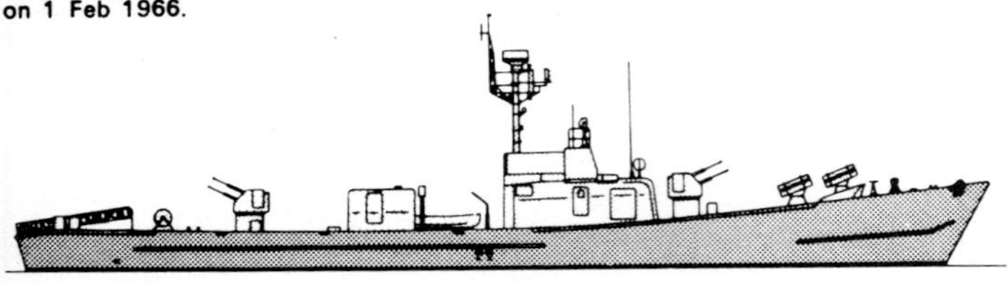
SOI *Class*

LIGHT FORCES

6 USSR "P 6" TYPE (TORPEDO BOATS)

Displacement, tons	66 standard; 75 full load
Dimensions, feet	84·2 × 20 × 6
Guns	4—25 mm AA (2 twin)
Torpedo tubes	2—21 in (single)
Mines	4
Main engines	Diesels; 4 800 bhp; 4 shafts = 45 knots
Range, miles	450 at 30 knots
Complement	25

Built in China and transferred in 1967.

P 6 *Class*

12 USSR "P 4" TYPE (TORPEDO BOATS)

Displacement, tons	25 standard
Dimensions, feet	62·7 × 11·6 × 5·6
Guns	2 MG (1 twin)
Torpedo tubes	2—18 in
Main engines	2 diesels; 2 200 bhp = 50 knots

Approximately a dozen aluminium hulled motor torpedo boats were transferred from the Soviet Union in 1961 and 1964.

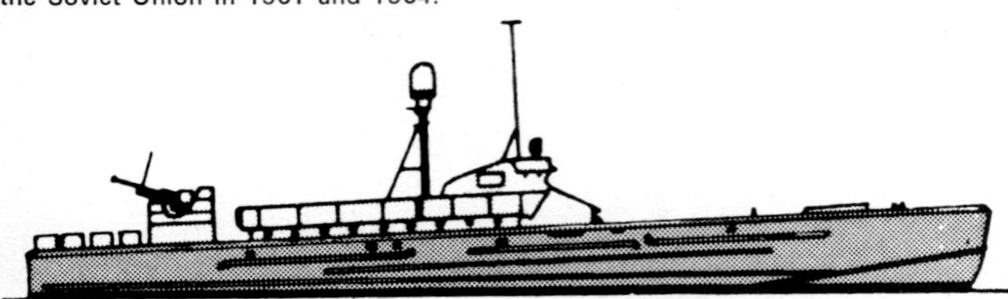
P 4 *Class*

Light Forces—*continued*

4 Ex-CHINESE "SHANGHAI" TYPE (GUNBOATS)

Displacement, tons	120 full load
Dimensions, feet	128·6 × 18 × 5·5
Guns	4—37 mm (2 twin mountings); 4—25 mm
Main engines	4 diesels; 5 000 bhp = 30 knots
Complement	21

Four motor gunboats were received from the People's Republic of China (Communist) Navy in May 1966.

SHANGHAI II *1972, Aviation Fan*

24 Ex-CHINESE "SWATOW" TYPE (GUNBOATS)

Displacement, tons	67 full load
Dimensions, feet	83·5 × 20·0 × 6·0
Guns	4—37 mm; 2—20 mm
A/S weapons	8 depth charges
Main engines	4 diesels; 4 800 bhp = 40 knots
Complement	17

Approximately 30 "Swatow" class motor gunboats built in China were transferred in 1958, and 20 were delivered in 1964 to replace those lost in action. Pennant numbers run in a 600 series.

MINESWEEPING BOATS

4 PATROL TYPE

Four vessels for sweeping, patrol and general purpose duties have been reported delivered in recent years.

PATROL CRAFT

30 MOTOR LAUNCH TYPES

Some thirty motor launches were reported to have been incorporated into the North Vietnam Navy before May, 1966, but not all are still in service.

SERVICE TENDERS

10 GENERAL UTILITY TYPES

Tenders and launches commandeered from private and commercial sources to serve the fleet and naval establishments.

LANDING SHIPS

7 US LSM TYPE

Displacement, tons	743 standard; 1 095 full load
Dimensions, feet	196·5 wl; 203·5 oa × 34·5 × 8·3
Guns	2—40 mm AA (1 twin mounting); 4—20 mm AA
Main engines	Diesels; 2 shafts; 2 800 bhp = 12 knots

One or two of these are reported to be out of operational service.

LANDING CRAFT

5 US LSSL TYPE

Displacement, tons	250 standard; 430 full load
Dimensions, feet	153·0 wl; 158·5 oa × 23·7 × 5·7
Guns	1—3 in; 4—40 mm AA; 4—20 mm AA
Main engines	Diesels; 2 shafts; 1 800 bhp = 14 knots
Range, miles	3 500 at 12 knots
Complement	71

There are also reported to be five of the LCI/LSIL type, one of the LCT(6) type, and six of the LCT (7) type.

AUXILIARY PATROL CRAFT

There are a substantial number of armed junks and similarly adapted craft.

VIRGIN ISLANDS

Mercantile Marine

Lloyd's Register of Shipping:

5 vessels of 713 tons

1 BROOKE MARINE PATROL CRAFT

VIRGIN CLIPPER

Displacement, tons	15
Dimensions, feet	40 × 12 × 2
Guns	3 MG
Main engines	2 diesels; 370 hp = 22 knots

There are a substantial number of armed junks and similarly adapted craft.

YEMEN

Mercantile Marine

Lloyd's Register of Shipping:
4 vessels of 2 844 tons

It is reported that up to 17 ex-Soviet patrol craft have been acquired.

YUGOSLAVIA

Administration

Assistant Secretary of State for National Defence for the Navy:
Vice-Admiral Branko Mamula

Commander-in-Chief of the Fleet:
Vice-Admiral Ivo Purisic

Personnel

1973: 27 000 (2 500 officers and 24 500 men)

Diplomatic Representation

Defence Attaché in London:
Captain Radomir Bogdanovic

Naval, Military and Air Attaché in Washington:
Colonel Milan Mavric

Naval, Military and Air Attaché in Moscow:
Colonel S. Krivokapic

Strength of the Fleet

1 Destroyer	12 Inshore Minesweeeprs
3 Corvettes	14 River Minesweepers
5 Submarines	29 Landing Craft
10 Missile Boats	2 Training Ships
44 Torpedo Boats	4 Oilers
25 Patrol Craft	1 Survey Vessel
4 Coastal Minesweepers	11 Miscellaneous

DISPOSALS

Destroyers

1971 *Kotor* (ex-*Kempenfelt*, ex-*Valentine*)
Pula (ex-*Wager*)

Frigates

1963 *Durmitor* (ex-*Ariete*)
1968 *Ucka* (ex-*Balestra*)
1971 *Biokovo* (ex-*Aliseo*)
Triglav (ex-*Indomito*)

Submarines

1971 *Sava* (ex-*Nautilo*)

Mercantile Marine

Lloyd's Register of Shipping:
364 vessels of 1 587 585 tons gross

DESTROYER

1 "SPLIT" CLASS

SPLIT (ex-*Spalato*, ex-*Split*) R 11

Displacement, tons	2 400 standard; 3 000 full load
Length, feet (*metres*)	376·3 (*114·7*)pp; 393·7 (*120·0*)oa
Beam, feet (*metres*)	36·5 (*11·1*)
Draught, feet (*metres*)	12·3 (*3·8*)
Guns, surface	4—5 in (*127 mm*)
Guns, AA	12—40 mm
A/S weapons	2 "Squids", 6 DCT, 2 DC racks
Torpedo tubes	5—21 in (*533 mm*)
Mines	Capacity 40
Boilers	2 watertube type
Main engines	Geared turbines; 2 shafts; 50 000 shp
Speed, knots	31·5 max
Oil fuel, tons	590 capacity
Complement	240

Built by Brodogradiliste "3 Maj", Rijeka. The original ship was laid down in July 1939 by Chantieres de Loire, Nantes, in 1939 at Split Shipyard. Launched in 1940. Completed on 4 July 1958. Ready for operational service in 1959. The original design provided for an armament of 5—5·5 inch guns, 10—40 mm AA guns and 6—21·7 inch torpedo tubes (tripled), but the plans were subsequently modified.

SPLIT *Aldo Fraccaroli*

SUBMARINES

3 "HEROJ" CLASS

HEROJ 821 **JUNAK** 822 **USKOK** 823

Displacement, tons	1 068 submerged
Length, feet (*metres*)	210·0 (*64*)
Beam, feet (*metres*)	23·6 (*7·2*)
Draught, feet (*metres*)	16·4 (*5·0*)
Torpedo tubes	6—21 in (*533 mm*)
Main engines	Diesels; electric motors; 2 400 hp
Speed, knots	16 on surface; 10 submerged
Complement	55

Heroj, the first submarine of this class, was built at the Uljanik Shipyard, Pula in 1968.

HEROJ

Submarines—*continued*

JUNAK 1972

2 "SUTJESKA" CLASS

NERETVA 812 **SUTJESKA** 811

Displacement, tons	820 surfaced; 945 submerged
Length, feet (*metres*)	196·8 (*60·0*)
Beam, feet (*metres*)	22·3 (*6·8*)
Draught, feet (*metres*)	16·1 (*4·9*)
Torpedo tubes	6—21 in (*533 mm*)
Main engines	Diesels; electric motors; 1 800 hp
Speed, knots	14 on surface; 9 submerged
Range, miles	4 800 at 8 knots
Complement	38

NERETVA *1969, Dr Giorgio Arra*

SUTJESKA *1963, Yugoslavian Navy*

Sutjeska was launched on 28 Sep 1958 at Uljanik Shipyard, Pula. The first submarine to be built in a Yugoslav yard. Commissioned on 16 Sep 1960.

CORVETTES

2 "MORNAR" CLASS

MORNAR 551 **BORAC** 552

Displacement, tons	330 standard; 430 full load
Length, feet (*metres*)	170·0 (*51·8*) pp; 174·8 (*53·3*) oa
Beam, feet (*metres*)	23·0 (*7·0*)
Draught, feet (*metres*)	6·6 (*2·0*)
Guns, dual purpose	2—3 in (single)
Guns, AA	2—40 mm single; 2—20 mm single
A/S weapons	2 "Hedgehogs"; 2 DCT; 2 DC racks
Main engines	4 SEMT-Pielstick diesels; 2 shafts 3 240 bhp
Speed, knots	20 max; 16 sustained sea
Range, miles	3 000 at 12 knots; 2 000 at 15 knots
Complement	60

BORAC ***Aldo Fraccaroli***

Mornar was completed on 10 Sep 1959. Her design is an improved version of that of PBR 581. *Borac* was launched in 1965.

1 "FOUGUEUX" TYPE

581 (ex-P6)

Displacement, tons	325 standard; 400 full load
Dimensions feet	170 pp × 23 × 6·5
Guns	2—40 mm AA; 2—20 mm AA
A/S weapons	1 Hedgehog; 4 DCT; 2 DC racks
Main engines	4 Pielstick SEMT diesels; 3 240 bhp = 18·7 knots
Range, miles	3 000 at 12 knots; 2 000 at 15 knots
Complement	62

USA offshore procurement. Ordered in France. Built by F. C. Mediterranee (Graville). Launched on 1 June 1954. Transferred to Yugoslavia in 1956.

581 *1972, Yugoslavian Navy*

LIGHT FORCES

10 USSR "OSA" CLASS (MISSILE BOATS)

301 302 303 304 305 306 307 308 309 310

Displacement, tons	165 standard; 200 full load
Dimensions, feet	128·7 × 25·1 × 5·9
Missile launchers	SSN 2A for Styx
Guns	4—30 mm (2 twin, 1 forward, 1 aft)
Main engines	3 diesels; 13 000 bhp = 32 knots
Range, miles	700 at 30 knots
Complement	26

Acquired between 1965 and 1969.

306 *1972, Yugoslavian Navy*

308 *1972*

14 USSR "SHERSHEN" TYPE (TORPEDO BOATS)

210 211 212 213 214 215 216 217 218 219 220 221 222 223

Displacement, tons	150 standard
Dimensions, feet	131·5 oa × 23 × 6·5
Torpedo tubes	4—21 in single
Guns	4—25 mm AA (2 twin)
A/S weapons	12 DC
Main engines	Diesels; 7 500 bhp = 40 knots
Complement	16

Acquired between 1965 and 1971, some from the USSR whilst the remainder were built in Yugoslavia.

TC 220 *1972*

9 TYPE "133" (PATROL BOATS)

132 133 134 135 136 137 138 139 140

Displacement, tons	85 standard; 120 full load
Dimensions, feet	91·9 × 14·8 × 8·3
Guns	2—20 mm AA
Main engines	2 diesels; 900 bhp = 13 knots sea speed

Used for coastguard duties. Armament varies in individual boats. Built in Yugoslavia 1967-68.

No. 134 *1968, Yugoslavian Navy*

30 Ex-US "HIGGINS" CLASS (TORPEDO BOATS)

Displacement, tons	55 standard; 60 full load
Dimensions, feet	69 pp; 78 oa × 21·3 × 7·8
Guns	1—40 mm AA; 4—12·7 mm MG
Tubes	2—18 in
Main engines	3 Packard motors; 3 shafts; 5 000 bhp = 36 knots
Complement	14

Some have had their torpedo tubes removed. As MGBs they mount 2—40 mm and either 2 twin 50 cal MG or 2—20 mm (singles). Two of the "108" class were transferred to Ethiopia in 1960 and renamed *Barracuda* P 22 and *Shark* P 21.

174 as MTB *Yugoslavian Navy*

16 "KRALJEVICA" CLASS (PATROL BOATS)

501-512, 519-521 and 524.

Displacement, tons	195 standard; 250 full load
Dimensions, feet	134·5 × 20·7 × 7·2
Guns	1—3 in; 1—40 mm AA; 4—20 mm AA
A/S weapons	DCs plus Mousetrap in some
Main engines	Diesels; 2 shafts; 3 300 bhp = 20 knots
Complement	50

Built in 1952-58. Six transferred to Indonesia in 1959 and two to Sudan in 1969.

PBR 512 *Yugoslavian Navy*

MINE WARFARE FORCES

4 "HRABRI" CLASS (CMS)

HRABRI M 151 (ex-*D* 25)
SLOBODNI M 153 (ex-*D* 27)
SMELI M 152 (ex-*D* 26)
SNAZNI M 161

Displacement, tons	365 standard; 424 full load
Dimensions, feet	140 pp; 152 oa × 28 × 8·2
Guns	1—40 mm AA; 1—20 mm AA
Main engines	SIGMA free piston generators; 2 shafts. 2 000 bhp = 15 knots
Oil fuel, tons	48
Range, miles	3 000 at 10 knots
Complement	40

Hrabri, Slobodni and *Smeli* were built in France by A. Normand as US "off-shore" orders, launched on 27 Feb 1956, 26 May 1956, 26 June 1956, respectively, and allocated to the Yugoslav Navy at Cherbourg in Sep 1957. *Snazni* was built in Yugoslavia in 1960 with French assistance.

SLOBODNI *1966, Yugoslavian Navy*

6 ML 117 TYPE (IMS)

M 117 **M 118** **M 119** **M 121** **M 122** **M 123**

Displacement, tons	120 standard; 131 full load
Dimensions, feet	98·4 × 18 × 4·9
Guns	1—40 mm AA; 2—12·7 mm MG
Main engines	2 GM diesels; 1 000 bhp = 12 knots

A small type of inshore minesweeper built in Yugoslav shipyards between 1966 and 1968.

M 121 *1968, Yugoslavian Navy*

4 BRITISH "HAM" CLASS (IMS)

Displacement, tons	123 standard; 164 full load
Dimensions, feet	100 × 21·8 × 5·5
Guns	1—40 mm AA or 1—20 mm AA
Main engines	2 Paxman diesels; 1 100 bhp = 14 knots
Range, miles	2 000 at 9 knots
Complement	22

Built in Yugoslavia 1964-66 under the US Military Aid Programme. Of same design as British "Ham" class.

M 142 *1968, Yugoslavian Navy*

2 TYPE 101

M 106 **M 105**

Displacement, tons	90 standard; 95 full load
Dimensions, feet	82 × 19·5 × 6·2
Guns	1—40 mm; 1—20 mm
Main engines	Diesel; 135-175 bhp = 12 knots

Built during 1950-56 in Yugoslav shipyards. M 101, M 102, M 104, M 107, M 108, and M 110 were scrapped in 1966, and the remainder by 1970.

Mine Warfare Forces—*continued*

14 RML 300 TYPE (RIVER MINESWEEPERS)

M 301 **M 303** **M 305** **M 307** **M 309** **M 311** **M 313**
M 302 **M 304** **M 306** **M 308** **M 310** **M 312** **M 314**

Displacement, tons	38
Guns	1—20 mm
Main engines	Speed = 12 knots

All launched in 1951-53. Serve on the Danube.

LANDING CRAFT

25 DTM 230 TYPE

DTM 230 onwards

Displacement, tons	*circa* 220
Guns	4—20 mm AA

Capable of carrying at least two, possibly three of the heaviest tanks. Unlike other tank landing craft in that the lower part of the stern drops to form a ramp down which the tanks go ashore, underneath the prow, which is rigid. It is reported that probably some 25 of these craft are operational. Ex German.

DTM 230 *B. Hinchcliffe, Esq*

CATAMARAN TYPE

Displacement, tons	*circa* 50

A smaller craft consisting of two pontoons some feet apart, secured to each other by cross-girders on which stand the bridge and cabins, etc. This vessel appears to be capable of carrying one medium tank, to be put ashore by two bridge members which can be seen quite clearly, folded back on the deck.

Catamaran type *B. Hinchcliffe, Esq*

DTK 221 TYPE

DTK 221

Displacement, tons	410
Dimensions, feet	144·3 × 19·7 × 7
Guns	1—20 mm AA; 2—12·7 mm
Main engines	Speed = 10 knots
Complement	15

DTK 221 *Yugoslavian Navy,*

MZ TYPE

D 206 (ex-*MZ* 713) **D 219** (ex-*MZ* 717)

Displacement, tons	225 and 239
Guns	1—20 mm AA; 2 MG AA
Main engines	Speed = 11 knots

Ex-Italian landing craft. Launched in 1942. Capable of carrying three tanks.

Ex-GERMAN TYPE

D 203 **D 204**

Displacement, tons	220
Guns	1—3·4 in (88 mm); 2—20 mm AA
Main engines	Speed = 10 knots

Ex-German landing craft.

TRAINING SHIPS

1 "GALEB" CLASS

GALEB (ex-*Kuchuck*, ex-*Ramb III*) M 11

Displacement, tons	5 182 standard
Measurement, tons	3 667 gross
Length, feet (*metres*)	384·8 (*117·3*)
Beam, feet (*metres*)	51·2 (*15·6*)
Draught, feet (*metres*)	18·4 (*5·6*)
Main engines	2 diesels; 2 shafts; 7 200 bhp
Speed, knots	17.

Ex-Italian. Launched in 1938. Refloated and completed in 1952. Now training ship. Also Presidential Yacht. Former armament was four 3·5 inch, four 40 mm and 24—20 mm (six quadruple) guns. The guns were landed.

GALEB — *1972, Yugoslavian Navy*

JADRAN

Displacement, tons	720
Dimensions, feet	190 × 29·2 × 13·8
Sail area, sq ft	8 600
Main engines	1 Linke-Hofman Diesel; 375 hp = 8 knots

Topsail schooner. Launched in 1932. Accommodation for 150 Cadets. Name means "Adriatic". While in Italian hands she was named *Marco Polo*. A photograph of *Jadran* appears in the 1966-67 to 1969-70 editions.

DESPATCH VESSELS

JADRANKA (ex-*Bijeli Orao*)

Displacement, tons	567 standard; 660 full load
Dimensions, feet	213·2 oa × 26·5 × 9·3
Guns	2—40 mm AA; 2 MG
Main engines	2 Sulzer diesels; 1 900 bhp = 18 knots

Built by C. R. dell Adriatico, San Marco, Trieste. Launched on 3 June 1939. Was used as Admiralty yacht and yacht of Marshall Tito. While in Italian hands was named *Alba*, for some days only, then *Zagaria*.

JADRANKA — *1970, Yugoslavian Navy*

VIS Also reported in service.

HYDROGRAPHIC VESSEL

1 NEW CONSTRUCTION

A. MOHOROVICIC PH 33

Displacement, tons	1 475 full load
Dimensions, feet	239·5 × 36·1 × 15·1
Main engines	2 diesels = circa, 15 knots (official figure)

Built in 1971 at the shipyard in Gdansk, Poland, and added to the Yugoslav Navy List in 1972.

A. MOHOROVICIC — *1972, Yugoslavian Navy*

SALVAGE VESSEL

SPASILAC PS II

Displacement, tons	740
Dimensions, feet	174 × 26·2 × 13
Main engines	Triple expansion; 2 000 hp = 15 knots

Built by Howaldt, Kiel. Launched in 1929. Name means "Salvador". While in Italian hands she was called *Intangible*.

SPASILAC — *1966, Yugoslavian Navy*

OILERS

4 PN 13 TYPE

PN 13 (ex-*Lovcen*) **PN 14** **PN 15** **PN 16**

Displacement, tons	695 standard
Main engines	Speed = 8·5 knots

PN 13 (ex-*Lovcen*) was launched in 1932. For fleet servicing and freighting. PN 17 was transferred to the Sudanese Navy in 1969.

TRANSPORTS

2 PT 71 TYPE

PT 71 **PT 72**

Displacement, tons	310 standard; 428 full load
Dimensions, feet	141·5 × 22·2 × 16
Main engines	300 bhp = 7 knots

The transport *Tuni* PT 21 (ex-*Krk*, ex-*Kt.* 6) was removed from the list in 1963.

TUGS

PR 52 (ex-*San Remo*)

Displacement, tons	170
Main engines	350 hp = 9 knots

Former Italian tug and multi-purpose vessel. Launched in 1937.

PR 58 (ex-*Molara*)

Displacement, tons	118
Main engines	250 hp = 8 knots

Former Italian tug. Launched in 1937, now used as general transport and towing vessel.

PR 51 (ex-*Porto Cohte*)

Displacement, tons	226

Former Italian tug. Launched in 1936. A photograph appears in the 1951-52 to 1957-58 editions.

PR 55 (ex-*Snazi*)

Displacement, tons	100
Main engines	300 hp = 10 knots

Launched in 1917. Name means "Strong". The Italian name was *Resistance*.

PR 54 (ex-*Ustrajni*)

Displacement, tons	160
Main engines	250 hp = 9 knots

Launched in 1917. Name means "Durable". The Italian name was *Duratero*.

LR II (ex-*Basiluzzo*)

Displacement, tons	108
Main engines	130 hp = 8 knots

Former Italian tug. Launched in 1915. There is also the very old tug PP 1.

WATER CARRIERS

PV 6 **PV 11** **PV 12**

There are 8 water carriers of various types. Also PT 12 and PO 54.

YACHT

ISTRANKA (ex-*Vila*, ex-*Dalmata*)

Displacement, tons	230
Dimensions, feet	40·4 × 5·1 × 2·1
Main engines	325 hp = 12 knots

Istranka means Nympth. Named *Fata* whilst in Italian hands during 1941-45. Built in 1896.

ZAIRE

CONGO (ex-*President Mobuto*, ex-*General Olsen*)
River boat, 260 ft oa, renamed 3 Sep 1967. A force for Lake Tanganyika was formed in 1967 consisting of two 50 ft patrol boats, four 21 ft speed boats and a converted trawler. Four small patrol craft were reported transferred by Communist China.

NAVAL AIRCRAFT AND MISSILES

NAVAL AIRCRAFT

Shipborne Aircraft
Helicopters
Land-based Aircraft

NAVAL MISSILES

Surface-to-surface
Air-to-surface
Surface-to-air
Air-to-air
Anti-submarine Systems

NAVAL AIRCRAFT AND MISSILES

NOTES.

(a) The details of the aircraft or missiles listed appear only under the country of origin or manufacture. For those countries using equipment acquired from abroad reference is made to the main supplier.

(b) In each country the equipment listed is split as follows:—

(A) Shipborne aircraft
(B) Helicopters
(C) Land-based aircraft
(D) Missiles:
  (i) Surface-to-Surface
  (ii) Subsurface-to-Surface
  (iii) Surface-to-Air
  (iv) Air-to-Surface
  (v) Air-to-Air
  (vi) Anti-Submarine

(c) In the Soviet section missile-systems are listed under their NATO numerical code with, where possible, the NATO codenames of the missiles of that system.

(d) Where two countries are involved in the production of an aircraft/missile it is listed under the first country alphabetically (e.g. Jaguar (France/UK)) appears under "France".

(e) Missiles are listed only under the country of origin e.g. in the case of Brazil the Exocet mounted in the "Niteroi" class are not listed).

ARGENTINA

(A) McDONNELL-DOUGLAS "Skyhawk" (A-4F).
GRUMMAN "Tracker" (G-89)
GRUMMAN "Albatross" (HU 16)

(B) BELL 47-J
SIKORSKY S-55
SIKORSKY S-58

(C) WESTLAND "Lynx" (WG-13)
AERMACCHI MB 326K (Trainers)
LOCKHEED Neptune (P2-H)

AUSTRALIA

(A) McDONNELL-DOUGLAS "Skyhawk" (A-4E)
FAIREY "Gannet"
GRUMMAN "Tracker" (G-89)

(B) BELL "Iroquois" (UH-IB)
WESTLAND "Wessex" (Mk 3)

(D) (vi) IKARA

Long-range anti-submarine weapon system

The actual weapon is a dual-thrust, solid-propellant rocket-propelled missile carrying an acoustic homing torpedo launched from a surface ship. It has short cropped-delta wings, elevon control surfaces and upper/lower vertical tail-fins. Target information from a ship's Variable Depth Sonar or a helicopter's Dunking Sonar feeds into the Action Data Automation system which, with radar/radio guidance, ensures that the American Type 44 accoustic homing torpedo, separated from the missile and lowered by parachute, enters the sea in the immediate vicinity of the target. It is operational in three "Perth" class and six "River" class destroyers of the Royal Australian Navy and will be fitted in certain "Leander" class ships and the HMS *Bristol*

Length	**11 ft 0 in (*3·35 m*)**
Wing span	**5 ft 0 in (*1·50 m*)**

Ikara missile in launcher on HMAS "Perth"

BELGIUM

(B) SIKORSKY "Alouette III" (HSS-1)

BRAZIL

(A) GRUMMAN "Tracker" (G-89)

(B) BELL 47 C2 and 47J
SIKORSKY S58
SIKORSKY SH 3D (Sea King)
WESTLAND "Wasp"
WESTLAND "Lynx" (WG 13) (in new destroyers)

(C) LOCKHEED "Neptune "(P2V-7)
BRÉGUET "Atlantic" (replacing "Neptunes")

CANADA

(B) SIKORSKY CH-SS22

(C) CANADAIR "Argus" (CP-107)

Fifteen-crew long-range maritime reconnaissance aircraft

Max speed at 20 000 ft (*6 100 m*)	**274 knots**
Cruising speed	**150-175 knots**
Service ceiling	**20 000 ft (*6 100 m*) plus**
Max range	**5 124 n. miles at 194 knots**
Equipment	Large nose radome, MAD in tail (for search role), searchlight
Armament	15 600 lb of weapons (bombs, torpedoes, missiles) stowed 8 000 lb internally and 3 800 lb under each wing
T-O weight	148 000 lb (*67 130 kg*)
Wing span	142 ft 3·5 in (*43·38 m*)
Length	**128 ft 9½ in (*39·25 m*)**
Height	36 ft 8·5 in (*11·19 m*)
Power plant	4 × Wright R-3350-EA-1 turbo-Compound radial piston engines of 3 700 hp each

In service with five squadrons (Nos. 404, 405, 407, 415 and 449 training Sqdns) of the Canadian Armed Forces in both Mk 1 and Mk 2 versions which differ in equipment.

Argus Mk. 2 maritime reconnaissance aircraft *Courtesy, B. M. Service*

CANADAIR CL 215 (Amphibian)

Cruising speed	158 knots
Max range	970 n. miles
T-O weight	43 500 lb (*19 731 kg*) (land)
	37 700 lb (*17 100 kg*) (water)
Wing span	93 ft 10 in (*28·6 m*)
Length	65 ft (*19·82 m*)
Height	29 ft 6 in (*8·98 m*)
Power plant	2 × 2 100 hp Pratt and Whitney

GRUMMAN "Tracker" (G-89)
LOCKHEED "Neptune" (P2V-7)
LOCKHEED "Orion" (P3)

CHILE

(B) BELL 47J and G
BELL "Jetranger" (206 A)
SIKORSKY HSS-1N

COLOMBIA

(C) PBY-5A (Catalina)

FRANCE

(A)

BR 1050 ALIZE Breguet

Carrier-borne 3-seat anti-submarine aircraft

Max speed at 10 000 ft (*3 050 m*)	254 knots
Patrol speed	210-320 knots
Service ceiling	26 250 ft (*8 000 m*)
Normal range	1 350 n. miles
Normal endurance	5 hr 10 min
Max endurance	7 hr 40 min
Armament	Internal Bay: 3 × 353 lb depth charges or one torpedo Inner wing racks for 2 × 353 lb or 385 lb depth charges Outer wing racks: 6 × 5-in rockets or 2 × AS12 ASM's
Max T-O weight	18 100 lb (*8 200 kg*)
Wing span	51 ft 2 in (*15·60 m*)
Width folded	23 ft 0 in (*7·00 m*)
Length	45 ft 6 in (*13·86 m*)
Height	16 ft 5 in (*5·00 m*)
Power plant	1 × 2 100 eshp Rolls-Royce Dart R.Da 21 turboprop

75 were built for the French Navy to equip three squadrons; 12 were supplied to the Indian Navy for service on board *Vikrant*.

CHANCE VOUGHT "Crusader" F-8E (FN)

These, embarked in *Clemenceau* and *Foch* are fitted to carry 2 MATRA R 500 missiles each.

ETENDARD IV-M Dassault

Carrier-borne single-seat interceptor and fighter bomber

Max speed at 36,000 ft (*11 000 m*)	Mach 1·02
Max cruising speed at 25,000 ft (*7 600 m*)	Mach 0·90
Service ceiling	49 200 ft (*15 000 m*)
Range (at 510 mph; 821 kmh with external tanks)	1 520 n. miles
Armament	Fuselage: 2 × 30 mm Cannon Wing Mounts (4): Up to 3 000 lb (*1 060 kg*) of rockets, bombs, Sidewinder AAM's or AS.30 ASM's
Max T-O weight	22 650 lb (*10 275 kg*)
Wing span	31 ft 6 in (*9·60 m*)
Width folded	25 ft 7 in (*7·80 m*)
Length	47 ft 3 in (*14·40 m*)
Height	14 ft 1 in (*4·30 m*)
Power plant	1 × SNECMA Atar 8B turbojet of 9 700 lb (*4 400 kg*) st

Entered service with French Navy for *Clemenceau & Foch* carriers in 1962. 75 aircraft were built. 21 additional aircraft were built as IV-P dual-role tanker and reconnaissance aircraft with nose and ventral camera positions and flight refuelling equipment.

SEPECAT JAGUAR M Breguet/BAC

Single-seat naval tactical aircraft

Max speed at S/L	729 knots
Range (ferry, with external fuel)	2 270 n. miles
Armament	2 × 30 mm DEFA 553 type cannon in lower fuselage aft of cockpit. One ventral attachment point on fuselage centre-line and two under each wing. Provision for wingtip attachments for air-to-air missiles. The centre-line and inboard wing points can each carry up to 2 000 lb (*900 kg*) of weapons, and outboard underwing points up to 1 000 lb (*450 kg*) each. Typical alternative loads include 2 × Martel AS 37 anti-radar missiles and a drop tank; 8 × 1 000 lb (*450 kg*) bombs; various combinations of freefall bombs, Sidewinder air-to-air missiles, air-to-air or air-to-surface rockets, including the 68 mm SNEB rocket; or a reconnaissance camera pack with two photo-flare pods.
Max T-O weight	29 762 lb (*13 500 kg*)
Wing span	27 ft 10½ in (*8·49 m*)
Length overall	50 ft 11 in (*15·52 m*)
Height overall	16 ft 0½ in (*4·89 m*)
Power plant	2 × Rolls-Royce/Turboméca Adour turbofan engines (each 4 620 lb = 2 100 *kg* st dry) and (6 950 lb = *3 150 kg*) with afterburning.

Under development for French Navy. Prototype first flew on 14 November 1969.

(C) BEECHCRAFT D-18S
GRUMMAN "Albatross" (SA-16A)

DENMARK

(B) SIKORSKY S55C
SIKORSKY SH 3D (Sea King)
SUD-AVIATION "Alouette III"

Alizé of the French Navy, with wings extending

Etendard IV-M of the French Navy, with wing tips folded

SEPECAT Jaguar M prototype *Courtesy Air Portraits*

FRANCE (continued)

(B)

SA321 SURER FRELON — Aérospatiale

Land-based two crew heavy assault and anti-submarine helicopter

Max (never exceed) speed at S/L	148 knots
Cruising speed	135 knots
Hovering ceiling in ground effect	6 950 ft (*2 120 m*)
Service ceiling	10 325 ft (*3 150 m*)
Range at S/L	442 n. miles
Range, ferry with two 220 imp gallon (*1 000 litre*) auxiliary tanks	549 n. miles
Capacity	30 troops, 15 stretchers and 2 attendants or 11 023 lb (*5 000 kg*) payload
Max T-O weight	28 660 lb (*13 000 kg*)
Main rotor diameter	62 ft 0 in (*18·90 m*)
Length of fuselage, incl tail rotor	65 ft 10¾ in (*20·08 m*)
Width folded	17 ft 0¾ in (*5·20 m*)
Height	21 ft 10¼ in (*6·66 m*)
Power plant	3 × Turbomeca Turmo IIIE6 shaft-turbine engines of 1 570 shp each

SA-321G Super Frelon—French Navy

Eighteen in service with the French Navy as the SA-321G for ASW duties.

ALOUETTE III — Aérospatiale

Seven-seat general-purpose helicopter

Max speed at S/L	114 knots
Max cruising speed at S/L	100 knots
Service ceiling	10 825 ft (3 300 m)
Range	290 n. miles
Armament	2 × AS12 missiles or 2 × Mk 44 torpedoes or 1 × torpedo and MAD equipment
Max T-O weight (standard version)	4 850 lb (*2 200 kg*)
Main rotor diameter	36 ft 1¾ in (*11·02 m*)
Length overall	42 ft 1½ in (*12·84 m*)
Length folded	32 ft 10¾ in (*10·03 m*)
Height	9 ft 10 in (*3·0 m*)
Power plant	1 × Turbomeca Artouste IIIB turboshaft engine of 870 shp derated to 550 shp

Developed from the standard Alouette III, this version is intended for "plane guard", ASW and attack duties aboard various classes of naval vessels.

Alouette III of the French Navy — *Courtesy of Peter R. March*

(C)

SIKORSKY HSS-1
VERTOL HUP-2
WESTLAND "Lynx" (WG 13)

BR 1150 ATLANTIC — Breguet

Twelve-crew long-range maritime reconnaissance aircraft

Max speed at high altitudes	355 knots
Max range	4 854 n. miles
Max endurance at 169 knots (patrol speed)	18 hours
Armament	Fuselage weapons bay: carries standard NATO bombs, 385 lb (*175 kg*) depth charges, homing torpedoes Wing mounts (4): HVAR rockets; or Martel ASM's
Max T-O weight	95 900 lb (*43 500 kg*)
Wing span	119 ft 1 in (*36·3 m*)
Length	104 ft 2 in (*31·75 m*)
Height	37 ft 2 in (*11·33 m*)
Power plant	2 × RR Tyne R.Ty.20 Mk 21 turboprop engines of 6 105 ehp each. (SNECMA built)

In service since 1966 with French Navy (38 aircraft), German Navy (20 aircraft), Netherlands (9 aircraft), Italian (18 aircraft)

Atlantic in French Navy insignia — *Courtesy of B. M. Service*

N262 — Aérospatiale

Light transport aircraft

Max speed	208 knots
Max and econ cruising speed	202 knots
Service ceiling	23 500 ft (*7 160 m*)
Range with max payload, FAA reserves	525 n. miles
Capacity	Max seating for 29
Max T-O weight	23 369 lb (*10 600 kg*)
Wing span	71 ft 10 in (*21·90 m*)
Length overall	63 ft 3 in (*19·28 m*)
Height over tail	20 ft 4 in (*6·21 m*)
Power plant	2 × 1 080 eshp Turboméca Bastan VIC turboprop engines (1 145 ehp Bastan VIIA in Series C and D)

Fifteen of these aircraft are used by the French Navy as aircrew trainers and light transports.

Aerospatiale N 262 transport of the French Navy

FRANCE (continued)

(C) (continued)

DASSAULT MD-312 (Transport)

DOUGLAS C47 R4D (Transport)
LOCKHEED "Neptune" (P2V-6 and 7)
MORANE "Paris" (MS-760)
POTEZ "Zephyr" (C.M. 175) (Trainer)

(D)
(i)

MM-38 EXOCET Aérospatiale

Surface-to-surface missile

Designed to provide warships with all-weather attack capability against other surface vessels. It can be fitted in all classes of surface warships, including fast patrol boats.
The Exocet missile is in the form of a streamlined body, fitted with cruciform wings and cruciform tail control surfaces indexed in line with the wings. Propulsion is provided by a tandem two-stage solid-propellant motor, and highly destructive warhead. The launch tubes, which are also used as store containers, can be installed in a fixed position or on rotatable mountings.

For operation of the weapon system, the launch ship must be fitted with surveillance and target indicating radar, a vertical reference plane gyro and a log, indicating its speed through the water. Also required is a fire control installation comprising a control panel, fire control computer and junction box.
The missile flight profile consists of a pre-guidance phase during which it travels towards the target, whose range and bearing have been determined by the fire control computer and set up in the missile pre-guidance circuits before launch, and a final guidance phase during which the missile flies directly towards the target under the control of its active homing head. Throughout the flight the missile is maintained at a very low altitude (reported to be 2 to 3 metres=6·5 to 10 ft) by an FM radio altimeter supplied by TRT. Its range is approximately 20 n. miles (23 miles; *37 km*), cruising at high subsonic speed, and Exocet is intended to operate efficiently in an ECM (electronic countermeasures) environment. The French, German, Greek, British Royal Navy and others operate Exocet.

Development firing of Exocet

Length	16 ft 9½ in (*5·12 m*)
Body diameter	1 ft 1½ in (*0·344 m*)
Span of wings	3 ft 3½ in (*1·004 m*)
Span of fins	2 ft 5¾ in (*0·758 m*)
Launch weight	1 587 lb (*719 kg*)
Warhead (over)	220 lb (*100 kg*)
Range	20 n. miles

OTOMAT SA Engines Matra/Oto Melara

Surface-to-surface missile

This weapon is powered by a Turboméca Arbizon III turbojet. It is launched with aid of two jettisonable booster rockets and flies the last 2 n. miles to its target at 50 ft above S/L, with the aid of a TRT type AHV-7 radio altimeter. It is fitted with an active Thomson-CSF homing head. Delivery began in 1973, and it is to be operated by the Italian Navy in the "Freccia" class of fast patrol boats.

Length	15 ft 9½ in (*4·82 m*)
Max	1 ft 6·11 in (*46 cm*)
Launch weight	1 543 lb (*700 kg*)
Max range	32-43 n. miles

Full-scale test version of Otomat in a wind tunnel

SS-11-(B1) Aérospatiale

Close-range surface-to-surface wire-guided missile

Developed from the AS-11 (B.1) ASM this missile is in use by French Navy and Army and differs from the AS-11 in launching systems only. It is powered by two-stage solid propellant rocket with cruciform swept wings on a cylindrical body and can be fitted with a range of warheads for anti-tank, perforating/exploding or anti-personnel work. The guidance is visual/manual, with a gyrostabilised optical sighting system, through wires from the control. Orders totalled 148 000 by the beginning of 1971, with the production at the rate of 600 per month.. France, USA, NATO countries and others use this misslie.

Length	3 ft 11 in (*1·20 m*)
Body diameter	6 in (*0·16 m*)
Wing span	1 ft 7.5 in (*0·50 m*)
Launch weight	**66 lb (30 kg)**
Range	**9 850 ft (*3 000 m*)**
Cruising speed	**313 knots**
Endurance	**20-21 secs**

SS-12M Aérospatiale

Close-range surface-to-surface wire-guided missile

A larger and more powerful derivative of the SS-11, it is used from a twin shipboard launcher. The warhead weighs about 66 lb (*30 kg*), which is four times as much as that of the SSII, and it is powered by a two-stage solid-propellant rocket motor. It is used aboard three Royal Libyan Navy patrol boats. Also used by France and the Royal Netherlands Navy.

Length	**6 ft 2 in (*1·875 m*)**
Body diameter	**7·1 in (*0·18 m*)**
Wing span	**2 ft 1·5 in (*0·65 m*)**
Launch weight	**167 lb (*75 kg*)**
Range	19 650 ft (*6 000 m*)
Endurance	32 secs
Impact speed	182 knots

SS-11 and SS-12

FRANCE (continued)

MSBS Aérospatiale
(D) (ii)

Submarine-borne intermediate range ballistic missile (IRBM)

Length	34 ft 1½ in (*10·40 m*)
Body diameter	4 ft 11 in (*1·50 m*)
Firing weight	39 683 lb (*18 000 kg*)

This two-stage solid-propellant missile with nuclear warhead was developed in France to equip the "Redoutable" class of nuclear-powered submarines from 1969 onwards, each of 4 submarines carrying 16 missiles becoming operational from 1971. The first stage has 22 050 lb (*10 000 kg*) of solid propellant in a PNSM P10 type 904 rocket motor; the second stage has 8 820 lb (*4 000 kg*) of solid propellant in a PNSM P4 Rita rocket motor. The MSBS has inertial guidance.
A second generation MSBS called the M2 is now in production and is different to the M1 by the replacement of the second stage Rita I motor by a Rita II. It will be operational in 1974, and by 1976 a thermonuclear charge will be incorporated.

MSBS missile

MASURCA Mk 2 Marine Francaise
(D) (iii)

Surface-to-air missile

Developed to equip the guided missile frigates *Suffren* and *Duquesne* of the French Navy this missile is a two-stage solid-propellant missile, the first stage being jettisonable. The second stage has controllable tail surfaces in cruciform configuration, in line with the low-aspect ratio wings. A high-explosive warhead with a proximity fuse is fitted. There are two versions of this weapon: Masurca Mk 2 Mod 2 (with a beam riding guidance system) and Masurca Mk 2 Mod 3 (with a self homing guidance system) now superseding Mod 2. In both cases the guidance systems are produced by CFTH/CFS

Length	28 ft 2·5 in (*8 600 m*)
Body diameter	1 ft 4 in (*0·405 m*)
Booster fin Span	4 ft 11 in (*1·500 m*)
Launch weight	4 585 lb (*2 079 kg*)
Range	21·7 n. miles plus
Max speed	Mach 2·5

MURENE

A small surface-to-air missile weighing only 165 pounds with a range of 16 miles.

Two Masurca missiles on the launcher of the French Navy's guided missile frigate Suffren

(D) (iv)

ALBATROS SA Engines Matra/Oto Melara

Air-to-surface missile

The Albatros will be operational in 1973, and can arm Atlantic and Nimrod maritime reconnaissance aircraft as well as helicopters like the Super Frelon. The rear half of the missile is similar to the Otomat, with a Turboméca Arbizon III turbojet engine, and the forward half to the Martel. It uses Thomson-CSF terminal guidance.
After being launched the missile maintains a very low cruising height, using a radio altimeter, until the target is approached, where it climbs for a final dive.

Range 32-43 n. miles

AS-12 missile under wing of Alize of French Navy

AS-11 (B1) Aérospatiale (France)

Airborne wire-guided missile

This is identical with the SS-11 (B.1) (which see) except that it is air-launched and this increases its range. It is carried by 14 different types of aircraft (fixed and rotary-wing) of 19 nations including all the ASW aircraft of the NATO countries.

AS-12 Aérospatiale (France)

Airborne wire-guided missile

This missile is a companion to the SS-12M (which see) and is already supplementing and replacing the AS-11 (B.1). It is being prepared for automatic guidance with the TCA system for the Harpon missile.

FRANCE (continued)

(D) (iv)

AS-30 Aérospatiale

Tactical air-to-surface missile

This missile has a two-stage solid-propellant power plant and is directed by a pilot-operated radio-command guidance system whereby the pilot steers the missile by means of a small control column in the cockpit. Alternatively this missile can utilise the TCA optical aiming/infra-red automatic guidance system. It is operational with the French Air Force, French Navy, German, Swiss, Israeli and South African air forces and the RAF. It normally carries a 510 lb (*230 kg*) HE warhead.

Length	12 ft 9 in (*3·885 m*)
Body diameter	1 ft 1·4 in (*0·34 m*)
Wing span	3 ft 3·5 in (*1·00 m*)
Launch weight	1 146 lb (*520 kg*)
Speed at impact	1 475/1 640 ft/sec (*450/500 m/sec*)
Range	5·9/6·5 n. miles

Aérospatiale AS-30 (inboard) and AS-20 (outboard)

AS-30L Aérospatiale

Tactical air-to-surface missile

A developed lighter version of the AS-30 for smaller, lighter aircraft. Warhead reduced to 253 lb (*115 kg*).

Length	11 ft 9·5 in (*3·60 m*)
Body diameter	1 ft 1·5 in (*0·34 m*)
Wing span	2 ft 11·5 in (*0·90 m*)
Launch weight	838 lb (*380 kg*)

AS-37/AJ168 MARTEL MATRA/HSD

Air-to-surface radar and television-guided missile

Developed jointly by Matra and Hawker/Siddeley Dynamics the Martel is in two forms, a passive radar homing missile or a television-guided missile operated by a weapon operator aboard the parent aircraft. The radar version can be launched in a variety of height and mission profiles. Immediately after launch the missile homes automatically on the target radar, the parent aircraft being independent. Its range of tens of miles gives it a stand-off capability. The TV version is guided in the final stages of its run by the weapon operator in the launch aircraft reading from a high brightness monitor in the aircraft displaying the missile's target field.

Martel is to be operational with the British Fleet Air Arm and RAF on Buccaneer aircraft and the French services on Mirage III-E, Jaguar and Atlantic aircraft.

Length	12 ft (*3·65 m*) teleguidance 13 ft 1½ in (*4·00 m*) anti-radar
Wing span	3 ft 8 in (*1·12 m*)
Body diameter	1 ft 3 in (0·*38 m*)

Martel development missiles under wing of Buccaneer aircraft

(D) (v)

R-550 MAGIC SA Engins Matra

Short/medium-range air-to-air missile

Started as a private venture in 1967, this missile is intended as a dogfight weapon. In 1969 the French Air Force took over sponsorship and the first guided firing of this missile took place on 11th January 1972. The missile itself is powered by a solid-propellant rocket motor and is infra-red guided. The body is cylindrical with cruciform movable foreplanes, fixed wings and tail-fins.

R-550 Magic air-to-air missile

MATRA R-530 Matra

All weather air-to-air missile

In quantity production for the French Air Force and Navy, which latter uses it on its F-8E (FN) Crusaders; it is also supplied to Israel and the South African and Royal Australian Air Forces. It has a cylindrical body with cruciform delta wings, two with ailerons and cruciform tail controls and is powered by a two-stage Hotchkiss-Brandt solid-propellant motor of 18 740 lb (*8 500 kg*) static thrust.

It has interchangeable Hotchkiss-Brandt warheads, each weighing 60 lb (*27 kg*) and fitted with a proximity fuse; with semi-active radar or infra-red homing heads.

Length	10 ft 9·25 in (*3·28 m*)
Body diameter	10·25 in (*0·26 m*)
Wing span	3 ft 7·25 in (*1·10 m*)
Launch weight	430 lb (*195 kg*)
Max speed	Mach 2·7
Range	9·5 n. miles
Operational heights	0-69 000 ft (*21 000 m*)

R-530 missile with semi-active radar head

FRANCE (continued)

(D) (v) (Continued)

MATRA R-511

A 396 lb weapon with a range of 15 miles.

NORD 5103

A 293 lb missile with a range of 8·5 miles

(D) (vi)

MALAFON Mk 2 Latecoere

Long-range anti-submarine weapon system

It comprises a cylindrical body containing a 21 inch (*0·533 m*) acoustic homing torpedo and with wings and tail, this weapon is ramp-launched by two solid propellant rocket boosters which jettison after 3 sec. The weapon then glides at a height fixed by radio-altimeter. Sonar-detected data is fed into the device so that 875 yards short of its target the torpedo is jettisoned by parachute enters the water and homes on its target. It is in service with the French Navy installed in the anti-submarine vessel *La Galisonniere* and subsequently the frigates *Suffren* and *Duquesne*, five T-47 class destroyers and three new corvettes of the "Tourville" class.

Length	19 ft 8 in (*6·00 m*)
Wing span	9 ft 10 in (*3·0 m*)
Launch weight	2 865 lb (*1 300 kg*)
Speed	447·2 knots
Range	9·5 n. miles

Malafon ASW missile on the French destroyer "Vauquelin"

GERMANY (FEDERAL REPUBLIC)

(B) BELL UH-ID
22 WESTLAND/SIKORSKY "Sea King" (SH-3D)
SIKORSKY S 58
SIKORSKY S 61

(C) BREGUET "Atlantic" (1150)
DORNIER 27A
DORNIER 28 D-2
GRUMMAN "Albatross" (SA-16A)
HUNTING "Pembroke" Mk 54
PIAGGIO P149D
POTEZ "Magister" (CM 170R)

(D) (iv)

KORMORAN Messerschmitt-Bölkow-Blohm

Air-to-surface missile

This missile is being developed against a German Navy requirement. Its guidance system has pre-guidance and homing phases, enabling it to approach the target at low altitude. The Kormoran will be carried by F-104G Starfighters of the German Naval Air Arm and by Sea King helicopters, but can be employed with all aircraft having modern navigation system.

Length overall (approx)	14 ft 5 in (*4·40 m*)
Wing span (approx)	3 ft 3½ in (*1·00 m*)
Launch weight (approx)	1 320 lb (*600 kg*)

Kormoran missile under wing of F-104G Starfighter.

INDIA

(A) 12 BREGUET "Alizé" (1050)
GRUMMAN "Tracker" (S2-A)

(B) 10 AÉROSPATIALE "Alouette III"
6 WESTLAND/SIKORSKY "Sea King" (SH 3D)

(C) HINDUSTAN HT 2
SHORT "Sealand"

NOTE. (a) The Indian Air Force includes a maritime squadron of L-1049 Super Constellations.
(b) The Indian Navy is considering the addition of LRMP aircraft—possibly Breguet "Atlantics".

35 SEA HAWK Hawker Siddeley (UK)

Carrier-borne single-seat fighter bomber

Sea Hawk Mk. 50 of the Indian Navy with underwing rockets

Max cruising speed at S/L	512 knots
Radius of action	**251 n. miles**
Armament	Fuselage: 4 × 20 mm cannon Wing mounts (4): 2 × 500 lb bombs and/or RP
Max gross weight	16 200 lb (*7 355 kg*)
Wing span	39 ft 0 in (*11·89 m*)
Width folded	13 ft 4 in (*4·04 m*)
Length	39 ft 8 in (*12·09 m*)
Height overall	8 ft 8 in (*2·64 m*)
Height folded	16 ft 10 in (*5·13 m*)
Power plant	1 × RR Nene 103 turbojet of 5 400 lb (*2 450 kg*) st

The type is operational with the Indian Navy for the carrier *Vikrant*.

INDONESIA

(B) AÉROSPATIALE "Alouette II"

(C) FAIREY "Gannet" (AS 4)
GRUMMAN "Albatross" (HU 16C)
ILYUSHIN "Beagle" (Il-28)

NOTE.
Very few of the above can be considered as operational.

ISRAEL

(C) SIKORSKY S-55

(D) (i)

GABRIEL Israel Aircraft Industries

Subsonic ship-to-ship missile

Operated in the "Saar" class and "Saar IV" class of the Israeli Navy. It is an automatic homing missile, using sophisticated electronic guidance system and has a high-explosive warhead. Gabriel is subsonic and travels a few metres above S/L to its target. It can be used in rough seas and adverse weather and in an electronic countermeasures environment.

Length	11 ft 0 in (*3·35 m*)
Max diameter	12·8 in (*32·5 cm*)
Wing span	4 ft 6½ in (*1·385 m*)
Launch weight	882 lb (*400 kg*)
Warhead	330 lb (*150 kg*)
Max range	11 n. miles

Gabriel missile leaving its launcher

ITALY

NOTE. The Italian Navy and Air Force work together in ASW matters. All aircraft concerned are listed below. Navy personnel fly with the Air Force and the operations and administration of these ASW squadrons are a naval responsibility.

(B) (all naval)
9 SIKORSKY SH-34
24 SIKORSKY SH-3D (Sea King)

(C) (all Air Force)

18 BREGUET "Atlantic" (1150) (delivery started July 1972)
30 GRUMMAN "Tracker" (S2 F)

30 AGUSTA BELL-204B Agusta

Utility helicopter

Max speed at S/L	104 knots
Cruising speed	96 knots
Hovering ceiling (out of ground effect)	4 500 ft (*1 370 m*)
Max range	340 n. miles
Equipment	Dipping Sonar and special electronic equipment for stabilisation etc (AB 204AS version)
Armament	2 × Mk 44 torpedoes (AB 204AS version)
Max T-O weight	9 500 lb (*4 310 kg*)
Main rotor diameter	48 ft 0 in (*14·63 m*)
Length overall	57 ft 0 in (*17·37 m*)
Power plant	1 × Lycoming T53-11A shaft-turbine engine of 1 100 shp; alternatively 1 × Rolls-Royce Bristol Gnome H.1200 of 1 200 shp or a General Electric T58-GE-3

In service with the navies of Italy, Spain and Holland.

Agusta-Bell 204AS anti-submarine helicopter of the Italian Navy

A special ASW version of the 204B known as the 204 AS has been built for individual or dual-role search and attack missions and is in service with the navies of Italy and Spain.

(D) (i)

SEA KILLER Mk 1 Sistel

Short-range surface-to-surface missile, ship-borne

This missile is installed in a five-round multiple launcher aboard the fast patrol boat *Saetta* of the Italian Navy. Single-stage solid-propellant rocket of 4 410 lb (*2 000 kg*) st thrust propels this missile which has movable cruciform control surfaces and stabilising tailfins. Guidance is from beam rider/radio command/radar altimeter-systems and the warhead is a high-explosive fragmentation type with proximity impact fuse.

Length	12 ft 3 in (*3·73 m*)
Body diameter	8·1 in (*0·206 m*)
Wing span	2 ft 9·5 in (*0·85 m*)
Launch weight	370 lb (*168 kg*)
Speed at burn-out	Mach 1·9
Min/max range	1·6/5·4 n. miles (*3/10 km*)

Sea Killer Mk I in flight

SEA KILLER Mk 2 Sistel

Ship-borne surface-to-surface missile

A two-stage version of Sea Killer Mk I, to increase operational range. The booster and sustainer are both solid-propellant rocket motors. After burn-out the booster is separated by an aerodynamic drag section.
The missile has the same specification as the Mk 1 except for length increased to 15 ft 5 in (*4·7 m*), launching weight to 594 lb (*270 kg*), and max effective range to over 13 n. miles. The missile is fully operational.

SEA KILLER Mk 3 Sistel

Surface-to-surface missile

Power plant	1 booster 2 sustainers
Launch weight	248·5 lb (*548 kg*)
Range miles	24+ (*45 km+*)

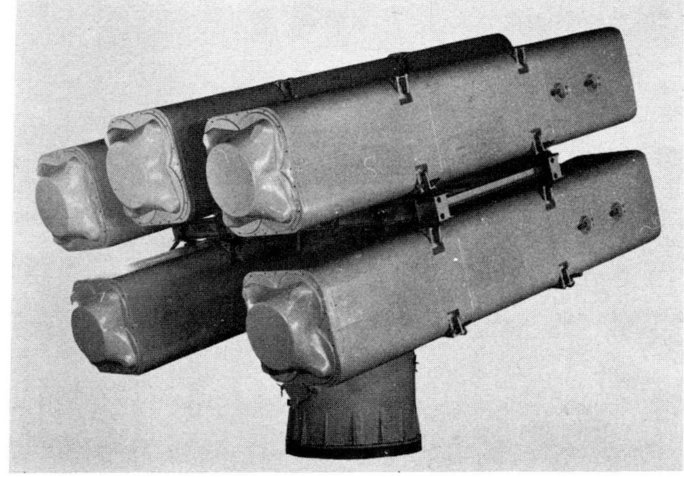

Sea Killer multi-round launcher

ITALY (continued)

(iii)
ALBATROS

Surface-to-air missile system

The system consists of a Ferranti GA-10 digital gun fire control system or an Elsag NA-10 system; Selenia Orion RTN 10 tracking radar; Sparrow missiles and a missile launching system with 1/2 anti-aircraft guns. The Sparrow missiles are modified with folding wings and cropped tail-fins, so as to fit into launcher.
The system gives Naval craft all-weather defence against aircraft and missiles.

Range (missiles) 5·2 n. miles

SEA INDIGO — Contraves Italiana/Sistel

Short-range Surface-to-air missile

This is a navalised version of the Indigo. It is intended to utilise an automatic reloading system when installed in ships of more than 500 tons displacement; manual reloading is specified when Sea Indigo is fitted in naval craft of less than 500 tons.
Main features of the missile are similar to those of the Indigo land-based version.

MEXICO

(B) 4 AEROSPATIALE "Alouette III"
6 BELL H-13

(C) 5 "Catalina" PBY-5
GRUMMAN J2F-6

NETHERLANDS

(B) 9 AGUSTA-BELL 204B AS
20 SIKORSKY "Sea King" (SH-3D) (For ASR duties)
9 WESTLAND "Wasp" HAS Mk I

(C) 12 BREGUET "Atlantic" (1150)
12 LOCKHEED "Neptune" (P-2V)

NEW ZEALAND

(B) WESTLAND "Wasp" HAS Mk I (in two frigates)

(C) 5 LOCKHEED "Orion" (P-3B) (LRMP aircraft operated by RNZAF)

NORWAY

(B) WESTLAND/SIKORSKY "Sea King" (SH-3D) (For ASR duties operated by Norwegian Air Force)

(C) 9 LOCKHEED "Orion" (P-3B) (LRMP aircraft operated by Norwegian Air Force)

(D) (i)

PENGUIN — Kongsberg Vaapenfabrikk

Surface-to-surface missile

Penguin uses an inertial guidance system with infra-red terminal homing, and has a 264 lb (*119 kg*) warhead. It has two-stage solid-propellant propulsion. 20 "Storm" class gunboats are fitted with 6 launchers on rear deck. 6 "Snogg" class torpedo boats are each fitted with four launchers, with others on the five Oslo class frigates.

Length	10 ft (*3·05 m*)
Max dia	11 in (*0·28 m*)
Wing span	4 ft 7 in (*1·40 m*)
Launch weight	727 lb (*329 kg*)
Range	10-15 n. miles

TERNE Mk 8 — Kongsberg Vaapenfabrikk

Anti-submarine missile

Produced by Kongsberg Vaapenfabrikk this anti-submarine missile was originated by the Norwegian Defence Research Establishment for the Royal Norwegian Navy, who now use it operationally. It is a rocket-propelled depth charge with a 110 lb (*50 kg*) warhead having an ogival nose cone, and cruciform stabilising fins. Propulsion is by two concentric solid-propellant rocket motors and detonation of the warhead by a combined acoustic proximity, impact and time fuse. The system is so installed operationally that a full salvo of six missiles can be fired in 5 seconds.

Length	6 ft 4·75 in (*1·95 m*)
Body diameter	8·0 in (*20·3 cm*)
Launching weight	298 lb (*135·2 kg*)

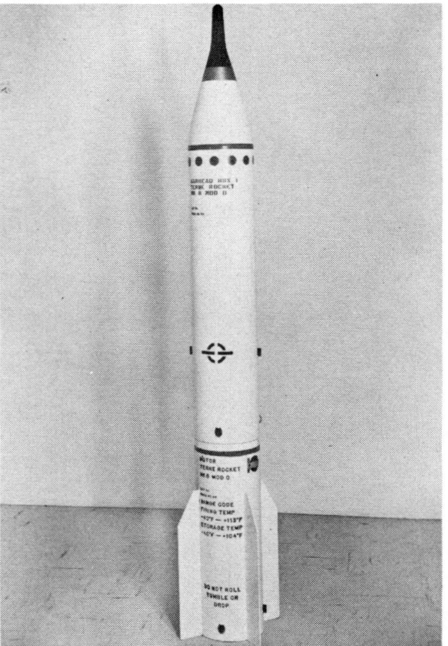

Terne Mk.8 surface-to-surface missile

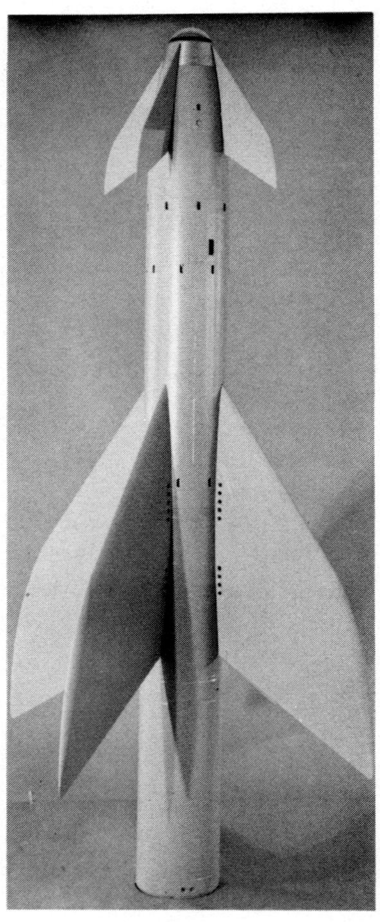
Penguin anti-ship missile

PAKISTAN

(B) 2 UH-19 (for ASR duties)

PERU

(B) 8 BELL 47G

(C) 6 GRUMMAN "Albatross" (HU-16A)
6 LOCKHEED "Harpoon" (PV-2)
(Both LRMP aircraft operated by Peruvian Air Force)

POLAND

(B) MIL "Hound" Mi-4

(C) 10 ILYUSHIN "Beagle" (Il-28)
45 MIKOYAN MiG-17

PORTUGAL

(C) 12 LOCKHEED "Neptune" (P-2V5)
(LRMP aircraft operated by Portuguese Air Force)

SOUTH AFRICA

(B) 6 WESTLAND "Wasp" HAS Mk I
(embarked in destroyers and frigates)

(C) 7 AVRO "Shackleton"
(LRMP aircraft operated by South African Air Force)

SPAIN

(B) 9 AGUSTA-BELL 204 AS
28 SIKORSKY S-61
(For embarkation in *Dedalo*)

(C) 12 GRUMMAN "Albatross" (HU-16B)
(LRMP aircraft operated by Spanish Air Force)

SWEDEN

(B) 10 AGUSTA-BELL 204B
10 BOEING-VERTOL 107-II

(D) (iv) (included because of their maritime application)

RBO4 **Robotavdelningen**

All-weather air-to-surface missile

This missile has been operational since early 1959 with the Swedish Air Force but has been under a continuous improvement programme to up-date it to modern needs.

It equips the four attack wings flying A32A Lansens as the RB.04D and will also be used with the Viggen in a later version, the RB.04E. It is powered by a solid-propellant rocket motor giving it a subsonic performance carrying a 660 lb (*300 kg*) warhead. Guidance is by a high-efficiency homing system.

Details apply to the RB.04C.

Length	**14 ft 7¼ in (*4·45 m*)**
Body diameter	**1 ft 7·75 in (*0·50 m*)**
Wing span	6 ft 8 in (*2·04 m*)
Launch weight	1 320 lb (*600 kg*)

RB.04E anti-shipping missile for the Viggen

RBO5A SAAB

Supersonic air-to-surface missile

Being developed for the Viggen and Saab-105, this missile is intended for the strike role but can also be used air-to-air. With long-chord cruciform wings and aft-mounted cruciform control surfaces it is powered by a pre-packed liquid propellant rocket motor built by Volvo-Flygmotor. Guidance is by radio command signals from a pilot-operated micro-wave radio link, based on simultaneous observation of both target and missile by the pilot.

Length	11 ft 10 in (*3·61 m*)
Body diameter	1 ft 0 in (*0·30 m*)
Wing span	2 ft 8 in (*0·80 m*)
Launch weight	675 lb (*306 kg*)

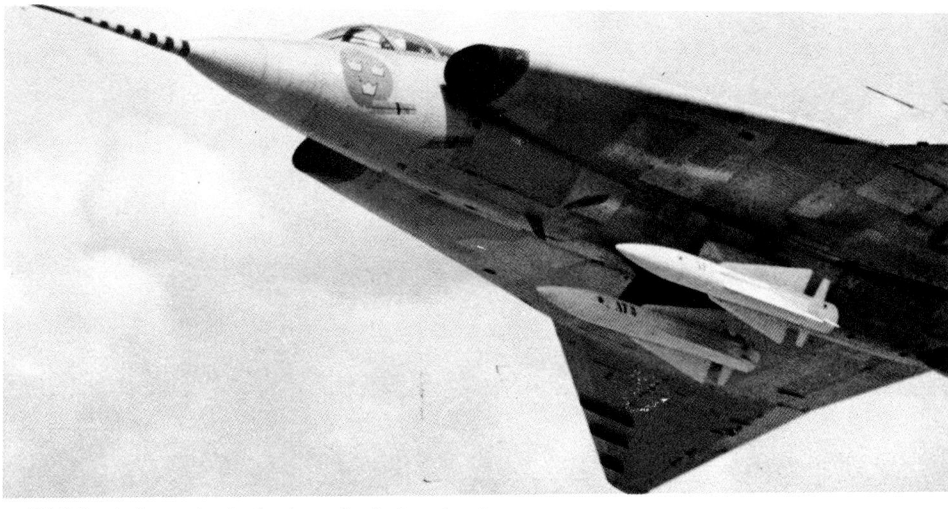

RB.05A missiles under the fuselage of a Draken aircraft used for development trials

TURKEY

(B) 3 AGUSTA-BELL 204 AS

UNITED KINGDOM

(A)

BUCCANEER S Mk 2 Hawker Siddeley

Carrier-borne and land-based 2-seat all-weather strike and reconnaissance aircraft

Max speed at 200 ft (*61 m*)	Mach 0·85 approx.
Tactical radius	1 000 n. miles plus
Armament	Internal Bay: Nuclear or conventional weapons (4 × 1 000 lb *453 kg* bombs) or camera pack; four underwing attachments for Bullpup or Martel missiles, 1 000 lb (453 *kg*) bombs (up to three on each pylon) or rocket packs
Max weapon load	**16 000 lb (*7,257 kg*)**
Max T-O weight	**62 000 lb (*28 123 kg*)**
Wing span	**44 ft 0 in (*13·41 m*)**
Width folded	**19 ft 11 in (*6·07 m*)**
Length overall	**63 ft 5 in (*19·33 m*)**
Length folded	**51 ft 10 in (*15·79 m*)**
Height overall	**16 ft 3 in (*4·95 m*)**
Height folded	**16 ft 8 in (*5·08 m*)**

Hawker Siddeley Buccaneer S.Mk.2

Power plant	2 × 11 100 lb (*5 035 kg*) st Rolls-Royce Spey turbofans

Only one squadron of the Fleet Air Arm, based on HMS *Ark Royal*, continues to operate the Buccaneer. Former FAA aircraft are operated by the Royal Air Force, for which production was continued. A land-based version, designated S.50, was built for the South African Air Force, to a total of sixteen.

SEA VIXEN (AN) Mk 2 Hawker Siddeley

Carrier-borne two-seat all weather fighter

Max speed at 10 000 ft (*3 050 m*)	560 knots
Service ceiling	Approx 48 000 ft (*14 630 m*)
Armament	Fuselage: 2 pods each containing 14 × 2 in rockets. Wing mounts: (6) Combination of Firestreak, Red Top or Bullpup missiles, bombs, rocket pods or air-to-surface rockets.
Max gross weight	**35 000 lb (*15 875 kg*) approx**
Wing span	**50 ft 0 in (*15·24 m*)**
Width folded	**22 ft 3 in (*6·78 m*)**
Length overall	**55 ft 7 in (*16·68 m*)**
Length folded	**50 ft 2·5 in (*15·30 m*)**
Height overall	**11 ft 0 in (*3·35 m*)**
Height folded	**14 ft 11 in (*4·55 m*)**
Power plant	**2 × RR Avon Ra.24 Mk 208 turbojets of 11 250 lb (*5 100 kg*) st**

With the Fleet Air Arm since 1959, it is still in first-line service. 4 squadrons.

Sea Vixen F(AW Mk. 2 of No. 766 Squadron, Royal Navy *Courtesy, Peter R. March*

UNITED KINGDOM (continued)

(A) (continued)

GANNET AEW Mk 3 — Westland

Carrier-borne three-seat early-warning aircraft

Max speed	220 knots approx
Endurance	5-6 hours at 120 knots
Equipment	Early-warning electronic for long-range ship and aircraft detection
Max loaded weight	24 000 lb (*10 886 kg*)
Wing span	54 ft 6 in (*16·61 m*)
Width folded	19 ft 11 in (*6·07 m*)
Length	44 ft 0 in (*13·41 m*)
Height	16 ft 10 in (*5·13 m*)
Power plant	1 × Rolls-Royce Bristol Double Mamba 102 turboprop of 3 875 ehp

Entered service with the Fleet Air Arm in 1959, equips No. 849 Squadron which provides early-warning flights on each carrier.

Westland Gannet AEW Mk 3 of the Royal Navy's No. 849 Squadron — *Courtesy Brian M. Service*

AV-8A HARRIER — Hawker Siddeley

Single-seat V/STOL strike and reconnaissance aircraft

Max speed	over 640 knots
Service ceiling	over 50 000 ft (*15 240 m*)
Range with one in-flight refuelling	over 3 000 n. miles
Ferry range, unrefuelled	nearly 2 000 n. miles
Armament	One under-fuselage and four under-wing attachments for up to 5 000 lb (*2 270 kg*) of bombs, 68 mm SNEB rocket pods etc. Under-fuselage strakes can be replaced by two 30 mm gun pods
Max T-O weight (GR Mk 1)	over 25 000 lb (*11 339 kg*)
Wing span	25 ft 3 in (*7·70 m*)
Length	45 ft 6 in (*13·87 m*)
Height	approx 11 ft 3 in (*3·43 m*)
Power plant	1 × RR Pegasus 10 (first ten aircraft for USMC) or 1 × Pegasus II of 21 500 lb (*9 752 kg*) st on later aircraft

Delivery of 60 aircraft for the USMC began in 1971. Others serve with the RAF.
(This aircraft is included in the hope that the long-delayed decision to use it in the Royal Navy may be reached during this year.)

Hawker Siddeley AV-8A Harrier of the US Marine Corps

PHANTOM F-4K — McDONNELL-DOUGLAS
2 squadrons

(B)

LYNX WG-13 — Westland

Frigate-borne anti-submarine search and strike helicopter

Max speed	179 knots
Hovering ceiling out of ground effect	above 12 000 ft (*3 650 m*)
Mission radius	154 n. miles
Accommodation	Two crew; 12 troops or freight for secondary capability
Armament	2 × Mk 44 torpedoes etc on cabin sides
Max T-O weight	8 550 lb (*3 878 kg*)
Main rotor diameter	42 ft 0 in (*12·80 m*)
Length overall	49 ft 9 in (*15·16 m*)
Width folded	9 ft 7¾ in (*2·93 m*)
Height overall	12 ft 3 in (*3·73 m*)
Power plant	2 × RR BS.360-07-26 turboshaft engines.

Prototype Westland Lynx. Naval version will have wheel landing gear

The Royal Navy is to receive the Lynx helicopter as a replacement for the Wasp. Lynx helicopters will also go to the French and Argentine Navies.

3 squadrons WESTLAND/SIKORSKY "Sea King"

WASP — Westland

Shipborne general purpose and anti-submarine helicopter

Max speed at S/L	104 knots
Cruising speed	96 knots
Hovering ceiling out of ground effect	8 800 ft (*2 682 m*)
Range with max fuel and allowances of 5 min for T-O and landing, 15 min cruising with 4 passengers	234 n. miles
Armament	2 × Mk 44 homing torpedoes
Max T-O weight	5 500 lb (*2 495 kg*)
Main rotor diameter	32 ft 3 in (*9·83 m*)
Length	40 ft 4 in (*12·29 m*)
Width folded	8 ft 8 in (*2·64 m*)
Height, tail rotor turning	11 ft 8 in (*3·56 m*)
Power plant	1 × RR Bristol Nimbus 503 turboshaft engine of 710 shp

In service with the Fleet Air Arm since 1963 aboard anti-submarine frigates. Also with the navies of Brazil, the Netherlands, New Zealand and South Africa.

Wasp of the Royal Netherlands Navy

UNITED KINGDOM (continued)

WESSEX Westland

Ship and carrier-borne two-crew anti-submarine assault and general-purpose helicopter

Max speed at S/L	115 knots
Cruising speed	105 knots
Hovering ceiling out of ground effect	HAS.1: 3 600 ft (*1 100 m*) HU.5: 4 000 ft (*1 220 m*)
Service ceiling	HAS.1: 14 000 ft (*4 300 m*)
Range with max fuel 10% reserves	HAS.1: 560 n. miles HU.5: 415 n. miles
Equipment	HAS.1: Doppler radar and dipping sonar HAS.3: as HAS.1 plus new search radar
Armament	HAS.1, 3: 1 or 2 homing torpedoes on fuselage side mounts, alternatively 4 × SS.11 ASM's, Machine guns or rockets HU.5: 4 × SS.11 ASM's alternatively various gun/rocket combinations
Capacity	In commando role can carry 16 troops or 8 stretchers or 4 000 lb (*1 814 kg*) of freight
Max T-O weight	HAS.1: 12 600 lb (*5 715 kg*) HU.5: 13 500 lb (*6 120 kg*)
Main rotor diameter	56 ft 0 in (*17·07 m*)
Length	65 ft 9 in (*20·03 m*)
Length folded	38 ft 6 in (*11·73 m*)
Width, folded	13 ft 4 in (*4·06 m*)
Height	16 ft 2 in (*4·93 m*)
Power plant	HAS.1: 1 × Napier Gazelle NGa. 13 Mk 161 shaft turbine engine of 1 450 shp HAS.3: 1 × Napier Gazelle NGa. 22 Mk 165 shaft turbine engine of 1 600 shp HU.5: 2 × RR Bristol Gnome 112/113 shaft turbine engines of 775 shp each

Westland Wessex HU Mk. 5—Royal Navy *Courtesy Peter R. March*

In service with the Fleet Air Arm on anti-submarine duties since 1961 (HAS.1) and 1966/67 (HAS.3). 8 squadrons.
With Royal Australian Navy as HAS.31, which is similar to the Mk 1 but with Gazelle Mk 162 engine of 1,540 shp, (27 aircraft, since modified to HAS-31B, with new search radar). The HU.5 version is a Marine Commando assault version, in service since 1964 with the Commando carriers.

WHIRLWIND Westland

Land-based and Carrier-borne two-crew rescue and general-purpose helicopter

Max speed	92 knots
Cruising speed	90 knots
Hovering ceiling	6 900 ft (*2 100 m*)
Service ceiling	16 600 ft (*5 060 m*)
Normal range	260 n. miles
Capacity	Up to 10 troops or 6 stretchers or freight
Max T-O weight	8 000 lb (*3 630 kg*)
Main rotor diameter	53 ft 0 in (*16·15 m*)
Length fuselage	44 ft 2 in (*13·46 m*)
Height	13 ft 2·5 in (*4·03 m*)
Power plant	1 × RR Bristol Siddeley Gnome H.1000 shaft turbine of 1 050 shp

This aircraft is in service with the Fleet Air Arm as the HAR.9 for plane guard and SAR duties and with RAF Strike Command as the HAR.10 for SAR duties. Also in service with the Brazilian Navy.

Westland Whirlwind HAR 10—Brazilian Navy

(C) (All operated by the Royal Air Force)

HS 801 NIMROD MRI Hawker Siddeley

Eleven-seat long-range maritime-reconnaissance aircraft

Max speed for operational necessity, ISA +20°C	500 knots
Ferry range	4 500-5 000 n. miles
Wing span	114 ft 10 in (*35·00 m*)
Length	126 ft 9 in (*38·63 m*)
Height	29 ft 8·5 in (*9·05 m*)
Power plant	4 × RR RB168 Spey Mk 250 turbofan engines of 11 500 lb st (*5 217 kg*) each
Armament	Forward bay for bombs, mines, depth charges and/or torpedoes 2 wing mounts for Nord AS.12 or Martel ASM Rear weapons bay for active and passive sonobuoys.
Equipment	Elliot nav-attack system, Sonar ASV-21 radar, Autolycus Ionisation detector, ECM gear, MAD and searchlight

Hawker Siddeley Nimrod MR.Mk.1

38 aircraft in service with RAF Strike Command and further orders have been placed.

UNITED KINGDOM (continued)

SHACKLETON MR Mk 3 Hawker Siddeley/Avro

Ten-seat long range maritime-reconnaissance and rescue aircraft

Max cruising speed	220 knots
Service ceiling	19 200 ft (*5 850 m*)
Range at 150 knots at 1 500 ft (*450 m*)	3 178 n. miles
Armament	2 × 20 mm cannon in nose (optional) Weapons bay for bombs, mines, depth charge torpedoes, etc Wing mounts (8) for unguided rockets on SAAF aircraft only
Gross weight	100 000 lb (*45 360 kg*)
Wing span	119 ft 10 in (*36·52 m*)
Length	92 ft 6 in (*28·19 m*)
Height	23 ft 4 in (*7·11 m*)
Power plant	4 × RR Griffon 57A in-line piston engines of 2 455 hp each RAF Phase 3 versions have additionally 2 × RR Bristol Viper 203 turbojet engines of 2 500 lb (*1 133 kg*) st in outboard nacelles

Hawker Siddeley Shackleton MR Mk 3 Phase 3 of the RAF *Courtesy, Peter R. March*

In service with the South African Air Force in the MR Mk 3 version and the RAF in the MR Mk 3 Phase 3 version and MR Mk 2 which is an earlier tail-wheel version with less tankage. Twelve AEW Mk 2 Shackletons have been delivered to the RAF for maritime airborne early-warning duties.

(D) (ii) The "Polaris" missiles carried by the SSBN's of the Royal Navy are equipped with UK designed and built warheads.

(iii)

SEACAT Short Bros & Harland

Short-range surface-to-air missiles

Seacat is in widespread service and production. It is standard armament aboard Royal Navy ships ranging from "Leander" class frigates to the aircraft carrier *Hermes* and is also ordered for the Royal Australian Navy, Royal New Zealand Navy, Royal Netherlands Navy, Royal Swedish Navy (with whom it is designated RB 07) Chilean, Brazilian, Federal German, Indian, Argentinian, Libyan, Venezuelan, Iranian, Royal Malaysian and Thailand navies. It is also under development for use from fast patrol-boats and in a surface-to-surface anti-shipping role. It is propelled by a two-stage solid-propellant IMI rocket and has a high-explosive warhead with contact and proximity fuses. A number of different fire control systems are in use:—Mk 20 Visual, Mks 21, 22 and 24, Radar Director, M4/3 Radar director and integrated with fire control system of guns. Normally mounted in a four-round launcher. In 1969 Shorts stated that successful trials had been completed of a system that replaces the optical sighting binocular with a closed-circuit TV system produced by Marconi Co. as the 323 Series.

Further developments now in progress include the use of CCTV for automatic missile tracking operations.

Length	4 ft 10·3 in (*1·48 m*)
Body diameter	7·5 in (*19·05 cm*)
Wing span	2 ft 1·6 in (*0·64 m*)

Seacat missile being fired from HMNZS Taranaki

SEADART Hawker Siddeley

Medium-range ramjet powered surface-to-air missile

Fitted in the Royal Navy's Type 82 and Type 42 destroyers, this missile is a two-stage vehicle with an IMI solid-propellent first stage booster and a second stage comprising the warhead powered by a Rolls-Royce Bristol Odin ramjet. The air duct is in the nose with interferometer aerials for the guidance systems around it. It employs semi-active radar homing using the Tracker illuminator radar Type 909. Sea Dart will also arm two type 42 destroyers ordered for the Argentine Navy.

Length	14 ft 3·5 in (*4·36 m*)
Body diameter	1 ft 4·5 in (*0·42 m*)
Wing span (max)	3 ft 0 in (*0·91 m*)
Range	14·8/19·5 n. miles

Hawker Siddeley Sea Dart

UNITED KINGDOM (continued)

SEASLUG Mk 1/Mk 2 Hawker Siddeley

Surface-to-air missile

The Seaslug, in its Mk 1 and Mk 2 forms, equips the "County" class destroyers of the Royal Navy. The Mk 1 was fitted in the first four ships although they will be retrospectively fitted with Mk 2 as are the last four "County" class ships now in service. During test firings a success rate of 90% has been achieved, by the Mk 1, at heights up to 50 000 ft (*15 250 m*) plus. It has a solid-propellant sustainer rocket which is made by ICI, with four solid-propellant booster rockets around the body. Its guidance system is beamriding in conjunction with Type 901M Radar. The Mk 2 also has transistorized electronics, longer range, better low-level capacity and an increase in length of 4 in.

Length (Mk 2)	20 ft (*6·10 m*)
Body diameter	1 ft 4·1 in (*0·41 m*)
Wing span	4 ft 8·6 in (*1·438 m*)
Tail span	5 ft 6·6 in (*1·69 m*)

Seaslug being launched from HMS "Kent"

SEAWOLF BAC

Short-range anti-aircraft missile

Being developed by BAC and Marconi (for the guidance and control system) the Seawolf, originally designated PX 430 is intended as the Royal Navy's Seacat replacement for the 1970's. It will give an improved defensive capability against supersonic anti-ship aircraft and missiles and will be an all-weather missile. The launch and guidance sequence will be automatic.

SLAM Vicker Ltd

Short-range surface-to-air missile

The system consists of six Blowpipe missiles in launchers around a central TV camera, gyro-stabiliser and control package.

An operator in the launch ship's control room guides each missile, by means of a joystick, by keeping the target and missile centred on a TV monitor.

It is being developed for close range defence against aircraft and ships, and can be fitted to "Oberon" class submarines and any light surface ship.

Dimensions of Blowpipe missile.

Length	4 ft 5·1 in (*1·35 m*)
Body diameter	3 in (*7·60 cm*)
Span of tail-fins	10·8 in (*27·4 cm*)

Blowpipe defence system for light surface ship

(v)

FIRESTREAK Hawker Siddeley Dynamics

Air-to-air missile

The current standard British air-to-air weapon is used by the RAF on Lightnings and the Fleet Air Arm on Sea Vixens. It has a cylindrical metal body, cruciform wings and tail. It is propelled by a solid-propellant rocket and is homed by an infra-red guidance system and controlled by a proportional navigation system. The 50 lb (*22·7 kg*) warhead can be detonated at a predetermined range.

Length	10 ft 5·5 in (*3·19 m*)
Body diameter	8·75 in (*22·5 cm*)
Wing span	2 ft 5·5 in (*0·75 m*)
Launch weight	300 lb (*136 kg*)
Cruising speed	Mach 2 plus
Range	0·65/4·34 n. miles

A Firestreak AAM being loaded on a Sea Vixen aboard HMS Victorious

UNITED KINGDOM (continued)

RED TOP — Hawker Siddeley Dynamics

Air-to- Air missile

This is in effect a vastly-improved Firestreak with larger wings and control surfaces and a new infra-red guidance unit not limited to pursuit-course attack. Warhead is increased in weight to 68 lb (*31 kg*). The rocket motor is increased in power also. This missile is used by the RAF on Lightnings and the Fleet Air Arm on Sea Vixen FAW Mk 2's.

Length	11 ft 5·7 in (*3·50 m*)
Body diameter	8·75 in (*22·5 cm*)
Wing span	2 ft 11·75 in (*0.91 m*)
Cruising speed	Mach 3
Range	6 n. miles

Red Top missile

UNITED STATES OF AMERICA
(A)

OV-IOA BRONCO — North American
Two-seat multi-purpose counter-insurgency aircraft

Max speed at S/L without weapons	244 knots
Combat radius, with max weapon load	198 n. miles
Ferry range	1 240 n. miles
Armament	4 × 0·30 in machine-guns in sponsons, which also carry maximum of 2 400 lb (*1 088 kg*) external ordnance; provision for one Sidewinder AAM under each wing, and for 1 200 lb (*544 kg*) load under fuselsge
Max weapon load	3 600 lb (*1 633 kg*)
Max T-O weight	14 466 lb (*6 563 kg*)
Wing span	40 ft 0 in (*12·19 m*)
Length	41 ft 7 in (*12·67 m*)
Height	15 ft 2 in (*4·62 m*)
Power plant	2 × Garrett AiResearch T76-G-10/12 turboprops each of 715 shp

96 built for the US Marine Corps, of which 18 were loaned to the US Navy for use in Vietnam. Two converted to YOV-10D configuration, with ventral turret and infra-red sensors, as night observation/gunships.

OV-10A Bronco light armed reconnaissance aircraft — *Courtesy of Duane A. Kasulka*

A7 CORSAIR II — Ling-Temco-Vought (USA)

Carrier-borne single-seat attack aircraft
Data for A-7E

Max speed at S/L	606 knots
Max range (ferry)	2 900 n. miles
Other performance details	Secret
Armament	Fuselage: 1 × 20 mm multi-barrel gun. Six underwing pylons and two fuselage weapon stations. Two outboard pylons on each wing can each accommodate a load of 3 500 lb (*1 587 kg*). Inboard pylon on each wing can carry 2 500 lb (*1,134 kg*). Two fuselage weapons stations, one on each side, can each carry 500 lb (*227 kg*). Weapons include air-to-air and air-to-ground missiles; general-purpose bombs; rockets; gun pods and auxiliary fuel tanks
Max T-O weight	42 000 lb (*19 050 kg*)
Wing span	38 ft 9 in (*11·80 m*)
Width folded	23 ft 9 in (*7·24 m*)
Length	46 ft 1·5 in (*14·06 m*)
Height	16 ft 0 in (*4·88 m*)
Power plant	A-7A 1 × P. & W. TF30-P-6 of 11 350 lb (*5 150 kg*) st A-7B 1 × P. & W. TF30-P-8 of 12 200 lb (*5 534 kg*) A-7E: 1 × Allison TF41-A-2 of 15 000 lb (*6 800 kg*)

A-7E Corsair II of squadron VA-195 of the US Navy

A-7A entered service with US Navy in November 1967, followed by A 7B. A-7E is a development of the A-7B, with TF41-A-2 engine. It was preceded by 67 similar aircraft, designated A-7C with TF30-P-8 engine.

F-8 CRUSADER — Ling-Temco-Vought
Carrier-borne single-seat fighter

Max speed	F-8A, B, C: 868 knots plus F-8D, E, H, J: nearly Mach 2
Combat radius (F-8A)	521·05 n. miles (*965 km*)
Other performance details	Secret
Armament	Fuselage: 4 × 20 mm Colt cannon and 2 × Sidewinder missiles (4 on F-8C/K, F-8D/H, F-8E/J) Provision for carrying Matra R 530 AAMs on F-8E(FN). Wing Mounts: (2) on F-8E, E(FN), H, J, K and L: 2 × 2 000 lb (*907 kg*) bombs or Bullpup A or B ASMs or 24 Zuni rockets
Max weight F-8E/J	34 000 lb (*15 420 kg*)
Wing span	35 ft 8 in (*10·87 m*)
Length	F-8E/J: 54 ft 6 in (*16·61 m*) Others: 54 ft 3 in (*16·54 m*)
Width folded	22 ft 6 in (*6·86 m*)
Height	15 ft 9 in (*4·80 m*)
Power plant	F-8A, B: 1 × Pratt & Whitney J57-P-4A turbojet of 16 200 lb (*7 327 kg*) st F-8C: 1 × P. & W. J57-P-16 of 16 900 lb (*7 665 kg*) st F-8D, E, H, J: 1 × P. & W. J-57-P-20 turbojet of 18 000 lb (*8 165 kg*) st

RF-8G Crusader, a remanufactured RF-8A

In service with the US Navy since 1957. F-8H, J, K and L are reworked D's, E's, C's and B's respectively.

F-8E(FN) is version for French Navy. Reconnaissance versions are RF-8A & RF-8G.

UNITED STATES OF AMERICA (continued)

(A) (continued)

EA-3B SKYWARRIOR McDonnell Douglas

Carrier-borne electronic countermeasures aircraft

(Data applies basically to standard A-3B)

Max speed at 10 000 ft (*3 050 m*)	530 knots
Service ceiling	45 000 ft (*13 780 m*)
Range, normal	2 520 n. miles
Armament	Fuselage: Weapons bay for bombs, torpedoes, etc. Tail-mounted barbette with 2 × 20 mm cannon (not always fitted)
Gross weight	73 000 lb (*33 181 kg*)
Wing span	72 ft 6 in (*22·07 m*)
Length	76 ft 4 in (*21·46 m*)
Height	22 ft 8 in (*6·91 m*)
Power plant	2 × P & W J57-P-10 turbojets of 10 500 lb (*4 760 kg*) st

McDonnell Douglas EA-3B Skywarrior ECM aircraft of the US Navy *Courtesy of AiReview*

Entered service with the US Navy in 1957, the A-3B has provision for flight-refuelling. Electronic countermeasures version (24 built) designated EA-3B with crew compartment in weapons bay and thirty RA-3B's with cameras in the weapons bay entered service. Also in service are KA-3 and EKA-3 tankers which will eventually be replaced by KA-6D's.

F14 TOMCAT Grumman

Carrier-borne two-seat all weather fighter

Max speed	Mach 2 plus
Max T-O weight	(with 4 Sparrow missiles) 53 500 lb (*24 262 kg*)
Wing span (max)	64 ft 1½ in (*19·54 m*)
Wing span (min)	32 ft 11½ in (*10·05 m*)
Length	61 ft 10½ in (*18·86 m*)
Height	16 ft 0 in (*4·88 m*)
Armament	1 nose-mounted M-61 six-barrelled cannon, Phoenix, Sidewinder and Sparrow missiles under fuselage and wings
Power plant	F-14A 2 × Pratt & Whitney TF30-P-412turbofans of 23 000 lb (*10 432 kg*) st F-14B: 2 × P and W F401-P-400 turbofans

Grumman F-14A variable-geometry fighter with its wings fully swept

This aircraft is at present at the advanced development stage as a replacement for the Phantom II in the US Navy. The prototype F-14A first flew on 21 December 1970. Present orders are for 12 development aircraft and 26 production aircraft, with plans for eventual procurement of 313, with first operational squadron in 1973. From the 67th aircraft, designation will be F-14B with P and W F401-P-400 turbofans.

E-1B TRACER Grumman

Carrier-borne four-seat early-warning aircraft

Max speed at S/L	230 knots
Endurance at 10 000 ft (*3 050 m*) at 156 knots	8 hr
Equipment	A 20 × 30 ft (*6·1 × 9·1 m*) radar antenna used in conjunction with the APS-82 early-warning system
Gross weight	27 000 lb (*12 250 kg*)
Wing span	72 ft 7 in (*22·04 m*)
Length	45 ft 4 in (*13·82 m*)
Height	16 ft 10 in (*5·13 m*)
Power plant	2 × Wright R-1820-82 piston engines of 1 525 hp

Developed from the S-2 Tracker, the Tracer entered service with the Navy in 1960. 64 aircraft remain in service.

E-1B Tracer early-warning aircraft of Squadron VAW-11, US Navy

S-2 TRACKER Grumman

Carrier-borne four-seat anti-submarine attack aircraft

Max speed at S/L	230 knots (S-2E)
Patrol speed at 1 500 ft (*450 m*)	130 knots
Service ceiling	21 000 ft (*6 400 m*)
Ferry range	1 128 n. miles
Max endurance	9 hrs
Armament (S-2D version)	Fuselage bomb bay: 2 × homing torpedoes or 4 × 385 lb depth charges or 1 × Mk 101 depth bomb Wing mounts (6): torpedoes or rockets or 250 lb bombs. Sonobuoys and marine markers in rear of engine nacelles.
Max T-O weight	29 150 lb (*13 222 kg*)
Wing span	72 ft 7 in (*22·13 m*)
Width folded	27 ft 4 in (*8·33 m*)
Length	43 ft 6 in (*13·26 m*)
Height	16 ft 7 in (*5·06 m*)
Power plant	2 × Wright R-1820-82WA piston engines of 1 525 hp each

Grumman S-2E of the Royal Australian Navy

The original variant, the S-2A, entered production in 1954; a total of about 500 were built including over 100 supplied to Japan, Italy, Brazil, the Royal Netherlands Navy and other countries. The S-2C (60 built) had enlarged weapons bay. The S-2D (215 built) had increased wing span and improved accommodation. The S-2E is an S-2D with improved ASW equipment, 14 of which were supplied to the Royal Australian Navy. This aircraft was built under licence in Canada with the designations CS2F-1 (S-2A equivalent) and CS2F-2, and CS2F-3 which are developed versions. These are in service with the Royal Canadian Navy and the CS2F-1 with the Royal Netherlands Navy. A new version, the S-2G, was being developed in 1972, with changed equipment, as an interim ASW aircraft for the US Navy, pending delivery of the S-3A.

C-1A TRADER

Developed from the S-2 Tracker is the C-1A Trader which is used by the US Navy as a COD transport with accommodation for nine passengers or 3 500 lb (*1 590 kg*) of freight.

UNITED STATES OF AMERICA (continued)

C-2A GREYHOUND — Grumman

Carrier-borne COD (Carrier On-board Delivery) Transport Aircraft

Max speed at 11 000 ft (*3 450 m*).	306 knots
Cruising speed at 27 300 ft (*8 320 m*)	258 knots
Range at cruising speed and height	1 432 n. miles
Capacity	39 troops, 20 litters with 4 attendants or 10 000 lb (*4 535 kg*) of freight
Max T-O weight	54 830 lb (*24 870 kg*)
Wing span	80 ft 7 in (*24·56 m*)
Length	56 ft 8 in (*17·27 m*)
Width folded	29 ft 4 in (*8·94 m*)
Height	15 ft 11 in (*4·85 m*)
Power plant	2 × Allison T56-A-8A turboprops of 4 050 ehp

A small number (17) of these COD transports were built, developed from the E-2A Hawkeye, for service aboard US Navy carriers. 8 more were ordered in 1970.

Grumman C-2A Greyhound of US Navy squadron VR-24 *Courtesy, B.M. Service*

E-2A HAWKEYE — Grumman

Carrier-borne five-seat early-warning aircraft

Max speed	320 knots plus
Service ceiling	31 700 ft (*9 660 m*)
Ferry range	1,654 n. miles
Equipment	Early-warning and command electronics including Airborne Tactical Data System (ATDS)
Max T-O weight	49 638 lb (*22 515 kg*)
Wing span	80 ft 7 in (*24·56 m*)
Length	56 ft 4 in (*17·17 m*)
Height	18 ft 4 in (*5·59 m*)
Power plant	2 × Allison T56-A-8A turboprops of 4 050 ehp

E-2C Hawkeye of the US Navy

59 produced for service with Squadrons VAW-11 and VAW-12 of the US Navy in 1964. A development, designated the E-2B with more advanced avionics, first flew in February, 1969, and E-2A's are being converted to E-2B standard. The E-2C with new electronics flew for the first time on 20 January 1971.

A-6A INTRUDER — Grumman

Carrier-borne two-seat strike and reconnaissance aircraft

Max speed at S/L	595 knots
Service ceiling	41 660 ft (*12 700 m*)
Max range (ferry)	2 800 n. miles
Armament	Weapon mounts (5): Each mount is of 3 600 lb (*1 633 kg*) capacity to carry bombs, Bullpup missiles and other stores.
Max T-O weight	60 626 lb (*27 500 kg*)
Wing span	53 ft 0 in (*16·15 m*)
Width folded	25 ft 2 in (*7·67 m*)
Length	54 ft 7 in (*16·64 m*)
Height overall	15 ft 7 in (*4·75 m*)
Height folded	15 ft 10 in (*4·82 m*)
Power plant	2 × P & W J52-P-8A turbojets of 9 300 lb (*4 218 kg*) each

KA-6D tanker version of the Intruder

This attack aircraft uses a digital integrated attack navigation system and serves with US Navy and Marine Corps squadrons. It has been developed into the EA-6A electronic countermeasures aircraft and further into the four-seat EA-6B for the same task. Developments are the A-6B, a special purpose missile carrier, the A-6C with forward-looking infra-red (FLIR) sensors and low-light-level television cameras, the KA-6D tanker version and the A-6E with multi-mode radar and an IBM computer.

F-4B PHANTOM II — McDonnell Douglas

Carrier-borne two-seat all-weather fighter

Max speed	Mach 2·5
Combat ceiling	71 000 ft (*21 640 m*)
Combat radius	781 n. miles
Ferry range	1 997 n. miles
Armament	Fuselage: 4 mountings for Sparrow III and/or Sidewinder AAM's Wings: 2 mountings for Sparrow III or Sidewinder AAM's Alternatively, 5 mounts for nuclear or conventional bombs and/or missiles up to 16 000 lb (*7 250 kg*)
Max T-O weight	54 600 lb (*24 765 kg*)
Wing span	38 ft 5 in (*11·70 m*)
Width folded	27 ft 6·5 in (*8·39 m*)
Length	58 ft 3 in (*17·76 m*)
Height	16 ft 3 in (*4·96 m*)
Power plant	F-4B, G: 2 × GE J79-GE-8 turbojets F-4J: 2 × GE J79-GE-10 turbojets of 16 500 lb (*7 485 kg*) st F-4K: 2 × RR Spey RB 168-25R Mk 201 turbofans of 12 500 lb (*5 670 kg*) st dry

Phantom FG.Mk.1 (F-4K) of Royal Navy taking off from HMS *Ark Royal* ***Courtesy, B. M. Service***

In service with the US Navy and Marines since 1962 in the F-4B form, together with the reconnaissance version the RF-4B. The F-4G is a development of the F-4B with AN/ASW-21 data link communications equipment; the F-4J is a developed F-4B with more powerful engines, control improvements and advanced electronics; the F-4K version, a developed F-4B, is in service as the Phantom FG Mk 1 with the British Fleet Air Arm.

A-4 SKYHAWK — McDonnell Douglas

Carrier-borne single-seat attack bomber

Max speed (with 4 000 lb *814 kg* bombs)	560 knots (A-4M version)
Max ferry range (at max TO weight, with max fuel and standard reserves)	1 785 n. miles (A-4M version)
Armament	Fixed: 2×20 mm cannon in wings. Fuselage and Wing Mounts (5): Up to 10 000 lb (*4 535 kg*) assorted bombs, rockets, Sidewinder AAM's Bullpup ASM's, Zuni or Mighty Mouse pods, gun pods, torpedoes or ECM equipment
Max T-O weight	24 500 lb (*11 113 kg*) (A-4M version)
Wing span	27 ft 6 in (*8·38 m*)
Length	40 ft 3·25 in (*12·27 m*) (A-4M version)
Height	15 ft 0 in (*4·57 m*)
Power plant	A-4A: 1 × Wright J-65-W-4 turbojet of 7 700 lb (*3 493 kg*) st A-4B, C: 1 × Wright J65-W-16A of 7 700 lb (*3 493 kg*) st A-4E: 1 × P & W J52-P-6A of 8 500 lb (*3 855 kg*) st A-4F, G: 1 × P & W J52-P-8A of 9 300 lb (*4 218 kg*) st A-4M, J52-P-408A 11,200 lb (*5 080 kg*) st

A-4M Skyhawk of the US Marine Corps

In service with the US Navy since 1956. A-4C and subsequent models have all-weather capability. A-4F improved controls. A-4G in service with the Royal Australian Navy since 1967. Delivery of about 50 A-4M's for the US Marine Corps with a more powerful J52-P-408A engine began in November 1970. Further orders placed for A-4M's in 1971.

UNITED STATES OF AMERICA (continued)

S-3A VIKING Lockheed

Carrier-borne anti-submarine aircraft

Max speed	430 knots plus
Ferry range	3 000 n. miles plus
Normal ASW weight	42 000 lb (*19 050 kg*)
Wing span	68 ft 8 in (*20·93 m*)
Length, overall	53 ft 4 in (*16·26 m*)
Armament	Provision for homing torpedoes, mines, depth charges, rockets, missiles and special weapons in fuselage weapon bay and on underwing pylons
Power plant	2 × General Electric TF34-GE-2 high by-pass ratio turbofan engines of approx 9 000 lb (*4 082 kg*) st

Lockheed S-3A Viking prototype

Lockheed have received contracts from US Navy to build 8 prototypes of a new anti-submarine aircraft under the designation S-3A. This four-crew aircraft will have improved sonobuoys and MAD equipment, enabling it to find the latest quieter, deeper-diving submarines. The first prototype flew on 21 Jan 1972.

RA-5C VIGILANTE North American Rockwell

Carrier-borne two-seat tactical reconnaissance aircraft

Max speed	Mach 2 (approx)
Service ceiling	64 000 ft (*19 500 m*)
Normal range	2 000 n. miles
Armament	Wing mountings (4): variety of weapons, including thermo-nuclear bombs
Max T-O weight	approx 80 000 lb (*36 285 kg*)
Wing span	53 ft 0 in (*16·15 m*)
Width folded	42 ft 5 in (*12·93 m*)
Length, overall	75 ft 10 in (*23·11 m*)
Length folded	68 ft 0 in (*20·73 m*)
Height	19 ft 5 in (*5·92 m*)
Power plant	2 × GE J79-GE-10 turbojets of 17 859 lb (*8 118 kg*) st

In service as the A-5A with the US Navy from 1961. The A-5B was a long-range version with extra fuel in the enlarged fuselage. The RA-5C is a reconnaissance version, carrying cameras and side-looking radar in a ventral fairing. All A's and most B's have been converted to RA-5C standard.

RA-5C Vigilante reconnaissance aircraft of the US Navy *Courtesy, AiReview (Tokyo)*

(B)

S-58 SEABAT, SEAHORSE, CHOCTAW Sikorsky

Carrier-borne and land-based anti-submarine and general-purpose helicopter

Max speed at S/L	107 knots
Cruising speed	85 knots
Hovering ceiling, out of ground effect	2 400 ft (*730 m*)
Service ceiling	9 000 ft (*2 740 m*)
Range with max fuel, 10% reserve	243 n. miles
Capacity	16-18 passengers
Max permissible weight	14 000 lb (*6 350 kg*)
Main rotor diameter	56 ft 0 in (*17·07 m*)
Length	56 ft 8¼ in (*17·27 m*)
Height	15 ft 11 in (*4·85 m*)
Power plant	1 × Wright R-1820-84B/D piston engine of 1 525 hp

Sikorsky S-58, Royal Netherlands Navy

In service with the US Navy as the SH-34G and SH-34J Seabat, the LH-34D for cold-weather operation, UH-34G and UH-34J utility aircraft. UH-34D is the US Marines version, also UH-34E amphibious version and VH-34D VIP transport. The S-58 is in service with other navies including the Belgian Navy (Sud-built), Federal German Navy, Italian Navy, Indonesian Navy, Royal Netherlands Navy and the French Navy, the latter's aircraft being built in France by Sud-Aviation.

AH-IJ SEACOBRA Bell

Two-seat close-support helicopter

Max speed	180 knots
Service ceiling	10 550 ft (*3 215 m*)
Hovering ceiling (in ground effect)	12 450 ft (*3 794 m*)
Range	311 n. miles
Armament	XM-197 three-barrel 20 mm cannon in forward lower fuselage turret. Four external attachment points under wings for 7·62 mm minigun pods and rockets
Gross weight	10 000 lb (*4 535 kg*)
Main rotor diameter	44 ft 0 in (*13·41 m*)
Length overall	53 ft 4 in (*16·26 m*)
Power plant	1 × 1 800 shp Pratt and Whitney T400-CP-400 coupled free-turbine turboshaft

The AH-1J SeaCobra is in production for the US Marine Corps, with 49 ordered initially. Also in service with the Marine Corps are 38 single-engined HueyCobras, designated AH-1G.

Bell AH-1J SeaCobra of the US Marine Corps

UNITED STATES OF AMERICA (continued)

(B) (continued)

SH-3 SEAKING — Sikorsky

Carrier-borne and land-based amphibious all-weather ASW and transport helicopter

Max speed	144 knots
Cruising speed for max range	118 knots
Hovering ceiling (out of ground effect)	8 200 ft (*2 500 m*)
Service ceiling	14 700 ft (*4 480 m*)
Range with max fuel, 10% reserve	542 n. miles
Equipment	Bendix AQS-13 sonar. Hamilton Standard autostabilisation equipment with sonar coupler. Ryan APN-130 Doppler radar
Armament	Up to 840 lb (*381 kg*) of weapons including homing torpedoes, Kormoran missiles
Max T-O weight	**20 500 lb (*9 300 kg*)**
Main rotor diameter	**62 ft 0 in (*18·90 m*)**
Length overall	**72 ft 8 in (*22·15 m*)**
Width folded	**16 ft 4 in (*4·98 m*)**
Height to top of rotor hub	**15 ft 6 in (*4·72 m*)**
Power plant	**2 × GE T58-GE-10 shaft turbines of 1 400 shp each.**

Westland Sea King in Royal Navy insignia

The original versions built by Sikorsky for the US Navy were the SH-3A, with GE T58-GE-8B engines which is also in service with the Japanese MSDF and, under the designation CHSS-2, with the Canadian Armed Forces; and the SH-3D which is in service with the US, Spanish, Brazilian and Italian Navies and built under licence by Westland Aircraft for the Fleet Air Arm, German and Indian navies, this latter using the RR Bristol Gnome 1400 engine. The Italian Sea Kings are built by Agusta. Nine SH-3A's were converted for mine countermeasures duty and designated RH-3A's. Also a number of SH-3A's are being converted into SH-3G Utility helicopters; and a new version of the G, designated the SH-3H, is a multi-purpose version with increased capabilities against submarines and low-flying enemy missiles.

SEA KNIGHT — Boeing-Vertol

Carrier-borne and land-based three-crew transport and utility helicopter

Data for UH-46D

Max speed	144 knots
Cruising speed	143 knots
Hovering ceiling out of ground effect	**5 750 ft (*1 753 m*)**
Service ceiling	**14 000 ft (*4 265 m*)**
Range at AUW of 23 000 lb (*10 433 kg*) with 6 750 lb (*3 062 kg*) payload, 10% fuel reserve	198 n. miles
Capacity	25 troops and troop commander or 15 stretchers plus 2 attendants or up to a 10 000 lb (*4 535 kg*) load
Max T-O weight	23 000 lb (*10 433 kg*)
Main rotor diameter (each)	51 ft 0 in (*15·54 m*)
Length, fuselage	44 ft 10 in (*13·66 m*)
Height to top of rear rotor hub	16 ft 8·5 in (*5·09 m*)
Power plant	2 × GE T58-GE-10 shaft-turbine engines of 1 400 shp each

In service with the US Marine Corps since 1962 as the CH-46A and US Navy for shore to ship and ship to ship duties as the UH-46A, uprated in 1966 to CH-46D and UH-46D. Three in service with the Royal Swedish Navy as the HKP-4 using Bristol Siddeley Gnome H1200, and six with the Japanese MSDF for mine countermeasures duties.

Boeing-Vertol UH-46D Sea Knight of US Navy Squadron HC-6 — *Courtesy, B. M. Service*

SEASPRITE — Kaman

Ship-borne two-crew all-weather rescue, ASW, anti-missile defence and utility helicopter

Data for UH-2A/B

Max speed at S/L	141 knots
Cruising speed	130 knots
Hovering ceiling out of ground effect	5 100 ft (*1 555 m*)
Service ceiling	17 400 ft (*5 300 m*)
Normal range with max fuel	581 n. miles
Capacity	11 passengers or 4 stretcher patients
Max T-O weight	10 000 lb (*4 535 kg*)
Main rotor diameter	44 ft 0 in (*13·41 m*)
Length (blades turning)	52 ft 7 in (*16·03 m*)
Height	15 ft 6 in (*4·72 m*)
Power plant	1 × GE T58-GE-8B shaft turbine engine of 1 250 shp

Entered service with the US Navy in 1962 as the UH-2A, followed by the UH-2B "fair weather" version. A twin-engined version, the UH-2C with two T58 engines, was introduced into service by retrospective modification of UH-2A's and B's. 6 UH-2C's redesignated HH-2C's, were converted into gunships with a chin Minigun, 2 additional machine-guns and additional armour. A total of 67 single-engined models were being converted into HH-2D's, similar to HH-2C but with armament and armour deleted. Ten SH-2D's are interim ship-borne ASW helicopters, with search radar, homing torpedoes and other equipment.

HH-2D Seasprite helicopter of the US Navy

UNITED STATES OF AMERICA (continued)

SEA STALLION — Sikorsky

Carrier-borne and land-based three-crew heavy assault and transport helicopter

Max speed	170 knots
Cruising speed	150 knots
Hovering ceiling out of ground effect	6 500 ft (*1 980 m*)
Service ceiling	21 000 ft (*6 400 m*)
Range, with 4 076 lb (*1 849 kg*) payload 10% reserve at cruising speed and 2 min warming up	223 n. miles
Capacity	38 passengers, 24 stretchers and 4 attendants or internal or external cargo
Max T-O weight	42 000 lb (*19 050 kg*)
Main rotor diameter	72 ft 3 in (*22·02 m*)
Length	68 ft 3 in (*26·90 m*)
Width, folded	15 ft 6 in (*4·72 m*)
Height	24 ft 11 in (*7·60 m*)
Power plant	2 × GE T64-GE-6 shaft turbine engines of 2 850 shp each

Entered service with the US Marine Corps as the CH-53A in 1966, becoming operational in Vietnam in January 1967. The later CH-53D has 3 695 shp T64-GE-412 engines or 3 925 shp T64-GE-413 engines. Under development are the RH-53D, for mine countermeasures operations, and the CH-53E, a three-engined version of the CH-53D.

Sikorsky CH-53A of the US Marine Corps

UH-IE

Land-based single-crew assault support helicopter

Max speed	140 knots
Cruising speed	120 knots
Hovering ceiling out of ground effect	11 800 ft (*3 595 m*)
Service ceiling	21 000 ft (*6 400 m*)
Range, max fuel	248 n. miles
Armament	2 × machine guns and 2 × rocket pods, on each side of the cabin
Capacity	8 passengers or 4 000 lb (*1 815* kg) of freight
Max T-O weight	9 500 lb (*4 309 kg*)
Main rotor diameter	44 ft 0 in (*13·41 m*)
Length	53 ft 0 in (*16·15 m*)
Height	12 ft 7¼ in (*3·84 m*)
Power plant	1 × Lycoming T53-L-11 shaft-turbine engine of 1 100 shp

Bell TH-IL trainer of the US Navy

Entered service with the US Marine Corps in 1964; the UH-1E is the Marine version of the Iroquois which is in widespread military service. Nine UH-1D's are in service with the Royal Australian Navy. Licence-built by Dornier, UH-1D's will serve with the German Navy. The US Navy is receiving 45 TH-IL trainers and 8 UH-1L.

QH-50 — Gyrodyne

Max speed	80 knots
Speed for max endurance	55 knots
Service ceiling	QH-50C: 16 400 ft (*5 000 m*) QH-50D: 16 000 ft (*4 875 m*)
Hovering ceiling (in ground effect)	QH-50C: 16 900 ft (*5 150 m*) QH-50D: 16 300 ft (*4 965 m*)
Max range	QH-50C 71 n. miles QH-50D 122 n. miles
Armament	2 × Mk 44 torpedoes or 1 Mk 46 torpedo
Max T-O weight	QH-50C: 2 285 lb (*1 036 kg*) QH-50D: 2 328 lb (*1 056 kg*)
Rotor diameter	20 ft 0 in (*6.10 m*)
Power plant	QH-50C: 1 × Boeing T50-BO-8A shaft-turbine of 300 shp QH-50D: 1 × Boeing T50-BO-12 shaft-turbine of 365 shp

The DASH System (Drone Anti-Submarine Helicopter) of which the QH-50 is the mobile weapon-carrying unit is carried aboard many US Navy vessels. The QH-50C went into service in 1962 and the QH-50D in 1965. Take-off and landing are visually controlled by the Deck Control Officer who hands the helicopter over to the control information centre in the ship which flies the drone to the target, actuates the arming and weapon release switches and returns the drone to the ship.

QH-50C drone helicopter, armed with two Mk. 46 torpedoes

UNITED STATES OF AMERICA (continued)

HU-16 ALBATROSS — Grumman

Land-based five-crew general purpose amphibian

Max speed at S/L	205 knots
Max cruising speed	195 knots
Service ceiling	21 500 ft (*6 550 m*)
Range	2 475 n. miles
Equipment (ASW version)	MAD gear, nose AS radome, ECM radome in wing, searchlight
Armament (ASW version)	Torpedoes, depth charges or rockets
Max T-O weight	37 500 lb (*12 500 kg*)
Wing span	96 ft 8 in (*29·42 m*)
Length	62 ft 10 in (*19·12 m*)
Power plant	2 × Wright R-1820-76A radial piston engines of 1 425 hp each

In service with the US Navy as HU-16D and Coast Guard as HU-16E, developed from earlier HU-16C, many of which were converted. Supplied to a number of foreign countries including Argentina, Brazil, Chile, Germany (West), Indonesia, Italy, Nationalist China, Japan and the Philippines. Spain, Norway and Greece use the ASW version.

ASW version of Albatross in service with the Greek Air Force — *Courtesy of S. P. Peltz*

C-130 HERCULES — Lockheed

Medium/long-range transport and reconnaissance aircraft

Max level speed	333 knots
Max cruising speed	320 knots
Service ceiling at 155 000 lb (*70 310 kg*) AUW	23 000 ft (*7 010 m*)
Range with max load	2 101 n. miles
Capacity	92 troops, 64 paratroops, or 74 stretchers and 2 attendants. Cargo of 26 640 lb (*12 080 kg*)
Max normal T-O weight	155 000 lb (*70 310 kg*)
Wing span	132 ft 7 in (*40·41 m*)
Length	97 ft 9 in (*29·78 m*)
Height	38 ft 3 in (*11·66 m*)
Power plant	4 × Allison T56-A-7A turpobrop engines of 4 050 eshp each

This transport is in widespread service with twenty air forces and with the US Navy as C-130E, C-130F and C-130D (for ski operation), the Marine Corps as KC-130F (with flight refuelling equipment) and with the US Coast Guard as HC-130B for SAR duties and EC-130E.

The US Navy has also ordered several LC-130R's which are basically C-130H's with wheel-ski gear and T56-A-16 engines of 4 500 eshp.

Lockheed KC-130F Hercules tanker refuelling two Phantom fighters

P-2 NEPTUNE — Lockheed

Seven-seat long-range maritime patrol aircraft

Max speed at 10,000 ft (*3 050 m*)	309 knots
Patrol speed at 1,000 ft (*305 m*)	150-180 knots
Service ceiling	22 000 ft (*6 700 m*)
Max range	3 200 n. miles
Armament	Fuselage Weapons Bay: Up to 8 000 lb (*5 000 kg*) of bombs, torpedoes, depth charges. Wing mounts (2): 16 × 0·5 in rockets. Optional dorsal turret with 2 × 0·5 guns
Max T-O weight	79 895 lb (*36 497·73 kg*)
Wing span (inc. tiptanks)	103 ft 10 in (*31·65 m*)
Length	91 ft 8 in (*27·94 m*)
Height	29 ft 4 in (*8·94 m*)
Power plant	2 × Wright R-3350-32W radial piston engines of 3 500 hp each Plus 2 × Westinghouse J34 turbojet engines of 3 400 lb st each

This aircraft is in widespread service with the US Navy as the P-2H and with the French Navy, Royal Netherlands Navy and Argentine Navy. With Brazil and Portugal it serves as the P-2E without the auxiliary turbojets.

A highly-modified version, the Kawasaki P-2J serves with the Japanese MSDF. It is powered by two 2 850 shp IHI/General Electric T64-IHI-10 turboprops plus two 3 085 lb st IHI J3-7C auxiliary turbojets. It has an extended front fuselage and new sensor systems.

Kawasaki P-2J of the Japanese MSDF

UNITED STATES OF AMERICA (continued)

P-3 ORION — Lockheed

Data apply to P-3C

Twelve-seat anti-submarine reconnaissance aircraft

Max speed at 15 000 ft (*4 570 m*) at AUW of 105 000 lb (*47 625 kg*)	411 knots
Patrol speed at 1 500 ft (*450 m*), same weight as above	206 knots
Max mission radius	2 070 n. miles
Equipment	A-NEW sensors and control equipment, with ASQ-114 digital computer.
Armament	Fuselage weapons bay: accommodates mines, depth bombs, torpedoes Wing mounts (10): torpedoes, mines or rockets singly or in pods
Max T-O weight	142 000 lb (*64 410 kg*)
Wing span	99 ft 8 in (*30·37 m*)
Length	116 ft 10 in (*35·61 m*)
Height	33 ft 8·5 in (*10·29 m*)
Power plant	4 × Allison T56-A-14 turboprop engines of 4 910 eshp each

EP-3B Orion of the US Navy — *Courtesy of T. Matsuzaki*

Produced for US Navy as P-3A (Allison T56-A-10W engines), P-3B and P-3C with A-NEW data processing system. P-3B also serves with Royal Australian Air Force, Royal New Zealand Air Force, Royal Norwegian Air Force, and the Spanish Air Force. Specially-equipped US Navy versions are the WP-3A for weather reconnaissance, the RP-3D for long-range flights to map the earth's magnetic field, and EP-3B/E for electronic warfare duties.

(D) (ii)

POLARIS A2 and A3 (UGM-27B and C) — Lockheed

Submarine-borne fleet ballistic missile

Length	A2/3—31 ft (*9·45 m*)
Body diameter	4 ft 6 in (*1·37 m*)
Launch weight	A2—30 000 lb (*13 600 kg*) A3—35 000 lb (*15 850 kg*)
Speed at burn-out	Mach 10
Max range	A2—1 500 n. miles A3—2 500 n. miles

Both versions are in service as long-range two-stage solid-propellant missiles with nuclear warhead. The first stage is powered by an Aerojet-General motor and the second stage by a Hercules Inc motor. Initially 41 US Navy nuclear-powered submarines were operational with 16 Polaris missiles, 28 with A3 and 13 with A2. The A3 serves in 4 Royal Navy submarines. The submarine is positioned by a Ship Inertial Navigation System (SINS), thereafter the missile, after firing relies on its own inertial-guidance system. The first stage ignites as the missile breaks surface, having been ejected by a pressure system forcing air or steam into the base of the launch tube. Polaris is no longer in production but a total of 1 452 missiles were built.

POSEIDON

POSEIDON CB UGM-73A — Lockheed

Submarine-borne fleet ballistic missile

Length	34 ft 0 in (*10·36 m*)
Body diameter	6 ft 2 in (*1·88 m*)
Launch weight	65 000 lb (*29 500 kg*) approx
Range	2 500 n. miles

This is a larger and twice as powerful missile to replace Polaris with twice the payload and increased accuracy. It became operational on the USS *James Madison* in March 1971 and is to equip 31 existing Polaris submarines. First test firing, at Cape Kennedy, was on 16 August 1968. The first stage is powered by a Hercules Inc or Thiokol solid-propellant motor and the second by a Hercules Inc solid-propellant motor.

(D) (iii)

AEGIS — RCA

This missile will be carried on board destroyers and frigates of a new class. The launcher for Aegis is equally suitable for Asroc missiles and will form the US Navy's main anti-aircraft system. The solid-propellant rocket motor is dual-thrust and guidance is by semi-active radar.
An electric (all-direction) scanning radar is part of the Aegis equipment, as well as the UYK-7 naval tactical data system computer and microwave radars for target illumination.
The prime contractor is Radio Corporation of America who are expected to flight-test this missile in 1973.

SEASPARROW — Raytheon

Short-range supersonic surface-to-air missile

This ship-launched version of the Sparrow AAM is operational with the US Navy. It is a single-stage rocket powered by a Rocketdyne Mk 38 Mod-2 solid-propellant motor and its guidance system is a Raytheon-built continuous-wave semi-active radar homing system. It has a cylindrical body with pivoted cruciform wings and tailfins. Successful test firings have been made from USS *Enterprise*. Canada is installing its close range system with Raytheon Canada Ltd as prime contractor. Norway, Denmark, Italy, Netherlands, Belgium and the US have joined together in the development of a NATO Sea Sparrow system. Raytheon is the prime contractor. Contractors in each European country developed significant portions of the system.

Length	12 ft 0 in (*3·66 m*)
Body diameter	8 in (*0·20 m*)
Wing span	3 ft 4 in (*1·02 m*)
Launch weight	450 lb (*204 kg*)
Speed	**over Mach 3·5**
Range	**7 n. miles plus**

STANDARD RIM-66A/67A — General Dynamics

Supersonic surface-to-air missile

This missile was developed in two versions, medium-range and extended-range, as a replacement for Tartar and Terrier on board 50 destroyers, frigates and escort vessels of the US Navy. Little modification was needed to fit it to the older launchers for the Tartar and Terrier. The MR version is a single-stage integral dual-thrust rocket whilst the ER version has a two-stage motor with jettisonable booster. Both versions have all-electric controls and solid-state electronics and an adaptive autopilot. Standard Missile has a semi-active homing system.

Length	ER: 26 ft (*7·92 m*) plus MR: 14 ft (*4·27 m*) plus
Launch weight	ER: 3 000 lb (*1 360 kg*) MR: 1 300 lb (*590 kg*)
Range	ER: 30·4 n. miles plus MR: 13 n. miles plus

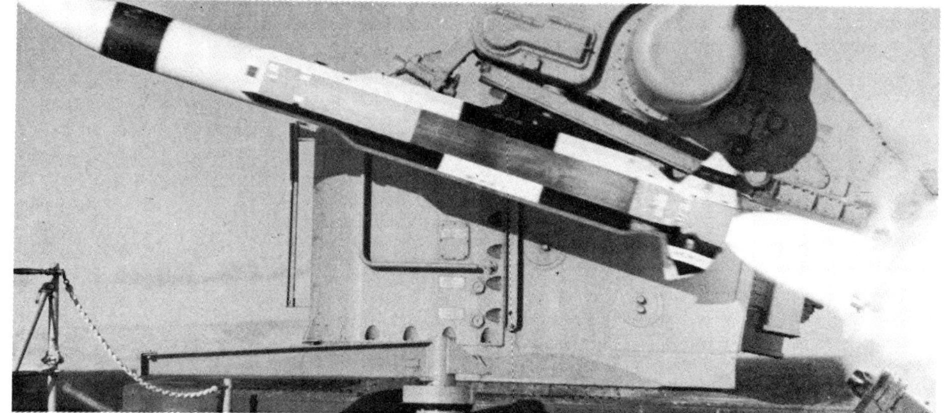

RIM-66A medium-range Standard Missile

UNITED STATES OF AMERICA (continued)

TALOS RIM 8G-AAW and RGM 8 H ARM

Bendix

Long-range ramjet surface-to-air / surface-to-surface missile

Entered service on USS *Galveston* in 1959 and has since equipped six other cruisers including USS "Long Beach" for which General Electric has developed a special launching and handling system using a computer mechanism by means of which all operations from selecting the particular warhead below decks to the firing of the missile are done automatically. It is a two-stage vehicle with a 40 000 hp Bendix 28 inch (*710 mm*) ramjet sustainer and an Allegany Ballistics jettisonable solid-propellant booster. It is a beam-riding missile using a semi-active Sperry SPG-49 "lamp" radar and can carry either a nuclear or high-explosive warhead.

It can also be used surface-to-surface. It was reported that the *Long Beach* destroyed two MiG's using Talos over North Vietnam in the summer of 1968, with intercepts in the 60 n. mile range.

Length	**38 ft 0 in (*11·58 m*)**
Body diameter	**2 ft 4 in (*0·71 m*)**
Wing span	**9 ft 6 in (*2·90 m*)**
Launch weight	**7 800 lb (*3 538 kg*)**
Speed at burn-out	**Mach 2·5**
Slant range	**60 n. miles plus**

Talos

TATAR RIM-24 General Dynamics

Supersonic surface-to-air missile

This weapon is in service with the US Navy, and equips many guided missile destroyers and several heavy cruisers. In addition it is aboard 4 French "Surcouf" destroyers, two Italian destroyers, three destroyers of the Royal Australian Navy and the Japanese destroyer *Amatsukaze*. It is secondary armament on the larger ships and primary on the smaller ships and has a dual-thrust solid-propellant Aerojet-General motor with an initial high-thrust firing followed by a longer low-thrust period maintaining a supersonic speed to the target. It employs a Raytheon guidance system of the homing type.

Length	15 ft 0 in (*4·57 m*)
Body diameter	13·4 in (*0·34 m*)
Launch weight	1 200 lb (*545 kg*) plus
Speed at burn-out	Mach 2·5 plus
Range	**10 n. miles plus**
Height effectiveness	1 000 to 40 000 ft (*305* to *12 200 m*)

Tartar on a twin-launcher

ADVANCED TERRIER RIM-2 General Dynamics

Supersonic surface-to-air missile

Developed from the Terrier the Advanced Terrier is in widespread service. As well as many ships of the US Navy, 3 cruisers of the Italian Navy and one of the Dutch Navy are equipped with this missile which is especially effective against low-flying aircraft. Allegany Ballistics supply both the solid-propellant sustainer and booster for this missile and it uses a beam-riding guidance system in conjunction with SPS-48 search radar, the Mk 76 fire control system and the Naval Tactical Data System (NTDS).

Length	27 ft 0 in (*8·23 m*)
Body diameter, missile	1 ft (*0·305 m*)
Body diameter, boosters	1 ft 4 in (*0·406 m*)
Wing span	1 ft 8 in (*0·51 m*)
Launch weight	3 000 lb (*1 360 kg*)
Range	**20 n. miles**

UNITED STATES OF AMERICA (continued)

(D) (v)

PHOENIX XAIM-7E Hughes

Long-range air-to-air missile

The F-111B aircraft was in mind when the Phoenix was being developed but now it is specified for the Grumman F-14A. It has a cylindrical body with long-chord cruciform wings and tail controls. It is powered by a Rocketdyne solid-propellant motor. It is radar-guided (AN/AWG-9) and all-weather operation is envisaged with particular application to long-range targets.

Length	**13 ft 0 in (*3·96 m*)**
Span	**3 ft 0 in (*0·91 m*)**
Max dia	**1 ft 3 in (*0·38 m*)**
Launch weight	approx 1 000 lb (*455 kg*)
Range	85 n. miles plus

Phoenix missile (extreme right)

SPARROW AIM-7E Raytheon

All-weather air-to-air missile

The Sparrow is in service with F-4B and F-4C aircraft of the US Navy and USAF respectively and equips the F-4K (Fleet Air Arm) and F-4M (RAF) versions in the UK. It is also carried by the F-104S of the Italian Air Force and will be carried by the McDonnell Douglas F-15 and the Grumman F-14 Tomcat for the USAF and US Navy respectively. Powered by a Rocketdyne Mk 38 Mod-2 solid-propellant motor, it is of standard cylindrical shape with pivoted cruciform wings and tail fins in line with the wings. Homing is by means of a Raytheon continuous-wave semi-active homing system and a 60 lb (*27 kg*) warhead is fitted.

Length	12 ft 0 in (*3·66 m*)
Body diameter	8 in (*0·20 m*)
Wing span	3 ft 4 in (*1·02 m*)
Launch weight	450 lb (*204 kg*)
Speed	Mach 3·5
Range	7 n. miles plus

An advanced version, designated AIM-7F, is being developed.

AIM-7E Sparrow IIIB missiles carried by F-4B of US Navy

SIDEWINDER IA AIM-9B and AIM-9H NWC

Air-to-air missile

Accent in the Sidewinder is on simplicity, with fewer than two dozen moving parts and unsophisticated radio equipment. It is powered by a Naval Propellant Plant solid-propellant rocket and has a 25 lb (*11·4 kg*) warhead. Control surfaces are at the nose in cruciform configuration, indexed by similar tailfins. It has had limited success in action. As well as being used by the USAF and US Navy it has been exported to Nationalist China, Australia, Japan, Philippines, Spain, Sweden and nine NATO countries, the Royal Navy, Royal Canadian and Royal Netherlands Navies, and is under licence production in Germany. The AIM-9H version is under development for the F-14 and other aircraft for the US Navy.

Length	9 ft 3½ in (*2·83 m*)
Body diameter	5 in (*0·13 m*)
Fin span	1 ft 10 in (*0·56 m*)
Launch weight	159 lb (*72 kg*)
Speed	Mach 2·5
Range	1·75 n. miles

Sidewinder missile mounted on an F-8 Crusader

UNITED STATES OF AMERICA (continued)

(D) (vi)

SIDEWINDER IC AIM-9C/D NWC

Air-to-air missile

A developed version of the 1A the 1C is in production for the US Navy and the UK. Power is from the Rocketdyne Mk 36 Mod-5 solid-propellant motor and the aerofoil surfaces have been revised. The AIM-9D version is equipped with infra-red homing guidance (the US Navy and UK version, in production by Raytheon) and the -9C with semi-active radar guidance, (Produced by Motorola).

Length	9 ft 6·5 in (*2·91 m*)
Body diameter	5 in (*0·13 m*)
Fin span	2 ft 1 in (*0·64 m*)
Launch weight	185 lb (*84 kg*)
Range	2 n. miles plus
Speed	Mach 2·5

All figures relate to AIM-9D version.

ASROC RUR-5A Honeywell

Surface ship-launched anti-submarine ballistic missile

The complete system comprises a Librascope precision fire control computer fed with data from a Sangamo Electric underwater sonar detector, the Asroc missile and an 8-missile launcher. The missile comprises a ballistic solid-propellant rocket with the weapon (General Electric Mk 44 Model O acoustic homing torpedo, Mk 46 Model O advanced acoustic homing torpedo by Aerojet-General, Honeywell Mk 46 Model 1, NWC and Honeywell nuclear depth charge) affixed by a frame. Following a ballistic trajectory after firing, the rocket is jettisoned at a pre-determined point and the weapon continues to its target. If a torpedo a parachute opens to lower it into the target area and when submerged behaves as any other homing torpedo. If a depth charge it sinks to a pre-determined depth before detonating.

It is operational aboard cruisers, destroyers and escort vessels of the US Navy and the Japanese destroyer *Amatsukaze*.

Length	15 ft 0 in (*4·57 m*)
Diameter	1 ft 0 in (*0·30 m*)
Fin Span	2 ft 6 in (*0·76 m*)
Launch weight	1 000 lb (*450 kg*)
Range	0·9/5 n. miles

Asroc anti-submarine missile

SUBROC UUM-44A Goodyear

Submarine-launched long-range anti-submarine missile

Subroc is part of a complex weapons system including advanced long-range detection equipment and a specially designed fire control system for use aboard many US Navy hunter/killer submarines. It is fired conventionally from a submarine's torpedo tube, after which the solid-propellant tandem booster ignites under water at a safe distance from the submarine. Thrust-vectoring controls set the missile on its course, its angle of emergence from the water and control its stability in flight. At a pre-determined range the rocket separates from the depth bomb which continues to its target supersonically, controlled by the inertial guidance system. Upon re-entering the water a shock-mitigating device cushions the impact, the bomb sinks and explodes. The production of Subroc has now finished.

Length	21 ft 0 in (*6·40 m*)
Max diameter	1 ft 9 in (*0·5333 m*)
Launching weight	4 000 lb (*1 815 kg*)
Max range	21·7/26 n. miles

Subroc anti-submarine missile.

USSR

(A) FREEHAND Yakovlev VTOL Experimental Aircraft

The NATO codename for an R & D VTOL aircraft first seen at the Domodedovo air-show in July 1967. The original version was clearly subsonic with a wide fuselage housing two turbojet engines, a stubby delta wing assembly and a high tail with a fixed tailplane mounted towards its top. Since 1967 development has clearly gone ahead—advanced versions have been flown at Ramenskoye, southeast of Moscow and the helicopter-cruiser *Moskva* has been fitted with a pad on the after-end of her flight deck, suitable for use by VTOL aircraft. The "Freehand" derivative will probably operate from the new Soviet aircraft-carrier *Kiev*.

Approximate dimensions:

Length, overall	58 feet
Wing span	27 feet
Height	15 feet
Max speed	400 mph

(B) HOUND MIL Mi-4

Land-based anti-submarine search and strike helicopter.

Max speed	90 knots
Normal cruising speed	75 knots
Service ceiling	18 000 ft (*5 500 m*)
Max range	Probably about 220 n. miles
Equipment	Search radar under nose. MAD (sensors in a towed "bird") Sonobuoys
Armament	Small stores can be carried on external fuselage racks. Main armament possibly depth-charges
Max T-O weight	17 200 lbs (*7 800 kg*)
Main rotor diameter	68 ft 11 in (*21·0 m*)
Length of fuselage	55 ft 1 in (*16·8 m*)
Height overall	17 ft (*5·18 m*)
Power plant	1—ASh 82V eighteen cylinder air-cooled radial piston engine — 1 700 hp.

This anti-submarine version of the "Hound" which in its other versions is in service with all Soviet air-forces, Aeroflot and foreign forces is with the Soviet and other Warsaw Pact navies. Has been operating from shore-bases for some years and is probably being replaced by "Hormone".

HORMONE Kamov Ka-25

Shipborne and land-based anti-submarine search and strike helicopter

Max speed	**119 knots**
Normal cruising speed	**104 knots**
Service ceiling	**11 500 ft (*3 500 m*)**
Range with max fuel with reserves	**351 n. miles**
Equipment	Search radar under nose. Dipping sonar
T-O weight	16 100 lb (*7 300 kg*)
Main rotor diameter	51 ft 8 in (*15·75 m*) (no tail rotor)
Length	32 ft 0 in (*9·75 m*)
Height to top of rotor head	17 ft 7½ in (*5·37 m*)
Power plant	2 × 900 shp Glushenkov GTD-3 shaft-turbine engines
Armament	An internal weapons bay with doors under the fuselage carries stores including A/S torpedoes. Smaller stores such as markers and flares can be carried on external racks, one either side of the fuselage

Kamov Ka-25 "Hormone" anti-submarine helicopters on the cruiser "Moskva"

In service with the Soviet Naval Air Force in a number of roles. The anti-submarine version (A) operates mainly from the "Moskva" class, although hangars are now provided in *Kara*, the "Kresta I" and "II" class and the latest Sverdlov conversion. Helicopter pads are becoming more common now in cruisers and destroyers. There is also believed to be a reconnaissance version of Hormone, presumably intended to operate with cruise-missile ships.

(C) BACKFIRE TUPOLEV

Max speed	Possibly Mach 2·5
Max range	Possibly 4 000 n. miles
Armament	? AS-6 system
Power plant	Possibly 2 Kuznetsov turbofans

A variable-geometry medium bomber which may shortly be entering squadron service with the Soviet Naval Air Force. Probably V-G only on outer wings and with engines built into fuselage with large air-intake either side of the cockpit.

BADGER TU-16

Long-range medium bomber/maritime reconnaissance aircraft

Max speed at 35 000 ft (*10 700 m*)	**510 knots**
Cruising speed	**417 knots**
Service ceiling	**42 650 ft (*13 000 m*)**
Range, max bomb load	**2 605 n. miles**
Max range at 417 knots with 6 600 lb (*3 000 kg*) bombs	3 450 n. miles
Armament	Defensive: 2—23 mm cannon in each of the dorsal, ventral and tail turrets. Some versions have one 23 mm cannon in starboard nose position
Bombs/ASM	Badger A. 19 800 lbs (*9 000 kg*) carried internally Badger B. 2 Kennel ASM—No bombs Badger C. 1 Kipper ASM—No bombs Badger G. 2 Kelt ASM—Can carry alternative bomb load
Normal T-O weight	150 000 lb (*68 000 kg*) approx
Wing span	110 ft 0 in (*33·5m*)
Length	120 ft 0 in (*36·5 m*)
Height	35 ft 6 in (*10·8 m*)
Power plant	2 × Mikulin AM-3M turbojet engines of 20 950 lb (*9 500 kg*) st each

The version of the Tu-16 known as Badger-F with underwing electronic pods

Badger A—Basic bomber, some tankers
Badger B—Kennel ASMs.
Badger C—Kipper ASMs.
Badger D, E and F—EW versions.
Badger G—Kelt ASMs or bombs

There are at least seven versions of this bomber serving with the Soviet Naval Air Force, probably more. First entered service in 1956. Some have been supplied to Egypt, Indonesia and Iraq.

USSR (continued)

BEAR TUPOLEV TU-95

Long-range Bomber and maritime reconnaissance aircraft

Over target speed at 41 000 ft (*12 500 m*)	435 knots
Cruising speed at 32 000 ft (*10 000 m*)	410 knots
Range with max bomb load	6 775 n. miles
Armament	Fuselage weapons bay: 25 000 lb (*11 300 kg*) of bombs (Bear-A) Fuselage external mounts 1 Kangaroo ASM (Bear B and C) 2—23 mm cannon in dorsal, ventral and tail turrets
Loaded weight	340 000 lb (*154 220 kg*)
Wing span	159 ft (*48·5 m*)
Length	156 ft (*47·6 m*)
Power plant	4 × Kuznetsov NK-12M turboprop engines of 14 795 shp each

At least four versions of BEAR are in service with the Soviet Naval Air Force and there are probably others:

Bear A—basic bomber
Bear B—ASM carrier with one Kangaroo
Bear C—As B with additional equipment blisters
Bear D—Maritime reconnaissance version without bomb-bay or ASM pylons

BEAR D—maritime reconnaissance version

BLINDER TUPOLEV TU-22

Medium-range supersonic maritime reconnaissance bomber

Max speed at 40 000 ft (*12 200 m*)	Mach 1·4
Service ceiling	60 000 ft (*18 300 m*) plus
Range	1 215 n. miles
Armament	Fuselage (Blinder B): "Kitchen" ASM part-recessed in bomb bay, alternatively internal bomb load. Blinder A has free-fall bombs only
Max T-O weight	184 970 lb (*83 900 kg*)
Wing span	90 ft 10½ in (*27·70 m*)
Length	132 ft 11½ in (*40·53 m*)
Height	17 ft 0 in (*5·18 m*)
Power plant	2 × unspecified turbojet engines developing 26 000 lb (*11 790 kg*) st with reheat

Blinder B in service with the Soviet Naval Air Force. A version with electronic countermeasures (ECM) equipment is now in service.

Tupolev Tu-22 "Blinder" of the Soviet Naval Airfleet

MAIL BEREIV M-12

Anti-submarine reconnaissance amphibian

Max speed	329 knots
Normal operating speed	172 knots
Max range	2 160 n. miles (*4 000 km*)
Max altitude (record attempt)	39 977 ft (*12 185 m*)
Gross weight	65 035 lb (*29 500 kg*)
Armament	Bomb-bay in bottom of hull, aft of step, and pylons for external stores under outer wings. Main armament probably torpedoes and depth charges.
Equipment	Nose radome and MAD gear in tail. Sonobuoys
Span	97 ft 6 in (*29·72 m*)
Length	99 ft 0 in (*30·18 m*)
Power plant	2 × Ivchenko AI-20D turboprop engines of 4 000 shp each

In service with Soviet Naval Air Force, some operating until recently from bases in Egypt.

Beriev M-12 "Mail" of the Soviet Naval Airfleet *Courtesy, Tass*

MAY ILYUSHIN IL-38

Anti-submarine reconnaissance aircraft

Max cruising speed	365 knots (*675 km/hr*)
Max operating height	32 800 ft (*10 000 m*)
Max operating radius	1 500 n. miles

Increasing numbers of this aircraft are in service with the Soviet Naval Air Force and some with the Polish. It has been encountered whilst operating from bases in Egypt and in the North Atlantic area. The MAY is based on the IL-18 (Coot) transport. The main changes seem to be a lengthened nose and a move forward of the complete wing-assembly. A radome, possibly with a new ASW radar, is placed under the nose and a MAD tail-boom has been added in addition to weapon-carrying equipment. Its A/S detection equipment is probably therefore, similar to that of MAIL (radar, MAD, sonobuoys) whilst its weapons are most likely the same (A/S torpedoes, depth-charges). Few details of performance are available but they are likely to be similar to those of the IL-18D from which the above figures are derived.

(D)

NOTES

a) This is the only navy with a full inventory of all types of missiles with the exception of a submarine-launched A/S missile and air-to-air missiles, which reflects their lack of carrier-borne aircraft.

(b) The NATO/US method has been used throughout this section. It should be noted that the numbered missile systems employ code-named missiles which may be used for other systems—e.g. the SA-N-2 system in *Dzerzhinski* uses the Guideline missile which is deployed by the Soviet army in a land-towed system, the SA-2.

(c) In all cases maximum range is given, (optimum and minimum range are given where possible).

(d) The figures in brackets after Launch Platform/ Aircraft indicate number of launchers.

(i) SS-N-1

Missile	Scrubber (Strela)
Launch Platform	4 Kildin's (1), 2 Krupny's (2)
Total launchers available	8
Number of stages	—
Power plant	—
Mach speed	1·0
Max range n. miles	130 (minimum 15)
Length, feet (*metres*)	25 (*7·6*)
Control	Radar with infra-red homing
Operational Date	1958

This obsolescent missile system remains something of an enigma—even whether the Scrubber and Strela are the same missile. Of the launchers two further "Krupny" class have been converted to SAM-carrying "Kanin" class. At maximum range external mid-course guidance is required.

USSR (continued)

SS-N-2

Missile	Styx A and B
Launch platform	25 Komar missile Boats (2), 65 Osa I missile boats (4)
Total launchers available	310
Number of stages	1 booster, 1 sustainer
Power plant	solid fuel
Mach speed	0·9
Max range n. miles	23 (minimum 6)
Length, feet (*metres*)	21·3 (*6·5*)
Control	Radar with active radar homing
Operational Date	1960

The Styx missile is in two versions of which A is probably the export model and B used in Warsaw Pact forces. In use by Algeria, China, Cuba, Egypt, East Germany, India, Indonesia, Poland, Romania, Syria, Yugoslavia. A Chinese version may be embarked in their new destroyers and be exported to Pakistan.

The missile itself has short delta wings and a triform tail-unit with control surfaces. It is carried in containers on a twin-rail launcher. This system proved its efficiency when used by the Egyptians to sink the Israeli destroyer *Eilat* on 21 Oct 1967 and by the Indians in a night attack on anchored merchant ships in Pakistan waters in Dec 1971.

"Styx" surface-to-surface missile

SS-N-3

Missile	Shaddock
Launch platform	4 Kynda's (8) 4 Kresta I (4) 16 Juliet's (4) 3 Echo I (6) 27 Echo II (8) 7 Whisky Long Bin (4) 5 Whisky Twin Cylinder (2)
Total launchers available	48 (surface), 336 (submarine)
Number of stages	2 Boosters, Ramjet or Turbojet sustainer
Power plant	Ramjet or Turbojet
Mach speed	1·5
Max range, n. miles	300 (optimum probably nearer 100)
Lenth, feet (*metres*)	35·7 (*10·9*)
Control	Radar with external mid-course guidance and, possibly, radar or infra-red homing
Operational date	1961-62

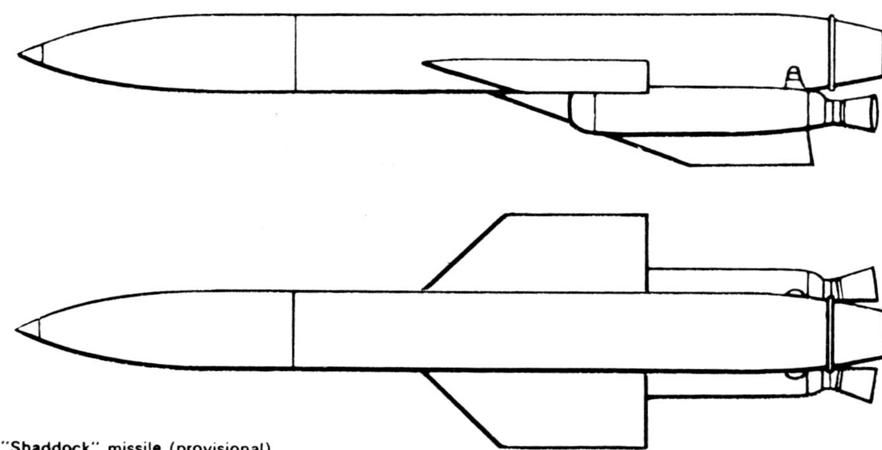

"Shaddock" missile (provisional)

For this medium-range system target information is probably obtained from reconnaissance aircraft or embarked helicopters in the case of cruisers. In the cruisers the launchers are trainable. The submarine version is carried in both nuclear boats (Echo I and II) and diesel boats (Juliet and Whisky). A road-mobile system using the Shaddock missile is also used by the Soviet Navy for coast-defence.

SS-N-7

Missile	—
Launch platform	11 Charlie submarines (8)
Total launchers available	88
Number of stages	—
Power plant	—
Mach speed	1·5
Max range n. miles	26
Length, feet (*metres*)	Possibly 25 max (7·6)
Control	—
Operational date	1969-70

Eight vertical launch-tubes forward are fitted in the Charlie class for dived launch of this new missile.

SS-N-9

Missile	—
Launch platform	6 Nanuchka (6)
Total launchers available	36
Number of stages	—
Power plant	—
Mach speed	1·0+
Max range n. miles	150 (optimum probably nearer 50)
Length, feet (*metres*)	Possibly about 32·8 (*10*)
Control	Radar with external mid-course guidance beyond horizon range
Operational date	1968-69

The Nanuchka's carry a triple launcher either side of the bridge. A derivative of the missile used here may be mounted in the Papa class submarine.

SS-N-10

Missile	—
Launch platform	1 + 2 Kara (8), 6 Kresta II (8), 5 Krivak (4)
Total launchers available	76
Number of stages	—
Power plant	—
Mach speed	1·2
Max range n. miles	29
Length, feet (*metres*)	approx 28 (*8·5*)
Control	Radar controlled
Operational date	1968

This system first appeared in the Kresta II where a group of four launchers was positioned either side of the bridge. In Krivak there is a four-launcher mounting on the fore-castle and in Kara the same arrangement as in Kresta II has been adopted.

SS-N-11

Missile	Probably modified Styx
Launch platform	55 Osa II (4)
Total launchers available	220
Number of stages	? 1 booster, 1 sustainer
Power plant	? Solid
Mach speed	·9
Max range n. miles	29
Length, feet (*metres*)	? 22 (*6·7*)
Control	? Radar with radar terminal homing
Operational date	1968

The above details are conjectural in places, although this must be a very similar missile to Styx, possibly with folding wings.

SS-N-?

Reports have been received of the development of a mach 4 cruise missile with a range of 400 n. miles.

SS-C-?

See remarks under SS-N-3.

USSR (continued)

SS-C-2

A coastal defence system using an adaptation of the Kennel ASM named Samlet. This has a probable range up to 55 n. miles and a speed of Mach .9 (see section D (iv)).

Samlet missile on launch ramp

(D) (ii)

SS-N-4

Missile	Sark derivative
Launch platform	11 Golf I (3), 2 Zulu V (2)
Total launchers available	37
Number of stages	? 2
Power plant	—
Max range n. miles	330
Length, feet (*metres*)	37·5 (*11·4*)
Operational date	Test firing 1955. Operational 1958.

The first ballistic system which, in the nuclear Hotel I class and the diesel boats of the Golf I and Zulu V classes, was fitted for surface launch. Now probably obsolete, all Hotel I's having been converted to II's and the Zulu V's almost certainly non-operational.

SS-N-5

Missile	Serb
Launch platform	11 Golf II (3), 9 Hotel II (3)
Total launchers available	60
Number of stages	Two
Power plant	Solid
Max range n. miles	650
Length, feet (*metres*)	35 (*10.6*)
Diameter (*metres*)	5 (*1·5*)
Operational date	Test fired March 1962. Operational 1963.

Possibly intended for a new SSBN class but retrofitted to the Golf II and Hotel II classes. Dived launch.

Serb submarine-launched missile *Courtesy of Novosti*

SS-N-6

Missile	Sawfly
Launch platform	32 Yankee (16)
Total launchers available	512
Number of stages	Two
Power plant	Solid
Max range n. miles	1 350
Length, feet (*metres*)	42 (*12·8*)
Diameter, feet (*metres*)	5·75 (*1·75*)
Operational date	1969

The first version of the missile was seen in the Moscow parade of 7 Nov 1967.

Sawfly missile

USSR (continued)

SS-N-8

Missile	—
Launch platform	4 Delta (12)
Total launchers available	48
Number of stages	? 2
Power plant	? Solid
Max range n. miles	4 000
Length, feet (*metres*)	Approx 46 (*14*)
Diameter, feet (*metres*)	approx. 7 (*2·1*)
Operational date	Tested 1971. Operational 1973

First test-fired at sea from the single Hotel III conversion and now operational in the Delta class. The fact of tripling the Sawfly range has brought a totally new problem into Western missile-defence planning.

(D) (iii)

SA-N-1

Missile	Goa
Launch platform	8 Sam Kotlin (2), 6 Kanin (2), 19 Kashin (4), 4 Kynda (2), 4 Kresta I (4)
Total launchers available	128
Number of stages	2
Power plant	Solid with booster
Slant range n. miles	15
Mach speed	2
Max effective ceiling, feet (*metres*)	44 000 (*12 200*)
Length, feet (*metres*)	19·3 (*5·9*)
Wing span, feet (*metres*)	4·0 (*1·2*)
Operational date	1961-62

The first embarked SAM in the Soviet fleet with a low-altitude short-range capability.

GOA in its land-based form

SA-N-2

Missile	Guideline
Launch Platform	Dzerzhinski (2)
Total launchers available	2
Number of stages	2
Power plant	Solid booster, liquid sustainer
Slant range n. miles	22
Mach speed	3·5
Max effective ceiling feet (*metres*)	60 000 (*18 300*)
Length, feet (*metres*)	34·7 (*10·6*) (27 (*8·25*) without booster)
Wing span, feet (*metres*)	main body 5·6 (*1·7*) Booster 8·5 (*2·6*)
Warhead	288 lbs HE
Guidance	Radar
Operational date	First reported ashore 1957. Fitted in *Dzerzhinski* in 1961-62

As this system went to sea slightly before SA-N-1 and has not been repeated it must be assumed to be unsuitable for maritime operations.

SA-N-3

Missile	Goblet
Launch platform	2 Moskva (4), 6 Kresta II (4), 1 Kara (4)
Total launchers available	36
Slant range n. miles	20

A larger and longer range follow-on of SA-N-1.

SA-N-4

Missile	—
Launch platform	2 Sverdlov conversions (1), 1 Kara (2), 5 Krivak (2), 6 Nanuchka (1), 11 Grisha (1)
Total launchers available	31
Slant range n. miles	20

A new SAM which is normally housed in a silo, is raised to fire and retracted for reloading or stowage. Associated with a new radar.

(D) (iv)

AS-1

Missile	Kennel
Aircraft	Badger B (2)
Total no. of aircraft	About 50
Stages	1
Power plant	Turbojet
Length, feet (*metres*)	27·9 (*8·5*)
Wing span	16·0 (*4·9*)
Max range n. miles	55
Mach speed	0·9
Operational date	? 1958

An obsolete system, possibly beam-riding. And adaptation of the German Komet missile. Launch height below 25 000 ft (*7 600 m*). Has been supplied to Indonesia and Egypt. The shore based version of this missile, Samlet, appears in section D (i) above, under "SS-C-2".

Two "Kennel" anti-ship missiles loaded beneath the wings of a Tu-16 bomber

(D) (iv) continued

AS-2

Missile	Kipper
Aircraft	Badger C (1)
Total no. of aircraft	About 50
Stages	1
Power plant	Turbojet
Length, feet	31 (*9·5*)
Wing span feet (*metres*)	16 (*4·9*)
Max range n. miles	115
Mach speed	1·2
Operational date	1960

This system imposes neither height nor speed restrictions on the parent aircraft. The missile itself has an underslung turbojet power plant.

USSR (continued)

(D) (iv) continued

AS-3

Missile	Kangaroo
Aircraft	Bear B and C (1)
Total no. of aircraft	About 20
Stages	1
Power plant	Turbojet
Length, feet (*metres*)	49·2 (*15·0*)
Wing span feet (*metres*)	29·8 (*9·1*)
Max range n. miles	350
Mach speed	2
Operational date	1961

The missile is very similar to a swept-wing fighter such as "Fitter", and is the largest in the Soviet naval armoury. It gives the Bear a long-range stand-off capability and is probably radar guided.

AS-4

Missile	Kitchen
Aircraft	Blinder B (1)
Stages	1
Power plant	Liquid rocket
Length, feet (*metres*)	37 (*11·3*)
Wing span feet (*metres*)	8·5 (*2·6*)
Max range, n. miles	170
Mach speed	2+

Apparently intended only for the TU-22 Blinder B on which it is belly-slung. Probably fitted with inertial guidance.

AS-5

Missile	Kelt
Aircraft	Badger G (2)
Total no. of aircraft	About 150
Stages	1
Power plant	Liquid rocket
Length, feet (*metres*)	30·8 (*9·4*)
Wing span, feet (*metres*)	15·1 (*4·6*)
Max range, n. miles	100
Mach speed	·9
Operational date	1968

Externally similar missile to Kennel with a variation of the nose and belly lines. The nose houses an active-homing radar.

AS-6

Missile	Unnamed
Aircraft	Badger ? G (2)
Total no. of aircraft	About 50
Stages	1
Max range n. miles	150
Mach speed	3
Operational date	1970-71

This system may also be fitted to Backfire.

(D) (vi)

The Moskva class mounts, as the first launcher of the three forward, a weapon which is probably an A/S launcher. This suggests either an increase in range of the ship-borne sonar or, more likely, an integration with the Hormone A helicopters embarked. The head could be torpedo or depth-charge.

URUGUAY

(B) 4 BELL 47

(C) GRUMMAN "Avenger" (TBM-IC)
2 MARTIN "Mariner" (PBM-5)

NAVAL STRENGTHS

NAVAL STRENGTHS

	Aircraft Carriers (L=light)	*Cruisers and Fire Support Ships*	*Destroyers*	*Frigates*	*Corvettes*	*Ballistic Missile Sub-marines (N= Nuclear D= Diesel)*	*Cruise Missile Sub-marines (N= Nuclear D= Diesel)*	*Fleet Sub-marines*	*Patrol Sub-marines*	*Missile Boats*	*Torpedo Boats*	*Gun Boats*	*Patrol Craft*	*Mine-layers*
ARGENTINA	1 (L)	3	10	3	2				2		2		14	
AUSTRALIA	1+1 (L)		7	6					4				20	
BELGIUM													6	
BRAZIL	1 (L)	2	13	5	10				3			8		
BULGARIA				2	8				2	3	12			
BURMA				2							5	72	2	
CANADA			4	18					4					
CEYLON				1								5	27	
CHILE		3	4	4					2		4		6	
CHINA			8	9	11	1			43	17	130	315	20	
COLOMBIA			4	5					2 (small)			4	22	
CUBA				3	20					20	24			
DENMARK				6	4				6	8	16		35	7
DOMINICAN REP				3	5								9	
ECUADOR				4	2						3	2	6	
EGYPT			5	3	12				12	18	36			
FINLAND				3	2					1	15		23	2
FRANCE	3 (L)	3	19	28		2			20	1			20	
GERMANY (DEM)				2	26					12	62		12	
GERMANY (FED)			11	6	6				12		38			
GREECE			9	4	5				6	4	12		5	2
INDIA	1 (L)	2	6	24					4	8			21	
INDONESIA			3	10	18				10	12	21	18	34	
IRAN			3	4	4								10	
IRAQ					3						12	4	18	
ISRAEL									2	13	9		30	
ITALY		3	10	11	11				9		18			
JAPAN			32	19	20				16		7			3
KOREA (N)					14				4	10	53	47		
KOREA (S)			5	10									36	
MALAYSIA				2						4		3 (bldg)	24	
MEXICO			2	9									10	
NETHERLANDS		1	2 (bldg)	22 (4 bldg)	11				6				6	
NEW ZEALAND				4									15 (4 bldg)	
NORWAY				5	2				15	26		20		4
PAKISTAN		1	4	2					3			6	1	
PERU		2	4	3	2				6 (2 bldg)			9	6+3	
PHILIPPINES				1								9	18+11	
POLAND			4						4	12	20		46	
PORTUGAL				8	23				4				36	
ROMANIA					3					5	8		3	
SOUTH AFRICA			2	7					3				5	
SPAIN	1 (L)	1	18	4	5				8		3		18	
SWEDEN			8	5					22		42		23	2
TAIWAN			19	12					2		6		4	1
THAILAND			1	9	7							13	10+20	2
TURKEY			12	2 (bldg)	9				13		11		6+43	9
UNITED KINGDOM	1+2 (L)	2+10 (5 bldg)		64		4		8	23				13	3
UNITED STATES	17 (3N) + 14+6(L)	17 (+16 res)	123 (+50 res)	100 (+35 res)		41 (N)	1 (D)	84 (23 bldg)	32 (+8 res)	3	17	14		
USSR	1 (L) (bldg)	33	108	54	70	45 (N) 22(D)	42 (N) 28 (D)	26	233	131	190			
VENEZUELA			4	6					4 (2 bldg)	12 (bldg)			22	
VIETNAM (N)					3						12	28	30	
YUGOSLAVIA			1		3				5	10	44		25	

* In addition there are 40 Cargo and Transport Ships (amphib), of which 32 are in reserve.

TABLE SHOWING THE NUMERICAL STRENGTH OF EACH COUNTRY

eet Mine- weepers	*Coastal Mine-sweepers/ Mine-hunters*	*Inshore Mine-sweepers*	*Mine-sweeping Boats*	*Assault Ships*	*Landing Ships*	*Landing Craft*	*Depot Repair Main-tenance Ships*	*Survey Research Ships (Large and Small)*	*Supply Ships*	*Large Oilers*	*Small Oilers*	*Hydrofoils and ACVs*	*Misc-ellaneous*	
	4+2				6	2+27		3			3		19	ARGENTINA
	6							6	2				6	AUSTRALIA
7	9	12						2	2				13	BELGIUM
	6				1		1	6+6		2			10	BRAZIL
2	4	4	24			20								BULGARIA
								2					11	BURMA
							2	6	5				40	CANADA
												1	1	CEYLON
					1	4		1					11	CHILE
	27					54						70	400	CHINA
								2			4		15	COLOMBIA
													34	CUBA
	8	4					2				2		6	DENMARK
	2					3		+ 2			2		10	DOMINICAN REP
					2			1	1				4	ECUADOR
	10	2				14							6	EGYPT
													24	FINLAND
14	61+5	10		2	5	14+33	4	13	5		9		114	FRANCE
12	41	10				22		10			4		24	GERMANY (DEM)
	24	50			2	22	17		14		19		42	GERMANY
	21				14	8		5		2	6		13	GREECE
	4	4			1	2	3	4	1		4		1	INDIA
6	20				8	9	4	4			9		58	INDONESIA
	4	2				2	2		2		1	16	10	IRAN
													3	IRAQ
						9							9	ISRAEL
4	37	20			1						1		144	ITALY
	39		10		7	48	2				1		10	JAPAN
														KOREA (N)
	12				20			1					13	KOREA (S)
	6						1	0+1					24 (Police)	MALAYSIA
	25							2			2		5	MEXICO
	35	16					2(1 bldg)	4 (1 bldg)					32	NETHERLANDS
	2							1+3						NEW ZEALAND
	10												14	NORWAY
	7							1					7	PAKISTAN
	2					7					6		14	PERU
4					11							4	2	PHILIPPINES
24			27		16			6			7		20	POLAND
4	12					66		7					9	PORTUGAL
	4	22	8			10							17	ROMANIA
	10							1					10	SOUTH AFRICA
11	12				6	8							47	SPAIN
	18	17				48		6					22	SWEDEN
	13		9		26	22							27	TAIWAN
	4				7	9		1					20	THAILAND
	16	4				72+18	4				7		16	TURKEY
	38	24		2	7	24+33	5	5+5	10	25	6	2	285	UNITED KINGDOM
25 * (18 res)	11 * (3 res)			13 (5 bldg+4 res)	*45 (+37 res)	100	28 (+24 res)	46 (2 bldg+5 res)	25 * * (+11 res)	37 (+9 res)		5 (2 bldg)	84	UNITED STATES
195	125				11	60	53	116	3	8	38	25	172+ 53 AGIs	USSR
					5			3					13	VENEZUELA
			4		7	5							100	VIETNAM (N)
	4	12	14 (river)			29		1			4		13	YUGOSLAVIA

* * In addition amongst logistic support ships there are 68 Cargo Ships (8 in reserve) and 16 tankers.

INDEX OF NAMED SHIPS

INDEX OF NAMED SHIPS

Abbreviations in brackets following the names of the ships indicate the country of origin

AbD	Abu Dhabi
Al	Albania
Alg	Algeria
A	Argentina
Aus	Australia
B	Bahamas
Ba	Bangla Desh
Bel	Belgium
Br	Brazil
Bru	Brunei
Bul	Bulgaria
Bur	Burma
Cam	Cameroon
Can	Canada
Cey	Ceylon
Chi	Chile
C	China (People's Republic)
Col	Colombia
Co	Congo
C.R.	Costa Rica
Cu	Cuba
Cy	Cyprus
D	Denmark
Dom	Dominican Republic
Ec	Ecuador
Eg	Egypt
ES	El Salvador
Et	Ethiopia
Fin	Finland
F	France
G	Gabon
Ger	Germany (Federal Republic)
GE	Germany (Democratic Republic)
Gh	Ghana
Gr	Greece
Ga	Grenada
Gu	Guatemala
Gui	Guinea
Guy	Guyana
H	Haiti
Hon	Honduras
HB	Honduras, British
HK	Hong Kong
Hun	Hungary
Ice	Iceland
In	India
Ind	Indonesia
Ir	Iran
Ira	Iraq
Ire	Ireland (Republic of)
Is	Israel
I	Italy
I.C.	Ivory Coast
Jam	Jamaica
J	Japan
Jo	Jordan
Ke	Kenya
Kh	Khmer Republic
Kor	Korea (Republic of)
K.N.	Korea (North)
Ku	Kuwait
L	Laos
Leb	Lebanon
Li	Liberia
Lib	Libya
Ma	Malagasy
Ml	Malawi
M	Malaysia
Mau	Mauritania
Mex	Mexico
Mor	Morocco
N	Netherlands
N.Z.	New Zealand
Nic	Nicaragua
Nig	Nigeria
Nor	Norway
O	Oman (Sultanate of)
Pak	Pakistan
Pan	Panama
Par	Paraguay
P	Peru
Ph	Philippines
Po	Poland
Por	Portugal
R	Romania
S	Sabah
St. L	St. Lucia
St. V	St. Vincent
Sau	Saudi Arabia
Sen	Senegal
S.L.	Sierra Leone
Sin	Singapore
Som	Somalia
S.A.	South Africa
S.Y.	Southern Yemen
Sp	Spain
Su	Sudan
Sw	Sweden
Sy	Syria
T.C.	Taiwan (Republic of China)
Tan	Tanzania
Th	Thailand
To	Togo
T & T	Trinidad & Tobago
Tu	Tunisia
T	Turkey
U.K.	United Kingdom
U.S.A.	United States of America
Rus	Union of Soviet Socialist Republics
U	Uganda
Ur	Uruguay
Ven	Venezuela
V	Vietnam (Republic of)
V.N.	Vietnam (North)
V.I.	Virgin Islands
Yem	Yemen
Y	Yugoslavia
Z	Zaire

ALMIRANTE CLEMENTE—BARROSO

BARROSO PEREIRA—CAPE HORN

C

D'ESTIENNE-D'ORVES—ÉTOILE

ETOILE POLAIRE—GRIBB

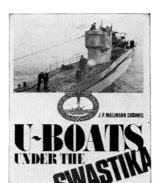

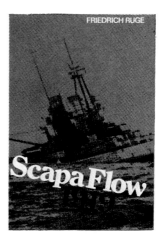

ILO—KOMSOMOLETS

KONDA—MADANG

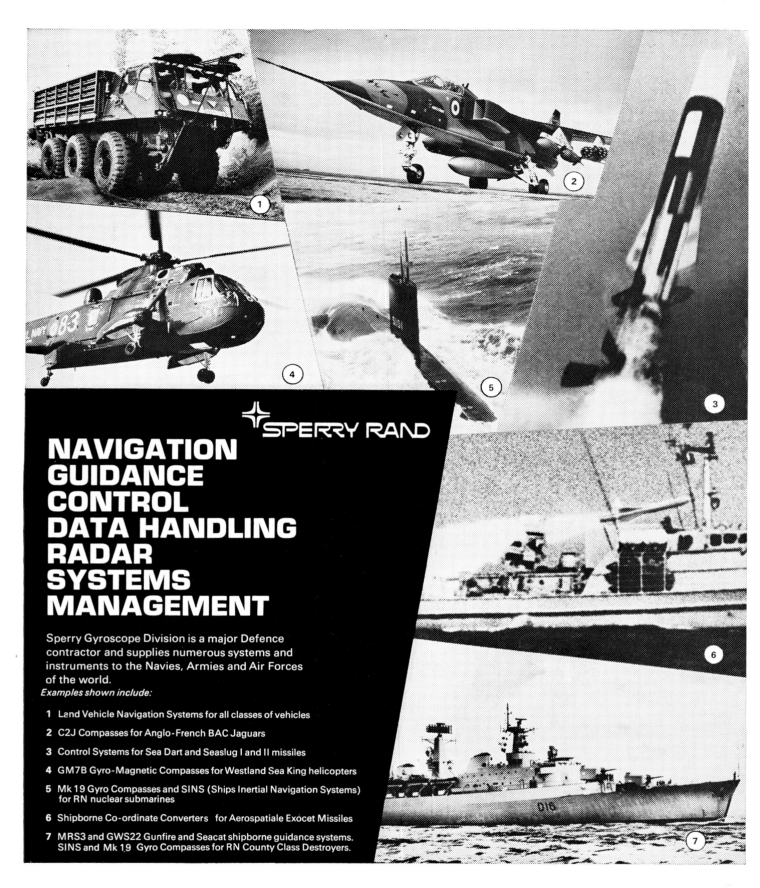

MADIDIHANG—NAPO

NAPORISTYJ—PARVIN

O

P

PASELBERG—PYRPOLITIS

SAPELE—STEADFAST

STEFAN MALYGIN—TORUGERO

T

TOSHIMA—WENATCHEE

WERRA—ZWROTNY

INDEX OF CLASSES

INDEX OF CLASSES

A CLASS—IZUZU

SOFIA—ZWAARDVIS

Printed in England by Netherwood Dalton & Co. Ltd., Huddersfield